# THE OXFORD
# COMPANION TO
# THE MIND

# THE OXFORD COMPANION TO THE MIND

EDITED BY

## RICHARD L. GREGORY

*with the assistance of*

## O. L. ZANGWILL

Oxford   New York

OXFORD UNIVERSITY PRESS

1998

Oxford University Press, Great Clarendon Street, Oxford OX2 6DP

Oxford New York

Athens Auckland Bangkok Bogota Buenos Aires Calcutta
Cape Town Chennai Dar es Salaam Delhi Florence Hong Kong Istanbul
Karachi Kuala Lumpur Madrid Melbourne Mexico City Mumbai
Nairobi Paris São Paolo Singapore Taipei Tokyo Toronto Warsaw

and associated companies in
Berlin Ibadan

Oxford is a registered trade mark of Oxford University Press

First published 1987
First published in paperback 1998

British Library Cataloguing in Publication Data
Data available

Library of Congress Cataloging in Publication Data
The Oxford companion to the mind / edited by Richard L. Gregory,
with the assistance of O. L. Zangwill.
Originally published: 1987.
Includes bibliographical references and index.
1. Psychology—Dictionaries.  2. Neurophysiology—Dictionaries.
3. Philosophy—Dictionaries.
I. Gregory, R. L. (Richard Langton)
II. Zangwill, O. L. (Oliver Louis), 1913- .
BF31.094  1998  128'.2'03—dc21  98-22974
ISBN 0-19-866124-X
ISBN 0-19-860224-3 (pbk.)

Printed in Great Britain
by Biddles Ltd.
Guildford and King's Lynn

# PREFACE

THIS Companion to the Mind has been companion to my mind, throughout her ten years of gestation. I am grateful for her friendship; and honoured by the trust accorded me by the Oxford University Press, without whose generous help and advice through this long time she would not have been born.

Her inception followed a gleam in the far-seeing eyes of Michael Rodgers, who was then an Oxford University Press editor. He approached me to take on the task of editing a Companion to the Mind, following a perhaps too-ambitious scheme that I had submitted a year or two before for an Encyclopaedia of Concepts, or ideas, to cover the whole of science and even more as it would extend into philosophy and perhaps the arts. This scheme unfortunately foundered in the planning stage, as it was deemed impracticable; but somehow this proposal must have led to the notion of a Companion to the Mind—to be written by a wide range of authorities on as many aspects of Mind as possible: to be interesting, useful, and understandable not only to experts but to anyone interested in normal or abnormal behaviour, human potentials that might be enhanced, the biological origins and evolution of man, the deeply difficult philosophical questions of relations between Mind and matter (both in brains and computers), and those perpetually puzzling questions of free will, and what is perhaps the main mark of Mind—intentionality. Some of this is necessarily technical, and much depends on certain key concepts which (and this is a criticism) are not familiar to us from our school-days.

In particular, the structure and function of the nervous system is important for considering perception, behaviour, skill, arousal and attention, thinking, effects of drugs and of brain damage, and a great deal more. For, in a physical sense, the structure and function of the nervous system are what we are. It was, also, clearly desirable to avoid the need to define technical terms (such as 'neurone', 'synapse', and so on) in each entry where they may occur. So early on it was decided to include (for the first time in an Oxford Companion) a *tutorial*, on the basic plan and function of the human nervous system, together with useful definitions of often-occurring technical terms which might be unfamiliar. This tutorial ('*Nervous System*') is written by the distinguished neurologist Peter Nathan, from the National Hospital for Nervous Diseases, Queen's Square, London. All the entries, including this introduction to the physical basis of mind, are specially written for this book.

The range is wide, as the concept of Mind accepted here is far broader than what may (at least at first) come to mind, as one thinks of Mind: especially thinking and consciousness. We do not, however, limit 'Mind' to consciousness, or awareness, for even long before Freud it was clear that a great deal goes on 'mentally' that is beyond (or beneath, or at least outside) our awareness. Here we present contributions from over a hundred experts on many aspects of the nervous system and its functionings—and all manner of malfunctions. These focus not only on such diverse and clearly very important topics as education; human, animal, and computer intelligence; sex; subnormalities; genius; learning; language; diminished responsibility in law; drugs; art; a great variety of philosophical accounts, and puzzles of Mind that can intrigue all of us; but also on more way-out topics (which some may reject out of hand but which we feel should be presented for discussion) such as parapsychology, and various widely held beliefs which are frankly outside science, such as blood myths and the origins of powerful fantasies such as Dracula and Frankenstein. Then there are state-of-the-art technical, and specifically medical, contributions on matters of concern for many people and indeed ultimately for all of us. All these, and much more, are presented and discussed here, as Mind is widely (and we hope in some depth) considered in this book.

A problem throughout has been the inclusion—or not—of biographies of the many philosophers, scientists, educators, doctors, and writers of all kinds who have contributed knowledge and advanced ideas over the centuries. As it has turned out, the selection of biographies is only partial, as this is not primarily a historical work and in any case makes no claim to completeness. Following misgivings, we finally decided against the inclusion of any biographies of living persons. This should at least protect us from some inevitable criticisms of omission! On the other hand, the *work* and *views* of very many people, both living and dead, are discussed in appropriate subject entries; their names can be found in the index (p. 821).

How were the contents planned? They were based on an initial list of topics of just about everything one could conceive of as relevant, having possible interest or use. Appropriate lengths were estimated, and authors (at first mainly friends and colleagues from around the world) were selected and invited to contribute. Then the fun started—and went on and on for years and years. The correspondence files grew even faster than the piles of manuscripts, and many were the bribes, threats, promises, and shared jokes (which were especially effective and mutually rewarding), which were vital stimuli for action—but now lie silent in the dark, their work done.

Angela Sainsbury, then Kate Tiffin, spent many evenings not only typing letters and sorting and filing, but suggesting new entries and improvements. Their careful work and enthusiasm is greatly appreciated. Following the vital initial work at the press by Michael Rodgers—who was both sounding-board and his own voice, as we walked in the meadows in Oxford, lunching at the Trout, while building up the book in our minds—the responsibility devolved upon Bruce Phillips, Dorothy McCarthy, Nick Wilson, and Christopher Riches, then finally on Pam Coote who focused the enterprise to completion— undertaking with wonderful effectiveness the intimidating task of cutting entries down to size, and with her colleagues going through the proofs. It is very important (as by now I have learned several times) for an editor, or author, to have ready understanding and mutual trust (which must, however, be based on evidence!) with his publishers. However it be for Nature, a vacuum is abhorrent to inspiration.

Thanks are due to John Cottingham who read all of the philosophy entries, suggesting and making many improvements; to Professor F. A. Whitlock who provided valuable help with the psychiatry entries; and to many other advisers.

It is most pleasant to record that several of my teachers have made major contributions to this book. Here I particularly record that one of my Cambridge teachers, Derek Russell Davis (now Emeritus Professor of Mental Health at Bristol) proved (as I expected) singularly adept at writing lucidly and instantly on any topic requested. Several of my students also are represented here; though just a few it must be confessed have not improved over the years in getting their essay in on time! Most of all, thanks and gratitude are due to my ex-boss at Cambridge, who succeeded my teacher Sir Frederic Bartlett in the Psychology Department: Professor Oliver Zangwill. Upon his retirement, Oliver Zangwill devoted a lot of his time and energy to going through the entire manuscript, pointing out inconsistencies, and suggesting and implementing many improvements and filling important gaps, often with his own writing. (These omissions were not like those a book reviewer once described: 'This book fills a much needed gap'.) Oliver Zangwill repaired inadequacies due to my lack of appreciation of several topics that he rightly saw to be significant and interesting.

Authorships are given for each entry, with initials to be identified from the list of contributors (p. ix). My own entries (which, when written, were often abandoned in favour of superior accounts as they came in) are left without initials; except for 'R.L.G.' on some for which I had no doubt unjustified pride, or (more often) regarded as controversial and so needing explicit authorship.

Some authors have, sadly, died since contributing. This includes the great Russian neuropsychologist, whom I had the pleasure of meeting at Cambridge and Moscow—Alexander Romanovich Luria—whose very last writings (which he tapped out on a portable typewriter on the shore of the Black Sea) now appear in this book. These he wrote in English, in which he was fluent. As he wrote with Russian sentence constructions, which can be quite hard to understand, Luria's last writings have been 'Englished', by a Russian scholar with a knowledge of psychology, Armorer Wason. By and large, editing has been light, as clearly each contributor should speak for him- or her-self; but occasionally I have cut sections I was perfectly certain were in error, and sometimes, in the cause of clarity, modified punctuation. Occasionally, for various reasons, entries have been 'dropped' at the final stage of editing; here apologies are due to their authors, which will I hope be accepted, as inevitably overlaps occurred which could not be allowed to remain.

It is hoped that this book, as it falls hot from the press, will be interesting and useful. It could be, however, that in a hundred year's time it will be even more interesting to the specialist—to see who wrote what and to guess why we think about Mind as we do now. There is no one way of thinking or writing about these many topics. I can only hope that encapsulated here—and not entirely limited to the Western tradition—there is a familiar sample of the facts and fancies, the perceptions and conceptions, of our past and present understanding of what we all recognize as deeply mysterious, though they are our reality—the many hidden faces of Mind.

RICHARD LANGTON GREGORY

*University of Bristol*

# CONTRIBUTORS

A.    Richard H. Adrian (Baron Adrian), Professor of Cell Physiology, University of Cambridge, and Master of Pembroke College, Cambridge, UK.

H.A.    Hans Ågren, Associate Professor of Psychiatry, University Hospital, Uppsala, Sweden.

P.A.    Peter Alexander, Emeritus Professor of Philosophy, University of Bristol, UK.

J.M.A.    John M. Allman, Professor of Biology, California Institute of Technology, Pasadena, USA.

M.A.A.    Michael A. Arbib, Professor of Biomedical Engineering, Computer Science, and Physiology, University of Southern California, Los Angeles, USA.

M.A.    Michael Argyle, Reader in Social Psychology, University of Oxford, UK.

D.M.A.    D. M. Armstrong, Challis Professor of Philosophy, University of Sydney, Australia.

R.A.    Rudolf Arnheim, Professor Emeritus of the Psychology of Art, University of Harvard, Cambridge, USA.

A.J.A.    Sir Alfred Ayer, formerly Wyndham Professor of Logic at the University of Oxford, UK.

A.D.B.    Alan Baddeley, Director, Medical Research Council, Applied Psychology Unit, Cambridge, UK.

H.B.B.    Horace B. Barlow, Royal Society Research Professor of Physiology, Cambridge, UK.

J.BA.    Jonathan Barnes, Fellow of Balliol College, Oxford, UK.

P.P.G.B.    P. P. G. Bateson, Director of the Sub-Department of Animal Behaviour, University of Cambridge, UK.

G.B.    Geoffrey Beattie, Lecturer in Psychology, University of Sheffield, UK.

J.BE.    John Beloff, formerly Senior Lecturer, Department of Psychology, University of Edinburgh, UK.

G.BE.    Glin Bennet, Consultant Senior Lecturer, Department of Mental Health, University of Bristol, and Consultant Psychiatrist, Bristol and Weston Health Authority, UK.

D.E.B.    D. E. Blackman, Professor of Psychology, University College Cardiff, UK.

S.J.B.    Susan J. Blackmore, Visiting Research Fellow, Brain and Perception Laboratory, University of Bristol, UK.

M.A.B.    Margaret A. Boden, Professor of Philosophy and Psychology, School of Cognitive Sciences, University of Sussex, UK.

I.B.W.    Ivan Bodis-Wollner, Professor of Neurology and Professor of Ophthalmology, Mount Sinai School of Medicine of the City, University of New York, USA.

J.BO.    John Bowlby, Honorary Consultant Psychiatrist, Tavistock Clinic, London, UK.

H.F.B.    H. F. Bradford, Professor of Neurochemistry, Royal College of Science, Imperial College of Science and Technology, London, UK.

J.B.    John Brown, Professor of Experimental Psychology, University of Bristol, UK.

# CONTRIBUTORS

P.T.B.    P. T. Brown, Consulting Clinical and Occupational Psychiatrist, Gwynn & Brown, London, UK.

B.L.B.    Brian Lewis Butterworth, Reader in Psychology, University College London, UK.

A.J.C.    Anthony J. Chapman, Professor of Psychology, University of Leeds, UK.

D.L.C.    Dorothy L. Cheney, Assistant Professor of Psychology and Anthropology, University of Pennsylvania, Philadelphia, USA.

N.C.    A. Noam Chomsky, Ferrari Ward Professor of Modern Languages and Linguistics, Massachusetts Institute of Technology, Cambridge, USA.

D.C.    David Cohen, Editor, *Psychology News*, UK.

J.CO.    J. Cohen, Department of Psychology, University of Manchester, UK.

S.C.    Steven Collins, Lecturer in the Study of Religions, University of Bristol, UK.

K.J.C.    Kevin J. Connolly, Professor of Psychology, University of Sheffield, UK.

D.A.G.C.    David Angus Graham Cook, Consultant Senior Lecturer in Mental Health, University of Bristol, UK.

A.R.V.C.    Arthur Cooper, Honorary Visiting Fellow, School of Oriental Studies, University of Durham, UK.

R.C.    Ray Cooper, Director, Burden Neurological Institute, Bristol, UK.

J.G.C.    John G. Cottingham, Lecturer in Philosophy, University of Reading, UK.

A.C.    Alan Cowey, Professor of Physiological Psychology, University of Oxford, UK.

J.M.C.    June Crown, District Medical Officer, Bloomsbury Health Authority, London, UK.

S.CR.    Sidney Crown, Consultant Psychiatrist (with special interest in Psychotherapy), The London Hospital, UK.

K.D.    Kurt Danziger, Professor of Psychology, York University, Toronto, Canada.

D.R.D.    Derek Russell Davis, Emeritus Professor of Mental Health, University of Bristol, UK.

E.DE B.    Edward de Bono, Lecturer in Medicine, University of Cambridge, UK.

D.C.D.    Daniel C. Dennett, Professor of Philosophy, Center for Cognitive Studies, Tufts University, Medford, Massachusetts, USA.

J.B.D.    J. B. Deręgowski, Professor of Psychology, University of Aberdeen, UK.

D.D.    Diana Deutsch, Research Psychologist, Department of Psychology, University of California, La Jolla, USA.

J.A.D.    J. A. Deutsch, Professor of Psychology, University of California, San Diego, USA.

A.D.    A. Dickinson, University Lecturer, University of Cambridge, UK.

R.W.D.    † Robert William Ditchburn, Emeritus Professor of Physics, University of Reading, UK.

N.F.D.    N. F. Dixon, Professor of Psychology, University College London, UK.

M.D.    Margaret Donaldson, Emeritus Professor of Developmental Psychology, University of Edinburgh, UK.

R.E.    Robert Epstein, University of Boston and Cambridge Center for Behavioral Studies, Cambridge, Massachusetts, USA.

G.E.    G. Ettlinger, Professor of Psychology, Universität Bielefeld, Federal Republic of Germany.

C.E. † Christopher Evans, late Principal Scientific Officer, National Physical Laboratory, Teddington, UK.

H.J.E. Hans J. Eysenck, Professor Emeritus, Institute of Psychiatry, University of London, UK.

F.J.F. F. J. Fitzpatrick, Education and Research Officer, The Linacre Centre for the Study of the Ethics of Health Care, London, UK.

K.A.F. K. A. Flowers, Lecturer in Psychology, University of Hull, UK.

D.F. Deborah H. Fouts, Adjunct Professor of Psychology, Central Washington University, Ellensburg, Washington, USA.

R.S.F. R. S. Fouts, Director of Friends of Washoe Foundation, and Professor of Psychology, Central Washington University, Ellensburg, Washington, USA.

C.F. Colin Fraser, University Lecturer in Social Psychology, University of Cambridge, UK.

M.F. Marianne Frankenhaeuser, Professor of Psychology, Head of Psychology Division, Department of Psychiatry and Psychology, University of Stockholm, Sweden.

N.H.F. Norman H. Freeman, Reader in Psychology, University of Bristol, UK.

R.M.G. R. M. Gaze, Biologist, University of Edinburgh, UK.

F.H.G. Frank George, Bureau of Information Science, and formerly Professor of Cybernetics, Brunel University, UK.

N.G. † Norman Geschwind, late of the Neurological Unit, Beth Israel Hospital, Boston, USA.

R.N.G. † R. N. Gooderson, late of St Catharine's College, Cambridge, UK.

R.L.G. Richard L. Gregory, Professor of Neuropsychology and Director of Brain and Perception Laboratory, University of Bristol, UK.

A.M.H. A. M. Halliday, Consultant in Clinical Neurophysiology, The National Hospital for Nervous Diseases, London, UK, and member of the External Staff of the Medical Research Council.

M.H. M. Hammerton, Professor of Psychology, University of Newcastle upon Tyne, UK.

C.H. Charles Hannam, Senior Lecturer, School of Education, University of Bristol, UK.

P.M.H. Pam Hannam, Chair of Avon Mencap Societies, Bristol, UK.

J.P.H. John Harris, Research Fellow, Department of Anatomy, University of Bristol, UK.

J.C.H. John C. Haugeland, Professor of Philosophy, University of Pittsburgh, USA.

D.H.H. Dorothy H. Heard, Honorary Lecturer, Department of Psychiatry, University of Leeds, UK.

L.S.H. Leslie S. Hearnshaw, Emeritus Professor of Psychology, University of Liverpool, UK.

A.W.H. Alice W. Heim, former MRC Research Psychologist, Psychology Department, University of Cambridge, UK.

V.H. Volker Henn, Professor of Neurology, University of Zürich, Switzerland.

B.H. Beate Hermelin, MRC Research Psychologist, University of London, UK.

P.H. Peter Herriot, Professor of Occupational Psychology, Birkbeck College, University of London, UK.

J.HI.     John Hick, Danforth Professor of the Philosophy of Religion, Claremont Graduate School, California, USA.

R.A.H.    Robert A. Hinde, Royal Society Research Professor, Department of Zoology, Cambridge, UK.

J.H.      Julian Hochberg, Professor of Psychology, Columbia University, New York, USA.

D.D.H.    Deborah Duncan Honoré, Research Worker, Oxford, UK and formerly of *The Oxford English Dictionary.*

D.H.      David Howard, MRC Senior Research Fellow, Psychology Department, University College London, UK.

I.P.H.    Ian P. Howard, Professor of Psychology, York University, Downsview, Ontario, Canada.

L.H.      Liam Hudson, Professor of Psychology, Brunel University, UK.

M.HU.     Miranda Hughes, Management Consultant in Human Resources.

O.J.W.H.  The Revd. O. J. W. Hunkin, formerly Head of Religious Programmes, BBC Television, UK.

I.M.L.H.  Ian M. L. Hunter, Emeritus Professor of Psychology, University of Keele, UK.

C.HU.     † Corinne Hutt, late of the Department of Psychology, University of Keele, UK.

A.I.      Ainsley Iggo, Professor of Veterinary Physiology, University of Edinburgh, UK.

L.L.I.    L. L. Iverson, Director Merck Sharp & Dohme Research Laboratories Ltd., Harlow, UK.

L.A.I.    Lawrence Alfred Ives, formerly Senior Lecturer at the University of Manchester and Consultant Psychologist.

M.A.J.    Malcolm A. Jeeves, Professor of Psychology, University of St Andrews, UK.

B.J.      Bela Julesz, Head of Visual Perception Research, AT & T. Bell Laboratories, and Continuing Visiting Professor, California Institute of Technology, USA.

R.J.      † Richard Jung, late of the Abteilung Klinische Neurologie und Neurophysiologie, Freiburg, Federal Republic of Germany.

H.K.      Harry Kay, Research Psychologist, formerly Vice-Chancellor of the University of Exeter, UK.

C.K.      C. Kennard, Consultant Neurologist, The London Hospital, UK.

R.E.K.    R. E. Kendell, Professor of Psychiatry, University of Edinburgh, UK.

P.A.K.    † Paul A. Kolers, late of the Department of Psychology, University of Toronto, Canada.

N.K.      N. Kreitman, Director, MRC Unit for Epidemiological Studies in Psychiatry, Edinburgh, UK.

R.D.L.    R. D. Laing, Psychiatrist, London, UK.

B.L.      Brian Lake, Consultant Psychotherapist, St James's University Hospital, Leeds, UK.

D.R.J.L.  Donald R. J. Laming, University Lecturer in Experimental Psychology, University of Cambridge, UK.

R.L.-H.   Richard Langton-Hewer, Consultant Neurologist, Frenchay Hospital, Bristol, and Director of Bristol Stroke Research Unit, UK.

| | |
|---|---|
| E.R.L. | Sir Edmund Leach, Professor Emeritus of Social Anthropology, University of Cambridge, and Provost of King's College, Cambridge, UK. |
| A.M.L. | Alan M. Leslie, MRC Cognitive Development Unit, London, UK. |
| G.E.R.L. | Geoffrey Ernest Richard Lloyd, Professor of Ancient Philosophy and Science, University of Cambridge, UK. |
| A.L.-B. | Ann Low-Beer, School of Education, University of Bristol, UK. |
| A.R.L. | † A. R. Luria, late Professor of Neuropsychology, University of Moscow, USSR. |
| W.C.M. | W. Cheyne McCallum, Senior Research Fellow in Neuropsychology, Burden Neurological Institute, Bristol, UK. |
| J.J.McC. | J. J. McCann, Adrian Land Research Laboratory, Boston, USA. |
| R.H.M. | R. H. McCleery, Edward Grey Institute of Field Ornithology, Oxford, UK. |
| D.J.M. | D. J. McFarland, Reader in Animal Behaviour, University of Oxford, UK. |
| C.M. | Colin McGinn, Wilde Reader in Mental Philosophy, University of Oxford, UK. |
| P.McG. | Peter McGuffin, Professor of Psychological Medicine, University of Wales College of Medicine, Cardiff, UK. |
| D.M.M. | † Donald MacKay, late Emeritus Professor, Department of Communication & Neuroscience, University of Keele, UK. |
| R.T.M. | Raymond T. McNally, Professor of History and Director of the Russian and East European Center at Boston College, Chestnut Hill, Massachusetts, USA. |
| G.M. | George Mandler, Professor of Psychology and Director, Center for Human Information Processing, University of California at San Diego, USA. |
| R.ME. | Ronald Melzack, Professor of Psychology, McGill University, Montreal, Canada. |
| P.A.M. | P. A. Merton, Professor of Human Physiology, University of Cambridge, UK. |
| D.M. | Donald Michie, Chief Scientist, The Turing Institute, Glasgow, UK. |
| T.R.M. | T. R. Miles, Professor of Psychology, University College of North Wales, Bangor, UK. |
| S.M. | † Stanley Milgram, late Professor at the Graduate School and University Center of the City of New York, USA. |
| M.M. | Michel Millodot, Professor of Optometry, University of Wales, Cardiff, UK. |
| P.M.M. | Peter M. Milner, Professor of Psychology, McGill University, Montreal, Canada. |
| B.C.J.M. | Brian C. J. Moore, Lecturer in Experimental Psychology, University of Cambridge, UK. |
| F.C.T.M. | Francis Charles Timothy Moore, Professor of Philosophy, University of Hong Kong. |
| P.M. | Patrick Moore, Astronomer, UK. |
| N.M. | Neville Moray, Professor of Industrial Engineering, University of Toronto, Canada. |
| M.J.M. | M. J. Morgan, Professor, Department of Psychology, University College London, UK. |
| R.M.M. | Robin M. Murray, Dean, Institute of Psychiatry, London, UK. |

# CONTRIBUTORS

P.W.N.     Peter W. Nathan, Neurologist, formerly of the National Hospital for Nervous Diseases, London, UK.

N.N.     Nigel Nicholson, Senior Research Fellow, MRC/ESRC Social and Applied Psychology Unit, University of Sheffield, UK.

J.N.     Joanna North, Postgraduate student, Birkbeck College, University of London, UK.

F.N.J.     F. Nowell Jones, Professor Emeritus of Psychology, University of California at Los Angeles, USA.

N.O'C.     Neil O'Connor, Research Psychologist, Medical Research Council, UK.

M.O'M.     Michael O'Mahoney, Professor of Food Science and Technology, University of California, Davis, USA.

R.W.O.     Ronald W. Oppenheim, Professor of Anatomy, Bowman Gray School of Medicine, Wake Forest University, North Carolina, USA.

A.O.     Andrew Ortony, Professor of Psychology and Education, University of Illinois at Urbana-Champaign, USA.

I.O.     Ian Oswald, Professor of Psychiatry, University of Edinburgh, UK.

J.M.O.     John Oxbury, Senior NHS Consultant Neurologist, Radcliffe Infirmary, Oxford, UK.

J.H.P.     John Hunter Padel, formerly Visiting Lecturer at the Tavistock Clinic, London.

R.C.T.P.     R. C. T. Parker, Tutor in Greek and Latin Languages and Literature, Oriel College, Oxford, UK.

C.M.P.     Colin Murray Parkes, Senior Lecturer in Psychiatry, The London Hospital Medical College, UK.

T.E.P.     Theodore E. Parks, Professor of Psychology, University of California, Davis, USA.

W.D.M.P.     Sir William Paton, Emeritus Professor of Pharmacology, University of Oxford, UK.

C.P.     Colin Patterson, Senior Principal Scientific Officer, Department of Palaeontology, British Museum (Natural History), London, UK.

D.F.P.     David Pears, Professor of Philosophy, University of Oxford, UK.

P.P.     Philip Pettit, Professorial Fellow, Research School of Social Sciences, Australian National University, Canberra, Australia.

O.T.P.     O. T. Phillipson, Lecturer, Department of Anatomy, The Medical School, University of Bristol, UK.

R.W.P.     † R. W. Pickford, late Emeritus Professor of Psychology, University of Glasgow, UK.

I.W.P.-P.     I. W. Pleydell-Pearce, Senior Lecturer in Psychology, University of Bristol, UK.

K.P.     Klaus Poeck, Professor of Neurology, University of Aachen, Federal Republic of Germany.

E.C.P.     E. C. Poulton, formerly Assistant Director of the MRC Applied Psychology Unit, Cambridge, UK.

M.A.P.     M. A. Preece, Professor of Child Health and Growth, Institute of Child Health, University of London, UK.

W.V.Q.     Willard V. Quine, Professor of Philosophy Emeritus, University of Harvard, Cambridge, USA.

P.R.     P. A. M. Rabbitt, Director of the Age and Cognitive Performance Research Centre, University of Manchester, UK.

| | |
|---|---|
| S.R. | S. Rachman, Professor of Psychology, University of British Columbia, Vancouver, Canada. |
| M.E.R. | Marcus E. Raichle, Professor of Neurology and Radiology, Washington School of Medicine, St Louis, Missouri, USA. |
| G.F.R. | Graham F. Reed, Chairman, Department of Psychology, Glendon College, York University, Toronto, Canada. |
| M.R. | Mark Ridley, Research Fellow, St Catharine's College, Cambridge, UK. |
| H.R.R. | H. R. Rollin, Emeritus Consultant Psychiatrist, Horton Hospital, Epsom, Surrey, UK. |
| F.G.R. | Graham Rooth, Consultant Psychiatrist, Bristol, UK. |
| S.P.R.R. | Steven Rose, Professor of Biology, The Open University, Milton Keynes, UK. |
| H.E.R. | Helen E. Ross, Reader in Psychology, University of Stirling, UK. |
| W.A.H.R. | † William Rushton, late Professor of Visual Physiology, University of Cambridge, UK. |
| C.R. | Charles Rycroft, Psychoanalyst, London, UK. |
| O.S. | Oliver Sacks, Associate Professor of Neurology, Albert Einstein College of Medicine, New York, USA. |
| B.S. | Barbara J. Sahakian, Institute of Neurology, The National Hospital, University of London, UK. |
| D.J.S. | D. J. Satterly, Senior Lecturer in Education, University of Bristol, UK. |
| F.S. | Francis Schiller, Clinical Professor of Neurology, Senior Lecturer History of Health Science Emeritus, University of California, San Francisco, USA. |
| C.SC. | Claudia Schmölders (formerly Henn) editor at Suhrkamp Verlag, BRD, Frankfurt am Main, German Federal Republic. |
| C.S. | Christopher Scott, Consultant Statistician. |
| B.SE. | B. Semeonoff, formerly Reader in Psychology, University of Edinburgh, UK. |
| R.M.S. | Robert M. Seyfarth, Assistant Professor of Psychology and Anthropology, University of Pennsylvania, Philadelphia, USA. |
| I.S. | The Sayed Idries Shah, Director of Studies, Institute for Cultural Research, Kent, UK. |
| N.P.S. | Noel P. Sheehy, Lecturer in Psychology, University of Leeds, UK. |
| A.M.S. | A. M. Sillito, Professor of Physiology, Head of Department, University College, Cardiff, UK. |
| B.F.S. | B. F. Skinner, Professor of Psychology Emeritus, University of Harvard, USA. |
| V.S. | Vieda Skultans, Lecturer in Mental Health, University of Bristol, UK. |
| N.SP. | Lady Spender (Natasha Spender), Pianist, formerly Lecturer at the Royal College of Art, London, UK. |
| R.W.S. | Roger Walcott Sperry, Trustee's Professor of Psychobiology Emeritus, California Institute of Technology, Pasadena, USA. |
| N.S. | Norman Stephenson, formerly Senior Lecturer in Education, University of Bristol, UK. |
| R.J.S. | Robert J. Sternberg, IBM Professor of Psychology and Education, University of Yale, New Haven, USA. |
| P.F.S. | Sir Peter Strawson, Waynflete Professor of Metaphysical Philosophy, University of Oxford, UK. |

# CONTRIBUTORS

N.S.S.  Stuart Sutherland, Professor of Experimental Psychology, University of Sussex, UK.

J.S.H.T.  Jeremy S. H. Taylor, Research Fellow, Department of Zoology, University of Edinburgh, UK.

G.T.  Georges Thinès, Professor of Experimental Psychology, University of Louvain, Belgium.

J.E.T.  J. E. Tiles, Lecturer in Philosophy, University of Reading, UK.

M.E.T.  Mary Elizabeth Tiles, Secretary, The Royal Institute of Philosophy, UK.

E.W.F.T.  E. W. F. Tomlin, formerly British Council Representative in Japan and Professor of English and Philosophy at the University of Nice, France.

C.T.  Colwyn Trevarthen, Professor of Child Psychology and Psychobiology, University of Edinburgh, UK.

T.T.  Tom Troscianko, Research Associate, Brain and Perception Laboratory, University of Bristol, UK.

J.R.U.  Julian R. Ullman, Professor of Computer Science and Head of Department of Statistics and Computer Science, Royal Holloway and Bedford New College, University of London, UK.

P.H.V.  Peter H. Venables, Professor of Psychology, University of York, UK.

P.E.V.  Philip E. Vernon, Emeritus Professor of Educational Psychology, University of Calgary, Alberta, Canada.

G.N.A.V.  Godfrey N. A. Vesey, Professor of Philosophy, The Open University, Milton Keynes, UK.

N.D.W.  Nigel D. Walker, formerly Director of the Institute of Criminology and Fellow of King's College at the University of Cambridge, UK.

R.C.S.W.  Ralph C. S. Walker, Fellow and Tutor in Philosophy, Magdalen College, Oxford, UK.

G.J.W.  Sir Geoffrey Warnock, Principal of Hertford College, Oxford, UK.

M.W.  Baroness Warnock, Mistress of Girton College, Cambridge, UK.

P.B.W.  Peter B. Warr, Director, MRC/ESRC Social and Applied Psychology Unit, University of Sheffield, UK.

P.C.W.  Peter Cathcart Wason, Emeritus Reader in Psycholinguistics, University College London, UK.

R.J.W.  Roger J. Watt, Scientist, MRC Applied Psychology Unit, Cambridge, UK.

L.W.  L. Weiskrantz, Professor of Psychology, University of Oxford, UK.

A.T.W.  A. T. Welford, Professor Emeritus of Psychology in the University of Adelaide, Australia.

M.J.W.  Martin John Wells, Reader in Zoology, University of Cambridge, UK.

G.W.  Gerald Westheimer, Professor, Department of Physiology-Anatomy, University of California, Berkeley, USA.

F.A.W.  F. A. Whitlock, Professor Emeritus of Psychiatry, University of Queensland, Australia, and formerly Honorary Consultant Psychiatrist, St Lawrence's Hospital, Bodmin, UK.

A.J.W.  Arnold J. Wilkins, Research Worker, MRC Applied Psychology Unit, Cambridge, UK.

M.WI.  Moyra Williams, formerly Principal Clinical Psychologist, Cambridge, UK.

C.W.  Colin Wilson, Author, Cornwall, UK.

J.H.W.  † John Wolstencroft, late Professor of Physiology, University of Birmingham, UK.

## CONTRIBUTORS

J.Z.Y.    J. Z. Young, Professor Emeritus, Department of Experimental Psychology, University of Oxford, formerly Professor of Anatomy, University College, London, UK.

O.L.Z.    † O. L. Zangwill, late Emeritus Professor of Experimental Psychology, University of Cambridge, UK.

Y.Z.    † Y. Zotterman, late of the Symposium Secretariat Wenner Gren Center, Stockholm, Sweden.

# NOTE TO THE READER

ENTRIES are arranged in strict alphabetical order of their headword, except that names beginning with Mc are ordered as if they were spelt Mac. Cross-references between entries are indicated either by means of an asterisk (*) in front of the word to be looked up, or by the use of 'See' followed by the entry title in small capitals. Cross-references are given only when reference will provide further information relevant to the subject under discussion; they are not given automatically merely to indicate that a separate entry exists. The comprehensive index at the back of the book, includes not only the subjects discussed within entries but also the names of the contributors and the principal author of each bibliographical reference.

# A

**ABACUS.** Ancient calculating instrument in which numbers and operations (especially adding) are represented by the numbers and positions of pebbles or (later) beads on strings or wooden rods; it may be regarded as an early form of *digital computer. Although it originated in prehistoric times, the abacus is still widely used especially in China and Japan. The fact that this 'mind tool' can vastly improve mental arithmetic might suggest that the unaided mind functions on very different principles (perhaps that thinking is analogical rather than a digital process). Just as, if fingers were like screwdrivers we would not need screwdrivers, so, if the brain worked like an abacus, bead-counters should not be so helpful. But perhaps the abacus serves as a memory.

Our language reflects the importance of the abacus throughout history. The word 'calculate' comes from the Latin word for a pebble, and the term 'Exchequer' derives from the chequered table on which counters or jettons were moved to reckon the nation's accounts (the abacus continued to be used for British governmental accounting into the eighteenth century). The mechanical calculating machine with geared wheels (invented by Blaise *Pascal in 1642) is a direct development of the abacus; and this in turn led to Charles *Babbage's programmable wheeled calculator and, eventually, to today's electronic computers.

Pullan, J. M. (1969). *The History of the Abacus*. New York.

**ABNORMAL** describes behaviour or an event that differs from the familiar or usual. Just how bizarre, unusual, or even antisocial behaviour must be in order to be classified as 'abnormal' depends on many factors that change with knowledge and with social preconceptions. Thus, for example, classification might depend upon whether or not the behaviour was socially acceptable or whether there were symptoms, however minor, of an underlying problem or disease already regarded as abnormal. Such classification is helpful when it leads to useful treatment, therapy, or special education, but it can also be dangerous, for in extreme cases it can take an unusual or gifted person away from society.

The probability of an abnormal event occurring against chance can be predicted from statistical tests. In scientific research such tests are important in establishing whether an event is unusual enough to require special explanation. In clinical situations, however, applicable tests are difficult to establish, because classification of abnormal events depends on factors that are changeable.

**ABRAHAM,** KARL, German psychoanalyst. See FREUDIANISM: LATER DEVELOPMENTS.

**ABREACTION.** A recalling or re-experiencing of stressful or disturbing situations or events which appear to have precipitated a neurosis. During the recalling the patient is encouraged to give an uninhibited display of emotion and afterwards it is hoped that the neurosis will have vanished. Abreaction was used by Josef *Breuer in the treatment of patients with *hysteria; in a modified form, it still finds some applications in modern psychiatry, especially in the treatment of battle stress.

**ACCELERATION.** Acceleration of the body is sensed in the inner ear by the otoliths, small weights of calcium carbonate suspended on stalks. Accelerated movements of the head produce deflections of the stalks, since the otoliths do not respond immediately to movement because of their inertia. Unaccelerated motion cannot be sensed intrinsically by any sense or by any physical instrument, but only by reference to external objects that may themselves be moving. So there is ambiguity, such as occurs when a stationary train appears, to one who is in it, to move when a neighbouring train moves past it. Here the visual sense of movement dominates the sensing of acceleration—or rather the lack of acceleration—for the observer in the stationary train.

**ACCIDENTAL PROPERTY.** See CONTINGENT PROPERTY.

**ACCIDENT PRONENESS** is a deceptively easy term. We all know what it means but we do not all mean the same thing. Since the ambiguities arise partly because of the way we speak about accidents, it may be helpful to clarify this term.

An accident refers to the results of an action, generally to an unplanned, even an unexpected result. It has been described as 'an error with sad consequences', but the relationship between the preceding behaviour and the consequences is not at all simple. A time-honoured example of an accident is a person falling flat as he slips on a banana-skin—an act, incidentally, that few have ever witnessed and which conveys the impression that the world at one time must have been littered with banana-skins. In such an example the person who slips has the accident for which he was partly responsible. But we also speak of someone having an accident when something falls on him. *A* spills a cup of tea over *B* and we say that *B* has suffered an accident. To add to the confusion, different kinds of action result in similar accidents, while the same act often has very different results. Hence, if we are to understand accidents we need to understand the preceding behaviour. But accident data are usually only records of the outcome of actions.

There is a further complication. It is a feature of accident statistics that the more severe the accident (particularly a fatal injury), the more accurate is the record. But the majority of accidents are relatively trivial, and in our society the greatest number occur in the home and often go unrecorded. The basis for extrapolation, therefore, is somewhat shaky. Nevertheless we can be confident that over the years the trend of incidence in different kinds of activities has shifted. Industrial accidents are no longer the major component; rather, the home and transport make up the bulk of the total. This shift is important, for a quick inspection of a nation's annual accident data shows such regularity from year to year that it might be concluded that accidents were an inevitable consequence of man's mobility. Closer scrutiny reveals that within the total of accidents the pattern has shifted from one class of accidents to another.

Within this general framework, it is accepted that the risks inherent in some activities are greater than in others and that the chances of accident also fluctuate with varying environmental conditions: changes in lighting, humidity, temperature, for example. The behaviour of the individual is the common factor, and inevitably explanation has been sought of the proneness to accident. The direct question has been asked: in the same circumstances, do individuals differ in their liability to accident? In everyday thinking about skilled actions, some individuals would be more proficient than others; conversely, some individuals would be less so, and to that extent they would have more accidents. This straightforward and rather simple line of thought presumed that a single measure of overall performance provided a reliable index of the skill of a performer. But a performer's degree of skill is not necessarily an index to his liability to accident. A palpably poor driver of a car may be aware of his fallibility and drive more cautiously, with the result that he has fewer accidents than a skilful but over-confident driver. It is necessary to analyse the skill in some detail if it is to provide a guide to accident liability.

Even so, accepting for the moment that we may use an overall measure, it is easy enough to demonstrate in statistical data that some individuals over a limited time-period incur more accidents than others. It is tempting to infer that this identifies those who are more liable to have accidents—the accident-prone. But, of course, such an inference is not necessarily justified. In a normal distribution of random events over a sample time-period, some will occur more frequently than others.

Early research workers, such as Greenwood and Yule (1920), were well aware of these statistically attractive fallacies and, though their data indicated

that some individuals had incurred a high proportion of the accidents in situations where other factors were equal, they stressed the need for caution. But in 1926 Farmer and Chambers suggested the term 'accident proneness' for this liability to incur accidents, and such is the power of an attractive label that it was universally accepted, not as a tentative guess to be examined by further research, as they proposed, but as an established fact. The concept of accident proneness was taken a stage further by Flanders Dunbar in America who claimed that a personality trait of accident proneness was proven fact. She gave psychodynamic interpretations which claimed that persons involved in repeated accidents had some unconscious need for physical trauma. Later she had to modify her original views about accident proneness being an enduring personality trait when it was pointed out that some of these so-called accident-prone personalities ceased to have accidents as they grew older.

The history is typical of what happens when scientific ideas are accepted on too little evidence. For a time accident proneness became the major explanatory concept in its field; then in the 1940s doubts began to creep in and by the 1950s careful assessments were pointing out that the evidence was insufficient. Soon opposition swung well beyond this point, as in the highly critical major review of Haddon, Suchman, and Klein (1964). During the 1960s, the fact that the statistical evidence failed to demonstrate the existence of accident proneness was interpreted as a refutation of all hypotheses relating to it. The pendulum had to swing back, and in 1971 Shaw published her comprehensive analysis of accident proneness. She avoided an extreme position. She conceded that many characteristics of behaviour change with age and that it is not true that most accidents are sustained by a small number of people. But she examined in detail earlier studies and demonstrated the importance of certain factors such as *attention (defined as the ability to choose quickly and perform a correct response to a sudden stimulus), the stability of behaviour, and the involuntary control of motor behaviour. She supported the study of car drivers—'a man drives as he lives'—and the finding that a bad civil record tends to indicate a bad accident risk.

Where does this leave accident proneness? In spite of, perhaps because of, much contentious writing the problem is still with us and becoming of increasing importance as accidents, the twentieth-century disease, assume an ever greater significance in mortality rates. Now, if accident data are not recording behaviour directly but its consequences, then the less the probability of an accident following an action, the more insensitive the data as an index of behaviour. Little can be inferred about, say, the behaviour of pedestrians at railway level crossings from accident data for, fortunately, there is little data—but what if behaviour could be recorded directly? In general the problem would be lessened, given guidance on the kinds of behaviour that cause accidents, or if the number of situations that have to be studied were reduced. Some beginnings have been made with detailed examinations of the behaviour of drivers on the roads, and these should be extended into the home and to other everyday situations. An understanding is required of the basis of human skills, and fortunately advances have now been made in this field of study. When a human operator is carrying out a skill, he is receiving signals from several sensory modalities and initiating responses to them. The whole process is conceived as an information loop. The operator is in the centre and the information is measured statistically in terms of the probability of the signals. Though this concept may seem at first sight a little removed from everyday thinking, a moment's reflection will show that it is not. We expect to see certain things under certain conditions and we know how we shall respond. For example, it is no surprise to drive round a corner and see another car; it would be to see an elephant. And evidence shows we respond more quickly to the car than we would to the elephant, or, to put it another way, the more certain the signal, the less information it carries in a statistical sense it carries. If, then, we conceive of a skill as processing information, one essential is for the operator to reduce the amount of information by anticipating the probability of different signals. It is a truism to say that accidents occur when the operator has too much information to process in too little time. One way to handle such situations is to know which events are likely to occur.

But although a sensitive analysis may be made of human skills, and insight gained into how a person's propensities vary with different tasks and at different stages of his life, knowledge of how performance is affected by the personality of the individual is still sketchy. Over and above the psychomotor skill itself, there is a further influence reflecting the personal qualities of the performer, and exactly how this affects accident proneness is not known. The influence differs according to the state of fatigue or the vigilance of the operator, to the difficulty or length of the task, to the importance of the occasion, and so forth. This area requires much more study, but we see its importance exemplified in the case of age. It is often said, 'Tell me a person's age and I will tell you what accidents he may have.' The under-25s contribute disproportionately to road accidents the world over (seen even when experience is held constant over different age-groups). Similarly the over-65s contribute a large proportion of the psychomotor accidents in the home, which are generally due to falls as control deteriorates. It is a question of coming to terms with the varying skills we possess as life advances. Finally, there is the puzzling and recurring example of accidents that turn out to be anything but accidental. Investigation into the antecedent history of the individual in these cases suggests that the behaviour causing the accident

was highly predictable and that the accident had the inevitability of Greek tragedy. It was fitting that Michael Ayrton added a new dimension to the classical myth of Daedalus and his son Icarus; under his interpretation it was no mischance that Icarus flew too close to the sun god, Apollo, and thereby caused the wax of his wings to melt: it was his act of challenge and defiance. H. K.

Dunbar, F. (1954; repr. 1976). *Emotions and Bodily Changes*, 4th edn. Philadelphia.

Farmer, E. and Chambers, E. G. (1926). *A Psychological Study of Individual Differences in Accident Rate*. Industrial Health Research Board, report no. 38, London.

Greenwood, M. and Yule, C. V. (1920). An enquiry into the nature of frequency distribution in repeated accidents. *Journal of the Royal Statistical Society*, **83**, 255.

Haddon, W., Suchman, E. A., and Klein, D. (1964). *Accident Research*. New York.

Shaw, L. and Sichel, H. S. (1971). *Accident Proneness*. New York.

**ACCOMMODATION** (OF THE EYE). The lens in the eye of land-living vertebrates focuses by changing the curvature of its surface, a process known as 'accommodation'. In fish the lens moves backwards and forwards as in a camera. Accommodation brings objects of interest, when fixated on the centre of the retinas in animals that have foveae, into sharp focus. This is achieved by 'hunting' for the sharpest image (or highest spatial frequency response of the eye), as there is no available signal indicating whether accommodation is set too *far* (insufficient curvature of the lens) or too *near* (too much curvature). Spectacles can correct for too great or too small a curvature of the lens, to give focused images when the eye's accommodation is incorrect or, as almost invariably happens in middle age, when the lens of the eye becomes too inflexible to change its shape to keep the image in focus for a wide range of distances of objects. Spectacles were invented in the thirteenth century in the West, and earlier in China. Several inventors have been suggested, especially Salvino d'Armato (d. 1312), and Roger Bacon (?1214–94), who also described the magnifying glass.

**ACETYLCHOLINE** (ACh). An important *neurotransmitter, liberated at nerve endings, that transmits nervous impulses to muscles or to other nerve cells. Once released, acetylcholine has a very short existence as it is quickly broken down by the enzyme cholinesterase. See NERVOUS SYSTEM.

**ACTION POTENTIAL.** See NERVOUS SYSTEM.

**ACUPUNCTURE.** See PAIN.

**ADAPTATION OF THE EYES.** See VISUAL ADAPTATION.

**ADDICTION.** For most people the concept of drug addiction is dominated by images of physical and mental degradation brought about by the use of heroin and cocaine. It is generally forgotten that the most widely used *drugs are caffeine (in tea and coffee), nicotine, and alcohol; and that the most successful drug 'pushers' are tobacconists and publicans. Of course the great majority of those who enjoy these drugs are not necessarily addicted, if addiction means a tendency to excessive use of the drug, a craving for it when it is not available, and the development of a variety of physical and psychological symptoms when it is suddenly withdrawn.

Addiction is a difficult word to define, and a WHO expert committee in 1970 substituted the words 'drug dependence'. This is characterized by psychological symptoms such as craving and a compulsion to take the drug on a continuous or periodic basis, and physical effects developing when the drug is withheld or is unavailable. Although many drugs will meet these criteria, those of overriding concern are the opiates, alcohol, and the sedatives, particularly barbiturates, all of which cause both physical and psychological symptoms of dependence. Other drugs of significance are stimulants such as cocaine and the amphetamines, the hallucinogens, of which mescaline, and lysergic acid diethylamide (LSD) are examples, and cannabis. Most of these drugs do not induce the symptoms of physical dependence associated with abrupt discontinuance, and it is their psychological effects which are the main driving forces behind their continued use. Glue sniffing and the inhalation of volatile solvents by children are probably increased by publicity. None of these substances can be regarded as addictive; apart from the risk of liver damage from the solvents, the chief danger is from asphyxia, should the user place the glue in a plastic bag and pull it over his head. Glue sniffing is a form of behaviour which usually ceases with adolescence—and possibly with legal access to alcoholic drinks.

Although government concern centres principally on the illegal use of heroin, the number of known 'addicts' is relatively small in comparison with the very large number of people who have become dependent on alcohol. Precise figures are impossible to obtain but, as the purchase of alcoholic drinks has increased considerably over the past few decades, so has the number of alcoholics. A well-known formula has related the estimated number of alcoholics in a community to the annual consumption of liquor calculated as pure ethanol per head of population. In Great Britain the overall consumption of alcohol between 1950 and 1976 increased by 87 per cent, and it was estimated that in 1979 there were at least 300,000 alcoholics in the country. Whereas in the past alcoholism and excessive drinking were mainly male attributes, over the past few decades there has been a sharp increase in the number of women damaged by intemperance, a phenomenon which is probably related to the ease of purchase of liquor from supermarkets and other retail outlets, and of its concealment.

The problem of addiction to alcohol is not peculiar to the twentieth century. The Romans passed laws to control drunken charioteers and Victorian philanthropy was well acquainted with the evils of drink. Now as then, excessive drinking results in medical and social damage. Research in Great Britain and Australia has shown that 15–20 per cent of hospital beds are occupied by patients suffering from diseases or injuries directly or indirectly brought about by excessive indulgence in alcohol. As its consumption has increased, so have deaths from cirrhosis of the liver and the other diseases it causes, while psychiatric hospitals are familiar with the acute and chronic psychoses due to it. The social damage is not always recognized or acknowledged. In Great Britain, Australia, and the USA, for example, some 50 per cent of deaths and injuries from car crashes and 20–40 per cent of other accidental deaths such as falls, drowning, and incineration can be attributed to the effects of alcohol. It is impossible to obtain accurate figures on the role of alcohol in occupational accidents but there is a striking correlation between the numbers of patients admitted to hospital with alcoholism and those of patients undergoing treatment for injuries sustained at work. The contribution of alcohol to antisocial behaviour is well known: violence in the streets, at football matches, and in the home; the battering of wives and of babies are all familiar examples of the phenomenon. Criminal behaviour such as rape and homicide can often be attributed to intoxication of the aggressor and, in some cases, of the victim as well. Yet in the West it continues to be a widely advertised drug; from it in 1983–4 the British government reaped tax of £3,900 million. As to nicotine, in recent years much publicity has been given to the contribution of tobacco to diseases of the heart and lungs to whose aetiology heavy smoking is an important contributor. Following the introduction of tobacco into England in 1565, James I wrote his trenchant 'Counterblaste to Tobacco' (1604). Wiser than some other rulers, however, he did not attempt to ban its use but placed a tax on it; and governments ever since have found it a singularly lucrative source of revenue.

The reputation of heroin with its addictive properties may mislead some people into thinking that other drugs are relatively trouble-free. But in the case of sedative drugs, the widespread use of barbiturates—predominantly by middle-aged women—in the 1960s was an epidemic which caused considerable ill health and an increase in the rates of suicide and attempted suicide. For therapeutic use they have been largely superseded by the safer benzodiazepines (Valium, Mogadon, etc.—see PSYCHOPHARMACOLOGY), though these are not so free from addictive potential as was believed initially. Sudden cessation of their regular use by an individual accustomed to them can cause a drug-withdrawal syndrome with both physical and psychological symptoms (Ashton, 1984). While their popularity for the control of anxiety, insomnia, and a variety of psychosomatic symptoms is testified to by Tyrer's estimate (1980) that some 40 billion doses were being consumed each day throughout the world, the publicity given to benzodiazepine dependence in recent years has probably influenced doctors towards greater caution in prescribing them for long periods of time. The greater the dose and duration of consumption, the greater is the risk of dependence developing.

Cannabis (also known as marijuana, pot, and hashish) grows wild as hemp in many parts of the world. It was used medicinally in China as long ago as 2737 BC, Herodotus (c.484–425 BC) mentions its being inhaled by Scythians as part of a funeral ritual, and the physician *Galen says that it was customary to give hemp to guests at feasts to promote hilarity and happiness. In recent times every kind of evil has been attributed to smokers of marijuana (see Schofield, 1971), but the evidence for these baneful effects is far from satisfactory and there are singularly few dangers to health that can be attributed to cannabis alone—though anyone driving while affected by cannabis is at risk, and even more so if alcohol has also been consumed. Few addicts confine their intake to a single substance, and interactions are often more hazardous than the effects of single substances; even so, the cultivation and possession of hemp products are generally prohibited by law. Whether such laws should continue has become a matter for continued debate.

The control of drug trafficking and misuse is based on the United Nations Single Convention on Narcotic Drugs (1961) to which most countries are signatories. This instrument wholly restricts the use of a wide range of substances and requires governments to enforce by punishment its regulations on the cultivation, manufacture, and sale of the drugs listed. Unfortunately, total prohibition of the recreational use of drugs which users are determined to obtain appears to be a singularly unsuccessful policy, as the USA discovered when alcoholic drinks were forbidden for nearly fourteen years from 1919. Attempts by governments to prevent their citizens from smoking tobacco have been equally futile: suppliers were liable to decapitation in ancient China; smokers were tortured to death or exiled to Siberia in Tsarist Russia, and had molten lead poured down their throats in Persia; and the popes from time to time threatened excommunication. Similarly, with suppliers and users of opiates and cannabis, the draconian laws of some countries seem not to inhibit those who are prepared to risk apprehension.

In the United Kingdom great emphasis is placed on the control of opiates. In many cities heroin addicts can be treated in special centres, where the main task of the therapist is to wean the addict off the heroin by reducing his daily intake or else to substitute a long-acting opiate, such as methadone, that will block the action of heroin if this continues to be used. In addition, much attention is paid to the addict's life circumstances, with counselling offered by social workers, psychologists, and other members of the centre's staff. Whereas withdrawal of the drug is comparatively easy, the task of ensuring continued abstinence is decidedly difficult, and relapses are commonplace. It is questionable whether young addicts 'mature out' of dependence on reaching an age even of 30–35, yet it is possible that a change in circumstances coupled with a desire to be free from the constant need for opiates and money for their purchase may persuade a sufferer to find other satisfactions in life.

The treatment of alcoholism is scarcely easier, largely because of the ready availability of alcoholic drink: a person persuaded to give up the drink habit in the clinic may suffer immediate relapse on returning to former surroundings. Yet there is evidence to show that some alcoholics can abstain sufficiently to permit a return to 'normal social drinking', an elastic-sided term that depends on the attitudes of a society to drinking behaviour.

F. A. W.

Ashton, H. (1984). Benzodiazepine withdrawal; an unfinished story. *British Medical Journal*, **1**, 1135–40.

Davies, D. L. (1962). Normal drinking in recovered alcohol addicts. *Quarterly Journal of Studies of Alcohol*, **23**, 94–104.

Schofield, M. (1971). *The Strange Case of Pot*. Harmondsworth.

Tyrer, P. (1980). Dependence on benzodiazepines. *British Journal of Psychiatry*, **137**, 576–7.

**ADLER,** ALFRED (1870–1937). Adler, the founder of the School of Individual Psychology, was born in Vienna, and qualified in medicine in 1895. He spent his early years in medical practice, and became increasingly interested in the environmental and psychological aspects of physical disorders. In 1902, Sigmund *Freud invited Adler and three other colleagues to discuss the psychology of the neuroses. The group was later to become the Vienna Psychoanalytic Society, with Adler as a president and co-editor of its journal. During this period he developed the theory of organ inferiority and compensation, based on his observation of the effects of different environments on the outcome of developmentally retarded organs. The purpose of compensation, either organic or psychological, was seen to make up a deficiency by increasing development or function. Compensation, which could be favourable or unfavourable, might, for example, in good enough circumstances bring about normal speech in cases of retarded speech development; while over-compensation in particular cases might lead a stutterer like Demosthenes to brilliant oratory. The theory led to the development of Adler's view that feelings of inferiority, determined by genetic, organic, or situational factors, were of fundamental importance in provoking the small, weak, and dependent child to conceive of weakness as analogous to both inferiority and femininity. The 'masculine protest' and the striving for power and superiority were thus the predictable outcome of compensation in a male-dominated society.

In 1911 Adler's theoretical divergence from Freud's views was forcefully expressed in his papers given to the Psychoanalytic Congress at Weimar. He disagreed with Freud's view of the sex instinct as the pre-eminent motivational drive and pertinently questioned whether *ego drives did not have a libidinal character: a position which Freud was later to entertain, and one which Carl *Jung regarded as a 'rather poky corner' in Freud's psychology. Adler criticized Freud's concept of repression, replacing it by ego-defensive safeguarding tendencies, and asserted that the neurotic's value system resulted from increased feelings of inferiority and the subsequent unfavourable over-compensation of the masculine protest, of which the *Oedipus complex represented a comparatively insignificant stage. Freud in his reply recognized this presentation as 'ego psychology deepened by knowledge of the unconscious', but saw it as an impediment to his development of an instinct and impulse psychology. Only one helmsman was required, and Adler left to form a society with the rebuking title of 'The Society of Free Analytic Research', which was, within the year, significantly renamed 'The Society of Individual Psychology'.

In 1911 Adler was profoundly influenced by Vaihinger's concept of 'fictions', i.e. mental constructs or early conceptions of what might now be called working models. This led him, in his first and essentially most significant book, *The Neurotic Character* (1912), to insist that human character and actions must be explained teleologically; separate goals coming under the dominance of, and oriented towards, the final purpose. This guiding fiction or purpose, developed by the age of five years, was to move feelings of inferiority to those of superiority—under the direction of the individual's unconscious but uniquely created self ideal—as a constellation of wishful thoughts and imaginings of being and becoming strong and powerful; or if over-compensation was present, in fantasies of god-like immutable supremacy. 'Counter-fiction forces', Adler's name for the correcting factors of social and ethical demand on the self ideal, led to mental health if mutual compatibility with the self ideal was achieved. However, devaluation of corrective factors (later seen to be the patient's overt or covert mode of dealing with the therapist), when combined with a high level of unfavourable over-compensation, led to the development of the more extreme personality traits and psychological disorders.

A major period of expansion in the influence of Individual Psychology took place between 1920 and 1935. Adler, whose work had been restricted during his service as a physician in the Austrian army in the First World War, was to extend and consolidate both his theory and his practice. In 1927 he established twenty-two child guidance clinics in Austria, a number which increased to thirty before they were closed down in 1933. He became a regular visitor to, and frequent lecturer in, the United States, where, as in Europe, Individual Psychology Societies increased in number, activities, and influence.

Freud was correct in thinking that Adlerian doctrines would 'make a great impression'. Adler's understandable, rational, and optimistic approach to interpersonal and social problems contrasted favourably with Freud's psychobiological, more mechanistic, pessimistic concepts, and with the more mystical and esoteric ingredients of Jung's theory. Later developments of Adler's theory of personality included his concept of the 'style of life', which comprised not only the person's 'fictive' goal but his plans and schemes to achieve it, including self-evaluation. He came to regard the origin of a neurotic disposition or style of life as the result of the overburdening of the child with physical disorders and illness; pampering (his wishes being treated as laws); neglect (not knowing what love and co-operation can be); marital disharmony, and certain dispositions of sibling arrangements. Mental disorders of every sort were conceived as having a common cause, constructed by individuals who determine themselves by the meaning they give to situations.

Adler's therapeutic method avoided, as he stated, 'tedious excursions into the mysterious regions of the psyche'. It was sensibly concerned with the prevention of adult maladjustment by the early correction of the mistakes of the child, a task which he attempted to accomplish through the training of teachers. It was their duty to see that children were not discouraged at school but were put in a position, by being given tasks which they could accomplish, to gain faith in themselves. His own therapy, based on his understanding of the symptoms, problems, and the specific life-style of the patient, insisted on explanations to the patient of the predictable effects of his life-style, and an encouragement and strengthening of his social interest, which was Adler's criterion of mental health. This was done in a relationship in which blame was excluded, and resistance (the depreciation tendency) reduced by repeatedly drawing the patient's attention to the similarity of all his behaviour, and disarming him by refusing to adopt a superior role or engage in a fight. Devices included what are now called paradoxical injunctions and the use of humorous models and historical instances. *Transference was recognized but avoided by teaching the patient to take full responsibility for his conduct. Aggression was recognized behind the patient's attempts to devalue the therapist, and blame others before himself. Narcissism resulted from the exclusion of obviously given social relationships or from not having found them. Symptoms were seen as attempts to safeguard self-esteem and the current life-style.

In 1935 Adler was appointed professor in medical psychology at the Long Island College of Medicine, and died in Aberdeen two years later, on the last day of a course of lectures given at the university. The influence of the School of Individual Psychology receded after his death. Many of his ideas, however, while rarely attributed to him, became common currency in the so-called neo-Freudian group of Sullivan, Horney, and Fromm, and are clearly recognizable in contemporary cognitive, problem-solving, and existential therapies. (See FREUDIANISM: LATER DEVELOPMENTS.)

Adler's writings are intuitively penetrating and frequently inspirational, but are at times confusing and lacking in objective rigour and refinement. It is a matter of regret that he took insufficient time to argue his ideas more closely and present them as a fully coherent alternative to those of Freud and Jung, although the Ansbachers' work (1956) has helped to correct this. It leaves him open to the criticism that while helping to lay the foundations of contemporary ego and social psychology his theories over-simplified the inherent complexity of their subject.                                    B. L.

Adler, A. (1935). The structure of neurosis. *International Journal of Industrial Psychology*, **3-12**, 303, 304.

Adler, A. (1929). *Individual Psychology* (rev. edn). London.

Ansbacher, H. L. (1985). The Significance of Alfred Adler for the Concept of Narcissism. *American Journal of Psychiatry*, **142:2**, 203–6.

Ansbacher, H. L. and Ansbacher, R. R. (1956). *The Individual Psychology of Alfred Adler*. New York.

Bottome, P. (1939). *Alfred Adler: Apostle of Freedom*. London.

Freud, S. (1957). *On the History of the Psychoanalytic Movement*. Standard edition of *Complete Psychological Works*, **14** (1914–16). London.

Guntrip, H. (1968). *Personality Structure and Human Interaction*. London.

Jung, C. G. (1953). *Two essays on analytical psychology*. Collected Works, vol. 7 (Bollingen series 20), first essay, Ch. 3. New York.

**ADOLESCENCE.** See HUMAN GROWTH; SEXUAL DEVELOPMENT.

**ADRENALINE** (EPINEPHRINE). One of the two main hormones released by the medulla of the adrenal gland, the other being the related noradrenaline. It produces effects similar to the stimulation of the sympathetic nervous system, increasing heart activity and muscular action, generally preparing the body for 'fright, flight or fight', hence the oft-quoted need for sportsmen 'to get their adrenaline going'.

See **NEUROTRANSMITTERS** AND NEURO-MODULATORS.

**ADRIAN,** EDGAR DOUGLAS, 1st Baron Adrian (1889–1977). Adrian was born in London and educated at Westminster School, where he became a King's Scholar at the end of his first term. Like his mentor at Cambridge, Keith Lucas (1879–1916), he at first studied classics but went over to science in his last year. He went up to Cambridge as a scholar of Trinity College, where he read medicine, and became a Fellow in 1913. On the outbreak of war in 1914, he completed his medical studies at St Bartholomew's Hospital, London. After qualifying, he obtained a resident appointment at the National Hospital for Nervous Diseases, Queen Square, London, following which he became Medical Officer at the Connaught Military Hospital at Aldershot. After the war he returned to the Cambridge Physiological Laboratory to continue the work he had started in association with Keith Lucas, who had died as the result of a flying accident in 1916. Keith Lucas's interest had centred on 'all-or-nothing' activity in skeletal muscle and in motor nerves, and there is no doubt that Adrian conceived it to be a pious duty to carry on and complete his work.

In November 1925 he succeeded in recording with Lucas's capillary electrometer the impulse traffic in a single afferent nerve fibre. He wrote of the experiment in this way:

At all events the great simplicity of the discharge from the sensory end organ came as an exciting and welcome surprise. Bitter experience does not encourage physiologists to suppose that their material will give predictable reactions except under the most rigorously controlled conditions, but the stretch receptors in the frog's muscle did not merely give a discharge which could be reproduced many times without variation, there was the added pleasure of finding that the discharge from each unit was a simple series of impulses varying only in frequency in accordance with the strength of the stimulus. It cannot be often that a general principle like this is as plainly revealed in the course of a single experiment.

This experiment finally proved that Lucas and Adrian's conception of the 'all-or-nothing' character of the propagated nervous impulse, based on indirect evidence, was true. The transmission in the nerve fibre occurs according to what today would be called impulse frequency modulation.

Adrian was always hunting big game: 'the unsatisfactory gap between two such events as the sticking of a pin into my finger and the appearance of pain in my consciousness', as he wrote in *Basis of Sensation* (1928). In this book he gives a summary of the experiments on the muscle spindle, on the cutaneous senses (touch, pressure, and pain), and on the optic nerve, which he performed within the course of only two years.

It is amazing to read today how at that early date he had arrived at the following fundamental view on the relation between the sensation and the impulse frequency in sensory nerve fibres:

The simplicity of the relation is at once very natural and very surprising. It means that our mind receives all the information which can be got out of the messages from those receptors which are in touch with it, but it means also that the mental correlate is a very close copy of the physical events in the sensory nerves. The only kind of distortion which takes place in the transference from body to mind (or in the parallelism of the bodily and mental events) is that the sensations rise and fall smoothly, whereas the nervous message consists of a series of discrete impulses with pauses in between. Somewhere on the way between the two there must be a smoothing process which converts the disconnected impulses into a change of much slower period.

Adrian's study of the adaptation in various

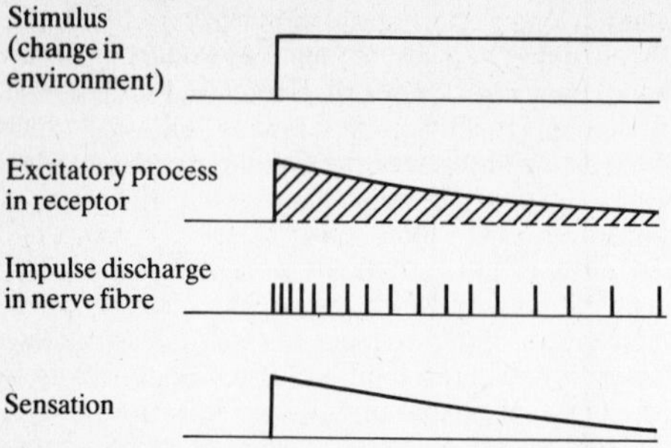

Stimulus
(change in
environment)

Excitatory process
in receptor

Impulse discharge
in nerve fibre

Sensation

**Fig. 1.** Relation between stimulus, sensory message, and sensation.

sensory receptors led him further to the suggestion, seen in Fig. 1, that the excitatory state in the receptor consists of a slow potential, the peak height of which varies with the strength of the stimulus. This receptor potential modulates the impulse frequency transmitted in the nerve fibre via relay stations (synapses) to the cerebral cortex, inducing there the '*evoked potential' which integrates the series of impulses into a 'quasi-steady effect', as Adrian suggested in 1928. 'The diagram (Fig. 1) does not bridge the gap between stimulus and sensation,' he concludes in *Basis of Sensation*, 'but at least it shows that the gap is a little narrower than it was before'. This was typical of his modesty. Recent parallel recordings in humans of the neural and perceptual responses to sensory stimuli have proved that there is a close linear relation between the two events, thus definitely confirming Adrian's pioneer conception of 1928.

From these early recordings followed a quick development. Adrian's simple amplifier and Keith Lucas's capillary electrometer and camera were gradually exchanged for new inventions—Matthews's iron-tongue oscillograph, cathode ray oscillographs, etc.—which enabled Adrian and the hundreds of his followers all over the world to study the inflow and outflow of nerve impulses and to record the bio-electrical events within the whole nervous system. In nearly all these fields Adrian was the leader who opened the field or who made the proper analysis and interpretation of bio-electrical phenomena: for instance, the cochlear microphonics first described by Wever and Bray, and the *electroencephalogram discovered by Hans *Berger in Germany.

Adrian used to work alone and had not more than a dozen co-workers through all his active period in the famous basement room of the Cambridge Physiology Laboratory, which covered nearly sixty years. He was Foulerton Research Professor of the Royal Society from 1929 to 1937, when he succeeded Joseph Barcroft as Professor of Physiology at Cambridge. In 1951 he was appointed Master of Trinity College, and from 1950 to 1955 he was President of the Royal Society. He shared the Nobel Prize in Physiology or Medicine with Sir Charles Scott *Sherrington in 1932, received the Order of Merit in 1942, and delivered the Waynflete Lectures at Magdalen College, Oxford, in 1946. These lectures were published by the Clarendon Press in the following year under the title of *The Physical Background of Perception*.

Although Adrian never thought of himself as a psychologist, he was a founder member of the British Psychological Society and greatly encouraged the growth of experimental psychology in the University of Cambridge; in particular, he held the young Cambridge psychologist, Kenneth *Craik, in high regard and commented on his achievement in the Waynflete Lectures. Adrian was by no means unsympathetic to psychoanalysis in spite of his firm belief that psychology should develop on the model of the biological sciences.

In 1955 he was created Baron Adrian, and in 1967 was elected Chancellor of Cambridge University. He died in his eighty-eighth year, in August 1977. At his funeral, the Master of Selwyn College, Professor Owen Chadwick, said: 'I am not sure what wisdom is, but whatever it is, Adrian had it.'

Y. Z.

O. L. Z.

**AESTHETICS.** Derived from the Greek verb *aesthanesthai* (to perceive), the term 'aesthetic' was until fairly recently used in connection with the philosophy of sensation and *perception. The present use of the label 'aesthetics' to refer to the study of criticism and taste in the arts is due to the German philosopher A. G. Baumgarten, whose *Aesthetica* (1750) dealt with art and the nature of beauty.

The earliest and still probably the most influential discussions of aesthetics, embracing the beautiful and the good, are in *Plato's Socratic dialogues. In the *Hippias Major* a distinction is drawn between what *appears* beautiful and what *is* beautiful. It is almost accepted that the beautiful is whatever is useful or powerful; but Socrates objects that power may be used for evil, which is not beautiful, so power and beauty cannot be the same. One may reply by making a qualification (e.g. power when used for good is beautiful); but this implies that the good and the beautiful are cause and effect and therefore different things. Yet this is absurd, given the ancient and long accepted identification of the beautiful and the good. It is then suggested that the beautiful is a particular species of the agreeable or pleasurable—comprising all things that give pleasure through the senses of sight and hearing. Socrates questions, though, why these pleasures should be so special compared with other pleasures, and, finding no answer, he rejects this account.

In the *Republic* Plato reveals his more metaphysical thinking, as he describes the beautiful as seen as approximating to the ideal forms of the timeless perfect reality of the universe hidden from mortal view. For Plato, the world as perceived is a rough and imperfect model of the hidden ideal world of the gods, as fully described in the early part of the *Timaeus*. In the *Republic*, Plato describes how works of art, and especially paintings, are at a still further remove from the ideal reality than are the objects of sense—which are but semblances of his perfect universe from which somehow spring truth and beauty. Thus:

... you may look at a bed or any other object from straight in front or slantwise or at any angle. Is there then any difference in the bed itself, or does it merely look different?

It only looks different.

Well, that is the point. Does painting aim at reproducing any actual object as it is, or the appearance of it as it looks? In other words, is it a representation of the truth or of a semblance?

Of a semblance [i.e. of the sensed object world].

The art of representation, then, is a long way from reality; and apparently the reason why there is nothing it cannot reproduce is that it grasps only a small part of any object, and that only an image. (*Republic*, Book X, 598)

Plato goes on to deny that artists or poets convey reliable truth, as they have neither knowledge nor correct belief, and he argues (*Republic*, Book X, 602C–605C) that the errors of the artist, at this third remove from reality, are somewhat similar to perceptual errors caused by optical illusions that distance the perceiver from reality.

Only the intellect of philosophers can, for Plato, correct the errors of art and poetry, and the errors of perception. Here geometry is especially important, for the diagrams of geometry most nearly represent the mathematically elegant and unchanging underlying forms, which are true, good, and beautiful. This is still echoed by physicists and mathematicians who seek and find mathematical elegance in nature—for example, the Cambridge mathematician G. H. Hardy in *A Mathematician's Apology* (1941): 'Beauty is the first test; there is no permanent place in the world for ugly mathematics.'

Plato's account of aesthetics has had the most profound effects on art and architecture, and perhaps on music. The close association between the beautiful and the morally good, together with his rejection of action and change in the ideal world, promoted distrust and even distaste for the living body and its normal activities, which is a basis of puritanism.

A worldly kind of Platonism was developed by the English painter Sir Joshua Reynolds (1723–92), who held that beauty is given by the central idea, or by representative examples of classes of things, including faces and the human figure, while the deformed is what is uncommon. Thus beauty is above singular forms, local customs, particularities, and details of every kind. It was objected to this idea that in fact there are many different particular forms and examples of beauty in each species, including man. Reynolds replied that individuals can represent subclasses, which can have distinct forms of beauty, and that 'perfect beauty in any species must combine all the characters which are beautiful in that species'. He thus

tried to bring Plato's ideal forms down to earth.

A theory entirely different from Plato's—based firmly on our bodily characteristics and sensations rather than on hidden ideal forms of the structure of the universe or the averages of classes—is the *empathy theory. An early exponent was the artist William Hogarth (1697–1764), who in his *Analysis of Beauty* (1753) suggests that twisted columns are elegant (he prefers waving lines because they are more varied) but they displease when they are required to bear a great weight. The notion is that we identify ourselves with the columns: when thin they look inadequate, as we, if thin, would be too weak to support a great weight; and when too thick they look clumsy, as we feel clumsy when too large for delicate work. This notion is no doubt related directly to the muscle sense of required effort. A golfer driving a ball high and long identifies himself with its flight by an empathy perhaps not so different from the power of art to take us out of this world.

The philosophers of mind of the eighteenth and nineteenth centuries, holding associationist theories, tended to believe that the beautiful is not intrinsic in the nature of things, or related to empathy, or to the muscle sense; but that it is given by associations with objects or concepts, such as whiteness associated with purity, or the grandeur of mountains with their creation by the superhuman power of gods or the magnificent forces of nature. On this account, what is associated determines what is seen as beautiful. So, there is a related fear that if belief, for example, in gods is abandoned the world will lose its beauty, and be drab and meaningless. No doubt scientific understanding imparts new beauties to the world; but this is surely no reason for it to destroy our appreciation of art, though it changes associations and the meaning of things so that we develop new appreciations.

Certain proportions have been regarded as intrinsically beautiful—that is, apart from associations with objects or concepts. This is especially so of the Golden Mean or Golden Section, the name given to a division of a line or figure in which the ratio of the smaller section to the larger section is the same as the ratio of the larger section to the whole. The notion can be traced back to Plato's obsession with the regular solids: cube, tetrahedron, octahedron, icosahedron, and their supposed association with the four elements. It is the root of much misty mysticism. There is no clear experimental evidence that the Golden Section is an aesthetically unique or specially preferred proportion; and it is suggestive that it is rarely found in the proportions of artists' pictures, or frames. Aesthetic proportions are often supposed to be based on the human form, as in the *Divina proportione* of Luca Pacioli (c.1445–c.1514), who was a Franciscan, a celebrated mathematician, and a friend of *Leonardo and Alberti. Pacioli tries to relate Euclidean geometry to Christianity, and describes the sacred ratio as 'occult and secret'— the three-in-one proportion of the Holy Trinity.

There are several biologically based theories of aesthetics, with various emphases on innate properties of mind (perhaps derived from ancient experience) and associations with things and situations that give individual pleasure in life or are important for survival. A subtle notion is that repetitions and symmetries, which are characteristics of all decoration, are appealing because we have had to search out repetitions and symmetries in nature in order to predict, control, and survive by intelligence. The Austrian physicist Ernst *Mach points out the biological importance of discovering order, in a lecture 'On symmetry' (reprinted in his *Popular Scientific Lectures*, 1894). This general view is developed in detail by Sir Ernst Gombrich (1979).

In *Art and Illusion* (1960), Gombrich relates processes of perception and representative art. He is, however, concerned here not so much with theories of beauty as with issues of the cultural basis of the visual arts. He takes 'illusion' to mean the techniques and aims of the artist in representing reality rather than the sense of misleading error that the word usually suggests. (See ILLUSIONS.)

Is beauty objective, or is it in the eye of the beholder? The notion that the universe is beautiful apart from man, and so objectively beautiful as well as good, was an essential of Platonism. But how can beauty be objective? Agreement of aesthetic practice and judgement between different societies and over long intervals of time may be taken as evidence of some kind of objectivity; but it must be remembered that all human environments, and the human form itself, have much in common in all societies throughout history, so commonality of experience might be responsible for similarities of art forms. Also, there was a surprising amount of trade (by the Beaker people, for instance) with dissemination of artefacts over Europe and Asia even in neolithic times. This, indeed, works against C. G. *Jung's argument (*Psychology and Alchemy*, 1944; *Man and his Symbols*, 1964) that the spontaneous emergence of 'archetypal' forms is evidence for the existence of innate symbols universally accepted as beautiful and especially significant, although not representational.

When Jung was writing, the extent of prehistoric and ancient trade routes was not appreciated. In addition, there is, perhaps, only a limited number of simple symmetrical shapes to choose from. What seems at least as remarkable as the frequent occurrence of certain formal designs is the local individuality and gradual changes of aesthetically accepted forms in particular communities, making it possible to date pottery and other artefacts with astonishing accuracy. Why should the craftsmen of a community or region accept current aesthetic standards or conventions? Why is art and design not a free-for-all—the individual expressing himself as he wishes? It has been suggested (Gregory, 1981) that there is a technological need for agreement over non-functional features of artefacts, if they are to be made co-operatively without endless arguments and disagreements that cannot be resolved or decided on functional grounds. Thus, the slope of a roof is, within limits, determined by the available building materials, and by the climate (for example, roofs for heavy snow are steep so that it slides off); but the proportion, if not the size, of windows is largely arbitrary. There are many features of boats, tools, pots, and other useful artefacts that may be varied over wide limits with no loss of function, but these have fixed conventional forms in given societies. Could it be that social leaders and artists set forms where discussion leads merely to argumentative waste of time and effort? Could this be so important that the aesthetic sense has developed over perhaps several million years as man has learned to make and use tools, and undertake effective co-operative projects? Could aesthetics be a by-product of tool using? This seems a far cry from the beauty of pictures and music; but possibly the roots of style and fashion lie in ancient technology rather than in pictorial and decorative art. From this start, it may have grown to evoke almost the whole range of human experience, and at the same time serve to comment and to judge, and to lift us beyond Nature while revealing our own natures: such is the power of art.                                R. L. G.

Gombrich, E. H. (1960). *Art and Illusion*. London.
Gombrich, E. H. (1979). *The Sense of Order: A Study in the Psychology of Decorative Art*. Oxford.
Gregory, R. L. (1981). *Mind in Science*. London.
Mach, E. (1894). *Popular Scientific Lectures* (trans. T. J. McCormack). Chicago.
Plato (1941). *The Republic* (trans. F. M. Cornford). Oxford.

**AESTHETICS: SOME PSYCHOLOGICAL APPROACHES.** There are five main ways in which psychological approaches are made to visual *aesthetics. First, there is the use of special experimental methods of dealing with judgements about art and aesthetic feelings and attitudes. Next there is the application of existing psychological facts and theories—for instance, as formulated in the psychology of perception—to illuminate problems of art and aesthetics. Thirdly, there is the study of cross-cultural and racial differences and similarities in aesthetic judgements and preferences. Fourthly, there is the study of the influences on the development of artistic styles and cultural changes in art exerted by the interaction of social groups. And fifthly, there is the approach to aesthetics and the understanding of art through the study of the lives of artists, and any influences which are due to personality qualities and psychiatric factors. These different approaches have been reviewed by Pickford (1972, 1976). The many aspects of psychology and the arts are discussed in O'Hare (1981). There has been an almost equally varied and extensive development in the psychology of musical aesthetics—as seen, for example, in the writings of Francès (1973) and Imberty (1976).

G. T. *Fechner (*Vorschule der Aesthetik*, 1876) is generally regarded as the founder of experimental aesthetics, and he established the first method of approach mentioned above. He put forward a number of principles on which aesthetics could be approached as an experimental science 'from below', in contrast to the philosophical approaches 'from above'. He was a major contributor to the development of psychophysical methods in experimental psychology, and he argued that such methods, especially the method of paired comparisons, could be used to measure preferences for colours, colour combinations, figures, shapes, proportions, and actual works of visual art or musical composition. The essential foundations of aesthetics could thereby be established on a factual basis. He cast a wide net, with five main and seven subordinate principles (Pickford, 1972, p. 18), and was not as restrictive as is often supposed.

For about fifty years after Fechner's work only a small number of researches based on it were published, but by the 1930s it had begun to become popular among experimental psychologists, and the study of aesthetic judgements and preferences was introduced into laboratory courses on experimental psychology. Since then experimental aesthetics, although not always tied strictly to Fechner's concepts, has expanded rapidly. Now it is a major branch of experimental psychology, applying itself not only to the visual arts but also to auditory and musical problems, and using factor analysis, the analysis of variance, the semantic differential and other statistical techniques, and *information theory (Moles, 1966).

With regard to the second method of approach mentioned at the start, it is clear that a very large part of visual art depends on (i) the representation of three-dimensional scenes and objects, viewed in perspective, upon two-dimensional surfaces; and (ii) the construction of solid shapes, in sculpture or architecture, in such a way that they create the best aesthetic impression when seen from one or even from many points of view. The representation of three-dimensional scenes and objects on flat surfaces has presented complex and interesting problems for artists, and, in turn, for psychologists in understanding and explaining how they worked. After the accurate handling of the geometry of perspective became important in Renaissance art, these problems came to be of outstanding interest (see Osborne, 1970).

Apparent depth perception in flat pictures is essentially monocular, and viewing is assumed to be from a particular point. Viewing flat pictures with two eyes, and from all sorts of positions and distances, tends to be a disadvantage. All distances or positions except one are unrelated to the perspective construction of the picture, and two eyes commit us to two viewing points, which, because the picture is flat, cannot contribute to stereoscopic vision. Monocular depth perception depends on shadows, the overlapping of distant by near objects, decrease in precision of outline as distance increases, changes of colour, usually towards less saturation and more blue-grey or purplish hues in the distance, the recession of parallel lines towards vanishing points, and on the automatic variation in focusing of the eye in spite of the picture being flat. When two eyes are used there is also a tendency to variation of convergence when looking at near or distant objects in a flat picture.

The branch of psychology which has given most illumination to aesthetics is *Gestalt psychology. Its phenomenological principles are almost a practical guide for the artist and the viewer. The first of its four basic principles is that of 'figure and ground', according to which every form or object perceived is experienced as a figure standing out against a ground or background. The second principle is that of 'differentiation' or 'segregation', by which presentations tend to organize themselves into perceptual structures. The third is that of 'closure', by which incomplete or partly occluded figures or objects tend to be perceived or experienced as wholes. (Thus a face partly occluded by shadow is seen as a full face, as every artist knows.) And the fourth principle is that of the 'good Gestalt', according to which a strongly emphasized or more complete or adequate pattern or configuration will take precedence over weaker or less adequate patterns. These principles operate phenomenologically even though the physiological theory of 'isomorphism', that the excitations in the brain's visual area are the same as those in outward experience, cannot be supported. Indeed few people would suspect that it could be supported, or that it would clarify perceptual theory even if it were supported, by experimentally established fact. After all, even if a solid stimulus object when perceived were known to be represented in the brain by a solid pattern of neurological excitations, we should be no nearer to understanding how such a solid neurological pattern would give rise to the perception of the stimulus object as a three-dimensional solid. The gap between neurology and experience cannot be bridged so easily.

Turning to the third psychological principle or approach, which deals with cross-cultural and allied matters, there have been numerous experimental researches on colour preferences, preferences for figures, shapes, and complete works of art such as pictures, sculptures including African masks, and musical works. The central aim of these researches has been to test the hypothesis that there are cultural or racial differences in aesthetic preferences. In the field of colour preferences, Eysenck (1941) showed that in sixteen studies of white people's colour choices and ten of choices by non-whites, there was a surprising degree of conformity. The average order for six saturated colours among the whites was blue first, then red, green, violet, yellow, and finally orange. The order for non-whites differed only in that yellow and orange changed places. Child and Siroto (1965), for instance, showed that, when

American art experts' judgements of BaKwele ceremonial masks were compared with choices by BaKwele judges, the least degree of agreement was found with tribesmen, most agreement with those who actually carved the masks, and an intermediate degree of agreement with the ceremonial leaders who used the masks. Similar results were found in other experiments, and it seems that, when competent judges of art are used, there is more cross-cultural agreement than is often supposed. Differences of material, style, subject-matter, or intention of the works of art do not necessarily imply basic differences of aesthetic evaluation (Pickford, 1972, 1976). A significant contribution to cross-cultural studies has been made by Segall (1976). (See also PERCEPTION: CULTURAL DIFFERENCES.)

The fourth approach of psychology to aesthetics is based on study of the interactions of groups and of individuals with groups in the history of art. F. C. *Bartlett's interesting and stimulating book, *Psychology and Primitive Culture* (1923), was based largely on the study of folk-tales and their changes and vicissitudes under varying cultural conditions. Sayce followed this with a study of primitive arts and crafts (1933), and Pickford attempted to apply a similar approach to movements in the history of painting (1943). Very interesting studies have been made by Brothwell (1976).

The fifth approach has been biographical and in the study of the relation of personality factors and differences to aesthetic judgements and preferences. Burt (1939) showed a relation between *extraversion/introversion on the one hand, and instability/stability of personality on the other, in aesthetic preferences for pictures. Unstable extraverts tended to prefer romantic art, while stable extraverts preferred realistic art; unstable introverts tended to prefer impressionistic whereas stable introverts preferred classical art. Eysenck (1940) showed a connection between introversion and liking for classical art, and between extraversion and liking for modern and colourful art. Many other researches have been carried out, and some of them are summarized by Pickford (1972).

The relations between various mental or psychiatric disturbances and aesthetic preferences have been studied experimentally, as by Katz (1931), Warner (1949), and Robertson (1952). Blue was the most preferred colour among mental hospital patients, as among normal people, but in one study male patients put green second while females put red in that position. Manic-depressives liked red, orange, and yellow more than did schizophrenics, who preferred green. Another study showed that anxiety neurotics preferred green to yellow, and also liked lighter colours. Male patients preferred cool hues more than did females. Robertson's study of paintings made by patients showed that red was more used by male than by female schizophrenics. It was also found that schizophrenics tended to be less aroused by

colours than were psychopaths, depressives, and psychoneurotics, and that the difference probably lay in a diminished reactivity to colour in the more seriously disturbed patients.

In recent years (1968, 1976), D. E. Berlyne with his concepts of 'aesthetic behaviour' and 'exploratory behaviour' has exercised great influence over psychological approaches to aesthetics, and his work has stimulated many important and interesting researches. His untimely death in 1976, while he was President of the International Association for Empirical Aesthetics, was a severe blow to all persons working in this field.    R. W. P.

Bartlett, F. C. (1923). *Psychology and Primitive Culture*. Cambridge.

Berlyne, D. E. (1968). Aesthetic behaviour and exploratory behaviour. In Aler, J. (ed.), *Proceedings of the Fifth International Congress of Aesthetics*, pp. 865–8. Amsterdam.

Berlyne, D. E. (1976). The new experimental aesthetics and the problem of classifying works of art. *Scientific Aesthetics*, 1, 85–106.

Brothwell, D. R. (1976). Visual art, evolution and environment. In Brothwell, D. R. (ed.), *Beyond Aesthetics*, ch. 3. London.

Burt, C. (1939). Factorial analysis of emotional traits, II. *Character and Personality*, 7, 285–99.

Child, I. L. and Siroto, L. (1965). BaKwele and American esthetic evaluations compared. *Ethnology*, 4, 349–60.

Eysenck, H. J. (1940). The general factor in aesthetic judgements. *British Journal of Psychology*, 31, 94–102.

Eysenck, H. J. (1941). A critical and experimental study of colour preference. *American Journal of Psychology*, 54, 385–94.

Francès, R. (1958). *La perception de la musique*. Paris.

Imberty, M. (1976). *Signification and Meaning in Music*. Montreal.

Katz, S. E. (1931). Colour preference in the insane. *Journal of Abnormal and Social Psychology*, 26, 203–11.

Moles, A. (1966). *Information Theory and Esthetic Perception*. Chicago.

O'Hare, D. (1981). *Psychology and the Arts*. Brighton, Sussex.

Osborne, H. (ed.) (1970). *The Oxford Companion to Art*. Oxford.

Pickford, R. W. (1943). The psychology of cultural change in painting. *British Journal of Psychology*, Monograph Supplement 26. London.

Pickford, R. W. (1972). *Psychology and Visual Aesthetics*. London.

Pickford, R. W. (1976). Psychology, culture and visual art. In Brothwell, D. R. (ed.), *Beyond Aesthetics*, ch. 10. London.

Robertson, J. D. S. (1952). The use of colour in paintings by psychotics. *Mental Science*, 98, 174–84.

Sayce, R. N. (1933). *Primitive Arts and Crafts*. London.

Segall, M. H. (1976). Visual art: some perspectives from cross-cultural psychology. In Brothwell, D. R. (ed.), *Beyond Aesthetics*, ch. 6. London.

Warner, S. J. (1949). The color preferences of psychiatric groups. *Psychological Monographs*, 301.

**AFFECT.** A term used in psychology for a feeling or emotion, particularly one leading to action.

**AFFERENT.** A word pertaining to the sensory neural inputs to the nervous system—the nerves and their signals (action potentials) running from the senses to the brain. (Efferent nerves and signals control the muscles.) See NERVOUS SYSTEM.

**AFTER-EFFECT.** See CONTINGENT PERCEPTUAL AFTER-EFFECT.

**AFTER-IMAGE.** An image seen immediately after the intense stimulation of the eye by light has ceased. For about a second, the after-image is 'positive', and then it turns to 'negative', often with fleeting colours. The positive phase is due to after-discharge of the receptors of the retina (see COLOUR VISION: EYE MECHANISMS); the negative phase is caused by loss of sensitivity of the receptors as a result of bleaching of the photo-pigments by the intense light. After-images can be annoying, but they are usually ignored or suppressed. They are technically useful for visual experiments as they are precisely fixed on the retina. They are seen to move with the eyes during normal eye movement. See also CONTINGENT PERCEPTUAL AFTER-EFFECTS; VISUAL ADAPTATION.

**AGEING.** Performance at many types of task studied in the laboratory rises to a peak somewhere between the late teens and late thirties, and then gradually declines into old age. It used to be assumed that the declines were due either to age effects in sense organs, muscles, and joints, or to older people being uninterested in, or out of practice at, the kinds of tasks set by laboratory experiments. Research since the 1940s has shown that, while peripheral changes may be important in later old age, central brain functions account for the main trends of performance in middle and early old age. The trends are by no means all adverse: certain kinds of 'mental agility', such as indicated by scores on typical *intelligence tests, decline from the early twenties—it has been estimated that by the age of sixty they have returned to their level at the age of ten—but the decline is offset, at least partly and sometimes more than fully, by increased knowledge gained in the course of experience. The age of peak performance is thus usually in the thirties, forties, or fifties rather than in the twenties, and varies with the balance between demands for 'mental agility' and for knowledge: for example, it comes relatively early among mathematicians, and relatively late among historians and philosophers.

It must be emphasized that these statements are of *average* trends and that some individuals achieve their peak performance much earlier or later than the majority. Indeed, the extent and rate of changes differ widely between individuals, so that performances tend to become more variable with age—some people in their seventies or eighties perform some tasks in a manner similar to that of people half a century younger, whereas others show profound differences. It is thus all too easy for ideas about old age to be coloured, for better or worse, by a few striking examples who are not typical of their contemporaries.

Psychological studies of ageing made during the last thirty years or so may be broadly divided into three areas.

**Speed of performance.** Perhaps the most characteristic age change is that performance becomes slower. The extent to which it does so is not, however, uniform for all tasks. For simple, aimed movements the change is comparatively slight—a loss of less than 10 per cent between the twenties and seventies. Slowing in sensory motor tasks is mainly in the making of decisions about what action to take—in other words, in cognitive and intellectual rather than in motor functions. When the relationships between signals for action and the corresponding responses are straightforward, as, for example, when the signals are a row of lights and response is by pressing a button under whichever comes on, the time to react increases typically by about 25 per cent from the twenties to the seventies. When the relationships are more complex, as, for instance, when lights on the right have to be responded to by pressing buttons on the left, and vice versa, increases of 50 per cent or more have been found between these ages. Slowing with age is also greater in continuous tasks, where each response immediately brings on the signal for the next, than in discontinuous tasks, where responses and ensuing signals are separated by an interval of a second or more. The reason appears to be that older people tend more than younger to have their attention diverted to monitoring the response they have just made, so that they cannot attend immediately to any fresh signal.

Much if not all slowing with age can be explained by the fact that signals from the sense organs to the brain and from one part of the brain to another become weaker, while at the same time random neural activity in the brain tends to increase. The latter blurs the former and leads to errors. The blurring can, however, be at least partly overcome by taking a longer time. This allows data to be accumulated, making the signals stronger and averaging out some of the random activity. As a result, older people, although slower, may be as accurate or more so than younger. With some highly complex tasks, however, such compensation is incomplete, so that the older tend not only to be slower but also to make more errors.

The laboratory findings accord well with studies of real-life situations. In industry, operatives tend to move before retiring age not only from physically strenuous work such as coal-mining, but also from lighter jobs where there is pressure for speed, such as on assembly lines. Industrial accidents sustained by older people tend to involve either being hit by moving objects or tripping and falling—in other words, slowness either in getting out of the way or in recovering balance—whereas younger people's accidents tend to be the result of either rashness or lack of experience. The same is true of road accidents and traffic offences: older people fail to react in time to rapidly changing situations, while younger people take undue risks. The problem of complexity is shown in difficulties often found by older industrial operatives with complex machinery and elaborate working drawings. It is also epitomized in the finding that some can no longer read a map while travelling south without turning it upside-down.

**Memory and learning.** A six- or seven-digit number heard once can be recalled immediately about equally well by people of all ages from the twenties to the sixties. With more items than this, older people recall less than younger. The reason appears to be that they have difficulty in transferring material from a limited and ephemeral *short-term memory to a more enduring long-term memory: some of the material is lost, and the traces of what is transferred are weaker. The strength of the traces can be increased by repetition, and with enough additional practice recall by older people can equal that by younger. Once material has been learnt, older people do not forget more rapidly than younger. Well-learnt facts, familiar events, and thoroughly practised motor skills such as riding a bicycle or driving a car are, therefore, retained well in old age even if there is difficulty in learning new facts and acquiring new skills.

Failure to register material in long-term memory probably accounts for many difficulties in *problem-solving and other tasks in which data have to be 'held in mind' while other data are gathered: for example, when multiplying, say, 57 by 38, the product $57 \times 3 \times 10$ has to be held while $57 \times 8$ is obtained. Calculating the second product will destroy the short-term memory of the first, so that it will be lost unless it has been transferred to long-term memory.

Probably the most successful method of training older people in industry has been the 'discovery method' whereby the trainee is given just enough information to enable him to discover accurately for himself how to perform his task. The active decisions required have the effect of facilitating registration in long-term memory, and the fact that the trainee can learn at his own pace means that he has time to sort out difficulties. It is fair to suggest that insufficient time devoted to mastering new facts and ideas is a reason why thinking often becomes hidebound in later middle age among those hard pressed by day-to-day activities and responsibilities, and that time set aside to acquaint themselves with new developments would be well repaid.

**Personality.** This often appears to change with age, yet scores on personality tests show small, if any, trends. The apparent changes seem instead to represent reactions to altered circumstances in old age which are not measured by the usual tests. For example, on the one hand retirement brings increased leisure and opportunities, while, on the other, changing capacities may restrict interests and activities and in extreme cases lead to dependency. The ways in which individuals adjust

to these circumstances vary greatly. Some welcome the new opportunities and accept the restrictions. Others find little use for leisure, resent restrictions, and become self-centred. This last reaction is well illustrated in many who complain of being lonely. Older people are understandably lonely for a time following *bereavement: however, complaint typically comes from those who are surrounded by relatives, neighbours, and others, but whose self-centredness makes normal social intercourse unrewarding. In all cases the manner of adjustment seems to have little relation to economic or material circumstances or, within limits, to health: it depends upon personality traits which have been present throughout life but which may not have had the opportunity to show earlier because of the exigencies of work or bringing up a family.

The changes in personality can perhaps be summed up by saying that old age is a revealing time, when the best and worst in us stand out in bold relief. As a recipe for contentment, we may cite a remark by Maurice Chevalier: 'Growing old is inevitable for all of us. The clever thing is to accept it and always plan your next move well in advance.'

See also AGEING: SENSORY AND PERCEPTUAL CHANGES.                                         A. T. W.

Birren, J. E. and Schaie, K. W. (eds.) (1977). *Handbook of the Psychology of Aging*. New York.
Bromley, D. B. (1974). *The Psychology of Human Ageing*, 2nd edn. Harmondsworth.
Charness, N. (ed.) (1985). *Aging and Human Performance*. New York.
Welford, A. T. (1958). *Ageing and Human Skill*. Oxford.

**AGEING: SENSORY AND PERCEPTUAL CHANGES.** Since a person can deal efficiently with his social and physical environment only if his sensory and perceptual processes are not unduly impaired or distorted, changes which might be attributable to the inevitable process of ageing assume considerable importance. In briefly reviewing this topic, two generalizations need to be kept in mind. First, it is not always clear that a given impairment is a natural result of advancing age rather than the result of disease, trauma, or disuse. Secondly, individual differences in general become more pronounced with age, so that some elderly may exceed the norms in a particular function.

Certain reductions in the efficiency of seeing appear to be inevitable with advancing age, although there are, of course, individual differences. Most obvious is the change in ability to focus on nearby objects, and the use of reading spectacles or bifocals is commonplace. To understand the importance of this change, consider the plight of an artisan doing fine work before the advent of spectacles! Fig. 1 shows the approximate distance from the eyes of the limit of clear focus for 'normal' eyes—or eyes corrected to normal by spectacles—as a function of age. Other apparently 'normal' changes are ordinarily not so obvious to the individual. These include a reduction in resting

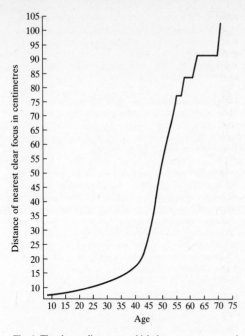

**Fig. 1.** The closest distance at which the average person of a given age can see clearly. There are no significant sex differences.

pupil size, an increase in yellow pigment in the eye media, some reduction in overall acuity, a slight narrowing of the visual field, some loss of colour discrimination, and increased susceptibility to glare. It can readily be appreciated that in our modern society these changes might have serious consequences for the automobile driver or pedestrian. However, tests of visual *efficiency*

show that many of the old surpass many of the young, so that knowing a person's age does not permit us automatically to assume that he is visually inefficient. It is also true that we cannot be certain how much effect training might have on the maintenance of visual skills; nor has our physiological knowledge so far led to any great advance in the treatment of the ageing eye.

Although the changes in seeing are, barring some actual disease process, rather generally regarded as 'normal' effects of age, the case for hearing is not at all decided. Fig. 2 illustrates the results of hearing surveys which find a progressive decline in the ability to hear the higher frequencies ('pitches') of sound. Fortunately, until the impairment involves frequencies below about 1,800 hertz (about three octaves above middle C), ability to comprehend speech, that basic ingredient of interpersonal interaction, is not significantly reduced. Of course we know that exposure to loud sounds will adversely affect the sensitivity of hearing, whether the exposure be in the boiler factory or the rock concert hall. The modern environment is rather noisy, and most if not all hearing loss is traumatically caused. In fact one investigator has found that persons living in a quiet, remote environment showed little or no loss. In any event, there are most certainly pathological causes of hearing loss or deafness, some of which (those involving conduction of sound to the inner ear) can be helped by 'hearing aids'. Also, lip-reading and other skills can partially compensate for any kind of loss, provided that the perceptual inefficiency is not of cerebral origin.

When we consider 'bodily sensibility'—the skin senses, position sense, and internal sensations—the picture becomes very blurred by the effects of vascular and nervous disorders. Reported changes in some persons in sensitivity to touch and tem-

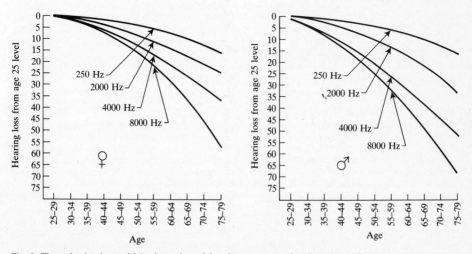

**Fig. 2.** The reduction in sensitivity for male and female persons as a function of age. Curves are shown for four sound frequencies.

perature are rendered ambiguous by these possible disorders. Even so, there does seem, with age, to be a reduction in sensitivity to vibration and to pain, and some loss of sensitivity to the detection of fine movements of various joints, although the practical implications of these results have not been fully explored. Indeed, here lies a rich field for research.

Since dietary problems can be important in the elderly, changes in tasting and smelling that might affect the choice or enjoyment of food are of potential importance. It appears that loss of sensitivity does occur, although, especially in the case of smelling, pathological processes as simple as the common cold may also affect sensitivity. In recognition of this decline, especially of smell sensitivity, flavour enhancers have been tried, with some degree of success. Also of considerable interest is the danger that loss of smell sensitivity may cause in the detection of warning agents such as the odorous agents added to domestic gas. Although some persons at any age are not sensitive to at least some of these agents, it has been shown that the elderly are particularly at risk.

It should be noted that demonstrably pathological states, such as senile *dementia, which affect sensory and perceptual processes, have not been considered. Although such conditions are relatively rare, they may affect 10 per cent of persons aged over 65, with the frequency increasing to 22 per cent among those aged 80 and over. Nevertheless, to reiterate a previously made point, it is entirely possible that many sensory losses now considered to be 'normal' decline may be found to result from exogenous influences, or to loss of perceptual skill through disuse.

See also AGEING.                                    F. N. J.

Corso, J. L. (1981). *Aging Sensory Systems and Perception*. New York.
Ordy, J. M. and Brizzee, K. R. (eds.) (1979). *Sensory Systems in the Elderly*, vol. 10, Aging Series. New York.
Sekuler, R., Kline, D., and Dismukes, K. (eds.) (1982). *Aging and Human Visual Function*. New York.
Thomas, A. J. (1984). *Acquired Hearing Loss*. London.
Van Toller, C., Dodd, G. H., and Billing, A. (1985). *Ageing and the Sense of Smell*. Springfield, Illinois.
Verillo, R. T. and Verillo, V. (1985). Sensory and Perceptual Performance. In Charness, N. (ed.), *Aging and Human Performance*. New York.

**AGGRESSIVE BEHAVIOUR.** Behaviour directed towards causing physical injury to another individual must clearly be labelled as aggressive; this is the hard core of aggression. Behaviour directed towards causing psychological harm is usually also included in the definition, and fantasies involving harm to others are closely related. The question of intent is crucial: accidental injury is not usually considered aggressive.

Since attack on another individual may involve risk of injury for the attacker, it is often associated with elements of self-protective and withdrawal responses. This is especially apparent in the case of animal threat postures, which often consist of a mosaic of elements of attack and withdrawal (see FEAR AND COURAGE). For this reason attack, threat, submission, and fleeing are often lumped together as 'agonistic' behaviour.

Aggressive behaviour often settles status, precedent, or access to some object or space. Some, especially psychiatrists, choose to define aggressive behaviour so widely that all behaviour that leads or could lead to such results is included. Thus common speech uses such terms as 'aggressive salesmen'; this loose usage makes 'aggressive' synonymous with 'assertive'.

**Heterogeneity of aggression.** However defined, the category of aggressive behaviour conceals considerable internal heterogeneity, and numerous attempts have been made to subdivide it. Two examples may be cited.

In studies of children, four categories have been useful (Feshbach, 1964; Manning *et al.*, 1978): (i) Specific or instrumental aggression, concerned with obtaining or retaining particular objects, positions, or access to desirable activities. (ii) Teasing or hostile aggression, directed primarily towards annoying or injuring another individual, without regard to any object or situation. (iii) Games aggression, occurring when playful fighting escalates to the deliberate infliction of injury. (iv) Defensive aggression, provoked by the actions of others.

Turning to adults, Ticklenberg and Ochberg (1981) have classified criminal violence as follows. (i) Instrumental violence: motivated by a conscious desire to eliminate the victim. (ii) Emotional: impulsive, performed in extreme anger or fear. (iii) Felonious: committed in the course of another crime. (iv) Bizarre: insane and severely psychopathic crimes. (v) Dyssocial: violent acts that gain approbation from the reference group and are regarded by them as correct responses to the situation.

Such distinctions have been useful in a number of ways: for instance, the several types of childhood aggression have different developmental courses, and differ in their prognostic value for adult or adolescent behaviour problems. However, difficulties arise, partly because the different categories are not always clearly distinguishable. This results in part from their motivational complexity.

**Motivational complexity.** Confronted with the astonishing range and diversity of aggressive (and courtship) behaviour in many non-human species, ethologists came to realize that the relations between the categories could be understood in terms of hypothesized underlying variables— aggression in terms of a motivation specific to the context (e.g. over food, or territory; see Moyer, 1968) and conflicting tendencies to attack and flee from the rival. These hypothesized motivations could be assessed by a number of methods, including analysis of the precise nature of the agonistic behaviour shown and the behaviour that immediately followed it. The diversity of the behaviour could be understood in terms of variations in the absolute and relative levels of the several motivations (Baerends, 1975). In a similar way it seems likely that the several types of human aggression can be understood in terms of different combinations of hypothesized underlying variables. Obvious candidates are 'specific acquisitiveness', or the motivation to acquire specific objects or situations; 'assertiveness', or the motivation to elevate one's position or push oneself forwards; and 'fear' (see below); as well as the propensity to behave aggressively (i.e. to harm others) itself (Hinde, 1985; Attili and Hinde, 1986).

**Proximate factors predisposing to aggression.** Whereas some writers have regarded aggression as dependent solely on emotional factors, others have regarded it as spontaneous and inevitably finding expression. The issue could be of importance, since it affects the solutions that are sought for excessive social violence. However, neither view is adequate. It is well established that, in many species, the tendency to show aggressive behaviour varies with hormonal condition, and considerable knowledge about the endocrine and neural mechanisms involved is now available (Svare, 1983): thus it is now realized that aggressive behaviour is not solely elicited. Neither is it solely internally generated: the catharsis view, proposing that aggression depends on spontaneously generated energy which must be dissipated in action, rests on an outdated model of motivation and has received no empirical support (Berkowitz, 1962). However, behaviour that serves to lower arousal level, specific acquisitiveness, or assertiveness may well also lower aggressive propensities.

Rejecting either one or the other of these views, research workers attempted to identify prime causes of aggression. Since by definition aggressive behaviour is directed towards other individuals an obvious candidate was the proximity of another member of the species. In animals the eliciting stimuli often proved to be quite simple—the red breast of a territory-holding robin is enough to elicit attack from an intruder (Lack, 1939). Of course situational determinants are also crucial: a male great tit will attack intruders if he is holding a territory, but flocks with other individuals if he is not.

Others emphasized frustration as a potent cause of aggression in man (Dollard *et al.*, 1939). Frustration has been demonstrated in animal experiments: a pigeon, trained to peck a key for food reinforcement, will attack another pigeon confined nearby during experimental extinction (Azrin *et al.*, 1966). One problem with this hypothesis is that practically any incident of aggression can be ascribed to frustration of acquisitiveness or assertiveness so the thesis is incontrovertible (Bandura, 1973), and another lies in identifying the precise nature of the factors that operate in a frustrating situation (Berkowitz, 1978).

Aggression can also be caused by pain or fear: for instance, rats confined together over a grid floor are likely to fight if the current is turned on. However, there is some doubt as to the similarity between natural aggression and that induced in these (often unnecessarily cruel) experiments (Ulrich, 1966).

So, rejecting any prime factor view, current research attempts to identify the spectrum of factors, internal and external to the individual, past and contemporaneous, that affect the incidence of aggression. These include constitutional factors and the current state of the individual (e.g. sex, genetic factors, hormones both prenatally and contemporaneously, temperament, and neural factors), current influences (e.g. frustration, peer example, the availability of weapons), and experiential factors. The latter include aspects of the family of origin (psychosocial disadvantage, unstable parental marriage, punitive and rejecting parents); details of family interaction patterns; and vicarious experience of aggression by others, especially if rewarded, including experience of violence on television (see, for example, reviews by Shaffer *et al.*, 1980).

It is clear that aggressive behaviour (like any other) has multiple causes, and that studies purporting to identify single, all-important causes are bound to be simplistic. A recent study found that the conditions related to the use by parents of harsh punishment were, in order of importance, perception of the child as difficult to handle, proneness to anger on the part of the parent, rigid parental power assertion, and intra-familial problems and conflicts. Perceived harsh parental punishment was associated with either conduct disorder or anxiety and helplessness (Engfer and Schneewind, 1982). Although this study was cross-sectional in design, it illustrates the manner in which aggressive behaviour can be seen only as one constituent of a complex causal nexus (see also Bandura, 1979).

**Intergroup conflict.** Most of the above concerns conflict between individuals. Different issues arise in conflict between groups. The most important are the degree of the actor's felt membership of his own group; the extent to which members of the other group are perceived (a) as individuals or as indistinguishable units and (b) as fellow human beings or as strangers, foreigners or even sub-human; and the extent to which reinforcement for the actor's behaviour comes from the approval of his own group or its effect on members of the other (see Tajfel, 1979, for example).

**Ultimate causes.** In addition to assessing what factors exacerbate or ameliorate an individual's propensity to aggression, we may ask why it is these factors that operate, rather than any others. Biologists seek answers in evolutionary terms, the hypothesis being that individuals have been shaped by natural selection to display or refrain from aggression in accordance with how it affects their own survival and reproduction and/or that of their close relatives. The data come mostly from animals, but there is growing evidence that the principles may be applicable to humans.

In the first place, in the course of evolution threat postures have become elaborated or 'ritualized' to make them effective as signals. At the same time, selection has modified the responsiveness of other individuals to the signals. The selection pressures on actor and reactor are of course distinct, as their interests are not the same. Threat can be seen as a process of negotiation with the rival about what to do next (Hinde, 1985). (See also NEGOTIATING.)

Now let us suppose that all individuals in a population used conventional threat signals but retreated from a context if there was any real danger. A new mutant who fought vigorously in every encounter would be clearly at an advantage, because he or she would be likely to win every encounter. However, if the mutant reproduced itself, vicious fighters would often meet vicious fighters. In such encounters someone would be liable to get hurt; if the gains of winning were less than the costs of losing (in terms of inclusive reproductive success), it might be better not to be a vicious fighter. Maynard Smith (1976) has shown that, given certain assumptions, a stable situation would arise when there were particular proportions of conventional and vicious fighters, or when each individual adopted each strategy for a particular proportion of the time. This is an example of an 'evolutionary stable state'.

In practice the advantages accruing to an individual from being a vicious fighter depend both on the benefits of winning encounters (and thus on the scarcity of the resources over which the encounters take place) and on the costs of engaging in them—benefits and costs being reckoned ultimately in evolutionary terms. The benefits will vary between individuals and between classes of individuals. One issue here concerns the differences between the sexes. Human sex differences, interpreted in the light of comparative data on other species, suggest that in our environment of evolutionary adaptedness males have competed for females (see Short, 1979). Selection would then have enhanced aggressiveness in males more than in females. (This in itself says nothing about the way in which it would have come about: for instance, selection could operate to make males inherently more aggressive than females, or to make parents encourage aggressiveness in boys more than in girls, or both, or in some other manner.)

Considerations of costs and benefits (in either evolutionary or more immediate terms) should also warn us against expecting any simple relations between exposure to aggression in development, either at home or in the peer group, and aggressiveness in adulthood, for the costs and benefits of aggressiveness vary with the probability of meeting other aggressive individuals and with the scarcity of resources. In a population containing few vicious fighters and plentiful resources, the advantages to individuals of co-operating in group living may detract from the advantages of being an egotistical vicious fighter. In a population containing a moderate number of vicious fighters and in which resources are scarce, it may be necessary to be a vicious fighter or succumb. But if nearly everyone is a vicious fighter, so that the costs of encounters are certain to be great, it may be better to contract out and seek another means of access to the resources. These speculations about crude caricatures of 'co-operators' and 'vicious fighters' must not of course be taken too seriously, but they are useful in sounding a warning against expectations of simple monotonic relations between childhood experiences and later characteristics.

R. A. H.

Attili, G. and Hinde, R. A. (1986). Categories of aggression and their motivational heterogeneity. *Ethology and Sociobiology*, **7**, 17–27.

Azrin, N. H., Hutchinson, R. R., and Hake, D. F. (1966). Extinction induced aggression. *Journal of Experimental Animal Behaviour*, **9**, 191–204.

Baerends, G. P. (1975). An evaluation of the conflict hypothesis as an explanatory principle for the evolution of displays. In Baerends, G. P., Beer, C., and Manning, A. (eds.), *Essays on Function and Evolution in Behaviour*. Oxford.

Bandura, A. (1973). *Aggression, a social learning analysis*. Englewood Cliffs, New Jersey.

Bandura, A. (1979). Psychological mechanism of aggression. In von Cranach, M., Foppa, K., Lepenies, W., and Ploog, D. (eds.), *Human Ethology*. Cambridge.

Berkowitz, L. (1962). *Aggression*. New York.

Berkowitz, L. (1978). Whatever happened to the frustration–aggression hypothesis? *American Behavioral Scientist*, **21**, 611–70.

Dollard, J., Doob, L. W., Miller, N. E., Mowrer, O. H., and Sears, R. R. (1939). *Frustration and Aggression*. New Haven, Connecticut.

Engfer, A. and Schneewind, K. A. (1982). Causes and consequences of harsh parental punishment. *Child Abuse and Neglect*, **6**, 129–39.

Feshbach, S. (1964). The function of aggression and the regulation of aggressive drive. *Psychological Review*, **71**, 257–62.

Hinde, R. A. (1985). Categories of behaviour and the ontogeny of aggression. *Aggressive Behavior*, **11**, 333–5.

Lack, D. (1939). The behaviour of the robin, I and II. *Proceedings of the Zoological Society of London*, A, 109, 169–78.

Manning, M., Heron, J., and Marshall, T. (1978). Styles of hostility and social interactions at nursery, at school and at home. In Hersov, L. A. and Berger, M. (eds.), *Aggression and Anti-social Behaviour in Childhood and Adolescence*. London.

Maynard Smith, J. (1976). Evolution and the theory of games. *American Scientist*, **64**, 41–5.

Moyer, K. E. (1968). Kinds of aggression and their physiological basis. *Communications in Behavioural Biology*, **2**, 65–87.

Shaffer, D., Meyer-Bahlburg, H. F. L., and Stokman, C. L. J. (1980). The development of aggression. In Rutter, M. (ed.), *Developmental Psychiatry*. London.

Short, R. (1979). Sexual selection and its component parts, somatic and genital selection, as illustrated by

ALGORITHM 19

man and the great apes. *Advances in the Study of Behaviour*, **9**, 131–58.

Svare, B. B. (1983). *Hormones and Aggressive Behavior*. New York: Plenum.

Tajfel, H. (1979). Human intergroup conflict: useful and less useful forms of analysis. In von Cranach, M., Foppa, K., Lepenies, W., and Ploog, D. (eds.), *Human Ethology*. Cambridge.

Ticklenberg, J. R. and Ochberg, F. M. (1981). Patterns of adolescent violence. In Hamburg, D. A. and Trudeau, M. B. (eds.), *Biobehavioral Aspects of Aggression*. New York.

Ulrich, R. E. (1966). Pain as a cause of aggression. *American Zoologist*, **6**, 643–62.

**AGNOSIA.** Originally Sigmund *Freud used the term agnosia to mean loss of perception. It is now applied to disorders whereby the patient cannot interpret sensory information correctly even though the sense organs and the nerves leading to the brain are operating normally. Thus in auditory agnosia, the patient can hear but he cannot interpret sounds (including speech).

**AGORAPHOBIA.** See PHOBIAS.

**AGRAPHIA.** The loss of the ability to write, which may or may not be connected with alexia, the loss of ability to comprehend the written or printed word. It is thought to be caused by a lesion in the cerebral cortex or by more generalized cerebral dysfunction.

**AKINESIA.** The severe reduction or absence of spontaneous movement, characteristic of the later stages of *Parkinsonism.

**ALCOHOLISM.** See ADDICTION.

**ALEXIA** (WORD-BLINDNESS). Inability to read the printed or written word, usually caused by damage of cerebral hemisphere. See DYSLEXIA.

**AL-FARABI** (Muhammad ibn-Muhammad ibn-Tarkhan ibn-Uzlagh Abu-Nasr al-Farabi, or Alpharabius) (870–950). Born in Farab, Sughd, now in Uzbekistan, he was the first great Turkic exponent of *Islamic philosophy. He studied at Baghdad and taught as a *Sufi at Aleppo, now in Syria. He states that he read *Aristotle's *De Anima* two hundred times; he was certainly so well versed in it that he gained the Arabic title of *Al-Mu'allim al-Thani*—the Second Teacher (after Aristotle). The author of over a hundred volumes, he lived simply, taking employment as a night-watchman so that he could work by the light of the lantern provided.

He harmonized Greek philosophy with Islamic thinking, thus continuing the work of *Al-Kindi and preceding *Avicenna; his considerations covered logic and rhetoric, geometry, psychology, and politics. Baron Carra de Vaux and others state that the logic of Farabi had a permanent effect upon the thought of the Latin schoolmen.

Farabi believed that God exists as the only ultimate reality and unity, intermediary agencies successively producing the world as we know it through conventional avenues of perception. Human society he regards as emerging through two impulses: a social contract not unlike that later proposed by *Rousseau, and an urge prefiguring the *Nietzschean will to power. Society, for Farabi, realizes its perfection (the Ideal City) through a ruler who has become a divine agent, or alternatively by the administration of a group of wise men, each specializing in one subject. The capacity to be detached from objects and concerns enables a human being to go beyond familiar dimensions, transcending the ignorance produced by regarding secondary phenomena, such as time and space, as primary.　　　　　I. S.

Hammond, R. (1947). *The Philosophy of Alfarabi and its Influence on Medieval Thought*. New York.

Sheikh, M. S. (1982). *Islamic Philosophy*. London.

**AL-GHAZZALI** (Imam Abu-Hamid ibn-Muhammad Al-Ghazzali, or Algazel) (1058–1111), born at Tus, Persia. Originally a theologian and scholastic philosopher, professor at the Nizamiyyah College in Baghdad, Ghazzali is known as *Hujjat al-Islam* (Proof of Islam) and is one of its greatest thinkers. He decided that ultimate truth could not be attained by intellectual means, and became a *Sufi. He influenced all subsequent Sufic thought as well as many Western philosophers and theologians. His *Ihya Ulum al-Din* (Revival of the Sciences of Religion) is a classic which is widely believed to have had a great (some believe determining) effect upon Europe, through Latin and Hebrew translations, especially in his method of criticizing hypotheses and assumptions. Jehuda Halevi (in his *Khazari*) follows the Ghazzalian method as found in the remarkable *Incoherence of the Philosophers*, and the first Hebrew translations of the influential *Maqasid al-Falasifah* (Aims of the Philosophers) were made by Isaac Albalagh, *c.*1292, and by Judah ben Solomon Nathan, *c.*1340. The Dominican Raymund Martin (d. 1285) used Ghazzali's arguments in his *Explanatio symboli apostolorum* and *pugio fidei*, continually quoting the devout Islamic thinker in support of Christian ideas. St Thomas *Aquinas (1225–74) also cites Ghazzali. Blaise *Pascal, writing on belief in God, echoes Ghazzali's *Ihya*, *Kimia*, and other writings, while Pascal's theory of knowledge (in *Pensées sur la religion*) closely follows Ghazzali's book *Al-Munqidh*. Ghazzali's work is as widely studied today as it ever was.　　　　　I. S.

Kamali, S. A. (trans.) (1963). *Tahafat Al-Falasifah*. Lahore.

Shah, I. (1964). *The Sufis*. London.

Sheikh, M. S. (1982). *Islamic Philosophy*. London.

Watt, W. M. (1953). *The Faith and Practice of Al-Ghazzali*. London.

**ALGORITHM.** A predetermined procedure or ordered sequence of instructions for carrying out an operation in a finite number of steps. Computer programming involves designing such procedures since computing is precisely the automation and execution of algorithms. Moving the decimal point for multiplication or division by multiples of 10 is a commonly used algorithm. The Euclidean algorithm is a method for finding the greatest common divisor of two numbers by continued subtraction.

The origin of the term is from the name of an Arab mathematician, al-Kuwārizmi (c.830), who wrote an extensive account of the Hindu system of numerals and numeration from which our current system evolved. Writing numbers and performing calculations using Hindu numbers became known through his account as 'algorismi', and competitions were held between the abacists, who favoured the abacus for calculations, and the algorists, who preferred pencil-and-paper calculations. To use an algorithm, perhaps as a rule of thumb, need not require an understanding of why it works, and algorithmic thinking can be a term used derogatively. Yet making some mental operations a matter of mechanical routine can free the conscious attention for other more demanding matters.

**AL-KINDI** (Abu-Yusuf Ya'qub ibn-Ishaq) (803–73). Born at Al-Kufah, now in Iraq, of a southern Arabian family, he worked mainly in Baghdad, and was the first Arab philosopher. He attempted to combine the views of *Plato and *Aristotle, and his collation of the *Theologia* ascribed to Aristotle had considerable influence on philosophy and theology in both East and West until the time of St Thomas *Aquinas.

Al-Kindi was a polymath, like almost all of the major Islamic philosophers: an optician, music theorist, pharmacist, and mathematician; he wrote 265 treatises, most of them now lost. He saw the universe as an architectonic whole, not as something to be observed piecemeal to discover causality. He asserted 'one of the most marked features of Islamic thought—the belief that there was only one active intellect for all humanity, and that every human soul was moved and informed by this separated active intellect' (Leff, 1958). More of his work survives in Latin (such as in the translations by Gerard of Cremona) than in Arabic. One of his major scientific contributions was *De Aspectibus*, on the *Optics* of *Euclid, which influenced Roger Bacon. His works show that mensural music was studied in his culture centuries before it appeared in the Latin West.                              I. S.

Abdulwahab Emiri (1976). *The Scientists of Islam*. Baghdad.
Hitti, P. K. (1951). *History of the Arabs*. New York.
Leff, G. (1958). *Medieval Thought*. Harmondsworth.
Sheikh, M. S. (1982). *Islamic Philosophy*. London.

**ALLOTROPY.** Variation of physical properties without change of substance. Thus diamond and graphite are the two allotropes of the element carbon. Both are composed of pure carbon but have different physical forms. In most early philosophy, there was supposed to be underlying substance which maintained the continuity of objects even when they changed. This same idea was often applied to mind—that the mind of an individual is a continuing substance even though, throughout life, the individual changes in his ideas, *emotions, and behaviour. David *Hume took the opposite view, arguing that the self is no more than a 'bundle of sensations'. See also PERSONAL IDENTITY.

**ALZHEIMER'S DISEASE.** See DEMENTIA.

**AMBIGUITIES IN PERCEPTION.** See ILLUSIONS.

**AMNESIA.** The popular conception of amnesia is probably typified by the occasional newspaper report of the appearance of someone who has mysteriously lost his *memory. The person has no idea what his name is, where he comes from, or indeed about any of his past. Such cases usually recover their memory within a day or two, and typically turn out to be people attempting to escape from some socially stressful situation by simply opting out through the mechanism of dissociation. The precise nature of their memory defect is variable and seems to depend very much on their own views about how the human memory system works. In this respect they resemble *hysterical patients suffering from glove anaesthesia, numbness in the hand which extends up to the wrist but not beyond and bears no relationship to the underlying pattern of innervation of the hand, indicating that it is of psychogenic origin rather than based on a physiological defect. The extent to which psychogenic amnesia represents genuine inability to recall, as opposed to conscious refusal to remember, is hard to ascertain. For further details see Pratt (in Whitty and Zangwill, 1977).

The most extensively studied form of amnesia is that resulting from damage to the *limbic system of the brain, typically involving the temporal lobes, hippocampus, and mamillary bodies. Such damage may occur in people suffering from *Korsakoff's syndrome, which results from a prolonged period of drinking too much alcohol and eating too little food, leading to a vitamin deficiency of thiamine (vitamin $B_1$). Such patients often go through a delirious confused state, before stabilizing. They may then show a range of symptoms extending from considerable general intellectual impairment with relatively little memory decrement to occasional cases in which a relatively pure memory defect occurs. A broadly comparable memory defect occasionally occurs following encephalitis, and may also be produced by other kinds of brain damage such as stroke, tumour, or coal gas poisoning. There is some controversy over whether such a wide range of patients have a common memory defect, or whether subtle differences occur but the broad pattern of symptoms is similar.

Such patients have no difficulty in knowing where they grew up or telling you about their job or family background. In the case of relatively pure amnesics at least, their ability to use language is unimpaired, as is their general knowledge of the world. Their *short-term memory also appears to be intact, at least in many cases. Their ability to repeat back a telephone number is just as good as would be the case in a normal person, and if you present them with a list of words, they show the normal tendency for the last few words presented to be well recalled. Their retention of the earlier words in a list is, however, likely to be very poor indeed.

The amnesic defect in the case of these patients appears to be one of episodic memory. They would be quite unable to tell you what they had for breakfast, and would very probably have no idea where they were or how long they had been there. If you had spent the morning testing them, by the afternoon they would probably fail to recognize you, and if asked for items of current information such as the name of the Prime Minister, would be likely to come up with a totally inappropriate response, naming a figure from twenty or thirty years ago. They have great difficulty in learning lists of words, whether you test them by recall or recognition, and have similar problems in remembering non-verbal material such as pictures of faces or objects.

There are, however, aspects of long-term memory which seem to be relatively unimpaired. Amnesic patients can learn motor skills, and one case, a pianist who was taught a tune on one day, had no difficulty in reproducing it on another. But characteristically such patients have no idea how or when they acquired the relevant information. A classic example is that cited by the Swiss psychologist *Claparède, who on one occasion secreted a pin in his hand before shaking hands with an amnesic patient. On a subsequent day when he extended his hand the patient withdrew hers. When asked why, she could give no justification other than the general comment that sometimes things were hidden in people's hands. As one would expect from this demonstration, amnesics appear to be quite capable of classical avoidance *conditioning. They are also quite capable of learning verbal materials under certain conditions. For example, Warrington and Weiskrantz used a learning procedure whereby subjects were presented with a series of words, and recall was tested by presenting the first three letters of each word and requiring the subject to produce the whole word. When tested in this way, amnesics were virtually normal.

What characterizes the long-term learning tasks that amnesics can do? This is still a controversial issue, but broadly speaking the tasks seem to be ones in which the patient simply has to use the information available in his memory store, without needing to worry about how it was acquired. The case where he is cued by being presented with the initial letters may be interpreted as simply a problem-solving task where he must find a word that fits these particular constraints. Having recently been presented with the relevant word will in fact make it more available, but he does not need to know this in order to take advantage of such an effect.

While classic amnesics like those just described are theoretically extremely interesting, patients having such a dense amnesia unaccompanied by more general intellectual deterioration are relatively rare. It is much more common for memory disturbance to stem from the after-effects of a blow on the head, as is often the case in road traffic accidents. Consider, for example, a motorcyclist who is involved in an accident involving a severe head injury. He is likely to lose consciousness for a period which may range from a few seconds to several months; if and when he regains consciousness he is likely to show a range of memory problems. It is usual to distinguish three separate types or aspects of such traumatic amnesia, namely retrograde amnesia, post-traumatic amnesia, and anterograde amnesia.

On recovery there will be evidence of loss of memory extending over the period between the injury and full return of consciousness. Following a head injury there will be a period of confusion characterized by the patient's inability to orient himself in time and place. The duration of post-traumatic amnesia, which will comprise the duration of total and partial loss of consciousness, provides a useful measure of the severity of the patient's injury and so permits some estimate of the extent of probable recovery to be made. On emerging from post-traumatic amnesia the patient is still likely to show considerable retrograde amnesia. This is indicated by an inability to remember events before the accident. In the case of a severe blow the amnesia may extend over a period of several years. Typically this blank period becomes less and less, with earlier memories being recovered first, although the process is far from systematic, with 'islands' of memory cropping up in periods that are otherwise still blank. Typically the retrograde amnesia shrinks up to a point within a few minutes of the accident. These final few moments are seldom ever recovered, possibly because the memory trace was never adequately consolidated. This point was illustrated rather neatly in a study of American football players who had been 'dinged' (concussed) during a game. As they were led off the field they were asked the code name of the play in which they had been engaged when concussed (e.g. 'Thirty-two pop'). Typically they were able to supply this information immediately on leaving the field, but when retested 20 to 30 minutes later they were quite unable to provide it. A subsequent study showed that this was not simply due to normal forgetting, nor to the mnemonic limitations of American football players, but suggests that failure of memory traces to consolidate during the concussed state may be an important factor.

The third memory disturbance associated with head injury concerns difficulty in learning and retaining new information. During the process of recovery from a closed head injury, memory problems are commonly reported, together with difficulties in concentrating and a tendency to become fatigued much more rapidly than was previously the case. While the memory problems of patients with head injuries have been rather less extensively investigated than those of the classic amnesic syndrome, we do know that they show some of the same characteristics. Typically short-term memory is not greatly affected, and if one presents an amnesic head-injured patient with a list of words, he is likely to do reasonably well on the last few presented, but relatively poorly on the earlier items in the list. Although not much work has been done in directly comparing such patients with other types of amnesics, it seems likely that the pattern will be somewhat different, since closed head injury appears to cause neuronal and vascular damage in large areas of the brain as opposed to specific subcortical damage in the classic amnesic syndrome. Furthermore, whereas the classic amnesic patient does not completely recover, head-injured patients typically do improve quite substantially from the time when they emerge from their initial period of post-traumatic amnesia. In many cases they return to performing at what appears to be their level before injury.

Amnesia is an important component in senile and pre-senile *dementia. In both these cases intellectual deterioration probably results from a substantial loss of cortical neurones, and in addition to showing memory problems such patients usually show a more general intellectual deterioration. This in turn increases the memory problem, since they seem unable or unwilling to use effective learning strategies.

We have so far discussed patients who have long-term learning problems but normal short-term memory. However, the reverse has also been reported. Shallice and Warrington (1970) describe a patient who had great difficulty in repeating back sequences of numbers, the longest sequence he could repeat back reliably being two digits. He was, however, quite unimpaired in his long-term memory as measured both by his ability to learn word sequences and by his memory for faces and for the events of everyday life. As is suggested in its entry, short-term memory is almost certainly not a single unitary function, and there is some evidence to suggest that there are other patients who have different defects of the short-term memory system.

Theoretical interpretation of the various ways in which memory can break down obviously depends crucially on one's interpretation of normal memory. As such, amnesia presents a theoretically important though difficult question. We have in recent years made progress in exploring and defining more precisely the amnesic syndrome, but are as yet some way from constructing a completely adequate interpretation at a psychological, neurological, or biochemical level.          A. D. B.

Baddeley, A. D. (1982). Amnesia as a minimal model and an interpretation. In Cermak, L. S. (ed.), *Human Memory and Amnesia*, pp. 305–36. Hillsdale, New Jersey.

Shallice, T. and Warrington, E. K. (1970). Independent functioning of the verbal memory stores: a neuropsychological study. *Quarterly Journal of Experimental Psychology*, **22**, 261–73.

Whitty, C. W. M. and Zangwill, O. L. (eds.) (1977). *Amnesia*. London.

**AMPUTATION, EXPERIENCE OF.** See NOTHINGNESS; SPATIAL CO-ORDINATION OF THE SENSES.

**ANAESTHESIA** may be described as a reversible loss of consciousness produced by a drug, from which arousal does not take place even with painful stimuli such as setting a fracture or surgical operation. In this latter respect it differs fom *sleep or the change in consciousness following sensory deprivation; and it is this that made it so revolutionary a discovery, opening the gateway to modern surgery and safer childbirth. The name is not quite exact, since loss of consciousness is not the same as loss of feeling; and a good anaesthetic in clinical practice should exert other actions, such as some analgesia (to diminish reflex responses to what would be very painful stimuli) and muscular relaxation (to facilitate the surgeon's work). When an anaesthetic such as ether or chloroform is given, there is a characteristic progression of effects, first described by Guedel in 1937: first analgesia, some loss of memory, and perhaps euphoria; then consciousness is lost, but the patient may struggle, breathes irregularly, is sweating and flushed; in the third stage, the patient becomes quieter with regular breathing, but the eyeballs move rhythmically and a good many reflexes are still present. As anaesthesia deepens, and the patient passes through the successive planes of the third stage, various reflexes progressively fall away, the breathing becomes shallower, and eventually death may ensue (the fourth stage). In modern practice anaesthesia is induced with a suitable barbiturate (such as thiopentone) injected intravenously: the patient then passes through the early stages within seconds; once 'under', anaesthesia is usually maintained by some other substance.

How do anaesthetics work? It is paradoxical that more is known at the molecular level than at any other. A remarkable feature is the astonishing range of substances that can produce anaesthesia: in addition to the classical anaesthetics and the barbiturates, nitrogen in the air (if given at high pressure) and many other gases, alcohols, dry cleaning fluids (such as trichloroethene), industrial solvents, and certain steroids can all produce typical anaesthesia. There is no common chemical structure such as would suggest a specific action on some particular part of the brain. Instead, as two pharmacologists, Overton and Meyer, pointed out over eighty years ago, anaesthetics all share the property of dissolving in fat; and it is remarkable that one can predict the potency of an anaesthetic quite accurately by measuring the pressure of a gas or the concentration of a vapour which will produce a given concentration (about 0·05 moles per litre) of the substance concerned in olive oil. Modern work has revealed the significance of this: the cell membrane, which defines the cell's limits, and across which an electric potential is maintained, consists of an ordered array of fatty molecules (mostly phospholipids and cholesterol); the anaesthetic dissolves in it, and slightly expands and disorders the membrane. Since the membrane also carries large protein molecules (enzymes, ion channels, receptors, transport mechanisms) which mediate its 'traffic' with its environment and with other cells, disturbance of their normal function becomes possible. A fascinating aspect is that very high pressures (which compress and reorder the membrane) cause recovery from anaesthesia. Conversely, a suitable amount of an anaesthetic can be used to neutralize the adverse effects of high pressure. The 'high pressure nervous syndrome', which includes tremor, bursts of 'micro-sleep', and convulsions, threatened to limit the depth to which *divers could go; but the addition of nitrogen (using it as a small dose of anaesthetic) to the diver's helium–oxygen mixture has extended that limit.

But if one asks, 'On what synapses, or on what cell groups of the brain, is this molecular action particularly exerted?', no satisfactory answer exists. The simple fact of surgical anaesthesia shows that higher brain functions are particularly sensitive, while respiration and simple reflexes, as well as other bodily processes like the heartbeat, are relatively resistant. Detailed analysis yields a bewildering variety of effects, with actions both pre- and post-synaptically, varying with the synapse and with the anaesthetic. A simple view is that the anaesthetic picks out any delicately poised nervous activity, and that the pattern of anaesthetic activity is simply that of reduced activity in the most vulnerable nervous pathways—particularly complex nervous functions rather than (for example) simple reflex movement. Theories include the idea of a specific effect on the 'ascending reticular activating system', in the absence of whose activity the cerebral cortex is believed to relapse into a sleeping state, or on cortical cells generally. Some recent drugs (such as ketamine), which produce the so-called 'dissociative anaesthesia', may help to throw light on the problem; these differ, both in having a specific chemical structure, and in producing a rather different pattern of anaesthesia.

There is an abundant literature on the effects of anaesthetics on mental function, short of anaesthesia, and Humphry Davy's description (in 1800) of the effect of nitrous oxide (*laughing gas) on himself and his friends (including Southey, Coleridge, Roget, and Wedgwood) reveals the salient features recorded many times subsequently: considerable variation with the individual; excitement; euphoria or sometimes dysphoria; compulsive movements or laughter; 'thrilling' sensations in the limbs; feelings of deep significance; rush of ideas; synaesthesiae; drowsiness; warmth, rapid breathing, palpitations, giddiness; and often a strong desire to repeat the performance. This last characteristic brings the risk of *addiction in its train, particularly for those (such as anaesthetists and nurses) with easy access to the drugs; and it shows itself again in 'glue-sniffing' in children, or with workers using some solvents in industry.

An important feature with all these volatile substances is the speed with which effects are produced by inhalation, by which the vapour passes very quickly into the circulation. More familiar to most people will be the effect of anaesthetics such as alcohol or barbiturates taken orally, with an onset delayed by circulatory absorption; and the fact that by this route some of the more dramatic effects are lacking (although euphoria and the risk of addiction remain) suggests that these effects are largely due to especially rapid access to, and uptake by, particular parts of the brain, producing a selective action which fades as distribution of the drug becomes general. With sustained exposure to any anaesthetic, the adaptation known as 'tolerance' develops, by which an increasing dose is required to produce the effect. 'Cross-tolerance' occurs between different anaesthetics—hence the difficulty often encountered of anaesthetizing an alcoholic! When exposure stops and the drug is withdrawn, characteristic symptoms appear: for example, insomnia after a short course of any sleeping pill, or delirium tremens (d.t.'s) after prolonged high exposure to alcohol, or convulsions after chronic barbiturate use. While some of the adaptive changes may be biochemical, some of them certainly represent a change in nerve cell function, and there are interesting indications that the composition of the cell membrane changes so as to reduce the effect of the anaesthetic.

One would like to think that experience with anaesthetics would deepen our understanding of consciousness, mood, sensation, pain, memory. Yet it is still impossible to move convincingly from the subjective phenomena to physiological understanding. Perhaps it is unreasonable to expect to do so until our knowledge of normal neurophysiology is more satisfactory, or perhaps pharmacology and physiology need to proceed, collaboratively, in parallel. Some areas may be picked out as potentially fruitful.

1. The effect on *sense of time*. There is a puzzle here: nitrous oxide and alcohol appear to reduce 'felt' time compared with 'clock' time, whereas ketamine (like cannabis) prolongs it. With the latter drugs, one can readily suggest, as William *James suggested, that 'disinhibition' in the brain, allowing a greater than normal sensory input, could give rise to an experience of more numerous mental impressions than usual per unit of 'clock' time, and hence a greater 'felt' time. But why should other anaesthetics differ?

2. The effect on *pain sense*. There is some evidence that enkephalins or endorphins may play

a part in analgesia produced by anaesthetics. (See NEUROPEPTIDES.) But there remain remarkable differences between anaesthetics, some with pronounced analgesic action, some potentiating the response to a painful stimulus. Bearing in mind its practical relevance, as well as the recent advances in our knowledge of the neuroanatomy and neurochemistry of the nociceptive pathways, and the successful application of decision theory to the study of pain, a systematic study of the action of a range of anaesthetics on pain discrimination and pain report seems well worth while.

3. The effect on *sensation generally*. An intriguing but neglected observation is that anaesthetics facilitate the generation of impulses in the vagal nerve fibres registering the inflation of the lung, which accounts for the ability of many anaesthetics to produce what is known as 'rapid shallow breathing'. It is an intriguing action, and exerted peripherally on the proprioceptive endings in muscles might account for the 'thrilling' sensation described by Davy. But more generally there might also be an important effect both on the pattern of sensory input to the brain, and on subsequent processing.

4. Effect on *memory*. With the recent advances in our knowledge of registration, consolidation, and retrieval, systematic study of the effect of a range of anaesthetics on memory is overdue, although the problem is complicated by 'state dependence'. An old method of anaesthesia for childbirth, 'twilight sleep', exploited the effect of the drug hyoscine on memory, so that even if pain was felt, it was not remembered. The method has been abandoned because of the effect on the baby, but the approach is still interesting.

5. The concept of *disinhibition* is constantly, and plausibly, invoked to account for phenomena such as the rush of ideas, synaesthesia, and electroencephalographic synchronization. The underlying idea is that the great complexity of mental activity does not merely need some neurones to be active, but also needs others to be actively 'switched off' (inhibited): if the latter process were interfered with (disinhibition), then differential activity and 'gating' of information transfer could become progressively impaired. Simple model systems exist, illustrating how depression of an inhibitory pathway can lead to release phenomena; but no serious attempt has been made to extend the idea to more complex systems. Yet if certain inhibitory mechanisms are particularly vulnerable, it should be possible, by careful choice of systems sharing common elements, to identify them more closely.

6. A tedious but necessary development is that of knowledge about the kinetics of *anaesthetic distribution* in the brain. Some knowledge exists of the rise and fall of the concentration of an anaesthetic during and after an exposure, for samples of brain containing thousands or millions of neurones. But this is merely a gross average, telling us nothing of local concentration in synaptic detail. Equilibrium with an anaesthetic is virtually never reached in clinical practice, and rarely in experimental work, so that (as mentioned earlier) there is ample scope for differential effects arising, not from the properties of the drug itself, but from varying access and uptake. For instance, evidence is accumulating that if any part of the brain becomes particularly active it consumes more energy, with a corresponding increase in blood-flow; that would at once open the way to differential access by an anaesthetic.

7. Finally one must recall that, despite all the advances in neuroanatomy, it is only a tiny minority of nervous pathways that can be precisely and completely described in anatomical and neurochemical detail, with the specific neurones and their connections specified. But some beautiful techniques now exist for mapping out these pathways, for recording the activity of single or groups of neurones, and for neurochemical analysis (see NEUROANATOMICAL TECHNIQUES): the new methods of anaesthesia that a deeper understanding will provide are not far away.                    W. D. M. P.

Miller, K. W. (1986). General Anaesthetics. In Feldman, S. A., Scurr, C. F., and Paton, W. D. M. (eds.), *Mechanisms of Action of Drugs in Anaesthetic Practice*. London.

Paton, W. D. M. (1984). How Far Do We Understand the Mechanism of Anaesthesia? *European Journal of Anaesthesiology*, **1**, 93–103.

**ANAGLYPH.** A picture that can be used to create a stereoscopic image. It uses two colours (in practice red and green, or sometimes red and blue) with corresponding colour filters, so that a picture with different colours can be presented to each eye. This method is used for presenting stereoscopic pictures in printed books, instead of using separate pictures that require a stereoscope to present one picture to each eye. See STEREOSCOPIC VISION.

**ANALOGUE.** See DIGITAL.

**ANALYTIC PROPOSITION.** The idea behind the notion of an analytic proposition is that at least some of our concepts can be represented as complexes of simpler concepts and that a proposition may state nothing more than what an analysis would reveal, namely a relation between a simple concept and a complex concept of which it forms a part. Thus *Kant, taking judgements expressed by propositions to have the form '*A* is *B*' defined an analytic judgement as one where 'the predicate *B* belongs to the subject *A* as something which is (covertly) contained in the concept *A*'. In more linguistic terms, if the criteria for calling something 'a body' include the criterion, being extended, then the latter is 'contained in' the former and the proposition 'a body is extended' is analytic. An analytic statement thus cannot be denied without contradiction and is logically necessary (*possibility). That this necessity can be seen simply from a grasp of the concepts or words involved leads to speaking of analytic propositions as true in virtue of the meanings of words.

Gottlob Frege freed the notion of analytic proposition from the assumption that the logical structure of all concepts is based upon conjunction of criteria, by taking as analytic any proposition whose proof rested only on general logical laws and definitions. This also made clear that whether a proposition is regarded as analytic is relative to what are recognized as legitimate means of definition and what general logical laws are accepted as valid.

A proposition that is not analytic is synthetic. The arguments of W. V. Quine showed that the analytic/synthetic distinction is not as sharp as had previously been assumed, but not that the distinction is wholly without foundation.          J. E. T.

Frege, G. (1959). *The Foundations of Arithmetic* (trans. J. L. Austin), Section 3. Oxford.
Kant, I. (1929). *The Critique of Pure Reason* (trans. N. Kemp-Smith), Preface and Introduction. London.
Quine, W. V. (1953). *From a Logical Point of View*, ch. II. Harvard.

**ANGELL, JAMES ROWLAND (1869–1949).** An American psychologist, James Angell worked at Harvard with William *James, then at Chicago, where he became a founder of the Chicago 'functionalist' school which stressed the importance of physiological processes (see FUNCTIONALISM). This was a direct development of much of James's thinking, and led to *behaviourism. The founder of behaviourism, J. B. *Watson, was a student of Angell's.

Angell showed that *reaction times have two components—sensory and muscular—and that unpractised subjects have greater individual differences in reaction time than when they are practised. This raises a curious question. Specially trained or skilled subjects give more reliable results—but they are not typical subjects. So, should subjects be given special training, to get more consistent results which look better on paper; or should relatively naïve subjects be used, as they are typical of most people and so represent normality? This is quite a general problem in experimental psychology, even for simple skills or tasks which seem close to basic physiological limits, such as designing and interpreting experiments on reaction time.

Boring, E. G. (1950). *A History of Experimental Psychology*, 2nd edn., ch. 24. New York.

**ANIMAL.** Although in its widest sense the term 'animal', as contrasted with vegetable and mineral, includes mankind, in common usage the term is restricted to 'lower' or non-human animals—the 'brutes' or 'beasts'. For *Descartes (whose *Discourse on Method*, 1637, examines the difference between men and beasts), the crucial point is that animals lack language: their 'utterances' are always elicited by a specific stimulus, and thus can never amount to genuine speech. It follows, on Descartes' view, that animals lack thought, and that their behaviour can be explained on purely mechanical principles—a view which led later Cartesians to the notorious doctrine of the '*bête-machine*' and that animals are merely mechanical automata. In recent times the linguistic theories of Noam Chomsky have reinforced the view that animals lack genuine (i.e. creative, stimulus-free) language; current empirical research, however, suggests that chimpanzees, at least, may have a degree of linguistic competence. Current work in moral philosophy has stressed the fact that animals, though they may lack thought, are at least sentient, and hence are entitled to moral consideration. (See PRIMATE LANGUAGE.)          J. G. C.

Singer, P. (1977). *Animal Liberation*. London.
Singer, P. and Regan, T. (1976). *Animal Rights and Human Obligations*. Englewood Cliffs, New Jersey.

**ANIMAL BEHAVIOUR.** See ETHOLOGY.

**ANIMAL–HUMAN COMPARISONS.** How far can animal data help us understand human behaviour and experience? We may consider the question in two stages. First, do animals resemble humans sufficiently closely for data derived from their study to be relevant? And second, in what ways could animal data be used?

With respect to the question of similarity, the human brain is very like those of the great apes, somewhat similar to those of monkeys, and is built on generally similar lines to those of other mammals. There is also a general structural similarity with the brains of other vertebrates, but very little with the nervous system of invertebrates. On anatomical grounds, therefore, we might expect similarities in behaviour between humans, non-human Primates, and perhaps other mammals, an expectation supported also by palaeontological evidence. (See PRIMATES, EVOLUTION OF THE BRAIN IN.)

The complexity of the behaviour of higher mammals confirms this view. Much of their behaviour can be interpreted only in terms of the trying out of alternative strategies to reach a goal. Problems requiring an animal to respond to the middle of three objects, to the odd one out, or to an abstract number of objects (up to about five), or to form concepts of categories of objects, have been demonstrated many times in laboratory studies of mammals, and also in some birds. Field studies show that chimpanzees not only use but also make tools, and that many Primates have an extraordinarily complex social organization based on elaborate signalling systems. Observation also indicates that chimpanzees have a concept of self and can dissemble and deceive others. Chimpanzees can co-operate in that one can learn to ask another for one out of six possible tools required to obtain food, which is then shared. It has even been claimed that they impute mental states to others. The evidence here is that a chimpanzee, shown pictures of a human actor struggling with a problem, can select from a series of photographs the one portraying the solution.

Although we can have no direct knowledge of animal affective states, there is strong evidence that dogs have pleasant and unpleasant dreams, and it seems likely that the greater the similarity in brain structure, the greater the similarity in affective experience.

The main difference, of course, lies in the complexity of human language. All animals communicate by a repertoire of signals, and chimpanzees can learn to use complex systems of signs or symbols for communicatory purposes. (See PRIMATE LANGUAGE.) However, these fall so far short of human language that the difference is best seen as one of quality rather than quantity. One immediate consequence of this is that anything corresponding to human institutions is virtually non-existent in animals, and cultural differences, though present, are minor. Local traditions can be acquired only through individuals' experience and their observation of the experiences of others, and perhaps to a limited extent by parental training. Lack of linguistic complexity no doubt also restricts animals' abilities to solve problems by the manipulation of symbols, to reflect on the past and future, and so on. In so far as our emotions are culturally influenced, it may limit the range of affective states animals can experience. Finally a human being, and perhaps a higher Primate, can interpret his own behaviour as goal-directed ('I am reading a book') or as impelled ('I fell asleep'), but it may be only a human being who monitors his own monitoring, seeing his behaviour as more or less efficiently goal-directed ('I was trying to read, but fell asleep').

Given, then, that the behaviour of higher mammals, and especially that of higher Primates, resembles that of humans in some respects while differing in others, in what ways can animal data help our understanding of the human case? In practice, there are three main ways of using such data.

First, one can search for an animal model, suitable for investigating the problem in hand. 'Suitable' in this context usually means 'resembling humans' in relevant ways; models are usually evaluated in terms of their similarity to the original. As we have seen, Primates resemble humans in brain structure more closely than do other mammals, and are thus more likely to produce relevant data about behaviour and brain function.

However, the value of models in science lies in part in their differences from the original. Three issues must be considered here. (i) Models are useful because, by virtue of availability or simplicity, they pose questions, suggest relations, or can be manipulated in ways not possible with the original. When a model becomes an exact replica, it loses its *raison d'être*. (ii) If a model is very like the original, it is easy for an investigator to assume that all the properties of the model exist also in the original, and to confuse the two in arguments in which the model is employed. (iii) The third issue is of crucial importance where animals are confined or experimented upon. The more closely related the experimental animal to humans, the more the infliction of suffering requires justification in terms of potential benefit to animals or humans.

For these reasons, the most useful animal models are not always those most similar to humans. Much of our knowledge of brain function is based on experiments with rodents and carnivores, for instance. For some purposes, relative simplicity is an advantage. Furthermore, for many problems resemblance to humans in a particular feature is more important than overall close evolutionary relatedness. For example, the sexual behaviour of chimpanzees is adapted to quite different social conditions from that of humans, and would provide a poor model. And some anthropologists have argued that the savannah-living baboon may provide a better model for the social structure of early man than the more closely related but forest-dwelling chimpanzee.

While animal models have been of great value in studies of brain function, their use can involve great dangers. The very act of comparing humans with animals may lead us to neglect the complexity of the human case. For instance, studies of animals have facilitated isolation of many factors conducive to aggression, such as proximity, male sex hormone, and 'frustration'. But animal studies alone will never permit us fully to understand human aggression in all its deviousness and complexity. A second danger arises from the fact that interactional influences between causal factors are ubiquitous. For instance, the effect of stimulation in infancy on the behaviour of adult rats in an open field depends on the sort of cages they are kept in both before and after weaning. Thus the finding that a given treatment does or does not produce a given effect in an animal may not be valid even for that species in all circumstances, let alone for man. A third danger, related to the last, arises from the multiplicity of animal species; so much depends on selecting the right models. For instance, the effects of temporarily separating mother and infant monkey vary between species, and thus extrapolations to humans might easily depend on which species was used. The problem is exacerbated by the diversity of human cultures; factors important in one may not be so in another.

A second way of using animal data can sometimes avoid these dangers. If we compare a range of animal species, and abstract principles, the validity of those principles to the human case can then be evaluated. For instance, in mammals the protein content of maternal milk is inversely related to the frequency of suckling; human breast milk composition suggests that new-born babies should be fed more often than the four-hour schedule often recommended in hospitals. Again, experiments with a number of species suggest that the long-term effects of separating mother and infant monkey depend primarily on the degree to which the mother–infant relationship was disturbed; this principle seems directly applicable to humans, although the treatments most disruptive of the mother–infant relationship differ between species and between human cultures. (See ATTACHMENT.) And, on a broader horizon, cross-phyletic comparisons suggest trends in brain evolution, extrapolations of which to humans can guide research endeavours.

A third but often neglected type of argument involves focusing not on the similarities but on the differences between animals and humans. For example, human social structure is usually described in terms of language-bound institutions—marriage, the monarchy, and so on. Yet monkeys and many other mammals have societies of extraordinary complexity. If complex social structure can exist without language, perhaps we should look also for non-language-based determinants in humans. Again, if mother–infant separation induces depression in infant monkeys, that depression must be explicable in terms of concepts applicable to the monkey level of cognitive functioning, and comparable depression in humans *may need* no additional ones. And, as a third type of example, the relative simplicity of the animal case can provide scope for the sharpening up of concepts which can then be applied with greater advantage to the human case.

In conclusion, animal models can provide data relevant to human behaviour and experience, but their use involves dangers of which the experimenter must be aware. Abstracting principles from comparative data, and assessing their relevance to humans, is often a safer course. And the differences between animals and humans can also be usefully exploited.                          R. A. H.

Gardner, B. T. and Gardner, R. A. (1971). Two-way communication with an infant chimpanzee. In Schrier, A. M. and Stollnitz, F. (eds.), *Behavior of Nonhuman Primates*, vol. 4, pp. 117–83. New York.
Premack, D. (1976). *Intelligence in Apes and Man*. Hillsdale, New Jersey.
Serban, G. and Kling, A. (eds.) (1976). *Animal Models in Human Psychobiology*. New York.

**ANIMAL MAGNETISM.** See MESMERISM.

**ANIMISM. 1.** The belief, common among primitive peoples, that all things in the world (including stones, plants, the wind, etc.) are imbued with some kind of spiritual or psychological presence; this may imply that things are 'ensouled' or 'animated' by a universal 'world soul', or by individual spirits of various kinds. **2.** The philosophical doctrine, sometimes known as 'panpsychism', that there is some spark or germ of consciousness present in all things. A version of this view was developed by the German philosopher G. W. Leibniz. (See LEIBNIZ'S PHILOSOPHY OF MIND.) For a recent attempt to take panpsychism seriously, see T. Nagel (1980), *Mortal Questions*, ch. 13, Cambridge.

**ANOESIS.** Literally, the absence of thought. It seems clear that there can be 'anoetic' mental states—that is, states in which there is some form of consciousness (for example, sensation), but no thought.

**ANOKHIN,** PIOTRE KUZMICH (1897–1974). Soviet psychologist whose work did much to place the work of Ivan *Pavlov and other reflexologists of his time on a broader biological foundation. Anokhin worked first under V. M. Bechterev, the self-styled reflexologist, and later under Pavlov before he became Head of the Department of Physiology in the University of Gorki, where much of his best work was done. He later became a senior professor in the University of Moscow.

Early in his career, Anokhin became convinced that animal behaviour cannot be satisfactorily explained in terms of a mere colligation of discrete unconditioned and conditioned *reflexes. It should be viewed, he contended, as a functional system, in which the separate links are related to a particular biological goal. Such a system plays a decisive role in the organization of behaviour involving the whole organism.

In support of his view, Anokhin devised a series of experiments in which the relations of the central and peripheral portions of a pair of nerves innervating an extremity, e.g. flexors and extensors, were interchanged so that the central parts of the extensors now innervated the flexors and vice versa. This led to a reorganization of the functional system such that its basic biological role was preserved, the new adaptations being executed by novel neural relationships.

These ideas of flexibility in nervous adaptation were followed up in conditional experiments. Anokhin devised a novel technique which combined salivary and motor responses while allowing the experimental dog freedom of movement. He pointed out that there is a preliminary stage of orientation to the situation before *conditioning begins and that the whole reaction, whether unconditioned or conditioned, does not end with a final reflex. The result of the action has to be evaluated and only if intention and final result are in accord does the action cease. If result and intention do not accord, further trials take place and behaviour continues. Thus the simple concept of a reflex arc is replaced by that of a system regulated by the results of its own actions, showing that functional systems are essentially self-regulating systems, as Norbert Wiener appreciated many years later (see CYBERNETICS).

To this formulation, Anokhin later added the idea of 'forward afference' or 'feedforward', i.e. a form of anticipation which serves to prepare the system for action (see FEEDBACK AND FEEDFORWARD). Anokhin later devoted much study to the physiological and biochemical processes which he believed to be involved in the functional systems of the brain that regulate its behaviour. For Anokhin's work on conditioning and its neurology, see his *Biology and Neurophysiology of the Condi-*

*tioned Reflex and its Role in Adaptive Behaviour* (1974), Oxford. This brings together 22 papers translated and edited by S. A. Curson and a translation panel.                                     A. R. L.
                                                                    O. L. Z.

Luria, A. R. (1980). *Higher Cortical Functions in Man*, pp. 27–36. New York. (For an explanation of Anokhin's concept of functional systems and its application in neurology.)

**ANOREXIA NERVOSA AND BULIMIA NERVOSA.** Many people are now familiar with the disorder of anorexia nervosa, which is diagnosed by the criteria of self-induced weight loss (which may be so severe as to result in amenorrhoea in female patients) coupled with a morbid fear of becoming fat and a relentless pursuit of thinness. Other distinguishing features of the condition include a denial of the subjective feelings of *hunger, a distortion of body image, and a desire to increase energy expenditure by elevated physical activity. It is potentially a fatal disorder, with mortality rates ranging from 5 to 15 per cent, mainly from suicide.

Anorexia nervosa most commonly occurs in middle-class females, although it has also been reported in males. The disorder appears generally during adolescence, though it has been known to begin prior to this period, or even during adulthood. In Britain, the incidence in young women has been estimated to range between 1 and 4 per cent. Many believe that it is a disorder of very recent origin; however, patients with such a disorder have been described by physicians practising from the seventeenth century onwards.

The related disorder, bulimia nervosa, is far less well known, perhaps partly because of its antisocial and somewhat shocking symptoms, which may have retarded its identification. Bulimia was not differentiated from anorexia and was not described as a distinct disorder until very recently. Like anorectics, bulimics have a distorted body image, are obsessed with their body weight, and have a tremendous fear of becoming fat. However, bulimics have an overwhelming desire to eat large quantities of food at a single sitting (termed 'compulsive' or 'binge' eating); they then immediately self-induce vomiting, abuse laxatives, or use both these forms of purging before the food has had time to be digested and absorbed. The majority of bulimics induce vomiting by pushing their fingers into the throat, thus producing the gagging reflex. Use of this method frequently results in calluses over the dorsum of the hand caused by its rubbing against the upper teeth (see Russell, 1979, Fig. 1). But some bulimics have developed their purging techniques to such a degree that they simply need to stoop over the toilet to vomit.

Thoughts about food and body weight are obsessional, and the behaviour related to food becomes compulsive. For example, some bulimics have as many as twenty or thirty episodes of bingeing and vomiting in a 24-hour period. The energy value of food consumed during frequent binges has been measured, and it was found that a bulimic subject may be eating food with an energy value of at least 26 megajoules (about 6,214 kilocalories) per day. Obviously, much of this energy would never be absorbed, because the partly digested food would be expelled by vomiting immediately following the binge. By contrast, women with no history of eating disorders and with comparable indices of body weight were eating food with an energy value of under 15 megajoules (approximately 2,585 kilocalories) per day.

Many bulimics have never been treated for their disorder, since many retain normal or slightly below normal weight through the use of these bizarre purging methods. Hence, unlike the painfully thin anorectic, whose illness is obvious to both her doctor and others around her, the bulimic may be ill for years without anyone discovering her secret disorder, not even her husband, parents, or friends.

The causes of these two disorders are not known; there is no convincing evidence for either inherited or biologically determining factors. Anorexia nervosa has been viewed in the psychodynamic sense as a struggle towards a self-respecting identity, as a 'defensive, biologically-regressed' attitude taken in response to pressures (especially sexual ones) experienced in puberty, and as an attempt to realize society's current view of the ideal feminine figure as sylphlike. Similarly, evidence has been provided that the development of bulimia is related to the struggle to attain a perfect stereotyped female image of beauty, helplessness, and dependence.

**Treatment.** Both anorexia nervosa and bulimia nervosa are very resistant to treatment, with a less favourable prognosis for bulimia nervosa than for anorexia nervosa. Thus physical complications, such as potassium depletion, urinary infections, and renal failure, are more frequent and dangerous, and the risk of suicide is greater for those suffering from bulimia.

Pharmacological treatment is possible, and the drugs that have been used exert their behavioural actions through the central monoamine and opiate *neurotransmitter systems. Certain drugs that have been shown to be effective in the treatment of other psychiatric or neurological disorders—for example, chlorpromazine used predominantly in treating schizophrenia and which appears to have had some success in combating compulsive behaviour—have been used to treat patients with anorexia or bulimia nervosa. In addition, tricyclic antidepressants have been tried in several studies. The results of these drug trials to date have been unconvincing, however, because of the small number of subjects studied and the failure in general to use control procedures. Indeed, in the few studies where the latter procedure has been implemented, pharmacological treatment has *not* been shown to be effective.

It has been reported in one study that in-patient treatment for anorexia nervosa was required in 80 per cent of cases. When the patient was separated from her family, weight was usually restored but only with some difficulty, using a combination of psychotherapy, capable nursing, and, in about half of the cases, treatment with chlorpromazine. Most patients were reported to take between one and five years to stabilize their weight at a reasonable level, to lose their fear of increasing weight, and to be considered fully recovered.

Some success has been reported in treating bulimic patients using a 'cognitive behavioural' approach. This focuses on increasing the patient's control of eating, eliminating food avoidance, and changing maladaptive attitudes. A recent approach, with some similarities to this, combines dietary and cognitive techniques. The patient is placed on a calorie-controlled diet that allows her to control her weight at an acceptable level while enabling her to eat a balanced diet, including food rich in carbohydrate, which is normally irrationally avoided. This dietary regimen is coupled with behavioural modification techniques, together with cognitive and self-control strategies. *Behaviour therapy is employed to help render normal the patient's eating patterns, while the cognitive techniques enable her to concentrate on other creative, positive aspects of her life, rather than on ruminations about her body weight and feeding behaviour.                              B. S.

Boskind-Lodahl, M. and Sirlin, J. (1977). The gorging-, purging syndrome. *Psychology Today*, March, 50–2, 82–5.

Bruch, H. (1978). *The Golden Cage: the enigma of anorexia nervosa*. London.

Crisp, A. H. (1977). Anorexia nervosa. *Proceedings of the Royal Society of Medicine*, **70**, 464–70.

Dally, P. (1977). Anorexia nervosa: do we need a scapegoat? *Proceedings of the Royal Society of Medicine*, **70**, 470–74.

Minuchin, S., Rosman, B., and Baker, L. (1978), *Psychosomatic Families. Anorexia Nervosa in Context*. Cambridge, Mass.

Russell, G. F. M. (1979). Bulimia nervosa: an ominous variant of anorexia nervosa. *Psychological Medicine*, **9**, 429–48.

Russell, G. F. M. (1983). Anorexia nervosa. In Weatherall, D. J., Ledingham, J. G. G., and Warrell, D. A. (eds.), *Oxford Textbook of Medicine*. Oxford.

**ANORTHOSCOPIC VISUAL PERCEPTION.** If a simple outline drawing or geometric figure is placed behind an opaque screen which contains a slit, and if that figure is moved quickly past the slit (thus exposing the figure 'slice by slice'), an observer will often experience a faint, brief glimpse of the pattern (Fig. 1). Thus, even under such poor ('non-proper') conditions, veridical *perception can be achieved (with the sole exception that the figure will appear to be foreshortened on an axis parallel to the direction of motion).

These facts were known to various nineteenth-century psychologists, but were, by and large, lost until their independent rediscovery in 1965, by

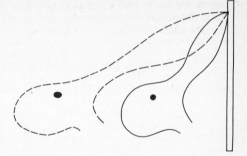

**Fig. 1.** The white rabbit reappearing out of his (very narrow) rabbit-hole. If a line drawing (dashed line above) is passed rapidly behind a slit in an otherwise opaque screen, viewers will often see that line faintly, briefly, and moving slightly, in the vicinity of the slit (solid line above). The screen extends far enough to the right, as well as left, that the figure is visible only through the slit.

which time visual methodology and theory had advanced to a point where it was possible both to assess, quite precisely, the conditions requisite to the effect and to appreciate, much more fully, its theoretical importance. As a result, extensive research made it obvious that not only was (almost) veridical perception under such conditions a most impressive feat of the visual system, but also that the manner in which that feat is accomplished represents an outstanding example of the cognitive, problem-solving nature of the visual system.

To appreciate the difficulty posed for the visual system, it is only necessary to reflect upon the precise nature of the input received by that system under these conditions. First of all, the various parts of the passing figure are received at (slightly) different times. This, however, is not a major (nor unique) difficulty, since several lines of evidence suggest that our experience of briefly presented stimuli persists beyond the presentation itself in the form of '*iconic images'. The major source of difficulty is the fact that the effect can be achieved even when all of the successive 'slices' strike the same strip of retinal receptors (as, for example, when the entire display apparatus is retinally stabilized by appropriate optical devices). In this event, not only must all of the slices persist, but they must persist somewhere other than within the retinal receptors and they must be tagged for relative time of arrival so that they can finally be reassembled in proper sequence.

Considering such difficulties, it is not surprising that a percept of the stimulus pattern is sometimes not achieved. Moreover, such failures, when they occur, are instructive both with respect to the phenomenological nature of success, when it occurs, and with respect to the operations of the visual system which underlie success. As to the former, some observers report a difficulty in deciding whether they merely come to 'know' the given pattern or whether they actually can be said to 'see' it. As Irvin Rock (1981) pointed out, however, subjects who have been exposed to very poor inducing conditions (who, for example, have been shown simply an oblique straight line with the result that, while they can understand that the hidden pattern is an oblique line, nevertheless experience a short line moving up or down the slit) have little difficulty in deciding that success, when achieved, is visual.

In addition, the conditions which lead to such failures (when contrasted with more effective circumstances) strongly suggest, as do many other phenomena, the presence of cognitive, problem-solving, preconscious processes within the visual system. To take just one example drawn from an extensive and incisive series of investigations carried out by Rock and his colleagues, if the oblique line mentioned above is replaced by an undulating line, it is more likely that success will occur and especially if the slit is widened; precisely the result that would be expected from a system faced with the problem of deciding 'what's there?' and governed (in part) by the principle that coincidence is to be eschewed as much as is possible. That is to say, if the display does not consist of an extended line being revealed through the slit, then the alternative is, again, that a small line is moving up and down the slit—and, in this case, is at the same time bending and curving in just such a way that, *coincidentally*, each part blends into the next in a smooth continuous fashion. Apparently, rejecting such coincidences as improbable (but not impossible—the display *is* sometimes seen that way), the system reaches the more 'reasonable' (and veridical) conclusion instead, and imposes that conclusion upon conscious visual experience.    T. E. P.

Parks, T. E. (1965). Post-retinal visual storage. *American Journal of Psychology*, **78**, 145–7.

Rock, I. (1981). Anorthoscopic perception. *Scientific American*, **244**, 145–53.

**ANOSMIA.** The loss of the ability to *smell. It may be congenital but can be caused by a variety of reasons, including the common cold and lesions in the olfactory tract incurred as a result of head injury.

**ANTICIPATION** (or PREDICTION). The development of the *nervous system through the evolution of species is characterized by increasing powers of anticipation—the ability to survive against nature and predators. Anticipatory behaviour is not initiated by stimuli; so a stimulus–response account of the behaviour of higher animals is essentially inadequate. Intelligent anticipation requires stored knowledge, and the ability to draw analogies from past situations, which may be in many ways different from the current situation. This ability is uniquely developed in humans. Its neural localization is essentially in the frontal lobes of the cerebral cortex; but it may be the case that damage to the frontal lobes produces personality changes such that the future is judged less important.

Anticipation allows organisms and societies to avoid danger before disaster strikes; it allows strategies to be devised and individual and communal plans to be made for overcoming nature and enemies, and for achieving goals. Such abilities are quite foreign to inanimate matter, and are beyond the capacity of many living things: anticipation requires a mind. Some would argue, however, that computers may reasonably be said to have the ability to anticipate and warn of situations and events, and hence to be 'mindful'.

**ANTIDEPRESSANT.** See DEPRESSION.

**ANXIETY.** The characteristics of anxiety as an *emotion are that it is distressing, and that its sources are indefinite. In the latter respect it is unlike *fear, which has reference to a specific aspect of the outside world. Fear with a more or less specific reference but out of proportion to the real danger is a *phobia. Agoraphobia, for instance, is a morbid fear of public places. An anxious person is in suspense, waiting for information to clarify his situation. He is watchful and alert, often excessively alert and over-reacting to noise or other stimuli. He may feel helpless in the face of a danger which, although felt to be imminent, cannot be identified or communicated. Hope and despair tend to alternate, whereas *depression describes a prevailing mood of pessimism and discouragement.

With the emotion of anxiety may be associated such bodily symptoms as feelings in the chest of tightness or uneasiness which tend to move upwards into the throat, sinking feelings in the epigastrium, or light feelings in the head which may be described as dizziness. The patient tends to be pale or, less often, flushed. His pulse is rapid, and his heart overacting. He shows effort intolerance, mild exertion producing an undue increase in pulse and respiration rate; he tires rapidly. His posture is tense, his tendon reflexes brisk. Sexual interest tends to be in abeyance. The function of every organ in the body is affected in some degree. Numerous studies have examined physiological changes associated with the experience of anxiety. Among the better known is the change in skin conductivity, the galvanic skin reflex (GSR) the basis of action of the so-called 'lie detector' (see ELECTRODERMAL ACTIVITY). Increased anxiety causes sweating and a sharp drop in the resistance between the two electrodes attached to the subject's finger. In an anxious person, however, spontaneous fluctuations of the GSR will be recorded. Such an individual, when tested by a lie-detector, would show even greater fluctuations in the tracing, sufficient, probably, to make an interpretation of the results invalid.

*Freud's psychoanalytic theory offers explanations of anxiety, which occurs in greater or lesser degree in almost every form of mental disorder. In his earliest formulation, Freud argued that anxiety is a vicarious manifestation or transformation of sexual tension (libido) not discharged through normal sexual activity. It might sometimes be a repetition of the experience of being born. In his later work he wrote of it as reflecting motives which, although excluded from consciousness by repression, threaten the dissolution of the ego. The contemporary explanation, although similar, is expressed in different terms.

Anxiety has also been used in a broader sense as a term for the drive aroused by a danger signal, i.e. a conditioned stimulus associated in previous experience with *pain, physical or psychological. To a danger signal a response is made which has proved effective in avoiding the pain. The pain is not experienced again, but the response is reinforced every time it reduces the anxiety aroused by the danger signal. Responding by avoidance has other consequences. It precludes further exploration of the danger situation, and, not being explored, the sources of the danger remain ill-defined, and other ways of coping with them are not learnt. Avoidance responses tend, therefore, to become firmly established.

The emotion of anxiety is felt whenever responses made to a danger signal appear to be ineffective. Because it is frustrated, the behaviour associated with anxiety tends to become vacillating and disorganized; also, destructive impulses occur. The anxiety is then mixed with anger. To these effects are due some of the special qualities of anxiety as an emotion.

The agoraphobic patient does not feel anxious while he succeeds in avoiding whatever dangers public places contain for him; otherwise he would feel helpless in the face of whatever demands being in a public place might make. These demands might represent threats to his conception of himself or to the assumptions he makes about the world. Akin to agoraphobia is 'separation anxiety', which arises when a person faces demands while being denied, as a result of separation, the reassurance and support of a parent or other significant person. Existentialist theory equates anxiety with the dread of being alone or of being nothing; without the reassurance given through a relationship with another person, the sense of self is threatened.

D. R. D.

**APHAKIA.** See EYE DEFECTS AND THEIR CORRECTION.

**APHASIA.** The ability to talk may not, as was once thought, be the crucial factor that distinguishes humans from the animals, but loss of the power of speech is one of the most distressing things that can happen to a human being. Aphasia (the disruption of speech) commonly follows a stroke—especially if the stroke also impairs movement of the right arm or leg. The loss of articulated language is not always or necessarily accompanied by loss of other linguistic functions, like reading and writing. Least of all is it necessarily accompanied by loss of comprehension: a sufferer often knows that the

words he is uttering are wrong, but he cannot correct or alter them ('Pass me the bread—no, not the bread the *bread*—no!'). However, where one of the linguistic skills is seriously disturbed, one or more of the others tends to be somewhat reduced as well. Neither does the disruption of speech mean that all aspects of it are obliterated, nor, even if it is seriously reduced in the early stages after the disrupting incident, that it can never be regained. But the recovery of abilities by an aphasic person does not follow the same principles of learning as the acquisition of learning a language by a normal, healthy child or adult. Asking the patient to repeat a word or phrase over and over again is not necessarily going to help him to say it later on; it is more likely merely to make him angry and depressed. Impairment of language does not necessarily imply loss of other faculties, such as intelligence or memory.

The three aspects of aphasia which have been studied most intensively are the manner in which speech breaks down, the causes of the breakdown, and treatment of and recovery from it.

**The manner of breakdown.** The different forms of breakdown can be classified in different ways, but most people nowadays consider just two major groups: non-fluent (or *Broca's) and fluent (or *Wernicke's), the names in parentheses being those of the neurologists who first described them. (See LANGUAGE, NEUROPSYCHOLOGY OF, for a fuller discussion.)

In non-fluent aphasia, the sufferer has difficulty finding words, particularly uncommon ones. He has difficulty naming objects, and his syntax is often faulty. He tends to talk hesitantly and gropingly, although he is often acutely aware of how stupid he sounds. The fluent aphasic, on the other hand, emits a stream of words the intonation of which is perfectly normal. Heard from a distance, they sound obscure or clever, but closer listening reveals meaningless jargon. Unlike the non-fluent aphasic, the fluent one seems undisturbed by, and even unaware of, his poor communication. In each of these conditions, concomitant disorders of reading, writing, and comprehension may be present in some degree, but are usually more severe in fluent than in non-fluent disorders.

**The causes of breakdown.** Aphasia is caused by damage to tissue within the brain. But whether injuries to different areas of the brain cause different types of disorder, and whether the same patterns of disorder occur in all individuals, is less certain. Each hemisphere of the brain not only controls movement and sensation of the opposite side of the body (the left hemisphere controls the right side, and the right hemisphere controls the left), but seems to specialize in particular mental functions. (See NEUROPSYCHOLOGY.) It is the left hemisphere that seems to be most closely concerned with language, although in left-handed people and those with a family history of left-handedness the association is not so strong. Moreover it is not inevitable. People whose left hemispheres are damaged in early infancy or childhood can 'learn to speak' perfectly adequately with their right. By and large, however, it is damage to the left hemisphere that most commonly causes aphasia; that to the anterior part causing non-fluent disorders, and that to the posterior part causing those of the fluent type. It is sometimes held, though, that in fluent aphasia there is also usually some damage to the right or non-dominant hemisphere as well as to the left.

An important factor relating to breakdown is the degree to which a person made use of language before his injury. Although after breakdown the words and phrases previously used most commonly can usually be found more easily than others, this does not necessarily mean that the first language of a bilingual or polyglot is the one best preserved: it is frequency of usage rather than recency that is important. Even so, there is a tendency for sufferers of non-fluent aphasia to emit swear-words and taboo-words when searching for those they cannot find. Here it is the words which have *not* been uttered in the past that appear before those which have. The reason for this is probably that inhibition or repression of an act gives it particularly strong emotional force; and the emotional aspects of mental behaviour are not controlled by the same areas of the brain as language. Indeed, they tend to be released when intellectual control is removed.

**Recovery.** The vast majority of aphasic people, especially in the younger age-groups, recover a good deal of speech as time goes on; and a few of the more literary ones have written accounts of their experiences. Unfortunately these seldom contain information about how the faculties were regained, probably because such processes—like many other forms of learning and remembering—occur at a level which is not available to normal consciousness. Psychologists who have been able to watch and study these people have, however, identified several factors which seem to be involved, especially in non-fluent aphasia.

1. Arousal of previous or common contexts. In most languages there are words that have different meanings in different contexts. In English, the word *hand* can be applied to a part of the human body, parts of a clock-face, a unit for the measurement of horses, a style of penmanship, a pledge of fidelity, a member of a ship's crew. The first usage here is undoubtedly the commonest, and aphasics can often name the body-part when asked to do so, even when they cannot find the word 'hand' in its other contexts. However, once a word has been found in its most common context, it can often be found in others too ('Of course, those are called "hands", aren't they?').

2. Narrowing of syntactical constraints. In most languages, words are uttered and understood in sequences rather than individually, and are con-trolled by those preceding them. For instance, in the sentence starting 'The man was bitten by——', there is a limit to the choice of words that can follow. Narrowing the field of possibilities by such means seems to be very helpful to the aphasic patient, who can often find words if they form parts of familiar sentences (or song phrases) when not able to do so otherwise.

3. The hesitancy seen in non-fluent aphasia is usually due to the patient's knowledge that the first words which occur to him are wrong and must be corrected. Yet if these words *are* uttered, they are usually far from random. Indeed, they tend to be closely related to the word being sought. They arise from the same semantic field or consist of functional descriptions of the object to be named ('They're the things that point to the time—the fingers—no, the pointers—no!').

Summing up, it seems that in non-fluent aphasia the difficulty is one of having lost not the ability to speak, but only the ability to find the right words at the right moment. Any stimulus which gives a 'lead in' to the general semantic field helps. After this, it is a matter of sifting through the various items until the target is found. (How one recognizes the target is a different problem, and although this ability seems to be intact in the non-fluent aphasic, it seems to be at fault in the fluent one, who does not try to inhibit or correct his 'near misses'.)

Experiments with normal, healthy humans indicate that the processes whereby they find and utter words are very similar to those seen in aphasia, but that the processes take place more quickly and efficiently. But rare words take longer to find than common ones; and if the sorting/sifting/correcting process is impeded by external factors (such as distraction) or internal ones (such as intoxication), 'near misses' of much the same sort as those given by the aphasic may be emitted.          M. WI.

Benson, D. F. (1985). Aphasia. In Heilman, K. M. and Valenstein, E. (eds.), *Clinical Neuropsychology*, pp. 17–48. Oxford.

Gardner, H. (1977). *The Shattered Mind*. London.
Luria, A. R. (1970). *Traumatic Aphasia*. The Hague.
Russell, W. R. and Espir, M. L. E. (1961). *Traumatic Aphasia*. London.
Wernicke, C. (1874). *Der Aphasische Symptomenkomplex*. Breslau.

**APHRODISIAC.** One of the ineluctable facts of life is that male potency reaches a peak in late adolescence and thereafter undergoes a slow decline, to be extinguished in most men in late old age. Unfortunately there is not a commensurate fall in sexual desire in the female, and it may even increase in middle life after the menopause. Understandably, therefore, there has been an age-long search for substances to restore male potency, but so far there is very little evidence that any of the more popular remedies are based on any factual demonstration of their efficacy. Aphrodisiacal properties have been attributed to many foods, including oysters, mushrooms, and various fishes.

In addition, on the basis of the ancient Doctrine of Signatures, it was believed that substances with similar appearances would have the same therapeutic effects. Consequently a symbolic likeness between genitalia and certain plants and animal parts led to the assumption that powdered rhinoceros horn (popular in China), mandrake, ginseng, and asparagus would produce the desired action.

Magic and suggestion are important contributions to the alleged aphrodisiacal properties of many substances, but certain drugs have been used, the most dangerous of which is cantharides, a powerful vesicant (causing blistering of the skin). When taken internally it causes acute inflammation of the urinary tract, resulting in painful priapism and the passage of bloody urine. Yohimbine, a central excitant which enhances the release of noradrenalin, has an unproven reputation as an aphrodisiac. Cannabis is said to increase the pleasure experienced by both sexes during coitus but has no effect on male potency. Treatment with androgens, the male sex hormones, does not generally produce the sought-after effects and is not without hazard as it may cause cancer of the prostate in the middle-aged man. Alcohol, the oldest and most often tried of aphrodisiacs, acts more as a disinhibitor of sexual drives than as a promoter of sexual capacity.                    F. A. W.

**APPARENT.** Appearance is traditionally contrasted with reality, and the 'apparent' qualities of things with their 'real' qualities. Thus (to use a time-honoured example) a stick in water 'appears' bent but is 'really' straight. The distinction between appearance and reality arises in at least four contexts. (i) The 'appearance' may be an optical illusion—due for example to the refraction of light rays when passing through water—or a perceptual illusion (see ILLUSIONS). (ii) More generally, a property may be ascribed to something, or its meaning defined, with reference to standard conditions: thus an object's 'true' colour is normally defined in terms of how it looks to a normal observer in ordinary light, even though it may appear differently under different conditions. (iii) Often, when we speak of 'apparent' qualities, there may be a 'perspectival' element involved—an implicit reference to the position or frame of reference of the observer. Thus the earth is *apparently* stationary (from the perspective of an observer on the surface) but is *really* rotating (i.e. from the wider perspective of an observer in space). (iv) Finally, even when all considerations about perspective, and standard conditions of application, have been taken into account, it may be thought that there is still an important gap between how we see the world and how it really is. Thus some of the qualities we ascribe to objects may be thought to involve an irreducibly subjective element which debars them from counting as 'real' qualities of objects. According to John Locke, our ideas of redness and sweetness, for example, do not resemble anything really in the objects themselves. For this issue see LOCKE, JOHN and QUALITIES.                    J. G. C.

**APPERCEPTION.**    When    experimental psychology became a fact towards the end of the nineteenth century, the only concepts available to it were those developed in either a philosophical or a biological context. 'Apperception' belongs to the former category, having played an important role in the German philosophical tradition since the beginning of the eighteenth century. Wilhelm *Wundt, who initiated the first systematic research programme in experimental psychology and trained many of its early practitioners, was steeped in this tradition and actively contributed to it. As a result, the concept of apperception occupied a prominent place in the early literature of experimental psychology.

The term was originally used by G. F. *Leibniz, particularly in his critique of Lockian sensationalism, as a way of emphasizing the distinction between a passive sensation and a mental content self-consciously 'apperceived'. It became the major technical term used by German philosophers to express what they considered to be the two fundamental features of the human mind: the fact that mental experience is not composed of separate bits but forms a unity, and the fact that this unity involves a constructive activity of the mind itself rather than a passive reflection of external events.

This usage is found in the highly influential philosophy of Immanuel *Kant, where a clear distinction is introduced between the empirically observed unity of experience and a *transcendental apperception*, a cognitive act, which makes this unity possible. This distinction devalued the introspective analysis of inner experience as being concerned only with effects and appearances, but it also acted as a challenge for nineteenth-century psychologists to find a more satisfactory explanation for the empirical unity of experience.

The challenge was taken up by Kant's successor, J. F. *Herbart, whose model of mental functioning involved the notion of ideas combining to form powerful 'masses' that dominated the mental life of the individual. Apperception occurred through the assimilation of new ideas by an existing complex of ideas. Herbart's concepts achieved wide popularity among nineteenth-century educationists, so that the concept of apperception began to descend from the lofty heights of philosophical speculation.

This process was continued in the work of Wundt, who proposed to subject the process of apperception to experimental investigation in the psychological laboratory. The original vehicle for accomplishing this was provided by *reaction time experiments which had been developed by physiologists. Wundt conceived the idea of using variations in reaction times that occur with different patterns of stimulus presentation as an empirical index of central apperceptive processes. Responses to sequences of stimuli or to distracting stimuli, for example, had to involve the kind of synthesizing cognitive activity that was traditionally referred to as apperception. These early experiments constituted the first systematic attempt to subject central psychological processes to precise laboratory investigation.

The notion that the process of apperception occupied measurable periods of time implied that it was not transcendental but involved physiological processes of definite physical duration. Wundt speculated that these processes were localized in an 'apperception centre' in the forebrain that co-ordinated the activity of lower sensory and motor centres.

This was the physical side of Wundt's psychophysical theory of apperception. The more prominent psychological side treated the phenomenon of *attention as the primary subjectively observable expression of the apperceptive process. While this provided further opportunities for experimental study, Wundt also used the theory of apperception to explain the structure of language, developing an early version of psycholinguistics (see NEUROLINGUISTICS, LURIA ON).

Thus, apperception became the major unifying concept in the first important theoretical system of modern psychology, attempting to synthesize evidence from psychophysiology, from laboratory studies of human *cognition, and from comparative studies of symbolic structures. It is noteworthy that, while the *effects* of apperception were generally investigated in the context of cognition, Wundt believed that its psychological *sources* lay in affective processes.

This theoretical *tour de force* proved to be premature. Wundt's successors, including his most prominent students, abandoned the concept of apperception, restricting themselves to observables, like attention. This generation of psychologists was anxious to cut psychology's ties with philosophy which Wundt had wanted to maintain. Apperception was rejected as excessively metaphysical. Possible practical applications of their findings became more interesting to many empirical psychologists than were broad theoretical syntheses, and from this point of view apperception was a redundant concept. For many years work on central integrative processes was neglected in favour of a more simplistic sensorimotor psychology. Some of the phenomena that apperception had been intended to explain were more effectively reinterpreted in the framework of *Gestalt psychology. Thus the term went out of use rather quickly and permanently. Contemporary cognitive science has revived an interest in many of the problems that the theory of apperception had been concerned with, but the term itself has not been resurrected.                                   K. D.

Leahy, T. H. (1980). *A History of Psychology*, ch. 7. New York.

Rieber, R. W. (ed.) (1980). *Wilhelm Wundt and the Making of a Scientific Psychology*, chs. 2–4. New York and London, 1980.

Wundt, W. (1911). *An Introduction to Psychology*, ch. 4. Reprinted 1973, New York.

**APRAXIA** is the inability to make purposeful skilled movements. Like the *aphasias, the apraxias are classical syndromes in human neuropsychology. Animals do not develop apraxia as a consequence of brain lesions, no matter where the lesion is located. In man, apraxia occurs, as a rule, after a lesion in the hemisphere dominant for language, usually the left hemisphere. In those rare instances where language is processed in the right hemisphere, apraxia might be expected after right-sided brain damage.

This observation might suggest that apraxia should be considered among those neuropsychological symptoms which are language-dependent. An inherent relationship between the two syndromes, however, has not been demonstrated. Both aphasia and apraxia vary independently. After left-sided brain damage there can be recovery of language functions in the presence of persisting apraxia, and vice versa.

There are two varieties of apraxia, traditionally termed ideomotor apraxia and ideational apraxia. These terms reflect late nineteenth-century views on the organization of psychological processes in the brain; in particular, they imply a two-stage model of motor processing, similar to the traditional two-stage model of sensory processing (*perception and *apperception) developed during the same period. Although these models have been abandoned in favour of a multi-step, multi-modal integration model of processing, it is still convenient to adopt the terms ideomotor and ideational in modern research provided they are used as neutral denominators and do not confer a priori theoretical implications.

**Ideomotor apraxia** is a common syndrome in which the execution of simple or complex, meaningful (or symbolic), or meaningless (or non-symbolic) movements with the oro-facial musculature and/or with the limbs is impaired in a characteristic way. The paramount feature is not clumsiness of movement or absence of execution, but rather a distortion of movements, which Hugo Liepmann termed parapraxia. Parapraxias are brought about by inadequate selection of the elements that contribute to a motor sequence, and/or by impairment in the sequential combination of these elements. Both aspects, impaired selection and sequencing of elements, are of equal importance. In order to arrive at the diagnosis of ideomotor apraxia, one has to make sure that the motor disorder is not explained by paresis, sensory impairment, disturbances in the co-ordination of movements, or by problems in understanding a specified task because of either language disturbance or impaired intellectual performance.

A striking feature of ideomotor apraxia is that the execution of movements is impaired only when they are required out of their natural context. Traditionally, the examination is done by making the patient perform certain movements, like whistling, sticking out his tongue, blowing out his cheeks, performing the sign of the cross or a military salute, or placing the back of his hand on his front. These and similar movements are required either on verbal command or by imitation after demonstration by the examiner. It is important to note that a patient with ideomotor apraxia is perfectly able to brush his teeth in the morning, in a natural setting, whereas he performs the same movement in a rather parapraxic way when required to do so in the doctor's examination room. A convincing explanation for this well-recognized feature has not yet been put forward. One could be tempted to entertain a disconnection model, specifying that movements are impaired when they are elicited by input from the language system or from the visual system, but not when the input is generated in the limbic system. The reliance of spontaneous, context-dependent actions on limbic input to the motor system, however, still has to be demonstrated in both physiological and anatomical terms.

The structure of apraxia has been investigated on the basis of qualitative analysis of the parapraxic errors. This analysis was based on studies by David Efron, who was the first to apply sophisticated methods for the description of expressive movements in a study of gestural behaviour. He used the term 'linguistic' to denote the referential aspect of symbolic movements. While his analysis was focused only on movements as a whole, single components of movements were systematically studied by Birdwhistel, who applied the methods of structural linguistics to the study of normal movements. He recognized posture and movement as patterned behaviour, and he developed a notation system which permitted a description of a hierarchy of motor elements similar to the description of speech elements in a linguistic hierarchy.

Stimulated by this research, Poeck and Kerschensteiner have developed a method permitting the quantitative and qualitative assessment of single components constituting the apraxic movements. A code has been elaborated which enables one to transcribe the characteristics of the single components of the motor sequence. Error analysis showed that the most characteristic behaviour in apraxia is perseveration (the inappropriate repetition of parts of speech or movement). In apraxia it occurs not only as the repetition of a whole movement or motor sequence but also, much more importantly, as the intrusion of motor elements that were part of a movement correctly or incorrectly performed many tasks before. To give an example, the patients not only repeated the military salute when they were asked to touch their chin but they perseverated on the rhythmic elements of the movement 'to show that somebody is crazy' when they performed the static movement of the military salute—i.e. they tapped their temple while their hand was in correct military salute position. The perseveratory tendency is so strong that when asked to imitate a movement, the patients were likely to repeat a movement or an element of a movement carried out earlier in spite of the visual evidence of the correct execution by the examiner.

In a systematic study with 200 apraxia tasks given to 88 patients with left-sided brain damage, 10 patients with right-sided brain damage, and 10 control subjects, no differences between the right and left limbs were found. Meaningful (i.e. practised, easily verbalized) and meaningless (i.e. unpractised and difficult to verbalize) tasks were equally impaired. The aphasic language disturbance did not explain errors on verbal command. No qualitative relation between aphasia and apraxia was detected, nor any subtypes of apraxia characterized by certain patterns of error.

Therapy is not necessary because ideomotor apraxia occurs only under the conditions of examination and does not impair the patient's spontaneous actions.

**Ideational apraxia** is a rare condition. It is observed in patients with lesions in the language-dominant hemisphere. There is only one case on record where the syndrome was the consequence of a right-sided brain lesion. This patient was left-handed and had right-sided or at least bilateral representation of language functions.

Patients with ideational apraxia are seriously impaired when they are about to carry out sequences of actions requiring the use of various objects in the correct way and order necessary to achieve an intended goal. These patients are conspicuous in everyday behaviour because they have problems in, for example, preparing or even eating a meal, or doing some professional routine they have performed for years. The behavioural disturbance of these patients is most frequently misinterpreted as indicating mental confusion—and all the more so since, in addition to ideational apraxia, they are regularly aphasic.

Patients do not fail these tasks because they have problems in the recognition of objects. In spite of their aphasia they frequently give pertinent verbal comments on the task, indicating that the language problem cannot be the determinant factor. Ideational apraxia is not a very severe degree of ideomotor apraxia; although both syndromes may occur in the same patient, they vary independently of each other. On the basis of a small number of observations it is suggested that the ideational apraxia syndrome is due to a disturbance in the associative elaboration of various inputs with motor programmes. This would be in line with modern concepts of the hierarchical organization of the motor system. Ideational apraxia is a great handicap for the patient, and therefore it is necessary to develop appropriate lines of treatment. Such treatment should first attempt to teach the patient to avoid perseverative behaviour.                K. P.

Birdwhistel, R. L. (1970). *Kinesics and Context*. Philadelphia.

Efron, D. (1941). *Gesture and Environment*. New York.

Geschwind, N. (1974). *Selected Papers on Language and the Brain*. Dordrecht and Boston.

Liepmann, H. (1908). *Drei Aufsätze aus dem Apraxiegebiet*. Berlin.

Poeck, K. (forthcoming). The relationship between aphasia and motor apraxia. In Oxbury, Wyke, Coltheart (eds.), *Aphasia*. London.

Poeck, K. (1984). Clues to the disruptions to limb praxis. Qualitative studies. In Roy, E. A. (ed.), *Disruptions to the Sequencing of Actions*. *Advances in Psychology*. Amsterdam.

Poeck, K. and Kerschensteiner, M. (1975). Analysis of the sequential motor events in oral apraxia. In Zülch, Creutzfeldt, Galbraith (eds.), *Cerebral Localization*. Berlin, Heidelberg, and New York.

**A PRIORI** is a term applied to statements to reflect the status of our knowledge of their truth (or falsehood). It means literally 'from what comes before', where the answer to 'before what?' is understood to be 'experience'. Loosely, one may speak of knowing some truth 'a priori' where it is possible to infer the truth without having to experience the state of affairs in virtue of which it is true, but in strict philosophical usage, an a priori truth must be knowable independently of *all* experience. *Kant held that the criteria of a priori knowledge were (i) necessity, for 'experience teaches us that a thing is so and so, but not that it cannot be otherwise', and (ii) universality, for all experience can confer on a judgement is 'assumed and comparative universality through *induction'. Gottlob Frege stressed that the issue was one of justification, and defined an a priori truth as one whose proof rests exclusively on general laws which neither need nor admit of proof, while a truth which cannot be proved without appeal to assertions about particular objects is a posteriori.

Statements such as 'A vixen is a fox', whose truth is *analytic are accorded a priori status without dispute. Kant held that in addition truths of arithmetic and geometry, and such statements about the natural world as 'Every event has a cause,' were not analytic but nevertheless had the hallmarks of being a priori. The central question that his philosophy addressed was how such synthetic a priori truths were possible, whereas the strategy of his twentieth-century empiricist critics has been to argue that there are no a priori truths which are not analytic.                J. E. T.

Frege, G. (1959). *The Foundations of Arithmetic* (J. L. Austin, trans.), Section 3. Oxford.

Kant, I. (1929). *The Critique of Pure Reason* (N. Kemp-Smith, trans.), Preface and Introduction. London.

**AQUINAS,** ST THOMAS (1224/5–74), the greatest of the medieval scholastics. Aquinas was primarily a theologian, but in his theological work he was led to develop a comprehensive treatment of the philosophical issues at stake; hence we can extract from his writings a philosophical psychology which he considered capable of standing on its own feet, without requiring support from Christian revelation.

St Thomas, the seventh son of Landulf, count of Aquino, was born at the family's castle of Roccasecca, near Aquino (about half-way between Rome and Naples). He was educated at the Benedictine abbey of Monte Cassino and at the University of Naples. In 1244 he decided to join the newly-established Dominican order, and afterwards studied at the University of Paris and at the Dominicans' institute in Cologne, where one of his teachers was St Albert the Great. Aquinas lectured at various times at the universities of Paris and Naples and at the papal court. He died while on his way to the Fourth Ecumenical Council of Lyons, and was canonized in 1323.

Aquinas rejected much contemporary Christian theorizing about man, based on the thought of St Augustine and, via Augustine, on *Plato and neo-Platonism, and instead took over and developed many of *Aristotle's conclusions. Like Aristotle, he viewed human activity as taking place on three levels, vegetative (comprising the powers of nutrition, growth, and reproduction), sensitive (comprising sensory activity and locomotion), and intellectual (comprising reason and will). Among bodily creatures, only man possesses reason and will, but these powers are found also in angels and, in a very much higher manner which we cannot adequately comprehend, in God; and it is because man shares, to some degree, in these divine attributes of reason and will that the Scriptures speak of man as made in the image and likeness of God (Genesis 1: 26–7).

Aquinas followed Aristotle in defining the soul of a living being as its substantial form, i.e. as that inherent principle by which it is the kind of entity or substance which it is; and he contrasted the soul as form with the matter which it organizes or 'informs': both soul and matter are necessary constituent principles of the living being. So, he believed, all living creatures have souls, but only human beings have spiritual souls. Aquinas rejected the medieval Augustinians' belief that in man there are three distinct souls, vegetative, sensitive, and intellectual, each accounting for human activity at its corresponding level. This view, he said, would destroy man's natural unity by breaking him up into three distinct entities; rather, there is just the one soul, which is responsible for all of a man's activities, regardless of the level to which they belong.

Following Aristotle, Aquinas distinguished the five external senses of sight, hearing, touch, taste, and smell, and four 'internal senses'. These latter are: the 'common sense' by means of which sense-impressions or 'phantasms' produced by different external senses are referred to a single entity existing outside the perceiver; secondly, the imagination (*imaginatio* or *phantasia*), which stores sense-impressions and can combine them into complex images of hitherto-unperceived things and events; thirdly, the 'cogitative power' (*vis cogitativa*), which corresponds to instinct in animals and by which we can apprehend things and events in the world as either beneficial or harmful to us; and finally the sense memory (*vis rememorativa*), in which information gained by the cogitative power is stored.

In sensory cognition we appropriate the sensible forms of objects, that is, their observable characteristics, without the matter of the objects themselves; so (for example) in seeing a silver coin I receive its colour into my sense organ, but not the actual matter of the coin. Likewise, he thinks, the two kinds of human activity at the rational level, thinking and willing, involve receiving into the soul the *intelligible* form of whatever one's thinking or willing is about. For an entity or substance in the external world is made to be the sort of thing that it is by possession of a certain nature or form—the form of oak tree, for example—and we understand and think about things by mentally receiving their forms: in this way, as Aristotle said, 'the mind is in a way all things'. But matter as such, considered in isolation from any determining form, is unintelligible, and so we can 'latch on' to a thing in thought only by mentally disengaging or 'abstracting' its intelligible form from the material conditions of sensation. This process of abstraction, Aquinas said, is carried out by a power called the agent intellect (*intellectus agens*); and another power, the receptive intellect (*intellectus possibilis*), then receives and stores the forms abstracted by the agent intellect. Thus the form of (say) cat which is present in cats themselves, thereby making them the kind of animal they are, is also present in the minds of human beings, thereby making them capable of thinking about cats. In this way Aquinas accounted for the fact of *intentionality, that is, the fact that our thoughts are *about* things. The form of something, as stored in the receptive intellect, is a concept. Unlike sensations, which are particular modifications of the sense powers, concepts are universals because they enable us to think about a potentially indefinite number of things of a given kind; and the receptive intellect employs these concepts in carrying out such intellectual operations as judging, reasoning, and deliberating. A form present in someone's mind as a concept is, Aquinas said, obviously present in a very different way from that of a form present in an external thing, and he called this mental mode of presence 'intentional being' (*esse intentionale*).

Against the Latin Averroism of Siger of Brabant and others, St Thomas denied that the agent intellect is a single entity which is distinct from all human beings but in which the latter somehow participate. Rather, he said, it is a constituent power of each human mind. There are, then, as many agent intellects as there are men.

Because he believed that human beings can acquire concepts only by abstracting forms from sense-appearances, Aquinas can be called an empiricist. He insisted that without some sensory input on which the mind's abstractive power could get to work, no concepts would ever be constructed, nor would any rational activity ever take place: there are no 'innate ideas'. Moreover, any actual use of concepts in thinking or willing must—at least in this life, in which the soul is embodied—be constantly referred to sense-contents, either of perception or memory or imagination. This necessary human orientation to sensory data is what Aquinas called 'conversion to sense-experience' (*conversio ad phantasmata*).

Since concept-formation involves the abstraction of intelligible forms from all material conditions, Aquinas concluded that the formation and utilization of concepts are activities which cannot in principle be performed by any physical organ or organism. For, he said, if there were a physical organ of thought it would be unable to do something which it obviously can do, namely, receive the forms of all physical objects, but would be restricted to receiving the forms of only one particular kind of object, as the eye is restricted to receiving colours. Nor would any physical organ be capable of that self-conscious awareness which is so prominent a feature of human thought. Our concepts are, then, present in us in a non-material way; hence that which performs mental acts must be a wholly non-material, that is, spiritual, principle. So the human soul, as well as being the substantial form of the body—that by which the human body *is* a body—must also be a spiritual substance in its own right.

Because man's soul is a spiritual substance, it can survive death. For it is not made up of physical parts and is therefore, unlike the body, free from corruption and dissolution. Admittedly, since man depends on his sense organs to provide him with appropriate objects of thought—things to think about—it seems that a disembodied soul will be unable to exercise its mental abilities without some special help from God; and in any case, since the human soul is the substantial form of the human body, disembodiment is clearly an unnatural condition for it. Thus, although we can have reason to accept the Christian doctrine of the resurrection of the body only on the basis of God's revelation, that doctrine is entirely appropriate to the human condition. For only if soul and body are eventually reunited will there be a fully-constituted human being once more; until then, the souls of the departed will exist in a condition which is abnormal, contrary to nature (*praeter naturam*).

For Aquinas, man is not the highest of all created beings, because angels far exceed him in intellectual power. But he is the highest of all bodily creatures, and as a partly material, partly spiritual being, man forms the bridge, so to speak, between the physical and spiritual realms.

How does a human being come into existence? Is he generated out of physical elements, as is a plant, or is some higher, non-physical agency required?

Aquinas replies that since the soul is a purely spiritual entity it must be created directly, out of nothing, by God. But there is no pre-existence of souls: when God creates a soul he immediately infuses it into the appropriate matter which is present in a woman's womb.

Just as man's cognitive powers are present on both sensory and rational levels, so it is with what Aquinas calls man's appetitive or striving functions. The latter include such activities as wishing, willing, desiring, intending, and feeling emotions. Here we shall concentrate on Aquinas's account of the will, which he defines as the rational appetite, that is, the appetite or tendency which belongs to the rational part of the soul. As rational, it is directed not to any particular good, as are the sensory appetitive powers, but rather to goodness as such: it is the power by which man strives towards that which he rationally apprehends as in some way good or desirable. Aquinas analyses the process of deciding to do something into a whole series of 'component' acts, some belonging to the intellect and some to the will. The decisive choice (*electio*) which results in some action's being performed is an act of the will, but the will cannot function without the intellect's aid; we can will something only if we have already recognized it to be good. However, Aquinas also believes that the will very often operates freely, i.e. without being determined to any particular outcome. For, he says, we choose to do one thing rather than another because our intellect apprehends the goodness of what is chosen; but nothing short of the supreme and final good of man (which, for Aquinas, ultimately consists in the vision of God in heaven) can irresistibly attract the human mind; everything other than this will be attractive in some respects but unattractive in others. Hence the will can choose freely among goods which fall short of the complete and ultimate good. This is St Thomas's principal argument for the freedom of the will, or 'free choice' (*liberum arbitrium*), as he calls it; but he also argues that unless man were capable of making free choices, 'advice, exhortations, precepts, prohibitions, rewards, and punishments would be in vain'.

While some of Aquinas's arguments rest upon outdated theses of Aristotelian science, his major conclusions concerning thinking, willing, and the nature and destiny of the human soul escape this limitation and still find defenders today. P. T. Geach's *Mental Acts*, for example, is a particularly interesting analysis of human mental activity which owes much to Aquinas.

Aquinas's account of the nature and workings of the mind is presented, above all, in the *Summa Theologiae* (English translation in 60 vols., ed. T. Gilby, London, 1963–75), especially vols. 11–13, and in the *Summa contra Gentiles* (English translation by A. C. Pegis et al., New York, 1955–7), especially vol. 2. A useful selection of readings is Pegis, A. C. (ed.), *Introduction to St Thomas Aquinas* (New York, 1948).　　　F. J. F.

Copleston, F. C. (1955). *Aquinas*. Harmondsworth.
Geach, P. T. (1957). *Mental Acts*. London.
Lonergan, B. J. F. (1967). *Verbum: word and idea in Aquinas*. Notre Dame.
Weisheipl, J. A. (1974). *Friar Thomas D'Aquino*. Oxford.

**'ARABI** or **AL-'ARABI, IBN** (1164–1240), Sufi teacher. See IBN 'ARABI.

**ARISTOTLE** (384–322 BC). Aristotle was born in the obscure Chalcidic village of Stagira, far from the intellectual centre of Greece. His father, Nicomachus, was court physician to King Amyntas III of Macedon; and it is pleasing to speculate that Nicomachus encouraged his son to take an interest in matters scientific and philosophical. However that may be, in 367 Aristotle migrated to Athens, where he joined the brilliant band of thinkers who studied with *Plato in the Academy. He soon made a name for himself as a student of great intellect, acumen, and originality.

On the death of Plato in 347, Aristotle moved to Asia Minor, where he spent some years devoted principally to the study of biology and zoology. In 343 he moved to Pella, where he served as tutor to King Philip's son, the future Alexander the Great. (What influence Aristotle may have had on that obnoxious young man is uncertain.) After further migrations, Aristotle returned to Athens in 335, and for the next decade engaged in teaching and research in his own school in the Lyceum. He fled from Athens on the death of Alexander in 323, and died a year later in Chalcis. His will, which has survived for us to read, is a humane and touching document.

Aristotle was a polymath: his researches ranged from abstract logic and metaphysics to highly detailed studies in biology and anatomy; with the possible exception of the mathematical sciences, no branch of knowledge was left untouched by him. His contributions were both innovatory and systematic: no one man has achieved more, no one man has had greater influence, and Aristotle remains, in Dante's phrase, 'the master of those who know'.

Aristotle's main contributions to the study of mind are to be found in his treatise *De anima* ('On the Soul' or 'Concerning Psyche') and in a series of short papers known collectively as the *Parva naturalia*. He regarded the study of psychology as a part of the general study of animate nature (see PSYCHE): there is no division in his thought between the study of mind and the study of matter, and his psychological writings are continuous with his overtly biological works.

An early work, the *Eudemus* (only fragments of which survive), betrays a juvenile interest in a Platonic account of the psyche: there Aristotle argued that the psyche was independent of the body, pre-existing it and surviving its death. But that separation of mind from body is foreign to Aristotle's mature works: in the *De anima* he defines the psyche as 'the first actuality of a natural organic body'; and he associates psyche with the animate functions of nutrition, perception, thought, and motion. Psychology is thus by definition linked to the biological sciences; and Aristotle explicitly states that the student of the psyche must investigate the behavioural and physiological aspects of his subject—he must know, for example, that anger is the boiling of the blood around the heart.

*Perception receives a lengthy discussion in the *De anima* and in the *De sensu*, a component treatise of the *Parva naturalia*. Aristotle regards perceiving as a special sort of change in the perceiver: objects of perception, acting via some medium of perception, causally affect the perceiver's sensory apparatus; the apparatus changes inasmuch as it 'receives the form of the object without its matter', and that change is perception. For example, if you look at a white piece of paper, your eyes (or some part of them) actually become white: the eyes are made white by the paper, although no material part of the paper enters them. Similar stories are told of the other four senses. (Aristotle thinks he can prove that there can be no more than five senses.) Each sense has its own 'proper objects' (colours for sight, sounds for hearing, etc.), but some objects (for example, shape, size, motion) are 'common' to two or more senses. Other objects (men or trees, say) are only perceived 'accidentally' or indirectly: you see a man by virtue of seeing something white and moving, which happens to be a man.

The different sense modalities are somehow unified by a 'common faculty', sometimes called the 'common sense'; that faculty, which is located in the heart, is employed to explain various perceptual and quasi-perceptual phenomena, the most important of which is the 'unity of consciousness'. Colours are perceived by way of the eyes, sounds by way of the ears; but nevertheless, both perceptions belong to one and the same unitary subject or perceiver, who can compare and associate the data given by the two senses. By my eyes I see the colour and shine of the trumpet; by my ears I hear its tones: but it is a unitary *I* who perceives the trumpet, and I perceive the trumpet as a unitary substance. That task of perceptual unification is performed by the 'common sense'.

Perception is fundamentally a physical change, and it leaves physical traces in the body. Aristotle refers to those traces as 'phantasms', and they constitute the objects of *phantasia* or the faculty of imagination. The imagination is invoked in a number of contexts: thus it has an important role to play in the analysis of memory, which Aristotle discusses in his *De memoria*, and in the account of sleep and dreaming which he gives in the *De somno* and *De somniis*. (All three works are parts of the *Parva naturalia*.) Most importantly, the imagination supplies the link between perception and thought.

Aristotle's account of thought or 'the intellect' (*nous*) is one of the most perplexing aspects of his mental philosophy. On the one hand, he tends to treat thought on the model of perception: thought, like perception, is a change, and in thinking of things the mind somehow 'becomes' what it is thinking of (as the eye becomes what it is seeing, for example, white). Less obscurely, Aristotle holds that thought is dependent on imagination, and hence on perception: phantasms are, or represent, or accompany, the objects of thought, and we cannot think without phantasms. Since phantasms are the traces of perceptions, it follows that we cannot think without having perceived, and that the scope of our thought is determined by the extent of our perceptual experience. On the other hand, that strongly empiricist approach to the problems of thought seems to be modified by some remarks in one of the most celebrated and painfully difficult chapters in the whole of the Aristotelian corpus: in *De anima*, iii. 5, Aristotle distinguishes between two types of intellect: one, the 'passive' intellect, is securely tied, by way of phantasms, to perception and the body; the other, the 'active' intellect, is pure and unmixed, free from physical trappings, and capable of independent and eternal existence. The 'active' intellect has been discussed for more than two thousand years, and scholars are no nearer understanding Aristotle's doctrine than was his own first pupil, Theophrastus. It is legitimate to suspect that Aristotle's brief notes on the two varieties of *nous* represent no more than a passing fancy or a temporary aberration; in any event, their presence in the *De anima* should not blind us to the fact that for the most part that treatise is uncompromisingly empiricist and materialist in its doctrines.

Movement is treated in the *De anima*, and also in certain of Aristotle's ethical and biological works. (The short treatise *On the Movement of Animals* is a particularly rich source for Aristotle's views on the subject.) Aristotle's treatment is remarkable for its attempt to combine a physiological explanation of animal locomotion (in terms of 'spirit' or *pneuma*, which runs through the body like current in an electric motor) with a psychological account in terms of desire and thought (imagination and perception). The physiology is inevitably crude, but Aristotle's aim is sophisticated: he thinks it possible to account for animal (and human) movements purely in terms of the physical events taking place in the body, while at the same time he wants to explain action, at a philosophical or analytical level, by way of the interaction of desires and beliefs. The attempt to combine those two approaches raises questions of their mutual consistency: Aristotle did not face up to those questions; but it is fair to observe that the issue is still a central and unresolved problem in the philosophy of mind.

An outline survey of Aristotle's psychological theories does scant justice to his contributions to the subject; indeed, it may have the unwanted effect of belittling those contributions, since it is bound to stress the more abstract or general elements in Aristotle's thought. It is above all in the detail—both scientific and philosophical—of his account that Aristotle's genius shines out: a single page of his own writings will reveal more clearly than any summary the perspicuity, the intellectual acumen, and the scientific richness which justify his pre-eminence in the history of the study of mind and its place in nature.                                    J. BA.

The standard translation of Aristotle, and the only complete English translation, was prepared by several scholars under the general editorship of J. A. Smith and Sir David Ross; usually known as the 'Oxford translation', it is now available in two volumes (revised by Jonathan Barnes) under the title *The Complete Works of Aristotle* (1984).

**AROUSAL.** Arousal differs from *attention in that it involves a general rather than a particular increase (or decrease) in perceptual or motor activity. There can, however, be quite specific 'arousal', such as sexual arousal. General arousal is mediated by a diffuse neural system, centred in the brain-stem, which not only sets a level from *sleep to wakefulness (and sometimes over-arousal) but also provides moment-to-moment changes of arousal which are usually appropriate to the prevailing situation, or task in hand. A great deal is known of the neurology of arousal (Milner, 1971), especially in the amygdala.

Subtle moment-to-moment changes of arousal are experienced, for example, while driving a car; arousal immediately increasing with any small unexpected event or situation. It has been suggested that *fatigue results from over-arousal; the blurring of *perception perhaps being due to raised 'neural noise', or increased randomness of neural signals (which may also occur in *ageing) in over-arousal. Experiments conducted on vigilance during the 1939–45 war found that radar operators and others looking out for infrequent signals or events rapidly became inefficient as their level of arousal dropped—errors or misses increasing in as short a time as half an hour. This loss of arousal in repetitive or boring situations (though it also occurs in the stress and danger of battle) can be distinguished experimentally from fatigue.

Arousal has been related to stress; indeed stress may be over-arousal. There is an optimal level of arousal, which has been thought of as following an inverted 'U', for performing a task. But the performance of skills at low arousal differs from that when arousal is 'over the top' of optimal arousal; this suggests that the arousal-function is not truly U-shaped. Errors under conditions of under-arousal tend to be omissions while over-arousal tends to lead to errors of commission or over-correction.

Learning is improved with increase of arousal—again up to an optimum level, when over-arousal becomes associated with distractions of various kinds (Bills, 1927; Sherwood, 1965). There is considerable evidence that long-term but not short-term recall is improved with increased arousal. This is presumably because the laying-down of memory traces is more efficient, perhaps with more

cross-associations for future reference, for learning while arousal is high. Many people learn to control and optimize their arousal level when working or studying, by varying the task, or perhaps with the aid of music, or (not to be recommended!) smoking. There is little point in working when arousal falls close to the level of sleep.

Bills, A. G. (1927). The influence of muscular tension on the efficiency of mental work. *American Journal of Psychology*, **38**, 227–51.

Broadbent, D. E. (1971). *Decision and Stress*. London.

Crawford, A. (1961). Fatigue and Driving. *Ergonomics*, **4**, 143–54.

Milner, P. (1971). *Physiological Psychology*. London.

Sherwood, J. J. (1965). A relation between arousal and performance. *American Journal of Psychology*, **78**, 461–5.

Welford, A. T. (1976). *Skilled Performance: Perceptual and Motor Skills*. Glenview, Illinois.

**ART AND VISUAL ABSTRACTION.** The following attempts to demonstrate the role played by abstractive processes of contour, areal contrast, body-axes, and movement in pictorial representation. Some of these abstractions show parallels with physiological mechanisms of the visual brain, as is demonstrated in Fig. 1. The treatment is restricted to the graphic arts in which mostly white–black contrasts are used. Colour effects are not treated, although they, too, may contribute to these abstractive processes.

In drawing, the artist uses a reduction to contours similar to that found in vision. A physiological basis of pattern perception in the visual system is the signalling of outlines signifying the contoured forms of the object seen. The draughtsman usually first sketches these linear outlines and later fills them in with hatching or wash to give the illusion of light, shade, and plastic form. In vision the eye receives the projections of bright and dark areas on the retina, and the neuronal systems code them for relative brightness or darkness respectively, and enhance their linear borders. During the transfer of visual information from the eye to the brain, the contoured borders are accentuated progressively in the retina, the lateral geniculate, and the visual cortex (Jung and Baumgartner, 1965). By means of this border contrast enhancement, the neurones of the visual cortex can signal visual complex patterns with linear contours. Fig. 1 shows the principles of this neurophysiological contour abstraction.

In sketching, the artist acts in accordance with the same visual laws, but proceeds in a direction opposite to the abstractive process of vision. He begins with the linear outlines and ends with a picture showing also the values of light and space (Jung, 1971). In addition, he can delineate the structures and movements of the human body graphically, using oriented lines without contours, as is illustrated in Fig. 6.

**Abstractions of contour, structure, and movement.** Three main kinds of linear abstraction can be distinguished in the graphic arts: (i) the enhance-

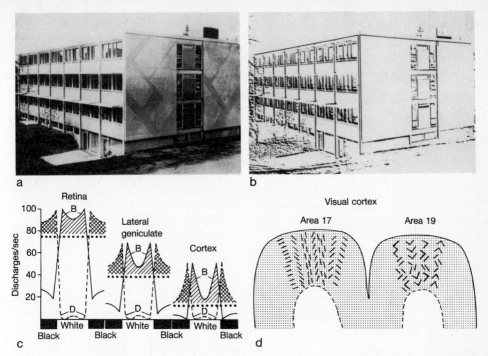

**Fig. 1.** Contour enhancement in the visual system by progressive effects of simultaneous contrast. The halftone picture (a) is transformed into the linear figure (b) by neuronal mechanisms of border contrast (c). The order of contour-signalling neurones in the visual cortex is shown in d.

a, b. Photographic imitation of contour abstraction, obtained by copying from displaced positive and negative photographic plates. a may correspond approximately to the retinal image, b to the information of the visual cortex. c. Neuronal responses to a light bar on black background show progressive contour enhancement from retina to cortex in the brightness system B (on-centre neurones signalling contrast brightness) and the darkness system D (off-centre neurones signalling contrast darkness). A comparison of the discharge rates of diffuse illumination (. . .) with contrast stimulation shows the contrast enhancement in the hatched and cross-hatched areas for the brightness and darkness systems respectively. d. Scheme of neuronal columns in visual cortex areas for information about contours and angles of certain orientations. In the orientation columns the retinal image is abstracted into linear contours similar to b.

ment of form and contour by linear outlines; (ii) the emphasis of the structural axes of the body, independent of contoured forms; and (iii) the representation of movement by schematic line drawings. To put it simply: outlines determine the form (Fig. 2), axial lines show the structure, and certain relations of structural axes signify a body in motion (Fig. 6).

Only the contour form of linear abstraction (i) can be explained by neurophysiological processes, as is shown in Fig. 1. Although the physiological basis of abstractions (ii) and (iii) is unknown, they may be characterized in *cybernetic terms as a reduction in redundant information about visual forms, in favour of information about axial orientation.

Figs. 2–6 show works of art, selected from different ages and cultures, in which the human body is predominantly depicted by linear contours, non-linear brightness contrast, or structural axes for the representation of motion. The figures demonstrate the power of linear expression in the graphic arts

and the truth of the ancient saying that drawing is the art of omission. This omission is effected by abstractions to the essential values of contour, light, and movement.

**Contour dominance.** Forms and individuals can be recognized from a few contoured lines without other brightness or colour information. The building in Fig. 1a is perceived almost as clearly in the linear abstraction of Fig. 1b. This linear simplification is used by caricaturists to characterize individuals or constructs. Contoured drawings or prints are examples of this contour dominance. They may provide both form perception and aesthetic value, as in Figs. 2a and 2b.

Thus it seems to be true that outlines give sufficient information to characterize a form and that areal and colour contrast provide only additional and redundant information. With more radical reduction of redundant information even contours may be renounced, information being limited to the axial lines of body and limbs, as is shown in

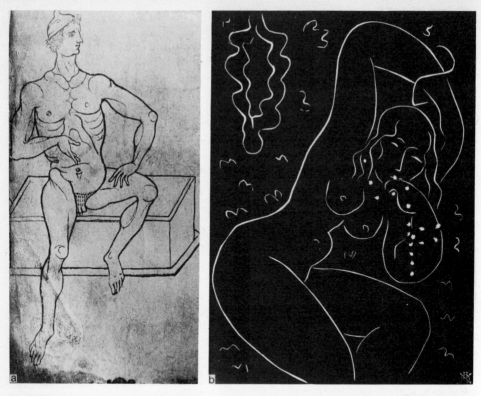

**Fig. 2.** Contoured representations of the human body from the thirteenth and the twentieth centuries. The examples show opposite contrasts: black on white (**a**) and white on black (**b**). **a.** Medieval drawing of a sitting man in Villard d'Honnecourt's sketch-book (*c.*1230). It is limited mainly to the body contour with a few added lines indicating muscles and ribs. Pen on parchment. Left side, 14 × 7 cm of a 14 × 22 cm page. **b.** Modern contoured print by Matisse in white lines on black background (1944). It shows the essential outlines of a sitting female nude wearing a pearl necklace and surrounded by some background decoration. Linocut. 24·3 × 17·7 cm.

Fig. 6. The Stone Age pictures of the Franco-Cantabrian group, for example in Lascaux, have mainly contoured outlines in the naturalistic style of ten to eight thousand years BC, whereas axial line reduction is mainly used in the late Stone Age rock painting of the sixth to fourth millennium BC in eastern Spain.

**Uncontoured brightness contrast.** Physiologists have demonstrated two kinds of visual contrast: one is border contrast, which enhances the contours by the so-called Mach bands (Ratliff, 1971); and the other is areal contrast, which exaggerates the brightness differences of large surfaces, as investigated by Ewald *Hering (1878). In Hering's contrast, a bright area is seen brighter in a dark surround; and vice versa: a dark area appears blacker when framed by bright areas relatively independent of contoured borders. Hering's contrast may be seen as non-linear brightness differences. Some artists, such as Seurat and Signac, avoided all linear contours in their drawings and pictures, producing only a pointillistic surface effect (Ratliff, 1971). This is demonstrated in

Fig. 3, a typical uncontoured drawing by Seurat. Contours may be seen, at the borders of non-linear bright and dark areas, as a linear illusion caused by Mach bands.

The special uncontoured technique of Seurat is exceptional in the art of drawing. Most artists combine lines with areal contrast by supplementing the linear design with added brushwork and wash in different halftone gradations of brightness. In etchings, these halftones may be added by the mezzotint technique as shown in Fig. 4. Here Turner designed the original contoured etching (Fig. 4a) and a professional engraver completed it with mezzotint (4b). Linear and areal contrast are also combined in the so-called *Craik illusion, resulting in border-induced brightness and darkness, which Ratliff (1971) discusses for East Asiatic brush paintings. The Craik effect may enhance areal contrasts.

**Wash and colour supplementing contour.** Visual forms and patterns are most easily reproduced as outline drawings. This linear contour abstraction may remain dominant, as in Fig. 2, or may be

**Fig. 3.** Non-linear drawing of a female nude made by G. Seurat in 1887 using pure bright–dark contrast. Light values, atmosphere, plastic form, and contour effects are obtained without lines by more or less dense rubbing of black chalk (*crayon conté*) on granulated paper. The black granules contrast with the white paper. Seurat avoided linear contours with his pointillistic technique, both in black–white drawings and in coloured pictures. This sketch for the painting *Poseuses* was preceded by a contoured outline-drawing. 29·7 × 22·5 cm.

supplemented by surface effects adding brightness and colour contrast (Fig. 4b). Both types are found in the pictorial art of all ages. The most ancient examples come from neolithic cave art, which produced many contoured and coloured drawings of animals. In this Stone Age naturalistic style, the first outline sketch either remains linear or is completed in colour. A linear style is also prominent in medieval pen drawings and in the earliest woodcuts. All woodcuts of the fifteenth century were contoured, before Dürer introduced more or less dense hatchings and cross-hatchings to the woodblock to depict the values of light and shade. The frequent colouring of the early woodcuts and the adding of wash to contoured drawings shows that there was a need for additional colour and surface values. These are often completed by refined brushwork, so that the subjects drawn appear as plastic forms in an envelope of light. Some artists also prefer linearity for light and shade and achieve these effects by the use of hatching and cross-hatching—for example, Dürer and Raphael. Others express non-linear values of light, shade, and colour by additional brushwork (e.g. Tiepolo), or by special techniques with chalk (Seurat, Fig. 3). All variations, including the soft shining surface of

the late Nazarene or Pre-Raphaelite drawings of the nude, and the vigorous linear or surface contrasts of modern art (which often deform or destroy the contours), have their special aesthetic appeal. In prints made as reproductions, aquatint and mezzotint techniques are used to represent surface values of bright and dark areas similar to brushwork and wash in the drawings (see Fig. 4b).

**Linearity, light effects, and style.** The linear and non-linear tendencies of the graphic arts vary in different style epochs, often alternating in a process of reaction and counter-reaction (Jung, 1971). For example, in the nineteenth century academic linearization and classicizing contour enhancement provoked the emphasis on light and colour in the Romantic movement and in Turner's aquarelles. Later the rather dry figure drawing of historical painters gave way to the impressionists' turbulent drawing style with dissolution of patterns and dispersed light. This again was followed by the sharply contrasting boundaries seen in art nouveau, the black–white areal contrast of the expressionists' woodcuts, the contour distortions of the fauvists, and the tendency to deformation in many modern artists following Picasso (Jung, 1974).

Although the neo-impressionists, such as Seurat, used physiological concepts of colour contrast for their art theories, the influence of these scientific tendencies on the pictorial arts was negligible. Discussions of art on the basis of science are limited to a few aspects of contrast and colour, already mentioned by *Leonardo da Vinci in his treatise on painting written around 1500. Many a limit can be transgressed in free artistic creation, but even the artists followed physiological laws of visual perception when they applied principles of contour and brightness vision almost instinctively in their work, as *Helmholtz remarked as early as 1871. The abstractive processes of vision in art receive little attention in the monographs on art and visual perception. Ratliff (1971) has depicted good examples of contour-induced brightness effects in oriental art.

**Dynamic linear structures.** Many purely contoured drawings from all historical periods—for example, the medieval Fig. 2a or the classicizing drawings by Flaxman and others—appear static, dry, and often somewhat boring. To avoid this the artist tends to vivify or dissolve these pure contours by interrupting them or adding a variety of line or light values. Dynamic effects may be obtained by irregular contours and lively hatching without wash and areal brightness contrast. Fig. 5 shows two modern drawings of human figures in which dynamic linear structures are added. In *information theory, these dynamic additions would be called redundant, since they do not supply further information about the forms, but they are aesthetically rewarding.

A vivid drawing technique and a dissolution of

**Fig. 4.** Linear contours of an etching by J. M. W. Turner (**a**) completed in 1812 as a mezzotint (**b**) in halftones of light and shade. 18·7 × 26·5 cm. **a.** The pure linear etching depicts the landscape mainly by contours, with a few hatchings at the trees and on the human figure. It was sketched by Turner himself and intended to be mezzotinted by a professional engraver. **b.** Completed mezzotint. The engraver, W. Say, has added the halftones, varying from a dark blackish brown in the foreground to light yellowish brown in the buildings of the background. The scraped, smooth parts of the plate ground are seen as light areas in contrast to the dark, roughened, unscraped areas.

contours may depict emotional values or physical movement. However, dynamic lines are not necessarily expressions of lively motion. In Fig. 5 the dynamically drawn women appear to move slowly from a standing or sitting posture, in Fig. 5a bending forward during the act of washing, and in Fig. 5b turning sideways. Slight modifications to this dynamic drawing technique are used to depict moving figures. Motion *per se*, however, can also be expressed without any linear redundancy by very simple drawings of the essential body axes in single lines, as is shown in Fig. 6. Here the redundancy is reduced, whereas in Fig. 5 it is increased.

In modern art the tendency towards contour distortion and expressionist deformation is counteracted by a tendency in the opposite direction, towards natural contour representation and calm. Matisse is a good example of this predilection for clean, simple, and balanced line drawings, avoiding extreme expression and wild movements or gestures. This return from excessive extravagance to the rules of classic art is marked more in the works of French than German or British artists of recent decades. From his Fauves period (1905), when he used contrasting surfaces or dissolved outlines, Matisse turned to clear and serene contours. The odalisque-like women of his pen drawings, etchings, and linocuts made in 1930–48 show sharp outlines without effects of light or movement. The background is usually formed by decorative additions at a distance from the body, as in Fig. 2b. His contoured bodies signify relaxed rest or perhaps quiet movement. Matisse himself remarked: 'Je veux un art d'équilibre, de pureté, qui n'inquiète ni trouble. Je veux que l'homme fatigué, surmené, éreinté, goûte devant mes peintures le calme et le repos.'

a                                                                          b

**Fig. 5.** Dynamic structures with dissolving contours in modern drawings of female bodies. **a.** Weisgerber's woman standing in front of a dressing-table is drawn with irregular hatching and restless contour lines. Hence body and objects appear more vivid than in pure contour drawings, but the impression of quiet stance bending forward prevails over movement. Pen black. *c.*1913. 20·7 × 15·3 cm. **b.** Friesz's sitting woman turned to the left, and the signature, are drawn in vivid lines. Quick and turbulent hatchings and interrupted contours enhance the impression of a turning movement from a quiet sitting posture. Pencil. *c.*1928. 39·6 × 29·0 cm.

**Structural axes and representation of movements.** The oriented axis of a body or limb can be drawn in a single line. The combined arrangement of these lines depicts characteristic postures of the human figure that can be recognized at a single glance. These axes are independent of body contours but are related to the position of the joints in various postures. When the limbs are drawn in positions of walking or running, the viewer immediately recognizes these movements in the immobile picture. Fig. 6 shows examples of this depiction of motion in various cultures, from Stone Age rock paintings down to modern art.

Axial structures have been used since prehistoric times to depict men and animals in motion. Linear human figures of this type are typical of the 'Levante' rock paintings in eastern Spain made about 5000 BC (Fig. 6a). Similar figures appear in Viking pictures in Scandinavia in the first centuries AD, in the later South African bushman drawings, and in Australian aboriginal rock pictures (Fig. 6b). Their use by these very different populations, who had no cultural relations with each other, demonstrates that the representation of axial structures and movement is a universal feature in the human visual arts. Such linear figures depicting running men are recognizable at a glance and are even understood by children as signifying movement.

**Perception of axial clues and motion.** The neuronal mechanisms of the visual abstraction of body axes are unknown. One can only presume that they may be related to *Hubel and Wiesel's orientation columns and direction-specific responses in the visual cortex (Hubel and Wiesel, 1959) (see VISUAL SYSTEM: ORGANIZATION). The perception of axial clues, however, has been well investigated since Marey began his chronophotographic analyses of body movements marked by axial lines of the limbs. G. Johansson (1973) has shown that we can recognize complex movements of human bodies in a film from a few dots positioned at the limbs. This extremely reduced information on spatio-temporal patterns is integrated into a *Gestalt perception of moving bodies.

**Conclusion.** We have come to the general conclusion that forms are determined by outlines, organic structures by axial lines, and bodies in motion by arrangements of structural axes. These principles of visual abstraction appear to be valid for both visual representation and cognition.

The few examples of visual abstractions in graphic art discussed with Figs. 2–6 show that the artist, albeit dependent on the physiological laws of vision, has some freedom of selection and variation. According to his concepts he can express what he wants to say by different techniques. In

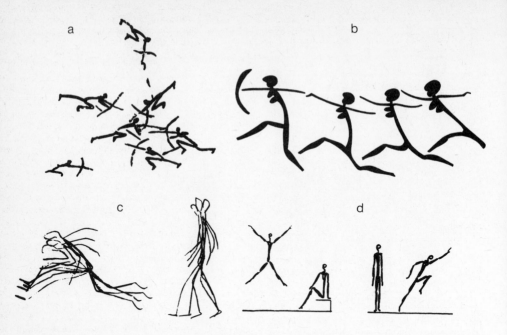

**Fig. 6.** Human motion depicted by oriented axial line patterns in Stone Age rock paintings and in modern drawings. **a.** A battle of archers (eastern Spain), painted in simple axial lines of limbs and trunk signifying moving and shooting men. Red lines on grey rock. *c.*5000 BC. 10·5 × 12·0 cm. **b.** Running and dancing women drawn in simple line figures by Australian aborigines. Red paint on grey rock. *c.* AD 1700 (?). 50 × 150 cm. **c.** Modern drawing of a running and walking man with multiple axial lines of body and limbs. Pen black. *c.*6 × 10 cm. **d.** Sitting, standing, jumping, and running men, with slightly thickened orientated lines indicating the limb postures. Pen black. *c.*6 × 10 cm.

spite of these various possibilities, art is not completely autonomous, since its effect on the viewer is processed by the viewer's visual system. The draughtsman can add colour and wash to contour drawings to obtain surface values in an envelope of light, but the effect on the viewer is determined by the mechanisms of contrast vision. The draughtsman can depict motion in a static picture by arranging contours and axial lines, but this is only an illusion of movement. We perceive moving figures in these drawings, although there is, of course, no real movement in them. Visual recognition, trained by experience and memory, helps us to see motion in the simple line figures of Fig. 6. A further information reduction to an immobile pattern of spots positioned at the joints, such as used by Johansson in his experiments, is not seen as moving. Only real motion of these spots, as seen in a film, transforms them into apparently moving bodies.

In general, the significance and the beauty of art are only apparent to those who can see and are trained in viewing. The artist himself is not interested in the process of seeing, and lets the physiologist investigate visual mechanisms. Leonardo, who discovered certain laws of contrast vision, was unique in being both an artist and a scientist. The vain attempts of the neo-impressionists to build a theory of painting on the physiology of colour contrast show the limits of the relation between physiology and art. Modern techniques of Op Art, deliberately using optical illusions to induce stereopatterns and movement perceptions, are confined to a narrow field.

Although it may be useful for the artist to know some of the principles of vision and their possible applications to the visual arts, the relevance of physiological laws to the visual arts and to *aesthetic values is limited. Art has a greater degree of freedom than science. Even if the scientist elucidates certain principles and limits of the visual perception of form, science cannot dictate to the artist what he should do. The frontiers of the visual arts must be set by the creative artist himself.

See also ART AS PERCEPTUAL EXPERIENCE.      R. J.

Arnheim, R. (1956). *Art and Visual Perception.* London.
Gombrich, E. H. (1962). *Art and Illusion,* 2nd edn. London.
Helmholtz, H. von (1871–3). *Optisches über Malerei.* Braunschweig.
Hering, E. (1878). *Zur Lehre vom Lichtsinne.* Vienna.
Hubel, D. H. and Wiesel, T. N. (1959). Receptive fields of single neurones in the cat's striate cortex. *Journal of Physiology*, **148**, 574–91.
Johansson, G. (1973). Visual perception of biological motion and a model of its analysis. *Perception and Psychophysics*, **14**, 201–11.
Jung, R. (1971). Konstrastsehen, Konturbetronung und Künstlerzeichnung. *Stud. Gen.*, **24**, 1,536–65.

Jung, R. (1974). Neuropsychologie und Neurophysiologie des Kontur—und Formsehen in Zeichnung and Malerei. In Wieck, H. H. (ed.), *Psychopathologie Musischer Gestaltungen*, pp. 29–88. Stuttgart and New York.

Jung, R. and Baumgartner, G. (1965). Neuronenphysiologie der visuellen und paravisuellen Rindenfelder. *Proceedings of the 8th International Congress of Neurology*, vol. 3, pp. 47–75. Wien.

Kleint, B. (1969). *Bildlehre, Elemente und Ordnung der Sichtbaren Welt*. Basle and Stuttgart.

Ratliff, F. (1971). Contour and contrast. *Proceedings of the American Philosophical Society*, **115**, 150–63.

**ART AS PERCEPTUAL EXPERIENCE. The objectivity of images.** For most practical purposes, human beings do not get into much trouble when they base their conduct on the conviction that the world they see is the world as it is. It is a reasonable simplification, and only occasional refinements call for minor corrections. 'This colour looks yellower than it is in the daylight.' 'In this dress she looks taller than she is.' 'The mountains are farther away than they look.' Corrections of this kind consist in revising a particular view on the basis of one's total perceptual resources. One may correct, for example, an observed size by comparing it with the length of a yardstick, or test a colour against a sample swatch.

These corrections are necessary as long as we use visual images as intermediary information for the purpose of getting along in what we call the physical world. The physical world, known to us through the totality of our perceptual experiences and the inferences suggested by these experiences, is governed by laws we cannot ignore with impunity. If one builds a house whose walls look vertical but are not, the house may collapse. Hence the need for correcting our images.

In the visual arts such corrections are inappropriate because a painting or piece of sculpture is not a stand-in for physical objects, to be subjected to physical handling. Rather a work of art is a statement *about* such objects and other facts of experience. Being perceptual statements, the images produced by art objects are final in all their properties. A giant in a painting by Goya is as large as he looks. The Rialto bridge in a view of Venice is, rightly or wrongly, as far away as we see it. The weightiness of a wooden figure by Ernst Barlach has little to do with the weight of the wood; and a certain orange in a painting by Matisse is orange, even though it might look red when put somewhere else. What *looks* vertical *is* vertical.

Are we then to say that the perceptual features of the mental images we call works of art are purely subjective? 'Subjective' is a dangerous term, to be used with caution. Those visual qualities are subjective in the sense that they require a pair of functioning eyes in the observer. Without eyes there is no picture. And yet, images have an objectivity of their own, which we acknowledge when we say that a tired tourist looking at Leonardo's cartoon of the Virgin with St Anne may see something pale, stiff, indifferent; but his image has to be discounted. The tourist has failed to see the picture. The cartoon contains objective qualities of expression and compositional relation that must be fully perceived to be appreciated. Only because art images are objective facts can there be critical dialogue about their nature. Only because images are objective facts can the eyes of a student be opened by a perceptive teacher.

Somebody may assert, 'In this etching by Picasso the head of the Minotaur is much too large in relation to his body', and be told, 'But in relation to all the other small figures in the picture, the large size of the head is exactly right!' The first judge has been convicted of misinterpretation caused by restricted vision. There is no way of avoiding the debate about the true perceptual structure of the picture by insisting on one's right to look subjectively.

The observer, however, has a mental structure of his own. When one of Picasso's paintings is used by psychologists in a personality test—as in fact has been done—someone who is being tested may report that the figures in the painting look at each other with bitter hatred. Such a response cannot be brushed aside as irrelevant. It may not do justice to the picture, but it describes the result of the encounter between two mental structures, namely the perceptual image received and the personal views, needs, attitudes of the beholder. Such encounters attain more general importance when a historian notes how differently certain cultural periods react to works of a particular style, for example to Gothic architecture, Roman portraiture, or the paintings of El Greco. The interplay between the viewer and the work of art viewed sheds light on the objective structures of both parties. These structures can be extrapolated from the context by a comparison between many different works seen by the same viewer or, vice versa, between many different responses to the same work. If you collect and compare the responses to the Laocoön group in the Vatican over the last five hundred years, you will learn something about the work's objective nature and qualities.

**The perception of images.** The ability to see visual representations at all cannot be taken for granted. At closer scrutiny this ability turns out to be a combination of two abilities. (i) The viewer can recognize the subject-matter, even though the image varies from the model in size, colour, spatial dimensions, etc. A primitive tribesman, confronted with a photograph for the first time, may see only a flat object with a mottled surface. But the same tribesman may recognize simply shaped outlines of human faces, fishes, or the sun. So may a monkey, looking at similarly simple pictures—a remarkable feat of perceptual abstraction. (ii) The viewer is able to conceive of images as representations of kinds of subjects existing elsewhere. Instead of, or in addition to, responding to a portrait by saying, 'A smiling woman is looking at me'—an experience that can lead in extreme cases to actual delusions—the viewer realizes, 'This picture is meant to look like someone who actually lived in Italy in the past.' A monkey, as far as we know, could not treat a picture in this way as a referential statement.

A picture may be called a *self-image* when it is taken as a visual expression of its own properties, and a *likeness* when it is taken as a statement about other objects, kinds of objects, or properties. The first conception, more elementary, can exist without the second; the second, more sophisticated, combines with the first.

Both abilities to deal with images may occur at various levels of abstraction. Man and animal would be unable to see a simple outline figure as a human face unless perception consisted in the grasping of general structural features rather than in the mechanical recording of all individual detail. In the arts, this fact is demonstrated to us, for example, when we step close to a portrait by Frans Hals and find that the face, moustache, and lace collar disintegrate into a qualitatively different pattern of brush-strokes. With changing distance, the level of abstraction has shifted.

Observe now that the structural features of shape and colour which make us see a Dutch cavalier on the canvas are perceptual generalities. The roundness of a face, the curliness of hair, the whiteness of a collar are examples of very general qualities, found everywhere. Hence, seeing a clearly shaped thing means also seeing a *kind* of structural behaviour. This sort of generality remains subordinated to the objects portrayed in the naturalistic paintings of a Van Eyck or Holbein. It comes increasingly to the fore in highly abstract styles, for example in the arts of our century. In such works the formal features predominate to such an extent that they subdue the vehicle of subject-matter. In a reclining woman by Henry Moore the particular shapes of a female body are reduced to very general although characteristic curvatures of surfaces and volumes. Viewed even more abstractly, the sculptor's piece of wood or stone becomes an image of man's relation to the earth, on which his body reposes; and finally one may go beyond the distinction between the organic and the inorganic and see a grouping of masses in which characteristics of living bodies and rolling hills combine indistinguishably in an image of the forms of nature.

When the references to natural subject-matter are entirely suppressed and representation is entrusted to purely 'abstract', non-mimetic shapes, colours, and movement, the artist probes the outer limits of the imagery which is accessible to man as a symbolizing animal.

See also ART AND VISUAL ABSTRACTION.    R. A.

**ARTIFICIAL INTELLIGENCE** (AI) is the science of making machines do the sorts of things that are done by human minds. Such things include holding a conversation, answering questions sensibly on the basis of incomplete knowledge, assembling another machine from its components given the blueprint, learning how to do things better, playing chess, writing or translating stories, understanding analogies, neurotically repressing knowledge that is too threatening to admit consciously, and recognizing the various things seen in a room—even an untidy and ill-lit room. AI helps one to realize how enormous is the background knowledge and thinking (computational) power needed to do even these everyday things.

The 'machines' in question are typically digital computers, but AI is not the study of computers. Rather, it is the study of intelligence in thought and action. Computers are its tools, because its theories are expressed as computer programs which are tested by being run on a machine.

Other theories of intelligence are expressed verbally, either as psychological theories of thinking and behaviour, or as philosophical arguments about the nature of knowledge and *purpose and the relation of mind to body (the *mind–body problem). Because it approaches the same subject-matter in different ways, AI is relevant to psychology and the philosophy of mind.

If we think of a program as a picture of a part of the mind, we must realize that a functioning program is more like a film of the mind than a portrait of it. Programming one's hunches about how the mind works is helpful in two ways. First, it enables one to express richly structured psychological theories in a rigorous fashion (for everything in the program has to be precisely specified, and all its operations have to be made explicit); and secondly, it forces one to suggest specific hypotheses about precisely *how* a psychological change can come about. For example, one might say that a person reacts to a policeman in a particular way because he sees him as an 'authority figure'. *Freudian psychologists suggest some ways in which this sort of interpersonal perception and attitude might function, and ways in which it might have developed in the person's mind—tracing it back to early infancy. But if one were to write a computer program that was able to recognize the analogy between a policeman and a father, one would have to specify the conceptual comparisons that underlie this recognition.

Of course, one could cheat: one could simply write into the program the information that 'All policemen may be treated as one would treat a father'; but this would both lead the program into some very strange behaviour—such as buying Christmas presents for the policeman—and fail to capture the general concept of an 'authority figure', so that the program had no inkling of the affinity between fathers, policemen, government ministers, and God. Clearly, a program able to recognize this general affinity would need to have a great deal of knowledge about interpersonal relationships in Western society, as well as being able to make subtle comparisons between various aspects of different concepts. The attempt to write such a program, even if it were unsuccessful, could not fail to indicate the richness of the equivalent psychological phenomenon in human minds.

Similarly, attempts to write programs that can interpret the two-dimensional image from a TV camera in terms of the three-dimensional objects in the real world (or which can recognize photographs or drawings as representations of solid objects) help make explicit the range and subtlety of knowledge and unconscious inference that underlie our introspectively 'simple' experiences of seeing. Much of this knowledge is tacit (and largely innate) knowledge about the ways in which, given the laws of optics, physical surfaces of various kinds can give rise to specific visual images on a retina (or camera). Highly complex computational processes are needed to infer the nature of the physical object (or of its surfaces), on the basis of the two-dimensional image.

In addition, 'visual' computer programs help to show how the perceptual system copes with ambiguity in the input, and how it is able to recognize certain inputs as pictures of 'impossible' objects. These achievements rest on the active interpretation of the picture-parts by reference to an implicit *schema or representation, where the 'parts' are largely identified by way of this over-all schema. Work in computer vision thus helps to clarify plausible but vaguely expressed notions in theoretical psychology, such as *Helmholtz's 'unconscious inference' and supports the *Gestalt psychologists' slogan, 'The whole is greater than the sum of its parts'.

Traditional philosophical puzzles connected with the mind–body problem can often be illuminated by AI, because modelling a psychological phenomenon on a computer is a way of showing that—and how—it is *possible* for that phenomenon to arise in a physical system. For instance, people often feel that only a spiritual being (as opposed to a bodily one) could have purposes and try to achieve them; and the problem then arises of how the spiritual being, or mind, can possibly tell the body what to do, so that the body's hand can try to achieve the mind's purpose of, say, picking a daisy. It is relevant to ask whether, and how, a program can enable a machine to show the characteristic features of purpose. Is its behaviour guided by its idea of a future state? Is that idea sometimes illusory or mistaken (so that the 'daisy' is made of plastic, or is really a buttercup)? Does it symbolize what it is doing in terms of goals and sub-goals (so that the picking of the daisy may be subordinate to the goal of stocking the classroom nature-table)? Does it use this representation to help plan its actions (so that the daisies on the path outside the sweet-shop are picked, rather than those by the gas station)? Does it vary its means–end activities so as to achieve its goal in different circumstances (so that buttercups will do for the nature-table if all the daisies have died)? Does it learn how to do so better (so that daisies for a daisy-chain are picked with long stalks)? Does it judge which purposes are the more important, or easier to achieve, and behave accordingly (if necessary, abandoning the daisy-picking when a swarm of bees appears with an equally strong interest in the daisies)? Questions like these, asked with specific examples of functioning programs in mind, cannot fail to clarify the concept of purpose. Likewise, philosophical problems about the nature and criteria of knowledge can be clarified by reference to programs that process and use knowledge, so that AI is relevant to *epistemology.

AI is concerned with thinking *in general*, not just with mathematics and logical deduction. Computers are not mere 'number crunchers', but are general symbol manipulators, systems which alter and combine symbols according to the instructions expressed in the program. Just as a spy could use numerals and arithmetical rules as a code to represent the information that the Prime Minister is having an affair with his secretary—which is semantic rather than numerical information—so the apparently 'numerical' symbols manipulated 'arithmetically' by computers can be given semantic meaning by the programmer. Thus computers are not limited to handling only information about numbers. Nor are they limited to purely deductive, or rigorous reasoning: like people, computer programs can use 'fuzzy' methods of reasoning which work fairly often, fairly well, although they may sometimes lead them into error. Visual programs, for instance, are in principle liable to visual illusion or mistake, just as humans are. Programs can even represent *inconsistent* beliefs and reasoning, much as some verbal psychological theories try to give an (internally consistent) explanation of why people often make logical errors. Indeed, AI has shown that to insist on logical rigour in the use of knowledge is often *not* the intelligent thing to do.

The main areas of AI include natural language understanding (see SPEECH RECOGNITION BY MACHINE), machine vision (see PATTERN RECOGNITION), problem-solving and game-playing (see COMPUTER CHESS), robotics, automatic programming, and the development of programming languages. Among the practical applications most recently developed or currently being developed are medical diagnosis and treatment (where a program with specialist knowledge of, say, bacterial infections answers the questions of and elicits further relevant information from a general practitioner who is uncertain which drug to prescribe in a given case); identification of unknown substances by spectroscopic analysis; teaching some subject such as geography, or electronics, to students with differing degrees of understanding of the material to be explored; the automatic assembly of factory-made items, where the parts may have to be inspected first for various types of flaw and where they need not be accurately positioned at a precise point in the assembly-line—as is needed for the automation in widespread use today; and the design of complex systems, whether electrical circuits or living spaces or some other, taking into account factors which may interact with each other in complicated ways (so that a mere 'check-list' program would not be adequate to solve the design problem).

The social implications of AI are various. As with all technologies, there are potential applications which may prove bad, good, or ambiguous in human terms. A competent medical-diagnosis program could be very useful, whereas a competent military application would be horrific for those at the receiving end; and a complex data-handling system could be well or ill used in many ways by individuals or governments. Then there is the question of what general implication AI will be seen to have for the commonly held 'image of man'. If it is interpreted by the public as implying that people are 'nothing but clockwork, really', then the indirect effects on self-esteem and social relations could be destructive of many of our most deeply held values. But it could (and should) be interpreted in a radically different and less dehumanizing way, as showing how it is possible for material systems (which, according to the biologist, we are) to possess such characteristic features of human psychology as subjectivity, purpose, freedom, and choice. The central theoretical concept in AI is *representation*, and AI workers ask how a (programmed) system constructs, adapts, and uses its inner representations in interpreting—and changing—its world. On this view, a programmed computer may be thought of as a subjective system (subject to illusion and error much as we are) functioning by way of its idiosyncratic view of the world. By analogy, then, it is no longer scientifically disreputable, as it has been thought to be for so long, to describe people in these radically subjective terms also. AI can therefore counteract the dehumanizing influence of the natural sciences that has been part of the mechanization of our world-picture since the scientific revolution of the sixteenth and seventeenth centuries.                                M. A. B.

Boden, M. A. (1977). *Artificial Intelligence and Natural Man*. New York. (2nd edn. revised, forthcoming, Cambridge. Mass.)

Boden, M. A. (ed.) (1990) *The Philosophy of Artificial Intelligence*. Oxford.

Charniak, E. and McDermott, D. V. (1985). *Artificial Intelligence*. New York.

Feigenbaum, E. A. and Feldman, J. (eds.) (1963). *Computers and Thought*. New York.

Feigenbaum, E. A. and McCordrick, P. (1984). *The Fifth Generation*. New York.

McClelland, J. L. and Rumelhart, D. E. (eds.) (1986) *Parallel Distributed Processing: Explorations in the Microstructure of Cognition*. 2 vols. Cambridge, Mass.

Marr, D. A. (1980). *Vision*. San Francisco.

Sloman, A. (1978). *The Computer Revolution in Philosophy: Philosophy, Science, and Models of the Mind*. Brighton.

Winograd, T. (1972). *Understanding Natural Language*. New York.

Winston, P. H. (1977). *Artificial Intelligence*. New York.

**ASTIGMATISM.** Defect of vision due to the radius of curvature of the optics of the eye—especially the cornea—being unequal at different orientations around the visual axis. Lines or bars at different orientations are not all simultaneously in focus, and there can be distortions for some orientations. It is well corrected by suitable spectacles, though not so easily by corneal lenses as they may be placed in the eye with any orientation.

See also EYE DEFECTS AND THEIR CORRECTION.

**ASTROLOGY.** Anyone who has taken even the most casual interest in astrology will have noticed that, contrary to all common sense, it *seems* to work. That is to say, the personal characteristics that are supposed to be governed by the 'sun signs' often appear curiously accurate. People born under Aries (between 21 March and 19 April) are supposed to have drive and enterprise; Tauruses are supposed to be practical and stubborn; Geminis clever but changeable; Cancers homelovers with a tendency to over-sensitivity; Leos dominant extraverts with a touch of egoism; Virgos hard workers who are obsessed by detail; Libras charmers who know how to get their own way; and so on. And most of us can, without much trouble, recall acquaintances who are typical Leos, Cancers, Geminis, etc.

Scientifically speaking, of course, this proves nothing; the sceptic can always point to untidy Virgos, modest Leos, timid Aries. Yet it is not difficult to feel that the 'hits' are striking enough to be worth closer investigation. In a case like this, the obviously sensible method is statistical—how many people can be shown to fit their astrological 'type'? In the early years of this century, a Frenchman, Paul Choisnard, tried the statistical approach, and his work inspired a Swiss mathematician, Karl Ernst Krafft, to even more ambitious efforts. Emphasizing his strictly scientific approach, Krafft preferred to call the subject 'astrobiology'; his immense *Traité d'astro-biologie* appeared (in French) in 1939; but the times were unpropitious, and it attracted little attention. It was Krafft who, in a letter of 2 November 1939 (to a member of Himmler's Secret Intelligence Service), predicted that Hitler's life would be in danger between the 7th and 10th of the month—he specifically mentioned 'assassination by explosive material'. When Hitler narrowly escaped death in the Munich beer cellar—he had just left when the bomb exploded—on 8 November 1939, Krafft's prediction was remembered and he was brought to Berlin. For a while he became a kind of semi-official astrologer to Himmler, but soon fell out of favour, and died in a concentration camp.

Krafft had attempted to 'prove' astrology by examining the birth certificates of thousands of professional men—he concentrated on musicians—and trying to show that their temperament corresponded to their sun sign. In 1950, a Sorbonne-trained statistician and psychologist, Michel Gauquelin, became interested in Krafft's *Traité*, and fed its results into a computer. His conclusion was that Krafft was deceiving himself when he believed his figures proved anything—he had allowed himself too much leeway of interpretation. Gauquelin's book, *Songes et mensonges de l'astrologie* (1969), was a scathing attack on astrology, as its title (*Dreams and Delusions of Astrology*) indicates. Yet the unsatisfactoriness of Krafft's experimental method led Gauquelin to devise a few simple tests of his own.

He concentrated his analysis on two straightforward questions. The first was whether astrologers are correct in stating that people born under 'odd' signs of the zodiac—Aries, Gemini, Leo, Libra, Sagittarius, Aquarius—tend to be extraverts, while those born under even signs—Taurus, Cancer, Virgo, Scorpio, Capricorn, Pisces—are likely to be introverts (see EXTRAVERSION–INTROVERSION). The second question was whether a person's choice of profession is in any way governed by the planet that is in the ascendant (coming up over the horizon) at the moment of birth.

Greatly to his surprise, the evidence in both cases was positive. The tests were repeated many times, in four European countries, and the results continued to favour these assertions of astrology. Professor H. J. Eysenck was asked to check the results. He agreed, apparently with the expectation that they would prove to be invalid; and was equally surprised to find that they were positive.

The method used by Gauquelin—and later by Eysenck (and two associates, Jeff Mayo and A. White)—was as follows. Certain professions were chosen—sports champions, actors, scientists—and their birth certificates consulted for the exact time of birth (which is recorded on the Continent, though not in England). The subjects were 'famous'—to be found in reference books—and the numbers ran into thousands.

Astrologers believe that the 'rising sign' (the sign coming up over the horizon at the moment of birth) and the rising planet are of basic importance in governing the subject's temperament. Gauquelin's computer analysis seemed to show that three other positions were equally important: directly overhead, sinking below the horizon, and directly underfoot—the four quarters of the heavens, as it were. The findings were perfectly clear. Sportsmen tended to be born when Mars was in one of these critical positions, actors when Jupiter was there, and scientists (and doctors) when Saturn was there. Eysenck (1979) states: 'The results were extremely clear-cut and so significant statistically that there is no question whatsoever that the effects were not produced by chance.' But Eysenck, like Gauquelin, is careful to state that he does not consider these results 'prove' astrology; rather, he says, they should be regarded as the possible foundation of a new science of astrobiology.

Now there can be no possible doubt that astrology, as traditionally practised, is a pseudoscience. Early astrology—as practised by the Sumerians

and Babylonians—was a jumble of old wives' tales. 'When a yellow dog enters a palace there will be destruction in its gates', says a Babylonian text; 'When the planet Mercury approaches Aldebaran the king of Elam will die', says another; and the two assertions sound equally absurd. But they are no more embarrassingly silly than modern popular books on astrology with titles like *Love Signs* and *The Stars and You*. How, then, is it possible to take seriously any 'science' that asserts a connection between 'the stars' and human destiny?

It must first be noted that the stars, as such, play no part in astrology. Because they are 'fixed', they can be used as reference points for the positions of the planets—that is to say, they could be regarded as the figures around the face of a clock, while the planets are the hands. It is the bodies in our own solar system that are believed to exert forces upon the earth, which, in turn, exerts forces on human beings. How? Astrology has never been concerned with this question, but Gauquelin suggests that the answer lies in the earth's magnetic field. In 1962, Y. Rocard, professor of physics at the Sorbonne, conducted an investigation into the claims of water-diviners, and demonstrated that the dowser's muscles react to weak changes in terrestrial magnetism caused by underground water, and that a capacity for detecting extremely small magnetic gradients is surprisingly common among human beings. It has long been widely accepted that the moon can produce emotional tension—hence 'lunatics'—and the statistical evidence has been documented by Arnold Lieber (1978). Leonard J. Ravitz, of the Virginia Department of Health, investigated the influence of moon cycles on mental patients in the late 1950s and found that the difference in electrical potential between the head and chest is greater in mental patients than in normal people, and increases at the full moon. In the late 1930s, Maki Takata of Tokyo discovered that when there is high sunspot activity, the 'flocculation index'—the rate at which albumen curdles in the blood—rises abruptly. It also rises before dawn, as the blood responds to the rising sun. At about the same time, Harold Burr of Yale observed that the electric field produced by living creatures—trees, for example—varied with the seasons, as well as with the cycles of the moon and sunspot activities.

So the basic medical facts may seem to be fairly well established. It may also be worth mentioning the discovery of John H. Nelson, an electronics engineer, that most magnetic storms (causing radio interference) occur when two or more planets are in conjunction, or at angles of 180° or 90° from the sun. This seems to establish a foundation for a science of astrobiology; what still remains to be discovered is how forces of terrestrial magnetism could influence a human being to the extent of predisposing him to one profession or another—or even what regular monthly cycle could possibly determine whether a person is introverted or extraverted.

I should emphasize that I am not now asserting that the claims of astrology must somehow be 'reduced' to a series of statements about the influence of magnetic fields on animal organisms. Even a sceptical historian of astrology like Ellic Howe (1967) concedes that a 'good astrologer' can produce results of astounding accuracy—describing not only a person's temperament, but the pattern of his life. Similarly, anyone who has ever investigated dowsing will feel that the dowser's powers of detection—of other substances besides water—go far beyond the results obtained by Rocard. When the old wives' tales have been sifted out, there still seems to be more to explain than science is at present willing to admit. Modern computer analysis of structures like Stonehenge, the stones of Carnac, and the Great Pyramid suggests that their original purpose was connected with astronomy, which in turn suggests that our neolithic ancestors (the outer ditch of Stonehenge was constructed about 2900 BC) had a far more precise knowledge of astronomy than we give them credit for. Incised reindeer bones dating back twenty thousand years earlier still, suggest that Cro-Magnon man went to the trouble of tabulating the phases of the moon. It is difficult to imagine why, unless our ancestors possessed their own primitive science of 'astrobiology'—undoubtedly involved with magic and religious ritual—which later degenerated into traditional astrology.

Eysenck has said: 'At the moment the only feedback that most research workers in the field get is to be shouted down by both sides—by the astrologers for daring to have any doubts, and by the scientists for daring to look at the alleged phenomena of planetary influences on humankind at all.' But this statement in itself indicates that some of the investigations he wishes to see are already beginning to take place.     c. w.

Burr, H. S. (1972). *Blueprint for Immortality: the electric patterns of life.* London.
Eysenck, H. J. (1979). Astrology—science or superstition? *Encounter,* December, p. 88.
Gauquelin, M. (1967). *The Cosmic Clocks.* New York.
Howe, E. (1967). *Urania's Children: the strange world of the astrologers.* London.
Lieber, A. L. (1978). *The Lunar Effect: biological tides and human emotions.* New York.
Lindsay, J. (1971). *Origins of Astrology.* London.
Marshack, A. (1972). *The Roots of Civilization.* New York.

**ASYLUMS: A HISTORICAL SURVEY.** In England the care of the insane in special asylums dates from the eighteenth century and institutional care on a large scale came to be practised in the nineteenth century. The origins of the madhouse system are probably to be found in the practice of boarding out lunatics and idiots to private households. This custom persisted until well into the nineteenth century and was, predictably, much abused. Abuse occurred in two areas: firstly in the unjust confinement of sane persons, and secondly in the quality of care provided. Illegitimate con-

finements were already feared in the eighteenth century. In a *Review of the State of the English Nation* (1706), Defoe described the convenient ploy which alleged insanity provided in the case of unwanted wives or other relatives, particularly where inheritance was at stake. This fear has haunted public imagination ever since the beginnings of confinement and has provided a favourite theme in nineteenth-century literature. (For example, *Jane Eyre, The Woman in White, Melmoth the Wanderer,* and *Hard Cash* all deal with unjust or, at least, mysterious confinement.)

The second area of abuse, namely the physical conditions of the insane, was brought to public notice by the vigilant activities of nineteenth-century philanthropists. Parliamentary reports on the condition of lunacy relied on the evidence of these men and described instances of lunatics kept for many years in chicken-pens or coal-sheds, and generally under conditions of extreme barbarity and neglect.

The law did not make separate reference to lunatics until 1714. This act (12 Anne, c. 23) distinguished between lunatics and 'rogues, vagabonds and sturdy beggars and vagrants'. It authorized two or more Justices of the Peace to detain a lunatic and confine him in a safe place. The cost of the detention was to be borne by the lunatic's parish of settlement. Although the Act did not require treatment to be provided, it at least exempted the lunatic from the customary whipping legally sanctioned for rogues, vagabonds, and vagrants. The Vagrant Act of 1744 (17 Geo. II, c. 5) added the cost of cure to the expenses to be defrayed by the parish.

During the time that separate legal provision was being made for lunatics, private madhouses and asylums grew up to cater for their needs. Evidence from newspaper advertisements and books written by madhouse proprietors suggests that the practice of confining the insane in private madhouses was well established by the beginning of the eighteenth century and that it grew steadily thereafter. In 1774 an act (14 Geo. III, c. 49) was passed for the regulation of private madhouses within a seven-mile radius of London. It made obligatory the licensing and inspection of private madhouses by five commissioners to be elected from the Royal College of Physicians. However, the Act was largely ineffective. For example, it had no influence over provincial madhouses, over single lunatics, or over public subscription asylums. The commissioners could refuse to license a house to which they had been denied admission, but ill-treatment and neglect were not grounds for refusal. Thus they had no powers to bring about improvements. Nevertheless, the Act marked the beginnings of state control of lunacy.

The illness of George III (1760–1820) played an important part in the development of public awareness and tolerance of insanity. George III suffered from several distinct episodes of what was thought to be insanity, and the state of his health became a matter of grave political consequence and a point of national discussion. (For a fuller discussion, see Macalpine and Hunter (1969), in which they claim that the king was, in fact, suffering from a rare metabolic disorder called porphyria, which is liable to cause phasic attacks of mental disorder.) What is important is that the king was thought to be insane and that the nation was much moved by his sufferings. During the latter part of his reign the lunacy reform movement got under way.

From the beginning of the nineteenth century parliamentary reports on the condition of lunacy followed one another in steady succession. The establishment of county lunatic asylums was prompted partly by moral outrage felt upon the discovery of the revolting and inhuman conditions of the insane and partly by the newly found faith in the possibility of cure. The committees submitting these reports consisted of well-meaning people who displayed some of the best features of Victorian philanthropy, namely, scrupulous attention to detail and a compassion for the destitute. They took it upon themselves to visit all workhouses and asylums where lunatics were kept. The committee of 1807 concluded that 'the practice of confining such lunatics and other insane persons as are chargeable to their respective parishes in gaols, houses of correction, poor houses and houses of industry is highly dangerous and inconvenient'. They therefore recommended that 'the measure which appears to your committee most adequate to enforce the proper care and management of these unfortunate persons and the most likely to conduce to their perfect cure, is the erection of asylums for their reception in the different parts of the kingdom'. The following year (1808) an act was passed recommending that each county erect an asylum for the care of the insane. The asylums were to be supported by public funds. The Act was a permissive one, since it had no powers to enforce its regulations. As a result few county asylums were built for the time being.

The following years saw the growth of 'a free market in lunatics' and private madhouses multiplied to cope with increasing demands. Although some asylums provided a high standard of care, many more kept lunatics in dreadful conditions. These were publicized by the reports of 1815 and 1828. In York Asylum, a series of tiny cells was discovered, each housing many filthy and incontinent patients. For example, one cell measuring 12 feet by 7 feet 10 inches ($3 \cdot 7 \times 2 \cdot 4$ m) housed thirteen incontinent women. At Bethlem the case of William Norris, who had been chained by the neck to a stone wall for nine years, was given much publicity. Throughout the 1815 report conditions are described as inhuman and the patients as animal-like. In Bethlem Hospital this was particularly true. For example, the report says, 'the patients in this room were dreadful idiots, their nakedness and their mode of confinement gave this room the appearance of a dog-kennel'. The 1828 committee looked into the conditions within metropolitan madhouses. Their findings include the earlier ingredients of darkness, overcrowding, filth, and stench. They provide a catalogue of abuses and horrors.

The idea of moral management provided theoretical support for asylum-based treatment (see INSANITY: EARLY THEORIES). It advocated the abandonment of physical restraint and an appeal to the will of the patient. It aimed to restore the dignity of the patient and to enlist him as an ally in the treatment process. Two requirements of moral management were the early detection of insanity and separation of the patient from the circumstances precipitating his attack, usually his home. Both these requirements, together with claims of a near 100 per cent recovery rate, favoured the growth of the asylum. Moral management also contributed towards the recovery of lunatics from workhouses. The lunacy reformers deplored the indiscriminate intermingling of lunatics with other destitute persons.

By 1844 the abuses within madhouses had been made public and the need for improvement was clearly established. Despite the recommendation of the 1808 Act only twelve county asylums had been built. The 1844 report of the metropolitan commissioners in lunacy provides a landmark. One of the most influential commissioners was Lord Shaftesbury. The report was comprehensive: it included domestic details of the running of asylums, information on the non-restraint system, a discussion of the nature of insanity, and comments on the admission of pauper lunatics from workhouses. It was based on 166 visits to public and private asylums. One of the less well-known themes of the report concerned the dangers of clogging up asylums with incurable patients, thereby 'converting them into a permanent refuge for the insane instead of hospitals for their relief and cure'. By the middle of the nineteenth century the paradoxical situation had arisen where asylums were not able to cure because of the large numbers of incurable patients. One major reason for the asylums' lack of success was that the problems which confronted them were not specifically medical, but had a large social component. The problems of lunacy were closely related to the problems of pauperism, as 75 per cent of the insane came under poor law authorities. The year following the report two acts were passed, one making compulsory the erection of county asylums and the other providing a more comprehensive system of asylum inspection. By 1847, 36 of the 52 counties had complied with the Act and built asylums of their own. However, within a short space of time it was found that the demand for asylum beds far exceeded supply. The size of the lunacy problem grew to fit and then exceed the provisions made for it. Interestingly, the vast increases in the lunatic population occurred among pauper and not private patients: between 1844 and 1870 the number of private patients increased by about 100 per cent whereas the number of pauper lunatics increased by about 365 per cent. Alongside this growth in asylums the numbers of curable patients declined. Superintendents of asylums estimated that roughly 90 per cent of their patients were incurable. No matter how many new beds were provided the promised cures never materialized. When the asylum failed to fulfil its initial promise a cheaper asylum system and a return to the workhouse were advocated, precisely the state of affairs which had earlier aroused so much horror.

Lunatic asylums deteriorated from being small family-based units to becoming large, custodial institutions offering little hope to their inmates. Emphasis moved from early detection and treatment to illegal detention. The next major piece of legislation, the Lunacy Act of 1890, was concerned with protecting the individual against wrongful detention rather than with cure and treatment. Physicians of the period already recognized the bad effects of increasing size and routine on the inhabitants of the asylum: 'In a colossal refuge for the insane, a patient may be said to lose his individuality and to become a member of a machine so put together, as to move with precise regularity, and invariable routine; a triumph of skill adapted to show how such unpromising materials as crazy men and women may be drilled into order and guided by rule, but not an apparatus guided to restore their pristine self-governing existence. In all cases admitting of recovery, or of material amelioration, a gigantic asylum is a gigantic evil and figuratively speaking a manufactory of chronic insanity.' Despite the pessimism which came to surround the asylum, its population continued to grow. Figures show a steady increase in the asylum population (excluding the two world wars) until its peak in 1954, and thereafter a dramatic decline. With the introduction and widespread use of the major tranquillizers from the mid-fifties onwards, the emphasis on community treatment, and the attacks by sociologists on the pernicious effects of institutional care, the asylum population has continued to decrease (see ASYLUMS: ARE THEY REALLY NECESSARY?). By 1980 the total number of beds in England and Wales for the reception and treatment of patients with mental illnesses had declined to about 92,000, of which some 4,360 were in psychiatric units in general hospitals. These beds are intended for short-stay patients, and the majority of psychiatrically ill persons are still admitted and treated in the old county mental hospitals. The asylum buildings remain as a robust testimony to the Victorian faith

**Table 1.** Total number of patients in public asylums in England and Wales

| Year | Number | Year | Number |
|------|--------|------|--------|
| 1850 | 7,140  | 1954 | 148,100 |
| 1870 | 27,109 | 1960 | 136,200 |
| 1890 | 52,937 | 1970 | 103,300 |
| 1910 | 97,580 | 1980 | 92,000 |
| 1930 | 119,659 | | |

in order and progress in the face of unreason and lunacy.

v. s.

Bynum, William, Porter, Roy, and Shepherd, Michael (1985). *Anatomy of Madness:* Essays in the History of Psychiatry. Institutions and Society. London.

Donnelly, Michael (1983). *Managing the Mind:* A study of Medical Psychology in Early Nineteenth Century Britain. London.

Macalpine, I. and Hunter, R. (1969). *George III and the Mad Business.* London.

Rothman, David (1971). *The Discovery of the Asylum.* Boston.

Scull, Andrew (1979). *Museums of Madness.* London.

**ASYLUMS: ARE THEY REALLY NECESSARY?** The odium surrounding our mental hospitals, or asylums—a synonym fallen into disrepute but worthy of resurrection in the light of the present situation—is best understood as a chapter in the continuing and complicated history of the care of the mentally disordered (see ASYLUMS: A HISTORICAL SURVEY).

During the nineteenth, and early part of the twentieth centuries, Britain's asylums underwent many vicissitudes. From time to time there were scandals leading to inquiries similar in many ways to those that take place all too frequently today and for the very same reasons. However, in the period between the two world wars the trend towards a more liberal approach was established, culminating in the Mental Treatment Act, 1930, the outstanding feature of which was the provision made for the admission of voluntary as opposed to certified patients. The same liberalism permeated the hospitals themselves and was reflected in the more imaginative decoration and furnishing of the wards, and an improvement in the clothing and diet of the patients. Of even greater importance was the evolution of the concept of the 'open door', thus acknowledging that the majority of mental patients are not dangerous, and that a prison-like regime is not necessary to contain them. The spirit of enlightenment was crowned with such success that Britain easily led the world. Visitors from far and near came to see what had been achieved.

But the pendulum swung too far. An extraordinary wave of optimism flooded the psychiatric scene in the 1950s, triggered off no doubt by the introduction of the phenothiazines, claimed by some to be as specific for the treatment of the *schizophrenias as, say, insulin is in diabetes, or thyroxine in myxoedema. In a way which is difficult to understand, the mental hospitals, so recently declared Good Objects, became, almost overnight, Bad Objects. Consonant with this changed attitude, a most seductive slogan, 'community care', was conjured up; but unfortunately adequate field-work had not been done to make quite sure that the community in fact did care. Nevertheless, the policy of 'discharge and be damned' prevailed, a policy which was to be given administrative blessing in the Mental Health Act, 1959. Then, stimulated by the statistical forecasts of Tooth and Brook (1961), the then Minister of

Health, Enoch Powell, in his Hospital Plan (1962), declared that there would be a very substantial reduction in the number of beds in mental hospitals, some of which would be razed to the ground and their function divided between psychiatric units in general hospitals and 'community care'. The local authorities were to provide certain facilities, such as hostels for discharged mental hospital patients, half-way houses, sheltered workshops, home visits, and so on. Unfortunately, no date was given for when these facilities had to be made available, and it is generally accepted that with a very few exceptions the overall response left a great deal to be desired.

The policy of discharge continued, however. In the twenty years 1960–80 there was a reduction of over 44,000 in the number of beds in British mental hospitals. This might in itself be an achievement if it could be guaranteed that the quality of life of those who might have occupied those beds was at least as good as it was when they enjoyed the 'asylum' offered by the hospitals. But is it? An examination of some of the evidence might lead one to believe that it frequently is not.

Failing adequate support in the community in general and from their families (if any) in particular, discharged patients may become vagrants and by one avenue or another return to the mental hospital. Berry and Orwin (1966) report on the steep rise in the number of patients of no fixed address admitted to their hospital in Birmingham since the Mental Health Act came into being. Their summary is worth quoting:

Their plight is evidence that the initial enthusiasm evoked by the new Act for the discharge of chronic psychotics into community care was premature in view of the resources available and has resulted in the overwhelming of existing community services.

The doss-house is, of course, another alternative focus of redistribution. Edwards, Williamson, Hawker, Hensman, and Postoyan (1968), in their study of inmates of Camberwell Reception Centre, London, showed that of a population of 279, 24 per cent had previously been in a mental hospital for reasons other than drinking, and of these 7 per cent had been out of hospital for six months or less. Other studies of 'dossers', for example Lodge-Patch (1970) and Scott, Gaskell, and Morrell (1966), paint equally gloomy pictures.

But of all the foci of redistribution perhaps the most socially undesirable is the exchange of a bed in a mental hospital for a cell in a prison. Mental disorder may and does at times manifest itself in offences against the criminal law. Such offences are for the most part trivial, but they are not necessarily so by any means. Criminal statistics show that the number of cases remanded for psychiatric report rose from 6,366 in 1961 (Home Office Report) to 11,057 in 1976 (Home Office Report), nearly doubling. It is known that 16 per cent at least had been discharged from mental hospitals less than one year before their arrest. Furthermore, it is safe to say that if the period were extended to two

years since discharge the number would be in the neighbourhood of 50 per cent. But of paramount importance in this context is the angry comment contained in the 1976 prison report referring to the growing difficulty in finding accommodation for mentally abnormal offenders in National Health Service psychiatric hospitals: '. . . mentally ill people are entering prisons and borstals in increasing numbers and people of previous good personality, whose offences frequently stem solely from their illnesses, are now being refused admission to psychiatric hospitals and are, instead, being received and detained in establishments'. Furthermore, the same report refers to an assessment made by prison medical officers of the number of prisoners in custody who were suffering from mental disorder within the meaning of the 1959 Act. It emerged that 'the prison system was then holding some hundreds of offenders who were in need of and capable of gaining benefit from, psychiatric hospital care, management and treatment in psychiatric hospitals'.

Moreover, the official statistics quoted give an account of mentally abnormal offenders dealt with after prosecution (Part V of the Act). But there is also a steep rise in the number admitted, or readmitted, to mental hospitals without prosecution. Of special importance in this respect is the use of Section 136 (Part IV of the Act), a method whereby the police can deal expeditiously with social crises occasioned by the mentally disordered and remove them to a place of safety, in practice almost invariably a mental hospital. For example, in the twelve mental hospitals administered until recently by the South-West Metropolitan Regional Hospital Board the number rose from 308 (1·9 per cent of all admissions) in 1965 to 709 (4 per cent of all admissions) in 1972, an increase of well over 100 per cent. Investigations by the writer (Rollin, 1969) indicate that no less than 66 per cent of unprosecuted mentally abnormal offenders have previously been treated in mental hospitals.

From what has been said thus far it would appear that it is those who have no homes, or whose homes are unsatisfactory, who are the ones worst affected by the inadequacies of 'community care'. But are ex-patients who are more fortunate in this respect necessarily better off? A leading article in the *British Medical Journal* (4 May 1974) reads:

As a corollary it might be assumed that a warm, welcoming home would offer optimum conditions for the returning ex-patient. 'No place like home for rehabilitation' could be another seductive slogan and mean as much or as little as its counterpart 'community care'. But even under optimum conditions the major psychoses usually persist in following their predetermined course. Schizophrenia in particular, still one of the major scourges of mankind, characteristically is a chronic disease with alternating remissions and relapses, producing in about half the cases evidence of ever-increasing damage to the personality. The potential for self-sufficiency or 'rehabilitation' will vary inversely with the degree of damage and directly with the support from the family and the community. If the family burden is too great or the community support inadequate, then not only will the patient suffer but the family may go under too.

Precisely these points have been made with telling and poignant effect in the first report of an organization—the National Schizophrenia Fellowship—which has the support of the Department of Social Psychiatry of the Institute of Psychiatry, London (*Living with Schizophrenia*, 1974). In his foreword John Pringle, the honorary director of the Fellowship, does not pull his punches. He castigates those whose duty it was 'to provide the community support, in replacement for custodial care, which many chronic sufferers [from schizophrenia], unable to fend for themselves, cannot do without'. He goes on: 'The closure of mental hospital wards, which at least provide the basic minimum shelter and life support, goes ruthlessly on, leaving nothing in their place.'

The body of the report contains a series of accounts of relatives, mainly parents, of what it is like to live with schizophrenia. The burning desire to do what is right shines through the pages, but if there is a common theme it is that there are promises and more promises of help from innumerable agencies but in the end the relatives must go it alone. 'The effect of having George at home on our home life has been disastrous' typifies several examples of the way one schizophrenic can wreck the social life of an entire family. 'I do not think "the community" exists' is the sad reflection of a mother whose daughter has encountered 'the sneers, no job, cold shouldering, impatience and general feeling of being out of step'. 'I have found that every hospital wants to discharge my son at the first opportunity' is a wry comment on the administrative policy obtaining in so many mental hospitals today. 'There is, therefore, virtually nothing available in the way of after care, rehabilitation or training for the schizophrenic in this immediate area' is a further caustic statement requiring no further comment.

The Mental Health Act 1983, which consolidated the provisions of the 1959 Act and those of the Mental Health (Amendment) Act 1982, has focused attention even more sharply on the divide between what may be described as the psycho-social as opposed to the medical model. The principal change in the legislation has been new provisions concerning patients' rights, in particular when compulsory detention is involved. The District Health Authority and local social services are charged as a mandatory duty with provision of treatment, care, and support for patients living in the community, employing a cadre of approved social workers with appropriate competence. However, at the time of writing there are few signs that adequate community care under the new Act is likely to be more of a reality than in the past. Isolated experiments, such as those accompanying the closure in 1986 of Digby Hospital, Exeter, may give some cause for hope for the future; but in the main the political will at local level to implement all of the requirements of the Act has been in as short supply as the necessary finance in a time of economic stringency.

It has been necessary to condense a very considerable body of evidence to substantiate the plea made by a not inconsiderable number of psychiatrists that the mental hospital—or asylum in the true meaning of the word—should be retained for the foreseeable future, or at least until satisfactory alternatives for the care of its patients are available. If we go on as we are, sacrificing the well-being of sick people for doctrinaire reasons, or for reasons of economic or political expediency, then we will have turned the wheel full circle and be back where we were at the beginning of the nineteenth century. There is this difference, however, that in our present industrialized, urbanized, heterogeneous society, the family may not be prepared to shoulder the burden of the psychotic in their midst, nor may the 'community' (analogous to the parish of bygone days) be prepared to shoulder the burden of adequate community services.

As a footnote it could be added that Britain is not alone in reaping the bitter harvest of policies which are both ill-considered and precipitate. In Italy, for example, laws were introduced in 1978 which, *inter alia*, forbade the admission of further new patients to mental hospitals which were themselves to be run down and eventually closed. This has led to a new class of vagrants—the *abandonati*—a host of homeless, mentally sick ex-patients who roam the streets and public places. The situation in the USA, where comparable policies have been put into effect, is no better. Dr Alan A. Stone, Professor of Law and Psychiatry at Harvard, writes in 1984: 'Yet madness has not gone out of the world as was hoped, in fact madness is more visible than ever before in this century. One can see chronic mental patients in the streets of every major city in the United States.'

See also MENTALLY ILL, SERVICES FOR THE.

H. R. R.

Berry, C. and Orwin, A. (1966). No Fixed Abode. A Survey of Mental Hospital Admissions. *British Journal of Psychiatry*, **112**, 491.

Edwards, G., Williamson, V., Hawker, A., Hensman, C., and Postoyan, S. (1968). Census of a Reception Centre. *British Journal of Psychiatry*, **114**, 1,031.

Lodge-Patch, I. C. (1970). A London Survey. *Proceedings of the Royal Society of Medicine*, **63**, 437.

Scott, R., Gaskell, P. G., and Morrell, D. C. (1966). Patients Who Reside in Common Lodging Houses. *British Medical Journal*, ii, 1,561.

Stone, A. A. (1984). *Law, Psychiatry and Morality: Essays and Analysis*. Washington, D.C.

Tooth, G. C. and Brook, E. M. (1961). Trends in the Mental Hospital Population and their Effect on Future Planning. *Lancet*, i, 710.

**ATAXIA.** The lack of co-ordination between muscles that causes unsteadiness in body posture and movement and affects eye movement and speech. Sensory (or proprioceptive) ataxia results from an impaired sense of joint position (proprioception). It is aggravated when the patient shuts his eyes, as some of the proprioceptive defect is compensated for visually. Motor ataxia results from cerebellar disorders.

**ATTACHMENT.** It is characteristic of human beings to make strong affectional relationships with each other and for some of their strongest emotions to depend on how these relationships are faring. Whereas stable relationships are a source of enjoyment and security, separation, loss, or threatened loss arouse *anxiety or anger, or else sadness and *depression.

There is much controversy about how the urge to form such relationships, or bonds, is to be best understood. Until the mid 1950s only one explicitly formulated view of their nature and origin was prevalent, and in this there was agreement between psychoanalysts and learning theorists. Bonds between individuals develop, it was held, because a person discovers that, in order to reduce certain drives, for example for food in infancy and for sex in adult life, another human being is necessary. The theory postulated two kinds of drive, primary and secondary; it categorized food and sex as primary and 'dependency' and other personal relationships as secondary.

Studies of the ill effects on personality development of deprivation of maternal care led the writer to question the adequacy of this traditional model. Early in the 1950s Konrad Lorenz's work on *imprinting, which had first appeared in 1935, became more generally known and offered an alternative approach. At least in some species of birds, he had found, strong bonds to a mother-figure develop during the early days of life without any reference to food and simply through the young being exposed to and becoming familiar with the figure in question. Arguing that the empirical data on the development of a human child's tie to his mother can be understood better in terms of a model derived from *ethology, the present writer outlined a theory of attachment in a paper published in 1958. Simultaneously and independently, Harlow published the results of his first studies of infant rhesus monkeys reared on dummy mothers. A young monkey, he found, will cling to a dummy that does not feed it provided the dummy is soft and comfortable to cling to.

As a result of these findings many behavioural scientists now believe that affectional bonds are better understood in terms of what has come to be known as attachment theory. Attachment theory deals with the phenomena hitherto explained in terms of 'dependency need' or of 'object relations'; and although it incorporates much psychoanalytic thinking, it differs from traditional theorizing by adopting a number of principles derived from ethology, control theory, and cognitive psychology. An affectional bond is conceived as being the consequence of certain pre-programmed patterns of behaviour becoming focused on another individual. Their effect is to bring the first individual close to the other and to maintain him there—hence the inclusive term 'attachment behaviour'.

While especially evident during early childhood, attachment behaviour is held to characterize human beings from the cradle to the grave. It includes crying and calling, which elicit care, following and clinging, and also strong protest should a child be left alone or with strangers. With age, the frequency and the intensity with which all these forms of behaviour are exhibited diminish steadily. Nevertheless, all of them persist as an important part of man's behavioural equipment. In adults they are especially evident when a person is distressed, ill, or afraid. The particular patterns of attachment behaviour shown by an individual turn partly on his age, sex, and circumstances, and partly on the experiences he has had with attachment figures earlier in his life.

As a way of conceptualizing proximity keeping, attachment theory, in contrast to dependency theory, emphasizes the following features†:

1. *Specificity*. Attachment behaviour is directed towards one or a few specific individuals, usually in clear order of preference.

2. *Duration*. An attachment endures, usually for a large part of the life-cycle. Although during adolescence early attachments may attenuate and become supplemented by new ones, and in some cases are replaced by them, early attachments are not easily abandoned and they commonly persist.

3. *Engagement of emotion*. Many of the most intense emotions arise during the formation, the maintenance, the disruption, and the renewal of attachment relationships. The formation of a bond is described as falling in love, maintaining a bond as loving someone, and losing a partner as grieving over someone. Similarly, threat of loss arouses anxiety, and actual loss gives rise to sorrow; while each of these situations is likely to arouse anger. The unchallenged maintenance of a bond is experienced as a source of security and the renewal of a bond as a source of joy. Because such emotions are usually a reflection of the state of a person's affectional bonds, the psychology and psychopathology of *emotion is found to be in large part the psychology and psychopathology of affectional bonds.

4. *Ontogeny*. In the great majority of human infants, attachment behaviour to a preferred figure develops during the first nine months of life. The more experience of social interaction an infant has with a person, the more likely is he to become attached to that person. For this reason, whoever is principally mothering a child becomes his principal attachment figure. Attachment behaviour remains readily activated until near the end of the third year; in healthy development it becomes gradually less readily activated thereafter.

5. *Learning*. Whereas learning to distinguish the familiar from the strange is a key process in the development of attachment, the conventional rewards and punishments used by experimental psychologists play only a small part. Indeed, an attachment can develop despite repeated punishment from the attachment figure.

6. *Organization*. Initially, attachment behaviour is mediated by responses organized on fairly simple lines. From the end of the first year, it becomes mediated by increasingly sophisticated behavioural systems organized cybernetically and incorporating representational models

of the environment and self. These systems are activated by certain conditions and terminated by others. Among activating conditions are strangeness, hunger, fatigue, and anything frightening. Terminating conditions include sight or sound of the mother-figure and, especially, happy interaction with her. When attachment behaviour is strongly aroused, termination may require touching or clinging to her and/or being cuddled by her. Conversely, when the mother-figure is present or her whereabouts well known, a child ceases to show attachment behaviour and, instead, explores his environment.

7. *Biological function*. Attachment behaviour occurs in the young of almost all species of mammal, and in a number of species it persists throughout adult life. Although there are many differences of detail, maintenance of proximity by an immature animal to a preferred adult, almost always its mother, is the rule, which suggests that such behaviour has survival value. By far the most likely function of attachment behaviour is protection, mainly from predators.

Thus attachment behaviour is conceived as a class of behaviour distinct from feeding behaviour and sexual behaviour, and of at least equal significance in human life. There is nothing intrinsically childish or pathological about it.

The concept of attachment differs greatly from that of dependence. For example, dependence is not specifically related to maintenance of proximity, it is not directed towards a specific individual, it does not imply an enduring bond, and it is not necessarily associated with strong feeling. No biological function is attributed to it. Furthermore, in the concept of dependence there are value implications the exact opposite of those that the concept of attachment conveys. Whereas to refer to a person as dependent tends to be disparaging, to describe him as attached to someone can well be an expression of approval. Conversely, for a person to be detached in his personal relations is usually regarded as less than admirable. The disparaging element in the concept of dependence is held to be a fatal weakness to its clinical use.

It was remarked that when mother is present or her whereabouts are well known, and she is willing to take part in friendly interchange, a child usually ceases to show attachment behaviour and, instead, explores his environment. In such a situation mother can be regarded as providing her child with a secure base from which to explore and to which he can return, especially should he become tired or frightened. Throughout the rest of a person's life he is likely to show the same pattern of behaviour, moving away from those he loves for ever-increasing distances and lengths of time, yet always maintaining contact and sooner or later returning. The base from which he operates is likely to be either his family of origin or else a new base which he has created for himself. Anyone who has no such base is rootless.

The behaviour of parents, and of anyone else in a care-giving role, is complementary to attachment behaviour. The roles of the care-giver are, first, to be available and responsive as and when wanted, and, secondly, to intervene judiciously should the child or older person who is being cared for be heading for trouble.

Evidence suggests that there is a strong causal relationship between an individual's experiences with his parents and his later capacity to make affectional bonds, and that certain common variations in that capacity, manifesting themselves in marital problems and trouble with children as well as in neurotic symptoms and personality disorders, can be attributed to certain common variations in the ways that parents perform their roles. The main variables are the extent to which a child's parents (i) provide him with a secure base, and (ii) encourage him to explore from it. Especially important is the extent to which parents recognize and respect a child's desire for a secure base and his need of it, and shape their behaviour accordingly. This entails, first, an intuitive and sympathetic understanding of a child's attachment behaviour and a willingness to meet it, and, secondly, recognition that one of the commonest sources of anger is the frustration of a child's desire for love and care, and that anxiety commonly reflects uncertainty whether parents will continue to be available. Complementary in importance to a parent's respect for a child's attachment desires is respect for his desire to explore and gradually to extend his relationships both with peers and with other adults.

J. BO.

† The description of these features draws with permission on the text of an article written for Volume VI of the *American Handbook of Psychiatry*, © 1975 by Basic Books Inc.

Bowlby, J. (1979). *The Making and Breaking of Affectional Bonds*. London.

Parkes, C. M. and Stevenson-Hinde, J. (eds.) (1982). *The Place of Attachment in Human Behaviour*. London.

**ATTAR, FARIDUDDIN** (abu-Talib/Abu Hamid Muhammad ibn-Abu-Bakr Ibrahim, ibn-Mustafa ibn-Sha'ban Farid-al-Din Attar, 'The Druggist', d. 1220/1230). Born at Kadkan, near Nishapur, Persia, one of the major *Sufi teachers, and acknowledged by Jalauddin *Rumi as one of his inspirers, Attar wrote at least thirty books. The most famous is the classical *Mantiq at-Tair* (the Bird Discourse, or Parliament), thought by some to have influenced Chaucer in his *Parliament of Fowls*. A major authoritative compilation is his *Tadhkirat al-Awliya* (Recapitulation of the Saints), with biographies of Sufi teachers down the centuries, partially translated by A. J. Arberry. Also highly esteemed is his *Pand-Nama* (Book of Counsel) and the *Asrar-Nama* (Book of Secrets). The *Ilahi-Nama* he composed while working at his pharmacy, where he had 500 patients; and it was this work which he presented to Rumi when, as a small boy, he passed through Nishapur with his father in 1212. The *Mantiq* is an allegory of human psychological reactions to the problems encountered on the Sufi way, with each individual bird in turn displaying his hopes, fears, and inadequacies. The birds of the world have elected the hoopoe as their leader in the spiritual quest, and he has to deal with their reactions, in the manner of a Sufi teacher. The purpose of the journey is to seek the king of the birds, the immortal Simurgh (Persian homonym for 'thirty birds'). Ultimately the pilgrims reach the throne and find, when a curtain is drawn aside, that they are looking into a mirror: the collective (human) soul is seen to be the divine one, which differentiation conceals from ordinary consciousness.  I. S.

Arberry, A. J. (trans.) (1966). *Muslim Saints and Mystics. Selections from the Tadhkirat*. London.

**ATTENTION.** The nervous systems of living creatures are subjected to far more stimulation than can be used. On the one hand, the sense organs receive stimuli of great variety. On the other, memories, images, and ideas arise internally and must be considered from moment to moment. Yet it is a commonplace that we are consciously aware of only a limited amount of this information at any moment. The operation by which a person selects information in attention, and its study, have twice been seen as central to research on our understanding of how information is processed by humans and animals.

The first great period was around 1900, when *James, *Titchener, *Wundt, and Pillsbury all wrote of attention at length. William James, on this as on so many other topics, described the main characteristics of attention with precision. Attention was, for him, 'the taking possession by the mind, in clear and vivid form, of one of what seem simultaneously possible objects or trains of thought'. Titchener and his students, in particular, carried out an extensive experimental programme into such topics as 'prior entry' and the conditions of binocular rivalry and fluctuations of attention. The first of these was the observation that of two simultaneous events, the one to which attention was diverted appeared to occur earlier than the other.

The fundamental property of attention was, for those workers, to make the contents of *consciousness appear clearer. It would have made little sense to them to discuss effects of attention of which the observer was not aware. Pillsbury's book *Attention*, published in 1908, contains many observations which modern work has confirmed, and is a remarkably insightful volume in many respects.

With the rise of *behaviourism, attention was relegated to the status of a mental function which could not be admitted as a suitable object for research. Indeed, for some thirty years it disappeared from indexes and reviews. The second golden age of attention research dates from the early 1950s, and received a particular impetus with the publication of *Perception and Communication* by Donald Broadbent in 1958. A major reason for the renewed interest was the need for the solution of new practical problems, such as the design of control towers and communication networks in the Second World War. A controller might receive several messages at once from different aircraft or ships, and be required to make appropriate responses to each. With an attempt to understand how humans behaved in such situations, modern work on attention began. It was aided by the invention of the tape recorder, which for the first time allowed the ready control and replicability of speech signals, while the phenomenon of stereophony provided an easy way of varying the content and amount of information in competing messages.

Broadbent's Filter theory tried to explain how the brain coped with the information overload caused by having many sense organs receiving information simultaneously. Drawing an analogy with electronic communication theory, he proposed that there is in the brain a single central information channel whose rate of information-processing is rather limited. This channel could select only one sensory input channel at a time, and could switch no more than about twice a second between input channels. To accept an input was equivalent to paying attention to that source of information, and information on unattended channels could be held in a *short-term memory for a few seconds. Broadbent called the selection mechanism 'the Filter'. While he drew on many fields of research, the most direct line of evidence was the 'split span' experiment. If three digits are read, at a rate of two per second, to the left ear of a listener, and another three to the right ear, so that the listener receives three synchronous pairs, he will recall them ear by ear, not pair by pair. Broadbent interpreted this to mean that the listener attended to one ear first and then switched to the memory trace of material in the other ear. By finding the fastest rate at which the listener could repeat the message as pairs, he believed he had measured the rate of switching of auditory attention. This concept of a single-channel, limited-capacity information processing system was central to much research in the next twenty-five years.

From about 1953 to 1963 'speech shadowing' was widely used by Broadbent, Neville Moray, Anne Treisman, and others. This technique had been introduced by Colin Cherry, and required a listener to repeat aloud a prose message in the presence of one or more distracting messages. It was found that major factors which aided selective attention included separation in space of the speakers, difference in voice timbre, and the statistical structure of the messages. In a series of elegant experiments Anne Treisman greatly extended our knowledge. Certain features of a distracting message proved to be potent sources of distraction, including emotional words (such as a listener's own name), contextually probable words, and—for bilingual listeners—the presence of a translation of the message to which they were listening.

However, these experiments also showed that some material, such as emotionally important words and contextually probable words, was perceived even when in the 'rejected' message.

This led to a series of modifications to Broadbent's Filter theory, notably by Anne Treisman, Anthony Deutsch, and Don Norman. Although differing considerably in detail, they all attempted to account for the fact that the Filter apparently did not block all information from the rejected channels, and that selection could be not only of sensory inputs, but of such features as language, class of word, colour (in the case of visual stimuli), and even classes of responses. Attention came to be seen as acting in a variety of ways, at a variety of levels, and on a variety of operations in the nervous system.

By the middle 1960s interest had grown greatly, and a wide variety of experimental techniques were developed. In addition to speech shadowing, simultaneous auditory messages were used, requiring much simpler responses than speech. In a series of studies Moray showed that, contrary to what the early shadowing experiments seemed to indicate, attention acted in the same way on non-linguistic as on linguistic material. Robert Sorkin and his co-workers in America explored attention to non-linguistic auditory material. Others, like Alan Allport and Peter McLeod in Britain, and Richard Shiffrin and Walter Schneider in America, found conditions where little or no interference between two messages occurred. These arose especially when messages were presented in different sensory modalities, where long practice had made performance almost automatic rather than conscious and voluntary, and when no competition between responses was required.

Visual attention was investigated by means of eye movements in such tasks as reading, by Paul Kolers, and in car driving and piloting aircraft, by John Senders. Very spectacular results were found using the 'Stroop test', in which attentional and perceptual conflict is induced by the nature of the stimulus. If the word 'red' is written in green ink, the word 'blue' in yellow ink, and so on, it is possible to read the word rapidly without the colour of the ink causing interference, but almost impossible to name the colour of the ink. Analogues of this effect provide a way of discovering which 'analysers' in the brain can be selectively biased by voluntary attention. (The word 'analyser' originated in a theory of learning and perception due to Anthony Deutsch, but its use in attention theory is largely due to Anne Treisman.)

Some attempts were made to investigate the physiological mechanisms underlying attention. For example, the 'Expectancy wave', or CNV, was discovered in *electroencephalographic records, a change in electrical brain activity which appears when the observer is concentrating on the imminent arrival of a signal he knows is probable. In the late 1970s Emmanuel Donchin and his colleagues began work on the 'P-300' component of the brain-evoked potential, and this seems very likely to be intimately connected with attention in the sense of decision-making. But to date our understanding of the physiological basis of attention lags a long way behind behavioural research.

More than a dozen theories of attention have been proposed since 1958, most of them strongly influenced by communication theory and computer technology. Their variety to some extent is due to the variety of phenomena which may be subsumed under the heading 'attention'. In addition to our ability to listen selectively to one message and ignore another, or to look at a picture in one colour in the presence of other colours, one may cite *vigilance* (or watch-keeping), in which an observer looks for very rare events, such as detecting the presence of a sonar or radar target. Some studies have been made of mental concentration on cognitive problems. The interference between internal images and incoming stimuli has been investigated, as has the ability of the brain of a sleeping person to respond selectively to the sleeper's name, even though the sleeper is not aware of the response.

Although no single theory has emerged as completely dominant, the influence of Broadbent's Filter theory remains strong, and what follows is a conflation of theories based on his suggestions. He assumed that an observer can block or weaken the strength of incoming messages to the brain, and there is ample evidence that this can happen. It is not known whether this is done by reducing the intensity of the messages or by switching them on and off rapidly. But some such blocking definitely occurs. In vision it can be done by closing the eyes or averting the gaze. In hearing the mechanism is not so clear. It seems probable that all information which impinges on the receptors of the sense organs reaches the pattern-analysing mechanisms of the brain. The Filter perhaps acts to prevent the output of these analysers from reaching consciousness, although behaviour may still be produced, as when we become aware that we have driven for some time 'without being aware of it' (see TIME-GAP EXPERIENCE). It seems likely that information from different sense modalities, or from different dimensions within a modality (such as colour and shape), can be attended to simultaneously, at least after practice; while tasks which are very similar (such as judging the loudness of two tones) cannot. One should note that in making these assertions we are far from William James's definition. Very often the observer is conscious of only one message, but it can be shown that the second is producing behaviour simultaneously with that produced consciously. (See also SUBLIMINAL PERCEPTION.)

A second way in which attention can operate is by biasing the interpretation of information proceeding from pattern analysis to consciousness. Thus a person expecting to see a bull in mist will see one, while a person expecting to see a rock will see a rock. This kind of bias is set by the probability of events, their subjectively perceived value, and contextual information derived from recent inputs and from memories. In earlier days this kind of bias was called 'mental set'.

The contents of consciousness as filtered by

attention are very limited: attention is frequently modelled as a 'limited-capacity information channel'. But with practice, quite dramatic increases in performance are seen, and some writers, among whom Daniel Kahneman is particularly influential, have proposed a 'parallel processing' model of attention, in which the main limit is on the total effort available, rather than on competition between separate analysers. Such models make extensive use of the concept of *arousal.

Recently, renewed interest in applications of attention has become apparent. Most of the laboratory research has been directed to understanding the internal mechanisms of attention in the brain. But as large and complex man–machine systems appear, and more and more automation is introduced, there is a tremendous need for a good understanding of man as a monitor of complex systems. How should the latter be designed so as to optimize the use of attention? (It is fairly clear that in real-life tasks attention is never switched more than about twice a second.) How should a man be trained so as to combine to best effect his limited conscious attention with his unconscious control of *skilled behaviour? The solution of such questions is necessary if accidents in power stations, aircraft, and industry are to be avoided. Attention theory has advanced to a point where it can give a real insight into the solution of practical problems, and there is likely to be a third age in which the precise experimental work of the 1950s to the 1970s is extended in more complex ways to solve the problems of man–machine system design in the 1980s and 1990s. We have come to see attention not merely as a single process concerned with enhancing the clarity of perception. Rather, it is a complex of skills. These include selecting one from several messages, selecting one from several interpretations of information, selecting one from several plans of action, and selecting one from several actions. But in our interactions with the rich dynamics of the world in which we live and to which we adapt, attention also models that world, and provides us with strategies and high-level control of our tactics of information sampling, optimizing our information-processing in the face of our limited processing capacities.

Developments in research since Donald Broadbent's work in the 1950s have emphasized both the conceptual richness of the concept of attention, and the practical importance of an understanding of its properties. One cannot do better than conclude with an early claim of Edward Titchener's: 'The doctrine of attention is the nerve of the whole psychological system, and that as men judge of it, so shall they be judged before the general tribunal of psychology.'                                    N. M.

Broadbent, D. (1958). *Perception and Communication*. London.
James, W. (1890). *Principles of Psychology*. New York.
Kahneman, D. (1973). *Attention and Effort*. New York.
Moray, N. (1969). *Listening and Attention*. Harmondsworth.
Titchener, E. B. (1908). *Lectures on the Elementary Psychology of Feeling and Attention*. New York.
Underwood, G. (1978). *Strategies of Information Processing*. New York and London.

**ATTENTION, LAPSES OF.** There are quite frequent short intervals of loss of *attention, technically called Bills' blocks after A. G. Bills. Their cause is unknown, but the explanation is possibly that brain circuits have multiple functions and so are not always available when multiple tasks are being carried out—much as fingers or tools cannot be used for more than one task at a time.

**AUDIOMETER.** Electronic instrument used for testing *hearing. A simple audiometer is an oscillator having about ten pre-set frequencies in the range 500 to 8,000 hertz, and a stepped attenuator so that tone detection thresholds can be measured in decibels. More elaborate instruments combine noise masking (for measuring recruitment, which is associated with sensory neural deafness). The most sophisticated is the *Békésy audiometer, in which the patient, or subject of an experiment, tracks a continuously changing tone, his responses being recorded with an automatic plotter. Audiometry may test for word recognition, and it may introduce more-or-less normal confusing sounds. It can be most useful for distinguishing various kinds of hearing impairment.

**AUDITORY ILLUSIONS.** Although many visual *illusions were discovered in the nineteenth century, interest in auditory illusions has developed only recently. Some of these illusions are paradoxical. Apart from their subjective interest they provide valuable information concerning the mechanisms that our auditory system (see HEARING) employs to interpret our environment.

One illusion demonstrates that separate and independent brain mechanisms exist for determining what we hear, and for determining where the sound is coming from. The combined operation of these two mechanisms may lead to the perception of a sound that does not exist, i.e. with its characteristics taken from one source and its location from another.

The configuration that produces this illusion is shown in Fig. 1a. This consists of two tones that are spaced an octave apart and repeatedly presented in alternation. The identical sequence is presented to both ears simultaneously through earphones; however, when the right ear receives the high tone the left ear receives the low tone, and vice versa. So in fact the listener is presented with a single, continuous two-tone chord, but the ear of input for each component switches repeatedly.

It can be imagined how this sequence should sound if perceived correctly. However, with very rare exceptions an illusion is always produced. The type of illusion obtained varies from listener to listener, but the most common one is shown in Fig. 1b. This consists of a single tone that switches

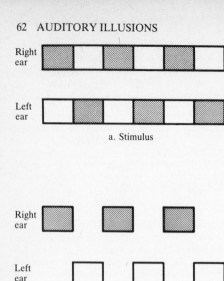

a. Stimulus

b. Percept

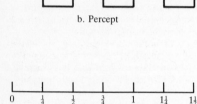

Time in seconds

**Fig. 1. a.** Pattern giving rise to the first illusion. Two tones that are spaced an octave apart are repeatedly presented in alternation. When one ear receives the high tone the other ear simultaneously receives the low tone. The filled squares indicate the high tone and the unfilled squares the low tone. **b.** Illusion most commonly obtained. This consists of a high tone in one ear alternating with a low tone in the other ear.

from ear to ear; and as it switches its pitch simultaneously shifts back and forth from high to low. That is, the listener hears a single high tone in one ear alternating with a single low tone in the other ear.

There is no simple way to explain this illusion. We can explain the perception of alternating pitches by assuming that the listener processes the input to one ear and ignores the other. But then both of the alternating pitches should appear localized in the same ear. Alternatively, we can explain the alternation of a single tone from ear to ear by supposing that the listener suppresses the input to each ear in turn. But then the pitch of this tone should not change with a change in its apparent location. The illusion of a single tone that alternates simultaneously both in pitch and in localization is paradoxical.

The illusion is even more surprising when we consider what happens when the listener's earphones are placed in reverse position. Now, most people hear exactly the same thing: that is, the tone that appeared to be in the right ear still appears to be in the right ear, and the tone that appeared to be

in the left ear still apears to be in the left ear. So it seems to the listener that the earphone which had been producing the high tone is now producing the low tone, and that the earphone which had been producing the low tone is now producing the high tone!

Experiments have shown that this illusion is based on the operation of two independent mechanisms; one for determining what pitch we hear, and the other for determining where the sound is coming from. To provide the perceived sequence of pitches, those arriving at one ear are heard, and those arriving at the other ear are suppressed. However, each tone is localized in the ear receiving the higher pitch, regardless of whether the higher or the lower is in fact heard. So, given a listener who hears the pitches presented to his right ear when a high tone is delivered to the right ear and a low tone to the left, this listener hears a high tone since this is the tone delivered to his right ear. Further, he localizes the tone in his right ear, since this ear is receiving the higher pitch. But when a high tone is delivered to the left ear and a low tone to the right, this listener now hears a low tone since this is the tone delivered to his right ear; but he localizes the tone in his left ear, since this ear is receiving the higher pitch. So the entire sequence is heard as a high tone to the right alternating with a low tone to the left. Reversing the position of the earphones would not alter this basic percept (though the identities of the first and last tones in the sequence would reverse); but given a listener who hears the pitches delivered to his left ear instead, keeping the localization rule constant, the same sequence would be perceived as a high tone to the left alternating with a low tone to the right.

Another auditory illusion demonstrates the importance of unconscious inference in auditory perception. This illusion also involves presenting two different tonal sequences through earphones. The configuration consists of a musical scale, presented simultaneously in ascending and descending form. When a tone from the ascending scale is delivered to the left ear, a tone from the descending scale is delivered to the right ear; and successive tones in each scale alternate from ear to ear. This sequence is repetitively presented without pause.

This configuration also produces various illusory percepts, which fall into two main categories. Most listeners perceive the correct set of pitches, but as two melodic lines, one corresponding to the higher tones and the other to the lower tones. Further, the higher tones all appear to be emanating from one earphone and the lower tones from the other. When the earphone positions are reversed there is often no change in what is perceived. So it appears to the listener that the earphone that had been producing the higher tones is now producing the lower tones, and that the earphone that had been producing the lower tones is now producing the higher tones! Other listeners perceive only a single melodic line, which corresponds to the higher tones, and they hear little or nothing of the lower tones.

How can we account for the first type of illusory percept? It must have a different basis from the illusion described earlier, since here all the tones are perceived; they are simply localized incorrectly. There are strong cognitive reasons for expecting such an illusion. In everyday life similar sounds are likely to emanate from the same source, and different sounds from different sources. Our present sequence consists of tones drawn from closely overlapping pitch ranges which are continuously emanating from two specific locations in space. So the best interpretation of this sequence in terms of the real world is that an object which emits sounds in one pitch range is located in one place, and that another object which emits sounds in a different pitch range is located in another place. This inference is here so strong as to override our actual localization cues, so that we perceive the sequence in accordance with this interpretation.

D. D.

Deutsch, D. (1975). Musical illusions. *Scientific American*, **233**, 92–104.

Deutsch, D. (1983). Auditory Illusions and Audio. Special issue of the *Journal of the Audio Engineering Society*, **31** (9).

**AUTHORITY.** See OBEDIENCE.

**AUTISM** is a very rare condition that was first named by Leo Kanner, an American psychiatrist, in 1943. It occurs in perhaps four out of 10,000 live births (for comparison, severe subnormality occurs about four times out of every 1,000 births); and the diagnosis is made four times more frequently among boys than among girls. The word means self-concerned, or independent, and the social withdrawal which is commonly associated with the condition resembles *schizophrenic withdrawal in adults. Despite its rarity and sex-selective quality, the condition may arise from several disorders masquerading as one. Although far more autistic children are of below normal *intelligence than would be expected if it occurred equally often at all levels of intelligence, none the less a small number of highly intelligent autistic people have been observed.

The autistic child characteristically appears to go through his or her early development normally, but a break in development occurs usually before two and a half years of age. At this stage, the development of speech may stop and social response does not develop. Bizarre behaviour may show itself, and stereotyped self-occupying movements may become more obvious. This characteristic pattern of arrest of growth generally results in a relatively poor intellectual development; more than two-thirds of autistic children have an IQ within the subnormal range (see SUBNORMALITY). Sometimes social response never develops at all, and a mother may notice that her infant does not cuddle normally from the beginning.

In later years some of the more marked disturbances of behaviour may become less marked and less bizarre. In this phase the children may become more like the mentally subnormal children whom they may match in intelligence. However, their speech may continue to be even more markedly handicapped.

In the past, certain investigators suggested that autism might have psychological origins, and parents classified as schizophrenogenic because of their supposed emotional coldness were caused unnecessary pain, through fear that they might have been responsible for the handicap of their autistic child. Such psychogenic hypotheses no longer win informed support, and psychiatrists now more frequently identify physical disorders as precipitating autism. As J. K. Wing (1966) pointed out, early onset with signs of brain damage, screaming, and feeding difficulties, the high male–female ratio, histories of complications of pregnancy or at delivery, and the nature of speech and perceptual difficulties, all point to an abnormality of the central nervous system.

The nature of this abnormality is undetermined, but one investigator, G. R. De Long (1978), has suggested a bilateral hippocampal lesion; and J. G. Small (1975), reviewing recent papers on electroencephalography (EEG) and reports of studies of *evoked potential in autistic children, states that there is a high incidence of abnormal EEGs and that the evoked potential studies showed the children to be less than normally responsive to stimuli. She pointed out that the high incidence of lowered intelligence may be indicative of central nervous damage. It has been suggested also that abnormalities in the limbic system and vestibular nuclei might be the basis for some elements of autistic behaviour. Tests of vestibular function and EEG sleep studies give some support for these theories and so favour an organic rather than a predominantly psychological cause of childhood autism.

While De Long pointed to the probability of a bilateral hippocampal lesion in these children, P. T. White *et al.* (1964) first noted the relatively high incidence of *epilepsy in adolescence. S. Folstein and M. Rutter (1977) also noted epilepsy in association with autism, but added their own observations on the genetics of autism. They reported complex findings that indicated a genetic contribution but also showed the importance of environmental factors, by which they meant the occurrence of brain injury, in a majority of cases. De Long has made some detailed studies of the effect of cortical lesions on cognitive development in children and has found considerable hippocampal deficits, especially when language deficits and certain autistic features of behaviour are present. Some evidence has suggested cortical atrophy, especially of the left temporal lobe. However, any serious and long-term reduction of language ability in children must involve bilateral damage to speech areas, because otherwise the undamaged hemisphere of the brain would probably take over the speech function—compensation which could occur in the developing nervous system at any time before ten years of age, that is before neurological development presumably becomes complete.

This conclusion, however, is uncertain, because it has been claimed that left unilateral hippocampal lesions even in adults may result in peculiarities of language and social behaviour without affecting visuo-motor learning.

One point concerning autistic features of behaviour that has not received as much attention as it probably deserves is the occurrence in children of nearly normal or even superior intelligence of a type of social behaviour closely resembling autism. M. Bartak and L. Rutter (1976) reported a clinical study comparing subnormal and normal groups aged eight and a half years, both of whom had difficulty in social relationships and showed little *eye-contact. Both groups withdrew from adults and did not make friends with other children. They did not adapt easily to new situations and seemed obsessive in their behaviour, being strongly attached to favoured objects. Both groups showed stereotyped hand movements and facial grimaces. The significance of this report is the large IQ difference between the groups, suggesting that we may be dealing with two different causes of autism, or perhaps the same cause in mild and severe forms. Bartak and Rutter do not discuss their findings in relation to Asperger's finding of autistic children with high IQs, but presumably they have identified a group of children of a similar kind (Asperger, 1944, Wing, 1981).

L. Wing and J. Gould (1979) on the other hand, in a very thorough population study, produce evidence in favour of an association between low intelligence and autistic symptoms, finding increasing percentages of children showing autistic behaviour towards the bottom end of the intelligence scale. Their results do not contradict those of Bartak and Rutter, but they do suggest a common cause for social and cognitive deficits. This common cause, if it exists, must, however, be differential in its effects because it seems from clinical observation that *Down's syndrome (mongol) children, although often of very low intelligence, are frequently sociable and certainly not withdrawn, although like autistic children they often have a severe language handicap.

Wing and Gould have made an interesting contribution to the study of autism by suggesting a classification or subgrouping of social as distinct from cognitive impairment. They find that many children other than those classified as autistic have social disabilities, although they regard these latter as associated with cognitive disabilities and low intelligence. The essence of their social classification is in terms of severity—from severe aloofness to social passiveness to oddity (mild)—and of course not all subnormal children are socially inept, although 'associated language and behavioural problems accounted for more than half of all children in the study with intelligence quotients below 50'.

Autistic children might be regarded as having especially severe social handicaps if some recent work of P. Hobson (1981) is confirmed. In this work autistic children matched with subnormals for their capacity to solve objective cognitive tasks proved much inferior to non-autistic subnormals in their capacity to classify representations of emotional displays, or even to classify the displays by the sex of the actor presented in them.

Study of this problem of social incompetence, and its relationships with (or independence of) intelligence, has gone through three historical phases. Leo Kanner first noticed the social withdrawal of certain children and called them autistic. Several authors—B. Hermelin and N. O'Connor (1970), V. Lotter (1974), and M. Rutter—noted the cognitive deficit associated with autism and interpreted autism in terms of this deficit. More recently attention has turned again to the social incompetence of autistic children, as distinct from their purely cognitive deficits. Whether, finally, this social incompetence will be shown to be independent of cognitive deficit or strongly associated with it remains to be seen. Recent research suggests that social withdrawal and social incompetence can occur in both more and less severe forms and may to some degree be independent of the intelligence level of the people in whom they are found.

The presence of a disability such as autism in a child inevitably presents society, but more especially the parents, with a very demanding problem. In the United Kingdom provision exists for the special education of autistic children, and the National Society for Autistic Children will inform members of schools available within their area.

Fewer educational than diagnostic studies have been carried out, because the educability of autistic children presented an initially daunting problem. Some technical approaches involving *behaviour therapy have been tried, such as those of O. I. Lovaas, B. Schaeffer, and J. Q. Simmons (1965) in the United States, but in a number of such studies diagnosis has been in doubt, and the method employed, sometimes using electric shock, would be thought highly undesirable in the UK. Bartak and Rutter investigated three schools in or near London, where each school was using a somewhat different educational approach. Rutter (1979) summarized the results of comparing Unit A (psychotherapeutic), Unit B (permissive), and Unit C (organized and structured), as he called the three approaches, as follows:

The follow-up findings showed that whether assessed in terms of educational attainment, on-task behaviour in the classroom or co-operative play with others, the autistic children at C had made most progress and those at Unit A the least. However, there were no differences between the units in terms of the children's behaviour at home, and although the children at C tended to have made more progress in language than those at the other two units, the difference fell short of significance.

In all three units the level of intelligence considerably affected progress made. While children profited educationally from a structured environment, they learned without generalization or understanding, that is, mechanically. Studies of home-based education have also been made, and although the results are uncertain, the effect of intelligence on learning progress is again seen as highly relevant.

To summarize, our present knowledge concerning autism is scanty. It is a rare condition that occurs mainly in boys and shows itself before the age of two and a half. It is marked mainly by social withdrawal and poor speech development, together with stereotyped behaviour patterns. It is associated with low intelligence, although exceptions occur, and may be associated with brain damage, which is most likely bilateral; there is also likely to be a genetic component. Such children, if they are of low intelligence, are unlikely to attend a normal school except as special pupils, but proper training can improve their social behaviour and elementary scholastic knowledge. The best educational approach is probably that of sympathetic but formal instruction.

See also CHILDREN'S UNDERSTANDING OF THE MENTAL WORLD.

N. O'C.

B. H.

Asperger, H. (1944). Die 'autistischen Psychopathen' im Kindesalter. *Archiv. für Psychiatrie und Nervenkrankheiten*, **117**, 76–136.

Bartak, L. and Rutter, M. (1976). Differences between mentally retarded and normally intelligent autistic children. *Journal of Autism and Childhood Schizophrenia*, **6**, 109–20.

De Long, G. R. (1978). A neuropsychologic interpretation of infantile autism. In Rutter, M. and Schopler, E. (eds.), *Autism: a reappraisal of concepts and treatment*. New York.

Folstein, S. and Rutter, M. (1977). Infantile autism: a genetic study of 21 twin pairs. *Journal of Child Psychology and Psychiatry*, **18**, 297–321.

Hermelin, B. and O'Connor, N. (1970). *Psychological experiments with autistic children*. Oxford.

Hobson, P. (1981). The autistic child's concept of persons. *International Conference on Autism*. Boston.

Kanner, L. (1943). Autistic disturbances of affective contact. *Nervous Child*, **2**, 217–50.

Lotter, V. (1974). Factors related to outcome in autistic children. *Journal of Autism and Childhood Schizophrenia*, **4**, 263–77.

Lovaas, O. I., Schaeffer, B., and Simmons, J. Q. (1965). Building social behaviour in autistic children by use of electric shock. *Journal of Experimental Research in Personality*, **1**, 99–109.

Rutter, M. (1979). Autism: psychopathological mechanisms and therapeutic approaches in cognitive growth and development. In Bortner, M. (ed.), *Essays in Memory of Herbert G. Birch*. New York.

Rutter, M. and Schopler, E. (eds.) (1978). *Autism*. New York.

Small, J. G. (1975). EEG and neurophysiological studies of early infantile autism. *Biological Psychiatry*, **10**, 385–97.

White, P. T., De Myer, W., and De Myer, M. (1964). EEG abnormalities in early childhood schizophrenia: a double-blind study of psychiatrically disturbed and normal children during promazene sedation. *American Journal of Psychiatry*, **120**, 950.

Wing, J. K. (1966). Diagnosis, epidemiology, aetiology. In Wing, J. K. (ed.), *Childhood Autism*, 1st edn. Oxford.

Wing, L. (ed.) (1976). *Early childhood autism*, 2nd edn. Oxford.

Wing, L. (1981). Asperger's Syndrome: a clinical account. *Psychological Medicine*, **11**, 115–29.

Wing, L. and Gould, J. (1979). Severe impairments of social interaction and associated abnormalities in children: epidemiology and classification. *Journal of Autism and Developmental Disorders*, **9**, 11–29.

**AUTOMATION.** The development and use of machines to replace human labour, wholly or in part, has ancient origins. Water and windmills for grinding corn and other uses are long-established examples, and early in the Industrial Revolution many machines, such as Arkwright's water frame, Crompton's mule, Hargreaves's spinning jenny, and Kay's flying shuttle loom, were introduced into the manufacture of textiles. Printing with movable type started just before 1450 and was probably the most important single invention that might at least loosely be labelled 'automation'.

Automation in this broad sense has immensely increased the wealth of societies and individuals, and has freed people from the bondage of repetitive work, allowing time for recreation. However, the use of automation in manufacturing led to large industrial units, and these tended to be grouped together to form urban areas. They created a regimented working environment, with the discipline of time being enforced by shift work. The gains and losses from the immense effects of automation are incalculable.

Psychologically there is always resentment at jobs or skills being taken over by machines, and there are harrowing stories of strong men dying while trying to compete with steam saws, for example. In our own time automation by computers is producing some decentralization of work with, in some cases, a relaxation of time-keeping and the opportunity of working at home which, as before the Industrial Revolution, greatly helps women. On the other hand, highly skilled and responsible jobs like those of air traffic controllers and radar operators cannot easily be automated, even when this is technically possible, because the controllers and operators lose both prestige—affecting their morale—and their skills, so that they may be unable to cope in an emergency. As automatic machines become more sophisticated, it may be that prestige will be attached to those who mind the machines.

R. L. G.

**AUTOMATISM** may be defined as a state in which the individual performs simple or complex actions in a skilled or relatively uncoordinated manner without having full awareness of what he is doing.

Such a definition excludes purely *reflex motor responses but includes well-developed skills, such as playing a musical instrument, where the individual carries out highly complex movements without detailed awareness of what he is doing. This kind of normal automatism increases with practice and the more expert the performer is, the greater will be the degree of automatism displayed.

Automatism is also associated with psychopathological conditions such as sleep-walking (see SOMNAMBULISM) and post-hypnotic states, when the subject may respond to signals in a manner suggested to him during the hypnotic trance (see HYPNOSIS). Of greater importance are post-epileptic automatisms. The term was introduced by Hughlings *Jackson to describe 'all kinds of doings after epileptic fits'. These are most often witnessed following psychomotor seizures and may take the form of continuing an action being performed before the onset of the fit, or of new behaviour, simple or complex, which may, although very rarely, be of such violence that serious harm is done to bystanders or anyone going to the patient's help. In cases where homicide has been the outcome of a post-epileptic automatism, a plea of non-insane automatism may be accepted in place of insane automatism (a circumstance when an individual, suffering from a disease of the mind, does not know the nature and quality of the act of which he is accused). With a plea of insane automatism, the accused is likely to be found not guilty on the ground of insanity, and sent to a special hospital. (See DIMINISHED RESPONSIBILITY for a discussion of the McNaghten Rules.)

Sane automatism might be adduced in persons committing offences following an epileptic fit or during a post-concussional state. It would have to be shown that the defendant was not suffering from mental illness—disease of the mind in legal parlance.

But in a recent case the accused, an epileptic, attacked an individual who came to his help when he was recovering from a seizure. He inflicted injuries sufficiently severe to warrant a charge of causing grievous bodily harm. A plea of not guilty on the basis of his automatism was offered, but the judge directed the jury to the effect that on the evidence given a verdict of not guilty on the ground of insanity would be appropriate. In this instance the judge considered that psychomotor epilepsy had to be classed as a disease of the mind. Although his ruling was challenged it was upheld by the higher Court of Appeal. The case was further considered by the House of Lords (*R*. v. *Sullivan*, [1983] 3WLR 123), which concluded that a person who committed an offence while in a state of post-ictal confusion, so that he did not know what he was doing and had no recollection of the event on recovering, was insane at law. This seems to rule out pleas of sane automatism in the future but one might surmise that more will be heard of this decision as it hardly makes sense to insist that a brief disorder of brain function as in epilepsy, is equivalent to a 'disease of the mind' in the McNaghten sense of the words.        F. A. W.

**AUTONOMIC NERVOUS SYSTEM.** Also known as the involuntary nervous system, it involves the smooth (rather than the striated) muscles, and is essentially the regulatory mechanisms of digestion, respiration, circulation of the blood, and so on (see NERVOUS SYSTEM). These processes are not normally under voluntary control, though they may be brought under control by *conditioning or by *biofeedback. The fact that much behaviour is involuntary and unconscious raises such questions as: why is some behaviour *voluntary*, and under conscious control? It seems that high rates of information-processing in unusual situations require consciousness, and are voluntary. The recent appreciation that many involuntary processes (such as heart-rate) can be brought under voluntary control is strengthening the claims and widening the range of *psychosomatic medical practice.

**AUTOSCOPY.** See DOPPELGÄNGER.

**AVERSION THERAPY.** Applying, or showing, situations or objects which frighten, or disturb, with gradually increasing nearness, or frequency of presentation, as a way of alleviating *phobias by gradually increasing familiarity with the frightening object or situation. See also BEHAVIOUR THERAPY.

**AVICENNA** (Abu 'Ali al-Hussein ibn-'Abdallah ibn-Sina) (980–1037). *Islamic philosopher and eminent physician, born at Afshana, near Bukhara, called by the Arabs *Al-Sheikh al-Rais*, 'Chief and Leader (of thinkers)'. His *Canon of Medicine* was the standard work, in Europe as in the East, until the seventeenth century. He was a royal physician at the age of 17.

Avicenna's philosophy exercised, through twelfth-century translations, a considerable influence upon Western thinkers, his major work being the eighteen-volume *Book of Recovery*, written in eighteen months. He follows *Al-Farabi in ideas, though his work is regarded by scholars as more lucid, dealing with the distinction between necessary and possible being. Among the terms and concepts that he bequeathed to human thought is *intentio* (*ma'qulat*), the intellectually intelligible. His theme is that the entire universe is constituted of *essences: all existing things have specific essences. 'A horse', he says, 'is a horse.' He holds that all the senses are secondary, being divisions of an inner sense, which is common to all. All reality as we know it derives from one ultimate, unitary reality: God—but not directly. There are agencies which, in a series of actions, cause the apparent differences between phenomena.        I. S.

Hitti, P. K. (1951). *History of the Arabs*. New York.
Wickers, G. M. (ed.) (1952). *Avicenna: scientist and philosopher*. London.

**AXIOM.** When, in any intellectual discipline, a theory is proposed, there will be some propositions that are regarded as fundamental, or first, principles of the theory. This is in contrast to other propositions which, although part of the theory, are consequences of, or follow from, these fundamental principles. According to *Aristotle, first principles will take the form of either definitions, postulates, or axioms. The Aristotelian definition of an *axiom* is that it is a principle common to all sciences, which is self-evidently true (and thus knowable *a priori) but incapable of proof. Thus we have as one of *Euclid's axioms, or Common Notions, 'The whole is greater than the part.' A *postulate* on the other hand is a principle specific to a given science which is assumed without proof and whose truth may not be self-evident. Thus we have Euclid's postulate that 'if a straight line falling on two straight lines makes the interior angles on the same side less than two right angles, the two straight lines, if produced indefinitely, meet on that side on which the angles are less than the two right angles'. In modern deductive formalizations of theories this distinction between axioms and postulates is retained, but in a slightly modified form as a distinction between logical and non-logical axioms. The non-logical axioms contain terms specific to the science in question. Where these terms are not explicitly defined, the set of axioms adopted is sometimes regarded as providing an implicit definition of the terms involved. Sets of axioms are also used, particularly in mathematics, as ways of characterizing, and hence providing a definition of, a kind of structure. Thus a group is defined as any structure of which a particular set of axioms, the group axioms, are true. (See also GEOMETRY and DEDUCTION.)

M. E. T.

**AXON.** A nerve fibre that transmits signals, sometimes over distances of a metre or more. The signals are action potentials from sense organs (*afferent fibres) to muscle (*efferent fibres). Axons transmit with a wide range of velocities up to about the speed of sound, the largest diameter fibres having the fastest conduction rate. Myelinated axons transmit fastest. The myelin sheathing, formed of the myelin-producing Schwann cells, serves not only to increase the conduction rate but also to isolate fibres from each other. This is important where axons run in bundles, which in the extreme case of the optic nerve contain as many as a million nerve fibres. See NERVOUS SYSTEM; NEUROTRANSMITTERS AND NEUROMODULATORS.

# B

**BABBAGE,** CHARLES (1792–1871). British mathematician and inventor, born in a wealthy West of England banking family and educated at Trinity and Peterhouse colleges, Cambridge. Babbage became Lucasian Professor of Mathematics at Cambridge (1823–39). He was not, however, a traditional academic: he was a gentleman of private means and he spent a large proportion of his own money, and funds he received from the government of the Duke of Wellington, developing and building the first programmable computing machine. In the 1830s he conceived the essentials of modern computers, realized by mechanical means. His Difference Engine was designed to compute tables, with its own print-setting to avoid human error. In his efforts to get it built, Babbage became a pioneer in developing both modern methods of machine drawing and the precision mass production of components. Much of the Difference Engine is preserved in the Science Museum in London, but it was never completed, as he conceived a far more ambitious project: the Analytical Engine. This was to have contained the essentials of the modern programmable digital computer, though it would, by comparison, have been extremely slow. It also was never completed.

We owe much of our understanding of Babbage's ideas to the account given by Ada, Lady Lovelace, who was Byron's daughter and Babbage's close friend and collaborator over many years. She was a mathematician in her own right. How much she contributed to the design of the calculating engines is uncertain but she was undoubtedly the first to understand the concepts they represented. As Babbage recognized, these concepts depended in part on earlier ideas, including binary arithmetic, of George Boole.

Babbage also invented the ophthalmoscope (anticipating *Helmholtz by two years), and the railway cowcatcher! He was also a pioneer in actuarial calculations. He ended his life a disappointed man; but the technology of his time was not quite adequate for his ideas to be fully realized in practice. His autobiography, *Passages from the Life of a Philosopher*, appeared in 1864 and was reprinted in 1969.

Hyman, A. (1982). *Charles Babbage*, Oxford.

**BABBLING.** The utterance or hearing of incoherent speech sounds. It is thought that the Greeks heard all other languages as 'babble', giving the word an onomatopoeic origin. Indeed unfamiliar languages do sound formless, with no clear demarcation between words. In a familiar language, word units are identified not by breaks in speech but from the continuous 'babble' of speech, much as separate objects are seen from the mosaic pattern of stimulation of the eyes.

It is believed that babies produce all the speech sounds of any language in their babbling, and that speech sounds or phonemes of the language of their environment are gradually selected, according to use (see LANGUAGE DEVELOPMENT IN CHILDREN).

**BABINSKI REFLEX.** The involuntary raising of the big toe upon stroking the side of the foot. The *reflex is present in adult apes and in human infants, but disappears in humans at about eighteen months, when it is inhibited by higher centres. The inhibition is lost in tabes dorsalis (the degeneration of the posterior ascending fibres of the spinal cord that occurs in tertiary syphilis) and in other diseases of the brain and spinal cord. It is believed that the reflex is useful for grasping the branches of trees with the toes, and that the inhibitory mechanism was developed late in primate evolution, when apes forsook the trees to walk on the ground. It is a useful diagnostic reflex, and was discovered by the French neurologist Joseph Babinski (1857–1932).

**BACON,** FRANCIS (1561–1626). British statesman and philosopher, born at York House in the Strand, London, the younger son of Sir Nicholas Bacon (1509–79), who was Queen Elizabeth's Keeper of the Great Seal—which office Francis later held. He became Baron Verulam, Viscount St Albans, a mark of his highly distinguished legal career culminating in his appointment as Lord High Chancellor in 1618. His public career ended sadly in 1621 when he was convicted on charges of bribery, charges that were probably unfair, given the contemporary professional morality.

Bacon is distinguished for setting out what was to be considered the technique and philosophy of modern science. He developed, from *Aristotelian beginnings, *inductive principles for amassing and interpreting data—especially for establishing *causes. Whereas Aristotle saw causes as the *essence of things, to be discovered by descriptive analysis, Bacon stressed the importance of enumerating instances where characteristics and events occur, or do not occur, in association. By setting out methods of induction, which included looking for exceptions and refutations of hypotheses, he separated science from philosophy. He saw his inductive methods as instruments for generating knowledge. The Royal Society was founded in London in 1660, essentially on the basis of Bacon's *The Advancement of Learning* (1605) and *Novum Organum* (1620). In his *Essays*, written throughout his life, Bacon appears as a highly literate and wise man. He was thus a philosopher in the fullest sense of the word, as well as having the vision to set out principles that greatly influenced the development of modern science.

The standard edition of Bacon's *Works* is edited by Spedding, J., Ellis, R. L., and Heath, D. D. (1857). London.
Quinton, A. (1980). *Francis Bacon*. Oxford.

**BAIN,** ALEXANDER (1818–1903). British psychologist, born in Aberdeen, where he spent most of his life. His books *The Senses and the Intellect* (1855) and *The Emotions and the Will* (1859) remained, with revisions, standard texts of psychology for half a century. They are still useful reference sources for their historical comments, and their structure remains as the skeleton of modern textbooks of psychology. Bain linked psychology with physiology; paid attention to reflexes; and discussed instinct and belief. Most important, he developed sophisticated views on the still difficult questions of voluntary action, or the will. His discussions of this topic are still worth reading.

**BAJJAH,** IBN (1106–38), Islamic thinker, poet and musician, scientist and mathematician. See IBN BAJJAH.

**BALINT,** MICHAEL, British psychoanalyst. See FREUDIANISM: LATER DEVELOPMENTS.

**BÁRÁNY,** ROBERT (1876–1936). Austrian physiologist, educated at the University of Vienna. He was appointed lecturer in otology at Vienna in 1905, and, after being captured by the Russians during the First World War, he moved to Sweden, where he ran the department of otology at Uppsala. His most valuable work was in unravelling the functions of the labyrinth of the ear (see HEARING), and in designing tests, still widely used, to check labyrinthine function. He was awarded a Nobel prize in 1914 for this work.

**BARTLETT,** SIR FREDERIC CHARLES (1886–1969). Born at Stow-on-the-Wold, Gloucestershire, where his father owned a small boot and shoe business. He read for an external London University degree, through the University Correspondence College, and took logic as one of his subjects. His success led to an appointment as tutor in philosophical subjects for the College, whose headquarters were at Cambridge. There he became an undergraduate at St John's College, and gained a First in the moral sciences tripos examinations.

At Cambridge he met the philosopher James *Ward, whose article on 'Psychology' in the *Encyclopaedia Britannica* (1886) had great influence on British psychologists and influenced him in turn. He also met C. S. *Myers and W. H. R. *Rivers. In his own account of the development of psychology in Cambridge from 1887 to 1937 (Bartlett, 1937) he gives a most interesting account of these three men and of their influence on him and on psychology in Cambridge. Ward, who foresaw the future psychology could and ought to have, did his best to advance it. Myers had a major influence in the establishment of experimental psychology in Cambridge, and Rivers brought to the university an outstanding and unique combination of sensory physiology and social anthropology, and later of social psychology.

At first Bartlett had wanted to work on social anthropology with Rivers, but joined with him, Ward, and Myers, who had been able to establish a laboratory for experimental psychology at 16 Mill Lane, Cambridge, under Myers's direction. Cyril *Burt assisted Myers with the laboratory work at first, and, when Burt left, Bartlett took his place. Rivers, who had done extensive pioneering work on sensory measurements in the course of his anthropological studies, considered that experience with psychophysical methods would be an advantage to Bartlett if he ever did social anthropology in the field. In due course the development of the Cambridge University psychological laboratory became Bartlett's life-work. The University chair of experimental psychology was established in 1931 and Bartlett became its first occupant.

The inspiration given by Ward, who developed a psychology altogether opposed to the atomistic–associationist psychologies such as that of Herbert *Spencer, must have strengthened Bartlett's discontent with associationist theories of sensation, *perception, learning, memory, and thinking prevalent in experimental psychology at the time. He also chimed in with William *James and the Würzburg school in their different ways. His discontent with the orthodoxy of the day no doubt led towards his extensive empirical research on perceiving, *imaging, recognition, and recall (see REMEMBERING), using definite (and sometimes not-so-definite) picture material, and also stories derived from folk tales instead of the usual and supposedly meaningless nonsense material (see EBBINGHAUS, HERMANN). The outcome of many years of research was published in his celebrated book *Remembering* (1932). In this he shows that perceiving, recognition, imaging, and recall are to be understood as the expression of active or dynamic processes dealing with the current situation of the organism and its current needs, always based on and related to its past experiences. To avoid the somewhat over-mechanical notion of 'memory traces', he used the concept of flexible '*schemas' which had been used by Henry *Head in connection with earlier work on *aphasia. Bartlett also used the expression 'effort after meaning' to good purpose in his studies of perceiving and the other psychological functions mentioned above.

The influence of Myers, apart from experimental psychology itself, is to be seen in Bartlett's keen interest in applied and industrial psychology throughout his life. This was apparent in his studies during the First World War, when submarine warfare was of paramount significance, of the problems of perceiving changes in underwater sounds which might indicate the presence of an enemy submarine approaching a ship.

During the 1920s and 1930s Bartlett continued to work on social psychology. His book *Psychology and Primitive Culture* (1923) was an interesting and original work. This and *The Study of Society* (1939), which was compiled during meetings of an informal group of which he was the mainspring and leader, never gained the attention they deserved. Bartlett once told a student that he always enjoyed committee, faculty, and senate meetings because of the fascinating opportunities they gave for the study of leadership, social and personal interactions, and the processes of group decision.

Two important factors then appear to have combined to bring about a change. One of these was the coming of the Second World War, with its tremendous demand for a better understanding of aircraft design and control, and the many problems of the flying personnel themselves and their training, and here Bartlett's interest in applied psychology came to the fore again. The other factor was the coming to Cambridge of Kenneth *Craik, Bartlett's most outstanding pupil, who combined an exceptional gift for theoretical work—seen, for instance, in his concept of the human operator viewed as a link in a control system, clearly relevant to the problems of aircraft control—with an equally astonishing skill in experimentation and the design and use of apparatus and equipment. He and Bartlett fused their powers in a way that made the applied psychology of wartime problems such as they dealt with a major force for success. Craik's sudden death, two days before the end of the war, must have been as severe a blow to Bartlett as Rivers's death had been more than twenty years before.

Myers had gone to London in 1922 to establish the National Institute of Industrial Psychology there. Bartlett then became the leading figure in psychology in Cambridge, a position which he filled at least until his retirement from the University chair of experimental psychology and the directorship of its psychological laboratory thirty years later.

In 1944 the Medical Research Council had established an applied psychology unit in Cambridge under Craik's direction, and Bartlett continued his association with it after his retirement. In later years he extended his earlier work on perceiving and remembering to the psychology of thinking, with the production of a book (Bartlett, 1958) in which he showed that the thinker, whether by interpolation or by extrapolation, deals with a present problem in terms of his past experience, and by a flexible activity brings about the completion of an open-ended situation. So thinking is a kind of skill, comparable with the skills seen, for instance, in ball games (which had always interested Bartlett); and it was thus brought into line with perceiving and remembering, which can also be regarded as kinds of skill.

Bartlett had very exceptional intellectual powers, sharpened and expanded by logic and philosophy. He could see to the heart of any problem and realize the many ramifications it might have. He could understand and express other people's ideas clearly alongside his own, and weigh their relative merits with illuminating impartiality, sometimes gravely but always with an engaging smile. Students felt that he treated them as equals, much to their astonishment, just as he tells us Rivers treated him. With Ward, Rivers, and Myers at his back, Mary Smith, an animal psychologist, as his wife, and Craik as his lieutenant, it is not surprising that he occupied the major position in British psychology for some forty years. He received numerous honours, including a knighthood and in 1922 fellowship of the Royal Society.

R. W. P.

Bartlett, F. C. (1923). *Psychology and Primitive Culture*. London.

Bartlett, F. C. (1932). *Remembering: A Study in Experimental and Social Psychology*. London.

Bartlett, F. C. (1937). Cambridge, England, 1887–1937. *American Journal of Psychology*, **50**, 97–110.

Bartlett, F. C. (1958). *Thinking: An Experimental and Social Study*. London.

Bartlett, F. C., Ginsberg, M., Lindgren, E. J., and Thouless, R. H. (eds.) (1939). *The Study of Society: Methods and Problems*. London.

Oldfield, R. C. (1972). Frederic Charles Bartlett, 1886–1969. *American Journal of Psychology*, **85**, 133–40.

Zangwill, O. L. (1970). Sir Frederic Bartlett (1886–1969). Obituary. *Quarterly Journal of Experimental Psychology*, **22**, 77–81.

**BASAL GANGLIA.** Large masses of grey matter embedded deep in the white matter of the cerebral hemispheres and the midbrain (see NERVOUS SYSTEM). The basal ganglia have very complicated connections with the central nervous system and are concerned with the control of movement. Degeneration of the basal ganglia can disturb the motor function of the body, as occurs, for example, in *Parkinsonism and *Huntington's chorea.

**BEDLAM.** A term used initially to describe a lunatic *asylum or madhouse, but now used figuratively to describe a general state of uproar. The word is derived from the Hospital of St Mary of Bethlehem (later the Bethlem Royal Hospital), which was founded in London in 1247 as a priory and which became a hospital specifically for the mentally ill in 1402. In the eighteenth century, the public, as an entertainment, could view the inmates, and the use of the word bedlam (from Bethlem) arose at this time.

**BEHAVIOUR GENETICS.** See GENETICS OF BEHAVIOUR.

**BEHAVIOURISM.** The central tenet of behaviourism is that thoughts, feelings, and intentions, mental processes all, do not determine what we do. Our behaviour is the product of our conditioning. We are biological machines and do not consciously act; rather we *react* to stimuli.

In 1913, John B. *Watson argued that human psychology could do without the concept of *consciousness and the technique of *introspection. Instead, people could be studied objectively, as are cats, monkeys, and rats, by observing their behaviour. Watson claimed that research on consciousness had led nowhere because investigators who contemplated consciousness could never really agree about what was going on 'in the mind'. Behaviour was public. Two scientists could time how long it takes a rat to get to the end of a maze or how much of an evening John spends dancing with Jane. This approach came as a shock because, in its early days, psychology was linked closely to philosophy. The assertion that human beings were observable like animals jolted many pioneers who assumed that humankind was a cut above the rest of nature. Watson, furthermore, did not want behaviourism to be just an academic theory. Its goal ought to be 'the control and prediction of behaviour'. If you could predict behaviour, it would show psychology was a science, just like physics; and if you could control behaviour, you could improve life.

The history of behaviourism has had its ironies. Though Watson was forced out of psychology because of a divorce scandal and temporarily reduced to selling rubber boots, behaviourism came to dominate Anglo-American psychology from the early 1920s to the mid 1950s. Moreover, though it came under increasing attack for neglecting not just consciousness but feelings, it has shaped much of psychology this century. We are all behaviourists now, it could be said. Even a psychoanalyst, Anna *Freud, explained in a late interview that it was well worth observing how children used toys, responded to tests, or ate meals. 'The analyst as behaviourist', she pointed out, 'can use pieces of behaviour to infer for example how a child deals with anxiety or frustration.' It is a mark of the success of behaviourism that even those who were radically opposed to it conceded that psychology has to involve studying actual behaviour. Watson and his followers were remarkable in claiming that psychology should study nothing else. Watson himself, however, did not quite stick to this extreme position: he was always willing to listen to what people said about what they did and, in *A Balance Sheet of the Self*, he suggested that psychology students ought first to analyse their own behaviour, reactions, and fears before being allowed to practise on anyone else.

Behaviourism has featured in political literature. Two nightmares and one Utopia were inspired by the notion that it is possible to condition people's behaviour. Aldous Huxley's *Brave New World* and George Orwell's *1984* both feared that advances in psychology had given the state the technology with which to control individuals. In B. F. Skinner's *Walden Two*, psychology is also in power. But Skinner, a behaviourist, firmly believed that its insights could be used to make people better and happier. In his community, there is harmony, love, co-operation, and creativity because human beings have been reinforced to behave that way to each other. Many critics of behaviourism have argued that *Walden Two* is, in its cloying, apple-pie harmony, just as oppressive as the Orwell and Huxley nightmares. Be that as it may, these three books bear witness to the cultural importance of behaviourism. The only other school of psychology to have impressed the twentieth century as much was *psychoanalysis.

Though it is now unfashionable to credit one man with a discovery, Watson was very much responsible for the initial success of behaviourism. He was born in Greenville, South Carolina, in 1878. His mother, Emma, was a zealous Baptist; his father, Pickens, was a misfit who enjoyed bourbon whiskey and eventually ran away from his pious wife to live with two Indian women. Religious Greenville was shocked and vitriolic; this helped make Watson detest religion, and was to prove important in his development—and that of behaviourism. After a difficult adolescence during which he was arrested for 'nigger bashing' and for firing a gun in the middle of Greenville, Watson went to Furman University; there 'I cut my teeth on metaphysics'. Having graduated, he went to the University of Chicago to study under the philosopher John *Dewey. But Watson soon became disillusioned with Dewey and turned to the study of animal behaviour. His doctoral thesis, 'Animal learning', looked not at how rats run mazes but at how they learn a variety of tricks including getting out of a box and opening a drawbridge.

In 1903, psychology was very young. Before the start of its first laboratories in 1879, it had often been called experimental philosophy, and in many universities psychologists still worked under the department of philosophy. It is not surprising that much of the discipline was rather abstract. Much effort was devoted to introspection and the unravelling of consciousness. In 1903, introspecting did not mean brooding on one's *psyche but rather trying to dissect what was going on inside one's mind. Psychologists believed that a trained observer could report on what was going on in his consciousness when he saw dots, waited for a tone, or was asked to respond to a picture by pressing a button. Taking their models from chemistry and physics, they hoped to work out what were the 'atoms' of consciousness; but different subjects reported very different mental processes.

Introspection made Watson acerbic. 'I hated to serve as a subject,' he wrote in an autobiographical note in 1936; 'I didn't like the stuffy artificial instructions given to subjects. I always was uncomfortable and acted unnaturally. . . . More and more the thought presented itself. Can't I find out by watching their behaviour everything the other students are finding out by using *O's*.' *O's* were introspective observers. Evidence that he began to be highly critical of orthodox ideas does not depend only on his memory. He raised the possibility of studying humans like animals with James *Angell, his doctoral supervisor. Angell told him to stick to animals. This dismayed Watson and, with the pressure of finishing his doctorate, it led to a short breakdown. But he did not abandon his critique. He vowed to a friend that he would remodel psychology.

By 1908, Watson had a national reputation as 'an animal man'. He took the professorship of psychology at Johns Hopkins University and began to read widely in human psychology. He tested some of his ideas in letters to Robert Yerkes, an animal psychologist. Yerkes warned that Watson was too extreme; yet, in 1912, in a series of summer lectures at Columbia University, Watson outlined his critique. The lectures were well attended, and Watson, given the radical nature of his ideas, was nervous about how they would be received. Angell, he had heard, 'thinks I am crazy. I should not be surprised if that is the general consensus of opinion.'

The lectures, published in 1913, remain the text for behaviourism. Psychology 'as the behaviourist views it is a purely objective branch of natural science. Its theoretical goal is the control and prediction of behaviour.' Introspection was no help and psychologists should not judge the value of their data by whether it shed any light on the intricacies of consciousness. The behaviourist 'recognises no dividing line between man and brute'. Watson's dislike of religion, learned in Greenville, made him hostile to the idea that human beings were superior organisms with souls.

He made much fun of the failure of introspection. 'If you can't observe 3–9 states of clearness in attention, your introspection is poor. If, on the other hand, a feeling seems reasonably clear to you, your introspection is again faulty.' Sweeping such mystical nonsense away would enable psychology to become a proper science linked to biology rather than to metaphysics.

Rejecting introspection was easy; developing a coherent theory of how human beings behaved was rather harder. Watson drew heavily on the work of *Pavlov, who had shown that you could condition dogs to salivate not just at the sight of food but at the sound of a bell that preceded food. A reflex-like salivation was malleable. Watson argued that human behaviour is built on just such conditioning. He claimed that almost all behaviour is learnt: if one gets up every time a lady enters the room, one is acting not out of politeness but because behaviour is a chain of well-set reflexes. Watson claimed that what determined the next item of behaviour a person 'emitted' was *recency* and

*frequency*—what had occurred just before and what, in the past, had been the response a person made to that particular stimulus: if one usually gets up when a lady enters the room, one is very likely, if a lady enters the room now, to get up again. The behaviour may be explained as a polite action, but it is a reaction that could have been predicted. In Watson's scheme, rewards and punishments were not crucial.

In 1916, Watson began to study how children develop. He wanted to isolate the most important early reflexes on which conditioning could build. He also examined the idea of applying such ideas to psychiatry. In the early 1920s, he reported a study of Little Albert, a child who was taught to fear rats and then not to fear them entirely through manipulating. This paper (whose integrity has been disputed) was an inspiration to behaviour therapists who aim to train people out of their phobias and neuroses.

The historian John Burnham has warned against being romantic about Watson. Other psychologists were inching towards behaviourism, too. Burnham stressed T. S. Kuhn's theory of scientific revolutions which states that scientific revolutions occur when the field is ripe for a new paradigm. According to this view, Watson prevailed because the prevailing mood was right. But Kuhn's theory may not fit psychology too well. In arguing for behaviourism, Watson wasn't so much making a new discovery as offering a new philosophy and methodology. Behaviourism was a self-conscious revolution against consciousness. Some traditional psychologists grasped its dangers very well and reacted with hostility: James Angell said privately that Watson should be 'spanked', while Watson said of E. B. Titchener that he 'roasted me'. There is some dispute about how quickly behaviourist ideas spread through American psychology, but by 1920 Watson was recognized as one of the leading American psychologists.

In the 1930s and 1940s, behaviourism became very much laboratory-based. B. F. Skinner (see next entry and SKINNER BOX) made his name through his studies of how to reward pigeons and other creatures; Clark *Hull, perhaps the leading behaviourist of the 1940s, devised immensely complicated models of animal behaviour. These developments make it easy to imagine that Watson was bent not only on making psychology scientific but on imprisoning it in the laboratory. Nothing could be further from the truth.

In *Psychology from the Standpoint of a Behaviorist* (1919), Watson argued passionately that psychology should be relevant to real life. Scientists should analyse what people did in the factory, the office, the home, and even the bedroom. He initiated studies on subjects as varied as how well one can throw darts while drunk and the effects of anti-VD propaganda on the sex lives of GIs. Behaviourism was to be a psychology of real life. But after the divorce scandal he had to resign from Johns Hopkins and could not see his programme through. Following his job as a travelling salesman, the advertising firm J. Walter Thompson employed him. Advertising was to benefit from his psychological skills—he pioneered many modern advertising techniques—but he was lost to serious psychology. He was only 42 at the time of his divorce, an age at which many psychologists begin doing their best work.

Behaviourism as it developed between 1913 and 1920 had many problems. It was a fluid theory. Watson tended to ignore the power of reinforcement. There was no convincing account of language, let alone of thought. B. F. Skinner later attempted to remedy this with his *Verbal Behavior* (1957); further research showed conclusively, however, that we do not just learn language but that we are innately 'wired' to speak. Then, from 1920 and into the 1930s, American universities expanded quickly and many new departments of psychology were set up. Behaviourism was in an attractive position because it seemed to ensure that psychology could be scientific. Most psychologists accepted Watson's methods though not his vision of applying psychology objectively to all of life. Behaviourism became narrower than it might have been if he had remained active.

The three major figures among those who developed behaviourism through the 1930s and 1940s were Edward Guthrie (1886–1959), Clark Hull, and Skinner. Guthrie followed Watson most closely but dropped frequency as an important determinant of behaviour. For Guthrie, 'a combination of stimuli which has accompanied a movement will on its recurrence tend to be followed by that movement'. He tried to show that all learning could be explained on this principle, ignoring rather how it might explain novel combinations of movements.

Clark Hull proposed a more systematic total behaviourist theory. He tried to link the external circumstances (such as the intensity of a pain stimulus or the size of a reward) with internal body states (hunger and thirst) and with specific behaviours such as the speed with which an animal will run a maze for a food reward. Hull wanted a theory of behaviour as formal as Euclid's theory of geometry, and he introduced theorems and postulates which could account for all behaviour. The scheme was a grand one, and defined precisely some internal states such as drive, and strength of habit. For example, a rat who had been deprived of food for seven hours was likely to be hungrier than a rat deprived of food for three hours, unless the seven-hour rat had been used to going without food for longer. Hull perfected his system over some twenty years, but it had its problems. First, some experiments had inconvenient results. For example, Hull argued that habit strength built up slowly. It could therefore be expected that, for an animal used to doing $X$ for reward $Y$, if the reward was reduced it would still tend to do $X$ because of the habit strength attached to $X$. In fact, diminishing rewards reduced the behaviour fast. Then, as

Hull tried to accommodate such results, internal inconsistencies in the theory began to creep in. He succeeded in offering a very grand vision of a theory that was precise and quantifiable. His books are full of equations. But by 1952, the year of his death, he knew that he had not quite succeeded, and it may be that his failure to make his system convince affected the ambitions of psychology. Perhaps it was too soon to attempt a comprehensive theory of behaviour.

B. F. Skinner now became the leading exponent of behaviourism. His first major theoretical contribution had tended to go against Watson's ideas. Arriving at Harvard in 1929 to work for his doctorate, Skinner was committed to a scientific and practical psychology. But he grew dissatisfied with basing everything on the reflex. It seemed to him not only that people respond to the environment but also that 'behaviour operates on the environment to generate consequences'. If a rat gets food every time it presses a lever, it is operating on the environment. Skinner argued, therefore, that most behaviour involves operant conditioning. We behave the way we do because of the consequences our past behaviour has generated. If every time a man takes his wife out to dinner, she is very loving, he is likely to learn to take her out to dinner if he wants her to be loving. Though this example (like many of Skinner's) involves description of behaviour in which motives, feelings, and intents appear to matter, Skinner himself was always scathing about what he described as 'the mentalists'. For Skinner, it is the history of reinforcements that determines behaviour. Consciousness is just an epiphenomenon, and feelings are not causes of actions but consequences. Behaviour can be predicted and controlled without reference to them.

Skinner made famous the notion of *shaping*. By controlling the rewards and punishments the environment offers in response to particular behaviours, you can shape behaviour. Pigeons can be 'shaped' even to play ping-pong. Psychiatric patients can be 'shaped' to behave in less anxious and more socially acceptable ways. Much of Skinner's detailed technical work was aimed at discovering the different effects of different schedules of reinforcement. Which are most effective: regular rewards, irregular rewards, or a mixture of the two?

The controversies Skinner has fuelled arise largely because, like Watson, he was not content to see behaviourism merely as a scientific method; rather it offers a way of organizing our lives better. Skinner has been accused of helping to perfect technologies of control, but the truth is more prosaic. In the 1950s and 60s, there was a vogue for trying out 'token economies' in penal and psychiatric institutions. Professionals tried to 'shape' the behaviour of inmates by giving them rewards for behaviour that was deemed good or appropriate. Usually, the inmates were not punished, a point Skinner liked to stress. But though some institutions continue to use such methods of 'behaviour modification', as it has been called, it would be an exaggeration to say they are widespread or entirely successful. The individual histories of human beings are too complex for their behaviour to be shaped like that of laboratory-reared birds. Moreover, Skinner claimed, human beings cling to illusions of being free to act because they think, wrongly, that without them they will lose all dignity. We are, in fact, controlled by our past and controlled by our environment. The more we realize that, the more we analyse the nature of that control, the better our situation. Herein there is a paradox that Skinner doesn't really explore in his enthusiasm to go against the importance of thoughts, intentions, and feelings. Skinner has certainly attracted much respect and fame but his form of classic behaviourism is now less and less in vogue especially as cognitive psychology has, since the late 1960s, suggested that it is possible to be objective about studying mental processes.

Behaviourism has been seen in different lights by different observers. The British psychologist Donald Broadbent argued (1961) that it offers the best method for rational advance in psychology, allowing one to weed out facts from fantasy and to replace armchair speculation about the nature of the soul or the mysteries of consciousness with repeatable results. In contrast, Nehemiah Jorden asked the question (1968), 'can one positive contribution towards any increased knowledge of man be pointed to since Watson wrote his famous paper?' And answered it: 'None such can be found.' Any assessment of behaviourism has to recognize such different opinions, but almost all psychologists and psychiatrists see merit in some of Watson's ideas, while very few are strict behaviourists. One needs to study behaviour objectively. There are close links between human and animal behaviour, and conditioning does play an important part in human development. Many would also applaud the original aim of establishing a scientific psychology of life in the factory, the office, and the home. On the other hand, seventy years of research have shown that consciousness cannot be dismissed as uninteresting in human psychology and that even introspection has its uses as one tool among many.                    D. C.

Broadbent, D. (1961). *Behaviour*. London.
Cohen, D. (1979). *J. B. Watson, the founder of behaviourism*. London.
Jorden, N. (1968). *Themes in Speculative Psychology*. London.
Skinner, B. F. (1961). *Walden Two*. New York.
Watson, J. B. (1919). *Psychology from the Standpoint of a Behaviorist*. Philadelphia.

**BEHAVIOURISM, SKINNER ON.** The scientific study of behaviour covers many fields, including ethology, psychology, sociology, anthropology, economics, and political science. Behaviourism is not one of these fields; it is a consideration of certain problems which arise in all of them.

Behaviour is most effectively studied in relation to the environment—the environment in which the species evolved and the physical and social environments in which the individual lives. It has been traditionally viewed, however, in other ways—for example, as the expression of feelings or states of mind, as the role played by a personality, or as the symptom of mental illness. Behaviourism is in part an attack upon these traditional interpretations. It is a philosophy of behavioural science, the roots of which are to be traced through the writings of J. B. *Watson and I. P. *Pavlov to Ernst *Mach, Henri *Poincaré, and Auguste *Comte, among others.

'Methodological' behaviourists often accept the existence of feelings and states of mind, but do not deal with them because they are not public and hence statements about them are not subject to confirmation by more than one person. 'Radical' behaviourists, on the other hand, recognize the role of private events (accessible in varying degrees to self-observation and physiological research), but contend that so-called mental activities are metaphors or explanatory fictions and that behaviour attributed to them can be more effectively explained in other ways. A few examples will be considered here to illustrate the latter position.

**Purpose, intention, expectation.** Most behaviour is selected by its consequences. For example, we tend to do the things we have successfully done in the past. Although it is the product only of past consequences, behaviour is useful because it may have similar consequences in the future. We refer indirectly to that future when we say that we act with a *purpose, intention, or expectation. Such 'states of mind' are not, however, the causes of our behaviour. We do not act because we have a purpose, we act because of past consequences, the very consequences which generate the condition of our bodies which we observe introspectively and call felt purpose. Natural selection raised the same issues. Has life a purpose? Is a given species the result of an intentional design? (See EVOLUTION: HAS IT A PURPOSE?) These concepts can be abandoned in both fields when the principle of selection by consequences is understood.

**Mental processes.** Many aspects of mental life are modelled upon the physical environment. The smell of a rose is said to 'remind us of' or 'bring to mind' the visual appearance of a rose because we associate one with the other. But the odour and the visual properties are associated in the rose. When we have been exposed to two physically associated stimuli, we may subsequently respond to one as we responded to the other, but the environmental association is enough to account for our behaviour. We have no introspective evidence of any internal process of association. Abstraction, concept formation, and many other so-called mental processes are also modelled upon complex arrangements of stimuli, and again the arrangements suffice to explain the behaviour without appeal to mental duplicates.

**Sensations, perceptions, and images.** Most people believe that when they look at a rose they construct an internal copy, called a sensation or perception, and that later, when they are reminded of a rose, they reconstruct that copy, now called a mental image, and look at it again. They do not observe themselves doing so; they simply see a rose. Under special circumstances, they may, in addition, observe that they are seeing one, but even so there is no evidence, introspective or physiological, of an internal copy. If seeing were simply constructing a copy of the thing seen, we should have to make another copy to see the copy, and then another copy to see that. At some point we must 'see a rose' in some other sense. What that means is not well understood—by anyone. Rather than look for internal representations, we should examine the ways in which a person learns to see things, in both the presence and absence of the things seen.

**Reasons and reasoning.** Three things must be taken into account in the study of behaviour: the situation in which behaviour occurs, the behaviour itself, and the consequences that follow. The relations among these things can be very complex, and only a careful scientific analysis will then untangle them. For practical purposes, however, we describe many of them with reasonable accuracy. When we give someone advice, for example, we specify a situation ('When you have a headache . . .'), an act ('take an aspirin . . .'), and (possibly only by implication) a consequence ('and you will feel better').

People profit from advice because by following it they can behave in ways which, without help, they would have to learn through a possibly long exposure to the conditions described. The social environment called a culture offers a vast store of rules, maxims, and governmental and scientific laws describing relations among situations, behaviour, and consequences, which enable people to acquire much more extensive repertoires than would otherwise be possible.

In taking advice or following rules we can be said to behave because of reasons rather than causes, and in what is called reasoning we formulate rules for our own use. Rather than explore a situation and allow our behaviour to be changed directly by it, we analyse the situation and extract a rule which we then follow. We sometimes extract rules from other rules, as in logic and mathematics.

**Introspection.** The world within a human skin is part of the physical world. It may seem that we should know it better because we are close to it, and we do, indeed, respond to private events with great precision in the normal functioning of our bodies. But *knowing* about our bodies, in the same sense in which we *know* about the world around us,

depends upon conditions which cannot easily be arranged with respect to a private world. We learn to tell $P$ from $Q$ because other people respond appropriately when we say '$P$' or '$Q$' when looking at a letter. Unfortunately they cannot respond as precisely when we name or describe a private event (such as those we call feelings or states of mind), because they lack the necessary contact. As a result, we never know our own bodies with any great accuracy. Moreover, we cannot know much about many important parts of them (for example, the physiological processes which mediate the complex behaviour called thinking) because we simply do not have nerves going to relevant places.

Behaviourism criticizes mentalistic explanations of behaviour in this way only to promote a more effective analysis. By dismissing mental states and processes as metaphors or fictions, it directs attention to the genetic and personal histories of the individual and to the current environment, where the real causes of behaviour are to be found. It also clarifies the assignment of the neurosciences, saving the time that would otherwise be wasted in searching for the neurological counterparts of sensations, stored memories, and thought processes. Behaviour is simply part of the biology of the organism and can be integrated with the rest of that field when described in appropriate physical dimensions.

At the same time behaviourism provides an overview which is particularly helpful in the social sciences. The experimental analysis of behaviour has led to an effective technology, applicable to education, psychotherapy, and the design of cultural practices in general, which will be more effective when it is not competing with practices that have had the unwarranted support of mentalistic theories.                                    B. F. S.

Skinner, B. F. (1974). *About Behaviorism*. New York.

**BEHAVIOUR MODIFICATION.** See BEHAVIOUR THERAPY.

**BEHAVIOUR THERAPY.** The term 'behaviour therapy' was coined towards the end of the 1950s by H. J. Eysenck to denote a method of treatment of neurotic disorders that was based on laboratory studies of *conditioning, and on modern *learning theory. Behaviour therapy is derived from a general theory of neurotic disorder which differs profoundly from psychoanalytic or orthodox psychiatric theories. Before presenting this theory (which is basic to the therapeutic application of the various methods comprised under the general term 'behaviour therapy'), it may be useful to distinguish behaviour therapy from *psychotherapy* and from *behaviour modification*, two terms which partly overlap with behaviour therapy, and are partly contrasted with it.

Psychotherapy denotes the use of psychological theories and methods in the treatment of psychiatric disorders; in its generic sense it therefore includes behaviour therapy as one of the methods used by psychologists and psychiatrists, and is partly synonymous with it. However, psychotherapy also has a narrower meaning, namely the use of interpretative (mostly *Freudian) methods of therapy; in this sense psychotherapy and behaviour therapy are antonyms, the former relying on verbal and symbolic methods, the latter on the direct manipulation of motor and autonomic behaviours. Thus psychotherapy in the wider sense can be usefully divided into psychotherapy in the narrower sense, and behaviour therapy. Both psychotherapy and behaviour therapy refer to a whole set of methods; they are not confined to one single method, as the terms used might suggest.

The terms behaviour therapy and behaviour modification are also partly synonymous, partly antonymous. In the United States, particularly, both terms are used indiscriminately to refer to two sets of rather different theories and methods. Both these sets do, indeed, make use of psychological theories of learning and conditioning, and to that extent there is some overlap. However, psychologists make a fairly clear (although probably not absolute) distinction between two kinds of conditioning: *Pavlovian or classical, and instrumental or operant. Behaviour therapy in the narrower sense is concerned with Pavlovian conditioning, behaviour modification with instrumental conditioning. In this sense these methods and theories are antonymous; and we may say that behaviour therapy in the wider sense can be usefully subdivided into behaviour therapy in the narrower sense, and behaviour modification. These complications of nomenclature are bothersome and annoying, but they have become so firmly entrenched that they have to be dealt with; clearly anyone writing about these various therapies should indicate in which sense the terms are being used.

Pavlovian conditioning forms associations between conditioned stimuli (neutral before conditioning) and unconditioned stimuli and responses by simple pairing: the animal or human being conditioned does not perform any act that would affect the outcome. Thus a dog may be conditioned to lift his paw upon a signal by fixing to his foot a device that delivers an electric shock and activating it shortly after giving a signal (the conditioned stimulus). The shock makes the dog lift his leg, and although this movement does not enable the dog to escape from the shock, nevertheless the movement becomes conditioned. Instrumental conditioning, pioneered by Pavlov's rival Bekhterev, is based on similar associations, but in this case the action performed by the animal or human is the crucial factor. Thus the shock to the leg of the dog may be delivered through a grid on which the foot of the animal rests; if he lifts his foot, in response to the conditioned stimulus, he avoids the shock. This is a profound difference, and E. L. *Thorndike, B. F. Skinner (see BEHAVIORISM, SKINNER ON), and other American psychologists have elaborated practical methods of using positive and negative reinforcements (rewards and punishments) in order to modify behaviour. These are usually related to explicit behaviour patterns: for instance they may be used to make schoolchildren less boisterous, criminals better behaved, or psychotic in-patients more responsive to the demands of society. In each case the stress is on segments of large-scale behaviour: the child may be required to learn to sit quietly for certain periods of time, the criminal to carry out a series of acts such as making his own bed, keeping his room clean, and working adequately for a certain period of time. The psychotic may be required to come to meals punctually, keep himself tidy, work in the laundry, associate with other people, and so on. Methods have been worked out for the optimum use of rewards ('token economies') according to the laws of operant conditioning, and many practical applications of these methods have been developed, particularly in the treatment of deteriorated psychotics. But little attempt has been made to use these methods in connection with the treatment of the far more widespread neurotic disorders, and in clinical practice there is little doubt that Pavlovian methods are much more frequently used, and much more efficacious.

Operant conditioning applies, for the most part, to motor activities and the performance of integrated activities. Pavlovian conditioning applies, for the most part, to the activity of the autonomic system, i.e. to emotions; thus it is no accident that neurotic behaviour, which is largely characterized by emotional upsets and difficulties, is more closely related to Pavlovian conditioning. (This distinction is not an absolute one, but it is very useful and far-reaching; most human activities, as well as most animal activities studied in the laboratory, partake of both operant and classical conditioning, and complex methods of analysis are required to sort out the respective contributions of these two processes.) The theory of neurosis from which behaviour therapy derives states that neurotic disorders are essentially *conditioned emotional responses*; they are acquired through some traumatic emotional event, or a series of subtraumatic emotional events, in which some previously neutral conditioned stimulus becomes linked (perhaps quite accidentally) with a fear-producing unconditioned stimulus. This theory is clearly different from psychoanalytic and other psychiatric theories, according to which the observed signs of the disorder are merely symptoms of some underlying 'complex'; according to Freud and his followers, this 'complex' must be eliminated before any permanent cure is possible. Behaviour therapists deny the existence of these alleged 'complexes', and they assert that the putative 'symptoms' are not in fact symptoms of anything— they *are* the disorder. The aim of behaviour therapy is to eliminate these 'symptoms'; if this can be accomplished, then no 'disease' or 'complex' will remain. Freud predicted that 'purely symptomatic treatment', which did not eliminate the 'complex' allegedly underlying the outward manifestations of the disorder, would lead to relapse or to symptom substitution, i.e. either the 'symptom' would return, or else another one would arise in its place. Behaviour therapists have been on the look-out for such effects, but although they have succeeded much more completely than others in eliminating the 'symptoms', relapse and symptom substitution have been notable mainly by their failure to occur.

The methods of behaviour therapy (in the narrower sense) derive from this general theory. If the manifestations of neurotic disorder are conditioned emotional responses, then a cure must consist in the *extinction* of these conditioned responses. Fortunately experimental psychologists, following the lead of Pavlov, have elaborated many different methods for attaining this aim, and these have been tried out very successfully in neurotic patients. The methods include *desensitization* or counter-conditioning (in which the conditioned stimulus that produces fear/anxiety responses in the patient is conditioned by the therapist to more positive anti-anxiety-producing unconditioned stimuli, such as relaxation or self-assertion); *flooding* (in which the patient is exposed for a lengthy period to the conditioned stimulus that produces fear/anxiety responses; by preventing the usual reactions of flight or whatever, the therapist forces the patient to face his fears, which then disappear quickly); and *modelling* (in which the patient is shown a 'model' who copes properly with his own difficulties and fears, and thus learns the absurdity of his conditioned responses). The effectiveness of these, and many other similar methods, is no longer in question; indeed, empirical evidence from clinical and experimental studies has shown that for no other therapy is there anything like as good evidence for speed and efficacy of cure. If we consider that, at the time of writing, these methods have been in existence for less than twenty years, their future development suggests even greater promise of effectiveness.　　　　H. J. E.

Eysenck, H. J. (ed.) (1973). *Handbook of Abnormal Psychology*. London.

Eysenck, H. J. and Rachman, S. (1964). *Causes and Cures of Neurosis*. London.

Kazdin, A. E. (1978). *History of Behavior Modification*. Baltimore.

Kazdin, A. E. and Wilson, T. (1978). *Evaluation of Behavior Therapy*. Cambridge, Mass.

Rachman, S. (1971). *The Effects of Psychotherapy*. London.

Ullmann, L. P. and Krasner, L. (1975). *A Psychological Approach to Abnormal Behavior*. Englewood Cliffs, New Jersey. (For a presentation of the theories and methods of behaviour modification.)

**BÉKÉSY**, GEORG VON (1899–1972). Hungarian physicist and physiologist, the son of a Hungarian diplomat. He spent his early years in Munich, Constantinople, Zurich, and Berne. He received his Ph.D. in physics from the University of Budapest, and remained in Budapest until 1946. After a year in Stockholm he moved to the psychoacoustic laboratory in Harvard, where he remained until 1966. He then moved to Honolulu to become professor of sensory sciences at the University of Hawaii. He continued in active research there until shortly before his death.

Békésy is most famous for his work on the inner ear or cochlea. He was the first to observe directly the patterns of vibration on the basilar membrane inside the cochlea. He found that sound evoked a pattern of wave motion which travelled from one end of the membrane towards the other, increasing in amplitude up to a certain point, and then decreasing. He found that the position of maximum vibration varied systematically with the frequency of the sound, thus providing the basis for the frequency-analysing power of the ear. He carried out this work first on models of the cochlea, and later on preparations of human temporal bones and on the cochleas of living animals. Most of his work in this field was carried out in Hungary. (See also HEARING.)

In Stockholm Békésy invented a new method for measuring thresholds of hearing, and devised a new *audiometer to go with it. The Békésy audiometer is still widely used in clinical hearing testing and in auditory research.

At Harvard the emphasis of his work shifted from the mechanics of the ear to biophysics, and particularly the mechanism by which mechanical vibration on the basilar membrane is transformed into neural impulses. Later still he conducted perceptual experiments on a number of different senses, including hearing, sight, smell, and taste.

Békésy's work on hearing is summarized in his fine book *Experiments in Hearing* (1962). The quality of his work was recognized by the award of the Nobel Prize for Physiology or Medicine in 1961, for 'discoveries concerning the physical mechanisms of excitation in the cochlea'. The award was celebrated by a special issue of the *Journal of the Acoustical Society of America* in 1962, which contained a series of papers dedicated to his work.　　　　B. C. J. M.

**BELL,** SIR CHARLES (1774–1842). British anatomist and surgeon, born in Edinburgh, the son of a Scottish Episcopalian clergyman. He was taught anatomy by his brother and was admitted to membership of the Royal College of Surgeons of Edinburgh in 1799, followed shortly by his appointment as a surgeon at the Edinburgh Royal Infirmary. In 1806 he moved to London, where he taught anatomy and surgery to his house pupils and, from 1811, at the Great Windmill Street School of Anatomy. From 1812 to 1836 he acted as surgeon at the Middlesex Hospital. In 1824 he accepted the senior professorship of anatomy and surgery at the Royal College of Surgeons of London, his lectures there forming the text of a book entitled *Animal Mechanics, or Proofs of Design in the Animal Frame* (1828) (see CYBERNETICS). In 1826 he was elected a Fellow of the Royal Society, and in 1828, on the founding of the University of London, he accepted the chair of anatomy and physiology, but after two years he resigned. On the accession of William IV he was knighted, and in 1836 he became professor of surgery at Edinburgh, where he remained until he died, while on a journey to London.

Bell's first claim to fame rests on his contributions to physiological psychology, of which the law bearing his name is the corner-stone. Throughout his published work he has much to say about the mind, and especially in his two favourite books, *The Hand* and *The Anatomy and Philosophy of Expression as Connected with the Fine Arts*, which testify to his capacity for shrewd observation. He delved into the art of antiquity, examined theories of the beauty of the human form, and critically studied the laws governing the expression of feeling, emotion, and passion in the movements of face and figure.

For nearly two thousand years no one had seriously ventured to question *Galen's conception of brain and nerves. Many anatomists, it is true, had suspected that the nerve fibres serving sensation and movement, though joined in the same sheath, might be distinct, and Thomas Willis (1621–75) had stated that some nerves were exclusively sensory and others exclusively motor. But, as Bell says in his preface to *The Nervous System of the Human Body* (1830), 'the (ancient) hypothesis that a nervous fluid was derived from the brain, and transmitted by nervous tubes, was deemed consistent with anatomical demonstration'. Furthermore, his contemporaries took it for granted that one and the same nerve fibre could serve the twofold function of conducting sensory messages and of transmitting the 'mandate of the will'.

Why, Bell asked himself, should sensation remain entire in a limb when all voluntary power over the action of the muscle is lost? And why should muscular power remain when feeling is gone? In seeking to answer these questions, he demonstrated the separate functions of the anterior and posterior roots of the spinal nerves. Some time between 1812 and 1821, his surgical and clinical 'experiments' led him to believe that movement is served by the anterior or ventral, and sensation by the posterior or dorsal, roots of the spinal nerves (Bell–*Magendie law); the respective fibres are distinct but bound within the same trunks, and terminate separately, both centrally and peripherally.

From this discovery, Bell moved to the suggestion that sensory and motor functions might be served by different parts of the brain. He recognized (before Johannes *Müller) the specificity of sensory nerves; identified (before C. S. *Sherrington) the muscle sense; and understood the facts of reciprocal innervation (relaxation of extensor muscle while the flexor contracts). No one before him had acquired such an understanding of the human hand, and of the manner in which it reveals its superiority over the homologous organs of other animals. By dwelling on the delicate musculature of the fingers, and on the sensibility of the skin, he came to see the hand as the special organ of the sense of *touch, while in the 'muscular sense' he detected a sixth sense which we now recognize as that which serves our powers of *haptic perception. He saw the function of the hand as adapted to the arm and shoulder. In studying their comparative anatomy, he drew striking comparisons with the shoulder of the horse, elephant, and camel, and with corresponding organs of the mole, the bat, the ant-eater, and other species, including many now extinct.

Bell felt that he was continuing in the tradition of what he called 'the English School of Physiology', in contrast to the French School, which represented life as 'the mere physical result of certain combinations and actions of parts by them termed Organization'. This was an oblique reference to the Cartesian conception of 'animal as machine' (see DESCARTES), which culminated in *La Mettrie's *L'homme machine*.

A simple principle governed his work, namely 'that design and benevolence were everywhere visible in the natural world'. The 'different affections of the nerves of the outward senses' were, for him, 'the signals which the Author of nature has willed to be the means by which correspondence is held with the realities'. Perfect symmetry of form and function, continuous renewal of the 'material particles', and the integrity of the body amidst the ceaseless changes to which it is subject, convinced him of the existence of a 'principle of life' which governed bodily structure and change.

Charles Bell must be counted among the leading men of science of the nineteenth century, and the most versatile of that illustrious group of men who raised Scottish medicine to pre-eminence. He combined a surgeon's intimacy with the human body with a profound understanding of its anatomy and physiology. To all this he brought considerable gifts as a writer, and as a consummate medical artist.                                    J. CO.

Boring, E. G. (1926). *A History of Experimental Psychology*. New York.
Carmichael, L. (1926). Sir Charles Bell: a contribution to the history of physiological psychology. *Psychological Review*, **33**, 188–217.
Cole, F. J. (1955). Bell's law. *Notes of the Royal Society of London*, **11**, 222–7.
Cranefield, P. (1974). *The Way In and the Way Out*. New York.
Gordon-Taylor, G. and Walls, E. W. (1958). *Sir Charles Bell: His Life and Times*. Edinburgh.
Le Fanu, W. R. (1961). Charles Bell and William Cheselden. *Medical History*, **5**, 196.

**BENHAM'S TOP.** Quite intense colours can be produced by pulsing coloured or white light. Flashing coloured lights can produce other colours: for example, flashing monochromatic sodium yellow light may produce any spectral hue (and brown,

**Fig. 1.**

which is not in the spectrum), though not usually with very high saturation. These phenomena are most easily seen with a spinning disc, or top, having black and white sector rings (as in Fig. 1). This gives intermittent stimulation to retinal regions as it is rotated, quite slowly, to give a flicker rate below the fusion frequency. The colours seen depend on the widths and arrangement of the black sectors and the rate of rotation. There are considerable individual differences for what is seen under given conditions.

Although generally called 'Benham's top', after C. E. Benham (1894), the basic effect goes back to a French monk, Benedict Prévost, who, in 1826, observed colours—like a heavenly light on his fingers—when he waved his hands about in the cloisters. Finding that this also happened with white cardboard, he realized that it has a physiological origin, in the eye, and attributed it to different rates of action of specific colour mechanisms of the retina. He was essentially correct. It is remarkable that Prévost's discovery was forgotten, and the effect was rediscovered no less than twelve times: by Gustav *Fechner in 1838 and then by others. John Smith, in 1859, thought that the effects were 'objective' by changing the light itself, and so he (incorrectly) challenged *Newton's account of light and colour. The third rediscovery was made by Sir David *Brewster in 1861. (The history is given fully in Cohen and Gordon, 1949). Hermann von *Helmholtz carried out systematic observations, noting that a white rotating sector is red on the leading edge and blue on the trailing edge, and in dim light the red becomes yellow and the blue violet. In very bright light the red becomes pinker and the blue greenish. Further observations were made by S. *Bidwell, who discovered a related effect, Bidwell's ghost.

These subjective colours have been shown successfully on black and white television, but they are a little too weak for commercial uses. They are due

to different time-constants of the colour receptor systems of the eye, but they are rather too variable for precise measurements. The effects are interesting but not particularly useful.   R. L. G.

Benham, C. E. (1894). The artificial spectrum top. *Nature*, **51**, 200.
Bidwell, S. (1896). On subjective colour phenomena attending sudden changes in illumination. *Proceedings of the Royal Society*, **60**, 368–77.
Cohen, J. and Gordon, D. A. (1949). The Prévost-Fechner-Benham subjective colours. *Psychological Bulletin*, **46**, 2.

**BENTHAM,** JEREMY (1748–1832). Born in London and educated at Westminster School, he entered the Queen's College, Oxford, at the age of twelve. Although he studied law at Lincoln's Inn and was called to the Bar in 1772, he never practised law; but he wrote on its theory. He held that laws should be socially useful and should not merely reflect custom, that men are hedonists (pursuing pleasure and avoiding pain), and that desires may be classified into self- and other-regarding: the function of law is to provide punishments and rewards to maintain a just balance between them. His famous dictum is that all actions are right and good which promote 'the greatest happiness of the greatest number', this principle being the basis of utilitarianism.

Bentham was a founder of University College, London, where his mummified body may still be seen, dressed in his own clothes. He collaborated closely with James *Mill, whom he met in 1808. He also founded the *Westminster Review*.

**BEREAVEMENT** is a common cause of grief, that 'fierce or violent sorrow' which Robert *Burton in his *Anatomy of Melancholy* referred to as 'the epitome, symptom and chief cause of melancholy'. The relationship between mourning and melancholia was explored in more detail by Sigmund *Freud who, in 1917, suggested that depressive illness (melancholia) differs from grief in the prominent part played by feelings of guilt and in the symbolic significance of the loss which preceded it. Subsequent research has confirmed the frequency of guilt and self-reproach among those who develop depressive illnesses after bereavement.

Despite Freud's claims, little attention was paid to bereavement by psychiatrists until Eric Lindemann described the symptomatology and management of acute grief following the Coconut Grove night-club fire in Boston, Massachusetts, in 1944. Lindemann showed that people who do not 'break down' and express feelings appropriate to a bereavement may suffer from delayed or distorted grief. Such pathological forms of grief, said Lindemann, could be restored to a more normal form in the course of six to eight weekly interviews in which the bereaved person was encouraged to give vent to the feelings of sadness, anger, or guilt which they had repressed. A recent development of this approach has been the use of 'flooding', a technique derived from *behaviour therapy in which bereaved people are pressed to vivid recollection of the sight, smell, sounds, and feelings associated with the dead person. R. W. Ramsay (1977, 1979), the originator of this method of treatment, has subsequently toned down the intensity of the approach, which, in its original form, could only be safely carried out in a psychiatric in-patient setting.

While there is now much agreement regarding the efficacy of Lindemann's approaches to delayed or avoided grief, their use in the treatment of the severe and protracted grief which sometimes follows the dissolution of relationships characterized by ambivalence or dependency is more controversial. Alternative strategies have been developed by C. M. Parkes, who has also advocated the introduction of bereavement counselling during the early phases of grief as a means of preventing later difficulties in those who are thought to be at risk. Recent random-allocation studies have confirmed the effectiveness of some counselling services of this kind (Parkes, 1972, and Raphael, 1984).

The application of Freud's libido theory to grief has been challenged by John Bowlby (1969), whose studies of the development of *attachment between mother and child led him to explain the intense pining or yearning of acute grief as a frustrated form of the urge to search for any loved person from whom one has become separated. This urge to search is thought to be an instinctually derived behaviour-pattern which conflicts with the awareness of the older child or adult that such a search is useless and bound to disappointment. Consequently attempts to avoid reminders of the loss, seek distraction, and inhibit thoughts of loss coexist alongside contrary impulses to cry aloud, to drop everything, and to focus one's mind upon the search for the lost person. Individuals, families, and cultures vary in the extent to which one or other aspect of the conflict is permitted, but some form of expression of sorrow is allowed for in the religious ceremonials of all cultures which have been studied (Rosenblatt et al., 1976). G. Gorer (1965) has claimed that the decline in ritual aspects of mourning which has taken place in industrialized countries since the First World War has removed an important source of support for the bereaved and encouraged pathological reactions to bereavement.

In most bereaved people the urge to search for the lost person is reflected in thoughts, actions, and perceptions. Thoughts about the dead person return repeatedly, and the bereaved tend to pine intensely and to go over in the mind the events leading up to the death as if, even at this time, they could find out what has gone wrong and put it right again. The search is reflected in acts concerned to 'keep alive' the memories of the dead, to visit graves or places associated with them, and to treasure possessions which will act as reminders. Clear visual memories of the dead person are kept in mind, and sights and sounds are commonly misperceived as evidence of his or her return.

In the normal course of events the intensity and duration of episodes of pining (the so-called 'pangs' of grief) grow gradually less, and attachment behaviour is extinguished. As this happens, people become more fully aware of the extent to which their basic assumptions about themselves and the world will have to change. The psychosocial transition which results necessitates lengthy revision of the individual's view of the world (world model), and, in the interim, the bereaved remain insecure and relatively helpless. Many withdraw from social relationships and become disengaged from their wider circle of interests and acquaintances. The elderly bereaved may never become re-engaged with the outside world. Younger people more often find their way through to a new identity which may be more mature than the one which preceded it.

Factors which predispose to a successful outcome of this transition include appropriate anticipation and preparation for bereavement, emotional support from friends and others (permitting expression of grief), psychological resilience and confidence in oneself, opportunities for personal growth, and faith in a religious or philosophical system of belief that gives meaning to death. Conversely the process of grieving may be impaired by sudden, unexpected, and untimely deaths, by the dissolution of relationships characterized by ambivalence or dependence, by social isolation or the presence of others who will block attempts to grieve or distract the griever, by the failure of previous attempts to cope with major loss (particularly in childhood), by lack of self-confidence, by physical or other obstacles to self-fulfilment, and by the absence of a system of belief that gives meaning to death.

Although bereavements are commonest in old age, their frequency and predictability reduce the chance that the bereaved will be unprepared for them. Also there is less need for old people to compete for a place in the world that remains to them, and many come through the stress of bereavement without experiencing the lasting distress which characterizes younger bereaved people.

Although most of the published work on bereavement has focused on bereavement by death, the phenomenon of grief follows many of the 'slings and arrows of outrageous fortune'. Hence an understanding of the psychology of bereavement is important to all those involved in the care of people who are undergoing psychosocial transitions.                                         C. M. P.

Bowlby, J. (1969, 1973, 1980). *Attachment and Loss*, 3 vols. London.

Gorer, G. (1965). *Death, Grief, and Mourning in Contemporary Britain*. London.

Lindemann, E. (1944). Symptomatology and Management of Acute Grief. *American Journal of Psychiatry*, **101**, 141.

Parkes, C. M. (1986). *Bereavement: Studies of Grief in Adult Life*, 2nd edn. London and Harmondsworth.

Ramsay, R. W. (1977). Behavioural approaches to bereavement. *Behaviour Research and Therapy*, **15**, 131–5.

Ramsay, R. W. (1979). Bereavement: a behavioural treatment of pathological grief. In Sjöden, P. (ed.), *Trends in Behaviour Therapy*. London.

Raphael, B. (1984). *The Anatomy of Bereavement*. London and Sydney.

Rosenblatt, P. C., Walsh, R. P., and Jackson, D. A. (1976). *Grief and Mourning in Cross-cultural Perspective*. London.

**BERGER,** HANS (1873–1941). German psychiatrist who spent most of his career at the University of Jena where, in 1929, he discovered the human *electroencephalogram. Influenced by his father, a physician, and his mother, the daughter of the poet Friedrich Rückert, Berger's interests spanned medicine, science, and philosophy. He sustained a lifelong preoccupation with the *mind–body problem and saw the electrical activity of the brain as a means of clarifying that relationship.

After a brief study of astronomy and an equally brief time in the German army he studied medicine. In 1897 he received his doctorate at Jena and was subsequently appointed to the University psychiatric clinic there. During the period up to 1910 he published work on the spinal cord, cranial blood-flow, and brain temperature changes. Underlying the physiological investigations were always questions of psychological state. He had also in this period attempted, less successfully, to record electrical activity from the cerebral cortex of a dog. In 1911 he married his technical assistant, Baroness Ursula von Bülow, with whom he had carried out work on the psychogalvanic reflex (see ELECTRODERMAL ACTIVITY).

During the First World War, Berger served on the Western Front as an army psychiatrist. On his return to Jena after the war he was appointed professor of psychiatry at the University and director of the clinic, where his duties also encompassed neurology. He resumed his research, but not until 1924 did time permit him to begin in earnest his search for cortical currents in the human brain which might relate to consciousness. In that year he observed from the head of a patient very small oscillations on his string galvanometer, although for a long time he retained serious doubts about their cerebral origins. However, by painstaking research he systematically eliminated most of the possibilities that they were due to extra-cerebral artefact. In 1929 he was sufficiently satisfied with their authenticity to publish his first paper 'On the electroencephalogram in man' in the *Archiv für Psychiatrie und Nervenkrankheiten*.

The world of neurophysiology remained unimpressed by the claims of this little known professor of psychiatry, who had only begun his serious investigations at the age of 51 and who seemed more at home in philosophy than in electrophysiology. Contemporary animal evidence provided little support for the human findings. It was not until 1934, when *Adrian and Matthews published their replication of Berger's findings, that neurophysiologists felt obliged to take account of their significance.

Once Berger had satisfied himself that the electroencephalogram (EEG) was a genuine brain phenomenon, he used it as a tool to study psychophysical relationships. The two main features of the EEG were termed 'alpha' and 'beta' waves. The former were represented by regular oscillations of about 10 hertz, seen when the eyes were closed and in states of relaxation. The latter were less synchronous forms of faster activity which replaced the alpha waves when the eyes were open or when the individual was engaged in mental activity such as arithmetic calculations.

For Berger, alpha waves represented a form of automatic brain functioning, a state of electrical readiness which exists when the individual is conscious, but inattentive. The desynchronous blocking of this activity was held to occur when attention was focused on one idea or sensory input. This was considered to result in a localized activation of the specific sensory-receiving area in the brain, coupled with a more generalized inhibition of the surrounding areas, manifesting itself as a blocking of the alpha waves. He postulated that consciousness depended upon the potential gradient between the localized active area and the surrounding area of inhibition. Although he made little attempt to utilize his findings in clinical contexts, he described abnormal patterns of EEG activity in a number of pathological conditions, most notably in epilepsy.

In his thinking Berger was much influenced by the notion of the conservation of energy. He regarded *dualism as inconsistent with that principle, but could not reconcile its alternative, materialism, with his belief in volition. His solution was a form of psychophysical parallelism which accepted transformation of physical energy to 'psychic energy' and vice versa, thus permitting causal interaction between the physical and mental domains.

He retired in 1938 at the age of 65. During his last years in Thuringia he developed a severe depression, and in May 1941 he took his own life. W. C. M.

**BERGSON,** HENRI LOUIS (1859–1941). French philosopher, born in Paris. He was professor at the Collège de France (1900–24), elected an Academician in 1914, and awarded the Nobel Prize for literature in 1927. Bergson follows *Heraclitus in arguing that change is the stuff of reality. He contrasts the ever-changing and yet unified world of consciousness with the world of things in space. He stresses the immediacy of experience, given by *perception, with the structure of things known only intellectually. His most important books are *Essai sur les données immédiates de la conscience* (1889), translated as *Time and Free Will* (1910), and *L'évolution créatrice* (1907), translated as

*Creative Evolution* (1911), in which he discusses the place of man in nature and his notion of *élan vital* as the force of evolution (rather than natural selection). He also wrote on aesthetics and the particularly interesting *Le Rire* (1900), translated as *Laughter: an essay on the meaning of the comic* (1911). Bergson's philosophy, which at best is poetical, is critically discussed by Bertrand *Russell in *The History of Western Philosophy* (1946).

**BERKELEY,** GEORGE (1685–1753), was born in Ireland, went to school at Kilkenny College, and in 1700 proceeded to Trinity College, Dublin, where he graduated in 1704 and became a Fellow in 1707. He retained his Fellowship, though with long periods of absence, until 1724, in which year he became Dean of Derry.

His intellectual development was strikingly precocious, and he was fortunate in his education. In 1700, although Ireland had so recently been the scene of prolonged turmoil and civil war, the state of learning at Trinity College was much livelier and more progressive than at either of the English universities at that time. It is clear that Berkeley was early and thoroughly acquainted with John *Locke's *Essay concerning Human Understanding* (published in 1690) and with the physical theories of Isaac *Newton and others which underlay that work. He learned much also—perhaps more than he afterwards cared to admit—from Malebranche's *Recherche de la vérité*. His own first book, *An Essay Towards a New Theory of Vision*, was published in Dublin in 1709, when he was 24; and his most important work, *A Treatise Concerning the Principles of Human Knowledge*, followed in 1710. He first visited England in 1713, and the third major work of his youth, the *Three Dialogues between Hylas and Philonous*, was published in London in that year. These are the works on which his fame securely rests, all written and well established before he was 30.

Berkeley was, with the zeal and confidence of youth, in a sense a reactionary figure. He rightly discerned, in the writings of Locke and his scientific mentors, the steady progress towards general acceptance of a certain scientific 'world-view', which he hated and believed that he could utterly confute. This was the idea that mathematics and mechanics are the keys to the understanding of nature—that all matter is fundamentally atomic, or 'corpuscular', in structure, and that its properties, on both the largest and the smallest scale, are ultimately a matter of mechanical interactions. Berkeley believed this idea to be fatal to religion and dangerous to morality; he thought also that he could show it to be philosophically absurd and untenable. His own sweeping solution, by which he believed that all could be set right at a stroke, was his denial of the existence of matter. For if there is no matter, there is nothing that mechanistic materialism can even pretend to be true *of*, and the pretensions of the physical scientist are completely undermined. Not surprisingly, a major theme of

Berkeley's writings is his struggle to persuade his readers that, by the denial of the existence of matter, no one—other than the sinister physicist— need be surprised or disturbed. At no time was this struggle particularly successful. Berkeley's contemporary readers, to his chagrin and surprise, were inclined to praise him for his dialectical ingenuity, but to dismiss his conclusions as the paradoxes of an amusing Irishman.

Berkeley's middle years, from about 1722 until late in 1731, were almost wholly given over to a project for founding a college in Bermuda, intended for both indigenous and white colonial Americans. For this project he secured a charter from the king, the promise of a large grant from the public revenues, and wide support from individuals—on this topic at least, his powers of persuasion, supported by what all observers agree to have been great personal charm, proved most efficacious. In September 1728 he set sail for Newport, Rhode Island, where he built himself a house (which still stands) and waited for his project to mature. But he was disappointed. The pragmatic Sir Robert Walpole had always regarded the scheme as visionary, and, once Berkeley's persuasive presence was withdrawn, he worked quietly against it. The crucial grant was found at last not to 'suit with public convenience', and after three years in America Berkeley returned, empty-handed, to London.

In 1734—in spite of having, it appears, never once visited the Deanery he had held for ten years—he was appointed Bishop of Cloyne, in the extreme south of Ireland. Here in 1744 he published his strange work *Siris*, a disquisition on the supposed medicinal virtues of 'tar-water', decked out—in a manner astonishingly unlike that of his graceful, rapid, and lucid early writings— with an oppressive bulk of miscellaneous scientific, medical, and philosophical learning. It has been held that his enthusiasm for tar-water was eccentric enough to catch the professional eye of the psychoanalyst; but it must be remembered that, if Berkeley's medical opinions were somewhat wild and uncritical, they differed little in that respect from those of many of his contemporaries.

Berkeley died in January 1753, while visiting Oxford to supervise his second son's entry to Christ Church. The memorial tablet erected in the cathedral there is noteworthy in that, presumably on his widow's authority, it records his date of birth as six years earlier than it actually was.

See also BERKELEY ON PERCEPTION; BERKELEY ON THE MIND.                                            G. J. W.

The complete and definitive modern edition is *The Works of George Berkeley* (ed. Luce, A. A., and Jessop, T. E.) (1949–57), 9 vols. London. The authoritative biography is Luce, A. A. (1949), *Life of George Berkeley*, London, published uniformly with the *Works*.

Bennett, J. (1971). *Locke, Berkeley, Hume*. Oxford. (An able, selective commentary on 'central themes'.)
Foster, J. and Robinson, H. (eds.) (1985). *Essays on Berkeley: a Tercentennial Celebration*. Oxford. (A valu-

able collection, issued to mark the tercentenary of Berkeley's birth.)

Luce, A. A. (1945). *Berkeley's Immaterialism*. London. (The work of a learned but somewhat uncritical partisan.)

Pitcher, G. W. (1977). *Berkeley*. London. (An unusually detailed scrutiny, step by step, of the particular arguments by which Berkeley sought to support his conclusions.)

Tipton, I. C. (1974). *Berkeley: The Philosophy of Immaterialism*. London. (A notably careful and scholarly work, particularly useful on those topics, for instance Berkeley's theory of the mind, which other commentators have tended to neglect.)

Warnock, G. J. (1969). *Berkeley*, 2nd edn. London. (A general analytical survey, perhaps over-stressing Berkeley's 'defence of common sense' and underplaying his very curious metaphysical and religious views.)

**BERKELEY ON PERCEPTION.** The principal sources for Berkeley's views on *perception are *An Essay towards a New Theory of Vision* (1709) and *A Treatise Concerning the Principles of Human Knowledge* (1710). The doctrines set out in these two works are not the same. But the explanation of that, according to Berkeley's own statement in the *Principles*, is not that he had changed his mind, but that in the *Essay*, the topic of which was specifically vision, he had deliberately suppressed—even misrepresented—his views on other matters, so as to avoid introducing too many novel doctrines all at once. The explanation seems odd, but there is no good ground for not accepting it.

In the *Essay* Berkeley has two principal aims. The first is negative. Raising the question how and why we make by vision—as on the whole we make pretty successfully—our everyday judgements of the sizes, distances, and positions of objects, Berkeley first contends—contrary to much current theorizing of his day—that such judgements are not made on the basis of a knowledge of optics. It may for example be true that, as an object recedes from us, the angle at which the optic axes converge upon it decreases; but since we do not see those axes or the angle at which they converge, that cannot explain why we judge the object to be receding. His point here, surely a correct one, is that the everyday visual judgements we all make of distance and size must be in some way based on how things look to us, not on theorems of optics which, however sound in their own sphere, cannot constitute direct visual evidence and for that matter are often totally unknown to persons of perfectly sound visual competence.

Berkeley then turns to the question of how it comes about that 'how things look' does enable us to make, on the whole, reliable judgements as to how things are. And here he offers the double contention that the connection between visual 'clues' and actual states of affairs, first, is learned only by experience, not calculable *a priori; and second, is completely *contingent, and indeed arbitrary. In support of this contention he argues that objects are, strictly speaking, tangible objects only; they are not, strictly, literally seen—or, for

that matter, heard. The 'proper objects' of hearing are sounds, and only indirectly or by inference the things that make sounds. Similarly, he holds, there are purely visual 'proper objects' of vision; and we learn only by experience to make inferences from these 'proper objects' to states of (tangible) things. States of things are, as we learn by experience, fairly reliably correlated with the occurrence of distinctive purely visual objects; but these correlations, however reliable, are fundamentally quite arbitrary—like, for instance, the link between the word 'red' and the colour red. God maintains these correlations for the benefit of his creatures, so that the objects of vision can be said to constitute a 'divine visual language' by which, once we have learned it, we are 'told' about the tangible things in our environment.

Readers of the *Essay* must have been struck, even in 1709, by one conspicuous omission from it. John *Locke's many admirers, for example, would have agreed with Berkeley that the direct objects of vision were purely visual 'ideas', and that these were properly quite distinct from what they would have called 'external bodies'. But why say that the connection between visual ideas and states of things is *arbitrary*, maintained purely at God's pleasure? For surely it is *causal*. Was there not a well-established, or at any rate widely accepted, theory as to the causation of perception, according to which visual ideas, and for that matter all 'ideas of sensation', were the causal products of states of things and of their action upon our sense organs? Why is this theory, which at least appears to offer a unified, non-arbitrary explanation of the connections between our ideas of sensation, not even mentioned by Berkeley?

Berkeley's total rejection of that theory—Locke's so-called 'causal' or 'representational' theory of perception—is made clear in the *Principles*. The theory was that the universe is, fundamentally, a system of solid bodies in mechanical interaction; that the objects of everyday experience are themselves systems of 'corpuscles', 'insensible particles', in mechanical interaction; and that, in perception, these bodies act mechanically upon our various sense organs, causing ultimately, by way of causal chains in nervous system and brain, 'ideas of sensation' to occur 'in the mind'. Such ideas are the 'immediate objects' of perception, and inform us—or, so Locke held, in some cases *mis*inform us—as to the existence and character of the 'external' bodies that are their originating causes.

Berkeley's chief grounds for rejecting this theory were these. First, he took it to be self-defeating—if true, it could not be known to be true. For if the contents, the 'immediate objects', of perception are all, and only, *ideas*, what ground could there be in perception for supposing the existence of anything else? Second, and for much the same reason, he regarded the theory as ontologically redundant. Given observers ('spirits') and the ideas that they have, that actually constitute their experience, why add a supposedly distinct 'external' world which forms no actual part of anyone's experience at all? *Experience* would be just the same if no such world existed: why, then, suppose that it does exist? Now the answer to that question was supposed to be that the existence of 'external bodies' *causes* and therefore *explains* the occurrence of ideas in our experience; but Berkeley's third contention is that that cannot be so. For, he asserts, only an active, animate being can be a cause; the only true case of causation is volition, intelligent agency, so that the mere mechanical happenings postulated in Locke's theory could in principle neither cause nor explain anything.

Berkeley's own views in the *Principles* could be said to take the form of a generalization, to all sensory modes, of the account of vision put forward in his *Essay*. He had held there that the 'proper objects' of vision are purely visual ideas 'in the mind', generated by the direct action of God so as to 'tell' us about tangible objects 'in circum-ambient space'. In the *Principles* he dispenses with those objects. Every sense, he now holds, even the sense of touch, has its own 'proper objects', all 'ideas', all 'in the mind'; there are (besides minds or 'spirits') *only* ideas; and God's work is now said to be, not merely that of informing his creatures by 'visual language' of independent things, but of so maintaining the complex correlations between *all* ideas, of *all* the senses, as to sustain in the experience of us all the apparent unity, continuity, and coherence of a common world. He claims for this extraordinary doctrine, first—surprisingly enough—that it accords with common sense. Locke, with his 'scientific' theory, had been obliged to shock us by concluding that the world is in many ways not as it appears; Berkeley holds that, on his view, the world is exactly as it appears—for, in fact, it *is* 'what appears', no more and no less. Then his doctrine is also, he claims, ontologically economical, non-redundant: to describe our experience we need nothing more than 'spirits' and 'ideas'; and Berkeley makes no further, gratuitous existential assumptions. Then, since the cause of ideas, in Berkeley's doctrine, is the will of God, he has, he claims, a real cause, a truly explanatory agency—and, last but for Berkeley not least, one that firmly entrenches theism in the nature of things, as the ground of all being.

What then of the 'scientific' theory of perception, according to which 'particles' acted on sense organs to cause sensation? Berkeley was at first inclined to dismiss all such talk as mere rubbish, to be simply abandoned. But later he contrived to accommodate this theory also, as not a genuinely causal theory, not really explanatory, and indeed not true, but a possibly *useful* purely theoretical construct to assist us in predicting how the true cause—God's will—was likely to operate in our experience. This was, indeed, his general account of all scientific theories which postulated entities not accessible to direct observation.     G. J. W.

**BERKELEY ON THE MIND.** The task of outlining Berkeley's theory of the mind is complicated by the fact that the work in which he was to treat at length of this topic was never published. His major work, *A Treatise Concerning the Principles of Human Knowledge*, as we now have it, was issued in 1710 as 'Part I'. Apparently its account of perception and our knowledge of the external world was to be followed by a second and even a third volume, one dealing with the mind, and another with the principles of morality. It seems that the second volume was at least partly written; for in a letter of 1729 Berkeley says that 'the manuscript was lost about fourteen years ago, during my travels in Italy'. But that manuscript was never rewritten, and Berkeley's views on the mind have consequently to be collected, partly from brief passages in his published works, and partly also from his surviving private notebooks of 1707–8, which give many clues to what 'Part II' of his *Principles* was intended to contain.

We may consider first a certain view of the mind by which Berkeley was, not surprisingly, tempted, though he eventually rejects it. His term—shared with John *Locke—for the successive actual contents of experience is, of course, 'ideas'; and early in his notebook he had laid down (with his theory of perception in mind) the general principle that 'Language and knowledge are all about ideas, words stand for nothing else'. If so, then clearly language and knowledge about the mind must be 'about ideas'; and accordingly in later entries we find Berkeley saying that 'the very existence of Ideas constitutes the soul. . . . Mind is a congeries of Perceptions. . . . Say you the Mind is not the Perceptions but that thing wch. perceives. I answer you are abus'd by the words that & thing: these are vague empty words without a meaning.' These remarks of course suggest a theory of the mind resembling that later put forward by David *Hume—and much later by William *James and Bertrand *Russell—in which the mind is, not a persistent entity distinct from the contents of experience, but a 'logical construction' out of those contents themselves. Such a view, however, is directly and flatly contradicted in the second paragraph of the *Principles*, where Berkeley writes: 'But, besides all that endless variety of ideas or objects of knowledge, there is likewise something which knows or perceives them; and exercises divers operations, as willing, imagining, remembering, about them. This perceiving, active being is what I call MIND, SPIRIT, SOUL, or MYSELF. By which words I do not denote any one of my ideas, but a thing entirely distinct from them, wherein they exist, or, which is the same thing, whereby they are perceived.'

It is perhaps clearer why Berkeley rejected the Humean 'logical construction' view than what the view actually was with which he sought to replace it. He held—and this was indeed crucial in his criticism of Locke's 'causal' theory of perception—that ideas, and indeed any other non-animate entities if any others exist, are essentially 'inert', inactive, incapable of *doing* anything; and he no doubt took it, reasonably enough, that a 'congeries' of such inactive elements could not but be itself inactive. He came to regard it, by contrast, as the fundamental truth about the mind that it is essentially active—and uniquely as well as essentially so, for he came to hold that mental agency was in fact the *only* case of real activity, of actual doing. That is why, in the passage quoted above, he was careful to speak of MIND as 'this perceiving, active being'; and it follows of course that he must regard such 'active beings' as 'entirely distinct' from ideas or any other inanimate items. It should be added that he does not mean to say that MIND is active in addition to perceiving; for he came to hold that perceiving, 'taking notice', is itself an act, not merely passive receptiveness. In one notebook entry he goes so far as to say, 'The soul is the will properly speaking', and in another asks 'Whether Identity of Person consists not in the Will'.

Since Berkeley held without question that we could speak intelligibly about, and have knowledge of, minds, then, since minds are 'entirely distinct' from ideas, he naturally had to modify his simple empiricist's maxim that 'language and knowledge are all about ideas'. He does little more, however, than concede that the case of minds is an evident exception to that principle. Though we have no idea of the mind, he says, we have—from our own case—a 'notion' of it; but what it is to have a 'notion' of the mind he then elucidates no further than to insist that 'we understand the meaning of the word'—which, though doubtless true, is unilluminating.

There is one further point, however, on which Berkeley is clear and explicit. While insisting that the mind is 'entirely distinct' from its ideas, he insists no less that it is *not* distinct from its 'acts'. Just as the existence of an inanimate thing consists in, *is*, its being perceived—just as its being perceived and its existing are not to be distinguished—so the existence of 'mind, soul, or spirit' is its acting, and so its acting and its existing are not to be distinguished. Hence Berkeley boldly asserts in the *Principles*, as if it were the most natural thing in the world, that 'it is a plain consequence that *the soul always thinks*'. Since the very existence of 'the soul' is thinking, the very notion of a mind not thinking, not active, is self-contradictory.

Now this conclusion, as Berkeley was of course aware, at least appears to fly in the face of very obvious facts: for it at least appears to be a fact of common experience that, in the history of 'myself', there are intervals of complete unconsciousness in which the mind is inactive. Remarkably, of the possible ways of attempting to get round this difficulty Berkeley seems quite deliberately to choose the most extraordinary of all. In theory, he might have argued that, while my mind does not exist continuously through periods of complete unconsciousness, *I* do; it is, however, not realistic

to suppose that Berkeley could have taken that line, since it requires a distinction between 'myself' and 'my mind' which (however wrongly) he would never have thought of making—like *Descartes, he took it for granted that a person is, and is only, a mind or 'spirit', a 'thinking thing'. Again, he might have argued that, through periods of what is commonly called unconsciousness, the mind is really in some way active after all; but that line has a decidedly *ad hoc*, unempirical look about it, and Berkeley seems never to have found it tempting. What he held at one time, boldly embracing the paradox, was that persons actually do not exist continuously; since the mind is active only intermittently, 'men die or are in state of annihilation oft in a day'. But that too he rejects; and the doctrine he finally adopts is the very extraordinary one that there can be in a person's life no periods of unconsciousness, since the passage of time itself is nothing but the succession of his 'perceptions'; we cannot ask what the position is *during* the mind's unconsciousness, for if the mind is not active there is no duration. It is clear that, in this strange doctrine of 'private times', with its evident rejection of any public, objective time-ordering, desperate paradoxes lurk; and one can only speculate how Berkeley might have tried to deal with them, or alternatively how he might have so modified his theory of the mind as to avoid them, if his projected second volume of the *Principles* had ever been completed.

See also LOCKE ON THE MIND.          G. J. W.

**BERNSTEIN,** NICHOLAS (Nikolai Alexandrovich, 1896–1966). Russian physiologist and founder of the school of the physiology of co-ordination and the 'physiology of activity'. Born in Moscow, the son of a well-known psychiatrist, Bernstein was a rare case of a scientist who practically devoted his whole life to one problem: the physiological mechanisms of human movements and motor actions.

A man of outstanding abilities, he started his work, when twenty years of age, with studies of human movements (gait, movements included in the process of work, etc.). The invention of a precise method for the recording of movements (a system of photographing lights fastened to the extremities, and interrupted by a rotating sector disc) made it possible to establish not only the trajectory of the movement but also changes of speed. These observations brought Bernstein to the statement that human movements have structures, and, though not repeating their form, always preserve their basic *scheme*, and that this scheme (clearly seen in writing movements) remains preserved, independently of which organ is involved in its production.

These studies of man's movements were followed by a careful analysis of the process of the development of motor skills. Bernstein observed that motor skills go through at least two basic developmental stages. In the first stage, motor action sometimes results in an inadequate movement, which is only secondarily corrected. During the second stage these 'secondary corrections' become 'primary corrections', when an adequate scheme of the movement is centrally elaborated and does not require a secondary correction of motor mistakes. As to the mechanism of regulation and co-ordination of movements underlying motor skills, Bernstein concluded that motor actions are based on the extremely complex apparatus of joints and muscles, which have practically infinite degrees of freedom, so that they change every moment according to changes in the position of the limbs and the density of muscles. Such complexity cannot be controlled by *efferent impulses only; it requires a permanent system of *afferent impulses, which give continual signals from the moving extremities and provide the basis for a self-regulatory movement system. This assumption, formulated by Bernstein in 1935, provided the starting-point for the development of the theory of self-regulated motor systems and different levels in their organization (see CYBERNETICS). It was found that the 'afferent fields' could be arranged at different levels of the nervous system—beginning with the reflex or spinal level, going through the thalamo-striatum level, or level of co-ordination, and ending at the cortical levels required for the changeable spatial, or object-linked and symbolically determined movements. These levels of organization of movements were described in Bernstein's *On the Construction of Movements* (1947), which gained him one of the highest prizes in the USSR.

The last part of Bernstein's work led him to a more complicated problem. As a physiologist, he had studied well-determined, reactive movements. However, the question of how to provide a scientific approach to man's *active* movements remained unanswered. Was a physiology of active processes possible?

Bernstein dedicated the remainder of his life to this problem and to creating a 'physiology of activity'. He supposed that feedback mechanisms are only a part of the regulating system, that 'feedforward mechanisms' have to exist, and he tried to explain their origin and their place in the organization of movements (see FEEDBACK AND FEEDFORWARD). Every movement starts with a *goal*, and that goal provides a model of the future result, or, as Bernstein called it, a '*Soll-Wert*'; the present position of the movement is reflected in an image of actual position—an '*Ist-Wert*'. The whole sequence of the movements required emerges from the comparison of both, and can be designated as '-*Wert*'. This '-*Wert*' is a leading factor in the determination of the further sequences of the movements.

Bernstein's attempts to create a 'physiology of activity' were only the first steps in this field, the first attempts to move physiology from elementary theory of passive (reactive) processes to a theory of man's active processes. Although he could not, in the short time left to him (he died before reaching 70), come to decisive conclusions on this very complicated problem, his attempts were highly regarded, and his ideas not only remained influential but became increasingly so among scholars of other countries.                    A. R. L.

Bernstein, N. A. (1926). *General Biomechanics* (in Russian). Moscow.
Bernstein, N. A. (1947). *On the Construction of Movements* (in Russian). Moscow.
Bernstein, N. A. (1967). *The Co-ordination and Regulation of Movements*. Moscow.

**'BESIDE ONESELF'** (with anger, grief, etc.). An English phrase suggesting that the individual is temporarily not, or is separated from, his usual self. The implication is that there are limits to how far the self can be different from or change from its usual character—before another self takes over. This is a possible basis for the notion of being *possessed*; and also of multiple personalities, as in the remarkable case of Sally Beauchamp, who was supposed to have several alternating selves or personalities. See DISSOCIATION OF THE PERSONALITY.

**BIDWELL,** SHELFORD (1848–1909). British physicist and barrister, born at Thetford, Norfolk, and educated at Cambridge. After practising as a barrister for a number of years he devoted himself to scientific research, especially in electricity and magnetism and physiological optics. He was elected a Fellow of the Royal Society in 1888 and was President of the Physical Society (1897–9). In 1899 he published *Curiosities of Light and Vision*, enlarging a series of lectures he gave at the Royal Institution. The so-called Bidwell's ghost is a visual phenomenon associated with *after-images produced by alternating flashing lights.

**BILINGUALISM,** or polyglossia, refers to a person's ability to communicate in two or more languages. The phenomenon is found commonly in border regions, especially in those whose geographical boundaries change from time to time. South-eastern Poland, for example, was formerly part of the Austro-Hungarian Empire, making Austrian the official language for a population whose native language was Polish but which was in contact with neighbouring Ukrainian, Belorussian, and Slovakian communities, and whose religious groups included Orthodox, Roman Catholic, and Jewish. Thus Church Slavonic, Greek, Latin, Hebrew, and Yiddish were all likely to be used to varying degrees by inhabitants of the region, in addition to the Slavic languages. The phenomenon is also found in small countries that participate extensively in international relations: the Netherlands and Switzerland are especially well-known examples. In the Netherlands, children characteristically have instruction in Dutch as a first language, begin a second, third, and fourth (English, French, or German) within a few years of each other, and, if they plan to go to university, add several years of Latin and perhaps some Greek. Most high-school graduates can manage to communicate in two foreign languages; fluency in three or four is common among university graduates. Bilingualism is encountered also in small countries experiencing substantial immigration or made up of disparate groups. It is estimated that peoples from more than ninety different language communities have emigrated to Israel since the 1930s. It is encountered in large countries also. In the Soviet Union, as in Iran, China, and India—countries comprising people of many different ethnic, linguistic, and religious backgrounds—a single 'national' language is inculcated as a unifying device, while the separate groups use their own languages for local communication. Even in a country where the languages share a common root, such as Italy, the regional variants may be almost mutually unintelligible. In all of these cases people who wish to communicate with others not in their immediate linguistic community are obliged to learn another language. The fact of two languages in a single person is commonplace in most parts of the world, but is still thought of as an oddity in many others. Most English-speaking countries seem to be among the latter group.

Bilingualism is actively studied by linguists who are interested in the way that speakers of one language accommodate the impact of another on their own; by sociologists and sociolinguists who trace change in social custom as a function of change in language; by teachers concerned to minimize the interfering effects of one language upon the learning of another; by psychologists who are interested in bilingualism as a natural laboratory for the study of the way the mind represents its knowledge; and of course by many others. The psychological issues are the most pertinent here.

One long-standing query has been whether instruction in a second language helps or hinders the student. The question seems not to have been asked when several years of Greek and Latin were customary constituents of the young scholar's programme. It has come to be asked largely following the development of linguistic nationalism. Although first undertaken in the context of educating children in Welsh or Irish, the studies have been extended to the education of many groups in their native language. The findings have been that educating a child in one language interferes with his or her ability to pass examinations in a second, and the interference is greater the more 'minor' the one language and the more elaborate the second. Initially interpreted as evidence that bilingualism interfered with or lessened intellectual capability, the data are now seen as supporting the view that particular skills acquired through one language may not be wholly available for transfer to a second, especially if the two languages are quite different. No evidence has been accumulated to suggest that intelligence is lessened or heightened by instruction in one language or another; what has

been shown is that skill in manipulating the dominant symbols of the culture is better acquired one way than another.

Languages are said to differ in their ability to express information in one or another area or on one or another topic. The classic examples have to do with the vocabulary for varieties of snow among some Eskimo, and for varieties of camel in Arabic. A considerable philosophy has been built on related observations. The term 'linguistic relativity' marks the view of the linguists E. Sapir and his student B. L. Whorf, which in its dogmatic form is called the Sapir–Whorf hypothesis: the language one uses controls the way one thinks about the world. This extends well beyond differences in vocabulary items of Eskimo and Arab—or of a vintner for wines, or a perfumer for smells, or any other specialized terms or jargon: the claim is that the mind works differently. In this claim Whorf seemed to identify language with thought—an equation few linguists, psychologists, or philosophers accept at present—and went on to confuse the ability to learn to make a discrimination with the readiness with which it is made. That is, Whorf used lexical and syntactic aspects of a language as evidence for procedures of mind, and in so doing seems to have used faulty reasoning to arrive at a plausible conclusion. The conclusion is that the *symbols the mind uses in its activities actually affect the way the mind works. The interaction of symbol systems and mental operations is under present active study.

Languages do seem to differ in the ease with which they lend themselves to certain topical areas. Italian and French are rich and subtle in the areas of interpersonal relations, German lends itself easily to metaphysics, English dominates modern science—to name a few related languages. The structure of language, it has sometimes been suggested, also influences the way the mind works, perhaps in the way that speaking a particular language tends to shape the face. Whether a language requires many qualifications of the action before the action is named, or whether it is named first and then qualified; whether disparate items are stuck together to make new composites or whether features are analysed out and put into contrast; whether word order is a fixed or a free variable—these and other questions have been related to 'national character' and to mental activity. The topics are rich in speculation and poor in data.

They attract the psychologist's attention because of their relation to the topic of representation. Psychologists not only study the fact of behavioural change as a function of experience, but also try to give a plausible account of the means by which behaviour is controlled. Since what a person knows somehow affects what he or she does, some formalism is sought by the psychologist to accommodate the knowledge. That is, how knowledge is represented in mind and how best to represent it can be taken as important aspects of the psychologist's study. In this respect bilingual individuals are interesting test cases, for they can learn something through one of their languages and be tested for the knowledge through another; changes in performance as a function of changes in language can then sometimes be used to make plausible inferences about the mental operations underlying the behaviour. The findings suggest that knowledge is often situational and specific and that something learned through one language is not known to the person generally but is available to him or her only through that language. Recent evidence on the effects of stroke and related cerebral accidents upon language performance tends to bear out the supposition that knowledge and skill may be interfered with selectively, according to interference with the means by which the knowledge or skill were acquired.                                   P. A. K.

Albert, M. L. and Obler, L. K. (1978). *The Bilingual Brain*. New York.

Haugen, E. (1974). Bilingualism, language contact, and immigrant languages in the United States: a research report, 1956–1970. In Sebok, T. A. (ed.), *Current Trends in Linguistics*, vol. 10. The Hague.

Kolers, P. A. (1978). On the representations of experience. In Gerver, D. and Sinaiko, W. (eds.), *Language Interpretation and Communication*. New York.

Weinreich, U. (1953). *Languages in Contact: Findings and Problems*. New York.

**BILLS' BLOCKS.** See ATTENTION, LAPSES OF.

**BINARY DIGIT.** See BIT.

**BINAURAL HEARING.** The use of both ears in order to locate the direction of sound sources. For frequencies lower than about 1,500 hertz the location is given by phase, or time, differences between the ears. For higher frequencies it is given by the different amplitudes of sound in the ears, as the head masks high-frequency sound from the further ear (see HEARING). (It is remarkable that the low-frequency phase detector resolves time differences between the ears of only a few microseconds.) The use of the two ears is important for understanding speech where there is an echo, as there is even in a normal room, the echo being suppressed by some unknown mechanism depending on binaural signals. For this and other reasons, binaural hearing-aids can be significantly better than the more usual monaural aids, and are especially useful for blind people with impaired hearing, who make much use of binaural location of the direction of sounds. (See also AUDITORY ILLUSIONS.)

**BINET,** ALFRED (1857–1911). French psychologist, born at Nice. He became director of the department of physiological psychology at the Sorbonne in 1892. With Theodore Simon, he was responsible for the design and standardization of the first formal *intelligence tests—the 'Binet scale'—originally devised at the request of the French Government in order to establish which children were or were not worthy to benefit from education.

He instigated the concept of intelligence quotient (IQ), i.e. chronological age divided by mental age, multiplied by 100, which has been widely used ever since to 'measure' the intelligence of children and, in somewhat modified form, that of adults too. Indeed, the notion that individuals are born with all potential ability assessed along a single continuum is widely regarded as one of the most notable achievements of modern psychology; and yet it may be both conceptually and socially misguided and has led to race and sex rivalries. In spite of extensive research, it still remains unclear how far the IQ score represents actual ability and whether it is genuinely predictive of intellectual accomplishment. At all events, the recent tendency is to interpret the results of intelligence tests only with extreme caution.

Binet's most important book was *L'Étude éxperimentale de l'intelligence* (1903). But he also wrote books on many other psychological subjects, including hypnosis and suggestibility, and the psychic life of micro-organisms.                    O. L. Z.

**BINOCULAR VISION.** The use of the two eyes, which in many animals and in man gives *stereoscopic or 3-D vision. Sensitivity to very dim light is also improved with two eyes instead of one, just as though the second eye belonged to another observer. The increased probability of capturing photons precisely describes the increase in visual efficiency. Stereo depth is given by neural computation of the slight shift in position of corresponding points in the retinas due to the separation, and so slightly different viewpoints, of the two eyes. This combining of the different signals from the two eyes to give a single (stereoscopic) perception is remarkable, and from recent experiments is now coming to be understood (see VISUAL SYSTEM: ORGANIZATION).

When the differences between the eyes' images are too great, fusion fails, and there is either 'rivalry' or rejection altogether by one 'lazy' eye.

**BIOFEEDBACK.** It is self-evident that many of our physiological processes are not under our voluntary control. We cannot, for instance, decide to alter our blood-pressure or our heart-rate and successfully accomplish the change in the direction and to the extent desired. One of the reasons why voluntary control is not possible in such cases is that we do not consciously sense their current state.

Biofeedback is a term used to describe a series of techniques that aim to provide us with such information, and hence enable us to exercise some degree of voluntary control over the particular physiological function under consideration. What these techniques have in common is that relevant information about the process involved, e.g. muscle tension, heart-rate, and blood-pressure, is monitored, usually by an electronic device of some sort, and displayed to the person himself, usually in a visual or auditory form, or less usually in some other modality.

The general term '*feedback' was coined by Norbert *Wiener, who defined it as 'a method of controlling the system by reinserting into it the results of its past performance'. Such feedback is common in biological systems and, indeed, no creature would survive were it not for such self-regulation. Through feedback we come to learn to co-ordinate and control our limbs, through sight and kinaesthesia for example, and to co-ordinate hand and eye by means of visual and propriocep-tive feedback, and, at a higher level, to solve problems mentally from the *memory systems without which we could not process linear inference. By means of equipment such as trans-ducers, amplifiers, and visual and auditory dis-plays, we can artificially extend such a principle to parts of the biological system that do not have such conscious feedback, in the expectation that the subject can learn to control a particular physiologi-cal function in a manner similar to the way he can in those parts of the system with integral feedback loops. How such control is achieved is still a matter of considerable controversy.

The beginnings of biofeedback go back to the late 1960s. As with other so-called departures in psychology, there were earlier examples. The work of Alexander Graham Bell (1847–1922), the inven-tor of the telephone, with the deaf, and his interest in using the visible display of speech sound, either by means of 'manometric' flames or by an early form of kymograph, in order to help the deaf to reproduce correct sounds, would seem to utilize feedback principles (Bruce, 1973). However, it needed a dramatic event to focus attention on the area of feedback control. This event took place at the 1967 annual meeting of the Pavlovian Society of North America in the form of a report by Neal Miller (1968). He introduced a technique that his colleague, Jay Towill, had first devised. This involved immobilizing animals with D-tubo curarine, artificially respiring them, and with electrodes placed in the so-called 'pleasure *centres' in the brain, operantly *conditioning various physiological systems. For example, it was reported that the animal could learn, through operant conditioning, to increase or lower blood-pressure, increase or decrease heart-rate, kidney flow, and so on. The reward was, in each case, a brief electric pulse delivered to the pleasure centres. The use of D-tubo curarine to produce paralysis of skeletal muscles was an attempt to avoid the possibility that the animal was modifying its autonomic responses via voluntary activities, such as changes in muscle tension or breathing pattern or rate. Research papers soon followed, and in a series of studies carried out with Leo DiCara on the curarized rat, the instrumental con-ditioning of heart-rate, blood-pressure, renal blood-flow and—in collaboration with A. Banu-azizi—contraction of the intestines, appeared to be demonstrated. Reports from other laboratories seemed to support Miller's findings.

These results conflicted with a prevailing bias in experimental psychology of *learning that divided learning processes into two classes: Pavlovian, classical or respondent conditioning, and instrumental or operant conditioning. The former applied to autonomic and visceral learning and the latter only to the external behaviours mediated by skeletal muscles. Miller's work, and that of others at the time, led to a less rigid distinction between classical and instrumental conditioning, and the different order of control of the skeletal nervous system and the autonomic nervous system. Hence it paved the way for an acceptance of the idea that autonomic functions could be brought under voluntary control.

Miller (1974) subsequently found that he could not replicate the results he had previously reported of operant autonomic control under curare, and finally admitted that he was uncertain as to whether he had ever genuinely demonstrated the instrumental conditioning of autonomic function in the rat.

From the time of Miller's early reports there has been an escalation of research work in, and clinical applications of, biofeedback techniques, together with a growing public interest. Three main factors have contributed to this: (i) the potential practical clinical application of biofeedback; (ii) the development of technical means for investigating biofeedback effects and for displaying feedback; and (iii) a belief among certain sections of the community, even some scientists, that it might provide a route to higher states of consciousness, to greater 'awareness' and 'fulfilment of life', to greater creativity and more efficient cognitive activity. So far, however, in spite of the continuing enthusiasm and the many claims made for its effi-ciency both as a clinical tool and when applied in normal psychology, as an experimental technique biofeedback has still not been thoroughly evalu-ated, and studies involving its clinical application have outstripped by far those concerned with fundamental research issues.

A typical example of applied biofeedback, and one which has generally been considered formative in one area, is the early work of Budzynski et al. (1973) on electromyographic (EMG) biofeedback and tension headache. It was based on the belief that tension headaches are associated with higher resting levels of frontalis muscle tension (measured by EMG methods). Consequently, since the immediate cause of pain with tension headache is usually sustained contraction of the muscles of the scalp and neck, patients would obtain alleviation of the pain if they could be trained to relax these muscles (the evidence concerning this supposed relationship between tension headache and fron-talis muscle activity is equivocal). Volunteer patients who suffered from tension headaches (characterized by a dull 'band-like' pain located bilaterally in the occipital region, although often

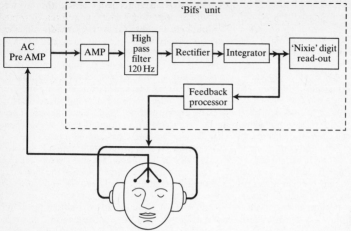

**Fig. 1.** Functional diagram of the EMG feedback system.

felt in the forehead region as well, which is gradual in onset and may last for hours, weeks, and even months) were trained to relax their frontalis muscles with the aid of biofeedback. This took the form of a series of clicks in the headphones that the patient wore during training sessions. The click-rate was proportional to muscle tension. The higher the tension in the forehead, the faster the click-rate. The patient had EMG electrodes applied to the skin over the area of the frontalis muscle and connected to an electronic feedback system, which transformed the EMG level as picked up through the electrodes into a series of clicks whose rate was proportional to the measured tension (Fig. 1). He attempted to lower the click-rate by progressively relaxing the muscle.

As this was intended to be a controlled outcome study, there were two other groups of patients included in order to test for placebo or suggestion effects. The members of one of these control groups received false feedback (i.e. clicks from a previous successful patient) which appeared to indicate their success in muscle relaxation; the other control group received no treatment. The results showed that the group receiving real biofeedback experienced a significant reduction both

in frontalis muscle tension and in headache activity (Figs. 2 and 3). Follow-up data reported a dramatic decrease in drug usage, tiredness, and insomnia, and a general increase in well-being, in the feedback group—and indeed some changes were also reported in the pseudofeedback group.

In spite of the reported success of this study, however, there were many theoretical issues which had not been resolved. The supposed causal relationship, e.g. between frontalis muscle activity and tension headache, had not been conclusively demonstrated, nor had it been shown that frontalis muscle tension reduction training was superior to general relaxation training. Subsequent studies have failed to resolve these issues unequivocally. The relative success of this study and the issues that it fails to resolve are typical of much of the extensive work carried out on biofeedback since the late 1960s. The studies have been very varied. Apart from the work on tension headaches, clinical applications of biofeedback have been used with patients suffering from *migraine headaches, peripheral vascular disorders such as Raynaud's disease, insomnia, cardiac arrhythmias, hypertension, asthma, epilepsy, anxiety, neuromuscular disorders, chronic pain, dental disorders, and

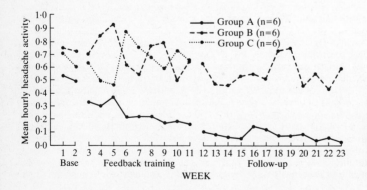

**Fig. 2.** Headache activity during feedback training (all three groups) and during the three-month follow-up (Groups A and B only). Group A, true feedback; Group B, pseudofeedback; Group C, no treatment.

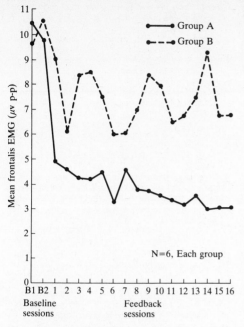

**Fig. 3.** Mean frontalis EMG levels across sessions. Group A, true feedback; Group B, pseudofeedback.

speech, hearing, and reading disorders. They have also been used with hyperactive and learning-disabled children. In most of the areas studied biofeedback therapy appears to work, but no reported study has so far demonstrated that the active element responsible for the observed change, when it occurs, is in fact biofeedback *per se*.

There are several reasons for this state of affairs. First, there is the enthusiasm from clinician and patient alike that greets most innovative therapy, especially if some success is apparent; and, as Miller (1978) has pointed out, there is a wonderful tendency on the part of the body to heal itself, with or without treatment. Thus, as many chronic conditions fluctuate, it is likely that the patient will seek treatment when he feels worse than usual and claim relief, if not cure, when he feels better than usual. Further, many patients show a profound placebo effect and are likely to feel better because they are receiving 'expert' attention. Such non-specific treatment effects are present in all clinical procedures and are likely to be particularly profound in all psychotherapeutic relationships. In general, in clinical biofeedback, there has been too great an emphasis on the widespread application of biofeedback therapy and too little attention paid to the models and underlying theoretical conceptualizations of the disorders and treatments.

Apart from those already mentioned, biofeedback studies have given rise to a number of theoretical problems. One of these, arising out of the reported evidence of instrumental learning of autonomic functions, is the so-called mediation

issue. This is concerned with whether the observed changes in autonomic functions are really learned or whether they are, for instance, mediated reflexively, consequent upon somatic or cognitive change. (It was in order to control for somatic mediation that Miller used D-tubo curarine to produce paralysis of the rats' skeletal muscles in his original feedback experiment.)

With regard to the possibility of cognitive mediation, several studies have shown that cognitive activity, such as internally generated thoughts, and expectations induced by the instructions given to the subject, may play a part in feedback training, although this effect probably varies with the specific function being trained. The relatively small number of studies in which imagery has been used have not as yet confirmed its popularly believed role as a mediator in some feedback learning. Certain logical considerations complicate the issue. These have to do with the direction of the supposed mediation. Is the cognitive state a determinant of the observed autonomic change, or vice versa? Or are they both consequent upon activity elsewhere?

Such complication is pertinent to the possible role of somatic mediation also, and several investigators questioning the legitimacy of the mediation issue as a criticism of studies indicating autonomic learning, have considered alternative models in which autonomic, cognitive, and somatic responses are all mediated at a higher neural level. The question then becomes 'what specific functions can be voluntarily controlled'? The role of muscular and respiratory activity (itself muscular) has been investigated. Biofeedback studies directed towards resolving this issue, in relation to attempts to control heart-rate, for example, generally indicate that somatic mediators can be utilized in heart-rate control, although whether they are necessary as well as sufficient is not known. This is a general problem.

Apart from the mediation issue, other problems remain unresolved. Does reinforcement play any role in the learning of voluntary control over those physiological functions not normally subject to such control? Does the information fed back to the subject act as a reinforcer which makes the voluntary control of the function more likely in the future, or is the role of reinforcement one of increasing motivation, the subsequent change being attributed to the feedback of information? This issue, like so many others, still remains to be resolved, although the weight of evidence at the moment would appear to support the latter view that there is feedback of information.

Yet another problem, and one related to the mediation issue, concerns the 'control' that biofeedback techniques are designed to help the subject learn. The use of biofeedback equipment which senses somatic changes and displays them to the subject in some form is a temporary device, later to be discarded when the subject has learned how to 'control' the function. In what way does he 'know' what to do when the equipment is withdrawn? Neither he nor the therapist or experimenter knows! He cannot say how he is exercising any control, nor can the therapist tell him. In short he appears to be learning some sort of functional body language which defies adequate description.

Perhaps we should not be surprised at this state of affairs because a very similar situation obtains in many of our natural so-called volitional functions. We do not, for instance, know 'how' we are doing it when we retrieve information from our memory store, nor indeed 'how' we are organizing our thoughts into sentences. If, as seems likely, the 'language' we learn involves processing at a higher nervous level (the brain presumably), then we may never completely resolve this issue.

Another difficulty, and one probably inherent in many biofeedback studies, has to do with the possibility of inherent biological constraints. Organisms can only learn to modify functions within possible physiological limits. Some limitations in control may arise because of such constraints. It has been suggested, for instance, that the greater incidence of success in studies aimed at accelerating the heart-rate than in those with deceleration as the aim, can be put down to a postulated constraint that works against the production of large-magnitude decreases in heart-rate (Schwartz, 1975).

Individual differences undoubtedly play an important role in biofeedback studies—although positive results abound there is a very large variability in the ability of subjects to achieve control. The factors underlying such individual differences have yet to be discovered. Non-specific or placebo factors undoubtedly play some part and confuse many studies, and they need to be investigated and controlled if the true nature of biofeedback control is to be exposed. Clarification of the issue would enable the clinician to utilize those factors to advantage in treatment—especially as it is unlikely that he will ever be able to remove them.

Finally, although the nature of biofeedback still needs to be elucidated, and the final evaluation of clinical biofeedback is still awaited, work directed towards the former will teach us much about the mechanisms of volitional control and the role of internal systems involved in an organism's adaptation to its environment, and work directed towards the latter may well indicate that in some circumstances biofeedback may become the preferred alternative to other treatments, especially where their efficacy is questionable or their side-effects undesirable. Further, clinical biofeedback has the great merit that it emphasizes the role of the patient in determining the course of the treatment and in taking an active role in it. This is likely to prove one of its most positive aspects.

See also CYBERNETICS; FEEDBACK AND FEEDFORWARD.                                    I. W. P.-P.

Barber, T. X., DiCara, L. V., Kamiya, J., Miller, N. E., Shapiro, D., and Stoyva, J. (1970). *Biofeedback and Self-Control: An Aldine Reader on the Regulation of Bodily Processes and Consciousness*. Chicago. (Contains vital work published before 1970.)

Barber, T. X. *et al.* (1971 onwards). *Biofeedback and Self-Control: An Aldine Annual*. Chicago. (Contains important studies during each previous year.)

Bruce, R. V. (1973). *Bell: Alexander Graham Bell and the Conquest of Silence*. London.

Budzynski, T., Stoyva, J. M., Adler, C. S., and Mullaney, D. J. (1973). EMG biofeedback and tension headache: a controlled autonomic study. *Psychosomatic Medicine*, **35**, 484–96.

Miller, N. E. (1968). Paper presented at the Annual Meeting of the Pavlovian Society of North America. *Conditioned Reflex*, **3**, 129.

Miller, N. E. (1978). Biofeedback and visceral learning. *Annual Review of Psychology*, **29**, 373–404.

Miller, N. E. and Dworkin, B. (1974). Visceral learning: recent difficulties with curarized rats and significant problems for human research. In Obrist, P. A. (ed.), *Cardiovascular Psychophysiology*, pp. 312–31. Chicago.

Olton, D. S. and Noonberg, A. R. (1980). *Biofeedback: Clinical Applications in Behavioral Medicine*. Englewood Cliffs, New Jersey.

Ray, W. J., Raizynski, J. M., Rodgers, T., and Kimball, W. H. (1979). *Evaluation of Clinical Biofeedback*. New York.

Yates, A. J. (1980). *Biofeedback and the Modification of Behaviour*. New York. (For a detailed evaluation and discussion of the literature on biofeedback.)

**BIOLOGICAL CLOCK.** Anybody who has crossed the Atlantic in an aeroplane knows about 'jet lag'. After a journey from London to New York it is difficult to stay awake, while after the return journey one tends to wake up late. Man's body is intolerant of changes in clock time and it takes several days to readjust to a new local time.

The same is true of practically all other animals, not very surprisingly, because we all live on the same planet and experience the same 24-hour cycle as the earth rotates. Mice, birds, and men eat and sleep at particular times of day, depending on their species, and if they are placed (or choose to place themselves) in unvarying habitats such as laboratories or down a mine they will generally retain these regular habits. The cycle tends to drift a little, with the animal waking a few minutes earlier or later on each succeeding day, but it remains amazingly constant in duration. The rhythm of the body's activities can be reset by a new time of sunrise, or by a series of night-shifts at a factory, but it cannot be substantially altered: man can be induced to live on a 23- or 25-hour cycle (by speeding up or slowing down his watch), but a 12- or 18-hour day seems impossible.

Shore-living invertebrates typically show an additional 'tidal' cycle, which has obvious adaptive significance, and many also show longer-term rhythms, coincident with the phases of the moon; species may spawn only at spring tides, or even only at spring tides at a particular time of year. Even annual rhythms may persist in constant conditions: weaver-birds, for instance, build nests and lay eggs at the 'correct' time of year for at least two years when deprived of day-length or temperature clues to the time of year.

There are also much shorter cycles—activities that are repeated every few seconds or minutes. Many sessile, burrowing, and boring animals lead monotonous lives in almost constant conditions and show these shorter rhythms very clearly. As with the circadian (*circa diem*, almost 24-hour) cycles, the rhythms tend to persist when all obvious sources of stimulation (even food) have been eliminated; they seem to be generated from within, rather than caused from outside.

The conclusion is that an animal contains one or more 'biological clock' (but the existence of several different rhythms in one animal does not necessarily imply several clocks—it could be a matter of gearing); and a great deal of research has gone into establishing the whereabouts of the mainsprings. A recurrent problem is that because a body's various activities are interrelated, most if not all of its tissues operate to a cycle, and how does one distinguish between the mainspring and the rest of the clockwork? One approach is to determine which of the tissues will continue to perform rhythmically in isolation, although it is difficult to keep most tissues alive in a test-tube, and even if one succeeds it is impossible to be certain that the tissue is behaving normally. The method is useful in the study of short-term cycles, however, and there are now a number of well-documented cases in which individual nerve cells have repeated regular patterns of electrical discharge over periods of hours or even days. The matter can be followed further into the cell, which may show cyclic changes in ribonucleic acid (RNA) content.

But where and how does the timing originate? Some argue that there is no endogenous clock and that the rhythms observed are driven from outside. It is impossible to disprove this, although in laboratories it is relatively easy to screen animals and plants (even potatoes show rhythmic cycles in respiration rates) from changes in lighting, temperature, and vibration. It is difficult, however, to screen them from daily changes in weak magnetic fields (and many are known to respond to these) and quite impossible to screen them from cyclic geophysical events such as the varying pull of the moon. Eventually the use of orbiting laboratories may help; in the meantime conventional wisdom holds that truly endogenous clocks are likely, even though it can offer no convincing models of how they may be engineered.   M. J. W.

Moore-Ede, M. C., Sulzman, F. M., and Fuller, C. A. (1982). *The Clocks that Time Us*. Cambridge, Massachusetts.

**BIRAN,** MAINE DE (1766–1824), French philosopher. See MAINE DE BIRAN.

**BIT.** The binary digit, or 'bit' as it is termed, is the primary unit for measuring information and uncertainty. The bit is a yes/no decision, which may be represented in an information system, or computer, by the two positions of a simple on-off switch. *Digital systems are based on 'bits', and their speed may be specified as their maximum 'bit rate'.

The 'Dictionary Game' illustrates very clearly how dividing a set of possibilities into two, and then this set into two again, then again, can lead very quickly to finding a particular item. Any word can usually be located with a dozen questions of the form: 'Is the word before "G"?' or 'Is it after "D"?' . . . But this works only when the items are arranged in some kind of order, such as alphabetical, or numerical. It is, however, just possible that at least some memories may be selected or accessed in this kind of way, by branching search strategies.

In *information theory (Shannon and Weaver, 1949), information is related mathematically to uncertainty; for it takes more information to specify a particular specific alternative item from many possibilities than from few possibilities. As the number of alternatives increases, so more bits are needed to select one of them. The number of bits required is the logarithm, to the base 2, of the number of alternatives. So for dice, there are six possibilities for a die, and the uncertainty for each face or number on the die is $\log 6 = 2 \cdot 58$. For drawing a card from a pack of 52 cards, $\log 52 = 5 \cdot 70$. Thus, for the die two or three questions will determine the number, and five or six questions will identify a card.

Many experiments have been aimed at measuring the 'bit rate' for human performance, first defined by W. H. Hake and W. R. Garner (1951). Their subjects identified positions of a pointer on a linear scale, with various possible positions for the pointer. With five positions the subjects lost no information, but with 10, 20, or 50 alternatives the transmitted information was effectively constant, at about $3 \cdot 0$ bits. People can only identify about nine points on a line; increasing the number of alternatives does not increase the amount of information transmitted. The human bit rate for choices along a single dimension is about $3 \cdot 0$ bits, but this rises with more dimensions (for example, recognizing positions of a dot on a square, with a short exposure time) up to about 8 bits. Long practice may raise the bit rate somewhat.

H. Quastler and V. J. Wulff (cited in Attneave, 1959) have estimated bit rates for various human skills. For a pianist playing random notes, the bit rate may be as high as 22 bits per second. The skilled pianist learns to '*chunk' notes into familiar chords—each being a single selection—so his effective performance may be much better. Typing is limited to about 15 bits per second. Speech can be as high as 26 bits per second, though around 18 is normal. It has been estimated that silent reading may be as high as 44 bits per second. Mental arithmetic by a 'lightning calculator' was estimated at about 24 bits per second: about the same as that of a pianist.

The pioneering experiment by Edmund Hick (1952), which measured the 'rate of gain of information' by getting subjects to press a key corresponding to a light, with various numbers of keys and lights, showed that *reaction time increases logarithmically as the number of choices (the number of lights and keys, one for each finger) increases. There is, however, a deep problem for this or any other technique for measuring the bit rate for the human nervous system—for we are never quite limited to the alternatives provided by the experimenter. Thus, the subject in Hick's experiment (actually the editor of this Companion to the Mind!) was not deaf, or blind, to everything except the lights to which he was responding, so that his range of possibilities was always greater than the experimenter knew, or could take into account. Possibly *attention serves, consciously or unconsciously, to limit possibilities to what are likely to be relevant: to make best use of our limited human bit rate.

Attneave, F. (1959). *Applications of Information Theory to Psychology*. New York.

Gregory, R. L. (1986). Whatever Happened to Information Theory? In *Odd Perceptions*. London.

Hick, W. E. (1952). On the rate of gain of information. *Quarterly Journal of Experimental Psychology*, **4**, 11–26.

Shannon, C. E. and Weaver, W. (1949). *The Mathematical Theory of Communication*. Urbana, Illinois.

**BLACK.** The visual sensation associated with lack of, or sudden reduction in, light. Black is not absence of visual sensation but is sensationally a colour. If we think of what is behind the head, we experience *nothing*—which is very different from black. (See NOTHINGNESS.)

**BLEULER,** EUGEN (1857–1939). Swiss psychiatrist, educated at the University of Zurich, where he became professor of psychiatry. He undertook major studies of *schizophrenia and suggested that this term, rather than *dementia praecox*, be used to describe the disorder.

**BLINDNESS, RECOVERY FROM.** What would an adult who had been blind all his life be able to see if the cause of his blindness was suddenly removed? This question was asked by several empiricist philosophers in the eighteenth century. John *Locke considered the possibilities of such a case in 1690, following the question posed in a letter from his friend William Molyneux:

Suppose a man born blind, and now adult, and taught by his touch to distinguish between a cube and a sphere of the same metal. Suppose then the cube and the sphere were placed on a table, and the blind man made to see: query, whether by his sight, before he touched them, could he distinguish and tell which was the globe and which the cube? . . . The acute and judicious proposer answers: not. For though he has obtained the experience of how the globe, how the cube, affects his touch, yet he has not yet attained the experience that what affects his touch so or so, must affect his sight, so or so. . . .

Locke comments in the *Essay concerning Human Understanding* (1690), Book II, Ch. 9, Sect. 8:

I agree with this thinking gentleman, whom I am pleased to call my friend, in his answer to this problem; and am of the opinion that the blind man, at first, would not be able with certainty to say which was the globe, which the cube. . . .

René *Descartes, in a passage in the *Dioptrics* (1637), considers how a blind man might build up a perceptual world by tapping around him with a stick. He first considers a sighted person using a stick in darkness. Descartes must surely have tried this for himself, and perhaps actually tested blind people. He says, of this experiment:

. . . without long practice this kind of sensation is rather confused and dim; but if you take men born blind, who have made use of such sensations all their life, you will find they feel things with perfect exactness that one might almost say that they see with their hands. . . .

Descartes goes on to suggest that normal vision resembles a blind man exploring and building up his sense world by successive probes with a stick.

George *Berkeley, in *A New Theory of Vision* (1709), Sect. lxxxv, stresses the importance of touch for seeing by considering that a microscope, by so changing the scale of things that touch no longer corresponds to vision, is of little use; and so, if our eyes were '. . . turned into the nature of microscopes, we should not be much benefited by the change . . . and (we would be) left only with the empty amusement of seeing, without any other benefit arising from it' (Sect. lxxxvi). Berkeley goes on to say that we should expect a blind man who recovered sight not to know visually whether anything was

high or low, erect or inverted . . . for the objects to which he had hitherto used to apply the terms up and down, high and low, were such as only affected or were in some way perceived by touch; but the proper objects of vision make a new set of ideas, perfectly distinct and different from the former, and which can in no sort make themselves perceived by touch (Sect. xcv).

These remained interesting speculations, until in 1728 an unusually expert and thoughtful surgeon, William *Cheselden, reported such a clinical case. Though generally distinguished as a surgeon his achievements were especially ophthalmic operations for cataract (Cope, 1953). In a celebrated case Cheselden gave sight to a boy aged thirteen or fourteen who was born with highly opaque cataracts. Cheselden reported that:

When he first saw, he was so far from making any judgment of distances, that he thought all object whatever touched his eyes (as he expressed it) as what he felt did his skin, and thought no object so agreeable as those which were smooth and regular, though he could form no judgment of their shape, or guess what it was in any object that was pleasing to him: he knew not the shape of anything, nor any one thing from another, however different in shape or magnitude; but upon being told what things were, whose form he knew before from feeling, he would carefully observe, that he might know them again; and (as he said) at first learned to know, and again forgot a thousand things in a day. One particular only, though it might appear trifling, I will relate: Having often forgot which was the cat, and which the dog, he was ashamed to ask; but catching the cat, which he knew by feeling, he was observed to look at her steadfastly, and then, setting her down, said, So, puss, I shall know you another time. He was very much surprised, that those things which he had liked best, did not appear most agreeable to his eyes, expecting those persons would appear most beautiful that he loved most, and such things to be most agreeable to his sight, that were so to his taste. We thought he soon knew what pictures represented, which were shewed to him, but we found afterwards we were mistaken; for about two months after he was couched, he discovered at once they represented solid bodies, when to that time he considered them only as party-coloured planes, or surfaces diversified with variety of paint; but even then he was no less surprised, expecting the pictures would feel like the things they represented, and was amazed when he found those parts, which by their light and shadow appeared now round and uneven, felt only flat like the rest, and asked which was the lying sense, feeling or seeing?

Being shewn his father's picture in a locket at his mother's watch, and told what it was, he acknowledged the likeness, but was vastly surprised; asking, how it could be, that a large face could be expressed in so little room, saying, it should have seemed as impossible for him, as to put a bushel of anything into a pint. At first he could bear but very little light, and the things he saw, he thought extremely large; but upon seeing things larger, those first seen he conceived less, never being able to imagine any lines beyond the bounds he saw; the room he was in, he said, he knew to be but part of the house, yet he could not conceive that the whole house could look bigger. Before he was couched, he expected little advantage from seeing, worth undergoing an operation for, except reading and writing; for he said, he thought he could have no more pleasure in walking abroad than he had in the garden, which he could do safely and readily. And even blindness, he observed, had this advantage, that he could go anywhere in the dark, much better than those who can see; and after he had seen, he did not soon lose this quality, nor desire a light to go about the house in the night. He said, every new object was a new delight; and the pleasure was so great, that he wanted words to express it; but his gratitude to his operator he could not conceal, never seeing him for some time without tears of joy in his eyes, and other marks of affection. . . . A year after first seeing, being carried upon Epsom Downs, and observing a large prospect, he was exceedingly delighted with it, and called it a new kind of seeing. And now being couched in his other eye, he says, that objects at first appeared large to this eye, but not so large as they did at first to the other; and looking upon the same object with both eyes, he thought it looked about twice as large as with the first couched eye only, but not double, that we can in any ways discover.

Evidently the sensory worlds of touch and vision were not so separate as at least Berkeley imagined they would be, and visual perception developed remarkably rapidly. This was discussed in terms of the Cheselden case by the materialist philosopher Julien Offray de *La Mettrie, in his dangerously challenging book, *Natural History of the Soul* (1745), where he argues that only education received through the senses makes man man, and gives him what we call a soul, while no development of the mind outwards ever takes place. A few years later, in his better known *Man A Machine* (1748), he says:

Nothing, as any one can see, is so simple as the mechanism of our education. Everything may be reduced to sounds or words that pass from the mouth of one through the ears of another into his brain. At the same moment, he perceives through his eyes the shape of the bodies of which these words are arbitrary signs.

The findings of the Cheselden case (which, though by no means the first, is the first at all adequately reported) are confirmed by some later cases, though in others the development of perception is painfully slow. R. Latta described a case of a successful operation for congenital cataract in 1904, which was broadly similar with almost immediately useful vision; but very often the eye takes a long time to settle down after a cataract operation. This may explain why so many of the historical cases described by M. von Senden (1932) showed such slow development. This is, however, a controversial matter. The Canadian psychologist Donald Hebb, in *The Organization of Behaviour* (1949), attributed the general slowness to see after operation as evidence that a very great deal of learning is needed. This, indeed, is now generally accepted, but it remains a question how far previously gained knowledge from exploratory touch, the other senses, and from the reports of sighted people helps new-found vision.

The case of a man who received corneal grafts when aged 52 (Gregory and Wallace, 1963) has the advantage over previous cases that a good retinal image is immediately available after corneal grafts as the eye is far less disturbed than by a cataract operation. In this case the patient, 'S. B.', could see virtually immediately things he already knew by touch; though for objects or features where touch had not been available a long, slow learning process was required, and in fact he never became perceptually normal. It was striking that he had immediate visual perception for things that absolutely must have been learned while he was blind, and could not have been known innately. Thus, from extensive experience of feeling the hands of his pocket watch, he was able, immediately, to tell the time visually. Perhaps even more striking, as a boy at the blind school S. B. had been taught to recognize by touch capital letters which were inscribed on special wooden plates. This was useful for reading street names, brass plates, and so on. Now it turned out that he could immediately read capital letters visually, though not lower-case letters, which he had not been taught by touch. These took months to learn to see. The general finding, of this case, was dramatic transfer of knowledge from touch to vision. So S. B. was not like a baby learning to see: he already knew a great deal from touch, and this was available for his newly functioning vision.

He had difficulties with shadows. When walking on steps on a sunny day he would quite often step on the shadow, sometimes falling. He was remarkably good at judging horizontal though not vertical distances. Thus while still in the hospital he could give the distance of chairs or tables almost normally; but when looking down from the window he thought the ground was at touching distance though the ward was several stories high. When he was shown various distortion *illusions it was found that he was hardly affected by them: they were almost undistorted. And he did not experience the usual spontaneous depth-reversals of the Necker cube—which appeared to him flat. Indeed, like the Cheselden case, he had great difficulty seeing objects in pictures. Cartoons of faces meant nothing to him. He also found some things he loved ugly (including his wife and himself!) and he was frequently upset by the blemishes and imperfections of the visible world. He was fascinated by mirrors: they remained wonderful to the end of his life. As for most of the cases, though, S. B. became severely depressed, and felt more handicapped with his vision than when blind.

A dramatic and revealing episode occurred when he was first shown a lathe, at the London Science Museum, shortly after he left hospital. He had a long-standing interest in tools, and he particularly wanted to be able to use a lathe.

We led him to the glass case, and asked him to tell us what was in it. He was quite unable to say anything about it, except he thought the nearest part was a handle. (He pointed to the handle of the transverse feed.) He complained that he could not see the cutting edge, or the metal being worked, or anything else about it, and appeared rather agitated. We then asked the Museum Attendant for the case to be opened, and S. B. was allowed to touch the lathe. The result was startling; he ran his hands deftly over the machine, touching first the transverse feed handle and confidently naming it 'a handle', and then on to the saddle, the bed and the head-stock of the lathe. He ran his hands eagerly over the lathe, with his eyes shut. Then he stood back a little and opened his eyes and said: 'Now that I've felt it I can see.' He then named many of the parts correctly and explained how they would work, though he could not understand the chain of four gears driving the lead screw.

Many of these observations have been confirmed by Valvo (1971) in half a dozen cases of recovery from blindness by a remarkable operation: fitting acrylic lenses to eyes that never formed completely. Tissue rejection of the artificial lenses was prevented by placing them in a tooth, which was implanted as a buffer in the eye. One of these Italian patients, wearing a lens in a tooth in his eye, is a philosopher! It is now possible to implant artificial lenses without tissue rejection, so perhaps more cases of adult recovery from infant blindness will now appear.                                        R. L. G.

Berkeley, G. (1709). *A New Theory of Vision* (ed. A. D. Lindsay, 1910). London.

Cope, Z. (1953). *William Cheselden*. Edinburgh and London.

Descartes, R. (1637). *Discourse on Method* (trans. E. S. Haldane and G. R. T. Ross, 1967). In *The Philosophical Works of Descartes* (2 vols.). Cambridge.

Gregory, R. L. and Wallace, J. G. (1963). *Recovery from Early Blindness: A Case Study*. Cambridge.

Hebb, D. O. (1949). *The Organization of Behaviour*. London.

Latta, R. (1904). Notes on a Successful Operation for Congenital Cataract in an Adult. *British Journal of Psychology*, **I**, 135–50.

Locke, J. (1690). *Essay concerning Human Understanding* (ed. P. H. Nidditch, 1975). Oxford.

Mettrie, J. O. de la (1748). *L'Homme* (trans. G. C. Bussey, 1953), in *Man A Machine*. Open Court, Illinois. (The *Natural History of the Soul* (1745) is well discussed by F. A. Langer in his *The History of Materialism*, 1925, London.)

Valvo, A. (1971). *Sight Restoration after Long-Term Blindness: The Problems and Behaviour Patterns of Visual Rehabilitation*. New York.

**BLINKING.** When the eye is irritated by a foreign body, such as grit or a fly, we blink to remove it. This is a *reflex, and there is also reflex closing of the eyes to prevent damage when we sneeze; but everyday blinking is not a reflex activity. A reflex needs an initiating signal; but if, for example, the eyes had to dry up to initiate blink signals, the blink would follow the beginnings of damage, due to the eyes drying, for it would be too late to protect the delicate corneas with a film of tears.

Normal blinking is initiated by signals initiating in the brain, probably from the *basal ganglia. Rather surprisingly, the rate of blinking is a useful index of general attention, as it tends to increase markedly at times of *stress or distraction and it falls below the normal resting rate during extended periods of high concentration. This is possibly related to its early use in conditions such as hunting, when the eye needs to be cleared and the fluid on the cornea smoothed out for maximum visual acuity. During a prolonged task, however, the eyes need to remain open for long periods. Blinking can then be so reduced that damage may result as the eyes dry. This is a hazard in some occupations: draughtsmen, for example, are apt to suffer from inflammation of the eyes, and over time from clinical problems with their corneas if they continue to concentrate for prolonged periods without blinking.

It is interesting that the rate of blinking is also affected by non-visual tasks, and may increase with anxiety or embarrassment. Most curiously, we are not normally aware of blinking, though the eyes are closed every few seconds. One might have thought that blinking would occur in one eye at a time so that we are not intermittently blinded; but it turns out that this seldom matters, as blinking is normally inhibited just prior to important anticipated events. It has been suggested that people having unusually high blink rates may be unsuitable as pilots, or be dangerous drivers; but experiments have shown that high individual blink rates are not a significant hazard for skills where short-term prediction of dangerous events is possible.

Ponder, E. and Kennedy, W. P. (1928). On the act of blinking. *Quarterly Journal of Experimental Physiology*, **18**, 89.

Poulton, E. C. (1952). Perceptual anticipation in tracking with two pointer and one pointer displays. *British Journal of Psychology*, **43**, 222.

Poulton, E. C. and Gregory, R. L. (1952). Blinking during

visual tracking. *Quarterly Journal of Experimental Psychology*, **4**, part 2, 57.

**BLOOD MYTH.** Always man has been fascinated with blood, and he has often associated it with the life force itself. Primitive man noticed that, when an arrow or spear pierced the skin of another human or animal, as the blood flowed out on to the earth so life gradually ebbed away. So he made the simple deduction that blood must be the source of life itself, since when it drains from the body, life also goes away. Blood is the life-sustaining substance.

In accordance with this belief, primitive man often smeared himself with blood, in order to give himself more life. It was thought that those who had a ruddy complexion, the 'bloody ones', had more health than those who were pale and had less blood in them. Today, the use of rouge and lipstick may be regarded as a sophisticated relic of this primitive practice.

In ancient Greece, humans gave blood to the gods of the earth, to heroes, and to the dead in general. The precious blood was spilled on the ground; sometimes there were deeply buried, makeshift pipes to carry it down into the bowels of the earth. The Greeks characterized the dead as 'bloodless' ones who needed blood. In Homer's *Odyssey* there is the famous passage in which blood of newly slaughtered animals is provided for the dead, so that they can drink and become conscious once again. The shades of the dead gather round the blood to drink it; only after they have drunk are they able to think and speak. Virgil, too, mentions how 'holy blood' was poured on Polydor's grave.

Sprinkling the altar with blood to honour the gods in heaven was also a common practice. In the Old Testament, priests had the duty of sprinkling the altar with the blood of victims.

In those civilizations where human sacrifice was customary, blood letting sometimes reached astounding proportions: every year in ancient Mexico, for example, thousands of humans were killed to honour the gods; their blood was smeared on godly images or collected in bowls for libations. Often these rituals were directed towards the sun god.

If one accepts the myth that blood is the source of life, it follows that blood must carry characteristics of the soul. Hence, drinking the blood of some person or animal of strength should communicate this strength to the drinker. In Lapland humans drink the blood of reindeer; in parts of Asia the blood of the tiger.

Whoever gives blood, gives up part of himself as well as life. This is the origin of the belief in the sacred character of blood pacts. A blood pact can be set up with God or with the Devil. Both deities seem to enjoy blood sacrifices, since the soul is in the blood.

In so-called 'higher religions' wine is often substituted for blood, but the symbolism of blood remains. In the Christian ritual the faithful drink the wine which has been changed into the blood of Christ, in order that they may become one with the Saviour. With the blood comes the promise of eternal life: 'Unless a man eats of my flesh and drinks of my blood, he shall have no life in him. But whosoever eateth of my flesh and drinketh of my blood, shall live forever, and I shall raise him up on the last day.'

In everyday language there is an association between the blood myth and life, as in the expression 'he gave his life's blood for his friend'. Blood is the most worthy gift of all. From life is life given. Friendship can be expressed in the blood ritual, in which both prospective friends cut themselves and mix their blood together, in order to become 'as thick as blood brothers'.

Tied up with the blood myth is the belief that there is 'good' blood and 'bad' blood. Until the late eighteenth century illness was often assumed to be the result of 'bad blood'. So the bad blood had to be let out; and medical doctors were often referred to as 'leechers' because of their practice of blood-letting.

In the act of sexual intercourse some humans like to bite their partners on the neck or shoulder. This may be a residue of the human sucking instinct developed while still a foetus. Carried to an extreme, this fixation on seeing human blood is part of sexual pathology. There are some humans who thrill at the sight of flowing blood; they are classified as 'living vampires'. For most of them it is not enough to draw blood, they must see the blood spurt. Apparently these patients confuse blood and spurting semen. To them the flowing blood is the main attraction, rather than genital pleasure, hence they are sometimes called blood fetishists.

R. T. M.

**BLUSHING.** Uncontrollable reddening of the cheeks, and sometimes the ears and neck, is associated with embarrassment and guilt. Charles *Darwin made the most interesting suggestion: that blushing is a warning that the individual who is blushing is not to be trusted, as he or she has violated the mores of the group or has committed some crime. This notion that blushing is a visible warning sign that an individual is not to be trusted, Darwin puts forward in *Expression of the Emotions in Man and Animals* (1872). Part of his evidence is that children before the age of understanding social rules do not blush, for 'the mental powers of infants are not yet sufficiently developed to allow of their blushing. Hence, also, it is that idiots rarely blush.' Blushing (and also weeping and sobbing) is found only in man and not in other Primates, who are generally supposed (in spite of some recent contrary evidence) not to have cognitive understanding of social mores or their violation. This is not to say that only humans have social mores, only that we alone appreciate and evaluate them, and act on our assessments of social situations, and monitor our successes and failures and the appropriateness of our behaviour in situations that had no precedence earlier in evolution. It seems that only humans have the understanding to be embarrassed—and so to blush.

For Darwin 'blushing is the most peculiar and the most human of all expressions'. He goes on to suggest a psychosomatic origin: 'we cannot cause a blush by any physical means . . . It is the mind which must be affected.' But this is not the *conscious* mind, for (writing nearly twenty years before Sigmund *Freud was born) Darwin points out that blushing is not under control and that, further: 'Blushing is not only involuntary; but the wish to restrain it, by leading to self-attention, actually increases the tendency.' That it is an innate sign of mental states is confirmed by blushing in blind people.

Women blush more than men. Darwin wished to discover how far down the body blushes extend, so he adopted the ingenious notion of asking his medical friends 'who necessarily had frequent opportunities for observation'. His friend Sir James Paget (1814–99, who wrote the standard texts, *Lectures on Surgical Pathology* and *Clinical Lectures*) reported that: 'with women who blush intensely on the face, ears, nape of the neck, the blush does not commonly extend any lower down the body'. He never saw an instance in which it extended below the upper part of the chest. Darwin considers whether it is the exposure of the face to temperature changes that makes the capillaries specially labile; but decides, rather, that the face is intimately associated with the brain and that the blushing is primarily facial, at least in Englishwomen, because of the 'attention of the mind having been directed more frequently and earnestly to the face than any other part of the body. . .'.

What we would now call the psychosomatic basis of blushing was pondered in astonishing depth by Darwin as he considered that its mental effects may be *reversible*. He refers to the observation that when patients are given nitrite of amyl they blush in the same restricted regions as with embarrassment. 'The patients are at first pleasantly stimulated, but, as the flushing increases, they become confused and bewildered. One woman to whom the vapour had been administered asserted that, as soon as she grew hot, she grew *muddled*.' Although all this was said well over a century ago there is little to add now, apart from its detailed physiology, to Darwin's comments on blushing.          R. L. G.

**BODY BUILD AND PERSONALITY.** The continuing debate on the relation between physical form and mental attributes, which goes back at least to Hippocrates, took on new life with the publication in 1921 of Ernst *Kretschmer's monograph *Körperbau und Charakter* (English translation, *Physique and Character*, 1921). Although the form taken by this debate has varied greatly from one century to the next, the most prevalent belief was that two types of temperament could be distinguished. Thus Shakespeare contrasted 'fat; Sleek-headed men and such as sleep o nights' with Cassius's 'lean and hungry look; He thinks too much: such men are dangerous.' In more modern times, C. G. *Jung wrote of extraverts and introverts and William *James contrasted tough-minded empiricists with tender-minded rationalists, while *Kraepelin drew the distinction between *schizophrenia and manic-depressive psychosis which still remains a cornerstone in psychiatric classification (see MENTAL DISORDERS: CLASSIFICATION). The question then arose: is there any correlation between these two classes of illness, predispositions to which are inherited individually, and particular features of body build? On the basis of clinical experience Kretschmer reached the conclusion that manic-depressive illness—or predisposition to develop it—and what he called psychotic temperament (i.e. proneness to either undue exuberance or depression) were associated with a round-bodied, so-called *pyknic* physique, whereas schizophrenia—or predisposition to develop it—appeared to be linked with a so-called *asthenic* physique.

Kretschmer was, however, careful to point out that any distinction between the abnormal and the normal, i.e. the pathological and the biologically healthy, is relative; and that between the main types that he recognized are the average men, those of athletic build and those of harmoniously balanced, so-called *syntonic* temperament. He recognized, too, that among patients are to be found many of anomalous physique (*dysplastic* types) differing markedly from the types already described and impressing as being 'rare, surprising, and ugly'. Kretschmer worked out detailed schemes for preparing an inventory of the entire body surface from head to foot. This involved systematic measurement with calipers and tape measures, photographing, and drawing. Extensive verbal descriptions of temperament were based on viva voce questioning in a concrete manner in order to get information about the 'simple, colourless psychic life' of his patients. Even so, although his work exhibited both thoughtfulness and care, it is too remote from experimental design and control to justify serious scientific consideration.

More satisfactory methods of classifying physique have since been devised, most notably by W. H. Sheldon, who based his investigation on the premise that the components of physique are normally distributed in the community. He was then led to postulate three supposedly primary aspects of physique for large-scale inquiry. The first, which he called *endomorphy*, refers to relative predominance of soft and rounded tissue throughout the body; the second, christened *mesomorphy*, is concerned with the relative predominance of muscle, bone, and connective tissue; and the third, *ectomorphy*, is marked by a predominance of linear dimensions and a relatively large surface area in relation to body-weight. These three components were viewed not only as normally distributed but also as varying independently in any given physique. In consequence they were chosen as basic variables and, with the aid of specially constructed check-lists of their main characteristics, a large number of photographs of young male physiques was arranged in rank order, one for each component. A seven-point scale was employed and a numeral assigned to each ordered series: thus the extreme endomorph was designated 711, the extreme mesomorph 171 and the extreme ectomorph 117. The pattern of morphological structure as represented by these three numerals is termed the *somatotype* of the individual. It is important to bear in mind that whereas over seventy individual somatotypes were distinguished, the three extreme types taken together make up only 1 per cent of the entire population sampled in the study.

Sheldon then proceeded to investigate whether significant correlation could be discovered between varieties of physique and qualities of temperament. To this end he selected fifty traits for study, and subjects were rated for each trait on a seven-point scale. Ratings were based on a combination of personal knowledge and observations of behaviour. It transpired that twenty of the traits studied fell into three well-defined clusters that were highly inter-correlated, suggesting that there might be three basic temperamental components, which Sheldon christened *viscerotonia*, *somatotonia*, and *cerebrotonia*. The first of these is marked by sociability and love of comfort, the second by self-assertiveness verging on aggression, and the third by self-consciousness and diffidence. Correlations as high as 0·80 were claimed between viscerotonia and extreme endomorphy, somatotonia and extreme mesomorphy, and cerebrotonia and extreme ectomorphy, though in the light of more recent studies these correlations are generally considered to be too high.

Sheldon's later work was largely concerned with the application of his methods to the study of clinical issues. This has been less successful, partly on account of methodological difficulties and partly through doubts as to how far physical characteristics in adult life reflect inherited constitution and how far they depend on eating habits, physical activity, or illness contracted at various stages of life.

Although there has been a good deal of criticism of the body-build–personality concept, there is some evidence of a correlation between ectomorphic body build and the personality trait of dysthymia. It has also been reported that young schizophrenic patients had a predominantly ectomorphic body build. This is essentially in agreement with Sheldon's findings, although older patients who develop paranoid schizophrenia were more often mesomorphic. As might be expected, delinquent boys in detention centres showed a high degree of mesomorphy, equivalent to measurements recorded on young men attending a physical training college. In spite of these interesting and suggestive findings there is no evidence that posses-

sion of a particular body configuration is of aetiological importance, and relatively little interest has been shown in this topic in recent years.   o. l. z.

**BODY LANGUAGE.** One important aspect of 'body language' is that people are supposed to exert an enormous degree of precise yet unwitting control over each other's movement in everyday social interaction. In the mid-1960s William Condon and W. D. Ogston of the University of Pittsburgh studied films (shot at 48 frames per second) of two people conversing. The films were analysed intensively, one frame at a time. When Condon and Ogston (1966) compared the movement flow analysis with the linguistic segmentation, they discovered that there were sustained configurations of body change which occurred isomorphically with the words uttered. They also claimed that the configurations of movement change of one individual were in precise synchrony with those of the other. The form of the behaviour displayed by the two individuals did differ, but the timing was precisely co-ordinated. Thus, a speaker was found to move his hand in time with his speech while the listener echoed the same rhythm with small head movements. They called the harmony between the speech and body motion of one speaker 'self-synchrony', and the harmony between speaker and listener 'interactional synchrony'.

In a subsequent study they analysed a segment of a film of a three-person interaction—a mother, father, and their four-year-old son at dinner. Here again, they identified self-synchrony and interactional synchrony, the father and son moving in precise harmony with the mother as she spoke. They also found that changes in velocity of movement were to some extent shared by all three individuals and identified the mechanism underlying this synchrony as the rhythmic structure of the speech. Thus, the father was seen to move his fork to and from his plate in precise cadence with the syllabic structure of the mother's speech.

Adam Kendon (1970) followed up this investigation of interactional synchrony using material from a film shot in a London pub. He noticed that other members of a group moved in synchrony with both the speaker and the direct addressee, but that their movements differed either in form or timing from those of the direct addressee. Kendon claimed that the addressee, by exactly mirroring the movements of the speaker, differentiates himself from others present and so heightens the bond that is established between himself and the speaker. He further noted that interactional synchrony occurs when people are not looking at each other, thereby indicating that the co-ordination of the listener's and the speaker's movements is brought about through the listener's response to the speech rather than through direct copying. Lastly, he claimed that interactional synchrony is not continuous during a period of interaction, and that its intention may be to signal rapport.

A phenomenon somewhat akin to interactional

synchrony, which has been described by Albert Scheflen (1964), is postural congruence shown by two or more individuals who adopt identical or mirror-image postures. This was particularly noted in group sessions and it is of interest that when one member of the group changes his posture, others are quick to follow suit. The outcome is that postural congruence is often maintained despite repeated changes in bodily posture. Scheflen has also reported that in family psychotherapeutic sessions, one child may maintain postural congruence wth one parent and the other child with the other. Possible interpretations of such behaviour are easily surmised.

Interactional synchrony and postural congruence are decidedly intriguing and have featured in a number of popular accounts of 'body language' and cognate phenomenon, of which the best known is undoubtedly that of Desmond Morris (1977). Unfortunately, certain errors and distortions have crept into both this and other popular studies, and too much is frequently claimed on the basis of anecdotal or poorly controlled observations. For example, Scheflen's accounts of his work are often too imprecise to allow replication or direct test. Again, the possibility that some, at least, of the instances of synchrony reported in earlier work may be no more than chance occurrences can seldom be excluded with complete confidence. Postural congruence, too, may in some cases at least be purely coincidental, as Scheflen himself has admitted.

Fortunately, a number of more recent studies have embodied more rigorous methods of investigation. In a carefully designed study by McDowall (1978), for example, micro-analysis was carried out on a film shot at 24 frames per second involving a six-person discussion group comprising both friends and strangers. Two observers each coded three boundary types of movement for each of the six participants. McDowall calculated the chance occurrence of frequency of interactional synchrony with which he compared the observed frequency of such synchrony. The results of this careful test were largely negative, only one pair of subjects displaying interactional synchrony at above chance level. Further, no difference was found in the amount of synchrony shown by friends as compared with strangers. On the other hand, studies of postural congruence, particularly those undertaken in a clinical context, have produced findings more closely in keeping with the results of earlier studies and provide more positive evidence both for the existence of postural congruence and its possible role in signalling rapport. A study by Beattie and Beattie (1981) carried out on a beach provides convincing evidence that postural congruence is definitely not a chance phenomenon.  G. B.

O. L. Z.

Beattie, G. W. and Beattie, C. A. (1981). Postural congruence in a naturalistic setting. *Semiotica*, **35**, 41–55.

Condon, W. S. and Ogston, W. D. (1966). Sound film analysis of normal and pathological behaviour patterns. *Journal of Nervous and Mental Disease*, **143**, 338–47.

Kendon, A. (1970). Movement co-ordination in social interaction: some examples described. *Acta Psychologica*, **32**, 100–125.

McDowall, J. J. (1978). Interactional synchrony: a reappraisal. *Journal of Personality and Social Psychology*, **36**, 963–75.

Morris, D. (1977). *Manwatching*. London.

Scheflen, A. E. (1964). The significance of posture in communication systems. *Psychiatry*, **27**, 316–31.

**BODY–MIND PROBLEM.** See MIND AND BODY; MIND–BODY PROBLEM; CONSCIOUSNESS AND CAUSALITY.

**BOGGLE.** It is said that 'the mind boggles' (meaning an extreme state of incredulity, or rejection of a situation or idea). Nothing but minds can boggle—except computers? Perhaps this depends on whether computers are accepted as having, or not having, minds.

**BONDING.** A term from ethology, meaning a special relationship developed by individuals, such as the pair-bonding of male and female birds. The ethological theories of bonding have been taken over to describe or explain human relationships. See ATTACHMENT.

**BORING,** EDWIN GARRIGUES (1886–1968). American psychologist, who became Edgar Pierce professor of psychology at Harvard. He won distinction for his *History of Experimental Psychology* (1929; revised edition 1942), which traces the genesis of experimental psychology from its origins in early nineteenth-century philosophy and physiology to its general acceptance as an autonomous academic discipline a century later. While placing the major stress on its German origins—more particularly the massive contribution of Wilhelm *Wundt—Boring was fair to the claims of the United States and Britain to have developed important brands of experimental psychology in which introspective analysis was less strongly represented and greater emphasis was placed on objective studies of behaviour in both animals and man. There was also wide recognition of the practical applications of psychological enquiry. Boring's book was, however, criticized in some quarters for its identification of scientific with experimental psychology and its correlated neglect of psychological medicine, in particular the work of Sigmund *Freud and his School (remedied, however, in the 1942 edition). None the less, in spite of some noteworthy limitations, Boring's *History* remains a scholarly record of the early days of experimental psychology.

Boring later published *Sensation and Perception in the History of Experimental Psychology*, a less ambitious though perhaps more satisfactory account of its subject viewed in historical perspective. It is fittingly dedicated to the memory of Hermann von *Helmholtz. A slighter book, owing much to its author's mentor, E. B. *Titchener, is the *Physical Dimensions of Consciousness* which, though dated, is still of some importance. o. L. z.

**BRADLEY,** FRANCIS HERBERT (1846–1924). English *idealist Oxford philosopher. He followed *Hegel in his ethics, and developed a metaphysics, based on a principle of monism, that truth must always be the whole truth. Bertrand *Russell's logical atomism has been described as 'Bradley turned upside down'. His chief works are: *Ethical Studies* (1876), *Principles of Logic* (1883), and especially *Appearance and Reality* (1893).

Wollheim, R. (1959). *F. H. Bradley*. Harmondsworth.

**BRAID,** JAMES (1795–1860), British physician and surgeon. See HYPNOTISM, HISTORY OF.

**BRAILLE.** A system by which the blind read from patterns of raised dots. The basic 'cell' consists of six dots in two vertical lines of three, from which can be derived letters, numerals, and punctuation marks (see Fig. 1). Most experienced Braille readers use their left index finger rather than their right to read Braille (see HANDEDNESS). The system was developed by Louis Braille (1809–52), simplifying the system of the army officer Charles Barbier, who wanted to use his system to pass messages silently. Braille became blind at the age of 3 and at 10 became a student at the Institution Nationale des Jeunes Aveugles in Paris, where he was later appointed a professor.

**BRAIN, ANATOMY OF THE.** See NERVOUS SYSTEM.

**BRAIN DEVELOPMENT.** The fabric of the brain has been discovered within the last 150 years. As recently as Charles *Darwin's day, nerve-cells and their delicate connections were almost unknown.

Darwin wisely spoke little of the brain, though he assumed it to be the evolved organ of the mind.

About 1870 an Italian psychiatrist, Camillo *Golgi, discovered that single nerve-cells could be stained black with silver or gold particles, so that their fine receptor branches (*dendrites) and output fibres (*axons) could be seen in brain slices under the microscope. In Spain, Santiago Ramon y *Cajal used silver-staining to lay the foundations of modern neuroanatomy. By the end of the nineteenth century the tissues of the brains of many animals had been mapped, showing in outline how the main parts had evolved. A common plan, evidence for common principles of growth and function, became clear.

Surgical experiments with animals located regions in the cortex necessary for perception in different modalities, and these researches were soon augmented by controlled electrical stimulation of territories from which movements could be elicited. Strangely distorted sensory and motor images of the body were found. These were evidence for the ordered growth of nerve systems that mapped perceptual and motor skills. Then, about the turn of the century, methods were developed for amplifying the minute electrical impulses by which neurones excite one another. Electrodes could be used to record nerve discharges, as well as to stimulate; and connections were followed with a totally new precision.

During the 1960s and 1970s, much closer inspections of the complex arrangements of brain tissues were made, by staining and by micro-electrode techniques capable of identifying inputs to a single cell and of following its projections to the furthest tips. (See NEUROANATOMICAL TECHNIQUES.) It is possible now to trace where a cell at one point projects to, and backwards, to locate cell bodies which send axons to that point. Micro-electrodes can excite a single cell and follow its discharges,

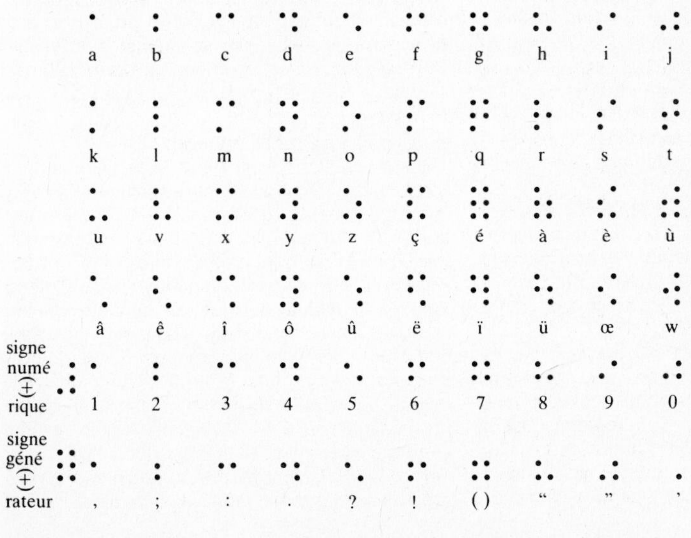

**Fig. 1.** A Braille alphabet.

pick up impulses in a single axon, and inject *neurotransmitters or blocking agents into a minute territory of the brain. With the electron microscope, nerve-cell membranes and the specialized contact points (*synapses), by which selective chemical communication is established from cell to cell, can be seen. The electron microscope can also reveal the intricately folded macromolecular membranes that control nerve-cell biochemistry: the synthesis of protein or of transmitter chemicals, and other processes. Biochemical and immuno-histochemical methods show up chemical differences between nerve-cells and reveal the location of chemical communication points on the cell surface. The anatomical patterns revealed by these methods testify to the formation of organized cell systems by a process of development and differentiation more complex than in any other tissue.

Cajal pioneered studies of how the brain develops from undifferentiated sheets of block-like embryo cells into the most amazing communication system in the universe. He imagined the growing tip of a nerve fibre probing its way with delicate filaments, like an amoeboid protozoon. He described it as, 'a sort of battering ram, possessing an exquisite chemical sensitivity, rapid amoeboid movements and a certain driving force that permits it to push aside, or cross, objects in its way'. He concluded that formation of the right patterns of connections in development or regeneration depends upon how this growth tip chooses a path through the densely packed tissues of brain and body. He also saw evidence of elaborate mass migrations of nerve-cells, resembling the manœuvres of an army for battle. He drew remarkably accurate conclusions about mature brain anatomy by studying the relatively uncluttered tissues of foetal mice and birds.

Recently, the use of radioactive or fluorescent tracers that are drawn into nerve-cell chemistry and carried throughout the protoplasm, and techniques of micro-electrode neurophysiology, have brought a new vitality to studies of brain growth. The brain is seen to lay the foundations of even the higher psychological processes before birth. Such discoveries prove that brain growth is inseparable from mental growth. Notions of how *consciousness, will, and human understanding came about can never be the same.

For most of the modern scientific era, descriptions of the human brain have been faithfully Cartesian (see DESCARTES). One set of anatomically fixed conduction pathways is imagined to be prewired innately, before birth. These govern essential 'biological' functions. Somehow, inside these pathways, probably at junctions between nerve-cells, plastic changes allow use and disuse to modify function. New connections make up new combinations of reflexes by *conditioning. This is the familiar theory of *Pavlov, based on his brilliant experiments on the formation of new connections between stimulus effects and movements or gland secretions in restrained dogs. His work gave the physiological foundation to *behaviourism, the belief that even the higher mental, moral, and cultural attributes of a human being are added by learning to the reflex biology of the brain.

Such a theory of how the mind is formed takes no account of how the brain actually develops. It is impossible to reconcile a simple reflex theory of integrative functions of the brain with the facts of brain growth as they now appear. In the first place, sensory and motor nerve-cells are in a minority, even in the spinal cord. Interneurones that link input to output, and determine changes in the possibilities of such links and how they will be grouped into co-ordinating systems, are a hundred times more numerous. Everywhere in the brain these intermediate integrative cells, some small, some reaching far in the brain, are organized to form systems that look much more like special machinery for formulating varied central states of nervous activity. Every type of neurone is capable of spontaneously firing impulses that may be transmitted through the nerve net. We have to take this into account in our theories of learning.

In foetal birds and mammals, varying movements and sequences of action can be formed before sensory cells are connected to the brain or in pieces of the central nervous system that have been cut off from sensory nerves by surgery. The movement programs are set up among the interneurones. On the input side, too, the fine branches of sense cells—from the retina, from the touch cells of the skin, etc.—grow millions of fine branches that end among already organized and active central networks. Then these afferent terminals sort themselves into precisely ordered arrays that map the body and the outside world into the pre-wired systems of the brain. In short, the way the human brain parts grow before birth suggests that the interacting nerve-cells might make up and co-ordinate basic rules for object perception, for purposeful movement patterns, and for motive states, without benefit of experience. This is confirmed by the behaviour of infants shortly after they are born (see INFANCY, MIND IN). We are therefore obliged to pay careful attention to the steps by which nerve-cells are linked up into communicating systems before birth.

The brain starts as a slab of cells in the upper layer of the embryo, which become irreversibly different from other cells about three weeks after gestation. Different parts are already designated to form specific relations with the body in the future. Both brain and body of the embryo have bilateral symmetry but hidden differences exist between left and right halves. Brain and spinal cord roll into a hollow cylinder, then, in a few days, cell multiplication occurs round the central cavity, and cells migrate outwards to form rudimentary brain nuclei in the wall of the tube. Some cells become neurones and others change into non-neural support cells (glia). Ventral cells in brainstem and cord grow axons out to the muscles of the trunk, limbs,

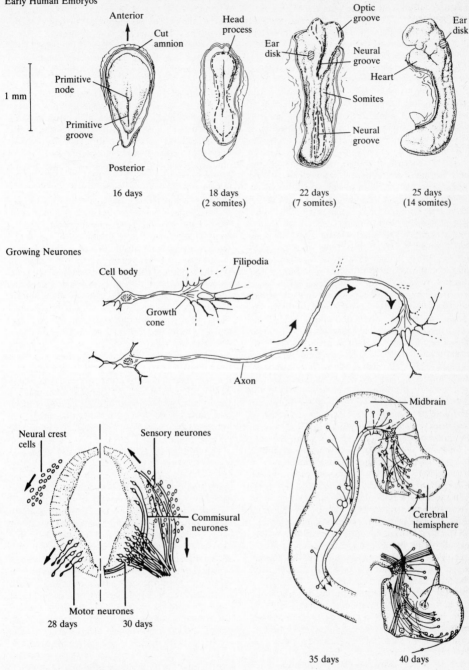

**Early Human Embryos**

Anterior

Cut amnion

Head process

Optic groove

Ear disk

Ear disk

Primitive node

Neural groove

Heart

1 mm

Somites

Primitive groove

Neural groove

Posterior

16 days

18 days
(2 somites)

22 days
(7 somites)

25 days
(14 somites)

**Growing Neurones**

Cell body

Filipodia

Growth cone

Axon

Neural crest cells

Sensory neurones

Midbrain

Commisural neurones

Cerebral hemisphere

Motor neurones

28 days

30 days

35 days

40 days

Embryo Spinal Cord

Embryo Brains

**Fig. 1.** The human central nervous system develops in the dorsal surface of the embryo (inside dotted line) and rolls up to form a tubular spinal cord and brain.

At one month after conception, nerve cell axons grow out, each headed by a growth cone: first away from the spinal cord, then up and down within the core of the brainstem.

and viscera after four weeks, the anterior-most motor cells innervating the muscles of the eyes, face, and mouth. Sensory cells grow shortly after motor cells, projecting their input to the dorsal half of the central nervous system.

The brain is soon much enlarged relative to the cord; its dorsal lobes receive axons from the special receptors of the head (nose, eyes, ears, and mouth). The hypothalamus, the foremost ventral component of the embryo brainstem, as well as being the 'head ganglion' of the viscera, controlling appetites and aversions, acts as a co-ordinator between activities of the central *nervous system and the endocrine system—glands that secrete hormones controlling growth, metabolic activity, and *sexual development. Among the earliest neurones inside the brain to send axons down the embryo brainstem to the cord and upward to the developing forebrain hemispheres are core interneurones, which will transmit a spectrum of messenger chemicals to other neurones and maintain the balance of integrative states in the central nervous system. These substances play a key role in the regulation of nerve cell growth and differentiation everywhere in the young brain. One set of cells from the ventral midbrain reticular system of embryo rats can be injected into adult rats to correct for the attentional and motor deficits that follow particular surgical removals of tissue from nuclei deep in the cerebral hemispheres. The 'brain grafts' penetrate the older brain and 'cure' its fault, rejuvenating nerve axons, finding the right sites, and terminating on cells that had lost input from cells of the same type as the graft. In the mature brain reticular neurones of the brainstem modulate perception, the formation and recall of memories, and motor co-ordination. By the end of the embryo period (eight weeks), when the cells of the future neocortex of the cerebral hemispheres first appear, the brainstem has an elaborate system of projections that will influence the migration and differentiation of cortical neurones (Fig. 1).

In the forty weeks of gestation a human brain grows to a two-thirds-sized likeness of the adult brain. Its anatomy at birth is remarkably complete. All the typically human cortical areas and nuclear masses of the brainstem are there, containing a million million nerve-cells in total. But this general impression is misleading in one important respect. The formation of intercellular connections, which take up little extra space but upon which the function of the brain depends, is far from complete. There is, in fact, a huge postnatal manufacture of fine branches where nerve-cells seek to form effective contacts with dendrites of other cells (Fig. 2). The number of contact points in the cerebral cortex increases astronomically. Each mature cortical cell is estimated to have, on average, about 10,000 synapses, the greater part of which develop a few months after birth. The total number of synapses in the cortex of one person ($10^{15}$) is about 200,000 times the population of humans on earth. Prolific branching of dendrites

and formation of synaptic contacts can be seen in microscope slides of the cerebral cortex of infants, and comparable developments occur in the cerebellum of infants and young children.

How are we to interpret these discoveries? How might specific connections be selected accurately to govern mental processes in this teeming array of minute living elements? On the selection of the right connections depends the development of skill in motor co-ordination, refinement of perception, retention of memories of all kinds, formation of a vocabulary, and development of increasingly critical and precise patterns of thought. The facts of brain growth do not imply that mental and physical abilities governed by the brain simply expand and elaborate independently of stimuli. Nor, on the other hand, do they give the brain a passive submissiveness to experience. True, even in foetal stages the selection of nerve connections depends upon input from the maternal environment. Serious mental deficiencies in children can arise if the mother is poorly nourished or under mental stress during critical brain growth periods in gestation. But the process of gaining experience is at all stages an active one. After birth, stimuli are sought and actively taken up by a baby, not just submitted to. Those stimuli which are assimilated cause selections to be made from among rival adaptive alternatives within general rules for brain formation. These ground rules, including rules for recognizing other persons and for detecting their emotions from their expressions, are innate in the sense that they are formulated in earlier stages where stimuli had no effect. The learning involved takes place as part of a most elaborate developmental strategy that must be ascribed to a continuous regulated unfolding of nerve-cell interactions from the embryo to the adult.

The principles of how stimuli and genes act together to control brain differentiation are beginning to come to light. When embryo nerve-cells migrate and form into patterned aggregates, and when they grow long, branching axons that sort themselves in an intricate criss-crossing array to make up patterned circuits, they communicate by biochemical expressions of regulator genes that can switch the actions of other genes governing nerve-cell development. There are message-emitting and message-receiving loci on the cell surfaces. These respond to hormones and growth substances that are produced by cells of all kinds. Once the network of nerve connections is formed, a new factor, conduction of nerve impulses, adds power and precision to this communication. The electrical discharges of neurones cause adjustments in their biochemistry because powerful intercellular chemical messages may be turned off or on by electrical excitation of the cell membrane.

In the 1940s, Roger Sperry performed surgical experiments with fish and amphibia to observe the regrowth of specific functional connections in the brain after nerves had been cut and rearranged (see NERVE CONNECTIONS: HOW THEY ARE FORMED; BRAIN

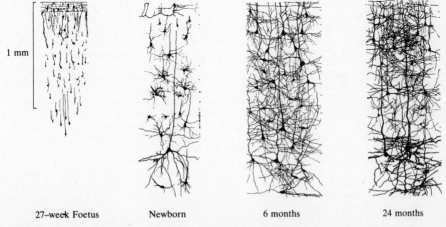

Embryo Brains

Early Foetal Brain

M
CH
H
BS
2 mm
5 weeks

M
CH
T
H
BS
2 mm
6½ weeks

M
CH
T
H
BS
5 mm
10 weeks

Newborn

Adult

Slow Maturation of Interneurones and Long Association Fibres

Foetus

2  4  6  8 10 12   2  3  4  5      10      15
        Months                              Years

Babbling

Protolanguage First Words

Fluent Speech

Fluent reading

Writing

Number of words in vocabulary

10  100  1000

Conception
0      2        4        6        8
                              Months

Embryo        Foetus        Infant        Child        Adult

Birth

Growth of Cells in Striate Cortex

1 mm

27-week Foetus        Newborn        6 months        24 months

**Fig. 2.** The cerebral hemispheres appear in the mid-embryo (one month gestation), expanding in mid-foetal stages when cortical neurones multiply. A second surge of hemisphere growth occurs shortly after birth when cortical dendrites grow and glia cells multiply—synapses form at this stage. Cell maturation continues throughout psychological development. CH = Cerebral Hemisphere; T = Thalamus; M = Midbrain; B = Brainstem; C = Cerebellum; H = Hypothalamus.

SCIENCE: SPERRY'S CONTRIBUTION). He proved that nerve networks could re-form well-ordered contacts, without benefit of learning by behavioural trial and error. He also ruled out a number of explanations of how this could happen, such as contact guidance and electrical field hypotheses, and concluded, as Cajal had done, that some unknown chemical 'landmarks' guided the nerve fibre tips to the right location. This 'chemoaffinity' theory has been upheld by subsequent studies, but it has been shown that no gene code can possibly specify, on its own, this cell-to-cell precision of nerve mappings in such well-ordered arrays as the projections of the visual field. The intricate interconnected anatomy of the brain is formed as a result of the multiplying effects of many choices in cell differentiation that are governed by genes acting in the context of development. To effect this, there is much negotiation—a sorting or editing of connections, with removal of many, so that the remainder take up exactly right neighbourhood relations inside an overall array oriented approximately by chemical field markers that were set out early in the embryo period.

Step-by-step, in a program that keeps reference to the polarized symmetry of the body, the cells of the embryo nervous system multiply, migrate, grow axons and dendrites, and then form synaptic contacts. At each step there is either a potential excess with selective activation of those chosen to develop, or an actual exhuberant over-production of elements, followed by a selective elimination that leaves an effective arrangement, as in Darwinian evolution of species. Some cell lineages divide more than others and leave more offspring; many cells die after migrating; axons branch out widely, then most of the branches are pruned off and digested by phagocytes; only a part of the huge population of cell contacts are retained to form mature synaptic junctions that can effectively transmit nerve discharges. The multiplication, migration, and survival of neuroblasts, the growth and pruning away of axons and the reinforcement or suppression of synapses are decided by the molecular compositions of the surrounding media and nerve cell membranes. Trophic or inhibitory factors are produced by many types of cell, including non-neural supporting cells (glia) in the central nervous system. The glia make up a scaffold that guides migrating neuroblasts and the creeping of axon growth cones, and they assist in the maturation of axons and synapses. Within this tapestry of interacting components, nerve-cells take many forms and become differentiated chemically. They come to contribute different patterns of electrical and chemical activity to the system.

The forces of selection that shape the nervous system and weed out unwanted elements are created at first inside the body and in the spontaneously active nerve net, but in foetal and postnatal stages the brain is increasingly open to selective influences that enter the electrical traffic of the young brain from outside, through the sensory nerves. Chemical communication with the mother through the placenta significantly affects brain development in utero, and subtle refinement of brain structures may also take place in response to gustatory, mechanical, touch, and auditory stimulation. The foetus begins to have some control of this stimulation by moving to change posture, to displace limbs, and to swallow amniotic fluid.

At first the intercellular 'talk' that animates nerve-cell interactions is spontaneously generated or intrinsic to the brain. Coupling or competition between active nerve-cells at one place can be reproduced at remote locations to regulate the layout of contacts being formed elsewhere in the brain. But recent research has shown that sorting out of the most refined precision in sensory and motor projection systems depends on the timing and spatial arrangement of external stimuli. When an animal orients a well-formed receptor array, like the retina of the eye, the patterning of stimuli due to structure in the environment is translated into patterns of nerve excitation. Features like the edges of objects and the velocities of patches of light give order to nerve activity. This order enters into the editing and sorting process that grows the finest sensory integrative connections in the young brain. This explains why soon after birth a baby is so avid for visual stimulation with a fair degree of pattern in it, and why babies regulate their looking behaviour as they do. The great improvement in selectivity and discrimination of looking during the first month and a half of a baby's life requires the extra information about the state of eye-to-brain connections which structured retinal stimulation provides.

At birth the human being enters a new world with vastly greater opportunities for experience. New forces on a body no longer floating, new levels and qualities of sound, new material taken in by mouth, air breathed by the lungs and bringing in new substances and micro-organisms, new stimulation of the surface of the body, and the immense range of new visual information give the unfinished circuits of the cortex a fresh set of criteria for selective retention of functional nerve connections. More changes occur in the cellular structure of the cortex in the first six months after birth than at any other time in development. A large proportion of the millions of axon collaterals spanning the hemispheres and bridging the gap between them are eliminated, segregating intra- and interhemispheric association systems (Fig. 3). Dendrites branch out from large cortical cells and receive astronomical numbers of synapses (Fig. 2). Connections by way of nerve tracts that link subcortical nuclei to cortex, cortex area to cortex area, and cortex to motor systems of the brainstem and cord are made more precise and more effective. These early postnatal building processes, and their continuation into childhood, create the essential anatomical and physiological basis for refined perception with precise and powerful motor con-

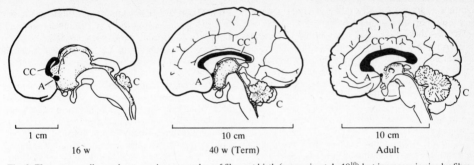

**Fig. 3.** The corpus callosum has a maximum number of fibres at birth (approximately $10^{10}$) but increases in size by fibre thickening, and myelin deposition, after a majority are lost in early infancy. A = Anterior Commissure; CC = Corpus Callosum; C = Cerebellum.

trol. They permit the elaboration of psychological representations or cognitive programs that give predictive mastery of events and objects in the world remote from the body.

Although these changes receive essential information from stimuli through sense organs, all of them continue to be guided by processes generated inside the brain. The control from within continues, as in embryo stages, to make selective hook-ups between converging neural elements that bear excitation from the receptors, leaving the greater part of potential linkages between convergent systems to be discarded. Thus, for example, in the selection of the precise cortical circuits necessary for binocular stereoptic perception of depth, which happens in a human baby about six months after birth, the choice of functional synapses that contribute to the detection of interocular disparities (differences between the retinal images) depends both on the coincidence of stimulus patterns from the two eyes and on a centrifugal activation of the receiving cell, by way of inputs to the cortex from the reticular formation of the stem of the brain. This corresponds to the observation that a baby has to be alert and seeking experience to benefit from the education that visual patterns give to the two eyes at this critical stage. Controlled movements of the eyes in precise unison are also vital to bring corresponding stimuli in register. It has been found that the visual cortex of girl babies gain binocular discrimination about two weeks ahead of boy babies, which indicates that, at some stage, sex hormones had an influence on the readying of these areas for visual information—possibly it is testosterone, produced in male infants for a few weeks after birth, that delays the process of cortical cell maturation.

The biggest developments in perception and in the formation of cognitive strategies that link perception to voluntary action, giving clear purpose to movements, undoubtedly occur in infancy or early childhood. That is the time when serious deprivation such as that due to blindness, deafness, limblessness, or to lack of affectionate care, can distort the growth of the brain most seriously. For example, defects in the optics or motor control of an eye (as in squint) cause the cortical connections of that eye to be pushed out of action by the more coherent and regulated input of the other eye. Deprivation of all humane care and emotional support may cause mental deformity—even large-scale anatomical abnormalities in the brain.

There is good evidence that the mechanism of brain growth operating before birth and in infancy is continuous with the mechanism for the longer and permanently impressionable function of learning from experience throughout life. Brain scientists are now hopeful that they may actually observe the anatomical changes that explain how we remember what we have experienced and how we keep the intricate images of movement that enable us to gain unconscious skill in the use of our bodies. But there is increasing evidence that the *self*-organizing processes of brain tissue formation continue to have a hand in even the most specialized and culturally elaborated acquisitions of learning. There are regions of the cerebral cortex in the foetus that appear to be specially formed to engage in cultural life and acquire traditional skills (Figs. 2 and 4).

The cerebral hemispheres, one of the last brain areas to develop, appear in the early foetus and increase rapidly in size in mid-foetal stages as nerve-cells are multiplied in the still membranous cortex. A second 4-fold increase in bulk takes place in the last two months of gestation and continues into the first few months of infancy (Fig. 2). This is due, not to multiplication of cortical neurones, but to their branching and to the formation of the first connections that integrate the powerful cortical integrating tissues with the rest of the brain to make conscious perception, voluntary action, and intelligent learning possible.

The cells of the neocortex, generated round the cavities of the cerebral hemispheres (ventricles), move into the cortex between fifteen and twenty-five weeks after gestation. This phase is a crucial first step in the building of higher psychological functions. Immature neuroblasts migrate in waves to make a stratum called the cortical plate, later arrivals passing through earlier migrants so that the youngest cells are towards the outside of the hemispheres. This flow of neuroblasts into the cortical plate proceeds at different rates in different parts, the last parts to receive a full complement of potential neurones, at six months after gestation, being areas that will attain mature tissue structure years later, towards adolescence. Cells in cortex and subcortex that are dedicated to one psychological role start as neighbours in the periventicular germ layer, or even derive from the same stem neuroblast cell.

Late migrating components of the hemispheres tend to left–right asymmetry (Fig. 4). How hemispheric asymmetry begins and how it relates to gene-controlled asymmetries in the chemistry and immunological properties of cells widespread in the brain remains to be worked out. It is known that abnormal migration, in the left hemisphere, of one late contingent of cortical and thalamic neurones related to the perisylvian area, where temporal and parietal lobes meet, can lead to *dyslexia, a defect in language ability that makes it very difficult for a person of otherwise normal intelligence to learn to read and write. This is an example of a brain development fault beginning before birth that shows up only years later, in school performance. Another late maturing area is the prefrontal cortex. Research with monkeys has shown that memorizing the spatial arrangement of things for future reference, when action must be delayed, is a mind function that changes with age; it completes as a monkey nears sexual maturity. Monkeys less than one year old use one mental strategy, in the lower lateral parts of the frontal lobe, to keep the memory of where they saw some food hidden. After three years, the same task needs the upper lateral prefrontal cortex, in combination with deep nuclei toward the midline of the brain. Transformation of psychological processes as new brain parts arrive at functional maturity confers a plasticity of function so that a child can partly recover from loss of brain tissue by injury or disease (SEE PLASTICITY IN THE NERVOUS SYSTEM). The developments also explain why injury of a given part of the cortex can have different effects in children and adults.

After birth, brain development depends on how patterns of stimulation from the outside world meet the varying inner states of brain activity. Stimuli to the infant are regulated both by the infant's movements and by the behaviour of caretakers who mediate between the environment and the infant, and the immature brain has powerful control of this caretaker behaviour, especially through emotional expression. Indeed, the most precociously mature functions of a young child's brain are those that communicate needs, feelings, and motives to other persons, and that lead them to present the world to the child in precisely regulated ways.

In future research, brain science will be concerned with breaking through the veil of ignorance that still conceals how developments in human brain tissue over the years of childhood relate to psychological maturation. In this phenomenon, unique in developmental biology, the state of morphogenetic regulators in an immature organism depends upon the affections and interests of more mature conscious beings, and upon the way the brains of these beings from the preceding generation have been programmed with cultural rituals and beliefs in an earlier childhood. Growing human brains require cultivation by intimate communication with older human brains. Thus are built the powerful collaborations of human society.

Anthropologists and psychologists consider language the hallmark of human kind. It permits symbolic communication without which traditions of belief and understanding could not be built up. It powerfully aids processes of thought and reasoning, even if it is not entirely responsible for these great glories of the human mind. There was, therefore, some surprise when brain scientists announced the discovery that territories of the left temporal and parietal lobes, which are essential for language understanding in the great majority of adult humans (Fig. 4), are already asymmetric in a human foetus of twenty-four weeks gestational age—four months before birth. Although quite indeterminate as to which language it will learn, the human brain is set to acquire some kind of language long before it hears a single word. Complementary pre-adaptations or readiness in structure are seen in different cortical regions of the right hemisphere which seems, indeed, to be slightly ahead of the left hemisphere in development during foetal stages. These underlie this hemisphere's subsequent superiority in perception of form, in visuo-constructive skills and in other schematic processes that are of obvious importance in the development of technology and habits of interpersonal and co-operative life. The nerve-cell interactions responsible for postnatal changes in left and right halves of the brain relate directly to those neuroembryogenic processes which form cortical territories in the late foetus and in infancy, when cultural experience is only a remote factor in a future environment.

In the mature brain, detailed information about perceptions, memories, and fine motor co-ordinations can only pass over the interhemispheric space by a massive bridge of fibres called the corpus callosum (see SPLIT-BRAIN AND THE MIND). This structure develops in foetal stages, increasing in size from its first appearance at ten weeks of gestation until it has over a billion ($10^9$) fibres at birth (Fig. 3). In the next three months, there is a decrease in size as a large proportion of this huge population of callosal axons is eliminated. This weeding out confines contacts between the hemispheres to certain cortical zones, separating groups of cells that send axons over the corpus callosum from other groups that send axons forward and backward, inside one hemisphere. In the mature brain, the cortex is composed of columnar territories of uniform size, and interconnections

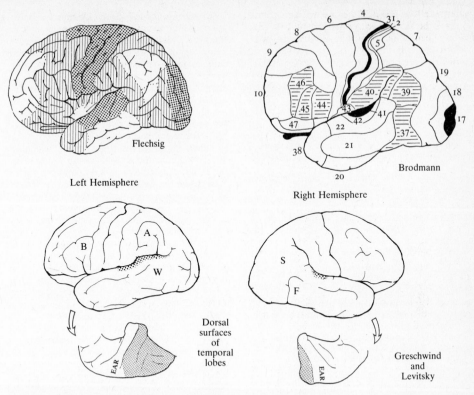

Flechsig

Left Hemisphere

Brodmann

Right Hemisphere

Dorsal
surfaces
of
temporal
lobes

Greschwind
and
Levitsky

**Fig. 4.** Top Left: Flechsig's map of cortical development (myelin deposition round nerve fibres). Stippled areas are mature at birth; shaded areas mature in early childhood; unshaded areas mature later.

Top Right: Brodmann's map of cortical areas. Shaded areas are unique to humans, tend to asymmetry, and are identified with learned cultural skills.

Below: Left and right hemispheres differ anatomically; auditory association areas (stippled) are larger on the left. Psychological disorders after brain lesion depend on the area and hemisphere damaged; A = Angular gyrus, important in reading; B = Broca's motor speech area; W = Wernicke's receptive speech area. The right hemisphere has territories more developed for spatial abilities (S) and for recognition of faces (F). The anatomic basis for these asymmetries is laid down in foetal stages.

between its parts, and with structures deeper in the brain, are arranged so they link columns into ordered systems. This orderly anatomy clears in infancy when redundant axons are eliminated and synaptic fields are sorted out, a process which forms the basis for sharp perceptions and precisely skilled movements. From four months after birth the interhemispheric bridge gains in bulk as its fibres receive a sheath of myelin. Interhemispheric communication matures in step with the development of mature synaptic arrays in different cortical areas over the first decade or so of childhood. Differences in the size and form of the corpus callosum in adults have been shown to relate to differences in hemispheric representation of cognitive abilities and to handedness.

It is now clear that the anatomy and function of human cerebral cortices are very variable. People differ in the pattern of their mental abilities because their brains grow in different forms. Males tend to differ from females, left-handers from

right-handers and architects from psychologists. Some of this diversity of human minds, and their temperaments and aptitudes, will be preprogrammed in a great variety of outcomes of gene expression in nerve tissue development, but the same processes are also influenced by intrauterine and postnatal environments. Among the influential factors are hormones, especially sex hormones, nutrition, and state of health of the mother during pregnancy, chemical and immunological factors, viral infections, epilepsy, and trauma. A pregnant woman who takes psychoactive drugs or alcohol can be changing the development of her child's brain. Particular risks are associated with birth— the brain of a foetus or premature infant is sensitive to its chemical and physical environment which must be regulated inside narrow limits.

We are brought by recent findings to see the brain with new interest. This bewildering part of us is difficult to observe. It is still largely a *terra incognita*, as remote as Mars but greatly more relevant to our being. The more we learn of brain growth the more trust we gain in the belief that even our most cherished human qualities have a self-maintaining fitness. The process of brain growth may reasonably be said to be the source of our motives. We need to know more about how experience and practice give fulfilment to these most remarkable products of evolution.     C. T.

Changeux, J. P. (1985). *Neuronal Man: The Biology of Mind*. New York.

Dobbing, J. (1981). The later development of the brain and its vulnerability. In David, J. A. and Dobbing, J. (eds.), *Scientific Foundations of Paediatrics*, 2nd edn., pp. 744–59. London.

Gaze, R. M. (1970). *Formation of Nerve Connections*. New York.

Goldman-Rakic, P. S. (1985). Toward a neuroembryology of cognitive development. In Mehler, J. and Fox, R. (eds.), *Neonate Cognition: Beyond the Blooming, Buzzing Confusion*, pp. 285–306. Hillsdale, New Jersey.

Mark, R. F. (1974). *Memory and Nerve Cell Connections*. London.

Rakic, P. (1972). Mode of cell migration to the superficial layers of foetal monkey neocortex. *Journal of Comparative Neurology*, **145**, 61–84.

Singer, W. (1986). The brain as a self-organizing system. *European Archives of Psychiatry and Neurological Sciences*. (Edition in Honour of D. Ploog.)

Sperry, R. (1965). Embryogenesis of behavioural nerve nets. In De Hann, R. L. and Ursprung, H. (eds.), *Organogenesis*, pp. 161–86. New York.

Trevarthen, C. (1986). Neuroembryology and the development of perceptual mechanisms. In Falkner, F. and Tanner, J. M. (eds.), *Human Growth*, 2nd edn., vol. 2, pp. 301–83. New York.

Trevarthen, C. (1979). Brain development and the growth of psychological functions. In Sants, J. (ed.), *Developmental Psychology and Society*, pp. 46–95. London.

Yakovlev, P. I. and Lecours, A. R. (1967). The myelogenetic cycles of regional maturation of the brain. In Minkowski, A. (ed.), *Regional Development of the Brain in Early Life*, pp. 3–70. Oxford.

**BRAIN FUNCTION AND AWARENESS.** It is something of a paradox that the most exacting studies of brain function are apt to come from research on animals, whose behaviour we can study with increasing sophistication, but who cannot communicate with us very fluently. In contrast, studies of human brain function derived from the clinic are apt to depend on just those methods of communication that we are precluded from using with animals. That is, most clinical tests of psychological capacity of human patients involve considerable verbal interchange between the patient and the examiner, often expressed in a form intended directly to reveal the patient's disorders. So, in a classical and routine examination of visual capacity, the patient is asked, 'Tell me what you see', 'How many spots do you see?', 'What letter is it?', and so forth. Or the patient with a memory disorder is asked, 'Tell me what you can remember from this morning', 'Do you recognize me?', 'What words can you recall from the list you just read?'

In studying animals' vision or memory, it is often assumed that we are simply transforming the questions we usually ask of human patients into an equivalent form, albeit one that is rather more cumbersome to transmit. Examined more closely, however, the resemblance is less than close. The animal reveals his capacity by displaying a discrimination between stimuli or events, which he has usually been trained to demonstrate by following some particular rule, and for which he is rewarded. The human subject also discriminates between stimuli or events, of course; but often the clinician does not study the discrimination as such, but rather the subject's commentary upon it, such as 'Yes, now I see the flash,' or 'I can see the letter A in the bottom line.' Even when the verbal response appears to be just an embellishment on, or a short cut to, the discriminative response, serious problems can arise if the subject is unable to render a commentary but nevertheless is capable of making the relevant discrimination—i.e. if he is restricted in the way that an animal is restricted when we study its visual capacity. We refer here not to the relatively trivial difficulty when a subject has, say, an impairment in the mechanics or the organization of speech. Even if a human subject is able to communicate freely and efficiently he may nevertheless be unaware of his own discriminative capacity and hence have nothing to communicate as a commentary.

It is only recently that this distinction, between a capacity and a subject's commentary upon it, has been recognized, and it has thrown light on some persistent puzzles in the comparative study of brain function in human and animal subjects. Two examples can be given. In both instances the differences between the results of research on humans and on other animals appeared to be so great that it was argued that the brains of animals must be organized in a qualitatively different way from human brains, despite the very close anatomical similarity between them.

First, if the region of cerebral cortex to which nerve fibres from the eye ultimately project is removed, animals (unlike humans) can still discriminate visual events, although not as well as normally. This in itself is not surprising, because the eye sends information not only to the so-called 'visual cortex' but also directly to a variety of other structures in the mid-brain and elsewhere. Indeed, the way in which vision is altered after blockage of one of the targets helps one to infer the type of capacity that the remaining targets must have. This residual visual capacity of animals has been studied over several decades, and techniques have been developed for yielding a good description of it. The paradox is that the human brain, while organized anatomically in a way that appears closely similar to the brains of other Primates, is said nevertheless to yield a state of blindness after removal of the 'visual cortex'. (Because the visual field projects upon the visual cortex in a well-known retinotopic manner (see VISUAL SYSTEM: ORGANIZATION), most blindness is in fact commonly restricted to just a certain portion of the visual field, depending upon which part of the visual cortex is damaged, it being rare for the entire visual cortex in both cerebral hemispheres to be damaged). For example, when a light is flashed in the blind field of a human patient, and he is asked whether he sees it, he will say 'no'. A monkey, in contrast, if appropriately trained, will reach out to touch a brief visual stimulus, can locate it accurately in space, and can discriminate between lines of different orientation and between simple shapes. He will pick up even quite minute specks of food if they contrast well with the background.

This difference in outcome puzzled investigators as long ago as the end of the nineteenth century. They appealed to a doctrine of 'encephalization of function' to account for it. This doctrine asserted that, in evolution, visual and other functions somehow migrated to higher and new structures in the brain, so that in man visual function had reached the highest level, namely the visual cortex, whereas in lower animals a greater degree of visual capacity was subserved by lower midbrain or even brain-stem structures. It was a somewhat curious doctrine, because the lower structures do not wither away in man, and therefore one wonders just what role they would have after they had been deprived of their earlier role. Be that as it may, it is only very recently that investigators have actually started to ask their human patients the questions in a form in which one is perforce obliged to ask them of animals. That is, the subject is asked to discriminate between stimuli, using a forced choice method—whether or not he says he can 'see' the stimulus. He is asked to guess, say, whether or not a stimulus occurred, whether it was located at position $A$ or $B$, whether it was a cross or a circle, and so on. Using this approach it has been found that some human subjects with damage to the visual cortex can perform about as well as animals in the absence of such cortex. The subjects themselves may be quite unaware that they are able to perform so well, and indeed surprised to learn that they can, because they say they did not actually 'see' the stimuli. This residual capacity is called 'blindsight'. Of course, pathology in man is varied, and more often than not when visual cortex is damaged, the surrounding tissue is also damaged. Therefore, not all patients with blind fields associated with brain damage show blindsight.

There is an additional aspect to this discovery. The residual capacity in the monkey actually increases as the animal continues to use it; significantly, this improvement does not occur spontaneously, but with practice the region of only partial vision actually contracts. Recently, some human patients with field defects have been shown to have the same benefit: their regions of blindness (if caused by damage to the visual cortex but not, of course, if caused by damage to the eyes themselves) also contract with specialized practice designed to make them give forced-choice responses to visual stimuli in their 'blind' fields. It is not clear how much of this recovery is mediated by the surrounding intact visual cortex, and how much by one of the parallel pathways from the eye to the midbrain. Probably both are involved.

A second example implying differences in the organization of Primates' brains comes from the field of memory defects. Damage to certain midline structures in the human brain can yield a persistent state of profound memory failure. Patients apparently cannot remember fresh experiences for more than a few seconds. Paradoxically, in animals it seemed for a long time that these same midline structures—apparently anatomically identical to those in man—could be dispensed with almost with impunity. No obvious losses of memory or learning capacity appeared to result. The story is similar in some respects to that of blindsight. It has emerged that the sorts of tasks that animals were traditionally taught to test their learning capacity, and which they succeeded in learning and retaining, can also be learned quite well by amnesic patients. Indeed, there is now a large catalogue of tasks that such patients are known to succeed in learning and retaining. They all share one property: in none of them is it necessary actually to ask the patient, 'Do you recognize this?' or 'What do you remember of the task we just saw?' Indeed a patient may acknowledge no memory for the task, even though he succeeded in it. For example, if shown a list of words, and later asked what the words were, he may well say he cannot remember even seeing a list of words. But if shown the first few letters of each of the words and asked to guess what words they stand for, he is likely to produce the very words for which he says he has no 'memory'. Or, to take another example, a patient will show a benefit of having solved a particular jigsaw puzzle by solving it faster the next day (but only the jigsaw he solved before). Amnesic patients can learn such tasks and show good retention over quite long periods—weeks or even months, in fact—although, again, as with blindsight, the capacity is distinct from an acknowledgement of it by the subject. It remains to be seen whether methods of retraining such patients, whose lives are severely crippled by memory impairment, can also be developed. There are at least serious efforts being made along these lines.

Both of these examples have come to light specifically in the context of a paradoxical and deep discrepancy between animal and human clinical research. But there are other examples that come directly out of clinical research. The best known are from work on commissurotomized patients, popularly referred to as '*split-brain' patients. In these, surgeons have severed the connections between the two cerebral hemispheres in order to try to control the spread of uncontrollable epileptic discharges throughout the entire brain. Such patients enable an investigator to direct perceptual information to one or other of the two cerebral hemispheres, and thereby to infer what its capacities are in isolation from the other hemisphere. (For example, by projecting a visual image on to the left half of the retina, only the visual cortex of the left hemisphere is stimulated.) Research with such patients has strongly reinforced an already well-established view, namely that the verbal commentaries require the participation of the left hemisphere (especially in the right-handed subject). But it has also shown, interestingly, that information directed to the right hemisphere can still be used by a patient, even in response to a verbal instruction from the experimenter and even though the patient does not acknowledge his success. Thus, a subject will deny recognizing an object (masked from view) presented to his left hand (which is controlled by the right hemisphere). But at the same time the left hand will correctly select an object from an array if 'instructed' to do so by flashing the name on to the right side of the retina, so that the right hemisphere has access to the word. Of course a vast amount of our everyday activity is carried out without direct awareness: indeed, it would be wasteful actually to reflect on processes that can be dealt with in an automatic way, once they become routine—for example, constriction of the pupil or accommodation of the lens of the eye. A great variety of skilled motor acts, some learned and some not, do not warrant introspection. It is also wasteful to reflect on each occasion when we stop at a traffic-light that we 'remember' red means stop, even though this clearly reflects retention of a learned association. The brain may well reserve for itself only a small proportion of its capacity for those activities that form the corpus of material for the introspector of mental processes. The study of patients with 'blindsight', or of memory without awareness, or of split-brain patients, not only highlights what regions of perception, memory, and other 'cognitive' capacities can be divorced from awareness, but also may allow an empirical analysis of the boundary conditions of those regions.

The examples taken from human clinical research go beyond anything that can be drawn from comparative research with animals. (Although, of course, corresponding regions of the brain can be studied, how can one ask an animal not to discriminate or select a stimulus from an array but to reveal to us whether or not he can 'recognize' it or 'characterize' it?) Even so, some progress along these lines can be seen. Animal investigators in recent years, spurred on in part by the paradoxical discrepancies between their findings and those from the human clinic, have been able to evolve new methods of testing recognition memory in animals. It appears that recognition can be altered independently of an animal's capacity to discriminate stimuli and form simple associations between visual events and reward. But work has scarcely begun on the more fundamental problem of how to allow an animal not only to discriminate or learn and to retain but to acknowledge these acts. And, therefore, while the paradoxical gap

between the results of animal and human brain research may have been reduced, we are left with the even more difficult problems: how would one know whether an animal possesses blindsight and when is an animal aware that he can discriminate? Is a frog or an insect ever aware of such a capacity? That question was raised in the nineteenth century by some of the pioneers of research on the visual cortex, but then afterwards largely ignored. For a long time it appeared that it could be ignored safely—that it might even be a pseudo-problem. But it is difficult to accept that animals, especially advanced Primates, differ so fundamentally from humans that they do not demonstrate the same division between automatic unmonitored acts and those acts that are so effectively monitored as to enable further action to be based upon the knowledge of them. To ask such a question of an animal would appear to require not only the standard methods used to study its discriminative and mnemonic capacities, powerful as they are, but the introduction of a parallel response which could serve as a 'commentary' response, by which the animal could signal its acknowledgement that it has indeed 'seen' the signals, and ultimately might even offer a confidence level. Perhaps the important contribution that animal research has made towards uncovering unsuspected capacities in human patients will be repaid by the development of techniques that will allow us to ask much deeper questions of our animal relations.          L. W.

Beninger, R. J., Kendall, S. B., and Vanderwolf, C. H. (1974). The ability of rats to discriminate their own behaviours. *Canadian Journal of Psychology*, **28**, 79–91.

Cowey, A. (1967). Perimetric study of field defects in monkeys after cortical and retinal ablations. *Quarterly Journal of Experimental Psychology*, **19**, 232–45.

Cowey, A. and Weiskrantz, L. (1963). A perimetric study of visual field defects in monkeys. *Quarterly Journal of Experimental Psychology*, **15**, 91–115.

Gazzaniga, M. S. (1970). *The Bisected Brain*. New York.

Humphrey, N. K. (1970). What the frog's eye tells the monkey's brain. *Brain, Behavior and Evolution*, **3**, 324–37.

Humphrey, N. K. and Weiskrantz, L. (1967). Vision in monkeys after removal of the striate cortex. *Nature*, **215**, 595–7.

Mishkin, M. (1982). A memory system in the monkey. In Broadbent, D. E. and Weiskrantz, L. (eds.), *The Neuropsychology of Cognitive Function*. Royal Society, London.

Paillard, J., Michel, F., and Stelmach, G. (1983). Localization without content: a tactile analogue of 'blind sight'. *Archives of Neurology*, **40**, 548–51.

Perenin, M. T. (1978). Visual function within the hemianopic field following early cerebral hemidecortication in man. II, Pattern discrimination. *Neuropsychologia*, **16**, 696–708.

Perenin, M. T. and Jeannerod, M. (1975). Residual vision in cortically blind hemifields. *Neuropsychologia*, **13**, 1–7.

Perenin, M. T. and Jeannerod, M. (1978). Visual function within hemianopic field following early cerebral hemidecortication in man. I, Spatial localization. *Neuropsychologia*, **16**, 1–13.

Pöppel, E., Held, R., and Frost, D. (1973). Residual visual function after brain wounds involving the central visual pathways in man. *Nature*, **243**, 295–6.

Singer, W., Zihl, J., and Pöppel, E. (1977). Subcortical control of visual thresholds in humans: evidence for modality specific and retinotopically organized mechanisms of selective attention. *Experimental Brain Research*, **29**, 173–90.

Sperry, R. W. (1974). Lateral specialization in the surgically separated hemispheres. In Schmitt, F. O. and Worden, F. G. (eds.), *Neuroscience: Third Study Program*. Cambridge, Massachusetts.

Squire, L. R. and Zola-Morgan, S. (1983). The neurology of memory: the case for correspondence between the findings for human and nonhuman primate. In Deutsch, A. (ed.), *The physiological basis of memory* (2nd edn.). London.

Travel, D. and Damasio, A. R. (1985). Knowledge without awareness: an autonomic index of facial recognition by prosopagnosics. *Science*, **228**, 1,453–5.

Torjussen, T. (1976). Residual function in cortically blind hemifields. *Scandinavian Journal of Psychology*, **17**, 320–2.

Warrington, E. K. and Weiskrantz, L. (1982). Amnesia: a disconnection syndrome? *Neuropsychologia*, **20**, 233–48.

Weiskrantz, L. (1961). Encephalization and the scotoma. In Thorpe, W. H. and Zangwill, O. L. (eds.), *Current Problems in Animal Behaviour*, pp. 30–58. London and New York.

Weiskrantz, L. (1972). Behavioural analysis of the monkey's visual nervous system. (Review lecture.) *Proceedings of the Royal Society*, Series B, **182**, 427–55.

Weiskrantz, L. (1977). Trying to bridge some neuropsychological gaps between monkey and man. *British Journal of Psychology*, **68**, 431–3.

Weiskrantz, L. (1980). Varieties of residual experience. (Eighth Sir Frederic Bartlett Lecture.) *Quarterly Journal of Experimental Psychology*, **32**, 365–86.

Weiskrantz, L. (1985). Introduction: categorization, cleverness, and consciousness. In Weiskrantz, L. (ed.), *Animal intelligence*, pp. 3–19. Oxford.

Weiskrantz, L. (1986). *Blindsight: a case study and implications*. Oxford.

Weiskrantz, L. and Cowey, A. (1970). Filling in the scotoma: a study of residual vision after striate cortex lesions in monkeys. In Stellar, E. and Sprague, J. M. (eds.), *Progress in Physiological Psychology*, Vol. 3, pp. 237–60. New York and London.

Weiskrantz, L., Warrington, E. K., Sanders, M. D., and Marshall, J. (1974). Visual capacity in the hemianopic field following a restricted occipital ablation. *Brain*, **97**, 709–28.

Zihl, J. (1980). 'Blindsight': improvement of visually guided eye movements by systematic practice in patients with cerebral blindness. *Neuropsychologia*, **18**, 71–7.

Zihl, J. (1981). Recovery of visual functions in patients with cerebral blindness. *Experimental Brain Research*, **44**, 159–69.

Zihl, J. and von Cramon, D. (1985). Visual field recovery from scotoma in patients with postgeniculate damage: a review of 55 cases. *Brain*, **108**, 335–65.

**BRAIN MANIPULATION, THE ETHICS OF.** Brain manipulation—the changing of people's motivation or personality by physico-chemical action on the mechanisms of the brain—is at least as old as the discovery of alcohol. The basic ethical and philosophical problems are as well illustrated in principle by the old-fashioned phenomenon of drunkenness as by the more subtle and bizarre changes that can be produced by modern drugs or brain surgery. In each case we have changes not just in the ability of the mind to make the body serve its purposes but also in the process and the purposes of 'minding' itself. The affected individual may find his priorities changed, his ability to think, remember, and plan disturbed, and his moods and relationships distorted or incoherent.

Such phenomena would be surprising if we thought of the mind as related to the brain in the way that, say, a driver is related to a car. Physical damage to the car might leave the driver unable to achieve what he wants; but it would not be expected directly to change what he wants, let alone his ability to think about it. With a different sort of thought model of the human being, however, the facts make sense in a way that attaches an even heavier responsibility to the manipulator. All the evidence to date suggests that the mind is much more intimately related to the brain than a driver to his car. The relationship is two-way, and has been likened to that between a message and the ink in which it is written, or between the equation being solved by a computer and the electronic workings of its transistors. Any change in the message must mean a change in the distribution of ink; any change in the equation must mean a change in the activity of the transistors. Conversely, some (though not all) of the physical changes we could make in the ink pattern would necessarily alter the message; and some (though not all) of the physical changes we could make in the computer would *ipso facto* alter the equation being solved. The one, we say, is 'embodied' in the other.

The working assumption of most brain scientists is that our conscious experience is 'embodied' in the activity of our brains in a rather similar sense: so that no change can take place in someone's conscious experience or personality without some corresponding physical change taking place in his brain. Conversely, it would be expected that some (though not all) of the physical changes we could make in his brain would *ipso facto* alter his conscious experience, or even the very structure of his personality. Thus the brain manipulator has the heavy responsibility of shaping not only what his patient can do, but also what sort of person he is.

Once this is recognized the ethical issues fall into place, in the same class as those raised by *education and other ways of shaping and reshaping personality and motivation. Physical manipulation of the brain can be classified as a drastic alternative to more conventional methods of determining what sort of people we are. The essential ethical constraints—over and above those governing surgical or pharmacological intervention in general—are those that should inform and limit the practice of education. The same deep-going tests of the manipulator's motivation are applicable, such as compassion, respect both for what the other is and for what he can become, and the absence of self-seeking hubris. These, if accepted, would rule out all dictatorial abuse of drugs or neurosurgery to enslave fellow human beings.

It should be added that although it is already possible to demonstrate animals made hungry, thirsty, maternal, or sexy by electrical stimulation of the brain, such techniques are bound in practice to be crude and poorly selective. According to the neuroscientist Elliot Valenstein, 'the belief that we can stimulate or destroy a given region of the brain and reliably produce only one type of behaviour is sheer fantasy'. It seems fair to say that if a dictatorial government wanted to control its population, it would be likely to find some of the older-fashioned methods more cost-effective than either mass brain-implantation or drug-administration.

Bracketing brain manipulation with education, rather than with something like heart surgery, should not blind us to one important difference between the two. In the upbringing and education of children the shaping process uses and (ideally) respects the subject's conscious mental processes; manipulation is exercised (quite ethically) at the *personal* level. Brain manipulation, however, whether by surgery, current injection, or drugs, is carried on at an impersonal level. Quite apart from the crudity of the means available, this introduces a factor of great ethical significance which has no parallel in education. It may be best illustrated by an analogy.

A human brain after many years of life can be compared with a chess-board (of gigantic complexity) on which the layout of the pieces reflects the history and identity of one particular game. Normal interpersonal communication, as in education, can be likened to the making of moves that respect the rules of chess, and so preserve the continuity and identity of the game. By contrast, physical brain manipulation can be compared with the removal or addition or displacement of chessmen without regard to the rules. The end result might or might not be a legitimately playable game; but, in a sense that could be important, the play would not in general be a continuation of the same game.

The corresponding question in any particular case of brain manipulation, then, is whether the individual who emerges from the exercise is still (for ethical purposes) *the same individual*. In the most radical (and purely fictional) case of complete 'brain transplantation', explored by H. G. Wells in 'The Story of the Late Mr Elvesham', the answer would presumably be 'no'. In general it would obviously be a matter of degree. All of our brains lose a small fraction of their nerve-cell population daily by natural decay, without disrupting the effective continuity of our personalities. (One might compare this with the amount of ink that can be lost from a written message without changing what it says.) The alternative, however, which may have to be faced in extreme cases of irreversible brain damage, would be that the life of the original

individual had effectively been terminated. In that case, even though a viable human being were to emerge from the operation, it is arguable that such brain manipulation should be bracketed for ethical purposes with homicide or murder.

See also DETERMINISM AND FREE WILL.   D. M. M.

Ellison, C. W. (ed.) (1978). *Modifying Man: Implications and Ethics*. Washington, DC.
MacKay, D. M. (1979). *Human Science and Human Dignity*. London.
Valenstein, E. S. (1973). *Brain Control: A Critical Examination of Brain Stimulation and Psychosurgery*. New York.

**BRAIN SCANS.** See IMAGES OF THE BRAIN IN ACTION.

**BRAIN SCIENCE AND THE SOUL.** See SOUL, BRAIN SCIENCE AND THE.

**BRAIN SCIENCE: SPERRY'S CONTRIBUTION.** Roger Sperry, Trustee professor emeritus of psychobiology at the California Institute of Technology, is famous for experimental studies of how brain circuits are formed, and for research on mental activities after the connecting tracts between the cerebral hemispheres have been cut. He worked for his doctorate in close association with the biophysicist Paul Weiss, who had developed surgery to analyse how connections between nerves and muscles are patterned, and had demonstrated that the movement patterns of amphibia develop spontaneously in the embryo. By transplanting limb buds and re-routeing motor nerves, Weiss found that salamanders could regain an excellent sequential control of their limb muscles, the nerves making connections that matched, not the locomotor usefulness of the movements, but the embryonic origins of the different muscles. Sperry felt there must be a more specific and refined control of the growth of nerve circuits than any existing theory could explain, and that the intricate networks of the brain must result from a highly differentiated genetic coding for nerve contacts. He transplanted the insertions of extensor and flexor muscles of rats, or cut and re-routed their nerve supply, and then observed their limb movements. He reported that the rats' motor system was almost completely lacking in plasticity: except for some editing out of false moves of the forelimbs, central motor command was inflexible. The rats' wrongly connected nerves or muscles continued to produce maladaptive movements.

In the early 1940s, with Karl *Lashley, Sperry published a paper on the effects of thalamic lesions on olfactory learning in the rat, yet his main endeavour now was to explore the laws that fitted nerves into functional networks in development. He confirmed the finding by Robert Matthey in Switzerland and Leon Stone at Yale that after a newt's eye had been dissected from the head and replaced, retina and optic nerve would re-connect to the brain and normal vision would return. Sperry observed the behaviour of the animals more closely; and he showed that when a transplanted eye had been rotated through 180°, movements to catch food after recovery of vision were precisely as predicted by the theory that cells at each retinal point had re-connected themselves to the same place in the brain as before surgery. All orienting reactions were the reverse of correct, like those of a person who has just put on inverting prisms, though for newts adaptive visuo-motor co-ordination was not regained. This proved that the routeing of nerves, beyond a random tangle in the re-joined optic nerve into the brain centres, was precisely guided by some pathfinding principle in which learning played no part.

Later experiments on amphibia showed that regeneration of links from eye to brain, and from brain to the muscles of the eyes and fins—both of which make intricate movements in these species—obeyed the law of innate specification of connections. With Norma Dupree, a fellow biologist, whom he married in 1949, he carried out an important study at the Lerner Marine Laboratory, Bimini, West Indies, which found evidence suggesting that motor nerves preferred to regenerate connections to their own muscles. This suggested that the salamanders Weiss had studied were atypical. Later Richard Mark, working with Sperry in California, showed this to be the case.

In 1950 Sperry reported that fish and newts with one eye removed and the other either inverted or transposed to the opposite side of the head behaved in a peculiar way. They remained quiet, if not caused to swim, but spun in accelerating circles as soon as they moved. This behaviour was affected only by removal of the midbrain, where the optic nerves terminate, and was unchanged by removal of the labyrinths (organs detecting accelerations and gravity) or severance of the oculomotor muscles. Sperry concluded that the midbrain is the site of a predictive adjustment of visual perception triggered by the impulse to turn. The signal on the retina that the external world was displacing relative to the animal's head, was now reversed along the front/back axis by surgery. It signalled that the world was receding, and the locomotor system then worked harder to catch up, like a kitten chasing the tail of another kitten running twice as fast. Sperry proposed that there is an internal brain signal, which he termed a 'corollary discharge from efference' that matches visual effects normally consequent on each locomotor displacement for its direction and speed. He pointed out that such a 'central kinetic factor' would help explain both perception of self-movement and the constancy of perception of the spatial layout of the world while in motion. He had independently and simultaneously discovered the integrative principle co-ordinating perception with movement that von Holst and Mittelstaedt in Germany had found in the reflex optomotor responses of the praying mantis. They called it the 'reafference principle'

and explained it, by the same mechanism as Sperry, under the name of 'efference-copy'.

Sperry then returned to his old idea that many fundamental laws of perception are reflections of inherent and precisely structured mechanisms for patterning movements. In an essay entitled 'Neurology and the Mind-Brain Problem' (1952) he argued that motor output in free behaviour gave better evidence of the neural basis of integrative behaviour than did the enumeration of simple and unnatural reactions by largely inactive subjects to physical variation in imposed stimuli. He also questioned the anticonnectionist views of Lashley and the *Gestaltists, and indicated that associationist *learning theories are to be attacked by examining how patterns of response are co-ordinated, rather than by postulating field-processes in the sensory cortex. He showed prophetic insight with regard to questions now being tackled by systems engineers and cognitive scientists trying to model *intelligence with computational machines, and also to those questions of interest to psychologists who seek to relate categories of perceptual processing to the problems the brain has to solve if it is to initiate movements that use terrain or objects efficiently.

Karl Lashley, Wolfgang *Köhler, and others believed form recognition to be the result of field effects or interference configurations generated in a random cortical net, or of transitory electrical or magnetic fields arising between nerve-cells in the grey matter. To test these ideas, Sperry and his students made minute criss-cross cuts under microscopic control throughout the visual cortex of cats, riddled it with tantalum wires to short-circuit any electrical fields, and implanted leaves of mica to interrupt local transverse currents. Then they subjected the cats to extreme tests of visual form discrimination. They found virtually no losses in vision, and concluded that form perception must depend on the passage of information in and out of small cortical territories, presumably by specific neuronal linkage with cells below the grey matter.

A graduate student, Ronald Myers, invented a delicate operation to cut the cross-over of visual nerves ('optic chiasm') under a cat's brain, so that each eye would lead to only one cerebral hemisphere. In 1953 Myers and Sperry reported not only transfer of the visual pattern memory between the hemispheres in chiasm-sectioned cats, but also that this transfer did not occur when the huge fibre bridge between the hemispheres, the *corpus callosum, was cut. The term *split-brain, with which Sperry's name is associated, refers to this operation and the research to which it has given rise. The operation proved that specific fibre connections could transmit learning, and further challenged Lashley's 'mass action' theory of brain systems.

Sperry and his associates made many experiments on the divided awareness and learning of split-brain cats, confirming the role of the commissural fibres in memory formation, and he also explored systems by which vision or touch controls voluntary limb movements. The investigations were extended to monkeys: like cats, these showed independent learning in the two brain halves after complete section of the corpus callosum, and experiments found that vision and touch crossed in different parts of the commissure. Colwyn Trevarthen showed that split-brain monkeys could learn two conflicting visual discriminations simultaneously; in other words, they could have double consciousness.

In the cat, each disconnected hemisphere directed movements of the whole body, but the motor system of split-brain monkeys was partly divided. They were both less willing to respond with movements of the hand on the same side as the seeing hemisphere and, if forced into action, were clumsy with this combination, as if they became blind each time they moved. Clearly, when the two halves of the cortex were disconnected, only crossed pathways linking each half of the cortex to the opposite hand could guide the fine exploratory and manipulative movements of a monkey's fingers.

Split-brain animals were used to reveal shifts of attention between the two separated halves of the cortex, and the effects on perception of *sets to move in particular ways. Thereby fresh interest was aroused in the global design of the mammalian brain for awareness, learning, and voluntary action. The minimum territory of cortex needed to retain learned control of the hands by touch or vision was determined by progressively removing all other cortex from one hemisphere of a trained split-brain animal around the primary touch or visual area until losses occurred. The other half brain was left intact, so that behaviour could continue as usual outside the training situation where experiences were confined to the operated side.

Between 1950 and the mid-70s Sperry continued to direct research on the formation of nerve circuits in lower vertebrates. He published some twenty articles explaining and defending his theory that most cerebral functions are determined genetically by some chemical or physiochemical coding of pathways and connections. New methods for following nerve growth have revealed competitive epigenetic processes involved in sorting out functional connections while they were growing, but so far every attempt to overthrow the chemoaffinity theory by experiment has reached a point where some such selective principle has to be invoked. Sperry has certainly won his battle against the theories of the 1930s that conceived complex psychological functions to be entirely the result of experiences which impose selective influences on random and infinitely plastic nerve nets.

General articles on experiments with cats and monkeys expressed Sperry's belief that learning itself is the consequence of submicroscopic modification in cerebral circuits whose anatomical design is pre-wired according to genetic instructions. The latter set adaptive goals and give the organism categories of experience as well as intricately coordinated forms of action.

Around 1960, a Los Angeles neurosurgeon, Joseph Bogen, observed with Sperry that the behaviour of split-brain monkeys outside test situations indicated that division of the commissures left motivation, consciousness, and voluntary action virtually unimpaired. Bogen pointed out that the operation offered promise of relief from debilitating epileptic fits which involved reverberation of discharges across the corpus callosum. In 1962 Bogen and Philip Vogel performed a total neocortical commissurotomy on a man who suffered frequent epileptic attacks, and Sperry and a graduate student, Michael Gazzaniga, were able to apply systematic psychological tests. After 1965 a growing team of researchers under Sperry's close direction, including Jerre Levy, Robert Nebes, Harold Gordon and Dahlia and Eran Zaidel, explored the state of divided and asymmetric mental activity in a small population of commissurotomy patients. The implications of the findings reached into all areas of human mental life, and excited immense public and scholarly interest. An account of the initial findings was given in Vinken, P. J. and Bruyn, G. W. (eds.) (1969), *Handbook of Clinical Neurology*, vol. 4 (Amsterdam).

From this research came support for concepts of inherent modes of thought and asymmetric involvement of the brain in rational/verbal thinking, non-verbalizable imagery, and conceivably also mystical experience (see SPLIT-BRAIN AND THE MIND). It stimulated studies of patients with lateralized injuries of the brain and research on the perceptual, cognitive, and motor asymmetries of function in normal subjects. Sperry's hypothesis that the hemispheres are so constructed as to display unlike psychological functions—genetic variation in *handedness, or the lateralization of language, being but two manifestations of human hereditary regulation—caused a reappraisal of the reasons for differences in intellectual and educational performance of different individuals.

Reflection on inherent mental processes in the human brain led Sperry to publish, in 1965, the first of a series of philosophical papers entitled 'Mind, Brain and Humanist Values'. He proposed a new monist theory of mind in which consciousness is conceived as an emergent, self-regulatory property of neural networks, which enables them to achieve certain built-in goals. These define requirements of the mind and psychological values which are given detailed form and direction by the rituals and symbols of tradition.

Sperry's philosophical ideas have proved somewhat controversial but derive great force from the range and depth of his experience in the field of psychobiology. Among his publications have been his chapter, Mechanisms of neural maturation, in Stevens, S. S. (ed.), *Handbook of Experimental Psychology* (New York, 1951); Neurology and the mind–brain problem (1952, *American Scientist*, **40**, 291–312); The eye and the brain (1956, *Scientific American*, **194**, 48–52); The great cerebral commissure (1964, *Scientific Ameri-*

*can*, **210**, 42–52); Embryogenesis of behavioural nerve nets, in Dehaan, R. L. and Ursprung, H. (eds.), *Organogenesis* (New York, 1965); In search of psyche, in Worden, F. G., Swazey, J. P., and Adelman, G. (eds.), *The Neurosciences: paths of discovery* (Cambridge, Massachusetts, 1975); Forebrain commissurotomy and conscious awareness (1977, *Journal of Medicine and Philosophy*, **2**, 101–26); and *Science and Moral Priority* (New York and Oxford, 1982).

See also BRAIN DEVELOPMENT.                                    C. T.

**BRAIN WAVES.** See ELECTROENCEPHALOGRAPHY.

**BRENTANO,** FRANZ (1838–1917). One of the most original figures in the history of philosophy and psychology. In character he was impressive, courageous, even reckless. He was a Roman Catholic priest, but rejected the Pope's infallibility; and his marriage at the age of 42 meant that he had to resign his professorship at the university of Vienna.

Brentano was a man of broad intellectual interests. He is best known for his work in philosophy and psychology, but he also wrote on theology, ethics, and politics. This, as we shall see, was not foreign to his great endeavour in the field of scientific psychology. Brentano was first interested in Aristotelian metaphysics and, though rejecting *Aristotle's system as a whole, he found in it an important starting-point for his later reflections on the value and meaning of knowledge. But, having done away with Aristotelian philosophy, he was also deeply aware of the weakness of the attempts of the psychologists of his time to develop scientific procedures within the framework of philosophical studies. These circumstances, as well as his personal convictions, led him to consider himself as being charged with the mission of reforming philosophy in a fundamental manner. In his view, this mission assumed an 'almost messianic sense' (Spiegelberg, 1960, p. 28).

This peculiar attitude was ultimately motivated by metaphysical concerns. As a result of his reflections on theology, Brentano developed a basically obsessive anxiety about time and eternity; having rejected his religious faith as far as dogmatic contents were concerned, he nevertheless remained deeply troubled by the problems of human destiny which such teachings necessarily raise. Since he could no longer rely on theology, he was bound to search for another life-reference. This he found in *experience*, i.e. in *consciousness. It is therefore not surprising tht he should have devoted his main philosophical effort to the epistemological analysis of the foundations of psychology.

The word 'experience' is misleading because it may be understood either as the content of consciousness in the sense of introspective psychology, or as the perceptual phenomena which make up our empirical knowledge of the external world. As a matter of fact, Brentano succeeded in transcending the classical opposition between immanentism and empiricism by developing an original theory of consciousness that allowed him to escape this well-known dualistic conception of the psychological subject. This he achieved by stressing the fact that the fundamental property of consciousness is *intentionality: every subjective experience can only make sense if it is understood as an *act* of consciousness referred to some object, the latter being either some perceptual content, or some mental construct independent of its object but, once again, necessarily referred to some kind of object. Within such a framework, psychological immanentism is condemned at the outset because, though internal *perception* readily exists in subjective experience, internal *observation* of the introspective kind is plainly impossible, since it requires that particular sort of dualism according to which the subject is at the same time an object for himself. If, further, this postulated 'object' is defined as a 'scientific' one, as in early experimental psychology, the study of experience amounts finally to paradoxical realism, because it is a realism devoid of any empirically definable 'reality'.

Given these difficulties, we must now ask ourselves in which sense Brentano claims to be an empiricist, as testified by his well-known contention that experience is his 'only teacher' and by the significant title of his main work, *Psychologie vom empirischen Standpunkt* (*Psychology from the Empirical Standpoint*) (1874). Empiricism, in this context, carries the meaning of a return to the only unavoidable experience, viz. the subjective one as constitutive of a relation to the world. We know from *Descartes's philosophy that his *Cogito ergo sum* led him to a similar attitude regarding the foundations of metaphysics and of science. The basic difference in Brentano's system lies in the fact that, unlike Descartes, he does not discard the relation to experienced objects for the sake of the so-called illusions of the senses but strives on the contrary to establish a firm world-reference for every conscious phenomenon. This is the reason why he speaks of *acts* of consciousness, designating thereby not the facts of actual behaviour but the constitutive power of the self as such.

In order to circumscribe the realm of psychic phenomena, empirical psychology must first proceed to a descriptive survey of subjective experience by way of intuition. This first phase is not meant to be introspective; it is in fact an attempt at delineating psychology's own field of investigation, i.e. at a pre-scientific level. This basic task of classifying the 'acts' is ultimately phenomenological and represents the epistemological moment of Brentano's endeavour. In the partial republication of his original work in 1911 under the title *On the Classification of Psychic Phenomena*, Brentano refers to it as 'psychognosis' or 'phenominognosis'. Once this has been completed, the second task of empirical psychology is to establish psychological science as such by evidencing the causal relations between phenomena, eventually up to the physiological level. Brentano refers to this part of his work as 'genetic' psychology. We see therefore that what he is aiming at is finally a kind of experimental psychology epistemologically well founded, i.e. relying firmly on actual subjective experience.

It is worth noting that the publication of *Psychology from the Empirical Standpoint* coincided almost exactly with that of Wilhelm *Wundt's Grundzüge der physiologischen Psychologie (Foundations of Physiological Psychology)*, both works appearing in March 1874. However, of these two founding treatises, for many decades only that of Wundt exerted a wide influence on the developments of psychology as a science. This was most probably due to the fact that in Wundt's system the relation of psychic events to physiological ones was more readily understandable, because Wundt took the existence of phenomena of consciousness for granted, under the form of introspectively accessible 'objects', whereas in Brentano's view the very concept of object could only be defined through the intentional founding acts. Historically speaking, it seems that the positivistic impetus given by Wundt to the new science of consciousness was much stronger than the epistemological warnings of Brentano concerning the *possibility* of a scientific psychology.

More than a century has now elapsed since the birth of experimental psychology, and we are in a better position to appreciate the results. Whatever tendencies made their appearance in psychology during this long period of experimenting and theorizing, we know that the debate is not closed. Brentano's teachings have made their way through the school of Graz and were responsible for the emergence of both *Gestalt psychology and *Husserlian phenomenology. The psychological positivism inherited from Wundt has evolved in its own way; it has not only yielded visible results, but has also given rise to a great deal of methodological and even epistemological reflection. This in itself testifies to the fact that the question of the *essence* of psychic phenomena, to use a phenomenological expression, is an unavoidable one. No doubt it would be careless to consider that a satisfactory answer to it will be found by merely increasing the quantity of factual results, since psychological *data* are the products of intentional acts of scientists. Today's psychologists are therefore indebted to Brentano—be it in an indirect fashion—for his early endeavour to lay the epistemological foundations which psychology needs, in order to exist as an adequate science of man's subjective experience.

See also PHENOMENOLOGY.                    G. T.

Brentano, F. (1874). *Psychologie vom empirischen Standpunkt*, vol. 1. Leipzig. Posthumous edn., Kraus, O. (ed.) (1924–8). Leipzig.
Spiegelberg, H. (1960). *The Phenomenological Movement: a Historical Introduction*, 2 vols. The Hague.
Thinès, G. (1977). *Phenomenology and the Science of Behaviour*. London.

**BREUER, JOSEPH** (1842–1925). *Freud described his close friend and collaborator, Joseph Breuer, as 'a man of rich and universal gifts, whose interests extended far beyond his professional activity'. For Breuer's professional activities and achievements extended from being a distinguished physician in Vienna, to discovering the significance of the vagus nerve for controlling breathing, and to establishing the essential functions of the semicircular canals for the sense of balance. He is, however, known best for his work on *hysteria—following the celebrated case of Frl. Anna O.

During her father's last illness Anna O. developed paralysis of her limbs, and anaesthesias, as well as disturbances of vision and speech. Breuer noted that she had two alternating personality states: one more or less normal, the other that of a naughty child. He found that the symptoms were reduced or disappeared after she described her frequent and terrifying hallucinations. This 'talking cure' or 'chimney-sweeping', as they called it, led Breuer to the use of hypnosis to speed things up, and to the concept of catharsis. Anna O.'s true name was Bertha Pappehheim (1859–1936). She was highly intelligent and unusually physically attractive. She became the first social worker in Germany and founded a journal. She never was entirely cured.

The Anna O. case made a deep impression on Freud, who heard of it shortly after Breuer terminated treatment in June 1882. Discussions of it with Breuer were a formative basis of Freudian theory and psychoanalytic practice; especially the importance of fantasies (in extreme cases, hallucinations), hysteria (which was first fully recognized by *Charcot), and the concept and method of catharsis which were Breuer's major contributions. Breuer also introduced the use of hypnosis as a clinical tool. Freud adopted it for a time but later gave it up in favour of *free association.    O. L. Z.

Jones, E. (1953). *The Life and Work of Sigmund Freud* (3 vols.), Bk. I, ch. 11. New York.

**BREWSTER, SIR DAVID** (1781–1868). Scottish physicist, born at Jedburgh and educated at Edinburgh University, of which he became vice-chancellor in 1860. He was elected a fellow of the Royal Society in 1815 and was active in the foundation of the British Association for the Advancement of Science. His main interest was optics, and in 1816 he invented the kaleidoscope. He also improved Wheatstone's stereoscope (or at least made it more convenient, by introducing lenticular prisms rather than Wheatstone's mirrors) so allowing pairs of large pictures to be presented, one to each eye, in spite of the small interocular distance and the inability of the eyes to diverge for fusion. He also made important discoveries on the polarization of light (notably Brewster's law, that when the polarization is at a maximum the tangent of the angle of polarization—Brewster's angle—is equal to the refractive index of the reflecting medium).

Wade, N. J. (1984). *Brewster and Wheatstone on Vision.* New York.

**BRIGHTNESS.** The sensation of light which is roughly associated with the intensity of light at the eye, or its luminance. The sensation of brightness is affected by the adaptation level of the eye and by various contrast phenomena—so brightness cannot be measured in physical units. (See VISUAL ADAPTATION.)

**BROAD,** CHARLIE DUNBAR (1887–1971). English philosopher, professor of moral philosophy at Cambridge (1933–53). He carried out detailed conceptual analyses of science (*Scientific Thought,* 1923), of mind (*Mind and its Place in Nature,* 1929), and of ethics (*Five Types of Ethical Theory,* 1930). His *Examination of McTaggart's Philosophy* (1933–8) contains interesting discussions on time.

See also EMERGENCE AND REDUCTION IN EXPLANATIONS and PARANORMAL.

**BROCA,** PAUL PIERRE (1824–80), French surgeon and anthropologist, professor of surgery and anthropology in Paris, was the only son of a doctor at Sainte-Foy-la-Grande, a small town in the Gascogne, on the river Dordogne, east of Bordeaux. He is remembered chiefly for establishing in 1861 that destruction of an area of grey matter not much larger than 4 square centimetres—'Broca's area'—makes a person unable to speak—Broca's (expressive or motor) *aphasia, by him first called 'aphemia'. In practically all right-handed people this area, he also found, lies in the left; hence it is called the 'dominant' hemisphere of the brain. His test case was a patient nicknamed 'Tan', because 'tan-tan' were the only syllables he could produce for an answer. By contrast, Tan's understanding of the spoken word was considered to be intact. For years Tan had also been paralysed on the right side—presumably through a succession of strokes—and had become Broca's surgical patient because of an infected bed sore. He soon died. At autopsy his brain showed the essential lesion situated at the hind end of the third, or inferior, of the three frontal lobe convolutions (or gyri). Here, for the first time, it was demonstrated with fair precision that a small set of muscles as well as a mental function—the expression of ideas through words—could be localized in a fairly circumscribed portion of brain tissue. The observation has been confirmed innumerable times since. (In 1870 Gustav Fritsch and J. L. Hitzig localized motor function, Carl *Wernicke three years later a receptive speech area.) Before Broca established this localization, only a few diehards had been upholding Franz Joseph *Gall's vague contention of half a century earlier that the frontal lobes generally 'preside over the faculty' of speech.

Broca's other major contribution to understanding the relationship between the structure of the brain and mental function concerns what in the 1950s was revived under the designation of the '*limbic system'. This comprises the convolutions of the inner wall of the cerebral hemispheres and part of the inferior aspect of the frontal lobes. Broca based his concept of the 'great limbic lobe' on the fact that it is relatively underdeveloped in aquatic mammals and Primates, including the human, as compared with lower mammals, which rely to a much greater extent on the sense of smell, and have otherwise less developed hemispheres. On this basis Broca contrasted a 'brute' part with an 'intelligent' part of the brain. Today the limbic (threshold) system is recognized for being concerned with emotion, instinct, and visceral control.

When in 1859—also the year of *Darwin's publication of *The Origin of Species*—Broca was prevented in the Société de Biologie from reading a series of his papers—considered too revolutionary as they negated the permanence of species—he founded the Société d'Anthropologie (the first under this name), and later a laboratory, museum, and institute. One of the papers was based on a study of fertile 'leporids', so-called in France because they were a cross between a hare and a female rabbit.

Broca also first described Cro-Magnon and Aurignacian, or palaeolithic, man, developed a large number of instruments for measuring skulls (craniometry), employed the novelty of statistical standardization, and lent the budding science of anthropology his eminently critical spirit. He inaugurated the study of prehistoric trephining of the skull, and exploded the 'Celtic myth' (that the Celts constitute a racial group with inherited characteristics) and other racial prejudices: 'Spread education, and you improve the race,' were his words. In his early years he belonged to a small group who used the microscope to detect cancer cells, and he discovered their spread via the venous system. He published some 500 papers but his only major book was a standard monograph on aneurysms.

He was also active in political life, holding radical views. He was elected to the French Senate in 1879, but died one year later having delivered only one memorandum, which pleaded to grant public high school education to females. He was sceptical about the prevalent view of equating female inferiority with the female's relatively smaller brain: 'An enlightened person cannot think of measuring intelligence by measuring the brain', he wrote.

F. S.

**BROWN.** Although perhaps the commonest colour, brown is not in the spectrum: it is not a spectral hue. It cannot normally be produced by a mixture of any three lights—as can the spectral hues (see COLOUR VISION: BRAIN MECHANISMS; COLOUR VISION: EYE MECHANISMS)—and is thus somewhat mysterious. It seems to depend on contrast, and on perceived surface texture, which may also affect other colours.

**BRUNSWIK,** EGON (1903–55). Austrian-American psychologist, born in Budapest and educated in Vienna. He intended originally to be an engineer but deviated to psychology and worked in the Psychologisches Institute in Vienna under Karl Bühler, where he obtained his doctorate and became a *privat-docent* in 1934. He spent the following year as a visiting lecturer at the University of California at Berkeley, to which he returned in the following year with the intention of becoming a permanent immigrant to the United States. He became an assistant professor in the department of psychology and in 1947 was promoted to full professor.

Brunswik's early interests lay almost exclusively in the field of visual *perception, and he published a scholarly monograph on object constancy based on experiments carried out in Vienna before he emigrated to the USA (*Wahrnehmung und Gegenstandswelt*, 1934). In America he extended and developed his interests in perception, in part as a result of his close friendship with E. C. *Tolman, with whom he published a joint paper on 'The organism and the causal structure of the environment' (*Psychological Review*, **22** (1935), 43–77). He also developed a strong interest in the design of psychological experiments, producing an original, though difficult, monograph on *Perception and the Representative Design of Psychological Experiments* (1956). He was also much interested in the philosophy of science and the history of psychology.                                      O. L. Z.

**BUDDHIST IDEAS OF THE MIND.** See INDIAN IDEAS OF MIND; CHINESE IDEAS OF THE MIND; JAPANESE CONCEPT OF MIND: TRADITIONAL VIEWS.

**BULIMIA NERVOSA.** See ANOREXIA NERVOSA AND BULIMIA NERVOSA.

**BURT,** SIR CYRIL LODOWIC (1883–1971). British psychologist, born in London, the son of a medical student who was later to become a general practitioner in Warwickshire. Burt is remembered primarily for his pioneering development of psychology in the fields of education and guidance. While still a schoolboy he met and came under the influence of Francis *Galton, who was a patient of his father's, and his whole life's work can be regarded as an attempt to uphold the Galtonian tradition of individual psychology. This tradition emphasized the importance of individual differences in ability and character, the role of heredity in determining these differences, and the need to develop statistical methods in order to handle quantitative measures and assessments.

Burt received a classical education at Christ's Hospital and Oxford University. It was at Oxford that he came under the influence of William *McDougall, who was at the time reader in mental philosophy. He assisted McDougall in collecting psychological measurements for a survey of the British people sponsored by the British Associa-

tion for the Advancement of Science. The data collected during this survey provided the material for his first important article, 'Experimental tests of general intelligence', and set the pattern for his life's work. After graduating in 1907, he spent some time in Oswald Külpe's laboratory at the University of Würzburg, and then took a lectureship in Liverpool under C. S. *Sherrington. He remained in Liverpool for five years, continuing to work on *intelligence, and constructing new types of verbal reasoning test. In 1913 he was appointed psychologist to the London County Council. This was a new appointment, and the first of its kind in Britain. Burt's job was to assist the Council's education committee in two main tasks; the identification of pupils requiring special treatment by reason either of mental subnormality or of behavioural maladjustment, and the selection of gifted pupils for secondary education. In furtherance of these aims he conducted a systematic survey of the distribution of educational abilities among London schoolchildren, and compiled and standardized a set of mental and scholastic tests that remained in use for more than forty years. In addition to his psychometric work Burt ran what was in effect the first child guidance clinic in Britain. The material he collected in this clinical work formed the basis of his classical treatises, *The Young Delinquent* (1925) and *The Backward Child* (1937).

Burt's routine duties with the London County Council occupied only part of his time. On the foundation of the National Institute of Industrial Psychology in 1921 he assisted C. S. *Myers in establishing a vocational guidance seryice; and in 1924 he became part-time professor of educational psychology at the London Day Training College. Aided by teachers, social workers, and students he collected during this period a large body of data, clinical and psychometric, including data on twins, which he was to make use of in his subsequent publications. In fact the bulk of Burt's data was almost certainly collected between 1913 and 1932, before he was appointed to the chair of psychology at University College, London, in succession to Charles *Spearman.

This appointment marked the climax of, and at the same time a turning point in, Burt's career. Until 1932 his energies had been directed primarily towards applied problems; after 1932 he turned mainly to theoretical and methodological questions, chief among which was factor analysis. Building on the foundation laid by Spearman, Burt introduced new mathematical techniques (by this time he had become a competent statistician), and provided new evidence for group ability factors to supplement Spearman's general factor, 'g'. His views were set out definitively in *The Factors of the Mind* (1940), and later in the pages of the *British Journal of Statistical Psychology*, which he edited, for a time with Godfrey Thomson, from 1947 to 1963. Burt never wavered in holding that there was a 'general factor' of cognitive ability, that this factor was largely innate, and that it roughly corresponded with what in popular language is called 'intelligence'. These views of Burt had considerable influence in the shaping of the educational system established by the Education Act of 1944. Burt had frequently been consulted by the official committees on education during the 1920s and 1930s, and during the Second World War he was an adviser to the armed services on matters connected with personnel selection and training. In recognition of this work he was knighted in 1946.

Burt retired from his chair at University College in 1950, and for the remaining twenty-one years of his life lived quietly in his London flat. His activities were restricted by attacks of Ménière's disease, which had commenced during the war. This prevented him from carrying out any field studies or research, but he continued writing, most of his publications being either of a theoretical nature or based on data collected in the early part of his career. Among the latter were his articles on the multifactorial theory of inheritance, which contained the results of his twin studies.

He had from very early days been interested in the question of inheritance, and was from the beginning a convinced Mendelian. Even prior to the First World War he had suggested that Mendelian genetics could be applied to the inheritance of mental qualities. By the 1930s he had become familiar with Ronald Fisher's work on quantitative genetics, and in a famous article written together with an alleged collaborator, Miss Howard, and published in 1956, he concluded on the basis of an analysis of the test scores of twin pairs reared together and apart that 'intelligence was to an overwhelming extent innate'. It is generally agreed that Burt was a pioneer in the application of multifactorial genetics to psychometric data, and his work in the area had a considerable impact. Further articles in 1966, written with another equally mysterious collaborator, Miss Conway, and backed up by a much larger twin population, appeared to lend additional weight to his earlier conclusions. There is little doubt that these articles were a response to the attacks to which his views on inheritance were increasingly subjected from the 1950s onwards. It was only after Burt's death in 1971 that serious discrepancies and flaws were detected in his data on twins, and it is virtually certain that he never in fact collected the additional twin material which he professed to have acquired during his retirement, or that he was assisted by any collaborators. Illness and disappointments may partly explain Burt's frauds, but cannot condone them. His reputation following this exposure suffered a catastrophic decline, so much so that there is a tendency to overlook the important achievements of his early years.

Burt was Britain's first applied psychologist. He laid the foundations of applied educational psychology, vocational guidance, and child guidance in Britain; developed many of the psychological tests that were employed widely during the first half of this century, and refined the techniques of statistical analysis. To a considerable extent he put applied psychology on the map, and made it seem relevant and practical. He was highly regarded by those most closely associated with him between 1910 and 1950. Nevertheless, there were always weaknesses in Burt. He was never at heart a scientist. Much of the data he collected were hastily gathered and of doubtful quality. He was an able and ambitious man, who early came to regard the Galtonian tradition almost as gospel truth and himself as Galton's heir. He was immensely erudite, industrious, and accomplished; to those who were prepared to look up to him, he was kind and generous. But he could not take criticisms or rebuffs; he could not brook opposition; and in the last resort he tragically chose to cheat rather than see his opponents triumph.                  L. S. H.

Burt, C. L. (1962). *Mental and Scholastic Tests*, 4th edn. London.

Burt, C. L. (1957). *The Young Delinquent*, 4th edn. London.

Burt, C. L. (1977). *The Subnormal Mind*, 4th edn. London.

Burt, C. L. (1961). *The Backward Child*, 5th edn. London.

Burt, C. L. (1940). *The Factors of the Mind*. London.

Hearnshaw, L. S. (1979). *Cyril Burt: Psychologist*. London.

**BURTON, ROBERT** (1577–1640), author of *The Anatomy of Melancholy*. Burton was born at Lindley in Leicestershire and went to Brasenose College, Oxford, in 1593, becoming a student of Christ Church in 1599 and vicar of St Thomas's, Oxford, in 1616. In about 1630 he also became vicar of Seagrave in Leicestershire, but for most of his life he lived a 'silent sedentary, solitary, private life' at Christ Church.

*The Anatomy of Melancholy* was first published in 1621. Melancholy was, he considered, an 'inbred malady in every one of us' and he wrote on it 'by being busy to avoid melancholy'. The book is divided into three parts: the first deals with the causes and symptoms of melancholy; the second with its cure; and the third with the melancholy of love and the melancholy of religion. He expanded the subject, however, to cover the whole of the life of man, and on every page there are many quotations and paraphrases from a very wide field of literature, giving the book the reputation of a storehouse of miscellaneous learning rather than a medical treatise.

**BUTLER, SAMUEL** (1835–1902). British author, painter, musician, and eccentric philosopher, born at Langar, Nottinghamshire, where his father was rector. He was a direct descendant of Samuel Butler (1612–80), the author of the satirical poem *Hudibras* (1663), which lampooned puritanism, and the grandson of Samuel Butler (1774–1839), classical scholar and Bishop of Lichfield and Coventry. Educated at Cambridge, he emigrated to New Zealand in 1859, where he ran a successful sheep farm, returning to England in 1865 to concentrate on writing and painting.

*Erewhon* (1872) is satirical romance set in the land of Erewhon (roughly nowhere backwards). In chapters 23–5 there is an extended discussion of the effects of machines on people, and of consciousness and intelligence considered in terms of actual or potential machines, as well as animals and plants. Thus:

There is no security against the ultimate development of mechanical consciousness, in the fact of machines possessing little consciousness now . . . who can say that the vapour engine is not a kind of consciousness? Where does consciousness begin and where end? The shell of a hen's egg is made of a delicate white ware and is a machine as an egg-cup is; the shell is a device for holding the egg as much as the egg-cup for holding the shell.

And considering fly-eating plants:

When a fly settles upon the blossom, the petals close upon it . . . but they will close on nothing but is good to eat; of a drop of rain or a piece of stick they will take no notice. Curious that so unconscious a thing should have such a keen eye to its own interests! If this is unconsciousness, where is the use of consciousness? . . . Shall we say that the plant does not know what it is doing merely because it has no eyes, or ears, or brains? If we say that it acts mechanically only, shall we not be forced to admit that sundry other and apparently very deliberate actions are also mechanical? If it seems to us that the plant kills and eats a fly mechanically, may it not seem to the plant that a man must kill and eat a sheep mechanically?

There is a prophetic account of *artificial intelligence, as Samuel Butler considers the rapid development, and imagines future machines:

There was a time when it must have seemed highly improbable that machines should learn to make their wants known by sound, even through the ears of man; may we not conceive, then, that a day will come when those ears will be no longer needed, and the hearing will be done by the delicacy of the machine's own construction—when its language shall have developed from the cry of animals to a speech as intricate as our own? . . . We cannot calculate on any corresponding advance in man's intellectual or physical powers which shall be a set-off against the far greater development which seems in store for the machines. Some people may say that man's moral influence will suffice to rule them; but I cannot think it will ever be safe to repose much trust in the moral sense of any machine.

Machines are outlawed in *Erewhon*—as potentially far too dangerous for man to live with.

In *Erewhon* and in some of his other writing, for example *Life and Habit* (1877), *Luck or Cunning* (1886), and in his *Notebooks* (1912, edited by H. Festing Jones), he expressed his views on *Darwinism. Though he accepted natural selection he protested against the banishment of mind from the universe and argued for the inheritance of acquired habits. The novel *The Way of All Flesh* (published posthumously in 1903) is largely autobiographical and explores family strife and morality in ways that affected Shaw and later writers.

# C

**CAFETERIA EXPERIMENTS.** The self-assessed dietary preferences or needs of animals (and perhaps humans), indicated by free-choice feeding from a large variety of their normal, or sometimes unfamiliar, foods or substances. There is some evidence that animals may choose substances containing vital minerals which have an effect only some days, or weeks, after eating. It is not clear how these preferences arise by learning when the effect is delayed for so long.

**CAJAL,** SANTIAGO RAMON Y (1852–1934), Spanish neuroanatomist. See RAMON Y CAJAL.

**CALCULATE.** To use numerical techniques to find the answer to mathematical problems by formal rules, such as those of arithmetic. The word is derived from the Latin *calculus*, meaning small stone, referring to the ancient, and indeed prehistoric, use of pebbles for counting, later formalized in the *abacus. The first gear-wheel calculating machine was built by Blaise *Pascal in the year of Isaac Newton's birth, 1642. It is odd that this and many later demonstrations of the calculations of 'mental arithmetic' being undertaken by machine did not, at once and generally, suggest that human thinking may be carried out by physical brain processes and may be largely or completely unconscious.

**CALCULATING GENIUSES.** The term 'calculating genius' describes anyone strikingly more able than normal to do numerical calculations mentally. Since the term is relative to what is regarded as normal, it is applied to people of three different types. (i) Children whose ability is precocious, i.e. exceptional for their age but not necessarily by comparison with many adults. (ii) Mentally retarded people in whom mental calculation is an 'island of ability'. Their ability is not usually outstanding by normal standards but contrasts with their general lack of ability in other respects. (iii) People whose ability is exceptional relative to the adult population at large, and among whom calculating geniuses, in the strict sense, are to be found.

In studying calculating geniuses, four general points merit emphasis. First, the ability rests on the individual's knowledge of numerical facts and short-cut methods. To illustrate, you can multiply by 25 by dividing by 4 and multiplying by 100: for example, 16 times 25 is 4 hundreds. The answer, 400, is attained so rapidly that it seems miraculous to anyone unfamiliar with the short cut. Now, there is literally no end to the numerical facts, interrelations, and short cuts that may be discovered; and when these are deployed in mental calculation, the resulting performances can be impressive, especially to the uninitiated. Mental calculators of high calibre skilfully deploy extensive, recondite knowledge of facts and methods which are largely unknown to, and unsuspected by, most people, and which have usually been discovered by the calculator himself.

Secondly, people who have acquired a small amount of numerical knowledge can go on by themselves to discover and elaborate new facts and methods, and progressively build calculating ability that is out of the ordinary. Self-taught and with no need for external equipment, they can, unaided and unobtrusively, build an ability which may be well developed before it comes to public notice or before they themselves become aware that they can do something unusual. It may easily be supposed that the ability blossoms abruptly and fully formed. However, there is no evidence that ability develops other than by prolonged, cumulative experience. Furthermore, ability atrophies with disuse.

Thirdly, calculating procedures taught at school are designed for use in conjunction with a written record of the various steps taken, and are not serviceable in mental calculation. To illustrate, multiply 123 by 456 using your accustomed paper-and-pencil method. Now repeat exactly as before but, this time, try to do the entire calculation in your head without writing anything. You lose track, don't you? So would mental calculators. They would use other methods—of which there are many—that lend themselves better to mental working. They would, also, generate the answer (56,088) in natural left-to-right sequence, not right-to-left as happens with your paper-and-pencil procedure. In brief, the numerical language needed for mental calculation is, in many respects, different from that taught in school. This explains why the unschooled are not necessarily disadvantaged in developing talent in mental calculation and why such people often claim, in retrospect, that schooling would have been a positive hindrance.

Fourthly, it is difficult to discover in minute detail how any individual calculates. A certain amount can be inferred from objective characteristics of performance; but reliance must also be placed on subjective reports which, apart from their inescapable limitations, encounter certain difficulties. When the calculator is highly educated and articulate, he may take his numerical knowledge so much for granted that he neglects to make it explicit, even if able and willing to do so, once the need for communication becomes apparent. When young or uneducated, he may lack vocabulary to describe his self-taught knowledge. George Parker Bidder (1806–78), for example, was a calculating genius who became a distinguished engineer and gave an autobiographical account of his talent. At six, when he began seriously to calculate, he could not read or write, had no notion of written numbers, and had never heard the word 'multiply'. He remarked, 'The first time I was asked to "multiply" some small affair, say 23 by 27, I did not know what was meant; and it was not until I was told that it meant 23 times 27 that I could comprehend the term.'

The difficulties are worse confounded when the calculator is a public entertainer who contrives theatrical effects and deliberately conceals the tricks of his trade. He may, for example, give the square roots of numbers called out by the audience. His swift, accurate answers are impressive because we all know how cumbersome it is to calculate square roots. What we do not realize is that he has no need to calculate at all. He assumes that the audience will, to save labour and be able to check his answer, take some number, square it, and give him the result. So, assuming a perfect square, he applies special numerical knowledge and, by merely inspecting the number and especially its last two digits, detects what the square root must be. With cube rooting, the inspectional technique is even easier, granted knowledge of certain numerical facts and the assumption that the given number is a perfect cube. Such an entertainer would be embarrassed if given a number which is not a perfect cube and asked to express its cube root to several decimal places.

Fairly full and reliable information exists about the biographies and abilities of several people who properly deserve to be called calculating geniuses. Of these, the ablest and best documented is A. C. Aitken (1895–1967), an outstanding mathematical scholar with exceptional all-round intellectual accomplishments. At the age of 13 he became fascinated by mental calculation, and then spent years exploring numerical facts and calculative methods. In middle age, mental calculation lost its intrinsic appeal, and for certain calculations, such as multiplication by very large numbers, he used electric calculating machines which had, by then, come on the market. However, he still found it convenient, in his mathematical research, to do some calculations mentally, and so he never lost his ability. His nimble deployment of deep numerical knowledge is illustrated by the two following commentaries, both transcribed from a tape-recorded session.

After expressing 1/851 as a decimal, he reported as follows

The instant observation was that 851 is 23 times 37. I use this fact as follows. 1/37 is 0·027027027, and so on repeated. This I divide mentally by 23. 23 into 0·027 is

0·001 with remainder 4. In a flash I can get that 23 into 4,027 is 175 with remainder 2. And into 2,027 is 88 with remainder 3. And into 3,027 is 131 with remainder 14. And even into 14,027 is 609 with remainder 20. And so on like that. Also, before I even start this . . . I know that there is a recurring period of sixty-six places.

He was asked to multiply 123 by 456, and gave the answer after a pause of two seconds. He then commented as follows

I see at once that 123 times 450 is 55,350, and that 123 times 6 is 738; I hardly have to think. Then 55,350 plus 738 gives 56,088. Even at the moment of registering 56,088, I have checked it by dividing by 8, so 7,011, and this by 9 gives 779. I recognize 779 as 41 by 19. And 41 by 3 is 123, while 19 by 24 is 456. A check you see; and it passes by in about one second.

The study of calculating geniuses gives insight into how people develop and deploy their varied talents, and how development depends on the interplay of potential ability, interest, and opportunity. It also shows how intellectual skills must be organized differently in order to meet special requirements, such as calculating mentally rather than by using external recording devices. It reminds us that there are many ways of calculating—for example, logarithms, electronic calculating machines, and several forms of *abacus, among which the Japanese *soroban* is especially efficient in expert hands. Each of these calculative systems has its own balance of strengths and weaknesses, and each requires its user to master a distinctive repertoire of skills.

Much of the literature about calculating geniuses is patchy and regrettably unreliable. This is not always because people are inclined to exaggerate, but because it is so easy to gather false impressions when care is not taken to consider each calculator individually and to make precise observations about his ability. We go seriously astray if we assume that every calculator works in exactly the same way, or by conventional procedures that are somehow speeded up. Each uses a knowledge of numerical facts and methods which is, in its details, largely self-taught and uniquely his own.

I. M. L. H.

Hunter, I. M. L. (1962). An exceptional talent for calculative thinking. *British Journal of Psychology*, **53**, 243–58.

Hunter, I. M. L. (1977). Mental calculation. In Wason, P. C. and Johnson-Laird, P. N. (eds.), *Thinking: readings in cognitive psychology*. Cambridge.

Mitchell, F. D. (1907). Mathematical prodigies. *American Journal of Psychology*, **18**, 61–143.

Smith, S. B. (1983). *The Great Mental Calculators*. New York.

**CALIBRATE.** To adjust or compare an instrument with a standard, which may be man-made or naturally occurring. The readings of instruments may be calibrated with correction tables, or curves, so that their errors can be compensated.

One can think of much sensory adaptation as setting the calibration of sensory systems—which can be upset by maintained stimuli or by distortions, such as prolonged viewing through deviating prisms or distorting lenses. (See, for instance, CONTINGENT PERCEPTUAL AFTER-EFFECT.)

**CALIBRATION ERROR.** See ILLUSIONS.

**CANNON, WALTER BRADFORD** (1871–1945). American physiologist, born at Praire du Chien, Wisconsin, and educated at Harvard, where he was George Higginson professor of physiology at the Harvard Medical School from 1906 until 1945. As a student of medicine he started by studying the phenomenon of swallowing; this led him to observe the motions of the stomach and intestines, and his observations were summarized in *The Mechanical Factors of Digestion* (1911). He gradually moved towards studies of emotion as related to bodily changes, and this resulted in the important book *Bodily Changes in Pain, Hunger, Fear and Rage* (1919; 2nd edn., 1929), and in the work which remains a classic, *The Wisdom of the Body* (1932). For further details, including his critique of the James–Lange theory of emotion, see EMOTION.

Cannon developed the concept of *homeostasis, which in modern terminology is the *feedback control of servo-systems. This concept was not mathematically expressed until the work of Norbert *Wiener in the 1940s, when it became the basis of *cybernetics. Cannon was the first to see the importance of such regulatory mechanisms, which now control complex machines as well as organisms. His work is also a basis of current ideas on *psychosomatic disease.

**CAPGRAS' SYNDROME.** This rare and unusual psychological disorder was first described by J. M. J. Capgras (1873–1950) and Reboul-Lachaux in 1923 under the title of 'L'illusion des sosies'. The patient comes to believe that familiar persons around him, usually close relatives, have been replaced by impostors who have assumed the exact appearances of those whom they have supplanted. Although this delusional belief has most often been described in patients suffering from schizophrenia or affective psychoses, it can also occur in the presence of organic disease of the brain. The poet Cowper, who suffered from recurrent bouts of manic-depressive psychosis, apparently was suffering from the condition when he came to doubt whether his friend, the Revd John Newton, was real or some phantom masquerading in his shape (Lord David Cecil, 1965).

Although 'L'illusion des sosies' is usually translated as 'the illusion of doubles', it is evident that the afflicted person is suffering from a fixed delusional belief and not simply a misinterpretation of appearances. The term 'sosies' derives from the story of Amphitryon and his servant Socias as recounted in the play by Plautus and later in revivals of the same story by Molière, Dryden and, most recently, Giraudoux. Robert Graves (1960) recounts how Zeus planned to seduce Alcmene, Amphitryon's beautiful wife, by imper-

sonating him during his absence at the wars. To add verisimilitude to the deception he persuaded Mercury to assume the shape of Socias (Sosie) and pretend that he had been sent ahead to announce Amphitryon's return. To prolong his enjoyment of Alcmene, Zeus arranged that the sun and moon should halt in their courses, so protracting one night to the duration of three. When the real Amphitryon finally returned he was not a little disappointed at Alcmene's lack of enthusiasm for his embraces. Nine months later she gave birth to Heracles.

Related to Capgras' syndrome is the Illusion de Frégoli, in which the victim claims that persons well known to him are impersonating others, usually individuals said to be persecuting him. Frégoli was a well-known actor, famous for his ability to represent others by changing his facial appearance. The Frégoli phenomenon seems to be even rarer than 'L'illusion des sosies'.

The psychopathology of Capgras' syndrome has been variously interpreted. Some have regarded it as an extreme form of depersonalization. Marked ambivalence towards the person thought to be impersonated allows the patient to project negative feelings on to the impostor while preserving normal feelings of affection towards the one who has been supplanted. Such formulations may serve to explain this phenomenon in persons suffering from one or other of the functional psychoses, but they are inadequate when the delusional belief appears as the result of some physical disease or injury of the brain. In many patients the delusion remains fixed and unchanging but in others the phenomenon may gradually fade, although it is probably true to say that, whatever is done to help the patient, some lingering doubts about the true identity of the alleged impostor will persist.

F. A. W.

Cecil, D. (1965). *The Stricken Deer*. London.
Enoch, M. D. and Trethowan, W. H. (1979). *Uncommon Psychiatric Syndromes*, 2nd edn. Bristol.
Graves, R. (1960). *The Greek Myths*. Harmondsworth.
Weston, M. J. and Whitlock, F. A. (1971). The Capgras Syndrome Following Head Injury. *British Journal of Psychiatry*, **119**, 25–31.

**CARMICHAEL, LEONARD** (1898–1973). American psychobiologist, educator, and administrator. He was born in Philadelphia, and educated at Tufts University and Harvard.

Beginning in his student days Carmichael was attracted to the fields of animal behaviour, neuroembryology, neuroanatomy, and neurophysiology. These were topics which guided his considerable research efforts early in his career and which remained central to his scientific interests throughout his life. He was the first academic psychologist to study the prenatal origins of behaviour. In a series of now classic experiments begun during his first academic post at Princeton in 1924–5, Carmichael (1926) attempted to determine whether the experimental suppression of all motor behaviour in developing frog embryos, by the use of a paralytic anaesthetic, would impair the normal development and manifestation of swimming in the hatched tadpole. He found that the treatment had little if any effect on later behaviour; the treated tadpoles swam as efficiently as normal frogs. This was one of the first scientific demonstrations that practice, use, or experience during early development are not necessarily critical for normal neurobehavioural development. In subsequent years Carmichael and his students conducted important and extensive pioneering studies on foetal behaviour and physiology in mammals.

In addition to his laboratory research, Carmichael made many scholarly contributions to the field of psychobiology. Paramount among these was his editing of two editions of a fundamental reference work in the field of developmental psychobiology, *The Manual of Child Psychology* (1946, 1954).

Over a period spanning more than fifty years, Carmichael was a strong proponent of a developmental and psychobiological approach to the study of behavioural problems, and as a result he had a vital influence in formulating, and fostering the development of, our modern conceptualization of these problems.

Carmichael was widely honoured during his career, and, in a brief autobiography published in 1967, he noted that 'if I were asked what thread seems to me to have run most consistently through my career, I could answer the question in one word, *Research*' (1967, p. 52). Despite having stopped his own direct involvement in laboratory research by about 1940, it is therefore fitting that it is his early research contributions that will remain as his most important and lasting legacy.   R. W. O.

Carmichael, L. (1926). The development of behavior in vertebrates experimentally removed from the influence of external stimulation. *Psychological Review*, **33**, 51–8.
Carmichael, L. (ed.) (1946, 1954). *The Manual of Child Psychology*. New York.
Carmichael, L. (1967). An autobiography. In Boring, E. G. and Lindzey, L. (eds.), *A History of Psychology in Autobiography*, Vol. 5, New York.

**CARR,** HARVEY (1873–1954). American psychologist, born in Indiana and educated mainly at the University of Chicago, gaining his doctorate in 1905. He replaced J. B. *Watson as an assistant professor when Watson left for Johns Hopkins in 1904, and remained in Chicago right up to his retirement in 1938, being chairman of his department for much of this period.

Carr's main interests lay in space perception, on which he published a useful book, and comparative psychology, the study of which had always been prominent in the Chicago laboratory. While Carr held to a *behaviourist line in the case of animal psychology, he remained convinced that human psychology could not be satisfactorily explained without reference to *consciousness. At the same time, he was distinctly sceptical of conventional

classification in psychology and always warned his pupils of the hazards of reification. He was even doubtful whether psychology justified its claim to be a fully fledged scientific discipline.   O. L. Z.

**CARROLL,** LEWIS (pseudonym of Charles Lutwidge Dodgson, 1832–98). British author and logician. He was mathematical lecturer at Christ Church, Oxford (1855–81). *Alice's Adventures in Wonderland* (1865) and *Through the Looking-Glass* (1872) introduced logical puzzles to children and to their parents. He also wrote serious logical and mathematical works: *Euclid and his Modern Rivals* (1879), *Curiosa Mathematica* (1888–93), *Symbolic Logic* (1896), and a paper on *Zeno's paradoxes, 'What the tortoise said to Achilles', in *Mind* (1895).

**CARTESIANISM.** See DESCARTES, RENÉ.

**CARTOON.** The fact that even very simple drawings convey facial expressions and other rich perceptions is excellent evidence of the creative power of *perception. Cartoonists, by discovering which features of drawings are important, have managed to latch on to the key features for normal perception. There must be a great store of knowledge of perception (if implicit) that artists use. See also ART AND VISUAL ABSTRACTION.

**CATECHOLAMINES.** The principal catecholamines found in the mammalian nervous system are noradrenaline (norepinephrine), *dopamine, and *adrenaline (epinephrine). The adrenal medulla, an endocrine gland which receives innervation from the sympathetic nervous system, contains the largest quantities of catecholamines body. This tissue was used in pioneer studies to determine the biosynthetic pathway for the catecholamines. This is as follows: TYROSINE → DIHYDROXYPHENYLALANINE → DOPAMINE → NORADRENALINE → ADRENALINE.

The ability of cells to synthesize catecholamines depends on the presence of enzymes which catalyse the conversion of tyrosine, taken up from the bloodstream, to dihydroxyphenylalanine, dopamine, noradrenaline, and adrenaline. Noradrenaline and adrenaline in the adrenal medulla function as hormones and are released into the bloodstream in response to activation of the input it receives from the sympathetic nervous system. This occurs during physiological responses to stressful stimuli such as sudden anger, fear, severe cold, or physical exercise.

In the peripheral nervous system, the postganglionic neurones of the sympathetic division of the *autonomic nervous system synthesize and release noradrenaline as a *neurotransmitter, thereby influencing the activity of smooth muscle cells in a wide variety of tissues. For example, they control the diameter of the pupil, the smooth muscle in blood vessels of the salivary glands (thus influencing glandular secretion), the rate of the heartbeat, the diameter of the coronary arteries, the diameter of bronchi in the lungs, the activity of smooth muscle in the bowel (thus influencing movement of intestinal contents), the smooth muscle activity in a variety of pelvic organs, and the diameter of small blood vessels and hence blood-flow in large areas of skin and muscle throughout the body. These diverse tissues can thus be influenced by the sympathetic nervous system to respond in a co-ordinated fashion to stressful stimuli. The well-known cold sweaty hands, fast heartbeat, dilated pupils, and pale complexion produced by fear are explicable in terms of the known hormonal and neurotransmitter actions of the catecholamines.

The brain contains another and separate family of neurones using catecholamines as neurotransmitters. These contain either adrenaline, noradrenaline, or dopamine. Adrenaline neurones are few in number and are located in the brain-stem. They send their axons down into the spinal cord and into the hypothalamus, as well as to a region of the brain-stem known as the nucleus of the tractus solitarius. (For a description of the structure of the brain, see NERVOUS SYSTEM.) There is evidence that adrenaline plays a role in this latter nucleus in the control of blood-pressure. Abnormally high blood-pressure is a common clinical problem, and it is therefore of interest that a genetically distinct strain of laboratory rat has been found in which there are abnormally high quantities of the enzyme that synthesizes adrenaline. These rats suffer from high blood-pressure.

Noradrenaline neurones are scattered in small groups throughout the brain-stem. The largest of these, the locus coeruleus, contains only a few thousand neurones, but they provide branching axons which together innervate a vast area of the brain and spinal cord. Furthermore, neurones may provide axons to innervate, for example, both cerebellum and cerebral cortex. Therefore these neurones may influence widely separate and functionally distinct brain areas simultaneously (see NEURONAL CONNECTIVITY AND BRAIN FUNCTION). Morphologically these neurones have many similarities to other parts of the brain-stem reticular formation, and make many functional contacts with other divisions of the reticular formation. All the evidence points to the fact that the synaptic actions (see SYNAPSES) of noradrenaline are relatively diffuse (or hormone-like) and act over a relatively slow time-course of seconds (compared to a time-course of milliseconds for *acetyl-choline), while the action of the transmitter is mediated by slow chemical changes rather than fast changes in ionic channels in the nerve-cell membrane. In most cases it seems that the action of the transmitter on single neurones is inhibitory, although it appears to operate without altering the responses of neurones to other specific input stimuli.

As would be expected from the very widespread distribution of noradrenaline fibres in the brain and spinal cord, they appear to influence a correspondingly large number of functions. There seems little doubt that they are involved in the regulation of general brain states such as arousal and sleep, and the co-ordination of the many brain functions appropriate to these states. It is of interest that drugs which appear to have clinical activity in alleviating depressive illness are able to act by altering the availability of noradrenaline at the receptor level. Noradrenaline fibres may also have a role to play during the establishment and selection of normal synaptic connections during development and in the recovery of function after damage to the nervous system.

The third main group of catecholamine neurones of the brain are those utilizing dopamine as transmitter. These neurones have been the subject of much research, because there are two common clinical conditions alleviated by drugs which interact with dopamine neurones—*Parkinsonism and *schizophrenia.

O. T. P.

**CATHEXIS.** See FREUD ON MENTAL STRUCTURE.

**CATTELL, JAMES McKEEN** (1860–1944). American psychologist born in Easton, Pennsylvania, the son of the Presbyterian president of a small East Coast university. He studied under Rudolf Lotze (1817–81) at Göttingen, following which he worked for three years with Wilhelm *Wundt at Leipzig and took his doctorate. He then spent a year at St John's College, Cambridge, and at this time made the acquaintance of Francis *Galton, by whom he was immensely impressed. Had he stayed permanently in Cambridge—which at the time he was strongly tempted to do—it is likely that he would have played an important role in the growth and development of experimental psychology in the University.

Cattell's work at Leipzig was largely concerned with measurements of reaction times, which he continued for some time at the University of Pennsylvania after his return to the United States, publishing an important paper with C. S. Fullerton on the perception of small differences. His next move was to Columbia University, where together with E. L. *Thorndike he built up the leading laboratory in America principally concerned with mental tests and the measurement of individual differences. It would thus appear that it was Galton rather than Wundt who had the major influence on his career.

O. L. Z.

Sokal, M. M. (ed.) (1981). *An Education in Psychology: James McKeen Cattell, Journal and Letters from Germany and England 1880–1888.* Boston.

**CAUSAL THEORY OF MENTAL CONCEPTS.** See MENTAL CONCEPTS: THE CAUSAL ANALYSIS.

**CAUSES.** The earliest treatments of causality link the concept firmly to that of explanation. Aristotle defines *aitia* (the Latin translation of which is *causa*, from whence our 'cause') as something which answers the question 'why?' (*dia ti?*). Such a question asks for an explanation of some kind, an answer beginning 'because . . .'. If one asks what distinguishes an explanation from other forms of information, such as a mere description, the answer implicit in Aristotle's discussion is that an explanation starts with what is taken to be a correct description of something and indicates what constrained or necessitated that thing to be as it is. An explanation, in other words, shows how the *possibilities were restricted so that things *had* to be that way, so that had one known the explanation he would have been justified in expecting things to be that way. This is a task which the citation of a cause is meant to perform. A cause is cited to explain, to show that something is or was in some way necessary.

It is a mark of how the concept of cause has taken on a meaning more specific than simply 'an explanation' or 'what explains', that the so-called 'four Aristotelian causes' are likely to strike a modern mind as having little to do with causes. Regarded as a fourfold classification of explanatory patterns, however, the doctrine is not at all implausible. (The following examples are not Aristotle's, but Aristotelian in spirit.) If one asks why a certain act which resulted in the death of a person counts as murder, one will be referred to an account of what murder is: an Aristotelian *formal* explanation. If one asks 'through what' (a more literal translation of *dia ti?*) means a murder was carried out—was it poison, gunshot, a blow to the head?—one will be referred to an Aristotelian *material* explanation. If one asks why the murderer committed the act, one may be asking for a motive, such as inheriting the victim's money, which is an Aristotelian *final* explanation. Or one may be asking what prompted the murderer to act just then (a short temper and an insult, or greed and the victim's threat to alter his will), i.e. for an Aristotelian *efficient* cause/explanation.

Of the four, it is most natural nowadays to speak of 'cause' in connection with the last of these and then only in connection with a subclass of what Aristotle termed 'a source of change or remaining the same'. For Aristotle gives as examples of such 'causes', human agents, their dispositional states, and also what may be called 'triggering events', i.e. events which set in motion some further event. It is examples of the last sort that set the pattern of contemporary discussions of causality. The historical reason for this lies in a shift in thinking about patterns of explanation which took place in the seventeenth century.

Aristotelian explanations of natural phenomena ultimately come to rest on the natures (forms, *essences) of things, which are expressed in terms of complexes of active and passive powers. Thus a concept of natural agency is central to Aristotelian explanations of natural phenomena; things cause changes to take place (or fail to take place) by virtue of the powers which constitute them as the

sorts of things they are. As a result of developments in the seventeenth century, explanations came to be thought of as resting on laws rather than on natural agencies. A law is a relationship between quantitative aspects of natural phenomena which can be expressed in the form of a mathematical function. What was explained was no longer the action of one thing on another, but the law-governed interactions which took place between things, such as the motions which resulted when one body collided with another.

But the notion of agency, which is almost certainly modelled on the way we account for the affairs of human beings, is deeply rooted in our thought; and as long as the implications of the shift in explanatory practices were unclear, there was a tendency to look for the powers which had belonged to agents in the events governed by laws, as though an event at the beginning of some law-governed interaction had by itself the power to effect what took place.

The eighteenth-century philosopher David Hume was able, without any deep familiarity with the science of his day, to reflect in his analysis of causality both the change in forms of explanation to patterns of interaction and the precarious position which the notion of agency had come to occupy. He concluded that a cause was an 'object' (a word which many read in this context as 'event') preceding and spatially adjacent to another (the effect) where we have observed objects resembling the first in 'like relations of precedency and contiguity to those objects that resemble the latter'. As for the limitation of possibility which is the function which cause performs in explanation, Hume dismissed the notion of power as without foundation in experience and concluded that our idea that what we identify as related as cause and effect are in some way necessarily linked is the product of feeling the habit of mind which has been formed by observing so many similar pairs of objects, the one preceding the other.

Hume's analysis does far less justice than does Aristotle's to the variety of forms of explanation which we still use with apparent success every day, and it has not gone unremarked that his approach to *necessity* undermines the hopes of science to establish for us what are the laws of nature. His analysis has, however, had the salutary effect of raising the question of the empirical foundation of our (supposed) knowledge of necessity, and the possibility of our giving explanations. One way of trying not to capitulate to Hume is to pre-empt the question and to argue along the lines suggested by *Kant that experience, i.e. anything that would constitute an empirical foundation for any knowledge, must use, if not the notion of cause, then that of natural possibility/necessity. There would, if this strategy were successful, be no question of our right to use these notions, only a question of how well we manage to use them.

See also MENTAL CONCEPTS: THE CAUSAL ANALYSIS.                                J. E. T.

Harré, R. and Madden, E. H. (1975). *Causal Powers*. Oxford.

Mackie, J. (1974). *The Cement of the Universe: A Study of Causation*. Oxford.

Sorabji, R. (1980). *Necessity, Cause and Blame: Perspectives on Aristotle's Theory*. London.

**CENTRES IN THE BRAIN.** Some neurologists believe that there are specific regions in which, in some sense, particular sensations are located. The 'pleasure centres', discovered by James *Olds, are regions that, when stimulated electrically, produce intense pleasure in man. When the stimulation is self-administered with a level switch by an animal, the animal may stimulate himself for hours on end, and will ignore food, sex, or other typically pleasurable stimuli or situations. It is interesting to find that this so-called brain-reward system depends upon the activity of biogenic amines, particularly dopamine (see CATECHOLAMINES). Observations have been made in the USA on patients with electrodes implanted in the septal region of the brain. When asked to comment on how they felt when the electrodes were stimulated, they reported having a 'good feeling', which appears to have had some of the qualities of sexual pleasure. Enjoyable feelings were also said to follow electrical stimulation of other parts of the limbic brain, but unpleasant feelings were caused by stimulation of the hippocampus and amygdala (see LIMBIC SYSTEM). The observations of Olds on animals with implanted electrodes that caused almost continuous self-stimulation have been considered as explanatory of the behaviour of some drug-dependent subjects who inject themselves repeatedly with opiates for pleasure (and in response to a conditioning process created by the drive of the nervous system to reinforce activities which provide satisfaction). This highly reinforcing self-stimulation activity in animals is blocked by drugs such as phenothiazines, although the ability to press the bar which stimulates the implanted electrodes is not lost.                    O. L. Z.

**CEREBELLUM.** The region of the brain (posterior below the striate cortex) mainly responsible for co-ordinating movement. See NERVOUS SYSTEM.

**CEREBRAL CORTEX.** The outer layer or 'bark' (from the Greek) of the brain, associated with sensory perception and the higher mental functions. It appeared late in evolution, and is especially developed in man. See NERVOUS SYSTEM.

**CEREBRAL DOMINANCE.** See HANDEDNESS; NEUROPSYCHOLOGY.

**CEREBROTONIA.** See BODY BUILD AND PERSONALITY.

**CHANCE.** See POSSIBILITY.

**CHANNELS, NEURAL.** One normally thinks of a channel as a physically existing and easily seen structure, such as a river course. Nerve fibres are, similarly, easily seen courses along which neural signals flow. The situation, however, is not at all simple in neurophysiology because a whole sensory modality, such as vision or hearing, may be called a channel, even though many thousands of nerve fibres comprise these 'channels'. Conversely, and even more tricky, a single physical channel may transmit several channels of information. Thus telephone systems employ a single high-frequency link along which many messages can be simultaneously transmitted, each on its own 'carrier frequency' which is modulated by the channel signals to keep the messages separate. Here the separation is given not in any obvious physical or visible way, but by splitting the very wide frequency range of the carrier into several frequency bands, which provide independent information channels. There seem to be somewhat analogous ways in which different signals are carried separately on shared nerve fibres. Also, by selective attention it is possible to switch from one signal source to another, so that that which is effective depends on selection rather than simply on laid down neural channels.

It is now believed that the visual system is organized into many more-or-less independent channels, not only for colour (which uses three channels) but also, and perhaps more surprisingly, for different orientations of lines or edges, directions of movement, brightness, and texture size. Isolating and studying channel characteristics is an important part of current experimental work on how the senses function. Just how the channels converge to a single unified perception (which used to be called the *common sense) is not yet understood.

What use are channels? If information transmission was the only requirement for designing sensory channels, then just one, covering all the physical information, might suffice. However, the information also has to be analysed and, if there are many different channels, they can sort the information into relevant categories to start the perceptual processing. Many of the objects in the environment are only recognizable in terms of a combination of different physical attributes (think how you would recognize bacon cooking). Likewise many of our actions are determined by the information from various different physical sources. These different physical attributes and sources have therefore to be distinguished and it is convenient to allow the selectivity of channels to make the distinctions. Conversely, sometimes a particular object can be partially specified by one source of physical information (think how you can search a crowd for a friend wearing a scarlet hat), and in this case a channel more-or-less specific to that information is very useful.

If I have a private channel from $A$ to $B$, the receiver at $B$ knows a great deal about the incoming messages in advance, such as their type and range, because these are simply inherent to channel.

The selectivity of a channel is a type of advance knowledge which allows the receiver to correct any systematic errors in the channel. Imagine a channel transmitting edge curvatures, which are physically as often curved one way as any other. If the receiver simply compares each incoming message with the distribution of messages that it has received in the past it will automatically *calibrate the channel for any distortions that it introduces.

All channels have physical limits on the amount of information that they can transmit, but some physical attributes, for example luminance contrast, can take a wide range of values. In such instances, it is useful to be able to split the whole range into a number of separate bands and assign one channel per band. This arrangement allows the transmission of a wide range of values with high accuracy.

Luminance contrast is an interesting case. Imagine a diffuse shadow lying across a finely chequered surface. The luminance contrast between any adjacent black and white squares will always be the same because the shadow will equally affect the two. However, the luminance contrast between a black and a white square that are separated will be affected by the shadow, which may lie over one but not the other. Long-range contrast is different in this case from short-range contrast, even though they physically overlap in space. A channel for contrast must work over some predefined spatial range, and a long-range channel would be indifferent to short-range contrast and vice versa. Therefore it is necessary to have several contrast channels each selective for a different spatial range.

Many physical aspects of our environment have this complicated overlap property. The wavelength of light is another instance: any physical surface reflects a wide range of different wavelengths. Sound and speech is another interesting case. In a room where several people are speaking at the same time, the air is vibrating in response to all of them together. The perceptual process has a problem, the *'cocktail party problem', because it has to break the air vibrations down in portions that will allow it to select one speaker's message. The hearing system has channels that are selective to frequency of sound and direction and these are thought to provide the basis for this selection.

It is sensible to have many channels for several reasons. They organize the overall sensory information into a structure which is suitable for subsequent cognitive processing. They also allow for automatic calibration and adaptation to prevailing conditions in the physical environment.

Empirically, it has so far proved easier to identify channels than to discover how their outputs are combined or used. Channels can be discovered by seeking interactions between the processing of very similar physical stimuli. Gazing at a periodic pattern of high contrast black and white stripes will make the visual system less sensitive to very similar patterns, but does not affect sensitivity to patterns where the stripes have a considerably different size or direction (see CONTINGENT PERCEPTUAL AFTER-EFFECT). Similarly, similar patterns will interfere when present simultaneously if they are processed by the same channel. In these observations the important point is the selectivity of the effect for a particular range of physical stimuli, and this range is thought to correspond to the selectivity of the channel itself.

R. L. G.
R. J. W.

Andrews, D. P. (1964). Error-correcting perceptual mechanisms. *Quarterly Journal of Experimental Psychology*, **16**, 104–115.

Braddick, O., Campbell, F. W., and Atkinson, J. (1978). Channels in vision: basic aspects. In Held, R., Leibowitz, H., and Teuber, H. L. (eds.), In *Handbook of Sensory Physiology*, Vol. 8. Berlin.

**CHARCOT,** JEAN MARTIN (1825–93). French neurologist, born in Paris, where he qualified in medicine. In 1853 he began to work at the Salpêtrière, becoming physician-in-chief in 1866 and professor of clinical neurology in 1882. He was a brilliant diagnostician and was the first to recognize a number of nervous diseases including multiple sclerosis and the 'lightning pains' of tabes dorsalis. Towards the end of his life, he became much interested in *hysteria and its treatment by hypnosis, in which he likewise became deeply interested. Among the many who studied with Charcot was Sigmund *Freud, upon whom he made a lasting impression.

O. L. Z.

Guillain, G. (1959). *J. M. Charcot, His Life, His Work* (trans. P. Bailey). London.

**CHESELDEN,** WILLIAM (1688–1752). British surgeon, born near Melton Mowbray in Leicestershire. He became surgeon at St Thomas's Hospital, and later at the Royal Hospital, Chelsea, where he organized the separation of the old Barber-Surgeons Company, to found the Corporation of Surgeons in 1745 by Act of Parliament. The foremost surgeon of his day, and an excellent anatomist, he was influential also on account of his birth, as his family was entitled to a coat of arms— an unusual advantage, as surgeons of his time were seldom socially acceptable. He was a close friend, among other intellectuals, of the poet Alexander Pope and the painter Jonathan Richardson, whose fine portrait of him hangs in the Council Chamber of the Royal College of Surgeons. Cheselden attended Sir Isaac Newton in his final illness, advising against an operation for stone.

Cheselden was the first to create by operation on the eye an artificial pupil; and he developed improved procedures and instruments for removal of cataract. A case of restoration of sight in 1728 remains famous: the removal of congenital cataracts by 'couching' in a boy 13 or 14 years old who had no previous vision except some indication of the colours of bright lights. (See BLINDNESS, RECOVERY FROM, for a full discussion of this case.)

Cope, Z. (1953). *William Cheselden*. Edinburgh and London.

**CHESS.** See COMPUTER CHESS.

**CHILD ABUSE.** Human beings can go to great lengths to care for and to protect children; yet since history began children have been abused. It was not, however, until the nineteenth century that social reformers in Europe and North America influenced legislation by showing that children employed under conditions accepted as normal were in fact being seriously abused.

Awareness that the two contradictory states, caring for children yet abusing them, could exist side by side was not apparent to members of the medical profession and many others caring for children until very recently. Despite a description in 1888 of the signs of child abuse, it was not until Henry Kempe and his associates published in 1962 the now classic paper, emotively entitled 'The Battered Child Syndrome', that professional eyes opened. Shock and initial disbelief were followed by a growing acceptance of Kempe's findings, leading to an extensive literature and registers of children at risk. This sharpening of awareness is illustrated by the paediatrician who, in a recent presidential address, while pointing out clear-cut and unequivocal signs of physical abuse in infants and young children, stated that over a period of seven years of general paediatric practice he had never seen a case of child abuse because he had not been looking for it.

The item 'child abuse' refers to a number of areas and is usefully considered under three headings. These cover (i) general neglect, systematic poisoning, and physical violence—which in recent years has been euphemistically relabelled non-accidental injury; (ii) sexual abuse, which since the late 1970s has become increasingly recognized and found to be widespread; and (iii) psychological abuse, a concept that is gaining ground. It is safe to work on the assumption that children subjected to any form of general physical or sexual abuse will also suffer psychological abuse. Moreover, many children who are not physically abused are deliberately made to suffer painful psychological states such as fear, rejection, and loneliness which constitute abuse. The statements that follow refer to findings on non-sexual physical abuse.

All figures on the extent of child abuse are at best imprecise estimates. Furthermore, findings from different studies are not easily compared because workers tend to focus upon different aspects of the subject and to express their findings in different ways. It can however be estimated that in the USA approximately one in every hundred children under 18 is physically abused, sexually molested, or severely neglected; the figure is probably about the same for England and Wales. It is a conservative estimate that up to 10 per cent of abused children die, and that at least 25 per cent suffer serious neurological damage with impairment of intelligence. The epidemiology of child abuse has been reviewed by Jack Oliver (in Smith, 1978). Since about 1960 the figures have tended to increase, but it is an unanswerable question whether this reflects greater recognition of the condition or an actual increase in its extent.

Child abuse is not a haphazard occurrence, despite evidence that anyone sufficiently stressed by adversity is liable to abuse a child judged uncooperative. As a group, abusers show certain characteristics, although many people with the same characteristics do not abuse children. For instance, abusers are most frequently parents, step-parents, or others in charge of the child. Parents who abuse tend to be young, unskilled, and often from lower social classes. Criminality, recidivism, and low intelligence are common; whereas mental illness, severe alcoholism, and drug addiction are less frequently found. There is evidence that many abusers show disorders of personality, or neuroses coupled with a sense of low self-esteem, but there is no homogeneous personality profile. They tend to have difficult relationships with their spouses or partners, family, and friends, and consequently have little support or help despite, frequently, suffering hardships such as poor housing and unemployment.

Abusing parents have themselves usually been abused as children. They frequently function at the emotional level of a young child, and the abuse occurs during outbursts of uncontrolled anger. They have, almost always, unrealistic expectations of the abused child, who is expected to be obedient and empathic to the parents' needs, and to have a degree of control over natural functions and behaviour appropriate to a much older child or to an adult. This feature is frequently so marked as to constitute a role reversal: it is as if the child is expected to be the parent of the parent.

There is no one set of characteristics that distinguishes children who are abused, although there is evidence that some groups are especially vulnerable: for instance, the youngest child, any under two years, the premature, and children with congenital deformities. Commonly one child in a family is abused more than the others.

There is now evidence that it is a common human characteristic for parents not to feel love immediately for their newly born offspring and that a loving, protective attitude becomes established as a result of social interaction between infant and parents, in which each plays a part—a process often referred to as 'bonding' (see ATTACHMENT). In many instances of abuse associated with difficult family relationships, the ability of parents to develop their capacities to protect and to care consistently for an infant appears to be limited. In such families particular dynamic patterns can be identified. For example, so long as the infant is an 'easy baby', rewarding to handle and healthy, all may be well; and while this state continues the infant may be protected and loved. Intense anger, associated with irresistible impulses to force the child to comply with the parents' wishes, is, however, aroused whenever the infant's behaviour leads one, or both, parents to feel inadequate (the irritable or sickly baby, the baby who is difficult to feed or to pacify), or to feel rejected by the baby (the unresponsive baby who seldom smiles). In other instances, anger is directed towards the baby because the relationship cannot be isolated from the relationships the parents have with each other or with other members of the family.

Some common examples of family dynamics associated with abuse are: (i) The parents feel they are in some way to blame, because the child is malformed, or because the child's physical attributes or sex do not meet with family or cultural expectations. (ii) One parent, usually the father, or a sibling, feels unloved and jealous because of the attention given to the baby by the other parent. (iii) Anger aroused by someone towards whom a parent cannot show anger is redirected towards the baby, who cannot retaliate. (iv) Abuse is a Medea-like attempt on the part of one spouse to take revenge on the other. The assumption is that it will hurt that spouse if the baby is hurt. (v) A love-hungry parent may demand an unrealistic degree of altruistic devotion, companionship, and love from a child—who is attacked because he or she cannot meet these expectations. An overview of the subject of child abuse has been edited by Ellerstein (1981).

We are still far from constructing a comprehensive theoretical model to explain social behaviour in man, and it may never be possible to explain all instances of child abuse by a single model. For example, abuse by parents who suffer recognizable mental illness—when the abuse is often bizarre—may have a distinctive origin. Nevertheless, many of the characteristics described above are seen frequently enough to suggest that it may be possible to find a theory that will allow useful predictions to be made in many instances of child abuse. The model would have to explain why intensely angry impulses towards a child are regularly aroused whenever the behaviour of the child results in a parent feeling inadequate, lonely, or rejected. Ethologists such as Konrad Lorenz have suggested that harmful behaviour to babies and young animals is inhibited by an innate releasing mechanism which responds to the total configuration characterizing 'babyishness'. For some unknown reason those who abuse their children are apparently not endowed with this innate response to their offspring's behaviour and morphological features. The most comprehensive theory available today postulates that anger as described above is an emotional response to rejection and to a sense of inadequacy. This is attachment theory, formulated by John Bowlby and elaborated by Mary Ainsworth.

Attachment theory has been described as 'programmatic', in that it acts as a guide to understanding data and to further research. It can be seen as a new paradigm for understanding social development. The theory has integrated several major trends in biological and social science. It is based on the assumptions (i) that behaviour is organized around plans to reach set goals, (ii) that in order to reach goals one has to have internal representations, or working models, of the world in which one acts, and of one's self in action in that world, and (iii) that behaviour is governed by control systems—kinds of mechanisms such that certain behaviour is evoked by specific circumstances and terminated by others. Using these basic assumptions, attachment theory postulates that the infant is born with the potential to develop an internal behavioural system mediating attachment behaviour. The goal of attachment behaviour is to attain physical closeness to and interaction with familiar, more experienced people (attachment figures). Attachment behaviour can be activated at any age, and is aroused whenever strangeness, fear, or physical states such as hunger, fatigue, or malaise are experienced. There is also a complementary inbuilt system, usually fully functional in adults, which mediates parental care-giving. Care-giving behaviour, when effective, terminates attachment behaviour in another person, and restores a child (or indeed another adult) to a state in which he or she is able to explore and to enjoy the surrounding world and relate to others in a care-giving way. Without such experience of care-giving the child, or adult, feels angry and rejected; angry protests then alternate with states of despair.

Child abuse is difficult to treat; but in many instances it is possible, after the first discovery of abuse, to promote the development of effective parental care-giving behaviour, by providing understanding helpers who act, as it were, as surrogate grandparents, taking an active part in supporting and educating parents so that they can achieve a sense of attainment about their lives and parental responsibilities.

Punishment of abusing parents is singularly ineffective. A reason for this can be predicted from attachment theory. Punishment, in so far as it evokes fear and feelings of rejection, arouses the parents' own attachment behaviour and leaves them disassuaged. Moreover, the parents are not helped to develop effective parental behaviour.

It is an important preventive measure to take steps to promote the development of affectionate parent–child relationships, by ensuring that the child and parents have the opportunity to interact right from birth onward, and so build up the new relationships. There is now growing evidence (Bretherton and Walters, 1985) that development of harmonious relationships between parents and child is facilitated first by close physical contact between them in a supportive, comforting environment immediately after birth followed by responsive, supportive, and companionable interaction thereafter.

Nevertheless, in some instances it is found that, even with help, a parent's capacity to care for a child reliably and consistently cannot be sufficiently developed. Then a second home, with consistent and loving surrogate parents, has to be found for the child, in order to ensure not only that he survives but that his development in all its aspects proceeds as well as possible. Without such measures an abused child is unlikely to become an effective parent when he grows up, and is liable to continue the tragic tradition of abuse into which he was born.                                        D. H. H.

Bretherton, I. and Waters, E. (eds.) (1985). *Growing Points of Attachment Theory and Research*. Monographs of the Society for Research in Child Development. Chicago.

Ellerstein, N. S. (ed.) (1981). *Child Abuse and Neglect*. A Medical Reference. New York.

Smith, S. M. (ed.) (1978). *The Maltreatment of Children*. Lancaster.

**CHILDHOOD.** The way societies treat their children, how they regard them, and how they order their lives reveal a great deal about the values of those societies. In Britain, a curious ambivalence about children has been displayed since the end of the First World War. There has been a flood of books on child-rearing, much discussion and theorizing about their upbringing and early education, and a plethora of educational toys. The general assumption has been that this is the golden age of childhood, an enormous lollipop that will last for ever. At the same time, though, there is much envy of children and aggression towards them: they are battered, beaten, and sexually exploited (see CHILD ABUSE) and in modern warfare they are killed and injured with impartiality.

In the twentieth century it looks as if childhood is celebrated more self-consciously than at other times. As Aries (1973) has pointed out, the concept of childhood as a phase of life existing in its own right is a relatively recent one. Children have always been appreciated as a means of continuing the family line, a way of achieving a kind of immortality, a source of labour, and an investment for the future. But since, in the past, means of contraception were inadequate, more children were born than could possibly be fed in times of food shortage or poverty. They were commonly killed off either by exposure in the open or by being subjected to lethal child-rearing practices. Disease, famine, and war carried off many more and kept the world's population in check. Christian fastidiousness about the preservation of life checked the practice of infanticide in Europe, but unwanted children were left at church-doors or outside almshouses. The foundling homes were a response to this practice. If the child was strong enough to survive, he was incorporated into the adult world and put to work as soon as possible. The chief distinction between adult and child was that the child being smaller and weaker was worth less and so paid less than the adult in his prime. The appalling incidence of infant mortality set limits to the relationship between parent and child. What was the use of becoming fond of a child who was almost certain to die? The duty of the middle-class parent was to prepare the child for the afterlife,

and the possibility of salvation, rather than for the world he was likely to inhabit for so short a time. A look at the readers and grammar of a Puritan family makes this point forcibly: 'Child, you will not live long so prepare to meet your God!' seems to be the predominant message. In an agricultural society where food was produced by labour-intensive methods, there was a place for the labour of those working-class children who survived. If they were set to work at the earliest possible age, this was not merely exploitation: their labour was an important contribution to the needs of the family. The Industrial Revolution too, is often stigmatized as a period of particular horror for children, and our attention is drawn to the small boy sitting for hours opening and shutting a trap-door in a coalmine, or the half-naked girl dragging a cart full of coal behind her, or to the child mutilated by unprotected machinery. All this happened, and was dreadful, but it must also be remembered the child was contributing to the survival of his family. Working-class families had no alternative and at least the child could take pride in his achievements. The almost desperate resistance to compulsory education when it was first introduced in the nineteenth century is evidence that many families needed their children's wages and could not afford to lose them to the schoolteachers. Even today many working-class children are eager to leave school as early as possible, in order to earn a living and support themselves. And this is at a time when changes in industrial practice make the employment of the young uneconomic.

The modern child is more likely to survive into adulthood than his predecessors (although the survival rate of working-class children is still lower than that of middle- and upper-class children); and with survival as a probability new attitudes have arisen. Moreover, now parents can control the number of children they have and can space out pregnancies. Together with children who are 'wanted' comes a belief in the goodness of childhood. Jean Jacques Rousseau's conviction that the child is born pure but is ruined by the impositions of civilization which fetter and corrupt, and William Blake's view of the child's innocence and beauty, have powerfully affected society's view of childhood, which has come to be treasured for itself. This new vision was celebrated widely in nineteenth-century painting and poetry: the innocent child was set alongside the 'noble savage' and on to both were projected society's yearning for a better state. (The strain of maintaining the purity of this image of childhood was perhaps partly responsible for the decline into the sentimentality about children characteristic of middle and late Victorian times.) Then Sigmund *Freud's theories of the powerful (but not specific) sexual drives in the small child undermined this unrealistic view of young innocence. And so two views of childhood have continued to exist side by side in our own time: the child as a beautiful and creative individual in his own right, and as one whose libidinous and chaotic energies must be harnessed and educated.

The 'permissive' view of child-rearing has become firmly established both in the USA and in Britain. Beneath the belief that it is wrong to give a firm structure to the life of the child, lurks the hope that life will be better for the child than it has been for the parent, even if there is no clear view of what is 'better' in terms of human security and happiness. Sometimes permissiveness has led to a disastrous abandonment of common sense and has caused much unhappiness to both parents and children. Respect for the child has, however, made family life less formal and has made schools happier places to be in; an appreciation of the creative abilities of children and closer attention to their ways of learning have been positive benefits of this new respect.

On the other hand, opposed to this belief in 'freedom' for the child, has run an undercurrent of envy, fear of the child's sexuality, and even a hatred, which is expressed in punishment and exploitation. Relegation of the child to the nursery or boarding school, baby batterings and scoldings, the feelings of guilt engendered by the prohibition of masturbation or the insistence of regular bowel movements have all taken their toll. A. S. *Neill wrote of this 'hatred of children' and insisted that it was the root cause of most of the problems of child-rearing—bedwetting, thieving, and the inability to learn. These represented the rebellion of the child against its restrictive upbringing. Life in our large cities brings further restrictions—many children have little mobility, are confined to the upper floors of tower blocks, and have inadequate facilities for play. Often their capacity to understand and to learn are under-estimated: they are assumed to be ignorant of the facts of death, sex, or race. It is hard to accept that children, like all human beings, are in their own terms engaged in the task of making sense of the world.

Finding that it is seemingly impossible to bring up children satisfactorily, many in the West have turned to other civilizations for hope and guidance. One thing is certain: the ills of Western civilization have not been cured by changes in child-rearing methods. Truby King's four-hourly feeding schedule did not cause the First World War nor Dr Spock the urban guerrilla!

Dispassionate evaluation of an activity as complex as parenthood is not easy. Children are at once relatively weak and vulnerable and also potentially disruptive of adult peace of mind. There is now a long period during which children have time to become adults; adolescence has been interposed between childhood and adulthood. It used to be that a Jewish boy was told at his bar mitzvah ceremony at the age of 13 that he had become a man; this is still so, but now he must be content, as all youths must be, with the prospect of years at school and possibly, if lucky, professional training before admission to adult society. Girls are in the same predicament: they may secure recognition by early motherhood, otherwise they may have to accept even lower status than boys at school and at work.

The problems associated with adolescence have long been recognized. A society that celebrates childhood, however equivocally, finds it exceedingly difficult to tolerate adolescents. Baby-faced charm gives way to gauche assertiveness, and the object of biologically triggered, parental protectiveness becomes a challenge to authority. Adolescents in Western society have a generally poor image. Aided and abetted by entrepreneurs for commercial gain, they tend to set up what seems to be a separate culture designed to exclude adults. In part this attempt to establish a separate identity is in reaction to a society unable to find a constructive place for them. In dress, in music, and in their general life-style, adolescents assert themselves by banding together—though preserving the class distinctions which characterize their parents: the middle-class 'hippy' drop-out is very different from the working-class punk rocker. Their activities are envied and feared. Some adults fear that the young may usurp their rights and privileges; others regret their own lost, though less liberated, youth; many envy the lack of obligations and the freedom of movement and expression that the young seem to enjoy. Adolescents are often the target of the moral panics that sweep society from time to time.

It has to be accepted that there never has been a golden age of childhood when children were cared for without question and when filial duties were carried out without protest. In recent times attitudes to childhood have changed in complex ways. Parents may enjoy their children more positively than those in other centuries have been able to do, but they still have to cope with the envy and inner conflict that is an inevitable part of their relations with the young. A proper balance between the care and the control of children remains difficult to achieve.                    C. H.
                                                N. S.

Aries, P. (1973). *Centuries of Childhood*. Harmondsworth.
Bettelheim, B. (1969). *Children of the Dream*. London.
Bronfenbrenner, U. (1974). *Two Worlds of Childhood*. Harmondsworth.
de Mause, L. (1974). *The History of Childhood*. London.
Erikson, E. H. (1965). *Childhood and Society*. Harmondsworth.
Miller, D. (1969). *The Age Between*. London.
Newson, J. and Newson, E. (1965). *Patterns of Infant Care*. London.
Spock, B. (1969). *Baby and Childcare*. New York and London.

**CHILDREN.** See BRAIN DEVELOPMENT; CHILDREN'S UNDERSTANDING OF THE MENTAL WORLD; HUMAN GROWTH; INFANCY, MIND IN; LANGUAGE DEVELOPMENT IN CHILDREN; REASONING: DEVELOPMENT IN CHILDREN; SEX DIFFERENCES IN CHILDHOOD.

# CHILDREN'S DRAWINGS OF HUMAN FIGURES.

Children's drawings are often very beautiful. As the article about them in *The Oxford Companion to Art* says, 'The art of children is not a vehicle for the greatest expression of the human mind, but within its limits it offers a rare perfection of feeling and expression.' Even the collection of decrepit monstrosities shown in Fig. 1 is beautiful. But of course, if these drawings are supposed to be realistic (as we must accept that they are) something is very queer. The realism concerned must be realism in rather a special sense. It results from a sensibility to which, it seems, all children intuitively aspire. The drawings have an undeniable underlying logic: they have been called the products of 'intellectual realism' as opposed to 'visual realism'. The question is, precisely what kind of logic they reveal. According to what kind of rules are these children operating? Recent books which discuss the results of detailed experimentation have been written by Freeman (1980), Gardner (1980), Golomb (1974), and Goodnow (1977).

Without a sophisticated theoretical model of the workings of the child's mind, we shall never know exactly what he or she intends to represent. We cannot rely upon the drawings to give us direct access to the inner world of the child, as though they were faithful reflections of 'body images'. First, it is debatable how far an activity which demands sophisticated motor control can ever be free of planning problems specific to the medium. Secondly, as Neisser (1970) explains, in order to use the concept of a mental image it is necessary to have evidence for its place in a mental system that is independent of the phenomena to be explained. Otherwise one falls into circular judgements whereby the form of the mental image is deduced from the drawing and then used to explain it. Thirdly, as Abercrombie and Tyson (1966) point out, it is necessary to have criteria specifying the standard of comparison. If a child who draws a disjointed human figure always draws incoherently, whatever the topic, one would say that the child could not draw adequately rather than that she had a fragmented body image. No research project to date has come near to solving these three linked sets of problems, though Shontz (1969) made a commendable attempt. Therefore, although the child's system of thoughts and feelings about himself and others undoubtedly influences many aspects of his drawings, there is no acceptable evidence that his conceptual system is necessarily the major determinant of the form of any particular drawing.

Faced with these difficulties, some authors have simply attempted to classify drawings. R. Kellogg (1970) produced an elaborate taxonomy of forms based partly on the mandala. Certainly some of the forms are extremely striking in that they seem to conform more to radial symmetry than to the elongated conventional figure whose progression towards visual fidelity is shown in Fig. 3. The ubiquitous 'tadpole' is shown in Fig. 2. But Kellogg's formal scheme does not appear in the development of individual children (Golomb, 1981). So if it is unsafe to assume an infantile urge

**Fig. 1.** Drawings of people done by nursery-school children, showing their different solutions to the difficult problem.

**Fig. 2.** The tadpole figure (*homme têtard*). The central one was produced by a severely mentally handicapped adult, the other two by pre-school children. Are the arms really attached to the head?

**Fig. 3.** Trend towards visually faithful drawings by Helen, between 4 years 6 months and 5 years 6 months, as she develops her characteristic stylization.

towards radial symmetry, perhaps radial forms such as the tadpoles represent the solution to a special kind of problem. The child may intend to produce an elongated figure but always slips up in the execution. According to such a view, the drawings would show us more about the child's mastery of spatial relations in laying out lines on a page than about urges governing mental imagery or aesthetic aims. One argument runs as follows.

First, in order to draw body parts and represent the relations between them, the child must have mental representations of them *available*. However, this does not guarantee that the representations will be *accessible* when they are needed. Performance in a task involving the active use of memory·can never be assumed to be com-

pletely efficient. If one wishes to investigate the contents of memory, it is common practice to 'prompt' the subject, using cues for recall, rather than rely upon unaided performance. So with drawings, if one dictates the parts of the drawing simply by naming them, the child will often produce a vastly improved drawing, showing that she had been aware of the parts but could not call them up for herself. Again, provision of an incomplete drawing often cues the child into producing new parts: even inveterate scribblers may suddenly demonstrate their knowledge, as in Fig. 4. Clearly we ought not to judge the child's ability on the basis of spontaneous drawings without considering the conditions under which she would draw differently.

**Fig. 4.** This pre-school child, who had never produced anything better than a scribble, responds excellently by adding limbs to an incomplete figure pre-drawn on the page.

Secondly, even if the child has access to all the necessary information, she cannot produce it all at once on the page. Drawing is sequential: one can only draw one thing at a time; and there are specific problems inherent in organizing serially ordered behaviour. One problem often manifests itself in a tendency towards end-anchoring: the ends of a series can often be recalled or responded to with greater reliability than intermediate items. The phenomenon is most marked with temporal series, but can apply to spatial series too. The end-items in the human figure are the head and legs. So we expect them to be produced more reliably than the body or arms. This is indeed the case. Indeed, when we consider the facial features alone, there is some evidence suggesting that the eyes and mouth are more reliably drawn than the serially intermediate nose.

We can now see how the tadpole figure might be generated. The child might even have available a full body image, but would preferentially access the terminal head and legs. It seems to be the case that most tadpole-drawers produce the body parts in the order: head, legs, arms. In such a case the arms are more often put on the head than on the legs. But what kind of rule guides arm-positioning here—is the child really aiming for the head? If we were to intervene and draw a body for him, would she then attach the arms to the body?

To put the argument formally, there are two possible responses. One is to attach arms to the head, the other to attach them to the body. The series in Fig. 5 presents two sets of stimuli (*a* and *b*), scaled according to head–body ratio, which might influence the relative strengths of the two response-tendencies. Experiment shows that it does so. The majority of tadpole-drawers do not consistently go for either the head or the body, but to whichever circle is the larger. The head–body

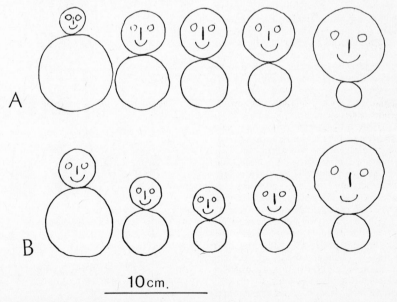

10 cm.

**Fig. 5.** Drawing-completion tasks involving stimuli scaled according to head–body ratio. Where will the children attach the arms?

**Fig. 6.** Human-figure drawings by Sarah Freeman, aged 3 years 2 months to 3 years 4 months, with spontaneous confident attempts at a cat, Tyrannosaurus Rex, and a leopard, which are clearly based on her method of drawing the human figure.

ratio reliably controls the locus of arm-attachments: the 'body-proportion' effect. So none of the simple accounts based on body image, which children have in their minds as a result of extended sensory experience, can be *quite* right, for they do not predict drawing behaviour associated with the tadpole stage.

The technique opens up the possibility of forcing children to make graphic decisions, in a way that is not possible if one confines oneself to collecting their spontaneous products. This applies most strongly to two-year-old children who cannot yet draw: they willingly undertake such a drawing-completion game, and it can be shown that they too reliably attach the arms to whichever shape is the larger. Interestingly enough, even when they progress beyond the tadpole stage in their drawings many children show this phenomenon for a time; so the transition from a tadpole to a more conventional figure may not represent a sharp break.

What does the drawing-completion evidence show? It may show that the children simply regard the larger circle as the *real* body, and they know that bodies have arms. However, the basic phenomenon appears even when the children have been asked to draw a nose or a navel immediately prior to attaching the arms. They do so correctly, treating the circles appropriately as head and body, but cannot avoid attaching the arms to the larger circle. Thus the body-proportion effect attests to a graphic production problem: a problem in organizing lines on the page and handling the interactions between what is already on the page and what is to come. Mastery of this for one topic may be generalized to tackle others (see Fig. 6).

The same approach may be used in analysing the representation of complex scenes involving the combination of separate forms (see Fig. 7). Psy-

chologists are now engaged on research into children's depiction of occlusion (hiding of further by nearer objects), elevation, relative orientation, and perspective. Already one new puzzle has

**Fig. 7.** Sarah's drawing of a car with passenger and driver: a first attempt at unification of separate forms, at age 3 years 7 months.

**Fig. 8.** 'Transparency drawings' by two children aged 5 years 6 months, in which a hidden object is shown in its entirety. Perhaps 'superimposition' would be a better term than 'transparency'. The first drawing shows a pirate in a lifeboat, the second shows a house with a bed and a person in it.

emerged. Given the striking nature of 'transparency representations' (see Fig. 8), which are often held to be the hallmark of 'intellectual realism', why are they so very difficult to obtain under experimental conditions? The status of this indication of drawing ability is one of the topics increasingly questioned as experimenters move away from the 'development of drawings' to the psychological development of the child drawer (Freeman and Cox, 1985). N. H. F.

Abercrombie, M. L. J. and Tyson, M. C. (1966). Body image and draw-a-man test in cerebral palsy. *Developmental Medical Child Neurology*, **8**, 9–15.

Freeman, N. H. (1975). Do children draw men with arms coming out of the head? *Nature*, **254**, 416–17.

Freeman, N. H. (1977). How young children try to plan drawings. In Butterworth, G. (ed.), *The Child's Representation of his World*. London.

Freeman, N. H. (1980). *Strategies of Representation in Young Children: analysis of spatial skills and drawing processes*. London.

Freeman, N. H. and Cox, M. V. (1985). *Visual Order: the nature and development of pictorial representation*. Cambridge.

Gardner, H. (1980). *Artful Scribbles*. New York.

Golomb, C. (1974). *Young Children's Sculpture and Drawing*. Cambridge, Massachusetts.

Golomb, C. (1981). Representation and reality. *Review of Research in Visual Art Education*, **14**, 36–48.

Goodnow, J. J. (1977). *Children's Drawing*. London.

Kellogg, R. (1970). *Analysing Children's Art*. Palo Alto.

Neisser, U. (1970). Visual imagery as process and experience. In Antrobus J. S. (ed.), *Cognition and Affect*. Boston.

Osborne, H. (1970). *The Oxford Companion to Art*. (Entries concerning Art Education, Children's Art, Psychiatric Art.) Oxford.

Shontz, F. C. (1969). *Perceptual and Cognitive Aspects of Body Experience*. London.

**CHILDREN'S UNDERSTANDING OF THE MENTAL WORLD.** One of the most important powers of the human mind is to conceive of and think about itself and other minds. Because the mental states of others (and indeed of ourselves) are completely hidden from the senses, they can only ever be inferred. Thinking about these unobservable states is a subtle business indeed, but in one way or another an essential part of our social life. One could be forgiven therefore for assuming that the deployment of such a 'theory of mind' must be a very late accomplishment of childhood and that it must require the benefit of education and tutoring. Recent research, however, is beginning to show that this 'theory' emerges during the pre-school years and depends upon specific innate mechanisms.

The most important kinds of mental state that we infer and attribute have a characteristic form. First, they have a *content*—they are about something; second, they take an *attitude* to the content—whether the content is believed, hoped, or desired; and third, they say who is taking this attitude to the content. So, for example, 'John believes it is raining' has John taking the attitude 'believes' to the content 'it is raining'. We use such attributions to explain and to predict behaviour. So, 'John jumped into the doorway *because* he believed it was raining and he will now put up his umbrella *because* he wants to remain dry.'

We can look experimentally to see whether a child can use such attributions in this way. A powerful test of this is when the child can predict someone's behaviour on the basis of an attributed false belief. This attribution will differ from and indeed contradict the child's own beliefs and so provides a stringent test of the child's ability to conceive of beliefs *as* beliefs.

For example, Sally hides a chocolate in a certain box, then goes out for a walk. Meanwhile, someone else, Ann, arrives, finds the chocolate and transfers it to a basket near by. Ann too then departs. A short time later Sally returns, wanting her chocolate. We can test a child who has been watching these comings and goings, to see if he (or she) understands the various events, and satisfy ourselves that he does. We can then go on to ask the child, 'well, where will Sally look for her chocolate?' If the child understands that Sally will still believe her chocolate to be in the box (while he himself knows it is in the basket), then he will point at the box. If, on the other hand, he cannot work out what Sally will believe, he will predict Sally's behaviour in terms of the actual situation and point to the basket.

Wimmer and Perner (1983) and Baron-Cohen, Leslie, and Frith (1985) found that most 4-year-old children can pass this test. On the other hand, most 3-year-olds will fail. Those who fail consistently point to where the chocolate really is, as if Sally too would know this. One way of understanding the 3-year-olds' failure is in terms of a fundamental logical ability which they, but not the 4-year-old, lack. For example, it may be that before about 4 years, children are not capable of simultaneously conceiving of and appreciating two alternative and contradictory models of reality.

Thus the very young child can work only with his own model of the situation as he perceives it and not at the same time with Sally's model, which is different from and contradicts his own. By 4 years of age this ability has appeared and the child can now successfully predict Sally's behaviour (where she will look) according to Sally's model of the situation.

Another task requiring appreciation of simultaneously contradictory models of reality occurs when an object appears to be one thing but is really another. For example, a child is shown a sponge which has been cleverly disguised to look like a rock. The child is allowed to discover that really it is a sponge, and is then tested to see if he can appreciate the contrast between what it looks like and what it really is. J. H. Flavell has tested children on this sort of task. Again it appears that most 4-year-olds succeed while most 3-year-olds fail.

Thus it seems that the appreciation that people can have different ideas about a situation develops between 3 and 4 years of age. But is this ability to conceive of alternative realities really absent at 3 years?

Consider what is involved when a 2-year-old child engages in pretend play. Let us suppose that the child sees a banana on a table in front of him. He decides to pretend that the banana is a telephone and accordingly picks it up, holds it at the side of his face, and simulates talking. It is most unlikely that the child has made an error and has wrongly identified the banana as a telephone, for he can see that the banana is a banana. So at one and the same time he is representing the situation as one which contains a banana and one in which the banana is a telephone. Isn't this child appreciating alternative and contradictory models of the same situation?

Consider also what happens when a child watches his mother pretending to take imaginary clothes off a teddy bear and throw them in a pile. She dips the teddy into an imaginary tub, splashes it with imaginary water, and 'soaps' it with a toy brick. What is the child to make of this? What his mother actually does is merely wiggle her fingers in the vicinity of the teddy, put teddy on the floor, accompany more finger wiggling with slurping noises, and rub the teddy with the toy brick. Clearly the child has to infer from this—from what he actually sees and hears—what it is that his mother is pretending.

The price of not being able to infer that someone is pretending something can be very high for a young child. A 2-year-old observing his mother at a telephone is able to acquire useful information about telephones and social practices, even though he does not yet really understand what is going on. But think of the same child seeing his mother pretend that a banana is a telephone. If he interprets this literally he may end up with some very funny ideas about bananas or his mother, or both. Moreover, at the same time as learning about objects and social practices from observing others, children at this age are also learning what words mean. So if a 2-year-old interprets 'Here, take the telephone' literally when what his mother is handing him is in truth a banana, language learning is put in jeopardy as well. The fact that such socially shared pretence does not have ill effects shows that young children can and do understand the alternative 'reality' of pretence while relating it to the literal reality of what they see before them.

If the 2-year-old is so expert at handling alternative and contradictory models in pretence, then why is the false belief situation (as exemplified in the chocolate box/basket test) so difficult? Why do so many children fail even at 3 years old?

The ability to *conceive* of alternative realities cannot be the breakthrough that brings success in false belief or appearance–reality tasks. But the critical change might be in the child's ability to *handle* such contradictory models—for example, in the ability to work out *precisely* what the alternative should be.

In pretence, the alternative model is essentially merely stipulated or invented. And even where the child has to work out what it is that someone is pretending, it is usually the case (*always* if the child is to succeed?) that the pretence can be read off from, or at least strongly suggested by, what the other person is literally doing. The false belief task, however, differs in both these respects, for here there is a right and a wrong answer—it has to be worked out and cannot be read off. In the chocolate test, for example, Sally's belief has to be worked out by the child on the basis of what Sally saw and did not see of the situation. Once that is done the child must deduce what Sally will do on the basis of that belief.

Even so, we may wonder if difficulty in working out the alternative model accounts entirely for the two-year lag in solving the false belief task. In the rock–sponge appearance–reality task, can the child not just 'read off' the appearance of the sponge that looks like a rock? Why is that so much more difficult than 'reading off' what someone is pretending?

Before we try to answer this, let us return to the 2-year-old and pretending. When the child works out that his mother is pretending that the banana is a telephone, he is attributing a mental state to her—the mental state of pretending (attitude) that a banana is a telephone (content). A 2½-year-old girl watches her brother who pretends to fill a cup with water and then turns this cup upside-down over the head of a doll. She reaches for a cloth and pretends to dry the doll, showing that she has worked out the consequences of an attributed pretence. This involves both attributing an alternative model and handling it cognitively.

Furthermore, analysis can show that being able both to pretend and to make attributions of pretence to others requires mastery of exactly the same *logical structures* as understanding mental states in others (Leslie, 1986). For a discussion of the peculiar logical properties of things which express mental states—for example, sentences about mental states or thoughts about thoughts—see CONSCIOUSNESS.

So even the very young child can handle the basic logic of mental states. Despite this, most children fail in false belief tasks until about 4 years of age. Our question is, why? So far we have suggested that the failure has something to do with not being able to work out what belief someone with a given exposure to a given situation will have.

Perner, Leekam, and Wimmer (forthcoming) took sixteen 3-year-olds who had failed the false belief task and showed them a Smartie box (for a confection well known to British children), asking them what they thought it contained. The children answered, 'Smarties'. They were then shown that in fact the box contained no Smarties, just a pencil. Nine of the children could tell the experimenter, 'I thought it contained Smarties, but I was wrong.' These children were then asked, 'When we bring your friend in and show him the closed box, what will he think is in it?' Amazingly enough, they all answered, 'A pencil'!

This shows that these 3-year-olds, despite their ability to model and report a false belief, were unable to understand where the belief came from. Despite the fact that they themselves had just undergone the process of acquiring that false belief, they were quite unable to understand and reconstruct the process, and were thus unable to predict what would happen to their friend.

Adults attribute mental states to machines and plants without actually believing that mental states really exist inside the machines or plants. For example, a person says that his central heating system *knows* when it's cold and *wants* to keep the house warm. He does this to describe its behaviour; but whatever it is that responds to the temperature and makes the heating come on, he never believes that it is a thought or anything like a thought. Can it be in a similar way to this that the young child attributes mental states to people and

that, under special circumstances, the child will even attribute mental states in order to understand behaviour, but without regarding them as *things which really exist*?

What would follow from the child's regarding mental states as real? It would allow the build-up of general knowledge to begin, with general knowledge about mental states. If mental states are real, they must exist somewhere (but where?) and most importantly, they must be part of the *causal* fabric of the world (but how?). It may not even occur to the very young child that mental states are actually caused by other things—by concrete events—and that they are in turn the *cause* of other real things such as behaviour. Without this insight, there is no reason for a child to look closely at situations and people's exposure to them, with mental states in mind. But once a child does, he or she will consider what events lead to what mental states. It seems that these developments begin to take place between 3 and 4 years, culminating in the cognizance that led to the 4-year-olds' remarkable success in the Wimmer and Perner false belief task reported in 1983.

Wellman (1985, 1986) showed that 3-year-olds have the beginnings of a cohesive and explanatory theory of mind that include ideas about the way mental states exist. For example, they understand quite clearly that while a banana can be eaten, the thought of a banana cannot. When explaining these differences even young children have recourse to mentalistic language and locate states of mind as being in the head. For example, in explanation of whether or not a dream is real, a child might say 'it's in his head, it's only pretend'. Indeed, it is striking how often in these contexts a child qualifies the mental state with 'just', 'just pretending', or 'only', 'only a dream'. Such qualification seems to contrast the mental state with concrete publicly observable objects and events. This focus upon the different reality status of mental events is a perfectly proper emphasis for the child to have and in itself demonstrates the subtlety of early human understanding.

This focus may, however, exact a price in obscuring the fact that mental states are real enough, only in a different way from the concrete world. Again, the crucial step in coming to think of mental states as real will be the linking of them *causally* with the concrete world: if mental states can be both the effect and the cause of something concrete then they must themselves at least be *real*, if not concrete.

The task then for the 4-year-old is to link his developing understanding of causal mechanisms in the physical world with his theory of mind. We know that by 4 years children have a good grasp of the essentials of physical mechanics (Bullock, Gelman, and Baillergeon, 1982). One aspect of this has to do with understanding when people are and are not in a position to see and hear things—Level 1 understanding in Flavell's (1978) sense. This then could provide the bridge enabling the 4-year-old to link up his causal understanding of the concrete world with his more abstract understanding of the mental world.

Understanding false belief requires the child to realize that Sally's exposure to the chocolate in the box will *cause* her to believe the chocolate to be in the box, while her non-exposure to its change of location will leave this belief unchanged. Thus when Sally comes back again it is this unchanged belief about the box that will determine her search behaviour. Likewise, in the rock–sponge example, understanding appearance–reality requires the child to figure out what mental state (belief) would result, given exposure to only some of the visual properties of the object. In a sense, the child could indeed just 'read off' the appearance. But what mental state would such an appearance cause in someone who does not know what the object really is (has not been exposed to the other perceptible properties as well)? This may be what provides the insuperable problem for the very young child.

We are suggesting, then, that children start with a causal theory of behaviour which admits only of concrete objects and events as causes of behaviour. Their ability to attribute mental states develops independently and in parallel with this, and is used only in special circumstances—for example, pretence, or reporting the fact of knowledge changes. But at around 4 years of age the two capacities are brought together and the child enlarges its notion of possible causes of behaviour to include mental states. From now on, mental states can cause behaviour, while (perceptual) exposure to situations can cause mental states (which then represent those causing situations). Now it becomes sensible, and indeed natural, for the child to pay attention to the causal relationships between situations, mental states, and behaviour. Mental states become part of the causal fabric of the world and will now therefore be predictable, reliable, and *learnable about*.

Finally, it seems that there are children who do not develop a theory of mind in the normal way. These are children who suffer from the syndrome of childhood *autism. Such children have severe impairments in their social skills. Baron-Cohen, Leslie, and Frith (1985) tested a group of autistic children of high ability with borderline to average intelligence on the false belief task. Their performance was compared with a group of *Down's syndrome children who were more severely retarded and with a group of much younger normal children. The Down's and young normal children performed remarkably similarly, with the vast majority of them passing the false belief task. However, the vast majority of the autistic children failed, pointing consistently to where they themselves knew the object to be.

Subsequently, as a follow-up, these children were tested with a picture sequencing task (Baron-Cohen, Leslie, and Frith, 1986). The pictures depicted various kinds of events. Whereas the autistic children performed very well indeed on picture stories depicting both causal mechanical events and social behavioural events, their performance with regard to events which crucially involved understanding the protagonist's mental state was extremely poor. This pattern of performance was quite different from both the normal and the Down's syndrome children.

The autistic child, then, appears to have a theory of mind impaired in a way that is not accounted for by general mental retardation. It is too soon to say with confidence precisely what is wrong, but it seems that such children are not simply like very young normal children—for the autistic child appears to show highly abnormal development in pretend play; indeed pretend play may even be entirely absent. Where that is the case it seems likely that the child has suffered a serious neurodevelopmental problem that unfortunately strikes at the innate basis of his theory of mind.

A. M. L.

Baron-Cohen, S., Leslie, A. M., and Frith, U. (1985). Does the autistic child have a 'theory of mind'? *Cognition*, **21**, 37–46.

Baron-Cohen, S., Leslie, A. M., and Frith, U. (1986). Mechanical, behavioural and intentional understanding of picture stories in autistic children. *British Journal of Developmental Psychology*, **4**, 113–25.

Bullock, M., Gelman, R., and Baillargeon, R. (1982). The development of causal reasoning. In Friedman, W. (ed.), *The Developmental Psychology of Time*, 209–54, New York.

Flavell, J. H. (1978). The development of knowledge about visual perception. In Keasey, C. B. (ed.), *Nebraska Symposium on Motivation*, **25**. Nebraska.

Flavell, J. H., Flavell, E. R., and Green, F. L. (1983). Development of the appearance–reality distinction. *Cognitive Psychology*, **15**, 95–120.

Leslie, A. M. (1986). Some implications of pretence for the child's theory of mind. Paper presented to the International Conference on Developing Theories of Mind, Toronto, Canada, May 1986.

Leslie, A. M. (forthcoming). Pretence and representation in infancy: The origins of 'theory of mind'. *Psychological Review*.

Perner, J., Leekam, S. R., and Wimmer, H. (forthcoming). Three-year-olds' difficulty with false belief: the case for a conceptual deficit. *British Journal of Developmental Psychology*.

Wellman, H. M. (1985). The child's theory of mind: the development of conceptions of cognition. In Yussen, S. R. (ed.), *The Growth of Reflection*. San Diego.

Wellman, H. M. (1986). First steps in the child's theorizing about the mind. Paper presented to the International Conference on Developing Theories of Mind, Toronto, Canada, May 1986.

Wimmer, H. and Perner, J. (1983). Beliefs about beliefs: representation and constraining function of wrong beliefs in young children's understanding of deception. *Cognition*, **13**, 103–28.

**CHINESE EVIDENCE ON THE EVOLUTION OF LANGUAGE.** Human language is the unique and most important possession of the human mind, yet thought about it has always proved extraordinarily difficult. It is suggested here that important new light on its evolution is to be found in an original way of representing it visually, i.e. writing it, developed gradually by the ancient Chinese.

The Chinese script (adopted by the Japanese and Koreans, whose own languages are unrelated to Chinese but who nevertheless use it, especially for the many loan-words they have incorporated from Chinese, much as English has from Latin and Greek, and who eke it out with their own phonetic symbols) differs from all others in wide use today by being logographic: that is, instead of aiming at recording segments of sound that strung together can notate speech, its symbols or characters each represent a *logos* or unit of meaning in the language's construction. In Chinese this is always a grammatically invariable monosyllable, which may be a word used independently, like 'house' or 'boat', or 'man' or 'kind'; or may be combined with other such monosyllables to form polysyllables, like 'houseboat', 'boatman', or 'mankind'. All words of more than one syllable in Chinese were at least originally of this type; word-forming syllables such as '-er' in 'farmer' and so on, which never existed as independent words, did not feature in Chinese word-making. Furthermore, grammatical inflexions which also had no independence as words, like our plural '-s' and past tense '-ed', had no place either. Chinese lacks the kind of grammar that makes them necessary: expression of plurality, tense, and the like in Chinese is voluntary, and when necessary is performed by means of independent syllables such as 'two-three', 'some', 'just now', 'long since', and so forth. Otherwise it is left to context. Chinese is therefore described by linguists as an extreme example of the 'analytic' as opposed to the 'synthetic' type (exemplified by Latin and Greek) of human language; and the logographic system of writing invented for it is possible and suits it, as it would not a language of less analytic nature. Because of its analytic nature Chinese has always resisted the importation of foreign words, which would be mere sounds resistant to analysis in Chinese terms; preferring to translate or otherwise find purely Chinese expressions for new ideas from abroad. Etymology, usually a learned subject to those with more synthetic languages and who import foreign words, is to a much greater extent self-evident to the Chinese and is recorded faithfully in their logographic script. The logograms themselves (or ideograms, but this name is ambiguous in so far as it is also used for certain kinds of them only) were devised in several ways. First, there are those most obvious, the *indicative*: for example, one stroke for 'one', two strokes for 'two', a dot above a line for 'above', a dot below a line for 'below', and signs such as 入 'to enter', 'to insert', which, in what became the standard brush-written script, are now respectively 一, 二, 上, 下, and 入. Secondly, there are those that were *pictorial*: for example like 人 or 个 or 大 for a 'human being, man(kind)', kneeling in a loop 卩 for a 'girl', 'young person', 'woman' (one not an adult man), 子 or 子 for a 'child', 田 for 'fields', which are now respectively 人, 大, 女, 子, and 田. In addition, there are characters which, though they depicted things, stood rather for their qualities than for themselves: for example 丿, an arm, for 'strength' (the mere cross for the hand showed it was not a focus of attention) is now much changed as 力. Thirdly, there are the characters called by the Chinese *combining meanings*, that showed two or more things together to suggest a meaning: for example, 好, a woman and child, for 'to love; lovely, good' and 男, strength and fields, for '(able-bodied) man, male, masculine'. Each of these logograms was invented to write a monosyllable, with its range of meanings and sometimes minor variations in pronunciation according to usage (for example, as between 'to love' and 'lovely, good'). They were tied to the language for which they were devised as a system of writing it, and did not otherwise depict things or ideas (even though they contained no indication whatever of pronunciation, any more than arabic or roman numerals show how they are pronounced). Finally there is the category, to which the great majority of Chinese characters belong, that do contain some indication of pronunciation. They are divided in two, as the so-called *borrowed characters* (i.e. any symbol belonging originally to any of the above categories but supposedly 'borrowed' only for its sound without respect to its meaning), and the so-called *phonetic compounds*, of which part was a *borrowed character* (called the 'phonetic' by Western scholars) according to traditional descriptions, and part (the 'determinative', 'signific', or 'radical', the latter because of its use as a key in arranging characters in dictionaries) serving to distinguish between words with similar pronunciation. Such words are inevitably legion in a monosyllabic language—like English 'bear', the animal, and 'to bear', to carry, be strong enough, endure. In a phonetic compound, the animal might be distinguished by having 'mammal', and the verb by having 'hand' (which is often used to indicate verbs in Chinese) added to a 'phonetic' which they would share.

In any Chinese text, although many of the characters may be formed by the other methods of character-formation (especially those for some common words), the great majority will usually be found to belong to the phonetic compound class, which is even said to account for 95 per cent of the characters listed in Chinese equivalents of the *Oxford English Dictionary*; and each, when etymologies are given, will be described merely as so-and-so 'determinative' with so-and-so 'phonetic'. Such character 'etymologies' do not seem as interesting as the analysis of the other, 'poetic' kinds of character-formation, and yet it is these very characters which, when examined afresh with the assistance of newly discovered ancient forms, throw light on the evolution of language. A simply phonetic explanation, though it seems to be universally accepted for most of these so-called phonetic compounds, encounters great difficulties. In the first place, they are by no means truly phonetic but allow extraordinary differences in pronunciation between the supposed phonetic element as a character itself and composite characters containing it: why then were they chosen? Reconstruction of ancient pronunciation, in which the great Swedish phonologist Bernhard Karlgren was a pioneer in the first half of the twentieth century, seems to have brought a degree of reason into these anomalies, showing that they were once somewhat *less* unlike than now; but why, if they were intended to represent pronunciation, should they have been unlike at all? As Karlgren said in his seminal *Analytic Dictionary of Chinese and Sino-Japanese* (1923), they cannot, by all experience of phonetic laws, once have been the same and then diverged. Why then should there be such anomalies in this supposed phonetic spelling as mixing *P* with *M*, or *N* with *T*, in characters sharing the same 'phonetic element'? Karlgren could only resort to a theory of 'homorganic spelling', whereby sounds made with the lips or sounds made with the tongue against the teeth could each be treated alike, as *M* and *P*, *N* and *T*, and so on; but why should the ancient Chinese, to whom the differences between these 'homorganic' sounds were as important as to anyone else, have done anything so perverse? Could they have read texts written by such a system? In short, does it make any sense to think of the compound class primarily as a phonetic system of spelling? And if it was not, what was it? There is a vast number of Chinese characters that can be used as supposed 'phonetic elements' in constructing others (much greater than is needed for a simply phonetic function, especially one so imprecise); yet there is remarkable consistency in the choice of one of them, even a very poor phonetic match, for the writing of a given word as a so-called 'phonetic compound'.

There is only one explanation for all this: that the 'phonetic element' also had a *meaning* and that that was even more important than how it was articulated. Let us look again at 入 'to enter', now written 入 and pronounced *rù* in Modern Standard Chinese but *yap* in Cantonese and reconstructed as **ñiəp** by Karlgren for the language of about 600 BC. The same drawing with a bar or bars behind it, 今 or 仐, is nowadays written 今, pronounced *jīn* in Modern Standard Chinese, *kam* in Cantonese, and means 'now'. The reconstructed pronunciation is **kiəm**: 'homorganic' with **ñ** because **ñ** represents a nasal sound made against the palate, so 'homorganic' with the **k** of **kiəm**, while the **-p** and the **-m** are also 'homorganic',

both being made with the lips. The meaning of 入 with a bar or bars behind can be seen as 'enclosed', conveyed in speech by the gesture of closing the mouth, hence 'included', 'contained', and so 'present'—used as in English for 'now'. The 'homorganic' qualities of the words 入 'to enter' and 今 'now', in their ancient pronunciations, would have arisen from their being derived from the same *root* which the 入 represents; the differences in pronunciation, from ancient word-forming modifications to that root. When one looks at other characters with 今 in them, one finds varying but also 'homorganic' pronunciations for meanings which all clearly relate to ideas of 'included', 'present'. As one example, with determinative 心 'heart, mind', 念 is '(to have) present in mind', 'to think about', 'to remember' (*nian* in Modern Standard Chinese, *nim* in Cantonese. Karlgren did not, in fact, treat these various characters as having the same 'phonetic' although, by his own rules, there was no good reason why he should not have done so.)

Another word for 'to have present in mind', 'to think' is written with determinative 'heart, mind' and a different so-called 'phonetic', 隹, which is said in dictionaries to mean 'a short-tailed bird' and, although obsolete now as a character on its own, occurs as the determinative in many characters for the names of birds. There are in fact two characters for 'bird', either of which is used as a determinative in characters for their names: 鳥, said to be a 'long-tailed bird', and this one; but ancient pictograms show them respectively as

and reveal a crowing cock and a squatting hen. Composite characters with the latter as 'phonetic' are used in writing words vaguely related to the hen and to one another phonetically, with a great variety of meanings: 'to be plump', 'isolated', 'stay in one place' (all like a broody hen) and to 'brood', 'think obsessively', as in English. Branching forth, as it were, from some of these ideas, which the hen illustrates, are others (given various determinatives) that can seem exceedingly remote from it: 'high' (of a mountain because isolated by its height) and metaphorical, noble meanings from that; 'moored' (of a boat); 'constant' (of a principle); even a particle with meanings like 'at' a place or time, or isolating a word or phrase for the purpose of drawing attention to it, and so on. The hen, her broodiness and sitting, are put on one side or forgotten, as conscious metaphors must be for language to develop freely from them; but there has to be a conscious metaphor *to start with* for a word to be created, because communication can only take place given a presumption of references shared in common between those endeavouring to communicate. Ultimately, these must be to common observation and experience of the world; and it is therefore not surprising to find close parallels in the etymologies of words in phonetically, grammatically, and historically unrelated languages. And even in cases where there are no such parallels, ultimate etymologies will very seldom not be comprehensible to any human being.

What about the name of the hen herself? In English it was just the feminine gender (something lacking in Chinese) of an old word for a cock, cognate with 'chant' (cf. 'chanticleer'); in Chinese it probably meant 'squatter', also relating it to a verb: in both cases something that could be acted, gestured, before a word was made.

The animal, a 'bear' has been mentioned. Etymologies in dictionaries of English ascribe this word to a root meaning 'brown': as a colour name, an abstraction certainly not amenable to acting. But a Chinese character suggests that it may have been one and the same with the root of the similarly pronounced verb 'to bear'. An early version of the character (on a bronze of the eleventh century BC)

is taken now by most scholars as a pictogram, a drawing of a bear, so contradicting the view of an early work (AD 100) on a contemporary version of it, which saw the 𠃌 in it as the 'phonetic' in a phonetic compound with the rest determinative. The 'phonetic', now 厶, in the modern form 能 of this character representing an old Chinese word for a 'bear', is seen on its own in the earliest, oracle bone script of the second millennium BC as an excellent one-stroke drawing of the profile of a hand in a carrying, *bearing* posture,

and meant 'bearing in the hand', hence 'taking with one', 'using as an instrument' and the like (now written with the addition of 'man' determinative as 以 and one of the commonest words in the language). Although this is now pronounced yĭ, reconstructed phonology shows that as **diəg** it could well have been the 'phonetic' (or represented the 'root') in 能, which is now pronounced **néng**! It is in fact the 'phonetic' or 'root' in an enormous number of characters with senses of bearing, enduring, being strong; and remarkably like the equally prolific Indo-European base **bher**—from which the English verb 'to bear' is derived, as well as (through Latin) 'fortitude', (through Greek) 'metaphor', and a vast number of other English words. The determinative elements added in the ancient Chinese character for the animal 'bear' were 𠕎: 'flesh, body, physical' (so 'physically strong'), and 𠬝, which was part of the drawing

of a stag, to represent a large animal. So 'a physically *strong* (the root of the word) large animal' was

the information conveyed in the Chinese character for a 'bear', which has been too readily supposed a crude and incompetent ('primitive') drawing. Moreover, Indo-European philologists may need to think again about the derivation of our name for the animal. Supposing it just to have meant 'brown', they assume 'beaver' (which was the same root reduplicated) to have meant 'very brown'—as if this were the best name our ancestors managed to think of! Might it not have been a *busy bearer* of materials for its dams? And might not 'brown' itself, certainly from the same root, have implied the colour of strength and health? That is an idea which can be acted, but metaphors do not provide meanings (intentions) in themselves, needing *context*.

This is well illustrated by a Chinese character with meanings now like 'to retire to rest', but in ancient texts also 'to go busily to and fro'. The character 栖, which was 'tree' plus 'bird's nest', illustrated the metaphor lying behind both. Birds 'nest' (go to roost) at sunset and 'nest' (build, go to and from their nests) in spring. Contexts would make it perfectly clear which sense was meant before the notion grew of 'words' possessing meanings in themselves: a notion that has given endless trouble to philosophers since, but which became necessary for human organization, government and institutions, and for the establishment of laws.

Two Chinese characters for 'words', now 言 and 詞 each reflect this history. Each in early forms of the script contained 𠮷, which, by studying characters containing it and their meanings, can be identified as 'a crying infant' (cf. 𠃊 for 'child')—whence 'complaint', with legal connotations in these and other characters incorporating it. Though both these characters now have only to do with speech and language, the first, augmented by 'mouth', represented originally *speech about a complaint*, including pronouncement of judgment; while the second, augmented by 'hands unravelling', represented *analysing the complaint*, pleading. (The hands unravelling showed them with a thread between them, on either side of a bar; so could indicate, according to context, *tying* the thread around the bar or *untying* it. In English the verb 'to ravel' can have similar opposing meanings, as will be seen in the *Oxford English Dictionary*. Again an image of an activity was shown, while the specific meaning depended on context.) Pleading is still its sense in ancient texts, whereas now it is like the *lexis* of 'lexicon' and used in the Chinese name for a dictionary.

In the purely metaphorical stage of language, there was no cause to think about its components individually as 'words' with fixed intentions: Chinese characters show legal processes, when they came to be important, as that cause. The revolution then brought about is the reason for misunderstanding now about the original nature of

Chinese script; as it is, too, for much of the confusion about the dual nature of human language, both natures vital now to thought and communication. The newer, artificial (logical) language strives for precision; but the original, natural (poetic) language remains necessary for creative thought.

A. R. V. C.

**CHINESE IDEAS OF MIND.** In traditional Chinese philosophy and science the psychological was almost never regarded separately from the physiological. The stance was holistic, in contrast to common Indo-European thinking stemming from ancient Greece, where *Plato and his school conveniently distinguished matter from ideas, and the soma from the *psyche. Yet the Western tradition has in the twentieth century given rise to an array of psychobiological monistic attitudes, which have as their *raison d'être* *idealism, reinforced by Judaeo-Christian tradition. (For further discussion, see MIND AND BODY; MIND–BODY PROBLEM; EVOLUTION: NEO-DARWINIAN THEORY.)

Philosophical anti-dualism in China can be traced to the Warring States period (481–221 BC), to Confucius (Kong Fuzi or Kong Qiu, 551–479 BC), and even earlier. Chinese rationalism of various schools generally opposed supernatural conceptualizations; and an organic outlook on interactions between man, nature, and government became firmly entrenched in the minds of literate people. Religious supernatural thinking nevertheless continued within popular Taoism.

Earlier Chinese sources demonstrate commonly held animistic modes of thinking—devils and spirits were thought to be able to possess the human body and soul and thus produce physical, behavioural, and social disorders. These supernatural factors were soon paralleled by the concept of natural factors such as cold, heat, wind, drought, and humidity, affecting the human body in much the same way. Confucians, on the other hand, created a highly rational, though metaphysical, system of thought characterized by numerology and what may be termed 'correlative' thinking. Objects and phenomena in the universe were seen as belonging together in groups and governed by superior principles. Numerological systems were used to analyse the phases of change that these groups, consisting of concrete as well as abstract things, went through, and the changes were believed to occur in resonance, or 'in correlation' with one another. Examples of these numerologies are the well-known yin and yang used in any analysis of paired relationships, the Five Phases (*wu xing*, earlier misleadingly rendered as the Five Elements) used in correlating anything divisible in fives, and the Ten Heavenly Stems and Twelve Earthly Branches used jointly mainly for calendrical purposes. In these contexts, they used terms, more usually applied to the supernatural, in borrowed and natural senses. Supernatural forces were disregarded—there is no way of gaining knowledge about gods; thus they are of no interest. Any dichotomy between the body and an intrapersonal soul was similarly disregarded.

Chinese literate tradition, dominated by Confucian rationalism, thus took a decidedly 'organic' point of view on psychological matters. It did not discriminate between physical, behavioural, emotional, or social cues when incorporating them into more general concepts used in medicine, psychology, or politics. This organic outlook appears to be deeply ingrained in the minds of Chinese, and other East Asians, and helps explain why their attitudes towards psychological explanations of human behaviour differ from those of Westerners. The Chinese never developed any psychology of the *unconscious.

Nevertheless, the history of Chinese philosophy is replete with arguments concerning 'principle' versus 'practicality', and 'idealism' versus 'empiricism'. One finds varying degrees of emphasis on *xin* ('heart' or 'mind'), as opposed to *wu* ('things'). For example, the most idealistic school of philosophy in the Song dynasty was that of Lu Xiangshan (1138–91), who wrote: 'Space and time are [in] my mind, and it is my mind which [generates] space and time' (Needham and Wang, 1962, p. 508). A somewhat later but more influential idealist thinker was the neo-Confucian Wang Yangming (1472–1528). Wang's *xin-xue* (study, or school of the mind) emphasized that man should endeavour to become a sage—regarding heaven-and-earth and all men and things as a unity of close relationship, and relying on [moral] principles (de Bary and Bloom, 1979). Wang wrote: 'The master of the body is the Mind; what the Mind develops are Thoughts; the substance of Thought is Knowledge; and those places where the thoughts rest are Things' (Needham and Wang, 1962, p. 509). Confucian *xin-xue* was distinct from its *shi-xue* (real or practical learning). The Japanese Buddhist-turned-neo-Confucian Hayashi Razan (1583–1657), influenced by the Wang school, held that 'principle [*li*] is prior and material force [*qi*, often transcribed as *ch'i*, the Chinese counterpart to the Greek concept of *pneuma* = vitality] posterior', but he came to experience difficulty in sustaining this position:

Principle and material force are one and yet two, two and yet one. This is the view of the Song [neo-]Confucians. However, Wang Yangming claims that principle is the regularity of material force and that material force is the operation of principle. If we follow the latter view, then there is the danger that everything will be chaotic. (de Bary and Bloom, 1979).

Buddhism, spreading from India to China in the second century AD onward, held a decidedly idealist position in declaring the visible universe an illusion: the world was nothing but mind, and the individual's mind was part of the universal mind. The Chinese Buddhists substituted *xing* ([subjective] nature) for *qi* (material force, or *pneuma*). They came to form one strand in neo-Confucian organic philosophy, but they failed to alter the fundamentally holistic outlook of indigenous Chinese thought patterns. (For further discussion of the Buddhist position, see INDIAN IDEAS OF MIND.)

The absence of a mind–body dichotomy is clearly seen in the traditional Chinese medicine of the literate classes. In the rational tradition, supposed pneumatic imbalances between internal organs were analysed in terms of a 'manifestation type' (*zheng*) of a disorder, according to specialized rules for diagnosis, including tongue inspection and pulse palpation. Widely differing disorders ('mental' as well as 'physical') would be shown to have a similar type of manifestation and thus receive similar treatment, such as herbal drugs or acupuncture.

For these reasons, psychiatry has no independent status in traditional Chinese medicine. Instead, concepts with a clearly psychiatric content are found widely dispersed in various fields of medicine. Not surprisingly, therefore, the Chinese word for psychiatry (*jingshenbingxue*: 'mental-disease-study') is a modern translation.

Psychology as a discipline (rendered in Chinese *xinlixue*: 'mind-principle-study') was introduced in Chinese universities around 1915. The subject has had a strongly practical application both before and after 1949. During the 1950s Soviet influence was dominant, with Pavlovianism the leading creed (see PAVLOV); a great deal of research attention was devoted to medical, labour, and educational psychology as well as to the development of moral character (Chin and Chin, 1969). Psychology, along with sociology, ceased to exist as an academic subject for a decade during the Cultural Revolution but was academically rehabilitated in the subsequent liberalization movement.      H. A.

de Bary, W. T. and Bloom, I. (eds.) (1979). *Principle and Practicality: essays in neo-Confucianism and practical learning*. New York.

Chin, R. and Chin, A. L. (1969). *Psychological Research in Communist China, 1949–1966*. Cambridge, Massachusetts.

Needham, J. and Wang, L. (1962). *Science and Civilisation in China*: vol. 2, *History of Scientific Thought*. Cambridge.

**CHOICE, BIOLOGICAL.** The concept of choosing is, of course, a notion that is primarily applied to human beings; and it may seem absurd to speak of a bacterium as exercising choice, for that is one of many attributes that humans like to reserve for themselves. But is this exclusive view either wise or justified? Of course there are many things humans do that other animals don't, but the biologist suspects that by looking carefully it may be possible to discover in nature something of the origins of even the most distinctive human features. Such influences, though remote, may be revealing if they show characteristics that special human features share with more humble life processes.

Choice implies the capacity to select from a set of possible actions those that are likely to achieve some end, given the circumstances. This involves a series of concepts very strange to a scientist. First, there must be a chooser. Next, given the conditions, he 'can' do more than one thing, i.e. he is not fully 'determined'. Most difficult of all, he acts in pursuit of some aim, objective, or end. It is said on all sides that such words should be used only of humans, and some scientists themselves have been among the leaders in decrying 'teleology'.

It may be difficult to discern 'ultimate' meanings in nature, but can even the wisest theologian do more than make guesses about ultimates anyway? What the biologist sees is that organisms show evidence that they act with a direction or aim, namely to ensure that life continues. As Monod (1972) expresses it, 'objectivity obliges us to recognize the teleonomic character of living organisms'. The life that is preserved is first of all that of the individual and then of his species. The fundamental fact about the acts of all living creatures is that they involve this tendency. This is an influence that should never be forgotten, even in the most abstract thinking of philosophers. The biologist can examine how living actions come to be so directed that they produce this effect. Is there evidence that in any clear sense organisms actually seek to maintain a given standard?

The continuity of life is ensured by a continuous series of selections among sets of possible alternatives. We do not know precisely how life began, but early on it involved a selection of only a few among all the ninety-two naturally occurring elements. The sets of nucleotides then established, with their mutants, have provided the raw material from which further selections have been made. Moreover, every organism during every second of its life is making repeated selections among the various metabolic pathways that can be followed.

This immense sequence of selections certainly has at least a formal similarity to what humans call choice, but where is the chooser? In enthusiasm over the discovery of the genetic code, biologists often imply that DNA and its replication is, as it were, the essence of life. This is to omit the living creatures themselves and the processes by which they are maintained. The whole 'function' of the DNA is to provide instructions that allow the individual life to continue. Genes alone can do nothing. They can produce a new organism only if they find themselves in a *system*, equipped with all the appropriate enzymes and other materials for synthesis. The very existence of such a system depends upon all the long, past history of the species and of life itself. When bacteria are placed in lactose, the decision to synthesize β-galactosidase depends not only on the presence of the relevant gene but on the whole system that detects the new sugar, communicates with the genetic material, and allows synthesis and the use of the enzyme. The whole organism is thus the chooser, and it is aiming at a previously defined target or standard, which is set in this case by the demand for energy. If this demand is not met, mechanisms are brought into action that detect any possible fuel and so alter the organism's own action that it can utilize whatever is available. Thus it is ensured that departure from the target through lack of sugar activates mechanisms that can correct the deficiency. So in a precise sense there is an individual chooser, acting to achieve a specific pre-set aim, even in this simplest of examples. It is an essential of any living thing that it must make such repeated decisions, using the best information available from outside and from within itself. And every human 'knows' that this is also what he must do throughout his life.

It may be objected that there is an essential difference between such 'selections' and human 'conscious' choice. This indeed raises great difficulties, but we are concerned here to emphasize the possible significance of similarities, which remain relevant even if there are also differences. Of course, the word 'choice' can be arbitrarily restricted to humans, but to do this for any type of activity is to give up the possibility of learning from man's animal ancestry. As Trevarthen says of language, 'Biological causes run deep. One does not find complex, highly evolved life processes showing no evidence of their origin from simpler adaptive functions.'

It may also be objected that given lactose the bacterium has no real 'choice', it *must* make β-galactosidase, and the action is as 'deterministic' and 'chemical' as any other. This objection points very clearly to the problems raised by discussions of choice and free will and the importance of an analysis that includes *both* human and other biological information. When we insist that our own choices are 'free', do we really mean that they are wholly indeterminate? Surely that would imply that they were the result of chance, the very opposite of our meaning. What we want to indicate by 'free choice' is decision made according to our own needs, aims, and standards and with our information, not made under duress to meet the needs of others. What the bacterium is doing is choosing the appropriate one from its own set of possibilities, rather than being forced to make some other protein, as it would if invaded by a virus. It is true that its set of alternatives is limited; it cannot decide to try to jump out of the culture and back into one containing glucose. But we do not have an indefinite range of choice either.

As organisms have become more complicated the number of possible lines of action open to them has increased; in human beings it is very great indeed. Making choice between so many nearly similar paths of action (for example, by speech) is our specifically human property. We cannot be fully human unless we operate it freely (and, incidentally, social systems that allow this freedom may well prove to be at an advantage over those where choice is limited by convention or compulsion). With the increasing complexity, organisms have developed very elaborate control mechanisms, each with its reference targets. The fact that they seek to achieve specific targets becomes very obvious. We now even have some knowledge of the operations in ourselves by which departure from reference standards is detected and corrected. Nerve-cells in the hypothalamus of the brain provide such references for control of temperature, eating, drinking, sex, and much else.

The realization that choice is a property of all living things gives us great help in understanding the world and our place in it. It shows that the activities of life do indeed have a direction and an aim. Life originated perhaps 3,500 million years ago, and since then there has been a definite progress, in the sense of the increasing information and order in organisms. The increase has been achieved as a result of repeated selections or choices made by organisms between alternative possible courses of action.

See also DETERMINISM AND FREE WILL.          J. Z. Y.

Monod, J. (1972). *Chance and Necessity*. London.

**CHUNKING.** The Scottish philosopher Sir William Hamilton (1788–1856), born in Glasgow (where his father and grandfather held the chairs of Anatomy and Botany) wrote: 'If you throw a handful of marbles on the floor, you will find it difficult to view at once more than six, or seven at most, without confusion.' This was confirmed by the English economist, William Stanley Jevons (1835–82), by throwing beans into a box and estimating their number. He found that he never made a mistake with three or four, was sometimes wrong when there were five, was right about half the time with ten beans, and was usually wrong with fifteen. These experiments are cited by the American psychologist George Miller (1956), the author of the famous paper 'The Magic number seven, plus or minus two' (1956). Miller found that more items can be remembered when they are coded, or 'chunked'. Thus, we can remember more numbers or letters when they are in recognized sequences or words. So chunking enormously increases effective memory and perception. One might think of perception of objects as 'chunking' the sensory and stored data into large units—which are objects as perceived.

Miller, G. (1956). Information theory, *Scientific American*, August.
Miller, G. (1956). The Magic number seven, plus or minus two. *Psychological Review*, **63**, 2, 81–97.

**CLADISTICS.** A system for classifying organisms. The word 'clade' was coined by Julian Huxley in 1957, to refer to characteristics that can be used as units for setting limits to classes and establishing hierarchies which may or may not be associated with evolutionary sequences. The cladistic system of classification—which, for some reason, arouses heated controversy—has three axioms. (i) Features shared by organisms (homologies) reveal hierarchical ordering in nature. (ii) Hierarchical orderings are economically expressed in branching diagrams, or 'cladograms'. (iii) The nodes in cladograms represent common features (homologies) shared by organisms—so cladograms can be used to represent and suggest biological classifications. The method can be used outside biology—for example, in geology, or linguistics, or wherever homologous characteristics can be recognized and there is no adequate structure of theoretical understanding for classification. The method demands explicit decisions on what are to be accepted as valid homologues, and this can be a useful exercise. Absence of characteristics (such as absence of teeth in birds) may be accepted for cladistic classification.

The current controversy over cladistics and Darwinian evolution seems to be based on the notion that cladistics is somehow opposed to or provides evidence against evolution; but this is mistaken. It can offer classifications which do not assume evolutionary sequences; but this is all to the good, as classifications which assume particular evolutionary sequences can generate vicious circular arguments in biology. See EVOLUTION: NEO-DARWINIAN THEORY.

Patterson, C. (1980). Cladistics. *Biologist*, **27**, 234–40.

**CLAIRVOYANCE.** See EXTRA-SENSORY PERCEPTION.

**CLAPARÈDE, ÉDOUARD** (1873–1940). Swiss psychologist and educationalist, who studied at Geneva, Leipzig, and Paris, and with his cousin Flournoy founded the journal *Archives de Psychologie* (1901). He became director of the experimental psychology laboratory at Geneva University and later founded the J. J. Rousseau Institute for Educational Science. He had strong clinical interests and made a number of studies of the psychological sequelae of injury to, and disease of, the human brain, including a seminal study of the partial preservation of recent memory in *amnesic states despite what appears to be total forgetting. He also published, in 1900, an important review on defects in the visual recognition of objects (visual *agnosia) in *L'Année Psychologique*, vol. 6, pp. 74–143. His books include *L'Éducation fonctionelle* (1921).          O. L. Z.

**CLASSICAL CONDITIONING.** See CONDITIONING.

**CLASSIFICATION, BIOLOGICAL.** See EVOLUTION: NEO-DARWINIAN THEORY.

**'CLEVER HANS'.** A famous horse once thought to possess powers of telepathy. The horse (of a Russian trotting-horse breed), which lived in Berlin at the beginning of the twentieth century, could apparently perform arithmetic in the presence of its owner by tapping a hoof on the ground to count out the answer. Fraud seemed unlikely since the owner and trainer, Herr von Osten, would allow people (free of charge) to watch the animal perform and even to question it themselves.

The phenomenon was investigated in 1904 by O. Pfungst, a student of the psychologist C. Stumpf, and Pfungst subsequently reported his findings in a book, *Clever Hans*. His conclusion was that the horse was receiving clues from *gestures made, probably unwittingly, by the owner and other questioners—an example of non-verbal communication which is easily taken for telepathy.

See also EXTRA-SENSORY PERCEPTION.

Pfungst, O. (1911). *Clever Hans* (trans. C. L. Rahn). New York.

**CLOCK, BIOLOGICAL.** See BIOLOGICAL CLOCK.

**'COCKTAIL PARTY' EFFECT.** The rejection of unwanted messages by the ears. This rejection depends largely on *binaural hearing, and allows signal sources to be localized. However, the quality of the voice, such as the sex of the speaker, can also be used to accept or reject messages. See ATTENTION and CHANNELS, NEURAL.

Carterette, E. C. and Friedman, M. P. (1978). Perceptual processing. *Handbook of Perception*, **9**. New York and London.

**CODE, CODING, AND DECODING.** When physical events or patterns, such as letters and numbers, represent a message, the message is said to be 'encoded' in the marks or events. Thus neural signals (action potentials, see NERVOUS SYSTEM) are coded activity from the sense organs and must be decoded to be useful. The amount of information that can be transmitted depends not only on the band width (the frequency response) of the *channel but also on the appropriateness of the coding. Morse code is efficient because the most frequent letters are the shortest—they have the fewest dots and dashes—and so occupy least time.

For *cognition—perception or behaviour based on knowledge—neural signals are 'read' on the basis of knowledge or assumptions, which may be false. See INFORMATION THEORY.

**COGNITION.** The use or handling of knowledge. Those who stress the role of cognition in *perception underline the importance of knowledge-based processes in making sense of the 'neurally coded' signals from the eye and other sensory organs. It seems that man is different from other animals very largely because of the far greater richness of his cognitive processes. Associated with *memory of individual events and sophisticated generalizations, they allow subtle analogies and explanations—and ability to draw pictures and speak and write. The word 'cognition' is probably related to 'gnomon'—the shadow-casting rod of a sundial—which measures the heavens from shadows.

**COLLECTIVE UNCONSCIOUS.** See JUNG, C. G.

**COLOUR-BLINDNESS.** See COLOUR VISION: EYE MECHANISMS.

**COLOUR SCALING.** See RETINEX THEORY AND COLOUR CONSTANCY.

**COLOUR VISION: BRAIN MECHANISMS.** In COLOUR VISION: EYE MECHANISMS William Rushton outlines the trichromatic theory that colour vision is mediated by three different kinds of retinal receptor, each responding best to light from a different part of the visible spectrum. The theory is based firmly on the empirically established trichromacy of colour-matching: given any four coloured lights, it is always possible to place three of them on one side of a foveal matching field and one on the other, or two on one side and two on the other, and by adjusting the radiances of three of them cause the two sides of the field to match. When the observer makes his adjustment he is thought to be equating, on the two sides of the field, the rates of quantum catch in the three classes of cone. If the two sets of quantum catches are identical, then we may suppose that subsequent neural events are also equivalent and the two sides of the field will look alike to the observer. However, the trichromatic theory limits itself to predicting whether or not two colours will *look alike*; it does not tell us how they will actually look to the observer.

**Opponent colour theory.** Historically, a number of rivals to the trichromatic theory have taken as their starting-point the phenomenology of colour. The most celebrated of these rivals is the 'opponent colour' or 'tetrachromatic' theory of Ewald *Hering. The trichromatic theory, in the form that it was advanced by Thomas *Young, James Clerk Maxwell, and Hermann von *Helmholtz, does not obviously account for the fact that a mixture of yellowy red and yellowy green can produce a yellow that is without trace of redness or greenness. Hering proposed that colour analysis depends on the action of two types of detector, each having two modes of response: one detector that signals either red or green, and a second that signals either yellow or blue. Finally he supposed that brightness depends on a system that signals white or black. Thus one can see a colour that looks greenish, and bluish, and dark; but not one that is both reddish and greenish, or both light and dark, and so on.

Nowadays it is generally held that a complete theory of colour vision must draw elements from both the trichromatic and the opponent colour theories. Indeed, Helmholtz himself proved that the two theories are not incompatible, since a simple transformation could change the three receptor outputs into two difference signals and one additive signal. Wasserman (1978, pp. 91–3) gives Helmholtz's argument. Unfortunately, this statement by Helmholtz appeared only in the second edition of his *Handbuch der Physiologis-*

*chen Optik* (1896) and was missing from the third edition (1909), the latter being the one translated into English (by the Optical Society of America, in 1924).

**Electrophysiological studies of opponent processes.** A transformation of the kind considered by Helmholtz probably occurs in the retina itself. In 1958, MacNichol and Svaetichin found that, at the level of the horizontal cells in the goldfish retina, light of one wavelength may depolarize (i.e. excite) a cell, whereas light from a different part of the spectrum may hyperpolarize (i.e. inhibit the cell). In the absence of stimulation the cell's electrical potential has an intermediate value, and this potential can be increased or decreased by stimulating the retina with different colours. Soon afterwards De Valois reported opponent responses in the lateral geniculate nuclei of macaque monkeys; and others have reported such responses at the level of retinal ganglion cells in the monkey, although it has so far proved difficult to obtain recordings from the more distal cells of the Primate retina. Thus De Valois was led to propose that colour information is transformed from a 'component' system (three cone types giving responses that increase with increasing intensity of stimulation) to an 'opponent' system in which some wavelengths cause an increase in a given retinal signal and other wavelengths cause a decrease. Such an opponent system effectively transmits colour difference signals: for example, a cell that increases its firing rate as a result of stimulation with red ($R$) light and decreases its firing rate with green ($G$) stimulation can be said to be signalling $+ R - G$.

If colour difference signals are transmitted, can we tell which combinations of receptor responses are 'differenced'? There is some doubt about this, since the electrophysiological reports are not entirely consistent; but by and large, if we call the three cone types $R$, $G$, and $B$, neural pathways have been found that signal $\pm (R - G)$ and $\pm [(R + G) - B]$. It should be noted that in the second of these expressions, the sum $(R + G)$ may be taken as signalling 'yellow'. This may be the explanation for why yellow is the fourth psychological primary—along with red, green, and blue. It seems that the responses from the $R$ and $G$ cones are added, thus generating a spare colour (yellow) that looks neither green nor red, and is complementary to blue. For details of the physiological evidence for opponent processing, see De Valois and De Valois (1975).

**Psychophysical studies of opponent processes.** There is good psychophysical evidence that opponent colour channels exist. Thus the efficacy of two adapting fields of different wavelength (or the detectability of two lights of different wavelength) may be less when the two are concurrently presented than when either alone is present (see Mollon, 1982). In these experiments the observer is asked only to detect a liminal (difference) stimulus; he is not asked to make subjective judgements about the quality of the colour appearance.

It is currently a controversial question how closely these psychophysically demonstrated opponencies are related to the phenomenological oppositions of red and green and of yellow and blue. The latter oppositions, however, can be systematically measured. This was classically done in the 1950s by Jameson and Hurvich (see Hurvich, 1978), using the method of *hue cancellation*: to measure, say, the amount of yellowness in a series of wavelengths from the long-wavelength part of the spectrum, the experimenter adds blue light of a fixed wavelength to each in turn of the long wavelengths. The long wavelengths would range from a slightly yellowish green to a deep red. For each of these test wavelengths, the observer is asked to adjust the added blue light until the mixture looks neither yellowish nor bluish. The amount of blue light required is the dependent variable and is taken as a measure of the yellowness, the 'yellow chromatic valence', of the test wavelength.

**Luminance.** The main tenet of opponent colour theory is that there are two independent '*channels' signalling colour information. One of these signals red or green, the other signals yellow or blue. But from trichromatic theory it is clear that we need three, not two, independent variables to describe colour appearance. Thus, a third channel is necessary. What does this channel signal? The answer is luminance. The signals from the $R$ and $G$ (but probably not $B$) cones are added, and the information is transmitted as luminance. But again, it is opponent coded. The channel signals 'brighter' or 'darker', but with respect to what? Simply with respect to other parts of the picture, or retinal image. The luminance channel signals comparative information, not about absolute local luminance but about how the local luminance compares with the rest of the scene. Comparisons are made not across colour but across space. The visual system places heavy emphasis on comparison across space. The impressive colour effects demonstrated by Edwin Land (see RETINEX THEORY AND COLOUR CONSTANCY) are a powerful example of long-range interaction in the visual system.

**An analogy with colour television.** Why should opponent coding of colour have evolved? It may be useful to draw analogies with colour television. About 1950, television engineers started looking for a means of transmitting an acceptable colour picture efficiently. This meant transmitting as little information as possible (i.e. keeping the band-width low), with a high level of resistance to extraneous noise, and in a way that was compatible with monochrome receivers, i.e. capable of giving an acceptable black-and-white picture.

Obviously this analogy cannot be pursued too far, since colour television aims to provide an image that is a good substitute for the original object; the visual system of each member of the audience must then get to work on the picture. However, the choice of how much importance to attach to different aspects of the information contained in the picture, and how to transmit the information most efficiently, seems to raise interesting questions for visual science.

The simplest system would 'look at' the original scene through three primary filters, transmit the three pictures separately, and recombine them in the receiver. Since the $G$ primary is most similar to the luminance signal, this would be the one that monochrome receivers would receive. But errors would result, reds being too dim and greens too bright. More importantly, three times as much information would have to be transmitted (so the band-width would be trebled) in comparison with monochrome transmission. This would be expensive, and impossible where many broadcasts must share a limited range of radio frequencies.

At the time when colour television was being developed, it was known that visual acuity was worse for colour than for brightness contrast. Since it was desirable to separate colour and luminance anyway (to allow monochrome sets to receive a true luminance signal) there now appeared a way of reducing the total transmission band-width: give the colour information less band-width than the luminance information. But how could colour and luminance be separated? A neat mathematical solution presented itself: opponent coding. If $R$, $G$ and $B$ are the signals from the red, green, and blue receivers respectively, then we can define luminance, $L$, as

$$L = 0.3R + 0.59G + 0.11B \qquad (1)$$

The weightings given to the $R$, $G$ and $B$ signals are commensurate with the relative contributions of the three primaries to luminance.

We can now derive two 'colour difference equations':

$$R - L = 0.7R - 0.59G - 0.11B \qquad (2)$$
$$\text{and} \quad B - L = -0.3R - 0.59G + 0.89B \qquad (3)$$

Equations (2) and (3) give 'chrominance' information. If $R = G = B$, then both chrominance signals are zero. Since the viewer's visual acuity is less for colour, less band-width need be used to transmit (2) and (3) than (1) (Sims, 1969).

There are other consequences of the colour difference operation that hold advantages for both television and the visual system. If three trichromatic signals were transmitted untransformed, then redundant information would be carried in the transmission. For the three signals would be correlated: they would necessarily be correlated because the spectral sensitivities of the three receptors overlap and because objects in the world have broad spectral reflectances. To avoid waste of valuable channel capacity the three signals should be orthogonal, i.e. should not be correlated with each other. By transmitting a luminance signal and two difference signals, visual systems may approach this ideal of communications engineering (Fukurotani, 1982).

Another advantage of the difference operation may lie in the preservation of neutral colours. Imagine that a television camera is looking at a neutral object. There will be a luminance signal, but the two chrominance signals will be zero, since the camera is set so that $R = G = B$. The chrominance signals are thus zero: all is well. But now imagine that the gains of the two chrominance channels are altered—that is, the $R - L$ and $G - L$ signals are each multiplied by a different number (as might arise from drift in the electronics). The two channels will still be signalling 'zero' for neutral scenes, since a product of any number and zero is still zero. The resistance of the neutrality of neutral objects to drifts in the gains of opponent channels is likely to be an important consideration in our visual system as well.

**Cortical analysis of colour.** A question of great interest, and still unsettled, is that of the extent to which colour is analysed separately from other attributes of the retinal image, such as form and movement. S. Zeki has identified in the rhesus monkey two adjacent regions of the prestriate cortex that he suggests are specialized for the analysis of colour: these regions (denoted '$V4$' and '$V4A$') lie on the posterior bank of the lunate sulcus and the anterior bank of the superior temporal sulcus (Zeki, 1977). He suggests that colour-specific cells are here more frequent than in other prestriate regions and, most interestingly, that the cells show colour constancy (see RETINEX THEORY AND COLOUR CONSTANCY) when one patch of a complex, multicoloured array falls within their receptive field; that is to say, they respond to the colour seen by a human observer despite large changes in the local spectral flux that falls on their receptive field. But as yet we have little idea of how the colour constancy is achieved or of how the hue of an object is referred to its other attributes, such as movement, shape, and distance.               T. T.

De Valois, R. L. and De Valois, K. K. (1975). Neural coding of color. In Carterette, E. C. and Friedman, M. P. (eds.) *Handbook of Perception*, 5, pp. 117–66. New York.

Fukurotani, K. (1982). Color information coding of horizontal-cell responses in fish retina. *Color Research and Application*, 7, 146–8.

Hurvich, L. M. (1978). Two decades of opponent processes. In Billmeyer, F. W., Jr., and Wyszecki, G. (eds.) *Colour 77*, pp. 33–61.

Mollon, J. D. (1982). Color vision. *Annual Reviews of Psychology*, 33, 41–85.

Sims, H. V. (1969). *Principles of PAL Colour Television and Related Systems*. London.

Wasserman, G. S. (1978). *Color Vision: an historical introduction*. New York.

Zeki, S. M. (1977). Colour coding in the superior temporal sulcus of the rhesus monkey visual cortex. *Proceedings of the Royal Society B*, 197, 195–223.

**COLOUR VISION: EYE MECHANISMS.** When things are seen, it is usually because light enters the eye and is focused upon the retina, that sensitive membrane at the back. Light consists of electromagnetic vibrations of minute wavelengths—one million waves to the half metre for green light.

Isaac *Newton, by his famous prism experiment, showed in 1666 that sunlight consists of a mixture of rays, each bent to a different degree in traversing the prism and thus falling at a different place upon the far wall. He showed that each ray was elementary in the sense that it could not be changed into a ray differently bent. Each elementary ray had a different colour, and the colour of objects depended upon the copiousness with which the various coloured rays were reflected or transmitted from the object to the eye.

Newton's conclusions, though true, met with fierce opposition. To *Goethe it was absurd to assert that the mere mixing of all the rainbow colours could appear white since white is without colour. And artists had long known that it was not necessary for them to have a set of seven rainbow paints; a judicious mixture on the palette of a few bright paints—perhaps only three—was sufficient for masterpieces of natural representation.

A person's perception of everything in the world outside him depends upon three factors: (i) the physical stimulus, such as vibrations of light or sound, (ii) the sense organs that respond to particular stimuli in special ways, and send corresponding messages along their nerves to the brain, and (iii) the mind that creates perception out of brain activity. Newton analysed correctly the diversity of light rays that constitute sunlight. But he did not consider the limitations of the eye in responding selectively to these divers rays. This was done by the physician Thomas *Young in 1801, at St George's Hospital, London. He saw that human perception of fine detail implies a 'fine grain' of photoreceptors in the retina, and thought it unlikely that each 'grain' would be selectively responsive to every wavelength of light. Nor was this necessary to explain colour discrimination. Young suggested that each grain consisted of a triad of resonators each thrown into vibration by light waves. The 'green receptor' was moved chiefly by waves from the middle of the spectrum (which looks green), though neighbouring spectral waves also acted upon it less vigorously. The 'red receptor' and the 'blue receptor' respond likewise to waves near either end of the spectrum. Thus light of any composition falling upon the eye will throw these three resonators, $R$, $G$, and $B$, into determinate amplitudes of vibration. Their sum, $R + G + B$ defines the brightness, and their ratio $R : B : B$ defines the colour.

This view, which is essentially what is believed today, is seen not to question Newton's physics but, by taking into account the limited discrimination of the eye, to explain the painter's experience that mixing a few paints will give the whole range of colour. Young's explanation should lead to a simple and striking result. Every colour (including white) should excite the *R*, *G*, and *B* receptors in a characteristic set of ratios. Consequently, a mixture of red + green + blue lights, adjusted to produce this same set of ratios, should appear white, or whatever the initial colour was. In 1854 this was systematically tested by James Clerk Maxwell (1831–79), the great physicist, while a student at Trinity College, Cambridge. He showed that every colour can be matched by a suitable mixture of red + green + blue 'primaries', although sometimes it is necessary for the experimenter to mix one of his three primaries with the colour to be matched rather than with the other primaries. This *trichromacy* of vision was confirmed by Hermann von *Helmholtz in Heidelberg and later measured with spectral lights and great accuracy by W. D. Wright at Imperial College London and independently by W. S. Stiles at the National Physical Laboratory, London.

**Visual pigments.** What does light do to the photoreceptors of the retina to make them send nerve messages to the brain? Willy Kühne (1837–1900), professor of physiology at Heidelberg, observed in 1877 that a dark-adapted retina removed from a dead frog in dim light and then observed in daylight, was initially pink, but bleached to pale yellow upon exposure to light. This showed that the retina contains a photosensitive pigment, i.e. one that changes its chemical constitution on exposure, as does a photographic film. This pigment, 'visual purple' or 'rhodopsin', is present in the photoreceptors called 'rods' that serve deep twilight vision, which is without colour. Therefore the pigments serving colour vision must lie not in the twilight receptors but in the daylight receptors called 'cones'. And Young was correct in supposing that these are of three types.

Researchers in Cambridge were the first to measure the visual pigments in the living human eye, applying the familiar observation that if at night a cat's eye is caught in the beam of a car's headlamps it shines back with reflected light (Rushton and Campbell, 1954). By knowing the incident light and measuring the reflected light, it is found what light has been absorbed in the eye. And if these measurements are made before and after the visual pigment has been bleached away with strong light, the change in absorption, resulting from the change in amount of visual pigment present, is learnt.

The same measurements may be made in human eyes, though here there is a very black surface behind the retina instead of the cat's shining *tapetum lucidum*. Since the measuring light sent in may not be made very strong (or it will bleach away the pigment that is being measured), the great sensitivity of a photomultiplier tube is needed to measure the faint light that emerges from the eye. Using this technique, it has been possible to measure the spectral sensitivity and kinetics of bleaching and regeneration in the living human

eye, first of rhodopsin, then of the red and the green cone pigments. There was never sufficient blue light reflected to measure the blue cone pigment.

This work has been confirmed and extended by Marks, Dobelle, and MacNichol at Johns Hopkins University, Baltimore. They used fresh retinas from monkeys' and human eyes removed at operation, and with superb technique measured the visual pigments in single cones. They found Young's three types of cone and specified the visual pigment in each, confirming the measurements made in Cambridge on living colour-blind subjects who possessed only one of the two cone pigments measurable by the Cambridge technique.

**Colour-blindness.** Almost all so-called colour defectives have some appreciation of colour, and generally resent being called colour *blind*. The common defective cannot distinguish well between red and green. This is a hereditary defect, something wrong with a gene carried on one (or rarely both) of the sex chromosomes in the female or on the single active sex chromosome in the male. If in the male the gene is missing or abnormal, colour vision will be defective; and 8 per cent of all males exhibit some defect. But in the female it needs *both* chromosomes to suffer the loss before her defect will show, and of course the probability of the double event is much smaller than that of the single one. In fact only 0·4 per cent of females show some abnormality. Even so, women who are abnormal in only one chromosome, though showing perfect colour vision themselves, have a fifty-fifty chance of transmitting their weakness to their children; and half their sons will be 'colour-blind', since the (normal) father holds his normal gene on the one sex chromosome that will make his child a daughter, and he has none for his sons.

*Dichromacy.* In the extreme conditions of the red–green defect, the subject cannot tell red from green and can match every colour of the rainbow exactly with a suitable mixture of only *two* coloured lights, for example red and blue. Such subjects are called dichromats, to distinguish them from ordinary people (trichromats) who need also a green primary if every colour is to be matched.

The cone pigments in the red–green spectral range of dichromats have been measured by a reflection technique. It has been shown that instead of the red- *and* green-sensitive cone pigments of normal vision, these subjects have only the red *or* the green. They lack one dimension of colour vision because they lack one kind of cone pigment.

*Anomalous trichromacy.* The majority of colour defectives are not true dichromats, but anomalous trichromats: like normal subjects, they require three variables in a colour-matching experiment, but the matches they make are different from those of the normal. Thus, in matching a monochromatic yellow with a mixture of red and green, some ('protoanomalous') observers require more red than normal in the match, whereas other ('deuteranomalous') observers need more green. Usually, though not necessarily, the abnormality of matching is associated with a reduced capacity for discriminating colours. It is thought that anomalous trichromacy arises when one of the cone pigments is displaced from its normal position in the spectrum.

**Adaptation.** Newton's physics of colour was inadequate because it did not take into account the selective physiological action of Young's three cone types. We are now on the way to understanding their selectivity and the sort of nerve signals they generate. But though light waves and nerve signals are factors that lead to colour vision, there is still the miracle of how some nerve signals generate a sensation in the mind. This sensation certainly does not depend exclusively upon the $R : G : B$ excitation ratios of the three cone types. We all know how adaptation to any strong-coloured light leaves the eye, as it were, fatigued to the colour so that some extra light of this colour must be added to any presentation if its appearance is to be the same as it was before adaptation. This adaptation is often called 'successive contrast' to distinguish it from the rather similar 'simultaneous contrast', where two different-coloured objects seen close together have their differences enhanced through their proximity. Some of these effects can be objectively measured by recording from nerves in the visual pathways of animals.

**Psychology.** Colours are so gay that those with total colour loss cannot but be pitied; and it must be wondered what it is that makes red produce the wonderful red sensation most people perceive. What has been said here explains only what cannot be discriminated, and nothing has been said about how sensations arise from what is seen. Let it be concluded that Newton ended his first paper with these strong words: 'But to determine . . . by what modes or actions light produceth in our minds the phantasms of colours is not so easie. And I shall not mingle conjectures with certainties.'    W. A. H. R.

Boynton, R. M. (1979). *Human Colour Vision*. New York.

Brindley, G. S. (1970). *Physiology of the Retina and the Visual Pathway*, 2nd edn. Monographs of the Physiological Society, Section 7. London.

Marriott, F. H. C. (1976). In Davson, H. (ed.), *The Eye*. New York.

Rushton, W. A. H. (1975). Visual pigments and colour blindness. *Scientific American*, 232, 64.

**COMMON SENSE.** The original meaning is a 'common centre', or neural pool into which all the five senses were supposed to contribute to give coherent perceptions, though the various senses are so very different. René *Descartes (1596–1650) used the term *le siège du sens commun* in this way. There is indeed still a problem over the co-ordination of the senses and just how the different sources of information are pooled (see, for example, SPATIAL CO-ORDINATION OF THE SENSES and CHANNELS).

Nowadays 'common sense' generally refers to practical attitudes and widely accepted beliefs which may be hard to justify but which are generally assumed to be reliable. Extreme deviations from common-sense beliefs may be evidence of psychological disturbance, but may, on the other hand, be the products of genius, sometimes becoming accepted later as common sense. Thus, although it is now common sense that the earth is round, only a few centuries ago a man believing this might have been regarded as mad.

There is indeed a vast body of unquestioned assumptions which is seldom questioned. Common sense is, however, frequently questioned by philosophers—with a curious ambiguity, for at least linguistic philosophy tends to assume that the 'common sense' of normal language is philosophically significant. This is discussed critically by Ernest Gellner (1979).

Gellner, E. (1979). *Words and Things*. Cambridge.

**COMPATIBILISM.** Traditionally, those who maintain the truth of determinism and believers in the freedom of the will have been regarded as taking up incompatible positions. Thus from one side it is argued that since all events, including human actions, are causally determined, the belief that we are free is an illusion; from the other side it is argued that we know we are free, and hence universal determinism must be false. Compatibilists maintain that both these arguments are invalid: since a free action is simply one that is not constrained by external forces, there is a perfectly ordinary and proper sense in which we act freely when we do what we want to do; and the existence of such freedom need not presuppose that determinism is false, or that human beings possess some contra-causal power. Defenders of the compatibilist or 'reconciliationist' position have included Leibniz and Hume. See DETERMINISM AND FREE WILL.    J. G. C.

**COMPLEX.** In experiments using the association method, C. G. *Jung observed that there are stimulus words about which the subject does not think quickly and surely. He attributed this disorder to a concealed cluster of ideas and feelings, which he called a complex, such signs as repetitiveness, uncommonness of the response word, and delay in responding, being complex-indicators. He showed also how these may reveal guilt over, say, having stolen. The complex-indicators on which the 'lie-detector', used in some courts in the USA, depends are the changes, recorded on a polygraph, produced by stimulus words or questions on the electrical resistance of the skin, the pulse-rate, and the rate and pattern of respiration (see ELECTRODERMAL ACTIVITY).

The term is also applied to the cluster of childhood fantasies underlying a neurosis. The *Oedipus complex has been said to be the 'nucleus-complex' in neurosis in males, the Electra complex in females (see INFERIORITY COMPLEX).        D. R. D.

Jung, C. G. (1917). The association method. In Long, C. E. (ed.), *Collected Papers on Analytic Psychology*, 2nd edn. London.

**COMPULSIONS.** See OBSESSIONS AND COMPULSIONS.

**COMPUTED TOMOGRAPHY (CT).** See IMAGES OF THE BRAIN IN ACTION.

**COMPUTER CHESS** is pursued in some cases for sport and in others to deepen scientific understanding of the kinds of knowledge that support mental skills. From specialized activities in both the sport and the science category, *artificial intelligence scientists have obtained insights of general relevance to *cognition and its computer simulation, including topics such as the following. How is a causal model of some problem domain to be exploited in solving particular problems within it? What principles characterize knowledge-based planning? What are the trade-offs between the use of calculation and the use of stored patterns during problem-solving? Can the fruits of past calculations be turned into summarizing patterns for future use; and can the fruits of past miscalculations also be utilized, and if so how? What are the limits to human codification of a skill, and can these limits be overcome in any way? What makes a pattern-directed representation intelligible, and what makes such a representation also executable 'in the head'?

The properties of chess which make it especially suitable for computer-based approaches to such questions are that the domain can be fully and exactly defined; it overextends the best human intellects; it demands calculation, learning, concept-manipulation, analogical thinking, and long-term judgement. Moreover master skill at chess is measurable on a universal scale, and over the centuries players and scholars have built a vast incremental literature of chess knowledge, as apprehended and improved by each generation.

In the theory of games chess is a two-person game with perfect information: both players have full sight of the board and of every move made. It is also zero-sum, i.e. what is good for one player is bad in precisely equal measure for the other. Further, the rule which declares a draw when 50 moves have passed without castling, captures, or pawn moves ensures that the game is finite. The space of legal positions is, however, rather large, having been estimated as exceeding 10 to the power of 46. The fraction of these which a chess-master would regard as capable of occurrence in serious play, and hence meaningful, is infinitesimal. Yet the number of distinct positions contained in that infinitesimal fraction has been estimated as exceeding 10 to the power of 23. This is still many billion times too many for complete solution by computer search and enumeration. Such an enterprise would also require mechanizable representations of chess meaning, in a language whose most primitive expressions would denote basic features from which the master builds his mental picture of a chess position.

Only a few descriptive clichés of the hypothesized language have been uncovered to date. The 'chunks' involve such relations as mutual defence between pieces, co-operation in attacking a common target, certain types of pawn chain, characteristic castled-king patterns, and the like. Relevant investigations began a century ago with Alfred *Binet's studies of chess memory in simultaneous blindfold chess, and were extended in the 1940s by Adriaan de Groot's analyses of players of varying strengths, including former world champions, 'thinking aloud' at given positions. More recent work by Herbert Simon and by Jorg Nievergeldt has yielded in addition estimates of the number of chunks, or basic patterns, stored by a master in long-term memory. (See CHUNKING.) This number, thought to lie between 30,000 and 50,000, corresponds to the size of the vocabulary employed by the hypothesized language. Little use has so far been made of studies of chess cognition by the mechanizers, who have mainly been content to apply brute force along lines mapped out, although not particularly recommended, by Claude Shannon in 1950. Current high-water marks are reviewed below.

*Brute force: tournament play.* The first world computer chess championship in 1974 was won by a program authored by M. Donskoy and V. L. Arlazarov of the USSR. It performed at the level of mediocre club play. Programs for playing under tournament conditions have concentrated on wringing the most out of the concurrent rapid advance of computing technology together with the use of short-cut tricks of programming technique (such as 'alpha–beta'—see below). The Shannon paradigm of searching large trees of possibilities, guided by simplistic but fast means of evaluating each possibility as it is thrown up, has dominated.

The principle of machine search resembles the strenuous 'thinking ahead' of an ambitious beginner, enhanced with miraculous speed, completeness and accuracy. Tens, or even hundreds, of thousands of variations per second are scored for features generally correlated with a position's strength, such as piece scores, mobility, control of centre, king safety, and pawn structure. From the positions located along the furthermost boundary of the forward search, position-values are backed up the levels of the look-ahead tree by a method known as minimaxing, until the immediate successors of the position under consideration have received backed-up values. Choice of the highest-scoring of these determines the machine move. A refinement of minimax known as alpha–beta pruning almost doubles the depth of analysis obtainable for given computational cost: modern tournament programs regularly search three to four moves ahead (six to eight 'ply'), pursuing capture–recapture or other unstable-looking sequences to as much as twice this depth.

As early established by de Groot, the chess mind follows a diametrically opposite regime. When asked how many moves ahead he looked, the great grandmaster and theorist Richard Reti replied 'One, the right one'. Even in correspondence chess forward calculations are highly selective, pruned and guided by criteria of strategic meaning not yet seriously addressed by the mechanizers.

In 1985 the strongest programs had reached the borderline of international master strength, as judged by their showing in regular human tournaments. When, however, obliged to play the same opponent repeatedly, they tend to fall to the human's ability to learn his enemy's weak points and exploit them. No tournament program of today has the power to learn from experience. Yet the final of the 1985 North American computer chess championship, in which Hans Berliner's 'Hitech' defeated Robert Hyatt's 'Cray Blitz', was recognizably master level. Both programs searched 20–30 million look-ahead positions per move. The equivalent figure for de Groot's grandmasters was 20–30 positions.

*Brute force: end-game analysis.* Given today's fast processors and large computer memories, exhaustive computation can be performed so as fully to solve and tabulate sub-games of chess which are not understood by grandmasters, or even (a taller order) by end-game specialists. The first such feat, by T. Strohlein in 1970, fully analysed the four-piece ending king and rook versus king and knight, thought until then to be in the general case a drawn game. Of the 1,347,906 legal rook's-side-to-move positions (neglecting positions equivalent under rotations and reflections of the board), almost half (651,492) turn out to be winnable by correct (though for the most part protracted) play. The two longest wins are represented by positions 27 moves from checkmate or knight-capture. Aided by knowledge that it could be done and by samples of the computer-generated material itself, the leading end-game scholar A. J. Roycroft was able to acquire and demonstrate complete mastery of optimal play of positions won for the rook's side (contrast the KBBKN case, below).

Kenneth Thompson has completed exhaustive data bases for all the interesting four-piece and five-piece pawnless endings. Of his factual discoveries one of the most spectacular has been the status of king and two bishops versus king and knight (KBBKN), previously believed to be drawable provided that the knight's side can attain the 'Kling & Horwitz' position (Fig. 1a). The position dates from 1851. The verdict that the defending side can draw positions like this (based on the

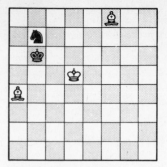

**Fig. 1a.** Either side to move.

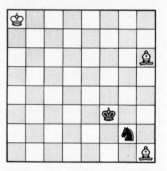

**Fig. 1b.** White to move.

placing of the two black men and largely ignoring the white placement) is repeated in all relevant chess end-game textbooks. In 1983 Thompson's exhaustive solution demonstrated the general win of this end-game in at most 66 moves, and the particular win in Kling & Horwitz positions in about 40–45 moves. Cases of this kind have led to a growing number of *ad hoc* modifications by the World Chess Federation of the 50-move drawing rule.

Not only does the Thompson data base, comprising some two hundred million legal positions, show that the bishops' side can win from all but a few freak starting positions, but its manner of doing so passes the comprehension of the ending's dedicated human students. The critical fourth stage of a 5-stage win from the starting position shown in Fig. 1b involves a procedure 'not to be found in any book and characterized by excruciating slowness and mystery' (Roycroft). Moreover, following a year's study by Roycroft and others, involving availability of a variety of computer aids, it seems that human mastery (as opposed to machine mastery) of this ending may never be attainable.

Data bases generated in this style can also be searched for positions which a master or end-game scholar would recognize as 'studies' or 'compositions'. Here a unique winning (or in appropriate cases drawing) line of play must exist, coupled with properties of elegance, surprise, didactic value and

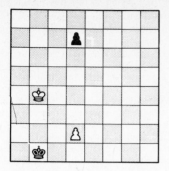

**Fig. 2a.** White to win.

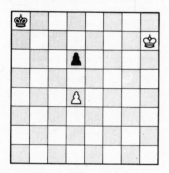

**Fig. 2b.** White to win.

Two computer-assisted study compositions in the KPKP domain. The natural-looking Pd4 for Fig. 2a, and Kg6 for Fig.. 2b, fail. Correct are Kc3 and Pd5 respectively.

even wit, not easy to define in programming terms. M. R. B. Clarke has conducted selective trawls with some success: two of his discoveries for king–pawn—king–pawn (KPKP) are shown as Figs. 2a and 2b.

*Automation of chess knowledge.* In addition to purely factual discoveries, computer programs could help the chess expert fill the gaps of which codified chess knowledge is now seen mainly to consist. Knowledge-directed programs can support his endeavours to outline the missing framework and by semi-automatic generation of descriptions from expert-supplied examples to fill empty slots in the framework as it takes shape. Using a technique of Alen Shapiro and Timothy Niblett known as 'structured induction', Shapiro was able to generate a complete human-readable codification for adjudicating positions in the king–pawn—king–rook ending (pawn's side to move, pawn on a7) where none pre-existed. A side-benefit subsequently extracted from this phenomenon was endowment of the program with the ability to document its own adjudications on demand with explanatory notes.

In the above-mentioned work the induction process was fuelled by hand-supplied examples. In some other cases success has been reported where

the examples have been quarried by the program itself from large pre-computed data bases. A recent *de novo* synthesis of knowledge in clinical cardiology by Ivan Bratko and colleagues employed just such an alternation between (i) exhaustive derivation of brute facts from a logical model and (ii) induction from these of an operational theory. Sparked initially by the chess work, application is beginning to place emphasis on factual compilations as raw materials for automating the codification of new knowledge as a commercial product. The need to better understand the cognitive invariants with which the designer of codification languages must now come to terms is also leading to closer involvement of professional students of mind. D. M.

Binet, A. (1894). *Psychologie des Grands Calculateurs et des Joueurs d'Echecs*. Paris.

de Groot, A. (1965). *Thought and Choice in Chess*, rev. edn. The Hague. (For mental representations of chess masters.)

Chase, W. G. and Simon, H. A. (1973). Perception in Chess. *Cognitive Psychology*, **4**, 55–81.

Hayes, J. E. and Levy, D. (1976). *The World Computer Chess Championship, Stockholm 1974*. Edinburgh. (For an introduction to chess cognition in relation to artificial intelligence.)

Michie, D. and Shapiro, A. (1986). Several articles in *Advances in Computer Chess*, **4**. (For the knowledge-synthesis approach.)

Shannon, C. (1950). Programming a Computer for Playing Chess. *Philosophical Magazine*, **41**, 256–75.

Simon, H. A. and Gilmartin, K. (1973). A Simulation Memory for Chess Positions. *Cognitive Psychology*, **5**, 29–46.

Thompson, K. (1986). Programs that Generate Endgame Data Bases. *End Game*, **83**, 2.

**COMPUTERS AND THE MIND.** See ARTIFICIAL INTELLIGENCE; PATTERN RECOGNITION.

**COMTE, AUGUSTE** (1798–1857). French philosopher and sociologist, and the founder of positivism. His main work is *Philosophie Positive* (6 vols., 1830–42), which was freely translated into English and condensed into three volumes by Harriet Martineau: *The Positive Philosophy of Auguste Comte* (1896).

Comte tried to organize knowledge of society and technology into a consistent whole. He argued that all human conceptions pass through a theological and then a metaphysical stage, and then into a positive or experiential form. The abstract sciences form a hierarchy, with mathematics at the top, then astronomy, physics, chemistry, biology, and finally sociology. Sociological development is from militarism to industrialism. Positivism is an expression of *humanism, in which there is no deity and the emphasis is entirely on man and on intellectual conceptions of the world and man's place in it.

**CONCEPT.** An abstraction or general notion that may serve as a unit (or an 'atom') of a theory. Some concepts can be powerful thinking tools even when they are not at all fully understood. Thus even simple concepts or procedures in mathematics (such as 'dividing by $x$', or 'taking the square root of $x$') allow problems to be solved even though they, or even the questions addressed, are not understood.

Concepts may be more or less clear, and a major part of philosophy is to clarify them. This can be extremely difficult: what is our concept of time—or of mind?

Perhaps most concepts are components of theories or explanations. At least they seem to give fairly direct insight into the nature of things. For example, the astronomer Johannes Kepler's concept of the planets moving in elliptical orbits was essential for *Newton's great synthesis in his *Principia*, which went virtually unchallenged as an account of the universe until Einstein's Special and then General Theory of Relativity. Evidently changes of theory change concepts; and new concepts, or revisions of old ones, can change theories —and so how we understand and see.

In psychology, concepts of mind must be invented or discovered, much as in physics, for we cannot see at all clearly into our own minds by introspection. So we need experiments in psychology; they sometimes suggest concepts far removed from *common sense, or what we *seem* to be like. If we could see 'directly' into our own minds by introspection perhaps we would not need explanatory concepts for understanding at least our own psychologies. But as it is, introspection tells us virtually nothing about how our minds work, or what they or we are. So we need experiments and concepts for psychological understanding. In this way concepts of mind are not so different from concepts of physics, except perhaps for concepts such as purpose: for both underlie appearances and are more-or-less helpful tools for thinking and understanding.

Boden, M. A. (1972). *Purposive Explanation in Psychology*. Harvard.

**CONCUSSION** can be defined as a clinical syndrome characterized by immediate and transient impairment of mental functions such as alteration of *consciousness, and disturbance of *vision or equilibrium, due to mechanical forces. Such results follow all but the mildest blows to the head. In the majority of instances loss of consciousness is of short duration, but severe injuries result in periods of unconsciousness varying from hours to weeks or even months. The greater the duration of unconsciousness and the subsequent post-traumatic *amnesia, the greater will be the period of post-concussional disability. Consequently it is important to record the duration of loss of memory following head injuries, not only as an index of severity but also as a guide to ultimate recovery.

It has been estimated that about 150,000 patients in England and Wales are admitted to hospital each year following head injuries. About 7 per cent of these cases are classed as severe, and the majority of severe cases are the consequences of road traffic accidents. Falls in the home make a significant contribution to the number of elderly cases, and injuries from violent assault have become increasingly common.

The cerebral damage is caused by rotational stresses within the brain, and is likely to be the more severe if the head is in motion at the time of impact. This causes minute haemorrhages and neuronal changes throughout the brain which may be of aetiological importance for the so-called post-concussional syndrome. At the same time it is clear that the principal features of concussion are caused by interference with vital centres in the brain-stem. If unconsciousness lasts more than a few hours, it is likely that permanent brain damage has been sustained, with the risk of major psychological disabilities and personality changes that may prevent the patient returning to his former employment or even living equably with his family. The pre-morbid qualities of the individual will greatly influence his capacity for attaining full recovery, but even the most stable of individuals may suffer to some extent from post-concussional symptoms. These may include headache, dizziness, fatigue, and intolerance of noise, as well as emotional instability and impaired memory and concentration.

Chronic psychological impairment is sometimes seen in professional boxers who have sustained repeated blows to the head without necessarily losing consciousness. In recent times a good deal of attention has been focused on this 'punch-drunk' syndrome, which has led to proposals that boxing should be banned. This is unlikely to happen but greater protection of the head and face of boxers and medical control of those taking part in the sport may do something to minimize the frequency of punch-drunkenness.                    F. A. W.

**CONDILLAC, ÉTIENNE DE** (1715–80). Born of an aristocratic family at Grenobles, Condillac was a proponent of the philosophy of sensationalism— that all knowledge is based on the senses. He was also one of the first to realize, after the discovery of the *retinal image (suggested by the astronomer Johannes Kepler in 1604, and observed in the ox eye by C. Scheiner in 1625), that we do not *see* retinal images (as we see optical images): what we see are external objects. The eye is not like a camera. Retinal images are just one cross-section of the visual channel, and are not objects of *perception (except for the special case of looking at the image in another's eye with an ophthalmoscope). Condillac concludes that perceptions are inferences from data from retinal images. This is the basis of current representational theories of perception, following Hermann von *Helmholtz, who stressed the importance for perception of 'unconscious inference'.

Condillac, É. de (1754). *Traité des sensations*, trans. Carr, G. (1930), *Treatise on the Sensations*. London.
Morgan, M. J. (1977). *Molyneux's Question*. London. (For Condillac's account of perception and comparison with Locke, Berkeley, Diderot, and other earlier and contemporary writers.)

**CONDITIONED REFLEX.** See PAVLOV.

**CONDITIONING.** The rudiments of conditioning are familiar to most people. After experiencing a number of pairings of a signal, for example a tone or light, and a reinforcer, in this case food, Ivan *Pavlov's (1927) dogs came to salivate to the signal much as they did to the food. Similarly, B. F. Skinner's (1938) rats (see SKINNER BOX) would readily perform some action, such as pressing a lever, that procured food.

Clearly, both these behaviours depend upon *learning, in that their development requires the animal to experience a relationship or association between the signal and food in the case of Pavlovian or classical conditioning, and between the action and food in instrumental or operant conditioning. Although the empirical phenomena themselves are not a matter of dispute, the significance of this type of learning is contentious. Traditionally, conditioning represented the cornerstone of the *behaviourist's analysis of learning, but with the increasing focus on *cognition and information processing, the study of this form of learning has been consigned to a backwater of psychology.

The current neglect seems to be based largely upon the assumption that conditioning is a simple, automatic, and unconscious form of learning that underlies the acquisition of relatively trivial behaviour. Following a thorough survey of human conditioning studies, W. F. Brewer (1974) concluded that there was no good evidence for conditioning in human beings. This surprising claim was based not on our failure to show the appropriate behavioural changes, but on the observation that whenever conditioning-like effects occur, we are aware of the association between the signal or action and the reinforcer. Underlying this argument there appears to be the assumption that, by definition, conditioning must be an unconscious process. But neither the empirical effect itself nor its associated terminology imply such an assumption. Pavlov referred to the signal and its associated response as a 'conditional stimulus' and a 'conditional response' respectively, simply because the acquisition of this reaction was conditional or dependent upon having experienced the relationship between the signal and the food. Similarly, the food can be identified as a reinforcer because, at an empirical level, it appears to be an important agent for strengthening, or reinforcing, the conditional response. However, this terminology has undergone a subtle change in the West, so that one now finds statements to the effect that people and animals can be 'conditioned' and 'reinforced'. Obviously such statements are a travesty of the Pavlovian terminology: a person cannot be conditioned or strengthened, at least not by a conditioning experience. These distortions are important, however, for they reveal a fundamental and widespread belief about the nature of conditioning, namely that it is a passive process to which a person or animal is subjected.

The origin of this belief lies not in the conditioning phenomenon itself, but rather with the initial behaviourist explanations of this type of learning. For instance, E. L. *Thorndike (1911) in his famous 'law of effect' argued that following an action by a reinforcer simply strengthens a connection between the stimuli present when the action is performed and the action itself, so that the action reoccurs as a response to these stimuli when they are again presented. This stimulus–response theory has at least two features that bolster the idea that conditioning is a simple and passive process. First, the conditions for learning, and by implication the process underlying such learning, appear simple: in essence, successful conditioning depends just upon the temporal contiguity between the response and reinforcer. Secondly, a conditional response occurs because it is automatically elicited by the appropriate conditional stimulus. Thus, a trained rat presses the lever not because it knows about the relationship between its action and the occurrence of the reinforcer, but rather because the sight of the lever automatically triggers lever-pressing. Both these claims turn out to be incorrect on further analysis.

It is a relatively easy matter to show that instrumental conditioning does not necessarily establish a simple habit released by the appropriate stimulus. Stimulus–response theory, by denying the animal any knowledge about the consequences of its actions, implies that conditional behaviour, once established, should be insensitive to any subsequent changes in the value of the reinforcer. We can test this claim by training an animal to perform an action for a particular food before devaluing the food, for example, by establishing quite separately an aversion to the food. This is readily done by inducing nausea shortly after consuming the food. If we now give the animal the opportunity to perform the action that had previously procured the food, stimulus–response theory would anticipate that the vigour of the action should be unaffected by the devaluation of the reinforcer. Not surprisingly, however, the animal is reluctant to perform this action (Adams and Dickinson, 1981), indicating that simple instrumental conditioning reflects the acquisition of knowledge about the relationship between an action and the occurrence of the reinforcer rather than establishing a reflexively elicited habit. The deployment of this knowledge in controlling behaviour can then be modified by other relevant information, such as the current value of the reinforcer. Given this perspective, instrumental conditioning can be seen to represent a relatively simple procedure for investigating learning about the consequences of our actions and general purposive and goal-directed behaviour.

Just as our view of the knowledge underlying conditioning has changed from that specified by Thorndike's 'law of effect', so have our theories about the conditions for the acquisition of this knowledge. The 'law of effect' states that simple temporal contiguity between an action and a reinforcer is sufficient for instrumental conditioning, and Pavlov himself argued that a classical conditional stimulus also acquires its properties as a result of contiguous pairings with a reinforcer. It has long been recognized that a system sensitive only to temporal contiguity would often fail to distinguish real causal and predictive relationships from purely fortuitous and coincidental conjunctions, and thus be prone to the development of superstitious beliefs and behaviour. It is now clear, however, that the conditioning mechanisms embody a number of subtle and complex processes designed to counteract the formation of superstitions. For instance, conditioning depends not only upon the temporal relationship between the conditional stimulus or action and the reinforcer, but also upon whether or not the occurrence of the reinforcer is surprising or unexpected. The role of surprise is demonstrated by L. J. Kamin's (1969) 'blocking effect'. If an animal receives conditioning trials in which a conditional stimulus, $A$, is paired with a reinforcer, it will subsequently show little conditional responding to a second stimulus, $X$, when a compound of $A$ and $X$ is reinforced. In the initial stage the animal learns to expect the reinforcer following stimulus $A$, so that its subsequent presentation following the $AX$ compound is fully predicted by stimulus $A$ and hence unsurprising. As a result, minimal conditioning accrues to stimulus $X$. Conversely, if stimulus $A$ is initially established as a predictor of the non-occurrence of the reinforcer, the presentation of the reinforcer following the $AX$ compound is very surprising and leads to enhanced conditioning to stimulus $X$ (Rescorla, 1971). This sensitivity to the surprisingness of the reinforcer will serve to protect us and other animals against the formation of superstitious beliefs and behaviour. Effectively, the conditioning mechanism appears to embody an assumption of minimum sufficient causation; an animal is less likely to attribute the contiguous occurrence of a reinforcer to the presence of a stimulus or the execution of an action if another adequate cause or signal for this reinforcer is also present.

In conclusion, the contemporary view of conditioning is considerably more complex and subtle than that expounded by the early behaviourists. We should not overplay, however, the importance of conditioning as a general model for all learning. There are many examples of non-associative learning that lie outside the scope of conditioning theory. Even so, conditioning studies appear to reveal universal mechanisms by which we and other animals intuitively detect and store information about the causal structure of our environment.                                    A. D.

Adams, C. D., and Dickinson, A. (1981). Instrumental responding following reinforcer devaluation. *Quarterly Journal of Experimental Psychology*, **33B**, 109–21.

Brewer, W. F. (1974). There is no convincing evidence for operant or classical conditioning in adult humans. In Weimer, W. B. and Palermo, D. S. (eds.), *Cognition and the Symbolic Processes*. Hillsdale, New Jersey.

Kamin, L. J. (1969). Predictability, surprise, attention and conditioning. In Campbell, B. A. and Church, R. M. (eds.), *Punishment and Aversive Behaviour*. New York.

Pavlov, I. P. (1927). *Conditioned Reflexes*. Oxford.

Rescorla, R. A. (1971). Variations in the effectiveness of reinforcement and non-reinforcement following prior inhibitory conditioning. *Learning and Motivation*, **2**, 113–23.

Skinner, B. F. (1938). *The Behavior of Organisms*. New York.

Thorndike, E. L. (1911). *Animal Intelligence: experimental studies*. New York.

**CONFUCIAN IDEAS OF THE MIND.** See CHINESE IDEAS OF MIND.

**CONSCIOUSNESS** is both the most obvious and the most mysterious feature of our minds. On the one hand, what could be more certain or manifest to each of us than that he or she is a subject of experience, an enjoyer of perceptions and sensations, a sufferer of pain, an entertainer of ideas, and a conscious deliberator? On the other hand, what in the world can consciousness be? How can physical bodies in the physical world contain such a phenomenon? Science has revealed the secrets of many initially mysterious natural phenomena—magnetism, photosynthesis, digestion, even reproduction—but consciousness seems utterly unlike these. For one thing, particular cases of magnetism or photosynthesis or digestion are in principle equally accessible to any observer with the right apparatus, but any particular case of consciousness seems to have a favoured or privileged observer, whose access to the phenomenon is entirely unlike, and better than, anyone else's, no matter what apparatus they may have. For this reason and others, not only have we so far no good theory of consciousness, we lack even a clear and uncontroversial pre-theoretical description of the presumed phenomenon. Some have gone so far as to deny that there is anything for the term to name.

The mere fact that such a familiar feature of our lives has resisted for so long all attempts to characterize it suggests that our conception of it is at fault. What is needed is not just more evidence, more experimental and clinical data, but a careful rethinking of the assumptions that lead us to suppose there is a single and familiar phenomenon, consciousness, answering to all the descriptions licensed by our everyday sense of the term. Consider the baffling questions that are inevitably raised whenever one turns one's attention to consciousness. Are other animals conscious? Are they conscious in the same way we are? Could a computer or robot be conscious? Can a person have unconscious thoughts, or unconscious pains or sensations or perceptions? Is a baby conscious at or before birth? Are we conscious when we dream? Might a human being harbour more than one conscious subject or ego or agent within one brain? Certainly good answers to these questions will depend heavily on empirical discoveries about the behavioural capacities and internal circumstances of the various problematic candidates for consciousness, but about every such empirical finding we can ask: what is its bearing on the question of consciousness, and why? These are not directly empirical but conceptual questions, and answering them is not an alternative or competitor to answering the empirical questions, but an essential preliminary—or at least accompaniment.

Our ordinary concept of consciousness seems to be anchored to two separable sets of considerations that can be captured roughly by the phrases 'from the inside' and 'from the outside'. *From the inside*, our own consciousness seems obvious and pervasive: we know that much goes on around us and even inside our own bodies of which we are entirely unaware or unconscious, but nothing could be more intimately known to us than those things of which we are, individually, conscious. Those things of which I am conscious, and the ways in which I am conscious of them, determine *what it is like to be me*. I know in a way no other could know what it is like to be me. From the inside, consciousness seems to be an all-or-nothing phenomenon—an inner light that is either on or off. We grant that we are sometimes drowsy or inattentive, or asleep, and on occasion we even enjoy abnormally heightened consciousness, but when we are conscious, *that* we are conscious is not a fact that admits of degrees. There is a perspective, then, from which consciousness seems to be a feature that sunders the universe into two strikingly different kinds of things: those that have it and those that do not. Those that have it are *subjects*, beings to whom things can be one way or another, beings it is like something to be. It is not like anything at all to be a brick or a pocket-calculator or an apple. These things have insides, but not the right sort of insides—no inner life, no point of view. It is certainly like something to be me (something *I* know 'from the inside') and almost certainly like something to be you (for you have told me, most convincingly, that it is the same with you), and probably like something to be a dog or a dolphin (if only they could tell us!), and maybe even like something to be a spider.

When one considers these others (other folk and other creatures), one considers them perforce *from the outside*, and then various of their observable or determinable features strike us as relevant to the question of their consciousness. Creatures react discriminatively to events within the scope of their senses: they recognize things, avoid painful circumstances, learn, plan, and solve problems. They exhibit *intelligence. But putting matters this way might be held to prejudge the issue. Talking of their 'senses' or of 'painful' circumstances, for instance, suggests that we have already settled the issue of consciousness—for note that if I had described a robot in those terms, the polemical intent of my choice of words would have been obvious (and resisted by many). How do creatures differ

from robots, real or imagined? They are organically and biologically similar to *us*, and we are the paradigmatic conscious creatures. This similarity admits of degrees, of course, and one's intuitions about which sorts of similarity count are probably untrustworthy. Dolphins' fishiness subtracts from our conviction, but no doubt should not. Were chimpanzees as dull as sea-slugs, their facial similarity to us would no doubt nevertheless favour their inclusion in the charmed circle. If house-flies were about our size, or warm-blooded, we'd be much more confident that when we plucked off their wings they felt pain (*our* sort of pain, the kind that matters). What makes us think that some such considerations ought to count and not others?

The obvious presumption is that the various 'outside' indicators are more or less reliable signs or symptoms of the presence of that whatever-it-is each conscious subject knows from the inside. But how could this be confirmed? This is the notorious 'problem of other minds'. In one's own case, it seems, one can directly observe the coincidence of one's inner life with one's outwardly observable talents for perceptual discrimination, introspective avowal, intelligent action, and the like. But if each of us is to advance rigorously beyond solipsism, we must be able to do something apparently impossible: confirm the coincidence of inner and outer in others. Their *telling us* of the coincidence in their own cases will not do, officially, for that gives us just more coincidence of outer with outer: perceptual capacities and so forth normally go hand in hand with capacities for 'introspective' avowal. If a cleverly designed robot could (seem to) tell us of its inner life (could utter all the appropriate noises in the appropriate contexts), would we be right to admit it to the charmed circle? We might be, but how could we ever tell we were not being fooled? Here the question seems to be: is that special inner light really turned on, or is there nothing but darkness inside? And this question looks unanswerable. So perhaps we have taken a mis-step already.

My use of 'we' and 'our' in the last paragraph, and your unworried acquiescence in it, reveals that *we* don't take the problem of other minds seriously—at least for ourselves and the human beings with whom we normally associate. The temptation then is to decide that, in so far as there is a serious, coherent question yet to be answered about the imagined robot (or about some problematic creature), it will turn out to be answerable by straightforward empirical means once we have better theories of the organization of our brains and their role in controlling our behaviour. This is to suppose that somehow or other the facts we individually get 'from the inside' reduce to facts publicly obtainable from the outside. That is to say, enough of the right sort of outside facts will *settle* the question of whether or not some creature is conscious. For instance, a recent attempt to define consciousness in objective terms is E. R. John's:

a process in which information about multiple individual modalities of sensation and perception is combined into a unified multidimensional representation of the state of the system and its environment, and integrated with information about memories and the needs of the organism, generating emotional reactions and programs of behavior to adjust the organism to its environment . . . (Thatcher and John, 1977, p. 294).

Determining that this internal process occurs in a particular organism is presumably a difficult but clearly empirical task. Suppose that with regard to some creature it were completed successfully: the creature is, by this account, conscious. If we have understood the proposal correctly, we will not find any room to wonder further. Reserving judgement here would be like being shown in detail the operations of an automobile engine and then asking, 'But is it *really* an internal combustion engine? Might we not be deluded in thinking it was?'

Any proper scientific account of the phenomenon of consciousness must inevitably take this somewhat doctrinaire step of demanding that the phenomenon be viewed as objectively accessible, but one may still wonder if, once the step is taken, the truly mysterious phenomenon will be left behind. Before dismissing this sceptical hunch as the fancy of romantics, it would be wise to consider a striking revolution in the recent history of thinking about the mind, a revolution with unsettling consequences.

For John *Locke and many subsequent thinkers, nothing was more essential to the mind than consciousness, and more particularly self-consciousness. The mind in all its activities and processes was viewed as transparent to itself; nothing was hidden from its inner view. To discern what went on in one's mind, one just 'looked'—one 'introspected'—and the limits of what one thereby found were the very boundaries of the mind. The notion of *unconscious* thinking or perceiving was not entertained, or, if it was, it was dismissed as incoherent, self-contradictory nonsense. For Locke, indeed, there was a serious problem of how to describe all one's memories as being continuously in one's mind, when yet they were not continuously 'present to consciousness'. The influence of this view has been so great that when Sigmund *Freud initially hypothesized the existence of *un*conscious mental processes, his proposal met widely with stark denial and incomprehension. It was not just an outrage to common sense, but even self-contradictory, to assert that there could be unconscious beliefs and desires, unconscious feelings of hatred, unconscious schemes of self-defence and retaliation. But Freud won converts. This 'conceptual impossibility' became respectably thinkable by theorists once it was seen that this way of thinking permitted one to explain otherwise inexplicable patterns of psychopathology. The new way of thinking was also supported by a crutch: one could cling to at least a pale version of the Lockian creed by imagining that these 'unconscious' thoughts, desires, and schemes *belonged to other*

*selves* within the psyche. Just as I can keep my schemes secret from you, my id can keep secrets from my ego. By splitting the subject into many subjects, one could preserve the axiom that every mental state must be someone's conscious mental state, and explain the inaccessibility of some of these states to their putative owners by postulating other interior owners for those states. This move was usefully obscured in the mists of jargon so that the weird question of whether it was like anything to be a super-ego, for instance, could be kept at bay.

It is easy to speculate, but hard to confirm, that Freud's expansion of the bounds of the thinkable was a major pre-condition for a much more pervasive, and much less controversial, style of theorizing in experimental, and especially cognitive, psychology in recent years. We have come to accept without the slightest twinge of incomprehension a host of claims to the effect that sophisticated hypothesis-testing, memory-searching inference—in short, information processing—occurs within us even though it is entirely inaccessible to introspection. It is not repressed unconscious activity of the sort Freud uncovered, activity driven out of the 'sight' of consciousness, but just mental activity that is somehow beneath or beyond the ken of consciousness altogether. Freud claimed that his theories and clinical observations gave him the authority to overrule the sincere denials of his patients about what was going on in their minds. Similarly the cognitive psychologist marshals experimental evidence, models, and theories to show that people are engaged in surprisingly sophisticated reasoning processes of which they can give no introspective account at all. Not only are minds accessible to outsiders; some mental activities are more accessible to outsiders than to the very 'owners' of those minds!

In the new theorizing, however, the crutch has been thrown away. Although the new theories abound with deliberately fanciful homuncular metaphors—with subsystems sending messages back and forth, asking for help, obeying, and volunteering—the actual subsystems are deemed to be unproblematically *non*-conscious bits of organic machinery, as utterly lacking in a point of view or inner life as a kidney or kneecap. (Certainly the advent of 'mindless' but 'intelligent' computers played a major role in this further dissolution of the Lockian view.)

But now Locke's extremism has been turned on its head; if, before, the very idea of *un*conscious mentality seemed incomprehensible, now we are losing our grip on the very idea of *conscious* mentality. What is consciousness *for*, if perfectly unconscious, indeed subject-less, information processing is in principle capable of achieving all the ends for which conscious minds were supposed to exist? If theories of cognitive psychology can be true of us, they could also be true of zombies, or robots, and the theories seem to have no way of distinguishing us. How could any amount of mere subject-less information processing (of the sort we have recently discovered to go on in us) add up to or create that special feature with which it is so vividly contrasted? For the contrast has not disappeared. Karl *Lashley once provocatively suggested that 'no activity of the mind is ever conscious', by which he meant to draw our attention to the inaccessibility of the processing that we know must go on when we think. He gave an example: if asked to think a thought in dactylic hexameter, most of us can readily oblige; but how we do it, what goes on in us to produce the thought, is something quite inaccessible to us. Lashley's remark might seem at first to herald the demise of consciousness as a phenomenon for psychological study, but its true effect is just the opposite. It draws our attention unmistakably to the *difference* between all the unconscious information processing—without which, no doubt, there could be no conscious experience—and the conscious thought itself, which *is* somehow directly accessible. Accessible to what or to whom? To say that it is accessible to some subsystem of the brain is not yet to distinguish it from the *un*conscious activities and events which are also accessible to various subsystems of the brain. If some particular and special subsystem deserves to be called the *self*, this is far from obvious. What feature of its particular traffic with the rest of the nervous system would make it a thing it was like something to be?

Strangely enough, this problem is the old chestnut, the problem of other minds, resurrected as a serious problem now that psychology has begun to analyse the human mind into its functional components. This comes out most graphically in the famous split-brain cases. (For details, see SPLIT-BRAIN AND MIND.) There is nothing very problematic in granting that the people who have undergone severing of the corpus callosum have two somewhat independent minds. It is not problematic because we have grown used to thinking of a person's mind as an organization of communicating sub-minds. Here the lines of communication have simply been cut, rendering the mind-likeness of the individual parts particularly salient. But what remains entirely problematic is whether both sub-minds 'have an inner life'. One view is that there is no reason to grant (full, 'inner-life') consciousness to the non-dominant hemisphere, since all that has been shown is that that hemisphere, like many other unconscious cognitive subsystems, can process a lot of information and intelligently control some behaviour. But then we may ask what reason there then is to grant consciousness to the dominant hemisphere, or even to the whole intact system in a normal person. We had thought that question was frivolous and not worth discussing, but this avenue forces us to take it seriously again. If, on the other hand, we grant full, 'inner-life' consciousness to the non-dominant hemisphere (or, more properly, to the newly discovered *person* whose brain is the non-dominant hemisphere), what will be said about all the other information-

processing subsystems posited by current theory? Is the Lockian crutch to be taken up again, at the expense of populating, quite literally, our heads with hosts of subjects of experience?

Consider, for example, the striking discovery by J. R. Lackner and M. Garrett of what might be called an unconscious channel of sentence comprehension. In dichotic listening tests, subjects listen through earphones to two different channels, and are instructed to *attend* to just one channel. Typically they can report with great accuracy what they have heard through the attended channel, but can say little about what was going on concomitantly in the unattended channel. Thus, if the unattended channel carries a spoken sentence, the subjects typically report that they heard a voice, and even a male or female voice. Perhaps they even have a conviction about whether the voice was speaking in their native tongue, but they cannot report what was said. In Lackner and Garrett's experiments, subjects heard ambiguous sentences in the attended channel, such as 'He put out the lantern to signal the attack'. In the unattended channel one group of subjects received disambiguating input (e.g. 'He extinguished the lantern'), while another group had neutral or irrelevant input. The former group could not report what was presented through the unattended channel, but they favoured the suggested reading of the ambiguous sentences significantly more than the control group did. The influence of the unattended channel on the interpretation of the attended signal can be explained only on the hypothesis that the unattended signal is processed all the way to a semantic level—that is, the unattended signal is comprehended—but this is apparently unconscious sentence comprehension! Or should we say it is evidence of the presence in the subjects of at least two different and only partially communicating consciousnesses? If we ask the subjects what it was like to comprehend the unattended channel, they will reply, sincerely, that it was not like anything to them—they were quite unaware of that sentence. But perhaps, as is often suggested about the split-brain patients, there is in effect someone else to whom our question ought to be addressed: the subject who consciously comprehended the sentence and has relayed a hint of its meaning to the subject who answers our questions. (See also ATTENTION; SUBLIMINAL PERCEPTION.)

Which should we say, and why? We seem to be back to our unanswerable question, which suggests we should find a different way of looking at the situation. Let us then entertain the hypothesis that what we had taken to be one phenomenon is actually two quite different phenomena: the sort of consciousness that is intrinsically connected to the capacity to say in one's natural language what is going on; and the sort of consciousness that is just a matter of intelligent information processing. On this proposal, adding the capacity to make 'introspective reports' *changes the phenomenon*, so when we wonder what a dolphin or dog could tell us, or what a non-dominant hemisphere could tell us, if only they could talk, we are wondering about a radically different phenomenon from the phenomenon that exists in the absence of such a linguistic capacity.

It is a familiar theme in discussions of consciousness that human consciousness is somehow tied to our capacity for language, and is quite different from animal consciousness. Developing this idea in a cognitivistic model of linguistic production and comprehension should clarify the conditions of this dependence of human consciousness on language. Of course many perplexities must be confronted along the way. How should we conceive of the gradual acquisition of language by children (or chimpanzees, perhaps!—see PRIMATE LANGUAGE), and what should we say about the 'experience' (conscious or unconscious) of the pre-verbal Helen Keller? A theory of consciousness that does justice to the variety of complications will almost certainly demand of us a revolution in our habits of thought about these issues, but we have already partially absorbed the first shocks of that revolution in the overthrow of the Lockian vision of the transparent mind.

See also CONSCIOUSNESS AND CAUSALITY; MIND AND BODY; MIND–BODY PROBLEM.          D. C. D.

Dennett, D. C. (1978). *Brainstorms: philosophical essays on mind and psychology*. Montgomery and Hassocks.
Farrell, B. A. (1950). Experience. *Mind*, 170–98.
Jaynes, J. (1976). *The Origin of Consciousness in the Breakdown of the Bicameral Mind*. Boston.
Lackner, J. R. and Garrett, M. (1973). Resolving ambiguity: effects of biasing context in the Unattended Ear. *Cognition*, **1**, 359–72.
Nagel, T. (1974). What is it like to be a bat? *Philosophical Review*, **83**, 435–51.
Thatcher, R. W. and John, E. R. (1977). *Foundations of Cognitive Processes*. Hillsdale, New Jersey.

**CONSCIOUSNESS, ALTERED STATES OF.** See HALLUCINATION; HYPNOSIS, EXPERIMENTAL; OUT-OF-THE-BODY EXPERIENCES; PSYCHOPHARMACOLOGY.

**CONSCIOUSNESS AND CAUSALITY.** The difference between mind and matter and how the two interrelate has challenged and baffled human understanding ever since man first began to reflect on his nature and the meaning of existence. The common, naïve impression that we use the mind to initiate and control our physical actions has long been rejected almost universally in science, following the doctrine of scientific materialism, which predicates that a full account of brain, behaviour, and reality is possible in terms purely physical without reference to conscious, mental, or subjective agents. The more progress neuroscience achieved in explaining the electrophysiology, chemistry, and anatomy of brain activity, the greater became the apparent dichotomy between mind and brain, and the more inconceivable that the course of brain function could be influenced in any way by the subjective qualities of inner experience.

In the 1950s materialistic philosophy was carried to a new extreme in the so-called 'psychophysical (or mind–brain) identity theory'. By involved semantics it was affirmed that no difference exists at all between mind and brain, that they are one and the same, and only seem like two different things because we have used different languages and perspectives in our objective and subjective descriptions. According to this identity theory, there is no mind–brain relation; only a pseudo-problem remains that allegedly can be resolved with a proper linguistic approach. The materialist position as developed through the late 1960s was expressed by D. M. Armstrong, a leading proponent, as 'the view that we can give a complete account of man in purely physico-chemical terms', in a 'purely electrochemical account of the workings of the brain'. 'The mind is nothing but the brain.' 'Life is a purely physico-chemical phenomenon.' 'It seems that man is nothing but a material object having none but physical properties.' (Armstrong, 1968). The accepted superfluousness of consciousness for neuroscience was expressed by Nobel laureate Sir John Eccles in 1964:

We can, in principle, explain all our input–output performance in terms of activity of neuronal circuits; and consequently, consciousness seems to be absolutely unnecessary! . . . as neurophysiologists we simply have no use for consciousness in our attempts to explain how the nervous system works.

In direct reaction against the materialist view, a modified, mentalistic concept of consciousness and the mind–brain relation emerged in the mid-1960s. In the course of attempts to account for the observed unity and/or duality of conscious experience following surgical disconnection of the cerebral hemispheres (see SPLIT-BRAIN AND MIND), favour was given to an interpretation of conscious mind in which subjective unity and subjective meaning generally were conceived to be primarily operational or functional derivatives. It was posited that a brain process acquires subjective meaning by virtue of the way it operates in the context of brain dynamics, not because it is a neural copy, transform, or an isomorphic or topological representation of the imagined object. This operational concept of subjective meaning necessarily involved a functional, and therefore *causal*, impact of subjective phenomena in the dynamics of brain control. Conscious phenomena were interpreted to be dynamic emergent properties of brain activity. The subjective phenomena by definition were 'different from, more than, and not reducible to' the neural mechanisms of which they are built.

The neural infrastructure of any brain process mediating conscious awareness is composed of elements within elements and forces within forces, ranging from subnuclear and subatomic particles at the lower levels upward through molecular, cellular, and simple-to-complex neural systems. At each level of the hierarchy, elements are bound and controlled by the enveloping organizational properties of the larger systems in which they are embedded. Holistic system properties at each level of organization have their own causal regulatory roles, interacting at their own level and also exerting downward control over their components, as well as determining the properties of the system in which they are embedded. It is postulated that at higher levels in the brain these emergent system properties include the phenomena of inner experience as high-order emergents in the brain's hierarchy of controls.

Interpreted as holistic high-level dynamic properties, the mental phenomena are conceived to control their component biophysical, molecular, atomic, and other sub-elements in the same way that the organism as a whole controls the course and fate of its separate organs and cells, or just as the molecule as an entity carries all its component atoms, electrons, and other subatomic and subnuclear parts through a distinctive time–space course in a chemical reaction. As is the rule for part–whole relations, a mutual interaction between the neural and mental events is recognized: the brain physiology determines the mental effects, as generally agreed; but also the neurophysiology, at the same time, is reciprocally governed by the higher subjective properties of the enveloping mental events. These interact at their own level and correspondingly move their subsidiary constituents in brain processing. Although determined in part by the properties of their neural components, the subjective properties are also determined by the spacing and timing of the components. Thus the critical, multinested space–time pattern properties of the neuronal infrastructure, as well as the mass–energy elements, must also be included in the causal account.

The resultant mind–brain model, in which mind acts on brain and brain acts on mind, is classified as being 'interactionist' in contrast to mind–brain 'parallelism' or mind–brain 'identity'. The term 'interaction', however, is not the best for the kind of relationship envisaged, in which mental phenomena are described as primarily *super*vening rather than *inter*vening, in the physiological process. Mind is conceived to move matter in the brain and to govern, rule, and direct neural and chemical events without interacting with the components at the component level, just as an organism may move and govern the time–space course of its atoms and tissues without interacting with them.

In the revised mind–brain model consciousness becomes an integral working component in brain function, an autonomous phenomenon in its own right, not reducible to electrochemical mechanisms. Exerting top-level causal influence in the direction and control of behaviour, the conscious mind is no longer something that can be ignored in objective neuroscience wherever an explanation of conscious activity is concerned. Subjective experience is given a use and reason for being as having a central, ineliminable causal role in brain function. A rationale is thus provided for the evolution of mind in a physical world.

The new mentalist view of consciousness as causal stands in direct opposition to the founding precepts of the behaviourist–materialist philosophy. The two explanatory frameworks are diametrically opposed and mutually exclusive. During the 1970s in the so-called 'consciousness' or 'mentalist' revolution (referred to also as the 'cognitive', 'humanist', or 'third' revolution) the new mentalist interpretation gained acceptance over behaviourism as the dominant paradigm of psychology. The shift from behaviourism to mentalism, or cognitivism, represents a shift to a fundamentally different form of causal determinism. The traditional micro-determinism of the materialist–behaviourist era emphasizing causal control from below upward, gave way to a paradigm in which primacy is given to emergent top–down control, exerted by the higher, more evolved forces in nature over the less evolved. In the brain this means a downward control of the mental over the neuronal. However, the principle of emergent downward control (referred to also as 'emergent interaction' or 'emergent determinism') applies, to all hierarchic systems in all science.

The new mentalism, combining tenets from previously conflicting views, tends to reconcile polar opposites of the past such as mind and matter, the physical and metaphysical, determinism and free choice, as well as 'is' and 'ought' and fact and value, in a unifying view of mind, brain, and man in nature. The new position appears metaphysical in its recognition of mental events as realities existing in their own form different from neural events, in endowing subjective phenomena with causal influence and in placing mind in a control role above matter in the brain. At the same time, the interpretation appears to be materialistic in defining mental phenomena as being built of physical elements and being inseparable from the neural substrate. Because it is neither traditionally dualistic nor physicalistic, the new mentalist paradigm is taken to represent a distinct third philosophic position. It is emergentist, functionalist, interactionist, and monistic.

In the new mentalist terms, science no longer postulates that all operations of the brain and behaviour are determined mechanistically or physio-chemically as in traditional materialist philosophy. Although the neuro-electro-chemical mechanisms sustain and help determine any given course of action, the choice of action is determined largely at higher levels by conscious mental events. Willed choice involves the causal influence of subjective value priorities wherein one's personal wishes, feelings, and other *mental* factors override the subsidiary forces of the neural substructure. In other words we do what we *subjectively wish* to do. Free-will decisions are still caused or determined in the new scheme but acquire degrees of freedom and of self-control far above those of classic mechanistic determinism.

The shift of the 1970s in the scientific status and treatment of conscious experience carries far-ranging philosophic and humanistic, as well as scientific, implications. The mind has been restored to the brain of experimental science. The qualitative, colourful and value-rich world of inner experience, long excluded from the domain of science by behaviourist–materialist doctrine, has been reinstated. The subjective is no longer outside the mainstream of objective science, nor something that will eventually be reducible in principle to neurophysiology. A logical determinist framework is provided for those disciplines that deal directly with subjective experience such as cognitive, clinical, and humanistic psychology. Scientific theory has become squared finally with the impressions of common experience: we do in fact use the mind to initiate and control our physical actions.

See also CONSCIOUSNESS; MIND AND BODY; MIND–BODY PROBLEM.                                    R. W. S.

Armstrong, D. M. (1968). *A Materialist Theory of the Mind*. London.

Sperry, R. W. (1966). Mind, brain and humanist values. *Bulletin of Atomic Science*, **22**, 2–6.

Sperry, R. W. (1976). Changing concepts of consciousness and free will. *Perspectives in Biology and Medicine*, **20**, 9–19.

Sperry, R. W. (1983). *Science and Moral Priority*. New York and Oxford.

**CONSTANCY SCALING.** See EMMERT'S LAW.

**CONTINGENT PERCEPTUAL AFTER-EFFECT.** A distortion occurring after prolonged sensory stimulation by alternating patterns. While there are early reports of effects which with hindsight we can see were contingent after-effects, there has been a growth in interest due to a paper published by Celeste McCollough in 1965. She presented human subjects with two alternating visual patterns: a grating of blue and black vertical stripes, and a grating of orange and black horizontal stripes. After her subjects had gazed at these alternating, adapting patterns for a few minutes (and so adapted to them), they were shown a test field of black and white stripes of the same size. In one part of the field the stripes were vertical, in the other horizontal. However, to the subjects the stripes did not appear black and white: where vertical they appeared pinkish and where horizontal they appeared bluish. This is now called the 'McCollough effect'.

Such effects are different from simple *after-images produced by staring at a bright, coloured surface. If one looks for half a minute or so at an unpatterned red field, for a few moments all subsequently viewed white objects will appear tinged with green. But in the McCollough effect, although the perceived colours are also the approximate complementaries of the adapting colours, they depend (or are contingent) upon the orientation of the stripes of the adapting and test fields. It is the orientation with respect to the retina which is important. McCollough's subjects were adapted and tested with their heads upright; but if while looking at the test field they tilted their heads sideways, by 45 degrees, the apparent colours disappeared, even though the stripes in the test field still looked horizontal and vertical. If they tilted their heads through 90 degrees the effects reappeared, though now the stripes which had appeared pinkish with the head vertical appeared bluish, and vice versa.

Interest in the McCollough effect, and related effects, has generated a large volume of research. It is worth asking why. The original interpretation of the effects seems to have been right for the *Zeitgeist* of the late 1960s. It was becoming clear from the discoveries of the neurophysiologists that cells in the visual cortex of the brains of cats and monkeys are specialized to respond to rather specific features of the sensory input. After-effects seemed to suggest a similar organization in man. For example, the movement after-effect (apparent motion of a stationary field in one direction, following prolonged viewing of real motion in the other) is consistent with the idea that there are specific *channels sensitive to particular directions of motion, whose outputs are reduced by prolonged stimulation and are compared to give perceived motion. The McCollough effect, as a complicated after-effect, might reveal how the human brain processes more complex patterns. This hope has, however, not been realized. Contingent after-effects have revealed little about how a face is recognized. Like other after-effects they seem to tell us only about the organization of early stages of visual processing.

Many other contingent after-effects (or CAEs) have been discovered since Celeste McCollough's original report. For example, coloured after-effects can be made contingent on the width of stripes, as well as on their orientation. Another effect, reported by H. J. Wyatt, is the size after-effect contingent upon orientation. After adaptation to coarse horizontal stripes, alternating with fine vertical stripes, medium stripes appear fine when horizontal, and coarse when vertical.

There are several ways for finding out where in the brain a particular effect is occurring (see Julesz, 1971, for a discussion of them). One trick is to induce a visual effect with one eye, and then see if it can be obtained with the other eye. For example, for the after-effect of movement: if one gazes for a time with one eye at a moving display, which is then stopped, the now stationary display will appear to move in the opposite direction—and this apparent motion can be seen not only with the eye which inspected the moving display but also with the other eye, when the adapted eye is closed. This phenomenon is known as interocular transfer. It implies (provided there is no activity from the closed eye) that the anatomical site of the after-effect lies at a point at or after the combination of the two optic tracts. Some CAEs transfer between the eyes; for example, the movement after-effect contingent on the orientation of a superimposed grating. However, the McCollough effect exhibits little, if any, transfer. It used to be thought that it was a purely monocular effect, whose site lay peripheral to binocular combination; but more recent studies have found evidence for binocular effects. One way to do this is to divide up colour and pattern information between the eyes so that, instead of coloured gratings, the subject sees a plain coloured field with, say, his left eye, and a black and white grating with his right eye. The alternate adapting stimulus used is another colour, seen by his left eye, and a grating at 90 degrees to the first, seen by his right eye. (These adapting conditions are shown diagrammatically in Fig. 1.) McCollough effects are then found, but they are of opposite sign in each eye. So when the subject views the test field with the eye that has seen colour, the perceived colours are the complementary colours to those paired with a particular orientation during adaptation. This is the normal relationship between the colours seen during adaptation and those which appear during testing. But, when the eye which has adapted to black and white stripes is tested, the perceived colours are the same as those with which that orientation was paired during the adaptation. Here the normal relationship is reversed. Perhaps when the left eye is flooded with green light while the right sees a black and white grating, the visual system treats the colour input as 'left eye greener than right'. At any rate, the apparently simple scheme suggested by the early interocular transfer results has now been complicated by such later work.

Although most work on contingent after-effects has been done in vision, they can be found in other sensory modalities such as touch. For example, contingent tactile adaptation can be obtained with a wedge-shaped block of wood, held with the tips of forefinger and thumb. If your hand moves from left to right as the finger and thumb slide from the thick to the thin end of the wedge, then, after some moments of sliding the hand right to left, and left to right, a rectangular block of wood will feel deformed. As the finger and thumb of the adapted hand are moved from left to right the block will feel to be getting thicker, and for the reverse direction of movement it will seem to be getting thinner. Here the tactile adaptation is dependent upon the direction of movement of the hand.

Although it is easy to generate CAEs within several (perhaps all) sensory modalities, no one has succeeded in generating CAEs across modalities. For example, the author failed to find a coloured after-effect contingent upon the frequency of sound, after staring at a red field while listening to a high tone, and alternating with a green field accompanied by a low tone. Absence of cross-modal links suggests that the underlying mechanisms lie peripheral to the site(s) where information from different modalities is combined. However, although vision and hearing have not been linked, different parts of the visual field will co-operate to give CAEs. For example, Michael

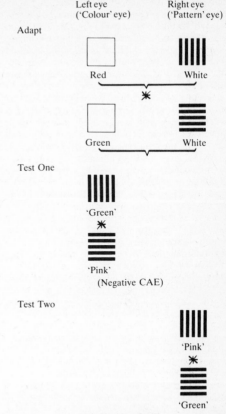

**Fig. 1.** Diagrammatic representation of the dichoptic induction of the McCulloch effect, reported by D. M. and V. MacKay. During adaptation, the subject's left eye always sees colour, and his right eye always sees black-and-white stripes. The colour and stripe orientations are systematically paired so that, say, red and vertical are always seen together, though by different eyes, and similarly green and horizontal. The pairs of stimuli alternate every 10 seconds or so during adaptation. To test for an after-effect, the subject views a black-and-white grating with one eye. If this is the eye that is adapted to colour, the after-effects are negative, but if it is the eye that is adapted to the gratings the after-effects are positive.

Potts and the author found that a movement after-effect contingent on colour can be obtained when the coloured adapting stimuli are not superimposed on, but surround the moving stimuli, so that no area of retina sees coloured moving patterns. This suggests some spatial spread of the mechanism linking colour and motion.

What do these striking and robust effects tell us about the brain? At present, there is still no generally accepted explanation for CAEs; but current theories are of two main types. One view likens CAEs to other after-effects supposed to result from adaptation in overlapping sensory channels. So, orientation would be coded by a number of neural channels: some tuned preferentially to vertical, some to, say, 10 degrees from vertical, and so on round the clock. Each group of channels tuned to a particular orientation would have members also tuned for red as well as vertical; others for green and vertical, and so on. During McCollough-type adaptation, gazing at a red vertical grating would reduce to below normal the output of channels tuned for both red and vertical. When the test grating is presented, channels tuned for vertical and other colours would give their usual output; but the red/vertical channels would be less active than normal. This imbalance in favour of the other channels would add an apparent green tinge to the vertical stripes. This is sometimes called a 'built-in' theory, since the mechanism producing the CAE is supposed already to exist in the subject's visual system before adaptation. It can be contrasted with a group of 'built-up' theories which propose that some kind of link is forged during the adaptation period, between previously separate mechanisms for processing colour and orientation. Different kinds of link have been proposed: some authors have suggested that an association is made like that in classical (Pavlovian) *conditioning (in which, after a bell has been presented together with food on several occasions, the bell alone comes to elicit salivation); others that a neural inhibitory link is formed, so that activity in, say, the orientation system reduces activity in the colour system. However, despite numerous attempts, no experiment has yet been reported which convincingly decides between 'built-in' and 'built-up' theories.

There are several important characteristics of CAEs which a successful theory will have to explain. First, the effects are usually 'negative'. That is, the value taken by a sensory quality in the after-effect is opposite to or shifted further away from the value of that quality during adaptation. So, in the McCollough effect the colour seen on a particular orientation (say, red) in the test field is the complementary to that viewed on that orientation during adaptation (in this case, green). Second, CAEs can be very long-lived. McCollough effects have been reported six weeks after adaptation; and reports that they can be re-evoked days after adaptation are common in the literature. Third, they do not decay during sleep. Indeed, there is some evidence that to remove the effects one has to look at the usual test field.

It is interesting to ask what the role is in normal perception of the mechanisms that produce the McCollough effect. Presumably, they do not exist simply to provide amusing perceptual demonstrations! One possibility is that if indeed the initial stages of human perception consist of banks of filters tuned to particular features of the sensory input, then there will be a need to keep the outputs of these filter-channels calibrated. For example, the gain of a particular sensory channel (that is, how much output it produces for a given input)

might be subject to unwanted drifts, or fluctuations, as, say, a blood vessel narrowed which supplied that area of cortex. The brain could attempt to distinguish between such internal changes and those introduced by stimuli in the external world, by sampling over time the outputs of all channels. On the assumption that red vertical stimuli are about as likely to occur on average as green vertical stimuli, it would turn down the gain of a channel whose output was abnormally high for a long period; or turn up the gain of one which was correspondingly low. Such an automatic gain control system would act to keep the gains of sensory channels roughly equal despite biological drift. It could also remove from the neural image false signals—such as colour fringes introduced by chromatic aberration in the optics of the eye—since these constant errors would be treated in the same way as the unvarying colour/orientation combination in the McCollough effect. But such a system would be misled by prolonged exposure to stimuli exciting only a very few channels. It would surely mistake the activity in these channels for internal drift, rather than external stimulation, and turn down their gain. This would give negative after-effects, since these channels would contribute less than their appropriate share to the final percept. The system would also require evidence that the gains of the adapted channels were too low before readjusting them. The best evidence of this would be for the subject to inspect (in the case of the McCollough effect) black and white gratings. Thus presenting the test field should cause CAEs to decay, but withholding it should produce longlasting after-effects, as is found. CAEs may, therefore, reflect the brain's usually efficient but sometimes erroneous attempts at self-calibration.

See also VISUAL ADAPTATION.                     J. P. H.

Julesz, B. (1971). *Foundations of Cyclopean Perception.* Chicago.

Potts, M. J. and Harris, J. P. (1975). Movement aftereffects contingent on the colour or pattern of a stationary surround. *Vision Research*, **15**, 1,225–30.

Skowbo, D., Timney, B. N., Gentry, T. A., and Morant, R. B. (1975). McCollough Effects: experimental findings and theoretical accounts. *Psychological Bulletin*, **82**, 497–510.

Stromeyer, C. F. (1978). Form–Color after-effects in human vision. In Held, R., Leibowitz, H., and Teuber, H. L. (eds.), *Handbook of Sensory Physiology*, vol. viii. Berlin, Heidelberg, New York.

**CONTINGENT   PROPERTY.**   'Contingent' (sometimes 'accidental') is applied to certain properties of a thing to suggest that they do not necessarily belong to that thing, either because of their dependence on some further cause, or simply to indicate that the thing need not have those properties to be the thing that it is. Thus a piece of wood may have the contingent property of being stained; however, the property of having been produced from a tree is necessary to its being a piece of wood.

The distinction between contingent and necessary properties is broadly the Aristotelian distinction between what a thing is in virtue of itself (*kath' hauto*) and what it is by accident (*kata sumbebēkos*). To sustain the distinction requires, on the one hand, a recognition that the very identity of a thing may be bound up with its being of a certain kind; otherwise all its properties are contingent (e.g. it would be thinkable that something which is a piece of wood might not have been a piece of wood). On the other hand, it must be allowed that a thing can alter some of its properties without changing its identity; otherwise all its properties are necessary (e.g. a piece of wood could not be stained without becoming a completely different thing).                                        J. E. T.

Kirwan, C. (1971). *Aristotle's Metaphysics Books Γ, Δ, E* (translated with notes). Oxford.

**CO-ORDINATION BETWEEN DIFFERENT SENSES.** See SPATIAL CO-ORDINATION OF THE SENSES.

**CORNEA.** The transparent window of the eye. It is the main image-forming structure in air-living vertebrates. (In fish, however, the crystalline lens produces the retinal image.) The cornea has no blood vessels, receiving its nutrients by absorption. It is for this reason that corneas can be transplanted without rejection. *Astigmatism is generally due to the cornea having a non-spherical surface.

**CORPUS CALLOSUM.** The very large bundle of fibres connecting the two cerebral hemispheres in the brain. It is occasionally sectioned as a treatment for *epilepsy, and the results have been used for 'split-brain' experiments, particularly associated with the American neurophysiologist Roger Sperry, who holds that the patient may then have two minds, or two selves. See NERVOUS SYSTEM; SPLIT-BRAIN AND MIND.

**CORRELATION.** An observed association between events (for example, that smoking is associated with lung cancer). It is not possible to assign causes directly from correlations: there must always be an underlying theory, or explicit or implicit assumptions, to set the causal 'arrow'. Discovering correlations is a principal aim of most scientific experiments, and much of learning may also be thought of as discovering correlations, which are useful when predictive.

**CORTICAL MAPS.** See LOCALIZATION OF BRAIN FUNCTION AND CORTICAL MAPS.

**COUÉ, EMILE** (1857–1926). French lay psychotherapist who founded a therapeutic method based on auto-suggestion (self-induced suggestion) that won considerable popularity in its day. He gained fame with his maxim 'day by day and in every way I am getting better and better'.

**COURAGE.** See FEAR AND COURAGE.

**COVERANT.** *Behaviourists have long relied on the concept of 'operant' or 'instrumental' behaviour: that is, behaviour which is modified by its consequences. The concept was applied almost exclusively to overt, observable behaviours such as speaking, walking, and lever-pressing, each of which may be considered 'operants'. But some behaviourists, such as B. F. Skinner, maintained that covert, unobservable behaviours—what most people would call 'thoughts', 'images', and other 'mental' events—work in the same way as overt behaviour. That notion eventually led to the concept of the 'coverant' (a contraction of 'covert' and 'operant'), which was introduced by the psychologist Lloyd Homme (1965). Homme suggested various means for controlling coverants as an aid to therapists dealing with problems such as obsessive thoughts. Control was said to be accomplished, for example, by training a patient to punish himself after an inappropriate thought. Though the theoretical underpinnings of this approach to therapy have been challenged, the coverant concept helped stimulate widespread interest among therapists in a behaviouristic approach to both self-control and cognition. See BEHAVIOUR THERAPY.
                                                        R. E.

Homme, L. E. (1965). Perspectives in psychology: xxiv. Control of coverants: the operants of the mind. *Psychological Record*, **15**, 501–11.

**CRAIK, KENNETH JOHN WILLIAM** (1914–45). British psychologist, educated at the Edinburgh Academy and the University of Edinburgh, where he graduated with first-class honours in philosophy. He then deviated to psychology, working for a year in Edinburgh under Professor James Drever, Sen., before moving on to Cambridge, where he became a research student in the psychological laboratory under Professor F. C. (later Sir Frederic) *Bartlett. Craik was awarded his Ph.D. in 1940 and elected to a fellowship at St John's College, Cambridge, in the following year.

During the Second World War, Craik was heavily engaged in applied research work on behalf of the Medical Research Council and the armed services, especially the Royal Air Force. In 1944 he was appointed the first director of the Medical Research Council's applied psychology unit at Cambridge and seemed well set for an active and productive post-war career. Unfortunately, his premature death in a road accident at the age of 31 deprived British psychology of one of its most promising figures. It can hardly be doubted that had he survived it would have become one of the ablest experimental psychologists of his time.

Craik's early work was concerned almost wholly with problems of vision. He was particularly interested in the adaptation of the eye to changes in the level of illumination and in the effects of such adaptation on visual efficiency. In a series of published papers, he described the effects of various levels of adaptation on differential brightness sensitivity, visual acuity, and subjective brightness, concluding that the efficiency of the eye was highest when at a level of illumination roughly equal to that to which the eye had been pre-adapted (see VISUAL ADAPTATION). In general, he viewed adaptation as a kind of 'range-setting' adjustment of the visual system and saw in it the first stage of the process whereby a degree of constancy is achieved in the apparent brightness of objects despite wide variations in the general level of illumination. Although he may have underrated the specificity of tuning of the adapted eye, his attempt to establish some general principles of perception on the basis of the simpler mechanisms of physiological response held high promise.

Craik was always much interested in the nature of dark adaptation, and some of his work in this field found important application during the war, particularly in relation to night flying. He also did important work on glare as a factor limiting visual efficiency in locating submarines from the air. On the basis of his impromptu experiments, he was able to evolve a simple experimental law relating intensity of glare to angle of light source and size of target. This led him to suggest a much improved method of visual scanning which was immediately adopted. Studies of anoxia (oxygen deficiency) in relation to aviation medicine stimulated him to undertake experiments, with himself as subject, on temporary blindness induced by mechanical pressure on the eyeball. In the course of these somewhat hazardous experiments, he established very convincingly not only that both light and dark adaptation are essentially retinal processes but that visual *after-images are likewise of peripheral origin.

Although vision may well have been Craik's foremost scientific interest, he shook off his earlier preoccupations with philosophy only with difficulty. In 1943 he published *The Nature of Explanation*, his only completed study of any length. Although this was in principle an essay in philosophy, it embodies a highly original attempt to develop a theory of thought along mechanistic lines. His point of departure is that thinking is undeniably predictive and that this predictive capacity is also characteristic of calculating machines, anti-aircraft predictors, and other devices which, at all events to this extent, can be said to operate in essentially the same manner as man himself. Craik therefore postulated that the brain makes use of mechanisms similar in principle to many of the artefacts of modern technology and that these mechanisms can model, or parallel, phenomena in the external world, just as a calculating machine can parallel the development, say, of strains in a bridge of given design and hence predict whether it will stand or fall. On such a view, Craik contends, our thought has objective validity because it is not fundamentally different from external reality and is especially suited to imitating it.

In assessing Craik's theory, it is important to bear in mind that modern computer technology was virtually in its infancy at the time that he was writing and that his model leans heavily on the principles of analogue devices. Had he been alive in the era of digital computers and lived to read A. M. *Turing's famous paper on *Computing Mechanisms and Intelligence*, which appeared five years after Craik's death, he might well have put forward a model of thought more in keeping with the capacity of digital computers to mimic any discrete-state machine. None the less, Craik's theory, and his concept of internal models in the brain, have had considerable influence on psychologists and neurophysiologists seeking mechanical analogues of intelligent behaviour in animals and man (see ARTIFICIAL INTELLIGENCE).

Craik's wide knowledge of general experimental psychology and the physiology of the senses had been appreciably expanded by his wartime work on human factors in tank and anti-aircraft gunnery. This work also fostered a lively interest in servo-mechanisms and automatic control principles, as is well shown in his two posthumous papers (1947, 1948) on the theory of the human operator in control systems. As the war neared its end, Craik began work on a systematic treatise on the mechanisms of learning and human action. This was never completed, although several chapters survived and have been edited for publication by Stephen Sherwood. They are to be found in a volume of Craik's essays, notes, and papers assembled by Sherwood on the initiative of Warren *McCulloch under the title of *The Nature of Psychology* (1966). As Sherwood rightly points out, Craik's draft embodies some of the earliest references to the relationships between learning, cyclical events in the nervous system, and servo-mechanisms. Indeed it foreshadows many of the arguments later developed *in extenso* by the mathematician Norbert *Wiener in his famous book on *Cybernetics* (1948) (see CYBERNETICS; INTERACTIONAL APPROACH).

His scientific talents apart, Kenneth Craik was an accomplished designer of technical equipment and derived enormous enjoyment from mechanical invention of all kinds. He was a skilled craftsman, and the set of miniature steam-engines, each one smaller than the last, which he made when still a schoolboy are now in the Royal Scottish Museum in Edinburgh. He was also an accomplished amateur violinist and had some talent for poetry.

O. L. Z.

Bartlett, F. C. (1946). Obituary Notice: K. J. W. Craik. *British Journal of Psychology*, **36**, 109–16.

Craik, K. J. W. (1943). *The Nature of Explanation*. Cambridge.

Craik, K. J. W. (1966). *The Nature of Psychology: a collection of papers and other writings by the late Kenneth J. W. Craik*, edited by Stephen Sherwood. Cambridge.

Craik, K. J. W. Theory of the human operator in control systems: I (1947). The operation of the human operator in control systems; II (1948). Man as an element in a control system. *British Journal of Psychology*, **38**, 56–61; 142–8.

Zangwill, O. L. (1980). Kenneth Craik: the man and his work. *British Journal of Psychology*, **71**, 1–6.

**CREATIVITY** is one of those terms (*intelligence is another) that psychologists use as though they refer to single human characteristics, but which direct us in practice to a number of concerns that are rather separate. Some of these, like 'innovation' and 'discovery', have a bearing on the ideas or objects that people produce; some, like 'self-actualization', refer more to the quality of the life an individual leads; and some, like 'imagination' and 'fantasy', point us, in the first instance, to what goes on inside a person's head. Despite its air of vagueness, the notion of 'creativity' has none the less served an important function among psychologists and teachers, acting as a banner under which ideological battles have been fought; and indicating, too, a somewhat disparate body of research, some of which is of real value.

What is now thought of as the 'creativity movement' had its first stirrings in America in the years after the Second World War. At one level, it was psychology's response to the challenge of Sputnik, and to the fact that little of the best space research was being done by home-grown American scientists—the implication being that there was something deadening about the education that clever young American scientists had received. At another level, it represented a liberal reaction, within psychology, against values which were seen as excessively manipulative and bureaucratic. Translated into the classroom, this concern for creativity expressed itself in a desire to shake education free of rote-learning and the set syllabus, multiple-choice examinations, and the IQ test, and to give children the opportunity to make discoveries for themselves.

Although hints of its existence were detectable as early as 1950, this movement was not in full swing until the early 1960s. It seems, in other words, to have been a portent of the liberal and anti-authoritarian mood that dominated university life towards the end of the 1960s, and which, in its turn, provoked its own reaction. By the early 1970s, the more self-consciously scientific psychologists had already begun to reassert the virtues of the IQ test, and to argue in favour of genetic rather than cultural explanations of individual and racial differences.

This symbolic war between 'soft' and 'hard' psychologists has tended to obscure genuine advances in our understanding of the ways in which the human imagination works. The founding fathers of psychology were keenly interested, Francis *Galton no less than Sigmund *Freud; and research has proceeded quietly for a hundred years or more. Two sorts of enquiry have been especially fruitful: straightforwardly descriptive studies of the lives that highly original men and women have led; and research on the processes of thinking itself.

In a sense, the evidence of the biographical studies has been largely negative. It has been found, time and again, that those who display great originality as adults were often, like Charles *Darwin, only mediocre as students. British scientists who become Fellows of the Royal Society show roughly the same distribution of good, mediocre, and poor degree results as do those who go into research but achieve little. The same holds for intelligence-test scores: above a surprisingly low level, there is little or no relationship between IQ and achievement in any sphere of adult endeavour yet studied. As a result, we would expect future Nobel prize winners to show roughly the same distribution of IQ scores as their fellow students at university. In the American context, the budding scientist of high renown seems typically to be a 'B+' student: one who works hard when a topic captures his (or her) imagination, but otherwise does the bare minimum. Science springs to life for such individuals when they discover that instead of assimilating knowledge created by others, they can create knowledge for themselves—and are hooked from that moment onwards.

It is the more detailed studies of thinking that indicate the tensions which underlie such creative effort. Some of the most vivid have concerned mathematicians; and a feature of them is the stress they place on the process of 'incubation'. Often, having struggled with a problem and then put it aside, mathematicians find that the solution comes to them quite unexpectedly, in a flash. The clear implication is that our brains are at their most efficient when allowed to switch from phases of intense concentration to ones in which we exert no conscious control at all.

There are many instances of such 'unconscious' work, one of the more dramatic being that of the German poet Rainer Maria Rilke. In 1912, in the midst of a long poem, the *Duino Elegies*, Rilke ran out of inspiration, and lapsed into a long period of frustrated depression. Interrupted in any case by the First World War, he was able to write little for a decade. When 'utterance and release' came to him in 1922, it took the shape of a series of poems, the *Sonnets to Orpheus*, that he had no intention of writing whatever. Eighteen days later, when he had finished both these sonnets and the *Duino Elegies*, he had produced some 1,200 lines of the pithiest and most carefully poised poetry ever written, and had done so largely without correction, as if taking dictation.

Such evidence encourages us to reconsider the popular idea that *genius and madness are closely allied. It is not true, of course, that great poets, painters, scientists, and mathematicians are mad; far from it. On the other hand, it may well be that they work as intensely and imaginatively as they do in order to remain sane; that they have access to aspects of the mind's functioning from which those who live more staid and conventional lives are excluded, and that it is this access which gives their work both its flair and its sense of risk. Rilke's lengthy depression may well have been necessary for the extraordinary burst of creative but also highly disciplined work that followed it.

It is such tensions as these which explain a remark once attributed to Einstein. He suggested that the creative scientists are the ones with access to their *dreams. Occasionally, a dream will actually provide the solution to a problem—as in the case of the chemist August Kekulé and his dream of the snake swallowing its own tail, the clue to the nature of the benzene ring. Einstein's point was less specific, though. As Freud realized, in establishing his distinction between primary and secondary process thought, the mind is capable of functioning both intuitively and according to the dictates of common sense. The implication of Einstein's remark is that, in order to innovate, the scientist, like anyone else, must break the grip on his imagination that our powers of logical-seeming story-telling impose. We must be willing to subvert the conventional wisdom on which our everyday competence depends.

It is here that the research done by the advocates of creativity in the 1960s now seems most relevant. Rather than straining to see whether tests of creativity can be devised, to stand side by side with IQ tests (a largely barren exercise, it seems), we can concentrate on an issue that Francis Galton identified over a century ago: the extent to which each individual can retrieve apparently irrational ideas, sift them, and put them to some constructive use. We know that individuals differ in their ability to *free associate, to fantasize, and to recall their dreams. We also know that these differences have a bearing on the kinds of work people find it comfortable to do: among the intelligent, it is those who are relatively good at free associating (the 'divergers') who are attracted towards the arts, while those who are relatively weak in this (the 'convergers') who are drawn towards science and technology. What we do not yet know is how the abilities to think logically and to free associate combine to produce work of real value: what qualities of mind, for example, a genuinely imaginative solution to an engineering problem demands, or how a sustained contribution to one of the arts is actually achieved.

See also LATERAL THINKING; PROBLEM-SOLVING; PROBLEMS: THEIR APPEAL.                    L. H.

Getzels, J. W. and Jackson, P. W. (1962). *Creativity and Intelligence*. New York.
Gruber, H. E., et al. (eds.) (1962). *Contemporary Approaches to Creative Thinking*. New York.
Hadamard, J. (1945). *The Psychology of Invention in the Mathematical Field*. New York.
Hudson, L. (1968). *Contrary Imaginations*. Harmondsworth.
Hudson, L. (1978). *Human Beings*. London.
Hudson, L. (1985). *Night Life*. London.
Koestler, A. (1959). *The Sleepwalkers*. London.

**CRETINISM.** Impaired physical and mental development due to lack of thyroid development. Appearing in early childhood, the problems can be largely avoided by treatment with thyroid extract—if diagnosed and treated sufficiently early in infancy.

**CRIMINOLOGY,** like medicine, is an amalgam of disciplines. In popular usage it even includes scientific methods of identifying criminals, although nowadays this is distinguished as 'forensic science' or—less elegantly—'criminalistics'. In stricter modern practice criminology comprises four kinds of study: descriptive, explanatory, penological, and nomological.

**Descriptive studies** are concerned with the frequencies of the various sorts of law-breaking; the situations in which they are most likely to occur; the kinds of people who are most likely to commit them; and the extent of the harm done. In the past such studies have relied chiefly or entirely on official statistics and police files. More recently, 'self-report' studies, in which samples (usually of teenagers) have told interviewers about their behaviour, have provided less superficial data, as have 'victim surveys'. These studies and surveys have yielded more valid estimates of the real incidence of violence, thefts, robberies, burglaries, and sexual crimes (but not yet of serious traffic offences, or of rare crimes such as homicide). They have shown that victims are selective in what they report to the police; that police are selective in what they regard as worth recording; and that fluctuations in recorded crimes can result from, or be greatly exaggerated by, changes in people's willingness to report them, as well as from variations in the interest which the police take in them.

**Explanatory studies** need to be subdivided into those which seek to offer explanations of particular breaches of law and those which try to account for especially high (or low) frequencies of law-breaking (or, better, of certain kinds of law-breaking), whether in different countries, in different social groups, or during different periods in their histories. Explanations of particular breaches usually attach importance to the disposition of the individual law-breaker, whether this is attributed to upbringing, to the influence of associates, or—less commonly nowadays—to genetic or perinatal misfortunes. Explanations of differing frequencies emphasize economic conditions, subcultural values that are in conflict with law, or inequalities of opportunity for legitimate acquisition or enjoyment. 'Histories' may figure in both kinds of explanation, whether they take the form of narratives about individuals or trace the origins of, say, violence in a country's past. Most explainers are highly selective, either because they are searching for some factor which can be manipulated so as to reduce the frequency of law-breaking, or because they want ammunition to support political or moral attacks on the current state of their society. What should not be overlooked, however, is the relevance of explanations when courts are trying to assess the culpability of an individual offender.

**Penological research** is concerned mainly with the effects of what is officially done to identified offenders, although it has also taken an interest in the social consequences of being labelled as an offender of one kind or another. Until recently most penologists concentrated on assessing the extent to which *desired* effects were achieved: reform, deterrence, rehabilitation, incapacitation. There have always been critics, however, who emphasized the unwanted side-effects of sentences; and when it became clear that the wanted effects were confined to a small minority of offenders (who could seldom be identified in advance) the importance of unwanted effects began to be appreciated. These too, however, have been exaggerated; and it is only in the last decade that attempts have been made to define and measure the sorts of damage which incarceration (for example) inflicts, and determine whether it is transient or lasting.

**Nomological studies.** What can be called 'nomological' studies—for want of a better term—concentrate on law-enforcement itself. Some offer answers to the question 'What kinds of conduct should be prohibited by the (criminal) law?' The kinds most frequently discussed are consensual sexual deviations, contraception and abortion, euthanasia, drug abuse, and obscene entertainment. Others are concerned with compulsory benevolence such as requirements to wear seatbelts in motor vehicles. Nomological work is also undertaken into the ways in which the criminal law as it stands is administered. Since police have to be selective—both because of limitations on resources and for the sake of good relations with the public— their selectivity has been subjected to very critical scrutiny in Britain and the USA, though much less in 'police states' for obvious reasons. Public prosecutors, who exercise considerable discretion in bringing people to court and in framing the charges against them, are also a subject of study. Another favourite subject is the criminal courts: chiefly summary courts and appeal courts. Where higher courts are concerned, it has been the jury which has been the focus of the spotlight. The behaviour of prison staff and administrators has also received much attention. Less attention has been paid to the behaviour of probation officers, hostel wardens, and other social workers, chiefly because their roles are seen as less coercive. Furthermore, penologists have interested themselves in 'theories of punishment': more precisely in the differing aims which are held to justify penalizing offenders. Until fairly recently this was regarded as a subject for moral philosophers; but penologists have been able to show that some philosophers' assumptions about the practicability of achieving their aims have been unrealistic.                     N. D. W.

Downes, D. and Rock, P. (1982). *Understanding Deviance*. Oxford.

Floud, J. and Young, W. (1981). *Dangerousness and Criminal Justice*. London.

Taylor, I., Walton, P., and Young, J. (1973). *The New Criminology*. London.

Thomas, D. A. (1979 edn.). *Principles of Sentencing*. London.

Walker, N. D. (1977). *Behaviour and Misbehaviour: explanations and non-explanations*. Oxford.

West, D. J. (1982). *Delinquency: its Roots, Careers and Prospects*. London.

**CRITICAL PERIODS.** Walking, language, sensorimotor co-ordination, and other skills are best learnt at certain 'critical periods' in the development of children, and similarly with other animals. Once the critical period is lost, it may be very difficult or impossible to learn the skill with full effectiveness. (See SPATIAL CO-ORDINATION OF THE SENSES; VISUAL SYSTEM: ENVIRONMENTAL INFLUENCES.) A major skill in teaching children is to recognize the advent of each critical period. Jerome Bruner speaks of readiness to learn, and Jean *Piaget has attempted to determine the ages at which various lessons are appropriate.

**CROSS-MODAL SENSORY INTEGRATION.** To the ordinary observer it is self-evident that an object he perceives remains unchanged even when on different occasions the same object is, say, seen (but not touched, heard, or smelled), or touched (but not seen, heard, or smelled), or heard (but not seen, touched, or smelled). Psychologists have increasingly during the recent past been posing questions with regard to skills of cross-modal recognition. Were *Berkeley, *Leibniz, and *Piaget correct in their supposition that at birth the perceptual systems relating to each sense modality are independent? Then, during development, do the perceptual systems become integrated, and does the infant learn through the experience of stimulus correlations that equivalences between sensory systems exist? Or, are others (e.g. Werner, Bower) right in arguing that babies have a primitive unity of the senses, so that early perception is 'supramodal' (i.e. the sense modality of the inflow is disregarded)? Then, during development, are the senses increasingly differentiated and does the child learn that the senses are distinct?

In addition, psychologists have been asking questions with regard to special populations. Is cross-modal recognition immediately proficient in patients whose sight has been restored at a later age after being virtually blind from birth on account of cataract (a question first raised by *Locke)? Is there evidence, from neurological patients, of a special brain area that acts as a structural bridge between the separate senses? Does language mediate cross-modal skills; and how do mammals lacking language but with their highly proficient perceptual capacities fare on cross-modal tasks?

Unfortunately, we have no certain answers to most of these questions. The originally posed issue (Piaget versus Bower) seems too broad to answer directly. In accordance with the particular task (which might involve objects or temporal sequences), and depending on the subject's prior experience and individual capacities, codes of processing are flexibly selected, irrespective of modality. Distinctions such as 'separateness' and 'unity' (of the senses) have no general validity: the particular task at a particular time is all-important. Moreover, demonstration of certain relatively primitive cross-modal skills in pre-verbal human infants, or in non-human animals, should not imply that symbolic coding is not the normal or preferred human strategy for processing information cross-modally once language has developed. The cross-modal capacities of the human infant (Meltzoff and Borton, 1979) and baby monkey (Gunderson, 1983) seem extremely crude in comparison with the skills shown (not in all tasks or comparisons, but none the less quite frequently) by children over the age of 8, or by adults.

A broad view of the current evidence suggests that a primitive kind of 'supramodal' perception is structurally given at birth in human infants (and also in apes and monkeys), possibly at a 'low' (subcortical) level of the brain. This system may be involved in stimulus–object identification and re-identification (i.e. recognition), but cannot serve when features of an object, as opposed to the identity of the object *per se*, have to be analysed (i.e. discriminated) and then recognized. Apes and monkeys have not progressed far beyond this stage (so that cross-modal 'transfer of learning' does not occur even in apes capable of immediate cross-modal 'recognition', and the greater the amount of experience given in the first sense modality, the poorer the cross-modal recognition in the second). With increasing age, the human child resorts to new strategies: it learns from lawful correlations (e.g. bi-modal exposure, when the stimuli are perceived simultaneously through different senses, so that feature analyses via different senses become possible); and even physically quite dissimilar properties can be assigned to the same stimulus on a conditional basis (e.g. the sound of the word 'apple' associated with the seen object 'apple'). (Such cross-modal conditional learning is also laboriously possible for non-human animals.) Finally, increasing through childhood, man tends to have recourse to symbolic mediation, where language serves as a cross-modal bridge, allowing for greater flexibility in judging equivalence. This tentative schema may well need to be revised as new evidence becomes available.

See also BLINDNESS: RECOVERY FROM; SPATIAL CO-ORDINATION OF THE SENSES.            G. E.

Gunderson, V. M. (1983). *Developmental Psychology*, **19**, 398–404.

Meltzoff, A. N. and Borton, R. W. (1979). *Nature*, **282**, 403–4.

**CULTURAL DIFFERENCES IN PERCEPTION.** See PERCEPTION: CULTURAL DIFFERENCES.

**CYBERNETICS, HISTORY OF.** The word 'cybernetics' was introduced by Norbert *Wiener (1894–1964), the distinguished mathematician. It was the title of a book, *Cybernetics, or Control and Communication in the Animal and the Machine*, published in 1948. The word is formed from the Greek *kubernetes*, 'steersman'. As Wiener explained: 'What recommended the term cybernetics to me was that it was the best word I could find to express the art and science of control over the whole range of fields in which this notion is applicable.' These words can also be used as a definition of cybernetics. It is a theory of *feedback systems, i.e. self-regulating systems, the theory being applicable to machines as well as to living systems. Today, after the introduction of computers, theoretical aspects of control analyses have become so sophisticated and their application to engineering, biomedicine, and economics so firmly rooted and self-evident that it is difficult to recapture the intellectual excitement brought about by Wiener and his publications. The roots of the application of control theory or feedback in engineering reach far back; so too, it was noticed by certain biologists that control or the maintenance of equilibrium is one of the basic properties of life. However, the unifying theory of control and communication as applicable both to living systems and to machines built by man was first generally recognized only in 1948 with the publication of Wiener's book.

It is not certain who was the first person to apply a feedback mechanism to regulate or control a machine. There is evidence that certain kinds of regulating devices, such as for regulating the level of oil in an oil-lamp or the outflow of water-reservoirs, were already being used more than 2,000 years ago, and were known in the Middle Ages and the Renaissance. However, knowledge was transferred orally from craftsman to craftsman, and only a few written descriptions exist, none of which treat the theoretical aspects of mechanical engineering. In the seventeenth century, machines that developed great power, like windmills and steam-engines, were first used. It then became essential to provide some mechanism to limit or control their power, so that it would not finally destroy the machine which produced it. One of the first patents granted to a feedback mechanism was for a 'whirling regulator' which controlled the speed of rotation in windmills by means of a centrifugal pendulum (T. Mead: Regulator for Wind and Other Mills, patent no. 1628, London 1787). The engineer James Watt (1736–1819) adapted it and used it as a 'governor' to regulate the velocity of rotation in steam-engines, where the output (i.e. the velocity of rotation) regulated the input (i.e. the steam). During most of the nineteenth century, although regulating devices were widely used in engineering, there were no clear concepts of the dimensions and mechanical properties they should have. They were built and simply had to be tried out—and often failed. There was no theoretical framework which allowed the performance of a given regulator to be calculated. Then James Clerk Maxwell (1831–79), a physicist, reduced the problems to mathematical formulae. However, it was not until the end of the nineteenth century that there became available the mathemat-

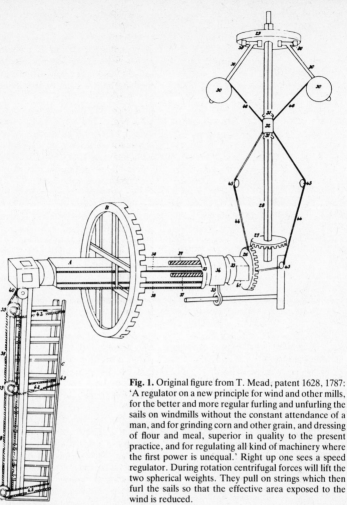

**Fig. 1.** Original figure from T. Mead, patent 1628, 1787: 'A regulator on a new principle for wind and other mills, for the better and more regular furling and unfurling the sails on windmills without the constant attendance of a man, and for grinding corn and other grain, and dressing of flour and meal, superior in quality to the present practice, and for regulating all kind of machinery where the first power is unequal.' Right up one sees a speed regulator. During rotation centrifugal forces will lift the two spherical weights. They pull on strings which then furl the sails so that the effective area exposed to the wind is reduced.

ical tools for giving easy and practical solutions to the equations suggested by Maxwell. Only then did the theory of feedback regulation become an established discipline that could be applied to all fields of engineering.

Similarly, in biology, the idea of control cannot be traced to a single person. Several steps, each focusing on special aspects, were important and necessary until it became apparent that the theory of feedback as applied to biological systems is structurally and mathematically the same as that used in engineering. Three physiologists of the nineteenth century deserve to be mentioned, because each of them drew attention to one important aspect of feedback control. The three aspects are the complex organization of organisms, the relative constancy of certain physiological parameters, and the description of animal behaviour using teleological terms.

In 1828 Charles *Bell, the Scottish anatomist

and surgeon, published *Animal Mechanics, or Proofs of Design in the Animal Frame*, in which he discussed the complex organization of organisms. He compared the structure which gives stability to bones with elements of architecture and building engineering. Similarly he compared the mechanism and efficiency of the heart and vascular system with pumps and pipes used in engineering. Although he did not go as far as actually to describe feedback mechanisms, by systematically comparing organisms with machines, and by using the same terminology, he was the first to widely use the concept of models. Models have since been generally employed, and have become an important element in biological cybernetics. One of their purposes is to isolate certain functional aspects of behaviour and to study their logic and limits of operation in order to better understand the mechanisms of biological design and development.

Claude Bernard (1813–78), a French physio-

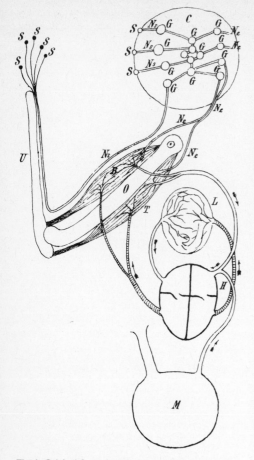

**Fig. 2.** Original figure from F. Lincke: Das mechanische Relais (the mechanical relay) VDI Zeitschrift 23, 509–24, 577–616 (1879). The 'indicators' are sensory nerves (*S*, *Ns*), the 'executive' organ (motor nerves *Ne* and muscle *B*), the 'transmitter' (brain with ganglion cells *G*), and 'motor' (stomach *M*, heart *H*, lung *L*). 'The activity we use to direct our human "machine" to its goal results from the difference between the will and the observed or imagined reality, i.e., the difference between the intention and the result of the execution.'

logist, introduced the concept of the constancy of the *milieu intérieur*. By that he understood that within certain limits blood, for example, has a constant composition independent of environmental changes. If the glucose level in the blood falls, animals as well as humans get hungry, eat, and by doing so raise the glucose level again. Bernard saw the results of feedback mechanisms and explored several examples, like the regulation of body temperature as well as glucose levels in the blood. In his book *Lessons on Phenomena of Life in Animals and Plants* (1878) he extended these experimental results and developed a general theory of how animals are able to maintain the constancy of their *milieu intérieur* (see HOMEOSTASIS).

The German physiologist Eduard Pflüger (1829–1910) considered the goal-directed behaviour of feedback mechanisms in biology. In 1877 he published a paper, *The Teleological Mechanics of Nature*. Teleology is defined as the study of final causes. Feedback mechanisms are characterized by the fact that the input is controlled by the output, and thus stabilizes the output, or makes the performance relatively independent from disturbing influences. One can consider the stability of the output as the 'goal' of the system. To turn the argument round, whenever a behaviour in biology is encountered that can be described as goal-directed, i.e. teleological, it is very likely that a feedback mechanism is involved.

The next step in combining biology and technology was taken by Felix Lincke (1840–1917), professor of mechanical engineering at the Institute of Technology at Darmstadt, Germany. He was probably the first who saw the outlines of a unifying theory of feedback control that is applicable to machines as well as to organisms. In 1879 he published a lecture, *The Mechanical Relay*, in which he classified the different feedback mechanisms used in mechanical engineering and listed the necessary elements of any feedback loop. These are: (i) the 'indicator', which continuously measures the output, (ii) the 'executive organ', which modifies the input of the feedback loop, (iii) the 'transmitter' which connects the 'indicator' and the 'executive organ', and (iv) the 'motor', which supplies the energy. Applied to an arm movement, the 'indicator' is the sensory nerve endings that sense the position of the arm, the 'executive organ' is the motor nerves with the muscles that perform the movement, the 'transmitter' is the brain which establishes a connection between the sensory and motor nerves, and the 'motor' is the alimentary tract supplying the energy for the whole system. The action of the indicator, executive organ, transmitter, and motor in a feedback loop can be described in the same way whether they are identified in biological systems or in machines. It is always the difference between the intended goal and the measurement given by the indicator that modifies the input to the feedback loop and thus brings the output of the system nearer to its goal. Although Lincke's paper was published in a widely recognized journal of engineering (*Zeitschrift des VDI*), and also as a book, nobody picked up his ideas and he was virtually unknown until well after Wiener's success in 1948.

In 1940, sixty years after Lincke's lecture, another engineer, Hermann Schmidt (1894–1968), a professor at the Institute of Technology in Berlin, published a series of papers in which he independently developed ideas similar to those of Wiener. Wiener focused his ideas more on the mathematical problems involved, while Schmidt based his theory more on the historical development of engineering. First, with primitive tools like an axe, man determines the exact action. In a second phase, energy is provided, but man still has to control the action by constantly monitoring the state of the machine, as in an automobile. In a third stage, energy *and* control over that energy is provided, as in aeroplanes with automatic landing control. (The pilot approaching the airfield makes only the decision to land; the exact monitoring of height, velocity, etc., is taken over by a computer). In this third stage of development, energy and the immediate control over it are transferred to a machine, even though man still has to determine the goal of action for the machine. Only in science fiction, like Samuel *Butler's novel *Erewhon*

(1872), is a fourth stage envisioned in which machines would develop to such a stage that they would determine their own goals—be it to the benefit of humans or not.

For a discussion of the application of cybernetics to human social behaviour, see also INTERACTIONAL APPROACH. V. H.

Mayr, O. (1970). *The Origins of Feedback Control*. Cambridge, Massachusetts.
Wiener, N. (1948). *Cybernetics*. Paris, New York.
Wiener, N. (1956). *I am a Mathematician*. Garden City, New Jersey.

# D

**DALTON,** JOHN (1766–1844). British chemist born in Cumberland, the son of a Quaker hand loom weaver. At the age of 15 he was teaching at the Quaker school in Kendal and in 1793 he moved to Manchester, where he remained for the rest of his life, supporting himself by teaching and tutoring. His atomic theory provided an explanation of the behaviour of elements and compounds and became one of the foundations of modern chemistry. He was also a keen meteorologist (recording over 200,000 observations), and a collector of butterflies and plants.

As a young man he discovered that a geranium appeared to him 'sky blue' by daylight but 'red' by candle-light. Finding that his friends did not experience this striking change (although his brother did), he came to realize that he had unusual colour vision. His detailed observations, reported to the Manchester Literary and Philosophical Society in 1794, suggest that he suffered from the type of dichromacy in which the long-wavelengths receptor is missing (see COLOUR VISION). His report excited widespread interest in Daltonism, as colour-blindness came to be known for many years.

**DANGER RECOGNITION.** Recognition of danger in animals requires that they distinguish dangerous stimuli from others, and distinguish among different sorts of danger that may require different escape responses. In many species there is a close relationship between fear and curiosity: confronted with a novel stimulus, or a change in environment, most animals respond first with flight and then with approach and investigation. The degree of novelty is crucial in determining which response will be given: familiar stimuli evoke little response, whereas a moderate degree of novelty elicits curiosity and approach, and fear is shown, by either freezing, flight, or alarm signals, when the stimulus is extremely novel. Thus, for a wide variety of stimuli the relation between stimulus novelty and response takes the form of an inverted U: positive interest is high at intermediate levels of stimulation, and fear responses, or the recognition of danger, appear only when stimuli are very unusual.

With many species certain sights, sounds, and smells are particularly effective in eliciting escape behaviour, and different stimuli may elicit different sorts of escape. Many birds and small mammals give acoustically distinct alarm calls when ground or aerial predators appear, and respond differently to each call type. In East Africa, vervet monkeys are preyed upon by leopards, two species of eagle, and pythons. Alarm calls given for leopards cause other monkeys to run up into trees; the different calls given for eagles cause animals to look up into the air or run into bushes; and those for pythons, acoustically distinct from both leopard and eagle alarms, cause animals to stand on their hind legs and peer into the grass around them (Seyfarth, Cheney, and Marler, 1980).

In some species, these highly specific responses appear fully formed, even when a stimulus is encountered for the first time: many birds give aerial predator alarm calls on their first encounter with such predators, and chicks of the same species freeze in their nests when they first hear the alarm. In other cases, recognition of specific classes of danger emerges gradually, apparently requiring some experience. While adult vervet monkeys restrict their alarm-calling to particular species, infants often make 'mistakes' and give alarms for objects that pose no danger to them. These calls are not entirely undiscriminating, however: leopard alarms are given for many animals other than leopards, but only for terrestrial animals; and eagle alarms are given for many non-predators, such as pigeons and geese, but only for objects flying in the air. Despite such early classification, however, the monkeys' use of warning calls does not emerge fully formed but requires further sharpening with experience.

Parallels in the way humans and other animals recognize danger are most evident in development. Upon first exposure to a novel stimulus, most animals exhibit fear, followed by curiosity and inspection, and then by disinterest. For each species some stimuli are particularly alarming, and faced with these an animal readily develops an ability to recognize different kinds of danger. Similarly, human infants are frightened by a variety of general stimuli, such as loud noises, bright lights, and being left alone; later, distress is caused only by more specific stimuli, such as separation from a particular person. Thus children learn to distinguish between different classes of danger.

R. M. S.
D. L. C.

Seyfarth, R. M., Cheney, D. L., and Marler, P. (1980). Monkey responses to three different alarm calls: evidence for predator classification and semantic communication. *Science*, **210**, 801–3.

**DARK ADAPTATION.** See VISUAL ADAPTATION.

**DARWIN**, CHARLES ROBERT (1809–82). British naturalist, born at Shrewsbury. His grandfather was Erasmus *Darwin, his father, Robert Waring Darwin, was a distinguished physician, and his mother was a daughter of Josiah Wedgwood. Charles studied medicine at Edinburgh, but, finding the operating procedures of that time extremely distasteful, went up to Christ's College, Cambridge, in 1828 in order to enter the Church. However, he was befriended by the botanist Professor J. S. Henslow, and his interests moved to botany and zoology. He graduated in 1831, and with Henslow's recommendation became naturalist to the survey ship HMS *Beagle*, bound on a voyage of scientific discovery. This changed the course of his life and the science of natural history.

Darwin sailed on 27 December 1831, and returned on 2 October 1836, after exploring Tenerife, the Cape Verde Islands, Brazil, Tierra del Fuego, the Galápagos Islands, New Zealand, Tasmania, and the coral reefs of the Keeling Islands. During the voyage he stocked his mind with knowledge, questions, and a hunch that species could not be separately created but must have evolved. He attributed the insight that evolution proceeds by selection of the fittest to reading the *Essay on Population* (1798, 1803) by Thomas *Malthus, which gave the pessimistic prediction that competitive society declines in spite of the individual's struggle for existence. Curiously, this same book later triggered the same concept of evolutionary development by natural selection (a phrase coined by Herbert *Spencer) in the mind of Alfred Russel *Wallace. The theory was presented jointly by Darwin and Wallace (though neither was present) at the Linnean Society in London, on 1 July 1858. It was received in silence, with no questions; and the president of the Linnean summed up 1858 as a year that 'has not been marked by any . . . striking discoveries'. Darwin showed remarkable character in maintaining friendship with Wallace and giving him due credit, though, unlike Wallace, he had spent twenty years collecting notes. He finally published *On The Origin of Species by Means of Natural Selection*, with the spur of Wallace's independent discovery, in November 1859. The entire printing of 1,500 copies was sold out in a day.

It was the science of geology that first cast serious doubt on the biblical account of special creation for each animal species, as it became clear that there had in the past been great changes in rocks, and so in the environment, and yet animals were adapted to the present environment. It also became clear that the age of the earth was very much greater than the biblical account taken literally allows; and, perhaps most important, unknown forms of life were discovered as fossils. These facts were set out in detail by Charles Lyell (1797–1875) in *Principles of Geology* (1830–3). Darwin began to develop an evolutionary theory with such thoughts in mind, and his first theory was very different from natural selection. He first thought (in the summer

of 1837) that species must change in order to remain adapted; and that, as species change, old species must die out, for the number of species to remain nearly constant. He supposed that simple living forms ('monads') appeared through spontaneous generation from inanimate matter, and evolved by direct environmental influences. The monads, he supposed, had a limited life-span, as do individuals, though presumably for different reasons. (See Gruber, 1974, ch. 5.) Although he soon abandoned this theory, he retained the notion of a continuous branching tree of evolutionary development, with the implication that we should not expect any simple sequence of evolving lifeforms to be found in the fossil record. There were enormous gaps in the fossil record that was available in his time, and this is still so, with controversial implications (See EVOLUTION: NEO-DARWINIAN THEORY.)

Darwin also made specific contributions to human psychology, tracing the origins of emotional responses and *facial expressions from prehuman species, in *The Expression of the Emotions in Man and Animals* (1872). This still unrivalled work contains accounts of the experiments he carried out on his own children, including—in spite of his extreme affection and gentleness—inducing fear to establish their responses.

He studied behaviour not only in animals and man (*The Descent of Man*, 1871, explicitly places man in the evolutionary sequence) but also in plants: *Climbing Plants* (1875), and especially *The Power of Movement in Plants* (1880), which describes not only elaborate movements of tendrils but also their selective sensitivity to appropriate or inappropriate stimuli. Darwin saw this as a precursor to control of animals by the nervous system, an idea yet to be followed up in detail.

Darwin's life after the voyage was spent with his talented family at Downe House, some twenty miles south of London, with its splendid garden and greenhouses in which he carried out many experiments while writing his books. Here he worked incessantly though dogged by ill health, possibly sleeping sickness (trypanosomiasis) contracted by an insect bite. The house and garden, with its famous walk, are preserved as a Charles Darwin museum. One can still see the study chair with wheels, in which he used to push himself around when too tired to stand among his zoological and botanical specimens and his books.

Darwin's principal regret was the pain his theory caused those of religious persuasion, including his beloved wife Emma. He was personally shy of controversy and debate, and T. H. *Huxley was his champion in public, disarming even the formidable Bishop of Oxford, Samuel Wilberforce, at a celebrated meeting of the British Association for the Advancement of Science, at Oxford, on 30 June 1860, when Wilberforce ('Soapy Sam') asked Huxley: 'Is it on his grandfather's or his grandmother's side that the ape ancestry comes in?' Huxley replied (in a verbal battle during which

Lady Brewster fainted) that 'a man has no reason to be ashamed of having an ape for his grandfather', and, 'if there were an ancestor whom I should feel shame in recalling, it would be a man of restless and versatile intellect who . . . plunges into scientific questions with which he has no real acquaintance, only to obscure them by an aimless rhetoric, and distract the attention of his hearers from the point at issue by eloquent digressions and skilled appeals to religious prejudice' (as reported by the historian J. R. Green twenty-two years later).

In addition to Darwin's books published in his lifetime, there are the notebooks that he kept to record and develop his ideas. Those named 'M' and 'N' record his growing ideas on mind, and man's place in nature. He was well aware that evolutionary accounts implied, or at least strongly suggested, that man's origin is in the animals that one may see in zoos. He ends the *Descent of Man*: 'with all his exalted powers—man still bears in his bodily frame the indelible stamp of his lowly origin'.

Realizing that mental characteristics can be passed on through generations, and assuming that only physical structures can be inherited, Darwin was forced to conclude that mind has a physical basis. On this ground he became a materialist—while aware that this would be painful to his wife Emma, to his friends, and more widely to all he would influence. He postponed for as long as possible his conclusions on the origin of man.

In Notebook 'N', writing at the time of his marriage, Darwin puts forward his theory of *blushing: that it depends on the person's awareness of the thought, or opinion, of another person. It is restricted to humans: 'animals, not being such thinking people, do not blush'. Darwin accepts blushing as evidence of *consciousness, and especially self-consciousness; but he rejects the notion of free will, saying that although we experience ourselves as causal agents, desires and purposes do not arise from some special endowment but only from natural laws of thought, as we would see if only we could stand outside ourselves. We cannot stand outside ourselves, so, 'on my view of free will, no one could discover he had not it' (N 49). The notebooks are fascinating both for their insights and as documents of the slow, painful development of Darwin's thought: for here are the germs of most of the ideas worked out often much later in his books.                      R. L. G.

There is an enormous literature on Darwin's life and work. See his *Life and Letters* (1887) and *More Letters* (1903), edited by his son, Sir Francis Darwin, and his autobiography edited by his granddaughter, Lady Nora Barlow (1958). The voyage of the *Beagle* is described in Darwin's own words in *Charles Darwin and the Voyage of the Beagle*, ed. Nora Barlow (1945), and with many illustrations in Alan Moorhead, *Darwin and the Beagle* (1969). An interesting account of Darwin's mental development (together with the previously unpublished notebooks) is Howard E. Gruber, *Darwin on Man: a psychological study of scientific creativity* (1974). An excel-

lent general study of his work and its implications is Gertrude Himmelfarb, *Darwin and the Darwinian Revolution* (1962).

**DARWIN,** ERASMUS (1731–1802). British physician and scientist, the grandfather of both Charles *Darwin and Francis *Galton. He was born near Newark in Nottinghamshire, studied at Cambridge and Edinburgh, and became a successful physician at Lichfield in Staffordshire. He was well known for his radical opinions, his eight-acre botanical garden, and for his books, including the long poem *The Botanic Garden* which appeared in two parts, *The Loves of the Plants* (1789) and *The Economy of Vegetation* (1791). His most important work was *Zoonomia, or The Laws of Organic Life* (1794–6), in which he anticipated *Lamarck's theory of evolution by the inheritance of acquired characteristics, and also, though somewhat vaguely, Charles Darwin's theory of evolution by natural selection. He was a founder member of the Lunar Society of Birmingham, the leading intellectual society of the Midlands, whose members included James Watt and Josiah Wedgwood.

King-Hele, D. (1963). *Erasmus Darwin*. London.
Krause, E. (1879). *Erasmus Darwin*. London. (Charles Darwin wrote an account of his grandfather for this volume.)

**DAY-DREAMING.** See HYPNAGOGIC HALLUCINATION.

**DE CONDILLAC,** ÉTIENNE (1715–80), French proponent of the philosophy of sensationalism. See CONDILLAC, ÉTIENNE DE.

**DEDUCTION.** In the more general sense any process of reasoning by means of which one draws conclusions from principles or information already known. Thus Isaac Newton talks of making deductions from his experiments with prisms, and G. K. Chesterton's Father Brown, after visiting the scene of the crime, deduces that Flambeau was responsible. But within logic and philosophy deduction is contrasted with *induction. Frequently the contrast is made by use of a directional metaphor: by induction one moves from particular to general and from the less general to the more general, ascending the theoretical ladder which terminates in first principles; by deduction one moves from more general to less general and from general to particular, descending the theoretical ladder which terminates in facts about particular individuals or events. This image of the ascent and descent of reason is to be found in *Plato, *Aristotle, in many medieval treatises on logic, and also in the works of Francis *Bacon.

In the logic of scholastic tradition, deduction is equated with syllogistic inference, for it was by means of the definition and study of syllogisms and their possible forms that Aristotle introduced a framework for both a codification and a theoretical discussion of the principles of valid deductive inference, the kind of inference that can be accepted as providing proofs or demonstrations. The central idea here is that in a valid deductive argument the truth of the premises guarantees the truth of the conclusion; in some sense the conclusion is already contained in the premises. Thus Aristotle defined a syllogism as 'a discourse in which, certain things being stated, something other than what is stated follows of necessity from their being so. I mean by the last phrase that it follows because of them, and by this that no further term is required from without in order to make the consequence necessary.' (*Prior Analytics*, 24b, 18–23.) But the further idea underlying the study of deductive inference, and indeed behind the notion of logic generally, is that this is a study of the principles of correct reasoning and that as such it must be independent of any particular subject-matter about which we might want to reason. The laws of logic, if they are to be universally applicable, must thus concern the forms or structures of arguments only, omitting all reference to content. On Aristotle's account, which was dominant for 2,000 years, all deduction is a matter of establishing connections between general terms. He defines a proposition as 'a statement affirming or denying something of something' (24a, 16). In other words, a (categorical) proposition is thought of as a statement that a certain relation holds between its subject *S* and its predicate *P*. Propositions are then classified according to the relation asserted to hold: Universal Affirmative—'All *S* are *P*' (*SaP*), Universal Negative—'No *S* are *P*' (*SoP*), Particular Affirmative—'Some *S* are *P*' (*SiP*), Particular Negative—'Some *S* are not *P*' (*SoP*). A syllogism is the making of a new connection between terms which goes via a third, or middle term. Syllogisms were traditionally classified into four figures according to the arrangement of their terms (although only the first three of these were recognized by Aristotle, who did not regard the fourth as a distinct figure). The figures are:

| (1) | (2) | (3) | (4) |
|---|---|---|---|
| $S - M$ | $M - S$ | $S - M$ | $M - S$ |
| $M - P$ | $M - P$ | $P - M$ | $P - M$ |
| $\therefore S - P$ | $\therefore S - P$ | $\therefore S - P$ | $\therefore S - P$ |

Thus an example of a valid first-figure syllogism would be:

*SaM* (All) whales are mammals.
*MaP* *(All) mammals are warm-blooded.*
$\therefore$*SaP* $\therefore$(All) whales are warm-blooded.

An example of a plausible but invalid first-figure syllogism would be:

*SaM* (All) larches are conifers.
*MiP* *Some conifers are deciduous.*
$\therefore$*SiP* $\therefore$Some larches are deciduous.

The invalidity of this form becomes obvious if 'Scots pine' is substituted for 'larch'. Any valid deduction will then be required to be reducible either to a syllogism or to a sequence of syllogisms

which traces a chain of connections between the subject and predicate terms of its conclusion.

In the seventeenth and eighteenth centuries, partly as a result of the increased hold of nominalism, partly as a result of the dominance of a (Cartesian) thinking-subject-centred approach to philosophy, the Aristotelian view of deductive reasoning was internalized. Instead of referring to classes or to universals, general terms were taken as standing for ideas (mental representations). (Categorical) propositions are thus interpreted as assertions about the relations between ideas, and deductive reasoning becomes a matter of perceiving the relations between ideas. From this perspective the laws of logic become the laws of thought, laws basic to the structure of the human intellect and constitutive of its rationality.

This conception finds perhaps its clearest expression in Immanuel *Kant's *Critique of Pure Reason*. But it is here also that the seeds are sown of the fundamental revisions both in logic and in conceptions of the nature and structure of thought which were brought about as a result of the work of Gottlob Frege and others working in the late nineteenth and early twentieth centuries. For Kant, in spite of his use of a very traditional Aristotelian framework for the construction of his table of judgements, (i) places primary emphasis on judgements as cognitive acts, rather than on ideas as the referents of general terms, and (ii) sees judgement as a matter of the application of a concept to an object according to a rule.

Frege strenuously rejected the idea that laws of logic are laws of thought. It was his view that if a valid deductive argument is to be one where the *truth* of its premises guarantees the *truth* of its conclusion, the laws of logic must be laws of truth, founded on the way in which language represents reality, not on the nature of the psychological processes by means of which human beings represent reality to themselves and then manipulate these representations. But Frege did retain and build on the Kantian emphasis on judgement which gives logical priority to propositions rather than to terms. Deductive argument is now seen to depend on establishing relations between the possible truth values of propositions (thoughts) expressed by (indicative) sentences; the proposition becomes the basic logical unit and truth the fundamental semantic notion. The simplest (atomic) propositions are regarded as expressing the application of a concept to an object (symbolized as '*Fa*'), where there is a fundamental asymmetry at both logical and ontological levels between concepts and objects. Concepts are treated by analogy with mathematical functions. This allowed Frege to develop a logical framework of much greater power and flexibility than Aristotle's. In particular it enabled him to incorporate arguments where the propositions involve relations and where the validity of the argument depends on the characteristics of the relation concerned, as, for example: '*A* is heavier than *B*. *B* is heavier than *C*. Therefore *A* is heavier than *C*.' In addition, by the device of introducing quantifiers and bound variables, Frege was able to treat such statements as 'Every natural number has a successor' and 'There is no largest natural number'. Present logical systems all exploit the basic Fregean innovations.                                    M. E. T.

Aristotle, *Prior and Posterior Analytics* (revised text with introduction and commentary by W. D. Ross, 1949). Oxford.

Kant, I., *The Critique of Pure Reason* (trans. by N. Kemp-Smith, 1929). London.

Frege, G. *Philosophical Writings* (selected and trans. by P. Geach and M. Black, 1960). Oxford.

Kneale, W. and M. (1962). *The Development of Logic*. Oxford.

**DÉJÀ VU.** 'It happened on my first visit to Paris. I was walking along one of those little streets in Montmartre, when I suddenly had the feeling that I'd been there before. It was all happening again . . .'

This is a characteristic account of *déjà vu* (literally: 'already seen')—the experience that one has witnessed some new situation or episode on a previous occasion. Perception of the scene is accompanied by a compelling sense of familiarity. Usually the sensation lasts only for a few seconds, but in some pathological cases it may be much more prolonged or, indeed, continuous. It is often accompanied by a conviction that one knows what is about to happen next—'When I reached the square, I knew what I was about to see . . .'

The *déjà vu* experience is often reported by patients suffering from psychiatric disorders. It is known to be associated with temporal lobe lesions, and is one of the 'dreamy state' experiences characteristic of focal *epilepsy. But the phenomenon seems also to be experienced occasionally by the majority of normal people. Most commonly it occurs in youth, or under conditions of fatigue or heightened sensitivity.

Understandably, the sensation of having previously experienced the event in question suggests to the individual that he is recalling a previous occurrence. The present event is taken to be a 'second' occurrence; mystification and interest is thus focused upon the 'first' one. As the crucial aspect of *déjà vu* is that the individual knows that he has not in fact previously experienced the event, lay explanations often posit psychic or magical processes. Such 'explanations' usually attribute unusual talents or powers to the individual concerned. Thus, one obvious 'explanation' is that the event has been 'revealed' to the individual prior to its occurrence. In that case he has demonstrated precognition, and is the fortunate possessor of the 'sixth sense' or the power of prophecy. More commonly, lay explanations make the presumption that the event has, in fact, occurred on a previous occasion, and focus on how the individual could have gained his knowledge of that 'first' occurrence. A common explanation is that the

individual experienced the 'first' event in a previous life. His *déjà vu* sensation may thus be taken as evidence for reincarnation. An associated view is that the 'first' event was witnessed by the individual but *through the eyes of another person*. He is therefore taken to possess telepathic gifts. The other witness may be hypothesized to have existed at another period in time. In that case the present individual is presumed to have mediumistic powers. A somewhat more subtle hypothesis is that the 'first' experience took place in a *dream, a proposition which accords well with the dream-like quality of the *déjà vu* experience itself. The individual himself may feel, not that he has previously witnessed the event, but that he has previously *foretold* it. But there is never any evidence of his actual foretelling, nor does he recall ever having done so. Thus he may speculate that the events were revealed to him in a dream, which would explain his failure to recall consciously his presentiment in the interim. Technically, this feeling is a *pseudo-presentiment*, so termed because the belief is held only at the moment that he witnesses the event. A number of serious writers have maintained this 'dream' hypothesis.

As noted above, the last four explanations presuppose that *déjà vu* is attached to a *second* experiencing of the situation in question—in other words, that the individual is *remembering*. Several psychological and psychiatric authorities have also taken this view, classifying *déjà vu* as an example of paramnesia. For them the question becomes one not of how the individual could remember something which he has not experienced before, but of why he should *think* he has not experienced it before. The obvious assumption is that the original experience aroused distress in the individual, so that its recall would prove painful to him. The standard psychoanalytic explanation of *déjà vu* is that the original experience has been repressed and so, by definition, is no longer accessible to *memory. Any repetition of the experience cannot elicit conscious recall of the original occurrence. But it does constitute a 'reminder' to the ego, and it is this which is reflected in the *déjà vu* feeling.

A more prosaic explanation of *déjà vu* is that, although the overall situation is novel, a number of its component features have in fact been experienced before. For example, the observer may know for certain that he has never walked along this particular street before—indeed, he may never previously have visited the town or even the country in question. But there are many features which all streets have in common, and it is the combination of these specifics which brings some familiarity to this newly visited street. However, this suggestion applies more directly to what has been termed 'restricted paramnesia'. (An everyday example of 'restricted paramnesia' is the frustrating experience of being unable to identify a person whom one knows but in some other context.) There are pronounced phenomenological differences between the preoccupying puzzlement which accompanies a restricted paramnesia and the *déjà vu* experience. In the former, one is well aware of those aspects of the situation which have been experienced previously (such as the other person's facial features, expression, and voice). The perplexity arises from the inability to reconstruct the totality of the previous experience (for example, the circumstances and context of previous encounters). In *déjà vu*, the *whole* of the new experience seems familiar, and so does the ensuing progression of events. Typically, the paramnesia experience is described in terms such as: 'I knew that I had met him before, but for the life of me I couldn't remember who he was . . .' Whereas *déjà vu* is described as: 'I felt that I had lived through it all before, but knew that I hadn't.'

Two other suggestions should be mentioned. The first one, once held by psychologists, stresses the affective component and classifies *déjà vu* as a paradoxical emotional experience. The argument would be that the sense of familiarity has reference, not to the characteristics of the situation, but to the observer's feelings. It is postulated that these are a carry-over of the emotional state associated with the preceding situation. The second suggestion is of more recent origin and focuses upon neurological function. Here the argument is that the two hemispheres of the brain may temporarily lose synchronicity. Thus the anomalous feeling of familiarity may be due to the fact that one side of the brain is receiving input a fraction of a second after the other.

A more fruitful psychological approach to the consideration of *déjà vu* may be to de-emphasize the recall aspect, with its presumption of a 'previous event', and approach the experience in terms of its other name: *fausse reconnaissance* (false recognition). Instead of 'Why is the observer unable to remember the previous situation?' the question now becomes: 'Why does the observer feel that he recognizes the present situation?' This, indeed, was the approach taken by Pierre *Janet, who was one of the first psychologists to identify, describe, and analyse the experience. He considered *déjà vu* to be one outcome of the obsessional incapacity for active and adequate response to the pressures of reality. The essence of *déjà vu*, he suggested, is not the 'affirmation of the past'; it is the 'negation of the present'. It is not a question of how the observer *remembers* a previous event, but how he *perceives* the present one.

At first sight, the classification of our topic as an anomaly of recognition rather than one of recall does not seem to offer any easier road to explanation. Certainly, conventional laboratory studies of recognition would seem to offer nothing which might throw light upon the *déjà vu* experience. However, consideration of the views of F. C. *Bartlett, as presented in his classic work, *Remembering*, may yield some clues. Bartlett's central point, which has been re-emphasized by contemporary cognitive theorists, was that long-term memory is a dynamic, constructive process. We do not recall an event in its original form, nor even in a merely attenuated version. We *reconstruct* it, drawing upon the *schematas or cognitive structures into which the perceived components of the event were organized. Thus, what is reconstructed during recall or reproduction shows not only omissions and abbreviations but elaborations and distortions.

On each occasion that we recall any given event, further distortions or elaborations are introduced. It could be said that in a series of recollections we are not recalling the original event at all, but our last recollection of it. The longer the series the more the remembered version will differ from the original, because each further recollection will involve distortions of distortions and elaborations of elaborations. If this line of argument (for which there is considerable experimental as well as observational evidence) is applied to the examination of recognition, some interesting implications emerge. Basically, recognition involves the acceptance of a 'good fit' or match of currently perceived material with recalled, imagined material. The better the level of match, the more pronounced will be the accompanying sense of familiarity. In the case of personal experiences, the familiarity includes an added dimension of personal identification. Clearly, the more often an original event has been recalled, the more modifications will have been introduced, and the weaker the subjective fit between our current recollection and any re-presentation of the actual original material. Conversely, the sense of familiarity may now be evoked by the perception of material which differs considerably from the actual original, given that the differences are in line with the distortions and elaborations present in our recollection. If we have good reason to believe that it would be quite impossible for us to have actually experienced this new material previously, then our feeling of familiarity is naturally highly perplexing. It may well be that this perplexity, resulting from the discrepancy between objective knowledge and subjective feeling, constitutes what is termed *déjà vu*.

In that case, why is the experience so rare? Perhaps the problem is not why *déjà vu* occurs, but why it does not occur more frequently. There are several possible answers. One is that perhaps it does occur commonly, but that we only register it under certain conditions. But at the same time, it is probable that there are relatively few occasions when we can be objectively certain that we have not experienced the criterion situation previously. A first visit to a geographic area is one such example. Other cases where the total situation may be labelled emphatically as a personal 'first time' event are often ones of a heightened emotive nature, where we are likely to be more sensitive to our subjective state and more vulnerable to feelings of anxiety and perplexity. It should be noted that while we may be acutely aware that a given situation is a personal 'first', we have almost certainly experienced it at second hand, through descriptions, literary accounts, or films. Perhaps the obvious examples are marriage ceremonies, job interviews, and funerals. And it is of interest that, after the 'strange town' example, these are the very situations in which people most commonly report experiencing *déjà vu*.

Purely psychological explanations of the kind discussed are hardly sufficient when the *déjà vu* experience is part of an epileptic aura. In this situation one might presume that the spontaneous electrical discharge in an area of the brain (the temporal lobe) particularly concerned with memory has reactivated a distant memory from the memory store, which is now perceived as something the patient has previously experienced—as, indeed, he probably has. *Penfield's brain-stimulation studies on patients undergoing neurosurgical operations might be considered as supportive of such an explanation of the *déjà vu* phenomenon, at least in cases when it is associated with temporal lobe *epilepsy. G. F. R.

**DELIRIUM.** A grossly disordered state of brain function characterized by restlessness, incoherent speech, and *hallucinations. Delirium is, as a rule, of toxic origin and is best known to the layman in its not infrequent link with delirium tremens, a condition resulting from chronic alcoholism. It may, however, also result from a wide variety of febrile conditions, or from drugs such as mescal, Indian hemp, cocaine, and bromide.

Hallucinatory states associated with toxic delirium are of considerable psychological interest. First, they may on occasion be associated with distortions of space and time; and secondly, they may give rise to *synaesthesia—a term first introduced by Sir Francis *Galton to denote phenomena such as 'coloured hearing', which is experienced from time to time by wholly healthy individuals.

The possible incidence of hallucinations in toxic delirium and in *schizophrenia has also been widely discussed, though it should be borne in mind that delirium is a wholly organic manifestation. O. L. Z.

**DELUSION.** A delusion is a fixed, idiosyncratic belief, unusual in the culture to which the person belongs. Unlike normal beliefs, which are subject to amendment or correction, a delusion is held to, despite evidence or arguments brought against it. Delusions are usually taken to indicate mental illness, but something akin to them is occasionally to be observed, at a meeting of scientists, for instance, when a person insists on the correctness of an idea he overvalues, and denies any significance to evidence appearing to refute it. There is a difference: usually he gets angry, whereas in mental illness the patient's emotional response when a delusion is challenged tends to be bland or otherwise inappropriate.

Extravagant ideas are relatively common at times of frustration. A driver, frustrated when his car does not start, may allege serious deficiencies in all the cars made in the same country as his. This is to over-generalize from the particular. Similarly, a student who has failed a test may feel for a while that he has failed as a student or, more generally still, as a person. Such feelings if they persist would amount to a delusion of unworthiness. Or he may conclude that his teachers are hostile to him, or that the world is against him. A persistent idea of this kind, especially if a person believes that there is a conspiracy or concerted action against him, is a delusion of persecution. A fixed belief that he is physically ill or, more extreme, that his organs are rotting or are destroyed, is a hypochondriacal delusion; that he does not exist or is nothing, a nihilistic delusion; that he has an exalted position or powers, a delusion of grandeur.

There is often sense in delusions, although it may be expressed extravagantly or confusingly. A man who declares that his wife is persistently unfaithful to him may be understood to mean that she has had sexual intercourse on many occasions with others. He is deluded if he insists unreasonably that this is so, in which case he is probably an example of the morbid jealousy syndrome; but he may only wish to convey his feelings that she no longer shows love or concern for him, feelings for which there might be some justification.

A delusion may persist because it explains what would otherwise cause *anxiety. Soldiers serving under stressful conditions occasionally express the belief that 'they' are putting bromide into the soup. The meaning of this belief emerges when added to it is the belief that aphrodisiacs are being put into the soup of other units. It serves to explain, for those who hold it, the changes produced by the stressful conditions in the pattern of occurrence of penile erections. Some bizarre delusions are unlabelled metaphors. A mentally ill girl says that she is the Virgin Mary. What perhaps she means is that she feels that she is still a virgin although she fears she is pregnant. The delusion, with its implication of her essential goodness, mitigates the intense anxiety which being seduced and becoming pregnant would otherwise evoke.

Why are delusions resistant to modification in the light of other evidence? In this respect they are similar to the behaviours, characteristic of neurosis, which persist although they appear to be maladaptive. It is supposed that they persist because, being instrumental in reducing anxiety, they are reinforced.

This is only part of an explanation of delusions, which, with *hallucinations, are the cardinal symptoms of some forms of mental illness. In cases of paranoid *schizophrenia, the patient may reveal, as well as hallucinations, a more or less coherent system of delusions of persecution and grandeur, without showing any awareness of how abnormal the ideas he expresses are. In other cases of schizophrenia, the delusions may be contradictory and incoherent. Severely disabling are hypochondriacal delusions, especially when they are associated with symptoms of *depersonalization, the patient then feeling that he has changed in personality with loss of his sense of identity; this may amount to a nihilistic delusion. Delusions of unworthiness occur in depressive illnesses in association with misery and hopelessness.

See also PARANOIA.                                    D. R. D.

**DEMENTIA** is defined by W. A. Lishman (1978) as 'an acquired global impairment of intellect, memory, and personality but without impairment of consciousness'. Although often considered to be an irreversible condition, recent studies have shown that about 10 per cent of patients with dementia have conditions for which treatment can reverse the otherwise inexorable decline of mental function. The progressive dementias are most often diagnosed in the elderly under the headings of senile dementia of the Alzheimer type and multi-infarct dementia. The former is caused by widespread degeneration of nerve-cells in the brain and their replacement by elements known as plaques and neurofibrillary tangles. Post-mortem studies of the brains of patients who have died from senile dementia have enabled correlation of the numbers of these elements with the degree of mental impairment shown by psychometric testing during life. Multi-infarct dementia, which is less common than senile dementia, is caused by loss of brain substance following repeated closure of small or large blood vessels, incidents which cause minor or major strokes. The older term, arteriosclerotic dementia, has now been superseded.

These areas of degeneration may be widespread and scattered, or concentrated in certain areas of the brain. If the latter, the mental changes will be much more severe in some functions than in others. For instance, the person may lose his speech (developing *aphasia) but not his memory, or vice versa. One of the last things usually to be affected is his basic personality, and some of the last skills to be lost are the social ones. Hence some demented persons will retain the major features of personality, remaining well-mannered, considerate, and responsive if these were the former characteristics. On the other hand, blunting of emotion and loss of control of social behaviour may lead to episodes of petulant and irritable behaviour or tactless and inappropriate remarks which would not have been uttered before the onset of the illness.

The difference between dementia and the more limited losses of mental ability due to focal injuries is that the demented person can seldom make compensations for his disabilities in the way the others do; and, indeed, very often seems to be unaware of them. He tends to live his life entirely for the present moment, although the present for him may be an era from his own distant past.

Although it is characteristic of the truly demented person that he has little insight into his defects, inability to cope with his environment may make

him severely perplexed, or trigger off a condition described by Kurt *Goldstein and called by him the 'catastrophic reaction'. The individual becomes tearful and angry; he may repeat non-adaptive stereotyped movements in a repetitive manner, or start sweating and becoming restless. The 'emotional lability' that accompanies dementia is one of its outstanding characteristics and helps to differentiate it from true *depression, in which the individual remains sad and retarded no matter how his circumstances alter. Dementia must also be differentiated from another, much less common form of emotional disorder: that accompanying bulbar palsy, in which the individual may respond to any sudden stimulus or strong effort by screwing up his face and bursting into tears, without any of the unhappiness which usually causes such outbursts. 'I just can't help crying,' he may be able to tell you between spasms. 'Don't pay any attention to me.' In contrast to both of these, the emotional state of the demented person seems to reflect exactly the situation of the moment. If he is faced with a problem too difficult for him to solve, he shows all the signs of distress, but if this is removed and he is presented with a simpler one, the next moment he will be laughing and cheerful. It follows that even severe dementia may not necessarily cause its sufferer any personal pain, depending on where and how he is cared for. If his environment is simple, cheerful, and constant (i.e. unchanging) he may to all outward appearances (and on his own admission) be perfectly cheerful and contented.

It is important to distinguish dementia from the other disorders which commonly affect the elderly, as although there is, as yet, no known method of retarding or reversing dementia, many of the other conditions are fully treatable. In the speech disorders of dementia, comprehension is usually just as badly affected as expression, whereas in the aphasia due to focal lesions this is very rare. Moreover, the errors made when trying to name objects are rather different. The aphasic person usually manages to indicate that he knows perfectly well what the object is even though he cannot find its name, but the demented person often seems to fail to recognize the object too. If asked to name different parts of his body, the aphasic person can usually name those parts which are commonly mentioned (such as feet, hands, and arms) but not those less frequently so (knuckles, eyebrows, ankles); in the demented there is seldom any difference.

The failure of memory seen in senile dementia is also different from that seen in normal old age (see AGEING) or in the organic *amnesic conditions. In the latter, cues or prompts very often help, but in the demented they seem rather to do the opposite. If one considers recall as being like searching for an item in a vast territory, a cue for the amnesic narrows the field of search and directs his attention to a specific area; for the demented, it seems to direct him to a new part of the field. For instance, if the target is the word 'cart', a useful cue for an amnesic would be the words 'Horse and ——'. A case of senile dementia might respond by saying, 'Horse? Yes, I remember we had many horses when I was a child, one particular one . . .'

The ability to handle and manipulate objects is usually little impaired in dementia. Those motor skills which were learned in the past are well retained, but since he is inclined to forget what he is aiming to achieve before he has half done it, the demented person gets himself into difficulties. At first appearance he may seem to be suffering from apraxia (the loss of such skills due to focal lesions), but closer study will reveal differences. For example, both apraxic and demented individuals often have difficulty dressing themselves, but in the case of the apraxic the difficulty is due to 'forgetting' how to tie knots, do up buttons, or put an arm into a sleeve; in the demented it is due to forgetting whether he is supposed to be getting dressed or undressed at the time. When preparing meals— even such a simple task as making a pot of tea—the apraxic forgets how to put tea into the pot or stir it with a spoon; the demented can do all these things, if reminded constantly of the task in hand, but if distracted at all is liable to lose track of how far he has got and start from the beginning again.

Finally, there are two conditions which may be easily mistaken for dementia. The first is a severe depressive illness which may produce the condition sometimes called *pseudodementia which only a skilled psychiatrist can distinguish from true dementia, but which responds to appropriate anti-depressant treatment. The second is a delirious state, triggered off in an old person by physical disorder such as pneumonia, a heart attack, or hypothermia. Unlike dementia, which usually comes on slowly over a long period, delirious states are likely to appear suddenly and will be accompanied by severe disorientation and even *hallucinations. These symptoms, however, clear up completely once the underlying physical disorder is rectified, and in former days it was quite common for an old person to 'wake up' after such an illness and find himself in a mental hospital labelled, to his great consternation, a case of senile dementia.                                    M. WI.

Lishman, W. A. (1978). Organic Psychiatry. Oxford.
Miller, E. (1977). Abnormal Ageing. London.
Roth, M. and Iverson, L. L. (eds.) (1986). Alzheimer's Disease and Related Disorders. British Medical Bulletin, vol. 42, no. 1. London.
Williams, M. (1979). Brain Damage, Behaviour and the Mind. Chichester.

**DENDRITE.** One of the branching small neural processes carrying signals to the cell body of a neurone (nerve-cell). See NERVOUS SYSTEM.

**DENOTATION** is one of several words (the most common alternative is 'reference') used by logicians and philosophers for the relation between a fragment of language and that part or aspect of the world which it is used to introduce into discourse. The paradigm of the relation is that of a proper name to its bearer, but it is a matter of dispute what to say about proper names (and other grammatical subject expressions) which lack a bearer; and it is a matter of dispute whether and how the relationship applies in the case of predicate expressions. It is common to identify the denotation (reference) of a predicate expression with its extension, i.e. the class of all things to which it applies. Those who are prepared to recognize the existence of universals are often inclined to treat predicate expressions as denoting these. For J. S. *Mill a general term like 'man' names the class of men, and denotes the indefinite number of individuals who belong to that class, while it connotes the attribute which is signified by 'humanity' (cf. 'white' connotes what 'whiteness' signifies), as well as any attributes implied by this, such as animal life and rationality. All such attributes comprise the connotation of 'man'.

Mill's distinction between denotation and connotation is often confused with Frege's distinction between reference (Bedeutung) and sense (Sinn); but for Frege the sense of an expression is the manner in which it refers, and this made it possible for him to hold that proper names have a sense, whereas Mill denied that proper names have a connotation.                                    J. E. T.

Frege, G. On Sense and Reference. In Geach, P. T. and Black, M. (1952), Translations from the Philosophical Writings of Gottlob Frege. Oxford.
Mill, J. S. (1879). A System of Logic. London.

**DEPERSONALIZATION.** A term applied in psychiatry to a complaint made by a patient that he feels himself to be changed, that the world appears different or unreal because he is different. If the world is seen as if in a dream, vague or unreal or, although familiar, as having no reference or significance to him, the state is called derealization. The essence of depersonalization is loss of identity or of the sense of the reality of one's self, accompanied usually by a sense of being divorced from one's body or having *out-of-body experiences.

Depersonalization and derealization may be experienced by healthy persons who have been going through periods of intense excitement in the face of danger. The onset is usually when they begin to relax as the danger recedes. In wartime, for instance, such states are occasionally reported by the crews of aircraft who have flown a sortie over enemy territory. Subsequently memory of the action has a dream-like quality.

Depersonalization and derealization tend to occur together, sometimes without, but more often with, other symptoms of mental illness, especially depression but also obsessional neurosis. Both depersonalization and derealization may be experienced in conjunction with the *déjà vu phenomenon, as part of an epileptic aura, especially in patients afflicted with temporal lobe *epilepsy. When associated with *hallucinations and *delusions, especially hypochondriacal delusions, depersonalization has been regarded as characteristic of true *schizophrenia and as a warning of disintegration of the personality. When combined with guilt, depersonalization and derealization may be ominous symptoms because they enable the patient to take cold-blooded steps to destroy himself without normal awareness of the significance and consequences of what he does.

'Depersonalization' has been used in a broader sense by psychiatrists who have come under the influence of existentialism. To depersonalize then means to negate another person by ignoring his feelings or by treating him as an object or thing. Depersonalization was experienced in an extreme form by inmates of the concentration camps in the Second World War. The passive, 'ontologically insecure' person, in R. D. Laing's phrase (1965), may feel under threat of being depersonalized or of losing his autonomy when he enters into a co-operative relationship with another person. Natural science depersonalizes when it adopts a determinist view of a person as a component of a system or as composed of a complex of organs or functions. In contrast is the existentialist view that each person is a free and responsible agent determining his own development by making choices, great or small. However, a healthy person accepts that his autonomy is limited by his responsiveness to the social and physical demands made on him.

See also INTERACTIONAL APPROACH; LAING'S UNDERSTANDING OF INTERPERSONAL EXPERIENCE.

D. R. D.

Laing, R. D. (1965). *The Divided Self*. Harmondsworth.

**DEPRESSION.** Psychiatry shares with general medicine a tendency to adopt words with commonly understood meanings and give them specialized, unfamiliar interpretations. Obsession, conversion, pervert, and depression are psychiatric examples of such words. In everyday language we speak of feeling depressed, thereby indicating a transitory downturn in mood whose origin can usually be traced to some set-back, even to the prospect of returning to routine living after too convivial a weekend. On the other hand, depression as an illness signifies a severe emotional disturbance whose source may or may not be traceable to external causes—misfortunes, bereavements, financial loss, illness, etc. Emil *Kraepelin distinguished two major psychotic illnesses under the headings of *dementia praecox* (*schizophrenia) and manic-depressive psychosis (SEE MENTAL DISORDERS: CLASSIFICATION). The latter condition takes the form of alternating periods of extreme melancholia and equally extreme periods of elation and excitement. But, as time has gone by, this relatively clear description has been complicated by the inclusion of persons suffering from recurrent bouts of severe depression without any periods of mania or, for that matter, major psychotic symptoms—the so-called endogenous depression. In addition, there are individuals who

experience less intense attacks with less clearly demarcated changes in mood, whose depression appears to be an understandable response in a vulnerable personality to lesser or greater degrees of adversity—a reactive or neurotic depression.

This simple dichotomy is unfortunately beset with difficulties. Indeed, the very terminology invites—and gets—criticism. To say that somebody has sunk into the depressive phase of a manic-depressive psychosis overlooks the obvious fact that many such cases do not develop psychotic symptoms. Delusions, hallucinations, and bizarre hypochondriacal beliefs about one's bodily functions may be, but often are not, present. More frequently the sufferer will manifest a state of deep despondency and hopelessness coupled, in some instances, with self-accusations and guilt over trivial misdemeanours previously ignored. The term *endogenous* depression seems to imply that the victim has some innate predisposition to this variety of mood disturbance; and there may be genetic evidence for such a predisposition, adding emphasis to the aetiological significance of the word 'endogenous'. On the other hand, speaking of *neurotic* (reactive) depression is probably saying as much about the quality of the symptoms as about their origin. To use more than one base for a classification hardly makes for clarity, and the word 'reactive' signifies that some external event is responsible for the onset of the individual's state of gloom. However, as some indubitable cases of endogenous depression and the depressive phase of manic-depressive psychosis can be preceded by psychological stresses such as bereavement and serious ill health, the distinction between endogenous and reactive depressions becomes distinctly blurred; and it would be erroneous to assume that in all persons with reactive depressions one can delineate external events determining the quality and time of onset of the illness.

For at least fifty years there has been controversy over whether endogenous and neurotic depressions are distinct and separate illnesses or merely alternative terms for severe and milder forms of mood change lying at the ends of what is essentially a continuum of affective disorder. Numerous attempts have been made to settle this dispute, with powerful statistical techniques being employed in the hope that mathematics will decide once and for all a debate which, some might think, has taken up more research time than the facts warrant. In the end the question of whether a person is suffering from a reactive or an endogenous depression will be decided on clinical grounds without recourse to statistics; and treatment will be given according to the judgement made at the time.

Numerous typologies aiming at a better classification of depression have been devised, but possibly a dimensional rather than a categorical approach to the problem is the most appropriate way of overcoming the difficulty of finding clear-cut natural boundaries between one type of depression and another. It is a fact that between patients with endogenous and reactive depressions lies a group with atypical symptoms who fail to fit neatly into one category or the other. This seems to presuppose a continuum of depressive disorders rather than a set of distinct classes of illness. But, as Kendell has written (1976):

The attempt to resolve our classification problems by the statistical analysis of clinical data has failed up to now and may continue to do so. We may have to live with our uncertainties and disagreements until we understand enough about the physiological or psychological basis of depression to construct a new classification on that basis.

Does it matter? Yes, but in all probability not so much as the protagonists in this debate might wish us to believe. The diagnosis of depression rests on consideration of the patient's symptoms, his previous history, and the course of his illness. Simple rating scales can be used, if required, to permit a fairly accurate diagnosis to be made. Treatment will depend on this clinical decision, for what may be appropriate in one type of depression may be ineffective in another. Electroconvulsive therapy (ECT) may be life-saving for patients with severe endogenous depression, when the risk of suicide can be high. But ECT rarely benefits those with neurotic depression, for whom drugs and psychological treatments are usually more effective. In recent years prominence has been given to a form of behaviour therapy, cognitive therapy; but it is clear that although this may be beneficial for neurotic depression, its impact on the symptoms of endogenous depression will be slight (Williams, 1984).

There is another complication introduced into the classification of depression that has a bearing on treatment. Persons with recurrent attacks of mania and depression (bipolar affective disorder) are more responsive to treatment with lithium salts than are those with recurrent attacks of depression only (unipolar affective disorder). Opinions differ on this point, but for the most part those with repeated attacks of endogenous-type depression appear to react best either to ECT or to tricyclic antidepressants, or to a combination of both. Neurotic (reactive) depression, on the other hand, is probably best treated with other types of drugs in conjunction with psychological methods designed to help the patient take a more realistic view of his situation.

In the end, in spite of many refined arguments, it appears that there are individuals who become severely depressed, sometimes losing touch with reality to a degree that warrants the label 'psychotic'; and there are those whose depressions are of a milder nature but, none the less, are sufficiently troublesome to interfere with enjoyment of life. One can for convenience designate the former as 'endogenous' and the latter as 'reactive' or 'neurotic'; but such labelling does not say as much about the origins of these mood disturbances as the terms themselves suggest. In both cases we are faced by illnesses requiring far more help than

will be derived from the admonition 'pull yourself together and snap out of it'. Although such advice may be beneficial for individuals with mild degrees of cyclothymia and an overdeveloped sense of self-pity, it is worse than useless for those whose depressed mood has gone beyond the limits of normal human variation.

Finally, one point of singular importance must be mentioned. All persons suffering from depression should be adequately assessed for the risk of suicide. Relatives, and some physicians, sometimes hesitate to enquire directly about suicidal thoughts lest such questions prompt the actions they are most anxious to prevent. This is not so. Most depressed patients answer truthfully to enquiries of this kind, and may even be relieved by the opportunity to discuss their innermost feelings of despair and dread of the future. It is sometimes believed, however, that those who mention suicidal thoughts never put them into practice. This is quite incorrect, and all mention of suicide by a depressed person must be taken with the utmost seriousness so that prompt admission to hospital for treatment can be arranged.          F. A. W.

Kendell, R. E. (1976). The classification of depression: a review of contemporary confusion. *British Journal of Psychiatry*, **129**, 15–28.

Mayer-Gross, W., Slater, E., and Roth, M. (1977). *Clinical Psychiatry*, 3rd edn. (revised). London.

Paykel, E. S. (ed.) (1982). *Handbook of the Affective Disorders*. Edinburgh.

Paykel, E. S. and Coppen, A. (eds.) (1979). *Psychopharmacology of Affective Disorders*. Oxford.

Silverstone, T. and Turner, P. (1978). *Drug Treatment in Psychiatry*, 2nd edn. London.

Williams, J. M. G. (1984). Cognitive therapy for depression: problems and perspectives. *British Journal of Psychiatry*, **145**, 254–62.

**DEPTH PERCEPTION.** The seeing of objects in three dimensions, although *retinal images are only two-dimensional. Depth is seen even with one eye by 'monocular depth cues'. These are the partial hiding of further by nearer objects, loss of fine detail through haze and the limited resolution of the eye with increasing distance ('aerial perspective'), geometrical perspective (especially the converging of parallel lines as optically projected on the retina), *accommodation of the lens of the eye (the anterior surface of the lens becoming more convex for near vision), and motion parallax (when the observer moves, objects are displaced according to his movements, the visual world rotating round the point of fixation in the direction opposite to his motion). We may say, following Hermann von *Helmholtz, that depth is unconsciously inferred from these cues, or clues; or, following J. J. *Gibson, that we 'pick up' depth information from these features.

*Stereoscopic depth is given by the comparison of 'corresponding points' of the retinal images in the two eyes. This requires remarkably powerful neural computation, which can now be carried out with computer programs, though far more slowly.

When depth cues are misleading, distortions of size can be generated. See ILLUSIONS.

Gibson, J. J. (1950; repr. 1974). *Perception of the Visual World*. Westport, Connecticut.

Gregory, R. L. (1970). *The Intelligent Eye*. London.

**DESCARTES,** RENÉ (1596–1650). Descartes was a pivotal figure in the great seventeenth-century revolution that marked the emergence of modern philosophical and scientific thinking. He was born at La Haye near Tours, and educated at the Jesuit college of La Flèche. He travelled in Germany during 1619, and on the night of 11 November he had a series of dreams which inspired his vision of founding a completely new philosophical and scientific system. In 1628 he moved to Holland, where he lived, with frequent changes of address, for most of the rest of his life. His philosophical masterpiece, the *Meditations on First Philosophy* appeared in Latin in 1641; and his *Principles of Philosophy*, a comprehensive statement of his philosophical and scientific theories, also in Latin, in 1644. He died of pneumonia in Stockholm, where he had gone to act as tutor to Queen Christina of Sweden.

Descartes made important contributions in many areas of human knowledge. His early work was in mathematics, and his *Rules for the Direction of the Understanding* (1628) provided a general account of scientific knowledge that was strongly influenced by mathematical models. His *Geometry* (published 1637) lays the foundations for what is now known as analytical *geometry. In the *Discourse on Method*, a popular introduction to his philosophy, published in French in 1637, Descartes developed his celebrated 'method of doubt': 'I resolved to reject as false everything in which I could imagine the least doubt, in order to see if there afterwards remained anything that was entirely indubitable' (see DOUBTING). This led to the famous affirmation 'I think, therefore I am' (*je pense, donc je suis*). On the basis of this 'Archimedean point' Descartes erected a comprehensive philosophical and scientific system which was to include both a general theory of the structure and working of the physical universe, and many detailed explanations of particular phenomena, such as the mechanics of human and animal physiology. Although the metaphysical foundations of his system depend heavily on the existence of an omnipotent, benevolent and non-deceiving God, Descartes aimed, in all areas of natural science, to provide explanations in terms of strictly mechanical models and mathematical principles. All phenomena, whether celestial or terrestrial, were to be explained ultimately by reference to the shapes, sizes, and motions of bits of matter: 'I freely acknowledge that I recognize no matter in corporeal things apart from that which the geometricians call "quantity" and take as the object of their demonstrations' (*Principles*, Part II).

Descartes's theory of the mind stands out as a striking exception to his general insistence on mechanical and mathematical explanations. Mental phenomena, for Descartes, have no place in the quantifiable world of physics, but have a completely autonomous, separate status. 'I am a substance the whole nature or essence of which is to think, and which for its existence does not need any place or depend on any material thing' (*Discourse*, Part IV). Developing the theory later known as 'Cartesian dualism', Descartes maintains that there are two radically different kinds of substance: physical, extended substance (*res extensa*)—i.e. that which has length, breadth, and depth and can therefore be measured and divided—and thinking substance (*res cogitans*), which is unextended and indivisible. Thus the human body—including the brain and entire nervous system—belongs in the first category, while the mind—including all thoughts, desires, and volitions—belongs in the second.

One of Descartes's reasons for supposing his mind to be essentially non-physical is that in his *Meditations* he found himself able to doubt the existence of all physical objects (including his body), but was unable to doubt the existence of himself as a thinking being. And from this he concluded that having a body was not part of his essential nature. But, as some of his contemporary critics pointed out, this argument seems invalid: ability to doubt that some item $X$ possesses some feature $F$ does not prove that $X$ could in fact exist without $F$. Descartes also argued that the essential indivisibility of the mind proves its non-corporeality; but this seems question-begging, since the premiss that the mind is indivisible would be disputed by those who maintain that the mind is some kind of physical system. Despite the shakiness of some of Descartes's arguments, his dualistic approach has continued to exert a dominatingly powerful influence on theories of the mind. As recently as 1977, for example, we find the eminent neurophysiologist Sir John Eccles and the famous philosopher Sir Karl Popper maintaining that Descartes was fundamentally correct. According to Eccles and Popper, the 'self'—the conscious being that is 'me'—is essentially non-physical. The self may make use of the brain in its operations, but its operations have separate and independent status over and above the occurrences in the brain.

As Descartes himself recognized, however, dualism faces considerable philosophical difficulties. The chief of these is the problem of 'causal interaction'. We know from experience that mind and body do not operate in total isolation, but interact with each other: if there is a physical change (e.g. my hand touches a hot stove), a mental change (e.g. pain) results; and, conversely, a mental event (a volition to raise my arm) leads to a physical event (my arm going up). Descartes acknowledges these facts by saying that in many cases mind and body 'intermingle' to form a kind of unit. Thus, sensations like hunger and thirst are, he maintains, 'confused perceptions' resulting from the fact that 'I am not merely lodged with my body, like a sailor in a ship, but am very closely united and as it were intermingled with it' (*Meditations, VI*). But exactly how there can be such a 'union' or 'intermingling' between two allegedly quite distinct and seemingly incompatible substances is left something of a mystery. Elsewhere (e.g. in the *Passions of the Soul*, 1649), Descartes suggests that the mind or soul, though incorporeal and indivisible, exercises its functions in one particular part of the brain, the *conarion*, or pineal gland. But this manœuvre seems not to solve but merely to re-import the problem of causal interaction: if there is a problem about how a non-physical soul can cause my arm to go up, there will be no less a problem about how a non-physical soul can cause movements in the brain by acting on the pineal gland.

Although in his psychological and physiological writings Descartes devoted great efforts to the problem of interaction between soul and body, it is worth remembering that in his system there are many areas where such interaction simply does not arise. First, in the case of animal physiology and a great deal of human physiology (e.g. that concerned with digestion, muscular reflexes, etc.), Descartes maintained that the soul is not involved at all: what occurs can be explained purely on mechanical principles. Second, in the case of human beings, though much of our activity (e.g. sense-perception) involves complicated transactions between soul and body, there are other mental acts (e.g. purely intellectual thoughts) which, according to Descartes, can occur without any physiological correlates at all; such 'ideas of pure mind' are, in Descartes's view, from start to finish non-corporeal. It must be said that advances in brain science have made this latter part of Descartes's theory increasingly difficult to defend.

Although substantive dualism, the doctrine that the mind is a separate, non-physical entity, now has ever fewer supporters, many philosophers have become attracted by a weaker version of Descartes's theory, which has been termed 'attributive dualism'. This is the view that, even if the mind is not a separate entity, there are none the less two distinct sets of properties or attributes that can be ascribed to human beings: psychological properties (thoughts, feelings, volitions) and physical properties (e.g. electrical and chemical properties of the nervous system). Attributive dualists maintain that even if all human activities must depend on some kind of physical substrate, there is none the less an important sense in which psychological descriptions of those activities cannot be reduced to mere physiological descriptions. This position on the one hand preserves Descartes's insight that what he called 'modes of extension' (size, shape, volume) are fundamentally different from 'modes of thought' (thoughts, feelings, volitions), while on the other hand resisting his conclusion that two separate entities, a 'thinking thing' and an 'extended thing' are

involved. This is similar to the hardware and software of a computer.

See also MIND AND BODY; MIND–BODY PROBLEM; PERSONAL IDENTITY.                                    J. G. C.

Haldane, E. S. and Ross, G. R. T. (trans., 1911, repr. 1969). *The Philosophical Works of Descartes*. Cambridge.
Popper, K. and Eccles, J. (1977). *The Self and its Brain*. London.
Williams, B. (1978). *Descartes, the Project of Pure Enquiry*. Harmondsworth.
Wilson, M. (1978). *Descartes*. London.

**DESENSITIZATION.** See BEHAVIOUR THERAPY; FEAR AND COURAGE; PHOBIAS.

**DESIGN, ARGUMENT FROM, FOR THE EXISTENCE OF GOD.** The universe appears designed; a design requires a designer; and so the universe was designed (created) by a designing intelligence. This of course raises the question: How was the Designing Intelligence (God) created? Therefore, although the argument by analogy—as human artefacts have human designers, so the universe must have a superhuman designer—is appealing, it lacks philosophical cogency, because how the Designer was designed remains unanswered. The design of organisms by natural selection shows that intentional mind is not required for designing. The most famous critique of the argument from design is in David *Hume's Dialogues concerning Natural Religion*.

**DESIGN IN NATURE.** Design generally implies the action of intentional intelligence. The 'design' of organisms is, however, on the theory of Darwinian evolution, produced without prior purpose or intention. In this sense evolution is 'blind'. It may be said, though, that random variation and natural selection form a kind of intelligence, as they produce designs which we would certainly rate as requiring high intelligence— indeed superhuman intelligence, as they are beyond us to produce or even to understand. See EVOLUTION: NEO-DARWINIAN THEORY; PALEY.

Dawkins, R. (1986). *The Blind Watchmaker*. London.
Gregory, R. L. (1981). *Mind in Science*. Harmondsworth.

**DETECTION.** In *perception, the term refers to the acceptance of selected patterns of energy by the sense organs—which are transducers producing neural signals. The retinal receptors can detect illumination down to the theoretical limit of one quantum. The ears detect sound energies down to the random motion of air molecules ($10^{-16}$ watts, or $0.00003$ dynes/sq cm).

Sensitivity is always limited by the fact that energies cannot be less than Planck's quantum of action, and because all detectors have residual random activity, or 'noise', against which signals must be discriminated.

**DETERMINISM AND FREE WILL.** Nobody can

predict how something as complex as the human brain would behave under all circumstances. With more than ten thousand million nerve-cells, each connected to thousands of its neighbours, the human nervous system would defy detailed prediction even if the matter of which it is made behaved according to classically determinate physical laws. To some people this may be a comforting thought. The idea is widespread that if any of our actions could be predicted from knowledge of the state of our brains, we would have to be denied (or excused) responsibility for them. Others might go further and argue that even if *in practice* nobody could make successful predictions of our actions, any suggestion that *in principle* they were physically determined would rule out the possibility that they could be determined by our conscious thinking and deciding. Our future actions in that case would be 'inevitable' (the argument runs), and we could take no more responsibility for them than for the future of the solar system. 'It ain't me fault, Judge, it's me glands', as the pretty girl is reputed to have said on an embarrassing occasion.

Plausible though it may seem, however, this conclusion does not follow. Consider first an analogy. To an electronics engineer, a computing machine set up to solve a mathematical equation is (for practical purposes) a physical system behaving according to determinate physical laws. In that sense, its behaviour is completely 'determined' by physical causes. To the programmer or user of the machine, however, what matters is that its behaviour should be 'determined' by the problem it is solving. Is there a conflict here? Must the user either prove that the engineer's explanations are faulty or leave 'gaps' in the chain-mesh of physical causes in order to justify his own claim? Of course not. The mathematical equation is not something outside the computing machinery that has to force its way in to exert an influence. It is something *embodied in* that machinery, in such a way that the computer's behaviour is determined *both* by physical forces *and* by the equation. The solving of the equation is the *significance* of the physical activity of the computer. So here the two different answers to the question 'What determines the behaviour?' are not rivals, but complementary. Each makes a point which is true and necessary in order to do justice to all the facts.

In the case of a human action, a similar argument applies. A complete physical explanation, showing how an action was determined by physical causes, would rule out determination by thought and decision only if these latter were some kind of external agencies that had to force their way into the chain-mesh of physical causes in the brain. If, however, our conscious thinking and deciding were *embodied in* the workings of our brains, in the sense in which an equation is embodied in those of a computer, there would be no contradiction in saying that our behaviour was determined by our thinking and choosing, even if our brain mechan-

isms were as physically determinate as the solar system (which they probably are not).

What then of the suggestion that physical determinism would make our future 'inevitable'? Suppose for example that some super-scientist S could examine every particle in the brain of Mr A, and all its environment. Suppose, on the basis of physical determinism, that he could work out (in principle, if not in practice) a completely detailed description (D) of the immediate future of A's brain, and of the body controlled by it. By definition D is then what the observer S would be *correct to believe*, and *mistaken to deny*, about A's future. In that sense, the future state described by D is *inevitable-for-S*.

So far, so good. But now what about Mr A? Is all of the future described by D in the same sense *inevitable-for-A*? Oddly enough it is not. The reason is simple. Mechanistic brain science works on the assumption that everything Mr A sees, feels, thinks, or believes is represented in some way in some part of his brain, in the sense in which all the data for a calculation are represented in some way in some part of a computer. This means that according to mechanistic brain science itself, no change can take place in what A believes without some change taking place in the detailed state of his brain. It follows that *no completely detailed description of the immediate future of A's brain can be equally accurate, whether or not A believes it.* (If it were accurate beforehand, A's believing it would necessarily bring about a change that would make it out of date. On the other hand, if it were 'corrected' so as to allow for the effects of A's believing it, then it would become accurate if—and only if—A believed it. But then A would not be mistaken to disbelieve it, since his disbelieving it would prevent his brain from taking up the state it describes!)

Thus, even on the mechanistic assumptions of brain science, there are some details of A's (present and future) brain-state for which there does not exist a single determinate specification that A would be both correct to believe, and mistaken to deny. In the sense used above, then, these details are *not* inevitable-for-A. They are for him to determine; and there is no complete specification of them, which unknown to A, has an unconditional claim to his assent (i.e. such that A would be correct to believe the specification, and mistaken to disbelieve it, if only he knew it). This situation clearly has an element of *relativity*. The view that a non-participant observer may be correct to take about someone's future is necessarily different in detail from the view that that person himself is correct to take. The two views are complementary, and do not contradict one another.

Notice that in this respect A's brain is distinguished from all the rest of the physical world, even assuming that its matter is subject to the same deterministic physical laws. For future events in any other parts of the world (such as eclipses or sunrises) which are not causally connected with A's brain, there would exist just one detailed description with an unconditional claim to his assent. Whether he knew it or not, or liked it or not, there would be one and only one future scenario that he would be correct to believe and mistaken to disbelieve. No such inevitable scenario, however, exists for the detailed brain-states we have been considering—nor for any events in the rest of the world (such as $A$'s bodily actions) causally dependent upon them. On the contrary, for these brain-states there may exist several (or an infinite range of) alternative scenarios, each of which $A$ would be equally correct to believe: for *his believing* would be one of the factors determining which scenario is correct. In that sense, these details of $A$'s future would not be inevitable-for-$A$, even on the strongest assumptions of physical determinism.

To guard against misunderstandings, two notes should be added. First, the above argument does not depend on assuming physical determinism to be true. It shows that even if determinism were true, it would be irrational to conclude from it that people's future actions were already inevitable-for-them, or to deny them responsibility for those actions on the grounds that they were predictable-by-others. But if, in line with present-day physics, the assumption of determinism is rejected, this would do nothing to weaken our argument. The point is that there is no *need* to invoke physical indeterminism in order to make room for human responsibility.

Secondly, our argument does not depend on whether $S$ in fact *tells* Mr $A$ his prediction $D$, nor on whether $A$ is psychologically suggestible or counter-suggestible. If nobody does tell $A$, then $D$ will presumably be fulfilled to the letter. Our aim has been to show that this does not mean that $D$ (unknown to $A$) had an unconditional *claim* to $A$'s assent. To prove this there is no need actually to offer $D$ to $A$. It is enough to show that $D$ could not have been embodied in $A$'s brain without causing changes that would render $D$ itself false in detail. This proves that even if $A$ does not hear of $D$ until afterwards, $D$ is not what $A$ rationally 'ought' to have believed unconditionally if only he had known. $D$'s later fulfilment merely proves that $S$ was correct in believing it. It does not prove that $A$ would have been correct to believe the same; for the truth is that if $A$ *had* believed it, both he and $S$ would have been mistaken.

See also BRAIN MANIPULATION, THE ETHICS OF; CONSCIOUSNESS AND CAUSALITY; and SOUL, BRAIN SCIENCE AND THE.                               D. M. M.

MacKay, D. M. (1971). Freedom of action in a mechanistic universe. Eddington lecture reprinted in Gazzaniga, M. S. and Lovejoy, E. P. (eds.), *Good Readings in Psychology*, 121–38. New York.
MacKay, D. M. (1974). *The Clockwork Image*. London.
MacKay, D. M. (1978). What Determines my Choice? In Buser, P. A. and Rougeul-Buser, A. (eds.), *Cerebral Correlates of Conscious Experience*. Amsterdam.

**DEWEY,** JOHN (1859–1952). American philosopher and educationalist, born at Burlington, Vermont. He went first to the University of Michigan (1884–94) and then to the University of Chicago (1894–1904), where he did much to promote a *functional point of view in psychology. This was well expressed in an influential paper on the reflex arc concept (1896) in which he laid stress on the function rather than the structure of *reflexes. In 1904, Dewey, whose interests had now shifted almost entirely to the philosophy of education, accepted the Chair at Teachers' College, Columbia, where he remained until 1930. His best-known books are *Democracy and Education* (1916), *Human Nature and Conduct* (1922), *The Quest for Certainty* (1929) and *Art as Experience* (1934).

**DIAGNOSIS.** The use of characteristic signs of a generally established disease or abnormality. This is based on the notion that diseases and typical abnormalities have grouped 'syndromes' of characteristics, such that recognition of some enables us to predict the others, and may also suggest the underlying cause and appropriate treatment. Typical clinical signs or symptoms are, however, sometimes 'seen' when not present, especially when they are likely to accord with the prevailing or probable diagnosis. This can lead to spurious confirmation. The philosopher Sir Karl Popper has emphasized the importance of looking for *negative* or *disconfirming* evidence to check diagnoses and to stop the generation of spurious syndromes when exceptions are overlooked.

**DICHROMATIC.** Literally 'two-coloured'. Usually applied to the (rare cases) of people who have only two, rather than the normal three, retinal colour channels. They can match any colour visible to them by adjusting the intensities of only *two* coloured lights, which are mixed. Thomas *Young showed in 1801 that normally *three* spectral colours (red, green, and blue) are needed to match all the spectral colours, and white, by adjusting the relative intensities of the three lights. Normal people are thus 'trichromats'. See COLOUR VISION: EYE MECHANISMS.

**DIGITAL.** From the Latin for 'finger'—hence 'digital' counting (on the fingers). 'Digital' essentially means representing states or carrying out mathematical or logical procedures in steps corresponding to the symbolic operations of a calculus.

A digital computer works in steps representing steps of logic or computing by means of a formal code. Because the symbols of logic or arithmetical calculation are discretely different from each other, digital computers require circuits having discrete states, which can be selected at great speed. Analogue computers, on the other hand, do not operate by coding into a symbolic system. Rather, they manipulate continuous physical variables, following a change or representing a function by an equivalent change or function but of a different physical form (such as the line of a graph).

Digital computers are far more versatile than analogue ones as, in principle, they can be programmed to perform any operation that can be stated. The same mechanism can readily be reprogrammed to perform very different operations; whereas, typically, analogue computers must be virtually rebuilt for different uses. Early analogue computers were relatively fast, because they did not go through many stepped operations, but modern digital computers can carry out up to $10^9$ operations per second.

It is an open question whether the brain is essentially analogue or digital. It is interesting that we are extremely weak at digital operations, such as complicated arithmetical problems, although these are easy to carry out mechanically, or electronically in pocket calculators, which far surpass human accuracy and speed. This may well suggest that the brain works analogically rather than digitally.

## DIMINISHED RESPONSIBILITY. The McNaghten Rules.

In English law until 1957 there was only one defence based on disease of the mind available to a defendant, that of insanity. In 1843 an authoritative pronouncement by all the judges answered questions put to them by the House of Lords in its legislative capacity. McNaghten had been tried for the murder of Sir Robert Peel's private secretary, Edward Drummond, under the mistaken impression that he was shooting at Sir Robert himself. He was acquitted by the jury on the ground of insanity. The acquittal aroused widespread controversy, and was debated in the House of Lords, with the result that their Lordships put abstract questions to the judges. The judges gave their answer to the second question in the following terms:

To establish a defence on the grounds of insanity, it must be clearly proved that, at the time of the committing of the act, the party accused was labouring under such a defect of reason, from disease of the mind, as not to know the nature and quality of the act he was doing, or, if he did know it, that he did not know he was doing what was wrong: (1843) 10 Cl. & F.200.

From the medical standpoint, this all-or-nothing approach to psychological functioning was already obsolete. It had also been shown that inability to distinguish between right and wrong was only one symptom of insanity, and that many mentally disturbed persons knew the difference between right and wrong. In 1838 Isaac Ray had published in the USA his work *A Treatise on Medical Jurisprudence of Insanity*, described in 1961 by a psychiatrist as the best book in the English language on forensic psychiatry: Diamond (1961) 14 Stan.L.R. 59, 63. Defence counsel had used this book at the trial of McNaghten, but to no effect.

### Doe–Ray tests of insanity.

In the United States the McNaghten Rules were adopted as the test of insanity in most states, but the state of New Hampshire was an exception. Judge Charles Doe, later chief justice of that state, began to correspond with Isaac Ray, an exchange of letters that continued from 1866 to 1872. One passage from Ray's work may be cited: 'Insanity is a disease, and, as is the case with all other diseases, the fact of its existence is never established by a single diagnostic symptom, but by the whole body of symptoms, no particular one of which is present in every case.'

Convinced of the inadequacy of the McNaghten tests, Doe came to regard the question of insanity as one of fact to be left to the jury, and by 1869 had converted his brother judges in the state to that view (*State* v. *Pike* 49 N.H. 399). In a letter to Ray he wrote: 'Giving this matter to the jury leaves the way open for the reception of all progress in your science. One jury is not bound by the verdict of another.' Doe and Ray are thus left in harmonious juxtaposition.

### Diminished responsibility in Scotland.

The McNaghten Rules had never been accepted unreservedly in Scotland, and in the very decade in which Charles Doe had wrought a transformation in New Hampshire, Lord Deas initiated a new defence, proof of which led not to an acquittal, but to a verdict of culpable homicide instead of murder. This was in *HMA* v. *Dingwall* 1867 5 Irv. 466. The development did not arise from close contact with medical writing, and seemed out of character for the judge himself, for his general attitude tended towards rigidity and severity. It has even been suggested that his direction to the jury may have sprung from a respect for Hogmanay, as the defendant's fatal attack on his wife had followed bouts of excessive drinking at that season, a time apparently when many a reasonable Scot will consume inordinate quantities of whisky. Whatever the reasons for the new idea, Lord Deas persisted in it. Before his retirement in 1885, he had contributed six of the first nine reported cases embodying the new doctrine. In the third case he instructed the jury that a weak or diseased mind, not amounting to insanity, might competently form an element to be considered in the question between murder and culpable homicide (*HMA* v. *Granger* 1878 4 Coup. 86, 103). In the last of the six, he said that *Dingwall* was now the recognized law of the land (*HMA* v. *Gove* 1882 4 Coup. 598, 599). The new defence received the name of diminished responsibility in *HMA* v. *Edmonstone* 1909 2 SLT 223, 224. In *HMA* v. *Savage* 1923 JC 49 a direction to the jury from Lord Justice-Clerk (Alness) has come to be regarded as a *locus classicus*. He stressed that the doctrine must be applied with care, and that there must be aberration or weakness of the mind, some form of mental unsoundness, a state of mind bordering on insanity, rendering the defendant only partially responsible.

It has been argued by some distinguished writers on the law of Scotland that diminished responsibility operates merely in mitigation of sentence, and does not affect responsibility. Such a view is certainly not tenable in England, where Parliament created the defence in 1957.

**Diminished responsibility in England.** In England the Royal Commission on Capital Punishment, 1949–53, heard much evidence on the operation of the defence of diminished responsibility in Scotland, but made no recommendation for its adoption, regarding the matter as outside its terms of reference. In 1956, however, during a debate in the House of Commons on capital punishment, the Home Secretary undertook to consider the question further. This led to section 2(1) of the Homicide Act 1957, whereby:

Where a person kills or is a party to the killing of another, he shall not be convicted of murder if he was suffering from such abnormality of mind (whether arising from a condition of arrested or retarded development of mind or any inherent causes or induced by disease or injury) as substantially impaired his mental responsibility for his acts and omissions in doing or being a party to the killing.

The defence is called diminished responsibility in a marginal note to the section. The burden of proof is placed on the defence, as in Scotland and under the McNaghten Rules. In such cases, as in all instances where a legal burden of proof is placed on the defence, the defendant has to establish the defence on a balance of probability, or in more homely language that it is more likely than not that his responsibility is diminished. If so proved, murder is reduced to manslaughter, just as in Scotland it is reduced to culpable homicide. It applies only to murder, following the predominant Scottish view. A successful defence of insanity leads to a verdict of 'not guilty by reason of insanity'.

The introduction of this new defence, coupled with the abolition of capital punishment for murder by Parliament in 1965, has led to the virtual disappearance of the defence of insanity.

From the outset difficulties were found in directing the jury on the question of fact they had to determine under section 2(1). In *R.* v. *Spriggs* [1958] 1 QB 270, the trial judge read the section to the jury, reviewed in detail the evidence relevant to the defence, made no attempt to explain the various medical terms that had figured in the evidence, and gave the jury copies of the section as they retired. The Court of Criminal Appeal quoted the charge to the jury from a Scottish case, which consisted largely of a quotation from the charge to the jury in *Savage* mentioned above as a *locus classicus*. The court considered that the case had been put to the jury in the only way it could be put, and affirmed the conviction.

In *R.* v. *Walden* [1959] 43 Cr.App.R. 201, the trial judge construed the section as meaning: 'Poor fellow, he is not insane, but not far from it; his mental condition is one which is bordering on, but not amounting to insanity.' He gave the jury copies of the section. The Court of Criminal Appeal refused leave to appeal. Parliament had not defined 'abnormality of mind' or 'mental responsibility'. The reference to substantial impairment connoted a question of degree, and questions of degree are questions of fact in each case.

At this stage English juries were not receiving the necessary guidance: Charles Doe, while insisting that the question of mental disease was one of fact for the jury, had also stressed that the jury must be given some help. Help was forthcoming from the Court of Criminal Appeal in *R.* v. *Byrne* [1960] 2 QB 396. The court gave a definition of two important concepts in the section. 'Abnormality of mind' meant a state of mind so different from that of ordinary human beings that the reasonable man would term it abnormal. It covered the mind's activities in all its aspects—not only the perception of physical acts and matters and the ability to form a rational judgement whether an act is right or wrong, but also the ability to exercise will-power to control physical acts. 'Mental responsibility' pointed to a consideration of the extent to which the accused's mind is answerable for his physical acts; this must include a consideration of the extent of his ability to exercise will-power to control his physical acts. Inability to exercise will-power to control such acts entitles the accused to the benefit of the section; difficulty in controlling such acts may do so, if great enough to amount to substantial impairment. The jury must decide, though there is no scientific certainty to guide them. Thus the court in *Byrne* clearly decided that an irresistible impulse falls within the concept of diminished responsibility, a status it never achieved under the McNaghten Rules.

The effect of *Byrne* was soon apparent. In *Rose* v. *Reginam* [1961] 45 Cr.App.R. 102, a summing-up that had passed muster in *Walden* now led to a successful appeal. In *R.* v. *Terry* [1961] 2 QB 314, a summing-up that failed to explain section 2(1) on the lines laid down in *Byrne* was held deficient. Further, the jury had been handed a transcript of volumes of medical evidence without explanation. It is of course the duty of the trial judge to take the jury through the evidence, trying to synthesize it and render it easier to digest. The conviction was in fact upheld as the crucial question was held to be whether the accused was shamming, and on this matter the summing-up was adequate. In *R.* v. *Gomez* [1964] 48 Cr.App.R. 310, a summing-up to the jury by Judge Paull on similar lines to that in *Walden* was again held inadequate: the proper course was to tell the jury what in law the section means, and what are the ingredients in the section, and then direct them on the evidence. The conviction was reduced to manslaughter. In *Walton* v. *R.* [1978] AC 788, the Privy Council put the clock back to *Walden* by indicating that the main question before the jury was whether the state of mind of the defendant was bordering on but not amounting to insanity, supporting this view by a quotation from *Byrne* itself. It is submitted that this is oversimplified, and regard should be had to the more thorough examination of the question demanded by *Byrne* rather than to an isolated passage taken out of context.

Although the question is one that the jury must decide, if they ignore unchallenged medical evidence that all points to substantial impairment, an appellate court may reduce the conviction to manslaughter, on the ground that the verdict of murder is unsafe or unsatisfactory, as in *R*. v. *Matheson* [1958] 42 Cr.App.R. 145. The verdict may, however, be allowed to stand if the medical evidence was challenged in cross-examination, as in *R*. v. *Latham* [1965] Cr.L.R. 434, or the solitary expert witness in the case, who considers the impairment to have been substantial, is unsupported by objective evidence of any history of mental disorder, as in *Walton* (above).

An issue of considerable importance is the position of one diagnosed as *psychopathic personality as defined by the Mental Health Act 1959. In the case of Fenton (1975, 61 Cr.App.R. 261) it was concluded that psychopathic personality was no defence under the terms of the Homicide Act 1957, regardless of whether the accused was affected by alcohol at the time of his offence. Furthermore, as intoxication with drink or drugs cannot be regarded as an 'inherent cause' of mental abnormality, an attempt to reduce the verdict to manslaughter in place of murder on the ground that the accused was drunk at the time of the killing will not succeed.

Nevertheless, the introduction of the defence of diminished responsibility has undoubtedly had beneficial effects. This is because psychiatrists have adapted themselves to giving opinions in accordance with the legal formula, vague and unscientific as it undoubtedly is.

**Proposals for reform.** The Butler Committee on Mentally Abnormal Offenders, in their report of 1975, Cmnd. 6244, recognizing the difficulties under which experts were labouring, proposed an alteration in the wording of section 2(1), substituting after the word 'murder', 'if there is medical or other evidence that he was suffering from a form of mental disorder as defined in section 4 of the Mental Health Act 1959, and if, in the opinion of the jury, the mental disorder was such as to be an extenuating circumstance which ought to reduce the offence to manslaughter'. The Committee claims that this amendment would provide a firm base for testifying psychiatrists to diagnose mental state. The claim is justified. The Mental Health Act 1959 contains definitions of mental disorder, psychopathic disorder, subnormality, and severe subnormality, so that the expert is now operating in a familiar field; and the Mental Health Act 1983 does not materially alter this situation. Although mental disorder includes psychopathic disorder as one of the defined components, as already mentioned, it is unlikely that this diagnosis will be admissible as a defence of diminished responsibility under the Homicide Act 1957.

The Criminal Law Revision Committee in its Fourteenth Report of 1980 (Cmnd. 7844) recommends that the Butler wording should be changed so that instead of the need for the jury to seek 'an extenuating circumstance' their quest should be for 'a substantial enough reason'.

The Fourteenth Report recommends, as the Committee had recommended in its Eleventh Report of 1972, and the Butler Committee in 1975, that there should be no burden of proof on a defendant raising a plea of insanity or diminished responsibility: the burden of proof should be on the prosecution to disprove the defence beyond reasonable doubt.

See also CRIMINOLOGY.                              R. N. G.

**DIOPTER.** Unit for the power of a lens or prism. For a 'positive' (convex) lens, 1 diopter brings parallel light to a focus at a distance of 1 metre from the centre of the lens; a 2-diopter lens a focal length of 0·5 metre, and so on.

**DIPLOPIA.** Double vision, resulting from failure to combine or 'fuse' the images from the two eyes. This often, though not always, gives total loss of stereoscopic depth perception. It may be due to squint (strabismus), or, temporarily, to tiredness, or to temporary or permanent disturbance of the central neural processes.

See also EYE DEFECTS AND THEIR CORRECTION.

**DISHABITUATION.** See INVERTEBRATE LEARNING AND INTELLIGENCE.

**DISPLACEMENT ACTIVITY.** During courtship a male three-spined stickleback (*Gasterosteus aculeatus*) is often observed to break off his display to the female. He swims to his empty nest on the substrate and fans water through it. He may also creep through the nest before returning to display to the female. These nest-directed activities are normally associated with the parental care of eggs (carried out by the male in this species) and as such are considered 'out of context' or 'irrelevant' to courtship. Behaviour of this kind is called a displacement activity.

Displacement activities often occur when an animal has a tendency for more than one incompatible behaviour, such as approach and avoidance (motivational conflict), or when it is prevented from reaching a goal such as an anticipated food reward (thwarting). In stickleback courtship it is thought that the female represents a stimulus for both aggression and for mating. Other examples are ground-pecking (feeding) during fights by red junglefowl (*Gallus gallus*), bill-wiping during fights by great tits (*Parus major*), and preening during approach–avoidance conflict by the common chaffinch (*Fringilla coelebs*). Many human actions, such as excessive drinking, nibbling food, or manipulation of the face in stressful social contexts, seem to be similar to the displacement activities seen in other animals. There is an extensive ethological literature on displacement activities because of the clues they are thought to provide about mechanisms of motivation, and because of their possible importance in communication displays (see also ETHOLOGY).

In many cases displacement activities have been found to have a function related to their context. For example, it has been shown that stickleback courtship does not proceed to a normal completion if displacement fanning is prevented. Similarly ground-pecking by red jungle fowl has an important influence on the outcome of a fight. In other cases the activity has a function even if not relevant to the context: for example, bill-wiping by great tits removes sloughed material from the beak, although this is not relevant to a territorial dispute. But our judgement of irrelevance may simply indicate ignorance of the true situation.

While the time of occurrence and duration of displacement activities is mainly dependent on causal factors relevant to the context (conflict or thwarting) in which they occur, their form and intensity is dictated largely by causal factors related to the displacement activities themselves. Thus displacement preening in chaffinches is more vigorous when the feathers are made dirty, but the timing of preening bouts is hardly affected. One explanation for this is that displacement activities are disinhibited, and it is based on the idea that during normal behaviour the current activity inhibits other incompatible activities for which the causal factors are also present. During a motivational conflict the incompatible tendencies suppress one another, leaving the displacement activity to occur by default, governed in performance by its usual causal factors but delimited in time by the context. An empirical test of this explanation involves showing that the amount of displacement activity seen, depends on the ratio of the conflicting tendencies rather than on their absolute value. This has been demonstrated in terns (*Sterna hirundo*), sticklebacks, chaffinches, and great tits; but there are other attributes of displacement activities which are not accounted for by this explanation. In chaffinches the precise preening movements seen during approach–avoidance conflict depend on the context as well as on causal factors relevant to preening. In great tits displacement activities during fights are affected by the absolute levels of competing tendencies as well as by the ratio.

Displacement activities often appear hurried, stereotyped, or incomplete when compared with similar behaviour occurring in its normal context. They share some of the characteristics of a variety of other behavioural effects seen when animals are thwarted. With rats, the omission of an expected food reward may lead to increased motivated behaviour towards the absent goal (e.g. increased running speed to the goal box of a runway), excessive performance of an alternative activity such as drinking or wood-gnawing, or a generalized increase in the rate of activities normally seen between deliveries of food. Such phenomena are sometimes attributed to a generalized state, frustration, caused by thwarting. The excessive behaviour induced by certain intermittent reward schedules (adjunctive behaviour) may also be a related phenomenon, though such schedule-induced activities differ in some respects from frustration effects: for example, they are not abolished by minor tranquillizing drugs. Displacement activities and frustration effects may represent a class of 'coping behaviour', enabling an animal to resolve a situation in which it is unable, due to inadequate or contradictory information, to decide what to do next.

Apart from intention movements and compromise postures, many of the displays seen in social behaviour, especially in the courtship or agonistic behaviour of vertebrates, appear to incorporate movements which are derived from activities not relevant to the context of the display. For example, in birds many threat displays are very similar to preening movements. This has given rise to the idea that displacement activities may have been important in the evolutionary origin of social communication. Because of what they can reveal about the motivational state of the performer, it has been thought probable that displacement activities are attended to by other individuals to whom such information might be useful, and that it is often advantageous to the performer to inform others of its motivational state. It has been argued that this 'tell-tale' of internal state has become established as a means of communication, with natural selection leading to emphasis of the original signal (ritualization) and probably to the emancipation of the activity from its original motivational mechanism. More recently it has been pointed out by those interested in the game-theoretical analysis of social transactions between animals, that the contestants often need to conceal their true motivational state (e.g. not show fear to an opponent) or to mislead others (e.g. threaten to attack while contemplating flight). The highly redundant nature of derived displays, which are usually stereotyped, rhythmic, and repetitive, is characteristic of persuasive rather than informative signals. Persuasive signals are to be expected where it is advantageous to the sender to manipulate recipients of the message, but advantageous to the recipients to avoid manipulation. Animals that co-operate in the exchange of reliable information to their mutual advantage might be expected to communicate in 'conspiratorial whispers', rather than by means of conspicuous announcements, since signals are likely to be intercepted by animals other than the intended recipient, to the disadvantage of the sender. For example, some predators make use of the courtship displays of their prey in order to locate them. This currently controversial area is discussed in detail by Krebs and Dawkins (1984). Whatever the explanation, any animal signals are, apparently, derived from other actions in the repertoire which have no connection with the motivational context of the display.                                                    R. H. M.

Krebs, J. R. and Dawkins, R. (1984). Animal signals: mind-reading and manipulation. In Krebs, J. R. and Davies, N. B. (eds.), *Behavioural Ecology*, 2nd edn., 380–402. Oxford.

**DISSOCIATION OF THE PERSONALITY.** Two—or more—mental processes can be said to be dissociated if they coexist or alternate without becoming connected or influencing one another. Prior to Sigmund *Freud and to the discovery of the *Unconscious, dissociation was a term much used by psychiatrists to describe and, by implication, to explain many neurotic symptoms; the underlying assumption having been that neurotics suffered from some inherent or constitutional weakness of the integrative function, as a result of which they were liable to perform actions, think thoughts, dream day and night dreams, which were unconnected with and dissociated from their usual, real, or true personalities. However, since Freud and the general abandonment of the assumption that the neuroses are the result of a 'functional', constitutional defect, the concept of dissociation has, with one exception, fallen into disuse, terms like 'repression', 'isolation', 'splitting' being preferred to describe those defence mechanisms by which a person, for specific though usually unconscious reasons, keeps wishes, actions, images, memories, etc., outside his self-image or *ego.

The exception consists of a group of phenomena which have it in common that the subject maintains for a considerable length of time some line or course of action in which he appears not to be actuated by his usual self—or, alternatively, his usual self seems not to have access to the recent memories that one would normally expect him to have. Contemporary psychiatry categorizes such phenomena as 'hysterical dissociations', the best-known examples being sleep-walking (see SOM-NAMBULISM), trances, post-hypnotic suggestions, fugues (in which the subject wanders off, not knowing who or where he is), loss of memory (hysterical *amnesia), in which the subject has a gap in his memory for some finite, recent period of time, and split, dual, or multiple personality, in which the subject appears to change from one person to another.

The last of these, dissociation of the personality, is a puzzling and, indeed, disturbing phenomenon, since it calls into question a basic assumption we all make about human nature, namely that for every body there is but one person; that each of us, despite the passage of time and changes in mood and activity, remains the same person, with a single biography and store of memories. Given the fact that all social relations and contracts presume consistency and unity of personality, it is hardly surprising that the occasional person who claims or appears to change into someone else becomes an object of concern to the police, of curiosity to the psychiatric profession, and of fascination to the general public.

Dissociation of the personality is not only bizarre but also extremely rare—so rare, indeed, that one has to take seriously the possibility that it may be a social and psychiatric artefact: i.e. that it can only occur if (i) prevailing views on the nature of personality make it conceivable that two personalities can occupy the same bodily frame, and (ii) the potential case of split or multiple personality encounters a psychiatrist who believes in, or is already interested in, dissociation of the personality.

In fact, the great majority of reported cases of multiple personality date from between 1840 and 1910—that is, from after demoniacal possession had ceased to be a plausible, scientifically respectable explanation of sudden, extraordinary changes in personality until the time at which psychoanalytical ideas began to have an impact. During this period two conditions existed which, it seems likely, must have facilitated the diagnosis of multiple personality. First, the prevailing Victorian conventions of reticence must have made it unthinkable that patients should tell, or that their doctors should enquire into, those intimate physical details of their lives which would have established continuity of bodily feeling despite massive changes in mental feeling; if *cogito, ergo sum* were the basis of identity, then indeed personality and identity could change if thought changed, in a way that could not happen if patient and physician believed that the ground of being is located in the body.

Secondly, there was obliviousness to what is nowadays called *transference and counter-transference, and in particular, to the fact that patients can and will produce symptoms to please their physicians. The great majority of the physicians reporting cases of multiple personality have been men, and the cases they have reported have been women younger than themselves. For instance, Dr Morton Prince of Boston, Massachusetts, was 44 when, in 1898, he was consulted by Sally Beauchamp, a young, single woman aged 23, who suffered from various nervous disorders. During the next seven years, three further personalities emerged in or from her, two of them while Dr Prince was hypnotizing her, and in 1908 he described his treatment of the foursome, whom he called collectively 'the family', in his classic *The Dissociation of a Personality*. In view of the fact that Dr Prince had already published papers on double personality and was widely known to be interested in the subject, and that Miss Beauchamp is on record as pleading to be hypnotized by him— 'And I do want you, please, please, to hypnotize me again. You know it is the only thing that has ever helped me . . .'—it is hard to resist the conclusion that Miss Beauchamp was obliging Dr Prince by formulating her experiences in terms that accorded with his known enthusiasms, and that both were erotically more attached to one another than the proprieties of New England at the turn of the century allowed either to realize. 'There was over her spine a "hypnogenetic point", pressure upon which always caused a thrill to run through her that weakened her will and induced hypnotic sleep.'

Rather similarly, most of the work done on multiple personality by the French neurologist Pierre *Janet was with women—notably Lucie, Léonie, and Rose—who regularly produced new or sub-personalities during hypnotic sessions. Janet, incidentally, distinguished clearly between 'roles' played by hypnotic subjects in order to please their hypnotist and new, unknown personalities which emerge spontaneously during hypnosis, particularly as a return to childhood. Presumably Janet was describing as dissociated personalities what contemporary psychiatrists and analysts would call revivals of repressed memories. Janet believed that the new personality emerging during hypnosis was more nearly the real person than the one which the patient originally presented, and that it was therapeutically helpful to name an emergent personality.

Both Prince and Janet believed that the self is not a pristine unity but an entity achieved by integration of 'simultaneous psychological existences', and that, therefore, multiple personalities and dissociated states generally were due to failures in integration. Contemporary psychoanalysis and psychiatry tends to take the opposite view: that the self is a pristine unity but uses defence mechanisms, notably repression, which make it unconscious of much of its total activity. As a result, many of the phenomena which Janet, Prince, and other nineteenth-century physicians described in terms of dissociation of the personality are nowadays described in terms of repression, splitting of the ego, etc.

This change seems to have occurred around 1910 and must presumably have been due to the impact of Freud's more dynamic, more biological, more sexual view of human nature. According to H. F. Ellenberger (1970), 'after 1910 there was a wave of reaction against the concept of multiple personality. It was alleged that the investigators, from Despine to Prince, had been duped by mythomaniac patients and that they had involuntarily shaped the manifestations they were observing.' And, although Ellenberger reports a slight revival of interest in the subject, contemporary textbooks of psychiatry are notably cautious and uncertain in their approach to dissociation of personality and to hysterical dissociation states generally. Henderson and Gillespie, in their *Textbook of Psychiatry* (9th edn., 1962), give only two paragraphs to multiple personality and the only two clinical examples they give date from the nineteenth century, while the emphasis in their paragraphs on hysterical dissociation states generally is on their rarity, on their purposiveness, which is usually transparent to observers but not to the subject himself, and on their dependence on gullibility. Explaining their rarity, Henderson and Gillespie remark, 'Both the public and their doctors have become more sophisticated.' Hysterical dissociation states, including dissociation of the personality, seem indeed to have more to do with the psychology of deception and self-deception than with any innate or acquired incapacity for integration. In the second half of the nineteenth century it seems to have been possible, in some circles at least, to evoke concern among friends and family and earn attention, if not effective treatment, from physicians by having trances, fugues, losing one's memory, or being taken over by another personality; but in the second half of the twentieth century less dramatic and more subtle signals of distress became the order of the day.          C. R.

Ellenberger, H. F. (1970). *The Discovery of the Unconscious*. London.
Prince, M. (1905, reprint, 1978, Oxford). *The Dissociation of a Personality*.
Sizemore, C. (1978). *Eve*. London.

**DISTORTION.** Strictly, nothing can be distorted—it is what it is. A ruler or straight edge is, however, said to be distorted when it produces aberrant measures, or curved lines when straight lines are required. 'Distortion' thus has a connotation of error or discrepancy from what is needed or desired.

Perceptual distortions include the classical visual 'distortion illusions' (see ILLUSIONS). Distortions of memory tend towards the familiar, and towards social norms (see BARTLETT, F. C., and his book *Remembering*, 1932). It is of course a deep question how far *all* perception and knowledge is a distortion, or discrepancy, from physical reality—as physics describes things very differently from how they appear.

**DISTRACTION.** See ATTENTION.

**DIVER PERFORMANCE.** The professional diver has probably the most hostile working environment on earth—or indeed off it, according to Scott Carpenter, who has been both an astronaut and an aquanaut and rates the underwater environment as the more hostile. Not only must the diver take along his own breathing mixture, but if he breathes air he is likely to suffer the dangerous intoxication of nitrogen narcosis at depths below 30 metres; if he breathes pure oxygen he is likely to suffer from convulsions at depths exceeding 9–12 metres; and even breathing oxyhelium he is liable to have problems in voice communication and to find his performance impaired if he goes much deeper than 300 metres. He must either carry his supply of breathing mixture with him on his back, and risk it running out, or must be attached by an umbilical cord to some more generous source, with all the attendant risks of snagging and tangling and the dangers resulting from having the umbilical cord cut.

He will be relatively weightless, which might seem to be an advantage when it comes to moving about, but this presents real problems. If he is required to exert any great physical pressure to turn a wrench or wield a hammer, it is all too likely that he will turn, the wrench remaining where it is. Underwater vision is severely restricted by the tunnelling effect of refraction through his face mask, if indeed he is fortunate enough to be working under conditions that allow him to see anything. He is often required to work under conditions of zero visibility, operating by touch alone.

A commercial diver will expect to have to work under very cold conditions. While suits heated by a constant flow of warm water may be available, they are by no means the rule. Similarly, although a wide range of diving gloves exists, none appears to be really adequate under near-freezing conditions. Communication presents a further problem. The diver's voice is likely to be distorted by pressure and even further distorted if he is breathing an oxyhelium mixture. Helium unscramblers help, but are very far from perfect.

Having successfully completed a job under water, the problems are far from over. As the diver breathes air or oxyhelium at pressure, the nitrogen from the air or the helium from the oxyhelium is absorbed by his blood and body tissue. If he surfaces too rapidly, the gas forms bubbles in his tissue and bloodstream, leading to decompression sickness, otherwise known as 'the bends'. These may range from relatively minor joint pains (the niggles) to symptoms associated with breathing (the chokes), and to impairment of the central nervous system, producing motor disability (the staggers), pain, and possibly death. The bends can be avoided provided the diver surfaces slowly enough, but if he has been working at a depth of several hundred metres, decompression is likely to take a matter of days. In order to cope with this problem it is common for divers having a major job to do at depth to live at pressure in a decompression chamber, being transported to and from the job every day by means of a submersible decompression chamber that can be locked on to or detached from the main chamber on board the ship or rig. After a week of living at pressure the diver will spend the next week or so decompressing before taking some well-earned leave.

Socially, a diver's life is likely to be a rather curious one: unless he limits himself to inshore harbour work, periods out on an oil rig or pipe-laying barge are likely to alternate with periods of leave. If he is working on a rig, he may have long periods of inactivity followed by an emergency and a requirement suddenly to dive to a considerable depth. If he is working on a barge, he may be required to operate under saturation for many days. Under these conditions it is essential to be able to maintain good relations with fellow divers.

Diving is a dangerous occupation even if the diver takes good care to breathe the right gas mixture and maintain the right working temperatures and the appropriate decompression schedule. He is working in an environment in which accidents are all too common, even out of the water. Under water, a minor accident can be fatal. Divers are very well paid—and so they should be.                                      A. D. B.

Godden, D. and Baddeley, A. D. (1979). The commercial diver. In Singleton, W. T. (ed.), *The Study of Real Skills: compliance and excellence*, vol. II. Lancaster.

**DODGE**, RAYMOND (1871–1942). American experimental psychologist, born in Wobern, Massachusetts, the son of a physician. He was educated at Williams College, where he obtained his degree, but failed to gain admission to Harvard. He then spent several years in Germany working with Benno Erdmann in Halle, where he obtained his doctorate and jointly with Erdmann published a book on the experimental psychology of reading (1898), which was a classic in its day. He returned to America in 1898 and became a professor at the Wesleyan University in Middletown, Connecticut, where he became well known among psychologists for his originality and skill in psychological instrumentation and research. (Erdmann told him that he should have become an engineer!)

Dodge saw service in the First World War and invented an instrument for testing, selecting, and training gun-pointers, which found wide application. He also worked on the psychological effects of alcohol. He later became chairman of the division of anthropology and psychology of the National Research Council in Washington.

After the war, Dodge became a professor at the Institute of Psychology at Yale and continued to pursue his early interests on the relation of eye movements to perception and on the conditions of human variability, about which he published several books, the best known of which is *Conditions and Consequences of Human Variability* (1931).                                      O. L. Z.

**DODGSON**, CHARLES LUTWIDGE (1832–98), British author and logician. See CARROLL, LEWIS.

**DOMINANCE, HAND.** See HANDEDNESS.

**DOPAMINE NEURONES IN THE BRAIN.** Dopamine neurones are one type of a class of neurones all of which use biogenic amines as *neurotransmitters. These have been identified as *adrenaline, noradrenaline, dopamine, and serotonin. A common feature of these groups is that a comparatively small number of neurones of each type in the brainstem give rise to a highly branched network of ascending and descending fibres of very fine calibre. These fibres carry action potentials (see NERVOUS SYSTEM) of low frequency and slow conduction velocity. The post-synaptic effects of their transmitters are slowly mediated by chemical reactions, in contrast to more 'classical' neurotransmitters such as *acetylcholine, which act extremely rapidly by means of the opening of specific ionic channels to carry current. Anatomically there appears to be a high degree of connections between some of these neurone groups, allowing for mutual interaction of function. The noradrenaline and serotonin neurones innervate a vast area of tissue throughout the brain and spinal cord. The adrenaline and dopamine groups on the other hand are somewhat more restricted in their anatomical distribution and their functions are likely to be correspondingly more specific.

The entire dopamine projection system arises from only a few thousand neurones located in the midbrain (see NERVOUS SYSTEM for a description of brain structure). One subgroup, the substantia nigra, innervates chiefly the caudate nucleus and putamen which lie in the basal ganglia—a brain region which controls movement. The substantia nigra also contains a non-dopamine neurone population by means of which it is brought into close relation to other sensory and motor brain regions. Degeneration of the dopamine neurones of substantia nigra has been found to occur in *Parkinson's disease, a condition characterized by poverty of movement (hypokinesia), tremor, and rigidity. It seems likely, then, that these symptoms are related to disturbance in the co-ordination of neural activity in these circuits. Several observations strongly suggest that in Parkinson's disease both the basal ganglia and thalamus are concerned with the appearance of tremor and rigidity. It is probable that globus pallidus (a subregion of the basal ganglia) is more concerned with the production of rigidity, while the thalamus is concerned with tremor. Successful neurosurgical treatment of these symptoms can be achieved by destroying small areas of these parts of the brain. On the other hand, it seems that the hypokinesia of Parkinsonism is due to degeneration of dopaminergic neurones. Thus it seems that there is a distinction between those symptoms in the Parkinsonian syndrome which are due to dopamine, and those due to non-dopamine neurones. Indeed, symptoms of hypokinesia can occur independently of rigidity and tremor. Hypokinesia can be successfully treated by giving the patient levodopa, an amino acid which is taken up in the brain and converted into the neurotransmitter dopamine in those dopamine neurones not affected by the disease.

The other main dopamine subgroup of neurones innervates various nuclei in the limbic system, including the amygdala. They are likely to be closely involved in the organism's emotional response to the environment. The same dopamine group also provides an innervation to important areas of the cerebral cortex—the frontal and temporal lobe cortex. Both these areas (particularly the latter) are targets for convergence of association fibres from extremely wide expanses of neocortex. They therefore provide potential anatomical structures in which the highest of cortical functions can be carried out. In man they are likely to be involved in the functions of memory, intellect, and personality. Dopamine neurones innervating these cortical regions also receive inputs from hypothalamic areas and the basal forebrain. These regions appear to be closely involved

in motivation, learning, and rewarding mechanisms. *Schizophrenia is a condition which appears to be sensitive to the action of drugs that act on brain areas innervated by dopamine neurones. Drugs which act more selectively on only the limbic and cortical dopamine systems are also antipsychotic. Thus it may be that disturbance of these neurones, particularly those related to the amygdala and the temporal lobe cortex, may play an important part in the development of this condition.

O. T. P.

*DOPPELGÄNGER,* or autoscopy, is the term given to the experience of meeting one's own 'double'. The apparition takes the form of a *mirror image of the viewer, facing him and just beyond arm's reach. It is life-sized and may move. Indeed, it usually replicates the viewer's posture, facial expressions, and movements as though it were his reflection. But beyond these features, reported experiences show several differences from the stereotype of popular imagination. First, the image is usually transparent: it has been described as being 'like jelly', or like a film projected on glass. (But it is not blurred or misty—its details are quite clear.) Secondly, it is generally monochromatic; if colour is observed, it is described as dull or 'washed out'. And thirdly, although the apparition may be inferred to include the whole figure, only the face, or head and trunk, are commonly 'seen'.

As reported by normal people, *doppelgänger* experiences occur most often late at night or at dawn. They are rare, occurring during periods of *stress or fatigue and in conjunction with disturbed consciousness. (However, the first recorded account, which is attributed to Aristotle, describes a man who could not go out for a walk without meeting his 'double'.) A *doppelgänger* episode is usually of very short duration with normal people, lasting only a few seconds. The experience is more common among delirious patients, among those with brain lesions in the parieto-occipital regions, or, most notably, among epileptics, where it may be part of a complex partial seizure. Autoscopy can occasionally be a feature of an attack of migraine, sometimes in association with a sense of distortion of a part of the body. The *doppelgänger* experience, when the subject sees himself standing behind his back or in another room, is referred to as an extracampine *hallucination.

The fact that an apparition is presumed in most cultures to be a visitor from the grave, a spirit of the dead, may well account for the morbid response accorded the *doppelgänger* experience. After all, the subject is apparently being accosted by his own ghost, which not only raises some knotty questions about the nature of time, but bears the distinct implication that the subject's own time is up. Indeed, the German folk-belief was that the *doppelgänger* was a harbinger of death. Like many old wives' tales, this superstitious belief may have had a factual basis; for in those cases where *doppelgänger* is associated with severe brain injury or cerebral thrombosis, the illness is often fatal.

The idea of a phantom 'double' has existed throughout recorded history, and still flourishes in superstitions, fairy-tales, and folklore throughout the world. It is taken seriously by some parapsychologists as an example of an *out-of-body experience. It figures in many primitive religions, where the 'double' is assumed to be the person's soul. Witches and shamans put their 'doubles' to good use, sending them on occult errands or as representatives or intermediaries. But the *doppelgänger* concept has also intrigued sophisticated people, and induced in them a dread of the unknown and a morbid assumption of doom akin to the responses of primitive groups. Autoscopic phenomena have frequently been described in the literature of the Western world, always in terms of sinister foreboding or impending tragedy. Descriptions have figured in the works of Dostoevsky, Kafka, de Maupassant, Edgar Allan Poe, Steinbeck, and Oscar Wilde. It is of interest that several of these suffered from epilepsy or cerebral disorder.

*Doppelgänger* experiences have attracted little medical or psychological study, despite widespread interest. Traditionally, the phenomenon has been classified as a visual hallucination, and its form can be examined in the same terms as other hallucinations. But an added dimension is that the experience is not limited to the visual modality; many subjects have reported that they could 'hear' and 'feel' their doubles. This multi-modality suggests the intriguing possibility that *doppelgänger* may in some way represent an externalization or displacement of Sir Henry *Head's 'body schema'. However, why should the apparition appear as a mirror image?　　　　　　　　　　　　　G. F. R.

**DOUBLE VISION.** See DIPLOPIA.

**DOUBTING.** The questioning of accepted beliefs or opinions. In Greek philosophy such doubting was erected into a philosophical system by the sceptics, such as Pyrrho of Elis (*fl. c.*300 BC), who argued that all truth is unknowable and that the only appropriate attitude for life is one of total suspension of belief. In the seventeenth century, *Descartes's famous 'method of doubt' involved withholding assent from all matters which allow even the smallest possibility of doubt. Thus all information derived from the senses is potentially unreliable; further, we cannot know whether we are awake or asleep, so that even such a simple statement as 'I am holding this piece of paper' is open to doubt; and, finally, there may be a malicious all-powerful demon who is bent on deceiving us, and so 'the earth, sky and all external things' may be merely delusions. Cartesian doubt is not, however, an end in itself, but it is designed to clear the way for the establishing of a secure system of knowledge built on indubitable foundations.

The questioning of accepted beliefs and preconceived opinions can be a valuable exercise both in philosophy and in science generally (SEE COMMON SENSE). It seems, however, that to insist on indubitability as a criterion of the acceptability of beliefs is to insist on an impossibly high standard. Immunity to all conceivable doubt is something that belongs to only a handful of very simple and relatively unexciting propositions, such as (perhaps) 'two and two make four', or Descartes's famous '*cogito*' ('I am thinking'); and it does not seem possible to construct any worthwhile system of knowledge on such meagre foundations.

The difficulty of seriously maintaining a position of philosophical scepticism has been highlighted by G. E. *Moore in the twentieth century, and earlier by David *Hume. Hume observed that 'Nature is always too strong for principle, and though a Pyrrhonian may throw himself and others into a momentary . . . confusion by his profound reasonings, the first and most trivial event in life will put to flight all his doubts' (*Enquiry Concerning Human Understanding*, 1748).　　　　　　　　J. G. C.

**DOWN'S SYNDROME.** Mental retardation due to a genetic abnormality which is believed to occur during the early stages of cell division during embryological development, some cells having too few or too many chromosomes. Cells having too few chromosomes generally die; but those with too many may survive and produce an individual with extra chromosomes in all the cells of the body. There are, however, severe mental and physical problems.

The characteristics of Down's syndrome (or 'mongolism') are: a flattened face, a thick tongue which may be too large for the mouth, extra folds of the eyelids, uncoordinated movements, and intelligence limited to an IQ of between 20 and 60.

Raised activity of the enzyme UR–NAP, indicates an 80% chance of Down's syndrome. The triple-marker test for Down's syndrome, and anencephaly and spina bifida, counts the alpha fetoprotein level. Best results are obtained at 16–18 weeks of pregnancy. The incidence of Down's syndrome is higher in children born of older parents, especially of an older mother.

See also MENTAL HANDICAP; PENROSE, LIONEL SHARPLES; SUBNORMALITY.

**DREAMING.** In our *sleep we all intermittently experience insanity. Some of our dreams differ so from normal awareness that they have often been attributed to the departure of the soul to another world, or to the visitation of alien beings, such as angels. Since earliest history, dreams have been interpreted in order to give guidance for the future, up to the dream books of the nineteenth century and punters' guides of the twentieth. In the 1950s Nathaniel Kleitman of Chicago, with E. Aserinsky and W. Dement, opened an era of laboratory techniques for studying dreams.

Dreams are often misleadingly defined as successions of visual images, but these are merely common accompaniments. A dream is an experience of living in a fantasy world in which things happen, emotions are felt, actions are carried out, people are present, with all the waking sensations coming and going. The congenitally blind have dreams that are no less vivid even though they see nothing. Visual images in dreams are as often in colour as in real life.

Dement and Kleitman introduced the technique of awakening and questioning volunteers about possible dreams at critically sensitive moments during sleep, and found that during periods of sleep accompanied by rapid eye movements (REMs) detailed dream reports could usually be elicited, whereas recall from other times during sleep was meagre. Dement wakened some further volunteers repeatedly as soon as their REMs began, and later found a compensatory increase of sleep with REMs. He proposed that he had deprived them of dreams, that they needed to dream, and that if they did not they might become insane. This notion achieved wide circulation but has not since been supported. We may need to dream, but no one has yet devised an experiment to see whether we have such psychological needs at night.

There are two kinds of sleep; they came to be called non-rapid eye movement (NREM or orthodox) and rapid eye movement (REM or paradoxical) sleep. In 1962 David Foulkes of Chicago asked of his subjects not the leading question, 'Have you been dreaming?' but instead, 'What was passing through your mind?' He found that NREM sleep allowed recall almost as often as REM sleep, but its less colourful content was more often characterized as 'thinking' and, despite considerable overlap, it was possible to distinguish between the 'dream' reports from REM sleep and those from NREM sleep. Typical dreams can be elicited especially easily from NREM sleep at the end of the night and when first falling asleep. The brief dreamlets that come as we drowsily drift to sleep are known as *hypnagogic hallucinations or images.

In subsequent research Molinari and Foulkes made awakenings from REM sleep both just after one of the intermittent bursts of REMs and when over thirty seconds of ocular quiescence had elapsed during REM sleep, and sought details of mental life just prior to waking. The first type of awakenings elicited many 'primary' visual and other experiences (for example, a little brother suddenly vomiting 'on my shoulder'), the second elicited 'secondary cognitive elaborations' resembling the thinking characteristic of NREM sleep. Jerky eye movements, limb twitches, face twitches, middle-ear muscle twitches, and sudden respiratory changes are all *phasic* components of REM sleep, whereas muscle relaxation and penile erections are *tonic* features. It seems that the special 'dream' elements are injected intermittently in company with the phasic components of REM sleep.

As the night progresses, the REM periods con-

tain a higher rate of phasic components, and dreams are more active and less passive in quality. Sleeping-pills diminish the phasic elements and dreams become more passive. There has been a lot of controversy about such relations between bodily events and the contents of a dream. While the majority of the REMs certainly cannot be ascribed to scanning the visual field of a dream-world, there are occasional large eye movements that do seem to bear a relation to described dream content. Closer correspondence has been found for movements of the limbs: Jouvet made lesions in the lower brains of cats so that they were no longer paralysed during REM sleep, and they rose up and appeared to the observer to be acting out their dreams. There is certainly a strong correlation between dream emotionality and heart-rate fluctuations or skin-potential fluctuations (see ELECTRODERMAL ACTIVITY), while in anxiety-ridden dreams there is loss of the usual penile erections.

The intensified dreaming qualities to the mental life that accompanies each REM sleep period about every 90–100 minutes led to findings that, while awake and in unchanging environments, people engage in intensified oral activity and have more day-dreaming qualities to their thoughts according to a daytime cycle of 90–100 minutes. Day-dreaming and night-dreaming are both associated with a 90–100-minute rhythm.

The term 'nightmare' is today used for dreams that occur during REM sleep, usually in the later night, and in which a series of events is associated with *anxiety. As the sleeper awakens from his nightmare, he is often aware of the inability to move that characterizes REM sleep. On the other hand, night terrors arise in the early night, from NREM sleep with large slow electrical brain waves. They involve brief and less elaborately detailed experiences of entrapment, of being choked or attacked, often with shrieking, sitting-up, or sleep-walking (see SOMNAMBULISM), and tremendous acceleration of the heart. Both nightmares and night terrors occur unpredictably in even the most emotionally stable people, but become more frequent when there is greater daytime anxiety; they are frequent among wartime battle evacuees and night terrors are commonly experienced by children aged 10–14. Likewise, those who are depressed by day have dreams by night that contain themes of failure and loss.

Environmental circumstances influence dream content. Dreams reported after awakenings by investigators in the home have more aggressive, friendly, sexual, or success-and-failure elements than those reported in the laboratory; but in both cases most are duller than would be supposed. Anxiety-provoking films seen prior to sleep can lead to dreams containing related themes. Events occurring around the sleeper during dreams are often incorporated, so that, for example, the words 'Robert, Robert, Robert' spoken to a sleeper led to his reporting a dream about a 'distorted rabbit'.

Dream reports from successive periods of REM

sleep in a single night can be distinguished from those of other nights, and the dreams of one individual are different from those of another: dreams thus reflect both day-to-day psychological variations and enduring individual traits. Sigmund Freud (see FREUD ON DREAMS), C. G. *Jung, and many others since, have sought hidden features of personality and understanding of an individual's emotional conflicts, through examination of, or *free association from, dreams described by day. Whatever the clinical value of such dream recollections, they hardly compare with the rich reports that can be elicited by awakenings at night. Despite the symbolism and fascinating condensation of ideas to be found in dreams, there is no evidence that a more useful understanding of personality can be gained from them than can be divined from the realities of waking behaviour.                    I. O.

Dement, W. and Kleitman, N. (1957). The relation of eye movements during sleep to dream activity, an objective method for the study of dreaming. *Journal of Experimental Psychology*, **53**, 339–46.

Foulkes, D. (1966). *The Psychology of Sleep*. New York.

Hall, C. S. (1953). *The Meaning of Dreams*. New York.

Kramer, M. (ed.) (1969). *Dream Psychology and the New Biology of Dreaming*. Springfield, Illinois.

MacKenzie, N. (1965). *Dreams and Dreaming*. London.

**DREAMS IN ANCIENT GREECE.** Belief in the dream as a revelation was widespread in the ancient Near East, and is present in our earliest Greek documents, the poems of Homer. Dreams may contain prophecy or binding instructions, because they come 'from Zeus'; but they are a mixed blessing, because they may be sent to deceive. Later authors distinguish between significant and non-significant dreams; a dream that simply reflects the anxieties or desires felt by the dreamer during the previous day is non-prophetic. This distinction does not imply a weakening of belief; anthropologists report that no society treats all dreams as significant, and evidence of the most diverse kinds shows that some dreams were widely regarded as god-sent or otherwise revelatory up to and beyond the end of the pagan Greek world. Of classical authors, the dream is noticeably absent only from Thucydides. *Plato describes *Socrates as composing poetry in obedience to a dream while in prison awaiting execution; the practical Xenophon twice records significant dreams of his own in the *Anabasis*; and the politician Demosthenes could claim to have received messages from the gods in sleep. Incubation, the practice of seeking significant dreams by sleeping in a sacred area, was a widespread oracular technique, and the incubation healing cult of Asclepius at Epidaurus became a centre of pilgrimage from all Greece. Dream interpreters are already mentioned in Homer, and from the fifth century BC there grew up an extensive literature on dream interpretation; this is represented for us by Artemidorus (second century AD), whose approach is, given his premises, cautious and practical, and shows that specialists in this sphere were not necessarily wild,

marginal figures. It should be noted that Greek dream interpretation, though it operated with symbols, was prophetic in aim, and thus has little in common with the system of Sigmund Freud (see FREUD ON DREAMS). Any dream that could be explained by the experiences or desires of the dreamer was dismissed as insignificant; many dreams, however, that would now be seen as psychologically revealing were regarded as externally motivated and therefore prophetic. For instance, the frequently reported dreams of incest (many men have dreamt of sleeping with their mothers, says Sophocles) were generally interpreted symbolically as auspicious, and Plato (*Republic*, 571–2) is unusual in censuring them as wish-fulfilment. Only a few passing remarks by Artemidorus on symbolic wish-fulfilment (*Onirocritica*, preface to Book 4) and the role of puns in dreaming suggest modern ideas.

Scientific theories of the dream were strongly influenced by these traditional beliefs in its veridical nature. For Democritus (fifth century BC), images emanating from distant persons and objects, somewhat distorted in transmission, impinge on the sleeper: images of people reflect their thought as well as their external shape. Aristotle in his early works spoke of the soul exercising special clairvoyant powers, in accord with its divine nature, when freed from the body's constraint in sleep. Later, much more sceptically, he denied the divine origin of dreams (the gods would not care to communicate with the animals, or lower classes) and suggested that veridical dreams, if they really occurred, should be explained by a modified version of Democritus's theory. Of later philosophical schools, the *Epicureans went still further in scepticism, but others much less far. Traditional belief in dreams of good and evil omen reappears, under a rather thin scientific disguise, in an anonymous medical treatise, perhaps of the fourth century. This distinguishes from 'divine' and wish-fulfilment dreams a third category, in which the soul, being 'master of its own house' in sleep, indicates symbolically the condition of the body, thus providing a valuable aid to medical diagnosis.

Though numerous Greek dreams, real and literary, are recorded, comparatively few strike the modern mind as very dreamlike, presumably because reported dreams tend to fall into stylized, culturally determined types. In one typical dream, familiar also from the Old Testament, a god, parent, or figure of authority stands over the dreamer's head and issues prophecy or instructions; when the god is Asclepius in an incubation dream, he performs an act of healing that on waking proves to have been effective. The fullest account of an individual's dreams is post-classical, the 'sacred discourses' in which the hypochondriac orator Aelius Aristides (second century AD) describes Asclepius's revelations to himself, and his own extraordinary obedience to the god's commands.                    R. C. T. P.

Aristotle, *On Dreams*, and *On Divination in Sleep*. In Ross, W. D. (ed.) (1931), *The Works of Aristotle translated into English*, vol. iii. Oxford.

Artemidorus, *The Interpretation of Dreams* (trans. R. J. White, 1975). New Jersey.

Behr, C. A. (1968). *Aelius Aristides and the Sacred Tales*. Amsterdam.

Dodds, E. R. (1951). *The Greeks and the Irrational*. Berkeley, California.

Dodds, E. R. (1965). *Pagan and Christian in an Age of Anxiety*. Cambridge.

Hippocrates, *On Dreams*. In Lloyd, G. E. R. (ed.) (1978), *Hippocratic Writings*. Harmondsworth.

Price, S. R. F. (forthcoming). The Future of Dreams: from Freud to Artemidorus. In *Past and Present*.

**DRUG.** The word 'drug', when used in ordinary conversation, often denotes a substance whose use is forbidden by law and which, if ingested, will cause the most serious consequences, both legal and medical, for the user. Alcohol and nicotine, which are as much drugs as are opiates, amphetamines, and cannabis, are often overlooked in this context, largely because both are legally permitted and widely used (see ADDICTION).

In more general terms a drug is any chemical agent that affects living processes. Pharmacology is the branch of science that studies these effects, particularly in the field of medicine. The development of clinical pharmacology, as a special area within the field of pharmacology, indicates the strong interest which is and always has been taken by doctors in the drugs they use. Until relatively recent times very little was known about the pharmacological effects of drugs and even less about their detoxification and excretion and distribution within the body. Although pharmacopoeias contained long lists of substances, most of these were of unproven efficacy. Many were presented in combination with other medicaments, usually in a liquid form—the 'bottle of medicine' without which a consultation with one's medical adviser was considered to be incomplete. Today most of the older drugs and mixtures have been superseded and replaced by powerful agents of known chemical composition designed to have specific effects on bodily organs and systems. Unfortunately, with the rise of modern pharmacology and pharmacy, has come a new science—the study of the so-called side-effects, or unwanted effects, or even unexpected effects, of many drugs used today. These iatrogenic disorders vary from the mildly inconvenient to the positively dangerous, and in some cases fatal. The greater the number of compounds that are prescribed, the greater will be the risk of adverse consequences. This is especially the case with older patients who, because of age, are likely to be suffering from more than one disorder, each of which requires treatment. Furthermore, the aged are less efficient at detoxifying and eliminating drugs, so that doses which may seem appropriate for younger patients will be greatly in excess of those required for patients approaching the *senium*.

Some orthodox and legal drugs may cause drug-dependence (addiction). In this respect one should mention pain-relieving drugs, sedatives, and preparations given to treat insomnia. Interestingly, opiates given for the relief of post-operative pain and of chronic pain in cancer patients do not usually cause dependence, a condition which more often occurs in younger persons. The study of drug dependence and its causes has become a major branch of pharmacology and psychology; but so far, it must be admitted, the amount of time and effort devoted to the subject have not been notably effective in controlling this psychosocial problem.

See also PSYCHOPHARMACOLOGY; and for the action of specific drugs on the brain, NEURO-PEPTIDES; SCHIZOPHRENIA: EVIDENCE FOR AN ORGANIC CAUSE. F. A. W.

**DUALISM.** The philosophical theory that supposes that mind is essentially independent of the brain, though mental events run parallel with physical brain events. This leads to several suggested (usually causal) relations: (i) Mental and brain events run in parallel without causal interaction (epiphenomenalism). (ii) The brain 'secretes' mental events, rather as glands secrete substances. (iii) Brain and behaviour are controlled by an essentially autonomous mind. (iv) The mind is an *emergent property of brain processes, rather as the properties of water emerge from the combined atoms of oxygen and hydrogen, which in isolation have very different properties. (v) Mind and brain are essentially separate but have some mutual interaction (interactive dualism). This last was the view of *Descartes. (vi) Mind is like 'software' of the brain ('hardware').

An account of the mind–brain relation which is not dualistic is the identity theory, of which there are various versions. These suppose that what we take to be mind and brain are different aspects of the same thing. See also MIND AND BODY; MIND–BODY PROBLEM: PHILOSOPHICAL THEORIES.

**DU BOIS-REYMOND,** EMIL HEINRICH (1818–96), German physiologist, the son of a Swiss father and Huguenot mother, was born and lived in Berlin. He was assistant to Johannes *Müller, and succeeded to his chair as professor of physiology at the University of Berlin in 1858, becoming head of the new institute of physiology there in 1877.

His work was of fundamental importance. It began with the investigation of electrical discharge in certain fishes; his discoveries related especially to electrical activity and chemical changes in the nerves and muscles generally. In 1845 he discovered the existence of a resting current in nerve. The value of this work was recognized early, and in 1851 he was elected to the Berlin Academy of Sciences. Later, in 1877, he suggested that nerve impulses might be transmitted chemically. His major published work was *Untersuchungen über thierische Elektricität* ('Researches on animal electricity', 2 vols., 1848 and 1860). D. D. H.

**DUNCKER,** KARL (1903–40). German psychologist with strong affiliations to the *Gestalt school. He worked for several years in Berlin as an assistant to Wolfgang *Köhler but spent a year at Clark University in 1928–9. He then went back to Berlin, but returned to America in 1938 after a short interlude in the department of experimental psychology at Cambridge. He committed suicide in America in 1940.

Duncker reported an important study on induced motion, in part translated by W. D. Ellis (*A Source Book of Gestalt Psychology*, 1938, pp. 161–73). But his best-known work was a monograph on the psychology of productive thinking (German, 1935; English translation: 1945).          O. L. Z.

**DUNNE,** JOHN WILLIAM (1875–1949). British inventor, and philosopher of time. He designed the first aerodynamically stable aeroplane (1906–7), but he is best known for his philosophical-psychological books *An Experiment with Time* (1927) and *The Serial Universe* (1934). These inspired many people to record their dreams, looking for dream-predictions, the notion being that time is an unfolding of pre-ordained events. Dunne's views are not now taken seriously, and there seems no substantive evidence for predictive dreaming.

**DYSLEXIA.** The term 'specific developmental dyslexia' is frequently used in neurological, psychological, and educational literature to describe a severe disability which reveals itself initially in difficulty in learning to read, and subsequently by erratic spelling and deficits which affect written as opposed to spoken language. The diagnosis of this condition in children has led to much controversy, and views range from neurologists who postulate a 'developmental dyslexia' said to be the consequence of a neurological delay in development which is of constitutional origin, to psychologists who doubt whether such a syndrome, with a specific underlying cause and specific symptoms, has been identified. Workers in the latter group acknowledge that it is possible to distinguish the minority of children with severe reading difficulty (and often spelling, writing, and number problems) who fulfil some of the criteria of dyslexia, but they prefer to place these pupils on a continuum spanning the whole range of reading skills from the most fluent to those with the most severe difficulties.

Let us, firstly, look at some general descriptions of this condition that would attract fairly wide agreement from medical and psychological specialists working with atypical children. It appears to be a cognitive disorder, possibly genetically determined, which concerns a linguistic coding disability. The condition is not due to intellectual inadequacy as such and is not open to explanation in terms of a lack of socio-cultural opportunity or inadequate teaching techniques. Secondary (reactive) emotional problems are frequently identified but the condition is not thought to be an outcome of a primary emotional resistance to learning. It is not due to any known structural brain defect and is possibly a specific maturational delay which will, in many instances, show positive responses to remedial help, especially if this is provided at a relatively early stage.

The term 'alexia' (word blindness) was initially used (and is still employed) by neurologists to describe very severe reading difficulties after a localized injury to the brain of an adult who was previously a competent reader. Towards the end of the nineteenth century, cases of children who seemed to have a similar disorder, although not caused by injury, were reported by physicians, and a number of papers were published in the *Lancet* and the *British Medical Journal* (for a summary of these articles see Hinshelwood, 1917). It was postulated that such children had a congenital disorder associated with a defect in the speech area of the left cerebral hemisphere which made learning to read extremely difficult, if not impossible. This was said to be a *specific disability* and as such could be distinguished from *mental deficiency*. Since this early work there have been numerous studies of children with severe reading difficulties, and the term 'specific developmental dyslexia' has been applied by some neurologists and a few psychologists to children who show at least some of the following difficulties within either one or both of the broad types of dyslexia outlined below.

The first type concerns children with what seems to be a form of language disorder. These pupils have a history of delayed receptive and expressive oral language acquisition and some may still have speech disorders. Although most will have overcome speech difficulties, they may have poor auditory discrimination (in the absence of any hearing loss) and find it hard to blend phonemes to form words. Such children have been found to score as many as 20 points fewer on verbal as compared with non-verbal intelligence tests.

Pupils in the second broad group have problems of visual *perception and *memory. Usually they can perceive simple material correctly but are deficient when asked to differentiate the parts of complex figures. Typically they reverse letters ('b' and 'd') and words ('was' and 'saw') when reading and writing. Cases of complete mirror writing have been reported. There seems to be a problem of directional confusion. Children in this group sometimes show a lack of firm unilateral cerebral dominance and are neither strongly right- nor strongly left-handed. It is not easy to estimate cerebral dominance, but a battery of tests could show some children to display crossed laterality, for example to be left-handed and left-footed but right-eyed.

In a number of cases pupils show problems associated with both types of specific developmental dyslexia, and although simple auditory and visual perception is only mildly affected, if at all, they do have clear difficulties when attempting to associate spatially ordered visual patterns (letters which combine to form words which, in turn, form sentences, etc.) and temporally ordered auditory patterns (the sound pattern of phonemes and spoken words). It could be said that the association between printed and spoken words is never completely regular and uinform in the English language, but visual/auditory association difficulties in pupils said to be suffering from specific developmental dyslexia are reported in countries (such as Italy) where spelling and letter-sounding *are* completely regular.

It may be asked how we are to distinguish dyslexia from other reading difficulties. It must be stressed that some eminent educationists refuse to accept that it is possible to differentiate this condition as an identifiable syndrome from other forms of reading backwardness (Morris, 1966). Other eminent workers recognize the condition but consider it difficult to draw any clear line of demarcation between constitutional dyslexia and reading difficulties due to environmental circumstances (Vernon, 1971). As the volume of research in this field has increased, the number of 'symptoms' has grown accordingly, and fourteen areas of deficit are indexed by Wheeler and Watkins (1979). Given this situation, it will be appreciated that no widely accepted estimate of the frequency of the condition has ever been achieved. Estimates as high as 10 per cent have come from the USA. Estimates in Britain have varied from 3 to 10 per cent. A wide age-range in the school population has been studied, and the symptoms said to indicate this condition have been shown to vary with age. One example will suffice to illustrate the problems encountered when an estimate of prevalence is attempted. Approximately 0·5 per cent of 11-year-old ordinary school pupils in Britain are reported to be illiterate, but not all these pupils are dyslexic. Further, it will be appreciated that not all dyslexic children are illiterate by the time they reach 11 years of age.

However, there have been recent advances in methods of assessment, and these include a comprehensive screening procedure which uses tests open to the class teacher (see Thomson, 1979). These measures provide a framework for teacher observation and cover a wide range of visual and auditory–vocal skills. Implicit in the employment of this technique is the assumption that the teacher will refer children who appear to have specific difficulties for a full investigation by an educational psychologist. It will be appreciated that there is much to be gained from the use of such screening measures by teachers, because their own knowledge and experience will be extended and they will be in a better position to advise parents of pupils with specific reading (and allied) difficulties.

It must be stressed that there is much that parents can do, particularly when they can obtain sound and sensitive advice. They must learn how to be patient and persevering, both in their pursuit of knowledge about the practical manifestations of the condition, and in their day-to-day contribution to their child's attempts to overcome what is seen to be, in conventional terms, 'educational failure'. It is essential that parents do not add to their child's anxiety. Direct and more formal attempts to help the pupil overcome specific difficulties are almost certainly best left to the specialist teacher. On the other hand, there are many relatively unobtrusive ways in which parents can help—always in close consultation with school staff. For example, they can use a structured oral language approach in visual/auditory–vocal games which, as well as being 'fun', are carefully devised to help at a precise level. The parents should be prepared to read to their child when, in the normal way of things, he would be able to read for himself. At a later stage, set books for examinations could be put on tape.

Co-operation of parents and teachers with an educational psychologist can be valuable. Sometimes the psychologist can help when a pupil's difficulties are such that special examination conditions are justified. For example, some dyslectics can be shown to be of good innate intelligence but to have abnormally slow reading speed—this being a specific difficulty arising from their reduced ability to synthesize polysyllabic words—thus losing free-flowing comprehension of passages. The present writer has intervened on behalf of several such students taking public examinations, and examining boards have allowed the candidates additional time for a paper. Thus what was an unfairly punitive *speed* test for an otherwise able student with a dyslexic history became a realistic *power* test, with speed playing a much reduced role.

Finally, reference is due to the assessment and teaching facilities established in Britain by the Dyslexia Institute, because these are making a valuable contribution towards our further understanding of this complex condition. The Institute itself is a useful resource centre for readers who wish to pursue this topic.

See also LANGUAGE AREAS IN THE BRAIN; LANGUAGE: NEUROPSYCHOLOGY. L. A. I.

Critchley, M. (1964). *Developmental Dyslexia*. London.

Critchley, M. and E. (1978). *Dyslexia Defined*. London.

Hinshelwood, J. (1917). *Congenital Word Blindness*. London.

Morris, J. M. (1966). *Standards and Progress in Reading*. London.

Thomson, M. E. (1979). Classroom screening: the Aston Index. *Dyslexia Review*, **2**, 2.

Vernon, M. D. (1957). *Backwardness in Reading: a study of its nature and origin*. Cambridge.

Vernon, M. D. (1971). *Reading and its Difficulties*. Cambridge.

Wheeler, T. J. and Watkins, E. J. (1979). Dyslexia: a review of symptomatology. *Dyslexia Review*, **2**, 1.

**DYSPHASIA.** See APHASIA.

# E

**EBBINGHAUS,** HERMANN (1850–1909). German experimental psychologist, born at Barmen, near Bonn, and educated at the University of Bonn. He obtained his doctorate in 1873 but thereafter worked for a number of years on his own. After a brief sojourn in Berlin, he travelled in France and England for three years, in the course of which he unearthed in a second-hand bookstall a copy of G. T. *Fechner's *Elemente der Psychophysik*, which evidently impressed him deeply and gave him the idea of applying Fechner's quantitative methods to the study of the higher mental processes.

Ebbinghaus thereupon embarked on a prolonged series of experiments designed to formulate the fundamental laws of human memory. As his experimental material, he laid great store on nonsense syllables in the belief that only by ridding his stimuli of conventional meaning could he treat them as constant and interchangeable units. Somewhat as Fechner had treated just noticeable differences in sensation as equivalent units of sensation, he carried out numerous, and—for the time—surprisingly well-controlled, experiments to establish learning curves under a variety of conditions. He hoped that this work would not only lead to advances in our understanding of the nature of learning and forgetting but also be of practical value in the field of education. His results were embodied in *Über das Gedächtniss* (1885), much of which was replicated and in certain respects amplified by, among others, G. E. Müller of Göttingen; and it was introduced to English psychologists by C. S. *Myers (1909). See REMEMBERING.

In more recent years, Ebbinghaus's methods have come under considerable criticism on the grounds that he was concerned with the acquisition of verbal repetition habits rather than with memory as it operates under the conditions of everyday life. In particular, the artificiality of nonsense syllables has been repeatedly stressed. F. C. *Bartlett, for instance, pointed out long ago that it is impossible to rid stimuli of meaning so long as they remain capable of eliciting any human response. He further insisted that the Ebbinghaus methods totally ignore those important conditions of recall which relate to pre-existing attitudes and response tendencies. None the less, the work of Ebbinghaus did much to convince the sceptical that quantitative methods were applicable to the higher mental processes.          O. L. Z.

Ebbinghaus, H. *The Intelligence of School Children* (1897); *Über das Gedächtniss* (1885; translated as *Memory*, 1913); *Textbook of Experimental Psychology*, vol. 1 (1902), vol. 2 (1908).
Myers, C. S. (1909). *Textbook of Experimental Psychology*. Reissued 1980, Wokingham.

**ECT** (electroconvulsive therapy). Applying a voltage, with surface electrodes on the head, across the brain. This is done under anaesthesia or muscle-relaxant, as it produces convulsions which can be dangerous. ECT is extensively used as a convenient and quick treatment for depression, though there is no theoretical basis to justify it. There is considerable criticism of its extensive use because it may produce permanent brain damage, especially losses of memory and intelligence, though the evidence is not entirely clear.

**ECTOMORPHY.** See BODY BUILD AND PERSONALITY.

**EDUCATION: THEORY AND PRACTICE.** The true nature of education, its goals, proper methods, and effects have long been a matter of argument; certainly since the time of *Plato (fourth century BC, see *Republic, passim*) and probably before, education has been a matter of concern, not only to the individual child who is to be educated, and to his parents, but to the whole society responsible for its provision. Though people sometimes urge that politics should be kept out of education (and they are right to hope that the extremes of party dogma may be avoided), the fact is that education is necessarily a political issue. For one thing, education itself is an expression of values, moral and political as well as academic. Moreover, what subjects children are taught, how and where they are taught, how many of them are taught and for how long, whether all are equally provided with education—all these questions are of interest to the whole of society, and the answers to them will determine the character of that society. No wonder, then, that politicians interest themselves in education, and if they are wise they will try to formulate a coherent theory, to justify the provision they decide to make.

In the eighteenth century the philosopher *Rousseau (1712–78) thought of education as child-centred. In *Emile* he propounded the theory that a child would flourish if allowed to grow freely in his own way and his own time, not forced or stunted by too much teaching. He was not concerned with who should be educated, but only with how a child, any child, should or should not be taught. He thought of education in the 'true' sense as a natural process, and therefore believed that all children, regardless of class or status, could benefit from it. His back-to-nature philosophy has had a considerable effect on later theories, if in nothing else then in the proliferation of all kinds of horticultural metaphors, according to which children, like plants, will flourish in the right soil, but may wilt or wither if either forced or neglected. In the early twentieth century this Rousseauesque philosophy was taken up and adapted by John *Dewey (1859–1952), who held that to educate a child was to provide him with experiences, out of which his thoughts and interpretations would flow; experience, and especially shared experience, was infinitely more educative than books. This anti-intellectual kind of educational theory had considerable effects in the development of British education in the 1960s.

However, at the time when Rousseau wrote, education was narrowly spread. It was a luxury to which by no means everyone could aspire. Though there had long existed charity schools and the provision for poor scholars, the beneficiaries were comparatively few. In the nineteenth century education came to seem more and more desirable, and therefore the question to be faced was not what education was, or what its best form was, but rather who should have it. The Utilitarians in particular valued education extremely highly, for they believed that people could, all of them, be taught to take pleasure in the right things, that is in things which would spread social advantages widely in society, and would in general raise the standards of life, both morally and materially. A man of education, John Stuart *Mill (1806–73) thought, would never wish to return to the enjoyment of the pleasures of the uneducated. Once introduce a child to the infinite resources of reading and learning, and his taste, his sensibility, and his understanding of true political goals would all inevitably be elevated. He needs must pursue the higher. This being so, Mill thought that it did not so very much matter what was taught, provided that education of some kind was universally available. Therefore in On Liberty (1859) he argued that the state should require all children to be educated, at least so that they could read, write, and calculate, but should not itself provide that education. If it were illegal to allow a child to go uneducated, demand would produce schools which could be inspected for efficiency by government servants, and the pupils of which could be publicly examined. Government could also subsidize those too poor to pay the fees. In this way he thought universal literacy at least would be ensured, while freedom to conduct educational experiments would also be preserved.

Mill's arguments were not accepted. But the goal of universal education gained ground, along with the conviction that the state must make provision for those whom it insisted should be educated. And at last, in the Education Act of 1944, all children in the United Kingdom became entitled to primary education, and to secondary education on up to the age of 15: such education as was, in the words of the Act, suited to their aptitude and ability. Only those children deemed to be too severely mentally handicapped to be able to benefit from education were excluded. Education was thus conceived as a right for everyone, but it was acknowledged that some kinds of education were better than others, not only in duration but in actual content. Success in life, in salaries, and the exercise of power all followed upon good education. What democracy demanded was that all children should have, not the same education, but the same chance of the best. So, in an admittedly competitive field, competition at the age of 11 for entry to the best schools, from which a child could proceed to university, was thought to be just, and also to be the best way of distributing an amenity which, by a marvellous natural harmony, was seen to be in short supply but also something from which only some members of the population would benefit.

But two things went wrong. First, the eleven-plus selection became suspect. It selected too many of the middle classes. Secondly, it became clear that the mere chance to enter the lists for selection was not sufficient. Those children who were not selected for the best education at 11 had virtually no further chances, and it began to be thought that one chance was not enough. And so gradually, during the 1950s and 1960s, it began to seem that what was wanted was not equality of opportunity to be educated, but something more like equality of education for all. Even the universities were not exempt from the demand that they should open their doors to literally everybody. (Financial considerations and a certain realism, however, prevailed.) But at school things were different. The comprehensive school, which had started as a convenient and often excellent way of educating a large number of children of very different abilities under one roof, began to be identified with a demand that all children should be given the very same education, so that neither their social nor their intellectual differences would distinguish one from another. During the 1960s, educational theory was predominantly concerned with such issues as these. The comparative affluence of the country, which allowed the establishment of new universities, also made it seem feasible to take the competitiveness out of education. Especially in the primary schools, the voice of Rousseau spoke again. Children must not be taught; they must discover things for themselves at their own pace. So an innate love of learning would find expression, and the old authoritarian style of education, which insisted that children be marked, graded, put in order of merit so that the best could get to the top, would finally disappear off the face of the earth. This was the kind of ideal incorporated in the Plowden Report (Children and their Primary Schools, HMSO, 1967). But it spread into the sphere of secondary education as well. In particular, it was linked with a Marxist view of the role of teachers (that the very concept of 'teaching' entailed the domination of one class over another, the perpetuation of a bourgeois value system, embodied in an insistence, for example, on reading, when books were predominantly middle-class productions). The very word 'teach' became suspect in the 1960s and early 1970s, and educational theory itself was difficult to separate from Marxist-dominated sociology.

However, while these influences were certainly important, in that they had a considerable effect on young teachers, and therefore on the actual educational provision within the comprehensive system, there was another element in educational theory which persisted from the 1950s onwards, and this was what may be called the Anglo-Saxon philosophical school. The theories of education that may be called, loosely, Marxist naturally linked theory with practice; and equally naturally were quite overtly political in their aims. Education is and ought to be a part of the armoury of the class-war. The philosophers, on the other hand, believed (I think wrongly) that education could be treated as a 'pure' subject; that it need have no connection with politics, and that, in so far as educational theory led to a change in practice, this would be practice based on totally rational considerations, concerned with the nature of knowledge and thus with the process of passing on knowledge from one person to another.

P. H. Phenix in America, and P. H. Hirst and R. S. Peters in the United Kingdom, were the most influential philosophers of education in the 1960s. They believed that there is a finite number of forms or kinds of knowledge, separable from each other by a process of logical analysis, and that no human being could be a full 'person' without some acquaintance with all these forms of knowledge. A school curriculum, therefore, must be so constructed that all of the forms have their place. Sometimes the august name of *Wittgenstein (1889–1951) was invoked in favour of this kind of theory, with the suggestion that each form of knowledge was naturally incorporated in its own 'language' or 'language-game'; and this was sometimes taken to prove that if the forms of knowledge were confused with each other, the result would be nonsense (but it can never have been taken to show that everyone ought to be able to speak in each of the different languages). This stipulation was, and must always have been, an independent judgement of value. The list of the forms of knowledge was intended to provide a value-free schema, arrived at a priori, within which education could be organized. The difficulty was that there exists no Platonic world of forms of knowledge. The list of forms, mathematical, historical, moral, literary, artistic, and so on, looked suspiciously like something derived from the timetable of an old-fashioned grammar school. And some of the items on the list could only very dubiously be counted as knowledge at all. Is it really the case that the moral education of children,

for example, consists in teaching them to know certain things? And how about religion? The difficulties were manifold; and the practical effect of such philosophical theories was not as great as the proponents hoped, for the very good reason that it is quite impossible, by the analysis of the concept of education, to derive any satisfactory or agreed guide to action.

Nevertheless the influence of this kind of exercise was not absolutely negligible. Especially in the contentious sphere of moral education, held, ever since the days of J. S. Mill, to be one of the most important aspects of education, and even to constitute a justification for increasing the spread of education among people in general, the analytic approach has had some consequences, in the kind of curricular material thought appropriate for school. It has been widely argued that, particularly in a multicultural society, it is impossible, and in any case undesirable, to lay down any actual moral principles for children to adopt. What must be done is to teach children to conduct moral arguments, so that they will be able both to determine what is and what is not a moral matter, and to make their own decisions rationally. Thus the analytic value-free educational philosophy at this point coincided with the anti-authoritarian theory of the neo-Marxists, and the result has been a considerable increase in some relativism among teachers. Nothing must be declared right or wrong; children must construct their own values, and are entitled to value anything high or low, provided they can argue on a rational basis to defend their evaluation.

Roughly, then, these two types of theory, the one overtly political and at first concerned with the distribution of education, the other supposedly value-free and concerned with curriculum content, dominated the field of educational theory and consequential practice until the late 1970s. Then a change came about. The affluent 1960s had passed; the financial climate was threatening; unemployment was beginning to be alarming. The days of student revolt, of permissiveness, of the excesses of the youth cult seemed to be over. Employers in industry were beginning to complain that young people coming out of school were ill-prepared for employment. Parents were becoming increasingly disenchanted with some of the educational theories of young teachers. In 1977, the Prime Minister, James Callaghan, instituted what was known as 'the Great Debate'. Everyone was encouraged to think about the proper goals and purposes of education, what should be taught, and in what state of preparedness for life children should leave school. A reform of the school curriculum, as well as of the public examination system which dominated the curriculum in most schools, began to be universally expected.

It had been clear for a long time that, despite the greater spread of education since the beginning of the century, in many ways the structure of the school curriculum had remained remarkably unchanged. Some schools, it is true, had invented interdisciplinary subjects to replace the old subjects of 'geography' or 'history'. But as long as universities demanded competence in classical languages, or even the ability to translate modern foreign languages though not to speak them, the old standards, according to which knowing Latin and Greek brought the highest prizes, were not wholly overthrown. Even when the universities relaxed their demands, the old domination of the classics remained to bedevil the teaching of modern languages, taught traditionally as if they were a kind of dialect of Latin; and the notion that a child must choose between language-learning and science, that if he was doing well with languages he could drop mathematics as early as possible . . . all these factors remained unchanged, and were ossified in the examination system and hence in the school timetable. Moreover, the children who did not take, or did not succeed in passing, public examinations had very little that was structurally different in their curriculum. A school devoted to the egalitarian ideal of the 1960s could not discriminate too blatantly between curricula of different children.

Meanwhile in the early 1970s another quiet reform had come about which had a significant effect. It was then that those very severely mentally retarded children, hitherto deemed ineducable, and therefore left as the responsibility of the health services, were brought under the educational umbrella. At last it became the duty of local authorities to provide education for all children without exception. It was inevitable that the notion of education itself should be re-examined now that it was supposed to be available for children of such totally different capabilities. The fact that these newly educable children had to have a curriculum, with curricular aims which could be achieved slowly and step by step, cast fresh light on the practical nature of teaching itself. Successful education depends on teachers who know what they are doing and what they are doing it *for*.

In the context, then, of economic recession and the widening scope of education, together with the general assumption of the 1970s and 1980s that government should be open, and provision or lack of it publicly justified, a new way of looking at education as a whole can gradually be seen to emerge. It is a mixture of pragmatism and idealism. All children are now legally entitled to education, not merely so that they may get better jobs (for some of them may get no jobs at all) but so that their lives may be of a decent quality. The old utilitarian belief in education is perhaps returning, but in a different form. Education is seen to have certain quite general goals, to increase the understanding, the independence, and the pleasure of the child who receives it; and if these aims are not to be frustrated, then as many obstacles to education as possible must be removed from the path of the child. The dominant question has become 'What does this child *need*, if he is to get from his education what he is entitled to?'

Of course, part of what a child needs is a sensible, useful, enjoyable curriculum. But the question of needs goes further. For a curriculum is futile, however well devised, if the particular child has no access to it, either because he cannot understand what he is being taught, or because the environment of the school where he is taught it is inimical to learning. Thus one of a child's essential educational needs is a good school, in the simple sense of a school where learning is possible. It has been increasingly recognized in the last few years that what has been called the 'hidden curriculum' is as important as the curriculum itself—the system of values, that is, which the school by its very existence as an institution hands on to its pupils.

Once the philosophy of educational needs is accepted, the criteria by which education is judged to be good or bad become immediately extremely wide and varied. It is no longer adequate either to raise the simple political question 'Is education justly distributed?' or the supposedly more philosophical question 'Is the curriculum appropriate to the common epistemological framework?' On the contrary, the first question must be 'Does this kind of education *work*? Is this child or that child actually learning anything?', and then the second question is the value-laden one: 'If he is learning something, what do we hope will come of it—exactly how will he benefit?' Increasingly, schools, and teachers themselves, are taking responsibility for answering these questions, with the more and more active co-operation of parents. There has never, perhaps, been any time when theory and practice have been so closely interrelated. The philosophy and the action can hardly any longer be separated.                                     M. W.

Frankens, W. (1965). *Three Historical Philosophies of Education*. Glenview, Illinois.
Hartnell, A. and Naish, M. (eds.) (1976). *Theory and the Practice of Education*. 2 vols., London.
Peters, R. S. (ed.) (1967). *The Concept of Education*. London.
Rutter, M. et al. (1979). *15,000 Hours*. London.
Young, M. (ed.) (1971). *Knowledge and Control*. Milton Keynes.

**EEG.** See ELECTROENCEPHALOGRAPHY.

**EFFERENT.** Pertaining to the motor nerves innervating the muscles. Efferent neural signals produce muscle contraction. (Afferent neural signals provide the brain with signals from the senses.)

**'EFFORT AFTER MEANING'.** See BARTLETT, F. C.

**EGO AND SUPER-EGO.** Sigmund *Freud supposed that three components make up the psychic structure: the id, the ego, and the super-ego. The id represents instincts and innate needs. The super-ego, manifest in conscience, shame, and guilt, is the agency by which the influence of parents and others is prolonged. Their judgements and prohibitions are internalized by the process of introjection in early childhood before the child is able to question them. The ego has been differentiated from the id through the influence of the external world, to whose demands it adapts. In so adapting it has to reconcile the forces of the id and super-ego in such a way as to maximize pleasure and minimize unpleasure. The development of ego-psychology as a branch of psychoanalysis, which reflected a shift of interest from the earlier instinct theory to the adaptive functions of the ego, in relation to other persons especially, facilitated some rapprochement between psychoanalysis and psychology.

See FREUD ON MENTAL STRUCTURE; FREUDIANISM: LATER DEVELOPMENTS.                            D. R. D.

Freud, A. (1937). *The Ego and the Mechanisms of Defence*. London.
Hartmann, H. (1964). *Essays on Ego Psychology*. London.

**EGO PSYCHOLOGY.** See FREUDIANISM: LATER DEVELOPMENTS.

**EGYPTIAN CONCEPTS OF MIND.** Whereas the people of other ancient civilizations believed that they were created by gods from matter, the Ancient Egyptians saw themselves as created directly out of nothing by the god who created the universe. They saw themselves as a divine nation, and their king as a god, though with a mortal body. They were uniquely religious. They had far more gods than any other country or civilization, their many gods reflecting their extremely animistic way of looking at nature—the heavens and everything on earth being seen as under the control of a great variety of often hostile beings. The most hostile spirits were often represented by dangerous animals: wolves, crocodiles, and venomous snakes, which overran Egypt in pre-dynastic times. The more powerful the threat, such as inundation of the Nile, the more powerful the responsible god; so the sun god was more powerful than the god of the moon. Many of the gods, however, were benevolent; or at least their goodwill might be sought by prayer or bought or bribed by gifts or offerings; or they might be made to help through the powers of magic and prayer. They might be persuaded to challenge the evil gods—so there were battles of good and evil in heaven, where the gods lived. Heaven was at first thought of as a rectangular ceiling, the earth (the land they knew) being this shape; later, it was thought of as the arched body of the goddess Nut, the stars being her jewels.

Many of the gods or spirits were occupied with carrying out the routine processes of nature, for everything in nature depended on the intentions of the gods; but as even these guardians, of what to us are natural laws, were open to suggestion or propitiation, magic was seen as immensely powerful. Perhaps this is why science was less developed in Egypt than in the contemporary Babylonia. Egyptian science lacked imagination and was essentially practical. From their experience of embalming the Ancient Egyptians had considerable knowledge of anatomy, and also of surgery and dentistry (their teeth were ground away by the sand in their food), but their knowledge of mathematics and physics was not sophisticated and their literature lacked incisive questioning or thoughtful discussion. Their knowledge and application of mechanical principles, for handling and carving stone and constructing vast buildings from blocks weighing several tons, is however uniquely impressive, and they did achieve much in the measurement of time, if again for practical purposes. For arithmetic, multiplication was done with a two-times table (much as with present-day *digital computers) and their geometry was simple and practical, without a system of proof. There were, nevertheless, a few enquiring minds: Imhotep, for example, wrote the mathematical treatise known now as the Rhind Papyrus (c.2600 BC); but even this lacks abstract notions or any concept of proof, which was the invention of the Greeks.

The gods of both Egypt and Babylonia were credited with speech, and with at least human intelligence, and human passions, and morality. The Egyptian judgement at death was not, however, entrusted either to gods or to men—but to a great mechanical balance on which the heart was weighed against the feather of truth. This balance in the hall of judgement was served by many gods, including the god of wisdom, learning, language, and number—the ibis-headed god Thoth (who was sometimes baboon-headed, baboons being seen as highly intelligent).

Egyptian hieroglyphic writing was fully developed by 3000 BC. It is a wonderful record of the use of pictures as formal symbols to represent meaning. Although pictures cannot at all directly convey opinions, beliefs, commands or requests, or logical or other relations, they were given such powers by referring to animal characteristics—such as the power and fecundity of the bull associated with the sun and controlling the Nile—and by representing human gestures. Thus 'not' was written as arms flung out, the hands later being left out, to become our negation sign '−'. It seems strange that, little or no attention has been paid by psycholinguists to ancient picture writings; for, surely, here lies invaluable 'fossil' evidence of the development of human communication and mind. (See, for example, CHINESE EVIDENCE FOR THE EVOLUTION OF LANGUAGE.)

The flowering of Egyptian literature occurred in the eighteenth dynasty (1570–1293 BC). In the writings of this period, especially in its second half, are to be found in many references to complex though not always consistent notions of mind, soul, personality, and their relations to the body. Throughout, there is a consistent and indeed dominating belief in eternal life. Man was believed to consist of several entities, each separate but each necessary for his welfare. These were the natural body, the spiritual body, the heart, the double, the soul, the shadow, the intangible casing of the body, the form, and the name.

The body as whole, the *khat*, is associated with things that decay. In early times the bodies of the dead were buried in the dry sand, beyond the agricultural land watered by the Nile, and they were preserved for thousands of years. But when the dead were placed in stone coffins, the flesh disappeared—supposedly eaten by the stone. Hence the Greek 'sarcophagus', meaning 'flesh-eating', which reflects the prehistoric notion of the body and soul of the dead entering and being preserved in stone.

For the Egyptians, the brain (being bloodless in death) was not important and was generally ignored; the heart was the power of life, and the source of good and evil. Thus, in their funerary literature, the *Book of the Dead*, the heart was weighed, against feathers, to determine the balance of good and evil at death. According to the Egyptologist Sir Wallace Budge (1895, in a most lucid account of this complicated psychology of gods and men, p. lxiii):

In close connection with the natural and spiritual bodies stood the heart, or rather that part of it which was the power of life and the fountain of good and evil thoughts. And in addition to the natural and spiritual bodies, man also had an abstract individuality or personality endowed with all his characteristic attributes. This abstract personality had an absolutely independent existence. It could move freely from place to place, separating itself from, or uniting itself to, the body at will, and also enjoying life with the gods in heaven. This was the *ka*, a word which conveys at times the meanings . . . image, genius, double, character, disposition, and mental attributes. The funeral offerings of meat, cakes, ale, wine, ungruents, etc., were intended for the *ka*; the scent of the burnt incense was grateful to it. The *ka* dwelt in the man's statue just as the *ka* of a god inhabited the statue of the god. In this respect the *ka* seems to be identical with the *sekhem* or image. In the remotest times the tombs had special chambers wherein the *ka* was worshipped and received offerings . . .

The *ka* . . . could eat food, and it was necessary to provide food for it. In the twelfth dynasty and in later periods the gods are entreated to grant meat and drink to the *ka* of the deceased; and it seems as if the Egyptians thought that the future welfare of the spiritual body depended upon the maintenance of a constant supply of sepulchral offerings. When circumstances rendered it impossible to continue the material supply of food, the *ka* fed upon the offerings painted on the walls of the tomb, which were transformed into suitable nourishment by means of the prayers of the living. When there were neither material offerings nor painted similitudes to feed upon, it seems as if the *ka* must have perished; but the texts are not definite on this point.

The *sekhem* was also thought of as the power, or vitality, of a man; but evidently it is very difficult to establish just what *sekhem* meant.

The Egyptians also accepted a more refined 'soul' named the *ba*. Again according to Wallace Budge (1895, p. lxiv):

To that part of man which beyond all doubt was believed to enjoy eternal existence in heaven in a state of glory, the Egyptians gave the name *ba*, a word which means something like 'sublime', 'noble', and which has always

hitherto been translated by 'soul'. The *ba* is not incorporeal, for although it dwells in the *ka*, and is in some respects, like the heart, the principle of life in man, still it possesses both substance and form: in form it is depicted as a human-headed hawk, and in nature it is stated to be exceedingly refined or ethereal. It revisited the body in the tomb and re-animated it, and conversed with it; it could take upon itself any shape it pleased; and it had the power of passing into heaven and of dwelling with the perfected soul there. It was eternal.

There is more: the shadow, or shade of a man—the *khaibit*—which may be compared with the *umbra* of the Romans. The *khaibit* is not so frequently mentioned as the *ka* and *ba*. Wallace Budge (1895, p. lxvi):

It (the *khaibit*) was supposed to have an entirely independent existence and to be able to separate itself from the body; it was free to move wherever it pleased, and, like the *ka* and *ba*, it partook of the funeral offerings in the tomb, which it visited at will . . . in later times at least the shadow was always associated with the soul and was believed to be always near it.

Little seems to be known, though, of the life of the shadow.

Now we come to human intelligence. The *khu* of a man could journey to heaven as soon as the prayers said over his dead body allowed it. Wallace Budge again (1895, p. lxvii):

Another and most important and apparently eternal part of man was the *khu*, which . . . may be defined as a 'shining' or translucent, intangible casing or covering of the body, which is frequenty depicted in the form of a mummy. For want of a better word *khu* has often been translated 'shining one', 'glorious', 'intelligence', and the like, but in certain cases it may be tolerably well rendered by 'spirit'.

Finally, there is the *ren* of a man—his name. This too had its own existence and could live in heaven among the gods.

The scholarship of Egyptologists tells us of past minds, and modes of thought and understanding. But clearly there are limits to modern understanding of what dead words such as '*ka*', '*ba*', and '*khaibit*' meant for there may be no anologies from our experience to read the past. Even now a word like 'soul'—or for that matter 'mind'—is exceedingly hard to define, and different writers may use it differently. Evidently the Egyptians saw *khaibit* as more than we see in the shadow of a man; for theirs could walk away and be its own self. Is it possible for scholarship to become so immersed in ancient ideas that such thoughts of long-lost minds can, through their dead language, enter our present understanding? Even though this is doubtful, the journeys of such scholarship are wonderfully rewarding.                              R. L. G.

Budge, E. A. Wallace (1895, reprinted 1967). *The Egyptian Book of the Dead: The Papyrus of Ani*. London.

Budge, E. A. Wallace (1891, reprinted 1971). *Egyptian Magic*. London.

Gardiner, A. (1957). *Egyptian Grammar: being an introduction to the study of heiroglyphs*, 3rd edn. Oxford.

Katan, N. J. (1985). *Hieroglyphs—The Writing of Ancient Egypt*. London.

Kramer, S. N. (1963). *The Sumerians: their history, culture, and character.* Chicago.

Simpson, W. K. (ed.) (1973). *The Literature of Ancient Egypt: an anthology of stories, instructions, and poetry.* New Haven, Connecticut.

**EHRENFELS,** CHRISTIAN VON (1859–1933). Austrian philosopher and psychologist, who was a student of Franz *Brentano in Vienna and is remembered as a precursor of *Gestalt psychology. His important paper *Über Gestalt Qualitäten* (On Gestalt Qualities) appeared in 1891. Although influenced to some extent by Mach's *Analysis of Sensations* (1896), this was an original and timely contribution to the psychology of *perception. Ehrenfels introduced the term 'Gestalt qualities' to denote the perception of form or melody which, though based on sensory stimulation, can in no sense be regarded as inherent in the pattern of stimulation. In his view, Gestalt qualities represent novel elements in the field of perception, and this is well brought out in the phenomena of transposition. For example, a form such as a square or circle is recognized as such even after changes in its size or colour. Similarly, a melody is recognized even when played in a different key. Indeed object-constancy, whether spatial or temporal, is perhaps the most basic property of a Gestalt quality.

Ehrenfels, and after him Alexius Meinong (1853–1920), elaborated the system further, pointing out for instance that a particular direction of change might be a potent source of Gestalt qualities, as when one observes a slowly spreading blush. Gestalt qualities may also combine with one another to produce superordinate Gestalt qualities, as commonly found in music. Although no precise theory was put forward to explain Gestalt qualities, Ehrenfels came very close to formulating the principle of isomorphism, which is usually attributed to Max *Wertheimer and Wolfgang *Köhler, and which played so important a role in the Gestalt theory.

The idea of Gestalt qualities was then little known outside Austria, but it seems to have inspired the English philosopher and psychologist George Frederick Stout to write his two-volume *Analytic Psychology* (1896).                    O. L. Z.

**EIDETIC IMAGERY.** See IMAGING.

**ELECTRA COMPLEX.** A son's hostility towards the parent of the same sex and sexual impulses towards the parent of the opposite sex make up the *Oedipus complex. Usually the same term is applied to the corresponding feelings of a girl; less often, but following C. G. *Jung, the term applied is the Electra complex. In the plays of ancient Greece, Electra, unmarried and still grieving for her father Agamemnon, who has been killed long before by her mother Clytemnestra and Clytemnestra's paramour, encourages her brother, Orestes, to kill them in retribution. Versions of Electra's story have been used by modern playwrights, notably T. S. Eliot, Jean Giraudoux, Eugene O'Neill, and Jean-Paul *Sartre.   D. R. D.

**ELECTROCONVULSIVE THERAPY.** See ECT.

**ELECTRODERMAL ACTIVITY.** The preferred general term for the electrical activity of the skin, replacing 'psychogalvanic reflex' (PGR) and 'galvanic skin response' (GSR). These earlier terms were confusing because although they referred to the phasic response patterns of electrodermal activity they were often used by implication to refer to longer-term changes (tonic activity). Furthermore, they did not distinguish 'endosomatic' responses (changes in skin potential) from 'exosomatic' responses (changes in the skin's resistance or conductance). The former are determined by measuring the potential difference between two electrodes, the one placed on the palm of the hand or sole of the foot and the other on an electrically indifferent site. In the case of exosomatic measurement, electrodes are normally placed on two active palmar sites, and the conductivity of the pathway between them is measured by passing a current through the pathway. If this current is less than 10 µA per square cm then the tissue of the skin obeys Ohm's Law and linear calculations of conductance can be employed. As the eccrine sweat-glands of the palms and the soles of the feet are the essential conducting pathways involved, and these can be viewed electrically as resistors in parallel, it is appropriate to use units of conductance rather than resistance in quantifying exosomatic tonic levels and phasic responses. (This is because resistances in parallel add as their reciprocal, and the reciprocal of resistance is conductance.)

The first work on electrodermal phenomena can be attributed to Vigouroux in 1879, but it is to Féré and to Tarchanoff that credit is usually given for really establishing work, respectively, in the fields of skin resistance (conductance) and skin potential activity. Féré's work, reported in 1888, states that 'irrigation of the tissues' caused a diminution in skin resistance and thus established the role of the sweat-glands in exosomatic electrodermal activity. This position is accepted today, in spite of attempts to suggest vascular or even muscular involvement. The sweat-glands are also responsible for a major part of skin potential activity, a fact that may be established by inactivating them by an anticholinergic drug such as atropine. Although the sweat-glands are innervated by the sympathetic branch of the autonomic nervous system only, and the sympathetic system may in general be considered to be adrenergic, the sweat-glands are unique in having acetylcholine as their peripheral *neurotransmitter, as shown by their inactivation by anticholinergic drugs.

The central control of electrodermal activity is evident at several levels. Stimulation of the brain-stem reticular formation (see NERVOUS SYSTEM) provokes an electrodermal response, although inhibitory modification of the response may be seen by stimulating the brain-stem area at a bulbar level (the brain-stem area below the activating system at reticular level). At the level of the *limbic system, bilateral removal of the amygdalae abolishes the skin conductance response, while ablation of the hippocampus retards habituation to repeated stimulation. The eccrine sweat-glands of the hands are only involved in temperature regulation when temperature reaches about 25 °C and at that point activity of the anterior hypothalamus is involved.

Until the 1950s only the amplitude of the electrodermal response and the level from which it started were measures of interest. Since that time three temporal measures have been shown to be of importance. These are latency, the time from stimulation to the inflexion of the recording at the point where the response first becomes evident; rise time, the time taken for the response to reach its peak; and half recovery time, the time taken for the response to decline to half its peak amplitude.

The main relevance of the electrodermal response is as a component of the response patterns known as the orienting and defensive responses. The former is seen, following Pavlov, when the organism responds to any change in its environment. The latter may be seen as having a protective role: one which prevents the organism from becoming overstimulated. While, for instance, pattern changes in heart-rate and vasomotor activity may signal differences between orienting and defensive responding, there is usually little difference in the amplitude of the skin conductance response to stimuli which would produce orienting (OR) and defensive (DR) responses (e.g. 70 dB and 95 dB auditory stimuli respectively). However, while the amplitude oɪ the response may not adequately differentiate ORs from DRs, the recovery time may be as much as three times as long in the case of the latter. Furthermore, the rate of habituation of the skin conductance response to weak stimuli which elicit ORs is very much quicker than to intense stimuli which elicit DRs.

The electrodermal response may be the subject of *conditioning procedures and, as one of the few readily measurable responses in man which reflect 'unconscious' activity, there has been a proliferation of skin conductance conditioning work. However, in spite of the fact that the immediate control of electrodermal activity is via the sympathetic nervous system, the accessibility to control from higher cortical levels results in modification of electrodermal conditioning by instructions, and the conditioning process in man cannot be viewed simply as parallel to that in animals.

Perhaps the most useful aspect of work using electrodermal activity is on individual differences and in mental illness. Some of the earliest work in this area was done by *Jung in Zurich at the turn of the century, when he used it as an adjunct to his word association studies. Since that time it has proved important in studies of neurosis and psychosis. In *schizophrenia, for instance, it is a well-replicated finding that some 40 per cent of adult patients show no electrodermal responsivity while a large proportion of the remainder respond excessively to weak stimuli. Measurement of electrodermal activity in the pre-morbid state has shown that these patterns of response are able to predict later breakdown; possible use as a screening device is thus indicated.

It is unfortunate that to many members of the public the use of electrodermal measurement is associated with the use of the so-called lie-detector. This 'technique', where electrodermal and other autonomic responses to 'critical' and 'non-critical' stimuli are recorded, has become an industry in the United States under the name of 'polygraphy'; but it has little scientific support, and the detection of true from false responses is probably not more accurate than 65–70 per cent as an average figure. It becomes a matter of political decision whether this small increase over chance level in the possibility of detection makes the use of the technique acceptable for the detection of those who might be security risks, or as evidence for court conviction. Clearly in the latter case the extent of inaccuracy makes its use unacceptable.

The potential interest of electrodermal activity is now apparent, even though at the end of the 1950s it appeared that half a century of experimentation had produced nothing useful. The turning-point came with improvements in technique that eliminated a large amount of the error introduced—for instance, by electrodes which polarized and produced random activity. The measurement of electrodermal activity is now a useful part of the experimenter's armamentarium.          P. H. V.

**ELECTROENCEPHALOGRAPHY.** A common aim of research of the normal brain and of clinical diagnosis of its disorders is to build a complete image of the living tissue and its activity. All practical techniques allow one to view only one aspect of it. The electroencephalogram (EEG) registers potential differences on the scalp which arise as a result of 'feeble currents' of the brain. Electrical activity of the brain was first reported in 1875 by Richard Caton, a British physiologist who studied it in monkeys, cats, and rabbits. Human EEG was first described by Hans *Berger, a German psychiatrist, in 1929, but not until E. D. Adrian (later Lord *Adrian) and Matthews in England published their work in 1934 did human EEG become a routine diagnostic test in neurology and psychiatry. It also became one of the widely used tools of brain research in humans.

For clinical purposes, most modern EEG machines register as many as sixteen *'channels' of brain activity. Many channels are used in order to be able to detect if there are different types of electrical activity in neighbouring brain areas.

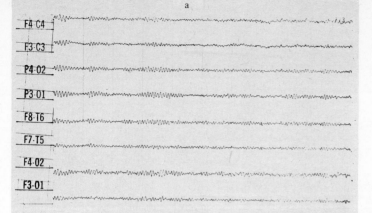

a

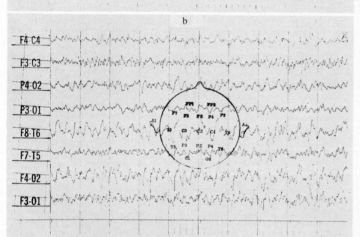

b

Fig. 1. a. Eight simultaneously recorded channels of normal EEG. Letters to the left of each trace represent electrode locations referring to a schematized drawing of a head. Notice on the right side of the figure the spindling of normal alpha range activity in several channels. b. Abnormal EEG of a patient with right cerebral lesion. Notice large amplitude slow wave activity in the even-numbered right-sided channels, especially in the frontotemporal ($F_8$-$T_6$) derivation. There was clinical evidence of focal seizure manifested by jerking of the left leg of the patient.

However, as will be explained later, spatial resolution of abnormal brain activity is not one of the strong points of clinical electroencephalograms. A 'channel' refers simply to the amplified record of the potential difference between two points on the skull and its changes. Since brain potentials change in time and do not usually measure more than 100 microvolts, the tiny signals need to be amplified and registered, usually with the help of an ink pen recorder. In most clinical EEG studies, discs pasted on the skull, or fine needles inserted into the scalp, will pick up the electrical activity of the brain. They are called electrodes, and each is connected to a powerful amplifier. A number of amplifiers, each with its pen recorder, constitutes the essence of an electroencephalographic machine. When the brain is alive, the potential difference between two recording electrodes changes 'spontaneously' as time goes on. When written out by the pen recorder, this is seen on the EEG record as undulations. By inspecting these one gains the impression that the brain produces waves. In fact, 'brain wave test' is a term used in the United States for the EEG. The wavy appearance provides a simple way of describing

and classifying the EEG by sheer visual inspection. The Greek letters alpha, beta, delta, and theta are commonly used for the different periodicities or wave frequencies apparent in the EEG. Alpha stands for brain waves with a periodicity of about 9 to 11 per second. Beta is a higher frequency 'component' of the EEG, while delta and theta are slower-changing brain potentials, or low-frequency waves.

Much interest has accompanied the nature of the alpha rhythm since it was shown by Berger that it appears when a human is resting quietly, but disappears when he opens his eyes. This disappearance is called 'alpha blocking'. Some people produce alpha waves even with eyes open, and in these people a flash of light is needed to block them. The presence of alpha is thought to be associated with a meditative, quiescent state, while its disappearance in the normal human is thought to be due to *attention and *arousal. Because of the relation of the alpha rhythm to vision, several investigators studied its presence or absence when patients suffer from abnormalities of their visual system. It has been reported that if a person has reduced vision due to some ocular abnormality but can see flashes of light, these are not enough to block his alpha rhythm. Apparently, not all visual activities block alpha. However, mental imagery, such as occurs when playing blindfold chess, can block alpha rhythm. Another pertinent observation has been that most patients who lose the ability to see as a result of a *stroke of the visual cortex on both sides of the brain do not have alpha rhythm. Stroke results from depriving a part of the brain of its blood supply, such as occurs when one of its supplying arteries is completely or partially occluded. Bilateral stroke of the visual cortex occurs when the so-called basilar artery or its branches receives diminished blood supply.

The slow waves of the EEG occur for short periods only in normal *sleep, but commonly when there is pathology of the brain—such as a stroke or a tumour. The electroencephalographer can sometimes diagnose the size and nature of brain pathology by comparing the simultaneous activity of many channels of the EEG. In some patients brain waves paroxysmally change their characteristics: they no longer appear as gentle waves of the sea, but become very sharp and spiky. (The appearance of such a 'brainstorm' unfortunately does not represent the occurrence of some sharp thought.) These abnormalities are seen in seizure disorders, called epilepsies. The EEG provides a major contribution to the diagnosis of epilepsy. Clinically different types of epilepsies have their individual EEG fingerprints, and these different types respond to different medications. Sometimes a medication which is good for one type of seizure disorder may be harmful in another. Thus for these patients EEG recording is indispensable.

The understanding of potential changes of the human brain has been helped by experimental recordings done in other animals. While their surface skull potential EEG is recorded, simultaneously an electrode is being advanced into the depth of the cortex and a third electrode may be held at a constant depth near to or within a single cortical cell. Thus surface EEG, intracellular potential changes, and extracellular spike activity can be recorded in the same animal at the same time. Studies by D. A. Pollen showed that slow surface potential changes (one of the main components of the EEG) are not influenced by spike generation of individual neurones; rather waves represent changes of potential differences between the bodies and processes of single neurones.

Using the electroencephalogram to reveal abnormal or even normal cognitive processes of the brain has been very disappointing. The attempt has been likened to trying to diagnose the problems of a computer by holding a voltmeter up to it. The EEG reveals the pathology of the human brain, but little about abnormal thinking. One reason may be that the EEG scalp electrode samples potential changes which arise in a large volume of the brain, and deficiencies of specific nerve-cells which may not all be in the same volume of tissue cannot be detected. The situation is different when, under surgery, the electrical activity of the brain can be directly recorded. With some patients there are medical reasons for putting electrodes on the surface or in the depth of the cortex, and exploring connections between distant areas of the brain. Surprisingly, under this condition, even a relatively large surface electrode samples only the activity of a small volume of tissue. Two intracranial surface electrodes, when spaced only 1 millimetre apart, can show different EEGs.

Resolution of brain pathology by EEG methods is limited by the organization of the human cerebral cortex itself. Sensory stimuli such as light through the eyes, tones through the ears, temperature and pressures, and other sensations, are first transduced and then transmitted to the cortex as changes in electrical activity along nerve fibres as a series of pulses. Often, as the nerves enter the cortex they branch like a tree and connect to many different cells (neurones) of the brain. In addition there are connections between various neurones in the immediate vicinity of each other, as well as long fibres connecting different parts of the brain. Consequently distant cells may register identical changes.

Modern diagnosis in clinical neurology relies less and less on registering spontaneous activity of the brain. Rather, one attempts to induce changes in specific brain areas devoted to one or another sensory modality, such as vision and hearing. Induced activity is of much smaller amplitude than the 'spontaneously' arising potential change and, to detect it, the averaging and summation of a large number of tiny signals is required. The technique is called '*evoked' (as opposed to spontaneous) potentials.

The conventional EEG is obtained through an alternating current (AC) coupled recording. Usually only changes in potentials which occur in less than 1 second are registered. Recordings that show the slower changes of so-called 'standing' potentials of the brain were made as long ago as the nineteenth century. 'Slow' in this context means a DC shift noticeable only over many seconds. Beck, a Polish investigator, was remarkably successful using the then available technique to record DC potentials. DC recording became clinically useful only with the development of transistorized amplifiers and better electrodes. DC potential changes of the brain may reveal more about cognitive processing than classical EEG does. For example, W. Grey *Walter, one of the pioneers of modern electroencephalography, has been able to show that DC potential shifts occur and may relate to *anticipation and decision-making by the human. A potential shift measured at the top of the head and called the contingent negative variation or CNV is the best-known example of a 'slow' potential change.                                    I. B. W.

Cooper, R., Osselton, J. W., and Shaw, J. C. (1974). *EEG Technology*. London.
Pollen, D. A. (1969). *Basic Mechanisms of the Epilepsies*. New York.

Walter, W. G. (1953). *The Living Brain*. 1968 repr. Harmondsworth.

**EMBARRASSMENT.** See BLUSHING.

**'EMERGENCE' AND 'REDUCTION' IN EXPLANATIONS.** A classical question of philosophy is the one/many problem: is everything in the universe ultimately one thing—or are there, as it certainly appears, many things? In another and more interesting form the question becomes: are there many *kinds* of things—or could there be a single unifying account of all the apparently various kinds of events and phenomena?

It is sometimes raised as an objection to science, especially to medicine, that reducing complex issues to simpler terms produces loss of significance of the whole, which like Humpty Dumpty cannot be put together again. This is the 'holistic' criticism of science's reduction of complex issues into simpler parts or concepts. The converse of reduction is that when parts are combined, surprising or mysterious 'emergent' properties may appear—mysterious because reduction-descriptions are inadequate. A familiar example is the creation of water by the combination of the gases oxygen and hydrogen.

Just as the properties of water are different from those of its constituent gases, so, it is sometimes suggested, mind may be similarly emergent upon physical brain structure or activity. Douglas Hofstadter (1979) makes effective use of an analogy—originating from a paper (1911) by William Morton Wheeler—that though ants build their nests they cannot reconstitute them when they have been disturbed and the structure has been destroyed. To conceive that the functioning ants' nest is more than the sum of the ants is helpful when thinking about brain-cells (which, also, individually do not understand); and it is helpful to conceive of the co-operative functioning of brain-cells in the process of understanding the mind. Knowledge of individual ants cannot explain nest behaviour and knowledge of individual brain-cells cannot explain the mind, even though the nest is no more than ants and the mind depends entirely on brain-cells.

Vitalist biologists such as Hans Driesch (1867–1941) have held that the functioning of organisms can never be explained from knowledge, however complete, of their parts because of a vital principle which relates to the whole but not the isolated parts. This doctrine precludes 'reductive' explanations drawn from analyses of the whole into parts that may be separately investigated and described. It implies that the biological and medical sciences are essentially outside the kinds of explanation by reductive analyses that have proved so powerful in the natural sciences. If this is so, biology (and psychology even more so) would seem to be essentially different in kind from physics. Is this holistic view of biology and mind justified? To consider this it is useful to look at simple *machines* and ask: do we find emergence when parts of a construction

set, such as Meccano, are combined to make a simple working model? Putting the parts together in various ways creates very different mechanisms: cars, cranes, clocks, and so on. It is indeed remarkable that the same differently arranged parts may move as a car, lift things as a crane, or keep time as a clock. This can look like emergence beyond explanation—much as for organisms—though here we clearly have simple mechanisms.

The Oxford philosopher Gilbert *Ryle tried (1949) to exorcise common concepts of mind that, implicitly or explicitly, dubbed the mind 'the Ghost in the Machine'. But even the simplest of Meccano mechanisms can look quite ghostly! Is this because they have emergent properties? If so, do they still appear ghostly in this way when they are fully understood? Or could it be that we do not yet completely understand simple machines reductively—though we may come to understand machines and organisms so fully that appearance of emergence vanishes, as analysis of the functions of their parts becomes complete?

A machine is assembled from component parts, yet how it functions may be explained by more or less abstract general concepts rather than in terms of its parts. Thus, how a clock keeps time is explained less by describing the parts and their mechanical interactions than from general principles, such as those stating why pendulums swing at a constant rate. We have to look beyond the parts of a mechanism to explain what the parts do. Moreover, there is no simple relation between a machine's structure and its function. A single part, such as the anchor of the clock's escapement, may have several functions, or several parts may combine to provide a single function. Similarly there is no simple correspondence of parts to functions in an organism. (Insights to relations between structures and functions of organisms are powerfully expressed by Robert M. Pirsig (1974)).

It is tempting to believe that the high-level properties of organic systems must somehow be present in a rudimentary or dormant form in their parts. But such belief does little to explain how organisms function, and can lead (as with inorganic mechanisms) to notions of molecules, atoms, or even fundamental particles such as electrons having *intention, or *consciousness. Such notions are without verification, however, and must surely be dismissed (see FALSIFICATION). We should prefer to say that mind emerges from brain function—if only because there is some hope of finding out what is so special about the brain. But it is hard enough to understand how organisms can be intelligent or conscious, even with all their interacting complexity; and to say that individual brain-cells (or, even more extreme, that the individual molecules, atoms, or electrons of which we are composed) have intelligence or consciousness merely pushes the question further beyond answer.

The Cambridge philosopher C. D. *Broad argued (1929) that the universe is inherently 'layered', to give emergences with increasing complexities that can never be predicted or explained from any knowledge of lower (generally simpler) 'layers' of reality. On this account, mind may remain beyond understanding despite knowledge of brain or other function—even though mind is causally given by physical functions. Moreover, most neurophysiologists, at least until recently, have held that brain and mind are essentially different—irreducibly two kinds of things—the causal connection (denied by *Leibniz) notwithstanding. (See also MIND AND BODY; MIND–BODY PROBLEM: PHILOSOPHICAL THEORIES.)

This duality may be criticized on the principle of Occam's razor, as postulating entities unnecessarily; though one might follow the physiologist Sir Charles *Sherrington's (1906, 1940) opinion: 'That our being should consist of two fundamental elements offers, I suppose, no greater inherent improbability than that it should rest on one only.' By contrast the neurologist Wilder *Penfield (1975) came to the view that the mind is the emergent characteristic of brain function and depends on physical processes of the brain. This is probably the prevailing view, though Broad's 'layers', limiting reductionist explanations, are largely ignored or denied.

Whether these dualist and emergent accounts of mind are so different, and just what each implies, depends on extremely difficult issues of what should be accepted as causal and what as emergent; and how emergence may be seen in causal terms. The answer seems to be that causal explanations require general concepts, or 'meta' accounts, and that these can remove the mysteries of emergence, though not simply by 'reduction' to the parts. But so far an adequate meta account for linking brain function to mind is lacking.

These issues have significance not only in science but also for anyone who wishes or needs to understand or apply scientific concepts; for the language, ideas, and aims of scientists differ according to the level of reduction in which they think and work. Thus a fundamental particle physicist or a cell biologist may find the concepts and aims of the neurologist alien and hard to appreciate—while the cognitive psychologist might as well be living in a different universe. And yet such universes of discourse have to be bridged for adequate understanding, and in many cases for effective research and action. Art and science have been described as 'two cultures'; but science is also divided within itself, with prestige accorded to the 'deeper', more 'fundamental' concepts—even though they may be inadequate to explain the way things are higher up the tree. And it is not clear even that this tree is rooted in the 'fundamental' sciences—for its 'levels' of explanation depend on the observations and intelligence of our minds, at the tree-top.

R. L. G.

Broad, C. D. (1929). *The Mind and its Place in Nature*. London.

Hofstadter, D. R. (1979). *Godel, Escher, Bach: an eternal golden braid*. New York and Hassocks.

Morgan, C. Lloyd (1923). *Emergent Evolution*. London.

Penfield, W. (1975). *The Mystery of the Mind*. Princeton.

Pirsig, R. M. (1974). *Zen and the Art of Motorcycle Maintenance: an enquiry into values*. London.

Ryle, G. (1949). *The Concept of Mind*. Oxford.

Sherrington, C. S. (1906). *The Integrative Action of the Nervous System*. New York.

Sherrington, Sir C. (1940). *Man on His Nature*. Cambridge.

Wheeler, W. M. (1911). The ant-colony as an organism. *Journal of Morphology*, **22**, 2, 307–25.

**EMMERT'S LAW.** It was reported by E. Emmert in 1881 that a visual *after-image appears to change in size, according to whether it is seen as lying near by or far away. This is easy to demonstrate by looking for a few seconds at a bright light, or a camera's flashlight, and then viewing the after-image as seen on a nearby surface (say a book held in the hand) and then on a distant screen or wall. The after-image is perceptually 'projected' on to the viewed surface, so that it appears near on the book and more distant on the wall. When near it looks small, and the more distant it is seen to be the larger it appears. Its apparent size—though it is actually a fixed-size 'photograph' on the retina of the eye—increases roughly linearly with its apparent distance. This linear increase of apparent size with increasing distance is Emmert's law.

Consider now a normal retinal image, of some object, rather than the local fatigue of a region of retina of an after-image. As the object increases in distance its image in the eye will correspondingly shrink—just as for a camera. But (and this is easily checked for oneself) as the viewed object recedes it does not appear to shrink anything like as much as the optical halving of the retinal image with each doubling of its distance. It normally *looks* almost the same size over a wide range of distances. This is due to a perceptual compensation called 'size constancy scaling'.

After-images are odd because they do not change in size at the retina. What we see in the *apparent* changes of size noted by Emmert is a compensation at work. It is compensating for what would normally be changes of size of the retinal image; but as the after-image remains unchanging, size constancy gives illusory changes of size.

Constancy scaling is set by several 'distance cues': convergence of the eyes, geometrical perspective, and the graded texture and falling of sharpness ('aerial perspective'), which are all associated with increasing distance of a viewed object. Correspondingly, after-images change their size with changes of convergence angles of the eyes, or with perspective—many *illusion figures having converging lines. Any cue to distance can set the compensatory size scaling mechanism, and when mis-set there is a corresponding size or shape distortion illusion.

Emmert himself thought that a visible screen, on which after-images are 'projected', is necessary for the size changes he described. This is not so, however, for these changes occur in the dark, if the observer moves backwards or forwards from an imaginary screen. This observation is important for it shows that Emmert's law is not due merely to relative size changes of the fixed after-image and the changing image of the screen, or its texture, but is indeed due to the brain's perceptual compensatory size constancy scaling, which, when inappropriate, produces illusions of size or shape.

Boring, E. G. (1942). *Sensation and Perception in the History of Experimental Psychology*, pp. 288–311. New York.

Emmert, E. (1881). Grossen verhalnisse der Nachbidder. *Klinische Monatsblätter für Augenheilkunde*, **19**, 443.

Gregory, R. L., Wallace, J. G., and Campbell, F. W. C. (1959). Changes in the size and shape of visual after-images observed in complete darkness during changes of position in space. *Quarterly Journal of Experimental Psychology*, **2**, Part 1, 54.

Thouless, R. H. (1931). Phenomenal Regression to the Real Object, 1. *British Journal of Psychology*, **21**, 339.

Thouless, R. H. (1932). Individual differences in Phenomenal Regression. *British Journal of Psychology*, **22**, 216.

**EMOTION** is a topic that, more than any other, has bedevilled students of mental life. The peculiar characteristics of emotional behaviour and experience have been repeated stumbling-blocks in the attempt to see human nature as rational, intelligent, and even sublime. From the earliest philosophical speculations to the present day, emotion has been often seen as interfering with rationality, as a remnant of our pre-sapient inheritance— emotions seem to represent unbridled human nature 'in the raw'.

In modern times the single most influential contribution to the study of the emotions is Charles *Darwin's work entitled *The Expression of the Emotions in Man and Animals* (1872). His general thrust represents a second major theme that has characterized the study of emotion—the notion that there are specific, fundamental emotions that find their 'expression' in the overt behaviour of humans and lower animals.

The current flux of speculations about the emotions started with a very specific event, the publication in 1884 of an article by William *James in *Mind* entitled 'What is an emotion?' James turned conventional wisdom completely around. Instead of the outward signs of emotions, such as facial expressions and visceral reactions, being the *result* of some prior emotional, neural signal, he insisted that 'our feeling of the [bodily] changes as they occur IS the emotion'. Similar points were made at about the same time by various other writers, the most important being the Danish physician C. G. *Lange, whose contribution appeared in Danish in 1885 and became generally available with its German translation in 1887. Since then, the theoretical position has been known as the James–Lange theory of emotion.

The theory dominated psychological thinking well into the first half of the twentieth century. It postulated that some external event, perceived by the individual, produces bodily responses, particularly specific avoidance or approach reactions, together with responses of the *autonomic nervous system. The perception of *these* events in their totality then constitutes the emotion that is experienced. Lange restricted the bodily reactions to the visceral, autonomic domain, but James stressed the total response of the organism. The obvious implication is that each specific emotional experience is generated by a specific and unique set of bodily and visceral responses.

The James–Lange theory remained dominant at least until the late 1920s, when W. B. *Cannon published a detailed and trenchant critique of its position. Briefly, Cannon noted that emotional behaviour was still present when the viscera were surgically or accidentally isolated from the central nervous system; that different emotions did not seem to differ in important ways in their accompanying patterns of visceral response; that perception of visceral response tends to be diffuse and non-specific; that autonomic responses are relatively slow and that emotional experience seems to occur faster than the visceral response; and that emotional states do not follow the artificial production of visceral response as a matter of course. Cannon's major contribution to the study of emotion was this critique; the theory he offered as an alternative to James never did achieve great popularity.

In the ensuing decades speculation about emotion abounded, much research being devoted to problems of special visceral patterning; but, until the middle of the century, few new advances were made. The question seemed to remain where James and Cannon had left it: do we experience an emotion because we perceive our bodies in a particular way, or are there specific emotional neural patterns which respond to environmental events and then release bodily and visceral expressions? Do we grieve because we cry, or do we cry because we grieve?

What did happen in the decades after Cannon was the (unfortunate) American interlude known as *behaviourism. With hindsight it appears that the main deleterious effect of behaviourism arose not from its insistence on dealing only with the objective and the observable as basic psychological data—in a sense all psychologists have become methodological behaviourists—but from the behaviourists' implicit dictum against complex theory, against the postulation of useful fictions to serve the explanation of behaviour. Uninhibited and expansive theorizing has generally characterized the cognitive theories, which implicate the knowledge and thought of the organism as determinants of action and experience. With the resurgence of cognitive theories, particularly in social psychology, came a concern with cognitive aspects of emotion. The single most important contribution in the form of both direction-changing theory and innovative experiments was made by Stanley Schachter, a psychologist from Columbia

University in New York. He postulated that only a general state of visceral arousal was necessary for the experience of emotion: i.e. that different emotional experiences arise out of the same visceral background. Next he assumed that, given a state of visceral arousal, an individual will describe his feelings in terms of the cognitions (thoughts, past experiences, environmental signals) available at the time. Schachter's contribution cut the Gordian knot in which James's theory and the Jamesian critics had been entwined. Visceral arousal was seen as a necessary condition for emotional experience, but the quality of the emotion depended on cognitive, perceptual evaluations of the external world and the internal state.

With the new insights into the possible nature of emotional experience, it was possible to raise new questions about the nature and function of emotions. If the emotional experience is a concatenation of visceral arousal and cognitive evaluation, what is the role of emotions in adaptive behaviour; what is the function of visceral, autonomic *arousal?

Rather than emotion appearing as an interfering, irrelevant, and chaotic state of affairs, it seems that different kinds of situations (and cognitions) become especially marked if they occur in the 'emotional' visceral context. This notion corresponds with the common experience that emotionally tinged events occupy a special place in our memories. The visceral component of the emotion may well serve as an additional cue for the retrieval from memory of specific events, and sets them apart from the run-of-the-mill catalogue of everyday events. The 'emotional' memory of a visit to a theatre is selected from among all the plays we have seen; it is 'special'. The memory of a friend with whom one interacted in the 'visceral' mode is different from the memories of people with whom one has interacted in non-arousing contexts. But if the visceral component of emotion has this special role of selecting important events, what are the conditions that give rise to the visceral reaction?

The best candidate for the psychological conditions for visceral arousal seems to be the occurrence of some cognitive or perceptual discrepancy. The notion that emotions, both positive and negative, have as their antecedents some discrepancy or conflict between the state of the world and the expectations which the individual brings to the situation has been bruited about for at least a century. The most eminent ancestors of the suggestion are the French psychologist F. Paulhan and the American philosopher John *Dewey. They implied that specific discrepancies and conflicts produce specific emotions. Current wisdom would suggest that any discrepancy, any interruption of expectations or of intended actions, produces undifferentiated visceral (autonomic) arousal. The *quale of the subsequent emotion will then depend on the ongoing cognitive evaluation (meaning analysis, appraisal) of the current state of affairs.

Thus, riding on a roller-coaster produces serious disturbances and discrepancies between our expectations and current feelings of balance and bodily support. Whether the ride is seen as joyful or dreadful depends on what we expect about the ride, who accompanies us, what we are told to expect, and whether we feel in control of the situation. Some love it, others hate it.

The notion that discrepancy or interruption produces a special visceral event suggests that in addition to the homeostatic function of the autonomic nervous system there are other adaptive characteristics ascribable to it. In fact there is good evidence that, with the initiation of autonomic arousal, attentional and scanning mechanisms are directed towards important aspects of the environment. In other words, in addition to the autonomic nervous system caring for the internal balance of the energy-spending and energy-conserving functions of the body, it also serves as an alerting and marking mechanism for events that are 'important'. The concept of discrepancy or interruption provides an independent criterion for what is 'important' for the organism. When the usual, habitual actions and experiences of the individual are interrupted, when expectations of the world fail, then attention is focused on the environment, and the event itself is subsequently stored in memory as special and easily retrievable.

The modern view answers the ancient concern about emotions. They are not necessarily remnants of our pre-sapient past, but rather they are important characteristics of an active, searching, and thinking human being. Novelty, discrepancy, and interruption generate visceral responses, while our cognitive system interprets the world as threatening, elating, frightening, or joyful. The human world is full of emotions not because we are animals at heart, but rather because it is still full of signals that elate or threaten, and replete with events and people that produce discrepancies and interruptions.                                   G. M.

Cannon, W. B. (1929). *Bodily Changes in Pain, Hunger, Fear and Rage*, 2nd edn. New York.

James, W. (1890). *The Principles of Psychology*. New York.

Mandler, G. (1979). Emotion. In Hearst, E. (ed.), *The First Century of Experimental Psychology*. Hillsdale, New Jersey.

Mandler, G. (1984). *Mind and Body*. New York.

Schachter, S. (1971). *Emotion, Obesity, and Crime*. New York.

Strongman, K. T. (1978). *The Psychology of Emotion*, 2nd edn. London.

**EMPATHY.** The feeling of 'belonging to', associating ourselves with, or 'being carried along' with something. Thus a golfer may feel that he is almost soaring into the air with the ball when he hits a good drive. It has been suggested that when we look at the columns of buildings, such as Greek temples, we identify ourselves with the columns: if they are very thin, we feel uncomfortable as though they, like us, must be inadequate to take the weight they support; and if they are very fat, we feel uncomfortable as some people do when large and clumsy. This application of the notion of empathy is a theory of *aesthetics due to the German philosopher and psychologist Theodore Lipps (1851–1914), professor at Bonn, Breslau, and Munich. 'Empathy' in this sense is a rough translation from the German *Einfuhlung*. The theory has been stated as: 'Aesthetic pleasure is an enjoyment of *our own* activity *in* an object.' This idea was developed by Vernon Lee (pen-name Violet Paget, 1856–1935), who applied it especially to studies of Renaissance architecture.

Carritt, E. F. (1949). *The Theory of Beauty*, 5th edn., especially chapter XI. London.
Lipps, T. (1907). *Ästhetik*. Berlin.
Lee, V. (1913). *The Beautiful*. Cambridge.

**ENCOUNTER GROUP.** During the Second World War and immediately after it, there were several initiatives intended to help individuals to become, through participation in groups, more sensitive to their own and other people's attitudes and emotions and more spontaneous in expressing feelings. The focus of 'T-groups' (training groups) was on issues of leadership and authority and the dynamics of change in organizations. 'Sensitivity' groups aimed at producing change by promoting 'interpersonal awareness'. Encounter groups, which became popular in the 1960s and 1970s, first in California and later in Britain, developed from Carl Rogers's 'client-centred' therapy, which emphasizes personal growth and communication. Encounter groups provide the conditions in which participants can be freed from a sense of isolation and alienation through self-discovery in a supportive, permissive, non-authoritarian group setting. The qualities to be induced are openness, authenticity, honesty in the physical, non-verbal expression of feeling, and 'actualization' as a person. Those who advocate them have resisted any attempt at scientific formulation and investigation of the processes involved, and claim that they are 'theory-free'. Nevertheless, several assumptions seem to be made—for example, that the physical expression of feeling in an unstructured setting is cathartic and beneficial. Participants probably do acquire certain social skills, which are transferable outside the groups. Whether the persona revealed in the group, although more congenial to the other participants, is more real or true than the one it replaces is open to question. A few participants are more confused than liberated, and there is a small risk of more serious ill-effects, especially if, despite the claim that groups are 'threat-free', a participant is confronted aggressively.     D. R. D.

Cheshire, N. M. (1973). Review of Carl Rogers's *Encounter Groups*. British Journal of Educational Psychology, **43**, 213–15.
Rogers, C. R. (1971). *Encounter Groups*. Harmondsworth.

**ENDOMORPHY.** See BODY BUILD AND PERSONALITY.

**ENDORPHINS** are one of the major classes of peptides that occur in the brain. They appear to take part in the transmission of chemical messages between nerve-cells by acting on receptors which have the characteristic property of binding opiate compounds such as morphine.

It has been known for a very long time that certain plant extracts contain opiates and that these compounds have powerful effects on behaviour, mood, and pain (see OPIUM). Only recently, however, was the question asked whether the presence of opiate receptor sites indicated the existence of naturally occurring opiate-like compounds in the nervous system itself. In 1975 the first successful extraction of such endogenous compounds was achieved. They were called encephalins (literally: in the brain). Originally two distinct forms were found. Both were peptides with five amino acid constituents in the sequence, differing from each other only at one site and named methionine-encephalin and leucine-encephalin.

Following this breakthrough, many more active endogenous compounds were found. They all contain the same opioid core of five amino acids found in encephalin. It is now clear that they can be grouped into three genetically different peptide families with different distributions in the nervous system. The situation appears to be similar to that found for another family of *neurotransmitter substances—the monoamines, where modification in the basic chemical structure is associated with their distribution in several anatomically distinct groups of neurones.

**Three opioid peptide families.** It has been known for some time that hormones secreted into the gut are synthesized initially as high molecular weight precursors, and that the active hormones are produced by cleavage of a fragment or several fragments from the precursor before they act at receptor sites. This same principle appears to hold true for hormones secreted from the pituitary gland and for the opioids in the brain and pituitary. The three precursors for the opioids are called pro-opiomelanocortin (POMC), proencephalin and prodynorphin. The POMC molecule, in addition to containing the encephalin sequence, contains another opioid peptide of very high potency, and two other hormone sequences, one for adrenocorticotrophic hormone (which stimulates the adrenal cortex) and one for melanocyte-stimulating hormone (which regulates skin pigmentation). Proencephalin contains several peptides all of which have opioid activity; while prodynorphin is a simpler precursor than the other two and produces three main opioids.

As is the case for many other neurotransmitters, there appear to be several types of receptor for the opioids. This may reflect differing mechanisms for translating opioid effects into different responses or the presence of several types of opioid compound within a given synaptic terminal, or the different anatomical distribution of the three main opioid families (see below) or all these possibilities together. For example, slight variations in the structure of the peptide sequence may result in subtly differing effects at the opiate receptor, particularly when these variations occur in the amino acids adjacent to the central encephalin sequence. It is possible to imagine a wide range of activity at receptors resulting from such modifications, which, when they act at different receptor subtypes, confer an enormous dynamic range of responsiveness. In addition, receptor super- or sub-sensitivity resulting from long-term functional adaptation may add further to the complexity of effects. The picture becomes even more complicated by the discovery that transmitters may coexist in the same synaptic terminal. It was thought that neurones used only one transmitter to exert their effects at chemical synapses, but this assumption collapsed. Many examples are now described where a low molecular weight transmitter such as acetylcholine or noradrenaline coexist with a peptide. One example is the co-presence of encephalin and noradrenaline in the adrenal medulla, an endocrine gland. The significance of the phenomenon of coexistence is unknown, but it may be related to the slow time-course of action of many neuropeptides. Thus the peptide may modulate the responsiveness of a neurone to its partner transmitter in some way perhaps to sharpen or broaden the time resolution of the synaptic message. These properties may confer further subtlety to neuronal events, which may allow us to transcend the simple idea that excitation or inhibition in a neural network is the only information subject to coding, translation and transformation.

*Anatomy of the opioid systems.* In the brain the main POMC cell group lies in the arcuate nucleus of the hypothalamus and it sends *axons to innervate many limbic and brain-stem regions. Another small group of neurones lies in the brain-stem centres that regulate autonomic functions (such as cardiovascular control). In the pituitary gland POMC is synthesized mainly in the intermediate lobe and in a few anterior lobe cells.

The most abundant type are neurones which synthesize proencephalin. They are distributed widely in the brain from the highest cortical to the lowest spinal levels, as both long axon and short axon pathways. In the peripheral neuroendocrine system, proencephalin-derived peptides are also found in the adrenal medulla, the gut, and many other structures.

Prodynorphin is found in the gut, posterior pituitary, and brain, where it is located chiefly in the hypothalamus, basal ganglia, and brain-stem.

**Functions.** The distribution of opioids indicates that they participate in many different brain functions and (in a broad sense) probably in every brain function. For technical reasons, however, some areas have received more attention than others. These are mechanisms of *pain sensation, cardio-

vascular regulation, hypotensive *shock, and endocrine activity. More complex systems controlling feeding, drinking, movement, motivation, reinforcement, memory, mood, and affect are also influenced by opioids but little is known of their effects in these difficult areas.

*Pain and stress.* The experimental finding that brain stimulation of specific sites produces a reduction in pain responses, which can be reversed by the specific opiate antagonist naloxone, suggests that endogenous opiates are involved in analgesic mechanisms (see ANAESTHESIA). Furthermore, pain relief is accompanied by increased opioid levels in the cerebrospinal fluid which circulates around the brain.

Analgesia may also be produced by repeated stressful stimuli. This is accompanied by a reduction in hypothalamic opioids, perhaps because the material is released by the stimulus. Stress-induced analgesia may also be counteracted by opiate receptor-blocking drugs. The site of action and neural circuits involved are far from clear, however, and they must involve non-opiate as well as opiate pathways. In addition, stress-induced analgesia may depend partly on opioids released from the pituitary gland or peripheral organs such as the adrenal glands. Thus the adrenal medulla stores and releases both the catecholamines and encephalin together in responses to stress.

An interesting finding has been obtained in relation to the phenomenon of placebo analgesia. Here subjects may report relief of pain even when given a dummy tablet. Those reporting analgesia following an inactive placebo show raised opioid concentrations in the circulation. No matter where the opioid is generated, the result suggests that physiological processes may be influenced by the belief of the subject that an analgesic substance has been given. The implications of this finding would appear to be quite far reaching.

*Circulation and endocrine control.* The anatomical distribution of the three opioid families suggests that they all play a role in the central regulation of cardiovascular functions. Thus, all three are present in neurones of the brain-stem cardiovascular regulatory centres. The POMC family is present in the anterior pituitary which influences the adrenal cortex and hence blood pressure, and the prodynorphin group act on posterior pituitary hormones to control blood volume. Furthermore, the encephalins of the sympathetic nervous system, via their control of the vascular bed, are well placed to regulate regional blood-flow and hence blood-pressure.

These fundamental discoveries feed through to applications of importance to medical treatment. For example, the state of shock resulting from loss of blood is a dangerous condition which is difficult to treat. Since naloxone, by blocking opiate receptors probably located in the brain, can reverse shock-induced reduction in blood volume, it is possible that more effective management of this condition will soon be available.

See also BRAIN ACTIVITIES RECORDED BY BLOOD FLOW; BRAIN FUNCTION AND AWARENESS; NEURONAL CONNECTIVITY AND BRAIN FUNCTION; PSYCHOPHARMACOLOGY.                                    O. T. P.

**ENGRAM.** A physical brain change, supposed to take place as a result of experience, and to represent memories. The physical basis of *memory is not, however, known. The problems of the concept are beautifully described by Karl *Lashley, In search of the engram, *Symposia of the Society of Experimental Biology*, **4**, 454–82.

**ENTAILMENT** is the relation that holds between one or more propositions $P_1 \ldots P_n$ and each proposition $C$ which follows logically from them. Thus $P_1 \ldots P_n$ entail $C$ (frequently symbolized $P_1 \ldots P_n$ $C$) if, and only if, the inference from $P_1 \ldots P_n$ to $C$ is logically valid. The further analysis of this relation has been extensively discussed and disputed both by logicians and by philosophers. It is generally agreed that whenever $A$ entails $B$ it must be impossible for $A$ to be true without $B$ also being true, in which case, according to the definition introduced by C. I. Lewis, $A$ strictly implies $B$ (see IMPLICATION). The further analysis of entailment has thus come to be linked to the account given of the logic of the modal notions of *possibility and necessity which is supplied in works on modal logic. Lewis, who produced the first axiomatized modal logic, proposed that the relation of strict implication should be regarded as the correct formal counterpart of the informal notion of entailment. Others, however, for example Anderson and Belnap, have argued that for $A$ to entail $B$ it is not sufficient merely that it be impossible for $A$ to be true without $B$ being true. On their view there must also be some connection between the meanings of $A$ and $B$, and the truth of $A$ must be relevant to the truth of $B$ (giving rise to the idea of developing what has been called a relevance logic). This would mean, for example, insisting that although a contradiction strictly implies any proposition whatsoever ('Grass is green and grass is not green' strictly implies 'The earth is flat') it only entails those propositions to which it is relevant ('Grass is green and grass is not green' entails 'Grass is not red').          M. E. T.

Anderson, A. R. and Belnap, N. D. Jr. (1975). *Entailment*, vol. I. Princeton.
Hughes, G. E. and Cresswell, M. J. (1968). *An Introduction to Modal Logic*. London.
Lewis, C. I. (1922). Implication and the Algebra of Logic. *Mind*, NS **21**, pp. 522–31.

**ENTELECHY.** The term *entelecheia* is first used in Greek philosophy to mean the actualization of something as opposed to its mere potentiality. Thus Aristotle in the *De Anima* (*Concerning the Soul*) defines *psyche (soul) as the 'entelechy of an organic body', viz. that which makes a body actu-

ally alive and functioning. Aristotle did not, however, regard the *psyche* as a separate non-material entity, but merely as the 'form' or organizing principle of the body.

In the philosophy of *Leibniz, 'entelechy' is used to refer to the active principle present in all created substances, which makes them complete, self-sufficient and changing only as a result of internal action. Later the term was used by *vitalists to refer to the (alleged) active principle responsible for organic life.                        J. G. C.

**EPICURUS** (341–270 BC) was born in Samos, and died in Athens. He founded a school in Athens whose members secluded themselves from the city and lived austerely, and included (most surprisingly) slaves and women. The second head of the school was a slave called Mys.

Of Epicurus's enormous literary output (about 300 rolls) most is lost, including his thirty-seven books *On Nature*. Although he lived frugally, his moral precept was: 'We say that pleasure is the beginning and end of living happily.' He argued that the pleasures of the soul—contemplation, and the expectation of bodily pleasures—are more valuable than bodily pleasures alone. The ideal is freedom from distraction; and the study of philosophy is the best way to achieve this ideal. Natural (physical) explanations of mind and soul free us from being distracted by the fear of the supernatural.

Epicurus maintained the notion of unchanging and indestructible atoms, from Leucippus and Democritus. He was unusual in holding an atomistic philosophy, which was revived only in the early nineteenth century, by John *Dalton, though in a rather different form. Most Greek philosophers thought that it could be made to explain anything, and therefore explained nothing. Epicurus also denied the power of gods, holding that natural motions explain all phenomena. He held a view of evolution that anticipates in some respects Charles *Darwin's theory of natural selection by survival of the fittest.

**EPILEPSY.** A person is said to suffer from epilepsy if he is prone to recurrent epileptic seizures. The epileptic seizure is a transient episode of altered consciousness and/or perception, and/or loss of control of the muscles, which arises because of abnormal electrical discharges generated by groups of brain cells. Many varieties of seizures are recognized. They differ according to the nature of their symptom content. Most last for no more than a few minutes, but occasionally they are prolonged beyond 30 minutes or else recur so rapidly that full recovery is not achieved between successive attacks—these conditions are labelled status epilepticus.

It has been estimated that 6–7 per cent of the population suffer at least one epileptic seizure at some time in their lives and that 4 per cent have a phase when they are prone to recurrent seizures (i.e. can be said to suffer from epilepsy). Between 0·05 and 0·1% of the population suffer from 'active epilepsy'—that is, they have had a recurrent seizure within the previous five years or are taking regular medication to prevent the occurrence of seizures. Seizures are particularly liable to occur in early childhood, during adolescence, and in old age.

The history of epilepsy is probably as long as that of the human race. The definition of the condition as a clinical entity is generally attributed to *Hippocrates. He recognized that it arises from physical disease of the brain. He also took the first step towards unravelling the intracacies of cerebral *localization of function with his realization that damage on one side of the brain can cause convulsions which commence on the opposite side of the body. Further significant advances in this direction, based on observations of seizures, were delayed more than 2,000 years until the nineteenth century, and in particular until the observations and deductions of Hughlings *Jackson.

William Gowers, writing towards the end of the nineteenth century in the same era as Hughlings Jackson, proposed a dichotomy with his suggestion that some people have epileptic seizures because of overt cerebral pathology whereas others have them because of some factor in their brains innate constitution unaccompanied by any detectable abnormality of structure. To some extent this is reflected in the current classification which divides epileptic seizures into the two main categories: 'primary generalized' and 'focal' (or 'partial' in the current terminology). However, further advance lay beyond simple clinical observation and was delayed until the technique for recording the electrical activity of the human brain (the electroencephalogram, EEG—see ENCEPHALOGRAPHY) was developed, first in the 1920s by the German psychiatrist Hans *Berger and then in the 1930s by the Cambridge physiologists E. D. *Adrian and B. H. C. Matthews. The technique was rapidly applied to the analysis of epilepsy especially by E. L. and F. A. Gibbs, W. G. Lennox, H. Jasper, and H. Gastaut. Their findings, and the findings of those who followed them, have supported the view that seizures can be broadly divided into the two main categories mentioned above. Primary generalized seizures are those in which the symptoms of the seizure, and the EEG if it is being recorded at the onset, indicate that the whole of the brain becomes electrically abnormal synchronously at the moment when the seizure commences. In contrast, focal (partial) seizures are those in which the symptoms, and the EEG if it is being recorded at the onset, suggest that the electrical abnormality commences in a restricted area, usually a part of the cerebral cortex, even though the electrical abnormality may then spread more or less widely.

The commonest forms of primary generalized seizure are the tonic-clonic convulsion without aura (the *grand-mal* convulsion), the *petit-mal* absence, and the myoclonic jerk. The convulsion commences with the tonic phase in which the muscles stiffen symmetrically on both sides of the body and this is followed by the clonic phase of muscle jerking. Consciousness is lost from the outset and the person falls to the ground if he was standing. There may be an epileptic cry at the outset, a blue coloration may develop around the lips (cyanosis) and the facial skin especially in the tonic phase when breathing is interrupted, the bladder and/or the bowels may be emptied and the tongue may be bitten. When consciousness is regained the person may be confused and may act in an automatic fashion (see AUTOMATISM); a period of sleep may follow. The *petit-mal* absence lasts only a few seconds. There is loss of awareness but the person does not fall to the ground; he stares blankly and any movement is confined to flickering of the eyelids and/or very slight twitching of the facial and/or arm muscles. There are a number of varieties of absence seizure, but the true *petit mal* absence is characterized by an EEG pattern consisting of spike-wave activity occurring at the rate of 3 cycles per second. The myoclonic jerk consists of a very rapid symmetrical upward jerk of the arms accompanied by a nod of the head and a forward bend of the trunk.

The true *petit-mal* seizure occurs very predominantly in childhood and adolescence. It is almost invariably a manifestation of constitutional epilepsy rather than due to cerebral pathology, and it is strongly associated with a hereditary factor. Children who are prone to *petit-mal* seizures may also have myoclonic jerks and tonic-clonic convulsions. *Petit-mal* absence seizures and myoclonic jerks tend to become much less frequent after adolescence but convulsions may continue. Primary generalized convulsions and myoclonic jerks are most often seen in childhood and adolescence when the epilepsy is usually due to a constitutional predisposition—idiopathic epilepsy—but they can be due to diffuse cerebral pathology.

Focal (partial) seizures commence with electrical discharges in a restricted area of the brain. The initial symptom of the attack depends upon the location of the focal discharges. Thus, when the focus is in the motor cortex the seizure usually begins with jerking in a restricted group of muscles on the opposite side of the body, especially those of the face, hand or foot, since these are represented by the largest areas within the motor cortex. As the electrical discharges spread to other parts of the motor cortex, so more and more muscles on the opposite side of the body are incorporated into the convulsion. This spread in a pattern corresponding to the homunculus mapped on the motor cortex is known as the Jacksonian seizure and indeed enabled Hughlings Jackson to predict such a map. When the electrical discharges extend beyond the motor cortex, and especially when they pass through the *corpus callosum to the opposite cerebral hemisphere, conciousness is lost and the convulsion may become generalized involving both sides of the body.

A particularly common variety of focal seizure originates from discharges in the structures of one or other temporal lobe—temporal lobe epilepsy. The demonstration, particularly by the Montreal school under the leadership of Wilder *Penfield, that some cases of temporal lobe epilepsy can be cured by surgery has been an enormous stimulus to detailed study of many of its facets. The seizures often commence with a visceral sensation or an alteration of thought processes and perception which can be remembered afterwards. This is the aura. Those who experience an aura often find the content very difficult to describe, partly because their awareness and memory systems are distorted by the seizure and partly because the appropriate words to convey the quality of these abnormal sensations do not exist. Common visceral sensations include a feeling of nausea in the stomach or chest which may rise to the throat or head, nausea felt elsewhere in the body, hallucinations of smell or taste, giddiness, and palpitations. The alterations of thought process and perception often have an emotional content and frequently involve a distortion of memory. Brief feelings of extreme fear, anxiety, or depression are common. Feelings of elation are much less so. The aura may contain a feeling of familiarity as if everything has happened before (*déjà vu), there may be a feeling of intense unreality, sensations of perceptual illusion such as macropsia or micropsia may occur, and occasionally a complex visual or auditory hallucination is experienced. The aura may be followed by an automatism (referred to as a complex partial seizure in the current terminology). That is a period of altered behaviour for which the person is subsequently amnesic and during which he appears to have only limited awareness of his environment, if any at all. The behaviour in an automatism is usually primitive and stereotyped consisting of, for instance, lip smacking, chewing, grimacing, and gesturing, but sometimes much more complex behavioural acts are performed. Very occasionally an automatism continues for a prolonged period—a state known as an epileptic fugue (see DISSOCIATION OF THE PERSONALITY).

Whereas primary generalized seizures are characteristic of epilepsy due to a constitutional predisposition (idiopathic epilepsy) focal seizures are attributed to a focus of pathology. It is usually impossible to define the precise nature of this pathology, but occasionally it is a tumour or an area of brain damage due to head injury. Some cases of the most severe temporal lobe epilepsy are due to loss of neurones in the hippocampus (a structure situated in the medial part of the temporal lobe) caused by a prolonged convulsion occurring in early childhood, and when this abnormality is restricted to one side of the brain there is a good chance that surgery will effect a cure. Regular medication can suppress the seizures of many people prone to epilepsy but unfortunately by no means all.

Lastly, mention must be made of the concept of an epileptic personality. It has been claimed that a particular personality type is associated with epilepsy. The matter is complicated because epilepsy is associated with many factors which themselves may affect not only personality but many other aspects of mental function. These include cerebral pathology, anti-epileptic medication, the depression to which many people with epilepsy are prone, and the restrictions which society imposes on them. It is difficult to find any evidence that a particular personality is associated with epilepsy *per se* after due allowance has been made for these factors.

J. M. O.

Hippocrates. The Sacred Disease. In *Hippocrates. Medical Works*, vol. 2 (Loeb Classical Library, no. 148). Cambridge, Massachusetts.
Hopkins, A. (1981). *Epilepsy. The Facts*. Oxford.
Penfield, W. and Jasper, H. (1954). *Epilepsy and the Functional Anatomy of the Human Brain*. Boston.

**EPIPHENOMENA.** Phenomena that occur in association with, or are supervenient upon, a given set of events, yet supposedly are not caused by those events. The term is applied particularly to the mind–brain problem. An epiphenomenal account of mind is that mental events, and especially *consciousness, occur during physical brain activity but are not caused by physical activity. They are supposed, rather, to run in parallel but to be autonomous. This, of course, leaves mind totally inexplicable and mysterious from the point of view of physiology and everything we know of the physical world.

René *Descartes narrowly avoided epiphenomenalism, holding that the bodies and brains of organisms are 'mere' machines and supposing that mind is causally linked to the brain at the pineal gland. Mind and brain were, for Descartes, largely independent, and this is also so for many more modern psychologists, philosophers, and neurophysiologists—such as William *James and Sir John Eccles (Popper and Eccles, 1977)—who hold forms of interactive parallelism. These are almost statements of epiphenomenalism, except for limited causal interaction between mind and brain. It is indeed often thought that mind (especially awareness of pain, colours, emotions, etc.) is more affected by physical brain states than it, considered as a largely separate entity, itself affects the brain. The common-sense view is that most behaviour is automatic (in physiological terms, controlled by *reflexes) without corresponding mental events, and that only when there is deliberate or conscious volition does mind affect behaviour.

Popper, K. and Eccles, J. (1977). *The Self and its Brain*. London.

**EPIPHENOMENALISM.** See MIND–BODY PROBLEM: PHILOSOPHICAL THEORIES.

**EPISTEMOLOGY.** The branch of philosophy concerned with the theory of *knowledge. One of the oldest of philosophical debates concerns the origin of human knowledge. Empiricists traditionally maintain that all knowledge is ultimately derived from sensory experience. According to John *Locke the mind at birth is a blank sheet, or *tabula rasa*: 'how then comes it to be furnished with that vast store which the busy and boundless fancy of man has painted on it? To this I answer in one word, from *experience*' (*Essay Concerning Human Understanding*, 1690). Rationalist philosophers such as Descartes, by contrast, insist on the doctrine of innate ideas—that the mind is furnished from birth with certain fundamental concepts which enable it to arrive at knowledge a priori, independently of the senses (see INNATE IDEA). The question of whether human knowledge can transcend the senses, and of whether, and in what sense, a priori knowledge is possible, is one of the major themes of the philosophy of Kant (see KANT'S PHILOSOPHY OF MIND).

A central epistemological issue that goes right back to *Plato is the question of what is the difference between knowledge and mere belief. In what sense does the person who has knowledge differ from one who has a belief that may happen to be true? Much recent work in epistemology has been concerned with answering this question by analysing the concept of knowledge, and attempting to formulate a precise set of necessary and sufficient conditions for the truth of statements such as 'S knows that P'. (See further, ENTAILMENT; ESSENCE; KNOWLEDGE; NATURALISTIC ANALYSES.)

J. G. C.

**ERGONOMICS,** the study of efficiency of persons in their working environment, sometimes called 'human engineering', received its first impetus during the First World War, when the problem was to increase the productivity of semi-skilled munitions workers. This led to work by the British Medical Research Council's Industrial Health Research Board in the 1920s and 1930s on the effect of fatigue and boredom in repetitive tasks, and on the effect of the environment at work: lighting, heat and humidity, and noise. The main thrust came during the Second World War, when men in the fighting services had to handle equipment which was a lot more complex than they were used to. The obvious alternative to long and difficult training was to make the work easier.

**Design of displays.** Late in 1945, as soon as the war was over, Paul Fitts of the US Aero Medical Laboratory at Dayton, Ohio, started a comprehensive investigation of the problems facing people using the new complex equipment. He and his colleagues asked wartime pilots to describe actual experiences in which errors were made in reading and interpreting aircraft instruments. Of the 270 critical incidents reported, 40 involved a misreading of a three-handed altimeter by 1,000 feet (300 metres) or more.

An altimeter tells the pilot how high he is flying. Its three hands are covered with luminous paint. One hand is for the 10,000s, one for the 1,000s, and the third for the 100s. A bedside clock has only two luminous hands; even so, when waking up at night it is possible to confuse the minute-hand for the hour-hand, when the minute-hand is pointing to a likely hour like 2 or 4 a.m. With three hands to confuse, the altimeter provides still greater opportunities for error. On a clear day, an error in reading the height will be realized because the pilot can see the ground below; but on a dark night, and when flying in or above cloud, the pilot has no external means of telling that he has misread his height. An investigation in the laboratory compared reading the three-handed altimeter with reading the same heights from a digital counter, like the counter showing mileage in a car. The three-handed altimeter took longer to read, an average of seven seconds, compared with about one second for the counter. It caused more errors of 1,000 feet or more, which could be fatal in an aircraft—10 per cent compared with less than 1 per cent for the counter. Three-handed altimeters were used by the commercial airlines for another twenty years and continued to result in accidents. But they are not used now.

**Design of controls.** Fitts and his colleagues also asked the wartime pilots about errors in operating the controls of aircraft. Practically all the pilots of the US Army Air Force who were questioned reported that they sometimes made errors. Of the 460 errors reported, 89 involved confusing the three engine controls which alter the throttle, the propeller speed, and the fuel mixture. This was because the three controls were located in three different orders in three of the standard aircraft in use at the time. A pilot who was used to flying one type of aircraft was particularly likely to make an error when he changed to flying one of the other two types. As Fitts remarked: 'Imagine the difficulty most car drivers would experience in learning to brake with the left foot and to use the clutch pedal with the right.' In aircraft the error can be serious if just after take-off the pilot inadvertently reduces the throttle or mixture, when he intends to reduce the propeller speed. Yet pilots are trained not to look at the controls they are operating: they have to look at their instruments, and at the world outside the aircraft. They should not need to look to see if they are operating the correct control.

These and other reports of confusion between the controls of aircraft also led to laboratory investigations. One question investigated was the distance between controls needed to prevent a person from operating the wrong control. Another was the shape of control-knobs needed, so that each could easily be identified and distinguished by touch. Following this work, the controls in aircraft are now separated and shaped to avoid confusion; and they are located in approximately the same position in each new type of aircraft. (See also TRANSFER.)

**Control–display compatibility.** Of the 460 pilot errors reported in operating controls, 27 involved moving the control in the direction opposite to that required to produce the desired result. Some of these moves would have been in the correct direction if the pilot had been in his accustomed type of aircraft, and they are avoided by standardizing controls between aircraft. But other errors involved moving the control in the 'natural' or 'expected' direction, which happened to be wrong.

This finding led Fitts to his principle of 'control–display compatibility'. The most compatible control is the display-marker itself. In setting the minute-hand of a clock, the minute-hand is clasped directly with the fingers and rotated to the desired time. The nearer the control–display relationship can approximate to this, the easier it will be for the person operating the control. If the clock-hand is controlled by a knob or key, the control should rotate in the same direction as the clock-hand, not in the reverse direction. Where a number of instrument displays and their controls are located on a single panel, each control should be next to its display. The controls should not be mounted on a separate panel far away from their displays, or the person may operate the wrong control in error.

**Layout of equipment.** The investigations of displays and controls led naturally to investigations of the optimal layout for a set of displays and their related controls. People have to be able to see the displays and to reach the controls. Yet people come in different sizes: from anthropometry, the systematic measurement of body heights and lengths of limb segments, it became clear that seats must be adjustable, both in height and in the distance from the working surfaces. With adjustable seats, most displays and controls are now located in positions suited to the people who use them. The strength of the limbs operating controls in various positions has also been measured, to ensure that a control in a particular position is not too stiff to operate.

The layout of individual work-places is now often part of the overall layout of a control room or factory department. Since equipment has to be maintained as well as operated, it is necessary to leave space behind the consoles for the maintenance engineers. The time spent maintaining equipment may be small compared with that during which it is operated but, when equipment breaks down, it is inconvenient, expensive, or in the case of military equipment unacceptable if repairs cannot be carried out quickly. Thus maintenance needs have to be considered in design, as well as the needs of operatives.

In planning a factory department, the ergonomist now usually considers the organization of the work to be done. Some functions can be performed automatically, while others require people. The layout of the machines and work stations is made to follow the sequence of operations to be carried out.

**The environment at work.** Equipment sometimes needs to be designed especially for the environment in which it is to be used. Driving farm tractors and harvesters over rough fields subjects both the driver and the equipment to vertical vibration and jolting. The vibration blurs the numbers on the instrument scales, and so they have to be larger than usual if they are to be read easily. The jolting may make the driver move a control accidentally: the chances of this happening may be reduced if the controls move horizontally—that is, at right angles to the vertical jolting.

It is particularly important for the equipment which a person is using in a noisy environment to be designed ergonomically. In quiet surroundings a person can usually hear when he is operating equipment correctly: switches may produce audible clicks when they are pressed, and the tap of a hammer has a higher pitch when it hits a nail or rivet than when it misses and hits wood or canvas. In noisy surroundings such cues may not be audible, or may be difficult to distinguish one from another. If in operating equipment a person has to use his eyes, or sense of touch, instead of his ears, and if these senses are already heavily engaged, he may fail to notice mistakes.

The medical problems of the environment at work are now giving ergonomics a new impetus. Loud noise causes industrial deafness, as well as masking sounds, and calls for noise control and hearing protection. Vehicles and aircraft crashing at speed cause injuries that call for better designs of safety-harness and seat-belts. Work under water, say on oil and gas installations, is carried out at pressures several times greater than atmospheric pressure, and requires foolproof equipment (see also DIVER PERFORMANCE). Industrial processes produce dusts, vapours, and gases which may cause cancer or other illnesses. Ionizing radiation, and electromagnetic radiation of short wavelength, like gamma rays, X-rays, ultraviolet light, and the microwaves used in cooking, can also damage human organism. Dosimeters have to be designed and worn. The more generally harmful effects of atmospheric pollution need to be reduced by changes in industrial activity. Ergonomists today require knowledge of chemistry and physics in addition to their traditional knowledge of displays and controls.

**Interface between user and computer.** Research has now expanded to study the interface between people and computers. At first a computer system was considered acceptable as long as it worked. To use the system, the operator had to learn to think like the computer engineers who designed the system. The few full-time computer operators learnt to do this, but it was too difficult for many of the non-specialists who wanted to use a computer to help them with their job. Research is now directed towards designing 'user friendly' interfaces, which are easy for the part-time and casual user to learn and use (Card, Moran, and Newell, 1983).

E. C. P.

Card, S. K., Moran, T. P., and Newell, A. (1983). *The Psychology of Human–Computer Interaction*. Hillside, New Jersey.

Fitts, P. M. and Jones, R. E. (1947). (i) Analysis of factors contributing to 460 'pilot-error' experiences in operating aircraft controls; (ii) Psychological aspects of instrument display: analysis of 270 'pilot-error' experiences in reading and interpreting aircraft instruments. Reprinted in Sinaiko, H. W. (ed.), *Selected Papers on Human Factors in the Design and Use of Control Systems* (1961). New York.

Parker, J. F., Jr. and West, V. R. (eds.) (1973). *Bioastronautics Data Book*, 2nd edn. (National Aeronautics and Space Administration special publication 3006.) Washington, DC.

Poulton, E. C. (1979). *The Environment at Work*. Springfield, Illinois.

Van Cott, H. P. and Kinkade, R. G. (eds.) (1972). *Human Engineering Guide to Equipment Design*, rev. edn. Washington, DC.

**EROTIC.** Evocative of sexual passion, from the name of the god of love in Greek mythology. Eros is not personified in Homer, although the word is used to describe the sexual desire that drives Paris to Helen, and Zeus to Hera. Hesiod describes Eros as the god who 'loosens the limbs and damages the mind', and makes him (together with Earth and Tartarus) the oldest of the gods and all-powerful.

The Greek philosopher Parmenides makes Eros (the power of love) that which joins contrasting things together. In fact, it is no exaggeration to say that love for the Greeks was a binding force in their physics. Magnets (loadstones) were described as male and female; according to Pliny (*Natural History*, xxxvi, 126–30) strong magnets are male and weak magnets female. *Plato discourses upon Eros in the *Symposium* and *Phaedrus*.

**ESSENCE.** The essence of something is what it is to be that thing as opposed to something else. Thus the essence of a triangle is three-sidedness. In *Aristotelian philosophy, a thing's essence is given by specifying its defining characteristics—its 'essential' as opposed to 'accidental' features. Thus, being a malleable metal would be an essential characteristic of gold, but being mined in South Africa would be an accidental characteristic (since if gold ceased to be mined in South Africa it would still be gold).

There is a celebrated philosophical debate about whether statements about essence reflect the real nature of things or merely human linguistic conventions. The former view is known as 'essentialism' or 'realism', the latter as 'nominalism'. Recently the American philosopher Saul Kripke has revived a version of essentialism according to which natural kinds (gold, water) possess real essences: that is, certain characteristics are necessarily true of these substances, and this is not a matter of linguistic convention but is a matter of the real structure which these substances necessarily possess.

Questions about essence ('what is X?', 'what is it to be X?') have traditionally been distinguished from questions about existence ('does X exist?'), and questions of the former sort have been supposed to be prior to the latter (thus we can raise questions about the essential characteristics of triangles without having to concern ourselves about whether triangles really exist). Existentialists such as *Sartre, however, maintain that, in the case of human beings, 'existence precedes essence'. On this view, the first truth of which a human is aware is simply that he exists; his freedom to choose how to live is not constrained by any predetermined 'nature' or essence.

J. G. C.

Kripke, S. (1980). *Naming and Necessity*. Oxford.

**ETHICS OF BRAIN MANIPULATION.** See BRAIN MANIPULATION, ETHICS OF.

**ETHOLOGY.** Modern ethology abuts on so many different disciplines that it defies simple definition in terms of a common problem or a shared literature. The subject started out as the biological study of behaviour. However, as Robert Hinde (1982) noted, those who *call* themselves ethologists are now to be found working with neurobiologists, social and developmental psychologists, anthropologists, and psychiatrists, among many others. Even classical ethology gave itself a wide remit. Niko Tinbergen (1963) pointed to four broad but separate problems raised by the biological study of behaviour, namely: evolutionary history, individual development, short-term control, and current function. Moreover, it was plain that he and the other grandmasters of the subject, such as Konrad Lorenz, were not only aware of these different problems, but were actively interested in all of them.

Inasmuch as ethology still has a distinctive flavour, much of it derives from this breadth of interest. For that reason it is worthwhile taking a closer look at the four central problems identified by Tinbergen. (i) *Evolution*. What is the ancestral history? What can be deduced about the ways in which the behaviour evolved and the pressures that gave rise to it? (ii) *Development*. How is the behaviour assembled? What internal and external factors influence the way it develops in the lifetime of the individual, and how does the developmental process work? (iii) *Control*. How is the behaviour controlled? What internal and external factors regulate its occurrence, and how does the control process work? (iv) *Function*. What is the current use of the behaviour? In what way does the behaviour help to keep the animal alive or propagate its genes into the next generation?

Many ethologists had strong childhood interests in natural history and subsequently received a training in zoology. This aspect of their personal histories explains their interests in the evolution and survival value of behaviour. Impregnated as their thinking has been with the Darwinian theory of evolution, they repeatedly speculate on the adaptive significance of the differences between species. Indeed, many ethologists are primarily interested in biological function. Others are wary of proceeding far in laboratory studies without first relating their findings to the context in which the behaviour naturally occurs. The functional approach has certainly helped those who are interested in the study of mechanism.

Understanding what behaviour patterns are for provides the scientist with an important way of distinguishing between different types of behaviour. Equally valuable, the background knowledge obtained in functional studies has been fruitful in guiding investigators to the principal variables controlling a behaviour pattern. Being able to distinguish the important causal factors is extremely useful when designing experiments—in which, inevitably, only a small number of independent variables are actually manipulated while the others are held constant or are randomized. While looking at animals in an unrestricted environment, the observer becomes aware of the context in which each pattern of behaviour occurs. This suggests some of the conditions necessary for its occurrence and the events that bring it to an end.

The preoccupation of many ethologists with function has led to many excellent studies of animals in natural conditions. The justification for field-work is that an animal's behaviour is usually adapted to the environment in which it normally lives, in the same way that its anatomical or physiological characteristics are adapted. A captive animal is usually too constrained by its artificial environment to provide a complete understanding of the functions of the great variety of activities which most animals are capable of performing. To observe the full richness of its repertoire and understand the conditions to which its behaviour is adapted, the animal must usually be studied in the field. The patient observer notices the circumstances in which an activity is performed and those in which it never occurs, thereby obtaining clues as to what the behaviour pattern might be for (that is, its function). Field studies also relate behaviour patterns to the social and ecological conditions in which they normally occur. This led to the development of an area of research known as behavioural ecology. Another subdiscipline, sociobiology, brought to the study of behaviour important concepts and methods from population biology and stimulated further interest in field studies of animal behaviour. As commonly happens, the announcements that a new discipline had been founded were accompanied by strenuous efforts to distance the newcomer from its roots (see Wilson, 1975). However, the eclectic wisdom of the classical ethologists seems to have prevailed, and the various subdisciplines are showing signs of merging into a unified approach to the study of the biology of behaviour.

Studies in unconstrained conditions of animals, and increasingly of humans, have been an important feature of ethology and have played a major role in developing the distinctive and powerful methods for observing and measuring behaviour. Even so, it would be a mistake to represent ethologists as non-experimental and merely concerned with description. The point of doing an experiment is to distinguish between alternative explanations of hypotheses. Field observation can also achieve this goal if, for example, naturally occurring events demonstrate associations between variables that previously seemed unrelated, or break associations between variables that previously seemed bound together. Moreover, many simple, well-designed experiments have been performed outside the laboratory.

For example, Tinbergen wanted to explain why the ground-nesting black-headed gull removes the eggshell from its nest site after a chick has hatched. A number of different functional explanations initially seemed possible—the chick might injure itself on the sharp edges of the shell; the shell might be a source of disease by harbouring micro-organisms; the chick might get trapped under a shell and suffocate; the white inner surfaces of the shell fragments might attract predators visually; or the smell might attract predators by olfactory means. Tinbergen and colleagues were able to exclude a number of these candidates at the outset, using comparative evidence. Another gull, the kittiwake, nests on cliffs where it is not vulnerable to predators and does not remove the eggshell from its nest. This suggested that the first three possibilities were unlikely to be of major importance. A simple test, which involved placing shells at different distances from the nest, was then used to show that the broken eggshell does indeed attract predators to the black-headed gull's nest. The egg is cryptically coloured on the outside, but the inside is white and therefore easy for an airborne predator, such as a crow, to spot. The study confirmed that nests with open shells lying near them were more likely to be raided.

Field experiments have also been used to understand how an animal's behaviour is controlled. For example, tape-recordings of predators or conspecifics (such as offspring or potential mates) have been played to free-living animals in order to discover how they respond (see DANGER RECOGNITION). Dummies of different designs have similarly been used to gauge responsiveness to a particular shape or colour, such as the pecking of gull chicks at different objects more or less resembling the bills of their parents. These and many other examples make the point that even core ethology involves a great deal more than passive observation. Moreover, a great many people who call themselves ethologists have devoted much of their professional lives to laboratory studies of the control and development of behaviour.

At a certain stage in the history of ethology, certain key concepts and theories were associated with it. They no longer form a central part of ethological thought, although they were important in its development. Two basic concepts were the 'sign stimulus' and the 'fixed action pattern'. The notion of the sign stimulus, such as the red breast of a robin releasing an attack from an opponent, was productive in leading to the analysis of stimulus characters that selectively elicit particular bits of behaviour. Fixed action patterns (or modal action patterns as they are sometimes more appropriately called) provided useful units for description and comparison between species. Behavioural characters were used in taxonomy, and the zoological concern with evolution led to attempts to formulate principles for the derivation and ritualization of signal movements.

Both the concept of sign stimulus, or releaser, and that of the fixed action pattern played important roles in the early ethological attempts to develop systems models of behaviour. Lorenz's lavatory cistern model was a flow diagram in more than one sense and provided a generation of ethologists with a way of integrating their thinking about the multiple causation of behaviour, from both within and without. Needless to say, the model was seriously misleading; and in some systems of behaviour, notably *aggression, performance of behaviour makes repetition *more* likely, not less as the model predicts. Another systems model has stood the test of time rather better. It was developed by Tinbergen and was concerned with the hierarchical organization of behaviour. Here again, though, its major role lay not so much in its predictive power but in helping ethologists to bring together evidence that would otherwise have seemed unrelated.

Another classic ethological concern was with the inborn character of much behaviour (see INSTINCT). Indeed, Lorenz saw adult behaviour as involving the intercalation of separate and recognizable 'learned' and 'instinctive' elements. Very few people share this view any longer, and the work by the developmentally-minded ethologists on such phenomena as song-learning and imprinting in birds has been important in illustrating how the processes of development involve an interplay between internal and external factors (see IMPRINTING). After the early abortive attempts to classify behaviour in terms of instincts, attention has increasingly focused on faculties or properties of behaviour that bridge the conventional functional categories, such as feeding, courtship, caring for young, and so forth. Consequently, more and more emphasis is being placed on shared mechanisms of perception, storage of information and control of output. As this happens the interests of many ethologists are coinciding to a greater and greater extent with the traditional concerns of psychology.

The modern work has also eroded another belief of the classical ethologists: that all members of the same species of the same age and sex will behave in the same way. The days are over when a field-worker could confidently suppose that a good description of a species obtained from one habitat could be generalized to the same species in another set of environmental conditions. The variations in behaviour within a species may, of course, reflect the pervasiveness of learning processes (see CONDITIONING). However, as in a juke-box, some alternative modes of behaviour may be *selected* rather than informed by prevailing environmental conditions. For instance, many adult male gelada baboons are very much bigger than the females and, once they have taken over a group of females, defend them from the attentions of other males. Other males are the same size as a female and sneak copulations when a big male is not looking. The offsetting benefit for the small males is that they have much longer reproductive lives than the big ones. It seems likely that any young male can grow either way, and the particular way in which it develops depends on conditions. Examples such as this are leading to a growing interest in alternative tactics, their functional significance, and the nature of the developmental principles involved.

In describing and analysing behaviour, it makes good sense to start by obeying the canon of Conwy Lloyd *Morgan and treat animals in the simplest possible way until there is good reason to think otherwise. Nevertheless, as in other fields, many ethologists have come to feel that slavish obedience to a methodological maxim tends to sterilize imagination. A person who studies behaviour and *never* treats the animal as though it were human is liable to miss some of the richness and complexity of what it does. Many experienced ethologists have found how much they are helped if they put themselves in the animal's place and consider how they would deal with the situation. They notice important influences on the animal's behaviour which they would otherwise have overlooked, and are led to perform experiments which they would not otherwise have done. For these reasons, terms such as 'intention', 'awareness' and 'reasoning' are being used with increasing frequency in studies of animal behaviour, despite the well-known pitfalls of excessive anthropomorphism and teleological argument. It seems likely that cognitive ethology will expand and, as it does so, start contributing to the study of mind.

P. P. G. B.

Hinde, R. A. (1982). *Ethology*. London.
Tinbergen, N. (1963). On aims and methods of ethology. *Zeitschrift für Tierpsychologie*, **20**, 410–33.
Wilson, E. O. (1975). *Sociobiology*. Cambridge, Massachusetts.

**EUCLID** (*c.*300 BC). Famous for his work on geometry, known as *Euclid's Elements* (modern English translation by T. L. Heath, 1956), Euclid was a Greek whose birthplace is not known. (In the Middle Ages he was known as Euclid of Megara, but this was the result of a confusion between him and a philosopher who lived around 400 BC.) It is thought probable that he received his mathematical training in Athens from pupils of *Plato. What is known is that he taught in Alexandria and founded a school there. From the writings of Greek commentators we learn that he wrote about a dozen works other than the *Elements*. Only five of these, the *Data*, the *Division of Figures*, the *Phaenomena*, and the *Optics*, have survived.

Aristotle described as elements of *geometry those propositions whose proofs are contained in proofs of most other geometrical propositions. In a similar vein Proclus (*c.*AD 412–85) likened the relation the elements of geometry bear to the rest of geometry to the relation the letters of an alphabet bear to a language. Euclid's was not the first exposition of the elements of geometry; we know of at least three earlier versions, including one by Hippocrates of Chios. But Euclid's seems to have so outclassed these that it alone has survived. His achievement was to have imposed a thorough systematic organization on geometry, one in which, starting from *axioms, definitions, and postulates, each proposition is proved either directly from these or from these together with propositions already proved. It thus provides an early example of a deductively organized body of knowledge, and it has functioned as a paradigm for all other sciences for at least 2,000 years.

The *Elements* is divided into thirteen books of which the first four concern basic plane geometry. Books V and VI develop a theory of proportions, generally credited to Eudoxus of Cnidos (*c.*390–340 BC), which overcomes the problem of incommensurable magnitudes, which are explicitly tackled in Book X. Books VII–IX deal with numbers and ratios between numbers, and Books XI–XIII are chiefly devoted to solid geometry. M. E. T.

**EUGENICS.** See GALTON, SIR FRANCIS.

**EVOKED POTENTIAL.** The study of evoked brain potentials arose as an extension of the interest in the spontaneous electrical activity of the brain, recorded in *electroencephalography. It was recognized even by Richard Caton, who first recorded the electrical activity of the brains of animals in 1875, that the voltages recorded from the brain's surface could be influenced by external events impinging on the senses.

Hans *Berger, who discovered the resting alpha rhythm of the electroencephalogram (EEG) in man some fifty years later, noted the disappearance of this oscillation, which had a characteristic frequency between 8 and 12 hertz, when the subject was stimulated by stroking the back of the hand (Fig. 1) or alerted by an auditory stimulus. He noted that the alpha rhythm could also be blocked by voluntary movement or mental arithmetic. This alpha-blocking reaction could be said to be the first of the evoked responses of the human brain to become the subject of scientific study.

Lord *Adrian in Cambridge demonstrated that the alpha rhythm arose particularly from the occipital areas of the brain and that its appearance was associated especially with visual inattention. Visual stimuli were much more effective in blocking the alpha rhythm than those of other modalities (Fig. 2). He also showed that a train of evoked potentials could be recorded from electrodes situated over the occipital lobe in response to a series of bright flash stimuli presented to the eyes. These photically evoked potentials were the first of the 'specific' sensory evoked potentials to be recorded in man.

The two decades following Berger's discovery of the alpha rhythm were marked by an increasing pace of advance in knowledge of the electrical activity of the brain. The potentials evoked by sensory stimulation in the specific visual, auditory, and somatosensory receiving areas in the cortex were studied in the exposed brains of animals and became accessible to study in man when methods of separating out the small potentials from the larger oscillations of the spontaneous background EEG were developed in the 1940s by George D. Dawson. Recorded from electrodes on the intact scalp, he was able to show that consistent responses of around 10 μV in amplitude could be recorded following electrical stimulation of peripheral nerve trunks through the skin in the conscious, intact human subject. The technique used depended on giving a large number of similar stimuli and adding the responses together, either by photographic superimposition or (in a later development) with an electronic averager. In this way, the consistent features of the response are reinforced, while the random variation in the background (noise) is minimized.

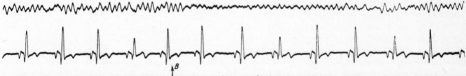

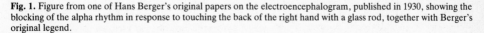

Dr. V., 30 year old physician. Double-coil galvanometer. Condenser inserted. Recording from forehead and occiput with chlorided silver needle electrodes. Electrocardiogram with silver foil electrodes from the left arm and the left leg. At the top: the electroencephalogram; in the middle: the electrocardiogram; at the bottom: time in 1/10ths sec. *B*: time at which the dorsum of the right hand was touched and stroking with a glass rod along the latter began.

**Fig. 1.** Figure from one of Hans Berger's original papers on the electroencephalogram, published in 1930, showing the blocking of the alpha rhythm in response to touching the back of the right hand with a glass rod, together with Berger's original legend.

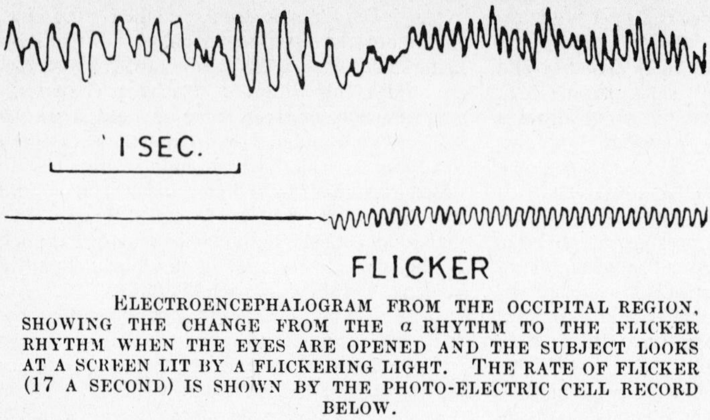

## FLICKER

ELECTROENCEPHALOGRAM FROM THE OCCIPITAL REGION, SHOWING THE CHANGE FROM THE α RHYTHM TO THE FLICKER RHYTHM WHEN THE EYES ARE OPENED AND THE SUBJECT LOOKS AT A SCREEN LIT BY A FLICKERING LIGHT. THE RATE OF FLICKER (17 A SECOND) IS SHOWN BY THE PHOTO-ELECTRIC CELL RECORD BELOW.

**Fig. 2.** An early recording of the visual evoked potential to flicker stimulation, from a paper by Adrian, published in 1944.

Small laboratory averagers became commercially available in the 1960s, enabling many centres to begin work on the clinical and scientific applications of evoked potential recording. As well as much further work with the types of stimulation used in the earlier studies, such as electrical stimulation of the limb nerves and stroboscopic flash stimuli, the responses to more 'natural' forms of stimulation were investigated, including tactile stimulation of the fingers and the visual responses evoked by sudden reversal of a black and white chequer-board pattern, which the subject viewed on an illuminated screen. The latter type of stimulus proved particularly successful in clinical work, as it transpired that marked abnormalities of the response were found in association with demyelinating lesions of the visual pathways in multiple sclerosis and in other disorders of vision associated with ocular or neurological disorders.

At about the same time, the scope of evoked potential research was greatly widened by an awakening interest in other event-related brain potentials associated, for instance, with preparing to make a response (readiness potential, *Bereitschaftspotential*, and motor potential) or expecting a stimulus to which one is to respond (contingent negative variation, CNV, or expectancy wave, E-wave).

The motor potential studies required the development of a new technique of opisthochronic averaging, 'averaging backwards in time', since interest was here focused on the events preceding an event, the response, whose exact time could not be predicted in advance. The latter is an example of a so-called endogenous potential as distinct from the exogenous sensory evoked potentials, whose occurrence and timing depended upon an external event, the sensory stimulus.

The *Bereitschaftspotential*, or readiness potential, which consisted of a slow build-up in negativity over the central regions of the cortex during the 1–2 seconds preceding a response, depended for its occurrence on the probability and predictability of the motor act, whether this was self-paced or made in response to an expected stimulus.

An even more interesting family of event-related potentials (ERP) can be recorded when a stimulus is sufficiently *im*probable and yet significant. These are the so-called P300 waves, which depend for their incidence on the unexpectedness of the relevant event. They were first described in two papers by Sutton and colleagues in 1965 and 1967 and have been extensively studied since that time. Even the unlooked-for absence of an expected event (Fig. 3) can elicit a P300, as in the case of a single missing stimulus in a long train of repeated tones.

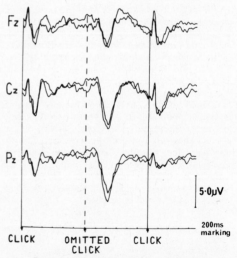

Evoked potentials to omitted stimuli. Clicks were presented regularly every 1.1 sec and occasionally a click was omitted; the subject was asked to count the number of omissions. The averaging computer was triggered by the click immediately preceding the omission. Evoked potentials are shown for three different scalp positions. Each tracing represents the average of 64 responses. Subject T.P.

**Fig. 3.** P300 evoked by a non-event, viz. the unexpected omission of one of a regular train of clicks. Note the large P300 wave, occurring with each scalp position.

*Semantic* improbability is associated with an N400 wave, a negativity occurring about 0·4 seconds following the unexpected word (e.g. when the sentence 'He spread the warm bread with socks' is presented, one word at a time, on a visual display, a large N400 wave occurs only in respect to the unexpected word 'socks'). No such response occurs to the sentences: 'It was his first day at work' or 'She put on her high-heeled shoes'. These language-related ERPs were first described by Kutas and Hillyard from San Diego in 1980. Work on linguistically related ERPs has also been carried out by Goto in Japan, who has studied the brain responses associated with the resolution of linguistic ambiguities.                                         A. M. H.

**EVOLUTION: HAS IT A PURPOSE?** If we agree that all organisms show something that may reasonably be called *choice, it implies that their actions are at least partly directed towards an end. Of course, if one reserves the words 'aim' and 'end' for something that is sought 'consciously' then they cannot be used for the 'teleonomic' actions of all living things. The biologist's plea should surely be that we seek for enlightenment from the similarities between species, as well as from their differences, and not allow terminology to interfere. It is amazing that many biologists should have so strongly maintained that they did not wish to consider aims, in the face of the obvious fact that organisms act so as to stay alive. Equally surprising is the unwillingness to admit that it is possible to see any sign of progress in evolution. Of course there are difficulties, but we can now put measures on the degree of complexity of organisms and can give a precise meaning to such statements as that man is the summit of an increasing process of collection of information. It is still conventional to say that questions of value cannot be decided by facts, and indeed everyone will agree that the meaning of 'good' is difficult to determine. Following G. E. *Moore, we are usually asked to hold that the only things that possess intrinsic value are human states of mind. The biologist can hardly accept that this is the last word. Surely our decisions about value are not wholly 'intuitive'. Whether we like it or not they are guided by the influences that have imposed themselves upon us, many of them biological, others social. Of course, to insist that it is nonsense to claim that judgements are wholly intuitive does not actually provide us with criteria for the meanings of 'good' and 'bad', still less for making ethical judgements and recommendations. Yet the general biologist can contribute marginally even to the characteristically human discussion of ultimates.

We do not know yet for certain how, when, or why life began or whether and when it will end. On such things indeed biologists are gaining some knowledge but can still only speculate. The anthropomorphic guesses of theologians have led people to hope for a certainty that we now realize to be unobtainable. But this does not mean that there are no signs of direction in human life. We can see that we have a long and wonderful history, involving an increasing collection of information and its use to allow life to invade regions not habitable before (Young, 1938).

Life probably began over 3,000 million years ago, perhaps in a probiotic soup of organic molecules (Bernal, 1967). We are uncertain what originally determined the ordering of specific nucleotides and proteins, but the subsequent course of evolution has certainly involved an increase of order. For perhaps the first 2,000 million years, life remained very simple. The few fossil remains that we have are of bacteria or algae. The evidence of the sedimentary rocks shows that by 500 million years ago there were already many complex invertebrates. Then came the first fishes and after them the amphibians, reptiles, birds, and mammals. The point of this now familiar story is that the whole sequence indubitably involves an increase of complexity of organization and of the information transmitted to ensure it. Under the pressure of natural selection, organisms have invaded ever new niches, made habitable by the development of special mechanisms. The examples are endless—to colonize fresh water an organism needs to pump out the excess that flows in. To colonize the land involves preventing loss of water and developing mechanisms for finding it. The skin, which in fishes is a relatively homogeneous tissue, becomes differentiated in mammals into perhaps 100 different sorts, all coded for in the DNA. And so on, through all the adaptions that pervade organisms. Of course the progressive increase of order is notoriously irregular. But the numbers of pairs of nucleotides give us a means of quantifying it. In a virus there are about $2 \times 10^5$ pairs, equivalent to 100 pages of 2,000 letters to the page. In a bacterium there are $5 \times 10^6$ pairs (2,500 pages) and in man $3 \cdot 5 \times 10^9$ (1,700 books of 1,000 pages each). There are many difficulties—for instance we cannot yet properly qualify the differences in complexity among mammals. But we do know that man has developed entirely novel methods of gathering information and storing and transmitting it outside the body.

These facts show that life has had a direction in the past and that man in the last million years has speeded it along its course. We cannot see direction or purpose when we look at the heavens, but we can see them in the progress of life on earth. Perhaps one day we shall be wise enough to see them in the stars too.

Meanwhile we can see that our wants and needs and ambitions are not in vain. They are there to guide us and we should not deny them. They tell us truly what is worth while to do for ourselves and for our species. If we look wider still we can see the implications of our very special place in nature. This shows the biological ethic, the imperative to increase variety and to collect further information with which to conserve life and even to create new ways in which it can continue.                         J. Z. Y.

Young, J. Z. (1938). The evolution of the nervous system and of the relationship of organism and environment. In de Beer, G. R. (ed.), *Evolution*. Oxford.

## EVOLUTION: NEO-DARWINIAN THEORY.

**History.** Charles *Darwin was by no means the first evolutionist. Ideas of transformation of species can be found in the classics ('It's all in Lucretius' was Matthew Arnold's comment on Darwin) and in the writings of eighteenth-century thinkers such as Buffon, Diderot, Goethe, and Charles's grandfather Erasmus *Darwin. But all those ideas are vague or covert. The French biologist (he coined that word) *Lamarck was the first to present an articulate and explicit theory of biological evolution in his *Philosophie zoologique* (1809). Other notable precursors of Darwin were the Scottish publisher Robert Chambers (1802–71) with his anonymous *Vestiges of the Natural History of Creation* (1844), and Alfred Russel *Wallace, whose independent discovery of the mechanism of natural selection prompted Darwin to abridge a vast, unfinished manuscript as *On the Origin of Species by Means of Natural Selection, or the Preservation of Favoured Races in the Struggle for Life* (1859). Natural selection, a materialistic explanation for adaptation and the diversity of life, was Darwin's main contribution. Coupled with a candid and persuasive argument, it was enough to convince most scientists of the truth of evolution, and to capture the imagination of most late nineteenth-century thinkers.

The latter part of the nineteenth century was a period of exploration of evolutionary theory. Its biological ramifications formed the mainspring of much late Victorian science, and Darwin's theory soon became influential in many other fields, notably anthropology, sociology, politics, philosophy, and psychology. As this list implies, Darwinism was seen by many as a coherent world view.

In 1900, Gregor Mendel's work on inheritance, originally published in 1866, was rediscovered, and the science of genetics was born. Mutation theory soon replaced natural selection as the most promising field of research into mechanisms of change, and for a while Darwinism was at a low ebb. But towards the end of the 1920s, mathematicians and geneticists—chiefly R. A. *Fisher, J. B. S. Haldane, and Sewall Wright—showed that genetic theory and natural selection were fully compatible, so founding population genetics, which became the central area of evolutionary research. The integration of population genetics with more traditional fields of evolutionary interest such as anatomy, palaeontology, and systematics (classification) was pushed forward in the late 1930s and early 1940s in books by T. Dobzhansky (a geneticist), E. Mayr (a systematist), and G. G. Simpson (a palaeontologist). Julian Huxley's *Evolution: the modern synthesis* (1942) gave an alternative name—the synthetic theory—for neo-Darwinism.

In 1953 Francis Crick and James Watson transferred interest to the molecular level with their model of the structure of deoxyribonucleic acid (DNA), the material basis of heredity. Exploration of the implications of the Watson–Crick model soon resulted in the breaking of the genetic code, unravelling of the mode of translation of the genetic message, and development of other branches of molecular biology. Ideas from molecular biology, though broadly consistent with neo-Darwinism, are one of many sources of a new ferment in evolutionary thought. Darwinism and its modern descendant are by no means fossilized theories, embedded as true foundations by scientific progress. Where the current ferment will lead, or end, is impossible to guess. But the ingredients of the brew can be matched with some of the main headings of Darwin's argument as presented in *The Origin*: variation, natural selection, instinct (behaviour), fossils, classification, embryology—and the origin of species, the title of his book, but a topic that he hardly tackled.

**Classification.** The basic unit in biological classification is the species. Attempts to define species have been made for centuries and no definition has yet been found to cover every case. Virtually all definitions emphasize reproduction—species are those aggregations of organisms within which mating and reproduction are normal and successful. The modern abstraction covering this concept is 'gene-pool': a species is a set of organisms sharing a set of genes, and the sharing is manifested in the mixing of the genes of two parents in the fertilized egg. Genes of one species are not mixed with those of another, because mating is not attempted, or is unsuccessful through the sperm failing to fertilize the egg, or through failure in development of the embryo, or through sterility of the hybrid offspring. The molecular basis for success or failure in reproduction is the exact matching of maternal and paternal chromosomes which is necessary in the cell division producing egg or sperm cells.

These criteria are broadly applicable in all sexual plants and animals. In asexual organisms, reproducing by simple fission, for example, it is difficult to form a rational concept of species, since the only link between organisms is a historical one of more or less remote common parentage (see Fig. 1). We recognize this by resemblance between the descendants.

The basic tenet of a theory of evolution is that the relation between species is also historical and due to past common ancestry, manifested in resemblances between species. To evolutionists, the distinct gene-pools of today's species are selected and modified fractions of the gene-pools of more or less distant common ancestral species. One central task of a theory of evolution is to explain how discontinuities in gene exchange may arise—how a species may split (see section headed 'Origin of species' below).

Above the species level, it is common experience that there are groups of species which seem to go

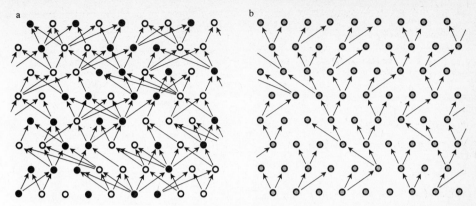

**Fig. 1.** Population structure in sexual and asexual species. **a.** A sexual species, like our own, in which each individual has two parents of different sexes (dark or light blobs). **b.** An asexual species in which the parent reproduces by dividing into two, as in simple plants and animals like amoeba; each individual has only one parent. According to the theory of evolution, the history of life is a pattern like this, in which blobs are species, not individuals. If the population is to remain constant from generation to generation, only half the individuals in **b** may reproduce. In **a**, a parent produces more than two offspring only at the expense of others.

together: birds, for example, or beetles or cats. Biological classification formalizes this fact of life by giving these groups Latin or Latinized proper names (birds are Aves, beetles are Coleoptera, cats are Felidae), and by ranking those names in a hierarchy of more or less inclusive categories (Aves is a class—category—within the phylum Vertebrata; Coleoptera is an order in the class Insecta; Felidae is a family in the order Carnivora and class Mammalia). These names and ranks are conventions, but from *Aristotle to Linnaeus (eighteenth century) to today, those who propose classifications usually believe that they express something real, an order in nature. Before Darwin, that order was commonly rationalized as 'the plan of the Creator' or the imperfect reflection of unchanging and ideal *essence. According to Darwin and his followers, the relation between birds, or between beetles, or between birds and cats is not abstract but historical or genealogical, due to common descent (see CLADISTICS).

The central concept of classification is *homology*. When a child learns to recognize birds, the criteria used are, at root, the same as those used by the scientist: the feathers, beak, wings, and so on are 'the same' in a sparrow and a swan, whereas the wings of a beetle or the beak of a turtle do not make those creatures birds—the 'sameness' is different or inessential; technically, it is analogy rather than homology. The task of biological classification is thus to distinguish homology (informative sameness) from analogy (misleading sameness). And the interest of classification to the evolutionist is that homologies, the characters of groups, are seen as evidence of common ancestry, so that the hierarchy reflects real historical relations. A research programme is implicit here, to reconstruct the history of life through the common ancestry inferred from homologies. Since Darwin first pro-

posed that 'Our classifications will come to be, as far as they can be so made, genealogies', this programme has been followed with enthusiasm. The programme concerns the main outlines of life's history; it integrates classification with morphology, palaeontology, and embryology. This work is an extrapolation from evolutionary theory, and the fact that the work can be carried out does not materially affect the theory itself. The theory depends on more basic matters, an explanation of how species originate. Darwin approached that problem first through his study of variation.

**Variation.** Lacking a sound theory of inheritance, Darwin studied it through the experience of those with a practical interest in it, animal and plant breeders. Of the manuscript, from which *The Origin* was abridged, the only part that Darwin actually published was the two-volume *Variation of Animals and Plants under Domestication* (1868). In *The Origin* Darwin argued by analogy. Under domestication, breeders observed variations and were often able to perpetuate them by selective mating. Over many generations, the breeds or varieties of dogs, cabbages, pigeons (Darwin's pets), and so on are the result. Darwin's opinions on the causes and inheritance of variation are chiefly of historical interest now. He wrestled with the problem of whether variation is spontaneous, or is provoked by the 'conditions of life' (i.e. the environment), and favoured the environment. And he tried to analyse the mode of inheritance, whether or not it is 'blending', offspring being intermediate between the parents. Blending seemed empirically true for many characteristics, and it has the consequence that a new variation would be swamped or diluted over the generations. These problems, of the origin of variation and its inheritance, were not solved until the twentieth

| | | | SECOND LETTER | | | | | | | |
|---|---|---|---|---|---|---|---|---|---|---|
| | | A | | G | | T | | C | | |
| **FIRST LETTER** | A | AAA Phenylalanine<br>AAG Phenylalanine<br>AAT Leucine<br>AAC Leucine | | AGA Serine<br>AGG Serine<br>AGT Serine<br>AGC Serine | | ATA Tyrosine<br>ATG Tyrosine<br>ATT Stop<br>ATC Stop | | ACA Cysteine<br>ACG Cysteine<br>ACT Stop<br>ACC Tryptophan | | A<br>G<br>T<br>C |
| | G | GAA Leucine<br>GAG Leucine<br>GAT Leucine<br>GAC Leucine | | GGA Proline<br>GGG Proline<br>GGT Proline<br>GGC Proline | | GTA Histidine<br>GTG Histidine<br>GTT Glutamine<br>GTC Glutamine | | GCA Arginine<br>GCG Arginine<br>GCT Arginine<br>GCC Arginine | | A<br>G<br>T<br>C |
| | T | TAA Isoleucine<br>TAG Isoleucine<br>TAT Isoleucine<br>TAC Methionine | | TGA Threonine<br>TGG Threonine<br>TGT Threonine<br>TGC Threonine | | TTA Asparagine<br>TTG Asparagine<br>TTT Lysine<br>TTC Lysine | | TCA Serine<br>TCG Serine<br>TCT Arginine<br>TCC Arginine | | A<br>G<br>T<br>C |
| | C | CAA Valine<br>CAG Valine<br>CAT Valine<br>CAC Valine | | CGA Alanine<br>CGG Alanine<br>CGT Alanine<br>CGC Alanine | | CTA Aspartic Acid<br>CTG Aspartic Acid<br>CTT Glutamic Acid<br>CTC Glutamic Acid | | CCA Glycine<br>CCG Glycine<br>CCT Glycine<br>CCC Glycine | | A<br>G<br>T<br>C |

THIRD LETTER

**Table 1.** The genetic code.
The letters A, G, T, and C stand for adenine, guanine, thymine, and cytosine, the four bases in DNA. The 64 possible triplet combinations of these letters are shown, together with their meaning—the named amino acid, or 'stop'. Most of the redundancy of the code is in the third letters of the triplets: AG-, GA-, GG-, GC-, TG-, CA-, CG-, and CC- each has the same meaning, regardless of the third letter.

century, with the development of genetics and, later, molecular genetics.

There is no space here to go into genetic theory, and its outlines must be baldly stated. The material basis of heredity is DNA, a ladder-like molecule which carries a message in the form of a 'four-letter' code, the letters being four chemical bases, each of which may occupy any rung in the ladder. The message is read in triplets, or 'three-letter words', and the words are of two kinds, 'stop' or 'amino acid X'. Twenty different amino acids are encoded by triplets, some by a single triplet, others by up to six different ones (see Table 1). Thus the genetic message specifies sequences of amino acids terminated by stop signs, and, when translated and acted upon, the result is proteins, which are chains of amino acids. Genes are sections of DNA which specify a discrete amino acid chain.

DNA is carried in chromosomes, in the nucleus of every cell. When sex cells (eggs or sperm) are produced, the chromosomes pair off very precisely, each pair containing one chromosome from each of the two parents, and within each pair parts are exchanged at random (crossing-over). The newly mixed chromosomes then separate in a cell division which produces sex cells containing one member of each pair, so that the number of chromosomes is halved. The number characteristic of the species is restored when the egg and sperm nuclei, each carrying a half set, unite in the fertilized egg. Inheritance is not blending: genes are passed on unchanged from generation to generation.

With that background, the sources of heritable variation can be specified. First, the genes of each new individual are a new assortment, because they

combine two half sets (from egg and sperm) each shuffled in the crossing-over between chromosome pairs in the parental cell divisions that produced them. This is a form of variation generated by shuffling existing material, as each deal of a shuffled pack of several thousand cards would be unique. Second, new variation may be introduced by mutations: accidents or mistakes in replication and repair of DNA or mishaps in cell division. Mistakes in DNA can alter one or more bases in the molecule (letters in the code), and may alter one or more amino acids in the protein specified. Mishaps in cell division may alter parts of chromosomes—lengths of DNA—which may be inverted, deleted, duplicated, or transferred to another chromosome. The effect of mutations on individual organisms ranges from negligible or indetectable to lethal. The effect of mutations on the reproductive capacity of an individual (i.e. the formation of viable eggs or sperm) also varies from indetectable to sterility. Known mutations in DNA turn up with frequencies from about 1 in $10^4$ to 1 in $10^8$: they are rare, but frequent enough for every human individual to carry several mutations which have arisen during his or her life. Most of these will be in somatic (body) cells, not in eggs or sperm, and so cannot be passed on to the next generation.

That statement recalls the other question that bothered Darwin—whether variations acquired during life can be inherited. The question refers to what is now called Lamarckian inheritance, for *Lamarck proposed that the effects of use and disuse and other changes during life are heritable, and are a cause of evolutionary change. In fact, Darwin held much the same belief. The orthodox answer to the question is no—acquired characters are not inherited. One reason for this is that offspring inherit only an egg or sperm from each parent, and at least in animals those cells are sequestered very early in embryonic life, before the environment takes its effect. A second reason is that translation of DNA into protein—construction of the organism—is held to be a one-way process, with no feedback from the organism to the DNA. This notion is the 'central dogma' of molecular genetics. The one known exception to that dogma is reverse transcriptase, an enzyme which transcribes RNA, the messenger nucleic acid, into DNA, the message store. But to get environmentally induced information into DNA requires more, a way of getting such information into RNA (reverse translation rather than transcription). No such mechanism is yet known. But there has been support for a neo-Lamarckian model of evolution, and various ways in which the environment might direct or influence the genes have been suggested.

Ideas on variation have gained impetus from techniques for separating variant protein molecules, and so estimating the proportion of variant genes in individuals and species. The result is surprising: there is much more hidden variation than was expected. Hidden genetic variation in one individual is due to different forms of homologous genes in the half set of chromosomes inherited from each parent. In humans, if the few that have been tested are a fair sample of the whole, the proportion of variant genes in each individual is at least 6 per cent, about normal for vertebrate species; in plants and invertebrates variation is often higher, 15 per cent or more. With the discovery that the genes of species are less uniform than expected, the problem has shifted from Darwin's—where does variation come from?—to a new one—why is there so much variation? Orthodox neo-Darwinism demands that it be due to natural selection.

**Natural selection.** Darwin's main contribution was natural selection, the survival of the fittest, a materialist explanation for evolutionary change. There have been several presentations of natural selection theory as a deductive argument. Here are three: (i) All organisms produce far more offspring than are necessary to replace them, yet numbers of each species remain roughly constant. Therefore, there is differential mortality, a struggle for existence. (ii) All organisms manifest hereditary variations. Therefore, those organisms inheriting variations useful in the struggle for existence will be more likely to survive to pass on those variations. (iii) The environment is not constant. Therefore, those hereditary variations advantageous in a changing environment will be selected, and species will change to remain in harmony with the environment. This is adapted from an 1870 formalization by A. R. Wallace. It emphasizes the effect of changing environments, and the observed constancy in numbers of individuals.

A briefer form, due to the philosopher A. G. N.

Flew, is: (i) Geometrical rate of increase + limited resources → Struggle for existence. (ii) Struggle for existence + variation → Natural selection. (iii) Natural selection + time → Biological improvement. This emphasizes the theoretical limits on environmental resources rather than constant populations and changing environments, and introduces the notion of 'improvement'. What is improved is not specified.

Another brief form: (i) All organisms must reproduce. (ii) All organisms exhibit genetic variation. (iii) Genetic variations differ in their effect on reproduction. (iv) Therefore, variant genes with favourable effects on reproduction will succeed, those with unfavourable effects will fail, and gene proportions will change. This emphasizes variant genes, and reproductive success rather than environmental factors.

If natural selection can be presented as a deductive argument in which the conclusion follows logically from the premises, then it must be true if the premises are true. If the premises in one, or all three, of these formulations are empirically true, natural selection must occur.

But we have to be clear about what is selected. Natural selection concerns differential survival or, the other side of the coin, differential extinction. What are the units that survive or become extinct: are they genes, or fragments of genes (e.g. triplets or single nucleotides), or chromosomes, or genotypes (genetic constitutions of individuals), or phenotypes (individual organisms, each expressing its own genotype), or groups of organisms, or species? Wallace's formulation of selection refers to species, Flew's perhaps to individuals, and the third form to genes: are they all correct? All descriptions of natural selection invoke interactions, of individual organisms with the inorganic environment, with other individuals in reproduction, with individuals of other species in predator–prey interactions, and so on. Descriptions of natural selection also invoke replication or multiplication, of genes, or of individuals carrying favourable mutations. DNA and chromosomes mutate and replicate, but since they do not interact with the environment, selection cannot act on them directly. It is individual organisms or phenotypes—life histories—that interact with the environment, but the genotype of every successful organism, the set of chromosomes, is broken up and reshuffled by crossing-over when it produces eggs or sperm, so that individuals (genotype + phenotype) do not reproduce themselves exactly.

In the network of ancestor–descendent relations over the generations (Fig. 1), the units that survive differentially, or are selected, are bits of DNA of unspecifiable length. If there is selective change over a number of generations, some bits of DNA in the original population will be represented by many copies in the final population, and others will not be represented at all, because they became extinct when the organisms carrying them failed to reproduce. In order to summarize the change, we have to use the abstraction 'gene-pool'. Over the generations, there is a change in the gene-pool of the population or species. Of course, no one has ever seen a gene-pool or dipped a finger in one, and the tangible effect of the change will be a change in the phenotypes in the population.

One definition of 'gene' is 'a portion of chromosome which survives enough generations to act as a unit of natural selection'. That definition may sound vacuously circular, as if we have to understand natural selection before we can understand genes, yet understanding natural selection depends on understanding genes. But it at least emphasizes the point that because chromosomes are randomly broken up in each generation by crossing-over, there is no particular unit that survives intact over many generations. Indeed, there is a theory of 'hitch-hiking' natural selection; a neutral or disadvantageous mutation may spread because it happens to be adjacent to an advantageous one, so that the two survive as a unit without being separated by the chances of crossing-over.

Because some organisms exhibit parental care, or social organization in which more or less extensive kinship groups take part, the family or kin-group may have sufficient cohesion to act as a unit of natural selection, kin selection as it is called. Beyond kin-groups, the next steps up the genealogical hierarchy are populations and species. Like kin-groups, they are linked by descent, by a shared gene-pool, and might act as units of selection, or of differential survival. It is doubtful whether populations of the same species ever interact so that one gene-pool becomes extinct: mixing of the gene-pools through interbreeding is the likely outcome (though some interactions between human populations may have resulted in extinction, by genocide without interbreeding). But different species do seem to interact in this way. One thinks of the extermination of native species in the Galápagos and other closed habitats after the introduction of animals like pigs and goats. In such cases, one speaks of species selection (see section headed 'Origin of species' below). This, on its own, can only decrease diversity, not generate it.

The observation explained by natural selection is adaptation, the apparent design of organisms for the environments in which they live. The 'argument from design' was one of the chief pre-Darwinian props for natural theology—evidence for a wise and benign Creator. Darwin's theory of natural selection cut the ground from that argument (see also HUME). In essence, neo-Darwinian selection theory is that mutations arise at random, with no feedback from the environment to direct or influence the type of mutation that is 'needed', and interaction between the environment and organisms bearing the mutation determines success or failure. Wallace's formalization of natural selection emphasizes changing environments as the driving force; but an alternative view is possible, of a static inorganic world which is explored by life through natural selection, so that the environment

is in a sense created by organisms. For instance, it is difficult to conceive environmental change which would lead originally aquatic plants first to colonize the land, or terrestrial animals to take to the air: the land and air were there, but not part of the habitable environment until organisms made them so. Of course, once there are plants on land, or insects in the air, we can easily conceive the advantage of becoming a cow or a swallow.

But talk of cows and swallows introduces the problem with natural selection. Two entirely distinct aspects of the theory must be distinguished. One is concerned with things like cows, swallows, and giraffes' necks. The other is concerned with selection in populations, the bread and butter of population genetics. As for this latter sort, there is no doubt that it works. The deductive form of the argument for it proves that it ought to work, and there is experimental and observational evidence that it does. Classic instances of natural selection in populations include bird predation of light and dark forms of the peppered moth in industrial and rural Britain; the development of resistance to antibiotics in bacteria, to insecticides in insects, and to rat poison in rats; and the relation between human sickle-cell trait and malaria in Africa. These instances cover two sorts of selection. In antibiotic or insecticide resistance, the gene-pool of the population is altered: genotypes to which the agent is lethal are eliminated, and those which can survive it increase. This is *directional* selection, where there is a shift from one state to another. Melanism in moths and sickle-cell trait are instances of *stabilizing* or *normalizing* selection, which results not in a shift, but in maintenance of the norm by elimination of variants. In both instances it happens that the norm maintained is a polymorphic population, and this is sometimes called *balancing* selection. Another type of selection is so obvious that it almost escapes attention; instances are the poor reproductive success of people suffering genetic defects which place them far outside the norm. Those defects are eliminated by *purifying* selection. The terminology seems varied and complex, but in general we can think of selection as either eliminating variation (purifying, directional) or maintaining it (balancing, stabilizing); and also as either promoting change (directional) or maintaining the status quo (purifying, stabilizing).

To neo-Darwinians, the important types of natural selection are directional selection (an explanation of inferred change) and balancing selection as an explanation of observed variation. The basis of change is the replacement of one form of a gene, or portion of chromosome, by a new (mutant) form. This will take place when the mutant form confers a relative advantage, and spreads through the population. The rate of spread depends on the degree of advantage or selection pressure (roughly the proportion of selective deaths per generation), and on whether the mutation is recessive (expressed only in those inheriting it from both parents—homozygous for it), dominant (expressed if inherited from only one parent—heterozygous), or intermediate (expressed more strongly if inherited from both parents rather than one). Change is irreversible only when the original form of the gene has disappeared; that is, the mutant becomes fixed, or universal in the population. Fixation is achieved most rapidly when the mutation is neither dominant nor recessive but intermediate, which is probably true for most mutations considered at the molecular or protein-producing level.

Balancing selection will occur when heterozygotes, inheriting different forms of a gene from each parent, are more successful than homozygotes. Here, selection will eliminate homozygotes in each generation, but will not alter the equilibrium proportions of the two (or more) forms of the gene. Balancing selection is the neo-Darwinian explanation for the high incidence (averaging 6–15 per cent of sampled proteins—see above) of heterozygosity observed in natural populations. The assumption is that heterozygotes are fitter than homozygotes because they have a wider array of resources to meet variations in the environment. An alternative explanation is the 'non-Darwinian' proposal that the observed protein variants are selectively neutral; they confer no real advantage or disadvantage and are maintained purely by chance, by random genetic drift. On this neutralist theory, harmless or even slightly deleterious mutations may spread and become fixed (or eliminated) purely by chance. As with natural selection, experiments show that genetic drift occurs, especially in small populations where biased samples are more likely, and there is a highly developed mathematical theory of how quasi-neutral mutations may behave in populations.

So far, it has proved impossible to discriminate between these two mechanisms, neo-Darwinian selection and neutralist drift, as general explanations, though neutralism has had remarkable recent successes. In essence, the neo-Darwinian expects that a given variation is correlated with some environmental variable, and the neutralist expects that it is not. When one such environmental variable is identified with one genetic variant, as malaria has been with sickle-cell trait (abnormal red blood cells) in humans, this may seem a triumph for neo-Darwinism, but a myriad protein polymorphisms remain to comfort the neutralist. The generality of balancing selection as an explanation for genetic variation took a sharp knock when it was found that bacteria, which lack sex and so cannot be heterozygous, are just as polymorphic as sexual organisms. At least the neo-Darwinist seems to have a task, or a research programme: to dissect the environment into factors correlated with variations in organisms. Neutralists have no such programme, and instead neutralism comes into its own in explaining evolution which is invisible to selection by the environment, changes in stretches of DNA which are not translated into the phenotype (see section headed 'Origin of species' below).

Natural selection, the idea that organisms are moulded or 'designed' by the environment, is also used as an explanation in quite a different sense, when applied to cows, or swallows, or giraffes' necks. Here, explanations are under virtually no empirical control, because the environmental factors invoked are necessarily in the past. In this mode, explanations take the form of conjectures or narratives, in which organisms are analysed in terms of function, and demonstration that one design is more efficient than another is sufficient to explain its origin by natural selection, or environmental conditions under which particular features could be advantageous are postulated or imagined. Critics argue that such exercises of the imagination demonstrate the emptiness of selection theory. In explaining everything, it explains too much; as an explanation of design in nature it seems hard to distinguish from the all-seeing Creator of *Paley and other natural theologians. On this view, natural selection is equated with a vacuous Panglossian optimism—'all is for the best in this best of all possible worlds'—or with the explanation of the action of opium by its content of 'dormitive principle'. One response to these critics is that they do not touch the status of natural selection: it could still be as effective in the global sense as it is in the experiments of population geneticists. Nevertheless, no one has yet reported the origin of a new species by means of natural selection.

**Origin of species.** Although this was the title of his book, Darwin scarcely addressed the problem of how new species arise. His mechanism, natural selection, concerns change or transformation of species through time, but this alone will not produce new species; it will merely modify and preserve old ones. New species appear only if the number of species increases, if a species splits into two or more. Darwin proposed what he called the principle of divergence: by analogy with artificial selection, and by appealing to 'many and widely different places in the economy of nature', he argued that the most divergent members of a species tend to be preserved, and gradually diverge into varieties, subspecies, and eventually into distinct species. The kernel of his explanation was gradual adaptive divergence.

The neo-Darwinian theory of the origin of species—of *speciation*—differs from Darwin's chiefly in the emphasis placed on geographic isolation as a necessary precursor of species formation, and in emphasis on genetic isolating mechanisms. Neo-Darwinian speciation theory is by no means monolithic, and there are arguments for speciation without geographic isolation, and without Darwinian gradualism.

That species can arise at one stroke there is no doubt. Doubling of chromosome number in a cell is a fairly common accident: it happens if the chromosomes divide, as before normal cell division, but the cell then fails to divide. Such cells are unable to give rise to normal eggs or sperm, because the chromosomes will associate in fours, not in pairs as is necessary in production of sex cells. But in a hybrid between two species, itself sterile because of incompatibility between the two sets of chromosomes, chromosome doubling will restore fertility (each chromosome now has a partner to pair with), and self-fertilization can then initiate a new species intermediate between the two parents of the hybrid. Many species of plants and a few of animals have evidently appeared in this way, and some have been created or re-created in the laboratory.

Speciation by multiplication of chromosome number (*polyploidy*) is instantaneous; the new species is descended from a single self-fertilizing individual; accident—macromutation—is the cause; and geographic isolation is unnecessary. In all these four ways, it differs from the classic neo-Darwinian model of speciation, which demands geographic isolation, gradual selective change over long periods of time, and involves populations, not individuals. Between these two extremes, there is a third model of speciation which has received much recent support and interest. This model is inelegantly called 'punctuated equilibrium'—'quantum speciation' is an alternative. One group with evidence bearing on this model includes geneticists who have found that similar or closely related species usually differ in chromosome arrangement, implying fixation of chromosome mutations during their history. For instance, human chromosomes differ from those of chimpanzees by inversions of parts of nine chromosomes, and fusion of two. Whereas identical point mutations in DNA recur at measurable rates, each chromosome mutation is virtually unique, for each depends on the coincidence of at least two accidental breaks in a chromosome, followed by rearrangement and fusion. Organisms heterozygous for a chromosome mutation (inheriting it only from one parent) usually show reduced fertility, but those inheriting it from both parents (homozygous) are potentially fully fertile. Chromosome mutations can therefore act as genetic isolating mechanisms, favouring mating amongst carriers of the mutation (hence homozygous offspring) and so initiating speciation. But since chromosome mutations are each virtually unique, the only way homozygotes can be produced is by inbreeding among the offspring of the individual in which the mutation originally occurred. This model—'chromosomal speciation'—resembles the chromosome doubling mode of speciation in several ways: no geographic isolation is necessary, accident rather than natural selection is the cause, inbreeding amongst the descendants of a single individual is necessary, and a new species may arise in a few generations, with the establishment of a population homozygous for the mutation.

A second set of arguments in favour of quantum speciation comes from palaeontologists, who generally fail to find evidence of gradual transformation in the fossil record. Instead, fossil species appear suddenly, persist unchanged over more or less long periods, and disappear as abruptly as they came. Data of the same sort were available to Darwin and his geological mentor, Charles Lyell (1797–1875). Lyell built a theory on them, of piecemeal creation of species by 'a power above nature'. Darwin, who believed natural selection was the power in question, appealed instead to imperfections in the fossil record, and hoped that future discoveries would show the gradual transitions he expected. Today, some palaeontologists have at last given up that hope and taken the fossils at face value, as a true record of the mode of evolution. They infer that speciation occurs rapidly, in small populations, so that transitions between species are evanescent. For if change does not occur during the recorded history of species, it must occur elsewhere, in the unrecorded history of small founder populations. From these ideas comes a theory of species continually and randomly throwing off small offshoots, of which most perish but a few succeed as new species (see Fig. 2). As in the chromosomal theory of speciation, natural selection is not responsible for the appearance of these offshoots, but operates at a higher level in selecting amongst them. In populations, random mutations throw up material on which selection acts; in just the same way, it is argued that random speciation throws up material—species—on which selection acts. Major evolutionary changes are not due to the action of selection on mutations of genes or chromosomes, but of species selection on a mass of species, thrown up by a random process.

A third group of scientists whose ideas fit in here are molecular biologists. Techniques recently developed make it possible to work out the

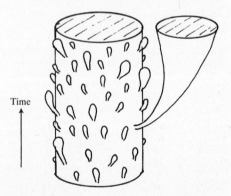

Time ↑

**Fig. 2.** Diagrammatic model of part of the history of a species, as envisaged by advocates of quantum speciation. The parent species is more or less stable through time, and is continually budding off potential new species in the form of small, inbreeding populations, which may be isolated by geography or by genetic accidents such as chromosome mutations. Most of these incipient species soon become extinct, but a few (one in this example) may succeed.

sequence of nucleotides in DNA and in the messenger nucleic acid, RNA. The letters of the genetic code may then be compared with the amino acid sequence in the protein synthesized on the message in the messenger RNA. The genetic code has a lot of redundancy. In eight of the sixteen boxes in Table 1 the third letter of the triplet makes no difference; the amino acid is specified by the first two letters alone. This means that mutations in the third position of many triplets will be 'silent' and will not alter the amino acid. Amino acids specified by triplets with different first (arginine, leucine) or first and second (serine) letters may also sustain silent mutations in the first and second positions. When the RNA and amino acid sequences are compared for human and rabbit beta haemoglobin genes, for instance, two-thirds of the differences between the RNAs are silent, not reflected in the protein; the same comparison between mouse and rabbit alpha haemoglobins gives virtually the same proportion of silent and non-silent changes. If all these differences represent mutations fixed during the history of the species compared, two conclusions can be drawn. First, the rate of 'silent evolution' must be greater than the rate of phenotypic change (we come back to this point later); second, the silent mutations must have been fixed by random drift, not by selection, since a change in DNA which is not reflected in the organism cannot be selected. If the majority of inferred change in DNA is due to mutations drifting randomly to fixation, then small populations should be frequent in the history of species, since drift is more effective in small populations, and most effective in inbreeding.

Thus three independent lines of enquiry— chromosomes, fossils, and molecular sequences— converge in a view of speciation which differs profoundly from neo-Darwinian orthodoxy. The nature of this difference or disagreement is interesting. It concerns three main things: time, or number of generations; number of individuals; and natural selection. But these three things, the first two in quantity, are the staples of population genetics. Neo-Darwinism depends on the synthesis of natural selection with experimental and mathematical population genetics, which themselves depend on avoiding random effects by considering many generations and many individuals. Population genetics can explain stability, or variety, or gradual change within species. The thrust of the above ideas on speciation is that those factors may all be irrelevant to the origin of species. In other words, the principles of population genetics are directed at the wrong level in the hierarchy: they explain the behaviour of genes in populations, but are inappropriate when extrapolated as an explanation of the history of life. It is, after all, a fairly fundamental criticism of neo-Darwinism to propose that natural selection is not relevant to the origin of species.

**Embryology.** Before Darwin, the word 'evolu-

tion' had a different meaning in biology. It referred to the unfolding of form in the development of the embryo, and in particular to the notion of preformation—that the adult organism is preformed in the fertilized egg. One complaint among Darwin's critics was that he and his followers misused and misappropriated the word 'evolution'. But in the neo-Darwinian theory, something approaching the doctrine of preformation seems to have reappeared. The theory is concerned almost exclusively with genes, but what interests most biologists is organisms and the form of organisms. Neo-Darwinism has, as yet, little to say on how form is generated; it is assumed simply to be programmed in the genes, as if the adult and its development are preformed in the DNA, or the four dimensions of a life history are mapped in the two dimensions of the linear information store.

Darwinism and neo-Darwinism are concerned with historical transformation of organisms. Despite more than a century of work in evolutionary biology, it remains true that the only transformations of which we have empirical knowledge are those observed in the life histories of organisms— the acorn into the oak tree, or the egg into the caterpillar, pupa, and then butterfly. It is remarkable that these transformations remain almost as mysterious today as they were in Darwin's time. The orthodox, genetic explanation of the genesis of form invokes control genes, which are thought of as switching on and off one or more structural (protein-specifying) genes. A hierarchy of control genes is envisaged, with 'master genes' which switch on batteries of lower-level control genes. Mutations in such control genes could obviously produce relatively large changes in the adult organism. But these control genes remain theoretical, and theoretical entities can, in theory, accomplish anything. Indeed, an immediate inference from the reductionist viewpoint of randomly mutating genes is that anything is possible, and it is natural selection which sorts out the actual from the possible.

Yet the regularity and uniformity of embryonic development in animals and plants seems to demonstrate that anything is not possible. One symptom of a reaction against the reductionist programme of neo-Darwinism and molecular biology is the insistence of some biologists that the transformations of embryology demand 'something more' than proteins and interactions between proteins: the miracle that demands explanation is not necessarily how the eye (for example) evolved in the ancestors of vertebrates, but how it evolves from nothing in every vertebrate today. The embryologists and others who take this stand have produced no fully coherent alternative to neo-Darwinism, but appeal to non-genic inheritance (through the cytoplasm of the egg, inherited from the mother), to possible neo-Lamarckian modes of change, or to the self-organizing and self-regulating powers of the developing organism. This revolt against the tyranny of the genes may be summed up as an interest in epigenetics (the sequence of events that happens in the embryo after fertilization).

A neo-Darwinian response is that these complaints are nothing new, smack of vitalism, and demonstrate a confusion between proximate causes, the embryologist's proper domain, and ultimate causes, the domain of evolutionary theory. Epigenesists might reply that neo-Darwinian theory offers no better explanation of the self-organizing capacity of the organism than contingency, a lucky chapter of irretrievable historical accidents. Like so much else in neo-Darwinism, the argument degenerates here into incommensurables, the conflict between chance and apparent necessity.

**Behaviour.** One of the modern growth areas within neo-Darwinism is sociobiology. It is concerned with evolutionary interpretation of behaviour, especially in social interactions within species. Darwin initiated work on these lines with explanations, in terms of natural selection, of insect societies (ants, bees) which entail self-sacrifice or altruistic behaviour by individuals or castes. Modern sociobiology is a fusion of population genetics, *ethology (study of behaviour), and game theory (see VON NEUMANN), interpreting behaviour in terms of strategies which will have selective advantage if they increase the chance of survival of individuals or their kin, who share their genes. Though relatively uncontroversial when applied to birds or butterflies, these ideas have raised a storm when, as was inevitable, they are extrapolated to human societies. The controversy, which has marked political overtones, centres over the extent to which behaviour is genetically determined, a topic on which agreement seems no more likely than in the argument over the relative contributions of heredity and environment to intelligence.

In order to be subject to natural selection, traits—whether behavioural or structural—must be heritable, or under genetic control. To bring some behavioural trait within neo-Darwinism, all that is necessary is to argue that it is adaptive under certain circumstances (few traits resist ingenuity), and to postulate a gene for it. There is little harm in theoretical genes for altruism or homosexuality, but critics of sociobiology see such exercises as examples of the reductionist tyranny of the genes, or of the emptiness of a theory which can explain anything.

**Current status of neo-Darwinism.** In the preceding sections, various new directions in, and criticisms of, neo-Darwinism were outlined. The basics of neo-Darwinism, as of Darwinism, are heritable variation and natural selection. Molecular and population genetics have supplied much insight into the source of variation and the mechanism of selection. There is no doubt that generation of genetic variation is an intrinsic property of sexually reproducing organisms as we know them. Nor can one doubt that natural selection censors variation,

and maintains organisms in harmony with their environments. That might seem to be the end of the matter. Nevertheless, there have been persistent arguments over the status of neo-Darwinism, both as legitimate science and as a comprehensive explanation of life.

In considering these arguments, it is essential to distinguish the two disparate aspects of neo-Darwinian theory. The first is that evolution has occurred: relations between species are material, not immaterial, and historical, due to common ancestry. This aspect is more general than Darwinism or neo-Darwinism. The particular contribution of those systems is a mechanism—natural selection—to account for evolution.

The general aspect of the theory, that evolution has occurred, has a curious philosophical corollary: acceptance of it entails a revolutionary change in the ontological status of its subject-matter. Concepts such as 'ravens' and 'swans' are traditionally considered classes or universals ('all swans are white' and 'all ravens are black' are classic statements about universals in logic). Evolution changes that. Biological species, and groups of species related in a closed system of descent, become individuals, and names like *Homo sapiens* or Mammalia become proper names, the names of individuals, or 'chunks of the genealogical nexus', a nexus which is necessarily unique. If evolution has occurred, it follows that there can be no real laws of evolution, for laws concern classes or universals, and evolution implies that all of life is one individual system, like the solar system. In other words, one consequence of evolutionary theory is that comparative biology becomes historical science, and there can no more be evolutionary laws than there are historical laws.

The general scientific method is to propose hypotheses about nature, and to test them by deducing what each hypothesis forbids, turning to nature to see if the forbidden consequence actually occurs. Then the question is what forbidden consequences, or potential tests, may be deduced from the proposition that evolution has occurred. Various possible observations have been suggested, such as the discovery of human fossils in Cambrian rocks, which could falsify evolution and so demonstrate its testability. But none of the potential tests that have been proposed appears to be directed exclusively at evolution. For instance, Cambrian human bones would falsify not evolutionary theory but the general comparative method in biology, codified before Darwin as the theory of 'threefold parallelism'—between the succession of fossils in the stratigraphic record, the transformations of embryonic development, and the hierarchy of natural classification, based on homologies. Evolution may seem to be an inescapable deduction from that theory, but the biologists who proposed and upheld it in the nineteenth century would not agree. Those who argue that evolution is falsifiable seem to demonstrate the weakness of that position by the conviction, which shines through their prose, that they know the truth. The only thing forbidden by evolution is that there should be species unrelated to others by descent, and since we have no access to unambiguous records of descent, no decisive test is forthcoming. Nevertheless, evolution explains important discoveries unforeseen by Darwin, such as the universality of the genetic code, and comparisons of nucleic acid and protein sequences.

One may reject testability as a criterion, and appeal instead to the fruitfulness of evolutionary theory as a research programme. That criterion has no necessary connection with *truth, for phlogiston chemistry and Ptolemaic astronomy were fruitful research programmes. Or one can point to the explanatory power of the theory, the quantity of disparate areas of knowledge it unites. Darwin used this argument: 'It can hardly be supposed that a false theory would explain in so satisfactory a manner . . . several large classes of facts.' A different strategy for evolutionists is not to analyse or defend their own theory, but to attack the opposition, alternative explanations of life. Only two seem to be on offer. The first is spontaneous generation or creation, necessarily on multiple occasions and locations rather than the one required by evolution. The second is the notion that Earth has been seeded from space, and again seeding on multiple occasions is required to distinguish this from evolution. The difference between the three explanations, when considered in terms of testable predictions, explanatory power, fruitfulness, or whatever, seems to come down to the principle of parsimony, or Occam's razor: evolution is superior because it does not multiply entities unnecessarily. For creation and seeding both imply repeated intervention (intelligent or not), whereas evolution implies no more than one such intervention. When treated as a criterion of truth, this has been called the 'best-in-field fallacy'. Fallacious it may be, yet evolution has no real competitors. (See FALSIFICATION.)

Turning to mechanism, the specifically Darwinian aspect of neo-Darwinism, we are on surer ground with natural selection. Darwin offered several potential tests of the mechanism: for example, 'If it could be proved that any part of the structure of any one species had been formed for the exclusive good of another species, it would annihilate my theory.' But he also wrote: 'I am convinced that natural selection has been the main but not the exclusive means of modification.' That is also the stance of modern neo-Darwinians, who allow genetic drift and other non-Darwinian means of modification such as polyploidy and less radical chromosomal saltations. In these terms, natural selection is clearly beyond criticism, for it is expected to explain only that which is explicable by it. Cases which are beyond the most ingenious selective explanation have another cause at hand, in random effects due to drift or inbreeding. Comparison of DNA sequences indicates that 'silent' substitutions are about four times as frequent as non-silent ones (with an effect on the phenotype): in other words, the majority of evolutionary change is immune to natural selection. This important conclusion is summed up in 'Kimura's rule' (Motoo Kimura is the father of the neutral theory of molecular evolution): Molecular changes that are less likely to be subject to natural selection occur more rapidly in evolution. One corollary of this is the 'molecular clock', the inference that in each lineage DNA evolves at a roughly constant rate. This contrasts with evolution of form or phenotype, which seems to occur in jerks in some lineages, hardly at all in others (so-called 'living fossils'), and never at a constant rate. If, at the molecular level, the majority of evolutionary change takes place in spite of natural selection rather than because of it, natural selection seems to be false as the general explanation of evolutionary change.

The effect of Darwin's theory was to give a mechanistic explanation of apparent intelligent design: the appearance was illusory, for the creative power was in natural selection. The effect of the large neutral or 'non-Darwinian' component discovered in molecular evolution is further to downgrade the role of design: the apparent creative power of natural selection was illusory, if it is outweighed by chance effects. In other words, the role of chance increases. It is this that seems to be the nub of the matter. The reductionist line of neo-Darwinism, aiming to reduce the diversity of life to the laws of chemistry and physics, leads to randomness. Instead of the relentless mill of natural selection, 'daily and hourly scrutinising, throughout the world, the slightest variations . . . silently and insensibly working . . . at the improvement of each organic being' (Darwin's words), buttressed by the equations of population genetics, modern neo-Darwinians seem to be turning on the one hand to pure randomness (neutral theory and the molecular clock), and on the other to explanations which approach the miraculous (to use a provocative word), unique events perpetuated by inbreeding. The latter has echoes in the biblical account of the genesis of mankind. Natural selection has been called a mechanism for generating the improbable, and if the role of natural selection is diluted, the improbability of the results increases. The ultimate in reduction is a recently fashionable idea, that the whole of life is an accidental excrescence, a by-product of selfish DNA, whose structure is such that it survives, multiplies, and diversifies. That view seems to lead nowhere, but there are two lines of research which might lead out of the impasse. One is into the structure of the genome (the genetic equipment of the individual), where surprising things like 'jumping genes' and spontaneous amplification of bits of DNA are being discovered. Perhaps the permanence we attribute to DNA is also illusory. The other line is in epigenetics, the link between the genes and the organism. It is here that the mystery of transformation can be approached most directly. C. P.

Bendall, D. S. (ed.) (1983). *Evolution from Molecules to Men*, Cambridge.

Bowler, P. J. (1984). *Evolution: the history of an idea*. Berkeley.

Futuyma, D. (1982). *Science on Trial: the case for evolution*. New York.

George, W. (1982). *Darwin*. London and Glasgow.

Gould, S. J. (1977). *Ever Since Darwin*. New York and Harmondsworth.

Gould, S. J. (1980). *The Panda's Thumb: more reflections on natural history*. New York and Harmondsworth.

Gould, S. J. (1983). *Hen's Teeth and Horse's Toes*. New York and Harmondsworth.

Gould, S. J. (1985). *The Flamingo's Smile*. New York and Harmondsworth.

Grene, M. (ed.) (1983). *Dimensions of Darwinism: themes and counterthemes in twentieth-century evolutionary theory*. Cambridge.

Howard, J. (1982). *Darwin*. Oxford.

Kimura, M. (1983). *The Neutral Theory of Molecular Evolution*. Cambridge.

Kitcher, P. (1982). *Abusing Science: the case against creationism*. Cambridge, Massachusetts.

Mayr, E. (1982). *The Growth of Biological Thought: diversity, evolution, and inheritance*. Cambridge, Massachusetts.

Mayr, E. and Provine, W. B. (eds.) (1980). *The Evolutionary Synthesis: perspectives on the unification of biology*. Cambridge, Massachusetts.

Midgley, M. (1986). *Evolution as a Religion: strange hopes and stranger fears*. London.

Milkman, R. (ed.) (1982). *Perspectives on Evolution*. Sunderland, Massachusetts.

Pollard, J. W. (ed.) (1984). *Evolutionary Theory: paths into the future*. Chichester.

Ridley, M. (1985). *The Problems of Evolution*. Oxford.

Ruse, M. (1986). *Taking Darwin Seriously: a naturalistic approach to philosophy*. Oxford.

Smith, J. M. (1986). *The Problems of Biology*. Oxford.

Smith, J. M. (ed.) (1982). *Evolution Now: a century after Darwin*. London.

Sober, E. (ed.) (1984). *Conceptual Issues in Evolutionary Biology: an anthology*. Cambridge, Massachusetts.

Stauffer, R. C. (1975). *Charles Darwin's Natural Selection*. Cambridge.

**EXISTENTIALISM.** See SARTRE, JEAN-PAUL.

**EXPERIENCE.** See CONSCIOUSNESS.

**EXTERNAL WORLD.** The very use of the phrase 'the *external* world' suggests that there may be something problematic about the existence and nature of the reality 'out there', beyond what is immediately given in subjective experience. This way of viewing the matter is probably due to *Descartes, whose philosophical starting-point was his conscious awareness of his own existence as a thinking thing; he was then faced with the difficulty of moving on from this subjective starting-point to conclusions about the existence and nature of the physical universe. Another source of the idea of the external world as problematic is the notion of a 'veil of perception' between our subjective experience and the world: if we are directly aware only of our own impressions (*Hume) or sense-data (*Russell and others), then the problem seems to arise of how we know that these immediate objects-of-experience resemble anything in the 'real world' outside us.

Twentieth-century philosophers have become increasingly dubious about the genuineness of many of these supposed problems about the 'external world'. First it has been argued that the idea of a 'veil of perception' rests on a philosophical confusion: the fact that we do not always see things as they are does not license the inference that all we ever see are subjective appearances. Second, the arguments of *Wittgenstein have suggested that the traditional, solipsistic presentation of these problems ('How do I, the lone isolated conscious subject, know that an external world exists?') may be incoherent. According to Wittgenstein's celebrated 'private language' argument (see WITTGENSTEIN'S PHILOSOPHY OF LANGUAGE), the use of the very linguistic concepts necessary for the raising of such questions already presupposes the existence of an objective world of public rules, and public criteria for the application of terms.

See also APPARENT; BERKELEY ON PERCEPTION.

**EXTINCTION OF CONDITIONED REFLEXES.** Also known as 'habituation', though 'habituation' may be used rather more generally, without reference to reflexes. Extinction is the gradual loss of the stimulus–response (SR) associative link (see CONDITIONING) in such situations as the reflex salivation given by the sight of food (unconditioned stimulus) being elicited by, for example, a buzzer (conditioned stimulus). Extinction occurs when the buzzer is repeatedly presented without the food. This is the classical experimental situation studied by the great Russian physiologist Ivan *Pavlov. Pavlov showed that conditioned reflexes remained intact over many years in animals kept in conditions where experimental extinction did not occur—for example in sheep allowed to graze normally outside the laboratory. This led to the view that *forgetting may not occur spontaneously, but that it is due to experimental extinction, by events occurring repeatedly without reward. This, however, seems too extreme a view: memories and skills can almost certainly fade spontaneously, though generally far more slowly than by extinction.

**EXTIRPATION.** The removal of parts, especially regions, of the brain.

**EXTRA-SENSORY PERCEPTION.** There are those who hold that man is an exclusively material being, living in an exclusively material universe; and there are also those who hold that he is a spiritual or psychic entity, inhabiting a material body in a universe which has both physical and non-physical aspects. The first view is a relative newcomer in philosophical terms: it has come to be widely held only since the advance of scientific materialism in the nineteenth century. The second view is of course much more venerable, lying at the heart of most systematized religions; and despite the fact that it is scientifically unfashionable, it nevertheless commands wider support, even today, among the population at large. Given our present very limited understanding of the brain and mind, it is possible to support this view without being in any way irrational or unscientific, though most scientists would probably lean toward a more agnostic position, which can be roughly summarized as: 'I will suspend belief in the existence of a non-physical entity such as mind, soul, or spirit until I have good evidence to indicate that it exists.'

Is there evidence that it exists? The non-materialistic view of the universe claims that there is, and that it comes from studies of the various types of phenomena clustered under the heading 'extra-sensory perception' (ESP). This phrase, which was coined by J. B. Rhine, one-time head of the world's first university parapsychology department, retains, despite popular usage, a fairly specific meaning. It refers to any mental faculty which allows a person to acquire information about the world without the use of the known senses. Such faculties are generally classified as (i) telepathy, (ii) clairvoyance, and (iii) precognition. A fourth phenomenon, (iv) psychokinesis, while not involving perception in the recognized meaning of the word, is almost always studied alongside ESP. The systematic investigation of these four faculties is the subject-matter of psychical research or parapsychology, whose history and achievements are considered in the articles on PARANORMAL PHENOMENA: THE PROBLEM OF PROOF, and PARAPSYCHOLOGY: A HISTORY OF RESEARCH. Here we will merely consider what each term implies.

(i) Telepathy refers specifically to the transmission of information from one mind to another, without the use of language, body movements, or any of the known senses. Because of the difficulty of ruling out normal sensory cues when humans are within sight or earshot of each other, most scientists are impressed by telepathic evidence only when it involves two people separated by a considerable distance or when at least one of them is isolated under the most stringent conditions. (ii) Clairvoyance refers to the acquisition by a mind or brain of information which is not available to it by the known senses, and, most important, which is *not known at the time to any other mind or brain*. To give examples, if one could read the pages of a closed book, or give the sequence of a shuffled but undealt pack of cards, then one would be demonstrating clairvoyance. (iii) Precognition refers to the acquisition of information about an event before it takes place. Common anecdotal 'evidence' for precognition comes in the form of dreams about the future which subsequently come true, but evidence in a laboratory setting is, for example, ability to predict the order in which cards will be dealt from a pack, with shuffling carried out *only after the prediction had been made*. As for (iv) psychokinesis, it refers to the supposed power of the mind to manipulate matter at a distance without any known physical means. At its crudest

and most dubious level, 'evidence' for this faculty comes from the performances of Uri Geller and others. More serious evidence comes from laboratory experiments into willing the fall of dice from a mechanical shaker.

Establishing the reality of one or all of these faculties would be of great interest to anyone engaged in studying the brain and nervous system. Not only would strictly mechanistic models of psychology—such as those exemplified by Skinnerian behaviourism (see BEHAVIOURISM, SKINNER ON)—have to be scrapped, but many of the assumptions and theories of physical science would need at least to be thoroughly overhauled. Perhaps the least challenging is telepathy, for all that is alleged is that information can pass from one mind to another without the *known* senses. There could be other senses, equipped with appropriate sense organs, hidden somewhere in the brain and acting as transmitters and receivers. It is now established that information can be sent across vast distances by radio—a fact which would have been considered highly improbable a century ago—and perhaps some parallel system, as yet unidentified, operates in human brains. But what of the remaining three faculties? What possible mental mechanism could allow the mind to inspect the sequence of a shuffled deck of cards *before the shuffling has taken place*? Or how could the mind physically operate on matter from a distance, causing a die to fall with one face rather than another uppermost?

Clearly, if ESP exists, in one or more of the forms discussed, then the idea of a non-materialistic component to the universe becomes more plausible. If the mind can roam more or less at will, then it would seem that man is, in part at any rate, a non-physical being, capable of exercising far greater control of his own destiny and of his environment than is usually assumed by science. Fortunately—or unfortunately—systematic laboratory research, once full of promise, has yielded little in the way of concrete evidence for ESP, while anecdotal evidence, however superficially convincing, so often withers away under close inspection.

C. E.

**EXTRAVERSION–INTROVERSION.** The terms 'extraversion' and 'introversion' entered popular use in England, with pretty much their current meaning, during the nineteenth century; they can be found in several popular novels, referring respectively to sociable, impulsive, carefree behaviour, and unsociable, responsible, thoughtful behaviour. C. G. *Jung popularized the terms on the Continent, and linked them with a very complex and difficult psychoanalytic set of theories; these theories are not now widely entertained, and the Jungian meaning of the terms is only accepted by a few followers of his. Jung suggested that there were links, in neurosis, between extraversion and hysterical symptomatology, and introversion and depressive/*anxiety symptomatology; this connection has been verified by later workers. The behavioural patterns which underlie the notion of extraversion–introversion were of course observed long before the nineteenth century; they go back at least to *Hippocrates and *Galen, the Greek physician who elaborated the earlier system of the four temperaments (choleric, melancholic, phlegmatic, sanguine) which has lasted in some form or other for two thousand years, and is still popularly used by many people.

The relation of this system to modern conceptions of personality was first suggested by Wilhelm *Wundt, the founder of modern psychology, just before the turn of the century. The four temperaments, until then, had been conceived of as qualitatively different types; you belonged to one or the other of these groups, but you could not show traits and qualities belonging to more than one group. This is patently untrue; many people do seem to belong to one or other of these types (otherwise the system would not have survived), but equally obviously others do not. Wundt pointed out that the melancholic and the choleric types had something in common that set them off against the phlegmatic and the sanguine types, namely a strong emotional reaction; this suggests a dimension of personality ranging from high to low emotional reactivity, or 'emotionality' (also often called 'neuroticism' or 'anxiety' by modern psychologists). Equally, the choleric and sanguine types have something in common which sets them off from the melancholic and phlegmatic types. Wundt called this quality 'changeableness', but we would nowadays call it extraversion, as opposed to introversion. Wundt was very perceptive: changeableness is indeed one of the most characteristic traits of the extravert—but it is not the only one, and consequently a less specific name for this personality dimension was required.

With this important change from four entirely discrete personality types to two separate dimensions of personality, with individuals located at any point on each scale, Wundt rescued the ancient scheme from oblivion and made it capable of reflecting the complexity of real life. The four Greek temperaments lie in the four quadrants generated by these two intersecting dimensions of personality. Melancholics are introverted and emotional (Jung's anxious and depressed neurotics), while cholerics are extraverted and emotional (Jung's hysterics, and, as modern research has shown, psychopaths and criminals as well). Phlegmatics are introverted and stable, while sanguinics are extraverted and stable. We can now measure the degree of emotionality–stability a person shows, or the degree of extraversion or introversion; and we can show that on both these scales the distribution of people is roughly in line with the Gaussian probability curve, i.e. most in the middle, with fewer and fewer towards the extremes. We do not, then, divide the population into extraverts and introverts: we measure the degree of extraversion or introversion shown, and allocate the person in question to some place along the continuum—very much as we would do if we measured his height, or weight, or *intelligence. When in what follows we speak of extraverts or introverts, we mean people falling towards one or the other end of this distribution; those in the middle are usually referred to as ambiverts.

Two problems are raised by the postulation of a concept such as extraversion–introversion. The first is a *descriptive* one: is it in fact true that the traits postulated to characterize the extravert, or the introvert, actually occur together? This is fundamentally a statistical problem, concerned with correlations. We can rate the degree of sociability, impulsiveness, changeableness, talkativeness, outgoingness, activity, liveliness, excitability, optimism, etc., of a few hundred persons, chosen at random, and determine whether all these traits are positively correlated—i.e. if a person showing one of these traits is also likely to show the others. We would not expect perfect agreement, of course, but we should expect reasonable correlation between these traits if the concept of extraversion were to have much meaning. Hundreds of empirical studies have shown that these various traits do indeed hang together to a degree which exceeds chance by a large amount; furthermore, these studies have demonstrated this general cohesion between traits for adults and children, men and women, different social classes, and different nations (including Japanese, Indian, European, and American). There is little doubt that descriptively the personality dimension of extraversion–introversion is amply supported by relevant research.

The second problem is the *causal* one—given that some people are extraverted, others introverted, others ambivert, can we say why these personality differences occur? The evidence suggests that genetic causes are very strongly implicated: something like two-thirds of the total variation in extraversion–introversion is probably due to heredity, with only one-third left for environmental causes. There is no evidence of dominance in the hereditary determination; this suggests that from the evolutionary point of view neither extraversion nor introversion is more successful in adapting to environmental *stress. But this answer is unsatisfactory: heredity cannot determine behaviour, only structure. Underlying extraverted or introverted behaviour there must be some physiologico-anatomical structure, presumably in the central nervous system, which mediates these personality differences. Recent experimental work has suggested that this is indeed so, and that extraversion is linked with resting states of low cortical *arousal, introversion with resting states of high cortical arousal. At first sight this would seem to be the wrong way round; one would have thought that the active, uninhibited extravert would be the person with high cortical arousal. However, the main function of the cortex is one of inhibiting lower centres; effective functioning of the cortex, due to high arousal, produces inhibited (introverted) behaviour. In the same way alcohol, a depressant drug which lowers the arousal of the cortical centres, produces extraverted, uninhibited behaviour; it frees the lower centres from cortical control. Cortical arousal in turn is determined by the so-called ascending reticular activating system, a group of cells lying in the brain-stem and responsible for reacting to incoming sensory messages by alerting the cortex so that it may be better able to deal with these messages. Here, theory suggests, is the causal locus of extraverted and introverted behaviour.

The evidence for this theory is by now quite strong. Part of it is direct, based on electro-encephalographic measurement of resting level brain waves and other psychophysiological measurements of arousal (see ELECTROENCEPHALO-GRAPHY). Part of it is indirect, based on laboratory investigations of certain psychological functions which are known to be determined in part by arousal level (conditioning, sensory thresholds, habituation, etc.). These studies are as yet not conclusive, but they do on the whole suggest that this theory is along the right lines. Unfortunately it is still impossible to record directly from the ascending reticular activating system in humans, so that the part played by this system must rest on work done on cats and other animal preparations in the laboratory; the evidence for the cortical part of the theory is much stronger. Certainly no other aspect of personality is as widely studied, or has given rise to such clear-cut theories and experimental investigation, as has extraversion–introversion; we probably know more about this trait (or system of traits) than about any other.          H. J. E.

A general survey of the field is offered in Eysenck, H. J. (ed.), *Readings in Extraversion–Introversion*, 3 vols. (London, 1970). The genetic and physiological theories of extraversion are discussed in detail, together with the evidence, in Eysenck, H. J., *Biological Basis of Personality* (Springfield Illinois, 1967). Alternative theories are considered in Nebylitsyn, V. D. and Gray, J. A. (eds.), *Biological Bases of Individual Behavior* (London, 1972). A more general approach will be found in Brody, N., *Personality: research and theory* (London, 1972). Jung's theory is described in detail by Hall, C. S. and Lindzey, G., *Theories of Personality* (New York, 1968). For the most recent summary of the evidence, see Eysenck, H. J. and Eysenck, M. W., *Personality and Individual Differences* (London, 1985).

**EYE-CONTACT,** or 'mutual gaze', occurs when two people look each other in the area of the eyes simultaneously. During conversation, two people seated 2 metres apart will each look at each other for about 60 per cent of the time (with wide individual differences), and there will be eye-contact for about 30 per cent of the time. This other-directed gaze consists of glances of 1–5 seconds in length, with mutual glances of about 1 second. Each glance in turn consists of a number of fixations of 0·3 seconds on different parts of the other's face, especially eyes and mouth, linked by saccadic movements; there are repeated cycles of such fixa-

tions. Eye-contact and glances can be recorded by observers who activate an interaction recorder, either observing directly or using a video-recording. The sequence of fixations requires an eye-movement recorder.

Eyes are responded to as a social signal by animals, some of whom have developed eye-spots as a threat signal. Human infants respond to their mother's eyes and establish eye-contact by the fourth week of life—which may be partly an innate response—and gaze plays a central role in the earliest sequences of social behaviour with the mother (see INFANCY, MIND IN). These gaze phenomena occur in all cultures, though they vary in the levels of gaze which are regarded as appropriate, and gaze may acquire special meanings, as in the case of the Evil Eye.

Gaze acts as a social signal: for example, if *A* likes *B* he will look at *B* a lot, and *B* correctly decodes this in terms of liking. In this situation, gaze is rewarding, and results in favourable evaluation of the person gazing. The basic effect of gaze is to show attention and to increase arousal, but the meaning can vary with the situation and facial expression—from threat to sexual attraction. Eye-contact is experienced as a special form of intimacy. Gaze is used and received as a signal for sexual attraction; couples who are in love have a high level of mutual gaze; girls enhance the stimulus properties of their eyes by cosmetics and dark glasses. Pupil dilation acts in a similar way, and can be produced artificially by drops of belladonna. The eyebrow flash is used in courting in many parts of the world.

The pattern of glances is closely co-ordinated with speech. Interactors look nearly twice as much while listening as when talking; they look during grammatical breaks and at the ends of utterances, and look away at the beginning of utterances. Glances act as signals of attention or emphasis, help to indicate the grammatical structure, and as 'terminal gazes' are one of the signals announcing the ends of utterances, but the same glances are also used to collect visual information. When relevant objects of mutual interest are present, a lot of gaze is deflected to them; there is more gaze at others when they are further away, less when intimate topics are discussed. Gaze plays an important role in greetings, farewells, and other ritualized social sequences.

There are large individual differences in amount of gaze. Autistic children scarcely gaze at all, for reasons not yet understood; *schizophrenics have a low level of gaze when talking to psychologists but not when talking to each other; depressives look little and look downwards; some neurotics avert gaze and some stare; extraverts gaze more than introverts (see EXTRAVERSION–INTROVERSION), females more than males, children and adults more than adolescents. Assertive or powerful people look as much while speaking as while listening. These findings help to explain the reasons behind gaze—it is a product of affiliative and other motivations—and various kinds of gaze aversion.

It is now realized that gaze plays a central part in social behaviour: the perception of others' reactions is essential, and gaze is necessary for this to occur. While the primary purpose of gaze is to collect visual information, it has acquired meaning as a social signal—in the course of evolution for animals, but mainly by learning for humans. While gaze is important for animals as well as humans, in human social behaviour it forms part of an intricate sequence in which it is closely co-ordinated with speech.

See also BODY LANGUAGE; FACIAL EXPRESSION.

M. A.

Argyle, M. and Cook, M. (1975). *Gaze and Mutual Gaze*. Cambridge.

**EYE DEFECTS AND THEIR CORRECTION.** We have become accustomed to marvel at the electronic miracles which made possible the pocket-size transistor radio and the small computer that fits into one's briefcase. But such great accomplishments are still not comparable to the extraordinary miniaturization of the complex structure of the human eye. Only about 24 mm in diameter, the eyeball contains several hundred millions of working parts, all carefully arranged to allow for a vast range of functions (such as vision of contrast, colour, form, and space) to be performed over many years and in all weathers. The optical system of that structure is no less remarkable although far simpler. The system often becomes faulty and errors of refraction such as myopia or hypermetropia occur. However, the other extraordinary aspect of the optical system of the eye is that its errors can be corrected simply and even relatively cheaply.

**Optics of the eye.** For a long time the eye has been compared to a camera but, although there are similarities since the eye is partially an optical instrument, the differences are fundamental. The camera gives an image which is the end result and has to be as perfect as possible. The eye, on the other hand, provides an image on the *retina which is only the beginning of an extraordinary process. (For further discussion, see VISUAL SYSTEM: ORGANIZATION.) This image is not to be looked at, as such. It sends coded neural signals to the brain where it is eventually decoded and perception emerges. Thus what the optics of the eye provide to the retina need not be as perfect or even similar to that formed by a traditional optical instrument. Indeed, when they are examined with the same criteria as are used for an optical instrument we find that the optics of the human eye are rather imperfect. *Helmholtz, the nineteenth-century giant of physiological optics, noted that if any optician were to build an optical instrument of such poor quality as the eye he would undoubtedly become bankrupt!

**Contribution of the surfaces of the eye.** The eye consists of a series of refracting surfaces (that is, surfaces which change the direction of light that traverses them) separated by clear media. These surfaces are the front and back surfaces of the cornea and of the lens (Fig. 1). The media are the *cornea, the aqueous humour, the lens, and vitreous humour. The dioptric power of each surface is a function of its curvature and of the differences in the index of refraction of the media on each side of that surface. The front surface of the cornea is the most refractive as it separates air from the corneal medium; whereas the back surface of

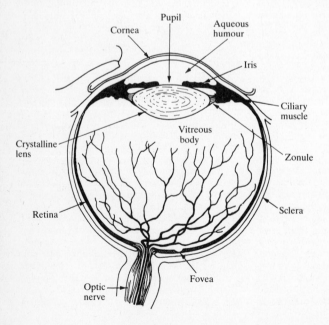

**Fig. 1.** Schematic diagram of the eye.

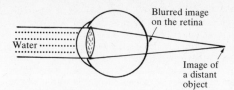

**Fig. 2.** Vision under water. Light is refracted by the crystalline lens only.

the cornea, with about the same curvature as the front, is the least refractive as it separates two media of about the same index of refraction. Specifically, the front surface of the cornea contributes about two-thirds of the power of the eye, the rest being provided by the surfaces of the crystalline lens. The optical power of the eye is equivalent to a magnifying lens with a magnification of × 15.

Thus when a person is swimming under water without a mask, the cornea is bathed in water of approximately the same refractive index and so its effective power is almost eliminated. This situation produces an out-of-focus retinal image and vision is hazy. In this case, the optical power of the eye depends only on the crystalline lens, which contributes only one-third of the total power. Hence the image of a distant object is formed very far behind the eye and only a blur circle appears on the retina (Fig. 2).

On the other hand, if the crystalline lens is removed, as happens following the surgical intervention for cataract due to old age or to an accident, the power of the eye is reduced by about one-third and the image of a distant object is also formed behind the eye (although not as far back as

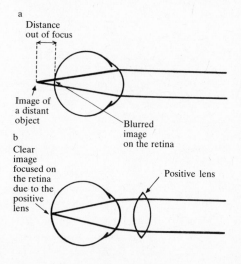

a

Distance
out of focus

Image of
a distant
object

Blurred
image
on the retina

b

Clear
image
focused on
the retina
due to the
positive
lens

Positive lens

Aphakic Eye

**Fig. 3. a.** Retinal image in an aphakic eye.
**Fig. 3. b.** Corrected aphake.

in the case of our swimmer). To correct such an eye, which has now become aphakic, a powerful lens of positive power (with a thick centre and thinner edge) is needed to replace the out-of-focus image onto the retina (Fig. 3). However, in the last few years, rather than using spectacle lenses to correct aphakia, an intra-ocular lens implant may be placed within the eye in lieu of the crystalline lens, during the surgical intervention. This method has proved to be very popular with a lot of people.

**Accommodation.** When the crystalline lens is missing, another important mechanism is disturbed and that is the *accommodation, or the auto-focus system of our 'camera'. Thus adjustment of the optical system to enable near objects to be seen is no longer possible: the eye is set for distance vision only.

The phenomenon of accommodation can be readily understood by making the following observations: Draw a small mark on a window with a felt-tip pen, then look at a distant object through that mark (cover the other one with your hand). You will notice that the mark on the window is blurred. Then look at the mark and you will notice that now the distant object has become blurred. In fact, to view the mark on the window you must make a conscious effort, whereas the eye seems to return naturally to the distant object. These observations demonstrate that the eye cannot be in focus at both distances simultaneously, the eye must accommodate to see the near object clearly. This complex involuntary mechanism is under the control of the central *nervous system which innervates the ciliary muscle inside the eye, and in turn produces accommodation by altering the shape of the surfaces of the crystalline lens (especially the front surface). Thus any interesting object in front of you which attracts your attention automatically triggers the accommodative reflex and in about 300 milliseconds the eye will be focused on that object.

**Presbyopia.** With age, the eye loses its ability to accommodate and there comes a time between 40 and 50 years when focusing on near objects becomes difficult, if not impossible. Presbyopia has set in and positive lenses are needed to enable near objects to be seen clearly.

Presbyopia is the most common eye defect in man. It affects everybody. Unsurprisingly, a lot of research is done to understand how it develops and how best to correct it. Yet presbyopia always comes as a shock to middle-aged people, who find their arms too short to hold reading material far enough away to still see it clearly. People who have worn corrective lenses for other eye defects need additional correction, often in the form of bifocals. Others who have never worn any correction and had perfect eyesight all their life are now faced with this new condition and need to wear spectacles to read and write—and to look at the screen of their visual display unit (often referred to among eye practitioners as a 'visual discomfort unit'). In a good number of cases the person has in fact had a slight eye defect for distance vision, which was insufficient to cause problems but now needs to be taken care of, as with age the visual system is far less adaptable; in such a case the person now has to wear spectacles continuously.

People react with various levels of *anxiety to presbyopia. Many feel handicapped, others will try to hide the fact and wear invisible contact lenses, others will simply ignore it and do without spectacles and perhaps occasionally use a magnifier surreptitiously. But inevitably in the very old, the acuity of vision even with the best correction may leave a lot to be desired, and many elderly people should begin to prize their insight rather than their sight. (For further discussion, SEE AGEING: SENSORY AND PERCEPTUAL CHANGES.)

**The errors of refraction.** Even when all the refractive surfaces of the eye are present, the image of a distant object may not be formed on the retina. If it does so, all is well and the eye is optically normal; it is then referred to as emmetropic. About half of the pre-presbyopic population is emmetropic. Considering the number of components of the optics of the eye (14 in fact) this figure is rather surprising, especially as a lack of harmony of the various optical elements needs only to be very slight to give rise to a lack of emmetropia, namely ametropia. For example, if the length of the eye varies by 1 mm, this produces a significant error of refraction of over 3 dioptres.

Thus, on the basis of chance alone the number of emmetropic eyes should be less than half of the pre-presbyopic population. The distribution, however, of errors of refraction in the general population is disproportionately peaked around the zero value. This phenomenon, in which nature seems to be on our side, has been called emmetropization. It refers to a presumed visual *feedback mechanism which would control the development of the optical components of the eye to maintain a state of emmetropia, whenever possible.

If the image of a distant object does not fall on the retina, the eye is said to be ametropic. There are three types of ametropia: myopia (or short-sightedness), hyperopia (or long-sightedness), and astigmatism, which may accompany either myopia or hyperopia. Presbyopia, which is an error of refraction occurring in near vision, is not usually considered among the errors of refraction (for distance vision) and has already been mentioned.

*Myopia.* This is a condition in which near objects appear clear while distance vision is blurred, with practically no other symptom except perhaps the discomfort of squeezing the eyelids, which does improve vision. From the optical point of view, the image of a distant object is formed not on the retina but in front of it (Fig. 4). In other words, the power of the eye is either too strong or the eye is too long;

the latter is usually the case. In some cases the amount of myopia does not stop at maturity but continues to progress. This is a pathological condition in which degenerative changes in the retina and other tissues occur and eventually vision is impaired even when corrected. It is important for these people not to engage in vigorous sports or activity (e.g. boxing or digging the garden) as the retina is liable to detachment with this condition.

Myopia usually develops in the early teens. However, an increasing number of people have been noted to acquire it in the late teens and early twenties, commonly in association with a great deal of visual stimulation, such as reading or working at a visual display unit. Hereditary influence as well as environmental factors both contribute to its development. In the general population approximately one person in five is myopic, although that figure varies with age, race, and geography (e.g. this figure doubles among Chinese and Japanese).

*Correction of myopia.* Correction of myopia, which can be done with either spectacles or contact lenses, is made by arriving at a negative lens which diminishes the power of the eye by an amount such that the image of a distant object coincides with the retina (Fig. 4). In the last few years, a surgical technique pioneered in the Soviet Union and called radial keratotomy has become relatively popular in some parts of the world (such as California). It consists of making incisions in the cornea, under anaesthesia, for the purpose of reducing its curvature and consequently its power. The optical result, however, is not very predictable and many patients (40 per cent in one report) still had to wear

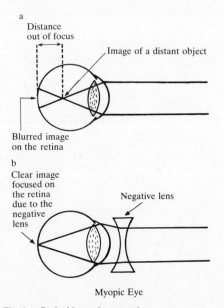

Fig. 4. a. Retinal image in a myopic eye.
Fig. 4. b. Corrected myope with a negative lens.

a
Distance
out of focus

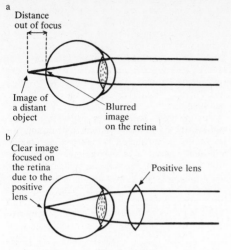

Image of
a distant
object

Blurred
image
on the retina

b
Clear image
focused on
the retina
due to the
positive
lens

Positive lens

Hyperopic Eye

**Fig. 5. a.** Retinal image in a hyoperopic eye.
**Fig. 5. b.** Corrected hyperope with a positive lens.

some corrective lenses after the intervention. In a small percentage of cases, vision was even made worse by the operation. Nevertheless, a great deal of research is being devoted to this subject and new techniques attempt to reshape the cornea without producing scars which hinder its transparency. In particular, experiments are carried out using ultra-violet lasers (called Excimer lasers) which can produce controllable, repeatable, and clear corneal incisions. Thus, in the next few years, we may observe considerable progress in the surgical correction of myopia, and even hyperopia.

*Hyperopia.* This is a condition in which the image of a distant object is formed not on the retina but behind it (Fig. 5). In other words, the power of the eye is either too weak or the eye is too short. The latter is usually the case, but in diabetic people the power of the eye can sometimes vary due to a transitory decrease in sugar concentrations in the blood, which results in a change of the index of refraction of the vitreous body, and consequently the quality of vision fluctuates. Hyperopes, unlike myopes, see objects clearly at all distances (provided they are not presbyopes) but they must accommodate continuously to increase the power of their eyes. This incessant effort often gives rise to eye-strain or even headaches. Where these symptoms are not evident, many hyperopes go without a correction, especially those with small errors.

Hyperopia usually develops soon after birth and strong evidence seems to indicate that hereditary factors play an important role in determining this ametropia. It is more frequent than myopia, affecting about one person in three in Western countries, but is very rare in Asia.

*Correction of hyperopia.* Correction of hyperopia, which can be done with either spectacles or contact lenses, consists of increasing the power of the eye with a positive lens of an amount such that the image of a distant object coincides with the retina (Fig. 5). This is in fact similar to the correction of presbyopia.

*Astigmatism.* In the perfect eye all refractive surfaces are spherical, with equal curvatures along all meridians. Alas, most human eyes do not fall into this category and the cornea, in particular, may have slightly different curvatures in various meridians, therefore it is astigmatic. As a result the image of a distant object will not be a single point but a complex image with two principal lines. Astigmatism is a term derived from the Greek: *a* meaning 'without' and *stigma* meaning a 'point'. A good example of an astigmatic surface is a rugby ball which is more steeply curved in one direction than the other. The amount of astigmatism represents the difference in power between the meridians of most and least curvature. Astigmatism is a condition which is superimposed on myopia, hyperopia, presbyopia, or emmetropia since it is a lack of symmetry of the surfaces of the eye irrespective of its total power.

The effect on vision is less marked than myopia of the same amount, as the eye probably sees clearly the features in one direction, namely that of the image closest to the retina. Small amounts of astigmatism do not usually reduce the quality of vision significantly, but often tend to produce visual discomfort as the eye keeps focusing on one part of the image or the other, always (involuntarily) attempting to improve vision. Large degrees of astigmatism produce blurred vision. Astigmatism is tested using a chart made up of black lines orientated in different directions (see Fig. 6). A person who has astigmatism will see some lines more sharply and others, at right angles, more blurred.

*Correction of astigmatism.* This is accomplished

**Fig. 6.** Bar patterns used to test astigmatism.

with a spectacle lens which has astigmatic surfaces producing astigmatism of the same amount but opposite sign as the eye; it therefore collapses the interval between the two images into a single one. The fact that the cornea may not have the same curvature in all meridians makes the fitting of contact lenses which rests on that surface somewhat delicate. However, because the tears fill the space between the lens and the cornea the front surface of the contact lens effectively becomes the new cornea and corrects astigmatism of the eye (at least that of the cornea) automatically with a new front spherical surface. When the astigmatism of the cornea is very large it may, however, be necessary to incorporate some astigmatism on the back surface of the contact lens as otherwise it is not possible to fit the lens.

**Binocular vision anomalies.** Defects and correction of the eye would probably be relatively simple if we had only one eye. However, in that case our perception of space would be distorted and the world would appear basically two-dimensional, although there are a few clues which help us appreciate depth with only one eye. In normal vision, the image of a distant object must not only fall on the retina of one eye (specifically on the fovea where the quality of vision is the greatest) but of both eyes. In many cases, however, the extra-ocular muscles (six for each eye) do not manage to synchronize perfectly and there is a tendency for one eye to converge too much or too little. But this is usually kept under control in normal vision and there is no obvious deviation. Such a condition is called heterophoria and some adjustment in the optical correction, with prisms in particular, or eye exercises, are sometimes necessary. Until the condition of heterophoria is diagnosed a patient, although sometimes already wearing an optical correction, may have visual discomfort and sometimes double vision or headaches.

*Strabismus.* In rare cases (about 2 per cent), the two eyes cannot turn toward the same object of regard, due to a paralysis of a muscle or very poor vision in one eye, or a difference in the refractive error of each eye, or cataract in one eye, or orbital fracture, etc., and one eye turns away from the other. This condition is called *strabismus* (or squint). The management of strabismus begins with the imperative need to correct, by optical means, whatever refractive error is present in the child and this should be done as young as possible so that clear images are provided to each eye. In babies, contact lenses are most appropriate. Otherwise an out-of-focus image in one eye may lead to cell degeneration in the brain such that optical correction in adulthood no longer restores quality of vision. The eye has then become amblyopic.

Eye exercises may also be necessary, but the child must be sufficiently mature to co-operate and these must be carried out not only in hospitals but at home as well. However, in some cases strabismus is not cured by either of the above methods and surgery must be undertaken, if only for cosmetic reasons. Following surgery, visual binocular function is not necessarily restored and more exercises and correction of refractive errors are often again needed.

**Conclusion.** We have reviewed briefly the most common optical defects of the eye and the means which are commonly used to correct them. Optical correction is essential as early in life as possible. It results in good vision with equal visual input to both eyes, elimination of visual discomfort, and often restoration of personal confidence. It hinders the development of amblyopia and strabismus, and facilitates the development of the three-dimensional sense of space.

In today's highly industrialized society where the use of the eyes predominates, optimum visual correction is a prerequisite for the enhancement of visual efficiency. To achieve this objective, the correction must not only be precise but appropriate for the distance, or distances, at which the eyes function; it must also be related to the wearer's occupation, for example tinted if the overall illumination is too bright, and must take into account whatever binocular anomalies may exist. The correction of the eyes may be an exact science, but to make the patient reveal his visual needs and wear and adapt to his new prescription is indeed an art, in which the mind of the wearer plays a major role.

M. M.

Bennett, A. G. and Rabbetts, R. B. (1984). *Clinical visual optics*. London.

Michaels, D. D. (1985). *Visual Optics and Refraction*. St Louis, Missouri.

Millodot, M. (1986). *Dictionary of Optometry*. London.

# F

**FABRE,** JEAN HENRI (1823–1915). French entomologist, born at St Leon, Aveyron. Fabre taught at Carpentras and Avignon before retiring to Sérignan, where he carried out remarkable investigations on the behaviour and sensory capacities of insects. He carried out controlled experiments: for example, by putting cotton wool, on which a female butterfly had spent some time, in a jar in one part of the room and the female herself in full view under a glass dome in another part of the room. He found that the males would fly straight to the jar, ignoring the female. This showed that the males were guided by a remarkable sense of *smell, dependent upon their antennae. Fabre is also celebrated for his work on the behaviour of the praying mantis and the hunting wasp, which he believed incapacitated larvae without killing them so that they remained available as food over long periods.

His fullest work is *Souvenirs entomologiques* (10 vols., 1879–1907, collected edn. Paris, 1925, with a *Life* by Lenoir).

**FACIAL EXPRESSION** is a primary source of information for judging another's mood, and even his character. Attempts to classify expressions and facial types were made by the *physiognomists. *Essays on Physiognomy* by John Lavater (1741–1801) appeared in many versions and editions from 1775 and throughout the nineteenth century. Much of it is based on comparisons of human faces and expressions with those of animals, as well as on Lavater's wide experience with people. It has little, if any, scientific validity, but the fact remains—we do, all the time, 'read faces'.

Charles *Darwin's *The Expression of the Emotions in Man and Animals* (1872) is a companion to, and was originally conceived to be part of, his great book *The Descent of Man* (1871). Both works are concerned with drawing conclusions from the hypothesis, startling at the time, that man as a species is derived by processes of natural selection from other species, and especially from his near relations, the great apes. Darwin argues that the facial expressions of man, which are now important as social *symbols*, were originally *functionally* important—often in ancient and even extinct species. For example, frowning shaded the eyes; drooping of the mouth rejected bitter or poisonous fruit; widening of the eyes improved vision for emergencies, and so on. His studies were meticulous, leading him to consider the development of particular muscles, and identifying reactions in his own children—sometimes even making them cry

for experimental purposes, though he was the kindest of men and most deeply attached to his family. *Expression of the Emotions* is well worth reading today: it has not been overtaken by later scholarship.

A popular treatment is *Manwatching* by Desmond Morris (1977), which brings out subtle and sometimes clear-cut regional and class differences. These are interesting in their own right and provide evidence of racial migrations. We are affected by other people's expressions; and our expressions affect our friends' and colleagues' behaviour to us—so expressions may not only influence responses to other people but also generate basic aspects of individual and social behaviour.

A curious logical point was raised by the philosopher C. D. *Broad (in *Mind and its Place in Nature*, 1925). He points out (p. 325) that we could hardly learn by association to read moods in others from their facial expressions by analogy with our own expressions and moods, because we only see our own faces and expressions in mirrors. He considers the possibility of some kind of telepathic association, or link, from which we know other people's moods from their expressions. An alternative and surely more plausible explanation is that expressions are largely innate (which would be Darwin's view), though, as Desmond Morris and others have shown, they are modified by social interaction.                                         R. L. G.

**FACTOR ANALYSIS.** See LEARNING AND LEARNING THEORY.

**FACULTY PSYCHOLOGY.** The theory, in vogue particularly during the second half of the eighteenth and first half of the nineteenth centuries, that the mind is divided up into separate inherent powers of 'faculties' such as *memory, *learning, *intelligence, *perception, and will. The faculties might be contrasted with those other powers which the individual could acquire through use, exercise, or study, and which were generally known as 'habits'. The theory was associated with *phrenology, which supposed that the various faculties were more or less represented in each individual according to the size of bumps which could be seen or felt on the skull. Similar divisions are still made in textbooks of psychology, but the notion that they are strictly distinct and localized individually in different regions of the brain has very largely been abandoned.

It is now held that abilities and skills result from

the interplay of very many brain mechanisms and that these do not show up as 'bumps'. Even if they did, it would be necessary to know a great deal about the organization of the brain to 'read bumps'. It is, however, the case that through the evolution of species some functional brain regions have grown and others have shrunk—with a general development of the cerebral cortex in mammals. (See PRIMATES, EVOLUTION OF THE BRAIN IN.)

A related objection to the notion of faculties is that, for example, perception involves memory and no doubt various kinds of intelligence. For convenience we separate perception, memory, and intelligence, even though each is involved with the others and it is hardly possible to see any one in isolation.

There has recently, however, been some return to the old notion of 'faculties', as the brain is now seen to be organized with many 'modules' of cells in small regions, each responsible for a particular ability (such as face-recognition) though of course many other parts of the brain must also be involved. The new ideas are fully discussed by the American philosopher Jerry Fodor (1983). R. L. G.

Fodor, J. A. (1983). *The Modularity of Mind*. Cambridge, Massachusetts.
Klein, D. B. (1970). *A History of Scientific Psychology*. London.

**FAIRBAIRN,** RONALD (1889–1964). British psychoanalyst, born and educated in Edinburgh. After graduating with honours in philosophy, he qualified in medicine and served in the First World War. Influenced by the work of Sigmund *Freud and by Anna *Freud's *The Ego and the Mechanism of Defence* (1936, English translation 1937), Fairbairn evolved a systematic theory of 'object relations'—i.e. inter-personal relationships—which involved an appreciable modification of the Freudian position (see FREUDIANISM: LATER DEVELOPMENTS). This is set out in his *Psychoanalytical Studies of the Personality* (1952), which has had considerable influence on psychoanalysis in Britain and further afield.

See FREUDIANISM: LATER DEVELOPMENTS.

O. L. Z.

**FALSIFICATION.** Scientists have generally been more concerned to justify their theories than run the risk of falsifying them with counter-evidence. This is a criticism of science which has been argued most powerfully by Sir Karl Popper (1902–94). Unusually for a philosopher of science, Popper with his comments and criticisms actually changed the way science is carried out, establishing especially that hypotheses should be formulated in such a way as to be falsifiable. Popper based his ideas on examples in early twentieth-century physics, especially on how Einstein's ideas challenged Newtonian physics, but his strictures are also applicable to biology and clinical hypotheses, as Sir Peter

Medawar has discussed most cogently (1967, 1969).

One usually thinks of science as producing new truths by observation and experiment, and the more secure the better—so Popper's idea that it should be possible to falsify a hypothesis, if it is to be acceptable as a 'good' hypothesis, came as a considerable shock. The point is not that a hypothesis cannot be good unless it is likely to be false; rather it is that a hypothesis should be conceived and formulated in such terms that experiments or observations could deal it a mortal blow. The hypothesis thus attacked might die or might be merely wounded, to recover in a changed form; but Popper prefers sudden death to hanging on to life. For him a hypothesis that staggers on, mutilated, generally does so because it was not formulated with sufficient vulnerability to die cleanly and be forgotten.

As an example of a hypothesis which refuses to die because inadequately formulated, we may consider Freud's notion of trauma at birth having significant effects in adult life. Suppose to test this we looked at adults who were born by Caesarean section, and suppose we found that they had, as adults, the characteristics that Freud attributed to birth trauma. If the post-Freudians accepted this as falsifying evidence for the birth trauma hypothesis, then in Popper's terms well and good—for the hypothesis was evidently set up in such a way as to be falsifiable. And in showing it to be false something has been learned: that these characteristics are not due to birth trauma. But the post-Freudians would have lost their hypothesis, and losing hypotheses can itself be traumatic. Popper would object to the post-Freudians responding by re-defining 'birth trauma'—so that, let's say, it is not the birth itself but the shock of coming into the world that produces the trauma—for then the hypothesis would have changed, rather than decently died, and it is hard to see how any evidence could count against it.

Popper would probably prefer that the whole idea be abandoned at this point; but it might be that such forced re-defining is a way in which science can work well, cumbersome though it seems. For could not some hypotheses be refined and improved in this way? There is surely a danger of throwing out the baby with the bath water.

Popper compared falsification as a way of gaining knowledge (and for him it was the *only* way, as he completely rejected *inductive generalizations*) with the deaths of individuals leading to improved species in evolution by natural selection of the fittest to survive. There is now, based on this analogy, an active school of epistemology led by Donald Campbell (1967) and Stephen Toulmin (1972). It goes back at least to the American philosopher Charles Sanders *Peirce (1839–1914) with the view that hypotheses die by competition, much as species die out when they are inadequate, for the cumulative good of life and science. There are objections, however, to saying that it is *only* by falsifying hypotheses that we gain new knowledge. It is very hard to believe that animals such as ourselves, with all the evidence of learning curves and so on, never actually learn by induction (Gregory, 1981).

It seems clear that, strictly speaking, hypotheses cannot be falsified by observational or experimental evidence alone, for all evidence has to be interpreted according to subjective background knowledge or assumptions which may be wrong. Thus, we take it as obvious that the stars appear to move across the sky because the earth is rotating daily on its axis; but before this was accepted the stellar observation was differently described. Aristotle thought he had falsified the hypothesis of daily rotation of the earth by jumping up and then finding that he landed on the same spot, when according to his assumption of earthly rotation he should have come down west of where he took off; and there should have been a continuous easterly wind.

Is there a fundamental difference between *falsifying* and *predicting* as a means of testing hypotheses? Isn't a successful *surprising prediction* excellent evidence for the hypothesis suggesting it? Perhaps there is no asymmetry between falsifying and predicting (logically, the failure of a prediction is no different from any other discordant evidence), except that dramatic true predictions may be rarer than equally surprising falsifications. Falsifications of the stationary and the flat earth hypotheses were extremely surprising—and so conveyed a very great deal of information. But there are comparably surprising predictions, such as the apparent shift of positions of the stars near the sun photographed during its eclipse in 1919, which *supported* Einstein's ideas against Newton.

R. L. G.

Campbell, T. D. (1974). Evolutionary epistemology. In Shilpp, P. A. (ed.), *The Philosophy of Karl Popper*. Illinois.

Gregory, R. L. (1981). *Mind in Science*. London and New York.

Medawar, P. (1967). *The Art of the Soluble*. London.

Medawar, P. (1969). *Induction and Intuition in Scientific Thought*. London.

Popper, K. R. (1959). *The Logic of Scientific Discovery*. London.

Popper, K. R. (1970). Logic of discovery or psychology of research? In Lakatos, I. and Musgrave, A. (eds.), *Criticism and the Growth of Knowledge*. Cambridge.

Popper, K. R. (1972). *Objective Knowledge: an Evolutionary Approach*. Oxford.

Toulmin, S. E. (1972). *Human Understanding*. Princeton.

**FARABI,** AL- (870–950), Turkic exponent of Islamic philosophy. See AL-FARABI.

**FATIGUE** in living beings refers to deterioration of their performance with the passage of time. It is associated with feelings of tiredness, slowing down, and making simple errors. More severe effects include disturbance of reasoning and judgement, depression, and disturbances in perception (mainly visual) leading to florid \*hallucinations. A broad view of fatigue in people involves consideration of the extremes of physical and psychological hardship, when they are trying to accomplish some task.

Fatigue most commonly occurs from lack of sleep. A deterioration in the performance of (albeit dull) laboratory tests after one night with only two hours of sleep, or after two consecutive nights with only five hours of sleep each, can be reliably demonstrated. Highly motivated people—such as doctors on duty, soldiers in battle, adventurers in hostile environments—are able to keep going longer, but after one night without sleep most of them will be functioning inefficiently, although they may not realize it themselves.

**The effects of fatigue.** The effects are increased by adverse conditions such as cold, excessive heat, hunger and thirst, noise and vibration, isolation, lack of oxygen, being wet or seasick, or being under the influence of alcohol or drugs. They may also be increased by anxiety, which can occur in people who doubt their ability to perform a task in hand, or who have worries about separate matters such as money, employment, or relationships.

The effects include:

*Simple errors, poor concentration, and forgetfulness.* The initial slowing down is not usually noticed by the individual, though it is plain to observers who are rested. Later on, tasks are started but not completed, things are put down and cannot be found afterwards, a cup of coffee is made and the fatigued person forgets to drink it. Doctors who have to work excessive hours can be shown, for example, to make errors in their interpretation of laboratory reports and electrocardiograph tracings.

*Faulty judgements and perceptions.* In practice it is not possible to determine whether an error of judgement exists directly as a result of, say, tiredness, or whether it is the consequence of a faulty perception. At a traffic junction where there are tired and frustrated motorists about, a driver wants to go straight ahead but the light is red. A green arrow lights up, permitting traffic to filter off to one side. The tired driver very much wants to see a green light, and so misperceives the filtering light as the signal for going straight ahead, and drives off. He will correct the error in a shorter or a greater time according to the degree of fatigue. Other such circumstances are the overhead railway gantries that carry signals for several adjacent tracks, and harbour lights with many opportunities for 'seeing' the lights a ship's navigator wants to see, indicating a particular channel.

As a second example, a driver when rested and relaxed takes in all relevant information—his car's speed and position in the road relative to other traffic, the condition of the road, proximity to junctions and other hazards, the mechanical state of the car, and weather conditions and visibility—and then responds in a logical manner, having evaluated the relative importance of the different factors; but the fatigued driver may instead concentrate exclusively on one aspect—such as his position in the middle lane—to the neglect of the other factors, and drive remorselessly along the middle lane without regard for speed, visibility, or other vehicles.

Either poor or extremely good visibility, moonlight, high vantage points (with nothing intervening)—all can lead to perceptual errors, especially among the fatigued, so that distances are overestimated or underestimated. Small objects seem to move in the distance, rocks high up on mountains appearing as people.

Ordinary phenomena can be misinterpreted by fatigued people. For instance, a very tired sailor thought the bow wave of his yacht was a flat fish, like a ray; another sailor, in mid-Atlantic, thought he saw a Ford car which later he realized was a small whale; another thought a sleeping-bag laid out on a bunk to be his wife. These are called misinterpretations because they are in due course corrected by closer examination.

A severely fatigued person will not be able (or try) to correct the initial impression. A dramatic example of an uncorrected illusion concerned Shackleton and his two companions as they struggled across South Georgia. All three felt there was a fourth person with them, a presence that was felt to be friendly and supportive. Such experiences are indicative of the limits of endurance.

*Ecstasy, depression, and frustration.* These are states which can afflict those who are fatigued, and increase the risk of danger.

Ecstatic states of mastery over, or of oneness with, all things are to be treasured, but they can lead to over-confidence if experienced, say, while climbing a mountain or piloting an aircraft. Depression is part of ordinary experience and commonly accompanies fatigue, especially if the person is isolated at the time, and can lead to lethargy and carelessness. Frustration, like depression, can be induced by inactivity, especially among the normally energetic. People accustomed to solving problems by increased effort can become very disturbed when no amount of physical effort is of any avail, as when becalmed in a small boat on the ocean or marooned in a tent in a blizzard. Then the ability to relax and go with events, rather than try to combat nature, has great survival value; the art is to cultivate a kind of alert inactivity.

*Disorganization and psychological breakdown.* Deprivation of fifty hours or more of sleep at one stretch is likely to lead to visual hallucinations and paranoid delusions, and to render the deprived person incapable of effective action. Experiments in which subjects are given impossible tasks—such as trying to fly a particular course in a trainer cockpit programmed to make the course impossible to steer—bring most subjects, eventually, to a state of complete incapacity.

A traumatic event such as seeing a relative or companion killed may lead to a period of shock-induced inactivity followed by acute distress or engagement in some activity which is useful only in that it distracts. Another response to traumatic crisis is denial of its happening at all: a ship may be sinking but the distressed person simply denies that he is at sea at all. These are instances of the psychological process compensating for circumstances to which the individual cannot adapt.

Panic is not a common reaction to a crisis unless there is imminent danger, as in the case of risk of escape routes closing in the event of fire or flood, or there is repetition of a crisis that has occurred.

**Lessening of effects.** Exceptional people (such as Shackleton) and ordinary people at times of extreme need can accomplish quite extraordinary physical feats. Most people on most occasions—say, those who have to make accurate observations, exercise rational judgements, or carry out complicated tasks over prolonged periods—can do something to maintain their efficiency. It helps to observe strict routines for rest and eating, especially when any prolonged activity is called for; and when in the middle of intense activity, to take every opportunity to rest and eat, rather than make a kind of virtue of keeping going. It is also useful for people to monitor themselves—to remain aware of how tense, tired, frightened, or hungry they are—and to make due allowances by taking extra care with observations and decisions.

See also STRESS. G. BE.

Bennet, G. (1983). *Beyond Endurance: survival at the extremes*. London.

**FEAR AND COURAGE.** Although the word 'fear' is used without difficulty in everyday language to mean the experience of apprehension, problems arise when it is used as a scientific term. It cannot be assumed that people are always able, or even willing, to recognize and then describe their fears. In wartime, admissions of fear are discouraged. Similarly, boys are discouraged from expressing fear. In surveys carried out on student populations, it has been found that the admission of certain fears by men is felt to be socially undesirable.

The social influences that obscure the accurate expression of fear complicate the intrinsic difficulties in recognizing and describing our own experiences or predicted experiences. For instance, it is regularly found that some people who state that they are fearful of a particular situation or object are later seen to display comparatively fearless behaviour when confronting the specified fear stimulus. Subjective reports of fear tend to be of limited value in assessing the intensity of the experience because of the difficulties involved in translating phrases such as 'extremely frightened', 'terrified', and 'slightly anxious' into degrees on a quantitative scale with stable properties.

For these reasons among others, psychologists have extended the study of fear beyond an exclusive reliance on subjective reports by including indices of physiological change and measures of overt behaviour. It is helpful to think of fear as comprising four main components: the subjective experience of apprehension, associated physiological changes, outward expressions of fear, and attempts to avoid or escape certain situations. When these four components fail to correspond, as they commonly do, problems arise. People can experience subjective fear but remain outwardly calm and, if tested, show none of the expected psychophysiological reactions. There can also be subjective fear in the absence of any attempt at avoidance. The fact that the four components do not always correspond, makes it helpful in speaking of fear to specify which component one is referring to.

In our everyday exchanges we rely for the most part on people *telling* us of their fears and then supplementing this information by interpreting their *facial and other bodily expressions. Unfortunately this kind of interpretation, when made in the absence of supporting contextual cues, can be misleading. Moreover, facial and related expressions register only certain kinds of fear, particularly those of an acute and episodic nature; diffuse and chronic fears are less visible. We may easily observe signs of fear in an anxious passenger as an aircraft descends, but fail to recognize it in a person who is intensely apprehensive about ageing.

While there are many types of fear, certain of them, such as neurotic fears, have understandably been studied more intensively than others. Among the many types, a major division can be made between acute and chronic fears. Acute fears are generally provoked by tangible stimuli or situations and subside quite readily when the frightening stimulus is removed or avoided (see PHOBIAS): the fear of snakes is an example. (A less common type of acute fear is the sudden onset of panic which seems to have no tangible source, can last for as long as an hour or more, and often leaves a residue of discomfort.) Chronic fears tend to be more complex but are like the acute types in that they may or may not be tied to tangible sources of provocation. The fear of being alone is an example of a chronic, tangible fear. Examples of chronic, intangible fears are by their very nature difficult to specify; one simply feels persistently uneasy and anxious for unidentified reasons—a chronic state of aching fear that has been better described by novelists than by psychologists.

Repeated or prolonged exposure to fearsome stimulation can give rise to enduring changes in behaviour, feelings, and psychophysiological functioning. Clear examples of such changes are encountered during war conditions and after. Adverse reactions can be classified in two broad categories: *combat neuroses*, which are persisting fear and related disturbances, and *combat fatigue* (far more common), which is a temporary disturbance readily reversed by rest and sedation. Wartime observations and research on animal subjects suggest that the fear and *anxiety experienced by many patients with psychological troubles may well give rise to enduring psychophysiological changes, as well as to the more obvious behavioural changes such as marked and persistent avoidance of the frightening stimuli. However, given the nature of chronic anxiety, it can be difficult to confirm causal connections between it and specific psychological and physiological changes (a major problem, incidentally, in studying *psychosomatic disorders).

A distinction is sometimes made between fear and anxiety: fear is taken to refer to feelings of apprehension about tangible and predominantly realistic dangers, whereas anxiety is sometimes taken to refer to feelings of apprehension which are difficult to relate to tangible sources of stimulation. Inability to identify the source of a fear is often regarded as the hallmark of anxiety; and, in psychodynamic theories such as psychoanalysis, is said to be a result of repression.

A clinically useful distinction can be made between focal and diffuse fears. Generally speaking, focal fears are more easily modified, despite the fact that they are often of long standing.

The distinction between innate and acquired fears is an interesting one, although it may be of little practical value. The impact of early behaviourism, with its massive emphasis on the importance of acquired behaviour, led to the demise of the notion that some fears may be innately determined. Even the possibility of such fears existing in animals was only reluctantly conceded. In recent years, however, the possible occurrence of innately determined fears in human beings has once again come under serious consideration.

The major causes of fear include exposure to traumatic stimulation, repeated exposure to subtraumatic (sensitizing) situations, observations (direct or indirect) of people exhibiting fear, and the receipt of fear-provoking information. Fears usually diminish with repeated exposure to a mild or toned-down version of the frightening situation. This decline in fear as a consequence of repetition can be facilitated by superimposing on the fearful reactions a counteracting influence, such as relaxation.

Fears can be thought of as existing in a state of balance, in which repeated exposures to a fear-evoking situation may lead to an increase in fear (sensitization) or, at other times and in other circumstances, to a decrease (desensitization). The balance tilts in the direction of increased or decreased fear according to the type of exposure, intensity of stimulation, the person's state of alertness, and other factors.

Fear and its first cousin, anxiety, play a major part in most neurotic disorders, and clinicians and their research colleagues have explored the effects of a variety of therapeutic means. Leaving aside the pharmacological methods which are often capable of dampening fear (but seldom of removing it), we are left with psychological methods. These can be divided into two main types: those which attempt to reduce the fear or anxiety directly (as in *behaviour therapy) and those which attempt to modify its putative underlying causes (as in psychoanalysis and related techniques). The direct methods are comparatively new and are largely products of experimental psychology. The best-established and most extensively used, desensitization, has been joined recently by *flooding* and by *modelling*, methods which involve repeated practice in confronting the frightening situation. Of the indirect methods, psychoanalysis is of course the most famous and influential, and it has spawned many derivations. Most of them, like psychoanalysis itself, were developed by psychiatrists or psychologists. The most widely practised is psychotherapy (a confusingly wide term covering many types of activity), and not psychoanalysis, which is a comparatively rare form of therapy. Although there are many different techniques, the indirect methods share the assumption that a thorough exploration of matters seemingly unrelated to the pertinent fear is a prerequisite for its reduction.

There is no generally accepted theory to account for the genesis and persistence of fears. The psychoanalytic theory, originally proposed by *Freud, has undergone little revision, despite a great deal of criticism. The *conditioning theory, derived from the work of *Pavlov, appears incapable of providing a comprehensive account. The conditioning theory postulates that any neutral object or situation which is associated with painful or fearful experiences will acquire fear-evoking properties. Although there is some evidence to support this theory, there remain important observations that cannot be accommodated by it, such as the non-random distribution of human fears, and the non-appearance of fears in predicted circumstances.

Although fearlessness is often regarded as synonymous with courage, there is some value in distinguishing it from a particular view of courage: the occurrence of perseverance despite fear, which is perhaps the purest form of courage—it certainly requires greater endurance and effort. Despite frequent exposure to dangerous and stressful situations, most people acquire few lasting fears. Wartime surveys testify to the resilience of people subjected to air-raids. Experimental analysis of programmes designed to train people in such dangerous tasks as parachute-jumping provides further information about the nature of courage. Although fear during or immediately after exposure to danger is a common reaction, we apparently have the capacity to recover quickly. And our capacity to persevere and adapt when faced by fear and stress is remarkable.

Training for courage plays an important part in preparing people to undertake dangerous jobs, such as fire-fighting or parachuting. One element of such training, gradual and graduated practice in the tasks likely to be encountered, seems to be of particular importance. This aspect of courage training is strikingly similar to the clinical method of reducing fear known as desensitization.

In the early stages of courage training, the probability of success is improved if the subject's motivation is raised appropriately, encouraging perseverance despite subjective apprehension. The successful practice of courageous behaviour should lead to a decrease in subjective fear and finally to a state of fearlessness. Novice parachute-jumpers display courage when they persevere with their jumps despite subjective fear; veteran jumpers, having successfully adapted to the situation, no longer experience fear when jumping: they have moved from courage to fearlessness.    S. R.

Freud, S. (1905). The analysis of a phobia in a five-year-old boy. In the *Collected Papers*, vol. 3. London.

Gray, J. A. (1971). *The Psychology of Fear and Stress*. London.

Marks, I. (1969). *Fears and Phobias*. London.

Rachman, S. (1978). *Fear and Courage*. Harmondsworth.

**FECHNER,** GUSTAV THEODOR (1801–87). German philosopher and physicist, the son of a village pastor. He took his degree in medicine in the University of Leipzig, where he remained for the rest of his life. Fechner's interests soon turned to mathematics and physics, and for a time he earned his living by translating scientific texts from French into German. He also undertook some research on electricity which won him the chair of physics at Leipzig at the early age of 33. Owing to a serious nervous breakdown, he resigned from his chair after a few years and, on recovering, with a deepened religious consciousness, he became a convinced pantheist.

Fechner's fame rests largely on his two-volume work *Elemente der Psychophysik* (1860). Basing his argument on E. H. *Weber's work on differential sensitivity, Fechner argued that, in a series of sensations of increasing magnitude, say brightness or pressure, the intensity of the stimulus must increase in geometrical proportion if a just noticeable difference (j.n.d.) in sensation is to result. Further, if such just noticeable differences could be regarded as units each greater by one than its predecessor, it follows that the intensity of sensation is proportional to the logarithm of the stimulus. This is known as the Weber–Fechner Law (also known as Weber's Law), which Fechner regarded as basic to our understanding of the relationship between body and mind. It is the first formulation of this relationship in quantitative terms (see PSYCHOPHYSICS for further discussion).

Fechner insisted that what he called 'outer psychophysics', i.e. the correlation of sensory magnitude with the intensity of physical stimulation, would eventually be replaced by 'inner psychophysics', i.e. the correlation of subjective magnitude with the intensity of the central excitatory process. He thought that ultimately it would make possible a quantitative treatment not only of sensory magnitude but also of images, feelings, and indeed states of consciousness generally. Unfortunately, techniques were not available in his time to achieve this aim, but developments in contemporary neuropsychology might at least suggest that such an aim is not wholly fanciful.                                    O. L. Z.

Fechner, G. T., *Elemente der Psychophysik*, vols. 1 and 2 (1860; vol. 1 translated by Adler, H. E., and edited by Howes, D. H. and Boring, E. G., 1967, New York).

Ross, H. E. and Murray, D. J. (1978) (trans.). *E. H. Weber: The Sense of Touch. De Tactu and Der Tastinn.* (Experimental Psychology Society.) New York.

**FEEDBACK AND FEEDFORWARD.** When we move to catch a ball, we must interpret our view of the ball's movement to estimate its future trajectory. Our attempt to catch the ball incorporates this anticipation of the ball's movement in determining our own movement. As the ball gets closer, or exhibits spin, we may find it departing from the expected trajectory, and we must adjust our movements accordingly. This is an example of the visual system providing inputs to a controller (our brain) which must generate control signals to cause some system (our musculature) to behave in some desired way (to catch the ball). *Feedforward* anticipates the relation between system and environment to determine a course of action; *feedback* monitors discrepancies which can be used to refine the actions. In general terms, therefore, a *control problem* is to choose the input to some system in such a way as to cause its output to behave in some desired way, whether to stay near a set reference value (the regulator problem), or to follow close upon some desired trajectory (the tracking problem). A control signal defined by its intended effect may not achieve that effect either because of the effect of disturbances upon the system, or because of inaccuracy in the controller's knowledge of the controlled system. Feedback is then required to compare actual and intended performance, so that a compensatory change in the input may be determined. Overcompensation yields instability; undercompensation yields poor adjustment to *'noise'. Thus, not only is feedback necessary, but it must be properly apportioned if the controller is to obtain smooth co-ordinated behaviour.

It is important to note that feedback can only be used effectively if the controller is 'in the right ballpark' in his (or its) model of the controlled system. However, in the real world the exact values of the parameters describing a system are seldom available to the controller, and may actually change (compare short-term loading effects on muscles and longer-term ageing effects and weight changes). To adapt to such changes, the outer, feedback, loop of Fig. 1 must be augmented by an *identification *algorithm*. The job of this algorithm

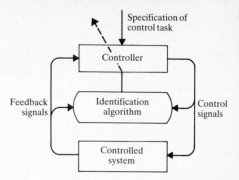

**Fig. 1.** To render a controller adaptive, an identification algorithm monitors control signals and feedback signals to provide the controller with updated estimates of the parameters that describe the controlled system.

is to monitor the output of the controlled system continually and to compare it with the output that would be expected on the basis of the current estimated state, the current estimated parameters, and the current control signals. On the basis of these data, the identification algorithm can identify more and more accurate estimates of the parameters that define the controlled system, and these updated parameters can then be supplied to the controller as the basis for his (or its) state estimation and control computations.

If the controlled system, or the disturbances to it, are sufficiently slowly time-varying for the identification procedure to make accurate estimates of the (system plus disturbance) parameters more quickly than they actually change, the controller will be able to act efficiently, despite the fluctuations in the system dynamics. The controller, when coupled to an identification procedure, is precisely what is often referred to as an 'adaptive controller': it adapts its control strategy to changing estimates of the dynamics of the controlled system.

Marvin Minsky (1961) has observed that it may also be necessary for the identification procedure to generate some of the input to the controlled system—in other words, to apply test signals to try out various hypotheses about the parameters of the controlled system—trading off the loss of control caused by an inaccurate estimate of the parameters against the degradation resulting from the controller intermittently relinquishing control.

Note that the identification algorithm can only do its job if the controller is of the right general class. It is unlikely that a controller adapted for guiding the arm during ball-catching will be able, simply as a result of parameter-adjustment, properly to control the legs in the performance of a waltz. Thus the adaptive control system of Fig. 1 (controller plus identification procedure) is not to be thought of as a model of the brain; rather each such control system is a model of a brain 'unit' which can be activated when appropriate. We may

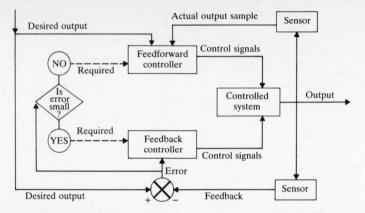

**Fig. 2.** Discrete-activation feedforward—one of various possible configurations in which feedback and feedforward controls are explicitly separated. Here feedforward is active for large errors to get the controlled system 'into the right ballpark', while feedback provides 'fine-tuning' in the presence of small errors. The dashed lines marked 'required' indicate the supply of necessary activation if the system supplied is to function. Non-dashed lines indicate 'data flow'.

think of it as a \*synergy. An important problem in analysing human movement is that of the co-ordinated phasing in and out of the brain's various synergies (control systems).

Feedforward is that strategy whereby a controller monitors a system's environment directly, and applies appropriate compensatory signals to the controlled system—rather than waiting for feedback on how changes in the environment have affected the system before giving compensatory signals. The advantage is speed—such changes may be compensated before they have any noticeable effect on the system—but the cost is paid in controller complexity: for the controller must have an accurate model of the effect of all such disturbances upon the system, if it is to compute controls which will indeed effect the necessary compensations.

Feedforward generates large control signals which rapidly correct large discrepancies from the desired output. The resultant change in output may be too fast for long-latency feedback paths to play a major effect.

Feedback and feedforward are separate control strategies and thus *may* have separate structural embodiments, as shown in Fig. 2 (which does not show the identification algorithms which may provide the adaptive components for each strategy). Note that feedforward is 'pulse-activated' in the hypothetical scheme of Fig. 2. It is activated when the error is not small. If well calibrated, the feedforward controller will, with a single brief time-pattern of control, return the system to the 'right ballpark', i.e. making the error small enough for feedback control to function effectively. The system should thus have a 'refractory period' based

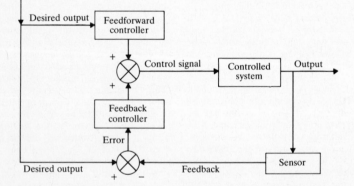

**Fig. 3.** Co-activation feedforward—one of various possible configurations in which feedback and feedforward are explicitly separated. Here the feedforward controller continually supplies a control signal which can maintain the output of the controlled system 'in the right ballpark', while the feedback controller utilizes error feedback to provide the necessary fine-tuning to compensate for inaccuracy in the feedforward controller's model of the controlled system, as well as for disturbances. Such a mode of control is appropriate only when the controlled system has a functional relation between maintained input and maintained output.

on the time-constants of the controlled system—it should not generate a second control signal before the control system has had time to respond fully to the first control signal. The reader should note what at first appears to be a semantic trick. The sample of the system's output is called 'feedback' when fed to the feedback controller, yet is called 'actual output sample' when fed to the feedforward controller. This looks like a way of avoiding the admission that feedforward requires feedback! But the difference is, in fact, a genuine one. A feedforward controller will, in general, need to know the actual state of the controlled system before generating its control signal) but need not monitor that output while the control signal is actually emitted. By contrast, the feedback controller continually monitors the error signal in generating its controls. As suggested by our ball-catching example, the situation in Fig. 2 might be refined so as to have the feedforward controller monitor the relation between the actual trajectory and a predicted trajectory, changing strategy if the discrepancy or error exceeds a threshold. But, again, we have a discrete-activation form of feedforward.

Fig. 3 shows a different strategy, which appears to describe better the control of muscle. Here, the control neurone must maintain a specific level of firing to hold a limb in a desired position—there is a functional relation between a desired output (e.g. muscle length) and a necessary input (e.g. maintained tension). In this case, the feedforward would be co-activated with the feedback system, so that feedforward sets and maintains the control level specified by the functional relationship, while feedback compensates for minor departures.

See also BIOFEEDBACK. M. A. A.

Fel'dman, A. G. (1966). Functional tuning of the nervous system with control of movement or maintenance of a steady posture—II. Controllable parameters of the muscles. *Biophysics* **11**, 565–78.

Greene, P. H. (1969). Seeking mathematical models of skilled actions. In Brodsky, R. (ed.), *Biomechanics*. New York.

MacKay, D. M. (1966). Cerebral organization and the conscious control of action. In Eccles, J. C. (ed.), *Brain and Conscious Experience*. Berlin, Heidelberg, New York.

Minsky, M. L. (1961). Steps towards artificial intelligence. *Proceedings of the Institute of Radio Engineers*, **49**, 8–30.

**FEMALE SEXUALITY.** Within the *Freudian tradition a good deal of controversy has arisen concerning the relevance of male sexual function as the model for female sexual function. As an example of theory going down a blind alley, creating a superstructure of assumptions around it, and then being rescued by the adequacy of more detailed clinical observation backed by discoveries in the parallel science of physiology, the Freudian statement on female sexuality bears some examination.

Freud's model of female sexual functioning is derived from the genital primacy of male functioning. In the male the reproductive act requires orgasmic release of seminal fluid. Hence, in the absence of contraception, ejaculatory orgasm and the reproductive act are not differentiated in the male.

In women such is not the case. There is no direct equivalent of ejaculation in the female, and she does not need to be orgasmic in order to be reproductive. This raised the theoretical problem of what should be thought of as constituting psychosexual maturity in women. In the psychoanalytic formulation, while the *process* for both men and women in reaching their psychosexual maturity is to reconcile their sexual drives with the requirements of their super-egos, the *experience* of that integration is not necessarily similar at all. Because of the different requirements concerning reproduction and orgasm, it might even be thought to be necessarily dissimilar. But if the only test of psychosexual maturity was the reported experience, and an experience of the male kind was not necessary to or possible for women, what was to be the test of the psychosexually mature female?

Freud recognized that the biology of the early twentieth century did not offer a satisfactory explanation of the physiology of female sexual response. So, in the absence of facts, he made the assumptive leap that the clitoris is a rudimentary male sexual organ—hence, *inter alia*, the penis envy of the female who can never aspire to the grandeur of the male, and the castration fears of the male that he might be left with a rudimentary female knob. In consequence it was reasoned that gratification arising from the clitoris must also be rudimentary or immature. Thus clitoral arousal became the province of the immature woman, while vaginal orgasm was the prerogative of the woman whose sexual conflicts were successfully resolved and the demands of her id integrated with those of the super-ego. Consequently the clitoris is to be abandoned as a source of gratification, and the desideratum of female gratification is to be from the vaginal experience of penile insertion. In further consequence, the woman knows herself sexually only through the presence of the male.

As a consequence of W. H. Masters and Virginia Johnson's studies (1966) it is now clearly understood that the clitoris and vagina are separate but mutually dependent parts of a continuous sexual process that is stimulated from a quiescent state through arousal to orgasm and a return to quiescence. They are thus *interdependent* rather than, as in the Freudian view, *independent* sites of sexual pleasure. Physical sexual stimulation is received via the clitoris (among other sexually responsive areas of the female body), while the orgasm is mediated by involuntary contractions of the pubococcygeal muscles surrounding the lower (outer) third of the vaginal barrel. The experience and perception of orgasm is widely different from woman to woman, and for many women from occasion to occasion. Thus the type of orgasm is not indicative of psychosexual maturity.

Interestingly, clinical observation had begun to

establish this view before the publication of Masters and Johnson's work, and such psychoanalytic observations were beginning to be incorporated in the revision of theory. Thus Helen Deutsch (1961) arrived at a clinical description of Masters and Johnson's subsequent physiological findings through her own analytical observations, when she expressed her conviction that

... the female sexual apparatus consists of two parts with a definite division of function. The clitoris is the sexual organ and the vagina primarily an organ of reproduction. The central role of the clitoris is not merely the result of masturbation but serves a biological destiny. Into it flow waves of sexual excitement which may more or less successfully be communicated to the vagina. The transition of sexual feelings from clitoris to vagina is a task performed largely by the active intervention of the man's sexual organ.

While the last part of this formulation would not now be accepted, as the transfer process is related to arousal threshold phenomena in the woman in which the penis may or may not play a part, the shift in assumptions from the male-dominated Freudian view is apparent. Therese Benedek (1961) asserted that there was a need for a theory of female sexuality which did not derive from the male model of sexual maturity, observing that when sexual sensations begin in the clitoris, spread to the vaginal walls, and finally encompass the whole body in orgasm, it is the woman's personality integration (her ego organization) that allows the clitoral stimulation to spread and be experienced as orgasm. Again, the latter part of this observation would now be questioned. W. C. Lobitz and J. LoPiccolo (1972) have shown that extensive masturbation may effectively produce orgasmic release where none has existed before, and in which the socially conditioned inhibitions of female sexual arousal appear to be much more dominant causal factors than personality integration.

In trying to integrate the physiological studies of Masters and Johnson into psychoanalytic thinking, Moore (1968) proposed that personal satisfactions deriving from sexual experience, rather than a continued preconception about desirable intensity and location of orgasmic experience, should be the criteria of adequacy/maturity in women, and the intrapsychic changes in the woman should be more the hallmark of personality integration than the presumed consequences of orgasm.

Finally, W. H. Gillespie (1969) provides the resolution of a debate that had been going on for over sixty years when, as an analyst himself, he observes that

... it seems probable that we must agree that an orgasm is an orgasm, and that one differs from another not in kind but in degree of completeness, or in the emotional satisfaction that accompanies it. I wish to propose that in future when the term 'vaginal orgasm' is used, we should no longer think of this as something excluding an outgrown clitoral erotogenicity; the term should instead be used exclusively to denote an orgasm that is *brought about* by thrusting movements in the vaginal barrel, whether or not such movements are indirectly producing excitation of the clitoris. The term 'clitoral orgasm' would then denote *orgasm produced by local stimulation* in the vicinity of the clitoris, not by thrusting movements in the vagina. Having in this way eliminated the probably misleading idea that female maturity necessitates an outgrowing or 'repression' (to use Freud's early description) of clitoral erotogenicity, we can proceed to consider what obstacles naturally stand in the way of vaginal orgasms as defined above; but here we shall find ourselves on familar psychoanalytic ground and shall be concerned with many psychological problems, such as fear of penetration or invasion, penis envy, masculine identification, and countless others, but one bogey will be out of the way, and I believe this will be a real advance in the psychoanalytic understanding of female sexuality.

See also SEXUAL DEVELOPMENT; SEXUAL PROBLEMS.                                                       P. T. B.

Benedek, T. and Deutsch, H. (1961). Participants in a panel discussion on frigidity in women, reported by Moore, B. E. *Journal of the American Psycho-Analytical Association*, **9**, 571.

Freud, S. (1905). *Three Essays in the Theory of Sexuality*. London.

Gillespie, W. H. (1969). Concepts of vaginal orgasm. *International Journal of Psychoanalysis*, **50**, 495–7.

Lobitz, W. C. and LoPiccolo, J. (1972). New methods in the behavioural treatment of sexual dysfunction. *Journal of Behavioural Research and Experimental Psychiatry*, **3**, 265–71.

Masters, W. H. and Johnson, V. (1966). *Human Sexual Response*. London.

Moore, B. E. (1968). Psychoanalytical reflections on the implications of recent physiological studies of female orgasm. *Journal of the American Psycho-Analytical Association*, **16**, 569–87.

**FERRIER,** SIR DAVID (1843–1928), British physician, was born near Aberdeen and went to university there. He graduated in classics and philosophy in 1863, having studied under Alexander *Bain, and went on to study medicine at Edinburgh in 1865–8. He was appointed physiology lecturer at the Middlesex Hospital in 1870 and in 1871 moved to King's College, London, where he spent the rest of his working life. The post of professor of neuropathology was created specially for him.

In 1873, Ferrier became interested in electrical excitation of the brain. He devised a method of faradic stimulation whereby he could explore the brains of various types of vertebrates including the monkey. The results confirmed his belief that cerebral functions were localized and enabled him to establish their areas. He noticed that if certain areas of a monkey's brain were destroyed, symptoms similar to those of a '*stroke' in humans were produced. He was now convinced that operations to treat brain injuries and diseases could be undertaken—if Lister's precautions against sepsis were observed—and these began to be successfully performed, thus changing the outlook in this field totally.

Ferrier was elected a Fellow of the Royal Society in 1876 and a lecture named after him was endowed.

See also LOCALIZATION OF BRAIN FUNCTION AND CORTICAL MAPS.                                                    D. D. H.

**FICTIONS IN PERCEPTION.** See ILLUSIONS.

**FIGURAL AFTER-EFFECTS.** These are changes in the appearance of a visual display consequent upon relatively prolonged fixation. These changes may affect size, shape, brightness, and location in space.

Figural after-effects were first described in 1933 by J. J. *Gibson, who observed that after fixating a curved line for several minutes it appeared to be curved in the opposite direction. Somewhat similar after-effects were studied in greater detail by the *Gestalt psychologists, Wolfgang *Köhler and Hans Wallach in 1944, and their work attracted considerable interest. Although these effects are often striking, unfortunately it cannot be said that their nature and mechanisms are fully understood.

Köhler's method of inducing figural after-effects in two dimensions may be briefly described. Two identical rectangles separated by about 25 cm. are displayed on a white ground and a fixation point provided midway between them. After the subject has satisfied himself that, when viewed from a distance of a few metres, the figures look identical, one rectangle, known as the Test or T-figure, is concealed by a screen, and the subject is instructed to fixate the remaining rectangle, known as the Inspection or I-figure, for three minutes. The screen is then swiftly removed and the subject is required to describe the appearance of the two figures. The typical response is to say that the I-figure appears smaller, dimmer, and lying further back in space than the T-figure. Although these effects vary appreciably as between subjects, very few fail to report them in whole or part. Furthermore, they may persist for a short period after the T-figure has been exposed.

Köhler satisfied himself that these after-effects are of central rather than peripheral origin. In particular, he claimed that if the I-figure is viewed with one eye and the T-figure with the other, the outcome is the same as with binocular vision throughout.

Köhler and Wallach attempted to explain figural after-effects in terms of an electrical field theory, often referred to as the 'satiation' theory. This theory is based in part on classical physics and in part on the tenets of Gestalt theory, in particular the concept of *isomorphism. Although ingenious, it can hardly be said that this theory carries conviction. An alternative theory, put forward by C. E. Osgood and A. W. Heyer, and owing much to W. M. Marshall and S. A. Talbot's excellent work on the mechanism of vision (1942), is altogether more plausible than Köhler's theory though not perhaps without difficulties of its own.

Köhler and his colleagues subsequently recorded some other varieties of figural after-effects, the most striking of which are figural after-effects in the third dimension, as described by Köhler and Emery in 1947. According to Osgood (1953), these find ready explanation if we assume that size changes are interpreted in terms of changes in distance. More perplexing are the accounts of figural after-effects in kinaesthesia reported by Köhler and Dinnerstein, also in 1947. These appear to continue very much longer than those reported in the visual experiments and may, it seems, persist for several days. Even Köhler was obliged to conclude that after-effects in the third dimension of visual space and those in kinaesthesis 'appear at present almost inaccessible to the theorist!' Indeed we are driven to conclude that whereas figural after-effects merit recognition as convincing perceptual phenomena, they still evade convincing psychological explanation.                                      O. L. Z.

Köhler, W. (1940). *Dynamics in Psychology*. New York and London.

McEwan, P. Figural After-Effects. *British Journal of Psychology* Monograph Supplement no. 31.

Osgood, C. E. (1944). *Method and Theory in Experimental Psychology*. New York.

**FIGURE–GROUND.** A term used in technical discussions on visual perception. In 'ambiguous figures', the *figure* alternates with the *ground* (Fig. 1) or with alternative figures or objects (see ILLUSIONS, Fig. 4). 'Figure' corresponds roughly to seeing *objects*. These important phenomena were investigated by the Danish psychologist Edward *Rubin, among others, and may be thought of as

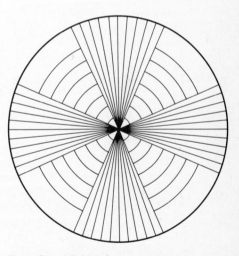

**Fig. 1.** One of Rubin's figure–ground reversing figures. Here there are two equally held figures, which in turn are relegated to ground. Regions accepted as figure are subtly changed perceptually in the process: if the concentric cross is seen as figure after the radial one, it is possible to note a characteristic change in the concentric markings, which depends on whether they belong to the figure or the ground. When they are part of the ground, they do not appear interrupted but seem to continue behind the figure. This is not noticed when the concentric cross is seen as the figure.

changing perceptual hypotheses. See also GESTALT THEORY; ILLUSIONS.

Gregory, R. L. (1970). *The Intelligent Eye*. London.

**FILMS, PERCEPTION OF.** See PERCEPTION OF MOTION PICTURES.

**FISHER,** SIR RONALD AYLMER (1890–1962). British statistician and geneticist, born in London and educated at Cambridge. While working on experimental methods in agricultural research at the Rothamsted Experimental Station, he developed the analysis of variance and the now standard methods of assessing statistical significance. He summarized this work in *Statistical Methods for Research Workers* (1925), a book whose many editions have been very influential. While at Rothamsted he also published *The Genetical Theory of Natural Selection* (1930), which became a classic of population genetics. In 1933 he became Galton professor of eugenics at University College London and in 1943 professor of genetics at Cambridge. His continued interest in statistics and experimental design led to two further important books, *The Design of Experiments* (1935) and *Statistical Tables for Biological, Agricultural, and Medical Research* (1938), the latter written jointly with F. Yates.

**FIXED ACTION PATTERN.** See ETHOLOGY.

**FLOODING.** See BEHAVIOUR THERAPY; BEREAVEMENT.

**FLOURENS,** (MARIE JEAN) PIERRE (1794–1867). French physiologist, born at Maureilhan, Hérault, and who studied medicine at Montpellier, qualifying in 1813. He moved to Paris, where he was helped by the anatomist Georges Cuvier. He became a member of the Académie des Sciences in 1828, professor of comparative anatomy at the Collège de France in 1835, and a member of the Académie française in 1840. He was a pioneer in techniques of ablation for investigating brain function.

An accomplished experimentalist, his findings led him to conclude that there is considerable diversification of function in the central nervous system: 'All sensory and volitional faculties exist in the cerebral hemispheres and must be regarded as occupying concurrently the same seat in these structures.' He likewise concluded that '. . . feeling, willing, and perceiving are but a single and essentially unitary faculty residing in a single organ (i.e. the cerebral hemispheres)'. These findings have been widely taken to imply that the various categories of psychological function are not discretely localized in the cerebral cortex—a view that held sway for some sixty years until Paul *Broca's claim that articulate speech in man is localized in a small area of the left cerebral hemisphere.

As might be anticipated, Flourens was a convinced opponent of phrenology and his work did much to discredit the standing of F. J. *Gall. And he is often held, not wholly with justice, of having anticipated the views of Karl *Lashley on the cerebral localization of psychological function. His important work on the effects of cerebral ablation in animals is *Recherches expérimentales sur les propriétés et les fonctions du système nerveux dans les animaux Vertélsnés* (1824).

**FLUGEL,** JOHN CARL (1884–1955). British experimental psychologist and psychoanalyst. Born in Liverpool, he became interested in psychology when, as a student at Oxford, he met William *McDougall, at that time Wilde reader in mental philosophy there. This led him to spend some months in Würzburg studying under *Külpe and, on his return, to becoming first assistant to Charles *Spearman at University College London. Here he carried out experiments on fluctuations of *attention under Spearman's direction and some years later published the monograph *Practice, Fatigue and Oscillation* (1928).

As well as being a dedicated university teacher, Flugel trained as a practising psychoanalyst and wrote several books on Freudian themes, among them *The Psychoanalytic Study of the Family* (1921), *The Psychology of Clothes* (1930), and *Men and Their Motives* (1934). He also produced *A Hundred Years of Psychology* (1933), a contribution to a series very popular in its day and still interesting.                                    O. L. Z.

**FORGETTING.** There are three possible causes of forgetting. First, relevant information may have been lost from the storage system of the brain—'storage loss'. Second, there may be failure to retrieve or to use stored information—'retrieval failure'. Third, insufficient information may have been put into storage to permit of differentiation between wanted and unwanted information—'encoding deficiency'. (Strictly, this is only one form of encoding deficiency. *How* information is encoded can also affect retrieval, as the success of *mnemonic systems testifies.)

Storage loss can occur in several ways. There may be decay of the physical representation of the information. Decay is a plausible explanation for the very rapid forgetting which takes place in the first second or so after an experience has occurred—for example, the fading perception of the visual world that occurs if you close your eyes. Another possibility is that information is displaced from storage by new information; the idea of displacement is used, for example, in the 'slot' theory of the memory span (see SHORT-TERM MEMORY). Or information may be modified by new information rather than be displaced by it, as in *Bartlett's '*schema' theory. Modification of schema may underlie the way our memory for a changing feature of the environment is updated, whether the feature is transient, such as our own location in space, or one that changes only slowly, such as the face of a friend. Schema provide a basis for recording abstractions from events without recording the events as such.

There is no direct evidence for storage loss. If such evidence is obtained it will be physiological. However, the total absence of storage loss would mean that, in a sense, nothing is ever really forgotten. This view was popularized by Freud but it is doubtful whether he meant that every trivial detail of every trivial experience remains stored. There is suggestive evidence of storage loss in post-encephalytic amnesia, since the *amnesia is characterized by unusually rapid forgetting. (Typically, amnesia is characterized by poor learning rather than rapid forgetting.) Suggestive evidence for storage loss, without any association with disease, comes from an extensive investigation of memory for school-learned Spanish: there was forgetting for the first 5 years after study, no forgetting for the next 25 years, and additional forgetting with the onset of middle-age. The interpretation of such evidence is, however, controversial.

Without physiological evidence it is impossible to be sure that storage loss occurs, for retrieval failure can never be excluded as a reason for forgetting. There is plenty of everyday evidence for retrieval failure: for example, we all forget names we know that we know and which we can later recall (the tip-of-the-tongue phenomenon). The likelihood of successful retrieval is greatly affected by the presence or absence of relevant cues—stimuli, logically or associatively related to the information to be retrieved—especially if they were present at the time of learning. Mood, which provides internal cues, has been shown to have quite a powerful effect on retrieval. It is easier to remember happy events when we are happy than when we are unhappy and vice versa (thus reinforcing a current mood state). Hypnosis can be used to alter mood state and can thereby affect retrieval. However, the common belief that hypnosis produces a dramatic increase in retrieval (thereby supporting the notion that there is no true forgetting) has been shown to be false, and the memories produced under hypnosis have proved to be highly unreliable.

An event is difficult to remember if it is one of a number of similar events (What did you have for lunch on Tuesday last week?)—a difficulty which has been extensively studied under the heading of proactive and retroactive interference. The difficulty probably arises partly because insufficient information has been stored to enable differentiation of one event from another—that is, from encoding deficiency. Immediately after an event has occurred, its recency is a sufficient basis for its identification, but later it can be distinguished from similar events only by some form of stored code of adequate precision. The difficulty also arises because retrieval failure becomes more likely; according to cue-overload theory, this is because retrieval of similar memories tends to depend on the same cues, and the effectiveness of a cue

falls as the number of memories associated with it rises.

We think of forgetting as undesirable. However, the difficulty of remembering similar events suggests that there is a positive advantage in forgetting, through storage loss, the great majority of our moment-to-moment experiences: such forgetting should reduce retrieval loss for information of importance to us. Can we, then, voluntarily discard information? Experiments suggest that the extent to which we can is very limited and probably confined to ceasing active maintenance of recently acquired information. Sadly, the mind does not seem to have at its disposal anything corresponding to the erase button of a tape-recorder.

See also MEMORY: BIOLOGICAL BASIS.                J. B.

Baddeley, A. D. (1976). *The Psychology of Memory*. London.

Bahrick, H. P. (1984). Semantic memory content in permastore: fifty years of memory for Spanish learned in school. *Journal of Experimental Psychology: General*, **113**, 1–29.

**FOURIER ANALYSIS.** A method of analysing into simpler components any complex sound or other waveform (whether it describes fluctuations over time or over place). The analysis uses the Fourier theorem, which states that any function or waveform can be described as a series of sine waves of multiple frequencies and various amplitudes. Conversely, the characteristic timbre of musical instruments can be produced by combining separate sine wave oscillations (Fourier synthesis).

Fourier analysis is useful for studies of electro-encephalography and *speech recognition by machine. The more recent notion that visual *pattern recognition may employ Fourier analysis is due largely to the work of F. W. Campbell at the University of Cambridge.

The Fourier theorem was formulated in 1826 by the French mathematician and physicist Jean Baptiste Joseph de Fourier (1768–1830), who was a professor at the École polytechnique in Paris from 1795 to 1798; he accompanied Napoleon to Egypt as scientific adviser and was for a time Governor of Lower Egypt. He was created baron in 1808 and in 1827 became president of the council of the École polytechnique.

Herivel, J. (1975). *Joseph Fourier: The Man and the Physicist*. London.

**FRANKENSTEIN.** The creator of a monster in a story, suggested in a dream, written by Mary Wollstonecraft Shelley (1797–1851) for her future husband, the poet Shelley, and their friend Lord Byron during a wet holiday on Lake Geneva in August 1816. The monster, created from parts of dead men, represented the fearful power of science to create uncontrollable beings and forces that threaten and might destroy us. The title-page of the novel (published in 1818) reads:

FRANKENSTEIN

or,

THE MODERN PROMETHEUS.

in Three volumes.

Did I request thee, Maker, from my clay
To mould me man? Did I solicit thee
From darkness to promote me?—
                              Paradise Lost.

Mary Shelley gives the full story of how it came to be written in the 1831 preface to the novel.

Frankenstein has been reborn in many films (Daniels, 1975), the first made in 1910 by the American inventor Thomas Alva Edison; sadly, this is lost, though there remain photographs of the first film monster: Charles Ogle. Boris Karloff played the monster in Universal Pictures' classic *Frankenstein* of 1931; his creator, Dr Frankenstein, vitalizes the monster most impressively by harnessing the powers of lightning with a wonderful apparatus. The same studio made seven sequels, while many other Frankenstein monsters appeared from other studios, demonstrating the power of a myth that represents fears of our time.

Daniels, L. (1975). *Living in Fear*. New York. (Reissued in 1977 as *Fear: a history of horror in the mass media*. London, Toronto.)

Grylls, R. G. (1938). *Mary Shelley: a biography*. London.

**FRANZ,** SHEPHERD IVERY (1874–1933). American neuropsychologist, educated at Columbia and Dartmouth, and best known as the man who was largely responsible for instructing the youthful Karl *Lashley in the techniques of cortical ablation, upon which Lashley relied exclusively in his later and celebrated studies of brain mechanisms and intelligence in the rat and monkey. Indeed Franz in some respects anticipated Lashley's claim that psychological functions are not controlled by small and strictly localized areas of the brain, and he collaborated with Lashley in several early studies of the effects of focal lesions of the cerebral cortex.

Unlike Lashley, however, Franz was active in studying the effects of brain lesions in human patients as well as in animals. He was particularly interested in the functions of the frontal lobes, on which he contributed several monographs and papers, several of them in collaboration with Lashley.

Franz was also interested in the variability of motor centres and in various aspects of *aphasia, and was one of the most distinguished early representatives of what is now known as clinical neuropsychology. His later work was based at the University of California.

**FRAZER,** SIR JAMES GEORGE (1854–1941). British social anthropologist and scholar of myths and comparative religions. Born in Glasgow, he graduated at Cambridge in 1878 and became a Fellow of Trinity College. His major work is *The Golden Bough* (1890; third edition, rewritten in twelve volumes, 1911–15; abridged 1922). He also wrote *Folklore in the Old Testament* (1918), *Belief in Immortality* (1913–24), *Fear of the Dead* (1933–6), and *Magic and Religion* (1944). He became professor of social anthropology at Liverpool in 1907, was knighted in 1914, and awarded the Order of Merit in 1925. Strangely, although his scholarship extended to the mythology of many countries, his sources were entirely from books, as he never travelled.

**FREE ASSOCIATION.** Sigmund *Freud gave a new direction to the study of the association of ideas as he developed his therapeutic techniques in clinical practice. He came to claim that the unforced remarks made by patients during treatment unwittingly revealed their wishes and motives, and thereby enabled the therapist to circumvent resistance to personal disclosure. In 1912, in *The Dynamics of Transference*, he described his fundamental principle of *psychoanalysis as the requirement that the patient repeats whatever comes into his or her head without criticizing it.

Interest in applying principles of organization to the headlong abundance of thoughts, images, memories, and *perceptions that distinguish mental life had previously overlooked the possible importance of personal experiences and preoccupations. *Aristotle's description of the formal (similarity, contrast) and accidental properties (contiguity in time or place) that linked thoughts, had been taken up by *Locke and *Hume to provide a detailed but highly abstract explanation of the contents of the stream of consciousness. No attempt to account for the individual colouring of associations was made by the British empiricists, even after an experimental approach had been introduced by Francis *Galton. Of course Freud's clinical findings had been intuitively anticipated by dramatists and novelists, and perhaps most powerfully realized in their depictions of suffering so great as to effect disintegration of syntax. Hamlet's word-play though dark is not impenetrable, and it has the effect of drawing the anxious listeners into the drama of his distress.

*Jung, who in so many of his researches followed where Freud led, had in fact begun to study free association before they met. He approached the subject from a different angle but also came to focus on the personal significance of associations. His interest had been aroused by his application, as an instrument of clinical investigation, of the word-association test invented by Galton. This test had provided a technique for putting the mechanism of association under scrutiny, although it suffered the limitation of being so atomistic as to produce highly artificial results. The procedure was very simple: the experimenter worked through a list of prepared words, perhaps fifty or sixty, calling out each one in turn. The subject was required to respond as quickly as possible with the first word that came into his or her mind, and the experimenter recorded this together with the time-lapse between stimulus and response. The early work looked at formal relations between word pairs and attempted a variety of classifications of responses. The vast amount of data collected, particularly by Wilhelm *Wundt and his associates, attracts little interest now, being regarded as a recalcitrant body of facts without practical application. Jung temporarily breathed new life into the procedure by noticing that the responses of psychiatric patients often revealed their most intimate concerns. He described a group of responses bound together by a pervasive feeling as a *complex, and transformed the test into a diagnostic tool. He also used it to make interesting observations on speech disturbances in psychotic states, regarding intense emotional preoccupation as a handicap to rational thought. In extreme disturbance, the Aristotelian principles of association became stronger than the influence of any particular directing idea, leading to a loosening of logical associations, and sometimes to a loss of any unifying feeling tone. Even so, beneath the fractured surface of psychotic communication, it was possible to find evidence of profound hurt and compensatory aggrandizement. That this early work made him receptive to the more sophisticated innovations of Freud is clearly indicated in the conclusion to his paper 'Association, Dream and Hysterical Symptom', published in 1906, a year before he met Freud. He wrote there that 'the interferences that the complex causes in the association experiment are none other than the resistances in psychoanalysis as described by Freud'.

Freud's approach to the treatment of neurotic disorders evolved over many years. In its final form, after he had abandoned the use of hypnosis, he would sit behind his patient who lay on a couch. There was no agenda of problems or topics to be discussed, and the session would be facilitated by Freud's non-emotive promptings. Although the therapeutic alliance required that the conscious attitude of the patient should be desire for change, Freud recognized that there would inevitably be unconscious resistance, as the abandoning of neurotic defences involved the renunciation of cherished illusions. The degree of resistance was a principal factor determining the length of therapy. The method of free association enabled him to capitalize on the unintended candour of the patient and make interpretations which could then be reflected on. Central to this endeavour was the examination of dream material, which provided a 'royal road to the unconscious' and a privileged glimpse of primary process thinking (see DREAMING). In this primitive style of thinking, the categories of space and time were said to be ignored and images tended to become fused and distorted by condensation and displacement. The key to understanding unconscious mental activity was the pleasure principle, which determined that all frustration of instinctual drives was repaired by hallucinatory wish-fulfilment. Freud regarded his

longest book, *The Interpretation of Dreams* (1900), as his seminal work, and thirty years after its first publication described it as containing the most valuable of all his discoveries. So it was that dreams, supplemented by recollections and anecdotes, provided the raw material which through interpretation revealed the motives and wishes of the patient. At first these were ill-discerned but later became clearer through the lessening of resistance and the resolving of transference feelings for the analyst. It was not uncommon for a powerfully charged and unusually lucid dream to coincide with a therapeutic breakthrough. Freud insisted on the objectivity of the method, contrasting his approach, in which the interpretation of associations is drawn from the patient by gentle probing, with the classical account of Artemidorus (2nd century AD), in which the adept authoritatively imposed his view on the dreamer.

Nowhere more clearly than in *The Interpretation of Dreams* does Freud display his extreme rationalism. It is as though he employs a psychological principle of sufficient reason, as every feature of a dream is explained in terms that illuminate the conflicts of the dreamer. While the sheer analytical power of his thinking is impressively demonstrated, there are perhaps few therapists today who would interpret with such complete confidence or not allow for undecidable or meaningless elements. Moreover, it is difficult not to feel that Freud's strength of personality imposed itself both on the material he analysed and on the patients themselves. Accounts by patients of their therapy with him tend to confirm this impression and contradict his own description of assumed emotional detachment during therapy. Perhaps Freud's patients tended to have Freudian dreams, as later Jung's patients had Jungian dreams. Nevertheless, the points of agreement between Freud and Jung seem much more profound than the points of difference. Jung subsequently developed his own therapeutic style to suit his temperament, and one of his innovations was to invite the patient to fantasize in the therapeutic sessions and thereby actively promote free association.

As psychotherapeutic practice has proliferated, so ways of conducting therapy have multiplied. The most important general feature of newer therapies has been the attempt to reduce the length of the procedure, from years to months, or even to a fixed number of sessions agreed in advance. In order to abbreviate therapy, various devices have been employed for breaking down resistance. Some examples of this trend are: structuring the therapy sessions, strategic focusing on specific problems, concentrating on patient–therapist interactions in the here and now, and more aggressive styles of interpretation. However, the common denominator in all these approaches is the use of the free associations of the patient to point up contradictions between unconscious attitudes, wishes and motives, and the self-image which unintentionally announces alienation from fundamental impulses.                                    D. A. G. C.

Freud, S. (1900). *The Interpretation of Dreams*, standard edition, **4–5**.

Freud, S. (1912). *The Dynamics of Transference*, standard edition, **12**, 99.

Galton, F. (1897). Psychometric Experiments. *Brain*, **2**, 149.

H. D. (Hilda Doolittle) (1956). *Tribute to Freud*. Manchester.

Jung, C. G. (1906). Association, Dream and Hysterical Symptom. *Collection Works*, **2**, 353.

**FREE WILL.** See CHOICE; DETERMINISM AND FREE WILL; INTENTIONALITY; MAINE DE BIRAN.

**FREUD,** ANNA (1895–1982). Born in Vienna, the sixth child of Sigmund *Freud, Anna was the only member of the family to follow in her father's footsteps and make her career in psychoanalysis. She was admitted to membership of the Vienna Psychoanalytical Society in 1922 and for a time became its chairman. After the Nazis occupied Vienna, she emigrated to England with her parents, and after the outbreak of the Second World War organized the Hampstead War Nurseries in co-operation with her close friend and admirer Dorothy Burlingham. In 1945, this enterprising venture was succeeded by the Hampstead Child Therapy Course and Clinic, which for long led the field in the training of child psychotherapists in the London area. Anna Freud's work, like that of her contemporary Melanie *Klein, was based not on the earlier Freudian ideas about child development, which derive largely from the analysis of adults, but on the direct observation of the behaviour of young children. This approach did much to make possible the remedial treatment of psychologically disturbed children.

Although she never held a formal medical or psychological qualification, Anna Freud's significant contribution to child psychology and psychiatry was acknowledged by her election to an Honorary Fellowship of the Royal College of Psychiatrists and the conferment of honorary degrees from a number of well-known universities, including Harvard, Yale, Sheffield, and Vienna.

Anna Freud is best remembered for her book on *The Ego and the Mechanisms of Defence* (German, 1936; English translation, 1937), which carried further some of the ideas developed by her father in his book on *The Ego and the Id* (1923) and played a very real part in the genesis of what later came to be known as 'ego-psychology' (see FREUDIANISM: LATER DEVELOPMENTS).          O. L. Z.

**FREUD,** SIGMUND (1856–1939). Sigmund Freud, who was born of Jewish ancestry at Freiberg in Moravia, was educated in Vienna, in which city he spent almost the whole of his long life. Here he enrolled at the university as a student of biology and medicine in 1873 and while still a medical student embarked on some research under the distinguished physiologist Ernst Brücke, whose interests lay predominantly in the vertebrate nervous system. In 1878, this work resulted in Freud's first published scientific paper, on the histology of the spinal cord in a primitive fish. He qualified in medicine in 1881 at the age of 26, somewhat tardily, and after working for a time in Theodor Meynert's Institute of Cerebral Neurology, decided to specialize in clinical neurology. He was appointed to a lectureship in neuropathology in 1885 and, soon after, was awarded a travelling fellowship to enable him to study in Paris with the world-famous neurologist J. M. *Charcot. This proved to be the turning-point in Freud's career; from it can be dated his metamorphosis from a clinical neurologist into a medical psychologist in the modern sense of the term.

While still active in neurology, Freud published several papers and two books. One of the latter, on disorders of speech (*aphasia) resulting from lesions of the brain, attracted considerable interest and has since been regarded as well in advance of its time. It has also been argued that his ideas about aphasia provided some basis for his later psychological thinking. It may be added that, as a young doctor, Freud only narrowly missed becoming the first to recognize the anaesthetic properties of cocaine.

In 1885, he arrived at the Salpêtrière in Paris, which then enjoyed a world-wide reputation as the Mecca of clinical neurologists. At this period, Charcot had become much preoccupied with the so-called functional nervous diseases, in particular *hysteria, in which no clear-cut somatic basis had been established. This protean disease was at that time widely treated by hypnosis, upon which Charcot held strong views. First, he maintained that only those of innate hysterical disposition are amenable to hypnosis; and secondly, that hypnosis provides a kind of laboratory for the induction and modification of hysterical symptoms. But whereas Charcot still believed that hypnosis had a physical basis, Freud became increasingly convinced of its psychological origin. It is not without interest that some years later he paid a special visit to M. Bernheim, of Nancy, who was perhaps the first to insist upon the overriding role of suggestion in bringing about hypnosis, and to stress its applicability to a wide range of individuals who sought his aid as a physician. Although Freud later repudiated hypnosis as a clinical tool, it is most improbable that, had it not been for Charcot's influence, he would have been led to collaborate with Josef *Breuer and ultimately to evolve the psychoanalytical method.

This work with Breuer began soon after Freud's return to Vienna. Breuer had been interested for some time in using hypnosis in the treatment of hysterical illness, and came to place great reliance on the therapeutic benefit of what came to be called abreaction. This was essentially a kind of re-enaction, during hypnosis, of stressful and disturbing experiences which appeared to have precipitated the illness, and the free and uninhibited expression of emotion was actively encouraged. While seeing some benefit in abreaction, Freud quickly came to realize not only that the structure of neurosis was much more complex than Breuer, at least, was prepared to admit, but also that it involved active processes of defence (repression) against the reproduction, or even the mere acknowledgement, of painful, distressing, or otherwise emotionally disturbing memories. He surmised that many of these had to do with sexual life, a conclusion which Breuer appears to have been ill-disposed to concede. Freud also came to appreciate that the understanding and disarming of these defences could often be achieved more effectively in the waking than in the hypnotic state. In consequence, hypnosis was replaced by the so-called method of *free association, from which psychoanalysis as a technical psychotherapeutic procedure gradually evolved.

Over the next few years, Freud was essentially concerned in developing his brilliantly original, if to many people extremely disconcerting, ideas about the causation and treatment of neurotic illness. He was led increasingly into study of the sexual life of his patients, at first believing that much neurosis is attributable to distressing sexual experiences in early adult life. Soon, however, he discovered that many of these supposed experiences existed only in imagination and were the products of fantasies evolved at a very much earlier age, often in quite early infancy. Analysis of these fantasies led him to believe not only that psychosexual life has its origins in early infancy but also that it involves intense and often complicated emotional relationships, both positive and negative, with the parents. These ideas were brought together in his *Three Contributions to the Theory of Sex* (1906), a book which shocked many people but which nevertheless had wide influence on modern conceptions of personality and its development. It also marks the transition from psychoanalysis conceived as a special theory of neurosis to psychoanalysis as a general theory of human personality.

This period, too, was marked by Freud's herculean attempt at self-analysis, using many of his own dreams to furnish clues as to his own early development and emotional relations with his parents. It further provided the occasion for the writing of what is often regarded as his greatest book, *The Interpretation of Dreams* (1900). As Freud's views on dreams are considered in a separate article, FREUD ON DREAMS, it is unnecessary to say more here than that dreams, in his view, have meaning and are largely the product of infantile wishes and thought processes, and that their personal significance can be assessed if their language can be understood and translated into the currency of adult, waking thought.

Although Freud's ideas incurred much odium in medical circles, his work none the less attracted a small but devoted band of followers, many of them neurologists who, like Freud himself, had felt challenged by the ubiquity of neurosis among their patients. Among them were Karl Abraham, Sandor Ferenczi, Alfred *Adler, Carl Gustav *Jung, Otto Rank, and the Welsh physician Ernest Jones, who became for many years Britain's foremost Freudian. Shortly before the outbreak of the First World War, this group was weakened by two major defections, those of Adler and Jung. Adler's defection was less important, as it is doubtful whether he was ever a committed Freudian, and Freud himself thought little of his ideas. (None the less, after Adler's death, some of his views, in particular those associated with the nature of aggression, came to exert considerable influence on neo-Freudian theory.) Jung, on the other hand, was a man of real distinction of mind and impressive literary productivity. As a psychiatrist, he did much in his early days to extend Freudian thinking to the psychoses, in particular *schizophrenia, and is remembered as the originator of the word-association test at one time much in vogue as a 'lie-detector'. There can be no question that Freud thought of Jung as his eventual successor in the leadership of the psychoanalytical movement, and his defection caused him very real chagrin. Subsequently, Jung wrote widely (if somewhat obscurely) on individual development, psychological types, and the cultural frontiers of psychology.

In his later writings, Freud displayed an admittedly speculative turn of mind, and though some of his ideas are of great interest, their empirical foundation became decidedly weaker. Among them are *Beyond the Pleasure Principle* (1922), *The Ego and the Id* (1923), *Inhibitions, Symptoms and Anxiety* (1936), and, finally, the work of his old age, *Moses and Monotheism*, published a year before his death. Some of the ideas expressed in these writings are discussed in the article FREUD ON MENTAL STRUCTURE.

Freud's work came to be widely known to the general reader, particularly through such works as *The Psychopathology of Everyday Life* (1904), *Wit and its Relation to the Unconscious* (1905), *Introductory Lectures on Psychoanalysis* (1922), and *New Introductory Lecures on Psychoanalysis* (1933). In America, the five lectures which he delivered at Clark University in 1910 (at the invitation of the veteran psychologist G. Stanley *Hall, then president of the University) subsequently appeared in English and enjoyed a certain vogue. But Freudian thinking did not seriously penetrate American psychiatry until after the end of the Second World War, when it came to dominate psychiatric practice for some years, possibly to the detriment of other and less doctrinaire approaches. It has also had wide influence on literature, particularly on biography, on some aspects of painting (for example, surrealism), and on much contemporary thinking in anthropology and the social sciences. Indeed many people nowadays regard psychoanalysis in the light of a social rather than a biological or medical discipline. Even so, its roots, as those of Freud himself, are wholly within the biological domain.

Following the Nazi invasion of Austria, Freud, by then a very sick man, fled from Vienna and lived quietly in London for the last year of his life. Shortly before his death, he was made a Foreign Fellow of the Royal Society, a belated though none the less imaginative tribute to his world stature and influence on modern thought. His daughter, Anna *Freud, a pioneer in the psychoanalytical study of children, became a leading member of the British psychoanalytical community. As a person, Freud is remembered by those who knew him as a man of some austerity but unchallenged personal integrity.

See also FREUD ON DREAMS; FREUD ON HYPNOSIS; FREUD ON MENTAL STRUCTURE.                    O. L. Z.

Freud, S. (1935). *An Autobiographical Study* (trans. J. Strachey). London.
Jones, E. (1953–7). *Sigmund Freud: life and work*, 3 vols. London.

## FREUDIANISM: LATER DEVELOPMENTS.

Sigmund *Freud's legacy of psychoanalytic theory and technique was essentially complete by 1926, when he turned 70, although until his death in 1939 he continued to re-present it, rethink its implications, and apply it in new ways. He had a small group of adherents from 1902, and in the twenty years 1906–26 a group of colleagues in Vienna and elsewhere developed along with him the concepts of psychoanalysis and their practical applications. By 1926 Freud's legacy itself owed much to them directly, as well as to their stimulation of his work and writing, sometimes by opposition but usually by their independent use of his and their ideas. This *was* a new way of thinking about man and his mental functioning and development; even though it had important roots in the work and writings of predecessors and contemporaries (see Ellenberger, 1970). In an amazingly short time Freud and his colleagues had applied psychoanalytic ideas beyond psychiatry in anthropology, sociology, and the criticism of art and literature, to biographical writing, and to the theories of mythology and of language.

Although Freud chose to think of psychoanalysis as a science, he often acknowledged the provisional character of statements of its findings, and even of its fundamental hypotheses. In an unfinished paper first published in 1940 he says of them, 'it is hard to say whether they should be regarded as postulates or as products of our researches'. The simple modesty of that remark is equal to the profundity of its truth: to verify psychoanalytic researches and to distinguish what one has found there from what one has put there are much harder things to do than, as a psychoanalyst, to relieve a patient's anxiety or, as a patient, to recover things forgotten and rework the significance of past experiences. Only the naïve and the obsessional will see it as a weakness rather than a strength of psychoanalysis that, like other

behavioural sciences (Devereux, 1967), its practice and theory operate with provisional concepts and with metaphors and sustained hypotheses rather than with accepted laws of a science.

Nearly fifty years after Freud's death it is possible to estimate what parts of his legacy later psychoanalytic practitioners and writers have found most useful and have accepted as valuable. Most important are the case-studies, full-length and vignettes; they are valuable both as accounts of what Freud hmself did, or said he did, with the kinds of patient one may still encounter, and as models of writing which give the psychoanalyst's thought and organization of material as well as his description of how the patients presented it. Along with the case-studies go the papers on technique, in which Freud's thoughts about the reasons for his own behaviour are matched with the behaviour of patients and with various statements of the aims and the mode of action of the treatment.

In psychoanalytic theory three sets of concepts have lasted: one set closely relates to practice and comprises *free association*, *symbolization*, *transference*, *identification*, *resistance*, and *interpretation*; another set relates to theories of mental structure and functioning and comprises *defence* (*repression* being one of the defences), *splitting of the mind* (and of its objects), and *unconscious mental processes*, including *fantasy* (not all now agree on using *Unconscious* as a noun); a third set comprises those concepts concerned with early human development, namely *infantile sexuality*, *fixation*, and *regression* (*separation-anxiety*, *castration-anxiety*, and the *Oedipus complex* are also largely accepted and used).

Freud's short book of 1923, *The Ego and the Id*, gave rise to two different schools of psychoanalytic thought, one known as 'ego-psychology' and the other as 'object-relations Theory'.

'Ego-psychology' has until very recently prevailed in the USA and in countries, such as Israel and Japan, which have derived their psychoanalytic teaching from the US. In Britain, Freud's youngest daughter, Anna, was the leading proponent of these views, which have concentrated interest on the ego, considered as a structure and as a set of mechanisms, and have seen the development of the personality and of 'ego-strengths' as due to successful defence against instinctual drives and to adaptation to social realities (Freud, 1937). These changes have meant less interest in the id, Freud's latest term for the Unconscious considered as a system, and in the super-ego, that part of the ego most closely identified with the parents at the end of the Oedipal period (age 5–6), since the very concept of adaptation meant that the external authority vested in society came to be of greater interest to ego-psychologists than the primitive internal authority developed during the individual's childhood. Accordingly the defences have been more emphasized than the splitting of the mind and of its objects, or than fantasies; but this school has kept the stress on the topographic metaphor to describe the mind (its division into the regions of conscious, preconscious, and unconscious), the dynamic metaphors to describe the opposed forces of the unconscious and of the preconscious maintaining repression, and the economic metaphors of psychic energy and its disposal.

Ego-psychologists have until recently given less attention than other psychoanalysts to processes of identification, and have in practice regarded transference (the carrying over on to the person of the analyst intensities of feeling originally developed towards parents and other important figures of childhood) chiefly as one of the inevitably met resistances to treatment. Interpretation, particularly of transference-feelings, is therefore used more sparingly by this group of psychoanalysts than by others.

Like other groups, ego-psychologists, in searching for the sources of psychopathology, have steadily concentrated their interest upon the early stages of childhood. One of their great contributions has been the annual publication (from 1945) of *The Psychoanalytic Study of the Child*. Infantile sexuality and the anxieties of early childhood have filled much of the picture, but this group has done its share in focusing the interest of clinicians and other workers on the processes of adolescence, and on the help which adolescents often need and the conditions upon which it may be tactfully offered and received.

A clear, sympathetic statement and examination of the tenets of this school was made by Roy Schafer, himself a former adherent of it, in a book which also contains a valuable bibliography (Schafer, 1969). *Aspects of Internalization* was for him a transitional work before he attempted a statement of psychoanalytic theory and technique eschewing metaphor; but it remains a most useful critique of ego-psychology.

In 1951 E. R. Dodds, then Regius Professor of Greek at Oxford, wrote *The Greeks and the Irrational*, inspired by Freud's writings and generally on the lines of ego-psychology; it has had an influence not only upon classical studies but more widely upon historical thinking.

One of the central weaknesses of ego-psychology is that ego as a set of mechanisms cannot be convincingly divorced from ego as self or personality. Ego cannot therefore be ultimately distinguished from id. Furthermore, since, according to *The Ego and the Id*, ego as personality has grown by the internalization of renounced love-relationships ('abandoned object-cathexes' was Freud's phrase in English translation), the ego cannot be clearly distinguished from its objects (or 'other persons') with whom it has identified, certainly in health and to some extent in pathology. (Freud himself occasionally acknowledged both the impossibility of distinguishing ego from id and also, in some normal circumstances, the lack of boundaries between ego and object.) For these and other reasons, American psychoanalysts are now showing a new interest in 'object relations', a term

used by Karl Abraham in a long and seminal paper (1924, in Abraham, 1927). Section II, the shorter section of that paper, is entitled 'Origins and Growth of Object-Love'; upon it as much as upon *The Ego and the Id* is founded the theory of 'object relations'.

The term 'object' had been used early by Freud to denote the person (or thing) required in order to mediate instinctual discharge. It has survived probably because in grammar it is complementary to the term 'subject', subject and object being joined through a verb in a context. It now means the person(s), or his (their) inner representative(s), with whom the subject is intensely concerned emotionally.

In Section I of his paper Abraham showed that severe *depressions and *obsessional neuroses, similar in many ways, could be distinguished in treatment by the different vicissitudes of their 'objects'; the obsessional lived on the verge of losing his but never did, while the depressive at the onset of a depression lost his and had to restore it. Melanie *Klein and Ronald *Fairbairn, both profoundly but differently influenced by Abraham, evolved theories of personal development based on the child's need of, and *attachment to, his mother. Donald Winnicott, during his first ten years as a paediatric consultant (1923–32), began to do likewise but independently of Abraham; his chief papers date from the period 1945–69, though 'The Manic Defence' is dated 1935.

By using, as the equivalent of free association, children's spontaneous play with suitable toys provided and kept in the treatment-room, Melanie Klein found a way to psychoanalyse quite disturbed children even as young as 3 or 4, interpreting their play particularly in terms of their implicit fantasies about their parents' bodies and their own. In her early papers sexual fantasies have first place but, having inherited from her second analyst, Karl Abraham, a deep interest in depression and its connections with the first pre-genital (the 'oral') stages of sexual development, she soon put the relationship of feeding mother and infant at the centre of the picture; later relationships came to be interpreted in terms of that one, by her and by her followers, who form a distinct group of the 'object-relations' school (Klein, 1975).

The characteristics of the Kleinian group are: (i) in technique, a concentration upon the two-person relationship and upon the interpretation of transference-manifestations, using frequent interpretations particularly of the mental defences of projection and introjection; (ii) a theory of infantile development in two stages. In the first stage, denoted the 'paranoid–schizoid position', the issue for the child is seen as the survival of the self against his own (projected) death-wishes; the defences of psychical 'splitting', 'idealization', 'projection', and 'introjection' make up the survival-technique he evolves. The second stage is called the 'depressive position', and the child enters it once he sees his mother as a whole, separate person; the issues for the child are now the survival and restoration of his 'object', the loved and needed figure upon whom he himself depends but whom, because of his ambivalence, in fantasy he damages or annihilates through envy of her or in anger with her.

Melanie Klein preferred the term 'positions' to 'stages' because she saw later pathology as due to failures to work through the different issues characteristic of them, to renounce inappropriate defences, or to overcome the ambivalence of love. In her attempt to explain both development and pathology in terms of forces within the individual child she kept a version of Freud's instinct-theory, and attributed behaviour, emotions, and attitudes to the action of his life-instinct and death-instinct (projected as destructive-instinct), ascribing to the second of these the innate envy which she held to be a crucial element in her patients' make-up.

The theoretical problem of the separateness of subject and object, a problem which makes it difficult to imagine how the infant makes the transition from the paranoid to the depressive position, is dealt with in Kleinian theory by use of the terms 'introjective' and 'projective identification', the latter a collective label for several defence-mechanisms previously described by psychoanalysts but now considered by Kleinians as tending both to jeopardize and to facilitate identification and object relationships.

Donald Winnicott (1965, p. 177) held that Melanie Klein was temperamentally incapable of allowing the importance of environmental provision to the child's early life and mental functioning, but he speculated that only somebody so incapable could ever have worked out as fully and as clearly as she did the very early forms of mental mechanisms in two-person relationships.

The other division of psychoanalysts who use 'object-relations' theory has formed the central core of the British Psychoanalytical Society, but the psychoanalysts composing it tend less to operate as a group than did the Kleinians and the ego-psychologists round Anna Freud (all three groups are component units of the Society, as Charles Rycroft describes in the introduction to his *Critical Dictionary of Psychoanalysis*).

All three groups understand the patient's present in terms of his past, and so interpret clinical material. But whereas the ego-psychologists have interpreted primarily in terms of the three-person, Oedipal relationship, and the Kleinians in terms of the two-person, 'pre-genital' relationship of child and mother, the so-called independent group interprets in terms of either the Oedipal or the pre-Oedipal relationship and operates more readily with the concept of identification. Transference for this group comes to mean the unconscious repetition and re-enactment in the psychoanalytic relationship of past relationships and not, as before, the transfer of psychic energy or primarily the carry-over of feeling or of images of past figures. The technique of the psychoanalyst is, as always, important in the successful development and undo-

ing of transferences, and this depends on his own (unspoken) free associations, on his capacity to recognize symbolization and to spot identifications, and on his respect for the patient's own insight and analytic work.

The four British psychoanalysts who by their writing and teaching have had the biggest influence on psychoanalysis since 1939 are Ronald Fairbairn, Michael Balint, John Bowlby, and Donald Winnicott. Balint, an immigrant to Britain of Hungarian origin and, like Melanie Klein in her first analysis, psychoanalysed by Sandor Ferenczi, took an early interest in the mother–infant relationship. In his book *Primary Love and Psycho-analytic Technique* (1952), a key paper on 'Primary Object-Love' dates from 1937. Later he took up an idea of John Rickman's (Rickman died prematurely in 1951) that mental function is quite different, and needs to be described differently, in three-person and two-person relationships, and different again in creative activity alone. Later still, Balint formulated an idea of what he called 'the basic fault': this was that there was often the experience in the early two-person relationship that something was wrong or missing, and this carried over into the Oedipal period (age 2–5); the resulting fault or flaw affected all subsequent dealings with people and also, of course, creativeness. Balint's books include one with that title (1968). He also applied psycho-analytic ideas in seminars with general practitioners, who took the opportunity to discuss with each other and with him aspects of their work with patients for which they had previously felt ill equipped. Since his death the continuance of this work has been assured by the formation of the Balint Society.

Ronald Fairbairn, a student of Hellenistic Greek and theology before he studied medicine and psychoanalysis in the 1920s, was piqued by Abraham's schematic account of child-development through six phases (two oral, two anal, and two genital) into a restatement of early development based on the notion of ego-splitting that resulted from tensions in the period of greatest dependence (the oral phases, which he accepted) and the period of lessening dependence. He reworked an account of the 'origin and growth of object-love', which was fully in the spirit of Abraham and Freud. Most of his papers were collected in his book *Psychoanalytic Studies of the Personality* (1952), but he continued to write, and in 1958 described the nature and aims of psychoanalytic treatment as a technique for the analyst's efforts to breach and turn into an open system that closed system which the neurotic patient did his best to maintain in his dealings with the world.

In rethinking the theory of defence and repression, Fairbairn described the 'moral defence' as the depressive neurotic's way of warding off a feeling of helplessness through the illusion of having himself been responsible for the failures of his early environment; the cost to him was a greatly increased sense of guilt, the advantage an illusory sense of independence. Fairbairn held that repression led to often crippling divisions in the self through keeping at bay two categories of internalized figures—highly sexualized ones, and strongly dominating ones that rejected sexuality; aspects of the self were closely associated with each of these and became repressed along with them.

Fairbairn's official work brought him in contact with assaulted children and with war-neurotics. He was a clear thinker and his writings have influenced all later thinkers. His own primary interest was in the early structuring of the mind, according to the various stages of dependence in which object relations were disturbed, and according to the defences that worked for the young child in his family.

In technique, Fairbairn argued for more flexibility than in classical psychoanalysis (this was not so different from the behaviour of Freud, who would sometimes give a patient tea or even food), and he pointed to the serious drawback for some patients in the use of the couch.

One of the chief exponents of all these ideas was Harry Guntrip. With his book *Personality Structure and Human Interaction* (1961) he gave the first synoptic, historical view of psychoanalytic schools and their development. In *Schizoid Phenomena, Object-Relations, and the Self* (1968) he applied Fairbairnian ideas to clinical work as well as to the development of theory. Although he himself never qualified as a psychoanalyst, he gave psychoanalysts a comprehensive view which filled a great need.

Here is the appropriate place to mention the work of John Bowlby. In *Attachment and Loss* (1969, 1973, 1980) Bowlby managed to replace the largely out-of-date and philosophical 'instinct-theories' of earlier psychoanalysis by studying the actual mother–infant and mother–child relationships and by considering the effects upon the child's behaviour when the bonds are unduly strained, prematurely broken, or not even allowed to form. He introduced ethological concepts into psychoanalytic theory and gave it fresh life. For further details, see his article on ATTACHMENT.

Donald Winnicott came to psychoanalysis from paediatrics, and not through reading Abraham but through his analysis with James Strachey, later the editor of the standard edition of Freud's collected works in English translation. In his paediatric clinics Winnicott studied mothers' relationships with their infants and small children, and eventually formulated his own views of the ways in which a child comes to be a separate individual. He never lost sight of the idea that for the infant at first his mother has a dual role: she is his environment and she is his object. Bit by bit she becomes a person.

Winnicott saw the attachment-bonds developing and then becoming loosened, while the mother responds appropriately, leaving the child at every stage to choose between living in his own illusions and acknowledging her provision for his needs. The 'ordinary devoted mother' who offers 'good enough mothering' will allow her child rights over his own first possessions. Many children use a 'transitional object' in one early stage of becoming independent. This is Winnicott's term for a child's indispensable possession, a thing which in use and possession stands for the dimly remembered unity of mother and infant-self. Contact with it both gives security and facilitates switches in identification between mother, self, and other people.

Winnicott's three volumes of collected papers (1958, 1965, 1971), replete with clinical experience and paradox, are an inexhaustible source of ideas for psychoanalysis. As theoretician he is often elusive, but partly because his writings up to 1960 often had the subsidiary aim of trying to get Melanie Klein to modify her views. The very title of the second volume, *The Maturational Process and the Facilitating Environment*, sums up his view of psychosexual development; the title of the third (posthumous) one, *Playing and Reality*, shows that he came to look upon the activity of playing as the basis of all creative and spontaneous living.

Like Fairbairn, Winnicott saw ego-splitting, consequent upon the parents' premature demands or failures, as the origin of many problems of personality. He saw classical psychoanalysis as designed to help neurotics, and Kleinian as developed for some depressives, but considered that only a technique which could allow and even facilitate regression might help people for whom the earliest experiences of being mothered had not been good enough.

From different starting-points and using mainly different terminologies, these four psychoanalytic writers evolved ideas that have a strong similarity to each other. In pathology, Winnicott's distinction between 'true and false selves' corresponds to Balint's 'basic fault' and to Fairbairn's 'compromised ego'. In health, Winnicott's concept of the 'transitional' (object, space, or experience), through which or in which the self–other boundary is transiently dissolved, corresponds in some ways to Fairbairn's repressed ego–object structures with their fluctuating states of fusion, bonding, and separation; this is not far removed from Balint's idea of re-experiencing primary love in states in which a third person is unthinkable. Bowlby describes behaviour rather than subjective experience, but for him even more than for Winnicott the adequacy of the early environment is all-important. Related ideas have been developed and applied by such writers as Marion Milner (1969) and Charles Rycroft (1968, 1968, 1979, 1985).

In Britain, intensive psychoanalysis is within the reach, economically and geographically, of only a very few people. But psychoanalysts are more and more giving personal help by psychotherapy, teaching, and supervision, as well as by full analysis, to many people who will apply it widely in the community—to young psychiatrists, psychotherapists, social workers, probation officers, teachers, civil servants, and managerial staff. (The London Clinic of Psychoanalysis has a limited number of vacancies for full psychoanalysis at reduced rates. Information about opportunities for psychoanalysis and for psychotherapy can usually be obtained from it.)

In 1974 a professorship in psychoanalysis was endowed and constituted. It is held at University College London and the aim stated in establishing the appointment was 'to promote the study and critical examination of psychoanalysis, including its theoretical aspects and its cultural implications.' It is intended also to facilitate studies and research into the subject (Lighthill and Jaynes, 1983).

From 1974 to 1984 the professorship was held annually but since then the appointment has been extended to a period of three to five years. The first holder of the Chair with longer tenure is Joseph Sandler, who, besides giving his own inaugural and other lectures, has invited psychoanalysts from Britain and abroad to present to the public their own work and ideas and to discuss its relevance to psychoanalysis.

Anybody intending to train in psychoanalysis in Britain, unless he does his best to discover the differences between the three groups of the Society (ego-psychologist, Kleinian, independent), will soon find himself having to make the judgement of Paris—to choose without knowing the basis for his choice. More hangs on this than at first appears, since psychoanalysts rarely change groups.

J. H. P.

Abraham, K. (1927). *Selected Papers on Psychoanalysis*. London.

Balint, M. (1952). *Primary Love and Psycho-analytic Technique* (enlarged edn. 1965). London.

Bowlby, J. *Attachment and Loss* (3 vols.: *Attachment*, 1969; *Separation*, 1973; *Loss*, 1980). London.

Devereux, G. (1967). *From Anxiety to Method in the Behavioural Sciences*. The Hague.

Ellenberger, H. F. (1970). *The Discovery of the Unconscious*. London.

Fairbairn, W. R. D. (1952). *Psychoanalytic Studies of the Personality*. London.

Freud, A. (1937). *The Ego and the Mechanisms of Defence*. London.

Guntrip, H. (1961). *Personality Structure and Human Interaction*. London.

Klein, M. (1975). *The Writings of Melanie Klein*, 4 vols. London.

Lighthill, James and Jaynes, David (1983). The Freud Memorial Professorship at University College London: a review of its development and future. *International Review of Psycho-Analysis*, vol. **10**, 227–230.

Milner, M. (1969). *The Hands of the Living God*. London.

Rycroft, C. F. (1968). *A Critical Dictionary of Psychoanalysis*. London.

Rycroft, C. F. (1968). *Imagination and Reality*. London.

Rycroft, C. F. (1979). *The Innocence of Dreams*. London.

Rycroft, C. F. (1985). *Psychoanalysis and Beyond*. London.

Schafer, R. (1969). *Aspects of Internalization*. New York.

Winnicott, D. W. *Collected Papers: Through Paediatrics to Psychoanalysis* and *Playing and Reality* (1958 and 1971 respectively); *The Maturational Process and the Facilitating Environment* (1965). London.

**FREUD ON DREAMS.** 'Find out all about dreams and you will find out all about insanity.' This prophetic remark was made by the English neurologist John Hughlings *Jackson, whose main contribution to its truth lay in establishing that certain curious alterations in *consciousness, in some respects akin to dreaming, might occur in a particular variety of epilepsy. But we owe almost entirely to Freud such little as we know regarding the relationship between dreams and the history and development of personality, normal no less than abnormal. Although Freud became interested in dreams largely in connection with psychoanalytical techniques, and more particularly in relation to his own self-analysis, it may be said that his work has given rise to the only theory of dreams which has so far won general acceptance (Freud, 1900).

Freud's approach to the interpretation of dreams was by way of the method of *free association he had evolved in the course of his early studies of neurosis as a substitute for hypnosis, with which he had become increasingly dissatisfied (see FREUD ON HYPNOSIS). As in psychoanalysis proper, the subject is required to relax and allow his mind to wander freely from elements in the dream to related ideas, recollections, or emotional reactions which they may chance to suggest. By this route, he is gradually led from the dream as recollected, which Freud termed the *manifest content*, to the underlying thoughts and wishes, called by Freud the *latent content*—this, he believed, is typically based upon wishes, recollections, and fantasies related to the deeper emotional reactions of early infancy. In short, the dream is a heavily disguised form of infantile wish-fulfilment expressed as a hallucinatory experience in the course of sleep.

The activity which transforms the latent into the manifest content is known as the *dream work*. This makes use of three principal mechanisms, known respectively as *condensation*, *displacement*, and *dramatization* (also known as *representation*). To these is sometimes added a fourth, *secondary elaboration*, or *revision*. The major function of the dream work is to evade what Freud picturesquely calls the *dream censorship*. This is envisaged as the continued operation of the mechanisms of repression which serve in waking life to protect the individual from the effects of potentially disturbing wishes and fantasies originating in early life. In spite of its name, the censorship was not envisaged as primarily of social or cultural origin, i.e. as an instrument of society. As Freud saw it, repression, whether operating during sleep or during wakefulness, is an essentially biological process, supervening after the age of 5 or thereabouts with the onset of the so-called latency period. *Inter alia*, it is responsible for the onset and maintenance of childhood amnesia, as a result of which very little can be recalled of the experiences or emotions of earlier infancy. At the same time, repression can of course be reinforced as a result of identification and social learning in childhood and after; and its derivative, the dream censorship, may in consequence be in some degree acquired.

Of the activities constituting the dream work,

the most familiar is almost certainly condensation, which few people fail to notice on occasions when recalling their own dreams. For example, a visual image in the dream may embody the features or manner of two or more quite distinct people, being evidently a composite figure. The same may also occur with places, buildings, and the like. Condensation also affects words; some neologisms in dreams are produced by condensing parts of two or more words or phrases. In a more general way, condensation of ideas may frequently be traced in dreams, often indicating that more than one theme or motive is being expressed in the same dream situation ('over-determination'). In view of the drastic ideational compression brought about by condensation, it is not surprising that Freud referred to the manifest content as 'meagre, paltry and laconic' as compared with the richness and variety of the latent dream content.

Whereas Freud regarded condensation as, in part at least, intrinsic to the dream process, displacement he attributed wholly to the effects of the censorship. It consists in attributing emotional significance to some element in the dream that, on analysis, turns out to be essentially trivial. For example, a dream image may recur for some hours after awakening and seem to possess a disturbingly haunting quality. Yet analysis may reveal that it is operating essentially as a decoy to lure the attention of the dreamer from more dangerous themes. In Freud's view, a great deal of the disguise making the memory of the dream so obscure originates from the vicissitudes of displacement.

The term 'dramatization' refers to the transposition of thoughts into imagery, largely, though not exclusively, visual. Inevitably, this mode of representation of thought is highly concrete, and it has therefore been disputed whether abstract ideas can feature in dreams. While dream thinking is certainly concrete in much the same sense as the thinking of the young child or the brain-damaged adult, this does not mean that abstract ideas may not be represented metaphorically in the dream by concrete images. At the same time, it seems unlikely that genuinely creative abstract thinking can take place in dreams.

Secondary elaboration refers to the further distortion or elaboration of the dream that occurs after awakening. As much of this proceeds by rapid and often progressive omission of elements in the manifest content, 'secondary revision' is probably a better term for it. Although it is often held that the power of *memory is intrinsically weaker in dreaming than in the waking state, the rapidity and completeness with which many dreams are forgotten only a few moments after awakening undoubtedly suggest that its basis is in part at least psychogenetic. It would be interesting to compare the repeated reproduction of dreams with that of stories or pictures in the manner described by F. C. *Bartlett (1932). In so far as the writer is aware, such an experiment has not been attempted.

Although Freud relied for the most part on free association to 'undisguise' dreams, i.e. to provide clues to the nature of the persisting wish or motive behind the dream, he noted that on occasion no relevant associations were forthcoming. In some cases, Freud considered it legitimate to appeal to what he called 'primal symbolism', i.e. modes of representation which occurred so consistently in dreams that he could attribute a meaning to them independently of associative context. Among these are the familiar symbols of the male and female genitalia, based quite evidently on association by similarity. But Freud, unlike Jung, always supposed that such symbolic devices were acquired through individual experiences and should not be regarded as inborn modes of symbolic representation, independent of history and culture. The Jungian universal symbols, or 'archetypes', found no place in his theory.

Freud's hypothesis of the dream as wish-fulfilment and as representing the 'primary process' of human thinking, unaffected by realities of space, time, and logic, underwent some modification in his later thinking. In particular, he came to accept the existence of a class of dreams which in no sense embody the fulfilment of infantile wishes. These are the repetitive dreams in which the dreamer re-enacts a traumatic episode in his recent experience. Freud was obliged to concede that dreams of this character, not infrequently associated with war neuroses, do not accord with the 'pleasure principle' and merit explanation in other terms. It is also of interest that W. H. R. *Rivers (1923), likewise on the basis of experience of war neuroses, was led to the view that many dreams could be interpreted in terms of an attempt in fantasy to resolve current emotional problems.

Although the respective parts played by infantile and adult experiences in the motivation of dreams remain controversial, and the concept of dream symbolism is undoubtedly treacherous, it is probably true to say that the dream is a mode of symbolic expression that has certain affinities with language. As Wollheim (1971) has pointed out, however, the dream lacks what is most characteristic of language: a grammar or structure. Moreover, it lacks any real communicative function. None the less, as a form of personal expression it merits attention as a modest manifestation of human *creativity.

See also DREAMING.                              O. L. Z.

Bartlett, F. C. (1932). *Remembering: a study in experimental and social psychology*. Cambridge.
Freud, S. (1900). *The Interpretation of Dreams*. In Strachey, J. (ed.) (1900–1). *Complete Psychological Works*, vol. V. London.
Rivers, W. H. R. (1923). *Conflict and Dream*. London.
Wollheim, R. (1985). *Freud*, 2nd edn. London.

**FREUD ON HYPNOSIS.** In spite of his repudiation of hypnosis as a clinical tool, Freud maintained his interest in the topic and returned to it many years later in connection with his speculative ideas concerning the structure of the mind. In his *Group*

*Psychology and the Analysis of the Ego* (1922), he drew an interesting parallel between hypnosis and the state of falling in love. 'From being in love to hypnosis', he wrote, 'is evidently only a short step.' In hypnosis, he continues, there is '. . . the same humble subjection, the same compliance, the same absence of criticism, towards the hypnotist as towards the loved object'. While the hypnotic relation reflects the 'unlimited devotion of someone in love', sexual satisfaction is of course excluded so that no lasting relation can be formed. But hypnosis, Freud urges, also bears a certain relation to the formation of social groups: the hypnotic relation can, indeed, be viewed as a group of two members. It is distinguished from other groups by the limitation of numbers just as it is distinguished from being in love by the absence of explicit sexual trends. The ultimate implication of Freud's argument seems to be that hypnosis involves a strong element of identification, the hypnotist being unconsciously equated with a significant figure, such as a parent who was both loved and admired, in the subject's early history. In other words, the hypnotist has been put in the place of what Freud at that time called the 'ego ideal'.

Freud of course concedes that this is by no means a complete explanation of hypnosis. As he points out, the manner in which it is produced and its relation to *sleep are far from clear. Further, his theory fails to account for individual differences in susceptibility to hypnosis or for the fact that some people resist it completely. It is of some interest that some later studies, for example that of Hilgard (1965), although supporting Freud's view that personal influences and identifications appear to play an important part in governing hypnotic susceptibility, do not find any very predictable relationship between these factors and the Freudian theory of psychosexual development. Indeed, resemblance in temperament to the parent of the opposite sex appears to favour hypnotic susceptibility equally in male and female subjects. Interestingly enough, it seems to be similarity in leisure activities that is important to identifications, rather than similarity in work or professional values. Where, however, there is no appreciable identification with either parent, the individual is likely to be little susceptible to hypnosis. These findings may be regarded as giving qualified support to Freud's view that the key to hypnotic susceptibility lies in the emotional relationships of early life.

See also HYPNOSIS, EXPERIMENTAL; HYPNOTISM, HISTORY OF.                                      O. L. Z.

Freud, S. (1922). *Group Psychology and the Analysis of the Ego*. Trans. Strachey, J. (1955) in *Complete Psychological Works*, vol. XVIII. London.
Hilgard, E. R. (1965). *Hypnotic Susceptibility*. New York.

**FREUD ON MENTAL STRUCTURE.** Freud's first essay in psychological theory was his draft *Project for a Scientific Psychology*, hastily written in 1895 under the stimulus of his eccentric friend Wilhelm Fliess, but published only many years after his death. This essay, which has proved to be very important for much of Freud's later thinking, might be described as a speculative theory of mental development envisaged in terms of the anatomy and physiology of the brain. Today, it might perhaps be called a neuropsychological model of the mind.

In the *Project*, Freud viewed the brain as composed of discrete nerve cells (neurones) organized in networks through which coursed an unspecified form of energy, presumably electrochemical. The operations of the system as a whole were governed by what, following G. T. *Fechner, he called the Constancy Principle, according to which the overall energy level is kept as low as the prevailing conditions permit, ideally zero. Two classes of neurones were distinguished. The first, constituting what Freud called the 'phi-system', was conceived to operate strictly in accordance with the *reflex principle, its energy being derived wholly from peripheral stimulation and immediately discharged in motor response. Some of these neurones relayed their input to a second system, the 'psi-system', in which *memories might be laid down and energy stored. This latter system, however, received its main input not from peripheral but from central sources, particularly those arising from internal bodily needs, such as hunger, thirst, or sex. In general, psi-neurones were thought to be more resistant to the outflow of energy than phi-neurones, i.e. less 'permeable', and in consequence more capable of storing energy and discharging it in a graduated fashion. This investment of neurones with energy Freud referred to as 'cathexis', a term which was later taken over into psychoanalysis, although with a very different meaning, namely investment of an object or idea with sexual energy or libido.

The psi-system was envisaged by Freud as the instrument of adaptive learning. Thus the degree of resistance of its neurones to the passage of excitation was conceived to depend on both the quantity of energy stored and the frequency of discharge. Following Theodor Meynert (and after him William *James), Freud held that the repeated passage of excitation along nervous pathways facilitated transmission, thus providing the neural basis of habit. For example, discharge of psi-neurones responsive to the bodily needs of a hungry infant becomes linked by association with the perception of the mother and thereby comes to initiate appropriate motor response, i.e. suckling. Regulation of this discharge, he supposed, is governed by the pleasure–pain (better 'unpleasure') principle, according to which pleasure attendant on the gratification of a biological need results from discharge of stored energy, and unpleasure either from an overload of the psi-neurones ('hypercathexis'), corresponding to frustration, or from failure of a protective mechanism (*Reizschutz*) which Freud (following Fechner) supposed to afford protection to the peripheral receptor system from excessive or unduly prolonged stimulation. (Such a mechanism was at one time widely held to provide the physiological basis of pain.)

As has often been pointed out, Freud's 'Psychology for Neurologists' (as the *Project* was subtitled) owed much to the writings of Brücke and Meynert, with whom Freud had worked as a young man, and the relevance of at least some of his ideas to contemporary thinking in the neurosciences has been touched on by Pribram and Gill (1976). What does *not* seem to have excited comment, however, is how much Freud's conception of the learning process in infancy has in common with the learning process in animals as formulated by E. L. *Thorndike (1898). Indeed Thorndike's 'law of effect', with its emphasis on the effects of pleasure and pain in respectively strengthening or weakening the nervous connections established by learning, may be regarded as closely analogous to Freud's pleasure–unpleasure principle in human development.

Although the *Project* remained unpublished in Freud's lifetime, several of the ideas embodied in it reappear in the development of psychoanalysis. For example, the reflex schema and the idea of perception and memory processes having different loci reappeared in the theoretical chapter (Ch. VIII) of the *Interpretation of Dreams* (1900). Further, the distinction between the primary process of thought, supposedly governed by the pleasure principle, and the secondary process, reflecting the demands of reality, both clearly foreshadowed in the *Project*, became basic to psychoanalytical thinking. In spite of the fact that Freud soon came to repudiate models of the mind based explicitly on considerations of anatomy and physiology, many of the concepts first introduced in the *Project* feature in his later 'metapsychological' writings. These include the concepts of force or energy, which reappears as libido (sexual drive), and cathexis, later redefined as emotional investment in an object or idea. Even the *Reizschutz* makes it return many years later in *Beyond the Pleasure Principle* (1922). Yet, notwithstanding this transition to purely mental models, Freud never wholly lost his early belief that psychology would one day have to be placed on its organic, i.e. bodily, foundations.

After the *Project* was written—and indefinitely put aside—Freud's work took him increasingly into the domain of neurotic conflict and the unconscious. Here his ideas have been much misunderstood. It must be clearly recognized that Freud at no time saw neurosis as a simple trial of strength between the conscious and the unconscious parts of the mind. As he saw it, certain emotion-laden memories, fantasies, or thoughts are subject to repression because they are too painful to dwell upon or are otherwise unacceptable to an individual's self-esteem. The associated emotion, on the other hand, is *not* repressed; it is only its links with the repressed material that are severed. Moreover, Freud insisted that the scope of the unconscious is far from restricted to that which is repressed. As he saw it, mental life is originally unconscious and only becomes conscious, or pre-conscious, i.e. potentially conscious, in the course of adaptation to external reality. In short, the evolution of consciousness is linked essentially with the development of perception, learning, and language, and is expressed pre-eminently through the medium of verbal communication.

Although the concept of the ego appears in the *Project*, it did not feature at all prominently in earlier psychoanalytical thinking. Its importance derived from Freud's increasing recognition of the facts that repression may be instigated without conscious knowledge or intention and that mental events of which the individual appears to have been at no time aware may undergo repression.

It was facts such as these that led Freud to undertake a systematic revision of the concept of the ego. In a short but important study (1927), he envisaged the ego as evolving gradually out of the unconscious substructure of infantile mental life. Like William James, he placed particular stress on the corporeal activities upon which the ego is built and which indeed constitute its primary components (James's 'material self': see James, 1891, vol. 2, ch. 10). But, in keeping with his general theory of sexual development, Freud's ego is to an important extent a product of infantile sexuality and its suppression during the 'latency period', and is to this extent heavily 'sexualized'. Indeed, investment of libido in the ego itself ('ego-libido') is conceived by Freud to lie at the roots of narcissism and its derivatives.

None the less, Freud's ego is far from being a mere product of the infantile unconscious. Although rooted in the corporeal ego, it develops from, and through, its transactions with the environment, both physical and social. The ego is viewed throughout as the agent of perception and learning and as the instrument of volitional activity. It reflects the operations of the reality principle and much of its activity is conscious, i.e. open to introspection.

It is at this point, too, that Freud introduces his concept of the 'super-ego'—a term that has since passed into everyday discourse. Referred to in his earlier writings as the 'ego-ideal', this entity is envisaged as an internal standard which acts as a crude regulator of moral conduct. It is thought to originate in early infancy and to derive from a process whereby feelings of hostility directed towards either or both parents are neutralized by a process of introjection, i.e. by becoming embodied in the child's own mind. This can be traced most convincingly in the male child, in whom hostility towards the father is often tempered by a degree of positive identification. The result is a crude amalgam of positive and negative feelings derived from the parent figures which evolves as an internalized controller of one's own behaviour. In Freud's famous phrase, the super-ego is the heir to the *Oedipus complex.

Obviously, Freud did not intend to give a complete explanation of the origins of conscience. He wished only to stress that conscience originates in the early identifications and repudiations of childhood and subsequently comes to embody influences derived from teachers, admired friends, and social and moral education generally. His ideas had value, however, in providing a measure of explanation of what we may call the pathology of conscience, i.e. the quite excessive sense of guilt or need for punishment provoked in some individuals by trivial transgressions. (As is well known, this is a common feature of depressive states.) Thus Freud's theory did to some extent account for the savagery of conscience, though not, perhaps, for its equally common deficiencies. This savagery is derived from the largely unconscious hostility shown by the very young child and the irrealistic character of his thinking.

Freud's recognition that the super-ego is in large degree unconscious and itself the principal instrument of repression led him to seek a new name for what he had previously called simply the 'unconscious'. The latter was essentially the instinctual substrate of conscious mental life and its associated memories and fantasies. These, for the most part infantile, strata of unconscious mental life Freud chose to name the 'id'—a term adapted from the work of a speculative Swiss philosopher, Georg Groddeck. But in Freud's later thinking, those unconscious activities of the id were no longer conceived as concerned exclusively with instinctual gratification and as operating wholly in accord with the pleasure principle. He came increasingly to appreciate the importance of certain repetitive and self-destructive elements in the pattern of human destiny that, literally, lay 'beyond' the pleasure principle (Freud, 1942). These constitute the Freudian 'death-wish', the deeply unconscious impulse to seek nirvana, the extinction of individual existence.

In short, the final Freudian model of mental structure is somewhat as follows. The *id*, wholly unconscious, embodies the instincts related to psychosexual gratifications (libido) and operates without relevance to the dictates of logic or external reality. While governed essentially by the pleasure principle, it incorporates certain regressive and destructive potentialities that are inherent in the biological make-up of the organism. The *ego*, wholly conscious, is essentially the mind as ordinarily conceived. It is the instrument of learning and of adaptive relationship to the environment. The ego is concerned essentially with perception, memory, and the control of speech and volitional activity. The *super-ego*, while closely related to consciousness, is in part unconscious and derives its energies vicariously from the id. It operates as a monitor of conduct and a major source of control through repression. The super-

ego constitutes the nucleus of conscience and provides the foundation of adult morality.   O. L. Z.

Bonaparte, M., Freud, A., and Kris, E. (eds., 1954). *The Origins of Psycho-Analysis*, London. This includes the *Project for a Scientific Psychology*; a revised and improved translation is available in Strachey, J. (ed.), *Complete Psychological Works*, vol. I (1966).

Freud, S. (1922). *Beyond the Pleasure Principle*. Trans. 1942, London; revised trans. in *Complete Psychological Works*, vol. XVIII (1955).

Freud, S. (1923). *The Ego and the Id*. Trans. 1927, London; reprinted in *Complete Psychological Works*, vol. XIX (1961).

James, W. (1890). *The Principles of Psychology*. London.

Pribram, K. and Gill, M. (1976). *Freud's Project Re-Assessed*. New York.

Thorndike, E. L. (1898). Animal intelligence. *Psychological Review Monograph Supplements*, vol. 2, no. 8.

Wollheim, R. (1985). *Freud*, 2nd edn. London.

**FREY**, MAX VON (1852–1932). German physiologist, best known for his investigations into the sensations of pain and touch. In 1882 he became a university lecturer in physiology at Leipzig, eventually being appointed to a professorship there, which he held from 1891 to 1898. He later taught for a year at Zurich, and then at Wurzburg. Developing the earlier studies of Blix (1882) and Goldscheider (1884), who had established that the skin has separate spots for cold, warmth, and touch, von Frey showed that pain is a special skin modality, separate from these sensations and also from pressure. He went on to map out 'pain spots'.

The set of hairs, carefully graded from soft to stiff (and including human hair), which he used in experiments investigating tactile senses became known as 'von Frey's hairs'.

Boring, E. G. (1942). *Sensation and Perception in the History of Experimental Psychology*, ch. 13. New York.

**FRISCH**, KARL RITTER VON (1886–1983). Austrian ethologist. Born of an academic family in Vienna, Karl von Frisch worked at several universities, in particular Breslau and Munich. His research was on the light sensitivity of sea anemones. He collaborated with his uncle Sigmund Exner (1846–1926), who became professor of physiology in Vienna and worked on both reaction times and cerebral localization. Von Frisch went on to show by behavioural experiments that fish are not, as had been thought, colour-blind. In more detail, he found that in dim light using 'rod' vision they are, like us, colour-blind; but with brighter light stimulating the retinal 'cone' cells, they do have *colour vision. He went on to demonstrate, by whistling to catfish, that fish are not deaf.

Having established unexpected sensory capacities in many animals, von Frisch carried out his celebrated experiments on how scout honey-bees convey information of where they have found nectar. He started by assuming that the other bees recognized the successful scout by odour; but he found evidence that the scout could convey information of direction and distance of the food source, which was surprising. Following experiments to discount the odour theory, he arrived at the wild conjecture that they signal by a symbolic dance, which he learned to interpret. Direction was normally signalled by reference to the sun; but on cloudy days it was established by the polarization angle of the light of the overcast sky, which the bee's compound eye can detect. Distance of the food source was signalled by different kinds of dance—a 'round' dance when near, and a 'waggle' dance when distant; and the speed of the dance was greater for greater distances. The direction of the food source with respect to the sun was signalled by taking the vertical of the honeycomb as, symbolically, the direction of the sun. This discovery (which has been independently confirmed) that bees use a symbolic language, was wholly unexpected; and it forces us to accept that man is not unique in organizing society by means of language.

Von Frisch shared the Nobel prize with Konrad Lorenz and Nikolaas Tinbergen in 1973. His books include: *You and Life* (1940), *Animal Architecture* (1974), and the celebrated *Dancing Bees* (1954).

O. L. Z.

**FROEBEL,** FRIEDRICH WILHELM AUGUST (1782–1852). Friedrich Froebel was born in Oberweissbuch, Thuringia. His father was a busy pastor, and his mother died soon after his birth, an event he regarded as crucial to his development. His early childhood was unhappy and he was thrown on his own resources, developing the passion for self-contemplation and self-education which he thought essential for all. Though he was moved by the mystical language of his father's hymns and sermons, he was critical of his schooling with its reliance on memorization of facts inculcated by stern teachers. At 15 he was apprenticed to a forester, and he wrote later of his religious communion with Nature at this period: 'I looked within myself and to Nature for help.' He began to develop his personal philosophy: a belief in the organic unity of man, God, and Nature. At the University of Jena he eagerly embraced the idealist philosophy of the time. He believed that all living things had an inherent form and purpose, not predetermined but developing through a kind of creative struggle with the environment. He studied the transcendental biology of the period, and was deeply impressed by the underlying pattern which seemed to unite all living things and by their growth from simple to complex structures. He had a romantic and mystical belief in universal harmony: 'Everything has a purpose, which is to realize its essence, the divine nature developing within it, and so to reveal God in the transitory world.'

Froebel early demonstrated an interest in education and in 1805 began in Frankfurt the work as schoolmaster and private tutor which was to occupy the rest of his life. Like *Rousseau he regarded man as essentially good, and his pedagogy starts from perceptive observation of chil-

dren's behaviour. 'Educators', he wrote, 'must understand their impulse to make things and to be freely and personally active; they must encourage their desire to instruct themselves as they create, observe and experiment.' The teacher was to guide the child in his self-discovery, not direct him. Each stage of development was critical and had to be fully experienced. Play was the young child's 'spontaneous expression of thought and feeling' and was central to learning. For this reason Froebel established the kindergarten, which provided the activities and materials needed by the pre-school child. He invented toys and exercises which became the basis of a pedagogic system whose formalism was curiously at odds with the permissiveness of his philosophy. He laid great emphasis on the relationship between teacher and pupil and on the need for continuity and connectedness in the school curriculum. The child had naturally a sense of the unity of life: it was the business of the school to make him conscious of it. Starting from the child's own experience, the study of religion, nature, mathematics, and language would encourage his awareness of self, the world, and God. The arts would enable him to express his inner life, and physical work teach him the dignity of labour. At all times the school was to maintain close contact with family and community; only so could it remain relevant and vital.

Froebel was a visionary as well as a gifted teacher. He had great ambitions for his educational programme, believing it would unify Germany as well as mankind generally. In fact his influence in his lifetime was limited—a year before his death in 1852, Prussia banned the kindergarten for its 'revolutionary' tendencies. Devoted disciples in Europe and America continued his work, however, and from the 1870s it profoundly influenced the training of teachers and the education of young children. The importance of play, the unified curriculum, links with home and community, and non-directive rather than authoritarian teaching remain live issues. But Froebel's 'organic' theory of human development led him seriously to underestimate social influences in individual lives. When he was asked to plan the education of the poor in Berne, he was at pains to point out that 'there need be no fear that individual pupils will want to improve their position and leave their own class. On the contrary, this system will produce educated men, each true to his calling, each in his own position.' N. S.

Froebel, F. (1825). *Menschenerziehung* (Eng. trans. 1877, *The Education of Man*. London).
Lilley, I. M. (1967). *Friedrich Froebel: a selection from his writings*. Cambridge.

**FRONTAL LOBE.** See 'The Spinal Cord and the Brain' under NERVOUS SYSTEM.

**FUGUE.** See DISSOCIATION OF THE PERSONALITY.

**FUNCTIONALISM.** An American school of

psychology based principally on the University of Chicago at the turn of the nineteenth century. It owes something to William *James but a great deal more to John *Dewey, who has been described by E. G. *Boring as the 'organizing principle' behind its emergence. Apart from Dewey, its principal advocate was James Rowland *Angell, for many years professor of psychology at Chicago, who stressed the functional significance of adaptive behaviour and viewed mind as mediating between the environment and the needs of the organism. As E. G. Boring wittily put it: 'Functionalism represented the Philosopher's approach to a science that had rebelled against Philosophy'; it was often contrasted with *Wundt's structuralism.

As an outcome of functionalism, experimental work on animal behaviour and its neurological foundations developed rapidly at Chicago, particularly at the hands of C. M. Child, G. E. Coghill, and J. B. *Watson before he became a doctrinaire behaviourist. Indeed functionalism did much to lay the foundations of biological psychology as we know it today.                               O. L. Z.

**FUNCTIONALIST THEORIES OF THE MIND.**
Recent functionalist theories of the mind, though they may be characterized broadly as 'materialist', can be seen as a reaction against the physicalist theories that baldly identified mental states with physically characterizable types of brain state. A difficulty with such theories is that there seems no reason to suppose that a particular type of mental state, such as being in pain, or having a given belief, will always be realized by a specific type of neurophysiological structure. Indeed, it is a well-attested fact that if a certain brain structure is damaged, resulting in mental impairment (e.g. after a stroke), the brain is often, after a period of time, able to utilize alternative neurological networks so that the relevant mental activity is eventually restored. These and other difficulties with straightforward mind–brain identity theories led to the suggestion that mental states should be identified not with the brain's physical states, but with its *functional* states. Such states, the functionalist argues, can be specified in purely formal terms—in terms of the logical and computational processes involved—and so are neutral with respect to the actual way in which the processes are physically realized. In computer terminology, functional descriptions are 'software' descriptions; and these can be given in a fairly abstract way, using logical symbols, transformation rules, organizational principles, and so on, without any need to be specific as to the precise design of the hardware needed to realize the functions involved. Many researchers into *artificial intelligence (AI) have adopted what may broadly be called a functionalist approach to the mind, which can encompass a variety of positions, from the radical thesis that mental states are nothing more than functional states of *Turing machines, to the weaker claim that the computational states of such machines may at least be used as helpful models or analogies to illuminate our understanding of the phenomena of mind.

Two difficulties for functionalism may be mentioned here. (i) First, since a functional system could clearly be instantiated by a wide variety of physical systems, e.g. a computerized robot, or perhaps even a complex telephone exchange, it seems that the functionalist would be committed to ascribing mental states to such systems, provided that they exhibited the relevant organizational complexity. Yet (the objection runs) there is obviously no human parallel to being a robot; robots have no inner mental life. Hence mental states must be more than mere functional states. Against this, functionalists have argued that if we could build a robot that was complex enough to instantiate the kind of enormously complicated program needed to model human mental states, and if moreover, the robot was able to interact causally with the environment in all the appropriate ways, then the assumption that the robot could not possibly have a 'mental life' might begin to lose much of its plausibility. (ii) A second objection concerns the phenomenon of *intentionality. Mental states have intentionality: they have representational content, or are 'about something'. Yet opponents of the strong AI programme (such as John Searle) have argued that functional specifications, being couched in terms of purely formal or syntactic operations, cannot possibly exhibit intentionality. A system might perform impeccably in manipulating symbols in accordance with complex operational rules, yet, for all that, it might be quite unaware of the meaning of the symbols, what they were 'about'; and hence (the argument runs) it could not be considered as having a 'mind' in the sense in which humans have minds. These matters are currently the subject of vigorous debate among philosophers and AI theorists.

See also HOMUNCULUS.                          J. G. C.

Boden, M. A. (1981). *Minds and Mechanisms*. Brighton.
Dennett, D. C. (1979). *Brainstorms*. Hassocks.
Searle, J. (1982). Minds, brains and programs. In Hofstadter, D. and Dennett, D. C. (eds.), *The Mind's Eye*. Harmondsworth.

**FUTURE SHOCK.** Term coined by the American writer Alvin Toffler, to mean the trauma experienced by rapid changes—for example, to the environment, including destruction of familiar buildings, or customs of childhood. The trauma is similar to that often experienced by *émigrés*, but is even less reversible as it is in time.

Alvin Toffler (1970). *Future Shock*. London.

# G

**GALEN** (CLAUDIUS GALENUS, second century AD). Greek physician, born at Pergamum in Mysia. He studied medicine there, and also at Smyrna, Corinth, and Alexandria, and became physician to Marcus Aurelius. He probably died in Sicily.

Galen wrote extensively on medical and on philosophical subjects and his extant works consist of eighty-three treatises on medicine and fifteen commentaries on *Hippocrates. He dissected animals and developed, to our minds, somewhat fanciful physiological theories. His clinical discoveries include diagnosing by the pulse. He was the authority from whom all later Greek and Roman medical writers quoted, with more or less accuracy.

Galen considered that the body worked by three types of spirit: natural spirit (located in the liver), vital spirit (located in the left ventricle of the heart), and animal spirit (located in the brain). He postulated several anatomical features, such as the *rete mirabile* (wonderful network) on the undersurface of the brain, which is found in some animals (especially those with hooves) but not in man, although on Galen's authority it was accepted as present in the human brain for over thirteen centuries. It was also believed on his authority that the septum of the heart contained minute pores—these were essential for Galen's physiological system as he believed that blood passes from the heart to the body from both the arteries and the veins, new blood being manufactured in the liver and supposedly burnt up in the tissues. The exhalation of breath, when concentrated, was known to be asphyxiating, and was compared to the smoke of fire. Galen made considerable discoveries in neurology and especially the kinds of paralysis associated with damage at various places to the spinal cord (see GREEK INVESTIGATIONS OF THE MIND AND SENSES).

Kühn, C. G. (ed.) (1821–33). *Opera omnia* (the only complete edition of Galen's surviving works).

**GALILEO** (Galileo Galilei) (1564–1642). Italian physicist, astronomer, and inventor, born at Pisa. He preferred to be known by his first name, rather than by his surname Galilei. When a student of medicine at the University of Pisa, in 1583, Galileo noticed that the oscillations of a suspended lamp in the cathedral kept the same rate whatever the amplitude of its swing. This at once suggested a timekeeper for the pulse, and much later (dictated on his death-bed to his son) the invention of the pendulum clock. He greatly improved the refracting telescope (which was invented in the Netherlands in 1608) and discovered the four 'Galilean' moons of Jupiter (1610), lunar craters, and sunspots, and he described the Milky Way as made up of countless stars. He was probably the inventor of the compound microscope (1610), and he was the first to see the seven photoreceptors in each optical element of the compound eye.

Much of his work challenged *Aristotle, initially by establishing that heavy and light weights fall at the same rate—though the story of dropping weights from the Leaning Tower of Pisa is most likely apocryphal, as the experiment would have been very difficult to perform reliably. He pointed out that if heavy and light weights were attached to each other with a string it would not stretch or break during the fall as one would expect if their rate of fall differed. For his experiments he effectively slowed down gravitational fall by rolling balls down sloping tracks; and little bells placed at intervals along the tracks told him of the speed of the balls by tinkling, so he made laws of nature observable. Some of his apparatus, including his telescope, can be seen at the Laurentian Library in Florence.

Galileo's challenge of Aristotle provoked such a reaction that as early as 1591 he was forced to leave Pisa and retire to Florence. A year later, however, he gained a professorship in mathematics at the University of Padua, where his lectures attracted immense attention and pupils from all over Europe, and where he remained for eighteen years (1592–1610). It was his book on sunspots (1613) that gave the explicit account of the earth moving round the sun which initiated the long tiring trial that cost him his freedom. This was a powerful defence of the Copernican view that the earth is not the centre of the universe, a view denounced in 1616 as a danger to the Catholic faith. Galileo's insistence on it was probably not intended as a deliberate attack on the Church, but rather as a defence of the right to make scientific observations and reasoned arguments, so saving the Church from the errors that science had revealed. After a long trial by the Inquisition he was imprisoned, and forced to recant his views, though probably he was not tortured.

Although Galileo wrote mainly on physics and astronomy (especially the work translated as *The Starry Messenger*, 1610) he also considered *sensation and *perception. His *The Assayer* (1623) has this passage:

To excite in us tastes, odours, and sounds I believe that nothing is required in external bodies except shapes, numbers, and slow or rapid movements. I think that if ears, tongues, and noses were removed, shapes and numbers and motions would remain, but not odours or tastes or sounds. The latter, I believe, are nothing more than names when separated from living beings, just as tickling and titillation are nothing but names in the absence of such things as noses and armpits. And as these four senses are related to the four elements, so I believe that vision, the sense eminent above all others in the proportion of the finite to the infinite, the temporal to the instantaneous, the quantitative to the indivisible, the illuminated to the obscure—that vision, I say, is related to light itself. But of this sensation and the things pertaining to it I pretend to understand but little; and since even a long time would not suffice to explain that trifle, or even to hint at an explanation, I pass this over in silence.

Having damaged his eyes with his telescopic studies of sunspots, in 1637 Galileo lost his sight. Five years later he died, blind, in the year Newton was born.                                        R. L. G.

Drake, S. (trans. and ed.) (1957). *Discoveries and Opinions of Galileo*. New York.

**GALL, FRANZ JOSEPH** (1758–1828). German anatomist and founder of phrenology, who was born in Baden and settled in Vienna (1785) as a physician. He was an anatomist of some distinction and the man to whom we are really indebted for the ideas we now hold on the relations which the constituent parts of the nervous system bear to one another. He was the first to distinguish clearly between the white matter of the brain, which consists of nerve fibres, and the gelatinous grey matter, which forms the cortex of the brain, and the ganglia. For the speculative ideas as to the cortical localization of human faculties, see PHRENOLOGY. Gall's most important work, written jointly with J. C. Spurzheim (1776–1832) is: *Anatomie et physiologie du système nerveux en général, et du cerveau en particulier, avec observations sur la possibilité de reconnaître plusieurs dispositions intellectuelles et morales de l'homme et des animaux par la configuration de leurs têtes*, 2 vols. (1810, 1819).                                        O. L. Z.

**GALTON, SIR FRANCIS** (1822–1911). Francis Galton pioneered the application of measurement and statistics to the study of human individual differences, and introduced several specific methods of enquiry which are now standard. Association of ideas, for example, had been discussed for centuries, but he was the first to devise an experimental approach. Again, in asking people to fill in questionnaires about their *mental imagery, he not only inaugurated the scientific study of imagery but also the systematic use of psychological questionnaires. In attempting to tease out the contributions of nature and nurture, he became the first to gather systematic data about the life-histories of twins, and about the family and educational backgrounds of people with exceptional talents in, say, literature or science or sport. He collected fingerprints, devised a method of classifying them, and introduced the fingerprint

system into police work. He invented the statistic known as 'the correlation coefficient', which is now a basic tool in education, biology, and psychology.

Born near Birmingham, Galton was the youngest of a large family which was wealthy, talented, and energetically involved with practical science and statistics. His intellectual precocity is shown by one of his early letters:

My dear Adèle, I am four years old, and I can read any English book. I can say all the Latin substantives, adjectives and active verbs, besides fifty-two lines of Latin poetry. I can cast up any sum in addition and multiply by 2, 3, 4, 5, 6, 7, 8, 9, 10, 11. I read French a little and I know the clock. Francis Galton. February 15th, 1827.

He attended private schools in England and France, studied medicine in Birmingham and London, and studied chemistry in Germany before entering Cambridge University in 1840 to read mathematics. During those early years, he developed strong interests in doing independent-minded scientific experiments, constructing gadgets, and keeping orderly records of numerical data. These interests foreshadowed his adult preoccupations and the guiding maxim of his mature years: Whenever you can, measure or count.

In 1844, the year Galton graduated from Cambridge, his father died and he found himself, at the age of 22, with a substantial financial inheritance and no clear plans. For six restless years he engaged in various enterprises, including a tour of the Middle East and an attempt to settle as a sporting English country gentleman. Then in 1850 he organized, financed, and led a scientific exploration of an unexplored part of Africa. When he returned from this two-year journey, he married Louisa Butler, and wrote reports of his travels which gained him, in his own words, 'an established position in the scientific world'. He now entered upon a settled way of life as a London-based scientist-at-large.

From 1854 until his death, Galton contributed to the scientific life of London. Although he never had or sought paid employment, he held various responsible posts in the Royal Society, the Royal Geographical Society, the Anthropological Institute, the Royal Institution, and the British Association for the Advancement of Science. At the same time, he privately undertook miscellaneous investigations of a characteristic style. He sought some issue which might lend itself to quantitative treatment; accumulated relevant data, often with single-handed ingenuity; systematized the data to extract their implications; and promptly reported his findings in a memoir to one of his scientific societies. He produced hundreds of these memoirs, and his several books were mostly edited collections of them.

Throughout his long and industrious life, Galton maintained interest in many branches of science: for example, in meteorology he invented the idea and the name of 'anticyclone' and devised the now-familiar weather map which first appeared in *The Times* in 1875. In studying the threshold for high-pitched notes, he invented the calibrated whistle which later bore his name and became a standard piece of equipment in psychological laboratories until it was replaced by electronic equipment. However, after 1859, when his cousin Charles *Darwin published *The Origin of Species*, Galton's dominant interest was to study, by measurement, the influences of heredity upon the mental and physical characteristics of human beings. He accepted Darwin's view that evolution was a trial-and-error process involving the inheritance, variation, and natural selection of organic characteristics. He applied this view to man, and conceived the enterprise of collecting the data necessary to understand human evolution. (See his books, *Hereditary Genius*, 1869; *English Men of Science*, 1874; and *Inquiries into Human Faculty*, 1883.)

This ambitious enterprise raised a host of challenging questions. What were the characteristics in terms of which people resembled, and differed from, each other? How might they be specified and measured? How far did they arise from genetic inheritance (nature) or environment (nurture)? What were the cumulative, generation-by-generation effects of the fact that individuals contributed differing numbers of offspring to the next generation? How did different environments and social practices exert natural selection by affecting fertility and breeding patterns and, thereby, affecting the composition of what, nowadays, would be called the 'genetic pool' of human populations? (See GENETICS OF BEHAVIOUR.)

Such questions inspired Galton to conduct many enquiries which, if viewed out of context, seem unrelated and even eccentric. He examined, for example, the number of children in different families, and he related these numbers to the age at which the parents married, the migration of families from rural to urban environments, and the social tendency for the eldest sons of aristocratic families to marry wealthy heiresses. He accumulated data about the tendency for outstanding talents to run in families (his own family tree, and that of his wife, were cases in point). (See GENIUS.) He devised gadgets and methods for recording any mental or physical characteristic that seemed measurable: for example, bodily proportions, fingerprints, strength of grip, sensory acuity, and mental imagery. He used unconventional photographic techniques (composite portraits) to record facial resemblances among different members of the same family, among criminals, tubercular patients, and various national groups. Some of his enquiries led nowhere. Some led to findings which have not been confirmed by later studies. Some led to findings that have been confirmed and extended, but given varying theoretical interpretations.

Galton hoped that human evolution would, one day, be understood in terms which were strictly materialistic, deterministic, and unaffected by unaccountables such as 'divine intervention' or 'free will'. In order to discount divine intervention, he conducted ingenious but controversial studies which showed, to his own satisfaction, that prayer was ineffective in bringing about the events that were prayed for. His experiments about association-of-ideas were aimed at discovering whether people may 'freely' choose what they think. He concluded against the intervention of 'free will'. Psychologists, who are nowadays familiar with the tradition of experiments about word-association and idea-association (see FREE ASSOCIATION), are usually unaware of the motive which led Galton to found the tradition.

Galton was imbued with nineteenth-century ideas about human progress and about science as the chief practical instrument of such progress. He envisaged his ambitious enterprise as leading, in the fullness of time, to nothing less than a body of scientific knowledge by which men could rationally direct the future course of human evolution. He invented the word 'eugenics' for this science which would provide such far-reaching practical applications. He was, like many Victorians, deeply interested in, but ambivalent about, religion; and he supposed that eugenics would supply a new, universal religion to supersede those that men had devised hitherto. In his autobiography, published in 1908, he wrote with high-minded passion about this elevating new religion, and he bequeathed £45,000 to establish the study of eugenics at London University.

As a person, Galton was socially reserved, preoccupied by scientific labours, and inclined to be aloof. Yet his courtesy, generosity, and gentle good-humour endeared him to the few people who knew him closely. He was widely respected, and honoured by, scientific circles, even though many scientists regarded him as crankish. He was knighted in 1909. Since his death, his eugenic ideals have remained deeply controversial and liable to misunderstanding. But his stature as a pioneering scientist has steadily increased. Modern genetics, mental measurement, and statistics owe much to the innovations which Galton introduced while pursuing his solitary enquiries into the human condition.                                          I. M. L. H.

Forrest, D. W. (1974). *Francis Galton: the life and work of a Victorian genius*. London.

Pearson, K. (1914–30). *Life, Letters and Labours of Francis Galton*, 3 vols. Cambridge.

**GALVANIC SKIN RESPONSE.** See ELECTRODERMAL ACTIVITY.

**GALVANIC STIMULATION.** Named after Luigi Galvani (1737–98), Italian physiologist born at Bologna who became professor of anatomy there in 1762. Galvani thought he had demonstrated animal electricity by showing that frog muscles twitch when touched by wires. He believed that the electricity flowed from the muscles to the nerve. We now know that the stimulation is produced by small currents applied to the nerve: the electricity in Galvani's experiment was produced by chemical reaction from acids present on the frog's skin. His work led, however, to the modern understanding of the electrical basis of neural activity.

**GAME THEORY.** See VON NEUMANN, JOHANN.

**GANSER SYNDROME.** See PSEUDODEMENTIA.

**GAUSS,** KARL FRIEDRICH (1777–1855). German mathematician, born at Brunswick. He was an infant prodigy, despite the fact that his father, a labourer, tried to keep him from an appropriate education; it was his mother who, though uneducated, encouraged him in his studies. His first great discovery was made just before he was 19 years of age, when he succeeded in constructing according to Euclidian rules the regular polygon of seventeen sides. He wished this to be inscribed on his tombstone, but the stonemason refused, saying it would be indistinguishable from a circle. Gauss kept a diary of his discoveries, which is a unique document of a genius, and establishes his priority in disputed cases as, except for a work on the theory of numbers which appeared in 1801, he published little of his work. He was among the first to realize the significance of non-Euclidian *geometries (especially from the work of Nikolas *Lobachevski). The Gaussian distribution (or 'normal' distribution) is the basis of statistics.

Dunnington, G. W. (1955). *Karl Friedrich Gauss, Titan of Science: a study of his life and work.* Baton Rouge, Louisiana. The diary was published by Felix Klein (1901), and with notes in *Gauss Werke* (1917).

**GENERALIZING.** The deriving of general statements from individual instances. Generalizing occurs in learning, and is essential for deriving knowledge from experiences and for skills of all kinds. It is the basis of predicting future situations from past experience and for drawing analogies. See also INDUCTION.

**GENETICS OF BEHAVIOUR.** Behaviour genetics is the study of the genetical basis of behaviour and of psychological characteristics such as *intelligence, temperament, *learning, and *perception. Long before the emergence of behaviour genetics as a science, man practised selective breeding for behavioural characters. The domestication of animals involved changing their behaviour in a number of respects by manipulating their genetic constitution (genotype) through selective breeding. The various breeds of dogs provide an interesting example, in that many breeds were produced for behavioural characteristics—for example, hunting dogs such as the spaniel and working dogs such as the sheep-dog. The ancient world was also concerned with the relationship between heredity and behaviour. The Greeks anticipated eugenics with their belief that young men who distinguished themselves in war or other socially valued activities should be encouraged to breed, whereas depraved persons should not.

The importance of hereditary components of behaviour was the subject of much dispute and theorizing in psychology during the first part of the twentieth century, but little sound empirical work was undertaken. The arguments centred around the nature vs. nurture controversy (see GALTON), or in other words whether the characteristic patterns of behaviour shown by an individual were learned or innate. Some believed with the eminent geneticist William Bateson that the natural genetic distinctions differentiated men into types—artists, actors, farmers, musicians, poets, scientists, servants, etc. At the other extreme J. B. *Watson, the founder of *behaviourism, made the proud boast that given a dozen healthy infants and the freedom to shape their environment he could train anyone to become any kind of specialist—doctor, lawyer, merchant, artist, etc. These sharply opposing viewpoints delayed a proper appreciation of the essential interdependence of genetic *and* environmental factors in the determination of behavioural and psychological characters. Both are essential, though the degree of contribution made by each depends on the character in question.

The effects of genes vary with differences in the environment in which the organism develops and lives. This can be appreciated by a gastronomic analogy. The taste, texture, and quality of a cake can be modified by both changing the ingredients and the way it is cooked, but it is not always easy to tell what has been changed by eating the cake. Both the ingredients and the cooking are essential to producing the cake, for without both there would be no cake. Much recent research in behaviour genetics has sought to identify the contributions of genetic and environmental factors in order to determine the causes of differences in behaviour, and to explore the mechanisms of behavioural development.

There are two broad areas of interest. The first involves tracing the pathways that link the genome (a set of chromosomes) with behaviour, and is consequently concerned with issues about how genes specify the properties and functioning of nervous systems. The second is about the genetic organization of behaviour itself, in the individual and in the population, and how genetically controlled differences in behaviour lead to population changes and ultimately to evolutionary change.

While the genetic constitution of an organism is called its genotype, the organism's form as perceived (or the character to be measured, such as height, personality, or intelligence) is called its phenotype. Genetics is concerned largely with examining the relationship between genotypes and phenotypes. A distinction is drawn between major genes (a single gene having a measurable effect on a phenotype) and polygenes (where many genes interact to produce phenotypic effects). Most of the known genetic effects on behaviour are due to polygenes: continuously variable characters such as intelligence or emotionality result from the effects of polygenes which individually have tiny effects but which cumulate.

Quantitative or biometrical genetics is concerned with studying the effects of polygenes in populations. In respect of a given phenotype, the amount of variability in a population which is due to genetic factors is called the heritability ($h^2$), and is given by the equation $V_g/V_p$, where $V_p$ is the sum of the phenotypic variance and $V_g$ the sum of the genetic variance. It is a characteristic of polygenes that their phenotypic expression—for example, measured intelligence—is subject to environmental modification. The interaction of genetic and environmental factors during development leads to the enormous variability observed in populations. A few examples of the effects of a single gene on behaviour have been described in man. About 30 per cent of the population are unable to taste a substance called phenylthiocarbamide in very low concentrations. Now the ability to taste this substance is known to be due to the action of a pair of genes designated $TT$, which are carried on homologous chromosomes. In people who cannot taste the compound, the genes exist in another form, $tt$. A heterozygote, having the genetic constitution $Tt$ at the relevant locus (address of a gene on a chromosome), can taste the compound. Thus in this case the effect of a single $T$ gene is said to be dominant over $t$, which is recessive.

Various methods have been used to study the genetics of behaviour. Broadly speaking, they may be divided into the phenotypic and the genotypic. In the case of the phenotypic approach the investigators begin with a behavioural character and attempt to find a relationship between it and genetic variation. In the genotypic approach the investigator starts with a standard genotype and examines the effects on behaviour of changing the components of the genotype. The principal methods are as follows.

*(i) Selective breeding.* The aim here is to change the population in specified directions, usually for 'high' or 'low' expression of the chosen phenotype. The method is based upon an assumption of correlation between phenotype and genotype and entails breeding together high/low scoring males and females. The method has been used extensively with animals, and lines showing divergences in behavioural characters such as learning or emotionality in rats have been produced. The existence of such lines allows further genetic and behavioural analysis of the phenotype.

*(ii) Inbred lines.* Long-continued inbreeding results in lines in which individuals are in effect genetically identical. Highly inbred lines, in which the members are genetically alike, but genetically different between lines, may be reared in identical environments and compared in respect of given behaviours. Observed differences between lines reared in identical environments will be genetic in origin. Many highly inbred lines of animals, par-

ticularly mice and fruit-flies, have been produced and provide valuable material for behavioural study. Certain inbred strains of mice drink a solution of alcohol in preference to water when offered a choice, whereas other strains take only water. Crosses between such lines enable analyses of the genetic architecture to be undertaken.

*(iii) Mutations.* These offer a way of changing the genetic instructions at a single locus. Comparisons are made between normal genotypes and genotypes carrying the mutant gene. If the experimental and control animals are genetically identical except for the mutant gene, and if they are reared in identical environments then any differences will be a consequence of the mutation. The effects of gene mutation can sometimes be highly specific, but more often they are part of a cascade of developmental effects, some of which have consequences for an animal's behaviour. A number of single gene mutations which have behavioural consequences have been identified. In man the best known of these results in a condition called phenylketonuria (PKU). Individuals who carry two abnormal PKU genes are unable to metabolize the amino acid phenylalanine because they congenitally lack the necessary enzyme phenylalanine hydroxylase. Babies carrying two PKU genes are of low intelligence, though the extent of the disability can be reduced by rearing the children on a diet lacking phenylalanine. Mutations can also be used to create animals with various abnormalities of the nervous system which provide another means of examining the relationship between genes, nervous system, and behaviour. By using, genetically, mosaic flies (individuals having male and female tissues where male tissues carry a mutant gene) and a technique called fate mapping, it is possible to locate sites in the nervous system for particular behavioural components.

*(iv) Family pedigree studies.* This approach provides the most direct way of studying the mode of inheritance of a character in man, and tracing the incidence of a trait down a family line provides a means of determining genetic dominance and recessiveness. Colour-blindness is a phenotype which has been studied in this way. (See COLOUR VISION: EYE MECHANISMS.)

*(v) Twin studies.* This is probably the best-known method of studying the genetical basis of behaviour in man. Twins are either identical (monozygotic, MZ) or fraternal (dizygotic, DZ). MZ twins are derived from the splitting of a single fertilized egg, whereas DZ twins derive from the fertilization of two eggs by two sperm. DZ twins are no more genetically alike than ordinary siblings, but since they share a common prenatal environment and usually grow up together they tend to be more alike than siblings born at different times. Differences within MZ pairs arise only from

environmental origins, whereas within-pair differences between DZ pairs are a consequence of genetic and environmental factors. Observations on MZ twins reared apart and hence in dissimilar environments provide information on the differentiating effects of the environment. In general the results of such investigations show that family environments can vary greatly without obscuring the basic similarities between MZ twins, though the importance of genotype varies for different psychological characters.

A very wide range of behavioural and psychological phenotypes are subject to genetic variation. In man, data from investigations of MZ twins, reared together and apart, and from DZ twins shows that the higher the degree of relationship between individuals the higher the correlation of intelligence-test scores. Thus the correlation for DZ twins reared together is 0·53, for MZ twins reared together 0·87, and for MZ twins reared apart 0·75. While this indicates that genetic factors play a major part in determining intelligence, there is also plainly an important environmental component. Studies with adopted children and their adopted and biological parents also provide support for this, since the correlation between children and their biological parents is higher and rises through early childhood. Measured intelligence is thought to be an aggregate of a number of primary mental abilities: verbal, spatial, number, reasoning, word fluency, and *memory. The available evidence indicates that genetic loadings on these vary, with verbal and spatial abilities having high loading, whereas memory has a lower loading. Many sensory and perceptual motor tasks show evidence of a substantial genetic component in man.

Evidence from multifactorial studies of twins indicates that the personality dimensions of *extraversion and introversion are both influenced by polygenic systems. There is also evidence which indicates that many psychiatric conditions have a substantial genetic component. Manic-depressive illness, for example, shows a concordance (agreement) rate of 95·7 per cent in MZ twins and 26·3 per cent in DZ twins. For *schizophrenia, one model has been put forward for a major gene effect, but the case for a polygenic constellation that leads some individuals to be prone to the condition when subjected to too stressful an environment is stronger: thus both genes and environment contribute in a significant way to its manifestation.                          K. J. C.

Abeelen, J. H. F. (1974). *The Genetics of Behaviour.* New York.

Burnet, B. and Connolly, K. J. (1981). Gene action and the analysis of behaviour. *British Medical Bulletin,* **37,** 107–13.

Hay, D. A. (1985). *Essentials of Behaviour Genetics.* Melbourne.

**GENIUS.** The word comes from the Latin *genius,* the male spirit of a household existing, during his lifetime, in the head of the family and subsequently in the divine or spiritual part of each individual; the English word 'genial' has the same root since the spirit was thought to be propitiated by festivities.

The notion that special gifts run in families was explored by the nineteenth-century polymath Sir Francis *Galton in *Hereditary Genius* (1896). Galton was a grandson of Erasmus *Darwin, and a cousin of Charles *Darwin. Extreme ability does run in some families—for example, the Bachs, the Darwins and their relations, including the Wedgwoods, the Huxleys, and the Barlows; and in a few political families, such as the Cecils (William, Lord Burghley, 1520–98; Robert, Earl of Salisbury, c.1563–1612; and successive generations in high positions of government in England until the present day), though this might just be chance. It is of course extremely difficult to distinguish heredity from effects of family tradition and upbringing; yet there does seem some evidence for genetic transmission of special abilities.

The genius of, for example, *Newton (whose ancestry was undistinguished) seems in part to lie in the ability to concentrate on particular problems for very long periods of time. The genius of Mozart seems different, in that his music seemed to pour from him almost without effort, and, compared to Beethoven, with remarkably little correction or rethinking.

Since geniuses are rare and there are very marked differences between each, it is extremely difficult to make generalizations or to explain genius beyond saying that there are wide individual biological differences on almost all dimensions, including such obvious ones as height. An important question is whether genius is a fortunate *combination* of characteristics, or whether there are 'genius genes'.

See also CALCULATING GENIUSES; CREATIVITY.

**GEOMETRY.** Even the earliest history of geometry as a theoretical study of spatial relationships and spatial structures reveals that it had, in addition, a powerful symbolic role in both imaginative and theoretically speculative thought. Thus, although the history of geometry can be told in purely mathematical terms, it is also, from another point of view, a history of forms of representation, of ways of thinking about the world and of views on the nature of thought itself.

We can never recapture the origins of geometry. Certainly there were in ancient cultures, such as those of the Babylonians and Egyptians, systematically codified empirical procedures relating to land measurement, the construction of temples, and astronomical observation which could be regarded as antecedents. But it is only with the Greeks that a sophisticated theoretical and demonstrative geometry of the kind we find in *Euclid's *Elements* emerges. It would be difficult to overestimate the impact of the emergence of geometry as a *deductively organized discipline, one in which it is shown that, for example, the internal angles of a triangle *must* equal two right angles, given the apparently undeniable truth of the kind of propositions which Euclid adopts as *axioms and postulates and the definition of a triangle. Such a demonstration provides knowledge not merely that something happens to be the case, but also an understanding of why it *must* be so, given the nature of the things concerned. Geometry thus provided, and to some extent continues to provide, the paradigm of what it is to have scientific knowledge or understanding, moulding, for example, *Aristotle's discussion in the *Posterior Analytics* of the demonstration of *causes.

But the very feature of geometry which singles it out as providing a conception of the ideal at which all other putative sciences should aim was also, from the outset, the source of philosophical problems concerning the status of geometrical knowledge and its relation to the ever-changing physical world. Many sketches of the history of geometry suggest that the Greeks regarded geometry as a theory of *physical* space and that they thus thought they had found a way of discovering truths about the *physical* world by mere contemplation. But this is to project on to the Greeks a way of thinking about geometry, physical space, and their relation which is a product of the Renaissance and of the new scientific outlook which emerged from it. For while geometry did provide the Greeks and subsequent generations of Western thinkers with their ideal of what it is to have scientific understanding (theoretical knowledge involving demonstrations from accounts of *essence), it is clear that geometry itself was not regarded as yielding a scientific understanding of the ever-changing *physical* world even though it finds application in that world, especially in the applied mathematical disciplines of astronomy, optics, and harmony; geometry deals with a timeless, unchanging world of pure shapes and sizes (forms).

From this point of view the problems raised by geometry concern the relation between forms and items in the physical world, how knowledge of forms is possible, and how this knowledge can be so useful in everyday dealings with the physical world. To the Pythagoreans and to *Plato the example of mathematics suggested that the knowable, intelligible reality must be an unchanging realm behind that of changing appearances. Aristotle, on the other hand, insisted that shapes and sizes have no existence except as aspects of physical, changeable things which are the things which have primary reality. The mathematician then deals with the possible shapes and sizes of physical things but *qua* measurable, not *qua* changeable, whereas the physicist, being primarily concerned with change and its explanation, seeks an understanding of natural objects *qua* changeable. Geometry is the science not just of spatial magnitudes but of all continuous magnitudes which, being represented by lines, can then be handled geometrically. Arithmetic is the science of discrete magnitudes.

Thus, far from taking geometry to be the science of physical space, the Greeks tended to see it as the science of continuous magnitudes, essentially concerned with ratios and proportions and with methods of construction enabling these to be determined. The physical space of the Aristotelian universe is not the infinite, homogeneous space of Euclidean geometry, but is the highly structured bounded set of nested spheres centred on the earth. It was the cumulative effect of a number of diverse factors operating from the beginning of the Renaissance that led, by the eighteenth century, to that identification of physical with geometric space which is most clearly apparent in the works of Isaac *Newton when he talks of absolute space. Perhaps the two most important of these factors were: (i) The co-ordinate development of geometrical theories of perspective and of geometrical optics in the work of Italian artists such as *Leonardo da Vinci, gave geometry a role in accounts of the mechanisms of visual perception. The geometrical treatment of problems of perspective, involving two-dimensional representations of three-dimensional spatial relationships, brings with it (a) a tendency to treat geometry as descriptive of both perceptual and physical space and (b) the development of the methods of projective geometry (needed to handle the various possible projections of three-dimensional solids into two dimensions). In projective geometry there is a shift of emphasis away from figures and their fixed shapes and sizes toward descriptions of the possible types of projections, the behaviour of shapes under such transformations, and a move toward a consideration of the more global, structural properties of spaces. (ii) The adoption of the Copernican, sun-centred view of the universe shattered once and for all the crystalline spheres, leaving the earth spinning through an infinite, homogeneous three-dimensional Euclidean space.

But if geometry is to be a theory of physical space then its axioms must be true of this space, and there is a problem of just how it is that we can come to recognize truths about physical space, the space of the world of experience, as necessary truths. To account for this necessity it would seem that they must be knowable *a priori, but without proof, for they are first principles. But then how can any truths about the world of experience be knowable prior to or independently of experience? There are two problems to be separated here. First there is a psychological problem of how we come by our grasp of spatial relations and spatial concepts and of what exactly we do acquire simply by experience. Secondly there is a philosophical problem which concerns not how we in the first instance come by our beliefs about space but how, if at all, these beliefs can be proved or justified.

So long as geometry was synonymous with Euclidean geometry it was possible to think that we have some innate knowledge, or a faculty of geometric intuition which makes it possible for us to recognize the Euclidean axioms as necessarily and self-evidently true. But Euclid's fifth postulate (which says, in effect, that parallel lines never meet however far they are extended) had never seemed entirely self-evident, and there is a long history of unsuccessful attempts to prove this postulate from the other four. In a work published in 1733, the Italian mathematician Girolamo Saccheri adopted a new strategy which was that of combining the first four of Euclid's postulates with the negation of the fifth, with the aim of deriving a contradiction and thus showing indirectly that the fifth postulate is a logical consequence of the remaining four. Although he thought he had succeeded in doing this, his proofs were faulty, as was shown by Bolyai, Lobachevski, Riemann and others who almost simultaneously demonstrated the existence of non-Euclidean geometries, ones in which the fifth postulate is false. These were shown to be consistent if Euclidean geometry is consistent, by interpreting them as the geometries of curved surfaces of various kinds (e.g. the surface of a sphere). When Einstein made use of non-Euclidean geometries in his theories of Special and General Relativity, treating space–time as a non-Euclidean four-dimensional space, it was no longer possible to regard the Euclidean axioms as self-evident, necessary truths concerning physical reality. This opened up once again questions concerning the nature and status of geometry and its role in physical theories. Some have argued that the choice of geometry is merely a matter of convention; it is just a question of the form of representation we want to use. Others argue that it is an empirical matter, a question of seeking empirically to determine a correct account of physical space.

It is possible, however, to articulate more sophisticated intermediate positions as a result of the work carried out in pursuit of Felix Klein's Erlangen programme (1872). Klein proposed that every geometry can be defined by specifying its group of transformations, and thereby its invariants. This leads to a hierarchy of geometrical theories of increasing generality: metrical geometry, affine geometry, projective geometry, topology (roughly speaking). Given these distinctions it is possible to ask more precise questions about which parts of the full metrical geometry we use could be regarded as factually constrained and which are a matter of convention.            M. E. T.

Boyer, C. B. (1968). *A History of Mathematics*. Chichester.

Koyré, A. (1957). *From the Closed World to the Infinite Universe*. Baltimore.

Lanczos, C. (1970). *Space Through the Ages: the evolution of geometrical ideas from Pythagoras to Hilbert and Einstein*. New York.

Nerlich, G. (1976). *The Shape of Space*. Cambridge.

**GESTALT THEORY** was developed in opposition to the classical theory of psychology best represented by J. S. *Mill and H. von *Helmholtz. In the classical account of *perception, our sensory receptors analyse the energies provided by the physical world into independent, simple, but *unnoticeable* sensations, and the world teaches us to perceive those objects and events that would, under normal conditions, most probably have produced any given set of sensations. Many perceptual phenomena, however, seem at first to defy analysis in terms of such 'atomistic' independent sensations. As an object moves laterally or sagittally in the field of view, its apparent shape and size remain unchanged (i.e. they display perceptual *constancy*) even though its projected image stimulates a changing set of visual receptors; a melody sounds the same although transposed to a new key and therefore to different auditory receptors; and the form depicted by any pattern can be completely changed by changing its context.

The most important example of this last point is the 'figure–ground phenomenon', i.e. that the same outline can be perceived as different alternative figures, with very different shapes. As E. J. *Rubin, a phenomenologist, noted in 1921, the region that is perceived as 'figure' appears to have hard surface, with a recognizable shape and definite boundaries; the 'ground' is usually less surface-like, and without definite boundary, extending indefinitely behind the figure's contour. In Fig. 1a, either the vase (Fig. 1b) or the pair of faces (Fig. 1c) can readily be perceived as figure, with the other possibility then relegated to ground. For a shape to be perceived or recognized, it must be figure. The perception of objects, of depth, and of scenes rests, in each case, on shape perception (for instance, on the shapes that comprise the *depth cues* of linear perspective). Yet the classical theory seemed unable to account for the figure–ground phenomenon and, therefore, for shape perception.

Such phenomena implicate a *Gestalt* (configurational) quality in addition to, or in place of, the individual elements composing the pattern of stimulating energies.

To Gestalt psychologists, notably Max *Wertheimer, Kurt *Koffka, and Wolfgang *Köhler,

a                    b                    c

**Fig. 1.** Figure and ground. The figure perceived in **a** can be either a vase (**b**) or a pair of faces (**c**).

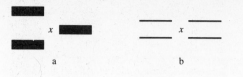

$x$

$x$

$x$

**Fig. 2.** Figural after-effects. **a.** Inspection figure. **b.** Test figure. **c.** Exaggerated sketch of appearance of **b** after staring at point $x$ in **a**.

a

b

c

*form* is the primitive unit of perception, taking its properties from underlying configured brain processes ('fields'). These brain processes were thought to be direct responses to the patterned energies acting on the sensory nervous system. The latter was variously conceived as an electrical network or a colloidal bioelectric medium. Brain fields might be studied indirectly by their effects on perceptual organization, an attempt pursued most concertedly by Köhler and H. Wallach (1944) through the study of the '*figural after-effect'. After staring at the fixation point, $x$, in an 'inspection figure' (Fig. 2a), a 'test figure' (Fig. 2b) appears distorted to subsequent viewing, as exaggerated in Fig. 2c; presumably the latter's contours are 'repelled' from regions previously 'satiated' by the brain fields (direct currents) involved in the perception of the inspection figure.

In point of fact, however, although there is ample evidence of organization in the nervous system (in that nerve fibres are arranged in patterns that constrain their function), there is no evidence for the direct-current, steady-state, whole-figure process models of the Gestalt theories. Indeed, such steady-state brain fields seem inappropriate even as metaphors, because in order to perceive any extended object or scene, the eye must direct the very narrow region of detailed vision (the fovea) at different places, so that different parts of the object are seen in succession by the same part of the eye at a rate of about four discrete glances per second. This basic fact would result in a superimposition of different fragments of the stimulus configuration in rapid succession on any hypothesized brain field. It is hard to see how this process could be represented by the holistic steady-state models of the Gestalt psychologists.

With no viable physiological model, the Gestalt theory consists primarily of the so-called 'laws of organization'. The figure–ground method for studying these 'laws' uses ambiguous patterns of either dots (Fig. 3a) or lines (Figs. 3b, 4c) which can be perceived as forming one shape or another, reversible pictures in which the contour that separates two regions gives only one of them recognizable shape as figure at any moment in time (Figs. 1, 4a, b), or reversible-perspective outline drawings (such as 'wire' cubes) which can be perceived as either flat or three-dimensional objects (Fig. 5). Configuration is varied to discover what factors lead one or another figure–ground organization to predominate.

One such factor is the 'law of good continuation', i.e. we perceive the organization that interrupts the fewest lines (for example, Fig. 3a, b is perceived as a square wave and a sine wave, not as

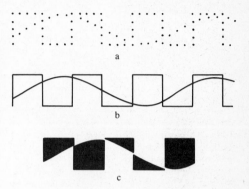

a

b

c

**Fig. 3.** Laws of organization, I.

the set of truncated squares in Fig. 3c). Another is the 'law of enclosedness', i.e. the enclosed region tends to be figure (for example, Fig. 4a is perceived as a set of convex shapes, Fig. 4b as concave ones). It is not merely that we perceive familiar as opposed to unfamiliar shapes: letters and numbers (surely familiar) can be concealed by embedding them in a completely unfamiliar set of squiggles, if the latter provide good continuation, as they do in Fig. 4c but not in Fig. 4e.

Many such 'laws' were proposed. They are potentially of practical importance because they seem to determine whether any shape that is presented (by artist, photographer, cartographer, architect, or computer) will in fact be perceived. They seemed potentially of the greatest theoretical importance, because they were taken to show that we perceive objects and events not by learning to interpret our sensations, but because evolution has provided nervous systems that yield three-dimensional perceptual organizations under appropriate conditions. In Fig. 5a the good continuation of the line i–ii would have to be broken in order to

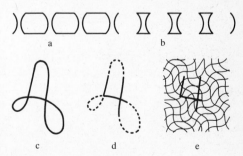

a

b

c

d

e

**Fig. 4.** Laws of organization, II.

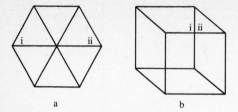

**Fig. 5.** Organization and tridimensionality.

perceive the pattern as a three-dimensional cube; in Fig. 5b, the edge i–ii must be broken to see the figure as flat.

For the most part, unfortunately, these 'laws' remain subjective demonstrations of unknown reliability. They can conflict: in Figs. 3a and 3b good continuation is in conflict with enclosedness. Because their relative strengths are unknown, they cannot be applied predictively. Many of them can, however, be subsumed under a single *minimum principle*, i.e. that we perceive the simplest or most homogeneous organization that will fit the pattern of sensory excitation. Fig. 5a, for example, is simpler (in terms of the number of different lines and angles that have to be specified) as a flat figure than is Fig. 5b, whereas they are equally simple as cubes (cf. Hochberg and Brooks, 1960). This formulation offered a unifying thread to Gestalt theory that the 'laws' themselves did not. Because the Gestalt demonstrations seem visually compelling, as far as they go, and because of their potential importance, various objective and quantitative treatments of the minimum principle continued to be attempted (notably by F. Attneave, J. Hochberg, P. C. Vitz, and E. Leeuwenberg), all of them quite dissociated from the Gestalt theory and its brain fields.

What was new about Gestalt theory is almost surely not true: aside from the speculations about brain fields, the main Gestalt notion was that the whole of any perceptual organization determines the appearance of its parts. Although the limits of this principle were never fully spelt out, both the individual laws of organization and the minimum principle were clearly intended to be applied to an entire figure. Thus, whether any intersection in a

reversible-perspective figure looks like a flat pattern or like a solid corner in space is presumably a function of the whole configuration. Such anti-elementarism surely goes too far. This point is *suggested* by the 'impossible pictures' devised by Penrose and Penrose in 1958, in which inconsistently oriented parts of objects combine in a single picture that is physically impossible as a three-dimensional organization yet nevertheless looks three-dimensional. Fig. 6a is such a picture. The same point is *proven* by making a single intersection in the cube irreversible, and observing that the other intersection continues to reverse spontaneously (Hochberg, 1978). Overall simplicity simply will not serve as even a vague and unquantitative explanatory principle.

What is true about Gestalt theory was not new. Not only were the Gestalt 'laws' never systematized or quantified: they were never explained by Gestalt theory, nor were the perceptual constancies, nor was the figure–ground phenomenon itself. In fact, the figure–ground phenomenon is most plausibly explained within the Helmholtzian framework, i.e. that we fit our perceptual expectations about objects and their edges to the relatively unusual situation of viewing lines on paper. If an outline is taken as an object's edge, even slight changes in viewpoint (such as head movements) from 2 to 1 in Fig. 7a would be expected to cause parts of the further surface (such as point i) to disappear behind the nearer surface; so that the definite shape of figure and the indefinite shape of ground, described in connection with Fig. 1, are characteristic of the expectations associated with the edges of objects. In this view, as

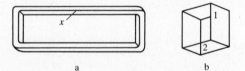

**Fig. 6.** Relative independence of wholes and parts. Object **a** looks three-dimensional even though the corners are inconsistently oriented and connected by an unbroken line (*x*). In cube **b**, the orientation is fixed at intersection 1, but perceived orientation reversals occur spontaneously at intersection 2 when the gaze is kept directed there.

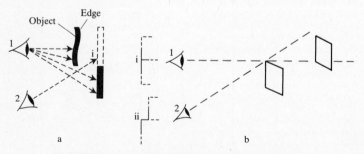

**Fig. 7.** Objects' edges, figural properties, and 'good continuation'.

Brunswik implied in 1956, the 'laws of organization' are merely assumptions about what parts of the visual field are most likely to belong to what object, under normal conditions. For example, because it is very unlikely that the viewer would be standing at that one precise point in space (point 1 in Fig. 7b) from which the edges of objects at different distances would be aligned (i) rather than offset (ii), the 'law of good continuation' simply reflects the probability that aligned edges belong to the same object.

The classical theory—that we perceive whatever most probably would produce the stimulation we receive, and that psychological structure therefore generally reflects physical structure—not only still accounts best for the perceptual constancies and illusions (Gregory, 1974) but it may account as well for Gestalt organization. The fact that we perceive impossible figures as three-dimensional, however, and that figures which are made non-reversible at one corner are free to reverse elsewhere (Figs. 6a and 6b respectively) surely does not reflect the constraints of physical structure, and therefore is not accounted for by Helmholtzian principles without more specific amendments and extensions than have yet been undertaken.     J. H.

Attneave, F. (1954). Some informational aspects of visual perception. *Psychological Review*, **61**, 183–93.

Brunswik, E. (1956). *Perception and the Representative Design of Psychological Experiments*. Berkeley.

Ellis, W. D. (ed.) (1938). *Source Book of Gestalt Psychology*. London.

Gregory, R. L. (1970). *The Intelligent Eye*. London.

Gregory, R. L. (1974). Choosing a paradigm for perception. In Carterette, E. C. and Friedman, M. P. (eds.), *Handbook of Perception*, vol. I. New York.

Hochberg, J. (1974). Organization and the Gestalt tradition. In Carterette, E. C. and Friedman, M. P. (eds.), *Handbook of Perception*, vol. I. New York.

Hochberg, J. (1978). *Perception*, 2nd edn. Englewood Cliffs, New Jersey.

Hochberg, J. and Brooks, V. (1960). The psychophysics of form: reversible-perspective drawings of spatial objects. *American Journal of Psychology*, **73**, 337–54.

Koffka, K. (1935). *Principles of Gestalt Psychology*. New York.

Köhler, W. (1929). *Gestalt Psychology*. New York.

**GESTALT THERAPY** is a non-interpretative psychotherapy which emphasizes awareness and personal responsibility and adopts a holistic approach, giving equal emphasis to mind and body. It began to achieve prominence towards the end of the 1960s. It is now one of the leading psychotherapies in the United States and is developing strongly in the United Kingdom. It is one of the several alternative therapies that comprise the Humanistic Psychologies of the Human Potential movement. Existing more as a style of practice than as a theoretical framework, its ideas are drawn from many sources, the precise boundary between Gestalt therapy and its neighbours is not always clear, and many practitioners use it in conjunction with other approaches.

*Gestalt* is a German word taken from the psychology of perception. A Gestalt is a figure or pattern which can be distinguished against the background or field of perception (see GESTALT THEORY). But the term has a wider meaning than the nearest English equivalents, 'shape' and 'form', and carries stronger connotations of significance and meaning. Moreover, its use extends over the whole range of perception: shapes and tunes are *Gestalten*, and so are certain aesthetic and causal phenomena. The term applies whenever a significant pattern or construct (the 'figure') emerges against the background scene or noise (the 'ground').

Fritz Perls (1893–1970), the German-born psychoanalyst, was one of the main founders of Gestalt therapy. His inspiration was to give the concept relevance to psychotherapy and use it as a hook on which to hang a number of therapeutic concerns. He saw the task of psychotherapy as one of enhancing the figure–ground differentiation of those Gestalten which reflect the patient's needs. The needs of a healthy person organize the field of experience into well-differentiated Gestalten which command the appropriate response. So, for example, a fluid-depleted person experiences the complex of perceptions which emerge into awareness as the Gestalt of thirst, and he gets himself a drink. An affronted person who is aware of his anger has a choice of responses; a person who is unaware or incompletely aware, on the other hand, may repress his anger and get a headache instead. The neurotic is continually interfering with the process of Gestalt formation. He is unable to deal effectively with certain needs because he interrupts and avoids the formation of the relevant Gestalten.

Much of Gestalt therapy is a training in awareness, in improving the individual's contact with himself and his environment. A commonly used exercise is to produce a series of observations, starting with 'Now I am aware that . . .'. Other exercises direct attention to specific experiences, and a distinction is drawn between observation and inference. 'I observe that you are smiling. I infer that you are happy.' Perls described Gestalt therapy as the psychology of the obvious, and he trained people to use what was immediately available by asking such basic questions as 'What are you feeling now?', 'What are you doing?' An important strategy is to increase the immediacy and completeness of any material used in therapy by bringing it into the here-and-now. This means that the patient describes his *dreams, *memories, and preoccupations in the present tense and, where possible, enacts them. 'Shuttling' is another method of increasing figure–ground differentiation. The subject moves his attention between different focuses. For example, if he shows confluence—i.e. lack of differentiation—between an emotion such as resentment and an associated symptom such as a headache, he might be asked to shuttle between his pain and his awareness of resentment.

A feature of Gestalt therapy is its ability to

incorporate and use complex ideas which were quite remote from experience in their original form. For instance, Perls took the psychoanalytic concept of repetition-compulsion and used it as 'unfinished business'. 'The patient feels compelled to repeat in daily life everything he cannot bring to a satisfactory conclusion.' In therapy, he is enabled to bring his unfinished business into awareness by acting out the meaning of selected aspects of his behaviour. The therapist may try to facilitate this, for example by getting him to repeat some characteristic behaviour, such as a gesture or statement, again and again until another level of meaning emerges.

Gestalt therapy explores the areas of conflict and confusion which result from failure to integrate aspects of the personality. 'Splits' occur when such aspects are in permanent and insoluble conflict. The attributes of a split-off part may be projected on to other people or the environment; or, in retroflection, one aspect of the personality influences another—in depression, for instance, resentment against others is often retroflected against the self. In therapy, these elements are repeatedly expressed and enacted. They become transformed into an expression of self, i.e. the patient becomes aware of, and able to identify with, the component in these experiences which belongs to him. For example, someone who complains that everyone pushes him around may be asked to reverse the statement to 'I push everyone around', and may be invited to go round the group enacting this verbally and physically. 'Re-owning projections' is a major theme in Gestalt therapy.

Clarifying the splits and polarities within the personality is another important area, and for this Perls used one of the most famous of Gestalt props, an empty chair. The subject may put feelings or a fantasy or a part of himself into the empty chair and begin a dialogue; in due course he moves into the empty chair and speaks as the other partner in the dialogue. It is a technique that illustrates a characteristic feature of much Gestalt work, which is to dramatize problems, thereby externalizing them and making them more accessible to the client.

In childhood, failure to cope effectively with certain kinds of experience may leave areas of impaired functioning which can be thought of as 'holes' in the personality. The child develops various strategies to avoid being overwhelmed by the distressing feelings associated with them—strategies that involve the ego defence mechanisms described by Anna *Freud. The child also learns, and becomes identified with, roles designed to manipulate other people into providing the support which he cannot generate from his own resources. So the goal of therapy is to enable people to stop their neurotic avoidance and to become fully self-supporting, in order that growth can take place. When the therapist succeeds in frustrating his client's defences and manipulations, the 'impasse point' is reached where the 'hole' in the personality is no longer protected and ordinary functioning breaks down. Movement in any direction seems impossible, and the subject may experience confusion and distress. Paradoxically this state, in which the feeling of being overwhelmed is again experienced, is also seen as 'the fertile void', offering the possibility of new growth through re-experiencing the old failure from an adult perspective.

According to one of its leading exponents, Irma Lee Shepherd, Gestalt is at its most effective with 'overly socialized, restrained, constricted individuals'; and she points out the dangers involved when inexperienced therapists use the powerfully confronting techniques of Gestalt to 'open up' unstable people with vulnerable personalities. Such people need time, support, and long-term commitment from their therapists. This warning is necessary because much of the public image of Gestalt therapy derives from Perls's dramatic performances, many of which were filmed and videotaped. His clients must have been fairly tough and self-secure to risk public exposure at the hands of a charismatic figure with an almost magical ability to penetrate defences.

Perls dominated Gestalt therapy during his lifetime. His years of experience and training and his extraordinary skill as a therapist made the work look deceptively easy; and it is this that was probably responsible for the overselling of both the theory and his particular model of its application to people lacking in experience. His mistrust of authority matched the anti-authoritarian spirit prevailing in the 1960s. Thus Gestalt therapy has a great deal to say about the harmful effects of the super-ego but says little about the positive value of discipline, and there is little emphasis on the steady, unremitting work between sessions that must be maintained by patients wishing to make significant changes in their lives. The Gestalt view—which is that of humanistic psychology in general—is that the organism has an innate tendency towards health and wholeness and the full expression of its potential, but in Perls's work there is more emphasis on removing obstacles to growth than there is on working to acquire and strengthen desirable traits.

There are other features of Gestalt therapy which are helpful and productive in moderation but unfortunately lend themselves to exaggeration and abuse. Intellectualization is rightly castigated as a major neurotic defence, but in the therapeutic process the intellect may be undervalued as a potential ally. In therapy, a challenging emphasis on personal responsibility can be a powerful antidote to feelings of futility and helplessness—but self-centredness and neglect of social realities may also be encouraged, together with insensitivity towards dependency needs in others. Emphasis on immediate experience, the here-and-now, can produce great therapeutic leverage—but it may lead to the discounting of historical perspective and to side-stepping round the issue of the unconscious in the developmental process.

Gestalt therapy with its characteristics of directness and flexibility developed at a time when there was widespread dissatisfaction with the available psychotherapies. Perls had the therapeutic skills and the charisma needed to sell the exciting new model, and he did so with courage and integrity. To him and his associates must go a lot of the credit for liberating psychotherapeutic practice from the dead weight of psychoanalytic technique. Gestalt therapy suggested new possibilities for the relationship between client, therapist, and symptoms. Traditional psychiatry and psychoanalysis take the patient's experiences and reinterpret them in terms of a system which remains the more or less exclusive property of the therapist. The patient's experiences become symptoms and instruments of diagnosis, something that only professionals can understand, and the process can increase his passivity and his sense of alienation from his inner experience. In this respect Gestalt therapy is radically different. The client works actively with his experiences under the therapist's guidance and there is a continual reference to what he is experiencing; therapist intervention is designed to clarify rather than interpret.

Research into psychotherapy has not yet reached a point where useful comparisons can be made between the effectiveness of different schools. It is therefore not possible to answer the question 'How effective is Gestalt therapy?' Even so, there are several indications of the worth of the Gestalt approach. (i) It has survived and expanded over a period which has seen the emergence, stasis, and collapse of many other therapies. (ii) It has survived the death of its charismatic founder. (iii) Most important, it is widely acceptable to many therapists, who apparently find Gestalt ideas valid and useful in their work.                    F. G. R.

Dusen, W. van (1975). Wu Wei, No-Mind and the Fertile Void. In Stevens, J. O. (ed.), *gestalt is*. Moab, Utah.
Passons, W. R. (1975). *Gestalt Approaches In Counselling*. New York.
Perls, F. S. (1947). *Ego, Hunger and Aggression*. New York.
Perls, F. S. (1969). *In and Out the Garbage Pail*. Lafayette, California.
Perls, F. S. (1969). *Gestalt Therapy Verbation*. Lafayette, California.
Perls, F. S. (1973). *The Gestalt Approach and Eye Witness to Therapy*. Palo Alto, California.
Shepherd, I. L. (1970). Limitations and caution in the Gestalt approach. In Fagan, J. and Shepherd, I. L. (eds.), *Gestalt Therapy Now*. New York.
Simkin, J. S. (1979). Gestalt Therapy. In Corsini, R. J. (ed.), *Current Psychotherapies*. Illinois.

**GESTURES** are movements of the body that signal intentions, commands, or comments—or suggestions, which may be rude or crude. Human gestures form a rich *body language. Some are innate, and probably derive from purely functional movements, such as picking something up, turning the head to look in a different direction, or hitting something hard. No doubt these functional movements were read by other members in a social group as indicating states and needs, and then they became developed as more or less conventional signs for conveying emotional states, intentions, commands, and so on. Although there is a genetic basis, the role of learning is clear because some gestures are specific to geographical regions, or to particular groups or families. People moving into a new area or marrying into a family will pick up some of their characteristic gestures.

The biological basis of gesture was pointed out in Charles *Darwin's masterpiece, *The Expression of the Emotions in Man and Animals* (1872), which suggests that many symbolic gestures are derived from functional behaviour. Their development may sometimes be traced through the use of individual or groups of muscles for purposes which changed in the evolution of species.

It is remarkable that artists, and especially cartoonists, can convey so much by recording a gesture even with just a few lines. It follows that gestures can be signalled and read from small changes of position of the limbs or body; some gestures may be recognized even at night or with the corner of the eye. Evidently we are well attuned in reading and responding to human gestures, which sometimes indicate vitally important intentions, sometimes a state of hope or fear, and sometimes doubt or confidence in those around us. It is necessary that it should be so, for the well-being and survival of any group.

Human gestures have been described and classified in considerable detail; for various regions, social classes and occupations, especially by Desmond Morris (1977, 1979). The range of social gestures is vast: 'the nose thumb', 'the eyelid pull', the vertical and horizontal 'horn sign', the 'palmback V-sign' and many more. It has also been shown how some of them have spread geographically, sometimes over several centuries.

Darwin, C. (1872). *Expressions of the Emotions in Man and Animals*. London.
Morris, D. (1977). *Manwatching: a field guide to human behaviour*. London.
Morris, D., Collett, P., Marsh, P., and O'Shaughnessy, M. (1979). *Gestures*. London.

**GHAZZALI,** AL- (1058–1111), Islamic theologian and scholastic philosopher. See AL-GHAZZALI.

**GHOST.** A manifestation of a dead person in human form, usually partially transparent and sometimes speaking (like Banquo's ghost in *Macbeth*). Ghosts, of various guises, are believed in to some degree in all societies.

Evidence from photography is dubious (if only because double exposures look remarkably as ghosts are supposed to appear), and there are plenty of possible explanations in terms of visual illusions. For example, *after-images of, say, candle flames or keyholes will appear very much larger when the gaze is transferred to a distant wall (see EMMERT'S LAW). There is a tendency to 'see' faces and human forms in even quite random shapes (such as 'faces in the fire') which, indeed, is a very great help to artists, and especially cartoonists, who can represent the human face complete with expression with a very few lines. It is possible that perceptual creations of this kind are occasionally elicited in states of *fear, and there do seem to be social factors determining to some degree the forms that ghosts take. There are, of course, less sceptical views; but lack of consistent evidence prevents general acceptance of ghosts.

Myers, F. W. H. (1903). *Human Personality and its Survival after Bodily Death*. London.

**GIBSON,** JAMES JEROME (1904–79). A distinguished American experimental psychologist, whose work on visual perception was and remains unusually influential. Following an appointment at Smith College, Northampton, Massachusetts, where as a young professor he was considerably influenced by Kurt *Koffka, who had recently emigrated from Germany, Gibson for many years ran a major department at Cornell University. His life-work was investigating visual perception of form and motion; his early work including the discovery that distorting lenses produce negative (reversed) adaptation to curvature even with free eye-movements. But his main work was to challenge the approach of *Helmholtz and suggest a very different account of perception.

Gibson first of all moved away from the traditional experiments with pictures, and what is seen with a single static eye, towards the observer moving around freely and viewing moving objects in natural conditions. He was led to this by considering pilots landing on fields, where the 'flow lines' of motion are important for seeing the landing-point and estimating height and speed. From such considerations of 'visual flow', and texture gradients, he developed what he called 'Ecological Optics'. This almost ignored retinal images, and active brain processes, in favour of regarding perception as 'picking up information from the ambient array of light'. This is very different from the Helmholtzian notion of perceptions as Unconscious Inferences from sensory data and knowledge of objects. Gibson tried to explain object perception by supposing that some 'higher order' features are invariant with motion and rotation and are 'picked up' with no perceptual computing or processing being required. His search for such invariances, and for just what the visual system uses under various conditions (though this was not Gibson's intention) has proved useful for developing computer vision. His general philosophy, however, that perception is passive pick up of information, present in the world, is hard for Helmholtzians to follow. His important books are: *The Perception of the Visual World* (1950), and *The Senses Considered as Perceptual Systems* (1966). Much of his work was done with his wife, Eleanor, a distinguished developmental psychologist.

**GNOSTIC.** Relating to knowledge, from the Greek *gnosis* (knowledge or investigation), which is also the root for 'cognitive' and 'cognition'. Gnosticism in general is a variety of religious belief, assuming privileged knowledge of the spiritual world—knowledge considered superior to the science of the day—and bringing with it the promise of salvation. It has taken many forms, having its origins in a variety of pagan sources, including Greek philosophy, Hellenistic mystery cults, and Babylonian and Egyptian mythology, and persisting into modern times in movements such as theosophy.

The best-known adherents are the Christian Gnostics, active during the second century AD. They appeared first as schools of thought within the Church, eventually mostly becoming separate sects; indeed much of early Church doctrine was formulated to counteract their heresies. The various groups widely differed in their teachings and practices but in common made a distinction between a remote and unknowable Divine Being and an inferior deity (the Demiurge) who was the immediate source of creation which was necessarily imperfect since he was held to be antagonistic to the truly spiritual. Some men, however, were thought to contain a divine spark and, through gnosis and the (often secret) rites associated with it, this spiritual element could be rescued from its evil material environment. Gnosis came from the Divine Being through the medium of Christ bringing redemption.

**GOALS IN LEARNING.** A technical term in *learning theories and experiments in animal learning. Goals are set up by rewards (usually food) to establish learning through consistent (goal-directed) performance. In 'latent learning' (especially associated with the American psychologist Karl *Lashley) animals are allowed to explore mazes before goals are set up. It is then found, when food is provided at a particular place, that the goal is reached with fewer trials than for a control group which has not had previous access to the maze. It follows that learning can occur without goal-seeking (or drive reduction), but it is difficult to establish or measure this since specific goals for scoring the successes and failures of performance cannot be used. For further discussion, see PURPOSE.

**GÖDEL,** KURT (1906–78). A mathematical logician, born in Czechoslovakia, who emigrated to the United States and held a position at the Princeton Institute for Advanced Study from 1940 until retirement. In the 1930s he proved three major theorems. The first of these, presented in his doctoral dissertation to the University of Vienna in 1930, was a proof of the completeness of first order predicate calculus. The second, published in 1931, was a proof of the incompleteness of formal systems of arithmetic, and the third, presented in lectures given during 1938–9, was a proof of the consistency of the continuum hypothesis with the basic axioms of set theory. Each of these results had a profound influence on all subsequent work in the fields of formal logic, number theory, and set theory. But it is the second result which has had the greatest impact outside mathematical circles. This is often known simply as Gödel's theorem (more precisely his first incompleteness theorem) and states that, given any formal system $S$ capable of expressing arithmetic, if $S$ is consistent then there exists a proposition $A$ of arithmetic which is not formally decidable within $S$, i.e. neither $A$ nor its negation is provable in $S$.

There are two aspects of this result which mean that its implications extend well beyond the domain of pure mathematical logic. (i) The theorem concerns formal systems capable of expressing arithmetic, but the notion of a formal (logical) system is closely associated with the idea of reducing reasoning to a mechanical, computational process. In preparing the ground for the actual proof of his theorem, Gödel did much to clarify the relation between a formal logical system and the notion of a recursive, and hence effectively computable, function. He showed, loosely speaking, that the functions representable in a formal system of arithmetic coincide with the recursively definable functions. This means that his result applies to all computer implementations of arithmetical reasoning based on recursive processes. Thus each such system will be incomplete in the sense that there will be sentences on which it can produce no decision. (ii) The proof works by providing a numerical coding (gödel-numbering) of formulae and sequences of formulae of the formal language which, since the sentences of the formal system were intended to be interpreted as statements about numbers, means that the system can also be interpreted as talking about its own formulae. This makes it possible to show that there must, for any such system $S$, be a sentence $P$ of $S$ which can be interpreted as saying '$P$ is not provable' or, more loosely, 'I am not provable'. It is then shown that if $S$ is consistent, neither $P$ nor its negation can be provable in $S$. Thus, it is frequently argued, since $P$ says '$P$ is not provable', $P$ must be true. On the basis of this last step it has then been claimed that Gödel's theorem shows that the human capacity to recognize arithmetic truths can never be fully captured in a formal system and hence, in view of (i), that men are superior to machines in that given any machine there will be an arithmetical proposition which men can prove but which the machine cannot. But this argument overlooks the fact that the proof of Gödel's theorem only allows one to conclude that *if $S$ is consistent*, neither $P$ nor its negation is provable in $S$. To go on to conclude that $P$ is not provable, and hence is true, requires that one show $S$ to be consistent. Because the proof methods Gödel used are, via gödel-numbering, themselves formalizable in $S$, one can argue that one machine $T$ *could* prove of another machine, or even of itself, that *if* it is consistent there exists a sentence which it cannot

decide. What a machine cannot do is prove its own consistency. To this extent the proof of Gödel's theorem does not of itself establish the superiority of minds over machines, but it shows that the issue here must be pushed back to the kinds of ground we have, or could have, for believing either a system of arithmetic or ourselves to be consistent.

M. E. T.

Gödel, K. (1962). *On Formally Undecidable Propositions*. New York.

Hofstadter, D. R. (1979). *Gödel, Escher, Bach*. Hassock.

Lucas, J. R. (1961). Minds, Machines and Gödel. *Philosophy*, **XXXVI**.

**GOETHE,** JOHANN WOLFGANG VON (1749–1832). Germany's most distinguished poet and a scientist, Goethe was born in Frankfurt-am-Main. He made discoveries in comparative anatomy, especially on the skull, and in botany showing that leaves are the characteristic form of which all other parts of plants are variations. He vigorously attacked Newton's theory of light and colour, and although here he was incorrect he did point out important colour contrast effects—'Goethe's shadows'. These are shadows cast by coloured lights, and they appear the complementary colour of the light. This is a starting-point of Edwin Land's *retinex theory of colour vision.

Goethe is best known for his *Faust* (Part 1, 1808, Part 2, 1832). It is based on the medieval legend of a man who sells his soul to the Devil. This became linked with the name and adventures of a sixteenth-century conjuror, Johann Faust. According to Goethe, Faust sold his soul to the Devil in exchange for superhuman powers of intellect and wisdom; and the Devil finally failed to claim his part of the bargain—Faust's soul. This story greatly affected *Freud in his early years, and it has passed into psychoanalytical folklore.

Matthaei, R. (ed.) (1971). *Goethe's Colour Theory*. London.

**GOLDSTEIN,** KURT (1878–1965). German physician and psychiatrist, who was born at Kattowitz, Upper Silesia, of Jewish origins and educated at Breslau and Heidelberg. His interest in *aphasia was kindled by Carl *Wernicke and, like Wernicke, he considered himself a psychiatrist rather than a neurologist. His knowledge of neuropathology he acquired at the feet of Ludwig Edinger (1855–1918).

On the outbreak of the First World War, Goldstein joined the staff of an institute concerned with research on the after-effects of brain injuries. Here he worked with Adhémar Gelb, a psychologist with strong *Gestalt leanings which Goldstein largely shared. Their collaboration was highly fertile and resulted in the issue of sixteen papers published under the general title of *Psychologische Analyse Hirnpathologischer Fälle*. Among these was a remarkable case of visual agnosia ('mind blindness') which was attributed by the authors to a failure to experience compactly organized visual impressions, i.e. a breakdown in Gestalt formation with partial compensation by 'tracing' movements with the head or hand. (It has since been objected, however, that this case may well have been in part psychogenic.)

In 1934, Goldstein published an important book expounding his mature views on the relations between general and localized brain functions and indeed the whole question of selective as opposed to global representation of psychological functions. An English translation of the book was published in 1939 as *The Organism: a holistic approach to biology*.

Goldstein delivered the William James lectures at Harvard in 1938–9, published in 1940 as *Human Nature in the Light of Psychopathology*. His short book on *The After-Effects of Brain Injuries in War: their evaluation and treatment* (1944) was found exceptionally helpful by many concerned with the assessment and rehabilitation of those who had sustained war wounds of the brain in the Second World War.                                    O. L. Z.

**GOLGI,** CAMILLO (1843–1926). Born at Corteno, Lombardy, he became professor of pathology at Pavia. In 1873 he described his method of using chromate of silver to impregnate neural tissue, so that a proportion of neurones show up in high contrast, enabling microscopic examination. Golgi used this method on normal and pathological material. The method was developed by Santiago *Ramon y Cajal (1852–1934) to study the fine structure of the brain. The two men were awarded the Nobel prize jointly in 1926. See NEUROANATOMICAL TECHNIQUES.

**GREEK INVESTIGATIONS OF THE MIND AND SENSES.** At what stage did the ancient Greek thinkers begin to realize the possibilities of carrying out empirical investigations in connection with their psychological theories, and at what stage did they actually do so?

Most of the terms used in Homer to refer to the seats of cognitive and emotional activity have strong concrete associations. Thus one of the words for a part of the body with which men think and feel is *phrenes*. Although this later came to be used of the diaphragm, it originally signified the lungs, as we can tell from a passage in the *Iliad* (xvi, 504) where, when a spear is withdrawn from a dead warrior's chest, his *phrenes* are described as prolapsing. But if we try to reconstruct in detail what was believed about the physical events corresponding to thoughts and feelings—about, for example, the movements of the blood and the breath and the changes taking place in parts of the body—much of the picture remains vague and unclear.

It has often been maintained that the first thinker who can be claimed to have undertaken dissections in connection with a theory of sensation is the pre-Socratic natural philosopher Alcmaeon (whose precise dates cannot be fixed but who appears to have been active some time around the middle of the fifth century BC). But that claim is probably unfounded. The chief evidence cited to support it is a reference to an investigation of the eye in the commentary on *Plato's *Timaeus* written by Calcidius in the fourth century AD. But even if—as Calcidius may suggest—Alcmaeon used the knife in this connection, it was almost certainly not to carry out a dissection of the eye, let alone to cut open the skull to study the structures communicating with the eye within the skull itself, but merely to excise the eyeball to show that the back of the eye is linked to the brain.

The admittedly very meagre fragments of other natural philosophers of the fifth and early fourth centuries BC (see PRE-SOCRATIC PHILOSOPHERS) show that they were interested in such questions as the constitution or substance of the soul (where we find such suggestions as that it consists of water or air or fire, or of all the elements or of atoms of a particular shape), in the seat of life and *consciousness (the heart and the brain were the favourite candidates), in whether sensation is by like apprehending like or by unlikes, and, sometimes, in the workings of the individual senses. They frequently cite analogies with objects outside the body to illustrate or suggest theories about its internal functioning, and some philosophers (Empedocles and Democritus especially) had some idea of the complexity of the structure of the eye, for instance. But our sources fail to yield clear and definite evidence that any of the natural philosophers employed dissection.

The possibility of opening the bodies of animals for investigative purposes is, however, occasionally mentioned in isolated texts from the fifth century. Herodotus (iv, 58) remarks that the fact that the grass in Scythia is exceptionally bilious may be judged by opening the bodies of cattle who have fed on it. Similarly the author of the Hippocratic treatise *On the Sacred Disease* (ch. 11) claims that his view that the sacred disease is due to the flooding of the brain with phlegm can be confirmed by inspecting the brains of goats who have suffered from the disease.

These texts establish that the idea of postmortem animal dissection had begun to be mooted long before *Aristotle. Yet the occasions when this possibility was suggested were restricted, and the dissections that were actually carried out were cursory and confined to a narrow range of questions. Our chief evidence for this negative conclusion comes from the Hippocratic corpus, a collection of some seventy medical treatises dating mostly from the fifth and early fourth centuries BC. With the exception of one much later treatise (*On the Heart*, now generally thought to belong to the third century BC), these works mostly ignore the method entirely. Their anatomical and physiological theories, when not purely speculative or traditional, were based on the evidence obtainable from the observation of lesions, or on what their authors discovered in surgical operations, or on what they believed could be inferred from such clinical practices as venesection.

Passages in Aristotle indicate, however, that some dissections had been undertaken by his predecessors, although the contexts in which they did so were limited (they included, especially, the investigation of the courses of the blood vessels), and although even in those contexts the method was still far from being generally accepted or employed. We have, in fact, to wait until Aristotle himself for good evidence of more than merely occasional use of dissection. His zoological treatises refer frequently to the method, and sometimes do so in sufficient circumstantial detail to make it clear that what is reported is, in part at least, the result of first-hand observation.

It may, therefore, reasonably be claimed that Aristotle and his associates were the first to begin to exploit the possibilities of animal (though not of human) dissection for the purposes of research—with beneficial results in many areas of anatomy especially. The extent to which he did so in connection with his complex and intricate doctrines concerning the soul and the activities 'common to soul and body' is, however, problematic. His view that the heart is the seat of life is supported by what he claims to have observed in embryos, notably in his comparatively detailed researches on the growth of the embryo chick, namely that the heart is the first part to develop and become distinct. On the other hand on many topics in psychology his discussion is, in parts, quite imprecise. Thus, although he claims (for example in *De Juventute*, 469 a 12 ff.) that the senses of touch and taste 'clearly' extend to the heart, he makes no attempt to identify and trace the connections. The various descriptions of the anatomy of the pores or channels leading off from the back of the eye to the brain are vague, and are evidently based in part on inferences from lesions. His account of the movement of substances between the brain and the heart (on which depends his explanation of the mechanisms of sleeping and waking) is also largely unclear, as also is his description of the structure of the brain. His anatomical and some of his physiological theories are supported by much more systematic empirical research than those of his predecessors had been. Yet in the particular context of psychology, where the starting-point of many of his speculations lies in certain traditional ideas and problems, it is often the case that his empirical investigations are not pursued beyond the point where he has satisfied himself that he has cited *some* evidence in favour of his own doctrine, or *some* to undermine those of his opponents.

The limitations of Aristotle's work in this area are evident when we compare it with what we know of that of the major Alexandrian biologists of the third century BC, Herophilus and Erasistratus. Although the evidence that they dissected—and indeed vivisected—humans as well as animals has often been doubted, there is no good reason to reject it. The results they obtained, in so far as these can be judged from the reports in Rufus and *Galen especially, were, in any event, impressive. They were responsible for the first detailed accounts of the structure of the brain (including its ventricles) and of the heart (including its valves); and they distinguished four main membranes in the eye, corresponding to (i) the cornea and sclera, (ii) the choroid, (iii) the retina, and (iv) the capsular sheath of the lens. Most importantly, from the point of view of psychology, they discovered the nervous system. Whereas earlier theorists had spoken vaguely of channels or pores as the routes by which sensation and movement were transmitted, and the term *neuron* itself had been applied indiscriminately to what we should call sinews and tendons as well as to the nerves, Herophilus and Erasistratus identified the nerves as such and began to classify them, distinguishing, for example, between the sensory and the motor nerves.

By the second century AD, as we learn from Rufus and Galen, human dissection had almost entirely ceased, and even the value of animal dissection was contested by different medical schools. Nevertheless, that did not stop Galen himself from engaging in extensive animal dissections and vivisections in connection with his physiological and psychological doctrines. Disclaiming any definite theory concerning the substance of the soul, he concentrated his efforts on an account of its faculties, and his work on the nervous system, particularly, goes appreciably beyond that of Herophilus and Erasistratus. Apart from many specific discoveries (such as that of the recurrent laryngeal nerves), he undertook a masterly series of investigations of the nerves of the spinal column. In *On Anatomical Procedures* (book ix, chs. 13 f.) he reports the results of systematic animal vivisections, where he made incisions either right through the spinal cord or through one side of it beginning with the vertebra next to the sacrum and working his way up the spinal column in order to reveal the effect that incision at each level had on the animal's faculties—the gradually increasing loss of movement, sensation, respiration, and voice. Although many of his own physiological theories, such as the doctrine of the various kinds of breath or *pneuma*, are highly speculative, these sustained investigations of the nervous system are the supreme example from the ancient world of the application of empirical methods to the understanding of vital functions. Although many of the disputes on the nature of the soul were not susceptible to resolution by such methods, from the Hellenistic period Greek theorists had available quite detailed information concerning many aspects of the functioning of the nervous system.            G. E. R. L.

Hippocrates, *On the Sacred Disease* and *On the Heart*, in Lloyd, G. E. R. (ed.) (1978), *Hippocratic Writings*.

Aristotle's psychological and zoological treatises are in Ross, W. D. (ed.) (1910–31), *The Works of Aristotle translated into English*, vols. iii, iv, v.

There are no adequate collections and translations of Herophilus and Erasistratus, but Celsus, *On Medicine*,

Spencer, W. G. (ed.), 3 vols. (1935–8), and the works of Galen provide much of our most important information. Three of the most important treatises of Galen are: *On Anatomical Procedures*, trans. C. Singer (1956), together with *Galen, On Anatomical Procedures, The Later Books*, trans. W. L. H. Duckworth and ed. M. C. Lyons and B. Towers (1962); *On the Natural Faculties*, ed. A. J. Brock (1916); and *On the Usefulness of the Parts of the Body*, trans. M. T. May, 2 vols. (1968).

**GRIEF.** See BEREAVEMENT.

**GUNTRIP,** HARRY. See FREUDIANISM: LATER DEVELOPMENTS.

# H

**HABITUATION** (ADAPTATION). In general, an aspect of learning, whereby an animal becomes accustomed to a situation that persists. In a narrower sense, habituation is the gradual loss of a *reflex behaviour by repetition of a stimulus without reinforcement—for example, continual tapping on the shell of a snail; after a few taps, it ceases to emerge from its shell. Habituation, or adaptation, allows animals to disregard irrelevant stimuli. (If the snail came out every time its shell got tapped, it would get worn out!) Some reflexes are highly resistant to habituation—such as blinking at loud sounds, or at air blown on the eye. This may be because these reflexes are particularly necessary to the survival of the organism, disregard of the stimuli being highly dangerous. See also INVERTEBRATE LEARNING AND INTELLIGENCE.

Hilgard, E. R. and Marquis, D. G. (1940). *Conditioning and Learning*. New York.
Humphrey, G. (1933). *The Nature of Learning in its Relation to the Living System*. New York.

**HALL,** GRANVILLE STANLEY (1844–1924). American psychologist who became Wilhelm *Wundt's first American student—and eventually president of Clark University, Worcester, Massachusetts. He was born at Ashfield, Massachusetts, and educated in New York and at Harvard. He obtained his doctorate under William *James with a dissertation on space perception. As president of Clark University, he was largely instrumental in inviting Sigmund *Freud and Carl *Jung to visit it in 1909 and deliver a course of lectures. His best known book is *Adolescence* (1904).

**HALLUCINATION.** Briefly defined as sensory perception in the absence of external stimuli, hallucination has three characteristics: thoughts or memory images, perhaps when they are as vivid and immediate as perceptions, are experienced as if they were perceptions; they are externalized, or projected, being experienced as if they came from outside the person; and the mistaking of imagery for perception is not corrected in the light of the other information available. The term *pseudo-hallucination has been used to describe imagery as vivid and immediate as perception but not mistaken as such. Pseudohallucinations are more likely to be perceived in response to isolation or an intense emotional need: for example, shipwrecked sailors may visualize boats coming to their rescue well before this actually occurs. The fanciful elaboration of perception of external stimuli—for

example, faces seen in the fire—is *illusion. The imagery of a vision is experienced as if it came from outside, although not from ordinary reality as perception does. These distinctions have little theoretical importance and are often difficult to make because they depend on evaluations of what a person says about what he has experienced.

Young children often fail to distinguish between imagery and perception and suppose that what they imagine is external and perceptible to others; but, as they grow older, they become better at making the distinction. Adults sometimes fail to make the distinction, especially at a time of high expectation or *arousal. A widow mourning her husband may see him or hear his voice or footsteps repeatedly after his death, resulting in a 'sense of presence', which fades with the passage of time. In a wood at night, dark shadows are seen as lurking beasts. Waking from a frightening dream, a person feels that what he has experienced has happened in reality.

Mistakes like these are corrected when the person recognizes that they conflict with other information or the views of others. Normally imagery is continually reappraised in the light of the further information becoming available; and further information is sought by testing reality. Hearing a noise, a person makes a small head movement and tests whether the change in the strength and character of the noise conforms to his expectation. Perceiving someone in a crowd as an acquaintance, a person looks again or asks a companion for confirmation. Macbeth in Shakespeare's play, while planning to murder Duncan, hallucinates a dagger, and asks: 'Art thou not, fatal vision, sensible to feeling as to sight? Or art thou but a dagger of the mind, a false creation, proceeding from the heat-oppressed brain?'

After a long period of wakefulness or busyness, attention tends to be withdrawn from the outside world, and the testing of reality to be impaired and reduced. Hallucination is relatively common under these conditions and remains uncorrected for longer. Sufficient information is available but is not used. On the other hand, the subjects of experiments on the effects of sensory deprivation, who are put into a darkened and sound-proofed room, do not get sufficient information to enable them to test reality and to reappraise their hallucinatory experiences. (See ISOLATION EXPERIMENTS.) Also, a person on his own is less able to test reality and to reappraise what he has experienced.

Hallucinations tend to be disowned, the person feeling that he has no control over the imagery, which he feels is imposed on him by an outside agency. They are often reported as distressing, threatening, or tormenting, only occasionally, for example by a widow, as reassuring; they may sometimes be accepted without any feeling being attached to them. There are other distressing phenomena, which are not hallucinations, although akin to them in some respects. Thus, some recurring images obtrude and cannot be stopped, but are accepted as belonging to the individual. Such images are termed *obsessions. Ringing in the ear ('tinnitus'), resulting, for instance, from disease of the ear, is sometimes described by a fanciful simile, e.g. as being like sea flowing over shingle, or as if there were nearby a machine crushing stones. What is being described may be thought mistakenly to be hallucination if the explicit comparison of the 'like' or the 'as if' fails to be noted.

Hallucination is common in patients who have suffered damage to the brain as a result of trauma, infection, or intoxication by drugs or alcohol. The association of hallucination, fearfulness, and agitation in these cases may be described as *delirium. A patient who suffers from delirium tremens as a result of alcoholism may see such frightening things as red spiders or pink elephants, or he may feel that lice are crawling over his skin, because hallucination although usually visual may be experienced through any of the senses. Indeed, hallucinations in functional psychoses are more often auditory than visual. *Schizophrenic patients may hear the voices of their persecutors, conversations about themselves between third parties, or their own thoughts spoken aloud (echo de pensée). Severely depressed patients may hear voices making derogatory remarks or threatening them with punishment or torture. Some schizophrenic patients even experience tactile hallucinations which give rise to delusional beliefs that they are being sexually assaulted. Olfactory hallucinations are sometimes perceived by severely melancholic patients who come to believe that they are giving off revolting odours from their bowels causing people to avoid them. Patients mistake hallucinations of all these kinds for perceptions coming from outside themselves, and attribute to others what they experience, usually without any testing of reality.

Explanations of hallucination refer to several processes. In delirium there tends to be a high level of arousal and at the same time a lowering of vigilance, impairment of perception, and impairment and reduction of reality-testing. Enhancement of imagery as a direct effect of drugs or toxins on nervous tissue is similar to that of electrical stimulation of the temporal lobes of the brain when it produces, in a conscious patient whose brain has been exposed during surgery, intense visual, auditory, or other imagery as 'strips' of experience. Poisoning by drugs may also, more importantly, increase the random activity of nervous tissue. Sensations then become blurred, to produce

background noise, which is then elaborated into illusion. A person poisoned by LSD may see visual patterns like lace curtains, usually coloured. In some illnesses in which there is hallucination, the functioning of peripheral nerves is affected by neuritis, and as a result the patient may experience numbness, pins and needles, or itching, which is elaborated into the illusion of lice. Similarly, the result of neuritis of the retina may be spiders dangling in front of the eyes, the elaborations of phosphenes. In schizophrenia, the patient has typically disengaged from social activities, and the testing of reality is reduced as a result, but this does not account for his disowning of what he experiences. It has to be supposed that thoughts and feelings have been dissociated as a psychological defence in order to reduce the *anxiety which would otherwise arise. The patient positively resists any reappraisal of what he has experienced.

D. R. D.

Galton, F. (1907). Inquiries into Human Faculty and its Development. London.

Siegel, R. K. and West, J. L. (eds., 1975). Hallucinations. London.

**HALO EFFECT.** A powerful social phenomenon, that reputation or belief affects judgement. For example, we may regard people wearing spectacles as especially intelligent. People distinguished in one field are often regarded—by the halo effect, and sometimes dangerously—as wise and learned in others. For example, the great inventor Thomas Alva Edison was consulted on political and philosophical matters. Wealth and fashionable clothes, and even opinions, can similarly confer unjustified prestige. The converse phenomenon is 'Give a dog a bad name . . .'.

**HAND.** The anatomist Wood Jones (1879–1954) proposed that 'man's place in nature is largely writ upon the hand'. There is a great deal of evidence that human *perception and the way in which we classify objects are very much determined by how we handle them, not only in infancy but also in the later development of perceptual and motor skills. So mind may depend as much upon the hands as it depends upon the senses for gaining knowledge, and so developing.

See BLINDNESS, RECOVERY FROM; HANDEDNESS; SPATIAL CO-ORDINATION OF THE SENSES; TOUCH.

**HANDEDNESS** is a characteristic peculiar to man. Only in man do individuals have a consistently preferred (and more skilful) hand for manual actions, and only man is predominantly right-handed. Other animals show paw preferences when freely picking things up, reaching into small spaces, pressing bars, or opening boxes, but they are less consistent within and across these activities, and are easily influenced by environmental variables such as training and object position. Moreover, in subhuman species tested (including mice, rats, cats, dogs, monkeys, and apes), one usually finds an even distribution of left and right preferences, without the typically human tendency to right-handedness. Man, by contrast, is predominantly dextral in all races and cultures, with most individuals' preferences remaining constant from an early age.

The inconsistency and lability of preferences in lower animals probably reflects their lack of an upper-limb dexterity comparable to man's. That is, the range of actions available to them—pushing, reaching for, or picking things up—usually involve whole-limb movements which require an accompanying postural body adjustment. Such movements are often stereotyped and appear to be controlled by lower centres in the brain. In man and the higher Primates, an individual's handedness becomes more marked the greater the manipulative skill required in an action, where movements independent of bodily position are controlled by higher cortical brain circuits.

Human handedness, therefore, appears to have developed along with, and to be a feature of, man's uniquely high level of finger dexterity and capacity to make and use tools. Anthropological evidence, although necessarily indirect, suggests that handedness first appeared in the lower Stone Age when tool-making became common. Some tools, for example, appear to have been made by right-handers for right-hand use.

By historical times the predominance of right-handedness was well enough known for its origin to be discussed and for sinistrality to be noted as exceptional. *Aristotle discusses ambidexterity as a problem for contemporary ideas of the inherent superiority of the right side of the body. The Old Testament notes two cases of left-handedness: a group of 700 sinistral sling-shooters in the tribe of Benjamin, and Ehud the Benjamite who stabbed an enemy king with his left hand.

Once established, manual asymmetry quickly attracted a potent mythology associating the right side of the body and the right hand with things that are good, strong, pure, and honourable, while the left in contrast was equated with evil of all kinds. This symbolism has pervaded nearly all cultures (except the Chinese) throughout the ages. Ancient Greeks and Romans regarded the left side as inferior and profane, and in medieval times use of the left hand was associated with witchcraft. Arabs still regard the left as the 'unclean' hand and forbid its use in normal human contact. The odium of the left remains today in terms such as sinister, gauche, and cack-handed.

Right-handedness is of interest to psychology and neurology in that the development of a consistent hand preference in relation to fine motor skills may be linked to the development of hemispheric specialization in the human brain for certain cognitive functions (see NERVOUS SYSTEM). It is known that in 95 per cent of dextrals language is mediated exclusively by the left hemisphere, that is, by the hemisphere controlling the right side of the body, including the preferred hand. Originally this 'cerebral dominance' for speech was thought to imply that the left hemisphere was the vehicle for all man's highest mental functions. Subsequently, however, it was established that the right hemisphere plays its own dominant role in tasks requiring spatial perception, reasoning, or memory, as in map-reading and the recognition of faces, patterns, and melodies. This complementary specialization of the two sides of the brain is, like strong right-handedness, peculiar to man, so they may have evolved together.

Handedness may, however, reflect more directly the cerebral basis of sensorimotor function. Clinical and physiological evidence suggests that in right-handers the left hemisphere has sensory and motor connections to both sides of the body, whereas the right hemisphere is almost exclusively unilaterally connected. The former may thus have a dominant role in integrating activity of the two sides of the body to make a co-ordinated behavioural unit. If so, voluntary control of the right hand may be easier, and a preference for its use in delicate manipulative skills may emerge as a result.

In accordance with this idea, although it is not yet known exactly what the difference is between the hands in terms of skill, the evidence to date suggests that it centres on timing and the co-ordination of movements into sequences. Single-finger contractions can be made as precisely or as fast with the left as with the right hand, and with practice either hand may run off pre-programmed sequences of movement (as in typing or piano-playing) equally well, provided they do not require adjustment during their execution. But tasks involving visual aiming (such as peg-placing or threading a needle) or serial adjustment (as in turning a crank handle or threading a nut on to a bolt) yield consistent differences in performance between the hands. Current theories of the basis of handedness include: (i) increased variability in the left arm's execution of movements, so that they require more frequent correction; (ii) longer time-lag in the correction of inaccurate movements when they occur, especially using vision; (iii) greater irregularity in timing of movements by the left hand; and (iv) a greater repertoire of movements available to the right hand because it has had more practice (this last being a rather circular argument).

Another explanation of dextrality is based on the predominant use of the right hand for gesturing, that is, for movements of communication rather than manipulation. This again links it with the development of speech, itself seen as man's most sophisticated form of communication. Certainly the neural motor systems of speech and the right hand are adjacent, and motor activity in the latter is strongly associated with speech generation. Talking in dextrals is accompanied by gestures mainly of the right hand and arm (whereas arm movements in other situations are not specifically dextral), and talking interferes with a concurrent motor activity in the right hand, such as balancing a rod on one finger, more than in the left. Musicians report that conducting rather than fingerwork is the most difficult action to perform with the non-preferred hand, implying that handedness consists of a 'closer, more immediate availability of the right hand as the instrument of the individual's conceptions and intentions' (Oldfield 1969).

Any theory of handedness has to account for the minority of left-handers found in all human societies, a proportion variously reported as from 4 to 36 per cent. The classification of subjects is itself a problem, because most sinistrals are less well lateralized than dextrals. Their preferences and usage are weaker and more changeable both within and across tasks, that is, they may prefer to use the right hand for any actions occasionally or for some tasks regularly. There seems, moreover, to be no hierarchy of preferences, nor any activity common to all sinistrals suitable for selecting them as such (although writing, throwing, shooting, and using scissors have been used for the purpose).

Nor is it clear whether handedness is a continuum (albeit an unusual J-shaped one) ranging from total dextrality to total sinistrality or comprises discrete categories and, if so, whether there are two groups (left and right) or a third 'ambilateral' (mixed-handed) group as well. Much variability in results between different studies of handedness stems from this ambiguity. The great variety of laterality measures used—including grip strength, touch sensitivity, eyedness, and writing hand—also adds to the confusion, especially as many have little relation to dexterity and do not intercorrelate.

On tests of manual speed, accuracy, and steadiness, the performance of pure sinistrals mirrors and equals that of dextrals, both showing a distinct superiority of the preferred hand. In ambilaterals of all kinds (including most self-professed left- and some right-handers) the two hands are more equal in skill, and neither perform quite as well as the preferred hand of the strongly lateralized.

Cerebral specialization and dominance in sinistrals is less clear cut than in dextrals. Speech is still represented in the left hemisphere in 70 per cent of left- and mixed-handers, but 15 per cent have right-hemisphere language and 15 per cent bilateral representation. Sinistrals may suffer *aphasia from damage to either hemisphere, but recover from it better than do dextrals. Similarly equivocal results are found for other skills, suggesting a bilateral brain involvement in all mental functions. Some investigators claim pure left-handers are the mirror opposites of dextrals while ambilaterals are a separate group. Others distinguish 'familial' left-handers (with sinistral relatives) from 'non-familials'. Others again classify all sinistral brains as 'imperfectly developed' or 'undifferentiated'.

Theories of the origins and distribution of handedness are of three kinds. (i) Learning-cultural theories claim that it is produced by social pressures or early experience, especially of tools designed for right-hand use. These (mostly older) theories are too imprecise to predict accurately the handedness of any individual or the distribution of handedness in any group. (ii) Genetic models (see GENETICS OF BEHAVIOUR) suggest handedness is inherited, although the exact mechanism is as yet unknown. Current theories include a two-gene model (Levy and Nagylaki, 1972) and a right-shift model in which pure right-handedness may be inherited from a dominant gene but, if not, the degree of laterality to either side is determined randomly by environmental factors (Annett). (iii) Brain-damage theories hold that neonatal injury shifts cerebral dominance and handedness or prevents normal hemispheric specialization. They explain thereby the higher incidence of sinistrality found in such pathological states as subnormality and epilepsy. Whether they account for left-handedness in the population generally is debatable.                                              K. A. F.

Annett, J., Annett, M., Hudson, P. T. W., and Turner, A. (1979). The control of movement in the preferred and non-preferred hands. *Quarterly Journal of Psychology*, **31**, 641–52.

Barsley, M. (1966). *The Left-Handed Book*. London.

Dimond, S. J. and Beaumont, J. G. (1974). *Hemisphere Function in the Human Brain*. London.

Hardyck, C. and Petrinovich, L. F. (1977). Left-handedness. *Psychological Bulletin*, **84**, 385–404.

Hicks, R. E. and Kinsbourne, M. (1976). On the genesis of human handedness: a review. *Journal of Motor Behavior*, **8**, 257–66.

Hicks, R. E. and Kinsbourne, M. (1978). Lateralized concomitants of human handedness. *Journal of Motor Behavior*, **10**, 83–94.

Levy, J. and Nagylaki, T. (1972). A Model for the Genetics of Handedness. *Genetics*, **72**, 117–28.

Oldfield, R. C. (1969). Handedness in musicians. *British Journal of Psychology*, **60**, 91–9.

Springer, S. P. and Deutsch, G. (1981). *Left Brain, Right Brain*. San Francisco.

Trevarthen, C. (1978). Manipulative strategies of baboons and origins of cerebral asymmetry. In Kinsbourne, M. (ed.), *Asymmetrical Function of the Brain*. Cambridge.

Zangwill, O. L. (1962). Handedness and dominance. In Money, J. (ed.), *Reading Disabilities*. Baltimore.

**HANDICAP.** A term now commonly applied to a person suffering from a physical or mental disability (as opposed to illness). The word probably comes from the phrase 'hand i' (in) cap', referring to a seventeenth-century sporting lottery in which the contestants deposited forfeit money in a cap or hat. Later, in horse-racing, it referred to the extra weight which various horses were required by the umpire to carry in order to penalize the superior animals and so even out the contest. Since the nineteenth century the term has been applied to any disability in a contest.

See also MENTAL HANDICAP; SUBNORMALITY.

**HAPTIC TOUCH.** Touching by active exploration, especially with the fingers. It is in contrast with 'passive' touch, in which structures are signalled by patterns impressed on the skin. Haptic touch has the advantage that large objects (much larger than any region of skin) can be discerned and identified, but is seldom used, except in the dark, or by blind people, when it is extremely useful. It is essentially *single-channel* scanning in time, whereas passive touch uses simultaneous *parallel* neural *channels. Since the sensitive nerve endings of the skin adapt with constant stimulation, movement and active touch are important for renewing their signals. See also TOUCH.

Iggo, A. (1982). Cutaneous Sensory Mechanisms. In Barlow, H. B. and Mollon, J. D. (eds.), *The Senses*. Cambridge Texts in the Physiological Sciences, 3.

**HARTLEY,** DAVID (1705–57). British philosopher and physician, born in Halifax and educated at Jesus College, Cambridge. While a medical practitioner in Newark, London, and Bath he developed an account of mind based on sound-like vibrations, which he used not only to explain transmission of messages in the nervous system but also association of ideas by a kind of resonance, as when one vibrating string activates another by sympathy. His associationism is highly important in the history of psychology. *Observations on Man* appeared in 1749.

**HAWTHORNE EFFECT.** A kind of experimenter effect which has been found in industrial research. There may be changes in productivity, etc., simply in response to attention from the investigators, rather than as the effect of any particular experimental treatments. It is so named because of a study at the Hawthorne plant of the Western Electric Company in Chicago in 1927–9 in which five girls were moved into a test room and subjected to various changes in rest periods and refreshments; it was found that output increased by about 30 per cent, this being unrelated to any particular experimental conditions. It was generally concluded that the increase was due to social factors within the group, although it could be accounted for by the change in group piece-work which was shared among a group of five instead of a larger group, the smaller variety of work done, the replacement of two of the girls by faster ones, the enthusiasm of the penurious operative number two, and the general expectation throughout the works that the experiment would be a 'success'.

Whether the result was correctly interpreted or not, this study had a profound effect on the subsequent development of research in industrial *social psychology. It was concluded that physical conditions of work might be less important than factors like the structure of groups and the style of supervision, and the study thus led to the 'human relations' movement.

It also led to greater care in later work to avoid errors of this kind. Sometimes it is possible to work from records, for example when studying the effect of group size on absenteeism. The Tavistock Institute of Human Relations has cultivated a strict neutrality and kept its distance both from managers and from workers. The effects of administering interviews or tests can be eliminated by means of elaborate designs with extra control groups. Industrial social psychology is still subject to various errors, nevertheless. For example, in follow-up studies of training it is rarely possible to keep raters 'blind' as to who has been trained.

M. A.

**HEAD,** SIR HENRY (1861–1940). British neurologist, born in London and educated at Charterhouse School and Trinity College, Cambridge. As a young man, he studied with Ewald *Hering in Prague. Later he joined the London Hospital, becoming consulting physician. He is best known for his work with W. H. R. *Rivers, Gordon *Holmes, and others on sensation and the cerebral cortex and for his studies on *aphasia, in which he cast doubt on the prevailing ideas regarding the cortical localization of speech. His concept of the *schema—a flexible representation of past experience in memory—greatly influenced the British psychologist F. C. *Bartlett. His books include *Studies in Neurology*, 2 vols. (1920) and *Aphasia and Kindred Disorders of Speech*, 2 vols. (1926).

**HEAD INJURY.** See CONCUSSION.

**HEARING.** When an object vibrates, pressure changes are set up in the surrounding medium, usually air, and these pressure changes are transmitted through the medium and may be perceived as sound. Sounds can be categorized into two main classes. Those for which the pressure changes have a random or irregular quality are perceived as noise-like: examples are the sound of a waterfall, or the consonants 's' or 'f'. Those which repeat regularly as a function of time are called periodic sounds, and generally have a well-defined tone or pitch: for example, a note played on a musical instrument. The size of the pressure change is related to the perceived loudness of a sound; the greater the pressure variation the greater the loudness. However, it is inconvenient to express the magnitude of sounds in terms of pressure changes, because the ear can perceive sounds over a huge range of pressures. Hence a logarithmic measure called the decibel (abbreviated dB) is used to express sound magnitude, or level; 0 dB corresponds roughly to the quietest sound which can be heard by a healthy young adult, normal conversation has a level of 60–70 dB, while sounds above about 100 dB tend to be uncomfortably loud and can damage our ears if heard for a long time. Sounds with a level above 120 dB can damage our ears within quite a short time, perhaps only a few minutes. When the level of a sound is increased by 10 dB, the subjective loudness roughly doubles, whereas the sound power actually increases by a factor of 10. The smallest detectable change in level is about 1 dB.

Periodic sounds can also be described in terms of

their repetition rate and the complexity of the pressure variation. The repetition rate is related to the subjective pitch; the higher the rate the higher the pitch. Complexity is related to the subjective timbre or tone quality; differences in timbre distinguish between the same note played on, say, the violin and the organ. One of the simplest pressure waves has the form of a sinusoid: pressure plotted against time varies as the sine of time (see the lower part of Fig. 3). A sine wave may also be called a pure tone or simple tone, since it has a very 'pure' or 'clean' quality, like that of a tuning fork or the Greenwich time-signal. For a pure tone the repetition rate, the number of complete cycles per second, is called the frequency. The unit of one cycle per second is called the hertz (abbreviated Hz). The Greenwich time-signal has a frequency of 1,000 Hz. The highest frequency we can hear varies from 16,000 to 20,000 Hz in young adults, but tends to decrease with increasing age. The lowest frequency which is heard as sound is about 20 Hz. Below that the pressure changes are felt as a vibration rather than heard as sound. We are most sensitive to frequencies around 1,800 Hz.

Sine waves, or pure tones, are particularly important in the study of hearing. Joseph Fourier showed that any periodic complex sound can be considered as composed of a sum of sine waves with different frequencies and levels. Conversely, any periodic sound can be synthesized by adding together sine waves with appropriate frequencies and levels. This can be very useful, since if we are investigating how some part of the auditory system works, it is often sufficient to measure only the way it responds to sine waves of different frequencies. The response to any complex sound can then be predicted from the response to the sine waves. The same philosophy lies behind the specification of amplifiers or loudspeakers in terms of their frequency response. It is assumed that if an amplifier faithfully reproduces any sine wave within the audible range, and amplifies each sine wave by the same amount, then it will also faithfully reproduce any complex sound composed of those sine waves.

A further reason why sine waves are important in the study of hearing is that the ear behaves as though it carries out a Fourier analysis, although it does not do this analysis perfectly, and is therefore said to have limited resolution. Thus when we are presented with two sine waves which are sufficiently separated in frequency, we are able to hear two separate tones, each with its own pitch. This contrasts with the eye, where a mixture of two different colours (frequencies of light) is perceived as a single colour. The process by which the different frequencies in a complex sound are separated in the ear is known as frequency analysis or frequency resolution.

If we subject a complex sound to Fourier analysis, and then plot the level of each sine-wave component as a function of frequency, the resulting plot is known as the spectrum of the sound. The spectrum is related to the complexity of the pressure variation: the simple sine wave has a spectrum composed of a single point, or vertical line, whereas musical instrument tones generally contain many sinusoidal components, and have a spectrum composed of many lines. The subjective timbre of sounds is more easily explained in terms of the spectrum than in terms of the pressure variation as a function of time. Sounds with many high-frequency components will seem sharp or strident, while those with mainly low-frequency components will seem dull or mellow. This correspondence between spectrum and timbre provides another example of the action of the ear as a frequency analyser. In the following sections we will discuss the physiological basis of this frequency analysis, and some of its perceptual consequences. We will also discuss the perception of pitch. Finally we will describe the major types of hearing impairments, and their perceptual consequences.

**The anatomy and physiology of the ear.** Fig. 1 illustrates the basic structure of the outer, middle, and inner ear. The outer ear consists of the pinna and the ear canal. The pinna is thought to play an important role in our ability to locate complex sounds. The spectrum of such sounds is modified by the pinna in a way which depends upon the direction of the sound source relative to the head. These spectral modifications are not perceived as changes in timbre, but rather determine the perceived direction of the sound source. They are particularly important in allowing us to distinguish whether a sound comes from behind or in front, and above or below.

Sounds impinging upon the eardrum are transferred by means of three small bones in the middle ear (the smallest bones in the body, called the malleus, the incus, and the stapes) to a membrane-covered opening (the oval window) in the inner ear or cochlea. The main function of the middle ear is to improve the efficiency of transfer of energy from the air to the fluids inside the cochlea. Small muscles attached to the bones contract when we are exposed to intense sounds, reducing sound transmission to the cochlea, particularly at low frequencies. This may serve to protect the cochlea, and it may also help to stop intense low frequencies, occurring in the environment or in our own voices, making higher frequencies inaudible.

The cochlea is filled with fluids, and running along its length is a membrane called the basilar membrane. This membrane is stiff and narrow close to the oval window (called the base), while at the other end (the apex) it is wider and less stiff. In response to sine-wave stimulation a wave appears on the basilar membrane travelling from the base towards the apex, at first increasing in amplitude and then decreasing. The position of the maximum in the pattern of vibration along the basilar membrane varies with frequency; high frequencies produce peaks towards the base, and low frequencies towards the apex. This is illustrated in Fig. 2. Thus the basilar membrane acts as a

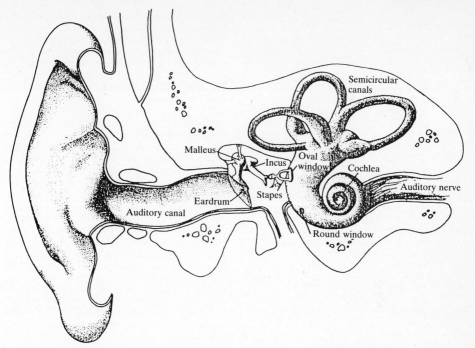

**Fig. 1.** The structure of the peripheral auditory system, showing the outer, middle, and inner ear.

frequency analyser, different frequencies producing activity at different places along the basilar membrane.

The patterns shown in Fig. 2 are rather broad to account for the frequency resolution which is actually observed in human subjects (see below). However, recent work has indicated that many of the early measurements may have been in error. The basilar membrane appears to be extremely vulnerable, so that even small impairments in the physiological condition of the animal being studied alter the responses and produce broader 'tuning'. It has recently been shown that the 'tuning' on the basilar membrane, i.e. its frequency resolution, can be extremely sharp if the animal and its cochlea are in good condition.

The information which is contained in the patterns of vibration on the basilar membrane has to be transmitted to the brain in some way in order for us to perceive sound. This transmission is achieved by an electrical 'code' carried in the auditory nerve. Each auditory nerve contains the axons or 'fibres' of about 30,000 individual nerves, or neurones, and information is transmitted in each of these in the form of brief electrical impulses, called spikes or action potentials. Thus transmission takes place in an all-or-none fashion; the size of the spikes does not vary, and only the presence or absence of a spike is important.

The vibrations on the basilar membrane are transformed to spikes by rows of special cells, called hair cells, which rest on the basilar membrane. The hair cells are among the most delicate structures in the cochlea, and they can be destroyed by intense sound, lack of oxygen, metabolic disturbance, infection, or drugs. They also tend to be lost with increasing age. Once lost they do not regenerate, and loss of hair cells is a common cause of hearing impairment.

The exact way in which information is 'coded' in the auditory nerve is not clear. However, we know that any single neurone is activated only by vibration on a limited part of the basilar membrane. Each neurone is 'tuned' and responds to only a limited range of frequencies. Thus information about frequency can be coded in terms of which neurones are active or 'firing' with spikes. This form of coding is called 'place' coding. Information about sound level may be carried both in the rate of firing (i.e. the number of spikes per second) and in terms of the number of neurones which are firing. Finally, information may also be carried in the exact timing of the spikes. For stimulating frequencies below about 5 kHz (1 kHz = 1,000 Hz), the time pattern of neural spikes reflects the time structure of the stimulus. Nerve spikes tend to occur at a particular point or phase of the stimulating waveform, a process called phase-locking, although a spike will not necessarily occur on every cycle. This is illustrated in Fig. 3. For a sine-wave stimulus with a frequency of, say, 1 kHz, the time for one complete cycle will be 1 millisecond (ms), and the time intervals between successive nerve impulses will be integral multiples of this, namely

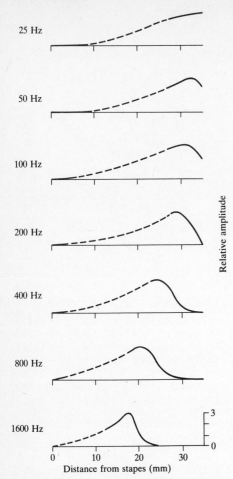

25 Hz

50 Hz

100 Hz

200 Hz

400 Hz

800 Hz

1600 Hz

Relative amplitude

0    10    20    30
Distance from stapes (mm)

**Fig. 2.** Envelopes or outlines of patterns of vibration on the basilar membrane for low-frequency sine waves of different frequencies. Solid lines indicate the results of actual experiments, whereas the dashed lines are extrapolations.

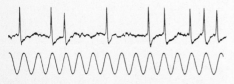

**Fig. 3.** The lower trace shows the waveform of a sine wave with frequency 300 Hz. The upper trace shows the response of a single auditory nerve fibre. Note that each impulse occurs at the same phase of the waveform, although an impulse does not occur on every cycle.

1, 2, 3, 4, 5, . . . ms. Thus phase-locking provides another way in which the frequency of a sound may be coded. Notice that a given neurone cannot 'fire' more than a few hundred times per second. It used

to be thought that the frequency of the stimulus at higher frequencies could be coded by co-operation between groups of neurones firing in volleys, the so-called 'volley' theory. In fact, the time pattern of response in a single neurone is sufficient to define the frequency of the input, provided that time *intervals* between firings are analysed, rather than overall firing rate.

**Theories of pitch perception.** The pitch of a sound is defined as that attribute of sensation in terms of which sounds may be ordered on a musical scale; variations in pitch give rise to the percept of a melody. For sine-wave stimuli the pitch is related to the frequency, and for other periodic sounds it is usually related to the overall repetition rate. Classically there have been two theories of how pitch is determined. The *place* theory suggests that pitch is related to the distribution of activity across nerve fibres. A pure tone will produce maximum activity in a small group of neurones connected to the place on the basilar membrane which is vibrating most strongly, and the 'position' of this maximum is assumed to determine pitch. The *temporal* theory suggests that pitch is determined from the time pattern of neural impulses, specifically from the time intervals between successive impulses (this used to be called the volley theory, but as discussed above, volleying is no longer considered necessary).

It is generally agreed that the place theory works best at high frequencies, where the timing information is lost, and the temporal theory works best at low frequencies, where resolution on the basilar membrane is poorest (see Fig. 2). However, the frequency at which the change from one to the other occurs is still a matter of debate. We can get some clues from studies of frequency discrimination, the ability to detect a small difference in frequency between two successive tones. For low and middle frequencies a change of about 0·3 per cent is detectable, but above about 5 kHz the smallest detectable change increases markedly. Furthermore, above 5 kHz our sense of musical pitch appears to be lost, so that a sequence of different frequencies does not produce a clear sense of melody. Since 5 kHz is the highest frequency at which phase-locking occurs, these results suggest that our sense of musical pitch and our ability to detect small changes in frequency depend upon the use of temporal information. Place information allows the detection of relatively large frequency changes, but it does not give rise to a sense of musical pitch.

We do not have space to deal with the pitch of complex sounds, but it is thought that relatively complex pattern-recognition processes are involved which depend upon both place and temporal information. For a review see Moore (1982).

**The ear as a frequency analyser.** We initially described how the auditory system functions as a

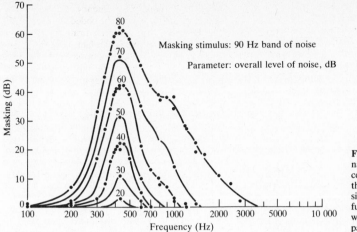

Masking stimulus: 90 Hz band of noise

Parameter: overall level of noise, dB

**Fig. 4.** Masking patterns for a narrow-band noise masker centred at 410 Hz. The threshold elevation of the sine-wave signal is plotted as a function of signal frequency, with masker level as parameter.

limited-resolution frequency analyser, splitting complex sounds into their sine-wave components. Although we have argued that place information is not the most important determinant of pitch, it seems almost certain that the place analysis which takes place on the basilar membrane provides the initial basis for the ear's frequency analysing abilities. We will now describe briefly some perceptual consequences of this analysis.

We are all familiar with the fact that sounds we wish to hear are sometimes rendered inaudible by other sounds, a process known as masking. Fig. 4 shows masking patterns produced by a masker containing only a small range of frequencies: a narrow-band noise. The threshold elevation of the sinusoidal signal (the amount by which the masker raises the threshold) is plotted as a function of signal frequency for several different masker levels. The figure illustrates two basic points. First, the greater the masker level, the more masking there is. Secondly, more masking occurs for signal frequencies close to the masker frequency than for those farther away. This makes sense if we assume that masking will be most effective when the pattern of vibration evoked by the masker on the basilar membrane overlaps that of the signal. If the place analysis on the basilar membrane is sufficient to separate completely masker and signal, then no masking will occur. (See also AUDITORY ILLUSIONS.)

As was described earlier, the subjective timbre of a sound depends primarily on the spectrum of the sound; the level of sound at each frequency. Presumably timbre is perceived in this way because the different frequencies excite different places on the basilar membrane. The distribution of activity as a function of place determines the timbre. Obviously, this distribution can be quite complex, but each different complex tone will produce its own distribution, and hence will have its own tone colour. This helps us to distinguish between different musical instruments, and to distinguish between the different vowel sounds in human speech.

**Hearing impairments.** Hearing impairments can be classified into two broad types. *Conductive* hearing loss occurs when the passage of sound through to the inner ear is impeded in some way, for example by wax in the ears, or by some problem with the bones in the middle ear. It can often be cured by simple medical treatment, or by surgery, and when this is not possible a simple hearing-aid can effectively alleviate the problem. *Sensorineural* hearing losses arise in the inner ear, or at some point 'higher up' in the auditory system. Cochlear hearing losses are often produced by damage to the hair cells and they are common in the elderly. Sensorineural hearing losses are not usually helped by surgery, and simple hearing-aids are of only limited use, since the percepts of the listener are 'distorted' in various ways.

One common problem in cochlear hearing loss is *recruitment*, an abnormally rapid growth of loudness with increasing sound level. Faint sounds may be inaudible to the sufferer, but high-level sounds are as loud to him or her as to a normal listener. A hearing-aid which amplifies all sounds will overamplify intense sounds, and these will be uncomfortably loud. One way round this problem is to use hearing-aids which 'compress' the dynamic range of sounds, by amplifying low-level sounds more than high-level sounds. Such aids are currently being evaluated, and have met with some success.

A second common problem in cases of cochlear hearing loss is an impairment in frequency selectivity. This has a number of consequences. First, the sufferer will be more susceptible to the effects of masking. Secondly, the ability to identify the timbre of different sounds, including speech, will be impaired. These two effects mean that the sufferer will have great difficulty in understanding speech whenever there is more than one person talking at once, or when there is background noise.

Present hearing-aids cannot compensate for this problem, and as a result many people with cochlear hearing losses never go to pubs or to parties.

Further research may clarify the nature of the defects in impaired ears, and suggest ways in which those problems can be alleviated. In the meantime we should remember that for most impaired people a hearing-aid does not restore normal hearing; it may make sounds louder but it does not bring them into focus.                                    B. C. J. M.

Békésy, G. von (1960). *Experiments in Hearing* (trans. and ed. by E. G. Wever). New York.

Moore, B. C. J. (1982). *Introduction to the Psychology of Hearing*, 2nd edn. London.

**HEDONISM.** Name for (i) the ethical doctrine that pleasure is the only good, and (ii) the psychological thesis that all actions are in fact directed towards the pursuit of pleasure in some form or another. Hedonism in both its forms has a long philosophical ancestry, but was especially prominent in the work of the utilitarians of the late eighteenth and the nineteenth centuries. Jeremy *Bentham argued that 'nature has placed mankind under the governance of two sovereign masters, *pain* and *pleasure*. It is for them alone to determine what we ought to do as well as what we shall do' (*Introduction to the Principles of Morals and Legislation*, 1789). For Bentham, pleasure was a purely quantitative notion, and the utility of an act could be calculated by measuring the amount of pleasure it produced in terms of intensity, duration, etc. J. S. *Mill, by contrast, distinguished between higher and lower pleasures, and argued that certain types of pleasure (notably those of the intellect) are qualitatively superior, irrespective of the actual amount of pleasure they produce (*Utilitarianism*, 1861). It seems, however, that this manœuvre involves a radical departure from hedonism, since it suggests that the value of an activity is not solely a function of the pleasure involved.

The psychological thesis that people only pursue pleasure seems false. It is a matter of common sense that people pursue a wide variety of goals in life (e.g. scientific truth, justice, religious enlightenment); and it does not appear that the pursuit of these differing goals can be exhibited as being 'really' the pursuit of pleasure—unless the concept of pleasure is defined so widely that the claim that only pleasure is pursued becomes trivially true. Ethical hedonism also seems untenable. The value of goods such as liberty and autonomy cannot, it seems, be explained solely in terms of the amount of pleasure which may be produced by securing them.                              J. G. C.

**HEGEL,** GEORG WILHELM FRIEDRICH (1770–1831). German philosopher born at Stuttgart. He studied theology at Tübingen, and became *privat-docent* at Jena and then headmaster of a school at Nuremberg, where he instructed the boys in his own, highly obscure, philosophy, which is a modification of *Kant's. He became professor of philosophy at Heidelberg in 1816 and finally at Berlin in 1818, where he dominated German philosophy.

Hegel is essentially mystical; he rejects the reality of separate objects, and of minds in space and time, and holds, rather, an all-embracing unity: the *absolute* which is rational, real, and true. To draw attention to a particular is to separate this from the whole; and so the particular is only partially true. Greater unity and truth are achieved by the dialectic of positing something (*thesis*), denying it (*antithesis*), and combining the two half-truths in a *synthesis*. It has been said that Karl Marx 'stood Hegel on his head' by making matter, and not reason, the ultimate reality. Hegel is the contrary of an empiricist, for he held that the whole has a greater claim to reality than the parts that may be observed; and (in societies) that the group has more reality than the individuals composing it. This came to justify extreme authoritarian political philosophies, from Fascism to Communism. It is also the mainspring of *idealist philosophies such as *Bradley's, which were finally abandoned with the impact of *pragmatism and *logical positivism, and the linguistic analysis and emphasis on 'atomic statements' of G. E. *Moore, Bertrand *Russell, and Ludwig *Wittgenstein.

Hegel's main philosophical work is *Phänomenologie des Geistes* (1807; English trans. *The Phenomenology of the Mind*, 1844).                    R. L. G.

**HELMHOLTZ,** HERMANN LUDWIG FERDINAND VON (1821–94). German physiologist and physicist, born at Potsdam. He was the son of Ferdinand Helmholtz, a teacher of philology and philosophy in the gymnasium. His mother's maiden name was Penne; she was descended from the Quaker founder of Philadelphia, William Penn. Hermann Helmholtz became the founder of the science of perceptual physiology. He carried out a vast number of observational experiments, often with himself as observer, as well as physiological experiments for explanations. He also formulated psychological concepts which have lasting significance. His immense range—he was one of the greatest physicists of the nineteenth century—even includes ideas on *aesthetics and art. He was also a director of research, and with his *Popular Lectures* a lucid presenter of science: by following a suggestion of his, his student Heinrich Hertz (1857–94) discovered how to confirm James Clerk Maxwell's theoretical prediction of radio waves. Helmholtz was professor of physiology at Königsberg (1849), Bonn (1855), and Heidelberg (1858). Then in 1871 he became professor of physics at Berlin, and from 1888 to 1894 was president of the Physikalisch-Technische Reichsanstalt, which he designed as 'an institute for the experimental promotion of exact science and the *technique* of precision'. It is, however, for his earlier work on the nervous system and especially on vision and hearing, and as the founder of the experimental study of *perception, that he concerns us here.

His first great achievement, in 1850, was to measure the rate of conduction of signals in nerves. It had been thought that sensory signals arrive at the brain immediately. Indeed, the founder of modern physiology, Johannes *Müller (1801–58) considered it to be beyond experimental possibility to measure the neural conduction rate, because nerves are so short, in comparison with the astronomical distances over which the velocity of light had been estimated, that no instrument could measure the very short time differences. But Helmholtz's friend Emil *du Bois-Reymond (1816–96), the originator of electrophysiology, suggested that there might be a molecular basis for neural conduction, so it could be a great deal slower than the velocity of light. Further, a new instrument, the chronograph, was invented in 1849, making it possible to record short durations and rapid changes with an electrically operated pen on a revolving drum. Helmholtz used this with frog preparations, and then on humans. The method with humans was to find the difference between *reaction times to a stimulus at, say, the ankle and the calf of the leg. Since the muscle action time (which he also succeeded in measuring) would be the same in either case, a longer reaction time from the ankle must be due to conduction time in the nerve of the leg. Helmholtz found it to be comparable to the speed of sound, rather than of light. His father commented in a letter to him: 'the results at first appeared to me surprising, since I regard the idea and its bodily expression not as successive, but as simultaneous, a single living act, that only becomes bodily and mental on reflection; and I could as little reconcile myself to your view, as I could admit that a star had disappeared in Abraham's time should still be visible'. This was, however, a misunderstanding which was for some time shared by the older physiologists; for as Helmholtz immediately pointed out to his father: 'the interaction of mental and physical processes is initiated in the brain, and consciousness, intellectual activity, has nothing to do with the transmission of the message from the skin, from the retina, or from the ear, to the brain. In relation to intelligence this transmission within the body is as external as the propagation of sound from the place at which it takes origin, to the ear.' The measurements did however lead Helmholtz to appreciate that the brain is quite slow, for reaction times are much longer than they should be from the speed of signals in peripheral nerves, and so he came to appreciate that a great deal of routeing and switching of signals must be going on during perception, and for decisions for muscle movement. This led to analogies between brain function and telephone exchange switching, and then computers.

Helmholtz was philosophically a thoroughgoing empiricist, believing that sensory signals only have significance as the result of associations built up by learning. We are essentially separate from the world of objects, and isolated from external physical events, except for neural signals which, somewhat like language, must be learned and read according to various assumptions, which may or may not be appropriate. This is the basis of Helmholtz's interest in perceptual and especially visual *illusions. More generally, it is the basis also of his notion, at that time disturbing, that perceptions are 'unconscious inferences'. This challenged the prevailing view that responsibility, and just blame and praise, depend on consciously held reasons and motivations. Sigmund *Freud's slightly later notion of an active unconscious mind is a rather different idea, though equally shocking to the Victorians. For Helmholtz it was simply that most of what goes on in the nervous system is not represented in consciousness. Physiological and psychological experiments are important, and often surprising in their findings, because we cannot experience or discover by introspection how we see or think, or even know on what data our perceptions and beliefs are based. Thus Helmholtz wrote of visual illusions, in his last paper on perception (1894):

Knowledge gained through daily experience, with all its accidents, does not usually have the range and completeness which it is possible to obtain with experiments. . . . We usually refer to incorrect inductive inferences concerning the meaning of our perceptions as *illusions of the senses*. For the most part they are the result of incomplete inductive inferences. Their occurrence is largely related to the fact that we tend to favour certain ways of using our sense organs—those ways which provide us with the most reliable and most consistent judgements about the forms, spatial relations, and properties of the objects we observe. . . . Unusual perceptions, concerning whose meaning we have no trained knowledge, occur with unusual positions and movements of our sense organs, and incorrect interpretations of these perceptions may result. We can, in fact, lay down the general rule that with abnormal positions and movements of the eyes, the intuitions which occur are those of the objects which would naturally have to exist in order to produce the same perceptions under the conditions of normal vision.

Then, after pointing out that ordinary plane mirrors produce illusions of this kind, though we are seldom actually misled, he adds: 'most observers know how to change an unusual kind of observation into one that is common and normal, thus causing the illusion to be recognized and to disappear'. Thus *after-images impressed on the retina by a flash of light are seen as external objects, even though we may realize they are illusory, as we move our eyes and find part of the visual world moving with them. The illusion persists but we are not fooled by it.

Helmholtz was remarkable in combining shrewd psychological accounts with extraordinarily powerful physical insights, as in his work on the conservation of energy. His experimental and inventive skills were also remarkable. They led to the ophthalmoscope (1851) for examining the retina; the ophthalmometer for measuring the curvature of the optical surface of the eye; and the Young–

Helmholtz trichromatic theory of *colour vision, which is the basis of current theories. In *hearing, he introduced the resonance theory of pitch discrimination. That he achieved his results before there were stable sources of light, or electronic instruments for producing and measuring sound waves, humbles the present-day investigator.

Helmholtz's *Treatise on Physiological Optics* (3 vols., 1856–67; trans. 1924–5 reprinted New York 1962) is the foundation of the science of visual perception and well worth reading today. His *On the Sensations of Tone* (1863; 4th edn. 1877 trans. New York 1954) was his main work on perception in hearing, and his *Popular Lectures* (1881; New York 1962) range from painting through perception to physics and the basis of geometry. R. L. G.

Kahl, R. (ed.) (1971). *Selected Writings of Hermann von Helmholtz*. Middletown, Connecticut.

Koenigsberger, L. (1906). *Hermann von Helmholtz*. Oxford. Reprinted New York, 1962, this is the fullest and best biography, with a good account of the development of most of his ideas.

McKendrick, J. G. (1899). *Hermann von Helmholtz*. London. More concerned with his work in physics than on perception or the mind.

Warren, R. M. and Warren, R. P. (1968). *Helmholtz on Perception: its physiology and development*. New York. A selection of Helmholtz's writings on perception, with a short life and excellent comments on his work and ideas.

**HELVÉTIUS,** CLAUDE-ADRIEN (1715–71). French encyclopaedist philosopher. In *De l'esprit* (1758) he set out to prove that sensation is the source of all intellectual activity. This work was denounced by the Sorbonne and condemned by the French parliament to be publicly burned. It was, however, translated into several European languages. His posthumous *De l'homme* (1772) is supposed to have influenced Jeremy *Bentham.

**HERACLITUS** (*c.*540–*c.*480 BC). Greek *Pre-Socratic philosopher, born at Ephesus; he founded a school in the Ionian tradition. Fragments exist of his *On Nature*, which is divided into 'On the Universe', 'Politics', and 'Theology'. It was placed in the Temple of Artemis, and it has been suggested that it was deliberately written so obscurely as to be intelligible only to aristocrats and scholars. Heraclitus's philosophy is based on unity in change; hence the famous remark of his follower Cratylus that 'you cannot step twice into the same river'. Apparent permanence of objects is attributed to conflicting movements or flows; the essential element is fire, out of which all else comes and perishes. In modern times this emphasis on change, and on permanence as illusion, is expounded by A. N. *Whitehead.

Barnes, J. (1982). *The Presocratic Philosophers*, 2nd edn. London.

Kirk, G. S. and Raven, J. E. (1957). *The Presocratic Philosophers*. Cambridge.

**HERBART,** JOHANN FRIEDRICH (1776–1841), German philosopher and educator, born at Oldenburg. He was professor of philosophy at Königsberg and Göttingen. His account of mind essentially followed the philosophy of *Leibniz. For Herbart the universe consisted of independent elements, called reals; though these were different from the Leibnizian monads, as the reals were not necessarily conscious. They were, rather, units of a causally interacting machine—which is very different from Leibniz's conception of pre-established harmony. Herbart defined psychology as the 'mechanics of the mind'; but at the same time he emphasized the importance of *consciousness, explaining mental states and thinking as interactions of ideas. They were supposed to interact somewhat as physical particles obey and represent or manifest the laws of physics.

Herbart believed that experimentation is impossible for psychology. He maintained that for psychology to be a science it must be mathematical. To this end he set up equations: for example, for how ideas are suppressed. He attempted to show how the mind could be atomic—with ideas as atoms, displaying attraction and repulsion as in Newtonian physics. Some ideas (such as a musical tone and a visible colour) would, however, not interact, except presumably in special cases of *synaesthesia.

For Herbart ideas were in themselves active, and could struggle with one another to cross the threshold into consciousness, rather as the most active molecules of water escape through the boundary of surface tension. His philosophy of mind may appear absurd, in giving ideas independent vitality, but it did introduce concepts of suppression which reappear in *Freud's account of the unconscious, and also, if more mundanely, in current theories of memory and forgetting by interactive inhibition.

His *Textbook in Psychology* was translated into English by M. K. Smith (2nd edn., 1891) and *The Science of Education* by H. M. and E. Felkin (1892). R. L. G.

Garmo, C. de (1896). *Herbart and the Herbartians*. Reprinted 1979, London.

Stout, G. F. (1930). *Studies in Philosophy and Psychology*. London.

**HERING,** EWALD (1834–1918). German physiologist, born and raised near the Bohemian border; the son of a pastor. He studied medicine in Leipzig in the 1850s. His contributions to sensory physiology contrast distinctly with the main current of German science of his time. The outstanding representative of the latter was Hermann von *Helmholtz, a thorough physicalist and empiricist. By careful attention to the findings in more basic sciences, coupled with thoughtful but still simple experiments, and rigorous application of mathematics, Helmholtz managed to place physiological optics and acoustics as well as thermodynamics on the solid foundations so magnificently utilized by twentieth-century science. But Helmholtz had strayed a long distance from the two giants of the German intellectual scene, *Goethe and *Kant. Their much more direct descendant was the physiologist Ewald Hering, who claimed also to have been influenced, as a student, by *Schopenhauer and *Fechner.

After gaining his MD, Hering stayed in Leipzig for several years, and before he was 30 had written a series of short monographs on *visual space and eye movement. They are slightly querulous in tone and do not now make the same impact as his contribution during the following decades, but they obviously marked the author as a rising young scientist of significance. His first major academic post, as physiology lecturer in the Vienna military medical academy (the Josephinum), brought him into contact with Josef Breuer, who was later to work with Sigmund *Freud on the foundation of psychoanalysis. Together Hering and Breuer showed that respiration was in part controlled by receptors in the lung, which signal excessive distension and cause cessation of inspiration: the Hering–Breuer reflex. The Josephinum was about to be dissolved, and in 1870 Hering accepted a call to be professor of physiology at the Charles University in Prague, where he stayed for twenty-five years, until returning to Leipzig as head of the physiology department in 1895.

In his physiological researches Hering sought a synthesis of physics and psychology. He epitomized his attitude to purely physical analysis in sensory physiology in his analogy of those who might understand a timepiece by dissecting it into component gears; would not a glance at its face and hands yield an indispensable insight into its function? Accordingly, Hering made the subjective phenomena of sensation full-fledged ingredients when assembling the bases for a physiological theory, most successfully in his theories of *brightness perception and *colour vision. In this he broke ranks with almost the entire materialist natural philosophy of his time, except indeed with *Mach, a colleague in Prague. Hering did not follow Fechner, who stressed a rather simple form of psychophysical parallelism. Nor was he entirely in the tradition of Goethe and Schopenhauer, who, while sponsoring opponent theories of colour vision, placed almost all the emphasis on the subjective elements. Hering's theories of light and colour postulated substances and neural processes that could go in two directions from their neutral point—anabolic and catabolic. To arrive at these formulations, he used not only the available data on colour mixture that had been basic to previous theories, but also the observations that subjectively yellow did not *appear* to be a mixture of green and red, that yellow was a stable hue with changes in intensity, and that *after-images and complementary colours fitted best into an opponent-colour scheme. It took seventy-five years before electrophysiologists demonstrated the existence at the cellular level of Hering's mechanisms: centre-surround organization of retinal

ganglion cells; and opponent, i.e. excitatory *and* inhibitory, coding of colour. However, Hering was still very much a creature of the science of the middle of the nineteenth century. His postulated sensory and neural processing may have been more advanced and more encompassing than that of his contemporaries, yet he also believed it to reside in the cells of the organism. Its universality and presence at an early stage of development (in the case of perfect conjugacy of the eye movements even at or shortly after birth) led him to conclude that the mechanism for this kind of processing (i.e. of eye movements, of colour and brightness detection) was inborn.

In his most widely read essay (1870), Hering dealt with 'Memory as a general function of organized matter'. Because memory survives periods of unconsciousness (see MEMORY: EXPERIMENTAL APPROACHES) and *sleep, it cannot be merely associated with our *consciousness but must be regarded as a capacity inherent in brain substance and hence must follow the rules of purely material processes.

Hering's acceptance of compelling perceptual impressions as pointers of how the organism processes sensory inputs, and his willingness to postulate for them physiological, i.e. to him material, channels, at one time had great influence. A whole generation of researchers in perception followed Hering's lead by basing their theories on rules derived from (to them) persuasive sensory judgements: *Gestalt psychology was a major force until well into the 1930s. While never popular with the physicalist researchers who have dominated sensory physiology and psychology from the 1930s to this day, Hering's theories had more unity of design and less of a dualistic component than those of, say, Helmholtz. The latter relegated certain visual phenomena, such as apparent contrast, to 'errors of judgement', whereas Hering looked at them as inevitable concomitants of the physiological organization that gives us good discrimination of colour or contrast or space. As the diversity and richness of neural connectivity of the mammalian brain is being displayed by modern neuroanatomy and neurophysiology, and the untold variety of possible pathways becomes evident, many scientists are turning again to Hering and his characteristically synthetic way of making theories.

G. W.

**HERMETIC.** Associated with alchemy, from the Greek god Hermes. This is the origin of 'hermetically sealed' jars, etc.

**HEROPHILUS** (*fl.* 300 BC). Greek anatomist, and founder of the medical school of Alexandria. He was the first person who is known to have dissected a human body and compared it with other animals. He described many bodily organs and was the first to distinguish between sensory (afferent) and motor (efferent) nerves. See GREEK INVESTIGATIONS OF THE MIND AND SENSES.

**HEURISTICS.** Serving to discover or solve problems, even when no *algorithms or rules exist, using rules which involve essentially a process of trial and error. An item of information or a rule used in the process is sometimes known as a heuristic for that problem. The term is especially important in *artificial intelligence and *cybernetics.

**HIPPOCAMPUS.** A region of the brain, in the lower part of the cerebrum. The old anatomists thought it looked like a sea-horse, hence its name. There are two parts: hippocampus major (or horn of Ammon), and hippocampus minor. It is especially associated with memory. See NERVOUS SYSTEM.

**HIPPOCRATES** (*c.*470–*c.*370 BC). Greek physician born on the island of Cos. He practised medicine in Thrace, Thessaly, and Macedonia, before returning to Cos, where a school of medicine gathered around him. It is not known how much of the Hippocratic collection, consisting of some seventy books in the form of notes, is his own work. Some is known to be much later and indeed the collection may have been the library of Cos. Like his contemporaries, Hippocrates believed that disease was the result of an imbalance of the humours (see for example, INSANITY: EARLY THEORIES), but his emphasis on objective observation and critical deductive reasoning was enormously influential in separating medicine from superstition. He and his followers were the first to record case histories—some of the descriptions of disease contained in their writings are so vivid that a modern diagnosis can be made. Of particular interest among the works is the treatise entitled 'On Wounds of the Head', which describes trephining—making holes in the skull. This is known to have been a prehistoric practice, probably usually intended as a means of releasing evil spirits from the heads of the afflicted, though Hippocrates describes trephining for what we would regard as rational medical usage. His ethical standards, largely embodied in the much later Hippocratic oath, have offered inspiration to the medical profession over the centuries and largely account for his reputation as the 'father of medicine'.

See also GREEK INVESTIGATIONS OF THE MIND AND SENSES.

Singer, C. and Underwood, E. A. (1962). *A Short History of Medicine*, 2nd edn. Oxford.

**HOBBES,** THOMAS (1588–1679). British philosopher, born prematurely at Malmesbury, Wiltshire, when his mother 'fell into labour upon the fright of the invasion of the Spaniards'; Hobbes was later to say that his life was dominated by a constitutional timorousness. Foreseeing the impending civil war he went over to France in 1640—the 'first of all that fled'; in Paris he met Mersenne, friend and principal correspondent of

*Descartes, who persuaded him to contribute the Third Set of Objections to Descartes' forthcoming *Meditations* (published 1641). Hobbes's masterpiece, the *Leviathan*, appeared in 1651. This work is famous for its investigation of the basis of political authority. The authority of the sovereign (whether an assembly, or, as Hobbes preferred, a monarch) depends on the fact that supreme power is used to provide for the citizens that stability and physical security without which life would be 'a war of every man against every man' and the condition of humanity 'nasty brutish and short'. Hobbes's other works include the *De Cive* (1642), *De Corpore* (1655) and *De Homine* (1658), dealing respectively with political theory, the nature of matter, and human nature.

Though Hobbes is best known as a political theorist, he made a major contribution to the philosophy of mind. He may be regarded as an early exponent of a physicalist or materialist approach to mental phenomena. First, the universe is purely material, and contains none but physical things: 'the universe, that is the whole mass of things that are, is corporeal, that is to say body' (*Leviathan*, ch. 46). Second, talk of the soul as an independent substance that could be separated from the body is absurd: to say that something possesses a 'soul' is simply to say that it is alive (ch. 42). Third, statements about mental or psychological properties can ultimately refer only to the motions of matter in the body: 'all qualities called sensible are in the object that causeth them but so many motions of the matter that presseth our organs diversely. Neither in us that are pressed are they anything else but diverse motions, for motion produceth nothing but motion' (ch. 1).

J. G. C.

**HOLMES,** SIR GORDON MORGAN (1876–1965), Irish neurologist, was born in Dublin and studied medicine there at Trinity College. He was awarded a scholarship which gave him two years' study abroad after qualifying and went to Germany to work under Karl Weigert and Ludwig Edinger, the neuroanatomist. In 1901 he was appointed house-physician at the National Hospital for Nervous Diseases in London, where he stayed until his retirement in 1941, and later in his career also held consultancies at the Royal London Ophthalmic and Charing Cross hospitals. In 1914 he became consulting neurologist to the British Army, and from 1922 to 1937 was editor of *Brain*.

For about ten years from 1901, Holmes was concerned mainly with improving the accuracy of neurological examination, and this he accomplished through research and stringent clinical observation. It led him to investigate the neurophysiology of sensory perception in the cerebral cortex and the location of sensations with (later Sir) Henry *Head. During the First World War, especially, his work on spinal and head injuries was of great importance.

Holmes was revered as a teacher and he inspired

the many postgraduates who came to work under him. His *Selected Papers* (edited by Sir F. M. R. Walshe) were published in 1956.                D. D. H.

**HOLT,** EDWIN BISSELL (1873–1946). American philosopher and psychologist, who was a strong supporter of the behaviourism of J. B. *Watson. He is best known as the author of a book entitled *The Freudian Wish and its Place in Ethics* (1915) which attracted considerable interest in its day. Holt was essentially a philosopher by temperament and training, and reflected the close links between philosophy and psychology which were virtually taken for granted in the later decades of the nineteenth century but scarcely exist today.

**HOME,** DANIEL DUNGLAS (1833–86). British *spiritualist medium, who was born near Edinburgh and went to America as a child. The phenomena for which he was to become famous there, and later in Britain and Europe (he was expelled from Rome as a sorcerer in 1864), included rappings, 'messages' from the dead, tables and chairs which apparently rose or tipped, musical instruments which seemed to play by themselves, and *levitation. He held many seances, some rigorously tested by scientists, for which he never accepted money, and while a few people who attended them remained unconvinced, none could find any evidence of dishonesty. See his *Incidents of My Life* (1863–72).

See also PARANORMAL and PARANORMAL PHENOMENA: THE PROBLEM OF PROOF.                D. D. H.

**HOMEOSTASIS.** The main concept of homeostasis is the principle of negative *feedback control, which was developed for military purposes in the Second World War. It is the basis of *cybernetics, whose founding fathers were Norbert *Wiener, Ross Ashby, and Grey *Walter. Producing stability in dynamic systems by negative feedback has, however, a history back to James Watt's governor for the automatic regulation of steam engines as their load varies, and the still earlier governor for windmills. There are even hints of the notion of feeding the output of a system back to its input for maintaining stability in some ancient Greek devices, described by Hero in the first century AD, especially for maintaining constant supply for water-clocks by a float and needle valve, as in modern carburettors.

The term 'homeostasis' was coined some years before cybernetics, by the American physician Walter B. *Cannon, in his germinal book *Wisdom of the Body*, 1932. It is interesting that Cannon stated the basic idea of feedback as a fundamental physiological principle before it was properly recognized by engineers, though it had been used as it were implicitly, without recognition or understanding. Cannon explained the regulation of body temperature by mechanisms such as perspiring when the body is too hot and shivering when it is too cold, as maintaining the body's equilibrium by feedback signals from *what* is needed to *how* what is needed can be attained. It is now clear that this is an extremely important principle for almost all physiological processes, and also for the guiding of skilled behaviour.

Ashby, W. R. (1952). *Design for a Brain*. London.
Cannon, W. B. (1932). *Wisdom of the Body*. New York.
Walter, W. G. (1953). *The Living Brain*. London.
Wiener, N. (1948). *Cybernetics*. New York.

**HOMUNCULUS.** Literally a 'manikin' or 'little man'. The term 'homunculus fallacy' is often used to condemn accounts of psychological processes which are vacuous or circular, because they ascribe to some internal device the very psychological properties which were being investigated in the first place. Consider, for example, a theory of vision which says that there is within the brain a 'soul' or 'sensorium' or whatever, that 'scans', 'views' or 'inspects' images on the retina: such a theory is vacuous, since 'viewing', 'scanning' and 'inspecting' are all instances of the very visual processes that the theory was supposed to be illuminating in the first place. At the crudest level such explanations invite us to imagine a 'little man' sitting inside the skull inspecting some neurological equivalent of a television screen on which images of the outside world are displayed. Such theories arguably commit the 'category mistake' of trying to locate, within the structure of the brain, events and processes that belong to a higher level of description.

The term 'homunculus' is also commonly used in *artificial intelligence theory to refer to a subsystem which executes functions specified entirely in formal terms. Whether reference to such homunculi is fallacious or circular hinges on the complexity of the functions they are supposed to perform. If the operations involved can be specified ultimately in terms of very elementary devices (e.g. very simple switching devices), then the role of homunculi in this context seems relatively benign. Thus D. Dennett: 'homunculi are only bogeymen if they duplicate entirely the talents they are rung in to explain. . . . If one can get a team of relatively ignorant, narrow-minded, blind homunculi to produce the intelligent behaviour of the whole, this is progress' (*Brain Storms*, p. 123).

See also FUNCTIONALISM.                J. G. C.

Dennett, D. C. (1979). *Brain Storms*. Hassocks.
Kenny, A. (1971). The Homunculus Fallacy. In Grene, M. (ed.), *Interpretations of Life and Mind*. London.

**HUBEL AND WIESEL: JOINT WORK.** Their work on the visual cortex opened a new chapter in our understanding of the mechanisms of the brain. It started when David Hubel joined Torsten Wiesel in Steve Kuffler's laboratory at Johns Hopkins in 1958, and continued for twenty years after Kuffler moved his laboratory to the neurobiology department of the Harvard Medical School. Their outstandingly successful collaboration produced a flow of important new discoveries year after year, and these will here be summarized under four headings: the pattern selectivity of single cortical neurones, their binocular connections, their anatomical arrangement, and their normal and abnormal development in early life.

**Pattern selectivity.** The striate cortex (area 17, or the primary visual area) contains some $10^8$ cells, and in 1960 many people felt that recording from them just one at a time would not reveal much about how it all worked. But Hubel and Wiesel claimed that for each cell there was a specific pattern of excitation that would reliably excite it, and this obviously had a major impact. They discovered that the most important characteristics of the stimulus were its orientation, size, contrast (darker or brighter than the background), and which eye it was delivered to. The idea of 'feature detectors' was already a familiar one at that time and examples were known in the frog retina and arthropod visual systems, but theirs were the first examples in the mammalian nervous system, and the implications were revolutionary. Instead of thinking of the striate cortex as a structure with myriads of cells, each taking part in the representation of every visual image, one was forced to recognize that each cell had its own specific stimulus requirements, and that consequently when it became active it 'said' something specific about the nature of the image in its own particular part of the visual field. Not all their ideas about the hierarchical connections of cells or the mechanisms whereby pattern selectivity was achieved have stood the test of time, but theirs were the results that put the idea of feature detectors into the psychological literature.

**Binocularity.** Cortical neurones are the first cells in the visual pathway that have access to information from both eyes. Hubel and Wiesel found that many of them could be activated through either eye or both together, and that in such cases the stimulus requirements were nearly the same, regardless of which eye was used. In other cases the cell could be activated only through one eye and not through the other, and there were yet other cells that could be strongly activated by one eye but only weakly by the other. They plotted the numbers of cells of each type as the 'ocular dominance histogram', and this turned out to be a sensitive tool for showing the influence of factors that disturb the normal development of cortical connections. It is, however, a potentially misleading tool, for we now realize that the main significance of the binocular connections of cortical neurones lies in the small differences of alignment of the connections from each eye; this is what makes different cells responsive to different disparities and hence gives information about the distance of objects from the eyes. The ocular dominance histogram tells one nothing about this aspect, and it is therefore wrong to deduce from a normal histogram that the cortex is in a normal functional state. Hubel and Wiesel may possibly have been misled by this when assessing the role of experience in formulating the properties of the mature cortex.

**Anatomical arrangement of cortical cells.** This is the area of their greatest success, for they revealed an orderly arrangement of cortical neurones, constituting a microstructure, that was previously unsuspected. They were fortunate in that many new anatomical methods became available while they were engaged in the task of mapping this microstructure, but they were in the forefront in developing these methods and demonstrating their usefulness. The existence of a map of the visual field on the striate cortex was well known before their work, but this map is only accurate to distances of about one millimetre on the cortical surface. Each square millimetre contains some quarter million cells, and Hubel and Wiesel found first that neurones were grouped according to ocular dominance, each eye supplying irregular, alternating strips of cortex about half a millimetre wide. Orientation was also organized, for the preferred orientation of successively recorded cells tended to shift regularly through a small angle as the recording electrode moved across the cortex, a complete cycle occurring every $\frac{1}{2}$ to 1 mm. It has subsequently been shown that cells preferring a particular spatial frequency (or size) are also clustered, as are those preferring particular colours. The final details of the arrangement of the cells according to their selective properties is not yet (1983) known, but there seems little doubt that Hubel and Wiesel have sketched the skeleton of this microanatomy.

**Development.** The clinical facts of amblyopia (poor sight not caused by defects in the visual system) have long suggested that visual experience has an important effect on the neural development of the visual system. As early as 1963 Hubel and Wiesel published their first results on this problem, showing that depriving a kitten of the use of one eye by closing its eyelids has the effect of permanently disrupting the connections that eye makes to the cortical neurones. This was shown by the bias of the ocular dominance histogram towards the eye that continued in use, and they were also able to modify the histogram by surgically induced strabismus (squint), and by occluding each eye on alternate days; both of these procedures leave many cells connected to each individual eye, but cause a marked reduction in the number of cells that receive connections from both of them, thus showing that these connections require associated use of both eyes to become firmly established. They later showed that these effects of deprivation only occur up to about 6 weeks of age in the cat, or 6 months in the monkey.

This was the first demonstration of a critical or sensitive period that has physiologically demonstrable consequences and is caused by changes to normal sensory messages. The results have been obtained consistently by many others and they are among the most robust and well-confirmed findings in a field where not all claims have been substantiated. It is interesting that Hubel and Wiesel have consistently argued that experience does no more than preserve innately formed connections, basing this on the apparently normal responses and ocular dominance histograms found in young, visually inexperienced animals. Later results have shown, however, that immature and inexperienced cortical neurones lack the disparity selectivity and fine spatial resolution of adult cells, and that the cortex is therefore far from normal. Hubel and Wiesel have thus provided some of the best evidence for the effects of experience on the cortex, while making some of the most dogmatic statements on the predominance of ontogenetic factors in determining its properties. (See also VISUAL SYSTEM: ENVIRONMENTAL INFLUENCES.)

Hubel and Wiesel's interpretations of their results have often been replaced by others which they, the pioneers, have vigorously resisted; even so, their results themselves have an enviable record of reliability. Furthermore, they led the field over a twenty-year period during which exceptionally rapid progress was made. It must be added, however, that their contribution cannot be finally assessed, for there is as yet no confident understanding of how the striate cortex helps us to see the world around us. David Hubel, Torsten Wiesel, and Roger Sperry received the Nobel prize for their work in neurophysiology, in 1981.

See also BRAIN SCIENCE: SPERRY'S CONTRIBUTION.

**H.B.B.**

**HULL, CLARK LEONARD** (1884–1952). American psychologist, born at Akron, New York. He originally intended to become an engineer but contracted poliomyelitis, and this obliged him to pursue a less taxing career. In consequence, he turned to psychology, obtaining his doctorate at the University of Wisconsin and eventually becoming a professor at Yale. His early work was concerned with the measurement of attitudes and with an important study of hypnosis—almost certainly the first in which the experimental procedures were fully controlled and the results submitted to statistical analysis (see HYPNOSIS, EXPERIMENTAL). His major work, however, lay in the field of systematic *behaviour theory, in which he won considerable renown, though his attempt to evolve a hypothetico-deductive model of the learning process in animals and man has not stood the test of time (see BEHAVIOURISM and REASONING: DEVELOPMENT IN CHILDREN). None the less, he brought much-needed rigour and control into research in experimental psychology. His books include *Hypnosis and Suggestibility* (1933), *Mathematico-Deductive Theory of Rote Learning* (1940), *Principles of Behaviour* (1943), and *A Behaviour System* (1952).

**HUMAN GROWTH.** A term which covers both the increase in size of individuals with increasing age, and change in shape during the same time. In considering either aspect it is fundamental to recognize the effects of sexual dimorphism in determining both change in size and differential change in shape between the sexes. See also SEX DIFFERENCES IN CHILDHOOD.

**Growth in size.** It is convenient to use growth in height as an example. Our knowledge of the pattern of growth can come only from repeated measurements on individual children as they grow. Fig. 1 shows the growth in height of a boy from 0 to 18 years of age, measured by his father every six months (see Tanner, 1978). The upper panel shows the actual height measurements at each age, the lower panel shows the rate of growth at the various ages. Growth is a form of motion, and the former can be considered as distance travelled while the latter shows velocity. Two principal facts are shown by this figure: firstly the marked regularity of growth, and secondly the existence of three important epochs. From birth to about 4 years of age the child is growing very rapidly, but slowing steadily from growth rates of 20 cm per year to nearer 6 cm per year. Over the next six to eight

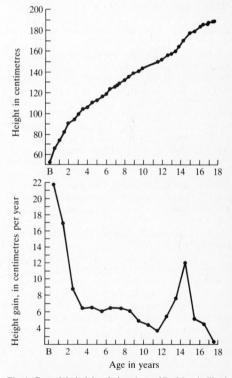

**Fig. 1.** Growth in height of a boy (son of De Montbeillard, during the years 1759–77): (above) distance curve, height attained at each age; (below) velocity curve, increments in height from year to year.

years the growth rate slows still further, but gently, so that the average velocity is about 5 cm per year. At 10 to 12 years of age the rate increases rapidly before finally slowing down to cessation of growth between 17 and 19 years. This general pattern holds for all muscular and skeletal measurements and for the more composite variables such as weight, but not for all body organs. Growth of the reproductive organs is quiescent for many years and does not start properly until the onset of puberty. Then there is very rapid growth to adult size over five or six years. Growth of the lymphatic organs, such as the tonsils and lymph nodes, is considerable in early childhood, so that between 8 and 12 their size is actually greater than in the adult, although at puberty these organs regress to adult size. Lastly, brain growth occurs very much earlier than general body growth, achieving some 95 per cent of mature size by the age of 6 years. (The growth and development of the human brain is discussed separately, under BRAIN DEVELOPMENT.)

**Sex differences.** On average, growth in height is little different between boys and girls until the onset of adolescence in girls, on average at about 10 years of age. Then the average girl starts her adolescent growth spurt and for one or two years she is taller than the average boy, who is still continuing to grow at a pre-pubertal rate. At about 12 years of age, by which time the average girl is at the peak of her growth spurt and starting to slow down again, the average boy starts his adolescent growth spurt. This is greater in intensity than in the average girl, so that not only does he reach equal height again but he goes further, to attain a greater adult height by some 12 cm. The excess of adult height in the male has two components. First there is the extra two years of growth at the pre-adolescent rate, and secondly there is the more intense growth spurt once adolescence begins.

A similar pattern is seen in other body dimensions, such as leg length, trunk length, and shoulder width. There are, however, some interesting sexual differences in timing and intensity. The growth spurt in shoulder width is more intense in the male than in the female, whereas that of pelvic breadth is rather similar between the sexes. The net effect of this is the greater shoulder breadth relative to pelvic width of the male. Thus the differential growth of these few simple dimensions is already beginning to produce differences in the characteristic shapes of the average male and female adult. Added to this are differences in the growth of subcutaneous fat. During adolescence the average male actually loses subcutaneous fat and increases muscle bulk under the influence of male sex hormones. In contrast, although the rate of gain of subcutaneous fat slows down in girls, they do not actually lose it. The effects of female hormones on the distribution of body fat produce the softer female profile, compared with that of the male.

**Differences between individuals of the same sex.** There are two principal differences: first, in size at a given age, and, secondly, in tempo—the timing with which each individual reaches the various stages of physical growth.

The range of variation in size at any age is surprisingy large. The height of a perfectly normal 10-year-old boy at the lower end of the range might be 124 cm, which is the same as that of an equally normal 6-year-old at the upper end of his range. This variation increases with age, so that the normal range of height for 2-year-old boys is about 14 cm, whereas for 10-year-old boys it is about 26 cm.

With tempo—the differences in speed with which a child passes through the various stages of development—it is slightly more complicated. Thus a child with a fast tempo, who is always advanced in his growth, seems large compared with his peers, goes through an early adolescence, and finishes growing early. This is in contrast with the so-called 'late developer', who passes each of the stages late compared with the average, and finishes growing much later. Such differences are most apparent in adolescence, and so are important when assessing individuals or groups of individuals at or after the onset of puberty: it is possible to find among boys of identical chronological age one who is pre-adolescent and another who is nearly mature. Clearly in such cases comparison is invidious and to be avoided; usually it is possible to relate growth to a maturity index, such as the stage of pubertal development.

Size at birth is generally related to maternal size; large women tend to have large babies. The size of the father is relatively unimportant, except in so far as, due to assortative mating, there is a tendency for large mothers also to have large husbands. It is believed that the dominant maternal influence is due to the environment within the uterus determining the intra-uterine growth of the child. After birth, the influence of the father's size gradually increases, until, from about the age of 2, the child's growth is related principally to the average of its parents' heights, both exerting an equal influence. This association between the child's and the parents' heights remains fairly constant from then until maturity, although during adolescence it becomes distorted unless the child matures at an absolutely average rate.

**Prediction of adult height.** Without knowledge of a child's tempo, it is very difficult to make any sort of prediction of his final height from heights at earlier ages. Given a measure of his skeletal maturity obtained from studies of X-rays, the possibility of prediction improves considerably, though there is still room for quite considerable error. For example, a prediction of the final height of a child of 9, with known skeletal maturity, is subject to a range of 14 cm in possible error. This range becomes progressively smaller the older the child is at the time of the prediction, but unless he is very near maturity it is always quite significant. A large part of scope for error arises from the great unpredictability of the size and the timing of the adolescent growth spurt.

**Environmental factors.** Thus far, genetic factors have been our main consideration. Chronic illness of any sort may affect growth, usually to reduce and very rarely to increase it, and there are some diseases, such as deficiency of growth hormone, which have highly specific effects. Disease apart, nutrition is the most obvious environmental influence, and it varies from extreme, starvation situations, where children's growth may be grossly stunted, to less severe, suboptimal situations. With suboptimal nutrition there is a tendency for growth in size to be reduced overall, but relative to reduced weight and reduced body fat. Tempo is usually affected first. Minor differences in diet, as between a child who is just rather 'faddy' about his food and one who eats heartily, do not produce significant effects on growth.

Socio-economic class has long been considered to be a significant determinant of physical size. Generally, children from families of higher socio-economic groups are taller than others. Part of the reason is nutrition, but it is probably due also to the general circumstance of the environment: children from better-off families are, for example, less exposed to recurrent infection. The fact that in the West such differences between socio-economic groups are getting smaller, and in Scandinavia have almost disappeared, presumably relates to family income and size. The more children there are in a family, in general, the smaller they are, but again these differences are tending to decrease.

Allied to the socio-economic effects are certain psychological problems. Without doubt, severe psychological stress may affect a child's growth. The condition may mimic organic disease, and severe growth failure may be apparent before it becomes clear that there are emotional difficulties. In such a situation resolution of the emotional problems leads to a prompt improvement in growth and usually to complete, or near complete, normality.

Although in general children appear to grow evenly over a span of years, in some cases there are quite marked variations within any one year. In about one-third of children there is a seasonal variation, most commonly with fast growth in the spring, and slower growth during the rest of the year. In a rather larger number there are less regular cycles, with the fast time not necessarily occurring at a fixed time of year; while in some children there is no variation at all. A child's growth should be considered over a whole period of one year; indeed, all growth standards are constructed on this criterion.

The most striking environmental effect of the last 150 years, called the secular trend, is the tendency for all children to grow to greater adult height and to mature earlier. Adult height has increased by approximately 1 cm per decade, while the first menstrual period has advanced from an average age in Norway of about 16½ in 1840 to about 13 at the present time. The cause of this secular trend is still obscure, but certainly includes improved nutrition (perhaps especially in infancy) and social circumstances.

Growth is the result of a continuing interaction between environmental and hereditary factors. It is a matter not of a simple additive effect of environment upon heredity, but of a complex interaction between the two that determines the timing of events and the degree to which various changes occur at different ages. The timing and degree vary between groups of individuals—between sexes, for example, or between ethnic groups—and in turn determine the final size and physical characteristics of the adult. But they do not materially alter the fundamental physique of an individual from that seen at a very early age. Thus it is that a child's ultimate adult appearance can largely be predicted from about the age of 5.

M. A. P.

Falkner, F. and Tanner, J. M. (1985). *Human Growth*, 2nd edn. New York.

Tanner, J. M. (1978). *Foetus into Man*. London.

**HUMANISM.** How does *humanism* connect with *humanity*? The dictionary doesn't help, both words have a cluster of meanings. The Renaissance humanists (for example, Petrarch and Erasmus) were so called because they felt that Christianity should be as much concerned with human affairs here on earth as with the afterlife in heaven and hell, and also because they were learned in the newly discovered literature of classical Greece and Rome, which was rated as 'the humanities' because it was the secular work of man whereas the Bible and the patristic commentaries were treated as the divinely inspired works of God.

Contemporary humanism is a morally concerned style of intellectual atheism openly avowed by only a small minority of individuals (for example, those who are members of the British Humanist Association) but tacitly accepted by a wide spectrum of educated people in all parts of the Western world. The essence of this modern humanism is summed up in the following quotation from Vico, who was an eighteenth-century Italian, though he wrote in the manner of the Renaissance humanists: '[it is] a truth beyond all question that the world of civil society has certainly been made by man and that its principles are therefore to be rediscovered within the modifications of our own human mind'.

Vico considered himself a Christian, but twentieth-century humanists have no use for God either as an external force which interferes in the processes of nature and the affairs of men or as an arbiter of moral judgements. Many things that happen are the consequence of pure chance, but there is no point in deifying chance and treating it as a disembodied mind which might respond intentionally to prayer. The only intentional force in the world is our own human mind.

But although modern humanists reject supernaturalism, they are not *behaviourists in any simple sense. They do not claim that all human action can be explained in terms of triggered responses to external stimuli. Humanists believe that we are capable of making choices, changing our minds, and telling lies. Men are therefore responsible for what they do. But this formula is less straightforward than it seems. Where is this 'I' located that can assume responsibility for what I do?

Let us go back to Vico, who was a thinker of great subtlety. Vico contrasted certainty (*certum*), which is what we learn from empirical observation, and truth (*verum*), which he thought of as a kind of structural model in the mind which we use to interpret the 'certainties' of our sensory experience. Hence history, that which we know as certain, is constantly transformed by the developing modifications of the mind through which alone we come to know what is true. Putting the same argument in a different way, Vico insisted that an external observer can never understand a product of human craft in the way that the craftsman himself understands it. Comparably we can understand human history not only because men made it but because our understanding comes from the truths which we hold in our mind rather than from the certainties which we obtain as external observers.

The relevance of all this to humanism is that it bears on what we might mean by the concept *humanity*. In what sense is this creature 'man', who makes his own history as a carpenter makes a chair, 'other than' just an animal caught up in the accidents of fate? How is man different? What makes him a human being?

The religious answer to this question is that man has a soul; the atheist–humanist answer is that man has a mind. But what do we mean by that? Significantly, both in German (*Geist*) and in French (*esprit*) soul and mind are covered by the same word.

Let us try to be more specific. Humanity is that which differentiates man from other animals. Where does that get us to? What can we do that they cannot do?

All animals have a limited capacity to discriminate and categorize other animals. They can recognize members of their own species and discriminate as to sex; they can distinguish food from not-food; they can recognize potential predators; some highly social species (for example, various insects, birds, rodents, baboons) can learn to discriminate neighbours from strangers. In man this last capability has been greatly elaborated. In the human case the development of a self-conscious 'I' which is contrasted with 'other' is closely linked with the formation of verbal concepts. The structure of speech, which is linear and segmented, encourages us to perceive our environment as consisting of separable 'things' and 'events' and 'categories' each of which can be described by a name. The discriminations which are indicated by such contrasts as 'I'/'other', 'we'/'they' are a part of this very general process.

But our thinking is not limited to this linear form in which we distinguish polarities, one thing after another. We also think by analogy (*metaphor), one thing superimposed upon another. Thus, while polarity may lead us to distinguish 'I'/'other', 'we'/'they', 'man'/'animal', 'tame'/'wild', 'cultivated'/'natural', analogy may lead us to feel that these pairs somehow resemble one another, so that 'we' are to 'they' is as 'man' is to 'animal', as 'tame' is to 'wild', and as 'culture' is to 'nature'.

The way we make discriminations and the way we make metaphoric associations seems to be largely arbitrary so that, overall, there are many degrees of freedom built into the way we perceive the environment in which we live. A great deal of this 'freedom' (arbitrariness) derives from our use of language in category formation; hence we may infer that other animals, which do not possess language, have a much more constricted perception of the world. To put it differently, because we have language we are able to convert sensory inputs into 'concepts in the mind' and we can play with these concepts in the imagination without reference to operations in the external world. We have persuaded ourselves that this is a human characteristic which is not shared by other animals.

The concepts which have been listed above all represent categories which derive from our experience of the external world, but language allows us to form other concepts which are wholly products of the imagination and which have no objective counterpart in the world out there. We can then use polarity to distinguish things in the world from products of the imagination, thus: 'man'/'God', 'mortal'/'immortal', 'imperfection'/'perfection', 'impotence'/'omnipotence'—and then, by the use of analogy, we may come to polarize 'impotent-imperfect-mortal-man' against 'omnipotent-perfect-immortal-God'. But this is precisely the dichotomy which modern humanists reject as superstition!

In some ways this is paradoxical since it is one of the peculiarities of our humanity that we should be capable of inventing such religious concepts at all. The point is however that whereas religion insists that God created man in his own image, humanist scepticism maintains that man created God in his own (mirror) image and that it is only self-deception which leads us to credit this mirror image with a potency which we ourselves lack. Humanists hold that religious faith is undesirable firstly because it encourages belief in what is false, namely that the human individual survives after death, and secondly because, by attributing omnipotence to God, it undervalues both the limited potency of man and the final responsibility that goes with it.

But God is more than a magnified non-natural man; he is also the source of moral judgement and here the humanists run into difficulty.

During the nineteenth century atheistical moralists believed that they could dispense with God the Moral Arbiter and substitute an equally metaphysical concept, Human Reason. At this stage in its development rationalist humanism was simply a variation of eighteenth-century deism and was itself a form of religion which even developed a church hierarchy. Modern humanism has largely abandoned ideas of this sort, though the central humanist thesis that human beings are what they are because of their education rather than because they were created to be that way by God has persisted right through. But 'education' must here be understood in the broad sense of socialization. The individual is created by the whole social milieu into which he was born; my consciousness of myself is coloured by my class consciousness, by my community consciousness, and by my national consciousness of what 'we' are as against the 'others'.

When it comes to morality, humanists now recognize that each individual's conceptions of what is right and wrong will depend upon the circumstances of his upbringing. And since humanists reject the idea that there can be any absolute criteria for making such distinctions they are led to put an unusually high valuation on the virtue of tolerance.

Many religions preach tolerance, but they do not practise it. The divine commandment 'Love thy neighbour as thyself' has never inhibited Christians from inflicting every imaginable barbarity upon their neighbours in the name of true religion. But it was a sixteenth-century humanist, Montaigne, who first complained that the contemporary treatment of heretics was far more horrible than anything that had been reliably reported of South American cannibals.

In this context the unique feature of humanism is that not only does it proclaim the virtue of tolerance but at the same time it denounces all forms of religious zeal, including zeal for humanism itself. In short, humanism is an intellectual attitude rather than the creed of a religious sect or political party; it provides us with a sceptical base from which to criticize the prejudiced certainties with which other people are prepared to proclaim the Will of God and the Destiny of Mankind, but it is not in itself a guidebook to any new kind of Utopia.                                    E. R. L.

**HUME, DAVID** (1711–76). Scottish empiricist philosopher, born in Edinburgh. He studied law at Edinburgh University, though he did not graduate, and took up commerce in Bristol, but without success. Indeed he came close to a nervous breakdown. In 1734 he moved to La Flèche in Anjou and there he wrote, while in his mid-twenties, *A Treatise of Human Nature*, his masterpiece. As Bertrand *Russell (1946) points out, in the later shortened version, *An Enquiry concerning Human Understanding* (1748)—which became much better known—Hume left out the best parts and most of the reasons for his conclusions. Even so, it was the later *Enquiry* that awakened *Kant from his 'dog-

matic slumbers': he does not seem to have known the *Treatise*. Hume also wrote *Dialogues concerning Natural Religion* (written in 1750, published posthumously in 1779), in which he discusses, with scepticism, proofs for the existence of God; on *Morals* (1751); and on politics and the history of England.

Hume is important for his systematic development of *Locke's and *Berkeley's empiricism; and for his critical discussions of *cause, and of the status of the self as no more than a 'bundle of sensations'. For Hume, the self is not an entity, for it is not an object of perception since there is no specific impression corresponding to 'I'. He somewhat similarly denies cause as usually considered, on the grounds that there are no logical connections between events.

Just as Berkeley banished *substance* from physics, as having no properties, so Hume banned *substance* from psychology. This follows in part from his view that there is no 'impression' of self, and so no 'idea' of self. In the *Treatise* (Book i, Part iv, Sect. 6) he writes:

For my part, when I enter most intimately into what I call myself, I always stumble on some particular perception or other, of heat or cold, light or shade, love or hatred, pain or pleasure. I never catch *myself* at any time without a perception, and never can observe anything but the perception.

Hume's graded distinction between *impressions* and *ideas* is fundamental to his philosophy. Thus (the opening sentences of Book i, Part i):

All the perceptions of the human Mind resolve themselves into two distinct kinds, which I shall call Impressions and Ideas. *The difference betwixt these consists in the degree and force and liveness with which they strike upon the mind, and make their way into our thought or consciousness.*

This leads to his treatment of belief (in Part iii): the 'force and liveness of the perception' is belief—and not inference, or the conclusions of inference. He argues this mainly from the example of causal beliefs; but he considers also belief in perceptions of objects. He accepts immediate experience of objects as absolutely certain. This is indeed a feature of all empiricists, for perceptions are taken as the basis of all knowledge, and some knowledge is supposed to be unquestionably true in order to give a basis for certain knowledge—although empiricist philosophers seldom agree as to what knowledge is certain. For *Aristotle, and the later Scholastics, the causal relation, *A causes B*, is a logical relation to be discovered by understanding the *essences of *A* and *B*. This, for Aristotle, is explanation. But Hume realized that it would not do as an account of cause, or as a theory of explanation. He writes: 'There is no object, which implies the existence of any other if we consider these objects in themselves, and never look beyond the ideas which we form of them.' He thus argues that cause is not a logical relation; and also that we do not experience causal relations, though we may perceive events and objects. He suggests that we infer cause from experiences of successions, of *B* following *A* in time. This takes cause—and inductive inference—outside logic and into psychology. Hume raised problems here which are still not fully resolved. One of the difficulties is that *A* and *B* may occur in regular sequence, or occur together through some other factor, *C*. It seems absurd to say, for example, that day causes night (or vice versa); or that winter causes summer, and yet they occur in regular succession. We would put the cause into our conceptual model of the solar system—the earth rotating with respect to the sun, and so on. But it remains a problem just why cause is supposed from some features of cognitive models—especially scientific accounts—and not from others.

Hume was disappointed by what he saw as his failure to justify knowledge as rational by showing that cause is not a logical relation, and that *induction is suspect. This 'failure' is the basis of all modern sceptical philosophy. Although Kant said he was awakened from his dogmatic slumbers by reading Hume, he did not succeed in countering Hume's scepticism as to whether knowledge based on induction from observed instances could be rational knowledge. Ultimately, Kant's a priori categories of perceived space and time are not justifiable, either on rational or on empirical grounds. Even more generally, there is no justification of any principle of uniformity of nature for giving logical status to induction and prediction, except by inductions such as 'predictions have worked in the past, so they will go on working in future'. But this use of induction to support induction is clearly circular, and so cannot provide rational grounds for empirical knowledge.

The appalling consequence of Hume's sceptical arguments is that, strictly speaking, any belief is as justified as any other. So, strictly, there are no grounds for distinguishing madness from sanity.

This conclusion has led to retreat from demands for rational certainty for empirical knowledge and belief, and towards essentially *relative* accounts of knowledge, in which even observations are accepted as being dependent upon assumptions, not all of which can be justified. This is well argued by the American philosophers Norwood Russell Hanson (1958) and Thomas Kuhn (1962; 1970). An alternative and very different approach is taken by Sir Karl Popper (1959, 1972). Popper takes the radical step of trying altogether to deny that there is any induction, in human or animal learning or in scientific discovery. He attempts this by suggesting that knowledge can only be gained by putting up and testing (by match or mismatch against the observed world) hypotheses, which must be framed so as to be testable.

For further discussion, see FALSIFICATION. R. L. G.

Ayer, A. J. (1980). *Hume*. Oxford.
Bennett, Jonathan (1971). *Locke, Berkeley, Hume: central themes*. Oxford.
Hanson, Norwood Russell (1958). *Patterns of Discovery*. Cambridge.
Kuhn, Thomas S. (1970). *The Structure of Scientific Revolutions*, 2nd edn., Chicago.
Popper, Karl R. (1959). *The Logic of Scientific Discovery*. London.
Popper, Karl R. (1972). *Objective Knowledge: an evolutionary approach*. Oxford.
Russell, Bertrand (1946). *History of Western Philosophy*. London.

**HUMOUR.** Most popular dictionaries when defining 'humour' include the psychologist's three usages—stimulus, response, and disposition. Hence, for example, the *Concise Oxford Dictionary of Current English* refers to 'comicality', the 'faculty of perceiving', and 'state of mind'. It is extraordinary, therefore, that Drever's *Penguin Dictionary of Psychology* (the best-known specialist dictionary for psychologists) provides a much narrower definition of humour and a provocative definition of laughter. Humour is defined as the 'character of a complex situation exciting joyful, and in the main quiet, laughter, either directly, through sympathy, or through empathy'; and laughter is said to be an 'emotional response, expressive normally of joy, in the child and the unsophisticated adult'. Drever's dictionary was published by Penguin in 1952, and it was revised in 1964. Today few psychologists, and perhaps no one currently researching humour and laughter, would endorse his definitions without substantial qualification. The psychological literature has burgeoned since the early 1970s, and we now know considerably more about humour, that ubiquitous phenomenon which most of us cherish so dearly.

Drever's reference to the 'unsophisticated adult' might startle many of us. Some would find it quaint, even amusing. It reflects a long period of history, finishing not so far back, when laughing was not so universally prized. In the eighteenth century, Lord Chesterfield, writing to his son, said '. . . there is nothing so illiberal, and so ill-bred, as audible laughter'; and others have said of laughter that it is 'the mind sneezing' (Wyndham Lewis), 'the hiccup of a fool' (John Ray), and that it '(speaks) the vacant mind' (Oliver Goldsmith). In the 1930s Ludovici argued that humour was a principal cause of the decadence of the times; and, for him, laughter was a sinister behaviour. More recently a number of writers have inferred from systematic analysis that it is only in contemporary times that humour and laughter have been regarded as important; and they point, for example, to the Bible, where there is scant mention of laughter, and such laughter as there is tends to be of a scornful kind.

Surveys indicate that these days nearly all of us believe that we have an above average sense of humour. That statistical impossibility might merely illustrate that 'sense of humour' has many shades of meaning, but in part at least it stems from the high value that society now places on humour. The possession of a good 'sense of humour', or the capacity to laugh frequently at pleasurable and amusing events, is regarded as thoroughly desirable by almost all of us. Far from being base and degenerate, fit solely for the trivial and ignorant, the appreciation of humour is now taken as a sign of health and well-being. Humour is valued as a way of preserving order, changing group esteem and cohesion, expressing allegiances and revealing attitudes with relative impunity, testing the standing of a relationship, maintaining or undermining a status hierarchy, and so forth. The quality of our exchanges with other people can be greatly enhanced by the use of humour, whether or not it is injected as a deliberate ploy. Across a wide variety of everyday encounters, humour can be a crucial tool in our social armoury, conscripted for attack and defence. Humour can be used by protagonists to precipitate an absorbing and pacifying digression: with little danger of rebuke, they can use it to defuse the threats of others by engendering a debilitating discomfort; and through it they can easily make light, or pretend to make light, of their own misfortunes and predicaments.

Beginning with Plato's *Philebus* in 355 BC, philosophers, essayists and others have provided a broad array of earnest and challenging statements concerning the nature of humour and laughter. Plato saw the weak as a justifiably prime target for humour. For Aristotle (in *Poetics*) the ludicrous was based in deformities, defects, and ugliness which are neither destructive nor painful. Notions such as these were revived in Hobbes's (1651) superiority theory: in *Leviathan* and *Human Nature* Hobbes presented laughter as a self-glorifying, triumphant gesture emanating from comparisons made with inferiors. The origins of incongruity theories can be traced back through Schopenhauer (1819) and beyond to *Kant (1790), who talked of 'an affection arising from the sudden transformation of strained expectation into nothing'. According to Schopenhauer, laughter is the expression of our recognizing an incongruity, and Spencer (1860) limited it to descending incongruity: laughter naturally occurs when 'the conscious is unawares transferred from great things to small'.

There are various other forms of theory, the most influential of which has been Freud's (1905, 1928). His was a synthesis of incongruity, relief and conflict theories. A sharp distinction was drawn between 'the comic', 'wit', and 'humour'; and humour was said to grant relief through diverting energy from unpleasant emotion. In 'joke-work' (i.e. making jokes) there is said to be a number of techniques each of which is also to be found in 'dream-work', and the principal two of which are 'condensation' and 'displacement'. Both of these techniques require deviations from normal thought and representation, and both entail an economy of thought and expression. It was Freud's contention that the ludicrous always results in a saving in the expenditure of psychic energy: not only is the joke expressed with brevity, but amusement is taken to be the most economical response to the joke. Freud also maintained that both forms of economy

could be false: energy can be liberated unnecessarily and then dissipated in expressing amusement. However, through techniques analogous to those of dreaming, humour can lift repressions; and in Freudian theory humour is amongst the most important defences.

The pervasive view of the classic Greek and Roman scholars that humour and laughter are rooted in shabbiness and deformity persisted in various guises for many centuries, but it has been largely discarded in recent years as empirical researchers, particularly psychologists, have begun to contribute significantly to knowledge. There has been a genesis and development of substantial strands of experimentation, and at the same time the quest for a grand theory has been generally abandoned. No one seems sanguine about there ever being a grand theory of humour which is capable of embracing adequately all aspects of creation, imitation, and reaction. Instead the new literature abounds with 'mini-theories' which, typically, address stimulus issues (e.g. content, structure, complexity), *or* individual differences (e.g. personality, cognitions, physiology), *or* overt expression (e.g. verbal and non-verbal reactions), *or* social influences (e.g. effects of companions and audiences), etc.

The mini-theories differ from the older, global theories in a number of salient respects (cf. Keith-Spiegel, 1972). For example, the older accounts, with few exceptions, were in effect statements of function or properties; they were little more than taxonomies of laughter-provoking stimuli, or descriptions of conditions under which laughter is sometimes evoked. The modern-day accounts draw more on general principles in psychology, and most of them tacitly or explicitly acknowledge that laughter can find expression when there is a total absence of humour. They recognize that it may not be possible to delineate any set of circumstances under which laughter is never to be found. It can prosper under conditions of deprivation, pain and oppression: seemingly it can be observed in persons experiencing any of mankind's diverse emotional states. In his book *The Sense of Humour* (1954) the English humourist Stephen Potter summed up laughter's ubiquity as follows:

We laugh when the sea touches our navel. . . . We laugh at something because it is familiar and something else because it is unfamiliar. . . . We laugh at misfortunes if they do not incur danger. . . . We laugh because other people are laughing. . . . Then there is the laugh which fills up a blank in the conversation. . . . The laugh of the older man talking to a girl, which can suggest: 'You are charming, but I am charming too.' The laugh to attract attention. . . . The laugh . . . which we hear in the hall from the new arrival not sure of himself, who wishes to appear sure of himself, and it makes us sure we are not sure of him. The laugh of the lone man at the theatre, who wishes to show that he understands the play or understands the foreign language which is being spoken, or gets the point of the joke quickest, or has seen the play. The laugh of creative pleasure. . . . The laugh of relief from physical danger. . . . We laugh at funny hats . . . we laugh at sex jokes. We do not laugh at sex jokes if they are not funny unless other people are present.

While it is important to be aware that any particular instance of laughter need not have been triggered by humour, it is disturbing to find that the vast majority of humour researchers opt to exclude laughter and other behavioural measures from their indices of humour appreciation. It seems that humour loses much of its splendour, infectiousness and power under laboratory scrutiny, to such an extent that exuberant laughter is rarely elicited from experimental subjects. There is a need for more trenchant empirical work, and particularly research in 'the field', rather than for any continuation in the escalation of asocial, laboratory studies. As far as theoretical progress is concerned, no one has made noticeable headway in answering questions of the sort, 'Why does humour produce laughter, rather than, say, a more quiescent form of behaviour?' and 'Why should the enjoyment of humour climax in any overt response whatsoever?' Then there are other questions, barely more tractable, to do with the conditions necessary for laughter to feature in the repertoire of behavioural responses. The label 'humorous laughter' is to some extent a misnomer because research indicates that the quality and quantity of laughter which, temporally, follows a joke is primarily governed by social aspects of the prevailing situation in which the joke is presented.

It is generally thought that in the early stages of an individual's development a 'safe' or 'playful' mood has to be generated for the infant to engage in 'humorous laughter'. Laughter maturationally precedes humour appreciation and first appears at about four months of age. An inevitable consequence of definitional disagreements is that distinguished scientific scholars (e.g. McGhee, 1979; Rothbart, 1980) dispute when humour is first experienced. Those who say that symbolism is an essential ingredient in humour (e.g. McGhee, 1979) report that humour does not occur until the second year of the child's life: only then does the child have sufficient capacity for fantasy and pretend activities. Others report that humour is experienced by children as young as four months (e.g. Pien and Rothbart, 1980). At that age they laugh when incongruous events are presented in safe situations, but then the cognitive resolution does not entail symbolic capacities. Rothbart (1976) observes that, for children this young, incongruity is limited as an explanatory principle: while the perception of an unexpected event may lead to laughter, it may instead lead to curiosity, fear, problem-solving or concept-learning. For laughter, the incongruous event must be safe or playful, and resolution, or partial resolution, of the incongruity must be feasible.

Incongruity is defined in terms of a disparity between what was perceived and what was expected, and such a disparity is usually taken to be a necessary but not a sufficient condition for humour. Resolution refers to the rendering of the disparity as meaningful or appropriate, or to the discovery of a rule which renders the incongruity explicable within the context of the joke. We still have no model which satisfactorily embraces both the perception and resolution aspects of incongruities. However, we do know from empirical work as well as from everyday experiences that incongruities can be too trivial or they can be too complex for humour to be experienced; and, independent of complexity, some themes (e.g. sex and aggression) are generally more comic than others.

A notable exception to the modern-day brand of mini-theory is that propounded by D. E. Berlyne. His was an 'arousal' theory which enjoyed considerable support in the 1970s. Like Freudian theory, however, it has been gradually discarded by empirical researchers as they have increasingly dedicated their investigations to cognitive dimensions of humour. Berlyne's analysis was founded upon the view that moderate levels of arousal ('non-specific drive') and changes in arousal are pleasurable, whereas high and low levels of arousal are not pleasurable. Humour was said to boost the individual's arousal to an unusual level until resolution of incongruity caused a sharp decline. Hence pleasure can result from the change *per se* and from the raising of arousal from an uncomfortably low level. It is not clear from Berlyne's writings whether arousal changes and humour appreciation are related in a linear, inverted U, or U-shaped fashion. Since it is possible to argue for any of these three possibilities, the theory is inherently untestable.

The superiority theories of yesterday were precursors of contemporary disposition theory (Zillmann, 1983), and that theory posits that humour emanating from disparagement depends upon a balance of affective dispositions towards the disparaged and non-disparaged parties. The theory predicts that humour appreciation will be strong when one is negatively disposed towards the disparaged party, and it will also be strong when one is positively disposed to the person purveying the disparagement. A principal difference between disposition theory and superiority theories (e.g. La Fave, 1977) is that the latter highlight both the debasement of an inferior and the enhancement of a superior, whereas in disposition theory the enhancement of the superior is a by-product and is not essential to humour appreciation. Disposition theory is especially useful when accounting for the success of jokes aimed at minority groups, such as the physically handicapped and psychiatrically disturbed. It is similarly useful when accounting for the pervasiveness of jokes aimed at demographic, political and ethnic minorities.

It has been claimed that women find jokes funnier when heard by the left ear, with the suggestion that this ear routes to the right hemisphere of the brain, which processes information more holistically than the left hemisphere, which is analytical. Could this be the basis for a biological explanation

HUNGER AND FOOD INTAKE 323

of sex differences in humour appreciation? Unfortunately, each ear is represented in both hemispheres (though with some contralateral preference) so this is hardly a serious suggestion. Clinical studies of patients with damage to the right hemisphere have identified correlated deficits in humour comprehension and appreciation. However, it cannot be assumed that a cerebral 'centre for humour' is located in the right hemisphere. The operation of the left hemisphere is crucial in providing and organizing relevant information necessary to resolve perceived incongruity.

The bias of psychological theory and investigation has been towards a characterization of *responses* to humour. We know little about factors bearing on the creation and initiation of humour. Also, researchers tend to neglect fundamental conceptual and measurement questions, and they are too often insular in their approaches and objectives. None the less there is now much evidence to the effect that humour reflects basic underlying trends in emotional, social, and cognitive development.

A. J. C.
N. P. S.

Freud, S. (1905). *Der Witz und seine Beziehung zum Ubewussten*. Leipzig and Vienna.
Freud, S. (1928). Humour. *International Journal of Psychoanalysis*, **9**, 1–6.
Kant, I. (1790). *Kritik der Urteilskraft*. Berlin.
Keith-Spiegel, P. (1972). Early conceptions of humor: varieties and issues. In Goldstein, J. H. and McGhee, P. E. (eds.), *The Psychology of Humor: theoretical perspectives and empirical issues*. New York.
La Fave, L. (1977). Ethnic humour: from paradoxes towards principles. In Chapman, A. J. and Foot, H. C. (eds.), *It's a Funny Thing, Humour*. Oxford.
Ludovici, A. M. (1932). *The Secret of Laughter*. London.
McGhee, P. E. (1979). *Humor: its origin and development*. San Francisco.
Pien, D. and Rothbart, M. K. (1980). Incongruity humour, play, and self-regulation of arousal in young children. In McGhee, P. E. and Chapman, A. J. (eds.), *Children's Humour*. Chichester.
Rothbart, M. K. (1976). Incongruity, problem-solving and laughter. In Chapman, A. J. and Foot, H. C. (eds.), *Humour and Laughter: theory, research and applications*. Chichester.
Schopenhauer, A. (1819). *Die Welt als Wille und Vorstellung*. Leipzig.
Spencer, H. (1860). The physiology of laughter. *Macmillan's Magazine*, **1**, 395–402.
Zillmann, D. (1983). Disparagement humor. In McGhee, P. E. and Goldstein, J. H. (eds.), *Handbook of Humor Research*. New York.

**HUMOURS, CLASSICAL.** See INSANITY, EARLY THEORIES FOR.

**HUMPHREY,** GEORGE (1889–1966). British psychologist, born at Westgate-on-Sea, Kent, and educated at All Souls College, Oxford, where he was one of the last of the 'Bible clerks'—as the four undergraduates admitted yearly to the College were then known. After graduating in classical studies, Humphrey moved into psychology, then non-existent in Oxford as a subject for undergraduate study. He studied first in Leipzig and subsequently at Harvard, where he obtained his doctorate in 1924. He was appointed to the Charlton professorship of psychology at Queen's University, Kingston, Ontario, where he built up a laboratory in which most of his own best work was done. Humphrey, whose special interest lay in the nature of *conditioning and *learning, did much to narrow the gap between German and American conventions in the approach to experimental psychology.

He returned to Oxford in 1947 as the foundation professor of psychology charged with setting up a new Honours school of psychology, philosophy, and physiology and with developing the then tiny institute of experimental psychology, which he took over on the resignation of the then director, Dr William Stephenson. From the start, therefore, psychology in Oxford evolved along clear-cut experimental lines. While there can be no doubt that Humphrey's contribution to its birth was indeed substantial, the task of establishing and guiding the new psychology school imposed a severe stress upon his health and vitality, and appreciably limited his output in research. None the less, it is largely due to him that a major department of psychology came into being in Britain's senior collegiate university.

Humphrey's most important books are *The Nature of Learning* (1935) and *Thinking: its experimental psychology* (1951).

O. L. Z.

**HUNGER AND FOOD INTAKE REGULATION.** That organisms need to ingest nutrient is obvious; but what the mechanism is that controls such ingestion is not, and that is a question of more than academic interest. Disorders of the hunger mechanism, of which obesity is the most common, are cosmetically disfiguring and pose a very considerable danger to health, curtailing the life span significantly. Because of the threat that obesity poses, a large dieting industry has sprung up, which, as a result of misconceptions and ignorance of the normal hunger mechanism, is almost totally ineffective.

Normal humans and normal rats (and we know much more about rats) regulate their caloric intake so as to maintain their weight within close limits. Further, they are able to select various dietary constituents so as to maintain themselves in good health. Infants given a choice of a variety of foodstuffs at each meal thrive better than those whose diet is prescribed by a dietician, and so do rats. There are two questions posed by these observations. The first is how do organisms manage to regulate the amount of food eaten, and the second is how do they know which dietary constituents to choose. Let us start with the first question. To regulate the amount eaten there must be an internal signal which initiates eating, the introspectible counterpart of which we call hunger, and another signal which terminates eating, which we call satiety. It is sad to report that we do not know what these signals are.

We have found that it is possible to induce eating through various interventions. Peripheral injections of insulin produce hunger, and injections of noradrenaline (norepinephrine) into the brain ventricles produce some increase in food intake. However, rats and people that do not secrete insulin still feel hungry and eat, and noradrenaline produces a drop in body temperature which itself will increase food intake. Secondly we have believed that we know where the biochemical change that produces hunger acts in the brain. Small lesions in the lateral hypothalamus in rats produce an animal that starves in the midst of plenty; and electric stimulation of the same area through chronically implanted electrodes induces vigorous eating in an already satiated animal. These experiments might seem fairly conclusive, but there are problems. A rat with a lateral hypothalamic lesion is a very sick animal, and a number of peripheral mechanisms are disrupted by the operation: the effect on eating might therefore be indirect. Similarly, stimulation of the lateral hypothalamic area may stimulate other mechanisms which then induce eating. But the most devastating objection is that it is also possible to induce eating simply by a sustained pinching of the rat's tail!

Although the exact identity of satiety signals still eludes us, some progress has been made in their discovery. The simplest idea was that termination of eating occurs when the changes that produce hunger are reversed. But such an idea must be incorrect because eating stops when the digestion of a meal has barely begun. Another idea has been that we learn to eat a certain amount of a particular food because such an amount has in the past eventually led to the reduction of hunger. Though there is some evidence that this can be a minor factor under some circumstances, it cannot by any means be the whole story, because when an animal eats and the food does not either reach or stay in the stomach, the animal may continue to eat until exhausted. This suggests that satiety signals are generated somewhere in the upper gastrointestinal tract, either in the stomach or in the upper part of the gut. Such a conclusion is supported by experiments in which food is placed directly in the stomach: great reductions in subsequent feeding are observed. Unfortunately, however, the reason for this result could be wholly artefactual, for it has been recently found that placement of food in the stomach causes nausea, which by itself could produce a reduction in eating.

As we have just seen, when food is not allowed to stay in the stomach, animals eat abnormally large amounts. One popular hypothesis for this has been that the nutrient does not reach the duodenum; and experiment has shown that if food is pumped into the duodenum and not allowed to stay in the stomach, then overeating does not take place. But this experiment also is not conclusive, for it has subsequently been shown that pumping of food into the duodenum causes discomfort or nausea. Secondly, the duodenum is sometimes considered to be the origin of satiety messages because it secretes the gastrointestinal hormone cholecystokinin, injections of which have been shown to reduce eating. But although this has been taken to indicate that cholecystokinin is a satiety hormone, subsequent research has shown that the same dose also causes nausea. Thus there is no compelling evidence that the duodenum or its hormones are involved in satiety.

There is now clear evidence, however, that satiety signals emanate from the stomach. It is possible to implant a pyloric cuff round the exit from the stomach of a rat, a cuff which, when inflated, prevents the escape of stomach contents into the duodenum, without causing distress to the rat. (The gut may be squeezed, cut or cauterized without producing pain or distress, while distension is aversive.) Also implanted in the stomach is a tube for the overflow when pressure in the stomach reaches the normal limit. Under these circumstances rats do not overeat, as they would if it was signals from the duodenum that produced satiety. A further experiment makes the same point in another way. A rat is allowed to drink nutrient to satiety and, after the pyloric cuff has been inflated, a certain amount of nutrient is drawn off through the stomach tube. The rat then begins to drink again, even though the content of the duodenum is unchanged. Moreover, if a rat drinks nutrient to satiety while the pylorus is occluded, and then nutrient is allowed to escape from the stomach to the duodenum, the rat will drink more nutrient, when it is presented, even though the cuff is inflated.

These experiments demonstrate that signals of satiety emanate from the stomach. However, we are not yet sure what such signals are. There are various possibilities. It may be that satiety arises when the stomach has been distended past a certain point. Or it could be that the stomach senses the total amount of nutrient in the volume ingested, and that it is this that signals satiety. We now have evidence that both may be true. Rats are allowed to drink under two conditions: in the first they simply drink nutrient to satiety; in the second they also drink to satiety but as the nutrient is drunk the same volume of saline is pumped into the stomach. If the stomach-distension hypothesis is correct, the rats in the second condition should on average drink only one-half the volume of nutrient. If the theory of absolute amount of nutrient is correct, on the other hand, the same volume should be drunk in both conditions. The truth is complex. Rats that drink very large volumes to satiety support the distension hypothesis, but those that drink small amounts behave as if the absolute amount of nutrient theory is true. So it seems that satiety at small volumes is regulated by nutrient. However, past a certain point distension becomes an important cue in causing a rat to stop eating.

There is other evidence that the stomach can sense nutrient when volume is kept constant. A hungry rat is given a choice between the contents of two tubes, each containing a different non-nutritive flavour. When it drinks from one of the tubes, nutrient made non-aversive by predigestion is placed in the stomach. When it drinks from the other, an equal volume of saline is placed in the stomach. Each training session lasts only ten minutes and a pyloric cuff is inflated during this period. The rat quickly learns to drink from the tube that produces nutrient in the stomach. We do not know as yet whether this sensitivity to nutrient is due to early absorption of small amounts of this nutrient or whether it is due to sense organs within the stomach. We do know, however, that the partial digestion is necessary for the nutrient to produce satiety signals. The rat secretes an enzyme at the back of its tongue which splits a portion of the fat or oil into its constituents. When a rat drinks oil and we place some of the same oil directly in the stomach, thus bypassing that part of the early digestive process due to the enzyme secreted by the tongue (lingual lipase), there is little or no reduction in the amount that the rat chooses to drink. On the other hand, an amount of predigested oil, drawn from the stomach of a donor rat, when placed in the stomach reduces the volume drunk by the same amount.

If, as seems likely, the sense organs are in the stomach, we do not know how they relay their messages to the brain. It is known that the stomach produces hormones which could affect the brain via the bloodstream, and it is also known that a large number of nerve fibres carry messages to the brain via the vagus and splanchnic nerves. But it has been found that sectioning of the vagus does not affect a rat's ability to monitor nutrients in the stomach: a rat with its vagus nerve cut still compensates accurately for any nutrient removed from the stomach during a meal. On the other hand, it no longer stops eating in response to overdistension of the stomach.

So far we have spoken of hunger as if it was a single phenomenon. However, in order to obtain an adequate diet most organisms must select a balanced mixture of foods, because they must satisfy not only their caloric needs, but their protein, vitamin, and mineral requirements as well. The mechanism of selection varies from one requirement to another. For instance, the appetite for common salt is 'wired in' or built in: when a shortage of sodium occurs, whether it be through dietary insufficiency or malfunction of the adrenal cortex, the shortage is directly translated into a craving for a particular *taste—the taste of salt— and the rat does not have to learn that the ingestion of salty tastes has beneficial consequences. There are other types of deficiency, on the other hand, where the rat has to learn what food will relieve the deficiency. The way this happens is rather curious. The deficient rat begins to prefer any novel foodstuff; it seems to develop an aversion to its normal diet. If the novel diet relieves the symptoms of deficiency the rat will then learn to consume it even if the relief is not immediate.

Generally learning occurs only if a few seconds at the most separate an act, or a signal, from its consequences; but this is not true in the case of eating. If a rat eats poison, it will learn to avoid its taste even if sickness due to the poison occurs between 10 and 24 hours later. Similar taste avoidance has been noted in children who have eaten ice-cream of a certain flavour before undergoing chemotherapy. Clearly organisms must learn what foods are good for them, although learning is not necessary in every case. In the same way as the example of salt, aversions can also be 'wired in'— and that is as true of sweet as of bitter substances.

'Wired in' aversions and preferences have consequences for weight control. It has been shown that rats fed palatable diets maintain much higher body weights than those whose diets are unattractive. Another finding is that rats fed diets low in calories compensate by eating more. Now the stock-in-trade of the diet food industry seems to consist of two main items. The first is the substitution of sugar as a sweetener by nonnutrient substances such as saccharin. The second is the sale of food that has a lower number of calories per unit weight or volume than normal food. Now, if calories per unit volume are reduced and there is no restriction on the volume that can be eaten we would expect from the results of research that the volume eaten would increase to compensate. And as for saccharin, when it was shown that it was carcinogenic, the major argument for its retention as a food additive was that it made dieting easier; but as we have seen above, making a food palatable, or less aversive, increases its intake. One of the major aims of food production and preparation is to make food more attractive both by the addition of substances which are palatable and by removing tastes and textures which are aversive. Such gastronomic practices have almost certainly led to much ill health and a curtailment of life span through a general increase in obesity and other disorders.

See also ANOREXIA NERVOSA AND BULIMIA NERVOSA.                                              J. A. D.

**HUNTINGTON'S CHOREA.** Several types of cerebral degeneration occur which lead to loss of mental powers in middle age. All are rare. One type is Huntington's chorea, which owes its name to George Huntington (1850–1916), an American physician, who first described the disease. Among its cardinal features Huntington mentioned 'a tendency to insanity and suicide'. In the early stages spontaneous movements give the impression of clumsiness and fidgetiness, but, as the disease progresses, the characteristic jerking and writhing movements become more prominent, particularly affecting the face, tongue, and upper limbs, although, ultimately, all parts of the body musculature may be involved. The disease runs in families, and its pattern of distribution within families shows it to be due to a single autosomal dominant gene. It survives because the average age of onset is in the middle thirties, late enough for most carriers of the gene to have begotten children. The patients described by Huntington were said all to be descendants of a family of three brothers who had emigrated from England.

Two expectations have to be met before a disease is attributed to a dominant gene. One parent must have been affected, and the proportion of children affected must not depart significantly from one-half. Cases of Huntington's chorea do occur occasionally in which neither parent seems to have been affected. In some of these, a parent has died young; in others, there is doubt about the identity of the father. The proportion of children affected has usually been found to be about one in three. The probable reason why this falls short of one-half is that a relatively high proportion of the sibship have died young; some of those affected die before birth.

The course is progressive, with increasing disability due to the loss of neurones leading to *dementia. The cerebrum atrophies and loses weight. The ventricles enlarge. The caudate nucleus and putamen of the midbrain are especially affected. Severe *depression is a common complication which may end in suicide attempts or actual suicide, which is the cause of death of 7 per cent of non-hospitalized patients.

Numerous attempts have been made to identify carriers of the gene before they enter the reproductive period of life but, so far, none has been of proven validity. In any case, predicting a progressive, incapacitating neuropsychiatric illness in somebody who may at the time be relatively healthy raises ethical problems which may outweigh the potential eugenic advantages.   D. R. D.

Myrianthopoulos, N. C. (1966). Huntington's Chorea. *Journal of Medical Genetics*, **3**, 298–314.

**HUSSERL,** EDMUND GUSTAV ALBERT (1859–1938). The name of the German philosopher Edmund Husserl is associated with one of the most important philosophical revolutions of recent times. If one had to name the major changes which occurred in philosophy at the end of the nineteenth century, Husserl's *phenomenology would doubtless be mentioned, together with the developments of Marxist thought and of early *logical positivism. The case of Husserl calls for special attention in view of his deep influence on the overall field of disciplines which we label today human sciences and which include psychology, sociology, and philosophical anthropology, as well as classical humanistic sciences such as history and philology. Linguistics, which also contributed to the transformation of human sciences, evolved autonomously and became important much later, as testified by the relatively recent developments of structuralism and semiotics. The striking fact in Husserl's case is that, starting from the philosophy

of mathematics, he succeeded in elaborating a radical philosophy of *consciousness, from which a general epistemology as well as a new kind of psychology developed in the course of time. For these reasons, it is impermissible to consider Husserl's phenomenology just as one philosophical system among others.

Husserl's investigations began with his *Philosophy of Arithmetic* (1891), which was intended to lay the foundations of a philosophy of mathematics. In this initial phase, Husserl analyses the concept of number from both the psychological and the logical points of view. From the psychological point of view, numbers do not only correspond to sets of elements liable to be counted, they constitute wholes beyond the capacities of immediate perception as soon as they include a large quantity of units. From this moment on, they only exist for consciousness as wholes expressed by symbols. This theory of symbolic wholes foreshadowed the basic principle which was to be fully developed by *Gestalt theorists in later years.

The second phase of Husserl's work began with the *Logical Investigations* (1900–1). His main concern was then to establish the foundations of logic outside psychology, namely against the empiricists' contention that the basic principles of logic could be ultimately referred to psychological laws. As a result, the main effort of Husserl's philosophy centred for many years on a fundamental criticism of *psychologism*, i.e. the conviction that not only logic, but every field of knowledge would be rooted in psychology, being the science dealing with consciousness. The reasons for rejecting psychology as *the* fundamental science are twofold. First, from the point of view of logic and of mathematics, the psychologistic postulate leads to internal contradictions within the theoretical systems because it can be established that psychology, *as a science*, is necessarily a subsystem of a more extensive one comprising at the outset the minimal postulates which psychology needs to proceed as an organized field of knowledge. Secondly, in Husserl's time, scientific psychology, then mainly represented by early psychophysics and experimental psychology, was not in a position to furnish sufficiently rigorous proofs of its supposed founding role within the general framework of the theory of knowledge.

Consequently, the *Logical Investigations* stressed the fact that the logical structures exist independently of their psychological correlates and that the search for the psychological aspects of the logical acts as subjective experiences must itself be conducted beyond the realm of psychological science. In other words, if we want to study adequately such experiences, we are bound to turn to a descriptive science of psychic acts. Such an enterprise needs a science of phenomena, i.e. a *phenomenology*. It is, however, clear that if phenomenology is to be such a basic 'descriptive psychology' it has to cope with the *essences* of our subjective experience and not with the concrete scientific facts as evidenced in experimental psychology.

We see, thus, that in his attempt to situate the phenomena of experience in their proper subjective perspective, Husserl broadens *Brentano's theory of *intentionality up to a general epistemology, amounting finally to a radical theory of subjectivity. This implies that the descriptive dimension of phenomenology should evolve towards a *transcendental* mode of analysis, in which the point of view of natural science is 'bracketed', i.e. left out of consideration, but not eliminated because every act of consciousness is intentionally directed towards some object. This is the sense of his so-called 'reduction'.

Husserl's search for an adequate science of phenomena, as outlined in the second part of his *Logical Investigations*, was further developed in his *Ideas* (1913). In the period between 1901 and 1913 he produced two major works: *Die Idee der Phänomenologie* (1907), and *Die Philosophie als strenge Wissenschaft* (1911), in which the philosophical dimension of his epistemological strivings is thoroughly developed.

Because of its radical standpoint, Husserl's phenomenology is in a sense an attempt at founding the philosophy of all possible philosophies, which amounts to raising the basic question of the ontology implied by every act of knowledge. At the beginning of his career, Husserl believed he could locate the science of phenomena by drawing a fundamental distinction between the natural standpoint and that of pure transcendental phenomenology, the latter being freed from psychologism by the process of 'reduction' ('bracketing' of the natural). Towards the end of his life, he left aside his first idea of founding pure phenomenology on a descriptive (or phenomenological) psychology and expected to find a more suitable starting-point in an analysis of man's life-world (*Lebenswelt*).

This last phase of his research is represented by his work entitled *The Crisis of the European Sciences and Transcendental Phenomenology* (German edn. 1935–7; English trans. 1970). The main thesis developed in this important book deals with the historical consequences of Western science for everyday experience. Husserl contends that in striving to build up an objective picture of reality, scientific practice has progressively cut off subjective experience from the life-world to such an extent that Western man is in a permanent state of crisis, i.e. he feels that science is the only source of facts and loses consequently his lived relation to the historical and social reality of life. In brief, Western man is deprived of the immediate evidence of his world considered as the realm of significant relations to objects and to his fellow men, and is condemned to rely only on intermediate abstract constructs: the life-world is concealed by the transcendental act of scientific elaboration. *The Crisis* shows with a wealth of detailed analyses how *objectivism* (i.e. the belief in the exclusivity of

science in reaching well-established truths) has replaced actual *objectivity*. Once again, if objectivity is to be established as the intentional result of the activity of consciousness, we need an a priori epistemological theory of phenomena. This brings us back to the necessity of phenomenology as the starting-point of every rigorous man-centred philosophy.

In attempting to appreciate Husserl's undertaking, we must not forget that his theory of transcendence was rooted in a basic analysis of logic, aiming at a radical refutation of psychologism and of the mistaken attempts of individual sciences to present themselves as the fundamental discipline governing the development of other fields of knowledge. It must also be pointed out that though Husserl stresses the necessity of an a priori theory of phenomena in order to lay the foundations of any human science, his philosophy calls for a 'return to things themselves', i.e. to the primary experience of the subject in his world. The meaning of experience as the founding fact of Husserl's philosophy is therefore radically opposed to the positivistic outlook, according to which the scientific constructs as such are the only basic facts.

Considering the specific case of psychology, it is certain that phenomenology has profoundly modified its epistemological situation as a potential rigorous science. As a consequence, scientific psychology is now evolving towards a man-centred discipline under the heading of *phenomenological psychology*, an expression which should not be confused with Husserl's own attempt at elaborating the preparatory phase of his critical analyses. Present-day phenomenological psychology is in search of a new kind of empiricism, in which the subject, the observer, and the methodology which allows them to communicate are situated within a new functional framework. This framework allows a more adequate formulation of experimental, clinical, and social problems, and avoids a mere transposition of naturalistic postulates to a field of research in which subjectivity must be considered as a founding fact of the human life-world.

G. T.

Giorgi, A. (1970). *Psychology as a Human Science*. New York.

Kockelmans, J. J. (1967). *Edmund Husserl's Phenomenological Psychology*. Pittsburgh.

Spiegelberg, H. (1960). *The Phenomenological Movement: a historical introduction*. The Hague.

Thinès, G. (1977). *Phenomenology and the Science of Behaviour*. London.

**HUXLEY**, THOMAS HENRY (1825–95). English biologist and palaeontologist, born in London. He studied medicine but failed to complete his degree. He served on the four-year cruise of HMS *Rattlesnake* (1846–50) and undertook detailed studies of marine life, for which he was elected a Fellow of the Royal Society. In 1854 he was appointed lecturer of natural history at the Royal School of

Mines (now Imperial College) in London. Huxley explicitly rejected the possibility of evolution until he read Charles *Darwin's *Origin of Species* (1859), upon which he became 'Darwin's bulldog', propounding the theory in public on many critically important occasions and thus protecting Darwin from the public appearances which he found onerous and tiring. Huxley was in his own right a first-rate scientist, and he also supported popular education. His essays *Man's Place in Nature* (1863) contain his philosophy. He coined the term 'agnostic', following *Hume in his theological questioning.

**HYPERAESTHESIA.** Extreme sensitivity to touch and a low pain threshold.

**HYPEROPIA.** See EYE DEFECTS AND THEIR CORRECTION.

**HYPNAGOGIC   HALLUCINATION.** An extremely vivid image, usually visual, which is often experienced when one is dropping off to *sleep, or, less commonly, immediately on awakening. Unlike fully fledged *dreams, hypnagogic states are to a large extent under the control of the will and can be described to a second person on, or immediately after, their occurrence. Hypnagogic images are often said to possess an overwhelming sense of reality, with much detail and supersaturated colour.

An interpretation of hypnagogic phenomena along the lines of Freud's celebrated theory of dreams (see FREUD ON DREAMS) has been put forward by a Belgian psychologist, J. Varendonck, to whose book on *The Psychology of Day Dreams* Freud himself contributed an introduction. Varendonck places much emphasis on the role of preconscious thought and wishful thinking in hypnagogic phenomena, but it might seem more probable that these possess a physiological basis related to the incipient onset of sleep or partial awakening.                                    O. L. Z.

**HYPNOSIS, EXPERIMENTAL.** In the course of the twentieth century, interest in hypnosis has largely passed from the physician to the experimental psychologist, whose concern is with its nature and mechanisms rather than with its therapeutic efficacy. While a few scattered experiments, such as those of D. R. L. Delboeuf, were reported towards the end of the nineteenth century, the modern era in the study of hypnotism may be said to have been ushered in by the work of Clark L. *Hull and his co-workers at Yale University in the early 1930s. While militantly disowning hypnotism's murky past, Hull insisted that hypnosis is an essentially normal phenomenon that can be studied in precisely the same way as any other mental capacity which varies from one individual to another. His book published in 1933 represents the first systematic attempt to apply the experimental and statistical methods of modern psychology to the study of hypnosis and suggestibility.

Hull's work was to a considerable extent designed to cast doubt on the extravagant claims current in some quarters that individual capacity in the hypnotic state might transcend the limits of the normal. Thus it has been argued that exceptional feats of sensory discrimination, of muscular strength, or of *memory might be performed in the hypnotic state, suggesting that hypnosis *per se* enhanced many aspects of human capacity. Hull and his co-workers were able to show that whereas hypnosis as such does not appear to confer any obvious advantages, it is none the less possible to influence human performance, sometimes dramatically, by hypnotic suggestion. For example, he produced evidence of some increase in muscular capacity, more especially in sustained resistance to fatigue, and alterations in threshold of a variety of sensory stimuli, whereby the lower limits of intensity of stimulation necessary to produce a conscious sensation were appreciably raised. As regards memory, whereas no improvement in the reproduction of recently memorized material under hypnosis could be demonstrated, there was some evidence that memories of childhood might become more readily accessible. Hull's work, while producing no real evidence of the transcendence of normal capacity in hypnosis, did undoubtedly demonstrate the reality of many classical hypnotic phenomena (for example, hypnotic anaesthesia or analgesia and post-hypnotic amnesia) under reasonably well-controlled experimental conditions. His work also served to bring out the essential continuity between the effects of suggestion in the waking and the hypnotic states.

Experimental hypnosis rapidly expanded in the 1950s and 1960s, some of its foremost representatives being F. X. Barber, E. R. Hilgard, M. T. Orne, and T. R. Sarbin. One of the main preoccupations at this period was the construction of standardized scales of hypnotic susceptibility, of which the best known and most widely used were the Stanford scales devised by A. M. Weitzenhoffer and E. R. Hilgard in 1961. The rationale of their construction and use was well described by Hilgard (1965) and one need only comment here on some of the more interesting findings. In the first place, contrary to traditional belief, there is no real evidence that women are more readily hypnotizable than men, or are capable of greater depth of hypnosis. In the second place, a *critical period seems to exist as regards hypnotic susceptibility. While it has long been known that children are in general more easily hypnotized than adults, it has been found that children between the ages of 8 and 12 are more easily hypnotized than either older or younger children. The advantage may lie in part in the fact that whereas children of 8 and below find sustained concentration difficult and are readily distracted, children above the age of 12 or so have developed greater powers of self-criticism and are consequently less suggestible. Although changes in hypnotic susceptibility over the adult life span do not appear to be striking, the natural history of hypnosis is certainly deserving of closer study.

From Hull onwards, experimental methods have been widely used to study such classical phenomena of hypnosis as hypnotic anaesthesia or analgesia (Hilgard and Hilgard, 1975) and sensory deceptions or *hallucinations. In some ingenious experiments, Hilgard has shown that it is not difficult to induce selective deafness for sounds of weak intensity—for example, the ticking of a watch—without interfering with the subject's perception of the experimenter's voice. In susceptible subjects, it may even prove possible to effect profound attenuation of sensation within a particular sensory modality, such as touch or pain. Experiments by A. M. Halliday and A. A. Mason (1964) have, however, shown that, in such cases, the nervous messages from the sense organs do in fact reach the relevant areas of the cerebral cortex, where they give rise to electrical responses ('*evoked potentials') of normal amplitude. It therefore seems that the conscious sensory responses with which these electrical activities are ordinarily correlated must undergo some form of suppression or dissociation. That this is so is strongly indicated by a dramatic experiment of Hilgard's, in which he showed that a hypnotized subject in whom a profound loss of pain sense had been induced by suggestion, and who entirely denied feeling pain when appropriately stimulated, did in fact admit to doing so when tested by automatic writing, the content of which was ostensibly unknown to him. This is a classical example of hypnotic dissociation of the kind much discussed by Pierre *Janet (see HYPNOTISM, HISTORY OF) and other early expositors of the relations between hypnosis and *hysteria. It strongly suggests that hypnotic anaesthesia and analgesia are true dissociative phenomena rather than mere exaggerations of ordinary suggestibility.

Sensory deceptions (illusions) and even hallucinations induced by suggestion have also been demonstrated on occasion, using healthy, volunteer subjects in an experimental situation, but only in those whose susceptibility to hypnosis is unusually high (Hilgard, 1965, pp. 129–49; Weitzenhoffer, 1947, pp. 153–7, 286–95). In such cases, a distinction should be made between the generation of behaviour appropriate to an imagined object, which is not difficult to induce, and the production of what is described by the subject as a true perceptual experience (hallucination proper). For example, Hilgard has shown that many subjects will react positively to the suggestion that a fly has alighted, say, on their face, by grimacing or brushing it off. This might almost be regarded as play-acting in the sense of T. R. Sarbin and others who stress the 'role-playing' element in hypnosis. Even so, a few such subjects will say when asked that the experience was very real and lifelike, suggesting a true positive hallucination. Further experiments, in which it is suggested that the subject will

perceive two dim lights, when only one is shown, likewise on occasion elicit surprisingly convincing reports of a hallucinated experience. It is possible in such cases that suggestion in alliance with the artificial hypnotic state has produced a condition akin to *dreaming, in which a visual image can assume the vividness and reality of an actual external object. At all events, such phenomena seem to magnify, if not transcend, the effects of suggestion in the ordinary waking state.

Similar considerations also arise in connection with so-called age-regression, in which a subject aged perhaps 20 is told that he will experience himself as he was when, say, 10 years old (Hilgard, 1965, pp. 167–75; Gill and Brenman, 1966). He will thereupon comport himself, superficially at least, in accordance with his suggested age. Without further or more specific suggestions being given, he will commonly write or draw in a strikingly more juvenile manner and may even develop an apparent disorientation, stating, for example, that he is in the school he attended at the age of 10 and that the experimenter is a schoolmaster at that time known to him. In such cases it is often difficult to decide whether the patient is an accomplished, if unintentional, actor or whether there is a genuine reactivation of long superseded attitudes and modes of behaviour, i.e. a true regression to an earlier state of the person and genuine re-enaction of the past. One simple test might be to suggest to him that he should progress rather than regress in age, and see to what extent he can duplicate the presumed behaviour of a very much older person. It is also entirely conjectural whether regression, as some believe, can be pursued into earliest infancy.

As might be expected, experimentalists have given much attention to the relationship between hypnosis and ordinary *sleep (see Hull, 1933, pp. 193–243). Although subjects often refer to lethargy, drowsiness, and diminished contact with reality as characteristic of hypnosis, it seems clear that this state, whatever its nature, differs categorically from normal sleep, with or without dreaming. As James Braid observed in the nineteenth century, the muscles do not relax as in ordinary sleep and the subject does not drop an object held in the hand as he becomes hypnotized. Further, *reflexes which disappear in sleep can be elicited normally in the hypnotic state. Finally, study of the electrical rhythms of the brain (*electroencephalography) shows that the electroencephalogram (EEG) in hypnosis in no way resembles that in any of the recognized states of sleep but is essentially identical with that of ordinary wakefulness. From the electrophysiological point of view, therefore, the hypnotized person is awake.

Let us now turn briefly to theories of hypnosis. William *James wrote in 1890 that the suggestion theory of hypnosis may be approved, provided that we regard the trance state as its essential prerequisite. Although the term 'hypnotic trance' is seldom used today, most people regard the hypnotic state as something *sui generis* with its own peculiar properties. In addition to greatly enhanced suggestibility, these are commonly said to consist in voluntary suspension of initiative, restriction of attention to a narrow field, and marked reduction in self-consciousness and critical appraisal. Some would add that the hypnotized person, much like the dreamer, is not fully in contact with reality and exhibits a facile mode of reasoning ('trance logic') in some respects characteristic of childhood. Although the state of hypnosis lacks definite physiological or biochemical criteria of an altered state of consciousness, it does not of course necessarily follow that no such criteria will ever be discovered. Indeed, it is only in comparatively recent years that firm physiological correlates of ordinary dreaming have been securely established.

None the less, this lack of physiological criteria of the hypnotic state, together with its resemblances to many phenomena in ordinary waking life involving the effects of suggestion, has induced some recent workers, in particular F. X. Barber, who has published much useful work in experimental hypnosis, to argue that the concept of a trance state is an unnecessary assumption (Barber, 1969). As he sees it, hypnosis is to be viewed as an essentially normal state of waking consciousness in which a voluntary compact between experimenter and subject enables each to exercise his respective role, which is, so to speak, enshrined in traditional expectation. Although such a view has the merits of parsimony, it fails to account for many features of the hypnotic state, such as spontaneous post-hypnotic amnesia in highly susceptible subjects, loss or diminution of pain sense, and the operation of post-hypnotic suggestion. Further, the production of sense deceptions and hallucinations is more reminiscent of the effects brought about in indisputably altered states of consciousness, such as may be produced by drugs or toxic agencies, than the ordinary operations of waking suggestibility.

To say this is not of course to deny that there are important psychogenic factors in hypnosis which are closely related to suggestion and fantasy in daily life. Josephine Hilgard, in particular, has emphasized the links between susceptibility to hypnosis and the propensity to become immersed in novels, plays, and films, and to participate in the fictional existence of the characters. She likewise stresses the element of identification with parents or other emotionally significant features in early life, and indeed calls attention to many aspects of hypnosis, among them the blurring of fantasy and reality, the ready involvement in games of pretence, and the tendency to believe uncritically in the pronouncement of others, which may be viewed as 'part and parcel of childhood' (Hilgard, 1965, pp. 343–74). But just as dreaming, in itself essentially psychogenic, presupposes the altered state of consciousness characteristic of a certain stage of sleep, so it may be argued that hypnosis, likewise essentially psychogenic, presupposes the less dramatic alteration of consciousness formerly known as the hypnotic trance.

In conclusion, one may ask whether experimental hypnosis presents any hazards. By and large, the procedure seems harmless enough, though medical men rightly warn that it can be dangerous if the subjects should happen to include emotionally disturbed individuals or those with a history of psychiatric illness. In such cases, the experimenter may well lack both the knowledge and the experience to handle the emotional relationships, positive or negative, which may unwittingly be generated in the process. A related question is whether experimental hypnosis calls for ethical guidelines. We know, for example, that certain types of psychological experiment involve calculated deceit, as in the work of Stanley Milgram on obedience. Milgram explained to his subjects that it was necessary for the purposes of his experiment to deliver shocks of potentially lethal intensity to other human beings, and he found, somewhat to his surprise, that many subjects were prepared to undertake this in spite of their ignorance of the deceit which was being practised upon them. (See OBEDIENCE.) If such an experiment were repeated under conditions of hypnosis, it is entirely possible that even greater conformity with the instructions of the experimenter would be forthcoming. While it remains true that, in general, hypnotized subjects cannot be induced to perform actions that are morally repugnant to them, and that the danger of crimes being committed as a result of hypnotic suggestion appears to be extremely small, there is no doubt that any form of experiment on the effects of suggestion, with or without hypnosis, must be regarded as open to potential abuse. It is to be hoped that the psychological fraternity will take due notice of these hazards and introduce appropriate ethical guidelines for the conduct of human experiments, in particular those making use of hypnosis.

O. L. Z.

Barber, F. X. (1969). *Hypnosis: a scientific approach*. New York.

Gill, M. M. and Brenman, M. (1966). *Hypnosis and Related States*. New York.

For the work of A. M. Halliday and A. A. Mason see The Effect of Hypnotic Anaesthesia on Cortical Responses (1964). *Journal of Neurology, Neurosurgery and Psychology*, **27**, 300–5.

Hilgard, E. R. (1965). *Hypnotic Susceptibility*. New York.

Hilgard, E. R. and Hilgard, J. R. (1975). *Hypnotism and the Relief of Pain*. New York.

Hull, C. L. (1933). *Hypnosis and Suggestibility: an experimental approach*. New York.

Milgram, S. (1974). *Obedience to Authority*. New York.

Weitzenhoffer, A. M. (1947). *Hypnotism: an objective study in suggestibility*. New York.

**HYPNOTISM, HISTORY OF.** The term 'hypnotism' was invented by a contemporary of John Elliotson (see MESMERISM), James Braid (1795–1860), who spent much of his life as a general physician and surgeon in Manchester. Like Elliotson, Braid was introduced to mesmerism by a visiting French magnetizer, but he seems from the start to have held no belief whatsoever in animal magnetism and was quite convinced that the phenomena he had witnessed at a mesmeric seance were attributable to natural causes. The so-called mesmeric trance (i.e. the altered state of consciousness into which the subject had passed) Braid attributed to prolonged fixation of the eyes on a bright object that the magnetizer had used to induce a sleep-like state. Indeed Braid repeated this induction procedure with a number of volunteer subjects—including his own wife—and became at once convinced that his explanation was in principle correct. He supposed that protracted ocular fixation brings about a state of fatigue in the relevant brain centres which eventually causes the subject to enter into a state which he called 'nervous sleep', allied to, but not identical with, natural *sleep. The doctrine of 'nervous sleep' as a condition in which functional nervous disorders could be successfully treated he called *neurhypnology*, and the state itself *neurhypnotism*, later contracted to plain *hypnotism*. The latter he defined as 'a peculiar condition of the nervous system induced by artificial contrivance'. Although Braid came later to specify 'contrivances' other than fixation which may be used to induce hypnosis—for example, sustained concentration on the hypnotist's voice—his initial idea that the hypnotic state is similar to natural sleep and, like it, of physiological origin, was widely accepted at the time. Braid also attempted treatment of certain conditions which are nowadays recognized as purely organic—for example, speech disorders resulting from strokes. Any success that may have attended his efforts in such cases can almost certainly be ascribed to the effects of hypnosis in reducing the patient's anxiety or self-consciousness in relation to his disabilities. There is no good evidence that any wholly organic nervous or mental illness responds favourably to hypnotic treatment.

With the passage of time, Braid's ideas about the nature of hypnotism underwent considerable modification. Although he never abandoned the concept of 'nervous sleep', he laid weight increasingly on the role of psychological factors in its origin. First, he came to stress the importance of sustained mental concentration rather than physiological fatigue in the induction of hypnosis, and in this connection laid great emphasis on the subject's restriction of consciousness while under hypnosis. The subject's attention is virtually absorbed by the words and actions of the hypnotist to the exclusion of all else, and this state Braid called *monoideism*. Secondly, he came to appreciate the obvious role of suggestibility in giving rise to the bizarre and on occasion dramatic phenomena that can be induced under hypnosis. In short, it is often said that Braid was the first person to appreciate that hypnotism is essentially a psychological phenomenon and cannot satisfactorily be explained wholly in terms of brain physiology.

Again like Elliotson, Braid made extensive use of hypnosis in his medical practice, and the variety of conditions he attempted to treat was indeed catholic. It was in surgery, however, that 'neurhypnology' (whether called mesmerism or hypnotism) made its most dramatic impact. As early as 1842, a Nottingham surgeon named Ward had amputated a thigh during a mesmeric trance, apparently without producing pain. Although his report gave rise to widespread incredulity and the patient was in some quarters branded as an impostor, similar cases were soon reported, some of them attested by Elliotson himself. The foremost exponent of hypnotism as a method of painless surgery was, however, the Scotsman James Esdaile (1805–59), who practised for many years in India. (See Bramwell, 1913, for an account of his work.) Esdaile reported over 300 cases in which he had performed major operations on hypnotized patients, apparently without causing pain. These included amputations of limbs and the removal of very large scrotal tumours. In spite of strong professional disapproval, his claims were endorsed by a special committee of investigation wholly composed of medical men, appointed by the deputy governor of Bengal. Indeed Esdaile continued to use hypnotism to induce analgesia until chloroform came into general use, and persisted until the end of his life in the belief that as an anaesthetic chloroform was much inferior to hypnosis. (In modern times, hypnosis has seldom, if ever, been used as an anaesthetic agent in surgery but has found some application in dentistry, particularly with children.)

After Braid's death, interest in hypnosis languished for some years. This undoubtedly reflected the received view of the medical profession that it failed to meet the criteria of 'legitimate medicine' and, in spite of the demise of animal magnetism, was still tarred with the brush of quackery. In the 1880s, however, there was a marked revival of interest in hypnosis (as hypnotism now came to be generally called), partly due to the appearance of Braid's writings in French and German translations, and partly to its endorsement by the great French neurologist J. M. *Charcot as a valuable technique in the study and treatment of *hysteria. Further, an interest developed among a number of Continental physicians, mainly French and German, in studying the phenomena of hypnosis in a relatively systematic way and without paying primary regard to its therapeutic implications. Among those who wrote widely on hypnosis at this time were Moll and Heidenhain in Germany, Forel in Switzerland (who was also an authority on the social insects), and *Binet and Féré in France. There was much discussion at this period of alleged alterations in sensory acuity and of illusions and *hallucinations, said to be evoked in highly susceptible subjects in the hypnotic state. Exceptional feats of sensory discrimination and memory were often described, although many of these claims have since proved to have been very much exaggerated. Post-hypnotic suggestion, first described by Moll and others, evoked great interest. This consists in particular actions or patterns of behaviour suggested under hypnosis but carried out by the subject some time after being awakened. It is shown by some subjects though not by all and is commonly explained or justified by the subject in terms of facile rationalization. The production of changes in nervous activities not normally under conscious control—for example, the raising of blisters in response to instruction under hypnosis—likewise attracted much interest and is still imperfectly understood. Although most of these experiments were carried out by medical men in the course of their clinical practice, it was in this period that the experimental study of hypnosis was born. Even in sceptical Britain, the results of an inquiry into the phenomena of hypnotism sponsored by the British Medical Association in 1891 left little doubt as to the genuineness of many of the phenomena hitherto described in the literature.

None the less, it was the medical applications that remained central to the study of hypnosis well into the twentieth century, and it was only then that interest largely passed from the physician to the experimental psychologist (see HYPNOSIS, EXPERIMENTAL). Here the lead was taken by the French. Charcot, who became interested in the nature of hysteria late in his career, was much struck by the ease with which many of the signs and symptoms of this illness could be duplicated in the hypnotic state. Indeed he quickly came to conclude that only those individuals with hysterical predisposition are susceptible to hypnosis, which in fact he regarded as a kind of 'artificial hysteria'. His pupil, the distinguished medical psychologist Pierre *Janet, argued that in both hysteria and hypnosis the patient is liable to *dissociation*, i.e. the splitting of certain mental capacities, skills, or memories from the central stream of consciousness which in consequence become inaccessible though in no sense genuinely lost. For instance, the patient may lose his memory as a result of a frightening or otherwise stressful experience but it can often be restored completely by hypnotic suggestion. Janet claimed that a dissociated activity, whether produced spontaneously in hysteria or artificially in hypnosis, may continue to exercise its effects even though these are not consciously appreciated. For example, a patient suffering from hysterical blindness who genuinely claims, and believes, that he can see nothing, is seldom observed to collide with obstacles; at an automatic level, therefore, his vision continues to guide his behaviour. Following from such observations, Janet did much to arouse interest in the conception of subconscious mental activity and to introduce methods of therapy which aimed at the reintegration of the dissociated aspects of the personality.

Another pioneer in the medical applications of hypnosis was A. A. Liébault (1823–1903), of Nancy, an unpretentious provincial physician who made much use of hypnosis in his general practice (see Bramwell, 1913). Although appreciating that individuals differ markedly in their susceptibility to hypnosis, Liébault's experience convinced him that everyone in principle could be hypnotized, given a sincere wish to co-operate with the hypnotist. (Indeed he considered that the nervous and hysterical were among the most refractory of his patients.) In this connection Liébault placed great emphasis on the factor of *rapport*, i.e. sympathetic relationship between doctor and patient, in the absence of which attempts at hypnosis are seldom successful. Although rapport as a rule involves an element of authority, it would be wrong to suppose that hypnotism is a wholly autocratic procedure. It involves very real mutual co-operation between the hypnotist and his subject, and may indeed be viewed as in some sense a product of their relationship.

Liébault also placed a good deal of emphasis upon the factor of *suggestibility*, which even more than Braid or Charcot he regarded as a key factor in generating the effects of hypnosis. In this respect, he owed much to H. Bernheim (1837–1919), a professor of medicine at Nancy, who viewed the exaggeration of normal suggestibility as an all-embracing explanation of hypnotism. This issue of suggestibility enjoyed a considerable vogue in French psychology, being adduced not only by Charcot as a dominant characteristic of the hysterical patient, but by psychologists such as G. le Bon in explanation of the social contagion characteristic of panic and mob rule. Attempts to measure suggestibility and its relationship to hypnotic susceptibility have much occupied contemporary psychologists.

As is well known, Sigmund *Freud studied with Charcot, and on his way home visited Nancy, where he met Bernheim. Although critical of his authoritarian manner, he later spoke with admiration of his 'astonishing arts'. Back in Vienna, Freud worked for some years with Josef *Breuer (1842–1925) and together they developed a method of treatment which involved the re-enaction of stressful experiences under hypnosis with full and uninhibited expression of emotion. This procedure was termed *abreaction* and is usually regarded as the precursor of the psychoanalytical method. It is still used sometimes today, especially when combined with intravenous sedation ('narco-analysis').

Freud turned against hypnosis for several reasons, of which the chief seems to have been his distrust of all psychotherapeutic procedures based on authority rather than rational analysis. As he saw it, the relief of neurotic symptoms by hypnosis and suggestion does nothing to help the patient to understand the nature of his symptoms or the resistances which deny him insight into their deeper significance. In short, only symptoms are relieved and the causes of neurosis are left untouched. Although not everyone agrees that direct suggestion is never effective or that insight necessarily ensures recovery, most contemporary psychotherapists share Freud's distrust of hypnosis as a therapeutic tool. (For a more detailed account of Freud's views, see FREUD ON HYPNOSIS.)

O. L. Z.

Bernheim, H., trans. Herter, C. A. (1886). *Hypnosis and Suggestion in Psychotherapy*. New York.

Braid, J. (1843). *Neurhypnology, or the doctrine of nervous sleep*. Reprinted in Waite, A. E. (1899), *Braid on Hypnotism*. London.

Bramwell, J. M. (1913). *Hypnotism: its history, practice and theory*, 3rd edn. London.

Breuer, J. and Freud, S. *Studies on Hysteria*. In Strachey, J. (trans. and ed.), *Complete Psychological Works*, vol. xviii (1955). London.

Janet, P. (1925). *Psychological Healing* (trans. E. and C. Paul). London.

**HYSTERIA,** long-supposed disease of women, was attributed by Hippocrates to the movement of the womb (*hystera*) from its normal anatomical site into other parts of the body. The feelings of constriction in the throat, so typical of hysteria (*The Suffocation of the Mother*, by Edward Jorden, 1603), were thought to be caused by the uterus becoming lodged in that region. It followed, therefore, that men, since they do not have a womb, would not be affected by this disease, although Thomas Sydenham (1682) maintained that they were able to suffer from the symptoms experienced by the opposite sex. The belief that hysteria was a disorder confined to women had a long innings, and *Freud's report to the Vienna Medical Society in 1886 that men too could be affected by it was not well received. As an elderly surgeon remarked, 'But my dear sir, how can you talk such nonsense? Hysteria means the uterus. So how can men be hysterical?' (Stafford Clark, 1967).

Like many other words used in psychiatry, hysteria has been given many meanings. The following list shows how a disease that was once considered to be a single entity has been given different interpretations according to the nature of the symptoms and the theories proposed to explain them: (i) Hysteria as a personality disorder: for example, histrionic personality, or attention-seeking personality. (ii) Conversion hysteria, presenting a variety of neurological disturbances such as paralysis, convulsions, losses of sensation, blindness, speech abnormalities, and ataxic gait. (iii) Hysteria as a dissociation phenomenon manifested as fugues, twilight states, amnesias and multiple personality. (iv) Hysteria as a disease entity affecting women. There is also (v) hysteria as a term of abuse.

**(i) Hysteria as a personality disorder.** Hysterical personality is one of those misnomers that bedevils the subject, largely because it is often assumed that individuals showing the features of it are liable to develop other forms of hysteria. On the whole, the evidence does not favour this belief, and the term should be discarded in favour of one of the synonyms. The dominant chracteristics are shallow, labile emotions, manipulative behaviour, a tendency to overdramatize situations, a lack of self-criticism, and a fickle flirtatiousness with little capacity for sustained sexual relationships. It has been said that these qualities add up to a caricature of femininity; and as men are rarely labelled hysterical personalities it is likely that the old association of hysteria with uterine disturbance is responsible for the transformation of hysteria as a disease into an adjectival description of a constellation of certain behavioural characteristics.

**(ii) Conversion hysteria.** Freud's theory of hysteria, based largely on his treatment of female patients in late nineteenth-century Vienna, proposed that repressed sexual conflicts, which, if brought to consciousness, would arouse anxiety and distress, were converted into physical symptoms that symbolized the repressed wish and permitted the anxiety to be dispelled—the so-called primary gain. As Fenichel (1955) wrote, 'In conversion, symptomatic changes of physical function occur which, unconsciously and in a distorted form, give expression to instinctual impulses that previously had been repressed.' The lack of emotional response of the patient to her symptoms, for example a paralysed limb, was referred to by *Janet as 'la belle indifference des hysteriques'. In fact hysterics are by no means as free from *anxiety as they might appear to be. Understandably, considering the time and place of Freud's original communications on hysteria, his emphasis on repressed sexuality in the female as a cause of neurosis aroused a good deal of hostility. But *Charcot, the great neurologist in Paris, whose clinic Freud had visited, once remarked, 'Hysterie, c'est toujours la chose sexuelle'—a point re-emphasized by Freud when he wrote, 'I do not think I am exaggerating when I insist that the great majority of severe neuroses in women have their origin in the marriage bed.'

As time has gone by this emphasis on repressed sexual drives as a cause of conversion hysteria has declined. Some writers have considered the roles of anxiety and *depression in the genesis of hysterical symptoms, and others have stressed the importance of secondary gain, particularly when symptoms persist in compensation cases following accidental injury. The hysteric is nothing if not suggestible; and susceptibility to suggestion, especially in those of a relatively unsophisticated nature, could be an important determinant of the site and type of a conversion symptom.

**(iii) Hysteria as a dissociation phenomenon.** Janet considered *dissociation to be an important component of some hysterical symptoms. These include fugues (wandering away from one's usual environment, with subsequent amnesia), trances, multiple personality and twilight states. The individual who enters into a fugue state is sometimes escaping from an intolerable situation or suffering from a severe depression. This wandering behaviour has been equated with an act of suicide, with the patient seeking some state of nirvana which will free him from his worldly cares and responsibilities.

Much attention has been given to the phenomena of multiple personality, and the famous case of Sally Beauchamp, described by Morton Prince (1854–1929), has been succeeded by other well-publicized examples. There is reason to think that the subject's suggestibility and the amount of attention focused on the alleged change of personality to some extent perpetuate and elaborate the phenomena. Multiple personality can sometimes be of forensic interest when the defendant blames her *alter ego* for the offences of which she is accused. Obviously it is difficult to prove beyond reasonable doubt claims of this kind. In any case, multiple personality is a rare condition, and only its dramatic and bizarre nature is reason for the disproportionate interest in it. See DISSOCIATION OF THE PERSONALITY.)

**(iv) Hysteria as a disease entity.** The old concept of hysteria as a disease peculiar to women was gradually abandoned in the face of evidence that a great variety of hysterical symptoms affect men as well as women. The revival of the disease entity concept by psychiatrists in St Louis, USA, under the label Briquet's syndrome—the name derives from a French author who published a monograph on hysteria in 1859—has been criticized on the grounds that it appears to be resurrecting the ancient myth of a sexually determined illness confined to women. Indeed, many of its symptoms are functional disorders of the female reproductive system. Multiple surgery to treat such symptoms, and a variety of other abdominal complaints of a psychogenic nature, result in what is known in some hospitals as 'the thick file syndrome'. This is largely because of the sheer number of the patient's records and reports on multiple investigations that accumulate over the years. It could be argued that 'thick files' could not develop in a society which did not have well-developed medical and surgical technology; but all the same such patients are not the most welcome in busy outpatient departments, not only because of the time required to unravel their histories but also because of the sense of therapeutic and diagnostic hopelessness that overcomes the examining physician.

**(v) Hysteria as a term of abuse.** The layman—and sometimes the medical practitioner—faced by tiresome, noisy and overdramatic behaviour may be inclined to react with 'Pull yourself together and don't be so d— hysterical'. As the behaviour that provokes this kind of response has much in common with the chief characteristics of the hysterical personality, it is more likely to arouse antipathy when the subject is a woman. An 'attack of the vapours' is an older term used to describe such 'hysterical' behaviour by women; when the 'wandering womb' hypothesis of hysteria was discarded, it was replaced by the notion that noxious vapours could rise up from the womb to the brain and produce symptoms which today would be called conversion hysteria, especially hysterical convulsions.

Although there can be no doubt that psychological disturbances play a considerable part in the genesis of hysterical symptoms, it is important to realize that in nearly two-thirds of patients presenting to hospital with such symptoms, there will be some evidence of pre-existing or developing brain injury or disease (Slater, 1965; Whitlock, 1967; Merskey and Buhrich, 1975). It has been suggested that the capacity for manifesting acute hysterical illness is something which is built into the central nervous system to protect it from overwhelming stress. If the brain is damaged or diseased, there is an increased possibility for this innate mechanism to spring into action, especially if an added psychological stress serves as a trigger. Thus hysterical symptoms may be the first indication that some hitherto unsuspected brain disease is developing. Conversion hysteria in older patients with no previous evidence of psychiatric morbidity should alert the physician to this possibility. Indeed, given the high incidence of brain disease in patients with hysteria, it has been suggested that the time has come for the word as a noun signifying a disease entity to be relegated to psychiatric history. But this is unlikely to happen for, as Lewis (1975) has written, 'A tough old word like hysteria dies very hard. It tends to outlive its obituarists.'

F. A. W.

Fenichel, O. (1955). *The Psychoanalytic Theory of Neurosis*. London.

Lewis, A. (1975). The survival of hysteria. *Psychological Medicine*, **5**, 9.

Merskey, H. and Buhrich, N. A. (1975). Hysteria and organic brain disease. *British Journal of Medical Psychology*, **48**, 359.

Slater, E. (1965) The diagnosis of hysteria. *British Medical Journal*, **1**, 1,395.

Stafford Clark, D. (1967). *What Freud Really Said*. Harmondsworth.

Whitlock, F. A. (1967). The aetiology of hysteria. *Acta psych Scand.*, **43**, 144.

# I

**IBN 'ARABI** or IBN AL-'ARABI (Sheikh Abu-Bakr Muhammad ibn-'Ali Muhyiuddin, called the Greatest Sheikh/Sheikh Al-Akbar/Doctor Maximus, 1164–1240). He was born in Murcia, Spain, a descendant of the illustrious Arabian family of Hatim Tai, and died in Damascus. His work influenced Western thought and literature: for example, Asín Palacios and others have argued for textual copying by Dante in the *Divine Comedy*. He was a most influential *Sufi teacher who wrote, according to *Jami, over 500 works, mostly in Mecca and Damascus; in 1234 he himself reckoned them at 298 volumes. About ninety are extant, mostly in manuscript. Ibn 'Arabi's *Tadbirat* (Managements) is an important manual of Sufi training. The *Fusus al-Hikam* (Bezels, or Phases, of Wisdom), written in 1230, is his best-known work. Each of its twenty-seven chapters is named after a prophet or teacher and deals with the Sufi principles which that teacher is said to represent. He is associated with the doctrine of Unity of Being (*Wahdat al-Wujud*), which is characterized by his critics as pantheism. Although he claimed to have no master and to have been initiated into Sufism by Khidr, a spiritual being, A. E. Affifi (1939) places him firmly in the context of the Spanish Sufi thought of his time. His work constantly appeals to the Koran and traditions of Muhammad, though his interpretations are idiosyncratic. Two other major works are *The Meccan Revelations* and *The Interpreter of Desires*, both attacked by pietists as mere love-poetry but successfully defended by the author as mystical allegories. By a curious tradition in the East, pious men sporadically assemble groups of students and charge them with the literary study of Ibn 'Arabi's works. The intention is either to exhaust their capacity for research, or for them to discover the authorities who state that Ibn 'Arabi's works are not meant to be understood but to produce bafflement. This realization, according to these Sufis, drives the students to seek the current living exemplar of the teaching who alone can explain the writings. I. S.

Affifi, A. E. (1939). *The Mystical Philosophy of Muhiyid Din Ibnul Arabi*. Cambridge.

**IBN BAJJAH** (Abu-Bakr Muhammad ibn-Yahya ibn-al-Sa'igh, *c*.1106–38). A major *Islamic thinker, poet and musician, scientist and mathematician, Ibn Bajjah was a forerunner of Averroës. Known to the Latin Schoolmen as Avempace, or Avenpace, he was born in Saragossa, Spain, and known in his lifetime as the prime exponent of Aristotelian thought after *Avicenna.

He follows *Al-Farabi and his work greatly influenced Ibn Tufail. Averroës himself states that his own ideas of mind are derived from Ibn Bajjah. His *'Ilm al-Nafs* (Science of the Soul) is the earliest text hitherto known that gives the gist of all the three books of the *De Anima* of *Aristotle, and he is known, among other things, to Western scholars for his theory of separate substances, which they adopted from him. In his *Guide to the Solitary* he deals with the soul's return to reality by detaching itself from matter. I. S.

Leff, G. (1958). *Medieval Thought*. Harmondsworth.

**IBN HAZM** ('Ali ibn-Hazm, 994–1064). A native of Córdoba, Spain, he was the first scholar of comparative religion, and Hitti (1951) characterizes him as anticipating theological problems only arising in Christian Europe in the sixteenth century. Guillaume (1949), in referring to this author of over 400 books, accepted in the west as the greatest scholar and the most original thinker of Spanish Islam (see ISLAMIC PHILOSOPHY), notes that he composed 'Europe's first *Religionsgeschichte* and the first systematic higher critical study of the Old and New Testaments'. This is his *Al-Fasl fi'l-Milal w'al-Ahwa' w'al-Nihal* (the Decisive Word on Sects, Heterodoxies, and Denominations); but he also wrote love-poems. In *The Necklace of the Dove* he extols platonic love, and his romanticism is regarded as related to the Spanish–Arabian influence on the formation of the troubadour mentality. I. S.

Guillaume, A. (1949). Philosophy and theology. In Arnold, T. (ed.), *The Legacy of Islam*. Oxford.
Hitti, P. K. (1951). *History of the Arabs*. New York.

**IBN KHALDUN** (Abu-Zaid Abd-al-Rahman ibn-Khaldun, 1332–1406). Born in Tunis, he was one of the greatest *Islamic scholars of Moorish Spain, Arab ambassador to Pedro the Cruel, judge and professor of jurisprudence at Cairo. Author of the *Muqaddima* (Introduction), the first analysis of history by political and social pattern, Ibn Khaldun is regarded as the 'father of the science of history' and one of the founders of sociology. A *Sufi by persuasion, he is buried in the Sufi cemetery near Cairo where he died.

'Ibn Khaldun was an historian, politician, sociologist, economist, a deep student of human affairs, anxious to analyse the past of mankind in order to understand its present and future . . . one of the first philosophers of history, a forerunner of Machiavelli, Bodin, Vico, Comte and Cournot'—

George Sarton, *Introduction to the History of Science* (1927–48; repr. in 5 vols. 1975), iii, 1262.

I. S.

Dawood, N. J. (ed.) (1967). *The Muqaddimah: an introduction to history* (Eng. trans. F. Rosenthal, 1967). London.
Gellner, E. A. (1981). *Muslim Society*. Cambridge.

**IBN SINA** (980–1037), Islamic philosopher and physician. See AVICENNA.

**ICONIC IMAGE.** If a visual pattern is presented only very briefly (for example, by flashing a light on it in a dark chamber) an image of that pattern will persist in experience beyond its physical termination. Such an image is called an iconic image (or, alternatively, the information is said to be in a 'sensory register') and, unlike the after-effects produced by very strong lighting, will appear very much like the pattern itself, though faded. Indeed, careful measurements have shown that observers often believe that the stimulus is still physically present when, in fact, it has been terminated a fraction of a second previously.

One implication of the latter point is that this record is remarkably complete (contains all or most of the detail of the original) especially as compared to the contents of other memory systems. George Sperling demonstrated this point directly by signalling his subjects immediately after stimulus-offset to report to him the contents of one of a set of rows of letters which he had presented on a screen for 50 milliseconds. No matter which row was randomly requested, the level of accuracy was quite high.

Interestingly, however, a slight variation on this procedure drastically reduces performance. That is, if a mixture of letters and numbers is presented and the observer is requested immediately thereafter to report, for example, the letters but not the numbers, fewer successes are achieved. The implication is that although all of the items are available, they have not yet been identified, and so, in order to perform the task, the subject must identify each item whether called for or not. This is time consuming and the image disappears before the task can be completed. Thus, while iconic images may be remarkably complete, they apparently exist in a sensory, rather than properly perceptual, form.

The very 'unprocessed' nature of such records of stimulation may provide a key to their importance. It may be that such records hold information so that further, relatively time-consuming, processes such as segmentation, *figure–ground organization, and identification can occur. However, such a proposal must be developed cautiously. In nature the conditions under which these images have been studied are extremely rare, the rule in nature being relatively long-lasting scenes which we tend to explore with our eyes by fixating upon first one place and then another. This latter point is especially significant since it is also known that any part of an iconic image can be destroyed if new contours appear. For example, in an experiment such as Sperling's, if a particular letter on the screen is followed very quickly by another, an observer will not be able to report the former and may even indicate that it did not occur at all. The potential problem is, then, that in ordinary viewing the image produced by one fixation would be destroyed by the next, so that it would not be available for further processing. For example, what is now in the centre of the eye would destroy the image of what had been there just before the eyes moved.

Actually, the strength of this objection depends upon two assumptions: first, an assumption that the image is located in a fixed position in the retinas and, secondly, an assumption that the specific part of an image, which will be destroyed when new information arrives, will be that part which used to occupy that same place on the retina, even if the eyes have moved in the meantime.

As to the first assumption, while it is clear that some component of iconic images might be within the retinas, there is also ample evidence of a non-retinal component. For example, if these images were retinal, then they ought to appear to move around the environment when the eyes move. On the contrary, however, Douglas Hall observed that when his subjects were requested to report a particular row of letters, they moved their eyes so as to scan the (now blank) area of the screen where those letters had been. This would hardly make sense if the image, too, had moved. Instead, those things 'seen' in the image seem to stay in their proper environmental locales. If it is further assumed that various parts of an iconic image will be destroyed only by new stimulation that occurs in the same environmental locales as those parts, then it will be appreciated that such destruction does not occur unless the scene itself changes in whole or in part. That being the case, several such images (each produced by a different fixation of the eyes) are perfectly free to coexist and may well add together in normal everyday viewing.

Whether such additivity actually occurs or not, the fact that not only do iconic images stay in place when they should, but also may appear to move when induced by moving stimulation (*anorthoscopic visual perception), suggests the involvement of some exceedingly sophisticated mechanisms.

T. E. P.

Averbach, E. and Sperling, G. (1961). Short-term Storage of Information in Vision. In Cherry, C. (ed.), *Fourth London Symposium on Information Theory*. London and Washington, D.C.
Hall, D. C. (1974). Eye Movements in Scanning Iconic Imagery. *Journal of Experimental Psychology*, **103**, 825–30.

**ID.** According to Freud, the unconscious reservoir of primitive instincts from which spring the forces of behaviour and the conflicts and guilts of neurosis. See FREUD ON MENTAL STRUCTURE; FREUDIANISM: LATER DEVELOPMENTS.

**IDEAL.** The concept of an ideal seems to come from extrapolating from that which is seen as inadequate to some relatively perfect state. There are thus 'ideals of manhood' and general 'ideals worth striving for'. In *metaphysics, ideals can be supposed to exist, in some kind of heaven. This holds for *Plato's ideal forms of objects, including mathematical fictions such as the ideal triangle.

For Plato, mathematical and indeed all significant knowledge is of ideal unchanging forms, of which we see only transitory and imperfect replicas paraded before the senses. (See PLATONIC FORMS.) It is likely that this Platonic view has deeply affected ethics, and set up moral standards directed towards static, unchanging ideals which, in practice, cannot be realized, and, if they were, would be death.

**IDEALISM.** Name given to a group of philosophical doctrines which suggest that what we know as the '*external world' or the 'material universe' is in some important sense created by the mind or mind-dependent. (i) According to the Berkeleian version of this view, nothing exists outside the mind. To exist (*esse*) is to be perceived (*percipi*); and what we perceive can be nothing but our own ideas or sensations (see BERKELEY ON THE MIND). Subsequent 'phenomenalist' theories, which maintain that physical objects are merely 'permanent possibilities of sensation' (in J. S. *Mill's phrase), have something in common with Berkeley's view. (ii) Kantian or 'transcendental' idealism maintains that the fundamental categories in terms of which we characterize the world are not objective features of things in themselves but are structures imposed by the mind; without such organizing structures experience would not be possible (see KANT'S PHILOSOPHY OF MIND). (iii) According to *Hegelian idealism, the whole of history consists in the progressive realization of a single 'self-positing' mind or spirit (*Geist*).                    J. C.

**IDEAS** might be called 'the sentences of thought'. They are expressed by language, but underlie language—for the idea comes before its expression. (Though it is sometimes said that one knows what one thinks only after one has said it!)

Philosophers have traditionally distinguished between 'simple' ideas and 'complex' ideas. Simple ideas are supposed to be directly derived from sensation. When combined, they can produce complex and abstract ideas far removed from sensory experience and expressed in shared language. Simple ideas are the 'atoms' of associationist accounts of the mind. In common speech, 'one idea leads to another': and it is this which was formalized by the eighteenth- and nineteenth-century associationists such as John *Locke, David *Hume, James *Mill, J. S. *Mill, and Alexander *Bain. But how does one have a new idea, if ideas can only follow from others, or from sensations? Is it by the *emergence—as in chemistry—of new and surprising properties of combined elements? This leads to

considerations of *intelligence, *creativity, and *genius.

**IDENTIFICATION PARADE.** See MEMORY AND CONTEXT.

**IDIOT.** A person representing the lowest grade of *feeble-mindedness*. An adult idiot is technically a person having a mental age of not more than two years, or an IQ not above 25. An *idiot savant* may have remarkable specific abilities (such as mental arithmetic), though otherwise he fits this classification. See MENTAL ILLNESS.

**ILLUSIONS** are discrepancies from truth. All the senses can suffer illusions; but because we know most about *visual* *perception, visual illusions are the best known and most fully understood—though even of these many remain mysterious and controversial. All perceptions are subject to errors of many kinds; but illusions pass unnoticed except when they are strikingly inconsistent with what is accepted as true, or when there are internal inconsistencies—such as contradictory sizes or shapes, ambiguities, or paradoxes—which provide wonderful opportunities for artists, as exemplified in the ambiguous and paradoxical pictures of Maurits Escher. (See also ART AND VISUAL ABSTRACTION.)

Illusions are an embarrassment for those philosophers who would like to hold that knowledge is based securely on perception. Such a view is part of the empiricist tradition, which is the basis of science, but it is easy to show empirically that perception is not reliable; for at least in the laboratory, and the art gallery where interesting illusions abound, it is easy to fool the senses systematically so that all observers agree on what they perceive, though all are wrong. And we can all suffer misperceptions which may be disastrous in real-life situations, such as when driving a car or playing golf, or when doctors misread X-ray pictures. For everyone, the moon appears far too near, just beyond the horizon, and only about the size of an orange (smaller when high in the sky); yet we *know* it to be a quarter of a million miles distant and far larger than any earthly object.

Illusions are 'subjective' in our experience, and they affect behaviour and skill. Distortions of appearance can be measured, much as objects are measured, by comparisons with rulers or other physical references (Fig. 1). They may also be measured by *nulling—by measuring the change in size or shape of the visually distorted object or figure necessary to compensate or 'null' the distortion, though in doing so there is a danger of changing the angles, or other parameters, responsible for the distortion (Fig. 2).

So many processes contribute to perception that it is often difficult to know which is responsible for an error, or illusion, and no doubt there are some processes going on that we know nothing about. Some illusions, such as the bright or dark *after-

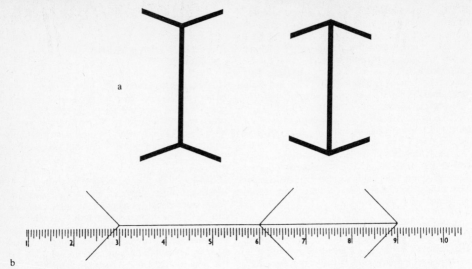

**Fig. 1. a.** Muller–Lyer illusion cancelled or 'nulled' by drawing the expanded (left) figure shorter than the shrunk (right) figure—no illusion is seen. **b.** Measuring a visual distortion by comparison with a ruler.

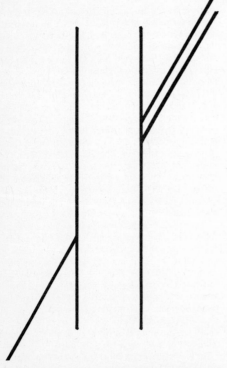

**Fig. 2.** Measuring a visual distortion by compensating or 'nulling' it. This can be a useful method, but it has the danger that features (such as critical angles) inducing the illusion are changed.

images that hover around after one looks at a bright light—owing to local loss of sensitivity of the retinas of the eyes following strong stimulation—are clearly due to physiological adaptation. Adaptation of physiological processes of visual systems in the brain are demonstrated by Fig. 3. Such illusions may be compared with errors made by instruments. Thus after-effects from prolonged stimulation by curved lines are calibration errors. They are useful for the experimental investigation of the signalling and representing of brightness, curvature, tilt, colour, movement, and so on; for these and many other characteristics are signalled by their own neural 'channels', which may be identified as they are individually adapted and so can be isolated quite simply, to find out how they work. (See also CONTINGENT PERCEPTUAL AFTER-EFFECTS; ILLUSORY FIGURES.)

Cognitive illusions are different. Their physiological bases are more subtle and more difficult to determine. In explaining any illusion the problem is how to select and concentrate on the appropriate 'level' of perceptual processing, and how to discover the particular process in which the relevant action has gone wrong. We can then ignore all the other processes, however important they may be for perception. This is not so simple for cognitive illusions, as for them there may be nothing abnormal or wrong with the anatomy, the physiology, or any of the underlying eye or brain processes. For just as any working tool, or knowledge, may be misapplied, normally functioning processes may be misdirected to produce errors, without fault of physiological function. This may occur whenever inappropriate knowledge or assumptions are

**Fig. 3.** Adaptation to curvature and tilt. Look at the short horizontal bar below the tilted lines for a few seconds, with the eyes moving left and right along it to avoid after-images. Then look at the vertical straight lines. Do they still look vertical? For a few seconds, they should look tilted—oppositely to the *adapting* lines. Similarly, following viewing the curved lines, the vertical lines should appear oppositely curved.

These adaptations are always opposite to the adapting stimuli—whether for shape, size, brightness, movement, or colour. It seems that specific neural channels are adapted (or fatigued), upsetting the balance of signals of position, movement, etc. The opposite colours are 'complementary' colours, such as adaptation to red producing green.

brought to bear in the 'reading' of sensory signals as evidence of an object's size, distance, colour, and so on. Thus physiologists and psychologists sometimes differ when accounting for particular illusions. Whereas, for example, the well-known *Müller-Lyer distortion illusion is generally explained by physiologists as due to some optical effect in the eye, or to disturbance of the signals from the retina by the angles of the 'arrowheads', very different explanations lie in the domain of cognitive psychology, as we shall see.

An undoubtedly cognitive effect is the *size–weight illusion: that a small object feels heavier than a larger object (for example soup tins) of the same scale weight. One anticipates a greater weight for the larger tin, because larger objects are usually heavier than similar smaller ones, and this sets up inappropriate expectations of the muscle-power required to lift them. Similarly, an empty suitcase flies up into the air (making one feel foolish!) when it is lifted, as too much force has been applied in lifting it, on the expectation that it will be heavy. This is a cognitive illusion because it is generated by an error of behaviour which is the result of a misleading assumption, or misleading knowledge.

For purposes of investigation, and discussion, cognitive illusions may be classified as *ambiguities*, *distortions*, *paradoxes*, and *fictions*.

**Ambiguities.** Some pictures, and sometimes ordinary objects, seem to change or turn into some other which may be quite different. Perception may switch between two or more alternatives (Fig. 4). What happens is that alternative hypotheses of what the object is (or where its parts lie in space) are entertained in turn. This occurs when the sensory data do not particularly favour just one possibility. A celebrated example of reversal in depth is the *Necker cube (Fig. 5). A three-dimensional wire cube is a fascinating object: when it reverses in depth it seems to stand up on a corner, and it rotates to follow one as one moves round it. This is because the motion parallax due to the movement is 'misread', as the apparent distances of the nearer and further faces are reversed. The cube also changes in shape. Such switches in depth—or from one object to another—can occur against the evidence of other senses. Thus, holding a small wire cube in the hand while seeing it depth-reversed is remarkably interesting; for when the hand is rotated the cube is seen to rotate—impossibly—against the hand's movement. The counter-information from touch does not correct the visual depth-reversal—and the wrist feels as if it is broken!

Perhaps all phenomena of ambiguity are essentially cognitive, for they depend on how sensory data are being interpreted, or 'read', in terms of

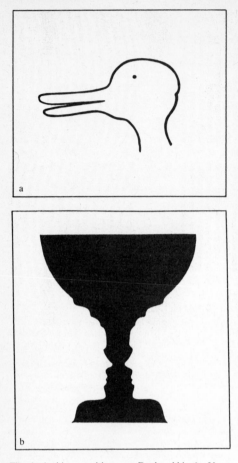

**Fig. 4.** Ambiguous objects. **a.** Duck–rabbit. **b.** Vase–faces. These can appear as alternative objects, according to selected rival perceptual hypothesis.

**Fig. 5.** Necker cube. This can be seen as switching in depth, the 'front' face reversing with the 'back' face.

objects. When there is one best bet, perception is stable; but when there are rival possibilities to be entertained, then perception becomes ambiguous, as each possibility is entertained in turn. Perception is intelligent, searching for solutions to the incredibly difficult problems of interpretation, that have to be solved hundreds of times every minute of the day.

**Distortions.** These are the best-known illusions: systematic distortions of size, and of length and curvature of lines or edges. Explanations remain controversial after a century of intensive investigation, by physiologists, opticians, neurologists, and psychologists—and more recently by computer programmers concerned with vision in *artificial intelligence. Many distortions were discovered by optical instrument-makers placing wires in the eyepieces of measuring instruments; their aim was to improve visual accuracy, but many attempts produced disastrous errors. For example, it was found

that converging lines produce distortions such as those of Fig. 6. These are large repeatable phenomena, which are easy to measure, and so are favourites for experiments. But what causes these distortions? There may be several causes, and there are certainly a score or so of (not all correct) theories.

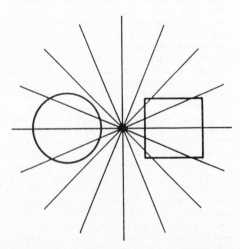

**Fig. 6.** Converging line distortions. One theory of why converging lines produce expansion, is that the convergence is read visually as perspective depth, or distance; this sets constancy of size for too great a distance.

**Fig. 7.** Café wall illusion. Named after a nineteenth-century café in Bristol which has this pattern of tiles. The long wedges are illusory. The distortion is unusual as it occurs in a figure (or object) having only right angles and parallel lines; it depends on the brightness–contrast of the 'tiles', and it only occurs when the brightness of the 'mortar' (which must be narrow) lies between the brightnesses of the tiles. There is no distortion with alternately different coloured tiles of the same brightness.

Many distortions—such as adaptation to the curves, or tilted lines, of Fig. 3—are straightforwardly physiological. And there may be optical distortions such as astigmatism. (See EYE DEFECTS AND THEIR CORRECTION.) A striking distortion illusion, which is almost certainly associated with physiological processes early in the visual system encoding the position of edges, is the 'café-wall illusion' (Fig. 7). A reason for believing that this effect occurs early in the visual system, prior to the cognitive processes of object recognition, is that (unlike most distortion illusions) it depends on brightness differences. When the tiles are alternately coloured, for example red and green, there is no distortion, providing the colours are set to equal brightness. Also, the distortion occurs only when the brightness of the mortar, which must be narrow, lies between the brightnesses of the dark and the light tiles. Illusions due to more 'central' cognitive processes are not likely to be affected by stimulus changes which do not alter the information provided by the picture, or object. It is often very difficult, however, to be sure whether an illusion is straightforwardly physiological, or has a cognitive cause through the brain misreading the significance of information-bearing features (Gregory and Heard, 1979).

Whether the distortions associated with (perspective) converging lines are straightforwardly physiological, or cognitive, remains controversial. The fact that they occur essentially unchanged for any brightness differences, for the colour-without-brightness contrast of isoluminance, and for any thickness of the lines, suggests that this is a cognitive phenomenon, which depends on certain features providing information that is misinterpreted. One theory is that depth-cues, such as perspective-convergence, set quite directly how far things appear to be, and will in some situations set distance or size incorrectly. An important depth-cue is perspective. The perspective shapes of retinal images are appropriate to the distances of objects only when given by objects of normal shapes, especially having parallel edges and right-angular corners. Odd shapes may be misleading: for example, the Ames room (designed by Adelbert Ames), which is not rectangular even though it gives the same image to the eye as a rectangular room, and the rotating trapezoid window which has marked perspective (as though viewed from an extreme angle), that disconcertingly persists as the window rotates.

All pictures that offer perspective challenge the eye with problems, as they present depth-cues of the objects they depict, in a space different from the picture plane. So it is hardly surprising if such pictures present problems that the visual system cannot solve without producing distortions. Pictures are essentially paradoxical, as they are flat while representing depth; so it is amazing that we see them as well as we do. These distortions obey certain rules. Features representing distance are perceptually expanded in compensation for the shrinking of the eye's images, for whereas actual objects normally look much the same size, whether near or fairly distant, their images shrink to half with each doubling of distance, just as for a camera. When the compensation for this optical shrinking is not set appropriately, it *must* produce such distortions (Gregory, 1963, 1968). A test is that when depth-cues are appropriate in these illusion figures, the distortions no longer occur (Gregory and Harris, 1975).

It is interesting to look at the wire cube that reverses in depth without change of the retinal image in the eye. When depth-reversed, its apparently further face looks too large, so that it seems like a truncated pyramid, expanding away from the observer (Gregory, 1970). But when not reversed it looks like a true cube. Size-constancy follows the apparent distance of the faces of the cube, an example of *Emmert's law. Visual size can be set in two ways—by perspective or other depth-cues, and by apparent depth—and it can be set wrongly by either. Thus there can be distortion 'bottom–up' from misleading depth-cues, or 'top–down' from inappropriate assumptions of distance.

**Paradoxes.** It is significant that, although we tend to see what is likely, we *can* see things that are so unlikely they appear impossible—even logically paradoxical. Striking examples are the 'impossible triangle' and 'impossible staircase' drawings of Lionel and Roger Penrose (Penrose and Penrose, 1958). But if we could see only probable objects, we would be blind to the unlikely; and this would be highly dangerous as unlikely events do sometimes occur. Indeed, if we could see only expected things there could hardly be perceptual learning. Nevertheless, it is strange that we can experience a paradox perceptually while knowing its solution conceptually, as with the 'impossible triangle' (Fig. 8). This is a simple unpainted object, made of three lengths of wood, yet from a certain point of view it looks impossible. This paradoxical perception occurs because the visual system assumes that the sides meet and touch at all three corners—though in fact at one corner they only touch *optically*, as here the sides are separated in depth. This is a cognitive effect, depending on a false assumption.

Not all perceptual paradoxes have such cognitive origins, however, for straightforward physiological errors can also produce them—as when signals arriving from one sensory channel disagree with signals from another channel, when they are differently adapted. As is well known, after one hand

**Fig. 8.** Impossible Triangle. **a.** From this viewpoint it looks paradoxical. **b.** When it is rotated, one sees the answer (but returning to **a**, it still looks impossible).

has been placed in hot water and the other in cold, tepid water will feel both hot and cold at the same time, when the differently adapted hands are placed in it. Movement after-effects (from a rotating spiral) are similarly paradoxical, as they can give sensations of movement though no change of position is seen. This shows that movement and position are signalled by different neural channels, which when they disagree can produce a paradox.

**Fictions.** On the general account of perceptions as predictive hypotheses which is assumed here (see PERCEPTION AS HYPOTHESES), it is not surprising that perceptions can be ambiguous, distorted, paradoxical, or even fictional. The *hallucinations of schizophrenia and drug-induced hallucinations apart, some striking examples of perceptual fictions are illusory edges and ghostly surfaces, which

occur in a wide variety of figures. The best examples are due to the Italian psychologist and
artist Gaetano Kanizsa (Kanizsa, 1979).

Again there are several theories that attempt to
account for these remarkable effects, and again
there may be more than one cause. The ghostly
surfaces occur in figures having surprising gaps.
They are, probably, postulated by the visual
system to account for the gaps, as due to occlusion
or eclipsing by some nearer object or surface. In
the normal course of events, parts of objects are
very often hidden by nearer objects; yet we continue
to recognize them as complete. The ability to recognize objects that are partly hidden is extremely
useful; but to postulate a nearer object or surface
on the evidence of gaps is bound to be hazardous,
for sometimes gaps are surprising (Fig. 9). The
tendency to postulate a surface that 'should' be, but
is not there, makes us see 'ghosts' in figures that
have unlikely gaps with the shapes of likely objects.

The three drawings in Fig. 9 show something of

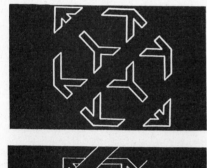

a

b

c

**Fig. 9.** Three cubes. **a.** This cube appears as separate
objects. **b.** Added parallel lines reveal a cube partly
hidden behind bars. **c.** Removing the parallel lines in **b** and
the end blocking lines in **a** produces illusory bars—with a
partly hidden cube behind them.

the subtlety of perceptual processes, and throw
light on how the world is seen as divided up into
objects. This is a basic perceptual problem, as very
often retinal images do not have clearly defined
edges for each object. The ear has the same problem in recognizing separate words in a sentence,
the sounds of speech being mainly continuous. We
cannot distinguish separate words in an unfamiliar
language; all we hear is an almost unbroken stream
of sound. So, in order to see what is an object, and
what is the space between objects, or words,
perceptual learning is important. (See also
AUDITORY ILLUSIONS; MUSIC, PSYCHOLOGY OF.)

Although one may know intellectually that one
is seeing an illusion, one still *sees* the illusion. This
difference between perceiving and conceiving,
which applies to all robust illusions, may be
because perception has to work very fast, for our
survival into the next second or so. Vision, hearing,
and our other senses must keep in step with
external events, which are often threatening, and
this requires a running prediction of what is likely
to happen in the immediate future. This remarkable speed could not be achieved if perception
drew upon all our knowledge. The access time
would be too long. Therefore, just as the strategy
of initial decision-making from a small data base is
becoming necessary for large computer systems, so
also is the intelligence of perception limited and
subject to illusions, as sensory data are not raw, but
cooked by assumptions that are often false. In
many ways it is different from our total understanding—anathema though this split between perception and understanding is to philosophers expecting certainty from the senses as premises for our
conceptual beliefs.                                R. L. G.

Gibson, J. J. (1950). *The Perception of the Visual World.*
New York.
Gibson, J. J. (1966). *The Senses Considered as Perceptual
Systems.* Boston. (This and the previous work listed give
a different account of perception and illusion from that
given here.)
Gombrich, E. H. (1956). *Art and Illusion.* London.
Gregory, R. L. (1963). Distortion of visual space as
inappropriate constancy scaling. *Nature*, **199**, 678.
Gregory, R. L. (1966; 3rd edn. 1977). *Eye and Brain.*
London. (Develops the account of distortion illusions
given in the previous work listed, together with the
notion of perceptions as hypotheses.)
Gregory, R. L. (1968). Perceptual illusions and brain
models. *Proceedings of the Royal Society*, **171**, 279.
Gregory, R. L. (1970). *The Intelligent Eye.* London.
Gregory, R. L. (1980). Perceptions as Hypotheses.
*Philosophical Transactions of the Royal Society*, **290**.
Gregory, R. L. and Harris, J. P. (1975). Illusion-destruc-
tion by appropriate scaling. *Perception*, **4**, 203–20.
Gregory, R. L. and Heard, P. (1979). Border-locking and
the café wall illusion. *Perception*, **8**, 365–80.
Kanizsa, G. (1979). *Organisation of Vision: essays on
Gestalt perception.* New York.
Penrose, L. S. and Penrose, R. (1958). Impossible
objects: a special type of illusion. *British Journal of
Psychology*, **49**, 31.
Robinson, J. O. (1972). *The Psychology of Visual Illusion.*
London. (For a comprehensive collection of illusion
figures.)

**ILLUSORY FIGURES.** Under some conditions, human beings, even as young children, possess a startling tendency to see a complete figure when only a small portion of its outline is actually delineated for them. For example, a white triangle can be seen in the centre of the first pattern.

This phantom triangle, far from being an after-thought to more primary experience, is emphatically 'seen', often in sharp delineation, very slightly in front of the line segments, and with a compelling glow. In fact, of course, except for the points at which it is touched by the black lines, the perimeter of the triangle is unmarked by any real change in stimulation—most of the border is simply not there in any physical sense. Such phenomena, as visually amusing to laymen as they are intellectually stimulating to theorists, occur in great variety and have come to be known as 'subjective' or, alternatively, as 'illusory' figures. Although the latter term is adopted here for convenience, either label, if taken too literally, is deceptive. It is instructive to consider why this is so.

First of all, while the triangle seen here obviously must be a subjective construction along most of its border, there are good reasons for believing that the perception of virtually any object involves a good deal of creative (*ergo*, subjective) activity. Visual perception can seldom, if ever, be accurately described as only a passive intake of environmental facts. In the same vein, illusory figures are decidedly not unbridled self-creations, but, like any percepts, are under the influence (although not the dictatorial control) of the stimuli presented. On the other hand, the phrase 'illusory figures' can also be misleading, suggesting, as it might, that the viewer is completely fooled. That is not the case—at any rate, not for long—with most observers. Even a child of 7 can assert (with wholesome candour considering the blatant contradiction involved) that the white triangle he sees is 'not *made* out of anything—it's just there'.

Rather oddly, widespread investigation of illusory figures developed only slowly. Early in the twentieth century F. Schumann made the pioneering observation that an appearance of a complete white square can be induced by partially enclosing a square area with half circles to each side and horizontal lines top and bottom (Fig. 1a). At the time, Schumann's publication was considered important enough to be made the leading article in the maiden issue of a new journal. As a goad to further studies, however, his work somehow failed to arouse much interest. Perhaps the particular example he presented was lacking in visual impact, or perhaps the uniqueness of his observation was not clear to most readers. At any rate, a few decades were to pass before another European, Walter Ehrenstein, produced illusory circles which should have been impressive enough for anyone's taste. Furthermore, he emphasized their theoretic novelty by showing that the brightness of these circles is lost when the area in question is physically outlined (Fig. 1b, far right). This latter point clearly distinguished Ehrenstein's figures from the more generally accepted notion that surrounding a white area with bits of black might tend to make that area appear whiter. If such 'simultaneous brightness contrast' were all that was involved here, then completely outlining one of the circular areas (thereby adding that much more nearby black) would have heightened the brightness rather than destroyed it. By now it should have been obvious that something new was here to be explored, but in the event interest in illusory figures did not begin to reach anything like epidemic proportions until yet another decade later when the work of Gaetano Kanizsa was published and received with enthusiasm.

Kanizsa's most famous stimulus pattern has already been shown in modified form, but can be seen in its original form in Fig. 1c. If the circle and line elements 'missing' from Kanizsa's pattern are presented instead (Fig. 1d), then the entire surround tends to become a bright illusory surface containing a triangular 'hole' through which the black pieces are glimpsed. Alternatively, a greyish triangle is sometimes seen lying over a whiter background. It is amusing to combine the previous two situations (Fig. 1e), in which case the window of Fig. 1d can be made to pierce through the surface of the illusory triangle of Fig. 1c, producing a thin white frame superimposed over the black elements.

While such displays can, therefore, be quite elegant, even more complex effects are possible. To a patient observer Fig. 1f reveals the impression of a cube formed of thin white members whose vertices are glimpsed through square holes in a nearer illusory surface. Even more impressively, Fig. 1G may produce an illusory figure which is, itself, a suggestion of a three-dimensional cube, complete, for some observers, with 'forward' edges. Nor are illusory figures found only in response to paper-and-ink presentations. John Kennedy and his colleague Colin Ware have devised ingenious three-dimensional constructions which, if held and viewed in normal surroundings, produce clear illusory lines and surfaces embedded *within* the constructions. Finally, the importance of illusory figures to our understanding of everyday experience becomes even more apparent when we realize, as Kanizsa himself did, that more naturalistic shapes can also be produced (Fig. 1h) and that more naturalistic elements may be employed

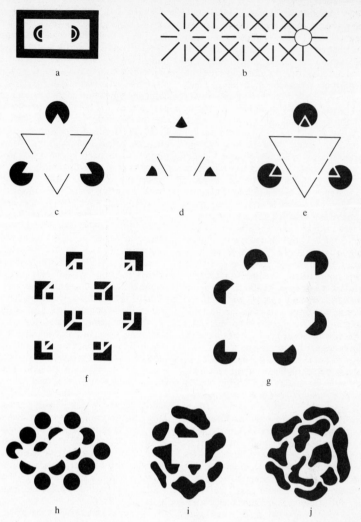

**Fig. 1.**

(Fig. 1i). Furthermore, such elements may be present within, as well as round, the area of the illusory figure (Fig. 1j).

These last examples make explicit what might only be suggested by more plane-geometric cases: that the tendency to see illusory figures might be closely linked to the ability to see natural objects in a normal environment—not only in detecting 'deliberately' camouflaged animate things, but in such common acts as discerning a gnarled and heavily grained stick lying on a forest floor as thatched with dead limbs and cross-hatched with shadows. By this argument, in order to understand the processes which yield illusory figures, it is first necessary to consider the enormous problems faced by the visual system when it seeks to delineate the natural visual environment into individual objects of certain shape and fixed dimensions. In other words, the suggestion is that the present laboratory stimuli are simplified examples of a general sort of challenge nature continuously presents. That challenge consists, in part, in the fact that a sharp difference in brightness or hue cannot always be taken as the extreme edge of an object of interest, since it might, instead, represent only a surface feature or an irrelevant shadow. Furthermore, those differences which do occur along an object's edge might be no more marked than differences produced by markings and shadows within the object. What then can be taken to be the extreme edge of 'an' object?

In the case of strongly three-dimensional situations, movement (of either the observer or the observed) provides useful information, as do such clues to relative depth as can be supplied by disparity, by changes in convergence and focus, or by systematic changes in texture. Inevitably, however, the system must make decisions and inevitably it must deal with probabilities. This, as Richard Gregory emphasizes (see ILLUSIONS), is the heart of the matter: those sharp changes in brightness or hue that *are* present and detected must form part of a pool of data upon which *hypotheses* are constructed as to the arrangement and shape of physical objects that *may* be present. Such hypotheses necessarily go beyond the given data if they are to be useful. They must, for example, accept only some observed differences as actually marking the perimeters of objects. Finally, once entertained, these hypotheses become as much the 'stuff' of visual experience as more mundane experiences of light and hue. That they are an integral part of seeing is, in fact, one of the most awesome senses in which vision is not merely photographic.

Going a step further, Irvin Rock argues that, in forming such hypotheses, a basic rule seems to be an abhorrence of excessive coincidence. Thus, while any particular part of the edge of any particular patch of dark might be completely ambiguous if taken alone, if too many patches terminate too abruptly and in too neat a fashion, it becomes increasingly reasonable to posit a single cause for that orderliness—which is to say, that an edge connects (and causes) that arrangement.

It will be apparent that Rock's principle is easily applied to the examples of illusory figures reviewed above, with only the added stipulation that an enclosing object contour, once hypothesized, might be expressed in experience through an alteration in brightness across the enclosed area relative to that which surrounds it. On the other hand, brightness alterations would not always be expected since not every object discerned in the natural environment seems to glow or glower, and, in fact, as Kanizsa himself discovered, neither do all illusory figures. For example, the lower right-hand corner of the triangle seen in the final pattern does not seem to glow and yet, quite remarkably, seems to retain a very real presence.

Similarly, some of the random-dot stereograms devised by Bela Julesz produce a substantial perceptual surface lying in front of a background surface, from which, however, it does not seem to differ in hue or brightness. (See VISION: THE EARLY WARNING SYSTEM.) Thus, shape, rather than always being expressed in terms of contrasting brightness or hue, is sometimes experienced as a quality which

may be called, for want of a better term, 'object-ness'. That is to say, a given area, while being seen as the same in brightness and hue as that which lies round it, may, nevertheless, be segregated and unified by the impression that that area is all *an* object. Of course, just as the perceptual system must disregard a shadow lying across any object in detecting the outline of that object itself, so here its proper business remains the business involved in the detection of objects rather than only patterns of light. As a result, the present phenomenon might even be called illusory 'objects'. After all, the impression induced by these demonstrations is one of a physical object (albeit a thin one) like, for example, a thin coat of white dusting powder.

On the other hand, it is equally important to recognize that any illusory figure is, in a different sense, distinctly unsubstantial. As has been said, the system seems to retain the knowledge that the hypothesis which posited the object is only tentative. Certain edges may be possible or even probable, but if not fully supported by the data at hand, further investigation (in particular the renewed search for physical brightness differences along all parts of the perimeter) eventually leads to rejection of the hypothesis. As a result, the experience of viewing illusory figures is one of their coming and going over time; depending, apparently, on which data are being weighed at the moment and, in each instance, on what the system 'makes of' (what it hypothesizes about) the data in question. If a great many irrelevant data are present—if, for example, Kanizsa's figure is surrounded by a random array of other lines and circle segments aimed this way and that—the triangular figure may emerge only gradually or never at all. On the other hand, by deliberately including conflicting (rather than merely distracting) elements, it is possible to destroy, with a longer look, the illusory figure that emerges during a shorter look.

In summary, illusory figures result from object hypotheses which are, all in all, closely analogous to scientific hypotheses formed in response to incomplete data. Not only are such hypotheses tentative and subject to rejection, and not only do they deal in probabilities in eschewing excessive coincidence, but, most importantly, they go beyond mere reiteration of the data in seeking, in effect, to explain them. Those explanations then become an integral part of concurrent visual experience so that any hypothesis which is supported by all, or almost all, of the data at hand becomes one that may be acted upon. That, of course, is what human vision is all about. See also PERCEPTION; PERCEPTION AS HYPOTHESES.   T. E. P.

Drake, R. and Petry, H. M., (1977) Organisational determinants of subjective contour: the subjective Necker Cube. *American Journal of Psychology*, **90**, 2, 253–262.

Julesz, B. (1971). *Foundations of Cyclopean Perception*. Chicago.

Kanizsa, G. (1955). Margini Quasi-percettivi in Campi con Stimolazione Omagenea. *Rivista di Psicologia*, **49**, 7–30.

Schumann, F. (1904). Einige beobachtungen über die Zusammenfassung von Gesichtseindrucken zu Einheiten. *Psychologische Studien*, **1**, 1–23.

**IMAGE, RETINAL.** See RETINAL IMAGE.

**IMAGE ROTATION.** Recent experiments by Roger Shepard, at Stanford, have shown that at least most people can 'rotate' mental images of fairly simple objects, and that this rotation can take place only at a limited rate, which varies between individuals. Remarkably, there is a precise linear relationship between the angle the mental image is rotated and the time required. What is being rotated may perhaps be some kind of analogue representation, as Shepard believes, or it may be changing parameters of a *digital description. This distinction between analogue and digital representations is a fundamental one, which is one reason why these experiments are so important. See also IMAGING.

Shepard, R. N. and Chipman, S. (1970). Second-Order Isomorphism of Internal Representations: Shapes of States. *Cognitive Psychology*, **1**, 1–17.

Shepard, R. N. and Metzler, J. (1971). Mental Rotation of Three-Dimensional Objects. *Science*, **171**, 701–3. New York.

**IMAGES OF THE BRAIN IN ACTION.** During the 1980s safe techniques for obtaining images of the living human brain have become widely available in clinical medicine. This revolution in diagnostic imaging began with the development of X-ray computed tomography (CT) in the early 1970s, followed by positron emission tomography (PET) and nuclear magnetic resonance (NMR; sometimes referred to as magnetic resonance imaging, or MRI). Each has made special contributions: CT and NMR to the production of refined, *in vivo* anatomical images, and PET to images of brain function measured in terms of local chemistry, metabolism (i.e., the use of oxygen and glucose), and blood-flow within the brain. It is the purpose of this entry to acquaint the reader with each imaging technique, but focusing primarily on PET and its potential to image the living brain in action.

**X-ray Computed Tomography (CT).** CT images are computer-generated images of tissue density, produced by tomographically measuring the attenuation of tissue to X-rays passed through the body at many different angles. These data have been analysed by a variety of increasingly sophisticated mathematical techniques to produce high quality images of the type shown in Fig. 1. The utility of such images for the clinical practice of neurology and neurosurgery can be recognized immediately. CT scans, almost overnight, replaced the need for more dangerous, unpleasant, and difficult-to-interpret diagnostic tests. The benefit to patients has been substantial through increased safety, accuracy, and promptness of diagnosis. The revolutionary nature of this type of imaging was recognized when the Nobel prize for physiology and medicine was awarded to A. M. Cormack and G. N. Hounsfield for work leading to the development of X-ray CT.

The primary contribution of X-ray CT to our understanding of human brain function has been to provide highly accurate ante-mortem data on the location of specific areas of injury affecting the human brain function. This has permitted accurate correlations to be made between the signs and symptoms of an illness and the specific brain structures involved. The literature now abounds with such observations. Many have provided valuable insights into the function of specific regions of the human brain.

Another important contribution of X-ray CT was to immediately kindle the interest of scientists in other types of neuro-imaging. For example, it was recognized that the mathematical techniques of X-ray CT, used to construct an image of the density of tissue to X-rays, could also be used to construct the distribution of a radiolabelled substance within the tissue from its emitted radiation. The development of X-ray CT was also a stimulus for the development of imaging techniques using the principles of NMR.

**Nuclear Magnetic Resonance (NMR)** is based on the fact that some atomic nuclei act like tiny bar magnets when placed in a magnetic field. When they are aligned in a magnetic field, they can be excited in controlled ways by irradiation with radio frequency energy. During recovery from such manipulations, these tiny bar magnets (or dipoles) emit radio frequency signals that contain a great deal of information about their chemical environment. Since discovery of this phenomenon by two independent investigative teams headed by Felix Block and Edward Purcell in 1946, for which they subsequently received the Nobel prize for Physics in 1952, it has been applied to the study of virtually any subjects from crystalline solids to living people.

Most NMR imaging of the brain of living human subjects makes use of the strong signal from the abundant hydrogen nuclei in tissue. These images provide exquisite anatomical detail of the human brain, varying in their appearance with the imaging strategy employed (Fig. 1). Abundant evidence now supports the use of such NMR images in clinical medicine as an excellent way to obtain anatomical information about the human brain *in vivo*. In many respects the images are superior in their anatomical detail to those produced by X-ray CT (compare images in Fig. 1). The primary contribution of proton NMR to our understanding of the human brain is similar to that of X-ray CT, providing accurate information for correlations between specific areas of brain injury and the signs and symptoms of illness. Many nuclei other than hydrogen can be studied with NMR (e.g., phosphorus, sodium, and carbon), portending biochemical and metabolic studies of the human brain

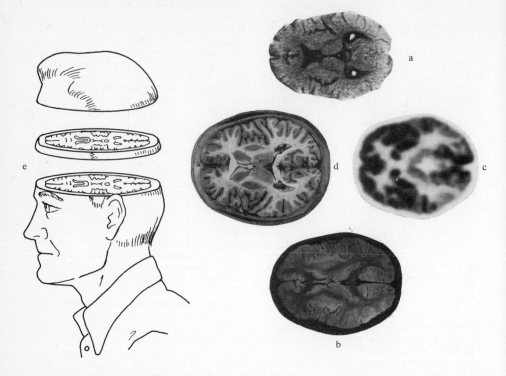

**Fig. 1.** Images of the normal adult human brain obtained with **a.** X-ray computed tomography; **b.** nuclear magnetic resonance (NMR); and **c.** positron emission tomography (PET). These images, obtained in living human subjects, are to be compared with a representative anatomical section of the human brain obtained in the same horizontal plane **d.** The approximate orientation of these images is shown in the line drawing on the left **e.** The CT image reflects the density of the tissue to X-rays, thus bone and calcified tissue appear most dense (white), brain parenchyma less dense (grey), and fluid bathing the brain least dense (black). The NMR image reflects the proton density of the tissue. In contrast to the CT image, bone is not visualized. Note the striking demarcation between grey and white matter in the brain and the exquisite anatomical detail as revealed by the presence of small blood vessels (fine black lines within the brain). The PET image represents a quantitative map of local glucose utilization in the structures depicted in the other images and the anatomical section. Areas highest in glucose utilization are dark. Areas with lower glucose utilization appear lighter.

with NMR (Prichard and Shulman, 1986). However, technical difficulties have so far precluded high spatial resolution biochemical and metabolic studies of the human brain *in vivo* (Raichle, 1986).

**Positron Emission Tomography (PET).** Emission tomography is a nuclear medicine technique that produces an image of the distribution of radioactivity in the human body, resulting from the administration of a substance containing radioactive atoms. Positron emission tomography (PET) uses the unique properties of radioactive atoms, that decay by the release of positively charged particles called positrons, to provide an image that is a highly faithful representation of the spatial distribution of radioactivity in selected planes through the tissue. The radioactive atoms most

frequently employed in PET are atoms with very short half-lives that are commonly utilized in the body's physiological processes, such as oxygen-15 (122 seconds), nitrogen-13 (10 minutes), and carbon-11 (20 minutes). Because of the development of ingenious labelling techniques, radio-chemists can incorporate these atoms into compounds utilized normally by the body, such as glucose or oxygen, permitting clinical investigators to monitor safely and accurately such important physiological processes as brain metabolism and blood-flow with PET.

PET images are based on the *in vivo* detection of two high-energy, annihilation radiation photons (511 kilo electron volts) that simultaneously emerge from tissue, after the local interaction of a positron with an electron (Fig. 2). Detection of the annihilation radiation is based on the use of

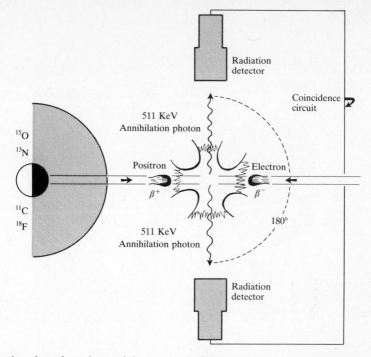

**Fig. 2.** Detection scheme for positron emission tomography (PET). Radioactive atoms employed in PET decay by emission of positrons. Positrons lose their kinetic energy in matter after travelling a finite distance (~1–6 mm) and, when brought to rest, interact with electrons. The 2 particles are annihilated, and their mass is converted to 2 annihilation photons travelling in opposite directions from each other with an energy of 511 kilo electron volts. Annihilation photons are detected by imaging devices using opposing radiation detectors, connected by electronic coincidence circuits that record an event only when 2 photons arrive simultaneously. (From Raichle (1983), reproduced, with permission, from the *Annual Review of Neuroscience*, 1983 by Annual Review Inc.)

coincidence circuits, in which two opposing radiation detectors record an event in the tissue between them only when two annihilation photons strike the detector coincidentally (Fig. 2). To optimize the efficiency of such a system, detectors are usually arrayed about the head in a circular fashion (Fig. 3). The use of several rings of detectors permits the simultaneous measurement of radioactivity in several tomographic slices of the tissue. A typical PET imaging device is shown in Fig. 4. A discussion of the process by which PET measurements of tissue radioactivity are converted into quantitative cross-sectional maps of local blood-flow, metabolism (Fig. 1), or other physiological variables is beyond the scope or intent of this entry. Several general reviews are available (Raichle, 1983; Leenders et al., 1984; Phelps and Mazziotta, 1985).

PET has demonstrated its capacity to contribute to a better understanding of normal brain function. This work, in its most sophisticated form, is based upon the relationship of local nerve-cell activity to brain blood-flow. Interest in the relationship between brain blood-flow and local functional activity has spanned nearly a century. The initial interest crystallized when Roy and *Sherrington

(1890) published their seminal paper in which they put forth the suggestion that there exists 'an automatic mechanism by which the blood supply of any part of the cerebral tissue is varied in accordance with the activity of the chemical changes which underlie the functional action of that part. Bearing in mind that strong evidence exists of localization of function in the brain, we are of the opinion that an automatic mechanism, of the kind just referred to, is well fitted to provide for a local variation of the blood supply in accordance with local variations of the functional activity.' (See LOCALIZATION OF FUNCTION AND CORTICAL MAPS.) The hypothesis of Roy and Sherrington has compelled investigators to pursue the envisioned relationships in order to better understand the function of the brain.

Even before the development of modern radiotracer methodology in the middle of the twentieth century, and nearly 50 years before the first PET scanners, several early experiments indicated the correctness of the hypothesis of Roy and Sherrington. In 1927 S. Cobb and J. H. Talbot performed tests in rabbits in which vigorous nasal stimulation with smelling salts produced increased blood supply to that portion of the brain serving the

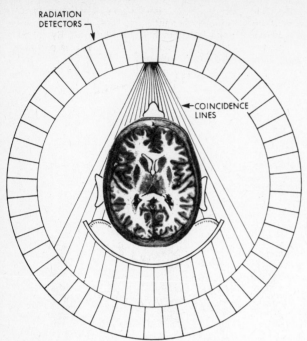

RADIATION
DETECTORS →

←COINCIDENCE
LINES

**Fig. 3.** Geometry employed in positron emission tomography (PET). Multiple radiation detectors (type depicted in Fig. 2) are arranged about the subject's head and connected by coincidence circuits. Data from coincidence lines between detectors are used to form a quantitative image of the distribution of radioactive atoms within the brain. From these images, it is possible to measure a variety of physiological processes depending upon the behaviour of the particular compound in which the radioactive atom is delivered to the subject.

**Fig. 4.** A typical positron emission tomography (PET) imaging device designed specifically for the study of the human brain (Super Pett IIH; designed and built by M. M. Ter-Pogossian and colleagues at Washington University, St Louis). The subject lies on the couch in the foreground with his head in a specially designed head holder. The subject is positioned with his head in the central aperture of the imaging device and is surrounded by the radiation detectors contained in the gantry.

sense of smell, whereas other areas of the brain remained unchanged. The first observations in humans were reported a year later by Fulton (1928) who studied a patient of the American neurosurgeon, Dr Harvey Cushing, at the Peter Bent Brigham Hospital in Boston. The patient was operated on for an abnormal collection of blood vessels located at the back of the brain, in the region of the cerebral cortex known to receive and process visual information. The blood vessels could not be removed and the patient was left with a small defect in the bones of the skull. By placing a stethoscope over the scalp in this area physicians could hear a pulsating noise as blood was pumped through the malformation by each heart beat. This noise was also heard by the patient who reported that the noise in the back of his head intensified whenever he used his eyes. Fulton pursued this

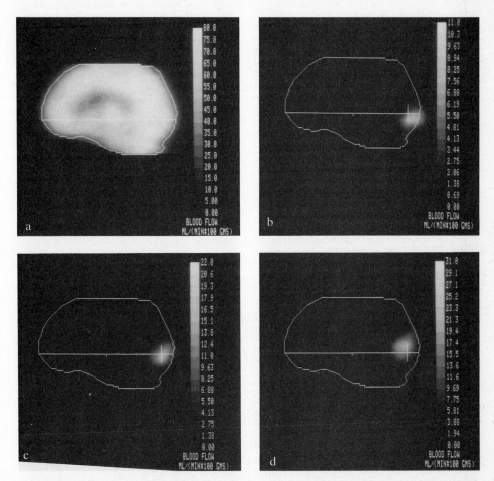

**Fig. 5.** Positron emission tomography (PET) images of local brain blood-flow during stimulation of visual centres of the human brain. The orientation of these images is best appreciated by reference to Fig. 6, which is an NMR image reconstructed in the same anatomical plane and contains the same fiducial markers for easy reference. **a.** Resting image of blood-flow in the brain. The scale on the right is callibrated in the units of blood-flow, i.e. millilitres (ml) of blood per 100 grams (gms) of brain per minute (min). **b.** An image of the difference in blood-flow between the resting and stimulated state obtained by subtracting image **a.** from the image obtained during the stimulation of the very centre of the subject's visual field. The centre of the area of increased activity is located at the back of the visual cortex. **c.** An image of the difference in blood-flow produced by stimulating the subject's visual field slightly away from the centre of the visual field. **d.** An image of the difference in blood-flow produced by stimulating the periphery of the visual field. All images were obtained in the same subject. The stimulus consisted of an annulus composed of red-on-black chequer-boards alternating colours 10 times per second, and presented to the subject on a television monitor visible to him while lying in the PET scanner. The size of the annulus was varied to stimulate various parts of the visual field. Note that, as the stimulus moved from the centre of the visual field to the periphery, the area of activation moved systematically along the visual cortex. This corresponds to a well-known map of visual space existing in this part of the brain. The centre of areas of activation such as these can be determined with an accuracy of approximately 1 mm (Fox et al., 1986).

observation and was able to confirm that the noise over the visual cortex increased during visual stimulation (for example, reading a newspaper) but not during any other type of activity. This unique observation provided the first direct evidence in a human subject of the close link between local neuronal activity and blood-flow.

Abundant evidence now indicates that functional brain activity of all types (for example, somaesthesis, hearing, movements of all types, vision, language, as well as covert cognitive activity) causes striking changes in local brain blood-flow and metabolism. Analysis of such images has progressed from simple, qualitative, uncontrolled demonstrations of anticipated changes to much more sophisticated studies using rigorously controlled experimental paradigms and precise analytical techniques (Raichle, 1987). A good example of such a study is shown in Fig. 5. By combining the physiological information from such PET images and the anatomical information from an NMR image (Fig. 6) it is now possible to visualize safely, and with considerable precision, the relationship between physiology and anatomy in the normal, living, human subject.

PET will also contribute to an understanding of brain function by providing a new understanding of the effect of localized areas of injury on the function of the brain. For many years neurologists have studied the effects of localized disease of the brain, usually *strokes and occasionally other diseases such as *epilepsy, on the function of the human brain. It was through many years of painstaking study of such lesions, first at the autopsy table, and more recently with CT and NMR imaging, that we have obtained our current understanding of such complex human functions as language and memory. What such lesion studies reveal is the relationship between an anatomical lesion and a patient's signs and symptoms. What they fail to reveal are areas of the brain remote from the lesion where function is significantly altered due to the disruption of normal relationships between regions within the brain. Because altered neuronal function causes alterations in blood-flow and metabolism, PET is ideally suited to detect these areas of altered function remote from the actual area of brain damage (Metter et al., 1985). A typical example is shown in Fig. 7 where a small stroke deep within the cerebral hemisphere causes a large metabolic abnormality in overlying cerebral cortex, in an area with no gross pathological abnormality. A systematic study of the clinical significance of these remote physiological effects of brain injury has yet to be conducted. It seems safe to say, however, that the availability of this new physiological information will enhance our understanding of human brain function.

Finally, some recovery of function often occurs despite irreversible injury to a particular region of the human brain (see BRAIN FUNCTION AND AWARENESS). One hypothesis is that such recovery is due to a reorganization of the brain, such that a new region of the brain now serves that particular function. Our ability to observe the local activity of the brain during the performance of the recovered function should permit a much better understanding of this process of reorganization and ultimately

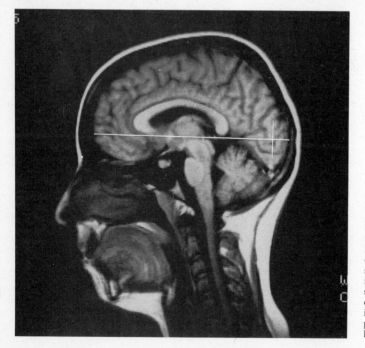

Fig. 6. A nuclear magnetic resonance (NMR) image of a normal human subject reconstructed in the midsaggital plane. The orientation of this image corresponds to the PET images shown in Fig. 5. The fiducial markers on the image correspond to similar markers on the PET images in Fig. 5. The intersection of these two lines corresponds, approximately, to the centre of the primary visual cortex in humans.

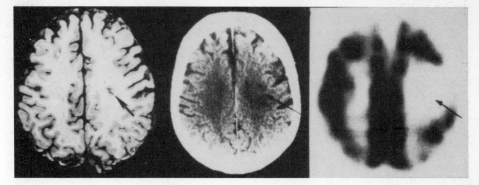

**Fig. 7.** Gross pathological section, X-ray CT scan, and corresponding PET study of glucose metabolism in a patient with a small subcortical stroke. The area of brain injury is clearly seen in the CT image and the section of brain obtained following the patient's death (arrow). This small area of brain damage resulted in a large area of functional impairment as demonstrated by the area of reduced cortical glucose metabolism remote from the stroke itself.

lead to more rational treatment of affected individuals.

It might be argued by some that, despite the developments described above in our ability to do functional mapping of the human brain, it is virtually impossible for PET to reveal the underlying neuronal elements participating in such changes, and hence they contribute little to our understanding of how the brain works. It seems fair to assume, however, that once PET has safely identified a specific area of human brain responsible for a well-defined type function, a task it is uniquely equipped to do, other neurobiological techniques can be brought to bear on the exact nature of the process. Complementary interaction of this type will benefit both clinical investigators and brain scientists.

M. E. R.

Cobb, S. and Talbott, J. H. (1927). Studies in cerebral capillaries. II. A quantitative study of cerebral capillaries. *Transactions of the Association of American Physicians*, **45**, 255–62.

Fox, P. T., Mintun, M. A., Raichle, M. E., Meizen, F. M., Allman, J. M., and Van Essen, D. C. (1986). Mapping the human visual cortex with positron emission tomography. *Nature*, **323**, 806–9.

Fulton, J. F. (1928). Observations on the vascularity of the human occipital lobe during visual activity. *Brain*, **51**, 310–20.

Leenders, K. L., Gibbs, J. M., Frackowiak, R. S. J., Lammertsma, A. A., and Jones, T. (1984). Positron emission tomography of the brain: new possibilities for the investigation of human cerebral pathology. *Progress in Neurobiology*, **23**, 1–38.

Metter, E. J., Mazziotta, J. C., Itabashi, H. H., Mankovich, N. J., Phelps, M. E., and Kuhl, D. E. (1985). Comparison of glucose metabolism, X-ray CT, and postmortem data in a patient with multiple cerebral infarcts. *Neurology*, **35**, 1,695–1,701.

Phelps, M. E. and Mazziotta, J. C. (1985). Positron emission tomography: human brain function and biochemistry. *Science*, **228**, 799–809.

Prichard, J. W. and Shulman, R. G. (1986). NMR spectroscopy of brain metabolism *in vivo*. *Annual Review of Neuroscience*, **9**, 61–85.

Raichle, M. E. (1983). Positron emission tomography. *Annual Review of Neuroscience*, **6**, 249–67.

Raichle, M. E. (1986). Neuroimaging. *Trends in Neuroscience*, **9**, 525–9.

Raichle, M. E. (1987). Circulatory and metabolic correlates of brain function in normal humans. In Mountcastle, V. and Plum, F., *Handbook of Physiology—the Nervous System*, V. Section Editor: Vernon Mountcastle. Forthcoming.

Roy, C. S. and Sherrington, C. S. (1890). On the regulation of the blood supply to the brain. *Journal of Physiology*, **11**, 85–108.

**IMAGING.** Most people can imagine the appearance of a loved person's face, of a familiar and often used room, or even, with the lights suddenly turned out, the approximate dimensions and organizations of the place they are in. Most people can report the reveries of a day-dream, the somewhat hallucinated state that often precedes sleep, or the dreams of sleep itself. Barring those who are neurologically damaged, people can with their eyes closed touch a finger to their chin or throw a dart with enough force just to hit a nearby wall; can hear the voice of the writer when they read a letter from a friend, or the voice of an adviser when in a situation of conflict; or taste a remembered food, or experience the aroma of an object not present. And, indeed, most people can rise from their chairs and walk across the room with their eyes closed, navigating the intervening space safely and accurately. In all these many conditions people can be said to be imaging. The nature of the mental image, its role in mind and behaviour, and even how to account for imagery in a theoretically satisfactory way, are all puzzles of great interest to a number of philosophers and psychologists.

Often the notion of mental image is taken as a 'picture in the mind', the richly pictorial evocation of a scene not present to view, so not all of the events listed above are customarily thought of as images. All of the sense departments—vision, hearing, touch, smell, taste—can be involved in the production of imagery, however, although some sorts of image may be evoked somewhat more readily than others. People differ in their preferred way of encoding the world; some say they learn a subject better by reading about it, whereas others claim that a lecture is more informative. An early division of people into audiles and visiles—those preferring listening to reading, for example—broke down when it was found that these allegedly constitutional differences were often a matter of strategy, or preference, or appropriateness to the occasion.

The way the image may function in mental life, and even its nature as an object of mind, are debated issues at present. Some investigators endow mental images, especially spatial images, with the very properties they are alleged to represent in mind; others maintain that the content of mind is not a suitable descriptor and assert that all mental experience can be captured with the structured propositional representation of the logician; and yet others maintain that imagery is best thought of as a kind of private *symbol system that people use for different purposes: to orient themselves in space, aid their recall of some event, or even, as on a sort of mental scratch-pad, to work out solutions to problems. Whereas the first two groups concern themselves with the question of what an image is and how best to describe it, the third group recommends studying how imaging may, among other kinds of symbolizing, function in mental life.

It is important to realize that an image of an experience is sometimes not readily distinguished from the perception of a physical encounter, a fact that has strengthened those concerned with identity of the image, although a few minor tests can quickly reveal the difference. The image is not readily manipulated (see IMAGE ROTATION), nor does it withstand the detailed scrutiny that a physical object can. In a test made many years ago a psychologist exposed matrices of letters and digits to people recognized as ready visualizers. After the people had examined each matrix for some moments it was removed and they were asked to form a mental image of it and to name the letters or digits in a row or column. If the matrix were present to view, the letters could be named in any direction in about the same amount of time, although a favoured reading direction might give a slight advantage. In fact, people were not able to manipulate their images of the matrix so as to read off its contents in unfamiliar directions without some sort of rehearsal. Thus, its appearance may not by itself allow one to judge accurately whether an event is stimulated by some object of the environment external to the person or is constructed by the person wholly from within; however, suitable tests of manipulation, scrutiny, and evaluation resolve the puzzle. Many different sorts of events can result in similar appearances, so that appearance alone can never be used reliably as a guide to identity.

Eidetic imagery seems to challenge some of the assertions made above. Found more readily in children than among adults, the eidetic image is said to have more of a richly pictorial quality than other images have. Shown a complex drawing for a few minutes, some children can subsequently report on many of its features, even seeming to re-examine it in detail when questioned about something not yet reported. Very little more is known about this ability.

The role of imagery in mental life has puzzled and entranced philosophers and psychologists alike for many years. One reason for this, stemming from the empiricist theory of mind, has to do with the way we acquire knowledge of the external world. An early, and recently revived, theory has it that the visual system forms brief images—'snapshots', so to speak—which the linguistic system then encodes and deposits in *memory. The image here serves as a first stage in some chain of information acquisition, a notion which is, however, questioned by many. Secondly, images are thought to sustain orientation and mobility in space. And for a third reason, the proposal has been made that the mental image serves as a personal symbol.

The lack of sure knowledge regarding the nature and function of imagery stems in part from the difficulty of saying much with certainty about the mind, and in part from the bad reputation that imagery has until recently suffered. For sculptors, painters, and other artists, the notion of a richly pictorial inner life has been assumed without saying—as much as a richly linguistic inner life must mark the essayist, judge, poet, and others concerned with the sense and sound of language, a mind full of sounds the musician, or a mind full of smells the perfumer. A vivid inner life must surely characterize anyone whose work requires invention, problem-solving, organization—anything beyond the stereotypy of mindless activity. The bad reputation developed because imagery was wholly subjective and so not available for public scrutiny. In the earliest days of experimental psychology, a proper experiment often consisted in describing as analytically as one could the bare 'sensations' that presentation of a stimulus or memory of it evoked. The contents of consciousness were thought then to be the principal data of psychology, and accounting for them to be the task of the psychologist; much as, in direct analogy, the contents of the world were taken as the data of chemistry and accounting for them—how combinations of elements yielded compounds—was taken to be the task of the chemist. Rejection of this view constituted part of the dogma of the 'behaviourist revolution' (see BEHAVIOURISM) and the enterprise of accounting for the inner life was discredited. Recent developments in psychology, philosophy, linguistics, and computer science (see ARTIFICIAL INTELLIGENCE) have restored interest, if not in the contents of mind, at least in its operations, of which imaging is one.

See also ICONIC IMAGE.                                    P. A. K.

Ferguson, E. J. (1977). The mind's eye: nonverbal thought in technology. *Science*, **197**, 827–36.
Kolers, P. A. and Smythe, W. E. (1979). Images, symbols,

and skills. *Canadian Journal of Psychology*, **33**, 158–84.

Sheehan, P. W. (ed.) (1972). *The Function and Nature of Imagery*. New York.

## IMMATERIALISM. See BERKELEY, GEORGE.

**IMPLICATION** is the fact of being involved or implied without being plainly expressed. Thus seeing the implications of a decision, or of a course of action, requires knowledge of its consequences, and seeing the implications of what someone has said requires a knowledge of the significance or meaning of his words, given the context in which they were uttered.

It is via the notions of consequence and meaning that implication has become a term of the logician's art and a focus of philosophical study and debate. Here it is treated as that relation between two statements or propositions $A$ and $B$ which obtains whenever the corresponding conditional statement 'If $A$ then $B$' is true: e.g. '$ABC$ is a triangle' implies 'The internal angles of $ABC$ add to $180°$' if, and only if, 'If $ABC$ is a triangle, then its internal angles add up to $180°$' is true. Thus $A$ implies $B$ if, and only if, it is that case that if $A$, then $B$. Philosophical and logical theories of implication are thus inseparably tied to analyses of conditional statements. In the most widely used formal propositional logic (that based on truth tables), conditional statements are represented by the (truth functional) connective '$\supset$' (or sometimes '$\rightarrow$'), where '$p \supset q$' is true if, and only if, it is not the case that '$p$' is true and '$q$' is false. Thus '2 is an even number $\supset$ 2 is a prime number' is true, since both '2 is an even number' and '2 is a prime number' are true, whereas '2 is an even number $\supset$ 3 is an even number' is false, since '2 is an even number is true' but '3 is an even number' is false. When '$p \supset q$' is true, '$p$' is said to *materially imply* '$q$', and '$\supset$' expresses the relation of *material implication*. This definition has the consequences (known as the 'paradoxes of material implication') that, for example, 'Snow is red' materially implies 'Pigs can fly', and 'Dodos ate fish' materially implies 'Snow is white', since a false proposition materially implies *any* other proposition, and a true proposition is materially implied by *any* other proposition.

These examples fly in the face of our intuitions both about implication and about the meaning of 'If . . . then . . .' and have thus been used to cast doubt on the legitimacy of using '$\supset$' to give formal, logical representations of conditional statements. But attempts to find alternative logical representations, for example by means of the relation of *strict* (or sometimes *logical*) *implication*, encounter similar problems. '$p$' strictly implies '$q$' ('$p \rightarrow q$') if, and only if, it is impossible that '$p$' should be true and '$q$' false (see ENTAILMENT). Hence if '$p$' expresses a contradiction, '$p \rightarrow q$' is automatically true for any $q$. Similarly, if '$q$' expresses a necessary truth, '$p \rightarrow q$' is true for any $p$. Several other notions of implication have been introduced with a view to avoiding these paradoxes but encounter problems of their own.                                          M. E. T.

Haack, S. (1978). *Philosophy of Logics*, chs. 3 and 10. Cambridge.

## IMPOSSIBILITY. See POSSIBILITY.

**IMPRESSION.** This term reflects the ancient notion that experiences are impressed on the 'wax' of the mind by the 'seal' of experience in *memory. This implies that memory is essentially passive; but modern work, following F. C. *Bartlett (*Remembering*, 1932), strongly suggests that memories are active constructions, and are often distorted towards the familiar or the wanted. So this notion of memories as impressions like seals on wax is not an appropriate model.

**IMPRINTING.** When recently hatched birds such as ducklings are hand-reared for a few days, they strongly prefer the company of their human keeper to that of their own species. This remarkable process, which can so dramatically influence the development of social relationships, is called 'filial imprinting'. A bird's experience later in life can also strikingly influence its sexual preferences. When exposed to another species at a certain stage in development, it may subsequently prefer to mate with that species. The process influencing mate choice is known as 'sexual imprinting'.

In many ways the term 'imprinting' is a misnomer since it implies an instantaneous stamping-in to the bird's memory of information that will determine its social preferences. In fact, the process is more gradual and is better likened to the painting of a portrait in which the broad outlines are first sketched and fine details are filled in by degrees. Furthermore, despite the remarkable distortions of social preferences that can occur under artificial conditions, some stimulus objects are much more effective than others. In general, objects that are most like the animal's own species are most effective in influencing its subsequent preferences.

The procedures used for studying imprinting are not associative. The experimenter merely exposes the bird at the right age to a single conspicuous object and subsequently shows that its preferences have become restricted to that object. Even so, the underlying process might be associative. If this were the case, initially significant and attractive features of the stimulus object would be linked to initially neutral features in the course of learning. Deciding whether or not this is really what happens is not easy. Even if the imprinting process that leads to the identification of parents (or future mates) is not associative, it operates simultaneously with both classical and operant *conditioning. What is more, the objects that work best for purposes of imprinting can be used with the associative procedures as rewards. Thus, the imprinting stimulus is highly effective as a reinforcer, and a young duckling can easily be trained to press a pedal that switches on a motor and brings an object into motion. However, enough is now known about the neural mechanisms to dissociate by lesions in the brain the operant conditioning which involves learning to press a pedal, from the imprinting which involves the narrowing of preferences to a familiar object.

As it happens, filial imprinting in domestic chicks has proved to be a useful model for studying the neural basis of *learning. Using biochemical measures of neural activity and autoradiography, a site in the intermediate part of the medial hyperstriatum ventrale (IMHV) has been found to be intimately involved in filial imprinting. When the neurones in this area are destroyed before imprinting, a chick fails to identify the object with which it has been trained; and furthermore, when they are destroyed immediately after imprinting, a chick no longer responds preferentially to the object with which it was trained. Nevertheless, lesioned birds are just as capable as intact animals of learning discriminations in which reward is involved, and will work just as readily for an imprinting object—even though they do not learn its characteristics.

Some other discoveries of the work on the neural mechanisms involved in imprinting are also striking. Storage only remains localized in the IMHV on the left side of the brain. On the right side, information is stored initially in the IMHV but within twenty-four hours it has dispersed to other, and as yet unknown, sites in the brain. In the left IMHV, where information about the imprinting object remains stored, the dendritic synapses increase in size. It would be an exciting, as well as demanding task, to discover whether the pattern of synaptic enlargement codes the information stored in the course of imprinting.

One of the striking features of filial imprinting is that it is easiest to get birds to learn about an object at a particular stage early in life. This stage is referred to as a 'sensitive period' in development. However, it is important not to confuse the descriptive evidence for such a period with explanations for how the evidence has been generated. The nature of the timing mechanisms has proved to be subtle, and the image of a clock, opening a window on to the external world and then shutting it again, is not good enough.

Generally, the onset of sensitivity is measured in terms of time after hatching. However, birds can differ by as much as thirty hours in the stage of development at which they hatch. In other words, when eggs have been incubated under identical conditions, the time from the beginning of incubation to hatching varies greatly. It is possible, therefore, to have birds of the same post-hatch age which are at different stages of development, and birds which are at the same stage of development but of different post-hatch ages. The influence on imprinting of the general stage of development can be separated from the influence of experience occurring at hatching and after it. It turns out that both the age from beginning of embryonic development and the age from hatching influence the results. In other words, it looks as though the general stage of development of the bird plays a part in the onset of sensitivity, but that the events associated with hatching, or experiences subsequent to it, also play their part. Part of the increase in sensitivity is attributable to the changes in the efficiency of the visual system. This being the case, the interaction between internal and external influences is particularly easy to understand. Visual experience with patterned light has a general facilitating effect on the development of visually guided behaviour. It also serves to strengthen connections in neural pathways. Thus, it is probable that the development of the visual pathways, on which filial imprinting must depend, can be accelerated by early hatching if this means that the bird receives more experience from patterned light than the bird which is still inside the egg.

The end of sensitivity to novel objects arises from a property of the imprinting process. When a bird has formed a preference for an object, as a consequence it ignores or even escapes from other objects. Therefore, imprinting with one object prevents further imprinting with other objects from taking place. While some objects are much more effective than others in eliciting social behaviour from naïve birds, domestic chicks can form social preferences for suboptimal stimuli such as the static cages in which they were isolated, although this takes several days. It follows, that if some birds are reared with near-optimal stimuli, such as their siblings, and some are reared in isolation, it should be possible to imprint the isolated birds with a novel object at an age when the socially reared birds escape from, or are indifferent to, new things. This is clearly the case with both domestic chicks and mallard ducklings. Investigators find it difficult to get older birds to respond socially to an object, because the birds have already developed a preference for something else.

It seems, then, that the end of sensitivity of a bird to a wide range of objects is generated by a runaway process in which the consequences of an initial change in state generate the conditions for further and more rapid changes. When the bird is poised to learn, all that is required is the presence of a suitable external stimulus to trigger the process. As a result of learning about a particular object, the bird escapes from those it can detect as being different. This escape from strange objects intensifies the young bird's contact with a familiar object, and the range of acceptable companions rapidly contracts so that in the natural world the bird ends up with a distinct preference for its own mother. Enforced contact with something other than the preferred familiar object may wear down the behavioural constraints to the point where the bird does form a new preference. Escape from novel objects can be habituated, and domestic chicks that have developed a preference for object A can be induced to prefer object B to object A by sufficiently long exposure to the second object. It turns out that the early preference is not forgotten and may resurface after isolation from both types of object. So, it would seem, the protection of preferences from subsequent disruption is accomplished not only by behavioural means, but also by internal processes as well.

For many years it was thought that imprinting enabled an animal to learn about its species. However, it is becoming apparent that imprinting serves a more subtle but equally important purpose, enabling the young to recognize one or both of their parents as individuals. The species that are feathered and active at hatching must learn the parental characteristics quickly because, on leaving the place where it was hatched, the young bird must stay near a parent. If it approaches another adult of its own species, it may be attacked or even killed. For this reason, as soon as the young animal is able to recognize its parent (or a substitute parent in an experiment), it escapes from anything that is noticeably different. The rapid attachment to the first conspicuous objects encountered after hatching is characteristic of the precocious species. In birds like the swallow, which are hatched naked and helpless, learning occurs later in development, and the young only respond selectively to their parents when they have left the nest about two weeks after hatching. Sexual imprinting probably occurs later in development because birds need to know the characteristics of their siblings' adult appearance when they come to choose a mate. The ideal mate must be a bit different but not too different from close relatives in order to avoid the dangers of inbreeding and, at the other extreme, the dangers of mating with a genetically incompatible partner such as a member of another species. Some animals are so careful in their choice of sexual partner that, having been reared with their siblings, they then choose first cousins as mates. This has been discovered in Japanese quail and also in mice. Indeed, it is becoming apparent that processes similar to those first described in birds are equally important in mammals. The biological need to recognize close kin, both early in life and when adult, is a general one.                                    P. P. G. B.

**INDIAN IDEAS OF MIND.** A short survey cannot do justice to the enormous range of ideas of the mind produced in India. In an unbroken cultural tradition of some three thousand years, which has given birth to Hinduism (itself the name not of a single religion but of a family of religions), Buddhism, and Jainism, one of the main topics of conceptual interest has been in philosophical psychology: how the mind is to be analysed, trained, and developed, in order to explain and obtain the religious goal of enlightenment and release from rebirth. Here it is possible only to indicate some of the main structures and attitudes of Indian thought; and certainly exceptions to everything said here have existed.

Among the many words which can be translated as 'mind' are: *manas*, from *man*, to think; *citta* or *cetas*, from *cit*, to perceive or attend to (these latter two are often better translated as 'heart', the Western term for the affective and intentional centre of personality. Indeed the word usually translated as heart, *hrdaya*, itself is often used to refer to cognitive acts); *buddhi*, from *budh*, to be awake or aware; *vijñāna*, from *jñā*, to know or be conscious; and, finally, in many philosophical contexts the term *antaḥkaraṇa*, literally inner activity or inner organ, is used to refer collectively to a variety of perceptual, intentional and cognitive functions or agencies. Often some or all of these terms are to be regarded as synonymous; in particular systems they can also be taken to refer to different things. In no case can we assume anything simply comparable to Western *mind–body dualism; nor has much attention been paid to the specific mind–brain problem. In so far as mind or *consciousness has been given a physical location, or at least been associated with particular locations in the body, it has been in terms of the mystical physiology of *cakras*, circles or centres of energy, twelve of which are thought to be located in various parts of the body; different kinds of consciousness are then associated with different *cakras*.

The first and most general point to make about Indian ideas of the mind is that they have been elaborated in a conceptual context derived from, or at least constantly in interaction with, religious concerns. The basic structure of the religious world-view is given by the following three terms. (i) *Saṃsāra*—'the round of rebirth'—is the idea that each person (however that is conceived) lives through a series of lives, which can occur in various forms both in this world and elsewhere. (ii) *Karma*—'action', 'moral retribution'—is the belief that it is action which causes this process of rebirth, and experience within it; the moral quality of actions performed previously—usually but not necessarily in past lives—determines the happiness or suffering experienced thereafter. This gives both one type of explanation of suffering and evil, and a possible rubric for religious and moral behaviour which tries to improve one's lot in the future. One may hope for rebirth in better circumstances, or for an escape from rebirth entirely. (iii) *Mokṣa*—'release', 'liberation' (in Buddhism usually called *nirvāna*)—refers to the escape from rebirth, to an ultimate state variously conceived, but usually involving some or all of the qualities of freedom, bliss, transcendental knowledge, and power.

This conceptual system is understood in at least two main ways. Firstly in a literal or mythological sense, it can be taken straightforwardly to refer to a sequence of births, lives, and deaths, and to escape from them. Secondly, it can be interpreted in a psychological or 'demythologized' sense—that is, as referring to different ways of perceiving and evaluating the temporal world, rather than to different life-histories or destinies within it or beyond it. In this sense, *saṃsāra* is best taken as something like 'differentiated perception', or 'unenlightened understanding'—that is, seeing the multiform and in itself unreal ordinary world as ultimately real and desirable, in contrast with *mokṣa*, which is seeing the world in its eternally true light (a true light, of course, very differently described by different systems). Here, instead of the religious goal of enlightenment being taken in a horizontal perspective—as something awaiting the holy man at the end of his earthly life—it is taken in a vertical perspective, as a possibility of moral-mystical experience *now*. (Of course, these two perspectives are not mutually exclusive; the symbolic, psychological sense can be, and is regularly taken to be, the means of operation of the literal, religious-destiny sense.) A very fine expression of the vertical, demythologized interpretation of these concepts is given by the tenth–eleventh-century theologian Abhinavagupta, for whom the ultimate subjective reality of the self and the objective reality of the experienced universe are both God, known as Siva or Bhairava. It is God's essential nature, as pure consciousness, constantly to manifest or emanate the individual selves and objects of the ordinary world (*saṃsāra*) as both its efficient and its material cause. Thus we read that

(Liberation *is* knowledge; it is not a separate phenomenon which knowledge produces), for liberation *is* the revelation of one's true identity; and the identity of the self is consciousness. . . . When one has established oneself in the sphere of prediscursive intuition one may become supreme Siva, through any of the levels of manifestation, from the grossest impenetrable matter to the subtlest Siva. One's awareness becomes supreme Siva by these (various inroads, by centredness) in the light which manifests itself as these ordered aspects as they shine in their primal brilliance. . . . One becomes Bhairava by the revelation that within one's own identity as the void of consciousness one is oneself causing the universe to appear and that as one creates it one is it. 'This entire system of the six parts of the cosmos is reflected in me alone and it is I that sustain its existence.' Thus shines forth one's identity with everything. 'This universe is dissolving into me as I roar with the fire of absolute awareness beyond time.' With this vision he comes to rest. The realization that one is Siva (is) the surging holocaust (which) burns to nothingness the dream-palace of *saṃsāra*, with its infinite, diverse and beautiful chambers. (*Tantrāloka*, I, 156; I, 211–12; III, 283–6, translated by Alexis Sanderson.)

In this general religious context, ideas of the mind depend on different notions of the enlightening realization, and specifically on different notions of what is the soul or self which is realized and liberated. Answers to this latter question vary greatly: there is the view, as we have just seen, that the single and ultimately real self is (a personal) god; the real self can be seen as the impersonal cosmic spirit or essence, usually called *brahman* (as in the *Vedānta*); it can be a separate, eternally monadic soul or person (as in Jainism and *Sāṃkhya*. These two systems are atheistic: elsewhere such a monadic soul is also related, devotionally, to a god); and finally, as in Buddhism, the ultimate realization is that there is no self at all.

In all these systems, what we call the human mind is *not* part of what is released; it is in itself either an obstacle to, or at most merely an instrument of release, on a par with the physical senses. One system which exemplifies this, and which was used in various developed forms by many later traditions, is the classical *Sāṃkhya* ('Discrimination'). It is a dualism, but not at all in the Cartesian sense. On the one hand, the real self is called *puruṣa*, 'person'; it is eternally inactive, a mere spectator at the show of existence. On the other hand, *prakṛti*, 'matter' or 'nature', evolves from within itself the whole drama of rebirth and release. From an undifferentiated state of equilibrium, at the start of each cosmic aeon, there evolve first something called *mahat*, the great, or *buddhi*, will, or determinative awareness, then *ahaṃkāra*, 'I-maker' or ego, and then *manas*, mind, conceived as a *sensus communis*, a cognitive organization and recognition of sensory activity and experience. (Subsequently there evolve five sense-organs, five organs of action—these, together with *manas*, in fact evolve together and are called the eleven faculties—five subtle elements, the 'sense-data' perceived by the senses, and five gross elements, the external substances thus perceived.) The first three evolutes are together termed *antaḥkaraṇa*, inner organ, or in a general sense 'mind'. This mind is constantly changing, moving and being moved in the ordinary world of action and experience. In itself it is unconscious and inanimate; it is only the presence of the static and inactive *puruṣa* which, as an animating catalyst, transforms mental activity into conscious experience. This conjunction of the *puruṣa* and the 'material' mental/sensory apparatus is likened to that of a lame man and a blind man: separately incapable of movement and sight, respectively, but together capable of progress (toward enlightenment) (*Sāṃkhya Kārikā*, XXI). Another image conveys the notion of a release which comes to the 'witnessing' person, entirely without activity on its part, but rather from the material mind's own cessation of action: a dancer, whose dancing-show, beautiful but temporary, is finished, gracefully withdraws from the stage, leaving the spectator free (ibid., LXV–LXVI).

Thus the religious context of Indian thought puts ideas of the mind into this sort of conceptual structure. Equally, it influences these ideas by its overriding moral and spiritual attitudes. Generally speaking, the senses and mind are regarded as appetitive, as desiring, grasping, and relishing their objects, in the very act of sensing or knowing them. In the unenlightened, this rapaciousness is wayward and uncontrolled; enlightenment requires the imposition of control on it, either to stop ordinary experience entirely, or to let it proceed seen in its true light, seen as it really is. The *Kaṭha Upaniṣad* (*c*.sixth–fifth century BC) uses an image familiar in the West, and widely used in India:

Know the self as the chariot-owner (i.e. he who is carried,

inactively, by it), the body as the chariot. Know awareness (*buddhi*) as the driver, the mind (*manas*) as the reins. The senses, they say, are the horses, sense-objects the path they range over. The self joined to mind and senses, wise men say, is the experiencer. He who is without understanding, whose mind is ever unharnessed, his senses are out of control, as bad horses are for a charioteer. (*Kaṭha Upaniṣad*, I, 3–5.)

In the *Bhagavad Gītā* (*c.* third century BC) India's most popular religious text, we read of the unenlightened that 'when a man's mind follows after the wandering senses, his wisdom is carried away, as the wind (carries away) a ship on water'. Contrastingly, 'when everywhere a man withdraws his senses from their objects like a tortoise (withdrawing) his limbs, then his wisdom is firmly established' (II, 67; II, 58). The Buddha taught that 'just as a monkey in a big forest seizes one branch, lets it go and seizes another, so too that which is called mind (*citta*), thought (*manas*), or consciousness (*vijñāna*) by night and by day at one moment arises as one thing, (the next moment) ceases as another' (*Saṃyutta Nikāya*, II, 94–5).

This last text embodies the Buddhist idea that the mind itself changes as rapidly as do its objects; and this points to a very general fact about Indian ideas of the mind. Whereas the true self, or whatever lies behind the ordinary experienced world (in Buddhism not a self or an 'absolute' of any sort, but the fact of emptiness) is unchanging and timeless, the mind and its temporal experiences are constantly changing; but further, the mind changes *together with* its objects, because the mind and the senses conform to the nature of what they cognize or perceive. A regular idea of perception, for example, is that a ray of light goes out from the eye, makes contact with, and takes on the form of its object, and then carries vision of the object back to the eye (see, e.g., the third-century BC *Nyāya Sūtras*, III, 32f.). In a medieval *Vedānta* text (cited from *Panchadasi: a treatise on advaita metaphysics*, trans. Hari Prasad Shastri, London, 1956) it is said that 'the mind, which is the illuminator of all objects, assumes the forms of the objects it perceives, just as sunlight assumes the forms of the objects which it illumines' (IV, 29).

From this notion that the mind assumes the form of its object arise various other Indian ideas. In certain devotional schools of Hinduism, since intense mental concentration of any sort on God will transform the mind into God, even intense hatred will produce God-realization and thus liberation in the hater's mind. Similarly, in certain meditation traditions in Buddhism and Hinduism, when the mind concentrates on a certain level of the psychological-cosmological hierarchy, it 'becomes' that level, and (particularly if the mind is in this state at death) the meditator will be reborn in the corresponding heaven. If, in contrast, an ordinary man's mind is regularly characterized by a predominant emotion, he will be reborn in an appropriate sphere—greed, for example, might produce rebirth as a dog. In the traditions of religious thought and practice known as the *tantra*, this pattern of ideas explains the attainment both of this-worldly pleasure and powers (*bhukti*) and of final release (*mukti*). In order to achieve a particular good (or, in what we call black magic, a harm), the religious specialist will concentrate his mind on the particular deity who controls the desired object, usually in that god's *mantra* form. (A *mantra* is a hymn, sound or 'spell'. Language—that is, Sanskrit—is regularly thought to be the ground of all thought and consciousness; so particular gods, and the supreme God, have two forms of representation, one visual and iconographic, the other sonic and 'bodied forth' in *mantras*.) In this way, the mind concentrates on and becomes the *mantra*, and thus becomes the god, and so gains control over the god's domain. When this technique is applied to lower-level gods, for this-worldly goods or harms, we tend to see it as magic; it becomes more recognizably religious when final release is sought, when the human microcosmic mind seeks identification with (or, as it is expressed, 'possession by') the macrocosmic supreme divinity. In both these contexts, an image regularly used is that of the god's seal, *mudrā*, impressing itself on the wax of the disciple's mind.

In all contexts, magical, religious and philosophical, the simple description of the workings of the mind is embedded in their moral evaluation. This can be seen in (though not proved by) the terminology used: the standard terms for the functioning of consciousness, regardless of its ultimate subject (or lack of one) are *grāhaka*, *grāhya* and *grahaṇa*, grasper, grasped and grasping, subject, object and (act of) knowing or perceiving. These three elements of consciousness may or may not be thought of as arising simultaneously or in one or other causal sequence. It is true that in most uses of these terms there is as little concentration on their etymologically literal meaning as there is in the case of their English translation; equally, the fact that Indian thought regularly uses concepts which do not distinguish factual description from moral evaluation does not show (what would be false) that it cannot do so. Nevertheless, these terms are used in systems where the unenlightened mind's 'grasping' its objects *is* seen as intrinsically connected with, or a function of, the foolish desire mistakenly to take the ordinary world for true reality, by grabbing hold of the pleasure and illusory permanence of the experience of the ordinary world. The earliest text of the *Vedānta* school, Gaudapāda's *Māṇḍūkyopaniṣad-kārikā* (*c.* seventh–eighth century AD?), demonstrates this:

It is consciousness (*vijñāna*), birthless, motionless and immaterial, (eternally) at peace and non-dual, which seems to be born, move and perceive substance. ... Just as the movement of a firebrand produces the appearance of straight and crooked (lines), so the vibration of consciousness produces the appearance of perception and perceiver. ... This duality of subject and object is just a vibration of mind (*citta*). ... (This) is the craving for what is (ultimately) non-existent, but in truth no (real) duality is found; he who realizes the absence of duality, beyond qualifications is not reborn. (IV, 45, 47, 72a, 75.)

Just as description and evaluation are conflated in these accounts of the mind, so too moral and religious explanations of character and destiny derived from the idea of karma, enter into the account of other kinds of mental activity. The key concept here is that of 'traces' or 'impressions' (the term is usually, but not always, *vāsanā*, 'perfuming'), and the notion is that each act, mental or physical, leaves behind it a trace which 'perfumes' or conditions the individual series of mental events which is the mind of the agent/experiencer, just as a sesame seed retains the smell of the flower after the flower has died. These traces in the mind can be representational—that is, a trace can be reactivated as a memory, a dream, or in some systems a perception—or they can be moral and psychological conditioning factors—that is, they may operate in the future as one of the various kinds of determining influence on an individual's character and behaviour in a particular lifetime. The location of these traces is differently described; it is often seen as a particular kind or level of the mind, for which the translation 'the unconscious' is tempting. The metaphor of depth, however, usual in (at least popular versions of) Western psychoanalysis, is not much stressed in India, even in the other image used to picture the mind's operation here, that of 'seeds' sown by action and experience, which ripen later into the 'fruits' of memory, character-disposition and so on.

In the case of the traces being representational, the realist *Vaiśeṣika* system holds that 'memory, dreams and dream-consciousness arise from a particular contact between the self and the inner organ, along with traces' (*Vaiśeṣika Sūtras*, IX, 22–3). In the idealist school of Buddhism, the *Vijñānavāda*, a comparable mechanism produces perception of a world mistakenly thought to be external, but in fact arising, just as do memory and dreams, from the traces kept in the 'store-' or 'base-consciousness' (*ālaya-vijñāna*) (e.g. in Vasubandhu's *Vimśatikā*). When the traces act as moral and psychological conditions, the overall effect of such 'perfuming' by previous unenlightened acts is to predispose the mind habitually to perform further desire-based and ignorant deeds. The general predisposition is specified in various ways. When rebirth at one of the various levels in the cosmic hierarchy takes place, particular kinds of trace in the mind are activated, so as to produce the appropriate mental dispositions for that kind of being (e.g. *Yoga Sūtras*, IV, 8–11, and Commentaries). These dispositions in each life are both general, as species-specific characteristics and instincts, and particular, as those patterns of motivation and behaviour which give rise to individual personality. These individual characteristics are usually described as the predominance of one or more kinds of emotion and attitude; often they are expressed in terms of

the 'humours' of traditional Indian ayurvedic medicine, which resemble the humours of ancient and medieval Western thought. Sometimes, individual character as a man is derived from the predominance of traces derived from species-specific characteristics in former lives; and this individual character can continue even after enlightenment (for although the enlightened man creates no new karma, he may well still have old karma to work off). Étienne Lamotte (in Cousins, *et al.* (eds.), *Buddhist Studies in Honour of I. B. Horner*, Dordrecht, 1974, p. 93) recounts the following story:

In Vaisali, a monkey met his death after having filled the Buddha's bowl with honey. He was reborn into a brahman family and as in recompense for his good deed he had as much honey as he needed, he received the name Madhuvasistha, 'Excellent-Honey'. As soon as age allowed he took up the robe [became a monk] and attained holiness. Nevertheless he retained his monkey habits and was often seen perching on walls and climbing trees.

Indian ideas of the mind, then, are influenced by their cultural context, both by the kind of conceptual structure in which they are cast, and the kinds of moral and religious attitude which arise from the various ways of construing the belief system of rebirth and release. What happens to the mind when release is achieved is variously imagined. The opening lines of the *Yoga Sūtras* declare uncompromisingly that 'Yoga is the cessation of mental activity', and frequently the religious training of the mind consists in an ever-deepening meditative absorption and implosion, in what Mircea Eliade (1958) has called ecstasy. The difference between this kind of quietistic vision of the enlightened mind and more activist conceptions can be illustrated by the following two examples of ocean imagery. In the *Vijñānavāda* school of Buddhism, objects of thought and perception, as well as the illusion of a real subject, are said to arise from within the mind, from the 'store' (*ālaya*). Thus we read that 'just as on the ocean, waves stirred up by the wind dance and roll unceasingly, so the (*ālaya-*) mind-sea, constantly stirred up by sense-objects, dances and rolls with its multiform consciousness-waves' (*Lankāvatāra Sūtra*, 46). The attainment of enlightenment here is then conceived as a calming of the storms of ordinary consciousness; and the mind-ocean finally stops at the 'further shore' of nirvana. In non-dualistic Saivism, contrastingly, while God (Siva) is the only reality, subjectively and objectively, he is not conceived as a quiescent and transcendent divinity, but as the radically immanent and active event of consciousness. Enlightenment consists then not in calming the mind to an absolute stillness, but in the full realization of God's nature in all its self-manifestation. Thus we read (*Tantrāloka*, I, 116; I, 5–6, trans. Alexis Sanderson) of Siva, whose nature is nothing other than self-transformation through the energies of consciousness (expressed mythologically as goddesses):

The undivided lord, consciousness, has creative awareness

as his innermost nature; (thus) the totality of the waves of this consciousness is contemplated and worshipped in various specific conformations, mild or wrathful.... (His) power of freedom, the impulse to project himself as order (in space and time) and his embodiment as this order: may this triad of goddesses, the all-inclusive glory of the all-pervading lord, shine within me revealing my ultimate nature. May Ganeśa, son of Siva's consort, the unique ego which controls the faculties of cognition and action, and whose inner nature is as the lord of the great rays which are the fullness of those three (great) goddesses—may Ganeśa, offspring of absolute awareness, radiant full moon, swell the tide of the ocean of my consciousness.

s. c.

Eliade, M. (1958). *Yoga, Immortality and Freedom*. London.

**INDUCTION** is a term encompassing a variety of forms of inference, commonly, but not always, in contrast to *deduction. If 'proposition' is defined as a thought expressible by a grammatical sentence having either prescriptive or descriptive force, 'inference' may be defined as a transition in thought between one or more propositions (premises) and a further proposition (conclusion), where the premises purport to be reasons for the conclusion. The conclusions of deductive inferences cannot be rejected without contradicting the thoughts contained in the premises, and in this sense are already contained in the premises. Deductive inferences were consequently classified by C. S. *Peirce as 'explicative', while inferences whose conclusions were not already implicit in their premises were called 'ampliative'. 'Induction' is sometimes used in the sense of 'ampliative inference'. Classically, however, following *Aristotle's use of '*epagōgē*' (from the Latin translation of which we have 'induction'), the term applies to a subclass of ampliative inferences, namely those in which the conclusion is more general (applies to a wider range of instances) than the premises.

The root idea of a movement in thought from particular to general has given rise to the practice of applying the term 'induction' to two forms of inference which are in fact deductive. The first of these is complete induction (in Aristotle, 'deduction from induction, *ex epagōgēs sullogismos*'), where the premises are all less general than the conclusion, but collectively exhaust the instances covered by the conclusion. If chimpanzees, gorillas, humans, etc., are found species by species to react in a certain way to a certain virus, and these species exhaust the class of Primates, one may conclude that all Primates react in this way to the given virus. The second is the large family of proof procedures used by mathematicians on a variety of order structures, the simplest example of which is numerical induction: if (1) $F$ is a property of the number one and (2) if $F$ is a property of the number $n$, then it is a property of $n + 1$, then (1) and (2) together *entail that $F$ is a property of all (natural) numbers.

The narrower classical idea of induction as

inference from particular to general excludes certain ampliative inferences involving probability, e.g. inferring that $x$ is $F$ from the high probability that a member of a class, $C$, to which $x$ belongs, will be $F$. It also excludes ampliative inference from one or more descriptions of an individual case to some further descriptions of that case. (Where the further description stands as the best explanation of why the first descriptions apply to that case, Peirce distinguished what he regarded as a scientifically vital form of inference, and which he called 'hypothesis' or 'abduction'.)

It is clear from this account that ampliative inferences are by definition not deductions and hence not deductively valid. Where, in other words, an induction is not complete—that is, the cases covered in the premises do not exhaust those referred to in the conclusion (e.g. when concluding that all chimpanzees react in a certain way to a certain virus on the basis of having examined any number, $n$, of chimpanzees)—the premises may all be true and the conclusion false, and the inference may be reasonable but unfortunately misleading. This gives rise to the so-called problem of induction, but from a purely logical standpoint it can appear to be a matter of lamenting the fact that not all of the inferences which we make have the rigour and compulsion of deductions, coupled, perhaps, with the insinuation that only deductive inferences are rationally grounded. But, against the insinuation, it is far from obvious why good reasons for a conclusion must preclude its negation on pain of contradiction. It is clearly possible to distinguish good from bad reasoning which is not in this way absolutely compelling.

From the standpoint of certain epistemological presuppositions, however, the problem is acute. If we assume, as is done in traditional empiricism, that all our knowledge is founded on (sensory) observations of individual instances, inductive inference presents itself as the only, however doubtful, means at our disposal for building on this modest foundation the vast edifice of our beliefs about the natural world. Unless there are general statements whose truth can be known *a priori, all premises of our deductions must be reached by induction; and every attempt to infer what holds for some unobserved or unobservable case on the basis of what has been observed must explicitly or implicitly appeal to a general proposition, which can only rest on induction from observed cases.

But the most, it is held, we are able to observe in individual cases are certain similarities among them, and it seems reckless in the extreme to expect such similarities to appear elsewhere unless we can identify some *cause or constraint which ensures that a pattern we have observed will occur elsewhere. However, in seeking such a causal constraint in what we observe, all we will find are further patterns of similarities in the features of what we observe which are constantly conjoined. We can find, in other words, no basis for a causal constraint which is not itself in need of the very justification which we are seeking to provide.

David *Hume, who is the classic source for this problem (although he did not formulate it using the word 'induction') considered whether a global principle such as the uniformity of nature could underwrite our inferences from observed to unobserved cases. But such a global principle seems a non-starter: nature is uniform only in certain respects, and in other respects is highly variable. This is reflected in our practice of making inductive inferences. In some cases it is reasonable to generalize on the basis of very few instances; in others a very large number of observed instances is no basis at all for a generalization. Traditional empiricism tends to obscure this difference because it presents all inductive inferences as ultimately proceeding by 'simple enumerations', which have to be assessed in the absence of any background of established beliefs and experimental techniques. Popular and oversimplified views of Karl Popper's response to Hume, namely that science does not rely on induction but on finding exceptions to its generalizations, are likewise based on the notion that induction is simply a matter of projecting a similarity in our experience of part of a class of cases on to the whole of that class (e.g. of expecting what we have observed in some chimpanzees to hold of all chimpanzees which have yet to be observed). In fact we move no closer to real science by saying that the aim is rather to find exceptions to such attempts at superficial generalization.

Francis *Bacon rejected the procedure of applying a global principle as 'childish', insisting that induction must proceed 'by proper rejections and exclusions'. The underlying principle of this genuine Baconian induction (known as 'eliminative induction') is the control we exercise over the circumstances of our observations. We must, in other words, move beyond simply projecting our observations to cases not yet observed and project in the form of experimental hypotheses, which ascribe a network of links between circumstances, that can be varied, and phenomena, which we can observe. We have observed a link between heavy smoking and lung cancer, but do not yet know how the circumstances may be varied so as to interfere with the link (and therefore cannot yet explain why many heavy smokers do not get lung cancer). In this spirit Peirce defined induction as 'the operation of testing a hypothesis by experiment'.

J. S. *Mill's 'four methods of experimental inquiry' were designed to help identify the laws and causal factors governing phenomena. We need (i) to find what is common among the differences in the instances which we have observed ('method of agreement') and (ii) to compare the instances in which the phenomena occur with those in which they do not ('method of difference'). We can (iii) 'subduct' from the phenomena all portions which we can assign to known causes, and the remainder will be the effects of causes still to be determined ('method of residues'). And we can (iv) look for functional relations between variations in phenomena ('method of concomitant variations'). The application of such methods and the testing of the hypotheses which they yield evidently involve a procedure of thought which goes well beyond the projection of superficial similarities (expecting future crows to be black because all observed crows have been black); it requires an account of the causal mechanism, which we can then test by creating circumstances which would very likely not occur in nature without our intervention.

Arguably, traditional empiricism generalized inadequately on the procedures by which all humans learn about their environment. Some things are learned by simple *habituation, developing a uniform response to similar stimuli, but a great deal of human learning involves interfering with the environment.

Such a response to traditional empiricism and the problem it has with induction, however, will appear to beg the question unless at the same time one calls into question the assumptions that observation consists in the passive reception of sensory qualities and that the concepts we apply to what we observe derive wholly from this source rather than, in a large and important part, from the control we are able to exercise over what we observe. Bacon, for one, saw that induction properly conducted (i.e. as experimental inquiry) needed to be used not only 'to discover axioms but also in the formation of notions'. If we allow that induction is a procedure through which we develop our concepts of what is or is not a (natural) *possibility, the traditional problem of induction appears in a quite different light.            J. E. T.

Bacon, F. (1620). *The New Organon* (especially bk. I). 1960 edn., New York.

Hume, D. (1739–40). *A Treatise of Human Nature*, bk. I, pt. iii. 1888 edn., Oxford.

Mill, J. S. (1843). *A System of Logic*, bk. III. 1879 edn., London.

Peirce, C. S. (ed. Buchler, J., 1955). *Philosophical Writings of Peirce*, chs. 11–15. New York.

Swinburne, R. (ed.) (1974). *The Justification of Induction*. Oxford.

**INFANCY, MIND IN.** Theories of mental life show their axioms in the way they describe the *intelligence of infants. Empiricists, who tend to be materialists, see *consciousness coming into existence through learning—by remembering experiences. They claim the infant to be a reflex organism, making adaptive responses to stimuli and possessing drives for survival, but inert mentally and amoral. With experience, representations of objects in the world are synthesized and new motivations are built up. A child gains thinking, perception of meanings, and values entirely through imitation and training—from parents and then from a wider society of peers and elders. Thus are collective knowledge and consciousness of meanings and purposes passed on from generation to generation. Individuality arises from each subject's unique voyage of experience.

Romantic nativists, however, have a quite different view. They assert that the infant is born with unspoken wisdom: a human spirit with awareness and feelings who has simply to grow in strength and skill and in knowledge of the specifics of reality while acting on inherent human impulses. All humans, they believe, have the same basic forms of consciousness and the same motives. In health human minds grow on the same overall specifications. The characters of individuals differ in their particular natural gifts, as well as in the opportunities these have had to grow.

Other ways of describing infants combine elements of the extreme philosophies. Psychoanalysis, by focusing on organizing processes of the self, created a new interest in the development of the child's separate mental identity: an individual motivation and consciousness crystallizing out from the protective mother–child relationship. Cognitivists emphasize the novelty-seeking and problem-solving tendencies of infants, and they explain development as a construction of increasingly complex cognitive programmes focused on mastery of physical reality and its patterns of change. The Swiss educational psychologist Jean *Piaget, who made meticulous observations of infants solving problems, is this century's great rationalist among developmental psychologists. He portrays the child as an autonomous experimenter who acquires representations of objects in the world and who gains rational awareness by recording the effects of his acts. For both Sigmund *Freud and Piaget the newborn infant has little but reflex powers of integration. Separation of 'self' from 'outside world' and from 'the other' who shares life with one is achieved by the learning of distinctions and forms of relationship that arise in interaction of subject with environment. This is called the 'object concept' and the formation of an 'object relation'.

Recent research with infants has cast new light on these questions. It has brought support for a more nativist position in opposition to a physiological empiricism that dates from Ivan *Pavlov. Beyond that, the increased detail of our knowledge makes a self-controlled process of differentiation in the child's mind, which tests experience, more and more obvious. The mind of the infant is neither simple nor incoherent. Children do not develop intentional integrity by the linking up of sensory-motor reflexes through conditioning, as the behaviourists said they did. They seem, rather, to be seeking to refine their reactions to particular events and formulate specialized skills within a coherent general ability to perceive and understand both physical objects and persons. They are born with several complementary forms of knowing, and they use these to develop experience of the particular world they are in, assisted by communicating. They do not, at any stage, confuse themselves with objects 'outside' nor do they fail to recognize that other persons are separate sources of motives and emotions.

Recent experimental studies give data for a rigorous presentation of this thesis. They prove that infants have organized cognitive activities that regulate uptake of experience in one mental time/space frame. Moreover, these activities are found to have remarkable foresightfulness. For example, babies no more than a few minutes old may adapt their orientations and states of alertness to fit the motion of objects that are remote from their bodies. New-borns can detect patterns in the recurrence of particular things, so it is obvious that they rapidly acquire rules for making perceptual distinctions, and they record the timing and location of recent happenings. Babies adapt, by co-ordinated movements, to the time, place, and nature of events that have importance for them. Events caused by human movements hold the greatest interest for them.

Conditioning tests, in which new-born infants have to react to and anticipate repeated events, show that they may generate predictive strategies, seeking new rules for keeping track of a changing world near them. These tests depend upon accurate observation of the infant's looking and listening behaviour, of breathing, or of sucking on a pressure-sensitive nipple. The latter two measures detect fluctuations in attending, since visual and auditory focusing compete with sucking and breathing. Evidence for complex reactions to events also comes from video and film studies of the facial expressions and hand movements of infants. Expressions of concentrated puzzlement, surprise, pleasure, and displeasure are clearly delineated, and arms and hands make movements that vary systematically with the other signs of attending. Evidently babies are ready to show a variety of feelings to others.

In the last few years there has been increasing effort to describe the first signs of mental activity in new-borns and development in early months. The neonate period, from minutes after birth to about three weeks old, is highly specialized. It is true that survival is the baby's main preoccupation then. Functions of suckling, breathing, and protective action against threatening variations of temperature or injurious contact with hard objects or dangerous animals are all adjusted quickly to an environment which has been radically transformed at birth. The quick and effective movements of new-borns to gasp air, to find the nipple, and to seek comfort and protection are remarkable. They are classically described as *reflexes and assumed to be due to relatively simple neural links from special receptor zones of the brain-stem and spinal cord to motor nerve centres. But a healthy baby born without complications is immediately capable of more than mere fixed responses to physical stimuli and much of the behaviour is spontaneous. Even the true reflex responses to artificial stimulation with touches, sounds, or flashing lights are powerfully modulated by central physiological processes (called 'state variables') that arouse the brain's activities, or quiet them down. Experiments with supposedly simple events produce highly variable and complex results, because the infant's state is changing.

Given quiet and gentle attention, a baby born without trauma or sedation is strikingly alert within minutes of birth to the new world of sights and sounds. The wide-open eyes make finely co-ordinated stepping movements (see SACCADES) aimed in different directions round the body. They may stop or change direction to fixate bright places, or track stimuli in motion. They also clearly orient to the face of a person who approaches close and speaks gently in a tone of greeting. The eye movements are coupled with small pulsating rotations of the head. Films of new-borns orienting to and tracking objects with their eyes reveal that a reach-and-grasp movement of arm and hand is inherently co-ordinated within a visual space–time field of awareness. The movements are a well-formed prototype of the movement an adult makes to take hold of an object. This automatic movement of prehension, linked to perception of the changing reality outside the body, is a necessary basis for the eventual consciousness of objects and intentional command of actions. If a higher mental command is to work, it must eventually decide about goals in a richly patterned world, and the lower-level problems of perceptual locating and motor patterning must be solved without reflection. Apparently some of the required solutions have been formulated in outline during foetal stages of brain growth. They are ready for adjustment to perceptions of certain goals very soon after birth. Critical tests show that the new-born has almost no capacity to modulate the form of the basic reach-and-grasp automatism, by changing its duration or size in relation to different kinds of object with different kinds of motion, but the old idea that visual field and aiming of the hand have to be linked together by experience is disproved.

Reactions to persons are the most remarkable. Tests show that new-borns will turn in the direction of a voice from a loudspeaker behind a curtain, orienting not only the head and ears but the eyes as well, as if searching to see the person who calls. Simultaneously, hands and face move in ways which indicate a total involvement of a co-ordinated expressive system in the brain. At birth a baby prefers to hear its own mother's voice. Her particular vocal characteristics have been learned *in utero*. In the first few days the sounds of different syllables in speech, as well as their emotional tone, are discriminated by the baby. Observations of face movements of both premature babies and full-term neonates prove that not only the musculature but also the nerve centres exciting the muscles are organized, so that a wide repertoire of well-formed expressions is present before the baby has had an opportunity to learn from adult exemplars of these human movements. Paediatricians and mothers unconsciously observe the infant's facial expressions, hand activity, and body posturings to make sensitive appraisal of a baby's state and needs; but the movements, which may be small and fleeting, are only now being accurately charted by developmental scientists.

Much of a neonate's life is spent in sleep. Although infants are usually wide awake and active just after birth, for two or three weeks thereafter the most common state of a baby is either one of sleep with eyes closed, or a vague open-eyed condition in which awareness of the outside world appears weak and fluctuating. The routine cycle of sleep and wakefulness is very weakly foreshadowed at birth. It needs shaping by the consistent behaviour of a responsive caretaker. Often a wakeful new-born is actively and effectively avoidant of experiences, and this is particularly noticeable in unfamiliar circumstances. It is important, in this connection, to note that the tissues of the brain undergo enormous developments in these few weeks (see BRAIN DEVELOPMENT). Intercellular connections are rapidly multiplying. There is evidence that nerve circuits in this condition powerfully limit their own excitation by controlling the motor functions which direct sensory pathways away from stimuli.

In spite of this avoidant state, which is comparable with the dark-seeking, closed-eyed condition of a nestling kitten, controlled observations show that new-borns are capable, like other newly born mammals, of rapid conditioning. With the assistance of a mother's routine, a new-born's sleep cycles become adjusted to time of day and night. The opinion of many mothers that a baby learns in a couple of feeds to find the breast with more skill, and that her baby soon knows her and the father as particular individuals, different from others, is confirmed. Olfactory, gustatory, visual, auditory, and body-contact senses have all been implicated in this recognition by familiar caregivers. The mother is known even when she takes the baby up silently in the dark. The individual appearance of her face is learned in two or three days.

Psychologists, and mothers alike, are astonished by recent demonstrations that babies less than a month of age are capable of imitating facial expressions. Indeed, with some babies, it is easy for a mother to see for herself that her new-born, just minutes old, may watch her mouth intently if she protrudes her tongue or opens her mouth wide, then move his mouth and appropriately poke out his tongue or open wide his mouth. The model is accurately copied. Expressions of happiness, sadness, or surprise are also imitated. With calling vocalizations, a similarly prompt imitation can be obtained, when the baby is a few weeks older. Imitation of movements of the hands opening or coming together has also been seen. All these movements, like the expressions of smiling, knitting of the brows, etc., and hand movements of gesture, including making a fist, extending all fingers, or pointing with the index finger, may occur also without a model—but prompt and well-differentiated imitation of some of them is undeniable. At the very least, this phenomenon proves that the infant has made a reasonably well-differentiated perceptual image of the model act of the mother's face, vocal apparatus, or hands. This image must be formed in close relation to the appropriate motor command which sets off the right imitative response almost immediately after focused attending to the model the first time it is presented. Denial of this ability to imitate reflects a strange, culturally induced belief that a new-born cannot have awareness of persons as such. Luckily, both mothers and doctors may act at variance with over-cautious scientific prejudices that have no obvious virtue. Mothers are certainly made happy by this simple test that shows their babies know them in a complex way. Clinically, systematic use of such relatively complex behaviours would seem to have potential value for diagnosis of sensory or motivational differences or abnormalities.

Besides imitating, neonates can smile and coo and make hand gestures when spoken to. A majority of new-borns raise the right hand more than the left. These signs to persons become much more responsive in the second month, after the perceptual systems of the cerebral cortex have developed, especially for vision. Contented facial expressions of a baby may be stimulated by soft handling and gentle speech; quite different patterns are evoked by loud, impatient, or aggressive speech and abrupt movements. The split-second timing of exchanges of expression between the infant and the mother have been analysed, to prove that both of them are actively controlling the exchange. A highly significant series of experiments has begun to examine infants' responses, in the second and third month, to broken or unreal communication, or to the attentions of a distressed mother. Threatening expressions or inconsistencies in a partner's behaviour cause the baby to make expressions of sadness or fear. When being spoken to in the normal way, babies show quickly changing patterns of face movement, alternating between the appearance of puzzled attending, with knit brows and mouth depressed, and a face full of pleasure and greeting with raising of the eyebrows and a smile. The subtlety of these positive expressions, and the speed of their disappearance when a mother holds her face artificially still on a prearranged signal proves that the baby is highly perceptive that 'something has gone wrong with mother'.

This work has helped determine how the baby may enter into control of the communication of moods and levels of awareness with another human being. But we have much description to do before we can give a full account of how the baby perceives other persons. Microanalysis of ordinary face-to-face play between mothers and their two-month-old babies reveals a precise conversation-like timing in the way they address one another and reply. Babies stimulate gentle and questioning 'baby talk' which has a regular beat and characteristic expression of mood in its changing intonation, rhythm, and accompaniment of movements of head, eyebrows, eyes, and so forth. The infant watches the maternal display intently and then makes a reply, on the beat, with a smile, head and body movements, cooing, hand movements, and even lip-and-tongue movements which are called 'pre-speech'. Photographic records suggest they are developmental precursors of actual speech. These attempts at vocal expression are synchronized with hand gestures. It is not claimed that babies have things to say, or that they can hear words as such, but they are certainly perceptive of certain identifying features in the sight and sound of human speech. They even appear to want to make rudimentary utterances themselves when persons excite them by friendly greetings. The outbursts of infant expressive movement last two or three seconds, with characteristic beginning, climax, and end. Sometimes they contain coos or calls—but often there is no vocalization at this age, merely activity of mouth and hands. Their regularly repeated form helps the mother give the right support and encouragement in her well-timed movements and speech (Fig. 1).

The intensity of interest and the delicacy of response of young babies to persons who speak to them also helps to establish an affectionate personal relationship, which has great importance in the baby's mental development. In the 'bond' (in the sense of a compact of mutual trust) which develops between them, infant and favourite companion begin to develop a shared repertoire of expressive tricks and exchanges of feeling (see BONDING). As the babies' cognitive powers increase by selective retention of mental rules that work better and better to control objects, and after actions have become more alert and discriminating, mutual interest with the mother undergoes a subtle but pervasive change. There develops a conflict between pursuit of purpose in subjugation of objects and ways of exploring them, on the one hand (i.e. development of an 'object concept'), and the sharing of interpersonal interest, on the other. But out of this complication appears a new kind of playfulness which offers a crucial bridge for sharing motives and, eventually, knowledge.

The nature of *humour and play has long baffled philosophers and psychologists. Whatever it is for, play certainly has a key role in the taking of this major developmental step in infancy. As soon as infants gain the ability to reach and grasp objects, so they become susceptible to gentle responsive teasing about their gropings after a changing target and to the mother's emotional attunement to everything the baby does. An affectionate mother of a blind baby will tease the gropings of her infant after an object heard or felt, with much lively vocalization, and cause her baby to laugh. Frequently, a six-month-old will try to grasp the mother's face or her hand. This leads to many games in which the mother moves the attractive

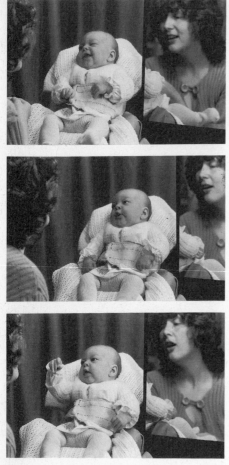

**Fig. 1.** A six-week-old girl smiles at her mother, coos and gestures, raising her right hand more than her left. Her mother is speaking gentle 'baby talk' on a steady beat and watching closely.

months old, he or she is clever at handling and mouthing objects, very alert to the sight and sound of happenings, including effects of their own manipulations, and clear about the distinctions between the familiar and the strange. Life with others is enlivened by humorous games and clowning, created mutually, and sometimes there are conflicts of purpose that the baby learns to adjust to with strong and unambiguous expressions of refusal or acquiescence. But there is rarely any sign of specific interest in another's wishes or intentions in regard to the shared reality before the baby is nine months old (Fig. 3). Then, within two or three weeks, this self-directedness (called egocentricity by some psychologists who see it as a limitation of immaturity, rather than a necessary process of development in autonomy) changes fundamentally. By one year a baby starts to both express and respond to a new kind of mental relationship, in which the purposes and experiences of another in

**Fig. 2.** Paul, at 36 weeks, plays happily with his mother trying to 'catch' a ball, but he is shy then sad with a friendly stranger.

part of her about, tempting and dodging the infant's interest. Games of 'peek-a-boo', 'pop goes the weasel', and creeping of the hands up the baby's body ('round and round the garden') will easily come to mind. Such games, with their well-marked patterns in time, all tease the infant's growing curiosity, and they give companionship. Traditional musical formulae in nursery songs, chants, and rhymes, found in all cultures, are purpose-built to entertain a baby at this age. They show that all babies gain a sense of fun and appreciation of musical communication long before they speak (Figs. 2 and 3).

Out of the intertwined and interacting developments of object-perceiving and communicating with persons emerge extremely powerful mental functions which pave the way for language, effective logical formulae for reasoning, and other key artefacts of human culture. Before a baby is nine

on others, but they do not make utterances about their experiences that are addressed to others as comments or enquiries that seek affirmation or complement. They do not make baby words to specify objects to others. Nor do they appear to recognize the mother's names for objects. But, by the end of the first year most babies everywhere do all of these things. They quickly learn intricate reciprocal or co-operative games where they purposefully share the effort to build something, look at a book, create an amusing effect. They become aware of and are interested in the changing directions of another person's interest. The motivation for this kind of co-operative play is strong, and people who know the baby well become aware of an intense companionship in it. It leads to a sharing of experiences, and of symbols, that is uniquely human.

**Fig. 3.** Emma, at 28 weeks, has learned to play a traditional hand game ('clappa, clappa handies') with her mother. Songs for infants have similar musical form in different cultures. Emma is a genetic left-hander; already she claps left hand over right. Esme, 40 weeks, enjoys playing with and exploring wooden dolls and a truck, but has to be physically 'persuaded' to obey the instruction 'Put the man in the truck'. She does not understand her mother's gestures and spoken instructions.

relation to the world outside both of them become of primary interest (Fig. 4).

Towards the end of the first year, the infant develops a clear awareness of the existence of objects in their own right, and a short-term memory that can direct a search for them when they have been hidden by someone in view of the infant. But there are other developments, too, that change the infant's communication. Before nine months, babies do not 'offer to give to' or seek 'to have help from' or 'point to direct the attention of' the person with whom they play. They gesture and babble in a highly expressive way, obviously playing with the postures and sounds, and with effects

**Fig. 4.** Basilie, one year old, co-operates. When her mother hands her the doll, saying, 'Put the man in the truck', Basilie does so immediately, then looks at her mother and grins. She understands her mother's wishes, and can use 'protolanguage' of gesture and vocal expression to influence others. Basilie is a right-hander.

Through the last six months of the first year babies show strong selective affection for their principal caretakers, usually mothers, and they become highly sensitive to approaches from strangers—acting afraid or distressed (Fig. 2). This sign of trust in the familiar, with matching anxiety about the unfamiliar, seems to relate to the great increase, at 9 months, in complexity of the baby's interest in the knowledge and skills that can be shared with steady companions. The familiar playmate is an integral and necessary part of the baby's developing consciousness.

There is much attention in contemporary developmental psychology to the start of spoken language when, properly, a child ceases to be an infant (*infans*: unable to speak). (See LANGUAGE: DEVELOPMENT IN CHILDREN, and LANGUAGE: LEARNING WORD MEANINGS.) Language, and the symbolic understanding of moods, purposes, and meanings, is central in human nature. Evidence from the interpersonal skills of infants strongly supports the idea that language skills are built on a sharing of motives that begins soon after a baby is born. The speedy and rich exchange of thoughts that is made possible when insubstantial words stand for all manner of actions and physical objects and events is preceded by the infant's ability to enter into the minds of others, first by their direct expression of interest and mood in affectionate relationship, then by their playful teasing, and finally by their willingness to share significant moments in the experience of surroundings and what may be done inside this joint experience.

A one-year-old does not merely want to keep close to mother. He or she wants to take note of comments, give and take, share the looking and handling of things, and try to follow the words that seem to be given special emphasis in these interactions. The baby will make vocalizations with gestures in order to mean something, or to give a deliberate message; a demand, a request, a refusal, etc. At two years the same baby is not only walking about, but also speaking. For speaking, objects of interest have to become significant, with conventional meaning and symbolic value. No regimen of conditioning can explain these transformations of a child's mind. They must be motivated within the child by growth of mental processes that are ready for the instructions and examples that come from older companions.

It would appear as if we are beginning to describe the fundamental form of human motive processes in the brain by gaining detailed evidence on how co-operative understandings emerge in infancy, from the sensitivity of the neonate to human care and human emotions to the intelligent co-operativeness of a two-year-old. In the process, we seem to be learning a new philosophy of mind that does not set the empiricist against the nativist, and that does not wholly segregate the material from the mental. How else can we attempt to conceptualize an inherent set of motives to share experience with others and to learn ways of communicating?

C. T.

Bower, T. G. R. (1974). *Development in Infancy*. San Francisco.

Bruner, J. S. (1975). The ontogenesis of speech acts. *Journal of Child Language*, **2**, 1–20.

Field, T. M. and Fox, N. (eds.) (1985). *Social Perception in Infants*.

Halliday, M. A. K. (1975). *Learning How to Mean: explorations in the development of language*. London.

Hubley, P. and Trevarthen, C. (1979). Sharing a task in infancy. In Uzgiris, I. (ed.), *Social Interaction and Communication in Infancy* (New Directions for Child Development, Vol. iv).

Mehler, J. and Fox, R. (eds.) (1985). *Neonate Cognition: beyond the blooming buzzing confusion*.

Stern, D. N. (1985). *The Interpersonal World of the Infant*.

Trevarthen, C. (1974). Conversations with a two-month-old. *New Scientist*, **62**, 230–5.

Trevarthen, C. (1979). Communication and co-operation in early infancy. A description of primary intersubjectivity. In Bullowa, M. (ed.), *Before Speech: the beginnings of human communication*.

Trevarthen, C. (1982). The primary motives for co-operative understanding. In Butterworth, G. and Light, P. (eds.), *Social Cognition: Studies of the development of understanding*.

Trevarthen, C. and Marwick, H. (1986). Signs of motivation for speech in infants, and the nature of a mother's support for development of language. In Lindblom, G. and Zetterstrom, R. (eds.), *Precursors of Early Speech*.

**INFERIORITY COMPLEX.** His view that *Freud had put too much emphasis on sexuality in the genesis of neurosis and too little on the 'will to power' was one of the reasons why Alfred *Adler broke away from psychoanalysis in 1911 and formed the more or less independent school of 'individual psychology'. According to Adler's theory an individual adopts a style of life which tends to relieve feelings of inferiority. Thus a boy feeling himself to be inferior in sports devotes himself to his studies. Demosthenes, finding a way to overcome his stammer by speaking on the sea-shore with pebbles in his mouth, became the greatest orator in Greece. Or a person may hold to conceited fantasies which falsify a discouraging reality. Striving for success, self-assertion, and self-aggrandizement thus reflect both the will to power and its obverse, a sense of inferiority. This has its roots in the circumstances of childhood. A child feels inferior if he lacks affection, acceptance, and approval. Physical or 'organ' inferiority may play an important part. Position in order of birth, in particular, as Adler pointed out, moulds a child's style in competitive situations.

Inferiority and *complex were put together to make a portmanteau phrase. This soon became popular because it offered an explanation, albeit a simplified one, of inappropriate or neurotic behaviour in terms of underlying ideas and feelings which are part of most people's experience.

D. R. D.

Ansbacher, H. L. and Ansbacher, R. (1956). *The Individual Psychology of Alfred Adler*. New York.

**INFORMATION THEORY.** The idea of measuring information might at first seem as senseless as that of weighing the Theorem of Pythagoras; but it was in fact among hard-headed communication engineers that the need to do so was first recognized. A communication channel exists (and is paid for) in order to 'transmit information'. In order to compare the efficiencies of alternative methods we must be able to estimate the 'capacity' of each to do the job.

In ordinary language we say we have received information when *what we know* has changed. The bigger the change in what we know, the more information we have received. Information, then, like energy, does *work*: but whereas energy does physical work, information does logical work. There are various ways of measuring the size of the logical job done when a communication signal is received. Different measures are relevant in different contexts. The main consideration is whether the output of the communication channel has to be *constructed* by the signal, or merely *selected* (identified) by it from a range of prefabricated forms. Some examples will make this clear.

**Construction.** When a camera shutter is opened, we say that 'information' is transmitted from the scene to the film. By this we mean that the image on the film is constructed by the action of the light signal received. In comparing results from two cameras, two quite different criteria may be relevant. (i) We might compare the number of distinguishable picture-elements, which is called the *structural information-content* of each picture. A picture taken with poor optical resolution would have a low structural information-content. (The unit of structural information-content, 1 *logon*, specifies one independent element or 'degree of freedom' of a signal.) (ii) Alternatively, or additionally, we might compare the statistical weight of evidence gathered by the two films, or their *metrical information-content*. A picture taken with too short an exposure, for example, would be deficient in metrical information-content. (The unit of metrical information-content, 1 *metron*, represents a certain minimum weight of statistical evidence.)

**Selection.** Although in many telecommunication systems (such as domestic telephones, radio, and TV) the signal has to construct the output, in other cases (such as telegraphy and teleprinting), where the range of possible outputs is small, and is known in advance, a much more economical approach is possible. This is known as encoding. Instead of transmitting a complete description of the output required, a code system transmits only instructions to select (identify) that output from a range of prefabricated outputs (for example, letters of the alphabet) available at the receiving end. Thus, whereas the construction of a television picture of a page of type might require several million independent signals, the same page of type can be specified by only a few thousand selective code signals controlling a teleprinter.

In this context, the size of the selective job done by a signal depends not on the size or complexity of the output as such, but on the number of alternative forms that it might have taken, and on the relative likelihood of each. The simplest selective operation is the identification of one out of two equally likely possibilities—as in the game of 'Twenty Questions'. This, in the jargon of communication engineers, has a *selective information-content* of one *bit' or *bi*nary digit. Selection of one out of four equally likely possibilities requires two bits; one out of eight requires three; and so on. In general, then, selective information-content measures the statistical unexpectedness of the event in question. The precise form of the event is irrelevant, except as it may affect its prior probability. The more improbable an event, the larger its selective information content. This way of measuring information flow was developed chiefly by the American engineer C. E. Shannon (Shannon and Weaver, 1949) and the mathematician Norbert *Wiener (1948). (Mathematically, the number of bits per event is $\log_2(1/p)$. Where events $1, 2 \ldots i$ have prior probabilities $p1, p2 \ldots pi$, the average selective information-content or 'entropy' $H = \Sigma pi \log(1/pi)$.)

The average unexpectedness or selective information-content per event is greatest when all possible events are equally probable. The communication channel is then being used with full 'informational efficiency'. If some events are much more or much less probable than others, the average number of bits per event is correspondingly reduced, and the sequence is said to have 'redundancy'. (Redundancy is defined as $1-H/Hmax$, where $H_{max}$ is the value of $H$ when all $p_i$ are equal.) A redundancy of 50 per cent means that the average number of bits per event is only half what it could be if all events were equally probable.

Despite its pejorative label, redundancy has one great merit. It allows a communication system in principle to tolerate a corresponding amount of random transmission error or 'noise'. If the right kind of code is used, it is even possible to achieve almost error-free transmission up to a certain rate, despite the presence of 'noise', by building in redundancy in such a way that errors can be identified and corrected. Although this may sound almost magical, it is similar in principle to what a human reader does when spotting and correcting printers' errors. The detection of misprints in an unfamiliar passage is possible only because the sequence of letters in typical English text is about 50 per cent redundant. With a table of random numbers, it would be impossible! Saying the same thing several times in different ways (a device familiar to teachers and public speakers) is another sensible way of building in redundancy, so as to make a message more resistant to distortion, either by noise in the communication channel or through misperception by the recipient.

By analogous reasoning, it has been proved that networks of computing elements can be constructed with redundant connections in such a way as to perform without errors, even if individual elements were to break down at random. Here again, the amount of malfunctioning that can be tolerated depends directly on the amount of redundancy built in. There is reason to believe that the amazing reliability of the human brain (despite a steady loss of nerve-cells throughout life) depends on a sophisticated use of redundancy on these lines.

Since the Theory of Information embraces communication processes of all kinds, whether in human societies, in nervous systems, or in machines, it inspired at first some exaggerated expectations. Early efforts to measure the flow of information through sense organs, or through human operators controlling machines, were sometimes frustrated because the probabilities attached to events by the experimenter were not the same as those represented in the subject's nervous system. In other cases, where there was no reason to believe that the neural systems concerned worked on a selective principle, the use of Shannon's measure gave irrelevant or trivial results.

On the other hand, the development and spread of information-theoretical ideas has made notable contributions to brain research by suggesting new ways of looking at the function of the nervous system and new kinds of experimental questions. To take one of the earliest examples, Hick (1952) found that the *reaction time of human subjects to a stimulus depended in a particularly simple way on

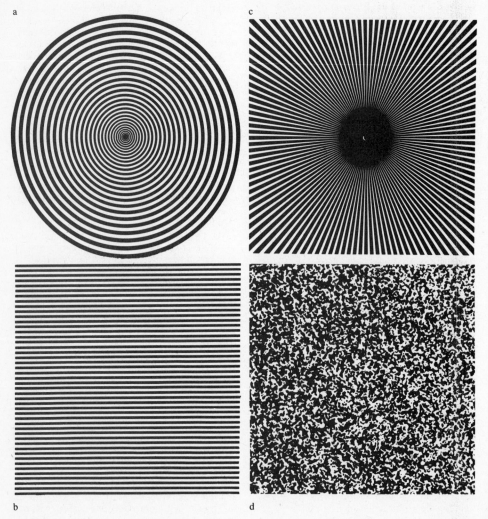

**Fig. 1. a** to **c**. Examples of visual stimuli incorporating a high degree of structural redundancy. **d**. A sample of 'visual noise' with minimal redundancy.

its selective information-content. In other words, what mattered in his experiment was not the form of the stimulus *per se*, but rather the number of alternative forms that it might have taken but did not. The idea that the range of forms *not* taken by the input might be an important part of its specification is typical of the shift in emphasis brought to psychology by information theory.

Again, both physiologists and psychologists now make extensive use of test signals originally developed by communication engineers to measure the performance of TV and radio channels. Both highly redundant signals such as regularly repetitive patterns (Fig. 1a–c), and completely non-redundant patterns of 'noise' (Fig. 1d), can induce the nervous system to reveal characteristics that might have remained unsuspected without their use.

It is now commonplace to regard the impulses that flow along nerve fibres as 'conveying information'; but just how information about the world is represented in the brain remains an unresolved question. Although nerve impulses do not function like the code signals in a *digital computer, the general ideas of information engineering are proving increasingly useful in suggesting experiments to throw light on the way they do operate. One of the chief advantages of these ideas is that they belong in a sense to both the psychological and the physiological levels. They thus offer an invaluable working link or 'conceptual bridge' by which data and questions at either level can be brought to bear on hypotheses at the other.

For the application of information theory to the visual system, see VISUAL INFORMATION RATE.

D. M. M.

Hick, W. E. (1952). On the rate of gain of information, *Quarterly Journal of Experimental Psychology*, **4**, 11–26.
MacKay, D. M. (1969). *Information, Mechanism and Meaning*. Cambridge, Massachusetts.
MacKay, D. M. (1970). Perception and brain function. In Schmitt, F. O. (ed.), *The Neurosciences: second study program*, pp. 306–16. New York.
Shannon, C. E. and Weaver, W. (1949). *The Mathematical Theory of Communication*. Urbana.
Wiener, N. (1948). *Cybernetics*. New York.

**INK-BLOT TEST.** See RORSCHACH, HERMANN.

**INNATE IDEA.** The philosophical theory of innate ideas has its roots in *Plato. In the *Meno*, Socrates manages to get a slave boy to recognize certain mathematical truths (the example concerns the properties of a square) simply by asking the right questions. The conclusion drawn is that the boy already has the knowledge within him; Socrates was merely 'drawing it out'. Innate ideas play a crucial role in the metaphysical systems of the seventeenth-century rationalists. For *Descartes, the mind possesses innate awareness of certain fundamental concepts (God, triangle, mind, body), and as well as of certain elementary propositions of logic (such as 'it is impossible for the

same thing to be and not to be'). The infant may be distracted by bodily stimuli from reflecting on these truths but 'nonetheless it has them in itself, and does not acquire them later on; if it were taken out of the prison of the body, it would find them within itself' (letter of 1641). Such theories receive short shrift from empiricist philosophers—notably John *Locke in the *Essay Concerning Human Understanding* (1690). According to Locke, talk of innate knowledge must imply conscious awareness; yet many people are obviously unaware of many of the allegedly innate principles: children, for example, 'have not the least apprehension or thought of them'. To this *Leibniz replies (in the *New Essays on Human Understanding*, written 1705, that 'we must not expect that we can read the eternal laws of reason in the soul as in an open book'. The ideas are present not in a fully developed form but as dispositions or *virtualités*.

In recent years the debate between rationalists and empiricists over innate ideas has aroused fresh interest in the context of the linguistic theories of Noam Chomsky. According to Chomsky, the ability of children to become language users, i.e. to acquire a set of highly complex and creative skills on the basis of very meagre sensory data, suggests that the child has innate knowledge of the principles of 'universal grammar' (see LANGUAGE: CHOMSKY'S THEORY). However, while the human ability to master language does suggest the presence of innate, genetically determined structures and predispositions in our brains, it is doubtful whether such structures should be said to amount to 'knowledge' of concepts or principles in anything like the sense supposed by the traditional theory of innate ideas.

J. G. C.

Stich, S. (ed.) (1975). *Innate Ideas*. Berkeley.
Hook, S. (ed.) (1969). *Philosophy and Language*. New York.

**INQUISITIVENESS.** Seeking knowledge without prospect of immediate gain or reward is a characteristic of higher animals, and is most marked by far in man. It implies a degree of risk-taking, since the unknown is explored, and is difficult to explain in theories of behaviour based on motivation and drive reduction; but it clearly has survival value, when combined with rapid learning. One might say that man is unique as a species through his extraordinary inquisitiveness.

**INSANITY: EARLY THEORIES.** Although attempts to find logically satisfactory definitions of insanity have been dogged with failure, their construction has given much scope to the imagination. Two broad and irreconcilable traditions can be discerned: the Galenic and the Aristotelian views of madness. *Aristotle is alleged to have asked, 'Why is it that all those who have become eminent in philosophy or politics or poetry or the arts are clearly of an atrabilious temperament and some of them to such an extent as to be affected by diseases caused by black bile?' Robert *Burton is firmly within this tradition when in *The Anatomy of Melancholy* (1621) he describes melancholy men as 'of a deep reach, excellent apprehension, judicious, wise and witty'. On the other hand, the tradition which stems from *Galen sees madness as due to an imbalance of the four humours. According to Galen the four bodily humours were blood, phlegm, choler, and black bile, and they were endowed with the elementary qualities of heat and moisture. The preponderance of a particular humour determined a person's temperament, thus providing an early schema of psychosomatic or constitutional types. The theory was a comprehensive one in that it was able to account for health, temperament, and the type of illness to which a person was likely to succumb. In the essential characteristics of their outlook these two traditions have persisted to the present day, and can be recognized in the writings of contemporary psychiatrists.

| Humour | Temperament |
| --- | --- |
| Blood (warm and moist) | Sanguine |
| Phlegm (cold and moist) | Phlegmatic |
| Choler (hot and dry) | Choleric |
| Black bile (cold and dry) | Melancholic |

Although it is possible to construct elaborate and exhaustive typologies of psychiatric terminology for each particular age—and, indeed, this has been done (see, for example, Karl Menninger's appendix to *The Vital Balance*)—at any one given period one diagnosis predominates and serves to describe a variety of ills. Alternatively, several terms are used interchangeably. For example, in sixteenth- and seventeenth-century England all varieties of psychological distress were described as melancholy. Renaissance psychopathology could be dealt with under a single rubric. No wonder that melancholy had many aspects! Robert Burton wrote: 'Proteus himself is not so diverse; you may as well make the *moon* a new coat, as a true character of a melancholy man; as soon find the motion of a bird in the air as the heart of a melancholy man.'

By the eighteenth century a new term, 'the spleen', had become fashionable. The spleen referred not only to the bodily organ of that name, but also to the disease associated with it. The spleen, being the source of black bile and hence of the melancholy temperament, is clearly a development of earlier Elizabethan melancholy and also a reaffirmation of links with the Galenic pathology of the humours. During the course of the century the spleen acquired a number of additional names: the vapours, hypochondriasis, hysteria, and the English malady. William Stukeley in his book *Of the Spleen* (1723) enumerates a long list of symptoms of the spleen:

When the head is attack'd, coma's, epilepsy, apoplexy, or the numbness of a part ensue, or talkativeness, tremors, spasms, head-ach; when the heart, palpitation, swooning, anxiety; when the breast, sighing, short-breath, cough; when the diaphragm, laughing; when the belly (and more frequently being the seat of the morbid minera) rugitus, cardialgia, colic, iliac passions, etc.

Thus the spleen could strike the unwary in myriad unsuspected forms. According to a physician, Thomas Dover (1732), the difficulty of detecting the spleen was accentuated by the fact that it could mimic the symptoms of other illnesses. Thus the accounts of many of these early concepts somewhat resemble the *Freudian view of hysteria. In view of the diversity of its symptoms, it is not surprising that preoccupation with the spleen spread rapidly throughout England and encouraged both a growth in the number of physicians and a diversity of opinion. Both in England and abroad the spleen earned the title of the English disease.

The fashionable and well-known physician George Cheyne (1671–1743) regarded the corrosive and viscid humour associated with splenetic disorders as being caused by 'the English climate, the richness and heaviness of our food, the quality of the soil, the wealth and abundance of the inhabitants, the inactivity and sedentary occupations of the better Sort and the Humour of living in great, populous and unhealthy towns'. However, he attached prime importance to diet and in his *Essay on Health and Long Life* (1724) he advocated a milk and seed diet. Nevertheless, madness continued to be associated with inner excellence and social quality. Cheyne himself suffered from depression and claimed that 'those of the liveliest and quickest natural Parts . . . whose genius is most keen and penetrating', were most prone to such disorders. Firstly, the spleen, unlike lowness of spirits, was an indicator of high social rank. Secondly, it also implied a degree of intelligence, imagination, and sensitivity in the sufferer. As a youth, David *Hume was in correspondence with Cheyne. After describing his symptoms, Hume was flattered and reassured to learn that his was no ordinary complaint, but 'a disease of the learned'. Thus, even a rank-order in illnesses was acknowledged. Eighteenth-century writers on the spleen are also concerned with the relationship between imagination and the spleen and, in particular, with the possible dangers of too much imagination. The fear of imagination developed from and is related to the fear of passion. Thomas Wright was able to voice these fears most clearly and forcefully (*The Passions of the Minde in Generall*, 1620). He described the evil effects of unrestrained passions as: 'blindness of understanding, persuasion of will, alteration of humours; and by them maladies and diseases and troublesomeness and disquietness of the soul'. The paradoxical demands of reason and imagination and the precariousness of their relationships were recognized well in advance of Freud's discussion of the dilemmas of civilized man. Foremost among the eighteenth-century distrusters of imagination is Samuel Johnson, who waged a lifelong battle against melancholy. Idleness and solitude were both to be avoided on the grounds that they provided a fertile breeding-ground for the imagination. Solitude 'is dangerous to reason, without being favourable to virtue. . . . Remember . . . that the solitary mortal is certainly luxurious, probably superstitious and probably mad: the mind stagnates for want of employment, grows morbid and is extinguished like a candle in foul air.' Idleness is condemned not because of its later associations with poverty, but because it promotes inner stagnation and decay.

Early nineteenth-century writing on insanity is dominated by the work of the moral managers. Their ideas developed from faculty psychology, according to which man possessed three souls: the rational, the sensitive, and the vegetative. The rational soul is concerned with understanding and the will; the sensitive soul is concerned with the imagination, memory, and perception; and the vegetative soul is concerned with growth, nutrition, and reproduction. Health depends upon the right relationship between the rational and the sensitive soul, namely one of dominance and control. The moral managers held that insanity was a 'lesion of understanding' and that the will could be trained to cope with the possibility of madness. John *Locke had first put forward the view that madness was a self-contained defect of reason and thus left open the possibility that other parts of the self could be enlisted to combat this weakness. In *An Essay Concerning Human Understanding*, Locke wrote that

madmen do not appear to have lost the faculty of reasoning, but having joined together some ideas very wrongly they mistake them for truths . . . as though incoherent ideas have been cemented together so powerfully as to remain united. But there are degrees of madness as of folly; the disorderly jumbling ideas together in some more, in some, less. In short, herein seems to lie the difference between idiots and madmen. That madmen put wrong ideas together, and so make wrong propositions, but argue and reason right from them. But idiots make very few or no propositions, but argue and reason scarce at all.

Now that the seat of madness had been isolated, optimism and cure became possible. In fact, much of the writing on insanity in the first half of the nineteenth century was concerned with delineating the strategic role played by the will. One such book which crystallizes the early nineteenth-century outlook is called *Man's Power over Himself to Prevent or Control Insanity*, published anonymously in 1843. The author assigns the following role to the will:

The affection of the brain which causes delusions is not madness, but the want of power or will to examine them, is. Nothing then but an extent of disease which destroys at once all possibility of reasoning, by annihilating, or entirely changing the structure of the organ, can make a man necessarily mad. In all other cases, the being sane or otherwise, not withstanding considerable disease of brain, depends on the individual himself. He who has given a proper direction to the intellectual force and thus obtained an early command over the bodily organ by habituating it to processes of calm reasoning, remains sane amid all the vagaries of sense.

Within asylums treatment consisted of the cultivation of character and the rediscovery and strengthening of will-power.

During this period there is one important change of emphasis in the accounts of madness. James Cowles Prichard, ethnologist and physician, first introduced the term 'moral insanity' in 1833, and defined it as follows: 'This form of mental disease . . . consists of a morbid perversion of the feelings, affections, habits, without any hallucination or erroneous conviction impressed upon the understanding; it sometimes coexists with an apparently unimpaired state of the intellectual faculties.' Thus the will was no longer the impenetrable stronghold against insanity, and madness had shifted from defective reasoning to the emotions. Given that the will in man was seen to be like a pilot in a ship, this reappraisal constituted a far more serious threat to man's supremacy over madness. Incidentally, the term 'moral insanity' is often, but erroneously, claimed to be the forebear of the modern *'psychopathic personality', whose cause still remains a matter for debate.

The theme of moral decline which lunacy represented was developed in a more systematic way and on a larger scale in the last third of the nineteenth century. Henry Maudsley published *Responsibility in Mental Disease* in 1873. Misleadingly titled, it was in fact a claim for nonresponsibility in mental disease (although not in any indulgent sense) and was largely an argument against the claims of the moral managers. Maudsley was not concerned with cure so much as with identifying and segregating the morally degenerate. Man's life is governed by *genetic laws, and thought and volition are determined by them as much as are all other aspects of human life. Maudsley called this genetic determinism 'the tyranny of organisation'. He writes:

Individuals are born with such a flaw or warp of nature that all the care in the world will not prevent them from being vicious or criminal, or becoming insane. . . . No one can escape the tyranny of his organisation; no one can elude the destiny that is innate in him, and which unconsciously and irresistibly shapes his ends, even when he thinks he is determining them with consummate foresight and skill.

Whatever the complex intellectual and social changes that contributed towards this position (see ASYLUMS: A HISTORICAL SURVEY), it is a startling reversal of earlier accounts. Maudsley brings the dialogue with the irrational to a bleak and abrupt close. His concept of the 'tyranny of organization' seems to have been taken to its logical conclusion by Johannes Lange in his book *Crime and Destiny* (1930). Later studies of twins involved in crime have given as much emphasis to environmental as to hereditary factors as causes of felony         v. s.

**INSPIRATION.** The use of this word both for 'breathing' and for 'a bright idea' is not accidental. It derives from the notion of the ancient Greeks that mind pervades the universe, and is a subtle vapour—the pneuma. (Pneumatic bliss is, indeed, a state of mind!)

**INSTINCT.** St Thomas *Aquinas wrote that animal judgement is not free but implanted by nature. Thus, from an early time, instinctive behaviour was regarded as the counterpart to voluntary behaviour. In everyday, though not in scientific, speech the term 'instinct' is still used to imply 'without thought'. For example, if I heard a taxi-driver say 'I instinctively stamped on the brakes', I would assume that he meant that his behaviour was *reflex or involuntary, and not that he was born with an innate ability to apply the brakes in motor cars.

The associationists believed that human behaviour is maintained by the knowledge of, and desire for, particular consequences of behaviour, and they looked upon notions of instinct with disfavour. However, John *Locke did concede that there was 'an uneasiness of the mind for want of some absent good. . . . God has put into man the uneasiness of hunger and thirst, and other natural desires . . . to move and determine their wills for the preservation of themselves and the continuation of the species' (*An Essay concerning Human Understanding*, 1690). Francis Hutcheson argued that instinct produces action prior to any thought of the consequences (*An Essay on the Nature and Conduct of Passions and Affections*, 1728). Thus Hutcheson made instinct into a kind of motivational force, and this concept was taken up by the nineteenth-century rationalists, such as William *James, who conceived of human nature as a combination of blind instinct and rational thought.

The irrational forces in man's nature were emphasized by *Freud, but the ideas of *McDougall probably had a greater influence upon the scientific development of the concept of instinct. McDougall regarded instincts as irrational and compelling motivational forces. He enumerated particular instincts, each of which was accompanied by an *emotion. Examples are: pugnacity and the emotion of anger; flight and the emotion of fear; repulsion and the emotion of disgust (*Instincts and their Vicissitudes, Collected Papers*, 1915). McDougall's views do not find favour with modern psychologists because they are derived from subjective experience and are therefore hard to verify. There is inevitable disagreement among psychologists as to the number of instincts that should be allowed.

A different line of thought was initiated by Charles *Darwin. In his *Origin of Species* (1859), Darwin treated instincts as complex reflexes that were made up of inherited units and therefore subject to natural selection. Such instincts would evolve together with other aspects of the animal's morphology and behaviour. Darwin laid the foundations of the classical ethological view propounded by Konrad Lorenz and Niko Tinbergen.

Lorenz maintained that animal behaviour included a number of fixed-action patterns that were characteristic of species and largely genetically determined. He subsequently postulated that each fixed-action pattern or instinct was motivated by action-specific energy. The action-specific energy was likened to liquid in a reservoir. Each instinct corresponded to a separate reservoir, and when an appropriate releasing stimulus was presented the liquid was discharged in the form of an instinctive drive which gave rise to the appropriate behaviour. Tinbergen proposed that the reservoirs, or instinct centres, were arranged in a hierarchy so that the energy responsible for one class of activity, such as reproduction, would drive a number of subordinate activities, such as nest-building, courting, and parental care.

The concept of instinct that is identified with classical ethology does not find favour with the majority of present-day behavioural scientists, for two main reasons. The first reason is connected with the idea that there are instinctive forces, or drives, that determine certain aspects of behaviour. Although the notion of drive as an energizer has been very influential in psychology, it involves a misuse of the concept of energy. In the physical sciences, energy is not a causal agent but a descriptive term arising from mathematically formulated laws. Analogous laws can be formulated for animal behaviour, but they do not lead to a concept of energy that corresponds to the notions of drive popular with the early psychologists and ethologists. Although the idea of drive as an energizer of behaviour has intuitive appeal, this is not nowadays regarded as sufficient justification for a scientific concept. In addition there are empirical problems. Early psychologists sought to identify a drive for every aspect of behaviour: a hunger drive responsible for feeding, a thirst drive, a sex drive, etc. It proved impossible to classify animal behaviour in this way without resorting to a *reductio ad absurdum* involving drives for thumb-sucking, nail-biting, and other minutiae of behaviour. A more modern view is that animals choose from among the set of alternative courses of action that is available at a particular time, in accordance with certain precisely formulated principles of decision-making. This approach obviates the view that animals are driven by instinctive forces to perform particular behaviour patterns.

The second reason for abandoning the classical concepts of instinct is an objection to the implication that certain aspects of behaviour are innate in the sense that they develop independently of environmental influences. Most scientists now recognize that all behaviour is influenced both by the animal's genetic make-up and by the environmental conditions that exist during development. The extent to which the influences of nature and nurture determine behaviour varies greatly from activity to activity and from species to species. For example, the vocalizations of pigeons and doves are relatively stereotyped and characteristic of each species, and are not influenced by auditory experience after hatching. The vocalizations of other birds, however, may depend heavily upon such experience, as in the strongly imitative birds, or they may be partly influenced by experience. For example, chaffinches will learn the song they hear during a particular sensitive period of early life, provided it is similar to the normal song.

While the influence of particular genes may be necessary for the development of a behaviour pattern, it is never a sufficient condition. All types of behaviour require a suitable embryonic environment for the correct nervous connections, etc., to develop. Normally, the physiological medium provided by the parent is designed to ensure that normal embryonic development occurs. Just as the parent provides an environment suitable for the development of the embryo, so it may provide an environment suitable for the development of a juvenile. Thus a chaffinch is normally reared in an environment in which it inevitably hears the song of other chaffinches, and so it develops the song that is characteristic of its own species.

Even apparently stereotyped activities may, upon closer examination, be shown to be influenced by the environment. For example, the newly hatched chicks of herring gulls peck at the tip of the parent's bill, which bears a characteristic red spot on a yellow background. The chick's behaviour induces the parent to regurgitate food. The behaviour is typical of all newly hatched chicks, is performed in an apparently stereotyped manner, and would appear to be a classic example of instinctive behaviour. Upon closer examination, however, it can be seen that the initial behaviour of individual chicks varies considerably in force and rapidity of pecking, angle of approach, and accuracy. As the chicks gain experience their pecking accuracy improves, and the pecking movements become more stereotyped. Some of these changes are due to maturation. The chicks become more stable on their feet as their muscles develop, and their pecking co-ordination improves. Some of the changes are due to learning. Initially the chicks peck at any elongated object of a suitable size. Although the red spot on the parent's bill is attractive to them, it is not their only target. Once the chicks begin to receive food they learn to exercise greater discrimination. It is not surprising that the behaviour of different chicks develops along similar lines, because in the natural environment they are all confronted with a similar situation. Practice and experience in similar situations lead to similar results, and the behaviour of the older chick consequently becomes more and more like that of its peers.

The concept of instinct has undergone many changes over the years. Whereas, at one time, instinctive behaviour was seen as inborn, stereotyped, and driven from within, the modern approach is to treat the innate, the reflex, and the motivational aspects as separate issues. While much animal and human behaviour is innate in the sense that it inevitably appears as part of the repertoire under natural conditions, this does not mean that genetic factors are solely responsible. Maturational factors and modes of learning that are characteristic of the species may be just as important. Much of the nature–nurture controversy, particularly that associated with sexual and racial differences among humans, results from a failure to recognize the vast complexity of developmental processes.                                    D. J. M.

**INSTRUMENTAL   CONDITIONING.** See CONDITIONING.

**INTELLECT.** Mental abilities, usually distinguished from feelings, *emotions, and also *perception—though perception, we now generally believe (following Hermann von *Helmholtz), in fact depends upon unconscious inferences. The word is seldom applied to animals; and an 'intellectual' person means someone concerned with problems requiring high *intelligence and much learning. The intellect is associated with cortical brain function.

**INTELLIGENCE.** Innumerable tests are available for measuring intelligence (see INTELLIGENCE: ITS ASSESSMENT), yet no one is quite certain of what intelligence is, or even of just what it is that the available tests are measuring. There have been any number of attempts to resolve these uncertainties, attempts that have differed in their approach to the problem, and in the outcome of applying each given approach.

One time-honoured approach to discovering the meaning of a construct is to seek expert opinion regarding its definition. This is exactly what the editors of a major psychological journal did in 1921, when they sought the opinions of experts in the field of intelligence regarding what they 'conceive "intelligence" to be, and by what means it can best be measured by group tests' ('Intelligence and its Measurement', 1921, p. 123). Fourteen experts replied, with definitions of intelligence such as the following: (i) the power of good responses from the point of view of truth or fact (E. L. *Thorndike); (ii) the ability to carry on abstract thinking (L. M. *Terman); (iii) having learned or ability to learn to adjust oneself to the environment (S. S. Colvin); (iv) the ability to adapt oneself adequately to relatively new situations in life (R. Pintner); (v) the capacity for knowledge, and knowledge possessed (V. A. C. Henmon); (vi) a biological mechanism by which the effects of a complexity of stimuli are brought together and given a somewhat unified effect in behaviour (J. Peterson); (vii) the capacity to inhibit an instinctive adjustment, the capacity to redefine the inhibited instinctive adjustment in the light of imaginally experienced trial and error, and the volitional capacity to realize the modified instinctive adjustment into overt behaviour to the advantage of the individual as a social animal (L. L. *Thurstone); (viii) the capacity to acquire capacity (H. Woodrow); (ix) the capacity to learn or to profit by experience (W. F. Dearborn). The other experts did not answer the question directly.

Viewed narrowly, there seem to be almost as many definitions of intelligence as there were experts asked to define it. Viewed broadly, however, two themes seem to run through at least several of these definitions: the capacity to learn from experience, and adaptation to one's environment. Indeed, an earlier definition often cited by these experts viewed intelligence as general adaptability to new problems and conditions of life. (For an update of the 1921 symposium, see Sternberg and Detterman, 1986.)

If one is dissatisfied with the heterogeneity in these definitions, one can attempt to answer the question of what intelligence is by begging the question. Edwin *Boring (1923) did just that when he defined intelligence as whatever it is that the tests measure. This definition tells us no more than we knew when we started, and it may tell us less: no two tests measure exactly the same thing, so that one is left with as many definitions of intelligence as there are tests (which is certainly a number greater even than that of experts in the field!).

A more recent and sohisticated version of the definitional approach to discovering what intelligence is has been suggested by Ulric Neisser (1979). According to Neisser, the concept of intelligence is organized around a 'prototype', or ideal case. One is intelligent to the extent that one resembles this ideal case:

There are no definitive criteria of intelligence, just as there are none for chairness; it is a fuzzy-edged concept to which many features are relevant. Two people may both be quite intelligent and yet have very few traits in common—they resemble the prototype along different dimensions. . . . [Intelligence] is a resemblance between two individuals, one real and the other prototypical (p. 185).

If there is a single prototype, or ideal case, Neisser's notion will give us a concept of intelligence validated by consensus, if not a concrete definition. There are at least two problems with Neisser's approach, however. First, there exist multiple prototypes, or ideal cases, not just a single one (Sternberg et al., 1981). Different groups of people have somewhat different prototypes. Which one do we use? If we use all of them, including those of various groups of experts and laymen, we end up with as many ideal concepts of intelligence as there are different prototypes, and we are no better off than we were when appealing to experts' definitions. Secondly, the 'ideal case' approach seems to be an excellent way of discovering what people mean by 'intelligence', but not of discovering what 'intelligence' means. Neisser would argue that the two are indistinguishable, but I suspect they are not. Suppose, for example, that people in some culture view their ideal case as able to harmonize with Kron, the god of nature. This description tells us what these people think intelligence is, but it doesn't tell us much about the nature of intelligence: we still have to find out what it means to harmonize with Kron. In our culture,

an analogous notion might be the ability to adapt to natural events. Again, we still need to find out what kinds of mental events and physical behaviours result in the ability to adapt. What is it that people who are able to adapt well do that people who are not able to adapt well do not do?

Questions such as this one have led some theorists of intelligence to seek the nature of intelligence by the analysis of individual differences. The question asked here, as above, is what aspects of mental functioning distinguish more intelligent people from less intelligent ones. The nub of this individual-differences approach is to have people perform a large number of tasks that seem to predict intelligent performance (in school, on the job, or wherever), and to analyse patterns of individual differences in task performance. These patterns of individual differences have usually been analysed through the use of a method of statistical analysis called 'factor analysis'. The idea is to identify the 'factors' of human intellect.

The earliest factorial theory of the nature of intelligence was formulated by the inventor of factor analysis, Charles *Spearman. Spearman's (1927) analysis of relations among the kinds of mental tests he and other psychologists had been administering led him to propose a 'two-factor' theory of intelligence. According to this theory, intelligence comprises two kinds of factors—a general factor and specific factors. General ability, or $g$ as measured by the general factor, is required for performance of mental tests of all kinds. Each specific ability, as measured by each specific factor, is required for performance of just one kind of mental test. Thus, there are as many specific factors as there are tests, but only a single general factor. Spearman suggested that the ability underlying the general factor could best be understood as a kind of 'mental energy'.

Godfrey Thomson's (1939) reassessment of Spearman's individual-differences data led him to accept Spearman's hypothesis of a general factor running through the range of mental ability tests; however, it led him to reject Spearman's interpretation of this factor. Thomson disputed Spearman's claim that the general factor represented a single underlying source of individual differences. Instead, he proposed that the appearance of a general factor was due to the workings of a multitude of mental 'bonds', including reflexes, learned associations between stimuli, and the like. Performance of any particular task activates large numbers of these bonds. Some bonds will be required for the performance of virtually any task requiring mental effort, and these bonds will in combination give rise to the appearance of a general factor.

L. L. Thurstone (1938), like Thomson, accepted Spearman's hypothesis of a general factor. But he disputed the importance of this factor. He argued that it is a 'second-order' factor or phenomenon, one which arises only because the primary or 'first-order' factors are related to each other. What are these primary factors, or, as Thurstone called them, 'primary mental abilities'? Thurstone suggested that they include verbal comprehension (measured by tests such as knowledge of vocabulary), word fluency (measured by tests requiring rapid word production—for example, a listing of as many words as a person can think of that have *c* as their third letter), number (measured by tests of arithmetical reasoning and computation), spatial visualization (measured by tests requiring mental manipulation of geometric forms), perceptual speed (measured by tests requiring rapid visual scanning, for example, proof-reading), *memory (measured by tests of recall and recognition of previously presented information), and reasoning (measured by tests such as number series, which require people to say which of several numbers should come next in a given series).

J. P. Guilford (1967) parted company from the majority of factorial theorists by refusing to acknowledge the existence of any general factor at all in human intelligence. Instead, he proposed that intelligence comprises 120 elementary abilities, each of which involves the action of some operation upon some content to produce some product. An example of an ability in Guilford's system is 'cognition of verbal relations'. This ability involves recognition of a conceptual connection between two words: for example, recognition that a *caboose* is often the last car in a *train*.

Probably the most widely accepted factorial description of intelligence is a hierarchical one. A good example of this class of descriptions was proposed by P. E. Vernon (1971). He proposed that intelligence can be described as comprising abilities at varying levels of generality: at the highest level of generality (the top of the hierarchy) is general ability as identified by Spearman; at the next level are 'major group' factors, such as verbal-educational ability (the kind of ability needed for successful performance in courses such as English, history, and social studies) and practical-mechanical ability (the kind of ability needed for successful performance in courses such as draughtsmanship and car mechanics); at the next level are 'minor group' factors, which can be obtained by subdividing the major group factors; and at the lowest level (the bottom of the hierarchy) are specific factors, again of the kind identified by Spearman. This description of intelligence may be viewed as filling in the gaps between the two extreme kinds of factors proposed by Spearman: in between the general and specific factors are group factors of intermediate levels of generality.

The factorial views of intelligence are unlike the definitional ones in that they are based on the analysis of intelligent functioning (on ability tests), rather than merely on the speculations of one or more psychologists or laymen. The factorial views are like the definitional ones, however, in their potential number and diversity. Is it the case that one of the factorial descriptions is right and the others wrong, or is it possible that a single entity or complex of entities, intelligence, can conform to all of these different descriptions? In other words, is there some level, or common denominator, at which these various descriptions all reduce to the same thing? It is here suggested that such a level of description exists, and that it can be found by analysing the ways in which people process information when solving problems of the kind found both on intelligence tests and in everyday life.

Information-processing psychologists have sought to understand general intelligence in terms of elementary components (or processes) used in the solution of various kinds of problems (Carroll, 1976; Hunt et al., 1973; Newell and Simon, 1972; Sternberg, 1979 and 1979). Let us distinguish five kinds of components that people use in the processing of information. *Metacomponents* are higher-order control processes that are used for planning how a problem should be solved, for making decisions regarding alternative courses of action during *problem-solving, and for monitoring one's progress during the course of problem solution. *Performance components* are processes that are used in the actual execution of a problem-solving strategy. *Acquisition components* are processes used in learning, that is, in the acquisition of knowledge. *Retention components* are processes used in *remembering—that is, in the retrieval of previously acquired information. *Transfer components* are used in generalization—that is, in the transfer of knowledge from one task or task context to another.

Consider, for example, how each of these five kinds of components might be applied in the solution of an arithmetical problem.

Mrs Smith decided to impress Mrs Jones. She went to a costume jewellery shop and bought three imitation diamonds of equal value. She received £4 in change from the ten-pound note she gave the assistant. (But as Mrs Smith was receiving her change, Mrs Jones walked into the shop!) How much did each imitation diamond cost?

Metacomponents would be used in setting up the equations for solving the problem, for example, in deciding that the problem can be solved by subtracting £4 from £10 and dividing the difference by three; the metacomponents must also decide what information is relevant to the problem at hand, and what information is irrelevant. Performance components would be used in the actual solution of these equations to obtain, first, £6 as the price of the three imitation diamonds and, then, £2 as the price of each item. Acquisition components were used in the problem-solver's past to learn how to set up the equations, how to subtract, how to divide, and so on. Retention components are used to retrieve this information from memory at the time that it is needed. Transfer components are used to draw an analogy between this problem and previous ones: the problem-solver has never learned how to solve this particular problem, and must generalize his or her learning from similar problems previously encountered to the problem presently being encountered.

How can this scheme account for the various factorial views of intelligence described earlier? According to this view, the general factor that appears in various theories of intelligence results from the operations of components that are general across the range of tasks represented on intelligence tests. For the most part, these are metacomponents—mental activities such as deciding upon the particular components to be used in the solution of problems, deciding upon a strategy for problem solution, monitoring whether the strategy that has been chosen is leading to a solution, deciding upon how quickly the strategy can be executed and still lead to a satisfactory result, and so on. Major group factors of the kind found in Vernon's theory, and primary factors of the kind found in Thurstone's theory, are obtained in factor analyses primarily as a result of the operations of performance, acquisition, retention, and transfer components. For example, verbal comprehension, as tested by vocabulary, is the product of past executions of acquisition components to learn new words, and of present executions of retention components to retrieve the meanings of these words. If vocabulary is tested by presenting the words in unfamiliar contexts, transfer components may also be involved in applying previously acquired information to the new contexts that are presented. Reasoning, as tested by problems such as numerical series completions (say, 3, 7, 12, 18, 25, . . .), requires the execution of various performance components, such as encoding the terms of the problem, inferring the relations between the given pairs of numbers, applying these relations to the last given number to obtain the next number, and the production of a response.

This information-processing view of intelligence seems to unify what were formerly a number of disparate views regarding the nature of intelligence. A number of important questions still need to be answered, however, and it is possible to consider only a small number of them here.

First, is the meaning of intelligence the same across different societal and cultural groups? On the view proposed, the answer is both yes and no. On the one hand, the components that would be applied to the solution of a given problem in one culture or society probably overlap to a large degree, although perhaps not completely, those that would be applied to the solution of the same problem in a different culture or society. On the other hand, the kinds of problems that need to be solved may differ widely from one culture or society to another. The mental (and physical) processes needed to corner game in a hunt are very different from those needed to balance accounts. Hence, the kinds of persons who are considered intelligent may vary widely from one culture to another, as a function of the components that are important for adaptation to the requirements of living in the various cultures.

Secondly, if intelligence tests measure, in greater or lesser degree, the components of infor-

mation-processing, why are they so imperfectly predictive of real-world performance? One reason is that they are fallible as measuring instruments: they measure only imperfectly what they are supposed to measure. Another reason is that they do not necessarily weigh most heavily those aspects of intellectual functioning that are most important for intelligent functioning in a given environment. Metacomponential functioning is probably underemphasized, for example, in the measurements made by most of these tests. Yet another reason, and probably the most important one, is that there is a great deal more to everyday living than what the intelligence tests measure, or even than what can reasonably be called intelligence. The tests fail to take into account such important aspects of functioning as motivation, social skills, persistence in the face of adversity, and ability to set and achieve reasonable goals. The tests provide reasonably good measures of limited aspects of functioning for most people. But even here a qualification is necessary, since there are some people whose anxieties, or inability to take tests, render their test scores meaningless or even deceptive.

Finally, is intelligence largely inherited, as has been claimed by some (for example, Jensen, 1969), or is it largely or exclusively determined by environment, as has been claimed by others (for example, Kamin, 1974)? Few bodies of evidence are more confused and confusing than that dealing with the heritability of intelligence. The probability is that heredity, environment, and the interaction between heredity and environment all play some role in intelligence as it has traditionally been measured, but it is not at all clear what the relative extents of these roles are. Nor is it clear what it means, in practical terms, to assign proportional values to the influence of each. No matter what the proportions are, there is good evidence that at least some aspects of intelligence are trainable (see, for example, Feuerstein, 1979; Sternberg, 1981a), and theoretical interest in the heritability of intelligence should not divert attention from questions about how intelligence can be modified in individuals of all levels of measured intelligence.

See also ARTIFICIAL INTELLIGENCE.        R. J. S.

Boring, E. G. (1923). Intelligence as the tests test it. *The New Republic*, 6 June, 35–7.

Carroll, J. B. (1976). Psychometric tests as cognitive tasks: a new 'structure of intellect'. In Resnick, L. B. (ed.), *The Nature of Intelligence*. Hillsdale, New Jersey.

Feuerstein, R. (1979). *The Dynamic Assessment of Retarded Performers*. Baltimore.

Guilford, J. P. (1967). *The Nature of Human Intelligence*. New York.

Hunt, E., Frost, N., and Lunneborg, C. (1973). Individual differences in cognition: a new approach to intelligence. In Bower, G. (ed.), *The Psychology of Learning and Motivation: advances in research and theory*, vol. vii. New York.

Intelligence and its measurement: a symposium (1921). *Journal of Educational Psychology*, **12**, 123–47, 195–216, 271–5.

Jensen, A. R. (1969). How much can we boost IQ and

scholastic achievement? *Harvard Educational Review*, **39**, 1–123.

Kamin, L. J. (1974). *The Science and Politics of IQ*. Potomac, Maryland.

Neisser, U. (1979). The concept of intelligence. In Sternberg, R. J. and Detterman, D. K. (eds.), *Human Intelligence: perspectives on its theory and measurement*. Norwood, New Jersey.

Newell, A. and Simon, H. (1972). *Human Problem Solving*. Englewood Cliffs, New Jersey.

Spearman, C. (1927). *The Abilities of Man*. New York.

Sternberg, R. J. (1979). The nature of mental abilities. *American Psychologist*, **34**, 214–30.

Sternberg, R. J. (1979). Stalking the I.Q. quark. *Psychology Today*, **13**, 42–54.

Sternberg, R. J. (1981a). Cognitive-behavioral approaches to the training of intelligence in the retarded. *Journal of Special Education*, **15**, 165–83.

Sternberg, R. J., Ketron, J. L., Bernstein, M., and Conway, B. E. (1981b). People's conceptions of intelligence. *Journal of Personality and Social Psychology*, **41**, 37–55.

Sternberg, R. J. and Detterman, D. K. (eds.) (1986). *What is Intelligence? Contemporary Viewpoints on its Nature and Definition*. Norwood, New Jersey.

Thomson, G. H. (1939). *The Factorial Analysis of Human Ability*. London.

Thurstone, L. L. (1938). *Primary Mental Abilities*. Chicago.

Vernon, P. E. (1971). *The Structure of Human Abilities*. London.

**INTELLIGENCE, INVERTEBRATE.** See INVERTEBRATE LEARNING AND INTELLIGENCE.

**INTELLIGENCE: ITS ASSESSMENT.** Definitions of 'intelligence' vary with the theoretical position (and also the political persuasion) of the definer. The biologist tends to stress concepts such as healthy adaptation, capacity for adjustment to the environment, and learning to learn. The more philosophically minded intellectual is liable to emphasize the element of abstraction: indeed, 'the capacity for abstract thought' was the definition offered by Lewis *Terman. But many would reject the implicit value-judgement that abstract thinking is in some way superior to—or, in any case, more intelligent than—concrete or practical thinking. (See INTELLIGENCE for a fuller discussion.)

'Intelligence' has sometimes been contrasted with *'instinct', the latter posited as being a feature of the lower animals, common to all members of a species and relatively immutable because unlearned, i.e. performed almost perfectly at its first manifestation. Intelligence, on the other hand, was assumed to be an attribute unique to mankind and evincing wide individual differences. Of recent years, however, such distinctions between man and beast have become blurred (as, in certain quarters, have those between man and machine). The concept of instinct has both increased in flexibility and diminished in scientific respectability, since it is held to encourage mere naming and to lack explanatory or predictive power.

The stature of 'intelligence' has, for several reasons, also declined recently. First, the assertions made by certain psychometrists as to its degree of innateness (cf. Cyril *Burt's 'innate, general, cognitive ability') and the alleged constancy of its nature/nurture ratio (cf. Hans Eysenck's '4 : 1') are now largely discredited, as are claims for the existence of 'culture-fair' intelligence tests. Secondly, the identification of tested intelligence with everyday intelligence is questionable, especially in view of the many so-called intelligence tests which lack cogency. Thirdly, the whole climate of opinion during the 1960s and early 1970s among 'progressives' was anti-assessment; and while this attitude persisted, intelligence testing was bound, rightly or wrongly, to be a target for attack.

The word 'intelligence' is indeed likely to give rise to misconceptions, partly owing to the above overtones and partly to the suggestion implicit in an abstract noun that the word refers to 'something'—perhaps to something which one either possesses or lacks. This is, of course, a gross oversimplification of the issue. To avoid perpetuating such reification of intelligence (or any other factor) let us consider a *description* of *intelligent activity* rather than a definition of intelligence: that intelligent activity consists of grasping the essentials in a given situation and responding appropriately to them. This purposely leaves open such questions as speed-versus-accuracy or abstract-versus-practical; as to whether the most intelligent is he who can solve the most diverse problems or he who can answer the 64,000 dollar question; as to the existence of people who grasp the essentials but fail to react, and of others who respond appropriately but cannot explain their action. This open-endedness is deliberate in order to stress the flexibility of the term 'intelligent activity' and to cover intelligence both as tested and as manifested in everyday life.

How then is this elusive quality appraised? And what are the purposes of such appraisal? The agreement on what an intelligence test actually assesses is far greater than that found among the definitions and the theories in this realm. An intelligence test is essentially a test of deductive reasoning. In fact, since 'intelligence' has become a dirty word, many psychologists prefer to talk of 'tests of reasoning'. More specifically, the phrases 'verbal reasoning' or 'numerical reasoning' or 'perceptual reasoning' may be used. Two examples of each of these are given in Fig. 1.

It may be seen from these examples that some element of acquired knowledge is assumed—i.e. the understanding of everyday words and of simple arithmetical concepts, the capacity to recognize certain features of formal shapes and to interpret representational pictures. A test which makes no such assumptions would be both impracticable and valueless. But, in so far as is possible, all the information required to solve each problem is contained within it, and the items are unambiguous in the sense that only one of the proffered responses is defensible.

1.  Which one of the six lower words means **either** the same as **or** the opposite of the top word ?

    **probable**

    | sure | likely | impossible | convenient | profitable | certainly |
    |------|--------|------------|------------|------------|-----------|
    | 1 | 2 | 3 | 4 | 5 | 6 |

2.  **seed** is to **plant** as **egg** is to . . .

    | tree | root | pollen | oats | potato | bird |
    |------|------|--------|------|--------|------|
    | 1 | 2 | 3 | 4 | 5 | 6 |

3.  In the following series, the fifth member is omitted. Which is it ?

    56  35  20  10  . . .  1

    | 2 | 3 | 4 | 5 | 6 | 7 |
    |---|---|---|---|---|---|

4.  42 people work in four shops. Half the people work in the big shop and the rest are divided equally among the smaller shops. How many work in each small shop ?

    | 7 | 5 | 21 | 6 | 4 | none of these |
    |---|---|----|---|---|---------------|

5.  Which one comes next ?

6.  Which one of the lower pictures is like the top two but unlike the other five ?

Fig. 1.

Such problems can be devised that are appropriate for people of almost every level of ability: for the seven-year-old (e.g. no. 5), for the young adolescent (e.g. no. 1), or for the sixth-former or older (e.g. no. 3). These tests are often good predictors of academic or vocational success but they differ from examinations in that they are less dependent on memory, diligence, and congenial teaching, as they are not primarily concerned with assimilated knowledge; and they are clearly more objective than *interviews or other methods involving direct personal judgement.

The purposes of assessing intelligence are manifold. Let us consider four of the uses to which such tests are put: selection, vocational guidance, clinical work, and research. First, selection: whenever the number of applicants exceeds the number of places—whether in education, or industry, or the Civil Service—some form of assessment is necessary, in order to determine which candidates to accept. Intelligence is only one of the factors to consider, but it is nearly always relevant and it is easier to assess than such traits as conscientiousness, sense of responsibility, and the ability to get on with people. The test scores, unlike interviews, are not liable to be influenced by such factors as the applicant's clothing or accent, or his willingness to appreciate his interviewer's sense of humour (though the *ability* to do this may well be related to intelligence!)

So much for selection. Vocational guidance is the other face of the same coin: here the psychologist advises the individual as to what kind of job is likely to give him most satisfaction and to make the best use of his talents. Advice is especially helpful in those cases where people have no idea what work would suit them or where, for one reason or another, they are in a state of conflict on the matter. Tests of aptitudes and of interests may also be helpful in vocational guidance.

Tests are used in clinical situations as an aid, sometimes to diagnosis and sometimes to assess the progress of a patient. They can help in determining whether brain-damage has occurred, and also in deciding whether one particular course of treatment is more appropriate than another.

In research, the intelligence test may be a valuable instrument either in its own right—in a study of 'slow developers', for example, or of the effects of environmental change, or of male/female intellectual differences (if such study is still within the law!)—or as a means to an end. Since it is rarely the case in human psychology that 'other things are equal', techniques such as matching members of pairs on intelligence-test performance may be usefully employed in the investigation of other psychological or social variables.

Equality of opportunity is as important as ever it was, and it is gradually becoming more of a reality—partly owing to the use of intelligence tests, since they often facilitate the recognition of an able child from an underprivileged background. But to insist, as some educationists do nowadays, that equality *of ability* is the rule—and to decry assessment of any kind—since if some are designated as brighter it follows that some must be designated as duller—is unhelpful to the individuals concerned as well as to their subsequent employers or instructors.

The intelligence test can yield valuable data, provided that it is devised with critical care, interpreted with understanding, and used always in conjunction with other procedures. Indeed, intelligence testing is most informative in those somewhat rare cases when its results are at variance with other relevant criteria.      A. W. H.

Burt, C. (1955). *The Subnormal Mind*, 3rd edn. London.

Butcher, H. J. (1968). *Human Intelligence: its nature and assessment*. London.

Heim, A. W. (1970). *Intelligence and Personality*. Harmondsworth.

Heim, A. W. (1975). *Psychological Testing* (Oxford Biology Readers, No. 76). Oxford.

Hinde, R. A. and Hinde, J. S. (1976). *Instinct and Intelligence* (Oxford Biology Readers, No. 63). Oxford.

Vernon, P. E. (1969). *Intelligence and Cultural Environment*. London.

**INTELLIGENCE: THE ART OF GOOD GUESSWORK.** We think that intelligence is a quality easily recognizable in other people's talk, deeds, or writings, yet the current trend among psychologists is to deny that it can be succinctly defined or described. This avoidance of the most interesting of all general questions about intelligence results partly from intellectual revulsion against the psychometricians' simplistic arrogance in promoting the IQ as an adequate measure of an individual's mind, and partly from moral revulsion at the degradation and insult to whole racial groups that has resulted from this approach. It is also partly a historical relic, for the early discussions of the topic were singularly inconclusive and unproductive (Thorndike *et al.*, 1921). However, intelligence is something to do with the way the mind processes information and handles data, and there have been great advances in information science since the early days of intelligence tests; for this reason one's intuition that intelligence is not only recognizable, but also definable, should now be given more theoretical attention. Heat, like intelligence, shows itself in many different ways: it gives the feeling of warmth, it melts solids and vaporizes liquids, it accelerates chemical reactions, it comes from the sun or the fireplace, and so on. Where would thermodynamics be if everyone had accepted the pervasive but pleomorphic manifestations of heat as proof that the theoretical problem of its nature was insoluble?

The notion that the biological role of intelligence is to produce good guesswork comes from a suggestion that it is the capacity to detect new, non-chance, associations (see Fatmi and Young, 1970; Barlow, 1970). Further consideration suggests that the most important use of newly detected associations is to improve the quality of the decisions that are made, and it is easy to see that anything that does this will be highly prized and sought after. It is reasonable to define intelligence in terms of the main benefits it confers, but the basic capacity is that of detecting new associations whose importance has long been recognized; here are some illustrations.

Consider the hungry (and intelligent) dog that leaps from its comfortable rug in front of the fire when it hears the sound of the refrigerator door being opened. That sound is associated with the availability of food, and the recognition of such associations has obvious value. But in pointing to this particular association of sensory stimuli with reward we have only skimmed the surface, for there is no unique component to the sound of the refrigerator door; what is unique is the collection of sounds made by the door, and to determine what makes up this collection is itself an associative task. Since we are primarily concerned with human intelligence we must also point to uniquely human aspects of the structure of associations: we have spoken language with words representing associations of sensory stimuli, written language compiling those associations into sentences, and books, libraries, and whole academies whose purpose is to explore and elaborate associations among mere words.

Two more points about spotting associations need emphasis. First, the *newness* of the associations that are detected is important, for we do not really grant that someone is intelligent because he is full of knowledge of past discoveries and as a result can point to associative structures that would otherwise have been missed. We feel intuitively that a bright mind discovers associations anew from direct experience, rather than relying on memory, hearsay, or the knowledge contained in books. 'New' in the definition must therefore be taken to mean new for the mind in question, not new in the sense of 'never previously detected'.

The second point is that the associations discovered must be genuine ones and not due to chance. The mind that seizes on any random coincidence and sees it as a sign of an important permanent association will not guess right and is not conceded to be intelligent, though it may at times be entertaining.

Linking intelligence to guesswork captures the common-sense view of intelligence rather than the psychometrician's, but it is worth pointing out that some of the questions in tests, empirically developed as they have been to probe the capacity of the mind thought to correspond with intelligence, do indeed probe the capacity to detect new associations and relationships. This is the case for questions that require the completion of sequences or recognition of analogies. Many other questions merely probe something more appropriately termed 'general knowledge'; however, these too would be justifiable in terms of the definition to the extent that general knowledge represents the result of past applications of the capacity to detect associations.

If guessing right depends on spotting new associations, and if this is central to intelligence, what do we learn about its measurement? In order to guess right there are three conceptually distinct tasks, namely formulating possible guesses (i.e. hypotheses about new associations), testing them to find the right ones, and working out the implications of those that escape disproof. Of these three, it is easiest to imagine an objective measure of the testing process, because the theory and practice of statistical tests for associations are well developed, and this makes it possible to compare the performance of an individual at an associative task with that of an 'ideal statistician'. The ideal will make the best possible use of the evidence, and a measure of 'associative efficiency' is obtainable from the ratio of the amounts of evidence required by the ideal and the individual being tested, when each performs at the same level of reliability; this is an absolute measure of how well the subject utilizes the information available—how well he guesses in fact. The concept of statistical efficiency (Fisher, 1929) has been used to measure human perceptual tasks (Rose, 1942; Tanner and Birdsall, 1958; Barlow and Reeves, 1979), but has not yet been applied to the associative tasks that underlie intelligence (nor to learning for that matter). It is satisfying that the definition allows one to point to one aspect of intelligence that could in principle be measured objectively and in absolute terms, knowing precisely what one was measuring.

The next question is 'How does the possibility of a particular association enter someone's mind?' One naturally attributes intelligence to a mind that generates its own array of plausible possibilities, and stupidity to a mind that produces inappropriate ones or has to be fed with suggestions in every new circumstance. Seeing possible solutions is an essential part of good guesswork, and the nature of this imaginative ability is a more difficult and interesting question than that of assessing statistically whether a given association is present or not. The main difficulty here is the astronomical number of possible associations: it is certainly *not* intelligent to point to any or all of them for testing, whereas it would, for instance, show a glimmer of intelligence to start looking for associations between those events which occur with approximately the same overall frequency. It would be a formidable task to specify a catalogue of good tactics for imaginative guesswork in order to measure how well an individual was able to devise them, and a single numeric measure of imaginative inventiveness is most unlikely to emerge from such an effort. One must also pay attention to the third distinct part of intelligence.

It is not intelligent to claim as a new association something that can readily be deduced from associations that are already known. Every moment we see sights and hear sounds that can be predicted from associations already established by our own minds, or implanted in them by others. To distinguish what is new, knowledge of these pre-existing associations must be organized so that they are taken into account. Thus the deductive reasoning required to use a background of general knowledge is a necessary part of intelligence on the current definition.

It will surprise no one that intelligence appears to be complex and requires imagination, judgement and reasoning. But this discussion has led to two novel conclusions: first, the part concerned with statistical judgement can in principle be measured on an absolute scale, using theoretical limits as a reference rather than population norms or anything like that; and second, the nature of intelligence is rather satisfactorily defined simply by stating its goal, namely guessing right. One must respect past psychometricians for their empirical development of practical tests of mental ability, but one should now hope that the theoretical basis will be strengthened and particularized (see Barlow, 1983; Sternberg, 1985). The diversity of minds and their aptitudes should not conceal the fact that there is a recognizable unity behind all the manifestations of intelligence. H. B. B.

Barlow, H. B. (1970). Definition of intelligence. *Nature*, **228**, 1008.

Barlow, H. B. (1983). Intelligence, guesswork, language. *Nature*, **304**, 207–9.

Barlow, H. B. and Reeves, B. C. (1979). The versatility and absolute efficiency of detecting mirror symmetry in random dot displays. *Vision Research*, **19**, 783–93.

Fatmi, H. A. and Young, R. W. (1970). A definition of intelligence. *Nature*, **228**, 97.

Fisher, R. A. (1925). *Statistical Methods for Research Workers*. Edinburgh.

Rose, A. (1942). The relative sensitivities of television pick-up tubes, photographic film, and the human eye. *Proceedings of the Institute of Radio Engineers*, **30**, 293–300.

Sternberg, R. J. (1985). *Beyond IQ*. Cambridge.

Tanner, W. P. jr. and Birdsall, T. G. (1958). Definitions of d' and n as psychophysical measures. *Journal of the Acoustical Society of America*, **30**, 922–8.

Thorndike, E. L. and twelve others (1921). Intelligence and its measurement: a symposium. *Journal of Educational Psychology*, **12**, 123–54 and 195–216.

**INTENTION.** This is one of the most difficult concepts to understand or discuss in academic psychology, although most 'common-sense' psychological explanations are in terms of intentions. Behaviour is commonly explained by intentions (such as: 'Why did the chicken cross the road . . .?'), but just what an intention is, in terms of brain processes or anything else, is exceedingly hard to say.

Intention seems to characterize mind; for we can hardly say that natural objects (atoms, molecules, tables and chairs, or planets or stars) have intentions. They are controlled, rather, according to natural laws. The forming of an intention seems to imply free will and the ability to choose. Whether such an ability is compatible with the operation of strictly causal laws at the physical level is a matter of philosophical debate.

Can a machine show intention? It has been argued for example by the philosopher Margaret Boden (1972) that *artificial intelligence machines can exhibit *purpose and intention.

Boden, M. (1972). *Purposive Explanation in Psychology*. Cambridge, Massachusetts.

**INTENTIONALITY.** Intentionality is *aboutness*. Some things are about other things: a belief can be about icebergs, but an iceberg is not about anything; an idea can be about the number 7, but the number 7 is not about anything; a book or a film can be about Paris, but Paris is not about anything. Philosophers have long been concerned with the analysis of the phenomenon of intentionality, which has seemed to many to be a fundamental feature of mental states and events. It should be clear that this use of 'intentionality' and 'intentional' is a technical use, and should not be confused with the more familiar sense (discussed in the entry, INTENTION) of doing something deliberately or on purpose. Hopes and fears, for instance, are not things we *do*, not intentional *acts* in the latter, familiar sense, but they are intentional phenomena in the technical sense, for they are *about* or *of* something.

The term was coined by the Scholastics in the Middle Ages (see, for example, AQUINAS), and derives from the Latin verb *intendo*, meaning to point (at) or aim (at) or extend (toward). Phenomena with intentionality point outside themselves, in effect to something else: whatever they are *of* or *about*. The term was revived in the nineteenth century by the philosopher and psychologist Franz *Brentano, one of the most important predecessors of the school of *phenomenology. Brentano claimed that intentionality is the defining distinction between the mental and the physical; all and only mental phenomena exhibit intentionality. Since intentionality is, he claimed, an irreducible feature of mental phenomena, and since no physical phenomena could exhibit it, mental phenomena could not be a species of physical phenomena. This claim, often called the Brentano thesis, or Brentano's irreducibility thesis, has often been cited to support the view that the mind cannot be the brain, but this is by no means generally accepted today.

There was a second revival of the term in the 1960s and 1970s by English and American philosophers in the analytic tradition. In response to seminal work by R. Chisholm and W. V. Quine, a vigorous attempt was made to develop an account of intentionality in harmony with the canons of modern logic and semantics. Since the phenomenological tradition, mainly on the Continent, has continued to exploit the concept of intentionality along rather different lines, the problem of intentionality is one of the best points of convergent concern in these two largely separate—and often antagonistic—research traditions.

In spite of the attention currently devoted to the concept, there is a striking lack of received wisdom about the proper analysis of intentionality. What agreement there is concerns the nature of the problems raised, and while some of the proposed solutions are forbiddingly technical, the problems themselves readily emerge on a little reflection.

If we make an initial rough catalogue of the things that can be about things, it will include a great variety of *mental* states and events (ideas, beliefs, desires, thoughts, hopes, *fears, *perceptions, *dreams, *hallucinations . . .), also various *linguistic* items (sentences, questions, poems, headlines, instructions . . .), and perhaps other sorts of *representations* as well (pictures, charts, films, symphonic tone poems, computer programs . . .). Many have thought that these linguistic and non-linguistic representations are only derivatively about anything. They depend for their intentionality on their being the creations and tools of creatures with minds, and particular representations derive their specific aboutness from the specific aboutness of the ideas, beliefs, and intentions of their creators. What makes the particular sequence of ink marks on the next line:

Napoleon was exiled to Elba

about Napoleon is its role as a sentence in a language used by people who know about Napoleon, or at least have beliefs about Napoleon, and wish to communicate about Napoleon. What *representations* mean depends on what *people* mean by using them. This suggests that the primary or underived intentionality of mental states and events is a very special feature indeed—the source of all meaning in the world. On this view, sentences, pictures, diagrams, and the like are in effect prosthetic extensions of the minds of those who use them, having no intrinsic meaning but only the meaning they derive from their utilization.

With regard to conventional representational artefacts, this is surely a plausible view; but it is not so plausible to claim that *all* intentionality is either the underived intentionality of (purely) mental phenomena or the derived intentionality of such artefacts. An exposed cliff-face might be said by a geologist to store information *about* the Triassic period; impulse trains in nerve bundles might be said by a neuroscientist to carry information *about* state changes in the inner ear. How is this sort of aboutness related to the aboutness discussed by philosophers under the rubric of intentionality? It is tempting to suppose that some concept of *information* underlies all these phenomena, and could serve eventually to unify mind, matter, and meaning in a single theory.

Identifying intentionality with aboutness nicely locates the concept, but hardly clarifies it, for the ordinary word 'about' is perplexing on its own. A belief can be about Paris, but a belief can also apparently be about phlogiston—and there is no phlogiston for it to be about. This curious fact, the possible non-existence of the *object* of an intentional item, may seem to be an idle puzzle, but in fact it has proved extraordinarily resistant to either solution or dismissal. Brentano called this the *intentional inexistence* of the intentional objects of mental states and events, and it has many manifestations. I cannot want without wanting something, but what I want need not exist for me to want it. It can be true that I now want a two-ton diamond even if there is not now and never has been or will be such a thing. People have believed in Poseidon, and children often believe in Santa Claus, and while in one sense we can say these believers all believe in nothing, their beliefs are quite different states of mind—they have different *objects*—and both are to be distinguished from the state of mind of the sceptic or agnostic who can be said in quite a different sense to believe in nothing.

It might seem that there is a simple and straightforward solution to these problems: although Poseidon does not exist, an idea of Poseidon surely exists in each of the believers' minds, and this idea is the object of their belief. This will not do, however, for it is one thing to believe in the existence of the *idea* of Poseidon—we can all believe in the existence of that mental item—and quite another to believe in Poseidon. Similarly, what I might want could hardly be the idea in my mind of a two-ton diamond, for that is something I already have. Moreover, when, as normally happens, the object of an intentional state does exist—for example, when I believe that London is crowded—that very object, London, the city itself and not my idea of it in my mind, is what my belief is about.

The relation, then, between a state of mind—or for that matter a sentence or picture—and its intentional object or objects is a very peculiar relation in three ways.

First, for ordinary relations, like *x is sitting on y* or *x is employed by y*, *x* and *y* are identifiable entities quite apart from whether they happen to be thus related to each other. The thing which is *x* would be the same *x* whether or not it were sitting on *y* or employed by *y*. But the same is not true of intentional 'relations'. One and the same belief cannot at one moment be about a frog (that it is green, say) and at another moment be about a house (that *it* is green). The latter is a *different* belief. What a belief is supposed to be about is crucial to which belief it is.

Second, for ordinary relations, each of the things related must exist (or have existed); but, as we have seen, intentional 'relations' can be to non-existents.

Third, ordinary relations obtain between things regardless of how they might be specified. If I am sitting next to Jones and Jones is the Mad Strangler, then it follows that I am sitting next to the Mad Strangler, whatever anybody may think. But if I believe that Jones is harmless, or hope that he will marry my sister, it does not at all follow that I believe that the Mad Strangler is harmless or hope that the Mad Strangler will marry my sister. Even if one is tempted to object that in this case *in one sense* I *do* hope the Mad Strangler will marry her, there is clearly another sense in which I *might* hope this and *don't*.

For these reasons the normal logic of relations cannot accommodate the presumed relation between an intentional state and its intentional object or objects, but it has also not proved comfortable for theorists to deny on these grounds that there are such things as intentional relations—to hold that mental states, for instance, are only *apparently* relational. This, then, is the unsolved problem of intentionality.

Faced with this problem, the Anglo-American tradition, characteristically, has tended to favour a tactical retreat, to a logical analysis of the language we use to talk about intentional states, events, and other items. This move, from the direct analysis of the phenomena to the analysis of our ways of talking about the phenomena, has been aptly called 'semantic ascent' by Quine, and its immediate advantages are twofold. First, we set aside epistemological and metaphysical distractions such as: 'How can we ever know another person's mental state anyway?' and 'Are mental states a variety of *physical* state, or are they somehow *immaterial* or *spiritual*?' The *things people say* about mental states are in any event out in the public world where we can get at them and study them directly. Second, switching to language puts at our disposal a number of sophisticated techniques and theories developed by philosophers, logicians, and linguists. Semantic ascent is not guaranteed to solve any problems, of course, but it may permit them to be reformulated in ways more accessible to ultimate solution.

In its new guise, the problem of intentionality concerns the semantics of the so-called *intentional idioms*—'. . . believes that $p$', '. . . desires that $q$', '. . . dreams that $r$', etc. (where $p$, $q$, and $r$ are replaced by clauses, such as 'frogs are green' or 'Labour is returned to power'. Linguistically and logically, intentional idioms are a subset of those that Quine calls 'referentially opaque'. What this means is that many normally valid logical moves are not valid for the clauses 'within the scope' of intentional idioms. For instance, normally, if two words happen to be words for the same thing, then one can freely substitute one for the other without affecting the *truth* of the whole sentence (although one may change its meaning, or effectiveness, or style). Thus, since 'Cicero' and 'Tully' are names for the same man, from the truth of 'Cicero was an orator' we can infer the truth of 'Tully was an orator'. By contrast, however, the same substitution is not always allowable in 'Tom believes that Cicero denounced Catiline', for Tom may believe that Cicero denounced Catiline but not believe that Tully did. So '. . . believes that $p$' is an opaque idiom.

Clearly this is just another (and more precise) way of putting the point made earlier, that intentional relations depend on how their objects are specified. The other points have analogues too. Thus, normally, a relational statement is false if one of the alleged *relata* doesn't exist; not so within the scope of opaque idioms. And, of course, the

fact that the identity of a particular belief depends on the object or objects it is supposed to be about, emerges on this treatment as the fact that the ascription of a particular belief depends crucially on the words used in the clause expressing it. We can see now that this condition is essentially the same as the first, and that the second condition (possible non-existence of the object) is also just a special case of opacity: believing that Santa Claus is generous and believing that Poseidon is generous are different beliefs, in spite of the fact that 'Santa Claus' and 'Poseidon' refer to 'the same thing', i.e. to nothing.

Seeing this unity in the various conditions of intentionality is one of the benefits of semantic ascent. Another is that it thus provides us with a relatively formal and uncontroversial test for the intentionality of idioms, and hence a test for appeals to intentionality in a theory. This is an interesting test, for theories relying on intentional idioms—such as classical 'rational agent' economics and cognitive psychology—cannot be formulated in any non-controversial way within standard logic, while it seems that other theories, pre-eminently in the physical sciences, can be so formulated. The logical oddity of intentional idioms, and their resistance to regimentation, led Quine and several other theorists to declare the bankruptcy of all intentional theories, on grounds of logical incoherence. The only sound alternatives within the social sciences, then, would have to be theories making no appeal to meaning or intentionality at all: purely *behaviouristic or purely physiological theories. This claim strikes a familiar note: many psychologists and brain scientists have expressed great scepticism about the utility or permissibility of 'mentalistic' formulations in their fields—while others of course have held them to be indispensable. The philosophical analysis of intentionality yields a clear logical characterization of this fundamental theoretical division in the social sciences and biology: 'mentalistic' theories are all and only those making ineliminable use of intentional idioms, and hence inheriting the *logical* problems of construing those idioms coherently.

Dispensing with intentional theories is not an attractive option, however, for the abstemious behaviourisms and physiological theories so far proposed have signally failed to exhibit the predictive and explanatory power needed to account for the intelligent activities of human beings and other animals. A close examination of the most powerful of these theories reveals intentional idioms inexorably creeping in—for instance in the definition of the stimulus as the 'perceived' stimulus and the response as the 'intended' effect, or in the reliance on the imputation of 'information-bearing' properties to physiological constructs. Moreover, the apparent soundness of information-processing theories, and their utility in practice, has strengthened the conviction that somehow we *must* be able to make sense of the ineliminable intentional formulations they contain without compromising thoroughgoing materialism.

One avenue currently being explored apparently challenges the thesis that the intentionality of linguistic entities is derivative, and, turning that idea on its head, attempts to explain the intentionality of minds by analysing minds as systems of 'mental representations'; our thoughts and beliefs exhibit intentionality *because* they are couched somehow in a 'language of thought' physically embodied in our brains. The intentionality of 'expressions' in the language of thought is held to be primary—the intentionality of expressions in natural language, for instance, is supposed to be derived from it—but the hope of this research strategy is that the impressive resources of formal theories of semantics in logic, computation theory, and linguistics can render the puzzles about aboutness more tractable, and lead to their eventual solution in cognitivistic or information-theoretic theories of the mind. If, for instance, the *theory of reference* for expressions in *public* (natural or formal) languages can be exploited to produce a theory of reference for expressions in the language of thought, the problem of what mental states are about might be solved.

It is far from clear, however, that this is not a fundamental error, leading, for instance, to a vicious regress of languages and language-users within the mind or brain, in spite of the beguiling constructions already devised and to some degree tested by the enthusiasts of this persuasion. It is too early to say, then, whether the semantic ascent of the analytic tradition in philosophy, and its ideological cousin, cognitive or computational psychology, will provide more durable solutions to the problems of intentionality than the more frankly metaphysical investigations of the phenomenologists.                          D. C. D.
                                             J. C. H.

Aquila, R. E. (1977). *Intentionality: a study of mental acts.* Philadelphia.
Brentano, F. (1874). *Psychologie vom empirischen Standpunkt.* Rev. edn. (1925). Hamburg. (An English translation of excerpts can be found in Chisholm, 1960.)
Chisholm, R. (1957). *Perceiving: a philosophical study.* New York.
Chisholm, R. (1960). *Realism and the Background of Phenomenology.* Glencoe, Illinois.
Dennett, D. C. (1978). *Brainstorms: philosophical essays on mind and psychology* (chs. 1 and 4). Montgomery, Vermont.
Field, H. (1978). Mental Representation. *Erkenntnis*, **XIII**.
Fodor, J. (1975). *The Language of Thought.* New York.
Quine, W. V. O. (1960). *Word and Object.* Cambridge, Massachusetts.
Searle, J. (1983). *Intentionality.* Cambridge.

**INTENTION TREMOR.** A neurological term meaning an increase in tremor, especially of the arms and hands, when close to picking up or manipulating objects. It is associated with various neurological disturbances, and is probably due (in engineering terms) to increasing the gain of the servo-control systems of the limbs, mediated by the gamma-efferent system: a small error in position (for example, when picking something up with the hand) produces an over-correction so that the hand overshoots; this is over-corrected in its turn to produce an oscillation, or tremor. It is common, though not inevitable, in *Parkinson's disease.

**INTERACTIONAL APPROACH.** Experiments in psychological laboratories tend to study correlations between stimulus variables and response variables. Responses are regarded as reactions to, and dependent upon, stimuli, which are independent, whether they are manipulated by the experimenter or not. This model proved too simple when, during the Second World War, psychologists took up the study of performance on skilled tasks. In such tasks, stimuli are not independent of responses. What the operator does, decides in part what happens next, and what stimuli then impinge on him. Outside the laboratory, stimuli often depend on what responses have been made. For instance, a person who reacts to a fall in room temperature by turning on a heater, changes the stimulus situation.

One of the first to point out that in skilled tasks human operator and machine form an interacting 'control system' was Kenneth *Craik, one of the most brilliant of F. C. *Bartlett's pupils. In papers written in 1945, Craik described the operator as behaving as an 'intermittent correction servo-mechanism'. Deviation in the display of the machine evokes corrective responses, and hence a change in display and further responses. The general effect of a sequence of responses is to regulate and to restore or maintain a steady state or *homeostasis, just as a person's intermittent responses to changes in room temperature tend to be thermostatic.

Craik's work anticipated the development of a new branch of science, to which Norbert *Wiener in 1947 gave the name *cybernetics, the Greek root of which means to steer or govern. Cybernetics, now defined as the science of control and communication in animals and machines, is concerned with *feedback processes. A response—the motor output—produces feedback of two kinds: internal, due to kinaesthetic and other stimuli from the operator himself, and external, from the changes produced in the machine.

Concepts derived from cybernetics, and the related and more comprehensive general system theory, have pervaded the study of social behaviour, which is made up of the responses of individuals to one another. The responses of one provide the external feedback of the other—that is, the behaviour of one controls, and is controlled by, the behaviour of the other. When this is so, the two form a 'system', by which is meant an organization of two or more units, i.e. persons, who interact with one another in a more or less consistent way. A system is typically open, i.e. it forms part of one or more larger systems. A couple such as a husband

and wife belong usually to the larger systems of a family and of a community.

Interaction between one person and another is made up of responses which are 'messages', i.e. items of communication. Messages, which may be verbal or non-verbal, convey information and feelings more or less openly. At one extreme are the peculiar, idiosyncratic messages which represent the symptoms of mental illness, and which convey information and feelings in paradoxical, disguised, or metaphorical terms. Messages provide feedback, which is *negative* when they preserve the relationship between two people. If the feedback is *positive*, a vicious circle is initiated, action and reaction then intensifying one another; this is usually referred to as 'escalation'. An angry reaction to anger—positive feedback—leads to escalation. Breakdown in the relationship is then averted if other regulatory mechanisms are brought into operation. A conciliatory reaction, on the other hand—negative feedback—restores the relationship.

The relationship between two people, which is based on the assumptions they make about each other, and hence their expectations of each other, tends to be stable, despite changing circumstances, because of the homeostatic tendencies shown by systems. Homeostasis may fail, and the system break down, when an event occurs of special significance or force. There is then a crisis, or turning-point. The relationship between a husband and wife may come to a crisis when the moving away or death of the wife's mother brings a structural change in the system, or when the discovery of the infidelity of one makes it necessary for each to revise assumptions about, and expectations of, the other.

The interactional approach supposes that mental illness arises out of a crisis in a significant relationship. The symptoms of the illness—the messages sent from one to the other—reflect either the instability before the relationship is restored, i.e. the system is reorganized, or the impasse when the relationship has become stabilized on terms which involve the disabling of one or both. The psychotherapist, who serves as a third party, mediates in order to bring about a reorganization of the system and the restoration of the relationship on terms more satisfactory than before. A crucial point in the interactional approach is the recognition that the behaviour of one person cannot be modified without concomitant changes in the behaviour of the other or others related to him.

D. R. D.

Bertalanffy, L. von (1968). *General System Theory*. London.

Craik, K. J. W. (1947–8). Theory of the human operator in control systems: (i) the operator as an engineering system; (ii) man as an element in a control system. *British Journal of Psychology*, **38**, (i) 58–61, (ii) 142–8.

Watzlawick, P., Beavin, J. H., and Jackson, D. D. (1968). *Pragmatics of Human Communication*. London.

Wiener, N. (1965). *Cybernetics*. Cambridge, Massachusetts.

**INTERNAL MODELS.** This term was coined by the Cambridge psychologist Kenneth *Craik, in his important book *The Nature of Explanation* (1943). Internal models are the supposed brain representations of reality (or imagination) as accepted for perception and for setting behaviour appropriate to the world. Craik thought of internal models as analogue representations—similar to F. C. *Bartlett's 'schemas', and Donald Hebb's 'phase sequences'. His notion was an important break from the prevailing emphasis on stimulus–response mechanisms of behaviour: it was a step towards psychological accounts based on the importance of stored knowledge; and it drew attention to the importance of control engineering, and later, computers, for understanding brain function. Craik wrote when analogue computers were in vogue, and just before the impact of *digital computing. His internal models are analogues rather than digital programs and so are rather inflexible and not explicitly formulated.

Bartlett, F. C. (1932). *Remembering*. Cambridge.

Craik, K. J. W. (1943). *The Nature of Explanation*. Cambridge.

Gregory, R. L. (1986). Kenneth Craik's The Nature of Explanation: Forty Years On. In *Odd Perceptions*. London.

Hebb, D. (1949). *Organisation of Behaviour*. London.

**INTERSENSORY CO-ORDINATION.** See SPATIAL CO-ORDINATION OF THE SENSES.

**INTERVIEWS.** People seek interviews with their bank manager or their doctor, they are interviewed for a job or for promotion, and at work they may have an annual 'appraisal interview'. Some are interviewed as they apply for social security or other benefits, and others may be interviewed by a journalist or a market researcher.

These different encounters all have as defining characteristics a certain formality and an asymmetry. Participants' roles are specified, in that one person is the interviewer and the other is the interviewee (although in practice more than two people may be involved) and each has a fairly clear idea of the type of behaviour which is expected. The objective is for the interviewer to obtain and interpret information from the interviewee in order to make a decision or take some action.

Let us look particularly at interviews in personnel selection, where an official of an organization has to decide which candidate to select for a job from among a number of applicants. Such interviews are often criticized on the grounds that different interviewers can reach different conclusions about the same candidate, and a number of experiments have examined the ways in which interviewers can be 'calibrated' so that they reliably form similar impressions. One approach has varied the degree of structure imposed upon the interview, in terms of the requirement to obtain certain kinds of information and to draw inferences only about pre-specified attributes or likely behaviours. Results indicate that increased structure yields significantly greater uniformity between interviewers. Similar outcomes can be achieved through training schemes which aim to make interviewers aware of possible biases and which stress the need to identify goals and important issues in advance. For example, the 'seven-point plan' encourages interviewers to define job requirements carefully and to obtain information about candidates in terms of physique, intelligence, aptitude, attainments, interests, disposition, and circumstances.

Although reliability can be enhanced in these ways, there remains the question whether interviewers can validly predict subsequent work behaviour. A major research problem is the difficulty of establishing acceptable measures of 'good' or 'bad' behaviour in an occupational role. Limited measures of skilled performance or of output levels may be available for some manual jobs, but professional and managerial work is much less open to quantification; and it is in those areas that interviews are particularly widespread. This problem, of adequately measuring the behaviour we wish to predict, is endemic in all areas of personnel selection, and is often referred to as 'the criterion problem'.

However, despite the commonly expressed doubts, selection interviews are here to stay, if for no other reason than that they provide an opportunity for the candidate to ask his own questions and to reach his own conclusions about a potential employer. The interpersonal processes at work during an interview are subtle, complex, and fascinating. Consider the ways in which an interviewer will search for and integrate information about the applicant. Research has established clearly that people form impressions of each other through the application of previously established expectancies or 'inference rules'. Evidence that a person has a certain characteristic (anxiousness in the interview situation, for example) sets up a network of inferences about other characteristics. These networks are sometimes referred to as 'implicit theories of personality', and perceivers apply their own implicit theories to even the most limited pieces of evidence. Indeed, some people take pride in 'summing him up as soon as he comes through the door', whereas others may devote their energies to fighting a similar form of stereotyped perception, where extensive inferences are drawn from single cues such as 'black', 'female', or 'handicapped'. In general terms, manifested features have been found to make their greatest impact during short encounters, when other evidence is meagre. Thus many perceivers initially take the wearing of spectacles to imply intelligence and thoughtfulness (cf. HALO EFFECT). Conventional wisdom has it that 'first impressions count', and research has looked in detail at this question. It seems that the initial impression is tested through subsequent investigation. However, there is often a predisposition in an interviewer to obtain *negative* information, material which suggests that the candidate should not be selected. This is understandable in the light of the interviewer's regular need to reject most of the applicants, but it is important for the 'first impressions count' thesis. This needs to be refined to suggest that an early negative impression is readily reached and is difficult to change, whereas an early positive impression is less easily made and is liable to be overridden if negative evidence becomes available subsequently.

One interesting research finding bears upon this issue. There is typically a significant positive correlation between the proportion of time during which the *interviewer* talks and the probability that a candidate will be offered the job. This may be interpreted in terms of an early implicit decision by an interviewer which tends to make later questioning redundant and perhaps suggests that the desirable candidate should be encouraged through conversation to maintain his interest in the vacancy.

The skills of interviewing extend to co-ordinating the interaction through verbal and non-verbal cues at the same time as gaining and integrating a variety of items of information. Recent research has placed emphasis on the non-verbal cues which contribute to impression formation and management: they may be relatively unchanging—as with general appearance, clothes, *facial expression, and so on—or they may be dynamic—as in *eye contact, bodily movements, or loudness of speech.

How can people learn to be good interviewers? We all have relevant experience, talking with and acquiring information from others, and there is a tendency to feel that we are quite competent. But experience without detailed feedback is often of limited value: we need to learn with some precision about the effects of our actions and impressions so that we can improve upon them. This requirement has been the basis of recent experiments in interviewer training, and powerful procedures are now available. These have as their core the use of feedback about performance, often through the replay of videotaped practice sessions. In this way, trainees are able to chart and improve their performance over a series of practice interviews, assisted both by their tutors and their fellow trainees. Behaviour category systems are often applied to generate profiles of an interviewer's style in a way which points up strong and weak points, providing in a striking manner the feedback which is necessary for learning.          P. B. W.

Anstey, E. (1977). *An Introduction to Selection Interviewing*. London.
Argyle, M. (1973). *Social Encounters: readings in social interaction*. Harmondsworth.
Mackensie Davey, D., and McDonnell, P. (1975). *How to Interview*. London.
Sidney, E., Brown, M., and Argyle, M. (1973). *Skills with People: a guide for managers*. London.

**INTROSPECTION.** Looking into one's own mind. Used as a psychological technique it has great dangers of misinterpretation, even though introspections may seem to provide the most direct knowledge of ourselves that we have. It has, however, become clear that very little that goes on in the brain associated with the mind is accessible to conscious introspection, and we regard the mind as a much broader concept than awareness, conciousness, or what is known by introspection.

**INTROVERSION.** See EXTRAVERSION–INTROVERSION.

**INTUITION.** This is, essentially, arriving at decisions or conclusions without explicit or conscious processes of reasoned thinking. It is sometimes thought that intuitions are reliable; and indeed we do act most of the time without knowing why or what our reasons may be. It is certainly rare to set out an argument in formal terms, and go through the steps as prescribed by logicians. In this sense, almost all judgements and behaviour are 'intuitive'.

The term is used in philosophy to denote the alleged power of the mind to perceive or 'see' certain self-evident truths (Latin *intueor*, to see). The status of intuition has, however, declined over the last century, perhaps with the increasing emphasis on formal logic and explicit data and assumptions of science.

'Woman's intuition' is, perhaps, largely the subtle use of almost subliminal cues in social situations from gestures, casual remarks, and knowledge of behaviour patterns and motives. Psychologists find these important matters for living almost impossible to formulate.

**INVENTION.** Inventions may be old ideas or techniques applied in new ways: they are very often combinations of old, and even highly familiar, ideas. To some degree almost all human behaviour is inventive, for it is seldom strictly repetitive and is aimed at contingencies which, though small and trivial, nevertheless require invention even if of a humble kind. The outstanding inventions, such as the phonograph of Thomas Alva Edison, represent the extension of abilities to some degree possessed by us all. Edison had remarkable perseverance towards imaginative goals; indeed he described invention as '99 per cent perspiration and 1 per cent inspiration'. The motivations, methods, and travails of inventors are described with case histories in *The Sources of Invention*, by J. Jewkes, David Sawers, and R. Stillerman (1958).

**INVERTEBRATE LEARNING AND INTELLIGENCE.** There are some signals to which an animal must respond, if it is to remain alive. It must pull back if it is hurt, and it must respond to extremes of hunger or thirst, heat or cold. One might add that it must, sooner or later, respond to the opposite sex and reproduce if the species is to survive.

Response to all other signals is optional. The fact that animals respond to a much wider range of events than those that immediately affect their physical well-being is a reflection of the non-random nature of the natural world. Stimuli of whatever sort may have predictive value, and a creature that responds appropriately can often avoid future unpleasantness and ensure the regular enjoyment of the better things in life, to the immediate benefit of itself and the ultimate survival of its species.

Learning is largely concerned with establishing the predictive value of stimuli that do not of themselves demand responses. We recognize other animals as intelligent when they predict effectively from these stimuli, and as highly intelligent when they begin to predict by analogy, generalizing to the point where they can take appropriate pre-emptive action without prior experience of the particular sequence of events to which they are reacting.

All invertebrate animals learn, many show glimmerings of *intelligence, and some would qualify as highly intelligent by the definitions employed above. A major problem, as we shall see below, is that we are often ourselves insufficiently intelligent to devise situations that will fairly test their performance. This problem becomes particularly acute when an invertebrate is making an elaborate response in an apparently complex situation, so it is perhaps most appropriate to begin by considering 'simple' forms of learning in which it does seem to be possible (i) to define the stimuli to which the animals are responding and (ii) to recognize the likely advantage of the behaviour in question.

One such category is *habituation*. Animals, in general, soon cease to respond to stimuli that prove to have no predictive value. A shadow passes. It could signal the approach of a would-be predator. In the past, individuals that played safe and ducked, or froze, lived to breed. Their offspring are liable to do the same; caution is genetically determined, natural selection having eliminated the unwary over countless generations in the past history of the species. But a shadow is not invariably dangerous. It may signal no more than a passing cloud, or the waving of a frond of seaweed. An animal that reacts to every moving shadow is doomed to a restless and economically hopeless existence, and cannot effectively compete with its less wary neighbours; in the long run the over-cautious are eliminated as surely as the foolhardy. Animals must habituate if they are to remain in business, and the best assumption with which genetics can equip them is that the immediate future is likely to resemble the immediate past. If a stimulus recurs regularly, unaccompanied by consequences of importance to the animal, it is well to ignore it. Rates of habituation vary, as we might expect, because the degree of built-in caution will vary from one sort of stimulus to the next; but caution is always present.

In an opposite direction, we find that nearly all animals will *sensitize*, becoming more rather than less responsive in circumstances where anything that happens *is* likely to have predictive value. If recent experience has revealed that something of importance is going on, it is well for the animal to remain more than usually alert, so that it responds to stimuli that it might otherwise have ignored. An animal that has just been hurt will flinch at stimuli that have nothing to do with the damage, and an animal that has just engulfed a tasty mouthful is more than usually attentive; any event could be a signal that more of the same is in the offing. It should be noticed that such effects can be quite unspecific: if things are going badly for the animal it will sensitize in the direction of caution, and take no chances over stimuli that would normally evoke a positive reaction; and if events are proving favourable, it becomes particularly responsive to stimuli that may indicate desirable objectives, like food, or sex. The animal, in either case, is responding to the sum of events (good and bad) in its recent past, and adjusting its response levels accordingly.

Taken together, habituation and sensitization will ensure that an animal behaves economically and opportunistically, cashing in when the going is good and lying low when conditions are unfavourable. The two interact: *dishabituation*, where a sudden change in circumstances re-establishes responses to a repeated stimulus that the animal has come to ignore, is a special case of sensitization. Between them the twin processes of habituation and sensitization will ensure better-than-even odds on an animal's responding appropriately, even under conditions where the creature is quite incapable of determining the precise nature of the stimulus to which it is responding. The system works, provided only that events occur in a non-random sequence—provided, in short, that the future is likely to resemble the recent past. Inside the laboratory it may, for various reasons, be desirable to randomize trial sequences so that an animal cannot predict what is going to happen without precise identification of the stimuli offered to it, but in the wild the animal is never likely to encounter a random sequence of events. Predators hang about, or go away; food comes in patches, scattered in time and space but never quite at random.

It is relevant to an understanding of invertebrate learning and behaviour to realize that cold-blooded animals in general can afford to be opportunists to an extent unthinkable in a homoiotherm. We poor warm-blooded creatures consume fuel so fast that we tend to discuss motivation in terms of imperatives: hunger must be satisfied or we die. We get thirsty because we live above the temperature of our surroundings and evaporate our body water; the need to replenish the water becomes an imperative because we overheat and die if we fail to do so. This personal experience distorts our thinking about invertebrates; we tend to assume that a starved snail or a thirsty cockroach will take risks to satisfy its needs as we would, becoming increasingly desperate as time passes. There is no evidence for this, at least on the sort of time-scales that one would expect from an experience of rats and people. A fed octopus is more, rather than less, liable to attack a strange but potentially edible object lowered into its tank; it cashes in while the going is good, and can starve for weeks if conditions suggest that it is unprofitable or even dangerous to respond to the unfamiliar. Sensitization is relatively unimportant in ourselves, because we can rarely afford to accept its dictates for very long; invertebrates can lie low for months, then stuff themselves, mate, and multiply when conditions improve.

One consequence of this is that it may be difficult to investigate invertebrate learning by conventional methods, forcing the animal to become active and solve problems because it is hungry or thirsty.

A further difficulty that confronts any biologist rash enough to examine learning in the lower animals is that most of them depend predominantly upon chemical stimuli, which we find awkward to classify and almost impossible to measure in the laboratory, let alone in the wild. Experimenters tend, in consequence, to set problems based on visual and spatial cues, so that their unfortunate subjects are more often than not tested with learning problems based on our sensory capabilities rather than theirs, a situation that can only lead to persistent underestimation of their learning abilities.

At a somewhat more subtle level, it is easy to forget that the bodily construction of animals may itself preclude certain forms of learning. Many of the things that we do, and believe simple, are based on an awareness of bodily position that is probably lacking in most invertebrates. When we move, we know how the position of our limbs is changing. If I pick up and examine an object, I am continually moving my fingers; each time I change my grip I know about the new positions adopted and, putting this information together with the feel of the contacts made, I can build up a mental picture of the shape of the thing I am holding. An octopus, for example, apparently cannot. It is quite as capable as I am of feeling over an object that it touches, and there is no doubt whatever that the animal can learn by touch, since it can be taught by simple reward and punishment techniques to distinguish between a wide variety of different textures and tastes (chemoreception again!), learning to perform such discriminations with great accuracy after a dozen or so trials. But it cannot manage shapes. A cube and a sphere are alike to it, apparently because the animal has no means of assessing the relative positions of its equivalent of our fingers, the many suckers arrayed along its flexible arms.

On reflection this is perhaps not very surprising. It is the animal's very flexibility that defeats it. We can compute the precise position of our hands because the human body only bends in a few places and is even there restricted to movement in a few directions. Sense organs in and around our joints can tell us about the angle adopted at each. No such easy computation is possible in a soft-bodied animal, where the position of each part depends upon the degree of contraction or relaxation of muscles all over the rest of the body. Muscle stretch receptors, which all have, are useless in this respect since they can only signal tension in the muscle concerned, not the position achieved as a result. The jointless animal perforce lacks any equivalent of our proprioceptive sense of position.

This divides the animal kingdom rather abruptly into two groups. On the one hand there are the jointed animals, the vertebrates and the arthropods, which seem to have a double (muscle and joint) set of proprioceptors. These creatures are potentially able to learn to manipulate; they can discover by trial and error precisely which movements it pays to repeat; they can monitor the number of steps they have taken and the angle of any turns that they have made. On the other hand there is the world of the soft-bodied, forever debarred from learning to make skilled movements, and faced with learning to find their way about entirely from exteroceptive cues. Arthropods, like vertebrates, can readily learn to run mazes, while many of the other things that they do or make (such as honeycombs and spiders' webs) necessitate accurate measurement of lengths and angles. A hermit-crab, investigating the inside of an empty shell with its claw, plainly learns about the size and the shape of the hole he is examining before risking exposure of his soft abdomen as he quits his old home in favour of the new. In marked contrast to all this, the soft-bodied snails and worms (and octopuses) rarely succeed in mastering any maze more complex than a T or Y, they never seem to create patterned structures, and they never, so far as we can assess the matter, learn to carry out a skilled movement. As a result we tend to assess their learning capabilities and their intelligence generally as exceedingly limited compared with arthropods and our fellow vertebrates, which find easy the same sorts of tasks as we do ourselves. It may well be, indeed it seems very likely, that the individual adaptive capacity of worms and snails *is* very limited; but it is well to remember that most of our present evidence comes from tests appropriate to ourselves rather than the creatures we have studied.

Granted, then, that we are almost certainly underestimating the capacities of most invertebrate animals, what generalities can be made in comparing higher forms of learning in vertebrates and invertebrates? Can we, for example, detect signs of *latent learning* ('the association of indifferent stimuli in situations without patent reward') or *insight learning* ('the production of a new adaptive response as a result of the apprehension of relations') among invertebrates, as we can among the higher vertebrates?

The answer appears to be 'yes', if one searches. Many invertebrates, inevitably, show little sign of these more complex forms of learning. Any animal that lives a highly specialized existence (an aphid

on a rose-bush or a lugworm in the mud of a saltmarsh) is unlikely to show conspicuous signs of intelligence. It does not need to: the same very limited range of problems have cropped up generation after generation for so long that almost the totality of its behaviour has come to be programmed genetically. Wherever this is possible, because the future has always rather precisely resembled the past, learning, with its inherent capacity for errors that could be dangerous or even fatal, is plainly a luxury that will be eliminated in the course of natural selection.

To discover what invertebrates can really do, one is obliged to examine cases where the animals live in complex environments. In general, also, it is necessary to look at predators, because predators must always be a little brighter than the prey they feed upon. Two such animals will be considered below, one soft-bodied (a cephalopod, of course), the other a jointed animal, an insect.

The octopus can be taught to make a wide variety of visual and tactile discriminations in the laboratory and it learns rapidly in these trial-and-error situations. It is also plain, from its life-style in the sea (where it returns to a home in the rocks after foraging expeditions that may carry it quite far afield) that it is capable of learning its way about a complex landscape, despite the restrictions already considered in relation to the consequences of flexibility. Observations of octopuses in the sea suggest that they can return home from any point in their range without retracing their outgoing steps, and this suggests a capacity for latent learning. In the laboratory octopuses will readily make detours to get at prey that they cannot approach directly; in a typical apparatus the animal was obliged to run out of sight of a crab, down an opaque corridor, and turn appropriately to reach its food. Even untrained octopuses manage this quite readily and will reach their goal with considerable reliability even if delayed for a minute or more by shutting them into the corridor. Plainly the animals are in some manner aware of the spatial relations of the crab and the various baffles that prevent them from reaching it—they show *insight*. (It is surprising how few vertebrates will detour successfully in similar circumstances.)

Performances that are in some ways even more impressive are shown by some of the hunting wasps. *Ammophila*, for example, hunts, paralyses, and stores caterpillars. Each mated female operates alone. She digs a hole in sand, covers it over, and after a brief orientation flight in the vicinity of the nest, departs to search for caterpillars. A caterpillar is paralysed by a sting in the central nervous system and is thus preserved as a living food-supply for the egg, which is subsequently deposited with it in the hole that the wasp has dug. The wasp's first problem, however, is to get the caterpillar home. Often the prey is too heavy to fly with, and the wasp sets off to drag it, often for many tens of metres, across the ground and round obstacles to the nest site. This performance is in itself remarkable because it implies a considerable knowledge of the geography of the district round the nest, apparently derived from the brief orientation flight carried out before setting out to hunt down a caterpillar—another nice example of latent learning. Extensive tests show that the cues used are entirely visual and more often than not precisely the sort of landmarks, skyline patterns and the like, that we would choose in the same circumstances.

More impressive still, however, is the discovery that *Ammophila* will run as many as three nests, in different stages of construction, at one and the same time. After the first egg and caterpillar have been deposited, she begins and provisions a new nest. A day or two later she returns to the first nest, checks whether the egg has hatched, and if it has, begins to stuff further caterpillars down the hole to feed her grub. Any spare time is spent digging out nest three, with a visit to nest two after a couple of days to see whether that egg has now begun to develop. Quite clearly the wasp not only remembers the precise position of each separate hole, but also recalls the state of play at each site, often delaying the response that she makes as a result of an inspection visit for two or three days on end.

Performances like those of *Ammophila* and the octopus leave no reason to doubt that learning by invertebrate animals can be every bit as complex as that found in vertebrates, which have been far more extensively studied. Whether one regards such creatures as 'intelligent' is largely a matter of taste, that is to say the precise definition of that somewhat elusive property one chooses to employ. We have come a long way from the proposition that the lower forms of life are automata, bereft of the ability to adapt and determine their individual destinies.                                            M. J. W.

Corning, W. C. *et al.* (eds.) (1973–5). *Invertebrate Learning* (3 vols.) London.
Hinde, R. A. (1970). *Animal Behaviour; a synthesis of ethology and comparative psychology*, 2nd edn. New York and London.
Wells, M. J. (1978). *Octopus: physiology and behaviour of an advanced invertebrate*. London.

**INVOLUNTARY ACTION.** See NERVOUS SYSTEM.

**INVOLUNTARY NERVOUS SYSTEM.** See NERVOUS SYSTEM.

**IRIS.** The coloured (usually blue or brown in man) ring round the pupil of the eye. It closes in bright light, and opens in dim light as a result of the action of light on the retina—including a reflex from one eye to the other. The small pupil in bright light reduces the optical aberrations of the eye, and gives maximal depth of field (focus over a wide range of distances). These qualities are sacrificed in dim light to give greater light-gathering power. Albinos, who lack pigment in their irises, have severe visual problems.

In mammals, the pupil is controlled involuntarily, with 'smooth' muscles, by the autonomic nervous system. In birds this is quite different: the pupils of their eyes are controlled by striate muscle and at least in some parrots the pupils respond to their level of arousal. Remarkably, the pupils of talking parrots open and close in apparent relation to their attention when producing, or listening to, sounds meaningful for them. The human pupil is affected, though far less markedly than the parrot's, by emotional changes, increasing in size with autonomic emotional arousal.

**IRRADIATION.** In vision, the apparently greater size of a white area than a corresponding darker area. Described in detail by *Helmholtz, it is still not fully understood.

**IRRITABILITY.** As a technical term in biology, the triggering of responses from small stimuli, such as gentle *touch. It is a defining property of living organisms—as through their 'irritability' they do not obey Newtonian mechanics—for they are active and wholly or partly autonomous, in a way that non-living objects (apart perhaps from some machines) are not.

**ISLAMIC PHILOSOPHY.** A traditional occidental theme is that the thinkers of Islam were mere synthesizers of Greek and other traditions (such as those of India and Persia) and made no original contribution to human thought. This simplistic view originates with the assumption that such work as that of *Avicenna was the totality of Islam's philosophy: which in turn is understandable when it is realized what a profound effect Avicenna had upon the Schoolmen.

The importance of Avicenna's thought for the West cannot be overestimated. Both in its negative aspect, such as the necessity of everything, and its more sympathetic notions, it offered a stimulus to the West. It was *par excellence* a combination of Neoplatonism and Aristotle, transforming the One into a first mover from whom all existence ultimately sprang. For Christian thinkers it offered especial attraction in distinguishing God from His creatures in terms of being; in holding essence to be the foundation of all existence; in making the effect dependent for both its being and its movement on what was prior to it; and in regarding all knowledge as the result of illumination (Gordon Leff, 1958; pp. 154 f.)

Characteristically, T. P. Hughes's massive *Dictionary of Islam* of 1885 (1964 edn., p. 452) baldly repeats: 'The whole philosophy of the Arabians was only a form of Aristotelianism tempered more or less with Neo-Platonic conceptions.'

More recently this generalization has been challenged with great vigour by both Muslim and Western scholars.

The Arab conquest and occupation of eastern and western lands from the early eighth century produced intense intellectual activity in centres of learning as widely dispersed as Baghdad and Spain, Bukhara and Egypt. The study and exercise of traditional knowledge were directly linked to the Prophet's dictum, accepted with the force of law:

'Seek knowledge even unto China.' During much of the thousand years of the period known as the Dark Ages in Europe, the Islamic centres of learning were major agents for the preservation and transmission of accumulated knowledge; those of Spain especially being a magnet for Christian scholars. 'The Christian West became acquainted with Aristotle by way of Avicenna, *Al-Farabi, and Algazel (*Al-Ghazzali). Gundisalvus' own encyclopaedia of knowledge relies in the main on the information he had drawn from Arabian sources' (Guillaume, 1949; s.v. 'Philosophy and Theology', p. 246).

Many Islamic theorists, including Al-Ghazzali, were even believed by European scholars of the time to be Christian divines. The widespread belief that the Arabian schools were the great source of wisdom, which arose at this time, was later replaced, particularly in Victorian thought, by the thesis that they were merely run by copyists of the Greeks. More comprehensive study from a wider perspective has indicated that original contributions began to appear as the period of translation of classics and the absorption of ancient teaching advanced, after the eighth century. Work published during the twentieth century has increasingly asserted unexpected anticipations of relatively modern Western thought by the major Islamic philosophers, especially from the ninth to the fifteenth centuries.

Typically, M. S. Sheikh (1982; x and *passim*) has propounded themes in the systems of Al-Farabi, Avicenna, Al-Ghazzali, Ibn Khaldun, and others as prefigurings of the ideas of *Descartes (methodological doubt and *cogito, ergo sum*) and *Spinoza (*idealism), of Cartesian occasionalism, of *Leibnizian pre-established harmony, of *Kant (antinomies of pure reason and metaphysical agnosticism), *Hegel (panlogism and the notion of the absolute), *Hume (denial of causality), of *Bergson's creative evolutionism, and even of logicism and positivism. The Indian Muslim poet and thinker Sir Muhammad Iqbal (1876–1938) is the best-known Islamic philosopher of modern times.

In the Islamic world, in addition to the many customary preoccupations of philosophy as expressed in logic, ethics, method, knowledge, and political thought, there were also a vast number of exponents and schools of religious philosophy and *metaphysics (seen as mysticism). Among the most important were the Islamic theologians and the *Sufis. The works of the latter are today increasingly studied by both East and West in newer disciplines such as psychology and sociology.

From the comparative point of view, the picture of the Islamic contribution which emerges indicates the relative freedom of speculation within the culture, as contrasted with the somewhat more restricted categories of the West in the same epoch. This may be because Islam has never had a central ideological disciplinary institution which could succeed in imposing dogmatic authority over large populations for long periods of time, and because the door of reinterpretation of the limits of philosophical speculation has remained open, being the responsibility of the courts, in the absence of a priesthood.                I. S.

De Boer, T. J. (trans. Jones, E. R.) (1961). *The History of Philosophy in Islam*. London.
Guillaume, A. (1949). *The Legacy of Islam*. Oxford.
Hashimi, A. Al- (1973). *Islamic Philosophy and Western Thinkers*. Cairo.
Hitti, P. K. (1951). *History of the Arabs*. New York.
Houtsma, W. T. et al. (eds.) (1908–38). *The Encyclopedia of Islam* and Supplement. Leiden.
Leff, G. (1958). *Medieval Thought: St Augustine to Ockham*. Harmondsworth.
Nicholson, R. A. (1966). *A Literary History of the Arabs*. Cambridge.
O'Leary, D. (1954). *Arabic Thought and its Place in History*. London.
Schacht, J. and Bosworth, C. E. (eds.) (1974). *The Legacy of Islam*, 2nd edn. Oxford.
Sheikh, M. S. (1982). *Islamic Philosophy*. London.

**ISOLATION EXPERIMENTS.** When people are cut off from communication with other people, or, in even more extreme cases, from almost all sensory stimulation, there is a strong tendency to develop *hallucinations and hallucinogenic drug-like experiences not altogether dissimilar from those of *schizophrenia. There are many accounts of delusions and loss of reality and personal identity in, for example, single-handed voyages, and many experiments have been conducted in isolation chambers in which subjects have only diffused lighting and a minimum of auditory or tactile stimulation. Many of these experiments have been carried out on students, of an age-group which is perhaps less stable than later adult life, and the effects may be less for older people; but nevertheless there is good evidence that loss of sensory inputs seems to free the active mind to generate fantasies which may be overwhelming. Also, upon re-entering the normal world there may be dramatic visual and other *illusions (which makes these experiments dangerous unless carefully controlled), suggesting that fairly continuous inputs are required to maintain the sensory system in calibration. The results strongly suggest that, for example, space flights should be made by several crew members and not individually, and that there may be isolation problems for divers and others working and living alone (see DIVER PERFORMANCE).

Similar principles may apply to all levels of neural activity—hence the beneficial stimulation of companionship and competition in sport and academic activities. There seem to be important implications for education, and generally for a satisfying and productive way of life (the rich introspections of mystics and monks may be due to being cut off from stimulation they see as irrelevant and trivial).

The first experimental studies were by W. H. Bexton, W. Heron, and T. H. Scott in 1954, in Donald Hebb's laboratory at McGill. J. C. Lilly in

1956 increased the sensory isolation of his subjects by immersing them in a tank of water maintained at body temperature. Apart from a mask which covered the head, they were naked and so deprived of the sensations produced by pressure from clothing. After variable periods of time, thinking became less directed, and was eventually replaced by highly personal fantasies and hallucinations which were usually visual. Subjects were unable to distinguish between sleeping and waking—a finding of some importance as, regardless of the psychological explanations, there is evidence that episodes of microsleep occurred in which there was an early onset of REM *dreaming sleep. None the less, hallucinations of a similar kind may be experienced by other persons deprived of sensory stimulation, examples being prisoners in solitary confinement. Although *sensory* isolation may not be a prominent feature, being cut off from normal human intercourse when coupled with a fair measure of intense anxiety seems to produce both real *hallucinations and *pseudohallucinations.

O. L. Z.

**ISOMORPHISM.** Literally 'equal form'. Used by the Gestalt writers to refer to supposed electrical brain states, or 'fields', of the same shape as perceived objects. This notion has now been abandoned. See GESTALT THEORY.

**ITERATIVE PROCEDURES.** A computing term meaning successive approximations to a good, or the best, solution.

# J

**JACKSON,** JOHN HUGHLINGS (1835–1911). Widely known as the 'father' of British neurology, he was born in Yorkshire and spent the greatest part of his life in London, where he was for many years consultant physician to the then newly founded National Hospital for Nervous Diseases, Queen Square. His conception of nervous and mental disease, which owed much to the writings of Herbert *Spencer, was formulated in terms of the evolution and dissolution of the nervous system and is perhaps the most thoroughgoing attempt to explain the breakdown of neurological functions along evolutionary lines.

Jackson's most important contributions were to the study of *epilepsy and *aphasia. As regards the former, he was the first to appreciate that the sequence of involuntary movements which characterizes focal epilepsy indicates the spatial layout of excitable foci in the motor cortex. This brilliant inference was confirmed soon after by the experiments of David Ferrier and others, who demonstrated in animals that electrical stimulation of individual cortical foci elicit discrete bodily movements. Jackson was also the first to describe perceptual illusions and other dream-like states of consciousness evoked by focal epileptic discharges in the temporal lobes. These have since been fully studied by Wilder *Penfield.

In his work on aphasia, Jackson laid great stress on the fact that the disorder is an affection of language rather than merely one of speech. In his view, aphasia is essentially an intellectual deficit marked by inability to formulate propositions, rather than by failure to recall individual words. He further pointed out that words or phrases may on occasion be uttered under stress of emotion when they cannot be spoken voluntarily. (See also LANGUAGE: NEUROPSYCHOLOGY.)

Although in agreement with Paul *Broca that aphasia almost invariably results from damage to the left cerebral hemisphere, Jackson suggested that visual and spatial disabilities might bear a comparable relation to the right cerebral hemisphere. Though long ignored, this idea of cerebral asymmetry of function has been widely accepted in contemporary neuropsychology.

Jackson's *Selected Papers* (2 vols, ed. James Taylor, 1931) is an indispensable source of his writings. His papers on aphasia were republished by Sir Henry Head in *Brain* (1915) **38**.          O. L. Z.

**JAMES,** WILLIAM (1842–1910). A towering scholar, talented communicator, individualist, celebrity in his day, and a warmly empathic man who inspired genuine affection and respect. His personal charm shows through his writings, most of which follow closely the spoken lectures he gave to students and intelligent non-specialists. His greatest work, the two-volume *Principles of Psychology* (1890), is still fresh and informative. Probably the best-known book in all psychology, it is a treasure-house of ideas and finely turned phrases which psychologists continue to plunder with profit.

James was an American who, for most of his adult life, was associated with Harvard, where he graduated in medicine and taught successively physiology, psychology, and philosophy. He was also very much a European. He first visited Europe before his second birthday, and almost every year of his life spent some time there, occasionally staying for a year or two at a stretch. He was fluent in German and French, competent in Italian, and personally acquainted with most of the leading intellectuals of his time, ranging from Ralph Waldo Emerson to Sigmund *Freud and Bertrand *Russell. His brother, the novelist Henry James (1843–1916), settled in England, where he, the novelist who wrote like a psychologist, often received William, the psychologist who wrote like a novelist. Both brothers were fascinated by the problem of expressing in words the phenomena of individual consciousness. Henry approached the problem through novels which exhibited the subtle uniqueness and partiality of individual people's perspectives. William approached the problem through psychology.

William was born in New York, the eldest of five children whose education was unconventional. His father, a brilliant conversationalist and writer on theology, enjoyed a large inherited fortune which enabled him to devote his time to travelling, meeting interesting people, and educating his children. Wherever father went, his wife and children went also, accompanied by a variable entourage of relatives, friends, and servants. The children were actively encouraged to absorb their surroundings, talk about their experiences, read, write, and paint. This lively nomadic troupe lodged in hotels and rented houses on both sides of the Atlantic. They everlastingly engaged in wide-ranging, self-analytic discussions which, often shared by visiting celebrities, dominated Jamesian life and education.

William was educated by short-stay tutors and brief attendances at private schools, but mainly by his father and family. The upshot was that he developed a formidably heterogeneous repertoire of academic, social, linguistic, and artistic talents. Between the ages of 18 and 30 he continued further studies and intensive programmes of private reading. He also became increasingly perturbed about what to do with his life. He was torn among so many possibilities. He suffered bouts of depression and neurotic malady, and family letters spoke of his 'ill health', 'the choice of a profession', and 'the awful responsibility of such a choice'.

At 18 he started training as a painter. He later switched to the study of science, then to medicine. Even after deciding on medicine he had doubts, and interrupted his studies to go on a geological expedition to Brazil and, again, to spend a year in Germany. He travelled in Europe in 1867-8, graduated MD from Harvard in 1869, and thereafter entered a period of black despair and took a decisive step toward resolving his existential crisis. This step averted suicide and began to heal what he later called his 'sick soul'; it also contained themes which he explored for the rest of his life and which dominated his mature work. On 30 April 1870, he wrote as follows in his private diary.

Yesterday was a crisis in my life. I finished the first part of Renouvier's 2nd Essay and saw no reason why his definition of free will—'the sustaining of a thought *because I choose to* when I might have other thoughts'—need be the definition of an illusion. My first act of free will shall be to believe in free will. For the remainder of the year, I will abstain from mere speculation and contemplative *Grübelei* [musing] in which my nature takes most delight, and voluntarily cultivate the feeling of moral freedom. . . . Today has furnished the exceptionally passionate initiative which Bain posits as needful for the acquisition of habits. . . . Now, I will go a step further with my will, not only act with it, but believe as well; believe in my individual reality and creative power. My belief to be sure can't be optimistic—but I will posit life, (the real, the good) in the self-governing resistance of the ego to the world.

Once his self-administered, existentialist cure began to work, he returned to Harvard, where he was offered a post as a teacher of physiology. He accepted and, at the age of 30, began his career as a university teacher. In 1878 he married, happily, and subsequently children were born in whom he and his wife took delight. Also in 1878, he contracted to write a book based on the lectures he was giving on psychology. The book took twelve years to write but, when *Principles of Psychology* appeared, it established James as the foremost psychologist of the day. The opening pages plunged into the recurrent Jamesian themes of individuality, *choice, and *purpose. Each of us is, within the limits of our biological potential and environmental circumstances, forever pursuing purposes, long-term and short-term, by making choices, great and small, which cumulatively shape every aspect of our individual being. As James said elsewhere, 'Sow an action, and you reap a habit; sow a habit, and you reap a character; sow a character, and you reap a destiny.'

These themes ran through all James's work. In *The Varieties of Religious Experience* (1902), he examined the biographies of people who reported a belief 'that there is an unseen order, and that our supreme good lies in harmoniously adjusting ourselves thereto'. Such beliefs were subjective, but none the less real to the experiencer, and they had manifest effects on the individual's conduct. When such effects were 'good', he argued, the individual was right to exercise the 'will to believe', although not to insist that others share the same belief. James's contributions to the philosophy of pragmatism were in the same vein. In brief, any hypothesis was true if the consequences of holding it were satisfactory to the individual concerned. The truth of which he spoke was not absolute but relative to each individual. The 'pluralistic and unfinished universe' had undiscovered potentialities which different individuals might make actual through the hypotheses they held, the choices they made, and the purposes they pursued.

Between 1878 and 1899, James vigorously enjoyed work, family life, and social life. He travelled, attended conferences, lectured, kept up a massive correspondence, and took unassuming pleasure in his growing international fame. In 1899 he suffered the first of many attacks of angina, which progressively impeded his vigour even though he still continued a formidable round of activities. On 11 August 1910, he and his wife left Henry James's home at Rye in England and made what William knew to be his last Atlantic crossing. He died in America fifteen days later.

During his life, James fostered much psychological discussion and enquiry; but he was precluded, by his artistic sensitivity to the many-sidedness of the human condition, from adopting any one view as final. His popular lectures inspired many people with a new sense of human worth and dignity; but he himself was never entirely free from bouts of depression. In 1875 he established at Harvard a laboratory for psychological experiment (see LABORATORIES OF PSYCHOLOGY); but he himself had insufficient patience to conduct experiments, make measurements, or use statistics. He was consistently protean.

His pluralistic vision is evident in the brilliant perceptiveness, intuitiveness, and inconsistency of the *Principles*. The book presents, in masterly language, a wealth of naturalistic observation about human behaviour and conscious experience, culled partly at first hand and partly from wide reading. It contains sharp intellectual analyses in which issues are turned over critically and open-mindedly. It makes clear that psychology concerns, and is of concern to, the lives of individual people. It is exploratory, not consistently scientific in spirit, and arrives at no coherent theory of psychology. However, it widens horizons and raises issues that have, in the twentieth century, been approached scientifically. It raises many issues that still challenge scientific enquiry.

See also EMOTION.                          I. M. L. H.

Allen, G. W. (1967). *William James: a biography*. London.

James, W. (1890). *Principles of Psychology* (2 vols.). New York.

James, W. (1907). *Pragmatism: A New Name for Some Old Ways of Thinking*. New York.

**JAMES–LANGE THEORY OF EMOTION.** See EMOTION.

**JAMI** (Mulla Nuruddin 'Abdurrahman ibn-Ahmad, 1414–92). Jami, who was born in Jam, Khurasan, and died in Herat, modern Afghanistan, is often called the last great classical poet of the Persian language. He was a most prolific writer and a great scholar, as well as being a mystic of the Naqshbandiyya ('Designers') School of *Sufis. For him, God alone is absolute truth, and human duty is to reach this truth through love. In his *Lawa'ih* (Flashes) are the short utterances which encapsulate his teaching, while *Nahfat al-Uns* (Fragrances of Companionship) is a considerable work treating of the lives of 611 male and female Sufi sages. His *Silsilat al-Dhahab* (Chain of Gold) resembles *Sanai's *Walled Garden*, and his *Baharistan* (Land of Spring) may have been suggested by Saadi's *Rose Garden*. In personality he was remarkably straightforward and free from cant, and he expected this behaviour in others: the traditional Naqshbandi attitude. His sense of humour was remarkable. When he was on his death-bed and Koran-readers had been brought in, he exclaimed: 'What is all this commotion—can't you see that I am dying?'                I. S.

Browne, E. G. (1964). *A Literary History of Persia.* Cambridge.

Davis, F. H. (1967). *Jami, the Persian Mystic*. Lahore.

**JANET,** PIERRE (1859–1947). Pierre Janet must rank with the handful of thinkers, including William *James and Wilhelm *Wundt, who established psychology as a discipline. Yet nowadays in Britain and America he is acknowledged merely as a contributor to early psychiatric studies of *hysteria. Remarkably little is known of his ideas, although many of them have passed into common usage. His systematic theorizing is ignored, and none of the current standard English-language textbooks in experimental, clinical, cognitive, or personality psychology makes more than a passing reference to his work. Even histories of psychology and medicine refer to him only as a 'pupil' of J. M. *Charcot who studied hypnotism in relation to hysterical phenomena (see HYPNOTISM, HISTORY OF). Such accounts fail to recognize Janet's work in many other fields, his encyclopaedic scholarship, his meticulous and subtle clinical observations, his intellectual stature, and the originality of his theorizing.

What went wrong? How is it that a great psychologist, who received international acclaim in his lifetime, should now be virtually ignored by English-speaking psychologists and psychiatrists? There are a number of plausible reasons—his most interesting works have never been translated into English, and several of his major propositions have been misunderstood. It is also generally recognized that his work was overshadowed by the more dramatic and controversial propositions of his contemporary, Sigmund *Freud.

Probably a more important reason is that Janet failed to establish a school of followers who might have propagated and developed his approach. To understand why this was so involves some examination of his career. In one sense, this is a story of sparkling and untrammelled success. But closer consideration suggests that it may be viewed as an interesting case-study in the subtleties of academic and professional power politics. It is also replete with sad ironies. Janet was the product of the reigning intellectual establishment of his youth. But later he was to be the victim of departmental intrigue, as a new establishment took over. Similarly, his early research won him immediate recognition because of its contribution to an area which was preoccupying the thinkers of the time. His later studies far transcended this, but when intellectual fashions changed he was stigmatized as a promulgator of outmoded thought. Lastly, he attained one of the most coveted academic positions in France. But this was destined to cut him off from any academic 'ground-roots' constituency.

Pierre Janet was born in Paris, where he was to remain for almost all of his long and active life. He came of an established, upper-middle-class family, his relatives being intellectuals and professional people. Throughout his career he was to maintain close contact with many of the leading intellectuals of metropolitan France. His immediate family was close and affectionate. He married Margaret Duchesne in 1894; they had three children, and remained happily married until Margaret's death in 1944. As a person, Janet was dignified and rather reserved but the possessor of a warm heart and dry wit.

Janet was educated at one of the oldest and most famous *lycées* in France, the Collège Sainte-Barbe. Despite a short depressive breakdown at the age of 15, he was successful in the intensely competitive admission examination for the École Normale Supérieure, which he entered in 1879.

'Normalians' were exempt from military service but were expected to teach for ten years. Thus, after graduating with distinction in 1882, Janet was posted to Châteauroux, but transferred after a few months to the more prestigious *lycée* of Le Havre, where he taught for the next six and a half years.

The person who exerted the most profound influence upon Janet's intellectual development was his uncle, Paul Janet the philosopher, who urged him to combine his study of philosophy with that of science and medicine. Thus Pierre Janet initially considered writing his doctoral thesis on the subject of hallucinations and perceptual mechanisms, and approached Dr Gibert, a local physician and psychiatrist, who was interested in 'animal magnetism' (see MESMERISM) and urged Janet to investigate hypnotic phenomena. He arranged for the young philosophy teacher to study a patient named Léonie, who had been a hypnotic subject in her youth (see also DISSOCIATION OF THE PERSONALITY).

The results of Janet's first series of experiments with Léonie were reported in a paper presented to the new Société de Psychologie Physiologique in Paris in November 1885. The paper was read by Paul Janet, and the meeting chaired by the Society's co-founder, the great Charcot. The findings were reported with admirable scientific caution. But they *could* be taken as evidence for hypnotism from a distance, which Janet deplored. Even so, the paper made a perfect match with the intellectual climate of the time and caused something of a sensation.

For the remainder of his period at Le Havre, Janet continued to study hysterical patients, being given facilities at the city hospital. His investigations were reported in a series of papers which formed the basis of his main doctoral thesis, *L'Automatisme psychologique*. This he successfully defended at the Sorbonne in 1889, and was appointed to a teaching position in Paris. At the same time he enrolled as a medical student, his studies being concurrent with his *lycée* teaching duties and the continuation of his research, much of which was carried out under Charcot's aegis. He graduated with distinction in 1893, and was promptly appointed by Charcot to direct a new experimental psychology laboratory at La Salpêtrière. Unfortunately, Charcot died only a few weeks later, to be succeeded by Fulgine Raymond, a neurologist not personally interested in neuroses, but who nevertheless continued to maintain the psychological laboratory and support Janet's researches. Janet also continued to teach philosophy until 1898, when he was appointed director of studies in experimental psychology at the Sorbonne.

In 1894 Janet published his textbook on philosophy. By the turn of the century he had published papers on a variety of psychological topics, and had established his reputation as a clinical teacher and outstanding expert on the neuroses. By then his interest had shifted from hysterical states to psychasthenia, a term he coined to cover what we would now call *anxiety states, *phobias, and *obsessional disorders. In 1898 he published *Névroses et idées fixes*, to be followed by *Les Obsessions et la psychasthénie* in 1903. Each of these was a massive work in which he developed a classification of the neuroses, together with an integrative theory which encompassed both hysteria and psychasthenia. These two books introduced, for the first time, terms and concepts such as 'dissociation', and 'narrowing of the field of consciousness', which are now in general use. Janet's distinction between hysteria and psychasthenia was directly responsible for the concepts of extraversion and introversion introduced by C. J. *Jung (who attended Janet's lectures in 1902–3 and made many references to him). Similarly, Alfred

*Adler's emphasis on inferiority feelings was directly derived from Janet's *Sentiment d'incomplétude*.

During this same period, Janet and his young colleague, Georges Dumas, were active in the establishment of a new international psychological society, and in 1904 the two men co-founded the *Journal de psychologie normal et pathologique*. In 1902, on the retirement of Theodule *Ribot, Janet was appointed professor of experimental and comparative psychology at the Collège de France, which he held until his own retirement in 1935. But despite the prestige of this appointment and the popularity of Janet's lectures, this post undoubtedly imposed constraints on his work and influence: Janet had no regular undergraduate or graduate students or research assistants. Furthermore, the Collège had no laboratories or clinics, and he was perforce obliged to rely for his case material on La Salpêtrière. Even this source disappeared when, after Raymond's death in 1910, internal political manœuvres led to the closure of the psychological laboratory, and with it the termination of Janet's hospital appointment and clinical teaching.

Janet's intellectual activity, however, continued unabated. He now devoted himself to developing a comprehensive psychological system taking account of normal, no less than abnormal, behaviour from childhood to old age. The general idea was that psychological function is hierarchically organized, with neurosis representing a reduction of integration. It was further postulated that optimal functioning requires an appropriate deployment of psychic energy: asthenia is to be regarded as an insufficiency of available 'psychological force', manifested in lassitude and feelings of inadequacy.

Janet then went on to define and analyse a more elaborate developmental hierarchy of increasingly complex levels of organization. At the most primitive level are the 'reflexive tendencies', which are unregulated and stimulus-bound. These are followed by 'tendencies' which reflect adaptation of an elementary kind, and these in turn by interactional social adaptations. The 'elementary intellectual tendencies' are at the level where actions develop into thinking: language, symbolic thought, and memory are beginning to develop. The next two levels involve the development of language, attitudes, and beliefs at the pre-logical stage. The final three 'tendencies' start with the growth of voluntary control, perseverance, and the function of work. These are followed by the development of value systems, the capacity for logical thought, and the achievement of self-identity, coupled with a responsive awareness of the needs of others. Abnormal behaviour and neurotic states are seen as failures to integrate 'tendencies' at an appropriate level; the individual may regress to, or be fixated at, an earlier stage.

In his old age, Janet continued to be active and, after the completion of his vast re-conceptualization, he applied himself to the study of belief and the development of a theory of conduct. He devoted much time to the revision and preparation for publication of his lectures at the Collège de France. The lectures appeared in the form of six major books between 1928 and 1937; none of them, unfortunately, was translated into English.

Unless the English student can read French with ease, it is very difficult for him to familiarize himself with Janet's thought or even capture the flavour of his writing. The small number of Janet's works which have been translated into English are not at all representative, and in any case they, like all his books, have long been out of print. His best-known books are *L'Automatisme psychologique* (1892), *Les Névroses* (1905), *The Major Symptoms of Hysteria* (15 lectures delivered at the Harvard Medical School, 1907), *Psychological Healing* (translated by Eden and Cedar Paul, 2 vols. 1925), and *L'Évolution de la mémoire et de la notion du temps* (1929).                                G. F. R.

Ellenberger, H. F. (1970). *The Discovery of the Unconscious*. New York. (An excellent biography of Janet with a scholarly summary of his theories appears as chapter 6.)

Ey, H. (1968). In Wolman, B. B. (ed.), *Historical Roots of Contemporary Psychology*. New York. (A brief biographical note, with a good account of Janet's work from the psychiatric viewpoint.)

May, E. (1952). *The Psychology of Pierre Janet*. London. (An introduction to some of Janet's ideas.)

## JAPANESE CONCEPT OF MIND: TRADITIONAL VIEWS.

The idea, associated with Lucien Lévi-Bruhl and E. B. Tylor, that primitive humanity passed through a pre-logical phase is no longer generally accepted. 'We now know that this is not how the most primitive of men behave; they have minds and reasons of their own' (G. S. Kirk, *The Nature of Greek Myths*, 1974, p. 74). Like the *Logos* of Heraclitus, reason is common to all mankind. There are no human communities which repudiate logical inference as the basis of their thinking, though the stages of the syllogism may be differently set out, as in the Nyaya doctrine (*darshana*) of Vedanta, and even though the exposition of a doctrine or myth may appear incoherent. But differences of mentality clearly exist. In order to understand the Japanese character and outlook, it is important to grasp certain tendencies for which Western psychology offers no parallels. One is summed up in the word *amae*, or 'dependency wish', i.e. the need felt by the average Japanese for psychological support not merely in childhood but at the adult stage, differentiating him in this respect from the Westerner, who strives for ever greater independence or individuality. (See Doi Takeo, *The Anatomy of Dependence*, a translation of his *Amae no kōzō*.) Secondly, there is the fundamental distinction in Japanese psychology between *omote* and *ura* (literally 'front' and 'rear'), namely 'outward thoughts' and 'innermost thoughts': what is said in public and what is thought in private. (See Doi Takeo, '*Omote* and *Ura*: concepts

derived from the Japanese two-fold structure of consciousness'—*Journal of Nervous and Mental Disease*, **157** (1973), 4, 258–61.) Such behavioural characteristics must entail in the end a different outlook on the world, a particular *Weltanschauung*. Again, if you believe that everything in nature possesses its own special divinity, your pantheon will tend to be overcrowded. Thus the ancestral religion of the Japanese, Shinto ('the way of the Gods') moulded their character, conditioned their everyday behaviour, and laid the basis for their view of the nature of mind or spirit. Indeed, *ura* was one of the ancient words for 'mind', though today the mental realm is conveyed by *kokoro*. And despite the growth of secularism, the Japanese still show the influence of these traditional beliefs.

An important clue to the Japanese understanding of the mind is the fact that in Japan there has been, until modern times, no tradition of thought comparable to the Western philosophical tradition from the time of *Socrates and *Plato. The Japanese tradition is mythico-religious. Although the origin of the Japanese as a race is still a matter of dispute, it is reasonable to suppose that Shinto developed in the Japanese archipelago, possibly from the fourth century. But during the sixth century—the key date is considered to be either AD 534 or 552—the influence of a 'higher religion', Buddhism, began to make itself felt. Buddhism was disseminated by missionary effort and by sponsored delegations from China and Korea. Despite the multiplication of Buddhist sects and a gradual accommodation with Shinto (the founder of the Shingon sect, Kukai or Kobo Daishi, maintained that the more exalted Shinto gods were incarnations of Buddhas), this faith of Indian origin influenced the Japanese character no less profoundly than did Shinto itself. For many centuries, most works of religious exegesis were written in Chinese, which, like Greek in the Occident, was pre-eminently the 'classic' language. Of Chinese origin likewise were Taoism and the *ethic* of Confucius, the impact of which should not be underestimated. Finally, the Christianizing work of the remarkable Spaniard, Francis Xavier (1506–52), though later subject to pitiless persecution, proved in many respects so durable that, with the provision of a measure of freedom of belief after the Meiji Restoration of 1868—see Muraoka Tsunetsugu, *Studies in Shintō Thought* (Japanese National Commission for UNESCO, 1964), pp. 227–8—many 'underground' Christians emerged into the open, especially in the Nagasaki area. Behind the Japanese tradition, therefore, lies China, and behind that India, with a distinct Christian influence first felt in the seventeenth century and renewed in the nineteenth.

It is not uncommon for a Japanese to profess several faiths at once. And even a Japanese who declares himself a total unbeliever—as a great many do today—may merely be displaying reluctance to subscribe to a particular creed or set of dogmas; for in any case he prefers non-verbal modes of communication. Indeed, his intense cult of aesthetic values, which has probably gained strength in an industrial society, may be his way of honouring the 'sacred' in another form. The holiness of beauty is for him a substitute for the beauty of holiness.

Interpreted philosophically, Shinto, though the least philosophical or theological of religions, implied a form of pantheism or pan-psychism. Although the world of the gods (*kami*) was an invisible world outside the spatio-temporal dimension, it had 'ingression'—to employ Whitehead's term—in terrestrial affairs. Of individuality, the human being enjoyed little: there is a Japanese proverb, 'A nail that sticks out will be hit hard'. The community, possessing a kind of group mind, took precedence; and the group mind, animated by *tatemae* or 'consensus', submitted at every moment to the influence and intervention of the countless divinities of the celestial hierarchy.

By contrast, Buddhism and Christianity tended to make a direct appeal to the individual conscience, where *ura* reigned; and Buddhism presupposed the existence of some kind of awareness at every level of creation. Among the voluminous Buddhist writings, one of the most attractive is that entitled *The Buddha's Law among the Birds* (trans. Edward Conze, 1955); and, according to Kukai, even trees and plants could attain to Buddhahood—the processes of budding, growing, yielding, and dying corresponded to aspiration, training, enlightenment, and nirvana. (See Sakamoto Yukio, 'On the "attainment of Buddhahood by trees and plants"'—*Proceedings of the Ninth International Congress for the History of Religions*, Tokyo, 1960, pp. 416–17.) In preaching the need to extinguish the blind life-instinct—sometimes called craving or attachment—and to discharge the accumulated burden of karma (a Sanskrit word meaning 'action' or 'fate') which had 'fed' that instinct, the Buddha was presupposing the traditional Hindu doctrine of rebirth; for only after the shedding of the karmic load was entry into nirvana possible. Where the Buddha's teaching differed from that of the tradition, and also from Western conceptions, was in his view of the mind or soul. (It is important to stress that the Buddha's sayings, as reported, are highly and no doubt deliberately ambiguous on this as on many other fundamental matters—see Bahm, A. J., *Philosophy of the Buddha*, 1958, ch. 10, 'Soul or no soul?', pp. 122–30.) The so-called Wheel of Becoming started from ignorance, which gave rise to desire-attachment; but although that which moved through this cycle was endowed with consciousness (*vijñāna*), it was not an ego-entity, or indeed an entity at all, but rather a psychic process (see Allen, G. F., *The Buddhist Philosophy*, 1959, pp. 40–3); and so the succession of rebirths was intended to lead to that form of enlightenment which entailed a total awakening from psychic sleep, with its tormenting dreams. Indeed, the word Buddha means the 'Enlightened' or 'Awakened' One. At the same time, this condition of spiritual awareness, which certain sects held to be attainable in a single lifetime, represented a final liberation from individuality and the merging in nirvana. It is often stressed that the doctrine or *dharma* preached by the Buddha was practical rather than metaphysical: 'Buddhism teaches the practical means of remolding the mind' (Kishimoto Hideo, 'The Meaning of Religion to the Japanese People', *Religious Studies in Japan*, edited by the Japanese Association for Religious Studies, Tokyo, 1959, p. 23). But in due course Buddhist teaching, especially as elaborated in the Mahayana or 'Great Vehicle', came to erect a system of metaphysical ideas of extreme refinement. No longer an atheistic creed, Mahayana theology elaborated the idea of the three bodies of the Buddha: the *Nirmānakāya*, or historical body of Gautama that existed on earth; the *Sambhogakāya*, or the transfigured body existing in paradise; and the *Dharmakāya*, or the transcendent, cosmic Buddha body, which was identical with ultimate reality itself. (Eliot, 1935, pp. 113–14. Certain sects, e.g. the Kegon, distinguished ten bodies of the Buddha.) Being above or outside all categories, this Buddha of Essence was apprehensible not by reason but by intuition (Eliot, p. 45). Such a faculty, in fact, was higher than that of reason—not supplementary or inferior to it, as in Western notions. Indeed, intuitive knowledge in this sense was identical with intellectual knowledge in the traditional sense. Another name for it might be 'unitive' knowledge or what J. H. Newman seems to have been striving to convey by his idea of the 'illative' sense (*An Essay in Aid of a Grammar of Assent*, 1870, ch. 9). Now such knowledge, the attainment of which presupposed prolonged meditation, involved, at its highest reach, 'oneness' with its object, that is to say, identification with the Buddha nature, the concept of which is common to all the Mahayana sects except the Amidist ones.

This conception of the structure of the mind as composed of (i) psyche, (ii) reason, and (iii) (intellectual) intuition was similar at base to that of the Hindu tradition, in the context of which Buddhist theology was of course elaborated; and as scholars such as René Guénon (in his *Introduction to the Hindu Scriptures*, London, 1954) have pointed out, it was a view expounded by *Aristotle in the Posterior Analytics* and part of the *Metaphysics*. And Aristotle too believed in the final identification of knower and known. Indeed, such identification was abandoned in the West only with the disintegration of Scholastic philosophy, the exaltation of *ratio* as the highest mental faculty—the instrument of mathematico-physical science—and the loss of the concept of intellect as a spiritual faculty.

Admittedly, such considerations on the nature of mind entered hardly at all into the everyday thoughts of the ordinary man. Nor were they entertained by most Buddhist priests, who concerned themselves chiefly with the performance of ritual, including the highly stylized reading of the *sutras*, and the doing of good works. Similarly, the visitor to an Indian temple, with its milling devotees and animal sacrifices, will see no obvious connection between what is going on and the recondite doctrines of the Upanishads. And in Amidism—a simple theism in which the devotee needed merely to call upon the name of Amida for salvation—the ordinary man and woman found a non-intellectual faith which they could easily grasp. (This was *Jōdo*, or Pure Land Buddhism, which began to flourish in Japan towards the end of the twelfth century.) But this is precisely where the Oriental distinction between esoteric and exoteric—inner and outer, *shruti* and *smriti*—knowledge applies. To speak of the philosophy, still less the theology, of Buddhism is misleading, since, as already implied, 'the purpose of Buddhist doctrine is to release beings from suffering, and speculations concerning the origin of the universe are held to be immaterial to that task' (Conze, 1951, p. 39). Nevertheless, the Mahayana is a metaphysical teaching of such comprehensiveness as to stand to Hinduism much as Christianity stands to Judaism; and its dependence for its basic metaphysical principles on Hinduism makes it easy to understand why many Hindus regard the historical Buddha as an *Avatara*, i.e. a divine manifestation, and in fact the ninth incarnation of Vishnu.

The Christian missions of the sixteenth and early seventeenth centuries introduced Christian theology to many Japanese, and even to some of the Ainu aborigines of the northern island of Hokkaido; but the Meiji Restoration of 1868 opened the floodgates of Western thought. True to form, the intellectually curious Japanese seized on what was novel, iconoclastic, and supposedly scientific. Thus the French positivists and the British utilitarians were greatly in demand, and later the German idealists. To the Japanese intelligentsia, Herbert *Spencer became as much a hero as he did to the 'interpreter' of Japan to the West, Lafcadio Hearn. (Spencer had in fact expressed the hope, in a letter to a Japanese baron, that Japan would continue her two-hundred-year isolation, or *sakoku*—see the Appendix of Hearn's *Japan: an Interpretation*, 1904.) Consequently, the philosophy taught in Japanese universities is now largely Western, and some Japanese have mastered this so successfully as to be able to teach it in Europe and America. On the other hand, there have been philosophers such as Nishida Kitaro (1870–1945) who have sought to combine schools of Buddhism such as Zen (virtually a blend of the Mahayana and Taoism) with Western thought, though this has resulted in some obscurity, not least because of the inherent ambiguity of the Japanese language. (See Nishida's early work, *A Study of Good*, 1904, Japanese National Commission for UNESCO, 1960.) The Japanese founder of Zen was Eisai (1141–1215), who also originated the mind-calming tea ceremony.

Through concentrating on paradoxes or *kōans*, Zen forms a technique for disciplining the mind for the purpose of attaining *satori*, or sudden illumination; and its apparent use of irrational means has endeared it to Westerners in revolt against rationalism. What its vogue seems to reflect, however, is that philosophy in the Orient is at heart not a matter of abstract speculation or analysis, but an experience, designed to bring with it enlightenment and knowledge. Whereas in the Occident the mind is treated primarily as an engine of perception and cognition, the Oriental regards his mental faculties as in need of training for the purpose of achieving, at best, a condition of what the Buddhists call 'self-luminous thought'. This condition is sometimes rather unhelpfully called 'emptiness', because the word nirvana literally means 'the extinction of breath or of disturbance'; but we should treat such a description as on a par with St John of the Cross's paradoxical 'ray of darkness': in short, nirvana is a condition of supra-individual 'fullness'. See Guénon's remarks on Buddhism in his *Man and his Becoming according to the Vedanta* (London, 1945), p. 173.

See also JAPANESE CONCEPT OF MIND: THE NEW RELIGIONS.                                    E. W. F. T.

The literature of Buddhism is so extensive and in many instances so recondite that a short reading-list is extremely difficult to compile. The following works are recommended for their comprehensive character:

Conze, E. (1951). *Buddhism, its Essence and Development*. London.

Eliot, Sir C. (1935). *Japanese Buddhism*. London.

Murti, T. R. V. (1959). *The Central Philosophy of Buddhism*. London.

Suzuki, D. T. (1948). *Introduction to Zen Buddhism*. London.

For Shinto, understood in its relation to Japanese culture, Tomlin, E. W. F. (1973), *Japan* (London) may be consulted.

For a general study and analysis of the Japanese character and mentality, Hajime, N. (1960), *Ways of Thinking of Eastern Peoples* (Japanese National Commission for Unesco, Tokyo) may be recommended.

## JAPANESE CONCEPT OF MIND: THE NEW RELIGIONS.

The catastrophic débâcle of Japan, which brought the Pacific War to an end in 1945, proved as much a psychological blow as a material disaster. According to the official 'myth', the Japanese people were descended from the gods—and ultimately from the sun goddess, Amaterasu Omikami—and they were in consequence invincible. A country accustomed to earthquakes was no stranger to physical destruction; but defeat inflicted by a people considered to be hardly less barbaric than the Mongols, who had *failed* in their onslaught on the coast of Kyushu in the thirteenth century, had been considered unthinkable. Consequently, in announcing his decision to surrender, the Emperor enjoined his people, in a familiar idiomatic phrase, to 'bear the unbearable'. Even today, the resulting shock has not worked its way out of the Japanese psyche. Moreover, the proximate cause of the breaking of the will to fight was the use by the Allies of a weapon involving the release of a particular form of *pollution*. And pollution (*tsumi*), defilement, or taint of any sort is something to which the Japanese have a particular aversion.

Much of the ritual of Shinto was concerned with lustral purification. When in the aftermath of defeat this ancestral religion lost a good deal of its hold—for it had become virtually a state religion, and the state had been in many ways discredited—and when Buddhism, too, suffered the fate of a higher religion which had seemingly failed its adherents, a communal psychic vacuum was created. Admittedly, since adherence to Shinto was all but compulsory, and since every family was obliged to be registered at a Buddhist temple, the nominal worshippers greatly exceeded in number the true believers; but even when, after the war and in consequence of the liberal provisions of the 'American' constitution, people were free to admit their unorthodoxy or their lack of religious belief, the mental release was often less than might have been expected, because the psychological *needs* previously met by the traditional faiths were still clamant. Nor could humanism or rationalism or the pursuit of material prosperity effectively satisfy them. It was at this critical juncture that the *Shinkō-shūkyō*, or 'new religious cults', either spontaneously arose or came into their own.

There had been a similar uprush of religious emotion in the 1920s. Some of the cults, then and later, were quite obviously bogus. General MacArthur's Religious Bodies Law of 1945, exempting religious organizations from taxation, caused hurried registrations from bodies such as restaurants and old clothes shops purporting to have a religious 'dimension' (see Blacker, 1975, p. 336). Even so, the number of new cults in present-day Japan runs to several hundreds (see Thomson, 1963; McFarland, 1967).

Although it is sometimes asserted that the Japanese lack religious instinct, the facts would suggest otherwise. Such apparent indifference as there is may be due to the absence in their lives of any fixed boundary between the sacred and the secular; it is to this distinction that they are indifferent. The success of the new cults is an indication of a permanent need to 'lean on' a *guru* in the 'dependency attitude' defined by the hardly translatable word *amaeru* (noun, *amae*: see JAPANESE CONCEPT OF MIND: TRADITIONAL VIEWS). The *shaman* (originally a Sanskrit word) or the sibyl (*miko*) fulfilled this function in ancient society, beginning perhaps with the mysterious virgin queen, Pimiko or Himiko, who is spoken of in the ancient chronicles. And it is a role which, still openly played in certain remote regions of Japan, may be exercised under various guises in more 'civilized' regions (cf. Blacker, 1975, ch. 6). If spiritual leadership were wielded by more than one empress (for example, the eighth-century Empress

Jingo), the sacred female role—surprising perhaps in a country otherwise male-dominated—could be assumed by far humbler individuals. Of these the most remarkable was undoubtedly Mrs Nakayama Miki (note that in Japanese the family name comes first), founder of the enormously successful cult of Tenrikyo (*tenri* = 'divine wisdom'). Born in poor circumstances in 1797, Miki acquired her first sense of mission in 1838 in a state of trance-like possession, during which she believed that her body had been 'occupied' by Ten-no-Shogun, god and saviour of mankind. Thenceforward so extraordinary were her actions and vatic declarations that a number of disciples, beginning with her bewildered husband, gathered round her and began to promote her teaching. Despite official persecution, her cult grew until, when she died in 1887 at the age of 90, it was recognized as a new and flourishing religion, though classified as a branch of Shinto. Her followers maintain that she is in the world as the 'parent' of mankind, and she is ceremonially put to bed every night in the huge temple at Tenri.

Tenrikyo remains the largest and one of the most active of the Japanese new cults, with many adherents among the Japanese overseas communities and with some foreign disciples. Not long after Miki embarked upon her mission, another poverty-stricken woman, Deguchi Nao (1837–1918), falling into a trance and declaring herself to be possessed by the god Ushitora-no-Konjin, received a similar summons to lead mankind to salvation. Out of this experience grew the Omoto ('teaching of the great origin') cult. Both Nao and Miki produced extensive 'scriptures', some of them apparently by automatic writing. Although many religious leaders were women (who nevertheless often attracted to their side a capable male administrator), the leader of the powerful Sekai Meshiakyo or 'World Messianity' sect, now about 700,000 strong, was Okada Mokichi, born in 1882. This strange man, who was at first a failure as well as a chronic invalid, announced that he was 'possessed' by Kannon, the goddess of mercy: thereafter he developed extraordinary psychic powers as well as the gift of healing.

Another more recent clamant claimant to divine status was Kitamura Sayo (b. 1900), foundress of the so-called 'Dancing Religion' (Tensho Kotai Jingukyo), who declared in 1944 that her body was inhabited by a snake. This creature not merely gave her commands, but inspired the homilies and songs which, without her bidding, poured from her lips and also the dance which her followers still perform. These followers today number something like 350,000, and they regard Kitamura Sayo as a true successor of the Buddha and of Christ.

Many of the cults place emphasis upon happiness and contentment in this world. To that extent they diverge from 'pessimistic' religions such as Buddhism, even in the case of cults with Buddhist affiliations, such as the well-known Soka Gakkai, with its political wing of Komeito, and also

Reiyukai, another cult founded by a woman, Kotani Kimi. Most of the others betray blends of all the higher religions, particularly Christianity. All stress the need for ritual purity. Indeed, the general aim seems to be to effect in their disciples a kind of psychic spring-clean, by expelling evil forces from the unconscious in order to achieve 'peace of mind'. In Japan, the extraordinary phenomenon called 'fox possession' was formerly an indication of the presence of some psychic obstruction: and just as in the field of psychiatry the patient can sometimes produce precisely the symptoms—such as dreaming the dreams—expected of him, what was formerly considered to be 'possession' by an animal might today be interpreted in terms more in keeping with psychoanalytical thinking. But even so, the Japanese psyche seems to have resisted psychoanalytical investigation more than that of the West, possibly owing to the strength of the 'dependency relationship' which would otherwise be undermined. The fact remains that psychic 'possession' of some kind, whether by another creature or by 'voices', seems a good deal commoner in Japan than in Western countries. Consequently, in the rural areas, the shaman or the ascetic is still much in demand, whereas these figures have no equivalent in the West save in the few ecclesiastically-licensed exorcists or freelance faith-healers.

We may sum up the significance of the *Shinkō-shūkyō* by reaffirming that the Japanese have traditionally regarded the mind not as an engine of perception and cognition, but as the psycho-spiritual part of the person which seeks identification with ultimate reality. If some of the new cults strive to achieve this identification by rather superficial means—for example, by the emotional and to some extent hypnotic appeal of mass gatherings—this may be due to their simplistic view of 'the end of life'. As with Aristotle—in the *Metaphysics* at least, and in that part of the *Metaphysics* which is concerned with 'being as such'—knowledge is an experience, not the accumulation of information. Granted, there are Japanese philosophers who, following the Western empiricists in their early and latterly in their linguistic form, believe in the identity of the mind and the brain—the one being an epiphenomenon of the other—and who consider philosophy not as an experience, leading to enlightenment, but as 'linguistic analysis' (not that some analytic thinking would come amiss on occasion). But this is mainly due to the tendency for the academic world in Japan to assume an attitude of excessive veneration for whatever happens in the West, and particularly in the Anglo-Saxon countries. Meanwhile, the cults undoubtedly meet a psycho-spiritual need which the decline of the higher religions has rendered all the more compelling. The persistence of such cults also raises for the student of mind the unsettled question of the nature of hypnotic and trance states, and of 'possession' by another 'self'—divine, daemonic, or

animal—to which other contributors to this volume have addressed themselves more directly. (See, in particular, DISSOCIATION OF THE PERSONALITY; HYPNOSIS, EXPERIMENTAL; HYPNOTISM, HISTORY OF; and MESMERISM.)                        E. W. F. T.

Blacker, C. (1975). *The Catalpa Bow: a study of shamanistic practices in Japan*. (London. Includes extensive bibliography.)
McFarland, N. (1967). *The Rush Hour of the Gods*. London.
Thomson, H. (1963). *The New Religions of Japan*. Tokyo.

**JASTROW,** JOSEPH (1863–1944). Polish perceptual psychologist, born in Warsaw and studied at John Hopkins University; became professor of pyschology at Wisconsin (1888–1927). He contributed to psychophysical methods, and wrote *Fact and Fable in Psychology* (1900), but he is remembered for his visually ambiguous figure, the duck–rabbit (see ILLUSIONS, Fig. 4a).

**JENNINGS,** HEBERT SPENCER (1868–1947). American zoologist, born at Tonica, Illinois; his studies of the behaviour of lower organisms, such as protozoa, convinced him that their reactions are too variable to find explanation in terms of mechanistic principles. He therefore promulgated the unfashionable view that mind extends to all levels of the evolutionary scale. His best-known book is *Contribution to the Study of the Lower Organisms* (1904). Jennings's views were strongly contested by the German-American zoologist Jacques *Loeb, who advocated a strictly mechanistic explanation of animal behaviour.

**JET LAG.** It is common experience that lengthy journeys involving time-zone changes (changes in longitude) are more disturbing than journeys of equal length where there is no local time change (journeys along one latitude). There is indeed very good evidence that disturbances of the rhythms of *sleep, digestion, and daily activity are unpleasant and impair performance, especially decision-taking; and that it takes several days to get into phase with the new diurnal cycle. This is, of course, a problem not only for airline crews and passengers, but also for people such as nurses working on night-shifts. It is likely that the disruption is not only of the sleep cycle but also of various *biological clocks, so that they become out of phase with each other. Whether this produces long-term or irreversible bodily damage, or mental impairment, is not known.

**JUNG,** CARL GUSTAV (1875–1961). Swiss psychologist, born at Kesswil, the son of a pastor of the Swiss Reformed Church; his paternal grandfather and great-grandfather were physicians. He enrolled at the University of Basle in 1895, where he took a degree in medicine, and then decided to specialize in psychiatry. In 1900 he went to the Burgholzli, the mental hospital and university psychiatric clinic in Zurich, where he studied under

Eugen Bleuler. It was while working at the Burgholzli that he published his first papers on clinical topics, and also a number of papers on the use of word-association tests, which he pioneered (see FREE ASSOCIATION). Jung concluded that through word association one can uncover constellations of ideas that are emotionally charged and give rise to morbid symptoms. The test worked by evaluating the patient in terms of the delay between the stimulus and his response, the appropriateness of the response word, and the behaviour exhibited. A significant deviation from normal indicated the presence of unconscious affect-laden ideas, and Jung coined the term 'complex' to describe this combination of the idea with the strong emotion it aroused.

In 1906, Jung published a study on dementia praecox, and this work was to influence Bleuler when he proposed the name *schizophrenia for the illness five years later. Jung hypothesized that a complex was responsible for the production of a toxin which impaired mental functioning and acted directly to release the contents of the complex into consciousness. Thus, the delusional ideas, hallucinatory experiences, and affective changes of the psychosis were to be understood as more or less distorted manifestations of the originally repressed complex. This, in effect, was the first psychosomatic theory of schizophrenia, and although Jung gradually abandoned the toxin hypothesis and thought more in terms of disturbed neurochemical processes, he never relinquished his belief in the primacy of psychogenic factors in the origin of schizophrenia.

By the time (1907) that Jung first met Sigmund *Freud in Vienna, he was well acquainted with Freud's writings, and from the success of this meeting there followed a close association until 1912. In the early years of their collaboration Jung defended Freudian theories, and Freud responded to this support from an unexpected quarter with enthusiasm and encouragement. In fact, at that time Freud felt the psychoanalytic movement to be isolated and under attack, and in 1908 wrote to another colleague: 'It is only his [Jung's] arrival on the scene that has removed the danger of psychoanalysis becoming a Jewish national affair.'

In 1910 Jung left his post at the Burgholzli to concentrate on his growing private practice and also began his investigations into myths, legends, and fairy-tales and the light that their contents threw on to psychopathology. His first writings on this theme were published in 1911 and indicated both an area of interest which was to be sustained for the rest of his life and an assertion of independence from Freud in their criticism of his classification of instincts as either self-preservative or sexual. Although Jung's dislike of the conceiving of the libido as essentially sexual was already apparent at this early stage, the significance became clear only much later, when he wrote about individuation. However, it was not only intellectual differences that led to the breach between Freud and Jung. Jung has recorded that he found Freud unduly concerned to preserve the tenets of psychoanalysis as articles of faith, immune from attack, and that this attitude diminished his respect for him. In fact, Jung's writings reveal that he too was prone to dogmatic assertions, but his fundamental assumptions run counter to those of Freud. Thus, while Freud, characteristically, established causal links stretching back to childhood which imply a mechanistic account of human behaviour, Jung was concerned to place man in a historical context which gave his life meaning and dignity and ultimately implied a place in a purposeful universe. In their later writings, both men became more concerned with social questions and also more metaphysical in the way they expressed their ideas. Thus Freud balanced the life-instinct against the death-wish, and Jung discussed the split in the individual between the ego and the shadow.

Whatever the factors involved, Jung records that after breaking with Freud he underwent a prolonged period of inner uncertainty. Although we are given glimpses of this episode in his writings, we do not have a detailed chronological account. It is clear, however, that the inner images, which he felt almost overwhelmed him, became the major inspiration both for his writings and for his clinical practice throughout the rest of his life.

The theme which unifies the large number of writings that Jung subsequently published is individuation, a process which he saw as taking place in certain gifted individuals in the second half of life. While he felt that Freud and Alfred *Adler had many valuable insights, he saw their field of interest as restricted to the problems that might be encountered during maturation. His particular concern was with those people who have achieved separation from their parents, an adult sexual identity, and independence through work, who may yet undergo a crisis in middle life. Jung conceived of individuation as being directed towards the achievement of psychic wholeness or integration, and in characterizing this developmental journey he used illustrations from alchemy, mythology, literature, and Western and Eastern religions, as well as from his own clinical findings. Particular signposts on the journey are provided by the archetypal images and symbols which are experienced, often with great emotional intensity, in *dreams and visions, and which as well as connecting the individual with the rest of mankind also point towards his own peculiar destiny. In his writings on the Collective Unconscious and the archetypal images which are its manifestation, it is clear that Jung feels that cultural spread cannot wholly account for the dissemination of mythological themes in dreams and visions. He writes of many patients who, while completely unsophisticated in such matters, describe dreams that exhibit striking parallels with myths from many different traditions. Indeed, Jung records an example from the time of the resolution of his own mid-life crisis. He had taken to painting representational pictures of his experiences, but under a new impulse began to paint abstract circular designs often divided into four or multiples of four. It was only later that he discovered that similar designs were found throughout the East, and that under the name 'mandala' were used as instruments of contemplation in Tantric Yoga. He came to see the mandala as an archetypal symbol of the self, the totality of which embraces not only the conscious but also the unconscious psyche. The appearance of the mandala symbol as a spontaneous psychic event is associated with the attempt to integrate the discordant elements within the personality at a time when disintegration is threatened.

However, there does seem to be a basic ambiguity in Jung's various descriptions of the Collective Unconscious. Sometimes he seems to regard the predisposition to experience certain images as understandable in terms of some genetic model. In effect he is doing no more than pass a normative judgement about the way human beings experience the world. But he is also at pains to emphasize the numinous quality of these experiences, and there can be no doubt that he was attracted to the idea that the archetypes afford evidence of communion with some divine or world mind. It is interesting to find that T. S. Eliot, who might himself be described as having experienced a mid-life crisis, wrote, 'We take it for granted that our dreams spring from below: possibly the quality of our dreams suffers in consequence.'

The latter part of Jung's life was relatively uneventful. He lived in Zurich, where he pursued private practice and also studied and wrote. It has been regretted that he left no detailed accounts of his clinical activities, although throughout his works there are scattered anecdotes from his professional experience as a psychotherapist. His great interest in religious questions is often treated as an embarrassment by practising psychotherapists, and certainly the problems with which he wrestles seem esoteric when compared with those encountered in a psychiatric out-patient clinic. Nevertheless, his popularity as a thinker derives from precisely this subject-matter and from his assurance that life is a meaningful adventure. He studied Eastern religions and philosophy, but saw himself as inescapably belonging to the Christian tradition although he was in no sense an orthodox believer. In a late work, *Answer to Job* (1952), he pictures Job appealing to God against God, and concludes that any split in the moral nature of man must be referred back to a split in the Godhead. The book is often obscure, and there is no easy solution to this problem, but in a letter he wrote subsequently about the book he said, 'I had to wrench myself free of God, so to speak, in order to find that unity in myself which God seeks through man. It is rather like that vision of Symeon, the Theologian, who sought God in vain everywhere in the world, until God rose like a little sun in his own heart.' Whereas Freud said, 'I have not the courage to rise up before my fellow men as a prophet and I bow to the reproach that I can offer them no consolation', Jung in contemplating the future found himself able to view the division in man as an expression of divine conflict. 'The outcome', he wrote, 'may well be the revelation of the Holy Ghost out of man himself. Just as man was once revealed out of God, so, when the circle closes, God may be revealed out of man.'

Such darkly impressive statements are common in Jung's writings. However, in his memoirs, which were written shortly before he died, he is more detached and agnostic and denies having any definite convictions. He concludes the book: 'The more uncertain I have felt about myself, the more there has grown up in me a feeling of kinship with all things. In fact, it seems to me as if that alienation which so long separated me from the world has become transferred into my own inner world, and has revealed to me an unexpected unfamiliarity with myself.' D. A. G. C.

Adler, G. (ed.) (1973). *C. G. Jung: Letters*. London.
Jacobi, J. (ed.) (1971). *C. G. Jung: Psychological Reflections, an anthology of his writings*. London.
Jung, C. G. (1953–71). *Collected Works*. London.
Jung, C. G. *Memories, Dreams, Reflections* (ed. A. Jaffe, 1967). London.
McGuire, W. (ed.) (1974). *The Freud/Jung Letters*. London.
Storr, A. (1973). *Jung*. London (Fontana Modern Masters series).

**JUST-NOTICEABLE DIFFERENCES.** Small changes of stimulus intensity (such as an increase in light or sound intensity) may go unnoticed, and in general will not be noticed unless the increase is greater than 1–2 per cent. The critical intensity change that is discriminated is known as the 'just-noticeable difference' (or 'j.n.d.'), and it may be called the 'threshold' of sensation. It was discovered by Ernst Heinrich *Weber that the just-noticeable difference increases in direct proportion with the stimulus intensity. Gustav *Fechner, having become interested in galvanism (see GALVANIC STIMULATION), turned to philosophy, and tried to relate physiology to psychology (in his *Elemente der Psychophysik*, 1860) by assuming just-noticeable differences to be equal units of sensations, over the entire intensity range, and so quantifying sensations as integrations of j.n.d.s. His arguments for measuring sensation, though ultimately unsound, essentially founded psychology as an experimental science.

See PSYCHOPHYSICS.

# K

**KANT, IMMANUEL** (1724–1804). German philosopher. Born in Königsberg, Prussia (since annexed by the USSR and renamed Kaliningrad), Kant never left the town and taught at the university there, where he became professor of logic and metaphysics in 1770. His earliest works were concerned with astronomy, and his great philosophical masterpiece, the *Critique of Pure Reason* (*Kritik der reinen Vernunft*) did not appear until 1781. This was followed by the *Critique of Practical Reason* (1788) and the *Critique of Judgement* (1790).

Kant gave the name 'transcendental idealism' to his philosophy (see IDEALISM); but in fact it is a brilliant and complex synthesis of rationalism and empiricism. On the one hand, he condemns the aspirations of the rationalists to ascend to a world of pure *a priori knowledge independently of the senses; on the other hand he rejects the empiricist notion that knowledge can be founded purely on sensory data. Kant argues that in order to experience the world at all the mind necessarily interprets it in terms of a certain structure; it is already armed with certain concepts of the understanding (*Verstandesbegriffe*). These concepts are derived from certain fundamental 'categories' (such as the category of substance and the category of causality); and the categories are a priori, not in the sense that they are independent of experience, but in the sense that they are presupposed by experience. In a complex chain of arguments called the 'Transcendental Deduction', Kant attempts to demonstrate the 'objective validity' of the categories. (See KANT'S PHILOSOPHY OF MIND).

In addition to his crucial and enduring contribution to the theory of knowledge, Kant was also highly influential in the field of ethics. In the *Groundwork of the Metaphysic of Morals* (1785), he puts forward his famous doctrine of the 'categorical imperative': 'Act only on that maxim through which you can at the same time will that it become a universal law.'                    J. G. C.

Bennett, J. (1966). *Kant's Analytic*. Cambridge.
Kant, I. (trans. Kemp Smith, N., 1929). *Critique of Pure Reason*. London.
Kant, I. *Groundwork of the Metaphysic of Morals*. Trans. in Paton, H. J., *The Moral Law*. London, 1948.
Kant, I. (trans. Lucas, P. G., 1983). *Prolegomena to any Future Metaphysics*. Manchester.
Scruton, R. (1982). *Kant*. Oxford.
Walker, R. C. S. (1978). *Kant*. London.

**KANT'S PHILOSOPHY OF MIND.** It is a commonplace that the character of our experience of the world, and hence the character of the world *as experienced by us*, while dependent in part on the nature of the objects we perceive, is also in part dependent on our own cognitive constitution, our physiological and psychological make-up. Experience is the causal outcome of objects affecting our constitution, and the causal mechanisms involved are matter for empirical investigation and discovery: the discovery of what it is about objects and about ourselves that makes them appear to us as they do. The distinctive feature of Kant's 'transcendental' philosophy is his transposition or transformation of this commonplace in such a way as to lift it out of the sphere of empirical investigation altogether.

Any empirical researcher, any natural scientist, takes as his field of investigation some aspect or selection of natural objects and events, located in space and occurring or persisting in time. Among these natural objects, of particular concern to biologists, psychologists, and physiologists, are our human selves. The scientist's business is to discover the laws of working which govern the behaviour and account for the characteristics of his selected objects. But those general features which constitute the very framework of such enquiries—the spatio-temporality of nature and the existence of discoverable law—are alike attributed by Kant to the constitution of the human mind; whence he contentedly draws the conclusion that empirical enquiry can yield us knowledge *only* of appearances—of the appearances that things present to beings constituted as we are. Of things as they are in themselves (including ourselves as we are in ourselves) experience and scientific investigation can yield no knowledge at all. The field of empirical enquiry is nature: but all the characteristics of natural things (including ourselves as natural objects) are thoroughly conditioned by features which have their source in the human subject.

Kant distinguishes two primary subjective sources of these features: the *sensibility* and the *understanding*. Sensibility is passive or receptive: it is the mind's capacity so to be affected by things as they are in themselves that mental contents or representations which Kant calls 'intuitions' or 'perceptions' are thereby generated. Within this receptive faculty of sensibility Kant distinguishes between 'inner' and 'outer' sense, saying that time is nothing but the form of the one and space nothing but the form of the other. The doctrine is that the temporal character of experience in general, and of its objects, and the possession by some intuitions of the character of spatiality which allows of their being so ordered as to count as perceptions of objects in space are due to the constitution of inner and outer sense respectively; and that, in particular, time, the form of inner sense, is the mode of ordering which results from the self-affection of ourselves as we are in ourselves. For, in addition to the passive or merely receptive faculty of sensibility, we have the active, affecting faculty of understanding. Understanding is the faculty which, acting on the sensibility, enables us to conceptualize our intuitions; and, more, it is the subjective source of those general principles of conceptualization (the Categories) which enable and require us so to conceptualize our intuitions as to give them the character of perceptions of a law-governed world of objects of which the governing laws are open to investigation by the methods of empirical science.

For this theory, as elaborated in the *Critique of Pure Reason*, Kant made great claims. He claimed that it provided the unique explanation of certain features of our empirical knowledge of nature (i.e. of the world of appearances), features which were necessary conditions of the very possibility of any such knowledge; that it supplied a salutary demonstration of the impossibility of theoretical knowledge of the supersensible realm of things as they are in themselves; and that, at the same time, it left room, not for theoretical knowledge, but for the morally based conviction that the requirements of moral responsibility and moral justice were somehow fulfilled in that realm inaccessible to our knowledge.

These claims we need not consider here. From the brief sketch given above, it seems hardly to be expected that Kant's transcendental theory of mind should have much in common with the firmly empirical theories current among psychologists and physiologists who concern themselves with the mind as a naturally given phenomenon; or, indeed, with the views of those philosophers of mind who concern themselves with the analysis or elucidation of the mental concepts which men and women employ in thinking about themselves and their fellows. When Kant speaks of the 'human mind' or of 'ourselves' as the subjective source of time, space, and the Categories, it seems that it must be of those mysteries, ourselves as we are in ourselves, that he is speaking and not of ourselves as we know ourselves; and when he distinguishes sensibility and understanding, we cannot take him as referring to such familiar objects of empirical study as sensory receptors and the day-to-day workings of human intelligence.

Kant distinguishes further faculties: notably that of imagination, which serves sense and understanding as their indispensable go-between, synthesizing the manifold and discrete data of sense in such a way as to make possible recognition of objects as falling under empirical concepts. In this doctrine of synthesis we may be tempted to find a near or remote analogue of some findings of empirical (including physiological) psychology.

But the qualification 'transcendental' standing before the phrase 'synthesis of imagination' should warn us to tread warily. The transcendental synthesis of imagination is not to be conceived as any kind of occurrent process which could be empirically studied. The doctrine is more intelligibly seen as reflecting an inescapable feature of sense-perception of a world of objects: the fact that we cannot, in general, veridically characterize even a momentary perception except by acknowledging that, for example, we see what we see *as* a dog, say, or *as* a tree—thus uniting, as it were, the instantaneous impression with other past or possible impressions (of the same object or of different objects of the same kind) which would similarly require, for *their* characterization, employment of the same general concept. This infusion or penetration of momentary sense-impressions by object-concepts which extend beyond (and 'combine') them, Kant saw as a necessary condition of experience of a world of objects; and thus he saw imagination as a necessary ('transcendental') mediator between sense, as merely receptive, and understanding as the faculty of concepts in general and in particular as the source of those very general a priori concepts (the Categories) which necessarily found a footing in experience in the use we make of our merely empirical concepts of types of object and event. (There are instructive parallels and contrasts to be drawn between Kant's doctrine of imagination and that of *Hume.)

To the faculty of 'reason' Kant assigns a role which includes, but goes beyond, those merely conceptualizing, judging, and generalizing operations of the understanding whereby empirical knowledge of nature is gained and extended. Reason typically demands more than this limited knowledge which always leaves room for further questions and thus is knowledge, as Kant puts it, only of the 'conditioned'; for reason sets before itself the ideal of ultimate explanations, of final and complete knowledge which would leave no room for further questions. In so far as this 'demand of reason for the unconditioned' encourages us to push our empirical researches in the direction of more and more comprehensive theories or into ever-remoter regions of the physical universe or of past time, its effect is wholly beneficial. But in so far as we are encouraged to believe that the demand can be met, that we can, by pure reasoning, attain knowledge of objects answering to reason's 'ideas' of the unconditioned, its effect is simply to generate illusion; for our knowledge is necessarily confined to the realm of experience, the realm of appearances, in which no such objects are to be found.

Rather less convincingly, Kant finds for pure reason a 'practical' role as the essential source and end of morality. He further suggests that though we are denied theoretical knowledge of the supersensible realm of things as they are in themselves, yet reason in its practical role may yield moral certainties, falling short of knowledge, regarding that realm. He argues that our recognition of the unconditional binding force of the moral law carries with it both a belief in freedom of the will—a power of free choice which we do not possess as natural beings subject to causal determination but may possess as we supersensibly are in ourselves—and a belief in the supersensible fulfilment of the demands of moral justice and hence in a supersensible divinity capable of securing the moral ideal.

A question naturally arises regarding the internal consistency of the 'critical' philosophy and in particular of the doctrines of 'transcendental idealism'. If the spatio-temporality and law-likeness of nature and all that is in it are to be attributed to a subjective source in the human mind, this source cannot be identified with the human mind as a part of nature, the topic of empirical psychology—a discipline which Kant rather dismissively describes as a kind of 'physiology of inner sense'. So when Kant speaks of *our* sensibility and *our* understanding as the source of space, time, and the Categories, it must be to ourselves as we (supersensibly) are in ourselves that he is referring. But this conclusion appears to be in direct contradiction to the doctrine that nothing can be known of things (including ourselves) as they are in themselves: a doctrine he is at pains to emphasize in his criticism of 'rational psychology' which seeks to argue from the bare fact of self-consciousness to the conclusion that the soul is a simple, immaterial, indestructible substance. The fallacies of 'rational psychology' Kant declares to be among those to which pure reason is prone in its search for the unconditioned which cannot be found in experience. It is not clear why Kant's own brand of what might be called 'transcendental psychology'—which is clearly distinguished from the empirical—does not fall under the same interdict that he places on 'rational psychology'.

These (and other) difficulties may tempt us to reconstrue, or reconstruct, the central doctrines of the critical philosophy, by (i) eliminating all reference to ourselves other than those natural selves which can be empirically studied and (ii) interpreting Kant's doctrine of the mind as concerned with certain powers and properties which we ordinary human beings (objects in nature) innately possess, and our possession of which is a necessary condition of our enjoyment of the type of experience which we do enjoy and of attainment of such knowledge of nature, including our own nature, as we do attain. Such a radically reinterpreted, such a *domesticated*, Kant would perhaps be more intellectually acceptable to us; but he would not be the great and difficult philosopher that he is in himself.

A final note may be added concerning Kant's treatment of *aesthetics in The Critique of Judgement*, where he turns his philosophy of mind to strikingly good account. The judgement of taste, the judgement that an object of art or nature is beautiful, is subjective in so far as it necessarily involves, and rests on, a subjective feeling of pleasure; and yet it claims universal or objective validity. This claim Kant declares justified in so far as the feeling of pleasure results from the fact that the formal properties of the object are such as to excite the harmonious free play of the faculties of understanding and imagination; for these faculties are common to all men. The functioning of these faculties in this connection is described as 'free play' just because it is not under the governance of concepts such as we employ in ordinary non-aesthetic empirical judgements; i.e. our aesthetic response is not to the object *as* being of some general kind, but rather to it as the unique individual that it is.                              P. F. S.

**KATZ,** DAVID (1884–1953). German psychologist, born in Kassel of Jewish extraction. He was educated at Göttingen, where he worked under G. E. Müller, though he was also much influenced by Edmund *Husserl's phenomenology. He obtained his doctorate in 1906 and in the following year became a *privat-docent* at Göttingen. In 1911 he published his first and best-known book, *Die Erscheinungsweisen der Farben*, abridged in English translation as *The World of Colour*. He served in the German army in the First World War and in 1919 became professor of psychology at Rostock, where he remained until 1933, when he went to England. He worked first in Manchester and later in London until he was offered and accepted the chair of pedagogy at Stockholm, where he died.

Katz was a man with wide, and on occasion, somewhat bizarre interests. After the First World War he wrote a monograph on phantom limbs, and while a refugee in Manchester he undertook research on the tongue as a primitive sense organ and on the feeding habits of captive monkeys.

His most important books were *The World of Colour* (1935) and its companion volume *Der Aufbau der Tastwelt*, 1925 (*The World of Touch*). Other books are *Animals and Men* (1937) and *Gestalt Psychology* (1950).                       O. L. Z.

**KELLER,** HELEN ADAMS (1880–1968). Born in Alabama, at 19 months she became deaf and blind. Educated by Anne M. Sullivan (Mrs Macy), she gradually learned to speak. She obtained a university degree in 1904, and achieved world-wide fame as a writer—a unique case of international recognition of a person with this double handicap. The story of how she discovered channels of communication and powers of expression is remarkable: see *Story of My Life* (1903, 1959, 1966).

**KEPLER,** JOHANNES (1571–1630). A key figure in the history of ideas, Johannes Kepler was both astronomer and astrologer to the Holy Roman Emperor Rudolf II, and later to Wallenstein, Duke of Friedland. Kepler combined medieval mysticism with the analytical power of a great scientist whose achievements encompass laws of planetary motion and the optics and visual functions of the eye—that it provides optical images.

In his *Mysterium cosmographicum* of 1596 he attempted a geometrical theory of the motions of the five known planets: that the five types of regular polyhedra control the planets. He was disappointed over this essentially Platonic notion, for the new highly accurate observations of Tycho Brahe did not fit this notion any better than much earlier observations. Kepler reconsidered his static geometrical models, to take into account and emphasize the importance of times and speeds. This new idea of relative speeds led to his *Harmonie mundi* (Harmony of the Universe) in 1619, which included the mathematical statement known as his third law: that the square of a planet's periodic time is proportional to the cube of its mean distance from the sun. Here by heroic arithmetic from the new data he discovered, with no prior hypothesis, an entirely surprising key to the universe; and he justified his astronomy with the aesthetics of music, believing that the harmony of the universe, which we may appreciate by science and by art, is in God's mind. Kepler in his account recognized seven good chords: octave, major and minor sixths, the fifth, the fourth, and the major and minor thirds. These musical ratios he conceived in terms of a vibrating string, thought of as bent round the sides of a polygon, so that each polygon is a musical conception based on Pythagoras's discovery that musical pitch is inversely related to the length of a vibrating string. Enjoyment of music is not just pleasurable stimulation of the ear, for 'the souls of men rejoice in those very proportions that God employed (in the Creation), wherever we find them, whether by pure reflection, or by the intervention of the senses . . . (or exercise of reason) by an occult, innate instinct'. So the astronomer should learn to match the harmony of the heavens with the harmony within his mind. Kepler applied this also to astrology, holding that the earth is an animated being. How the soul of the body perceives planetary influences was for him no more mysterious than how retinal images in our eyes give us conscious perceptions. And yet he wrote (in a letter to Herwart): 'My aim is to show that the heavenly machine is not a kind of divine, live being, but a kind of clockwork (and he who believes that a clock has a soul, attributes the maker's glory to the work), in so far as nearly all the manifold motions are caused by a most simple, magnetic, and material force, just as all motions of the clock are caused by a simple weight.'

Kepler's first law, that planets move in ellipses, and his second law, that planets describe equal areas in equal times, were both published in 1609. The notion that planets move in ellipses took a great deal of working out, and it was not intuitively likely or aesthetically acceptable. The ellipse was seen as inelegant, as only one focus is filled—by the sun—the other being empty. Kepler could not even be sure that the planets revolve with constant angular (or rather swept area) velocity round the sun-filled focus, rather than the empty focus, and indeed there were rival claims that the empty focus was the key to planetary movements, rather than the massive sun. It still seems amazing that *conic sections* provide a master key to the heavens!

In his strange book, which is fanciful science fiction while also providing thinking tools, *Somnium* (A Dream, or astronomy of the moon; first draft 1611), Kepler wrote an allegory in which he protected himself against attack for holding the Copernican notion of the earth moving round the sun. He described what things would look like from the moon, which was well known to be in motion. He was able to point out that the stars would seem to move from a moving base, and thus to imply that, against appearances, the earth may be moving and so produce the movements of the 'fixed' stars. He had heard of Galileo's discoveries with the telescope in 1610, of lunar craters and the four bright moons of Jupiter, and he very soon had the use of a telescope to which he added optical improvements. He supposed that as the lunar craters are circular, they must have been made by intelligent moon-dwellers, to shield them from the heat of the sun; but he also supposed that as the lunar mountains are irregular, they are natural and not constructed by intelligence. This criterion for extraterrestrial intelligence was also accepted by NASA in the early years of space exploration with planetary probes; they looked for circular or straight-line structures as evidence of intelligence. It was the reason also for the American astronomer Percival Lowell believing there to be intelligent life on Mars, as he saw straight 'canals'; these turned out to be, a not yet fully understood, visual illusion.

The *Somnium* portrayed Kepler's own mother as an enchantress; it may have contributed to the calamity of her being prosecuted for witchcraft. (She died a year after being released from custody.) Be that as it may, he describes, in this first science fiction, how to get to the moon and suggests that the best space travellers would be 'dried up old crones who since childhood have ridden over great stretches of the earth at night in tattered cloaks on goats or pitchforks'. To avoid being shrivelled by the great heat of the sun they must travel during the four brief hours of a lunar eclipse, in the shadow of the earth, and be pulled up to the moon by the sun's power that raises the tides of the sea. From prehistoric times tides had been seen as evidence of the harmony of the universe with life on earth. This strange work has been translated by Edward Rosen as *Somnium: the dream, or posthumous work on lunar astronomy* (1967; Madison, Milwaukee, and London).

R. L. G.

Armitage, A. (1966). *John Kepler*. London.

Caspar, M. (1958). *Johannes Kepler*, 3rd edn. Stuttgart. (Trans. Hellman, C. D. 1959, London and New York.)

Koestler, A. (1961). Kepler and the psychology of discovery. In *The Logic of Personal Knowledge: essays presented to Michael Polanyi*. London.

Koestler, A. (1959). *The Sleepwalkers*. London.

**KIERKEGAARD,** SØREN AABY (1813–55). Danish philosopher, founder of existentialism. He read theology but did not take orders. Suffering ill-defined guilt, he broke off his engagement to Regina Olsen and lived as an obsessive bachelor, on capital which was exhausted the day he died. Rejecting philosophical systems, he argued that subjectivity is truth. He attacked official Christianity; he also attacked his own books in anonymous reviews. His principal works are *Either/Or* (1843), *Philosophical Fragments* (1844), and *The Concluding Unscientific Postscript* (1846).

Allen, E. L. (1935). *Kierkegaard: his life and thought.* London.
Collins, J. D. (1953). *The Mind of Kierkegaard.* Chicago.

**KINAESTHESIS.** See SPATIAL CO-ORDINATION OF THE SENSES.

**KINDI,** AL- (803–73), Arab philosopher. See AL-KINDI.

**KLEIN,** MELANIE (1882–1960) née Reizes, British psychoanalyst, was born in Vienna. Marrying early, she moved to Budapest. Her interest was aroused by the writings of Sigmund *Freud, and she underwent analysis with Sandor Ferenczi, later working in his children's clinic. In 1921 she moved to Berlin for further analysis with Karl Abraham and continued her work with children. She decided to move to London in 1926 and duly was naturalized.

She was much influenced by Abraham's object-relations interpretation of Freud's theories (see FREUDIANISM: LATER DEVELOPMENTS). Her own particular contribution to psychoanalysis, however, lay in her work with children. She believed that emotions—love, fear, hate, concern—were present in children from very early infancy and that it was possible to interpret the child's behaviour and the emotional states to which it could not give coherent expression by observing it play. She therefore undertook the analysis of children at a much earlier age than others had thought possible, and gradually built up a picture of the inner world and emotional needs of both normal and abnormal children. She was also noted for her work with paranoid-schizoid and manic-depressive adults.

Much of Klein's work has aroused fierce controversy, but many of her ideas have been absorbed into the greater understanding that now exists of mental states. Her publications have been collected in *The Writings of Melanie Klein* (London, 1975). D. D. H.

Mitchell, J. (ed.) (1986). *The Selected Melanie Klein.* Harmondsworth.
Grosskurth, P. (1986). *Melanie Klein, Her World and Her Work.* London.

**KLÜVER** HEINRICH (1897–1979). German-American psychologist, born in Schleswig-Holstein and educated at the universities of Hamburg and Berlin. He emigrated to the United States in the 1920s and obtained his doctorate at Stanford in 1925. A great admirer of Karl *Lashley, he went to the University of Chicago in order to work with him. Although Lashley soon moved on, Klüver remained in Chicago for the rest of his life.

Klüver's best known work is his monograph on *Behaviour Mechanism in Monkeys* (1933), which owes much to Lashley, who wrote the Introduction. He is also known for his description, with P. C. Bucy, of the Klüver–Bucy syndrome, observed in monkeys after bilateral excision of the temporal lobes. This syndrome is marked by failure to recognize objects by sight, hypersexuality, compulsive oral behaviour, and a striking diminution in fear and aggression. In so far as this last is concerned, it is now known to result from damage to the amygdala, a part of the limbic system lying deep in the temporal lobes.

O. L. Z.

**KNOWLEDGE** may be described as representations of facts (including generalizations) and concepts organized for future use, including *problem-solving. There is 'useless' knowledge, such as which is the third, or the thirteenth, longest river in the world; on the other hand there is also knowledge that far transcends even what is necessary for immediate survival. It is on this latter that civilization's future depends, and in our possession of it we are, surely, outside the biological stream of natural selection.

It is useful also to distinguish 'knowing how' from 'knowing what', for knowledge includes the skills of knowing how to make effective use of individual facts and generalizations. When appropriately organized, it allows us to transfer experience from the past to the future, to predict and control events, and to invent new futures. It is, thus, a crucial component of *intelligence.

**KNOWLEDGE: NATURALISTIC ANALYSES.** Philosophers have generally, if not invariably, held that to know that something is the case entails a true belief that that thing is the case. If A knows that *p*, then it is *entailed that A believes that *p* and that *p* is the case. However, it is not possible to maintain that every case of true belief is a case of knowledge. A paranoiac might believe, without good grounds, that a certain person was trying to injure him. But even paranoiacs have enemies, and it might be that in this particular case the paranoiac's belief was correct. Such a case of true belief would not be a case of knowledge. The question arises, therefore, what further condition or conditions must be added to true belief to yield knowledge?

A traditional answer to this question is that A knows that *p* if, and only if, his true belief that *p* is supported in his mind by the possession of sufficiently good evidence. A difficulty for this traditional answer is that this evidence, to be sufficiently good, will itself have to consist of a proposition or propositions, $q$, which $A$ *knows*. (For suppose it be given that $A$'s evidence is $q$, but it is not the case that $A$ knows $q$. We will hardly think that $A$'s true belief that $p$ is sufficiently supported for $A$ to know that $p$.) Now, however, the problem arises of what it is for $A$ to know that $q$. If the same traditional answer is given, still further knowledge will be required to back up $A$'s true belief that $q$, and so *ad infinitum*. The traditional analysis appears to be involved in a vicious infinite regress.

This difficulty has exercised philosophers for a long time and various remedies have been proposed. In recent years, various *naturalistic* accounts of knowledge have been suggested which show promise of evading the difficulty. The general outline, if not the detail, of a naturalistic account of *belief* is rather easy to discern. Beliefs will be some sort of complex structure, a structure purporting to represent reality, found within the minds (brains?) of human beings and, presumably, higher animals. These structures will stand in various naturalistic relations to the states of affairs which they purport to represent. Some of these relations may be such that, if a belief has such a relation to the world, it is not simply belief but is knowledge. Three suggestions about the nature of these relations are worth consideration.

(i) *The 'Proper channels' account.* It is clear that we are equipped by nature with certain reliable 'channels' for the receipt of information. We gain knowledge of the current state of the physical world, including our own bodily state, by means of our senses. We gain knowledge of our own current state of mind by means of introspection. We do not *acquire* knowledge by *memory, but memory is a reliable means of conserving it. If we restrict ourselves to simple, 'self-evident' steps we can by reasoning acquire knowledge in such fields as logic and mathematics. These facts lead up to the suggestion that knowledge is simply a true belief acquired (and/or conserved) through such channels.

This suggestion has to meet the difficulty that it is possible to have cases of true belief acquired and/or conserved in these ordinarily satisfactory ways, but for these beliefs not to be cases of knowledge. Consider, for instance, a person who begins by knowing that a certain telephone number is 328–6693. At a later time, as a result of alterations in the person's memory-trace, he comes to believe firmly but falsely that the number is 382–6963. The memory-trace continues to alter, but, by sheer chance, the next alteration happens to reinstate the original (true) belief: that the number is 328–6693. Here we have a case of true belief, yielded by memory, which we would not account a case of knowledge.

(ii) *The Causal account.* A second suggestion is that when a state of affairs brings it about that we believe that that state of affairs obtains, then and only then do we have knowledge. This is what generally happens in *perception. There is a bird in the tree; this state of affairs acts upon my sense organs; and, as a causal consequence, I come to *know* that there is a bird in the tree.

The Causal analysis has this advantage over the previous suggestion: it requires no independent stipulation that the belief be true. If the state of affairs, $p$, brings it about that $A$ believes that $p$, then, automatically, the belief is true. The definition is, however, a limiting one. For instance, it makes it impossible to have knowledge of *future* states of affairs except under the difficult and perhaps self-contradictory supposition of 'backward causation': that such states of affairs can have effects upon our minds at an earlier time.

It may be possible to sophisticate the Causal analysis in such a way as to bypass this objection, but the analysis also faces a difficulty similar to the one brought against the 'Proper channels' account. Cases can be conceived where a state of affairs brings about a belief that that state of affairs obtains, but where we would deny that the case was one of knowledge. Consider a man whose nervous system is so deranged that any sharp sensory stimulus makes him believe that he hears a loud sound. Bright light, a cut, a strong smell, a blow, all have this one effect. Now let the stimulus be a loud sound. He will believe that he hears a loud sound, but it is clear that he does not know it.

(iii) *The Reliability or Nomic (Law-like) account.* A final suggestion is this. If $A$ believes that $p$, and if it is impossible, given the natural laws which govern the world and the situation which $A$ is in that his belief should be false, then his belief constitutes knowledge. A reliable thermometer or a watch in good working order supplies a good model for this situation. If such a thermometer or such a watch, placed in a normal environment, gives a certain 'reading' (which corresponds to a belief), then, given the actual laws of nature, it must be the case that this reading is correct. One who knows is one whose belief stands to the world in the same way that the thermometer-reading stands to the actual temperature or the watch-reading stands to the actual time.

A major advantage of this particular approach is that it can be extended to cover beliefs which fall short of knowledge, but which are nevertheless reliable to a high degree. If the laws of nature make it objectively very probable that a certain belief held on a certain occasion is true, then that belief, even if not knowledge, will still be a reliable belief. It is possible to hold that no belief ever reaches the very high (but not logically unreachable) standards which the Reliability approach sets for knowledge. The biological value of beliefs with a high degree of reliability of the sort indicated is obvious enough.

It may be objected to this account that it can give us no practical help in deciding in actual cases whether a particular belief is or is not a case of knowledge. However, this is a complaint that can be directed against all naturalistic definitions of knowledge, indeed, against all definitions of knowledge whatsoever. It is in fact a misguided complaint. No definition can be expected by itself to pick out actual instances falling under the definition. No definition of knowledge can answer the sceptic who doubts the existence of knowledge. It can only tell us what knowledge is like *if* there is knowledge.

A more legitimate complaint against the Reliability account of knowledge is that it may turn out to be too restricted. It can perhaps give an account of knowledge of particular, spatio-temporally limited, states of affairs. But what of knowledge of laws of nature, or knowledge of logical and mathematical truth? A law-like connection between a belief in an individual mind and such general states of affairs as arsenic being poisonous, or 7 + 5 being equal to 12, is not easy to understand. This difficulty is one which may threaten any naturalistic account of the nature of knowledge.          D. M. A.

Armstrong, D. M. (1973). *Belief, Truth and Knowledge*, part III. Cambridge.

Dretske, F. I. (1981). *Knowledge and the Flow of Information*. Cambridge, Massachusetts.

Goldman, A. I. (1967). A causal theory of knowing. *Journal of Philosophy*, 64.

**KNOWLEDGE BY ACQUAINTANCE, AND KNOWLEDGE BY DESCRIPTION.** This distinction was made by Bertrand *Russell (see especially Russell, 1914, p. 151). Knowledge by acquaintance is 'what we derive from sense', which does not imply 'even the smallest "knowledge about"', i.e. it does not imply knowledge of any proposition concerning the object with which we are acquainted. For Russell knowledge is primarily—and all knowledge depends upon—the 'knowledge by acquaintance of sensations'; but when this is expressed in language, and organized by common sense or science, we have knowledge by description. It is a deep question how we learn to name objects of common experience (stones, tables and chairs, etc.) from our private 'knowledge by acquaintance'.

More recently, theories of *perception have blurred Russell's distinction by suggesting that there is no *direct* knowledge by the senses, but that perceptions are essentially descriptions (though by brain states rather than language) of the object world. This follows from the view that perception is knowledge-based and depends upon (unconscious) inference, as suggested in the nineteenth century by Hermann von *Helmholtz and now very generally, if not quite always, accepted. Clearly this philosophical issue is bound up intimately with theories of perception, though it is central for epistemology.          R. L. G.

Russell, B. (1914). *Our Knowledge of the External World*. London.

**KOFFKA,** KURT (1886–1941). *Gestalt psychologist, born in Berlin. With *Wertheimer and *Köhler, Kurt Goldstein, and Hans Gruhle, he founded the journal *Psychologische Forschung*. This survived for 22 volumes, until 1938 and the rise of Hitler. Koffka spent much of his academic life after 1924 in America. His main works are *The Growth of the Mind* (1924), and many important papers on *perception.

**KÖHLER,** WOLFGANG (1887–1967). Co-founder and leading member of the Gestalt school of psychology, Köhler was born in Reval on the Baltic and educated at Tübingen, Frankfurt, and Berlin. While at Frankfurt, he became acquainted with Max *Wertheimer, and both he and Kurt *Koffka acted as subjects in Wertheimer's classical experiments on apparent visual motion. Between them, they evolved what became known as *Gestalt theory.

In 1913, Köhler went to Tenerife to study the behaviour of anthropoid apes and was perforce obliged to remain there for the duration of the First World War. His celebrated book describing his observations and experiments appeared in German as *Intelligenzprüfungen am Menschenaffen* (English translation *The Mentality of Apes*, 1925). In this book, Köhler developed the important thesis that problem-solving involving detours or simple tool-using comes about through sudden insight, and does not depend on fortuitous trial and error as E. L. *Thorndike had contended. (This controversy was further reviewed by Koffka (1921), who strongly defended Köhler's standpoint.)

Although the Gestalt view of *problem-solving as due to sudden insight has often been questioned, the idea of a 'restructuring' of the field of perception to enable key features previously hidden or unnoticed to be literally 'seen', undoubtedly describes aptly some types of problem-solving—in particular visual–spatial—in both higher animals and man. Köhler further laid stress on the ways in which differences of size or brightness might apparently be perceived directly, irrespective of the actual value of the differences themselves.

Köhler was appointed to the chair of psychology at Berlin in 1921, largely on the strength of an important work on aspects of modern physics which he held to be relevant to psychological issues (*Die Physische Gestalten in Rühe und Stationären Zustandt*; translated in abridged form by W. D. Ellis, *A Source Book of Gestalt Psychology*, 1938, pp. 17–55). Though exhibiting high intellectual quality, this work is often dismissed as a *synthèse manquée*; none the less, Köhler believed implicitly that the road to scientific advance in psychology is by way of physics, and he attempted to justify this view in many of his later books and papers (cf. *The Selected Papers of Wolfgang Köhler*, ed. by Mary Henle (New York, 1971)). All his books are essentially inspired by Gestalt thinking. The most important are: *Gestalt Psychology* (New York, 1929; London, 1930; rev. edn. 1947); *The Place of Value in a World of Facts* (New York, 1938); *Dynamics in Psychology* (New York, 1940 and 1960).

Köhler felt obliged for reasons of conscience to abandon Hitler's Germany in 1934 and emigrated to the United States, where he found a congenial home at Swarthmore College, where he remained for nearly all the rest of his long life.   O. L. Z.

**KONORSKI,** JERZY (1903–73). Polish neurophysiologist and behavioural scientist, born in Lodz. After studying medicine at the University of Warsaw, he visited Ivan *Pavlov's laboratory before returning to Poland to work at the Nencki Institute of Experimental Biology. At the time of his death he was both the director of the Nencki Institute and head of its department of neurophysiology.

Konorski's studies of the relationship and interaction between classical and instrumental *conditioning in the 1930s antedated comparable research in the West by more than a decade. Unfortunately, even the belated English publication of his first monograph, *Conditioned Reflexes and Neuron Organization* (1948), was largely ignored in the West at the time. This book attempted to provide an interpretation of Pavlovian and instrumental conditioning in terms of Sherringtonian neurophysiology. Although his second book, *Integrative Activity of the Brain* (1969), in which he extended his ideas to cover perception and motivation, received more attention, Konorski's full influence on Western psychology became apparent only after his death. The influence of his work and ideas on current research on conditioning and related areas is secondary only to that of Pavlov himself.   A. D.

**KORSAKOFF SYNDROME.** Sergei Korsakoff (1854–1900), a Russian neuropsychiatrist, published in 1887 the first of several papers on a special form of psychic disorder which occurs in conjunction with peripheral neuritis. He mentioned as characteristic such symptoms as irritable weakness, rapid fatiguing, sleeplessness, *memory disturbance, preoccupation with fantasy, and fearfulness. In its modern use the term 'Korsakoff syndrome' refers to a group of symptoms—known alternatively as the amnesic syndrome—which includes inattentiveness, memory defect for recent events, retrograde *amnesia and other disorders of recall and recognition, and disorientation in time, place, and situation. Confabulation, grandiose ideas, and an inappropriate cheerfulness are prominent symptoms in some cases. The syndrome can occur without peripheral neuritis, for example as a stage in recovery after trauma to the brain. When it is combined with peripheral neuritis, the term Korsakoff psychosis tends to be used.

The Korsakoff syndrome develops most often in chronic alcoholics who fail to take an adequate diet. This may cause an acute deficiency of thiamine (vitamin $B_1$), which produces an acute delirious illness known as *Wernicke's encephalopathy. When or if the patient recovers he will probably be left with the typical features of the Korsakoff syndrome.

The syndrome has seized the interest of neurologists and psychologists because it throws light on normal processes of recall and recognition, although many of the questions it raises have yet to be given precise answers. The memory defect is revealed in the difficulty the patient shows in finding his way about, his forgetfulness in simple matters, and especially his failure to retain information. Also, presented with an object he has been shown a few minutes before, he tends to respond to it as not identical or as in some manner changed. A learning disability can readily be demonstrated in such tests as 'paired associates' and in the delayed recall of pictures of everyday objects. There is a tendency to persist in giving wrong answers, and to fail to 'unlearn'. The deficiency in recalling recent events has been attributed to partial or total derangement of the consolidation of sensory impressions as a permanent memory trace, or engram, or, to put it another way, to a failure to transfer information from a short-term to a long-term memory store. Explanation along these lines has to be qualified by the observation that the patient sometimes recalls after a few hours what he has not recalled after a few minutes.

Some of the symptoms have been attributed to lack of insight or lack of self-critique. A patient with severe memory loss will generally confabulate when questioned about recent activities. That is to say, he will answer incorrectly by describing events that could not possibly have happened. This may give the impression that he is fabricating replies to cover the gaps in his memory. In fact he is doing nothing of the kind. His replies are often accounts of occasions in his more distant past life which are now transposed into the immediate past. He is unaware of the absurd nature of his replies as he is unconscious of the fact that he is answering incorrectly. As Barbizet so neatly put it, 'Confabulation is due to the patient's inability to remember that he can't remember'. If his memory improves he ceases to confabulate and merely replies that he does not know the correct answer to the question which has been put to him.

The lack of self-critique is shown too when he 'entertains incompatible propositions'. He says, for instance: 'I am fifty-two years old. I was born in 1920. It is now 1975.' The item most likely to be correct is the year of birth. He does not apply tests to check the correctness of what he has said, as a healthy person tends to do. One reason may be indolence or passivity. However, by insisting on the incompatibility of the propositions the observer may provoke a 'catastrophic reaction', and this suggests that false propositions are held to as a defence against *anxiety.

Neuropathological studies of patients who have shown the syndrome have contributed to knowledge of the brain structures concerned in memory processes. The floor of the third ventricle is usually affected. The lesion tends to be localized in subcortical structures. The hippocampal region and the mamillary bodies are involved, it has been claimed, in all cases. Recent work has shown that damage is not confined to these structures. There is also evidence of atrophy of the frontal lobes and dilatations of the cerebral ventricles. This structural damage of the brain has been reported not only in chronic alcoholics but also in young heavy drinkers and may help to explain why it is so difficult for these subjects to learn new ways of dealing with their drinking problems.  D. R. D.

Victor, M. and Yakovlev, P. I. (1955). S. S. Korsakoff's psychic disorder in conjunction with peripheral neuritis. *Neurology*, **5**, 394–406 (a translation of Korsakoff's original article).
Whitty, C. W. M. and Zangwill, O. L. (1966). *Amnesia*. London.

**KORTE'S LAWS.** A. Korte was a student of the *Gestalt psychologist Kurt *Koffka, who with Max *Wertheimer and others described various kinds of 'apparent movement' elicited by lights switched alternately. The following kinds of movement were distinguished.

φ-movement:  pure movement from pairs of flashing lights.

β-movement:  movement of an object from one position to another.

α-movement:  change of size with successive presentation (e.g. of the two arrow figures in the *Müller-Lyer illusion).

γ-movement:  expansion or contraction with, respectively, increasing or decreasing illumination.

δ-movement:  'reversed' movement occurring when the later stimulus is much brighter than the earlier. This movement is in the opposite direction to the order of presentation.

Korte's laws refer to the time interval and separation of alternating pairs of stimuli for giving optimal apparent movement. Perhaps, though, 'laws' is too strong a word for such variable effects.

Boring, E. G. (1942). *Sensation and Perception in the History of Experimental Psychology*, pp. 596–7. New York.

**KRAEPELIN,** EMIL (1856–1926). German psychiatrist, educated at Würzburg, who became professor of psychiatry at Dorpat (1886), Heidelberg (1890), and Munich (1903). He was probably the only psychiatrist of his day to study with Wilhelm *Wundt, thereby acquiring considerable understanding of experimental methods. This he passed on to many of his early students of psychiatry, some of whom carried out experiments with their patients, in particular, studies of *reaction times and *mental disorders. Kraepelin is best known for the fundamental distinction which he drew between manic-depressive psychosis and *schizophrenia (then known as dementia praecox). His textbook of psychiatry, which went into several editions, was for many years the standard text.
  O. L. Z.

**KRAFFT-EBING,** RICHARD VON, Baron (1840–1902). German neurologist, born at Mannheim and educated at Prague; he became professor of psychiatry at Strasbourg in 1872, at Vienna in 1889. He established that general paralysis of the insane can be a late manifestation of syphilitic infection. This was one of the first clear examples of severe personality change and, finally, loss of mental abilities and behaviour from a specified organic brain disease. It led to identifying the effects of chronic intoxication with alcohol, lead, and other substances which may be pollutants.

**KRETSCHMER,** ERNST (1888–1964). German psychiatrist, educated at the University of Munich, where he studied under Emil *Kraepelin. He worked at Tübingen and then at Marburg, where he was appointed professor of psychiatry and neurology. He is best known for his books *Körperbau und Charakter* (1921; English trans. *Physique and Character*, 1925) and *Geniale Menschen* (1929; English trans. *The Psychology of Men of Genius*, 1931). Although his attempts to correlate *body build with types of psychosis proved to have little importance in psychiatric diagnosis, Kretschmer's work did much to reawaken interest in the relations between body build and qualities of temperament or personality.  O. L. Z.

**KÜLPE,** OSWALD (1862–1917). German philosopher and psychologist born at Kandau in Courland, at that time part of Russia and later Latvia, where he had strong German connections. He was educated at the universities of Leipzig and Berlin, where he studied history, but his major interests soon turned to philosophy and psychology, in large part due to the influence of Wilhelm *Wundt. After studying experimental psychology for a time with G. E. *Müller, Külpe returned to Leipzig, where he obtained his doctorate under Wundt. Thereafter he divided his interests more or less equally between philosophy and psychology, both of which he taught for the rest of his life, first at Würzburg, where his most important work in experimental psychology was done, and later at Bonn and Munich.

Külpe produced a large number of books, of which the best known are his *Grundriss Der Psychologie* (1893) of which an English translation was published in 1905, and *Einleitung en Die Philosophie* (1898), which was likewise translated into English and became highly popular in its day. His *Vorlesungen Über Psychologie* was published posthumously in 1922. In addition he published a book on Kant and wrote widely on issues in *aesthetics and ethics and even wrote a book on *Psychology and Medicine* (1912).

It was as a professor at Würzburg that Külpe established what came to be known as the Würzburg School of Experimental Psychology, which offered a strong challenge to Wundt's contention that the thought processes lie beyond the scope of experimental study. As an example of the Würzburg method one may, for instance, refer to an experiment in which the subject was asked to read a series of unrelated words and in each case to produce a spoken word logically related to the stimulus word—e.g. 'bird': 'wing'. *Reaction times were measured and introspective reports recorded in detail. In such an experiment it was found that the subject invariably made a kind of generic preparation for the task in hand. The preliminary instruction orientated him towards the general theme, e.g. that of subordination, which produced a kind of pre-selection from among all possible responses available to the subject. In Würzburg jargon, what came to be called the 'determining tendency' was released by the task (*aufgabe*) which enabled a pre-existing reproductive tendency to be raised to supraliminal strength. It was further supposed that the determining tendency was seldom represented directly in consciousness, and that a selective and facilitating influence on certain pre-existing associations took place, leading to what is essentially an act of constructive recall.

Although this interpretation of a very simple act of reproduction might sound unduly elaborate, it does provide an advance on the classical conceptions of association by continuity or similarity which were taken over from the philosophy of mind; indeed it may be said that Külpe's thinking had some of the originality—as well as the obscurity—which characterized the work of Sigmund *Freud.

A second advance which we owe to Külpe is likewise reminiscent of Freud in his insistence on the reality of so-called 'imageless thought'. Again and again in the experiments of Külpe and his colleagues, states of mind were reported in which no images could be detected, in spite of the fact that most of the subjects, including Külpe himself, were highly intelligent and well practised in introspective self-observation. It was alleged by almost all these subjects that no amount of introspective sophistication enabled such states as confidence or doubt to be brought under the rubric of sensation, image, volition or feeling which, in the view of Wundt and others of his time, were regarded as primary and irreducible.

The question of whether or not thought without images really exists became one of the most controversial issues in experimental psychology. A number of ingenious experiments, which it was hoped would settle the matter for good, were reviewed by George Humphrey (1951) without any clear-cut solution being found. All the same, Humphrey was right to conclude that the fundamental thesis of the Würzburg School had been well sustained by a majority of the experimentalists working on the problem. Moreover, as Humphrey pointed out, among the great names of philosophy it would be hard to find one, apart from Hume, who states unequivocally that thinking can be described in terms of images.

O. L. Z.

Boring, E. G. (1950). *A History of Experimental Psychology*, 2nd edn. New York.
Broadbent, D. E. (1961). *Behaviour*. London.
Humphrey, G. (1951). *Thinking: an introduction to its experimental psychology*. London.

# L

**LABORATORIES OF PSYCHOLOGY.** The first laboratories for carrying out experiments under controlled and isolated conditions were devised by the alchemists, and much of their apparatus is to be found almost unmodified in modern chemical laboratories. The first laboratory of experimental psychology was founded by Wilhelm *Wundt at Leipzig in 1879, in an old building which has not been preserved. Many celebrated psychologists received their training at this first laboratory: A. Lehmann and O. *Külpe; and from America G. Stanley *Hall, J. *Cattell, E. W. Scripture, Frank *Angell, E. B. *Titchener, G. M. Stratton (famous for his inverting spectacles experiment), and C. H. Judd, also a pioneer in the study of visual *perception.

In America, William *James, although not himself much of an experimenter, introduced physiological psychology to Harvard in 1875. He persuaded Harvard to spend $300 on 'physiological' apparatus and to set aside two rooms in the Lawrence Scientific School, where he held a class on 'the relations between physiology and psychology'. In 1877 he added space in Harvard's Museum of Comparative Zoology.

In Russia, Vladimir Bekherev (1857–1927) founded a laboratory at Kazan, where learning, psychopathology, and alcoholism were investigated. The first officially recognized institute of psychology, at Moscow University, was not, however, founded until 1911, and this was based on German psychological theory of the 1880s.

The first psychological laboratory in Britain was founded at Cambridge in 1879, under the direction of W. H. R. *Rivers. It became effective under C. S. *Myers from 1913, and was directed by Sir Frederic *Bartlett from 1931 to 1952 and by Oliver Zangwill until 1981, then by Nick Macintosh.

The Oxford Institute of Experimental Psychology was founded in 1936. It is now the largest psychological laboratory and teaching department of psychology in Britain. Only three years before its foundation, William Brown (then the Wilde Reader in Mental Philosophy) wrote, in the *Oxford Magazine* of 11 May 1933: 'Psychology has encountered more difficulty breaking away and finding its own level in Oxford than in any other university . . . Oxford is the only great university in the world which still has no laboratory in experimental psychology.'

The post of Wilde Reader in Mental Philosophy was founded by Henry Wilde in 1898. It was first held by G. F. Stout, then by William *McDougall—who violated the original stricture that no

experiments were to be undertaken. It has been suggested that this bizarre restraint reflected the comment of a Cambridge mathematician, that it 'would insult religion by putting the human soul in a pair of scales'. However this may be, Wilde's bequest required that: 'The Reader shall from time to time lecture on illusions and delusions which are incident to the human mind. He shall also lecture, as far as may be practicable, on the psychology of the lower races of mankind . . .' This statute has since been changed.

The present laboratory owes its creation to a student of McDougall's, Mrs Hugh Watts, who in 1935 donated £10,000 to the University for this purpose, thus inspiring the university to action. The Second Chair of Psychology—which was held by Jerome Bruner, and then by Peter Bryant—is named after Mrs Watts.

Experimental psychology was not a subject for undergraduate teaching in Oxford until 1947. The first professor was George Humphrey, who came to Oxford from Queen's University, Ontario. (He said that he first learned of Oxford's interest in him when he read of his appointment in *The Times*.) He was succeeded by Carolus Oldfield. The institute was housed in a medley of small buildings (the professor's office was a converted lavatory) in Banbury Road; then in a large Victorian house in South Parks Road. It changed its name from 'Institute' to 'Department' upon moving into its present magnificent specially designed building, which is shared with zoology, in South Parks Road. The professor and head of the department, Laurence Weiskrantz, who moved from America to Cambridge before his appointment at Oxford, supervised this vast expansion and built up a wide-ranging department which is internationally in the top league for teaching and research. R. L. G.

Boring, E. G. (1950). *A History of Experimental Psychology*. 2nd edn. New York.

**LABYRINTHS (OF THE EAR).** A complex organ for attaining balance, provided by a fluid in three orthogonal circular tubes (the semicircular canals; see HEARING), which moves beads of calcium carbonate suspended on hairs, and so activates special nerves sending signals to the brain of movement of the head. In Ménière's disease, these signals occur inappropriately, through damage of the hair cells, to produce dangerous unpleasant dizziness. The condition is most frequent in middle life and it generally subsides of its own accord.

**LADD,** GEORGE TRUMBULL (1842–1921). Pioneer American psychologist whose lifelong interest lay in the relations between the nervous system and mental phenomena. A professor of philosophy at Bowdoin College and later at Yale, his principal work was *Elements of Physiological Psychology* (1887).

## LAING'S UNDERSTANDING OF INTERPERSONAL EXPERIENCE.

The British psychiatrist R. D. Laing's contribution to the understanding of the mind operates in a field that can be broadly characterized as empirical interpersonal phenomenology, which is a branch of social *phenomenology. The field of social phenomenology has been cultivated from the standpoints of anthropology, sociology, psychology, and philosophy. Any work of social phenomenology from any one of these points of view has implications for all the other perspectives which are knit together by the common discipline of phenomenology.

At present there is no overall definition or system of phenomenology agreed upon by all self-styled phenomenologists, and even someone who disclaims phenomenology, such as the French historian Michel Foucault, may nevertheless be regarded as embodying much phenomenology in his theory and method.

Laing has been mainly concerned to see and to describe what goes on in people's experience, as mediated by their interactions.

Everyone knows that our feelings are affected by how our nearest and dearest feel about us. But this is a devilishly difficult area to study for many reasons. 'Galilean' natural science, in which we are all brought up, is a theory especially and explicitly designed to see the world without reference to personal passions. This theory and method is as irrelevant to the study of interpersonal experience as interpersonal experience is to it. But what then shall be our method? Is such a project possible by any method?

The philosophy, anthropology, sociology, and psychology of interpersonal relations are all in an unsatisfactory state despite the *aperçus*, insights, and intuitions of *Hegel, Dilthey, Buber, Goffman, *Husserl, Sigmund *Freud, Schultz, Marx, *Nietzsche, Scheler, Heidegger, *Sartre, Foucault, Merleau-Ponty, Bateson, MacMurray, and others, in and out of phenomenology, who have influenced Laing's work.

The philosophical foundations of a 'dialogal knowledge' have not so far been comprehensively and systematically laid down. The epistemological status, for instance, of the nature of the knowledge we derive from the study of how we affect each other remains unclarified; and, within some current ways of seeing and modes of thought, the very possibility of persons is hardly conceivable other than as the ghost of a category already *dépassé*.

Not only is there an absence of such desirable philosophical foundations but the problems of method are as vexing as they are unresolved. In some respects they have not yet even been explicitly formulated. Nevertheless, Laing has studied various facets of very disturbed and disturbing personal relations.

These studies grew out of, and have moved away from, his work as a psychiatrist and psychoanalyst. From the beginning he did not look at what he saw as a psychiatrist from the usual psychiatric point of view. The attribution of the absence in the other of the capacity to form good enough personal relationships is the basis for the diagnosis of *schizophrenia. This diagnosis is both an attribution (he is incapable of forming a personal bond; he is cut off) and a causal theory to account for this attribution (the reason he is cut off is because he is suffering from a mental or physical illness).

In *The Divided Self* Laing construed this attribution as a function of an extremely disjunctive relationship between the person who is in the role of a depersonalized—and depersonalizing—diagnosing psychiatrist and the person who has become a depersonalized, and sometimes depersonalizing, diagnosed patient. This construction is a contribution towards a personal understanding (*Verstehen*) of what is going on between psychiatrist and patient, in contrast to a scientific explanation of what is going on in the patient alone. In fact, he offered a personal understanding of the psychiatrist's scientific explanation and construed it as, unwittingly, a way of cutting off the cut-off person from the possibility of reunion and renewal.

The psychiatric, diagnostic look is itself a depersonalized and depersonalizing cut-off look. It is an application of a highly sophisticated scientific look that is culturally deeply conditioned. It is a way of seeing *things*, and the relation between things, by subtracting all personal experience. However, a person is not a thing, nor is a thing a person. It is a look which is cultivated with the express intention of not seeing intentions out there. Things have no intentions. It is the exact opposite of a sensibility cultivated with the express intention of recognizing and sympathetically understanding the intentions of others, and their interconnections.

The scientific, psychiatric, and medical look is an acquired technique, adapted to the elimination of the conditions of the possibility of understanding. To understand what is going on in and between people it is necessary to place the interpersonal happenings within their social context.

In a series of studies, Laing investigated the family contexts of diagnosed schizophrenics. The theory behind this work was largely influenced by Sartre's *Critique of Dialectical Reason*; in particular, the distinction made there between praxis and process, and the relation between them. There is an interplay between the dynamic structure of any human multiplicity and the intentions and actions of its members. When the psycho-social interior of the families of schizophrenics was looked at from the twin perspectives of praxis and process, instead of looking at the schizophrenic alone, it appeared that those experiences and actions which are regarded as the signs and symptoms of a pathological process within one individual were much more socially intelligible than they had been taken to be by most psychiatrists.

This claim is quite uncontentious and nonexclusive, but it has led to a lot of controversy, and to a lot of contentious misunderstanding. It does, however, keep open the rationality of a response to a quintessentially personal type of suffering, with its confusions, terrors, mystifications, and disarray, based on a personal understanding of it.

As Chairman of the Philadelphia Association, London from 1965 to 1982, Laing was involved in the provision of social contexts where people in disturbed states of mind could live, at their own choosing, on their own discretion, in their own way. Some of the experiences that emerged in these contexts were very unusual. In contemporary psychiatric practice they had never been allowed to happen. A notable feature of some of the accounts is the way some people's minds go through transformations which, if they are allowed to continue and if they do not lose their own momentum, seem to eventuate in a clear, balanced state of mind. Reports of similar experiences from comparable contexts, suggested in the first place by the London experiment, point in the same direction. Reports from the National Institute of Mental Health and elsewhere have shown that when these transformations are allowed free rein, in a socially facilitating, endorsing, validating, encouraging context, the 'results', viewed from the objective statistical standpoint, look as good as or better than those of conventional psychiatric treatment.

In the years since 1970 Laing's work has been concerned with all aspects of *biopolitics*: namely, the issues of power which cluster and accrue to all phases of the human life-cycle, from conception to death. Who makes and whence comes decisions about who can, must, cannot, must not, do what to whom, and in what circumstances? By what diktat is it determined what may or may not be done to us before we are born, when we are giving birth, or being born? Who says, of mothers and babies, who can be with whom? What can or cannot be done to us when we are in a state of mental, emotional, or physical collapse? How do we treat each other when we are helpless? Who says how and where and in what company we must, or may, or may not die? What happens between us at the interface of maximum and minimum power, as during a surgical operation?

There is so much that goes on between us which we can never know. The necessity of this ignorance, and the impossibility of any satisfactory criteria of decidability when it comes to the validation of particular attributions of a personal and interpersonal order, have led those who wish to cultivate the art of the soluble to abandon this area of uncertainty and enigmas. However, this domain does not evaporate because the objective look does not see it. The great divide between fact and feelings is a product of our own schizoid constructions.

In reality, the reasons of the heart and the physiology of the brain coexist and must be interdependent. We cannot construe this reality, however. We cannot explain it, much less can we understand it.

Many people recognize themselves in Laing's descriptions, but when they feel his constructions are correct it may simply be that they share with him their illusions. Those who disagree with his constructions and do not recognize his descriptions (of psychiatrists and patients, husbands and wives, parents and children, lovers, and others) regard his work with reserve and suspicion. There has been a lot of confusion.

However, it has always been part of Laing's method to attempt to depict his way of seeing as a contribution to the understanding of what comes into view or not, is seen or not, from whatever point of view. This methodological reflexivity is necessarily reflected in his own style of depiction. It therefore may turn out that the main significance in Laing's work lies in what it discloses or reveals of a way of looking which enables what he describes to be seen.

Laing's principal works include: *The Divided Self* (London, 1960); *The Self and Others* (London, 2nd edn., 1969); *Knots* (London, 1970); *Sanity, Madness and the Family* (with A. Esterson, Harmondsworth, 1970); *The Politics of the Family* (London, 1971); *The Politics of Experience* (London, 1978); *The Voice of Experience: Experience, Science, and Psychiatry* (Harmondsworth, 1983); and *Wisdom, Madness, and Folly: the Making of a Psychiatrist* (London, 1985).    R. D. L.

**LAMARCK**, JEAN-BAPTISTE DE (1744–1829). Born at Bazantin, he joined the French army in Germany at the age of 17, and while stationed at Toulon and Monaco became interested in Mediterranean flora. He resigned after an injury and worked on botany, publishing a *Flore française* in 1778. He became Keeper of the Royal Garden—the nucleus of the Jardin des Plantes—where he lectured for a quarter of a century on invertebrate zoology. He began to consider the origin of species about 1800; the result was his *Philosophie zoologique* (1809), and his *Histoire naturelle des animaux sans vertèbres* (1815–22). By stressing the variation of species he was a pioneer, before *Darwin, of an evolutionary account. His view that characteristics acquired by individual experience can be inherited was popular politically, and educationally, even though variation of species was opposed to religious belief in special creation. Darwin accepted *Lamarckianism (inheritance of acquired characteristics), but apart from occasional claims it has now been abandoned. Lamarck's evolutionary views were opposed particularly by Cuvier, who effectively destroyed him. Lamarck became blind, and died in poverty. Shortly after his death he was honoured by a vast monument, which still stands.

**LAMARCKIANISM** is the doctrine that what is learned by individual experience can be inherited by the offspring. It is named after the distinguished French anatomist Jean-Baptiste de *Lamarck, whose books had considerable influence. Charles *Darwin accepted the Lamarckian thesis, even to the extent of advising young women to learn as much as they could (including manly skills!) before starting their families (in *The Descent of Man*, 1888).

Inheritance of acquired characteristics appeared highly unlikely following the acceptance of Mendel's laws of inheritance, first appreciated in 1900, and with the development of the gene theory of inheritance in the 1920s. Many experiments have been conducted to test the issue, but none have convincingly shown inheritance of memories or learned skills. The collapse of Lamarckianism has consequences for accounts of ethics which may be upsetting—for, however hard one struggles to be good or wise, one's virtue as acquired by one's own efforts dies with one. Possibly the neo-Darwinianism which rejected inheritance of acquired characteristics—arguing that evolution depended entirely upon random genetic variation and selection of the fittest to survive and pro-create—was resisted largely because of its moral implications: it might reduce motivations towards good behaviour. (See EVOLUTION: NEO-DARWINIAN THEORY.)

Lamarckianism was the basis of Russian agricultural policy under Lysenko, though with unfortunate results. It is still not dead: every few years claims are still made of inheritance of acquired characteristics, and to a limited extent it just might be possible.

**LA METTRIE,** JULIEN OFFRAY DE (1709–51). French philosopher and army surgeon. His courageously expressed mechanistic ideas became so unpopular that he lived in exile in Leiden, where he published perhaps the first clear account of man as a machine: *L'homme machine* (1748); English version, Gertrude C. Bussey, *Man a Machine* (1953).

**LAND COLOURS.** The American inventive genius Edwin Land (inventor of 'instant' photography, and polaroid filters) discovered (following some early experiments by C. H. Judd) that although, as Thomas *Young showed in 1801, three spectral colours are required to match any spectral hue (see COLOUR VISION), a remarkable range of colours is produced by only two colours, for patterned or picture displays. Thus, a pair of photographs taken one with a red and the other with, say, a yellow or a green filter, or even white with no colour, give almost perfect colour pictures when combined with a pair of slide projectors each fitted with its appropriate filter. This led Land to develop his Retinex theory of colour vision, which suggests that colours are seen by ratios of different intensity regions, which may be quite widely separated, rather than only from the relative stimulation of neighbouring 'red', 'green', and 'blue' cone receptor cells. These Land effects are related to the well-known colour contrast phenomena, which were investigated by *Goethe, but they are gradually forcing a revision of understanding of colour vision. See RETINEX THEORY AND COLOUR CONSTANCY.

Land, E. H. (1977). The Retinex theory of color vision. *Scientific American*, **237**, 6, 108–28.
Matthaei, R. (ed.) (1971). *Goethe's Colour Theory*. London.

**LANGE,** CARL GEORG (1834–1900). Danish psychologist and materialist philosopher working in Copenhagen. Independently of William *James, he arrived at an almost identical theory of *emotion, i.e. that emotion consists of the bodily changes evoked by the perception of external circumstances. Lange, however, placed far greater stress on the role of the cerebrovascular system in the genesis of emotion than did James. None the less, their views are so similar that the theory has always been known as the James–Lange theory of emotion. Lange's principal work first published in Denmark in 1885 became widely known in German translation as *Über Gemustsbewegungen* (1887). The respective contributions of James and Lange were brought together in a book entitled *The Emotions* (ed. K. Dunlap, 1922).          O. L. Z.

**LANGUAGE, CHINESE EVIDENCE FOR THE EVOLUTION OF.** See CHINESE EVIDENCE FOR THE EVOLUTION OF LANGUAGE.

**LANGUAGE: CHOMSKY'S THEORY.** In undertaking the study of mind, it is useful to consider the less controversial question of how we study a complex physical system such as the human body. We assume that the species is characterized by a certain biological endowment. The embryo grows to the adult as its genetic programme unfolds, under the triggering and controlling effect of the environment. The organism does not 'learn' to grow arms or reach puberty. Rather, the general course of maturation is genetically determined, though the realization of the genetic plan depends in part on external factors. The result is a system of interacting organs—the heart, the visual system, etc.—each with its structure and functions, interacting in largely predetermined ways.

It is fortunate that we have such a refined and specific innate endowment. Were this not so, each individual would grow into some kind of amoeboid creature, merely reflecting external contingencies, utterly impoverished, and lacking the special structures that make a human existence possible. Naturally, the same innate factors that permit the organism to transcend environmental factors, reaching a remarkable level of complexity of organization that does not 'mirror' the limited environment, rule out many possible courses of development and limit drastically the final states that can be reached in physical growth.

Little is known about how any of this happens, but no one seriously doubts that something of roughly this sort is true. Why? Because of the vast qualitative difference between the impoverished and unstructured environment on the one hand, and the highly specific and intricate structures that uniformly develop, on the other.

Turning to the human mind, we also find structures of marvellous intricacy developing in a uniform way with limited and unstructured experience. Language is a case in point, but not the only one. Think of the capacity to deal with abstract properties of the number system, common to humans apart from gross pathology, and, it seems, unique to humans. The essence of this system is the concept of adding one, indefinitely. The capacity is not 'approached' by the ability of some birds to match patterns of $n$ objects for some finite (and small) $n$, just as human language with its discrete infinity of meaningful expressions constructed by abstract rules crucially involving operations on phrases is not simply 'more' than some finite system of symbols imposed on other organisms— or, for that matter, just as the ability of a bird to fly, though finite, is not simply an extension of the human ability to jump; whatever the evolutionary history may have been, quite different mechanisms are involved. The capacity to deal with the number system or with abstract properties of space—capacities that lie at the core of what we might call the human 'science-forming faculty'—are no doubt unlearned in their essentials, deriving from our biological endowment. One can think of many other examples.

These systems have many of the relevant properties of physical organs. We might think of them as 'mental organs'. Thus the human language faculty might well be regarded on the analogy of the heart or the visual system. It develops in the individual under the triggering effect of experience, but the mature system that grows in the mind (that is 'learned', to use the standard but misleading term) does not 'mirror' the contingencies of experience, but vastly transcends that experience. True, there are differences among individuals contingent on experience; some know English, others Japanese. Similarly, onset of puberty varies over some range, as does body size, or the ability to pole vault, or the distribution of cells of the visual cortex specialized to respond to lines of particular orientation in the visual field. But the pole vaulter will never fly like a bird (even a chicken), and the human language faculty will never grow anything but one of the possible human languages, a narrowly constrained set.

In brief, our genetic endowment provides for the growth and maturation of special mental organs, the language faculty being one. The development of these systems is essentially uniform among individuals. Two people from the same speech community can converse freely on some topic new to them despite substantially different experience, despite the fact that the sentences they produce and understand bear no direct analogy to anything that they have heard. Their minds contain roughly comparable rule systems of highly specific structure determined in general character by some property of the human species. These rule systems cannot be derived from the data of experience by 'induction', 'abstraction', 'analogy', or 'generalization', in any reasonable sense of these terms, any more than the basic structure of the mammalian visual system is inductively derived from experience.

As in the case of the physical body, we are fortunate to have this rich innate endowment. Otherwise, we would grow into 'mental amoeboids', unlike one another, merely reflecting properties of the impoverished environment, lacking the finely articulated structures that make possible the rich and creative mental life that is characteristic of all humans who are not severely impaired by individual or social pathology. These same innate factors provide the basis for a social existence in common with others whose capacities are not unlike our own despite accidents of individual history. We live in a world of shared understanding that extends far beyond the limited experience that evokes cognitive structures in the mind.

Again, the very same innate factors that provide for the richness and variety of mental life, shared with others comparably endowed, impose severe bounds on what the mind can achieve. Scope and limits are intimately related. Our inability to fly like birds derives from the same innate properties that enable us to become humans rather than amoeboid creatures. Comparably, the fact that there are many imaginable languages that we could not develop through the exercise of the language faculty is a consequence of the innate endowment that made it possible for us to attain our knowledge of English or some other human language. Similarly, the fact that there are no doubt many systems of musical organization that we simply could not comprehend or enjoy should be a source of satisfaction, because it reflects the same innate endowment that enables us to appreciate Bach and Beethoven. And the fact that many possible branches of science lie beyond our cognitive reach should cause no dismay when we realize that it results from that innate science-forming capacity that permits the construction of intelligible explanatory theories on weak and limited evidence in at least some domains of thought. And so on.

This talk of 'mental organs' should not mislead. We can discuss a physical organ—say the visual system—in terms of its abstract properties, knowing little about its physical realization. Nothing more than this is implied when one speaks of the mind as a system of mental organs, or when one studies these organs and their interaction as systems of mental representation and mental computation.

How can we proceed to gain insight into the specific properties of particular mental organs?

Consider the case of language. There are three basic questions that arise: (i) What do we know when we are said to know a language? (ii) What is the basis for the growth of this knowledge? (iii) How is this knowledge put to use?

The answer to the first question seems to be that knowledge of a language is mentally represented as a 'grammar'—that is, a finite system of rules and principles that interact to determine ('generate') an infinite class of expressions, each with a phonetic form, meaning, and associated structural properties (for example, an organization into words and phrases). As for (ii), it seems that many of the fundamental properties of these grammars are part of innate endowment, so that the child in effect knows in advance what kind of grammar he must construct and then must determine which of the possible languages is the one to which he is exposed. Study of (iii) leads to the construction of 'performance models' that have access to the grammar—the knowledge of language—represented in the mind.

To illustrate with a simple example, consider the reciprocal construction in English: such sentences as 'The men saw each other', 'I asked them about each other', 'We shot arrows at each other', etc. The rule of grammar governing these constructions specifies that the expression 'each other' requires a plural antecedent. Once the antecedent is found, we apply the dictionary rule of interpretation to fix the meaning: roughly, that each of the men saw the other men (or man), etc. However, it is not always so easy to select an antecedent. Sometimes it lies in a different clause, as in 'The candidates wanted [each other to win]' or 'The candidates believed [each other to be dishonest]'. In these sentences the bracketed expression is a subordinate clause with 'each other' as its subject, just as in 'John wants [Bill to be successful]' 'Bill' is the subject of 'be successful' in the bracketed subordinate clause. The antecedent of 'each other' lies outside the clause. But we cannot always select an antecedent outside of the subordinate clause. Consider 'The candidates believed [each other were dishonest]' (compare 'The candidates believed [their opponents were dishonest]') or 'The candidates wanted [me to vote for each other]' (compare 'The candidates wanted [me to vote for them]').

Such facts as these are known to all speakers of English, and analogues appear to hold in other languages. The facts are known without experience, let alone training. The child must learn that 'each other' is a reciprocal expression, but nothing more, so it seems. No pedagogic grammar would mention such facts as those described above; the student can be expected to know them without instruction. The principles that determine selection of an antecedent, it seems reasonable to assume, belong to 'universal grammar', that is, to the biological endowment that determines the general structure of the language faculty. From another point of view, these principles form part of a deductive, explanatory theory of human language.

Proceeding in this way, we can attempt to construct grammars that answer question (i), a theory of universal grammar that in part answers question (ii), and performance models that incorporate grammars, answering question (iii). In so far as it succeeds, this quest provides the theory of a particular mental organ. Others can be studied in the same way, and in principle we should be able to proceed to the study of the interaction of such systems—a central topic as soon as we turn to the study of word meaning, for example.

This seems to be a reasonable paradigm for the study of mind, one that has achieved a certain measure of success and holds much promise for the future.                                                   N. C.

Chomsky, N. (1965). Knowledge of Language: its nature, origin and use. New York.
Jackendoff, Ray (1985). Semantics and Cognition. Cambridge, Massachusetts.
Lightfoot, David (1982). The Language Lottery. Cambridge, Massachusetts.

## LANGUAGE: LEARNING WORD MEANINGS.

It may seem at first sight easy to tell when a child knows what a word means. When a little girl of thirteen months sees a ball, says 'ball', and then at once goes to pick it up, the obvious conclusion may appear to be that the meaning of the word is now known to her. But if, during the next month or so, she is heard to say 'ball' on seeing a balloon, an Easter egg, a small round stone, and so on, doubts must begin to arise; and it may then seem wiser to replace the first conclusion by the more guarded one that the word 'ball' has now entered her lexicon and that her knowledge of its meaning has begun to grow.

The above example is not invented. It is provided by Bowerman (1978) from a study of her daughter, Eva. And many similar instances have been recorded by Bowerman and others. So it is clear that, even in the case of 'simple' words like 'ball', the acquisition of word meaning is not an all-or-none affair. Word meanings grow and change—a fact stressed by *Vygotsky (1962), who regarded it as central to an understanding of the development of thought and language. Thus it is by no means so easy as one might suppose to give a straightforward answer to the question: how large is a child's vocabulary, on average, at different ages? Differences in the manner of collecting and handling the data (whether, for instance, the past tense of a verb is to be treated as a separate word or not) have led to widely differing estimates. However, normal children certainly have several thousands of words which are in some sense in their vocabulary by the age of 5. This means that some very rapid and efficient learning must go on.

Although nouns which name familiar objects—or people—are frequently among the earliest words that a child produces, the vocabulary, even in the beginning, need not be limited to words of this kind. Expressions such as 'all gone', 'more', and 'bye-bye' are common. Nelson (1973) reports marked individual differences in this respect among the children she studied: some used many object names, others were more inclined to use words expressing feelings and needs. However, some later studies (e.g. Benedict, 1979) suggest that children have early vocabularies that represent all word classes. It is in any case a problem to know how to classify words in this stage of a child's development, since even a common noun, when used by a very young child, appears to function not just as a label but rather as a substitute for some more complex utterance (expressing a limited range of communicative acts such as interest, desire, intention, etc.) of which the child is not yet capable.

Commonly, when a young child begins to use a word, the meaning is 'overextended', as in Eva's use of 'ball': that is, the range of referents to which the child applies the word is wider than in normal adult usage. Sometimes the extension is to objects all of which share with the original referent some common perceptual feature. All Eva's 'balls' have rounded contours. But the rule that governs extensions need not be of this straightforward kind. Vygotsky (1962) reports a principle of grouping known as a 'chain complex', where each new referent has a feature in common with some other, but where no single feature is common to them all. Thus the word 'quah' may be used first of a duck in a pond; then of any liquid; then of a coin with an eagle on it; then of any round object resembling the coin.

Bowerman did not find that chaining was common in the speech of her daughters; but she reports frequent occurence of a kind of extension, also noted by Vygotsky, where the first referent serves as a nucleus or 'prototype', so that later referents all have some feature in common with it, though, as in 'chaining', they may not have any feature in common with one another. Thus for Eva the word 'close' had as its nucleus the act of closing a drawer or a box and was later used for the act of folding a towel (shared feature: bringing two parts into close contact) and of turning the knob on the TV set till the picture darkens (shared feature: hiding or concealing something).

Some theorists have suggested that a prototype or central exemplar may function as a kind of unanalysed image or 'schema'. But, as Bowerman and others have pointed out, there is no reason to think that the existence of prototypes makes featural analysis unnecessary; and there is every reason to think that such an analysis must actually occur on some level even at very early stages in language acquisition.

A second kind of departure from Eva's overextension of 'ball' involves extension to objects which share with the original referent not some perceptual feature but some function. Thus the word 'ball' might be applied not to other round objects but to other objects able to be bounced or thrown. Nelson (1974) argues that, when the children are developing their first word meanings, function is more important than form. But this claim has been disputed and is certainly not proven. What is clear is that, from a very early stage, a child may use either perception of similar form or knowledge of common function (or both) as the basis for a generalization of word meaning—a generalization which may go beyond the limits of the accepted adult norm.

There is nothing surprising in the fact that children initially make such mistakes. It would indeed be astonishing if they were to arrive at a knowledge of the limits of adult usage by one simple assimilative move. It is much more reasonable to think of them as entertaining hypotheses—though these are unlikely to be consciously articulated—and modifying them progressively as more evidence is obtained.

So far we have considered only evidence that comes from observation of a child's *use* of language. However, knowledge of word meanings must also manifest itself in understanding. The problem is that when one considers both the evidence of how young children use language and the evidence of how they understand it, there is often a lack of accord between the two.

For instance, though children are apt to overextend meanings when they produce words, they do not consistently do the same thing when they interpret the words of others (Huttenlocher, 1974). If anything, a child may initially interpret a word more narrowly than an adult would do. Thus Reich (1976) reports that his son, Adam, in response to 'Where's the shoes?' would crawl only to the shoes in his mother's shoe cupboard, bypassing shoes on the floor to get there. Later he would also crawl to shoes in his father's cupboard; then to shoes on the floor, but not to shoes on someone's feet; and finally to shoes wherever they happened to be.

The assumption that there is a single 'word store' drawn on in the same way for comprehension and for production is thus called in question; and a related challenge arises when one considers evidence about the interpretation of words in longer utterances by older children. If a child understands an utterance, it may seem obvious that the words which compose it are 'known' and that, in the process of making sense of the utterance, each of these words is given 'its meaning'. But this is to suppose that a child interprets the language in isolation from its immediate context, which is not what typically happens. Macnamara (1972) argues that it is only to the extent that children understand *situations* that they are able to begin to work out the meaning of the language that is used in them; and this view is now widely accepted. Thus a child can begin to learn the meaning of 'Do you want some milk?' because when someone picks up a jug and holds it over a cup the intention to offer milk is understood. On this view it is to be expected that for a long time the interpretation of language should remain, for the child, embedded in, and powerfully dependent on, the context of occurrence.

There is now clear experimental evidence that this is so. What a child takes an utterance to mean is liable to be determined not just by knowledge of the language but also by an assessment of what the speaker intends (as indicated by non-linguistic behaviour) and by the impersonal context in which the language is being used. In one study, Donaldson and McGarrigle (1974) found that children aged between 3 and 5 who correctly judged that a row of five cars contained more cars than a row of four might reverse this judgement a moment later when the four cars were enclosed in a row of four garages (so that this row was 'full') while the five cars were enclosed in a row of six garages (so that one garage was left empty). One is tempted to say, then, that these children gave 'more' a different meaning on the two occasions; and yet to put it this way is probably to suggest a more analytic, word-by-word, interpretation than actually occurs, at any rate at the level of the child's conscious awareness. (It seems that children have only a limited awareness that the flow of language is broken up into words at all; and yet of course if they did not break it up this way, at some level, how could they produce, in their turn, words organized into new utterances which they have never heard before? Much that goes on in language learning is clearly not conscious.)

Attempts have been made to study children's ability to arrive at word meanings by giving them 'nonsense words' in linguistic contexts so devised that inferences as to meaning are possible. A classic study by Werner and Kaplan (1950) used such sentences as

A corplum may be used for support.

A wet corplum does not burn.

You can make a corplum smooth with sand-paper.

Children proved to be very bad at deriving the meanings of isolated words from a series of examples of this kind. (See also Campbell and Bowe, 1978.)

It seems clear, then, that non-linguistic contexts are essential for the early stages of the growth of word-meaning. And recent work has emphasized also the early importance of *conversational* contexts, within which the child's use of single-word utterances gradually shifts from a limited to a wider range of communicative acts, and eventually to the *predicative* function (as in uttering a comment on an adult-introduced topic) that appears to mark the threshold into early word combinations (Dore, 1985; Griffiths, 1985). But it is perhaps only with the advent of literacy that language starts to become sufficiently 'disembedded' to be considered and reflected upon as a system in its own right (cf. Donaldson, 1978 and Perera, 1984), so that linguistic contexts alone can begin to provide the basis for additions to the mental lexicon.

See also LANGUAGE DEVELOPMENT IN CHILDREN.

M. D.

Benedict, H. (1979). Early lexical development: comprehension and production. *Journal of Child Language*, **6**, 183–200.

Bowerman, M. (1978). The acquisition of word meaning: an investigation of some current conflicts. In Waterson N. and Snow, C. (eds.), *Development of Communication: social and pragmatic factors in language acquisition*. New York.

Campbell, R. N. and Bowe, T. (1978). Functional asymmetry, in early child language. In Drachman, G. (ed.), *Salzburger Beiträge zur Linguistik*, **4**. Salzburg.

Donaldson, M. (1978). *Children's Minds*. London.

Donaldson, M. and McGarrigle, J. (1974). Some clues to the nature of semantic development. *Journal of Child Language*, **1**, 185–94.

Dore, J. (1985). Holophrases revisited: their 'logical' development from dialogue. In Barrett, M. D. (ed.), *Children's single-word speech*. New York.

Griffiths, P. D. (1985). The communicative functions of children's single-word speech. In Barrett, M. D. (ed.), *Children's single-word speech*. New York.

Huttenlocher, J. (1974). The origins of language comprehension. In Solso, R. C. (ed), *Theories in cognitive psychology*. Hillsdale, New Jersey.

Macnamara, J. (1972). Cognitive basis of language learning in infants. *Psychological Review*, **79**, 1–13.

Nelson, K (1973). Structure and strategy in learning to talk. *Monographs of the Society for Research in Child Development*, **38**, Nos. 1–2, Serial No. 149.

Nelson, K. (1974). Concept, word and sentence: interrelations in acquisition and development. *Psychological Review*, **81**, 267–85.

Perera, K. (1984). *Children's writing and reading*. Oxford.

Reich, P. A. (1976). The early acquisition of word meaning. *Journal of Child Language*, **3**, 117–23.

Vygotsky, L. S. (1962). *Thought and Language*. Cambridge, Massachusetts.

Werner, H. and Kaplan, E. (1950). Development of word meaning through verbal context: an experimental study. *Journal of Psychology*, **29**, 251–7.

## LANGUAGE: NEUROPSYCHOLOGY.

In the psychological analysis of the breakdown of language and speech in neurological disorders the main emphasis is on acquired *aphasia (disorders of language in patients brain-damaged as adults, although there are also studies of patients with acquired *dyslexias (disorders of reading), dysgraphias (disorders of writing), and *dementias, as well as children (and adults) with the corresponding developmental disorders. The studies have centred around two main aims: the development of models of language processing that will account for the observed patterns of language breakdown, and the identification of the neural substrates of language processing.

Since H. C. Bastian (1869) and Carl *Wernicke (1874) demonstrated that, as well as problems in language production, some aphasic patients have problems in language comprehension, it has been evident that there is no single problem of aphasia. At the same time, the close relation between language and thought has led some theorists to maintain that underlying the language deficit was a more general impairment of cognitive function, in particular of symbolic thinking (Head, 1926), or of abstract reasoning (Goldstein, 1948), or of the ability to form propositions (Hughlings Jackson, 1878). Although many aphasic patients perform poorly on non-verbal tests of intellectual function, some do not (Zangwill, 1964); demanding non-verbal tasks may be performed quite adequately—there are cases of aphasic musicians, bridge players and painters.

The earliest comprehensive theory to account for aphasias was proposed by Lichtheim (1885); he showed that a model with three centres—one for storing auditory word images, one for motor word images, and one for the word concepts—could predict a number of distinct subtypes of aphasia.

In the second half of the twentieth century, advances in linguistics that emphasized the relationships between thought and language brought a renewed interest in aphasia and especially awareness of its linguistic dimensions. The Wernicke–Lichtheim classification system was revived and extended by Geschwind and Goodglass working in Boston, USA (for a summary see Albert, et al., 1981). They suggested that there are five main types of aphasia, together with some less frequent forms. These are classified in terms of the characteristics of their spontaneous speech, and the degree to which language comprehension and sentence repetition are impaired. Each of the types is believed to be associated with lesions in particular parts of the dominant cerebral hemisphere, and to represent a disruption at a different level of linguistic description. In *Broca's aphasia* spontaneous speech is non-fluent and sometimes dysarthric (slurred), with short sentences consisting mainly of nouns and main verbs; comprehension is relatively well preserved except with sentences which can only be understood with syntactic analysis. The underlying disorder is said to be (mainly) syntactic, and Broca's aphasia is associated with lesions in the inferior part of the left frontal lobe. In *Wernicke's aphasia* speech is fluent with many correctly-used grammatical structures, but some inappropriate nouns and main verbs; auditory language comprehension is severely affected. The deficit is thought to be mainly at a semantic level, and the lesion usually involves the superior part of the left temporal lobe. *Conduction aphasics* have poor repetition despite relatively well-preserved comprehension and fluent language production, although phonemic errors may be common in their spontaneous speech. It has been argued that their problem is (primarily) phonological, and the lesion responsible may lie on the borderline of the frontal and temporal lobes. In *anomic aphasia*, language comprehension and repetition are good, but spontaneous speech shows difficulty in finding words, and circumlocutions despite normal syntactic structures. Anomic aphasia, which is not associated with any well-defined areas of damage, is considered to be a disruption at a lexical level. In *global aphasia* all aspects of language are severely affected due to large lesions in the left hemisphere.

While this classification scheme is widely used in the English-speaking world, in other countries somewhat different approaches have been adopted. In the Soviet Union, A. R. *Luria (1947) developed a classification system based on his analyses of the aphasias of men with bullet wounds to the head, adopting the linguistic theories of the Prague School. In France and Germany the more classical theories of Wernicke and Lichtheim were maintained and developed.

Attempts to localize the lesions causing different types of aphasia have met with several criticisms. *Hughlings Jackson (1878) argued that aphasic symptoms were not the result of a missing, or damaged portion of the brain, but were rather the consequence of the activity of the whole of the undamaged part. He pointed out that language which might appear to be lost in purposive, propositional speech, could still be accessible in more 'automatic' uses (e.g. swearing and singing). Language functions could not be localized to one area of the brain without considering the operation of the rest of the brain as a whole. This dispute—between localizationists (e.g. Kleist and Nielson) and antilocalizationists (e.g. Pick, Head, and Goldstein) has been a recurring theme. Earlier studies relied for information on the localization of lesions by post-mortem examination of the brain. Since 1970, advances in techniques for examining the location of damage in the brains of living patients—e.g. computerized axial tomography (CAT scan) and positron emission tomography (PET scan)—have allowed many more patients to be examined. While different aphasia types can be shown to have a general correspondence to areas of damage, in large-scale studies there may be no single part of the brain that is affected in every one of a group of patients with aphasia of a particular type. (SEE IMAGES OF THE BRAIN IN ACTION.)

Systematic psychological testing was first introduced by Weisenburg and McBride (1935). They established test norms to enable comparisons to be made between aphasic patients and normal subjects on a range of verbal and non-verbal tasks, and also between the different aphasic patients. Modern test batteries used to classify patients into the diagnostic subtypes of the kind described above have depended on this methodological innovation.

Since the 1950s most investigations in the neuropsychology of language have used groups of patients with aphasia of these types in attempts to characterize their basic problems. But there is increasing evidence that the aphasia types of the Boston School are not unitary syndromes. For example, there are Broca's aphasics who are non-fluent but have no problem with grammar, and others who cannot generate syntactic structures but have no dysarthria; there are conduction aphasics who have problems in list and sentence repetition but do not make phonemic errors in their speech, and others who make many phonemic errors, but have no particular difficulties in list repetition.

One response to these problems is to reject the presupposition that proper, homogeneous aphasia types can be found, and instead to investigate single patients. This has led to the development of a cognitive approach to the neuropsychology of language; this approach, whose primary focus was disorders of reading and writing, has recently extended to other aspects of aphasic language, as well as developmental language problems in children. Workers in this field have adopted detailed information-processing models of language drawn from investigations of normal people, and applied these to the analysis of aphasic language by identifying the defective components of the processing system in individual patients. They have argued that, at best, questions of localization are secondary; they can only be approached once models have been developed that are rich enough to account for the language behaviour of every aphasic patient (see, e.g., Coltheart, Patterson, and Marshall, 1980).

See also SPEECH AND BRAIN PROCESSES.    B. L. B.

D. H.

Albert, M. L., Goodglass, H., Helm, N. A., Rubens, A. B., and Alexander, M. P. (1981). *Clinical Aspects of Dysphasia*. Vienna.

Bastian, H. C. (1869). On the various forms of loss of speech in cerebral disease. *British and Foreign Medical and Surgical Review*, 209–36, 470–92.

Coltheart, M., Patterson, K. E., and Marshall, J. C. (eds.) (1980). *Deep Dyslexia*. London.

Goldstein, K. (1948). *Language and Language Disturbances*. New York.

Head, H. (1926). *Aphasia and Kindred Disorders of Speech*. Cambridge.

Jackson, H. J. (1878). On the affections of speech from disease of the brain. *Brain*, **1**, 304–30.

Lichtheim, L. (1885). *Ueber Aphasie. Deutsches Archiv fuer klinische Medizin*, **36**, 204–68. (English trans., 1885. *Brain*, **7**, 433–85.)

Luria, A. R. (1947). *Traumatic aphasia*; English trans. from the original Russian edition by D. Bowden, 1970. The Hague.

Weisenburg, T. H. and McBride, K. (1935). *Aphasia: a clinical and psychological study*. New York.

Wernicke, C. (1874). *Der aphasischer Symptomenkomplex; eine psychologische Studie auf anatomischer Basis*. Breslau. (English trans. by G. H. Eggert, 1977. In G. H. Eggert (ed.), *Wernicke's Works on Aphasia; a sourcebook and a review*, pp. 91–145. The Hague.)

Zangwill, O. L. (1964). Intelligence in aphasia. In de Rueck, A. V. S. and O'Connor, M. (eds.), *Disorders of Language*. London.

**LANGUAGE AREAS IN THE BRAIN.** The study of the neurological basis of language began in 1861 when Paul *Broca published his findings from the brain of a patient who had suffered from one form of *aphasia. The superiority of one side of the brain for a particular function is called *cerebral dominance*. Each half of the brain is dominant for several functions—for example, the left side is usually dominant for language, the right side for certain musical and spatial abilities (see also NEUROPSYCHOLOGY). Dominance has usually been regarded as a unique biological feature of humans, but it is now known to be present in other species.

Thus bird-song is much more severely affected after damage to one side of the brain.

The basis of dominance was unclear for many years. It has recently been established that certain areas of the cortex are much larger on one side of the brain. In particular, one of the major speech areas has been found to be usually of greater extent on the left than on the right. This anatomical asymmetry is found in the foetus at thirty-one weeks of intra-uterine life, suggesting that dominance is genetically determined. Left-handers show less anatomical asymmetry than right-handers, a finding concordant with other data showing that functional dominance is less marked in left-handers. (See HANDEDNESS.) Asymmetries have also been observed in the brains of great apes, a finding of interest since recent studies support the thesis that chimpanzees have certain capacities for language. (See PRIMATE LANGUAGE.)

The human skull is also asymmetrical since its shape is moulded to that of the underlying brain. The long-rejected ideas of the *phrenologists are thus partially justified. Skulls of ancient humans (dating back as much as 300,000 years) exhibit similar asymmetries, so that cerebral dominance for language was probably present early in human evolution.

Our knowledge of the speech areas and their functions has been based on several techniques: post-mortem study of brains of aphasic patients; electrical stimulation of the exposed brain during neurosurgical operations; recording of changes in the electrical activity of the brain during language activities; and injection of radioactive substances into the bloodstream which permits measurements of changes in blood-flow in localized brain regions during speech. (See IMAGES OF THE BRAIN IN ACTION.)

The major language areas, named after two of the great pioneers in the study of aphasia, lie along the lateral (or Sylvian) fissure of the left side of the brain. We do not know the full extent of these areas. Broca's area lies in the frontal lobe above the lateral fissure. It is just in front of the region of the cortex, stimulation of which leads to movements of the muscles involved in speech. Broca's area may be thought of, as a simple first approximation, as the region which contains the learned programmes for control of the musculature of speech. After destruction of this region, speech is slow and hesitant and the sounds of language are badly produced. In addition the speech is agrammatic, i.e. prepositions, conjunctions, and auxiliary verbs are often omitted, and incorrect endings may be used in verbs or nouns (for example, 'President live Washington'). These findings suggest that Broca's area has a major role in the production of grammatically correct language. The Broca's aphasic also produces defective writing which is agrammatical. His comprehension of spoken and written language may be excellent. Although the Broca's aphasic produces defective speech, he usually sings melodies well. The programmes for production of musical sounds appear to lie elsewhere in the brain, probably on the right side. In a few cases, singing actually facilitates the production of words and this has been used as the basis of an experimental method of speech therapy.

The second major speech area lies in the left temporal lobe below the lateral fissure and is named after Carl *Wernicke. This area lies adjacent to the primary auditory cortex, which is the end-station for auditory input to the brain. The speech of the Wernicke's aphasic is quite different from that of the Broca type. The patient may speak very rapidly, with good articulation and melody and a normal grammatical structure. He has, however, great difficulty in finding the correct word and uses imprecise words (such as 'it' or 'thing') and circumlocutions. He may use words incorrectly. Such improperly used words are called paraphasias and may bear a close relation in meaning to the desired word (for example, 'knife' for 'fork') or no obvious relation at all (for example, 'Argentinian rifle' for 'coin'). He may use non-existent words, which are called neologisms (for example, 'flieber').

There are other areas involved in language functions, damage to which may lead to other distinctive language disorders. Furthermore, there are bundles of nerve fibres (called tracts) which connect the language areas to each other and to other parts of the cerebral cortex on the same or the opposite side of the brain. The corpus callosum is the largest and most obvious collection of such tracts. Destruction of a group of connecting fibres may prevent intact portions of the brain from communicating with each other. The resulting disorders are called disconnection syndromes. They demonstrate the fact that different portions of the brain may carry on complex functions without the awareness of activities in other portions.

A great variety of other aphasic syndromes can result from damage to the language areas or their connections. 'Pure alexia', 'pure word-blindness', and 'alexia without agraphia' are synonyms for a nearly isolated loss of the ability to understand written language while other language capacities are intact. 'Pure word-deafness' is an isolated loss of the ability to comprehend spoken language. 'Pure agraphia' is the isolated loss of the ability to write correct language (in the absence of paralysis). 'Apraxia' is the loss of the ability to carry out movements to verbal command despite good comprehension, and despite preservation in most cases of correct movements in response to non-verbal stimuli. Some remarkable patterns of loss of function are often seen. Thus, the pure alexic may fail to read words and to name colours, but he may read numerals and name objects without difficulty. A patient with callosal damage may write correct language with the right hand, but with the left hand he may produce legible but aphasic, i.e. linguistically incorrect, language. The mechanisms of many of these dissociations of function are well understood, but others still remain

obscure. They are of course important clues to the intellectual processes of the brain. (See LANGUAGE: NEUROPSYCHOLOGY.)

In the adult, extensive damage to one of the primary language areas leads in most instances to permanent disability. However, children who sustain gross damage to the left hemisphere before the usual age of language acquisition will go on to acquire language. The right hemisphere thus has the potential to become the major seat of language. Similar findings are found in birds who sustain unilateral damage on the dominant side before song appears.

If the left hemisphere is damaged after the appearance of language but before the age of 8 or 9, the child nearly always recovers language in a period ranging from a few months to three years. The mechanisms of this plasticity or recovery by means of the right hemisphere are not clearly understood. Their elucidation may help to lead to more effective means of therapy for that majority of older patients who do not recover adequate function spontaneously.                    N. G.

**LANGUAGE DEVELOPMENT IN CHILDREN.** How does a child acquire his native language? Perhaps this question presupposes a more basic one: what is it that a child has to know in order to be said to have acquired his native language? All the current answers to this question suggest that the child has to have competence. Some claim he needs linguistic competence, others that he needs cognitive as well as linguistic competence, and others again that he needs communicative competence, which adds a strong social component to the other two. Before we discuss these three alternative theoretical approaches, we must first clarify the notion of competence.

What does it mean when we say a person has competence? The first aspect of competence is that it is abstract knowledge. An example of linguistic competence is the general rule that to form a plural in English you add an 's' to the noun. Of course, you do not need to be consciously aware of this rule in order to use it—children aged 2 or 3 use it reliably, but cannot describe it. The fact that they *are* using a general rule is, however, clear from their errors. They are highly unlikely to have heard of 'sheeps' or 'mans' from someone else, so it is clear they are constructing these words themselves from a rule they have overgeneralized.

This brings us to the second feature of competence—it is generative. That is, knowledge of general rules means that we can generate new examples, new instances of those rules. 'Sheeps' and 'mans' are, for the child who spoke them, completely new instances, his own creations. The sentence I am writing now is a completely novel one, based on my knowledge of the rules whereby one constructs sentences.

But when we consider a child speaking, or, for that matter, an adult writing a sentence for *The Oxford Companion to the Mind*, we are unwilling to attribute these performances simply to linguistic competence. Putting it crudely, we know that the child has to have something to say before he expresses it, and that, hopefully, so does the adult. In other words, a certain cognitive competence as well as a linguistic competence is a necessary condition for successful linguistic performance; we have to mean something when we speak, and we have to go some way towards understanding what the other person means when he speaks to us.

This feature was somewhat underemphasized until the late 1960s and early 1970s. During the early 1960s, Noam Chomsky's account of generative linguistics dominated the research scene (see LANGUAGE: CHOMSKY'S THEORY). Investigators audio-taped young children in dialogue with their parents, transcribed the tapes, and analysed the transcripts linguistically. That is, they performed a *structural* analysis, whereby they treated the child's utterances as though they were a novel language. This analysis resulted in a description in terms of classes of words which did not correspond to adult-form classes (such as noun, verb). Children might say 'car gone', 'Daddy gone', 'lettuce gone', 'that red', 'that bow-wow', 'that man', demonstrating use of a class of pivot words (gone, that), which each occur frequently in one position only in a two-word sentence, and upon which other, open-class words are hung. Generative psycholinguists tried to extend these findings both back and forwards in the child's development. First, they suggested that these two-word utterances embodied the linguistic universals with the knowledge of which the child had been innately endowed. That is, every infant is preprogrammed, they maintained, with the capacity for using features which are common to all languages, such as the distinction between subject and object or that between qualifier and noun. The generative psycholinguists also tried to trace the ways in which the early two-word sentences subsequently develop into full linguistic performance. They attributed this development to the acquisition of more and more complex transformation rules—that is, rules that transform the deep underlying structure into the surface structure.

Soon dissatisfied with a purely linguistic approach, investigators started to videotape as well as audio-tape the child's conversations with his mother. When they did so, they found that a *functional* analysis was appropriate for the data collected. It is only from a videotape that one can discover whether, when a child said 'Mummy shoes', he was meaning 'Those are mummy's shoes' (possessive) or 'Mummy, put my shoes on' (actor, action, object). Clearly, the child has meanings he wishes to express, and functional analysis soon revealed a corpus of about a dozen or fifteen other such relationships which were expressed in the utterances of children aged 2. From this point of view, language development lags behind cognitive development—the child has to understand what he wants to say before he can say it. Or, as Dan Slobin has put it more elegantly, 'New forms first express old functions, and new functions are first expressed by old forms'.

In some cases, though, linguistic development lags far, far behind cognitive development. The four-year-old child has long since acquired the notion of himself as an individual. Yet the linguistic forms he uses to refer to himself develop painfully slowly. He may use his own name all the time to begin with—'Adam go hill', 'Pick Adam up'. Next he uses 'I' in the initial sentence position only, 'me' in all other positions—'I Adam do that', 'Why me spilled it?' Finally, he grasps the subject and object functions of I and me—'That what I do' and 'You want me help you?' This example shows that while a certain level of cognitive development is a necessary condition for linguistic performance, it is not a sufficient condition: there are certain specifically linguistic competences which also have to be acquired. What is more, some languages make it very hard to be linguistically competent—how does the French child acquire the right gender for all his nouns?

The mechanisms by which linguistic competence develops, and the nature of its dependence on cognitive development, have been the subject of much speculation; little, however, is really known. *Piaget and his followers suggest that the grammatical expression of such structures as action–object and actor–action is dependent upon the sensorimotor development of the child. The child has to act upon his own environment before he can conceive of the notions of actor, action, and object and subsequently express them.

More recently, psychologists have stressed the social context of the percursors to language. At a very early stage of his life indeed the child can direct his mother's attention to something in his environment simply by focusing his gaze upon it. Subsequently in his development he may make grasping movements towards it, and later still gesture or point towards it. Jerome Bruner suggests that it is by this manipulation of his *social* environments that the child is laying the foundations for competence. And it is *communicative* competence that is being acquired; he is acquiring the rules relating to how we refer.

See also LANGUAGE: LEARNING WORD MEANINGS.

P. H.

Cromer, R. (1974). The development of language and cognition: the cognition hypothesis. In Foss, B. M. (ed.), *New Perspectives in Child Development*. Harmondsworth.

Fletcher, P. and Garman, M. (1986). *Language Acquisition: Studies in First Language Development*, 2nd edn. Cambridge.

Greene, J. (1975). *Thinking and Language*. London.

Slobin, D. I. (1972). Seven questions about language development. In Dodwell, P. C. (ed.), *New Horizons in Psychology*, *II*. Harmondsworth.

Wanner, E. and Gleitman, L. R. (eds.) (1982). *Language Acquisition: The State of the Art*. Cambridge.

**LASHLEY,** KARL SPENCER (1890–1958). American neuropsychologist, educated at Johns

Hopkins University, Baltimore. While still relatively junior he began to work with Shepherd Ivery *Franz, a pioneer in the application of physiological methods to the study of brain mechanisms and intelligence in animals. Lashley later worked closely with J. B. *Watson and may indeed be regarded as a co-founder of *behaviourism. Indeed his understanding of neurology was a good deal more sophisticated than that of Watson and he soon abandoned Watson's reliance on *reflexes and conditioned reflexes (see CONDITIONING) as the building blocks of behaviour. At the same time, he held strongly to Watson's insistence on objective methods and the abandonment of consciousness in the explanation of behaviour.

Lashley's best-known work involved study of the effects of lesions of the cerebral cortex on intelligence and learning in the rat and monkey. He was a most competent experimenter and the first to apply statistical methods to the analysis of the results of brain lesions and to ascertain their locus and extent by post-mortem anatomical study. He published two important groups of studies, the first concerned with cerebral function in learning (1920–35) and the second on the neural mechanisms of vision (1930–48). His important monograph on *Brain Mechanisms and Intelligence* appeared in 1930.

Lashley's work convinced him that although sensory and motor functions are in some sense localized, the effects of cerebral lesions involving the so-called association areas do not indicate clear-cut functional *localization. Indeed it was far more in keeping with his experimental findings to denote the association cortex as substantially equipotential as regards the acquisition and retention of habits and to view the impairment of learning and memory which resulted from cerebral lesions as dependent on the extent rather than the locus of the excision. This relationship has become known as the law of mass action, and although it has been much criticized in recent years, it remains an important principle of cerebral organization.

Lashley was a figure of high standing in the field of physiological psychology and although, unlike his early colleague Franz, he never extended his studies to brain injury in man, he had great influence on the evolution of contemporary *neuropsychology. Among his students were Donald O. Hebb and Karl Pribram. He was a Foreign Fellow of the Royal Society of London.

O. L. Z.

Beach, F. A., Hebb, D. O., and Morgan, C. T. (eds.) (1960). *The Neuropsychology of Lashley*. New York.
Orbach, J. (1982). *Neuropsychology after Lashley*. Hillsdale, New Jersey, and London.

**LATERAL THINKING.** There may not be a reason for saying something until after you have said it. That statement does not make sense in the world of logic, where each step has to rest securely on the preceding step: reason must come before a conclusion, not after it. Yet the statement makes perfect sense in the world of lateral thinking, of perception, of patterning systems, of poetry, and of hypothesis. Philosophers and scientists have always complained that we have no logical way of generating hypotheses. We do have such a way, but it cannot be logical for logic involves analysis of what we know. Instead of analysis we need provocation, and that is what lateral thinking is about.

Suppose we are looking for a new idea for a cigarette product. We use one of the more provocative lateral thinking techniques and we bring in a random word as provocation. The word can be picked from a dictionary with a table of random numbers so that no unconscious selection takes place. Does this mean that any word whatsoever may be used as a provocation with any problem whatsoever? It does. There is no connection at all between the random word and the problem. The word is 'soap', and from this comes the idea of freshness, and of spring, and of putting flower seeds in the butt of cigarettes so that when the butts are thrown away a flower will grow from each one and beautify the surroundings instead of polluting them. It is very difficult to see how such an idea could ever come purely from *analysis* of a cigarette since there is no part of it which would suggest this type of idea. Another time the provocation is 'traffic-lights' and from this comes the idea of putting a red band round the cigarette about two centimetres from the butt end to indicate a danger zone and so give the smoker a decision point. Now this idea is very logical in hindsight and could possibly have come through analysis. In hindsight it is often difficult to tell how an idea actually came about since the aim of lateral thinking is to produce ideas that are logical in hindsight.

The first stage of thinking is the perception stage: how we look at the world; the concepts and perceptions we form. The second stage of thinking is the processing stage: what we do with the perceptions that have been set up in the first stage. Logic can only be used in the second stage since it requires concepts and perceptions to work upon. So what can we do about the first or perception stage? We can rely on chance, circumstance, experiment, or mistake to change our perceptions, or we can try to do something more deliberate. That is where lateral thinking comes in.

A perception is a particular way of looking at some part of the world. It is the grouping together of certain features or the isolation of a certain relationship. Perceptions are the patterns which form in our minds after exposure to the world at first or second hand. These patterns are only some among the *many possible patterns* that could have formed. Moreover, because of the nature of patterning systems, we may be unable to use one perception because we are led away along another. So the type of processing we want to do in the first stage of thinking is concerned with *changing perceptions*. It is concerned with forming new perceptions and with uncovering the perceptions we have but are unable to use.

If we accept that the mind is a pattern-making

and pattern-using system, at least in the perception stage (and all the evidence suggests it is), then we need to develop some deliberate habits of provocation if we are to move from established patterns to open up new ones. Our usual mode of thinking is, quite properly, based on judgement. But judgement only serves to reinforce existing patterns, not to change them. Instead of judgement we need something more provocative. Instead of judgement we need movement, and that is what lateral thinking is about.

There is nothing mystical or magical about lateral thinking. As soon as we accept that perception is based on patterns (rather like the streets in a town) then we need some method for getting out of the familiar patterns—some jolting or provoking system. If our ideas are only a summary of what we already know, then how are we to get new ideas? Certainly we can get some by analysing more fully the implications of what we do know, but the really new ideas depend on new hypotheses, on new conceptual jumps. In a patterning system it is perfectly logical to be illogical. In the example given earlier there is no connection between a cigarette and soap, but one quickly forms along one of the many association pathways we have. Our ideas can now start to move out along this track—and it is a different track from the one they would otherwise have moved along. So the reason for juxtaposing cigarette and soap only appears after the juxtaposition has been made and has proved useful.

We need some indicator to show that we are not operating in the usual judgement system. Otherwise, if we make a statement like 'The hands of a watch should move backwards', we would be judged as unhinged. So from *po*etry, hy*po*thesis, and sup*po*se we extract the syllable *po* which indicates that we are using an idea in a provocative manner in order to open up new ideas. So we now say, 'Po the hands of a watch should move backwards', and using that as a stepping-stone we might come to consider the idea of having the numbering of the hours running from twelve down to one so that by glancing at our watch we can tell how many hours are *left* to the day rather than how many have passed.

The use of random juxtapositions and provocative stepping-stones is only part of the process of lateral thinking—there are many other techniques, some of which are more analytical than provocative. With all the techniques the aim remains the same: the changing of concepts and perceptions. Occasionally the changed perception gives a solution or a valuable new idea. More often lateral thinking only gives a new starting-point which has then to be developed in the usual logical manner. For instance, in a fish-processing plant the starting-point that it might make more sense to take the bones away from the flesh instead of the more usual method of taking the flesh away from the bones led to a new process which saved a great deal of money.

In general our mental tools for judging and processing and analysing are very good. But we have been very poor at generating new ideas and hypotheses because we have failed to realize that in a patterning system provocative methods are required. It was necessary to invent the term 'lateral thinking' because creativity is too vague a word, simply meaning the production of something new. Lateral thinking is concerned with changing concepts and perceptions. Some of artistic creativity has to do with lateral thinking but much of it does not. The term 'divergent thinking' only covers a small part of lateral thinking: that is to say the generation of alternatives as a method for changing perceptions. Indeed some of the lateral thinking processes are not divergent at all. Lateral thinking is concerned with the changing of concepts and perceptions by provocative and other means.

A young toddler is upsetting granny's knitting by playing with the ball of wool. One suggestion is to put the child into the playpen. Another suggestion is to leave the child outside and put granny into the playpen.

See also CREATIVITY; PROBLEM-SOLVING.  E. DE B.

de Bono, E. (1977). *Lateral Thinking*, 2nd edn. London.
de Bono, E. (1971). *Lateral Thinking for Management*. London.
de Bono, E. (1970). *The Dog Exercising Machine*. London.

**LAUGHING GAS** (nitrous oxide). The effects of breathing nitrous oxide were first investigated by the distinguished chemist Sir Humphry Davy (1778–1829). In Bristol, as a young man, Davy joined the Pneumatic Institute, which was run by Dr Thomas Beddoes (1760–1808). Here experiments were undertaken on the effects of breathing gases. They were frequently dangerous, but were an important step towards the discovery of *anaesthetics. The 'subjects' included some of the most famous men of letters of the day, for example Robert Southey and Samuel Taylor Coleridge, who wrote:

The first time I inspired the nitrous oxide, I felt a highly pleasurable sensation of warmth over my whole frame, resembling that which I remember once to have experienced after returning from a walk in the snow into a warm room. The only motion which I felt inclined to make, was that of laughing at those who were looking at me.

Davy first tried the experiment on 11 April 1799, when he obtained nitrous oxide in a pure state. He describes a later experiment in these words:

A thrilling, extending from the chest to the extremities, was almost immediately produced. I felt a sense of tangible extension highly pleasurable in every limb; my visible impressions were dazzling, and apparently magnified, I heard distinctly every sound in the room, and was perfectly aware of my situation. By degrees, as the pleasurable sensations increased, I lost all connection with external things; trains of vivid visible images rapidly passed through my mind, and were connected with words in such a manner, as to produce perceptions perfectly novel. I existed in a world of newly connected and newly modified ideas: I theorized, I imagined that I made discoveries. When I was awakened from this semi-delirious trance by Dr Kinglake, who took the bag from my mouth, indignation and pride were the first feelings produced by the sight of the persons about me. My emotions were enthusiastic and sublime, and for a minute I walked round the room perfectly regardless of what was said to me. As I recovered my former state of mind I felt an inclination to communicate the discoveries I had made during the experiment. I endeavoured to recall the ideas: they were feeble and indistinct; one collection of terms, however, presented itself; and with a most intense belief and prophetic manner, I exclaimed to Dr Kinglake, 'Nothing exists but thoughts! The universe is composed of impressions, ideas, pleasures and pains!' (Kendall, 1954, pp. 44–5).

Davy realized that the gas might be useful as an anaesthetic, for he wrote in 1800: 'As nitrous oxide in its extensive operation appears capable of destroying physical pain, it may probably be used with advantage during surgical operations in which no great effusion of blood takes place.' It was not, however, until 1844 that Horace Wells, an American dentist, first employed nitrous oxide for this purpose—for the extraction of one of his own teeth. (See ANAESTHESIA.)

Kendall, J. (1954). *Humphry Davy, Pilot of Penzance*. London.

**LAW OF EFFECT.** The law of effect is a kind of hedonism of the past: actions that lead immediately to pleasure are learned, remembered, and repeated as habits; whereas actions leading to pain are not remembered, or are suppressed so that later painful behaviour is avoided. This is a reversal of the moralist's hedonism which suggests that we seek pleasure in the future. The concept of the law of effect is a basic tenet of *behaviourism, which eschews *purpose or *intention. It is now held to be correct, although not to be accepted as accounting for all learning and behaviour.

The concept derived from E. L. *Thorndike's experiments with cats placed in puzzle boxes, from which they escaped by trial-and-error behaviour. The escape was the reward that produced the learning, though without understanding.

Thorndike, E. L. (1898). *Animal Intelligence*. New York.

**LAW OF MASS ACTION.** See HANDEDNESS.

**LAWS OF NATURE.** Perhaps the most mysterious issue in the whole of science is the origin and logical status of the laws of physics. Why do they continue to hold without change? Did physical laws 'exist' before matter? Do they change, through the history of the universe? Are they, even, derived by a kind of natural selection of the inorganic world—as suggested by the American philosopher Charles Sanders *Peirce? These impossibly deep questions are discussed in the works listed below.   R. L. G.

Feynman, R. (1965). *The Character of Physical Law*. London.

Hartshorne, C. and Weiss, P. (eds.) (1931–58). *The Collected Papers of Charles Sanders Peirce*. Harvard.

Peirce, C. S. (1958). *Values in a Universe of Chance* (selected writings). New York.

**LAWS OF THOUGHT** have traditionally been linked with, and sometimes identified with, laws of logic. (This tradition was challenged by, among others, Sigmund *Freud, who held that there are highly irrational, powerful laws determining behaviour and how we perceive the world and ourselves.) The English mathematical logician George Boole (1815–64) was perhaps the first, since *Aristotle, to develop the idea that laws of logic are rules by which the mind works. Thus,

that which renders Logic possible, is the existence in our mind of general notions—our ability to conceive of a class, and to designate its individual members by a common name. The theory of Logic is thus intimately connected with that of language. A successful attempt to express logical propositions by symbols, the laws of whose combinations should be founded upon the laws of mental processes which they represent, would, so far, be a step toward a philosophical language (Boole, 1847, Introd.).

For Boole, it seemed possible to discover how the mind works by looking at rules of logic. This idea is remarkably similar to Ludwig Wittgenstein's account of the procedures of language as generating concepts according to the chosen 'language games'. Language, for Wittgenstein, is a kind of machine which by operating generates understanding—and sometimes confusions, which need to be made explicit and sorted out by philosophers. (See WITTGENSTEIN'S PHILOSOPHY OF LANGUAGE.)

A deep question is how far laws of thought are innate (and, together with this, how far the structures of language are innate, as Noam Chomsky holds with his Deep Structure theory of language: see LANGUAGE: CHOMSKY'S THEORY) and how far they are learned, and are products of particular cultures, societies, and technologies. Here there is an enormous range of opinion, from Immanuel *Kant's notion that our ideas of space and time are innately given, to the extreme empiricism of *Helmholtz, for perception, and the earlier empiricist philosophers, who believed, following *Locke, that all we have to start with is the ability to associate sensations to generate ideas and understanding.

If laws of thought are *innate—inherited—it now appears that they can be modified: there are few, if any, limits to how or what we may think.

At present, it seems that we shall not be able to specify effective laws of thought in detail before there are adequate computer programs for solving problems—including problem-solving that is not strictly and explicitly logical. (See ARTIFICIAL INTELLIGENCE.)   R. L. G.

Boole, G. (1847; repr. 1948). *The Mathematical Analysis of Logic: being an essay towards a calculus of deductive reasoning*. Oxford.

**LEARNING AND LEARNING THEORY.** The study of learning has been prominent in psychology for more than eighty years. Since the pioneering work of Ivan *Pavlov and E. L. *Thorndike, its importance has consistently been reflected empirically through experimental investigations and conceptually through interpretative theories.

Pavlov demonstrated empirically the ways in which dogs develop acquired *reflexes, and thus identified the basic phenomena of what is now termed classical *conditioning. As the result of a temporal association with a stimulus which already elicits a response, a previously neutral stimulus comes to elicit a similar, conditioned, response. Thus, for example, a bell paired with food elicits conditioned salivation. At an empirical level, Pavlov's extensive research was remarkably effective in producing robust data relating to a psychological phenomenon. At a theoretical level, Pavlov introduced an important element of plasticity into the Russian reflexological tradition which interpreted all behaviour, including that of humans, as the result of environmental stimuli. Pavlov regarded conditioned behaviour as a reflection of higher nervous activity set in train by stimuli.

Thorndike also used experimental methods and animal subjects, studying 'intelligence' by investigating, for example, how cats learned to escape from a puzzle box to obtain food. He too obtained pleasingly orderly behavioural data which indicated gradual changes in behaviour rather than sudden 'insightful' changes. Thorndike argued that the gradual changes occurred because the 'satisfying state of affairs' which followed the correct response made it progressively stronger or more probable. Through his *law of effect Thorndike emphasized that patterns of behaviour can be selected by their consequences, rather as advantageous taxonomic form is selected by evolutionary pressures on species. In both cases, apparent purpose can be reinterpreted in terms of the effects of consequences. Thorndike originally believed that behaviour followed by an 'annoying state of affairs' became weaker; but his own research, here largely with human subjects, did not demonstrate this. Thorndike therefore retained a truncated form of his law of effect which emphasized the selective strengthening effects of what are now termed reinforcers in instrumental conditioning.

The impact of subsequent empirical studies of learning was for some time largely reflected by theories which were in effect general theories in psychology. This is illustrated in J. B. *Watson's writing. He exploited his familiarity with early empirical studies which related changes in behaviour to environmental conditions in order to advocate that psychology as a whole should be reformulated as the science of behaviour rather than of mental life and experience. Watson's *behaviourism has contributed to the widespread adoption of behavioural studies in psychology, but his more negative views about the relevance of mental life to the refocused discipline of psychology have been less influential. Like subsequent theorists, Watson used the empirical data of studies of learning as a platform for his approach to psychology in general. In particular, he extended the principles of classical conditioning to emotions in humans through his famous studies with 'little Albert', and emphasized environmental influences on behaviour to the neglect of inherited differences.

Edward *Tolman carried out ingenious experiments on learning in animals, and demonstrated patterns of behavioural change which were not so readily interpreted in simple stimulus–response terms. For example, he showed that rats learned to run to a particular place for food rather than to make a stereotyped response such as turning right at a choice point. He also investigated latent learning, shown through savings when animals were allowed simply to explore a maze before being required to run through it to a specific goal box. Tolman used the methods of behavioural investigations, but extended the complexity of the environmental arrangements whose effects on behaviour were studied. He was drawn to use intervening concepts, such as expectancies or cognitive maps, to deal with the relationships he observed between environment and behaviour. In this regard, Tolman was a precursor of contemporary cognitive psychology.

The most detailed and systematic account of learning yet developed was that of Clark *Hull. Yet again based on controlled experiments with animals, Hull's theory was presented in formal terms, with postulates giving rise to precise behavioural predictions expressed in quantitative terms through equations with intervening variables. These variables, which in Hull's theory were such concepts as drive, habit strength, and reaction potential, were more tightly tied to empirical measurements than were Tolman's more cognitive terms. Hull's theory is often cited as the best example in psychology of the hypothetico-deductive method of scientific enquiry, and in this sense it is a further example of a learning theory which has implications for psychology reaching far beyond the empirical studies of learning on which it is based. The theory also strove for a general explication of learning, emphasizing similarities between classical and instrumental conditioning and across species, though incorporating quantitative differences.

In the thirty years 1950–80 the emphasis on formal global theories of learning diminished. Empirical research on conditioning and learning has continued to flourish, however. The methods of free-operant conditioning developed by Skinner have been extremely beneficial in this respect, making it possible to study more effectively the effects of intermittent reinforcement, discriminative control, punishment, and so on. Indeed operant conditioning has become a technology for the experimental analysis of behaviour. One systematic use of the data of operant conditioning has been to support the general behaviouristic approach to psychology favoured by Skinner, with its emphasis on explanations of behaviour couched in terms of its relationships with environmental events in applied contexts with humans as well as with animals in the laboratory (functional analysis of behaviour). (See BEHAVIOURISM, SKINNER ON.) However, the behavioural data obtained from operant conditioning may be evaluated in terms of other theories.

In recent years a number of trends have emerged from empirical studies of conditioning. First, conventional distinctions between classical and instrumental conditioning have been further challenged. One important factor here has been the suggestion that activities of the autonomic nervous system such as heart-rate and blood-pressure, previously thought to be affected only by classical conditioning procedures, can be modulated by instrumental reinforcement, a possibility that encouraged the use of so-called *biofeedback techniques with patients in clinical practice. Secondly, greater interest has been shown in biological or phylogenetic influences on conditioning and learning. It seems that some patterns of behaviour are more readily affected by conditioning procedures than others: animals appear, for example, to be biologically prepared to associate novel tastes and nausea, no doubt because of the implications of such preparedness for survival. Similarly, species-characteristic patterns of behaviour may intrude even in the controlled environment of the conditioning laboratory. These findings have raised some doubts about the generality of the laws of learning established thus far, but they emphasize that behaviour must be interpreted in terms of interactions between inheritance and experience. Thirdly, the increasingly complex relationships between environment and behaviour studied in conditioning experiments have led some contemporary learning theorists (e.g. N. J. Mackintosh) to reintroduce cognitive explanations even of animal behaviour.

The field of learning has consistently been one of the most active areas of experimental psychology. The empirical data which have been produced have consistently demonstrated the power of experimental and comparative methods in psychology. In turn they have given rise to theories which, though designed primarily to accommodate the phenomena of animal learning, have implications for psychology in general, in terms of human as well as of animal behaviour. These theories have therefore reflected (or perhaps led) changing perspectives in psychological science. Learning and learning theory can be said to offer an insight into the empirical and theoretical development of psychology as a whole.

See also MEMORY: BIOLOGICAL BASIS.          D. E. B.

**LEAST EFFORT, PRINCIPLE OF.** This asserts that minimal energy will be expended, sufficient for survival. As a 'complacent cow' description of

behaviour, this is not true even for complacent cows! Some degree of more or less random searching—apparently having a basis of curiosity—is characteristic of virtually all organisms, and is exceedingly highly developed in man. We by no means take least effort as our maxim for behaviour: hence the ziggurats of Babylon, the pyramids of Egypt, the temples, statues, and paintings as well as the philosophy of Greece, and the science which has come to mould Western civilization. The effort involved in building a city—be it Athens or New York—is truly remarkable. It provides the clearest evidence that behaviour is not passive, initiated by stimuli, and that we are not organisms content to exist with least effort. On the other hand, least effort *is* a criterion for the intelligent planning of an enterprise: we set up goals difficult to achieve, and with intelligence reach them without wasted effort.

**LEFT-HANDEDNESS.** See HANDEDNESS.

**LEIBNIZ,** GOTTFRIED WILHELM, FREIHERR VON (1646–1716). Born in Leipzig and trained as a lawyer, Leibniz depended for his livelihood on the patronage of German princes, for whom he worked as a counsellor, diplomatist, and historian. Much of his life was spent as librarian to the Electors of Hanover; George I, who disappointed him by not taking him to England when he became king in 1714, called him a 'living encyclopaedia'. There were few areas of learning to which he did not make important contributions.

He is best known as a philosopher and mathematician. He shares with *Newton the honour of discovering the calculus; their discoveries were effectively independent, though Leibniz was bitterly attacked by Newton's followers, who accused him of plagiarism. He attempted to apply the mathematical type of reasoning as widely as possible, and in so doing can be said to have invented symbolic logic; though because he did not publish his work it had to be invented again 150 years later. He wanted to create a perfect language, which would reflect in its grammar and word-structure the full logical complexity of what we say; this idea has been very fruitful in recent philosophy, especially through the work of Bertrand *Russell, who was much influenced by Leibniz. But Leibniz was also interested in how actual languages worked, and was a pioneer of systematic philology.

He was a leading critic of the physics of *Descartes, which left no place for the force he considered to be inherent in matter; this was one of the things that led to his remarkable philosophical theory of matter as built up out of little minds (monads). He was heavily influenced by Descartes and *Spinoza, who are usually classed with him as rationalists; he in turn was to be a major influence on *Kant. Popularly he was perhaps best known for maintaining that this is the best of all possible worlds, a view Voltaire satirized in *Candide.* But

Voltaire was unjust in treating him as a shallow optimist: he did not believe this world is obviously perfect, but only that because a good God exists this *must* be the best world possible, however evil it may seem.

He invented a calculating machine, and a machine for pumping water out of mines. He founded the Academy of Sciences at Berlin, and had Peter the Great found one at St Petersburg. Himself a Protestant, he did his best to achieve a reunification of the Churches, though without success. He worked extremely hard, and carried on an enormous correspondence on intellectual matters; but his life seems to have lacked an emotional side. He did write poetry, which was admired at the time, but it was dreary, formalistic stuff. He never married; it is said that he proposed at the age of 50 but changed his mind before it was too late.

See also LEIBNIZ'S PHILOSOPHY OF MIND.

R. C. S. W.

Broad, C. D. (1975). *Leibniz: an Introduction*. Cambridge.

Joseph, H. W. B. (1949). *Lectures on the Philosophy of Leibniz*. Oxford.

Leibniz, G. W. *Logical Papers* (a selection of his writings, trans. and ed. G. H. R. Parkinson, 1965). Oxford.

Morris, M. and Parkinson, G. H. R. (eds.) (1973). *Leibniz: Philosophical Writings*. London.

**LEIBNIZ'S PHILOSOPHY OF MIND.** Although he never published it in complete form, *Leibniz's philosophy is a closely knit system of speculative metaphysics, with a neatness and story-book attractiveness which led *Kant to say that Leibniz had built 'a kind of enchanted world'. Subsequent philosophers have generally found the system as a whole too strange to be taken seriously, but some of the individual ideas have been extremely influential.

It could all be described as philosophy of mind, for it is Leibniz's opinion that only minds exist. There are endlessly many of them, all different, and what we take to be inert matter is made up of nothing but minds of a rather stupid variety. There is no difference of kind between them and ourselves, only a difference of degree. They can be thought of as coming low on a scale of gradually increasing intelligence, with microbes and insects and animals and men above them. Above men come angels, and right at the top, God. God is rather a special case, being infinite and the creator of everything else; all other minds are finite minds, of more or less intelligence. Leibniz calls them 'monads'.

Monads have perceptions and desires; according to Leibniz, when mental states are analysed it turns out that fundamentally they all come down to these two kinds. Each monad continually seeks its own improvement, which consists in coming to perceive things more clearly and distinctly. The awareness that one's perceptions have become more clear and distinct is called pleasure, while the awareness that the opposite has occurred is called pain. This leads

to so implausibly intellectual a view of the feelings and emotions that only a philosopher could have adopted it. Leibniz probably derived it largely from *Spinoza, and does not work it out in much detail, but he does provide a few analyses—love, for example, is pleasure at the pleasure of another, pleasure itself being defined as above.

Perceptions may be more, or less, clear and distinct; it is in respect of the clarity and distinctness of their perceptions that minds differ. What makes one mind more intelligent than another is just that it can perceive things better. Leibniz includes as perceptions both thoughts and sense-experiences, for he sees no essential difference between them; sense-experiences are one variety of clear but not very distinct perception. A perception is clear when one understands what one is perceiving, but distinct only to the extent that one can analyse the concepts involved. Many of our thoughts are obscure and confused perceptions, but a few are clear and distinct: the thought that $2 + 2 = 4$, for example, and our apprehension of the two principles Leibniz thinks fundamental to all reasoning: the Principle of Contradiction ('No proposition can be both true and false at once') and the Principle of Sufficient Reason ('Nothing occurs without adequate reason'). These things are not learned from sense-experience, as *Locke and the empiricists maintain; our knowledge of them is innate, though experience is required to bring them ' to consciousness. Leibniz also rejects Locke's claim that all our concepts are acquired from experience by abstraction. No experience could give us concepts like those of God or of mathematical equality, and these must be inborn in us in the same way. Recently the defence of *innate knowledge has been taken up by Noam Chomsky (SEE LANGUAGE: CHOMSKY'S THEORY); but it is one of the things that mark Leibniz off as a rationalist, and it leaves him with the perennial problem of rationalist philosophers: why should an inborn propensity to believe certain things be any guarantee of their truth?

Leibniz was the first to introduce the idea of the *unconscious*. He points out that one can often recall having perceived something—some detail of a familiar scene, perhaps—although one did not notice it at the time: clearly one must have perceived it without being aware of doing so. And in listening to the sea breaking, one is conscious only of the sea and not of each individual drop of water; yet the sound of the sea is made up of the sounds of the drops, so that one must in some way be perceiving each of them. Such unconscious perceptions he calls 'little perceptions'; they differ from conscious perceptions only in degree—degree of clarity and distinctness. Unconscious perceptions are highly obscure and confused, and Leibniz thinks we have far more of them than we might ever suspect; for each monad continually perceives the entire universe, though we are never conscious of more than a small part. Those monads which come very low on the scale, so low that we normally fail to recognize them as minds at all, have only unconscious perceptions, and there are times when we are in this state ourselves—in *sleep, for example, and in death. For when someone dies his mind loses its clearer and more distinct perceptions, but does not cease to exist or lose its identity; it sinks down, temporarily at least, to a lower position on the scale.

No monad wants its perceptions to become less clear and distinct; on the contrary, all its actions are directed towards moving further up the scale. Leibniz regards an action as an event directly caused by the will of a monad, and this is much too crude an account of action. But it is over freedom that Leibniz gets into particular difficulties; he is anxious to defend free will against the determinism of Spinoza, yet it is hard to see how he can. Since every monad must will its own improvement, it can exercise *choice only over how to achieve this. But it is bound to choose whatever means seem the best available—the Principle of Sufficient Reason guarantees that no choice can be made without adequate grounds. So the choice is completely determined by the monad's beliefs about what the best means are. Leibniz ties himself up in knots over this, and attempts various solutions, but he usually says that its beliefs *incline* it, without *necessitating* it, to make the choice it does. Since they incline it quite irresistibly this constitutes a memorable attempt to have your cake and eat it.

The difficulty is made even more acute by a further part of his theory. For he holds that God programmed into every monad at the creation the whole course of its future development, including every action and every thought. We would hardly describe as free, a robot all of whose behaviour had been determined in advance by its designer.

Leibniz actually holds that created monads never produce effects in one another. They only appear to. They are like different clocks, which strike the hours together. God has so designed them that whenever an event we regard as a cause occurs in the career of one monad, the events we think of as its effects will occur in the histories of the others. So the monads keep time with one another, and appear to act on one another, but really do not: there is a 'pre-established harmony' between them. In virtue of the harmony there is a correspondence between each monad's perceptual states and how things are outside it, so that it can be said to 'mirror' the universe even though its perceptions are not caused by the things outside.

Leibniz's reason for this remarkable theory is that if monads could act on one another he thinks they would not be genuinely independent things, substances. Indeed, he goes so far as to maintain that monads cannot really stand in any relations to one another at all. This leads him to deny the reality of space, for he thinks that space can only be a system of relations between things. Things do appear to be spatially related, but really there are no relations between them and therefore no space. Nevertheless, the appearance is 'well founded' in the perceptual states of the individual monads; for they each differ in the clarity with which they mirror different parts of the universe, and our idea that they have positions in space is a confused awareness of these differences. Roughly speaking, I appear closest to those things I most clearly perceive. But one cannot do other than speak roughly here, for the theory is not properly worked out, and could not be. I can perceive the Pleiades, after all, more clearly than the back of my head.

Clarity and distinctness are being given too much work to do. They cannot provide the reality behind our awareness of spatial relationships, nor is it really our sole aim in life to get more of them. Leibniz's overvaluation of them is characteristic of an age intoxicated with the recent successes of rational thought and its apparent capacity to solve every problem; it does not detract from the brilliance and originality of many of his ideas.

R. C. S. W.

**LEONARDO DA VINCI** (1452–1519). Italian sculptor, painter, architect, and engineer–inventor, born at Vinci near Florence, the natural son of a notary. He was apprenticed to Verrocchio (about 1470) in Florence and in 1482 settled in Milan, working with Lodovico Sforza. In 1502 Leonardo entered the service of Cesare Borgia, as architect and engineer. The *Mona Lisa* was painted about 1504.

Leonardo's *Notebooks* are of great interest in describing his work and ideas on hydraulics, the casting of statues, and many inventions, as well as in giving his advice to painters and clear accounts of perspective and the use of shadow. He did not, however, appreciate that the two eyes give perception of depth (by stereopsis); and he wrongly thought that light must cross twice in the eye to produce a right way up retinal image, for perception to be non-inverted. He was also confused on why mirrors normally reverse left and right but not up and down—see MacCurdy (1938), vol. 1, ch. 9. Leonardo recognized, however, many properties of the eye, such as 'irradiation'—bright objects appearing larger than dark ones; and his anatomical drawings are masterpieces, even though they sometimes incorporate features which he believed present when in fact they are not. Leonardo is generally recognized as the most universal genius of all time. (See MIRROR REVERSAL.)

A feature of Leonardo's *Notebooks* of particular psychological interest is that these manuscripts were consistently written in mirror-script. As is well known, mirror-writing is not an altogether uncommon accomplishment, particularly among the left-handed. Although Leonardo's handedness is not reliably known, some experts have claimed that careful study of the detail and shading of his marginal sketches indicate that—at all events before he sustained a partial left-sided paralysis in later life—the pen was held in his left hand. It appears probable, therefore, that Leonardo was naturally left-handed and, like some other left-handed individuals, had a particular facility in mirror-writing.                                    O. L. Z.

Critchley, M. (1928). *Mirror-Writing*, pp. 11–13. London.
MacCurdy, E. (1938). *The Notebooks of Leonardo da Vinci*. London.

**LEUCOTOMY.** The removal of small regions of the frontal lobes of the brain, for extreme depression. The operation is now seldom, if ever, performed. See also PSYCHOSURGERY.

**LEVITATION.** A *paranormal phenomenon which has been claimed to occur in the open air (at a garden party and witnessed by perhaps a hundred guests), and, by the nineteenth-century medium Daniel Dunglas *Home, at a party when he was reported as gliding out of an upstairs window and into another without material support. There appear to be no recent reports of levitation.

An interesting party game is to press down on the head and shoulders of someone blindfolded and seated in a chair, and then to release the pressure. He will then (with some added verbal suggestion) feel that he is floating up to the ceiling. The experience can be extremely convincing, and frightening, though of course he remains seated in the chair.

**LIBIDO.** For Sigmund *Freud, the libido was essentially the sexual drive, which could be sublimated into the great variety of human creative expressions. The evidence that all *creativity beyond *least effort is sexual in origin is now generally regarded as too narrow, and Freud probably exaggerated the sexual basis of creativity. See FREUD ON MENTAL STRUCTURE.

**LIE DETECTOR.** See ELECTRODERMAL ACTIVITY.

**LIMBIC SYSTEM.** The term 'limbic system' derives from the concept of the 'limbic lobe'. It was first used by the French anatomist Paul *Broca in 1878 to describe that part of the brain surrounding the brain-stem and lying beneath the neocortex. A generally accepted modern definition of the 'limbic system' has, however, never been given. Some neuroanatomists believe that the term should be abandoned. Nevertheless it is a widely used 'shorthand' term and most authors would include the following structures within its definition: the hippocampal formation, olfactory regions, hypothalamus, and amygdala.

Functionally, the limbic system is generally said to be concerned with visceral processes, particularly those associated with the emotional status of the organism. Both experimental and clinical data indicate that the amygdala is involved in emotional experiences and reactions, particularly those associated with fear and anger, flight and defence. Stimulation of the amygdala in conscious animals can give rise to quite integrated response patterns evolving over time and involving a wide variety of motor and autonomic responses which are integral parts of the overall behaviour pattern. Although the amygdala would therefore appear to be involved in these responses, it may not be the only such area. Thus changes in aggressiveness can be obtained by stimulation or ablation of septum, certain areas of cerebral cortex, and the grey matter of the mesencephalon. This emphasizes the importance of considering the interaction of connected brain areas rather than the activity within particular 'centres', as effectors of functions.

The hippocampus has been the object of much experimental work, and theories about the nature of its function have multiplied. One possibility which has attracted attention from *behaviourists is that it may be involved in *memory. However, at present no clearly formulated results can be stated. This is in consequence partly of the anatomical complexity of the region and partly of the semantic difficulties surrounding the words 'memory' and 'learning'. Since the hippocampus is richly connected to many other brain regions, it is, as in the case of the amygdala, probably misleading to think of such a structure as a 'centre' of such a function. Physiologically one of its most striking properties is seen in relation to activity in the cerebral neocortex. When the neocortex is 'desynchronized' (i.e. shows low-voltage rapid potentials) the hippocampus becomes 'synchronized' and shows rhythmic sinusoidal waves of 4–7 per second ('theta waves': see ELECTROENCEPHALOGRAPHY). When the neocortex is synchronized, on the other hand, the hippocampus is desynchronized. The functions of this reciprocal relationship are not understood, but it appears to be related to the activity of the reticular formation and the state of attentiveness of the subject. Recent work strongly suggests that serotonin and noradrenaline are closely involved in the switching of mechanisms between these two states.

Another division of the 'limbic system', the entorhinal area, is closely related anatomically to the hippocampus, providing its main cortical source of afferent fibres. Recent anatomical work has shown that it also receives fibres from the frontal, temporal, and cingulate neocortex as well as the olfactory cortex, indicating that it is the final cortical link between the sensory systems of the neo- and transitional cortex on the one hand and the hippocampus and dentate gyrus on the other. It would seem from an anatomical point of view that the sensory information arriving at the entorhinal area is probably highly refined (see DOPAMINE NEURONES IN THE BRAIN).

The information derived from the entorhinal area interacts with hippocampus and amygdala. These structures deliver further messages both directly (from amygdala) and via septum and nucleus accumbens to regions of the hypothalamus concerned with motivational and rewarding mechanisms.

Thus interaction of all the structures in the complex, from the entorhinal area to hypothalamus, is probably of great importance in deciding the final actions of an organism in a particular environment, and in the formation of adaptive behaviour patterns.                                                    O. T. P.

**LOBACHEVSKI,** NIKOLAI IVANOVICH (1793–1856). Russian mathematician, founder of non-Euclidian *geometry. This was extremely important in epistemology as it showed that *Euclid's axioms are not known with certainty, a priori, but are hypotheses which may or may not correspond to physical space. His work is published in *Über die Principien der Geometrie* (1829–30).

**LOCALIZATION OF BRAIN FUNCTION AND CORTICAL MAPS.** One of the echoing controversies in psychology concerns localization of function, the notion that the control of different aspects of behaviour resides in different parts of the brain. Although it is difficult to say exactly when the dispute arose, it certainly became prominent with the work of *Gall in the early nineteenth century. From first observing at school that the mental characteristics of his friends appeared to be related to the shape of their heads, Gall believed that traits like cautiousness and mirthfulness were localized and that their degree of development was indicated by the size and shape of the overlying part of the skull. Gall's *phrenology enjoyed a brief

ascendancy until about 1820 when *Flourens, noting that damage to different parts of the brain often had similar and diffuse effects on behaviour, concluded that the brain acts as a whole. It was only after 1861, when *Broca first showed that speech impairment followed damage to a restricted part of the left frontal lobe, that localization of function acquired scientific respectability. And the dispute seemed settled in 1870 when Gustav Fritsch and J. L. Hitzig reported their observations on the effects of electrically stimulating different parts of the exposed brain, first in soldiers with head injuries and then in animals. They found that stimulating discrete parts of what is now known as the motor cortex produced movements of different regions of the body. Eighty years later, in 1950, W. G. *Penfield and Theodore Rasmussen published the results of similar observations made on fully conscious patients awaiting brain surgery under local anaesthetic. By electrically stimulating small regions along the central fissure, they showed that there was a map of bodily movements in front of the fissure and a map of sensation from the skin behind it (see Fig. 1). Meanwhile, in the intervening years, Gordon *Holmes had discovered that the eye is mapped on to the back of the brain. His method was to look for small areas of blindness in the visual field of patients with gunshot wounds at the back of the head. He found that the part of the

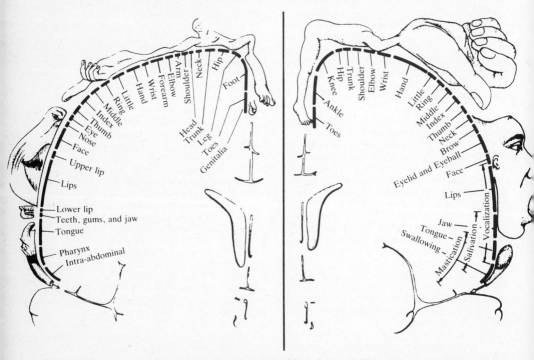

**Fig. 1.** The diagram on the left shows a slice through one side of the brain, roughly between the ears and through what is called the somatosensory cortex. There is a map of the body surface here. Note that some areas, like face and fingers, have a much larger cortical representation than others, i.e. the map is distorted. The diagram on the right shows the map of the muscles in the motor cortex on a slice of the other side of the brain and at a more anterior portion.

eye that was blind depended on the part of the visual cortex that was damaged.

Despite this apparently irrefutable evidence of regional specialization in the brain in connection with speech, movement, seeing, and the sensations from the skin, *Lashley produced abundant evidence in the 1930s and earlier that Flourens' position was not untenable with respect to some forms of behaviour. By studying maze-learning in rats, Lashley showed that the deleterious effects of removing parts of the cerebral cortex depended on the amount of tissue removed rather than on its exact location, a finding enshrined in the principles of mass-action and equipotentiality. Lashley's views struck a sympathetic chord with many psychologists of the following generation, who likened the brain to a computer which can become increasingly unreliable as more of its components are damaged, but which rarely suffers a severe breakdown when a small number of specific localized components are removed.

With hindsight we can see that the often bitter controversy was unnecessary. The view that the brain acts as a whole stems from investigation of complex phenomena, such as learning and remembering complicated tasks involving several of the senses. It is small wonder that a good deal of the brain is involved in such behaviour and therefore that damage to any part of it has some effect. The evidence for regional specificity came, by contrast, from investigations of relatively simple actions such as moving a finger, seeing a light in one part of space, or detecting that a particular part of the skin had been touched. The latter are all examples of sensory discrimination or voluntary movements, the former of higher-level cognitive and intellectual behaviour. To return to the analogy with a computer, we can say that the circuit controlling one of the bulbs on its visual display, or part of the keyboard used to type a program, is localized. But the function the computer performs, from arithmetic to guiding a spaceship, is not so localized.

The resolution of the apparently contradictory evidence concerning localization of function had one particularly interesting but unfortunate effect. It came to be taken for granted that the senses of touch and vision were mapped on the surface of the brain and that there was a similarly orderly representation of the muscles, as shown in Fig. 1. But why there is a map at all ceased to be recognized as a question of fundamental importance, despite the fact that nature had to go to a great deal of trouble to evolve a set of genetic instructions which ensured that the retina of the eye and the surface of the body are represented on the surface of the brain in an orderly map and not higgledy-piggledy. Furthermore, a computer programmed to recognize patterns does not need within its components anything like a map of the original scene. So why does the brain have one?

It became increasingly difficult to avoid the question with the demonstration from 1970 onwards of multiple maps of the retina in the brain. A map is usually demonstrated by recording the electrical activity of single nerve-cells or clusters of them, determining where a visual stimulus must lie on the retina for it to excite these particular cells, and then moving the recording electrode to another group of cells. Using this procedure in anaesthetized animals, it has been shown that the retina is mapped not once but over and over in the cortex. The cat has at least thirteen mapped representations of the retina, the owl monkey at least eight, and the rat has six. As shown in PRIMATES, EVOLUTION OF THE BRAIN IN, Fig. 8, the posterior third of the cerebral cortex in the owl monkey is concerned with the multiple mapped representations of visual space.

What is the possible purpose of such an arrangement, which is not confined to vision for there are now known to be several topological representations of the surface of the body and the musculature in monkeys? The most plausible explanation concerns a well-known physiological phenomenon called lateral inhibition. In the eye itself, adjacent differences in the brightness of the image are given prominence in the nerve signals that leave the eye. This is accomplished by a system of lateral inhibitory connections in the retina which ensure that nerve-cells tend to inhibit their immediate neighbours. In an area of uniform illumination, all cells are equally excited by the light and equally inhibited by their neighbours. But where there is a sharp difference in illumination, as at the image of a contour, the highly illuminated cells exert a powerful inhibition on their neighbours in the shade, and the difference in signals sent by the two groups of cells is enhanced. Lateral inhibition cannot create something out of nothing, but it can enhance one feature of the visual image at the expense of another. Lateral inhibition of the kind just described ensures that edges and contours are prominently coded in the signals from the eye.

There is now excellent evidence from physiology and anatomy that lateral inhibition works in the brain as well as in the eye, and this provides the major reason for the existence of a map of the retina on the cortex of the brain. If the differences in illumination of adjacent parts of the eye are to be given further note in the cortex, then the sensory connections between the nerve-cells concerned with the two adjacent parts of the image should be close together. In a map they are as close together as possible, and lateral interactions will be maximally efficient. If there were no map at all, so that nerve-cells concerned with adjacent parts of the image were often far apart in the brain, the problem of interconnecting the cells would be formidable and the average length of a connection could be much greater. In a map of the sensory surface the lateral interconnections between cells can all be local, and anatomy has shown this to be so.

But why are there many maps rather than just one? The answer is really the same. Inhibitory connections between neighbouring nerve-cells of the cortex are now believed to be involved in coding many attributes of the visual image, such as colour, movement, disparity, orientation, size, and spatial periodicity. If all of this were to be attempted within one map, the local interconnections would again have to be longer and the problem of interconnecting the right cells would increase. By having many maps, each of which is small and contains nerve-cells concerned only with one or a few of the stimulus attributes just mentioned, the lateral interconnections can be kept as short as possible and the problem of interconnecting the right type of cell is minimized.

This simple idea has much to support it. First, although there are long fibre connections from one part of the brain to another, electron microscopy has shown that the connections within a particular map are very short and predominantly inhibitory. Second, physiology has shown that nerve-cells within a particular cortical representation of the retina tend to be concerned with a restricted range of stimulus qualities, such as orientation and size, or colour, or movement. Different representations deal with different stimulus qualities. Third, there are many examples of very selective effects on visual perception of localized brain damage. Although they are rare, some patients suffer a highly selective disturbance of the perception of colour or position or depth, as would be expected when the damage is occasionally restricted to one of the visual maps.

Although the different sensory qualities of the visual scene may initially be coded in separate visual areas, our visual perception is unitary not fragmented, which means that the timing of the activity of cells in different visual areas must be precisely co-ordinated. If we look at a moving, spinning coloured object and the nervous signals in one visual area were to be out of phase with all the others, some distortion should occur in what is seen. Indeed, fever, toxicosis, and brain damage may all lead to temporary visual perceptual dislocations. For example, in one part of the visual field objects may appear too large or too small, smooth movement may look jerky, contours may be multiplied, position and orientation be greatly misperceived.

Multiple brain maps of sensory and motor systems are now established. They permit the maximum efficiency and economy in the myriad interconnections between nerve-cells responsible for analysing sensory signals. Their existence also throws light on what is now seen as an unwarranted controversy about localization of function. The cortical representations of the sensory attributes of some stimuli, such as colour, may be confined to a few areas. The cortical events underlying complex and cognitive actions are probably so widely dispersed that no brain damage, however great, can either destroy them entirely or leave them wholly unimpaired.                                          A. C.

**LOCKE,** JOHN (1632–1704), born at Wrington, Somerset, the first son of a lawyer whose father was

a clothier. He was educated at Westminster School, where he was a King's Scholar, and Christ Church, Oxford, where he obtained a scholarship in 1652. His first published work was a complimentary poem for Oliver Cromwell, written while he was an undergraduate.

He took degree courses in logic, metaphysics and classical languages, but he was dissatisfied with the peripatetic philosophy he was taught. Even so, he developed an interest in experimental philosophy which led him to the study of medicine and the foundations of empirical philosophy. Through this he met Robert Boyle, probably the strongest influence on him, and became his close friend, student and unofficial assistant. He graduated as an MA in 1658 and was elected a Senior Student of Christ Church and then a lecturer in Greek.

After a brief excursion into diplomacy in 1665/6 he returned to Oxford to study medicine and collaborated with the great physician Thomas Sydenham. In 1667 he left Oxford to become personal physician to Lord Ashley, later first Earl of Shaftesbury, whose life he was credited with saving by an operation. He was elected Fellow of the Royal Society in 1668. On the third attempt he gained a doctorate in medicine in 1674 and was appointed to a medical studentship at Christ Church. In the 1670s he spent periods in France and drafted his first *Letter Concerning Toleration* and *Essay Concerning Human Understanding*.

In 1682 he met Damaris Cudworth, daughter of the Cambridge Platonist Ralph Cudworth. They became close friends and wrote poems and love letters to one another, but their romance never blossomed and in 1685 she married Sir Francis Masham and went to live at Oates in Essex. They remained firm friends and Locke spent his last years at Oates.

Under the influence of Ashley and his friends, Locke's political views became more liberal and he was involved in Whig and Protestant struggles against the power of the king. The first of his *Two Treatises of Government*, probably written in 1681, may be seen as a justification of Shaftesbury's revolutionary movement for a Protestant succession. Shaftesbury fled to Holland in 1682 and, after the Rye House Plot to kidnap the king in which a number of his friends were implicated, Locke followed in 1683. A year later, at the command of Charles II, he was deprived of his studentship at Christ Church.

While in Holland Locke worked at his *Essay*, sending it for publication in 1686. He also wrote letters, later published as *Thoughts Concerning Education*, to his cousin Mary Clarke, wife of Edward Clarke, about the upbringing of her son. He also had contact with William Penn, of whose constitution for Pennsylvania he had criticisms. In 1688 Penn secured a pardon for Locke from James II, which Locke rejected, but he returned to London on the accession of William III in 1689. William offered him more than one ambassadorship, which he refused partly because of his inability to drink as deeply as such a post demanded. Instead he became a commissioner of appeals. His *Essay* was published in 1689 (dated 1690) by Thomas Bassett, who paid him £29 for the privilege. Locke met Isaac *Newton in 1689 and corresponded with him for the rest of his life, mainly on theological matters.

Finding that the London air was bad for his asthma, a lifelong complaint, he went to live with the Mashams at Oates, but his appointment as a commissioner for trade and plantations in 1695 involved him in much work in London, including the appointing of governors for New York and other American colonies, and the preparation of some vicious proposals, fortunately not accepted, for the combating of pauperism. He also worked on new editions of the *Essay*, and corresponded with admirers and critics, especially Edward Stillingfleet, bishop of Worcester. Perhaps his greatest mistake was to dismiss *Leibniz's criticisms as trivial. In 1698 the king offered him an important diplomatic post in Paris, possibly the one later held by David *Hume, but he refused. From 1700 until his death he lived in retirement at Oates. He is buried in the churchyard at High Laver in Essex. In spite of his many close friendships with beautiful women he had remained a bachelor.

Among his lesser known works were his editing of Boyle's *General History of the Air*, published in 1692, an edition of Aesop's *Fables* designed to help children to learn Latin, a book on money and interest rates, and the invention of a truss.   P. A.

Cranston, M. (1957). *John Locke: a biography*. London

**LOCKE ON THE MIND.** In an early scholarly book on Locke, James Gibson (1917, p. v) said that it is too often assumed that the *Essay Concerning Human Understanding* 'can be understood without being studied and that its full significance can be summed up in a small number of simple propositions'. This assumption is still made in spite of recent efforts by scholars. Locke is often spoken of as a precursor of modern psychology, but his view of the mind and its influence is seldom studied in detail. It is said that for Locke the mind was a mere passive receptor of sensations, that he espoused a crude *faculty psychology, and that he was an important initiator of associationist psychology. When these allegations are not plainly false they are seriously misleading.

Locke begins by saying (*Essay*, I.i.1, 2) that the understanding, like the eye, makes us 'see and perceive all other things' but takes no notice of itself; 'Art and Pains' are required to discover its nature. However, he says that he does not intend to enquire into the physical concomitants of the mind or to 'examine wherein its Essence consists'. What he does propose to examine is the relations between the mind and its objects.

A central conception of Locke's philosophy is that of *ideas*. This word is used to refer to various different things, including sensations or sense-data, memories, and concepts: when I see a yellow daffodil I am having, *inter alia*, an idea of yellow, when I remember the colour I am having a memory-idea of it, and when I think about democracy I am operating with an idea (i.e. concept) of democracy. None of these ideas should be thought of as mental *images*, but an idea *may* be an image. It is usually clear from the context which of these meanings is intended. The term 'idea', Locke says, stands for 'whatsoever is the Object of the Understanding when a Man thinks' or 'whatever it is which the Mind can be employ'd about in thinking' (*Essay*, I.i.8).

All ideas originate in experience. Locke devotes the whole of Book I to arguing directly against the conception of *innate ideas, and then says that the whole of the rest of the *Essay*, based as it is on the hypothesis that there are no innate ideas, shows that we can do without this conception.

There are two sources of ideas: sensation and reflection. Ideas of sensation occur when we observe external objects, and ideas of reflection when we observe the operations of our minds. Thus we come by ideas of yellow, cold, square, sweet, and of perceiving, believing, willing (II.i.2–4).

Ideas may be simple or complex. Complex ideas are analysable into, or constructed out of, simple ideas, but simple ideas are unanalysable and unconstructed. The mind is passive in its reception of simple ideas; it cannot prevent simple ideas from being impressed on the mind, or alter them, or choose to have a particular simple idea in the absence of the appropriate stimulus. However, this passivity is limited, and in the reception of simple ideas the mind may be active in attending to, or noticing, different things. The reception of simple ideas is not regarded by Locke as a purely physical process but involves also a mental element, logically distinct from the physical elements. He says that 'in bare naked *Perception*, the *Mind* is, for the most part only passive' (II.ix.1), but he also says that 'whatever impressions are made on the outward parts, if they are not taken notice of within, there is no Perception' (II.ix.3). If we are concentrating on a difficult book we may fail to notice even a loud noise and so not receive the idea even though our sense organs are stimulated (II.ix.4). It is similar with simple ideas of reflection (II.ix.7, 8).

However, the mind is active in operating upon its ideas as it does in remembering, discriminating, comparing, combining and enlarging, and abstracting them. By *combining* simple ideas the mind makes complex ideas, by *comparing* the mind arrives at ideas of relations, and by *abstracting* them from other ideas with which they occur it makes general ideas (II.xii.1).

Locke refers to thinking and willing, 'the two great and principal Actions of the Mind', as 'faculties' (II.vi.2), but he warns us against thinking of them as 'real Beings in the Soul, that perform[ed] those Actions of Understanding and Volition'. They are not separate mental agents each with its own task to perform; it is *the mind* that performs all these actions (II.xxxi.6).

Locke devotes a whole chapter to 'the association of ideas'. If it is true that this chapter was an important influence on the creators of associationist psychology then it is likely that those creators were among the many who have misunderstood Locke. This chapter, the last in Book II, was included only in the fourth and fifth editions of the *Essay* and the central conception is put to a very limited use: that of explaining one of the ways of going wrong in thinking, which Locke describes as 'a sort of madness'.

The sort of unreasonableness shown by a person who argues obstinately for his view in the face of all the 'evidence of reason' is often thought to result from education, presumably faulty, and prejudice. Locke, says,

Education is often rightly assigned for the Cause, and Prejudice is a good general Name for the thing it self: But yet, I think, he ought to look a little farther who would trace this sort of Madness to the root it springs from, and so explain it, as to show whence this flaw has its Original in very sober and rational Minds, and wherein it consists (II.xxxiii.3).

Locke calls this 'Madness' because it is 'opposition to reason', which he sees as one, but not the only, form of madness. What particularly concerns him includes arguing from false premisses provided by the association of ideas.

Some ideas are 'naturally' connected. An example that he might have given is the ideas of shape and size, which are essential properties of matter. However, besides this 'natural connexion',

there is another Connexion of Ideas wholly owing to Chance or Custom; Ideas that in themselves are not at all of kin, come to be so united in Mens Minds, that 'tis very hard to separate them . . . and the one no sooner at any time comes into the Understanding but its Associate appears with it . . . (II.xxxiii.5).

Locke then proposes a possible explanation for this which resembles a 'brain-trace' theory (see ENGRAM). Custom may 'settle' trains of motion in the 'animal spirits', 'which once set a going continue on in the same steps they have been used to, which by often treading are worn into a smooth path, and the Motion in it becomes easy and as it were Natural' (II.xxxiii.6). Thus two ideas may be connected by accident and then, by the strength of the original impression or frequent repetition, appear to be necessarily connected. If an adult is surfeited with honey, the very idea of honey may call up the ideas of dislike and vomiting. He can trace this association to its origin. However, if this happens to a very small child the cause may not be noticed and the child may be thought to have a 'natural antipathy' to honey (II.xxxiii.7). We should, in educating children, strive to prevent the undue connection of ideas that are in themselves 'loose and independent' of one another. Children may, for example, become afraid of the dark because goblins are, unnaturally, associated with darkness.

Associationism, seen primarily as the attempt to reduce all mental activity, including rational thinking, to the association of ideas, or sensations, is very far from Locke's conception of association. However, other aspects of Locke's philosophy of mind, and matter, might be more plausibly related to one idea of 'mental chemistry' espoused by some associationists. He was greatly influenced in his discussion of physical phenomena by chemistry and the corpuscular hypothesis of Robert Boyle. Locke accepted that physical objects are composed of minute corpuscles having just a few simple, intrinsic, 'primary' qualities, and that the more complex 'secondary' qualities of the physical objects may be explainable in terms of the primary qualities of the constituent corpuscles in their many different arrangements. There are suggestions in Locke's works that if he had gone on to consider mental phenomena in more detail he would have arrived at a view similar to his view about physical phenomena, namely that complex mental states or activities could be analysed into, or explained in terms of, simple mental entities. He does appear to have supposed that there is mental as well as material substance, and he might well have distinguished between primary *mental* qualities (simple) and secondary *mental* qualities (complex). There is a parallelism between the concepts of simple physical corpuscles combined to form complex physical bodies—primary qualities so arranged as to produce secondary qualities—and simple ideas combined to form complex ideas. Applied to mental as well as physical phenomena, this suggests a form of 'mental chemistry', according to which mental compounds may be analysed into simple mental elements, such as sensations (Woodworth, 1931). Locke does not, however, show any signs of attributing the combining of ideas involved to *his* conception of the association of ideas; he reserved that for the explanation of the involuntary connecting of ideas and held that the *reliable* connections of ideas were the result of natural or chosen connections (*Essay*, II.xii.2). There are, of course, problems about what 'natural' means, about how the ideas of natural connections and voluntary connections would relate to one another and to the combining of primary mental qualities to give secondary mental qualities, and how far the analogy with the corresponding physical combinings would hold.

P. A.

Aaron, R. I. (1971). *John Locke* (3rd edn.). Oxford.

Alexander, P. (1974). Boyle and Locke on Primary and Secondary Qualities. Reprinted in Tipton, I. C. (ed.) (1977), *Locke on Human Understanding*. Oxford.

Alexander, P. (1985). *Ideas, Qualities, and Corpuscles*. Cambridge.

Brown, T. (1820). *Lectures on the Philosophy of the Human Mind*. Edinburgh.

Drever, J. (rev. Wallerstein, H.; 1964). *A Dictionary of Psychology*. Harmondsworth.

Gibson, J. (1917). *Locke's Theory of Knowledge*. Cambridge.

Locke, J. (1690; 5th edn. 1706). *An Essay Concerning*

*Human Understanding.* (References in the text above are to the edition of P. H. Nidditch, Oxford, 1975.)

Murphy, G. (1962). *An Historical Introduction to Modern Psychology.* London.

Peters, R. S. (ed.) (1962). *Brett's History of Psychology.* London.

Woodworth, R. S. (1931). *Contemporary Schools of Psychology.* London.

Yolton, J. W. (1984). *Perceptual Acquaintance from Descartes to Reid.* Oxford.

**LOEB,** JACQUES (1859–1924). German biologist, born in Mayen. Educated in Berlin, Loeb emigrated to America in 1891, and finally became head of the general physiology division of the Rockefeller Institute for Medical Research (1910–24). He worked on comparative physiology, and on artificial parthenogenesis, but he is perhaps best known for his elegant experiments on the 'forced movements' of tropisms in simple animals and for his 'tonus hypothesis' to explain this highly ordered behaviour. The tonus hypothesis is that paired receptors, such as the eyes, send signals to paired muscles which when in balanced tension make the animal move in a straight line either towards the source of the stimulus (positive tropism) or away (negative tropism). Loeb's work on quantifying tropisms, and combining and opposing them to find their relative strengths and interactions, is important in its own right, and it is historically a basis of *behaviourism, as it suggested that there might be simple laws for the behaviour even of higher animals. The tonus hypothesis is now abandoned for even simple animals, and the behaviour of higher animals is not stimulus determined.

Loeb's books include *Dynamics of Living Matter* (1906); *Artificial Parthenogenesis and Fertilisation* (1913); and *Forced Movements, Tropisms, and Animal Conduct* (1918).

**LOGICAL POSITIVISM.** Philosophical school, based on linguistic analysis (to clarify the meanings of statements and questions) and on demands for criteria and procedures of empirical verification (for establishing at least in-principle truth or falsity of statements, by observation or experiment). Logical positivism is essentially a systematic attack on *metaphysics by demanding observations for conferring meaning. Metaphysics is rejected as nonsense. Many positivists (such as Bertrand *Russell) were influenced by the doctrines of 'logical atomism', which claimed that the world is a collection of atomic facts describable by simple propositions, the truth of which is independent of the truth of all other propositions. The positivist analogue of this doctrine is the idea that every basic statement must, in order to be meaningful, be verifiable in isolation. This argument has, however, largely been abandoned, as many clearly important statements in science are not individually verifiable; and it has proved impossible to formulate consistent criteria of verification which are not either too 'weak' (failing to reject metaphysics) or too 'strong' (rejecting important statements in science or other knowledge). See also VERSTEHEN.

The book which introduced and most clearly formulated logical positivism in the English language is A. J. Ayer, *Language, Truth and Logic* (1936).

**LUNACY.** The term was originally used to denote an individual subject to intermittent bouts of insanity thought to be influenced by the phases of the moon. According to Hugh Farmer (1775), in Greek and Roman times it was synonymous with epilepsy, and the evangelist St Matthew also appears to have considered lunacy and epilepsy as one and the same condition (Matt. 17:15).

In English law, lunacy implied such mental unsoundness as interfered with civil rights and transactions. The word was used in Britain throughout the nineteenth century in titles of the numerous Bills and Acts brought into Parliament for the regulation of persons suffering from mental illness. The general currency of lunacy and lunatic is shown in the title of a book published in 1850, *Familiar Views of Lunacy and the Lunatic Life.* If, as is probable, the author was Dr John Conolly of Hanwell Asylum, a man with the deepest concern for the welfare of patients committed to his care, evidently he did not consider the book's title to be derogatory but simply an apt description of conditions in his hospital. As time has gone by the words 'lunacy' and 'lunatic' have dropped out of medical parlance, to be replaced by mental illness and mental disorder in the last two 'Lunacy' Acts, the Mental Health Acts of 1959 and 1983.

**LURIA,** ALEXANDER ROMANOVICH (1902–77). Soviet psychologist, probably the only one to become generally known outside the USSR after the Second World War. Born in Kazan of Jewish extraction, Luria was educated at the University of Kazan and graduated in social sciences in spite of his father's wish that he should qualify in medicine, which in fact he did several years later when his career in psychology underwent an unexpected check. His interest in psychology developed rapidly and while still a student he had the temerity to found a psychoanalytic circle in Kazan which he brought to the attention of Sigmund *Freud himself—though later he repudiated psychoanalysis.

In 1925 Luria was appointed to a junior post at the Moscow Institute of Psychology, where, under the direction of N. K. Kornalov, he carried through an ambitious research programme on the effects of emotional stress on human motor reactions recorded under experimental conditions. This work owed something to Ivan *Pavlov's work on experimental neurosis in dogs, though it should be stressed that while Luria had the highest regard for Pavlov as a physiologist, he never accepted his view that complex human behaviour could ever be satisfactorily explained in terms of reflexes and conditioned reflexes. (His adherence to this view caused him great difficulty in later life and nearly brought his career to an untimely end.) Luria wrote up his experimental findings in a massive book which was published in English translation as *The Nature of Human Conflicts* (1932).

In 1924, Luria had made the acquaintance of Leo Semionovich *Vygotsky, originally a language teacher who deviated to psychology and came to exert a remarkable influence on the younger generation of Soviet psychologists. Although a convinced Marxist, Vygotsky was far from doctrinaire and had wide interests in human development and the role of education and culture in shaping it. Also he developed a lively interest in the effects of nervous disease on human intellectual capacities and was almost certainly responsible for redirecting Luria's interests towards *neuropsychology. He agreed strongly with Luria in deploring Pavlov's rejection of mind and consciousness in the human sciences.

Partly as a result of Vygotsky's influence, Luria successfully qualified in medicine, and in 1941 he was pressed into service as a medical officer with special responsibilities for the assessment and rehabilitation of brain-injured servicemen. His background in psychology, together with a more recently acquired knowledge of linguistics, enabled him to devise some simple, yet effective, methods of assessing deficits in higher psychological capacities and of retraining the patients whenever possible. This work was later transferred to the Institute of Neurosurgery in Moscow, and Luria continued to work there until 1950, when he was summarily dismissed from his post, apparently for ideological reasons, in particular his somewhat feeble enthusiasm for Pavlovian methods and theory. Fortunately, he was restored to his post some years later and was able to return to his neuropsychological studies virtually until his death.

Luria was a prolific writer, many of whose books and scientific papers were translated into English. He visited Britain and the United States on many occasions in the 1950s and 1960s to attend conferences and give lectures, and he made numerous friends in psychological and neurological circles, many of whom visited him in Moscow on occasion and came to know him well. His posthumous autobiography, *The Making of Mind: a personal account of Soviet psychology*, edited by Michael and Sheila Cole (Harvard, 1979), provides a brief but evocative account of his life and work.

Luria's principal books in English translation are *The Nature of Human Conflicts* (trans. W. H. Gantt, 1932), *The Role of Speech in the Regulation of Normal and Abnormal Behaviour* (1961), *Traumatic Aphasia* (trans. Basil Haigh, 1970), *Basic Problems in Neurolinguistics* (trans. Basil Haigh, 1976), and *Higher Nervous Functions in Man* (2nd edn. trans. Basil Haigh, 1980).                    O. L. Z.

**LYCEUM.** The name of the gymnasium and covered garden adjacent to the temple of Apollo Lyceus in Athens where Aristotle taught his students.

**LYING.** Deliberate falsification of the truth in order to confuse or mislead. This is an essential weapon for self-protection; and for societies, especially in war, to put an enemy off his stroke. Although condemned by moralists, lying can have high survival-value.

# M

**McCULLOCH,** WARREN STURGIS (1899–1969). American neurophysiologist, cybernetician and philosopher of mind. Born in Orange, New Jersey, his first degrees were from Yale (1921) and Columbia (1923), and his MD was from Columbia in 1927, where he was an instructor in physiological psychology following an internship at Bellevue Hospital in New York. He did his classic work with Dusser de Barenne at Yale, which led to the book *The Isocortex of the Chimpanzee.* Moving to the University of Illinois in 1941, he started the collaboration with Walter Pitts, which provided two of the foundation papers of brain theory, 'A logical calculus of the ideas immanent in nervous activity' and 'How we know universals: the perception of visual and auditory forms'.

From 1952 he was a member of the Research Laboratory of Electronics at the Massachusetts Institute of Technology, where he devoted himself full-time to leading a research group working on models of neural networks. This was the period that produced the work (with Jerry Lettvin and Humberto Maturana) 'What the frog's eye tells the frog's brain', a series of papers (with Jack Cowan, Sam Winograd and Manuel Blum) on the construction of reliable neural networks from unreliable components, and an interest (largely stimulated by the philosophy of C. S. *Peirce) in the construction of a logic of triadic relations.

See also McCULLOCH'S CONTRIBUTIONS TO BRAIN THEORY.                                      M. A. A.

## McCULLOCH'S CONTRIBUTIONS TO BRAIN THEORY. Warren *McCulloch was a central pioneer figure of cybernetic and computational models of brain function. The year 1943 saw the publication of 'A logical calculus of the ideas immanent in nervous activity' by McCulloch and Walter Pitts, in which they offered their formal model of the neurone as a threshold logic unit, building on the neurone doctrine of *Ramon y Cajal, and the excitatory and inhibitory synapses of *Sherrington.

A major stimulus for their work was the *Turing machine, an imagined device which could read, write and move upon an indefinitely extendible tape each square of which bore a symbol from some finite alphabet. Alan Turing (1936) had made plausible the claim that any effectively definable computation (i.e. anything that a human could do in the way of symbolic manipulation by following a finite and completely explicit set of rules (in 1936 the referent of 'computer' was still a human!) could be carried out by such a machine equipped with a suitable program. What McCulloch and Pitts

demonstrated was that each such program could be implemented using a finite network, with loops, of their formal neurones.

In another classic paper 'How we know universals: the perception of auditory and visual forms', Pitts and McCulloch (1947) sought 'general methods for designing nervous nets which recognize figures in such a way as to produce the same output for every input belonging to the figure'— just as we recognize a figure such as a square, despite changes in position or size.

Thus they sought to explain how we know universals. Lettvin, Maturana, McCulloch, and Pitts (1959) turned to the frog for experimental answers to the questions set by the earlier paper, noting that the frog is normally motionless, and that its visually guided behaviour can be adequately described in terms of recognition of two universals, *prey* and *enemy*. (Subsequent research has complicated this picture considerably—Fite, 1976.) Lettvin et al. (1959) found that the majority of the axons of the frog's retinal ganglion cells could be classified into one of four groups, on the basis of their response to visual stimuli, and that moreover the axons of the four groups ended in four distinct layers of the tectum (part of the frog's midbrain), with the four layers being in registration, in that vertically arranged cells in the tectum would signal the presence or absence of the four features in the same region of the visual field. The four feature detectors described in this celebrated paper, 'What the frog's eye tells the frog's brain', were:

(i) *Sustained contrast detectors* yield a prompt and prolonged discharge whenever the sharp edge of an object, either lighter or darker than the background, moves into its receptive field and stops there (or appears there when light is turned on).

(ii) *Net convexity detectors* respond to a small or convex edge of a large dark object passed through the visual field; the response does not outlast the passage; a smooth motion across the visual field has less effect than a jerky one.

(iii) *Moving-edge detectors* respond to any distinguishable edge moving through its receptive field.

(iv) *Net dimming detectors* respond to sudden reduction of illumination by a prolonged and regular discharge.

The essential point of this is that 'the eye speaks to the brain in a language already highly organized and interpreted, instead of transmitting some more or less accurate copy of the distribution of light on the receptor' (Lettvin, et al., 1959, p. 1,950). Further, the encoding is such as to aid the frog in finding food and evading predators—in recognizing the universals *prey* and *enemy*.

We now turn to McCulloch's consideration of the question 'How is the central nervous system structured to allow co-ordinated action of the whole animal when different regions receive contradictory local information?'. McCulloch suggested that the answer lay in the *principle of redundancy of potential command*, which states, essentially, that command should pass to the region with the most important information. He cited the example of a naval fleet, where the behaviour of the whole (First World War) naval fleet is controlled at least temporarily by signals from whichever ship first sights the enemy—the point being that this ship need not be the flagship, in which command normally resides. McCulloch suggested that this redundancy of potential command in vertebrates would find its clearest expression in the reticular formation (RF) of the brain-stem. W. L. Kilmer and McCulloch then made the following contributions toward building a model of RF. Firstly, they noted that at any one time an animal is in only one of some twenty or so gross *modes* of behaviour (e.g. sleeping, eating, grooming, mating), and they suggested that the main role of the core of the RF (or at least the role they sought to model) was to commit the organism to one of these modes. Secondly they noted that anatomical data (of the Scheibels, 1958) suggested that RF need not be modelled neurone by neurone, but could instead be considered as a stack of 'poker chips', each containing tens of thousands of neurones, and each with its own nexus of sensory information. Thirdly they posited that each module ('poker chip') could decide which mode was most appropriate to its own nexus of information, and then asked: 'How can the modules be coupled so that, in real time, a consensus can be reached as to the mode appropriate to the overall sensory input, despite conflicting mode indications from local inputs to different modules?'

In this framework, Kilmer et al. (1969) designed and simulated a model, called S–RETIC, of a system to compute mode changes, comprising a column of modules that differed only in their input array, and that were interconnected in a way suggested by RF anatomy, as the anatomy was at that time described.

The overall effect of the scheme is to decouple the modules initially, after an input change, in order to accentuate each 'poker chip's' evaluation of what the next mode should be, and then through successive iterations to couple them back together, in order to reach a global consensus. Computer simulation showed that S–RETIC, at least with the coupling patterns they studied, would converge for every input in less than 25 cycles, and that once it had converged it would stay converged for a given input. When the inputs strongly indicate one mode, convergence is fast; but when the indication

is weak, initial conditions and circuit characteristics play an important role. Although the anatomical picture of S–RETIC has now changed, this is the start of the important concept of 'co-operative computation' for brain function.

Let us now briefly examine the general implications of these papers for brain theory. For Pitts and McCulloch, the point of their model of the superior colliculus (the mammalian analogue of the frog's tectum) was that it gave an implementation of their conceptual scheme that did justice to neurophysiological data. However, the scheme has far greater significance than this, for it shows how to design a *somatotopically organized network in which there is no 'executive neurone' that decrees which way the overall system behaves; rather, the dynamics of the effectors, with assistance from neuronal interactions, extracts the output trajectory from a population of neurones, none of which has more than local information as to which way the system should behave*. In other words, the Pitts and McCulloch model of the superior colliculus showed how 'the organism can be committed to an overall action by a population of neurones none of which had global information as to which action is appropriate'. This is the organization (and sometimes disorganization!) of a democracy. The study of co-operative computation in somatotopically organized networks now provides a central paradigm of brain function.

M. A. A.
R. L. G.

Apter, J. (1945). The projection of the retina on the superior colliculus of cats. *Journal of Neurophysiology*, **8**, 123–34.

Apter, J. (1946). Eye movements following strychninization of the superior colliculus of cats. *Journal of Neurophysiology*, **9**, 73–85.

Fite, K. V. (1976). *The Amphibian Visual System*. New York.

Kilmer, W. L., McCulloch, W. S., and Blum, J. (1969). A Model of the Vertebrate Central Command System. *International Journal of Man–Machine Studies*, **1**, 279–309.

Lettvin, J. Y., Maturana, H., McCulloch, W. S., and Pitts, W. H. (1959). What the frog's eye tells the frog's brain. *Proceedings of the Institute of Radio Engineers*, **47**, 1,940–51.

Pitts, W. H. and McCulloch, W. S. (1947). How we know universals: the perception of auditory and visual forms. *Bulletin of Mathematical Biophysics*, **9**, 127–47.

Scheibel, A. B. and Scheibel, M. E. (1958). Structural substrates for integrative patterns in the brain stem reticular core. In Jasper, H. et al. (eds.), *Reticular Formation of the Brain*.

Turing, A. M. (1936). On computable numbers with an application to the Entscheidungs-problem. *Proceedings of the London Mathematical Society*, Ser. 2, **42**, 230–67.

**McDOUGALL**, WILLIAM (1871–1938). British psychologist, born in Lancashire. After studying at Weimar, Manchester, and Cambridge, he became a medical student at St Thomas's Hospital, London. In 1898 he accompanied an important anthropological expedition to the Torres Strait. Having held the Wilde readership in mental philosophy at Oxford from 1904 to 1920, he emigrated to America, going first to Harvard, and then, in 1927, to Duke University, North Carolina.

McDougall rejected *behaviourism and made *purpose the centre of his philosophy of psychology. He wrote extensively and was very widely read. Of particular interest are *Body and Mind* (1911), *Outlines of Psychology* (1923), *The Energies of Man* (1933), and *An Outline of Abnormal Psychology* (1926), which has an account of hypnosis. McDougall held a theory of mind involving monads, somewhat similar to *Spinoza and *Leibniz (see LEIBNIZ'S PHILOSOPHY OF MIND). He suggested that the mind is a kind of interacting network of monads linked by telepathy, and that brain damage can have little effect provided these links remain. His hydraulic analogies of purpose were taken over by the early ethologists. Late in life, McDougall espoused *Lamarckianism, carrying out with an assistant (who probably falsified the results) experiments in which rats' tails were cut off to demonstrate inheritance of an acquired characteristic. These experiments damaged his reputation; but his books remain worth reading today for their clarity and verve. The significance of some of his concepts for current thinking is well brought out by Margaret Boden in *Purposive Explanation in Psychology* (1972). In particular, his account of *emotions as the experience of thwarted drives remains important; as, more generally, does his attempt to use purpose as an explanatory concept in psychology.

**MACH**, ERNST (1838–1916). Austrian physicist and philosopher of science. Born in Moravia, he studied at Vienna, and became professor of mathematics at Graz in 1864; of physics at Prague in 1867; and of physics at Vienna in 1895. His experimental work was largely on the flow of gases. His philosophical writings both laid the foundations for *logical positivism and were a basis for Einstein's theory of relativity. (Mach's Principle suggests that effects of accelerated motion, including rotation, are absolutely related to the mean mass of the universe; in practice, to the 'fixed' stars.)

Mach contributed to knowledge of *perception, especially in his *Beiträge zur Analyse der Empfindungen* (1897; trans. C. M. Williams, *The Analysis of Sensations; and the Relation of the Physical to the Psychical*, 1959). He was among the first to use visually ambiguous figures as research tools, for separating what we now call 'bottom-up' and 'top-down' processing. (See ILLUSIONS.)

He tried to base the whole of physics on the observer's sensations. This was important philosophically, as it is an extreme form of operationalism which led to logical positivism and criteria of verification (as set out in A. J. Ayer's *Language, Truth and Logic*, 1936). The attempt has, however, turned out to be unsuccessful—unless, at least, we allow very large gaps with many unverified steps between observations (and especially sensations) and accepted facts of the world.

Further, the relation between sensation and perception remains far from clear, for—as Mach himself showed—how we perceive objects affects sensations, such as surface colour and brightness. So, though important, sensations can hardly be the building blocks of perception or of physics.

Other works by Mach available in English are: *Space and Geometry: in the light of physiological, psychological and physical inquiry*, trans. T. J. McCormack (1960); *The Principles of Physical Optics: an historical and philosophical treatment*, trans. J. S. Anderson and A. F. A. Young (1926); and *The Science of Mechanics: a critical and historical account of its development*, trans. T. J. McCormack (1960).

**'MAD AS A HATTER'.** This expression probably derives from the fact that mercury, used in the manufacture of felt, which in turn was used to make hats, produces loss of memory and other symptoms of the *Korsakoff syndrome when absorbed by the skin. The idea is immortalized in the Mad Hatter in Lewis *Carroll's *Alice's Adventures in Wonderland*.

**MAGENDIE**, FRANÇOIS (1783–1855), French physiologist, was born at Bordeaux and died at Sannois. He studied and practised medicine in Paris, researching in many fields and lecturing on experimental physiology; he was appointed professor of medicine at the Collège de France in 1831.

In 1809 he demonstrated that poison from the plant *Strychnos* was carried in the bloodstream and not by the lymphatics. This led to the isolation of strychnine in 1818, and he introduced it, as well as emetine, morphine, iodides, and bromides into medical usage. He also studied nutrition scientifically, and realized the importance of proteins.

Magendie's discovery in 1822 that the dorsal root of a spinal nerve was sensory and the ventral root motor was also claimed by Sir Charles *Bell: It is generally accepted that Magendie gave the final proof and description to work originated by Bell. His wide interests included research on the cerebellum, on olfaction, and on the circulation.

See also REFLEX ACTION.                              D. D. H.

**MAINE DE BIRAN** (Pierre-François Gonthier de Biran, 1766–1824). A French philosopher, son of a doctor from Bergerac, he held public office after the Revolution, under the Consulate and the Empire, and after the Restoration. For most of his mature life, he pursued the project of producing a single major work devoted to the Science of Man. Though he wrote extensively, this central project was never fulfilled, and he published very little during his lifetime. Most of the works subsequently published are (sometimes misleading) editorial reconstitutions and compilations. However, the historical place of his work and the main lines of development of his thought can readily be seen.

Biran marks an important transition in man's attempt to explore and understand his own mind.

We must place him on the one hand in the introspective tradition of those like Montaigne and *Pascal who gave prominence to the analysis and exposure of the intimacies of their own souls, and on the other hand in the empiricist tradition stemming from *Bacon, especially as it emerged through *Locke and the British empiricists in the sensationalism of the eighteenth century propounded by authors like David Hartley, *Condillac, and Charles Bonnet. He represents not only an intersection of these traditions, but also a source of later very divergent approaches to the mind, in experimental psychology, in psychoanalysis, and in *phenomenology.

His works fall into three main periods: an exploratory period in which he read and wrote very widely and in which his ideas were beginning to take shape, a mature period in which 'Biranian' theses found their clearest and most systematic expression, and a late period in which he stepped beyond his central psychological concerns to a consideration of questions of transcendent metaphysics and to an exploration of the nature of religious experience.

A main task which Biran set himself, above all in the mature period, was to explicate the notion of the will, holding that we should not understand anything in psychology if we did not understand the phenomenon of willed action; while if we did understand it, we should already have a framework for the understanding of other psychological notions. Willed action was in this sense the 'primitive fact' of psychology.

This contention already contains his central critique of the traditional empiricist view of the mind. Though the empiricists had, he thought, been right in respecting the empirical methodology of the natural sciences, and right also in giving the role which they often did give to introspective experience, they went disastrously wrong in adopting a passive model of the mind, in which *perception was thought of as simple reception of data, and action became either the mechanical result of accumulated inputs, or an arbitrary intrusion in the causal nexus.

For Biran, the operation of the will was known through immediate introspective experience; this experience was centrally the experience of willed *effort*—especially muscular effort—and the phenomenon of the will like all other mental phenomena was essentially *relational* ('Rien n'est dans la conscience qu'à titre de rapport').

This last claim represented another important break with the classical empiricists and foreshadowed phenomenology. But what is its force? It may seem that a case of willed action such as my raising my arm will be rightly analysed into two components—an act of will, followed by a bodily movement. The act of will would then presumably be an inner event known introspectively to the agent. But Biran denied the existence of such inner objects of attention: 'The inner sense has no object.' By this he meant that what is present to the inner sense is always properly a *fact*, and never an *object*—in this case, the fact of deliberately raising one's arm. This fact is *understood* as a relation between two terms, the active self, and the action performed, a relation occurring in the effort exerted. But these two terms are inseparable. When I deliberately raise my arm, the action is willed; but it does not contain a component of willing which might occur without the movement, and of which I could be independently aware through my inner sense. Thus, if in the natural sciences we observe independent events between which we attempt to discover a causal relation, using hypotheses of an underlying causal mechanism, in psychology, on the other hand, it is the causal relation which is given (in the central case of willed activity), and the extrapolation to a separate mental act of willing (whose causal link with the movement would then become problematic) must be resisted.

What then of the underlying physiology? Biran had an extensive knowledge of and respect for contemporary work in physiology and related empirical disciplines. However, he denied the reductivist thesis that psychological statements could be reduced, for instance, to physiological ones. This thesis encouraged absurdities like Cabanis's claim that the brain 'digests impressions' and 'secretes thought'. What then was the relation between psychological events and physiological processes? Biran denied that a thought was identical with, or caused, or was caused by such a process. He claimed rather that the relation between a physiological and a psychological statement was *symbolic*, meaning by this that the two kinds of account were partially isomorphic: they corresponded systematically, without corresponding in full. Thus we could pass from a statement that I deliberately raised my arm to a statement that certain physiological processes occurred in me, and thereby attain a greater understanding of human action; but we could not *translate* the one into the other without loss.

However, there is a further complexity in willed action: for I cannot act deliberately without knowing what I am doing. More generally, the separation of reason and will, or action and cognition, is a fundamental error. To act is to know, and vice versa. The first act of will is the origin of humanity: it is the birth, not only of the will, but of the intellect, of *consciousness, of language and knowledge. Just as acting must in part be an exercise of cognition, so perception, for instance, is an active faculty, and not a mere receptivity.

However, though Biran thought that will, consciousness, thought, and knowledge were inseparable features of the active life, he also claimed that this life came into being by raising to its level materials drawn from a complex passive underlayer of our experience—a vast subconscious, which, though sometimes drawn up into our conscious life, nevertheless lay broadly untapped, mysterious in its fashioning of our conscious being.

Biran wrote in his diary of 'an inner New World to be discovered one day by a Columbus of metaphysics'; the task would require one to 'plunge into the subterranean caverns of the soul', and would require a partnership of introspection and physiological knowledge.

This striking prediction of the nature and importance of psychoanalysis, together with his extensive anticipations of crucial areas of research in empirical psychology, whether on the influence of drugs (see PSYCHOPHARMACOLOGY), the nature of *conditioning, the application of *educational research, the study of the mechanisms of *dreaming, or the interplay in clinical psychology of abstract theory and pragmatic cure, and, thirdly, the equally striking anticipation of the programme of phenomenology—all these things should lead us to correct Biran's own estimate of his work. Near the end of his life, he reviewed his life's work in his diary. It had been, he felt, too schematic and too limited. It had ignored the religious and the social dimensions of human experience. 'I despise what I have been doing,' he said; 'I have spent my life erecting a mere scaffold.' That scaffold has served for the construction not of one theory but of a multiplicity of theories of the nature of the human mind. For that reason alone, it should command our respect and our attention.          F. C. T. M.

Azouvi, F. (ed.) (1984). *Discours à la société médicale de Bergerac*, Oeuvres de Maine de Biran, nouvelle édition, tome V. Paris.

Gouhier, H. (1948). *Les Conversions de Maine de Biran*. Paris.

Hallie, P. P. (1959). *Maine de Biran, reformer of empiricism*. Cambridge, Massachusetts.

Henry, M. (1965). *Philosophie et phénoménologie du corps: essai sur l'ontologie biranienne*. Paris.

Moore, F. C. T. (1970). *The Psychology of Maine de Biran*. Oxford.

Moore, F. C. T. (ed.) (1984). *Sur les Rapports du physique et du moral de l'homme*, Oeuvres de Maine de Biran, nouvelle édition, tome VI. Paris.

Tisserand, P. (ed.) (1920–49). *Oeuvres de Maine de Biran* (14 vols). Paris.

Voutsinas, D. (1964). *La Psychologie de Maine de Biran*. Paris.

**MAKARENKO,** ANTON SEMYONOVITCH (1888–1939), Russian educationist. Already a trained teacher, he took on the task of working with homeless juvenile delinquents left behind after the upheavals of the 1917 revolution and the civil wars which followed it. The numbers were never firmly established, but Lenin's wife estimated there were as many as seven million who were homeless and forced to survive by crime and violence. Makarenko was unimpressed by the Rousseauist educational theories of the early revolutionaries (see ROUSSEAU AND EDUCATION), who were in favour of leaving the child to educate himself by his own efforts. He thought the theorists were too distant from the masses and in particular from the *besprizornye* (waifs, homeless children)

he had to face. He found inspiration in the writings of Gorky, particularly *My Childhood*, *My Universities*, and *The Lower Depths*.

His approach to young people was based on actual observation and an awareness of the material necessities of their situation. When he set up his first colony he had almost single-handedly to find food and accommodation, and he displayed a concern which gained the respect of the young people who were brought to him. He ignored the elaborate police dossiers which accompanied them, preferring, like the children themselves, to forget past misdemeanours and to make a new start. He realized that their basic necessity was security. As a Bolshevik he saw the collective as a mode of organization giving security to the individual but also developing a sense of obligation to others. He had no compunction about enforcing conformity: 'The individual has to be incorporated into the collective in such a way that he believes himself to belong to it freely and without compulsion.' He believed in self-discipline as the goal of moral education but thought that the teacher had a responsibility to develop it. Children learned through being given responsibility: a persistent thief would be sent to collect money for the colony, and the children had to grow their own food.

The colonies were organized into 'detachments', each with a student leader, and all jointly responsible for running the whole community. Workshops were set up to produce goods which could be sold outside. There were large numbers of cultural activities, among them drama, model-making, pantomime, and brass bands, as well as conventional school-work. However, the school was not simply a place where knowledge and skills were acquired, but a way of life where members learned initiative and self-respect through the discipline of working for each other and through self-government. Each member of the youth collective belonged to the group not as a faceless cipher but as one who takes responsibility, not only for his own actions but also for those of his fellows. Because the collective provided support for the individual, it could also make demands which enlarged his capacity as a human being. Respect for the individual led Makarenko to challenge his pupils with difficulties to overcome. In his relationship with pupils, he argued that a balance had to be kept between kindness and severity; sentimental indulgence was to be avoided. His intention was not simply to rehabilitate but to prepare for life in a Communist state. It is arguable that his influence on Soviet education inspired the almost incredible self-sacrifice demanded and obtained by Russia during the war against Germany.

Makarenko was an idealist, one of the few who survived the Stalinist purges of the 1930s. Although influential, his work has not prevented social stratification in the USSR, and it would seem, too, that youthful hooliganism and delinquency are still a problem. Despite the totalitarian implications of his work, Makarenko's practicality and humanity are still relevant, even outside the USSR.

C. H.<br>N. S.

Bronfenbrenner, U. (1974). *Two Worlds of Childhood*. Harmondsworth.
Goodman, W. L. (1949). *A. S. Makarenko, Russian Teacher*. London.
Lilge, F. (1958). *Anton Semyonovitch Makarenko*. Berkeley.
Makarenko, A. S. (1954). *A Book for Parents*. Moscow.
Makarenko, A. S. (1951). *The Road to Life*. Moscow.

**MALTHUS,** THOMAS ROBERT (1766–1834), English economist and mathematician, born at Dorking, Surrey, and educated at Jesus College, Cambridge. His *Essay on the Principle of Population* (published anonymously in 1798; enlarged, 1803) inspired, or triggered, both Charles *Darwin and Alfred Russel *Wallace to develop the theory of evolution of species by natural selection.

**MANIA.** A form of mental disorder manifested by uncontrolled excitement, over-activity, and obsessive behaviour.

**MANIC DEPRESSIVE.** A personality oscillating between over-activity and inability to summon up energy or make decisions. In extreme form, it is *manic-depressive psychosis*. In a controlled form it can be useful for creativity. The writer Samuel Johnson was supposed to be manic depressive, using the manic phase for writing and the depressed phase for self-criticism. See DEPRESSION.

**MANNERS.** Rules of manners can be found in every culture. They are meant to regulate the behaviour of the individual in everyday life and social intercourse. There are rules for walking, sitting, laughing, eating, speaking, greeting, etc. Manners are not identical (though closely related) to either rites or morals. Although some of them are very refined and change with fashion, manners probably reflect a more primitive level of behaviour than rites such as sacrifice (see BLOOD MYTHS), or moral commandments such as the Ten Commandments. In general, rules of manners focus either on neatness (which may have hygienic origins) or respect: two examples of the latter are elaborate systems of salutation, and a rule not to stare into another person's eyes. Francis *Bacon has given one of the best definitions: 'The whole of decorum and elegance of manners, seem to rest in weighing and maintaining, with an even balance, the dignity betwixt ourselves and others' (*The Advancement of Learning*, 1605).

Many of these aspects of behaviour can also be found in higher animals. Dogs and cats have elaborate rules of greeting which also determine the order of rank. Many animals—for example, rhesus monkeys—interpret fixating the eyes as aggressive behaviour. A subordinate animal would instantly turn away with some submissive gesture, while an animal with a higher rank might start an attack. Monkeys display such behaviour not only towards other monkeys but also towards man. The existence of certain basic modes of behaviour which can be instantly understood by man and by some higher animals suggests genetic determination. However, one should not conclude that manners are genetically fixed; rather, the potential that manners develop seems to be genetically fixed in man. The individual rules are determined by tradition and can differ widely. Also, rules of manners for men usually focus on ideals, which may be very different from actual behaviour.

**History.** European antiquity does not have special books on manners. There are, however, several hints in the Bible as well as in writings on morals by Plutarch, Epictetus, and Cicero. Two concepts characterize the ancient ideal of the good-mannered man: the concept of propriety and the concept of urbanity.

Acting 'properly'—that is, with propriety—means doing the right thing at the right time in the right place. The Greek idea of propriety belongs to the ideal of universal harmony; the rule itself seems to arise from the more primitive rules of obeisance and submission to society. That the definition of 'proper' could be a matter of public opinion and therefore be changed is a discovery of later times.

Urbanity may be defined as the courteous and elegant and therefore charming behaviour of (educated) citizens. The frequent social intercourse of those who live closely together might have made it a necessity that people should not only respect but also please each other. The aim to please is reflected in the ancient art of rhetoric, which acquired so much importance during the urban democracies of ancient Greece and Rome. It was a work by Cicero, *De oratore* (On the Orator), which inspired the Renaissance author Baldassare Castiglione to write one of the first widespread books on manners: *Il Libro del Cortegiano* (The Courtier, 1528), stressing the courtier's duty not only to submit to the rules of propriety but to do so gracefully. Indeed, in most of the conduct books following *Il Libro del Cortegiano* the art of good behaviour has been reduced more or less to an 'art of pleasing'. At court the meaning of propriety sometimes changed to simple conformity; and since the decisions of the monarchs were often influenced by sudden humours or moods, the art of pleasing degenerated to open flattery. Consequently the art of compliments—which forms an important part of the older books on manners—was later heavily criticized, and even banned, during the ages of bourgeois democracy.

Life at court also for the first time set forth rules to respect and even worship women, an idea unknown to ancient moralists. From the Middle Ages women had an increasing influence on the refinement of manners, though there can also be observed a strong tradition of misogyny, especially in England.

The first important books on manners for the bourgeoisie were written by Erasmus, *De civilitate morum puerilium* (On the Civility of Boys' Manners, 1528), and Giovanni della Casa, *Il Galateo* (1558). Both books were translated into the main European languages and often imitated. Rather detailed rules were given, such as: comb your hair, clean your ears and nose, wash your hands, lift your hat. In the English tradition of conduct books of the sixteenth and seventeenth centuries, a puritanical attitude towards 'pleasing' manners predominated; the books mostly taught moralistic and religious maxims or principles, and the first American books on manners were based on this tradition. In the age of Louis XIV (1638–1715), France became the leading nation on questions of conduct. Several treatises were translated into most of the European languages, for example the *Art de plaire dans la conversation* (The Art of Pleasing in Conversation, 1688) by Pierre d'Ortigue. The moral pressure of court life 'to please' was even apparent in the famous *Letters* by Lord Chesterfield (1694–1773), who wrote to his son: 'By *manière* I do not mean bare civility; everybody must have that, who would not be kicked out of company: but I mean engaging, insinuating, shining manners: a distinguished politeness, an almost irresistible address . . .' (19 April 1747). Since the nineteenth century, books on etiquette, which were simply guides in how to conform to the rules of society, have enjoyed a wide distribution. Good manners were no longer considered to be an 'art'.

**Manners at table, and in conversation.** To select two of the many possible aspects of manners, *table* and *conversational manners* will be described: two forms of civilized behaviour which were closely connected in the ancient institution of the symposium. From the fifteenth century the upper class developed highly restrictive rules, not only for the more natural needs but also for the use of napkins, handkerchiefs, and cutlery. Many table-books were published, in which detailed instructions for the use of spoons and especially of knives were given. By the end of the eighteenth century the use of individual plates and cutlery (knife, spoon, and for the first time also fork) was general. Until then it had been quite usual to eat communally from the same plate. Similarly the manner of how meat was served changed considerably. In the Middle Ages the entire animal (often decorated with its own fur or feathers to suggest the illusion that it had been hunted down on the spot) was presented and carved in front of the family or the guests, either by the host or somebody especially trained. Whole books on the art of carving were written—strangely enough sometimes combined with the 'Art of Compliments', as if hungry people could have been calmed down only by compliments while waiting. Then, later, the carving of the meat was largely banned from the table and delegated to the cook in the kitchen or even to the butcher himself.

Conversational manners also has a well-documented history. Characteristic human behaviour has been described by types: the chatterer, the flatterer, the silent man, all of whom are familiar in all societies. One of the most influential works in antiquity was Cicero's book *De officiis* (On Duties). Cicero reprimands those who speak too long, too loud, or too aggressively, and those who praise themselves or criticize others. He also stresses an important point of good conversational manners: respecting the right of everybody to take part. Interest in the *theory* of conversation awoke only in the Renaissance, i.e. around 1500. Castiglione in *Il Libro del Cortegiano* differentiates between conversation with monarchs and with equals. Conversation with monarchs should consist mainly of information, flattery, or respectful silence—witticisms are allowed only in conversation with equals. The bourgeois conduct books give Ciceronian rules and prescriptions: Do not interrupt other people, Do not speak in riddles, Do not hurt anybody with jokes (the last-mentioned rule became a typical bourgeois taboo). At the time of Louis XIV, conversation meant the opposite of 'talking on serious matters'; in the drawing-rooms of French gentlewomen, it degenerated to more or less brilliant chat. Since the rules of conversation have always aimed at the protection of mutual respect, conversation theory consequently tends to demand not only social but also intellectual equality in those who converse with each other. In fact in the eighteenth century the ideal of Henry Fielding gained increasing influence: 'Certain it is, that the highest Pleasure which we are capable of enjoying in Conversation is to be met with only in the Society of Persons whose Understanding is pretty near on an Equality with our own . . .' (*Essay on Conversation*, 1742). Real development of conversational ideals in the nineteenth century seems to have taken place only in so-called intellectual circles. At least in America and Germany a certain distrust of conversation began to prevail: 'Good as is discourse, silence is better, and shames it', wrote Ralph Waldo Emerson (*Circles*, 1841). On the other hand there was a tendency to confine conversation not only to equals but to the privacy and intimacy of dialogue: 'The best conversation probably takes place between two persons' (Emerson, *Clubs*, 1847).

Conversation in all its possible forms has never ceased. Books on conversational manners are written nowadays as never before. The concentration of theoretical interest towards the end of the nineteenth and the beginning of the twentieth centuries on the most private dialogue (and even the soliloquy) may have been due to the development of a democratic society, in which conversation between equals, i.e. public discussion, is now taken for granted.                                          C. SC.

**'MAPS' IN THE BRAIN.** See LOCALIZATION OF BRAIN FUNCTION AND CORTICAL MAPS.

**MARR,** DAVID COURTENAY (1945–80), British psychologist, born at Woodford in Essex.

In his short life, David Marr made a contribution to the psychology of vision that could be regarded as more important than that of anyone since Hermann *Helmholtz. He was educated at Rugby School and Trinity College, Cambridge. He put his mathematics to use in the construction of a model of the function of the cerebellum. Despite its ingenuity, it was at best oversimplified and he himself became dissatisfied with it. After a junior research fellowship at Trinity College, he moved to a senior research fellowship at King's College, which he held from 1972 to 1976. He became increasingly aware of the promise of computer simulation for modelling brain function, and while still a Fellow at King's made a protracted visit to the artificial intelligence laboratory at the Massachusetts Institute of technology (MIT) in order to learn the techniques of computer modelling. In 1975 he again visited MIT and decided to remain there permanently. The last five years of his life were marked by an outburst of creative energy that culminated in a book entitled *Vision*, which was posthumously published in 1982.

Marr's main work was on three topics: first, the method by which the visual system recovers lines and edges, which, although they look so clean to the viewer, are extremely hard to reconstruct from the messy retinal image; second, stereopsis, particularly the correspondence problem, that is the method by which the brain matches a point in the image on one eye with the equivalent point in the other eye's image; and third, the problem of how objects are represented in the brain in such a way as to facilitate recognition. Although he made highly original and important contributions to all three problems, he will probably be remembered less for the details of his research than for the style of his approach. Before Marr, most computer programs in vision dealt only with very restricted 'toy' worlds, for example plane-sided blocks. Marr set out to model vision as it operates in the real world in all its complexity. Moreover, he was the first person to construct computer models that took account of neurophysiological and psychological findings. He did not want to produce just any model—he wanted to uncover the way the human visual system actually works. Finally, he saw more clearly than almost any of his contemporaries that in order to build an adequate model of how the brain executes a certain task, it is first necessary to obtain a clear understanding of that task: his mathematical ability helped him to achieve this kind of understanding. In addition to carrying out his own research, Marr through his intelligence, charm, and liveliness attracted around him a group of outstanding research workers drawn from all over the world. Inspired by him, they made important contributions of their own, many of which are recorded in his book.

David Marr's move to MIT seemed to lead to a remarkable flowering of his imagination and personality. Part of his vitality over the last few years of his life may have come from the fact that he

knew he had not long to live. Three years before he died he contracted leukaemia, a disease that necessitated repeated and painful stays in hospital. He faced his illness with quiet courage and no matter how weak he felt, he went on working: his fascination with his work was so great that however ill he was he never had to force himself to do it. His attempt to grapple with the deepest problems of vision was for him a source of spontaneous enjoyment. As he writes at the beginning of his book, 'This book is meant to be enjoyed'. One can be sure he enjoyed writing it.

See also PERCEPTION.                    N. S. S.

**MASOCHISM.** Pleasure (especially sexual) from being subjected to pain or cruelty. It is named after Leopold von Sacher-Masoch (1835–95), an Austrian writer and lawyer who wrote *Der Don Juan von Kolomea* (1866) and other books describing sexual pleasure derived from pain. The converse is *sadism—sexual pleasure from inflicting pain.

A curious problem arises as to whether one could say that an animal is motivated by masochism—for normally motivations for behaviour are supposed to be pleasurable. Pleasure might, of course, be deferred, but how far these subtle and important distinctions can be made on purely behavioural grounds, as in animal experiments and observations of animal behaviour, is an open and difficult question.

**MATERIALISM.** See MIND–BODY PROBLEM: PHILOSOPHICAL THEORIES.

**MATTER.** The distinction between mind and matter is as old as philosophy and as controversial. Both are ultimately mysterious. On the view known as *dualism (developed by *Descartes), matter has spatial extension and non-mental properties such as divisibility, while mind is not extended in space and does not obey the laws of physics. According to the *idealism of *Berkeley, the notion of matter existing independently of mind is incoherent. As physics has advanced, its accounts of matter have grown even further from the 'common sense' knowledge given by perception. This has given rise to 'two worlds' of physical reality and perceived experience. With this development matter seems to be more and more different from mind, whereas in mythology and early science mind and matter are hardly separated, and matter is seen as alive and intelligent. See also MIND AND BODY.

**MEANING.** The concept of meaning is every bit as problematic as the concept of mind, and for related reasons. For it seems to be the case that it is only *for a mind* that some things (gestures, sounds, marks, or natural phenomena) can *mean* other things. The difficulties which we have understanding the place of mind in nature spill over, and create problems for, our understanding of the phenomena of meaning. Anyone who conceives of science as objective, and of objectivity as requiring the study of phenomena (objects and relations between objects), which exist and have their character independently of human thought, will face a problem with the scientific study of meaning.

One might attempt to overcome this problem by finding a natural relation holding between things which have meanings (i.e. signs) and the things they mean (or signify). The idea that meaning is, or needs to be, founded upon a natural relation is responsible for the lure of causal, picture, and onomatopoeic theories. Cause and effect and similarity of shape are thought to be relations which hold independently of being recognized by a mind.

*Plato (*Cratylus*, 432–5) argued against the idea that the meaning relation could be founded purely on a natural relation of similarity. No signs, he observed, can be exactly similar to the thing signified without duplicating that thing in all respects. What counts as sufficiently similar is governed by convention (*nomos*) and there must, therefore, be an element of convention in every use of a thing as sign.

But while it appears unavoidable that meaning should have some component of convention, it does not seem unreasonable to seek a theoretical account of the general conditions under which such conventions, established for a relatively small number of linguistic elements (a basic vocabulary), would fix the meanings of complex terms and sentences constructed out of these elements. It would be the work of that branch of the science of logic known as compositional (or recursive) semantics to determine these general conditions, and the result would constitute an objective account of how parts of a language can mean something. If one added assumptions about how it is proper to fix the meanings of the basic elements—say they had to be tied in some way to sense experience—one could test any piece of discourse for meaningfulness by applying the principles of logic to analyse the discourse until it became clear whether its elements had been properly constituted or legitimated by experience, and hence whether it was a meaningful piece of discourse.

Early efforts in this direction were made by the classical British empiricists (*Hobbes and *Hume), but the important advances in logical technique at the turn of the nineteenth century gave those attracted to this approach a new self-consciousness and self-confidence, and they emerged as 'logical empiricists' (or 'logical positivists'). These were the philosophers (A. J. Ayer, Rudolf Carnap, and Moritz Schlick) who challenged the 'cognitive meaningfulness' of metaphysics, theology, and ethics, and whose slogan was 'the meaning of a sentence is its method of verification'; for the analysis of a sentence would, if carried out, also show how one could go about verifying the sentence. (See FALSIFICATION.)

The logical empiricists, however, differed over the way basic elements should be tied to sense experience. One group (including Ayer, Schlick, *Mach, and Bertrand *Russell) saw basic elements as grounded in subjective experience; another (including Otto Neurath and Carl Hempel) did not regard it as proper to anchor scientific discourse in subjective experience, and urged instead publicly accessible outcomes of publicly accessible (e.g. laboratory) procedures as the proper foundation for cognitive meaningfulness. The approach of this second group underwent a development as a result of the realization that what constitutes a test of something in science is not independent of the constellation of theories which scientists accept. The result was the abandoning of the idea that some elements of a language can be treated as basic with regard to the verification of all other sentences of that language. Hempel proposed instead a 'translatability criterion' according to which a whole body of discourse would be regarded as cognitively (i.e. scientifically) meaningful if it could be translated into a logically regimented language whose primitive vocabulary consisted of either 'logical locutions' or 'observation predicates'. None of the sentences, however, were to be regarded as basic for the purposes of verifying the sentences of the body of discourse thus translated. Instead of individual sentences confronting experience, the body of discourse as a whole stood or fell in the face of experience.

W. V. Quine and Donald Davidson developed further the line of this second group of positivists, by shifting attention from the attempt to say what it is to be cognitively meaningful to what is involved in one person understanding another person's (or culture's) language. In each case, they maintained, the interpreter has to work as a scientist works. The interpreter has to collect data, which consists in observations of the conditions under which the people whose discourse is to be interpreted will assent to, and dissent from, certain sentences. The interpreter also has to select basic elements (by proposing 'analytic hypotheses') and has to construct a theory which assigns truth conditions to basic elements and, through this, truth conditions to all the sentences of the language in such a way as to conform to the data. (Since the development of the logical apparatus, the compositional semantics, thought to be needed for this theory building, is due to Alfred Tarski; his name is often mentioned in this context.) As in Hempel's account, which is supposed to reflect the actual practice of natural scientists, the theory constructed stands or falls by its ability to accommodate the data taken *as a whole*.

As Quine and Davidson acknowledged, indeed urged, this approach to interpretation in an important sense undermines the idea that sentences or fragments of sentences have a meaning, or that names have a reference. The body of data is never adequate to determine uniquely one system of interpreting a language. There is no sense to the question what a noun *really* refers to, or what a speaker *really* means. In effect we should, in order to treat language as a natural phenomenon, abandon the notions of meaning and reference, and make use only of the concept of truth.

It was in the context of this challenge to the conceptions of meaning and reference that the 'causal theory of reference' was advanced by Saul Kripke and Hilary Putnam. According to this theory, *A* refers, for example, to a liquid chemical composed of two parts hydrogen and one part oxygen as 'water', because *A* heard *B*, *C*, *D*, etc., refer to it by that name, and they did so because they heard others do so; and so on back to an 'initial baptism' of that stuff with the name 'water'.

Although the phrase 'initial baptism' suggests a conscious attempt to establish a conventional pattern of linguistic response (as in a genuine christening), the initial baptism need not be regarded in this way. It could be treated as an unspecified natural occurrence, which under the circumstances holding at that time established a pattern of response to all essentially similar features of the environment. The similarity of feature, which is the basis of the pattern of response, need not be understood by those conforming to the pattern, although understanding could be achieved later by scientific investigation. This account thus underwrites the possibility of saying that what Aristotle *meant* by '*to hudor*' was $H_2O$, even though it is obvious that Aristotle did not possess our understanding of the composition of water. It is clear from this illustration how the notion of meaning can be conceived as a relation which obtains independently of what humans think.

To its critics, the causal theory failed to provide a historically plausible account of the mechanisms by which reference is secured and maintained. But to those sympathetic to it, it offered an alternative to abandoning the use of these notions and accepting the conclusion drawn by Quine and Davidson that meaning and reference are too indeterminate for scientific study. (A corollary of this conclusion, to the effect that mind is insufficiently determinate for proper scientific study, was subsequently drawn by Bernard Williams.)

One might also try to escape Quine's conclusions by calling into question the positivist conception of science which underpins them. Those prone to read the theoretical pronouncements of scientists literally, i.e. 'realists', brush aside the possibility, which is frequently stressed by Quine, that any body of scientific evidence, e.g. electrical phenomena, can be accounted for in a variety of incompatible ways, not just by postulating the existence of electrons. They insist that we are often justified in selecting one of the competing accounts as *the best explanation*, and this outlook can be applied to the phenomena of language to endorse, as perfectly respectable scientific reasoning, the idea that the best explanation of linguistic phenomena will postulate mental states as the causes of those phenomena.

Although the word 'idea' no longer figures prominently, this approach in effect returns to the position of John *Locke, who held that '*words, in their primary or immediate signification, stand for nothing but the* ideas *in the mind of him that uses them*,' (*Essay*, III,ii,2). Instead of ideas, the internal states most commonly appealed to are beliefs and desires, but the approach would still fall under the strictures of those philosophers and logicians who, since Frege, have indicted such theories on a charge of 'psychologism'; for such theories do indeed shift the attention of those studying meaning away from the relationship between signs and the things they signify to the relationship between the (minds of) sign-users and the things they signify.

Recent developments along these lines begin with an analysis of speaker's meaning advanced by H. P. Grice. We do quite often use the word 'meaning' to label what a speaker intended or was trying to do with his words. Thus Spooner's audience recognized that he *meant* to refer affectionately to the monarch when he used the words 'our queer dean'. This complex intention was analysed by Grice in terms of an intention to modify the beliefs or behaviour of the audience via the audience's recognition of that intention; and the presence of such intentions, Grice held, was what distinguished the ('non-natural') meaning of linguistic phenomena from the ('natural') meaning of natural phenomena (such as in 'those spots mean measles').

Criticisms of Grice's analysis focused on the difficulty of bridging the gap between this notion of (speaker's) meaning and the notion of word (or linguistic) meaning, for which we still need an account. Spooner's *words* after all *meant* something quite at variance with his intention; his words referred slurringly to a college official. Jonathan Bennett attempted to bridge the gap by integrating Grice's analysis with a sophisticated account of convention, which was devised by David Lewis. Under Lewis's analysis, a convention need not be established by conscious agreement (something which would presuppose, and hence could not explain, the existence of language) but is nevertheless more than a mere regularity because, however it was established, it is maintained by the recognition on the part of those who conform to it that conformity to it solves a 'co-ordination problem', i.e. eliminates certain disadvantages which would occur unless activities were co-ordinated. Bennett's account in effect rested linguistic meanings on the hardening into convention of speakers' meanings.

Bennett's approach has been criticized for not providing a convincing account of how what are essentially unstructured and unrelated primitive signalling acts (acts which express communication intention without presupposing a language) come to have the structure evident in all languages; viz. that by which each speech act is composed of elements which make a similar contribution to a variety of different speech acts. A second criticism called into question the sense of crediting non-language users with intentions sufficiently complex to count as (Gricean) communication intentions. The first of these criticisms rests on an important feature of meaning, its systematic nature. Different theoretical traditions give different accounts of this essential structure, but agree at least on the principle of systematic relatedness. (In the controversy over whether chimpanzees in acquiring the use of Ameslan signs had achieved *linguistic* mastery, a crucial point was whether they had the ability to form signs of sufficient complexity.) (See PRIMATE LANGUAGE.)

Compositional semantics offers an account of this structure based on the principle that the meanings of complex expression are functions of the meanings of elementary components. In fashioning the central concepts of this approach Frege had insisted that a sentential (or propositional) unit is primary to language, that singular terms and predicate expressions made radically dissimilar contributions to sentences, and that one must not ask for the meaning (*Bedeutung*) of a word outside the context of a sentence. Bennett's account seems in particular to lack resources to explain how a set of internally unstructured and logically homogeneous signalling acts could yield expressions with the different logical functions of subject and predicate. Frege's ideas were transmogrified in the hands of Quine, and, as the importance Frege attached to reference decayed, Quine replaced Frege's maxim about looking for the meaning outside the context of a sentence by a stricture against seeking the meaning of an expression outside the context of a whole language.

A radically different account derives from the work of the linguist Ferdinand de Saussure, who saw as relevant to meaning not only the relation between sign and thing signified, but also the 'value' of the sign (word). The value of a word is a function of the words that can in some contexts be exchanged for the word ('strike' and 'hit' are interchangeable only in some contexts) and the words that stand in contrast to it. 'Sheep' and 'mutton' are used for the animal and its meat in English, where the French use '*mouton*' for both. Thus the latter could have the value of neither of the former words.

Saussure's work provided an important inspiration for the movement known as structuralism. In the hands of the structuralists the relation between signified and signifier was virtually discarded, leaving the meaning of a sign resting on the structure of values constituted by the language as a whole. Coming from a different direction, the structuralists arrived at a linguistic holism which bore a number of striking similarities to that advanced by Quine and Davidson. In neither case could one look to some definite aspect of the world outside of discourse for what an expression meant or signified. If it made any sense to ask for the meaning of an expression, one had to look for it in its connections to other expressions.

Were this a viable account of linguistic meaning, it would support the idea that linguistic mastery (the ability thought by many to be essential to the possession of a mind) can be modelled in computer programs. A program, if it has the power to generate the right syntactic structure and vocabulary, could represent the way expressions interact with each other to constrain the formation of expressions and the assent to or dissent from sentences. Computer modelling along these lines has tended to draw more on the tradition which Frege founded than on that which Saussure founded. Such computer modelling leads to a second application of the 'realist' strategy mentioned above. Instead of postulating beliefs and intentions (in the head) to account for linguistic acts, what is postulated is an internal configuration formally isomorphic to a computer program (one we have yet to write) which accounts for what is conceived of as human linguistic 'print-out'. Many cognitive scientists see their task as the writing of such a program, or possibly working in conjunction with physiologists to determine which of several possible programs the human mind actually runs. (See also ARTIFICIAL INTELLIGENCE.)

There are, however, several doubts about the aspirations of such cognitive scientists. If these aspirations are based on a thoroughgoing holism, it is difficult to see how language mastery can be acquired (as humans evidently acquired it) in stages. For the whole of language would have to be mastered in order to have mastered any part of it. It is difficult also to see how two adult human beings could communicate with one another, so long as their vocabularies did not precisely coincide. For it would be impossible to determine whether a difference of opinion was based on one person being misinformed or the two speakers at cross purposes because they in effect spoke different languages.

Computer modelling need not rest on a holistic approach, but if there is thought to be some component of the meaning of an expression which is independent of its relationships to other expressions in the language, this component would seem to have to be sought in the relation that the expression bears to things outside the language. Computer models can be extended by connecting the machinery and software to 'external sensors', so that the print-out bears an appropriate relation to the world. But this expedient leaves open the possibility that different sensors responding to different external features (or even direct interference from the programmer) could produce the same internal states and the same print-out; and in so far as this is possible, the computer fails to model the meaning of the words on the print-out. Those, such as Jerry A. Fodor, who are convinced of the adequacy of computer models have tried to make a virtue of this difficulty and have advanced 'methodological solipsism . . . as a research strategy in cognitive psychology'. Others, such as John Searle, have turned these difficulties into an a priori argument against the possibility of computer modelling of human languages and against the claim that the human mind is in all essential respects a computer.

So far we have considered approaches to meaning which look either to the relation between language and the world or to the relation between language and mind. (The latter may seek to preserve the meaning relation as a fit subject for scientific study by treating mental structures or intentions as natural, possibly purely physical, phenomena.) A third approach would argue that the difficulties of the first two arise from not recognizing that meaning must be studied in the context of a (three-term) relation between mind and the world and language, where the last of these is conceived of as a social phenomenon. This was an important feature of Saussure's theory, for he insisted that 'language never exists apart from social fact', but it is also an important principle of the outlook of such diverse thinkers as *Hegel, Marx, *Dewey, Mead, *Vygotsky, and *Wittgenstein.

It is from this perspective that Bennett's programme would be criticized for assuming that non-language users could have, and recognize in others, intentions as complex as required for Grice's analysis of (even) a simple act of signalling. Thought, from this perspective, cannot exist without (or prior to) language.

According to the social behaviourists, George Herbert Mead for example, it would be acceptable to regard social animals as affecting the behaviour of one another in the following complex way: the beginning of a pattern of behaviour (a gesture) on the part of one animal elicits from another a pattern of behaviour which modifies the development of that pattern as it unfolds in the behaviour of the first animal. But to behave as a human does in such a social interaction, the second animal would have to respond not only to the gesture, but to the relationship between the gesture and the object, which had acted as stimulus to the gesture, *and to do so from the standpoint of the first animal*. This is what is required for the second animal to respond to something as meaningful, the concept of meaning implied here being 'an individual reaction which an object may call out'. For the meaning of an object to be 'ours' we must have adapted ourselves to a comprehensive set of reactions toward it, which we can not only adopt ourselves but do so also in the role of others who can respond in that way. Meaning is not, on this account, primarily a property of objects, John Dewey observed, it must be primarily a property of behavioural responses and derivatively of the objects that enter into those patterns.

Another development of an essentially social approach to meaning will be found in the later work of Wittgenstein. Wittgenstein interpreted Frege's suggestion that a word has a meaning only as part of a sentence, as a way of saying that things cannot have names except in a 'language game' (*Investigations*, I, 49), a label which Wittgenstein

applied to social contexts in which words are used in structured ways of interacting with the world. All three, language, language users, and the world are bound up in this concept, and its implications were spelled out in the advice, 'Don't ask for the meaning, ask for the use.' Wittgenstein, moreover, mounted controversial and much debated arguments against the possibility of a person assigning a meaning to a word on the basis of an intention to use that word to apply to something experienced privately. The use of language to describe subjective experience is dependent on and derivative from linguistic practices in which several people co-ordinate their interactions with each other. (See also WITTGENSTEIN'S PHILOSOPHY OF LANGUAGE.)

Whether one treats this third approach as conforming to or repudiating the demand for a scientific approach to language depends on whether one conceives the study of human social interaction as (at least potentially) continuous with the scientific study of nature. A tradition going back to Giambattista Vico in the early eighteenth century regards the study of human institutions and artefacts as the province of a study which, if scientific, involves methods quite discontinuous with the natural sciences. More recent developments in this tradition insist upon the need for the imaginative re-creation of the experience of other human beings, of the need for empathy or sympathy in grasping the meaning of a text, and generally refer to their methodology under the rubric 'hermeneutics'. Not all those, however, who insist on the importance of the social in the study of meaning adopt this methodological dualism. Whether or not one does adopt a dualist approach is related in an important way to the conception one has of scientific knowledge. This in turn rests on the way one conceives the relationship between human beings (in particular their minds) and the rest of nature.                                    J. E. T.

Ayer, A. J. (ed.) (1959). *Logical Positivism*. London.
Bennett, J. (1976). *Linguistic Behaviour*. Cambridge.
Davidson, D. (1984). *Inquiries into Truth and Interpretation*. Oxford.
Fodor, J. A. (1981). *Representations*. Hassocks.
Frege, G. (ed. and trans. Geach, P. T. and Black, M. 1952). *Philosophical Writings*. Oxford.
Kripke, S. (1980). *Naming and Necessity*. Oxford.
Mead, G. H. (ed. Reck, A. J., 1964). *Selected Writings*. Chicago.
Quine, W. V. (1960). *Word and Object*. Cambridge, Massachusetts.
Saussure, F. de (trans. Baskin, W. 1960). *Course in General Linguistics*. London.
Wittgenstein, L. (trans. Anscombe, G. E. M. 1958). *Philosophical Investigations*. Oxford.

**MEASUREMENTS IN MIND.** See PSYCHOPHYSICS.

**MEDIUM.** See SPIRITUALISM.

**MEDULLA.** The inner part of an organ; or the abbreviation for 'medulla oblongata' (or 'bulb') at the top of the spinal cord. See NERVOUS SYSTEM.

**MEMORY.** When we learn something there must be a change in the brain, but no one knows what the change is. Until quite recently the concept of memory was used only in mentalistic contexts. Few dictionaries contain any reference to memory as a feature of a physical system, though we now have the language of computer scientists to help us in thinking about our own memories, as physical records in the brain. In computer language the memory is an instrument in which is placed a store of whatever information is to be used for calculation. This information is thus a representation of some set of events, embodied in a code. How does the nervous system come to contain useful representations of its environment?

The code of the nervous system is provided basically by the fact that each nerve fibre carries only one sort of information. In such a system learning must consist in a change in the connection pattern of the pathways from input (say the eyes) to output (say movement). The initial basis of the nervous memory is thus provided by heredity (the genetic memory), which establishes the nervous pathways of the new-born. Natural selection has ensured that at birth each individual is provided with potentialities suitable for its future type of environment. A young kitten already has the connections which ensure that each cell of its visual cortex responds mainly when a particular contour moves in front of its eyes, though the responses are less vigorous than they are in an adult. If the kitten is only allowed to see vertical lines then it will later be found to have lost the power to respond to horizontal (or other) lines. Meanwhile the response to vertical contours has become much stronger. (See VISUAL SYSTEM: ENVIRONMENTAL INFLUENCES). Memory thus depends upon selection from the original multiplicity of possible actions of those that represent useful responses to the environment. Other work with kittens shows that normal capacities only develop if there is appropriate input at certain short *critical periods. (See SPATIAL CO-ORDINATION OF THE SENSES.)

A human child similarly is born with a range of capacities, and given the right stimulus he then learns to take those actions that are appropriate (see INFANCY, MIND IN). Thus from twelve months onwards he learns to speak whatever language he hears, making certain vocal movements and rejecting others. All skills involve such selection. As development proceeds we thus build a model in the brain that ensures appropriate behaviour. The problem of memory is to find the mechanism that increases the probability of use of some pathways and decreases that of others.

The decision as to whether a nerve-cell is to send a signal depends upon the synapses that it receives from other nerve fibres. It was early suggested by the histologist *Ramon y Cajal that memory depends upon forming synapses. By contrast, Ivan *Pavlov, who pioneered the physiological study of learning, attributed the 'conditioned reflexes' in his dogs to vague processes of spread of excitation and inhibition in the cortex. These two types of theory persist to the present. The majority of neuroscientists probably believe in a synaptic change, but there is little direct evidence of the details of it.

The nervous system contains many pathways that re-excite themselves, and it was suggested that these might serve for memory in the brain, as in some computers. This is not likely to be true for long-term memories, which must surely be physically embodied, since they can endure for up to a hundred years, in spite of shocks and anaesthetics and (in rats) even freezing. But it frequently happens that immediately after a shock there is no memory, say of an accident (see AMNESIA). It is therefore postulated that memory is recorded on two or more time-scales. The *short-term memory is transient and easily interrupted. Perhaps it is carried by the chains that re-excite themselves. It must endure for long enough to allow a record to be 'printed' in the long-term memory. This may involve synaptic change, perhaps by some sort of growth process. Parts of the brain concerned with memory contain many very small nerve-cells ('amacrine cells' or 'microneurones'). One suggestion is that these serve to produce an inhibitory substance whose action closes the unwanted pathway. This would allow the other one to be used: its synapses would then become more effective and those of the other pathway would wither away. All such changes would involve synthesis of new protein, and there is evidence that, if a substance inhibiting protein synthesis is given shortly after a learning occasion, no memory is established. This does not mean that the new protein carries the memory. It alters the probability of use of one set of channels rather than another. Information in the brain is coded by channels not molecules. Not appreciating this, biochemists have sought for a memory molecule, on the mistaken analogy of DNA. They have even claimed that memory can be transferred by injecting extracts from a trained brain, or even by the cannibalism of worms. Many injected substances will indeed change brains, but the claims of transfer of specific memories have not been substantiated. The attraction of the idea of cannibalism tells more about human psychology than about the biology of memory.

The capacity to change nervous pathways, that is to learn, is quite widespread. A cockroach without its head will learn not to dip its leg into water from which it gets a shock. From such simple learning systems it has been discovered that various changes in the electrical and chemical properties of the nerve-cells are involved. But memories like our own usually store more complicated information, and this involves special nervous equipment. In each species the brain has a memory system suitable to its special way of life. Memories are not parts of a generalized computer system but specific analogue devices. In octopuses we have been able to find two anatomically distinct memory mechanisms. In one are stored records of objects seen and in the other records of objects touched or tasted. The decisions that an octopus makes are rather simple—whether to attack a particular object or to draw in an object touched with its arms. It can learn to attack a horizontal rectangle and avoid a vertical one or to discriminate between rough and smooth spheres. (See INVERTEBRATE LEARNING AND INTELLIGENCE.) Such choices are typical of the selections between alternatives that are the essential features of recording in memory. The animal or man must be provided with feature detectors that can allow the performance of two or more actions. Learning which action to perform must depend upon a system that allows for information about past results to alter the probabilities of the use of the pathways in the future. We believe that this is done by initially reducing the effectiveness of the wrong pathway and then increasing the right one—perhaps by new synaptic growth. Many special features are required to make such a system effective, and it is not surprising that neuroscientists have not yet fully unravelled the secret of the memory mechanism. And, of course, in mammals memory does not depend upon switching single neurones, say in the visual cortex, but somewhere the pathways are changed when we learn.

There must be nervous tracts that bring information such as that of *taste or *pain together with signals from the outside world. In mammals there is evidence that these come through the reinforcement pathways, which can be activated by self-stimulation for reward. These lead through the hypothalamus to the hippocampus, which is a part of the brain particularly concerned with memory.

Another special need is for mechanisms of generalization in the memory, and here the octopus has proved most helpful. It does not have to learn everything eight times over. Martin Wells was able to show that what is learned by one arm can be performed by the others—but not if a particular piece of the brain is removed. This piece, the median inferior frontal, has a web-like structure that allows signals from the different arms to interact. This is one small example of how study of parts of the brain can tell us about the memory mechanism. Again, in an octopus the visual memory can be removed without damaging the touch memory, and vice versa. So the memory record in the octopus brain is localized. In mammals it has proved difficult to find where the record is, so that the psychologist Karl *Lashley, after his lifelong 'search for the *engram', could not decide whether it was nowhere in the brain or everywhere.

The model of the mnemon, or unit of memory, can be considered either as an anatomical reality, as I believe it to be in the octopus, or as a logical schema representing the much more complex situation in man. The essence of it is that establishing a permanent memory record involves selection from an initial set of possible pathways. Selection is made on a basis of the rewards that follow from different actions. The particular type of memory of each species depends upon modification of the connections of an inborn feature-detector system. In man these detectors are particularly tuned to respond to features of human behaviour. The child is specially sensitive to human speech sounds even at two months, long before he can talk or understand speech (see BRAIN DEVELOPMENT). By learning to react in appropriate ways to particular features he then builds a model in his brain that allows him to live in his human environment.

J. Z. Y.

Baddeley, A. D. (1976). *The Psychology of Memory*. New York. (For a comprehensive bibliography.)
Bartlett, F. C. (1932). *Remembering*. Cambridge.
Young, J. Z. (1978). *Programs of the Brain*. Oxford.

**MEMORY: BIOLOGICAL BASIS.** For materialist theories of the mind, it is axiomatic that in some way there must be brain representations of memory. This may not be intuitively obvious when we consider our own individual memories, for we can clearly rehearse in our minds the histories of past experience (the memories of a childhood birthday party, the image of an absent friend's face, the opening notes of a Beethoven symphony, or the taste of a roast dinner) without these rehearsals affecting our external behaviour in any obvious way. However, for an experimenter studying memory in others, whether human or non-human animal subjects, what is observed is a change in behaviour—a human showing a new skill, or an animal traversing a maze correctly and thereby finding food or avoiding electric shock—and it is from this change that memory is inferred. Indeed memory is a portmanteau expression which includes within itself two processes and, by hypothesis, a thing. The processes are the *learning of some new skill, behaviour pattern, or piece of information (sometimes called the *acquisition* of the memory) and, at some later time, the recall and re-expression of the skill or information (sometimes called *retrieval*). The thing that connects the two processes of learning and recall is a change in the properties of the brain system so as to store the new information which the learning represents, in such a form that it can subsequently, in response to appropriate cues, be searched for and retrieved. This change is known as the memory trace, or *engram*. The relationship between the language used to discuss these phenomena in the brain and that used in the description of the properties of computers and their memory stores is not accidental, for much of our present-day thinking about biological memory is directed—and constrained—by a framework of analogies from computer technology and *information theory.

For experimental science, the question is how far memory and its brain representation are amenable to experimental analysis rather than to logical and philosophical enquiry. Over recent decades, this has been one of the central problem areas for psychology and neurobiology. However, the nature of experimental method in these disciplines is such that most attention has been focused on a study of the processes of learning and recall; the engram which links them has been inferred rather than demonstrated. Research has concentrated on asking questions concerning the strategies and temporal processes involved in learning and recall—what and how much can be learned, how fast, and over what period—and concerning the brain systems, at the biochemical, cellular, and physiological levels, that subserve these processes. This research may be conducted either by a direct comparison of the brains of experimental animals which have learned, with those of controls which have not, or by examining, in humans or other animals, the effects of procedures which enhance or retard learning or recall.

The major obstacles to advance in this area are on the one hand conceptual—the need to develop clear and testable alternative models—and, on the other, experimental—the development of appropriate control procedures. As will become apparent shortly, it is relatively easy to perform experiments which show that in experimental animals particular drugs and treatments prevent learning or recall from occurring, or that when learning occurs, particular changes in brain-cell properties accompany it. The problem is to be sure that observed biochemical, anatomical, and physiological changes which accompany learning form the necessary, sufficient, and exclusive representations of that learning at the biological level, rather than being merely the correlates of other phenomena which occur at the same time as the learning. For example, in order to motivate experimental animals to learn it may be necessary to subject them to mild stress (hunger, electric shock); in order to learn, the animals may need to be rather active in the exploration of a particular environment. The challenge is to design experiments which eliminate the possibility that any observed change to be studied is a correlate or consequence of stress, activity, sensory stimulation, or whatever, rather than of the learning itself. Rigorous control of all alternative possibilities is virtually impossible to achieve in a single experiment; rather, the goal must be a balance of probabilities on the basis of a number of separate approaches.

There is ample evidence that the learning process is not a simple one-step process. The most popular hypothesis is that there are at least two separate stages, involving different physiological mechanisms and in all probability different brain regions. The first process is short-lived, the second slower but of longer duration, and they are conventionally referred to as *short-term (STM) and long-term (LTM) memory respectively, though some would claim that short-term memory itself embraces more than one process. The distinction between STM and LTM is illustrated by an experiment in which a list of seven numbers is read out to a subject, who is asked to repeat them back. Most people can repeat the numbers with accuracy if asked to do so within a few minutes of hearing

them, but will fail if asked an hour or so later. However, if the numbers are of importance to the subject (for example, if they form a telephone number) they can generally be recalled days or even years later. Many items are placed in short-term store—numbers, names, this morning's breakfast menu—but only a few find their way into the permanent memory system. This is obviously functionally desirable from the biological viewpoint, as the utility of recalling most short-term stored items for more than a brief while is very limited, and there must be a finite capacity to any store and to the retrieval mechanism.

STM, then, is labile, and in the normal course of events, decays over a period of minutes to hours. If the item to be recalled is not, over this period, transferred from STM to LTM, it is irretrievably lost as STM decays. A variety of drugs and other treatments can affect the memory while it is in STM. Substances which interfere with the brain's electrical activity, or treatments like electroconvulsive shock or the infliction of injury, such as a blow to the head resulting in concussion, will effectively obliterate all items in STM at the time, so that the individual on recovery will have no recall for the events leading up to the injury (see AMNESIA). Certain drugs also appear to enhance STM or facilitate transfer from STM to LTM. These include strychnine and amphetamine (the former having even more considerable and undesirable effects than the latter!). We are led to the hypothesis that the form in which STM is held within the brain involves transient changes in the electrical properties of the brain as a system, very likely a result of a reversible modulation of the firing properties of particular neurones or their *synapses. There is suggestive evidence, based on studies utilizing microinjection of drugs, electrical stimulation or recording, and ablation techniques, as well as the study of human patients with STM deficits, that the hippocampal region of the brain is closely involved in the mechanism of STM and its transfer to LTM. Yet this is a relatively simple model of the relationship between STM and LTM, and the situation is probably a good deal more complex. Not every item which cannot be retrieved from LTM has been lost for ever by STM decay: it may have been overlaid or suppressed, and can be recovered under appropriate circumstances, sometimes by re-creating the context in which the memory was first formed. Such observations have led some psychologists to argue that the terms STM and LTM be replaced by new concepts of 'active' and 'labile' memories. However, for the purpose of studying the cellular mechanisms of memory formation, the exact phenomenological features at the behavioural level are of relatively minor importance.

What matters here is that memories, when fixed, are notoriously difficult to erase (indeed they are the most durable features—other, perhaps, than scar tissue—acquired during a person's lifetime). Their durability has led to the widely shared hypothesis that they must be coded for in terms of some equally lasting change in brain structure, with a consequent effect on physiological processes. There is good evidence that LTM is a cortical function in mammals generally, and that in humans the temporal lobes are likely to be involved in memory processes, but what sort of changes in brain structure might one envisage as being able to code for memory? Since at least the 1940s there has been a long-running controversy among physiological psychologists over the localizability or non-localizability of the memory trace. Localized models essentially suggest that particular memories are coded for in terms of particular pathways, or neuronal circuits, and were given theoretical substance by Donald Hebb, who postulated the existence of a class of neurones whose connections were in the form of synapses which could be modified by experience, thus opening or closing unique pathways. Particular circuits or pathways could correspond to particular memory traces; learning resulted in the modification of synapses and recall resulted from the passage of impulses along the particular pathway concerned. Hebb's modifiable synapse theory found support in the clinical studies of the neurosurgeon Wilder *Penfield, who observed, in human patients being treated for epilepsy, that electrical stimulation of particular regions of the temporal lobe of the cortex regularly caused the patient to recall specific, if fragmentary, memory sequences.

The rival memory model suggests that, rather than there being localization of memory circuits, the storage of information is a molar property of the mass of cortical cells, a 'field' rather than a 'point' representation being involved. Experiments which lead in this direction derive from the studies of Karl *Lashley, who, also in the 1940s, showed that when rats had been trained to particular maze-running skills, these skills could not be obliterated by removal of particular cortical areas; rather the results of such ablations were generalized deficits proportional to the amount, but not the region, of cortex removed. The theoretical rationale for this model was not available until more recently, in the form of analogies with the non-localized storage of information on a photographic plate provided by the hologram.

It is probably true that holographic memory theories have found more favour with mathematical theorists than with experimental neurobiologists, most of whom favour a modifiable synapse/ neuronal circuit model, with the proviso that it is likely that any individual memory will have multiple representations in the brain, involving numerous different circuits. Could a neuronal circuit model account for the information storage capacity of the human brain? The number of neurones of the human cortex is often quoted as $10^{10}$, and direct counts of synapses would suggest upwards of $10^4$ synapses for each neurone. $10^{14}$ synapses would seem to give ample storage potential for the information acquired in a human lifetime.

How about the direct demonstration of synapses or neuronal circuitry being modified by experience and during learning? Physiological, biochemical, and anatomical evidence on this score has accumulated over the last two decades, though it is fair to say that no fully systematic model exists and rigorous proof that observed changes are the necessary, sufficient *and* exclusive correlates of learning is lacking; we have to make do with indicative rather than conclusive demonstrations.

At the anatomical and physiological levels, most of the evidence concerns long-term changes in the structure and properties of particular neurones or their synapses in response to experience. For instance, the visual cortex of experimental animals responds to the input of new visual information by lasting changes in the number and dimensions of synapses, including changes in the contact areas between pre- and post-synaptic sides of the synapse and of the storage vesicles which contain transmitter substances. The physiological response properties of visual cortex neurones are modulated in a predictable manner by the environment in which the animal, for example a cat, is reared (see VISUAL SYSTEM: ENVIRONMENTAL INFLUENCES). The neurones are thus 'learning' to recognize and respond to characteristic features of the environment.

Such plastic brain responses to environmental change are regarded as analogies of what happens, on a much more precise scale, during learning. But they are only analogies. To move to greater precision a learning 'model' is required. This is not as easy as it sounds. Psychologists explore memory in rats learning to run mazes, or pigeons pressing levers for reward. Such tasks often require training animals over a long period, and encouraging them to learn by keeping them either hungry or thirsty so that they may be rewarded with food or drink for correct responses, or by punishing them—for instance, by mild electric shocks—when they make mistakes. In such situations, if one trains an animal and finds a subsequent biochemical or cellular change, how can one be sure that the change is not the result of the shocks, or the motor activity involved in the running of the maze, or the sensory stimulation, or the stress?

Although biochemists could and did know in the 1960s and in the 1970s that training animals under these conditions affected the rate of protein synthesis in particular brain regions, the interpretation of such experiments was open to doubt. Other experiments used drugs which affected the rate of protein synthesis in the brain. In general, drugs which speed protein synthesis enhance the rate of learning of complex tasks, whereas those which inhibit protein synthesis are without effect on STM or the recall of acquired memories, but prevent the development of LTM. None the less it was argued that the effects of these drugs on memory formation and on protein synthesis were independent, both being the consequence of other types of central effect of the drugs concerned. More precise models and methods, at both behavioural and biochemical levels, were required.

In more recent years, three types of experimental system have begun to yield particularly revealing information about the cellular mechanisms involved in learning processes. In the first, the learning 'model' is the young chick. Day-old chicks readily learn a number of tasks—for instance, they become '*imprinted'—learning to distinguish their mother (or, in the experiments, a mother substitute) from all other objects in their environment, and following her subsequently. The chicks also continually explore their environment by pecking, and learn to distinguish food objects from inedible or distasteful items. For Pat Bateson and Gabriel Horn in Cambridge and Steven Rose's group at the Open University, these spontaneous forms of learning proved particularly amenable to cellular study. When a bird pecks at a distasteful object which it learns to avoid, there results a series of biochemical changes in very specific regions of the forebrain. The changes involve first the mobilization of certain key enzyme systems which modulate synaptic transmission, and then, as part of a longer-term process, the synthesis of new glyco-proteins, which are transported from the nerve-cell bodies in which they are made to the synapses, where they become incorporated into the synaptic membranes. As a consequence of these biochemical modifications, synapses in at least three separate but connected left hemisphere regions of the brain of the chick change in their structure in ways which can be detected at high magnification in the electron microscope; in particular, the number of synaptic vesicles—the transmitter containing bodies at the synapse—increases and the region of the synapse that directly apposes the pre- and post-synaptic cell changes in length. All this looks uncommonly like what might be expected if synaptic connectivity were being modulated and new pathways being formed. Over the period of hours following learning, the electrical properties of the cells in at least one of these forebrain regions also change dramatically, with large increases in the rate of neuronal firing. Such changes occur only in birds which remember the aversive stimulus. If they are trained but made to forget, the changes in physiology and biochemistry do not occur. Moreover, as Gabriel Horn has shown, using imprinting, these regions of synaptic change are *necessary* for memory formation to occur; if one particular region is excised from the chick brain before training, learning the imprinting task becomes impossible. If the bird is trained and then the region is immediately excised, the chick behaves as if it is naïve and has no recall for the task. In other respects it behaves normally, and sham operations do not produce the memory deficits.

The young chick may seem a simpler organism in which to study memory than the psychologists' traditional beasts, but the other two recent types of experimental system have even greater simplicity. For Eric Kandel and his colleagues in New York, the organism of choice was the seemingly unpromising sea slug, *Aplysia californica*. These large molluscs have a limited repertoire of behaviour, and do not even have brains in the vertebrate sense; their nerve-cells are distributed through their body in a variety of groups of cells known as ganglia. What makes them attractive to the neurobiologist is that whereas vertebrate brains have many thousands of millions of smaller cells, *Aplysia* have fewer than a million neurones, and many of them are large—up to a millimetre in diameter as opposed to the vertebrate size of 10–100 micrometres. Individual nerve-cells are thus amenable to physiological study: the 'same' cell can be located in many different individuals; it can be dissected out, and its connections studied. The entire ganglion plus its inputs and outputs can be isolated from the rest of the organism and maintained in physiologically functional condition for several days. Kandel studied in particular the nerve-cells involved in a number of cellular systems active in the processes of *habituation and sensitization of reflexes. When they are lightly touched, regions of the surface of the animal around its gill contract vigorously, as part of an escape and withdrawal reflex. This response diminishes if the same region is repeatedly touched (habituation) but may be extended to form a reaction to previously neutral stimuli if they are coupled with potentially noxious ones (sensitization). Kandel has mapped in some detail the neural pathways involved in these processes and has been able to record physiologically, from the pre- and post-synaptic cells involved in the responses, the changes that occur as habituation or sensitization takes place. He has been able to show the direct involvement of transmitters such as serotonin in the process, and has followed a number of key biochemical steps in the synapse—especially the role played by a combination of a synaptic membrane protein, capable of being reversibly phosphorylated in response to external stimuli, and the intracellular 'second messenger' substance cyclic AMP. These molecular processes are involved in regulating the entry of calcium ions into the cells; the calcium ions alter the membrane potentials and directly modulate synaptic connectivity. Kandel argues that such changes in the electrical properties of individual synapses as a result of experience both occur and underlie at least relatively short-duration memory processes.

The third experimental approach has been to abandon living organisms altogether in searching for a system in which to study the molecular biology of neuronal plasticity. It is well known that if thin slices of brain tissue—no more than a third of a millimetre in thickness—are cut and placed in a warm, oxygenated, glucose-containing medium, they retain their biochemical properties and some physiological properties for a period of several hours. If the slices are cut appropriately they can be made to retain at least some of their nerve inputs. Recording electrodes can be placed among the cells of the slice, and the effect on the cells of electrically stimulating the inputs can be followed. A particularly interesting brain region to study in this way is the mammalian hippocampus, for long considered to be involved in aspects of the process of transfer of short- to long-term memory. Gary Lynch and his colleagues at Irvine, California, among others have shown that if hippocampal slices are electrically stimulated from their appropriate nerve inputs, there can be long-lasting (up to an hour or more) changes in the electrical outputs from these cells—the so-called hippocampal potentiation. This phenomenon *in vitro* is known to mimic the *in vivo* properties of the cells of this brain region, which were found to show such potentiation by Bliss and others in the early 1970s. *In vitro* the biochemical mechanisms involved can be studied in detail, and shown to involve, as in *Aplysia*, phosphorylated membrane proteins, cyclic AMP, glutamate receptors, and calcium ion channels in the membrane. Lynch argues that hippocampal potentiation is an *in vitro* analogue of memory processes.

All this may seem a long way from Marcel Proust's evocation of youthful memory, *À la recherche du temps perdu* with its sense imagery. Are young chicks, sea slugs, or slices of brain tissue really going to reveal the molecular mechanisms of such a durable if elusive property of the human brain? It is an act of faith perhaps, to claim that they are. Complex phenomena are not merely the result of the additive properties of simpler ones, because as systems increase in complexity their properties change qualitatively (which is why we may speak of human consciousness, but are much more doubtful about animal consciousness despite the similarities in basic brain structure). Nevertheless, the general principles of organization that underlie these brain systems are similar. Biochemically, nervous and hormonal systems of body regulation involve similar chemical processes subserving different ends. The organization of nervous transmission is almost identical over a range of living organisms from insects and molluscs to humans. There seems no reason to doubt that the mechanisms involved in nervous system plasticity will turn out also to be related, even though the complexity and richness of the plastic response will vary qualitatively as we move from small-brained and rather 'hard-wired' organisms into the immensely plastic and flexible brain of the human.

However, it is important to emphasize what it is that such studies will not reveal. Some years ago there was wide publicity for experiments which purported to show that particular memories were encoded in particular molecular structures—substances which could be extracted from a trained animal and then injected into a naïve one, carrying the memories with them. This type of experiment, always theoretically dubious, has since been largely discredited in practice as well, as being

based on fallacious and artefactual errors of experimental design. What the biochemical and anatomical studies show is *not* specific 'memory molecules', but general cellular systems which underlie all plastic responses of the brain to experience. Although it is not known whether such mechanisms occur in all types of neurones in all organisms, a general parsimony principle which does not multiply processes needlessly would suggest that this is likely to be the case. If it is so, then the specificity of a memory—as when the brain distinguishes between remembering a telephone number, a friend's face, and a childhood recollection—does not lie in the particularity of the biochemical substances concerned. Rather it depends on which cells are involved in the circuits, where in the brain they are located, and with which other cells they are connected.

In this respect, analysing the biochemistry and anatomy of memory is like studying the chemistry and design of the recording head of a tape recorder and a cassette of magnetic tape. To know how a tape recorder works, these things must be studied. But no amount of information revealed by such study will enable one to predict the message on the tape. For that, one has to play the machine. This is likely to remain true for analysis of the cell biology of memory as well.                                    S. P. R. R.

Hebb, D. O. (1961). *Organisation of Behavior*, 2nd edn. New York.

Horn, G. (1985). *Memory, Imprinting, and the Brain.* Oxford.

Kandel, E. R. and Schwartz, J. H. (1982). Molecular biology of learning: modulation of transmitter release. *Science*, **248**, 433–43.

Lashley, K. S. (1963). *Brain Mechanisms and Intelligence.* New York.

Luria, A. R. (1969). *The Mind of a Mnemonist.* London.

Rose, S. P. R. (1976). *The Conscious Brain.* Harmondsworth.

Rose, S. P. R. (1981). What should a biochemistry of learning and memory be about? *Neuroscience*, **6**, 811–21.

Rose, S. P. R. (ed.) (1982). *Towards a Liberatory Biology.* London.

Squire, L. R. and Butlers, N. (eds.) (1984). *Neuropsychology of Memory.* Greensboro, North Carolina.

**MEMORY: EXPERIMENTAL APPROACHES.** One of the problems in the study of psychology is that it deals with the familiar. And the familiar, being taken for granted, provokes little curiosity. It is therefore often easier to perceive scientific problems when we are confronted with unexpected malfunction. The study of memory is a case in point. The failure of memory, or *amnesia, not only excites interest but also reveals unsuspected facets of the memory process. The form of amnesia which we will first discuss often occurs after blows to the head have produced unconsciousness. Upon recovery the subject cannot remember certain events that occurred in the past. However, it is not the events in the distant past, the memory of which is normally dim, that are most severely affected. It is precisely those events whose memory would be sharpest at the time of the accident that cannot be recalled—the events which occurred closest in time to the accident. For instance, in car accidents the injured person cannot remember the accident itself. The last thing he may remember is being at a place many miles from where the accident occurred. In severe cases the memory of weeks before the accident is unavailable. However, with the passage of time the blank in the memory shrinks, those episodes farthest away in time from the accident returning first. The extent of recovery is variable but a short period of about one second before the accident seems always to remain inaccessible to memory.

From this quite common type of amnesia (retrograde amnesia) some quite surprising consequences follow. It is obvious that some change occurs at the moment of the registration of a memory. Not so obvious is the observation that such a change is more vulnerable to trauma the more recent the change is. Apart from anything else, this 'age-dependence' indicates that the physiological change underlying memory is not all-or-none but alters in a continuous manner with time. The remarkable length of time over which such alterations occur can be most clearly seen in the *Korsakoff syndrome, a condition which sometimes occurs in association with alcoholism. The patient here also suffers from retrograde amnesia. However, the memory blank may be very extensive, perhaps extending over many years and often spreading further and further back until the patient can only remember events in his early youth or childhood. This indicates that the changes in memory we spoke of above must continue over decades.

Unfortunately the physiological changes that occur to produce amnesia clinically are somewhat obscure. A blow on the head can hardly be considered to be a delicate biochemical or anatomical dissecting tool. Consequently scientists have attempted to produce amnesia in animals using more controlled methods. One such method produces amnesia through the use of electroconvulsive shock. A brief surge of current is passed through the nervous system of a rat so as to produce unconsciousness. Twenty-four hours later the rat appears not to recall habits it learned just before the application of such a shock. However, other habits acquired a little while before the shock survive unscathed. These results encouraged theorists to postulate that memory existed in two stages—a labile short-lived stage, disruptible by electric shock, and a permanent stage invulnerable to such interference. Two main problems with such an interpretation are that slightly different experimental circumstances produce widely varying estimates of the duration of the time during which a memory is vulnerable. The second and more severe difficulty emerged when rats were tested at other times besides the traditional twenty-four hours after learning. It emerged that if rats were tested four hours later they did remember,

though matched animals would not remember twenty-four hours later. Further rats, given electroconvulsive shock five minutes after training, would remember well twenty-four hours later, but remember nothing a week later, when untreated rats showed good retention. Such findings are difficult to square with a two-stage theory of memory, but suggest instead that electroconvulsive shock causes an acceleration of forgetting. However, such forgetting may not be permanent because there exist well-authenticated cases of recovery of memory after such amnesia. In any case it turns out that passing a large current across the head is hardly more sophisticated as a research tool than a sharp blow to the skull.

In an effort to increase the specificity of physiological interference, various chemical agents have been administered after a learning task, and some of these, such as potassium chloride, flurothyl, and barbiturates, were found to have effects qualitatively similar to electroconvulsive shock. Nevertheless, no specific process in the central nervous system could be pin-pointed, and the conclusion seems to be that almost any agent capable of producing a profound interruption in the working of the brain will also induce retrograde amnesia.

Because of advances in the understanding of the storage of genetic information, attention became focused on the possibility that some analogous processes carried information in memory, and attempts were made to affect memory by administering RNA, DNA, and protein synthesis inhibiting drugs. While there is no doubt that these drugs do have effects similar to electroconvulsive shock, interpretation of the way they achieve those effects is in doubt. Even if we accept the premiss that amnesia is caused as a result of protein, RNA, or DNA synthesis inhibition by the drug and not by one of its side-effects, this does not necessarily mean that memory itself is coded by what the drug inhibits. Protein synthesis inhibition might very well interfere with some other changes that underlie memory. Suspicious also are the facts that the amnesic consequences of the above treatments may be countered by the administration of stimulants and that the memories that should lack a physiological substrate have in several experiments been shown to return. In any case the idea that the information stored in memory is encoded in a large molecule seems rather unlikely. While such a molecular hypothesis would solve the problem of storage, it fails when it comes to an equally important characteristic of the memory system—namely fast access. It is difficult to see how the nervous system would find the information once it was stored.

A more likely hypothesis than the molecular, concerning memory storage, that was put forward as early as the end of the nineteenth century, is that the change underlying memory consists of synaptic modification. Synapses are the gaps across which neurones communicate with each other, and it is easy to envisage how changes in the facility of transmission across such gaps could be used to store easily accessible information. Even so, in spite of its plausibility, such a hypothesis has received no experimental support till recently. The test that was made utilized a fact already mentioned above, that of a rather slow change in the substrate of memory. If this change is in the transmission capacity of a synapse, or a group of synapses, then pharmacological tools are available to show the existence of such changes. Poorly conducting synapses react differently to the same dose of drug from normally conducting synapses. A good example of this occurs in myasthenia gravis. In this condition the patient has great difficulty in contracting skeletal muscles. The neural pathways to the muscles are intact and so are the muscles themselves. What is impaired is the junction between the neurone and the muscle. This junction is a type of synapse. For reasons that need not concern us here, the transmitter substance, acetylcholine, which is ejected from the neurone, has a much smaller effect on the muscle than normal. When the patient is given a certain dose of the anticholinesterase group of drugs, the destruction of acetylcholine which normally occurs is slowed, and so more acetylcholine becomes available to cause muscle contraction. As a result, movement is facilitated and normal functioning is made possible. However, the same dose of drug administered to a normal person produces paralysis instead, as a consequence of too much transmitter. In a similar manner, we might expect new or weak memories to be facilitated and older or strong memories to be blocked, if the substrate of memory was a synapse that varied in efficiency. As a test of this, rats were trained to perform a habit. The rats were then divided into a large number of groups and made to wait different lengths of time before being retested. They were injected with anticholinesterase in the same dose at the same time, before being tested on their memory of the habit. Any effect of the drug on performance should therefore have been the same. However, the memory of the task was strongly affected by the age of such memory. Little effect of the drug was seen on memories of up to three days. Almost complete forgetting was manifest when the habit was seven to fourteen days old. However, when the habit was twenty-one to twenty-eight days old and almost forgotten by rats not treated with the drug just before retest, the treated rats showed very good retention. It was thus possible in a simple experiment to show both block and facilitation of a habit using a synaptically active drug.

These experiments strongly suggest that memory is based on a change in synaptic function. As a result of learning, a synapse begins to transmit, then transmits more strongly, and eventually such transmission attenuates to express itself as *forgetting. Because of the changes in susceptibility to drugs, it became important to look for changes in the strength of memory that these changes in susceptibility suggested. As a result it

has now been found that when the memory for a habit is tested at various times after learning, such memory does get progressively stronger before forgetting sets in. For instance, rats are placed in a box consisting of two compartments, one lit and the other dark. These are connected by a hole in a partition. When rats are placed in the lit compartment they invariably, after a certain average time, enter the dark compartment. Upon entering the dark compartment they are given an electric shock. On being placed in the lit compartment again, the time it takes the rats to enter the dark compartment is greatly increased. It is the magnitude of this increase that gives us an index of the strength of memory. It has been shown that the time that rats stay out of the dark compartment increases with the time since they were shocked in it. Interestingly enough, the longer the time that rats stay out of the dark compartment the greater the effect of anticholinesterase in reducing memory strength, again as measured by the time that rats choose to stay out of the dark compartment. So that, as memory improves, so does its susceptibility to anticholinesterase, confirming the notion that the physical change in memory occurs at a cholinergic synapse.

Separate from the question of what the change is that underlies memory is the problem of where in the nervous system the change occurs. Is there a place in the nervous system whose destruction abolishes memory? The answer is complex. During operations for removal of epileptogenic foci it is necessary for the surgeon to stimulate the brain while the patient is conscious. Such a procedure, while it may seem extreme, is actually quite innocuous and quite painless. During stimulation of the temporal lobe, complex memory-like imagery arises. However, while such local stimulation triggers recall, the memory does not reside within this locus, because surgical removal of the locus does not abolish later recall of the same memory. Bilateral lesions in the same general area do produce memory disorders, but again these are not due to the destruction of existing memories. Rather, the disorder closely resembles the Korsakoff syndrome, mentioned above, in which old memories survive while new memories are strangely transitory.

There seems to be no particular area in the nervous system that functions as a memory store, as no lesion so far has abolished all memory. There has been an assumption, now shown to be false, that the cortex somehow mediates memory and learning. However, totally decorticate animals, while diminished in the capacity to discriminate, show good learning and retention. This of course does not mean that each particular memory is diffusely stored all over the brain. It probably implies that the specialized capacity to change is a characteristic of most neural tissue. There is also suggestive evidence that memories are stored in those parts of the brain which mediate the perceptions on which those particular memories are based. For instance, patients with lesions of the visual cortex are blind, but unlike people whose blindness is due to an injury to more peripheral organs of sight they cannot even remember what it was like to see. Further, it has been shown by experiments on how items in memory inhibit each other that it is those items that are represented as neighbours in the sensory part of the brain which interfere with each other most. Such a pattern of interference would be expected if memory storage occurred in the parts of the brain devoted to perceptual processing.                    J. A. D.

**MEMORY AND CONTEXT.** A popular stand-by of writers of detective stories over the years has been the witness who is unable to recall some crucial piece of information until the cunning detective hits on the idea of reconstructing the exact situation in which the incident occurred, whereupon all comes flooding back. Such a device did indeed play a central role in the first ever detective novel, *The Moonstone* by Wilkie Collins. But is there any foundation to the belief that context may have such powerful effect? In fact there is.

A number of studies have been carried out in which subjects learn material, typically lists of words, in one environment and attempt to recall it in either the same or a different environmental context. There is usually a tendency for recall to be better when it takes place under conditions identical to those in which the material was learnt. The effect is, however, typically rather small, and certainly not enough to suggest—for example— that examinees should do all their revision in the examination hall. With really dramatic shifts in environment, however, quite large effects can be obtained.

Godden and Baddeley (1975) used divers as subjects and had them learn a list of words either on the shore or on the ocean bed at a depth of about 6 metres. The divers then attempted to recall either in the same environment or in the other one. A drop of about 40 per cent occurred when divers who had learnt under water were required to recall on land, or vice versa, indicating that it was crucial to reinstate the context if good recall was required. A subsequent experiment showed that if instead of asking the subjects to recall the words, they were given a recognition task in which they simply picked out the words they had seen before from a list comprising both presented and non-presented words, no such decrement occurred. This seems to suggest that context dependency is a retrieval effect, with context helping the subject to locate the relevant information in his memory store. Under recognition conditions, the presentation of the word itself acts as an excellent retrieval cue which dispenses with the need for environmental context to assist in locating the relevant memory trace.

A phenomenon which is closely related to that of context-dependent memory is that of state-dependent memory in which, instead of varying the environmental context, the internal state of the organism is manipulated, for example by means of drugs (Kumar et al., 1970). Goodwin, Powell, Bramer, Hoine, and Stern studied the role of state dependency in alcoholics. They cite (1969) clinical evidence of heavy drinkers who, when sober, are unable to find alcohol and money which they hid while drunk, but who remember the hiding-places once they are drunk again. They attempted to test this, using a group of heavy drinkers and studying the learning and recall of a series of tasks, including memory for words, and for pictures, which included both neutral pictures taken from a mail-order catalogue and 'emotional' pictures from a nudist magazine. They found clear evidence of context dependency in all the tasks involving recall, but no effect for picture recognition. A similar lack of effect has subsequently been shown for word recognition. As in the case of environmental context, an effect occurs for recall, but disappears when the retrieval component is diminished by using recognition testing.

One very powerful source of context effects is that of mood. In one series of experiments, subjects were hypnotically induced to feel either happy or sad during the learning of a list of words, and to be either happy or sad during recall. Words that were learnt when sad were recalled best when sad and vice versa (Bower, 1981). Similarly, quite powerful effects have been observed in the case of depressed patients who have great difficulty accessing memory for pleasant and happy events during periods of depression, while they are well able to recall sad incidents. This tendency of course tends to reinforce their depression, locking them into a vicious circle of increasing sadness and increasing difficulty in remembering anything not associated with sadness. Breaking away from this cycle has obvious therapeutic potential, and forms one component of the cognitive treatment of depression.

We have so far been concerned with the role of *extrinsic* or environmental context in memory. As we have seen, this typically occurs in the case of recall but not of recognition. Much more dramatic contextual effects can be obtained by means of *intrinsic* context, that is contextual cues which change the interpretation of the material to be remembered. To take an extreme example, suppose I ask you to remember the word 'jam'. I can bias the way in which you encode and remember the word by preceding it with the word 'traffic' or with 'strawberry'. If I have initially biased your interpretation of the word in the direction of traffic jam, you are much less likely to recognize the word subsequently if it is accompanied by the word 'raspberry', which biases you towards the other meaning of jam. This effect occurs even though the subject knows full well that he is only supposed to remember the word 'jam' and not the contextual or biasing words. As Tulving and Osler have shown, this effect is not limited to words that have more than one meaning. If one takes a word like 'city', and presents it alongside a weakly associated word such as 'dirty', then recognition is substantially impaired if the test item is accompanied by another but different weakly associated word such as 'village'. This suggests that the subject is not remembering the word 'city' in and of itself, but is creating some representation which is biased by the context. For example, he may be thinking in terms of the dirt and litter associated with a busy city. When 'city' is subsequently presented with another biasing word such as 'village', he may well be thinking of some secluded district within a city, a district which has many of the neighbourhood characteristics of a village, and which would therefore be very different from the original encoding of a busy, dirty city. Note that this intrinsic context effect differs from that of the environmental context effect in that the intrinsic context determines what is learnt by the subject during the initial presentation, whereas the extrinsic or environmental context merely assists the subject in accessing a particular memory trace. Since the effect of intrinsic context is on learning rather than simply retrieval, it shows up both with recall and recognition.

Most of the instances we have discussed have been concerned with remembering words. However, there are clear and important examples of the role of intrinsic context in other areas, and in particular in the recognition performance of witnesses. The Australian psychologist Donald Thomson has extended the original verbal studies into this particular area, and has shown that the probability of a witness falsely identifying someone in an identification parade, as the person observed at the scene of a crime, can be dramatically increased by changing irrelevant contextual features, such as having the suspect wear similar clothes or showing him in a similar contextual environment. He has shown that even careful and experienced witnesses such as police or lawyers are very subject to bias of this type. His work adds to the considerable evidence that eyewitness identification is very much less reliable than juries typically realize. We do not perceive or remember in a vacuum. The context within which we experience an event will determine how that event is encoded and hence retained. What we *have* learned, we are not always able to call to mind, particularly if we try to recall it when our internal or external environment is dramatically different from the conditions during learning.                    A. D. B.

Bower, G. H. (1981). Mood and Memory. *American Psychologist*, **3b**, 129–48.
Godden, D. R. and Baddeley, A. D. (1975). Context-dependent memory in two natural environments: on land and underwater. *British Journal of Psychology*, **66**, 325–31.
Kumar, R., Stolerman, I. P., and Steinberg, H. (1970). Psychopharmacology. *Annual Review of Psychology*, **21**, 595–628.

**MENTAL CONCEPTS: THE CAUSAL ANALYSIS.** In recent years analytical philosophers have become increasingly aware of the importance of causality (see CAUSES) in the logical analysis of mental concepts. Consider, for instance, what it is for somebody to *infer* one proposition from another. A person, A, believes that p is the case, and, on that basis, infers q is true (whether reasonably or unreasonably is of no concern), so acquiring the belief that q is true. It seems clear that A's believing that p is true brings about, that is, causes, the acquiring of the belief that q is true. For consider the case where A, believing that p is true, later acquires the belief that q is true, though the original state of belief is in no way causally responsible for acquiring the belief that q is true. In such a case we should not allow the possibility that A had inferred q from p. It is a necessary condition of A's making such an inference that the belief that p is true give rise to the belief that q is true.

Similar considerations may be adduced in the case of other mental concepts. When we *remember* an event, that event must play a part in bringing about the later recall. When we *perceive* an object, that object must play a part in bringing about the perception of it.

Awareness of the ubiquity of causal conditions in analyses of mental concepts has led some philosophers to make a more ambitious, though more speculative, proposal. They suggest that a logical analysis can be given of all the mental concepts in purely causal terms. This proposal, or research programme, in logical analysis constitutes the Causal theory of the mental concepts.

As models for the proposed undertaking, consider the ordinary language concept of 'brittleness' and the scientific notion of 'gene'. To say that something is brittle is to say that it is in a certain state. If, in addition, the object is struck sharply, then the combined influence of the two factors, the state and the blow, brings it about (generally) that the object shatters. The state of brittleness is defined simply in terms of what it causes. The concrete nature of the state cannot be elicited simply from its definition, but may be established by further scientific research.

Genes were originally conceived of simply as a set of causal factors at work within the organism. These factors, acting and interacting in a certain way, bring it about that the organism has certain hereditary characteristics (the notion of a hereditary characteristic being itself causally definable). The further nature of genes cannot be elicited simply from the notion as originally introduced. It is a later scientific discovery that genes are in fact DNA molecules. The original concept of the gene is simply the concept of that, whatever it may be, which brings about certain effects.

The causal analysis of the mental concepts asserts that all mental concepts are of the same general sort as the concepts of 'brittleness' and 'gene'. The mental concepts are concepts of states, events, processes, etc., which are definable purely in terms of their *causal role* (the phrase is due to D. K. Lewis). The causal role of brittleness is constituted by the fact that, in conjunction with striking, it produces shattering. The causal role of the gene is constituted by its production of hereditary characteristics. The causal role assigned to mental processes, etc., by this analysis is primarily the production of certain sorts of physical behaviour by the organism. As a rough characterization of that behaviour, it is the most flexible and sophisticated behaviour exhibited by the organism. An account of *purposes, for instance, is sought for along the following lines. The purpose to do $X$ is a state of the organism, whatever that state may be, which initiates and sustains those trains of physical activity which, in favourable circumstances, bring $X$ to be.

Minds are the most complex and sophisticated systems known to exist. It is to be expected, therefore, that the concepts which we have evolved for dealing with mental processes should be among the most complex and sophisticated concepts that we possess. Given that the causal theory is correct, it is quite certain that the causal roles involved will be exceedingly complex and correspondingly difficult to spell out. What was just said about purposes, for instance, can be no more than the crudest first sketch for an analysis. It turns out, in particular, that the different causal roles which constitute different mental processes are of an interlocking sort, so that it is not possible to give an account of one sort without giving an account of others, and vice versa. For instance, purposes and beliefs involve a package-deal so that, although their causal roles in the production of behaviour are different, the one causal role cannot be described without reference to the other. This reflects the familiar point that actual behaviour is always a joint product of purposes and beliefs.

Those who have actually proposed the causal analysis have been materialists. They wished to give a purely physicalist account of mental processes. The causal analysis makes it easy to do this, because the nature of that which plays these complex roles is not determined by the analysis. The causal theorist can then go on to maintain, on grounds of general scientific plausibility, that mental processes are in fact ordinary physical processes in the brain. This yields the doctrine of *central-state* (as opposed to *behaviouristic) materialism. However, it may prove possible to uphold a materialist view of the mind without accepting the causal analysis of the mental concepts. Furthermore, the causal analysis is entirely compatible with an anti-materialist view of the mind. A causal theorist could maintain without contradiction, for instance, that mental processes are, in their own nature, processes in a spiritual substance, processes which produce certain bodily effects.

The causal analysis of the mental concepts is far from having been completed. It remains a research programme. How promising a programme it is, is a matter for controversy among those philosophers who seek a general view of the mind. No full-scale critique of the causal theory has yet been developed, but various difficulties have been raised.

First, a property such as brittleness or an object such as a gene is a *theoretical* entity. It is something which is postulated as an explainer of certain phenomena: shattering after being hit; the recurrent patterns of characteristics in organisms related by descent. To give an account of mental concepts in terms of the causal role of the entities involved seems therefore to assimilate mental entities to theoretical postulations. Yet, unlike the case of brittleness or the gene, when we introspect we are directly, though no doubt not infallibly, aware of some of our own mental processes. We observe them. But could the content of our introspective observation be confined simply to this: the presence of something playing a certain causal role?

Secondly, all or almost all mental processes have the property of pointing beyond themselves to something which, nevertheless, need not exist. We may desire and pursue that which is unattainable, we may think of and believe in that which does not exist. Franz *Brentano spoke of this phenomenon as the *intentionality of mental processes. Can mere causal role, however complex and sophisticated, fully explain the intentionality of mental processes? If this objection can be made good, it may pose a threat to a materialist doctrine of the mind as well as to the causal analysis of the mental concepts.

Thirdly, by introspection we appear to become aware of certain mental *qualities*. Having an itch is introspectively different from having a pain, having a sensation of something green is introspectively different from having a sensation of something red, being angry is introspectively different from being afraid. In all these cases, it is quite plausible to assert, we are introspectively aware of a difference in the qualities of the mental processes involved. But it is difficult to see how a purely causal analysis of the mental concepts could account for such an awareness of qualitative difference. This objection is attractive to many philosophers working within what may be called the 'British empiricist' tradition.

It is an interesting question whether this objection, supposing it well taken, refutes not only the causal analysis but also a materialist account of mental processes. Such introspected qualities are in prima facie conflict with materialism, but perhaps the conflict is prima facie only.   D. M. A.

Armstrong, D. M. (1968). *A Materialist Theory of the Mind* (Part II). London.

Campbell, K. K. (1970). *Body and Mind* (chs. 5 and 6). London.

Lewis, D. K. (1966). An argument for the identity theory. *Journal of Philosophy*, **63** (repr. in Rosenthal, D. M. (ed.) (1971), *Materialism and the Mind–Body Problem*).

**MENTAL DISORDERS: CLASSIFICATION.** An agreed classification of mental disorders and the nomenclature which goes with it are essential to a scientific psychiatry. Among other things, they provide the common language in which professional colleagues can inform each other about individual patients, and enable investigators in different centres and countries to collate their research findings. Without them epidemiological studies would hardly be possible. The system now in use in Britain is the ninth revision, in 1978, of the International Classification of Diseases: ICD–9. It divides mental disorders into three classes: psychoses (see MENTAL ILLNESS); neurotic disorders, personality disorders, and other non-psychotic mental conditions (see MENTAL ILLNESS); and mental retardation (see MENTAL HANDICAP). The psychoses are subdivided into organic psychotic conditions, which include various types of dementia and other brain syndromes; other psychoses, which include schizophrenic psychoses, affective psychoses, and paranoid states; and psychoses with origins specific to childhood. The neurotic disorders, in the second of the classes, include anxiety states, hysteria, phobic state, and obsessive-compulsive disorders. Also in this class are several types of personality disorder, sexual deviations, alcohol and drug dependence, non-psychotic disorders specific to childhood and adolescence, and a variety of other syndromes. Mental retardation, in the third of the classes, is subdivided according to its degree.

A more advanced system, elaborated by the American Psychiatric Association, was published in 1980 in *The Diagnostic and Statistical Manual of Mental Disorders*: DSM–III. It starts from a definition of mental disorder in which the key phrases are 'a clinically significant behavioural or psychological syndrome or pattern', 'in an individual', and 'not only in the relationship between the individual and society', which is 'associated with either a painful symptom (distress) or impairment in one or more important areas of functioning (disability)'. Mental disorders exist as separate entities, not as gradations from normal to abnormal. DSM–III evaluates each case on five axes, the first three of which—(I) clinical syndromes, (II) personality disorders and specific developmental disorders, and (III) physical disorders and conditions—constitute the diagnostic assessment. This may be supplemented by ratings on axes IV and V, on a seven-point scale, of 'severity of psychosocial stressors' and 'highest level of adaptive functioning during past year'. The classification on I–III is broadly similar to that of ICD–9 although with numerous modifications in nomenclature and in criteria, which, widely tested before DSM–III was published, are more stringent.

The classification of mental disorders has evolved gradually over many years, going back at least to Philippe Pinel, who in 1798 divided them into four groups, mania, melancholia, dementia, and idiocy—while remarking that medical science was not sufficiently advanced to warrant a more detailed scheme. (A rougher classification of persons *non compos mentis* was proposed by Sir Edward Coke in 1604. His four categories were the idiot or fool natural; he who was of good and sound memory and by the visitation of God has lost it; the lunatic who enjoys lucid intervals; and he who was rendered *non compos mentis* by his own act as a drunkard. Obviously the first three categories correspond to our present-day ideas of subnormality, the dementias of old age, and the remitting and relapsing psychoses. Although drunkenness could be classed as an acute toxic psychosis, it would be unusual for this condition to be listed among that group of mental disorders today unless there was some additional evidence of abnormality.) In the second half of the nineteenth century distinctions were made between acute, primary, and curable dementia, on the one hand, and chronic, secondary, and incurable dementia, on the other. Secondary dementia, although sometimes attributed to syphilis, was regarded as hereditary and progressive. Emil *Kraepelin, after studying thousands of case-histories, proposed a comprehensive system of classification, much of which has been carried over into contemporary classifications. In particular, he distinguished between the endogenous disorders, caused by inherent constitutional factors, and the exogenous, caused by external conditions. The pattern of a disorder, he noted, depends also on the age at which it starts. In 1896 he made the crucial distinction between *dementia praecox*, which begins in adolescence or early adult life, is endogenous, and tends to show a progressive deterioration, and manic-depressive psychosis, the course of which tends to be cyclic, with intervals of normality between attacks. *Dementia praecox* was renamed schizophrenia in 1911 as a result of *Bleuler's revision of the clinical description; its course is not now regarded as inevitably progressive. The various forms of manic-depressive psychosis are now called affective psychoses.

Support for the distinction between the two disorders has been found in the raised incidence of schizophrenia, but not of manic-depressive psychosis, in the families of patients suffering from schizophrenia, and the raised incidence of manic-depressive psychosis, but not of schizophrenia, in the families of patients suffering from manic-depressive psychosis. These findings also support the hypothesis that the genes, and therefore the underlying metabolic defects, are different. (See SCHIZOPHRENIA for further details.) Attempts to confirm that there are two forms of affective psychosis corresponding to the endogenous and exogenous (or reactive) have not been conclusive. Statistical analysis of the correlations of symptoms has not produced consistent evidence that the symptoms fall into two patterns. The distinction made between organic and non-organic psychoses, however, is strongly supported on clinical grounds.

Supposing the disorders to arise from metabolic or other defects, Kraepelin described their manifestations as if they were neurological signs—'soft' signs, they have been called—and certainly not as reflecting continuing and changing processes of adaptation. This bias still influences the criteria on which contemporary classifications are based. Their strength, and their weakness, lies in that they are 'generally atheoretical with regard to aetiology', as has been claimed for DSM–III. This avoids the difficulty that the correlations between the forms taken by disorders and the external causes to which they might be attributed are small. In DSM–III the ratings on axis IV of the 'severity of psychosocial stressors' and on axis V of the 'level of adaptive functioning' are significant innovations which do something to compensate for the bias. However, the main concern in the international collaboration of the last two decades has been so to define the criteria that they provide a consistent and reliable basis for the collation of research findings. In this some success has been achieved. Evaluations of ICD–9 and DSM–III continue, and new revisions are to be expected in due course.

D. R. D.

Cooper, J. E., Kendell, R. E., Gurland, B. J., et al. (1972). *Psychiatric Diagnosis in New York and London.* London.

Task Force on Nomenclature and Statistics of the American Psychiatric Association (1980). *Diagnostic and Statistical Manual of Mental Disorders.* Washington, DC.

World Health Organization (1978). *Mental Disorders: glossary and guide to their classification in accordance with the ninth revision of the International Classification of Diseases.* Geneva.

**MENTAL HANDICAP.** It is estimated that about one in every thousand children in the United Kingdom and the United States of America is mentally handicapped. It is not easy to judge the total number because of the various definitions of mental handicap. The American Association on Mental Deficiency (AAMD) describes retardation as 'sub-average general intellectual functioning which originates during the developmental period and is associated with impaired adaptive behaviour'. 'Sub-average' means more than one standard deviation below the normal average level of intelligence commonly accepted (in the UK, 100; in the USA, 90–100); 'developmental period' means from birth to about 16 years of age; and 'impaired adaptive behaviour' means failure to mature, to learn, or to adjust socially.

This definition has been challenged because it does not take account of environmental and social factors, both of which may have an important influence on retardation. The lack of a clear definition has significance, for failure to diagnose may lead to failure to treat.

The problem of mental retardation emerged in the nineteenth century. Before that time, the retarded were assimilated into the general background of rural societies or they did not survive at all. The percentage of children who were mildly mentally retarded increased with the growth of towns, because of poor housing, lack of care before, during, and after birth, malnutrition, poverty, and poor working conditions for mothers. These causes remain, but, with the improvement of general standards of living and literacy, children retarded in this way are now among the 'ablest' of the mentally handicapped. As societies become more complex and technologically oriented, the number of people unable to cope with life increases, and the burden on the working population is correspondingly increased.

In the nineteenth century many schemes to train and educate the mentally retarded were begun and found to be successful. Possibly the first attempts at education were made by Jean-Marc-Gaspard Itard, who described his work with a wild boy found in the woods of Aveyron. Truffaut's film *L'Enfant sauvage* is an account of Itard's attempts to socialize and educate the boy Victor, who was, however, probably already retarded when he was found.

Since the success of treatment depends very much on the cause of the illness, improved skills in diagnosing mental retardation have also meant improved chances of rehabilitation. The aetiology of mental retardation is divided into two parts: intrinsic and extrinsic causes.

**Intrinsic causes.** These are biological, mainly genetic. One of the commonest is *Down's syndrome (mongolism), which results from a chromosome abnormality. One birth in 250 will have a chromosome abnormality, which can be diagnosed by counting the chromosomes taken in smears. Unfortunately the cause of the damage to the chromosome structure that produces Down's syndrome has not yet been identified, although a connection with infective hepatitis has been suggested. Genetic counselling may reduce the incidence of one type of Down's syndrome, for if one or both parents has an abnormal chromosome structure there is a greater likelihood that their child will have an abnormality. The chances of an abnormal birth increase with the age of the mother, and after the age of 35 special attention should be paid to the chromosomal compatibility of the parents.

Other intrinsic causes are metabolic. In phenylketonuria (PKU), which occurs in one in 10,000 births, failure to metabolize the amino acid phenylalanine results in a toxic condition which affects the brain and causes retardation unless a phenylalanine-free diet is given to the child. In the United Kingdom, every new-born baby is now tested for PKU, and so a dangerous condition is prevented by early intervention. Osteogenesis imperfecta ('brittle bones'), Tay–Sachs disease, and Duchenne's muscular dystrophy (both degenerative killing diseases) are other intrinsic causes of mental retardation. The causes of many intrinsic diseases are not yet known. The American Association on Mental Deficiency and the American Psychiatric Association maintain lists of most of the categories of intrinsic causes of retardation, and these lists are updated as knowledge extends.

**Extrinsic causes.** These are mental handicaps

that result from infections, accidents, poisoning, or other brain damage. Difficult or premature births may cause brain damage because of anoxia (shortage of oxygen supply to the brain). Babies may be born blind and/or mentally retarded if the mother is infected with rubella (German measles) before the fourth month of pregnancy. Congenital syphilis can also damage the child. (It used to be thought that this disease was the cause of Down's syndrome. The misery and anxiety such a mistaken belief must have caused parents whose children suffered from Down's syndrome can hardly be imagined.) Smoking, excessive use of alcoholic drinks, poor prenatal care, malnutrition, infection, or poisoning from environmental pollution (such as mercury or lead) may lead to immature or damaged babies.

During the neonatal period, factors such as high fever, jaundice, failure to breathe properly, or inadequate or unsuitable nutrition may cause retardation. The child's brain may be damaged by poisoning from sucking toys painted with paint containing lead monoxide or cadmium, or by baby battering (see CHILD ABUSE), or by falls. One category in the AAMD list should be looked at with particular attention: diseases and conditions due to unknown or uncertain factors with structural reaction alone manifest—a category into which the 'wild boy' of Aveyron might well fit. It is known that a child deprived of tender loving care will grow, up with deficient sensory and social ability. If the impoverishment and lack of stimulus in a child's upbringing are not remedied early, he will grow up with reduced social and intellectual capacity and may be diagnosed as a case of 'mild' (category I) retardation. *Autism is a condition which may fit into any of the categories of retardation, from I to V, and which causes great distress—particularly, perhaps, as at first sight the child may seem to be quite normal. There continues to be much debate about the nature and causes of autism.

**Treatment and provisions.** The amount of retardation in individual cases varies as much as intelligence does among 'normal' people, and this range makes management and discussion complex and difficult. Diseases caused by poisoning (intoxication) may be halted or even cured by removing the source of the poison, and eliminating the poison already in the child, before there is irreversible brain damage. Diseases caused by social factors—such as malnutrition, lack of care before, during, or after birth, poor stimulus, or infection of the mother—could be eliminated or at least reduced by social welfare programmes (for example, inoculation against measles and rubella) and by the education of parents to help counter retardation of this kind.

Treatment of intrinsic causes is more difficult because the damage is irreversible. However, prevention is beginning to be possible. Amniocentesis can be used to detect chromosome abnormalities while the child is still in the womb. The tech-

nique cannot be used until the fourth month of pregnancy, and, as the fluid has to be taken out of the uterus, there is the possibility of damage to a normal foetus and the risk of natural abortion; also it must be practicable to offer induced abortion as an alternative. Once a child is born with irreversible brain damage, drugs can help to prevent fits and special programmes can help to develop existing intelligence and mobility. The Doman–Delacato course of treatment may improve the abilities of some children, although it demands tremendous dedication and energy on the part of the parents, while the cost to the family as a whole should not be disregarded. More usually, brain-damaged children go to nursery schools and then to special schools where attention is paid to individual differences and needs. If this sort of help is given from birth onwards it may be possible to educate the child and support the family who look after it. In the United Kingdom such programmes have been devised by Mr R. Brinkworth, the founder of the Down's Babies Association.

In some parts of the world there are excellent provisions, while in others they are sadly lacking or even non-existent. At best the mentally handicapped may be helped to lead relatively normal lives, to do some sort of work, and to live in sheltered housing with some support. Whether the work is in workshops or on the land, it will give the moderately handicapped a sense of individual dignity and purpose. The severely handicapped will have to spend their lives in hospitals and will need dedicated nursing as well as support from all the other social services. It is important to distinguish here between the mentally handicapped and the mentally ill (see MENTAL ILLNESS). In the popular mind these two conditions are often confused, leading to much ill-informed fear and prejudice. None the less, there is good evidence that the mentally handicapped do have a higher incidence of neurotic and psychotic disorders.

Wherever adequate provision is made for the mentally handicapped, it will be found that the cost is great. Against this cost must be set the cost of *not* providing. The incidence of broken marriages is ten times higher where there is a mentally handicapped child. There are risks to physical and mental health—mothers typically suffer more than fathers, while the normal children in the family are also under pressure. Widows and deserted wives figure prominently in surveys.

In the past the mentally handicapped often died at birth or in early childhood. They survive into mature adulthood with the help of care before and after birth and the widespread use of antibiotics. Should doctors perhaps not strive 'officiously to keep alive' if spina bifida has been diagnosed and the child, and later the adult, is condemned to a crippled and handicapped life after operations which may relieve the symptoms but cannot cure the condition? How can we balance, for instance, the cost of keeping a mentally handicapped child against the cost of a kidney machine for a working man who supports a family? In a sensitive and civilized society, euthanasia is an emotive and difficult subject. Doctors need guide-lines and support to avoid accusations of murder when they must make decisions which affect not only the individual family but society as a whole.

See also SUBNORMALITY.                          P. M. H.

Adams, M. (1971). *Mental Retardation and its Social Dimensions*. New York.

Cuckle, H. S. and Wald, N. J. (1984). Maternal Serum Alpha-fetoprotein Measurement: a Screening Test for Down's Syndrome. *Lancet*, 28 April 1984, pp. 926–29.

Grossman, H. J. (ed.) (1983). *Classification in Mental Retardation*. Baltimore.

Heston, L. L. (1982). Alzheimer's Dementia & Down's Syndrome: Genetic Evidence Suggesting an Association. *Annals of New York Academy of Science*, **396**, 29–37.

Kemp, R. and Henry, C. (1978). *Child Abuse*. London.

Kurtz, R. (1977). *Social Aspects of Mental Retardation*. Lexington, Massachusetts.

McNamara, J. and B. (1977). *The Special Child Handbook*. New York.

Stone, J. and Taylor, F. (1977). *A Handbook for Parents with a Handicapped Child*. Newton Upper Falls, Massachusetts.

Warnock, M. (1978). *Meeting Special Educational Needs*. London.

**MENTAL HEALTH.** Answers given nowadays to the question 'What are the characteristics of a mentally healthy person?' are likely to refer to such signs as the capacity to co-operate with others and sustain a close, loving relationship, and the ability to make a sensitive, critical appraisal of oneself and the world about one and to cope with the everyday problems of living. At other times or places, different qualities would have been mentioned, according to the values prevailing in the culture. For the English middle class at the turn of the nineteenth century, *mens sana in corpore sano*—a sound mind in a sound body—would have included a disciplined intelligence, a well-stocked memory, qualities of leadership appropriate to the person's station, a respect for morality, and a sense of what life means. There was at that time an absolute refusal, as Clouston (1906) put it, 'to admit the possibility of a healthy mind in an unsound body, or at all events in an unsound brain'. Nowadays we regard mental health as attainable by even the severely crippled. Brain injury may put limits on the degree to which social capacities can be developed, but it does not prevent their development altogether; the influence of the milieu may be as strong as that of the severity of the injury. For a vigorous critique of the concept of mental health one can hardly do better than turn to Barbara Wootton's review (1960) in which, after commenting on a number of proposed definitions, she concluded that 'whichever way, therefore, the problem may be approached, no solid foundation appears to be discoverable on which to establish the propositions (as) formulated'.

The shift in emphasis from intellectual ability to harmonious relationships as the criterion of mental health can be partly attributed to the recognition that, whatever part physical inheritance plays in determining intelligence, intellectual development depends largely on learning in the setting of a relationship. The publication in 1951 by the World Health Organization of John Bowlby's monograph *Maternal Care and Mental Health* was a landmark because it made it widely known that an essential condition for the mental health and development of the child is 'a warm, intimate, and continuous relationship with his mother in which both find satisfaction and enjoyment'. 'Sound cognitive development', it has been said, 'occurs in a context of communication.' The abilities which enable the child to play the roles appropriate to a boy or girl are acquired through the learning engendered by the expectations of the family. Interruption, or disturbance, during early childhood in the relationship with the mother has been shown to retard or distort the development of language and the skills related to it, and to lead in some circumstances to an impairment in social relationships which lasts into adult life. The effects depend on the character of the 'support' or 'security' system, of which the mother is usually the chief member. The father, the grandparents, older siblings, and family friends contribute to the system. The young child is vulnerable if the system is weak or fragile.

The young child tends to attach himself to one person especially, usually the one who mothers him, and this relationship, established in the second half of the first year of life, prepares him for a monogamous relationship when sexual maturity is reached, and influences then his choice of partner. (See ATTACHMENT.) Social training of other kinds, in the family and outside it, prepares him for the several roles he is to play in adult life. A boy tends to take his father as a model, and a girl, her mother. Of importance too is membership of a peer group in the early teenage years. From his experience in relationships with his mother and father, peers of the same sex, and then a peer of opposite sex, the young person discovers what sort of person he is—i.e. he forms a conception of himself, or establishes his 'identity', especially his sexual identity. His education and early experience in a job establish his occupational identity. This conception of himself is tested out by further experience which confirms or modifies it. The first *affaire* confirms or, if it goes badly, confuses his sexual identity. He becomes emancipated in greater or lesser degree from his parents, and free to form relationships outside the family. The rapid intellectual development at the time of puberty helps the young person to understand, and in some degree gain control over, the world around him.

The social training he has had during childhood is put to the test at turning-points in circumstances, or 'crises', which require old habits to be abandoned, new habits to be developed. Crises are conveniently divided, following Erikson (1968), into 'developmental' and 'accidental'. By developmental crises are meant those decisive changes in circumstances ordinarily expected to occur in the life cycle—for example, being born, going to school, leaving school, getting married, becoming a parent, or retiring from work. Examples of accidental crises are the untimely loss of a member of the family, a spouse or other loved person, the loss of a job, or illness. If he is prepared for the new circumstances, as is usual when the crisis is developmental, a person acquires new habits quickly through the processes of learning. If not prepared, because the crisis is untimely, or social training has been lacking or inappropriate, a person may go through a period of instability and distress while he works out new ways of coping.

In studies of *bereavement—for example, by C. M. Parkes—are to be found illustrations of the differences between mental health and illness. After the loss of a loved one, one person mourns for a time. While doing so, he is able to express to others his grief and distress openly and authentically, and thus to review his relationship with the person lost. He soon re-engages in relationships with others, which change and develop. Another person becomes preoccupied by his fantasies about the person lost. These may be out of keeping with the realities, which are denied. He withdraws from other relationships, and shows a general contraction of activities and interests. He feels diminished and depreciated. Withdrawing from relationships, and unable to communicate his distress, his conception of himself remains uncorrected, and he does not work out a new pattern of relationships. This kind of severe reaction to bereavement occurs especially when the loss has been sudden or unexpected, or there have been distressing circumstances: for instance, if the death was due to *suicide, or to the negligence or misconduct of others. Such a reaction may also reflect the personality of the bereaved person and his relationship with the person lost. He may have been unaccustomed to taking decisions for himself, or have had limited personal resources, or have been unduly dependent, or the relationship may have been discordant and fraught with unresolved difficulties.

The features of the reaction of the latter person are the antithesis of mental health, and amount to mental illness if he also claims exemption from normal social responsibilities. Yet they reflect psychological processes which are part of the organism's normal reactive equipment, and which are adaptive in that they serve to reduce *anxiety. They can be described as due to 'the renunciation of functions which give rise to anxiety' (which Sigmund *Freud said was the essence of neurosis). The psychological processes are maladaptive in the particular circumstances in that they do nothing to remove the sources of the anxiety. There is thus a deadlock. By avoiding a situation or staying out of relationships in which he has experienced pain or anxiety, a person does not explore and re-evaluate the situation, or learn to cope wth it in more effective ways. Other characteristics of behaviour

in mental illness are persistence or repetitiveness and resistance to modification by experience, whereas behaviour in mental health tends to be flexible and modifiable.

To break the deadlock, and to restore mental health, a therapist creates conditions in which the testing of reality and learning can be resumed. New habits can then be acquired which are more appropriate to the circumstances. The person's conception of himself can be corrected by further experience. He is encouraged to re-enter into relationships. In other words, the therapist intervenes or mediates in order to bring about reconciliation, and to enable communication with others to be reopened.                                    D. R. D.

Bowlby, J. (1969, 1973, 1980). *Attachment and Loss* (3 vols.). London.
Caplan, G. (1964). *Principles of Preventive Psychiatry*. London.
Clouston, T. C. (1906). *The Hygiene of Mind*. London.
Erikson, E. H. (1968). *Identity: youth and crisis*. London.
Parkes, C. M. (1972). *Bereavement*. London.
Wootton, B. (1960). *Social Science and Social Pathology*. London.

**MENTAL ILLNESS.** Most people think of mental illnesses as strange and frightening conditions which can affect other people but not themselves or their families. But in the average family doctor's surgery psychological symptoms are surpassed in frequency only by common colds, bronchitis, and rheumatism. In the course of a year, about one in every eight people in Britain consult their general practitioners for problems which are predominantly or completely psychological in nature. General practitioners refer about 10 per cent of such patients to a psychiatrist; most of these will be treated as out-patients but some will need admission to hospital, which in Britain is nearly always on a voluntary basis. Thus, out of all those who seek medical help with psychological problems, only a small minority become psychiatric in-patients. It is then a striking indicator of the extent of such problems that psychiatric patients occupy nearly half of all the hospital beds in Britain and in most other industrialized nations.

Arguments continually rage over the exact limits of mental illness. Some authorities regard the concept of mental illness as a myth while others, by contrast, consider that the majority of seemingly normal people suffer, often unknowingly, from psychiatric abnormalities amenable to treatment. Furthermore, some believe that psychiatric disorders are simply mental equivalents of physical diseases, while others argue that there are as many sorts of psychological problems as there are individuals who suffer from them.

In practice it is possible to discern certain recurring patterns of complaints and disabilities which can be regarded as reasonably discrete entities. These disorders can be divided into two broad groups: organic disorders, in which some demonstrable physical illness including brain disease underlies the psychological symptoms, and functional disorders, where no definite physical abnormality has yet been replicably demonstrated. Since most forms of mental illness fall into the latter category, the classification of psychiatric disorders is generally based on the clinical distinction between different clusters of symptoms each with a characteristic outcome. (See MENTAL DISORDERS: CLASSIFICATION.) In general medicine, advances in classification occurred when technological progress allowed the elucidation of the underlying causes of illnesses. Unlike their colleagues practising general medicine or surgery, however, psychiatrists are unable to rely on laboratory or other tests to refute or confirm their clinical diagnoses. Recent attempts to develop specific diagnostic investigations, such as the dexamethasone suppression test for depressive illness, have yet to produce a procedure of proven value. Unfortunately other mental illnesses show the same response that was found with a proportion of depressed patients, but the search for laboratory tests to aid with the diagnosis of affective disorders and other conditions continues.

In the meantime it is useful to distinguish between the neuroses and the psychoses. Neurotic symptoms correspond to what is commonly called 'nerves' and comprise feelings and thoughts which most normal people have experienced at some time or other, albeit in a relatively minor form. However, if they become persistent and severe, such symptoms can become markedly disabling, and result in a frank neurotic illness or 'nervous breakdown'. Psychotic symptoms, on the other hand, are not part of normal experience and are almost invariably severe. The picture of psychotic illness is quite distinct from normality and corresponds to what in popular usage is called 'madness' or 'insanity'. Women outnumber men among neurotics by about two to one, but psychosis is equally frequent in the two sexes.

Neurotic problems account for about two-thirds of those consulting family doctors because of psychological symptoms, the remainder being made up by a variety of conditions including *psychosomatic complaints, abnormalities of personality, alcoholism, and the psychoses. Most neurotics are treated by their general practitioners, but individuals with psychotic illnesses are almost always referred on to psychiatrists. Thus, while those with psychoses form only about 4 per cent of patients consulting GPs because of psychological problems, 25 per cent of psychiatric out-patients and more than half of all psychiatric in-patients suffer from psychotic illnesses.

Table 1 lists the expectancies of being affected at some time during life by the different psychiatric conditions for (i) a member of the general population and (ii) someone who has a first-degree relative (i.e. parent, sibling, or child) with one of the disorders.

**Neuroses.** *Anxiety states* are among the most common of all psychiatric disorders and are characterized by persistent apprehension and fear, at times amounting to panic. They are often accompanied by sensations caused by over-activity of the *autonomic nervous system: these include excessive sweating, tremor, faintness, choking or breathlessness, and 'butterflies' in the stomach. (See ANXIETY for further discussion.)

*Phobic neuroses* have much in common with anxiety states in that the predominant symptoms are again of fear or panic together with autonomic over-activity. But in phobic neuroses the symptoms are provoked by certain specific stimuli, such as dogs, spiders, the sight of blood, or having to talk to strangers. The most common variety is agoraphobia, which literally means fear of open spaces. The agoraphobic is afraid of leaving home and subject to panic attacks in crowded public places such as supermarkets. He or she often dreads travelling on public transport, especially underground trains, and has great difficulty in tolerating lifts or rooms from which there is no ready exit. Since these symptoms considerably limit normal life, agoraphobic patients may become totally house-bound. (See PHOBIAS for further discussion.)

Obsessive-compulsive neurosis is much rarer, but nevertheless the symptoms which form its core are phenomena with which, in milder form, most people will be familiar. There can be few people who have not at some time been unable to stop a

**Table 1.** *Lifetime risk of developing the disorder*

| | In the general population | | In the first-degree relatives of individuals affected (per cent) |
|---|---|---|---|
| | Males (per cent) | Females (per cent) | |
| Schizophrenia | 1 | 1 | 10 |
| Manic-depressive psychosis | 2 | 3 | 15 |
| Neurotic depression | 6 | 12 | 11 |
| Anxiety states | 3 | 6 | 15 |
| Obsessive-compulsive neurosis | 0.05 | 0.05 | 10 |
| Alcoholism | 7 | 2 | 15 |

*Source:* E. Slater and V. Cowie, *Genetics of Mental Disorders* (OUP, 1971), and T. Helgason, 'Prevalence of the Incidence of Mental Disorders', *Acta Psychiatrica Scandinavica*, 58 (1978), 256–66.

song going round in their head, or had an irrational urge to avoid stepping on cracks in the pavement, or rechecked windows and doors which they know they have already secured. In obsessive-compulsive neurosis, such thoughts or practices become pathologically exaggerated. Fears of having been contaminated by dirt, or of having harmed someone, may preoccupy the sufferer for most of the day even though he recognizes that they are silly. Similarly, he may wash his hands or check taps a hundred times a day, while all the time trying to convince himself that his behaviour is ridiculous. Such repetitive thoughts and compulsive acts become so intrusive that productive activity becomes impossible. (See OBSESSIONS AND COMPULSIONS for further discussion.)

The predominant features of depressive neurosis are gloom and despondency. Bouts of weeping are common, as are edginess, irritability, and a tendency to tire easily. There is a general loss of ability to concentrate and in particular a lack of interest in things which were previously enjoyed. The symptoms tend to vary in intensity, but often cause difficulty in getting off to sleep. (See DEPRESSION for further discussion.)

A variety of neurosis which was formerly common but is now much less so is hysteria, which in its classical forms beguiled nineteenth-century physicians such as J. M. *Charcot and Sigmund *Freud. Indeed, it was while studying a hysterical patient, the celebrated 'Anna O.', that Freud and *Breuer developed many of the concepts upon which psychoanalysis came to be based. The essence of hysteria is that, in the face of intolerable stress, symptoms develop which provide a defence against the stressful circumstances. Characteristic symptoms include a paralysed limb, loss of speech, convulsions, or blindness, and are often called conversion hysteria because the psychological trauma has figuratively been 'converted' into a bodily form. Some forms of hysteria involve a different mechanism called dissociation, in which an individual may forget even his own identity. He may wander off in a 'fugue state' which carries him many miles from home, or he may take on some new identity or switch from one identity to another—the 'split personality' of popular films, such as *The Three Faces of Eve*. (This phenomenon is discussed under DISSOCIATION OF THE PERSONALITY.) Although hysterical mechanisms are usually unconscious, many psychiatrists doubt the genuineness of some of the more theatrical forms. Indeed one of the problems confronting psychiatrists in legal work is where to draw the dividing line between hysteria and conscious simulation or malingering. Fortunately, hysterical symptoms are becoming less common due to improved education and awareness of psychological matters; this allows the expression of emotional difficulties for what they are, and renders the communication of suffering via hysterical symbolism redundant. None the less, it is important to remember that conversion hysteria can develop against a background of serious organic brain disease, either pre-existing or unsuspected, in a considerable percentage of cases. (See HYSTERIA for further discussion.)

In contrast to hysteria, anorexia nervosa appears to be on the increase, particularly among adolescent girls and young women. The central feature is self-imposed starvation, which frequently starts with a slimming diet and occasionally ends with complete inanition and death. Weight loss, physical over-activity, cessation of menstrual periods, and the growth of downy hair on the face and back are the cardinal symptoms. Surprisingly, most patients shun treatment and instead show considerable ingenuity in avoiding weight gain. Thus they hide food or secretly throw it away, and abuse laxatives. Like the obsessive-compulsive, the anorexic often recognizes the pointless irrationality of her behaviour but nevertheless feels bound to continue. Psychoanalysts have suggested that anorexia is a desperate unconscious attempt to stave off imminent sexual maturity, but a simpler explanation is that the anorexic has a distorted perception of her body which causes her consistently to overestimate her own size. The rise in anorexia has been attributed to increasing pressure on women to diet, as over the past thirty years or so the ideal female shape has become thinner and less buxom. All anorexics can be shown to have abnormalities of function of the hypothalamus, a part of the brain which controls appetite and many hormonal responses, but it is unknown whether this is cause or effect of the illness. (See ANOREXIA NERVOSA AND BULIMIA NERVOSA for further discussion.)

*Causes and treatment of neurosis.* Everyone is probably capable of experiencing neurotic symptoms in some form or degree, but individuals differ in their susceptibility to *stress. Some neurotic patients develop their symptoms without obvious precipitating factors, whereas others only become ill after major tragedies, such as the loss of a husband or child. Vulnerability to anxiety states and to phobic and obsessional neuroses appears to be partly influenced by hereditary traits such as introversion, general nervousness, and the reactivity of the autonomic nervous system. But it is generally agreed that life experiences play a major role. What is not generally agreed is which life events are crucial, and how they produce their effects. According to psychoanalytical theory, neurosis is an outward manifestation of deep-seated intrapsychic conflicts which were set up in early life. Treatment, which is necessarily prolonged and intensive, aims to make this unconscious material accessible to consciousness, and the resultant insight is expected to produce resolution and relief. The *behaviourists, however, think that the symptom *is* the neurosis and that it is the result of faulty learning processes. Theoretical assumptions concerning unconscious mechanisms and insight are regarded as irrelevant. Instead the aberrant behaviour is examined closely and broken down into its component parts, and the goal is then to persuade or educate the patient into adopting more appropriate and adaptive patterns of behaviour. This approach is particularly useful with phobias and obsessive-compulsive neurosis. (See BEHAVIOUR THERAPY.)

Psychoanalytically-based psychotherapy, behaviour therapy, or an eclectic mixture of the two are the approaches favoured by psychiatrists. However, in practice most patients with milder neuroses never see a psychiatrist, but are instead treated by their general practitioner with a combination of simple support and minor tranquillizers of the benzodiazepine group (such as Valium® and Librium®). These drugs are very useful in allaying anxiety over a few weeks, but their effectiveness tends to diminish over longer periods. Unfortunately, they are often prescribed for inappropriate reasons, with the result that their consumption is increasing at a rate alarming to all—bar the manufacturers. Antidepressant drugs like Tryptizol® and Tofranil®, which are effective against discrete episodes of depression, are less likely to be misused, although they can be very dangerous when taken in overdosage by someone with suicidal intent.

**Organic psychoses.** *Acute.* A variety of physical illnesses may produce an acute reversible mental disorder called delirium; the causes include fever or disturbance in body chemistry as well as infections of the brain. Delirium may also follow intoxication with drugs or withdrawal from barbiturates or alcohol ('DTs'). The most striking feature is the rapid onset of confusion. The patient has no idea where he is or what day it is, and only the most tenuous grasp of what is going on around him. He may see or hear things which are not really there (*hallucinations), or experience distorted perception of things which are there (*illusions). He is often very fearful and may believe he is being attacked or persecuted. Evelyn Waugh's *The Ordeal of Gilbert Pinfold* is an excellent, presumably first-hand, account of an acute organic psychosis which could possibly have been an example of alcoholic hallucinosis complicated by the taking of other drugs. Most delirious patients recover completely when the cause of the insult to the brain is corrected.

*Chronic.* By contrast, dementia refers to chronic insidious organic psychoses which are usually progressive. Loss of memory for recent events is often the first symptom. Thus, an elderly woman may be able to describe vividly the days of her childhood, but be unable to recall what she has just eaten for breakfast. She then begins to forget the faces of friends and relatives, and may be unaware of where she is or what year it is. Deterioration in intellect and personality may show itself as a lack of propriety, lack of attention to personal appearance, and loss of normal social niceties and inhibitions. In about 10 per cent of cases dementia in later life is caused by remediable conditions such as benign

brain tumours and hypothyroidism, but the great majority of cases are due to degenerative disease of the brain or its blood vessels. The ageing of Britain's population has rendered these disorders, senile and so-called multi-infarct dementia, so common that the increase has been called 'the quiet epidemic'. Sadly, there are at present no effective cures. (For further discussion see DEMENTIA.)

**Functional psychoses.** *Schizophrenia.* In 1898 Emil *Kraepelin made the now classical distinction between the two major types of functional psychosis. He contrasted manic-depressive psychosis with its recurrent gross swings in mood with a more severe and progressive illness starting in young adulthood which he termed *dementia praecox*. This distinction still holds, although *dementia praecox* is now termed schizophrenia because this better describes the characteristic disintegration of mental life. Most schizophrenics suffer at some point from hallucinations which usually take the form of voices talking to or about them. Occasionally these voices are friendly but in the main they are disparaging and abusive. The schizophrenic is beset with strange beliefs (*delusions). He may think, for example, that he is the victim of a plot, that everyone can read his thoughts, or that alien forces are inserting or removing thoughts from his head or controlling his body.

Schizophrenia is only correctly diagnosed when these beliefs are unshakeable and totally out of keeping with the ideas and philosophies of the sufferer's own class and culture. Thus, a West Indian who believes he is a victim of a voodoo spell, or a spiritualist receiving instructions from the dead, is unlikely to be schizophrenic. But an Englishwoman who is absolutely convinced that her every action is personally controlled by a famous pop singer through a radio receiver he has installed in her mind may well be.

About 80 per cent of schizophrenic patients make a good recovery from their first attack. Unfortunately, many patients later relapse and require further admission to hospital, and in the long term only about 50 per cent remain quite free of any disability. More severely affected people become so preoccupied with their delusions and hallucinations that they tend to withdraw from social contact, and lose touch with reality. As a result their social and occupational functioning deteriorates, and about 10 per cent of all those initially affected become long-term hospital in-patients. In spite of the disorganized and irrelevant speech and disintegration of personality of such severe schizophrenics, their basic intelligence is usually unaffected and improvement can still occur after many years of hospitalization.

If, as some claim, schizophrenia is a myth, then it is a myth with a strong hereditary component! The risk of the identical twin of a schizophrenic also developing the disorder is about 50 per cent, whereas the risk for a non-identical twin is less than 15 per cent; this difference presumably reflects the greater genetic similarity of identical twins. Similarly, children of schizophrenic parents who were adopted and raised by normal families still have an increased risk of schizophrenia, whereas children born to normal parents and by mischance raised by a schizophrenic do not. The precise way in which liability to schizophrenia is transmitted is not known, but biochemical factors may be important. Some drugs, such as amphetamines, can in excess produce a mental state mimicking schizophrenia; this has led to the suggestion that schizophrenics could be endogenously producing some aberrant chemical.

The once fashionable theories that abnormal childhood experiences could by themselves induce schizophrenia can now be discounted, but environment is undoubtedly important. Traumatic life experiences or intense intrafamilial pressures can precipitate breakdown in the susceptible individual. For example, in many recovered schizophrenics, prolonged contact with excessively critical and over-involved relatives can cause relapse into florid psychosis.

In treating schizophrenia, the two essential elements are antipsychotic drugs and social rehabilitation. Intrusive therapies such as psychoanalysis are harmful, but a long-term supportive relationship with a concerned psychiatrist or social worker can be invaluable. Phenothiazine drugs are effective against florid symptoms such as delusions and hallucinations, and are needed to induce an initial remission and in some cases to retain it. (See SCHIZOPHRENIA: EVIDENCE FOR AN ORGANIC CAUSE.) Thereafter, a variety of social measures are used to provide a social and work environment to suit each patient's individual need. Rehabilitation may involve occupational therapy, attendance at a day hospital, or residence in a half-way hostel. The aim of such measures is, of course, to help the patient to find a satisfying role in the community and to stop him becoming institutionalized in hospital. Voluntary organizations such as the Schizophrenia Fellowship often play a major role in this. (See also SCHIZOPHRENIA.)

*Manic-depressive psychosis.* In its full-blown form, this is a cyclical disorder in which opposite extremes of mood are successively shown. Mania is characterized by an extraordinary sense of well-being, over-activity, and elation and is usually accompanied by a conviction of great self-importance which causes the individual affected to make grandiose pronouncements—for example, that he is the most talented and intelligent person in the world. He may consequently enter into wild and ruinous business ventures, or indulge in other unaccustomed excesses of spending, eating, drinking, or sex. His talk is profuse and prolix, flitting from topic to topic with an unstoppable stream of ideas interspersed with puns and feeble witticisms. His jollity may initially be infectious, but before long he becomes overbearing and tiresome. Not surprisingly most manics eventually dissipate their energy and return to normal, but an unfortunate minority descend straight into depression with no intermediate period of normality.

Mania is much less common than depressive psychosis, the predominant symptoms of which are profound gloom and despair. Life appears futile and hopeless and suicidal ideas are usually entertained, and, not infrequently, successfully acted upon. Depression produces a marked depletion in self-confidence and self-regard and the depressive may see himself as the most evil and wicked individual who ever lived. Racked with guilt, the previously blameless character becomes convinced that he has committed some grave infamy or that he is to blame for all the sin and misery which exists in the world. Less commonly he may believe that he has been stripped of all his possessions, or that his body has become hideously diseased and is rotting and decayed. Real bodily disturbance of a less bizarre nature does usually occur. Appetite is poor, weight loss ensues, and there is often constipation and loss of sex drive. Some depressives physically slow down, and their talk may decrease or altogether cease, a condition known as psychomotor retardation: occasionally such a patient develops a state of mute, immobile stupor. In others restlessness and edginess may culminate in severe agitation.

Manic-depressive illness, like schizophrenia, is partly determined by genetic factors. Again there is evidence that biochemical factors are important: for example, drugs which deplete the brain of chemical messenger substances called monoamines can induce depression, while drugs which raise the level of monoamines relieve depression and can precipitate mania. Despite the importance of these biological components, the part played by psychological factors can in no way be discounted. Adverse life circumstances or *bereavement or other forms of loss are known to result frequently in depression, and psychoanalytical theory considers that it is the turning-in on the self of the consequent feelings of hostility and annoyance which produces the illness. Some behaviourists on the other hand have stressed the importance of learning experiences, such as exposure to inescapable mental trauma which produces a feeling of helplessness. This, they believe, forms the basis of the depressed state.

Manic-depressive illness is a serious condition, not just because of the misery and the disruption it causes, but because about 15 per cent of sufferers eventually die by suicide. Fortunately, treatment is effective. Antidepressant drugs are of proven efficacy in the majority of typical cases, and although the manner in which it works remains obscure, electroconvulsive therapy can often relieve depression which has proved resistant to other treatments. Hospital admission, which is the general rule for cases of mania, provides a temporary sanctuary for many depressives, and is essential when the risk of suicide seems great. Psychotherapeutic help is invaluable and, in people who have recurrent episodes of illness, the chemical element lithium may be used on a long-term basis to prevent further relapses.   P. McG.

R. M.

Brown, J. A. C. (1963). *Freud and the Post-Freudians*. Harmondsworth.
Clare, A. (1980). *Psychiatry in Dissent*, 2nd edn. London.
Hill, P., Murray, R. M., and Thorley, R. A. (1985). *Essentials of Postgraduate Psychiatry*, 2nd edn.
McGuffin, P., Shank, M. F., and Hodgson, R. (1984). *Scientific Principles of Psychopathology*. London.
Marks, I. (1969). *Fears and Phobias*. London.
Stafford-Clark, D. (1973). *Psychiatry Today*. Harmondsworth.

**MENTAL IMAGERY** was first investigated and described in useful detail by Francis *Galton (1883). Galton asked his academic and less academic friends and acquaintances to describe, for example, the colours and patterns of the cloth on their breakfast table, from memory. He reported that the more intellectually gifted, the less vivid was the imagery. Several Fellows of the Royal Society were surprised to learn of imagery in other, lesser mortals—as they denied it for themselves.

Galton describes how for some people numbers are mentally imaged and 'seen' in space, in some fixed and often queer order. They may also be 'seen' in colours. Many examples are quoted by Galton, and perhaps no later study has much to add.

There are experiments attempting to show whether mental images are useful. Consider, for example, the following: a 6-centimetre cube of wood is painted all over with red paint. Now the cube is cut into 1-centimetre cubes. How many of these have (i) three red sides; (ii) two red sides; (iii) one red side; (iv) no red sides? Most people solve this by *imagining* a red cube; this they 'cut' into 1-centimetre cubes which they then 'examine' mentally. It is, however, an open question whether the images we experience (rather than the brain processes presumably producing them) are causally important for solving this problem, or for anything else. This is indeed the problem of awareness, or *consciousness; for what it does, if anything, is totally unknown.

See also IMAGE ROTATION; IMAGING.

Galton, F. (1883). *Inquiries into Human Faculty*. London.

**MENTALISM.** See MIND–BODY PROBLEM: PHILOSOPHICAL THEORIES.

**MENTALLY ILL, SERVICE FOR THE.** The provision of proper care for the mentally ill has been a problem for centuries (as is described in the article ASYLUMS: A HISTORICAL SURVEY). There is no right solution, for the size and nature of the problem changes according to society's definition of mental illness and its tolerance of unusual behaviour among its members. Therefore, before embarking on detailed planning of services for the mentally ill,

it is necessary to establish the need for such services.

It is traditional in Britain to adopt the medical model of *mental illness. This means that the disability is seen in terms of symptoms and signs arising from a pathological process (which may be undefined) for which medical diagnosis and treatment are appropriate. This model has been challenged by those who consider that much mental illness is related to adverse social or environmental factors. Doctors have not rejected this view, but have tended to extend their areas of interest to incorporate such fields as marital disharmony for which a purely medical model is inappropriate. This extension of medical activity into fields which would previously have been the province of other groups such as priests, with its implied extension of the range of 'mental illness', has to be taken into account when planning medical services.

The development of psycho-active drugs has had a major effect on the need for services for the mentally ill. The ability to control pharmacologically some of the symptoms of severe illnesses such as *schizophrenia and manic-depressive *psychosis has reduced the need for long-term residential care. On the other hand, there has been a massive increase in consultations with general practitioners on account of some form of mental illness. This is partly associated with the ready availability and comparative safety of drugs which affect mood. People have learned that they can be relieved of the discomfort of *anxiety or *depression by means of tablets, and acknowledgement of these conditions is no longer associated with social stigma. The evidence that some drugs which were initially considered 'safe' can in fact be addictive has not reduced the demands for treatment, but has increased the need for non-drug approaches, such as counselling and *psychotherapy. These changes at both ends of the mental illness spectrum, which appear likely to continue, have to be taken into account when planning, so as to develop the appropriate balance of facilities for care.

The demand for medical services for the mentally ill is not determined entirely by the activities of doctors and the opportunities for medical treatment. Society itself contributes to the equation by setting the somewhat arbitrary line which distinguishes between abnormal, though tolerable, behaviour and mental illness. The position of this line varies, both with time and between nations. In Britain at present, people are still relatively intolerant of even mild psychotic symptoms, whereas there is increased acceptance of sexual deviance, especially homosexuality. In some countries, disagreement with the governing regime is considered so deviant as to merit the label 'mental illness'. These differences predominantly affect the requirement for residential care, since the demand is usually for the deviant to be removed from the community at large, and there is indeed an overlap between those labelled mentally ill who are sent to hospital and those who contravene the law and receive prison sentences. Another influence on the way mental illness is viewed stems from changes in mental health legislation. Undoubtedly the UK Mental Health Act of 1959 led to a far greater acceptance by members of the community of the need for treatment of both major and minor psychiatric disorders. It remains to be seen what effect the Mental Health Act of 1983 will have on this trend.

The needs of the elderly have to be considered separately because of the different nature of their illnesses. It is, of course, not unusual for people over 65 years of age to suffer from the common psychiatric disorders for which the generally available treatment is appropriate; but with advancing years, the incidence of *dementia increases, and it is often accompanied by physical illness or handicap. Special account of the needs of such patients must be taken in planning services, both for assessment in order to ensure that remediable complicating factors are dealt with, and for their long-term care. Greater longevity has increased the need for psychogeriatric facilities, and governments in most Western developed nations have become concerned over the need to provide care for increasing numbers of aged patients, many of whom are suffering from irreversible dementia. How to relieve the strain on existing facilities is one of the problems to be faced over the next decade.

The planning of medical services demands quantification of future needs and knowledge of the resources which will be available to meet them. However, whereas the size of the population to be served can be calculated with reasonable accuracy on an actuarial basis, the proportion who will be suffering from mental illness is much more difficult to estimate. It depends on guesses about future patterns of designation of mental disorder and future therapeutic developments. Moreover, assessment of the treatment requirements of the mentally ill, upon which provision must be based, is dependent on further guesses about future social attitudes and about opportunities for care in the family when increasing numbers of women work outside the home.

Having reached an estimate of the quantity of service which will be needed, the way in which it will be provided has to be determined. The balance of care between medical and non-medical agencies, between psychiatrists and general practitioners, between large psychiatric hospitals and units in general hospitals, and between residential and non-residential facilities has all to be decided. Decisions cannot be reached entirely rationally: in many cases, there is little evidence to support one view or another. The enthusiasms of local practitioners, current government policy, and the necessity of modifying rather than replacing existing facilities may all take precedence over projections of future needs and opportunities, which in any case will be somewhat theoretical. It is important, however, that the factors which are taken into account are recognized and recorded, so that planning decisions taken now can be properly evaluated in the future and the quality of decision-making thus improved. In addition, it is essential that the full implications of each option are explored before a decision is reached. For example, expansion of care for the mentally ill in the community inevitably means that the most ill patients with the least likelihood of improvement in their condition will remain in the large hospitals. Realistic proposals for the maintenance of standards and for the recruitment of staff at these hospitals, by such means as rotation of posts with other units, in-service training programmes, and research projects, must be put forward before plans are implemented, in order to prevent serious problems of morale and an unacceptable fall in the standards of patient care.

The change in the balance of care poses problems in the community as well as in the institution. It is difficult to provide mentally ill people living in small groups with the range of supporting staff and activities which can be offered in institutions. When it is practical to offer such facilities in the community, the dispersal of the patients means that the cost of the services is much higher than the cost of an equivalent level of care in a hospital. The policy of transfer from hospital to community care is based on clinical and humanitarian arguments, but much support for it derives from the assumed financial savings. It is now clear that mentally ill people based in the community, receiving services funded at a lower level than hospital services, are at grave risk of 'community neglect' rather than 'community care'.

The prevention of mental illness is a complicated issue to which little attention has been paid in the past. It is unlikely that simple methods like vaccination will ever be appropriate in this field. Like other common non-communicable diseases such as coronary heart disease, any advances in the prevention of mental illness are likely to require changes in patterns of behaviour, which are extremely difficult to achieve and may raise ethical problems. Epidemiological evidence on topics such as suicide (see SUICIDAL BEHAVIOUR) and *bereavement and on the effect of important life events on the development of mental illness do, however, give clues about possible future activity in this field.

The rehabilitation of the mentally ill is of major importance and has also been somewhat neglected in the past. If, in general, the objective of treatment is to maximize the patient's independence, it is clear that exclusively medical services are inadequate, and must be complemented by help with social and employment problems. It is highly desirable that all the agencies which patients may need should be involved in the preparation of service plans.

The detailed planning of services must take place at a local level if they are to meet the needs of the local community. In Britain, however, the money for health care is not raised locally but comes from central government. The local planning therefore has to be undertaken within the framework of national policy. This determines what proportion of the Gross National Product will be allocated to health and, within that, the apportionment between services. At present, mental illness is a priority service and can expect an increased proportion of the health budget to be allocated to it. It is not, however, always possible to achieve such transfers of resources, especially in a time of economic stringency, because of the difficulties of making cuts in other services.

Planning has also to take account of government policy with regard to medical manpower. In Britain the aim at present is to remove the inequalities in staffing levels across the country and between specialties. Current initiatives to expand the consultant grade and to control entry of junior doctors into training posts in the popular acute specialties may attract more doctors into psychiatry, which has not historically been a popular career of first choice among medical graduates.

Planning of services for the mentally ill is an activity dependent on estimates of future medical, pharmacological, and social changes, but the range of such estimates is inevitably wide, and the interaction between the different factors imprecisely defined. It is not possible to predict with any accuracy the level of the financial or manpower resources that will be available in the next decade. Even so, it is important that planning should continue on as rational a basis as possible and that facts, assumptions, and arguments should be recorded. It is only in this way that planning can move from meeting vocal demands to meeting true needs. Meanwhile, all service plans should maintain the maximum flexibility, so as to minimize constraints on future developments.

See also ASYLUMS: ARE THEY REALLY NECESSARY?

J. M. C.

**MESMERISM.** It is often said that hypnosis was discovered by the controversial Viennese physician Franz Anton Mesmer (1734–1815), whose name gave the word 'mesmerism' to the English language. While it seems certain that some of Mesmer's patients indeed became hypnotized, it must be borne in mind that no formal concept of hypnotism existed at the time, and Mesmer attributed his therapeutic successes to a hitherto unknown physical agency to which he gave the name 'animal magnetism'. Greatly influenced by Newtonian physics—which he evidently misunderstood completely—Mesmer envisaged animal magnetism as a physical force or 'fluid', somewhat akin to gravitation, which permeates the universe and to which the human nervous system is somehow attuned (Mesmer, 1779). Nervous illness, he believed, results from an imbalance between the animal magnetism in the patient's body and that in the external world at large, which can be redressed by human agency. This Mesmer sought to achieve by channelling animal magnetism through his own

body to that of the patient, either directly by applying his hands to the affected part ('passes') or indirectly by requiring the patient to grasp an iron bar or other object which he had previously 'magnetized' by direct contact. Although magnets or magnetized iron filings were sometimes used as intermediaries, Mesmer insisted that animal magnetism is quite different from physical magnetism and in itself possesses no curative properties. None the less, the term 'magnetizer' long persisted as the popular designation of those who made use of Mesmer's methods for therapeutic ends.

Although Mesmer's theory of animal magnetism was rejected by scientists even in his own lifetime, there can be no doubt that he won many disciples and not a few grateful patients. Indeed his colourful personality and robust self-confidence created a distinct stir, first in court circles in imperial Vienna and later in the fashionable salons of pre-Revolutionary Paris. Inevitably, perhaps, he incurred the odium of the medical establishment, and the French government was eventually led to appoint a royal commission to conduct an inquiry into animal magnetism under the chairmanship of Benjamin Franklin. Among its members were Lavoisier, the famous chemist, and Guillotin, who gave his name to the instrument of decapitation that a few years later claimed the head of Lavoisier himself. This commission examined exhaustively not only the alleged medical benefits of mesmerism but also the evidence for the existence of animal magnetism itself, to which it quite properly adopted an experimental attitude. Although Mesmer did not give personal evidence to the commission (the brunt of cross-examination falling on one of his followers, Dr Deslon), there can be no doubt that it was in effect Mesmer himself who was on trial.

The commission published its report in 1784 and came out strongly against the existence of animal magnetism as a physical force. It did not, however, deny that in some cases mesmeric treatment brought therapeutic benefit. This the commissioners had no hesitation in attributing solely to the powers of imagination, which is hardly surprising when it is borne in mind that Mesmer, in his Paris days, made his patients sit in groups round a large barrel-like object known as a *baquet*, each grasping an iron rod protruding from the interior (which contained water and iron filings, sometimes magnetized), while he himself, splendidly attired, treated them by magnetism to the accompaniment of soft music. Also it is interesting that, in a section of the report apparently suppressed at the time but published over a century later by *Binet and Féré (1887), the Commissioners directed special attention to the moral dangers attendant on mesmeric treatment, evidently reminding the reader that a high proportion of those seeking it were of the female sex. This provides a striking anticipation of Sigmund *Freud's contention that sexual factors are of great importance for our understanding of the hypnotic state (SEE FREUD ON HYPNOSIS).

In consequence of the royal commission's

findings, mesmerism was officially discredited for many years and Mesmer himself disappeared into obscurity. None the less, a small number of 'magnetizers' continued to ply their trade. One of these was the Marquis de Puységur, who is credited with the first account of a case of *somnambulism evoked by mesmerism, with the subject showing a complete loss of memory for the events of the trance after being awakened. This would nowadays be called post-hypnotic *amnesia. Among other magnetizers, several of whom visited England and America, was Dupotet, who first introduced John Elliotson (1791–1868), professor of the practice of medicine at University College, London, to the phenomenon of mesmerism (see Bramwell, 1913). Elliotson soon became convinced of its value in medical practice, particularly in the treatment of what were then (as now) called functional nervous disorders, i.e. disturbances of bodily or mental functions for which no physical pathology can be established. Like Mesmer before him, Elliotson was to suffer greatly from the hostility of the medical establishment, but he had the courage to resign from his professorship rather than comply with the ruling of the College council forbidding the practice of mesmerism in the hospital. His temerity was also shown by the fact that, when invited by the Royal College of Physicians to deliver the Herveian Oration, he chose mesmerism as his subject. Whereupon the *Lancet* dubbed him a professional pariah and asserted that his lecture would strike a vital blow at legitimate medicine. None the less, Elliotson duly delivered his lecture, which was received in stony silence, and did much thereafter—if in slightly eccentric ways—to advance the cause of what is nowadays known as psychological medicine.

Thereafter, the history of mesmerism merges into that of hypnotism and, more broadly, into that of psychological medicine. Indirectly, however, it is linked with a number of broader issues in social history, not least that of faith-healing and Christian Science. Mary Baker Eddy, the founder of Christian Science, is thought to have first conceived its tenets through being cured of a hysterical paralysis when a girl, by a faith-healer who had been inspired by a visiting French magnetizer. (For the metamorphosis of mesmerism into hypnotism, see HYPNOTISM, HISTORY OF.)     O. L. Z.

Binet, A. and Féré, C. (1887). *Le Magnétisme animal*. Paris.

Bramwell, J. M. (1913). *Hypnotism: its history, practice and theory*, 3rd edn. London.

Mesmer, F. A. (1779; repr. 1971). *Le Magnétisme animal*. Paris.

Walmsley, D. M. (1967). *Anton Mesmer*. Paris.

**MESOMORPHY.** See BODY BUILD AND PERSONALITY.

**MESOPIC VISION.** Twilight vision. Vision is poor in the 'half-light' between the scotopic black–white vision given by the retinal rods, and the *colour vision given by the cones (photopic vision). It is important to know for driving that mesopic conditions are essentially dangerous and require extra care.

**METAPHOR.** The topic of metaphor has a history dating back at least to *Aristotle, but not until the twentieth century did it come to be regarded seriously as a problem relevant to the general study of language and thought.

Aristotle took the use of metaphors to be evidence of a superior intellect. At the same time, he seemed to believe that their use was primarily the prerogative of poets and politicians. For philosophers and scientists, they were potentially too misleading. In limiting the use of metaphors to the ornamental, rather than concentrating on their communicative value, Aristotle essentially elevated metaphor from the prosaic to the esoteric. The unfortunate result was that attention to the topic came to be largely restricted to rhetoricians. Indeed, during the nineteenth century, the principal activity of rhetoricians became the interpretation of particular metaphors (and other tropes) in literary texts—an obsession that was largely responsible for the demise of rhetoric as a serious discipline.

In spite of limiting what he presumably considered to be the legitimate uses of metaphor, Aristotle's analysis of the underlying logic of metaphor has always dominated thinking on the topic. He believed metaphors to be implicit comparisons based on the principles of analogy. It can be argued that this view has had the undesirable effect of blurring the distinction between metaphor, analogy, and similarity—more will be said of this later.

Around the turn of the century there appeared an English translation of Michel Bréal's *Essay de semantique*. In this influential work, Bréal claimed that metaphor was a linguistic device, widespread in its use, and of great importance in linguistic change. Then, in 1936, metaphor was revitalized in the study of the language of literature by I. A. Richards. Richards introduced useful terminology for talking about metaphors (topic/tenor, vehicle, ground, and tension)—terminology which has come to be fairly standard.

In 1962 Max Black's book *Models and Metaphors* appeared. In it, Black rejected the Aristotelian 'comparison' view wherein metaphors are merely elliptical comparisons, and he questioned the generality of the 'substitution' view wherein metaphors are merely ornamental substitutes for literal language. Instead, elaborating on the views of Richards, he proposed an 'interaction' view. On this view, the *tenor* (or topic, or subject) of a metaphor is seen as interacting with the metaphorical *vehicle* to produce a kind of emergent meaning for the entire sentence—one that could not have resulted from the combination of the tenor with some other predicate, literal or metaphorical. Thus, in the metaphor 'man is a wolf', 'man' is viewed, as it were, through a 'wolf' filter. Our interpretation of both terms is altered.

By the mid-1970s, an active interest in the topic had spread to all sorts of disciplines, most relevant of which, in the present context, was cognitive psychology. Psychologists became interested in questions such as: Does the comprehension of metaphors involve special processes not normally involved in the comprehension of literal language? Do metaphors play a role in the development of language? Why do people use metaphors? What is the relationship between metaphor, analogy, and similarity? Many of these questions have their counterparts in philosophy, but the empirical techniques that psychology brings to bear may throw more light on them.

The principal dispute over comprehension mechanisms is about whether or not metaphors are understood by first unsuccessfully attempting to impose a literal interpretation. According to one view, when people encounter metaphors they recognize that a literal interpretation is incompatible with the context and then proceed to reinterpret the metaphor figuratively. According to the other view, ordinarily people interpret the metaphorical meaning directly, without even entertaining a literal interpretation. Flatly stated in this way, each view has its problems. One problem with the reinterpretation account is that it does not specify the basis upon which a reinterpretation is made. Many linguistic forms require 'reinterpretation': sarcasm ('That was a clever thing to do', said of an obviously foolish act), hyperbole ('There were millions of people at the party', said to indicate that there were many—but obviously not millions), and indirect speech acts, such as indirect requests ('Do you know what time it is?', meant as a request to be told the hour of the day), are just some of the many examples. Reinterpretation theories need to be able to characterize the differences between these (and other) kinds of non-literal uses of language. They need both to specify the different rules that underlie the comprehension of different types, and to offer an account of how people are supposed to know in advance which rules to employ on a particular occasion: it hardly seems likely, for example, that the rules for reinterpreting sarcasm are applied, or even considered, in the ordinary interpretation of a metaphor.

The direct comprehension view finesses this last question. However, as stated, it suffers from underspecification. It amounts to little more than a statement to the effect that when people encounter metaphors, they understand them; on its own, it has no answer to the question, How? A more general theory of language comprehension is needed to answer this question. The theory (or theoretical framework) that is most often appealed to is one based on the notion of *schemas* (or scripts, or frames). The idea is that comprehension in general proceeds by finding a schema that 'fits' the input. Then, the argument goes, the difference between understanding literal and metaphorical language turns out to be simply one of quality of fit.

Data from experiments suggest that elements of both views are correct. Experiments measuring (for example) the time taken by people to indicate that they have understood a sentence (either metaphorical or literal) show that, with sufficient preceding context, subjects do not require the additional time to process metaphors that the reinterpretation theory predicts. On the other hand, when a metaphor is encountered with very little prior context, the predicted increase in *reaction time is found. In such cases, it seems, people have to 'work out' what the sentence means, whereas in other cases what they do seems more like confirming contextually generated expectations. Of course, 'working out the meaning' is something that is often required for literal uses of language too. Furthermore, there are many 'frozen' metaphors in the language, often idioms, that, once known, never require special processing. Thus, the evidence suggests that extra processing is required by language that is not well integrated into the context, be it literal or metaphorical, and that under appropriate circumstances metaphorical language is processed as quickly and easily as literal language.

Observant parents, as well as developmental psychologists, have often noticed that quite young children (2 to 3 years of age) appear to be very creative in their use of language. When the young child tries to express something for which he has not learned the conventional word, he often uses some other word that succeeds in realizing his communicative intentions, even though the choice may not be literally appropriate. This activity is described by developmental psychologists as 'semantic over-extension' (see LANGUAGE: LEARNING WORD MEANINGS), but some have claimed that this behaviour in fact reflects the use of metaphor by young children, and that the use of metaphor is a fundamental ingredient in language development.

Attractive though this view might be, it seems to suffer from some rather serious drawbacks. First among these is the evidence that such young children are unable to understand metaphors. Estimates of the age at which children begin to understand metaphors properly vary considerably. Some investigators claim that it is not until early adolescence, while others claim that by the age of 7 or 8 many children can deal with metaphors. The variations in these estimates are the result of several factors, the principal ones being fluctuating and often rather atheoretical criteria for what is to count as a metaphor, and for what is to count as evidence of its comprehension. However, most investigators agree that 3-year-old children cannot understand metaphors. Since it is well established that children's language comprehension is far ahead of their language production, if 2- and 3-year-old children were producing metaphors it would be the only known example of behaviour contrary to the comprehension-before-production rule. A second problem is that the claim that such young children produce metaphors fails to recognize that an utterance could be metaphorical from an adult's perspective, but not from that of the child who produces it. In other words, the claim may be excessively 'adultocentric'.

Doubtless part of the attractiveness of claiming that very young children produce metaphors is that an important function of metaphors is to permit the expression of ideas that might otherwise be (literally) inexpressible for a particular speaker in a particular language. In some cases the lack of words in the language has resulted in entire domains being mapped into other domains so that the language itself incorporates now unnoticed metaphorical means of description—this is one of the ways in which, as Bréal pointed out, metaphors are important in linguistic change. A familiar example of such a mapping is the use of temperature terms to describe personality characteristics—we talk of people in terms of their being warm, or cool, cold, or icy. When such metaphors are embedded in the language to fill systematic gaps in the lexicon, they often go unnoticed. But the same principle operates at the level of the individual speaker, except that if the language does not supply conventional resources (be they literal or metaphorical), the speaker may have to create his own. In such cases he uses a novel metaphor.

The expression of the otherwise inexpressible is not the only communicative function that metaphors serve. They also achieve a certain communicative compactness, since all the applicable predicates belonging to the metaphorical vehicle are implied succinctly through the vehicle itself. Thus, even if what a metaphor expresses may have been more or less expressible without the metaphor, its use may be more economical and hence more effective than the long list of predicates that it entails.

The relationship between metaphors and similarity is a complex one. Without having to commit oneself to one of the various theories about how metaphors work, it is apparent that at some level, and in some way, metaphors capitalize on a similarity between the term used metaphorically (the vehicle) and the thing that the metaphor is a metaphor for. Thus, even though it may be incorrect to claim, as some have, that a metaphor is *merely* a statement of similarity, it is probably not incorrect to say that a metaphor is *largely* a statement of similarity. Clearly, if one says of jogging that it is a religion, the metaphor would not work if jogging and religion were not in some way similar. On the other hand, it is obvious that in many ways jogging is not in the least bit like a religion. It could be argued, in fact, that jogging is not really like a religion at all; if we want something that is really like a religion, a cult is. The interesting thing is that if one now considers the two similarity statements 'Jogging is like a religion' and 'A cult is like a religion', the latter, while appearing to be really true, has no metaphorical potential. This suggests

that if metaphors are based on similarity statements, only some similarity statements can fulfil the required role. The similarity statements that seem to fit the bill are those that themselves seem to be metaphorical. According to this view, that is why one can say 'Metaphorically speaking, jogging is like a religion', but not 'Metaphorically speaking, a cult is like a religion'. Now, if the only similarity statements that can form the basis of metaphors are metaphorical similarity statements, two important consequences follow. The first is that it is futile to attempt to *explain* metaphors by reducing them to similarity statements because the statements to which they get reduced still have the characteristic of being metaphorical. The second is that, as a research strategy, the examination of similarity statements may be the best way to uncover the difference between the literal and the metaphorical.

Psychological discussions about the nature of metaphor often seem to use the terms 'similarity', and 'analogy' as though they were interchangeable. It is possible, however, to be more precise about the relationship between the two by arguing that an analogy is a similarity between relations rather than between single-place predicates. On this view, an analogy is a particular kind of similarity statement, and, from a psychological perspective, whether a particular comparison is or is not an analogy may depend on the way in which the entities being compared are conceptualized or represented at the time. A simple example will illustrate the point. Suppose we are told that cigarettes are like time bombs. If we entertain this proposition in terms of a simple similarity statement, we might say that both cigarettes and time bombs share the property of (potentially) causing death after a delay. In other words, considered in this way we would have something to the effect: 'Being a cigarette is like being a time bomb.' On the other hand, suppose one conceptualizes the statement in the following way: 'People smoking cigarettes are like people exposed to time bombs.' Now what we have is something roughly equivalent in meaning, except that it is stated as a similarity between two relations—it is an analogy. Again, from a psychological perspective, how the terms in a similarity statement will be represented is likely to depend on the context, it is not fixed by the linguistic structure of the statement itself. Thus, again, the point is not whether metaphors are built on similarity or on analogy, since both are forms of comparison. The point is that metaphors are built on comparisons which are themselves metaphorical, be they analogical or not.          A. O.

Black, M. (1962). Metaphor. Black, M. (ed.), *Models and metaphors*. Ithaca, N.Y.

Bréal, M. J. A. (1897). *Semantics: Studies in the science of meaning* (trans. Crust, H. 1964). New York.

Honeck, R. P. and Hoffman, R. R. (1980). *Cognition and figurative language*. Hillsdale, New Jersey.

Lakoff, G. and Johnson, M. (1980). *Metaphors we live by*. Chicago.

Ortony, A. (ed.) (1979). *Metaphor and thought*. New York.

Richards, I. A. (1936). *The philosophy of rhetoric*. London.

## METAPHYSICS

is generally taken to mean philosophical speculation beyond the current or even seemingly possible limits of science, and the development of more or less abstract systems intended to explain origins and purpose, phenomena of mind and matter, and the place of man in the universe. The word 'metaphysics' has its origin simply from those books of *Aristotle which were placed in sequence after his *Physics*. The pejorative sense of 'obscure' and 'over-speculative' is recent, especially following attempts by A. J. Ayer and others to show that metaphysics is strictly nonsense.

It is a moot point how far science is, or can be, free of metaphysics. There may always be untested and even for-ever untestable theoretical assumptions which are necessary for interpreting experiments. These assumptions are (by definition) metaphysical, for they are not testable by observation or experiment and so are essentially speculative.

Metaphysics is associated especially with idealist and rationalist philosophers, chief among whom is Immanuel *Kant. Kant argued, for example, most clearly in his *Prolegomena to Any Future Metaphysics* (1783), that time and space are categories of mind, and that it is impossible to conceive the physical world without such *a priori categories. Empiricism, on the other hand, is often thought to be free of metaphysical assumptions—at any rate for operationalist philosophers, who hold that all knowledge is derived from observation, and especially from observed matches and mismatches against formally defined test procedures and measurements. This is essentially Karl Popper's aim and claim for objective knowledge.

A very different current view, which is developed especially by the American philosophers Norwood Russell Hanson and Thomas Kuhn, is that there is no such thing as a neutral theory-free observation language which simply records 'the facts'; even the simplest observations and experiments must be made within the context of complex theoretical assumptions (see PARADIGMS). Given that these assumptions cannot be objectively verified or tested operationally, they may be said to be metaphysical; and this leads to a more or less extreme relativism which rejects the notion of 'brute facts' and 'objective' observational data.

R. L. G.

Hanson, N. R. (1972). *Patterns of Discovery: an inquiry into the conceptual foundations of science*. Cambridge.

Kuhn, T. S. (1970). *The Structure of Scientific Revolutions*, 2nd edn. Chicago.

Popper, K. R. (1972). *Objective Knowledge: an evolutionary approach*. Oxford.

Popper, K. R. (1959). *The Logic of Scientific Discovery*. London.

**METEMPIRIC(AL).** Knowledge of, or supposed knowledge of, things outside or beyond experience or experiment. (See also METAPHYSICS.)

**METEMPSYCHOSIS.** When a living thing dies, its 'soul' or *psyche takes up a new residence in some other body, which it thereby vivifies: for the psyche, bodily death means emigration, bodily birth immigration. That is the ancient doctrine of 'metempsychosis' or the transmigration of the soul.

Among the Greeks, the followers of *Pythagoras were particularly associated with the doctrine—indeed, it is one of the few beliefs that can confidently be ascribed to Pythagoras himself. (In *Twelfth Night*, 'Sir Topas' asks the imprisoned Malvolio: 'What is the opinion of Pythagoras concerning wild fowl?' And Malvolio rightly answers: 'That the soul of our grandam might haply inhabit a bird.' Empedocles, too, subscribed to the doctrine; one of his poems contained the following couplet:

For already have I once been a boy, and a girl,
and a bush, and a fish that jumps from the sea as it swims.

(Bushes are living things, and therefore have a psyche. The jumping fish is the dolphin.)

Note that the psyche is a principle of individuality for living things: since Empedocles's psyche once inhabited a fish, Empedocles himself once was a fish—metempsychosis is about the personal survival of bodily death. We are told that Pythagoras 'passed a dog that was being whipped; he took pity on it and said: "Stop! don't beat it—it is the psyche of a friend of mine; I recognize him by his voice."'

Different thinkers composed variations on the metempsychotic theme: for some, the process of transmigration went on for ever; some imagined a cycle of incarnations; some spoke of a hierarchy of lives; in some versions of the theory, incarnations are separated by periods of non-corporeal existence, during which divine Judgement may take place. The doctrine was sometimes associated with a theology or with a quasi-religious way of life; and Empedocles based a moral theory upon it: if one and the same psyche may animate now a man, now a lion, now an eagle, then living creatures are all akin; and we should have moral scruples about maltreating our psychic kinsmen. Empedocles denounced all bloodshed and advocated a form of vegetarianism; for if you kill and eat a sheep, you may be killing and eating your own father. ('Sir Topas' counsels Malvolio to 'fear to kill a woodcock, lest thou dispossess the soul of thy grandam'.) Strictly speaking, if you eat a parsnip, you may be eating your father; but Empedocles did not have the strength of character to insist upon a wholly inanimate diet.

Metempsychosis may seem at best an irrational form of mysticism, at worst a risible piece of nonsense. To some Greeks, at least, it appeared to be an empirical theory; and its empirical basis lay in memory. Thus, according to Heraclides Ponticus, a pupil of *Plato's, Pythagoras

says about himself that he was once Aithalides, and was deemed a son of Hermes; and Hermes told him to choose whatever he wanted except immortality: so he asked that, both alive and dead, he should remember what happened. Thus in his life he remembered everything, and when he died he retained the same memory. Some time later, he passed into Euphorbus, and was wounded by Menelaus. ... And when Euphorbus died, his psyche passed into Hermotimus. ... And when Hermotimus died, he became Pyrrhus the Delian diver; and again, he remembered everything—how he had first been Aithalides, then Euphorbus, then Hermotimus, then Pyrrhus. And when Pyrrhus died, he became Pythagoras, and he remembered all the events I have mentioned.

Pythagoras claimed to have memories of his earlier lives; and those memories supported the theory of metempsychosis—or at least, they constituted evidence that Pythagoras himself was a migratory psyche. Sceptical Greeks dared to doubt Pythagoras' claim to remember being wounded under the walls of Troy; but Pythagoras was prepared to back up his claim:

They say that, while staying at Argos, he saw a shield from the spoils of Troy nailed up, and burst into tears. When the Argives asked him the reason for his emotion, he said that he himself had carried that shield in Troy when he was Euphorbus. They didn't believe him, and thought he was mad; but he said he could provide a true sign that this was the case: on the inside of the shield they would find written in archaic letters: EUPHORBUS'S. Because of the extraordinary nature of his claim, they all urged him to take down the offering. And the inscription was found on it.

Thus transmigratory claims are supported by an appeal to memory; and memory claims are supported in their turn by practical demonstration. The stories about Pythagoras's abilities are doubtless apocryphal, but the moral they point is not: even in their most extravagant moments, the ancient Greek psychologists did not lose all touch with reason and empirical reality.          J. BA.

**MICHOTTE**, ALBERT (1881–1965), Belgian experimental psychologist of high reputation. He is best known for his investigations of perceptual causality. By combining with remarkable ingenuity various types of real object movements (such as coloured rectangles moving on a screen and visible through a slit), he was able to demonstrate that, in certain spatial and temporal conditions, the subjects reported a causal action of one moving object on another, such as 'launching', 'entraining', and the like. These perceptual effects were described by Michotte with a wealth of detail and framed within an overall theory of dynamic relationships between objects. If we were to confine ourselves to the historical developments of Michotte's ideas, we should only refer to this aspect of his work at the end of our analysis; however, his extensive investigations of perceptual causality are too typical of his conception of experimental psychology to be mentioned solely as the last productive moment of his exceptionally creative career.

From 1905 to 1908, Michotte was active in experimental psychology under *Wundt and *Külpe and tackled various experimental problems ranging from the study of tactile sensitivity to that of so-called superior functions, viz. thought and will processes. There is no doubt that Külpe's *Denkpsychologie* (thought psychology) exerted a considerable influence on him, namely by introducing him to the descriptive techniques of subjective impressions, a major feature of the early German laboratories of experimental psychology. In addition to this, Michotte was exceptionally gifted mechanically. His great skill in designing and even building laboratory devices specially conceived in view of particular effects greatly helped him in realizing numerous original experiments.

In 1906 Michotte became a lecturer at the University of Louvain and was entrusted with the task of developing the laboratory of experimental psychology which had been founded in 1892 by Cardinal Mercier and whose first director was A. Thiéry, himself a direct collaborator of Wundt at Leipzig (1892–4). Through the work of Külpe on thought processes, Michotte became acquainted with act psychology (the school of Graz), especially with the work of Carl Stumpf and Ernst *Mach. Stumpf was the founder of a new kind of psychology, partly descriptive and partly experimental, which he called *experimental phenomenology*. According to his theory, experiments in psychology should be elaborated on the basis of a description of subjective phenomena as related to objects, *phenomenology proper being supplemented by a theory of contents (eidology) and a theory of relations between contents (logology).

In view of these influences, it may be said that Michotte's theoretical and experimental position was the joint result of the teachings of Wundt and of Stumpf. To this should be added the fact that, from 1912 on, Michotte became influenced by *Gestalt theory, which itself was greatly indebted to the theories of the school of Graz. However, to the end of his life he resented being called a Gestaltist, because he rejected generalized isomorphic theory, preferring to call himself an experimental phenomenologist. Summarizing the main trends of his research work, he wrote in 1962:

When *The Perception of Causality* was published, I used the language which was then used by numerous psychologists and by Gestalt psychologists in particular. It seems however that in spite of precautions which may have seemed sufficient at the time, certain expressions and certain wordings are liable to cause some misunderstandings concerning our theoretical standpoint in the study of perception. I therefore consider it necessary to state exactly here the point of view of psychological (or experimental) phenomenology as I conceive it (Michotte, 1962, p. 10).

This kind of experimental phenomenology rests on two methodological hypotheses. (i) The verbal reports of experimental subjects may be considered as the dependent variable of the stimulation systems. If the latter change in their spatio-temporal organization, changes will be observed in the categories of responses (as, for instance, causal against non-causal ones). (ii) The changes observed in the responses are not only quantitative (as expressed by frequencies), but also qualitative (as referring to contents). As a consequence, a theory of subjective impressions may be established on the basis of the descriptive proper-ties of verbal responses. It is this second hypothesis alone that qualifies this type of analysis as belong-ing to experimental phenomenology; and that explains, among other things, why Michotte re-flected unceasingly on the role of language in the analysis of perceptual phenomena. He may be best characterized by saying that he was an experiment-alist who succeeded in studying with great accur-acy the dynamic organization of the perceiver's phenomenal world. In this sense, he is more akin to Gestalt teachings than to phenomenological issues as expounded by *Husserl, i.e. within the frame-work of transcendental philosophy. The Graz school, which emerged from *Brentano's inten-tional theory of *consciousness, split at the begin-ning of the twentieth century into Gestaltism and transcendental phenomenology.

As a laboratory researcher deeply concerned with the analysis of subjective phenomena, Michotte is one of the few psychologists of the time who were able to bring Stumpf's experimental phenomenology to a high level of scientific accom-plishment. Because of his early training in scholastic philosophy, Michotte did not develop the epistemological implications of his researches on perception, a task which would have required a comparative analysis of Stumpf's and Husserl's respective phenomenologies. In Michotte's con-ception, the phenomenological is always equated with the phenomenal. However, it was his achieve-ment to demonstrate that an accurate experimental analysis of the perceptual world is a kind of phenomenological research which leads in some cases to more fruitful theoretical constructs than mere phenomenological descriptions in the clas-sical sense. His outstanding contribution appears therefore as a strong argument in favour of the fairly recent idea that phenomenological psy-chology may include controlled scientific work.

G. T.

Michotte, A. (1946). *The perception of causality* (trans. Miles, T. R. and E. 1963). London.

Michotte, A. (1959). Réflexions sur le rôle du langage dans l'analyse des organisations perceptives. *Acta Psychol*, **15**, 70–91.

Michotte, A. (1962). *Causalité, permanence et réalité phénoménales*. Louvain.

Thinès, G. (1968). *La Problématique de la psychologie* (esp. ch. II). The Hague.

**MIGRAINE** (from a French word derived from the Greek ἡμί meaning half and κρανίον meaning skull) is a transient disorder of brain function which is commonly associated with headache. The diagnosis is usually made when discrete headaches are accompanied by two or more of the following features: unilateral *pain, nausea or vomiting, focal cerebral symptoms (e.g. visual phenomena), and a family history of the condition. Attacks usually start to occur before the age of 30 and decrease in frequency with advancing age. Sixty per cent of sufferers are women.

The headache is often preceded by a variety of warnings. Days or hours before its onset there may be a change of mood (usually elation), or an alteration in behaviour, in wakefulness, appetite, bowel activity, or fluid balance. In 'common migraine' these are the only warnings but in 10 to 15 per cent of patients (those who suffer 'classic migraine') the headache is immediately preceded by disturbances of sensation. These disturbances are usually visual in character, taking the form of flashing coloured lights, zigzag lines, or distortions of visual perception, with or without areas of blind-ness that begin near the centre of gaze or at the periphery, and then move, usually expanding in size. Less commonly sensations of tingling or numbness occur, usually on one side of the body, particularly in the arm, and even less frequently there can be disturbances of speech and language. In rare forms of migraine other focal neurological deficits may precede the headache: for example, when vertigo, slurred speech, and unsteadiness of gait suggest brain-stem dysfunction ('vertebro-basilar migraine'), when there is dysfunction of the nerves that control eye movements ('ophthalmo-plegic migraine'), or when there is a unilateral weakness of the limbs (familial 'hemiplegic migraine').

The disturbances, sensory or otherwise, usually last for 20–30 minutes and are followed by a head-ache which, although often unilateral, may involve both sides of the head, and which is often severe and pulsating in character. When both the sensory disturbances and the pain are unilateral they can involve the same or opposite sides of the body. The pain is often accompanied by nausea (occasionally leading to vomiting) and by an aversion to light and noise. Recovery is almost invariably complete within hours, but can take days. Very rarely an acute attack may result in a permanent neuro-logical disturbance, for example a defect of vision.

Attacks can be precipitated in a number of ways. Perhaps the most common cause is *stress of a non-specific kind, as in the case of loss of sleep or overwork, and in some people attacks tend to occur in the period of relaxation that immediately follows the stress. There are many visual triggers, such as glare, flashing lights, and striped patterns. Attacks may also occur in relation to the menstrual cycle and sexual activity. In about 20 per cent of sufferers certain foods, especially chocolate, cheese, and citrous fruit, can precipitate attacks. The agents responsible may include biogenic amines and, when attacks are precipitated by red wine, complex phenols.

The origin and nature of the brain disorder are

not known with any certainty. Changes in cerebral blood-flow, alterations in *neurotransmitter levels, and electrophysiological disturbances found before, during, and after attacks have led to a variety of hypotheses. The fact that attacks are often precipitated by a strong sensory input suggests that a neurological disturbance leads to the development of the attack (and the role of non-specific stress would be consistent with such a viewpoint). The onset and progression of visual disturbances in classical migraine suggest the propagation of a wave through the visual cortex of the brain, at a velocity of 3mm/min with abnormal excitation at the front of the wave, followed by a depression of activity. It is not clear whether this neurological dysfunction is due to a progressive loss of cortical blood supply or to a disturbance of the neurochemical composition of the environment that surrounds nerve-cells (as in the spreading depression of Leao). (For a description of brain structure and how the nervous system functions, see NERVOUS SYSTEM.) These two alternatives are not mutually exclusive, but any possible relationship between them is unclear. Specific changes in neurotransmitters have been found during migraine attacks, particularly with regard to serotonin (5-hydroxytryptamine), a vasoactive monoamine. Although these changes relate mainly to reduced levels in circulating plasma, it has been suggested that there is also depletion within the brain, which is of interest in view of the role of serotonin-producing neurones in the perception of pain. Nevertheless it goes without saying that many other neurotransmitters (known and as yet unknown) are undoubtedly involved.

The mechanisms of pain in migraine may involve dilatation of the meningeal and scalp blood vessels, which are known to be pain-sensitive. This dilatation is associated with a sterile inflammatory response in and around the vessels and with the release of a number of pain-producing substances such as the neurokinines. There are persistent abnormalities in the pulse of scalp arteries in between attacks of unilateral pain on the affected side.

Treatment of migraine is twofold: medication for relief of the acute attack and, for those individuals who suffer frequent attacks, daily treatment to prevent their occurrence. The pain of an acute attack can be reduced by common analgesics or paracetamol, and the nausea by metoclopramide. In addition, it has been common in the past to use the ergot alkaloid derivatives (e.g. ergotamine) which cause constriction of blood vessels and may alleviate pain for this reason. Frequent attacks can be prevented with a variety of drugs, some of which antagonize serotonin (among other neurotransmitters). These drugs include methylsergide, pizotifen, amitriptyline, and propanolol. Relaxation therapy and *biofeedback may have a role in treatment and claims have been made that the herb feverfew may help prevent attacks.                                          C. K.
                                                        A. J. W.

Peatfield, R. (1986). *Headache*. Berlin.
Olesen, J. (1985). Migraine and regional cerebral blood flow. *Trends in Neurosciences*, **8**, 318–21.
Pearce, J. M. S. (1984). Migraine: a cerebral disorder. *Lancet*, **II**, 86–9.

**MILITARY INCOMPETENCE.** An apparently inescapable feature of human progress is the toll in lives and money that occurs through our imperfect management of the institutions and technologies which we develop. The histories of railways, flying, bridge-building, communications, and political institutions, to name but a few of man's inventions, are replete with examples of costly disasters and harrowing chapters of human misery—part of the price for growing complexity. If an increasing ability to wage war—to kill more people at a greater distance more quickly—can be considered as a manifestation of human progress, then we have here what is probably the best and certainly the most expensive illustration of this principle. Judging from the recent spate of books that have been devoted to martial mishaps, the military case is also probably the most interesting, for three reasons.

First, despite the fact that the professionalizing of human intraspecific aggression has a longer history than most other human enterprises, the record of incompetence in this sphere is far the worst. As T. E. Lawrence said in criticism of British military endeavour, 'With 2,000 years of examples behind us we have no excuse when fighting for not fighting well.' Secondly, an explanation of the psychological causes of faulty generalship is usually in terms of a single factor—stupidity. (In the writer's opinion this so-called 'bloody fool' theory of military incompetence reflects no more than a natural preference for simple explanations of what are in fact very complex phenomena. If the phenomena are unpleasant and the simple explanation abusive then so much the better.) Thirdly, a feature of military incompetence which, incidentally, belies the 'bloody fool' theory is the recurrent and relatively unchanging pattern of military ineptitude.

If incompetent generalship resulted from stupidity (i.e. low intelligence) then we might expect to find the history of war revealing a random miscellany of errors. This is not the case. Indeed, it is just because military incompetence constitutes a syndrome that it is necessary to seek an alternative theory of underlying causation.

As a first attempt towards providing a viable theory, a study was made of military disasters occurring between the 'imbecilic' Walcheren expedition of 1809 and the Vietnam war. They included the retreat from Kabul in the first Afghan war; episodes in the Crimean war; the Franco-Prussian war, the Indian mutiny and Boer wars; the siege of Kut, Verdun, and the third battle of Ypres in the First World War; the events leading up to Dunkirk, the attack on Pearl Harbor, the losses of Tobruk and Singapore, and the abortive attempt to capture the road bridge at Arnhem in the Second World War; the siege of Dien Bien Phu and the Tet offensive in the Indo-China and Vietnam wars; and the Bay of Pigs fiasco. While all these episodes share the distinction of being classed as costly military disasters, the question arises as to whether they reveal a common pattern of errors. The following summary of frequently recurring factors suggests that they do:

1. A serious wastage of human resources and failure to observe one of the first principles of war—economy of force. This failure derives in part from an inability to make war swiftly. It also derives from certain attitudes of mind which we shall consider presently.

2. A fundamental conservatism and clinging to outworn tradition, with an inability to profit from past experience (owing in part to a refusal to admit past mistakes). This also involves a failure to use, or a tendency to misuse, available technology.

3. A tendency to reject or ignore information which is unpalatable or which conflicts with preconceptions.

4. A tendency to underestimate the enemy and overestimate the capabilities of one's own side.

5. Indecisiveness and a tendency to abdicate from the role of decision-maker.

6. An obstinate persistence in a given task despite strong contrary evidence.

7. A failure to exploit a situation gained and a tendency to 'pull punches' rather than push home an attack.

8. A failure to make adequate reconnaissance.

9. A predilection for frontal assaults, often against the enemy's strongest point.

10. A belief in brute force rather than the clever ruse.

11. A failure to make use of surprise or deception.

12. An undue readiness to find scapegoats for military set-backs.

13. A suppression or distortion of news from the front, usually rationalized as necessary for morale or security.

14. A belief in mystical forces—fate, bad luck, etc.

Contemplation of these 'symptoms' suggests that, far from being a product of ordinary stupidity, military incompetence stems from complex interactions between three things—the hazards of professionalizing violence, the nature of military organizations, and the personalities of some of those who are attracted to, and then for a time prosper in, a military career.

The theory which attempts to outline and explain these interactions starts from the premiss that in professionalizing violence man set himself the task of legitimizing and then controlling patterns of behaviour which are normally taboo in a civilized society. To achieve this difficult contortion there gradually evolved that system of rules, conventions, incentives, and punishments which constitutes militarism, a subculture of controls and constraints which may be likened to those precautionary measures adopted by any imaginative explosives expert to ensure that his particular stock-in-trade goes off only when and where he wants it to. Now, since many of the components of militarism bear more than a superficial resemblance to those personal defences which some people erect against their own anxieties and aggressive impulses, it is hardly surprising that a minority of men are attracted to joining organizations which not only provide legitimate outlets for controlled aggression but also have perfected an elaborate set of rules for maintaining order and discipline within their ranks. On the one hand, as I. L. Janis remarks, 'The military group provides powerful incentives for releasing forbidden impulses, inducing the soldier to try out formerly inhibited acts which he originally regarded as morally repugnant.' On the other hand, in so doing, militarism provides a therapeutic gain for some of its members. Thus, according to Robert Holt,

It was a common clinical observation during the war that military service was an unusually good environment for men who lacked inner controls. . . . The combination of absolute security, a strong institutional parent-substitute on which one could lean unobtrusively, and socially approved outlets for aggression provided a form of social control that allowed impulses to be expressed in acceptable ways.

Some confirmation of this relationship between personality and liking of a military career has been forthcoming from those recent researches which have found a relationship between authoritarianism and liking of a military ideology. When it is considered that authoritarianism, as measured by the Californian F (Fascist) scale, correlates positively with rigidity and the possession of obsessive traits, a personality type emerges which is remarkably similar to traditional descriptions of the military mind. (The F scale measures anti-Semitism, ethnocentrism, political and economic conservatism, and implicit anti-democratic trends or potentiality for Fascism.) In its most extreme form such a person would be conventional, conforming, rigid, and possessed of a closed mind. He would also be one who is orderly, obstinate, and unimaginative. Finally he would be the sort of individual who believes in force and toughness, is lacking in compassion, and is prone to stereotype out groups (i.e. the enemy) as less gifted than himself. Obviously there are, among this miscellany of characteristics, traits which are no handicap to those seeking advancement in their military career. Such a person would do well because in many ways he fitted in so well.

Unfortunately, however, those very traits which would facilitate his promotion up the military hierarchy are not conducive to competence at the highest levels. Being inflexible and unimaginative, predisposed to 'bull', excessively obedient and having a mind closed to unpalatable information, conservative and conformist, are not the characteristics for handling, let alone fathoming, the great uncertainties of war. Needless to say, attempts at applying this theory of incompetence to actual military disasters and particular military commanders encountered the difficulty that we have no personality measures of the characters concerned. However, a comparison between the best and the worst of military commanders, in terms of their military performance and what is known of their personalities and childhood, strongly suggests that failure of leadership and decision-making are due less to stupidity than to the fact that militarism attracts a proportion of people whose personalities are ill suited to warring behaviour.

See also MILITARY MIND.                    N. F. D.

Dixon, N. F. (1976). *On the Psychology of Military Incompetence*. London.
Holt, R. R. (1971). *Assessing Personality*. New York.
Janis, I. L. (1963). Group Identification under Conditions of External Danger. *British Journal of Medical Psychology*, **36**, 227–38.

**MILITARY MIND.** Consideration of whether human beings as a species have an innate tendency towards aggression among themselves has generated a massive literature and negligible evidence: the question remains completely open. Whatever the answer, it is certain that few people lack the qualities required to make at least an adequate member of an armed force: during the wars of the last hundred years, tens of millions of men, and many millions of women, have been taken into the forces of many nations; and very few—for good reasons or bad—have proved wholly unsuitable. Thus virtually any mind is more or less 'military' on the lower level; and consequently, when discussing the 'military mind' *per se*, it is usual to refer to the qualities needed for, or associated with, high command.

Any serious examination of the commanders of history (see, for example, Windrow and Mason, 1975) reveals at once that the range of character and personality, even among the successful, is very wide; and this is the case even if we look only at those traits loosely called 'aggression' in individuals: the humane Wellington, the callous Bonaparte, and the sadistic Chingis (Genghis Khan) immediately spring to mind. Can either history or modern experimental studies cast any light, then, on the main qualities of the military mind?

Every successful commander—every great commander, even more—has had to take decisions of grave consequence upon partial and more or less uncertain information, in circumstances of great psychological pressure and often of great physical danger. Small wonder, then, that Wavell (1941) considered '. . . the first essential of a general [to be the possession of] the quality of robustness, the ability to withstand the shocks of war . . . a high margin over the normal breaking strain'. High intelligence, professional competence, and imagination are naturally desirable; but those who sneer at the failure of commanders to grasp *at the*

*time* solutions which seem simple and obvious in the quiet of a study (see, for example, Dixon, 1976), should ever remind themselves of the circumstances in which the problems were faced. Very often, what was wanting when they failed was a sufficiently 'high margin over the normal breaking strain'.

In modern times all major armed forces have attempted to set up rational selection and training procedures for potential commanders, but difficulties stem from the fact that much has to depend on theory. Whereas the young doctor or engineer can practise under guidance on real patients or bridges, the young officer cannot train in real battle. The solutions adopted differ in detail from one nation to another.

Validation presents considerable problems (Reeve, 1972), but that used by the British army appears to be at least as successful as any. Psychological tests are used first in the process of elimination: for example, with the prospect of combat there is good theoretical reason for rejecting candidates who appear introverted (Corcoran, 1965). Then there is an ingenious technique invented by Major R. Bion and known as the 'Leaderless Group Test' (Bidwell, 1973, esp. ch. 8). Candidates are randomly assigned to groups of about ten, and a fairly difficult practical task, whose solution is not obvious and which requires co-operation within the group, is set ostensibly as a test for the group as a whole. No instructions are given, and no leader appointed: the testing officers simply stand and watch. It is set in as reasonably stressful a situation as can readily be set up, and no importance at all is attached to whether or not the group actually succeeds: the real object is to observe how the several members respond to the situation—who can co-operate, who can induce co-operation, who 'puts people's backs up', and who simply follows along. Such tests select those who become junior officers.

At a later stage, after some years of experience with their units, officers are given training for higher command at staff college or equivalent institution. The techniques now generally known as 'management gaming' were invented for this purpose and are intensively used. Trainees are placed in groups of eight to ten, known as 'syndicates'. Sometimes these are 'leaderless groups', as described above, and sometimes roles (such as C.-in-C., divisional commanders, and so on) are allotted to the members. The syndicates tackle a succession of exercises based on carefully prepared (and often very entertaining) 'scenarios' produced by the directing staff. In British staff training there are no predetermined 'best solutions' to these exercises—as there are, for example, in both the American and Russian equivalents; instead, the general virtues of simplicity and flexibility are sought. Solutions produced by syndicates or by individuals within them are subject to thorough and uninhibited criticism by both teaching staff and peers.

As with the selection of junior officers, this training for the higher ranks involves a considerable degree of pressure and stress. Not only are the problems faced difficult in themselves, and to be solved in limited time; but those taking part know that their careers are at stake, and that every word they write or utter is likely to be 'shot down' by rivals or tutors. It is thus a selective as well as an instructive mechanism, and, as far as can be discerned, a highly successful one. The students emerge not only with the vast amount of procedural knowledge that any modern officer needs but also with practical experience of solving difficult command problems under harassing conditions. They gain experience, too, in leading teams of equals without being able to rely upon the formal compulsions of military discipline.

Thus, by the time an officer is appointed to senior command he has passed through, first, a rigorous and well-validated selection procedure, and, second, a rigorous and highly competitive 'higher education' in his profession. There is thereby as much certainty that he possesses the necessary abilities and skills and as much evidence that he possesses the 'quality of robustness' under stress as can reasonably be obtained. Since the 'mind' of any profession requires a combination of general ability, special skills, and particular aptitudes, it seems difficult, in the present 'state of the art' to go much further than this.

See also MILITARY INCOMPETENCE.　　　M. H.

Bidwell, R. G. S. (1973). *Modern Warfare*. London.
Corcoran, D. W. J. (1965). Personality and the Inverted-U Relation. *British Journal of Psychology*, **56**, 267–73.
Dixon, N. (1976). *On The Psychology of Military Incompetence*. London.
Reeve, E. G. (1972). *Validation of Selection Boards*. London.
Wavell, A. (1941). *Generals and Generalship*. Harmondsworth.
Windrow, M. and Mason, F. K. (1975). *A Concise Dictionary of Military Biography*. London.

**MILL, JAMES** (1773–1836), British writer and political economist, born near Forfar, Scotland, and educated for the ministry at Edinburgh. In 1802 he moved to London to start a literary career, editing and writing for various periodicals. He also worked for the East India Company after writing a *History of British India* (1818). Having written *Elements of Political Economy* (1821–2) he produced *Analysis of the Phenomena of the Human Mind* in 1829 and *A Fragment on Mackintosh* (1835).

He was closely associated with Jeremy *Bentham and was one of the founders of utilitarianism. His remarkable personality is recorded with rare insight by his son, John Stuart *Mill, in his *Autobiography* (1873).

**MILL, JOHN STUART** (1806–73). British philosopher and political economist, born in London, the son of James *Mill. He was brought up by his father to be a genius—which indeed he became—being taught Greek at the age of 3, Latin and arithmetic at 8, logic at 12, and political economy at 13. His only recreation was a daily walk with his father; and during this he was given oral examinations. Perhaps not surprisingly he suffered a severe mental crisis, but he recovered to become one of the outstanding intellects of his generation. In his *System of Logic* (1843) he provided, among other things, a systematic account of inductive reasoning (see INDUCTION, and, for Mill's predecessors on this matter, ARISTOTLE and BACON, FRANCIS).

Mill also wrote extensively on political economy, and morals and ethics, developing his father's and Jeremy *Bentham's utilitarianism. His essays on *Representative Government* and *Utilitarianism* both appeared in 1861. He disagrees with the earlier authors by admitting qualitative differences between pleasures, and so raising doubts as to whether pleasure can be equated with right action. In his *On Liberty* (1859) he provides a famous principle (the 'harm' principle) which severely limits the extent to which individuals may be coerced by government. He was an early supporter of liberal campaigns for women's suffrage, and his *The Subjection of Women* (1869) provoked antagonism at the time, but heralded equality.

**MIND AND BODY.** Until quite recently most philosophers have held a *dualistic view of the relation between mind and body. This dualism has, however, taken several different forms. There have been those, like *Descartes, who ascribe mental attributes to spiritual substances which are supposed to be logically independent of anything physical but to inhabit particular bodies in a way which it has not proved easy to define. Others, like *Hobbes, have admitted only a duality of properties, ascribing both mental and physical attributes to human bodies. Others again have recognized an ultimate category of persons, differentiating them from physical objects just on the ground that they possess mental as well as physical attributes. Exactly what constitutes a mental attribute is itself not easy to define, but it can perhaps be sufficiently illustrated by examples, which may be chosen so as to cover the different varieties of sensation, perception, imagination, feeling, and thought.

For the most part, those who have subscribed to one or other form of dualism have also held that there is causal interaction between mental and physical events. The main opposition to this view has come from those who conceive of the physical world as a closed system, in the sense that every physical event must be explicable in purely physical terms, if it is explicable at all. If they also accept the existence of irreducibly mental occurrences, they regard them as accompanying and perhaps being causally dependent on physical events, but as not themselves making any causal intrusion into the physical world.

This refusal to admit psychophysical interaction does not seem justified, especially if one takes a *Humean view of causation as consisting basically in nothing more than regular concomitance. Even if there were a physical explanation for every physical event, this would not preclude there being alternative forms of explanation which relied at least in part on mental factors. It is, however, unlikely that such psychophysical correlations would be nearly so stringent as the laws of physics, and the same would apply to any generalizations that were couched in purely mental terms.

The difference in the type of causal laws to which they are subject is one of the ways in which mental and physical events are distinguished in the theory of neutral monism, which was advanced by William *James and subsequently by Bertrand *Russell. According to this theory, the elements of our experience consisted of actual or possible sense-data out of which the physical world was supposed to be constructible. These elements were also regarded as entering into the constitution of minds so that one and the same sense-datum might as a member of one group be a constituent of some physical object and as a member of another group be a constituent of a mind in whose biography a perception of the object occurred. Apart from the fact that there were also images and feelings, which entered only into the constitution of minds, the difference between mind and matter was represented not as a difference of substance, or content, but as a difference in the arrangement of common elements, involving their participation in different forms of causality. This was in many ways an attractive theory, but it met with serious difficulties. Though there may be a sense in which physical objects can be generated out of the immediate data of perception, an outright reduction of one to the other seems not to be feasible. Neither did the exponents of the theory succeed in giving a satisfactory account of *personal identity or of the special relation in which the elements that make up a person's mind stand to the particular physical object which is that person's body.

Similar difficulties beset the attempt made by *Berkeley to eliminate matter in favour of mind, by representing physical objects as collections of sensible qualities, which he termed ideas. In Berkeley's case, the want of a criterion of personal identity is especially flagrant, since he followed Descartes in treating minds as spiritual substances. It is, indeed, one of the principal objections to this view of the mind that it is incapable of furnishing any such criterion.

In recent times, monistic theories have mainly taken the other direction. They have gone beyond the older forms of materialism in that they not only ascribe mental attributes to certain physical objects, but also treat these attributes themselves as physical. The strongest theory of this type is that in which it is maintained that propositions which would ordinarily be construed as referring to mental states or processes are logically equivalent to propositions which refer only to people's overt behaviour. This theory may be allied to a verificational theory of meaning. Since the only way in which we can test the truth of the propositions in which we attribute experiences to others is through observation of the ways in which these other persons behave, it is deduced that this is all that such propositions can legitimately be taken to refer to. Then, since it can be shown that one cannot consistently combine a behaviouristic treatment of propositions about the experiences of others with a mentalistic treatment of propositions about one's own experiences, the conclusion is drawn that all references to one's own experiences are to be construed behaviouristically, even when they are made by oneself.

This argument can, however, be turned on its head. One can start with the premiss that the knowledge which one has of one's own experiences cannot be fully set out in any series of propositions which refer only to one's overt behaviour and then use the fact that the analysis of propositions about a person's experiences must be the same, whoever asserts them, as a ground for rejecting a purely behavioural account of propositions which refer to the experiences of others. And, indeed, unless one is prepared to feign anaesthesia, it would seem undeniable that this premiss is true. The advocates of logical behaviourism were indeed able to show that references to behaviour are often comprised in the use of what are classified as mentalistic terms. They were even justified in claiming that intelligent thought and action do not necessarily require the occurrence of inner processes. Nevertheless we do very often have thoughts that we keep to ourselves, and the existence of such thoughts cannot be logically equated with any disposition to report them. Neither, on the face of it, is there any logical equivalence between a person's having such and such sensations or perceptions and his dispositions to engage in any form of overt action.

In recent years logical behaviourism has given way to the less radical theory in which mental occurrences are held to be not logically but only factually identical with states of the central nervous system. On this view, for a person to have such and such an experience *is* for his brain to be in such and such a state, in the way in which lightning *is* an electrical discharge or temperature *is* the mean kinetic energy of molecules. As in those other cases, the suggested identity is supposed to be established not through the analysis of concepts but on the basis of empirical research. It rests on the assumption that there is a perfect correlation between a person's experiences and events which take place in his brain. In fact, this assumption goes further than the evidence yet warrants. There is, indeed, very strong evidence of a general dependence of mental occurrences on the functioning of the brain, but it has still to be shown that the correspondence is so exact that from observation of a person's brain one could arrive at a knowledge of his experiences in every detail.

Even if we make this assumption, it is not clear that it justifies the postulation of identity. If events which appear from their descriptions to belong to different categories are capable of being empirically correlated, the implication is rather that they are distinct. It is only on the basis of some theory that we can proceed to identify them. In this case the theory seems to be linguistic. It is thought that a general acceptance of the hypothesis that mental events are causally dependent upon events in the brain will lead to the denial of their separate existence. It has even been suggested that the use of psychological terms will be given up altogether.

This does not seem probable. Even if we were aware of what was going on in people's central nervous systems, it is unlikely that we should cease to find a use for explaining their behaviour in terms of their conscious thoughts and feelings. Nor is it likely, in a case in which an inference drawn from one's physical condition conflicted with one's awareness of one's own experience, that one should not continue to treat this awareness as the better authority.

If we have to adhere to dualism, the most defensible form of it would seem to be that in which we admit only a duality of properties. Unhappily, the problem of showing how these predicates combine to characterize one and the same subject has not yet been adequately solved.

See also MIND–BODY PROBLEM: PHILOSOPHICAL THEORIES.                                        A. J. A.

## MIND AND BRAIN: LURIA'S PHILOSOPHY.
The relation between brain and mind has been for many centuries one of the most difficult problems, both of philosophy and of science. Two approaches to the problem have been proposed—and both have failed.

The first was a mentalistic, the second a naturalistic approach.

For many centuries philosophers and other scholars supposed that the brain was a *detector* of mind, which itself was seen as an inner, subjective state of *consciousness. It was supposed that mind was a primary quality of the inner life whereas all external experience could be thought of as a secondary kind, consciousness of self being treated as the immediate existence of the soul. According to this spiritual approach, the brain was merely a device connecting a man's existence with his inner subjective experience, or—as some other scholars thought—with the objective spiritual reality. This theory—now out of date, it seems—persisted in some modern studies: Sir Charles *Sherrington and Sir John Eccles postulated brain units as special kinds of detectors of the spiritual life. It is easy to see, however, that such a theory was not amenable to proof.

The second approach was of a naturalistic kind. Brain was supposed to be the highest product of the natural history of evolution, during which special forms of apparatus of great complexity emerged, resulting in the appearance of internal sensations, memory, and—last but not least—a series of associations that gave rise to the appearance of the most complicated forms of subjective experience.

So, it was supposed, very specific groups of nerve cells (neurones) existed, each having some special function, each serving a special purpose to evoke sensations, images, ideas, motives, and voluntary actions. The hope of this group of scholars was to find *special* mechanisms serving to create *special* mental states.

Unfortunately this is not the case: the oversimplified naturalistic hypothesis of cerebral units creating complex subjective images could no more be verified than could the over-simplified mentalistic hypotheses—and all attempts to postulate that sensations, or images, or ideas, could be found in single units of the brain were as unrealistic as trying to find an image inside a mirror or behind it. They originated in archaic notions of mental functions as elementary, primary properties or 'capacities' of the brain. Whereas two or three centuries ago it seemed obvious that sensations and images, thoughts and voluntary impulses, were kinds of 'capacities', or immediate functions of specific brain organs—thinking of the brain as a system of specialized 'micro-organs'—such a concept is no longer acceptable. It is better to suppose that mental processes are complex information-processing activities, reflecting reality. Instead, mind is now considered to be a product of active processing of the flow of information working through elementary drives, or complex motives, set to single out important information about reality, relating bits of information and synthesizing them, and constructing plans and programmes of behaviour, which are expressed through speech.

In other words it is implausible to think of the brain as a 'generator of mind'. Quite a different approach to the brain–mind problem is needed. The human brain can be supposed to be a complex working system which consists of different functional blocks or units, every one of which plays a part in reflecting the external world, in complex information-processing, in establishing plans and programmes of behaviour, and in conscious control of actions.

It is now known that the deep structures of the brain (the higher brain-stem, the old cortex of the *limbic system) have a decisive role in the active state of the cerebral cortex. When this functional system is deranged the activity of the cortex is reduced. A dreamy state is observed, selectivity of the cortical processes is no longer possible, and the first and most important condition for the normal working of the brain—its vigilance—breaks down.

A second functional system, associated with the posterior parts of the cerebral hemispheres, can be considered as the system receiving, preserving, and elaborating information the brain accepts from the external world. This system consists of a series of highly specialized ('modality-specific') units: the occipital lobes dealing with visual, the temporal lobes with acoustic, and the post-central lobes with cutaneous information-processing. Each of these parts of the cortex has a clearly organized hierarchical structure. The primary parts are believed to be central receptor devices consisting of highly specialized neurones, which are activated by particular signals (for example, in the primary visual cortex some neurones react to lines of specific orientation, others react to specifically oriented movement in certain directions, and so on). The combination of single excitations, with the creation of complex patterns reflecting complex features of images, only becomes possible by transition to the secondary parts. Transition to the tertiary parts (which are seen only in the human brain) allows the separate, modality-specific areas of the cortex to work together; a co-operative functioning of different modalities is provided, and successive series of excitations are reorganized into simultaneous spatial (or quasi-spatial) schemes.

A third functional system includes the anterior parts of the human brain—the frontal and prefrontal areas, which are responsible for the retention of stable motives, the establishing of complex plans and programmes of actions, and control of their execution. It is the pinnacle of cerebral organization: when it is deranged, elementary forms of activity can be preserved but there are no stable motives, no goal-directed plans or programmes can be executed, and no higher forms of action control, including language, are possible.

Thus the co-operative working of the different systems of the brain supplies humans with information-processing, provides active and plastic adaptation to the immediate environment, and links human conduct to particular goals. It is a complex of functional systems, organized according to plans and programmes created by man's social history. As an alternative to both mentalistic and naturalistic theories, such a concept provides a significant step towards analysis of the intimate mechanisms of the brain as an organ of mind.          A. R. L.

Luria, A. R. (1966). *Higher Cortical Functions in Man*. New York.

Luria, A. R. (1972). *The Working Brain*. New York

Luria, A. R. (1976). *Basic Problems of Neurolinguistics*. The Hague.

Magoun, M. H. (1963). *The Waking Brain*. Springfield, Illinois.

Walter, W. G. (1953). *The Living Brain*. New York.

Young, J. Z. (1978). *Programs of the Brain*. Oxford.

## MIND–BODY PROBLEM: PHILOSOPHICAL THEORIES.

Classifications of theories are bad masters, but may be useful servants. In the following classification of the main theories of the mind–body relationship upheld by philosophers, it is to be understood that the positions sketched are 'ideal types' to which actually held positions may approximate in different degrees.

If we think of mind and body as two opponents in a tug-of-war, then we can distinguish between theories which try to drag body, and matter generally, over into the camp of mind; those which try to drag mind over into the camp of body; and those theories where an equal balance is maintained. This yields a division into mentalist, materialist (physicalist), and dualist theories.

It is convenient to begin by considering *dualism. The major position here is *Cartesian dualism*, named after *Descartes, the central figure in post-medieval philosophical discussion of the mind–body problem. For a Cartesian dualist the mind and body are both substances; but while the body is an extended, and so a material, substance, the mind is an unextended, or spiritual, substance, subject to completely different principles of operation from the body. It was this doctrine that Gilbert *Ryle caricatured as the myth of the ghost in the machine. It is in fact a serious and important theory.

Dualist theories are also to be found in a more sceptical form, which may be called *bundle dualism*. The word 'bundle' springs from David *Hume's insistence that when he turned his mental gaze upon his own mind, he could discern no unitary substance but simply a 'bundle of perceptions', a succession or stream of individual mental items or happenings. Hume thought of these items as non-physical. A bundle dualist is one who dissolves the mind in this general way, while leaving the body and other material things intact.

Besides dividing dualism into Cartesian and bundle theories, it may also be divided according to a different principle. *Interactionist* theories hold, what common sense asserts, that the body can act upon the mind and the mind can act upon the body. For *parallelist* theories, however, mind and body are incapable of acting upon each other. Their processes run parallel, like two synchronized clocks, but neither influences the other. There is an intermediate view according to which, although the body (in particular, the brain) acts upon and controls the mind, the mind is completely impotent to affect the body. This intermediate view, especially when combined with a bundle theory of mind, is the doctrine of *epiphenomenalism*. It allows the neurophysiologist, in particular, to recognize the independent reality of the mental, yet acknowledge the controlling role of the brain in our mental life and give a completely physicalist account of the brain and the factors which act upon it.

Mentalist theories arise naturally out of dualist theories, particularly where the dualist position is combined with Descartes's own view that the mind is more immediately and certainly known than anything material. If this view is taken, as it was by many of the greatest philosophers who succeeded Descartes, it is natural to begin by becoming sceptical of the existence of material things. The problem that this raises was then usually solved by readmitting the material world in a dematerialized or mentalized form. *Berkeley, for instance, solved the sceptical problem by reducing material things to our sensations 'of' them. Berkeley thus reaches a mentalism where the mind is conceived of as a spiritual substance, but bodies are reduced to sensations of these minds.

It is possible to combine Berkeley's reduction of matter to sensations with a bundle account of the mind. In this way is reached the doctrine of *neutral monism*, according to which mind and matter are simply different ways of organizing and marking off overlapping bundles of the same constituents. This view is to be found in Ernst *Mach, William *James, and was adopted at one stage by Bertrand *Russell. The 'neutral' constituents of mind and body are, however, only dubiously neutral, and the theory is best classified as a form of mentalism.

Just as Cartesian dualism may move towards mentalism, so it may also move towards materialism. Surprisingly, Descartes's own particular form of the theory lends itself to this development also. Descartes was one of the pioneers in arguing for an anti-Aristotelian view of the material world generally and the body in particular. First, this involved the rejection of all teleological principles of explanation in the non-mental sphere. Second, it involved taking the then revolutionary, now scientifically orthodox, view that organic nature involves no principles of operation that are not already to be found operative in non-organic nature. Human and animal bodies are simply machines (today we might say physico-chemical mechanisms) working according to physical principles.

A view of this sort naturally leads on to the suggestion that it may be possible to give an account of the mind also along the same principles. In this way, a completely materialist account of nature is reached, and so a materialist account of the mind.

The word 'materialism' sometimes misleads. The materialist is not committed to a Newtonian 'billiard-ball' account of matter. Keith Campbell has spoken of the 'relativity of materialism'—its relativity to the physics of the day. Materialism is best interpreted as the doctrine that the fundamental laws and principles of nature are exhausted by the laws and principles of physics, however 'unmaterialistic' the latter laws and principles may be. Instead of speaking of 'materialism' some writers use the term 'physicalism'.

Materialist accounts of the mind may be subdivided into *peripheralist* and *centralist* views. A more familiar name for the peripheralist view is *behaviourism*: the view that possession of a mind is constituted by nothing more than the engaging in of especially sophisticated types of overt behaviour, or being disposed to engage in such behaviour in suitable circumstances. Behaviourism as a philosophical doctrine must be distinguished from the mere methodological behaviourism of many psychologists who do not wish to base scientific findings upon introspective reports of processes that are not publicly observable.

Very much more fashionable at the present time among philosophers inclined to materialism is the centralist view, which identifies mental processes with purely physical processes in the central nervous system. This view is sometimes called *central-state materialism* or, even more frequently, the *identity* view. Unlike behaviourism, it allows the existence of 'inner' mental processes which interact causally with the rest of the body.

It remains to call attention to one important variety of theory intermediate between orthodox dualism and orthodox materialism. It is a 'one-substance' view, denying that minds are things or collections of things set over against the material substance which is the brain. But it does involve a dualism of properties, because brain processes, besides their physical properties, are conceived of as having further non-physical properties which are supposed to make the brain processes into *mental* processes. Such views may be called *attribute* or *dual-attribute* theories of the mind–body relationship. A theory of this sort could be said to be a variety of identity view, since it also holds that mental processes are identical with certain brain processes.

According to the doctrine of *panpsychism*, not simply brain processes but all physical things have a mental side, aspect, or properties, even if in a primitive and undeveloped form.

Although the dual-attribute view is important, it inherits the considerable difficulty and confusion which surrounds the philosophical theory of properties. There are many difficulties in giving a satisfactory account of what it is for a thing to have a property, and these difficulties transmit themselves to this sort of theory of the mind–body relationship.                                   D. M. A.

Armstrong, D. M. (1968). *A Materialist Theory of the Mind*, ch. 1. London.
Broad, C. D. (1925). *The Mind and its Place in Nature*, chs. 1–3. London.
Campbell, K. K. (1970). *Body and Mind*. London.

**MIRROR REVERSAL.** It is surprising how few people can give an intelligible answer to the question: 'Why are mirror images reversed sideways, but not up and down?' Even physicists, and experts in visual *perception, can be shaken by this apparently simple question, and find no ready answer; though 'mirror writing', and lateral reversal of objects—including oneself—seen in mirrors is an everyday experience.

This is best seen with writing. For example, ⅄⅂Oƃ⅁ꓕↃ is quite difficult to read. It is inverted laterally—as in a mirror. Vertical inversion is: ꓱ⅂ꓱꓭOⅼ⅄. Double inversion looks like this: ꓥ⅂ꓭꓱↄⅼ꓌.

Distinguishing left from right has been held, especially by *Kant, to depend upon an observer, and not to be a physical distinction of the world. Kant uses this as evidence for his mental categories of knowledge (*Prolegomena to any future Metaphysics*, 1783).

The mirror reflects top as top, bottom as bottom, right as right, and left as left: the mirror does not reverse right to left or up to down. All this is entirely symmetrical, so where does the asymmetry come from? That there is no asymmetry of the mirror round the line of sight may be demonstrated by rotating the mirror (or rotating it in imagination) in its plane. Clearly it is optically the same for any angle of rotation: there is no asymmetry here. To explain horizontal but not vertical reversal with optical ray diagrams is doomed to failure, for they cannot distinguish horizontal from vertical, as they are symmetrical and equally valid when held in any orientation.

Is the asymmetry of 'mirror reversal' related to the fact that we have a pair of horizontally separated eyes? This is sometimes suggested; but close one eye, and the 'reversal' is unchanged. Consider also a man born blind in one eye: would he not suffer 'mirror reversal' as we do? Yes, he does. The reversals (both upside-down and right–left) of the *retinal image by the optics of the eye cannot be relevant either; for this would affect *all* vision. (The inversion produced by the eye's image-forming optics is of no consequence, for the retinal image is not seen by the brain as a picture by some internal eye. Provided its (doubly inverted) relation of external objects remains unchanged, the inversions have no effect, and do not present any special difficulty for babies during perceptual learning. Experiments with inverting spectacles show that we can *adapt* to changed touch–vision relationships even when we are adult, which is remarkable, but this is not relevant here.)

It is sometimes said of 'mirror reversal' that it is 'merely verbal—how we *speak* of right and left' (Bennett, 1970). But 'mirror writing' is difficult to read: it *looks* very different from 'normal' writing. If the difference is difficult to express, it is present before we attempt to describe it; so it cannot be due to the way we use words, such as 'left' and 'right'.

If 'mirror reversal' is not in the mirror, not in the eyes, and not due to how we use words—can it be some *cognitive* perceptual effect? This kind of explanation has been put forward by recent writers (Gardner, 1964). It is suggested that since we appear behind the mirror, facing ourselves, we make a cognitive rotation—as a mental perceptual act—selecting rotation around the vertical axis because our bodies are nearly symmetrical left–right but not vertically, so this is the easier mental operation to perform. It is remarkable that this explanation appears to have gone unchallenged. If true, it would be of the greatest interest as a dramatic perceptual phenomenon, somehow specifically associated with mirrors. Mental *image rotation is possible, though it is slow and often inaccurate. It is very different from mirror rotation.

If mirror inversion were a cognitive rotation it would have to depend on knowledge that a mirror is involved. Suppose we hide from the observer the fact that he is looking in a mirror. He is shown a large, very clean, wall-to-wall mirror with no frame, so there is no information or knowledge that he is looking in a mirror—but the usual 'mirror reversal' still occurs. Consider, further, a photograph taken by reflection from a frameless mirror: the lateral 'reversal' still occurs in the photograph, and yet there is certainly no informa-

tion here that a mirror was involved. We may also consider introducing false information that there is a mirror when in fact there is not—a typical mirror frame but with no reflecting glass. Does the world reverse when we look through what *appears* to be a mirror but is not? There is no reversal. Since absence of knowledge that there is a mirror does not remove mirror reversal, and introduction of 'false' knowledge that there is a mirror when in fact there is no mirror does not produce it, we may rule out such cognitive explanations. What then is the answer?

It is remarkably easy to forget that the reflected object has to be rotated, to face the mirror, for us to see it in the mirror. Now we generally rotate objects, including ourselves, around a *vertical* axis. This produces the right–left reversal. The 'mirror reversal' is not in the mirror; or in the optics; or in ourselves as a cognitive reversal: it is the rotation of the object from our direct view of it, to face the mirror, which produces 'mirror rotation'. What is odd about mirrors is that they allow us to get a front view of objects though we are behind them. But for this, the object must be rotated from facing us to face the mirror. The reversal of the mirror image is right–left only when the object is rotated around a *vertical* axis. It is entirely possible (though often less convenient) to rotate objects around their *horizontal* axis. When, for example, a book is rotated around its horizontal axis to face a mirror, it appears upside-down, and not in 'mirror writing'.

If we stand on our head before a mirror, then we are upside-down and not right–left reversed. But this is a confusing case because, quite apart from mirrors, the world continues to look its normal way up though we are upside-down. Here there is indeed a perceptual phenomenon; but this is quite different from mirror reversal, though it may be confused with it. In the case of a room seen laterally inverted in a wall mirror, we see the room from the point of view of the mirror, though we stand opposite to it. The inversion occurs as we walk round the room and so rotate to face the mirror.

It is worth pointing out that if we place a transparent glass sheet with writing on it in front of a mirror, we see the writing on the front of the sheet, and its reflection from its back from the mirror, and they both look the same. This is because we have not had to rotate the transparent sheet for the writing to be reflected from the mirror, as we do have to rotate writing on opaque paper for it to be visible in the mirror. In all cases, it is *object* rotation that produces these mirror reversals in plane mirrors. Mirrors are not even required: the same considerations apply to lateral reversal of type in printing, as the paper is rotated when removed from the type—so type is made left–right reversed.

There is another kind of reversal of mirror images. We see objects *behind* the mirror though we are *in front* of it. This does have an immediate optical explanation; though this is not quite the whole story. Optically, the light path is from the object to the mirror and back to the eye, so we see reflected objects (and ourselves) according to the total length of the light path, which is always longer than the distance of the mirror from the eyes. So it is not surprising that we see objects *through* the mirror: except that we continue to see this though we know intellectually that the objects (and we ourselves) are in front of the mirror. So here our knowledge does not affect what we see. This is an interesting limitation of our cognition, which allows us to *see* ourselves through the mirror, as we are optically, though we *know* we are in front of it. Knowledge of the situation does not correct perception of where we are or which way round we are.

Although we see ourselves in a different place from where we know ourselves to be, we seldom mistake our image for that of another person. This appears not to be true for animals, other than the higher primates and human infants in their first year of life (Gallup, 1977). Almost all animals respond to their own images as to another individual of the same species. Gordon Gallup placed marks on one side of animals' faces, and did the same for infants, and found that even after lengthy experience with the mirror there was no tendency for the subjects to refer the mark to their own face. He suggests that this is an objective criterion for testing for awareness of self.

Somewhat similarly, tactile writing on the forehead may be read as from the *outside* or from the *inside*. It has been suggested that women tend to 'see' touch writing on their forehead from the point of view of an observer in front of them, while men generally 'see' the touch writing laterally inverted as though from inside their own head. Possibly this difference, if real, is because women spend rather more time concerned with their own faces and with how others see them while men look out.  R. L. G.

Bennett, J. (1970). The difference between right and left. *American Philosophical Quarterly*, 7, 3.

Gallup, G. G. (1977). Self-recognition in primates. *American Journal of Psychology*, 32, 329–38.

Gardner, M. (1964). *The Ambidextrous Universe*. Harmondsworth.

**MNEMONICS.** Consider the mnemonic sometimes given to a right-handed child who has difficulty in remembering which hand is called 'right' and which 'left'. 'When you write, you write with your right hand, and the hand that is left over is left.' The puns appropriately link the confused items of knowledge, and the whole is anchored to the act of writing, which the child can readily carry out or imagine (even if he or she can only draw!). The mnemonic organizes the information in a way the child can grasp, and provides a procedure for working out, when in doubt, which is 'right' and which 'left'.

In general terms, mnemonics are mental techniques aimed at helping us to learn and remember specific items of information. They provide

organization in terms of which we can more easily comprehend and remember information that has, as we say, little rhyme or reason for us. Mnemonics contrive meaning, sometimes of a quixotic sort, for information we find relatively meaningless and, because of this, they are sometimes called 'artificial memory'.

To illustrate further, consider the problem of remembering the number of days in each month of the year. A commonly used mnemonic runs, 'Thirty days hath September; April, June and November; all the rest have thirty-one; excepting February alone; which has twenty-eight days clear; and twenty-nine in each leap year.' This jingle helps by rearranging the information, categorizing it, compressing it, and introducing rhythm and rhyme. A less widely used mnemonic consists of counting each successive month on our knuckles. Long months fall on the knuckles, short months on the hollows between. Once more, organization makes the information easier to grasp and remember.

The mnemonics just mentioned achieve organizations which are relatively conventional and publicly comprehensible. But many mnemonics devised by individuals for private use achieve an idiosyncratic organization involving the person's unique background of experiences, visual imagery, and other features that are not readily communicable. Sir Donald Tovey, for example, was a highly accomplished musician who happened to assign a number to each location on the musical stave. When he wanted to memorize any telephone number, he translated each successive digit into the correspondingly numbered location on the stave, and remembered the resulting tune. Idiosyncratic mnemonics may work well for the individual concerned, but if he tries to explain them publicly they seem tortuous, arbitrary, and even laughable. They also imply that he cannot easily comprehend the information. Because of this, mnemonics are discussed less than they are used, and there is lack of systematic data on their uses and abuses in everyday life.

The most familiar mnemonics are *ad hoc*, opportunistic, and contrived by or for an individual who is having difficulty with some specific information. However, throughout history, mnemonic *systems* have been devised to provide standard, generalizable techniques for memorizing such things as random lists of words or historical dates. Each of these systems is paradoxical: it enables anyone who masters it to carry out impressive feats of memory, but of a kind that is rarely useful in everyday life. Such systems have been used mainly for entertainment, and their strengths and weaknesses are best illustrated by the Method of Loci.

The Method of Loci was known in classical Greece, described by Cicero in 55 BC, and discussed critically by Quintilian a century later. Used by stage performers into the present day, it has, in recent years, been studied experimentally by psychologists. It enables us to accomplish the kind of memory feat in which a randomly chosen list of nouns is read out one at a time, memorized at a single hearing, and later recalled in exact sequence. Under appropriate conditions, the Method works spectacularly well. But it is useless for most practical purposes.

The Method has two main ingredients, *loci* (places) and *imagines* (images). The *loci* are mentally pictured places arranged in a strict sequence with which we make ourselves familiar—for example, distinctive landmarks on a journey. The first landmark might be a particular church, the second a baker's shop, etc. These *loci* provide the pre-arranged topography into which the list of nouns will be pigeon-holed, one at a time. When we hear the first noun, we mentally picture the thing it represents and relate this, by interactive imagery, to the first landmark.

Suppose the first noun is 'tiger'. We might visualize a huge tiger scrambling over the façade of the church and ripping off the roof with its powerful claws. The many, perceptual-like attributes of the imaged tiger and the imaged church facilitate our bringing the two together into lively interaction. We are free to devise whatever interactive imagery best suits us, but the more animated and distinctive, the better. Having thus associated the first noun and *locus*, we dismiss the scene from mind, and deal likewise with the second noun and the second *locus*. And so on.

Memorizing is thus broken down into a succession of small sub-tasks. Each sub-task involves interactive imagery which associates a presented noun with its *locus*; and the several sub-tasks are held in sequence by the pre-arranged *loci*. When the time comes for recall, we revisit each landmark in turn. When we mentally picture the church, this brings to mind the tiger which is attacking it. When we move to the baker's shop, this prompts recall of the second image, and hence the second noun. The entire procedure may seem absurd. But its efficacy has been repeatedly demonstrated, not only by stage performers but also by ordinary people who have been instructed in the Method and given a little practice in applying it.

The Method has limited utility because it requires certain task conditions, of which three deserve mention. The presented words must be readily translatable into mentally pictured objects. The words must be presented slowly, not faster than one every three or four seconds. The Method breaks down if we depart from considering, at any one time, only one imaged object and its corresponding *locus*—for example, if we allow ourselves to notice relationships among the presented words. Now, such task conditions rarely arise in real life—for instance, the Method cannot be used in the word-by-word memorization of naturally spoken speech. In brief, the Method is an exhibition piece which, as Francis *Bacon observed in 1605, is 'not dexterous to be applied to the serious use of business and occasions'.

The Method is of psychological interest on two main counts. First, it shows that mental imagery is a powerfully effective means of learning and remembering, at least under certain conditions which have not yet been fully explored. Second, it sheds light on how people handle information. It shows that intellectual skills may be redeployed so as to accomplish unfamiliar feats: the Method does not require us to master any new component processes, but merely to select existing processes and sequence them in a new way. Again, if the Method is modified, new accomplishments become possible, such as our being able to recall instantly the noun which occupied any given location in the list. It is also surprising that an individual can, without confusion, use the same set of *loci* to memorize different lists; but, although such has been demonstrated to be the case, the explanation is not yet known.

In general, mnemonics take many forms, all aimed at contriving some comprehensibility for information that is relatively incomprehensible to the individual concerned. On a theoretical level, the chief importance of mnemonics is that they illumine, almost in caricature, what is involved when someone is said to 'comprehend' something, or find it 'meaningful', or 'understandable'. On a practical level, mnemonics clearly have both uses and limitations. Some of these are highlighted by the abilities and inabilities of S. V. Shereshevskii; he was a skilled professional mnemonist who tended to use the Method of Loci off-stage as well as on it (see Luria, 1969).

The best way to learn and remember information is to 'understand' it. Most people appreciate this fact. But they may sometimes want to have in their head information which is not readily 'understandable'. When this happens, the trick is to recognize that a mnemonic is indeed a substitute form of comprehension; and to deploy and devise our mnemonics intelligently, with due regard for what they enable us, and do not enable us, to achieve. Unfortunately, but not surprisingly, it is generally the case that the people with most need of mnemonics tend also to be the least able to devise them intelligently and evaluate their advantages and disadvantages.

See also REMEMBERING.     I. M. L. H.

Ericsson, K. A. (1985). Memory Skill. *Canadian Journal of Psychology*, **39**, 188–231.

Hunter, I. M. L. (1964). *Memory*. Harmondsworth.

Luria, A. R. (1969). *The Mind of a Mnemonist*. London.

**MODELLING.** See BEHAVIOUR THERAPY.

**MODELS, EXPLANATORY.** Essentially analogies, drawn from engineering or other physical systems, to explain e.g. behaviour and brain function. The prevailing technology has throughout history been drawn upon to provide explanatory models of mind. For *Descartes it was hydraulics (fluid in the supposed nerve tubes). For the ancient Greeks, marionettes controlled by strings (*neuron* is the Greek word for 'string') provided the model.

Recently the complex switching of telephone exchanges has served as a (too passive) model of brain function. Currently, digital computers are the main inspiration.

The highly important notion that behaviour is controlled by internal models (cognitive, mental models) was first effectively put forward by Kenneth *Craik, in his *Nature of Explanation* (1943).

**MONAD.** See LEIBNIZ'S PHILOSOPHY OF MIND.

**MONGOLISM.** See DOWN'S SYNDROME.

**MONTESSORI,** MARIA (1870–1952), Italian educationist, born at Chiaravalle, Ancona. Maria Montessori can take much credit for the things that are best in primary schools and in pre-school education. When the creative energies of children are allowed free expression, when classrooms are no longer full of the cast-iron-framed desks in which children were once confined, when the teacher is a helper and an enabler rather than a dictator of notes and purveyor of inert knowledge, credit must be given to the Montessori method and the influence of her work which has pervaded our thinking about children and their *education. Like the man who discovered to his great surprise that he had been talking 'prose' all his life, most workers in the education field have been advancing the ideas of the Montessori method without being fully aware of the debt due to her. By the same token, much of the criticism levelled against modern teaching methods—that children only work when they want to, that they are *supposed* to enjoy themselves in school nowadays, that there are no punishments, no rewards—is in essence criticism of Montessori principles.

Maria Montessori became the first woman in Italy to receive a medical degree. She was a doctor in medicine at the University of Rome at a time when the education of women was still unusual, and she excelled in a field which had been a male preserve. Had she simply continued to work as a doctor her life would have been remarkable enough. Her early work was with feeble-minded children. Between 1898 and 1901 she ran a special school, trained teachers, and lectured internationally on her methods of achieving results with her charges. She came to the conclusion that the same transformation she had been able to achieve with the feeble-minded was needed, and possible, in ordinary schools. Her work with the 'idiots' had been thought to be miraculously effective: they had learnt to read and they passed examinations. She wrote, 'While everyone was admiring the progress of my idiots, I was searching for the reasons which could keep the happy, healthy children of the common schools on so low a plane that they could be equalled in tests of intelligence by my unfortunate pupils.'

With her medical and scientific training, Dr Montessori observed children rather as an anthropologist watches the customs of a tribe, and free from the limiting views of childhood held by the traditional educators. Her approach was democratic, and it is interesting to note that in Russia after the Revolution and in Italy and Germany during the totalitarian regimes, Montessori schools were closed down. Her method was to treat children not as adults in miniature or as objects to be moulded in some 'correct way' but as individuals in their own right. She maintained that she had 'discovered' the child. This was not a just claim, because the child had already been seen in his own right by *Rousseau, Blake, and the Romantics—though, as Aries has shown us, *childhood itself is a relatively new concept (P. Aries, *Centuries of Childhood*, 1973).

Discovering the child also means acceptance of his relative helplessness, and in Montessori schools the apparatus and whole environment of the classroom are structured with the child's needs in mind. The role of the teacher is based both on respect and on confidence that learning will take place without formally set tasks; the child is assumed to want to learn because he has a creative spirit and wishes to discover the world for himself. Like the Freudian psychoanalyst, the teacher should not intervene unless the moment is right. Parallels between psychoanalysis and teaching were recognized by Dr Montessori.

There are limits to her methods. They demand particularly well-trained and sensitive teachers; for authoritarian personalities cannot flourish in a Montessori environment. Middle-class children will probably do better than others, as will children of parents more interested in individuality than in the corporate state. A society that values skill and conformity more highly than creativity and sensitivity is likely to reject or modify the Montessori principles.

C. H.

Montessori, M. (1936). *The Secret of Childhood*. London.
Montesori, M. (1976). *Education for Human Development*. Tel Aviv. (The publishers, Schocken, have produced a wide range of books on her work and her own writings.)

**MOORE,** GEORGE EDWARD (1873–1958), British philosopher, born in London. He was educated at Dulwich College, and read classics at Trinity College, Cambridge, where he became a Fellow in 1898 and was professor of mental philosophy and logic from 1925 to 1939. He was editor of the philosophical journal *Mind* from 1921 to 1947. He was awarded the Order of Merit in 1951.

As a philosopher Moore was extremely important for attacking *Hegelianism with common sense. For example, in a famous lecture he raised his arm and said, 'I *know* this is a hand'—meaning that no conceivable evidence or argument could be brought effectively to challenge the statement. The key essay is 'The nature of judgment' (1899), which served to emancipate Bertrand *Russell from his early philosophical *idealism. Moore's writing now appears over-detailed and somewhat fussy; but this was an essential palliative to the windy metaphysics of Hegelianism, represented in England—with commendable clarity—by John McTaggart (1866–1925). Indeed McTaggart, who was also at Trinity College, provoked Moore and Russell to counter Hegelianism by developing and demanding criteria for meaning: which in its extreme form became 'logical atomism', in which no statement is allowed that cannot be individually justified by some kind of test. This is the basis of *logical positivism.

Moore's *Ethics* (1912) was a key work which pointed out that moral philosophers, and particularly the utilitarians, were logically confused: for the word 'good' cannot be defined in terms of natural qualities, as it always makes sense to ask whether anything possessing natural qualities is good. Moore accepted that goodness is a simple, unanalysable, non-natural quality. This is, however, to give up a theory of the good. (As an example of a simple quality he took the sensation yellow; but unfortunately this is, physiologically, always a mixture of red–green neural signals!)

**MORGAN, CONWY LLOYD** (1852–1936), British psychologist, born in London. He first intended to make a career as a mining engineer, and entered the School of Mines and Royal College of Science in London. There he came under the influence of T. H. *Huxley, who encouraged his interest in biology and put him to study the instinctive behaviour of animals. After five years in South Africa as a college lecturer, he returned to England and became professor of geology and zoology in the University College of Bristol in 1884, and then principal of the College. He was elected a Fellow of the Royal Society in 1899, the first Fellow to be elected for psychological research. This was in recognition of the distinction of two books— *Animal Life and Intelligence* (1890) and *An Introduction to Comparative Psychology* (1894)— as well as numerous papers in scientific journals. When in 1909 the College became the University of Bristol, he served for a short time as vice-chancellor. In 1910 his chair was renamed the chair of psychology and ethics; and he continued to hold it until his retirement in 1919.

Modern animal psychology grew out of the work of Lloyd Morgan in England and the early work of E. L. *Thorndike in America. Lloyd Morgan established a tradition of careful observation of behaviour in natural settings, with systematic variation of the conditions. He enumerated some of his findings, for example when he showed that the proportion of limpets accomplishing a return home is in inverse ratio to the distance they have been removed. His caution in theorizing is exemplified in the canon named after him—the law of parsimony—which was a corrective to the anecdotalism and anthropomorphism of G. J. Romanes (1848–94): 'In no case may we interpret an action as the outcome of a higher psychical faculty, if it can be interpreted as the outcome of one which stands lower in the psychological scale.'

In 1894 Lloyd Morgan introduced the term 'trial-and-error learning' to describe what he had observed while his fox-terrier, Tony, learnt to carry a stick with a heavy knob at one end, and to open a gate by putting his head under the latch. Trial and error, which constitutes the method of *intelligence, he remarked, continues until a happy effect is reached. In order to understand a clever performance, one must have observed how it has developed. With this purpose he observed the development of the behaviour of birds after they were hatched—for example, the effect of practice on instinctive pecking, and of experience on the choice of object.

The term 'trial-and-error learning' came into general use when E. L. Thorndike put forward in 1911 the *law of effect, which explains the selection or rejection of responses as due to the retroactive strengthening or weakening of connections by the effects. However, one of the neatest experiments, and the first in a fully controlled laboratory setting, on the strengthening of responses by reward— instrumental conditioning—was made in 1932 by G. C. Grindley, a pupil of Lloyd Morgan's who had moved from Bristol to F. C. *Bartlett's laboratory in Cambridge. By this time, research into detour behaviour and maze-learning, prepared for by Lloyd Morgan's work, was in full flood.

D. R. D.

Grindley, G. C. (1932). The formation of a simple habit in guinea-pigs. *British Journal of Psychology*, **23**, 127–47.
Morgan, C. L. (1900). *Animal Behaviour*. London.
Thorndike, E. L. (1911). *Animal Intelligence*. New York.

**MÜLLER, JOHANNES PETER** (1801–58). German physiologist and anatomist, widely regarded as the founder of modern physiology. Born and educated in Koblenz, he studied medicine at Bonn (1819–22), where he became professor of anatomy and physiology (1830), before moving to take up a similar chair in Berlin (1833). He remained in Berlin for the rest of his life. As rector of the university there in 1838–9 and again in 1847–8, he was inevitably involved in the serious student disturbances during the 1848 revolution, events which troubled him deeply and caused a serious breakdown of his health.

He taught human and comparative anatomy, embryology, physiology, and pathological anatomy, and made important contributions in all these fields. His work included an explanation of the colour sensations produced by pressure on the eye, confirmation of the *Bell–Magendie law, and studies of *reflex action; he was also one of the first to use the microscope in pathology. His *Handbuch der Physiologie des Menschen* (2 vols., 1833–40; English trans. 1840–9) became the standard text in physiology. Among a generation of brilliant physiologists taught by Müller are *Helmholtz and *Du Bois-Reymond, the latter of whom succeeded him in the chair of physiology at Berlin after his premature death in 1858.

**MÜLLER-LYER, FRANZ CARL** (1857–1916), discoverer of the most famous of all the visual *illusions—the Müller-Lyer illusion: that a line terminated at each end with inward-pointing arrowheads appears longer, and a line with outward-pointing arrowheads appears shorter, than a 'neutral' comparison line (Fig. 1). He reported and described this distortion and many related examples, with detailed experiments, in two papers dated 1889 and 1896. Müller-Lyer is not a well-known psychologist, in spite of the enormous literature and the many attempts to explain the illusion that bears his name.

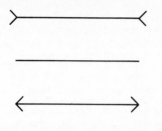

**Fig. 1.**

Born in Baden-Baden, he studied medicine at Strasburg, and at the age of 24 became assistant director of the Strasburg Psychiatric Clinic, where he remained until 1883. He visited and worked with E. *Du Bois-Reymond and J. M. *Charcot. He ended his career in private practice in Munich. His major work, in extent though not in fame, was in sociology, in which he wrote a seven-volume book, arguing a somewhat Marxist thesis of direction and inevitable development of societies (Salomon, 1959).

Müller-Lyer offered as the explanation of his distortion illusion that 'the judgement not only takes the lines themselves into consideration, but also, unintentionally, some part of the space on either side'. This is known as the principle of confluxion. So, for him, it is not the angles of the figure, but rather the spaces bounded by the lines (or by dots corresponding to the ends of the lines) that produce the distortion. He counters some rival theories in his second paper (1896).

Müller-Lyer's two papers, 'Optical illusions' (1889) and 'Concerning the theory of optical illusions: on contrast and confluxion' (1896), are translated by R. H. Day and H. Knuth, *Perception*, 10.2 (1981), 126–49. For his sociology, see entry by F. Salomon in *Encyclopaedia of the Social Sciences*, ed. R. A. Seligman and A. Johnson, Vol. ii (1959), pp. 83–4.

**MULTIPLE PERSONALITIES.** See DISSOCIATION OF THE PERSONALITY.

**MUSCULAR ACTION.** Muscle power has served man's needs for far longer than more recent, and apparently more abundant, sources of power. And even with those additional sources, doing work with muscles remains essential to most human activity. But it is so commonplace that we easily

forget how complex are the processes which make chemical energy from food available to us as mechanical energy. Not only has the energy derived from the oxidation of food to be stored so that it can be released when needed as mechanical energy, the release must be precisely controlled in order to make movements co-ordinated and purposeful.

The contractile properties of a muscle reside in the cells (muscle fibres) of which it is composed. Each muscle fibre is a long cylindrical cell which may be several centimetres long and is nearly a tenth of a millimetre in diameter. As cells go it is very large, and it is almost wholly specialized as a generator of mechanical force. By far the greater part of the constituents (apart from water) of each muscle fibre are two proteins, actin and myosin, whose interactions provide a means of generating a force. Actin is a moderately sized protein (molecular weight 60,000); myosin is substantially larger (molecular weight about 250,000), but both molecules have the property of aggregating with themselves into rods between 1 and 2 micrometres in length. These rods of actin and myosin are arranged within the muscle fibre in a very highly ordered array: transverse bands of actin rods and myosin rods alternating in the length of the fibre, and overlapping in such a way that each type of rod can slide along rods of the other kind. Small quantities of additional proteins are incorporated into the arrays of actin and myosin rods; their functions are to give order to the arrays of rods and to regulate the interactions of actin and myosin.

When a muscle is relaxed, the protein rods slide without hindrance past each other, allowing easy stretching of the muscle fibre by an applied force. When a muscle is contracting, the actin rods are pulled towards the centre of each myosin rod, and if the force generated by the pulls of all the myosin rods exceeds the external force the fibre will shorten.

How do the myosin rods move the actin rods and, in so doing, do work? From the sides of the myosin rods short flexible arms (about 200 on each myosin rod) can swing out and form cross-bridges between the myosin rod and an adjacent actin rod. Provided calcium ions and adenosine triphosphate are present, a cyclical process occurs, triggered by calcium ions and powered by the hydrolysis of adenosine triphosphate to adenine diphosphate and inorganic phosphates, a reaction which is well known as an immediate source of energy in living systems. The adenosine triphosphate is synthesized in the muscle fibre with energy derived from the oxidation of food. The cycle of events appears to involve a myosin cross-bridge attachment to a site on an actin rod; a multi-stage and progressive change in the cross-bridge attachment which results in a small but finite movement of the actin site past the myosin rod; and finally cross-bridge detachment. The cycle may be repeated and the actin rod moved on by another small distance. Hydrolysis of adenosine triphosphate is involved at each turn of the cycle because, however small the movement of the actin rod, if it is achieved against an external load mechanical work is done, and even if no net movement is achieved there will still be some stretching of elastic structures in the muscle. In any actual muscle fibre there are, of course, very many cross-bridges (approximately $5 \times 10^{12}$), and in any short time-interval many will become detached from, and many will become attached to, actin: the net result is a smooth movement of the actin rods along the myosin rods and a smooth shortening of the fibre. If movement is prevented by an external force, the repeated attaching and detaching exerts a steady tension which is proportional to the degree of overlap of the actin and myosin rods, that is to the number of the myosin side-arms which find an actin site for attachment.

In each fibre, contraction depends on the presence of a sufficient concentration of calcium ions (about $10^{-6}$ molar), and it is turned on and off by the release of calcium from, and uptake of, calcium ions into an intracellular compartment, which is separate from the main part of the cell containing the contractile proteins. This special compartment for calcium storage is called the sarcoplasmic reticulum, and it is bounded by a membrane containing a special protein capable of transporting calcium ions from the sarcoplasm—which is the main part of the fibre and contains the actin and myosin rods—to the interior of the sarcoplasmic reticulum, from which the calcium ions cannot normally escape.

This calcium-pumping protein does work by scavenging calcium ions from the sarcoplasm and concentrating them within the sarcoplasmic reticulum. It therefore also requires an energy source. As with contraction, the energy is provided by the hydrolysis of adenosine triphosphate. The calcium-pumping by the membrane of the sarcoplasmic reticulum can account for the normally relaxed state of a muscle fibre and for relaxation following a contraction. What events lead to a release of calcium ions into the sarcoplasm and thereby to a contraction?

Muscles (with the important exception of the heart and visceral muscles) only contract when there are nerve impulses in the nerve fibres which run from the spinal cord to the muscle. Skeletal muscle contraction is initiated and controlled entirely by the brain and spinal cord by impulses in these motor nerve fibres. All movements, whether skilled and voluntary or postural and apparently automatic, are organized and initiated in the central nervous system, and a nerve going to a muscle is the pathway by which executive instructions for contraction are passed to the muscle fibres and by which sense organs in the muscle (muscle spindles) signal information to the central nervous system about the results of the contraction and the effects of external loads on the muscle. The nerve contains many nerve fibres carrying impulses to the muscle and a separate set of fibres carrying nerve impulses from the muscle spindle to the spinal

cord. The nature of these nerve impulses is the same, but the directions and fibres in which they travel as well as their purposes differ.

Impulses in nerve fibres going to a muscle produce from the end of each nerve fibre, where it is in close contact with a muscle fibre (at the neuromuscular junction), the release of a small molecule, acetylcholine. The release of acetylcholine is brought about by a small entry of calcium ions into the nerve terminal, resulting from the propagation of the nerve impulse into the terminal. Acetylcholine has the role of a chemical transmitter because it is released by the nerve terminal and reacts with a special receptor protein in the membrane of the muscle fibre. As a result of this transmitter–receptor interaction, a propagated electrical change occurs in the entire surface membrane of the muscle fibre, and this action potential in the muscle fibre is very much akin to the nerve impulse in the nerve fibre. The acetylcholine has served to bridge the gap at the neuromuscular junction between the propagating electrochemical changes in the nerve fibre and the very similar propagating electrochemical changes in the surface of muscle fibre. In the case of the muscle fibre, its surface includes a network of very fine tubules which are invaginated from the outer surface of the fibre and ramify in the entire cross-section and length of the fibre interior. By means of this transverse tubular system the electrical changes initiated at the neuromuscular junction spread rapidly to all parts of the volume of the fibre; the transverse tubular system enables contraction to be started more or less synchronously in the entire muscle fibre. Not only do the transverse tubules extend throughout the fibre—they also make special and intimate contact with parts of the sarcoplasmic reticulum. Just as the nerve fibre contacts the muscle fibre at a special neuromuscular junction, so the transverse tubule comes very close to the sarcoplasmic reticulum at a recognizable structure called a triad junction.

We know in some detail about the release and role of acetylcholine at the neuromuscular junction; our knowledge of the physiological events at the triad is as yet sketchy. But we do know that an appropriate electrical change at the wall of the transverse tubule at the triad results in the rapid release of stored calcium ions from the sarcoplasmic reticulum and therefore triggers a contraction of the fibre.

We have traced the sequence of events between the spinal cord and the contraction of a muscle fibre, but this tells us nothing about the organization of a co-ordinated movement. We can say that any voluntary movement has its origin in the cerebral cortex. Such a statement begs many questions. One can, however, within the central nervous system trace pathways of nerve fibres in which impulses give rise to muscular movements. In a very general way there are two kinds of pathway in the spinal cord which can cause muscles to contract. Descending impulses from the brain may directly excite the nerve-cell (motor neurone) in the spinal cord whose main process is the nerve fibre going to a group of muscle fibres in a muscle. Alternatively, descending impulses may excite the motor neurones whose fibres go to special muscle fibres which form part of the muscle spindles. In a normal muscle there are so few of these spindle muscle fibres that they themselves generate no detectable tension in the muscle, but their contraction increases the frequency of nerve impulses going from the spindle to the spinal cord. These impulses in turn may be able to excite the main motor neurones and make the muscle contract. Stretching a muscle also increases the frequency of impulses from a muscle spindle in that muscle and can produce a contraction which resists the stretch. It is possible, too, that the sensitivity of the motor neurones to the incoming signals from the muscle spindles may be under the control of the higher parts of the central nervous system, providing a variable gain to the feedback pathway made up of the muscle spindle and its sensory nerve fibre.

Any actual muscular movement probably results from complicated temporal sequences of descending impulses; these play with varying intensities on the neurones which send fibres to the ordinary muscle fibres and to the spindle muscle fibres. Many parts of the brain interact and co-operate in the generation of any particular movement or sequence of movements. Interference with the functioning of the cerebral cortex, the basal ganglia, and internal capsule and the cerebellum diminishes motor performance in varying but characteristic ways; however, the precise roles of each part are still matters of speculation (see NERVOUS SYSTEM).

One can describe in some detail the cellular and even molecular events associated with muscular action, but gaps in the account are more obvious when it concerns the role of the mind, or even of the brain, in originating and organizing movement.

A.

**MUSIC, PSYCHOLOGY OF.** Music has existed in all human cultures, as far as we know, and all scale systems are based on the octave, which suggests a neurological factor. This suggestion is supported by the fact that animals conditioned to respond to a certain pitch will do so almost equally to its octave, whereas the intervening notes will evoke either much less response or none at all. However, only the Western tonal system originated in the Pythagorean division of the octave into intervals according to the frequency ratios of small whole numbers by which the harmonic series of overtones in a complex tone are related. This ratio basis of the 'chord in nature' was given theological significance and determined the early history of concerted music, which developed from octave ensemble (ratio 2:1), to perfect fifth (3:2), perfect fourth (4:3), and major third (5:4). These intervals occur in the first four overtones of the series and were deemed consonant. After the great development

of polyphonic music their ratios were adjusted to very complex ones in the eighteenth-century compromise of equal temperament tuning, yet our experience of the tension of dissonance and the repose of consonance survives in these newer complex interval ratios. Moreover, people prefer an octave tuned slightly larger than the exact 2:1 ratio, whether of pure tones (Ward, 1954) or complex tones (Sundberg and Lindquist, 1973), and this applies whether they are trained in the Western tonal system or in the Indian system of twenty-two śrutis (microtones) to the octave (Burns, 1974). Sensory theories of consonance, which attribute it to the ear's special sensitivity to the harmonic series, must reckon with these anomalies, and also with all the non-harmonic, complex ratio scale systems of other cultures. Thus, psychologists recognize that ultimately they must span the chasm between psychoacoustics and ethnomusicology. They must also endeavour to account for the whole response to music, not only sensory and cognitive, but also emotional and aesthetic. This latter task is beset with difficulties of method, and at present the main concern is with perception and memory in the Western tonal system, and its later development (using the same intervals) towards atonality.

In seeking to understand how the listener makes sense of music, should psychologists treat it as a set of arbitrary conventions (as David Hilbert views mathematics), or as a description of reality (as *Plato sees both mathematics and music), or as a property of mind (as Chomsky regards language)? All three approaches are essential, since all three characteristics—pattern-structural, acoustic, and grammatic—play their part; moreover they function interdependently in musical perception. Though a musical grammar may have been culturally evolved, acoustic characteristics and the constraints of performance will have contributed to its formation. That we perceive music phrase by phrase is not only because of repeated practice in hearing conventional design, but also because phrase length, as in sentence structure, has been historically constrained by what can be managed in one breath. The human auditory system evolved not only to be receptive (as are those of other species) to the sounds of nature, but also apparently to be 'wired for speech'. Vowel perception, like that of musical pitch and timbre, depends on the spectral characteristics of the complex wave form. Even so, perception phoneme by phoneme is not totally an acoustic process, for it also depends on knowledge of phonological constraints. In both speech and music, this 'wiring' for sequential processing of meaningful acoustic events must form the basis for the subsequent, more specialized expansion of perceptual skill through experience.

**Music as pattern.** Nevertheless, the Hilbertian approach is relevant, since the brain is biased towards detecting regularities, the non-random organization of pattern, irrespective of sense modality. Experiments on auditory temporal pattern (Garner, 1974; Jones, 1978), treat music as arbitrary design, evoking perception of features such as symmetry, repetition, and imitation, which occur also in other non-musical symbolic or visual design. The span of short-term memory sets a limit to the perception of auditory pattern; musical palindromes are difficult to perceive for this reason, whereas visual perception of bilateral symmetry is immediate. Listeners tend to impose structure and to discover or unconsciously apply the rule by which a pattern is defined. Formal transformations of melodies used in serial music are perceptible (depending on their length) in an ascending order of difficulty from exact repetition, to inversion, retrograde, and retrograde inversion. Perceiving retrograde tunes is a particular tax upon short-term memory, and the strong salience of forward temporal order is apparent if one plays backwards the tape of a well-known piece, even one of equal note values, where rhythm plays no part. In experiments where subjects are asked to identify the starting-point and the segmentation pattern of a sequence which is continually recurring, like auditory wallpaper, their perception tends to conform to *Gestalt principles of organization. Patterns of eight or ten recurring events, composed of only two pitch elements, seem to evoke a *figure–ground perception, sometimes reversible, as in an Escher picture. A slow tempo of presentation affords active coding into memory, whereas a fast one yields a more passively received Gestalt. The formal devices of composition are amenable to this approach, often presented by psychologists in terms of *information theory. But such an approach can only give an inadequate account of musical perception where it disregards the listener's use of an implicit tonal grammar in perceiving even quite simple melodies.

**Music and psychoacoustics.** The second approach, the acoustic one, is the study of constraints imposed upon the perceptibility of musical phrases by psychoacoustic factors. Throughout musical history these constraints have been intuitively respected or exploited by composers, even when not yet scientifically defined. For instance, tonal proximity in melodic steps is an important perceptual organizing principle. The ear requires some milliseconds of extra processing time to monitor large pitch-intervals in melody. This need has been explained as due either to the 'critical band' (the theory that the ear functions neurally as a series of band-pass filters), or to the brain's momentary conflict between integrating the frequency change as one of pitch or of timbre (this also is a neurological theory). Palestrina and other sixteenth-century composers observed the rule that, after a melodic leap in polyphonic music, that voice must return by step-wise motion within the compass of the leap—an intuitive recognition of the ear's need of extra steadying time. Even a well-known tune, when transposed note by note into disparate octave registers, becomes unrecognizable. Yet this very widely spaced layout is a characteristic device of twentieth-century serial music, and either of the two psychoacoustic theories mentioned would suggest why it is notoriously difficult to perceive. The salience of tonal proximity in perceptual organization is also apparent when two tunes, each consisting of large ascending and descending leaps, are presented one to each ear (Deutsch, 1975). They are heard as consecutive by the tonal proximity of the notes arriving alternately at each ear, and not, as might be expected, as a left ear tune and a right ear tune. A similar perception by tonal proximity which overrides that by separate sources occurs with the layout between violin parts in Tchaikovsky's Sixth Symphony (see Fig. 1).

J. S. Bach, in his solo violin partitas, exploits a related phenomenon now called 'auditory stream segregation' (McAdams and Bregman, 1979), where alternating notes will appear to separate into two coexistent tunes, depending on the tempo and on the pitch separation between the alternate notes. An eight-note tune, continually recurring, will perceptually separate into more than two streams of ever more restricted frequency ranges: the faster the tempo, the more streams are heard. Prestissimo gives the experience of eight coexistent streams forming a continuous chord or an inharmonic timbre. (See Fig. 2.) However, streaming does depend on what is being listened for, whether streaming itself or coherence, so it cannot be entirely attributed to neural factors. In some sequences, one of the eight notes may be 'captured' by either of two adjacent streams; the brain makes the best bet on the basis either of tonal proximity or of harmonic pleasingness. This latter criterion, however unconsciously it is used, reflects the listener's internalized musical grammar, derived from past experience, which will affect his performance in all experimental tasks, however musically neutral they may be. In general, the validity of explaining perception as due to acoustic rather than attentional processes rests on the experimenter's selection of subjects, how rigorously he distinguishes between non-musicians, musicians, those with absolute pitch, and acoustic engineers, for experience endows each group with demonstrably different coding processes.

The drawback of many psychoacoustic experiments hitherto has been their endeavour to regard perception as context free. Furthermore, the functions—amplitude, duration, frequency, and spectral complexity of the waveform—of the four main attributes of music—loudness, rhythm, pitch, and timbre—have often been treated independently of each other. This has perpetuated the philosophical notion of 'raw sense data'. For music the notion originated in the Pythagorean naïve realism concerning sensory coding, which assumed that sensory processes exactly matched physical events in the world. It survived in the assumptions of classical music theory (e.g. that of Rameau and Tartini)

**Fig. 1.** A section of the violin parts of Tchaikovsky's Sixth Symphony, showing **a** the music as it is actually played, and **b** how it is perceived by the listener.

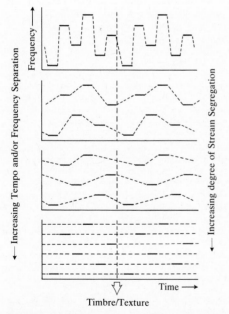

**Fig. 2.** The decomposition of an acoustic sequence into smaller and smaller perceptual streams as the frequency separation between the tones or the tempo of the sequence increases. In the latter case, a point is ultimately reached where one can no longer perceive individual tonal events; a texture or timbre is heard instead.

and in *Helmholtz's model of the ear as a frequency analyser which coded each discriminable pitch by its specific nerve. Combination or difference tones were thought to be manufactured in the waveform in the ear, rather than neurally. But the four attributes are by no means independent, loudness also depends on frequency, pitch is affected by amplitude, and timbre by frequency. Paul Divenyi (1971) shows that perception of time intervals is affected by the frequency separation between notes, and this has obvious importance for rhythm. Then also, there is no clear distinction between pitch and timbre, but rather a continuous dimension from the unequivocal pitch of pure tones to the spectral inharmonicity of church bells (though their fundamental pitch is distinguishable), to the vague 'pitchiness' of noise within a narrow band of wavelength (Erickson, 1975). Timbre is of course multidimensional, being also affected by fluctuations of harmonics or of pitch (in vibrato), and by the non-pitched starting noises of instruments, or 'transients'. A similar continuous dimension can be traced from the single complex tone to the chord, for if a single harmonic of a complex tone is sufficiently amplified it separates from the fundamental, and a chord is heard. This property is exploited in the chant of a Tibetan monk when he sings alone in two-part harmony. (Smith et al., 1965).

The fact that the fundamental may be perceived when no energy is present at its frequency level, and that the three or four adjacent harmonics which best give rise to this percept fall within a certain middle frequency range (the 'existence region'), whatever the fundamental involved, totally alters the picture of sensory coding inherited from Helmholtz. He held that we have to learn to combine the separately received harmonics of a complex tone, yet most people are unable to regain Helmholtz's supposed primal state of hearing even the first five harmonics separately (the rest of the higher ones, the 'residue', are not separately distinguishable in any case). The problem is to explain how we hear the components of sound as 'belonging' together, whether in hearing the harmonics of a complex tone as fused, or in hearing distinctly each separate stream of all the orchestral instruments in single waveform from a mono loudspeaker. How far does this ability depend on innate neural mechanisms which fuse the spectral components, and how far on mechanisms which have been built up by repeated experience? The limited resolution power of the ear is a psychoacoustic factor which is particularly important to the perception of rhythm. Although hearing is the most accurate temporal sense, there are nevertheless limits (in milliseconds) to the perceptibility of synchrony, successiveness, and 'flutter', i.e. rapid repetition.

The rise of computer and electronically synthesized music has greatly expanded the vocabulary of music so that, as the American composer Milton Babbitt has remarked, the limits are no longer those of sound production, but rather those of the human auditory system. Rapid changes of timbre are difficult to follow, just as speech recorded syllable by syllable in different voices is incomprehensible. Richard Warren and his colleagues (1972, 1974) have shown that subjects have great difficulty in identifying the order of recurring sequences of sounds which are unrelated in timbre (for instance, a high tone, a hiss, a lower tone, and a buzz) although they are presented at a slower speed than that necessary for auditory temporal resolution. Yet if the two tones are placed adjacently within the four-event sequence, performance is improved. That continuity of timbre is important to perceptual organization is also apparent where a single, pure tone is interrupted by noise, the cessation of the tone being exactly synchronized with the start of the noise, and vice versa. (See Fig. 3.) The pure tone is heard as continuing through the noise, much as in vision one object is seen as existing behind another by which it is occluded. (See ILLUSIONS.) Computer music is easily perceived in the degree to which the sounds resemble or are systematic near distortions of natural sounds. Composers of computer music are able not only to use these parameters of sound from experience but, in collaboration with psychologists, are able also to assess the reasons for the limits to the listeners' perceptual skills (IRCAM Reports).

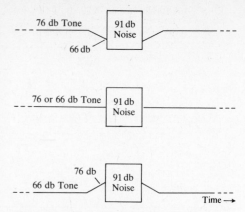

**Fig. 3.** The stimuli used by Bregman and Dannenbring (1977) consisted of a pure tone interrupted by noise. The level of the tone leading into and coming out of the noise burst was varied as shown. The greatest degree of continuity was found in the centre case where there was no change in level.

**Music as language.** The third approach, the grammatical one, treats music as analogous to language, since music also is hierarchically organized and makes selective use of the same neurally close-knit system of voice, ear, and brain. Though without denotative meaning, music is both syntactic and communicative (of subjective states). Its two linguistic elements, melodic phrasing which reflects the intonations of speech, and the formal, syntactic devices of composition, imply that the listener understands both the expressiveness of contour and the 'argument' of musical form. Even the musically untutored listener acquires a musical grammar, a system of rules unconsciously applied, by which he makes sense of music, and would detect 'wrong notes' in an unfamiliar work in the tonal idiom, though unable to name the notes or to state the rules. This grammar implies that the single note is characterized not only by its tone-height, and its chroma (all B flats sound alike), but also by its grammatic function (e.g. whether it is, at a particular point, functioning as a tonic, leading note, or unaccented passing note). As a word in a sentence is defined by its context, even more so is a note in music.

Formal theories of music and artificial intelligence models seek to define how the listener correctly perceives rhythm, key, tonal modulations, and thematic organization. Some models are based on traditional music theory and linguistics (Winograd, 1968, Longuet-Higgins, 1971), or on Gestalt principles (Tenney and Polansky, 1980). A more recent theory (Lerdahl and Jackendoff, 1981) covers formal, acoustic, and quasi-linguistic aspects, and accommodates the fact that a musical phrase might admit of more than one correct parsing, by distinguishing 'well-formedness' rules from those 'preference' rules which can account for conscious and unconscious organizing principles of musical perception. Its emphasis on the interactions between rhythmic and tonal aspects provides a useful antidote to some research where such interactions have hitherto been disregarded.

Experiments show that, as with language, salience of originally perceived or imposed rhythmic groupings is very strong in subsequent recognition memory; and tunes ending in cadence are easier to remember than those which are harmonically inconclusive. Most musicians would agree that tonal grammar is dominant, that it is not easy to eradicate entirely one's tonal habits of listening when hearing non-tonal idioms.

However, the swiftly moving innovations in the history of tonal music, particularly of the last two centuries, undermine the analogy of its grammar with that of language, which is anchored by semantic meaning. Any ancient Greek who conversed with Socrates could equally well have done so with Wittgenstein, but having heard only the musical grammar of the Delphic hymns he would not naturally make sense of Boulez, Beethoven, or even Byrd. Musical style and comprehensibility have increasingly depended upon the listener's developing tolerance of protracted dissonance through his grammatical understanding of its possible resolution in consonance, implicit in his familiarity with past and present idioms. That his long-term memory store, upon which present comprehension depends, is more idiosyncratic than it could ever be for language, presents a difficulty to the psychologist in testing general theories of musical grammar.

In psycholinguistics the experimenter tests a linguistic theory which treats grammaticality as paramount (i.e. whether a string of words constitutes a sentence), whereas ambiguity plays a much lesser role in the whole theory (i.e. whether a sentence is susceptible of more than one meaning and consequently of more than one structural description). But phrases in music frequently admit of differing interpretations and may be ambiguous. Indeed, the performing musician's enduring task is to choose, between the various possibilities of phrasing, the one that to him seems to represent the composer's message most faithfully and eloquently, and his interpretation is to a large extent judged by its internal coherence. Thus the psychologist of music must work with a grammar which can accommodate the latitude of perhaps many equally 'correct' parsings of a musical structure.

The three approaches outlined here, each concerned with an essential factor operative in musical cognition, remain at present more experimentally distinct than is warranted by their interrelation in the perception of musical structure. In making sense of music, its attributes of contour, interval, tonality, modulation, rhythm, symmetry, repetition, inversion, imitation, and the like, must in turn and at different moments assume different shares of the total cognitive process, and must influence the nature of perceptual grouping or coding processes. Exactly how this fluctuating process operates remains the fundamental question.

**Music and performance.** Musical perception and performance are both dependent on short-term memory and expectancy. 'The practically cognised present is no knife-edge but a saddleback, with a certain breadth of its own, on which we sit perched, and from which we look in two directions into time' (William *James, 1890). From this perch the performer monitors and constantly corrects the flow, shape, and tone-quality as it occurs, by a highly integrated system of coexistent codes: auditory, visual, and kinaesthetic. Implicit vocalizing may underlie musical perception, much as Liberman holds that we perceive speech by 'internal generation' at some neural level below that of overt response. But the acquired codes of the musician instrumentalist are more complex, including visual ones for musical notation and for instrumental fingering, and kinaesthetic ones for fingering and more general muscular movement. Kinaesthetic imagery for one's own instrument can also underlie one's perception while only listening. Karl *Lashley (1951) cites the musician's performance when he emphasizes that all human serial behaviour (speech, gesture, and perceptual motor skill) is grammatically structured, on hierarchically ordered levels of organization. Well-practised sequences occurring too fast for monitoring at the level of individual events are perceived and executed at a higher level of pre-planned groups. In music (unlike, for instance, Morse code) the flow of 'information' to be monitored or executed is not constant. Not only the number of consecutive events but also the denseness of harmonic texture may vary from moment to moment, yet the performer maintains a steady flow of action and perception through these variations in information load. The basis here is principally the intrinsic feedback of the nervous system, amplified by the extrinsic feedback of sight and sound, e.g. of the conductor's beat and the sound of other instruments.

Although the appropriate model for research on performance may well be the cybernetic one, it is not surprising that little has yet been done to tease out the components and interactions in this very complex skill. Seashore's research (1938) on intonation and vibrato anticipated the present experimental technique of wiring up musical instruments to computers which record the infinitesimal variations in tone and rhythm that distinguish live performance from computer deadpan accuracy, and one artist from another. Analysis of these recordings shows the variation to be consistent in respect of some general principles of rhythmic displacement, or differences of intonation according to the function of a particular note within a tonality. Some experiments on sight-reading indicate that good sight-readers take in and hold in short-term memory (the eye–hand span) phrase-length chunks (see CHUNKING), rather than a steady bar-by-bar succession of chunks at the rate of their performance.

A promising source of evidence as to how the components of musical skill may be integrated, is the clinical evidence on amusia, the breakdown of a previously established capability for music due to brain pathology. Although there are strong indications that in right-handed people music is stored in the non-dominant hemisphere of the brain, this is by no means invariably so, nor are musical and linguistic functions entirely lateralized. There are many mental abilities common to both speech and language, for instance perception of rhythm and of temporal order, and these seem to be processed in the dominant hemisphere. In left-handers, either hemisphere can mediate many musical functions, and in some professional musicians a dominant life-work may be stored in the dominant hemisphere. The distinctions between the roles of each hemisphere have been oversimplified in investigations hitherto, although broadly they are apparent. Nevertheless, research which correlates a patient's performance with damage to a particular brain structure, is gradually building up a picture which illuminates our understanding of the nature of musical skill.

An equally promising area is that of developmental psychology, an area which has been largely centred on aptitude tests. The early acquisition of the unconscious ability to operate the rules of musical grammar can be as rich a source of psychological theory as that of the child's acquisition of language. Teplov (1966) finds that children will complete half-finished musical phrases presented to them, with a fine sense of their tonality, rhythmic character, and implied harmonic cadence. The special aptitude of absolute pitch, the possession of which correlates with the early age at which the names of the notes were learned, illustrates the power of category systems in expanding musical intelligence. If more parents were equipped to teach note names as easily as colour names, it is possible that music might more easily resemble an artistic lingua franca.

**Music and aesthetics.** Most musicians would agree that, as well as the sensory and cognitive aspects we have discussed, aesthetic and emotional factors also play a part in perceiving and remembering music, but it is less easy to see how these can be approached experimentally. The belief that memory for melodic contour and implicit harmony is allied to its affective character is well described by Deryck Cooke (1958), whose theory gives general principles why, for instance, we all experience, with Browning, 'those minor thirds so plaintive, Sixths diminished sigh on sigh'. This characterization is, of course, dependent not on pitch intervals alone, but also on rhythm, phrasing, and tempo (for instance, descending couplet-phrasing is a particularly plaintive use of minor thirds). The music of non-Western cultures, based on quite different scale systems, no doubt has different aesthetic and emotional significances which are nevertheless experienced to similar degrees in those cultures. In Western music, the factor of musical imagery is partly understood universally by musical people, and is partly idiosyncratic to each composer and listener. Composers have self-consistent mood associations with key colour and timbre. Bach's use of the brazen timbre of the D major trumpet associated that key, for him, with jubilance, and the D major open string basis of tone colour enhances this characterization for most composers and hence for most listeners.

Hitherto experiments on aesthetic aspects have centred largely on subjects' ratings for a certain attribute, or for the more general 'pleasingness'; they were often directed to whole works, or to very large segments of them, rather than to phrases (Schoen, 1937). There are also correlations of measures of autonomic arousal with hearing or performing certain music, including one such study with the conductor Herbert von Karajan as subject (Harrer and Harrer, 1977). Sometimes responses are related to a measure of the information content of a work (Berlyne, 1974). Psychologists may well feel that judgements of whole works do not yield data that are specific enough, and they may be daunted by the great number of confounding variables, such as social, cultural, or fashion determinants of taste.

As yet no systematic experimental study of Deryck Cooke's theory has emerged, relating it to musical education, though a pilot study (Gabriel, 1978) showed that, for twenty-two non-musician students, Cooke's characterizations of musical phrases were not experienced. This evoked a music theorist's objection to the theory itself (Cazden, 1979), and another to the validity of using 'dead-pan' sine-wave sequences as an experimental test of a theory concerning real live music (Nettheim, 1979). To these one must add an objection to the restricted choice of subjects. A study using real live music, and musician subjects, to test Leonard Meyer's theory of the perception of certain melodic characteristics which he calls 'archetypes' attributes the variability of response to the degree of complexity in the underlying hierarchic phrase structure (Rosner and Meyer, 1981). It would seem that experimental musical aesthetics may have to await further progress in the rapprochement between experimental psychology and the theories of musical grammar discussed earlier.

Is it possible for the analytic methods of science to contribute a comprehensive account of the flexible, living performance and enjoyment of music? At the sensory and cognitive levels there has been substantial and illuminating progress. On the other hand, at present the aesthetic level of the musician's use of imagery, particularly with contour, key colour, tone quality, and emotional association seems, like the painter's idiosyncratic choice of palette, to be outside the realm of experimental psychology. N. SP.

Berlyne, D. (1974). *Studies in the New Experimental Aesthetics*. New York.

Bregman, A. and Dannenbring, G. (1977). Auditory Continuity and Amplitude Edges. *Canadian Journal of Psychology*, **31**, 151–9.

Burns, E. (1974). Octave adjustment by non-Western musicians. *Journal of the Acoustical Society of America*, **56**, 25–6.

Cazden, N. (1979). Can verbal meanings inhere in fragments of music? *Psychology of Music*, 7, 2, 34.

Cooke, D. (1958). *The Language of Music*. Oxford.

Deutsch, D. (1975). Musical illusions. *Scientific American*, **233**, 4, 92.

Divenyi, P. (1971). The rhythmic perception of micro-melodies. In Gordon, R. (ed.), *Research in the Psychology of Music*. Iowa City.

Erickson, R. (1975). *Sound Structure in Music*. Berkeley.

Gabriel, C. (1978). An experimental study of Deryck Cooke's theory of music and meaning. *Psychology of Music*, **16**, 1, 13–20.

Garner, W. (1974). *The Processing of Information and Structure*. New York.

Harrer, G. and Harrer, H. (1977). Music, emotion and autonomic function. In Critchley, M. and Henson, J. (eds.) *Music and the Brain*. London.

Helmholtz, H. (1863, trans. 1954). *On the Sensations of Tone*. New York.

IRCAM Rapports, Pompidou Centre, Paris.

Jones, M. Reiss (1978). Auditory patterns: studies in the perception of structure. In Cartarette and Friedman, *Handbook of Perception*, **8**, 255–88.

Lashley, K. (1951). The problem of serial order in behavior. In Jeffries, L. (ed.), *Cerebral Mechanisms in Behavior*. New York.

Lerdahl, F. and Jackendoff, R. (1981). *A Generative Theory of Tonal Music*. New York.

Longuet-Higgins, C. (1971). On interpreting Bach. *Machine Intelligence*, **16**, 221–41.

McAdams, S. and Bregman, A. (1979). Hearing musical streams. *Computer Music Journal*, **3**, 4, 26–60.

Nettheim, N. (1979). Comment on a paper by Gabriel on Cooke's theory. *Psychology of Music*, **17**, 2, 32–3.

Rameau, J. P. (1750, trans. 1971). *Treatise on Harmony*. New York.

Rosner, B. and Meyer, L. (1981). *Melodic Processes and the Perception of Music*. London.

Schoen, M. (1927). *The Effects of Music*. London.

Seashore, C. (1938, repr. 1967). *The Psychology of Music*. New York.

Smith, H., Stevens, K., and Tomlinson, R. (1965). On an unusual mode of chanting by certain Tibetan lamas. *Journal of the Acoustical Society of America*, **61**, no. 5, 1,262–4.

Sundberg, J. and Lindquist, J. (1973). Musical octaves and pitch. *Journal of the Acoustical Society of America*, **54**, 922–9.

Tenney, J. and Polansky, L. (1980). Temporal Gestalt perception in music. *Journal of Music Theory*, 205–39.

Teplov, B. (1966). *Psychologie des aptitudes musicales*. Paris.

Tobias, J. (1970, 1972). *Foundations of Modern Auditory Theory*, 2 vols. New York.

Ward, W. D. (1954). Subjective musical pitch. *Journal of the Acoustical Society of America*, **26**, 36.

Warren, R. (1974). Auditory temporal discrimination by trained listeners. *Cognitive Psychology*, **6**, 237–56.

Warren, R. and Obusek, C. (1972). Identification of temporal order within auditory sequences. *Perception and Psychophysics*, **12**, 86–90.

Winograd, T. (1968). Linguistics and the computer analysis of tonal harmony. *Journal of Music Theory*, **12**, 2–49.

**MUSIC PERCEPTION: HISTORY OF THOUGHT.** The study of music perception has a fascinating history. From the time of Pythagoras in the sixth century BC, thinking on the subject was heavily influenced by two factors. One was a profound distrust in the evidence of our senses (particularly our sense of *hearing), and the other was an obsession with numerology. As Boethius, the leading music theorist of the Middle Ages and a strong follower of Pythagoras, wrote: 'For what need is there of speaking further concerning the error of the senses when this same faculty of sensing is neither equal in all men, nor at all times equal within the same man? Therefore anyone vainly puts his trust in a changing judgement since he aspires to seek the truth.'

Matters were made even worse by the strong theoretical link, also stemming from the Pythagoreans, between music and astronomy. It was argued that the planets as they moved must surely produce sounds which would vary with their speeds and their distances from the Earth. It was further argued that the distances between the Earth and the different planets were such that the combination of sounds emitted must form a harmony. Fig. 1 shows the Pythagorean view of the distances of the planets relative to each other, and the musical intervals formed thereby. (This was the prevailing view in ancient and medieval times.) The distance from the Earth to the Moon formed a whole tone, from the Moon to Mercury a semitone, from Mercury to Venus another semitone, from Venus to the Sun a tone and a half, from the Sun to Mars a tone, from Mars to Jupiter a semitone, from Jupiter to Saturn a semitone, and finally from Saturn to the Supreme Heaven a semitone.

Considerable discussion centred on the issue of why, if the heavenly bodies do indeed produce this harmony, we cannot hear it. One suggestion, fielded by Censorinus (*fl. c.*238), was that the loudness of this sound is so great as to cause deafness. Another, more sophisticated view was that since this sound is present at all times, and since sound is perceived only in contrast to silence, we are not aware of its presence (perhaps this was one of the first suggestions concerning auditory adaptation).

At all events, the link between music and astronomy in ancient and medieval times was so great that the scientific half of the programme of higher education developed into the Quadrivium: the related studies of geometry, arithmetic, astronomy, and music. And even very recently Paul Hindemith in his book *A Composer's World* endorsed this association, writing that Johannes Kepler's 'three basic laws of planetary motion, expounded at the beginning of the seventeenth century, could perhaps not have been discovered, without a serious backing of music theory'.

The Copernican revolution did, however,

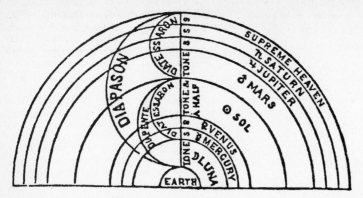

**Fig. 1.** Pythagorean view of the universe, in musical intervals.

weaken the link between music and astronomy, since it became clear that the planets did not in fact form a harmony. Nevertheless, the strong rationalistic and numerological approach to musical issues persisted. A few enlightened thinkers pleaded for empiricism (notable among these was Galileo's father, Vicenzo Galilei). However, their writings had little impact; and Hermann von *Helmholtz in 1862 felt impelled to express his concern on this matter in his book *On the Sensations of Tone*. He wrote: 'Up to the present time, the apparent *connection* of acoustics and music has been wholly external, and may be regarded as an expression given to the feeling that such a connection must exist, rather than its actual formulation.' And yet, despite Helmholtz's writings, the numerological approach has prevailed right up to very recent times.

However, we are now witnessing a most interesting phenomenon. The advent of electronic music and the increasing use of the computer as a compositional tool has caused a profound change in the thinking of many music theorists, particularly those who are also composers. If they are to make effective use of this new technology they need to obtain answers to various questions in perceptual psychology. For instance, they need to know the characteristics of a complex sound spectrum that result in a single sound image, and those that result in several simultaneous but distinct sound images. Given that sounds of any spectral composition can now be generated, they wish to characterize the dimensions underlying the perception of timbre, so that they can create sounds that vary systematically along these dimensions. Given the potential to generate any sequence of sounds, they need to develop an understanding of the perceptual and mnemonic constraints of the listener, so that their music will not fall on uncomprehending ears.

This same technological development has provided psychologists with the tools with which to explore the mechanisms underlying our processing of music. Such studies, apart from their implications for music, are of considerable value to our understanding of perceptual systems, mechanisms of memory and attention, and even abstract cognitive activity. Music is unique in that it involves an elaborate and highly organized processing system where verbal labelling plays a very minor role.

Given this new interest on the part of both psychologists and musicians, we are at present witnessing an explosion of collaborative work between the two disciplines. This type of interaction is quite recent, but already it has considerably advanced our understanding of the brain mechanisms underlying music perception.

See also MUSIC, PSYCHOLOGY OF.            D. D.

Boethius, *De institutione musica*; trans. Bower, C. M. (1967), *Boethius' The Principles of Music*. Ann Arbor, Michigan.

Hawkins, Sir J. (1853; repr. 1963). *A General History of the Science and Practice of Music*. London.

Helmholtz, H. von (1862). *On the Sensations of Tone* (4th edn., 1877; trans. Ellis, A. J., 1885; repr. 1954, New York).

Hindemith, P. (1961). *A Composer's World*. New York.

Hunt, F. V. (1978). *Origins in Acoustics*. New Haven.

**MYERS,** CHARLES SAMUEL (1873–1946), British psychologist, born in London. He qualified in medicine at Cambridge but his interests lay in the natural sciences. After a brief period as professor of psychology at King's College, London, he returned to Cambridge, where he took over the lectureship in experimental psychology from W. H. R. *Rivers. With the assistance of members of his family, he founded the Cambridge psychological laboratory, of which he became director in 1913. His *Text Book of Experimental Psychology* (1909, 3rd edn. 1925) was for long the standard introduction to students of psychology at Cambridge, though it was criticized in some quarters for the perhaps excessive weight which the author placed on the special senses, psychophysics, and the work of Hermann *Ebbinghaus.

During the First World War, Myers served as a physician in the Army. Many years later, in 1940, he published *Shell-shock in France, 1914–18* based upon his wartime experiences. After the war he moved to London and founded the National Institute of Industrial Psychology, of which he was the first director.

Myers's books include *Mind and Work* (1920), *Industrial Psychology in Great Britain* (1926), and *In the Realm of Mind* (1937).                    O. L. Z.

**MYERS,** FREDERIC WILLIAM HENRY (1843–1901), British writer, born at Keswick. He was a Fellow of Trinity College, Cambridge, where he became friendly with Edmund Gurney, and Henry Sidgwick who became the first president of the Society for Psychical Research in 1882. Myers was interested in \*spiritualism several years before the SPR was founded. Professionally, he was a school inspector, and a voluminous if not particularly good poet. His *magnum opus* is the remarkable *Human Personality and Its Survival of Bodily Death* (2 vols., 1903). Here he discusses hundreds of cases of phenomena such as 'fantasms of the dead', 'automatism', 'trance states', 'possession', and 'disintegrations of personality', as well as hypnotism and other phenomena.

Hall, T. H. (1964). *The Strange Case of Edmund Gurney.* London.

**MYOPIA.** See EYE DEFECTS AND THEIR CORRECTION.

# N

**NATIVISM.** The doctrine that certain capacities or abilities, especially of sense perception, are inherited rather than acquired by learning.

It can be surprisingly difficult to establish what is inherited and what learned, for much that is inherited develops, sometimes over several years, by maturation, and this is hard to distinguish from development by experience and learning. Often there is a mixture of maturation from inheritance and learning from experience—as in the infant's development of crawling and walking. Even for *language development in children there may be innateness, gradually maturing, and—as obviously there is—learning from experience of adult speech. As is well known, Noam Chomsky has suggested that natural human languages are based on a common 'deep structure', which is inherited and makes the infant's learning task possible (see LANGUAGE: CHOMSKY'S THEORY). Part of the evidence for inherited deep structure is indeed the apparent impossibility of the task with which the infant is faced, that of discovering the structure of language.

There is a similar controversy over how much visual and other *perception develops in the individual by maturation from inherited brain structures and how far (if at all) the physiology is developed or modified by early experience. It has been suggested that linguistic deep structure might be a pre-human, pre-language, perceptual classifying system developed by natural selection, over hundreds of millions of years, for perceiving and behaving appropriately to various kinds of objects. If that is so, it would explain how the deep structure could have developed so rapidly, on the biological time-scale, for human language.

See also INNATE IDEA.

**NATURAL SELECTION.** See EVOLUTION: NEO-DARWINIAN THEORY.

**NECESSITY.** See POSSIBILITY.

**NECKER CUBE.** A drawing of a wire cube (drawn without perspective) which spontaneously reverses in depth (Fig. 1). It was first described by the Swiss naturalist and crystallographer L. A. Necker in a letter to Sir David *Brewster in 1832. Necker discovered it while looking at rhomboid crystals with a microscope and drawing them: the drawings switched in depth and no longer seemed to compare with the crystals as seen with the microscope. There are many other depth-ambiguous figures.

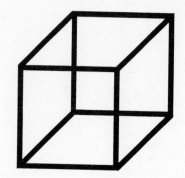

**Fig. 1.** Necker cube. This can be seen as switching spontaneously in depth, the front face reversing with the back face.

A true wire cube will also reverse in depth, and then shows a marked change of shape. The true front, but apparent back as it is reversed, appears too large; though the back and front faces appear almost the same size when unreversed. This shows that size scaling, normally producing size constancy, can operate from apparent distance, as in *Emmert's law for *after-images which increase in apparent size when seen 'projected' on screens of increasing distance, though without any change of the retinal image.

See also ILLUSIONS.

Gregory, R. L. (1970). *The Intelligent Eye*. London.
Necker, L. A. (1832). Observations on some remarkable phenomena seen in Switzerland; and an optical phenomenon which occurs on viewing of a crystal or geometrical solid. *Philosophical Magazine*, 3rd ser., **1**, 329–37.

**NEGOTIATING,** the use of communication between parties to reach agreement, is both a highly specialized social skill and a part of everyday dealings between people. It is a highly complex proceeding, involving the full range of human motives, attributes, and behavioural skills.

At its most commonplace, negotiation can be said to take place in all social encounters. When two people are getting to know each other they are consciously or unconsciously transacting. Each is 'performing' for the benefit of the other, and each is employing cue perception and skills of interpretation to understand the other's meanings. At the same time each conveys to the other the impression the other has created, and each is motivated to conform to the mirror-image received from the other, or to correct distortions. The continuance of the encounter depends on the creation of a coherent pooling of meaning, albeit one that may be collusive, sustained by deception of self and the other. Each 'actor' needs two sets of cognitive and behavioural skills: the ability to project or imagine himself in the role of the other, and the ability to improvise a performance that will convey the desired self-image.

In formal negotiation, this interactive process is embedded in a complex system of rules and relationships. The parties may be bargaining on behalf of constituents, or principals, to secure agreement over some decision, joint action, or form of words. The negotiator's role is then considerably complicated by forces such as the known position of his principals and their expectations of his behaviour, the dictates of wider social norms and values, and the pressure generated by the encounter to reach agreement. The nature of the pressures is unlikely to be the same for both parties: in industrial negotiation the union representative is typically constrained most of all by the demands of his membership. Such negotiation becomes very much a question of mutual attempts at influence, where the 'fate' of each protagonist is dependent on the moves made in the game by the other. The basic ploy usually takes the form of coercive threats, though these have to be exercised with care. Threats of too great a magnitude may well elicit a reaction that terminates the negotiation or engenders an escalating series of hostile exchanges, while threats that are too mild will be ineffective and damage the negotiator's credibility. On the other hand, participants also have the capacity to reward one another, principally by means of concessions. The dilemma here for the negotiator is how to make concessions that will not compromise his bargaining position, or damage his image, by indicating weakness or lack of commitment to earlier positions.

The reason why such conflicts, in most cases, do not end in stalemate or breakdown is that parties set out with the aim of reaching agreement and the pressure to settle mounts as negotiation proceeds. Moreover, negotiation takes place in a normative climate of shared expectations. The most powerful expectation is the 'norm of reciprocity': trust and good faith in bargaining, which are highly correlative with outcomes satisfactory to both parties, are dependent on the understanding that the behaviour of one side is likely to be reciprocated by the other.

Most formal negotiations have a strong 'distributive' component: what one side gains the other loses. Each party has a 'target' settlement point and a minimum 'sticking' point in mind, and each tries to find out about his opponent's targets and limits while concealing his own. If the two ranges within these two points are seen to overlap, both parties will aim at a point closest to their opponent's sticking point. If they do not overlap, then each will strive to shift his opponent's limits or be forced to shift his own; the inevitable alternative is breakdown of negotiations. Since the costs of breakdown are unequal, much tactical behaviour is geared to de-emphasizing the cost to one's own side and emphasizing the cost to one's opponent.

The opening moves of a negotiation are crucial. It is common to witness 'blue sky' bargaining, where extreme demands are progressively retreated from by the use of concessions, though this is an extravagant strategy that can lead to considerable 'image loss'. The extreme alternative—a 'final-offer-first' strategy—is risky: it deprives one's opponent of any credit with his principals for gain in negotiation, and so to be successful it demands that the offer involve a sufficiently large concession in order that a mutually acceptable bargain be struck.

But negotiation is seldom purely distributive: often it also contains 'integrative' components, i.e. the aim is not just to divide up the cake, but also to see if the size of the cake can be enlarged to the benefit of both sides. For this type of objective to be achieved, it is necessary that parties co-operate in a creative, trusting, and open manner—conduct which may be inimical to the distributive goal of preventing one's opponent from acquiring a disproportionate share of the enlarged cake.

A good deal of strategic purpose in negotiating is less palpable. Effort may be directed at changing the attitudes of the other side. The promise of rewards and punishments may be deployed to create changes in the relationship, the level of trust, the motivation of one's opponent, or his legitimacy.

The most difficult and delicate task for the negotiator as representative is 'intra-organizational bargaining': maintaining a positive relationship between the changing parameters of the negotiation and the wishes of his principals. Depending on how amenable his principals are, he may adopt an active or a passive approach to the task; but in any case he will be well advised to set his principals' initial expectations at a realistic level, for he may need to persuade them into revised expectations as negotiations proceed. He may also need to conceal or rationalize discrepancies between his actions and their demands, and sell the deal at the end. Tacit collusion is common between opposing negotiators cognisant of the pressures to which each other is subject—for example, by engaging in set-piece conflicts and reconciliations in which neither goals nor achievements are highly valued in reality but which will 'sweeten' the principals.

Formal negotiations are generally public affairs, conducted by two teams rather than two individuals. The effect of an audience is usually to make the team wish to appear dominant, and this is likely to lead to aggressive behaviour. Studies of intergroup conflict show how a team tends to overvalue its own products, devalues those of the opposing team, polarizes towards extreme positions, distorts or restricts communication between the teams, and allows 'group think' to dull its ability to search for divergent or creative solutions. Small teams of negotiators who know and like each other are more likely to reach agreement—a fact frequently demonstrated in the conduct and outcome of international negotiations.

Finally, negotiations do not take place in a temporal vacuum, but usually are governed by time pressures. Early in the bargaining process the differences between the sides often appears vast; subsequently, a period of informality develops in which the parties explore for openings and leads, often amid rising conflict within each group. As the pressure to settle increases, the parties concentrate on tractable issues, with (in the case of successful negotiations) a trade-off of the remainder in a final 'decision-making crisis'. Transition through these stages is often helped by the mediation of a third party, associating concessions with minimum loss of face. The process of reaching agreement is never simple, but is often and skilfully achieved for the sake of social order.                         N. N.

Fisher, R. and Vry, W. (1983). *Getting to Yes*. London.
Morley, I. E. and Stephenson, G. M. (1977). *The Social Psychology of Bargaining*. London.
Morley, I. E. (1981). Negotiation and Bargaining, in Argyle, M. (ed.) (1981), *Social Skills and Work*. London.
Rubin, J. Z. and Brown, B. R. (1975). *The Social Psychology of Bargaining and Negotiation*. London.
Strauss, A. (1978). *Negotiations*. San Francisco.
Walton, R. E. and McKersie, R. B. (1965). *A Behavioral Theory of Labor Negotiations*. New York.
Warr, P. B. (1973). *Psychology and Collective Bargaining*. London.

**NEILL,** ALEXANDER SUTHERLAND (1883– 1973), British educator, born at Forfar. He described his growing-up near Dundee in his last book, *Neill! Neill! Orange Peel*. His father was a village schoolmaster and they lived in a poor, hardy, farming community. His mother strove for respectability, cleanliness, and godliness. A. S. Neill wrote vividly about his Scottish Calvinistic upbringing: there was the gruesome Sabbath, designed to instil fear of the Lord and guilt about sexual matters. Their mother found Neill and his sister 'investigating' each other's genitals when they were small children and they were severely thrashed and locked up. In Neill's life there are often indications of neuroticism: the 'learning block' as a student, the fact that the Army was prepared to discharge him on medical grounds (an act of compassion that probably saved his life), his psychoanalysis with the educationist Homer Lane and Stekel, his relationship with Wilhelm Reich (1897–1958), and his difficulty in coming to terms with sex and authority. His considerable intellectual ability, together with his intuitive love for children, in whom he probably invested a desire to compensate for his own blighted childhood, produced one of the most influential educators of modern times. His school, Summerhill, was overrun with visitors until the children complained, his books have been read by millions, and there is

rarely a debate on educational principles when his name is not mentioned.

Beating children has been declared illegal by the European Court of Human Rights, and in the UK many local authorities have now forbidden the use of corporal punishment. The doubts about beating children and the restraints placed on teachers owe a great deal to the debate first fuelled by Neill's passionate advocacy of the rights of children. He defended the rebellious and the 'problem child'. At Summerhill he took on children expelled from their conventional schools. He saw that the liar, the thief, and the bed-wetter had become what they were because they had received no love from their parents or their teachers. When a boy broke a window, Neill stood by his side and broke another window and so seemed to say to the child, 'I approve of whatever you may do; you are more important than a broken window'. But there were limits to his permissiveness: what a disturbed child might do was not permitted to everyone. There were rules when the safety of children was at stake, and he could get very cross when a child misused his woodworking tools. He did not allow sexual freedom at Summerhill in case a child became pregnant, or, and this was possibly more important to Neill, in case the whole school was closed down by the authorities. The example of Homer Lane's Commonwealth and the allegations of scandal that ended it may have cast a shadow over Neill. He was rarely allowed to work with 'normal' children; most of his pupils came to Summerhill as a last resort.

Educationally the teaching methods employed at Summerhill were overtaken by progressive methods elsewhere. The pupils were largely middle-class and came from families prosperous enough to pay for the education of their children. There was not enough money to pay good salaries and staff turnover was high. Neill seemed much better at understanding the needs of children than those of adults. The great liberator of the young could also be strangely authoritarian with his staff. But the school continues, as does Neill's influence in the world outside, his love for children, his respect for their needs and rights. His reaction to the unfeeling authoritarianism of the Scottish educational system and the more barbaric aspects of conventional public schools has made a great number of schools less oppressive and more creative. It should be added that there have been times when a false 'permissiveness' has been unjustly ascribed to Neill. It has been used as an abdication from adult responsibility, a sentimental incapacity to accept that children need boundaries and a control which is not necessarily harsh. Excessive indulgence of the child has nothing to do with freedom and can be as destructive as the forces which Neill attacked so effectively in his lifetime.                         C. H.

Croall, J. (1983). *Neill of Summerhill*. London.
Croall, J. (1983). *All the best, Neill* (a collection of his letters). London.

Neill, A. S. (1961). *Summerhill: a radical approach to education*. London.

Neill, A. S. (1977). *Neill! Neill! Orange Peel*. London.

Skidelski, R. (1969). *English Progressive Schools* (contains a comprehensive bibliography on Neill and others involved in the progressive movement). London.

Wills, W. D. (1964). *Homer Lane: a biography*. London.

**NERVE CONNECTIONS: HOW THEY ARE FORMED.** In the mature vertebrate nervous system there is a very large number of neurones ($10^{12}$ is the figure frequently quoted for man) and these are extensively interconnected by nerve fibres to form highly complex patterns, which are remarkably constant from one animal to another. These patterns frequently show topographic order, in the sense that one particular set of neurones (for example, the ganglion cells of the retina) 'project' their nerve fibres to a second set of neurones (for example, the cells of one of the primary visual centres of the brain), in a fashion which preserves the organization of the first set of cells in the pattern of the connections that they form with the second set. In this manner the first set of neurones can be said to 'map' on to the second. This phenomenon, whereby the neighbourhood relationships of cells in one set are maintained in the connection pattern formed with the other set, is common within the *nervous system. It is known that many of the functions of the nervous system depend on the existence of these orderly mappings, and here we are concerned with how such nerve connections may be established during development.

Ideally, we would like to be able to investigate the development of all the individual constituent nerve fibres that comprise a particular set of orderly interconnecting neurones, together with the micro-environment through which they grow and the cells they eventually contact. This sort of approach, where the developing system is followed in detail at a single cell level, is possible only in certain 'simple' invertebrate nervous systems, where small numbers of individually identifiable neurones exist. In more complex vertebrate nervous systems, where the numbers of neurones involved may be very large and most of the cells cannot be individually identified, a useful approach has been to study *classes* of neurones which have orderly projections and to try to find general rules which govern the formation of their connection patterns.

The nervous system develops over a certain time, beginning in embryonic life and continuing for a period which depends on the species examined. Within any animal the development of the nervous system is not uniform; different types of neurones develop and form their connections at different times (see NEURONAL CONNECTIVITY AND BRAIN FUNCTION). At any particular time a neurone can only form connections with other neurones that have already developed sufficiently to be able to receive such connections. As a neurone

develops, its surrounding environment of glial cells, other neurones, and axons, will be unique at any given instant, and the role of this environment is crucial. What are the cues in the environment which tell the axonal growth cones where to grow and ultimately how to find their correct target structures? Various mechanisms have been proposed to account for the specific patterns of axonal outgrowth that may be observed in development. For instance: (i) There may occur the expression of particular sets of molecular components in the cell membranes of certain cells along the fibre pathway, which are recognized and preferentially responded to by the growing axons. (ii) Fibres may grow preferentially along specific extra-cellular substances in the environment which are manufactured by cells along the appropriate pathway and not, or to a lesser extent, elsewhere. (iii) There may be passive guidance by certain structural or spatial aspects of the environment which could lead axons towards the correct target regions. (iv) The direction of outgrowth of nerve fibres may be influenced by the differential distribution in their local environment of substances produced elsewhere in the system.

The recognition by growth cones of certain cell-surface molecular markers is the basis of the chemo-affinity hypothesis expounded by Roger Sperry in the 1940s (see BRAIN SCIENCE: SPERRY'S CONTRIBUTION) and foreshadowed by the work of Cajal and Langley at the end of the nineteenth century. This idea is that fibres are guided to their targets along specific pathways by recognizing cellular cues expressed on either glia or other neurones. At the simplest level, these cues need only be expressed at a very few choice points along the pathway to be followed by the fibres. Once the fibre has reached the general region of its target structure, the recognition of a specific set of cell surface molecules could determine which cell, or cells, the fibre will *synapse with.

The observations which led to this hypothesis involved the remarkable precision with which the optic nerve fibres of lower vertebrates are able to regenerate, after injury, to their original target sites in the main visual centre of the brain, the optic tectum. In these experiments the optic nerve fibres became disorganized at the point of the lesion and regrew as an abnormally ordered array, yet they nevertheless returned to their original target sites. Although numerous studies have evoked this hypothesis as a controlling mechanism for development, there is still very little direct evidence to support it. A major argument cited against the idea of individual cytochemical labelling of neurones is the vast array of molecules which could be needed to specify all connections in the nervous system. More plausible are the ideas that specific molecules are expressed in gradient fashion such that comparatively few molecular types would be needed to establish any one topographic projection. An alternative idea is that, by modulating the expression of surface molecules, target neurones could be made transitorily attractive to particular ingrowing axons at an appropriate time in development.

Some of the best examples of cell recognition by neurones exist in invertebrate nervous systems. Studies in the developing insect nervous system have shown that growing axons do respond to specific cells in their immediate environment. Axons growing in the developing limb are found to contact and positively respond to a series of cells which lie along their route. It has been postulated that these cells may form a series of 'stepping-stones' guiding the axons towards their targets in the central nervous system (Bate, 1976). It is as yet unclear whether these cells are specifically responded to by particular axons or whether they form a more generalized set of pathway cues which could be used by any axon which might encounter them. It has also been found that, in some cases, although selective destruction of individual 'stepping-stones', or 'guide-post' cells can prevent the normal sequence of fibre growth at that time (Bentley and Caudy, 1983), it may still be possible for an approximation to the normal connection pattern to be achieved by other mechanisms (Berlot and Goodman, 1984). Thus it is likely that there is an overlapping series of contingency plans available to the system, whereby if one mechanism fails, another can take over.

Another variant on the concept of specific cytochemical recognition is the idea that sub-populations of the growing neurones may have different cell-surface, and thus axon-surface, properties. By recognition of these differences, a growing axon could select an appropriate route along neighbouring axons, within a common nerve pathway. Some good evidence exists for this idea of selective fasciculation. An example, again from the insect nervous system, is that the growth cones of certain fibres called the $G$ axons in the locust are able to distinguish between the neurones they encounter. These growth cones grow as a part of a bundle of axons, but within the bundle they preferentially contact only one particular type of axon, the $P$ axon. If the preferred $P$ axons are eliminated before the $G$ growth cone reaches the bundle, the growth cones will not fasciculate with other axons in the bundle and cannot extend to their targets (Raper et al., 1983). A good example of selective fasciculation within growing fibre populations has been found in the chick visual system, where experiments in tissue culture have shown that fibres from temporal retina tend to fasciculate with other temporal fibres, whereas fibres from nasal retina have no such selective preferences (Bonhoeffer and Huf, 1985).

An extension of the selective fasciculation hypothesis is the idea that ingrowing axons could establish a topographic projection by referring only to information expressed on the surfaces of adjacent axons. In other words, each axon would be able to recognize the axon surface of its neighbour neurones, and terminate in adjacent positions. For the correct orientation of a projec-

tion formed in this manner, some form of cue would be required in the target structure. This could simply be the sequence of growth or maturation of the target cells, the position at which the first axons enter the target field, or a simple gradient function complementary to a particular subset of labels in the population of growing axons.

In the spaces that surround the cells of the developing nervous system there exists a matrix of various secreted molecules. This extra-cellular matrix (ECM) has been found to contain molecules which form very favourable substrates for axonal growth and for cell migration. Of these, laminin and fibronectin have been most extensively studied. Isolation and purification of these substances has enabled their axon-guiding properties to be investigated in tissue culture. More recently, with the development of appropriate monoclonal antibodies, the roles of various ECM components in the guidance of axons in certain parts of the intact developing nervous system have been investigated. Since these are secreted molecules, variations in the levels of production by cells which lie along pathways subsequently to be followed by growing axons, could induce and later guide the outgrowth of the axons. The transitory expression of certain ECM components along the migration routes followed by cells from the neural crest (Thiery et al., 1982), and along axon pathways in advance of the growth cones, provides compelling evidence for such a guidance system. However, the cellular mechanisms which underlie the production of these molecules, the blueprint which would be necessary to define the positions of enhanced secretion, and the orchestration of the expression of these molecules by the cells lying along a particular pathway, are still largely a mystery.

The development of the nervous system occurs as a series of closely timed events and, as discussed above, for a particular set of axons the pathway along which they normally grow is unique for that instant. It is therefore possible that, in some cases, specific and orderly nerve connections could be formed by defined sequences of axonogenesis. Thus for a particular system the neurones could differentiate in an orderly sequence, producing waves of growing axons which then pass along a specific pathway delineated by those cells which exist at that particular time of nervous system development. This pathway could then lead the axons towards a simultaneously and sequentially differentiating target population of cells, with which they could connect in the sequence of their arrival. In this fashion the first arriving axon would connect with the first differentiated target neurone, the next arriving axon would connect with the next differentiated target neurone, and so on throughout the development of the system. The delineation of the boundaries of the pathway could rely on the physical arrangements of cells. It is known that the physical morphology of the substrate of a growing axon may influence the direction in which the growth cone extends. Alternatively, the cells that line the pathway may transiently express ECM components which are favourable for axonal growth.

This idea of spatio–temporal control may seem oversimplistic, but there is good evidence for such a system in the formation of ordered connections by optic axons in the water flea *Daphnia magna* (Flaster et al., 1982). In the more complex systems of higher animals, where extensive rearrangements of axons have been shown to occur, such ideas may seem improbable. However, in many 'complex' systems the initial formation of connections occurs over a relatively short distance, through a relatively uncomplex terrain, and involves few axons. Once an initial pattern of topographically ordered pathways and connections has been established, then subsequent growth of the vast numbers of axons in such systems could follow, using selective fasciculation as the main guidance mechanism.

A further possibility, particularly in early development, is that direction of outgrowth of nerve fibres may be partly controlled by the influence of substances released from the target structure. It has been shown that embryonic mouse sensory neurones in tissue culture may grow selectively towards their appropriate targets, cultured in the same dish, and ignore inappropriate target tissue (Lumsden and Davies, 1983).

Once a growing axon has reached its target structure, how does it know precisely which cell to make contact with? We have already outlined one widely accepted theory, that each axon recognizes a specific set of cell-surface molecules on the appropriate target cell. However, there is considerable evidence that nerve connections are not that specific. Indeed, each ingrowing axon will form many synapses with a variety of target cells, each of which will receive contacts from numerous incoming axons. Furthermore, there is good evidence to show that these connections are continually being broken and re-formed, not only as systems develop, but also in what, in the past, has been considered to be the adult, 'hard-wired' system. The idea of specific connections must therefore be seen as relative and not absolute. It seems that axons are directed to certain regions of their target structures, producing there a roughly ordered array. When the axons reach the region of their target group of cells, some unknown signal instructs them to stop extending as single axons and to produce multiple branches, each of which bears a mini growth cone. These axon arborizations explore the target region, forming connections with many cells in the appropriate area. This initial exuberant pattern of connections will be topographically ordered, but only at a somewhat coarse level. As development proceeds, the pattern of connections is refined by retraction of the most exuberant branches and the consolidation of synaptic contacts with cells in a very localized region. In this fashion each axon will form contacts with target cells also contacted by axons which arise from its neighbouring neurones.

The mechanisms which are responsible for this fine tuning of the initial connection pattern are believed to involve the function of the system. One idea is that synchronous nerve impulse activity may stabilize connections. If an array of neurones is locally stimulated, neighbouring neurones will initiate impulses at the same time, while other cells in the array will be silent. If several of the stimulated neurones contact the same target cell, then it will receive an increased number of simultaneous impulses and it is highly likely to respond. In contrast, a target cell which has only few contacts from the stimulated neurones and many contacts from unstimulated neurones, will remain silent. In time, contacts which rarely cause their target cell to respond may become redundant to the function of the system and eventually be withdrawn, so that each neurone then concentrates its contacts on those cells where it achieves maximal effect. Such a mechanism could gradually consolidate the contacts made by neighbouring neurones on neighbouring target cells.

Evidence for these ideas comes from studies of the development of nerve connections in the mammalian visual system. Initially the fibres from each eye form superimposed (Rakic, 1977) but topographically ordered projections to the lateral geniculate nucleus. During the early life of the animal, these overlapping projections segregate to form eye-specific bands of terminations. If nerve impulse activity is blocked during this phase of development, the normal segregation of optic axon terminal arbors does not occur (Schmidt and Tieman, 1985). More evidence comes from studies of regeneration in the lower vertebrate visual system. As previously discussed, regenerating optic axons in fish are able to re-form precise retinotopic connections. This process occurs gradually, with the initial connections forming a grossly retinotopic projection which is refined over a period of weeks. The blocking of nerve impulse activity during this period has been shown (Meyer, 1983) to impair the normal sequence of refinement of the retinotectal projection map.

R. M. G.
J. S. H. T.

Bate, C. M. (1976). Pioneer neurons in an insect embryo. *Nature*, **260**, 54–5.

Bentley, D. and Caudy, M. (1983). Pioneer axons lose directed growth after selective killing of guidepost cells. *Nature*, **304**, 62–5.

Berlot, J. and Goodman, C. S. (1984). Guidance of peripheral pioneer neurons in the grasshopper: adhesive hierarchy of epithelial and neuronal surfaces. *Science*, **223**, 493–6.

Bonhoeffer, F. and Huf, J. (1985). Position-dependent properties of retinal axons and their growth cones. *Nature*, **315**, 409–10.

Cajal, S. Ramon y (1892). *The Structure of the Retina*. English translation 1972, Springfield, Illinois.

Flaster, M. S., Macagno, E. R., and Schehr, R. S. (1982). Mechanisms for the formation of synaptic connections in the isogenic nervous system of *Daphnia magna*. In Spitzer, N. C. (ed.), *Neuronal Development*, 267–96. New York.

Langley, J. N. (1895). Note on regeneration of prae-ganglionic fibres of the sympathetic. *Journal of Physiology*, **18**, 280–4.

Lumsden, A. G. S. and Davies, A. M. (1983). Earliest sensory nerve fibres are guided to peripheral targets by attractants other than nerve growth factor. *Nature*, **306**, 786–8.

Meyer, R. L. (1983). Tetrodotoxin inhibits the formation of refined retinotopography in goldfish. *Developments in Brain Research*, **6**, 293–8.

Rakic, P. (1977). Prenatal development of the visual system in rhesus monkey. *Philosophical Transactions of the Royal Society, London B*, **278**, 245–60.

Raper, J. A., Bastiani, M. J., and Goodman, C. S. (1983). Guidance of neuronal growth cones: selective fasciculation in the grasshopper embryo. *Cold Spring Harbor Symposia in Quantitative Biology*, **48**, 587–98.

Schmidt, J. T. and Tieman, S. B. (1985). Eye-specific segregation of optic afferents in mammals, fish and frogs: the role of activity. *Cellular and Molecular Neurobiology*, **5**, 5–34.

Sperry, R. W. (1943). Visuomotor coordination in the newt (*Triturus viridescens*) after regeneration of the optic nerve. *Journal of Comparative Neurology*, **79**, 33–55.

Thiery, J.-P., Duband, L.-P., Rutishauser, U., and Edelman, G. M. (1982). Cell adhesion molecules in early chicken embryogenesis. *Proceedings of the National Academy of Science, Washington*, **79**, 6,737–41.

**NERVOUS SYSTEM.** For the neurologist, there is no such thing as the mind. There are certain activities of the brain endowed with *consciousness that it is convenient to consider as mental activities. Since one expects to find a noun adjoined to an adjective, one supposes that there must be a mind expressing itself in a mental way. But the requirements of language and of logical thought are not always the same; demands of syntax may lead to errors in thinking.

The central nervous system is the physical substance that provides its possessor with genetically determined ways of behaving and also ways of changing this behaviour. What has been inherited is structure, studied as anatomy, and the working of this structure, studied as physiology. It is often convenient, and often misleading, to categorize some parts of the functioning as mental activities. But this does not imply that behind this functioning is a structure that could be called the mind.

The life of animals consists of receiving and responding to information. In animals made up of more than a few cells, this requires a nervous system. In vertebrates, the nervous system consists of three parts: afferent nerve fibres with their receptors, efferent nerve fibres with their muscles and glands, and the central nervous system, formed by the spinal cord and the brain.

**The neurone.** The nervous system is made of cells, like every animal tissue. The essential cell is a nerve-cell or neurone. Neurones are the largest cells in the body. A small neurone may measure about 3 micrometres, but a large one stretches for over 1 metre, and far more than that in a whale or an elephant.

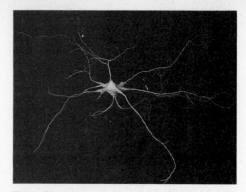

**Fig. 1.** Photograph of a three-dimensional model of a neurone, showing the cell-body and dendrites.

The neurone is considered to have three parts: the cell-body, the dendrites, and the axon. The dendrites are thin prolongations of the cell-body (shown in Fig. 1). Most sorts of neurone have one prolongation far longer than the others; this is the axon, the telegraph wire of the neurone, taking the message from one neurone to another or else to the muscle or gland that it supplies. The boundary of the neurone is a membrane, having certain properties on which the functioning of the nervous system depends. The axon with its surrounding membrane is called a nerve fibre. The ending of the nerve fibre is called, quite simply, the nerve ending or nerve terminal.

Fig. 1 is a photograph of a scale model of a neurone; it gives a better idea of the three dimensions of the cell than does a photograph taken down a microscope. The cell-body and the dendrites in actual fact would be covered with the nerve endings of other neurones.

All the neurones in the central nervous system of man are present at birth. As the baby grows, they enlarge and grow, the dendrites spread further, and the axon lengthens; but neurones, unlike most cells, do not divide and reproduce. Thus they are irreplaceable; and any neurones that we lose from accident or disease are lost for ever and we are so much the poorer.

Vertebrates have two kinds of neurones, those with myelinated and those with non-myelinated nerve fibres. Myelinated fibres have layers of a lipoprotein called myelin folded round the axon; non-myelinated fibres do not have these layers of insulating material. The myelin sheath is not continuous throughout the length of a nerve fibre; it is broken at little gaps, called the nodes of Ranvier or just nodes (shown in Figs. 2 and 3). Fig. 2 shows a myelinated fibre dissected out of a nerve of a baboon. It is the same as one from a human being. The arrows point to the nodes of Ranvier. Myelinated nerve fibres are shown at far greater magnification and with a good indication of three dimensions in Fig. 3. This photograph is focused on the external surface of a node of Ranvier, which is in the large fibre in the middle.

**Fig. 2.** Photograph of nerve fibre dissected out of a nerve of a baboon.

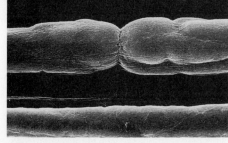

**Fig. 3.** Five myelinated nerve fibres shown by scanning electron microscopy.

**Receptors.** The way into the central nervous system is through the receptors. They are connected to the central nervous system by peripheral nerves; and peripheral nerves also connect the central nervous system to the muscles, to allow the animal to stand and move. The central nervous system of vertebrates is made up of the spinal cord and the brain. The spinal cord does not fill out the length of the vertebral column, for it is only about 40 centimetres long. The brain is an immensely complex and convoluted development of the cranial end of the spinal cord.

Receptors are natural transducers, converting the kinds of energy that they can receive into electric current. They can be classified as exteroceptors, reporting events in the outside world, and interoceptors, reporting the inside world of the body itself. They include receptors in muscles, tendons, and joints, the alimentary canal, and the bladder. There are receptors recording a steady state and changes occurring in that state; these include thermoreceptors, which report warmth and cold. Other receptors are silent until something new occurs. Among these are the receptors of the skin, which take notice of pressure and touch, pulling and stretching. All over the body are nociceptors, receptors reporting events that are liable to damage the body. There are chemoreceptors. Some of these are in the alimentary canal, including the nose and tongue. They report the arrival of molecules of substances that provide us with *smell and *taste. Further along the alimentary canal, they work without involving our conscious awareness; they serve to adjust the correct enzymes for the digestion of food.

Some receptors are formed of special cells; others are the nerve fibres themselves, unattached to any special end-organ. In the skin many receptors are naked nerve fibres, others are nerve endings surrounded by capsules of cells, looking like the layers of an onion surrounding the growing tip. Some receptors are massed together to form a sense organ, such as the eye or the ear. Others are scattered over a large area, for instance those of the skin or the viscera. If it is desirable to know the source of distant stimuli, one needs to have two separated sense organs. They then form the base of a triangle, the apex of which is the distant stimulus. When we are uncertain where a sound is coming from, we alter the angles of the base of the triangle, by turning first one ear and then the other in the supposed direction of the sound (see BINAURAL HEARING).

Not everything that a receptor receives is sent on to the higher levels of the central nervous system. Processing of the data begins in the sense organ and continues at the entrance to the spinal cord or brain and throughout the central nervous system. The brain itself controls its own input. The manner and purpose of this control is not yet known and can only be guessed at. It may be that if a certain location of the input is important at a particular moment—say something is damaging or hurting the back of the left hand—then the input from this region might have to be facilitated and that from other regions reduced or blocked. A mechanism such as this could form the first link in the chain of mechanisms of paying *attention.

All that the receptors report does not come to consciousness. Because we are occupied with what is happening around us, we tend to forget that many parts of the spinal cord and the brain are being informed about stimuli which reach no conscious level. Merely to maintain an upright posture depends on the reporting of the receptors of joints, muscles, the skin, and the organs of balance in the inner ear; this is going on all the time and none of it usually becomes conscious.

Not all of the information that the eye supplies to parts of the central nervous system makes us see something. There are visuo-motor reflexes that contribute to walking. In many birds and mammals, the cycles of life depend on the amount of light received. Lengthening periods of daylight or the days drawing in have their effects on the arrival of puberty and periods for procreation. They also cause hibernation or aestivation, and tell the animal when it is time to wake up and get moving. Somehow the amount of light is recorded and appropriate behaviour is brought about.

The sense of smell is so important to many animals that it is used for communication. Odoriferous substances, put out by animals in order to signal to others, are called pheromones. Sex pheromones are very commonly used. They may play a minor role in human sexual signalling. Certainly the attraction of the female rhesus monkey for the male depends entirely on her smell, and the male monkey emits a smell attractive to the female. Man has about thirty million olfactory receptors in each nostril, and they can respond to about twenty to thirty primary odours. The other smells that we can smell are thought to be mixtures of these primary odours.

**How the nervous system sends messages.** The behaviour of the central nervous system consists of passing messages from one lot of neurones to another. The message itself is sent in the form of a Morse code consisting only of dots. As the dots are always grouped together, they are usually referred to as a volley of nerve impulses, or just as a volley. The nerve fibre conducts impulses in one direction only. Afferent nerves outside the central nervous system conduct impulses towards the spinal cord and brain, and efferent nerves conduct them away from the central nervous system to the muscles and glands. Within the central nervous system, each nerve fibre is a one-way street.

One can talk of taking messages, for the nerve impulse is an instruction to the cell that receives it to do something. The message or impulse is an electric current, somewhat like the current sent along a telegraph or telephone wire. In the system invented by man, the electrical events take place in metal, in long thin wires. In natural systems, the electric current is carried by a flow of ions in fluid. In the telegraph, the current is carried passively along the wire; in the natural system, the nerve fibre itself generates the current that spreads along the fibre. The nerve impulse depends on the physical characteristics of the membrane surrounding the axon. This membrane is a semi-fluid lipid, permeable to certain hydrated ions and not to others. It is very permeable to potassium ions, less permeable to chloride ions, and far less permeable to sodium ions. These differences in permeability cause a different concentration of ions on the two sides of the membrane; and the different concentration gives rise to a difference in potential between the inside and outside of the axon. This potential difference, the inside being electronegative, the outside electropositive, is called the *resting potential*. The nerve impulse is a sudden, rapid, transient change in the permeability of the membrane to sodium ions. These positively charged ions pass through the membrane of the axon from the extracellular fluid, reversing the charge on the membrane from negative to positive. In this state, the membrane is more permeable to potassium ions, and so they flow out of the axon, through the membrane into the extracellular fluid—a process that brings back the former state with the inside negative and the outside positive. If this did not occur, the membrane could not be excited again. The passage of sodium ions carrying a positive charge is referred to as depolarizing the membrane, and the return to resting conditions is called repolarizing the membrane.

What has so far been described is how a nerve fibre at rest is excited. The next question is how this minute region of excitation spreads along the nerve fibre. The transient increase in permeability is induced by a potential change coming from a receptor or from the nerve endings of another nerve fibre. The increase in permeability causes current to flow between the spot that has become more permeable and the adjacent region of membrane. This circuit of current allows positively charged ions to pass through the membrane at the adjacent region; and so the cycle of events occurs in these neighbouring regions of the membrane. By such minute steps, the current spreads along the membrane of the axon. This spreading depolarization is called the *action potential*. The process takes place in one direction only, ahead of the region that has just been activated. The reason is that the membrane cannot be depolarized until it has been repolarized: in other words these electrochemical events cannot be repeated until the previous resting state has returned. Thus it is inevitable that the spreading permeability change will pass along the membrane only in front of the region that has just been active.

Similar events occurring at the receptor are called the generator potential or *transducer potential*. They are set off by the stimuli to which that receptor is sensitive. The generator potential starts off the action potential along the afferent nerve fibre.

The most primitive and smallest animals consisted of only a few cells with nerve-nets formed of only non-myelinated fibres. The faster conduction of impulses that became necessary as animals became larger, was not achieved by making nerve fibres with greater diameters: a new step in evolution occurred, the covering of nerve fibres with myelin sheaths. The conduction of the nerve impulse in myelinated fibres is different from that in non-myelinated fibres, and the continuous spreading of the current so far described is the mode of conduction in non-myelinated fibres. Conduction in myelinated fibres is called *saltatory conduction*, as the current jumps from node to node.

In saltatory conduction (illustrated in Fig. 4b) the current is also due to the passage of ions through the membrane; but in this case the membrane is covered by lengths of insulating material, the myelin sheath. The nodes are little breakages in this insulation. The current spreads along these fibres by passing through the non-insulated nodes, in through one and out through the next. This is a much faster way of conducting impulses than continuous conduction.

Once the electrical events have been started in a nerve fibre, they spread along it to its end. They are self-propagating, and nothing stops them, short of damage to or cutting the nerve fibre. A nerve fibre always produces the same amount of current; for the current is related to the resistance, and the resistance is inversely related to the radius of the fibre. The rate at which the impulses are conducted is between 0·5 and 2 metres per second in the case of non-myelinated fibres and from 2 to 120 metres per second in the case of myelinated fibres.

There are two ways in which nervous systems differ in principle from telephones and cables. They consist of inhibitory as well as excitatory neurones; and they are spontaneously active. The communication systems invented by man are excitatory: either you send a message or you don't. If you were to receive an inhibitory telegram, it would just say 'Keep quiet!' In the central nervous system, excitation and inhibition tend to cancel each other out. A neurone fires off an impulse when its threshold of excitability has been exceeded. Excitatory neurones tend to fire an impulse, inhibitory ones tend to stop it firing.

The nervous system starts being spontaneously active from an early moment *in utero* and continues until death. In man-made communication systems, nothing is happening until a message is sent. Into the mass of active neurones of the central nervous system, volleys of impulses are sent. It will be seen that inhibitory neurones are needed: the spontaneous activity may need to be quietened down as well as be increased.

Between the nerve endings of one neurone and the cell-body and dendrites of the next, there is a minute gap; it is about 200 nanometres wide in most cases. This region where the message is passed from one neurone to the next is called the synapse, after the Greek word for 'clasp', and the gap is called the synaptic gap or cleft. Structures and functions are spoken of in relation to the synapse as pre-synaptic and post-synaptic. The synapse is like a diode, conducting in one direction only. Any change in a message has to be made at a synapse, for once the impulse is travelling along a nerve fibre, it generally continues to the next synapse.

Many factors have an influence on the firing of a neurone: there is its threshold of excitability, its local chemical environment, and the sum of excitatory and inhibitory impulses it receives within a brief period of time. Each nerve impulse delivers a constant amount of excitation or of inhibition. The amounts of both are increased by increasing the number of impulses sent in a brief time. Once the post-synaptic neurone has fired an impulse, its excitation has to be raised to make it fire again. The excitatory effect of an impulse arriving on a motor neurone that works a large muscle of a cat's limb lasts 5 milliseconds. In this neurone, the relation between the intensity of current supplied to the neurone and the neurone's rate of firing off impulses is linear. In some other neurones, the relation is that of an S-shaped curve. In some places in the central nervous system, arriving excitatory impulses keep the post-synaptic neurone always ready to fire; only a few more impulses arriving will then fire it off.

The cell-body, like the human body, is not equally excitable all over. Out on the ends of the dendrites, the membrane is relatively inexcitable. Excitation delivered there may never fire the neurone but it may be sufficient to increase the excitability momentarily; thus impulses continually delivered far out on dendrites may keep the membrane of the cell-body at a certain threshold of excitability.

The kinds of excitation and inhibition discussed so far are called *post-synaptic potentials*. Another kind of inhibition is pre-synaptic inhibition. It is named pre-synaptic as it stops a nerve fibre delivering

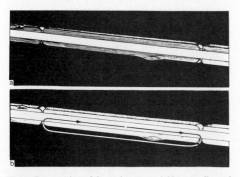

**Fig. 4.** Propagation of the action potential in a myelinated nerve fibre. **a.** Diagram of the axon with its myelin sheath and two nodes of Ranvier. **b.** Current circuit through the nodes.

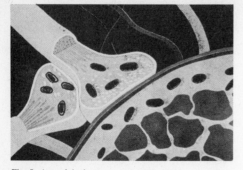

**Fig. 5.** A model of nerve terminals to show pre-synaptic inhibition. The nerve terminal coming from the left lower corner inhibits the nerve terminal on which it is ending before this nerve fibre can deliver its impulses to the cell-body on which it is ending.

its full amount of excitation just before it reaches the synapse where it ends. It is illustrated in Fig. 5. The fibre coming in from the bottom left corner inhibits the fibre on which it ends before that fibre delivers its quantum of excitation to the cell-body. Its effect is to cause partial or even complete blocking of the message. This blocking of the message in a fibre is an exception to the statement made above—that once the nerve impulse is travelling along a fibre, it continues to the end. As far as is known, pre-synaptic inhibition is a function only of excitatory neurones; there is no pre-synaptic inhibition of inhibitory neurones. Recent investigations lead one to conclude that dendrites of different neurones in juxtaposition can also influence each other.

With such a limited repertoire of interaction between neurones, it is surprising how complicated the total picture of neuronal activity can be. There are two common patterns of relations between neurones and groups of neurones. Messages can be spread far and wide from a few neurones or they can be channelled into a few pathways and sent on to only a few neurones. The first is called divergence and the second convergence. To give some idea of the figures involved, one might take as an example the large neurones known as Purkinje cells, after the anatomist who first described them early in the nineteenth century. On to each of these neurones there come 200,000 nerve endings from many other neurones: this is convergence. And a single neurone called a granule cell sends branches to 300–450 Purkinje cells: that is divergence.

There are other patterns of organization. One is surround or lateral inhibition. When a central or linearly arranged group of neurones is excited, there is concomitant inhibition of the surrounding neurones. This inhibition is strongest for the neurones immediately adjacent to those being excited and becomes weaker for the more distant neurones. The more strongly the central group of neurones is excited, the stronger will be the inhibition of the surrounding neurones. This kind of

organization has the effect of emphasizing contrasts. It was first discovered in the retina, where it is probably used to accentuate the edges and boundaries of what is seen. This reciprocal organization is not static. If the source of the central excitation is, for instance, a stimulus moving along the skin, then the line of excitation and surrounding inhibition will move; the moving stimulus on the skin excites new neurones as it moves, and these excited neurones inhibit different surrounding neurones as they themselves are turned on and off.

Excitation and inhibition at the synapse are electrical occurrences similar to those in the nerve fibre. There is a sudden increase in permeability of the post-synaptic membrane, and hydrated ions pass through it. Pre-synaptic inhibition is due to the flow of ions into the pre-synaptic fibre just before the nerve ending.

The response of any neurone depends on the following factors: the region of the membrane that receives nerve impulses, the temporal scatter of arriving impulses, the previous effect of hormones and endogenous peptides, and the chemical composition of the fluid surrounding the neurone. All these factors together determine the binary response of the neurone, to send an impulse or to remain silent.

Even though inhibition and excitation of the next neurone at the synapse depends on the passage of ions through the membrane in a fashion similar to the events of transmission along the nerve fibre, there are important differences. When an impulse reaches the end of a nerve fibre, a chemical substance is put out into the synaptic gap. This substance unites with the protein of the post-synaptic membrane, and the membrane with this substance becomes permeable to some hydrated ions and not to others; according to which ions pass, depolarization or excitation, or hyperpolarization or inhibition occur. The regions of the post-synaptic membrane where these chemical substances act are known as receptor sites; and the substances are called neurotransmitters or transmitters. The transmitters are synthesized in the cell-bodies of neurones; they are then passed along the nerve fibre and stored in vesicles in the nerve endings, remaining there until a nerve impulse arrives. The impulse liberates a constant amount of neurotransmitter into the synaptic gap; this passes across the gap and unites with the receptor site of the post-synaptic membrane. Whether excitation or inhibition occurs is determined by the size and shape of the pores of the receptor site. Smaller pores allow potassium and chloride ions to pass, resulting in inhibition, and larger pores allow sodium and chloride ions to pass, resulting in excitation. Once the transmitter has reacted with the post-synaptic membrane, it is inactivated and/or taken up again into the pre-synaptic nerve ending.

Neurones and their nerve fibres are often named according to the transmitter substance they synthesize and emit at their endings. So, for instance, one has cholinergic neurones, releasing acetylcholine, and noradrenergic neurones, releasing noradrenaline. Acetylcholine is the transmitter that works the muscles of the body; noradrenaline works muscles of the uterus and the blood vessels. The muscles of the alimentary canal are made to contract by many transmitters, including acetylcholine, noradrenaline, and many peptides.

In vertebrates, it appears that all nerve fibres act by putting out transmitters at their endings. At the various synapses in a chain of nerve fibres in the central nervous system different transmitters will be emitted. Also, outside the central nervous system, different neurones exert their effects by putting out their transmitters, making muscle fibres contract or glands secrete. A purinergic neurone, which has a short axon about 1·5 centimetres long, may be excited by a cholinergic nerve fibre, secreting acetylcholine; and the cholinergic neurone will have been excited by noradrenaline.

Parts of the nervous system working together to carry out a certain function often use the same transmitter for all the neurones concerned. Dopamine, for instance, is secreted by neurones concerned with waking the brain from *sleep. Noradrenaline is the transmitter used in the hypothalamus for controlling body temperature. Neurotransmitters are being discovered all the time, and an important research territory is that of peptides and hormones formed in the body that can act as neurotransmitters. (See DOPAMINE NEURONES IN THE BRAIN, and NEUROPEPTIDES, for further discussion.)

**Moving.** Plants are fixed, animals move. Here we discuss the activities of animals and the movements of various parts of their bodies.

Movement is due to the contraction of muscle fibres, and muscle fibres are caused to contract by impulses arriving in the peripheral nerves. If the nerve running to a muscle is cut, the muscle is paralysed. The nerve fibre goes to the neuromuscular' junction, which is a synapse between the nerve ending and the membrane covering the muscle fibre. From this region, electrical events similar to those of the nerve impulse spread over the membrane of the muscle fibre, causing the proteins of muscle to contract.

In vertebrates, the basic patterns of movement are organized in the spinal cord. For most quadrupeds—and this includes the crawling baby—the spinal cord arranges the basic pattern of running or walking: when a forelimb flexes, the opposite hindlimb extends, the other forelimb extends, and the remaining hindlimb flexes. During a movement, the muscles around a joint work according to a pattern of reciprocal innervation; when the limb is used for standing, the muscles around the joint tend to keep contracting together. Reciprocal innervation is organized so that as one group of muscles, say the flexors, contract, the

antagonist group, say the extensors, are relaxed. It is the same with the muscles used for breathing. When the muscles used for breathing in, contract, those for breathing out are relaxed.

Whether we stand, run, hop, or crawl, all the activity of the central nervous system finally ends with activating, or not activating, motor neurones. For this reason C. S. *Sherrington called the motor neurone the final common path. Whatever happens to the body, impulses are sent to the central nervous system, they go round and round in the brain, and they come out there, at the final common path of motor neurones.

All animals have inherited certain ways of responding to the situations they are likely to encounter. The more simple an organism, the more inevitable the behaviour will be; and the observer would not think of the animal as choosing how to behave. A minute organism endowed with positive phototaxis must go towards a light; another species, inheriting negative phototaxis, must escape from it.

The simplest and most automatic response to stimulation is a reflex movement. The word 'reflex' was introduced early in the nineteenth century by a British neurologist, Marshall Hall. He chose this word as he thought of the muscles as reflecting the stimulus, much as a wall reflects a ball thrown against it. By 'reflex' he meant the response of a muscle or several muscles to a stimulus that excites an afferent peripheral nerve. Since that time the meaning has been enlarged. It is now used to mean an inborn, immediate response of muscles or glands to a particular stimulus, involving the central nervous system.

Even a simple reflex, with only one synapse, such as the monosynaptic stretch reflex, is not the same on every occasion. This has been realized, and often forgotten, for about a hundred years. There are many factors influencing the one synapse between the afferent and the efferent nerve. There is the local and general state of excitability, and the number of reflex responses that have preceded the one being observed. For instance, if an identical stimulus to evoke a reflex response is repeated regularly several times a second, the response either increases or decreases. If the stimulus is repeatedly applied for many minutes, the local reflex response decreases and finally stops altogether.

There are many kinds of behaviour seen in animals lower in the evolutionary scale than mammals that in fact are reflex responses, though they appear not to be. The toad, for instance, has only two kinds of behaviour in its repertoire towards any moving object that it sees: it either turns towards it to snap it up, or else it turns away to escape. These are both reflex responses; which one occurs is related to the size of the object seen. Snapping-up-food behaviour is the answer to small objects moving in the field of vision, and avoiding and fleeing is the answer to large moving objects. To the naïve observer, these actions might well appear as behaviour based on choice, the animal making a decision what to do.

Most kinds of behaviour of the higher vertebrates are neither entirely reflex nor entirely subject to deliberation and decision: they have elements of both. When someone inadvertently burns you on the leg with a cigarette, a volley of impulses is sent off to the spinal cord from the skin, and nerve impulses continue to fire off for thirty minutes or so. From the local region of spinal cord, impulses are sent to many other parts of the spinal cord and brain. Some regions get the information before others, and some centres react automatically while others react only after impulses have been received from various higher parts of the brain. The sending of information to various parts of the brain is the physiological substratum for the functions classified as psychological, such as making a decision after pausing for deliberation. The first response to the burning cigarette is likely to be a flexion and withdrawal of the burnt leg with extension of the opposite limb to support the weight of the body. The lower parts of the brain are informed of the rapid movement of the lower limbs so that they adjust the posture for standing on one leg to remove the other from the damaging stimulus. A further necessary part of the reaction is to cause pain. In the brain all sensory information is integrated, the input from the eyes, the ears, the nose, the skin. The brain recognizes that the object causing the burn is a cigarette. The highest levels of the brain are needed to arrange behaviour related to the circumstances. The brain relates the new event to remembrances of things past. *Memory is used. Parts of the brain compare this new event with previous experience and note whether it is new and unfamiliar or something already known.

The first reflexes develop in the womb, as the structures are formed. The very earliest reflex responses occur around the mouth; the lips are turned towards the point stimulated. After birth, other reflex responses are added to the repertoire.

The essential reflex for maintaining posture is the stretch reflex; it is a servo-mechanism used to keep the muscles contracting to the right degree. When the muscle is pulled on and stretched, receptors within the muscle are excited and send impulses to the spinal cord. The nerves from the receptors of these muscles go to the motor neurones working the muscle and make it contract. When the stretch is removed, the receptors stop firing, the stimulus to the motor neurones of the muscle has gone, the motor neurones stop firing, and the muscle relaxes. Thus stretching a muscle makes it contract, and releasing it allows it to relax. In the stretch reflex, there is only one synapse, that between the afferent nerve fibres from the muscle receptors and the motor neurones working the muscle.

A baby learns to sit up when the organs of balance in the internal ear have established reflexes with the motor neurones working the muscles of the trunk and limbs. The basic reflexes

for standing, crawling, sitting, walking, and running depend on built-in circuits of neurones in the spinal cord, connected to circuits in the centre of the cerebral hemispheres and the cerebellum. The cerebellum is kept informed about the activity of all muscles, about acceleration and deceleration affecting the whole body, and about all other inputs to the central nervous system. As soon as the spinal cord starts performing a movement, impulses are sent up to the cerebellum and continue to be sent throughout the movement, so that the cerebellum is kept informed how the movement is progressing. For the cerebellum is an error-measuring device that compares the actual performance with the programme which it receives from the cerebral hemispheres.

Most movements are programmed by the brain, and they use lower-level reflex arrangements as their components. When you do touch-typing, the impulses leave the brain, programmed in time and place to hit the keys in order. Once the impulses are on their way, they cannot be interrupted. You know when you are going to type the wrong letter or the letters in the wrong order, and out they come, wrong; the knowledge comes too late to interrupt the planned movements. (See CHUNKING.)

The movements organized by the cerebral hemispheres depend on impulses sent down tracts of nerve fibres to the spinal cord. Some of these tracts have synapses on the way; others have no synapses until they are near the motor neurones. There is one large tract called the corticospinal tract; it is shown in Figs. 9 and 11. It is mainly a motor tract, though some of the fibres go to the posterior horn, which is an afferent part of the spinal grey matter. A recent development in evolution, it has reached its highest development in man and is used for carrying out the finest and most delicate movements of hands and feet, fingers and toes.

**The spinal cord and brain.** It is now necessary to describe some of the anatomical features of the spinal cord and brain. The spinal cord consists of a central region of grey matter, made up largely of the cell-bodies and dendrites of neurones, and a surrounding ring of white matter. The white matter consists of tracts of nerve fibres descending from and ascending to the brain. The input from the peripheral nerves of the body is delivered to neurones of the grey matter of the spinal cord. These data are then processed at this level, and the resultant nerve impulses are sent along the spinal tracts to various regions of the brain. The input from the organs of the special senses—as vision, hearing, smell, and taste are called—goes to the grey matter of the brain. The brain, like the spinal cord, consists of grey and white matter, but most of the grey matter is on the outside and the white matter inside; though there are some large masses of grey matter inside the cerebral hemispheres and cerebellum as well.

The brain is really an enlargement and opening out of the cranial end of the spinal cord. The first,

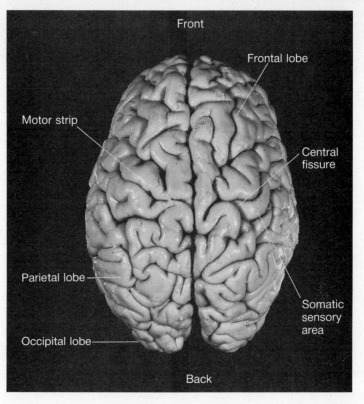

**Fig. 6.** Human brain seen from above.

slightly enlarged part is called the medulla oblongata (Figs. 7 and 8); the Latin term for the spinal cord is medulla spinalis. The medulla oblongata and the pons (Fig. 8) make up the hindbrain. From the roof of the hindbrain the cerebellum developed, first becoming large and important in birds. Further forwards or, to use the anatomical term, further rostrally (towards the beak) is the midbrain, and rostral to the midbrain comes the forebrain. When you take the brain out of the skull, what you first see are the two cerebral hemispheres. Each cerebral hemisphere is divided into lobes; they are called frontal, temporal, parietal, and occipital. Many anatomists also recognize a limbic lobe, which will be referred to later. The lobes are shown in Figs. 6, 7, 8, and 11.

The most posterior ridge or gyrus of the frontal lobe is the motor strip; it is the main source of the corticospinal tract. Most of the fibres of this tract go to the opposite side of the spinal cord, for each cerebral hemisphere mainly controls the opposite limbs. Many of the fibres marked as going to and coming from the cerebral cortex in Fig. 9 would be the fibres of the corticospinal tract. As they descend through the brain, they become collected into a narrower space; most of them cross over from one side to the other as they enter the spinal cord. The gyrus from which most of these fibres

come is called the pre-central gyrus; behind it is the post-central gyrus, and between the two is the central fissure (marked in Fig. 6). The post-central gyrus is the most anterior part of the parietal lobe. It is the somatic sensory area, a primary area for tactile and kinaesthetic input. There is another fissure, more prominent than the central fissure, the lateral fissure, shown in Fig. 7. It is the boundary between the temporal lobe below, and the frontal and parietal lobes above.

Once the cranium has been sawn through, the brain is easily lifted out of the skull. To remove it, one has to cut through the stalk of the pituitary (Fig. 8) and all cranial nerves, and also divide the medulla oblongata from the spinal cord. The cranial nerves were described and numbered from the front backwards by Thomas Willis in the seventeenth century. The first nerve cannot be seen in Fig. 8, as it was cut through when the brain was removed. It is the olfactory nerve, and is made up of thousands of nerve fibrils running vertically up from the cavity of the nose into the olfactory bulb (shown with most of the structures mentioned here in Fig. 8). From the olfactory bulb, impulses for smell are sent along the olfactory tract to the deeper parts of the temporal lobe. In Fig. 8, the second or optic nerve and the fifth or sensory nerve from the face can be seen. The pituitary gland is

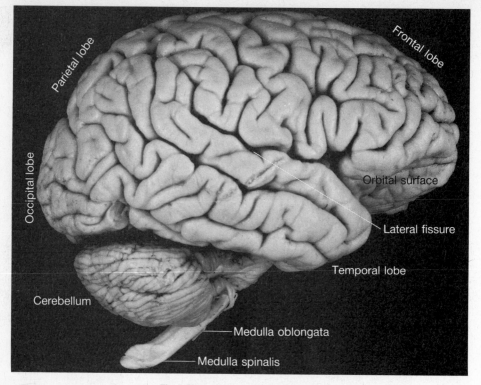

**Fig. 7.** Human brain seen from the right.

just behind the optic nerve. Tumours of the pituitary are liable to press on the optic nerve fibres and cause disturbances of vision, and, if they are not removed, blindness.

The cortex of the cerebral hemispheres is made up of six layers, the neurones being arranged in most places in columns of six. Vast numbers of nerve fibres run into these layers, and similar vast numbers leave them. The tracts in which these bundles of nerve fibres are collected are shown in Fig. 9. This figure shows another large mass of fibres, the optic radiations, passing backwards from the midbrain to the occipital lobe, to reach the primary visual area of the cortex. The pons is cut through the midline in this dissection; it is a bridge taking fibres from one side of the hindbrain to the opposite cerebellum. The great mass of fibres going to and coming from the cerebellum is also seen in this figure, as a large white band in the centre of the cerebellum.

There is a mass of interconnecting neurones with short axons throughout the core of the brain, named the reticular formation; a part of it is shown in Fig. 9. This is a very old part of the brain, being an essential structure for working vital functions. It organizes breathing, controls the heart, blood vessels, blood-pressure; it is concerned with sleeping and waking, with relaxation, and with the opposite state—vigilance and alertness. This system stops

all the input from receptors reaching the anatomical substrate of consciousness during sleep; it wakens us when the input is apparently urgent.

The two cerebral hemispheres are not equal and identical, neither morphologically nor physiologically. There is probably an inborn propensity for the two hemispheres to develop differently, and these differences are increased by experience and learning.

Each cerebral hemisphere organizes the movements of the opposite limbs, and the activity of each is co-ordinated by fibres passing across the large bridge, formed of nerve fibres, called the corpus callosum (shown in Figs. 11, 12, and 13). The two hemispheres are not equal partners in organizing movements; the left is the leading one, just as it is for speech. It keeps the store of learned skills. It programmes most movements, and it directs the right hemisphere to control the left limbs while it controls the right ones. If the great bulk of nerve fibres through the corpus callosum is divided, the movements of the right limbs, controlled by the left hemisphere, remain normal, but programmed movements of the left limbs become abnormal in a strange way. The afflicted person cannot comb his hair when asked to do so, for instance, but makes vague movements similar to combing movements, perhaps in the air above his head. When asked how he would point the way, he

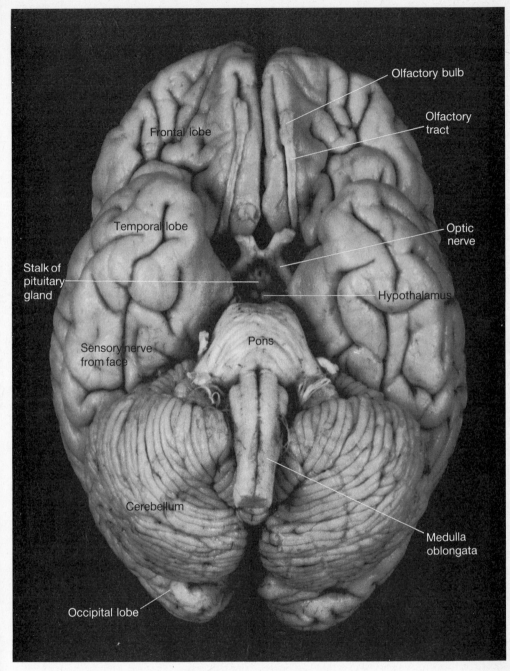

**Fig. 8.** Human brain seen from below.

may move his arm in an inadequate manner or just raise it vaguely in some direction. Although he can carry out more automatic and reflex movements, such as standing and sitting, quite normally, he cannot trace a circle on the ground with his foot nor point his toe when asked to do so. But all of these movements are performed quite normally by the right limbs. As the right hemisphere does not direct the left hemisphere, a lesion of the right hemisphere causes some paralysis of the left limbs but

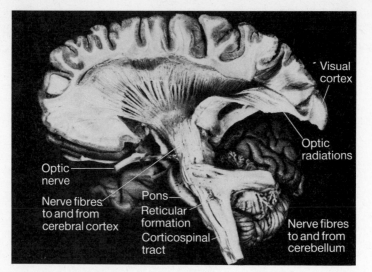

Visual cortex

Optic radiations

Optic nerve

Nerve fibres to and from cerebral cortex

Pons

Reticular formation

Corticospinal tract

Nerve fibres to and from cerebellum

**Fig. 9.** The human brain dissected to show the tracts of nerve fibres going to and coming from the cerebral cortex and the cerebellum, and the optic radiations, which are fibres running from the midbrain to the visual cortex of the occipital lobe.

has no effect on the limbs controlled by the left hemisphere. (For further discussion, see SPLIT-BRAIN AND THE MIND.)

**Types of muscle.** The movements of the body are not only the movements of the whole body in space; there are the movements of organs of the body, movements of the heart, the intestines, the bladder, the pupils of the eyes. The muscles working these organs are different from those making up the trunk and limbs.

There are two main kinds of muscle, smooth muscle and striated muscle, the names describing their appearance under a light microscope. One may make the generalization that smooth muscles work entirely automatically, without our having much influence on them; and striated muscles are the muscles we use when we intend to do something like getting out of bed or jumping over a fence. As we have seen, muscles are made to contract by receiving impulses from nerve fibres. Striated muscles are supplied by somatic nerve fibres, and non-striated muscles by nerve fibres of the autonomic nervous system.

**The autonomic nervous system.** This consists of two parts, the sympathetic and parasympathetic systems, which cannot be classified as being either central or peripheral, as they are both. The autonomic system is always active, though at any time one part may be more active than the other, each being activated by *emotion and behaviour depending on emotion. The sympathetic system is responsible for temperature regulation, contributes to the behaviour of threat and aggression, dilates the pupils and makes the hair stand on end, and controls the distribution of blood throughout the body by dilating or constricting blood vessels.

When the person has to be active, it distributes the blood, so that the muscles of the limbs get a lot and those of the alimentary canal little. When the body is active, the sympathetic system cools it by making the sweat-glands secrete sweat, for heat is lost by evaporating sweat. The parasympathetic system organizes micturition and defecation, and it is the main controller of the alimentary canal. Sexual functioning is mainly parasympathetic, with minor, but in the male essential, contributions from the sympathetic system.

**Perception.** Animals are active; they are not usually sitting around waiting to be stimulated. They spend a lot of time seeking information, engaging in what ethologists call exploratory behaviour; they are curious and are trying to satisfy their curiosity. They ask the question, 'What is this?' as we can see from cursory observation of domestic pets and of cows in the field. But curiosity has to be tempered with caution, the amount of each depending on the species of animal, and mainly on whether it is a herbivore or carnivore. Some sorts of stimuli are prepotent, particularly the dangerous ones. The first question to be answered is whether the newly found object is familiar or strange, something the animal knows about or something that has to be approached with circumspection. Such perception may need knowledge, and knowledge involves memory. A rose is a rose only when compared with the memory of previous roses; but recognition usually takes place so quickly that we do not know we have put up the hypothesis—this is a rose—and have then confirmed or refuted it. Even so, just as we may need time to test a hypothesis, so a cat or a dog faced with a strange object may be seen to exercise caution in determining whether it is familiar or new, related or unrelated to something already known, before reaching a decision on what to do with it.

Sometimes we behave as if we know about certain objects and situations when we have had no previous experience of them. How much of such built-in knowledge the human being has is only just being found out. In many higher vertebrates, visual patterns passing across the field of vision produce behaviour. When a young animal has never seen a shape before and yet knows what to do about it—this is the essence of knowledge. The human baby has more interest in human faces than in random lines and shapes and takes more notice of the sound of human speech than that of passing motor cars or the wind in the trees. The brain is constructed so as to receive and respond to the more significant kinds of stimulus. (See INFANCY, MIND IN.) So, from the mass of stimuli always affecting it, the animal selects those that are important to its needs of the moment. When it is hungry, it neglects background noise and looks for food and all the signs that indicate food.

The brain can increase one sort of input and play down another. Selection starts at the receptors, continues where the nerve fibres enter the brain and spinal cord, and can operate at any synapse within the central nervous system. In order to concentrate on listening, we may find it helpful to close our eyes; to concentrate on a pain, we may want people to stop talking. One can learn to neglect an input habitually. When researchers used to use microscopes with one eyepiece, they did not close the eye that was not looking down the eyepiece, they just did not record what it was sending into the brain. Ballet-dancers learn to suppress the input from the organs of balance in the inner ear, in order to avoid vertigo when pirouetting.

All inputs to the central nervous system, gustatory, auditory, visual, and from the skin, the organs of balance, the bladder, the alimentary canal, the muscles and joints, go to the cerebellum, the reticular formation, and the thalamus (Figs. 11 and 13). Those that can eventually become conscious and cause a sensation go to certain neurones of the thalamus and thence to the cortex. In the thalamus each input has its own territory, though there is also some mixing, with different sorts of inputs going to the same region.

Each kind of sensation depends on a primary sensory area of the cortex. Next door to or surrounding the primary area is its secondary sensory area. After the secondary sensory areas, there are the association areas; and finally the motor areas. Nerve fibres of the primary areas go to the secondary surrounding areas and nowhere else. Each secondary area connects with the corresponding area of the other hemisphere, with every other secondary sensory area of its own hemisphere, and with association areas. The association areas would seem to be concerned with elaborating sensory information, and with joining the various kinds of input to make a meaningful whole. It looks like a

fish, it smells like fish, it tastes like fish, and so it must be a fish. The association areas are interconnected; and finally they are connected to motor areas. The motor areas also receive other inputs— for example, to the neurones of the corticospinal tract there come fibres from the thalamus and from the somaesthetic area of the post-central gyrus, as well as fibres from other motor areas of the frontal lobe. The connections are laid down when the central nervous system is formed, according to the pattern of the species. They are then elaborated further during the experience of living.

Fig. 10 is a photograph of the brain dissected to show the optic pathways. The two optic nerves meet in the optic chiasm. There, half of the optic nerve fibres cross over to the opposite side and half remain on the same side as the retina from which they arise. The fibres then continue posteriorly, as the optic tract, going to a part of the midbrain. There is a relay there, and then fibres continue posteriorly to the visual areas, as the optic radiations (Figs. 9 and 10).

The primary area for hearing is in the upper part of the temporal lobe and cannot be seen until the brain is dissected. Near this region is the area for vestibular sensations, sensations which occur only under unpleasant circumstances, as when we feel giddy after spinning round and round or when we are rocked mercilessly on the sea. The area for smelling is also in the temporal lobe, and also in an older part of the forebrain, near the septal and preoptic areas (Figs. 11 and 12). The primary area for tactile feeling is in the post-central gyrus.

When a primary area is destroyed in man, the sense served by that area is not completely removed. In a few unusual cases, the primary visual cortex has been destroyed without damage to the surrounding visual parts of the cortex. The patient is blind but he can still point quite accurately to things he is shown. He knows where something is in the visual field, but he cannot say what it is. This produces the amazing situation of the patient being unable to see something but being able to put a finger on it, at the same time insisting that he sees nothing. In a sense, we may conceive of vertebrates as having two visual apparatuses, one to tell what a thing is, and another to tell where it is (see BRAIN FUNCTION AND AWARENESS).

In front of the secondary visual areas are the visual association areas. That in the right hemisphere is essential for the recognition of people's faces. In this region or in nearby regions of the cortex, the position of things in the environment in relation to ourselves is appreciated by means of connections with other parts of the hemispheres, parts concerned with knowledge of right and left, first on our own bodies and then in the world around us. If this region is badly damaged—and we know more about the effects of lesions than about how parts of the cortex normally function—then the patient cannot get any meaning out of the hands and numbers of a clock and thus cannot tell the time; neither can he understand the meaning of

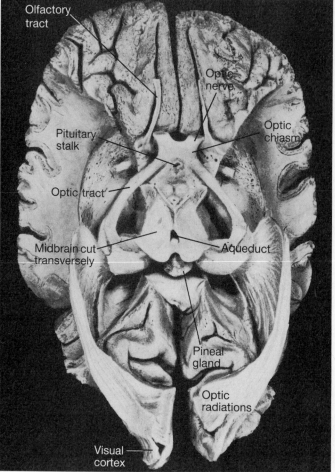

Olfactory tract

Optic nerve

Pituitary stalk

Optic chiasm

Optic tract

Midbrain cut transversely

Aqueduct

Pineal gland

Optic radiations

Visual cortex

**Fig. 10.** The human brain dissected from below, especially to show the visual pathways. The two optic nerves fuse at the optic chiasm and then continue as the two optic tracts to the midbrain. From relays in the midbrain, fibres run posteriorly as the optic radiations to the visual area of the occipital lobes.

the points of the compass, or of maps, or of the plans of architects. Nor can he plan a journey, for he cannot visualize the route and has no idea which road to take whenever there is a choice. For this region of the right hemisphere of the brain is the bump of locality—and note that we still use the terms of *phrenology.

Destruction of the primary area for hearing does not cause complete deafness; there is only a loss for high tones. Bats, for whom hearing is essential for life, can hear quite well with the primary auditory area destroyed.

The association areas are the important ones for all the activities we call thinking, remembering, imagining, or working things out. The ability to calculate, for instance, depends mainly on an association area of the left parietal cortex and the nerve fibres connecting to that area. This region is also essential for appreciating the relations of the fingers one to another. When this region is destroyed, the patient gets muddled in showing

which of his fingers is which, and he cannot recognize, say, the index or the ring finger of the right hand of someone else. In addition, he gets confused about right and left. It is very likely that our ability to calculate is related to our knowledge of our own digits; and it is not coincidence that as we have ten fingers we use a decimal system. The cognizance of spatial relationships comes into arithmetic as well as into geometry. There are congenital defects of the cerebral cortex in which a child can learn to deal with figures up to ten but is unable to transfer a figure laterally to the next column.

Most parts of the brain are paired. For paired structures to work together, they have to be connected; the connecting links in anatomy are called commissures. The largest of the commissures connects the two cerebral hemispheres together; it is the corpus callosum, and it is made up of about 145 million nerve fibres. It is shown in Figs. 11, 12, and 13.

From this rapid survey it will be realized that the brain is divided into separate regions with separate functions. This was first proposed by F. J. *Gall, who founded phrenology on this concept in the early nineteenth century. He called the different regions of the cerebral cortex the organs of the brain.

**Needs and desires.** For an animal to carry out correct behaviour, it is provided with drives, desires, emotions, rewards, and punishments—functions which are a feature of the working of the brain. Correct behaviour means satisfying not only the demands of metabolism but also the demands made on the individual by other members of the group—it means correct social behaviour. Both kinds of demands, or needs, are always changing. At one moment food is required, at another drink, or shelter; at some stage a mate of the opposite sex is needed; after mating, life has to be adjusted to care for the offspring. The reward for proper behaviour is pleasure and satisfaction; the penalty for not seeking and not finding stimulation is boredom. The punishment for biologically wrong behaviour is unhappiness, and failure to satisfy essential needs is followed by discontent, which may be demonstrated in agitated activity. Thus the behaviour of human beings, like that of all other gregarious animals, is aimed at satisfying the desires that have come from the needs of both the individual and the group. Being aware, consciousness of purpose, thought, and programming and planning for the probable future are to be seen as a part of fulfilling these aims. The development of these higher cerebral mechanisms reaches its greatest extent in man.

There are many experiments showing how mammals that do not think and plan make correct choices. For instance, rats choose a correct diet when they are presented with a large variety of substances to choose from. They are placed in a sort of cafeteria where they can choose what to eat from a large variety of foodstuffs. When deprived of an essential ingredient of diet, they choose those foods that supply the missing elements. Deprived of a certain vitamin, they choose foods rich in that vitamin. Female rats take more fat when they are lactating, and return to their usual amounts when the litter has been weaned. When pregnant, they take more calcium and phosphorus, protein and fat. Human babies and young children behave similarly when they are left to their own devices. Thus, in rare cases of atrophy of the adrenal glands, in which the body cannot retain salt, the child demands salt and eats great quantities of it. That the brain can make the child choose the right food comes as a surprise, for we tend to think of it as the organ of thought; and a two-year-old cannot work out what food it requires when deprived of a necessary hormone.

The needs of individuals are not only the usual ones stressed in biology and physiology. There are the needs that one may call social: the need for companionship, the need to be part of a group with a hierarchical structure, the territorial needs of the group of which one forms a part. To satisfy these needs, the brain provides feelings and emotions, instinctual drives, and it puts energy at the disposal of these drives. Knowledge of what parts of the brain are involved in these social needs is still inadequate; our conceptions of the physiological and anatomical bases of behaviour await improvement as further knowledge is gained.

Just as some regions of the brain produce sensations and others organize movement, so parts of the temporal lobes are involved in generating emotion. The main evidence for this comes from the electrical stimulation of the brains of patients with epilepsy during operations under local *anaesthesia. In some cases of *epilepsy, fits are caused by scarring in the cortex of the cerebral hemisphere, and occasionally good effects come from removing the scar tissue. During the operation, the surgeon has to stimulate the brain electrically so as to know if he is operating in the right part of the hemisphere. Excitation of certain parts of the temporal lobes produces in the patient an intense fear; in other parts it causes a strong feeling of isolation, of loneliness; in other parts a feeling of disgust; and in others sorrow or strong depression. Stimulation of some parts causes a feeling of dread rather than of fear, a dread without object, the patient being unable to explain what it is he dreads. Sometimes there is intense anxiety and sometimes a feeling of guilt. Often such stimulation causes stronger and purer emotion than occurs in real life. Whereas it is the nature of the human situation that feelings of delight and joy come more rarely than feelings of misery, an ecstatic feeling that all problems are soluble can be brought about by electrical stimulation of parts of the temporal lobe.

Certain total acts of behaviour are organized by the hypothalamus. This small region (Fig. 11) organizes the metabolism of the body, heat production and the control of body temperature, the production and circulation of hormones, and the states of being awake or asleep and of aggression or timidity. It organizes mating and sexual behaviour and it controls the sympathetic and parasympathetic nervous systems.

But the hypothalamus does not initiate behaviour. The cerebral hemispheres do this—in so far as one may abstract one part from the whole and see it behaving independently. The cerebral hemispheres receive information arriving from all input channels, form a total and meaningful picture of it, the meaning including emotion, and organize a programme of behaviour. In response to such and such an occurrence, one must threaten or even attack; to a different one, be submissive or hide or flee. Stereotyped patterns of response organized by small groups of neurones in the hypothalamus can be modified or totally changed by the cerebral cortex.

The parts of the cerebral hemispheres most directly connected to the hypothalamus are regions

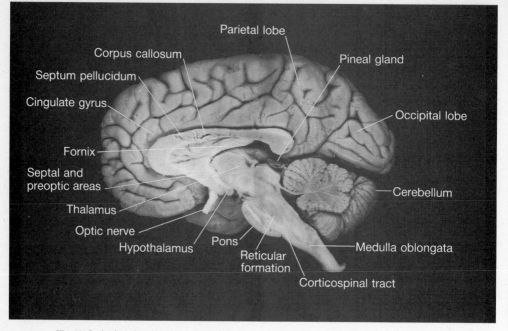

**Fig. 11.** Sagittal section through the human brain; it is cut through the midline and seen from the left.

within the temporal lobe sometimes called the limbic lobe. The limbic lobe is the most ancient part of the cerebral hemispheres and is already well developed in primitive fish. In mammals, it includes the hippocampus, the amygdala, the cingulate gyrus, the fornix, and the septal and preoptic areas (shown in Figs. 11, 12, and 13). The amygdala is a large mass of neurones deep in the

anterior part of the temporal lobe; this mass of grey matter, like other masses of archaic origin, lies within the white matter of the hemispheres. The cingulate gyrus surrounds the corpus callosum. The fornix is a connecting band of nerve fibres between the amygdala and hippocampus, and the septal and preoptic areas and hypothalamus. Beneath the corpus callosum there is a septum

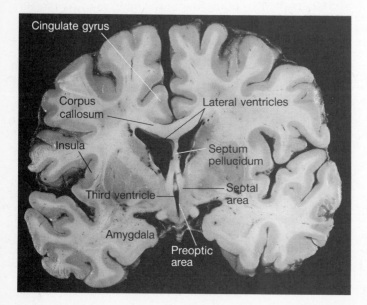

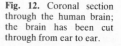

**Fig. 12.** Coronal section through the human brain; the brain has been cut through from ear to ear.

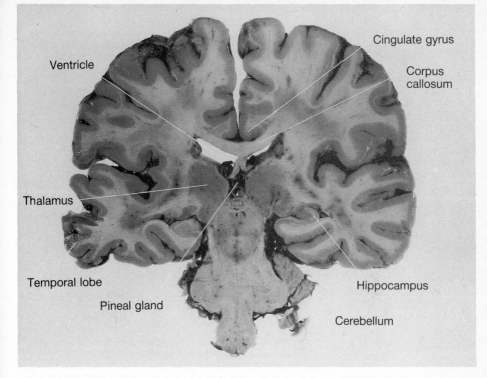

**Fig. 13.** Coronal section through the human brain; it is cut in the same plane as Fig. 12 but further posteriorly.

which is almost transparent, hence its name of septum pellucidum. It separates the two ventricles of the hemispheres (Figs. 12 and 13). Beneath the septum, the two ventricles connect through a hole to the third ventricle, which divides the hypothalamus into two. In front of the third ventricle are the septal and preoptic areas. The main centres of the autonomic nervous system are in the hypothalamus.

R. G. Heath, operating on conscious, psychotic patients in New Orleans, stimulated the septal area by means of electrodes and also by dripping in neurotransmitters. In some patients,

Expressions of anguish and despair changed precipitously to expressions of optimism and elaborations of pleasant experiences, past and anticipated. Patients could calculate more rapidly than before stimulation. Memory and recall were enhanced. One patient on the verge of tears described himself as somehow responsible for his father's near-fatal illness. When the septal region was stimulated, he immediately terminated this conversation and within fifteen seconds exhibited a broad grin as he discussed plans to date and seduce a girl friend. When asked why he had changed the conversation so abruptly, he replied that the plans concerning the girl had suddenly come to him. . . . Another patient, an epileptic, was one day agitated, violent and psychotic. The septal region was then stimulated without the patient knowing it. Almost instantly his behavioural state changed from one of disorganization, rage and persecution to one of happiness and mild

euphoria. He described the beginning of a sexual motive state.

Heath's patients could not account for their changing the subject to sex; they would say that the ideas just came into their minds. Now, electrical or pharmacological excitation of the parts of the brain related to certain functions causes the subject to have the thoughts and emotions associated with those parts of the brain, and the act of copulation is organized in the front end of the hypothalamus and the nearby septal area. The neurones organizing this behaviour and accompanying emotional states do so only when they receive the right hormones in their blood supply. Somehow the hormones must change the neurones, but it is not yet known what they do or how they do it. The septal area inducing sexual thoughts, emotions, and action is either the same region or quite near the region that causes pleasure when it is excited. This region may be damaged in professional boxers, as it is vulnerable to head injuries. Some boxers become impotent and lose any interest in sex. The neurones are near those organizing micturition; and some boxers also have difficulty in controlling their bladders.

Neurones of the hypothalamus organize aggression with the accompanying emotions. When these neurones have been stimulated electrically in experiments in various kinds of animals, the animals show manifestations of rage and attack any living being in sight. A pigeon stimulated in this way and alone in a cage behaves as if it sees another bird; it circles threateningly round the hallucinatory bird, preparing to attack it.

The brain and spinal cord are not isolated within the body, encased within walls of bone though they are. They are bathed in blood; and the constituents of the blood reach all parts of the brain and have an effect. The food and drink we take soon reaches it: not only alcohol but fish and chips, and hamburgers—all contribute. The hypothalamus controls the production of hormones, which are taken by the blood to the spinal cord and to all the tissues of the body. It is a part of the brain and functions in relation to the rest of the brain. It is related closely to the parts of the cerebral hemispheres that organize emotions and total acts of behaviour such as aggression, fear, and sex. Acts such as these need hormones with their effects on neurones and other tissues of the body.

If we think of nerve fibres as like telegraph wires, we can think of hormones as like radio messages. The programme is sent out; it can be picked up by anyone who has a radio to receive it. The hormone is poured into the bloodstream and it can be picked up by any cell capable of receiving it. Most hormones are made by endocrine or ductless glands. The glands are controlled by nerve fibres from the central nervous system and also by circulating hormones of other kinds. The brain orders and controls the secretion of hormones; and the brain itself is subjected to the action of hormones.

Many factors influence the secretion of hormones. The pineal gland (Figs. 11 and 13) is affected by light. In most animals, nerve fibres connect it to the retinae. In those few species that have a third eye in the top of the skull, the nerve fibres connecting the pineal with this eye are very short; the two structures are almost touching. Light affecting the pineal gland makes it release the hormone melatonin into the bloodstream. The pineal also prevents the pituitary from secreting gonadotrophic hormones. When this control is relaxed, these hormones act on many tissues of the body, including the central nervous system, and bring about the physical and psychological characteristics of adolescence. In some birds and some small mammals, the cycle of reproduction depends on the duration of daylight. Long days allow the parents time enough to find food for the young. When autumn comes, the days draw in and the pituitary rearranges its release of hormones. With shorter days, birds fly off to a warmer climate and small mammals settle down to a quiet and boring winter of chastity and hibernation.

Some hormones act on the genes. As genes control and organize the structure and function of cells, they can change the character of the cells completely. When the gonads secrete their hormones at puberty, most of the tissues of the body are changed: the genital organs enlarge and, in the male particularly, the larynx enlarges too. These hormones also act on the neurones of the nervous system, changing the function of cells. And so one sees that the male dog, reaching puberty, cocks a leg to urinate; if he is castrated, he never does this, but passes urine in the semi-sitting position common to puppies. Hormones acting on certain neurones in the brain give us mental pictures. The amount of sexual desire is much influenced by the secretion of hormones acting on neurones of the brain.

**Thinking.** When one is asked what part of the brain does the thinking, one has to answer in the usual way that appears to prevaricate: it all depends on what you mean by thinking. For the word is used to mean solving problems, remembering, planning what one is expecting to do, planning what one is about to say, imagining things, considering opinions, and making judgements. Much thinking makes use of words, of internal speech. But one can have auditory thoughts, thoughts without words. The composer conceives a melody without using words. The painter pictures things without using words, seeing them in his mind's eye. One remembers faces, things one has seen, and can imagine shapes and scenes when closing the eyes. Thinking of a smell is not helped at all by speech.

The parts of the brain concerned with the activity we categorize as mental are the cerebral hemispheres. The various kinds of intellectual activities are carried out by different parts of the cerebral hemispheres. The ability to think spatially depends on a region of the right hemisphere between the occipital, parietal, and temporal lobes; and a main region for mathematical thinking is in a similar part of the left hemisphere. Neurologists imagine that the higher levels of the brain make a model of the actual world, a mental picture that parallels the world, though no doubt with distortions; it is a symbolic representation of reality (see CRAIK, KENNETH). The model is made by the neurones, and the connections between the neurones, of the cerebral hemispheres. There are more than ten billion neurones in the human cerebral cortex. How connecting up regions of the cortex actually brings a memory into consciousness or allows us to imagine an event that has never occurred, we really do not know. We may conjecture that, in remembering a scene, the regions of cortex that were active when the original external stimulation occurred are brought into activity again. If this is so, and it is likely to be at least a part of the truth, there has to be some difference between the original activation of the region and the later pale image of the memory. It is obvious that a main function of the brain is to provide higher vertebrates with such mental images derived from the surrounding world. And it is customary to say that when one evokes these images, one has the picture in one's mind. Why we are unable to put all of this together is that our methods of research are apt for analysis but very poor at synthesis. (See the articles on

MEMORY and THINKING: HOW IT CAN BE TAUGHT for further discussion.)

**Speaking.** A baby starts by listening to the sounds of speech. Endowed as he is with acute hearing for the frequencies and overtones used in speech, he comes to notice the subtle differences between these sounds. He then learns to associate meanings with the sounds; he also imitates and learns to make the sounds himself and to stop the babbling that has no meaning to those around him. Just as he moves his limbs, he makes controlled movements with the muscles of the larynx, palate, lips, and tongue.

One supposes that something like this is happening. Volleys of impulses from the inner ears reach the lower centres for hearing in the lower parts of the brain. From there, volleys are relayed to various specific parts of the brain, including the auditory regions of both temporal lobes. Surrounding each primary auditory region is a secondary auditory region in which heard phonemes are turned into sound symbols. These are sounds with meaning. The secondary auditory regions of the temporal lobes are connected to many other cortical areas that contribute to speech. One is an area of the frontal lobes that organizes the actual movements of the respiratory muscles, larynx, and mouth to produce speech.

When a child learns to read, he organizes connections to the visual cortex, where recognition of the seen shape of letters and words occurs. Reading is associating the visual representation of the word with its auditory representation, and associating the auditory representation with the actual object. 'Associating' is a psychological term for the physiological activity of sending volleys of impulses between various cortical areas. When the child learns to write, he says the sound out loud to himself, and then draws the visual representation of that sound that has been accepted by the conventions of his society. This entails learning sequences of movements needed to draw the agreed symbols. All of it happens in milliseconds once it has been practised.

Neurologists have had to learn from observing the effects of damage to parts of the brain. When certain regions are destroyed, then such and such defects are found. From deducing what a destroyed region might have done, tentative guesses are made as to how the brain works. Learning about the brain in this way provides answers to many anatomical questions; but given the structure one still needs to understand how the rapid passage of nerve impulses results in all the activities we call thinking.

**Total behaviour.** The kinds of people we are depends primarily on our brains. The parts of the brain making each of us ourselves and different from everyone else are the higher levels of the brain: higher anatomically, towards the top of the head, and higher physiologically, in that their operations are least automatic and reflex, and most delayed in action and complicated. One spinal cord, one medulla, one brain-stem is much like another. But we differ in our cerebral hemispheres. They certainly start different; and they become more different on account of everything we have put into them or not put into them.

The temporal lobes are the main regions of the cerebral hemispheres for memory. The limbic lobes are the main parts for organizing the essential drives, which are kindled by emotions. They have rapid connections to both parts of the autonomic nervous system: sympathetic for activity and parasympathetic for relaxation. The hypothalamus has many functions. It organizes hormonal control of the body, total acts of behaviour, circadian rhythms, food and drink intake, and excretion and elimination among other things. It seems far too small a structure and to have far too few neurones to do all these things. Its smallness contrasts with the size of the cerebral hemispheres with their row upon row of neurones. From the whole extent of the hemispheres, one imagines, commands are sent to the limbic lobes, and from there are funnelled down to the hypothalamus. One supposes that a situation is apprehended by the cerebral hemispheres, is then related to previous experiences, probably in the hippocampus, and labelled as familiar or novel and strange. What is likely to happen next is then anticipated, and behaviour to meet it is planned. This requires not only action, but also emotions, desires, and the entire mental state that is necessary for the programme.

The more rostral parts of the frontal lobes and their connections to the thalamus, to the hypothalamus, and to the septal areas are the regions of the brain most concerned with social behaviour. Maturation of these regions takes years, and development of the anatomical connections continues until puberty. Experiments on dogs and monkeys in which connections between the frontal lobes and other parts of the brain were cut through, has demonstrated that animals losing social knowledge cannot relearn social behaviour. Animals subjected to the operation would go casually up and take food away from animals of higher rank, and would fail to learn not to do this in spite of being repeatedly punished by the other animals. Man's case is similar, though seldom extreme since lesions are not usually extensive. Large lesions in the front parts of the frontal lobes lead to lack of attention to the feelings and the behaviour of others. In 1868, Harlow of Boston reported a famous case in which a crowbar was blown through a man's frontal lobes without killing him:

His equilibrium, or balance, so to speak, between his intellectual faculties and animal propensities, seems to have been destroyed. He is fitful, irreverent, indulging in the grossest profanity (which was not previously his custom), manifesting but little deference for his fellows, impatient of restraint or advice when it conflicts with his desires, at times pertinaciously obstinate, yet capricious and vacillating. . . .

Early attempts at leucotomy cut many of the connections between the frontal lobes and the thalamus and resulted in apathetic beings with no energy, no interests, and no ability to concentrate on anything for long. The patients became uninhibited, their behaviour insensible to its effect on other people and unaltered by criticism. Less extensive operations resulted in less damaging effects.

The frontal lobes play an important role in determining our energy, and thus our interests, but are not primarily concerned with intellectual functions. They are concerned with mood, and with inherited and acquired behaviour in social groups, as we have seen. Connected as they are with the septal areas, it is likely that right behaviour is learned, by both man and other gregarious animals, from reward with pleasure. Conversely, wrong behaviour must be corrected, and there must therefore also be connections with aversive centres, if there are such centres in the limbic lobes. It may be that without such connections learning would not occur.

**Total conceptions of the central nervous system.** It has been apparent to investigators of the nervous system that one learns a few things about a small part, even about many different parts, but one comes no nearer to a conception of the functioning of the total system. A broad view of its anatomy, physiology, and pathology was the achievement of the clinical neurologist John Hughlings *Jackson, whose conception took into neurology the ideas about evolution current in the second half of the nineteenth century. Renaissance thinkers had removed man from the centre of the universe; he was put back by Charles *Darwin and Herbert *Spencer. In Jackson's concept the nervous system has evolved, both anatomically and physiologically, in hierarchical stages. When it becomes impaired or damaged by pathological processes, it degenerates in the reverse order to its evolutionary development; Jackson called this degenerating process dissolution. Evolution and dissolution accounted for its functioning in health and decay. The lower levels are the older, more primitive and simple; the higher levels more complex, less firmly established, and so more liable to suffer from toxic or pathological processes. This organization decreed that a higher level was constantly suppressing or inhibiting the functioning of its immediately lower level. During dissolution the higher level was seen as being damaged first and most, leaving the next level manifesting its activity in an uninhibited and excessive manner.

The lowest level was the spinal cord; above it were the lower levels of the brain, and above them the higher levels. It is unfortunate that Jackson indicated precise anatomical levels in the hierarchy, as his conception could otherwise be maintained. For example, he regarded the motor strip of the pre-central gyrus together with the kinaesthetic region of the post-central gyrus as the middle level, and the frontal cortex rostral to the pre-central gyrus as the highest. But the frontal cortex is not a sensorimotor region; most of it is concerned with behaviour in relation to the social group and with the totality of behaviour. Such ideas could not have entered into Jackson's nineteenth-century view, however, for the prevailing concept of psychology of the time was one of stimulus and response, of the sensorimotor reflexes of a single, isolated human being.

Jackson conceived of the lower levels as the most automatic, with stereotyped reflex behaviour, and proposed that the highest levels—with mental, intellectual, and psychological functions—be regarded as the least automatic and least stereotyped. One of the canny features of his conception was to see differences between neural levels as differences of degree rather than as of kind. It fitted in with the material of biology; and it enabled him to avoid the difficulties inherent in using terms such as 'voluntary', a term derived from the will, or terms such as 'psychic'.

Jackson saw a baby's life as ruled by primitive reflexes. As the baby grew and developed, more complicated and less stereotyped behaviour was superimposed on the stock of reflexes. Finally, in the adult, reflexes formed only a small and hidden part of the repertoire of behaviour, the rest relying on consciousness, apparent choice, and accompanying emotions. When dissolution occurred, the parts oldest in evolutionary terms survived longest, while the most recently acquired degenerated first. The early signs of dissolution of the cerebral hemispheres are a loss of finer sensibilities and indifference to social requirements. The senile person does not become different; he becomes more like himself than before. The choleric person loses his temper more readily, the obsessional becomes bound by compulsive rituals, the humorous becomes fatuous. As the higher levels of the cerebral cortex degenerate, an early loss is the ability to think with symbols. This may be detected in such banal examples as a person being unable to see the meaning of a proverb. He will explain that a rolling stone gathers no moss because the conditions during rolling are unsuitable for the growing of moss: the meaning, as a proverb, is not understood.

Jackson's way of thinking about the nervous system was based on the reflexes that Charles *Sherrington was investigating at the time. But reflexes, no matter how elaborate they become, do not constitute even a small part of the behaviour of higher animals. Even moving is not organized only by reflexes. Most of our movements are organized from above, being programmed by the cerebral cortex, though this was not known to Sherrington and Jackson. If something as essential to Jackson's conception as the organization of movement is not hierarchically built up, then his scheme falls to the ground. What also appears unsatisfactory today is that the conception was based, as it could only have been at the time, on a simple stimulus–response idea of neural organization. This view of behaviour saw an organism as waiting for events to occur. Something in the outer world eventually stimulates the animal, and the animal responds. It was not then realized that occurrences originate mainly from within. What was being neglected in psychology and neurology was the make-up of the nervous system itself. That the stimulus to behave originates within the central nervous system has been realized by twentieth-century biologists, though more from the contributions of ethologists than from observation of spontaneous activity within the system. We higher animals continually show purposive behaviour, seeking to satisfy internally originating needs. Animals are goal-seeking organisms.

A less all-embracing way of seeing the nervous system was that of W. R. Hess (1881–1973). His view took its origin from the basic behaviour of the animal. He was the first anatomist or physiologist to investigate the anatomy of the central nervous system in relation to total acts of behaviour such as attacking, escaping, digesting, and defecating. He implanted electrodes in small regions of the hypothalamus and produced total acts, as mentioned, when he stimulated them electrically. Thus he found that there are centres for rage, for fight and flight, for threatening and submissive behaviour, for digestion, for repose, sleep and maintaining wakefulness, for micturition, defecation, and copulation. These centres are in the hypothalamus and they are excited and inhibited by the cerebral hemispheres. What is meant by a centre in neurology is a small region of the central nervous system devoted to one function. Hess thought of the functions as consisting of two opposite forms of behaviour; he called them ergotropic and trophotropic. Ergotropic behaviour is going out and actively doing things; it includes both parts of the defence reaction—that is, fighting and fleeing—seeking food, and looking for a mate. When it is maximal, the pupils are dilated, respiration is increased, and blood-pressure rises. Ergotropic centres are in the more posterior part of the hypothalamus. Trophotropic behaviour is reposing and building up the body. It includes sleep with the anabolic functions that occur during sleep, the activities of the alimentary canal and the bladder, replenishing the supply of glucose, and the building of the cells of the body from protein and fat. When trophotropic behaviour is maximal, the pupils are small, respiration is slow, and the glands of the alimentary canal are secreting. The centres of trophotropic organization are in the rostral part of the hypothalamus and the septal and preoptic areas. The regions of the cerebral hemispheres most closely concerned with trophotropic behaviour are the posterior part of the orbital surface of the frontal lobes (Fig. 7), the insula, which is a part of the cerebral hemisphere (Fig. 12) lying deep to the temporal, frontal, and parietal lobes, and the anterior parts of the temporal lobes, with the evolutionary regions of old grey matter within them, including the amygdala (Fig. 12). The trophotropic system works mainly via the parasympathetic nervous system, whereas the regions of the cerebral hemispheres more closely concerned with ergotropic behaviour are the anterior nucleus of the thalamus, the hippocampus, and the connections of these structures, working mainly via the sympathetic nervous system.

Hess's scheme, like Jackson's, was developed before there was an adequate view in biology of man as a gregarious animal; and so it also is a scheme that describes the nervous system of an isolated person, as if he had no social relationships and no inherited social instincts and ways of behaving. Any total conception of the nervous system must rather see man as genetically endowed to function as a member of a group, with built-in drives and propensities to behave as we know human beings do behave. To omit an animal's relations with other members of its group is to leave out almost everything.

**The mind?** Should one think that the materialist view of the neurologist is inadequate or wrong, the best way to criticize it may be to attack it on its own ground. Such criticism would go something like this: 'Although you have explained the anatomy and physiology, you have said almost nothing. You tell me that when you hear me speaking, pressure waves reach your inner ear, and that they cause the physico-chemical events called nerve impulses in the auditory nerve. Further groups of nerve impulses finally reach the speech area of the left cerebral hemisphere, you say, and from there more impulses go to other parts of the brain, to regions where strangeness or familiarity are recognized, where memories are evoked, and where various emotions are induced. But you have chosen to leave everything out except the structure, the anatomy of the brain. *How does the activation of neurones at synapses make me feel frightened?* You answer that if during an operation the electrical stimulation of parts of the limbic lobes makes the patient feel frightened, then we may assume that fear is normally caused by the excitation of that part of the brain. But that is merely showing me a location, a bit of anatomy. Your explanation is no explanation at all.'

As we should have no preconceptions about what effects the activation of groups of neurones have, we can merely take note of what effects they do have. In one case, we have the feeling of fear; in another case, we hear a sound. These experiences are a part of the constant effort of an animal to remain alive, a station on the pathway towards activity in the world. Thus attacks on the present attempts of students of the nervous system to understand behaviour are most effective where ignorance of neural events is greatest; and they tend to fail where knowledge of neural functioning is adequate. In the example of movement, we know much of the neural events that occur, although of course gaps in our knowledge remain. Neurologists can point to the physical and chemical events that occur when we put our right foot forwards. Nerve impulses pass from the left frontal hemisphere along various circuits of neurones in the brain; and finally they come down to motor neurones working the muscles of the right lower limb, exciting some and inhibiting others. The result of this is that muscles used in putting the foot forwards are caused to contract, and opposing muscles to relax, the muscles of the trunk and upper limbs behaving similarly. There are no occurrences but physical and chemical ones, nothing but the events we study in anatomy and physiology, chemistry and physics; and therefore, in this case, the critic cannot say that the neurologist has not shown him everything. It follows that if what happens when we move can be more or less explained, any inadequacy in the ability to account for what happens when we feel fear or remember a past event is likely to be due only to insufficient knowledge of the physiology concerned.

Put at its most superficial, it is a matter of vocabulary. In the context of neurology the adjective 'mental' is in order but the noun 'mind' is not; so it is acceptable to say that perception is a mental occurrence but bad terminology to say that perception occurs in the mind. Once one is aware of the dangers of using the word 'mind', however, one may use it most acceptably. For 'let me not to the marriage of true minds admit impediments'.

P. W. N.

**NEUMANN,** JOHN VON (1903–57), Hungarian-born mathematician. See VON NEUMANN.

**NEUROANATOMICAL TECHNIQUES.** Although it is possible and productive to study the mind without knowing anything about the structure of the brain, rather as one can drive well and be knowledgeable about the performance of motor vehicles without understanding the internal combustion engine, few doubt that mental events are related to the activity of the brain and that the structure can give clues about how the brain works. Unfortunately, however, the brain is so complex that its detailed structure is only beginning to be understood. For example, in humans it contains about ten thousand million nerve-cells, and each one may make and receive several thousand contacts with other cells. The following describes the principal methods of obtaining information about the most complex circuit in existence.

Even before the invention of the microscope it was possible to say something about gross brain structure by post-mortem dissection. The nerve

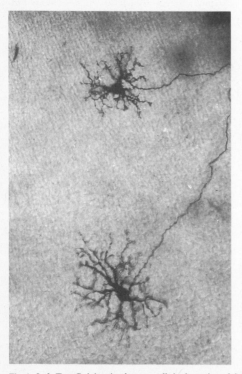
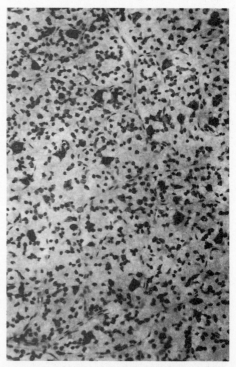

**Fig. 1.** *Left*. Two Golgi-stained nerve-cells in the retina of the eye of a rat. Each has a cell-body with branching dendrites that make connections with other cells. The long thin process is the cell's axon. The hundreds of other cells are unstained and therefore invisible. *Right*. A photograph of a similar region of the eye using a conventional stain, which shows up all the cell-bodies but none of the dendrites or axons.

bundles carrying information from the eyes, ears, nose, and skin can all be followed to their first and major destination in the brain. But from here we are lost, and in any case dissection has never revealed the course and connections of individual nerve fibres, which are often less than one-thousandth of a millimetre thick. The first great step forward came in 1873 when Camillo *Golgi discovered that a small proportion of nerve-cells could be stained with black silver chromate so that they became readily visible against the background of unstained, transparent cells. Why the Golgi method selects a few cells apparently at random is still unknown, but for over a hundred years it has been the principal tool in revealing their precise shape. It was the only method that let us see the trees instead of the wood (Fig. 1), and showed that most nerve-cells, or neurones, consist of a cell-body and an axon (fibre) which may vary in length from less than a millimetre to several metres in large mammals.

Although the Golgi method is excellent for revealing local details, it is highly impractical for showing whether two widely separated areas of the brain are directly connected by nerve fibres. A solution to this problem was that of 1870 by Gudden, who observed that when axons are cut their cell-bodies often die and disappear. When the tissue is sectioned and stained, the cells that gave rise to the cut axons are conspicuous by their absence (Fig. 2). The method of retrograde cell degeneration was widely used in the early part of

the twentieth century to show which parts of the thalamus in the centre of the brain sent axons to particular parts of the cerebral cortex on the surface of the brain. The resulting map is shown as Fig. 3. But the method produces too many false negative results. Some cell-bodies do not die when their axon is cut, perhaps because of regrowth of the axon. Other axons may branch, and only if all branches are cut will the cell die. Therefore the absence of cell degeneration following axon cutting does not prove that two regions lack connections. Nerve-cells may also degenerate in the opposite direction—that is, when the cell-body is damaged the axon and its terminal connections die. In the 1950s Nauta and his colleagues at the Massachusetts Institute of Technology developed what are known as the Nauta techniques for selectively staining degenerating axons and their terminal branches with silver, and an entirely new set of nerve connections was discovered. For example, the visual cortex at the back of the brain is now known to send axons to at least eight different regions of the cerebral cortex and subcortex (Fig. 4). None of these pathways is demonstrable by retrograde degeneration.

So far we have mentioned only histological methods. But nerve-cells can be stimulated by a natural agent such as light in the eye, or by brief pulses of electricity delivered through electrodes in the tissue. The electrical activity evoked in the nerve-cells can then be recorded as it is propagated in the brain along axons. For more than fifty years

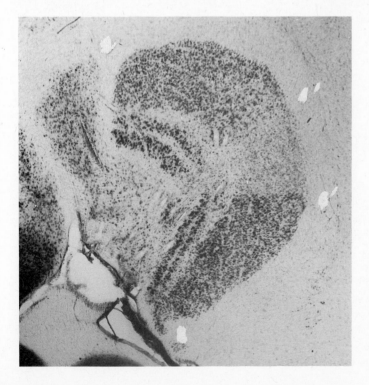

**Fig. 2.** Section through part of the thalamus in a monkey's brain showing the lateral geniculate body, whose cells send axons to the visual cortex. The cells in the centre have disappeared because a small part of the cortex was damaged. This method of retrograde degeneration shows which thalamic cells send axons to the damaged area.

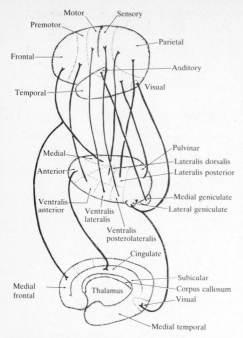

**Fig. 3.** The thalamus of the brain (shown much enlarged in the centre of the figure) consists of discrete groups of cells. By the method of retrograde degeneration the parts of the cerebral cortex to which they send their axons have been discovered. The lines show these pathways from the thalamus to the lateral surface of the brain (*top*) and to the medial surface of the brain (*bottom*).

this method has been used to map pathways in the brains of animals. One notable advantage of it is that the electrical activity crosses the junctions or synapses between cells, so that the entire route can in principle be revealed. For example, the impulses from the eye travel to the dorsal lateral geniculate nucleus of the thalamus, thence to the primary visual cortex, and from there to several other so-called secondary visual areas.

Such physiological methods reveal a great deal about the general route followed by axons of a particular sensory system and about the areas where the axons terminate, but they reveal little about the connections of individual cells. One way of overcoming this is to record the activity of a cell-body with a micropipette and then inject the cell with a dye. When the tissue is then sectioned the dyed cells and all their processes are visible microscopically. This method is tedious and can never reveal more than a few cells at a time, but it has successfully shown, for example, which of the thousands of cells in the visual cortex are the first to receive impulses from the eye, and how many brain-cells an incoming fibre can contact.

The methods described so far had reached their peak by the early 1960s, and radically new discoveries about the connections of the brain seemed impossible. How wrong this was! Neuroanatomy

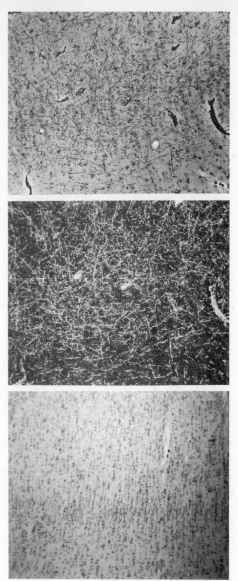

**Fig. 4.** *Top.* Degenerating axon terminals revealed by the Nauta technique in the cortex of the temporal lobe after damaging cells in a distant part of the occipital lobe. *Centre.* The same slide with the contrast reversed so that the degenerating fibres are even more conspicuous. *Bottom.* The same region of cortex stained conventionally. Only cell-bodies are visible.

was on the threshold of major advances. Since 1948 it had been known that the axoplasm inside a nerve fibre flows along the fibre. By injecting radioactive amino acids inside the eye of a mouse it was shown in 1965 that the amino acid was absorbed by nerve cell-bodies and incorporated into proteins, which were then passed along the axons. In 1968 it was

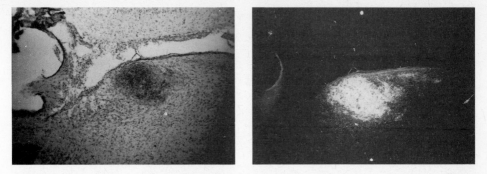

**Fig. 5.** *Left.* Autoradiograph of a group of cells in the midbrain of a rat after radioactive amino acids have been absorbed by the eye and transported to the brain. The dark patch shows the radioactivity. *Right.* The radioactivity is even clearer when the contrast is reversed.

shown that if the brain tissue was sectioned and the sections coated with photographic emulsion, the radioactivity that had reached the axon terminals could be detected by its effects on the photographic film. Since then, this technique of autoradiography has been widely used to study the course of axons from several groups of cells that have been bathed in minute injections of radioactive chemicals, which can now be delivered through a micropipette to any part of an animal's brain. Not only does the technique take advantage of a normal biological process without damaging the injected cells, it is far more sensitive than degeneration techniques. For example, autoradiography has shown that the nerve-cells in the eye send fibres to at least six different parts of the brain, whereas only four were known previously (Fig. 5).

When a nerve fibre is squeezed tight, axoplasm accumulates on *both* sides of the obstruction, implying that there is active transport in both directions. If that is the case, it should also be possible to apply chemicals to the terminals of axons and trace them back to the parent cell-bodies elsewhere in the brain. Such a technique, called retrograde marking, has been in use since 1970. The commonest tracer is horseradish peroxidase, which is rapidly conveyed from nerve axon terminals back to the cell-body, where its presence can be revealed by histochemical treatment of thin slices of the tissue (Fig. 6). However, a variety of materials can be used so long as they can be chemically attached to a transportable substance. For example, colloidal particles of gold, which show up well in light and electron microscopes, can be attached (conjugated) to transportable wheat-germ-agglutin.

New transportable substances are continually being discovered, and one class has already proved to be especially useful. When bathed with light of a particular wavelength some chemicals absorb the light and emit light of a very different colour, i.e. they fluoresce. It is now known that several fluorescent dyes are transported in the axoplasm. If such labelled nerve-cells are observed under a

fluorescence microscope where they are illuminated by light of one wavelength (which, like ultra-violet, may be invisible to the human eye), they fluoresce at visible wavelengths—for example, blue—and stand out against a dark background. By injecting two different fluorescent tracers in separate parts of the brain it was first shown in 1978 that some cell-bodies accumulated both tracers because they glowed red or blue according to the

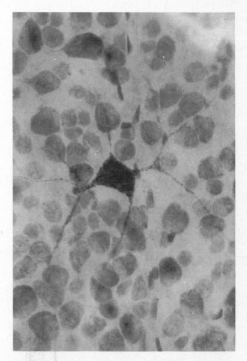

**Fig. 6.** Photograph of part of the retina of the eye of a rat. The dark cell in the centre has accumulated horseradish peroxidase tracer injected in minute amount into a small part of the brain, showing that this and other similarly labelled cells send their axons to this part of the brain.

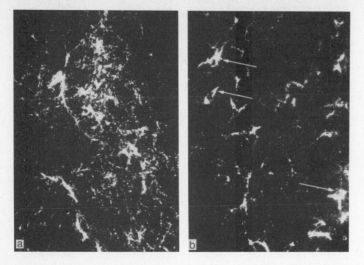

Fig. 7. a. Fluorescence in the septum of the rat brain after treating the tissue with formaldehyde. Both adrenaline and noradrenaline fluoresce. b. The same region from a different brain treated to make the fluorescence specific for a different transmitter, dopamine. The arrows show that the transmitter is concentrated round cell-bodies.

wavelength of the illuminating light. This proved conclusively that some cells give rise to an axon which branches and reaches entirely different areas of the brain.

Although nerve-cells transmit information as electrical impulses along their axons, the communication between cells at their points of contact, or synapses, is chiefly chemical. The terminals of an axon release minute quantities of the chemical, or transmitter, which then stimulates the membrane of adjacent cell-bodies. Although many different transmitters exist, any cell releases predominantly only one type. If that type can be selectively stained in some way it should be possible to display all the pathways which use that particular transmitter. This was achieved in 1962 by the discovery that nerve terminals secreting catecholamines fluoresced with a greenish hue after the tissue was treated with formaldehyde vapour (Fig. 7). Since then several other transmitter-specific pathways have been demonstrated, but the most precise and exciting development is the technique called immunohistofluorescence. When cells containing a particular transmitter are injected into another animal of a different species, the host develops antibodies to the transmitter just as it would to other foreign tissue like bacteria. These antibodies can be isolated from a blood-serum sample taken from the host. A fluorescent dye is now chemically attached to the antibodies, which are then applied to fresh sections of brain tissue, where they attach themselves to the type of cell producing the original transmitter (Fig. 8). In this way several cell groups and their fibres have recently been shown to act by secreting dopamine, adrenaline, noradrenaline, substance P, or tryptamine, a discovery that could not be made simply by studying their structure or electrical activity. Nor is the discovery of mere academic interest. Disturbances in the metabolism of specific transmitters have been implicated in several neurological and psychiatric conditions, for example dopamine in *Parkinson's disease, acetylcholine in senile *dementia, and gamma-aminobutyric acid in *epilepsy. To pin-point such pathways is therefore of great potential value to medicine. (For further discussion see DOPAMINE NEURONES IN THE BRAIN.)

So far the brain has been discussed as if it were a fairly static piece of machinery. The connections

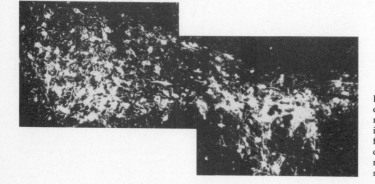

Fig. 8. Immunofluorescence in the substantia nigra of a rat brain after incubating the tissue with fluorescent antibodies to an enzyme which controls the metabolism of the transmitter tyrosine.

may be discovered by a variety of means, but what do they do and under what behavioural circumstances are they active? If only the brain were semi-transparent with pathways that lit up when they were in use, we might more easily relate structure with mind. This dream is not as outrageous as it may seem, as two examples show. Nerve-cells need glucose, and the more active they are the more glucose they use. The glucose is normally metabolized rapidly but, if an injection of a closely related radioactive chemical, carbon[14] 2-deoxyglucose, is given to an animal, the brain-cells fail to detect the disguise and absorb it as if it were glucose, but they fail to metabolize it. The chemical sticks in the cells and can be demonstrated by the autoradiographic method described earlier. By these means it has been shown which cells in an animal's brain are the most active when it looks through one eye, gazes at vertical lines, moves about, or listens to sounds (Fig. 9). This is a drastic and irreversible procedure, of course, because the brain has to be sectioned. However, regional activity at a grosser level can be demonstrated in the living brain without harming it. If a subject inhales radioactive xenon, the gas enters the bloodstream, where it circulates for a few minutes before gradually being lost again in the breath. As those parts of the brain that are most active at any particular time receive the greatest blood supply, they contain the most radioactivity, which can be detected by sensors outside the skull. The method is used clinically to pin-point brain abnormalities that may require surgery, but it also successfully shows which regions are most active when we are looking, listening, talking, moving a limb, problem-solving, or just day-dreaming.

To describe the bare bones of some of the techniques now available for studying the structure and connections of the brain may seem a far cry from understanding the mind. It is. But we are certainly much closer to saying something about the physical counterparts of perception, action, and mood than was St Thomas *Aquinas, who saw mind as those faculties which in their operation dispense entirely with matter.                        A. C.

Cowan, W. M. and Cuenod, M. (1975). *The Use of Axonal Transport for Studies of Neuronal Connectivity.* Amsterdam.
Heimer, L. and Robards, M. J. (eds.) (1981). *Neuroanatomical Tract Tracing Methods.* New York.
The Brain. (1979). *Scientific American*, **241**, 3.

**NEUROLINGUISTICS.** This term is used mainly in Europe and in some centres in the USA, to describe the application of linguistic theories to the classification and analysis of acquired disorders of language or speech in patients with brain damage (for example, *aphasia). Some work has also considered the corresponding developmental disorders of speech, reading, and writing in children (see LANGUAGE DEVELOPMENT IN CHILDREN), as well as the dissolution of language in dementing diseases.

While ideas from linguistic theories have been applied to aphasia for many years (e.g. Steinthal, 1871; Pick, 1913; Isserlin, 1922; Jakobson, 1956), the term neurolinguistics and more systematic application of linguistic ideas has only become widespread since 1970.

In 1969, the neurologist Henri Hécaen and the linguist Armand Dubois declared the object of neurolinguistics to be, first, the establishment of 'a purely linguistic typology' of neurologically caused verbal disorders, and second, the achievement of an experimentally verifiable correlation of lesion sites with the linguistic types. In practice, however, it has proved difficult to use solely linguistic criteria of classification, and Hécaen's own 1972 scheme classifies patients on the basis of clinical and psychological, as well as linguistic features: 'sensory aphasia', for example, has three aspects—a disorder of semantic relations, a failure of auditory decoding at a phonemic level, and a disorganization of attention.

Neurolinguistic researchers have used various types of linguistic theory: e.g. *Luria's (1947) linguistic theories come from the structuralism of the Prague school (see following entry); Lecours and Lhermitte (1979) use Martinet's theories, while Weigl (1981), Whitaker (1971) and others adopt

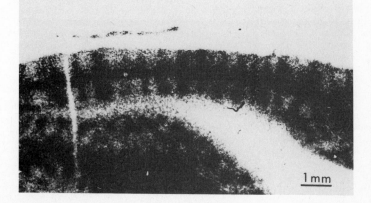

**Fig. 9.** Deoxyglucose autoradiograph of a section through the visual cortex of a monkey after the animal was looking at a pattern of stripes. The array of vertical stripes in the cortex shows which groups of cells were activated by the stimulus.

1mm

the perspectives of transformational generative grammar (see LANGUAGE: CHOMSKY'S THEORY).

Progress towards the secondary aim of discovering the anatomical substrates of various functions has not proved impressive, partly because of the lack of agreement on what constitutes a proper classification of aphasia in linguistic terms. It is becoming clear that the relationship between linguistic theories and brain structures will not be simple; many workers would now see the development of a neuropsychology of language as a prerequisite for the further advance of neurolinguistics.

See LANGUAGE: NEUROPSYCHOLOGY; SPEECH AND BRAIN PROCESSES.

D. H.<br>B. L. B.

Hécaen, H. and Dubois, A. (1971). La neurolinguistique. In Perren, G. E. and Trim, J. L. M. (eds.), *Applications of Linguistics*. Cambridge.

Hécaen, H. (1972). *Introduction à la Neuropsychologie*. Paris.

Isserlin, M. (1922). Über agrammatismus. *Zeitschrift für die gesamte Neurologie und Psychiatrie*, **75**, 332–416.

Jakobson, R. (1956). Two aspects of language and two types of aphasic disturbances. In Jakobson, R. and Halle, M. (eds.) *Fundamentals of Language*. The Hague.

Lecours, A. R. and Lhermitte, F. (1979). *L'aphasie*. Paris. (English edn. 1983, *Aphasia*. London.)

Luria, A. R. (1947). *Traumatic aphasia*. (English trans. D. Bowden, 1970. The Hague.)

Pick, A. (1913). *Die agrammatischen Sprachstoerungen*. Berlin.

Steinthal, H. (1871). *Einleitung in die Psychologie und Sprachenwissenschaft*. Berlin.

Weigl, E. (1981). *Neuropsychology and neurolinguistics; selected papers*. The Hague.

Whitaker, H. A. (1971). *On the Representation of Language in the Human Brain: problems in the neurology of language and the linguistic analysis of aphasia*. Edmonton, Alberta.

**NEUROLINGUISTICS, LURIA ON.** During the last few decades the sciences of language and speech have undergone a remarkable development.

A few decades ago linguistics was supposed to be a science concerned with general laws of the formal codes employed by language—its phonetic (or phonemic), lexical, syntactical structures. The goal of comparative and structural linguistics was to describe ideal codes of the language, their interrelations, and their formal organization. During the 1950s and 1960s the development of transformational grammar converted linguistics into a very precise science using systems of basic rules which could be expressed by mathematical means.

The discovery of these rules brought linguistics very close to basic psychological questions. The way in which initial motives and thoughts lead to inner speech, abbreviated in its structure and predicative in its function, and then towards extended speech utterances, appeared as a fundamental problem. The process of encoding the initial thought (generation of the speech utterance) and of decoding it (understanding of the speech utterance, its general meaning, and its deep sense) became the most important area for investigation. Leo *Vygotsky's classic work *Thought and Language* appeared, and started the development of a new branch of language science—that of psycholinguistics, which abandoned the formal description of the basic laws of the language and began to follow up carefully the steps of the semantic rules of speech, the conversion of the thought into a verbal intention. Problems associated with the actual psychological generation of verbal utterances, of dialogue and monologue, and of verbal and written speech (as well as their decoding) appeared, and a group of gifted scholars (among them G. Miller, D. E. Broadbent, J. Mehlez, T. Bever, R. Brown, T. Fodor, D. McNeill, and D. Slobin) made a series of really important contributions to this field.

In spite of the considerable progress associated with psycholinguistics, one important question remained unsolved. Psycholinguistics was scarcely able to single out basic factors in speech; nor was it able to analyse basic forms of speech composed of separate units, each dealing with a different factor underlying the form. To solve this problem a new step was needed, and this step was provided by a new branch of linguistic science—that of neurolinguistics.

The general method of neurolinguistics is to follow all changes in language and speech that are associated with local lesions of the brain, and to describe as carefully as possible the different forms of breakdown of the processes of encoding of verbal utterances and of their decoding which appear in cases of differently localized brain lesions.

It is thought that speech, as well as other kinds of mental activity, is really a functional system based on the co-operation of many cortical and subcortical regions, each contributing its own part to the whole processing of information or the establishing of plans and programmes of behaviour. This is why analysis of the derangement of speech processes associated with separately localized brain lesions provides a unique opportunity to single out factors included in language and speech, and to describe different kinds of language disorders each involving different factors in its manifestation.

Observations have shown that the process of speech, which includes mastering language codes and processing their encoding and decoding, can be impaired differently with lesions of different parts of the brain. As a rule, in lesions of posterior ('gnostic') regions of the major (left) hemisphere the process of acquisition of language codes can be disturbed. Lesions of the verbal–acoustic areas of the left temporal lobe evoke a derangement of phonemic organization of the sounds perceived, and as a secondary result considerable disturbance of the lexical units of the language is seen: words which are acoustically similar can be confused, and 'alienation of word meaning' takes place. This can result in marked difficulty in understanding single words, while the whole prosodic and partly syntactic structure of the phrase is preserved, and the patient remains able to understand the sense of the whole phrase in spite of lacking stable recognition of single lexical units.

It was found that lesions of the most complex 'tertiary' regions of the left hemisphere (inferoparietal or parieto-occipital regions of the cortex) are associated with different forms of impairment of language. Phonemic organization of language remains intact and the understanding of separate lexical units is preserved. Trouble appears when separate lexical parts are related in simultaneous 'paradigmatically' organized structures which require processes of simultaneous synthesis and perception of logico-grammatical relations. This is why in patients with lesions of these regions, fluent 'syntagmatically' organized verbal utterance, or simple 'communications of events' (such as: 'The house is burning', 'The boy hit a dog', 'Mother went to a movie and the children remained at home') are preserved, while complex 'communications of relations' resulting in logico-grammatical structures (such as: 'Brother's father', 'The triangle under the circle', 'Mary is fairer than Ann'), phrases, or complex distant constructions that need a series of additional transformations for their understanding, are severely deranged.

A careful description of these disturbances makes it possible to divide all utterances into two basic groups—one which is 'syntagmatically' organized and remains intact, and a second which is 'paradigmatically' organized and breaks down.

The general statement of neurolinguistics is that in differently localized brain lesions, verbal utterances can be broken down into different links (phonemic, lexical, logico-grammatical, etc.). This is of great importance for increased knowledge of the basic rules involved in language acquisition and linguistic performance, and is the reason why neurolinguistic studies can contribute to a better understanding of the basic structure of language. What we have described here are new ways of studying some linguistic structures, their components, and the basic types of their breakdown.

But speech comprises more than the mastering of the codes of the language. The generation of speech utterances, as well as their understanding, requires a long journey, starting from motives and intentions, including inner speech, and ending with extended verbal utterances—or, in the case of understanding, starting with perception of extended utterances and finally arriving at an understanding of the basic sense. Last, but not least, there is the motive of the whole verbal communication. This complex journey includes some important psychological, extra-linguistic factors, such as: retention of motives and intentions; constructing plans and programmes of verbal constructions ('realizations') of these plans; and building a 'closed semantic system' which has to remain stable and which can resist distracting factors.

This requires an adequate 'tone' of the cortex (it is impossible to retain goal-linked programmes in dreamy states) and an active participation of the frontal lobes of the brain, which should be considered as a special apparatus for retaining stable programmes and for permanent control of the information-processing. If the mechanisms ('apparatuses') of the brain-stem are deranged and the 'tone' of the cortex becomes low, or if the frontal lobes are injured and do not provide the control needed, 'closed semantic systems' are broken down and replaced by 'open semantic systems', i.e. by systems open to every distraction, or to inert stereotypes (perseverations). These extra-linguistic conditions result in a special kind of pathology, in which the subject becomes unable to use syntactical codes of language, or to generate extended verbal programmes, or to single out the meaning of complicated verbal constructions, which easily become deranged by external influences of immediate impressions, fixed stereotypes, etc.

The application of neuropsychological methods (i.e. the careful study of change in behavioural processes associated with local brain lesions) opens up new techniques both for linguistics and for the psychology of speech. This new field of science can be used with success to improve our knowledge of the inner mechanisms of language.

See also LANGUAGE: NEUROPHYSIOLOGY. A. R. L.

Luria, A. R. (1960). *Traumatic Aphasia*. The Hague.
Luria, A. R. (1976). *Basic Problems of Neurolinguistics*. The Hague.

**NEUROMODULATORS.** See NEUROTRANSMITTERS AND NEUROMODULATORS.

**NEURONAL CONNECTIVITY AND BRAIN FUNCTION.** The nervous system is made up largely of nerve-cells (neurones), with their associated neuronal processes, and glial cells. The role of the glial cells in the mature brain is believed to be supportive to the neurones, but in development their involvement in establishing organized connections, and in the formation of differentiated brain structures, appears to be most important. Here we concentrate on the neurones, which, with their axons and dendrites interconnecting the cells in a formidably complex fashion, are thought to carry out the main business of the *nervous system. This business, the primary function of the nervous system, is information-processing in the most comprehensive sense of the term. For many years there has been discussion on the relationship between the structure (here meaning connectivity) of the nervous system, and its function. If this discussion is to be more than a series of guesses and counter-guesses, we need to have a clear idea of what the structure and function of the system actually are; and here, because of recent advances in neuroanatomical techniques, we are in a much stronger position in relation to neural structure than to function.

We have a fairly extensive, though far from complete, knowledge of the connections that exist within both the vertebrate and the invertebrate nervous systems. About parts of the system in various vertebrates (the main sensory pathways, the main motor pathways, the cerebellum, the hippocampus, and certain regions of the spinal cord) our knowledge of connectivity is pretty comprehensive; about other parts of the system (many cortical regions of the cerebrum, the reticular core of the brain-stem, and numerous other parts) our knowledge of the patterns of connectivity, although increasing rapidly, is still very limited.

Many invertebrate nervous systems have a relative simplicity, in which not only are the classes of neurones fewer, but also the total numbers of cells, and concomitantly of connections, are less than in vertebrates. In such invertebrate systems this reduced complexity has enabled a fuller picture of connectivity to be obtained. As a result of technical advances in recent years investigators are now in a relatively strong position to start examining how connectivity in small circuits, in which the identities of the individual constituent neurones are known, is related to their function. The extent to which such systems model the circuitry of the more complex vertebrate nervous system awaits clarification.

In contrast to these 'simple' nervous systems, those of the vertebrates are impressively complicated. The brain of man is often quoted as comprising some $10^{12}$ neurones. Since, at any given time, an unknown number of these are probably altering their connections, and may be altering their basic characteristics, our attempts to obtain any sort of complete description of neural connectivity are fraught with practical and also theoretical difficulties. The numbers being dealt with are so large and so uncertain that, as was pointed out by Horridge (1968), no statement of the complete structure of the nervous system can ever be correct; by the time the statement is made, it will be out of date.

This gloomy thought need not deter us, however. In practice, we can get a long way by concentrating on *classes* of connections. When we do this, a most significant fact emerges. To the extent that we are able to demonstrate patterns of neural connections from one part of the nervous system to another, or to the rest of the body, we find that these patterns are closely similar from one animal to another within the same species, and in some instances are found to be remarkably similar in animals of widely different species.

These similarities in neural connection patterns between different animals indicate two things. First, they tell us that neural connections are not random but are formed in a controlled fashion. Second, they suggest that orderly connections have relevance for the function of the system. Teleologically speaking (and teleology is, after all, essential in any meaningful consideration of the nervous system), it would seem pointless for evolutionary mechanisms to perpetuate and refine the vastly complicated (and highly ordered) networks of neural connectivity, if these were purely decorative, so to speak.

When we consider neural function we find ourselves beset with far greater difficulties than in the study of neural structure. This is because, except for its most obvious roles, we do not really know what the function of the nervous system actually *is*. The above definition of neural function as 'information-processing' merely hides our ignorance behind a term which is presently popular without explaining anything. With man-made information-processing machines we know what the mechanism is and the nature of the operations performed by it, because we construct the machines in a particular way and for a particular purpose. With the nervous system we did not construct the mechanism, and we have not been able, so far, even to define some of its operations.

There are multiple levels of function in the nervous system and the only ones we know much about are those at the bottom. Some of the simpler spinal *reflexes we can both understand in terms of function and account for (almost) in terms of the connectivity underlying this function. At a higher level of complexity, we also have a fairly good understanding of many of the connection patterns that underlie the arrangement of sensory inputs and motor outputs. It is readily demonstrable at these levels of the nervous system that there is a close relationship between structure and function.

In the adult nervous system it is customary to consider that function is highly dependent upon structure. However, there is now good evidence that it also works the other way round, that structure may depend upon function, particularly during development. Experiments have shown that the refinement of the connection patterns formed between arrays of neurones is dependent upon normal stimulation of the system. If the normal pattern of stimulation is altered during crucial stages of development, the connection pattern can be modified, which in turn changes the functional capabilities of the circuitry.

The existence of a relationship between structure and function in the formed nervous system is readily demonstrated experimentally. Thus one can alter spinal reflexes in an accurately predictable fashion by switching nerve pathways; one can cause people to feel bodily sensations, to hear or see things by electrical stimulation of the appropriate parts of the brain; and one can alter the position of the apparent external stimulus by altering the point of stimulation in the brain. Observations such as these tell us that there are maps of the outside world, as perceived by our various sensory apparatuses, which extend across specific parts of the brain. The visual world, the auditory world, the sensitive surface of the body, are all represented in particular areas of the *cerebral cortex. All this is common knowledge and has been for many years; yet to a large extent the central mechanisms which are responsible for the motor outputs we associate with these sensory inputs remain unknown.

Even at the relatively low organizational level of sensory inputs and motor outputs, however, things are only fairly straightforward as long as we confine our attention to the three-dimensional geometry of the nervous system; as soon as we try to include the fourth dimension, taking into consideration the effects of such things as *learning, *memory and previous experience, the study of sensory inputs moves into another class of complexity.

The main difficulties we find in attempting to relate high-level neural functions to neural structure are tied up with the problems we have in defining these functions. *Pattern recognition is an easy one and we can almost see how it could work. *Intelligent behaviour is more difficult. We all know what we mean by the term intelligent, but there are almost as many definitions as there are people prepared to define it. Perhaps the most difficult function is language, since it may be very closely related to the very mechanisms of thought. What indeed *is* thought?

The brain is the organ of the mind. There can no longer be any doubt about this in the light of recent neurosurgical observations. The intimacy of the relationship between the brain and the mind is very clearly brought out by the personality changes which occur following surgical lesions of the frontal parts of the brain; and perhaps even more dramatically by the occurrence of two separate minds, or spheres of consciousness, one related to each side of the brain, in patients who have undergone *'split-brain' surgery (Sperry, 1966).

What we do not yet know is whether a form of in-built connectionist mechanism exists to underlie the highest neural functions. Here, the mind boggles (and we would indeed be far advanced if we knew what we meant by mind and if we could usefully define the term 'boggle'). However, while it is in no sense explanatory, a computer analogy may be useful. Simple computers can be wired up to do specific jobs. The larger the computer, and the wider the variety of tasks it can perform, the smaller is the emphasis placed upon specific patterns of wiring and the greater the emphasis on the programming. In the most powerful machines the wiring is in essence relatively simple, whereas the programs are highly complex. We may look on the brain as a form of computer, extensively hybrid, and containing many more elements, more complexly interconnected, than any man-made machine. It seems likely that, in the brain, connections are not pre-specified for the highest orders of function. Perhaps these latter depend upon programs which may themselves be either built in or, maybe more likely, acquired during the development of the individual, through the interaction of environmental factors on a genetically transmitted potential.

Although we do not know the nature of the relationship between neural connections and, for instance, intellectual and linguistic activities, we do know that such a relationship exists. It seems likely that many of the intractable difficulties we encounter in attempting to find out about the relationship between the brain and the highest neural functions, follow from the self-referential nature of the inquiry. The brain is the organ of the mind, of *intelligence, and yet we use the brain to investigate its own activity in these fields. Since modes of thought (including modes of *perception) are conditioned by the structure of the brain, it is hardly surprising, in principle, that we find that our thoughts on these matters tend to run in tight philosophical circles.

See also LOCALIZATION OF BRAIN FUNCTION AND CORTICAL ACTIVITY. R. M. G.
J. S. H. T.

Horridge, G. A. (1968). *Interneurons*. London.
Sperry, R. W. (1966). Brain bisection and mechanisms of consciousness. In Eccles, J. C. (ed.), *Brain and Conscious Experience*, 298–308. New York.

**NEUROPEPTIDES.** The study of neuropeptides, i.e. peptides occurring in the nervous system, is one of the fastest growing areas in neurobiology today. Novel peptides from the brain with actions related to functions such as *pain, analgesia, *sleep, etc., are being discovered at an increasing rate. There are probably two reasons for this neuropeptide 'explosion'. One is that methods for the identification of peptides in very small amounts, such as are present in the brain, have been developed and greatly improved in recent years. The other is the growing realization by neuroscientists of the importance of peptides in brain function, based on the ability of neuropeptides to relay messages selectively between particular groups of cells.

Peptides are made of amino acids joined together to form a chain, and since eighteen different amino acids are found in animals there are 306 ways of putting these together to make a dipeptide and, theoretically, there is an astronomical number of different decapeptides (with ten amino acids). Different peptides can be distinguished because many brain-cells, and cells elsewhere in the body, have receptors on their surface which can 'recognize' a particular peptide. Thus each peptide used by the brain can carry a particular message if it can travel to a nearby or distant site to interact with its receptor. The combination of the peptide with its receptor will induce a change in the cell, for example a nerve-cell may be excited or inhibited. In this way a peptide can be used by one group of cells to influence or control another group. There are several types of control. A peptide which is released into the bloodstream and acts on distant cells is a hormone: this type of action tends to be slow and long-lasting. A peptide released from the fibre terminal of one neurone into the synaptic cleft to act on the membrane of another neurone is a neurotransmitter: this type of action is relatively fast and short-lasting.

The first important neuropeptide to be identified chemically was the hormone vasopressin, shown by Vincent Du Vigneaud and his colleagues at Cornell Medical School in 1953 to be a peptide with nine amino acids. Vasopressin is made by a particular group of neurones in the hypothalamus and is transported to their terminals in the posterior pituitary gland, or neurohypophysis. When these hypothalamic neurones are activated, vasopressin is released from their terminals into the bloodstream and is carried all round the body. Reaching the kidney it recognizes receptors and acts on them and, in effect, commands the kidney to conserve fluid. Thus its function is to act as a messenger between the brain and the kidney in the control of water balance in the body.

Following this discovery, it was some years before it was realized that there are peptides which can relay messages within the brain. Evidence is now accumulating that some peptides act as neurotransmitters at synaptic junctions. It is also possible, though by no means established, that some peptides are released into the cerebrospinal fluid to act at a variety of distant neuronal sites. Research into these possibilities is being eagerly pursued.

The strongest evidence for a neurotransmitter role for a peptide comes from the study of substance P, which was known to be a biologically active peptide, present in brain extracts, as long ago as 1936, although its chemical identity was not established until 1970. Substance P is present in fine sensory fibres which inform the nervous system of painful stimuli, for example it is found in fibres from the tooth pulp. There is a body of evidence to suggest that it is released from the terminals of such fibres at synapses, where it excites sensory neurones which transmit the message that noxious stimulation has occurred to higher parts of the brain concerned in pain sensation and in behavioural responses to pain.

There are also peptides which can produce analgesia. These are the encephalins and β-endorphin, which are known as opioid peptides because their action resembles that of morphine and other derivatives of opium. Their discovery in 1975–6 was a major advance in our knowledge of brain function. These peptides occur in particular groups of neurones and their best-known action is to produce analgesia by inhibiting neurones which are attempting to transmit the message that pain-producing stimulation has occurred.

Is there a sleep peptide? This intriguing possibility has spurred the activity of several research groups. Certainly a substance of peptide composition with sleep-inducing activity can be extracted from the brain, or cerebrospinal fluid, or cerebral venous blood, of sleeping or sleep-deprived animals. However, different groups of workers are not yet in agreement on the identity of this peptide,

and identification is necessary before its role in sleep can be determined.

One group of peptides made in hypothalamic neurones are transported via local vascular channels to influence the release of hormones from the anterior pituitary gland. These include thyroid hormone releasing factor (THRF), luteinizing hormone releasing factor (LHRF), and growth hormone release-inhibiting factor (somatostatin). These three peptides are also found in neurones in many other areas of the central nervous system, where their functions are as yet unknown.

Peptides that occur in the alimentary canal and various other naturally occurring peptides have been found to be distributed in particular groups of neurones in the central nervous system, but little is known about their possible functions. Some peptides have been shown to influence behaviour, and a recently discovered tripeptide, containing pyroglutamate, histidine, and glycine, has been obtained from the urine of patients with one type of anorexia nervosa: given to mice it acts to reduce food intake, but it is likely that this peptide is only present under pathological conditions.

How are neuropeptides made? Nerve-cells are different from other cells in that they possess large amounts of RNA (Nissl substance) in the cytoplasm. The RNA makes proteins with a sequence of amino acids that depends on the sequence of bases in the RNA in each cell; these proteins are then cleaved at particular points by peptidases. The short-chain peptides thus produced can be transported to the fibre terminals of the neurone and released when required. During evolution, mutations occur which change the base sequence in the DNA in the genes, and therefore in the RNA, and this results in changes in the amino acid sequence in the proteins and peptides. These changes may be unimportant, resulting in minor differences between species in closely related peptides with the same function. Alternatively the changes may be more significant, resulting in the development of different peptides which, although related to their ancestral peptide, have become specialized for different functions. Thus vasopressin has the same function in different mammals even though in some species a particular amino acid in the sequence has been changed. On the other hand, vasopressin and another hypothalamic peptide, oxytocin, are related in that they both have nine amino acids, seven of which are identical, but the difference is sufficient for them to have different actions. Some mutations may throw a spanner in the works by preventing the formation of a particular peptide or by producing a peptide which interferes with normal function. In this way some pathological defects of genetic origin may arise.

For the future, we know that there are many peptides in the brain and spinal cord whose chemical identity and actions remain to be determined. Since some peptides have been shown to have actions related to specific functions we can speculate that this may be true also for many other peptides. Does each peptide supply the chemical code for particular types of activity? Within the next decade we can expect to know much more about the role of peptides in brain function. For better—it is hoped—or for worse, this work will lead eventually to the development of important new drugs with effects on brain and behaviour. One might also hope that better understanding of the functions of neuropeptides in the brain will yet produce a non-addictive analgesic. For example, β-endorphin, when injected, has effects similar to those of morphine. Unfortunately tolerance to and physical dependence upon both β-endorphin and metencephalin have been demonstrated as well as cross tolerance between these peptides and exogenous opioids.

See also NEUROTRANSMITTERS AND NEUROMODU-
LATORS. J. H. W.

Barker, J. L. (1976). Peptides: roles in neuronal excitability. *Physiological Reviews*, **56**, 435–52.

Cooper, J. R., Bloom, F. E., and Roth, R. H. (1978). *The Biochemical Basis of Neuropharmacology*, 3rd edn. New York.

Gainer, H. (ed.) (1977). *Peptides in Neurobiology*. New York.

Pappenheimer, J. R. (1976). The sleep factor. *Scientific American*, **235**, 24–9.

Wolstencroft, J. H. (1978). The neurophysiology of transmitters in relation to pain and analgesia. In Taylor, A. and Jones, M. T. (eds.), *Chemical Communication within the Nervous System and its Disturbance in Disease*, 135–60. Oxford.

**NEUROPSYCHOLOGY.** The first issue of the international journal *Neuropsychologia*, in January 1963, contained an editorial which defined the term 'neuropsychology' as 'a particular area of neurology of common interest to neurologists, psychiatrists, psychologists and neurophysiologists'. It added that 'this interest is focused mainly, though not exclusively, on the cerebral cortex', that 'topics of particular concern are disorders of language, perception and action', and that 'although certain of these disorders can, of course, be studied only in man, we are none the less convinced that information of great value to human pathology is to be obtained from animal experiment, which may be expected to throw valuable light on the basic mechanisms of cerebral organization'. An editorial in the same journal nearly twenty years later commented that 'there is still no better definition available'. The developments which led up to the emergence of an autonomous discipline of neuropsychology have a long and chequered history and provide insights into the perennial issues which still occupy neuropsychologists.

Attempts to localize mental processes to particular bodily structures can be traced back at least to the fifth century BC, when Hippocrates of Cos identified the brain as the organ of intellect and the heart as the organ of the senses. Empedocles (about 490–430 BC), concerned with the same central and enduring philosophical problem of the relationship of mind to body, located mental processes in the heart. For the next two thousand years, the relative merits of what have been called 'the brain hypothesis' and the 'cardiac hypothesis' were debated. The natural successor to Hippocrates was the anatomist *Galen, who, in describing aspects of brain anatomy, argued for the brain hypothesis. There is little doubt that both Hippocrates and Galen drew heavily upon their experiences as physicians. Galen as a surgeon tending gladiators was doubtless well aware of some of the consequences of brain damage. His views contrast with those of *Aristotle, who, having decided that the heart was warm and active, saw it as the source of mental processes, whereas the brain was relegated to the minor role of serving as a mechanism cooling the blood of the heart. Galen believed that the mind was located in the fluid found in the large ventricles of the brain, a view which continued to be canvassed until it was refuted by Vesalius (1511–64). *Descartes, continuing the debate, adopted a quite explicit dualist position, seeing the body and the mind as separate but nevertheless able to interact. By the eighteenth century, some of the issues that were to represent major viewpoints in what was to become neuropsychology were already being identified—the principal one being whether, and to what extent, particular mental functions could be localized in particular parts of the brain.

The detailed argument for localization of function is usually associated with the phrenological theory of *Gall and with his contemporary J. C. Spurzheim (1776–1832). Both Gall and Spurzheim were anatomists and made important contributions to their discipline by which they were assured a place in the history of science. Regrettably, once they went beyond anatomy and attempted to locate functions in different parts of the brain, they indulged in speculation which led them wildly astray. From their observations of the external structure of the skull, they developed the view that such external features might correlate with important aspects of behaviour. Despite the conceptual ingenuity of their views, they failed to produce evidence which was even reasonably objectively based and could be regarded as convincing support for their main hypothesis. The demolition of their views was brought about by the work of the French anatomist Pierre *Flourens, who ablated parts of the brains of pigeons and studied the changes that occurred post-operatively in their behaviour. He concluded that there was no evidence for localization of function within the cerebrum but that any loss that was observed simply reflected the extent of damage to brain tissue.

The possibility of demonstrating localization of function took a decisive step forward on 21 February 1825, when J. Bouillaud (1796–1881) read a paper to a scientific meeting in France in which he argued from his clinical studies that speech was localized in the frontal lobes, a view already suggested by Gall. Shortly afterwards, in 1836, Marc

Dax read a paper in Montpellier, also reporting a series of clinical cases; these he believed demonstrated that speech disorders were linked with lesions of the left hemisphere. It was not, however, until 1865 that Dax's manuscript was published, by his son. Meanwhile, in 1861, Paul *Broca, founder of the Anthropological Society of Paris, heard Bouillaud's son-in-law report the case of a patient who had ceased to speak when pressure was applied to his exposed anterior lobes. Soon afterwards, he saw a patient who had lost his speech and could say only one word, 'Tan', and utter oaths. Results of the post mortem on this patient indicated left frontal pathology. It is usual to credit Broca with describing this syndrome, which consisted of the inability to speak despite normal understanding of language, and also as the person who elaborated the concept of cerebral dominance of language in the left hemisphere. The other outstanding figure at this time was *Wernicke. To him is attributed the discovery that there is more than one language area in the brain.

The history of thought on *aphasia over the past 150 years and more illustrates the continuing debate about how mental functions are related to brain structure. Thus, one group of workers on aphasia, taking their lead from the early phrenologists, maintained that specific mental functions were subserved by separate areas of the brain. Those who opposed this 'localizationist' view believed that mental capability reflected total intact brain volume. While Broca and Wernicke lie in the localizationist tradition, Hughlings *Jackson and Kurt *Goldstein represent the so-called holistic approach to aphasia.

In view of these early observations on the relations between brain and behaviour, it remains something of a puzzle why a separate discipline of neuropsychology did not develop by 1900 rather than by 1949. Perhaps part of the reason was the intervention of the world wars, part was the suspicion of any views that seemed to indicate a retreat to the localizationist views of the phrenologists, and part was the strong presence of the so-called *Gestalt theories in psychology. All of these, it would seem, led to the localizationist approach being abandoned in favour of a more holistic approach. Henry *Head (1926) was dissatisfied with the classical neurologists' attempts to deduce schemes from clinical observations, believing that they were, as he put it, 'compelled to lop and twist their cases to fit the procrustean bed of their hypothetical conceptions'. He attempted to bring some order to the field by devising a standard list of tests to be used in the study of aphasia, an idea developed by Weisenberg and McBride (1935). Earlier (1933), Weisenberg and McBride had made the important discovery that individuals who do not understand spoken language, although their hearing is intact and they can identify nonverbal sounds (e.g. a telephone ringing), may have damage in two different locations. Around the same time, the influence of Karl *Lashley, who published his paper 'In Search of the Engram' in 1938, is usually seen as significant. Lashley proposed a theory of mass action, contending that the behavioural result of a lesion depends on the amount of brain removed more than on the location of the lesion.

During the second half of the twentieth century and, in particular, immediately after the Second World War, there was a reawakening of interest in the brain/behaviour relationship, and, as often happens in science, it was not so much the discovery of new ideas but the rediscovery of old ones. In this case it was the views of some of the classical neurologists, combined with the development of the new behavioural techniques of the experimental psychologists which were to give the necessary impetus to lead to the development of neuropsychology as such. Recent research (Bruce, 1985) suggests that the term 'neuropsychology' was first used in 1913 by Sir William Osler in an address he gave at the opening of the Phipps Clinic at the Johns Hopkins Hospital. In his address entitled *Specialism in the General Hospital* Osler expressed the hope that 'time may be found for general instruction of the senior class in the elements of neuropsychology'. Bruce speculates that Lashley, who was appointed research professor of neuropsychology at Harvard in 1937, may have heard Osler give his address at the Phipps Clinic since Lashley was a graduate and postdoctoral student at Hopkins from 1911 to 1917. Subsequently in 1949 the term 'neuropsychology' was given wide publicity when Donald Hebb published a book under the title *The Organization of Behaviour: A neuropsychological theory*. Nine years later, Heinrich *Klüver, in the preface to his book on *Behaviour Mechanisms in Monkeys*, suggested that it would be of interest to 'neuropsychologists'. In 1960, Karl Lashley's collected writings were published under the title *The Neuropsychology of Lashley*. At no point, however, thus far, was the term 'neuropsychology' used systematically, nor was it carefully defined in the text. Hans Lucas *Teuber, one of the early pioneers in neuropsychology, argued that the task of neuropsychology is twofold. First, to help the patient with the damaged brain to understand his disease and, secondly, by carefully studying such experiments of nature, to provide essential insights into the physiological basis of of normal brain function. Although such study draws information from several disciplines, including anatomy, biophysics, ethology, pharmacology, and physiology, nevertheless its central focus continues to be the development of a science of human behaviour based upon the study of the function of the human brain. Teuber showed elegantly and convincingly how the precise methods traditionally used by experimental psychologists in the study of psychophysics could be applied to problems in neuropsychology. His monograph entitled *Visual field defects after penetrating missile wounds of the brain*, published in 1960 and written jointly with

Battersby and Bender, illustrates the success of such methods.

Thus by 1963 the time seemed ripe for the launching of *Neuropsychologia*. The editorial of the first issue traced its background to regular meetings of a small group of European neurologists and psychologists who had first gathered in Austria in 1951 to discuss disorders of higher mental functions associated with injury or disease of the brain.

Today there are several different approaches to the study of the brain/behaviour relationships, but the method which has figured most prominently is the one that is the natural successor or complement to the work of the early neurologists, namely study of the effects of lesions in specific areas of the brain by carefully observing associated changes in behaviour. It is noteworthy that the results of carefully controlled animal studies have been very important in the development of neuropsychology. In studying patients, one must, for obvious ethical reasons, take what comes and thus accept that the limits of any brain damage are not precisely known. By contrast, in animal studies, the locus and extent of lesions can be precisely defined and pre- and post-operative behaviour carefully studied and measured. In human studies, experimental psychologists have contributed significantly by devising ingenious techniques to be used under controlled conditions and by proposing theoretical concepts to account for the deficits in behaviour observed in brain-damaged patients: for example, the distinction between short-term memory and long-term memory and models of their interrelationships.

Neuropsychologists study our awareness of the world in which we move. What we see, hear and touch are dependent upon the proper functioning of the intact central nervous system. Likewise, how we respond by taking action is dependent on the intactness of those parts of the nervous system concerned with initiating and sustaining co-ordinated motor activity. But it is not only sensory and motor processes that may be altered by changes in the nervous system: higher functions such as language, thought, and memory may also be changed. The human brain is well endowed with so-called association cortex. These are regions of neocortex not specialized as primary sensory or motor regions. Thus, *memory, for long a topic of interest to philosophers, was a central concern of Lashley, who, after years of animal experiment-ation, concluded that 'it is not possible to demonstrate the isolated localization of a memory trace anywhere in the nervous system'. Only three years after Lashley reached this conclusion, a neurosurgeon, William Scoville, in 1953, operated on a patient known as H. M. and left him unable to remember virtually anything that occurred after his operation. It appeared that the surgical bilateral removal of the hippocampus and adjacent structures had not touched H. M.'s stored memories but had made it impossible for him to store or retrieve new memories. The detailed study of H. M. changed the emphasis in the study of memory from searching for a location for memories to analysing how memories are stored and retrieved. Today, the roles of the temporal, frontal, and parietal lobes in memory form part of a wider study of the complementary specializations of the left and right hemispheres, to which we now turn. Since studies of cerebral asymmetries have been a major part of research in neuropsychology for several decades, they illustrate well the methods used by neuropsychologists, how their results are presented, and the controversies and uncertainties that remain.

**Cerebral asymmetries.** The discovery by Dax and Broca in the nineteenth century that damage to the left hemisphere resulted in inability to talk, whereas damage to the right hemisphere did not affect speech production, led to the general acceptance of the view that the left hemisphere plays a special role in language which is not shared by the right hemisphere. Language, however, is not the only special function of the left hemisphere. At the beginning of the twentieth century, H. Liepmann demonstrated that the left hemisphere has a special role in controlling complex movements. Nevertheless, the special functions of the right hemisphere remained a comparative mystery until the early 1950s when, following the work of Zangwill, Hécaen, and Milner, it became clear that it was more involved in the analysis of visual and spatial dimensions of the world than was the left hemisphere.

The potential for some behaviours, it would seem, is virtually wired into the structure of the nervous system. These include not only reflex and instinctive behaviours, but also behaviour as complex as language. In this sense, psychological asymmetry is based upon micro-anatomical asymmetry. In 1968, Geschwind and Levitsky reported gross anatomical asymmetries following their study of a large series of human brains. They reported that the part called the 'planum temporale' was larger on the left-hand side of 65 per cent of the brains they studied and that it was larger by nearly 1 cm than on the right. Subsequent studies have confirmed Geschwind and Levitsky's findings and have shown, moreover, that these structural differences are in evidence very early in life.

In addition to those studies of neurological patients with lesions on one side or other of the brain, there are studies of those who have had the brain stimulated during surgery and of those receiving temporary anaesthetization of one side of the brain before surgery. Most recently, studies of regional blood-flow have added another technique for the study of functional asymmetry. Studies of healthy people have also added significantly to neuropsychological knowledge. One widely used technique is to present sensory information selectively to one or other cerebral hemisphere and to ask for some kind of verbal or non-verbal response. Electrical recordings from the two hemispheres have also been studied. Even so, the method that has proved most powerful in demonstrating lateralization is that called, by Teuber, 'double dissociation'. Having demonstrated that lesions in the left hemisphere of right-handed patients produce difficulties in language, including speech, writing, and reading, and that such difficulties do not follow from lesions in the right hemisphere, we may say that the functions of the two hemispheres are dissociated. By contrast, difficulties which follow right-hemisphere damage are found with spatial tasks, with singing, and with playing musical instruments; such abilities are thus more disrupted by damage to the right than the left hemisphere. It is then said that the two hemispheres are doubly dissociated.

Another approach which has proved important in identifying cerebral asymmetries has been study of the results of an operation carried out on a small number of patients to whom *epilepsy had become a problem unresponsive to other forms of therapy. In some such cases, neurosurgeons resorted to cutting through the major fibres which interconnect the two cerebral hemispheres, known as the neocortical commissures. These include the corpus callosum and the anterior commissure, and their complete sectioning is known as 'total commissurotomy'. After the operation, the two hemispheres behave as if they are virtually independent. Because of the particular way in which sensory inputs are connected to the cerebral hemispheres, we know that information coming from the left visual field or the left hand is directed to the right hemisphere, and vice versa for the right visual field and the right hand. From numerous studies of such so-called 'split-brain' patients, it is now acknowledged that when the left hemisphere has access to information it can initiate speech and thus talk about the information, whereas the disconnected right hemisphere cannot. The right hemisphere apparently is good at recognizing things but is unable to initiate speech because it cannot get access to the speech mechanisms in the left hemisphere. By presenting stimuli such as pictures or words to the left visual field and thus the right hemisphere, or the right visual field and left hemisphere, and asking the patients to name or otherwise act upon what is seen, it has been possible to carry out careful studies of the functions of the isolated right and left hemispheres (see SPLIT-BRAIN AND THE MIND).

The technique of selectively presenting information to one or the other hemisphere, whether through the eyes or through the ears or through the sense of touch, has also been applied to normal people. The results indicate relative differences between the two cerebral hemispheres, but it is difficult to repeat such experiments and get the same results each time.

Another approach to the study of brain function arises at times in the course of major brain surgery when a neurosurgeon may briefly stimulate the exposed surface of the brain electrically in order to ascertain which part of the brain he is treating and also to establish with as much certainty as possible on which side of the brain speech is lateralized. Using such stimulation and asking the conscious patient to report what he feels or to answer questions, further information is gained about the functions of particular areas of the brain.

There is yet another source of neuropsychological knowledge associated with the study of neurological patients. To discover as precisely as possible in which hemisphere speech and language are lateralized, a neurosurgeon may temporarily inactivate one or the other hemisphere by injecting sodium amylobarbitone selectively into the carotid artery supplying one or other side of the brain. In this way, it is possible to study what one side of the brain is able to do in the temporary absence of help from the other side. Recently it has been assumed that the flow of blood to the neocortex increases in areas where the neurones are particularly active, and in this way, by injecting a solution of a radioactive substance into the blood, it has been possible to examine where it accumulates when particular cognitive activities are taking place. (See IMAGES OF THE BRAIN IN ACTION.)

The auditory system (see HEARING) is not completely crossed, as both hemispheres receive projections from both ears. It appears that the connections from each ear have a preferred access to the opposite hemisphere, so that sounds to the right ear are principally handled by the left hemisphere and vice versa. Kimura showed that when words are presented simultaneously to the two ears through headphones, the material that is entering through the right ear is more easily analysed than that coming in through the left ear. The converse seems to be true with musical material similarly simultaneously presented. Observing this difference, it has been inferred that the left hemisphere specializes in the analysis of language and the right hemisphere in music. A similar technique can be used to study sensation through *touch. For example, two flat stimuli can be represented simultaneously, one to each hand, and the subject is asked to identify the objects that are being palpated. In all such experiments the results show that in normal subjects, hemispheric asymmetry is relative rather than absolute. In the normal subject, since the two hemispheres are intimately interrelated through the corpus callosum, any information that is put into one hemisphere can rapidly be transferred to the other hemisphere. Thus, the most likely reason for the observed asymmetries is that the direct route into the left hemisphere is much more efficient than the indirect interhemispheric route.

Neuropsychologists recognize that such talk about lateralization of function begs a number of important questions. What, for example, is it that is lateralized? On this issue there are a number of competing theoretical arguments. For example, there are those who take the view that the two hemispheres are organized differently. Thus,

Josephine Semmes in 1968 suggested that the left hemisphere functions as if there is a collection of discrete regions, whereas the right hemisphere functions in a much more holistic and diffuse manner. Others take the view that the two hemispheres have distinct ways of processing information, and they argue that the left hemisphere works in a much more analytic way, as it processes information sequentially and abstracts out the relevant details, whereas the right hemisphere synthesizes what comes in. The possibility of different forms of cerebral organization is well illustrated by the continuing debate about how speech and language are organized in the brains of left-handers. Thus some (e.g. Zangwill, 1960), noting the higher incidence of aphasia in unilaterally brain-injured left-handers, have postulated an incomplete functional lateralization of speech in the vast majority of left-handers, resulting in greater sensitivity to brain lesions.

As the young science of neuropsychology has grown up in different parts of the world, so it has developed its own distinctive emphases and techniques. In the USA, the emphasis has been on quantitative and psychometric techniques. In some cases batteries of tests have been applied to large groups of patients in an attempt to analyse quantitatively the patterns of deficits that emerge between the different brain-damaged groups. In the UK, the approach has been more qualitative and less psychometric and has paid more attention to the in-depth study of crucial single cases, from which a great deal can be learned and any one of which may, properly studied, call into question an existing neuropsychological hypothesis. The case of H. M. cited earlier is a prime example of work in this tradition, including the work that has been done in Canada. In the USSR also, under the leadership of *Luria, qualitative and non-psychometric techniques have had pre-eminence. For Luria, the preferred techniques were simple, often using only pencil and paper which could be administered at the bedside and not requiring the full panoply of the experimental psychologist's laboratory. Commenting on Luria's contributions to neuropsychology, Teuber described them as 'monumental', noting that they spanned a third of a century and, in addition to being concerned with the major syndrome of man's left cerebral hemisphere, encompassed 'a detailed and brilliant analysis of the syndrome of massive frontal-lobe involvement'. The publication in 1965 of an English translation of his book, The Higher Cortical Functions in Man, made available to the West a wealth of neuropsychological theory and practice.

Each of these distinctive approaches to neuropsychology has contributed significantly to its development and will continue to do so. From time to time, excessive claims have been made for the young discipline, and simplistic accounts have been given of results. In the case of cerebral asymmetries, wide generalizations have been made, speculation going far beyond the relatively limited

data and not always helping the development of the subject. One of the major growth areas in recent years has been application of the results of detailed studies of patients to cognitive models of behaviour rather than to the neurophysiological and neuroanatomical substrate of behaviour. M. A. J.

Bruce, D. (1985). On the origin of the term 'neuropsychology'. Neuropsychologia, 23, 813–14.
Gazzaniga, M. S. (1970). The Bisected Brain. New York.
Gazzaniga, M. S. and Le Doux, J. E. (1978). The Integrated Mind. New York.
Geschwind, N. (1972). Language and the brain. Scientific American, 226, 340–8.
Hécaen, H. and Lateri-Laura, G. (1977). Evolution des Connaissances et des Doctrines sur les Localisations Cerebrales. Paris.
Kimura, D. I. (1973). The asymmetry of the human brain. Scientific American, 228, 70–8.
Kolb, B. and Whishaw, I. Q. (1980). Fundamentals of Human Neuropsychology.
Luria, A. R. (1972). The Man with the Shattered World. New York and London.
Luria, A. R. (1968). The Mind of a Mnemonist. New York.
Luria, A. R. (1973). The Working Brain. New York.
Milner, B. (1971). Interhemispheric differences in the localisation of psychological processes in man. British Medical Bulletin, 27, 272–7.
Osler, W. (1913). Specialism in the general hospital. Bulletin of Johns Hopkins Hospital, 24, 167–71.
Pribram, K. H. (1971). Languages of the Brain. Englewood Cliffs, New Jersey.
Sperry, R. W. (1964). The Great Cerebral Commissure. Scientific American, 210, 42–52.
Zangwill, O. L. (1960). Cerebral Dominance and its Relation to Psychological Function. Edinburgh and Springfield, Illinois.

**NEUROPSYCHOLOGY OF LANGUAGE.** See LANGUAGE: NEUROPSYCHOLOGY.

**NEUROSIS** is a habit that is either maladaptive in some obvious respect and/or distressing, yet more or less fixed and resistant to modification through the normal processes of learning. Its original meaning was a circumscribed disorder or loss of function of a bodily organ that was attributed, mistakenly, to disorder in the function of peripheral nerves or nervous tissue. It is only diagnosed nowadays when any disease or disorder in the nervous system seems improbable. Examples of neurotic habits are persistent anxiety out of keeping with the immediate circumstances, *phobias, obsessive thoughts, compulsions, and such losses of function as the paralysis of a limb or erectile impotence. (See OBSESSIONS AND COMPULSIONS.)

Therapeutic investigation of a neurosis turns on the mental mechanisms involved, its origins in past experience, and the current circumstances determining its persistence. These tend to lie in the benefits, often hidden, that the habit confers. Thus the essence of the neurosis may be, as Sigmund *Freud argued, the renunciation of a function whose exercise would give rise to anxiety. The neurosis then persists because, keeping away from a situation that would arouse anxiety, the patient is denied opportunities to learn more constructive ways of dealing with the sources of the anxiety.

Compare PSYCHOSIS.　　　　　　D. R. D.

## NEUROTRANSMITTERS AND NEUROMODULATORS.

The soft warm living substance of the brain and nervous system stands in stark contrast to the rigid metal and plastic hardware of a modern day computer, but at the fundamental level there are clear similarities between these two apparently disparate organizational systems and, of course, one is a product of the other. Not only are the nerve cell units (neurones) self-repairing and self-wiring under the grand design built into our genes, but they can also promote, amplify, block, inhibit, or attenuate the micro-electric signals which are passed on to them, and through them, and thereby give rise to signalling patterns of myriad complexity between networks of cerebral neurones, and this provides the physical substrate of mind. Such key processes of signalling by one group, or family, of neurones to another is achieved largely by the secretion of tiny quantities of potent chemical substances by neuronal fibre terminals. These neurotransmitters stimulate selected neighbours, with whom they junction, into producing electrical responses which both qualitatively (i.e. by excitation or inhibition) and quantitatively (i.e. by frequency of neurotransmitter release) reflect the patterns of presynaptic stimulation.

In this way, the nerve impulses are passed on from cell to cell. This continuous alternation between electrical and chemical conveyance of signals on their journeys through the pathways of the brain and nervous system, provides a special opportunity for the traffic of electrical impulses to be modulated or blocked as they attempt to jump the gap between one neurone and the next at their junctions, transposed into pulses of chemical substances. This is the point where selected constellations of neurones from the vast array of neuronal populations can effectively interact, one with another, to filter, edit, integrate, and add precise direction to their interplay of communication. Thus, neurotransmitters and their functional partners, the *neuromodulators*, play a cardinal role in controlling the flow of information through the nervous system.

**Neurones as information receivers and transmitters.** The extensive web of branching *dendrites which characterizes so many neurones in the brain (see NERVOUS SYSTEM) is primarily an adaptation to provide maximal surface area for receiving inputs from other nerve cells with which they make contact. *Interaction* is very much the principle theme which underlies the shape and cellular anatomy of neurones. Each pyramidal neurone in the vertebrate brain is likely to be receiving up to some 100,000 contacts from the neurones to which they are wired, and the dazzlingly complex and extensive multi-branched dendritic tree of the Purkinje cells of the *cerebellum, concerned with learning co-ordination tasks, probably extends to some 300,000 neuronal contacts. The *axons, the single output line of the neurone, can be rather short (e.g. in so-called *interneurones*) or very long, perhaps 12 metres in cortical pyramidal cells of the giant blue whale, which course from brain to lower spinal cord. At various points along its length, the axon may branch to make contact with local neuronal communities, though most of its contacts are made towards its terminal region. Thus, it is not surprising that the cell-body region of the neurone is

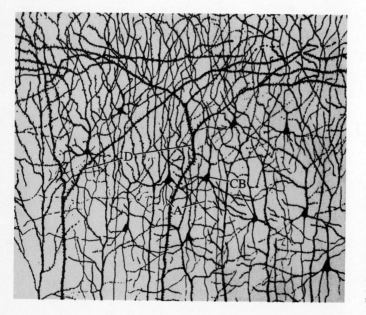

**Fig. 1.** Golgi preparation from the visual cortex of a human infant, showing the vertical orientation of many neuronal processes. Dendrites (D) can be identified by the spine processes which give their surface a rough, granular, appearance. In contrast axons (A) and cell bodies (CB) are smooth-surfaced.

estimated to take up only 5 per cent or less of the cellular volume of the brain, the greater part comprising the dense fibrous feltwork of dendrites and axons (Fig. 1).

Sometimes the neurone-to-neurone contacts or

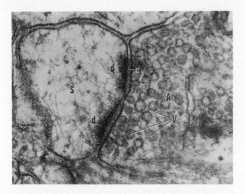

**Fig. 2.** Electron micrograph of nerve-ending (synapse) of the 'tight-junction' variety in rat brain. The pre-synaptic region (axon, A) synapses onto the post-synaptic region, (dendrite spine, S). Note the synaptic cleft (C), synaptic vesicles (V), and post-synaptic densities (d). The latter are double because the density forms a 'doughnut-like' ring and is seen as a cross section through this ring. This arrangement of the density, is not uncommon. Note synaptic vesicles exocytosing (*arrow*). Compare with Figure 3.

*synapses*, as they are termed, are highly organized junctions allowing an extremely close approach between the two cells so that they are separated only by a very narrow gap or *cleft* (typically 20 nanometres wide) (Figs. 2 and 3). In this case, neurotransmitters are delivered at a very precise location when their secretion is triggered by the incoming nerve-terminal. In other cases, the axon produces long chains of swellings (so-called *varicosities*) towards its terminal branching regions, and these provide multiple sites for neurotransmitter release as the nerve-impulse courses through them on its passage towards the distal regions of the neurone (Fig. 4).

These varicosities, whilst containing synaptic vesicles and granules of the type characteristic of the 'tight-junction' synapses described above, do not exist in highly organized apposition to other neurones, and the highly structured synaptic cleft (gap between neurones) or post-synaptic thickenings typical of 'tight-junction' synapses are rarely present (compare Figs. 3 and 4). The neurotransmitter is probably released from the whole bulbous surface of the varicosity as a miniature cloud which will diffuse away, diminishing in concentration, until it encounters the appropriate neurotransmitter neuroreceptors at which it can bind and act. These varicose modifications of nerve axons were first discovered in the peripheral nervous system, but in the past decade they have become established as a common feature

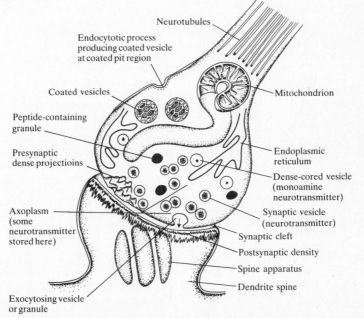

Neurotubules

Endocytotic process producing coated vesicle at coated pit region

Coated vesicles

Peptide-containing granule

Presynaptic dense projectioins

Axoplasm (some neurotransmitter stored here)

Exocytosing vesicle or granule

Mitochondrion

Endoplasmic reticulum

Dense-cored vesicle (monoamine neurotransmitter)

Synaptic vesicle (neurotransmitter)

Synaptic cleft

Postsynaptic density

Spine apparatus

Dendrite spine

**Fig. 3.** Diagrammatic version of an axon terminal forming a synapse on a spine apparatus of a dendrite. The structures shown are not to scale. Endocytosis produces complex vesicles consisting of a hexagonal basketwork of fibres (cytonet), which form part of the inner surface of the nerve terminal membrane at regions called 'coated pits'. In this diagram, vesicles containing monoamines, neuropeptides, and other neurotransmitters are shown. A vesicle is shown expelling neurotransmitter into the synaptic cleft by exocytosis.

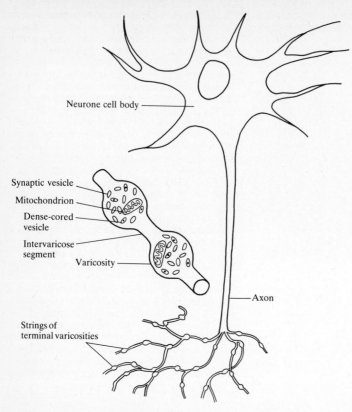

Neurone cell body

Synaptic vesicle
Mitochondrion
Dense-cored vesicle
Intervaricose segment
Varicosity

Axon

Strings of terminal varicosities

**Fig. 4.** Diagram of a neurone with terminal varicosities.

of the synaptic organization of the brain itself, and provide a semi-localized form of neurotransmitter release called *paracrine* neurosecretion.

**How many neurotransmitters are there?** The search for chemical agents which could transmit the activity of peripheral nerves onto their target organs began early in the twentieth century. In the 1920s and early 1930s, after a long trail of research *acetylcholine* was unequivocally demonstrated to be mediating the inhibitory influence of the vagus nerve on the heart, as well as the excitatory action of motor nerve terminals on voluntary muscle. At that point, acetylcholine became the first chemically identified neurotransmitter substance. *Adrenaline*, too, was an early candidate as neurotransmitter in the peripheral nervous system at ganglionic sites, but after long accumulation of evidence its unmethylated derivative, *noradrenaline*, was finally shown in the mid 1940s to be the actual agent responsible. *Dopamine*, a closely related amine (monoamines), followed a similar history, with doubt and then certainty following its progress to acceptance as a neurotransmitter in the 1950s (see CATECHOLAMINES). In the 1940s another neuroactive monoamine, *serotonin*, first isolated from blood was accepted as a neurotransmitter in the brain and peripheral nervous system.

Thus, in the 1950s only four compounds,

together with a few other unlikely candidates, including a peptide (*substance P*), were the full armoury of agents known to be acting as neurotransmitters. They were found to be localized to the neurones from which they were released. These substances seemed to be specialized for their task as neurotransmitters and were not involved in other biochemical activities. At that time, it seemed likely that, together, they provided the principal means of chemical neurotransmission throughout the nervous system. However, it was also in the 1950s and later in the 1960s that four amino acids (*glutamate*, *aspartate* as excitatory agents, and *GABA* and *glycine* as inhibitory agents), also amines (but carrying an acidic group as well), were being considered as new and important contenders as neurotransmitters in the brain and spinal chord. They were most unlikely candidates, being found ubiquitously in all cells and organs in high concentrations, and being involved in a wide range of metabolic pathways and biosyntheses in the general biochemical economy of the cell.

The first members of yet another entirely different biochemical category of neurotransmitters became serious contenders in the 1970s, namely the *neuropeptides* (2 to 50 residue oligo-peptides). Unlike the amino acids, the neuropeptides are mostly present in extremely small quantities in localized regions of the nervous system. The earliest candidates proved to be already operating in the brain as local *neurohormones* in the hypothalamus and anterior pituitary gland. One example is thyrotropin-releasing-hormone (*TRH*, a tripeptide). During the 1970s and 1980s many or most of the peptides known to be serving an endocrine or neurotransmitter role in the gastrointestinal system were found to be also serving as neurotransmitters in the brain. The significance of the dual existence and bioactivity of these peptides is not clear, but specific neuroreceptors for them exist in both brain and gastrointestinal systems, allowing the possibility of brain–gut interactions at the neurohormone level, and giving rise to the concept of the '*brain–gut axis.*'

Some of these neuropeptides seem to evoke rather more complex responses than simple synaptic excitation or inhibition (both of which they also mediate). For example, very small quantities of TRH can induce euphoric states, and it can act as an antidepressant drug for the treatment of affective disorders. Another neuropeptide, β-*endorphin*, causes muscular rigidity and immobility (catatonia), whilst *luteinizing-hormone-releasing-hormone (LHRH)* is reputed to stimulate the libido, and has been used to cure oligospermy. *Cholecystokinin (CCK)* promotes feelings of appetitive satiety and causes cessation of feeding in animals. *Bombesin* dramatically lowers body temperatures, controls many aspects of gastric secretion, and stimulates appetite by actions at sites within the brain. The *endorphins and *encephalins* not only produce fairly complex and sophisticated behavioural effects, they also induce analgaesia, behaving like endogenous 'morphine-like compounds'. Unfortunately, they (and their active synthetic derivatives) are also addictive when given in quantity as analgesic drugs. The endorphins seem to serve a neuro-humoral role as well as that of neurotransmitter (see PSYCHOPHARMACOLOGY).

Peptide-releasing neurones show certain special features in their organization. Thus, cholinergic (i.e. 'worked' by acetylcholine), monoaminergic, and amino acidergic neurones synthesize neurotransmitter principally in their nerve terminals, by simple enzymatic processes. Peptidergic cells in contrast, synthesize their peptide neurotransmitters as sub-components of large 'mother' proteins by protein synthesis processes occurring in the cell body. These are then loaded into large granules and transported down the length of the axon to the terminal regions of the neurone. During this journey, the active neuropeptides are 'snipped' off the mother protein by specific enzymes (proteases), and the peptide neurotransmitters are then ready for release on arrival (Fig. 5). Inactivation of the released peptide neurotransmitter is by enzymatic hydrolysis, as for acetylcholine, and unlike most other neurotransmitters—which are rapidly reabsorbed back into the terminals, and into surrounding glial cells.

When one surveys the current (1987) list of neurotransmitters (Table 1), it can be seen that apart from the simple amines and amino acids discovered during the first seventy years of this century, some fifty neuropeptides must be included. The latter serve in hybrid capacities as neurotransmitters-neurohormones-neuromodulators, and in this way trigger off complex patterns of behaviour.

In order to be accepted as a neurotransmitter, the substance must satisfy some seven key criteria. Until they satisfy all criteria, they are called *putative* neurotransmitters. Most of the compounds listed in Table 1 have satisfied these criteria and are fully fledged neurotransmitters. Many of the neuropeptides listed are of putative neurotransmitter/neurohormone status.

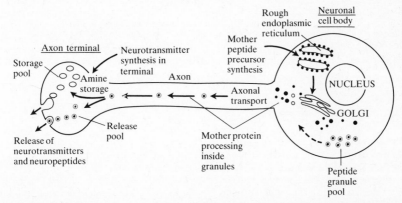

**Fig. 5.** Diagram illustrating the biosynthesis, packaging, and release of peptides and other neurotransmitters in neurones. The peptides are generated from large precursor molecules (pre-proproteins) produced in the rough endoplasmic reticulum (RER) of the neuronal cell body. These are packaged into secretory granules or vesicles in the Golgi membrane stacks. The granules are then transported out of the cell body (*axonal transport*) to the terminals, where upon stimulation, they release their contents by exocytosis. Other neurotransmitters are produced in the cytosol of the cell body, axon, and principally in the nerve terminal, and they are packaged by uptake into preformed granules or vesicles.

**Table 1.** *Neurotransmitters, putative neurotransmitters, and neuroactive peptides*

| System | Compound |
| --- | --- |
| Amino acidergic | γ-Aminobutyrate (GABA) |
| | Aspartate |
| | Glutamate |
| | Glycine |
| | Taurine |
| Cholinergic | Acetylcholine |
| Histaminergic | Histamine |
| Monoaminergic | Adrenaline |
| | Dopamine |
| | Noradrenaline |
| | Serotonin |
| | Tryptamine |
| Peptidergic | Angiotensin |
| | Bombesin family (2 members) |
| | Bradykinin |
| | Calcitonin gene related peptide (CGRP) |
| | Carnosine |
| | *Caerulein |
| | Cholecystokinin family (5 members) |
| | Corticotropin |
| | Corticotropin releasing hormone (CRF) |
| | Dynorphin family (5 members) |
| | *Eledoisin |
| | Endorphin family (2) |
| | Encephalin family (2) |
| | Gastrin family (2 members) |
| | Luteinizing-hormone-releasing-hormone (LHRH) |
| | Melatonin |
| | Motilin |
| | Neurokinins (2 peptides) |
| | Neuromedin family (4 members) |
| | Neuropeptide K |
| | Neuropeptide Y |
| | Neurotensin |
| | Oxytocin |
| | Peptide Histidine Isoleucine (PHI) |
| | *Physalaemin |
| | Sleep-inducing peptides (4 peptides) |
| | Somatostatin |
| | Substance K |
| | Substance P |
| | Thyroid hormone releasing hormone (TRH) |
| | Vasoactive intestinal peptide (VIP) |
| | Vasopressin |
| Purinergic | Adenosine |
| | ADP |
| | AMP |
| | ATP |

*found mainly in lower vertebrates.

**How do neurotransmitters work?** These highly potent substances are released from their storage sites in the close apposition synapses, or in terminal varicosities (or dendrites—see below), and diffuse shorter or longer distances until they encounter neurotransmitter receptors with which they are designed to specifically interact. Once bound to the neurotransmitter in question, the neuro-receptor, which is a large glycoprotein molecule, spanning the membrane thickness (10 nanometres), undergoes conformational or other struc-tural change, and this results in one of two known categories of response. The first of these is called an *ionotropic* response, and results in the appearance of a 'hole' or 'passage' right through the neuroreceptor protein molecule from outside to inside the membrane, through which only a particular charged ion can pass ($Na^+$, $K^+$, or $Cl^-$). The specific ion in question proceeds to move through the neuroreceptor molecule either into or out of the cell interior, driven down its concentration gradient, and attracted or repulsed by the prevailing electric field across the membrane, according to the nature of its own net charge (Figs. 6 and 7). Each neuroreceptor channel may be open for only a very brief period (e.g. 1 microsecond) as the neurotransmitter rapidly dissociates and is inactivated, or may remain open for much longer periods (e.g. 1 sec.) depending on the ion channel concerned. As the post-synaptic membrane is densely packed with these structures, the net effect is a substantial movement of charged ions across

the membrane. This movement generates excitatory or inhibitory synaptic potentials and, from this pattern of impingement of electrical signals (information) onto its dendrites and cell body (inhibitory inputs), the target neurone will be triggered to fire its own action potential, or remain quiescent, as appropriate according to the intensity of the excitatory and inhibitory signals received. Individual neuroreceptor channel-opening and -closing events can now be distinguished by

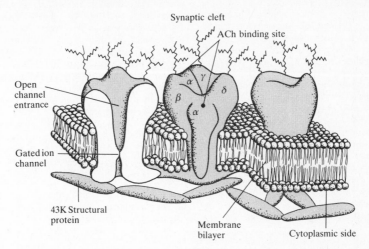

**Fig. 6.** Three-dimensional models of the nicotinic acetylcholine receptor from the electric ray fish *Torpedo californica* depicted as membrane proteins in the post-synaptic membrane of the synapse between the nerve and the electric organ which works essentially like a neuromuscular junction and employs acetylcholine as neurotransmitter. The sub-unit arrangement around the central channel is tentative. The sites on the two α subunits that bind acetylcholine, and other related substances are shown as dark patches. The proposed shape of the central channel can be seen in the vertical section. Also shown is the membrane structural protein of mol wt 43,000 often found in association with the receptor in *Torpedo*.

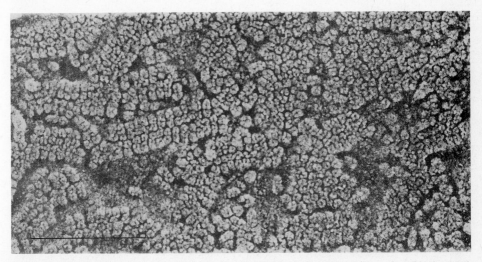

**Fig. 7.** Acetylcholine-activated neuroreceptors densely packed in the post-synaptic membrane of a cell in the electric organ of *Torpedo*, the electric ray fish. Note the central channel or hole through the neuroreceptor. This electron micrograph shows the platinum-plated replica of a membrane that has been frozen and etched. The size of the platinum particles limits the resolution to features larger than about 2 nanometres (scale bar equals 100 nanometres).

so-called 'single channel recordings' by 'patch clamping' electrophysiological recording techniques where neurotransmitter is perfused onto the postsynaptic membrane and the properties of small patches of membrane are studied.

The second category of neuroreceptor response is known as *metabotropic* because enzymes are involved. These enzymes are buried in the lipid membrane close to, and linked permanently or temporarily (depending on the cellular location) to, the neuroreceptor protein molecule. Following neurotransmitter-receptor activation there are conformational changes in the neuroreceptor-enzyme complex, which cause activation of the enzyme. The latter consequently acts upon its substrate, which is situated on the inner surface of the membrane, to produce a soluble product which diffuses into the neuronal cytoplasm and evokes responses which mostly lead on to produce a change in local membrane potential, usually resulting in the generation of a synaptic potential. These soluble enzyme products are called *second messengers*, as they produce actions which are secondary to the primary action of the neurotransmitter. Examples of such metabotropic, second-messenger, neuroreceptor-enzyme systems would be (1) the cyclic nucleotide system and (2) the phosphoinositide system:

(1) The key enzyme here is *adenylate cyclase* which produces the soluble product cyclic AMP (adenosine monophosphate). This catalyses a cascade of protein phosphorylations and dephosphorylations resulting in the secondary opening of particular ion channels with accompanying generation of synaptic potentials (Fig. 8). In this system coupling of neuroreceptor to adenylate cyclase is via a so-called *G-protein* (because it requires guanylate-triphosphate for its activation) which can convey either a stimulatory ($N_s$) or inhibitory ($N_i$) influence from the neuroreceptor to adenylate cyclase (Fig. 9). There is a parallel system which employs *guanylate cyclase* linked to neuroreceptors, which is particularly prominent in the cerebellum.

(2) The key enzyme in the phosphoinositide system is a particular molecular subtype of *phospholipase C (phosphoinositidase C)* which is buried in the lipid membrane in close association with particular neurotransmitter receptors (Fig. 10). When this enzyme is activated indirectly via a G-protein following binding of neurotransmitter to neuroreceptor, its substrate, triphosphoinositide (actually, phosphatidylinositol (4,5) diphosphate), is hydrolysed to release water-soluble *inositol triphosphate* ($IP_3$, Inositol (1,4,5)-triphosphate) (Fig. 10). This $IP_3$ molecule has the ability to release calcium from intracellular stores, and the calcium (which can be regarded as a *third* messen-

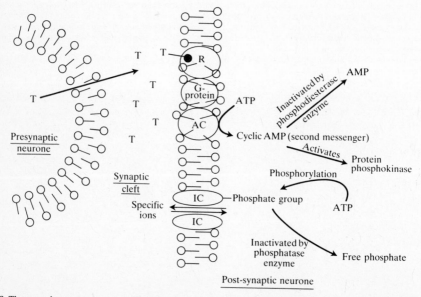

**Fig. 8.** The second-messenger concept: The adenylate cyclase system. Neurotransmitter receptor (R), buried in the post-synaptic membrane, interacts with neurotransmitter (T) and initiates cyclic nucleotide formation via the adenycyclase enzyme (AC) which is also in the membrane. The cyclic nucleotide (cyclic AMP) is the second messenger. It stimulates phosphorylation of a membrane protein (IC) via a protein phosphokinase enzyme. This protein is an ion conductance channel through the membrane and is opened by being phosphorylated, allowing ions to move in or out of the cell. This leads to a membrane potential change (synaptic potential). The effect is reversed first by a phosphoprotein phosphatase, which dephosphorylates the ion channel, and secondly by a phosphodiesterase which inactivates the cyclic AMP. Coupling between R and CA is known to involve guanylnucleotide binding protein (G-protein). See Fig. 9 for details.

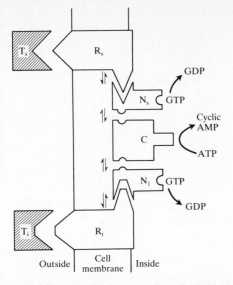

**Fig. 9.** Scheme showing the proposed coupling inside the post-synaptic membrane between neurotransmitters or hormones and adenylate cyclase via guanine nucleotide binding proteins (G-proteins). Key: T, neurotransmitter or hormone; R, receptor protein; N, guanine nucleotide binding protein (G-protein); C, catalytic sub-unit of adenyl cyclase. Subscript s indicates a stimulatory action; subscript i indicates an inhibitory action. The coupling between the three membrane components is shown as reversible. The binding of GTP by N enhances the interaction, which can result in either stimulation or inhibition of adenylate cyclase, as shown, depending on the category of N involved. GTP is removed by its hydrolysis. Refer also to Fig. 8.

ger in this case) then initiates a series of other biochemical events, particularly phosphorylations of key proteins in the cell. Such phosphorylations can switch on various ionic movements into the cell through channels (e.g. potassium ions) and thereby cause synaptic potential changes by this delayed and indirect route (Fig. 10).

The other product of phosphoinositidase C hydrolysis is a special neutral fat (diglyceride, containing arachidonic acid, a rather long fatty acid) which, in concert with calcium and a phospholipid, activates another enzyme, *protein kinase C*. This enzyme initiates a series of protein phosphorylations. These can result in the opening of local ion channels, and can therefore generate membrane or synaptic potentials (Fig. 10) on a par with those initiated by adenylate cyclase activation (see (1) above and Fig. 8).

These metabotropic responses to neurotransmitter-neuroreceptor activation are necessarily much slower (10 to 30 times) than their ionotropic counterpart, because they involve enzyme activation and subsequent cascades of biochemical responses, which are intrinsically slower than direct 'gating' of ion flow through membrane channels.

**Neuromodulators.** It is now emerging fairly clearly that the synaptic action of a neurotransmitter may be modulated (i.e. made more or less efficient) by a third party, a *neuroregulator or neuromodulator substance*, thereby amplifying or attenuating the action of the neurotransmitter. This seems to be achieved by more than one mechanism. Thus, the neuromodulator has the capacity to enhance or decrease the extent of release of the neurotransmitter following action potential invasion of the nerve terminal. For example, adenosinetriphosphate (ATP), secreted together with the neurotransmitter, will decrease noradrenaline or acetylcholine release from some adrenergic or cholinergic nerves, respectively. In other cases, the neuromodulator will alter the *efficiency* with which the neurotransmitter interacts with its neuroreceptor and allow the inward or outward flux of more ions per opening period, or a greater activation of neuroreceptor-linked enzymes.

Another, rather curious, neuromodulator substance is of considerable interest because of its links with *benzodiazepine* anxiolytic (anxiety-reducing) drugs. In fact, the existence of this naturally occurring neuromodulator has been *inferred* from the potent facilitatory actions of anxiolytic drugs, such as diazepam (Valium), on the most widespread inhibitory neurotransmitter system in the nervous system, namely the GABA (γ-aminobutyric acid) system. These benzodiazepine drugs both increase the affinity of GABA for GABA neuroreceptors located on synaptic membranes, and enhance GABA-mediated behavioural responses and synaptic potential generation. Moreover, there are neuroreceptors present in the brain which very specifically bind to the drugs. The endogenous benzodiazepine receptor protein (or binding site) is thought to form part of the GABA receptor complex. When released from its nerve endings (or co-released with GABA from GABAergic nerve endings) it is postulated to increase the extent, or period, of opening of GABA-operated chloride ion channels (Fig. 11). Although there are various candidates, as yet no endogenous benzodiazepine-like substance has been isolated which completely mirrors the properties of the endogenous neuromodulator—hence its chemical structure remains a mystery, and it is simply referred to as the '*endogenous benzodiazepine*'.

A precise definition of a neuromodulator is difficult to produce, since the same substance may act as a neurotransmitter in one synapse, and a neuroregulator at another synapse. Therefore, a definition must represent the category of neuroactivity at a particular site, rather than the identity of the substance itself. For instance, ATP, ADP, AMP (adenosine tri-, di-, and mono-phosphates), or adenosine itself, may function as a neurotransmitter or as a neuroregulator according to the nature of the neuroreceptors with which it interacts.

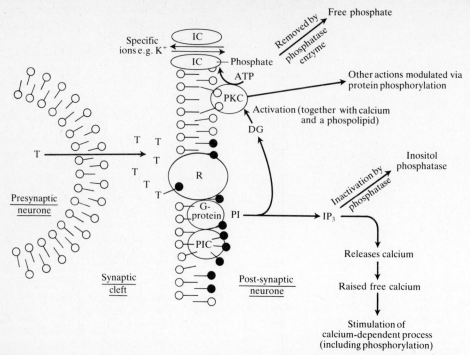

**Fig. 10.** The second messenger concept. The phosphoinositide-inositol triphosphate system. Neurotransmitter receptor (R), buried in the post-synaptic membrane, interacts with neurotransmitter (T) and initiates formation of inositol (1,4,5) triphosphate ($IP_3$), the second messenger. This is achieved by activation of the enzyme phosphoinositidase C (PIC, also in the membrane) via G-proteins, with the consequent hydrolysis of a membrane phospholipid (PI, phosphatidylinositol (4,5) diphosphate) which is located close to the enzyme and is indicated by the black heads. $IP_3$ releases calcium from intracellular stores and thereby raises the level of free calcium in the cytoplasm of the neurone. The second messenger ($IP_3$) is inactivated by another enzyme, inositol phosphatase. The other product of PI hydrolysis is diglyceride (DG). This activates another enzyme inside the cell, protein kinase C (PKC), which begins to phosphorylate proteins. This phosphorylation activity causes a wide spectrum of responses, including the opening of specific ion channels (IC) through the membrane, e.g. for potassium ion, thereby generating synaptic and other kinds of electrical membrane potential change. PKC activity can also influence neurotransmitter release rates, as well as produce profound effects on cell growth and development. Since a large part of the protein kinase C is found in nerve terminals, the larger proportion of the PKC response is likely to be the result of neurotransmitters acting at pre-synaptic receptors located on nerve terminals, rather than in dendrites on cell bodies.

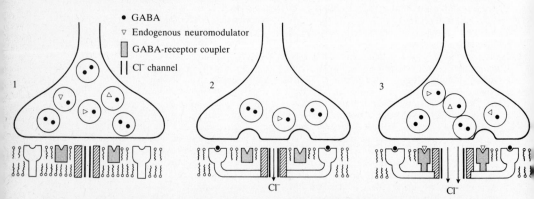

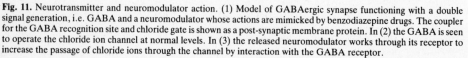

**Fig. 11.** Neurotransmitter and neuromodulator action. (1) Model of GABAergic synapse functioning with a double signal generation, i.e. GABA and a neuromodulator whose actions are mimicked by benzodiazepine drugs. The coupler for the GABA recognition site and chloride gate is shown as a post-synaptic membrane protein. In (2) the GABA is seen to operate the chloride ion channel at normal levels. In (3) the released neuromodulator works through its receptor to increase the passage of chloride ions through the channel by interaction with the GABA receptor.

**Co-existence and co-release of neurotransmitters.** The long-held dictum, enunciated by H. H. Dale and developed by J. C. Eccles, that 'only one and the same neurotransmitter is released by each neurone, at each of its terminals' (Dale's principle), is no longer universally tenable. We now have many examples where the newly discovered neuroactive peptides co-exist with longer standing ('classical') neurotransmitters, such as acetylcholine, noradrenaline, serotonin, and GABA. The co-existence of other relatively newly established, neurotransmitters, such as ATP within cholinergic and adrenergic neurones is also now fairly clear and well founded. For the most part, the different neurotransmitters appear to be contained in different categories of storage vesicle or granule within the nerve terminals concerned, and can be released independently of one another. Thus, *Vasoactive Intestinal Peptide (VIP)* co-exists with acetylcholine in parasympathetic nerves supplying the cat salivary gland, each being contained in its own vesicle type. High frequency stimulation of the nerve releases VIP, whilst low frequencies release acetylcholine. Each neurotransmitter can act as a neuromodulator to influence the extent of release or post-synaptic actions of the other (Fig. 12).

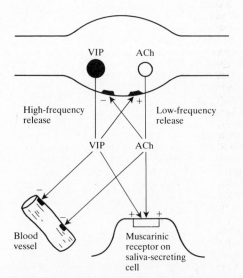

**Fig. 12.** Proposed scheme for co-transmission at a synapse where a classical neurotransmitter, acetylcholine (ACh), co-exists with vasoactive intestinal polypeptide (VIP) in parasympathetic nerve terminals supplying the cat salivary gland. Note that ACh and VIP are stored in separate vesicles, they can be released differentially at different stimulation frequencies to act on acinar cells (producing saliva) and blood vessels supplying the gland. Co-operation between the two neurotransmitter systems is achieved by selective release of ACh at low-impulse frequencies and of VIP at high-impulse frequencies. The two neurotransmitters are also seen acting as neuromodulators mutually influencing their extent of one another's release and postsynaptic action.

**Post-synaptic and pre-synaptic neuroreceptors.** Post-synaptic neuroreceptors represent the longer established category of neuroreceptor, and provide the conventional feed-forward of electrical and trophic influences of neurone on neurone. The past decade has seen the discovery of *pre-synaptic* neuroreceptors which serve a modulatory function in neurotransmission, being primarily concerned with controlling the *extent* of neurotransmitter release. These neuroreceptors respond to the principal neurotransmitter released by the nerve-ending concerned (so-called *autoregulation*), or to the actions of co-released, or extraneous, neurotransmitters or neuromodulators of different identity (so-called *heteroregulation*), by *reducing* or 'shutting down' the release of that neurotransmitter. This *negative feedback* action is the more common consequence of pre-synaptic neuroreceptor activation (e.g. noradrenaline release from heart, spleen, vas deferens, and also centrally in the brain). A minor category of pre-synaptic neuroreceptors actually mediate *enhancement* (positive-feedback) of neurotransmitter release. It seems that both negative and positive feedback control can be exercised in the same synapse at a few particular central and peripheral axonal endings, particularly of adrenergic nerves. In this case, integration of their actions is achieved as follows: when low levels of neurotransmitter (e.g. noradrenaline) are present in the synaptic cleft, the facilitatory (usually beta-type) neuroreceptors are activated, leading to increased release of neurotransmitters. When higher concentrations are reached in the cleft, the inhibitory (usually alpha-type) adrenoreceptors come into play, resulting in a reduction in the level of noradrenaline release. Thus, differential sensitivity to neurotransmitter concentration allows a delicate balance to be maintained between the opposing actions of the two categories of pre-synaptic neuroreceptor.

**How are neurotransmitters released?** Calcium ions are the critical factors in triggering neurotransmitter release. Normally these ions are at almost undetectable levels in neuronal cytoplasm ($10^{-9}$M), but rapidly flood into the terminals from the surrounding fluid through special channels during nerve-terminal depolarization caused by the action potential. Equally rapidly, the raised cytosolic levels of calcium are cleared by transport into mitochondria and endoplasmic reticulum within the terminal.

It has been demonstrated that neurotransmitters can also be released from the *dendritic tree* of the neurone as well as from nerve *terminals* as classically conceived. Indeed, the dendrites show localized accumulations of synaptic vesicles which are characteristic of all neurotransmitter release sites (e.g. synapses, terminal varicosities). Such release has been unequivocally demonstrated to occur in the dopaminergic neurones of the substantia nigra of the brain (see BASAL GANGLIA) and also by the mitral cells and GABAergic axonless granule cells of the olfactory bulb. It may be that neurotransmitters can be released from other regions of the neuronal cell surface, including the unmyelinated regions of axons, and from the cell bodies themselves, though the greater proportion of neurotransmitter is localized to the nerve terminals.

Whether neurotransmitter is actually released from these various sites by a single process remains unclear. Certainly the traditional view envisages an exocytotic process involving the fusion of neurotransmitter-filled synaptic vesicles with the nerve terminal wall, resulting in the expulsion of about 1,000 molecules (one quantum) of neurotransmitter into the synaptic cleft from each vesicle. Many multiples of such quanta are released as the nerve impulse invades the nerve terminal, and this involves fusion and exocytosis by equivalent multiples of vesicles. However, the synaptic vesicles involved must already be in contact with the terminal membrane and ready to release their content as there is less than 200 microseconds between first entry of calcium and first detectable appearance of neurotransmitter in the cleft. It is likely that the vesicles which release neurotransmitters are positioned on, or close to, the calcium channels.

An alternative view is that neurotransmitter is released not from synaptic vesicles, but directly from the cytoplasm through membrane pores or membrane 'shuttle' devices which require calcium to open or operate. By opening for a predetermined short period (microseconds) a quantum of neurotransmitter could be expelled into the synaptic cleft via these 'vesigates' or 'operators' as they have been called. The dispute is far from resolved, but the balance of evidence is in favour of the vesicular release hypothesis, though this may not be exclusive, and both or either process could be occurring according to the neurotransmitter in question.

**Why are there so many neurotransmitters?** The answer to this question is far from resolved. Certainly, sub-groups of the fifty or so neurotransmitters produce different categories of effect in both qualitative and quantitative respects, and many will co-exist in different neuronal populations. First, there is the differential speed of response following receptor activation, with ionotropic being some 10- to 30-fold faster than metabotropic responses. Another dimension is provided in the *variety* of second-messenger activation of *different* cascades of biochemical sequelae, with particular metabotropic neurotransmitter actions being mediated by one or other second messenger system. Further possibilities for adding to the qualitative features of the response could come through the range of distances through which the neuroactive compounds exert their influence once released. This may be 20 nanometres within the synaptic cleft but several millimetres fom varicosities or unstructured release points, and of course the concentration of neurotransmitter diminishes rapidly with the distance travelled. Actions ranging over a greater volume of tissue would activate specific neuroreceptors sited on a larger variety of neurone types, producing complex sequences of neuronal triggering, and therefore a greater spectrum of overall responses (so-called *trophic* actions). Continuous (*tonic*) release of neurotransmitter, as opposed to discrete and occasional release, would also provide a basis for variation in the patterns of activation of targeted neurones due to changes in sensitivity, accommodation, and desensitization of neuroreceptors which ensues during continuous neuroreceptor stimulation.

Thus, the large number and the chemical variety of neurotransmitters, together with their tendency to activate anatomically distinct neuronal pathways, often in pairs, and the evidence that they provide many palpable possibilities for variation in response, can be seen to provide a chorus of informational voices, each adding tonal colour or timbre to the final output of the brain and nervous system.                                                    H. F. B.

Bradford, H. F. (1986). *Chemical Neurobiology*. New York.

Cooper, J. R., Bloom, F. E., and Roth, R. H. (1982). *The Biochemical Basis of Neuropharmacology*, 4th edn. New York.

Downes, C. P. (1983). Inositol phospholipids and neurotransmitter; receptor signalling mechanisms. *Trends in Neuroscience*, **6**, 313–16.

Downes, C. P. (1986). Inositol phosphates: concord or confusion. *Trends in Neuroscience*, **9**, 394–6.

Kaczmarek, L. K. (1987). The role of protein kinase C in the regulation of ion channels and neurotransmitter release. *Trends in Neuroscience*, **10**, 30–4.

Kruk, Z. L. and Pycock, C. J. (1983). *Neurotransmitters and Drugs*, 2nd edn. London.

Miller, R. J. (1985). Second messengers, phosphorylation and neurotransmitter release. *Trends in Neuroscience*, **8**, 463–5.

Miller, R. J. (1986). Protein kinase C: a key regulator of neuronal excitability. *Trends in Neuroscience*, **9**, 538–41.

*Scientific American*: special edition, vol. **241**, No. 3, *The Brain* September 1979.

Stephenson, A. F. (1986). A new endogenous benzodiazepine receptor ligand. *Trends in Neuroscience*, **9**, 143–4.

*Trends in Neuroscience*: special edition, vol. **6** (8) *Neurotransmitters and their Actions*, August 1983.

**NEUTRAL MONISM.** See RUSSELL'S PHILOSOPHY OF MIND: NEUTRAL MONISM.

**NEWTON ON MIND.** Sir Isaac Newton (1642–1727) was born in the small manor house which still stands in the village of Woolsthorpe, near Grantham, Lincolnshire, where as a boy he made elaborate models (a windmill, a water-clock, and so on). In 1661 he became a student at Trinity College, Cambridge, and in 1665, while back at Woolsthorpe as the University was closed on account of the plague, he formed the outline of the ideas that dominated him for the next thirty years of incomparable achievement. The story that he thought of the moon circling the earth by continual gravitational attraction may indeed have been suggested by the falling of an apple in the Woolsthorpe orchard.

Newton became Lucasian professor of mathematics in 1669, when the first holder of the chair, Isaac Barrow, resigned in his favour. The fact that he did not take holy orders prevented him from becoming the head of a Cambridge college, and partly for this reason he left Cambridge. In 1696 he became warden of the mint in London, and, in 1699, its master. He was elected president of the Royal Society in 1703, and thereafter was re-elected annually. In 1705 he was knighted by the Queen for his services at the mint. Twice he was a member of parliament.

Newton's major work, the *Philosophiae Naturalis Principia Mathematica*, usually known simply as the *Principia* (1687), is generally regarded as the greatest scientific triumph of the human mind. He did not accept that space is absolute without the most careful consideration of the alternative, that all motion is relative to surrounding objects with no absolute reference provided by a 'fixed' space. He employed simple experiments, including thought experiments: especially the famous 'bucket argument'. He considered the behaviour of the surface of water in a bucket suspended from the centre of its handle by a rope, and allowed or made to spin. The water remains level as the bucket spins in relation to the water, when the water is stationary with respect to the room (or to the 'fixed' stars); but as the water speeds to rotate with respect to the room or the stars, but rotates *with* (and so becomes stationary with respect to) the bucket, it becomes concave. So the reference is not arbitrary: it is concave only by rotation with respect to the universe, and not with respect to the bucket. This is the basis of Ernst *Mach's principle, that the average mass of the stars provides an absolute reference for accelerated (including rotational) motion. However this may be, Newton had a reason that seems curious to us for accepting absolute space— he held that space is, and we live in, God's sensorium, or God's mind; we may thus appreciate laws of the universe by thought and mathematics, though the eyes and other senses are needed for transferring facts of the world to our minds.

In the Queries in his *Opticks* (1704) Newton writes (Query 12): 'For because dense Bodies conserve their Heat for the longest, the Vibrations of their parts are of a lasting nature, and therefore may be propagated along solid Fibres of uniform dense Matter a great distance, for conveying into the Brain the impressions made upon all the Organs of Sense.' And in Query 13: 'Do not several sorts of Rays make Vibrations of several bignesses, which according to their bignesses excite Sensations of several Colours, much after the manner that Vibrations of the Air, according to their several bignesses excite Sensations of several Sounds?' Touching upon aesthetics of colours and sounds (Query 14): 'May not the harmony and discord of Colours arise from the proportions of the Vibrations propagated through the Fibres of the optic Nerves into the Brain, as the harmony and discord of Sounds arise from the proportions of the Vibrations of the Air? For some colours, if they be view'd together, are agreeable to one another, as those of Gold and Indigo, and others disagree.' Although Newton held a vibration account of neural conduction he maintained a corpuscular theory of light. He did, however, see that this was not fully adequate (for example, in his long discussion of double refraction by feldspar, in Queries 28 and 29).

Newton sums up his general picture of man's place in the universe at the end of the *Opticks*:

... it seems probable to me, that God in the Beginning form'd Matter in solid, massy, hard, impenetrable, moveable Particles, of such Sizes and Figures, and with such other Properties, and in such Proportion to Space, as most conduced to the End for which he form'd them. ...

It seems to me farther, that though these Particles have not only *vis inertiae*, accompanied with such passive Laws of Motion as naturally result from that Force, but also they are moved by certain active Principles, such as is that of Gravity, and that which causes Fermentation, and the Cohesion of Bodies. These Principles I consider, not as occult Qualities, supposed to result from the specifick Forms of Things, but as general Laws of Nature, by which the Things themselves are form'd; their Truth appearing to us by Phaenomena, though their Causes be not yet discover'd. For these are manifest Qualities, and their Causes only are occult. And the *Aristotelians* gave the Name of occult qualities, not to manifest Qualities, but to such Qualities only as they supposed to lie hid in Bodies, and to be the unknown Causes of manifest Effects. ... To tell us that every Species of Things is endow'd with an occult specifick Quality by which it acts and produces manifest Effects, is to tell us nothing. ...

Now by the help of these Principles (of Natural Law) all material Things seem to have been composed of the hard and solid Particles above-mention'd, variously associated in the first Creation by the Counsel of an intelligent Agent. For it became him who created them to set them in order. And if he did so, it's unphilosophical to seek any other Origin of the World, or to pretend that it might arise out of a Chaos by the mere Laws of Nature; though being once form'd, it may continue by those Laws for many ages.

Here, surely most curiously, Newton gives up his mechanisms of nature as complete descriptions— first for the astronomical universe, and then for animals. He introduces, at this point, the notion of *choice* into the physics of the stars. This he does while considering eccentric comets:

For while Comets move in very excentric Orbs in all manner of Positions, blind Fate could never make all the Planets move one and the same way in Orbs concentrick, some inconsiderable inconsistencies excepted, which may have risen from the mutual Actions of Comets and Planets upon one another, and which will be apt to increase, till this System wants a Reformation. Such a wonderful Uniformity in the Planetary System must be allowed the Effect of Choice.

So, having built the self-perpetuating mechanism of the *Principia* Newton sets limits to its perpetual autonomy—to bring back into the universe the mind that his predictable mechanism had banished.

This leads at once to consideration of the forces of living organisms.

And so must the Uniformity in the Bodies of Animals, they having generally a right and a left side shaped alike, and on either side of their Bodies two Legs behind, and either two Arms, or two Legs, or two Wings before upon their shoulders . . . and the Instinct of Brutes and Insects, can be the effect of nothing else than the Wisdom and Skill of a powerful ever-living Agent, who being in all Places, is more able by his Will to move the Bodies within his boundless uniform Sensorium, and thereby to form and reform the Parts of the Universe, than we are by our Will to move the Parts of our own Bodies.

A little later Newton writes: 'The Organs of Sense are not for enabling the Soul to perceive the Species of Things in its Sensorium, but only for conveying them thither; and God has no need of such Organs, he being every where present to the Things themselves.'

Thus we live in the space of God's mind. Newton goes on to say that God might create particles of various sorts, and might change the laws of nature—or even have different laws working in several parts of the universe without contradiction, for the laws are God's ideas.

The starting-point of Newton's theory of light and colours was Barrow's notes on colour, which Newton edited. According to Barrow (as recorded by Newton's biographer Sir David Brewster):

White is that which discharges a copious light equally clear in every direction—Black is that which does not emit light at all, or which does it very sparingly—Red is that which emits a light more clear than usual, but interrupted by shady interstices—Blue is that which discharges a rarefied light, as in bodies which consist of white and black particles arranged alternatively—Green is nearly allied to blue—Yellow is a mixture of much white and little red—and Purple consists of a great deal of blue mixed with a small portion of red. The blue colour of the sea arises from the whiteness of the salt which it contains, mixed with the blackness of the pure water. . . .

It was Newton's genius to see that all the colours are contained in white light, and that they are separated by refraction of white light. He did not of course discover the spectrum, but he did see its significance; and he showed (probably) how colours can be built up as mixtures by spinning a disc of coloured segments, whose relative areas could be varied to control the mixture. Although the familiar and beautiful series of prism experiments are described in the *Opticks* as a progression of axioms, self-evidently true, it is clear from various notes that they occupied some eighteen months, and that Newton frequently changed his mind, only gradually coming to be sure of his conclusions. Controversy with Robert Hooke was partly responsible for postponing publication of the *Opticks* until 1704, after Hooke's death. Written in English, rather than the Latin of the *Principia*, it is well worth reading today.

Newton's work on colour bordered upon psychological experimentation. He described per-sistence of vision by noting the luminous path behind a glowing coal whirled around in the dark, which he explained as being like the gradual dying out of ripples on water; and he discusses \*after-images. This was inspired by his staring at the sun, which left an after-image lasting several days, greatly disturbing him so that he spent some days in bed. He noted that after-images transfer from one eye to the other eye, and concluded that the origin must be in the brain and not in the stimulated eye. This argument is not, however, sound, for the stimulated eye may continue to send signals to the brain and it is not possible to say which eye is providing signals—although each eye is 'known' to the stereoscopic mechanisms of vision. It is odd that Newton did not think this simple matter out, though he described the universe in terms that met all challengers until Einstein, 250 years later.

For Newton the mathematical laws of nature concern space rather than objects—for non-living objects, such as planets, would otherwise move around of their own accord, without universal law applying (at least in astronomical conditions) to all kinds of objects. He was, however, highly interested in chemistry, which is the study of the matter of objects, and even more interested in alchemy as a key to the design of the universe. Though he spent a great deal of time and wrote a million or more words on chemical and alchemical experiments and theories, he did not publish on these topics.

Why it was that such genius flowered in Newton, whose ancestry and upbringing were not out of the ordinary, has been a matter ever since for somewhat fruitless debate. Psychological reasons for Newton's genius have been most fully discussed by F. E. Manuel (1968; 1980), who offers a Freudian-type explanation, based on the effect of his mother, whom Newton adored, leaving him with his grandmother while very young when she went to live in a neighbouring parish with her second husband. (Newton's father had died before he was born.) Newton himself never married. He was a strange, irritable, and jealous man, who explored many paths to knowledge, sought immortality, and found it.                           R. L. G.

Brewster, Sir D. (1831). *Life of Sir Isaac Newton*. London.

More, L. T. (1934; 1962). *Isaac Newton*. New York.

Turnbull, H. W. and Scott, J. F. (eds.) (1959–77). *The Correspondence of Isaac Newton*. Cambridge.

Westfall, R. S. (1973). *Science and Religion in Seventeenth-century England*. 2nd edn., Ann Arbor, Michigan.

Westfall, S. (1980) *Never at rest: A Biography of Isaac Newton*. Cambridge.

**NIETZSCHE, FRIEDRICH WILHELM** (1844–1900). Born at Röcken, Saxony, and brought up the son of a Lutheran pastor, he was a brilliant undergraduate at Bonn and Leipzig; and accepted the professorship of classical philology at Basle before graduating. He was a disciple of \*Schopenhauer; and Schopenhauer's 'will to power' was a basis of his philosophy that only the strong ought to survive, while sympathy perpetuates the unfit. His *magnum opus* is *Also Sprach Zarathustra* (1883–91; Eng. trans. *Thus Spake Zarathustra*). It develops the idea of the 'superman', which was taken up by George Bernard Shaw in his play *Man and Superman* (1903). Nietzsche died insane at Weimar.

**NITROGEN NARCOSIS** is the term used to describe the apparent drunkenness experienced by deep-sea divers. Jacques Cousteau has termed it 'l'ivresse des grands profondeurs' (rapture of the deep), while divers typically use the rather more prosaic term 'the narks'. As its name implies, the primary source of intoxication in air breathed at pressure comes from nitrogen. One might expect therefore that breathing pure oxygen would alleviate the problem. Unfortunately, however, when the partial pressure of oxygen exceeds that obtained at a depth of 9–12 m it produces oxygen poisoning, resulting in convulsions and loss of consciousness.

Nitrogen narcosis first becomes detectable at a depth of about 30 m, while below a depth of 60 m the effects are sufficiently marked to make working risky even for an experienced diver. The symptoms are not unlike drunkenness: the diver may become euphoric, his ability to reason reduced, and his manual skill impaired, with a tendency to make errors of judgement that can be disastrous at depth. For example, a diver taking part in an open-sea experiment at 60 m noticed that he had insufficient air to complete the dive; he reasoned that he had enough air left either to do a decent job and complete the experiment or to get to the surface, but not both. He opted to complete the experiment. Fortunately, being a strong swimmer with a clear head, and having a good life-jacket, he managed to make the surface and was able to collect a fresh supply of air without suffering from 'the bends'—compressed air illness which may occur on return to normal atmospheric pressure, nitrogen dissolved in the bloodstream expanding to form bubbles which lead to pain, and possibly paralysis and death.

Most research on nitrogen narcosis has been carried out in dry pressure chambers, which are safer and allow better control over conditions than open-sea studies. Do they, however, provide an adequate simulation of the real thing? An experiment conducted by Baddeley (1966) suggests that they may not. He studied the manual dexterity of divers using a simple brass plate containing 32 holes and 16 nuts and bolts. The diver simply had to transfer the nuts and bolts from the holes at one end of the plate to the other, and was timed as he did so. Subjects performing this task in a dry pressure chamber showed a small but reliable decrement in performance (5 per cent) when they were performing under an air pressure equivalent to pressure at a depth of 30 m of sea water. A parallel experiment tested the performance of subjects at a depth of 3 m, and at a depth of 30 m, in the open sea. The experiment was carried out in the Mediterranean, ensuring good visibility and with no problems of cold. Simply testing a subject under water slowed him down by approximately 28 per cent, while testing him at a depth of 30 m caused a drop of 49 per cent as compared to dry-land performance.

Note that the decrement in performance observed at 30 m is greater than would have been predicted by simply adding the effects of water (16 per cent) and pressure (5 per cent). Why should this be? A clue was given by a later experiment which used the same task, and again tested at a depth of 30 m, but on this occasion resulted in a decrement of only 5 per cent. The difference between the two studies was as follows: the first was carried out in the open sea from a ship, the divers being required to go straight down. The second was carried out close inshore, where the diver could swim straight down from the jetty to a site populated by many other divers. It seems reasonable to suppose that the divers in the first experiment were much more anxious than those in the second, and subsequent studies have supported this conclusion. They reveal relatively small decrements when divers are tested in the relatively safe conditions of a 'wet' pressure chamber, and under open-sea conditions with divers who show little evidence of anxiety, while much greater decrements are shown by anxious divers and under relatively threatening open-sea conditions.

The nature of the anxiety effect is still far from clear. Performance on a reasoning task does not show the interaction with anxiety, suggesting that the anxiety effect may result from some factor such as muscular tension, impairing motor rather than cognitive skills. The point remains, however, that while initial work is best done in the pressure chamber, generalization to open-sea performance must proceed with caution.

How can nitrogen narcosis be prevented? The standard procedure at present is to have the diver breathe a mixture of oxygen and helium (heliox). Using this, dives have been made to as much as 600 m without the diver losing consciousness. For a while it seemed as though there might be no psychological decrement. Although a tendency to tremor and nausea, which was termed HPNS (High Pressure Nervous Syndrome), did occur, it was thought to result from compressing the diver too rapidly so that it could be avoided provided the rise in pressure was gradual. It has, however, subsequently become clear that more general intellectual and performance decrements do occur and are detectable at depths in excess of 300 m. The effect observed is almost certainly different from that obtained with nitrogen, and it is possible that some more complex mix of gases may allow greater depths to be achieved. Heliox has two further disadvantages: it conducts heat very efficiently, making it harder to keep the diver warm, and it distorts the voice. If you take a lungful of helium at normal pressure and speak, you sound like Donald Duck, while at pressure the effect is even further exaggerated. A number of helium speech unscramblers have been designed, and do improve communication. However, the existing commercial models still leave a great deal to be desired.

In recent years there has been increasing interest in operating with Trimix, a mixture of oxygen, helium, and nitrogen. Such a mixture has a possible advantage in terms of narcotic potency. However, this is still a controversial issue. At a pharmacological level we still seem to be some distance from understanding the mechanism of inert gas narcosis; theories exist, but it is probably true to say that no theory has yet won broad acceptance.

See also DIVER PERFORMANCE.                    A. D. B.

Baddeley, A. D. (1966). Influence of depth on the manual dexterity of free divers. *Journal of Applied Psychology*, **50**, 81–5.

Logie, R. H., Baddeley, A. D., and Williams, P. (forthcoming). Simulated Deep Diving and Cognitive Performance. *Progress in Underwater Science*.

**NOTHINGNESS.** Nature abhors a vacuum—and so do we. The idea of a void—of emptiness, nothingness, spacelessness, placelessness, all such 'lessness'—is at once abhorrent and inconceivable; and yet it haunts us in the strangest, most paradoxical way: 'Nothing is more real than nothing.'

For *Descartes there was no such thing as empty space. For Einstein there was no space without field. For *Kant our ideas of space and extension were the forms our 'reason' gives to experience, through the operation of a universal 'synthetic a priori'. The nervous system, intact and active—*Leibniz's stream of 'minute perceptions'—was envisaged by Kant as a sort of transformer, forming ideality from reality, reality from ideality. Such a notion has the virtue—very rare in metaphysical formulations—that it can instantly be tested in practice; specifically, in neurological and neurophysiological practice.

Let us proceed at once to examples. If one is given a spinal anaesthetic that brings to a halt neural traffic in the lower half of the body, one cannot feel merely that this is paralysed and senseless; one feels that it is wholly, impossibly, 'nonexistent', that one has been cut in half, and that the lower half is absolutely missing—not in the familiar sense of being somewhere, elsewhere, but in the uncanny sense of *not-being*, or being nowhere. The terms that patients use communicate something of this incommunicable nothing. They may say that part of them is 'missing', 'evacuated', 'gone': that it seems like dead flesh, or sand, or paste; devoid of life, of activity, of 'will'; devoid of the organic, of structure, of coherence—without materiality or imaginable reality; cut off or alienated from the living flesh (with which, none the less, it forms an impossible continuity). One such patient, trying to formulate the unformulable, finally said that his lost limbs were 'nowhere to be found', and that they were 'like nothing on earth'. Hearing such phrases, as one will hear from every patient who finds himself in such a situation—or, more properly, 'situationless'—and from every patient who can articulate this ultimate abhorrence, one is irresistibly reminded of the words of *Hobbes: 'That which is not Body . . . is no part of the Universe: and since the Universe is all, that which is not Body . . . is Nothing, and Nowhere.'

Spinal anaesthesia is common—perhaps a million women have had it for painless childbirth—but descriptions are most rare, partly because the experience is so abhorrent that it is instantly banished from the memory and mind, and partly because the experience (or non-experience) is an experience of *nothing*. How can one describe nothingness, not-being, nonentity, when there is, literally, nothing to describe? This paradox is pungently expressed by *Berkeley, in his denunciations of the nothingness of 'matter': 'It neither acts, nor perceives, nor is perceived . . . it is *inert*, *senseless*, unknown . . . a definition entirely made up of negatives.' Spinal anaesthesia provides a striking and dramatic example of a *transient* 'annihilation' (although it does not seem transient, but endless, when it occurs—a part of its peculiar horror).

But there are many simpler examples of annihilation in everyday life: all of us have sometimes slept on an arm, crushing its nerves and briefly extinguishing neural traffic; the experience, though very brief, is a terrifying one because (it seems to us) our arm is no longer 'our arm', but an inert, senseless nothing which is not part of ourselves. *Wittgenstein (following *Moore) grounds 'certainty' in the certainty of the body: 'If you can say, *here is one hand*, we'll grant you all the rest.' When you wake up, after nerve-crushing your arm, you cannot say 'This is my hand', or even 'This is *a* hand', except in a purely formal sense. What has always been taken for granted, or axiomatic, is revealed as radically precarious and contingent; having a body, having *anything*, depends on one's nerves.

Yawning is the abyss of nothing. It is only 'by favour of nature' that there are countless other situations—physiological and pathological, common or uncommon—in which there is brief, or prolonged, or permanent annihilation. Strokes, tumours, injuries, especially to the right half of the brain, tend to cause a partial or total annihilation of the left side—a condition variously known as 'imperception', 'inattention', 'neglect', 'agnosia', 'anosognosia', 'extinction', or 'alienation'. All of these are experiences of nothingness (or, more precisely, privations of the experience of somethingness).

Blockage to the spinal cord or the great limb plexuses can produce an identical situation, even though the brain is intact but deprived of the information from which it might form an image (or a Kantian 'intuition'). Indeed it can be shown by measuring potentials in the brain during spinal or regional blocks that there is a dying away of activity in the corresponding part of the cerebral representation of the 'body-image'—the empirical reality required for Kantian ideality. Similar annihilations may be brought out peripherally, either through nerve or muscle damage in a limb, or by simply enclosing the limb in a cast, which by its mixture of immobilization and encasement may temporarily bring neural traffic and impulses to a halt.

To conclude. Nothingness, annihilation, is a reality in this ultimately paradoxical sense. There is, indeed, no space without field; but there are conditions in which the 'field' may be lost—a perceptual-ideal 'Kantian' field which is closely analogous to an Einsteinian field. One's sense of *being* is entirely contingent upon, co-extensive with, and contained in such a field. And anything which produces 'fieldlessness' (or field-defect, or scotoma) is certain to produce a corresponding nothingness.                                           O. S.

Sacks, O. (1985). *The Man Who Mistook His Wife for a Hat*. London.

## NUCLEAR MAGNETIC RESONANCE (NMR).
See IMAGES OF THE BRAIN IN ACTION.

**NULLING.** An important technique for precise measurement, by cancelling an unknown against a known standard. When the unknown and the standard cancel, or 'null', then they are equal. The most familiar example is weighing with a balance: when the known mass balances the unknown mass they must be equal, so the unknown mass has been established by a simple nulling technique. A Wheatstone bridge determines electrical resistances with great precision and over a wide range in a similar way. Nulling methods are particularly useful for instruments as they do not require precise linearity of the apparatus, though the results can be extremely accurate over a wide range.

It has been suggested (Gregory, 1968) that the nervous system may employ nulling for sensory discrimination (especially for weight), by comparing an *expected* against a *sensed* value. This could help to explain how discrimination can be so good over a very wide range, from a few grams to ten or even a hundred kilograms, though neural components are far less stable than the components available for electronic weighing devices, which would probably have to adopt a nulling method to do as well. There is some evidence from the *size–weight illusion that mass discrimination works by nulling, and this might, possibly, explain the *Weber–Fechner law.

Gregory, R. L. (1968). Perceptual Illusions and Brain Models. *Proceedings of the Royal Society*, **171**, 279.

# O

**OBEDIENCE.** Among the more perplexing problems of human nature is this: how is it possible that a decent, kindly person may, in a short time, find himself killing others with ease? Preposterous? No, the transformation occurs routinely in society as young men are inducted into the armed services and are sent to kill the young men of another society. This is not intended as a moralistic statement against war, but as a source of genuine scientific puzzlement. How is such a transformation possible? The answer would seem to lie in an understanding of the psychology of obedience.

For the psychologist, obedience is neither a good nor an evil, but a neutral mechanism whose moral and adaptive aspects depend on the circumstances in which it occurs. Failure to obey the law in order to satisfy selfish interests is the hallmark of criminality; yet an excess of obedience may also present grave moral problems.

To the parents of small children obedience is, no doubt, perceived as a good thing. And indeed, much energy is expended teaching children to do as they are told. This process of socialization is indispensable to producing persons who can function in the everyday world; and humans are born into an overwhelmingly social world, which possesses a structure and order to which they must adapt. Indeed, human society as we know it could not exist unless a capacity for obedience were present in its members.

Obedience is often rational. It makes good sense to follow the doctor's orders, to obey traffic signs, and to clear the building when the police inform us of a bomb threat. But the habit of obedience may be so deeply ingrained that it overrides rationality. Indeed, for the fully socialized adult there is a readiness to defer to authority that is astonishingly powerful.

Obedience is not limited to human beings. Dominance hierarchies are found in many species. But its expression in human beings occurs in a uniquely symbolic field. We recognize a general category of individuals who, by virtue of status, have a right to direct our behaviour, i.e. we recognize authority. And people respond to abstract designations of authority such as insignia, rank, and title. Frequently, the transaction with authority benefits the person and the larger society. But this is not always the case.

In recent times, the widespread acceptance by the German people of a system of death camps that destroyed millions of innocent people has raised some profound questions about the way human nature is conditioned by obedience. Most heinous deeds were carried out by people who asserted they were merely obeying orders. What is the implication for our picture of human nature? Did their behaviour reveal a potential that is present in all of us? An experiment was set up to explore the response of ordinary people to immoral orders.

The experiment was relatively simple: a person comes to the laboratory and, in the context of a learning experiment, he is told to give increasingly severe electric shocks to another person—who, unknown to the subject, is a confederate, and does not actually receive the shocks. This arrangement provided an opportunity to see how far people would go before they refused to follow the experimenter's orders.

A scenario is needed to grasp the flavour of the experiment. Imagine you have answered an advertisement to take part in a study of memory and learning, and are arriving at the university at a time agreed upon. First, you are greeted by a man in a grey technician's coat, and he introduces you to a second volunteer, and says you are both about to take part in a scientific experiment. He says it is to test whether the use of punishment improves the ability to learn. You draw lots to see who is to be the teacher and who the learner. You turn out to be the teacher, the other fellow the learner. Then you see the learner strapped into a chair and electrodes are placed on his wrist (Fig. 1). The experimenter says that when the learner makes a mistake in the lesson his punishment will be an electric shock.

**Fig. 1.** Learner is strapped into chair and electrodes are attached to his wrist. Electrode paste is applied by the experimenter. Learner provides answers by depressing switches that light up numbers on an answer box.

**Fig. 2.** Shock generator used in the experiments. Fifteen of the thirty switches have already been depressed.

**Fig. 4.** Teacher breaks off experiment. On right, event recorder wired into generator automatically records switches used by the subject.

As teacher you are seated in front of an impressive-looking instrument, a shock generator (Fig. 2). Its essential feature is a line of switches that range from 15 volts to 450 volts, and a set of verbal designations that goes from slight shock to moderate shock, strong shock, very strong shock, and so on through XXX—danger, severe shock. Your job, the experimenter explains to you, is to teach the learner a simple word-pair test. You read a list of words to him, such as 'blue day', 'nice girl', 'fat neck', etc., and he has to indicate by means of an answer-box which words were originally paired together. If he gets a correct answer you move on to the next pair; but if he makes a mistake, you are instructed to give him an electric shock, starting with 15 volts (Fig. 3). And you are told to increase the shock one step each time he makes an error. In the course of the experiment the 'victim' emits cries of pain and demands to be set free, but the experimenter orders you to continue. The question is: how far will you proceed on the generator before you turn to the experimenter and refuse to go any further?

Before the experiment was carried out, people were asked to predict their own performance. The question was put to several groups: psychiatrists, psychologists, and ordinary workers. They all said virtually the same thing: almost no one would go to the end.

**Fig. 3.** Teacher receives sample shock from the generator.

But in reality the results were very different. Despite the fact that many subjects experienced stress, despite the fact that many protested to the experimenter, a substantial proportion continued to the last shock on the generator. Many subjects obeyed the experimenter no matter how vehement the pleading of the person being shocked, no matter how painful the shocks seemed to be, and no matter how much the victim pleaded to be let out. This was seen time and again, and has been observed in several universities where the experiment has been repeated.

But there is more to the experiment than this simple demonstration of obedience. Most of the energy went into systematically changing the factors to see which increased obedience, and which led to greater defiance: the effects of the closeness of the victim were studied, as was the importance of the sponsoring institution, and how the sight of other people obeying or defying an authority affected obedience. All of these factors had a powerful effect on whether subjects obeyed or defied the malevolent authority, showing that how a person behaves depends not only on his 'character' but also on the precise situational pressures acting on him.

A person who obeys authority does not see himself as responsible for his own actions, but rather as an agent executing the wishes of another person. In the experiment subjects frequently turned to the experimenter, saying: 'Am I responsible?' And as soon as he said they were not, they could proceed more easily.

Even if the conflict between conscience and duty gives rise to strain, there are psychological mechanisms that come into play that help to alleviate this strain. For example, some subjects complied only minimally: they touched the switch of the generator very lightly; they had the feeling that this really showed that they were good people, whereas in fact they were obeying. Sometimes they would argue with the experimenter, but argumentation did not necessarily lead to disobedience; rather it served as a psychological mechanism, defining the subject in his own eyes as a person who opposed the experimenter's callous orders, yet reducing tension and allowing the person to obey. Often the person became involved in the minute details of the experimental procedure; becoming engrossed, he would lose all sight of the broader consequences of his action.

When the results of the original experiments were published, opinion about them was sharply divided. On the one hand, the American Association for the Advancement of Science awarded the work its annual socio-psychological prize. At the same time the experiments attracted fierce criticism, centring mainly on the ethical issues of carrying out the research. The experiments that it was hoped would deepen our understanding of how people yield to malevolent authority, themselves became the focus of controversy.

But the problem of authority remains. We cannot have society without some structure of authority, and every society must inculcate a habit of obedience in its citizens. Yet this research showed that many people do not have the resources to resist authority, even when they are directed to act callously and inhumanely against an innocent victim. The experiments posed an age-old problem anew: what is the correct balance between individual initiative and social authority? They illuminated in a concrete and specific way what happens when obedience is unrestrained by conscience.                                                       S. M.

Arendt, H. (1963). *Eichmann in Jerusalem: a report on the banality of evil*. New York.
Comfort, A. (1950). *Authority and Delinquency in the Modern State: a criminological approach to the problem of power*. London.
Fromm, E. (1941). *Escape from freedom*. New York.
Koestler, A. (1967). *The Ghost in the Machine*. New York.
Milgram, S. (1974). *Obedience to Authority*. New York and London.
Milgram, S. (1974). *Obedience* (a filmed experiment). New York University Film Library; distributed in the UK by the British Universities Film Council.

**OBJECT-CONSTANCY.** See ILLUSIONS; OBJECT PERCEPTION; PERCEPTION.

**OBJECT PERCEPTION.** Although, for convenience, physiologists and psychologists tend to study *perception with controlled stimuli presented to the sense organs, man and the higher animals are adapted to recognize and behave in ways generally appropriate to objects of the external world. To understand how objects are perceived it is necessary to appreciate how the sensory inputs of stimuli are 'read' as evidence of objects and where they lie in surrounding space. This ability is in many ways the most remarkable that the higher organisms ever accomplish. The fact that we perceive objects from stimuli without even seeming to try is extremely misleading—for in fact it requires computations by neural mechanisms which at present can only be carried out very

inadequately by the most powerful available computers.

When objects change in position, or rotate to present a different view, they provide very different stimulus patterns—yet, remarkably, they are still seen as the same object. This is accomplished visually in part by perceptual selection of invariant features, such as corners, whose retinal images do not change much with changes of orientation. It is also a useful technique for computer-based object recognition: internal descriptions of useful identifying features are built up, these descriptions being perceptions.

**OBJECT-RELATIONS THEORY.** See FREUDIANISM: LATER DEVELOPMENTS.

**OBSESSIONS AND COMPULSIONS.** To say that an individual is obsessed with an idea, a pursuit, or a particular person usually implies, often with more than a hint of disapproval, that he is thus wholly preoccupied. But such obsessions may not necessarily be unhealthy or neurotic, even though, as Kräupl-Taylor (1979) comments, they have an element of compulsion attached to them. They have to be distinguished from obsessive-compulsive neuroses, or the psychotic's absorption with his delusions. A person may say that because of his beliefs, religious, political, or philosophical, he has to act in a certain manner: he is compelled by convictions which, if ignored, would cause him unease or anxiety. Such a person is not necessarily obsessional. The term obsessional personality is rather applied to one who is conventional, conscientious, reliable, scrupulous, or punctual well beyond average. He may find it necessary to check and re-check his work to assure himself that no errors have been committed; he may adhere rigorously to a routine which, if disrupted, will cause him considerable unease; and he will probably be singularly competent at clerical work, proof-reading, typesetting, or other tasks requiring attention to detail. The characteristics of the obsessional personality are not to be despised: they could be essential qualities for anyone engaged in precision work, and much scientific research could not be carried out without them.

In comparison, the individual who suffers from an obsessional-compulsive neurosis is a sick person. The late Sir Aubrey Lewis (1967) appraised the subject. With some reservations he adopted Carl Schneider's definition of obsession as 'contents of consciousness which, when they occur, are accompanied by the experience of subjective compulsion, and which cannot be got rid of, though on quiet reflection they are recognized as senseless'. Usually 'the contents of consciousness which preoccupy the obsessional neurotic are concerned with ideas of harm, contamination, sex, and sin, although repetitive ruminations about abstract problems and manipulation of words and numbers are not infrequent'. These may be obsessional *symptoms* which can occur independently of the neurosis proper. Fortunately the neurosis is rare, affecting about 0·05 per cent of the general population in Britain and the USA, for example, although obsessional symptoms crop up from time to time in the lives of otherwise perfectly normal individuals. (The symptoms can also complicate other psychiatric disorders, particularly severe depression.) Children, as is well known, engage in repetitive games and rituals such as avoiding treading on the cracks between paving stones; and, as any parent knows when reading a familiar story, an attempt to vary or skip a part of it may be resisted by the child. Many minor compulsions can be discerned in adult superstitions: failure to touch wood or avoid walking under a ladder, for instance; and a sense of mild anxiety may briefly follow the breaking of such rituals. Anxiety is indeed a main driving force in the life of the obsessional neurotic. Resisting a compulsion may arouse acute distress, which can be assuaged only by bowing to the inner need and going back to complete a ritual.

Lewis divides obsessions into primary and secondary. 'An example of the first,' he wrote, 'would be the insistent feeling that one is dirty . . . and then there is the impulse to wash—the secondary phenomenon, developed in order to obtain relief from the primary disturbance. The secondary phenomenon can be regarded as defensive and aimed at preventing or relieving tension.'

Standard textbooks of psychiatry give detailed accounts of the many varieties of symptoms which can cripple performance of the everyday activities of the obsessional neurotic. For example, the patient who fears contamination may wash his hands repeatedly only to find himself having to restart the whole process on account of a fear that chance contact with the tap may have again soiled his fingers. Such compulsions can occupy a large part of his waking day, as can the checking of rituals of those who fear that they might inadvertently harm somebody close to them. A sufferer may spend hours checking and re-checking gas taps, electric switches, and the contents of kitchen drawers to ensure that sharp objects such as knives have not been left lying where they could injure another person. Mothers of young children are sometimes tortured with the idea that some carelessness on their part could seriously injure a recently born infant.

There are many examples of well-known persons who have found it necessary to engage in compulsive rituals. Boswell described such a ritual performed by Samuel Johnson:

He had another particularity, of which none of his friends even ventured to ask an explanation. . . . This was his anxious care to go out or in at a door or passage, by a certain number of steps from a certain point, or at least so as that either his right or his left foot . . . should constantly make the first actual movement when he came close to the door or passage. Thus I conjecture: for I have, upon innumerable occasions, observed him suddenly stop, and then seem to count his steps with a deep earnestness; and when he had neglected or gone wrong in this sort of

magical movement, I have seen him go back again, put himself in a proper posture to begin the ceremony, and, having gone through it, break from his abstraction, walk briskly on, and join his companion. (*Life of Johnson*, Aetat. 55.)

John Bunyan in *Grace Abounding* gave a good example of an obsessional phobia: 'Sometimes again, when I have been preaching, I have been violently assaulted with thoughts of blasphemy and strongly tempted to speak the words with my mouth before the congregation.' But there is no reason for thinking that either Johnson or Bunyan suffered from obsessional neuroses, though clearly they did have troublesome symptoms; for fortunately the symptoms did not detract from their competence and genius. Obsessional doubts about religious observance are phenomena well known to confessors and theologians. Such scruples certainly tormented Bunyan as they did Martin Luther.

Successful treatment of patients suffering from obsessional neurosis is far from easy; and this despite the fairly obvious psychopathology—in psychoanalytic terms—of the neurosis. The frequent association of depression with the neurosis implies that appropriate treatment of the affective disorder might well mitigate the full impact of the patient's disabilities. In many cases supportive psychotherapy and behaviour therapy as well as the passage of time seem to ensure that the patients will come to terms with their symptoms sufficiently well to enable them to lead relatively normal lives. In about 60 per cent of the cases of patients who are severely afflicted, one of the modern forms of psychosurgery will bring relief. It may not entirely eliminate the symptoms, but they become less obtrusive and no longer dominate the patient's life.                                    F. A. W.

Kräupl-Taylor, F. (1979). *Psychopathology: its causes and symptoms*, rev. edn. Sunbury-on-Thames.
Lewis, A. J. (1967). 'Problems of Obsessional Illness' and 'Obsessional Illness' in *Inquiries in Psychiatry*. London.

**OEDIPUS COMPLEX.** Sigmund *Freud's first mention of the Oedipus complex was in a letter written in 1897, while he was reviewing his relationship with his father, who had died six months before. In *The Interpretation of Dreams*, written at about the same time, he referred to 'being in love with one parent and hating the other' as being 'among the essential constituents of the stock of psychical impulses' formed in childhood, and as important in determining the symptoms of later neurosis. These psychical impulses, which he called the Oedipus complex, retain their power to determine neurotic symptoms, he supposed, only when there is fixation at the Oedipal level of development. This happens when rivalry with the parent of the same sex is not resolved through identification with this parent or when sexual feelings for the parent of the opposite sex are not transferred to a sexual partner outside the family. In Jung's theory, the essential process in neurosis is not the fixation of the complex, but its revival when a new adaptation is required. Modern theories of neurosis attach more importance to the quality of the relationship between mother and child before Oedipal impulses develop (see ATTACHMENT).

Freud claimed some confirmation of his theory in the universal appeal of the legend of Oedipus Rex in Sophocles' play. The Thebans are told by an oracle that the plague will cease when the murderer of Laius, the former king, has been driven from the land. The play gradually reveals, in the manner of psychoanalysis, Freud remarked, that Oedipus is the murderer, and that he is the son of Laius and Jocasta, whom he married after Laius' death. Freud's formula, which is based, as is usual in psychoanalysis, on the child's feelings towards his parents, gives a one-sided and too simple an account of the complex interactions in a family. The son is the transgressor whereas in the legend the father, feeling threatened because he has been told by the oracle that he will perish at the hands of his son, instructs the mother to destroy him at birth. Instead she abandons him. The father later starts the quarrel which ends in his death. In the story of Hamlet, in Shakespeare's play, which psychoanalysts regard as similar to that of Oedipus, the stepfather, not the son, is the aggressor.

See also FREUDIANISM: LATER DEVELOPMENTS.

D. R. D.

Freud, S. *Introductory Lectures on Psychoanalysis* (trans. Strachey, J. 1974). Harmondsworth.
Jones, E. (1949). *Hamlet and Oedipus*. London.

**OLDS,** JAMES (1922–76). American psychologist who received his degree in 1947 from Amherst College and his doctorate from the laboratory of social relations at Harvard in 1952, working with Richard Solomon. At Harvard he attempted to combine the neurological views of Donald Hebb with E. C. *Tolman's model of learning.

In 1953 he went to McGill as a postdoctoral Fellow to learn physiological techniques and to work more closely with Hebb. It was during this time that he discovered that electrical stimulation of the septal area, lateral hypothalamus, and some other brain areas could act as a reward, one of the most significant physiological contributions to learning, and one that turned the attention of students of the neural bases of learning from the cortex to the brain as a whole. See also MEMORY: BIOLOGICAL BASIS.

After a further two years' postdoctoral research at the Brain Research Institute of the University of California at Los Angeles, Olds became a member of the psychology department of the University of Michigan, where he continued to explore the anatomy, pharmacology, and behavioural features of brain-stimulation reward.

In 1967 he moved to the California Institute of Technology, where he remained until his death in 1976 of a heart attack. Here his main energy was devoted to the study of learning by recording the activity of cells in different areas of the brain during conditioning.

P. M. M.

**OPERANT CONDITIONING.** See CONDITIONING.

**OPIUM**—the word is derived from the Greek for poppy juice—is obtained by incising the fruit and collecting the exudate from the opium poppy, *Papaver somniferum*. The plant appears to have originated in the lands bordering the eastern Mediterranean, whence it spread both eastwards and westwards. The psychological effects of opium may have been known to the Sumerians, but the first clear reference to poppy juice is found in the writings of Theophrastus in the third century BC, and Discorides in the first century BC gave the first description of modern opium.

During the subsequent centuries opium appears to have enjoyed both medicinal and recreational uses. Medically it was known to relieve pain and suppress dry coughing, and it was given for a wide variety of other complaints, including epilepsy and colic. Its sleep-inducing properties were well known to Greek and Roman writers; the Greeks appear to have taken opium cakes and sweetmeats for relaxation and recreation. Whereas opium-smoking has been most widespread in the Far East, consumption of the drug in the form of its tincture—laudanum—became fairly commonplace in Western Europe. Its addictive properties were well recognized and described in England at the end of the seventeenth century by John Jones, a physician in Windsor, who, in his book *The Mysteries of Opium Reveal'd* (1700), gave a clear account of the effects of intoxication and sudden withdrawal of the drug in one habituated to it. None the less, regardless of its recreational use, it was as a sovereign remedy for pain that it was most widely prescribed. As Thomas Sydenham wrote, 'Among the remedies which it has pleased Almighty God to give to man to relieve his sufferings, none is so universal and efficacious as opium'. In the nineteenth century many patent medicines, freely available to the public both in Britain and the USA, contained opium. Virginia Berridge (1977) has described how easily opium was obtained in the Fenland area of England. Opium pills were sold openly in Cambridge on market-day and many a person bought 'a ha'pennard o'elevation' to last for the week. Although opium was mainly imported in the nineteenth century from Turkey, the medical profession showed a preference for opium from poppies grown in fields near to the village of Winslow in Buckinghamshire.

Opium is a crude preparation containing at least twenty different alkaloids of which the best known are morphine, first isolated by F. W. A. Sertürner in 1803, and codeine, identified by Robiquet in 1832. Heroin is not a naturally occurring alkaloid but is derived from morphine by acetylation (the addition of an acetyl group). It is at least three times as effective as morphine for the control of pain, and when first synthesized in 1898 it was hoped that it would be less addictive than the parent drug. In fact, as the history of heroin has shown, it has proved to be the most addictive of all the opiates, both natural and synthetic, although none is free from this potential.

In spite of the free availability of opium medicines to the public in the nineteenth century, there is little evidence to show that addiction to the drug was particularly widespread. None the less, the giving of opium to small children as a sedative was a pernicious practice and a not infrequent cause of wasting and premature death. Although somewhat conflicting opinions were expressed by the medical profession, eventually restrictions were placed on the sale of opium to the public. In the twentieth century these restrictions have been tightened, the main impetus for strict control of the sale of opium and its derivatives coming from the USA, at first through the Harrison Narcotic Act of 1914 and later through the League of Nations and the United Nations Commission on Narcotic Drugs. It was hoped that international control of opium and heroin production would reverse the steady increase in the number of persons addicted to these substances. Unfortunately there is very little evidence that intense legal and law enforcement activity have made much difference, as the use of these drugs has become more extensive both in the USA and elsewhere.

**Addiction.** Statements about opium and its derivatives tend to be overshadowed by the problem of addiction to such a degree that concern over this single issue has led to restrictions on their medical use. As a result some doctors avoid their use even for the control of severe *pain in terminal illness, lest the patient become addicted. Fortunately, however, their medical use is not a common cause of addiction. Even so, if a patient is dying from cancer it is hardly a matter of importance if the drug that ensures freedom from pain also makes him addicted to its continued administration.

Although those who misuse opiates and other types of drugs are generally referred to as addicts, the term 'drug addiction' was replaced by 'drug dependence' by a WHO expert committee report in 1970. Dependence can be both physical and psychological. Opiates, like some other drugs of dependence, can, if taken repeatedly, result in the development of tolerance, so that some drug-dependent persons can build up a tolerance which allows them to take massive doses of the drug without immediate harm. De Quincey was well aware of this phenomenon, describing it in his *Confessions of an English Opium-Eater*. Sudden withdrawal of the drug will cause an abstinence syndrome: the 'cold turkey' in the slang jargon of the junkie's world. To a high degree of physical dependence will usually be added a compulsion to use the drug on a 'continuous or periodic basis in order to experience its psychic effects' (WHO, 1970).

See also ADDICTION.                    F. A. W.

Berridge, V. (1977). Fenland Opium Eating in the 19th Century. *British Journal of Addiction*, **72**, 275–84.
Goodman, L. S. and Gilman, A. G. (1980). *The Pharmacological Basis of Therapeutics*, 6th edn. New York.
Jones, J. (1700). *The Mysteries of Opium Reveal'd*. In Hunter, R. and Macalpine, I. (1963). *Three Hundred Years of Psychiatry*. London.
WHO Expert Committee on Drug Dependence (1970). *Technical Report*, Series 460. Geneva.

**OTHER MINDS.** The classical problem of why we believe that other people (and perhaps at least the higher animals) have sensations, thoughts, and so on, essentially similar to our own. It seems that we draw a widespread analogy from our own behaviour, and related internal affective states, to the internal states of other people (and sometimes animals), especially when their behaviour is similar to ours. Some clinical states, especially coma, are very difficult to interpret or 'read', as behaviour is no longer typical or at all like our own.

Given that computers are developing some abilities until recently thought specifically human, the question of whether computers can have minds is rapidly becoming a significant issue. As Alan *Turing suggested, we may say that a computer is as 'intelligent' as a human if it answers questions as a human does; but would we say that the computer is *conscious*, or *aware*, as we are? It is this doubt that gives *behaviourism its prima facie scientific validity—though behaviourism rejects what we take to be the most important fact of at least *our* minds: *consciousness.

Dennett, D. C. (1978). *Brain Storms*. Chicago.
Wisdom, J. (1952). *Other minds*. Oxford.

**OUT-OF-THE-BODY EXPERIENCE,** or OBE, may be defined as an experience in which a person seems to perceive the world from a location outside his physical body. OBEs have been reported from diverse ages and cultures by old and young, educated and uneducated, and those who have prior beliefs about the experiences and those who know nothing about them.

Some of the most dramatic OBEs have been reported as part of the near-death experience, for example in those who are resuscitated from cardiac arrest or who survive life-threatening accidents. However, very similar experiences can occur during resting, meditation, when taking certain drugs, or even during normal everyday activity. A few people claim to be able to induce the experience at will and to control it when it occurs (Muldoon and Carrington 1929; Rogo 1983).

Those who have experienced OBEs claim typically that they seemed to float out of their body and were able to see and move without it. Some seem to possess a duplicate body, or double, but many seem to take on other shapes or seem to be no more than a perceiving point in space. This point, or form, can then move about and observe what appears to be the normal physical world—but often with subtle differences from normal. It may contain odd errors, and objects may be strangely illuminated on the darkest night. It is possible to see and to travel at will through walls and other objects, though not usually to affect them physically. Sometimes completely different 'worlds' are visited, some merely bizarre, others of mystical quality. In addition there are controversial claims that people have actually influenced objects or acquired information paranormally during their 'travels'.

Whether or not one accepts that something does leave the body, a consistent feature of the experience is that it is described as totally vivid and realistic, and quite unlike a dream or day-dream. Very often people who have OBEs feel that the experience affected them deeply and even changed their beliefs and values.

OBEs have been investigated by case collections, surveys, experiments, and personal experience. Case collections show that the experience is very variable, as are the conditions under which it occurs. Muscular relaxation, exhaustion, monotonous sounds, and certain drugs are often implicated. These may all have in common the fact that they tend to disrupt both sensory input and the normal body image (Blackmore, 1982).

Surveys have shown that anywhere between 8 and 34 per cent of respondents report having had an OBE at some time during their lives, depending on the population sampled. There seem to be no obvious differences between those who have experienced OBEs and others, although recent studies have begun to find differences in imagery skills (Cook and Irwin, 1983).

Experiments have mostly been of three types. First were attempts to detect the double during the OBE, which began early this century. It is probably true to say that the size of any effect detected has decreased with increasing experimental sophistication. Most recent studies have used magnetometers, thermistors, ultraviolet and infra-red detectors, and so on, as well as humans and animals. There has been limited success with animals, but no reliable detector has yet been found (Morris et al., 1978).

The second type aims to determine whether a person having an OBE can actually bring back information from a distant location. Many such claims have been made but the experimental evidence is weak. Subjects have been asked to view target letters, numbers or pictures, placed in distant rooms. One subject correctly 'saw' a five-digit number, but such clear success has never been repeated. Other studies have tried to discover whether subjects seem to be looking from a specific location during OBEs; however, the results have been inconclusive (see Rogo, 1978). Generally these studies provide very mixed results and it is not clear that any paranormal process is involved.

The third type of experiment is studies of the physiological state associated with the OBE. No unique physiological state seems to be necessary. Rather, the experience may occur in a relaxed waking state, or in something resembling stage 1 sleep (Rogo, 1978).

Finally, personal experience should be mentioned as a useful adjunct to the other types of research—for the unique experiential qualities of the OBE demand explanation.

There have been three main types of theory of the OBE. The most popular are those suggesting that we all have a double that can act independently of the physical body. This notion can be traced back to ancient Egypt and to Greek philosophy, and can be found in folklore and mythology; it is an essential part of some religious teachings. A popular modern version is the doctrine of 'astral projection', according to which the astral body is capable of separating from the physical body and travelling without it on the astral plane. In life the astral body is joined to the physical by a 'silver cord'; but at death the cord is broken and the astral body freed, taking consciousness with it. There are numerous problems with this kind of theory. It cannot specify what the astral body consists of, in what sense it is conscious, how it perceives and interacts with the world without any perceptual apparatus and without being detected, or why the world appears so strange. In addition, many surveys have shown that astral bodies are rare and 'cords' even rarer (e.g. Green, 1968). In other words, these theories seem neither to make sense nor to fit with the evidence.

The second type of theory is that the OBE is imagination plus ESP (*extra-sensory perception). This can, potentially, avoid the problems of 'other bodies' and separate worlds while allowing for the claims of paranormal abilities in the OBE; but only in the weakest possible way. Since the term 'imagination' is so broad and we know next to nothing about how ESP functions—if indeed it does—it is hard to test this theory.

The final type of theory is that the OBE is a purely psychological phenomenon, involving no other bodies and no paranormal abilities (Blackmore, 1982; Palmer, 1978). There have been comparisons with the experience of birth, and suggestions that the OBE is a way of denying death. Some have suggested that it is no more than a kind of dream; but physiological studies show that the OBE need not take place during sleep, and certainly not in REM (rapid eye movement, or *dreaming) sleep (Rogo, 1978). Also, it does not seem like a dream. Consciousness seems absolutely clear, memory seems normal, and things are seen extremely vividly. If it is like any kind of dream, it is most like a 'lucid dream'—that is, one in which you know at the time that it is a dream (Gackenbach and LaBerge, 1985). Some aspects of the OBE resemble certain types of *hallucination. For example, tunnels are frequently rushed through at the start of an OBE or in near-death experiences, as well as in drug-induced hallucinations. The psychological theories attempt to integrate these features of the experience and to explain why it seems so real.

One possibility is to view the OBE as an altered state of consciousness in which an imagined model or representation of the world replaces the normal perceptual model. If sensory input is reduced or disrupted, the normal input-based model of the world may start to become unstable and break down. In this case the cognitive system will try to get back to normal by creating a new model of the world from imagination. If this model is more convincing than the degraded perceptual model, it may take over and seem real. Imagined models are often constructed in bird's-eye view, as though from above. So if a model like this takes over then an OBE will have occurred.

The theories obviously differ in their implications for survival after death. Some researchers have seen the OBE as one method of investigating 'survival', and to this end have tried to confirm that there is an objective double which leaves the body and is capable of independent thought and action. But this is in no way implied by the occurrence of the experience itself. Even if it is under stress the physical body is still alive, often quite well, and there is no reason to suppose that it is not responsible for the organized thought and consciousness involved.

All the evidence suggests that, rather than hunt down the elusive 'other body', we shall get closer to understanding the OBE by treating it is a psychological response to unusual conditions. What we need is a better understanding of subjective experience—including mystical experience and other altered states of consciousness—within which the experience of seeming to be outside one's body makes sense.                        S. J. B.

Blackmore, S. J. (1982). *Beyond the Body*. London.

Cook, A. M. and Irwin, H. J. (1983). Visuospatial skills and the out-of-body experience. *Journal of Parapsychology*, **47**, 23–35.

Gackenbach, J. and LaBerge, S. (1985). *Lucid Dreamings: new research on consciousness during sleep*. New York.

Green, C. E. (1968). *Out-of-the-body Experiences*. London.

Morris, R. L., Harary, S. B., Janis, J., Hartwell, J., and Roll, W. G. (1978). Studies of communication during out-of-body experiences. *Journal of the American Society for Psychical Research*, **72**, 1–22.

Muldoon, S. and Carrington, H. (1929). The Projection of the Astral Body. London.

Palmer, J. (1978). The out-of-body experience: a psychological theory. *Parapsychology Review*, **9**, no. 5.

Rogo, D. S. (1978). *Mind beyond the Body*. New York.

Rogo, D. S. (1983). *Leaving the Body*. Englewood Cliffs, New Jersey.

**OWEN**, SIR RICHARD (1804–92). British physician and naturalist, born at Lancaster, he studied medicine at Edinburgh and at St Bartholomew's Hospital, London, and became curator in the museum of the Royal College of Surgeons, producing splendid catalogues. In 1856 he became superintendent of the natural history department of the British Museum. He accepted evolution before *Darwin but maintained a lengthy dispute, especially with T. H. *Huxley, criticizing Darwin's principle of natural selection. They finally made up the quarrel. An important essay is *On Parthenogenesis* (1849). There is a splendid statue of Owen in the British Museum (Natural History), South Kensington, London.

# P

**PAIN.** Pain research and therapy have long been dominated by specificity theory which proposes that pain is a specific sensation subserved by a straight-through transmission system, and that the intensity of pain is proportional to the extent of tissue damage. Recent evidence, however, shows that pain is not simply a function of the amount of bodily damage alone, but is influenced by attention, anxiety, suggestion, prior experience, and other psychological variables (Melzack and Wall, 1982). Moreover, the natural outcome of the specificity concept of pain has been the development of neurosurgical techniques to cut the so-called pain pathway, and the results of such operations have been disappointing, particularly for chronic pain syndromes. Not only does the pain tend to return in a substantial proportion of patients, but new pains may appear. The psychological and neurological data, then, force us to reject the concept of a single straight-through sensory transmission system.

In recent years the evidence on pain has moved in the direction of recognizing the plasticity and modifiability of events in the central nervous system. Pain is a complex perceptual and affective experience determined by the unique past history of the individual, by the meaning to him of the injurious agent or situation, and by his 'state of mind' at the moment, as well as by the sensory nerve patterns evoked by physical stimulation.

In the light of this understanding of pain processes, Melzack and Wall (1965) proposed the gate control theory of pain. Basically, the theory states that neural mechanisms in the dorsal horn of the spinal cord act like a gate which can increase or decrease the flow of nerve impulses from peripheral fibres to the spinal cord cells that project to the brain. Somatic input is therefore subjected to the modulating influence of the gate *before* it evokes pain perception and response. The theory suggests that large-fibre inputs (such as gentle rubbing) tend to close the gate while small-fibre inputs (such as pinching) generally open it, and that the gate is also profoundly influenced by descending influences from the brain. It further proposes that the sensory input is modulated at successive synapses throughout its projection from the spinal cord to the brain areas responsible for pain experience and response. Pain occurs when the number of nerve impulses that arrives at these areas exceeds a critical level.

Melzack and Wall (1982) have recently assessed the present-day status of the gate control theory in the light of new physiological research. It is apparent that the theory is alive and well despite considerable controversy and conflicting evidence. Although some of the physiological details may need revision, the evidence supporting the concept of gating (or input modulation) is stronger than ever.

The subjective experience of pain clearly has sensory qualities, such as are described by the words throbbing, burning, or sharp. In addition, it has distinctly unpleasant, affective qualities which are described by words such as exhausting, wretched and punishing. Pain becomes overwhelming, demands immediate attention, and disrupts ongoing behaviour and thought. It motivates or drives the organism into activity aimed at stopping the pain as quickly as possible. On the basis of these considerations, Melzack and Casey (1968) have proposed that there are three major psychological dimensions of pain experience: sensory-discriminative, motivational-affective, and cognitive-evaluative. Psychophysiological evidence suggests that each is subserved by specialized systems in the brain which interact to produce the multidimensional qualities of pain experience.

Recent recognition of the complexity of pain experience has led to the development of a paper-and-pencil questionnaire (the 'McGill Pain Questionnaire') to obtain numerical measures of the intensity and qualities of pain (Melzack, 1975). The questionnaire consists of twenty sets of words that people use to describe pain. Ten sets describe sensory qualities, five describe affective qualities and one is an evaluative group. Four sets consist of miscellaneous words. Since each word has a numerical value, patients asked to check those words that best describe their pain provide quantitative measures for each of the major dimensions of pain. The power of the questionnaire has been demonstrated in many quantitative, controlled studies of the effects of different forms of pain therapy (Melzack, 1983). In addition, the questionnaire has been shown to discriminate among different types of pain. Distinctive patterns of words discriminate between migraine and tension headaches, between low-back pain of organic and that of functional origin, and between dysmenorrhoea and pain caused by an intra-uterine device.

Drugs, especially *opium and its derivatives, are among the oldest methods for controlling pain. Thomas *Sydenham in 1680 wrote: 'Among the remedies which it has pleased Almighty God to give to man to relieve his sufferings, none is so universal and efficacious as opium.' Since then, more effective derivatives of opium, notably morphine and heroin, have been discovered. The invention of the hypodermic needle and syringe not only stimulated the search for pure, injectable analgesics but also, unfortunately, increased the risk of drug dependence. The quest for preparations free from addictive properties has proved to be fruitless, but withholding such pain-relieving drugs from the terminally ill lest they become 'addicted' is as ridiculous as it is inhumane. Other drugs said to have analgesic properties include the antidepressants, but it does not appear that relief of depression is their mode of action. Possibly this may be by blocking the re-uptake of serotonin and so potentiating the effect of encephalins in the brain (see NEUROPEPTIDES).

Many new methods to control pain have been developed in recent years (Melzack and Wall, 1982). Sensory modulation techniques such as transcutaneous electrical nerve stimulation (TENS) and ice massage are widely used in the attempt to activate inhibitory neural mechanisms to suppress pain. These techniques have a long history but were not understood until recently. Acupuncture, for example, is an ancient Chinese medical procedure in which long needles are inserted into specific points at the skin. The traditional Chinese explanation is that the needles bring Yin and Yang (which flow through hypothetical tubules called meridians) into harmony with each other. It has been discovered, however, that the sites of insertion correspond to myofascial 'trigger points' which are well known in Western medicine. It has also been found that acupuncture and electrical stimulation through electrodes placed on the skin (TENS) are equally effective in relieving low-back pain and several other forms of pain, including pains due to peripheral nerve injury. The neural mechanisms which underlie the relief produced by these forms of stimulation are not entirely understood, but evidence suggests that the intense stimulation produced by acupuncture or TENS activates an area in the brain which exerts a powerful inhibitory control over pathways which transmit pain signals.

Psychological techniques that allow patients to achieve some degree of control over their pain have also been developed. These techniques include *biofeedback, hypnosis, distraction, and the use of imagery and other cognitive activities to modulate the transmission of the nerve-impulse patterns that subserve pain. Psychological techniques are being used increasingly and provide relatively simple, safe approaches to pain control. They represent a significant advance over the earlier tendency to treat pain by neurosurgical operations intended to cut the 'pain pathway' and which so frequently ended in failure.

The techniques of sensory modulation and psychological control work well in conjunction with each other. A large body of research demonstrates that several of these procedures employed at the same time—'multiple convergent therapy'—are often highly effective for the control of chronic pain states, particularly those such as low-back pain which have prominent elements of tension, depression, and anxiety.

While great strides have been made in the control of pain, there are still many pain syndromes which are beyond our comprehension and our control. Back pains, especially of the lower back, are the most common kind of pain, and literally millions of sufferers are continually seeking help. Sometimes they obtain temporary relief, but most continue to suffer. *Migraine and tension headaches similarly plague millions of people. Perhaps the most terrible of all pains are those suffered by some cancer patients in the terminal phases of the disease. In recent years, specialized medical units have been developed to cope with these problems. Their major feature is that physicians and other health professionals from many different disciplines work together in the attempt to alleviate the pain of each individual patient. Pain clinics have been set up in every major Western city to cope with benign chronic pain, and hospices or palliative care units in hospitals have been developed to control pain (and other miseries) of patients who are terminally ill with cancer.

The development of pain clinics and hospices represent a breakthrough of the highest importance in the clinical control of pain. They are radical, new approaches to old problems. Chronic pain and terminal pain are major challenges to the scientist and clinician. But the giant step has been the recognition that they are special problems. The challenges ahead are clear: to conquer pain and suffering in all their forms.

See also ANAESTHESIA. R. ME.

Melzack, R. (1975). The McGill Pain Questionnaire: major properties and scoring methods. *Pain*, 1, 277–99.

Melzack, R. (ed.) (1983). *Pain Measurement and Assessment*. New York.

Melzack, R. and Casey, K. L. (1968). Sensory, motivational and central control determinants of pain: a new conceptual model. In Kenshalo, D. (ed.), *The Skin Senses*, pp. 423–43. Springfield, Illinois.

Melzack, R. and Wall, P. D. (1965). Pain mechanisms: a new theory. *Science*, 150, 971–9.

Melzack, R. and Wall, P. D. (1982). *The Challenge of Pain*. Harmondsworth.

**PALEY,** WILLIAM (1743–1805). British philosopher, born at Peterborough. He was a Fellow of Christ's College, Cambridge, from 1766 to 1776. His *Principles of Moral and Political Philosophy* (1785) propounded a form of utilitarianism, while *Evidences of Christianity* (1794) was required reading for entrance to Cambridge University for many years. Paley is celebrated for his formulations of the argument from *design for the existence of God, and his arguments (especially in *Horae Paulinae*, 1790) that the New Testament is not myth.

Dawkins, R. (1986). *The Blind Watchmaker*. London.

**PANPSYCHISM.** See ANIMISM.

**PARADIGM.** 'Paradigm' has become an important technical term in the philosophy of science following the publication of *The Structure of Scientific Revolutions* by Thomas Kuhn (1962; 1970). Kuhn's thesis is that 'normal science' operates within a largely unquestioned framework governed by fundamental theoretical models, or 'paradigms'. These ruling paradigms determine the way in which experiments are designed and observational results are interpreted. Once a theory gains the status of a paradigm (an example is Darwin's principle of natural selection by the survival of the fittest) it remains unchallenged until a scientific 'revolution' occurs and it is overthrown in favour of a new paradigm (cf. the switch from Newtonian to Einsteinian physics); when this happens even old-established observations and experiments change their significance. This has been likened to a *Gestalt switch in perception of an ambiguous figure. An important part of Kuhn's view is the assertion that different scientific paradigms are 'incommensurable': there is no common body of neutral observation which can be used to decide between two competing theories—a notion which may be thought to cast doubt on the claims of science to objectivity and rationality.

Kuhn's view of paradigms has been criticized in detail by Margaret Masterman (1970), but it has proved of great importance by emphasizing the role of general conceptual models in science and thinking. Psychology may be a somewhat unsatisfactory science because it lacks effective unifying paradigms. Although the great theorists, such as Sigmund *Freud and B. F. Skinner (following the lead of J. B. *Watson), are important partly because they did provide paradigms, found to be useful clinically and by experimenters, these paradigms have never gained the degree of general acceptance achieved by paradigms in the physical sciences. R. L. G.

Kuhn, T. S. (1962; 1970). *The Structure of Scientific Revolutions*. Chicago.
Masterman, M. (1970). The nature of a paradigm. In Lakatos, I. and Musgrave, A. (eds.), *Criticism and the Growth of Knowledge*. Cambridge.

**PARADOX.** See ILLUSIONS.

**PARALYSIS** is loss of motor function. Thought processes and *perception may be subtly modified or impaired. It is an interesting question whether perception (which almost certainly depends primarily on active learning in infancy) and *emotion (which may largely be sensations of bodily changes, for example to perceived danger) can remain normal with extensive paralysis. William *James described the case of a woman paralysed almost from the neck down following a hunting accident, who yet experienced emotions when visited by her family. This has been used as evidence against the James–Lange theory of emotion, which is essentially that emotions are visceral sensations, and should therefore cease with sufficiently general paralysis. It was the observation, in classical times, that head wounds are associated with paralysis on the opposite side of the body, that led to concepts of *localization of brain function, with the left hemisphere controlling the right side of the body, and vice versa.

Paralysis is usually organic, due to brain damage or loss of peripheral nerve function, but it can occur as a functional symptom of *hysteria.

**PARANOIA.** Although paranoia today is a diagnosis used to describe patients who exhibit systematized delusions of grandeur and persecution, its original meaning, as the etymology of the word indicates, was 'being out of one's mind'. Heinroth in 1818 appears to have equated paranoia with *verrüchtheit* (madness); Kahlbaum in 1863 was the first psychiatrist to give it its modern meaning, and although he regarded paranoia as a persistent, chronic condition, he believed that paranoid patients suffered from a disorder of intellect. The term survives as the name given to one type of functional *psychosis, viz. that in which the patient holds a coherent, internally consistent, delusional system of beliefs, centring round the conviction that he (or, more rarely, she) is a person of great importance and is on that account being persecuted, despised, and rejected. As Henderson and Gillespie's *Textbook of Psychiatry* (9th edn., 1962) puts it: 'A person so affected believes that he is right, that he is justified in his beliefs, and that anyone who opposes his point of view is behaving maliciously or at least non-understandingly towards him.' Such a person does not subscribe to the view that he is ill, does not accept treatment, does not enter hospital voluntarily, and may do great harm to himself and others: to himself by coming into active collision with a world that does not subscribe to his own exalted view of himself, and to others by attacking those he conceives to be persecuting him. Paranoiacs on occasion commit murders, not infrequently engage in futile litigation, and generally make an infernal nuisance of themselves, quarrelling incessantly with their neighbours and falsely accusing people of trespass or their spouses of infidelity.

True paranoia is, fortunately, rare; it has a bad prognosis and is not amenable to any known treatment. However, despite its rarity, it is for a variety of reasons of considerable interest and importance.

First, incoherent, internally consistent delusions of grandeur and persecution occur in other psychoses, notably in *schizophrenia, where they form part of a clinical picture that includes *hallucinations, emotional withdrawal, and autistic thinking (in which syntax is disrupted). These are three classes of symptom which are conspicuous by their absence in true paranoia. Most but not all textbooks of psychiatry list 'paranoid schizophrenia' as one of three varieties of schizophrenia, the other two being hebephrenic schizophrenia, which is characterized by withdrawal, bizarre mannerisms, and neglect of the person, and catatonic schizophrenia, characterized by periods of excitement and stupor.

Secondly, many people who are not regarded as mentally ill, and who do not come under the care of psychiatrists, display a cluster of personality traits which can be, and nowadays often are, described as paranoid. These people are opinionated, touchy, and have an idea of their own importance which the rest of the world does not endorse. Such people patently suffer from a disorder of self-esteem, not of intellect—their opinions must be correct because they hold them; their families, their careers, their lives must be especially important because they are *their* families, *their* careers, *their* lives—and the same must presumably be so for true paranoia. According to classical psychoanalytical theory, paranoia and paranoid traits generally are narcissistic disorders, the implication being that they indicate fixation at some infantile stage of development during which the self is its own love object; but many contemporary analysts hold that narcissistic self-overestimation is a compensatory reaction to humiliation in infancy and childhood. Later research (Schatzman, 1973) has shown that Daniel Paul Schreber (1842–1911), the subject of *Freud's classic paper 'Psycho-analytical Notes on an Autobiographical Account of Paranoia (Dementia Paranoides)' (1911), was from birth subject to gross mechanical restraints by his father, who was determined to nip in the bud all signs of self-will and 'innate barbarity' in his infant son. Freud, however, made no enquiries into his subject's childhood, took his expressed devotion to his father at its face value, and interpreted his delusions of being persecuted by God as a reversal and projection of repressed homosexual longings for his father.

Thirdly, paranoiac delusions bear a disconcerting, embarrassing resemblance to the beliefs held and propagated by founders of religions, by political leaders, and by some artists. Such people often make claims on behalf of themselves, their religious ideas, their country, their art, which would be regarded as grandiose and delusional if their ideas did not harmonize with the needs of their contemporaries and thereby achieve recognition and endorsement. Nowadays anyone who claimed to be the Messiah, who addressed God as his personal father, and asserted that 'he who is not for me is against me' would be at risk of being referred to a psychiatrist and diagnosed a paranoiac. But presumably in the first century AD His Word spoke to many—as indeed it continues to this day to do. Similarly, any politician who asserted the innate superiority of his own race and claimed that his country was the victim of an international conspiracy would today raise doubts as to his sanity, but in Germany in the 1930s Hitler found all too many people prepared to agree with him. There must, it seems, be some as yet unformulated relationship between the psychology of paranoia and that of prophets and leaders.

Fourthly, the adjective 'paranoid' is sometimes used by psychoanalysts to describe anxiety and ideas that are inferred to be projections of the subject's own impulses, so that, for instance, a person who is unaware of his own hostility may suffer 'paranoid anxiety', imagining that everyone else is hostile towards him, or a person who is unaware of his own homosexual tendencies may have the 'paranoid idea' that other men are always about to make a pass at him. This usage derives historically from Freud's idea that the psychology of paranoia hinges on reversal and projection of unconscious homosexual impulses.

Finally, it must be mentioned that the word 'paranoid' has slipped into general use to refer to enhanced suspiciousness, often with the implication that such suspiciousness is evidence of unusual sensitivity and perceptiveness. Hence the catch-phrases 'Paranoia is total awareness' and 'The fact that you're paranoid doesn't mean that you aren't being followed'.                                      C. R.

Freud, S. (1911). Psycho-Analytical Notes on an Autobiographical Account of Paranoia (Dementia Paranoides). In *Complete Psychological Works*, vol. xii. London.

Schatzman, M. (1973). *Soul Murder*. London.

**PARANORMAL** is the adjective used for phenomena lying outside the range of normal scientific investigations. Among other things it includes communication without physical links, telepathy, clairvoyance, movements of objects without known causes, and extrasensory perception (ESP). What these phenomena have in common is not only the lack of accepted explanations but the much stronger claim—essentially difficult to justify—that there never will be acceptable explanations, even for any future science.

It is said of paranormal phenomena (and it is these suggestions that seem to lie outside science) that they demonstrate powers of disembodied minds, are associated with some kind of consciousness, and occur without physical force or material stimulus. They thus have implications for psychology, and for our views of the mind and its relation to the physical world. Many of the claimed phenomena are commonplace events, such as objects falling off shelves, for which no natural cause can be established. If any explicable reason can be supposed, then the claim vanishes, however bizarre the event, for the onus is always to show that the event *is* paranormal. Although paranormal intervention is nowadays seldom accepted as the reason for any other but very unusual events, except perhaps in *astrology, this has not always been so: 'primitive' explanations of everyday events were often in terms of the direct action of mind on matter, or on other minds.

Research on claims of paranormal phenomena has been and still is active in many countries; but the most influential body organizing experiments and examining such claims is the British Society for Psychical Research. After a century of work, by many highly distinguished people, including scientists of the first rank, there is probably less confidence now in the existence of paranormal phenomena than when the society was founded. As experiments designed to test for extrasensory perception, telepathy, telekinesis, 'fork-bending', and so on are tightened up, the phenomena tend to disappear or turn out to be clearly fraudulent. Of course one cannot say that every case is mistaken or fraudulent; but it is hardly to be taken lightly that, for example, the conjuror James Randi is able by conjuring methods to duplicate Uri Geller's fork-bending and other phenomena which only recently were widely accepted as paranormal. There are, however, a few cases of dramatic demonstrations of claimed paranormal abilities which have never been explained in terms of known or conceivable physics, or as cheating: especially those of Daniel Dunglas *Home (1833–86) who, among other inexplicable reported events, was 'seen' by many people at a party in London to levitate—passing out of one window and through another into a different room—and to perform many other dramatic 'paranormal' feats over many years without ever being 'found out'. On the other hand, there have been several accepted conjurors whose methods, though never ascertained, are assumed not to be paranormal abilities. In any case, it has come as a shock to discover how easily even the best observers and experimenters can suffer *illusions and be mistaken and misled into errors of observation and reporting. Even if all claims of paranormal phenomena are totally rejected, as they have been by such sceptics as David *Hume in his famous 'Essay on Miracles' (1755) and more recently C. E. M. Hansel (1966), it is interesting nevertheless to consider such claims, as they do highlight weaknesses of observation and experiment (for science depends on the reliability and honesty of its practitioners). They may also highlight some extremely difficult questions concerning the relation of mind to matter, and suggest what kinds of evidence might be useful for settling philosophical questions by scientific means, as discussed for example by S. E. Braude (1978).

The Cambridge philosopher Charlie Dunbar *Broad (1887–1971) suggested that we have beliefs which are deeper and more general than scientific theories, and that it is when these 'basic limiting principles', as Broad called them, of acceptable belief are violated that we move into the domain of the paranormal. Broad did not attempt to give an exhaustive list of these limiting principles, beyond which acceptable science cannot go, nor did he say how the limits of scientific acceptance might be determined. No doubt some people do believe that the paranormal is somehow 'beyond' science, and that science is blind to paranormal truths. This may however be difficult to maintain when we consider that many 'paranormal' phenomena are simple and well-known kinds of events—apart from their explanation. So, whether they appear to be within the bounds of science or beyond it depends on showing that they cannot be explained in normal terms in those particular conditions. The difficulty

is to establish that some kind of 'trick' conditions are not in operation, such as a child pushing objects off a shelf with a knitting needle poked through the wall from the next room. For example, there is the famous case of the 'telepathic' boys, who communicated with supersonic whistles hidden in their pockets—with air bulbs which they squeezed according to a code. The high-pitched signals were inaudible to the elderly investigators, who assumed that a paranormal explanation was necessary—until the trick, for trick it was, was found out. But suppose that telepathy can occur by some kind of scientifically acceptable though at present unknown radiation, analogous to radio. (And, after all, radio must seem magical to people with no understanding of its principles—it is amazing enough to those who do!) Telepathy would, then, no longer be regarded as paranormal as it could be explained by science. This brings out the difficulty in defining 'paranormal' as lying outside accepted science—for with new discoveries and theories science often changes dramatically and unpredictably—so what once seemed mysterious or 'paranormal' may become accepted science, as science changes to take account of it. This is so for several past mysteries, which have moved from being regarded as occult or paranormal to being accepted by and even to becoming central in science: such as thunder and lightning being once considered to be the wrath of the Gods, but now understood as the same electricity that we generate and use for wonders of our technology.

While electricity was seen as an occult life fluid—which it appeared to be with its ability to shock and convulse, its frenzied sparks, and its sinuous ethereal glow in discharge tubes responding wonderfully to magnets and to a near-by human hand—both electricity and magnetism were supposed to effect cures, and produce trances and other mental states. Franz *Mesmer (1734–1815) convinced many highly intelligent people with his demonstrations of such vital powers of magnetism, seeming to act directly upon mind. As we see it now, Mesmer was demonstrating hypnotism. He worked with histrionic skill, and most effectively. He made wooden pretend-magnets, which worked as well as the real steel magnets—provided they looked like steel magnets. Mesmer attributed this to some far more general, and indeed all-pervading, spiritual magnetism, acting on mind, though obeying laws of physics (such as being reflected from mirrors). The curious trance states and other phenomena, which Mesmer demonstrated, were gradually distinguished from 'spirit' or 'animal magnetism'—especially after the clinical demonstrations of the French neurologist Jean Martin *Charcot (1825–93)—when hypnotism was finally seen to be a psychological phenomenon, and it was used as a tool for probing the unconscious mind, by Sigmund *Freud who was a pupil of Charcot's.

However all this may be, we remain uncertain about the powers and limits of mind; so claims of paranormal powers can hardly be dismissed out of hand. What seems to underlie accounts of the paranormal is the notion of mind affecting matter, or other minds—but this is exactly what most of us believe happens whenever we do anything at all, even just waggling a finger. This is part of the deep problem of dualistic accounts of 'mental' mind and 'material' brain (see DUALISM). A way out for psychology is to suppose that minds are not entities which control behaviour, or brains, but are generated by brain activity. Hence the significance of the various kinds of mind–brain identity theories (see THEOLOGY and MIND–BRAIN IDENTITY), which deny a causal relationship between mind and brain; it should be recognized, however, that mind–brain identity accounts are controversial and are hard to formulate. Clear-cut paranormal phenomena demonstrating disembodied mind might conceivably show identity theories to be untenable. So paranormal accounts do have empirical consequences, even though—in spite of the immense work of controlled experiments, especially on telepathy, and the collections of accounts of bizarre phenomena by Frederic *Myers (1903) and later writers—we may seriously doubt whether there are any such phenomena.

For further discussion of the paranormal see EXTRA-SENSORY PERCEPTION; PARANORMAL PHENOMENA IN ANCIENT GREECE; PARANORMAL PHENOMENA: THE PROBLEM OF PROOF; PARANORMAL PHENOMENA AND THE UNCONSCIOUS; PARAPSYCHOLOGY: A HISTORY OF RESEARCH; PARAPSYCHOLOGY AND THE MIND–BODY PROBLEM.                                                    R. L. G.

Braude, S. E. (1978). On the Meaning of 'Paranormal'. In Ludwig, J. (ed.), Philosophy and Parapsychology, 227–44.
Broad, C. D. (1962). Lectures on Psychical Research. London.
Hansel, C. E. M. (1966). ESP: A Scientific Evaluation. New York.
Hume, D. (1748). Of miracles. In Enquiry Concerning Human Understanding, Section X.
Ludwig, J. (ed.) (1978). Philosophy and Parapsychology. Buffalo.
Myers, F. W. H. (1903). Human Personality and its Survival After Bodily Death. London.

**PARANORMAL PHENOMENA: THE PROBLEM OF PROOF.** By the late nineteenth century the spectacular success of science as an explanatory system was drawing attention to a corresponding failure: the inability of science to cope with a wide range of reported phenomena called 'supernatural'. These ranged from *ghosts to *levitation, and included thought-reading, seance-room 'materialization', water-divining, communications with the dead, precognition, hypnosis (arguably), and a long list of others. Did these phenomena really exist, and if they did why did they seem to stay so stubbornly outside the scientific worldview? In 1882 a group of British scholars and scientists founded the Society for Psychical Research with the aim of tackling these questions in a scientific spirit and removing this 'intellectual

scandal'. In the ensuing hundred years or so, a steadily growing body of research, of gradually increasing sophistication, has been devoted to the challenge in universities and laboratories all over the world. A century later may be an appropriate time to take stock of the position and to consider how far the aims of these early parapsychologists have been fulfilled.

Perhaps the only non-controversial statement that can be made about the present position is that the controversy continues. On the one hand we see results continuing to be reported. Several journals more or less regularly publish positive findings from respectable laboratories, written by people with scientific training and (often) higher degrees. On the other hand, with the single exception of hypnosis, not even the existence of one of the phenomena originally classed as supernatural, or later as paranormal, has achieved general acceptance among the scientific community; not one demonstrable, or repeatable, paranormal effect has been discovered; not one characteristic or law has been found which turns up in all those experiments that claim a positive result.

What are we to make of this situation? Should we argue that, since results continue to appear in such a wide range of circumstances in space and over time, there must be at least something there— for there's no smoke without fire? Or is it more reasonable to argue that, if the effects were real, such an intensive search over such a long period would surely have turned up something demonstrable?

If we are to choose between these two interpretations, we need to look rather carefully at the nature of the evidence that is being produced for and against the paranormal, and in particular at the social and psychological setting within which the controversy occurs.

First, it is important to note that paranormal phenomena are not claimed to be repeatable at will. Therefore, in order to claim evidence against the paranormal it is not sufficient to report that an experiment was done and no paranormal effect was obtained, for this proves nothing. In fact the only evidence *against* consists of criticisms of the evidence *in favour*. This situation weights the scales against the sceptic.

It is constructive to consider a case history. The Soal–Goldney experiments, with Shackleton as mind-reader (or 'percipient'), were carried out in 1941–3 under S. G. Soal, a London University lecturer in mathematics. They were widely quoted at the time, and for many years thereafter, as a model of rigorous experimentation, and stood for long as the backbone of the evidence for precognition. So strict were the conditions, with multiple witnessing and numerous changes of personnel and of experimental design, that they were held to be proof against fraud not only on the part of the percipient but by the experimenters themselves. Yet, over the years, the experiments gradually crumbled under the assaults of sceptics.

In 1955, G. R. Price showed that several methods of fraud were possible if collusion were assumed between Soal and two other participants.

In 1960, Hansel showed that only one other participant needed to be in the trick. Some statistical features of the data seemed to lend some support to such a hypothesis, though far from conclusively.

In 1956, pressure from sceptics obliged Soal to reveal that, contrary to the published report, the original records were not available for study because he had lost them. Handwritten copies, however, were still available.

In 1960, further pressure from sceptics obliged him to publish a more serious admission, which had been known to some of them by hearsay. During the experiments one of the participants had reported seeing Soal improperly 'altering the figures'—specifically, changing '1's into '4's and '5's. A full contemporary report had been kept by his collaborator Goldney, but Soal had up to that point refused to allow publication, using the threat of a libel action.

In 1971, Medhurst reported a computerized attempt to identify the sequence of target digits that Soal had used. He was unable to trace the sequences in any relevant sources and concluded that Soal's account of the way in which the targets were prepared must be incorrect.

In 1973 and 1974, Scott and Haskell showed that there was strong statistical evidence in the experimental records supporting the allegation that Soal had 'altered the figures', changing '1's into '4's and '5's among the target digits in such a way as to turn misses into hits. This evidence appeared in three of the forty sittings (including the one in which this manipulation had apparently been observed) and could account for all the above-chance scoring in these three sittings. (There was no sign of such an effect in the remaining sittings.)

The *coup de grâce* came in 1978, when Markwick published the results of an astonishingly tenacious pursuit of the line opened earlier by Medhurst. She first showed that the target digits contained a considerable number of runs of consecutive digits that were repetitions of runs used in earlier sessions, and that this could not have arisen by chance. This in itself was not particularly serious. However, she also showed that in many such cases the repetition was not exact but there were *intrusions*—digits inserted in the sequence—and that these intruded digits *were nearly always hits*. The implication of improper manipulation seems almost inescapable.

The lesson that this story teaches us is not simply that Soal's defenders were wrong and that a respectable academic *can* cheat in his own experiments. Equally significant is the time and effort that was required to demonstrate this conclusion. If we confine ourselves to the authors mentioned above, six researchers were involved over a period of thirty-five years. Yet the Soal–Shackleton experiments have received more attention from sceptics than any others. Such an effort of destructive criticism is simply not generally available for tackling the mass of less striking experiments that are regularly published. In our society, destructive work is not regarded favourably, and an institution devoted to criticism would have difficulty attracting funds. An experimenter working to demonstrate a new scientific phenomenon may be fired with enough enthusiasm to last him a lifetime; he may see himself as a pioneer on the frontier of knowledge and potentially a figure whose name will go down in history. But where is a sceptic to find his motivation? At the very moment when the researcher begins to lose his belief in the phenomena he begins to lose his interest in the issue.

Once again the scales are weighted against the sceptic.

The Soal–Shackleton exposure is exceptional in another respect. Very few parapsychology experiments have been so well documented. Detailed records of the procedures are available for study, including copies of the score sheets, and these proved to contain hidden but ultimately damning evidence of manipulation. In far more experiments only minimal records are kept. It is possible that in many cases errors or deceptions were made which left no trace in any subsequent record, so that their detection after the event is literally impossible. Once again, the sceptic's task is rendered more difficult.

For these reasons the argument that there is no smoke without fire—that the continuing flow of positive results proves the reality of the phenomena since the evidence has not been systematically disproved—is scarcely compelling. If the paranormal did not exist the situation could well be very close to that which we observe today. We have only to assume a small but continuing flow of researchers ready to deceive themselves, or perhaps to deceive others, victims of wishful thinking or conscious frauds. That such people are rare is no doubt true—but so are successful parapsychologists. If the paranormal does not exist then a parapsychology experiment is a selection procedure for finding such people among the overwhelming majority of genuine scientists. On this hypothesis the evidence will continue to flow in, from all countries and perhaps all centuries to come. As for the sceptic, he may expose the more important cases but he can never hope to catch up; the dice are loaded against him.

The characteristic symptom of this situation would be a continuing failure to build up any solid body of accepted knowledge in the area of the paranormal. For the time being this is the position we observe. As long as this situation persists it will be reasonable to regard the case for the paranormal as not proven, though outright disproof is certainly unattainable.　　　　　　　　c. s.

Hansel, C. E. M. (1979). *ESP and Parapsychology: a critical re-evaluation*. New York.

Markwick, B. (1978). The Soal–Goldney experiments

with Basil Shackleton; new evidence of manipulation. *Proceedings of the Society for Psychical Research*, **56**, 211.

Scott, C. and Haskell, P. (1974). Fresh light on the Shackleton experiments? *Proceedings of the Society for Psychical Research*, **56**, 209.

Soal, S. G. and Goldney, K. M. (1943). Experiments in precognitive telepathy. *Proceedings of the Society for Psychical Research*, **47**, 21.

Wolman, B. B. (ed.) (1977). *Handbook of Parapsychology*. New York.

## PARANORMAL PHENOMENA AND THE UNCONSCIOUS.

In 1972, the Toronto Society for Psychical Research, under the direction of A. R. G. Owen, began an experiment that has already become a classic of *parapsychology. What they did was to attempt to *create* a ghost. One member of the group invented the life story of a seventeenth-century nobleman named Philip, including a jealous wife and a gypsy mistress who was falsely accused of witchcraft and burned at the stake. The group then sat around, meditated, and attempted to 'conjure up' Philip. After long effort they succeeded. The table began to vibrate, then there were raps; using a code of raps, the 'spirit' identified itself as Philip, and told the life story that had been invented for it. On a later occasion the experiment was performed in front of a television audience; the table waltzed up on to the stage and performed its antics before the cameras.

The experiments seem to confirm a theory long held by many parapsychologists: that psychical phenomena originate in the subconscious minds of human beings (although we should also admit the possibility that the group conjured up a real 'disembodied entity' that chose to masquerade as Philip). Ever since the late nineteenth century, psychical researchers have recognized that poltergeist phenomena usually centre round a disturbed child or adolescent: that is to say, the bangs and crashes and unaccountable movements of objects associated with poltergeists seem to be in some way caused by the juvenile 'focus' of the disturbances. Yet in the majority of cases, the 'focus' is unaware of being the cause. Which in turn seems to suggest that the phenomena are 'caused' by the unconscious mind.

This clearly raises more problems than it solves. By what mechanism does the unconscious mind move objects around? Does it, for example, possess invisible pseudopodia? Why should such powers be beyond the reach of the conscious mind? What precisely do we mean by the 'unconscious mind'?

Now, for all practical purposes, the concept of the unconscious was invented by Sigmund *Freud, although it can be traced back as far as *Leibniz. And it is worth considering how Freud came by the idea. In Paris in the early 1880s, J. M. *Charcot was intrigued by the phenomena of hysteria—women whose stomachs swelled up in phantom pregnancies, or whose limbs were frozen by hysterical paralyses. He observed that hysteria was

closely related to hypnosis: for example, a hypnotist could sometimes cause a blister by telling the subject that he had been touched by a red-hot poker. It was Freud, who studied with Charcot in 1886, who saw the tremendous implications of these observations. The *conscious* mind cannot make the stomach swell up, or cause stigmata to appear on the hands of religious 'somnambules'. If the unconscious part of the mind can do this, then clearly its power is in some ways greater than that of the conscious mind. We are all familiar with the simpler manifestations of the unconscious mind—someone talks about itching and we itch; someone talks about coughing and we feel the need to clear our throats. What Freud recognized was that the unconscious mind can be persuaded to perform astonishing feats by means of suggestion—either of a hypnotist, or of the conscious mind.

Charcot apparently failed to grasp the import of his discovery; so, oddly enough, did Freud. He had, in effect, stumbled upon the mechanism of *neurosis. My conscious mind scans and assesses the world, and reacts accordingly. If it decides that the tasks confronting it are unutterably tiresome, we experience a kind of inner collapse, a feeling of 'Oh no'. What has happened is that the unconscious has responded instantly to a suggestion of futility by a *withdrawal* of vitality. This in turn gives the conscious 'self' a deeper sense of futility, and the continual 'feedback effect'—a kind of vicious circle—produces neurosis. Anyone who has seen the old Laurel and Hardy films has observed the same mechanism. Whenever they find themselves in some preposterous situation, Stan looks at Ollie's face to see how he is reacting. If Ollie looks cheerful, Stan grins broadly; if Ollie looks unhappy, Stan is plunged into gloom. He always *over-reacts*. The unconscious mind is Stan, and it takes its cues from Ollie. The psychiatrist Viktor Frankl tells a story of how prisoners at Auschwitz were moved by train to Dachau. The journey took three days, during which time they were frozen and half-starved. At Dachau they had to stand in the freezing rain all night because someone had missed the roll-call; and yet, Frankl said, they were all relaxed and happy, laughing and joking, *because Dachau had no incinerator chimney*. This is an example of the sustaining power of the unconscious. Ollie grins broadly because Dachau has no incinerator, and Stan positively dances with delight. Here we have an immensely powerful 'feedback' mechanism, capable of explaining all neurosis—and perhaps a great deal of physical illness too. The unconscious is nothing less than our *vital support system*. Yet it responds to suggestions from the conscious 'self'. Freud, it seems, failed to recognize this, and went on to create his own essentially sexual theory of neurosis.

Now it is fairly easy to accept that the unconscious mind can produce 'psychosomatic' effects, like phantom pregnancies and miracle cures; but it is altogether more difficult to see how it could produce 'psychokinetic' effects, like causing a table to waltz around the room.

The question begins to seem a little less baffling if we clear up certain linguistic confusions. For example, as soon as we ask, 'Why should the unconscious mind possess powers that the conscious mind doesn't possess?', we see that it is not a question of the mind 'possessing' anything. *I* possess certain powers—for example, I can waggle my toes. In the same sense, I also possess *consciousness; it is an attribute, or power. The term 'unconscious' seems to refer to another area that includes intuitions and buried memories; by the same rules of grammar, one assumes that it is also one of my 'possessions'.

If (for the sake of argument) we assume a central 'I' or self, which is responsible for acts of will, we can also see that these acts can be more or less 'conscious'. Digestion and breathing seem to involve an unconscious form of will; they certainly take place without my conscious volition. The kind of will involved in urinating seems to be partly conscious, partly unconscious; I apparently control the mechanism, yet if it is inhibited by nervous tension there is very little I can do about it.

The 'unconscious theory' of psychic phenomena suggests, quite simply, that the 'I' possesses powers of psychokinesis: the ability to move physical objects through an unknown form of energy. Recent experiments in psychokinesis involving such 'psychics' as Nina Kulagina and Felicia Parise would seem to indicate that even the conscious will is able to exert a slight degree of psychokinetic force—enough to move very small objects. The implication, apparently, is that, once again, the unconscious will is far more powerful.

There is, of course, no agreement about the nature of the force involved. Professor John Taylor is on record as believing that it could be analogous to radio waves. Most 'psychics' are inclined to feel that this is too simplistic. One obvious objection is that simple physical models cannot explain other paranormal phenomena such as precognition. *If* it is possible to have precognitive glimpses of the future—for example, in *dreams, as recorded by J. W. *Dunne—then there must be some sense in which the future has already taken place; moreover, there must be some part of the mind— or self—that exists 'outside time', and is capable of 'scanning' these future events. Common sense cannot suggest a 'model' to explain precognition; it can only flatly deny that such a thing is possible. Yet there are as many well-authenticated cases of precognition as of telepathy, psychokinesis, or second-sight. If time is so radically different from our conceptions of it, then the same may apply to space, and Professor Taylor's attempts to provide models for psychokinesis may be, at the very least, irrelevant.

The basic question, clearly, is of the nature of the 'I' to whose common sense we so frequently appeal. This common-sense 'I' is my measure of the possible; if he tells me something is nonsense,

it is almost impossible not to be convinced. Yet experiments in brain physiology (see Sperry, 1970) have shown that this confidence may be misplaced. The right and left sides of the brain are virtually two different personalities or selves, the left side controlling language and logical functions, the right side concerned with intuition and insight. When the nerves connecting them are severed, the right side of the brain knows nothing of what the left side is doing. (See SPLIT-BRAIN AND THE MIND.) A patient who is shown an obscene picture in the left half of his visual field (which is seen by the right side of the brain) shows signs of embarrassment. Asked why he is blushing, he replies truthfully: 'I don't know.' The 'I' who responds is the 'talking I'; yet he considers himself the rightful occupant of the head—in fact, the only occupant. Yet the intuitive half of the brain has just as much reason for regarding itself as the seat of the 'legitimate I'.

All of which raises the obvious speculation that when we speak of the 'unconscious', we are actually speaking of this right side of the brain (or of the 'I' who inhabits it). But this conveniently simple picture of a 'dual self' is brought into question by the widely observed phenomenon of multiple personality—studied, for example, by Freud's great contemporary Pierre *Janet. (See DISSOCIATION OF THE PERSONALITY.) This seems to suggest that we may all contain dozens of 'I's. What is so startling about so many of Janet's case histories—and more recent ones like the famous 'three faces of Eve'—is that the same body or brain appears literally to be taken over by distinct personalities, like a car with several drivers. And Janet noted that, in most of these cases, the personalities can be arranged in a hierarchy, with the maturest at the top, the most rudimentary at the bottom. The picture that seems to emerge is of a kind of 'ladder of selves', in which the person we call 'I' is merely the rung of the ladder on which my conscious awareness happens to be resting at any particular moment in time. C. G. *Jung even made the startling suggestion that the person into which we may eventually evolve—if we live long enough—may be already present from birth.

Devising methods to test such theories raises, of course, methodological problems. In science, the basic aim is to *observe* as accurately as possible, then to try to interpret the observations. It is important not to allow 'interpretation' to sneak into the act of observation, for we all know how easy it is to distort conclusions by allowing them to embody expectations. If parapsychological phenomena—or some of them—originate in acts of unconscious will, then it looks as if the mind is already involved before it starts observing.

Here, at least, the answer may be close to hand. There *is* a philosophical method aimed at preventing unconscious prejudices from slipping into the perceptual processes; its creator, Edmund *Husserl, called it transcendental *phenomenology, and its basic recognition is that *all* acts of perception are 'intentional'. (See INTENTIONALITY.) If present trends in parapsychology are anything to go by, the next generation of investigators could do worse than take a course in Husserlian philosophy.

It would, no doubt, be an exaggeration to say that parapsychology is at last entering its 'Newtonian' phase, when masses of disconnected observation can be unified by a single theory. But it is worth bearing in mind that *Newton arrived at his theory by asking the right questions. At least parapsychologists like A. R. G. Owen, who conjured up Philip, seem to have stumbled on some of the right questions.                              C. W.

Ellenberger, H. F. (1970). *The Discovery of the Unconscious: the history and evolution of dynamic psychiatry*. New York.

Frankl, V. (1963). *Man's Search for Meaning: an introduction to logotherapy* (originally *From Death Camp to Existentialism*). New York.

Jaynes, J. (1977). *The Origin of Consciousness in the Breakdown of the Bicameral Mind*. Boston.

Jung, C. G. (1957). On the psychology and pathology of so-called occult phenomena. In *Collected Works*, vol. 1: *Psychiatric Studies*. London.

Owen, I. M. and Sparrow, M. (1976). *Conjuring up Philip: an adventure in psychokinesis*. Toronto.

Sjöval, B. (1964). *Janet and the Psychology of Tension*. Uppsala.

Sperry, R. W. (1970). Perception in the absence of neocortical commissures. In *Perception and Its Disorders* (Association for Research in Nervous and Mental Diseases), **48**.

**PARANORMAL PHENOMENA IN ANCIENT GREECE.** Modern investigators and practitioners of so-called paranormal phenomena feel themselves to be operating in a dubious but exciting fringe area of human experience. In ancient Greece, many objectively similar phenomena were embedded in the traditional religious structure, and were thus, until that structure came into question, quite differently perceived. A translation intended to convey in Greek the content of the modern term would introduce the notion of the gods, and would therefore exclude the notion of supernormality, the gods being part of normal experience. Greece's most important and respected centralized religious institution, the oracle at Delphi, operated by trance mediumship. The priestess, an uneducated woman, seems to have entered an auto-suggestive trance induced by prescribed ritual acts, and in this condition—which was understood as possession by the prophetic god Apollo—to have answered the questions put to her. There followed some degree of editing and interpretation by the temple priests. Two typical features of the finished responses, their verse form and notorious ambiguity, may reflect an occasional (or original) practice of the prophetess, but in the majority of cases were probably due to the priests. Trance mediumship was also practised at various other oracles, and by the less respectable marketplace prophets known as 'words in belly'. The normal Greek word for prophet seems to derive from the verb 'to be mad', in reference to ecstatic trance. Unlike the modern medium, the ancient

trance prophet sought contact with the gods, not the dead, and his aim was the practical one of securing prophecy or advice.

Other paranormal prophetic states are less important in Greek culture. Divination by mirror-gazing (the mirror functioning like the modern crystal ball) is probably referred to by Aristophanes in the fifth century BC; subsequently, water-gazing seems, under Oriental influence, to have become more popular. We may perhaps recognize the widespread phenomenon of glossolalia in two isolated references, one to an oracular priest who answered a foreign enquirer in his own language, the other to priestesses credited with a universal gift of tongues. *Socrates was guided by a divine voice that always dissuaded him from action and never instigated it; like most things about Socrates, this was an exception, an enigma to the Greeks themselves.

Oracular practice was of course founded on the belief that knowledge of the future, or of distant contemporary events, was obtainable; but such knowledge was attributed to divine revelation, not telepathy, clairvoyance, or precognition on the part of humans. Some moderns might wish to reinterpret in these terms certain phenomena that were claimed by the ancients as proof of divine power—prophecies successfully delivered before the enquiry had been voiced (priestess's telepathy), for instance, or the dream revelation of a lost person's location (dreamer's clairvoyance); unfortunately the evidence for the phenomenon will seldom bear much weight. This is equally true of the relatively few early cases where a man rather than a god is explicitly credited with these powers. We do, however, find interesting theories of paranormal psychic powers in certain accounts of the dream that attempted to preserve its veridical character while excluding divine intervention (see DREAMS IN ANCIENT GREECE). It was argued either that the dreamer received images or vibrations from the person or object he dreamed of, or that the soul exercised special powers while released from the trammels of the sleeping body. Stoic philosophers add an explicit explanation of precognition (as distinct from clairvoyance): it is the soul's inference from perceptible present causes of future events. Such subtleties are, of course, very far removed from popular religion. In the early period, belief in direct divine revelation was so strong that mortals claimed to have experienced actual epiphanies of the gods, usually in wild country regions.

Popular stories told how those violently killed or improperly buried haunted houses or graveyards. There may be an allusion to a poltergeist in a speech of 400 BC, but the phenomenon is otherwise unattested throughout antiquity. The paranormal physical phenomena that are reported are, in general, cult miracles—the spring that regularly flowed with wine at a festival of Dionysus, doors flying open at the (invisible) approach of a god, and the like. But to collect all the paranormal feats attributed to gods would be an endless task, because gods by definition perform with ease tasks impossible for men.                                    R. C. T. P.

Dodds, E. R. (1973). Supernormal phenomena in classical antiquity. In his *The Ancient Concept of Progress*. Oxford.

**PARAPSYCHOLOGY: A HISTORY OF RESEARCH.** The term 'parapsychology' was introduced in the 1930s to refer to the scientific investigation of *paranormal phenomena—in particular the allegedly extra-sensory powers of the mind (see EXTRA-SENSORY PERCEPTION). Previously this interesting but highly questionable area of science had generally been described as 'psychical research'.

Man has always been fascinated by the possibility that his mind may be capable of exercising unusual powers not apparently linked to the physical senses—telepathy, the capacity to see the future, etc.—and it has to be admitted that mythology, religion, and much of art and literature are on his side in this respect. Furthermore there exists a great body of anecdotal evidence and personal testimony to the effect that such powers exist—almost everyone has had an experience which could be interpreted as having been telepathic, and most people have listened to friends or relations giving superficially convincing accounts of precognitive dreams they have had or of paranormal occurrences that have changed their lives. The history of psychical research or parapsychology in fact reflects the attempts of three or four generations of scientists to convert this intriguing anecdotal material into something more tangible—specifically to trap it in the laboratory. Throughout the course of this history, there has been a continuing shift of emphasis in the focus of research, but for the sake of simplicity it can be conveniently divided into three overlapping phases or periods: spiritualistic research, psychical research, and modern parapsychology.

**Spiritualistic research.** (See also SPIRITUALISM.) The great achievements of nineteenth-century science seemed to be unfolding a picture of a universe of a depressingly materialistic kind, a vast and rather pointless cosmos made up of tiny billiard-balls known as atoms and with no trace of souls or spirits. But most Victorian scientists brought up in the ethos of orthodox Christianity were expected to believe in the reality of an immortal, non-physical soul. For this reason a substantial body of them became involved in the minority religion of spiritualism, taking the line that if souls or spirits survived the death of the physical body then these spirits must exist *somewhere* in the universe, and should, in principle, be contactable. This remarkable period of science saw some of the outstanding brains of the time—the physicists Sir Oliver Lodge and Sir William Crookes, the Nobel prize-winning biologist Charles Richet, the anthropologist Alfred Russel

*Wallace, and numerous others of equivalent calibre—solemnly attempting to induce spirit forms to materialize in their laboratories. No better testimony could be offered of the simple logic and unbounded optimism of Victorian scientists, but their unbridled enthusiasm for their findings led other, more critical and sceptical colleagues to conduct their own experiments. The result was that medium after medium was exposed as fraudulent, the pioneers were shown up to be gullible, incompetent, or both, and this phase of psychical research, which had fleetingly looked as though it might have almost revolutionary importance, came to an inglorious end. Crookes, Lodge, Wallace, and others, having committed themselves to spiritualism, not unnaturally remained steadfastly loyal to it, but by 1900 scientific interest was moving away from seances and was concentrating on 'more plausible' aspects of the paranormal.

**Psychical research.** Put quite simply, the second phase was the era of the 'ghost hunter', a period when scientists and affluent amateurs turned their attention to such phenomena as manifestations in haunted houses, poltergeist activity, demonic possession, apparitions, premonitions, and other such spectacular and supposedly paranormal events. It also included a large number of casual studies of telepathy and precognitive dreams. The open-minded, amateurish, and 'gentleman scientist' approach of the time is epitomized perhaps by J. W. *Dunne's book *An Experiment with Time*, an influential work, which plotted the author's *ad hoc* investigation into his own dream-life and its supposedly precognitive content. Almost equally representative were the popularized investigations and writings of Mr Harry Price, who made a decrepit Suffolk rectory world-famous as 'The Most Haunted House in England'. Price's research findings, and indeed those of all amateur, non-quantifiable psychic investigations, took a heavy blow when he was exposed by members of the Society for Psychical Research for faking phenomena at Borley. Since then (he was exposed in 1955) it is probably true to say that 'ghost hunting' is no longer considered to be anything much more than crank or fringe science.

**Modern parapsychology.** The third phase was ushered in by the opening of a special university department devoted to the investigation of ESP at Duke University in North Carolina. The department was headed by a young biologist, Dr Joseph Banks Rhine, who, much influenced by the great British psychologist William *McDougall, was convinced that the supposedly paranormal powers of the mind were essentially psychological phenomena, and should thus be investigated with the tools of traditional psychological research. The failure of the pioneers of psychical research to achieve anything concrete he assumed to be not because they were investigating ephemera, but because they had not attempted to quantify the phenomena they were supposed to be studying. Throughout the 1930s, therefore, Rhine and his co-workers embarked on a lengthy series of quantifiable experiments, mainly using decks of specially designed cards (Zener cards) for the ESP tests, and automatically thrown dice for the psychokinesis (PK) tests. The admirable rationale for these studies was that they allowed the experimenter to compare the results achieved with what would have been expected by chance. For example, in a deck of twenty-five cards containing five each of five distinct symbols, one would expect, on average, five to be guessed right 'by chance'; persistent deviations above chance over a long series of trials would suggest that the guesser was receiving some information about the test cards. This in turn would imply that if the experiments had been so rigorously controlled as to exclude all normal or known sensory cues, then the information must be coming via 'extra-sensory perception'.

Rhine's early results in fact yielded just such sustained 'above-chance' scores and he swiftly claimed that he had established ESP as a legitimate phenomenon, or set of phenomena. As might be expected, however, his claims were met with considerable opposition from the psychological establishment. Were his subjects physically completely isolated from the experimenter so that information could not be passed over unwittingly—for example, by unconscious whispering or other non-deliberate cues? Were checks on the data and records precise enough to ensure that minor errors were not made, either unconsciously or deliberately, to bias the results in a pro-ESP direction? To do him justice, Rhine tightened up his procedures on both these accounts—separating subject and experimenter in different buildings, for example, and arranging independent verification and analysis of the results. As a consequence, the above-chance results became rarer, but still remained sufficiently common for them to constitute apparently inarguable evidence for ESP. But then came another, and more fundamental, criticism. When psychologists not committed to a belief in ESP attempted to repeat the Duke findings in their own laboratories, they simply failed to come up with any positive results. The Duke team replied with more sets of positive findings, but the critics again failed to replicate them. Aware that this non-repeatability was a cardinal weakness in their armour, the parapsychologists came up with the ingenious argument that a significant factor in ESP might be the attitude of the experimenter to the phenomena; if he was inclined to be unduly sceptical or dismissive, he might have a 'negative effect' on the results. This is a plausible but also a glib argument which seems to imply that only those who believe in ESP are fitted to investigate it—a point of view which cuts across the main spirit of scientific research. More recently, however, parapsychology received a severe blow when the director of research at Rhine's laboratory (Rhine had himself retired) was caught flagrantly modifying experimental results to provide pro-ESP data, thus offering up to the critics of parapsychology evidence for an argument they had frequently advanced in the past—that no researcher, however distinguished, can be exempted from suspicion of fraud, minor or major, in this controversial field. Since this rather cataclysmic exposure, new evidence has appeared which seems to imply that one of the most distinguished British parapsychologists, Dr S. G. Soal, was also guilty of falsifying data in a key experiment. (See PARANORMAL PHENOMENA: THE PROBLEM OF PROOF.)

At the time of writing, it looks as though the third phase of research in this area is coming to a close without parapsychology having demonstrated ESP to the general satisfaction of science. Indeed there appears to be a swing back to the study of poltergeist phenomena, paranormal healing, and the spectacular claims of Uri Geller and others, almost as though the failure of the strictly experimental approach has been implicitly recognized and agreed upon by all workers in the field. In sum, while it is true that many feel that parapsychology or psychical research is still a legitimate area of study, most scientists who have studied the topic in any depth are inclined to the view that a hundred years of fairly dedicated research has yielded disappointingly little in an area which should have offered great riches.

C. E.

**PARAPSYCHOLOGY AND THE MIND–BODY PROBLEM.** The scientific study of the *paranormal, originally 'psychical research' but nowadays generally known as parapsychology, is, historically speaking, a product of the conflict between science and religion that came to a head in Victorian England. It was then that the belief in an immaterial soul that animated the body when alive and survived its dissolution at death, which had been so central to most of the world religions, had to contend against an increasingly self-confident scientific materialism. The new psychophysiologists and experimental psychologists who followed in the wake of Hermann von *Helmholtz were particularly anxious to explain behaviour in terms that did not require the intervention of any kind of inner occult entity. Moreover, the *Darwinian revolution, which stressed the continuity of living things, seemed to make nonsense of the idea of an immortal soul that was the special prerogative of man, as *Descartes, who is credited with formulating the mind–body problem in its classic form, had taught.

The group of scientists and scholars who came together in 1882 to found the Society for Psychical Research in London, of whom Frederic *Myers was, perhaps, the most important in this connection, were all acutely aware of the materialistic implications of contemporary science and were no less convinced of the futility of trying to counter it with a reaffirmation of the dogmas of revealed religion. They believed, however, that it might still be possible to defend the autonomy of mind, as distinct from brain, if the objective methodology of science were to be deployed in the study of so-called paranormal phenomena. These phenomena, which defied a conventional scientific explanation, had been part of popular belief down the ages and, later, after the rise of *mesmerism and then *spiritualism, had been reported as occurring under controlled conditions. From the start, two classes of paranormal phenomena were recognized: (i) the paraphysical, which meant, originally, manifestations of physical mediumship such as the levitation of objects and the materialization of human figures, or else the effects observed in the course of poltergeist disturbances, and (ii) the paracognitive, which meant the awareness of external events otherwise than via the known sensory channels, i.e. telepathy, clairvoyance, precognition, etc. Later, when, under the influence of J. B. Rhine, statistical-type tests became the standard method of studying the phenomena, the former class came to be subsumed under the heading of PK (psychokinesis) and the latter under the heading of ESP (*extra-sensory perception), the two together being technically referred to by the generic term 'psi'.

Of particular importance to the pioneers of psychical research, and especially to Myers, was the search for proofs of survival, usually by examining ostensible communications from the deceased received through a medium. Had such proofs been forthcoming, nothing could well have afforded a more absolute vindication of a full-blown dualist solution of the mind–body problem, but this was not to be. At most it could be claimed that the simplest interpretation of the evidence demanded the survivalist hypothesis—yet, paradoxically, the greater the success of the psychical researchers in adducing evidence for the various paranormal powers of mind, the more alternative possibilities they opened up for reinterpreting the survival evidence. At all events, at the present time, the problem of survival is a peripheral rather than a mainstream concern of parapsychologists.

From the standpoint of the mind–body problem, perhaps the two salient features of the 'psi process' are, first, that it does not appear to be governed by constraints of space, time, or material screening such as delimit normal physical communication and, secondly, that it appears to achieve its results with an immediacy that suggests some kind of teleological rather than mechanistic causation. According to one current theory, proposed by Thouless and Wiesner (1947), psi is to be understood as an extension, directed on to an external target-system, of a power which, normally, we use to control our own brain when engaged in ordinary perception or in voluntary movement.

It should not be thought, however, that all parapsychologists are necessarily committed to a dualist interpretation of the mind–brain relationship. At the present time especially, many exponents prefer to think of psi as essentially a function of the brain, or of some special brain-mechanism or process. The importance of parapsychology, as they see it, lies not in the vindication of a dualist metaphysic, but in the extended scope of physics which it suggests, so that, eventually, what we now refer to as paranormal will be understood as no less lawful or physical than any other natural phenomenon. Recently a number of physicists who have been attracted to the field have been attempting to build a theoretical bridge between psi phenomena and one possible interpretation of quantum theory. Whether or not their efforts will prove fruitful, it could be a mistake to suppose that parapsychology as such, any more than any other body of empirical knowledge, could ever settle the philosophical issues raised by the mind–body problem.

Nevertheless, just as certain facts inevitably strengthen the plausibility of a materialist interpretation, so other facts, if accepted, would tend only to enhance the plausibility of a mentalist interpretation. The position which could, probably most fairly, be described as the current orthodoxy in philosophical circles of the English-speaking world is to accept some variant of the 'mind–brain identity thesis', the view that mental events and processes are no more than a particular aspect of brain events and processes. This view draws its empirical support partly from the achievements of the brain sciences, especially with regard to the detailed effects of brain lesions on mental functioning (see NEUROPSYCHOLOGY), and partly from the new sciences of *cybernetics and *artificial intelligence which seek to demonstrate rational and purposeful behaviour in machines. Indeed, the computer analogy which now dominates cognitive psychology has created a conception of man as an information-processing system which has become the mainstay of the modern materialist view of mind. On the other side, parapsychology alone can provide empirical support for the transcendent view of mind. So long, however, as the parapsychological evidence is open to question, the contest is bound to be an uneven one. It is an astounding fact that, a century after the founding of the Society for Psychical Research, there is still a total lack of consensus regarding the actuality of any parapsychological phenomenon. (See PARANORMAL PHENOMENA: THE PROBLEM OF PROOF.)

J. BE.

Broad, C. D. (1953). The relevance of psychical research to philosophy. In his *Religion, Philosophy and Psychical Research* (and repr. in Wheatley and Edge, op. cit.). London.

Burt, C. (1967). Psychology and parapsychology. In Smythies, J. R. (ed.), op. cit.

Edge, H. L., Morris, R. L., Rush, J. H., and Palmer, J. (1986). *Foundations of Parapsychology*. London.

French, P. A. (ed.) (1975). *Philosophers in Wonderland*. Saint Paul, Minnesota.

Ludwig, J. (ed.) (1978). *Philosophy and Parapsychology*. Buffalo, New York.

Myers, F. W. H. (1903). *Human Personality and its Survival of Bodily Death*, 2 vols. London.

Price, H. H. (1949). Psychical research and human personality. *Hibbert Journal*, **47** (repr. in Smythies, J. R. (ed.), op. cit.).

Smythies, J. R. (ed.) (1967). *Science and ESP*. London.

Thouless, R. H. and Wiesner, B. P. (1947). The psi process in normal and 'paranormal' psychology. *Proceedings of the Society for Psychical Research*, **48**, 177–97.

Wheatley, J. M. and Edge, H. L. (eds.) (1976). *Philosophical Dimensions of Parapsychology*. Springfield, Illinois.

Wolman, B. B. (ed.) (1977). *Handbook of Parapsychology*. New York.

**PARASUICIDE.** See SUICIDAL BEHAVIOUR.

**PARIETAL CORTEX.** The region of cerebrum between the frontal and occipital lobes, and above the temporal lobe. Associated with stored information, mechanisms mediating language, and learning and memory, it is a key region for human intelligence. See NERVOUS SYSTEM.

**PARKINSONISM** is the name given to a syndrome, or characteristic set of symptoms, shown by patients with lesions to certain subcortical areas of the brain. From the patient's point of view the main complaints are of involuntary tremor in the limbs together with a difficulty in initiating and controlling voluntary movements, and some general changes in posture, mood, and level of activity. There is no pain, little loss of sensation or awareness, and the mental state often remains well preserved. From the scientific point of view Parkinsonism is of interest because of the insight it gives into the processes involved in translating thoughts and intentions into the appropriate actions for their overt expression. It produces a number of behavioural changes stemming from a disruption of the brain mechanisms that mediate these processes.

Originally called the 'shaking palsy', the syndrome was first described by the surgeon James Parkinson in 1817. Nowadays it is termed 'idiopathic paralysis agitans' in recognition of its status as a naturally occurring degenerative disease of the nervous system of late middle or old age, and of its main features of impaired voluntary movement and a noticeable, continuous, induced shaking of the limbs at rest. The disease has an insidious onset, and there is a tendency for the patient's condition to deteriorate slowly, but it may remain stable for long periods. This is Parkinson's disease proper, for which no cause is yet definitely known—it is almost certainly not hereditary, but no definite link has been established with any slow virus, dietary deficiency, chemical toxin, or other suggested environmental cause.

The characteristic features, however, may occur as 'symptomatic Parkinsonism' in adults of any age as a result of a wide range of damage to the brain, including metal poisoning, anoxia (oxygen deficiency), strokes, certain drug overdoses, and infec-

tions. One special instance of the last category was the epidemic viral disease of the 1920s called 'encephalitis lethargica', which is often held to be the cause of a certain kind of Parkinsonism in that generation. Recently a dramatic series of cases occurred in California in young heroin addicts who injected themselves with a designer drug containing the toxic side-product MTPT, which destroys the same cells in the brain as are affected in idiopathic Parkinsonism.

The main defining features of Parkinsonism involve the motor system, and comprise *tremor* of the limbs at rest, a relatively slow repetitive oscillation which disappears during sleep or deliberate movement; *increased rigidity* of the limbs to passive movement; and *akinesia*, an impairment of the voluntary control of movement. Other symptoms which may be associated with these include difficulties in maintaining or adjusting posture; difficulties in walking steadily or with normal-size steps; an immobile facial expression; loss of strength in and modulation of the voice; eye-movement abnormalities; and an inability to get up out of a bed or low chair without help. The disease in fact affects all the forms of action, communication, and expression by which we interact with the environment and with each other.

In all Parkinsonian disorders the parts of the brain affected are groups of cells lying in the centre and at the base of the forebrain—the *basal ganglia. These nuclei have extensive and complex connections, and form part of several circuits through different levels of the brain. Neural activity in these circuits involves the neurotransmitter dopamine, whose progressive depletion underlies the disease, at first disrupting, and ultimately blocking, transmission through the pathways. A number of drug therapies are now available to patients to help them regain biochemical balance in the system and restore normal movement.

Pathways through the basal ganglia include some to and from the *autonomic nervous system (which controls bodily functions), the cortex, and the limbic system. So it is not surprising that other symptoms often associated with the disease include autonomic changes such as excessive sweating or trouble with digestion; cognitive changes, with impaired memory and thinking ability; and personality changes, most notably depression and lethargy or increased irritability. Although the latter may be a reflection of the patients' reaction to their impaired movement or embarrassing tremor, some observers think that they stem directly from the effects of the disease on the working of those circuits in the brain concerned with an individual's cognitive and emotional state. On this view Parkinsonism has a widespread effect on behaviour, and may be seen as a neuropsychological and neuropsychiatric disease.

**Motor symptoms: the role of the basal ganglia in movement.** While tremor is obvious and embarrassing, the impairment of voluntary movement is the disabling symptom of Parkinsonism. In its extreme form, untreated, it results in an immobile 'frozen' state where the patient remains fixed in a catatonic, typically crouching, posture. Even mild cases sometimes experience 'freezing' when walking or shifting posture.

More often, however, the mild form results in a subtle disturbance of movement, involving both a retardation in initiating movements (akinesia) and slowness and clumsiness in carrying them out (bradykinesia). There is an obvious lack of control, with patients complaining that their hands and fingers 'won't do what I tell them to'. Movements are slow and appear uncoordinated, as if the patient has lost the art of automatically performing familiar skills and has to think about and monitor his actions all the time as he carries them out. But the limbs are not numb, nor paralysed, although the grip may be weak and writing become small and spidery. When doing things slowly movements may be reasonably accurate, and visual control is still precise enough to allow fine adjustments of the fingers—patients who continue (on a good day) to mend watches or carve wood have been known. Moreover, the muscles themselves, and their immediate control from the motor cortex (see Fig. 1) are still intact, because they respond normally to direct stimulation.

Thus the components of movement appear to be intact in Parkinsonism, but patients have difficulty in co-ordinating them so as to produce effective actions. There is a dissociation of some kind between thought and action, suggesting that the basal ganglia play a crucial role in the neurological systems that underlie perceptual motor co-ordination. Parkinsonism disrupts the process at the very centre where the orders for movement are formulated; the patient's difficulty stems from faulty instructions being sent to the motor system, rather than from the motor system responding inaccurately.

Recently, anatomical studies have shown that the basal ganglia provide a connecting link between those areas of the brain mediating thought and those directly initiating movement. They receive inputs from the association cortex of the forebrain (frontal and parietal areas especially) and send their main outputs to the motor cortex and the red nucleus which innervate spinal motor neurones. In this respect they are similar to the *cerebellum, another structure known to be concerned with the control of movement. The two subcortical areas are in fact connected in parallel between association and motor cortex (Fig. 1).

On this model it may be postulated that the idea or initial plan for a movement takes place in the cortex, that this is passed on to the basal ganglia and cerebellum where some kind of 'programming' of orders for the contraction of muscles takes place, and that these are then passed on to the motor cortex for transmission to the muscles. The subcortical structures may thus be a kind of 'general staff' of the motor system, organizing the force, duration, timing and co-ordination of various kinds of movement.

This physiological model reinforces the notion of the basal ganglia and cerebellum as interface mechanisms between cognitive and motor systems of the brain, providing the means by which general intentions and ideas for action are translated into specific programmes of movement for their fulfilment. If either is damaged, therefore, connections through one pathway will be impaired, but those through the other will still be intact. So patients will not be paralysed, but will lose some aspect of control according to the function disrupted by the lesion. Exactly how the two structures divide control is not known, but there are several possibilities. Some workers have suggested that each is concerned with a different kind of movement (the cerebellum generating visually-controlled and the basal ganglia proprioceptively-controlled movements); others that each controls a different parameter of movement (for example, the basal ganglia determining the strength to be put into a muscle contraction while the cerebellum regulates its spatial position or timing). These, and other, possibilities are open to experimental test—showing that the disturbed nervous system may be a good proving ground for theories of how the normal system works.

Experimental investigations of Parkinsonian movement, by the author and others, have found

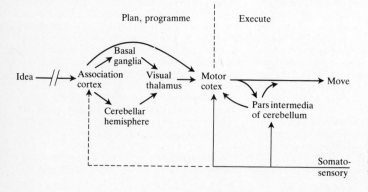

Fig. 1. The pathways concerned in the planning, execution, and control of voluntary movement.

that Parkinsonian patients asked to hit a visual target with hand or arm movements from a stationary starting-point have difficulty executing quick, large-amplitude aiming movements which are pre-programmed and executed as discrete units (ballistic movements). They can, however, perform small or slow movements under continuous visual correction reasonably well. Patients with cerebellar action tremor show just the reverse. Parkinsonian subjects tend not to increase the amount of force they put into large-amplitude ballistic movements appropriately, so that their movements undershoot the target point (hypokinesia) and are more erratic. Similar dissociable effects between 'ballistic' and visually guided movements have been found in monkeys who, in an experiment, track a target while output from either the basal ganglia or cerebellum is temporarily inactivated by cooling. These features may underlie the slowness and clumsiness in executing movements which characterize bradykinesia in Parkinson's disease.

If bradykinesia reflects a difficulty in programming individual muscle actions appropriately to achieve an intended movement, akinesia reflects a difficulty in the accurate selection and initiation of responses, that is, in the formation and implementation of 'motor plans'. This is the point at which a general decision or intention is specified as a particular set of actions to achieve it—in computer terms an 'algorithm' for movement. Often it involves switching in a repertoire of well-learnt sequences of movement (as in playing scales or chords on a piano) but it may involve assembling new patterns and sequences for the immediate task in hand. It also involves timing (when to start and stop movements) and whether to control movements through vision, touch, or proprioception—or without *feedback—in short, what strategy to adopt to achieve the goal originally set.

There is some evidence that Parkinsonian patients lose their facility in such higher-level aspects of a motor plan. They are slow in initiating movements of any kind, even when not aiming at a target but just responding to a signal as quickly as possible. They take longer to switch from one movement or movement sequence to another, even when using different limbs where there is no overlap of musculature involved. They have difficulty doing two things at once, and in running off rapid sequences where they cannot monitor each movement separately. They sometimes 'freeze' while walking or getting up out of a chair, as if unable to co-ordinate and synchronize an action involving several groups of muscles. They have difficulty tracking a continuously moving target on a screen if the target disappears for even short periods, as if they need continual visual information to initiate successive actions. (Tremor patients carry on through such gaps in visual data quite well.) And they tend not to make use of any available advance information about impending movements to reduce their reaction time or events, as normals do, as if the initiation of movements has to

be done from an external trigger signal, Parkinson subjects being unable to begin them spontaneously.

Such rather curious Parkinsonian characteristics suggest that the basal ganglia are especially involved in the assembly, selection, and triggering off of sequences of action, which explains why Parkinsonian subjects may tire quickly with repeated movement, be unable to do two things at once, or find difficulty in switching from one action to another. The functions disrupted are at the transition point between cognition and action, and are central to the control of behaviour. It is not surprising, therefore, that Parkinson's disease affects other aspects of behaviour as well, both mental and social.

**Cognitive and personality changes: the role of the basal ganglia in general behaviour.** In his original definition of the disease, Parkinson specifically excluded mental changes, declaring 'the senses and intellect being uninjured'. Since then, many observers have disagreed with him, and associated Parkinsonism with dementia or other psychological disturbances. In this they possibly mistake the outward appearance of the untreated advanced stage, with its profound motor immobility and unresponsiveness, for an inner mental deterioration. Nowadays it is generally agreed that Parkinsonian patients may show impairments on a range of cognitive activities, and personality changes too. But their nature is not certain, nor what are the crucial underlying changes in the brain.

Some studies emphasize certain subtle perceptual-motor difficulties in Parkinsonism. The only sensory deficit reported is a slight blurring of vision, possibly due to a retinal dopamine deficiency; otherwise there seems to be little disturbance of the ability to register and identify sensory information. But patients are reported as showing perceptual difficulties in the ability to use sensory information to guide their actions, especially where this involves orientation in space. Thus they have been reported as showing deficits in locating parts of the body correctly from diagrams; in following a given route round a room from a map; in setting a tilted rod to the vertical with the body itself tilted; and in correctly copying or making up gestures with the arms. In all these cases, the difficulty appears to lie in keeping track of one's own movements so as to maintain one's orientation in space, and results from a loss of the re-afferent information that one gets from one's own movements. But perceptual judgements of external objects and space are still intact.

Thus the Parkinsonian difficulty is not a cognitive deficit *per se*, but rather a deficit in the use of knowledge for action. It raises the intriguing possibility that motor and behavioural systems use a different sensory input from that, through the cortex, which underlies our conscious perception, so that one's actions may be initiated by signals and controlled by systems not directly amenable to

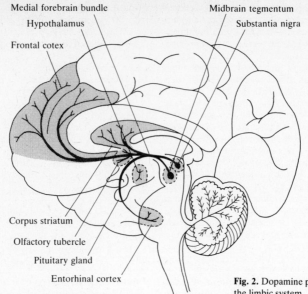

Medial forebrain bundle
Hypothalamus
Frontal cotex
Midbrain tegmentum
Substantia nigra

Corpus striatum
Olfactory tubercle
Pituitary gland
Entorhinal cortex

**Fig. 2.** Dopamine pathways through the limbic system.

awareness, which is a dissociation commonly found in motor-skills learning and performance.

On standardized tests of intellectual function, Parkinsonian patients often do badly, but this is probably at least partly due to motor difficulties on timed tasks which require manipulation of materials. On many tasks of perception, memory, and reasoning, Parkinsonian patients show little deficit. Or they may have lower scores than normal without showing any qualitative differences typical of *dementia, indicating rather a slowness in thinking (bradyphrenia). Where there is often a specific impairment is in what is termed mental 'set' (that is, the ability to choose one behavioural or mental strategy when several alternatives are available, and then either to maintain it or to switch to another strategy, as appropriate). This deficit in mental control parallels some of the motor difficulties described above, implying that the mental and motor effects of Parkinsonism are similar.

Some years ago, attention was drawn to the existence of ascending dopamine pathways through the basal ganglia from cell bodies in the reticular core of the brain to forebrain areas, especially the prefrontal cortex and the limbic system of the temporal lobes (Fig. 2). Disturbance of these diffuse projections might well interfere with the activity of the innervated structures, producing cognitive impairments, or emotional changes respectively. There are several theories of this kind.

(i) *Parkinsonism and dementia as diseases of a common core.* According to this theory, a loss of neurones in the reticular core of the brain will at first produce symptoms appropriate to whichever structure first loses its input. As neuronal losses increase, symptoms typical of other diseases of old

age (dementia, depression, and Parkinsonism) will appear as all three systems are affected. This theory is supported by a number of anatomical and biochemical studies showing similar neuronal changes in Parkinsonism and dementia, and clinically there is often overlap of symptoms too. But not all advanced Parkinsonian patients show signs of dementia, so the overlap may be coincidental.

(ii) *Loss of arousal.* On this theory, ascending projections through the basal ganglia are necessary to activate or initiate cortical activity. Loss of this facility means that patients show lethargic thinking and behaviour because they lack arousal, resulting in inefficient mental activity, although the mechanisms of thought, memory, and thinking are themselves still intact. Undoubtedly lethargy and a lack of spontaneous activity are often observed in Parkinsonism, particularly in the advanced stages, and increasing motivation can improve performance (although it does not always do so).

In the past, advanced cases deteriorated into a 'frozen' state of rigid immobility and unresponsiveness to external stimuli. The discovery in the 1960s of drugs which rectified the biochemical deficiency of Parkinsonism led to dramatic increases in the level of spontaneous activity, even in long-standing catatonic cases. The effect has been appropriately described as 'awakening' by Oliver Sacks (1973) in a vivid and moving account.

(iii) *Frontal syndrome.* This theory proposes that Parkinsonian patients show behavioural effects similar to those of frontal cortical damage, that is, personality and behavioural symptoms rather than loss of intellectual capacity and awareness. The mental set effects described above would fit this description, as would other observations of such frontal signs as perseveration—being unable to change an adopted strategy or sequence of behaviour if conditions change during a task, as for example, in perceptual adaptation or on tasks where the requirements or rules change on different trials. The theory emphasizes the close mutual interconnections of parts of the basal ganglia with prefrontal cortical areas, and it is likely that cortical and subcortical areas of the brain work together as an integrated unit, such that disruption at any point in the circuit impairs the function of the whole.

An extension of this theory attributes the personality changes often found in the disease (notably depression and irritability), as well as the autonomic changes, to basal ganglia connections with the *limbic system. The limbic system is a complex circuit of pathways connecting up structures on the inside borders of the cortex with central structures in the brain-stem and cerebrum, and is often described as the cerebral mechanism of emotional behaviour. Parts of the frontal lobes form an important link in this circuit, so frontal symptoms might well be accompanied by disturbances of mood and personality. Some authorities, therefore, describe Parkinsonian behavioural changes as frontal-limbic dementia, or subcortical dementia, to distinguish them from senile dementia (Alzheimer's disease) with its global deterioration in memory, thought, and language.

Of particular interest is the finding that while a deficiency of dopamine is associated with Parkinsonism, over-activity in the dopamine system produces schizophrenia-like behavioural effects (see DOPAMINE NEURONES IN THE BRAIN). This opens up the possibility that it is the biochemical status of the nervous system that underlies psychological and psychiatric changes in Parkinsonian patients and schizophrenics. It also holds out hope for the continued development of effective treatment, but as with studies of the biochemical basis of *schizophrenia, the exact relation of the mechanisms of the nervous system to the characteristics of the mind remains elusive. Progress in this problem may well depend as much on advances in our understanding of the latter as of the former.

K. A. F.

Divac, I. and Öberg, R. G. E. (eds.) (1979). *The Neostriatum*.

Flowers, K. (1976). Visual 'closed-loop' and 'open-loop' characteristics of voluntary movement in patients with Parkinson's disease and intention tremor. *Brain*, **99**, 269–310.

Flowers, K. (1978). Lack of prediction in the motor behaviour of Parkinsonism. *Brain*, **101**, 35–52.

Flowers, K. and Robertson, C. (1985). The effect of Parkinson's disease on the ability to maintain a mental set. *Journal of Neurology, Neurosurgery and Psychiatry*, **48**, 517–29.

Hallett, M. (1979). Physiology and pathophysiology of voluntary movement. In Tyler, H. R. and Dawson, D. M. (eds.), *Current Neurology*, vol. ii. Boston.

Sacks, O. W. (1973). *Awakenings*. London.

Siegfried, J. (ed.) (1973). *Parkinson's Disease: rigidity, akinesia, behaviour* (2 vols.). Bern.

Yahr, M. D. (1975). The extrapyramidal disorders. In Beeson, P. B. and McDermott, W. (eds.), *Textbook of Medicine*, 14th edn. Philadelphia.

Yahr, M. D. (ed.) (1976). *The Basal Ganglia*. New York.

**PASCAL,** BLAISE (1623–62). French mathematician and philosopher. Brought up in Paris by his father to be a mathematician, he worked out for himself when 11 years old the first twenty-three propositions of *Euclid, and at 16 published a paper on solid geometry that *Descartes refused to believe had been written by one so young. With his father he confirmed Torricelli's theory that nature does not abhor a vacuum—by carrying mercury barometers up a mountain and showing that the column of mercury varied in length. This finally disposed of Greek notions of air, pneuma, and the void. In 1642 he built the first metal-tooth-wheeled calculating machine, later to be developed by *Leibniz.

Pascal was also an influential Christian thinker. He contested the view of Descartes that human reason reigns supreme, arguing that it is unable to deal with ultimate *metaphysical problems. 'The heart has its reasons of which reason knows not.' His religious writings were published after his death as *Pensées* (1670; Eng. trans. A. Krailsheimer, 1966).

**PATTERN RECOGNITION** has become the name of a technology that includes automatic recognition and analysis of patterns by machines, and usually excludes the study of *perception in animals. (For pattern recognition by humans, see GESTALT THEORY; VISION: THE EARLY WARNING SYSTEM.)

One of the uses of pattern recognition is in reading-machines; and since the 1920s many such machines have been patented. Although there is still no complete and definitive solution to the problem of making machines recognize characters, reading-machines with worthwhile though limited capabilities are commercially available and widely used. Their practical value arises mainly from their high speed of reading, which is typically in the range 200 to 1,000 characters per second.

Each of the 2s in Fig. 1 would be regarded technically as a somewhat different pattern. To 'recognize' a given numeral, a machine has to determine whether this numeral belongs to the class of patterns that are called '2' or to the class of patterns that are called '3', and so on. In this context, 'recognition' means 'classification'.

Clinically normal electrocardiograms are not always exactly the same, but instead are somewhat different waveforms, that is, different patterns. 'Recognizing' an electrocardiogram as 'normal' means assigning it to the class of patterns that are

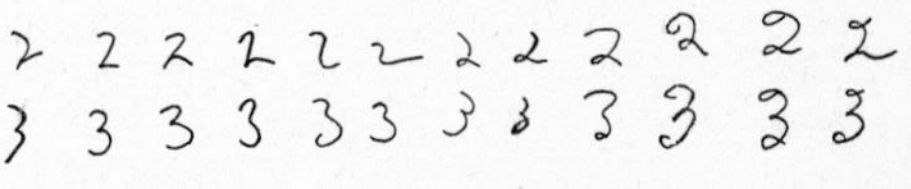

**Fig. 1.** Copies of 2s and 3s written by different people.

considered normal. This general idea holds in many applications: for instance, a blood-pressure wave should be recognized as normal if it belongs to the class of normal waves. Fingerprints from the same finger may have somewhat different patterns due, for instance, to different pressures on the skin, yet these patterns should all be classified as belonging to the same finger.

In nuclear physics laboratories, machines that assist humans in the visual processing of events in bubble-and-spark chamber photographs are required to do more than classify configurations of line-like tracks. Relevant configurations have to be picked out from a morass of irrelevant detail, and then not only classified but also measured. In metallurgy there are established applications in which a machine is required to find, count, and measure the area of many objects in a picture, but not to classify their shapes. Machines that check optically for cracks in glass, or fractures of bones in radiographs, or defects in printed circuits are attempting to recognize defects whose shape is not known in advance.

Machines which became commercially available in about 1976 for recognizing and counting the different types of white blood cell actually take account of colour and texture, as well as shape. Colour and texture are also often important in the automatic interpretation of satellite photography and other remotely sensed imagery, and various techniques for recognizing (i.e. classifying) colour and texture have been devised.

The automatic analysis of television pictures of natural scenes and other three-dimensional compositions is known as computer vision. Computer vision may have as its source of data a single static monocular image, or a stereo pair of images, or a sequence of images of moving objects. Typical practical objectives are to determine three-dimensional disposition of surfaces, and possibly also parameters of motion. In computer vision, recognition—that is, the automatic assignment of names to objects—often appears less important than 'reconstructing' the scene from one or more visual images. It is not yet clear to what extent a scene can be reconstructed, particularly from a single image, without some kind of recognition of known objects.

The classical approach to the recognition of separate isolated objects has two stages. The first consists of detecting various attributes or features of patterns. For instance, the number of closed loops, the number of line-ends pointing roughly leftwards, and the number of junctions of lines might be chosen as features of written characters. The square of the perimeter divided by the area, and the diameter of the largest inscribed circle, might be among the chosen (orientation-independent) attributes of a blood cell. The ratio of light flux through a red filter to total light flux might be chosen as one attribute of colour; and variance of grey-level is a simple example of an attribute of texture.

If the attributes or features found in the first stage of recognition have numerical values, then the list of attributes can be treated as a vector. For instance, such vectors might be obtained from, say, 1,000 specimens of '2' and averaged. If the attribute vector obtained from a given character is sufficiently close to this average in multidimensional space, then the given character can be classified as '2' in the second and final stage of recognition. Many more sophisticated techniques of vector classification are explained in pattern-recognition textbooks.

Instead of detecting, in the first stage of recognition, a fixed number of attributes or features constituting a vector, *linguistic* systems detect variable numbers of features or primitives that constitute strings. The final stage of recognition now consists of classifying strings by the syntactic methods of Chomskyan linguistics (SEE LANGUAGE: CHOMSKY'S THEORY). There might, for instance, be at least one separate grammar for '2', one for '3', and so on; and a pattern would be classified as '2' if it were syntactically accepted as '2'.

In the progressions illustrated in Fig. 2, the distinction between '4' and '9' depends upon the proportions of lines that constitute a character. It has been usual to deal with proportions, in the first stage of recognition, by attempting to choose features that will remain almost invariant when a pattern is subjected to limited deformation. Indeed the first stage of recognition ideally eliminates all unwanted variations of patterns (such as noise), but preserves distinctions between different classes. Careful design of the first stage has proved to be essential in the most successful of the vector-classification and linguistic-recognition systems.

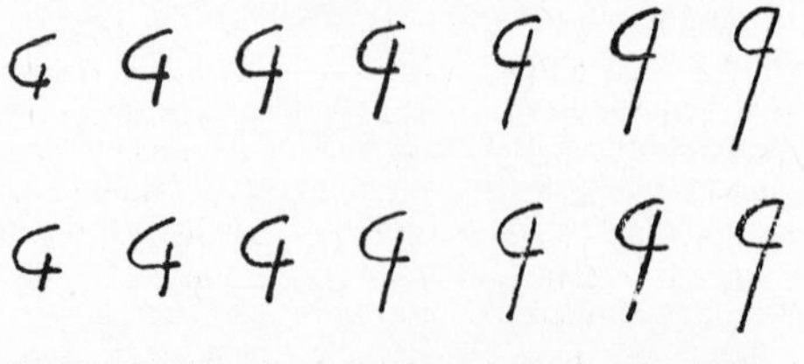

Fig. 2. Transition from 4 to 9 caused by lengthening the central upright stroke. In the lower row the transition may appear to occur further to the right because the horizontal stroke protrudes further rightwards.

The large literature reports cases where automatically selected features or attributes have proved more useful than randomly selected ones. Best of all, however, are features carefully chosen and worked out by humans using an intuitive trial-and-error process.

In Fig. 1 there are many pairs of 2s such that one 2 looks like a distorted or deformed version of the other. Similarly, one clinically normal electrocardiogram might look like a somewhat distorted version of another. Such limited distortions preserve positional relationships within some sort of tolerance. Relational matching techniques,

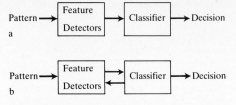

**Fig. 3. a.** Classical block diagram for pattern recognition. **b.** Block diagram in which there is a two-way exchange of information between the blocks.

which depend upon consistency of contextual constraints instead of relying only on judicious choice of features to deal with distortion, have a structure more like Fig. 3b than the classical structure shown in Fig. 3a. In Fig. 3b there is essentially an iterative interplay between the processes of classification and feature detection, these being best regarded as a single integrated monolithic process. Various systems that use context in recognition also have the Fig. 3b structure, and the recurrence of this structure is important because it shows the danger of presupposing, as many workers did unquestioningly in the 1960s, the optimality of the Fig. 3a structure.

In Fig. 1 there are some 2s and 3s that have almost the same top curve. Similarly, one can think of many pairs of words that contain the same letter, many pairs of sentences that contain the same word, and so on. In general, processes of analysis and recognition may be facilitated by subdividing patterns hierarchically into parts, just as a map may be subdivided into countries subdivided into counties subdivided into parishes. In principle the recognition of parts may be easier than recognition of wholes, particularly if the parts are features that remain almost invariant when a pattern is subjected to limited deformation, as mentioned previously. In practice, segmentation, which is the business of dividing up a pattern into hopefully relevant parts, may be difficult or impossible to achieve reliably until *after* a pattern has been recognized as a whole.

When a pattern has been successfully segmented into parts, for instance when an aerial photograph has been partitioned into fields, lakes, forest, etc., the parts may have interdependences that cannot be overlooked. For instance, the angle of the sun may be similar for neighbouring parts of an aerial photograph. The dialect or accent may be similar for different parts of one spoken utterance; and characters written by one person tend to have similar graphology. Machines may not be able to compete with humans in pattern recognition without taking account of such dependences.

A more firmly established use of context in pattern recognition is in precluding combinations of objects that are known to be impossible (or very unlikely). For instance, if a machine reading English words classifies a four-letter word as QOIT, which is absent from the dictionary, then the machine should make a second attempt at classifying the individual characters, particularly the second. But some of the contextual techniques described in the massive literature do not yield enough practical improvement to justify their cost.

It is worth remarking that contextual knowledge can be useful in segmentation. If a pattern is segmented into parts that are subsequently classified, and if the combination of classifications of parts is known contextually to be impossible, then the pattern can be segmented differently, and the process repeated until contextually acceptable segmentation is achieved. Instead of relying on contrast to segment a pattern into parts as a preliminary step that precedes recognition, segmentation can be integrated with recognition by using knowledge of contextual relationships between segments. This can be regarded as an iterative process, more like Fig. 3b than Fig. 3a. Processes of this type have been developed for the analysis of pictures of outdoor scenes, using, for instance, contextual knowledge that sky should be above a mountain, not below it. In several speech-recognition systems (see SPEECH RECOGNITION BY MACHINE), lexical, syntactic, and semantic contextual knowledge is used in choosing between alternative possibilities in segmentation and in the early stages of classification. In these sophisticated systems, pattern recognition tends to fuse with *artificial intelligence. The design of these systems in which segmentation increases contextual knowledge, which improves segmentation, and so on iteratively, is mainly *ad hoc*.

There is a tantalizing possibility of using practical pattern recognition to clarify various philosophical problems. For instance, how can a machine recognize all triangles as a triangle without having a 'general idea' of a triangle that is 'neither oblique, nor rectangle, neither equilateral, equicrural, nor scalene, but all and none of these at once'? The problem of recognizing the 2s in Fig. 1 is like this, and one can seek in clear practical systems for some useful abstraction corresponding to a 'general idea'.                J. R. U.

Ahuja, N. and Schachter, B. J. (1983). *Pattern Models*. New York.

Ballard, D. H. and Brown, C. M. (1982). *Computer Vision*. Englewood Cliffs, New Jersey.

Castleman, K. R. (1979). *Digital Image Processing*. Englewood Cliffs, New Jersey.

Chen, C. H. (ed.) (1976). *Pattern Recognition and Artificial Intelligence*. New York.

Devijver, P. A. and Kittler, J. (1982). *Pattern Recognition: a Statistical Approach*. Englewood Cliffs, New Jersey.

Duda, R. O. and Hart, P. E. (1973). *Pattern Classification and Scene Analysis*. New York.

Fu, K. S. (1974). *Syntactic Methods in Pattern Recognition*. New York.

Fu, K. S. (1982). *Syntactic Pattern Recognition and Applications*. Englewood Cliffs, New Jersey.

Fukanaga, K. (1972). *Introduction to Statistical Pattern Recognition*. New York.

Gonzalez, R. C. and Wintz, P. (1977). *Digital Image Processing*. Reading, Massachusetts.

Hall, E. L. (1979). *Computer Image Processing and Pattern Recognition*. New York.

Meisel, W. S. (1972). *Computer-orientated Approaches to Pattern Recognition*, vol. 83, Maths. in Science and Engineering. New York.

Niemann (1981). *Pattern Analysis*. Berlin.

Pavlidis, T. (1977). *Structural Pattern Recognition*. Berlin.

Pratt, W. K. (1978). *Digital Image Processing*. New York.

Rosenfeld, A. (ed.) (1976). *Digital Picture Analysis*, vol. 11, Topics in Applied Physics. Berlin.

Rosenfeld, A. and Kak, C. A. (1982). *Digital Picture Processing*, 2nd edn. New York.

Tou, J. T. and Gonzalez, R. C. (1974). *Pattern Recognition Principles*. Reading, Massachusetts.

Ullmann, J. R. (1973). *Pattern Recognition Techniques*. London and New York.

Young, T. Y. and Calvert, T. W. (1974). *Classification, Estimation and Pattern Recognition*. New York.

**PAVLOV,** IVAN PETROVICH (1849–1936), Russian physiologist. His importance for the study of animal behaviour is mainly due to his work on conditional reflexes; this work provided the basis for much of the subsequent research on *learning. Pavlov also conducted significant research on the physiology of digestion and on neurosis.

**Brief life.** Pavlov was born in Ryazan, Russia, and attended the religious school and seminary there, where he studied natural science. He did not complete his studies, but entered St Petersburg University in 1870, where he continued to study natural science, and decided to make his career as a physiologist. After graduation in 1875, he went to the Military Medical Academy to pursue his research. He completed his doctorate there in 1883, and then went to Germany (1884–6), where he studied in Leipzig with Carl Ludwig, and in Breslau. In 1890 he was appointed professor in the department of pharmacology in the Military Medical Academy, and in 1895 he moved to the department of physiology. In 1904 he received the Nobel prize for his work on the physiology of digestion. He remained professor of physiology until 1925, when he resigned in protest against the expulsion of sons of priests from the Academy (he himself was the son of a priest, but would not have been expelled). Initially Pavlov was outspokenly opposed to the Bolsheviks, even though they supported his research. In 1922 he asked Lenin's permission to transfer his research abroad, but was refused: Lenin wanted prestigious scientists. However, during the last few years before his death (in Leningrad) Pavlov increasingly accepted and approved of the Bolsheviks. From 1925 to 1936 he worked mainly in three laboratories: the institute of physiology of the Soviet Academy of Sciences (which is now named after him), the institute of experimental medicine, and the biological laboratory at Koltushy (now Pavlovo), near Leningrad.

**Physiology of circulation and digestion.** Pavlov held that physiologists should study 'the actual course of particular physiological processes in a whole and normal organism'. He also held that the main problems for experimental research were the mutual interactions of organs within the body, and the relation of the organism to its environment. The method of working on the whole, healthy body of an animal contrasted with the mainstream of physiology in the latter half of the nineteenth century; most investigations then were on isolated organs and prepared specimens.

Pavlov's work on the physiology of circulation (*c.*1874–88) was mainly concerned with the mechanisms that regulate blood-pressure. His experimental animal for this, and for most subsequent research, was the dog. He was mainly interested in nervous mechanisms. He discovered, for instance, that the vagus nerve controls blood-pressure, and that there are four nerves controlling the heartbeat, which can vary the heartbeat's rhythm and intensity (work on the nervous control of the heart had formed his doctorate).

Pavlov's work on the physiology of digestion began in about 1879, and culminated in his book *The Work of the Digestive Glands* (1902, a translation of *Lektsii o rabotie glavnych pishchevaritel'nykh zhelez*, 1897). He investigated the nervous mechanisms controlling the secretions of the various digestive glands, and how these nervous mechanisms were stimulated by food. He had to expose the structures of interest surgically, and work on them in a healthy animal, so it was crucial to his success that he was also a brilliant surgeon. (Similar experiments had been attempted in the laboratory in Breslau that he visited in the mid-1880s, but had failed because the experimenters lacked Pavlov's surgical skill.) Once he had exposed part of the gut, Pavlov could directly insert food or chemicals, and observe the effects on the activity of the digestive glands. The method of sham feeding was a related development. A slit is made in the animal's throat so that food entering through the mouth falls out through the neck before reaching the stomach. The animal can be fed through a second opening made into the stomach. By sham feeding, Pavlov could observe the effect of food in the mouth on the secretion of digestive juices elsewhere in the gut; he found that the *taste of food in the mouth causes the release of gastric juices in the stomach. A smaller quantity of juice is released if food is put directly into the stomach. Sham feeding has been used and developed extensively by later workers.

Pavlov's own theory for the control of digestive secretions postulated control exclusively by nervous mechanisms. Subsequent research has shown this theory to be incomplete: control by hormones also occurs. He made many other important discoveries while working on digestion. Two of the most important were the enzyme *enterokinase*, which controls the activity of another digestive enzyme, and the connection between the properties of the saliva and the type of food being eaten (the Pavlovian curves of salivary secretion).

N. P. Shepovalnikov and Pavlov were co-dis-coverers of enterokinase.

Pavlov's work on the physiology of digestion is important for understanding his work on animal behaviour, for his explanations of animal behaviour are similar to those of the control of digestion. In addition, his methods were similar in all his studies.

**Conditional reflexes.** While at the seminary in Ryazan, Pavlov had read I. M. Sechenov's *Refleksy golovnago mozga* (Reflexes of the Brain), which argued that mental events were reflexes. Then, while working on the physiology of diges-tion, he had noticed 'psychic' salivation: when the dog was confronted by a *stimulus that customarily preceded feeding, it salivated even before being fed. This psychic salivation could be induced, for example, by the animal's food container, or by the presence of the attendant who normally fed the animal, or even by the sound of the attendant's approach. Armed with these incidental observa-tions and with the reflexology of Sechenov, and stimulated by Charles *Darwin's evolutionary arguments about animal behaviour (which encouraged materialistic analyses of mental events), Pavlov set out to investigate the psychic salivation of dogs. This was a simple extension of his earlier studies on the control of digestive secre-tions, and once again it was the nervous reflex that he looked to for his explanation. He worked on conditional reflexes from about 1902 until his death.

A typical Pavlovian experiment on psychic salivation would be as follows. On several occa-sions a bell is rung just before the dog is fed, and the dog salivates on receiving its food. Then the bell is rung without presentation of food. It is observed that the dog salivates in response to the bell's ringing. Pavlov termed the food the *uncon-ditional stimulus*, the sound of the bell the *con-ditional stimulus*, the salivation to the food the *unconditional reflex*, and the salivation to the bell alone the *conditional reflex*. ('Conditional' is what Pavlov actually wrote, but the early mistranslation of 'conditioned' is now widespread in the psycho-logical literature.)

Many of the fine details of the conditional reflex were studied by Pavlov and his collaborators. First, there is the temporal sequence of stimuli. Pavlov found that it is much easier to form a conditional reflex if the unconditional stimulus (food) follows the conditional one (bell) than if they are simultaneous, or if the conditional stimulus follows the unconditional. Second, there is the time delay between stimuli. Here he found that a discrete conditional stimulus is more effective in forming a conditional reflex if it occurs near in time to the food than if it occurs a long time before. However, if the conditional stimulus starts a long time before, but continues right up to when the unconditional stimulus is presented, then it is as effective as a conditional stimulus which starts just before the food is given. Third, there is the intensity of the stimuli. A dog salivates more if it is trained on bigger pieces of food; and similarly, it salivates more to a louder bell. Fourth, Pavlov studied generalization of the conditional stimulus. If the animal has been trained on a stimulus of one pitch, it can then be tested for a response to a stimulus of another pitch. This leads to a method of investigat-ing the animal's powers of sensory discrimination, which again was originated and developed by Pavlov.

Pavlov was not only interested in how condi-tional reflexes were gained; he also studied how they were lost. He classified factors causing loss of a conditional reflex into cases of either *external inhibition* or *internal inhibition*. If an animal, con-ditioned in one way, is moved into a new environ-ment, or is exposed to new stimuli before being fed, it loses its original conditional reflex; this is called external inhibition. There are several forms of internal inhibition. The most straightforward is the gradual loss of the conditional reflex if the food is withheld after the conditional stimulus; the con-ditional reflex requires regular reinforcement (to use Pavlov's term) by the unconditional stimulus.

Pavlov thought of the conditional reflex as similar to any other kind of reflex. The flow of digestive juices is stimulated by the mechanical and chemical properties of food, through the mediation of a nervous (unconditional) reflex. Similarly, salivation could be induced by some environmental indicator of food, again by a nervous (conditional, in this case) reflex. The conditional reflex, however, is easily modifiable by the environment, according to whatever the local indicators of food happen to be. So, Pavlov regarded the formation of conditional reflexes as an adaptation whereby the animal could survive better in a changing environment.

Pavlov also speculated on the fine details of the formation of a conditional reflex. He suggested that the cells of the central nervous system must change structurally and chemically when a con-ditional reflex is formed: 'the locking in, the formation of new connections, we attribute to the functioning of the separating membrane, should it exist, or simply to the branching between neurones'. This idea has subsequently been confirmed.

Although nearly all his research was on dogs, Pavlov also showed that conditional reflexes can be formed in mice and monkeys, and he was in no doubt that they occur in man, and in all other animals. He wrote: 'A temporary nervous connec-tion is a universal physiological phenomenon in the animal world and exists in us ourselves.' He also showed that more or less any environmental factor can act as a conditional stimulus (though this con-clusion has been slightly modified by later re-search). Pavlov was aiming at truly universal laws of learning, and that is why his discoveries are so fundamental to modern theories of associative learn-ing. One branch of psychology—*behaviourism—

went so far as to attribute all human behaviour to *conditioning and reinforcement. Pavlov, however, made no such extravagant claims for the conditional reflex, and ridiculed the claims of behaviourism to scientific status. The most famous expression in English of Pavlov's work on conditioning is his book *Conditioned Reflexes* (1927). In psychiatry, conditioning is used in *behaviour therapy.

**Experimental neurosis and personality.** In a famous experiment (1921) by Shenger-Krestovnika a circle was used as a conditional stimulus before feeding, and the dog was also trained to associate an ellipse with not being fed. By small steps the ellipse was then made more and more like a circle. When the ellipse was almost round, initially the dog could usually distinguish it from a circle. But after a few weeks the dog became neurotic: it ceased to be able to recognize obvious ellipses and circles, became very excited, and was no longer calm during experiments. Pavlov termed the animal's abnormal condition experimental *neurosis, and he attributed it to a disturbance of the balance between excitatory and inhibitory processes in the *nervous system. This explanation of experimental neurosis is grounded in Pavlov's theory of personality. He explained personality by variation in the excitation of the nervous system. He did not, however, attribute neurosis solely to external factors, such as contradictory stimuli. His experiments on experimental neuroses showed that dogs with different 'personalities' were differentially susceptible to the treatment: the same treatment on different dogs could produce quite different neuroses. In the 1930s Pavlov decided to work on the *genetics of behaviour, and his government built him the biological station at Koltushy for this research.

There is an underlying unity to all Pavlov's work. In his earliest work on blood circulation he established his method (intervention in unanaesthetized, whole dogs) and his paradigm explanation: nervous control. The same procedure was used in his work on the control of digestive secretion, and he started research on conditional reflexes as just another kind of nervous control of digestion. Late in his life, he saw how conditioning could be used to analyse personality and neurosis, and once again he was able to carry over his theoretical framework into a new field.     M. R.

Babkin, B. P. (1951). *Pavlov: a biography*. London.
Gray, J. A. (1979). *Pavlov*. Brighton.
Grigorian, N. A. (1974). *Pavlov, Ivan Petrovich*. Moscow.

**PEIRCE,** CHARLES SANDERS (1839–1914). Considered by many to be the most original of American philosophers, Peirce is remembered principally for his teleological account of truth, for founding *pragmatism, for contributions to formal logic, and for pioneering work in the theory of signs (semiotics). His early published work attacked the idea, dominant in the nominalist tradition from William of Occam onward, that a proposition is true if it corresponds to a reality which is the efficient cause of our sensations. In place of this Peirce gave (1871) an account based on the idea of 'a final conclusion, to which the opinion of every man is constantly gravitating'. Peirce, however, understood this gravitational attraction strictly in terms of the operation of rigorous scientific method, and as a practising experimental scientist he was impressed by the way a scientific concept is made precise by being tied to observable consequences of concrete operations. It was along these lines that he formulated (1878) a general maxim for achieving clear ideas, which he later came to identify as the core of his pragmatism. From the outset the centre of Peirce's philosophic concerns was logic, and he made important contributions to the logic of relations and devised, a few years after, but independently of, Gottlob Frege, the theory of quantification. Both his pragmatism and his work on logic were embedded in a theory of signs based on the idea that the *meaning of a sign is its power to determine observers of it to interpret it in a determinate fashion.

Peirce had mixed feelings when in 1898 William *James drew attention to him as the founder of pragmatism but at the same time advanced under this label a doctrine of truth (seen by many as the crude idea that truth is what works or what is useful) to which Peirce was quite antipathetic. As a result Peirce tried (in vain) to change the name of his approach to 'pragmaticism'.

Peirce's father, a professor at Harvard, was the leading American mathematician of his generation, but the son, largely through an inability to get on with people, failed to secure a permanent academic appointment. Apart from five years teaching at Johns Hopkins University, Peirce was employed as a scientist by the US Coast Survey. He published voluminously (estimated total of twenty-four volumes) on science, mathematics, and philosophy but never succeeded in giving his logical and philosophical ideas a systematic treatment in book form.

One extensive selection of Peirce's work is *Collected Papers* (vols. 1–6 edited by C. Hartshorn and P. Weiss, and vols. 7 and 8 by A. W. Burks), Cambridge, Massachusetts, 1931–58. Another selection, *Writings of Charles S. Peirce: a chronological edition* (edited by M. H. Fisch, *et al.*), Bloomington, Indiana, began to appear in 1982. Two one-volume selections are available: *Charles S. Peirce: selected writings* (edited by P. P. Weiner), New York, 1966, and *Philosophical Writings of Peirce* (edited by J. Buchler), New York, 1955. Two useful introductions to his thought are *Peirce and Pragmatism* by W. B. Gallie, Harmondsworth, 1952, and *Peirce* by C. Hookway, London, 1985.     J. E. T.

**PENFIELD,** WILDER GRAVES (1891–1976). American neurosurgeon, born in Spokane, Washington, and educated at Princeton and

Oxford, where he held a Rhodes scholarship. At Oxford, he came to know C. S. *Sherrington and returned to work with him for two years after qualifying in medicine at Johns Hopkins University, Baltimore. He also made contact with Gordon *Holmes and other neurologists at the National Hospital for Nervous Diseases in London, where David *Ferrier had pioneered brain surgery. On his return to America, Penfield specialized in neurosurgery and worked in both New York and Baltimore before moving to Montreal, where he was largely responsible for setting up the Montreal Neurological Institute, erected with the support of the Rockefeller Foundation and of which he became the first director. It has since led the world in the field of neurosurgery.

Penfield was remarkable not only for his high surgical accomplishment but also for his belief that neurosurgery made possible important advances in our scientific understanding of the functions of the brain. This, in its turn, made possible important progress in surgical treatment and rehabilitation. He made extensive use of advances in neurophysiology, in particular electroencephalography, and later of techniques in experimental neuropsychology, in ascertaining the localization and extent of brain lesions. He also undertook important work on the surgical treatment of focal *epilepsy.

Penfield was elected a Fellow of the Royal Society in 1943. He was a man of varied accomplishments, who wrote several novels in addition to an informative autobiography, *No Man Alone: a neurosurgeon's life* (1977). Of particular interest is his book with Theodore Rasmussen on *The Cerebral Cortex of Man* (1950). O. L. Z.

**PENROSE,** LIONEL SHARPLES (1898–1972). British physician, born in London. Penrose's father was a portrait painter and both his parents were members of the Society of Friends. After serving in the Friends' Ambulance train of the British Red Cross during the First World War, he went in 1919 to St John's College, Cambridge, where he wanted to study mathematical logic with Bertrand *Russell. He obtained his degree in 1921, and then studied with F. C. *Bartlett and at the University of Vienna, where he did work on *memory and *perception in E. Buhler's laboratory and met Sigmund *Freud. At this time, Penrose was very interested in the problems of abnormal psychology and mental disorder and realized that he would be advised to qualify in medicine in order to pursue this interest. He therefore went to Cambridge in 1925 and subsequently to St Thomas's Hospital in London. He presented his MD thesis on the subject of *schizophrenia in 1930 and the following year applied for, and ultimately obtained, an appointment as research medical officer at the Royal Eastern Counties Institution at Colchester.

From this time on, the chief interest of his life, namely the study of mental deficiency, began to dominate his work, and when he left Colchester in 1939 to go to Canada, as director of psychiatric research for Ontario, he had already produced his classic *A Clinical and Genetic Study of 1,280 Cases of Mental Defect* (1938). This work alone would have established him as a leader in the subject, and at the time it advanced the study of mental deficiency very considerably. In addition, before leaving for Ontario he had developed a test which he believed might aid the diagnosis of schizophrenia, and had been instrumental, according to his own statement, in proposing the idea and outline of the test that subsequently became generally known as the Raven's Progressive Matrices (1936).

In 1945 Penrose was appointed to the Galton professorship of eugenics at University College London. He retired in 1965 but continued to work at the Kennedy–Galton Centre, which he set up at Harperbury Hospital, St Albans. He remained a leader in the field of subnormality and genetics, especially in relation to *Down's syndrome (mongolism). He was elected a fellow of the Royal Society in 1953 and received many other awards. Other details of his career are given by Harris (1973).

Penrose's great contribution to the study of *subnormality was to lift the subject from the realms of speculation and myth and give it a respectable place in the field of psychiatry, biochemistry, and genetics where it properly belongs. He achieved this by his two major investigations, the first into the 1,280 cases which he studied from Colchester and secondly through his application of measurement to the study of Down's syndrome. In the first study Penrose was able to investigate not only the 1,280 patients in the Royal Eastern Counties Institution but also their numerous sibs and relatives. The patients were graded on the basis of Stanford–Binet and Porteous Maze tests and classified according to intellectual grade. They were also classified according to diagnostic categories, and their family histories were investigated. An immense amount of data was collected by very limited staff. Over all, the survey indicated the continuity of subnormality with normal intelligence and the very considerable heterogeneity of mental defect and the multiplicity of its causes. The figures concerning incidence also reliably contributed to knowledge concerning mental defect. Finally the survey demonstrated that mental defect was more common among parents and relatives of patients of IQ 50 and above than in the parents of more severely handicapped patients. Arising from this work, Penrose was able to make observations concerning the genetics of epiloia (or tuberous sclerosis) and also Down's syndrome. In all this and subsequent work, he developed the mathematical theory of genetics applied to human populations, and always showed himself ready to collaborate with leaders in the field of statistics, such as R. A. *Fisher. At the same time, because of his considerable ability in mathematics, he was able to demonstrate a maturity of judgement not only in the field of human genetics concerning specific disorders, such as epiloia, but also in relation to the much more confused field of the inheritance of intelligence. In the latter area, he was one of the very few people who made the correct prediction concerning changes in intelligence in Scottish schoolchildren, in his Godfrey Thomson lecture in 1959. In this respect he differed from Cyril *Burt and most other psychometricians.

Penrose had been interested in Down's syndrome from his first days at Colchester, and in his work from the Galton laboratories he was able to pursue this interest. In the work at Colchester he showed great ingenuity in assessing the relative contributions of maternal and paternal age as causative factors in the birth of Down's children, controlling for such questions as birth order in sibs. He was thus able to demonstrate ultimately the significance of maternal age and the relative unimportance of paternal age. He also interested himself in the familial incidence of Down's syndrome, though without providing a satisfactory explanation, but at the same time through these studies developed the concept of palmar dermatoglyphics in relation to Down's syndrome, by extensive studies involving 235 sufferers and 698 of their relatives as well as over 2,000 controls. Later, during his time in Canada and during his occupation of the Galton professorship, he was able to take advantage of the discovery of chromosomal anomalies in Down's syndrome, and as a result of this work, combined with his observation of dermatoglyphic deviations among the relatives of Down's children, he was able to note that although maternal age might account for one group of Down's syndrome births, the births which occurred to mothers of a comparatively young age might show particular chromosomal anomalies.

It is impossible in such a short account to give a comprehensive view of all Penrose's many achievements. His interests in abnormal and subnormal psychiatry notwithstanding, he displayed at different times initiative and inventiveness in the areas of models of inherited intelligence, topological illogicalities, chess problems, mechanical models of genetic succession, mathematics, epistemology, art, the genetics of dermal ridges in association with sex chromosomes, and in many other things.

His character appealed strongly to many colleagues and also to young children. The view of one of these latter, committed to an essay included at the end of Harris's survey, presents him as a genial professor with a generous, warm attitude to encouraging cognitive skills in everyone he met, both young and old. He was never the sharp and contentious intellectual with an incisive and startling clarity of ideas, but more the gentle but widely and acutely aware observer.                    N. O'C.

Harris, H. (1973). *Lionel Sharples Penrose, 1898–1972.*
   Biographical Memoirs of Fellows of the Royal Society.
Penrose, L. S. (1938). *A Clinical and Genetic Study of*
*1,280 Cases of Mental Defect.* Medical Research Council Special Report, ser. no. 229. London.
Penrose, L. S. with Raven, J. C. (1936). A new series of perceptual tests: a preliminary communication. *British Journal of Medical Psychology*, **16**, 97.
Penrose, L. S. (1959). *Problems of Intelligence and Heredity.* Godfrey Thomson Lecture.

**PEPPER'S GHOST.** A simple optical effect which is used for stage ghosts and in optical instruments, such as the *camera lucida* for drawing from the microscope, and the tachistoscope, which presents pictures for controlled duration in visual experiments. A part-reflecting mirror superimposes one picture (or object) which is *reflected*, by another seen *through* the glass. By brightening one while dimming the other, one is seen to appear as the other disappears—and when roughly equally illuminated both are seen, superimposed, as transparent ghosts. The effect often occurs in window panes, especially at night, though curiously it is seldom noticed unless attention is drawn to reflected lampshades, etc., floating outside. This effect may produce 'flying saucers'.

**PERCEPTION.** Our senses probe the external world. They also tell us about ourselves, as they monitor positions of the limbs and the balance of our bodies, and through pain they signal injury and illness. More subtly, there are innumerable internal signals monitoring physiological activities, and conveying and maintaining our well-being; though little of this enters our *consciousness. It may surprise the non-scientist just how little of the day-by-day, second-by-second perception that allows us to survive in a threatening world is conscious. But although the processes are generally unconscious, through investigating them experimentally we can discover a great deal about the physiological basis of perception and how, as babies and later, we discover the world of objects and come to read meanings in pictures and symbols. In perception, as Sir Ernst Gombrich (1950) realized to such good effect, art and science meet.

Just how we know things through sensory experience is a question that was discussed by the Greek philosophers and has been ever since. But, perhaps curiously, planned experiments in the spirit of the physical sciences were hardly attempted much earlier than the mid-nineteenth century. Since then, the experimental study of perception has yielded fundamental knowledge for physiology and psychology, especially from the outstanding work of Hermann von *Helmholtz (1867). It has revealed many surprises in the form of processes of which we are unaware, though they can often be demonstrated simply and dramatically. The study of perception, especially of vision and hearing, has allowed psychology to grow from its philosophical roots into an experimental science; yet deeply puzzling philosophical questions remain—especially over the role of consciousness. It is puzzling, both that we are aware of so *little* of perception— and that we have *any* awareness!

There is a long-standing tradition in philosophy that perception, especially touch and vision, gives undeniably true knowledge. Philosophers have generally sought certainty and have often claimed it, whereas scientists, who are used to their theories being modified and upset by new data, generally settle for today's best bet. Philosophers have a heavy investment in perception. They stake their all on the certainty of knowledge from the senses because they need secure premises for their arguments from experience. Scientists, on the other hand, who are used to errors in measurement and observation by instruments, and have consequently found it necessary to check and compare and repeat experiments, do not so readily expect reliability from the senses. Indeed, many scientific instruments have been developed precisely because of the limitations of the senses and the unreliability of perception: for it is, after all, easy to produce and demonstrate all manner of dramatic *illusions which could hardly occur if perception constituted direct reliable knowledge. Yet although illusions of object perception have been discussed by philosophers from *Aristotle to *Berkeley (1709), and more recently as well, philosophy generally has paid more attention to errors of logic and ambiguities of expression than to the fallibilities of perception.

Philosophers are particularly impressed by the undeniability of the 'raw experience' of *sensations, such as colours and tickles and *pain. The sensation of toothache may be undeniable—but are perceptions similarly as infallible? One will necessarily think so if one believes that perceptions are simply sensations; but we now regard perception as giving us knowledge, albeit surprisingly indirectly, of the causes or *sources* of sensations—such as the states of our bodies and objects in the environment—rather than of the sensations themselves. It is now clear that there are vast and still largely mysterious jumps—intelligent leaps of the mind, which may land on error—between the sensation and the perception of an object. One can indeed be wrong about the cause of toothache!

It is worth asking why we have both *perceptions* and *conceptions* of the world. Why is perception somehow separate, and in several ways different, from our conceptual understanding? Very likely it is because perception, in order to be useful, must work very quickly, whereas we may take years forming concepts, since knowledge and ideas are in a sense timeless. It would probably be impossible for perception to draw upon all of our knowledge, as it has to work so fast. Rather, it employs a rapid but not deep intelligence with a small knowledge base.

Perception is not traditionally thought of as an intelligent activity, even though the power, especially of vision, to probe distance gains the time needed for intelligent reactions to on-going events. It can be argued (Gregory, 1970) that the development of distance perception freed organisms from the tyranny of reflexes, and was the necessary precursor of all intelligence. The special intelligence of perception has more recently been discussed by the psychologist Irvin Rock (1984). However, an earlier account portrayed sensory perception very differently as a passive undistorting window through which the mind accepts sensations which were considered to be 'sense-data' of perception, selected and assembled somewhat like the pieces of a jigsaw puzzle. On this kind of account sense-data may be selected according to need or *attention; for vision, the brain (or mind) has little to do except select and 'pick up' features of the 'ambient array' of light (Gibson, 1950, 1966).

But are sensations, such as colours and shapes and sounds, *picked up* by the senses, or are they *created* internally by the perceiver? This question about the passiveness or activeness of perception is a long-standing one which is still debated and has significant implications; for if sensations are created by the brain—a notion that receives strong support from recent physiology (Zeki, 1977, 1980)—they can hardly be data for perceiving the object world, whereas if they are in the world, to be 'picked up', they must exist apart from us.

This raises the question: what is 'objective' and what 'subjective'? The philosopher John *Locke (1690), who was well aware of the new science of his time, suggested that there are two kinds of characteristics: *primary* characteristics, such as hardness, mass, and extension of objects in space and time—being in the world before life, and quite apart from mind—and *secondary* characteristics, which are created by mind. Thus colours are not in the world, but are created within us, though they are related in complex ways to light and the surfaces of objects.

It is generally accepted that Locke's 'primary' characteristics are present independently of mind; and it is clear that his 'secondary' characteristics are affected by states of the sensing organism—for colours change as we look through haze, or wine, and everything appears tinged with yellow if we have jaundice. It is such considerations that bring to mind the distinction between appearance and reality; even so, it is important to note that sensations do have a kind of reality, although they are created by and within us. Thus Isaac *Newton, writing on sensations of colour in *Opticks* (1704), agreed with his friend Locke, saying that red light is not itself red, but is 'red-making'. Spelling this out, he said of light rays: '. . . there is nothing else than a certain power and disposition to stir up the sensation of this or that colour. For as sound in a bell or musical string . . . is nothing but a trembling motion.' Then (in Query 23) he specifies something of the neural mechanism of vision that leads to the mysterious seat of sensation: 'Is not vision perform'd chiefly by the Vibrations of this (Eatherial) Medium, excited in the bottom of the eye by Rays of Light, and propagated through the solid, pellucid and uniform Capillamenta of the optic Nerves in the place (the "Sensorium") of Sensation?'

The empiricist school, of which in their different ways Locke and Newton were founders, rejected the notion that had been the basis of much philosophy, that minds can receive knowledge by direct intuition, quite apart from sensory experience. Mind was now regarded as essentially isolated from the physical world: linked only by tenuous threads of nerve. At the same time there were attempts to discover 'laws' of mind, corresponding in some ways to the laws of physics though seldom, if ever, seen as being in quite the same category. Newton did however write (in a letter to Henry Oldenburg, secretary of the Royal Society): 'I suppose the *Science of colours* will be granted *Mathematicall* and as certain as any part of Optiques.' Laws of colour mixture were developed later, especially following the work of Thomas *Young, who made the important discovery in 1801 that all the spectral colours can be produced by mixture of various intensities of only three coloured lights. This took the sensations of colour somewhat outside the realm of physics, and yet they were seen as bound by certain laws. So evidently there could be a lawful science of sensation, and so of mind. Newton fully appreciated that colour sensations are not always given by light, as he said (*Opticks*, Query 16): 'When a Man in the dark presses either corner of his Eye with his finger, he will see a Circle of Colours like those of a Peacock's Tail.' At the same time, much like Pythagoras linking music with the physics of vibrating strings, Newton tried to describe aesthetics according to physical principles (Query 14):

May not the harmony and disacord of Colours arise from the proportions of the Vibrations propagated through the Fibres of the optick Nerves into the Brain, as the harmony and discord of Sounds arise from the proportions of the Vibrations of the Air? For some Colours, if they are view'd together, are agreeable to one another, as those of Gold and Indigo, and others disagree.

So we find attempts to explain perceptual experience, from sensation to aesthetics, by physical principles of the natural sciences. But though, for example, colour mixture is linked to the physics of light, it is not derivable from optical principles. As the direct realism of immediate experience of the object world has been (almost universally) abandoned, we are left with having to devise bridging theories of perception, to relate mind to matter.

It is now generally accepted that perception depends on active physiologically based processes, but this notion is non-intuitive, for we know nothing of such processes or mechanisms by introspection. Moreover, perceiving objects around us seems so simple and easy! It happens so fast and so effortlessly it is hard to conceive the complexity of the processes that we now know must be involved. The notion takes us, however, to concepts familiar to engineers. It is not misleading to describe the organs of the senses—the eyes, ears, *touch receptors, and so on—as 'transducers' that accept and signal patterns of energy from the external world as coded messages, which are read by the brain to infer the state-of-play of the world and of the body's own states. (For detailed information on sensory mechanisms and processes, see Barlow and Mollon, 1982.) Another useful engineering concept is that of 'channels'. The various senses—touch, vision, hearing, and so on—are each subdivided into channels which can be discovered only by experiment. Thus, for example, although this was not at all realized before Young's (1801) colour mixture experiment, *colour vision works with just three channels responding to red, green, and blue light, respectively. All the hundreds of colours we see are neurally mixtures from these three colour channels. Then there are channels representing the orientation of lines and edges, and channels for movement, as shown by direct physiological recording from the visual cortex, and demonstrated dramatically by *Hubel and Wiesel (1962). By less physiologically direct methods, such as selective *adaptation, it has been found that there are more or less independent channels for spatial frequency and many other visual characteristics. The ear has many frequency channels, and there is a score of channels for touch, various kinds of pain, tickle, and for monitoring the positions of the limbs and setting muscle tensions for moving them appropriately. Somehow the outputs from the many channels are combined to give consistent perceptions. Small discrepancies—such as the delay in sound between seeing a ball hit a bat and hearing the impact—are rejected, or pulled into place, to maintain a consistent world.

For signalling by the senses, as from instruments, it is important to appreciate the range of likely or possible objects that may be present. The eye receives all sorts of irrelevant stimuli which are mainly disregarded, just as unwanted data and random disturbances are rejected whenever possible by scientific instruments and in computer signal-processing. Sometimes, though, what is rejected turns out to be just what is needed! The immense difficulties encountered in current attempts to program computers to recognize objects from signals provided by television cameras indicate the incredible complexity and subtlety of animal and human perception.

David *Marr (1980) suggested that object shapes are derived from images via three essential stages: (i) the 'primal sketch'(es), describing intensity changes, locations of critical features such as terminal points, and local geometrical relations; (ii) the '2½-D sketch', giving a preliminary analysis of depth, surface discontinuities, and so on, in a frame that is centred on the viewer; (iii) the '3-D model representation', in an object-centred co-ordinate system, so that we see objects much as they are in 3-D space though they are presented from just one viewpoint. Marr supposed that this last stage is aided by restraints on the range of likely solutions to the problem of what is 'out there', the information-processing restraints being set by assuming typical object shapes—for example that many objects, such as human beings, are modified cylinders. Interestingly, the painter Paul Cézanne came close to this notion in 1904: 'Treat nature by the cylinder, the sphere, the cone, everything in proper perspective so that each side of an object or a plane is directed towards a central point . . . nature for us men is more depth than surface. . . .'

The limited variety of typical objects may set restraints that are useful, both for the artist representing objects and for the *artificial intelligence endeavour to program computers to see; but although it can be difficult to represent or see some atypical objects (or even familiar objects from atypical viewpoints) perhaps it is not clear that these difficulties reflect accepted restraints based on cylinders, spheres, and cones—for many other very different shapes can be depicted and seen without special difficulty.

Looking 'inwards' by introspection, we *seem* to know that perceptions are made of sensations, although from physiological and psychological experiments—as well as from this essentially engineering approach—it has to be denied that sensations are the data of perception. The data are neural *signals* from the transducer senses, analysed by many parallel channels to generate immediately useful predictive hypotheses, which are our perceptual reality of the object world.

It has usually been thought that perception occurs *passively* from inputs from the senses. It is now, however, fairly generally accepted that stored knowledge and assumptions *actively* affect even the simplest perceptions. The relative importance of what are called (especially in artificial intelligence) passive 'bottom–up' processes to active 'top–down' processes is a central controversy. Some evidence bearing on this is presented in the entry *illusions. The changes of shape of wire cubes which reverse spontaneously in depth (Fig. 5 in ILLUSIONS) is clear evidence of subtle 'top–down' processes affecting what used to be regarded as simple characteristics such as size and brightness. But these must be knowledge-based, 'top–down' effects because there are no changes of input from the eyes with depth-reversals of ambiguous figures. These are examples of how illusory phenomena can reveal processes of the perception we depend upon for our knowledge of the world and ourselves.

See also PERCEPTION AS HYPOTHESES.        R. L. G.

Barlow, H. B. and Mollon, J. D. (eds.) (1982). *The Senses*. Cambridge.

Berkeley, G. (1709). *A New Theory of Vision*. (Lindsay, A. D., ed., 1910) London.

Cézanne, P. (March, 1904). Letter from Aix-en-Provence. In Rewald, J. (ed.) (1941), *Letters*, and in Goldwater, R. and Trèves, M. (eds.) (1976), *Artists on Art*, pp. 363–4. London.

Gibson, J. J. (1950). *Perception of the Visual World*. Boston.

Gibson, J. J. (1966). *The Senses Considered as Perceptual Systems*. Boston.

Gombrich, E. (1960). *Art and Illusion*. Oxford.

Gregory, R. L. (1970). *The Intelligent Eye*. London and New York.

Helmholtz, H. von (1867). *Handbuch der Physiologischen Optic*. Hamburg. (Third edn., 1909–11, translated 1924 by Southall, J. P. C., with additions by other hands, as *Helmholtz's Treatise on Physiological Optics*, repr. 1962, New York.)

Hubel, D. H. and Wiesel, T. N. (1962). Receptive field, binocular interaction and functional architecture in the cat's visual cortex. *Journal of Physiology*, **160**, 106–54.

Locke, J. (1690). *Essay Concerning Human Understanding*. (Nidditch, P. H., ed., 1975, Oxford.)

Marr, D. (1980). Representing and computing visual information. In Longuet-Higgins, H. C. and Sutherland, N. S. (eds.), *The Psychology of Vision*. London.

Newton, I. (1704). *Opticks*. (4th edn., 1730, ed. 1952 by Nidditch, P. H., New York.)

Rock, I. (1984). *Perception*. New York.

Zeki, S. (1977). Colour coding in rhesus monkey prestriate cortex. *Brain Research*, **53**, 422–7.

Zeki, S. (1980). The representation of colours in the cerebral cortex. *Nature*, **284**, 412–18.

**PERCEPTION: CULTURAL DIFFERENCES.** Cross-cultural studies in perception arose from speculations on whether different patterns of behaviour and linguistic usage indicated differences in perception. For example, the difficulty of translating colour terms suggested that the ancient Greeks perceived colours differently from present-day observers, and reports from travellers and missionaries suggested that there might be differences in perception between Western and non-Western populations.

The growth of anthropology as an empirical discipline, and the development of psychological techniques modelled on those of physics (sometimes by scientists whose interests spanned both disciplines, such as G. T. *Fechner and E. *Mach), encouraged systematic research and led to several research projects, of which the Torres Straits expedition (1899) is probably the most significant. The object of this expedition was in part to assess the perceptual characteristics of remote groups. The scope of its investigations included acuity of vision, colour vision, visual illusions, and visual perception in general, which were studied by W. H. R. *Rivers; cutaneous sensation and discrimination of weight, studied by W. *McDougall, and hearing, smell, taste, and reaction times, studied by C. S. *Myers.

Although such studies as these, where hypotheses are selected by a worker from an alien culture, have been criticized for restricting the choice of hypotheses and introducing a bias, they are by far the most common and have provided some interesting results.

The effects that have been investigated subsume forms of social usage (for example, the economic structure of a group, child-rearing practices, and nutritional habits), purely environmental influences such as the topology of the terrain, the effect of cultural artefacts such as architectural style, and even genetic factors. Such is the plethora of factors which may influence perception that an entirely convincing isolation of one of them and a demonstration of its effects is not generally achieved. The results to hand strongly suggest, however, that although isolation of causes of the observed cross-cultural differences may be difficult or even impossible, such differences probably do exist.

**Visual perception.** The differences seem to be most pronounced in the visual modality (although this observation may be a result of the experimental bias described above). For example, an extensive study of simple *illusions conducted by Segall, Campbell, and Herskovits showed that certain illusion figures, such as the *Müller-Lyer and the Sander parallelogram, did not evoke such strong effects in the cultures where rectangular objects and arrangements of objects were rare as in those more 'carpentered' cultures where such phenomena abounded. The more carpentered the culture in which the observers lived, the higher was their susceptibility to these illusions. Another influence was found to affect the magnitude of the horizontal–vertical illusion. Observers living in open vistas, such as savannah, experienced the illusion more strongly than those living in more visually confined environments, such as tropical rain forests.

Cross-cultural differences have also been noted in the ability to perceive shape and the orientation of simple geometrical patterns and in the magnitude of shape constancy scores. The latter issue is thought by some to be related to the characteristics of art styles, since these differ in the manner in which they employ constancies. Similarly the ability to *interpret* pictorial material is found to differ with culture. This finding is of some practical consequence, since such materials are used as primary means of communication in illiterate cultures. Specifically it was found that pictures which to a Westerner appear unambiguous are often misunderstood in non-pictorial cultures. However, detailed, but unfortunately sparse, follow-up investigations offer no evidence to sustain the claim that single clearly depicted objects are likely to be consistently misperceived in these cultures. Even in a culture entirely devoid of graphic art, when large drawings of familiar objects printed on cloth were displayed, these were recognized, albeit with difficulty and rather slowly. There is, on the other hand, sufficient evidence to show that *relationships* between various items in the same picture are likely to be misperceived. Thus an observer may maintain that an elephant is nearer to a man than an antelope simply because the elephant is drawn nearer to the man (by perspective) in the plane of the picture, notwithstanding the fact that the elephant is drawn smaller than the antelope and hence, if the implied depth cue is taken into account, should be seen as being further away.

Such failures in correct interpretation of pictorial depth cues were first investigated systematically by W. Hudson, whose work has proved seminal to a large number of studies which confirm the existence of cross-cultural differences. The likelihood of such a misinterpretation varies both with the characteristics of the observer and the nature of the picture. Neither a correct interpretation nor a misinterpretation of any particular picture can therefore be regarded as an index of the observer's ability to perceive pictorial depth.

Considerations of such basic phenomena as the implicit-shape constancy in abstract figures show that the differences observed are not confined to depictions of lifelike scenes. A drawing of a square on a face of a drawn cube, both of which are, in a strictly geometrical sense, diamonds, leads to an impression of a figure whose 'squareness' appears to vary with culture, being greater, for example, in Scottish than in African observers.

Consistent with the above observations, the extent to which pictures can be regarded as object substitutes varies with culture. For example, the ability to categorize objects does not predicate an ability to categorize pictures of these objects equally well.

Perception of colour has traditionally formed a testing ground for linguistic hypotheses, such as the Sapir–Whorf hypothesis which argues that any grouping of colours is entirely determined by linguistic labels extant in any given culture. However, studies of grouping of colours by people drawn from a variety of linguistic communities have put such an interpretation in question. It seems that the same colours are regarded as *focal* (or archetypal) whether a language has a very rudimentary or a sophisticated colour vocabulary. Yet the linguistic cause cannot be said to be entirely routed, for language may exercise influence within the valleys between such focal peaks.

Another issue which has been studied is the perceptual outcome of binocular rivalry, when two different stimuli are presented separately to the two eyes. When the stimuli used were derived from two different cultures, it was observed that the subjects tended to describe the stimuli derived from their culture and ignore the alien stimuli. Ambitious but unfortunately inconclusive studies of eidetic imagery have also been carried out.

**Other perceptual modalities.** Perceptual modalities other than the visual one have received but scanty and unsystematic attention in cross-cultural studies. Of the more complex issues, perception of time has been studied; but here, too, the effects observed can be more readily attributed to the social values that are attached to activities occupying time rather than to time itself.

**Theoretical approaches.** Two theoretical frameworks, deriving from the work of *Piaget and from that of H. A. Witkin, dominate the research. The former is concerned with the stages through which a child passes as it gradually acquires cognitive concepts needed for the effective handling of perceptual information. Such stages as defined by Piaget have also been reported in other cultures and are said to occur in similar sequence. The age ranges within which they occur are, however, said to differ between cultures. Witkin links the style of child-rearing and therefore of general social structure and ecological conditions with the extent to which members of a culture show field dependence. The effects of dependence are apparent not only in perception of social relationships but also in perception in general. Subjects with higher dependence find it more difficult to perceive parts of the perceptual field as discrete from the field as a whole, than do subjects with lower dependence. This distinction in ability affects greatly performance on such tasks as reproduction of simple geometric designs (block design test), detection of a figure embedded in a matrix of irrelevant lines (embedded figure test), or adjustment to the true vertical of a luminous rod presented within a tilted luminous frame in a darkened room. In addition, there are a number of more *ad hoc* hypotheses attempting to interpret the way in which various factors combine to affect perception. One group of these, whose popularity owes more to their appeal to the sense of charity or justice than to empirical evidence, are the 'compensatory hypotheses'. These suggest that rather poor performance by a cultural group in one perceptual modality (such as vision) is likely to be compensated by (generally as the result of ecological or cultural adaptation) a relatively superior performance in another modality (such as hearing or touch).

**Problems.** Although cross-cultural comparisons provide an excellent ground for testing the universality of postulated theories or of observed phenomena, they also present the experimenter with greater than usual methodological obstacles. The main problems are the difficulty of 'distinguishing differences of perception from failures of communication' (D. T. Campbell), and the lack of adequate control groups, since generally populations not only differ in culture but also live in different ecological conditions and are of different genetic stock. Indeed so intertwined are these three variables that many of the studies which are now classified as cross-cultural would, in the not-so-distant past, have been seen as studies of differences in racial characteristics.       J. B. D.

Deregowski, J. B. (1980). *Illusions, Patterns and Pictures: A Cross-cultural Perspective*. London.
Jahoda, G. (1982). *Psychology and Anthropology*. London.
Segall, M. H., Campbell, D. T., and Herskovits, M. (1966). *Influence of Culture on Visual Perception*. Indianapolis.
Triandis, H. et al. (eds.) (1980). *Handbook of Cross-cultural Psychology*, vol. 3. New York.

**PERCEPTION: EARLY GREEK THEORIES.** The *Pre-Socratic philosophers attempted to explain the phenomena of perception, and to show how sensory interactions with the external world differ from non-sensory interactions. Of the several theories they produced, that of Empedocles may stand as typical. Empedocles' views are summarized for us by *Plato in his dialogue the *Meno*:

SOCRATES. Do you agree with Empedocles that existing things give off a sort of effluence?

MENO. Certainly.

SOC. And that they have pores into which and through which the effluences travel?

MENO. Yes.

SOC. And of the effluences, some fit some of the pores, while others are too small or too big?

MENO. That's right.

SOC. And there's something you call sight?

MENO. There is.

SOC. From this, then, 'grasp what I say to you', as Pindar puts it: colour is an effluence from things which is fitted to sight and perceptible.

The book in front of you is constantly emitting 'effluences' (streams of minute particles) differing one from another in kind; as they strike your body, some fit snugly into various of its 'pores' or openings, others do not; one kind of effluence (call it 'colour') fits precisely into the pores of your eyes—and thus you see the book. To see the book is simply for your eyes to receive colour-effluences sent out by the book. Similarly with the other senses; so that, in general, to perceive an object is to receive from it effluences of a kind to fit the organs of perception.

This theory is thoroughly 'materialistic': it makes no mention of non-physical objects of perception (immaterial 'sense-data'), and it does not invoke a peculiarly 'mental' relation of 'experiencing' or 'being aware of' an object; rather, one physical object reacts with another. The theory was criticized for just this reason: Theophrastus observes that 'one might wonder . . . how inanimate objects differ from the rest with regard to perception; for things fit into the pores of inanimate objects too'. Empedocles himself used the mechanics of pores and effluences to explain various non-perceptual phenomena (reflection, magnetism, deciduousness): how, then, can his theory distinguish between perception and other, non-sensory, pore-and-effluence interactions with the world? (Suppose a modern psychologist were to say that perception was a discriminatory capacity, nothing more; then we might ask him how he proposed to distinguish genuinely perceptual activity from, say, the performance of a potato-sorting machine which discriminates among potatoes according to their size.)

Theophrastus remarks that, in Empedocles' view, perception comes about 'by likes'; and a surviving fragment from Empedocles' own pen confirms the point:

For by earth we see earth, by water water,
by air bright air, and by fire brilliant fire.

Thus for perception to take place, the effluence

must not only 'fit' the appropriate pore: it must also be 'like' or homogeneous with (some parts of the walls of) the pore. I see red when a red effluence slots neatly into a red-edged pore in my eye. Perceptual interactions differ from non-perceptual interactions just because they require homogeneity, as well as a good fit between effluence and pores.

There are two points to note about this suggestion. First, it is pretty crude: as a physical theory of perception, it will not do; and Theophrastus tells us that Empedocles himself, in his detailed accounts of the modes of perception, did not in fact assign much work to the notion of 'likeness' or homogeneity. But secondly, and more importantly, the notion of homogeneity is thoroughly materialistic: in order to distinguish perceiving from other, non-perceptual, activities, Empedocles does not leave the hard land of matter. He does not appeal to some soft 'mental' or 'experiential' aspect of perceivers to mark them off as beings of a unique kind; rather, he supposes that the crucial difference between perceiving and non-perceptual activity can be characterized in physical terms: biology and physiology (we might now add: neurophysiology) will suffice to give a complete account of the phenomena of perception.   J. BA.

**PERCEPTION OF MOTION PICTURES.** The explanatory power of perceptual theories and the generality of perceptual research findings are both strongly challenged by the sensory phenomena on which motion pictures and television are based, and by the perceptual devices that they employ.

Motion pictures are possible because we perceive continuous movement in response to a rapid succession of static views. The phenomenon is often called *apparent movement* (or stroboscopic movement). Writers about cinema routinely appeal to 'visual persistence' to explain this fundamental phenomenon. Such persistence, however, although real enough (see AFTER-IMAGES) simply cannot explain apparent movement. At best, it names the fact that we do not detect the brief periods (c. 1/80 sec.) during which the motion picture screen is dark. At worst, persistence would result in the superposition of the successive views. In fact, we have only begun to explore the sensory mechanisms (including direct motion detectors, retrograde masking, and fast and slow neural channels) that must contribute to the phenomenon of apparent movement by eliminating the superposition of successive disparate views that mere visual persistence would provide, and to consider the cognitive processes that fit compelling perceptual meaning to those views (Hochberg and Brooks, 1978).

Some of these mechanisms and processes must also be engaged when we build up a continuous percept of our physical environment by taking successive discrete and discontinuous glances at it. Motion pictures and television differ in significant ways, however, from the information provided by glances taken at the real world. When the viewer looks over his environment, his knowledge of where in space his eye is directed during each successive glance is at least potentially informative about how the separate glimpses fit together into a single coherent object or scene. Considerable thought and research have been devoted to this matter of 'taking eye direction into account', but motion picture and television usage assures us that more elaborate integrative processes are available to the viewer than have been the subject of such research. When different camera shots of an object or scene are projected successively on the screen, the viewer's knowledge of where his eye is directed could not possibly tell him how the successive views are to be put together. At best, by taking his eye direction into account, the viewer could learn only that all of the partial views of the scene have been presented at the same place in space, i.e. on the viewing screen.

Changes in camera viewpoint are made for many purposes, and in several distinct ways. Such view changes serve to direct the flow of thought, emphasizing specific objects or events; to provide visual rhythms analogous to those of poetry and music; to recapture visual attention once a view's content has been identified and the viewer's visual interest wanes; and to provide narrative economy by 'skimming' lengthy events and presenting only the essential features. Most importantly, by changing camera viewpoints, the film-maker can present a scene that is vastly larger than each view on the screen, and can present scenes that do not really exist in any one place, or that are too large to display all at once on the screen in sufficient detail.

View changes can be continuous or discontinuous. That is, the camera may move continuously, as shown by the solid arrow in Fig. 1, from one station (1) to another (2), moving perpendicular to the line of sight (as in the *tracking shot*, Fig. 1a), or moving in the direction of the line of sight (as in the *dolly shot*, Fig. 1c). These movements, or their combinations, usually offer visual information about the depth relationships within the scene (for example, *motion parallax*; note the different displacements of near and far objects between the first and last shots as shown in Figs. 1a and 1c). Keeping the camera stationary, but changing the direction in which it is pointed from 1 to 2 in the *pan shot* of Fig. 1b, or changing its focal length in a *zoom* which merely imposes a uniform magnification on the field of view (Fig. 1d), achieves changes in view that are superficially similar to the track and dolly shots respectively, but provide no motion parallax and therefore no depth information.

Theoretically, because they lack depth information, pans and zooms should look very different from dolly and track shots, but for reasons of convenience and economy film-makers often use the former instead of the latter, with results that appear to be acceptable to the viewer. Although our ability to detect motion parallax in the

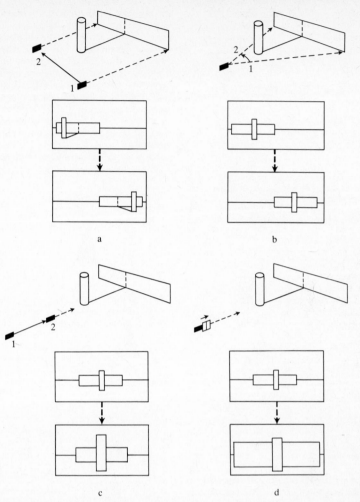

**Fig. 1.** Continuous transitions. **a.** Tracking shot: at top, the camera (black rectangle) moves from station 1 to station 2 (solid arrow); the dotted arrows show the camera's line of sight at beginning and end of section. Below: view from point 1 over view from point 2. Note effects of parallax. **b.** Pan shot: camera rotates (solid arrow) around stationary point. Note absence of parallax in resulting views. **c.** Dolly shot: camera approaches from station 1 to 2. Note parallax (i.e. change in relative size of nearer and further objects). **d.** Zoom shot: camera remains stationary, but focal length is increased. Note that magnification, but no parallax, is obtained.

laboratory is astonishingly good, how much we actually use it in motion pictures or in real life is an unexplored question of some importance to film-makers and of considerable theoretical interest to psychologists.

Part of its theoretical interest rests on the following issue: in recent years, several perceptual theorists have proposed that our visual systems are *directly* sensitive to the spatial information that is provided by transformations over time within the light that reaches the eye of a viewer who is in motion relative to a scene. In the case of track and dolly shots, this includes the three-dimensional relationships within the scene; in all of the transformations, the overlap between successive views

provides information about the loci of objects in the scene and the order in which the successive views were obtained. This is true of *discontinuous* sequences of overlapping views, as well: the sequence in Fig. 2 specifies that W is to the left of Z even though the two are never shown at the same time.

It is proposed that both in normal saccadic glances (rapid changes of regard between which the eye remains static for about 200 milliseconds), and in motion picture transitions, we respond directly to the visual information about spatial layout that the view sequences contain. At least in the case of discontinuous motion picture cuts, however, the perceptual process appears to be

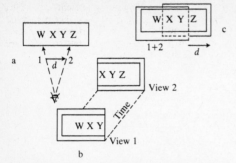

**Fig. 2.** Overlapping view sequence specifies the relative loci of parts of the scene (W, Z) that are not on the screen at the same time, and also specifies the direction of change in view (*d*) of eye or camera. **a.** Scene. **b.** Successive views. **c.** Information theoretically available in the view sequence at **b.**

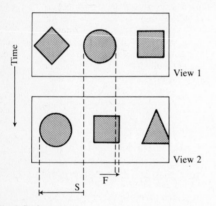

**Fig. 3.** Bad cut, 1.

neither as automatic, direct, nor veridical as the preceding analysis implies. The relationship between successive views may be grossly misperceived, even though those views overlap substantially. In Fig. 3, for example, although successive views 1 and 2 are in fact displaced leftward (vector S), rightward movement (F) is perceived (except at very slow presentation rates) because objects in one view have been incorrectly 'identified' by the viewer's perceptual system as being quite different objects in the preceding view. There is a great deal of laboratory work showing that apparent motion occurs, in this way, even between unlike but contiguous shapes or parts of shapes (Hochberg and Brooks, 1978; Kolers, 1972; Orlansky, 1940). And these are not merely laboratory phenomena: film-makers distinguish good and bad cuts, and most examples of the latter result from an unwanted apparent movement that may be completely independent of the actual displacement between views (Vorkapich, 1972), or indeed result from an apparent absence of displacement where a large displacement in fact exists. For example, when the camera direction

changes by approximately 180° ('crossing the camera axis', as in Fig. 4), there is a brief but upsetting impression that the people remain on the same places on the screen, but change their shape (as signified by the dotted arrows in that figure). Similarly changes in focal length in the traditional sequence of Fig. 5a should be large ones, for if they are small, as in Fig. 5b, the apparent movement between contours in successive views is perceived as a rapid expansion or approach, rather than as the changes in the field of attention that we discuss below.

Successive views of different objects or people

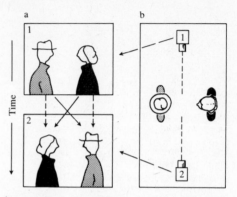

**Fig. 4.** Bad cut, 2. **a.** Sequence of two views taken from camera positions 1 and 2 in **b.**

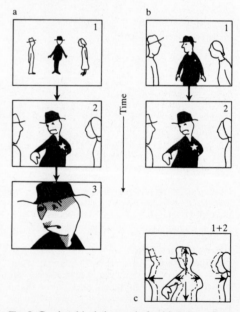

**Fig. 5.** Good and bad changes in focal length. **a.** Good sequence of long shot, medium shot, and close-up. **b.** Cut from 1 to 2 is bad because with small change in focal length, unintended movement occurs between successive views. **c.** Perceptual consequence of the sequence in **b.**

are often aligned deliberately in order to avoid the apparent 'jump' that occurs between successive non-aligned contours, and thereby to achieve a cut that is smooth and unaccented. Such cuts probably take longer to comprehend, however, because no adequate signal has been given to the eye that the view has been changed.

The factor of apparent movement between unrelated but contiguous successive shapes is of practical importance in that its various cinematic manifestations are evidently used by film-makers (through rules of thumb, and by trial and error in film editing) to achieve comprehensibility, and to control the accents in the cutting rhythm (or montage). It is theoretically important in showing that the overall relationship between discontinuous overlapping views is not directly and automatically perceived. Where the local factors do not change to provide apparent movement that conveys the intended spatial relationship, the film-maker must allow the viewer sufficient time to construct the spatial relationship using other sources of information. Those responses (i.e. 'readings' of any sequence) that depend on factors that are relatively local, but undetailed, like the phenomena in Fig. 3, seem to be rapid, effortless, and transient, and tend therefore to determine how sequences of brief views are perceived. Responses that depend on more detailed identification, or on more involved 'visual inferences', as discussed below, are slower, and perhaps more sustained. The same sequence of views may therefore be differently comprehended at different cutting rates. For instance, Fig. 3 appears to move rightward at rapid rates (less than a second per view) and leftward at slow rates (such as three seconds per view).

Why don't these local factors cause noticeable confusions in the course of normal saccadic glances as they do in cinematic view sequences? Several factors may account for this difference. In saccades, the entire field of view (well over 100°) is translated as a whole, as compared to the relatively small regions (c.45°) within which translation occurs on the motion picture or television screen; a brief but significant period of partial visual suppression accompanies each saccade, and this may

prevent the local apparent movements that afflict cinematic cuts, and may perhaps thereby permit invariant information in overlapping saccadic glimpses to be correctly used. Furthermore, we know that the viewer can take some account of the direction in which his or her eye has been ordered to move. Perhaps most important of all, in the case of saccadic glances, the viewer has asked the visual question that motivated the eye movement, and to which the resulting glimpse comes as an answer.

Such perceptual question-asking or 'hypothesis-testing' (a central feature in current perceptual theories: see Gregory, 1974; Hochberg, 1979) cannot readily be studied in the course of normal saccades, nor even with motion picture cuts that overlap substantially (e.g. Fig. 2), because of the purely visual information such events contain, and the possibility of the direct use of such information. But the fact is that *many or even most motion picture cuts occur between views that do not overlap at all*. It is these that allow the film-maker to construct scenes and events that never existed. No purely sensory information within such transformations could provide the basis for their combination in the mind's eye of the viewer, nor make the view sequence comprehensible. The film-maker connects such non-overlapping shots either by leading the viewer to ask the visual question, to which the next view is an answer, or by providing a context that identifies the relative locations of subsequently presented views. Fig. 6a is an example of the former: an actor looking leftward in one view naturally leads the viewer to expect that the next shot shows the object of the actor's regard, i.e. to the viewer's left. Fig. 6b is an example of the latter: in the sequence of a long shot followed by a medium shot and close-ups (views 1–4, respectively), the long shot acts as an *establishing shot* within which the non-overlapping close-ups take their appropriate places. (Note that the factor at work in Fig. 6a would reverse the relative locations of views 3 and 4, were the latter presented without the first two shots in their sequence.) After a sequence of non-overlapping close-ups has gone on for a while, or after a *cutaway shot* has shown

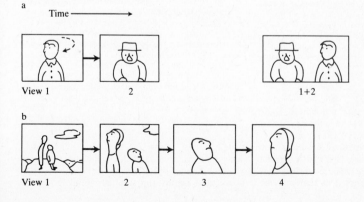

a

Time ⟶

View 1      2                1+2

b

View 1      2      3      4

**Fig. 6.** Typical devices for providing meaning to successive views.

*parallel action* going on elsewhere, *re-establishing shots* (like view 1) may again be needed.

Some of the film-makers' devices are clearly mere conventions (for instance: dissolves, indicating parallel action; calendar leaves, indicating elapsed time); some are simply logical inferences that follow from the viewer's legitimate assumption that the film sequence was created with a coherent narrative or expositional purpose (recent attempts to analyse the maxims of spoken discourse, notably by Grice, 1968, and Searle, 1969, may suggest ways to study such inferences). Some methods probably tap more general cognitive processes: for example, in the sequence from long shot to close-ups in Figs. 5 and 6, the viewer's attention is directed first to a general survey of the scene and then constrained to smaller regions and details that take their meaning from the preceding context.

Research in this area has barely begun. The cognitive skills by which the information from successive glances is integrated—skills that are of the utmost importance to any perceptual theory that aspires to apply beyond the momentary glance—are open to study through the medium of motion picture cutting. Since *Leonardo da Vinci, perceptual research and theory have been primarily concerned with the still picture. For both practical and theoretical reasons, we should turn our attention to motion pictures.          J. H.

Gregory, R. L. (1974). Choosing a paradigm for perception. In Carterette, E. C. and Friedman, M. P. (eds.), *Handbook of Perception*, vol. I. New York.

Grice, H. (1968). Utterer's meaning, sentence-meaning and word-meaning. *Foundations of Language*, **4**, 225–42.

Hochberg, J. (1978). *Perception* (2nd ed.). Englewood Cliffs, New Jersey.

Hochberg, J. (1979). Sensation and perception. In Hearst, E. (ed.), *The First Century of Experimental Psychology*. Hillsdale, New Jersey.

Hochberg, J. and Brooks, V. (1978). The perception of motion pictures. In Carterette, E. C. and Friedman, M. P. (eds.), *Handbook of Perception*, vol. X. New York.

Kolers, P. A. (1972). *Aspects of Motion Perception*. Oxford.

Orlansky, J. (1940). The effect of similarity and difference in form on apparent visual movement. *Archives of Psychology*, **246**, 85.

Reisz, K. and Millar, G. (1968). *The Technique of Film Editing*. New York.

Searle, J. R. (1969). *Speech Acts: an essay in the philosophy of language*. Cambridge.

Vorkapich, S. (1972). A fresh look at the dynamics of filmmaking. *American Cinematographer*, February 1972.

**PERCEPTION AS HYPOTHESES.** Philosophers have generally considered *visual* perceptions to be closely related to, or even to be samples of, surfaces of surrounding objects. Thus, vision was thought to be rather like *smell, and as direct and immediate as *touch. However, with the invention of the camera obscura, and the related discovery that the object world is imaged optically in the eyes, it became clear that patterns of light in the eyes (retinal images) are transmitted to the brain by coded electrical signals (action potentials), which are then, somehow, read as objects having very different and far richer properties than the optical pictures in the eyes. It became clear, at least to physiologists, that there must be a great deal going on in the brain in order to produce perceptions from sensory signals: that our perceptions are created in us, and that they may be very different from the corresponding objects of the external world, as described by physicists.

Physical accounts of objects have changed greatly over the centuries, but without, in general, corresponding change in the appearance of the objects in question. Objects *look* much the same whether they are believed to be made of billiard-ball atoms, or probability distributions of wave functions; so there must be discrepancies between the appearance and the scientific description—even though science depends on observation. Futhermore, there are *illusions, of many kinds, which are hard to reconcile with a 'direct' or 'immediate knowledge' account of *perception.

The notion that perceptions are *hypotheses*—perhaps much like the predictive hypotheses of science—derives from the account of perception given by Hermann von *Helmholtz (1821–94), who suggested that perceptions are *conclusions of unconscious inductive inferences*. Introducing this idea, he compared visual perception with language, and how we learn language (see LANGUAGE: LEARNING WORD MEANINGS). Thus, Helmholtz (1866) points out that, as with meanings of words, 'the concept of the normal meaning of frequently repeated perceptions can come about with immutable certainty, lightning speed and without the slightest meditation.' Helmholtz continues:

The example of language is instructive in another respect, for it affords an explanation for the problem of how such a certain and conventional understanding of a system of signs may be obtained, considering that these signs can have only a quite arbitrarily selected effect upon the individual observer . . . The child hears the usual name of an object pronounced again and again when it is shown or given to him, with the same word. Thus the word becomes attached to the thing in his memory more firmly the more frequently it is repeated. . . . The same name may become attached to a class of objects similar to each other, or to a class of similar processes. . . . I conclude from these observations that by frequent repetition of similar experiences we can attain the production and continual strengthening of a continually recurring connection between two very different perceptions, or ideas, e.g. between the sound of a word and visible and tactual perceptual images, which originally need not have had any natural connection; and that when this has happened we are no longer able to report in detail how we have arrived at this knowledge and on what individual observations it is based.'

Helmholtz stresses that the association of word with meaning, and of sensation with meaning in perception, comes from regular experiences of the connection with no (or few) exceptions. In this way, meanings are built up *inductively* (from many instances to a conclusion that is not logically necessary), both for language and for perceptions. These associations are, presumably, built up largely by interaction with objects—so that, for example, the patterns of the grain of wood become associated with a hard substance which can be dropped without breaking, and which can be cut with a saw; and the transparency of glass becomes associated with potentially dangerous brittleness; in consequence, we behave very differently with wooden as opposed to glass objects. Helmholtz suggested that we come to our ideas of the physical form of objects inductively, by combining visual experiences from many viewpoints, following the rules of perspective. Comparing these 'inductive conclusions' with the scientific method, Helmholtz says: 'Inductive conclusions are never so reliable as well-tested conclusions of conscious thought. . . . False inductions in the interpretation of our perceptions we tend to label as illusions.' Of these he says (1894) 'Obviously, in these cases there is nothing wrong with the activity of the organ of sense and its corresponding nervous mechanism which produces the illusion . . . It is, rather, simply an illusion of the judgement of the material presented to the senses, resulting in a false idea of it.' He goes on to say, 'These unconscious conclusions derived from sensation are equivalent . . . to [his italics] *conclusions from analogy*'. He attaches a lot of weight to active structuring of perception, which is especially evident in conditions of dim illumination, or when complex crystals or other structures are viewed stereoscopically:

a visual impression may be misunderstood at first, by not knowing how to attribute the correct depth-dimensions; as when a distant light, for example, is taken to be a near one, or *vice versa*. Suddenly it dawns on us what it is, and immediately, under the influence of the correct comprehension, the correct perceptual image also is developed in its full intensity. . . . Similar experiences have happened to everybody, proving that the elements in sense-perceptions that are derived from experience are just as powerful as those that are derived from present sensations.

In this connection, phenomena of *ambiguity* (which occur especially with vision and hearing) are clearly very important: 'Without any change of the retinal images, the same observer may see in front of him various perceptual images in succession, in which case the variation is easy to recognize.' For these and other reasons, Helmholtz thinks of perception as given by learning, and as *empirical*. It is not passive acceptance of stimulus patterns, but rather *projection* (though not merely geometrical projection) from internally organized knowledge of objects and processes. In current terminology, this may be termed use of stored knowledge 'top–down', for interpreting or reading sensory signals, as originating from particular objects. Similarly, we project our meanings of words on what we describe. The emphasis on processes searching for the best reading, or inter-

pretation, on the available evidence, we call 'active'; in comparison with 'passive' accounts, such as that of J. J. *Gibson.

It seems a natural development, to extend Helmholtz's account, by calling perceptions (which, not altogether happily, he called 'perceptual images'), rather, *perceptual hypotheses* (Gregory 1970, 1981). This suggests useful analogy with hypotheses in science, and the ways in which they are developed, used, and tested. That is not to say that perceptual hypotheses and scientific hypotheses are formed, or used, or tested identically; but they do seem to share strikingly significant similarities. Since the methods of science are open to inspection, they may provide a basis for considering processes of perception, which (as Helmholtz realized) are exceedingly hard to discover by direct methods, because they are hidden in brain processes that are only beginning to be understood; and also because they are unconscious.

It is generally accepted that science starts with inductively discovered associations and regularities, which may be conditional (glass breaks if it is dropped). These generalizations are used for *prediction* (the glass will break if it is dropped; it will rain when the temperature falls), and so for anticipating and planning—allowing intelligent behaviour. Only primitive behaviour is reflex from stimuli (see REFLEX ACTION); behaviour that follows the identification of objects is appropriate to their characteristics and potentialities—and these are generally not able to be sensed at the time. For example, the fact that glass is brittle has been established (at some cost) by experience in the past—and this fact is available now as knowledge, allowing appropriate perception of, and behaviour towards, it. It follows that a soap film or a perspex sheet, mistaken for glass, may be treated and seen inappropriately. Powers to predict are vitally important uses of hypotheses, both in science and in perception. In each case, prediction involves the application of analogies top–down from stored knowledge. In each case, also, it allows behaviour to continue with only partial, or even *no*, available sensed information, such as when we cross a familiar room in the dark. And the predictive 'look ahead' registers the speed needed, for example, to return a fast moving tennis ball, so that behaviour is not generally delayed by the physiological *reaction time (which Helmholtz was the first to measure).

The present is read from the past, to enable prediction and planning for the future. But, for perception, this applies only to the immediate future, generally less than one second ahead in time. Perception is remarkably fast, and needs to be, because unexpected events do happen, and they can be dangerous. In this respect, perception differs from science—and differs from our conceptual understanding. Indeed, it may be said that we have perceptual hypotheses and conceptual hypotheses of the world (and of ourselves), which are different, and which work on different time-scales. The factor of differing time-scales provides a clue to why perceptual and conceptual hypotheses differ, and why they may conflict. For it would be impossible to access the entire corpus of our knowledge for each perception, occuring in a fraction of a second. (This principle of small computers with restricted knowledge bases, without access to the main database, for rapid if tentative and approximate decisions, is now of necessity used in large computer systems.)

Perhaps the most dramatic separation between perceptual and conceptual hypotheses occurs in conjuring (Gregory, 1986)—a subject which, though extremely interesting, is not well studied by psychologists. During a successful conjuring trick, which may unfold quite slowly, the spectator sees events occurring which are either divorced from his understanding or are linked to some false understanding which generates predictions that fail to materialize.

We relate perception to conception by perceptually guided activities requiring understanding, such as making and mending things. Thus, the new development of hand-on science centres (such as the Exploratorium in San Francisco, the Toronto Science Centre, the Launch Pad gallery of the Science Museum in London, the Exploratory in Bristol, and others in France and in India) may help to enrich the perception of participants, by developing their understanding so that they appreciate in depth what they see, and so that they see more fully because they understand what they are handling and looking at. This has exciting implications for *education.

Hypotheses in the sciences are not only selected according to data: they also affect how data are selected and interpreted. This is true, also, for perception. Thus, the eyes are directed to what may be needed next, and to checking current perceptions, especially by checking predictions. But more subtly, as was shown by Ernst *Mach, apparently raw sensory data may be affected by the prevailing perception, with no change of stimulation involved—as in depth-ambiguous figures, or objects, such as Mach's card. This may be seen by folding a piece of card to form a corner, standing it on a table, and viewing it from a few feet away. It should be placed so that an inside surface is in shadow. The card will 'flip' in depth. When depth-reversed, the shadow will appear as a mark or stain, and considerably darker. This is because it is unlikely that an *outside* surface (as the inside shadowed surface now appears to be) would be in shadow. It is more likely that it is truly darker (has lower albedo) and this is how it appears when depth-reversed as shadows are minimized by the perceptual system. So a basic, relatively simple sensation such as brightness, is affected top–down by the prevailing perception—or hypothesis—of the objects before the eyes. Top–down knowledge of specific classes of objects also has clear perceptual effects. For example, a hollow mask of a face, seen from a few feet away, and viewed with both eyes in normal lighting, does not *look* hollow, but appears instead as a normal nose-sticking-out face. Here, evidently the stored knowledge about faces is forcing rejection of the many and powerful 'bottom–up' depth-information cues (from stereoscopy, texture, shadows, and so on) signalling that the mask is hollow, in order to maintain what is usually a correct (though in this case incorrect) perception of a face. This happens only with very familiar objects which are virtually never reversed in depth, so this is a specific effect of 'top–down' knowledge. The same tends to happen in science when data contradict a well-established hypothesis—for it may be more likely that the data are incorrect than that the hypothesis is wrong. This is one reason why it is (rightly) very difficult to refute firmly held hypotheses—and why prejudices can be useful.

Helmholtz wrote of the importance in perception of rules (such as the laws of perspective, for seeing distance and form), and rules and laws are of course central in scientific hypotheses. Rules of perception are emphasized in much of the recent work in computer vision (Marr, 1982), as *algorithms for handling data. Such rules can produce even clearly impossible perceptions when they are applied from misleading data, or false assumptions. A simple example is the Impossible Triangle picture (Penrose and Penrose, 1958) and the corresponding three dimensional object (Gregory, 1970). (See ILLUSIONS, Fig. 8.) There are also many examples in Maurits Escher's pictures. These paradoxes are produced by the (false) assumption that features, which from a given viewpoint are seen as touching, are lying at the same distance or in the same plane, though in fact they are not. It may be noted that when similar juxtapositions in depth occur with separate objects (as in William Hogarth's engraving, the *Fisherman*, (1754), in which the woman leaning out of the window with a candle is apparently lighting the pipe of a distant walker on the hill, behind the house), this is not seen as a visual paradox—but rather an explicable joke. (See ART AND VISUAL ABSTRACTION.) It seems that such visual paradoxes from false assumptions only occur *within* objects and not *between* objects. Similarly, paradoxes from false assumptions in science probably only occur within a single descriptive system.

On this essentially Helmholtzian account, mind is seen as consisting of hypotheses of perception and understanding: hypotheses (as perceptual illusions) may be ambiguous, distorted, paradoxical, or fictional, and perhaps never close to truth; nevertheless the private hypotheses of perception and the shared hypotheses of conceptions make up our reality.                                    R. L. G.

Gregory, R. L. (1970). *The Intelligent Eye*. London.
Gregory, R. L. (1981). *Mind in Science*. London.
Gregory, R. L. (1986). Conjuring. In *Odd Perceptions*, pp. 59–62. London.
Helmholtz, H. von (1896). The Origin of the correct

interpretation of our sensory impressions. In *Treatise on Physiological Optics*, 2nd edn.

Helmholtz, H. von (1866). *Treatise on Physiological Optics*, vol. 3, 3rd edn. Trans. edited by Southall, J. P. C., Optical Society of America, New York, 1925, section 26. (Reprinted by Dover, New York, 1962.) (Also given in Warren, R. M. and Warren, R. P. (1968), *Helmholtz on Perception: Its physiology and development*. New York.

Mach, E. (1897; 5th edn. 1959). *The Analysis of Sensations*, New York.

**PERLS,** FRITZ (1893–1970), German-born psychoanalyst. See GESTALT THERAPY.

**PERSONAL EQUATION.** Several important characteristics of the human observer have been discovered by astronomers. Most clebrated is the 'personal equation': corrections applied to individual differences in response time in observing stars crossing graticule lines in transit telescopes. This was extremely important as clocks were set by these measures; in 1799 the Astronomer Royal at Greenwich, Nevil Maskelyne, dismissed his assistant, D. Kinnebrook, because Kinnebrook recorded stellar transit time almost a second later than Maskelyne did. The method used was James Bradley's (1693–1762) 'eye and ear' method. The observer looked at the clock, noting the time to the nearest second, and then counted seconds as he heard the beats of a pendulum while watching the star cross the telescope field. As it crossed the field, he noted the position of the star in relation to each of a series of parallel threads in the eyepiece. This task involved co-ordination between eye and ear, and judgement of the position of each thread. The method was supposed to be accurate to one- or at least to two-tenths of a second—so Kinnebrook's difference of eight-tenths of a second appeared as such a gross error that Maskelyne concluded he had fallen into 'some irregular and confused method of his own'. However, the German astronomer Friedrich Bessel (1784–1846) at Königsberg eventually heard of the incident and realized that there may be large personal differences. In 1820 Bessel compared himself with a colleague, Walbeck at Königsberg, by taking observations of ten stars on alternate nights, for five nights. Bessel observed them earlier than Walbeck, there being an average difference of 1·041 seconds between them. This difference was so large that there may have been an error of method—but nevertheless it stimulated research. When the chronograph was invented in 1859 absolute response times could be made; and observations were corrected accordingly.

It seems clear that, in this complicated task at least, there is a major element of *anticipation in response to a stimulus. If the importance of anticipation had been generally realized, the history of experimental psychology would have been very different—for the immensely (indeed seductively) powerful stimulus–response paradigm would surely not have been accepted as the basis of perception and behaviour. See also REACTION TIMES.                                    R. L. G.

Boring, E. G. (1929; 1950). *A History of Experimental Psychology*, ch. 8. New York.

Gregory, R. L. (1981). *Mind in Science*. London.

**PERSONAL IDENTITY.** In ordinary everyday affairs we are sometimes concerned with questions of personal identity. The police, for example, may want to know whether the man they have detained is the man who broke into the cricket pavilion. It may be a difficult question to answer. Perhaps the fingerprints on the door-jamb were smudged. But the difficulty is not of a sort which calls for reflection on what is meant by 'personal identity'. For the police, questions like 'Is this the same person?' are practical questions, not conceptual ones. The questions and answers involve the criteria of personal identity, but they are not about the criteria.

Conceptual questions about personal identity may arise either from philosophizing which throws in doubt our ordinary practice with 'Is this the same person?' question, or from extraordinary cases, real or imaginary, where the 'Is this the same person?' question cannot be answered on the basis of our ordinary practice. It is not unusual for philosophers writing on personal identity to refer to extraordinary cases with a view to persuading their readers that one sort of consideration should be treated as decisive. The contrast is usually between a mental criterion, such as *memory, and a bodily criterion.

The philosophizing which pre-eminently throws in doubt our ordinary practice with 'Is this the same person?' question is that of *Descartes, though the questions about personal identity to which his philosophy gave rise came to the fore only in the writings of his successors, in particular John *Locke (*Essay concerning Human Understanding*, bk. ii, ch. xxvii) and David *Hume (*Treatise of Human Nature*, bk. i, pt. iv, sect. 6). To understand how Descartes came to set the scene for Locke, Hume, and subsequent philosophers writing on personal identity, it is necessary to sketch, very briefly, the relevant part of his philosophy.

Descartes was concerned, among other things, to replace the medieval, largely Aristotelian, conception of the world as inhabited by a multitude of things programmed teleologically according to their various fixed intelligible essences. For *Aristotle, as for *Plato, the paradigm of explanation was mathematical. The relations of numbers are necessary relations, and knowledge is of what is necessarily, and therefore unchangingly, the case. But despite their efforts, possibly inspired by the Pythagorean discovery of the numerical basis of musical concordances, to bring numbers and nature together conceptually, they remained distinct, with the result that science was not proof against scepticism. Descartes saw a way of reading the necessity of number-relations into nature. He had invented analytical geometry, which shows how every geometrical object or relation can be given numerical expression. It follows that if the extension of spatial, i.e. physical, objects is the extension of geometrical objects, and if 'matter' is defined in terms of this extension, then matter is thereby brought into the domain of what is necessarily true. Nature, *qua* matter, becomes through and through numerical. There were problems—such as how one bit of matter can exclude another bit of matter from the same place if there is no more to matter than extension—but Descartes thought they could be dealt with without having to add something non-numerical to the definition, such as solidity. But one major problem remained. It does not follow from the truths of arithmetic and geometry being necessary that science is proof against scepticism. There is still a gap between justified subjective certainty and objective necessity. Descartes needed to find a criterion whereby he could recognize those things of which he could justifiably claim to be certain. He found it via the intuition 'I think, therefore I am'. This, he thought, is true without a shadow of doubt. What assures me of its truth is my clear and distinct perception of it. Provided there is not an all-powerful malicious demon who makes things appear clear and distinct to me which are not, I can therefore adopt this as my criterion.

Now, Descartes thought that someone who thinks 'I think, therefore I am' is certain not only that this thought is occurring but also that there is a being which thinks the thought. He went on to consider whether there is more, essentially, to this being than that it is capable of thought. Specifically, is it essentially a being with a body? He argued (fallaciously, according to many critics both contemporary and present-day) that it is not. Accordingly, he dismissed, as philosophically naïve, what he described as 'that notion of the union of soul and body which everybody always has in himself without doing philosophy—viz., that there is one single person who has at once body and consciousness'. His own notion of a person was that of a particular thinking being which happens to be, but could equally well not be, united with a particular body. The significance of his replacement of our ordinary notion of a person with that of a thinking being which just happens to be united with a body is that it allows for the question 'How are such beings to be identified, and re-identified, if not by reference to the bodies they happen to occupy?'

Our ordinary practice with 'Is this the same person?' question is geared to the notion everybody always has of themselves, the notion that there is one single person who has at once body and *consciousness. It is not geared to the notion of a person as a being for whom a body is not conceptually necessary. Assuming that the question still makes sense, we need a new practice with 'Is this the same person?' to go with the new notion. Obviously it will be a very different practice. Given the origin in Descartes's philosophy of both questions, we may expect it to be rather like trying to find a meaning for 'Is this the same bit of matter, or has another, of exactly the same shape and size, taken its place?', with 'matter' defined solely in terms of extension.

Probably the most revealing attempt to find a meaning for 'Is this the same person?', with 'person' defined in the new, non-body-implying way, is that by Hume. He reformulates the personal identity question as the question 'whether in pronouncing concerning the identity of a person, we observe some real bond among his perceptions, or only feel one among the ideas we form of them'. This is revealing precisely because the question has been transformed into one a person can ask only about himself. Only he is aware of 'his perceptions'. So it is no longer the sort of question that could, on occasion, truthfully be answered with 'No; it is somebody else'. The sort of answer now catered for is 'There is a real bond among my perceptions' or 'There is no real bond, only a felt one'. It has become a question about the unity of a person's consciousness rather than what we ordinarily understand as a question about someone's identity.

Hume opts for there being only a felt bond. There is felt to be a bond because causal relations exist between a person's experiences. 'The true idea of the human mind, is to consider it as a system of different perceptions or different existences, which are linked together by the relation of cause and effect, and mutually produce, destroy, influence, and modify each other.'

Ordinarily we would think of any causal relations between different experiences as following from their being the same person's experiences, with telepathy as a possible exception to the rule. Hume, if the question about the unity of consciousness is regarded as being one about personal identity, tries to reverse that conceptual order. It is hardly surprising that (in the Appendix to the *Treatise*) he should write: 'Upon a more strict review of the section concerning personal identity, I find myself involved in such a labyrinth, that, I must confess, I neither know how to correct my former opinions, nor how to render them consistent.' He has reaped the harvest sown by Descartes.

Locke says that 'personal identity consists . . . in the identity of consciousness'. By 'consciousness' he means something that can be 'interrupted by forgetfulness', but also something that can be 'extended back' to actions done by people long since dead and buried. Locke says that a person who extends his consciousness back to actions done by someone in the distant past 'finds himself the same person' as the person who performed the actions. Exactly what he means by this is debatable, and has been debated at considerable length, but there is no doubt what question is most frequently raised by what Locke says on the subject. It is: 'Could memory be the sole criterion of personal identity?'

The standard argument against an affirmative

answer is one which draws attention to the conceptual grammar of the word 'remember'. If a child says he 'remembers' being in a certain place at a certain time, and he was seen to be somewhere else at that time, we say he is wrong. It is part of the concept of remembering that we take what can be seen, the physical presence or absence of a person, as relevant to whether or not he really remembers something. Hence memory could not be the sole criterion of personal identity.

Given that our talk of personal identity is against the background of using a bodily criterion, what should we say if someone claimed to remember having been at some place before he was born, and his memories of it proved to be uncannily accurate? Can there be exceptions to the rule? We can have exceptions to the rule that promises are kept, and still understand what it is to make a promise. Is it the same with personal identity? Is reincarnation conceivable? This is only one of many extraordinary cases, real or imaginary, which may be said to call for decisions that are not implicit in our ordinary practice with 'Is this the same person?' questions. Another whole range of such cases arises if we consider the possibility of transplanting brains, and, especially, of bisecting a brain and performing a dual transplant, so that two people claim to remember doing what one person did. Are they both identical with the earlier person, and so with one another?

Two distinct approaches to such extraordinary cases are possible. We can regard the concept of personal identity as being like an Aristotelian essence, that is, such that if only we had sufficient intellectual insight into it we could see what the answer should be. Or we can say that the concept of personal identity we have is one which goes with the criteria we employ, coinciding in the vast majority of cases, and that if they were to start failing to coincide then the concept we have would become incoherent. Whether the conditions would exist for us to have a new concept, perhaps 'psychological continuity', which took over some of the uses of the old one, is debatable. There are lessons to be learnt from Hume in this regard.

G. N. A. V.

Perry, J. R. (ed.) (1975). *Personal Identity*. Berkeley, California.

Shoemaker, S. and Swinburne, R. (1984). *Personal Identity*. Oxford.

Williams, B. (1973). *Problems of the Self*. Cambridge.

**PERSONALITY, DISSOCIATION OF.** See DISSOCIATION OF PERSONALITY.

**PERSONALITY DISORDER.** F. H. Allport in *Personality: a psychological interpretation*, reviewed some fifty definitions of normal personality, and it will come as no surprise to learn that definitions and typologies of personality disorder are almost as diverse. Generally the concept of abnormal personality refers to the affective and conative qualities of the individual, the mentally handicapped being omitted from further discussion. The boundary between personality deviation and *neurosis is not easily defined, as most neurotics will have shown abnormalities of temperament that are relevant to the onset and form of their illnesses. Karl Jaspers made a distinction between personality development and disease process or *psychosis. Those who have claimed some measure of continuity between personality and psychosis overlooked the lack of relationship between the *form* of the psychosis and the individual's premorbid qualities. Anxious personalities, for example, may well develop an *anxiety or *phobic neurosis but their symptoms do not progress to psychotic *delusions and *hallucinations. Like most attempts at making clear-cut distinctions and definitions, the separation of psychosis from personality disorder on the one hand and the continuity of personality and neurosis on the other does not cover all the possible variants of psychiatric illness. The *paranoid personality, whose suspicions and accusations may border on the delusional, may develop a psychosis whose content and form appear to be directly related to the subject's premorbid temperament.

Two measures of normality can be applied—the statistical and the ideal. Reliance on the latter results in some of the unattainable states of mind covered by the term '*mental health'. Hence one falls back on statistical measures which make the assumption that human traits and characteristic modes of behaviour are normally (Gaussianly) distributed in the population. For example, it is natural to feel moderate anxiety when faced by a threatening situation. Some individuals, however, presumably placed at the top end of the Gaussian curve of the distribution of the trait for anxiety, respond to stresses, however slight, by the generation of excessive amounts of fear—the anxiety-prone personality. None the less, definitions of what is abnormal must be made, taking into account the cultural background of the individual whose behaviour may be unremarkable in one society but grossly deviant in another. For example, the degrees of paranoia and suspiciousness which appear to be endemic amongst the Dobu (Ruth Benedict, *Patterns of Culture*, 1946) would be quite abnormal in most Western civilizations. But, then, the Dobu are very efficient poisoners . . .

K. Schneider (1958) described ten varieties of abnormal or psychopathic personality. The degree of overlap between these subgroups is considerable and the differences at times are not easy to discern. For example, the major traits of the affectionless and the explosive *psychopath clearly have much in common. For the purposes of discussion, the rather simpler classification of abnormal personality suggested by Curran and Mallinson (1944) seems preferable to Schneider's. They recognized three major classes of psychopathic personality: the vulnerable, the unusual or abnormal, and the sociopathic. The term 'unusual', omitting those with deviant sexual behaviour, relates to five major anomalies of personality: the schizoid, the cyclothymic, the hysterical, the obsessional, and the paranoid. None of these subdivisions is wholly separate from the others as they tend to overlap, as they do with neurosis and psychosis. The predominant characteristics of these variants of personality are described in most textbooks of psychiatry and psychology but some further comments are required to clarify some of their meanings.

Vulnerable personalities are individuals with a low capacity for coping with ordinary stresses and strains of everyday life. Sometimes the word 'inadequate' is applied to this kind of constitutional weakness but its use will obviously vary according to the individual's circumstances and the attitudes of the person who employs it. It is a word carrying overtones of disapproval and, therefore, best omitted from clinical nomenclature. As might be expected, the vulnerable personality is more liable to suffer from neurotic illness, particularly anxiety and phobic states. The word 'hysterical' in this context is unfortunate as persons so labelled do not necessarily suffer from the classic forms of hysterical neurosis (see HYSTERIA). Schneider preferred the term 'attention-seeking' and others have used 'histrionic' to indicate the self-dramatizing qualities of the person with this variety of personality disorder. It is a word more often used to describe women than men. Indeed, the qualities of the hysterical person are sometimes said to be a caricature of femininity.

Various mental mechanisms have been invoked to account for the different personality disorders. For example, the mechanism of projection is generally held to be basic to the behaviour and thinking of the paranoid personality. Repression and dissociation may be more important for the development of the symptoms of classic conversion hysteria, but such a formulation is probably less relevant to the characteristic behaviour of the hysterical personality. Obsessional personalities show a rigidity of mental structure which may be regarded as a defence against strong instinctual drives. (See also OBSESSIONS AND COMPULSIONS.)

Although some individuals with marked personality disorder suffer on that account, this is by no means an invariable consequence. For example, an obsessional temperament may be vital for the successful prosecution of enterprises requiring meticulous attention to detail. The sociable, energetic qualities of the cyclothyme may enable him to push through profitable schemes in industry which are beyond the scope of his more cautious colleagues.

The psychopathic or sociopathic personality has been discussed elsewhere and will not be described in detail here beyond noting that German authors use the word 'psychopathic' to denote all varieties of abnormal personality. F. A. W.

Allport, F. H. (1938). *Personality: a psychological interpretation*. London.
Benedict, R. (1946). *Patterns of Culture*. London.
Curran, D. and Mallinson, P. (1944). Psychopathic Personality. *Journal of Mental Science*, **90**, 266 ff.

**PERSONALITY TEST.** There is a long tradition of attempts to define the more or less permanent characteristics, or temperaments, of individuals which arise out of their physical constitutions, and to which the behaviour tendencies observed in them can be related. Interest in this field was revived as a result of the work in the 1930s of R. B. Cattell, who distinguished the two groups of temperament traits, surgent and desurgent, corresponding to what C. G. *Jung had called extravert and introvert, and in the 1950s of H. J. Eysenck, who developed methods for assessing degrees of 'neuroticism' and 'extraversion'. (See NEUROSIS and EXTRAVERSION–INTROVERSION.) Both used tests in the form of questionnaires or rating scales that required subjects to respond to carefully phrased questions about themselves, the data thus assembled being analysed by elaborate statistical techniques to provide scores indicating the strength of the factor in each individual. However, the results of research in this field have had little impact on the development of psychology, whether in the laboratory or in the clinic. One reason for this has been the relatively low reliability (i.e. reproducibility) of the data; another, the controversial nature of the statistical techniques. There are formidable difficulties too in generalizing from responses made in the miniature situation of a test to make predictions about behaviour in the complex social setting of real life. D. R. D.

Cattell, R. B. (1936). *A Guide to Mental Testing*. London.
Eysenck, H. J. and Eysenck, S. B. G. (1969). *Personality Structure and Measurement*. London.

**PHANTOM LIMB.** See SPATIAL CO-ORDINATION OF THE SENSES.

**PHENOMENOLOGY** is a term used in philosophy to denote enquiry into one's conscious and particularly intellectual processes, any preconceptions about external causes and consequences being excluded. It is a method of investigation into the mind that is associated with the name of Edmund *Husserl, as it was he who did most to develop it, although when Husserl's system appeared on the philosophical scene, the word already had a long history and had undergone a conspicuous semantic evolution.

The first use of it goes back to Johann Heinrich Lambert (1728–77), a disciple of Christian Wolff (1679–1754). Lambert published in 1764 a treatise on epistemology dealing with the problem of truth and illusion, under the rather pedantic title of *Neues Organon oder Gedanken über die Erforschung des Wahren und der Unterscheidung von Irrtum und Schein* (New Organon, or Thoughts on the Search for Truth and the Distinction between Error and Appearance), in the fourth part of which he outlines a theory of illusion that he calls 'phenomenology or theory of appearance'.

Although he belongs to a period in the history of philosophy in which the question of the intuition of essences had not yet been raised, his implicit definition of phenomenology, taken literally, does not sound odd to the post-Husserlian reader; except that to him, Lambert, an appearance (or phenomenon) is necessarily an illusion. More important, Lambert was acquainted with *Kant, and Kant in 1770 was writing to him about the need for a 'general phenomenology' which he conceived as a preparatory step to the metaphysical analysis of natural science. According to Spiegelberg (1960), what Kant called phenomenology was in fact synonymous with his idea of the critique of pure reason, though nothing allows us to suppose that he specifically used the term forged by Lambert to qualify phenomena as antithetic to noumena or things in themselves.

It is, however, with *Hegel's Die Phänomenologie des Geistes (Phenomenology of the Mind), published in 1807, that the term is used explicitly for the first time to label a philosophical work of fundamental importance. A significant step in its evolution from Lambert to Hegel may be found in J. G. Fichte's Wissenschaftslehre (Theory of Science), in which its role is to establish the origin of phenomena as they exist for *consciousness; and in Hegel's elaborate system, its basic task is primarily historical since it aims at discovering the successive steps of realization of self-consciousness from elementary individual sensations up to the stage of absolute knowledge through dialectic processes.

The few authors worth mentioning who dealt with phenomenological problems between Hegel and Husserl are William Hamilton (1788–1856), who in fact equates phenomenology with psychology as opposed to logic, Eduard von Hartmann (1842–1906), whose studies on religious, ethical, and aesthetic consciousness were greatly inspired by Hegel's phenomenology, and, to some extent, Charles Sanders *Peirce, though his work on the classification of phenomena belongs more to *metaphysics than to an actual phenomenology of subjective experience. Except in the case of Hegel, phenomenology was not a major field of reflection until Husserl's monumental work.

Since Husserl's transcendental phenomenology is discussed in some detail in the entry under his name, it will suffice here to underline its distinctive features. In contrast with pre-existing philosophies, it is no mere, closed, abstract construct that theoretically allows the philosopher to pronounce on the conditions of principles of experience; it is rather an endless attempt to stick to the reality of experienced phenomena in order to exhibit their universal character. In order to succeed in the endeavour, Husserl has to discard the classic dualistic view, according to which the knowing subject reaches the world only through representation—a position typical of rationalistic and idealistic systems. Hence he refers, after *Brentano, to the intentional character of con-

sciousness, and condemns psychologism (the theory that psychology is the foundation of philosophy) in view of the contradiction it brings about: that the supposedly universal laws of logic and mathematics would be dependent on the concrete functioning of psychological mechanisms.

The Husserlian standpoint is thus a radical one, since it aims at 'going back to the things themselves' by claiming that there is no reason to suppose that phenomenon and being are not identical. In other words, the noema (object content) and the noesis (knowing act) are directly related by the *intentionality of consciousness, so that every phenomenon is intuitively present to the subject. However, phenomena, as they are grasped by the subject, are always given under a particular profile. No object whatsoever is given in its totality as a simultaneous exhaustible whole, but every profile conveys its essence under the form of meaning for consciousness. In order to reach the essence of any object, one is bound to proceed to unceasing variations around the object as thematic reality, i.e. to discover the essence through the multiplicity of possible profiles. This procedure applies to all phenomena, ranging from current perceptual experience to the highly intricate constructs characterizing the various fields of knowledge, such as physics and psychology.

Every phenomenon belongs to a regional ontology by virtue of its essence, as revealed by the so-called eidetic intuition, the essence (eidos) being the sum of all possible profiles. In the course of this process, consciousness operates as a constitutive moment, i.e. its activity in grasping the essence of phenomena is, perforce, part of the process of their emergence. Thus Husserl overcomes the classic dualism of subject and object. Reaching the universal essence of an object through eidetic intuition, i.e. discovering the basic structure implied by its very existence, is a process which Husserl calls eidetic reduction. This being granted, the next step consists in referring phenomena to subjectivity without falling back into psychologism, since the empirical subject, as referred to psychology's own regional ontology (or *Descartes's res cogitans), belongs to a realm of contingent being, which cannot furnish by itself the necessary foundation for the organization of the absolute principles governing universal essences. Husserl is therefore bound to exclude belief in the natural world as the ultimate reference of all our intentional acts. This process is termed phenomenological reduction. It presupposes, in Husserl's terms, a provisional 'bracketing' (Einklammerung) of the natural and a description or explication of our intentional acts as referred to pure noematic structures. The final accomplishment of this process is the transcendental reduction, by which the fundamental conditions of every possible meaningful intentional relation must be elucidated. This is the core of Husserl's theory of transcendental subjectivity or transcendental ego.

Thus Husserl's phenomenology reconsidered

the philosophical problem of consciousnes in a radical fashion and contributed thereby to the placing of psychology—and the human sciences in general—within a new epistemological framework. Criticism of the one-sidedness of both empiricist and idealistic standpoints could be developed so that the shortcomings of dualistic views, with all their derivatives such as mechanicism, parallelism, and phenomenalism, became more apparent. As a fundamental theory of phenomena ranging from perception to creative thinking, it has provided a firm starting-point for the integration of concepts of the subject at different levels: hence phenomenologically inspired hypotheses such as those which guided F. J. J. Buytendijk and V. von Weiszäcker in anthropological physiology. The French philosopher Maurice Merleau-Ponty's analyses of the experienced body (1942) and perception (1945) were phenomenological works that contributed to the transforming of the classical standpoints in psychology.                                G. T.

Farber, M. (1943). *The Foundations of Phenomenology.* Cambridge, Massachusetts.
Kockelmans, J. J. (1967). *Edmund Husserl's Phenomenological Psychology: a historico-critical study.* Pittsburgh.
Misiak, H. and Sexton, V. S. (1973). *Phenomenological, Existential and Humanistic Psychologies.* New York and London.
Spiegelberg, H. (1960). *The Phenomenological Movement: a historical introduction*, 2 vols. The Hague.
Strasser, S. (1963). *Phenomenology and the Human Sciences.* Pittsburgh.
Thinès, G. (1977). *Phenomenology and the Science of Behaviour.* London.

**PHOBIAS.** Persons to whom the label 'phobic' is applied fall into two main groups: (i) those who respond with unusually intense *fear to a specified situation, for example to animals of a certain species, but who show no other symptoms; and (ii) those who exhibit unusually intense fear in a number of situations, often difficult to specify. Whereas those in the first group are in general emotionally stable, those in the second are not; they are prone to bouts of fairly acute *anxiety and *depression which may last weeks or months. They are often reluctant to leave home, and are described as agoraphobic if adult or as school phobic if children.

Attempts to explain the origin of phobias have been of two main kinds. One, the learning theory approach, holds that when a person is intensely afraid of something that others do not particularly fear, it is because the object or situation in question has become associated in his mind with a childhood fear, as of loud noises or falling. The other, the psychoanalytic approach, holds that the feared object or situation has become symbolic of something feared unconsciously. In the case of the 5-year-old boy, Little Hans, who was afraid to go out of the house for fear that a horse would bite him, the explanation offered by Sigmund *Freud was that Little Hans's fear resulted from the repression and subsequent projection of his aggressive impulses, comprising hostility directed towards his father

and sadism towards his mother, and that 'the motive force of the repression was fear of castration'. Empirical studies have given little support to either of these theories.

Research shows that specific and limited phobias have usually been present from early childhood but are normally diminished during adolescence. Since the fear is specified, treatment by means of desensitization is often appropriate. (See BEHAVIOUR THERAPY.)

The states of mind labelled agoraphobic, or school phobic, are much more complex than the specific phobias. These two conditions are closely related and are probably due to the same causes. Children who are school phobic, and nowadays referred to as school refusers, generally express much anxiety when pressed to attend school, their non-attendance being well known to their parents. Not infrequently their truancy is accompanied by, or masked by, *psychosomatic symptoms of one kind or another: anorexia, nausea, abdominal pain, or feeling faint, for example. Fears of many kinds are expressed—of animals, of the dark, of being bullied, of mother coming to harm, of being deserted. Occasionally a child seems to panic, and anxiety, tearfulness, and general misery are common. As a rule, the children are inhibited and well behaved. Most come from intact families, have not experienced long or frequent separations from home, and have parents who express great concern for them and their refusal to attend school. Relations between child and parents may be close, sometimes to the point of suffocation.

There is now general agreement that the refusal is much more to do with anxiety about leaving home than fear of what might happen at school. Why do they have this fear of leaving home? Among the many explanations suggested, those best supported by evidence point to trouble within the family. For example, in some cases one or the other parent, most often the mother, is a sufferer from chronic anxiety and is glad to have the child at home as a companion. In others a child becomes alarmed about what might happen at home during his absence and stays there to prevent it. In some cases both these influences are active. We examine each further.

A mother (or father) who retains a child at home may do so deliberately and consciously or may be completely unaware of what she is doing—and why. In either case she is commonly found to have had a difficult childhood and to be seeking from her child the affection and security she herself had lacked. In doing this she is inverting the normal parent–child relationship—requiring the child to act as parent whilst she becomes the child. To someone unaware of what is going on, it may appear that the child is being spoiled, but a closer look shows the reverse: the mother is in fact placing a heavy burden on her child. It is sometimes found, moreover, that a parent who is treating her child in this way swings abruptly from a genuine concern for his welfare to hostility and threats. Thus, if the child is to be helped, the parent must be helped to change. How best to do this is considered later.

In cases of a child staying at home for fear of what might happen while he is away—for example, he may be afraid of some harm coming to his mother—the problem is one of explaining why a child should think like that. Among psychoanalysts it has been usual to attribute the trouble to the child's harbouring unconscious hostile wishes towards his parent and being afraid lest his wishes come true. An alternative explanation is that the fear arises from actual events to which the child is being exposed: for example, (i) an illness of his mother's which the child is afraid may prove serious or even fatal; (ii) the death of a close relative or neighbour that leads the child to fear his mother might die also; (iii) threats or even attempts by the mother to commit suicide (which occur far more frequently than is usually realized); (iv) threats by a parent to abandon him, used as a disciplinary measure. (Little Hans's mother is reported to have used various threats to discipline him, including threats that she would go away and never return.)

A first task in helping a child who remains at home is to get his parents to recognize any part they may be playing and to change their ways. Depending on the part played and on the nature of their own problems, this may be easy or difficult. A mother prone to invert her relationship with her child can often be helped to release him if she is treated with sympathy. When encouraged to talk about her own childhood, she is likely to tell of unhappy experiences of certain specific kinds: for example, the loss of her mother by death or desertion; long absences from home in an institution, hospital, or foster home; having been an unwanted child; being threatened with abandonment; or witnessing a parent threatening or attempting suicide. She has grown up anxious not to lose anyone to whom she becomes attached and tends therefore to cling tightly to them. A person who has developed in this way is often called 'over-dependent' or 'immature' but is far more appropriately described as anxiously attached (in contrast to securely attached; see ATTACHMENT). Similarly, in cases of mistaken disciplinary measures, a parent may be helped to stop threatening the child when he or she appreciates the ill effects this has.

Most of the research on adults who are diagnosed as agoraphobic has neglected systematic study of what is happening in their families. In such study as has been undertaken, it is commonly found that the sufferer, usually a woman, is being subjected to the same sorts of pressure as the school-refusing child, and usually from the same source, namely her mother (though sometimes it is from the father or husband). Once established, the condition may persist even after the pressures that led to it have ceased.

One variety of adult agoraphobia was described by M. Roth in 1960 under the title of the phobic-anxiety depersonalization syndrome. The majority of victims were middle-aged housewives who, often after a sudden traumatic experience, developed intense anxiety associated with feelings of unreality and depersonalization. Thereafter their ability to go shopping alone was severely curtailed, especially if they were required to travel by public transport. Once inside a large store or supermarket they would become assailed with intense panic requiring their immediate departure from the shop. Their fears of travel and situational phobias could to some extent be allayed if accompanied by another person, even one of their children. The term 'housebound housewife syndrome' has come to be used for this variety of phobic-anxiety. Further study of the family experiences, past and present, of these women is called for.     J. BO.

Bowlby, J. (1975). *Attachment and Loss*, vol. 2, *Separation: anxiety and anger*. Harmondsworth.
Marks, I. M. (1980). *Fears and Phobias*. London.

**PHONETICS,** the science of speech sounds, is traditionally divided into two branches: *acoustic*, concerned with the structure of the acoustic signal itself, and *articulatory*, concerned with the way these sounds are produced. The most important initial impetus was to develop a standard means for the accurate and convenient transcription of the sounds of various languages and dialects. Proper transcription was regarded as an essential tool for field linguists and missionaries dealing with new languages, and for recording dialectal variations of known languages (and 'correcting' them—e.g. Henry Sweet, 1908). The idea of an International Phonetic Alphabet (IPA), suitable for all languages, was first suggested by Otto Jespersen in 1886; the International Phonetic Association (which included Paul Passy and Sweet, as well as Jespersen) published the first IPA in 1888. This was based on the articulatory features of the sounds: the place of maximum constriction of the vocal tract, the manner of the constriction (completely closed for consonants like /p/; with the nasal passage open for consonants like /m/, etc.) and the onset of voicing (immediate in the case of /b/, but delayed for /p/). Daniel Jones's classification of the 'cardinal vowels' was similarly based on articulatory features, the height of the tongue, front or back of the mouth, with lips rounded or unrounded. The IPA system enables the transcription of sound distinctions which have no significance for the speaker of one language, though they do for the speaker of another. Thus the initial consonants in 'key' and 'cool' can be heard, and felt, to be different but do not, in English, constitute different phonemes (units of significant sound); in Arabic they do.

Although methods of analysing the frequency components of the acoustic signal had been known since *Helmholtz in 1862, no convenient way of plotting frequency, energy, and time was available until the development of the 'sonograph' in the 1940s by R. K. Potter and others. The analysis of the movement of the vocal organs during speech has in recent years been advanced by the use of high-speed film to record the opening and closing of the vocal folds during phonation (though the earliest use of this technique can be traced back to 1913) and by cineradiography (Perkell). Two surprising and paradoxical results have emerged from these methods of acoustic and articulatory analysis: first, there is no simple correspondence between acoustic parameters and the phenomenological sound. The English phoneme /d/, for example, has a quite different sound depending on the vowel that follows it. Second, there is no simple correspondence between the sound and vocal action used to produce it. These fundamental puzzles have motivated the growth of experimental phonetics, which combines sophisticated analysis and synthesis of speech-like sounds with the investigative procedures of experimental psychology, with the aim of discovering which abstract characterizations of acoustic dimensions are critical in determining the sound contrasts meaningful in language (A. Liberman; K. N. Stevens). That is to say, what kinds of representation underlie the perception and production of spoken language?

B. L. B.

**PHRENOLOGY,** from the Greek words for 'mind' and 'discourse', is about reading character from the shape and especially from the 'bumps' of the skull. This has also been called 'cranioscopy', 'craniology', 'zoonomy', and '*physiognomy', though the last usually refers to reading character from faces. Phrenology was popular from the middle of the eighteenth to the middle of the nineteenth centuries; its principal proponents were Franz Joseph *Gall (1758–1828), who was a physician in Vienna and a more than competent anatomist (he was the first to distinguish the functions of the 'white' and the 'grey' matter of the brain); and Gall's student, Johann Kaspar Spurzheim (1776–1832), who with the controversial Scottish moral philosopher George Combe (1788–1858) spread the doctrine to England and America. It had such a vogue that by 1832 there were twenty-nine phrenological societies in Britain, and many journals in Britain and America, including the *Phrenological Journal*, a quarterly edited by Combe at Edinburgh from 1823 to 1847. There was, however, much criticism, such as from the philosopher, and early proponent of associative psychology, Thomas Brown (1778–1820), and phrenology was often lampooned in verse and on the stage.

Gall claimed to have discovered his phrenological principles inductively from people (and animals) of his acquaintance who had marked character traits associated with distinctive skull shapes, or 'bumps' that could be felt with the fingers. For example, the region he numbered as 1—Amativeness (*Instinct de la génération*), at the back of the head below the inion—he identified from its heat in a hysterical widow. Just above this region is No. 2—Philoprogenitiveness (*Amour de la progeniture*)—which Gall selected as the organ for the love of children because this occipital part of the skull is prominent in women and apes, in whom the love of infants is supposedly stronger than in men. To take an intellectual example: No. 22 (individuality), immediately above the nose, was named as the organ for recognizing external objects and for forming ideas from being large in Michelangelo and small in the Scots.

The twenty-six regions identified as personality organs by Gall (increased to as many as forty-three by later phrenologists) were based on very few instances. Implausible excuses were made for exceptions; and for such matters as inability to distinguish the skulls of saints from those of sinners. Phrenology does, however, have considerable importance in the history of psychology and brain studies. Even its obvious failures are revealing.

Phrenology is based on the notion that mind is intimately related to physical brain function. It is thus opposed to Cartesian mind–brain dualism, and is in line with much modern neurological thinking, and with 'identity' accounts, which suppose that mind is an aspect of brain structure and function. Phrenology implies some kind of *localization of brain function; though what are thought to be localized in the brain, as read from the 'bumps', are *complete traits* of ability and character, rather than *processes* generating characteristics of behaviour and intellect. The implied notion of brain 'organs', such as Veneration, Wonder, Wit, Tune, Language, Memory, Vanity, Cautiousness, and so on, is misleading, because these depend on many underlying processes which, as we now know, are widely separated and in many cases never appear in the 'output' of the brain. Nevertheless, we do still speak of 'speech centres' (see LANGUAGE AREAS IN THE BRAIN), and evidence for speech in pre-human and early human skulls is sought from bumps in casts corresponding to those anatomical features associated with language in modern man.

Phrenology made psychological classifications which still survive. Spurzheim grouped human faculties in the following way:

I. *Feelings*, divided into:
  1. Propensities (internal impulses to certain actions).
  2. Sentiments (impulses prompting emotions as well as action).
     (i) Lower: those common to man and the lower animals.
     (ii) Higher: those proper to man.
II. *Intellectual faculties*, divided into:
  1. Perceptive faculties (knowledge by observation and through language).
  2. Reflective faculties (knowledge by intuition and reasoning, especially by noting comparisons).

Although the phrenologists accepted and formulated *faculty psychology, they did not contribute to brain anatomy. This, in part, was because they did not say, simply, that the larger the 'bump' the greater the characteristic. Thus Spurzheim writes, in *Phrenology: in connexion with the study of physiognomy* (1824), under the heading 'Of the Heads of the Sexes':

The body and face vary in the two sexes. Do their brains differ likewise? The talents and feelings of the male and female are commonly considered as dissimilar; indeed it is proverbially said that women feel and men think. The majority of modern authors, however, have attributed the phenomenon to the modified education which the sexes receive. The female head is smaller than that of the male; it is commonly narrower laterally. The female cerebral fibre is slender and long rather than thick.

He continues:

Lastly, and in particular, the organs of philoprogenitiveness, of attachment, love of approbation, circumspection, secretiveness, ideality, and benevolence, are for the most part proportionately larger in the female; while in the male those of amativeness, combativeness, destructiveness, constructiveness, self-esteem, and firmness predominate.

But he then argues:

I say that the heads of men are wider than those of women, and then I state that I consider circumspection and secretiveness, whose organs lie laterally, as more generally active in the female than in the male. They who make this objection do not understand the phrenological principle, according to which the organs which are most largely developed in every individual display the greatest energy, and take the lead of all the other powers. Now, although the female head be so commonly narrower than the male, the organs of secretiveness and circumspection are still the most prominent, and thus contribute essentially to the formation of the female character.

Spurzheim concludes that phrenologists examining innate dispositions 'do not compare the heads of the sexes together, nor even those of the same sex; they judge of every head individually, and form conclusions in regard to the dispositions generally, according as the respective faculties are developed'.

The phrenologists generally stressed innateness of faculties. Spurzheim, while admitting that the education of the girls of his time was inferior to that of boys, argues that 'girls are more commonly instructed in drawing, painting, and music than boys', and often spend much time at these occupations; 'nevertheless, no woman has hitherto produced such works as those of Handel, Mozart, Haydn, Titian, Rubens, Paul Veronese, Canova, and so many others'. He adds: 'The female sex appears to greater advantage in actions which result from feeling.' Now this argument depends on the assumption of faculty psychology, that skills such as painting are developed simply by practising that particular skill. But it is possible that other, and perhaps traditionally male, activities transfer knowledge and abilities to give males an advantage even for skills such as painting which are frequently practised by girls. This possibility could hardly have been considered by proponents of a faculty psychology based on localized organs of behaviour and personality.

Phrenology seemed to give promise of objective assessments and judgements of people; it was even proposed to select Members of Parliament from candidates having propitious bumps. It was suggested, as a joke, by the distinguished editor of *Blackwood's Magazine* and professor of moral philosophy at Edinburgh, John Wilson ('Christopher North'), that children's heads should be moulded—to accentuate their good qualities and remove evil. The suggestion was taken up by several practising phrenologists.

With the advent of experiments in which small regions of brain were removed, by careful operations pioneered by the French physiologist Pierre *Flourens, and by electrical stimulation with fine wires, electrodes, pioneered by Gustav Theodor Fritsch (1838–97) and Julius Eduard Hitzig (1838–1907) on the 'motor cortex' of dogs (1870), it at last became obvious that functions are localized; but that localized functions are not simply related to behavioural skills, or to mental attributes or abilities. However, although this became clear to many physiologists towards the end of the nineteenth century, it was resisted by some, and especially by the members of the *Gestalt school of psychology, who held that the brain works holistically, with perception given by perceived objects represented 'isomorphically' as brain traces like pictures; so that circles are represented by circular traces, houses by house-shaped traces, and so on. This was a rejection of functionally interacting processes of analysis and of inference-generating perceptions, in favour of notions more like those of the phrenologists. And such ideas die hard. One might say

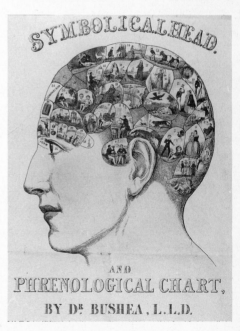

Fig. 1.

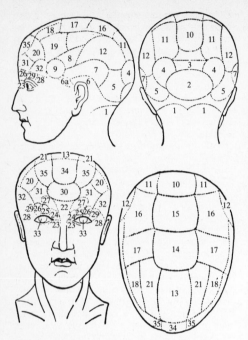

**Fig. 2.** The regions identified as personality organs, according to the classification of Gall, with additions by Spurzheim and Combe, were:

1. Amativeness
2. Philoprogenitiveness
3. Concentrativeness
4. Adhesiveness
5. Combativeness
6. Destructiveness
6a. Alimentiveness
7. Secretiveness
8. Acquisitiveness
9. Constructiveness
10. Self-esteem
11. Love of approbation
12. Cautiousness
13. Benevolence
14. Veneration
15. Conscientiousness
16. Firmness
17. Hope
18. Wonder
19. Ideality
20. Wit
21. Imitation
22. Individuality
23. Form
24. Size
25. Weight
26. Colour
27. Locality
28. Number
29. Order
30. Eventuality
31. Time
32. Tune
33. Language
34. Comparison
35. Causality

that the current interest in 'cerebral dominance', with the left hemisphere of the cortex supposedly 'analytic' (responsible for skills such as arithmetic and logical thinking) and the right hemisphere 'synthetic' or 'analogue' (responsible for intuitive and artistic skills), is the dying kick of phrenology. (See SPLIT-BRAIN AND THE MIND.) Physiological experiments on localizing functions give very different functional maps from those of the phrenologists, (Figs. 1, 2) and are highly revealing and of great use in brain surgery; yet they too are subject to logical difficulties of interpretation. For ablation especially, there are difficulties in inferring from loss, or change in behaviour, what the missing

region does in the normal intact brain. It is extremely difficult to isolate functions in interactive systems, and in systems where parts can take over the functions of other parts when these are overloaded or damaged. Moreover, it is logically necessary to appreciate what the functions are before they can be named or localized. Physiological functions are not units of behaviour, and so are not to be discovered simply from observation. What is required is an adequate theoretical understanding—an adequate conceptual model—of brain function, which is something very different from the localized mental faculties of the phrenologists.

Recently, however, the (Fodor, 1983) brain has been seen to be organized in 'modules' carrying out complex functions, such as face recognition. This is something of a return to phrenological ideas.                                                            R. L. G.

Fodor, J. A. (1983). *The Modularity of Mind*. Cambridge.

**PHYSIOGNOMY.** The word 'physiognomy' is a compound of two Greek words meaning 'nature', and 'an interpreter'. Francis *Bacon described it as 'discovery of the disposition of the mind by the lineaments of the body'; and indeed this is the aim of portrait painting. *Aristotle wrote extensively on physiognomy, with many comparisons between human and animal characteristics, and many Latin authors discuss it as a descriptive science; but in medieval writings, physiognomy becomes linked with *astrology and necromancy. It was made illegal by George II, in 1743, and earlier Queen Elizabeth had decreed that 'all persons fayning to have knowledge of phisiognomy or like Fantasticall Ymaginacions' were liable to be 'stripped naked from the middle upwards and openly whipped until his body be bloudye'. Nevertheless, Elizabeth set much store on delineation of character in paintings. Our own view, now, is surely as paradoxical, for we generally hold that physiognomy as a science is unfounded and yet we spend a great deal of time reading character from faces and pictures.

There are many examples, from Aristotle onwards, of people looking dull but being bright (and Aristotle admitted it of himself, saying that it was the practice of philosophy that brightened his native dullness); while the converse can also be true. But there are good grounds for associating expression with character traits and habits of thought. The point is that groups of muscles are associated with emotions, moods, and activities; and the use of facial muscles both modifies the countenance and produces permanent changes, such as lines and wrinkles. The first scientific study of this notion was by the distinguished Scottish anatomist-surgeon and neurologist Sir Charles *Bell, whose *Essay on the Anatomy of the Expressions* (1806) related specific muscles to *facial expressions.

The idea was developed, with strong evolutionary implications, by Charles *Darwin in his still highly important book *The Expression of the Emotions in Man and Animals* (1872). Darwin dismisses earlier writers on expression and physiognomy, such as the French painter Charles Le Brun (1619–90), who wrote *Conférence sur l'expression des différents caractères des passions* in 1667, and the Dutch anatomist Peter Camper (1722–89), but he does give full and just praise to the work of Bell. He also refers to the best-known of the physiognomists, Johann Kaspar Lavater (1741–1801), born in Zurich, whose *Physiognomische Fragmente* (1775–8; translated by Thomas Holcroft as *Essays on Physiognomy* in 1793) went into many editions and was widely read. Lavater is interesting for his many drawings of faces, and his astute comments on the characters and lives of his examples, but there is a total absence of system or theory. Darwin refers also to Burgess's *The Physiology or Mechanism of Blushing* (1839), which points out that *blushing cannot be caused 'by any physical means', but that it must be the mind that is affected, 'for if we try to restrain blushing, this increases it'. Finally, Darwin refers to the French pioneer in electrophysiology, Guillaume Duchenne (1806–75), who was the first to describe locomotor ataxia, and was the founder of techniques using electrical stimulation for therapy. Darwin refers to Duchenne's *Mécanisme de la physionomie humaine* (1862), in which he 'analyses by means of electricity, and illustrates by magnificent photographs, the movements of the facial muscles'. Duchenne lent and allowed Darwin to copy his photographs, many of which appear in *The Expression of the Emotions*. He succeeded in showing the effects of contraction of individual muscles of the hand, and their effects in producing creases in the skin; and, perhaps most significant, in showing which muscles are and which are not under voluntary control. Both he and Darwin were well aware of the problem of how it is that groups of muscles are innervated for behaviour, gesture, and expressions. This could not be investigated experimentally before techniques of cortical stimulation were developed.

The philosopher Herbert *Spencer contributed an account of facial expression and emotion somewhat similar to Darwin's (in *Principles of Psychology*, 1855), and Darwin quotes from it with approval:

Fear, when strong, expresses itself in cries, in efforts to hide or escape, in palpitations and tremblings; and these are just the manifestations that would accompany an actual experience of the evil feared. The destructive passions are shown in a general tension of the muscular system, in gnashing of the teeth and protrusion of the claws, in dilated eyes and nostrils, in growls; and these are weaker forms of the actions that accompany the killing of prey.

Darwin's essential point is that the facial muscles of monkeys are similar to ours, but, as he puts it, 'no one, I presume, would be inclined to admit that monkeys have been endowed with special muscles solely for exhibiting their hideous grimaces'. Rather the 'grimaces' were originally of functional importance—and in many cases still are in us—as when muscles surrounding the eyes contract to protect the eyes from increased blood-pressure or from the blow of an assailant. Frequent use of such sets of muscles, either in action or in the simulation of imagination and emotion, will produce, gradually, permanent changes of expression. So there is strong evidence and a consistent theory for a biological basis to physiognomy. It is, however, very far from clear how accurately it is possible to read the subtleties of human character from facial forms and expressions having pre-human functional origins.

It is most curious that expressions of extremely different emotions can be so similar that they are indistinguishable in photographs—unless the context of the situation is available. Pictures of reactions of horror and uncontrollable laughter are easily confused when presented out of context. In normal life, no doubt, it is facial and verbal reactions to events—speed and appropriateness—that are crucially important signals for evaluating character and ability. This is the power of the cinema, for it presents the context of situations, and the timing of responses. There remains a considerable mystery just why and how static portraits convey so much of the character of individuals by their physiognomy.          R. L. G.

**PIAGET,** JEAN (1896–1980), Swiss psychologist born at Neuchâtel, Switzerland, became professor of child psychology at the University of Geneva, and director of the Centre d'Épistémologie Génétique; he was also a director of the Institut des Sciences de l'Éducation. He was the great pioneer of the study of cognitive development through childhood, and he virtually founded *epistemology as an experimental science. He wrote a vast number of books, using writing as his principal aid to thought and inspiration for new experiments. The best are highly important, and are clearly written to be read, but some are clumsy vehicles of his thinking, though no doubt useful for the author and immediate colleagues at the time of writing.

J. H. Flavell (1963) describes how Piaget worked on and published some twenty-five papers on molluscs, of which about twenty were in print before he was 21. Piaget's early studies in zoology and the behaviour of simple organisms evidently gave rise to his interest in comparing external with internal organizational principles, and in the nature of intelligence, which crystallized out as he worked in *Binet's laboratory in Paris on standardizing intelligence tests for children.

Although Piaget became one of the most famous psychologists of his time, psychology was not his main aim or interest; rather this was to unify biology and logic. To this end he investigated the development of concepts and language, and interactive behaviour with objects in children, and their internal mental manipulations of symbols. He saw knowledge as providing 'self-regulating' symbolic structures, developed by processes of 'assimilation' and 'accommodation'. There is something of *Hegel in his manner of discussion and thinking, which he calls 'dialectical constructivism': passing from *thesis* to its contradictory *antithesis* to the next step, the *synthesis*. This in its turn might serve as a new thesis, so his thinking climbs in a kind of staircase. It is however a spiral staircase, for the contextual premises are re-examined each time the 'spiral' sweeps round, from successively higher levels of consideration. Piaget sees psychological development as this kind of spiral, with interacting antitheses generating new knowledge, rather than as an unfolding of innate properties by maturation, triggered or released by experiences, which is perhaps a more usual view. He thus adds empiricism to Hegel's a priori idealism for cognitive development.

'Assimilation' is the modification of perceptual inputs by existing knowledge-structures, while 'accommodation' is modification of the knowledge-structures to adapt to the input. The result is a lifelong quasi-stable equilibrium which is maintained by climbing to new generalizations along the spiral of the growth of mind. This is, essentially, a dynamic model of mind, with active exploration seen as the basis for learning and understanding and discovery.

The child goes through various stages of learning and development, and he is unable to proceed to later stages before critically important earlier stages have been passed, or lessons learned, or discoveries created by new syntheses. Piaget sets specific ages to some of these stages, but it appears that these tend to be somewhat late for most children. Paradigm experiments include the famous 'mountain' test, in which the child is asked to describe a model of mountains from the point of view not of himself but of someone in a different location—the tester, or a model person placed in the scene. He found that young children find this impossible. Equally celebrated experiments concern predicting what will happen to the levels or slopes of liquids, as glass jars are tilted or liquid is poured into jars of various diameters. These are extremely interesting tests of understanding, and may be pre-verbal. There are, however, difficulties in ensuring that very young children understand exactly what is asked of them, and later experimenters have sometimes found that inability to perform the tests is due to lack of understanding of the instructions. (See REASONING: DEVELOPMENT IN CHILDREN.)

Broadly, children seem to go through a phase of *Aristotelian physics before they understand acceleration, inertia, and so on, as these are now understood by scientifically educated adults.

Piaget's work is important for considering *education, communication of ideas, and epistemology. By applying *cybernetic concepts of dynamic stability it may have implications and applications at several levels, for programming computers to be intelligent (see ARTIFICIAL INTELLIGENCE) as well as for teaching children.

Among Piaget's main works are *The Language and Thought of the Child* (1923; Eng. trans. 1926); *The Child's Conception of the World* (1926; Eng. trans. 1929); *The Child's Conception of Physical Reality* (1926; Eng. trans. 1960). His theory of visual illusions based on his notion of assimilation is described in *The Mechanisms of Perception* (1961; Eng. trans. 1969).                    R. L. G.

Boden, M. (1979). *Piaget*. London.
Flavell, J. H. (1963). *The Developmental Psychology of Jean Piaget*. Princeton, New Jersey.

**PIAGET AND EDUCATION.** Piaget's work on children's intellectual development owed much to his early studies of water snails. *Limnaea stagnalis* spends its early life in stagnant conditions. On transfer to tidal waters and in order to remain on the rocks the snail is forced to engage in motor activity, and this activity directly influences the development of the size and shape of its shell. This model of development through active adaptation has become the prototype for learning. Inherited patterns of motor activity (such as sucking, grasping) enable the infant to interact with the world but are themselves transformed as a result of this interaction. So too with knowledge. The complementary processes of 'assimilation' and 'accommodation' (see PIAGET) are invoked by Piaget to describe the course of adaptation and the stage-like nature of the development of understanding as the child strives for stability between new learning and old at successively higher levels ('equilibration').

Piaget insists on the fundamental importance of the child as agent of his own learning throughout development. In the early years knowledge of the outside world is assimilated to the structure of elementary actions, and later involves the reconstruction in thought of operations performed in action. This restricts the child's ability to think logically. By middle childhood (the junior school period) greater co-ordination of thought is achieved but is limited in its sphere of application to objects rather than to verbal propositions. According to Piaget's theory of stages, it is not until early adolescence that children become capable of formal reasoning and hypothetico-deductive thinking.

Although Piaget did not systematically apply his theory to teaching, his account of intellectual development has been used to reinforce and provide theoretical justification for aspects of earlier theories of education and practices, such as those advocated by *Montessori and *Dewey. His theory stresses that knowledge and understanding are derived from the active adaptation of children to their environment and not through direct instruction, and consequently that schools should provide children with opportunities to invent and to discover; it recommends a sequence of intellectual demands compatible with the forms of thought which define the stages of development described. Direct application of the theory has proved difficult, partly because Piaget's interest was in skills not normally taught and partly because of lack of clarity or inconsistency on certain fundamental points. There is, for example, no empirical support for equilibration as a mechanism of learning, and Piaget was generally indifferent to more parsimonious accounts of the phenomena he described. Recent research to train children on various concepts has been more successful than the theory would predict. Piaget's account also underestimates social interaction and cultural transmission as constituents of education.

Nevertheless, some specific curricula derived from Piaget's work have been devised, notably by Lavatelli in the USA for children aged 4 to 7, by Weikart and others at Ypsilanti in Michigan, by Kamii and De Vries for pre-school children, and in the Schools Council science 5–13 project in Britain. Stage theory has also been used to develop techniques to assess intellectual capacity (as in the British ability scales) in skills that are, according to Piaget, only minimally influenced by teaching, if at all. Although Piaget's theory provides possible guidelines as to reasonable demands for children at different age-levels, to ascribe to his influence alone the idea that children learn by manipulation, comparison, and reconciliation of discrepant events (proceeding from the equilibration concept) is mistaken. Despite the conscious extension of Piaget's ideas into education by the few mentioned above, many more have employed his theory to justify practices already in vogue with educationists seeking to emphasize discovery-learning.

D. S.

Meadows, S. A. C. (ed.) (1983). *Developing Thinking*. London.

**PIERON,** HENRI (1881–1964), founder of French experimental psychology. He was trained in philosophy and physiology, and became a leader in physiological studies of sensation and perception. He designed several ingenious optical and other instruments, and also was influential in personnel selection, vocational guidance, and animal psychology, as well as in psychophysics.

**PLASTICITY IN THE NERVOUS SYSTEM.** In everyday usage, when we say something shows plasticity we imply that it can be moulded or readily made to assume (and to retain) a new shape. Probably the term should not really be used in relation to living systems, since plasticity is something found in inert, inanimate material. The *nervous system is living and changing all the time; and while it can readily be induced to change shape, by surgical or other traumatic means, it cannot be induced to maintain a new shape without being killed. Yet the concept of plasticity is used in relation to other growing systems; one talks about moulding the character of a young person, or moulding the shape of a tree by selective pruning. What is meant by such cases is that constraints are applied so that the form of the organism changes and future growth is differently channelled.

Plasticity in the nervous system means an alteration in structure or function brought about by development, experience, or injury. Such a statement is not sufficiently precise, however; in relation to the nervous system, we commonly imply a further restriction of meaning. We do not mean just *any* alteration. For instance, a massive and disorganized malfunction associated with extensive injury would not be referred to as plasticity. To qualify for this name, an alteration has to show pattern or order. Plasticity here means patterned, or ordered, alteration of organization; one that makes some sort of sense biologically or to the investigator.

Neural plasticity can be mainly of structure or mainly of function. To the extent that the function of the nervous system reflects its structure, we assume that any plastic change in structure is associated with a change, at some level, in function and vice versa. In some cases, where our functional tests are inadequate, plasticity will appear to be mainly of structure; and in other cases, such as *learning and *memory, where our structural knowledge is inadequate, plasticity will appear to be mainly of function.

The term plasticity also implies that the changes are in some sense positive; we would normally mean more than just an ordered deficit following a localized lesion. When we say that the nervous system is showing plasticity after injury, we imply that the structures or functions under discussion alter in some way to make up for this deficit; or to provide a new and abnormally ordered pattern. Comparably, when the plasticity takes the form of learning or memory, the functional alteration resulting from the input experience must be organized, this time in a functional sense. Functional changes that were merely chaotic would qualify for neither the term plasticity nor the term learning.

We now describe three situations in which parts of the nervous system show forms of plastic alteration: changes in eye–brain connections (i) induced experimentally in adult fish and (ii) during the initial development of the visual system, and also (iii) changes in the connections between the left and right optical tectum. These examples all come from the visual system in lower vertebrates and illustrate some of the changes that may occur in different situations.

**Changes in eye–brain connections induced experimentally in adult fish.** The ganglion cells of the retina are distributed in a two-dimensional array across the back of the eye. In lower vertebrates (including fish) optic nerve fibres from these ganglion cells form the optic nerve connecting the retina to the main visual centre of the brain, the optic tectum. Here, the fibres distribute their endings across the surface of the tectum in such a way that neighbourhood relationships between adjacent ganglion cells in the retina are reproduced in the relationships between the endings of their

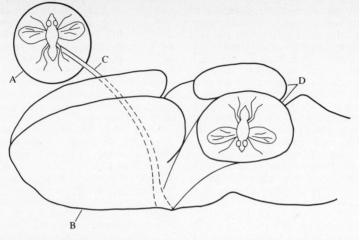

**Fig. 1.** Diagram showing the right eye (A) and the brain (B) of a *Xenopus* frog. Ganglion cells in the retina of the eye send their nerve fibres via the optic nerve (C) to the main visual centre, the optic tectum (D). These fibres form a 'map' of the retina on the surface of the optic tectum, and the way the retinal surface is represented on the tectum is indicated by the relative orientation of the flies. Ganglion cells underlying each particular part of the fly on the retina send their fibres to terminate at the corresponding part of the fly on the tectum.

fibres on the tectum (Fig. 1). The entire sheet of retinal ganglion cells thus forms, through the distribution of its nerve fibres on the tectum, a neighbourhood-preserving 'map' of the retina across the entire extent of the tectal surface.

If half the retina is removed and the optic nerve is cut in a fish, when the retinal fibres regenerate (as they do, in lower vertebrates, within a few weeks) back to the tectum, they form a map of the remaining half of the retina across the appropriate half of the tectum (Fig. 2). The regenerating fibres will even ignore available, but inappropriate, termination sites left unoccupied by the part of the retina which has been removed (Attardi and Sperry,

1963). A similar phenomenon of the precise re-establishment of connections is demonstrated when half the tectum is removed (Gaze and Sharma, 1970). In this case, it is again only fibres from the appropriate half of the retina that are found to have re-established connections (Fig. 3). This shows, therefore, that the factors controlling the initial re-establishment of the nerve connections are acting in a quite unplastic way; no change results other than that directly attributable to the surgical treatment. Removal of part of the retina or tectum always produces a corresponding gap in the retinotectal map.

If, however, one examines the result some considerable time (several months) later, one finds

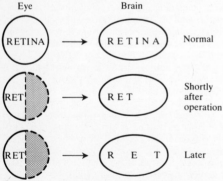

**Fig. 2.** The result of removal of half the retina in a fish. At first, fibres from the remaining half retina form a partial map over the corresponding half of the tectum. Later, fibres from the remaining half retina spread out to form an expanded, but still properly ordered, map across the whole of the tectum.

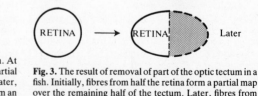

**Fig. 3.** The result of removal of part of the optic tectum in a fish. Initially, fibres from half the retina form a partial map over the remaining half of the tectum. Later, fibres from the whole of the retina form a compressed, but properly ordered, map over the remaining half tectum.

that the connection pattern between retina and tectum has now changed. Where only half a retina innervates a whole tectum, fibres from the half retina are found to have spread their terminals, in an orderly fashion (Fig. 2), across the whole of the tectum (Schmidt *et al.*, 1978). In similar fashion, where half the tectum has been removed (Gaze and Sharma, 1970), it is found that ganglion cells from the entire extent of the retina now form an organized but compressed map across the available tectal surface (Fig. 3).

**Changes in eye–brain connections during the initial development of the visual system.** In amphibia and fish the retino-tectal system continues to grow for much of (in some cases, all of) the animal's life. The retina grows by the addition of rings of cells at its periphery, so that the oldest part is at the centre of the eye, close to where the optic nerve fibres leave the retina, and the youngest part is at the edge of the retina. The optic tectum, on the other hand, grows from front to back.

In the earliest stages of development, when both the retina and the tectum are very small, the few optic nerve fibres that then exist connect the early retina to the early tectum and make a 'map' which is properly ordered and properly oriented on the

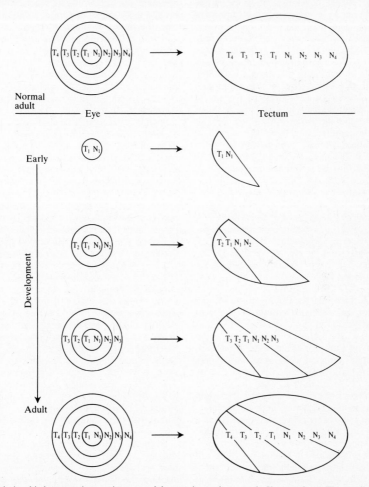

**Fig. 4.** The relationship between the growing eye and the growing optic tectum in *Xenopus* frogs. The top diagram shows how the horizontal (temporo-nasal) axis of the retina maps on to the antero-posterior axis of the tectum in a normal adult animal. The most temporal ganglion cells in the retina (T4) send their fibres to the front of the tectum and the most nasal ganglion cells (N4) send their fibres to the back of the tectum. When the retina first forms, it has very few cells (T1, N1) and these connect with the small tectum then existing. The *order* of the map is correct (i.e. similar to that in the adult) from very early stages of development. Next, a further ring of retinal ganglion cells develops (T2, N2) and these connect with tectum in the same relative order: most temporal fibres (T2) to the front, most nasal fibres (N2) to the back. And so on. The result of the different modes of growth of eye and tectum is that there occurs a continual shift of fibre connections across the tectum as the system grows.

tectum. The orientation of the map formed by the retinal fibres on the tectum is such that fibres coming from ganglion cells at the temporal margin of the retina (i.e. furthest away from the nose) connect to the front-most part of the tectum; while those at the nasal edge of the retina (nearest to the nose) connect towards the back edge of the tectum. This orientation persists throughout life, despite the continuing growth of the system (Fig. 4).

This would present no problems if the retina and the tectum were growing in a similar fashion. However, the fact that the retina grows in rings while the tectum grows from front to back in bands means that, during development of the visual system, there has to be not merely the addition of new fibres between the eye and the tectum, but also a continual shift of those fibre connections already existing on the tectum (Fig. 4). Thus during growth of the eye there is a continual addition of new ganglion cells round the retinal margin, including the temporal edge. Fibres from these new temporal ganglion cells must connect with the front-most part of the tectum, which is where the problem arises. The front of the tectum is the oldest part and already holds connections from the preceding group of temporal fibres. Fibres from the nasal edge of the retina have no such problem. They grow to the back of the tectum where new cells are being added and so have plenty of room to connect. Obviously, as the system grows, something has to give; and what happens is that, on the arrival of new temporal fibres, all the previous fibres shift backwards across the tectum to make room for the newcomers (Gaze, Chung, and Keating, 1972). This type of shift of nerve connections during development has been demonstrated both in amphibians and in fish.

**Changes in the connections between the left and right optic tectum, associated with the development of binocular vision in *Xenopus* frogs.** In adult *Xenopus* there is a binocular visual input to the optic tectum on each side of the brain. From each eye the retinal ganglion cell axons send fibres directly to the tectal lobe on the other (the contralateral) side of the brain (Fig. 5a). The input to the tectal lobe on the same side, the ipsilateral visual input, is indirect, involving some form of second order nerve connections between the two lobes of the tectum (Fig. 5b). This intertectal connection system itself shows topographic order, such that terminations of retinal ganglion cell axons which arise in complementary positions in each eye (i.e. look out at the same point in visual space), are interlinked. The development of this intertectal fibre system occurs at a later stage than the direct contralateral visual input, and appears to be linked to the onset of metamorphosis, during which the initially laterally projecting eyes migrate dorsally and rostrally, providing partial binocular vision in the adult frog.

If, in embryonic life, one eye is surgically rotated by 180°, the connections that it forms with the contralateral tectal lobe are unaltered (Fig. 5c); but since the eye is now upside-down and back-to-front the visual information coming from the outside world through that eye will be inverted along both axes. If one examines the ipsilateral intertectal fibre pathway at around the time of metamorphosis in such an animal, one finds that, while the visual field map established through the *rotated* eye on its contralateral tectum is rotated as expected, the ipsilateral map from that eye is *normal*; and conversely, the contralateral map from the *normal* eye is normal while the ipsilateral map from the *normal* eye is rotated (Fig. 5d). This remarkable phenomenon has the effect (which could be closely related to its cause) that, after rotation of a larval eye, the binocular inputs to each tectum remain congruent. The result is that we obtain a plastic alteration in the intertectal connections underlying the ipsilateral visual input, and this change in connectivity is dependent upon the existence of binocular visual input during a formative period. In this case, therefore, we have a change in functional connections initiated by a *functional* interaction following a *structural* alteration to the eye (Gaze, Keating, Szekely, and Beazley, 1970).

In contrast to these observations in the lower vertebrates, observations concerning structural plasticity in the mammalian central nervous system have mainly been made during embryonic and neonatal life. In the mammalian central nervous system there appears to be a loss, at a specific time period in development, of the ability of axons to grossly alter their connections. This time limit for structural plasticity may be related to changes in the ability of axons to regenerate, believed to be caused by changes not in the neurones themselves but in the surrounding glial cells. Technical advances have made it possible to demonstrate that more subtle changes in the fine details of the connection pattern are occurring even in young adult animals. These changes involve the production and retraction of dendritic arbors, altering the morphology of the neurone and, in consequence, its synaptic relationships to those cells which have made functional connections with it. This ability for subtle alteration of what has generally been considered an apparently rigid structural connectivity pattern, adds even further complexity to the study of the formation of nerve connections.

Even more elusive are functional changes occurring in the 'established' nervous system. These may include changes in synaptic type, thereby altering the signal communicated to contacted neurones; or alteration in the 'strength' of synapse—which in turn may profoundly change the relative effect of one neurone on another. It is perhaps these latter mechanisms which are more important in the vastly more complex nervous systems of the higher vertebrates. Such functional plasticity may be a form of evolutionary trade-off, where the smaller degree of variable 'wiring' is

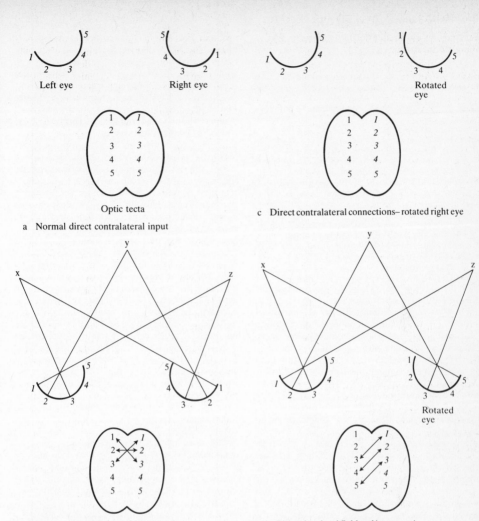

Left eye · Right eye · Rotated eye

Optic tecta

c   Direct contralateral connections– rotated right eye

a   Normal direct contralateral input

b   Binocular visual field and intertectal
     connections – normal

Rotated eye

d   Binocular visual field and intertectal
     connections – rotated right eye

**Fig. 5. a.** In a normal adult *Xenopus* frog fibres from ganglion cells distributed along the horizontal (temporo-nasal) axis of the retina send their fibres to the opposite (contralateral) optic tectum, as shown. Most temporal retinal cells (*1* and 1) connect to most anterior tectum, while most nasal retinal cells (*5* and 5) send their fibres to posterior tectum.

**b.** *Xenopus* frogs can see part of the visual field with both eyes. Except for parts of the visual field along the mid-line of the animal, each point in visual space that can be seen by both eyes will be represented at a relatively different position on each eye to the tectum. For instance, point X in the visual field is 'seen' by ganglion cells at position *3* in the left retina and position 1 in the right retina. These ganglion cells send fibres respectively to position *3* on the right tectum and position 1 on the left tectum. *Experiment shows that these positions, on right and left tecta, are interconnected.* This means that, in addition to the direct contralateral connection of each eye to its opposite tectum, there is also an *indirect* connection from each eye to the tectum on the same side (ipsilateral). Position *3* in the left retina, for example, sends fibres directly to position *3* on the right tectum. But position *3* on the right tectum itself connects, through other nerve fibres, with position 1 on the left tectum. The pattern of intertectal connections is as shown by the arrows.

**c.** When one eye is rotated by 180° in embryonic life, each part of the *retina* still connects, later in development, with the proper part of the tectum. Thus retinal position 1 still connects with anterior tectum, although the position of the eye has been altered. But, since the eye is rotated, the map of the *visual field* on the tectum is back-to-front and upside-down.

**d.** When one eye has been rotated in embryonic life, experiment shows that, later, the representation of the visual field seen through the *rotated eye* is rotated on the contralateral tectum. Thus point X in the visual field is *seen* by ganglion cells at position *3* in the left retina, but is now seen by ganglion cells at position 5 in the rotated retina. However, the map of the visual field on the ipsilateral tectum, as seen through the rotated eye, is *normal*. Conversely, the visual field-map seen through the *normal eye* is normal on its contralateral tectum but *rotated* on the ipsilateral tectum. Any point in the binocular visual field-maps, through each eye, to one position only on each tectum. This means that the pattern of intertectal connections is different from normal, as shown here.

exchanged for a greater flexibility in the 'programming' of the system.

R. M. G.
J. S. H. T.

Attardi, D. G. and Sperry, R. W. (1963). Preferential selection of central pathways by regenerating optic fibers. *Experimental Neurology*, 7, 46–64.

Gaze, R. M., Chung, S. H., and Keating, M. J. (1972). Development of the retinotectal projection in *Xenopus*. *Nature*, 236, 133–5.

Gaze, R. M., Keating, M. J., Szekely, G., and Beazley, L. (1970). Binocular interaction in the formation of specific intertectal neuronal connections. *Proceedings of the Royal Society London B*, 175, 107–47.

Gaze, R. M. and Sharma, S. C. (1970). Axial differences in the reinnervation of the goldfish optic tectum by regenerating optic nerve fibres. *Experiments in Brain Research*, 10, 171–81.

Schmidt, J. T., Cicerone, C. M., and Easter, S. S. (1978). Expansion of the half retinal projection to the tectum in goldfish: an electrophysiological and anatomical study. *Journal of Comparative Neurology*, 177, 257–77.

**PLATO** (427–347 BC). Plato was born into a distinguished family whose members played a prominent part in the political life of Athens. It is probable that he himself expected to follow a political career, but at some point he came under the influence of that charismatic talker, *Socrates: Socrates was put to death in 399 BC, and it may have been this which changed the course of Plato's life and turned him to philosophy. He did not give up all political aspirations—indeed, he later meddled with unhappy results in the affairs of Sicily—but he seems to have had little to do with the politics of his native city.

His celebrated school, the Academy, probably opened its doors in about 385; and it soon attracted the brightest ornaments of intellectual Greece, among them *Aristotle. Little is known of the structure and nature of Plato's Academy; but it is not implausible to think of it as an institute for advanced research. A comic poet portrays the young academicians as attempting to classify the pumpkin: is it a species of tree? a kind of grass? a vegetable? The caricature suggests that the natural sciences were studied in the Academy; there is good evidence for the study of mathematics; and of course philosophy, in all its branches, was the centrepiece. Plato himself doubtless spent much of his time in teaching and lecturing to his disciples and colleagues, and there are stories of a public lecture in which he managed to bemuse most of his lay audience.

Plato left behind him a body of philosophical writings, in dialogue form, unsurpassed for their literary elegance and their profundity. The notion of the *psyche exercised him throughout his life, and reflections upon one aspect or another of psychology can be found in most of his works; but the primary sources for his psychological theories are the *Phaedo*, the *Republic*, the *Phaedrus*, and the *Timaeus*.

Two topics concerned him especially: the question of the immortality of the psyche, and the problem of its unity. The two questions are closely linked; for Plato, like many thinkers after him, believed that only a unitary and indivisible item could be eternal—anything divisible would at some time actually be divided and hence destroyed. A psyche with parts cannot be immortal; and since Plato held both that the psyche has parts and that it is immortal, he found himself in a perplexity from which he never really escaped.

The *Phaedo* represents Socrates, on the day of his death, talking to his friends about the nature of the psyche: he is determined to discover whether the psyche survives death, or whether, as certain theories dictate, it perishes when the body perishes. The dialogue produces a battery of arguments, developed with great sophistication, to show that the psyche is indeed immortal. The arguments—together with subsidiary reflections produced in the *Republic* and the *Phaedrus*—repay close study. They are none of them cogent, and they are too complex to be profitably summarized, but one point about them is worth mentioning: in arguing for the immortality of the psyche, Socrates is arguing for his own immortality—in the *Phaedo* he believes that he has proved that *he* will survive his death. In other words, Socrates' psyche is the very same thing as Socrates: the one survives if and only if the other does. That is thoroughly consistent with the general Greek notion of psyche, and it shows that Plato, unlike many Christian thinkers, did not regard the person as a compound of body and soul, only one component of which can achieve immortality. My soul may be a *part* of me; my psyche *is* me.

The doctrine that the psyche has 'parts' is expounded in the *Republic*, the *Phaedrus*, and the *Timaeus*. According to the *Republic*, the psyche is composed of an appetitive, an emotional, and a rational part. Plato argues for this tripartite division from the existence of certain types of psychological conflict; for example, a desert traveller may feel thirsty and experience a strong desire to drink from a well, while at the same time his reason (observing that the well is insanitary) urges him not to drink. Since one and the same thing cannot at one and the same time possess opposite properties (a single and undivided psyche cannot at the same time both urge the traveller to the well and hold him back from the water), it follows that the psyche contains at least two distinct parts.

Plato's tripartition of the psyche has been compared to *Freud's distinction among the id, the ego, and the super-ego; and certainly it is very different in style from Aristotle's division of the various psychological faculties. Moreover, the basis of Plato's tripartition is logically dubious, and it is not clear if the tripartition is meant to be exhaustive or even exclusive. (Plato himself hints at a more refined and numerous partition, and elsewhere in the *Republic* he assigns appetites to the rational part of the psyche itself.) The fact is that Plato is not primarily concerned, as Aristotle was, with analytical psychology: his interest in the psyche centres on its role as a source of human behaviour, and in particular of moral action. The 'rational part' of the psyche is the morally superior part—the part which ought to govern our actions; and Plato singles it out, not from a desire to develop a detailed psychological theory, but because he wants to attend to the place of reason in the ethics of human action.

In the *Timaeus* (and also in a short passage in the *Theaetetus*) Plato offers accounts of the psychological faculties which are similar in style and motivation to those of the *Pre-Socratics and of Aristotle. But those contributions to analytical psychology are not particularly original: *moral* psychology—the study of the psychological conditions of moral activity—was the focal point for Plato's interest in the affairs of the psyche.

Plato's dialogues have often been translated into English. The best complete translation is still the Victorian masterpiece of Benjamin Jowett (now available, in a revised and more accurate form, in paperback).                                   J. BA.

For an introductory discussion, see Hare, R. M. (1982). *Plato*. Oxford.

**PLATONIC FORMS.** The so-called 'theory' of Forms or Ideas is the name given to a group of Platonic doctrines, found in the *Republic* (c. 380 BC) and elsewhere. The central notion is that, over and above the particular objects that are, for example, beautiful, there is a separate Form—'the beautiful itself'. And in general, wherever a single term is applied to a group of particulars (e.g. beds, tables) there is a corresponding Form. Unlike particulars, which are subject to change and decay, the Forms are eternal and unchanging, and possess their properties in an absolute unqualified way. *Plato argued that true knowledge or understanding relates to the Forms alone; and the Forms must be apprehended not by the senses but by the intellect. Hence, the mind must be drawn away from the senses if it is to apprehend ultimate reality (a doctrine which had considerable influence on subsequent philosophy). *Aristotle criticizes the theory of Forms, arguing that what makes a man a man, for example, is a set of essential characteristics which do not have a separate existence, but must always be instantiated or embodied in particular individuals. Commentators sympathetic to Plato have suggested that the doctrine of Forms contains an important insight: that true scientific understanding must always attempt to go beyond particular observation and ascend to the more universal realm of theoretical models and mathematical laws.                          J. G. C.

Annas, J. (1980). *An Introduction to Plato's Republic*. Oxford.
Plato. *The Republic* (trans. Cornford, F. M., 1941). Oxford.

**PLEASURE CENTRES.** See CENTRES IN THE BRAIN.

**PLEASURE–PAIN PRINCIPLE.** See FREUD ON MENTAL STRUCTURE.

**POINCARÉ,** JULES HENRI (1854–1912). French mathematician and philosopher, born at Nancy. The range of Poincaré's work was so great that the obituary number of the *Revue de Metaphysique et de Morale* (September 1913) devoted 130 pages—written by a philosopher, a mathematician, an astronomer, and a physicist—to outline his contributions. Bertrand Russell, in his introduction to the English translation of Poincaré's collected essays *Science and Method* (1908), contrasts Poincaré's writings on science with most professional philosophers as having 'the freshness of actual experience, of vivid contact with what he is describing', which shows, for example, in his vivid account of mathematical invention. As Poincaré says in his essay 'Mathematical Discovery': 'This is a process in which the human mind seems to borrow least from the exterior world, in which it acts, or appears to act, only by itself and on itself, so that by studying the process of geometric thought we may hope to arrive at what is most essential in the human mind.' This leads him to ask how it is that many people do not understand mathematics, as it is founded on logic and principles common to us all. For his own discoveries Poincaré describes: 'appearances of sudden illumination, obvious indications of a long course of previous unconscious work', and he gives interesting first-hand examples. He holds that most creative work consists of unconscious selection of possibilities, the selection being guided by subtle rules for rejection which may be worked out during conscious activity. The result is direction and purpose, with a minimum of thinking-time wasted on dead ends. Analogies are important for guiding (conscious or unconscious) thinking, but Poincaré holds that the ultimate guide for creative mathematics is a sense of aesthetic elegance. This, however, does have the snag that it can bias thinking towards errors when the truth is less than elegant.

Poincaré was concerned with how sensation and perception relate to physics; or rather, how physics is *derived* from our experience. Here his thinking in some ways paralleled that of Einstein, who derived some of his ideas from these deep questions of how knowledge can be gained, and how observations can suggest and test theories. Poincaré stressed the importance of hypotheses in science, and he was content to see truth as the unattainable end of a convergence.

Poincaré, H. (1905). *Science and Hypothesis*. London.
Poincaré, H. (1908). *Science and Method*. London.

**POLYGRAPHY.** See ELECTRODERMAL ACTIVITY.

**POSITIVISM.** See COMTE.

**POSITRON EMISSION TOMOGRAPHY (PET).** See IMAGES OF THE BRAIN IN ACTION.

**POSSIBILITY.** The concept of possibility can be firmly related to that of necessity, but very little else pertaining to these two concepts is a matter beyond dispute. If we take for granted that we understand what it is for a statement to be true, a statement is possibly true (states a possibility) if it is not necessary that it is not true.

At least one class of statements might be thought to be necessarily not true, namely those which involve an explicit contradiction. There is, however, a tradition in Western philosophy, stretching from *Heraclitus to *Hegel, which holds that there are real contradictions in nature, and that hence a contradiction sometimes states a possibility. *Aristotle (*Metaphysics*, Gamma 4–6) argued strenuously against the followers of Heraclitus on behalf of the principle of non-contradiction, and by far the bulk of Western philosophers, rationalist and empiricist alike, have accepted that contradictions are necessarily not true. For them, there is firm foundation for a concept of logical possibility: any statement which does not involve a contradiction states a logical possibility. Two questions then arise: how far can one build on this foundation, and is there any more to (real) possibility than absence of contradiction?

The first question arises because not all contradictions are apparent. If one does not realize that a rooster is a male chicken, it will not be apparent that there is a contradiction involved in saying that a rooster has laid an egg. Such examples encourage the thoughts that non-apparent contradictions are all rendered obscure by linguistic ignorance and that ultimately possibility and necessity reflect only arbitrary rules for the use of words. To find out whether a statement is necessary, all that anyone who is fully in command of what words mean needs to do in order to establish the consistency of any description (and hence the logical possibility of what is described) is to *imagine* the state of affairs described.

Hume was thus able to develop a general strategy for undermining claims that some event $A$ was the *cause of event $B$ (i.e. made the occurrence of $B$ necessary) by inviting his reader to imagine $A$ not followed by $B$, thereby showing '$A$ and not $B$' to be consistent and hence the description of a possibility. (This was the foundation of the argument in *Hume which gave rise to what is known as the problem of *induction.) The strategy assumes that we have nothing more to learn about $A$, which would reveal that for $B$ not to follow would be a contradiction; and this in turn rests on the assumption that what we are talking about when we refer to $A$, or to any object, can be adequately conceptualized on the basis of how objects appear.

If we drop this assumption and make use of a framework (not unlike that found in Aristotle) in which our concepts of things have to be framed in terms of how the powers and capacities of those things restrict what is possible elsewhere, we must address the second question, i.e. that of further sources of restriction on what is a possibility. We can imagine (what appears to be) the sun standing still in the sky; but to think this out fully in the light of our knowledge of nature requires us to register the effects of halting the earth's rotation. Science reveals that such an event is not (naturally) possible without certain concomitant events. We can describe without (apparent) contradiction a world in which these events do not follow, and we can also speak without (apparent) contradiction of a world in which there is a perpetual motion machine; but if our science is well founded, neither of these is our world. Science, it seems, is engaged in spelling out for us what is naturally possible and naturally impossible.

It is evident from this that the issue of whether possibility and necessity are purely a matter of how we use language, or are also a matter of how the world is, is an issue closely bound up with what is thought to be involved in the scientific understanding of the natural world. Any approach such as that of traditional empiricism which bases knowledge on immediate appearances will be deeply suspicious of the notion of natural possibility or impossibility. But at the opposite pole an extreme realist may invite us to view the universe from the standpoint of a being (e.g. God) whose knowledge is complete. From such a standpoint there might seem to be no place for a notion of possibility beyond something like that defined by Diodorus Cronos (*c.*300 BC): whatever is or will be true, which entails that no possibility is not at some time actualized. All other notions of possibility, in other words, only reflect our limited perspective on the universe and should be treated as kinds of epistemic possibility, i.e. defined as what is consistent with some state of our knowledge.

There is, however, another way to conceive the position of a being whose knowledge is complete, particularly if He is also to be thought of as an all-powerful Creator. In *Leibniz's view, God had knowledge of all the possible ways the world might have been, each a 'possible world', and He chose one of those to be the actual world. This concept has given rise in recent decades to a notion in formal logic of a possible world, and a definition of a possible truth as one true in at least one possible world and of a necessary truth as one true in all possible worlds.                J. E. T.

Hume, D. (1739–40). *A Treatise of Human Nature*, bk. I, pt. iii. Oxford (repr. 1888).

Kneale, W. and M. (1962). *The Development of Logic.* Oxford.

Leibniz, G. *Philosophical Writings*, ed. G. H. R. Parkinson, 1973. London.

Pap, A. (1958). *Semantics and Necessary Truth.* Princeton.

**POSTULATE.** See AXIOM.

**PRAGMATISM** is a largely American philosophic tradition, too divergent in doctrine to constitute a school, which stresses the purposive nature of cognition and seeks in practical consequences the key to the meanings of concepts or the correctness of belief. The term was coined by the philosopher C. S. *Peirce, who applied it to a method, first published in 1878, for determining the meanings of 'intellectual concepts'. This method counselled us to consider the effects likely to have practical bearings which 'we conceive the object of our concept to have', for in those lie 'the whole of our conception of the object'. (Peirce thus anticipated verificationist themes which were to be prominent in quite different forms in logical positivism.) Peirce's method attracted the ready sympathy of his close friend William *James, who wrote in 1879 that a conception 'is a *teleological instrument* . . . a partial aspect of a thing which *for our purpose* we regard as its essential aspect, as the representative of the entire thing' (*Principles of Psychology*, II, 335 n.).

Peirce, however, resisted the way James widened pragmatism to incorporate a theory of truth. This theory, which provoked intense controversy in the decades prior to the First World War, appeared to suggest that truth is nothing more than what works in practice. Doubtless James's vivid way of expressing his views (speaking of 'cash value' and of truths as having in common only the quality 'that they *pay*') contributed to the tendency of his opponents to father on him hopelessly crude views; but it remains exceedingly difficult to extract a coherent theory of truth from James's writings. The reason may be that truth as we commonly use the notion points to a divorce of cognition from purposive activity, so that a pragmatic spirit is best developed by leaving the notion of truth behind. This was the path taken by John *Dewey (e.g. in his *Logic* of 1938), who abandoned the notion of truth in favour of 'warranted assertibility'.

J. E. T.

Thayer, H. S. (1968). *Meaning and Action, A Critical History of Pragmatism*. Indianapolis.

**PRECOGNITION.** See EXTRA-SENSORY PERCEPTION.

**PRE-SOCRATIC PHILOSOPHERS.** The term 'Pre-Socratic' is conventionally applied to a heterogeneous collection of Greek thinkers who lived and worked in the period from *c*.600 to *c*.400 BC. These men in no sense formed a single sect or school; but they wrestled, each in his own way, with a common set of problems—problems which we would now classify as scientific or philosophical.

None of their writings (some of which were in verse, some in prose) has survived intact: what we know about them is gleaned from the reports of later authors, and from the short quotations contained in those reports. Our knowledge of Pre-Socratic philosophy is thus fragmentary; and the interpretation of those fragments is generally subject to scholarly controversy. Moreover, many Pre-Socratic opinions and theories were certainly primitive, ill-informed, and simple-minded. For all

that, the Pre-Socratics are of primary importance to any student of Western intellectual progress: they first posed the questions which *Plato and *Aristotle later attempted to answer; and they thereby determined, indirectly, the whole course of Western science and philosophy. Above all, they began the tradition of rational enquiry which disdains any appeal to authority (whether human or divine) and which insists that observation and inference are the twin pillars of knowledge.

The Pre-Socratics were all polymaths, and their studies left few fields of human knowledge unsurveyed. They made precocious investigations into most of the issues which now fall under the heading of psychology or philosophy of mind: thus they discussed the nature of the 'soul' or *psyche and of the various psychological faculties; they developed theories of perception (see PERCEPTION: EARLY GREEK THEORIES) and of thought; they pored over the related phenomena of memory, dreaming, and sleep. Aristotle's pupil, Theophrastus, wrote a critical appreciation of Pre-Socratic theories of the mind: a large part of his book has survived, and it gives us some idea of the scope and detail of those early intellectual adventures.

The main Pre-Socratic thinkers were these (the dates are at best approximate): *Thales (620–550 BC), Anaximander (610–550), and Anaximenes (570–500)—all from Miletus in Asia Minor; *Pythagoras (570–500); *Heraclitus (540–480); Parmenides (520–430), *Zeno (500–440), and Melissus (480–420)—the 'Eleatics'; Anaxagoras (500–430); Empedocles (490–430); Democritus (460–370). Thales, the founder of Western thought, reflected on the nature of psyche, and argued that the magnet has a psyche (since it can initiate motion). Pythagoras advocated the doctrine of *metempsychosis. Heraclitus, an enigmatic thinker, avowed that the psyche was too profound to be fathomed by human thought—but he nevertheless offered certain speculations on its fiery nature. Empedocles and Democritus, the atomist, produced detailed theories of perception and of other psychological activities. Two minor figures deserve mention: Alcmaeon (510–440), a doctor, taught that the various sense modalities are unified in the brain; and he produced an argument, which Plato later adopted, for the immortality of the psyche. Philolaus (470–390), a follower of Pythagoras, suggested that the psyche is nothing more than an attunement or harmony of the body: a creature has a psyche (or: is alive) just so long as his physical constituents are harmoniously interrelated.

The fragments of the Pre-Socratics are translated in Jonathan Barnes, *Early Greek Philosophy* (1986); for discussion see Jonathan Barnes, *The Presocratic Philosophers* (2nd edn., 1982).

J. BA.

**PRIMATE LANGUAGE.** Is only man, *Homo sapiens*, capable of communicating by language? Clearly the answer must depend on what is meant by 'language'—for all the higher animals certainly communicate with a great variety of signs, such as gestures, odours, calls, cries and songs, and even the dance of the bees. Yet animals other than man do not appear to have structured grammatical language. And animals do not, which may be highly significant, draw representational pictures. At best they only doodle. If animals (other than ourselves) could speak, or gesture with comparable effectiveness—or draw pictures—we would have immediate access to non-human minds. As it is, investigators of animal learning, understanding, and perception are forced into undertaking experiments which, however ingenious, are difficult to carry out and to interpret. Apart from anything else, it is not possible simply to ask an animal to press a button, or search for a solution to a puzzle, let alone ask it what it sees or hears or smells; or what it thinks of its cage-mates, or of us and our experiments.

There are several historical attempts to teach animals human language; but until 1966 no such attempts yielded positive results. Then R. A. and B. T. Gardner, in extensive studies carried out in America, considered the possibility that although primates might be unable (for anatomical reasons) to vocalize speech, perhaps they could learn to communicate by a human sign language. So they set out to teach an eleven months old female chimpanzee—Washoe—the American sign language used by deaf people, Ameslan.

After fifty-one months, Washoe had acquired 132 signs of Ameslan, being able to use them for indicating general classes as well as specific objects or events. Thus the sign for *dog* was used to refer to live dogs and pictures of dogs of many sizes, breeds, and colours, and for the sound of barking (Gardner and Gardner, 1978, p. 38). She would use the signs spontaneously, and it was estimated that her use of combinations of signs was comparable to that of the early word combinations of human children. (For a discussion of human development of language, see LANGUAGE DEVELOPMENT IN CHILDREN and LANGUAGE: LEARNING WORD MEANINGS.) Washoe was brought up as nearly as possible in a child's environment, as the Gardners assumed that this would be conducive to human-like development and learning. So her days were like a child's, with baths, play, schooling, and outings to interesting places. She had furniture, toys, tools, a kitchen, a bedroom, and a bathroom. It should, however, be noted that the Ameslan sign language is constructed differently from spoken or written language; generally having larger 'units' of meaning, so direct comparison with human, and particularly infant speech is not easy.

In 1972 the Gardners added four more young chimpanzees—Moja, Peli, Tatu, and Dar, who were only a few days old—to study signing *between* animals. Washoe was nearly a year old at the beginning of her language-learning, but the newcomers started a few days after birth: 'After seven months of exposure to the conditions of the project, her (Washoe's) vocabulary consisted of the signs, *come-gimme*, *more*, *up*, and *sweet*. By contrast, both Moja and Peli started to make recognizable signs when they were about three months old.

For example, Moja's first four signs (*come-gimme*, *more*, *go*, and *drink*) appeared during her 13th week. The Gardners (1978) comment that though the acquisition of first signs for chimpanzees may seem early compared with children's first speech, this is not so for deaf children exposed to sign language from birth; for parents report that these deaf children's first signs appear between the fifth and sixth months.

The Gardners (1978) compared the five chimpanzee's 10-sign and 50-sign vocabulary acquisition with reports in the literature of hearing children's 10-word and 50-word acquisition: 'The age for ten-sign vocabulary was five months for Moja, Peli and Tatu, and six months for Dar, but 25 months for Washoe; in the case of children, the age at ten words ranged from 13 to 19 months, with a mean of 15 months' (p. 50).

The Gardners report that the chimpanzees modified or extended their sign language, such as by signing *tickle* on the hand of another chimpanzee, or a human, and sometimes to give an object to a human who is then expected to tickle the chimpanzee with the object. Eye gaze and facial expression are also important adjuncts to the signs, and may be used to distinguish between a declaration and an interrogation. Repetition is also used, for example when a sign is ignored.

Although syntax is important in adult human language, sign order is much less in evidence in early child language, and is not important in the American sign language (Klima and Bellugi, 1979). So the application of syntax is hardly appropriate as a criterion for the chimpanzees' sign language. But it does not follow that order is beyond their capacity. Fouts, Shapiro, and O'Neill (1978), report that order can be trained, with production (by their chimpanzee Ali) of novel prepositional phrases for objects. This was in double-blind experimental conditions (the stimulus objects being hidden from the experimenter) which were also used by the Gardners. The essential claim is that as novel combinations of signs were used, and were used to 'describe' conceptually related novel stimuli, there was more going on than conditioning or instrumental conditioning. Suggestive here is *errors*. Most errors fitted two categories: semantic error, in which a sign of similar meaning was incorrectly used, such as *comb* for *brush*; and form errors, such as confusion between the signs *meat* and *oil*, which though very different in meaning are similar in their physical form.

There is criticism of these and further claims for language acquisition by chimpanzees, including: (a) the chimpanzees are cued to make the signs by the humans (the *Clever Hans phenomenon); (b) the chimpanzees do not sign spontaneously, which is quite unlike children; (c) the chimpanzees sign only for rewards; (d) humans are needed to teach them; they don't develop signing by themselves.

The author's experiments, with Loulis, were designed to answer at least some of these criticisms. The signs used were limited to seven: *who*, *what*, *want*, *where*, *which*, *name*, and *sign*. Apart from these, vocal English was used to communicate to the chimpanzee, to ensure that he could not acquire extra signs from humans. These experiments suggest that chimpanzees can communicate with each other, for not only has Loulis acquired signs from Washoe and the other signing chimps he lives with, but Washoe and the other chimps have acquired new signs from each other in their chimpanzee-to-chimpanzee signing conversations. It was observed that a chimp would teach another chimp by demonstrating, for example the *chair-sit* sign, several times, with a toy chair. Fouts (1984) has made video records, over randomly selected twenty minute periods, of what appears to be (612 occurrences of signs) chimp-to-chimp sign conversation. The use of video recording prevents cuing by humans. Also, spontaneous signing has been observed many times (Fouts, Fouts, and Schoenfeld, 1984), and many of these were for social communication rather than (only 5 per cent) for food reward.

Some investigators, however, such as Terrace, Petitto, Sanders and Bever (1979) and Savage-Rumbaugh, Rumbaugh, and Boysen (1980), have failed to achieve evidence of language acquisition in chimps. Possibly they used ineffective procedures, such as inappropriate rewards. It has been suggested that language-learning (and, for children, drawing) is intrinsically rewarding, for chimps as it is for human children; and that for both, extrinsic rewards such as food can impair performance and learning.

Language and cognitive understanding (Premack, 1971) in chimps is controversial, some authorities altogether denying chimp language; but the possibility challenges any sharp break between human and animal cognition, which raises moral issues for how we should consider and treat animals even though normally we cannot talk to them.

R. S. F.<br>D. H. F.

Fouts, D. H. (1984). Remote video taping of a juvenile chimpanzee's sign language interactions within his social group. Unpublished master's thesis, Central Washington University, Ellensburg, WA.

Fouts, R. S., Fouts, D. H., and Schoenfeld, D. (1984). Sign language conversational interactions between chimpanzees. *Sign Language Studies*, **34**, 1–12.

Fouts, R. S., Shapiro, G., and O'Neil, C. (1978). Studies of linguistic behavior in apes and children. In Siple, P. (ed.) *Understanding language through sign language research* (pp. 163–85). New York.

Gardner, R. A. and Gardner, B. T. (1978). Comparative psychology and language acquisition. *Annals of the New York Academy of Sciences*, **309**, 37–767.

Klima, E. and Bellugi, U. (1979). *The signs of language*. Cambridge, MA.

Premack, D. (1971). On the assessment of language competence in the chimpanzee. In Schrier, A. and Stollnitz,

F. (eds.), *Behavior of non-human primates*: Vol. 4 (pp. 183–228). New York.

Savage-Rumbaugh, E., Rumbaugh, D., and Boysen, S. (1980). Do apes use language? *American Scientist*, **68**, 49–61.

Terrace, H., Petitto, L., Sanders, R., and Bever, T. (1979). Can an ape create a sentence? *Science*, **206**, 891–902.

## PRIMATES, EVOLUTION OF THE BRAIN IN.

The earliest placental mammals were small, nocturnal, insectivorous animals that lived in the Cretaceous period more than 100 million years ago (Fig. 1). They possessed acute senses of smell and hearing and long, sensitive snouts bearing vibrissae. Their eyes were small, laterally directed, and possessed very limited acuity. Their brains were somewhat larger than those of similarly sized reptiles, but the neocortex, which was to become the great focus of mammalian brain evolution, had undergone only very limited development (Fig. 2). The telencephalon was largely devoted to the olfactory bulbs and olfactory cortex. The early placental mammals lived in a landscape dominated by reptiles, but this was to change radically with the massive extinctions that devastated the ranks of reptiles at the end of the Cretaceous. A host of theories has been advanced to explain the sudden extinctions. Perhaps the most compelling, because of its strong support from geophysical data, is the theory advanced by L. W. Alvarez and his collaborators that a large asteroid struck the earth, resulting in the release of enormous quantities of dust into the atmosphere and thus a great reduction in sunlight reaching the earth's surface. The nocturnal, warm-blooded mammals would have been much better equipped for survival during a period of sudden climatic cooling than were their reptilian contemporaries. Whatever the cause, 65 million years ago at the beginning of the Cainozoic era, the 'age of mammals', a large number of ecological niches lay vacant that formerly had been occupied by reptiles.

During the next 10 million years the basal stock of placental mammals began to differentiate into the various orders of mammals. The fossil remains

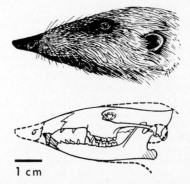

1 cm

**Fig. 1.** Skull and restored head of the Cretaceous placental mammal *Zalambdalestes lechei*.

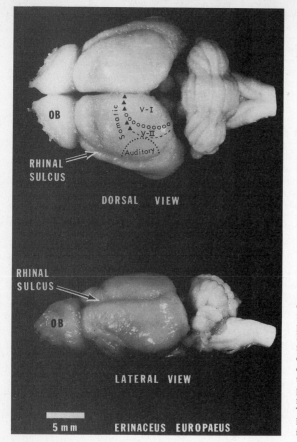

DORSAL VIEW

RHINAL SULCUS

OB

Somatic

V-I

V-II

Auditory

RHINAL SULCUS

OB

LATERAL VIEW

5 mm   ERINACEUS EUROPAEUS

**Fig. 2.** Dorsal and lateral views of the brain of the European hedgehog (*Erinaceus europaeus*), a modern insectivore that has retained many features characteristic of the primitive placental mammals. The neocortex lies dorsal and medial to the rhinal sulcus. V-I, first visual area; V-II, second visual area. The circles indicate the representation of the vertical meridian (mid-line) of the visual field; the triangles indicate the representation of the far periphery of the contralateral half of the visual field. Note the large olfactory bulbs (OB). The cortex ventral to the rhinal sulcus is largely devoted to the processing of olfactory input.

of the earliest Primates that bear a close resemblance to living Primates have been recovered from early Eocene deposits approximately 55 million years old. The skull and cranial endocast of one of these early Primates, *Tetonius homunculus*, is illustrated in Fig. 3. *Tetonius* possessed large bony orbits that completely encircled its eyes, and a cranium containing a large brain compared with its similarly sized contemporaries. The relative size and position of the orbits in *Tetonius* closely resemble living nocturnal prosimians such as *Galago* (Fig. 4). As can be seen in Fig. 5, *Galago* possesses large, frontally directed eyes with virtually as much binocular overlap, in the order of 120° to 140°, as is present in monkeys, apes, and man. The great similarity in the size and position of the orbits in *Galago* and *Tetonius* suggests that *Tetonius* also possessed large, frontally directed eyes and was crepuscular or nocturnal. The cranial endocasts of *Tetonius* and other Eocene Primates show that their brains possessed a conspicuous enlargement of the neocortex in the occipital and temporal lobes, which in modern Primates are known to be devoted mainly to the cortical processing of visual information (Fig. 4). Thus, by the

early Eocene, there appeared in Primates the concomitant development of large, frontally directed eyes with improved acuity and an expanded visual cortex. The sensitive snout of the primitive placental mammals was greatly reduced in the early Primates. The functions of the snout as a tactile probe and an apprehender of insect prey were taken over by the hands. The olfactory system in the early Primates retained a comparable degree of development to that present in the early placental mammals. The size of the olfactory bulbs did not diminish relative to body size, but the occipital and temporal neocortex expanded so greatly that the olfactory bulbs became small by comparison (Figs. 2, 3, and 4).

These developments must reflect fundamental changes in ecological specialization that occurred in the evolutionary progression from the earliest placental mammals to the early Primates. Two theories have recently been advanced to explain the basic adaptations that served to differentiate Primates from the early placental mammals. In the first, R. D. Martin has suggested that the early Primates, like the smaller living prosimians they closely resemble and the small arboreal marsupials

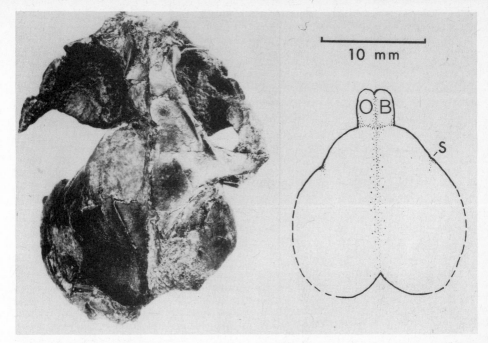

**Fig. 3.** *Left*. Dorsal view of the skull of *Tetonius homunculus*. (A.M.N.H. No. 4194.) *Right*. Dorsal view of L. B. Radinsky's cranial endocast of *Tetonius*. OB: olfactory bulbs. S: sylvian sulcus.

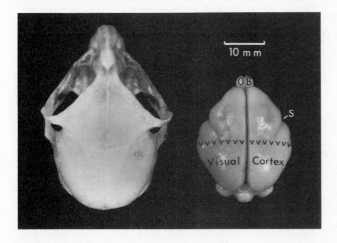

**Fig. 4.** *Left*. Dorsal view of the skull of *Galago senegalensis*. *Right*. Dorsal view of the brain of *Galago senegalensis*. The visual cortex corresponds to approximately the posterior half of the neocortex. The Vs demarcate the anterior border of visual cortex. OB: olfactory bulbs. S: sylvian sulcus.

of Australia and South America, adapted to a 'fine branch niche'; the prehensile hands and feet found in these animals developed to grasp the fine terminal branches of trees. Most arboreal mammals, such as squirrels, run on the trunk and larger branches but are unable to grasp the finer branches. The second theory is based on the observation that, outside the order Primates, animals with large frontally directed eyes (owls and felids) are nocturnal, visually directed predators, which has led M. Cartmill to propose that visually directed

predation was the ecological specialization responsible for the developments in the early Primates. Cartmill's visual predation hypothesis is supported by the fact that the tarsier, the living Primate that most resembles the early Primates of the Eocene, is exclusively a predator (Fig. 6). It appears that both hypotheses have considerable merit. It seems probable that the early Primates did invade the 'fine branch niche', where they gained access to a rich array of insect and small vertebrate prey.

What are the advantages that frontally directed

**Fig. 5.** Close-up of the face of *Galago senegalensis*. Note the mid-line cleft in the upper lip, which is a feature present in all strepsirhine Primates but absent in haplorhine Primates.

**Fig. 6.** Tarsier seizing a lizard. The tarsier is exclusively a predator; it eats no fruit or vegetable matter. Of the living Primates, the tarsier most closely resembles the early Primates living in the Eocene.

eyes afford nocturnal, visually directed predators? Predators generally orient so that the prey is located in front of them so that they can propel themselves forward rapidly and carry out a co-ordinated attack with forelimbs and jaws, and it is likely that frontally directed eyes provide maximal retinal image quality, for the central part of the visual field where the prey is located, in the crucial moments before the final strike is made. Image distortion tends to increase the further an object is located off the optical axis of the lens system, and thus it is advantageous to a visually directed predator to have frontally directed eyes in which the optical axes are directed toward the central part of the visual field, so that the predator can utilize the maximum quality retinal image in the crucial moments before the strike, when it is evaluating the prey's movements, the prey's suitability as food, and the prey's ability to defend itself. The dimly illuminated nocturnal environment makes these optical factors particularly important, and rules out other mechanisms for improving retinal image quality such as stopping down lens aperture.

Frontally directed eyes also provide a large binocular field over which binocular summation can be achieved, which may be of particular value in conditions of low illumination. The binocular input is also used to reconstruct a stereoscopic view of a large portion of the visual field. The advantages of stereoscopy to a predator are that it provides information about the distance of prey, and as B. Julesz has pointed out, it helps the predator to discriminate camouflaged prey from background (cf. VISION: THE EARLY WARNING SYSTEM).

Almost all of the distinctive features of the Primate visual system relate to the frontal direction of the eyes and binocular integration, and since these features are present in all Primates, it is likely that they developed in the early Primates. These features include: (i) a high concentration of retinal ganglion cells in the central retina, and the greatly expanded representation of the central retina in the neural maps of the visual field in the brain; (ii) the representation restricted to the contralateral half of the visual field in each side of the optic tectum, differing from complete representation of the field of view of the contralateral retina found in each side of the optic tectum in all other vertebrates that have been investigated (Fig. 7); (iii) a relatively large retinotectal projection, which together with the unique visuotopic organization found in the Primate tectum, suggests that the optic tectum in the early Primates developed capacities related to the integration of binocular input; (iv) a distinctly laminated dorsal lateral geniculate nucleus in which inputs from the two retinae are brought into precise visuotopic register before being relayed to the primary visual cortex (VI); and (v) a greatly expanded visual cortex containing a number of neural maps of the visual field (see LOCALIZATION OF BRAIN FUNCTION AND CORTICAL MAPS).

Why does the visual cortex contain a series of separate representations of the visual field rather than a single map? In attempting to develop computer analogues of visual perception, D. Marr elaborated the principle of modular design. Marr stated that any large computation should be broken into a collection of smaller modules as independent as possible from one another. Otherwise, 'the process as a whole becomes extremely difficult to debug or improve, whether by a human designer or in the course of natural evolution, because a small change to improve one part has to be accompanied by many simultaneous changes elsewhere'. This modular principle has many counterparts in other biological systems. The palaeontologist W. K. Gregory noted that a common mechanism of evolution is the replication of body parts due to genetic mutation in a single generation which is then followed in subsequent generations by the gradual divergence of structure and functions of the duplicated parts. An analogous idea has been advanced by a number of geneticists. They have theorized that replicated genes escape the pressures of natural selection

## VISUAL FIELD

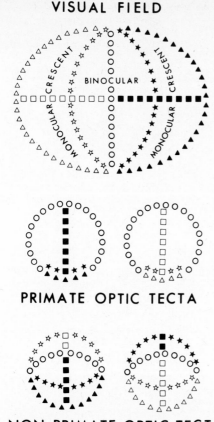

**Fig. 7.** Schematic plan of the representation of the visual field in the optic tectum of Primates and non-Primates. Circles indicate the vertical meridian (mid-line) dividing the two halves of the visual field; squares, the horizontal mid-line; triangles, the extreme periphery of the visual field; stars, the division between binocular and monocular portions of the visual field.

operating on the original gene, and thereby can accumulate mutations which enable the new gene, through changes in its DNA sequence, to encode for a novel protein capable of assuming new functions. Many clear-cut examples of gene replication have been discovered, and DNA sequence homologies in replicated genes have recently been established. Using this analogy, the author and J. H. Kaas have proposed that the replication of cortical sensory representations has provided the structures upon which new information-processing capabilities have developed in the course of evolution. Specifically, it has been argued that existing cortical areas, like genes, can undergo only limited changes and still perform the functions necessary for the animal's survival, but if a mutation occurs that results in the replication of a cortical area, then in subsequent generations the new area can eventually assume new functions through the mechanisms of natural selection while the original area continues to perform its functions.

The primary visual cortex (VI) and the adjacent second visual area (VII) are present in all mammalian species that have been investigated. Thus, VI and VII were probably present in the early placental mammals that were the common ancestors of the various living mammalian orders. The full complement of cortical visual areas varies in different mammals from a minimum of two in a basal insectivore, the hedgehog (Fig. 2), to a maximum of twelve found in cats by Palmer, Tusa, and Rosenquist. At least nine cortical visual areas are present in the owl monkey, the Primate which has been mapped most completely (Fig. 8). Beyond VI and VII it is very difficult to establish homologies among the visual areas present in mammals belonging to different orders. The last common ancestor of the different mammalian orders lived no more recently than the late Cretaceous period more than 65 million years ago, and this ancestral mammal had only a very limited development of its neocortex. In addition, the adaptive radiation of mammals into different ecological niches with widely divergent behavioural specializations serves to make very difficult the discovery of diagnostic similarities among potentially homologous cortical areas in different mammalian orders.

Within the order Primates, it is easier to determine homologous areas in different species. The highly distinctive middle temporal visual area (MT) is present in prosimians and in both New and Old World monkeys and thus probably existed in the early Primates. MT neurones are selective for the direction of movement of visual stimuli and often are particularly responsive to moving fields of visual texture. MT may have developed as a specialized mechanism for detecting and tracking moving prey. MT may also participate in visuomotor co-ordination by analysing the visual flow patterns that the animal sees as it moves through its environment; MT projects via the pontine nuclei to the cerebellum, a major centre for the control of body and eye movements. The evolutionary development of this system may be related to the special demands of locomotion in the 'fine branch niche'.

The dorsolateral visual area (DL) lies adjacent to MT and also appears to be part of the basic complement of visual areas common to all living Primates and thus probably existing in the early Primates. In DL about 70 per cent of the neurones are selective for the spatial dimensions (length and width) of visual stimuli within excitatory receptive fields that generally are much larger than the preferred stimulus dimensions. The dimensional selectivity of DL neurones is independent of the sign of contrast in the receptive field, as they are equally selective to both light-on-dark and dark-on-light stimuli, the amount of contrast, and the position of the stimulus within the excitatory receptive field. It suggests that DL contributes to *form perception*. This hypothesis is consistent with the

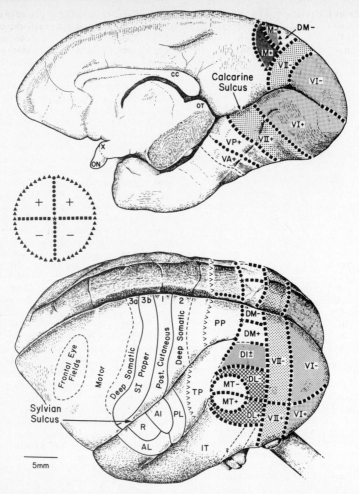

**Fig. 8.** The representations of the sensory domains in the cerebral cortex of the owl monkey. Above is a ventromedial view of the right hemisphere, below is a dorsolateral view of both hemispheres. On the left is a perimeter chart of the visual field. The symbols in this chart are superimposed on the surface of the visual cortex. Pluses indicate upper quadrant representations; minuses, lower quadrants. The row of Vs indicates the approximate border of visually responsive cortex. AI, first auditory area; AL, anterolateral auditory area; CC, corpus callosum; DI, dorsointermediate visual area; DL, dorsolateral crescent visual area; DM, dorsomedial visual area; IT, inferotemporal cortex; M, medial visual area; MT, middle temporal visual area; ON, optic nerve; OT, optic tectum; PL, posterolateral auditory area; PP, posterior parietal cortex; R, rostral auditory area; VI, first visual area; VII, second visual area; VA, ventral anterior visual area; VP, ventral posterior visual area; X, optic chiasm. The main connections of the visual areas are as follows. VI projects to VII and MT. VII projects to DL, which in turn projects to IT. MT projects to all visual areas except VII and IT. MT and PP project to the frontal eye fields.

fact that DL, of all the visual areas, has the most expanded representation of the central visual field where the most acute recognition of form takes place, and with the discovery (by Weller and Kaas) that DL is the main source of input to inferotemporal cortex. Inferotemporal cortex (IT) has been strongly implicated in the analysis of complex visual stimuli and the learning of visual form discriminations.

The small amount of neocortex possessed by the early placental mammals and the great variation in the number of cortical visual areas reported for different mammalian species suggests that some of the areas beyond VI and VII developed at different stages in evolution and independently in different lines of descent. One clear example of variation within the order Primates is among the areas immediately anterior to VII. In the prosimian *Galago*, only one map of the visual field, the dorsal area (D), is located in the position occupied by three separate maps, M, DM, and DI, in the owl monkey (see Fig. 8). The existing data suggest that there exists a core of areas including VI, VII, MT, and DL and possibly one or two others that are common to all Primates, but that there also exist areas present in some species but not in others. It is probable that each area performs a distinct set of functions in visual perception and visuomotor co-ordination, and that an area possessed by one species (or larger taxon) and not by another will endow its possessor with behavioural capacities not present in the other. A major task for the future will be to determine what are the distinctive functions of these cortical areas and how they relate to the behavioural and ecological specializations of their possessors.

The early Primates probably were small nocturnal predators living in the fine branches; some Primates have retained this mode of life, but most have become larger, diurnal folivores or frugivores. Frugivorous diet is correlated positively with brain size and the amount of neocortex relative to body size in Primates. This association between frugivorous diet and enlarged brain and neocortex may be related to the special demands imposed because a fruit-eater's food supply is not constant, since different plants bear fruit at different times and at different locations in the complex matrix of the tropical forest. It is clear that an animal guided by memory of the locations of fruit-bearing trees can more efficiently exploit the available fruit resources than would be possible otherwise. Thus natural selection would have favoured the development in frugivorous Primates of capacities for visuospatial memory, which may be localized in a particular area or set of areas.

Another, even more significant behavioural specialization is the development of complex systems of social organization in many Primate species. The neural substrate for the mediation of social communication is bound to be an important focus of evolutionary change in the brains of Primates. The order Primates is divided into the strepsirhines (lorises, lemurs, galagos), which tend to have relatively simple forms of social organization, and the haplorhines (tarsiers, monkeys, apes, and humans), in which social organization tends to be much more complex. In strepsirhines, as in most mammals, the rhinarium, the space between the upper lip and the nostrils, is furless, moist mucosal tissue that is tightly bound to the underlying maxillary bone and is divided along the mid-line by a deep cleft (Fig. 5). Since strepsirhines share this type of rhinarium with most other mammals, it is very likely to have been the primitive condition in Primates. By contrast, haplorhines possess a furry rhinarium and a mobile upper lip that is capable of participating in *facial expression. Strepsirhines, like most primitive mammals, have scent glands and scent-marking behaviours that play a very important role in their social communication, and while haplorhines also use olfactory cues to some extent, they rely much more heavily on the use of visually perceived facial expressions and gestures, which allow much more rapid and subtle communi-

cation. Strepsirhines also tend to have much larger olfactory bulbs than do haplorhines. Thus it appears that as complex systems of social organization evolved in haplorhine Primates, social communication was increasingly mediated by the visual channel at the expense of the olfactory. One expression of this evolutionary development is the sensory input to the amygdala, which controls the neuroendocrine functions of the hypothalamus and thus emotion. Primitively, the main input to the amygdala was from the olfactory bulb, but in haplorhines the main input is from the temporal lobe and particularly from inferotemporal cortex, which is a high-level processor of visual information. Neurones responsive to the specific configurations of faces have been recorded in the amygdala and temporal cortex. The clinical condition prosopagnosia, the inability to recognize familiar faces with relatively little impairment of other visual functions, which is usually associated with lesions located near the occipital temporal junction (see SPLIT-BRAIN AND THE MIND), suggests the development of a specialized system for processing the information in faces. Finally, in man, another system of social communication, language, has developed along with specialized cortical regions in the temporal and frontal lobes (see LANGUAGE AREAS IN THE BRAIN).                J. M. A.

Allman, J. M. (1977). Evolution of the visual system in the early primates. In Sprague, J. M. and Epstein, A. M. (eds.), *Progress in Psychobiology and Physiological Psychology*, vol. vii, 1–53. New York.

Cartmill, M. (1974). Rethinking Primate origins, *Science*, **184**, 436–43.

Clutton-Brock, T. H. and Harvey, P. H. (1980). Primates, brains and ecology. *Journal of Zoology*, **190**, 309–23.

Gregory, W. K. (1951). *Evolution Emerging*. New York.

Jerison, H. J. (1973). *Evolution of the Brain and Intelligence*. New York.

Julesz, B. (1971). *Foundations of Cyclopean Perception*. Chicago.

Martin, R. D. (1979). Phylogenetic aspects of prosimian behavior. In Doyle, G. A. and Martin, R. D. (eds.), *The Study of Prosimian Behavior*. New York.

Penfield, W. and Roberts, L. A. (1959). *Speech and Brain Mechanisms*. Princeton.

Polyak, S. (1957). *Vertebrate Visual System*. Chicago.

Radinsky, L. (1979). *The Fossil Record of Primate Brain Evolution*. New York.

**PROBLEMS: THEIR APPEAL.** People enjoy the mental stimulation of a good problem, and for some it becomes a powerful need—a cerebral restlessness epitomized in fiction by Sherlock Holmes. It makes little odds whether the problem is trivial or profound, vague or precise, so long as it tempts us to resolve a state of puzzlement or contradiction. Harlow et al. (1950) have shown that even monkeys spend considerable time in the manipulation of puzzles, without any extrinsic reward when left to their own devices. Does curiosity constitute a biological need? White (1959) and Berlyne (1971) have developed the theory that one reason for seeking the stimulation of novelty is to ward off boredom. The challenge of the problematic is manifested in a wide variety of forms, and here we contrast the response to two problem situations of a very different kind in order to see what they have in common.

The solution to a formal problem generally demands the postulation of a hypothesis, the assumption that something is true without knowing whether it is true. Its consequences can then be tested to see whether they fit the facts. The following is a very precise problem which critically requires this ability (Wason, 1977). (For a fascinating development of this problem, see Smyth and Clark, 1986.) If the individual does not think about it hypothetically he finds himself in a looking-glass world where everything seems the wrong way round.

In front of you imagine four designs made up of two colours and two shapes:

| | |
| --- | --- |
| *Blue diamond* | *Blue circle* |
| *Red diamond* | *Red circle* |

The problem is this: 'In these designs there is a particular shape and a particular colour such that any of the designs which has one, and only one, of these features is called a THOG. If the *blue diamond* is a THOG, could any of the other designs be THOGS?'

The problem hardly seems difficult. The *red circle* obviously could not be a THOG, and the other two could be THOGS because each has one feature of the *blue diamond*. That is the common-sense solution and it is wrong; it is the mirror image of the correct solution. If the *blue diamond* is a THOG, then the *red circle* is a THOG, and neither the *blue circle* nor the *red diamond* could be THOGS.

There is more than one path to the solution, but the following one is probably the clearest. Postulate a hypothesis about the pairs of features consistent with the *blue diamond* being a THOG. It could not be ['blue' and 'diamond'] and it could not be ['red' and 'circle']. These hypotheses have both, or neither, of the features contained in the *blue diamond*, and the problem states that a THOG has just one. Try ['blue' and 'circle'] as a candidate. It would stop the *blue circle* being a THOG (it has both features) and also the *red diamond* (it has neither feature), but it would make the *red circle* a THOG because 'circle' is one of its features. The only other hypothesis compatible with the blue diamond being a THOG is ['red' and 'diamond']. By the same argument it would rule out both the *red diamond* and the *blue circle* but it also would make the *red circle* a THOG because 'red' is one of its features. The solution is rather elusive because the reasoner has to keep clear the distinction between the designs and the features which constitute them.

Elsie Mimikos showed that students with a science education do better on this problem than students with an arts education. A subsequent experiment convincingly replicated this result. Twenty-five out of thirty-two science graduates solved it compared with only three out of thirty-two arts graduates. It would seem that the precise hypothetical thinking which is involved may be

alien for the latter group, although there is no imputation that the problem is in any way a test of intelligence.

The formal elegance of the 'Thog problem' prevents it from resembling most of the problems we encounter in daily life. It tests a highly specific skill—that is all. Problems do not generally come like this, in neatly packaged form. They have to be discovered, and it is difficult to investigate this process experimentally. Moreover, the problems used by the psychologist to study thinking usually have one right answer. In real life problems are seldom like this; they have many different grades of adequate answer. Art, furthermore, provides a realm in which problems do not have right answers at all. It may be objected that this is to stretch the meaning of the word 'problem' metaphorically, but artists (and poets) do often discuss their work in these terms.

In a unique longitudinal study of artistic creativity, Getzels and Csikszentmihalyi (1976) were struck by the fact that students of fine art seemed primarily motivated by self-discovery. It might be expected that they would discuss the rewards of the artist in aesthetic terms, in terms of 'beauty', 'harmony', or the creation of 'order'. Instead they talked about them much more in terms of 'discovery' and 'understanding', and this suggested that their work was structured around 'discovered problem situations'. The investigators developed an ingenious technique to test this idea. Thirty-one fine-art students were asked to compose a still-life drawing based on a selection from a number of objects which were placed on an adjacent table. The first task of each student was to choose some of these objects, and arrange them on another table to form the subject of his composition. The investigators made the assumption that the choice of objects corresponded to a 'problem-finding' stage. They observed the number of objects chosen, the way in which the student explored and handled them, and their uniqueness, i.e. the extent to which each had been chosen by the other students. These indices were assumed to reflect the characteristic ways in which a person approaches an unstructured aesthetic task. They were used to test the hypothesis that individuals who considered more problematic elements, explored problematic elements more thoroughly, and selected the less common among them, would formulate a visual problem which would result in a more original drawing. Five art critics, who knew nothing about the experiment, then independently rated each drawing for originality, aesthetic value, and craftsmanship. The main result confirmed the prediction. The problem-finding process results in drawings which are judged to be more original, but not necessarily of higher craftsmanship. In fact, the correlation between the problem-finding scores and 'originality' was highly significant.

This result is really surprising: the quality of the final product is related to behaviour *before* the drawing started. It was corroborated by subsequent interviews. Those artists who stated that when they started to work they had no clear idea about what they would do, produced drawings which were highly rated for aesthetic value and originality; those who stated they already had a problem in mind when they approached the task were rated low on the same dimensions. It was corroborated by measures of time taken during the experiment. The only such measure significantly related to the quality of the drawings was time spent in choosing objects, as opposed to time spent in arranging or drawing them.

In science the result would hardly be surprising because its theories are based on explicitly formulated problems, while the products of art are based on the attempt to come to grips with unformulated private problems. Copernicus's questioning of the common-sense observation that the sun revolves around the earth was also highly original. But in the long run his doubts would have had no more value than a delusion had they not also been shown to be true. After problems have been discovered in science the testing of possible solutions can proceed deductively in order to see whether they can be falsified. It is precisely this ability which the 'Thog problem' attempts to catch in a small way. A scientist would probably regard it as trivial because skill in solving it involves no imagination. And yet this skill involves an analysis of the structure behind the surface of things. Without it, a person finds the solution incredible in its outrageous assault on common sense—the *red circle* has *nothing* in common with the *blue diamond*. How different it is from the production of a work of art subject only to aesthetic appraisal! We should not allow the difference to conceal a more fundamental similarity. In both science and art the individual is driven by an insatiable curiosity which refuses to accept things as they are, and which forces us to think about them in a new way. The origin of this curiosity is manifest in the appeal which artificial problems exert upon us.   P. C. W.

Berlyne, D. E. (1971). *Aesthetics and Psychobiology*. New York.

Getzels, J. W. and Csikszentmihalyi, M. (1976). *The Creative Vision: a longitudinal study of problem-finding in art*. New York.

Harlow, H. F., Harlow, M. K., and Meyer, D. R. (1950). Learning motivated by a manipulation drive. *Journal of Experimental Psychology*, **40**, 228–34.

Smyth, M. M. and Clark, S. E. (1986). My Half-Sister is a THOG: Strategic Processes in a Reasoning Task. *British Journal of Psychology*, **77**, 275–87.

Wason, P. C. (1977). Self-contradictions. In Johnson-Laird, P. N. and Wason, P. C. (eds.), *Thinking: readings in cognitive science*. Cambridge.

White, R. W. (1959). Motivation reconsidered: the concept of competence. *Psychological Review*, **66**, 297–331.

**PROBLEM-SOLVING.** A great deal of the art of problem-solving is to understand the kind of question that is posed and the kind of answer that is demanded. It is for this reason that psychologists prefer problems with unique solutions, and that they try to ensure that individuals understand what they have to solve.

There are several theoretical points of view about problem-solving, but none are really complete because each tends to be restricted to different problem domains, and there is little definitive agreement about what constitutes a problem. The *Gestalt theorists (e.g. Wertheimer, 1969) believed that a problem occurs because of the way in which a situation is initially perceived, and that its solution emerges suddenly from reorganizing it in such a way that its real structure becomes apparent. On the other hand, many contemporary psychologists have been impressed by ideas borrowed from research on *artificial intelligence. They conceive the mind as analogous to a computer program which operates in discrete steps ('information-processing') to reduce the difference between existing states and 'sub-goals'. Their pioneering efforts were devoted mainly to a small number of computable games and puzzles, and they were not deterred by the fact that computer programs played poor chess. See Newell and Simon (1972), and, for criticism, Dreyfus (1972) and Weizenbaum (1976); and COMPUTER CHESS for recent improvements. For an account of the fundamental difficulties of computer chess, see Hartson and Watson (1983, ch. 6). My own interest has been to devise problems in which the initial response may ensnare the capacity to see the point.

The difficulty of writing about problem-solving is that one may either insult the reader's intelligence, or create states of frustration. Hence I shall not report the solution to my first problem. Instead I shall take the reader by the hand (if he will pardon the condescension) and ask him to solve with me two related, simplified problems. These may alter the way in which he conceived the original problem. Of course, he may find the first problem trivial, but then I hope his boredom will be alleviated by the knowledge that others find it rather puzzling. I could say a lot more at this point, but that would be to lay all my cards on the table. Consider the first problem.

*Problem 1.* I formulated this problem in 1966, and the present version was devised for the 1977 Science Museum Explorations Exhibition in London. Earlier versions contained some confusing features. The problem is generally known as 'the selection task'.

You are shown a panel of four cards, A, B, C, D (Fig. 1), together with the following instructions:

Which of the hidden parts of these cards do you *need* to see in order to answer the following question decisively? FOR THESE CARDS IS IT TRUE THAT IF THERE IS A CIRCLE ON THE LEFT THERE IS A CIRCLE ON THE RIGHT? You have only *one* opportunity to make this decision; you must not assume that you can inspect cards one at a time. Name those cards which it is absolutely necessary to see.

Please record your solution, and then consider the next problem.

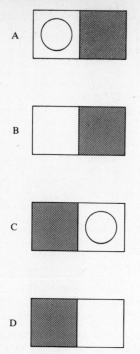

**Fig. 1.** Problem 1: the Science Museum Problem.

*Problem 2.* This problem is based on Johnson-Laird and Wason (1970). A more recent, intensive investigation of the issues may be found in Wason and Green (1984). In front of you are two boxes, one labelled WHITE and the other labelled BLACK (Fig. 2). There are fifteen white shapes in the white box and fifteen black shapes in the black box, and the only shapes are triangles and circles. Your problem is to prove the following sentence true, as economically as possible, by requesting to inspect shapes from either box: IF THEY ARE TRIANGLES, THEN THEY ARE BLACK.

The students who were tested in this experiment tended to ask first of all for a black shape—they were handed a black triangle. The task turned out to be fairly easy; on average only six black shapes were requested. Of course, when individuals asked for a white shape they were always handed a white circle. Somebody in my class said recently: 'The best strategy is to alternate your choices between the two boxes.' This would have been a perverse strategy, especially if one were to apply it consistently by exhausting the contents of both boxes. In fact, insight came rapidly, and all the individuals

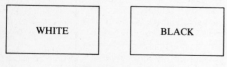

**Fig. 2.** Problem 2.

exhausted the supply of fifteen white circles, and requested no more than nine black shapes. Moreover, they tended to do so with a broad grin, as if they had penetrated a secret, or seen the point of a joke. In order to prove the truth of the sentence 'If they are triangles, then they are black', it is merely necessary to establish the absence of a white triangle. The contents of the black box are gratuitous.

What is the connection between problems 1 and 2? In the first place, problem 2 is only concerned with half the amount of information in problem 1. In problem 2 no decision has to be made about 'triangles' and 'circles' which corresponds to the presence and absence of a 'circle on the left'. Secondly, problem 1 involves a single and ultimate decision for its solution, but problem 2 involves a series of decisions so that an earlier error can be corrected. Thirdly, problem 2 involves a number of concrete objects rather than the consideration of symbols positioned on cards.

Are you still satisfied with your solution to problem 1?

*Problem 3.* This problem is based on Wason and Shapiro (1971). There are four cards on the table in front of you, showing (respectively) 'Manchester', 'Leeds', 'Train', 'Car' (Fig. 3). The students who were tested in this experiment had first of all examined a larger set of cards (from which these four had been selected), each of which had on one

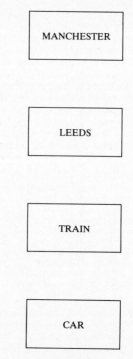

**Fig. 3.** Problem 3.

side a town (e.g. Chicago), and on the other side a mode of transport (e.g. aeroplane). They had been asked to satisfy themselves that this condition obtained on every card. The four cards were then placed on the table, and the individuals were instructed to imagine that each represented a journey made by the experimenter. They were then presented with the experimenter's claim about her journeys: EVERY TIME I GO TO MANCHESTER I TRAVEL BY TRAIN.

The problem is to state which cards need to be turned over in order to determine whether this claim is true or false. The solution is 'Manchester' and 'Car' because only 'Manchester' associated with a transport other than 'Train', or 'Car' associated with 'Manchester' would disprove the claim. This thematic problem proved much easier than a standard, abstract version which was structurally equivalent to problem 1. However, recent attempts to replicate this effect have not been at all clear. For a general discussion, see Griggs (1983).

What is the connection between problems 1 and 3? In both a single decision has to be made about four cards, so in this sense they are both unlike problem 2. But in problem 3 the cards are not simply cards. They represent four different journeys and their two sides are connected intrinsically in this respect. This means that the material of the problem is intimately related to experience, and the solution can be guided by it. For a more detailed account of these, and similar, experiments see Wason and Johnson-Laird (1972).

Still happy about the solution to problem 1? If it did cause any difficulties, it seems fairly likely that any error will now have been corrected because that particular problem has been broken down into two much simpler ones, each of which eases the original burden of thought. But suppose, just for the sake of argument, that the solution to problem 1 is still wrong—for instance, it might be cards A and C. In the original experiments based on it I devised therapies which induced contradictions between the first attempted solution and a subsequent evaluation of the material. The card, corresponding to A, which everybody had (rightly) selected, would have been revealed thus:

A

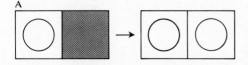

'What does this tell you about the answer to the question?' ('For these cards is it true that if there is a circle on the left there is a circle on the right?') Everybody said that this told them the answer is 'yes'.

Then the card, corresponding to D, which nearly everyone had (wrongly) omitted, would have been revealed thus:

D

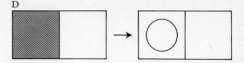

Conflict: a card which had been chosen allowed the answer 'yes', but now a card which had been ignored indubitably forces the answer 'no'. The majority of individuals remained unmoved—they refused at this point to incorporate D into their solution. When prompted, they made remarks like, 'It's got nothing to do with it', and 'It doesn't matter'. All the available evidence is present, but the correction tends not to be made.

We went on informally to discuss the potential consequences of B and C which were never fully revealed. B had nearly always been omitted (rightly) and C selected (wrongly).

'Can you say anything about the answer from this card [B]?':

'It's got nothing to do with it because there's no circle [on the left].'
'Can you say anything about the answer from this card [C]?':

'There has to be a circle under it for the answer to be "yes".'
'What if there is no circle?'
'Then the answer would be "no".'
What could be the selfsame card has a different meaning according to whether it had been selected initially. The individual is confronted with the possibility of both cards being like this:

But only when this contingency derives from C is it assumed (wrongly) to be informative. It is evidently the individual's intention to select a card which confers meaning on it.

Reality, for the individuals who made these kinds of error, is determined by their own thought. That is not, perhaps, surprising. What is very surprising is that this reality is so recalcitrant to correction. See Wason (1977) for further discussion. For a recent and much more comprehensive account of the issues raised by this problem, see Wason (1983). It is as if the attention mobilized in the initial decision is divided from their subsequent attention to facts, or possibilities. The solution, cards A and D, is systematically evaded in ways which are not yet properly understood. There is even the finding that the origin of the difficulty might arise through differences in the functioning of the two hemispheres of the normal brain. When corrective feedback is induced in the left ('analytic') hemisphere it is more effective than when it is induced in the right ('synthetic') hemisphere.

Our basic paradigm (problem 1) has the enormous advantage of being artificial and novel; in these studies we are not interested in everyday thought, but in the kind of thinking which occurs when there is minimal meaning in the things around us. On a much smaller scale, what do our students' remarks remind us of in real life? They are like saying 'Of course, the earth is flat', 'Of course, we are descended from Adam and Eve', 'Of course, space has nothing to do with time'. The old ways of seeing things now look like absurd prejudices, but our highly intelligent student volunteers display analogous miniature prejudices when their premature conclusions are challenged by the facts. As Kuhn (1962) has shown, the old paradigms do not yield in the face of a few counter-examples. In the same way, our volunteers do not often accommodate their thought to new observations, even those governed by logical necessity, in a deceptive problem situation. They will frequently deny the facts, or contradict themselves, rather than shift their frame of reference.

Other treatments and interpretations of problem-solving could have been cited. For instance, most problems studied by psychologists create a sense of perplexity rather than a specious answer. But the present interpretation, in terms of the development of dogma and its resistance to truth, reveals the interest and excitement generated by research in this area.                    P. C. W.

Dreyfus, H. L. (1972). *What Computers Can't Do*. New York.

Griggs, R. A. (1983). The Role of Problem Content in the Selection Task and in the THOG Problem. In Evans, J. St. B. T. (ed.), *Thinking and Reasoning: Psychological Approaches*. London.

Hartston, W. R. and Wason, P. C. (1983). *The Psychology of Chess*. London.

Johnson-Laird, P. N. and Wason, P. C. (1970). Insight into a Logical Relation. *Quarterly Journal of Experimental Psychology*, **22**, 49–61.

Kuhn, T. S. (1962). *The Structure of Scientific Revolutions*. Chicago.

Newell, A. and Simon, H. A. (1972). *Human Problem Solving*. New Jersey.

Wason, P. C. (1977). Self-contradictions. In Johnson-Laird, P. N. and Wason, P.C. (eds.), *Thinking: readings in cognitive science*. Cambridge.

Wason, P. C. (1983). Realism and Rationality in the Selection Task. In Evans, J. St. B. T. (ed.), *Thinking and Reasoning: Psychological Approaches*. London.

Wason, P. C. and Green, D. W. (1984). Reasoning and Mental Representation. *Quarterly Journal of Experimental Psychology*, **36**, 597–610.

Wason, P. C. and Johnson-Laird, P. N. (1972). *Psychology of Reasoning: structure and content*. London.

Wason, P. C. and Shapiro, D. (1971). Natural and contrived experience in a reasoning problem. *Quarterly Journal of Experimental Psychology*, **23**, 63–71.

Weizenbaum, J. (1976). *Computer Power and Human Reason*. San Francisco.

Wertheimer, M. (1969). *Productive Thinking*. London.

**PROGRAMS AND PLANNING.** It is safe to predict that concepts of computation will play an increasing role in the articulation of theories of the mind. Here we introduce the basic notion of a 'program' which underlies computation and relates it to the mental activity of planning. It is emphasized that computer science is an evolving subject, and that the analysis of mental activity is already feeding back into computer science to yield notions of programs of increasing subtlety and flexibility.

A program for an ordinary electronic computer executes one instruction at a time: to transfer inputs to memory, to combine pieces of data, to control output devices, and—crucially—to choose the next instruction on the basis of a test. Because of these tests, the 'overt behaviour' of the program—the temporal sequence of reading of inputs and emission of output values—will depend on both the input values and data values already stored internally. This dependence yields the basic logical property of *algorithms: a program can be specified in a form shorter than any normal execution upon particular data.

By contrast, normal English usage often takes 'pre-programmed' as a synonym for 'stereotyped', and for many people, the word 'program' is synonymous with the notion of a 'fixed sequence', so that each fixed behavioural sequence is a different program. However, for the computer scientist, it is the program that provides the formal description of the process which generates different output sequences on the basis of differing values of inputs and internal parameters. To take a simple example, consider a man walking to the door. Depending on where he starts, his overt behaviour might require three steps or thirty—and each such sequence would constitute a 'program' in the fixed-sequence sense. But it seems more insightful to hypothesize that a single program in the computer scientist's sense underlies all these behaviours. In one formalism, we might represent it as:

DO *advance one step* UNTIL *door is reached*.

(This can be recognized as a notational variant of the TOTE unit—Test–Operate–Test–Exit—of Miller, Galanter, and Pribram, 1960, p. 26.) Here we explain all behaviours of the class in terms of a program with one action, *advance one step*, whose execution is repeated under the control of a single test, *is door reached?*

If we regard this program as a hypothesis about human behaviour, we turn attention from the release of patterns with fixed numbers of steps to the study of ways in which perceptual mechanisms testing *is door reached?* may 'gate' motor mechanisms. At a simple level, such 'gating' differs little from negative *feedback, but when we move to planning behaviour in a complex environment, the loops within loops seem to call for the richer vocabulary that computer science can help to provide. We turn then to a look at this vocabulary.

For certain motor tasks, a sufficiently high-level choice of strategy need not involve specification of the details of execution at the muscular level. For example, *Lashley (1929, p. 137) notes that animals which have learned a maze prior to injuries to the motor system continue to traverse it, although muscular activity may be changed completely—one animal had to roll over completely in making each turn, yet made no errors in traversing the maze. Again, in writing a word, we use a completely different set of muscles, depending on whether the instrument available is a pencil or whether it is a paintbrush on the end of a long pole. How is it that we can still produce our characteristic mode of writing with these two different systems? Computer scientists find it expedient to program a computer not in the machine language that directly controls the basic operations of its machinery but rather in terms of some high-level language. They provide the computer with a translation program called an 'interpreter' that will enable the computer to translate each instruction from the high-level program and then execute it. In much computing, the process of translation is relatively straightforward—multiplication of matrices, or sorting a sequence of numbers into a histogram can be carried out by standard procedures which (once the size of the matrices or the length of the sequence is given) do not depend on the idiosyncracies of the situation. However, the study within AI (*artificial intelligence) of *planning*—programming a computer to go from goal specifications to a plan for achieving the goals—may be viewed as the study of *context-dependent* translation. Consider, for example, our program above as one way of compiling the higher-level instruction *go to the door*. Such a compilation is appropriate only if the system is facing the door and there are no obstacles *en route*. Otherwise, the position of the 'organism' and the layout of obstacles within the room must be taken into account in determining a path.

We shall illustrate the AI approach to high-level planning of movement by considering a mobile robot equipped with a television camera and wheels. The planning problem for this robot enables it to respond to a command such as 'Push the large cube to the door' by (i) forming a plan that will take it to the cube without bumping into obstacles, and then will allow it to push the cube to the door without bumping into obstacles; and, then, (ii) executing the plan. A separate problem, then, is the design of a visual system (Hanson and Riseman, 1978) to locate the obstacles.

To simplify the planning problem for the mobile robot, we may schematize its task as that of selecting a number of intermediate points (called nodes) to pass through in sequence, *en route* to its goal. A path is then a trajectory that links up these nodes in order. Clearly, the nodes must be so chosen that, in moving from one point to the next, the robot does not bump into any obstacle. When given a task specified in a high-level language, the robot must find a path that achieves the task and that is also, ideally, as short as possible.

The simplest form of this problem is to find the shortest path from one specified place to another. What makes the problem interesting is that the space may be so complicated that it is impossible to consider all alternatives. Instead, workers in AI have sought ways to 'grow' paths, considering for each point along a possible trajectory a limited number of candidates for the next segment. It should be emphasized that this process of path-growing is made within the computer during the *planning* stage. At the completion of this path-growing process, a single path results, and it is this that directs the actual movement of the robot. In most AI research projects, all relevant details about the 'search space' are represented in the 'internal model' within the computer. In biological organisms, the internal model is only approximate, and sensory input must be used in model updating and, where necessary, replanning. In building on such AI approaches to model the neural control of movement in animals and to build more adaptable robots, we study the extent to which planning and execution would be interwoven within the action–perception cycle (see SCHEMAS).

Doran and Michie (1966) proposed a path-growing program that used the idea of a *heuristic distance*, which is defined as an indication, rather than a guaranteed measure, of distance to the goal. For example, the straight-line distance is a heuristic distance for the real distance when one avoids the obstacles. The Doran–Michie approach proceeds by exploring alternative paths, giving first preference to the exploration of paths whose next node has the least heuristic distance to the goal node. However, while this algorithm always yields a path from the start node (which represents where the system is) to the goal node (which represents where the system is to be), it cannot be guaranteed that the path obtained is the shortest. This problem was overcome by Hart, Nilsson, and Raphael (1968), who developed an algorithm that gave first preference to the exploration of paths whose next node had a minimal sum of distance already traversed from the start node plus heuristic distance to the goal node.

In later work, Fikes, Hart, and Nilsson (1972) studied generalized robot plans. Very briefly, the idea is to store information about the changes in the relationship between the robot and the environment brought about by a sequence of actions that are part of a successful plan. As time goes by, and other plans are made, various constants within both the sequence of operations and the prescription of its effects are replaced by variables, in such a way that the robot has available a number of MACROPs: high-level operations that will let it meet many familiar planning problems. Sacerdoti (1974) has built on this study to define a problem solver called ABSTRIPS, which uses planning in a hierarchy of abstraction spaces. It usually proves far more efficient to plan the overall stages of a series of movements, and then refine the plan with greater and greater detail, making modifications only when necessary, than to grow the overall plan step by step, with each step defined at the lowest level. The importance of these studies is clear. The first shows how AI provides techniques which we may refine into a theory of 'learning from experience'. The second gives us a clue as to how to analyse the relation between a 'plan' in its colloquial sense of a high-level 'strategic' specification of a course of action, and the detailed step-by-step unfolding of that action when the plan is executed.

With those programs written by AI researchers to explicitly embody aspects of the planning process, we are well on our way to an even more abstract type of program—a *program synthesizer*, which takes as its input samples of behaviour (e.g. input–output relations) and generates programs that can yield this type of behaviour. In fact, we may regard the generation of MACROPs as an example of program synthesis. To summarize, then, we have the following levels of program sophistication. (i) Straight-line program: executing a fixed predetermined sequence. (ii) Program: executing a sequence of actions whose composition may depend on on-line testing of internal and external values. (iii) Planning (= context-dependent interpretation): knowing what to do, in general terms, find a solution tailored to the current situation. (iv) Program synthesis from examples: starts by finding out what is the problem to be solved.

Yet another style of programming comes with the study of *concurrent programming*, stimulated by the technological concern with playing out computation over a network of concurrently active, communicating, computers. In brain theory and AI we speak of *co-operative computation*. A classic example in brain theory is the Kilmer–McCulloch (1968) model of the reticular formation of the brain as a set of interacting modules that could reach a global consensus without any single module having executive control. To put the AI problem in picturesque terms, consider that you have a library of books, and need to get the references to solve a problem. The co-operative computation approach is the analogue of having each book become an *active* process, with the books responding to user questions, and 'talking' to each other, until they agree on what is required. Arbib and Caplan (1979) have analysed the relevance of such techniques to the study of language mechanisms in the human brain.

And this is only the beginning of the evolution of computing concepts relevant to the construction of theories of mind and brain.                M. A. A.

Arbib, M. A. and Caplan, D. (1979). Neurolinguistics must be computational. *Behavioral and Brain Sciences*, **2**, 449–83.

Hanson, A. R. and Riseman, E. M. (1978). *Computer Vision Systems*. New York.

Kilmer, W. L., McCulloch, W. S., and Blum, J. (1968). Some mechanisms for a theory of the reticular formation. In Mesarovic, M. (ed.), *Systems Theory and Biology* (New York), 286–375.

Lashley, K. S. (1929). *Brain Mechanisms and Intelligence*. Chicago.

Miller, G. A., Galanter, E., and Pribram, K. H. (1960). *Plans and the Structure of Behavior*. New York.

**PROJECTIVE TECHNIQUES** derive their name from the psychoanalytic concept of *projection*, the mechanism whereby psychological states or processes in the self are seen as pertaining to an object in the outside world. Projection is most commonly regarded as a defence mechanism, a means whereby the *ego protects itself from anxiety, associated with unpleasant or unacceptable thoughts and feelings, by attributing them to others. This aspect of projection, however, is not part of the rationale of projective techniques, which can be used without necessarily accepting the tenets of psychoanalytic theory. A more helpful definition of projection in this context is the process whereby the individual 'projects' something of himself or herself into everything he or she does, in line with Gordon Allport's concept of expressive behaviour. The aim of projective techniques is, then, to provide stimuli or situations, to which variations in response may be interpreted in accordance with a set of rules.

The two best-known projective techniques are the *Rorschach ink-blots and the Thematic Apperception Test (TAT).

The Rorschach test consists of a series of ten symmetrical ink-blots, five in black and white only, and five introducing colour. The subject is asked to report what he or she sees in each blot in turn; at the end of the series an 'inquiry' allows for clarification of the responses. Responses are classified within each of three 'scoring' categories: *location*, *determinants*, and *content*. *Location* refers to how much and which part of the blot area has been used; *determinants* to the structural qualities, namely form (shape), colour, shading, and inferred movement; *content* to the types of object seen, with particular emphasis on human, animal, and anatomical percepts. Total incidence of each type of response is noted, and various ratios and percentages calculated. Traditionally considerable importance is attached to scoring, but recently there has been a move towards increased interest in content, treated in the same way as other material obtained in clinical interview.

Material for the TAT, devised by the American psychologist H. A. Murray as an adjunct to his 'need–press' theory of motivation, consists of black-and-white pictures representing personal and interpersonal situations, the subject being required to make up a story about each in turn. In its original form the test is administered individually, in two series of ten pictures each; the response is given orally, with provision for prompting, if required. More recently there has been a trend towards a single shorter series and group administration with written response; non-standard pictures are also sometimes used. Since relatively little importance is attached to formal scoring, such flexibility is permissible, and indeed thematic apperception is probably best regarded as designating a group of procedures rather than a specific test.

Murray's own system of analysis rests on his concepts of *need*, a hypothetical force or process in the organism, and *press*, a force or other element in the environment which activates a need in the perceiver. Incidence of the expression of need and press variables, as well as others, such as 'outcome', in the subject's TAT material may be compared with norms, which will obviously vary with populations and circumstances of testing. For this reason, among others, many users of the TAT prefer to use systems of analysis which they consider better suited to the purpose in hand.

Other projective methods include Word Association (in which the subject speaks or writes the first word that comes to mind in response to a stimulus word), Sentence Completion, and various 'activity' methods, principally drawing (most commonly of the human figure) and structured play, as in the sand-tray procedures familiar in child guidance and child psychiatry settings.

In all of these, as well as in the Rorschach and the TAT, it is possible to achieve some measure of quantification of the data, and so to claim that measurement has taken place. Measurement, however, is not a primary concern of projective psychology, a fact reflected in the choice of the term 'techniques' rather than 'tests' in the title of this entry. Interpretative hypotheses are, of course, attached to Rorschach variables, and to other projective 'indicators'. In some cases, as in the formulation of a set of 'signs' of brain damage, criteria for validation are available, and would appear, in that particular case, to have been met. In others, particularly when a form of response relates to experience rather than to behaviour, demonstration of validity presents more serious problems. In the cognate field of reliability, test–retest reliability presupposes personality to be static, and in statistical terms can be applied only to single category scores; whereas the projective standpoint has always been that a protocol must be interpreted as a whole. 'Tester effects' may also be quite powerful, but may be understood if one regards projective testing as a channel of communication between particular individuals in a specific situation. Free expression is impeded by use of a forced-choice format, or by the imposition of statistical control, as in the Holtzman Ink-blot Technique, a variant of the Rorschach, in which the number of responses (itself a variable considered important in standard Rorschach practice) is controlled by limiting the subject to a single response to each of a longer series of stimuli.

Attempts to make projective testing conform to psychometric standards have in general met with relatively little success; many projectivists indeed believe that such an aim is illusory. Projective techniques are properly regarded as an aid to, rather than an instrument of, diagnosis or other decision-making process. They may be found useful in counselling, in psychotherapy, particularly of the type known as client-centred, and in some forms of personnel selection—in short, in any situation in which 'understanding' is regarded as relevant. In English-speaking countries they have declined in popularity from their peak in the 1950s, partly perhaps because they are on the whole unamenable to computer analysis. In continental Europe, on the other hand, interest continues to be high.                                                              B. SE.

**PSEUDODEMENTIA.** Some deeply depressed, elderly people may appear to be suffering from a progressive *dementia. This impression is created by the general slowness of thought and activity and loss of interest in everyday pursuits which may accompany depressive illness. It may be difficult to engage such a person in a meaningful conversation because of the effect of the illness upon ability to attend and concentrate on what is being said. Similarly, self-neglect and loss of weight may be attributed to a dementing process rather than to a functional psychosis. But although psychological tests of cognitive function may be poorly performed, the overall results are not likely to be consistent with the picture of general decline in mental function typical of a true dementia. Moreover, treatment of the depression can result in a rapid restoration of mental abilities, a development incompatible with true dementia.

People with *Parkinson's disease can undoubtedly develop dementia of varying degrees of severity, but some are so slowed up by the illness that they may give an impression of dementia when a diagnosis of bradyphrenia (slowness of mind) is more correct. These patients manifest a loss of concentration, a decreased ability to associate ideas, and a general slowing of thought processes that will include difficulty in concept formation and slow *short-term memory scanning. Bradyphrenia is usually associated with *depression, which will contribute to the picture of psychomotor retardation.

A more controversial variety of pseudodementia is referred to as hysterical pseudodementia. Strictly speaking the term 'dementia' is inappropriate, as individuals so diagnosed may give the impression of suffering from a mental illness which does not necessarily involve a progressive decline of all mental functions. Relatives may say that the individual 'acts silly' by making absurd remarks or behaving in a bizarre or stupid manner. Making a distinction between this kind of conduct and straight malingering is far from easy, but Lishman

(1978) comments that hysterical pseudodementia is most often seen in persons of limited intellectual endowment. The behaviour is most likely to surface when the individual finds himself in a situation beyond his comprehension or in a new and unpalatable environment which he cannot handle. For example, dullards finding themselves drafted into one of the armed services may well have difficulty in coping with the demands of discipline and other exigencies of military life. Their capacity for carrying out the normal activities of everyday life may be unimpaired, and any 'hysterical' symptoms that appear will rarely persist once discharge from the service is ordered.

In considering the problem of simulated illness, it must be remembered that diagnosis in psychiatry is very largely based on what the patient says about his symptoms. Moreover he may exhibit certain kinds of behaviour from which it could be inferred that he is mentally ill. Psychiatry suffers from an absence of laboratory tests, and cases lack physical evidence to confirm or refute an original diagnosis. If a person says that he is anxious, depressed, and contemplating suicide, or is hearing hallucinatory voices, it would be an unwise physician who turns him away rather than admit him as a patient. In any case, it is difficult to simulate mental illness consistently, even for an individual who is fairly knowledgeable about psychiatric topics.

One variety of what is sometimes erroneously classed as a pseudodementia is the Ganser syndrome. This rare condition was originally described by S. J. M. Ganser in Germany in 1898—a description based on three patients awaiting sentence in prison. For this reason it has often been called a prison psychosis, although there is no evidence to show that it is peculiar to prisoners; indeed, it certainly occurs in individuals not involved in criminal proceedings. The characteristic features include a clouding of consciousness, a tendency to give 'approximate answers', with elaboration that seems inappropriate. This so-called 'talking past the point' or 'vorbeireden' is sometimes found in patients recovering from head injuries. The 'approximate answers' seem to indicate that the subject knows the correct reply but is feigning mental illness: for example, when asked how many legs a cow has, he will reply 'three' or 'five'; he seems to be perfectly aware of the correct answer and to deliberately avoid saying it. In some instances the answers appear more random than approximate. Although the *syndrome* is rare, the *symptoms* are not uncommon and may feature in a number of mental disorders, but particularly when there is a history of recent brain damage. Assertion that the Ganser syndrome, or its symptoms, are varieties of hysterical pseudodementia is incompatible with the fact that those who display them have genuine psychiatric illnesses. These are often found to be organic in origin or, in some cases, prove to be symptoms of *schizophrenia.

F. A. W.

Lishman, W. A. (1978). Pseudodementia. In his *Organic Psychiatry*. Oxford.
Whitlock, F. A. (1982). The Ganser syndrome and hysterical pseudodementia. In Roy, A. (ed.), *Hysteria*. Chichester.

**PSEUDOHALLUCINATION.** The term was first used in 1885 by Kandinsky and was elaborated by Karl Jaspers in his book *Allgemeine Psychopathologie* (1913), in which he described a pseudohallucination as lacking 'leibheftigkeit', variously translated as 'concrete reality', 'substantiality', or 'corporeality'. Jaspers claimed that true *hallucinations are corporeal and appear in objective space, while pseudohallucinations lack corporeality and appear in subjective space. It has been suggested that the hallmark of a pseudohallucination is that it is accompanied by insight into the lack of an objective counterpart, and it is certainly recognized that pseudohallucinations are by no means confined to the mentally ill. Thus examples include long-distance lorry drivers at night, seeing non-existent objects or animals in their paths and swerving automatically to avoid them, but realizing their mistake immediately afterwards. Monotony combined with prolonged solitude can produce pseudohallucinations and may be experienced by lonely explorers or by single-handed sailors on long voyages. Sedman (1966) defined pseudohallucinations as hallucinations perceived through the senses but recognized by the patient as not being a veridical perception. Sedman found that such experiences were closely linked to the ego, and recognized as being of the self and not true percepts. In most instances the contents were meaningful, giving comfort and helpful advice. His investigation was based on psychiatric patients and not on normal populations, so his findings do not include the pseudohallucinations of the recently bereaved, who may hear the voice of the deceased or have a 'sense of presence' which is, however, quickly realized as erroneous. (See BEREAVEMENT.)

F. A. W.

Fish, F. (1967). *Clinical Psychopathology*. Bristol.
Kandinsky, V. (1885). *Kritische und klinische Bethrachtung in Gebiete der Sinnentäuschungen*. Berlin.
Kräupl Taylor, F. (1979). *Psychopathology: its causes and symptoms*. 2nd edn., Sunbury on Thames.
Sedman, G. (1966). A Comparative Study of Pseudohallucinations, Imagery, and True Hallucinations. *British Journal of Psychiatry*, 112, 9–17.

**PSYCHE.** The Greek word *psyche*, from which our terms 'the psyche' and 'psychology' derive, is generally translated by 'soul'; but the translation is in several respects misleading. *Psyche* is intimately connected to the notion of life: all and only living things possess a psyche; and to have a psyche is to be alive. (To have a psyche is to be *empsuchos*; and *empsuchos* is appropriately translated by 'animate'. Note that 'animate' derives from the Latin *anima*, which, like *psyche*, is conventionally Englished as 'soul'.) Thus a psyche is a principle of life, or an 'animator'. In addition, a psyche is a principle of individuality for living things; that is to say, anything which possesses my psyche is the very same living thing as I am—Socrates and Socrates' psyche are identical. The psyche, in sum, is the living self.

Different Greek thinkers offered different accounts of the nature of *psyche*: most of the *Pre-Socratic philosophers were materialists, primitive or sophisticated—they held that psyche was a special portion of air or fire, or perhaps a special parcel of particles or atoms. *Plato supposed that the psyche was an entity quite distinct from such crass corporeal stuffs: his view of the nature of *psyche* is comparable to *Descartes's notion of the soul as a separate spiritual substance.

Of all Greek theories, that of *Aristotle is the most refined (though some of its features are anticipated in Philolaus's doctrine that the psyche is an attunement). Aristotle offers two connected definitions of *psyche*. The first, couched in the terminology of his metaphysics, runs thus: 'If we are to say something which applies in common to every psyche, it will be the first actuality of a natural organic body.' (Roughly speaking, he means that to have a psyche is to be a natural body, equipped with the organs of life, and capable of functioning.) His second definition reads as follows: 'A psyche is a principle of the aforesaid things [i.e. of the various faculties of living things] and is defined by them—by the faculties of nutrition, perception, thought, and motion.' (Roughly: to have a psyche is to be capable of self-nourishment—including growth and reproduction—of perception, of thought, and of independent motion; or rather, to have a psyche is to have at least some of those capacities.)

Aristotle's first definition emphasizes the connection between *psyche* and the body; his second definition indicates the existence of interdependent psychic 'parts' or faculties—and those faculties, in Aristotle's view, turn out to be hierarchically ordered. Both definitions fit well with Aristotle's predominantly biological and physiological approach to the notion of *psyche* (though it is a celebrated and perplexing aspect of his psychology that thinking, or some special type of thinking, is to some extent untouched by corporeal contamination).

In one important respect at least, the Greek notion of 'psychology' is strikingly different from the modern notion. For the Greeks, all living things, including plants and the lower animals, have, by definition, a psyche; so that the general study of 'psychology' will aspire to give a unified account of all that distinguishes animate from inanimate objects. Modern psychologists may be said, at the risk of oversimplification, to deal with 'the mind': for the Greeks, the primary distinction is between what is alive and what is not alive (and the primary problem is the connection between living and non-living matter); for the moderns, the primary distinction is between what possesses mind and what does not (and the primary problem is the connection between 'the mental' and 'the physical'). Despite that fundamental difference, the particular problems discussed by ancient psychologists frequently overlap with those of their modern successors; but the difference is significant—and it prompts an intriguing question: did the ancient Greeks hit upon a more fruitful and unitary way than ours for tackling the problems of the mind?                                                    J. BA.

**PSYCHIATRY** applies knowledge from the biological and social sciences, e.g. genetics, pharmacology, and psychology, to the care and treatment of patients suffering from disorders of mental activity and behaviour. It emerged as a branch of medicine in the first half of the nineteenth century when some of those kept under social control for the protection of society in workhouses and other institutions were recognized as curable, i.e. susceptible to moral treatment, or requiring the firm although therapeutic use of restraint, and as lying therefore within the province of medicine. One of its first tasks was to classify mental disorders. After the First World War its practice, hitherto based in Britain on the county *asylums, was extended, although still based on the hospital services, to provide treatment for those living in the community and suffering from disorders not requiring admission to hospital. The term, usually restricted in Britain to the work of suitably qualified medical practitioners, is used more widely in North America to cover the work of other mental-health professions such as clinical psychology and psychotherapy.                                       D. R. D.

Doerner, K. (1981). *Madmen and the Bourgeoisie: a social history of insanity and psychiatry*. Oxford.

Bynum W. F., Porter, R., and Shepherd, M. (eds.) (1985). *The Anatomy of Madness: essays in the history of psychiatry*, 2 vols. London.

**PSYCHOANALYSIS.** During the last years of the nineteenth century *Freud gave up the use of hypnotism, because its effects proved capricious and encouraged dependency, and developed a new method, which he referred to at first as psychical analysis. This method, which relies on the interpretation, or analysis, of what a patient says or omits to say, while freely associating under instruction to report his thoughts without reservation, is the essence of what became the specialized form of psychotherapy known as psychoanalysis (see also FREE ASSOCIATION). The first volume of papers on psychoanalysis, *Studies in Hysteria*, published in 1895, brought together a series of case-histories, including that of Fräulein Anna O. which have subsequently been much discussed, an account of a new method of examining and treating hysterical phenomena and of the 'cathartic method', and some 'theoretical reflections', which introduced the concepts of unconscious ideas, ideas inadmissible to consciousness, and splitting of the mind. (For a discussion of the Anna O. case-history, see BREUER.)

Freud immediately applied his new method to the study of dreams, and published in 1900 an account of his analysis of his own dreams in *The Interpretation of Dreams*, which he came to regard as his most important book. 'Insight such as this', he remarked, 'falls to one's lot but once in a lifetime.' It presented the concepts that became the essence of a comprehensive theory of mental life: the meaningfulness of seemingly chaotic and absurd mental activity, wish-fulfilment, the *Oedipus complex, infantile sexuality, regression, the *Unconscious, resistance, *repression, defence, projection, and symbolism, as well as the similarities of dreams and mental disorders (see FREUD ON MENTAL STRUCTURE). The decisive step lay in the demonstration that phenomena which might be dismissed as accidental, capricious, or meaningless products of disorder in the brain can be explained by reference to past experience and the motives revealed by psychoanalysis. He elaborated on the essential concepts in *Introductory Lectures on Psychoanalysis* (1922).

Freud gathered round him in Vienna a group of colleagues who shared his views and who published accounts of their own experiences in psychoanalytic practice. There were notable defections, Alfred *Adler in 1911, who led the development of 'individual psychology', and Carl Gustav *Jung in 1913, who led the development of 'analytic psychology'. The Clark Lectures in 1909 in America by Freud and Jung brought psychoanalysis to the notice of the English-speaking world, but psychoanalysis did not become widely known in England until the 1920s. It then aroused as much interest among scholars in the humanities as among physicians. Notable among those who made distinctive contributions to psychoanalysis in Britain was Melanie *Klein, who explored the development of relationships in early infancy and showed how fantasy and the inner world are built up. In the twenties and thirties Freud examined civilization, religion, and literature in the light of the findings of psychoanalysis.

Psychoanalysis was dominated in its early development by the biological ideas of the time, e.g. the derivation of energy from instincts. The shift in emphasis, starting in the 1930s, from biological or intrapsychic, to social or interpersonal, processes and object-relations, and from the origins of symptoms to those circumstances of the 'here and now' determining their persistence, reduced greatly the differences in method and theory from other schools of psychotherapy, from which, however, psychoanalysts still maintain their independence.

Since it requires several sessions a week over two or three years with a trained therapist, psychoanalysis is a lengthy and therefore expensive form of treatment that is available to few patients. Its effectiveness is open to question. Its original purpose was to circumvent the resistances to the recall of the painful experiences thought to underlie *neurosis. Later, greater importance was attached to the transference of feelings into the relationship with the therapist. There has been little systematic research to evaluate the benefits achieved in these ways. Comparisons made of the effects on symptoms and attitudes produced by psychoanalysis with those produced in other ways have so far proved controversial and inconclusive.

See also FREUDIANISM: LATER DEVELOPMENTS.

D. R. D.

Freud, S. (Pelican Freud Library): *1. Introductory Lectures on Psychoanalysis* (1973); *3. Studies on Hysteria* (1974); *4. The Interpretation of Dreams* (1976); *12. Civilisation, Society and Religion* (1985); *14. Art and Literature* (1985). Harmondsworth.
Jones, E. (1961). *The Life and Work of Sigmund Freud*, abridged edition. Harmondsworth.
Roazen, P. (1974). *Freud and his Followers*. London.
Wyss, D. (1966). *Depth Psychology: a critical history, development, problems, crises*. London.

**PSYCHOGALVANIC REFLEX.** See ELECTRODERMAL ACTIVITY.

**PSYCHOKINESIS.** See EXTRA-SENSORY PERCEPTION; PARANORMAL PHENOMENA AND THE UNCONSCIOUS.

**PSYCHOLOGY.** *Psyche, personified by the ancient Greeks as the goddess loved by Eros, means breath and hence soul or mind. Psychology, when introduced as a term in the eighteenth century, described the branch of philosophy covering the study of the phenomena of mental life, i.e. what is perceived, through *introspection, as taking place in the mind, and of such activities as perceiving (see PERCEPTION), *remembering, *thinking, and reasoning.

'The science of mental life, both of its phenomena and their conditions' was William *James's definition. The strength of his classic *The Principles of Psychology*, published in 1890, lies in its descriptions, as the result of 'looking into our minds and reporting what we there discover' of 'feelings, desires, cognitions, reasonings, decisions and the like'. For half a century *The Principles* provided much of the material for textbooks such as R. S. *Woodworth's *Psychology: the study of mental life*, which went on into the 1950s as a standard text. The main chapters of contemporary texts are still about perceiving, remembering, thinking and language, and concepts and reasoning, as well as emotions, needs, and motives, learning, coping behaviour, and conflicts, skills, and attitudes and beliefs in relation to social and cultural factors.

Herbert *Spencer had given in 1874 a wider definition of 'objective psychology', which he said forms with physiology the two subdivisions of zoology, this and botany being the two divisions of biology. Objective psychology 'deals with those functions of the neuromuscular apparatus by which organisms are enabled to adjust inner to outer relations' and includes 'the study of the same functions as externally manifested in conduct'.

'Subjective' psychology 'deals with the sensations, perceptions, ideas, emotions, and volitions that are the direct or indirect concomitants of this visible adjustment of inner to outer relations'.

Spencer and James both struggled with the ancient problem of the relation between *mind and body. James accepted dualism as a strategem, not as a conviction. Certain mental processes cannot be reduced to physical processes, he insisted; otherwise there would be no science of psychology. 'When the brain acts a thought occurs.' 'Mental phenomena lead to bodily processes.' 'No mental modification ever occurs that is not accompanied or followed by a bodily change.' Contemporary explanations in psychology sometimes reduce the phenomenon or the behaviour to what is regarded as the essential physiological or biochemical process (see REDUCTIONISM IN PSYCHOLOGY); more often they relate it to the conditions or the contexts in which it occurs or to the system of which it is a part.

In James's time there were turning-points in the development of several branches of psychology. Wilhelm *Wundt had founded in 1875 the first laboratory devoted to the experimental study of sensation, memory, and learning. Francis *Galton's Inquiries into Human Faculty, first published in 1883, had opened up the study of individual differences in mental functions. Lloyd *Morgan's Animal Life and Intelligence, published in 1890, and E. L. *Thorndike's Animal Intelligence, published in 1911, pioneered comparative studies of learning. Studies of the effects of lesions of the brain on mental functions were being pioneered by David *Ferrier, Herman Munk, and Hughlings *Jackson. *Psychoanalysis with its concept of the unconscious was just over the horizon.

Soon after James's death in 1910, attention was drawn away from his work by the emergence of several confident schools, particularly *behaviourism, physiological psychology, *Gestalt psychology, psychoanalysis, purposivism (see MCDOUGALL and PURPOSE), factor analysis (see SPEARMAN), and *ethology. Behaviourism especially narrowed the definition of psychology so as to exclude subjective psychology, on the grounds, based on a narrow definition of science, that the phenomena of mental life are not susceptible to scientific study—that is, psychology should restrict itself to the study of those aspects of behaviour that can be directly observed and measured or graded.

For nearly half a century few scholars, except in the older universities in Britain, engaged with the formidable problems of method in psychology, which James had admitted could be no more than the hope of a science. Interest in mental phenomena revived again in the 1960s, partly as a result of the emergence of schools of *phenomenology, such as *Husserl's.

The meaning given to the term psychology changed gradually, first to insist that the study should be systematic, observations being made under pre-arranged conditions that allow reliable conclusions to be drawn, and, secondly, to include the responses of the subject to external events or stimuli, whether these occur naturally or are manipulated by an experimenter. Interest grew, under the influence of Kenneth *Craik, in an *interactional approach, in which behaviour is seen as exchanges between man and machine or man and man (see CYBERNETICS). The dividing line between objective and subjective psychology became blurred.

In most universities there is now a department of psychology, in which an assortment of research methods is applied in the study of the behaviour, including the mental activity, of intact organisms, humankind especially. Comparative studies of the behaviour of animals (see ETHOLOGY) are shared with the department of zoology. The psychology department is likely to have a place in the faculty of science, with links with other departments of biology, with which it shares work on the physiological mechanisms of behaviour, in the faculty of social sciences, in which it shares work on the behaviour of individuals in social groups, in the faculty of education, in which it shares work on mental development and learning processes in childhood, and in the faculty of medicine, in which its work lies in applications in the diagnosis and care and treatment of the sick.

It is one of several branches of science applied in *psychiatry to the care and treatment of the mentally disordered. Psychopathology is the branch of psychology that seeks to explain disorders of mental activity and behaviour in terms of psychological processes, whereas neurology and *neuropsychology relate them to the site, extent, and character of faults in the structure or function of the central *nervous system. Psychology contributes to many other branches of knowledge, among them, in the faculty of engineering, to *ergonomics, and in the faculty of law, *criminology. Since the 1920s, students of the humanities, such as literary critics and historians, have increasingly turned for their interpretations to psychological and, especially, psychoanalytic theories.　　　　D. R. D.

**PSYCHOMETRICS.** See PSYCHOPHYSICS; QUANTIFYING JUDGEMENTS.

**PSYCHOPATHIC PERSONALITY.** Strictly speaking, this term should be applied to all varieties of abnormal personality (see PERSONALITY DISORDER). Schneider (1958) defined the psychopathic personality as an abnormal personality who either suffers because of his abnormality or makes the community suffer because of it. In the UK and the USA greater emphasis has been placed on the second part of this definition, mainly because of the frequent involvement of such persons in breaches of the law. American authors prefer the terms 'sociopath' and 'antisocial psychopath' which more clearly define the individual by virtue of his criminal propensities. In the UK, before the Mental Health Act of 1959 the psychopath was an entity unrecognized by law, but the Act defined psychopathic disorder as 'a persistent disorder or disability of mind (whether or not including subnormality of intelligence) which results in abnormally aggressive or seriously irresponsible conduct on the part of the patient, and requires or is susceptible to medical treatment'. Although a good deal of controversy surrounds the last seven words of this definition, quite clearly the Act considered psychopathic disorder to be a form of mental illness. If such a person is 'ill'—and he would be the last person so to regard himself—it is up to the medical profession to treat him. The Mental Health Act of 1983 apparently recognizes the questionable value of medical treatment, as the phrase is omitted from its definition of psychopathic disorder. None the less, the term stays under the general heading of mental disorder.

Numerous attempts have been made to identify the principal characteristics of the psychopath. The term in a general sense is often applied to adolescent or young adult males who appear unable to conform to the rules of society. The qualities of this sort of person's psychological make-up include an inability to tolerate minor frustrations, an incapacity for forming stable human relationships, a failure to learn from past experiences, however unpleasant they might have been, and a tendency to act impulsively or recklessly. Henderson (1939), in a well-known essay on the subject, divided psychopathic personalities into three categories: the predominantly inadequate, the predominantly aggressive, and the creative. They are by no means mutually exclusive but, whereas the first two have gained general acceptance and receive more psychiatric attention, far less has been heard about the creative psychopath, whose sometimes erratic behaviour may seem less significant than the creations of his fertile imagination. He is less likely to come before the courts or to the attention of the mental health services, for his eccentricities are not usually regarded as indicative of mental disorder.

The question of whether, in the long run, psychopaths do learn from experience was considered in a follow-up study of children who showed persistent antisocial behaviour in St Louis (Robins, 1966). Of those who survived—there was a high mortality from accidents, suicide, and alcoholism—a significant number appeared to be keeping out of trouble by middle life, finding that relative conformity was preferable to constant conflict with society and the law. Whether maturation or learning from experience was the more responsible for this beneficial change is uncertain, but it does appear that some so-called antisocial psychopaths do ultimately learn to mend their ways. There was little evidence that medical treatment had made much contribution to this outcome.

It is often said—erroneously as it happens—that our present-day concept of psychopathic personality originates from the introduction of the diagnosis of moral insanity into English medical and legal theory and practice by J. C. Prichard, a Bristol physician, in 1835. At the time, Prichard and many others were considerably influenced by *Gall's writings on *phrenology which localized human propensities to specific parts of the brain. Among these propensities was included the moral faculty, and it was widely assumed that moral insanity was caused by a derangement of that part of the brain concerned with making a choice between good and evil. Prichard, however, was using the term moral insanity to denote emotional disturbances—delusions and hallucinations—that were devoid of the usual hallmarks of insanity. None of his cases bore the remotest resemblance to the present-day psychopath, but because he used the word 'moral' it was widely believed that this form of insanity was responsible for the actions of individuals who exhibited a persistent tendency to indulge in criminal behaviour. Hence the plea of moral insanity in the courts in attempting to exculpate the offender from the full penalties of the law. Understandably, it was not an excuse which found much favour with the judges of the day. As they reasonably pointed out—and it has continued to be pointed out—it was impossible to decide whether a crime had been caused by the innate wickedness of the offender, or whether it resulted from a fit of moral insanity.

The Mental Deficiency Act of 1927 softened the term 'moral imbecile'—incorporated in the earlier Act of 1913—to 'moral defective', but retained in its definition the words 'mental defectiveness coupled with strongly vicious or criminal propensities', and added, and 'who require care, supervision and control for the protection of others'. This was the forerunner of the psychopathic disorder definition in the Mental Health Act of 1959. Because many of those so constrained were not devoid of normal intelligence, placing them in hospitals for the mentally defective was neither appropriate nor beneficial.

Why *psychopathic* personality? As already mentioned, Schneider used the term to denote all varieties of abnormal personality, but his subgroups of explosive, affectionless, and weak-willed come close to Henderson's categories of aggressive and inadequate psychopaths. Koch in Germany in 1891 introduced the term 'psychopathic inferiority' as a catch-all phrase implying a constitutional predisposition not only to neurosis but also to abnormalities and eccentricities of behaviour. At the time of his writing, psychiatric thought was dominated by concepts of degeneration and the hereditary transmission of 'the taint of insanity'. As such degeneration was often attributed to parental excesses, particularly alcoholism and sexual profligacy, it is understandable that what at first sight appeared to be persistent immoral or criminal behaviour became linked with the prevailing notions about psychopathic inferiority and moral insanity. Although in Britain the Royal Commission on the Law relating to Mental Illness, 1954–7, repeatedly used the word 'psychopath', it avoided making any precise definition of what the word meant. Baroness Wootton (1959) considered that the modern psychopath is the linguistic descendant of the moral defective, which takes us back to nineteenth-century writings on moral insanity. Whatever word is used, it has to be admitted that making clear distinction between the mentally healthy offender and the presumably mentally abnormal one is not an easy task.

The question thus arises whether psychopathic personality should be classed as a form of mental disorder. Opinions differ widely; but as the psychopath now has legal status the existence of such a condition has understandably been put forward in criminal proceedings as a plea for mitigation of sentence. In some cases of homicide, the verdict has been reduced from murder to manslaughter on the basis of *diminished responsibility as defined in the Homicide Act of 1959. But many psychiatrists would have reservations about claims that psychopathic disorder is a mental illness on a par with neurosis or psychosis. While it could be argued that it amounts to an abnormality of mind which could seriously impair the responsibility of an offender for his alleged homicidal act, what is 'abnormality of mind' in this context? The subject was clarified by Lord Chief Justice Parker, who said that it meant 'a state of mind so different from that of ordinary human beings that the reasonable man would term it abnormal'. He went on to indicate that such an opinion applied to a person's acts, his ability to decide whether they were right or wrong, and his capacity for exercising will-power to control such behaviour in accordance with rational judgement. None the less, as Nigel Walker (1965) comments, 'It is clear . . . that while a diagnosis of psychopathy is now recognized by English courts as an acceptable basis for a defence of diminished responsibility, the psychopath's chances of succeeding in this defence are by no means high'.

The causes and treatment of psychopathic disorder are as contentious as its legal implications. Theories of aetiology have included brain damage in childhood, late maturation of the central nervous system, and adverse circumstances of upbringing, particularly difficult relationships with parents and those in authority. As far as treatment is concerned, there is little evidence that a purely psychiatric approach to the problem has been successful. Controlled studies are hard to come by, but one such investigation found that firm but sympathetic handling in a disciplined environment was better than a more permissive approach based on group therapy and a self-governing type of regime. As the psychopath appears to lack the inner controls normally developed during childhood and adolescence, this result is hardly surprising. Time, however, seems to be a significant factor in treatment, an observation which could be interpreted as favouring the late maturation theory of psychopathic disorder. But in all probability learning over a period of years may also play a part in this process of maturation.          F. A. W.

Craft, M. J. (1965). *Ten Studies into Psychopathic Personality*. Bristol.

Henderson, D. (1939). *Psychopathic States*. New York.

Robins, L. N. (1966). *Deviant Children Grown Up*. Baltimore.

Schneider, K. (trans. Hamilton, M. W., 1958). *Psychopathic Personalities*. London.

Walker, N. (1965). Liberty, liability and culpability. *Medicine, Science and the Law*, January 1965.

Whitlock, F. A. (1967). Prichard and the concept of moral insanity. *Australian and New Zealand Journal of Psychiatry*, **2**, 72–9.

Wootton, B. (1959). *Social Science and Social Pathology*. London.

**PSYCHOPHARMACOLOGY.** The use of drugs that act on the mind is as old as the recorded history of man. Alcohol in the form of fermented beverages such as mead was probably already popular in the Palaeolithic age, about 8000 BC, and grape wine from about 400–300 BC. *Opium is referred to in Sumerian tablets of around 4000 BC, and marijuana was known in China at 2737 BC. The hallucinogenic properties of the magic mushroom (teonanacatl) were known from 1000 BC in Mexico, while in Northern Europe and Asia the inebriant properties of the fly agaric mushroom, *Amanita muscaria*, feature in Norse legends. The concept that drugs can be used medically to restore mental health is, in contrast, the result of a very recent revolution in pharmacology, following the discovery in the 1950s of new classes of drugs, the tranquillizers and antidepressants, and their widespread use in the treatment of mental illness.

Staggering quantities of psychoactive drugs are now consumed for medical purposes. About half of the female population of the United Kingdom over the age of 60 regularly uses sedative drugs to put them to sleep each night. Benzodiazepines in the form of Valium (diazepam) and related substances by day, and Mogadon (nitrazepam) and Dalmane (flurazepam) for night sedation, have largely replaced barbiturate sedatives and hypnotics. The success of these 'tranquillizers' can be gauged by the astonishing quantity consumed, amounting to tens of billions of doses throughout the world each year. These substances have a definite although mild calming effect, they relieve anxiety and diminish aggression, and they are relatively safe— in contrast to the barbiturates, which all too commonly lead to death from overdose. Because these newer drugs are relatively safe, and since almost all of us feel anxious from time to time, the extravagant success of the benzodiazepines during the 1960s and 1970s is not hard to understand. More recently, with the recognition that prolonged use of benzodiazepines can lead to addiction, there has been a growing reaction to their widespread use.

The most remarkable modern development in this field, however, is the discovery of drugs that are successful in the treatment of some of the fundamental symptoms of psychosis and depression. The first drug found to have such effects in schizophrenic patients was chlorpromazine

(Largactil, Thorazine), and from this a large number of other so-called 'major tranquillizers' with similar effects have been developed. Since the first favourable reports on chlorpromazine appeared in France in 1952, such drugs have been adopted widely for the treatment of schizophrenia. More than 100 million schizophrenic patients have been treated with chlorpromazine since 1953. The major tranquillizers have definite beneficial effects on some of the most fundamental symptoms of schizophrenia: patients show less disordered thinking, suffer from fewer delusions and hallucinations, exhibit more appropriate emotional behaviour. They are not simply quietened or sedated, and indeed other sedative drugs such as the 'minor' tranquillizers (benzodiazepines) do not exhibit these effects. It is not surprising that the massive use of chlorpromazine and similar drugs has had an enormous impact on the treatment of schizophrenia. (For further discussion, see SCHIZOPHRENIA: EVIDENCE FOR AN ORGANIC CAUSE.) The mental institutions have been transformed from sombre places with a largely custodial function to hospitals with open doors in which community therapy and rehabilitation techniques have been introduced. The number of patients so severely ill as to need more or less permanent hospitalization has also diminished strikingly—to the extent that separate psychiatric hospitals may no longer be necessary in future.

Other groups of drugs have been discovered to have beneficial effects in treating the melancholia of depressed patients. Two major classes of antidepressants have been introduced since the late 1950s—one derived from the substance iproniazid and the other from imipramine. Both groups of compounds have beneficial effects in depression, although these actions are usually less dramatic than those seen with the anti-psychotic drugs. A remarkable discovery, made by Dr John Cade in Australia in 1949, has been that the symptoms of mania can often be treated very effectively by administration of small doses of an inorganic salt—lithium carbonate. Continued treatment with lithium carbonate reduces the frequency of recurrence of manic episodes in individuals who would otherwise show a regular cycle of such illness.

The problems of madness have not been solved by the drugs—we still do not understand what causes schizophrenia or depression, or even the nature of these illnesses. The idea that abnormalities in brain chemistry may underlie mental illness has, however, derived strong support from the finding that psychosis can be treated with simple chemicals. Much research effort is currently directed towards discovering precisely how the antipsychotic and antidepressant drugs alter brain chemistry. It is now widely accepted that antipsychotic drugs act by blocking the effects of one of the chemical transmitter substances used by braincells to transmit signals to one another. The transmitter blocked by chlorpromazine and related drugs is dopamine, and this finding has suggested the possibility that in schizophrenia excessive amounts of dopamine secreted in the brain might represent an immediate causative factor for the psychotic state. (See DOPAMINE NEURONES IN THE BRAIN.) On the other hand, antidepressant drugs seem to act by enhancing the effects of other chemical transmitter substances, noradrenaline and serotonin, in the brain—suggesting that these chemicals may be available in abnormally low amounts in the brains of depressed people.

In general, however, our knowledge of the mode of action of many psychoactive drugs is limited. This applies particularly to nicotine, cannabis, and the hallucinogens, but both barbiturates and alcohol act as central nervous system depressants. With respect to barbiturates and benzodiazepines it is likely that their depressant effects on neural activity are mediated by the neurotransmitter gamma-aminobutyric acid (GABA), but other *neurotransmitters may also be involved. Rather surprisingly, less is known about the precise mode of action of alcohol on the brain beyond the fact that it appears to depress synaptic transmission.

The fact that simple chemical substances can have such profound influences on the state of the mind, as between madness and sanity, between depression and euphoria, between normal perception and the vivid hallucinations induced by lysergic acid diethylamide (LSD), has obvious philosophical implications for the relation between the mind and the chemistry of the brain. It is clear that subtle changes in brain chemistry can have profound effects on the state of consciousness, and it behoves us to understand more of such subtleties.

Drugs are also consumed very widely for non-medical reasons. Of these alcohol, nicotine, and caffeine are relatively universal—others, whose use is strictly controlled by legislation, such as the hallucinogens, barbiturates, amphetamines, marijuana, phencyclidine, cocaine, and opiates, are, nevertheless, also quite widely taken. These compounds have a bewildering variety of different psychic effects. Alcohol and barbiturates are depressants, leading to a feeling of relaxation, loss of inhibition, and to inebriation and sleep. Others are stimulants, such as nicotine and the more powerful amphetamines; these are performance-enhancing drugs. LSD, mescaline, phencyclidine, and the many other hallucinogens are in a class apart because these compounds can produce bizarre changes in perception—they replace the present world with another that is equally real but different, often with vivid sensory hallucinations. There are other drugs whose actions are primarily euphoriant, notably cocaine, morphine, heroin and other opiate drugs, and—in a milder form—marijuana. They replace the present world with one in which the individual experiences no problems, and often intense pleasure. The most powerful euphoriants, the opiates and cocaine are medically dangerous drugs—largely because their continued use leads inevitably to tolerance and *addiction, i.e. larger and larger doses become necessary to achieve the desired effects, and the organism becomes physically dependent on continued drug use, so that stopping the drug may precipitate very unpleasant withdrawal symptoms. It should be remembered, however, that morphine and related opiates still have important medical uses in the control of pain. Opium has long been regarded as a sovereign remedy for the relief of pain and other symptoms. As Thomas Sydenham, the English physician, wrote at the end of the seventeenth century, 'I cannot forbear mentioning with gratitude the goodness of the Supreme Being who has supplied afflicted mankind with opiates for their relief.' Almost certainly it is the insanitary habits and unsterile modes of use as well as the actions of the drugs as such, that make opiates such a hazard to the life and health of the addict today.

We may one day discover how to eliminate the problem of addiction, and we will then be faced with the difficult decision as to whether 'safe' euphoriant drugs should be allowed widespread availability and use. Several millennia of experience with alcohol suggests that strict control of the availability of such substances would inevitably be needed. The 'soma' of Aldous Huxley's *Brave New World* may be nearer than is generally realized. There is little doubt that legislation controlling the use of marijuana will gradually become less prohibitive, and that modern plant breeding could work wonders with the Indian Hemp plant to produce 'super-pot'. It is also clear that society has not yet decided what its attitudes should be to the general availability of chemically induced pleasure.                                      L. L. I.

Iversen, S. D. and Iversen, L. L. (1981). *Behavioral Pharmacology*, 2nd edn. New York.
Iversen, L. L., Iversen, S. D., and Snyder, S. H. (eds.) (1975–84). *Handbook of Psychopharmacology*, vols. 1–18. New York.
Ray, O. S. (1972). *Drugs, Society and Human Behavior*. St Louis.

**PSYCHOPHYSICS** originally meant the study of the sensations evoked by physical stimuli. As an example to illustrate the distinction between a stimulus and a sensation, the amount of light reflected by this page is its luminance, and can be measured with a light meter such as photographers use; the sensation evoked by that reflected light is the experienced brightness of the page, and may be deceptively related to the luminance, as photographers know well. Psychophysics is concerned with the *brightness* of the stimulus, and its other subjective qualities, and, secondly, with the relation of that brightness to the physical luminance.

The term 'psychophysics' was introduced by Gustav *Fechner in his *Elemente der Psychophysik* (1860), in which he conceived an indirect method of measuring sensations. If a luminance $L_2$ can just be distinguished as greater than $L_1$, then, to a close approximation, $L_2/L_1$ is constant; this is Weber's law (formulated as the Weber–Fechner law). If one supposes that all *just noticeable differences (e.g. between $L_1$ and $L_2$) are subjectively equivalent, then the *sensation* (in this case, of brightness) must increase as the logarithm of the physical stimulus magnitude; for if $L_2/L_1$, is constant, so also is log $L_2-\log L_1$.

Fechner's logarithmic measure was universally accepted until the 1930s, at which time it was questioned for a purely practical reason. At that time the decibel scale for the measurement of auditory intensity was newly developed. On this scale 20 dB represents a 10-fold increase in the amplitude of modulation of sound pressure, or a 100-fold increase in acoustic power; and, since the range of acoustic powers to which the ear may be exposed is typically $1:10^{12}$, a logarithmic scale is convenient. Decibel measurements are always relative to a reference point, which is usually taken as about equal to the faintest sound that the ear can detect. So, a naïve application of Fechner's law would suggest that 50 dB should sound half as loud as 100 dB; but it is generally agreed that 50 dB sounds much quieter than that. To enable acoustic engineers to communicate meaningfully with their customers, the 1930s saw some research on how people assign numbers to ratios of sound levels and this research led to the development of the sone scale by S. S. *Stevens in 1936. Loudness in sones grows as the 0·3 power of the physical sound power.

Subsequently, in the 1950s, S. S. Stevens and his collaborators developed the methods and ideas of the 1930s to devise power law scales of the sensations, evoked by more than thirty different sensory attributes, substantially those for which Weber's law holds. When subjects judge the ratios of stimuli, the numbers assigned vary as $N = aX^\beta$, where $X$ is the magnitude of the stimulus being judged and $\beta$ is an exponent characteristic of the attribute. This exponent varies from 0·33 for luminance to 3·5 for electric shock.

Inspired by Fechner's use of the just noticeable difference as a unit of sensation, there has evolved a very great body of experimental work and practical knowledge about human discrimination of all kinds of sensory attributes; and following from Stevens's power law, there has developed a comparable body of facts and figures about human judgement. For practical purposes, psychophysics has come to refer to these two large accumulations of data and models. But, notwithstanding its long history, basic theoretical principles are only just beginning to emerge.

On mature consideration it can be seen that sensation is not, in fact, measurable independently of the physical stimulus from which it is derived. Fechner's logarithmic transform exists only as a mathematical construction, having no operational validity; and conformity to Stevens's power law depends on getting the experiment 'right'. These two assertions can be supported by a demonstration and a simple experiment.

Panel a of Fig. 1 shows a black and white

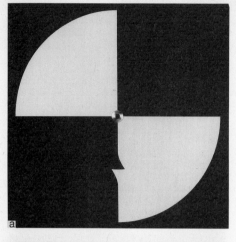

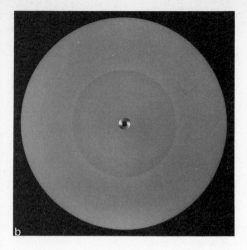

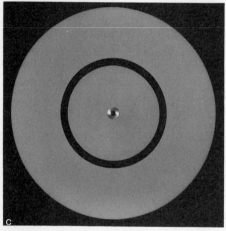

**Fig. 1.** The Craik–Cornsweet illusion. Plates b and c have been made from the same photographic negative which was taken while the sectored disc was rotated a high speed. The inner disc has the same average luminance as the outer annulus, but in plate b it appears darker because only the sharp step in luminance at the boundary is perceptible.

sectored disc which, when spun rapidly, appears as in panel b. Intermittent illumination interrupted at a sufficiently rapid rate is not distinguishable from uniform illumination of the same time-average illuminance. So the centre and periphery of the rotating disc must have the same luminance—but their brightnesses are manifestly different. Now if the boundary between the centre and periphery of the rotating disc be covered with an opaque annulus (panel c), the brightnesses of the centre and the periphery are immediately seen to be equal. Remove the annulus (panel b) and they are again different. This phenomenon is known as the Craik–Cornsweet illusion. It depends on the kinky profile of luminance at the boundary of the figure, which may be appreciated from the shape of the black sector on the stationary disc. There is an abrupt step in luminance which is easily perceived, and two ramps which are not. And so the centre appears darker than the periphery. When this profile is obscured by the annulus, centre and periphery appear equally bright. It follows that we

do not see relative brightness only from a comparison of the two luminances in question, but from the *perceived change* in luminance at the boundary. That is, the sensation of brightness is obtained by a differential process from the physical stimulus. This idea was first proposed as long ago as 1865, by Ernst *Mach.

The Craik–Cornsweet illusion is known to have analogues in the attributes of sound intensity and frequency, and in the length and spacing of lines. It is probably a general feature of human sensory perception. And the differential process which it reveals explains Weber's law, why the just noticeable difference increases in direct proportion to the stimulus magnitude. The logarithmic transform is a matter of the imagination only.

If our sensory experience is differentially coupled to the physical world, what of Stevens's power law? An elegant experiment by W. R. Garner addresses this point. Thirty subjects listened to a standard tone at 90 dB and then a comparison tone. The comparison tone was to be judged 'more' or 'less' than half as loud as the standard, and from each subject's judgements of a series of such comparisons was estimated that intensity of tone that would have been judged 'more' and 'less' equally often—a subjective half-loudness value. One group of subjects listened to comparison tones varying between 75 and 85 dB, and having half-loudness values within that range. Another group listened to comparison tones between 65 and 75 dB which all had half-loudness values within *that* range; and likewise for a third group listening to tones between 55 and 65 dB. Only one subject complained that the comparison tones presented did not straddle the half-loudness value, and she was happily reassigned to the third group.

It is apparent that most people have no idea what 'half as loud' means. Not wishing to appear foolish, the subjects in Garner's experiment assumed that some comparison tones must be more, and some less, than half as loud as the standard (else the experiment made no sense) and adjusted their criteria of judgement accordingly. They were conned. Their judgements depended on the immediate context rather than on the loudness of the stimulus. In experiments on the estimation of sensations the influence of context is very powerful and the accuracy of judgement is typically poorer by one to two orders of magnitude compared to that accuracy revealed in the measurement of just noticeable differences. The accuracy of judgement of single stimuli has been found, with many different attributes, to be equivalent to the identification of no more than five different stimulus levels.

In conclusion, there is no way to measure sensation that is distinct from measurement of the physical stimulus. Sometimes we are deceived—Fig. 1 presents an example—and such examples present intriguing problems to the experimental psychologist. Attempts to 'measure' sensation have taught us that judgements of quantity are astonishingly poor. For this reason photographers use exposure meters; and cars are fitted with speedometers, so that the driver merely has to judge that the needle is adjacent to the mark representing 30 m.p.h., rather than 25 or 35—a 'Yes or No' kind of judgement that is reliable. We habitually make our judgements of quantity with the aid of a measuring instrument, a ruler or scale-pan, and, in practice, problems arise only with those attributes which we feel intuitively ought to admit a continuum of values, but for which no measuring instrument exists—attributes like the merit of essays written in an examination or the aesthetic value of a painting. Such problems are nicely illustrated by the auction prices of Old Master paintings. The authenticity of such a painting can often be determined with great reliability; but sometimes the provenance is re-appraised and the market value of the painting, physically the same, with its aesthetic qualities entirely unchanged, can vary at least 30-fold in consequence. In the auction room aesthetic merit is of very little account, precisely because it cannot

be accurately assessed; in its stead, provenance, a 'Yes and No' matter, is almost everything.

D. R. J. L.

Gescheider, G. A. (1985). *Psychophysics: method, theory, and application*, 2nd edn. Hillsdale, New Jersey.
Laming, D. (1986). *Sensory Analysis*. London.

**PSYCHOSIS.** The word 'psychosis' seems to have been coined in the mid-nineteenth century and to have meant originally any kind of mental disturbance arising from whatever cause. But after the turn of the century its meaning was restricted by excluding both the mental consequences of familiar physical illnesses (such as *delirium associated with fever) and the neuroses. In contemporary psychiatric terminology, 'psychosis' is a classificatory and descriptive term, referring to a specific range of illnesses and symptoms, the illnesses being those in which the patient's basic competence as a person is called in question, the symptoms being those which seem to indicate some gross disorder of perception and thought (such as *hallucinations and *delusions). A psychosis is, therefore, any mental illness which is liable to render its victim *non compos mentis*, and unfit to plead in a court of law; and a symptom is 'psychotic' if it betrays misapprehension and misinterpretation of the nature of reality.

If, for instance, someone asserts that he is Napoleon, or emperor of Canada, or has had sexual intercourse with God, he is psychotic, since such assertions are by common consent untrue and anyone making them seriously must be misapprehending the nature of reality and failing to distinguish between his fantasies and the facts of the case. In contrast, if someone asserts that he spends time imagining that he is Napoleon, or day-dreaming that he has established an empire in Canada, or that he has dreamt he was emperor of Canada or has had intercourse with God, he is not psychotic, for he has correctly distinguished between his own imaginings and the nature of the external world. Similarly, if someone asserts that he has committed terrible crimes (when he hasn't) and deserves lifelong imprisonment for having done so, he is psychotic, but someone who complains of feeling irrationally guilty is not; nor is a religious person who has a lively sense of original sin.

The International Classification of Diseases 1955 (see MENTAL DISORDERS: CLASSIFICATION), published by the World Health Organization and used by the National Health Service in Britain, lists eight specific psychoses. Four of these, the so-called organic psychoses (senile, pre-senile, arteriosclerotic, and alcoholic), are generally agreed to be the result of degenerative changes in the brain. They excite little interest within the psychiatric profession and practically none at all with the general public. The other four, the so-called functional psychoses—*schizophrenia, manic-depressive psychosis (see DEPRESSION), involutional melancholia, and *paranoia—arouse considerable controversy within the profession and great interest with the general public, partly because their symptoms are dramatic, but more importantly because research has (as yet) failed to discover any convincing, as opposed to plausible, causes for them—and in the absence of any specifiable physical causes it is possible and legitimate to question even whether the medical model is the appropriate one to apply to psychosis.

However, the majority of psychiatrists do seem to believe that the functional psychoses are true medical diseases and that, one day, physical causes will be found for them—and that as a result, rational, effective treatments will become available. If they are right, not only will an enormous amount of suffering be relieved, but the claims of the medical profession to be the appropriate people to care for and treat the mentally disturbed will finally be vindicated. In fact, the advent of effective drugs for the treatment of schizophrenia and manic depressive psychoses has given considerable support to the possibility that biochemical rather than structural changes in the brain could be causes of these diseases. The medical model therefore gains some plausibility from these discoveries.

But, it must be stressed, at least two non-organic, non-medical conceptions of psychosis are also in circulation. One, held by some but not all psychoanalysts, argues that the functional psychoses are not in principle all that different from the neuroses; it is merely that the fixation points are earlier, the regressions deeper, the infantile traumas more massive, the defence mechanisms more primitive. If the analysts who hold this view are right, the functional psychoses are psychogenic, not organic, illnesses, and their symptoms require interpretation in terms of their concealed meanings, not explanations in terms of cerebral dysfunction.

The other, non-organic conception, held by anti-psychiatrists, 'family process' therapists, and the post-Laingian counter-culture generally, explains the functional psychosis of any single individual as the end-result of complex and skew interactions within his family that have driven him into bizarre and incomprehensible behaviour, which is then 'disauthenticated' by being labelled 'mad' or 'psychotic'. This theory exists in more than one form. In one the psychotic patient is the victim of a villainous schizophrenogenic parent, usually the mother; in another he is the overt casualty of a deeply concealed family tragedy. This last is a socio-political theory which locates pathology not in the body or the mind of the individual patient but in the power politics of society and the family.

C. R.

Bateson, G. (1956). Towards a theory of schizophrenia. In *Steps to an Ecology of Mind*. London.
Fairbairn, W. R. D. (1952). A revised psychopathology of the psychoses and psychoneuroses. In *Psychoanalytic Studies of the Personality*. London.
Laing, R. D. (1971). *The Politics of the Family*. London.
Laing, R. D. and Esterson, A. (1964). *Sanity, Madness and the Family*. London.

**PSYCHOSOMATIC DISEASE: A MEDICAL VIEW.** The successes achieved in the 1920s and 1930s in the treatment of diabetes mellitus with insulin, of pernicious anaemia with liver-extract, of malnutrition with vitamins, and of infectious diseases with antitoxin and their prevention by immunization, all encouraged the reductionist view that the objective of scientific medicine should be the discovery of the essential internal disorder underlying the symptoms, and the specific treatment for it. However, this model was soon recognized to be too simple. For many diseases the causes appear to be multiple and complex, some lying in internal and some in external conditions and others being, in a loosely defined sense, psychological. The interest in psychological processes grew in the 1930s, as the psychodynamic theories derived from psychoanalysis became more widely known. The term 'psychosomatic' was then applied to diseases in which disorder in the function of an organ was thought to be due to, or associated with, psychological factors. A definition of psychosomatic medicine was given in 1939 in the editorial introducing the first number of the journal *Psychosomatic Medicine*. Its object was 'to study in their interrelation the psychological and physiological aspects of all normal and abnormal bodily functions and thus to integrate somatic therapy and psychotherapy'. The journal's intention was to promote an approach to causes and treatment, rather than to make distinctions between classes of disease. Nevertheless, certain diseases were identified as psychosomatic—for example, atopic dermatitis, anorexia nervosa, bronchial asthma, essential hypertension, gastric and duodenal ulcer, myocardial infarction, and ulcerative colitis. It should be said, however, that the inclusion of some of these conditions under the rubric of psychosomatic disorders has been questioned.

The stress/strain analogy became popular. Just as stress, an external force, produces strain in a material, so forces in the physical, biological, or social environment produce strain in the mental and physical functions and behaviour of organisms. The strain effects are potentially adaptive, the form taken by the adaptation depending on the organism's constitution and past experience, and hence they are idiosyncratic. The analogy is, however, misleading in one respect at least. For whereas the effects constituting strain in a material cease as soon as the stress ceases, there is no return in the organism to the status quo, because stress causes reorganization or 'reprogramming' of the adaptive mechanisms. The organism acquires new habits, for instance, or a new immunity.

Support for the psychosomatic approach comes from epidemiological studies of the incidence of diseases among those subjected to more or less defined stresses. Gastric ulcer, for instance, was noted in the First World War to be unduly common among soldiers who had recently been in action in the trenches. Recorded deaths from gastric and duodenal ulcer rose in the Second World War during the period of heavy air raids. When stocks go down in New York, diabetes goes up, it was remarked. The survivors of fires and floods and of imprisonment, and the *bereaved, among others, have been shown to have rates of morbidity and mortality greater than those in comparable populations. Many diseases not directly related to the known effects of the stress are then unduly common—for example, heart disease, cancer, disease of the gastro-intestinal tract, and pulmonary tuberculosis, as well as suicide and accidents. So many diseases have now been included in such lists as to discourage any inclination to distinguish between those diseases which are psychosomatic and those which are not.

Experiments on mammals have shown that such stresses as confinement, restraint, and frustration affect the function of almost every organ. The temporary separation of new-born mammals from their mothers results in high rates of morbidity and mortality. It is well known that in man emotions such as anger, *fear, and *anxiety tend to be accompanied by changes throughout the body in almost every function. The effects of various stresses on functions of the stomach, colon, skin, and cardio-vascular system in particular have been studied experimentally in healthy human subjects. Some of the effects are mediated by the autonomic nervous system, some by the endocrine system, and others through behaviour such as refusing food or eating to excess. Some create the conditions in which the disease arises—for example, by affecting the resistance to infection—while others form an inherent part of the disease. Research has tried to give some definition to the psychological factors, although this has proved difficult, and to elucidate the processes involved in each pattern of disease. There is no distinctive psychosomatic process, but rather a wide variety of processes. For this reason the use of the term 'psychosomatic' has declined.

The pattern of responses has been shown in experiments on mammals to vary with the character of the stress. In human patients, on the other hand, there tends to be a remarkable consistency in the psychosomatic disease, which tends to recur in a stereotyped form. The pattern is peculiar to each patient and more or less fixed. It could be argued that a genetic predisposition as, for example, in the asthma–eczema syndrome, to some extent determines the type of psychosomatic disorder that is likely to recur. Evidence from studies of children suggests that the pattern is laid down before the child is 6, 'organ-vulnerability' being decided by this age. From time to time there may be a 'syndrome-shift'. Thus a patient who has had several attacks of atopic dermatitis develops bronchial asthma, or perhaps, later in life, rheumatoid arthritis. A sufferer over many years from migraine develops ulcerative colitis, or a patient who has had a recurrent peptic ulcer develops essential hypertension. It has often been suggested that each pattern of disease is associated with particular traits of personality, but systematic studies have largely failed to show correlations. However, recurrent diseases like asthma and ulcerative colitis may be held to influence the style of life a person adopts and so indirectly affect his medical state.

See also PSYCHOSOMATIC DISEASE: PHILOSOPHICAL AND PSYCHOLOGICAL ASPECTS; STRESS.          D. R. D.

Alexander, F. (1950). Psychosomatic Medicine. New York.

Hill, O. W. (ed.) (1976). Modern Trends in Psychosomatic Medicine—3. London.

Tanner, J. M. (ed.) (1960). Stress and Psychiatric Disorder. Oxford.

## PSYCHOSOMATIC DISEASE: PHILOSOPHICAL AND PSYCHOLOGICAL ASPECTS.

Diseases are designated as psychosomatic if two conditions are fulfilled: if (i) the symptoms are accompanied by demonstrable physiological disturbances of function and (ii) the illness as a whole can be interpreted as a manifestation or function of the patient's personality, conflicts, life history, etc. The first condition distinguishes psychosomatic illness from psychoneurosis, particularly conversion hysteria, in which, by definition, the physical symptoms are not accompanied by demonstrable physiological disturbances. The second condition distinguishes psychosomatic illness from physical diseases pure and simple, which are explicable solely in terms of bodily dysfunction without reference to the psyche of the patient.

Although the word 'psychosomatic' was used by Coleridge, and its reversed form 'somapsyche' occurs in the original Greek of the New Testament, the concept of psychosomatic disease dates properly from the first half of the twentieth century, when it became necessary to have a concept that cut across the division of diseases into physical (somatic) and mental (psychical) which had been established by *Freud and *Breuer's demonstration that the psychoneuroses were not functional disturbances of the central nervous system but symbolic expressions of psychical conflict. Given the resulting tendency to assume that illnesses were either physical and all in the body, or mental and all in the mind, the term 'psychosomatic disease' became necessary to categorize illnesses resembling psychoneuroses in being expressions of psychical conflict but yet had solid, demonstrable physical signs and symptoms.

As the preceding two paragraphs perhaps reveal, psychosomatic disease is logically and philosophically speaking a most tricky concept, since its meaning and precise implications necessarily depend on each particular user's basic assumptions about the relationship between body and mind. Presumably a materialist must hold that all diseases, including so-called mental ones, are ultimately somatic, and an idealist must hold that all physical illnesses are ultimately mental, while those who hold that physical and mental events belong to different causal sequences have to explain, if they believe in the possibility of psychosomatic disease, how the leap from one to the other is effected. However, in actual practice, the term is only used to categorize illnesses which present with physical signs and symptoms but none the less require the clinician to explore the patient's biography and state of mind. It is never used to refer to illnesses which present with mental symptoms but are none the less due to physical causes as, for example, depression caused by a brain tumour.

Georg Groddeck (1866–1934), the maverick German psychoanalyst, is often regarded as the father of psychosomatic medicine. His way of formulating the relationship of body and mind was to assume that both are the creations of a third, impersonal force, *das Es*, the It:

the body and mind are a joint thing which harbours an It, a power by which we are lived, while we think we live. . . . The It, which is mysteriously connected with sexuality, Eros, or whatever you choose to call it, shapes the nose as well as the hand of the human, just as it shapes his thoughts and emotions. . . . And just as the symptomatic activity of the It in hysteria and neurosis calls for psychoanalytical treatment, so does heart trouble and cancer.

Rather similarly, another maverick psychoanalyst, Wilhelm Reich (1897–1957), held that all illnesses were the result of imprisonment of spontaneous bio-energy within character-armour imposed by a repressive, authoritarian society. More soberly but less imaginatively, many workers during the last fifty years have produced evidence, much of it statistical, suggesting that many physical illnesses occur predominantly in individuals who have rigid personalities, who are subject to stress, who have recently experienced upheavals in their life-style, or who have lost all connection with other people. Psychoanalysts such as Franz Alexander and Flanders Dunbar in the USA attempted to relate specific psychosomatic disorders to specific emotional conflicts and personality patterns. This theory of psychosomatic illness has not been generally supported by recent work, although there is some evidence that coronary artery disease occurs more often in individuals with a particular personality make-up—the so-called type A personality. This concept is still controversial and the mode of interaction between personality and cardiac disease is not fully understood.

However, psychosomatic disease remains an elusive concept. Many, perhaps most, clinicians feel that there is something in it, but the problem of formulating correctly the nature of the relationship between body and mind implicit in it has proved recalcitrant.

See also PSYCHOSOMATIC DISEASE: A MEDICAL VIEW.                                                                    C. R.

Bakan, D. (1968). *Disease, Pain, and Sacrifice*. Chicago.
Dunbar, F. (1954). *Emotions and Bodily Changes*. New York.
Groddeck, G. (1923). *Das Buch vom Es*. (English trans. 1935, London.) *The Book of the It*.
Grossman, C. M. and S. (1965). *The Wild Analyst*. London.
Higgins, M. B. (ed.) (1960). *Wilhelm Reich: Selected Writings*. New York.
Totman, R. G. (1979). *Social Causes of Illness*. London.

**PSYCHOSURGERY.** This term is used to denote operative procedures on the brain specifically designed to relieve severe mental symptoms that have been unresponsive to other forms of treatment. Although surgery for mental illness had been attempted sporadically—mostly in the form of trephining—since early times, it was not until 1935 that the Portuguese neurologist Egas Moniz, in association with the surgeon Almeida Lima, performed the first systematic series of operations known as prefrontal leucotomy, severing the connections between the prefrontal cortex and the rest of the brain. Although the operation was crude, of the first twenty cases seven recovered and seven improved. The best results were obtained in cases of agitated *depression, a finding which has been repeatedly confirmed by later workers. Unfortunately, some patients developed adverse personality changes, an effect which could have been predicted from the case of Phineas Gage, a competent worker in the USA who, in 1847, had the misfortune during a rock-blasting operation to have an iron bar blown through the front part of his head. He survived this extremely violent form of prefrontal leucotomy but, on recovery, was found to have undergone a profound change in personality. He swore in the grossest manner, behaviour not previously indulged in, and his overall qualities as a likeable individual were severely impaired. Despite these changes to his character he did not show any decline in intelligence or memory. Although patients treated by prefrontal leucotomy did not usually show such severe impairment of personality as Gage did, it is undeniable that adverse alterations in behaviour occurred sufficiently often to arouse opposition to the operation.

None the less, it was taken up enthusiastically in the USA by Freeman and Watts (1942) and with rather less vigour in the UK, where it was carried out on 10,365 patients suffering from mental illnesses between 1942 and 1954 (Tooth and Newton, 1961). It was stated that only 3 per cent showed undesirable side-effects and that more than 40 per cent had been ill for at least six years. The operation was performed in only a few centres, a fact which seems to imply that, regardless of its alleged usefulness, attitudes opposing it were strongly held by medical staff in many hospitals. By 1961 the annual frequency of leucotomy had fallen substantially.

As time has gone by there have been many modifications of the original operation, and today it has been almost entirely replaced by exact stereotactic procedures which allow very small lesions to be placed in certain key areas of the brain. Such methods are designed to alleviate symptoms without causing undesirable changes in personality. Comparatively few patients are treated each year by psychosurgery, largely because of the development of more effective drugs (see PSYCHOPHARMACOLOGY) and behavioural (see BEHAVIOUR THERAPY) methods for the treatment of mental illness.

What kinds of symptoms are most susceptible to surgical intervention? The phrase 'tortured self-concern' is often quoted to indicate the degree of distress which has failed to respond to less drastic treatments. The best results have been obtained from patients suffering from severe chronic *anxiety, agitated depression carrying a high risk of suicide, and those afflicted with incapacitating *obsessive-compulsive disorders.

Although there is every indication that, with careful selection and post-operative management, many patients with these apparently intractable symptoms have benefited from the more precise forms of psychosurgery, very strong opposition has been mobilized in some quarters against any form of surgery for the relief of psychiatric symptoms. Such opposition has been most vigorously expressed in the USA, where in some states these operations are forbidden by law. Peter Breggin, a psychiatrist in Washington, has claimed that there is no scientific justification for the operation and that the price paid in terms of blunted emotions and other personality changes is too high. Furthermore he has argued that psychosurgery could be used as a means for controlling antisocial behaviour and the activities of political dissidents. While there may be too few skilled in stereotactic surgery to permit its extensive use for political and social reasons, in India and Japan operations on the amygdaloid nucleus of the brain have been performed to control 'hyperactivity' in children. Although there is no doubt that outbursts of unbridled violence can be caused by diseases of the limbic brain, there is very little evidence that psychosurgery has been systematically applied to control such symptoms in the UK. And at present the requirements of Section 57 of the Mental Health Act of 1983 would almost certainly prevent any form of brain surgery being carried out expressly for the purpose of controlling antisocial, aggressive, or politically dissident behaviour.

Others have been concerned not only about the irreversible nature of the operation and permanent alteration of the personality, but also that in some way the patient's immortal soul would be damaged. Perhaps such considerations are best left to the theologians and the Almighty. A charitable view might be taken of man's efforts to relieve his fellow creatures of suffering. Be that as it may, given the safeguards that limit psychosurgery to the alleviation of distress, there seems to be a place for it as one form of effective treatment.

Although psychosurgery has been used for the treatment of deviant sexual behaviour, drug dependence and alcoholism such methods can only be condemned partly because they are unlikely to be effective but also because of uncertainty over whether such kinds of behaviour fall within the ambit of psychiatric illness. In any case they are unlikely to cause 'tortured self-concern' to those who are so afflicted although the disturbing effects of these behaviours upon relatives can not be denied. But psychosurgery to allay the anxieties of relatives has not yet achieved whole-hearted support even from its most enthusiastic practitioners.

See BRAIN MANIPULATION, ETHICS OF.          F. A. W.

Clare, A. (1976). Psychosurgery. In *Psychiatry in Dissent*. London.

Smith, S. J. and Kiloh, L.G. (1977). *Psychosurgery and Society*. Oxford.

Tooth, G. C. and Newton, M. P. (1961). *Leucotomy in England and Wales, 1942–1954*. London.

**PSYCHOTHERAPY, ASSESSMENT OF. What happens to untreated patients?** It must surely always have been true that a proportion of neurotic difficulties eased, or resolved, or were adapted to, in relation to the happenings of everyday life. Paradoxically, an issue only arose because, following Sigmund *Freud, a group of persons claimed special expertise in the curative role and this expertise tended to be somewhat uncritically accepted, especially in the USA. However, it was the English psychologist H. J. Eysenck who in 1952 turned the issue into a challenge.

Eysenck suggested that psychoneurotic difficulties tended to resolve 'spontaneously', i.e. regardless of treatment. Backed by an analysis of data such as the discharge rates of neurotics from mental hospitals and the outcome of insurance claims for psychological disability, he suggested that approximately two-thirds of neurotics recovered without treatment. Both his statistics and his basic analysis of data were challenged. An influential paper (Bergin and Lambert, 1978) suggested that, while spontaneous recovery certainly takes place, the likely figure was nearer 46 per cent. The exact figure is intrinsically unknowable because it depends on the type of patients considered, the disorders from which they suffer, the length of follow-up, the criteria of recovery used, and the objectivity of their assessment. Considering only severe hospitalized neurosis, for instance, Simms (1978) made a careful twelve-year follow-up of 146 neurotic former in-patients and compared their symptomatic and social status (work, marital, sexual) with a matched control group of patients operated upon for varicose veins. A satisfactory outcome was achieved by only 42 per cent of the neurotics compared to 90 per cent of the surgical group. Thus the figure for neurotics is not dissimilar to that of Bergin. Malan et al. (1975) developed this trend further, being concerned to assess in detail the *quality* of recovery of untreated patients. Forty-five untreated neurotic patients were followed up and carefully assessed symptomatically and psychodynamically. Fifty-one per cent were judged improved symptomatically and 24 per cent showed at least partial psychodynamic improvement.

It seems probable, therefore, that one-third to one-half of neurotic patients who have no systematic psychotherapy improve symptomatically. A smaller percentage, perhaps one-quarter, show constructive personality changes. In any case, the outcome of this debate has been wholly constructive. Psychotherapists of all allegiances now tend to look more critically at their therapeutic results. In particular, from a research point of view, the necessity of including adequate control groups, either untreated or treated by another type of therapy, is accepted.

**The assessment of psychotherapy.** Psychotherapy and psychotherapists faced up to, and recovered from, the crisis of identity induced by Eysenck's challenge. Comprehensive examination of available objective data by Bergin (1971), Malan (1973), and Luborsky et al. (1975) suggests that the results of psychotherapy, even if not as outstanding as enthusiasts would hope, demonstrate that it is effective and has a valued place among psychiatric treatments. It is also now clear how complex and difficult is the assessment of psychotherapeutic outcome.

Bergin contrasted the spontaneous remission rate of 30 per cent with 65 per cent for all forms of psychotherapy other than psychoanalysis and with the 83 per cent which is the overall rate for psychoanalysis. But these were, admittedly, rough figures. Others attempted the double task of assessing outcome studies for the adequacy of their design, and noting the therapeutic results, particularly from controlled trials. Malan, discussing these reviews of control studies, concluded that the evidence for the effectiveness of psychotherapy was relatively strong, especially for *psychosomatic conditions. However, for the neuroses and personality disorders—for which this form of therapy was developed—the evidence was weak. His own careful studies at the Tavistock Clinic in London over a period of many years, and repeated on two groups of patients, established the effectiveness of brief psychodynamic psychotherapy. He also made explicit a number of the criteria for selection of patients, as well as points of therapeutic technique.

Luborsky et al. critically reviewed comparative studies of psychotherapy. When comparisons were made between different psychotherapies, most studies failed to show significant differences in the proportion of patients who improved. However, controlled comparative studies indicate that a high percentage of patients who go through any of the psychotherapies do gain from them. From both individual and group psychotherapy, about 80 per cent of the studies show positive results. In addition, combined treatments (for psychosomatic conditions such as peptic ulcer or asthma) often did better than single treatments—a further plea for eclecticism rather than rigid ideology in psychotherapeutic practice. Luborsky et al. emphasized, as Frank et al. (1978) had for many years, the components common to psychotherapies, especially the helping relationship with the therapist. Luborsky et al. also stressed that the quality of outcome from therapy to therapy is important, as well as the amount of improvement.

Again, this is an area for further careful consideration in the future.

It seems clear that research into psychotherapy needs to become more analytic, and must try to assess the multiple and interacting factors involved, such as the therapist, the patient, their relationship, the social situation, the type of treatment, the type of disorder, and the experience of the therapist.

A study by Sloane et al. marks a significant advance. Ninety-four persons suffering from moderately severe neuroses and personality disorders were carefully assessed clinically, using structured rating scales, and also on psychological tests. A close friend or relative was also interviewed, for an outside informant's view. Patients were randomly assigned to a waiting list or to one of three experienced behaviour therapists (see BEHAVIOUR THERAPY) or analytically oriented psychotherapists. The controls were promised therapy in four months and were kept in touch. Patients were treated for four months (an average of fourteen sessions) and then re-interviewed and tested. Two measures of psychological change were used, one aimed at symptom assessment and the other at work and social adjustment. The assessors who had originally seen the patients re-assessed them, and were 'blind' as to which treatment had been used. Informants were also interviewed, and re-assessed the patients. Further follow-up was done one and two years after the original assessment. Major trends were: symptomatic improvement in the control group, and the two experimental groups at four months showed the treatment groups to be significantly more improved; but there was no difference between psychotherapy and behaviour therapy. On work and social adjustment, there was no significant difference in amount of improvement between the three groups. Assessment of overall improvement showed 93 per cent of the behaviour therapy group, compared to 77 per cent of the waiting list, or psychotherapy groups, improved or recovered. After one year, improvements were maintained or continued in most patients. Sixty-one patients were seen at the two-year follow-up; the great majority in all groups increased or maintained symptomatic improvement and personality adjustment. Special interest attached to the control group which had contact and interest maintained but no formal therapy. Both of the formal therapies were, however, more effective than this minimal therapy.

The conclusion of this study was that psychotherapy, in general, works, and its effects are not entirely due to non-specific effects such as arousal of hope nor to spontaneous recovery. The general effectiveness of psychotherapy has been confirmed by a new statistical research technique, meta-analysis, in which the outcome from active psychotherapy is compared to the variation in a control treatment (Shapiro and Shapiro, 1982).

**Are some patients made worse by treatment?**
When critical attention first began to be paid to
outcome studies, especially to those which
reported no difference in average outcome
between patients and waiting-list controls, it was
noted that there was significantly greater variation
of outcome among treated patients. It became
apparent that some patients were actually being
made worse by psychotherapy.

Any practising psychotherapist must recognize
the truth of this observation—we do make some
patients worse. A systematic attempt was made,
therefore, to note the incidence of deterioration
effects and also possible causes. Strupp *et al.* (1978)
systematically reviewed the problem of negative
effects. The best quantitative estimate of deterioration effects, both from dynamic and from
behavioural psychotherapy, is 3–6 per cent. Possible sources of these negative effects include:
poor preliminary assessment; personality factors
in the patient, the therapist, or their interaction;
inadequate training of therapists, leading to clumsy
or rigid therapeutic techniques; misguided or
erroneous choice of therapy or of treatment goals.
This is an area of current interest and importance:
further investigation is necessary.         S. CR.

Bergin, A. E. and Lambert, M. J. (1978). The evaluation
of therapeutic outcome. In Bergin, A. E. and Garfield,
S. L. (eds.), *Handbook of Psychotherapy and
Behaviour Change*. New York and London.

Eysenck, H. J. (1952). The effects of psychotherapy: an
evaluation. *Journal of Consulting Psychology*, **16**,
319–24.

Frank, J. D., Hoehn-Saric, R., Imber, S. D., Liberman,
B. L., and Stone, A. R. (1978). *Effective Ingredients of
Successful Psychotherapy*. New York.

Luborsky, L., Singer, L., and Luborsky, L. (1975). Comparative studies of psychotherapies. *Archives of
General Psychiatry*, **32**, 995–1,008.

Malan, D. (1973). The outcome problem in psychotherapy research. *Archives of General Psychiatry*, **29**,
719–29.

Malan, D., Heath, E. S., Bacal, H. A., and Balfour,
F. H. G. (1975). Psychodynamic changes in untreated
neurotic patients. *Archives of General Psychiatry*, **32**,
110–26.

Shapiro, D. A. and Shapiro, D. (1982). Meta-analysis of
Comparative Therapy Outcome Studies: a Replication
and Refinement. *Psychology Bulletin*, **92**, 581–604.

Simms, A. C. P. (1978). Prognosis in severe neurosis.
*Current Themes in Psychiatry*, **1**.

Strupp, H. H., Hadley, S. W., and Gomes-Schwartz, B.
(1978). *Psychotherapy for Better or Worse: the problem
of negative effects*. New York.

**PULFRICH'S PENDULUM.** This famous stereo-
phenomenon, first described by Carl Pulfrich
(1858–1927), is easily observed, by those with normal binocular vision, with the help of a pair of sun-
glasses and a length of string with a weight such as a
teacup attached to one end. The string and weight
are used to make a pendulum attached to a convenient point on the ceiling, and oscillating slowly
from side to side. If the pendulum is viewed with
the sun-glasses covering one eye, the other eye
remaining open, it will appear to move through an

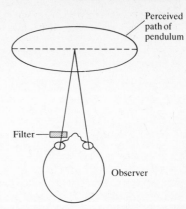

**Fig. 1.** A plan view of an observer looking at a horizontally
oscillated pendulum, the actual path of which is shown by
the dotted line. When the observer's left eye is covered by
a sun-glass filter, the pendulum appears to move in depth
along the trajectory represented by the solid line. The
direction of movement is opposite if the right eye is
covered.

elliptical path in depth (Fig. 1). The direction of
movement in depth is clockwise (as if viewed from
above) when the sun-glass filter is covering the left
eye, and counter-clockwise if the dark glass covers
the right eye. The function of the sun-glass is
simply to reduce the amount of light reaching the
eye, and any light-attenuating filter will serve just
as well. The depth illusion applies not just to a
pendulum but to any object in horizontal movement with respect to the eyes. In an ordinary
television picture, for example, objects moving
from left to right will appear displaced in front of
the screen if the right eye is covered by a filter.

In his 1922 paper Pulfrich (who was blind in
his left eye and never saw the phenomenon himself) describes previous observations of the effect
by astronomers using stereo-comparators. He
attributes to Fertsch, an optical engineer with the
Zeiss company in Jena, the now generally accepted
'delay line' explanation. Fertsch proposed that the
filter causes a delay in the transmission of signals
from the retina to the brain. Since the target is
moving, a temporal delay corresponds to a spatial
displacement: the covered eye is seeing the target
with a delay in time, and thus at a spatially lagging
point on its trajectory. The lag produces a stereoscopic disparity, and therefore a shift in depth
(Fig. 2). Fertsch's hypothesis is now well established
by direct electrical recording of the latency of the
retinal response to light, and the geometrical
reasoning can be verified by using a haploscopic
display in which one eye's target is subjected to an
actual delay. The cause of the delay is that the filter
induces the covered eye to adapt to a reduced
general level of illumination, which is a visual
mechanism (like increasing photographic exposure
time) for gaining sensitivity in dim light. The converse effect can be achieved by shining a bright pen
torch into the corner of one eye: this eye now

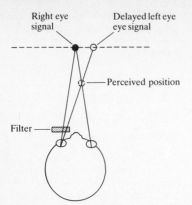

Right eye signal    Delayed left eye eye signal

— Perceived position

Filter —

**Fig. 2.** Fertsch's 'delay line' explanation of Pulfrich's effect. The signals from the covered eye are effectively delayed so that the eye signals an earlier point on the target's trajectory; the delay therefore produces a stereoscopic disparity, and the target is seen as shifted in depth.

adapts to a higher level of illumination and thus responds more quickly, with a consequent depth shift in the reverse direction to the normal Pulfrich effect (i.e. if the left eye illuminated depth shift is anti-clockwise).

Technical interest in the phenomenon was rekindled by the finding that Pulfrich's effect can be observed with stroboscopically lit targets, and even when viewing an 'electronic snowstorm' on a detuned television set. In the latter case the snowstorm appears to rotate horizontally in depth when one eye is filtered. Since there is no real motion in the display, the delay line explanation needs to be supplemented by spatio-temporal averaging of target position.

A clinical use of Pulfrich's phenomenon has several times been suggested, on the basis of the finding that it may arise spontaneously, without the use of a filter, as a result of demyelinating disease of the optic nerve.                                M. J. M.

Christianson, S. and Hofstetter, H. W. (1972). Some historical notes on Carl Pulfrich. *American Journal of Optometry*, **570**, 944–7.

Morgan, M. J. and Thompson, P. (1975). Apparent motion and the Pulfrich effect. *Perception*, **4**, 3–18.

Sachs, E. (1946). Abnormal delay of visual perception. *Archives of Neurology and Psychiatry*, **56**, 198–206.

Tyler, C. W. (1974). Stereopsis in dynamic visual noise. *Nature*, **250**, 781–2.

**PURPOSE.** We commonly explain what people (and perhaps animals) do by assuming they have some purpose in doing it, some idea in mind which guides their activity towards their goal in an intelligently flexible fashion.

We say, for instance: Why is Mary buying arsenic?—Maybe she intends to poison Martha, but more likely she needs it to get rid of the rats. Why did the chicken cross the road?—To get to the corn on the other side. What made Jill insult Joan?—I don't know, but she must have had some reason. As these examples suggest, we rarely use the word 'purpose' itself; perhaps this is why the Mock Turtle got the word wrong when assuring Alice that 'No wise fish would go anywhere without a porpoise. . . . Why, if a fish came to *me*, and told me he was going a journey, I should say "With what porpoise?" ' But we assume that we can explain or make sense of what people do by referring to their intentions, goals, aims, interests, ambitions, desires, wants, motives, needs—in a word, to their purposes.

Despite this universal acceptance of the concept of purpose in our everyday thinking about why people do what they do, it is not universally accepted by theoretical psychologists. On the contrary, throughout the history of psychology this concept has been, and remains, one of the most controversial of all. (It follows that the position argued in this article would not be endorsed by all current psychologists, although it is an increasingly accepted view.) People do not merely disagree about purpose, but get more than usually heated in discussing it, often ascribing gross irresponsibility of one sort or another to their opponents in debate.

Some psychologists refuse point-blank to admit the concept of purpose into their theories, regarding it as not merely unhelpful but positively mystifying. Others are content to use it as a convenient shorthand, but believe that purposive explanations of behaviour could in principle be replaced by complicated stimulus–response or neurophysiological explanations in which the concept of purpose would not appear. Yet others insist that psychology must give a central role to purpose, that action and experience cannot possibly be explained without it; usually, they add that what it is to be a *human* being cannot be understood without this notion, so that to reject it is to adopt an essentially dehumanizing image of mankind.

Theoretical resistance to purpose arises primarily from its close connection with the *mind–body problem. It is difficult to understand how purposes can function as guiding factors in behaviour—for how can an idea affect bodily action? (There is no help in identifying the purpose with the actual goal-state, rather than with the subject's idea of the goal; for the goal-state is always in the future until the action has been completed, and is often not achieved at all. How can a not-yet-existent state, which may in fact never exist, cause anything to happen here and now?) The *behaviourists, with the exception of *Tolman, rejected purposive explanation, because they avoided all reference to *consciousness, subjectivity, ideas, or mind. And neurophysiology, at least at first sight, seems to leave no place for purpose, since it deals with brain-cells and brain functions whose physical description does not involve reference to ideas.

However, with the work of Kenneth *Craik, neurophysiology gained the concept of a cerebral model, or inner representation of the world.

According to Craik, we possess physical mechanisms in the brain that function as inner models of the world—by which we perceive, think about, and act upon the environment. Explanations of psychological phenomena must refer to these models, since it is only via these internal representations that action and experience can take place. But inner models may sometimes be misleading: the fact that there are no unicorns does not prevent people from developing internal representations of such mythical beasts. Similarly, an inner model may represent a state of affairs that does not yet exist, or a plan of action that cannot be fully carried out; the person can nevertheless use this model to guide present behaviour in various ways. So there is no radical difficulty in understanding how it can be that a person acts with the purpose, or goal, of finding a unicorn—even though this purpose can never be achieved.

Cerebral models correspond to the *'schemas' described by the psychologist F. C. *Bartlett. They are essentially subjective, in that they constitute the psychological subject's view of the world—and of itself. This is why action and experience possess what *Brentano and *phenomenologists call *intentionality. Many psychologists and philosophers have claimed that intentionality could not possibly be explained in terms of a physical system, so that physiology is in principle incapable of helping us understand how psychological phenomena arise. In any case since very little is known about the detailed physiological basis of cerebral models, neurophysiologists cannot yet offer precise explanations of specific psychological characteristics.

But the concept of internal representation has entered *artificial intelligence, the science of writing computer programs which enable computers to do the sort of things that are done by human minds. Programs using different inner models of cubes, for instance, recognize (and misrecognize) cubes in different ways—and on different occasions. (See PATTERN RECOGNITION.) Each program has its own view of the world; and its behaviour (saying that *this* is a cube whereas *that* isn't) can be fully understood and explained only by reference to its inner schemata or models. Even though electronic engineers know precisely how the underlying mechanism works, it is the representational functions of the program which explain the 'psychological' characteristics of the programmed computer. Whether or not every aspect of human psychology could in principle be simulated on a computer is irrelevant here. The important point is that even though the computer's 'physiology' is fully understood, its 'psychology' can be explained only in terms of its subjective (internal) models of the world.

By analogy, then, even if neurophysiologists knew everything there is to know about the brain, *psychological* explanations would still be required to understand psychological phenomena. So psychology is not reducible to physiology, if by that it is meant the claim that with sufficient physiological knowledge we could stop talking about purposes, ideas, beliefs, mistakes, and the like. (See REDUCTIONISM IN PSYCHOLOGY.) Psychology is reducible to physiology only in the quite different sense that psychological features like purposes are generated by cerebral mechanisms, rather than being mysteriously inexplicable features outside the scope of science. A faith in the second kind of reducibility need not entail a faith in the first kind. It follows that the concepts in terms of which we express everything specifically *human* about human beings would still be needed, even if we understood in detail how purposes are embodied in brain mechanisms.                    M. A. B.

Boden, M. A. (1972). *Purposive Explanation in Psychology*. Cambridge, Massachusetts.
Woodfield, A. (1976). *Teleology*. Cambridge, Cambridgeshire.

**PYTHAGORAS** (*c.*570–*c.*500 BC). Born in Samos, he founded a school at Croton in Magna Graecia, which combined asceticism, strict traditional rules of conduct and taboos (such as smoothing out the imprint of the body upon leaving the bed, and not eating beans), and an emphasis on reason and mathematics. Although *Plato wrote a book on Pythagoras (lost in antiquity), all that has come down to us are a few doctrines, including that of the transmigration of souls (see METEMPSYCHOSIS); a list of ethical rules; and some mathematics, including his famous theorem (which has Babylonian origins), and especially number theory, which, so far as is known, he founded. See also PRE-SOCRATIC PHILOSOPHERS.

# Q

**QUALIA.** This Latin plural term (of which the singular is *quale*) has come into philosophical use by analogy with the term *quanta* (singular *quantum*). A *quantum* is an amount: to specify a *quantum* involves reference to an amount of energy, mass, momentum, or whatever. The notion of a *quale*, by contrast, is, as the name implies, a qualitative rather than a quantitative one. To specify a *quale* is to say what something is *like*; and an irreducible reference to the phenomenological character of our experience, to the way in which things appear to the conscious subject, may be involved here. Examples of *qualia* are the smell of freshly ground coffee or the taste of pineapple; such experiences have a distinctive phenomenological character which we have all experienced but which, it seems, is very difficult to describe. An investigation of the nature, phenomenology, and possible causation of *qualia* has become an important concern of recent philosophy of mind. According to reductionists, *qualia* can be fully explained in terms of the neurophysiological events in the brain and its interactions with the environment. According to the view known as epiphenomenalism, *qualia* are causally dependent, or 'supervenient', on brain events, but cannot straightforwardly be identified with such events. According to dualism, *qualia* are independent of physics, and belong in the essentially autonomous, non-physical realm of the mind. See further under QUALITIES; and MIND–BODY PROBLEM: PHILOSOPHICAL THEORIES.                                J. G. C.

**QUALITIES.** The universe, as described by modern science, is conceived largely in quantitative terms. Mass, energy, velocity, length, breadth, and height are all expressible as mathematical quantities or amounts—as answers to the question *Quantum*? or 'How much?' But it is striking that most of the ordinary ways in which we describe our environment are not quantitative but qualitative: the descriptions involved answer the question *Quale*?, 'What is it like?' Such \*qualia, or qualities, include redness, softness, sweetness, rankness, shrillness (of the five types of so-called 'sensible qualities' of sight, touch, taste, smell, and hearing, respectively). There is a long-standing philosophical debate about whether such qualities really inhere in objects or whether they are simply subjective effects in the mind of the observer. John \*Locke systematized (though he did not invent) a distinction between primary and secondary qualities. Primary qualities (roughly corresponding to the scientifically measurable *quanta* mentioned above) include shape, magnitude, and number, and are supposed to inhere in objects, so that our ideas of size, etc., actually resemble genuine features of the objects in question. But secondary qualities, such as redness, sweetness, etc., are rather different: our ideas of them do not, according to Locke, directly resemble anything in the object themselves, but are merely the result of the way objects affect our senses by means of their primary qualities.

Some philosophers have been suspicious of the primary/secondary distinction, pointing out that our attributions of colour, no less than our attributions of size, are a function of perfectly straightforward and objective rules of language, so that it is as correct to say that the sun is 'really' yellow as it is to say that it is 'really' spherical. But there remains a special subjective or phenomenological character to our sensation of qualities like yellowness which seems to depend in part on the particular sensory apparatus with which our species is equipped—and it is not the same for all individuals. Thus it is possible to imagine that aliens equipped with different kinds of organs would perceive light of a certain wavelength in radically different ways from us, to the point where the human notion of 'yellowness' would be inaccessible to them. This line of thought lends support to the idea that there is indeed something 'subjective' about sensory qualities such as redness and sweetness; the notions of squareness or sphericity, by contrast, do not seem similarly tied to the particular sensory 'mode' in terms of which they are experienced.

Apart from questions of subjectivity, there is a problem about whether *qualia* such as redness or sweetness can usefully figure in scientific explanations. Robert Boyle, writing in the 1650s, pointed out that if you want to know why snow dazzles the eyes it is no help to be told that it has the 'quality of whiteness'. Similar charges of explanatory vacuity were levelled against the scholastic theory that bodies fall because of an inherent quality of *gravitas* or heaviness. It was for this kind of reason that we find \*Descartes insisting that scientific explanations should invoke 'nothing apart from that which the geometricians call quantity, and take as the object of their demonstrations, i.e. that to which every kind of division, shape and motion is applicable' (*Principles of Philosophy*, 1644). Nevertheless, while this quantitative approach has undoubtedly been fruitful for physics, its application to psychology is more controversial. Sensible qualities are, after all, an inescapable part of the psychological landscape; any understanding of our mental life must, it seems, include some account of *what it is like* for us to see colours, smell smells, and so on.                                                    J. G. C.

**QUANTIFYING JUDGEMENTS.** Human judgement is so fallible that, in assessing magnitudes, objective physical measures need to be used wherever they are available. There are cases, however, where physical measures are not available: some magnitudes lack them. The loudness of noises, for example, cannot be measured directly in physical units because loudness is a subjective quantity which depends on the ear and the brain. A noise is likely to sound less loud to a partially deaf person than to a person with normal hearing. Similarly, the likeableness of people cannot be measured directly. In these and comparable cases it is necessary to resort to quantitative subjective judgements.

**Theoretical issues.** *Two kinds of stimulus magnitude.* It is important to distinguish between stimulus magnitudes with familiar physical units and those without (Poulton, 1981). Lengths, weights, and durations can be measured in physical units learned at school. In judging differences in magnitude or ratios between different magnitudes measured in familiar units, observers have merely to perform the appropriate arithmetical operations. Such judged differences and ratios are thus related by the rules of arithmetic, and the average of the findings of, say, several people in a group will be a reasonably accurate one.

Here we will consider only stimulus magnitudes which observers are unable to measure in familiar physical units and for which they have to develop and use their own, subjective units. Such units of discriminability do not have, at the sensory threshold, an obvious zero from which absolute magnitudes can be judged; and therefore they cannot be used to judge ratios of magnitude. Even so, they can be used to judge differences between magnitudes, because where two magnitudes are the same size the difference between them is zero.

*Two kinds of quantitative judgement.* There are two ways of quantifying subjective judgements. One method uses a restricted range of responses with specified upper and lower limits: category ratings are the most frequently used examples. In contrast, the other method uses direct numerical magnitude judgements, which can provide the judge with a potentially infinite range of numbers.

Category ratings characteristically give a logarithmic relation between stimulus magnitude and subjective magnitude:

$$R = k + n \log S \qquad (1)$$

where $R$ is the response, $S$ is the stimulus, and $k$ and $n$ are constants. By contrast, direct numerical magnitude judgements characteristically give a loglog relation (Stevens, 1975):

$$\log R = \log k + n \log S \qquad (2)$$

Taking antilogs, Equation (2) becomes a power function:

$$R = kS^n$$

where $n$ is the exponent.

S. S. *Stevens (1906–73) was the main protagonist of direct numerical magnitude judgements. Most technologists or others who need to quantify subjective judgements use category ratings, on the other hand, because their restricted range makes judging easier and provides less variable averages.

*Logarithmic response bias.* There has been controversy over whether Equation (1) or Equation (2) better represents the observers' perceptions of magnitude. It is now tacitly accepted that Equation (1) is correct. Stevens's Equation (2) incorporates a logarithmic response bias which occurs when observers use for responses a range of numbers containing a change in the number of allowed digits. After responding with numbers up to 10, observers have two alternative ways of proceeding. They can continue 11, 12, 13, 14 . . ., using numbers linearly. Or they can go more logarithmic and continue 20, 30, 40 . . . . The average of a group of observers is likely to be a compromise between a pure linear and a pure logarithmic use of numbers, but closer to logarithmic.

Once Stevens had obtained his loglog relation, he instructed his student observers to use for responses a scale of numbers calibrated in ratios, like a slide rule. But this ensures that a loglog relation will be found, because it changes the $R$ on the left side of Equation (1) to the log $R$ on the left side of Equation (2).

There are two main lines of evidence that support the linear relation of Equation (1). In providing the first, Poulton (1986) asked separate groups of uninitiated observers to judge the difference between the loudnesses of two noises. The less intense noise he called 1·0. The observers were told to respond with a higher number that represented the loudness of the more intense noise. When the medians of the very first judgements were numbers less than 10, they were linear in decibels.

The medians of the very first judgements showed a logarithmic response bias only when they were greater than 10, and so median responses were taken from a range of responses that contained both single-digit and two-digit numbers. A logarithmic response bias was found, also, when observers made a series of judgements of different loudnesses; but this was because the logarithmic response bias from using a range of responses which contained both one-digit and two-digit numbers transferred to the responses using only single digits.

*Judged differences and ratios of magnitude have the same underlying relation.* The second main line of evidence comes from several comparable investigations using different stimulus dimensions, which are summarized by Birnbaum (1980). In an investigation of the likeableness of people, described by single adjectives, Hagerty and Birnbaum (1978) compared judgements of differences, $(A-B)$, with judgements of ratios, $A/B$. The median difference judgements (of their 23 undergraduates) showed a linear relation to the stimulus magnitudes, following Equation (1). The median ratio judgements showed a logarithmic relation, following Equation (2).

Yet the rank orders of the sizes of the median difference judgements can be compared with the rank order of the sizes of the median ratio judgements, using Kruskal and Carmone's computer program Monanova. This program maximizes the fit of all the rank orders to the linear model, without changing the orders. When this is done, the two rank orders are found to fit almost exactly the same subtractive model. This should not happen if the difference and ratio judgements represent genuine differences in perception because, for example, $(7-3)$ is greater than $(4-1)$, yet $7/3$ is less than $4/1$. Clearly the subjects' difference and ratio judgements are simply two ways of describing the same perceptual relation between the stimuli of a pair.

*Judged ratios of magnitude are simply judged differences with a logarithmic response bias.* In the Hagerty and Birnbaum investigation, the relation perceived and judged must be a difference, not a ratio, because there are no familiar physical units of likeableness. The experimental subjects could use only their own improvised subjective units of discriminability. But these have no zero corresponding to a sensory threshold, which would have enabled ratios to be perceived and judged. When they were instructed to judge ratios, they were given a scale described in ratios; but it turned out that they could not perceive and judge the ratios. However, they could use their subjective units of discriminability to judge the differences, because differences become zero when the two members are equal. Thus, differences were judged, but by using a scale of ratios.

In confirmation of this, Hagerty and Birnbaum presented adjectives representing pairs of people. The undergraduates were instructed to judge the ratios of the two differences in likeableness, $(A-B)/C-D$. Both differences having obvious zeros, the undergraduates could judge their ratio. For the differences $(A-B)$ in the numerator, the median judgements changed from positive to negative as $A$ changed from being more likeable than $B$ to being less likeable than $B$. This indicates that the median of the subjects perceived the difference in likeableness between $A$ and $B$. For the ratios, reducing the size of the difference $(C-D)$ in the denominator magnifies the median differences $(A-B)$ in the numerator. This indicates that the median of the subjects judged the ratio of the perceived differences.

Since the ratios of the differences in likeableness bear the appropriate arithmetic relation to the magnitudes of the differences, the Monanova program cannot fit a simple model to all the medians taken together. To produce a simple acceptable linear fit, the ratios have to be excluded. The medians for each size of difference in the denominator have to be fitted separately. For the same reason, when all the medians are taken together, a nonmetric scaling program cannot fit a simple multiplicative relation either.

The important point is that it is the *differences* in likeableness that are perceived and their *ratios* that are judged, not vice versa. There is no corresponding condition where ratios are perceived and their differences are judged. In a crucial control condition, the undergraduates were instructed to judge the differences of the ratios, $A/B - C/D$, and their median judgements showed a linear relation to the stimulus magnitudes. When subjected to the Monanova program, these median judgements fit almost exactly the same subtractive model as do the median judgements of a *differences* of *differences* condition $(A-B) - (C-D)$. Thus, the subjects must have judged the differences of the differences, not the differences of the *ratios* as they were instructed to do.

*Theoretical conclusions.* The general rule is that in dealing with stimulus magnitudes that do not have familiar physical units, people perceive only differences in magnitude. People can judge the ratios of the perceived *differences*, because they can use their improvised units of discriminability. But they cannot perceive the *ratios* of the magnitudes directly, because this requires an obvious zero at the sensory threshold, which units of discriminability do not have.

By contrast, in dealing with stimulus magnitudes that do have familiar physical units, observers can calculate both differences and ratios. The differences and ratios are related by the rules of arithmetic. Thus it is not possible to tell whether the observers actually perceive the differences and ratios, or simply calculate them. Presumably they perceive differences as they do in dealing with stimulus magnitudes that do not have familiar physical units. But they may or may not perceive ratios as well.

**Avoiding biases.** Biases found in quantifying judgements are illustrated in Fig. 1. The biases are considerably larger when stimulus magnitudes cannot be judged directly in familiar physical units. The centring bias, a, and the stimulus spacing and stimulus frequency biases, e, are most often recognized in judgements using category ratings. The logarithmic response bias, f, and the stimulus and response range equalizing bias, b, occur most frequently in direct numerical magnitude judgements (see below). The contraction bias, c, and transfer bias (not shown) occur with all kinds of quantitative judgements. The local contraction bias, d, is seldom reported.

*Centring bias or adaptation level in rating.* In rating, people tend to use a symmetric distribution

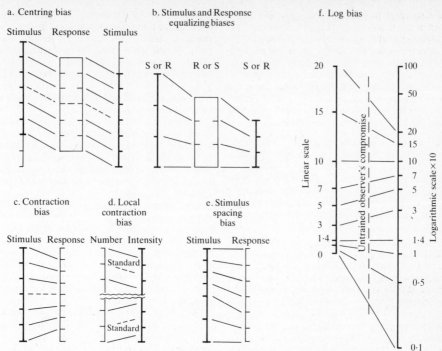

**Fig. 1.** Biases in quantitative judgements. S = stimulus. R = response. (Poulton, 1979.)

of responses. This centres their range of response ratings on the mid point of the range of stimuli, as is illustrated in Fig. 1a. Thus, in judging a series of road vehicle or aircraft noises, the just acceptable noise level in the centre of the rating scale is found to lie close to the middle of the range of noises—at whatever intensity level that happens to be. This means that in a quiet residential area the loudest noises will continue to be judged too loud, however much they are reduced in intensity.

In designing an investigation, this bias is avoided by presenting a range of stimuli with an unbiased mid point which corresponds to the centre of the rating scale. The unbiased mid point can be determined by presenting separate groups of people with ranges of stimuli that bias the centre of the rating scale in one direction. Other groups of people are presented with ranges which bias the centre of the rating scale in the opposite direction. The stimulus range with the unbiased mid point can then be determined, by interpolation.

The centring bias affects most kinds of judgement. In judging how hard up they are, people are likely to judge their present income against what they are used to spending, or what their neighbours spend. The relatively unstressful events in a relaxed period of people's lives are likely to appear at the time almost as stressful to them as the most stressful events in a stressful period of their lives.

*Stimulus spacing and stimulus frequency biases.* The stimulus spacing and stimulus frequency biases are produced by using all parts of the response scale about equally often. In the stimulus spacing bias, people judge a set of stimuli to be more equally spaced subjectively than they really are, as is illustrated in Fig. 1e. The stimulus frequency bias can be treated as a special case of the stimulus spacing bias. The observers behave as if all the stimuli were equally probable. When one stimulus is presented more frequently than the others, the observers treat the more frequent stimuli as if they had almost, though not exactly, the same magnitude. Thus three identical stimuli one quarter of the way from the top of the stimulus range are treated as three closely spaced stimuli of slightly different size, as is illustrated on the left of Fig. 1e. This bias increases the amount of the observers' response range that is allocated to the identical stimuli. In designing an investigation, the *stimulus spacing* bias is avoided by spacing the stimuli at subjectively equal intervals. The *stimulus frequency* bias is avoided by presenting all the stimuli equally often.

The stimulus spacing bias may influence the choice of the candidate for a job. There may be a few very good candidates who are all close together in order of merit, like the stimuli at the top on the left of Fig. 1e. Yet, owing to the stimulus spacing bias, all the candidates are judged to be about equally spaced. As a result, the candidate who is only marginally the best may be selected, whereas if all the very good candidates were known to be almost equally good, the choice between them could be made in part on other criteria that are important.

The stimulus frequency bias may influence the interpretation of a situation or object represented as a branching tree, which is sometimes used to help make decisions, or to find faults in equipment. People assume that all the branches represent equal frequencies or probabilities and so are equally important, whereas some branches may be much more important than others.

*Logarithmic response bias.* The logarithmic response bias is the cause of the theoretical controversy discussed above. The bias is avoided by taking two precautions: (i) Do not provide for responses a range of numbers which includes a change in the number of digits; (ii) Do not instruct the judges to use a scale of numbers calibrated in ratios.

*Stimulus and response range equalizing bias.* When judged magnitudes are plotted on the ordinate of a graph against physical magnitudes on the abscissa, smaller stimulus ranges give steeper slopes. People start their judgements with what they believe to be a sensible range of responses. They distribute these responses over the range of stimuli presented to them. With a smaller range of stimuli, the responses are spaced more closely, as is illustrated on the right of Fig. 1b. Thus the slope is steeper. This bias is usually unavoidable.

*Contraction bias.* People underestimate large sizes and differences, and they overestimate small sizes and differences. Once they know the range of responses that is available, they select a response that lies too close to the middle of the range, as is illustrated in Fig. 1c. The figure shows that the range of responses is contracted when compared with the range of stimuli. Hence the name 'contraction bias'. Stevens (1975) calls it the regression effect.

The contraction bias can be counterbalanced by reversing stimuli and responses. The dimension previously used for the stimuli is now used for the responses, and so has the contracted range. Averaging the results of the two investigations should counterbalance the contractions.

The contraction bias occurs in every kind of judgement. In giving people references, exceptional people do not usually receive as good references as they should do. Dreadful people do not usually receive as bad references as they should do. At universities, the bias is likely to result in too many students being awarded second or third class degrees, while too few students are awarded first classes or failed. Small risks are usually overestimated, whereas large risks are underestimated. When respondents specify the range of confidence within which a statement is judged to lie, the extent of the range is likely to be underestimated at both ends, as in Fig. 1c.

*Transfer bias*: the influence of a condition on the performance of subsequent conditions. Transfer biases are likely to occur in any investigation where people perform more than one condition, especially if they are free to choose their strategies. Transfer biases are particularly common and powerful when uninitiated people have to judge several magnitudes in turn. Once a person uses a particular range of numbers in direct magnitude estimation, he or she is likely to use a similar range in subsequent investigations. If the instructions mention a range of possible numbers or ratios, they are likely to influence the numerical magnitude judgements of uninitiated people. Transfer bias occurs both between successive judgements within an investigation and between successive investigations.

Investigators who use balanced Latin square designs assume that transfer is symmetric; but it may be asymmetric. The effect of performing Condition *A* on the subsequent performance of Condition *B* may be different from the effect of performing Condition *B* on Condition *A*. If so, comparing the average of the two *A* conditions with the average of the two *B* conditions does not remove the transfer bias.

Worse still, adding conditions *C* and *D* to the Latin square may reverse the differences found between conditions *A* and *B*. This happens when conditions *C* and *D* require a new strategy. The strategy may transfer to conditions *A* and *B*, and change the way in which the observers approach the task (Poulton, 1982). Transfer bias can be avoided for certain only by using separate groups of uninitiated people for each investigation or judgement.                                        E. C. P.

Birnbaum, M. H. (1980). Comparison of two theories of 'ratio' and 'difference' judgments. *Journal of Experimental Psychology: General*, **109**, 304–19.

Hagerty, M. and Birnbaum, M. H. (1978). Nonmetric tests of ratio vs. subtractive theories of stimulus comparisons. *Perception and Psychophysics*, **24**, 121–9.

Poulton, E. C. (1979). Models for biases in judging sensory magnitude. *Psychological Bulletin*, **86**, 777–803.

Poulton, E. C. (1981). Schooling and the new psychophysics. *Behavioral and Brain Sciences*, **4**, 201–3.

Poulton, E. C. (1982). Influential companions: effects of one strategy on another in the within-subjects designs of cognitive psychology. *Psychological Bulletin*, **91**, 673–90.

Poulton, E. C. (1986). Why unbiased numerical magnitude judgments of the loudness of noise are linear in decibels: a rejoinder to the Teghtsoonians. *Perception and Psychophysics*, **39**.

Poulton, E. C. (in preparation). Bias in quantifying judgments.

Stevens, S. S. (1975). *Psychophysics: introduction to its perceptual, neural, and social prospects*. New York.

**QUETELET, LAMBERT ADOLPHE JACQUES** (1796–1874). Belgian statistician and astronomer, born at Ghent. He was a pioneer in developing and applying statistics to social and human characteristics, especially in relation to the average man. His works include *Sur l'homme* (1835) and *L'Anthropometrie* (1871).

# R

**RAMON Y CAJAL,** SANTIAGO (1852–1934). Spanish neuroanatomist, born at Petilla, Navarra, in the Pyrenees. He studied medicine, and after army service in Cuba he returned to Spain to teach, becoming professor of anatomy at Valencia (1883), of histology at Barcelona (1887), and of histology and pathological anatomy at Madrid (1892–1922). Cajal improved Camillo *Golgi's method for staining nervous tissue with silver and undertook a systematic study of the microscopic structure of the brain. He established that adjacent nerve-cells did not join each other however close their fibres might be and suggested that nerve impulses passed from the axon of one neurone to the dendrite of the next, and not in the opposite direction (see BRAIN DEVELOPMENT; NERVOUS SYSTEM). In 1906 he shared a Nobel prize with Golgi for their work on the structure of nervous tissue.

**RAPID EYE MOVEMENT (REM).** See DREAMING.

**REACTION TIMES.** Like all other animals, humans can only *experience* the immediate past. Many scores of milliseconds must pass before any change in the world can be registered by a sense organ or interpreted by a brain. This perpetual lag behind the world, measured from the moments at which changes actually occur and the moments at which we can apprehend them, has become known as 'reaction time'.

Philosophies that attributed human consciousness to incorporeal entities whose rates of apprehension were infinitely fast ('the speed of thought') delayed recognition of this simple fact until very late in human history. In 1799, Nevil Maskelyne, then British Astronomer Royal, sacked his assistant Kinnebrooke because their timings of stellar transits always disagreed. Friedrich Bessel (1784–1846), a more considering scientist, noted that discrepancies between measurements made by individual astronomers were widespread and substantial. For the first time someone saw the necessity of calibrating human observers, as well as the equipment that they used. Each astronomer, thenceforth, determined his personal, characteristic lag and used it as a corrective constant in his work.

By 1858 *Helmholtz had recognized a further implication of this lag, seeing that one factor limiting human reaction time must be the speed with which electrical impulses travel along nerve fibres. To measure this speed he asked a human observer to bite on a contact switch as soon as he felt an electric shock, which might be delivered either to his foot or to his face. Responses to foot shocks were slower. Assuming that this difference occurred because impulses from the foot have further to travel before they reach the brain, Helmholtz measured the difference to obtain the first estimate for the velocity of transmission of nerve impulses. The phrase 'swift as thought' took on a potentially exact, if rather humble, value.

Helmholtz's brilliant insight, that measurements of human reaction times may be used to make deductions about the nature of otherwise unobservable neural processes, provided impetus for a next step. In 1868, F. C. Donders, a Dutch ophthalmologist, reasoned that a human must recognize a new stimulus before he can begin to organize a response to it. As we shall see, this is not quite true. However, Donders argued that since a stimulus must be recognized before a response to it can be chosen and executed, lags for these two processes must seem to give overall observed reaction times. By appropriate techniques reaction times may therefore be decomposed to give independent estimates for times taken to recognize signals and for times required to choose responses to them.

To obtain such estimates Donders required his observers to carry out each of three different tasks. In the '*a*' task (simple reaction time task) they always had to make the same response as fast as possible every time a single signal occurred. In the '*b*' task (choice reaction task) any one of five different signals might occur in unpredictable order and the observer made a different response to each. In the '*c*' task (Go/No Go task) any one of the same five stimuli might occur, unpredictably, but the observer responded only to occurrences of one of them and ignored the others. Donders argued that differences in observed reaction times '*c*'–'*a*' would provide estimates of how much longer a person needed in order to distinguish among five different signals than to make a response without having to discriminate which signal had occurred. Similarly, the difference '*b*'–'*c*' would give an estimate of how long an observer needed to select among five different responses, rather than merely to always choose whether or not to make a particular response, after making the same discrimination. Donders's experiment gave him estimates for perceptual discrimination times (less than 50 milliseconds) which were far shorter than his estimates for response selection times (over 150 milliseconds), and he began to hope that his technique would allow independent estimates for other, more complex 'unobservable internal mental processes'.

Donders's results were reasonable in principle, but the logic of his experiment was flawed in two ways: first, in his '$c$' task his observer never had to discriminate each of five signals from all of four others, as in the '$b$' task. In the '$c$' task the observer merely had to discriminate one 'Go' signal from all of another set of four 'No Go' signals. There was thus no requirement to discriminate any 'No Go' signal from any other 'No Go' signal. Thus the '$b$' task involved both a more complex perceptual discrimination and a more complex response choice than the '$c$' task, and the '$b$'−'$c$' estimate for discrimination time confounded these factors.

A more interesting weakness of Donders's experiment was that, like all other successful animals, human beings overcome their temporal lag behind events in the external world by learning to predict what will happen next. When they can do this they can have reaction times of zero milliseconds, responding to events just as soon as they occur, or they can even take leaps into the future, gaining an edge over a rapidly changing environment, or over rapidly moving adversaries, by anticipating events which have not yet occurred. In Donders's '$a$' task his observer could set himself, in advance, to identify the same, recurrent, signal on every trial, and on every trial he could also safely prepare to make the same response to it. Thus the neural processes timed in the '$a$' task have much more to do with anticipation and expectancy than with the processes of discrimination and choice that underlie the '$b$' and '$c$' tasks, in which observers must always wait until after something happens before their sense organs and brains can begin to work out what has occurred.

It is now widely recognized that reaction-time measurements make little sense unless we bear in mind that, although all living things can *experience* only the past, animals like ourselves have gained our success in the world by continuously, and accurately, predicting the very immediate future. A good cricketer has to predict, before the ball leaves the bowler's hand, the precise point in space at which it will be intercepted by his bat. A squash player who could not anticipate would founder hopelessly behind the game. Reaction times do not provide us with measurements of the time necessary for sets of nerve impulses generated in the sense organs to activate those parts of the brain that, in turn, activate our muscles. They rather measure the duration of operation of processes of active, predictive control, by means of which we organize responses that anticipate, and pre-empt, very fast changes in the world.

This point was only very slowly recognized. In Leipzig, in 1879, *Wundt set up the first laboratory of experimental psychology. His research programme was largely concerned with criticisms and extensions of Donders's work. It is sad that his many years of heroically dull experimentation now merely provide a textbook moral that conscious introspection can tell us little about the nature of decisions that may take us less than a fifth of a second to make.

As is often the case in experimental psychology, unpretentious calibrational studies proved the most fruitful in the long run. In 1892, von Merkle showed that an observer's reaction times increase regularly with the number of signals among which he has to discriminate, and with the number of responses among which he must, consequently, choose. In 1931 Henmon showed that as pairs of signals become more similar to each other, people take longer to discriminate between them. Observations such as these are very simple, and unsurprising, but their consequences are not at all trivial. From experiments based on von Merkle's results, Hick (1952) and, separately, Henmon (1952) developed models for human reaction times that were the first, and the most influential, demonstrations that the new sciences of *cybernetics and information theory, which had been developed during the 1940s, have very fruitful applications as abstract descriptions of the way in which the human brain arrives at decisions. From data similar to those gathered by Henmon, later workers such as Audley (1961), Crossman (1956), Falmagne (1976), Laming (1969), Luce (1969), and Vickers (1978) have shown how reaction-time measurements may be incorporated into a new *psychophysics of signal detection (see BIT). Nonspecialists may capture something of the importance of this endeavour if they reflect that human experimental psychologists can only measure two things about human performance: how accurately people do things and how long they take to do them. Metrics and models that allow us to discuss speed and errors as complementary indices are basic tools of research.                    P. R.

**REALISM** as a philosophical term generally refers to the doctrine that objects exist independently of sensory experience. The essential problem of *perception is to account for how we experience things which exist in the time and space of the real world. 'Naïve' or 'direct' realism suggests that we experience objects as they are by a kind of direct awareness comparable with intuitive understanding of mathematics. This is very different from theories which suppose that perceptions are hypotheses (perhaps essentially like predictive scientific hypotheses) about, or 'about the nature of', or 'descriptive of' physical reality. Realism may be contrasted with *idealism.

**REASONING: DEVELOPMENT IN CHILDREN.** It is commonly claimed that, until the age of 6 or 7, children are very limited in their capacity for deductive reasoning. This claim is made largely on the basis of research carried out within two main traditions: that based on the thinking of Jean *Piaget in Geneva, and that based on the thinking of Clark *Hull in the United States.

The theories of Piaget and of Hull are in most

respects opposed, and their conceptions of the nature of inference are very different. It is all the more striking that their work has led to agreement about young children's lack of competence; and indeed this agreement has seemed to many to be conclusive. More recent research, however, makes it necessary to reopen the debate.

Piaget's claims may best be illustrated by his studies of 'class inclusion'. These have demonstrated that, if young children are shown a group of, say, six flowers, comprising four red ones and two yellow ones, and are then asked whether there are more red flowers or more flowers, they are likely to answer: 'More red ones.' And they will probably justify the answer by pointing out that there are 'only two yellow ones'.

Piaget's explanation is that at this stage a child's mind is lacking in a certain kind of flexibility, a kind crucial for reasoning. Piaget points out that the child who replies 'more red flowers' will normally have no difficulty in recognizing that if you take away the yellow flowers the red ones will be left; and further that if you take away all the flowers none will be left. To reach these conclusions, however, children need only think of the class and the sub-classes successively. What they cannot do, according to Piaget, is think of them *simultaneously* (as they must, of course, if they are to reason as to the relations between them); for when they 'centre' on the whole class they mentally lose the subdivisions, and when they centre on the subdivisions they mentally lose the totality. So the seemingly simple comparison of whole with part is impossible for them. They have no mental structure representing a hierarchy of classes, with some included in others and these again included in still broader groupings, this being of course precisely the kind of structure with which logicians have traditionally been much concerned.

The deficiency in thought that is manifested by young children in the class inclusion task is held by Piaget to be quite general. Until it is overcome children's thinking is said to consist largely of a succession of separate 'moments', poorly co-ordinated with one another, so that the current one is too dominant. According to this argument, young children are not good at seeing their own momentary 'point of view' as one of a set of possible points of view co-ordinated into a single coherent system within which reasoning as to relationships can freely take place.

Piaget claims that the process of overcoming this deficiency is one of building 'cognitive structures', for which the original 'building-blocks' are overt actions—acts of combining, ordering, etc., carried out on the real world. According to him, such actions, once they have been internalized (so that they can be performed 'in the mind') and organized into systems, are the very stuff of reasoning. It is then interesting to find that, in the other major tradition within which experimental studies of children's reasoning have been carried out— namely, the *behaviourist tradition, as exemplified in the thinking of Clark Hull—there appears the same emphasis on actions that are initially overt and subsequently internalized. Beyond this, however, the theories of Hull and Piaget have little in common.

For Hull and his followers, the essence of reasoning lies in putting together two 'behaviour segments' in some novel way, never actually performed before, so as to reach a goal. For instance, one 'behaviour segment' might consist in pressing a button, which act would release a marble from a little slot; a second might consist in putting a marble in a hole, which act would open a little door and allow access to a toy. An act of inference would consist in combining these (separately learned) acts in order to get the toy. Such an inference would obviously have the form: if A leads to B and if B leads to C, then A leads to C.

Work by Kendler and Kendler (1967) has shown that young children who have learned these separate 'behaviour segments' do not readily integrate or combine them. So these investigators, like Piaget, conclude that children under the age of 7 are very limited in their capacity for inference.

There is now reason to think, however, that this conclusion needs to be modified. Simon Hewson has shown that if the apparatus and the procedure used by the Kendlers are changed in certain ways that do not alter the basic structure of the problem, then 5-year-old children can perform as well as did the college students in the original studies.

Hewson replaced the button-pressing mechanism in the first 'segment' by a drawer which the child could open. Also he played a 'swapping game' with the children to help them to understand the functional equivalence of different marbles as means of opening the little door (so that they would realize there had been nothing special or 'magic' about the marble used in their original learning of the second 'segment'). These two modifications produced a jump in the 5-year-old success rates from 30 per cent to 90 per cent.

It seems then that, whatever was the nature of the children's difficulty with the original task, it did not consist in a radical inability to make the inferential link. The conclusion that there is no such radical inability is supported by Peter Bryant (1974). Bryant argues that, in their perception of the world, young children continually make comparisons which depend on reasoning in the form: if A = B and if B = C then A = C. Thus they combine two separate pieces of information to reach an inferred conclusion.

Hewson's demonstration that the difficulty of the Kendlers' task can be greatly altered by inessential modifications has its parallel in studies of class inclusion. These have established that very slight changes in Piaget's class inclusion task can enable many young children to perform it successfully (see, for instance, McGarrigle, Grieve, and Hughes, 1978). It now appears that much of the difficulty with this and other similar Piagetian tasks lies in the fact that children are powerfully influenced by context, so that they do not interpret the experimenter's words alone with the strictness and rigour which—by adult standards—a reasoning task demands. It should also be noted that evidence obtained from observation rather than experiment suggests the presence of considerable reasoning skills in children as young as 3 or 4. An example is provided by a comment from a 4-year-old who was listening to the story of Cinderella and looking at a picture of Cinderella marrying the prince. In the picture the prince looked effeminate, and the child thought it was a picture of two women. He called out, 'But how can it be (that they are getting married)? You have to have a man too!' He appears to have been using two premises:

1. If there is a wedding there must be a man.
2. There is no man.

And he concludes validly:

So there is no wedding.

The general conclusion which we are now justified in drawing seems to be that young children have a considerable capacity for reasoning deductively about topics related to ongoing activities in which they are spontaneously engaged. What is hard for them is to accept verbal premises which are 'set' for them by someone else in the absence of a meaningful, supportive context. Young children do not readily constrain their thinking in this way. Cross-cultural studies (for instance, Cole et al., 1971) indicate that the same tends to be true of unsophisticated, illiterate adults.

With increasing age, and especially with the advent of literacy, people tend to become better able to turn their minds deliberately to a reasoning task and respect its constraints. But at all ages this kind of rigorous, disciplined inference is difficult for the human mind (see Henle, 1962).          M. D.

Bryant, P. (1974). *Perception and Understanding in Young Children*. London.

Cole, M., Gay, J., Glick, J. A., and Sharp, D. W. (1971). *The Cultural Context of Learning and Thinking*. London.

Henle, M. (1962). The relationship between logic and thinking. *Psychological Review*, **69**, 366–78.

Hewson, S. N. P. (1977). Inferential problem solving in young children. Oxford University: unpublished doctoral dissertation.

Kendler, T. S. and Kendler, H. H. (1967). Experimental analysis of inferential behavior in children. In Lipsitt, L. P. and Spiker, C. C. (eds.), *Advances in Child Development and Behavior*, vol. iii. New York.

McGarrigle, J., Grieve, R., and Hughes, M. (1978). Interpreting inclusion: a contribution to study of the child's cognitive and linguistic development. *Journal of Experimental Child Psychology*, **26**, 528–50.

**RECEPTIVE FIELD.** This term is widely used in sensory neurobiology. It refers to the 'region' from which a particular sensory neurone can be activated. The sensory nerve fibres concerned with cutaneous sensation provide a simple illustration of the concept (Fig. 1). A nerve fibre mediating, for example, touch sensation terminates in one or more processes in a restricted area of the skin.

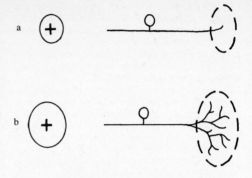

**Fig. 1.** Receptive fields of cutaneous afferents. **a.** Receptor is single terminal at the end of a cutaneous afferent. **b.** Receptors occur at the ends of all the terminals of an afferent which branches extensively in the skin.

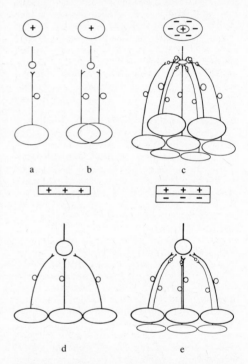

**Fig. 2.** This illustrates the way in which neurone complex receptive fields may be produced by convergence of the inputs from a number of afferents on to a second-order (or third-order) neurone. **a.** Simple one-to-one relay of input from afferent fibre to second-order sensory neurone. **b.** Convergence of two inputs on to one second-order neurone, resulting in the second-order neurone having a larger receptive field than either of the afferents. **c.** Formation of a 'concentric receptive field' with inhibitory region surrounding the excitatory zone. **d.** Organization of inputs to produce an oblong receptive field best activated by a bar, as in the visual cortex. **e.** Similar situation to **d** but with aditional inhibitory side band to enhance the selectivity of the cell to the orientation of the bar. (For further details, see VISUAL SYSTEM: ORGANIZATION.)

These terminal processes together with any ancillary structures are the receptors relating to the nerve fibre in question. Touching the skin distorts these receptors, which depolarize and initiate an action potential discharge in the nerve fibre. The region of the skin surface which when touched results in activation of these receptors is known as the 'receptive field' of the nerve fibre. Taking this example further, individual nerve fibres are generally sensitive to one modality of sensation. Their receptive fields thus may be said to exhibit modality specificity and, in the case illustrated, this specificity is to mechanical distortion of the skin.

Receptive fields at higher levels in the *nervous system can be much more complex (Fig. 2). Here the inputs relayed from a number of receptors may converge on to a single neurone. Moreover, these inputs may be organized to form a specific spatial pattern and some may relay via inhibitory interneurones, thus forming inhibitory zones in the receptive field. Furthermore, because of widespreading interconnections in the brain, some higher-order sensory neurones may be slightly influenced by a wide variety of inputs in addition to the main input. At this level it can be difficult to decide where the receptive field boundaries are.

A. M. S.

# REDUCTIONISM IN PSYCHOLOGY—Luria's Philosophy. 

For a very long time reductionism remained the generally accepted philosophical aim of the natural sciences as well as of psychology. It was supposed that the basic goal of science is to reduce complex phenomena to separate simple parts, and that such reduction provides significant explanations of phenomena.

Reductionism had its origin in the middle of the nineteenth century, and in biology it was closely associated with Rudolf Virchow's cellular anatomy and pathology, which supposed that the organism is a complex of organs—and the organs a complex of cells. So to explain basic laws of the living organism we have to study as carefully as possible the features of separate cells.

The same principle of reductionism was seen in psychology. It was supposed that the basic goal of the behavioural sciences is to reduce the whole wealth of human behaviour to associations of separate elementary events. This was the aim of *Pavlovian physiology and also the direction of *behaviourism, which tried to reduce behaviour to the simple laws of conditioning.

Although the philosophy of reductionism was accepted as a general principle in the natural sciences and psychology, there are grounds to suppose it may be false.

To study a phenomenon, or an event, and to explain it, one has to preserve all its basic features: one must be able to describe their rules and their mechanisms without the loss of any individual characteristics. It can easily be seen that reductionism may very soon conflict with this goal. One can reduce water ($H_2O$) into H and O, but—as is well known—H (hydrogen) burns and O (oxygen) is necessary for burning; whereas water ($H_2O$) has neither the first nor the second quality. This is why the outstanding Soviet psychologist Leo *Vygotsky stated that reduction can only be done up to certain limits. In order not to lose the basic features of water, one must split it into *units* ($H_2O$), not into *elements* (H and O). The same is true for the psychological analysis of human conscious behaviour.

Although this may seem obvious, psychology as a science followed, for many decades, a different view. During the period of associationist psychology, it was supposed that all forms of mental processes could be reduced to simple sensations (or ideas) and their associations. Even after *Gestalt psychology had made its well-known criticisms of the associationist point of view, the basic tenets of reductionism did not change: the only difference was that the Gestalt group of psychologists continued their attempts to reduce complex mental phenomena to physical or quasi-physical Gestalts, which were larger elements than single sensations or associations. It remained evident that the wealth and diversity of mental events was being lost through expression in the too-generalized terms of Gestalt psychology, just as it had been in the former associationist theory. This situation remained unchanged in the twentieth century, when attempts were made to reduce complex forms of man's conscious behaviour to conditioned reflexes (see CONDITIONING), or to over-generalized laws of conditioning.

Of course, human behaviour can be reduced to reflexes and their combinations; and general rules of conditioning are often supposed to be the most elementary rules for establishing new forms of connection. But it is evident as well that a reduction of human conscious behaviour to these 'elements' does not preserve the whole wealth of conscious behaviour. This means that the procedure of such kinds of reductionism is futile; and that real 'units' of conscious behaviour have to be found, which can preserve all the richness of the behaviour while at the same time pointing out models for it which can be the subject of an accurate study. Now we come to the basic question: what can serve as a real *model* of human conscious behaviour, as the 'unit' which includes all its essential qualities?

Vygotsky supposed that higher mental processes are of a social origin; and that the basic unit of human conscious behaviour is not to be found in unconditional or conditional reflexes (the latter being rather general physiological 'elements', not psychological 'units' which preserve all the essential features of conscious actions). He suggested that the simplest form of such behaviour can be found in tool- or sign-using, where a tool (or a sign) can be used to reach a certain goal. Instead of the elementary scheme of $S \rightarrow R$ ('S' for stimulus, 'R' for reflex), he proposed a new scheme, $S_{\searrow x \nearrow} R$, where $S$ stands for stimulus or situation, $x$ for means (tool or sign), and $R$ for reaction. Some decades later this scheme was improved, and a new component—that of feedback (see CYBERNETICS)—was added. This provides the formula $S \underset{x}{\overset{\frown}{\searrow}} \overset{\frown}{\nearrow} R$, essential for a self-regulating system.

This assumption changed significantly the general philosophy of reductionism. New components were added. Instead of attempting to reduce complex psychological phenomena to biological (or physiological) 'elements', a new method was proposed—to step outside the organism itself and to try to find the basic units of human conscious behaviour in the relation of the subject with the social environment, treating these *relations* as an essential feature of human mental processes.

Such an attempt radically altered the classical attitude of reductionist philosophy. The goal of psychology became not to try to explain the essence of complex phenomena by reducing them to elementary parts, but rather to find *new relations* in which the organism is involved. This became the ultimate goal of science. The more of these essential relations that can be found, the closer we come to the whole wealth of the phenomenon, and to its explanation. *The explanation of the phenomenon is supposed to lie not in its reduction to single elements but rather in its inclusion in a rich net of essential relations.*

This attitude has basic significance for every science, and for psychology especially. It is the way Marx calls 'ascending to the concrete', as opposed to the classical way of 'ascending to the abstract', based on singling out definite features and progressing to more and more general categories, such as 'dog' (opposed to 'cat')→'tame animal' ('wild animal')→'animal' ('plant')→'living being' ('inanimate nature')→'natural' ('unnatural') →'something' (as opposed to 'nothing'). Such a way of 'ascending to abstractness', a kind of inverted reductionism, inevitably leads to an over-generalized nullity, in which the whole richness of concrete events is lost. The way of 'ascending to the concrete', i.e. the inclusion of the event in a rich net of relations, preserves the whole complexity of events, while at the same time revealing new and essential relations and thus providing the most important steps to the discovery of the *essence* of the phenomenon or the event, as opposed to its scientific explanation.

It may be supposed that such a method can serve as an alternative to dry reductionism, and that it can open new and productive ways for the scientific analysis of human conscious behaviour.    A. R. L.

Leontiev, A. N. (1959). *Problems of Mental Development*. Moscow. (In Russian.)

Leontiev, A. N. (1979). *Activity; Consciousness; Personality*. Moscow. (In Russian.)

Vygotsky, L. S. (1956). *Selected Psychological Studies*. Moscow. (In Russian.)

Vygotsky, L. S. (1960). *Development of the Higher Mental Functions*. Moscow. (In Russian.)

Vygotsky, L. S. (1962). *Thought and Language*. Cambridge, Massachusetts.

**REFLEX ACTION.** Reflexes are the automatic reactions of the nervous system to stimuli impinging on the body or arising within it. They are more easily described than further defined. The knee jerk (one of the 'tendon jerks') is a familiar instance. The tendon below the kneecap is struck sharply with a rubber hammer and the muscles of the kneecap in the thigh are caused to give a brief twitch-like contraction which extends the knee joint and causes a little kick of the foot. The latency, the time between the blow and the first sign of muscular contraction, is about a fiftieth of a second, not much longer than is required for nerve impulses to travel from the sense endings excited by the blow to the central nervous system (here the spinal cord) and back down to the muscle.

The word 'reflex' comes from the idea that nerve impulses are 'reflected' in the central nervous system. *Descartes instances the constriction of the pupil when a light is shone in the eye. In the eighteenth century, Robert Whytt and Stephen Hales showed that the integrity of the central nervous system is, indeed, essential for 'reflection' to occur. In the next century the subject was greatly clarified by the discovery of *Magendie and *Bell that the nervous system uses separate *channels (nerve fibres) for input and output so that 'reflection' must occur centrally. With minor exceptions ('axon reflexes') the dorsal spinal nerve roots are exclusively sensory and the ventral roots exclusively motor in function. Detailed knowledge of the connections between the sensory and motor nerves in the grey matter of the spinal cord dates only from 1951, when Eccles obtained records from a microelectrode inside a motor nerve-cell—the first time this had been achieved with any central neurone.

The tendon jerk is the simplest and fastest mammalian reflex known and its neuronal mechanism (although not its function in everyday life) is still the best understood. Endless other reflexes exist of greater complexity and longer latency. Commonly instanced are responses to injury or irritation: sneezing and coughing, the withdrawal of a foot in a frog or quadruped, the scratching of a dog. There are very many reflexes concerned in the vital functions: blood-pressure is reflexly affected by pressure receptors in the walls of the aorta, breathing by reflexes from stretch receptors in the diaphragm, and so forth. Reflexes from receptors in the muscles of the limbs and trunk (of which the knee jerk is one) are a large class, of still controversial function in the control of bodily movement.

Although the experimental investigation of reflexes in animals is traditionally carried out on the spinal cord after severing it from the brain, or on the lower parts of the nervous axis after removing the cerebral hemispheres (decerebrate preparation), there are many reflexes whose pathway is through the cerebral cortex. The involuntary blink to a threatening gesture is one. And the elaborate learned responses called 'conditioned reflexes' (see CONDITIONING) are cortical or usually so.

C. S. *Sherrington, to whom we owe much of our knowledge of reflex action, regarded the reflex as the unit of nervous action and suspected that complex sequential acts, such as walking, were in the nature of chain reflexes, in which one element reflexly caused the next: in walking, for example, the movement of the leg forward excited receptors in the leg which reflexly caused it to move back again, and so on. There is now evidence that the nervous mechanism for performing such acts as walking or breathing, exists in the central nervous system and can function, after a fashion, without reflex inputs; but that, normally, reflexes modify and regulate these actions and adapt them to changing circumstances.

The point at which an animal's responses to stimuli cease to be regarded as reflex and are called deliberate or voluntary, or by some similar term, is ill-defined. A mild cough can be suppressed by an effort of will during a concert; but such coughing would be regarded as reflex. A similar suppression of the urge to pass water is more easily achieved and passing water is normally to be considered a deliberate act; the underlying reflex element is dominant only in infancy or when self-control is impaired.                                    P. A. M.

Eccles, J. C. (1957). *The Physiology of Nerve Cells*. Baltimore and London.

Liddell, E. G. T. (1960). *The Discovery of Reflexes*. Oxford.

Merton, P. A. (1979). The central nervous system. In Lippold, O. C. J. and Winton, F. R. (eds.), *Human Physiology*, 392–427. Edinburgh, London, and New York.

Sherrington, C. S. (1900). The spinal cord. In Schäfer, E. A., *Textbook of Physiology*, vol. ii, 783–883. Edinburgh and London.

Sherrington, C. S. (1906). *The Integrative Action of the Nervous System* (new edn. 1947). Cambridge.

**REFRACTORY PERIOD OF NERVE.** Nerves conduct information from the senses, and send commands to muscles, by trains of electrical spikes—the 'action potentials'. For sensory nerves, the stronger the stimulation the higher the frequency of spikes; but this never exceeds about 800 spikes/seconds, for following a spike there is a short period of inactivity—the 'refractory period'—which sets an absolute limit to the maximum frequency of spikes. This limits the amount of information that can be transmitted down a single nerve fibre. This is far lower than electronic *channels—which, no doubt, is a reason for the large number of fibres in nerves and the rich parallel processing of the nervous system. See NERVOUS SYSTEM.

**REID,** THOMAS (1710–96). Scottish philosopher, born at Strachan Manse, Kincardineshire. He succeeded Adam Smith as professor of moral philo-

sophy at Glasgow (1764–80). He reacted sharply to the scepticism of David *Hume's *Treatise of Human Nature* (1739), and defended intuitive common sense knowledge and belief. His principal work is *Inquiry into the Human Mind on the Principles of Common Sense* (1764); also important are his essays on the *Intellectual Powers* (1785) and *Active Powers* (1788) of man.

Reid was influential in developing *faculty psychology, which supposed that human abilities can be considered in separate units, probably localized in specific brain regions. This is a basis of *phrenology—which on the whole had unfortunate consequences for nineteenth-century neurology.

There is a strong orthodox theological streak in Reid, who argued that our perception of the existence of external objects is given directly though with help from God, whereas sensation, as the raw data of experience, is given directly by physical objects. Reid's distinction between sensation and perception is still frequently used (though with God left out); but recent accounts of perception tend to blur this distinction, as sensation can be affected by processes of object perception, and it is far from clear that sensations are given at all directly by neurally peripheral or simple physiological processes (see PERCEPTION).

**REINFORCER.** See CONDITIONING.

**RELIGION.** John Macmurray used to say that the obvious difference between science on the one hand and art and religion on the other is that science is intellectual, while art and religion are peculiarly bound up with the emotional side of human life. Failure to make this distinction has led to much confusion. Some have simply dropped religion as no longer worthy of a thinking man's attention. Others, in extreme contrast, have turned a blind eye on contemporary doubts, and entrenched themselves in traditional dogma. But the twentieth century has been essentially the age of the half-believer—the person who is not without intuitions about the meaning of life, but is baffled by the dead weight of theology which has been accumulated.

The so-called five proofs of God's existence have never carried as much conviction as the personal encounters with God which religious people have claimed to have. 'Dieu d'Abraham, Dieu d'Isaac, Dieu de Jacob, non des philosophes et des savants.' So said *Pascal. And it is significant that all the great religions do appear to stem from some shattering personal experience. The Buddha achieved enlightenment as he sat in meditation beneath the Bodhi tree. As a result, he believed that he had found the cure for all human sufferings and dissatisfactions. The Old Testament prophets had experiences which, they alleged, told them profoundly important things about God—even suggesting that what passes for religion can be a bar to finding Him. There is always this gap between the religious founder and what the faith has become. We see it in Jesus's denunciation of the religion of *his* day, in contrast with his own sense of intimate closeness to the Father. One cannot read the Upanishads, the main source of Hindu doctrine, without feeling the writer's sense of union between the self and the Holy Power. And it was alone in the desert that Muhammad received his call to preach. True, these key figures quickly gathered round them a band of disciples; and other elements, such as a sense of common purpose and a sense of fellowship, accrued. Religion ministers to the group mind as well as to the individual. For all that, what has been said about literature may equally be said about religion in its essence: 'The best in each kind comes first, comes suddenly, and never comes again.'

Is it the *same* basic experience that all religions are seeking to interpret? Making every allowance for the divergencies of time and place, it would seem a strong possibility. A study of so-called primitive people may offer useful clues. Their world is alive and shot through with elemental unseen power. This power is thought to take possession of certain of their chieftains, priests, and medicine men. One group of special interest are the shamans. In Siberia an aspiring shaman has to pass many hours in a cabin of snow, contemplating his own skeleton. He ends, we are told, by obtaining the 'flash' or 'illumination'—'a mysterious light that the shaman suddenly feels in the interior of his head'. He is now able to discern things hidden from other human beings.

Is the experience of conversion, as we know it in the West, so very different? Problems of language make it hard to judge. Here is a witness, quoted by Rudolf Otto: 'The more I seek words to express this intimate intercourse, the more I feel the impossibility of describing it by any of the usual images.' However, William *James analysed it as consisting of two elements—an uneasiness and its solution. Carl *Jung said that 'it gives a human being that sense of wholeness, which he had as a child, but loses when he leaves his parents'. And its common characteristic is a sense of something not earned, or even asked for—a sense of something 'given'. This led men naturally to infer a Giver; and therefore the postulation of a 'Someone', not ourselves, wholly other, out there in the void, may be directly connected with the origin of religion.

The human race, on the whole, has found no difficulty in filling that void with an endless variety of deities. Considering that no one could really have supposed that they had been *seen* by anybody, it is amazing the number of forms these gods have taken—from Rongo, the Polynesian god of agriculture, to Shiva, the Hindu lord of the dance, and from the Zeus of Greek mythology to the Jehovah of Michelangelo. From earliest times man has sought to establish some sort of working relationship with these powers that be—some enlistment of their aid against the evil all round him. The many and bloody sacrifices, which the Hebrew prophets denounced, were believed to open up communication between the sacred and the profane, and the idea of sacrifice has not yet ceased to be an important element in religion. (See BLOOD MYTHS.) Men have also believed that 'mercy and *not* sacrifice' was what was required: that personal values count, when it comes to being right with God. Religion has always been closely linked with morality—even though it has given rise to some curious anomalies. Today the questions are still being asked. Is celibacy, or virginity, really demanded of us, if we are to be numbered among the saints? Are there absolute standards of conduct, applicable at all times and in all places? Or is everything relative?

As to our ultimate chances and the possibility of judgement after death, these remain beyond our logical apprehension. But Jung has suggested that our unconscious, which is free from the categories of space and time, may be the part of our make-up which 'knows' about these matters. Responses are set up in the unconscious by the use of certain symbols. Rituals give a sense of 'timeless moments', and myths of flight and ascension suggest escape from one mode of being to another. The rites of spring around the world celebrate the rhythm of rebirth. Jung has furthermore maintained that the crisis of the West is in part due to the fact that the Christian myths and symbols are no longer lived by. They have become fossilized and irrelevant to most of the population. To some extent this must be true of Eastern religions as well—despite all their genuine holy men and all their various techniques for quieting the mind. A recent traveller to Bodh Gaya, where the Buddha was enlightened, was disheartened to see so many Buddhists, in his opinion, missing the point. If the truth lies within the self, why so much noisy ceremonial?

What then of the future? The twentieth century has certainly been a crisis for mankind. The sheer achievement of science has caused modern man to claim that 'what no God did for his worshippers in thousands of years, he has by his own efforts succeeded in bringing about'. For authentic existence from now on, so the existentialists say, we shall have to face up to the absence of God. Nobody can give us directions. We are alone in the cosmos. But the history of religions shows that they have an uncanny capacity for revival, even when they have seemed to be most dead.

Hinduism was at a low ebb at the time of the establishment of the British Raj, and it was thought that the educated Indian would soon reject it. But far from rejecting it, he has done much to reinstate it. Its strength lies in the recognition of different levels of spiritual development, and it has a special attraction for men alienated from the religion of their own society. One of the great texts of the Upanishads is: 'God does not proclaim Himself. He is everybody's secret.' An old prophecy says that after 2,500 years Buddhism will either fade away or enjoy a renaissance. It does not involve belief in God, over which many Westerners today have intellectual difficulties, and is undogmatic and experimental. One day a Zen master may deliver a sermon. Another day, if a bird begins to sing, the master will say nothing, and everyone will listen to the bird. Islam has been steadily increasing in influence and numbers, till there are over 817,065,200 Muslims at the latest count. In Christendom, the Roman Catholic Church is by far the largest, with 872,104,700 members. Its discipline is stricter than that of the Protestant Churches, and its appeal lies in its unbroken tradition. Protestants, by comparison, have broadened their outlook, yet they continue to preach to an anxiety-ridden world that 'sin' means separation from the ground of one's being, and that, as a matter of urgency, wholeness must be restored.

It is hard to be objective where religion is concerned. Objectivity suggests lukewarmness. It is easy for the agnostic to be objective, for there is nothing much at stake for him. It is very difficult for the man who claims that he has been vouchsafed a vision of the truth. 'Woe *is* me! for I am undone . . . for mine eyes have seen the King, the Lord of hosts.'

See also HUMANISM; THEOLOGY AND MIND–BRAIN IDENTITY.                                        O. J. W. H.

Eliade, M. (1960). *Myths, Dreams, and Mysteries.*
James, W. (1902). *The Varieties of Religious Experience.*
Jung, C. G. (1933). *Modern Man in Search of a Soul.*
Macmurray, J. (1961). *Reason and Emotion.* London.
Otto, R. (1923). *The Idea of the Holy.* Oxford.
Pascal, B. (1670). *Pensées.*
Smart, N. (1971). *The Religious Experience of Mankind.*

**REMEMBERING.** If one asks teachers, students, or the proverbial man or woman in the street for the best available techniques for remembering something, the answers will be quite varied. However, one recurrent theme is sure to be: 'Repeat it!' A psychologist is likely to comment: 'Yes, but . . . repetition by itself, mere repetition, does not help.' Yet the history of experimental investigations of *memory is to a large extent concerned with mere repetition. In fact, the father of the experimental psychology of memory, Hermann *Ebbinghaus, started his investigations in Germany in the last quarter of the nineteenth century by focusing almost exclusively on the effect of repetition. How many repetitions did it take to learn a list of words (or nonsense syllables)? How many trials were saved in relearning some list as a function of its prior repetition?

Both the common lore about repetition and the influence of Ebbinghaus dictated a preoccupation with the effect of repeated rehearsals. After all, it is well known that repeating a telephone number between looking it up and dialling it protects it from disappearance. And handsome, negatively accelerated learning curves resulted from numerous experiments that studied the effect of repetition on retention. But repetitive activities do not lead to effortless retrieval. Actually, when we try to remember an address, a name, the title of a book, or the plot of a play, we seem to engage in rather complicated search operations. The success of these operations depends not so much on how often we have repeated the required information in the past as on the proper embedding (the organization) of the target information within the larger flux of our knowledges and memories. When shopping for the weekend meals, we might retrieve the meats to be bought as a single memorial 'chunk', and liquid refreshments in another. Or another shopper might organize a mental shopping list by remembering what to buy in terms of what is where in the local supermarket. Both of these schemas are kinds of organizations of the to-be-remembered things, and both require effort. Trying to recall the plot of a play, the rememberer might first recall vaguely the gist ('It was about a family who were always arguing') and then more and more details within coherent subdivisions ('Yes, there was the unhappy daughter and her pitiful suitor').

The notion that organization and structure are essential for memory retrieval is not novel. Extensive *mnemonic techniques date at least to ancient Greece, where orators constructed complex spatial and temporal schemata as an aid in rehearsing and properly presenting their speeches (see Yates, 1966). In modern times the associationism of British empiricism and German experimentalism was seriously questioned during the first half of the twentieth century by the *Gestalt psychologists in general and by the British psychologist F. C. *Bartlett in particular. Today we know in some detail what it is that repetition makes possible, what it is that is needed in addition to *mere* repetition.

A set of objects, events, or mental representations is said to be organized when consistent relations among the members of the set can be identified and specified. The result of such organization is called a structure. Structures may exist among events in the world as well as among mental events. A special kind of structure is the *schema which is a mental structure, specifically an organized representation of a body of knowledge. Thus, schemata determine the expectations people have about events to be encountered, and about the spatial and temporal structure of those events.

The organization of to-be-remembered material takes time and conscious capacity. If we are told to remember a luncheon appointment while reading a book or watching our favourite television programme, conscious capacity is taken up by these primary activities and little organizational action will result. In order to remember the luncheon appointment we need to retrieve other plans (schemata) about the specific day and 'fit in' the appointment. For example, we need to store such things as 'After the dentist, go to work, but go to the luncheon an hour later'. In the temporal organization of that day's plan, dentist, work, and luncheon will form an appropriate mental schema. And thinking about these plans (repeating them) will make their proper retrieval on the appointed day more likely. But again it is not mere repetition that provides a better schema, rather it is the anchoring of the relevant events within better, richer, and more accessible events that provides the more effective schema. Thus, each repetition provides an opportunity to relate the target event (the luncheon) to other events and thoughts. We may store the fact that our best friend will be at the luncheon, that it is held at a favourite restaurant, etc. etc. Each of these additions produces a more elaborate structure, and the more elaborate the retrieval opportunities for a target event the more likely it is that it will be recalled. Repetition provides opportunities for the organization of the to-be-remembered events.

While it is the case that most events are stored in long-term memory in complex, multistructured forms, certain frequently used structures can be identified. First there is the categorical or subordinate kind of structure in which a list of instances is stored under a general concept or label. To recall all the animals we know requires the use of such subordinate structures within a hierarchy of categories. Typically we gain access to some general animal category and then generate its subcategories such as domestic animals and cat-like animals. Second there are co-ordinate structures of a few, usually less than five, events or things that are related to one another. Spatial structures, such as the directions of the compass, are one good example; another is the set of things called a table-setting. Whereas in the categorical structure the higher-order label or node retrieves the lower instances, in the co-ordinate structure the members of the set act as retrieval points for one another. The third kind of structure is a serial or pro-ordinate structure in which a string of events is organized, usually in a temporal or spatial form. An excellent example is the way we retrieve the alphabet, another is the structure that represents the route we take to work from home. Parts of the serial string act as retrieval cues for subsequent things or events.

These idealized structures usually interact within any complex memorial event. More important, they are incorporated within the more general spatio-temporal schemata mentioned earlier. Thus the understanding of a conversation involves the kinds of expectation inherent in our schemata for social conversations, story schemata tell us to look for crucial aspects and themes of a story, restaurants require that we have the proper schema for ordering from menus, talking to waiters, and so forth. The episodes of our daily lives are organized within such schemata, which in turn incorporate the three kinds of structures described above.

Up to now the description of memory systems has focused on the recall of information. Another important kind of memory feat involves the recognition of previously encountered events. We are able to determine that people, rooms, foods, tunes are events that we have previously met, seen, tasted, heard. Not only do we know that we have encountered them before but we usually also know who or what they are. Conversely we sometimes know only that the event is familiar without knowing exactly who that person is, where we have seen that room before, what kind of food it is, what the name of a tune is. It is the latter phenomenon that has generally been studied by psychologists under the rubric of recognition.

The recognition of prior occurrence is a two-stage process involving two distinct mechanisms. One of them is a judgement of familiarity, the other a retrieval process essentially identical to that discussed for the recall of information. The judgement of familiarity is an automatic process, requiring no conscious effort and occurring as an immediate response to the event. However, the familiarity of information available of the event may be inadequate to make a confident judgement of prior occurrence. In that case a search process queries the long-term memory system whether the event in question is in fact retrievable. If such an attempt is successful then the event is considered to be 'old', i.e. having been previously encountered. Thus, recognition involves a judgement of familiarity which is supplemented by a retrieval attempt. For example, we meet someone who looks vaguely familiar, but the definite judgement that we 'know' that person is not made until we can recapture the place or context where we have previously encountered him or her.

The process of judging familiarity brings us back to the problem of repetition, because mere repetition does affect familiarity. The more frequently an event has been observed the more likely it is to be recognized on the basis of familiarity alone. Thus, repetition does have a function, but not for the retrieval of information. Repetition affects the process of integrating the representation of an event; it establishes its familiarity independent of its context or its relations to other mental contents.

Finally, errors of memory can obviously be of two kinds, retrieval errors and, less frequently, errors of familiarity judgements. Given the structural, schematic organization of memory storage, it is obvious that some events that 'fit' into the appropriate schema are likely to be retrieved even though they were not originally encountered. One might remember having witnessed an argument in a play because the structure of the play is stored under some general schema of 'family conflict', or one might 'recall' having seen a particular red armchair before, because it was stored as 'striking looking furniture'. Thus, errors of memory are often even more instructive about the nature of mental structure than the normal recovery of information. See also DÉJÀ VU.                    G. M.

Baddeley, A. D. (1976). *The Psychology of Memory*. New York.

Bartlett, F. C. (1932). *Remembering*. Cambridge.

Mandler, G. (1985). *Cognitive Psychology*. Hillsdale, New Jersey.

Norman, D. A. (1976). *Memory and Attention*, 2nd edn. New York.

Yates, F. A. (1966). *The Art of Memory*. London.

**REPRESSION,** a key concept of *psychoanalysis, is a defence mechanism that ensures that what is unacceptable to the conscious mind, and would if recalled arouse anxiety, is prevented from entering into it. Akin to denial, which tends to refer to current events, it was invoked to account for a patient's failure to recall, in the course of *free association, events of significance in the past. Painful memories, being kept out of consciousness by repression, achieve 'psychic autonomy' and become fixed. Derivatives of what has been repressed may evade the censorship and enter into consciousness in a disguised form as strange or seemingly irrational thoughts. Or they may be recalled in dreams or in other states, e.g. those due to alcohol or drugs, or hypnosis, with what *Freud described as 'the undiminished vividness of recent events'.

The method of psychoanalysis creates conditions for the undoing of repression, i.e. the making conscious what has been repressed. Painful experiences when so recalled are ranged alongside other related experiences which perhaps contradict it; they then undergo correction by means of other ideas.                                        D. R. D.

Freud, S. and Breuer, J. (1974). *Studies on Hysteria* (Pelican Freud Library, vol. 3). Harmondsworth.

**RESPONSIBILITY AND MENTAL STATES.** In ordinary discourse some people are spoken of as 'not responsible' for acts or omissions, but there are several uses of the term 'responsible'. For example, not only people but things or events also are spoken of as 'responsible' for occurrences or non-occurrences, when all that is meant is that they had a part in the physical causation of them. Again, people are said to be 'responsible' for other people—such as their children—or for organizations, in the sense that they are morally or legally culpable if the latter misbehave. In the sense, however, with which we here are concerned, 'responsible' means 'to some extent culpable (either morally or in law, according to the context) for *one's own* acts or omissions'. The ascription of responsibility in this sense depends on what we believe to have been the person's mental state at or before the time of the act or omission. 'Premeditation' usually makes an objectionable act seem more culpable. If the actor foresaw a real possibility of his causing harm—for example by his way of driving—his act or omission will be called 'reckless', and blamed accordingly. If he did not foresee it, but we think that he should have, he may be called 'negligent', and blamed accordingly—usually less than for 'recklessness'. The law, too, makes distinctions of this sort, although with more subtlety (for example, civil law takes into account 'contributory negligence' by the person harmed).

More often it is the actor's state of mind at the time of the act—or more precisely what it is believed to have been—that determines the degree to which he is regarded as blameworthy. If the act seems to have been quite accidental—if for instance he knocks over a child whom he did not see in his path—he is not blamed, unless we think that he should have been aware of this as a real possibility. Again, if his physical movements that did the harm were of a kind which are not willed, then he is not blamed: examples are the movements of a sleep-walker, or of a man who is sneezing. This excuse is called '*automatism' by English lawyers. Criminal courts usually demand medical evidence before accepting it, since it is usually based on abnormal cerebral conditions, such as an epileptic fit, or a hypoglycaemic state (which may occur in diabetics).

In certain situations, however, lawyers—and ordinary people—regard intentional actions as excused. Violence may be excused by the belief that one is about to be killed by the other person and that there is no alternative (such as escape). 'Necessity' is an excuse in the US Model Penal Code, although English judicial decisions are hostile to it. 'Duress'—acting under threats of death to oneself or one's family—is sometimes accepted. About 'superior orders' there is even more disagreement. An official executioner who carries out a lawful sentence of death is not legally culpable, but is morally condemned by many people for accepting the task. Carrying out an order which one knows to be unlawful usually incurs moral—and sometimes legal—blame, unless one does so in the knowledge that one would suffer death or a severe penalty for disobedience.

Even uncoerced intentional acts, however, may be excused, or at least mitigated, by other explanations. Provocation, if sufficient, is accepted by English law as lessening culpability rather than excusing the act completely, although courts are sometimes persuaded by it not to penalize the convicted person. Less transient mental states may also mitigate or even excuse. An example is an abnormal inability to control desires or impulses, especially if given a psychiatric label such as '*psychopathic'. Other mental states, such as depression, frequently persuade courts to forgo penalties, and, if a hospital or clinic is willing to accept the sufferer, to entrust him to psychiatric care and treatment. The extent to which such states protect the sufferer against moral censure varies with the circumstances and the viewpoint of the censurer. The English Homicide Act of 1957 (following Scots common law) allows a person charged with murder (but paradoxically not attempted murder) to offer a plea of '*diminished responsibility': if successful this reduces the crime to manslaughter, and allows the judge freedom to impose a less severe sentence than life imprisonment. (The Infanticide Act of 1938 allows a somewhat similar plea of 'disturbed balance of mind' to a mother who kills a baby to whom she has given birth within the previous twelve months.)

Some kinds and degrees of mental disorder are regarded as excusing offenders completely. English law recognizes an 'insanity defence'. To qualify, the offender must, at the time of his act or omission, have been suffering from a 'disease of the mind' (in more modern language, 'mental disorder') such that he did not 'know the nature and quality' of the act, or alternatively know that it was 'wrong' (which is now interpreted in England as meaning 'against the law'). A third qualifying possibility is that he was suffering from a *delusion which, if true, would have legally justified what he did: for example a deluded belief that his life was threatened. In other common-law countries which have adopted and adapted this defence the exact definitions of the sufficient conditions vary, so that, for instance, 'wrong' can mean 'morally wrong'. In countries which follow the Code Napoléon the rule is simpler: no crime has been committed if the accused was suffering from *démence* at the time; but *démence*—or its equivalent—is defined very restrictively in practice. Most such countries also recognize 'partial insanity' or its equivalent as grounds for reducing the severity of the penalty; definitions of states which amount to this vary greatly.

Moral or political convictions are often regarded—especially by those who share them—as excusing behaviour which would normally be condemned, such as assassinations, violent demonstrations or even genocide. Few legal codes allow for such a defence, although it has been proposed, for example by Moran (1981).          N. D. W.

(English) Homicide Act 1957, s. 2.

Hart, H. L. A. (1968). *Punishment and Responsibility*. Oxford.

Hart, H. L. A. and Honoré, A. M. (eds.) (1985). *Causation in the Law*, 2nd edn. Oxford.

Moran, R. (1981). *Knowing Right From Wrong*. New York.

*Report of the Committee on Mentally Abnormal Offenders* (1975, Cmnd. 6244), chs. 18, 19. London.

Walker, N. D. (1984). Psychiatric explanations as excuses. In Roth, M. (ed.), *Psychiatry, Human Rights and the Law*. Cambridge.

**RETINA.** The screen at the back of the eye on which *retinal images are projected. The word derives from the medieval Latin *rēte*, meaning 'net'. In human and many other eyes there are closely packed 'rod' light receptors which signal levels of brightness (giving *scotopic vision), and considerably fewer 'cones' which allow colours to be identified: photopic vision. Photopic vision occurs only in fairly bright light. The evidence suggests that mammals have very little colour vision, and that most almost certainly have none—except for primates including man. In the human eye there are about 100 million rods and about 5 million cones. Curiously, they lie at the back of the retina, so light has to pass through the vascular system, a mesh of nerve fibres and three layers of cell-bodies, before it reaches the light-sensitive cells. It is possible to see the arterial system in another person's eye with an ophthalmoscope. It is also possible to see one's own retina by holding a torch bulb close to the closed eye and waggling it about—a tree of blood vessels becomes visible as

their shadow image moves across the underlying receptors. The central, foveal region of best vision can be seen in one's own eye by waggling, in front of the pupil, a piece of cardboard containing a small hole, and looking at a blank screen—a faint pattern of nerve fibres (the blood vessels do not cover the fovea but pass round it) are revealed.

**RETINAL IMAGES, STABILIZATION OF.** The eye is continually moving—even when a person tries to fixate a well-marked point as steadily as he can. The small residual movements of the eyeball cause irregular oscillations of the retinal image across the *retina and fluctuations in the light falling on retinal receptors near to boundaries (Fig. 1). W. H. Marshall and S. A. Talbot in the early 1940s worked out a detailed theory of the visual process based on the hypothesis that the receptors respond primarily to *fluctuations* of illumination and little, or not at all, to steady illumination—as indicated in the 1920s by the neurophysiological experiments of E. D. *Adrian and R. Matthews, and of H. K. Hartline and R. Granit and their co-workers. According to this theory, the retinal-image movements are essential to vision. An opposed view was that the eye movements were an unavoidable imperfection of the neural control of the eye muscles and that the retinal-image movements effectively blurred the boundaries, causing a loss of visual acuity—so that vision would be better if the retinal-image movements were stopped.

The crucial experiment to decide between these views is to make the eye movements control the movements of a target so that its image remains on the same part of the retina even when the eye moves, i.e. to produce a stabilized retinal image. The simplest way to do this is to attach the target (and a lens which focuses it) on to a tightly fitting contact lens (Fig. 2). The whole system then moves with the eye and the retinal image is fixed on the retina. A more elaborate apparatus (Fig. 3) enables a wider range of targets to be used. The target is in the projection system P. The beam from P is reflected from the mirror M, which is attached to a contact lens worn by the subject. It enters the eye after passing through the telescope T. When the eye rotates through an angle θ, the beam from

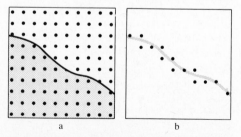

**Fig. 1. a.** Light–dark boundary superposed on a schematic regular array of retinal receptors. **b.** Receptors that receive fluctuating signals when boundary is given a small oscillation.

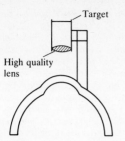

Target

High quality
lens

**Fig. 2.** Direct attachment apparatus with external contact lens mounted on a stalk.

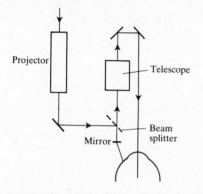

Projector

Telescope

Mirror

Beam
splitter

**Fig. 3.** Telescopic system involving a mirror that is caused to rotate by the eye.

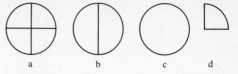

a          b          c          d

**Fig. 4. a.** Target. **b, c, d.** Fragments seen at different times when the retinal image is stabilized.

the mirror M rotates through an angle $2\theta$. If the telescope T has an angular magnification of $\frac{1}{2}$, the beam which enters the eye rotates through $\theta$ and its image falls on the same part of the retina even when the eye moves.

When a person views a stabilized image, the structure of the target fades out in two or three seconds and the field appears dark grey or black. If the target has no sharp boundaries between areas of high contrast, the field remains black so long as stabilization is maintained. Thus the retinal-image movements are essential to normal vision, as was suggested by Marshall and Talbot.

If the target does contain sharp boundaries between areas of strong contrast, it reappears intermittently. These reappearances are usually hazy and sometimes fragmentary. There has been some controversy whether these reappearances are due to imperfect stabilization or to a weak visual signal which remains even when the image is stationary on the retina. Sharp *after-images may be imprinted when a target with sharp boundaries is illuminated with a brief, but strong, flash of light. These after-images, which are certainly stationary on the retina, exhibit the same hazy, fragmentary, and intermittent reappearances. This strengthens the view that a weak secondary signal remains even when the retinal image is accurately stabilized.

When a target consists of a line pattern (Fig. 4a),

fragmentation of the stabilized image is observed (Fig. 4b, c, d). Fragmentation is not purely random, but the factors which determine what part of a pattern is seen at a given moment are not understood. Pattern units which are seen—or not seen—as a whole can be identified. The circle is one such unit and a complete circle may be seen even when the target is an incomplete circle. Fragmentation supports the ideas of those who have postulated the existence of pattern units (including the *Gestalt school) but does not support any previously proposed scheme in detail. It seems probable that the human visual cortex contains cells which respond to particular pattern elements. The signals which reach these cells when the image is stabilized are very weak and difficult to distinguish from a background discharge of 'noise'. From time to time the signal in one cell is recognized as greater than the noise, and the corresponding pattern element is 'seen'. Only very rarely do sufficient of these cells have signals above threshold simultaneously so that the whole target is seen.

Suppose that a target consists of a red centre surrounded by a green annulus (Fig. 5), with the outer boundary unstabilized and the inner boundary stabilized. Then the whole field appears green. The signals from the outer boundary give information that immediately within this boundary the field is green. Little or no information is received from the inner boundary, so the logical

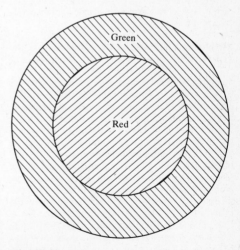

Green

Red

**Fig. 5.** Target with inner boundary stabilized, outer boundary unstabilized.

deduction is that the whole field is green. The target is 'completed', as happens in normal vision with a target which extends over the blind spot.

A more subtle example of the same process is obtained when a subject views a stabilized image of a large circle—15in (38cm) or more—divided by a diameter into two parts, light and dark. The boundary may fade first in the outer region while it is still seen in the central region. The available information cannot then logically be reconciled, because it is possible to go from a light to a dark region without crossing any perceived boundary. In this situation, the brain struggles to reconcile the irreconcilable. Various shapes of hazy boundaries appear briefly. Finally the whole field goes grey—and a 'logical', but useless, picture is obtained.

If eye movements operate in the way indicated by the experiments we have described, then the main visual information accepted by the visual system comes from receptors near to boundaries between strong contrasts of illumination or of colour—if there are any such boundaries. This may account for the extent to which an artist can convey both form and sensuous feeling by means of a drawing in which just a few lines indicate the boundaries (see ART AND VISUAL ABSTRACTION).

An animal, in order to survive in a natural situation, needs to keep in mind prominent features of the area in which it is placed and to give instant attention to any movement in the visual field which may reveal predator or prey. The visual receptors that respond mainly to *changes* of illumination filter the visual information so as to retain the permanent background but to give great prominence to any change, even in the periphery of the field. There is thus an in-built bias in favour of the information which is most important for survival.

See VISUAL SYSTEM: ORGANIZATION.     R. W. D.

Ditchburn, R. W. (1973). *Eye-movements and Visual Perception*. Oxford.
Yarbus, A. L. (1967). *Eye-movements and Vision* (translation). New York.

**RETINEX THEORY AND COLOUR CONSTANCY.** As we view an object from different distances, at different angles, and in different illuminations, there occur vast changes in the physical image on our retina; but our sensations prove much more stable than would be expected from our changeful retinal image. One of the several 'constancies' that characterize our sensory experience is colour constancy. Just as our visual system is built to tell us about the permanent size of objects rather than about the ever-fluctuating size of our *retinal image, so too it is built to tell us about the permanent colours of objects rather than about the spectral composition of the light falling on a local area of retina. The spectral composition of the light, that is, the relative proportions of the different wavelengths it contains, will depend on two factors: (i) the spectral reflectance of the object, its tendency to reflect some wavelengths more than

others, and (ii) the spectral composition of the illuminant, the relative proportions of different wavelengths in the light that falls on the object. When we pass from, say, tungsten illumination, which is rich in long wavelengths, to the bluer environment of daylight, our perception of an object's colour remains dependent on the object's spectral reflectance, and we are aware of little change. To achieve this constancy, the visual system must be taking into account not merely the local absorptions in the three classes of cone cell (see COLOUR VISION: EYE MECHANISMS) but also the pattern of absorptions in other parts of the visual field. For the *local* absorptions can depend only on the local spectral flux; and the latter, being dependent on factors (i) and (ii) above, will vary greatly as the illumination changes.

A particularly impressive and instructive demonstration of colour constancy has been provided by Edwin Land. He performed an experiment in which a single mixture of red, green, and blue light produced many different colour sensations. Observers reported white, pink, green, red, brown, yellow, purple, blue, and black sensations from identical mixtures of red, green, and blue lights. The experiment used a large, complex display that Land called a 'colour Mondrian'. The display had approximately 100 different matt papers arranged arbitrarily so that each colour was surrounded by several others. The display was illuminated with three projectors, each with a different broad-band interference filter. One filter transmitted long-wave, or reddish light; one transmitted middle-wave, or greenish light; and one transmitted short-wave, or bluish light. Each projector had an independent brightness control. The observers picked an image segment—say a white paper—and the experimenter measured the amounts of red, green, and blue light coming from the white paper. Then the observers picked a second paper—say a red one—and the experimenter measured the amounts of red, green, and blue coming to each observer's eye from the red paper. The measurements showed that roughly the same amount of red light and much less green and blue light are reflected from a red paper. The experimenter then changed the illumination so that the red light from the red paper was exactly equal to the red light from the white paper. This was a small change. The experimenter then substantially increased the brightness of the other two projectors so that exactly the same amounts of green and blue light came from the red paper as had previously come from the white paper. When all three projectors were turned on together, each observer reported the sensation red despite the fact that the physical properties of the light from that image segment were the same as that from the white with the previous illumination. In this manner, Land went from paper to paper and showed that nearly the full gamut of colour sensations can be produced from a single mixture of red, green, and blue light.

This experiment led Land to propose that the information from the long-wave receptors is intercompared to compute a biological analogue of reflectance from the long-wave light across the entire image. Similarly, the information from the middle-wave receptors is intercompared to form the biological analogue of middle-wave reflectance, and short-wave information for short-wave reflectance. The information from each of the sets of receptor mechanisms generates a separate lightness image; the comparison of three lightnesses is the determinant of colour. In Land's theory, which he called the retinex theory, these three lightnesses provide the co-ordinates of a three-dimensional space. Whereas a colour space based on the absolute absorptions in the three classes of receptor will predict only whether or not two physical stimuli will match, a space based on the three lightnesses of retinex theory will predict how colours actually look. For, between them, the three lightnesses give the reflectance of the object in different parts of the spectrum—in other words, its spectral reflectance.

The formation of lightnesses and their comparison could occur in the retina or in the cortex. Land coined the word retinex—a combination of retina and cortex—to designate the mechanism that generates independent long-, middle-, and short-wave lightness images. This system independence does not require that the retinal receptors with the same spectral sensitivity are directly connected to each other. Instead it argues that the retinal–cortical structure acts in total, as if all the colour mechanisms of the same sensitivity form independent lightness images.

McCann, McKee, and Taylor described a series of quantitative experiments that were patterned after Land's. In these experiments they measured the sensations of each area in a 'Mondrian' using a series of different illuminants. In each situation they measured the sensation by matching each area in the display to a Munsell book of colours in constant illumination. Secondly, they tested how well the sensations correlated with the reflectance of the papers as measured with spectrophotometers. They showed that there was an excellent correlation between sensation and reflectance measured with light meters that had the same spectral sensitivity as the three human cone pigments. (This correlation was particularly good when the reflectance numbers were scaled by Glasser's Munsell lightness function.)

Land and McCann proposed a lightness model that is based on the comparison of receptor-mechanism responses from all parts of the image. This lightness model does not use local averages or global averages, but rather comparisons that are based on the relationships of image segments. Local relationships are calculated by the visual system using the ratio of energies at nearby points, and this information is propagated to other parts of the image by multiplying ratios to form products. These products propagate relationships across the entire image. The mean of many different products is used as the prediction of lightness.

McCann, McKee, and Taylor showed that the ratio–product lightness model combined with retinex colour-mechanism independence accurately predicted the colour sensation reported by the observer in the 'colour Mondrian' experiments.

The rods provide an opportunity to study sets of receptors forming an image in terms of lightness. With the appropriate low-intensity light source it is possible to see, below cone threshold, that the rods interact to form a lightness image—just as above cone threshold, lightness of an image segment is dependent on the relationship of objects in all parts of the image. With a low-intensity light that is very rich in long-wave light, it is possible to see a wide variety of colour sensations from rod and long-wave cone interactions. Colour is determined by the lightness of the image generated by the rods and the lightness generated by the long-wave colour mechanism.

In summary, Land's retinex theory proposed that colour is determined by three lightnesses—each computed from comparisons using intensity information from the entire image. Each lightness is computed independently using intensity information from each spectral region. The Land and McCann lightness model uses the multiplication of ratios to form products that relate each image segment to each of the others. The mean of many different normalized products is used to predict lightness. Quantitative tests have shown that retinex colour-mechanism independence and the ratio–product lightness model can predict colour sensations in experiments with unknown changes in the spectral distribution of the illumination.

J. J. McC.

Land, E. H. (1964). The retinex. *American Scientist*, **52**, 247–64.

Land, E. H. (1977). The retinex theory of color vision. *Scientific American*, **237**, no. 6, 108–28.

Land, E. H. and McCann, J. J. (1971). Lightness and retinex theory. *Journal of the Optical Society of America*, **61**, 1–11.

McCann, J. J. (1973). Human color perception. In *Color Theory and Imaging Systems*, pp. 1–23. Washington, DC.

McCann, J. J. and Houston, K. L. (1983). Color sensation, color perception and mathematical models of color vision. In Mollon, J. D. and Sharpe, L. T., *Colour Vision*. London.

McCann, J. J., McKee, S., and Taylor, T. H. (1976). Quantitative studies in retinex theory. *Vision Research*, **16**, 445–58.

**RIBOT**, THÉODULE (1839–1916). French psychologist who did much to advance the subject in both its experimental and its clinical aspects. In 1885, he was made responsible for a course of experimental psychology at the Sorbonne and was later given a chair of experimental and comparative psychology at the Collège de France. His best-known work is *Les Maladies de la mémoire* (1884), translated as *Diseases of Memory* (1885), in which he put forward a theory of the progressive loss of memory brought about by brain disease along the evolutionary lines adumbrated by Hughlings *Jackson.                                    o. l. z.

**RIVERS, WILLIAM HALSE RIVERS** (1864–1922). British physiologist, psychologist, and ethnologist, born in Luton, Kent. After qualifying in medicine, he was appointed to a lectureship in experimental psychology and the physiology of the senses at Cambridge, but his interests moved increasingly towards ethnology, partly because of the celebrated expedition to the Torres Straits in 1899 in which he took part, along with his fellow psychologists C. S. *Myers and William *McDougall, and the anthropologists C. G. Seligman and A. C. Haddon. As an experimental psychologist to the expedition, Rivers was particularly active in measuring sensory thresholds and visual illusions in what was probably the first cross-cultural study ever carried out.

Notwithstanding his concern with anthropology, Rivers never wholly forsook his physiological interests, collaborating with the neurologist Henry *Head in an important study of the changes in tactile sensation resulting from the severance of a cutaneous nerve, Head himself being the subject. Their findings led them to the theory that there are two forms of cutaneous sensation, one relatively crude ('protopathic') and the other highly discriminative ('epicritic'). Although raising much interest at the time, this theory has since been wholly discarded.

At the outbreak of the First World War, Rivers's interests were largely centred on medical psychology, and he did important work in the treatment of war neuroses, then known as shellshock. Among his patients was the writer Siegfried Sassoon, who has painted an unforgettable portrait of Rivers in *The Complete Memoirs of George Sherston* (1937). After the war, Rivers wrote widely on issues in medical psychology and, though he remained eclectic in his views, his ideas were evidently much influenced by Freud.

Rivers, who died relatively young, was elected a Fellow of the Royal Society in 1908, and was for many years a Fellow of St John's College, Cambridge. His books included *Kinship and Social Organization* (1914), *The History of Melanesian Society* (1914), *Instinct and the Unconscious* (1920), and *Conflict and Dream* (1923).    o. l. z.

Slobodon, R. (1978). *W. H. R. Rivers*. New York.

**RORSCHACH, HERMANN** (1884–1922). Swiss psychiatrist, born at Zurich, who devised the famous standardized ink-blots (made by placing a blob of ink on paper, then folding the paper to produce symmetrical patterns) that have been widely used as an 'open-ended' test for personality traits and disorders. The Rorschach test has, however, turned out to be extremely difficult to validate objectively, and its success depends very

much on the intuitive grasp of the psychologist who interprets the patient's responses or comments. (See PROJECTIVE TECHNIQUES.)

Klopfer, B. and Davidson, H. H. (1962). *Rorschach Technique: an introductory manual*. New York.

**ROUSSEAU, JEAN-JACQUES** (1712–78). Born in Geneva, his mother dying at his birth and his father deserting him when he was 10 years old, he was brought up by relations and had no formal education, except for reading Plutarch's *Lives* and Calvinist sermons. He had an extraordinarily ramshackle early life, taking up with an illiterate maid-servant by whom he had five children—whom he committed to the foundling hospital even though he became famous for defending the natural goodness of man while blaming institutionalized life for the ills of the world. His *Confessions* (1781–8) are noted for their frankness. He died insane; and indeed his sanity throughout his life has been questioned in spite of his remarkable achievements and literary fame. See also ROUSSEAU AND EDUCATION.

Grimsley, R. (1973). *The Philosophy of Rousseau*. London.

**ROUSSEAU AND EDUCATION.** In *Émile* (1762) Rousseau presented a view of *childhood and human nature which continues to inform educational thinking. In contrast to the Christian doctrine of original sin, he asserted that human nature was essentially good. He argued that it was the institutions of society which corrupted man. He reacted against the coercive nature of the authoritarian society of his time. 'From the beginning', he writes, 'to the end of life civilized man is a slave. At birth he is sewn up in swaddling bands, and at death nailed down in a coffin.' At a time when many children could not be expected to live for long, he argued powerfully that such life as they did have should be enjoyed. The memory of his own unhappy childhood made him acutely aware of the needs of children and insistent on their right to happiness. He argued for the transformation of child-rearing: mothers were to breast-feed their own children, infants were to wear loose clothing and generally to enjoy freedom of movement and a closeness to nature. He viewed the child as a child and not as an inadequate adult, believing that it had the potential within itself to develop almost unlimited talents.

This kind of optimism is central to Rousseau's view of human nature and to his revolutionary ideas about society and education. The role of the teacher was not to restrain or to indoctrinate but so to arrange the child's environment that it could learn for itself. He attacked the education of his time on the grounds of its 'verbalism'; rote learning and textbooks were anathema to him. It was from things that they could actually experience that children best learned. His attitude was not anti-rational: 'I am far from thinking that children have no kind of reasoning. On the contrary, I notice that they think very well on everything which bears on their present and obvious interest.' From observation and his intuitive sympathy for children he was led to conceive of stages in their development towards adulthood, a notion which Jean *Piaget, another Genevan, later developed more scientifically.

Rousseau did not question contemporary *faculty psychology (the theory that various capacities—moral, aesthetic, reasoning—exist discretely in the human brain and develop separately), but his developmental view led him to recognize that children need to be childish and adolescents adolescent. He notes that the adolescent becomes ever more curious about the world, and eager for knowledge, but stresses that this knowledge must be his own, based on his own experience. Even at this stage he is sceptical of the educative value of books, except for *Robinson Crusoe*, which showed a man learning from nature and hard necessity. Rousseau understood adolescence, the moods and instability associated with the urgency of *sexual development. His views about sex education are still pertinent: 'If your pupil cannot be kept ignorant of sex differences up to 16 make sure he learns about them before 10.' This strength of Rousseau's, his trust in an intuitive understanding of the nature and needs of children, remains a positive stimulus to educational thought and practice. His belief in the essential goodness of human nature may be a myth but it is a more sustaining one than its converse. There are also dangers: a distrust of accumulated human knowledge, an anti-intellectualism that can lead to the worship of unreason, an over-reliance on feeling as a sufficient basis for sane human action. His profound distrust of institutions, however, has proved well justified: we are still struggling to make schools good places for children to learn in. (See EDUCATION: THEORY AND PRACTICE for a discussion of the influence of his views.)

C. H.
N. S.

Boyd, W. (1956). *Émile for Today*. London.

**RUBIN,** EDGAR (1886–1951). Danish psychologist, born and educated in Copenhagen, where he studied with Harold Höffding and Alfred Lehmann. He then worked for three years with G. E. Müller in Göttingen, returning to Copenhagen in 1922 to succeed Lehmann as professor and director of the psychological laboratory. Apart from some early studies of tactile sensitivity, his interests lay mainly in visual perception. His work on 'figure' and 'ground' in the visual perception of form had considerable influence and was viewed by Gestalt psychologists as basic to their treatment of figural organization (see GESTALT THEORY).

O. L. Z.

Beardslee, D. C. and Westheimer, M. (eds.) (1958). *Readings in Perception*. New York. This contains a translation of large sections of Rubin's *Visuell Wahrgenomener Figuren*.

**RUMI,** JALALUDDIN (Jalaluddin Muhammad Ibn Bahauddin Walad al-Khatibi al-Bakri al-

Balkhi, 1207–73). One of the greatest *Sufis and a major Persian poet and thinker. Born of a royal and caliphial line of distinguished scholars in Balkh (present-day Afghanistan), he taught and died in Iconium (Konya, today Asiatic Turkey). His pen-name (literally 'of Rome' or 'the (eastern) Roman') was chosen, by poetic substitution-cipher, because it represented both the town of his adoption and the Perso-Arabic word *Nur* ('light'). He acknowledges the Sufi masters *Attar and *Sanai as his 'two eyes', and they are undoubtedly his spiritual precursors. His major work is the *Mathnawi-i-Maanawi* (Poem of Inner Meaning), which was something like forty years in the writing. His theme as a guide to mystical experience is that man in the ordinary state is cut off ('veiled') from higher perceptions by lower, usually emotional, stimuli. This state is often found in both the learned and the emotionalist: addiction to vice or to imagined virtue are both forms of idolatry, which cause 'veiling'. Teaching people to hate evil and covet sanctity is training in hatred and covetousness more than an approach to goodness or holiness. Bad things cannot be avoided, nor good ones approached, he insists, by such crude and ignorant methods. The following major themes give an idea of his teaching.

*Conventional religious systems are secondary, imitative, and limited*: 'Do not attach yourself to the brick of the wall—seek instead the eternal original.' *A teacher is essential*: 'Water needs a medium between it and the fire, if it is to heat correctly.' *Laymen cannot evaluate mystical masters*: '"This ruin may seem a prosperous place to you: for me, the better place is on the King's wrist," said the Hawk. Some owls cried, "He is lying to steal our home!"' *Sufi knowledge involves escaping from familiar dimensions*: 'You belong to the world of dimension: but you come from non-dimension. Close the first "shop", open the second.' *Knowledge of Objective Truth (God) is developed through love and self-knowledge*: 'Ultimate Truth is reached by Love, that special love of which worldly love is a crude analogue: HE is within you!'

I. S.

Nicholson, R. A. (1926). *The Mathnawi of Jalaluddin Rumi*. London.
Shah, I. (1966). *Special Problems in the Study of Sufi Ideas*. London.
Shah, I. (1974). *The Elephant in the Dark*. London and New York.
Shah, I. (1978). *The Hundred Tales of Wisdom: materials from the life and teachings of Rumi*. London.
Whinfield, E. H. (1974; 1975). *Teachings of Rumi*. London; New York.

**RUSSELL,** BERTRAND ARTHUR WILLIAM (third Earl Russell, 1872–1970). By general consent the most distinguished philosopher of the twentieth century, Bertrand Russell made fundamental contributions to logic, and influenced equally academic and popular philosophy, as also appreciation of psychological issues and social questions. Starting from a broadly *idealist philosophical position (*The Problems of Philosophy*, 1912), he became a thoroughgoing empiricist, after the manner of John *Locke, in later books such as *Human Knowledge: its scope and limits* (1948). His work on the place of the individual in society included the first of the BBC Reith lectures, *Authority and the Individual* (1949).

Russell also wrote on the philosophy of physics (*The A. B. C. of Relativity*, 1935; 1958). His main works on the basis of logic and mathematics are *The Principles of Mathematics* (1903) and, with A. N. *Whitehead, *Principia Mathematica* (1910–13), which attempts to derive mathematics from logic and to resolve Frege's contradictions by means of the celebrated Theory of Types, or Theory of Classes. Among his most important philosophical contributions is his theory of descriptions, given in an article in the philosophical journal *Mind* (1905), 'On denoting'. This distinguished between the logical and grammatical subject of propositions, and developed a theory of meaning which was able to avoid the hitherto widespread view that the grammatical subjects of all meaningful propositions must refer to objects which in some sense exist. This is fundamental for an account of language that does not populate the world with a bizarre zoo of entities, such as glass mountains, female Popes, and all else that we can speak about, whether true or false.

Russell attempted to base physics on sensory—perceptual—experience. For him *sense-data (such as sensations of red, hard, extension, and so on) are the basis of all knowledge of the world and the ultimate justification and test for all empirical statements. It is perhaps unfortunate that he did not consider phenomena of perception in any detail; for if he had, he would surely have concluded that much that we experience perceptually is not given at all directly by the senses of the eyes, the ears, and touch, but is rather itself created, much as we create explanatory concepts.

Russell will be remembered not only for his own outstanding philosophical achievements but also for the crucially important personal encouragement that he gave to his student Ludwig *Wittgenstein, who might very well have abandoned philosophy had not Russell seen the importance of the *Tractatus Logico-Philosophicus*, which appeared in 1922 and for which Russell wrote a highly significant introduction. In later life Russell gradually withdrew from his logical studies, and then from his philosophical work, towards political concerns and, especially, dedication to the cause of nuclear disarmament.

Bertrand Russell revelled in and inspired controversy: his *Autobiography* (3 vols., 1967–9) has the frankness one should expect from a man exulting in all aspects of life and intellect, while totally free of humbug. In spite of his unorthodox views and behaviour he received the highest honours: Fellowship of the Royal Society (1908) and the Order of Merit (1949).

Russell's main works include *An Essay on the Foundations of Geometry* (1897); *The Principles of Mathematics* (1903); 'On denoting', *Mind*, n.s. xiv (1905), 479–93; with A. N. Whitehead, *Principia Mathematica* (vol. i, 1910; 2nd edn., 1935); 'Knowledge by acquaintance and knowledge by description', *Proceedings of the Aristotelian Society*, n.s. xi (1910–11), 108–28; *The Problems of Philosophy* (1912); *Our Knowledge of the External World* (1914); *The Analysis of Mind* (1921); *The Analysis of Matter* (1927); *An Outline of Philosophy* (1927); *An Inquiry into Meaning and Truth* (1940); *The History of Western Philosophy* (1946); *Human Knowledge* (1948); *My Philosophical Development* (1959).

See also RUSSELL'S PHILOSOPHY OF MIND: DUALISM; RUSSELL'S PHILOSOPHY OF MIND: NEUTRAL MONISM.                                              R. L. G.

Ayer, A. J. (1972). *Bertrand Russell as a Philosopher*. London.

Pears, D. (1967). *Bertrand Russell and the British Tradition in Philosophy*. London.

Pears, D. F. (ed.) (1972). *Bertrand Russell*. London.

**RUSSELL'S PHILOSOPHY OF MIND: DUALISM.** When *Russell wrote about the mind, his gaze was also fixed on the physical world beyond it, because he wanted to explain how minds can acquire knowledge of what lies outside them. This gave his philosophy of mind an outward-facing character. He was especially interested in what happens at the point of contact between mind and matter when knowledge is acquired. What he says about the mind's output is less detailed except when the output is language and the language expresses knowledge or belief about the physical world. Emotions, intentions, and actions are treated in a more perfunctory way.

He shared *Hume's view that psychology is the central science, because all the data of physics and physiology are somehow passed into the mind and one of psychology's tasks is to explain how this is done. However, he did not share Hume's tendency to scepticism about the physical world. He believed that science gives us a rich and extensive knowledge of what lies outside minds and that a philosophy of mind which denies, belittles, or jeopardizes that knowledge is unacceptable.

His main contribution to the subject was *The Analysis of Mind*, which he published in 1921. The theory that he there proposes about what happens at the point of contact between mind and matter is not one that appeals to common sense. Common sense might endorse the theory that there is a mysterious interaction between two irreducibly different kinds of things, the mental and the physical (dualism). But the theory proposed in *The Analysis of Mind* is that at the point of contact there occur events which are in themselves neither mental nor physical, but which are the basic components out of which we construct both the mental and the physical world (neutral monism). This is the kind of conclusion that could be reached only at the end of a long philosophical investigation. So perhaps the best way to explain it is to describe its development out of the dualism which Russell espoused first.

The leading idea in his early, dualistic philosophy of mind is that all knowledge is based on acquaintance. In his philosophical classic *The Problems of Philosophy* (1912) he defines acquaintance as the mind's relation with those objects that directly confront it. He explains that the kind of confrontation that he means occurs in sense-perception, introspection, and certain kinds of memory. Sense-perception gives us our knowledge of the external world, and the crucial question is whether the direct objects of perceptual acquaintance lie outside the mind. His answer is that they do. However, he does not think that they are the physical objects which the unphilosophical take themselves to perceive. They are sense-data, external to the mind, unlike mental images, but phenomenal, unlike physical objects. Their intermediate status is hard to formulate, and his specification of examples, such things as patches of colour and sounds, does not make it much easier to understand.

The construction of the physical world out of such components does not belong to the philosophy of mind. But the difficult task of specifying the components themselves does belong to it. There was also another difficulty that faced Russell at this point. *Sense-data, which are by definition appearances presented to minds, do not provide a sufficient basis for constructing the physical world, in which much of what goes on is never presented to any mind. So he had to enrich the basis with unsensed appearances (sensibilia). He could then treat a physical event as a centre from which lines of appearances radiate outwards in physical space and only a small proportion of these appearances would be presented to minds and so become sense-data. The introduction of unsensed appearances put a constraint on his philosophy of mind: it had to explain the difference between mere sensibilia and sense-data.

At first the distinction did not give him any difficulty. A sense-datum was simply distinguished by the fact that it was presented to a mind, or, to put this the other way round, by the fact that a mind was acquainted with it. But later, when this reliance on the mind as the subject of acquaintance (ego) began to strike him as illegitimate, he had to explain the difference between unsensed and sensed appearances in another way.

He finally gave up the ego in 1921, when he was converted to neutral monism, which constructs the mental world out of the very same components as the physical world and, therefore, cannot admit the ego. The construction of the physical world out of these components—the other side of neutral monism—was developed by him eight years earlier in *Our Knowledge of the External World*, and it did not produce a crisis in his philosophy of mind, as the abandonment of the ego did.

Russell's dualism lasted just so long as he refused to construct the mental world out of the same components as the physical world. In that period the main lines of his philosophy of mind were very simple. Acquaintance was a relation connecting the ego with its objects. At that time his main adversary was *idealism, which in its extreme form maintains that we never make any contact with anything outside our own minds. Acquaintance seemed to offer a way of escape from this restriction. It was a relation, and he conceded to the idealists that it was a mental relation. But he rejected their inference that, therefore, its objects must be mental too. His early theory of sense-data attempts to exploit the possibility that they are sometimes physical. However, the attempt would succeed only if he could give an acceptable account of sense-data, which would not only show that they are the same kind of thing as unsensed appearances but also explain what distinguishes them from unsensed appearances.

If he could do these two things, he would have a realist theory of knowledge and a realist theory of meaning, and he would have thrown off the cramping restrictions of idealism. For though sense-data would be the only physical objects of acquaintance, all our knowledge of the physical world could start from them and the meanings of all our descriptive words could be derived from them.

This ambitious enterprise ran into two difficulties, one on each of its two main fronts. His reaction was to give up the dualistic theory that mental and physical things are irreducibly different and to take up neutral monism, which reduces both to the same basis.

The first difficulty was that he could rely on acquaintance only so long as he believed that the mind was, or contained, an ego, or subject. In fact, even in 1912, he felt unsure about the ego. It was too vulnerable both to Hume's criticism, endorsed by William *James, that introspection reveals no such thing, and to *Kant's criticism, foreshadowed by Hume, that no empirical meaning can be attached to the hypothesis that there is such a thing. So Russell gave up the ego, and then had to find another explanation of the awareness that distinguishes sense-data from mere sensibilia. The new explanation could not be that sense-data are related by acquaintance or by any other relation to an ego. It had to be that sense-data and other directly presented objects are related in certain ways to one another.

The second difficulty concerned the status of sense-data. How could they be the same kind of thing as unsensed appearances? If, as he believed, unsensed appearances exist as actual things at points in physical space, they are unequivocally physical, and the word 'appearance' merely alludes to the possibility that they might acquire a relation with a mind. Sense-data, on the other hand, could be physical only if they occurred in the nervous systems of percipients. Now there is no doubt that in his early philosophy of mind he did ascribe this kind of physical existence to them. But that left many mysteries unsolved. How exactly did the mental relation, acquaintance, manage to reach out to them? And how exactly did they themselves manage to represent their causes outside the percipient's body, as he implied that they did, when he specified them as things like patches of colour and sounds?

The neutral monism which he adopted in 1921 was intended to answer these questions. (See following entry.)                D. F. P.

## RUSSELL'S PHILOSOPHY OF MIND: NEUTRAL MONISM.

The philosophy of mind adopted by *Russell in his middle period was neutral monism, which denies that there is any irreducible difference between the mental and the physical and tries to construct both the mental world and the physical world out of components which are in themselves neither mental nor physical but neutral. He adopted this theory because he believed that there was no other way of solving the problems that beset his earlier dualism (see previous entry). The book in which he developed the theory, *The Analysis of Mind* (1921), is an unusual one. The version of neutral monism defended in it is qualified in several ways and it is enriched with ideas drawn from his reading of contemporary works on *behaviourism and depth psychology. The result is not entirely consistent, but it is interesting and vital especially where it is least consistent.

The aim of neutral monism is to show that the difference between the physical and the mental is not a difference of components but only a difference in the way in which the components are put together. An analogy can be found in the difference between the division of a country's population into groups living in different areas and its division into the categories used by tax-collectors. In both cases the same human material is used, and the difference lies in the method of selection. Similarly, according to neutral monism appearances are grouped in one way to form physical objects and in another way to form minds. In order to get a physical object, you take all the appearances that radiate outwards from its position in physical space. In order to get a mind, you take all the appearances that start from surrounding objects and converge on its position in physical space. The difference is based on the distinction between output and input. However, a physical object is not the separate source of its output of appearances, but only the group of all the appearances sent out, and similarly a mind is not the separate recipient of its input of appearances, but only the group of all the appearances received.

This theory was devised to solve the problems of perception, and its generalization to cover not only sensations (received appearances) but also such things as beliefs and desires was bound to lead to difficulties. But first, did it solve the problems of perception?

There were two such problems which Russell's earlier dualism had failed to solve. First, he had to explain the difference between an unsensed appearance (sensibile) and a sensed appearance (sense-datum), and his earlier explanation was that a sense-datum is presented to a subject (ego) which is then acquainted with it. But when he ceased to believe in the ego, he was no longer in a position to appeal to its acts, and he could not even use the word 'sense-datum', because it implies that something is given to a recipient. So he used the words 'sensation' or 'sensum' instead, and he had to find some other distinguishing mark of sensa. Second, he had to show that sensa really are the same kind of thing as sensibilia, and, what is more, that they are both in themselves neither physical nor mental but neutral.

The neutral monist solution to the first of these two problems was that sensed appearances are distinguished from unsensed appearances by the fact that they are related to other appearances in ways in which unsensed appearances are not related to other appearances. For sensed appearances produce later memories, and at the time they produce beliefs with the help of memories of earlier appearances. These networks of relations cannot be found among unsensed appearances and so they can be taken as the distinguishing mark of sensed appearances. The difference becomes more striking when we add the behavioural effects of memory and belief and all the stratified processes of learning. The details are complicated, but the essential point is that the analysis of *consciousness does not rely on a relation between subject and object, but relies, instead, on distinctive relations between sensed appearances and other appearances.

At this point Russell qualifies his neutral monism. The theory in its pure form would claim that these distinctive relations provide the complete explanation of consciousness. But he avoids this extreme position. In fact, the philosophy of mind of anyone who adopted it would be like *Hamlet* without the Prince of Denmark. More specifically, it would be vulnerable to two objections. Depth psychology shows that the distinctive relations are not always accompanied by consciousness, and common sense suggests that, conversely, consciousness is not always accompanied by the distinctive relations.

The neutral monist response to the second of the two problems amounted to little more than an assertion that sensed appearances really are the same kind of thing as unsensed appearances. But sensed appearances are sensations, and sensations are already mental and do not need any distinctive relations in order to make them constituents of minds; and so their basic neutrality is a pretence. Indeed, the only plausible theory that is at all like neutral monism is the theory that sensations are a special kind of physical occurrence in the nervous systems of observers. It is, therefore, not surprising to find Russell adopting this position in *An Outline of Philosophy* (1927) and in *My Philosophical Development* (1959). However, this is not neutral monism but the kind of materialism that identifies the mental with the physical. In subsequent decades many philosophers have subscribed to this identification in the general form that covers everything mental. When Russell suggested the theory in the special case of sensations, he put them in the same category as unsensed appearances only by giving them a physical aspect as well as a mental aspect. In any case, unsensed appearances would have nothing to match the mental aspect of sensations, but only the possibility of becoming sensations. In general, Russell construed the world, in a way that was always *Leibnizian but never *idealist, as a constellation of radiating views each of them something like what would be recorded by a photographic plate at the appropriate point in physical space. But neutral monism is not the right metaphysic to accommodate this idea.

Outside the area of perception it is even harder for a neutral monist to demonstrate that the basis of the mental world is neutral. The two most difficult cases are beliefs and desires. Neither of them can be constructed entirely out of sensa, and Russell's strategy is to call in images. But are images really like sensa? Certainly most images are quite unlike what is recorded on a photographic plate, and the use of an image is often more like drawing a picture than looking at one. In any case, images at best could supply only the content of a belief, and there is also assent to the content. Since Russell was committed to avoiding acts of mind, he adopted *Hume's theory that assent is a feeling. However, such a feeling would be completely unlike a sensum and at this point neutral monism has been left far behind.

Quite apart from neutral monism, it is questionable whether Russell's analysis was on the right lines. Assent may not be an act of mind, but it is directed on to a content and this feature (*intentionality) is not easy to include in a theory that treats assent as a feeling. Intentionality is *Brentano's idea rather than Hume's, and *Wittgenstein put it at the centre of his philosophy of mind. When Russell gave up the ego and its acts, he ought to have retained the essential feature of its acts, intentionality.

In his analysis of desire, his rejection of intentionality is deliberately provocative. His main point, derived from depth psychology, is that people often do not know what they want. Now it is undeniable that people often do not know what they need. So he assimilates desires to needs, and defines desire as a feeling that starts a line of behaviour and defines satisfaction as another feeling that terminates it. The name of the initial feeling is 'discomfort' and the name of the terminal feeling is 'removal of discomfort' or 'pleasure'. However, he is inclined to define these feelings not by their introspectible qualities but by their places in the pattern of behaviour. In fact, his whole analysis is very behaviouristic. The object of a desire is whatever would cure the discomfort, and conscious desire is merely desire accompanied by a true belief about the cure. If this were correct, it would certainly explain why people do not always know what they want.

The three main theories of *The Analysis of Mind* have had very different fates. Its neutral monism, already heavily qualified, has not survived, and materialism is the only monistic theory that seems to have any hope of replacing it. Russell's rejection of intentionality appears to have been a mistake. On the other hand, his critique of the assumption that all the contents of a mind lie open to inspection has produced an enduring effect. This critique is a characteristic Russellian achievement. It uses ideas taken from behaviourism and depth psychology with panache, and it threatens to destroy the Humean framework in which it is set.   D. F. P.

Borst, C. V. (ed.) (1970). *The Mind/Brain Identity Theory*. New York.
Pears, D. (1967). *Bertrand Russell and the British Tradition in Philosophy*. London.
Quinton, A. (1972). Russell's philosophy of mind. In Pears, D. (ed.), *Bertrand Russell*. London.
Wittgenstein, L. (Eng. trans. 1975). *Philosophical Remarks*. Oxford.

**RYLE**, GILBERT (1900–76). British philosopher, commonly characterized as a leading member of the school of 'linguistic philosophy' which was prominent at Oxford in the years following the Second World War. This description of him is questionable, however. He regularly made clear to students that he had no wish to be the founder of any philosophical 'school', and philosophical terms such as 'materialism', 'idealism'—and even perhaps the expression 'linguistic philosophy' itself—were sometimes described by him, almost dismissively, as 'hustings' words.

A central part of his programme was to classify concepts according to their 'category' or 'logical type'. His most famous work, *The Concept of Mind* (1949), is an attempt to show that philosophers have misled themselves by assigning concepts which purport to refer to minds and mental qualities to the wrong category. (One assigns words to categories according to their 'logical behaviour'; thus 'know' does not behave like 'read'—at least in some respects—since one can read carefully or carelessly but one cannot know something carefully or carelessly; similarly one can do some reading for half an hour but one cannot 'do some knowing' for half an hour.) *Descartes, according to Ryle, had correctly recognized that men were different from machines but had mistakenly characterized the difference by suggesting that some human movements were the result of 'non-material' or 'non-mechanical' causes. A second 'world' had therefore to be invented—a 'mental' world—to house such entities; it belonged in the same category as the 'physical' world but contained non-spatial and non-mechanical happenings. The postulation of such a 'world' is scathingly referred to by Ryle as 'the dogma of the Ghost in the Machine'. He is not saying that there is *no* such world, since this would be to repeat the same category mistake; he is arguing that the counting of 'worlds' is misguided and that we are misleading ourselves if we raise questions couched in 'ghost-in-machine' terms. He argues instead that many mentalistic words are dispositional in character: thus to describe a person as intelligent does not imply that occult events going on 'in the mind' are influencing other events going on 'in the body'; it indicates some of the things which he is disposed to do if particular circumstances arise. Other mentalistic words, such as 'solve', 'detect', and 'see', are 'achievement' words: that is to say, they are used when certain processes or activities have been brought to completion and do not relate to shadowy processes or activities going on 'somewhere else'.

In his later writings (see *Collected Papers*, 1971, and the posthumously published *On Thinking*, 1979) he argues that when a person is described as thinking (like Rodin's *Le Penseur*) it does not follow that there is a single activity, for example operating with words or symbols, that is invariably going on. Other published works include *Dilemmas* (1954) and *Plato's Progress* (1966).

Ryle's views have sometimes been described as 'behaviourist', and they do indeed have a certain amount in common with the radical *behaviourism of B. F. Skinner. In particular both thinkers are in agreement in their opposition to methodological behaviourism: neither wishes to say that 'mental events' exist *alongside* 'physical events' but are not suitable objects for scientific study. Skinner's attack on 'autonomous man', however, is less sophisticated than Ryle's attack on 'the Ghost in the Machine'; mental-conduct words, for Skinner, are 'perquisites of autonomous man' (*Beyond Freedom and Dignity*, 1972, p. 15), and the suggestion that such words are not all of the same logical type is not considered. In addition Skinner writes

at times like a traditional determinist, whereas Ryle correctly recognizes that the question, 'Does this action merit praise or blame?' is of a different logical type from the question, 'What were this action's causal antecedents?' An extension of Skinner's position might be to say that for its own purposes a science of behaviour requires a language without the explanatory superstructures implied by disposition words, and that it is for this reason—not simply for doctrinaire behaviourist reasons—that mentalistic words should not figure in scientific reports on human and animal behaviour. Ryle, however, unlike Skinner, is concerned with the use of mentalistic words for workaday purposes; and, apart from his admonition to philosophers, he is not attempting to argue that our ways of talking require revision.

The final chapter of *The Concept of Mind* offers an account of the subject-matter of psychology. Its main thesis is that psychology should not be regarded as though it were a kind of counterpart to Newtonian physics, concerned with 'mental' phenomena as opposed to 'physical' ones.

The Cartesian picture left no place for Mendel or Darwin. The two-worlds legend was also a two-sciences legend, and the recognition that there are many sciences should remove the sting from the suggestion that 'psychology' is not the name of a single homogeneous theory. Few of the names of sciences do denote such unitary theories, or show any promise of doing so.

For those interested in psychology perhaps the most important message from Ryle's work is that insufficient attention to correct categorization can lead to false contrasts, to misleading analogies, and indeed to downright bad theorizing. It is a message which, up to now, not all practising psychologists have fully taken to heart.                T. R. M.

Lyons, W. (1980). *Gilbert Ryle: an introduction to his philosophy*. Brighton.
Wood, O. P. and Pitcher, G. (eds.) (1970). *Ryle: a collection of critical essays*. London.

# S

**SACCADES.** Rapid movements, punctuated by brief fixations of the eyes, during searching eye-movements. The saccades (or saccadic flicks) of the eyes do not occur when a person is following a moving object with his eyes, or with eye-movements due to the head turning as an object is fixated. Thus, there are two kinds of eye-movements—'saccadic' and 'smooth'—given by different neural mechanisms. The world remains fixed only during saccadic movements, and not during smooth eye-movements; this is probably because the *efferent commands to move the eyes for searching are cancelled against the movement signals from the retinas: when the eye-movement command and retinal-movement signals are equal and opposite, the world remains stable (unlike a panning cine camera) but only while the eyes move saccadically.

The successive fixations between the saccadic jumps refresh the borders of retinal images, as the receptors adapt (fatigue) with constant stimulation, giving rise to *after-images. Visual acuity for resolving fine detail is, however, slightly impaired by the small saccadic movements, as is shown by a slightly improved acuity, for a second or so, in flash after-images, which are 'photographed' fixed on the retinas, although they move.

The word 'saccade' derives from an old French word meaning the sudden flicks of a sail.

**SADISM.** Term first used by *Krafft-Ebing to describe sexual pleasure gained by the infliction of pain or cruelty on others. He derived the word from the name of the Marquis de Sade. De Sade was condemned to death by the *parlement* at Aix-en-Provence for sexual vices, but had his sentence commuted by the king to imprisonment. While in the Bastille he wrote scandalous novels based on fact: *Justine* (1791), *La Philosophie dans le boudoir* (1793), *Juliette* (1797), and *Les Crimes de l'amour* (1800).

**SANAI,** HAKIM (Khwajah Abu-al-Majd Majdud ibn-Adam Sanai, *c.*1046–?1141). A native of Ghazna in present-day Afghanistan, he was a major *Sufi teacher and author, acknowledged by *Rumi as one of his inspirers. He wrote an enormous quantity of mystical verse, of which his *Hadiqa* (Walled Garden of Truth, 1131) is his master-work and the first Persian mystical epic of Sufism. He taught that lust and greed, emotional excitement, stood between humankind and divine knowledge, which was the only true reality. Love and a social conscience are for him the foundation

of religion; mankind is asleep, living in what is in fact a desolate world. Religion as commonly understood is only habit and ritual.                I. S.

Sanai, Hakim. *The Walled Garden of Truth* (trans. D. Pendlebury, 1976). New York.

**SARTRE,** JEAN-PAUL (1905–80). Sartre's father, a naval officer, died two years after Jean-Paul was born, whereupon he and his mother went to live with her parents. Sartre thus grew up under the supervision of his grandfather, Charles Schweitzer (uncle of Albert Schweitzer), who exercised a powerful and not altogether benign influence on the boy's development. He was sequestered at home, and there encouraged in precocious literary aspirations until the age of 10, when he was sent to school, to enjoy for the first time the companionship of other children. Sartre's own account of his childhood in *Les Mots* (1964) is mostly negative, and his grandfather is subjected to extremely unfavourable criticism. In the course of his adolescence he studied at the prestigious École Normale Supérieure, met Simone de Beauvoir, qualified to become a *lycée* philosophy teacher, and did national service in the meteorological section of the Army. He nurtured strong literary ambitions and ideals, which came to fruition with the publication (1938) of his first novel, *La Nausée*, the first existentialist novel. In subsequent years he published several plays and novels, notably *Huis clos* and *L'age de raison*, in which his philosophy is given concrete dramatic expression. This work was combined with more purely philosophical productions, dealing with the imagination, the emotions, and *Husserl's notion of the transcendental ego; in this he was much influenced by the works of the German *phenomenological school. These studies culminated in his most systematic and ambitious philosophical work, *L'être et le néant* (1943), which powerfully integrated his philosophical concerns and his controlling literary themes. In later years he became increasingly occupied with political matters, both practically and intellectually, thus attracting by his outspoken heterodoxy the obloquy of both Church and state.

The subtitle of *L'être et le néant* is 'an essay on phenomenological ontology', and this aptly describes the method and content of that difficult but rewarding book. For Sartre's aim is to give a systematic descriptive account of the fundamental categories into which reality divides—an architectonic of being—and of their interrelations, by means of a phenomenological enquiry into the structures that *consciousness displays. This is designed to elucidate the basic character of man's existence in the world, and so expose the underlying principles of his various modes of conduct. The starting-point and pivot of the enquiry is, in the spirit of the phenomenological tradition, an insistence upon the constitutional *intentionality of consciousness—its directedness on to outer objects—and from this Sartre's whole philosophy ultimately derives. It is first observed that consciousness is, of its very nature, consciousness *of* things other than itself. These things exist independently of consciousness, and are thus transcendent to consciousness, inasmuch as their being is never exhausted by their presentations to consciousness. The objects of consciousness comprise the realm of being Sartre calls the 'in-itself'.

The in-itself, for Sartre, is wholly outside of consciousness: intentional objects are not (as they were for Husserl) in any sense constituents of, or in, consciousness. But consciousness itself, by contrast, is a dependent entity in that it cannot be conceived to exist independently of the in-itself, since it is essentially intentional; it is therefore supported in its being, as Sartre puts it, by something other than itself. (His position is thus the reverse of *idealism.) Indeed, consciousness just *consists* in the intentional positing of transcendent objects; it has no other being. Yet—and this is the crucial point—it does not thereby collapse into the in-itself: it remains distinct from its intentional objects, and in a special way. Consciousness is not distinct from its objects in the way the ink-well is distinct from the table, since the being of these things is independent and the relation in which they stand external. Rather, consciousness stands off from the in-itself as a kind of pure emptiness, whose concrete being, such as it is, is exhausted by the objects it cannot but intend. Sartre characterizes the structure of intentionality, and thereby of consciousness itself, by saying that the relation incorporates a kind of negation: consciousness is at a distance from its objects by *not* being those objects, and at the same time what is intended constitutes all that is *positive* in the being of consciousness. Sartre is thus able to conclude that, in virtue of the structure of intentionality, the being of consciousness consists in its unalloyed negativity, i.e. its intrinsic nothingness. The directedness of consciousness is then not the directedness of any *thing*, since that would have to be an in-itself and hence an object for consciousness. So this evacuation of consciousness does not stop at ordinary objects of perception or memory; it includes one's character, past, body, and even one's ego, which for Sartre (unlike Husserl) is intelligible only as an object of consciousness, not as its immanent unifying and constitutive essence. In general, nothing that is an *object* of consciousness can be *within* consciousness. As a result of this nothingness, says Sartre, we are apt to apprehend small pockets of negativity in the world. This occurs in the attitude of questioning and is revealed in the experience of *lack*, which characterizes human reality; the

phenomenon is most famously illustrated by the example of the expectant man apprehending the *absence* of Pierre in the café. Sartre's contention is that consciousness of negation, which is integral to human experience, is possible only on the ground of the nothingness of consciousness itself.

But consciousness is not only engaged in the world by virtue of its intentionality and correlative nothingness; it is further distinguished from the in-itself by possessing the characteristic of *self*-consciousness. Consciousness is thus a being, as Sartre says, that exists for itself. The primary mode of self-consciousness is what Sartre calls 'pre-reflective' self-consciousness, i.e. the awareness of its own directedness on to transcendent beings. It is important to Sartre that the structure of this primitive self-consciousness does not recapitulate within consciousness the intentional relation: there is not, between consciousness and itself, the kind of distance that separates consciousness from the in-itself. For if there were, consciousness, in taking itself as object, would be self-transcendent; which is impossible. Pre-reflective consciousness is what Sartre calls 'non-positional' self-awareness. Indeed, if this self-consciousness were positional there would be the threat of an infinite regress, since the positing consciousness must always be transparent to itself. Consciousness is, paradoxically enough, entirely coterminous with itself, yet at a kind of distance from itself: there is, in Sartre's phrase, an 'impalpable fissure' within consciousness. This characteristic of self-consciousness implies that whatever is a property of consciousness is a conscious property of it. Sartre's thesis now is that the properties of consciousness which are thus revealed to consciousness are not tolerable to it, and that we seek, by a variety of stratagems, to conceal these properties from ourselves. (Some of these conditions of consciousness appear also on the reflective plane, which is to say the kind of self-consciousness that is genuinely positional, as when we take up the stance of another with respect to our own being.)

We can now formulate and locate Sartre's conception of freedom: freedom is precisely the nothingness of consciousness as it stands off from its objects. Specifically, one's character or past or body—what Sartre calls one's *facticity*—transcend one's consciousness of them, and are symmetrically transcended *by* consciousness. Choice consists in exploiting this distance in the formation of projects: the for-itself has possibilities because it *is not* its facticity. Imagining and questioning and doubting thus become models of human freedom. But, according to Sartre, consciousness is appalled by its freedom; it is therefore appalled at its own being, which is nothingness. The outcome is that consciousness tries to conceal its own nothingness from itself by denying its freedom: this is the condition of *bad faith*. Bad faith is, however, doomed to failure because of the principle that what is true of consciousness is consciously true of it: there is thus no escaping the anguish that is consciousness of freedom. Moreover, in so far as bad faith represents the aspiration of the for-itself to become an in-itself, it characterizes the attitude of *sincerity* as well as the attitude of refusing to acknowledge to oneself what in fact one is. In both cases bad faith consists in a denial of freedom, either by conceiving of one's choices as externally determined or by trying to collapse the transcendent for-itself into its facticity, as with sincerity. We refuse to acknowledge our actions as our own by trading upon our transcendence from them, or we represent them as inevitable by denying this transcendence. And behind this mode of conduct is the basic structure of intentionality, now taking facticity as object. Good faith would be an undistorted conception of the relation between free consciousness and all that one *is* in the way of body, character, actions, past, and so forth.

In addition to the in-itself and the for-itself, Sartre discloses, by attending to the structures of consciousness, a third category of being, namely 'being-for-others'. So far, consciousness has been characterized as a pure point of view on the world, rather than as an item within it; but the revealed existence of other consciousnesses alters this solipsistic picture radically. The body has hitherto been considered as *my* body, as it is lived by me; but it is also the medium through which I exist for the other, and the same is true of other facets of my facticity. According to Sartre, consciousness takes on the structure of being-for-others—it becomes an object *in* the world—when it is subjected, via the body, to the *look* of the other. In experiencing the look I can establish a new relation to myself, as in the attitude of *shame*: I am ashamed of myself as I appear to the other, and my body mediates for me the formation of this attitude. (It is to be noted that, for Sartre, the primary mode of recognition of others is affective, not cognitive: it is not a relation of knowledge.) In being-for-others consciousness presents itself to itself as an object in the field of another subjectivity, and this on the pre-reflective plane. The fundamental character of interpersonal relations is thus a confrontation of freedoms, which Sartre sees as generating relations of *conflict*. As with bad faith, this arises from an inherently unstable oscillation between freedom and facticity. Thus, for Sartre, the basic modes of human relationship embody self-defeating projects. Love, he says, is the wish to possess the other's freedom, for the other to be freely enslaved; but this is not possible, so the project of love is futile. Similarly the conducts of *sadism and *masochism involve, in their different ways, the possession or appropriation of a freedom: but in the end the possession self-defeatingly implies an exercise of freedom. In sex, too, the aim is to induce the identification of the other with his or her body; but the being of the other, as an incarnated consciousness, cannot but transcend the facticity that invades the desiring consciousness.

What is not clear in all this is whether Sartre thinks that his bleak and pessimistic account of human relations is essential to them or whether, like bad faith, they are conditions of consciousness from which we might conceivably be liberated. It does not seem, at any rate, that they issue from the constitutive structure of consciousness as it relates to the subjectivity of others.

It is important to bear in mind, in coming to grips with *L'être et le néant*, that Sartre's philosophy does not take the form of a series of unconnected but insightful commentaries on the human condition; it consists, rather, of a systematically articulated body of doctrine, ostensibly derived from certain basic tenets of phenomenological ontology, and is to be evaluated as such. In particular, one should be aware that familiar terms—'freedom', 'shame', 'nothingness', 'anguish', etc.—are employed with a specific theoretical content which can only be grasped by coming at the work as an organized whole. Nor should such paradoxical-seeming dicta as 'the being of the for-itself is defined as being what it is not and not being what it is' be taken at face value, but should be construed as dramatic expressions of thoughts whose meaning, often relatively sober, can only be grasped in context.

Next to *L'être et le néant*, Sartre's main philosophical works are *La transcendance de l'ego* (1936); *L'imagination* (1936); *Esquisse d'une théorie des emotions* (1939); *La Critique de la raison dialectique* (1960). Arthur C. Danto, *Jean-Paul Sartre* (1975) contains a bibliography of English translations of Sartre's works.　　c. m.

**SCANNING.** Used loosely, this word is sometimes used to describe the searching movements of the eyes, but a usefully restricted technical sense is conveying information by movement (as of the flying spot in a television camera and a corresponding electron beam in the receiver) down a single channel. The receptors of the eyes, the ears, and the skin are parallel channels and do not employ scanning in this technical sense. There is, however, a creature with a single channel scanning eye—a copepod, *Copilia quadrata*. See SACCADES.

Gregory, R. L. (1986). *Odd Perceptions*. London.

**SCANNING OF THE BRAIN.** See IMAGES OF THE BRAIN IN ACTION.

**SCHEMAS.** In walking down the street with a friend, one simultaneously engages in at least five movement processes: walking (including maintaining posture), breathing, talking, gesticulating, and scanning the shop windows and passers-by. But each of these processes involves the co-operation of multiple processes: for example, stepping is determined *inter alia* by high-level route-selection processes ('turn left at the town hall'), visual *feedback about the location of obstacles, and tactile feedback from the soles of the feet. And each of these in turn requires activity in a neural network linking an array of receptors with an array of motor neurones.

These behaviours involve not only 'externally directed' movement, but also a variety of 'exploratory' movements that help update an 'internal model of the world' (Craik, 1943). In a new situation, we can recognize that familiar things are in new relationships, and use our knowledge of those individual things and our perception of those relationships to guide our behaviour on that occasion. It thus seems reasonable to posit that the 'internal model of the world' must be built of units which correspond, roughly, to domains of interaction—a phrase carefully chosen to include objects in the usual sense, but to include many other things besides, from some attention-riveting detail of an object all the way up to some sophisticated domain of social or linguistic interaction for purposeful beings. We shall use the word 'schema' to correspond to the unit of knowledge—the internal representation of a domain of interaction—within the brain.

The intelligent organism does not so much respond to stimuli as select information that will help it achieve current goals—though a well-designed or evolved system will certainly need to take appropriate account of unexpected changes in its environment. To a first approximation, then, planning is the process whereby the system combines an array of relevant knowledge, to determine a course of action suited to current goals. In its fullest subtlety, planning can involve the refinement of knowledge structures and goal structures, as well as action per se. While an animal may perceive many aspects of its environment, only a few of these can at any time become the primary locus of interaction.

In general, our thesis is that *perception of an object (at least at the pre-verbal level) involves gaining access to routines for interaction with it, but does not necessarily involve execution of even one of these sub-routines. Our image for the control of the ensuing behaviour is context-dependent interpretation (in the sense described in PROGRAMS AND PLANNING), in that new inputs (such as coming upon an unexpected obstacle) can alter the elaboration of the high-level structures into lower-level tests and actions which in turn call upon the interaction of motor and sensory systems. We study programs which are part of the internal state of the system prior to action, and which can flexibly guide that action in terms of internal goals or drives and external circumstances.

To better appreciate the intimate relation between perception and action, consider the perceptual cycle (Neisser, 1976). The subject actively explores the visual world—for example, by moving eyes, head, or body (or manipulating the environment). Exploration is directed by anticipatory schemas, which Neisser defines as plans for perceptual action as well as readiness for particular kinds of optical structure. The information thus picked up modifies the perceiver's anticipations of certain kinds of information which—thus modified—direct further exploration and become ready

for more information. For example, to tell whether or not any coffee is left in a cup we may reach out and tilt the cup to make the interior visible, and keep tilting the cup further and further as we fail to see any coffee, until we either see the coffee at last or conclude that the cup is empty.

Head and Holmes (1911) were perhaps the first to study systematically patients' perceptions of the spatial aspects of their own bodies. They referred to the basis of this perception as the 'postural schema'. This integrated representation of prior movements was held to be updated by each change of position, and to provide a postural model into which all incoming sensations might be integrated. F. C. *Bartlett (1932), who had been much influenced by H. *Head, introduced the term 'schema' into the psychological literature in the sense of an active organization of past reactions, or of past experiences, which must always be supposed to be operating in any well-adapted organic response. With this, the emphasis shifts from the postural frame to cognitive aspects as revealed in Bartlett's memory experiments.

Workers in *artificial intelligence organize their schemata for 'understanding', separating the problem of sensory representation from that of directing action (see Bobrow and Collins, 1975, for a sampling of approaches). Minsky (1975) has advanced his concept of 'frames' as a unification of these studies. Here, the stress on recognition of overall contexts which subsume the particularities of the current situation complements the schema-assemblage emphasis on the building up of a representation from familiar subparts.

Neisser (1976), influenced by Gibson, takes a holistic approach with little concern for mechanism and with the schema usually viewed as corresponding to a total situation rather than some localized element of it. He takes explicit account only of those actions which are directed to sampling sensory data. Neisser's use of schema seems to be that of Bartlett, augmented by the Gibsonian view of information pickup and the resultant stress on the perceptual cycle discussed above.

Another root of the use of 'schema' in current psychology is found in the work of Jean *Piaget. The Piagetian schema is the internal representation of some generalized class of situations, enabling the organism to act in a co-ordinated fashion over a whole range of analogous situations. Reviewing his approach to the genesis and development of knowledge, Piaget (1971) relates his schemas to the innate releasing mechanisms of the ethologists and thus, via Konrad Lorenz, to the schemata of *Kant in the Critique of Pure Reason (1787). Yet Oldfield and Zangwill (1942) assert that the Head–Bartlett concept of schema has no connection with that of Kant!

The concept of schema has also developed a special meaning in the motor skills literature—for instance, in the work of R. A. Schmidt. Schmidt's schemas seem suited to the performance of a single motion in the laboratory or in sports (such as swinging a bat) rather than to a complex manipulation or to goal-oriented performance in a dynamic environment. Each such schema is broken into two parts: The *recall schema* seems akin to feedforward (cf. Fig. 2 in FEEDBACK AND FEEDFORWARD), being responsible for the complete control of a rapid movement, even though environmental feedback may later signal errors. The *recognition schema* is responsible for the evaluation of response-produced feedback that makes possible the generation of error information about the movement. It thus seems to combine on-line feedback and identification procedures which may operate even after a movement is completed to better tune the schema for its next activation.                     M. A. A.

Arbib, M. A. (1972). *The Metaphorical Brain*. New York.

Bartlett, F. C. (1932). *Remembering*. London and New York.

Bobrow, D. G. and Collins, A. (1975). *Representation and Understanding: studies in cognitive science*. New York.

Craik, K. J. W. (1943). *The Nature of Explanation.* Cambridge.

Gibson, J. J. (1977). The theory of affordances. In Shaw, R. E. and Bransford, J. (eds.), *Perceiving, Acting and Knowing: toward an ecological psychology*. Hillsdale, New Jersey.

Head, H. and Holmes, G. (1911). Sensory disturbances from cerebral lesions. *Brain*, **34**, 102–254.

Minsky, M. L. (1975). A framework for representing knowledge. In Winston, P. H. (ed.), *The Psychology of Computer Vision*, 211–77. New York.

Neisser, U. (1976). *Cognition and Reality: principles and implications of cognitive psychology*. San Francisco.

Oldfield, R. C. and Zangwill, O. L. (1942; 1943). Head's concept of the body schema and its application in contemporary British psychology. *British Journal of Psychology*, **32**, 267–86; **33**, 58–64, 113–29, 143–49.

Piaget, J. (1971). *Biology and Knowledge: an essay on the relations between organic regulations and cognitive processes*. Edinburgh.

**SCHIZOPHRENIA.** Towards the end of the nineteenth century Emil *Kraepelin suggested that most of the variegated forms of insanity familiar to his contemporaries were manifestations of two major disorders, which he named *dementia praecox* and manic-depressive insanity. His claim was based on a meticulous study of large numbers of patients followed for many years and it had a profound effect on the subsequent development of psychiatry. *Dementia praecox* was a progressive illness which started in adolescence or early adult life and followed an inexorable downhill course; recovery, if it occurred at all, was always incomplete. Manic-depressive insanity, on the other hand, was a phasic illness. Although in the course of a lifetime a patient might have several episodes, and spend many years in hospital, individual episodes always ended in recovery and full restoration of the previous personality. The term schizophrenia, meaning 'split mind', was coined by Eugen *Bleuler, the medical director of the Burgholzli Hospital in Zurich, during the period of ferment that followed this seminal innovation. Bleuler's schizophrenia was an expansion and elaboration of Kraepelin's *dementia praecox* and he believed that its protean manifestations were due to a 'splitting', or loss of co-ordination, between different psychic functions, particularly between the cognitive (intellectual) and conative (emotional) aspects of the personality. The monograph he published in 1911 was so influential that within a generation Kraepelin's original terminology was forgotten, and for the last fifty years schizophrenia has been recognized throughout the world as the most important single cause of chronic psychiatric disability.

The subjective experiences and observable alterations in behaviour which characterize schizophrenia are both very variable; but there is a central core of symptoms which, though occasionally seen in the presence of brain disease of various kinds, are in practice highly specific. The subject ceases to experience his mental processes and his will as under his own control; he may insist that thoughts are being put into his mind or removed from it by some alien force, or suspect that he is being hypnotized. He hears voices telling him what to do, commenting on or repeating his thoughts, discussing him between themselves, or threatening to kill him. In the acute stages of the illness other *hallucinations and *delusions of varied kinds may be present. His thought processes also develop a characteristic vagueness and illogicality. At first he simply keeps wandering off the point, but in some chronic patients there eventually ceases to be any logical connection between one idea, or phrase, and the next; so their speech becomes almost incomprehensible. Although *intelligence and *memory remain relatively intact, the whole personality is affected by the illness. Above all, the patient loses his vivacity and drive; he loses his interest in and capacity to respond emotionally to other people; and he becomes increasingly more apathetic, eccentric, and isolated.

Schizophrenia is a relatively common condition, affecting nearly 1 per cent of the population. Although its onset is usually in adolescence or early adult life, it may develop in childhood, or be delayed until middle age or even later. There is no good evidence that its incidence has changed in the past 150 years, and it occurs in much the same forms and with much the same frequency throughout the world, regardless of environmental differences or differences in language, creed, or social structure. Neither do wars nor other catastrophic events appear to influence its incidence. Although it is well established that some people may, even in the absence of treatment, have a single attack from which they recover completely and permanently, it is more common for a series of psychotic episodes to lead to some degree of lasting emotional impoverishment, even though the subject may still be capable of supporting himself and earning his living.

Of all mental illnesses schizophrenia is the most feared, and the most fascinating, and it is the model for the layman's concept of madness. It causes great suffering, not only to the patients whose lives and personalities it slowly destroys but also to their families, and its high incidence and chronicity make it a greater burden on health services than any other single illness. The fears and frustrations it engenders are also a fertile breeding-ground for worthless treatments and fanciful theories of causation. In the last twenty years there have been claims that schizophrenia can be cured with novel forms of *psychotherapy, by special diets, and by massive doses of vitamin B. Others have asserted that it is not an illness at all. To R. D. Laing it is the only rational way of coming to terms with an insane world (see LAING'S UNDERSTANDING OF INTER-PERSONAL EXPERIENCE); to some sociologists it is merely a convenient label used by society for coping with troublesome deviants; to Thomas Szasz (*Schizophrenia. The Sacred symbol of psychiatry*, 1979) it simply 'does not exist'.

Despite much research, the cause or causes of schizophrenia remain elusive and no specific neuropathology has ever been identified. It is well established that the lateral ventricles of the brain are often modestly enlarged, but it is still unclear whether this is a direct manifestation of the disease process, or merely a predisposing factor. It has also been established, by postmortem studies, that the number of dopamine receptors in parts of the basal ganglia of the brain is increased in chronic schizophrenia, but again it is uncertain whether this is a fundamental abnormality or a secondary consequence of neuroleptic treatment. Psychological and psychophysiological researches have not been any more successful, though it is clear that the eye movements of schizophrenics are abnormal, and also that there is often a disturbance in the distribution of functions between the two cerebral hemispheres. There is also evidence to suggest that schizophrenics have difficulty processing incoming information, both auditory and visual; they find it hard to distinguish the relevant from the irrelevant, and their performance on a variety of perceptual and other psychological tests differs from that of other people. But the range of variation is wide and there is always a considerable overlap between them and normal people. There is no doubt, however, that schizophrenia is, at least in part, transmitted genetically. Several studies in Europe and North America have shown not only that the illness runs in families, and that the concordance rate is consistently higher in uniovular (identical) than in binovular (non-identical) twins, but also that the offspring of schizophrenic parents have a high risk of developing the illness even if they are separated from them soon after birth and adopted by other people. The mode of transmission remains uncertain, but is probably polygenic, like height and hypertension. (See GENETICS OF BEHAVIOUR.)

There is also no doubt that environmental factors are important. Uniovular twins, being derived from a single fertilized ovum, are genetically identical, but if one of the pair develops schizophrenia, there is less than a 50:50 chance that the other will do the same, and this fact alone is proof of the importance of environmental influences. But we have little idea what these environmental factors are, or whether they act in childhood or shortly before the onset of the illness. In the 1960s there were claims that the childhood relationship between the patient and his mother, and emotional strains within the family as a whole, were the crucial factors—that some mothers or families were so pathological that they eventually drove their children into madness. However, the few established facts in this area are all capable of alternative explanations, and it is irresponsible and heartless to suggest to a distraught parent that she is responsible for her child's illness, when there is no real evidence to that effect. There is evidence, though, that the onset of the illness is often preceded by stressful events (like being called up for military service or spurned by a girl-friend) and also evidence that relapses are commoner in schizophrenics living with relatives who nag or criticize them than in those living in more tranquil settings. So it is clear that emotional or psychological factors must be involved, directly or indirectly, in causation.

Because so little is known about its aetiology, schizophrenia has to be defined, and diagnosed, largely on clinical grounds. In consequence, as with other diagnoses which cannot be confirmed by laboratory tests, usage of the term is liable to vary from place to place. Indeed, major international differences in usage were identified in the 1960s, American and Russian psychiatrists, in particular, using the term much more freely and loosely than psychiatrists elsewhere. (It was mainly in these same two countries, and this was probably no coincidence, that psychiatrists were accused of abusing the diagnosis and labelling as schizophrenic people who were really perfectly sane, but who were a nuisance to their families or the state, and incarcerating them in hospitals to receive treatments they did not require.) In the last decade, the adoption of unambiguous operational definitions, at least for research purposes, has reduced the confusion; though the coexistence of several alternative ways of defining the term still means that a diagnosis of schizophrenia may have a somewhat different meaning in different centres.

In the past, most schizophrenics spent most of their lives in hospital, but since the 1950s the course of the illness has been greatly improved by the discovery of the tranquillizing effects of the phenothiazines. The efficacy of these and other neuroleptic drugs, both in controlling the acute illness and in reducing the risk of relapse, is well proved and almost certainly depends on the fact that they inhibit transmission in dopaminergic neurone systems in the brain. Unfortunately, because dopaminergic neurones (i.e. brain cells which use dopamine as their transmitter substance) are also involved in the extrapyramidal motor system, these drugs are all liable to produce troublesome restlessness in the legs (akathisia), involuntary movements (tardive dyskinesia) and *Parkinsonism as side effects. (For a more detailed discussion, see SCHIZOPHRENIA: EVIDENCE FOR AN ORGANIC CAUSE.)

There have also been important social changes in the last thirty years which have probably contributed as much to the improved outlook as these neuroleptics. Partly as a result of legal changes embodied in the Mental Health Act of 1959, partly as a result of increased public tolerance, and partly because of the growing realization by psychiatrists themselves that life in the huge asylums (which they inherited from their Victorian predecessors) increased rather than reduced the disabilities of their patients, the last two decades have seen a substantial change in policy. Instead of being allowed, or compelled, to remain in hospital as long as their illness persisted, patients are now discharged as soon as possible, and if they relapse and have to be readmitted they are discharged again as soon as their acute symptoms are controlled. In this way the evils of 'institutionalization' are avoided, and many schizophrenics who in the past would have spent forty or fifty years in an asylum are now able to live useful and even happy lives. There are times, however, when contemporary enthusiasm for 'community care' (and for closing hospitals in order to save money) is taken too far and the emotional and practical burdens which a chronic schizophrenic may place on a family are too readily overlooked. There are still situations in which the most humane course is to provide the patient with asylum from a world he can no longer comprehend or cope with. (See ASYLUMS: ARE THEY REALLY NECESSARY?) R. E. K.

Bleuler, E. (1950). *Dementia Praecox of the Group of Schizophrenias* (trans. J. Zinkin). New York.
Wing, J. (ed.) (1975). *Schizophrenia from Within.* London.

**SCHIZOPHRENIA: EVIDENCE FOR AN ORGANIC CAUSE.** Important recent advances in the understanding of the neural mechanisms involved in schizophrenia have come from discoveries of the mode of action of drugs used in its treatment. Chlorpromazine has been known as an antischizophrenic drug since the mid-1950s, but not until 1963 was there a good pharmacological explanation for its action. Measuring the rate of formation and metabolism of the neurotransmitter *dopamine, it was possible to suggest that this and other clinically effective drugs block dopamine receptors in the brain. Chemically related drugs that were not clinically effective did not have this property. This suggestion was later confirmed by direct measurement of the binding of drugs to dopamine receptors. The receptor-blocking property is specific to dopamine receptors at low concentrations of the drug, since other neurotransmitter receptors are not powerfully blocked, and even closely related receptors (e.g. noradrenaline receptors) are not sensitive to the drug. In addition, the

potency of these drugs as blockers of dopamine receptors closely parallels their clinical potency. Thus it seems that brain areas innervated by dopamine neurones are the main sites of the clinically effective actions of anti-psychotic drugs. Of course, dopamine neurones, by means of their high degree of connectivity with other neural systems, are not the only ones involved in schizophrenia, but it does seem that they form an active link in the neural circuitry necessary for this condition.

The involvement of dopamine neurones is also suggested by evidence that two drugs which increase the release of brain dopamine, amphetamine and levodopa, may worsen schizophrenic symptoms; and that amphetamines may produce a condition, in previously healthy volunteers, that is indistinguishable from acute paranoid schizophrenia.

Although the pharmacological evidence for understanding schizophrenia in this way is encouraging, direct evidence from postmortem schizophrenic brain tissue is less so. The technical difficulties of studying transmitter chemistry in poorly preserved tissue are formidable and render interpretation of results very difficult. Most evidence has been unable to demonstrate clear abnormalities in dopaminergic function, partly because of the difficulty of excluding treatment-induced changes. However, some evidence does suggest that the amygdala (a phylogenetically ancient part of the brain buried deep in the temporal lobe) contains abnormal quantities of dopamine in schizophrenics. Since the amygdala is closely related to the temporal lobe cortex and the symptoms of temporal lobe epilepsy closely resemble some schizophrenic symptoms, this finding is of some interest.

The general problem of how to determine which of the many brain dopaminergic systems may be disturbed has been given a new perspective by recent neuropathological and brain-scan techniques. These appear to show atrophic change in brain-stem structures, in the periventricular system: the thalamus, basal forebrain, and temporal lobe (amygdala and hippocampal region). Further progress in understanding this condition will hardly be possible until there is a clearer understanding of precisely how these brain areas are connected, and how these connections underlie normal brain function. O. T. P.

**SCHOPENHAUER,** ARTHUR (1788–1860). German philosopher, born at Danzig, now Gdansk. His father was a banker and his mother a novelist. He was educated at Göttingen and Berlin, where he became *privat-docent*. As a challenge, he held his lectures at the same time as *Hegel, but without success. He retired to Frankfurt-on-Main as a lonely and unloved bachelor, befriended only by his poodle Atma, 'World Soul'. He was a personal and professional pessimist. He held a subjective idealism that the world is a personal fantasy, while will is primary as creating (subjective) reality. He is thus a kind of solipsist. His main book is *The World as Will and Idea* (1819).

**SENSATIONALISM.** See CONDILLAC, ÉTIENNE DE.

**SENSATIONS.** Traditionally *perceptions have been thought of as made of sensations: sensations such as colours, touches, smells, and sounds being accepted as 'bricks' of which perceptions are made. Hence the now somewhat out-of-date term *'sense-data'. But now we generally think of physical *stimuli at the organs of sense (the eyes and ears, and so on) or the neural *signals* from the sense organs as the data of perception. This change of thinking is from regarding sensations such as colours as being in the world of external objects and detected by the senses, rather than as being generated by the brain, or produced in the mind. Sir Isaac *Newton contributed the important notion that light itself is not coloured, but that the sensations of colours are generated in us, according to what sort of light strikes the eyes.

Some regions of the brain have been identified as specially important for various sensations; but just how, or indeed why, certain brain activities in critical regions produce sensations remains mysterious. It is not even clear that sensations are necessary for perception, at least as perception is defined behaviourally by recognizing and handling objects. And as an object is differently identified, so sensations of colour or brightness may change. So perception is not simply built up of 'brick'-like sensations, as sensation bricks are modified and even entirely created by what objects are (correctly or not) identified. Effects of perception on sensation were appreciated by Ernst *Mach, whose book translated as *The Analysis of the Sensations* (1897) remains interesting and important. Mach pointed out that the seen brightness of a surface may change, in ambiguous figures, when the surface 'flips' in depth though there is no change in the stimulus, as is seen in Fig. 1.

This effect appears dramatically with a card bent to this kind of shape. In general, when a region is accepted or is likely to be a shadow, it looks lighter than when seen as a surface. This shows that sensations such as brightness and colour are not

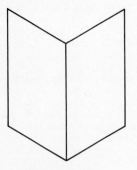

**Fig. 1.** Mach figure.

simply given by stimulation of the eye, or the other sense organs, but may be drastically changed and enriched by 'higher level' perceptual processes. A most dramatic example of this is Edwin Land's demonstrations of a rich variety of colours given by only two colours, by combining a pair of otherwise identical photographs, one taken, for example, with a green filter and the other with a red filter, and projected with the same filters. This can be done even with one picture unfiltered (white) and the other with a red filter—when greens, blues, and many other colours are seen. Another dramatic example is the appearance of illusory surfaces and contours, which seem to be created perceptually, as postulated nearer masking objects, to account for surprising gaps when the gaps are likely object shapes. The best known examples are due to the Italian psychologist Gaetano Kanizsa (1979). (See ILLUSIONS.)

Because sensations are essentially private, we have no way of knowing how the world appears to other people. Thus, strictly speaking, we have no way of knowing whether their 'red' is our red—which may bother painters. At least for some colour-blind people it may well be that sensations are individually different, and surely (if they are conscious) bats must have sensations very different from any of ours when detecting objects by sound-ranging. These issues are explored most imaginatively in philosophical papers collected by Hofstadter and Dennett (1981).

Having said that strictly speaking we cannot know another person's sensations, it may seem impossible to *measure* sensations. There have however been many attempts to relate stimuli to sensation in quantitative ways, following the pioneer work of *Fechner and *Weber. Fechner measured the smallest difference of stimulus intensities that could be discriminated, and with a mathematical treatment he tried to derive measures of sensations. This involved certain assumptions which are very difficult to justify, but the approach remains of great interest (see PSYCHOPHYSICS). Also interesting are attempts to 'scale' sensory dimensions. Thus, for example, if there were two lights one brighter than the other, how would one set the intensity of a third light to lie half-way between the other two? Or could a picture be said to be twice as beautiful as another? The American psychologist S. S. *Stevens spent many years trying to scale sensations and judgements of various kinds, and claimed that each psychological dimension obeys a power law, with an empirical component that differs for the various senses, or kinds of judgement being made. There are methodological difficulties in this, but again the attempts to measure aspects of mind are interesting. (See QUANTIFYING JUDGEMENTS.) A full discussion of many of these issues is given by Savage (1970).

Although sensation is ultimately mysterious, as *consciousness is mysterious, it is worth pointing out that much the same holds for *matter. If a physicist is asked, 'What is an electron made of?' he has no answer. Indeed he may say that it is nothing but a probability distribution, or some such. In any case he will not say that it is made of matter, for physics is concerned ultimately only with relations and not with substances. Perhaps this is so also for mind—perhaps there is no 'mind stuff'—and in any case sensations should not be thought of in such terms. The trouble is, though, the kinds of relations that have been found and that are so powerful in physics are exceedingly hard to discover or measure in psychology. Although the attempts to measure sensation are intriguing we cannot feel that they are satisfactory, so psychology remains apart from the physical sciences.                                    R. L. G.

Bradley, I. J. (1971). *Mach's Philosophy of Science*. London.

Hofstadter, D. R. and Dennett, D. C. (1981). *The Mind's Eye: fantasies and reflections on self and soul*. New York.

Kanizsa, G. (1979). *Organisation of Vision: essays on gestalt psychology*. New York.

Land, E. H. (1959). Experiments in colour vision. *Scientific American*, **5**, 84.

Mach, E. (1886). *The Analysis of Sensation* (Eng. trans. Williams, C. M. 1897). New York.

Savage, C. W. (1970). *The Measurement of Sensation: a critique of perceptual psychophysics*. San Francisco.

**SENSE-DATA.** A philosophical term referring to the experience, of patches of red, heat, hardness, and so on, which have been supposed to be the data by which objects are known. This concept has given way, with increasing physiological knowledge, to the very different account that objects are signalled via patterns of received energy (*stimuli) and represented at the brain via the neural signals of action potentials. Where the *experience* or *consciousness* of sensations comes in—or what it *does*—is highly mysterious, for it no longer seems to be data. (See CONSCIOUSNESS; PERCEPTION; SENSATIONS.)

**SENSORIMOTOR   CO-ORDINATION.**   See SPATIAL CO-ORDINATION OF THE SENSES.

**SENSORY DEPRIVATION, EFFECTS OF.** See ISOLATION EXPERIMENTS.

**SET.** In psychology, the intention to act in a particular way or to accept certain kinds of information. The term is linked to the concept of *attention, or attending to what may be needed in a given situation; for example, one has a set for laying the table for a meal. The set may be evoked by an external stimulus, or be self-initiated.

**SEX DIFFERENCES IN CHILDHOOD.** Distinctively male and female development begins soon after conception, and the eventual degree of human sexual dimorphism exceeds that in many Primate species. The twenty-third pair of chromosomes in females is XX, while in males it is XY. In the presence of the Y chromosome, cell division of the zygote is accelerated, and the medulla of the initially bipotential embryonic gonad differentiates during the seventh week into a testis. The secretion of androgenic hormones from the foetal testis organizes both the development of the genitalia and of the brain according to the male pattern. Female differentiation always occurs in the absence of the male hormones. Circulation of androgens *in utero* is known to increase the amount of aggressive behaviour and gross physical activity in Primates, and it is likely that these hormones predispose the human male to greater physical activity.

At birth, males are heavier and longer than females, and from the second month their calorie intake is greater; boys have a consistently higher basal metabolism than girls and greater vital capacity. However, in terms of bone age the new-born girl is equivalent to a four- to six-weeks-old boy, and growth velocity in the boy lags about two years behind the girl. Puberty is attained roughly two and a half years later in males than in females. (See HUMAN GROWTH.)

In addition to their relatively retarded postnatal physical development, males are characterized by a greater susceptibility to a variety of adverse conditions. They are more vulnerable to both postnatal and perinatal complications that can lead to death or long-term disability. In developing countries, where infant mortality rises at weaning due to intestinal complications, again it is the male who is more at risk. Throughout life, males remain more prone to a variety of diseases—respiratory, cardiac, infective, and neurological, as well as the sex-linked recessive disorders.

Thus cultural and social pressures that influence sex-typed behaviours act on organisms which, biologically at least, are distinctively male or female. A crucial issue for psychologists is the extent to which these different biological substrata may predispose males and females to different abilities or behaviours. Male and female babies do behave differently—boys are more restless than girls. They are also treated differently by those who care for them; it is therefore difficult to disentangle the relative influences of socialization and biological predisposition. It is none the less illuminating to document cultural influences on behaviour and to speculate upon their possible effects on sex differences.

In the early months of life boys tend to be handled more than girls, but new-born girls are spoken to and smiled at more during feeding sessions. These differences in care-giving behaviour have been attributed to the babies' differential responsiveness, and it is important to stress that any adult–infant interaction is a two-way process, and depends on far more than the adult's perception of the infant's sex. A recent comprehensive review of parental behaviour in laboratory studies concludes that there is 'a remarkable degree of uniformity in the socialization of the two sexes'.

Against this finding, though, stands evidence from observations of a more general nature. Consider, for example, a study of 96 middle-class homes—in the 48 boys' rooms there were 375 vehicles, whereas in the 48 girls' rooms there were only 17; over half the girls possessed a baby doll, compared to just 3 of the boys. In general, the boys' rooms contained more educational materials and more sports equipment than the girls' rooms. The agents of socialization are, evidently, insidious.

Books and television are also factors which can strongly influence children's perceptions of sex-appropriate behaviours. In a study of children's literature, it was found that most children's books were about boys, men, and male animals; in nearly one-third of the books which won literature prizes (over a five-year period) there were no women at all. Boys were portrayed as active and adventuresome, girls as passive and immobile. This highly exaggerated presentation of sex-stereotypes is repeated in the medium of television, where females are very much in the minority. Males are portrayed as aggressive, constructive, and helpful; females as deferential and passive.

Despite the restricted range of female roles presented by the media, adults appear to tolerate a wider range of behaviour from girls than from boys—thus, whereas it is perfectly acceptable for a girl's behaviour to be tomboyish, a boy who engages in female typical behaviour would be labelled with the more pejorative term 'cissy'. None the less, the preferred play activities of boys and girls are very different: boys play more outside, they are more physically active, and they play less with dolls. Parents tend to allow boys of school age greater freedom to roam the local neighbourhood and are more likely to encourage girls to stay at home. Investigators who have observed young children in play-groups and nursery schools have found that boys initiate more aggression than girls (approximately two-thirds of all aggressive acts are initiated by boys) and their aggressive encounters are more prolonged than those of girls. Even before they reach school age, girls tend to be more nurturant and protective than boys, and this is evident in their increased readiness to comfort a distressed child or to help a younger child in some activity.

The evidence for sex differences in cognitive abilities is equivocal, and this may be partly due to the fact that many tests are specifically designed to ensure that groups of males and females obtain the same mean score. There are, however, two types of tests in which boys do excel: mazes of the kind frequently seen in children's comics, and Koh's blocks (where a set of coloured blocks have to be assembled to match a pattern). Both these are tests of spatial ability and reflect boys' greater facility in understanding concepts of orientation and perceptual configuration. Girls tend to use verbal strategies for solving these types of problems—though this does not affect their accuracy, it slows down their performance relative to boys and

accounts for their lower scores. More boys than girls have reading difficulties, and it has been thought that this is due to relatively poor language ability; it is now considered more likely that there is no sex difference in general language abilities, but that boys' greater restlessness at school makes them more difficult to teach! In studies of arithmetical ability, boys have usually achieved slightly better scores than girls; however, it has recently been shown that girls perform better when the problems are phrased in terms of 'female' objects (such as dolls and clothes) than they do when the same arithmetical computations are phrased in terms of 'male' objects (such as rockets and cars).

It is known that in adult males the right hemisphere of the brain is specialized for visuo-spatial skills, whereas the left hemisphere is specialized for language skills. Thus, if a male adult sustains damage to the left side of the brain his language ability will be impaired. In adult females there appears to be language representation in both hemispheres, and damage to the left hemisphere does not have such a profound effect as it does for the males. These sex differences in lateralization develop during childhood years, and the superior performance of boys on tests of visuo-spatial skills has been attributed to the earlier specialization of the right hemisphere for these abilities.

The fact that boys show a slight but consistent advantage in visuo-spatial abilities is insufficient to account for their vastly superior performance in science subjects during adolescence. It is well established that visuo-spatial ability is correlated with mathematical ability, and it would not be unexpected to find slightly more males than females preferring to study science-based subjects. There is now evidence that girls' reluctance to study science is due less to their lack of ability than to the fact that they perceive science subjects as 'masculine', and therefore inappropriate to them.

In conclusion, the following four statements summarize our understanding of psychological sex differences in childhood: (i) There are biological sex differences which predispose males and females to some behavioural differences. (ii) Caregivers respond differentially to males and to females, but these responses are to the child's behaviour rather than to his or her sex. (iii) There are sex differences in brain organization, but it is not established beyond doubt that these are related to sex differences in intellectual ability. (iv) Cultural influences act to persuade children to conform to sex-stereotyped expectations.

The overwhelming importance of cultural influences in shaping sex-typed behaviour is evidenced by data from studies of cultures where male and female sex-roles are characterized quite differently from those in our own culture. The biological dichotomy of the sexes should not be seen as necessarily implying an equally rigid dichotomy of abilities and behaviour; it would none the less be unhelpful to deny that biological differences will interact with environmental influences.

C. HU.<br>M. HU.

Maccoby, E. E. and Jacklin, C. N. (1975). *The Psychology of Sex Differences*. Stanford and Oxford.

Wittig, M. A. and Petersen, A. C. (1979). *Sex-Related Differences in Cognitive Functioning*. New York.

**SEXUAL DEVELOPMENT.** Human sexual development has been described as the last frontier of psychological knowledge. Until quite recently it has been a subject surrounded in myth. Popularized Freudian concepts of the repressed libidinous forces of the id have fuelled the kinds of fantasies that have discouraged serious research. Only the cumulative influence of *Freud (1905), Kinsey and his colleagues (1948, 1953), and Masters and Johnson (1966, 1970), in building up a coherent body of clinical, sociological, and scientific knowledge over the course of the larger part of a century, has at last established a climate of opinion in which sexual function and development have been widely accepted in the scientific community as a proper area of systematic research.

Medical science has traditionally concentrated on the processes connected with birth and the diseases surrounding venery. It is the psychological and sociological sciences that have considered the totality of human sexual experience, and thereby established a core around which physiological and anatomical knowledge about sexual function can be set in its place. Such has been the development in recent years that the mainstream psychiatric view, expressed by Mayer-Gross, Slater, and Roth in 1969—'. . . a sexual activity is usually regarded as perverse if it has no immediate connection with reproduction, and still more so if it tends to lead to a sexual activity which could replace reproduction'—is no longer supportable. Sexual activity is now seen as a multiply functional part of human potential, in which the intention to reproduce is one among a number of valid intentions, such as pleasure, or the deepening of a bonding relationship, which the sexual act may properly subserve.

As a body of knowledge becomes established, so its operational concepts become increasingly elaborated. What was previously self-evident becomes redefined. That the study of human sexual development has reached this phase is perhaps best exemplified by considering first the biological basis of sexual development and then its psychological basis. It will be seen that the psychological, especially in regard to the development of male and female identity, intrudes continuously upon the biological as the means of making sense of it.

The simple idea that male and female is an unvarying dichotomy, from which much else springs, has been observed by Haeberle (1978, to whose thoughtful writing this contributor is happy to acknowledge an especial debt) to be more complicated than the Latin root of sex (*secare*: to cut, divide, or separate) implies. At least seven different factors have to be taken into account.

In the first place is *chromosomal sex*. The male body cells contain one X and one Y chromosome, whereas female cells contain two X chromosomes. Recently other combinations have been recorded, at least one of which (XYY) may be linked to severe aggressive tendencies. Nevertheless, chromosomal sex appears to be the most basic distinction between male and female.

Secondly, there is *gonadal sex*. The male's testicles and the female's ovaries are their primary anatomical sexual characteristics, but in rare cases tissues of both may occur in the same body.

Thirdly, *hormonal sex*—the balance of the androgens and oestrogens—which starts sex differentiation in the second month of foetal life, and continues through puberty and adult sexual maturity to old age, affecting all stages of growth and differentiation, has a wide range of characteristics of its own. The balance considerably affects essential sex-linked physical features during maturation, such as body shape and hair distribution, as well as controlling the reproductive process.

Fourthly, the *anatomical structures of reproduction* in the male and female may be less than fully developed, giving rise to variations of sexual classification.

Fifthly, the *external sex organs* may in some instances be missing, malformed, or inappropriate to chromosomal sex. Thus a child with the chromosomal structure of a male may be brought up as a female, the absence of a penis at birth giving rise to the assumption that a girl child has been delivered. There is evidence that the presence or absence of a penis is the most marked sign upon which sex is assigned to a child, with considerable social consequences.

Whether or not there is anatomical cause, a child of one sex may be reared as a child of the opposite sex, so that the *gender* or *social role* normally assigned to one sex is transferred, usually by parental influence. Instances are recorded in which early traumatic loss of the penis, through surgical accident for instance, have resulted in a child male by all usual tests being brought up as a female.

Finally, and in seventh place, but by no means least, the individual may assume a *gender identity* other than the gender role assigned during early development. In cases of transsexualism, for instance, the gender identity a person wishes to assume is the opposite of the gender role that has been assigned socially. Sex reassignment surgery may change the anatomical structures very successfully, creating a functioning penis or lubricating vagina, but the individual who encourages psychiatrist and surgeon to co-operate in such a process of elective change cannot change the chromosomal identity of their sex, which has usually been that of their gender role up to the point of reassignment surgery.

For the vast majority of individuals there is no conflict in any of these variables. The XY male has functional testicles, the appropriate hormonal balance of androgen and pituitary hormones, adequate reproductive mechanisms, an apparent penis responsive to sexual stimulation, is raised as a male, and feels himself to be such as he moves through adolescence into adult life. *Per contra* the female. The complexity of that apparent normality, however, and its dependence upon hormone production at the critical time, master-minded, as it were, by the pituitary, is a cause for marvel as hormone assay methods become increasingly refined. It should perhaps be recorded in passing that, embryologically, all human life is female. In the first month of uterine existence the embryo is sexually undifferentiated. Towards the end of the second month testosterone in the potentially male embryo begins to circulate, which causes the gonads that would otherwise have grown into ovaries to become testicles, and the penis and scrotum to form from the tissue that in the woman remains the clitoris, vagina, and labia of the genital structures.

Given this physiochemical developmental process, which by birth is usually responsible for clearly differentiated male and female sexual organs as the *primary sexual characteristics*, two other stages of development can be observed.

Hormonal influences produce the *secondary sexual characteristics* of puberty, confirming the maleness or femaleness of the individual in varying degrees by varying emphasis on anatomical structures. Fifteen secondary sexual characteristics have been noted, ranging from differences between the sexes in body hair distribution, shape of breasts, and muscular size, to the carrying angle of the arm and leg, which in the male is straight and in the female forms an angle at the elbow and the knee.

Finally, *tertiary sexual characteristics* are those gender role qualities of being masculine and feminine that cultural or subcultural conditioning emphasizes as appropriate to one sex or the other. It is clearly in the area of tertiary characteristics that there is most room for change, as the primary and secondary are physiologically determined whereas the tertiary are determined by socio-psychological forces. The feminist movement, which has arisen in part from the separation of the sexual and reproductive processes in consequence of reliable contraception, and advances in medical technology such as artificial insemination, is an excellent example of a social process that has a profound effect upon tertiary sexual characteristics.

Tertiary characteristics are of course always influenced by the family subculture and the larger social context of an individual's growth. It might be assumed that the gender roles of men and women would change only slowly; or, conversely, be changed quickly only by violent or radical means, because of their very fundamental purpose in the identity-stabilizing process of the sequence of the generations. (The psychological theories of *transactional analysis*, as developed by Berne and his followers (e.g. Harris, 1970), describe especially the means by which the wisdom, or prejudices, of the generations is transmitted onwards and received.) The involvement of women in the combat forces of many countries is a particular example of a radical process shifting tertiary characteristics suddenly and widely.

As with the gradual and sequential development of the physical sexual characteristics, so the psychological and social tertiary characteristics are established over many years. In reviewing this process, Haeberle (1978) observes that '. . . the realization that adult human sexual behaviour results from a long, complex, and often hazardous development is relatively new'. While sex may be perfectly natural, it is clear that it is not always naturally perfect. The Freudian challenge of the early twentieth century begins this clarification.

In traditional psychoanalytic thinking, the three phases of early and infantile sexual development (oral, anal, and phallic) are more or less successfully passed through and repressed until, after the quiescent period before puberty, puberty itself provokes the awakening of early adolescent sexual urges, which may or may not attach themselves to appropriately mature heterosexual relationships and behaviours. This process of attachment depends upon whether early fixation at one of the infantile stages has taken place, or whether those erotic stages have been integrated; and also upon how the child's attachment to its parent of the opposite sex (the resolution of the so-called *Oedipus or *Electra complexes) has been managed.

Cultural variations in these processes, described by anthropologists from Margaret Mead onwards, suggested that the Freudian view was not universally appropriate. In considering the tertiary aspects of sexual development, it is now widely accepted that cultural influences are both significant and variable. The work of Money at Johns Hopkins (Money and Green, 1969), as well as that of Kinsey, and Masters and Johnson, can be held to provide firm support for this view.

In the end, it is the sum of the biological processes and the development of gender role and identity, in whatever circumstances that takes place, that results in sexual orientation—whether this be heterosexual, homosexual, bisexual, or object-related as in fetishistic behaviours.

In a society that can reconsider long-held aversions to some sexual behaviours—such as admitting that homosexual behaviour can be the basis for both pleasure and long-term relationships—questions of what is normal or abnormal inevitably arise. Such questions have particular relevance for those concerned in an educative or clinical way with the developmental process. As the boundaries alter, so moral and ethical questioning properly arises too. In such circumstances, what are clearly in a developmental sense aberrant behaviours need specifying clearly. In the current state of knowledge it is possible to state without fear of informed contradiction that sexual practices between adults and children (paedophilia) are harmful to the development of children; and that any sexual acts which seek to expose another person unwillingly to the demands of a close aggressor (rape) or more distant aggressor (the *frotteur* or the exhibitionist) do physical and/or psychological violence of a personally intrusive kind that a mature society finds reprehensible. The open sale of pornographic material might come under such a rubric. In addition there are clearly some sexual behaviours, such as the sado-masochistic, which, in their more extreme forms, contain elements of violence that would lead them to be considered symptomatic of a disturbed personality. However, the range of sexual behaviours which are now tolerated and openly advocated (see Comfort, 1974) includes mild degrees of fetishism and sado-masochism. The question of when the normal becomes the abnormal is difficult to resolve in principle, but in specific cases can reasonably easily be determined by a skilled enquiry into the total sexual value system of an individual or partnership. As clinical dependence upon alcohol is considerably distant from the majority of alcohol users, who have personality structures sufficiently robust to be able to enjoy its disinhibiting effects yet control the limits of the experience, so if a person's generally preferred sexual behaviours involve no compulsive quality, and if no manifest physical or psychological harm results to the individuals involved, then such behaviours should be classed as proper and within the realm of private and responsible action.

It is apparent from the above that in considering matters of human sexual development it is not possible to ignore the maturation, or regression, of the society in which the development takes place.

Since Freud drew attention to infantile sexual development, the broad acceptance of such development as natural and proper has become firmly established, even if all the psychoanalytical assumptions deriving from it are not so firmly accepted. Infant boys will have spontaneous erections, and infant girls the equivalent in vaginal lubrication. General body and specifically genital exploration and stimulation is now happily recognized as establishing later adult comfort with sexual matters. The untoward effects of inhibiting such exploration and its consequent discoveries are more strongly acknowledged than was even quite recently the case.

By and large the explorations of the child are sensually diffuse rather than erotically specific, though well before the onset of puberty both boys and girls may masturbate to some kind of orgasmic experience without there being, in the boy, any ejaculatory consequences. Masturbation is itself now recognized as a valid sexual experience throughout the whole life-span, and the nineteenth-century horrors with which it was invested are rapidly fading from popular culture. (It might be noted in passing that this statement refers to Western cultures, and even so would not be true of many countries of southern Europe where there is a specifically Catholic cultural tradition. In many Third World countries there are often still severe, and perhaps surgical, prohibitions against sexual activities that would be considered a natural part of the developmental process in most of northern Europe and North America).

Adolescence, started by the hormonal triggers that create the secondary sexual characteristics, is the beginning of sexual fertility. It carries the individual from childhood through to increasing separation from parents and emerging independence in the adult world. Adolescence is a period that is very variable from culture to culture, and where education is extensive it may be considerably prolonged. In the last hundred years or so in Britain, as the period of education has increased and the age of the onset of puberty has decreased, so the time between actual sexual fertility and the opportunity for independent existence in a continuing relationship of adult choice can become surprisingly long. Haeberle observes that there may now be as many as twenty years from the age of puberty to establishing full economic independence, while ten years is very common. In contrast, '. . . many of the great romances of the world celebrate the passionate love-affairs of the young. . . . Margarethe was a teenager when she fell in love with Faust, Helen was only twelve when she left her husband Menelaus and followed Paris to Troy. Narcissus was sixteen when "many youths and maidens sought his love". Ganymede was even younger when Zeus made him his favourite.' The contentious age of Juliet is well known to generations of schoolchildren.

The prolonged changes of adolescence, which occur at different ages for different individuals, and may take one or several years, begin rather earlier for boys than girls. Heredity, diet, climate, and cultural and emotional influences may all be implicated in the start and duration of this period between the ninth and fourteenth years. The development of adult sexual organs, fertility, the enlargement of breasts in the girl, and the obvious development of male and female body shapes in this period all serve to concentrate adolescent awareness on the increasing differentiation into men and women. The typical same-sex gang behaviour of the early teens begins to give way by the mid-teens to overt sexual awareness of, and increasing interest in, members of the opposite sex. Boys' sexual interest appears to focus on overt sexual activity earlier than girls', a difference in sexual awareness and responsiveness that persists through early adult years. Men are at their most sexually active and interested in the late teens and through the twenties, whereas women's sexual responsiveness and interest appears to increase to a peak in the middle thirties. It is then capable of being sustained for the next thirty years or more, whereas male sexual responsiveness tends to decline from the late twenties onwards. There are of course wide individual variations in this overall pattern. Whether the different rates of growth of interest and responsiveness and decline are physically or sociopsychologically determined is not yet clear. The differences are, however, clearly observed. Changing social roles and expectations may have a particular effect on this tertiary aspect of male and female sexual development.

While the adolescent male is generally encouraged, in Western society, to view himself in a specifically and overt sexual way, the adolescent female is encouraged to be undemanding sexually but attractive socially. It is the adolescent boy's task to push at the boundaries of what sexual experimentation his adolescent girl-friend will permit, and it is her social task to set the limits. 'Nice girls say "No!"', while boys are not discouraged from sowing wild oats: which rather unfairly requires that there must be some girls who are not nice. These differentiated tasks, previously strongly reinforced by social conditioning and the necessity of avoiding unwanted pregnancy, are under attack by feminists and modern sexologists as potentially harmful to the female in limiting her awareness of her own sexuality, and harmful to the male in encouraging an achievement-oriented view of sex. Only time will demonstrate whether there is a fundamentally passive aspect of being female and an essentially aggressive aspect of being male, of which these different tasks of sexual development in adolescence are the consequence; or whether they are only the result of social value systems and will yield to new values in due course.

It is during adolescence that boys experience their first discharge of seminal fluid, either through masturbation or through spontaneous nocturnal emission. There is no parallel to this in the sexual development of adolescent girls: some girls may experience spontaneous orgasm during sleep, but such an event is very rare. Indeed many girls do not discover masturbation spontaneously at all, and in the absence of specific information about it from reading, or adults, or their peer group may not be conscious of overt sexual arousal, and may enter marriage and their first experience of coitus without being at all informed of their sexual responsiveness. Whereas at one time it was thought that this was a proper state for a young woman, it is now recognized that this not only lays responsibility on the man for the development of female sexuality—a burden for which men are developmentally not prepared—but denies the woman responsibility for the awareness and control of her own body and its responses. It remains the case, however, that many girls do not receive specific information even from their peer group, as evidenced by the lack of a slang word among girls for masturbation, in comparison with the extensive vocabulary that boys have for the same activity. Again this seems to be related to cultural conditioning, and we may expect the influence of such books as *Our Bodies, Ourselves*, and Dodson's *Liberating Masturbation*, as well as the female pre-orgasmic workshops that have begun to make their appearance quite extensively in the USA and to some extent in the UK (Hooper, 1980), to have a beneficial effect upon undue inhibition of sexual development. The modern trend of adolescent sex education is to make facts that were previously not known or not generally discussed much more widely available, and to stress responsible choice rather than avoidance in matters of personal sexual practice and experience. Kaplan (1979) and Cousins (1980) are excellent examples of this approach.

Homosexual fantasy and/or contact is not at all uncommon among boys and girls in adolescence. In the vast majority of cases it appears to be part of the transition from the sexually undifferentiated responses of childhood to increasingly articulated adult heterosexuality. Characteristically, in the adolescent homosexual phase, boys tend to be sexually attracted to (have crushes on) younger boys, while girls have crushes on older girls. Overt physical contact may or may not be present in these adolescent phases. The presence or absence of overt physical or sexual contact appears to bear no relationship to subsequent adult homosexual or bisexual behaviours.

It is at present a matter of controversy as to whether adult homosexual behaviour should be regarded as normal or not. In statistical terms it is infrequent but not abnormal. The temper of the times suggests that to raise the question at all is to convey narrow-minded prejudice or bigotry. However, Stoller (1976) has convincingly argued the case for considering adult sexual behaviours that are not heterosexual, and indeed some that are, as 'perversions'—in the technical sense that the biologically determined recipient of the sexual process must be the person of the opposite sex so that the survival demands of the species are met through mating and consequential reproduction. Acts that do not serve such a function should properly be considered as having had their focus turned away, and hence perverted, from the biological intent.

The range of heterosexual contacts during adolescence is very variable. It is however now thought that the large majority of couples will have experienced sexual intercourse prior to marriage. This is a significant shift in the sexual practices of the population in little more than a generation.

Adulthood is a period with its own characteristic phases that are only just beginning to receive detailed descriptive attention. In delineating the phases of adult life, Levinson (1978) has remarked that the period from early adulthood to the onset of old age—a span of about forty years—has been ignored as if it were a tranquil period. Clearly it isn't. It is the period sexually when the pleasures and difficulties of the marital and child-bearing years subordinate sexual development into limited expectation and less discovery. It is also the period when sexual difficulties become manifest. The current tendency is to assume that sexual development will have taken place by the early adult years, but that sexual experience and discovery may lag considerably behind physical maturation.

The work of Masters and Johnson has made it quite clear that sexual activity can happily persist well into the seventh and eighth decades of life. The needs and urgencies of a couple may change, yet the reassurance and confirmation of existence that comes from the close physical intimacy of sexual contact can be pleasurable in itself to an advanced age and highly beneficial in the process of adjustment to increasing years. There is a growing though as yet limited professional interest in the relation between poor marital and sexual adjustment and a high incidence of demands for the resources of medicine by way of gynaecological distress, *psychosomatic distress, and psychiatric breakdown, suggesting that much might be prevented by more successful adaptation earlier on.

In the male entering his fifties and sixties, the vasocongestive responses of sexual arousal become less, even in the presence of effective physical or psychological sexual stimulation. Erections become harder to establish. It is important at this stage for a couple to know from within their own experience that sexual involvement is not simply dependent upon the act of intercourse, but involves a wide range of pleasurable behaviours of which coitus may be only one. Sexual desire may remain high in the absence of strong erectile response, and the male urgency to ejaculate upon sexual arousal correspondingly diminishes too. The lack of erection should not be taken as the sign of lack of sexual interest and desire for sexual expression of affection.

In the female some corresponding changes in the tissue of the vaginal barrel may occur after the menopause. Changing hormone supply may cause some thinning and drying of the walls of the vaginal barrel, the same occurring after surgical removal of the ovaries. Hormone replacement therapy has been advocated after such operations and after the menopause to counter the adverse effects of the absence of ovarian hormones, but it is not yet clear what the long-term effects of such replacement are. As in the male, however, the absence of one physical sexual response, vaginal lubrication, does not in later years necessarily indicate loss of sexual desire. As with all bodily functions, the rate of change varies enormously from individual to individual. There is some suggestion that the rate of loss of physical sexual function is less in those who have had a generally continuous and satisfying sexual life.

Quite clearly the doubts, urgencies, and discoveries of adolescent and young adult sexual development give place to sexual function coming more under the influence of increasing life stresses as the thirties and forties merge into the later adult years. In positive caring in relationships, however, sexual development subserves not only the continuation of the species but the most vital existential discovery—that physical encounter with a person of the opposite sex, and perhaps of the

same sex too, sustains, supports, and heals in the individual life journey (Dominian, 1977). P. T. B.

Boston Women's Health Book Collective (1976). *Our Bodies, Ourselves*. New York.

Comfort, A. (1972). *The Joy of Sex: a gourmet guide to lovemaking*. New York.

Cousins, J. (1980). *Make it Happy. What sex is all about*. Harmondsworth.

Dodson, B. (1974). *Liberating Masturbation*. New York.

Dominian, J. (1977). *Proposals for a New Sexual Ethic*. London.

Freud, S. (1905; 1953). *Three Essays in the Theory of Sexuality*. London.

Haeberle, E. J. (1978). *The Sex Atlas*. New York.

Harris, T. A. (1970). *I'm OK—You're OK*. London.

Hooper, A. (1980). *The Body Electric*. London.

Kaplan, H. S. (1979). *Making Sense of Sex: the new facts about sex and love for young people*. London.

Kinsey, A. C., Pomeroy, W. B., and Martin, C. E. (1948). *Sexual Behaviour in the Human Male*. Philadelphia.

Kinsey, A. C., Pomeroy, W. B., and Martin, C. E. (1953). *Sexual Behaviour in the Human Female*. Philadelphia.

Levinson, D. J. (1978). *Seasons of a Man's Life*. New York.

Masters, W. H. and Johnson, V. (1966). *Human Sexual Response*. London.

Masters, W. H. and Johnson, V. (1970). *Human Sexual Inadequacy*. London.

Mayer-Gross, W., Slater, E., and Roth, M. (1969). *Clinical Psychiatry*, 3rd edn. London.

Mead, M. (1935). *Sex and Temperament in Three Primitive Societies*. New York.

Money, J. and Green, R. (eds.) (1969). *Transsexualism and Sex Reassignment*. Baltimore.

Stoller, R. J. (1976). *Perversion: the erotic form of hatred*. Hassocks, Sussex.

**SEXUAL PROBLEMS** in marriage became a matter of particular clinical and popular interest with the publication in 1970 of Masters and Johnson's *Human Sexual Inadequacy*. This was an account of an eleven-year period of clinical work and research, conducted at the Reproductive Biology Research Foundation in St Louis, Missouri, involving the treatment of a group of sexual difficulties that Masters and Johnson classed together as sexual dysfunctions. Over the eleven-year period, 790 instances of sexual difficulty were seen, the majority (733) presenting in 510 marital partnerships where one or both of the partners were experiencing a sexual problem. The treatment of single individuals is referred to later.

This clinical work was itself based upon a research programme into the physiology of human sexual response that Masters and Johnson had started in 1954, and which they had published in 1966 as *Human Sexual Response*. Unlike Kinsey's pioneering work of twenty years previously, which had asked people in considerable detail what they did in their sexual lives, Masters and Johnson established laboratory conditions for observing how people reacted sexually in terms of their physiological mechanisms under specific conditions of stimulation. It was their avowed intention to make the field of sexual function academically and professionally respectable. There is now no doubt that they achieved this aim in a quite signal way, though probably with consequences for the effective use of the knowledge that they supplied which are not yet fully appreciated.

Until the appearance of their works, sexual problems had been seen clinically within the framework of psychopathology, and no distinction was made between difficulties of normal function and variations of normal function. Freudian thinking generally underpinned this view, and there was overall pessimism about the possibility of help for specific sexual problems. Sexual difficulties were themselves seen as symptoms of deeper, underlying problems, and moreover clinicians generally had no clear diagnostic framework within which to consider sexual difficulties that might not be deeply rooted in psychopathology. The most optimistic views of treatment had been presented by Friedman in *Virgin Wives*, where he reported the work of Balint at the Tavistock Clinic in the mid-1950s. Balint had developed a form of brief psychotherapy, particularly for the disorder of vaginismus, which is a spasm contraction of the outer third of the vaginal barrel that effectively prevents intercourse by presenting such a constricted vaginal entrance that penetration by the male is not possible. Standard psychiatric texts of the 1960s and early 1970s, however, hardly touched sexual difficulties *per se*, beyond the blanket terms 'frigidity' in women and 'impotence' in men, and '*ejaculatio praecox*' also for men who complained of too rapid an ejaculation. In any event, both 'frigidity' and 'impotence' had acquired considerable pejorative overtones in popular usage by the 1960s, and (as had previously happened with such terms as 'idiot' and 'imbecile') required redefinition for clinical usage for that reason if no other.

It was the particular achievement of Masters and Johnson to shift thinking about difficulties of sexual function from considerations of psychopathology to those of learning and the failure to establish effective learning, and it is in this context that sexual difficulties are now first regarded upon presentation at a clinic. It is only when they appear to be unresponsive to treatment based upon educative concepts that considerations of psychopathology and inner psychic conflict are introduced. It is moreover quite possible now to separate sexual difficulties from sexual perversions—which is not to say that the two might not coexist.

Masters and Johnson also made the startling observation, which had previously passed most clinicians by, that sex tends to happen between two people. They concluded therefore that it might be best to see a couple in therapy rather than the single individual, as the focus of treatment is most likely to be upon the couple's pattern of sexual communication—what exactly happens between them—and not so directly upon the specific presenting difficulty of function, which is seen as a consequence of, or as being maintained by, the limitations of the couple's communication. The logic of this observation was also carried through by observing that a male clinician can never fully understand the female sexual experience, nor a female clinician the male. In consequence it might be helpful to have both a male and a female therapist present. This creates the situation of co-therapy—the treatment of a couple by a couple in a therapeutic foursome.

In defining the group of difficulties with which they were concerned, Masters and Johnson also made it possible, as noted briefly above, to distinguish the sexual dysfunctions from the sexual deviations. The sexual dysfunctions are often experienced by the majority of individuals in a transitory fashion, becoming dysfunctions by their persistence or their adverse effect upon the sexual relationship. For instance, most men will experience difficulties of erectile function in their adult life, and most women may have intermittent difficulty establishing a climax, even when these functions are generally satisfactory for the individuals concerned.

The description of the sexual dysfunctions is, briefly, as follows. In the man, primary or secondary impotence, premature ejaculation, and ejaculatory incompetence. That is to say, men who fail to establish and/or maintain an erection of sufficient strength for effective vaginal insertion, either throughout the whole of their adult sexual experience (primary impotence) or temporarily (secondary impotence); and men who ejaculate too quickly for their own and their partner's satisfaction (premature ejaculation), or too slowly, or not at all (ejaculatory incompetence). In the woman, the dysfunctions were classified by Masters and Johnson as being primary orgasmic dysfunction or situational orgasmic dysfunction. The first specified a situation in which the woman had never been orgasmic by any means (intercourse, masturbation, or any other method) throughout the whole of her sexually mature life, while the second described the conditions under which a woman might be orgasmic by coitus but not by masturbation (masturbatory orgasmic dysfunction), by masturbation but not by coitus (coital orgasmic dysfunction), or only occasionally orgasmic and without any feeling of certainty or predictability (random orgasmic dysfunction). Additionally they considered problems of pain upon intercourse in both men and women (dyspareunia) and vaginismus in women. They made a particularly strong case for encouraging physicians to believe in and thoroughly investigate a statement of pain during sexual intercourse, and not simply to dismiss it as 'hysterical' or 'psychogenic' because it was related to the sexual act. They also considered problems of low sexual drive.

In their physiological studies, Masters and Johnson had observed the processes of sexual arousal, from original quiescence through arousal and climax to quiescence (resolution) again, in a total of 694 male and female volunteers in the age range 18 to 89. In doing so they had made it clear that the sexual physiology of men and women is essentially the same even though the specific sexual anatomy is markedly different—bearing in mind, in regard to this latter statement, that in the embryo eventual male and female both start out as female, and are only differentiated as a consequence of hormonal effects, from about the sixth week of intra-uterine life, so that it is not until the third month of gestation that anatomical differences are apparent.

The first physiological change to arise as a consequence of effective physical or psychological sexual stimulation is that blood begins to flow more rapidly around the body as heart-rate increases, so that specific tissues become engorged. This process, called vasocongestion, creates an erection in the male of which the exact equivalent in the female is vaginal lubrication. Both are the early signs of sexual arousal and/or interest. In the female, increasing vasocongestion in the tissues of the vaginal wall creates a type of sweating response on the surface of the walls of the vaginal barrel (the transudorific reaction) which accumulates to form the lubrication of sexual arousal. Masters and Johnson observed this process by the simple expedient of introducing a clear plastic dilator into the excited vagina, illuminating the interior, and filming the process. Not only did they thereby dismiss the assumption that vaginal lubrication came from the glands of Bartholin at the vaginal entrance, or that it was a product seeping through the neck of the womb, but they also observed the continuing process of arousal, which was that after lubrication had established itself the vaginal barrel lengthened and increased its diameter considerably, ballooning in its upper third. The vagina was thus seen to produce changes which were the effective analogue of the male erection. As the limp penis is a potential erection, so the vagina in its unaroused state was seen to be potential space.

One immediate consequence of these observations of vaginal lubrication was that the processes of arousal in the woman began to be seen as equally important to those of the male, if the sexual act was to be mutually satisfying, and that it made as little sense to tell a sexually unresponsive woman to use a cream in order to make male insertion possible as to tell a man without an erection to tie a splint on his penis.

Apart from the vaginal and penile reactions of erection, other marked changes take place in the erectile tissues of the female sexual organs, including the clitoris, and in the breasts, which are all dependent upon vasocongestion. Not only is the sexual response of the body more widespread and complex in the female than in the male, but a wide variety of cultural influences make it possible for the female to value and enjoy the feelings of her body whereas the male is often taught to discount feelings of all kinds. Thus the woman may especially enjoy and value the experience and complexity of feelings in a sexual relationship, while the male may be more concerned with the performance of the act. Difficulties in a sexual relationship

frequently arise from this difference, as the man's interest may centre more on achieving climax than upon the pleasure of the encounter. It is also the case that the complexity of the woman's sexual responses is more vulnerable to adverse social conditioning; this may teach her that sexual acts are connected with excretory acts and menstruation which, if they themselves are adversely loaded emotionally, may make it difficult for her to value her sexuality positively and enjoyably.

At a specific point in the process of sexual arousal, involuntary muscular responses are triggered which in the male result in ejaculation of seminal fluid, and in the female in the experience of orgasm. In the male the sites of sexual sensation and orgasm are essentially the same, occurring in both cases around the tip of the penis, the glans. In the female, however, there is relatively little specific sensation inside the vagina, where the muscular spasm of orgasm is experienced. The main site of sexual stimulation on the input side, for the majority of women, is the clitoris, and ineffective clitoral stimulation is one of the main contributors to orgasmic difficulties. The separation of the clitoris and vagina in the sequence of sensory input and orgasmic experience has been a considerable theoretical dilemma in the development of Freudian thinking, giving rise to the now-redundant clitoral–vaginal transfer theory of adult female sexuality.

Their physiological observations led Masters and Johnson to conclude that the sexual response cycle of arousal and climax is a natural physiological property of the intact adult human being and responds predictably to adequate stimulation. However, it is also under the potentially inhibitory control of higher centres, and has the singular property for an *autonomic process that its function can be effectively inhibited for the whole of a lifetime. It is therefore distinguished from other autonomic processes, such as respiration, heart-rate, digestion, and so on. In consequence, Masters and Johnson's treatment procedures have been developed to aid the establishing of normal function. The goal of therapy is not to teach couples how to function sexually, but to help them discover how to stop stopping their natural functioning.

The therapy format which Masters and Johnson developed was a rapid, fourteen-day programme of intensive, therapist-guided development of effective sexual communication, using all senses but especially touch, the basic source of sexual pleasure. The early stages of treatment involve guided exercises (sensate focus) which the couple build up in discussion with the therapists and then undertake in the privacy of their own lives. Out of the shared experience of sexual responses occurring under the right conditions, specific techniques may become useful for specific difficulties. For instance, in the case of premature ejaculation, the woman in the partnership eventually becomes the therapeutic controller of the ejaculatory experience by applying a specific squeeze upon the glans penis just prior to an ejaculation provoked by masturbation, thus inhibiting the ejaculation and helping the man acquire the kind of reflex arc control that he acquired as a small boy in learning to control the passing of urine by discriminating internal signals.

Not only did Masters and Johnson's therapy proceed upon systematic lines, illuminated by a clear understanding of the expected physiological effects of an increasingly skilled sexual encounter between the couple in treatment, hence commending itself instantly to a planned therapeutic approach previously absent in this field; they also established treatment effects of a very high order. At best, 97·8 per cent of 186 premature ejaculators responded to treatment; at worst, 59·4 per cent of primary impotence cases recovered. Over all disorders, male and female, the initial successful outcome rate was 81·1 per cent, a figure of an extremely high order for any therapy. Five-year follow-up on 313 marital units showed a relapse rate of only 5·1 per cent. In consequence it can be claimed that Masters and Johnson developed not only a very systematic treatment procedure but also a highly effective one, for difficulties not previously responsive to treatment nor properly understood.

The publication of their treatment results in 1970 led to a considerable surge of popular and professional interest, occurring as it did at a time when reliable and readily available contraceptive measures in the USA and northern Europe had become established aspects of the sexual life of these cultures. With the separation of the act of intercourse from the act of reproduction, the increasingly discussed concept of sex-for-pleasure *for both partners*, responsibly undertaken, suddenly acquired an authoritative knowledge base. This reached an elegant if early apotheosis in Alex Comfort's *The Joy of Sex* in 1972. Clinics for the treatment of sexual difficulties sprang up throughout the United States, so that within five years of the publication of *Human Sexual Inadequacy* it was reliably rumoured that over 3,000 such clinics had established themselves.

This mushroom development sprang in part from a small amount of work which Masters and Johnson had done with single individuals, where, for 41 males, a female partner, called a 'surrogate', was made available by the therapists to co-operate in providing psychological and physical involvement during therapy. Masters and Johnson themselves abandoned this approach to therapy in view of the considerable administrative and ethical issues which their bold exploration of it raised. It led to a good deal of sexual 'therapeutic' licence in the States, a process eventually controlled by the development of a professional association for surrogate partners in sex therapy. Reputable schools of practice did also develop using a much more physically involved approach by therapists than Masters and Johnson had advocated, Hartman and

Fithian being one example and McIlvenna at the Institute for the Advanced Study of Human Sexuality another. Apart from a treatment series conducted by Dr Martin Cole at Birmingham, the use of surrogates in therapy has not become common in Britain. Therapy for women to explore their own sexuality has become so, however, and there are some accounts of this (e.g. Hooper, 1980), though no clinical trials in a formal sense.

Indeed, the whole field of sexual function therapy is notable for its enthusiasm rather than systematization, and it is often difficult to distinguish therapy from sexual enrichment work. Perhaps at times there may be no useful distinction to be drawn. Be that as it may, no systematic replication of Masters and Johnson's work has been attempted, and it is possible that such a task could not now be accomplished. Their work has itself dramatically altered the levels of information available in the population about sexual matters; their personal therapeutic effectiveness as the outstanding pioneer authorities in the field is an element that could not be replicated; the nature of their fourteen-day, vacation-based therapy programme is not one that is easily re-created once a variety of more local centres becomes available; and their criteria for selecting couples for therapy has never been clearly stated.

Despite a flood of literature following their work, of which LoPiccolo and LoPiccolo (1978) is a good summary, the only two studies to have investigated components of their treatment procedures have originated in England, where J. Bancroft and his colleagues at Oxford and P. T. Brown on behalf of the National Marriage Guidance Council at Rugby considered the co-therapy situation, among other aspects, in clinical trials. In both these cases therapy was modified to weekly-attendance procedures, and spread out over ten to twelve weeks instead of fourteen days. This is now the typical pattern for sexual function therapy in Britain, a development that has in part been systematized through the establishing of a multi-disciplinary Association of Sexual and Marital Therapists in 1976.

Kaplan in the United States has been the strongest source of clinical thinking to integrate Masters and Johnson's work into the established psychological therapies, and she has been particularly concerned to distinguish disorders of sexual desire from the dysfunctions, as well as clarifying other aspects of the diagnostic statements of Masters and Johnson. Brown (1977) has summarized Masters and Johnson and Kaplan into a diagnostic schema which lists in a simple fashion the categories of the sexual dysfunctions, and makes it clear that they are now readily distinguishable from those difficulties of sexual expression which were once called 'perversions', then 'deviations', then 'variations', and most recently by the *behaviour-ists 'excesses', but which Stoller has argued should properly be called 'perversions'. Their characteristic, to distinguish them from the dysfunctions, is that they are not difficulties of sexual expression, but contain choices of sexual object other than the familiar acts associated with heterosexual arousal and response.

Treatment for sexual dysfunction, both for couples and individuals, is now available throughout the UK, though more so in some areas than others. Both the National Health Service and the National Marriage Guidance Council have developed specialist clinic facilities, and there is a limited private field. Therapy typically involves an exploration of not only what the problem is, but why in the particular partnership or individual it has arisen or been maintained; and this is followed, usually on a weekly basis, by guided exploration of effective sexual stimulation. Thus the couple and the individual are helped to become increasingly expert and effective in their own sexual well-being.

P. T. B.

Brown, P. T. and Faulder, C. (1977). *Treat Yourself to Sex*. London.

Comfort, A. (1972). *The Joy of Sex; a gourmet guide to lovemaking*. New York.

Friedman, L. (1961). *Virgin Wives*. London.

Hartman, W. E. and Fithian, M. A. (1972). *Treatment of Sexual Dysfunction*. California: Center for Marital and Sexual Studies.

Hooper, A. (1980). *The Body Electric*. London.

Kaplan, H. S. (1974). *The New Sex Therapy*. London.

Kaplan, H. S. (1979). *Disorders of Sexual Desire*. New York.

Kinsey, A. C., Pomeroy, W. B., and Martin, C. E. (1948). *Sexual Behaviour in the Human Male*. Philadelphia.

Kinsey, A. C., Pomeroy, W. B., and Martin, C. E. (1953). *Sexual Behaviour in the Human Female*. Philadelphia.

LoPiccolo, J. and LoPiccolo, L. (1978). *Handbook of Sex Therapy*. New York.

Masters, W. H. and Johnson, V. (1966). *Human Sexual Response*. London.

Masters, W. H. and Johnson, V. (1970). *Human Sexual Inadequacy*. London.

Matthews, A., Bancroft, J., Whitehead, A., Hackmann, A., Julier, D., Bancroft, J., Gath, D., and Shaw, P. (1976). The behavioural treatment of sexual inadequacy. *Behaviour Research and Therapy*, **14**, 427–36.

Stoller, R. (1976). *Perversion: the erotic form of hatred*. Hassocks, Sussex.

**SHERRINGTON, SIR CHARLES SCOTT** (1857–1952). British physiologist, born in London and educated at Ipswich grammar school and at Cambridge; he qualified at St Thomas's Hospital in London in 1885. As a physiologist he anticipated *Pavlov in attempting to uncover the structure of the *nervous system by looking at input and output. Moreover, his discoveries stand up better than Pavlov's because he worked mainly on a comparatively simple aspect of the nervous system, spinal reflexes, whereas Pavlov was attempting to investigate the workings of the brain using the same techniques. This work on nervous integration and brain functions resulted in a neuroanatomical theory of behaviour that prefigures ethological models and, unexpected as it may seem, converges with some basic teachings of *phenomenological

psychology. Yet his originality is not limited to his master-work *The Integrative Action of the Nervous System* (1906, 2nd edn. 1948); it is equally patent in his two late works, *Man on his Nature* (1940; 2nd edn. 1952) and *The Endeavour of Jean Fernel* (1946), which deal with man's place in the world as a living being endowed with *consciousness and reflective power, and involve fundamental issues in the fields of philosophy of science, ethics, and the theory of values. To complete the picture, one should remember the great physiologist's interest in the humanities and literature, as evidenced, among other things, by his publication in 1925 of *The Assaying of Brabantius, and other verse*.

Sherrington's career was exceptionally brilliant. He was Brown professor of physiology, London (1891), Fellow of the Royal Society (1893), Holt professor of physiology, Liverpool (1895), and in 1913 he became Waynflete professor of physiology at Oxford, a post he held until 1935. In 1932 he shared the Nobel prize for medicine with E. D. *Adrian. His physiological investigations, which began with the study of nerve degeneration in the decerebrate dog (1884), developed into a manifold and steady production covering a great diversity of topics, ranging from anatomy to perceptual processes. However, the guide-line in the vast majority of his works is analysis of the functional properties of the nervous system. Important discoveries within this framework are the reciprocal innervation of antagonistic muscles, decerebrate rigidity, and the basic features of peripheral reflexes. In addition to *The Integrative Action of the Nervous System*, he produced *Mammalian Physiology* (1919; rev. edn. 1929), *Reflex Activity in the Spinal Cord* (1932), and some 300 specialized articles. He opened an era of experimental research and theory by clarifying the functional relations between reflexes and behaviour patterns. This is one of the major objectives, if not *the* major one, of neurophysiology, comparative physiology, physiological psychology, and, most recently, neuroethology. It is therefore necessary to ask where exactly Sherrington's originality lies.

First, his experimental studies of reflexes on decerebrate animals allowed him to discover both the complexity of spinal reflexes and the control effected on them by superior (or 'higher') brain centres. This he could achieve by decerebrating the animal at the mesencephalic level, a technique which proved most appropriate and led him to clear evidence of integrative processes. Secondly, he was able to establish a now classical distinction between different categories of receptors—interoceptors, exteroceptors, and proprioceptors—according to the sites where they gather information as required by the organic processes actually in course. For the connections between neurones, the term *synapses was introduced by Sherrington and Michael Foster in 1897.

These and other important contributions to the systematic and accurate knowlege of the anatomo-physiological structures and functions of the nervous system amounted progressively to a general interpretation of the organism's activity which is present on every page of *The Integrative Action of the Nervous System* and is fully developed in the last two chapters of that work. Sherrington succeeds in explaining the emerging properties of behaviour patterns by referring to the *continuity* that exists between anatomo-physiological substrates and overt behaviour, thus doing away at the outset with classical dualistic views. Moreover, the question of internal causation of behaviour is viewed not in the form of extrinsic mechanical links between acts and supposedly corresponding internal organic events: it is systematically related, rather, to the structural constraints of the body as a spatio-temporal system within the process of evolution.

In brief, physico-chemical changes inside the body and bodily changes at the behavioural level occur within subsystems included in overall organic activity. Continuity therefore implies integrative action, for causal factors to be at work between one level and the other in order to ensure survival. This comprehensive philosophy of the organism is exceptionally well outlined in the penultimate chapter of *The Integrative Action of the Nervous System*. After discussing the main features of the reflex-arc, Sherrington goes on to describe the central nervous system as a synaptic network. He then turns to the analysis of *receptive fields, contrasting the richness of the exteroceptive field with the relative poverty of the interoceptive one. This is apparently due to the fact that receptors of a special kind, the distance-receptors, initially appeared in relation to locomotion requirements, and are located for this reason in the leading segment of an animal. The distinctive functional advantage of the distance-receptors lies in their unique power of dissociating the stimulus from its physical source, thereby enabling the organism to develop around itself peculiar space–time relations in perceptual activity. This may be observed in various degrees in vision, hearing, and smell, as well as in some less widespread mechanical and thermal receptors. The distance-receptors are said to be 'precurrent'—i.e. they can gather information about the animal's surroundings without requiring a direct physical contact between the source of a stimulus and the body surface. This important feature is not to be found in the proximal receptors, namely those of touch and taste.

The high survival value of precurrent responses is evident, since it allows for explorative appreciation of, for example, *potential* prey and predators. If food could be detected only by taste, or enemies only by mechanical contact, an organism would be unable to make any preparatory decision as to the positive or negative nature of any biologically important stimulus. In other words, the subjective spatio-temporal field would be practically nonexistent and the autonomy of the animal would be drastically limited (as is the case, to some extent, in so-called 'primitive' living forms). Clearly, the

product of evolution we call the 'superior' animal is that type of organism which has evolved towards an increasing explorative autonomy, due to the potentialities of the distance-receptors and the corresponding development of a highly complicated brain capable of integrating a great diversity of sensory information. Considering the time sequences of behaviour patterns, anticipatory responses, which allow for an extension of subjective space and consequently for an increase in reaction-time and duration of response, have the fundamental function of preparing the responses of the immediate receptors, i.e. the reactions triggered by proximal stimuli in contact with the body.

Sherrington's account of these active relations established by the organism with its surroundings converges to a great extent with later ethological teaching, a fact which is still hardly recognized in ethological circles. The expression 'consummatory reaction' appears in *The Integrative Action of the Nervous System* twelve years before Wallace Craig introduced the term 'consummatory act', to which ethologists refer as the first formulation of the concept. The main difference is that Sherrington's outline of the role of anatomical structures in exteroceptive communication emerged from his neurophysiological experiments, whereas the corresponding topic was developed in ethology on the basis of naturalistic descriptions of behaviour patterns in the social life of animals within the framework of phylogenic studies.

Finally, there exists a definite affinity between Sherrington's analysis of the precurrent receptive fields and the phenomenological descriptions of bodily subjectivity. Phenomenological themes, such as the lived experience of bodiliness in the active constitution of a meaningful world, or even descriptive studies of animal subjectivity referring to the perception of bodily limits in the actualization of observable behaviour patterns, may conveniently be set against Sherrington's theory of the biological significance of the body's 'interface' as meeting-point of exteroceptive and interoceptive experiences. His interpretation of the subjective field as a result of his experimental studies on reflex activity also laid the foundations of a physiologically inspired psychology which is in many interesting respects at variance with the Pavlovian model. In Sherrington's view, *behaviour* must be considered as that sector of overall biological activity which is initiated by the precurrent receptors and which ceases to exert itself as soon as the subsequent activity of non-precurrent receptors comes into play. Concerning feeding behaviour, for instance, he writes: 'The morsel vanishes from an experience at the moment when our choice in regard to it becomes inoperative. The psyche does not persist into conditions which would render it ineffective.' In Pavlov's view, on the contrary, behavioural processes are conceived as events resulting from stimuli which impinge on the organism without any previous activity in the behavioural field. Whatever the case may be, the careful reader of Sherrington's writings will readily be convinced of the founding character of his contribution to the biology of behaviour.   G. T.

Straus, E. (1935). *Vom Sinn der Sinne*. (Eng. trans. Needleman, J. (1963), *The Primary World of Senses: a vindication of sensory experience*. London.)
Thinès, G. (1977). *Phenomenology and the Science of Behaviour*. London.

**SHOCK.** This term is sometimes applied to an event of special force or significance that causes disruption or collapse of mental or physical functions or behaviour, and sometimes to the effects of such an event. After the impact, a usually short-lived attempt to restore the position is followed by reduction in activity and in responsiveness to the external world. After a serious accident, for instance, a person becomes apathetic and largely unresponsive to what goes on around him. He lacks initiative and is compliant, sometimes to a degree of child-like dependence on others. These effects protect him from further stimulation. If he has suffered serious physical injury, and his state is one of surgical shock, he is pale, his skin is cold, and his peripheral pulses feeble. These effects reflect the shunting of blood from the skin to organs more essential for survival. The adaptiveness of the effects has not always been recognized: for instance, surgical shock used to be treated by warming the patient in an attempt to restore the circulation to the skin.

The term 'shell-shock' was used in the First World War to describe a variety of bizarre hysterical symptoms which were attributed to the pressure effects of exploding shells. It was superseded in the Second World War by 'battle neurosis' or 'exhaustion', implying a psychological rather than a physical cause for the condition.   D. R. D.

**SHORT-TERM MEMORY.** \*Memory for what happened an hour ago or a year ago fulfils an obvious function in our lives. However, our capacity to store information for periods measured in seconds is equally if not more important to our integrity as human beings. This capacity is referred to as short-term memory (STM). \*Descartes asserted, 'I think, therefore I am'. It is equally true to say 'I think, therefore I have short-term memory'. Indeed any mental activity extended in time, including the production and comprehension of language, must involve STM. It is certainly fortunate that STM is robust and, unlike long-term memory, is seldom affected by old age, drugs, or brain damage.

The most familiar fact about STM is the existence of the so-called span of immediate memory. A rough definition of the span is that it is the longest sequence of items that can be reproduced correctly following a single presentation. However, the same individual may manage a sequence of seven items on one occasion and make a mistake with a sequence of only five items on another. Accordingly, the span is in fact defined as

that length of sequence for which the chance of correct reproduction is fifty-fifty. The span has a number of interesting properties. Two are as follows. First, for items in random order, the span is about seven, plus or minus two. This is surprising in that the amount of information per item has little effect on the span. For example, the span for binary digits (0,1) is only slightly longer than for decimal digits (the digits 0 to 9), although the latter contains over three times as much information. Second, within wide limits, the span is almost unaffected by the rate at which items are presented, and is therefore relatively independent of the time elapsing between the presentation of an item and its recall. These two facts are nicely explained by the so-called slot theory. On this theory, the span reflects the capacity of an information store in the brain with about seven 'slots'. Each slot is capable of storing a single item or unit. Once the store is full, new items can only be stored by displacing existing items. Variation in the span is attributed on this theory to the fact that a unit can sometimes comprise more than one item. For example, two or more digits can sometimes be recoded as a familiar number which can then be stored as a unit. Indeed, if an individual has an exceptional familiarity with numbers he may have a digit span of fifteen or more. However, recoding digits into familiar numbers cannot account for the digit span of eighty recently achieved by one individual after extensive practice, who reported using both recoding and a hierarchical grouping strategy. At best, therefore, the slot theory describes the mechanism which *normally* determines the span.

Two other interesting facts force another qualification to the slot theory. The span is reduced if the items of the sequence sound similar. For example, the sequence B V T G P is more difficult than the sequence S K L R N. If reproduction of the sequence involves retrieving the items from separate slots, why should this be so? Similarly, the span is smaller for long words than for short words, which is puzzling if each word is a unit and occupies a separate slot. With visual presentation, both the effect of similarity of sound and of word length vanish if the subject is asked to count aloud during presentation of the sequence. (At the same time, the counting task somewhat reduces the span.) This suggests that normally there is sub-vocal rehearsal of earlier items during presentation of later items of the sequence and that such rehearsal contributes to the span as normally measured.

Since the slot theory postulates a special store for STM, by implication there must be a different store for long-term memory (LTM). Evidence for a two-store view of memory comes from memory pathology. \*Amnesia due to brain damage can take one of two forms. In the common form, STM is intact but LTM, in the sense of the ability to form new permanent memories, is impaired. In a rare form, which has only been identified quite recently, the reverse is found, wth LTM intact but

STM impaired. Clearly independent impairment of STM and LTM is highly consonant with the two-store theory. However, recent theory tends to postulate not one but several stores for the temporary storage of information. Indeed, evidence from the study of patients with impaired STM suggests that there are separate temporary stores for auditory speech sounds and for non-verbal sounds.

Other evidence has been interpreted as showing that there are also temporary stores associated with touch and vision, although information from the latter fades in less than a second. There is also the possibility that the brain has temporary stores concerned with making responses. In the case of speech, for example, such a store might hold in readiness the codes for articulating several words and would substantially assist the smooth production of speech. Accordingly, the span of immediate memory (and STM generally) may reflect the output of one or more temporary stores, depending on circumstances. The common characteristic of these postulated stores is that each is of limited capacity and new information displaces old information. The slot theory of the span therefore seems too simple, although the facts it explains need to be accommodated in more complex accounts of the mechanisms underlying STM. If short-term memory depends on specialized stores holding information over short intervals of time, the question arises of how information reaches the store responsible for LTM. One possibility is that there is a process of information transfer from these stores to the LTM store. If so, this process is presumably successful for only a proportion of the information entering the temporary stores, since we forget more than we remember. A second possibility is that information enters the LTM store directly at the time of perception, although at a slower rate than it enters the temporary stores. On this hypothesis, STM as we observe it may depend both on information retrieved from temporary stores and on information retrieved from the LTM store. At present, there is no decisive evidence favouring either possibility. Indeed, some theorists prefer to view memory as a single complex system. For example, the different properties of STM and LTM can be held to reflect, not the operation of different stores, but factors affecting the ease of retrieving stored information. This sort of theory is not implausible in view of the fact that problems associated with the retrieval of information from a storage system often imposes major constraints on efficiency. However, the detailed facts about STM do seem to favour the view that specialized temporary stores are involved. Ideally, there would be physiological evidence to show how many stores underlie memory, but at present the evidence is indirect and difficult to interpret.

See CHUNKING; INFORMATION THEORY; MEMORY: BIOLOGICAL BASIS; MEMORY AND CONTEXT.　J. B.

Baddeley, A. D. (1976). *The Psychology of Memory*. New York.

Ericsson, K. A., Chase, W. G., and Faloon, S. (1980). Acquisition of a memory skill. *Science*, **208**, 1,181–2.

**SIGN STIMULUS.** See ETHOLOGY.

**SIZE CONSTANCY SCALING.** See EMMERT'S LAW.

**SIZE–WEIGHT ILLUSION.** Lifting weights was a favourite activity of experimental psychology in its early days; but now, although these experiments involve much of interest, they are unfashionable and are seldom even mentioned in textbooks. This may change, however, as manipulative skills in space at zero g give rise to new problems in relation to *perception (see SPACE PSYCHOLOGY). One of the most theoretically significant of perceptual *illusions, which also has practical importance, is the size–weight illusion: when objects are lifted by the hand, a *larger* object feels and is judged to be *lighter* than a smaller object of the same scale weight. This makes a nice kitchen experiment, which can easily be carried out, with a pair of tins of different size, partly filled with sugar or salt (or lead or sand) to have the *same* scale weight. When lifted, a few inches from the table, the *larger* tin will feel *lighter* than the smaller tin—though they both have the same scale weight. Ideally, the tins should be lifted by identical handles or wire loops, so that there are no significant touch signals from the different sizes of the tins—for the whole point is that sensory signals of weight are the same for both tins, though the smaller feels heavier. This illusion is interesting because it shows very clearly that the sensation of the weight—which one might think is directly and simply given from forces on the hand and arm—is markedly affected by the assumption of how heavy it 'should' be. Further, it turns out that it is the *surprise* that the larger weight is not the heavier (as it would usually be) that produces the illusion. (Weight illusion also arises from the colours and shades of objects—darker objects being accepted as probably heavier than lighter ones.)

Even the 'purest' sensory signals must be 'read' or interpreted according to general knowledge or assumptions in order to provide information, sometimes fallible, about the objects handled. Thus, sensed weight is not given simply by skin and muscle receptors, but also from our knowledge that larger objects are usually heavier than smaller objects. Anticipated weight is important when lifting objects, since the muscle force must be set to give a reliable smooth lift and avoid injury. That we do not always correctly anticipate the force required is obvious from the familiar 'empty suitcase' effect: that is, when we pick up an empty suitcase assumed to be full, it flies up in the air! For, then our anticipation of its weight was wrong—which shows that we *do* anticipate weight before we lift things.

The size–weight illusion is a large (up to about 30 per cent), stable, and repeatable effect, which offers an opportunity to challenge an assumption of *psychophysics—that our ability to discriminate between small differences depends, simply, on relative stimulus intensities. It is possible to test whether the *Weber–Fechner law depends (as is generally assumed) simply on the weight stimuli, or whether it is related also to our knowledge and assumptions of what objects are like. We can test this by finding out whether it is more difficult to distinguish differences between weights of small objects than it is in the case of larger ones. It turns out that there *is* an effect of size, and so of *apparent* weight; but it is not merely a matter of an increase of the Weber fraction in proportion to apparent weight. Rather, weight discrimination is best—that is, the Weber fraction is smallest—when the density of the lifted weights is about 1, which is roughly the average density of objects. Both lower and higher densities give impaired weight discrimination.

Why should this be so? A possible reason is that the neural signals for weight are compared with expectations, and that the *signalled* and *anticipated* weights are *nulled*—as in delicate measuring instruments such as Wheatstone bridges. Cancelling of received input against anticipated values is useful as a way of gaining sensitivity over a wide range of input values, even when the components (whether electronic or those of the nervous system) have only small dynamic ranges. A *nulling arrangement gives high stability even if the components are liable to 'drift' or fatigue, as neurones are. That our weight-sensing system is labile is obvious—for after carrying a heavy object even for a short time the arm, and even the whole body, feels light when it is released. And the arm may float up, almost out of control. This is the basis of the party 'levitation' trick: after someone's shoulders have been pushed down in the dark, that person may have the impression of rising towards the ceiling, for such is the lability of the nervous system.                                         R. L. G.

Ross, H. E. (1969). When is a weight not illusory? *Quarterly Journal of Experimental Psychology*, **21**, 346.

Ross, H. E. and Gregory, R. L. (1964). Is the Weber fraction a function of physical or perceived input? *Quarterly Journal of Experimental Psychology*, **16**, part 2, 116.

Ross, H. E. and Gregory, R. L. (1970). Weight illusions and weight discrimination—a revised hypothesis. *Quarterly Journal of Experimental Psychology*, **22**, 318.

**SKILL, HUMAN.** In everyday parlance, 'skill' is used to denote expertise developed in the course of training and experience. It includes not only trade and craft skills acquired by apprenticeship, but high-grade performance in many fields such as professional practice, the arts, games, and athletics.

The psychological study of skills came to the fore during the Second World War with the need to match the demands of new equipment such as radar, high-speed aircraft, and various sophisticated weapons to human capacities and limitations. More recently, the growth of sport as

highly lucrative entertainment and as a medium of national pride and international diplomacy has raised competitive standards and led to studies of human performance at games and athletics in order to extract maximum physical and mental effectiveness.

The common feature running through all these types of skill is that the performer has to match the demands of a task to his capacities. He does this by applying some *method*, or, as it is often called, 'strategy' of performance. For example, a tradesman will select tools and manipulate them in ways which match his capacities for exerting force and exercising fine motor control to the requirements of the metal, wood, or other material he is using. Similarly, a barrister or negotiator will order the questions he asks in a manner which he judges will best enable his powers of persuasion to secure the outcome he desires. These strategies, it should be noted, are not typically concerned with single responses to stimuli, but with chains or programmes of action which look ahead from the situation that initiates them to a future goal or end result. Some strategies are more efficient than others, in that less capacity, time, or effort has to be deployed to obtain the results required. *Skill consists in choosing and carrying out strategies which are efficient.*

Almost every skilled performance involves the whole chain of central mechanisms lying between the sense organs and the effectors, but different types of skill can be distinguished according to the link in the chain where their main emphasis lies. For this purpose, the central mechanisms can be broadly divided into three functional parts: perception of objects or events; choice of responses to them; and execution of phased and co-ordinated action giving expression to the choice made. An example of perceptual skill is the ability of musicians to judge 'absolute pitch'. It depends upon the possession of a conceptual scale against which any note heard can be placed. The ability is sometimes claimed to be inborn, but studies have shown that it can be acquired, or at least greatly improved, with practice. Analogous skills occur in other occupations which require the making of fine discriminations, such as dyers distinguishing subtle shades of colour, steel furnacemen deciding when the colour of molten metal indicates that it is ready to pour, wool- and other fibre-graders assessing thickness by 'feel', cheese-graders judging softness by pressure, and wine- or tea-tasters using a 'sensitive palate'.

Skills in making choices, or, as they are sometimes termed, 'decisional' skills, include the expertise shown in various intellectual pursuits, and also in games such as chess and cards. In all these cases, the perceptual data are usually clear and the precise manner of executing the actions required is unimportant: the essential for success is to decide upon the correct actions to take.

Examples of motor skills include sitting on a horse, riding a bicycle, or manipulating the controls of a car. Their essential characteristics lie in motor co-ordination and timing. They have attracted somewhat less research than other types of skill, probably because the knacks involved are largely unconscious.

Industrial and athletic skills display the characteristics of all three types. Perceptual factors enter into trades and crafts in the assessment and judgement of materials, and in observing the effects of tools such as drills and lathe-cutters. In ball games they are concerned in the observation and assessment of the flight of the ball and of the moves made by other players. Motor skills are obviously involved in the fine manipulation of tools in trade and craft work, and in bowling, catching, or kicking and making strokes with bat, racquet, or club in various games. However, the core of all these skills, especially at higher levels of expertise, lies in processes of choice and decision. Thus high-level skill in craft and trade work lies less in the ability to execute particular manual operations, such as shaping clay on a potter's wheel or cutting cleanly through a piece of metal with a hacksaw, than in deciding what shape is needed or exactly where the cut should be made. Similarly, high-grade athletic skill lies more in the strategy of the game than in the ability to make accurate individual strokes or in sheer muscular strength. Again, in music, the soloist's skill transcends the mere playing of the instrument to the interpretation of the score.

Strategies are developed and become more efficient in the course of practice, and it is these rather than basic capacities that are amenable to training. Four points should be noted.

1. For improvement to occur with practice, some knowledge of results achieved by previous action (*feedback) is required, and, broadly speaking, the more precise and direct this is the better. Early in practice feedback needs to be detailed, but when comprehension and action become organized into larger units the need for feedback within these is reduced. In extreme cases the units become 'automatic' in the sense that conscious attention to feedback no longer occurs and the performer has little awareness of what he is doing. When this stage is reached two results follow. First, because each decision covers a larger unit of performance, fewer need to be made, so that action becomes smoother and less hurried—the skilled performer 'seems to have all the time in the world'. Secondly, performance becomes highly efficient, but may also become rigid in the sense that it cannot be adjusted to meet changing circumstances. A high-grade yet versatile expertise involves a nice balance between such efficiency and flexibility.

2. Strategies and information acquired in training for one task may *transfer to others: for example, techniques learnt when mastering a foreign language can be applied again when studying another language. Such transfer usually results in the later task being mastered more easily than it would otherwise be, but occasionally the reverse is true: for instance, the co-ordination between tilt and movement needed to ride a bicycle leads to gross oversteering if applied when riding a tricycle, and must be inhibited before the tricycle can be ridden successfully.

3. Improvement with practice is typically rapid at first, then more gradual but continuing over long periods: for instance, the speed of some repetitive work in factories has been shown to rise with time on the job over several years.

4. Once high levels of skill have been attained, they are usually well preserved over periods of many years. The fine edge of performance may be lost without continual practice, but can usually be regained relatively quickly.

Most discussions of skill have been concerned with men or women interacting with machines, tools, or other objects in their environment. It has recently been recognized that the concepts of skill can be applied also to the interaction of one human being with another. *Social skill* includes all the three types already distinguished. It includes perception of the needs and desires of others and of the effects upon others of one's own actions; decisions about how to react to the behaviour of, and communications from, others to achieve rapport and to influence them in ways desired; and on the motor side it includes the making of gestures, kissing, and modulations of the voice in expressing feelings such as sympathy. Social skill applies not only to relationships between individuals, but is essential for efficient leadership and communication in industry and other organizations, and is indeed necessary for living satisfactorily in any society.                                              A. T. W.

Argyle, M. (1967). *The Psychology of Interpersonal Behaviour*. Harmondsworth.

Legge, D. (ed.) (1970). *Skills*. Harmondsworth.

Singleton, W. T., Spurgeon, P., and Stammers, R. B. (eds.) (1980). *The Analysis of Social Skill*. New York.

Welford, A. T. (1968). *Fundamentals of Skill*. London.

Welford, A.T. (1976). *Skilled Performance: Perceptual and Motor Skills*. Glenview, Illinois.

**SKILLS, MEMORY FOR.** One apparently never forgets how to swim or ride a bicycle. Is this really the case? If it is, does it mean *memory for skills is in some fundamental way different from other kinds of memory?

What is the evidence? The fact that one does not immediately fall off a bicycle when remounting after an interval of several years does not necessarily mean that no *forgetting has occurred, it simply means that *something* has been retained. Fortunately we do have an answer to the question, based on studies of specialized skills under relatively controlled conditions.

The answer turns out to depend on the type of skill involved. Here we must distinguish between continuous and discrete skills. A continuous skill involves the performer in continually varying his response to a continuously varying stimulus. An example of this would be the steering response involved in driving a car, or the balancing involved in riding a bicycle, or for that matter simply maintaining an upright posture while walking. Such skills can be contrasted with discrete skills in which a discrete individual response is made; typing or manually changing gear in a car would be examples of such skills.

There was a good deal of interest in the acquisition and retention of continuous skills during the Second World War, since the skill of flying a plane clearly has a continuous component, as indeed does learning to control a missile using a joystick. Over the years, a number of experiments have studied the retention of continuous tracking performance, typically using a task in which the subject is given a joystick and required to control the movement of a spot of light on a cathode ray tube. Usually an analogue computer is used to simulate the control characteristics of the plane or missile, with a movement of the joystick changing the velocity of the missile or its acceleration, and producing a response that may be immediate or may follow only after a lag.

Fleishman and Parker (1962) studied a very difficult version of such a task. It involved three-dimensional tracking under conditions which simulated the problem of flying a plane on the attack phase of a radar intercept mission. They trained their operators over a six-week period, giving them 357 separate one-minute trials, by which time they were performing the task well. The operators were then split into three groups and given no further access to the apparatus. Retention of the skills was then tested, with one group returning after nine months, one after fourteen months, and one after two years. In all conditions, after a single warm-up trial to refamiliarize the subjects with the situation, performance was virtually as good as it had been immediately after the end of training. A number of subsequent studies have replicated this and shown that even the warm-up decrement shown on the first test trial can be reduced if the subject is sufficiently highly practised.

In the case of discrete motor skills, forgetting does occur. Consider, for example, the study by Baddeley and Longman (1978) in which a large number of postmen were trained to use a typewriter. The purpose was to familiarize them with the typewriter keyboard, which was subsequently to be used as part of a letter-sorting machine. Since the equipment was not ready at the end of the training experiment, it proved possible to study the retention of the skill under conditions where no subsequent practice was occurring, an unusual situation in the case of typing. Even after a warm-up period, clear forgetting occurred, with the average rate of keying dropping from about 80 strokes per minute at the end of the training session to about 70 per minute after one month, and to about 55 per minute after a nine-month delay. At the same time errors increased from about 1 per cent of keystrokes to somewhere in the region of 3 per cent.

Why the difference between the two types of skill? At present we can only speculate, but one possible interpretation is as follows. One source of forgetting is that of retroactive interference. A person learns to associate a particular stimulus with a particular response or action: for example, he learns that a bathroom tap with the letter C on it is likely to produce cold water if turned on. After a while such an association will become relatively automatic. If the situation then changes—for example, if he goes on holiday to Italy where C stands for *caldo*, 'hot'—then he will probably make a number of mistakes before adjusting. On returning to 'English-speaking' bathrooms he is likely to find that, to begin with, the previous habit interferes with his response, causing him to make at least one or two initial errors, although the massive amount of prior learning will mean that it takes very little time to revert. In brief, what has happened is that the person has learned two separate responses to the same stimulus, and at times he will recall the wrong one.

It seems likely that at least some, and some theorists would claim all, forgetting occurs because of interference from other learning (cf. TRANSFER OF TRAINING). In the case of a discontinuous or discrete skill, the same stimuli probably occur in a range of situations where the relevant motor response cannot or should not be made. For example, our trainee typists would clearly go on being in a situation where they were responding to printed text by reading or writing rather than by hitting the appropriate key. This would be expected to cause some interference and hence some forgetting, although the amount of interference would depend very much on the precise conditions involved in the two interfering tasks. One might contrast this with a continuous skill in which the operator is functioning as if in a closed loop, with his own responses and their interaction with the environment producing the stimulus for further response. In any situation other than that of performing the skill, the essential stimulus situation is simply not evoked, and hence no interference can occur.

Having presented this view, it should be pointed out that there is very little evidence either for or against it, and our knowledge of the detailed operation of interference effects is certainly not sufficiently great to allow one to regard it as more than a speculation. The basic phenomena, however, are reasonably well established, so you can assume with some degree of confidence that you will not forget how to ride a bike, or perhaps even more importantly, how to swim.    A. D. B.

Baddeley, A. D. and Longman, D. J. A. (1978). The influence of length and frequency of training session on rate of learning to type. *Ergonomics*, **21**, 627–35.

Fleishman, E. A. and Parker, J. F., Jr. (1962). Factors in the retention and relearning of perceptual motor skill. *Journal of Experimental Psychology*, **64**, 215–26.

**SKINNER**, B. F., American psychologist (1904–    ).
See BEHAVIOURISM, SKINNER ON.

**SKINNER BOX.** A type of experimental chamber often used in the laboratory analysis of behaviour, named after the American psychologist B. F. Skinner. As a graduate student at Harvard in 1929, he invented the first such chamber to facilitate the study of eating behaviour in rats, and he later developed many versions.

The prototypical Skinner box for, say, a rat (Fig. 1) would be cubic in shape, a foot (30 cm) long on each edge, and would contain the following elements: (i) an 'operandum', such as a lever that protrudes from one wall, and (ii) an opening in that wall where the rat could obtain a small pellet of food, delivered by a mechanical feeding device. The box would be light- and sound-proof to minimize distractions and maximize the effectiveness of events that occur inside the box. If lever-pressing produces a pellet of food in this situation, a hungry rat will typically press the lever repeatedly and thereby eat.

Since its invention, the Skinner box has been adapted to study many organisms besides the rat, behaviours other than bar-pressing, and consequences other than food presentation. Behaviour has been studied in the context of auditory and visual stimuli, such as coloured lights and pure tones, as well as more complex stimuli, such as other organisms and slides of the natural environment projected on a screen inside the chamber. In general, the term is now applied to almost any experimental chamber used in the study of the relationships between behaviour, its antecedent stimuli, and its consequences.

The use of the term probably began with Clark *Hull, who made use of what he called a 'modified Skinner box', described in his *Principles of Behavior*. Skinner himself objected to the use of

**Fig. 1.** The interior of a typical Skinner box. A hungry rat is poised over a lever protruding from the front wall. Pressing the lever one or more times will operate a feeder; the rat can retrieve a pellet of food which is dispensed at the small opening in the wall. The rat can easily learn to make discriminations—for example, to press the lever when a light is on and not to press it when the light is off. Chambers for other animals may vary considerably from this one.

the term and in particular to its erroneous extension to the 'air-crib', an enclosed crib for human infants that he invented in the 1940s.        R. E.

**SLEEP.** A third of our lives is spent in sleep. Of the remainder, some is spent in wishing that our small children would sleep longer, and, during our later years, some is spent wishing that our sleep was less broken. What is sleep? It is a healthy state of inertia and unresponsiveness that is recurrently imposed by unknown mechanisms within the nervous system. In most animals the sleep–wakefulness rhythm is coupled to the twenty-four-hour light–dark environment, as are the rest–activity cycles of lower life forms; there is no sharp demarcation between creatures which can be said simply to have rest phases and animals which certainly sleep. In animals possessing developed brains there are electrical rhythms that differ in sleep and in wakefulness, being generally slower during sleep.

The *biological clock that makes us sleepy every twenty-four hours means that shift workers and those who have just flown to different time zones are often tired and inefficient while they are trying to be alert (see JET LAG). If it is a long time since we last slept then that too makes us sleepy. Monotony, warmth, restricted movement, and a sense of waiting for something that cannot happen yet—all of these make us sleepy. A sleep-like state of 'animal hypnosis' can also follow extreme stimulation.

The amount of sleep each species takes is proportional to the need for restoration, i.e. to the waking metabolic rate, but is in part also determined by predator status: those animals who sleep safely sleep longer. Among human beings there are wide variations. A few are happy and healthy with under three hours' sleep a night; a minority of others will take as many as ten hours. In general those who habitually sleep longer have shorter *reaction times and higher body temperatures by day. Infants sleep a lot, but the sleep of ageing people becomes more and more broken with the years. A person sleeps less if he gets thin and sleeps longer if he gets fat.

There are two kinds of sleep that in man alternate with each other about every 100 minutes. Orthodox sleep (non-rapid eye movement, or NREM sleep) occupies 80 per cent of the night, and paradoxical sleep (rapid eye movement, or REM sleep) about 20 per cent. The amount of paradoxical sleep is greater in the new-born, but in adults is proportional to body weight, and among mental defectives to *intelligence. It is diminished by *anxiety and by many drugs.

Neither of the two kinds of sleep should be thought of as deeper than the other: they are different. Mental life continues in both, but whereas awakenings from orthodox sleep and questions about preceding mental life, generally lead to reports of 'thinking', awakenings from paradoxical sleep are generally followed by detailed descriptions of '*dreaming'. However, the recall of dreams is much diminished if as little as five minutes of orthodox sleep intervenes prior to awakening. In paradoxical sleep most body muscles are profoundly relaxed and many reflexes are lost, the blood flows faster through the brain than during wakeful rest, and in men the penis is erect.

Talking may also occur in both kinds of sleep, and reports made after prompt awakenings show concordance between the words and what was being thought or dreamt about. Sleep-walking (see SOMNAMBULISM) and 'night terrors' arise from orthodox sleep early in the night, as do most episodes of bed-wetting. The shriekings of a night terror often occur with sleep-walking, and liability to them runs in families. They are never remembered in the morning.

Indeed, memory of the events of sleep is always very poor. 'Sleep learning' by means of a tape-recorder playing lessons all night is ineffective: although what has been heard while still awake may be remembered, nothing of what was played during sleep will be recalled; to remember we must have paid *attention, and in sleep we do not pay attention. Even so, sleep is important for memory. If a list of nonsense words is learned, and memory of them is tested eight hours or twenty-four hours later, more of the list will be remembered after twenty-four hours, given an intervening period of sleep, than after eight hours without sleep. It seems that memory-traces are strengthened during sleep, maybe especially by paradoxical sleep; and since they presumably depend upon the durable molecules of brain protein, this can be understood.

Protein synthesis is favoured by sleep and so sleep enhances growth and restoration. Tissues such as the skin are restored by growth of new cells, and this growth proceeds faster during sleep. Throughout the body's tissues there are protein molecules being broken down and being synthesized all the time. There is a twenty-four-hour variation in the rate of synthesis, the rate being fastest during the period of rest and sleep. In the cerebral cortex, and the retina, protein synthesis is faster during sleep, and in the anterior pituitary there are more cell divisions. The fact that the balance shifts away from degradation towards greater net protein synthesis is a consequence of a lower rate of cellular work during sleep.

In higher animals there are hormones that reinforce the more fundamental effect of the lower rate of cellular work. In man, growth hormone is specifically released by orthodox sleep with the largest continuous slow electrical brain rhythms ('slow-wave sleep': see ELECTROENCEPHALO-GRAPHY). Growth hormone promotes protein synthesis. On the other hand, adrenaline and corticosteroids are hormones which are plentiful during wakefulness and which increase protein breakdown. In the blood during sleep, these latter hormones are diminished, and that means that the growth hormone is even more effective. Slow-wave sleep is not merely the time of growth-hormone release, it is the time when responsiveness to

meaningful sounds or to an itchy skin is minimal, when the body's oxygen consumption is lowest, and cellular work is lowest, and therefore slow-wave sleep is 'worth more' than lighter (more responsive) stages of orthodox sleep. If there is a greater need for restoration, as after sleep-deprivation, or after an athlete has trained hard, then the next night there is a higher proportion of slow-wave sleep and extra growth hormone.

Sleep-deprivation causes sleepiness. It is difficult to keep awake anyone who has been deprived of sleep for 60 hours. Such a person has frequent 'microsleeps' and recurrently fails to notice things he ought to notice, being unable to sustain a high level of attention. Sometimes visual *illusions or *hallucinations are experienced or the individual becomes *paranoid. After about 240 hours there are signs of adaptation to a more uniform but inert and dulled state.

People who complain of lack of sleep (insomnia) actually sleep more than they suppose. Indeed, the most distinguishing feature of their sleep is the degree to which it exceeds their own estimates—but we cannot yet measure its relative restorative value. Complaints are commonest among women, among those of nervous temperament, and among older folk; and it is they who account for most of the sleeping pills consumed. Although most sleeping pills today belong to the benzodiazepine class and are safe and effective, prolonged use leads to dependence, and attempts to stop them are accompanied by heightened anxiety, nightmares, and poor sleep for a week or two. Regular physical exercise; a good-quality, firm mattress; a warm but ventilated room; a malted milk drink, and sexual satisfaction at bedtime—all these promote good sleep; but they will not cure everyone's complaints. It has to be accepted that broken sleep is as normal a part of growing older as are grey hairs or wrinkles, though insomnia of sudden onset can be the result of mental depression, an illness amenable to treatment.

Finally, let it be emphasized that sleep is not a slothful habit. Its study as a necessity encompasses the whole functioning of the body and, with the study of dreams, some of the mind's most intriguing qualities. I. O.

Adam, K. and Oswald, I. (1983). Protein synthesis, bodily renewal and the sleep-wake cycle. *Clinical Science*, **65**, 561–7.

Kety, S. S., Evarts, E. V., and Williams, H. L. (eds.) (1967). *Sleep and Altered States of Consciousness*. Baltimore.

Luce, G. G. and Segal, J. (1970). *Insomnia*. London.

Oram, J. and Barnes, C. D. (eds.) (1980). *Physiology in Sleep*. New York.

Oswald, I. (1980). *Sleep*. Harmondsworth.

**SLEEP-WALKING.** See SOMNAMBULISM.

**SMELL.** Although all living things, both plant and animal, respond selectively to at least some of the chemicals in their environments, what we ordinarily mean by smell is more limited than this.

There are really two ways of deciding whether or not we are dealing with smelling rather than some other chemical sense. In the vertebrates—fishes, amphibians, reptiles, or mammal—we define smell as involving the stimulation of the first cranial nerve, the olfactory nerve. In the invertebrates, however, we refer to smell when the stimulating substance is airborne. Thus, for example, a moth finds his mate by means of smell. This inclusion of the invertebrates is important because much of the best controlled (and economically important) study has been and is being done on insects. In man, of course, both these qualifications apply and we speak of smell as involving the first cranial nerve and as having airborne molecules as its stimuli.

In man and other mammals the receptors for smell lie in the mucous membrane at the top or back of the air passages in the nose. These sensitive cells are in a constant state of decline and replacement. They are equipped with hair-like projections, the cilia, which protrude into the mucus and are the probable sites of odorant–receptor interaction. In man, the region of each nostril that they occupy is about the area of a postage-stamp—small compared with, say, that in the dog. The cells send their axons directly into the olfactory bulb, which is also relatively small. (Smell is unique among the senses in not having connections through the thalamus to the 'new cortex' or neocortex that has developed in relation to the other sense departments. In fact, the older portion of the forebrain of mammals is called the 'rhinencephalon', or 'smell brain', because of this.) There are many fewer transmission cells in the bulb than there are receptors, and this fact, in addition to the preservation of spatial distribution from receptor surface to bulb, is thought to be important in the perception of odour quality. The system is sensitive and compares well, even in man, with most laboratory methods of analysis: for example, one form of musk can be detected by a 'normal' person at a dilution of less than one ten-millionth of a milligram per litre of air.

Attempts to understand the manner in which odorous molecules affect the receptor cells have led to considerable theorizing without conspicuous success. The problem to be solved is similar to that for any of the senses: how a stimulating agent so alters a cell as to set in play the series of events that result in one or more nerve impulses being transmitted to the central nervous system. In man it is obvious that the molecules either make their way through the mucus and affect the receptor directly in some way, or act at a distance. Both means have been proposed. In explanation of action at a distance, it has been suggested that the characteristic infra-red absorption spectrum of a molecule leads it to absorb radiation from certain of the matching receptors. Unfortunately, this is thermodynamically impossible. Other absorption theories, such as the Raman spectrum and ultraviolet, seem aimed more at classifying the molecules than at implying action at a distance.

Theories supposing action directly on the receptor are better supported by modern research. Many have been developed with pharmacological or immunological models in mind. The current conception of the receptor cell membrane as a lipid (fatty) double layer in which protein molecules are embedded in mosaic fashion is compatible both with the suggestion that the molecules actually dissolve in (or 'puncture') the lipid, rather like the anaesthetic action of ether, and with the notion that adsorption takes place on the proteins. Evidence of molecules that differ only in being 'right-' or 'left-handed' implies that the proteins are involved, and the theory provides a simple basis for understanding the selectivity of different cells. Precisely what energy transfer is involved is uncertain, but with modern membrane research methodology, including the use of radioactive tracers, resolution of this problem should be forthcoming.

The pervasive role of smell in everyday life is often overlooked. Many unpleasant smells, such as of garbage and offal in the city of not so long ago, have been got rid of. Highly sophisticated methods of washing, filtering, and incinerating odorous discharges have been developed, and there is a host of personal deodorants and air 'purifiers'. On the other side of the coin, the flavours of foods are pretty largely determined by odour—a fact recognized by the international flavour industry. Closely related is perfumery, with its long history.

In the fashions that have surrounded perfumery, sexual attractiveness may be involved. Certainly in many species, particularly the insects, naturally secreted odours, pheromones, play a sexual role. In mammals, pheromones also play an important role in the establishment of territories: the 'marking' activities of dogs are well known, and in other species special glands—for example, the cheek glands of the rabbit—produce marking chemicals. In the mouse the sexual and marking functions come together—the female will ovulate after smelling a male, and will, if pregnant, abort upon smelling a strange male. While some Primates—the baboon, for instance—seem to have female pheromones secreted during receptivity, it is not presently clear what role, if any, such secretions might play in man.

One function of smelling is well known: the detection of leaking gas. To non-odorous gases, a warning agent such as ethyl mercaptan is added. In mines, the ventilating system is used to carry the warning. An apparent over-representation of older people among the victims of a gas leakage in London led to useful research on the effect of age on sensitivity to smell. (See AGEING: SENSORY AND PERCEPTUAL CHANGES.)

For smell, unlike colour, there is no satisfactory classification scheme. One difficulty is the absence of truly abstract terms such as red or blue; rather, the terms refer to objects (for example, lavender or fruity) or condition (burnt or rotten). Possibly no simple scheme will be found, for the basic scale along which we place odours is from pleasant to unpleasant—a scale that may reflect the approach–avoidance nature of behaviour in evolutionary history. It may be the only way for the organism to classify odours.

Three other topics need mention. First, there are considerable differences between the smell sensitivity of individual persons. Some even, because of disease or trauma, cannot smell anything at all—they are anosmic—while others lack sensitivity for specific odours—they are partially anosmic. Second, adaptation (that is, temporary loss of sensitivity with exposure) proceeds fairly rapidly for smells. This is largely a matter of reduced transmission in the brain, rather than fatigue of the receptors. It makes some jobs tolerable; but sensitivity to warning agents is reduced. Finally, it may be that sensitivity declines with age. If this is in fact so, and it is not certain, then among the important consequences would be diminished stimulation from flavours (see TASTE). Possibly some of the nutritional problems of ageing are ascribable to declining sensitivity.                                   F. N. J.

Amerine, M. A., Pangborn, R. M., and Roessler, E. B. (1965). *Principles of Sensory Evaluation of Food*. New York.

Engen, T. (1982). *The Perception of Odors*. New York.

Proceedings of the Eighth International Symposium on Olfaction and Taste, Melbourne, Victoria (Australia), 23–26 August, 1983 (1984). *Chemical Senses*, **8**, no. 3. Oxford.

**SOCIAL PSYCHOLOGY** studies how individuals relate to the societies they live in, particularly in so far as those relations are mediated by face-to-face interaction. Children first learn languages, moralities and positions in class structures, not by encountering abstract entities labelled 'institutions' or 'social structures' but primarily through everyday intercourse with others. When, as adults, we are in contact with economic, legal or religious institutions, the contacts in practice are usually with employees or agents of the institutions.

Social psychology should continually be interrelating three levels of analysis: the individual, the interpersonal, and the social structural (which should be taken to include economic and political structures). According to this view, it is something of an interstitial science: it aims to link the study of the individual by general psychology and the biological sciences to that of society by sociology and the other social sciences, and it is thus a very challenging and potentially pivotal social science. Its practitioners, however, have not always fully recognized either the challenge or the potential. To understand why not, a little history is necessary.

The historian of social psychology (e.g. Allport, 1985) can manage without difficulty to appropriate as progenitors of social psychology most of the major thinkers of Western civilization from Plato and Aristotle onwards. But the term 'social psychology' did not appear, as the title of a book for instance, until 1908, when it was used twice, by

W. *McDougall, a British psychologist, and by E. A. Ross, an American sociologist. Even so, the immediate origins of what has come to be social psychology are apparent for about half a century before then. Many of the originators were European. Le Bon, Tarde, and Durkheim in France; Simmel, *Weber, and *Wundt in Germany; *Freud in Austria, and *Darwin, *Spencer, and McDougall in Britain can all be seen, in part at any rate, as contributors to the emerging discipline. Had their contributions prevailed, then social psychology would have emerged as a biologically based—or at least 'instinct'-based—theoretically oriented endeavour. But they did not. Whether because a psychologically inclined social analysis was more congenial to the pervasive individualism of American social and political life, or because it proved easier for social psychology to become institutionalized in newer American than in ancient European universities, the subject established itself more readily in the United States, where it rapidly adopted the environmentalism of American sociology and the empiricism of American psychology. The main sociological influences were those of the Chicago school of symbolic interactionism, derived in turn from American pragmatic philosophy. G. H. Mead's (1934) analysis of the social construction of an individual's sense of self must be given pride of place, but other contributors within that tradition have included C. H. Cooley, W. I. Thomas, and, more recently, E. Goffman. American psychologists who exerted influence on the beginnings of social psychology included J. M. Baldwin, G. S. *Hall, and W. *James, but it has been less the ideas of particular psychologists and much more the practices of psychology in general that have proved most influential. A very early—perhaps the first—line of sustained empirical enquiry started from a study by N. Triplett in 1898. In order to examine the impact of the presence of others on the efficiency of individual performance, he had children wind in string on fishing reels on their own and competitively in pairs. From this study there developed a tradition of research on the consequences of the presence of others which today is still actively pursued as 'social facilitation'. This tradition has asked apparently limited questions and has been content with small-scale theories; its questions appear to be readily answerable and lend themselves to experimental studies in laboratories; it takes universality for granted and hence need only study undergraduates in Ann Arbor. Each of these can be regarded as a legacy from American psychology, and the general approach has been and is typical of most social psychology in North America. The approach reached its zenith with the self-conscious creation in the 1960s of a movement towards 'experimental social psychology', whereby prestigious work would be virtually confined to elegant experiments conducted in sophisticated laboratories and interpreted in terms of carefully formulated mini-theories; this latter-day methodological purification would demonstrate that social psychology could be (almost) as rigorous as the asocial parts of experimental psychology.

A decade of such endeavours was enough to provoke numerous criticisms. Two complementary critiques merit mention, those of method and scope. Micro-sociologists in America, as well as R. Harré in Britain, questioned the appropriateness of laboratory experiments for studying human social experience, because of their artificiality and the mechanistic views of man which, it was claimed, they imply. The main criticisms from resurgent social psychology in Europe, as voiced by S. Moscovici, H. Tajfel and others, were directed at the narrowness of American experimental social psychology: it studied individuals and sometimes inter-individual influences, but had ceased to be social; society must be brought back into social psychology. Despite some soul-searching, mainly about the ethics of experiments, the critiques had a limited impact in the United States. 'Experimental social psychology' was up-dated, thinly disguised and renamed 'cognitive social psychology'; the detailed psychological examination of individual attributions and judgements contrasted with the poverty of social analysis, and technical rigour was far more obvious than social relevance. If for no other reasons than numbers and resources, this narrow view of social psychology became the dominant one, but it has had to compete with a broader, if more diffuse perspective, derived in part from social psychology in Europe, in part from sociology and other social sciences. This broad view, which has been able to incorporate much of the narrower one, has organized the substance of social psychology around three interlocking sets of issues, each set demanding all three levels of analysis but highlighting one or other of them.

First, there is the social nature of the individual. How has biological inheritance been acted upon so that, within about twenty years, the microscopic egg has become an effective, fully functioning member of society, and over a life span the individual personality or self, while maintaining coherence and continuity, has also adapted to changing situations and roles? In part the self emerges through interaction with others. Parents imputing intentions to the infant help purposiveness and intentionality to develop in the child; and the ever-increasing expectations of the child encourage more and more complex, intelligent actions to appear. But the self is, in a sense, a product of social structure as well as of face-to-face interaction. In large part one's personal self is made up of one's views of the salient social categories to which one belongs. As a result, the study of differences and supposed differences between the sexes, classes, ethnic groups and the like is intrinsic to a properly social conceptualization of the individual.

The second substantive focus is social interaction. Here the social psychologist studies the acquisition and use of language and the non-linguistic communication systems not just as an achievement or skill of an individual but as the means whereby dyads and groups can succeed, or fail, in creating an intersubjectivity, or temporarily shared world which makes possible the transmission of information, the exchange of feelings, and the creation and fulfilment of common tasks. And once some understanding of the details of interaction has been achieved, the details themselves can be used to illuminate the operation of larger-scale social processes. Who is addressed as 'Sir' and who as 'Bill' can quickly tell us much about the operation of status and power within a community; the willingness, or reluctance, of a speaker of one language, or dialect, to switch to another for the benefit of a stranger can be very informative about the relations between communities. In addition to the details and dynamics of interaction, social psychologists increasingly study the sustained interactions that are interpersonal relationships, their initiation and development through dating, mating and marriage, their maintenance over time, and their dissolution or collapse through, for example, bereavement or divorce.

The third focus consists of representations of the social world. How do we view and think about the social world around us, and what effects do these 'pictures in our heads' have on our actions? Some representations concern individuals and interpersonal processes. Currently a major concern of American social psychology is the attributions to, or inferences about, others that we make—especially whether and how we decide if someone's behaviour is intentional or not. Many complex representations, on the other hand, concern larger-scale social phenomena: ethnic groups, work, unemployment and the unemployed, to mention only a few. Particular representations held by specific individuals may of course be in large part idiosyncratic, but the representations that merit systematic study will usually be those that are socially shared. Whether idiosyncratic or widespread, representations have traditionally been studied in social psychology via the concept of 'attitude'. For the study of shared representations, European social psychologists have recently shown interest in the French conception of 'social representation' (Moscovici and Farr, 1983), and even the notion of 'ideology' which hitherto they had largely eschewed (Billig, 1976).

The broader, largely European, view of social psychology underlay the definition with which we started, and it is with that view that the best hopes of realizing the potential of the discipline appear to lie.                                                    c. f.

Allport, G. W. (1968). The historical background of modern social psychology. In Lindzey, G. and Aronson, E. (eds.), *The Handbook of Social Psychology*, 2nd edn. Reading, Massachusetts.

Billig, M. (1976). *Social Psychology and Intergroup Relations*. London.

Brown, R. (1986). *Social Psychology: The Second Edition*. New York.

Deaux, K. and Wrightman, L. S. (1984). *Social Psychology in the 80s*, 4th edn. Monterey, California.

Lindzey, G. and Aronson, E. (eds.) (1985). *The Handbook of Social Psychology*, 3rd edn. New York.

Mead, G. H. (1934). *Mind, Self and Society*. Chicago.

Moscovici, S. and Farr, R. (eds.) (1983). *Social Representations*. Cambridge.

Tajfel, H. (ed.) (1983). *The Social Dimension: European developments in social psychology*. Cambridge.

Tajfel, H. and Fraser, C. (eds.) (1978). *Introducing Social Psychology*. Harmondsworth.

## SOCIOBIOLOGY. See ETHOLOGY.

## SOCIOPATHIC PERSONALITY. See PSYCHO-PATHIC PERSONALITY.

**SOCRATES** (469–399 BC). The son of Sophroniscus, a sculptor, and Phaenarete, a midwife, Socrates distinguished himself for bravery in three campaigns at Potidaea, Amphipolis, and Delium. He wrote no books, though the Delphic oracle declared in his own time that he was the wisest man in the world. Physically, he was, as he himself admitted, ugly, with a snub nose. The shrewish temper of his wife Xanthippe is now legend and was probably fact.

Socrates is immortalized in many of *Plato's dialogues, including the *Apology*, which gives his defence when he was charged in 399 BC with corrupting the young, as 'an evil doer and a curious person, searching into things under the earth and above the heaven; and making the worse appear the better cause, and teaching all this to others'. He was condemned to death, by a majority of six in a jury of perhaps 500. His friends planned his escape; but he refused to break the law, and in their company he drank hemlock and, still talking philosophy, died. His last days are most poignantly described in Plato's *Phaedo*.

Socrates is celebrated both for his personal qualities of courage and for maintaining the highest moral standards while yet being susceptible at least to wine and no doubt to the other traditional temptations. He was no recluse, or monastic; but lived to the full the life of a man. Philosophically, he represented, at the highest, values of questioning and discussion without bigotry or preformed conclusions, thus exposing feeble arguments and prejudice.

Guthrie, W. K. C. (1971). *Socrates*. Cambridge.

**SOMATOTOPICAL.** A term referring to brain-maps or representations of the body surface, especially by signals from the skin receptors indicating touch. The somatotopic maps in the brains of vertebrates, including humans, are upside down—so that the feet are represented at the top and the head at the bottom of the map, which can be explored with micro-electrode recording from the exposed brain surface. This curious arrangement is probably due to the need for rich relations between visual and touch mapping in the brain. As the retinal image is upside down (and laterally reversed) due to the optics of the eye, the touch maps are similarly inverted to simplify and shorten cross-sensory neural connections.

See also LOCALIZATION OF FUNCTION AND CORTICAL MAPS.

**SOMATOTYPE.** See BODY BUILD AND PERSONALITY.

**SOMNAMBULISM.** A sleeper may engage in a variety of more or less coherent activities. He may talk, for instance, or move purposefully, or get up and walk. He then appears dazed, preoccupied, and unresponsive to much that goes on round him. He tends to avoid obstacles, but may incur danger because he is clumsy and unreliable. He may return to bed on his own. After waking he has no memory of the incident. A child may walk half-asleep to the lavatory and return to bed, but usually somnambulism is less purposeful. Sometimes, but not typically, a sleep-walker appears to be acting out, like Lady Macbeth, fragmentary and irrational dream experiences.

Somnambulism is not uncommon among children. It may be repeated several times over a short period and then not occur again. It is said to run in families. It tends to occur early in the night, during 'orthodox' sleep, when large, slow waves are to be seen on the *electroencephalogram. *Dreaming, on the other hand, occurs typically during 'rapid eye movement' (REM) sleep. Somnambulism is distinct from the night terrors shown by children. When it is associated with persistent and severe disturbance of behaviour, as in the case of Lady Macbeth, it may be regarded as a manifestation of the 'twilight state' which occurs in some forms of mental illness.

Although it is very unusual for a sleep-walker to harm anyone else, there are cases on record where it has been claimed that acts of homicide have taken place during an episode of sleep-walking. In some of these the accused person had been drinking before falling asleep, only to wake later to find that he had killed his bed-mate. It is difficult to believe that sleep-walking in an undrugged state could possibly persist throughout a violent struggle such as would occur if the victim of a homicidal assault made every effort to resist. Furthermore, because sleep-walking takes place during orthodox sleep, and not during dreaming REM sleep, the sleep-walker who acts violently would be unlikely to be acting out a dream in which he might believe that he is defending himself against attack. None the less, pleas of somnambulism have been accepted as defences against charges of murder both in Great Britain and in the USA.   D. R. D.

Oswald, I. *Sleep* (1980). Harmondsworth.

**SOUL, BRAIN SCIENCE AND THE.** Mechanistic brain science proceeds on the working assumption that every bodily event has a physical cause in the prior state of the central nervous system. Traditional moral and religious thought, on the other hand, has always presupposed that some at least of our behaviour is determined by our thinking and deciding. This apparent conflict has given rise to suggestions that unless some parts of our nervous system are found to be open to non-physical influences, brain science will effectively debunk all talk of man as a spiritual being, and oblige us to accept a purely materialistic view of our nature. Many people seem to expect a battle to be fought between religion and the neurosciences like that waged by some theologians in the nineteenth century against evolutionary biology.

How justified is this impression? It is true that the seventeenth-century French philosopher–mathematician René *Descartes held that the mind or soul would be powerless to influence bodily action unless some part of the brain could act as a transmitter–receiver for its controlling signals. He considered that the pineal gland, in the middle of the head, was ideally suited to the purpose. 'In man', he says,

the brain is also acted on by the soul which has some power to change cerebral impressions just as those impressions in their turn have the power to arouse thoughts which do not depend on the will. . . . Only [figures of excitation] traced in spirits on the surface of [the pineal] gland, where the seat of imagination and common sense [the coming together of the senses] is . . . should be taken to be . . . the forms or images that the rational soul will consider directly when, being united to this machine, it will imagine or will sense any object.

In recent years the neurophysiologist Sir John Eccles and the philosopher Sir Karl Popper have advanced theories of the 'interaction' of mind and brain, which, though they differ in important respects from that of Descartes, agree with him that the brain must be open to non-physical influences if mental activity is to be effective.

At first sight this might indeed seem obvious common sense; but a simple counter-example throws some doubt on the logic of the argument. We are nowadays accustomed to the idea that a computer can be set up to solve a mathematical equation. The mathematician means by this that the behaviour of the computer is *determined* by the equation he wants to solve; were it not so, it would be of no interest to him. On the other hand, if we were to ask a computer engineer to explain what is happening in the computer, he could easily demonstrate that every physical event in it was fully *determined* (same word) by the laws of physics as applied to the physical components. Any appearance of conflict here would be quite illusory. There is no need for a computer to be 'open to non-physical influences' in order that its behaviour may be determined by a (non-physical) equation *as well as* by the laws of physics. The two 'claims to determination' here are not mutually exclusive; rather they are *complementary*.

The analogy is of course a limited one. We (unlike our computing machines) are conscious

agents. The data of our conscious experience have first priority among the facts about our world, since it is only through our conscious experience that we learn about anything else. Our consciousness is thus not a matter of convention (like the mathematical significance of the computer's activity) but a matter of fact which we would be lying to deny. Nevertheless the logical point still holds. If we think of our mental activity as embodied in our brain activity, in the sense in which the solving of an equation can be embodied in the workings of a computer, then there is a clear parallel sense in which our behaviour can be determined by that mental activity, regardless of the extent to which our brain activity is determined by physical laws. The two explanations, in mental and in physical terms, are not rivals but complementary.

Note that we are here thinking of mental activity as *embodied in* brain activity rather than *identical with* brain activity. The latter is a notion favoured by what is called 'materialist monism', at the opposite extreme from the 'interactionism' of Eccles and Popper. This would simply identify 'mind' and 'brain', and would go so far as to attribute 'thinking' and other mental activities to the matter of which the brain is composed. The objection to this extreme view can be understood by once again considering the example of a computer. It is true that the solving of an equation is not a separate series of events, running in parallel with the physical happenings in the machine. It is rather the mathematical significance of one and the same series of events, whose physical aspect is well explained by the engineer. On the other hand it would be nonsensical on these grounds to identify equations with computers as physical objects, or to attribute mathematical properties (such as 'convergence' or 'being quadratic') to the physical matter in which the equation is embodied.

By the same token, even if we regard our thinking and deciding as a 'mental' or 'inner' aspect of one and the same (mysterious) activity that the neuroscientist can study from the outside as brain activity, this gives no rational grounds for taking the material aspect as more 'real' than the mental, still less for identifying the two and speaking of thinking and deciding as attributes of matter. This would be a confusion of categories belonging to different logical levels, for which nothing in brain science offers any justification.

It might appear that thinking of our conscious experience as 'embodied' in our brains would still be incompatible with the Christian concept of 'life after death'. What we have seen in the case of the computer, however, shows that there need be no conflict. The physical destruction of a computer is certainly the end of *that particular embodiment* of the equation it was solving. But it leaves entirely open the possibility that the same equation could be re-embodied, perhaps in a quite different medium, if the mathematician so desires. By the same logic, mechanistic brain science would seem to raise equally little objection to the hope of eternal life expressed in biblical Christian doctrine, with its characteristic emphasis on the 'resurrection' (not to be confused with resuscitation) of the body. The destruction of our present embodiment sets no logical barrier to *our* being re-embodied, perhaps in a quite different medium, if our Creator so wishes.

See also THEOLOGY AND MIND–BRAIN IDENTITY.

D. M. M.

Popper, K. R. and Eccles, J. C. (1977). *The Self and Its Brain*. London.
MacKay, D. M. (1979). *Human Science and Human Dignity*. London.

**SPACE PSYCHOLOGY.** The early astronauts were required to be very experienced test pilots, very healthy and resistant to stress, and morally fit to represent the nation. In 1958 the records of 500 qualified men were reviewed, and seven were eventually selected to fly in the Mercury programme, after much psychological and medical screening. Some of the early tests—such as keeping the feet in iced water for seven minutes—now seem bizarre. The validity of the early psychological screening is not known, since the 'failures' were not allowed to fly. Orbiting in a capsule sent up by a rocket was thought by some to be rather degrading in comparison with piloting an aircraft. Monkeys had been sent up first, so why send a human? It was soon evident that humans had a vital role in space: they could make observations, report back, make decisions, avert disasters, conduct experiments, and make repairs. And on the ground they were national heroes.

Many more candidates were trained for the Gemini, Apollo, and Skylab programmes. The emphasis shifted towards academic qualifications, and scientist-astronauts were accepted in addition to pilot astronauts. The advent of the space shuttle in the 1980s made space flight almost routine, and civilians were now allowed to fly as passengers with relatively little training. Indeed, instead of going to war, the Soviets and Americans now vied with each other to offer rides in space to political allies and 'minority' groups—rather as Solomon bearing gifts to the Queen of Sheba. The official route into space for a Western bloc civilian has been as a payload specialist (PS), his or her job being to look after some specialist aspect of the mission, such as a scientific or industrial experiment. The PS normally trains for one mission only, and should not expect to become a career astronaut. Much of this training is carried out in the laboratory of the payload developer, and relatively little time is spent learning how to operate the shuttle orbiter systems. PS applicants have had to go through the screening procedures of their own countries and those of NASA (the National Aeronautics and Space Administration) or ESA (the European Space Agency), a small number then being selected to train for a particular mission. Final selection has usually depended partly on performance in training, and partly on political and other considerations.

The number of scientific experiments conducted in space has increased enormously, as many as 70 being carried on Spacelab 1 in 1983. Civilian scientists have a correspondingly greater role in controlling space experiments. They, too, must expect to spend some time training to play their part in the complexities of a scientific mission. They must participate in 'timeline' simulations, and learn how to use the communication systems. Only then can they make full use of the space crew.

**The mission.** Many of the difficulties of living in space occur in other confined environments. These include isolation from the normal world and limited communication with it; problems of living in a small space; lack of privacy; social interactions within a small group; artificial day–night cycles and shift of circadian rhythms (see BIOLOGICAL CLOCKS); anxieties about the life-support system and a safe return to the normal world; tiredness due to long work schedules; delays in completing assigned tasks and coping with apparatus failures; and boredom on long missions. All of these difficulties are shared by deep-sea *divers operating from submersible chambers.

The unique aspect of space travel is weightlessness. An orbiting spacecraft is in a state of free fall, because the earth's gravitational acceleration is exactly balanced by the radial acceleration produced by the curved flight path of the spacecraft. The resulting microgravity (near zero gravity) causes various physiological changes, such as a shift of body fluids to the head, loss of calcium in the bones, muscular atrophy, and changes in blood composition. One of the most distressing effects is that of space motion sickness, which has affected roughly half of all space travellers during their first two to four days in space. This was not a problem on early NASA missions, but the incidence appears to have increased. One reason for the increase is that crew members move around more in larger spacecraft. The other reason is increasing detail in reporting symptoms: for example, a crew member of Spacelab 1 gave magnitude estimates of his feelings of discomfort during the first fourteen hours in orbit (Fig. 1).

Space motion sickness—like other forms of motion sickness—is probably due to sensory conflict. The normal correspondence between visual, vestibular, and tactile stimulation breaks down, and the traveller may feel disoriented and nauseated until his brain learns to reintegrate the sensory information. It is perhaps remarkable that this learning can occur within two or three days. There is, as yet, little evidence for a relationship between susceptibility to motion sickness on the ground and in space. This may be because astronauts usually avoid subjecting themselves to provocative movements in space, and may not fully report their symptoms. Alternatively, it may be because the nature of the sensory conflict is slightly

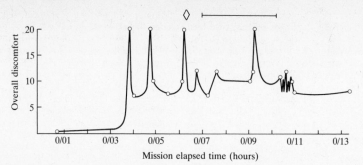

**Fig. 1.** Magnitude estimate of discomfort for one subject during the first fourteen hours in orbit. A score of 20 indicates vomiting. Curves between data points were interpolated by the subject. Diamond represents medication (scopolamine and Dexedrine), followed by horizontal bar representing period of maximal effectiveness.

different in space. Passengers on earth are passively subjected to unusual changes in acceleration, whereas space travellers move in an environment that effectively lacks the force of gravity.

The vestibular system consists of the semicircular canals (whose sense organs respond mainly to rotary acceleration) and the otolithic organs (which respond mainly to linear acceleration and gravity). Head movements on earth produce a familiar combination of signals from the canals and otoliths. Under weightless conditions the canals operate normally, but the otoliths do not. They can no longer indicate head orientation with respect to gravity, but only linear acceleration fore–aft or left–right or up–down. The space traveller must therefore learn to reinterpret otolithic information. Pitch and roll head movements seem to be particularly provocative, as are ambiguous visual stimuli such as seeing another crew member 'upside-down' or being inverted oneself in relation to the spacecraft. Unlike the terrestrial traveller, the astronaut can remove himself from provocative stimulation: he can wedge himself into a corner, close his eyes and keep his head still. Drugs that protect against terrestrial motion sickness also reduce the symptoms of space motion sickness, though they may produce unwanted side-effects such as drowsiness or dry throat.

Current experiments centre on the way in which humans adapt to altered gravitational cues. It seems that, early in a mission, they rely more heavily on visual cues to determine bodily orientation and the direction of gaze. Reflex eye movements of vestibular origin may be reduced, as may vestibulo-spinal reflexes. Humans learn how to move themselves around in space, using the hands and arms rather than the legs. They learn new patterns of hand–eye co-ordination: ballistic movements must be reprogrammed so as not to over-reach in the absence of gravity. They must adapt to their own loss of arm weight, and learn to judge the mass of objects through inertial cues rather than weight. This appears to be difficult to do, since objects continue to feel light, and mass-discrimination remains poor, even after several days in space.

Astronauts report good visual acuity for details seen on earth, and current research shows no consistent changes in near vision or the visual contrast sensitivity function.

**The return to earth.** The returning astronaut is rather like a swimmer staggering ashore after a long swim. He feels heavy and clumsy. In addition, his vestibular co-ordination is disturbed, and he may see the world swing round in an unusual manner when he moves his head. 'I felt like my gyros were caged,' explained one astronaut. These effects can cause difficulties for pilots who want to fly the shuttle back to earth manually. It takes a surprisingly long time for complete readaptation to the earth's gravity. For example, after the ten-day mission of Spacelab 1 some crew members were still showing some types of after-effect a week later. There are a lot of individual differences in this, and it is not clear whether prolonged after-effects are correlated with slow or rapid adaptation in space.

Some after-effects may be due to the continued reinterpretation of otolith signals as linear accelerations rather than as head tilt, which results in postural instability with the eyes closed, and an increased reliance on visual orientation cues. There may also be some changes in sensitivity to linear acceleration in different body axes. Other effects may be due to changes in proprioceptive and tactile sensations, such as feelings of heaviness, under-reaching for objects, reduction of weight discrimination (Fig. 2), and reduction in awareness of limb position.

Readaptation to gravity is not the astronauts' only problem. They may be short of sleep, or be required to shift their circadian rhythm to local time. They may face several long days of medical, physiological and psychological tests, debriefing sessions and press publicity. They must then face the reality of readjustment to normal life, and of difficult career decisions. The life of the astronaut is not quite as rosy as it is sometimes pictured.

**The future.** The Challenger disaster in January 1986 has reduced the West's enthusiasm for

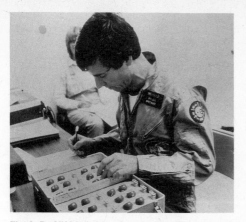

**Fig. 2.** Dr Ulf Merbold, a European payload specialist, tests himself on return from the Spacelab 1 mission, and shows impaired weight discrimination.

manned spaceflight, and has emphasized the advisability of launching satellites by remote control. Nevertheless, NASA's shuttle programme is likely to continue, but at a slower rate. Man's usefulness in space has been amply demonstrated, and NASA and ESA are planning to build a manned orbiting space station by the year 2000. The crews will probably include more scientists and technicians, and will stay in space for weeks or months at a time. Research on the psychology of man in space is likely to move away from the causes of motion sickness (which ceases to be a problem after about four days) to the longer-term effects of living in space and returning to earth. Simultaneously, research will go on into the automation of astronauts' tasks, and efforts will be made to replace men with robots or teleoperators. This is unlikely to be practicable for many tasks, and we can expect to keep the 'man-in-the-loop' for the foreseeable future.                                          H. E. R.

Benson, A. J. (1982). The vestibular sensory system. In Barlow, H. B. and Mollon, J. D. (eds.), *The Senses.* Cambridge.

Johnston, R. S. and Dietlein, L. F. (eds.) (1977). *Biomedical Results from Skylab*. NASA SP-377, Washington DC.

Nicogossian, A. E. and Parker, J. F. (1982). *Space Physiology and Medicine*. NASA SP-447, Washington, DC.

Reason, J. (1974). *Man in Motion: the psychology of travel*. London.

Ridpath, I. (1983). *Life off Earth*. London.

Ross, H. E. (1974). *Behaviour and Perception in Strange Environments*. London.

Sharpe, M. R. (1969). *Living in Space: the astronaut and his environment*. London.

Various Papers by Young et al., Von Baumgarten et al., Reschke et al., Ross et al., Quadens and Green (1984). *Science*, **225**, (No. 4658), 205–22.

Wolfe, T. (1980). *The Right Stuff*. New York.

**SPATIAL CO-ORDINATION OF THE SENSES.** Almost everything that a human being does involves the *perception of the spatial locations of objects. The senses used in perceiving spatial locations are known as the spatial senses: they are vision, hearing, touch, and kinaesthesis. Kinaesthesis is the sense which enables us to appreciate the positions and movements of limbs, and depends on receptors in muscles, tendons, and joints, as well as on the sense of muscular effort involved in moving a limb or holding it in a given position. Movements of the head are detected by a set of specialized sense organs in the head, known as the vestibular sense organs.

The task of judging the spatial location of an object is complicated by the fact that sense organs are attached to mobile parts of the body. For instance, the receptive surface of the eye (the *retina) is attached to a mobile eyeball, which in turn is attached to a mobile head. If we wish to know the direction of a seen object with respect to the torso, the position of the eyes and of the head must be taken into account, along with information about the retinal position of the image of the object. This type of process is here referred to as sensory integration.

The position of an object is often detected by more than one sense organ at the same time. For instance, we may hold an object which we can also see and hear. Furthermore, we usually see with two eyes and hear with two ears. Spatial information must be co-ordinated between different sense organs, either two organs of the same type or belonging to different spatial senses. This is the process of intersensory co-ordination.

Finally, after we have located an object we may wish to reach for it. This requires that sensory spatial information be co-ordinated with the motor commands which control the movements of limbs. This is the process of *sensorimotor co-ordination*.

Performance of any spatial task has an accuracy and a precision. 'Accuracy' is the extent to which the mean of a set of judgements deviates from the true value. 'Precision' is the extent to which spatial judgements are scattered about their mean position. A darts player is highly accurate, if the throws are evenly distributed about the target, even though the player is very imprecise because the throws are widely scattered. Another player is very inaccurate if the throws are well to one side of the target, even though all the throws land on the same spot.

**Sensory integration.** As an example of sensory integration, consider the act of estimating the direction of a seen object with reference to the body. Such a task involves estimating where the object is with respect to the eyes, how the eyes are oriented in the head, and how the head is oriented on the body. The visual direction of an object with respect to an eye is indicated by the position of its image on the retina. However, this task is simplified by the fact that we normally direct our gaze towards an object of interest and bring its image on to the centre of the retina (the *fovea*).

Information about the direction of the eyes in

the head is provided by motor signals sent to the muscles that move the eyes, or hold them in a given position. An eye never has to move against a variable load, so that the muscular forces, and hence the motor signals, are always the same for a given position of an eye. There is no need for sense organs to indicate the position of the eyes; their position is always indicated by the sense of effort required to move them or hold them in position.

The direction of the head with respect to the body is indicated by sensory receptors in the muscles and joints of the neck; motor signals are unreliable indicators of head position because the effort required to hold the head in a given position on the body depends on the posture of the head with respect to gravity.

For the total task of judging the visual direction of an object, the information from these three components must be summed, or integrated. Since the eye and the head rotate about approximately the same vertical axis, one would expect the algebraic sum of the angular inaccuracies of the three components to equal the inaccuracy of the total task and the sum of the variabilities (precision) of the component tasks to equal the variability of the total task. This is why this case is referred to here as 'sensory integration'.

A similar state of affairs holds when we judge the direction of a hidden object which we touch with the finger. In this case information from the various joints of the arm is summed in estimating the direction of the object relative to the body. An extra factor is involved in this example because, in addition to summing information about the angular positions of the joints, it is also necessary to know the length of each segment of the limb.

Implicit knowledge about the spatial properties of our own body is known as the 'body schema'. This knowledge seems to be stored in the parietal lobes of the brain; damage to these areas results in anomalous experiences of the body (Critchley, 1969). A patient with parietal lobe damage may complain that one of his arms does not belong to him, even though he is able to move it and feel with it, or he may feel that his arm is distorted, or not attached to the body. The body schema for a limb changes as the body changes during growth and persists after the limb has been amputated and this creates the illusion that the limb is still present. An amputee will attempt to use his phantom limb when doing habitual things.

**Intersensory co-ordination.** In intersensory co-ordination an object is detected by at least two sense organs and the person is required to co-ordinate the spatial information derived from these different sources. Consider the act of picking up a small handbell, looking at it, and ringing it. The direction of the bell is sensed by the eyes, by the ears, and by the hand, and yet these separate impressions normally seem to originate from one and the same bell.

Interesting things happen when the spatial in-formation from the various sense organs is not in agreement, that is, when there is a sensory discordance. Such a situation may be induced arti-ficially in several ways. For instance, a person may view a ringing bell through prisms which displace the retinal image to one side. A ventriloquist pro-duces a sensory discordance by moving the lips of his dummy and keeping his own lips still. The same thing happens in the cinema, where the sound that seems to come from the actors actually originates from loudspeakers to one side of the screen. In other words, we misperceive the direction of a sound to make it conform to the direction of a visual object with which the sound is associated; an effect known as ventriloquism or visual dominance. C. V. Jackson (1953) did an experi-ment to determine how far a visual object has to be separated from an associated sound before the discordance becomes noticeable. Subjects reported that a hidden whistle appeared to origin-ate from a silent steaming kettle if the kettle and whistle were separated by less than 30°. A move-ment of an isolated sound source by this amount is easily detected.

An experiment by I. Rock and J. Victor (1964) provides a nice example of the dominance of vision over kinaesthesis. Subjects looked through a lens which caused a square object to appear rect-angular. They selected a matching object from among a set of objects they could feel but not see and from a set they could see but not feel. Most subjects selected an object which matched the shape as seen rather than the shape as felt, and few subjects were aware of any conflict.

The conflict between audition and touch-kinaes-thesis was studied by H. L. Pick, D. H. Warren, and J. C. Hay (1969). Blindfolded subjects pointed with one hand to the felt position of the other hand which touched a loudspeaker that was emit-ting clicks. At the same time, subjects wore a pseudophone which apparently displaced the clicks by 11° to one side. Subjects pointed to the true position of the other hand and ignored the dis-cordant auditory information.

Thus, in a conflict situation, when the person is convinced that the object detected by one sense organ is the same as that detected by another, vision dominates audition and kinaesthesis, and kinaesthesis dominates audition.

If one wishes to determine how precisely a per-son can bring stimuli detected by different sense organs into coincidence, one must use stimuli which do not evoke a dominance effect. In the procedure shown in Fig. 1 a light, a small loudspeaker, and a small tactile-kinaesthesis 'but-ton' are each mounted on a boom at arm's length. The subject is presented with pairs of stimuli in various positions and reports which member of each pair is to the left of the other. The subject also judges the position of each stimulus presented on its own. In an ideal system—one which makes best use of the available information—the variability of judgements about the relative positions of two

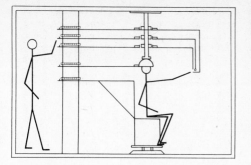

**Fig. 1.** Schematic representation of an apparatus used to measure the accuracy and precision of intersensory localization.

stimuli should equal the sum of variabilities of the judgements about the positions of each stimulus taken separately. C. Auerbach and P. Sperling (1974) showed that the performance of human subjects on an auditory-visual localization task, with an apparatus like that shown in Fig. 1, conformed closely to the ideal.

When we direct our gaze towards an object which is straight ahead, it is objectively to the right of the left eye and to the left of the right eye, and yet we experience one object straight ahead. This is because the part of ourselves which we use in making directional judgements is somewhere on a line passing through the bridge of the nose and the centre of the head. This point is known as the visual *egocentre*. Fig. 2 illustrates a simple procedure for demonstrating that lines which extend out from each eye are perceived to lie in a plane midway between the eyes, which is to say that they are referred to a common egocentre in the median plane of the head.

*Stereoscopic vision is a special case of intersensory co-ordination. In this case objects are seen by the two eyes, but in slightly different directions, because the two eyes are not in the same place. As long as the disparity in the relative positions of the two images is not too large, we experience only one object, but at the same time use the spatial disparity as a clue to the relative distances of objects.

Another interesting case of intersensory co-ordination is provided by the way we use information from the two ears to judge the direction of sound sources. This is a highly sophisticated mechanism which depends on the detection of relative intensities and times of arrival of sounds at the two ears (see BINAURAL HEARING).

**Sensorimotor co-ordination.** White, Castle, and Held (1964) described the normal development of visual motor co-ordination. During the first month the child is able to pursue objects with the eyes and head, and by the second month these movements become more refined and show sign of predicting the future position of moving objects. Arm movements are unrelated to vision at this stage. The grasp reflex is present but is wholly under tactile control. Infants under one month of age do not attend to objects within arm's reach, probably because of inadequate accommodation and convergence. In the second and third months the infants visually attend to near objects and begin to take a visual interest in their own arms. The first visually directed swiping movements of the arm develop, but the child grasps an object only if the hand touches it. In the third month the swipe gives way to a more directed arm movement, and the child looks back and forth between object and hand. In the third and fourth months, the child watches the two hands as they contact and manipulate each other, thus producing a double feedback experience. In the fifth month, this double arm action comes under visual control and gradually gives rise to the ability to reach rapidly and grasp an object. White (1970) reported that, for infants nurtured in an environment enriched by a variety of objects hanging within reach, the onset of sustained observation of the hand occurred at a mean age of 50 days, rather than at 60 days as in infants reared in a 'normal' environment.

The spatially co-ordinated behaviour of adult humans can be adjusted to the changing size and shape of parts of the body during growth, to the demands of novel environments, and to compensate for injury. Because of their intelligence, humans have dispensed with narrowly specialized sense organs and limbs and have instead evolved highly flexible mechanisms that reach their highest expression in learned skills. There are several ways of studying the flexibility of spatially co-ordinated behaviour. One way is to rotate or transplant sense organs or tendon insertions surgically: a method applicable to humans only when radical surgery is required for medical reasons. A second procedure is to study animals reared in anomalous sensory environments, or people with severe sensory

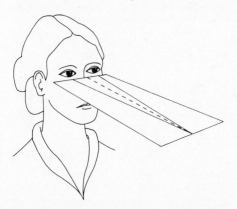

**Fig. 2.** Procedure for demonstrating that visual directions in the two eyes are referred to a common egocentre. Each line must point accurately to the pupil of an eye, and fixation must be maintained on the point where the two lines meet. When this is done a 'fused' image of the two lines is seen extending towards the bridge of the nose.

deficits from an early age. Finally, the flexibility of spatially co-ordinated behaviour may be studied by temporarily distorting the visual input by placing prisms or lenses in front of the eyes. Some representative experiments of each kind will now be described.

*The effects of surgical rotation of the eye.* As part of a treatment for a detached retina, R. R. Barrios, E. M. Recalde, and C. Mendilaharzi severed each rectus muscle of one eye in several human patients, rotated the eyeball through 90°, and sutured each muscle back on to a stump of tendon which was 90° away from the muscle's normal insertion. The patients were allowed to use both eyes during the six-month recovery period. At the end of this period, when tested using only the rotated eye, the patients reported that the visual scene appeared rotated 90°. Furthermore, pursuit eye movements and visually directed movements made with the unseen hand occurred in a direction at right angles to the movement of the visual targets. The total absence of adaptation in these patients was probably due to suppression in vision in the rotated eye during the recovery period. Human beings are certainly able to compensate behaviourally for the rotation of the visual scene produced by optical means, as the pioneering work of G. M. Stratton (1897) demonstrated. When a similar experiment was done on cats, the animals showed accurate visually guided paw placement and obstacle avoidance when seeing with the rotated eye, but only if, during training, the good eye was kept closed. In this experiment, the projection of nerve fibres from the retina of the rotated eye on to the visual cortex was found to be unchanged. The behavioural compensation was obviously due to changes at a higher level.

*The effects of restricted rearing on visual motor co-ordination.* One can study the kinds of sensorimotor experience required for the development of visual motor skills by rearing animals in environments which restrict experience in specific ways. In the most famous of these experiments (by R. Held and A. Hein) pairs of kittens were reared in darkness, except for a certain period each day when they were placed in an illuminated striped carousel apparatus, as shown in Fig. 3. One kitten of each pair was always placed in the box so that its feet did not touch the ground, and the other kitten was always placed on the other end of the rotating lever so that it could walk and thereby cause itself and its passive partner to be moved round inside the striped drum. Both kittens had the same visual experience, but only for the active kitten was this related to the act of walking. Sensory stimulation which results from self-produced movements is known as reafference, and sensory stimulation which occurs independently of self-produced movements is called exafference. Held and Hein found that only the active kitten developed the ability to avoid a cliff, blink at an approaching

**Fig. 3.** Apparatus used by Hein and Held for equating motion and consequent visual feedback for an actively moving animal (*A*) and a passively moving animal (*P*).

object, or extend its paw to a surface. They concluded that reafference is necessary for the development of visual motor skills.

Held, Gower, and Diamond subsequently showed that the paw-placing response developed in immobilized kittens which had experienced only diffuse light. The passive experience in the carousel must have interfered with the maturation of this response, which undermines the claim that reafferent stimulation is necessary for development of visual motor skills.

Held and Hein developed tests for abilities which, they claimed, do not develop without reafferent visual experience. They reared kittens with opaque collars round their necks which prevented them from seeing their limbs (Fig. 4). These kittens could extend their paws towards prongs (Fig. 5) but could not hit them, except by chance, and they could not strike a ball dangled in front of them. Held and Bauer conducted a very similar experiment with monkeys, who for the first 35 days after birth wore a collar which occluded their arms. When the arms were allowed to come into view the

**Fig. 4.** Kitten wearing a collar that prevents sight of limbs and torso.

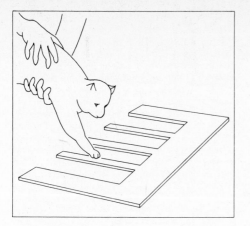

**Fig. 5.** Apparatus for testing the accuracy of visually guided paw placement in the cat.

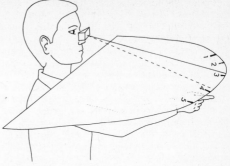

**Fig. 6.** A simple apparatus for demonstrating adaptation of pointing to displaced vision.

monkeys could not reach accurately towards a bottle. It was concluded that '. . . an infant Primate initially fails to reach accurately for attractive visible objects with a limb that it has never previously viewed'.

Note that the monkeys were not allowed to touch the bottle before the collar was removed, and therefore had not learned to relate seen objects with anything that the unseen arm did. R. D. Walk, and E. K. Bond repeated the experiment but allowed the monkeys to touch one end of a rod, the other end of which they could see projecting above the edge of the collar which occluded the hand. After this exposure, visually guided reaching was tolerably accurate after the collar was removed. Therefore, sight of the hand is not required for the development of visual motor co-ordination, only some experience that links its motion to a seen object.

Thus, visual motor skills seem to develop in the presence of any type of information which informs the animal about the accuracy of performance. Certain types of early deprivation have a general debilitating effect, but visual motor learning is usually very specific to the conditions under which it occurs.

*The effects of visual distortions on visual motor co-ordination.* When stimuli impinging on one sense organ are spatially distorted with respect to those impinging on the other sense organs, there is a sensory discordance. The types of visual distortion that have been studied include sideways displacement, tilt, inversion, left–right reversal, magnification, and curvature.

Anyone with a wedge prism can perform the following simple experiment. A few numbers are marked on the edge of a piece of card which is then placed horizontally under the chin as in Fig. 6. With the prism before one eye and the other eye closed, the finger is directed towards a number on

the far side of the card and allowed to come into view. This arm is then returned to the side of the body, after which the aiming movement is repeated several times to each of the numbers in random order. The error in pointing will be very evident for the first few trials, but accuracy is soon restored. When the prism is removed, it will be found that the first few aims will be off target in the opposite direction to the error first experienced when the prism was in place. This after-effect illustrates that adaptation to a visual distortion is not merely a question of deliberate compensation.

*The nature of the changes underlying adaptation to displaced vision.* It is agreed that visual motor adaptation to distorted vision does not involve changes in the sense organs, or in the muscular system which controls arm movements. The change must be in the way sensory or motor signals are coded in the central *nervous system. There is no evidence of a change in the internal calibration of the position of the retinal image. This is not surprising because, when a person points to an object, its image falls on the fovea, which is a very distinctive landmark. Other experiments, reviewed in Howard (1981), have failed to reveal any significant effects of visual motor learning on the apparent directions and shapes of objects, even when the objects are not fixated. It seems that simple visual sensations are insulated from events outside vision. There is an old theory, known as the motor theory of perception, in which it is claimed that the way we see is determined by motor behaviour. It would seem that this theory is wrong with respect to simple visual sensations.

Visual motor adaptation has been found sometimes to involve a change in the sense of eye position. For instance, B. Craske (1967) found that the objectively determined position of the eyes, when the subject was attempting to look straight ahead in the dark, was shifted after exposure to displacing prisms. Similar experiments have demonstrated that there may also be a change in the felt position of the head on the body.

If training one arm with prisms affects the way

the other arm points, the adaptation is said to show *intermanual transfer*. Intermanual transfer indicates that the change must have occurred in the sense of position of the head or the eyes—parts common to both arms. There is general agreement that intermanual transfer is only partial, so that most of the adaptive change to displaced vision must involve a change in the sense of position of the trained arm—a change in the way information from joint receptors is coded, or in the spatial coding of motor commands.

Evidence that motor learning may contribute to adaptation of the visual motor system comes from experiments by E. Taub and I. A. Goldberg on monkeys in whom the sensory roots of the spinal cord had been severed. These monkeys could be trained to reach with the unseen arm towards visual targets and to adapt their pointing when viewing the targets through displacing prisms. This must have been motor learning because the animals lacked sensory inputs from the arm.

Thus it seems that all systems beyond the most peripheral processes in sense organs and muscles are capable of adapting to unusual circumstances, given the correct set of constraints and demands. The one exception seems to be that the central calibration of the position of the retinal image is immutable.

*The conditions under which adaptation to displaced vision occurs.* Held proposed that sensations arising from active movement (i.e. reafferent stimuli) are necessary for visual motor adaptation to displaced vision. In one experiment A. Hein and R. Held asked subjects to watch one of their own hands through a displacing prism as the hand was waved from side to side, either actively by the subject or passively by the experimenter. Only after the active condition did subjects show evidence of having adapted to the prisms when they were tested in an aiming test. They concluded that self-produced movement coupled to visual reafferent stimulation (sight of the moving arm) is necessary for a change of visual motor co-ordination. However, subjects probably paid more attention to what they were doing when moving their own arms and, with this factor controlled, other investigators have demonstrated that self-produced movement is not necessary for visual motor adaptation.

Howard and Templeton (1966) argued that adaptation occurs in response to many forms of discordant information: the important thing is that salient information regarding the discordance (not necessarily consciously perceived) should be available to the subject. The sensory consequences of self-produced movement may be a particularly potent source of information, but the most reasonable general conclusion is that any consistent relationship between stimuli within a given sense or between stimuli in different senses, or any relationship between stimuli and responses, will be learned and the system changed accordingly.

The posterior parietal lobe of the cerebral cortex is well placed to serve as a centre for the higher control of co-ordination between vision, somaesthesis, eye movements, and limb movements. It has been shown that cells in this region of the monkey's brain respond when the animal sees an object of interest, such as food, towards which it is likely to reach. Many of the visually responsive neurones also respond when the eyes move, and some also respond to stimulation of touch receptors.

Subcortical centres in the brain are also involved in sensorimotor co-ordination. For instance, it has been shown that cells in the *basal ganglia, which receive highly processed spatial information, probably from the parietal lobes, are active when the animal is tracking a moving visual object. Damage to the basal ganglia in humans, such as is associated with *Parkinsonism, results in *akinesia, or an inability to initiate movements towards a visual object. This disorder is manifest only in certain contexts, which suggests that the basal ganglia are concerned with organizing responses to specific visual information. Our knowledge of the neurology of sensorimotor co-ordination is very fragmentary. Perhaps the development of artificial automata will help to provide theoretical insights which will guide future work.                                    I. P. H.

Aldridge, J. W., Anderson, R. J., and Murphy, J. T. (1980). The role of the basal ganglia in controlling a movement initiated by a visually presented cue. *Brain Research*, **192**, 3–16.

Auerbach, E. and Sperling, P. (1974). A common auditory-visual space: evidence for its reality. *Perception and Psychophysics*, **16**, 129–35.

Bailey, J. S. (1972). Arm–body adaptation with passive arm movements. *Perception and Psychophysics*, **12**, 39–44.

Barrios, R. R., Recalde, E. M., and Mendilaharzi, C. (1959). Surgical rotation of the eyeball. *British Journal of Psychology*, **43**, 584–90.

Blakemore, C., van Sluyters, R. C., Peck, C. K., and Hein, A. (1975). Development of cat visual cortex following rotation of one eye. *Nature. New Biology*, **257**, 284–7.

Craske, B. (1967). Adaptation to prisms: changes in internally registered eye position. *British Journal of Psychology*, **58**, 329–35.

Critchley, M. (1969). *The Parietal Lobes*. New York.

Fisher, G. H. (1960). Intersensory localization in three modalities. *Bulletin of the British Psychological Society*, **14**, 24–5.

Held, R. and Hein, A. (1958). Adaptation of disarranged hand–eye coordination contingent upon re-afferent stimulation. *Perceptual Motor Skills*, **8**, 87–90.

Howard, I. P. (1981). *Human Visual Orientation*. London.

Howard, I. P. and Templeton, W. B. (1966). *Human Spatial Orientation*. London.

Jackson, C. V. (1953). Visual factors in auditory localization. *Quarterly Journal of Experimental Psychology*, **5**, 52–65.

Pick, H. L., Warren, D. H., and Hay, J. C. (1969). Sensory conflicts in judgements of spatial direction. *Perception and Psychophysics*, **6**, 203–5.

Rock, I. and Victor, J. (1964). Vision and touch: an

experimentally created conflict between the two senses. *Science*, **143**, 594–6.

Stratton, G. M. (1897). Upright vision and the retinal image. *Psychological Review*, **4** 182–7.

Templeton, W. B., Howard, I. P., and Lowman, A. E. (1966). Passively generated adaptation to prismatic distortion. *Perceptual Motor Skills*, **22**, 140–2.

White, B. L. (1970). Experience and the development of motor mechanisms in infancy. In K. Connolly (ed.), *Mechanisms of Motor Skill Development*, pp. 95–113. London.

White, B. L., Castle, P., and Held, R. (1964). Observations on the development of visually-directed reaching. *Child Development*, **35**, 349–63.

**SPEARMAN,** CHARLES EDWARD (1863–1945). Formerly a cavalry officer, Spearman studied psychology in Germany, taking his doctorate at Leipzig. Thereafter he worked in London, becoming Grote professor of mind and logic at University College, where he remained until his retirement in 1931. He was elected a Fellow of the Royal Society in 1924.

Spearman is remembered as a pioneer in statistical psychology and a convinced believer in the two-factor theory of *intelligence, which he advocated in a paper written jointly with Bernard Hart in 1904. Making use of factorial analysis, Spearman claimed that the correlations between the measurement of different abilities in man tended towards a particular arrangement that could be expressed in a definite mathematical formula. This became known as the tetrad equation. Wherever this equation held throughout any table of correlation, every individual measurement of each ability could be divided into two independent parts, one called by Spearman g—i.e. the *general factor*—which, though varying freely from individual to individual, remains the same for any one individual in respect of all the correlated abilities, while the other part—known as the *specific factor*—not only varies from individual to individual, but even in any one individual from one ability to another.

Thus arose what soon became known as the 'two-factor' theory which aroused wide interest but sharp controversy in Britain and further afield. Although Spearman tended to interpret g in terms of a vague and unconvincing concept of 'mental energy', most psychological workers in this field who shared Spearman's views preferred to identify it with 'general intelligence'.

Spearman's work attracted much interest but many critics, among them Godfrey (later Sir Godfrey) Thomson, who advocated instead of a general factor a number of overlapping group factors. Later the interpretation of factorial analysis was extended and discussed with much statistical sophistication by Maxwell Garnett, Cyril *Burt, William Stephenson, L. L. *Thurstone, and many others on both sides of the Atlantic.

The outcome appears to be that whereas factorial analysis has evident value in classifying individuals for educational or occupational purposes, it does not materially contribute to our understanding either of the nature of intelligence or of the rationale of individual differences. It is therefore unlikely to make a decisive contribution to psychological theory.

Spearman wrote two major works: *The Nature of 'Intelligence' and the Principles of Cognition* (1923) and *The Abilities of Man* (1927).          O. L. Z.

**SPEECH AND BRAIN PROCESSES.** Natural speech is a communication of information by means of the codes of language. This means that, to communicate, man has to have a definite motive or intention (knowing what and why he has to communicate) and to use for his purposes a particular language, its phonemic, lexical, and syntactic codes (the last relating to the question *how* to communicate).

Systems of language can have different complexities. It was the Swedish linguist Svedelins (1897) who described two basically different classes of verbal communication: *communication of events* ('The house is burning', 'The boy hit a dog') and *communication of relations* ('Socrates is a man', 'That is the father's brother', 'Mary is fairer than Cathy', 'The triangle under the circle', etc.). These basic kinds of verbal communication are different both in content and in linguistic structure. Communication of events can be represented in concrete images; communication of relations cannot. Communication of events can use comparatively simple forms of linguistic codes; for the communication of relations, more complex linguistic codes are required, including complex case markers, and auxiliary words that express relations ('on', 'under', 'before', 'after', etc.). In the communication of relations, special grammatical codes (incorporation of one phrase into another, relational means, inversion, etc.) can be used as well.

These basic linguistic differences in the two forms of verbal communication are related to different psychological structures. The first class of constructions (which is most typical for the communication of events) is associated with an (immediate) sequence of words which constitutes a phrase. This kind of construction can be considered as a *syntagmatic* type, which is sometimes quite simple, and does not necessarily require any transformation for understanding. Communication of relations generally requires more complex grammatical rules and includes a kind of *paradigmatic* organization (Jakobson, 1971). The process of decoding these structures (or their understanding) very often requires a certain transformation, and the meaning of this form of logico-grammatical communication often becomes clear only after such transformations have been performed. So, the understanding of the construction 'brother's father' requires a chain of transformations and a series of additional grammatical or semantic markers, such as: 'That is my brother. He has a father. His father is my father too'; while the understanding of the construction 'Mary is fairer than Cathy' requires analogous transformations:

'Cathy is fair; but Mary is even more fair; so she is fairer than Cathy', etc. The loading with these additional transformations is much greater for communicating relations than events.

The most important fact observed in *neuropsychology (i.e. in the analysis of the changes of psychological processes associated with local brain lesions) is that the two kinds of verbal communication require different cortical mechanisms, and are based on different cortical systems. In cases where the lesion is situated in posterior ('gnostic') parts of the brain, acquisition of the language codes suffers: both the production and the understanding of paradigmatically organized verbal utterances become difficult, sometimes even impossible; whereas fluent, syntagmatically organized speech remains preserved. This is why patients who are unable consciously to make all the transformations needed for the understanding of complex linguistic structures remain able to use these forms in practice. They are unable to decode the construction 'father's brother' but are still able to include it in a practically preserved syntagmatic system, saying: 'Oh, well, that's my father's brother'. The breakdown of one of the levels (phonemic, lexical, or logico-grammatical) of paradigmatically organized language codes is typical of verbal disorders associated with lesions of the posterior parts of the speech regions of the left hemisphere; in all these cases, practical fluent speech, expressing communication of events or well-imprinted syntagmatic structures, remains basically preserved; that is why these forms of language impairment are called 'fluent aphasias' (see APHASIA).

Conversely, damage to the anterior parts of the 'speech areas' of the left hemisphere results in the opposite kind of deterioration of language. The performance needed for the acquisition of language codes (phonemic, lexical, logico-grammatical) and the systems of opposition these codes include remains basically intact; but the combination of words into fluent sequential (syntagmatic) structures, as well as all kinds of 'kinetic melodies' included in skilled movements, breaks down. This is why patients of this group can easily grasp phonemic oppositions, lexical meanings, and even paradigmatically organized structures—while fluent speech becomes impossible, and may be replaced by separate naming of objects, taking the form of 'telegraphic style'.

The basic brain mechanisms underlying these two forms of verbal utterance are not sufficiently clear, but it seems very probable that the posterior parts of the human brain are associated with the process of transformation of successively arriving information in simultaneous (spatial or quasi-spatial) schemes, whereas the anterior parts of the brain deal with the 'serial organization' of the processes providing skilled movements or successively organized 'kinetic melodies'. This is why a breakdown of the posterior, 'gnostic' regions of the cortex results in a derangement of the acquisition of complex, paradigmatically organized codes of language, while a breakdown of the anterior parts of the cortex (in both cases, of the major hemisphere) results in disturbance of 'serial organization' of the processes, and in a breakdown of syntagmatic organization of verbal utterances.

A. R. L.

Jakobson, R. (1971). *Kindersprache und Aphasie*. The Hague.
Luria, A. R. (1966). *Higher Cortical Functions in Man*. New York.
Luria, A. R. (1970). *Traumatic Aphasia*. The Hague.
Luria, A. R. (1972). *The Working Brain*. New York.
Luria, A. R. (1976). *Basic Problems of Neurolinguistics*. The Hague.
Svedelins, C. (1897). *L'Analyse du langage*. Uppsala.

**SPEECH RECOGNITION BY MACHINE.** Until recently, recognition of speech by a machine has seemed impossible—though machines have been talking and singing for the last hundred years. Speech recognition has immense theoretical and practical importance. An example of a now established commercial application for automatic speech recognition is in the sorting of baggage at airports. A human operator reads a destination from a baggage label into a microphone. The spoken destination is automatically recognized and the baggage is routed accordingly. This use of automatic speech recognition has the advantage that it leaves the operator's hands free to handle the baggage.

Speech is a succession of voiced sounds that originate from the vocal chords, interspersed with consonant sounds such as 's' which originates from the hissing of air between teeth and 't' which is produced by an explosive release of air pressure by the tongue. Speech waveforms are often very complicated, and tend to be roughly periodic during short (e.g. ten-millisecond) periods.

Automatic speech recognition is usually a multi-stage process, in which the first stage is intended to yield a representation of speech that is simpler and less repetitive than the original acoustic waveform. The first stage typically performs various measurements on each successive ten-millisecond portion of the acoustic waveform. For example, in the *Fourier spectrum for each such portion, the energy in various frequency bands spanning 200 to 6,000 hertz may be measured. Alternatively, linear predictive coding coefficients may be taken as measurements. Zero-crossing rates, glottal frequency, and total energy are further important examples of measurements.

For the simplest kind of automatic speech recognition systems, speakers are required to leave silences before and after isolated words. These isolated-word recognition systems usually work by matching the sequence of measurements obtained from a spoken word against various sequences of measurements stored in memory. These stored sequences of measurements are known as speech templates; and there is at least one such template for each different word that the machine can recognize. A spoken word is *recognized* as being the same as the template word that it matches best. Preferably the template words are obtained from the same speaker whose speech is to be recognized. A template can be obtained by having this speaker pronounce the word several times, and in some way averaging the resulting sequences of measurements to make a template. The process of obtaining a stored template from several utterances of one word can be regarded as a *learning* process.

A spoken word is generally a sequence of phonemes, and for example the third phoneme of a spoken word should be matched against the third phoneme of that word's stored template. The total duration of a spoken word may be different each time the word is uttered, and elongation or compression of the time-scale may impair the alignment of phonemic data. For short words this problem can be mitigated by measuring the duration of a spoken word and then elongating or compressing the time scale to standardize the duration of the word before matching it with templates that have been similarly standardized. Speech recognition machines working on these principles became commercially available in the 1970s, and could learn to recognize about thirty-two words spoken quite carefully by a single speaker.

More sophisticated template-matching technology allows elongation or compression of a word's time-scale to vary while the word is being spoken. Time-scale variations can be accommodated by dynamic time-warping, which has become popular in the 1980s because of the decreasing cost of computation, and because it yields more accurate recognition of larger vocabularies than can be recognized by less sophisticated matching techniques. Dynamic time-warping techniques have been developed to recognize whole sentences composed of words not separated by silences. Templates for whole sentences are composed of single-word templates, and the time-warping technique that time-aligns phoneme-like parts of a single word has been developed to time-align whole-word parts of a single sentence. After matching, it is easy to find which part of the spoken sentence corresponds to which part of a template sentence, and thus find when each spoken word begins and ends.

Except for specialized applications, it is not practical to store or synthesize sentence templates, and radically different techniques are required for automating the work of a typist who types unrestricted text that is dictated without silences between successive words. Instead of attempting to recognize whole words directly by template matching, it is usual to attempt to classify successive subword portions, known as segments. A segment may, for instance, be a portion during which the results of measurements on the acoustic waveform do not change by more than a threshold amount. Alternatively, successive ten-millisecond portions of the utterance may be regarded as segments. Segments may be classified, sometimes erroneously, by means of classical *pattern recog-

nition techniques, which yield one or more plausible labels for each segment. A speech recognition machine contains a dictionary which, for each recognizable word, stores one or more than one combination of segment labels for segments of that word. This stored lexical knowledge is generally not sufficient to cope with erroneous subdivision of speech into segments and erroneous classification of these segments. To bring further order out of this chaos it is usual to employ knowledge of syntax and semantics in addition to lexical knowlege.

In the mid-1980s, automatic recognition of unrestricted multispeaker connected speech is an unsolved problem that is receiving attention in many countries because of the commercial value of a viable solution. There is steady progress in the growth of phonetic knowledge and in the development of expert systems techniques, to bring together and apply the relevant knowledge in an orderly manner.                                J. R. U.

Fallside, F. and Woods, W. A. (1985). *Computer Speech Processing*. Englewood Cliffs, New Jersey.

Lea, W. A. (1980). *Trends in Speech Recognition*. Englewood Cliffs, New Jersey.

Witten, I. (1982). *Principles of Computer Speech*. New York.

**SPENCER,** HERBERT (1820–1903). British philosopher. The influence of Herbert Spencer in his lifetime was immense. It was not only in intellectual circles that his books were read, and their popular appeal in America and Asia, as well as in Britain, was enormous. But since the nineteenth century his reputation has suffered an uncommonly severe eclipse, and it is necessary to recall the extent of his influence.

Henry Holt, an influential publisher, declared, 'About 1865 I got hold of a copy of Spencer's *First Principles* and had my eyes opened to a new heaven and a new earth.' And Andrew Carnegie, prototype of the self-made American, publicized Spencer as 'the man to whom I owe most'. For thirty years, from the 1860s, Spencer's thought dominated American universities. The last of those decades, the 1890s, produced the revolution in educational thought and psychology led by William *James and John *Dewey, Stanley *Hall, and E. L. *Thorndike, all influenced by Spencer. In Britain, J. S. *Mill backed financially the subscription scheme that launched Spencer's work, and the scientists supported him too. Charles *Darwin wrote, 'After reading any of his books I generally feel enthusiastic admiration for his transcendental talents', but added that 'his conclusions never convince me'. (He also wrote, somewhat ambiguously, 'I feel rather mean when I read him: I could bear and rather enjoy feeling that he was twice as ingenious and clever as myself, but when I feel that he is about a dozen times my superior, even in the master-art of wriggling, I feel aggrieved.') In 1863 Alfred Russel *Wallace visited Spencer, commenting, 'Our thoughts were full of the great unsolved problem of the origin of life . . . and we looked to

Spencer as the one man living who could give us a clue to it.' And as late as 1897 Beatrice Webb noted that '"Permanent" men might be classed just above the artisan and skilled mechanic: they read Herbert Spencer and Huxley and are speculative in religious and political thought'.

In the 1880s Spencer was consulted by the Japanese government on education. And in Chekhov's short story 'The Duel' (1891) a female character recalls the beginning of an idyllic relationship: '. . . to begin with we had kisses, and calm evenings, and vows, and Spencer, and ideals and interests in common'. And, finally, a letter arrived at Spencer's home in the early 1890s addressed to 'Herbt Spencer, England, and if the postman doesn't know where he lives, why he ought to'.

Spencer's fame was based entirely on his books. He rarely appeared in public, save for one triumphant tour of America late in life. He was born in Derby, the only surviving son of a schoolmaster, and he was educated informally at home by his father and later in the family of an uncle. The family was staunchly Nonconformist, with a radical tradition and a keen interest in the social issues of the day. For some years the young Spencer was a railway engineer, but by 1841 he had decided against this career. He became a journalist in London, attended meetings, and was formulating ideas on politics and education. He began to write, and became known for his radical opinions and self-confidence, traits tempered by great honesty. If in old age he became idiosyncratic, in youth he was a shrewd iconoclast who delighted in argument. Perhaps it was these qualities which led him to some influential and lifelong friendships. He got to know the young T. H. *Huxley; they had interests in common and walked together on Hampstead Heath in London. George Eliot was a fellow journalist who fell in love with him, before he introduced her to G. H. Lewes. It was a remarkably tight-knit intellectual group in which Spencer moved, and it extended into the next generation. In 1877 when William James was attacking Spencer's books at Harvard, William's brother Henry, the novelist, wrote describing his meeting with Spencer at George Eliot's, and comments: 'I often take a nap beside Herbert Spencer at the Athenaeum and feel as if I were robbing you of the privilege.'

Spencer's first books were published in the serene mid-century. His essays on *Education* (1861) remained a standard text in colleges training teachers for many decades. By 1858 he had conceived the plan of writing a major synthetic philosophy, and the prospectus appeared in 1860. Small legacies, publications, and the support of friends, enabled him to give up journalism and for the rest of his life he was an independent author. He never married, and he devoted his life to completing the philosophy as he had originally planned it. The whole massive project, with volumes on biology, psychology, sociology, and ethics, together with

the initial *First Principles* (1862) was finally complete in 1896.

Today one point of pursuing Spencer lies precisely in trying to understand something of the reasons for his great appeal in his own time. The social milieu in which he moved is significant. The immense popularity of his work is due to a rather special way in which it reflected some of the preoccupations of his own generation. In his thirties Spencer suffered a severe breakdown in health. He shared the Victorian syndrome, which Darwin and Huxley also endured, of a crisis in health as a young man and thereafter constant hypochondria, insomnia, and headaches; it suggests some of the tensions in their thought and background.

Spencer had no formal education. He believed this to be a great advantage which 'left me free from the bias given by the plexus of traditional ideas and sentiments', and he adds, 'I did not trouble myself with the generalisations of others. And that indeed indicated my general attitude. All along I have looked at things through my own eyes and not through the eyes of others.' In later life he was never able to work for long, and his reading was severely curtailed. In fact he had never read a great deal; he observed, made biological collections and mechanical inventions, and he enjoyed intelligent conversations and his own thoughts much more than reading books. Although he believed this gave him an independent attitude, it in fact left him more than usually open to the influences around him.

When *Darwin's *Origin of Species* was published in November 1859, evolutionary theories were not new—they had been the subject of of speculation for half a century. Darwin's achievement was to make the elements of the theory coherent and to demonstrate, by massive evidence, that it must be taken seriously.

One man needed no conversion. Seven years earlier, in 1852, Spencer had published an essay on the 'Development Hypothesis', and coined the term of the *survival of the fittest*. Years later Huxley recalled that before Darwin's publication, 'The only person known to me whose knowledge and capacity compelled respect, and who was at the same time a thoroughgoing evolutionist, was Mr Herbert Spencer . . .'. Spencer first came across evolution in a secondary work discussing the ideas of Lamarck, whose theory was partly intuitive and had never convinced professional naturalists (see LAMARCKIANISM). Spencer was won over, before there was convincing evidence, for a characteristically mid-Victorian reason: 'The Special Creation theory had dropped out of my mind many years before, and I could not remain in a suspended state; acceptance of the only conceivable alternative was peremptory.'

An important feature of Spencer's generation of intellectuals is that they had discarded orthodox religion. Spencer himself was never religious, and he enjoyed setting out for Sunday rambles walking provocatively in the opposite direction to the church-goers. But unconsciously, the agnostic mid-Victorians searched for some other system of thought which could answer their doubts and give them clear first principles. Science was one alternative which was widely seized on, hence the battles over evolution and religion. Evolution offered, it seemed, an alternative conceptual framework, universally operating laws of cause and effect. The 'new heaven and the new earth' which Spencer's philosophy opened up to many of his contemporaries was essentially a systematic metaphysical cosmology: everything from the stars to the embryo, from civilizations to the individual, was in process of development, interaction, change, growth—and progress. For Spencer's conception of universal evolution was optimistic, a view which seemed natural to successful mid-Victorians. 'Progress, therefore, is not an accident but a necessity. Instead of civilisation being artificial, it is a part of the embryo or the unfolding of a flower.' Late eighteenth-century *laissez-faire* individualism is thus reconciled with the revolutionary changes of nineteenth-century society.

Naturalistic organic conceptions of society gained a new importance with the addition of evolutionary laws. Spencer was the first to pursue the study of such laws operating in society, and to call his analysis sociology. His book *The Study of Sociology* (1873) was as popular as *Education*. A similar but more dynamic conception was being developed in the same period by Karl Marx.

Fundamentally the reverence for nature which pervades all Spencer's work goes back to *Rousseau. It is romantic, not scientific. Spencer's conception of evolution owes nothing to Darwin. Although greatly impressed by science, Spencer never really grasped scientific method: his method was inductive—he generalizes laws without proof, draws facts haphazardly from his own experience, and is fond of asserting his beliefs as 'obvious'. Spencer understood his own romantic, speculative, and basically unscientific attitude, and recounts against himself the witticism of his friend Huxley that 'Spencer's idea of a tragedy is a deduction killed by a fact'. Not until almost a generation later was it realized that evolutionary theories cannot supply an ethical code for human societies. Spencer's only quarrel with Huxley was in the 1890s, when Huxley first publicly dissented from the view that the law of nature in human society was neither just nor good.

The origins of Spencer's philosophy owe much to the provincial dissenting background of his youth. By the 1880s his individualistic *laissez-faire* views were already anachronistic, though his book *Man versus the State* (1884) had enormous sales. Essentially, Spencer is a Janus figure looking as much backwards as forwards. He only partly understood evolutionary theory and used it considerably to give a systematic framework for the individualistic ethics and organic view of the state prevalent in his youth. John Dewey, in an excellent essay, came to the conclusion that Spencer was

essentially a transition figure, preserving the ideals of late eighteenth-century British liberalism in the only way possible: in 'the organic, the systematic, the universal terms which report the presence of the nineteenth century'.

Yet Spencer really did seize and propagandize the leading idea of his own day. It was Spencer, not Darwin, who opened up the horizons of the evolutionary theory in psychology, sociology, anthropology, and education. He did perhaps more than anyone else to persuade others that the implications of the evolutionary theory were important, and he did it in a thoroughly Victorian manner: energetic, confident, systematic, universal, which a modern scientist, Sir Peter Medawar, salutes with respect:

I think Herbert Spencer was the greatest of those who have attempted to found a metaphysical system on naturalistic principles. It is out of date, of course, this style of thought, it is philosophy for an age of steam. . . . His system of General Evolution does not really work: the evolution of society and of the solar system are different phenomena, and the one teaches us next to nothing about the other. . . . But for all that, I for one can still see Spencer's System as a great adventure. . . .

A. L.-B.

Medawar, P. (1967). *The Art of the Soluble*. London.
Peel, J. D. Y. (1971). *Herbert Spencer*. London.

**SPERRY, ROGER WALCOTT.** See BRAIN SCIENCE: SPERRY'S CONTRIBUTION.

**SPINOZA,** BENEDICT (BARUCH) DE (1632–77), Dutch philosopher, one of the last great metaphysical thinkers of the 'rationalist' period in philosophy. In his major work, *The Ethics*, he starts from supposedly self-evident truths and rigorously develops them through the use of reason and deductive argument. His commitment to the power of reason and to the view that man can gain knowledge of reality through the powers of the mind alone culminate in a profound vision of the world and of man's place within it.

Spinoza was born in Amsterdam of Portuguese Jewish stock. He was educated initially in the Jewish school, but later received Latin lessons from a private tutor, Van Den Ende, who introduced him to the scientific and philosophical developments of the day. Spinoza's growing commitment to secular thought and philosophy brought him into conflict with the Jewish authorities, and in 1656 he was expelled from the synagogue for his 'heretical' views. His Hebrew name, Baruch, he abandoned for its Latin form, Benedictus. The remainder of his life was spent developing his philosophical system while earning a living from polishing and grinding lenses. His reputation as a heretic and atheist did not prevent him carrying on an extensive correspondence with other major thinkers, but only one of his works, the *Theological-Political Treatise*, was published (anonymously) during his lifetime. His other works—*A Short Treatise on God, Man and his Well-being*, the *Treatise on the Emendation of the*

*Intellect, The Ethics,* and the unfinished *Political Treatise*—were collected and published by his friends shortly after his death, from consumption.

Spinoza developed his theory of the mind partly in an attempt to solve the problems raised by *Descartes's account of the mind and body as two fundamentally different substances. For Descartes the mind and body are independent and mutually exclusive systems, and it is well known that this strict dualistic theory made it extremely difficult to explain the apparent causal interaction between mental and physical items (see DUALISM).

Spinoza rejected Descartes's dualistic account and replaced it with a theory of 'substance monism'. This may be explained as follows. Substance is that which is self-dependent—needing nothing other than itself in order to exist. So far, both Descartes and Spinoza are in agreement. But where Descartes asserts that there are many such substances (including each finite mind and body), Spinoza argues that there can be only one being which has the character of substance, and this being is God or nature itself. All finite things, ourselves included, are dependent upon other things for existence. Only God—the being beside whom there *is* nothing else, for He is infinite—has the nature of substance. This being so, all finite things, in particular minds and bodies, are not substances but 'modifications' or 'modes', that is, beings that are manifestations or fragmented expressions of the one reality. Mental and physical items alike have no reality save that which they have as parts of substance.

God or nature (these are synonymous terms for Spinoza) may, however, be viewed in two ways. We may think of the one substance either as a thinking being, or as extended in space. For Descartes, thought and extension constitute the essence of mental and physical substances respectively. In contrast, Spinoza regards thought and extension as two ways of *conceiving* one and the same reality. He is committed not to mental and physical *things* but to things that may be *conceived* in two different ways. He claims that whether we conceive of God in mental terms or in physical terms, we are thinking of just one being in either case. He then applies this 'conceptual dualism' to all items in the world. Every finite thing or 'mode' can be viewed in two ways, either as mental or as physical. Whatever there is, is fully explicable in either way. But, as in the case of God, there is only one thing that is being described.

When Spinoza came to speak of the human mind and body he said: 'Mind and body are one and the same individual conceived now under the attribute of thought, now under the attribute of extension.' This seems to amount to an identity claim—there is just one thing, which may be viewed and described either as a mind or as a body. This approach to the *mind–body problem has some adherents today. Many accept that a human being can be described in two fundamental ways, attributing to him both psychological and physical properties, while also accepting that there is only one being—the human person—which is being so characterized.

With Spinoza's monistic theory, Descartes's problem—that of explaining causal interaction between disparate items—vanishes, for there are not *two* things at all; the mind and body do not interact, for one thing cannot interact with itself. Anything that occurs in the body can be explained in mental terms and anything that occurs in the mind may be explained and described physically. Spinoza would therefore be sympathetic to those materialist or physicalist philosophers who claim that mental states just *are* physical happenings in the brain. But they would be less happy with Spinoza's reverse claim—that any physical occurrence may be fully explained in mental terms.

Spinoza speaks of the mind as the 'idea' of the body. As such it is aware of the body and of the things that happen to it. When light rays hit the retina of the eye, for example, the physical process may be described in mental terms as an image or sensory idea. But Spinoza thought that such sense perceptions are invariably confused or 'inadequate', because we take them to be the true representations of external objects whereas in reality they are merely reflections of our own bodily processes. (See PERCEPTIONS AS HYPOTHESES; ILLUSIONS; SENSATIONS.)

Spinoza claims that all finite things endeavour or strive to maintain themselves in being and to perfect their existence. Thus the body will try to avoid those things which are harmful to it and will pursue those things that it needs in order to survive. The mind too, in Spinoza's view, exhibits this endeavour (or *conatus*, as he calls it) in its attempt to resist ideas which are inadequate and confused and to grasp those that help it to understand itself, the body and the external world. Spinoza thinks the mind will be aware that its sense perceptions are inadequate, for they will lack the clarity, distinctness and self-evident character of all true ideas. This being so, the mind will naturally try to replace sense perceptions with more adequate ideas, through a process of reasoned reflection and the application of self-evident principles. Once this stage is reached the mind is active rather than passive: it pursues and grasps the truth through its innate power of understanding, rather than remaining at the mercy of arbitrary and confused images and sense impressions.

This process of replacing sense impressions with adequate conceptions can also be applied to the emotions. For Spinoza, emotions are merely confused and inadequate ideas which befuddle the mind and which, for the most part, make us extremely unhappy. He thinks that to the extent that we allow our emotions to rule us we are in a state of slavery or bondage: 'When a man is a prey to his emotions, he is not his own master, but lies at the mercy of fortune.' Our emotions can be overcome by replacing the inadequate ideas on which they are grounded with a clear and distinct understanding of their causes. If emotions are confused ideas and if they arise from inadequate understanding, it seems to follow that increased knowledge will change them, and enable us to become free of their power over us. As Spinoza says: 'An emotion therefore becomes more under our control, and the mind is less passive in respect to it, in proportion as it is more known to us.' This account of active self-improvement through the analysis and clarification of ideas has led some commentators to greet Spinoza as an early precursor of Freudian psychoanalysis.

For Spinoza, the mastery of emotions, and the state of improved understanding achieved through the mind's reasoning powers, enables us to become more active and free. But the freedom which Spinoza grants us has seemed to some to be no freedom at all. When the mind understands things adequately it perceives them as necessary, and sees that they could not have been otherwise. Reason, Spinoza tells us, perceives things 'under a certain form of eternity', and we then see that nothing could have been different, because everything results from God, who Himself is a necessary and eternal being.

Our freedom consists in recognizing the necessity of our nature, understanding ourselves as expressions and manifestations of God's power and laws, and as having no existence save that which He grants us. Viewed rightly, we see ourselves and all things as in a sense eternal, for we no longer judge things as contingent happenings in time, but as determined by immutable laws. This understanding, which Spinoza calls 'intuition', constitutes the mind's highest achievement and its complete fulfilment. Knowing itself and other things in this manner, the mind achieves a certain immortality, and with true contentment realizes that death, which is a mere temporal event, cannot destroy it.

Spinoza thus ends his *Ethics* on a note of almost religious fervour which has encouraged some in the view that he was a mystic. Although his philosophy has influenced many, and has been hailed by idealists, materialists, atheists and theists alike, his vision is perhaps most pertinent today to all those who wish to find a place for spiritual fulfilment in a world governed by natural laws.

A translation by R. H. M. Elwes, *Basic Works*, was published in two volumes in New York in 1955, and *The Correspondence of Spinoza*, trans. A. Wolf, appeared also in New York in 1966.    J. N.

Hampshire, S. (1951). *Spinoza*. Harmondsworth.
Scruton, R. (1986). *Spinoza*. Oxford.

**SPIRITUALISM.** Belief in a world of spirits has been a constant feature of all human societies. However, systematic communication with that world through spirit mediumship and possession is a central feature only of certain peripheral cults in primitive societies, and of spiritualism in the Western world since the middle of the nineteenth century. In pre-literate societies, spirit possession cults have been described as deprivation cults,

attracting women and other downtrodden and depressed categories of person (Lewis, 1971). Through membership of the cult, a measure of lost status and esteem may be regained. In Western society communication with the spirits of the departed has been spasmodic. The voice of God, and intimations of divine presence, though central to the tradition of Christian mysticism, fall outside the province of strictly spiritualist experience.

As an organized movement, spiritualism has a quite precise time and place of origin. Historians of spiritualism trace its beginnings to March 1848, when unaccountable noises were heard by two young sisters in an isolated farmhouse in New York State. The rappings were attributed to the spirit of a travelling salesman murdered there some years earlier, and were interpreted as his attempts to establish communication with the living. Whatever the significance of the original rappings, within two years of their being heard the Fox sisters and their mother had established themselves as successful mediums with huge followings in New York city. Spiritualist circles and seances mushroomed along the east coast of America, and thence spread in two directions: westwards across the American continent and eastwards across the Atlantic to Europe.

The most striking characteristic of early spiritualist experience is precisely its non-religious quality: messages from spirits are peculiar for their concreteness, triviality and a certain mundane bizarreness. Conan Doyle, a historian of spiritualism, and himself a spiritualist, was sensitive to the bad impression which such trivial preoccupations might create. He therefore reminded his readers that the first message transmitted by cable across the Atlantic was a commonplace enquiry from a testing engineer. 'So it is that the humble spirit of the murdered pedlar of Hydesville may have opened a gap into which the angels have thronged' (1926, p. 56).

The movement which developed was quite remarkable in a number of ways. First, it accorded a very special role to women in that mediumship was thought to be primarily, though not exclusively, a feminine art. Secondly, it involved a startling array of events such as *levitations, ectoplasmic apparitions, telekinesis, and apports. Thirdly, it led to an alliance between spiritualists and scientists which is unique in the history of religion. While feminine stereotypes have always attributed greater intuitive and mystical powers to women (as they saw it at the time), their alleged passivity, lack of high intelligence, and lack of education made them seem peculiarly fitted to become mediums. In this connection Conan Doyle wrote: 'Great intellect stands in the way of personal psychic experiences. The clear state is certainly most apt for the writing of a message' (1926, p. 2). This congruity between stereotypes of femininity and the requirements of mediumship opened up career opportunities for women. The circles or seances were frequently held in the houses of mediums. However, in addition to its domestic setting the concerns of spiritualist messages were also of an intimately domestic and familial kind. The intrusion of scientists into this scene of cosy domesticity seems an unlikely event. The Society for Psychical Research was founded in February 1882 in order to make 'an organized and systematic attempt to investigate that large group of debatable phenomena designated by such terms as mesmeric, psychical and Spiritualistic'. Members of the society included philosophers, scientists and politicians. Among the famous names are Henry Sidgwick, Lord Balfour, William *James, Sir William Crookes, Andrew Lang, Henri *Bergson, Gilbert Murray, and William *McDougall. Although both science and religion are concerned with the ultimate nature of reality, only in the case of spiritualism were scientific criteria thought to be relevant for the establishment of religious truth and falsehood. This overlap of interests and techniques is perhaps to be accounted for by, on the one hand, the concreteness of spiritualist claims, and on the other hand by the direction of much scientific research during the 1880s, which was concerned with radiation physics.

In contrast to the respectable scientific solidity of the psychical researcher, the mediums tended to be young, vulnerable, beautiful, and possessed of a certain childlike naïvety. The relationship between Sir William Crookes and Florence Cook is in many ways typical of the relationship between scientist and medium. Florence Cook's spirit guide was an ectoplasmic apparition called Katie King. It was claimed that this materialization could move and talk quite independently of Florence. However, in 1874 the medium's reputation was dramatically threatened by allegations of fraud and trickery. Florence Cook decided to throw herself at the mercy of Sir William, who was known to have an interest in psychical research, having investigated the Scottish medium, Daniel Dunglas *Home. The move proved highly prudent since Sir William wasted no time in jumping to Florence Cook's defence. The precondition of his investigating her gifts was that he should remove her from her parents' house to his own, in the north of London. From the very outset he felt it his duty to defend Florence, particularly if he could remove 'an unjust suspicion which is cast upon another. And when this other person is a woman—young, sensitive and innocent—it becomes especially a duty for me to give the weight of my testimony in favour of her whom I believe to be unjustly accused' (quoted in Hall, 1962, p. 35). Hall puts forward the hypothesis that Sir William and Florence became lovers and that he extended scientific respectability to her in return for sexual love. Hall's interpretation appears to be highly plausible but, even if he were proved to be wrong in detail, the alliance is illuminating from a sociological perspective. Whereas most religious roles for women provide an exalted status and liberation for women at the cost of rejecting traditional femininity, spiritual mediumship capitalizes on existing relationships and transfers them to a spiritual plane. Spiritualism enthrones women in their traditional roles and relationships.

Although there have been many charges of fraud and counter-fraud, spiritualist belief has by and large remained impervious to such exposures. The late nineteenth century was the high point of dramatic apparitions and events. The First World War with its large numbers of bereaved provided yet another peak in the growth of the spiritualist movement. Thereafter, spiritualism gradually reverted to its earlier unassuming concerns. Essentially a domestic religion, it provides women with the opportunity of a religious life without transgressing the norms of traditional femininity. It also provides that much sought-after kind of work, work based at home—and the spiritual attention of circles is directed towards problems associated with marriage, family, and illness.

See also PARANORMAL.                                    V. S.

Doyle, A. Conan (1926). *The History of Spiritualism*. London.

Hall, T. (1962). *The Spiritualists*. London.

Lewis, I. (1971). *Ecstatic Religion*. Harmondsworth.

Nelson, G. K. (1969). *Spiritualism and Society*. London.

Skultans, V. (1974). *Intimacy and Ritual: a study of spiritualism, mediums and groups*. London.

**SPLIT-BRAIN AND THE MIND.** The problem of how the mind relates to the brain stands as the greatest challenge to a scientific age which seeks an objective explanation for all nature. Our physicalist world view and our pragmatic approach to social problems may both be transformed by significant discoveries concerning the way human experience and human social consciousness arise in cerebral activity.

Much has been learned by observing how physical damage to the brain in different locations causes losses or distortions of motives, wishes, skills, feelings, and conscious experiences (see NEUROPSYCHOLOGY). Perhaps the most striking results have come from a brain operation that segregates the highest brain functions into two unlike sets: by cutting some 800 million nerve fibres that connect one half of the cerebral cortex with the other it is possible effectively to divide the mind.

It is a principal characteristic of the mind to exhibit a harmonious unity and a coherent command—to make the *consciousness of an individual person. Ever since nerve conduction was understood it has been speculated that the great interhemispheric bridge, the corpus callosum (meaning 'thick-skinned body'), is essential for mental unity (Fig. 1). When it and other smaller interhemispheric connections are cut, communication between the two sides must pass by the stem of the brain, which is normally considered unconscious, or through external relations of the body with the world of stimuli and the effects of actions.

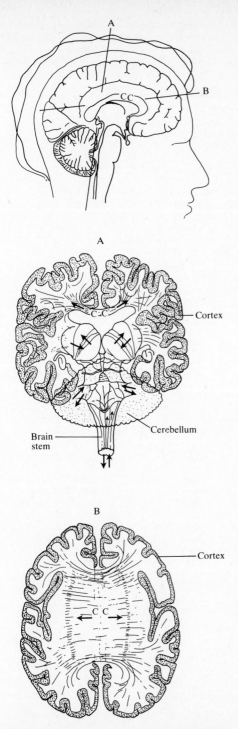

**Fig. 1.** The corpus callosum (CC) is the principal integrator of mental processes which are carried out differently in the two halves of the cortex. It complements connections through the brain stem.

Famous psychologists, including G. T. *Fechner and William *McDougall, have wondered what would happen to *consciousness if the brain were divided in this way. McDougall, it is said, even tried to persuade the physiologist C. S. *Sherrington to undertake to divide his, McDougall's, corpus callosum if he became incurably ill. Nerve connectionists tended to think conscious experience would be destroyed or divided, but McDougall, a mentalist, believed consciousness would remain unified. It was frustrating that, for a long time, studies of animals, and a few human cases, with corpus callosum sectioned gave no interesting evidence. Consciousness appeared to be slightly depressed and there were transitory lapses in voluntary co-ordination, but that was all. In irony, Karl *Lashley suggested that the corpus callosum might serve simply to hold the hemispheres together. Warren *McCulloch said its only known function was to spread *epilepsy.

Cerebral commissurotomy, the split-brain operation, has been performed with varying completeness on a small number of human beings since the mid-1940s, always in hopes of checking crippling epilepsy, to stop the non-functional neural discharges reverberating between the hemispheres and severely damaging the cortical tissues. The breakthrough in estimation of the mental effects of this operation came from investigations in Roger Sperry's laboratory at the California Institute of Technology, following the first effective experiments on the consequences of commissurotomy in cats and monkeys. The animal studies had established new methods. They revealed simple explanations for why all previous research had observed only trivial and uninformative consequences of so great a change in brain structure. With control for orienting, and of information exchange between the hemispheres through transactions with the external world, the split-brain animals were found to have totally divided perception and learning. When free, their movements, alertness, and general motivation were entirely normal.

In Los Angeles, the neurosurgeons Philip Vogel and Joseph Bogen concluded that selected epileptic patients would benefit from the surgery and suffer no serious mental loss. Between 1962 and 1968, nine complete operations were performed with success in reducing fits. Psychological tests performed by Michael Gazzaniga, Sperry, and Bogen at the California Institute soon revealed that, while the general psychological state and behaviour was, in most cases, little affected, there was a profound change in mental activities. Other studies with commissurotomy patients carried out since, in the U.S., France, and Australia, have produced similar findings.

For the commissurotomy subject (Fig. 2), direct awareness is no longer whole. An object felt in the left hand out of sight cannot be matched to the same kind of object felt separately and unseen in the right hand. As long as the eyes are stationary,

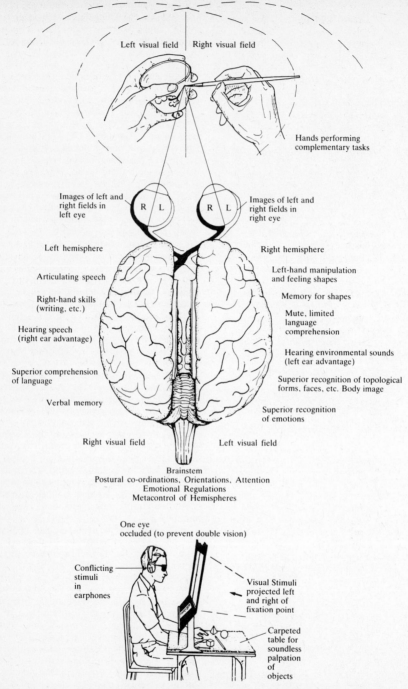

**Fig. 2.** Commissurotomy, division of the corpus callosum to relieve epilepsy, causes separate awarenesses in left and right halves of the visual field and for objects in left and right hand. Integrations through the brain stem keep the behaviour of the person coherent, but do not permit unification of consciousness. Testing a split-brain patient involves control of orienting movements, with one eye covered and stimuli flashed for 1/10th second on a screen, or objects felt out of sight on a carpet so no tell-tale sounds are fed back to the subject's ears. Using conflicting auditory stimuli in earphones, division of hearing may be demonstrated.

something seen just to the left of the fixation point cannot be compared to something seen on the right side. Comparable divisions in olfactory and auditory awareness may be demonstrated. Furthermore, although sight and touch communicate normally on each side, left visual field to left hand or right visual field to right hand, the crossed two-hemisphere combinations fail, as if experiences of eye and hand were obtained by separate persons. There is no evidence that perceptual information needed to identify an object can cross the mid-line of the visual field, or between the hands, to unify the patient's awareness. While the division of sight for detail is extremely sharp at the centre of the field, as long as the patient keeps his eyes still, with freedom to look to left and right and to see in both halves of vision what both hands are holding, the division of awareness ceases to be apparent. Indeed, the subject himself seems unaware of anything amiss, except when evidence is presented to him of an inconsistency in his conscious judgement. Then it would appear he feels some lapse of concentration, or absent-mindedness.

With stimuli on arms, legs, face, or trunk, there is some transfer of feeling between the sides. These less discriminatory parts of the body are represented in duplicate, with both sides in each hemisphere of the brain, and their functions, sensory and motor, are cross-integrated at levels of the brain below the hemispheres. Interesting results have been obtained with large, long-lasting stimuli moving in the periphery of vision. Seeing the spatial layout in surroundings at large, called 'ambient vision', is vital in steering on a confined or irregular route or in a cluttered environment, and even in maintaining the balance of standing or walking. It also functions to give approximate location to off-centre targets of attention before the eyes move to fixate. Evidently the semi-conscious appreciation of the location and orientation of major features in outside space, mainly picked up from dynamic transformations of the visual image, is not divided by commissurotomy. Indeed, the general background or context of body co-ordination and orienting must be intact for commissurotomy subjects to retain the freedom of action and coherence of awareness they ordinarily exhibit. To this degree the operation does not divide the agency of the subject, or the experience of whole-body action. The two halves of the neocortex are kept in functional relationship, co-ordinated through ascending and descending links with the sub-hemispheric regions of the brain stem (Fig. 1).

By far the most dramatic finding of the early tests was the total failure of the right cerebral cortex on its own to express itself in speech. It could not utter words to explain its awareness or knowledge. In contrast, when stimuli were given to the left cortex the subject could say perfectly normally what the experience had been like. Objects were named, compared, and described, and the occurrence or non-occurrence of stimulus events was correctly reported. Yet similar tests of the right half of the brain, with stimuli in the left visual field or left hand, totally failed. The subjects often gave no response. If urged to reply, they said that there might have been some weak and ill-defined event, or else they confabulated experiences, as if unable to apply a test of truth or falsity to spontaneously imagined answers to questions.

These events not only confirm a division of awareness, but they raise important questions which have been debated in clinical neurology since the discovery, over a century ago, that muteness or disturbance of language comprehension can result from brain injury confined to the left hemisphere. Could the right hemisphere comprehend spoken or written language at all? Could it express itself to any degree in signs, by writing, or by gesture? Could it make any utterance? Could it reason and think? Was it really conscious? The commissurotomy patients offered a wonderfully direct approach to these questions, and ingenious experiments were designed by Sperry and his students Jerre Levy, Robert Nebes, Harold Gordon, and Dahlia and Eran Zaidel to interrogate the unspeaking right hemisphere.

Some comprehension of spoken and written language was certainly present in the mute side of the brain. Information about how the right hemisphere should perform a test could be conveyed by telling it what to do, and if the name of a common object was projected to the right cortex only, the patient could retrieve a correct example by hand, or identify a picture of it by pointing. The right hemisphere could solve very simple arithmetic problems, giving its answer by arranging plastic digits out of sight with the left hand. Nevertheless, it was clear that both the vocabulary as understood and the powers of calculation of the right hemisphere were distinctly inferior to these abilities in the left hemisphere of the same patient. Rarely, a patient was able to start an utterance or begin to write a word with the right hemisphere, but, in these tests, the vigilance of the more competent left hemisphere blocked all such initiatives after the first syllable or letter. In general only the left hemisphere could speak, write, or calculate.

When Levy applied non-verbal *intelligence tests, the results indicated that there were some functions for which the left hemisphere did not dominate: for some modes of thinking the right hemisphere was superior. All these right brain tasks involved visual or touch perception of difficult configurations, judgements involving exploration of shapes by hand or manipulative construction of geometric assemblies or patterns. It appeared that the right hemisphere was able to notice the shape of things more completely than the left. Taken with evidence that systematic calculation and forming logical propositions with words were better performed by the left hemisphere, these results favoured the idea that the right hemisphere is better at taking in the structure of things synthetically, without analysis, assimilating all components at once in an ensemble, figure, or *Gestalt. Nebes discovered that the right hemisphere may have a clearer memory of the appearance of things, in the sense that it was better able to recognize familiar objects with incomplete pictorial data, and better able to perceive whole shapes from parts seen or felt in the hand.

The way hands are normally used hints at differences in awareness of the hemispheres. (See HANDEDNESS.) In normal manipulation, a right-hander supports and orients an object in the grasp of the left hand, to facilitate discrete moves of the right fingers that are more finely controlled. Consider such a simple act as taking the last drop of soup from a bowl with a spoon. To grasp, support, and orient objects, the left hand must 'understand' the dimensions and distribution of matter in an object, and usually this kind of judgement does not need visual inspection. In contrast, the discrete and precise acts of the right hand require a succession of decisions that are aimed or guided by a sequence of brief visual fixations. Writing is a cultivated skill that uses the right-hand endowment for rapid repeated cycles of action in the service of language. It may be a learned adaptation of the brain mechanism for gestural communication, the right hand of most persons being dominant for expressive gesticulation. In many tests, the left hand of the commissurotomy patients was more efficient than the right at feeling shapes that resist analysis into highly familiar elements. The left hand palpated complex raised patterns as wholes, as if sensing shape directly. In contrast, the right hand tended to feel the contours, corners, etc., one-by-one, as if trying to build up an inventory of discrete experiences along a line in time. Recently, experiments with the same subjects have demonstrated that the right hemisphere tends to be superior at metaphorical rather than literal perceptions, and that it perceives the emotions or moods in facial expressions or vocalizations better than the left.

To further explore the processes that direct awareness in the hemispheres, Levy, Trevarthen, and Sperry gave split-brain subjects a free choice of which hemisphere to use to control responses in tests. Halves of two different pictures were joined together down the vertical midline to make a double picture called a stimulus chimera. When this is presented to the split-brain patient with the join on the fixation point, information about each half is received in a different hemisphere. The tasks are designed so that in every trial the correct choice may be obtained by using the experience of either the left or right hemisphere. Preference for one half of the chimera depends on one-sided mental strategies that arise in response to the test instructions. With this kind of test, preferred modes of understanding of the hemispheres can be sensitively determined, as well as the cerebral functions that allocate attention between the two hemispheres.

The choices of the commissurotomy patients with chimeric stimuli confirm that thought in words favours the left hemisphere. Single words can be read by the right hemisphere, but the left is always preferred if the meaning of the words must be understood and not just their visual appearance or pattern. Further tests show that the right hemisphere is virtually unable to imagine the sound of a word for an object seen, even a very common one like an 'eye', so it cannot solve a test requiring silent rhyming 'in the head' (for example, 'eye' matches 'pie', 'key' matches 'bee'). It seems as if the habitual, and inherently favoured, dominance of the left hemisphere for speaking is tied in with a one-sided ability to predict how words will sound. The right hemisphere can know the meaning of a word from its sound, but it cannot make a sound image for itself from sight of the word, or from sight of the object the word stands for.

Preference for the right hemisphere in matching things by their appearance becomes strong when meaningless or unanalysable shapes are used, especially if these are not representing familiar objects, with a simple name. An extraordinary superiority of the right hemisphere for knowing a face, especially when it lacks bold distinctive features such as glasses, moustache, hat, or birthmark, relates to a rare consequence of damage to the posterior part of this hemisphere. This inability to recognize even the most familiar faces, called prosopagnosia, can greatly embarrass social life. With split-brain persons and stimuli restricted to the left hemisphere, face recognition is poor and identification is achieved by a laborious check-list of distinctive semantic elements to be memorized and searched for. There is obviously a stark contrast in hemisphere cognitive style, reminiscent of differences described in the way the two hands go about knowing or using objects. In addition to these apparently fixed differences in the organization of hemispheric cognitive structures, commissurotomy patients show a varying activation of the hemispheres under brain-stem control that can favour one or other side independently of task requirements. Sometimes the 'wrong' hemisphere is active in doing a task, and performance suffers. This 'metacontrol' may cause differences in the way normal individuals process cognitive problems; i.e. it may determine differences in mental abilities—for example, making one person skilled at visuo-constructive tasks while another is gifted at verbal rationalizations.

There are still many questions concerning the complementary styles of intelligence and conscious awareness revealed by commissurotomy and about how hemispheric functional states are co-ordinated. Some of the findings blur classical distinctions. Not all linguistic or propositional functions are confined to the left hemisphere, and though the right hemisphere is better at perceiving resemblances between complex forms, the left can perceive and recognize. In neither case is the monopoly of cognitive style complete, and cerebral asymmetry of function is now regarded as a matter of degree. However, as the chimera studies

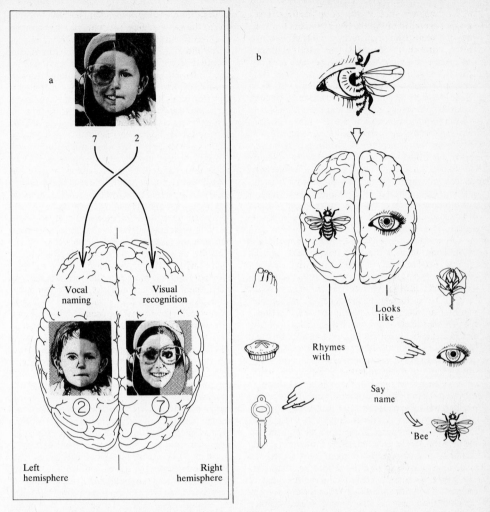

**Fig. 3. a.** Stimulus chimeras, joining left and right halves of different pictures, permit study of preferences in cognitive processes of the hemispheres. The stimuli are flashed in the precise centre of the visual field in a tachistoscope. If asked to say what was seen, the split-brain subject identifies the right half of the chimera, signifying preferential use of the left hemisphere. If pointing to match the picture that looks most like the stimulus, the left half is selected, indicating that the right hemisphere assumes control of this response.

**b.** By varying instructions one can obtain three different kinds of response from one stimulus. Saying the name or pointing silently to a picture of an object with a name that rhymes with that of the stimulus causes the left hemisphere to take charge. Visual matching engages the right hemisphere.

Note that in both these diagrams, the awareness of a half stimulus is shown as completed. Indeed experiments indicate that the subject imagines freely over the midline, presumably because there is no information at variance with imagined parts in the hemisphere doing the imagining.

showed, there are some factors, not necessarily simple in their relationship to conventional psychological tests, but more involved in the strategy by which the brain as a whole allocates mental operations or motivates consciousness, for which left and right hemispheres do have markedly different capacities and preferences. Since the hemispheres of commissurotomy patients become progressively more alike, or less differentiated, by post-surgical learning or other changes compensating for their

separation, they probably can reveal to us only weakened forms of hemisphere specialization.

Eran Zaidel has developed a method for blocking off half of the visual field of one eye of a commissurotomy patient. He attaches to the eye a contact lens which carries a small optical system and a screen. The patient can cast his eye over a test array in a normal way while picking up visual information by only one hemisphere. The subject has to interpret a story or picture or solve puzzles, many involving choice of the one picture from a group that will identify a concept to which he or she has been cued by a preceding stimulus. These tests prove that both hemispheres have elaborate awareness of the meanings of words and pictures. Metaphorical relationships form an important component of consciousness of meaning in both of them. Objects may be linked in awareness by their abstract properties or customary usefulness and social importance as well as by more obvious features. The usual names, colours, temperatures, and many other properties of things may be correctly identified when each thing is represented by a simple black and white picture. The tests of Zaidel and Sperry have shown that both hemispheres of commissurotomy patients have awareness of themselves as persons and a strong sense of the social and political value, or meaning, of pictures or objects.

Comprehension of words, spoken or written, is surprisingly rich in the right hemisphere, and all grammatical classes of words may be comprehended; but its consciousness does fail with relatively difficult, abstract, or rare words. When words are combined in a proposition, the comprehension of the right hemisphere falls drastically. When simplified items of no particular identity, such as plastic chips of differing size, form, and colour, are used as tokens for arbitrary grouping defined by short descriptions (for example, 'Point to a small red circle and a large yellow triangle'), this too proves difficult for the right hemisphere. A token test of this description was discovered by the Italian neuropsychologists Di Renzi and Vignolo to be extremely sensitive to left hemisphere lesions. The linguistic abilities of the right hemisphere thus resemble those of a nursery school child who understands language best when it is fitted into the world of objects, interpersonal acts, and events, all of which sustain the meaning of what is said. Disembedded or context-free propositions lacking interpersonal force require concentration of the mind on categories, critical formulae, or rules for action. These processes of thought may be developed by transformation of inherent human skills for establishing precise identity or harmony of purpose between thinking agents. Such propositions are difficult alike for young children and the disconnected right hemisphere of an adult.

Commissurotomy patients have helped us understand how consciousness, intention, and feelings are generated in activity at different levels of the brain. Thus separated cortices may experience and learn separately, but each may command coherent activity of the whole body. Feelings of dismay, embarrassment, or amusement, generated in one hemisphere by perceptions of threat, or risk, or teasing, invade the brain-stem to cause expressions and *emotions of the whole person, in spite of the operation. Levels of attentiveness and the shifting aim of orientation and purpose are also patterned within brain-stem regions, which can transmit no detailed evidence of experience. The precautions needed to reveal divided awareness after brain bisection emphasize how, in normal active life, information about the world is constantly reflected to all parts of the brain as it and the body engage in changing relations with the external world. It does not appear necessary to imagine that the 'self', which has to maintain a unity, is destroyed when the forebrain commissures are cut, although some of its activities and memories are depleted after the operation.

The evidence on hemispherical differences reveals inherited motive structures for speech and rational thought that have evolved to establish intentional and experiential communion between persons. The brain is adapted to create and maintain human society and culture by two complementary conscious systems. Specialized motives in the two hemispheres generate a dynamic partnership between the intuitive, on the one side, and the analytical or rational, on the other, in the mind of each person. This difference appears to have evolved in connection with the human skills of intermental co-operation and symbolic communication.

Research with normal subjects stimulated by the commissurotomy studies shows that individuals vary greatly in the development of asymmetrical functions in their brains and in the ways the hemispheres are habitually activated. Such diverse factors as sex, age, handedness, education, and special training correlate with psychological and physiological measures of cerebral lateralization and hemispheric activation. The evidence is that human kind is not only very diverse in outside appearance: minds in any race, even in a single family, are inherently different in cognitive bent. It is not hard to perceive advantages of such psychological diversity in the most highly co-operative of beings, in whom mind and the experiences of society and culture become inseparable.     c. t.

Bogen, J. E. (1969). The other side of the brain: II. An appositional mind. *Bulletin of the Los Angeles Neurological Society*, **34**, 135–62.

Levy, J., Trevarthen, C., and Sperry, R. W. (1972). Perception of bilateral chimeric figures following hemispheric deconnexion. *Brain*, **95**, 61–78.

Levy, J. and Trevarthen, C. (1976). Metacontrol of hemispheric function in human split-brain patients. *Journal of Experimental Psychology: Human Perception and Performance*, **2**, 299–312.

Levy, J. and Trevarthen, C. (1977). Perceptual, semantic and phonetic aspects of elementary language processes in split-brain patients. *Brain*, **100**, 105–18.

Sperry, R. W. (1970). Perception in absence of the neocortical commissures. *Research Publications of the Association for Nervous and Mental Diseases*, **48**, 123–38.

Sperry, R. W. (1974). Lateral specialization in the surgically separated hemisphere. In Schmitt, F. O. and Warden, F. G. (eds.), *The Neurosciences: third study program*. Cambridge, Massachusetts.

Sperry, R. W. (1977). Forebrain commissurotomy and conscious awareness. *Journal of Medicine and Philosophy*, **2**, 101–26.

Sperry, R. W., Gazzaniga, M. S., and Bogen, J. E. (1969). Interhemispheric relations: the neocortical commissures; syndromes of hemispheric disconnection. In Vinken, P. J. and Bruyn, G. W. (eds.), *Handbook of Clinical Neurology*, Vol. 4. Amsterdam: North-Holland.

Trevarthen, C. (1974). Analysis of cerebral activities that generate and regulate consciousness in commissurotomy patients. In Dimond, S. J. and Beaumont, J. G. (eds.), *Hemisphere Function in the Human Brain*. London.

Trevarthen, C. (1984). Hemispheric specialization. In Darian-Smith, I. (ed.), *Handbook of Physiology*, Section 1: *The Nervous System*, Vol. III: *Sensory Processes*. Bethesda, Maryland (American Physiological Society).

Zangwill, O. L. (1974). Consciousness and the cerebral hemispheres. In Dimond, S. J. and Beaumont, J. G. (eds.), *Hemisphere Function in the Human Brain*. London.

**SQUINT.** See DIPLOPIA; EYE DEFECTS AND THEIR CORRECTION.

**STEREOSCOPIC VISION.** It is remarkable that the use of the two eyes to provide 'stereoscopic' depth was not appreciated by the Greeks, or indeed at all generally before Charles Wheatstone's invention of the stereoscope in 1832 (published in 1836). Although it was forgotten, and is still not at all well known, the power of the two eyes working together to give three-dimensional perception was appreciated as early as 1677 by a French Capuchin friar, le Père Cherubin of Orleans. (This is described with a drawing of the instrument by Jabez Hogg, 1854.) Wheatstone made pairs of drawings from slightly separated points of view, which he presented one to each eye, by means of a pair of mirrors placed close to the eyes (Fig. 1). Wheatstone realized that each eye has a slightly different image because of its horizontal separation from the other; so that the 'corresponding points' of the images of the two eyes have a greater separation for near objects than for distant ones. These 'stereograms' he found are combined into a single perception—of objects in depth. More convenient optical systems were developed in 1849 by the Scottish physicist David Brewster and stereoscopic photographs became popular in the early days of photography.

More recently, it has been discovered by Bela Julesz that it is not necessary for there to be recognizable objects or line features for stereoscopic fusion and depth. He showed that if a region of one of a stereo pair of otherwise identical random dot patterns is displaced sideways, the region appears to lie in front of (or if reversed to the eyes, behind) the rest of the pattern. It is remarkable that each eye system can discover the corresponding dots, because all the dots are identical and featureless (see VISION: THE EARLY WARNING-SYSTEM). This discovery has led to a wealth of new knowledge about the visual system. For example, it has made it possible to show that the distortions of many well-known *illusions have their origin not at the retina (as had often been thought) but considerably further up the system—at or after the layer of the striate cortex where the signals from the two eyes are combined. This is shown by presenting illusion figures as stereo pairs of random dots, so that neither eye can see the figure or even any line of it; but when the two random dot figures are combined by stereo fusion, then the illusion figures are seen—and they have their normal distortions. The point is that since neither eye alone receives the shapes or contours of the figures, but only meaningless random dots, the origin of the distortion must be at, or after, the neural fusion of the dot patterns in the brain.

Normally stereopsis is important for perceiving random shapes, or objects such as leaves on a tree. It is interesting, however, that some of the 'monocular' depth cues can actually cancel stereoscopic

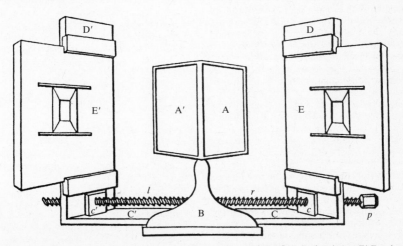

**Fig. 1.** Diagram of Wheatstone's stereoscopic apparatus. Two mirrors at A′,A reflect the drawings at E′,E and produce a 'solid' image when viewed simultaneously from very close range. (From *The Stereoscope*, by Sir David Brewster (1856).)

depth, when pitted against it. Thus a perspective scene viewed in stereo but with the images switched between the eyes (with a pseudoscopic optical system) will generally continue to appear in normal depth—the perspective beating the stereo. Also, stereoscopy will not allow highly unlikely reversals of depth, or correct perception of objects which have unlikely depths—such as the hollow mould of a face. Such a mould will continue to appear as a normal face, though it is hollow, in spite of considerable stereoscopic information when it is viewed from some distance with both eyes.

It is now known that most of the cells in the visual cortex are 'binocularly driven' from the two eyes, and the way in which the signals from the eyes are combined for stereo vision is becoming clear. It is also becoming possible to simulate or produce the equivalent of stereo perception with computer vision (Marr and Poggio, 1976, 1979) though at present this is very much slower than the brain's stereo computing.

See VISUAL SYSTEM: ORGANIZATION.

Hogg, J. (1854). *The Microscope: its history, construction and application*. London.

Julesz, B. (1971). *Foundations of Cyclopean Perception*. Chicago.

Marr, D. and Poggio, T. (1976). Cooperative computation of stereo disparity. *Science*, **194**, 283–7.

Marr, D. and Poggio, T. (1979). A computational theory of human stereo vision. *Proceedings of the Royal Society of London*, **B 204**, 301–28.

Ogle, K. (1950). *Researches in Binocular Vision*.

**STEVENS,** STANLEY SMITH (1906–73). American psychologist, professor of psychophysics at Harvard University, where he spent all his professional career. He is known, above all else, for the power law which relates physical stimulus magnitudes to the numbers assigned to them in magnitude estimation experiments. During the last twenty years of his life he and his many collaborators replicated this experimental result many times over with more than thirty different stimulus attributes. The same power relation applies when stimulus magnitudes are adjusted to match a given number and to match the magnitude of some other attribute (e.g. matching loudness to brightness). Stevens regarded the numbers uttered by his subjects as direct estimates of the magnitude of the sensation experienced, though this has always been a controversial issue (for technical considerations, see QUANTIFYING JUDGEMENTS).

During the Second World War, Stevens was engaged in studying the effects of intense noise in military aircraft, being then director of the psychoacoustic laboratory at Harvard. About that time he conceived his neural quantum theory, the idea that sensory discrimination is limited by the discrete nature of neural conduction. He also edited the 1,400-page compilation *Handbook of Experimental Psychology*, which appeared in 1951. But his most enduring contribution to science will probably prove to be his early work on measurement.

The names he proposed for different kinds of measurement—'nominal', 'ordinal', 'interval', and 'ratio'—have become so universally used that few people are now aware of their origin.

See PSYCHOPHYSICS.                    D. R. J. L.

For a posthumous summary of Stevens's work, see Stevens, S. S. (1975). *Psychophysics*. New York.

**STIMULUS.** Stimuli are patterns of energy received by the senses; they evoke behaviour and are the basis of *perception. Even so, they may not be noticed or experienced, or they may be only part of what we experience and accept as signals or data for behaviour and perception. In particular, *retinal images may be thought of as patterns of energy from the external world; but we do not see them. We see objects, partly as the result of signals from these optical stimuli and partly from our knowledge of what objects are like.

The role of stimuli is rather differently described in various biological and psychological accounts. 'Stimulus–response' theories for behaviour emphasize the importance of received stimuli rather than internal processes—a line of argument most radically worked out in behaviourism (see CONDITIONING). Such an approach, perhaps, had its initial plausibility as a psychological theory from observations of highly predictable tropisms (responses to or away from light, chemical concentrations, etc.) found in many lower organisms. The German-born American physiologist Jacques *Loeb (1859–1924) explained the 'forced movements' in simple animals in terms of the 'tonus hypothesis', namely that the muscular tone on each side of the body is affected by the relative intensity of signals from paired sense organs, especially the eyes, the animal moving towards the side having the strongest muscular tension. This view has been largely abandoned as a theory of tropisms in animals, but a similar explanation *is* accepted for plants as they grow towards the light, or grow upright by geo-tropisms. It is believed that, whereas stimuli can have quite direct effects on plants, their effects on even simple animals are seldom direct, as they are 'read' or interpreted according to the situation and the needs of the animal.

See also PSYCHOPHYSICS.

Loeb, J. (1918). *Forced Movements, Tropisms and Animal Conduct*. Philadelphia.

**STIMULUS-RESPONSE     THEORY.** See CONDITIONING.

**STRABISMUS** (SQUINT). See EYE DEFECTS AND THEIR CORRECTION.

**STRESS.** Why has the problem of stress become a major issue of our time? Can it really be that life conditions in our society are more stressful, more taxing, than those experienced by our ancestors? From a material standpoint the answer to this question is, of course: no. The conditions in contemporary society are less stressful than those that have been experienced by any previous generation. But our age has its own problems, many of them psychological and social in nature; and we do not need to be starved, or cold, or physically exhausted for stress to occur. Life in technologically advanced societies imposes new demands which trigger the same bodily responses that helped our ancestors to survive by making them fit for fight or flight—responses that may be totally inappropriate for coping with the stresses of life today.

Stress may be regarded as a process of transactions in which the resources of the person are matched against the demands of the environment. The individual's appraisal of the importance of the demands are reflected in the bodily resources mobilized to meet them.

**Man as a 'stressometer'.** One of the notions underlying the use of physiological and chemical techniques in human stress research is that the load that a particular environment places on a person can be estimated by measuring the activity of the body's organ systems. Technological advances, together with progress in the biobehavioural and biomedical sciences, have made new methods available for investigating the interplay between mental and physical processes. Much of what was previously the subject of speculation can now be recorded and measured, and as more of what happens in the different bodily organs becomes accessible to measurement, the effects that mental and physical processes have on one another become increasingly clear. We can record changes in heart-rate that accompany changes in the environment. We can show how psychological processes are reflected in the activity of the brain, in cardiovascular functions, in hormonal activity, etc.; and we can see how hormonal changes reflect changes in mood, how blood-pressure rises to challenge, and how the alertness of the brain varies with the flow of impressions transmitted by the sense organs.

Since feelings and *perceptions are reflected in the activity of many of the body's organ systems, individuals can themselves be regarded as 'stressometers', instruments which help to identify factors in the environment that tell hard on their mind and body. The environmental factors may be physical or chemical, such as noise or smell; or social and psychological, such as monotonous work, excessive information flow, or interpersonal conflict.

With the development of chemical techniques that permit the determination of small amounts of hormones and transmitter substances in blood and urine, neuroendocrinology has come to play an increasingly important part in stress research. Two neuroendocrine systems, both of which are controlled by the brain, are of particular interest in the study of stress and coping with stressful situations. One is the sympathetic-adrenal medullary system,

with the secretion of the *catecholamines adrenaline (epinephrine) and noradrenaline (norepinephrine). The other is the pituitary-adrenal cortical system, with the secretion of cortisol. These substances have several important functions: as sensitive indicators of the mismatch between the person and the environment, as regulators of vital bodily functions, and—under some circumstances—as mediators of bodily reactions leading to disease.

What do we know about the environmental conditions that activate these two systems?

**Underload and overload.** Stimulus underload and overload are typical features of modern society, and both of them trigger the adrenal medullary and adrenal cortical response. In order to function adequately, the human brain requires an inflow of impulses from the external environment; but both lack and excess of stimulation threaten the *homeostatic mechanisms by which the organism maintains an adequate degree of *arousal. The optimal level of human functioning is located at the mid-point of a scale ranging between very low and very high levels of stimulus input. At the optimal level, the brain is moderately aroused, the individual's resources are mobilized, and full attention is given to the surroundings; he is emotionally balanced and performs to the best of his abilities. At low levels he tends to be inattentive, easily distracted and bored. Conditions of extreme understimulation, involving both sensory and social deprivation, are accompanied by a state of mental impoverishment with loss of initiative and loss of capacity for involvement. When the brain is over-aroused, on the other hand, the ability to respond selectively to the impinging signals is impaired. Feelings of excitement and tension develop, followed by a gradual fragmentation of thought processes, a loss of ability to integrate the messages into a meaningful whole, impaired judgement, and loss of initiative.

**Helplessness.** Psychological theories of helplessness emphasize the role of learning in the development of active coping strategies. A sense of hopelessness, paired with a reduced motivation to control, is likely to develop when people realize that events and outcomes are independent of their actions. Empirical evidence from many sources, including both animal and human experiments, show that the organism responds differently to conditions characterized by controllability on the one hand, and lack of control on the other. On the whole it is consistent with the view that increased controllability reduces physiological stress responses, such as adrenaline and cortisol secretion, thus presumably decreasing bodily wear and tear.

**Is stress dangerous to health?** There is general agreement that mental stress may increase the risk of ill health and affect the course of both somatic and mental disorders. But the biological mechanisms by which stress translates into disease are still obscure. Relationships exist between stress and diseases such as myocardial infarction, high blood-pressure, gastro-intestinal disorders, asthma, and migraine; however, it is only occasionally that a particular mental factor can be identified as the specific cause of a disease. As a general rule the psychological aspect is merely one thread in a complex fabric in which genetic components, environmental conditions, and learned behaviours are also interwoven.

This lack of a clear picture of the links in the causal chain between stress and disease hampers our efforts to prevent harmful stress responses. However, we know a great deal about the mobilization of stress hormones under conditions of underload and overload, and although it is still not known when such stress responses lead to ill health it is agreed that they should be treated as early warning signals. Moreover, we also know a great deal about how stress that is liable to impair health can be counteracted. Stress responses can be dampened, for instance, by providing opportunities for personal control, which can then serve as buffer, warding off potentially harmful effects of, for example, overload at work.

In short, stress research has already contributed knowledge that can be used to shape the external environment so as to fit human abilities and needs. Such insights are being utilized more and more, particularly in working life, both in the organization of work and in the application of new technology.                                                         M. F.

Frankenhaeuser, M. (1979). Psychoneuroendocrine approaches to the study of emotion as related to stress and coping. In Howe, H. E. and Dienstbier, R. A. (eds.), *Nebraska Symposium on Motivation 1978*. Lincoln, Nebraska.

Frankenhaeuser, M. (1980). Psychobiological aspects of life stress. In Levine, S. and Ursin, H. (eds.), *Coping and Health*. New York.

Frankenhaeuser, M. (1981). Coping with stress at work. *International Journal of Health Services*, **11**, 491–510.

**STROKE** is the third major cause of death in the Western world. It is also the commonest cause of severe physical disability occurring in people living in their own homes. It has major financial implications both for individuals and for nations.

The term 'stroke' is used to describe an acute disturbance of the brain due to an abnormality of blood supply. The onset is usually sudden and, indeed, it is this suddenness which is one of its principal characteristics. The most common initial event is weakness of the arm and leg on one side of the body (hemiplegia). About 15 per cent of 'cases' are accounted for by spontaneous bleeding into the substance of the brain—cerebral haemorrhage—usually the result of rupture of minute aneurysmal weaknesses, on one of the small arteries deep inside the brain. In the remaining 85 per cent, the underlying pathology involves 'infarction' (death of tissue), resulting from partial or complete block-age of an artery, with the resultant cutting-off of arterial blood-supply.

The term 'cerebrovascular disease' is used to describe abnormalities of the arteries in the brain. The pathology of cerebral haemorrhage has been mentioned above. In the majority of cases, however, there is infarction due to arterial blockage. The underlying process involves atheroma, in which there is deposition of fatty substances on the wall of the blood vessel. The three principal results of this process are stenosis (narrowing), occlusion (blockage), and embolism, which involves the formation of a blood clot on the damaged arterial wall; this becomes dislodged and may itself produce blockage of an artery 'further on' in the arterial circulation. Cerebrovascular disease is often associated with degeneration of arteries elsewhere—particularly in the heart (cardiovascular disease).

**Who gets strokes?** The overall incidence (number of new cases each year) of stroke is about 2 per 1,000 persons. About 75 per cent of acute stroke cases occur in people aged 65 or more, but this still leaves 25 per cent occurring in people under 65, many of whom are still working at the time of the stroke. About 35 per cent of patients will die within the first three weeks.

The prevalence (number existing at any one time) of stroke survivors is about 5 per 1,000, about half of whom will be disabled. Thus, in British terms, the average health district of a quarter of a million people will contain about 1,250 who have survived a stroke, about 620 of whom will be disabled. The majority of disabled stroke-survivors will have a paralysed arm and many will be unable to walk normally.

**Can strokes be avoided?** Much attention has been given in recent years to identifying 'risk factors', with a view to setting up programmes of stroke prevention. The major treatable factor is hypertension (high blood pressure). There is now clear evidence that the effective treatment of hypertension can reduce (although not eliminate) the risk of an acute stroke. This places considerable logistical demands on general practitioners and others who have the responsibility of both detecting and treating the condition.

Other risk factors are of less importance and include diabetes, cardiac disease (particularly disorders of the heart valves and of cardiac rhythm), an increased number of red blood cells (raised haematocrit), and an excessive intake of alcohol.

There has been a steady decline in the death rate from cerebrovascular disease in many parts of the world during the last thirty years. The reason for this, however, is unclear.

**The acute phase.** The precise effects of a stroke are determined by a variety of circumstances, including the pathology (haemorrhage or infarction), and the extent and location of the damage. The majority of strokes involve one of the cerebral hemispheres, but a minority (10 per cent) affect the 'brain stem'. The initial insult involves local tissue damage and this is later followed, in many instances, by secondary swelling (oedema). This produces a mass-effect within the cranium which, if sufficiently large, may cause a marked elevation of pressure. This, in turn, may lead to pressure on the vital centres of the brain stem (coning), causing drowsiness, unconsciousness, respiratory paralysis, and ultimately death.

The diagnosis of 'stroke' can, in appropriate instances, be confirmed by a CT (computerized tomography) brain scan (see IMAGES OF THE BRAIN IN ACTION). This test reliably distinguishes between haemorrhage and infarction. In addition, it detects those few instances of brain tumour which masquerade as a stroke.

In most countries, patients with an acute stroke are admitted to hospital. A recent study in the UK (Wade et al., 1985) showed that 75 per cent are admitted within the first 1–2 weeks. None the less, patients *can* be managed at home if the appropriate support services (general practice, physiotherapy, district nursing, etc.) are well developed.

A few patients are suitable for some form of surgery—usually involving the removal of a blood clot within the cranium. There have been attempts to reduce brain oedema by using steroids, mannitol, dextran, and glycerol, but these agents have not been shown to produce consistent benefits. Anticoagulants can be used to prevent intravascular blood clotting, but are rarely of benefit. Lowering of blood pressure in the acute stage of the stroke is rarely indicated. A variety of other drugs are currently being evaluated, but at the moment no specific medication is helpful in the majority of instances.

During the first week, stroke patients require much skilled nursing care with particular attention to swallowing, hydration, and the prevention of pneumonia and pressure sores.

**Assessment of neurological deficits.** The patient usually becomes 'medically stable' within the first ten days. At the end of this time, he or she is likely to be fit enough to start the process of 'rehabilitation'. Most patients will have weakness or paralysis of the arm and leg on one side of the body (a hemiplegia). In many instances, this 'motor' loss is accompanied by impairment of sensation in the limbs. The paralysed limbs require careful positioning, and it is essential to avoid excessive pulling and stretching of the affected joints. A variety of other deficits may occur:

*1. Hemianopia.* A homonymous hemianopia occurs if the visual pathways in the affected hemisphere have been damaged (see VISUAL SYSTEM: ORGANIZATION). If the disturbance is severe, the patient will not see objects on one side. Thus, a patient with a right homonymous hemianopia may not react to his wife and family, if they are sitting at his bedside on his right side. If mobile, he may walk into door-frames and other objects on the right side.

*2. Aphasia* (in this context, the terms *'aphasia' and 'dysphasia' are used synonymously) involves a disturbance of *language* function, and usually results from damage to the left cerebral hemisphere. In its mildest form, it may simply involve the inability to name objects such as a table, clock, or pen. In most instances, however, there is a disturbance of comprehension, and reading is impaired. In the worst cases, the patient has almost complete loss of the ability to comprehend language, and cannot speak, though happily, the problem is rarely so severe.

*3. Visuo-spatial disorders.* Damage to the right cerebral hemisphere often produces disorders of spatial orientation (see SPATIAL CO-ORDINATION OF THE SENSES) and perception. These can be complicated and difficult to understand, but are of enormous importance to those who are caring for the stroke patient. Some patients neglect one side of the body (usually the left), and may even deny the existence of the left arm. Occasionally, the patient's perception of the arm is distorted so that it appears much longer or shorter than normal, or appears to be covered in hair. Patients with a severe disturbance of spatial function may be, for instance, unable to draw symmetrical objects, such as a house, or a clock-face, the left side of the object being usually less well drawn than the right. Such people are frequently unable to dress because they cannot organize their clothes, and may, for instance, try to don a jacket which is inside-out and back-to-front.

A variety of other deficits may be mentioned. *Apraxia involves a defect of motor programming, so that the person is unable to undertake tasks, although there is no paralysis of the affected part. Thus, the person may be unable to stick out his tongue when asked to do so, although he has no difficulty with licking his lips involuntarily. A patient with visual *agnosia may be unable to recognize common objects, such as a pen or a torch, although his eyesight is satisfactory. The range of scope of cerebral disorders resulting from a stroke is large; their recognition, quantification, and management are discussed in detail in Wade et al. (1985).

Patients with an acute stroke usually remain in hospital for 4–6 weeks and are then allowed home. Their rehabilitation involves physical therapy, designed to help the patient regain lost functions, and to avoid unnecessary complications such as stiff and immobile joints, and fractures (which are often due to falling, associated with premature attempts at walking).

**How much recovery will occur?** There is now considerable literature on the subject of recovery after stroke (for example, Skilbeck et al., 1983, and Barnett et al., 1986). The three adverse factors occurring in the first few days are unconsciousness, urinary incontinence, and deviation of the eyes to one side. Only 5–10 per cent of patients who are unconscious in the first week will survive, and those that do survive will usually be left very severely disabled.

About 75 per cent of disabled stroke survivors learn to walk again, though only about 20 per cent can walk at a normal speed. Many cannot, for example, get to the shops or pub. Only 15 per cent of those with a paralysed arm eventually regain normal arm function. Dysphasic patients may be expected to make about a 25 per cent improvement between three weeks and six months. In general, the amount of recovery is largely dependent upon the severity of the initial deficit: those who are severely disabled initially will usually remain with a severe permanent disability, although some recovery usually occurs; and similarly, those with a mild initial deficit may eventually make a full recovery.

**Long-term adjustment.** We have already indicated that many stroke survivors never make a full recovery. These unfortunate people are faced with trying to rebuild their lives. A few of the younger patients return to work, but most do not. Some stroke patients learn to drive again, often using a car with modified hand-controls. Many can enjoy everyday activities such as shopping, social visiting, and swimming. A full and worthwhile life is regarded as being the goal of rehabilitation.

Depression is present in about one-third of patients, though they may respond to appropriate treatment with drugs or counselling. Furthermore, the strain on the spouse can be very considerable, and depression and chronic unhappiness on their part are, again, common.

**The future.** There is increasing interest in the problem of cerebrovascular disease. Future research is likely to concentrate on prevention (including, particularly, ways of detecting symptomless hypertension), the development of techniques to reduce brain swelling in the acute phase, and the trial of different methods of encouraging recovery in the damaged *nervous system. Increasing attention is being given to helping stroke survivors rebuild their lives, and this is being done partly by a national network of voluntary Stroke Clubs which have been pioneered in Britain, for instance, by the Chest, Heart, and Stroke Association.

Stroke and its manifestations are subjects of great scientific interest. The present position has been dealt with extensively by Barnett et al. (1986). Until recently, in Britain the amount of money spent on research into the subject was extremely small compared with the sums devoted, for instance, to cancer and heart disease. However, there is now an increasing awareness of the problems of cerebrovascular disease, and it is to be hoped that in the years to come we shall see a much increased research effort.                R. L. H.

Barnett, H. J. N., Stein, B. M., and Mohr, J. P. (1986). *Stroke: Pathophysiology, Diagnosis and Management.* Edinburgh.

Skilbeck, C. E., Wade, D. T., Langton Hewer, R., and Wood, V. A. (1983). Recovery after Stroke. *Journal of Neurology, Neurosurgery, and Psychiatry,* **46**, 5–8.

Wade, D. T., Langton Hewer, R., Skilbeck, C. E., Bainton, D., and Burns-Cox, C. (1985). Controlled Trial of a Home-Care Service for Acute Stroke Patients. *Lancet,* Feb. 9, 323–6.

Wade, D. T., Langton Hewer, R., Skilbeck, C. E., and David, R. M. (1986). *Stroke: A Critical Approach to Diagnosis, Treatment, and Management.* London.

**STUMPF,** CARL (1848–1936). German psychologist, born in Wiesenfeld and educated in the University of Würzburg, where he was strongly influenced by Franz *Brentano. After studying with R. H. Lotze (1817–81) at Göttingen, he turned towards psychology, in particular the psychology of tone and music, which, since he was a dedicated musician, remained a lifelong interest. Thereafter he held a number of important academic posts, culminating in the chair of psychology at Berlin, which he held until 1921, when he was succeeded by Wolfgang *Köhler. Among Stumpf's many distinguished students were E. G. *Husserl, the founder of modern phenomenology. Stumpf's best-known work is his *Tonpsychologie* (two vols.; 1883, 1890).                O. L. Z.

**SUBJECTIVE COLOURS.** See BENHAM'S TOP.

**SUBJECTIVE FIGURES.** See ILLUSORY FIGURES.

**SUBLIMATION** is the term used in *psychoanalysis for the defence mechanism by which the energy derived from an instinct when it is denied gratification is displaced into a more socially acceptable interest or activity. Aggressive impulses are said to have been sublimated when they are expressed in competitive sports. Dancing may represent the sublimation of sexual impulses.

D. R. D.

**SUBLIMINAL PERCEPTION.** Few hypotheses in the behavioural sciences have occasioned so much controversy as the suggestion that people may be affected by external stimuli of which they remain wholly unaware. This notion of *perception without awareness, evidently taken for granted by such philosophers as Democritus, *Socrates, *Aristotle, and *Leibniz but still strenuously resisted by some academic psychologists, concerns a unique and non-commonsensical relationship between brain, *consciousness, and behaviour.

As depicted in Fig. 1, it implies that the brain processes underlying conscious experience differ from those that mediate between incoming stimuli and outgoing responses. It implies that information may be transmitted through the organism without

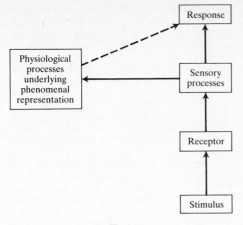

**Fig. 1.**

ever achieving conscious representation. Three sorts of evidence support this view: that based upon subjective experience, that stemming from neurophysiological studies, and, most specifically, that relying upon the data from behavioural research on subliminal perception. Let us consider these in order of specificity.

The occurrence of *dreams and *hallucinations unrelated to ongoing external stimuli attests to the fact that conscious perceptual experience depends upon brain processes that may operate independently of those subserving the receipt of information from the external world. Conversely, in *skilled behaviour, in situations involving divided attention, in *somnambulism, and in many of the body's involuntary regulatory responses to changes in external stimulation, information may be received, processed, and initiate responses without conscious registration. Taken together these observations suggest that consciousness and information transmission depend upon different systems which may, under certain circumstances, operate independently.

Since 1948 the existence of these two systems, a *sine qua non* of subliminal perception, has been confirmed by neurophysiological research (see Moruzzi and Magoun, 1949; Samuels, 1959; and Dixon, 1971 and 1981). Whereas the receipt and onward transmission of sensory information, initiated by external stimuli, depends upon the classical sensory pathways linking peripheral receptors with their cortical projections, *awareness* of this sensory traffic—perceptual experience—relies upon sufficient contribution from the ascending fibres of the reticular activating system, that dense network of cells which arises in the brain stem and then spreads upwards and outwards to infiltrate the cortex. If the reticular system is blocked by surgery or drugs, the arrival of sensory information at the cortex still occurs but the owner of the cortex remains oblivious of the fact! This finding, of considerable significance for proponents of subliminal

perception, accords with data from research by Libet and his colleagues (1967). Recording from the exposed brains of fully conscious human subjects, they were able to detect electrical potentials initiated by tactile stimuli of which their subjects remained totally unaware. *Pari passu* with intensifying the external stimulus, the recorded waveform became more complex and the subjects reported, 'I can feel something.' It seems reasonable to assume that the additions to the waveform reflected those contributions from the reticular system upon which consciousness depends.

In a subsequent experiment it was found that the amplitude of an electrical response, recorded from the visual receiving area and initiated by a flash of light to one eye, could be reduced by subliminal presentation of an emotional word to the other eye. Since this effect did not occur for emotionally neutral words, we must assume that the brain could analyse and respond to the meaning of words of whose presence the recipient remained unaware. Yet other studies (Dixon, 1971 and 1981) have shown, by its electrical response, that the human brain will respond to the meaning of words presented to the ears during sleep. It is interesting to note that even in the deepest sleep, and without awakening the subject, such words may also evoke dreams that are relevant to their meaning.

The researches involving human brain responses to subliminal stimuli have their counterpart in studies of lower animals. Thus it has been shown that a monkey's recognition threshold for a meaningful pattern may be significantly altered by direct electrical stimulation of the animal's reticular system. It has also been found that even the surgically isolated forebrain of a cat will respond to a previously learned pattern when this is presented to the preparation's one remaining eye. Since what is left of the animal in this experiment could hardly be capable of consciousness, this finding illustrates a simple and direct instance of subliminal perception.

One of the most extensively researched examples of subliminal perception occurs in connection with the fact that the awareness threshold for threatening words or pictures may be significantly higher or lower than that for more neutral material. Experiments which involved the simultaneous recording of EEGs (brain rhythms—see ELECTROENCEPHALOGRAPHY), heart-rate, and perceptual thresholds suggest that, prior to awareness of a visual stimulus which is gradually increasing in brightness, the brain may analyse the latter's meaning and, as a result, modify its own level of arousal to hasten or retard awareness of the information that it carries.

That the brain monitors and analyses subliminal stimuli, receives support from many comparable investigations. Thus, emotional words, presented below threshold to the eye, have been found to change auditory sensitivity, and vice versa. By the same token, during binocular rivalry, in which the subject perceives either with the left eye or with the right but never with the two together, the introduction of a subliminal stimulus to the 'blind' eye produces immediate transfer of perception to that side. Such a mechanism which automatically switches into consciousness a stimulus array that has changed (i.e. one that constitutes a potentially important *new* stimulus) has obvious survival value.

It can be argued that a capacity for subliminal perception came about with the evolution of attentional mechanisms. Since the span of consciousness is severely restricted, selective processes evolved whereby only a limited proportion of available sensory information could be admitted to consciousness. Subliminal stimuli constitute some part of the remainder—stimuli which, though insufficiently strong or important to warrant entry into consciousness, may nevertheless be received, monitored, and reacted to. A number of recent pieces of research attest to this view. In one (Corteen and Wood, 1972), people were asked to report a stream of prose presented to one ear while words of which they remained unaware were presented to the other ear. It was found that those 'subliminal' words (on the unattended-to ear), which had previously been associated with electric shock, produced an emotional response (i.e. a change in skin resistance due to sweating) without interfering with the attentional task of 'shadowing' prose on the other ear. In another experiment (Henley and Dixon, 1974) imagery evoked by music presented to one ear, above the conscious threshold, was shaped by subliminal words to the other ear. Considered together, these two sets of data suggest that, at a preconscious level of processing, the brain can 'decide' whether or not information on a subsidiary or unattended-to channel should be kept isolated from, or used to, facilitate responses evoked by material to which the recipient is devoting his conscious attention.

That a subliminal stimulus can bypass the moderating, rationalizing effects of consciousness has given rise to a number of useful applications of stimulation below awareness. These include the investigating of processes underlying such psychiatric disorders as *anorexia nervosa and *schizophrenia. Perhaps the most clearly useful application to date has been in the selection of pilots for the Royal Swedish Air Force. In the Defence Mechanism Test (Kragh, 1962a & b) the candidate for a flying career has to describe what he sees when flashed a composite picture, consisting of a central human figure which is flanked by a subliminal threatening male face. Numerous applications of this test have shown that those candidates whose responses show characteristic distortions as a result of the subliminal threat are likely to make accident-prone pilots. By using this test to eliminate undesirable trainees, the Air Force has succeeded in making a significant saving in lives and aircraft.

Despite the very great weight of evidence from many disciplines, there are still those who cannot bring themselves to accept the reality of subliminal perception. In the writer's opinion this carefully sustained prejudice is itself a psychological defence against the threat of possible manipulation which is implied by subliminal effects. There is the suggestion here of an unwarranted equation of consciousness with such nebulous properties of mind as will, self-control, and conscience. Evidence of many kinds, including that from studies of behaviour under hypnosis, suggests that this particular conceit is, to say the least, mistaken.

Besides being used in a diagnostic capacity, subliminal stimulation has now been employed in a therapeutic context. For example, by reducing anxiety through the subliminal presentation of reassuring messages it has been found possible to reduce neurotic overeating in cases of obesity (Silverman et al., 1978), and improve performance at mathematics (Ariam, 1979). Other techniques involving stimulation below the conscious threshold have proved useful in the treatment of phobias (Tyrer et al., 1978).

From the evidence to date, it seems that all the sensory modalities shown in Fig. 2 have a subliminal range within which excitation can occur without conscious representation. Of particular interest in this connection is the finding (Cowley et al., 1977; Kirk-Smith et al., 1978) that even subliminal olfactory stimuli—e.g. pheromones—may have a significant effect. Even though unable consciously to detect the smell of female pheromones, their inhalation by male subjects made the latter perceive photographs of women as more attractive than they would otherwise have been.

The subliminal range for each modality is still not clear but probably depends upon the relative importance, from a survival point of view, of the modality in question and the extent to which its response system can function adequately without the aid of consciousness. Thus, while *pain might be expected to have a very short range (i.e. it would be important to be immediately aware of noxious stimuli) the interoceptive senses (i.e. those concerned with internal 'automatic' bodily responses) remain almost entirely subliminal (as indeed we know they are).

Hardly less interesting than the phenomena of subliminal perception has been the resistance to

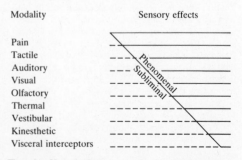

| Modality | Sensory effects |
|---|---|
| Pain | |
| Tactile | |
| Auditory | Phenomenal |
| Visual | Subliminal |
| Olfactory | |
| Thermal | |
| Vestibular | |
| Kinesthetic | |
| Visceral interceptors | |

**Fig. 2.** Hypothetical extents of subliminal and phenomenal effects for different sensory modalities.

accepting its validity. Since the whole idea of being influenced by things of which one is unaware is repugnant to some people—presumably because it seems to threaten notions of free will and personal autonomy—various arguments have been put forward to discredit demonstrations of the phenomenon. One of the favourites has been to view subliminal perception as merely a watered down version of normal conscious perception. According to this argument, so-called subliminal effects have been explained as no more than responses to consciously perceived fragments of the stimulus array. However, a recent study by Groeger (1984) invalidates this suggestion. Subjects were asked to choose either the word 'SMUG' or the word 'COSY' as a completion for the mutilated sentence 'She looked . . . in her new fur coat'. It was found that if they received a liminal (i.e. barely audible) presentation of the word 'SNUG' they chose 'SMUG' as their completion. But if the same cue was given at a *subliminal* level they preferred the completion 'COSY'. In other words, the subliminal response resulted from unconscious semantic analysis while responses to structural features occurred only at or about the threshold of awareness.

See also ATTENTION.                    N. F. D.

Ariam, S. (1979). 'The effects of subliminal symbiotic stimuli in Hebrew on academic performance of Israeli High School Students.' (Unpublished PhD Diss., New York University.)

Corteen, R. S. and Wood, B. (1972). Autonomic responses to shock associated words. *Journal of Experimental Psychology*, **94**, 308–13.

Cowley, J. J., Johnson, A. L., and Brooksbank, B. W. L., 1977. The effect of two odorous compounds on performance in an assessment of people test. *Psychoneuroendocrinol*, **2**, 159–72.

Dixon, N. F. (1971). *Subliminal Perception: the nature of a controversy*. London.

Dixon, N. F. (1981). *Preconscious processing*. Chichester.

Groeger, J. A. (1984). *Preconscious influences on language production*. (PhD Thesis) Belfast.

Henley, S. H. A. and Dixon, N. F. (1974). Laterality differences in the effect of incidental stimuli upon evoked imagery. *British Journal of Psychology*, **65(4)**, 529–36.

Kragh, U. (1962a). Precognitive defense organisation with threatening and non-threatening peripheral stimuli. *Scandinavian Journal of Psychology*, **3**, 65–8.

Kragh, U. (1962b). Predictions of success of Danish attack divers by the Defence mechanism test. *Perceptual and Motor Skills*, **15**, 103–6.

Kirk-Smith, M., Booth, D. A., Carroll, D., and Davies, P. (1978). Human social attitudes affected by Androstenol, Res. Commun. Psychol. *Psychiat. Behav.*, **3**, 379–84.

Libet, B., Alberts, W. W., Wright, E. W., and Feinstein, B. (1967). Responses of human somato-sensory cortex to stimuli below the threshold for conscious sensation. *Science*, **158 (no. 3808)**, 1,597–1,600.

Moruzzi, S. and Magoun, H. W. (1949). Brainstem reticular formation and activation of the EEG. *Electroencephalography and Clinical Neurophysiology*, **1**, 455–73.

Samuels, I. (1959). Reticular mechanisms and behaviour. *Psychology Bulletin*, **56**, 1–25.

Silverman, L. H. (1975). An experimental method for the study of unconscious conflict—a progress report. *British Journal of Medical Psychology*, **48**, 291–8.

Silverman, L. H., Martin, A., Ungaro, R., and Mendelsohn, E. (1978). Effect of subliminal stimulation of symbiotic fantasies on behaviour modification treatment of obesity. *Journal of Consultative Clinical Psychology*, **46(3)**, 432–41.

Tyrer, P., Lee, I., and Horn, P. (1978). Treatment of agoraphobia by subliminal and supraliminal exposure to phobic cine film. *The Lancet*, 18 Feb. 1978, 358–60.

**SUBNORMALITY** and severe subnormality are legal terms which were defined in the UK Mental Health Act of 1959. In the Mental Health Act of 1983 they have been replaced by the words 'mental impairment' and 'severe mental impairment' which are defined as follows. Mental impairment means a state of arrested or incomplete development of mind (not amounting to severe impairment) which includes significant impairment of intelligence and social functioning, and is associated with abnormally aggressive or seriously irresponsible conduct. Severe mental impairment means a state of arrested or incomplete development of mind which includes severe impairment of intelligence and social functioning and is associated with abnormally aggressive or seriously irresponsible conduct.

Incompleteness of the development of the mind has been observed for a very long time, and has been recognized in English law since 1325, whereas subnormality of intelligence is a concept which depends on the meaning given to the word intelligence by Alfred *Binet, in 1909, i.e. ability to learn. Thus the inclusion of the concept of a minimum level of intelligence in the Act of 1959 was meant to complement and limit the definition of subnormality according to social incompetence. Before 1959 social incompetence was the prime definition of subnormality. In addition, in medieval times the legal definition included the idea of incurability, and was distinguished from mental illness in so far as the 'natural fool' was supposed to be incurable, whereas the lunatic was recognized as a person who might perhaps recover from his illness. These legal definitions were of course related to the protection of the property of those involved. They were also the basis for decisions made on the criminal responsibility of persons accused of serious offences.

Subnormality today is regarded as a condition which, when associated with very low intelligence—for example, below IQ 55 or IQ 50—will have a relatively permanent character, whereas when associated with a level of intelligence between 55 and 70 will less frequently be combined with permanent social incompetence. In fact some authors have claimed that in mild subnormality of this kind IQ levels can be considerably increased by early and continuous educational attention. Whether this can be said with certainty or not, a great deal of research has shown that above IQ 55 ability to survive in the community is not very closely related to intelligence. Below this IQ level a relatively small proportion of people will be found to be socially independent, possibly between 10 and 20 per cent.

**The prevalence of subnormality.** At the beginning of the twentieth century, the prevalence of subnormality was thought to be increasing, because the views of Francis *Galton (*Hereditary Genius*, 1869) and Karl Pearson were uncritically applied to the concept of intelligence. It was supposed, therefore, that because of differential fertility more children would be born to those with less intellectual endowment and that, as a result, the average level of intelligence would decline. Few authorities, with the exception of L. S. *Penrose, disagreed with this view, though today few would agree with it. As a result of later studies, the prevalence of severe subnormality is now better understood and we know more about the intelligence level of the children of the mildly subnormal. If we were to define the prevalence of subnormality solely in terms of the level of intelligence, and if all below IQ 70 were assumed to be subnormal, then, further assuming distribution according to Karl Pearson's 'normal' curve, 2·28 per cent of the population would be expected to be subnormal. The great majority of these cases would be between IQs 70 and 55, say 2·14 per cent of the total population. The remaining 0·14 per cent (67,200 in England and Wales) would have IQs in the range of severe subnormality, i.e. lower than IQ 55. When investigations were made, however, fairly firm figures began to emerge for the severely subnormal. These figures were 3·88 per thousand (E. O. Lewis), 3·45 per thousand (N. Goodman and J. Tizard), for age ranges 7 to 14 years, and 3·75 per thousand (A. Kushlick) for the 15 to 19 age range. Obviously the actual findings, which for a population of 48 million people would yield a total prevalence of approximately 180,000 severely subnormal cases on the basis of Kushlick's figures, very much exceed the number which would be expected if the definition were based on intelligence level and the normal curve. The difference was accounted for long ago by Pearson and G. A. Jaederholm (*On the Continuity of Mental Defect*, 1914), the excess of severely subnormal subjects being assumed to be due to the pathological conditions so frequently found at this IQ level.

If we turn our attention to the prevalence of the subnormal as distinct from the severely subnormal we find that, between IQ 70 and 55, 21·4 persons per thousand would be predicted on the basis of the normal curve of IQ, which for England and Wales would give an estimate of approximately 1,027,000 cases. In point of fact, the estimates for the mildly subnormal in England have ranged from 1·39 per thousand to 6·73 per thousand. An intervening figure, that obtained by Kushlick in 1961 in Salford, was for an estimate of 2·60 per thousand. This figure yields a prevalence rate for England and Wales of 124,000 cases. In this instance the discrepancy is in the opposite direction and is easily explained by the fact that the mildly subnormal very often survive in the community despite their relatively low intelligence. As a result they do not attract the attention of the available services, and the actual prevalence rate is found to be much below that which might be expected on the basis of intelligence alone. In this particular group, as was initially pointed out by Penrose (1949), the prevalence is most marked during school years because of the special scholastic demands made at that time. A number of studies since W. R. Baller's initial research in 1936 have shown that, on follow-up, the mildly subnormal are frequently shown to have succeeded very well in social and occupational situations. They often marry and conduct their own businesses, show stability in their job experience, and in normally favourable social circumstances do not fall foul of the law in a serious way or come to represent a social problem in their later years. A variety of theories possibly explaining the relative success of the adult subnormal have been reviewed by Clarke and Clarke (1974).

While the tendency during the early years of the century was to consider that the prevalence of mental subnormality was increasing, N. Goodman and J. Tizard have argued, on the basis of their survey and by comparison with Lewis's earlier survey, that perhaps it is declining so far as the severely subnormal are concerned. The argument rests on two opposite trends, one being the decrease in infant mortality in England and Wales between 1900 and 1959 and the resulting possibility of a decrease in birth injuries, and the other being the likelihood that better birth conditions might lead not only to increasing survival of the fit but also to increasing survival of the unfit. Goodman and Tizard argue that since many of the severely subnormal, perhaps as many as 25 per cent, suffer from *Down's syndrome (mongolism), and since this group now survive longer than hitherto, an increasing number of the severely subnormal might be Down's syndrome cases. Down's syndrome is of genetic origin and perhaps little influenced by external factors except maternal age. If this were so, then it is possible that the number of the severely subnormal who were not Down's syndrome cases either remained the same or declined slightly between the Lewis survey in 1929 and the Goodman and Tizard survey in 1962.

Obviously, so far as the initial fears that gave rise to the UK Mental Deficiency Act of 1913 are concerned, a decline in national intelligence is no longer thought probable by those who are well informed about the prevalence of mental deficiency. This does not mean, of course, that there is no genetic element contributing to prevalence of subnormality. Perhaps today fewer severely subnormal children are being born, and fewer mildly subnormal adults need care; but of course those severely subnormal children who are born tend to live longer. B. W. Richards found that from 1949 there had been a steady trend towards ageing in the population in a mental deficiency hospital in Surrey. There was an especially great increase in the number and mean age of residents with Down's syndrome, even though the mean age of the Down's syndrome patients was lower than that of their comparable non-Down's syndrome fellow patients. B. Kirman (in Kirman and Bicknell, 1975, p. 57) presented a table showing the trend of ages in National Health Service hospitals between 1954 and 1969. The main feature of this table is the relative increase in the number of patients aged over 55 as compared with those aged below 14. There is, however, some evidence that Down's syndrome cases continue to die somewhat earlier than non-Down's syndrome cases of the same IQ level. It is interesting to note that practically all Down's syndrome patients over 35 years of age show the same pathological changes in their brains as are seen in the brains of subjects who develop the clinical features of senile *dementia of the Alzheimer type.

Clearly, therefore, the tendency is for fewer severely subnormal children to be born but for more of those who are born to survive over longer periods, and for fewer of the mildly subnormal to come to the notice of social aid services. These trends are probably matched by similar trends in the normal population, and it might be said that the subnormal, like the normal, are profiting from the general increase in the standard of living as well as from the improvement in medical care, especially in relation to birth conditions, since the beginning of the century.

For discussion of the causes of subnormality, and the care of mentally handicapped adults and children, see MENTAL HANDICAP.    N. O'C.

Clarke, A. M. and Clarke, A. D. B. (eds.) (1974). *Mental Deficiency: the changing outlook*. London.
Kirman, B. and Bicknell, J. (1975). *Mental Handicap*. Edinburgh.
Penrose, L. S. (1949). *The Biology of Mental Defect*. London.

**SUFISM.** Sufi individuals and groups became publicly known in Arabia in the eighth century. As mystics, esteemed for religious piety, they were able to exercise the role of mentors of devotion and conduct in the theocratic community of Islam. Observers have been attempting, for a thousand years, to categorize them, but conventional assessment has proved extremely difficult. Accepting Muhammad the Prophet as the originator of the current phase of Sufi manifestation, they also regard Jesus as a Sufi: while one of the greatest of all Sufis, Jalaluddin *Rumi, openly declared that many non-Muslims understood Sufism better than ordinary Muslims. *Al-Ghazzali, one of the foremost Sufis, is credited with having saved Islamic thought from dissolution by Greek philosophy. From his time (d. 1111) all Islamic thought may be regarded as being indebted to Sufism. Like all gnostic systems, Sufism regards conduct as secondary, and divine illumination primary. Sufi masters are therefore those who, having experienced the 'path' to such cognition, are able to guide others along it and also to relate it to terrestrial social needs.

There are three distinct ways in which assessment of this powerful and extraordinary movement has been approached. (i) The largely Western, scholarly approach, which has sought to analyse literature, seek origins, and identify affinities. The multiplicity of resemblances between Sufi thought and practices and those of other systems has led many of the followers of this technique to 'proof by selected instances'. According to which expert one reads, therefore, one will find Sufism attributed to Christian, Jewish, Buddhist, animist, or other origins. A listing of the proofs invoked by such students shows that they cancel one another out. (ii) The conclusions reached by Muslim non-Sufis, mainly in the East, over the centuries. Nasrollah Fatemi (1976) provides a summary:

To some it denotes humanitarianism, tolerance, harmony . . . love of mankind and the attempt to achieve spiritual fellowship. To a few, the Sufis are dreamers, rebels and meddlers who interfere with the serious rituals of the church and the business of the state. To others, they are the conscience of society and the antennae of the community, who exhibit in their activities a pronounced concern for humanity [and] the values that lie at the core of society, and who accuse the civil and religious authorities of lacking social conscience. The Sufis felt the need to resist the corrupt, tyrannical and arrogant, to ridicule the cruel rich and merciless might, to exalt the low and to help the helpless.

(iii) The assertions made by the Sufis themselves about what they are and what they do and why they do it.

Although it cannot be expected that the Sufis' contentions about themselves will be accepted by those with different assumptions, it can be seen that the Sufi rationale provides a better explanation than has been offered heretofore by members of the outside observing groups. The Sufis say that they have no history, because Sufism is experience, not recording information. Their goal is attaining knowledge of a higher reality, of which familiar religion is a lower level: that of social and psychological balance. When the goal is attained, the Sufi acquires not only knowledge of the divine (and of extra-dimensional reality) but also functions associated with it which are not to be confused with repetitious observance or emotional stimulus. Those alone who have reached this stage may properly be called 'Sufis'. Anyone else is 'on the Path', or a 'dervish', roughly equivalent to a monk or friar. It is this belief that gnosis commands action of all kinds that explains, according to the Sufis, why they are found in so many branches of literature, philosophy, science, administration, and so on. Their instrumental intervention is directed from beyond conventional limitations and, the doctrine continues, cannot be imprisoned in repetitious activity. Although this assertion is not necessarily acceptable to contemporary Western workers, the rich writings of the Sufis have in recent years interested psychologists and sociologists. Sufism itself was 'named' by August Thöluck, in his *Ssufismus, sive Theosophia Persarum Pantheistica*, published in Berlin in 1821. Before that it was known as Islamic mysticism and by a number of other names, such as Divine Wisdom (extracted by letter–number substitution cipher from the Arabic).

Sufi 'orders' came into being much later than teachers and schools; and they clearly resemble traditional orders in, for example, Christianity. The orders are therefore regarded as secondary, and few, if any, of their putative founders, famous Sufi masters, were really connected with their establishment. Their practices are mostly of a devotional autohypnotic nature, and produce conditioned states which are much at variance with essential Sufi theory relating to the need for individual and specific teaching. Most groups which employ the name Sufi in the Middle and Far East and Africa are in fact Islamic prayer-congregations of the enthusiast type. Many closely resemble formal churches of whatever religion, and hence have an attraction for people brought up in parallel systems.

The Sufis enjoy, on the whole, a high reputation in the East, and have been extensively appreciated by non-Islamic religionists and scholars, including Western mystics. The numerous extra-sensory manifestations which have always been associated with Sufi activity are regarded by the Sufis themselves as undesirable and preliminary (at best) phases; although they continue to excite those who attempt to study such things. At the present time, self-deluded and spurious 'Sufis' abound, in the East and West, as in the case of all enterprises of this nature.                                              I. S.

Burke, O. M. (1973). *Among the Dervishes*. London and New York.

Eastwick, E. B. (1974). *The Rose-Garden of Sheikh Muslihu'd-Din Sadi of Shiraz*. London and New York.

Fatemi, N. S. (1976). *Sufism*. South Brunswick, New York and London.

Lewin, L. (ed.) (1976). *The Elephant in the Dark*. London and New York.

Shah, I. (1968, 1971). *The Way of the Sufi*. London and New York.

Shushtery, A. M. A. (1966). *Outlines of Islamic Culture*. Lahore.

Subhan, J. A. (1938). *Sufism: its saints and shrines*. Lucknow.

Whinfield, E. H. (trans., 1975). *Teachings of Rumi*. London and New York.

Williams, L. F. R. (ed.) (1973). *Sufi Studies: East and West*. London and New York.

**SUICIDAL BEHAVIOUR.** Man's ability to kill himself has been a source of fascination since the beginning of human society. Philosophers from Marcus Aurelius and Seneca to Camus, writers (especially poets) from Virgil to Sylvia Plath, and sociologists from the beginning of the nineteenth century to the present day, have all contributed voluminously to its study. This widespread preoccupation has, if anything, obstructed the scientific investigation of suicide in two distinct ways. Firstly, the long-standing theological taboo against suicide, still discernible in many legal phrases and public attitudes, has tended to make the rational consideration of the subject difficult. Secondly, speculation on the theme has tended to spread over all forms of human activity which are potentially harmful or self-defeating, with a consequence that there is remarkably little that people can do which has not been interpreted as concealing some measure of suicidal intent. Clearly for scientific purposes it is necessary to use a much more precise definition.

In the first place, attention is confined to acts in which self-destruction is the essential component and not simply a hazard incurred in the course of pursuing another goal. Thus the religious martyr, or the soldier who has volunteered for a dangerous mission during which he dies, are not usually considered as suicides. Secondly, suicide is taken to refer to the behaviour of an individual and not a group, so that expressions such as a suicidal policy being pursued by a nation are to be understood as metaphorical. And lastly, present-day usage restricts the term to human beings; the notorious lemmings are firmly excluded.

Though often difficult to assess, intention thus becomes a central issue in categorizing deaths in which the deceased was an active agent. The law in most European countries requires clear demonstration not only that an individual caused his own death, but that he fully intended to do so. Psychiatrists and behavioural scientists would in general assert that this criterion is too narrow and that assessment should be made on the balance of probabilities, recognizing that a certain number of deaths will be unclassifiable. The important practical point is that official statistics tend markedly to underestimate the incidence of suicide according to psychiatric criteria. Additional reasons for under-reporting are a desire by families and general practitioners to conceal suicidal deaths in some cases, and a reluctance of coroners to reach the decision in an open court for fear of causing offence or having their verdicts challenged in, or reversed by, a higher court. Various studies suggest that the order of magnitude of under-reporting is in the region of between 50 and 100 per cent. Nevertheless, official statistics have been widely used and have proved valuable for certain types of enquiry. (For a fuller discussion of the validity of statistics, see SUICIDE: INTERNATIONAL STATISTICS.)

A great deal of literature exists on the epidemiology of suicide. Virtually throughout the world the rate for men exceeds that for women, with the former tending to use more violent methods such as shooting or jumping from heights, and the latter more passive procedures such as taking an excess of drugs. However, these differences are rapidly disappearing in most European countries. Where the rate for males is falling, that for females tends to remain stationary or fall more slowly; conversely, where the rate for males is increasing, that for females increases even more rapidly. Either way the net effect is towards equality, often interpreted in a rather vague way as reflecting the tendency in recent decades for the social roles of the two sexes to become more similar.

The effects of age are complex and interact with those of sex. In the United Kingdom the rates for males rise linearly with age, though in most developed countries, the curve resembles an inverted U, with the peak in the late fifties or sixties. For women, both in the United Kingdom and elsewhere, this latter pattern has always been the one most commonly reported. In general, suicide is very much a phenomenon of later life, suggesting that Shakespeare was correct in asserting that 'men have died . . . and worms have eaten them, but not for love'. Furthermore, old age is often accompanied by painful illness and chronic impairment of health. Such misfortunes may well precipitate a state of severe depression, when suicidal thoughts and acts commonly occur.

But what is currently true for Europe is not necessarily true for all times at all places. In Japan before the Second World War, for example, there was a distinct peak in the suicide rates for people in their late twenties and early thirties, which then fell away before the rate increased again among the elderly. Commentators ascribed this early peak to the complex and often contradictory social obligations which befell young married Japanese *vis-à-vis* their respective families. With the Americanization of Japan following the war, this early age peak virtually disappeared, and the general shape of the curve now approximates that of the United States.

In the United Kingdom suicide became increasingly common from 1945 until the early 1960s. There then followed a decline in the rates for all age–sex groups, entirely attributable to the progressive elimination of carbon monoxide from domestic gas, and the virtual disappearance of suicide by this method. This dramatic decline was unexpected. One might have supposed that anyone intent upon killing themselves would use any method to hand and that lack of availability of one particular agent would scarcely make any difference. The facts, however, point in the contrary direction. Extensive research, including for example studies on immigrants from different countries to Australia, has shown that the mode of suicide is strongly influenced by cultural attitudes which appear to favour one method in preference to others. More recently the UK rates have resumed their upward trend.

The role of cultural proscription or prescription has already been hinted at, and a number of sociological theories have been proposed which might account for the differences between societies in their suicide rates, differences which often remain surprisingly stable for sustained periods of time. Of the numerous hypotheses that have been advanced, the social cohesion theory developed by Durkheim and his followers still retains the widest support. On this view social cohesion minimizes the risk of suicide, whereas situations in which individuals are dissociated from their groups (leading to *egoistic* suicides), or live in communities that have no adequate normative values and beliefs to meet current social realities (*anomie*), conduce to suicide. The precise meaning of notions such as social cohesion or anomie is debatable, but it is empirically true that the suicide rates are particularly high among the divorced, among childless women, among those living alone, the retired or unemployed, and where populations are highly mobile or subject to economic uncertainty. Conversely, situations which promote social cohesion tend to lower suicide rates, and of these the classical example is the threat of war. In both World Wars suicide rates fell in practically all countries, both belligerent and neutral.

While social factors undoubtedly influence suicide rates, patients with conditions such as severe depression, alcholism, or epilepsy all have increased risks of dying by suicide. Reviews of comprehensive series of suicidal deaths have now established that the great majority of such individuals were suffering from a clearly recognizable psychiatric illness at the time of their death. In England and Wales the commonest such disorder is the depressive phase of manic-depressive psychosis (see MENTAL ILLNESS), often triggered by *bereavement. In Scotland and in the United States alcoholism is almost as prominent as depression. It also appears that social factors act as additional determinants *within* groups of depressives or alcoholics. Thus among all depressives those who are socially isolated, etc., have an appreciably higher risk of suicide than the remainder. It appears that social and psychological factors are necessary (though not sufficient) causes of suicide.

Such a sweeping statement begs the question of whether there exists such a thing as a rational suicide. The formulation which comes nearest to such a possibility is Durkheim's description of 'altruistic suicide', which he believed occurred only in communities that had extremely rigid codes of conduct, such as the Army in the nineteenth century. The notion that death was to be preferred to dishonour, a sentiment which goes back at least to Roman times, was not simply an empty phrase. It is also said that elderly Eskimos kill themselves in times of food shortage to help preserve the family. However, it appears that under normal circumstances rational suicide is exceedingly rare, if indeed it exists at all. The nearest approach is possibly the not uncommon phenomenon of an individual who kills himself during the course of a painful terminal illness in order, presumably, to put an end to intolerable suffering. Even so, many such individuals show an impaired ability to adjust to their disorder as compared with the majority of sufferers. Severe depression (or alcoholism) may of course also be features of a painful and chronic illness.

Whatever the social and clinical context, the meaning of the suicidal act may vary considerably between individuals. For some, death represents simply a termination. For many others the situation is more complex; suicide notes frequently reflect a theme such as reunion with someone who has already died, or imply that the individual will in some way continue and be able to monitor the activities of his survivors. A desire to inflict revenge on others through their guilt and remorse over the death is often evident. Indeed, a multiplicity of motives which, from a narrow logical point of view, may be mutually incompatible may be displayed. The supremely 'personal' action of suicide may, at the same time, be intensely 'interpersonal' or social. (Some psychologists would aver that ultimately there is no distinction between the two.)

Nothing has been said so far of so-called 'attempted suicide', which in the United Kingdom, at least, is overwhelmingly represented by drug overdoses. The term 'attempted suicide' is profoundly misleading; for the majority of such patients suicide is not what they are attempting. Indeed, advances in the study of the phenomenon have only become possible since it was realized that these individuals do not represent failed suicides, but rather something which, though having a loose behavioural analogy with suicide, should be viewed as a more or less distinct variety of behaviour. To this end the term 'parasuicide' has been introduced.

From the epidemiological point of view suicide and parasuicide are markedly different. Whereas suicides tend to be male, and in the second half of life, the great majority of parasuicides are female and in their teens or twenties. Suicide is prevalent among the widowed and the single, whereas parasuicide tends to be commonest among the married. Suicide is notable among the physically infirm and the socially isolated, whereas parasuicide has no such association with physical illness, and tends to be commoner among those who are living in congested, overcrowded conditions. Depressive illness and alcoholism certainly figure prominently among parasuicides, but are usually much less severe than among suicides; while lesser emotional disturbance, induced by interpersonal conflicts and other intercurrent events, assumes a much greater significance: an appreciable minority of parasuicides appear to be free of any kind of psychiatric disorder, unless of course the act itself is taken as sufficient evidence of disorder. Whereas, according to the latest figures, suicide shows no obvious social class gradient, parasuicide is very much less common in the upper than in the lower social classes.

Parasuicide is vastly more frequent than completed suicide, and from what has been said it will be appreciated that the magnitude of the ratio varies by age and sex. Thus, among men aged 55 and over, the excess is approximately threefold, while for young women below the age of 35 it is in the region of two-hundredfold.

From a clinical-descriptive viewpoint, the typical parasuicide tends to have had a disrupted and disadvantaged childhood, often in a broken home. She will be living in a state of conflict with her family of origin, or of procreation, or both; among men a story of trouble with the law and of interpersonal violence is common, as is excessive drinking. In association with these difficulties the patient becomes anxious and depressed, and in response to a crisis or a quarrel takes an overdose of pills (or more rarely deliberately causes self-injury).

The details of the psychological processes involved in the genesis of the act are still unclear, and often the patient herself is confused as to what, if anything, she intended. But certain broad themes can be discerned. A wish for a temporary respite, analogous to getting blind drunk, is one common component. In a minority, a desire to die or an indifference to survival will be reported, or may be inferred. Another very important aspect of parasuicide is its communication function, the much-cited 'cry for help'. Unfortunately the cry so produced may or may not lead to the hoped-for response, since families and friends may as readily pick up the aggressive overtones of the act—the hint of 'I'll die, and then you'll be sorry'.

Parasuicide may, thus, serve a number of purposes; but it is perhaps the communication aspect which is of particular interest. If the act does indeed serve as a means of conveying information, then it can be argued that it is a form of 'language' of a rather special kind. Consequently it could be predicted that the patient would commonly be found among a group of individuals who share a propensity to parasuicide when under stress. This supposition has been empirically confirmed. The concept also points the way to the study of parasuicide as a social institution, and here too the evidence suggests that communities exist in which parasuicide appears to have a more or less standard preformed 'meaning'.

Finally, having stressed the numerous differences between completed suicide and parasuicide, it is necessary to point out that there is also an important overlap between the two. About half of all completed suicides are preceded by a parasuicide. Conversely, if a representative sample of parasuicides is followed up, about 1 per cent would be found to die by suicide in the ensuing year (which is about a hundred times greater than would be expected for the general population), and the increased risk of an eventual suicide persists for many years. Subgroups at high and low risk of later suicide can be identified, but no parasuicide should be dismissed a priori as trivial.     N. K.

Durkheim, E. (1952). *Suicide: a study in sociology.* London.

Kennedy, P., Kreitman, N., and Ovenston, I. (1974). The prevalence of suicide and parasuicide in Edinburgh. *British Journal of Psychiatry*, **124**, 36–41.

Kreitman, N. (ed.) (1977). *Parasuicide.* Chichester.

Robins, E., Murphy, G., Wilkinson, R., Gassner, S., and Kayes, J. (1959). Some clinical considerations in the prevention of suicide based on a study of 134 successful suicides. *American Journal of Public Health*, **49**, 888–99.

Stengel, E. (1964). *Suicide and Attempted Suicide*. Harmondsworth.

## SUICIDE: INTERNATIONAL STATISTICS.

All civilized countries compile statistics on their suicides; many have done so for over a century. These deaths are usually investigated in detail by legal authorities and forensic medical experts even in the many countries where suicide is no longer a criminal offence, if only to establish the mode of death in people who might have died because of accidents or homicide. A mass of tabulations has resulted, containing details of age, sex, occupation, agent of death, etc., which appears to constitute an invaluable source of firm data, waiting at the student's elbow for employment. Some of the earliest theorists on suicide, such as Durkheim in *Le Suicide* (1892), unhesitatingly drew on this store, and subsequently Hendin (1964) has used such data in rather speculative studies concerning the susceptibility to suicide of the 'national character' of three Scandinavian countries. All the same, the number of studies that have exploited international statistical material has been relatively modest, probably because of lingering uncertainties as to the exact comparability of the figures.

These doubts were forcibly expressed by Douglas (1967) in bold, not to say polemical, tones. His argument, in essence, was that the classification of a death as suicide is effected not by God but by a judicial structure, and a 'verdict' is a social act rather than a scientific observation. Douglas pointed to the pervasive importance of attitudes and stereotypes in the minds of all concerned—families who might suppress or distort the information given to their doctors, who in turn maltreat the information before it is notified to the authorities, the coroner's officer who prepares the material for the inquest according to informal but powerful normative values, and finally the coroner himself, with his socially given definition of what a suicide ought to be like. He also emphasized the severe social stigma attached to suicide in some countries, which must inhibit coroners, or their equivalents, from making public pronouncements. Douglas concluded that the social scientist seeking confirmation of standard theories of suicide would always find them demonstrated by suicide statistics, since these very theories had determined the manner in which the data were derived. There was, he concluded, no point in using official statistical material.

This attack evoked a dual reaction. On the one hand, it was readily conceded that suicide has always been under-reported in official figures, since there must be some instances in which the evidence is more or less suppressed, but few where it is spuriously manufactured. It is also evident that a coroner does not like to upset grieving relatives, and in cases of doubt would incline to some altern-

ative verdict; in the United Kingdom his ruling is also subject to appeal to a higher court. Moreover, the legal definition of suicide is a very narrow one, and requires proof beyond reasonable doubt that the deceased not only caused his own death but that he fully intended to do so; whereas the traditional psychiatric viewpoint would stress, rather, the balance of probabilities. For the United States, Dublin's (1963) investigations suggested to him that a further 30 per cent of suicides went unrecognized, while in Eire McCarthy and Walsh (1975) thought that a figure of 100 per cent would be more appropriate.

Attempts to correct for under-reporting have taken the form of adding to the official suicide figures all those deaths in adults which are officially classified as 'undetermined', i.e. where the coroner is unable to come to a decision, plus deaths due to self-administered poisoning in adults, irrespective of the declared intent of the individual. The rationale for these procedures is that detailed case-studies have shown that according to psychiatric criteria the great majority of such individuals should be regarded as suicides. Interestingly, their aggregation to the official suicide figures makes no difference to trends occurring over time, nor does it materially influence the pattern for age and sex subgroups.

On the other hand, the assertion that official statistical data are of no value at all has been hotly contested. Critics point out that Douglas's attack on the role of ideology in determining the figures was advanced without any empirical evidence. It is a truism, which may be generally accepted, that all data reflect the conceptual organization of the observer as well as the natural world, but this is probably true for all science. More specifically, studies have been carried out to determine whether differences in legal procedures and the like do make any material difference to suicide statistics. One of the best-known of these (Sainsbury and Barraclough, 1968) showed that for immigrant groups to the United States, the rank order of their suicide rates closely correlated with that of their home countries, despite the fact that they were being assessed by a completely different set of social agencies. This work has been broadly supported by other studies in Australia. Another study considered the effect of a change in coroner on the suicide rates for his district, arguing that if personal bias played much of a role, then a greater variation in rates should occur at such transitions than in control groups where the same individual remained in office. In fact no differences emerged. Other studies have looked into the training of coroner's officers, with the broad conclusion that this makes virtually no difference to the way in which they prepare information for the coroner's court, or to the final suicide statistics derived from these proceedings.

Another type of investigation has exchanged data between two or more countries and compared the classifications of death that emerge. Evidence was found, in a study comparing Danish and English coroners, of considerable disagreement at the individual case level and, worse, that almost as much disagreement existed between the officers within each country as between the two nations as a whole. This particular series, however, was not meant to be a representative sample, so it is not yet clear how far the results can be generalized. Another investigation, in which records were exchanged between the Scottish Crown Office and a sample of English coroners (the two systems are really very different), again showed that there was appreciable misclassification at an individual level, but that the net effect of this was mutually cancelling and that the final discrepancies were trivial (Ross and Kreitman, 1975).

What, then, can be concluded? There is undoubtedly considerable, and variable, under-reporting. Even after allowing for this, however, consistent differences do persist and are not modified to any great extent by alternative statistical classifications or legal procedures. The data, then, are usable, a conclusion much strengthened by their uniformity in certain respects. For example, it is almost universally the case that the rates are higher among men than among women; among the middle-aged and the elderly rather than the young; in urban centres rather than rural regions; among the *bereaved; among the widowed, divorced, and childless; and possibly in populations undergoing rapid industrialization. Without data of this kind from many sources, the student can never be sure that his own findings reflect more than a purely local scene.

Even so, it would be wise never to accept international statistical data as *proof* for any particular hypothesis. Their prime role, rather, should be to suggest ideas which could be explored in more closely controlled investigations. This conclusion is particularly relevant when one turns away from the much-belaboured question of validity to the problems attendant on the interpretation of these statistics. Table 1 shows the rates by sex, for a sample of countries, calculated after corrections to allow for differences in their age structure. Most published statistics are based on total population figures, but as in most countries suicide by children aged less than 15 years is a rare event, the figures in the table give the suicide rate among adults, with due allowance for age variation between populations.

These figures pose the immediate question of why, within Europe, Hungary should have a (male) rate nine times greater than that of Greece, and thirteen times that of Mexico. Clearly differences between these areas are legion, and, as with any other type of cross-cultural comparison, there are so many discrepancies between pairs of countries or cultures that to propose any one of these as the cause of a difference in suicide rates is a highly hazardous exercise. What is required, rather, are general hypotheses that might explain the over-all pattern. Some are mentioned below.

**Table 1.** Standardized suicide rates (ages 15 and over) in thirty selected countries or areas, 1965–9

|  | Suicides per 100,000 | |
|---|---|---|
|  | Males | Females |
| Mexico | 4·44 | 1·20 |
| Greece | 6·38 | 2·77 |
| Italy | 10·19 | 4·04 |
| Netherlands | 11·78 | 6·87 |
| Yugoslavia | 11·97 | 4·16 |
| UK: Scotland | 12·00 | 7·44 |
| Israel | 12·74 | 8·42 |
| UK: England and Wales | 14·71 | 9·42 |
| Norway | 14·75 | 4·40 |
| Bulgaria | 18·32 | 8·69 |
| New Zealand | 19·11 | 9·31 |
| Canada | 20·63 | 7·45 |
| Hong Kong | 21·40 | 15·55 |
| Portugal | 22·44 | 5·60 |
| United States | 22·98 | 8·44 |
| Poland | 24·51 | 5·01 |
| Japan | 24·71 | 18·88 |
| Australia | 25·43 | 13·70 |
| Belgium | 25·43 | 10·85 |
| Singapore | 27·50 | 15·22 |
| France | 30·20 | 9·74 |
| Denmark | 31·84 | 17·01 |
| Switzerland | 34·69 | 12·20 |
| Federal Republic of Germany | 35·64 | 16·29 |
| Sweden | 36·81 | 13·84 |
| Austria | 41·48 | 15·87 |
| Czechoslovakia | 45·18 | 16·47 |
| Finland | 47·98 | 12·07 |
| Hungary | 58·46 | 22·34 |
| West Berlin | 63·90 | 31·65 |

Source: Ruzicka, WHO (1976)

There remains the use of international data analysed for longitudinal trends. Data collected over the years within a particular country are free from many of the hazards already cited; it can reasonably be assumed that such biases as operate will remain reasonably constant. It is thus possible to venture certain generalizations. For example, the effect of war on suicide rates has been studied in some detail, and has invariably been found to be associated with a steep decline, especially at the outbreak of hostilities. This decrease is not due to suicide masquerading as death in combat, as it affects all age-groups, to varying degrees, and women as well as men. Interestingly, the decline can also be shown for neutral countries faced with the threat of war but never actually engaged in conflict. A likely cause of the decrease is thought to be an increased sense of national cohesion, coupled with a decrease in unemployment. (Without data of international scope this important conclusion would have been difficult to establish.)

A similar type of analysis has been applied to economic recessions. Sainsbury (1963) showed, by an ingenious series of trend analyses, that economic reverses and unemployment both conduced to higher suicide rates, but that poverty *per se* was not particularly relevant. Again, conclusions of this kind require information from many sources, if the effects of numerous confounding influences are to be dissected out. More recently, similar techniques have begun to be used to elucidate the effects on suicide of improved psychiatric services, the availability of lethal agents, such as guns or toxic domestic gas, the increased deployment of social work services, the role of alcohol abuse, and similar influences.                                     N. K.

Douglas, J. (1967). *The Social Meaning of Suicide*. Princeton.

Dublin, L. (1963). *Suicide: a sociological and statistical study*. New York.

Hendin, H. (1964). *Suicide in Scandinavia*. New York.

McCarthy, P. and Walsh, D. (1975). Suicide in Dublin: I. The under-reporting of suicide and its consequences for national statistics. *British Journal of Psychiatry*, **126**, 301–8.

Ross, O. and Kreitman, N. (1975). A further investigation of differences in the suicide rate of England and Wales and of Scotland. *British Journal of Psychiatry*, **127**, 575–82.

Ruzicka, L. T. (1976). *World Health Statistics Report*, **29**(7), 364–413.

Sainsbury, P. (1963). The social and epidemiological aspects of suicide, with special reference to the aged. *Processes of Ageing*, **2**, 153.

Sainsbury, P. and Barraclough, B. (1968). Differences between suicide rates. *Nature*, **220**, 1,252.

**SUPER-EGO.** See EGO AND SUPER-EGO.

**SUPPRESSION.** In psychoanalytical (especially *Freudian) theory, the pushing down of painful memories, so that they are unavailable in consciousness. It is, however, supposed that they may in some sense persist in the unconscious, sometimes to create psychological havoc.

**SYDENHAM,** SIR THOMAS (1624–89), British physician, born at Wynford Eagle, Dorset, studied medicine at Oxford and Montpellier. He was remarkable in his time for insisting on accurate and detailed descriptions of disease, thereby making important contributions to medical classification. In his Epistolary Dissertation to Dr Cole (1682), entitled 'De Affectione Hysterica', he made some timely observations on *hysteria, a disorder with protean manifestations which, he believed, affected one-sixth of his patients.

At the time of his writing, two main theories dominated thinking about hysteria. Firstly there was the ancient belief that the condition was confined to the female sex, being caused by a disturbance of the womb, which it was alleged caused symptoms by becoming displaced into the affected part of the body—see Edward Jorden (1603), 'The Suffocation of the Mother'. A contrary opinion came from Thomas Willis, the anatomist, in 1667 when he denied that the uterus and humours were responsible for hysteria, claiming that the condition arose from disturbances of 'the Brain and Nervous Stock'. He observed similarities between hysteria in women and hypochondriasis in men, conditions which Sydenham likened 'as one egg to another'. Willis emphasized the importance of

'hysterical' convulsions, most of which today would probably be diagnosed as epileptic; but he firmly rejected the wandering womb hypothesis, when he wrote, 'As to the cause of these symptoms, most ancient and indeed Modern Physitians, refer them to the ascent of the womb and vapours elevated from it' and went on to point out that the womb was 'so small in bulk in virgins and widdows, and so strictly tyed by the neighbouring parts round about it, that it can not of itself be moved, or ascend from its place. . .'.

Sydenham, like Willis, repudiated the uterine theory of hysteria, although he considered that women were more prone to the disorder than men; none the less he agreed that men, particularly those 'who lead a sedentary life and study hard, are afflicted by the same'. His other major contribution was his observation that hysteria was more likely to follow 'disturbances of mind which are usual causes of this disease'. He also noted that hysterical symptoms were often accompanied by depression, but could coexist with physical disease.

In making these observations Sydenham placed hysteria firmly in the category of the psychological disorders that could be said to be the forerunners of the psychoneuroses today. No doubt he tended to diagnose hysteria as a psychological disorder far too frequently, and many of the signs and symptoms he described would probably be more indicative of physical than of neurotic illness. None the less, despite his emphasis on psychological causes for hysteria, the ancient uterine hypothesis has continued to influence medical thinking over the past three centuries. Freud faced opposition and ridicule when he described hysteria in men, and the revival of the notion of hysteria as a women's disease, under the title of Briquet's syndrome (1859) shows that Sydenham's observations have not been so influential as one might have hoped.

When it came to treatment, Sydenham was very much a man of his time, and prescribed bleeding and purging to purify the blood; but he made a point of enquiring whether his patients had suffered from 'fretting, or any disturbances of the mind'. He and his contemporary Dr Thomas Fuller, both of whom had seen service in the cavalry during the Civil War, strongly recommended horse-riding as a therapeutic measure for hysteria and hypochondriasis, although probably not for 'slender and weakly women, that seem consumptive, and girls that have the green sickness. . .'. No doubt—unless the patient fell off—horse-riding was safer and more beneficial than some of the other widely used remedies of the time.    F. A. W.

Dewhurst, K. (1966). *Sir Thomas Sydenham*: his life and original writings. London.

Hunter, R. and Macalpine, I. (1963). *Three Hundred Years of Psychiatry, 1553–1860*. London.

**SYMBOLS.** A symbol, broadly speaking, is something that stands for something else. Subordinate questions arise: what sorts of things can stand for things? for what sorts of things? and how do they do so? Also, certain reservations need to be made.

A five pound note once stood for five gold sovereigns, serving the same purposes. Usually a symbol stands for its object in a less robust way: it reminds us of it. It may do so by resembling it, or by standing to it in a known causal relation, or by some conventional connection of whatever origin. Hence C. S. *Peirce's trichotomy of 'signs' into 'icons' (e.g. a diagram), 'indices' (e.g. a thermometer), and 'symbols' in a narrower sense (e.g. a name).

Whereas association itself is symmetrical, the relation of symbol to object is not; it is limited to situations in which the object commands more interest than the symbol. The fish symbolizes Jesus, because the Greek ἰχθύς is an acrostic of a five-word description of Jesus; but it does so in churches, not kitchens. The relation is asymmetrical and intermittent.

A physical object, or state, may stand for a physical object or state: a fish for a man, an inscription for a man, a map for a province, a mercury level for a temperature. Often, the symbol is better seen as a whole class, such as that of ichthyomorphic carvings. A name, indeed, may be seen as the class of its inscriptions and utterances. Sometimes, as when gods are said to have symbolized seasons, or Janus to have symbolized wholeness, the symbols are evidently neither physical objects nor states nor classes of such; it is hard to categorize them otherwise than as ideas. A better account might take nominalistic lines, appealing to visual patterns and linguistic expressions.

The heat and wind activate their symbolic indices, the thermometer and weathervane. But primitive peoples have believed, conversely, in an efficacy of symbols upon their objects. Thus effigies and the magic of names. Thus also, presumably, the cave-paintings of thirty thousand years ago.

Fanciful subconscious resemblances must be assumed between symbol and symbolized, if we are to make sense of iconography or of Sigmund *Freud. The flights of creative imagination in our *dreams are undeniable, but their mechanism remains a mystery. Such symbolism must have figured in the origins of language. Paget had an imaginative theory of private gestures within the mouth, private muscular contortions that bore a subjective resemblance to some visible traits of objects. It is in language, at any rate, that symbolism attains the age of discretion. Let us look to its workings.

One way in which a linguistic expression often stands for something is by *designating* it. Designation is the relation that the names 'Plato' and 'Wales' bear to Plato and Wales, and that the phrases 'the author of *Waverley*' and 'Whittington's cat' bear to Sir Walter Scott and Whittington's cat. Symbols that purport to designate are *singular terms*. Some fail—for example, 'Pegasus'—for want of a designatum.

A way in which symbols more commonly stand for things is by *denoting* them. A *general term*, typically a common noun or adjective or intransitive verb, denotes each of the things it is true of. Thus 'horse' denotes each horse, 'green' each green thing, 'swim' everyone who swims.

There has been since antiquity an urge to view general terms as designating. Thus 'horse' was seen as designating some trumped-up abstract object, a universal—the property equinity—besides denoting each horse. This facile positing of universals was deplored by the medieval nominalists, as a confusion.

It was in part a happy confusion. In mathematics, and to some degree elsewhere in science, abstract objects serve theoretical purposes that cannot, evidently, be served by just talking of general terms and denotation. Classes do suffice in lieu of properties, but they are next of kin. Still, there is no need to view the general terms themselves as designating universals in addition to their job of denoting. If properties or classes are to be designated, we do have singular terms for the purpose: 'equinity', 'horsekind'.

General terms are meaningful, surely; and the urge to accord designata to them was due partly to confusing designation with meaning. Meaning is not designation, even among singular terms. The terms 'the Evening Star' and 'the Morning Star' (Frege's example) designate the same thing but differ in meaning. 'Pegasus' is meaningful, though designating nothing.

The notion of meaning is elusive. Jeremy *Bentham appreciated that meaning accrues primarily to whole sentences, and only derivatively to separate words. Setting aside emotive or poetic meaning, and looking only to the cognitive meaning of declarative sentences, we may say that the meaning of a sentence consists in its truth conditions. We know the meaning of a sentence in so far as we know in what circumstances the sentence counts as true. To understand a sentence is to know when to affirm it.

There are sentences, such as 'It's raining', 'This is red', 'That's a rabbit', that count as true only in circumstances observable at the time of utterance. Their meanings can be learned by conditioning, unaided by auxiliary sentences. To proceed from these beginnings to higher levels of language, unaided by translation from another language already known, is an impressive feat, but the child achieves it. He exploits analogies: from the apparent role of a word in one sentence he guesses its role in another. Also, he discovers that people assent to a sentence of some one form only contingently upon assenting to a corresponding sentence of some related form. Exploring, thus, the interrelations of sentences, and corrected by his elders, he learns how to compose innumerable sentences and when to affirm them.

Once he is well started, we could teach him harder sentences by constructing a dictionary along the following lines. Each entry explains some word—for example, 'putative'—by general systematic instructions for paraphrasing all possible sentential contexts of 'putative' into sentences lacking 'putative'. Each word in the paraphrase is either a word of the old sentence or a word more frequently heard than 'putative'. Words very frequently heard are left unexplained. Thus, though meaning belongs to sentences, words serve in generating it. The concept of a dictionary, just presented, shows how.

The sentential contexts of some words can be paraphrased simply by substituting some more frequent word, or some phrase. That word or phrase is then said to have the same meaning as the original word; and thus it is that the notion of word meanings is derivable from that of sentence meanings. Two expressions have the same meaning if substituting one for the other never disturbs truth conditions of sentences.

We saw that singular terms have their designata, when all goes well, and general terms their denotata. Many words claim neither—thus 'or', 'to', 'however', 'which', 'very'. Scholastics called these syncategorematic: lacking in intrinsic meaning, and meaningful only derivatively, through their contribution to the meaning of the containing sentences. There is a trace here of the confusion between meaning and designation, or denotation; words were thought to forfeit intrinsic meaning by not purporting to denote or designate. But let us take it that words generally are meaningful only through their contribution to the meaning of the containing sentences. Then we may keep the term 'syncategorematic' for the words that do not purport to denote or designate, but without thereby imputing any distinctive shortage of meaning.

Consisting, as it does, primarily in the truth conditions of sentences, meaning is pretty thin stuff. In the special case of observation sentences, it can be inculcated by sensory conditioning, or direct demonstration; for the rest, only by other sentences, paraphrases. We give the meaning of a sentence by explaining the sentence, and the meaning of a word by explaining how it works in sentences. Serious confusions could have been avoided if a practice had been made of speaking thus of explanatory activities, rather than of meanings as somehow separable entities that symbols might stand for.

The meaning of a symbol was often confused, we saw, with the designatum. When it was not, it was usually viewed as an idea. This circumstance doubtless delayed the demise of an uncritically mentalistic psychology. Meanings had to be admitted, it seemed, on pain of rendering language meaningless; and it was not easy to see what meanings could be, if not ideas. Hence a dualism of symbol and idea, language and thought.

John Horne Tooke denounced this dualism as early as 1786, protesting that John *Locke would have done well to write 'word' in place of 'idea' throughout his *Essay*. The way was opened for J. B. *Watson to identify thought primarily with language, subvocal speech. The medium becomes, in Marshall McLuhan's phrase, the message. The incipient muscular tugs that constituted the thinking process, according to Watson, were not indeed wholly confined to the speech apparatus; the inarticulate painter or engineer must think partly in his fingers. Without language, however, thought would be meagre.

Mathematics affords the ultimate example of the power of notation as a way of thought. In school, when we did problems about rowing across the current, the hard part was putting them into equations; that was the programming, and algebra was the computer. The boon of arabic numeration goes without saying, and the mere use of brackets to unify a complex expression is a cornerstone of mathematics. It is the use of brackets, together with the variable, that enables us to extrapolate our laws and iterate our operations beyond all finite bounds.                                        W. V. Q.

Cirlot, J. E. (1962). *A Dictionary of Symbols*. London.
Frege, G. (1892). Über Sinn und Bedeutung (Eng. trans.: On sense and reference). In Frege, *Philosophical Writings* (Geach, P. and Black, M., eds., 1952). Oxford.
Ogden, C. K. (1932). *Bentham's Theory of Fictions*. London.
Paget, Sir R. (1930). *Human Speech*. London.
Peirce, C. S. (1932). *Collected Papers*, vol. 2, 134–73. Cambridge, Massachusetts.
Quine, W. V. (1973). *The Roots of Reference*. La Salle, Illinois.
Tooke, J. H. (1786). *The Diversions of Purley*. London.
Watson, J. B. (1919). *Psychology from the Standpoint of a Behaviorist*. Philadelphia.

**SYNAESTHESIA.** Confusion between the senses: for example, some musicians experience colours for particular notes. The effect can become dramatic in some drug states, presumably through loss of normal inhibitory mechanisms which isolate the central processing of the senses.

**SYNAPSE.** A junction between two nerves. Synapses contain 'transmitter substances', of which it is now known there is a remarkable variety. The synapses allow the action potentials in axons to cross in one direction only into contiguous nerves. They are set by the activity of many other nerves (up to 2,000) and by chemical signals, especially hormones. See NERVOUS SYSTEM; NEUROTRANSMITTERS AND NEUROMODULATORS.

**SYNDROME.** In medicine, a typical grouping of features of a physical or mental disease. Thus the syndrome of measles includes spots, a high temperature and photophobia (dislike or fear of bright light). This raises the question: Is a disease more than its symptoms? The symptoms are what are apparent, and used for diagnosis; there is much that is hidden and causative in diseases, beyond symptoms.

**SYNERGIES.** There are two related approaches to the 'units of control' employed by the brain in controlling movement. Both are called synergies. The first, formulated by C. S. *Sherrington, posits a reflex unit above that of the motor unit; while the second, formulated by Nikolas *Bernstein, suggests that a restricted number of programs may underlie most of our behaviour.

To understand Sherrington's views we must start with the notion of a reflex. To take two familiar examples: in the knee-jerk reflex, the tap of the physician's hammer stretches a tendon, and this is sensed by a sensor (proprioceptor) which activates a motor neurone which contracts the extensor muscle (which had 'appeared' to be too long) so that the foot kicks out. In the scratch reflex, an irritant localized to part of the skin activates receptors which in turn activate motor neurones which control muscles to bring a foot or hand to the irritated skin and rub back and forth. In each case, we have a reflex-loop which mediates direct stimulus–response behaviour: from external world via receptors to the spinal cord, where motor neurones respond by controlling muscles to yield movement in the external world.

Now consider the scratch reflex more carefully. We may see it as made up of two components. The rubbing component needs the limb movement to ensure that it contacts the (right place on the) skin, the limb movement is tuned into contact by feedback from the rubbing movement. The two reflex actions 'synergize', or work together. More generally,

The executant musculature . . . provides a reflex means of supporting or reinforcing the co-operation of flexors with flexors, extensors with extensors, etc. The proprioceptors of reaching muscles operate reflexly upon other muscles of near functional relation to themselves. Active contraction (including active stretch) and passive stretch in the reaching muscles are stimuli for reflexes influencing other muscles, and the reflex influence so exerted is on some muscles excitatory and on others inhibitory; it is largely reciprocally distributed, knitting synergists together (Creed et al., 1932, p. 129).

Thus, for Sherrington, the synergy is an anatomically based reflex linkage of a group of muscles.

The Bernstein school is informed by notions of control theory. The brain is to generate control signals which will cause the muscles to contract with just the right timing to bring about some desired behaviour. But there are so many muscles, they suggest, that to control every muscle independently to its optimum would be a computationally unmanageable problem. They thus see the crucial problem in the 'design' of a brain which controls movement to be that of reducing the number of 'degrees of freedom', i.e. the number of independent parameters which must be controlled.

In order for the higher levels of the central nervous system to effectively solve the task of organizing motor acts within a required time, it is necessary that the number of controlled parameters be not too large, and the afferentation, requiring analysis, not too great. [This is achieved] by the so-called synergies. . . . Each synergy is associated with certain peculiar connections imposed on some muscle groups, a subdivision of all the participant muscles into a small number of related groups. Due to this fact, to perform motion it is sufficient to control a small number of independent parameters, even though the number of muscles participating in the movement may be large (Gel'fand et al., 1973, p. 162).

So far, the general framework is consonant with Sherrington's synergies. But these are restricted to stimulus–response patterns. Bernstein had a more general concern with dynamic patterns changing over time during some motor act: '[A] complex synergy is involved in walking. . . . "The bio-dynamic tissue" of live movements [appears] to be full of an enormous number of regular and stable details. . . . [In old people] the synergy existing in normal walking between the action of the arms and legs is destroyed' (Bernstein, 1967, pp. 67, 93).

However, this was too global a view of synergy, and later work of the Moscow school came to view synergies as the functional building-blocks from which most motions can be composed:

Although synergies are few in number, they make it possible to encompass almost all the diversity of arbitrary motions. One can separate relatively simple synergies of pose control (synergy of stabilization), cyclic locomotive synergies (walking, running, swimming, etc.), synergies of throwing, striking, jumping, and a certain (small) number of others (Gel'fand et al., 1973, p. 162).

One thus comes to see a synergy in general as a program for controlling some distinctive motor performance extended in space and time, built upon synergies of co-ordinated reflexes as substrate. The entry FEEDBACK AND FEEDFORWARD places this notion in a control-theoretic perspective. See also SCHEMAS.                    M. A. A.

Bernstein, N. A. (trans., 1967). *The Coordination and Regulation of Movements*. Oxford.

Creed, R. S., Denny-Brown, D., Eccles, J. C., Liddell, E. G. T., and Sherrington, C. S. (1932, repr. 1972). *Reflex Activity of the Spinal Cord*. Oxford.

Gel'fand, I. M., Gurfinkel, V. S., Shik, M. L., and Tsetlin, M. L. (1973). Certain problems in the investigation of movement. In *Automata Theory and Modeling of Biological Systems*, 160–71 (trans. from the Russian *Models of the Structural-Functional Organization of Certain Biological Systems*, 1966). New York.

# T

**TACHISTOSCOPE.** An instrument used for studying visual pattern and object recognition, by controlling viewing time. It may be merely a shutter placed before the eyes; but sophisticated instruments switch pictures alternately with blank fields of similar intensity in order to maintain adaptation (see VISUAL ADAPTATION) and minimize *afterimages. Some instruments allow successive presentation of pairs or up to six or so alternative pictures. These can be used for studying 'masking' and many other phenomena of visual perception.

**TAOIST IDEAS OF THE MIND.** See CHINESE IDEAS OF THE MIND.

**TASTE.** Flavour is usually defined as the overall sensation of taste and *smell. Taste refers to sensations arising from the taste receptors in the mouth and throat while smell arises from receptors in the nose. When a person has a cold or blocks his nose, he will taste but not smell food adequately, so the flavour is reduced. It is unfortunate that in everyday language the words 'taste' and 'flavour' are used interchangeably. Taste and smell, together with texture, visual appearance, and sound will give the overall sensory percept of the food, which is important in its choice and enjoyment. People who cannot perceive the flavour of food will often not maintain an adequate diet.

There are two main groups of scientists who are interested in understanding taste. The first group consists of food scientists within the food industry, who are interested in discovering the precise mechanisms of flavour perception so as to be able to maintain and control the flavour of the products being manufactured. Furthermore, food scientists use human judges to measure the physical and chemical characteristics of foods that are important for the flavour, texture, appearance, and sound of the food. They exploit the fact that the human senses are often more sensitive than laboratory instruments, to the minute quantities of chemicals present in a food that endow it with its characteristic flavour.

The second group of scientists are more interested in the workings of the senses and the brain *per se*. Knowledge of how a taste stimulus reacts with the membrane of a taste receptor would provide information not only about mechanisms of flavour, but also about other similar chemoreceptive functions involved in drug, hormone, brain, and cell mechanisms. Changes in taste perception are beginning to be utilized as diagnostic tools in medicine, while further research is providing insights into areas ranging from genetics to the working of insect and animal attractants and repellants. For this reason, taste, along with smell, is of vital interest to a broad range of scientists.

The behavioural measurement of taste, whether for the sensory evaluation of a food flavour or for elucidating taste mechanisms, can pose problems. People do not pay as much attention to taste as they do to vision and are thus less practised at assessing the taste sensations that they experience. One consequence of this is difficulty with language, for our language is largely concerned with visual stimuli. There are many adjectives available to describe colour but few for taste. Furthermore, parents teach their children to name colours but do not do so for tastes, so that, while young children are fairly skilled at colour-naming, even adults can misname common sweet, sour, salty, and bitter stimuli. In particular, the terms 'sour' and 'bitter' are often confused, but this is merely a matter of definition. The confusion can be remedied by giving tasters citric acid and quinine to compare and informing them that the correct descriptions are 'sour' and 'bitter' respectively.

Aside from these common descriptions, there is little agreement on the use of taste adjectives and individuals usually acquire their own sets of definitions or taste concepts. For precise evaluation and communiction of the taste or flavour of a foodstuff, however, a precise language has to be invented, for which the breadth of use of the taste adjectives has to be precisely controlled and agreed upon by those using the language. Usually, *ad hoc* languages are invented for a given food, so that although say, expert tea-tasters may be able to communicate amongst themselves, their language would be 'foreign' to expert wine- or mayonnaise-tasters.

The method of language invention generally adopted is to follow the way that children learn colours: words are paired with appropriate sensations. Thus, languages are invented to describe the tastes, odours, and textures of foods, using a set of physical taste standards which are always available to define the adjectives used. These methods fall under the general heading of flavour-profiling. There are problems, however, in ensuring that judges have the same breadth of use of the words in their invented language and this is still a subject of research. Without any special training, our command of vocabulary for taste is so poor that the merest suggestion of a word denoting a taste, in the instructions to a person judging a taste, will bias him to use that word. In fact, the power of suggestion is so strong that people have reported experiencing smells that they were told had been transmitted by television.

Different cultures have their own, idiosyncratic languages and confusions about taste, dependent probably on their dietary habits. Just as 'sour' and 'bitter' are confused in English, so it was reported at the beginning of this century that the islanders of the Torres Straits confused 'sour' and 'salty'. Many tribes of North American Indians were unfamiliar with salt until they had contact with Europeans, when they described salt as 'sour'. Some inhabitants of Polynesia and New Guinea had only one word to describe sweet, sour, and bitter. Recent studies have shown a tendency among Malay speakers to qualify taste adjectives. Thus, *masin* meaning 'salty', is often qualified: *masin ayer laut* (salty like seawater), *masin garam* (salty like salt), or *masin kitchup* (salty like soy sauce). It is not clear why Malay speakers should spontaneously volunteer more detail, though it may be because mothers teach their daughters to cook by telling them to add the various ingredients until the food has a specific taste, rather than to add pre-measured amounts of ingredient according to recipes. The need for precise communication about taste would encourage the development of a precise language. Whatever the reason for such precision, it would be a useful strategy for flavour-profiling techniques.

Spanish has three words for sour and bitter: *amargo* (bitter), *acido* (sour), and *agrio* (sour or bitter). Spanish dictionaries vary in their definition of *agrio*, and Spanish speakers, although eager to explain the correct usage as they see it, are generally inconsistent in the use of this word. The Japanese have words for 'sweet' (*amai*), 'sour' (*suppai*), 'salty' (*shiokarai*), and 'bitter' (*nigai*), and, in addition, a commonly used taste-word that is absent from the English language: *umami*—the taste encountered in several broths that are used as a stock, in which foods are cooked and to which they give their characteristic *umami* taste. Such *umami*-tasting broths can be made from *kombu* (a type of seaweed: *Laminiaria japonica*), from *katsuobushi* (dried bonito flakes), or from *shiitake* (a large mushroom, *Lentinus edodus*). Nowadays, the taste principles of these foods are commercially available as *umami* seasonings such as monosodium glutamate. Although the scientific term for the taste is *umami*, many Japanese call it the 'Ajinomoto' taste, after the name of the company that first made monosodium glutamate commercially available. Although English speakers can perceive the taste, they do not have an appropriate word to describe it, unless they are specially trained, and will often call it 'salty', with the qualification that it does not taste like common salt. The situation is rather as if there were no word in English for 'orange' and people had to describe the colour as 'sort of red'.

Interestingly, the idea that there are four primary tastes, sweet, sour, salty, and bitter, is quite arbitrary. In any case, what is meant by the term 'primary taste' has not been defined. It could mean the unit of types of reaction that can take place on the membrane of the taste receptor, or of types of neural code that can communicate sensations to the brain, or even of processes that can take place in the cortex which result ultimately in the sensation of taste. Whichever of these candidates for primacy is adopted, the operative number is not known, for the idea that there are *four* primary tastes came into the taste literature by misunderstanding and accident. In spite of the absence of any firm physiological evidence, some scientists still cling to the idea. The notion is often reflected in the way that taste experiments are designed: the taste stimuli used in research studies being limited to just four, or judges being allowed to use combinations of only four words to describe their whole range of taste experience.

Measurement of taste, as with the other senses, can produce difficulties. One interesting problem is the effect of adaptation. The brain tends to protect itself from having to cope with too much information, by simply 'turning down the volume control' on stimulation that is unchanging (see HABITUATION). There is no point in paying attention to a message that is merely repeating itself. This phenomenon of sensory adaptation is often experienced with smell. Should a person enter a room that smells of sweat or perfume, the smell receptors will send corresponding smell messages to the brain. However, because the person does not leave the room, the same smell message will be repeated and the smell sensation will gradually vanish. Should the person leave the room and return, the smell sensation will reappear. Another way of envisaging this is to think of the smell mechanism as re-setting the 'zero-level' for smell—the concentration at which the smell stimulus is perceived as odourless.

Taste receptors are bathed in saliva, which is secreted from the salivary glands, and contains low concentrations of taste stimuli such as sodium chloride or potassium chloride; these can come from the blood and reflect the physiological state of the organism. The taste receptors adjust so that the zero-level for taste (or taste zero) is set at the stimulus level in the saliva. For example, the level of salt in saliva is highest in the morning, drops until the afternoon, and then rises again to the high morning value. The taste zero appears to do the same, so that these salivary changes cause no sensation of taste; rather, the taste zero changes with the slow rise and fall of secreted salivary constituents. This constant adjustment is a useful way of ensuring that tastes are registered only when sudden large changes take place, such as when foods are placed in the mouth. Salivary concentrations can vary tenfold in value and may form the basis for changes in taste sensitivity connected with various diseases; however, they are comparatively unimportant compared to the effect described next.

When, during an experiment, a taste stimulus

like salt is tasted, it is sipped and then expelled from the mouth by spitting. However, spitting will not expel all the stimuli and while the person is spitting out the residual stimulus, his taste zero is rising to a higher level to render the residual tasteless. Thus, when the subject believes he has expelled all the residual stimulus, because his mouth feels tasteless, there will still be considerable amounts remaining and these will maintain a higher taste zero. The next stimulus will then be tasted with this new, higher taste zero; the taste system will not be as sensitive. This constant zero-drift has caused considerable trouble in taste measurement; the resulting changes in salivary concentration can be 100-fold and highly significant. If the residual stimulus is continually expelled from the mouth by a regime of water rinses between tastings, a lower average taste zero will be maintained. This confers a greater sensitivity, as well as ensuring that given stimuli taste more intense. Thus, the practice of rinsing between tastings, once thought to be an unimportant experimental detail, can be shown to have a major effect on taste sensitivity, and accounts for major variations in experience reported in the taste literature. One way of circumventing the problem of zero-drift in taste measurement, is to flow taste stimuli over the tongue. This prevents any residual taste stimuli from remaining in the saliva and affecting taste sensitivity. It also allows the taste receptors to be re-set to a constant zero level, between each tasting, by using a standard adapting flow. The taste receptors can adapt to tastelessness in this standard flow, thereby resetting the taste zero to the same level before tasting each new stimulus. The technique is powerful enough to allow tasters to distinguish between once- and twice-distilled water. However, little is yet known about the mechanisms of taste adaptation; even the extent to which taste receptors can 'zero-adjust' has not been explored.

Thus, a stimulus becomes tasteless to the extent that it can resemble saliva. Certainly the osmotic properties of saliva are nearer to those of tapwater than to distilled water, so distilled water has more of a taste than tapwater. The flat taste of distilled water is a sub-zero or subadapting taste; in fact, pure water can appear to have a whole range of tastes depending on the adaptation state of the taste receptors. Changes in taste zero for a range of receptors during eating or experimentation will lessen or accentuate certain aspects of the taste of other stimuli. This may form the basis for the choice of certain wines with certain foods. A sweet wine may be more suitable for drinking with a sweet dessert because adaptation to one would lessen the sweetness of the other.    M. O'M.

Beidler, L. M. (ed.) (1971). *Handbook of Sensory Physiology* vol iv: *Chemical Senses*, 2. 'Taste'. Berlin.

Meiselman, H. L. and Rivlin, R. S. (eds.) (1986). *Clinical Measurement of Taste and Smell*. London.

Miller, G. A. and Johnson-Laird, P. N. (1976). *Language and Perception*. Cambridge.

O'Mahony, M. (1984). How we perceive flavor. *Nutrition Today*, **19**, 6–15.

O'Mahony, M. (1979). Salt taste adaptation: the psychophysical effects of adapting solutions and residual stimuli from prior tastings on the taste of sodium chloride. *Perception*, **8**, 441–76.

O'Mahony, M. (1978). Smell illusions and suggestion: Reports of smells contingent on tones played on television and radio. *Chemical Senses and Flavor*, **3**, 183–9.

O'Mahony, M. and Ishii, R. (1986). A comparison of English and Japanese taste languages: Taste descriptive methodology, codability and the umami taste. *British Journal of Psychology*, **77** (in press).

O'Mahony, M. and Manzano Alba, M. del C. (1980). Taste descriptions in Spanish and English. *Chemical Senses*, **5**, 47–62.

O'Mahony, M. and Muhiudeen, H. (1977). A preliminary study of alternative taste languages using qualitative description of sodium chloride solutions: Malay versus English. *British Journal of Psychology*, **68**, 275–8.

O'Mahony, M. and Thompson, B. (1977). Taste quality descriptions: Can the subject's response be affected by mentioning taste words in the instructions? *Chemical Senses and Flavor*, **2**, 283–98.

**TAUTOLOGY.** In logic, saying the same thing in a different way, often unwittingly. For example, 'A fair-haired blonde' is tautologous if 'fair-haired' and 'blonde' are taken to have the same meanings. But if 'blonde' means the natural hair colour, then a dark-haired girl who is fair because her hair is dyed fair could be fair but not a blonde, and then 'fair-haired blonde' is *not* a tautology. Tautology always depends on accepted definitions.

When black, swan-like birds were discovered in Australia, there was doubt as to whether they could be 'swans'—for swans were supposed to be white. But it was allowed that though black they were swans—so 'black swan' was not contradictory. Conversely, it is not tautologous to call a swan white—though it would be if the quality of whiteness was part of the *definition* of a swan.

**TELEKINESIS.** Movement of objects from a distance by supposed *paranormal means. The alleged forces are generally acknowledged to be small; but if they exist at all it is exceedingly hard to understand why it is possible to carry out delicate experiments and operations, with galvanometers and so on: surely eager experimenters would exert their telekinetic powers, though unwittingly, to affect the results of experiments; and this would produce nonsense in science, and much else. Such negative evidence brings strong weight to the opinion that there is no such thing as telekinesis.

See PARANORMAL PHENOMENA.    R. L. G.

**TELEPATHY.** See EXTRA-SENSORY PERCEPTION; PARANORMAL PHENOMENA AND THE UNCONSCIOUS.

**TERMAN,** LEWIS MADISON (1877–1956). American experimental psychologist, and professor of psychology at Stanford University (1916). He introduced the Stanford–Binet test and the Terman Group *intelligence tests into the US

Army in 1920. He is particularly known for his studies of gifted children. Perhaps his best-known book is *The Measurement of Intelligence* (1916).

**TERROR** is the specific *fear that some evil event or action is going to occur. Its origins go back to the notion of trembling. Strictly speaking, it should be distinguished from horror in that horror implies something disgusting and negative, whereas terror does not.

In the field of myth, terror has often been associated with visitations from an all-powerful god controlling life and death in a seemingly indiscriminate manner. The Delphic oracle went into a kind of trance or frenzy, during which the awesome god spoke through the prophetess. All this, even the ambiguities of the prophecies themselves, was designed to inspire fear of the god in the onlookers. (See PARANORMAL PHENOMENA IN ANCIENT GREECE.)

Terror appears to fit into the category of instinct-response which humans share with most animals. For example, most humans and animals fear the sight of mutilated bodies. Experiments with chimpanzees during which the animals were shown pictures of chimpanzees with their heads or limbs cut off elicited instinct-responses of extreme trepidation. This fear of violence done to the body is at the basis of the terror process.

In the ancient world terror was the basis of tyranny, as in Rome under Marius and Sulla. Historically many political leaders have chosen to rule by terror tactics rather than customary, legal means—that is, by the systematic use of violence to inhibit political opposition. Present-day 'acts of terrorism' bear a different sense, as they are designed to disrupt a given system by violent actions.

While the causes of terror have changed over the centuries, the human mind continues to be highly susceptible to it. Our ancestors gathered round lighted fires not only to keep warm but to ward off 'the terror by night': there were terrifying animals lurking in the darkness. The 'night-light' in a child's room reflects this fear of darkness, of the unseen and the unknown. Even so, most humans seem to enjoy the feeling of terror under controlled conditions. Grandmothers have traditionally told tales of terror around the fireplace to countless generations of children, in a role which today has been supplanted by the so-called horror film. Perhaps the monsters who march across the screen are designed to purge the real monsters within the human psyche. (See FRANKENSTEIN.)

Contemporary science and technology have created new sources of terror, such as the threat of nuclear annihilation and highly sophisticated means of electronic surveillance and control of human behaviour. Modern adult human beings may no longer fear the presence of huge animals in the darkness, but most humans experience terror born from technology. R. T. M.

**TEUBER,** HANS-LUKAS (1916–77). German-American psychologist, born in Berlin, who studied in the University of Basel until 1941, when he emigrated to the United States. He took his doctorate at Harvard in the field of social psychology but his interests thereafter deviated to neuropsychology, in which his reputation became firmly established. He was a full professor at Bellvue Medical Center, 1947–51, and thereafter head of the department of psychology at the Massachusetts Institute of Technology, until his untimely death by drowning.

Teuber had a wide scholarship and he was an inspiring leader of research. His own work was mainly concerned with the psychological effects of war-wounds of the brain, studied wherever possible through the use of quantitative methods, many of which he devised himself. His most important books were *Somatosensory Changes after Penetrating Brain Wounds in Man* (1960) and *Visual Field Defects after Penetrating Missile Wounds of the Brain* (1960). O. L. Z.
R. L. G.

**THALES** (*c.*620–*c.*550 BC). The first named Western philosopher and scientist. Of the Ionian school, he was born at Miletus and travelled widely in Egypt and to Babylon, where he learned techniques of land surveying ('geometry') and astronomy. He is said to have invented formal *geometry as we know it, by formalizing empirical measuring techniques. He is also supposed to have predicted the solar eclipse of 585 BC. He held that all things are made of water; and he investigated magnets (loadstones) suggesting that they were alive, with mind, as they moved each other.

See also PRE-SOCRATIC PHILOSOPHERS.

Burnet, J. (1955 edn.). *Greek Philosophy, Thales to Plato*. London.
Kirk, G. S. and Raven, J. E. (1957). *The Presocratic Philosophers* (for Thales's recorded sayings). Cambridge.

**THEMATIC APPERCEPTION TEST (TAT).** See PROJECTIVE TECHNIQUES.

**THEOLOGY AND MIND–BRAIN IDENTITY.** If a human individual's mental life, conscious and unconscious, is identical with the functioning of that individual's brain, it is clear that when at death the brain ceases to function the mental life must thereby come to an end. And if by the soul we mean the mind, then clearly there can be no immortality of the soul. In *Plato's apt analogy, as the music ceases when the musical instrument which produces it is destroyed, so the soul ceases to exist when the bodily organism which produces it dies (*Phaedo*, 85–6). And so it might well seem that the mind–brain identity theory is directly incompatible with Christian belief in 'the life everlasting'.

The relationship of the identity hypothesis to Christian belief is more complex than this, however. The reference to Plato is a reminder that the idea of the immortality of the non-physical soul was developed, in the West, in Greek philosophy (see PSYCHE), particularly Platonism. And Platonism undoubtedly powerfully influenced the growth of Christian thought. But Christianity grew even more directly out of ancient Judaism, and it is from this source that it received its other main idea in this area, the idea of resurrection. The full phrase in the Apostles' Creed is 'the resurrection of the flesh and the life everlasting'.

The background of this belief is the ancient Hebrew view of the human being as, in modern parlance, a psychophysical unity. Generally speaking, a person was not thought of in the Hebrew scriptures (comprising the 'Old Testament' of the Christian Bible) as a non-material spirit inhabiting a physical organism, but as a completely corporeal being, 'an animated body, and not an incarnated soul' (H. W. Robinson in *The People and the Book*, ed. A. S. Peake, 1925, p. 362). Made out of the dust of the earth, at death we return to dust. We have no natural immortality, such as Plato believed the soul to have. If we live again beyond death, this can be only because God raises us up again on 'the last day' as bodily beings. This is the basic meaning of 'resurrection'; and it is in principle compatible with mind–brain identity.

But again the full picture is more complex. For we have to ask both what resurrection meant in the ancient scriptures and what it might mean today. The idea of the resurrection of the dead only developed within Hebrew religion during the last two or three centuries prior to the Christian era. In its popular form it was the belief that, at the end of the Age, God would raise the dead from their graves to a renewed life on this earth—a belief reflected in the statement in Matthew's Gospel that at the time of Jesus's death 'the tombs also were opened, and many bodies of the saints who had fallen asleep [i.e. had died] were raised, and coming out of the tombs after his resurrection they went into the holy city [Jerusalem] and appeared to many' (Matt. 27: 52–3). But a tendency was also developing to think in terms, not of a reanimated and transformed physical body, but of a 'spiritual' body inhabiting a different and 'heavenly' environment. St Paul spoke of a spiritual body (*soma pneumatikon*) as well as the natural or animal body. Using the analogy of the seed which is buried in the ground and the plant that later springs up, he says, 'It is sown a physical body, it is raised a spiritual body' (1 Cor. 15: 44). There has been much discussion of St Paul's meaning; but the most generally held view is that, according to St Paul, the individual in the resurrected state will be embodied, with a 'spiritual' rather than an earthly body, and that this body will express the inner self in relation to the world of which it is a part as the physical body now expresses it in relation to the present world. (See Dahl, 1962, ch. 1.) Thus, without attempting to say what the resurrection body will be like, St Paul is suggesting that it will be appropriate to the heavenly world; and presum-

ably, that different resurrection bodies will have individual characteristics appropriate to the different personalities which are thus embodied.

Can such an idea be further spelt out? If resurrection bodies have size and shape, and thus occupy space, it is a tempting option to postulate two (or more) spaces, in the sense of systems within each of which objects are spatially related to one another but such that each system is spatially unrelated to the other system(s). Within a resurrection world, constituting another space, the simplest model for a resurrection body would be an exact 'replica' of the former earthly body, including its detailed brain state. (More generally on the notion of replicas, see Parfitt, 1984.) A 'replica' is to be distinguished from a replica: there can be many replicas of the same original, and these can coexist with the original; but, we must stipulate that there can be only one 'replica' of a person and that the 'replica' and the original person cannot exist at the same time. That is to say, while there are many other kinds of possible universe, a universe in which resurrection, as here construed, takes place is one in which an individual's death on earth is succeeded by the coming into existence of his or her 'replica' in another space. In such a universe the identity of the 'replica' person with the earthly person consists in a total similarity of all attributes, with the consequent continuity of consciousness, character, and memory. The question, debated in discussions of the idea of *personal identity (such as Williams, 1973, ch. 1), 'What if there were two or more replicas of the same person?' no more arises in such a universe than it does in our present world; and, as in our present world, if there suddenly began to be such duplicates all that we can say is that they would disrupt our present concept of personal identity.

However, this notion of the post-mortem 'replica' provides only a starting-point, from which any building up of the idea of resurrection has immediately to diverge. For the exact 'replica' of a dying person would be a dying person, who would then proceed to die! Thus, while we have to postulate sufficient continuity as a basis for personal identity, we also have to postulate sufficient change, within this continuity, to make possible renewed life and indeed qualitatively better life. A number of the older Christian writers, including St Augustine (*City of God*, bk. 22, chs. 15–16) and St Thomas *Aquinas (*Summa Theologica*, part iii (suppl.), q. 81, art. 1), suggested that in the resurrection men and women would revert, or advance, to their optimal age, which was taken to be about 30. This is no doubt one possible way of meeting the problem. But whatever the follow-on, the 'replica' theory provides a starting-point for a conception of resurrection. Indeed, apart from the popular notion of the literal raising of buried corpses to a new life, something like this would seem to be the only intelligible interpretation of the idea of resurrection which is compatible with mind–brain identity. (See Hick, 1976, ch. 15.)

According to a very different conception, resurrection bodies are mind-dependent images. On this view the resurrection world has a status like that which *Berkeley, in his *Principles of Human Knowledge* (1710), attributed to our present world. Such a hypothesis is not, however, compatible with mind–brain identity. For on this theory consciousness survives the death of the body and forms its own 'world' by the mechanism through which *dreams are produced; though conceivably such an image world might be common to a number of percipients as a result of telepathic interaction between them (see Price, 1953).

A number of contemporary theologians and philosophers of religion have offered conceptions of 'the resurrection of the dead' other than the 'replica' conception—which presuppose some form (whether or not strict mind–brain identity) of the view that man is an indissoluble psychophysical unity, so that there can be no mental life without a living brain. Very briefly, these are: the theory that eternal life consists in one's endless preservation, as a bodily historical being, within the divine memory (Hartshorne, 1962, ch. 10); the theory that it consists in sharing the eternal divine view of one's present earthly existence (Pannenberg, 1962); and the theory that 'eternal life' is a moral quality of one's present life and does not entail any further existence after death (Phillips, 1970). These theories have in common the exclusion of any continuation of conscious life involving responsible decisions and actions through which the human person might continue to develop and change. There are however other theologians and philosophers of religion who hold that a coherent religious interpretation of life requires us to postulate the continuation and completion of the person-making process in a further life, or lives, whether involving the survival of mind after the death of the body, or the resurrection in some form of the body–mind complex, or both.

See also SOUL, BRAIN SCIENCE AND THE.     J. HI.

Dahl, M. E. (1962). *The Resurrection of the Body*.
Hartshorne, C. (1962). *The Logic of Perfection*.
Hick, J. (1976). *Death and Eternal Life*.
Pannenberg, W. (1962). *Was ist der Mensch?* (trans., 1970, *What is Man?*).
Parfitt, D. (1984). *Reasons and Persons*, part iii. Oxford.
Phillips, D. Z. (1970). *Death and Immortality*.
Price, H. H. (1953). Survival and the idea of 'another world'. *Proceedings of the Society for Psychical Research*, vol. 1, pt. 182. (Repr. in Smythies, J. R., ed. 1965, *Brain and Mind*.)
Williams, B. (1973). *Problems of the Self*.

**THERAPY.** See BEHAVIOUR THERAPY; ENCOUNTER GROUPS; GESTALT THERAPY; INTERACTIONAL APPROACH.

**THINKERS, INDEPENDENT.** On the whole, *Homo sapiens* tends to be conventional: that is, very few people have revolutionary ideas. At an early age, for instance, virtually every child is taught that the earth is a globe, revolving round the sun in a period of one year—and he (or she) will believe it. Yet a mere six hundred years ago, children who were taught at all learned that the sun goes round the earth, and they believed that with equal fervour.

Of course, there have always been rebels who have opposed what may be termed official doctrine. A Greek, Aristarchus, did so, long before the time of Christ, when he maintained that the Earth was not the centre of the universe. Nobody persecuted him, but very few people believed him. Some of the later protagonists of the Sun-centred theory were not so lucky; one of them, Giordano Bruno, was burned at the stake in Rome as recently as 1600 (though it is true that this was not his only crime in the eyes of the Inquisition, and the Church of those days was not noted for its kindliness).

Obviously, Aristarchus and Bruno were right. Bruno was to all intents and purposes following in the footsteps of Copernicus, a Polish churchman who had scandalized his contemporaries in 1543 by publishing a book in which he rejected the idea of a central earth. One of Copernicus's fiercest critics was Martin Luther, who referred to him as a fool who wanted to turn everything upside-down—a comment which cannot have worried Copernicus, who had prudently withheld publication until the last days of his life, but which faithfully reflected official views of the time. It is fair to call Copernicus an 'independent thinker', because he had no respect for orthodox science, and it is equally fair to say that throughout history there have been men of similar calibre who have been responsible for tremendous advances in knowledge. On the other hand, most modern rebels against scientific orthodoxy are not only wrong but so clearly irrational that it is by no means easy (or kind) to argue with them.

Consider, for instance, the Flat Earthers. The belief in a world shaped like a pancake is very old, but the fact that it lingers on is strange. A few decades ago there was a kernel of flat-earth believers in Zion, Illinois, presided over by one Wilbur Glenn Voliva, who believed that the world was disc-shaped, with the North Pole in the middle and a wall of ice all round. (To forestall any questions, let it be added that in Voliva's universe there was no South Pole!) Below the earth there was a kind of bargain basement inhabited by the spirits of a race of men who lived on the surface of the world before the arrival of Adam and Eve. Voliva died in 1942, but the International Flat Earth Society is more modern, and was for years controlled by the late Samuel Shenton, whose views were of the same overall type as Voliva's. Even the Apollo flights to the moon did not daunt him, and he continued to maintain that the moon is a very small body, while even the sun has a diameter of a mere thirty-two miles. He also maintained that the space-pictures of earth were deliberately faked by those who were intent on suppressing the truth.

This is highly significant. One of the modern

hallmarks of the Independent Thinker is that he is convinced that Orthodoxy is persecuting him. Generally, of course, he has no official support—but this is not an invariable rule, and there are a few rebels who have made their mark. Of these, the classic example in recent years has been Academician Lysenko, in the Soviet Union. He was (or claimed to be) a pioneer geneticist, and he produced a whole crop of revolutionary theories, together with experiments which signally failed to work. Yet he remained in favour with the Soviet authorities for an amazingly long time, and to disagree with him was to court official disapproval. All in all, Lysenko managed to put Soviet genetics back at least half a century.

Another case, less extreme but still important, was that of Hans Hörbiger, an eccentric Austrian engineer who believed that the most important material in the universe was, simply, ice. To him almost everything was icy; the stars were gigantic ice-blocks, and the moon an ice-globe which would eventually spiral down and hit us—as at least six other moons had previously done.

Hörbiger's book, *Glazial-Kosmogonie*, was published as long ago as 1913, and is regarded as a classic of pseudoscience. It is lengthy, heavy in style, humourless, and entirely without value except as a curiosity, but it led on to what was called WEL (*Welt Eis Lehre*, or Cosmic Ice Theory)—a cult which became popular in Germany between the wars, and continued to be so even after Hörbiger's death. Hörbiger himself was absolutely typical of his type; to him, everyone who disapproved of cosmic ice was to be treated as an enemy.

Most scientists were sceptical, but not all; one near-convert was Philipp Fauth, who had a considerable reputation as an astronomer, and who had compiled a large, albeit rather inaccurate, map of the moon. Some of the politicians were impressed, though they did defer to convention sufficiently to issue a statement that it was still possible to be a good National Socialist without believing in WEL. There is still a Hörbiger Institute with a British branch, though its members cannot have failed to be discouraged when the Apollo astronauts landed on the moon and had no need to use skates.

Yet another Independent Thinker who has met with a surprising amount of support is a psychoanalyst, Dr Immanuel Velikovsky, who was born in Russia but made his home in the United States. Velikovsky's book *Worlds in Collision*, published in 1950, is fully up to Hörbiger's standard. He believed that planets can turn into comets, and vice versa; that Venus used to be a comet, and that it made several close approaches to the earth in biblical times, on one occasion stopping the earth's rotation and leaving the Red Sea dry for long enough to allow the Israelites to cross.

Velikovsky's theories, elaborated in subsequent books, are so full of scientific absurdities that it is hard to see how even the most naïve reader could take them seriously. None the less, many people did—and still do. The extensive biblical references are quite correct, and the trouble is that one cannot argue—because there is no common scientific ground at all. Anyone who maintains that, for instance, the sun is 193,000,000 miles away instead of 93,000,000 can be challenged and disproved; but Velikovsky's whole theory is based on the possible interchange between planets and comets, which is no more rational than believing the earth to be flat (in fact, rather less on the whole).

There are two cults which are even more widespread: *astrology and flying saucers. Both have not mere hundreds of supporters, but millions. Astrologers are found everywhere, both on seaside piers and in lavish offices. Many are quite sincere, and when asked to explain how the apparent positions of the sun, moon, and planets can affect human destiny generally have the grace to admit that they do not know. Here, too, there is no rational basis for argument. It is useless to point out that a 'constellation' is merely a line-of-sight effect, and that the patterns are made up of unassociated stars at wildly different distances from us; it is equally useless to comment that the patterns themselves are arbitrary, and that anyone who can see the outline of two fishes in Pisces, or a sea-goat in Capricornus, must have a lively imagination by any standards. And now and then, of course, an astrologer makes a correct observation or prediction; it is impossible to be always wrong.

Astrologers are linked with the flying saucer enthusiasts, who now call themselves UFOlogists, and of whom there are two definite types. Type I follows men such as the late George Adamski and the rather mysterious Cedric Allingham, who published books describing their meetings with men from other worlds—a Martian in Allingham's case, and initially a long-haired Venusian in Adamski's. Even more astounding are the members of the Aetherius Society, who believe that they are in constant touch with Mars, Venus, and other worlds, and that messages of vital importance are telepathically relayed. Everything is regulated by the Interplanetary Parliament, which meets on Saturn and whose representatives look like huge ovoids perhaps forty feet in diameter (one might even describe them as large balls). Among various contactees are Confucius and Jesus Christ. On one occasion the earth was under attack from fish-men living on the far side of the Galaxy, though fortunately the Interplanetary Parliament took prompt action and the oncoming missile was blown to pieces by something equivalent to an Olympian thunderbolt.

The Type II UFO-believers have no faith in the Adamskis, the Allinghams, or even the Interplanetary Parliament, and content themselves with maintaining that various phenomena seen in the atmosphere are due to visiting spacecraft. Unfortunately, no saucer pilot has yet shown himself to the world at large, and most UFO pictures look so strikingly like lampshades that people with critical minds go so far as to suggest that they *are* lampshades. There is a real problem here, but psychological rather than astronomical. Nobody will deny that there are atmospheric phenomena which are difficult to explain (ball lightning is one), but to suppose alien spacecraft is frankly irrational. Moreover, recently there have been even weirder theories, some UFOlogists believing that the saucers come from inside the earth—popping out from a hole at the North Pole with the intention of keeping a watchful eye on us.

Quite apart from all this, the idea of a hollow earth lingers on—an echo of the episode of 1823 in which an American Army officer, Captain John Cleves Symmes, asked Congress for funds to send an expedition to the north polar entrance. (Congress declined, but it is on record that twenty-five members voted in Symmes's favour.) And in Germany, the present-day Society for Geocosmical Research believes that the Earth is nothing more nor less than the inside of a hollow globe; the sun is in the middle, with Australia and Britain on opposite sides, while the solid ground below our feet extends infinitely in all directions.

Such examples of independent thought could be multiplied almost *ad infinitum*. There are those who believe the sun to be cold; those who fear that the accumulation of ice at the North Pole will make the world tilt over, producing disastrous floods; and those who have a profound disbelief in evolution, preferring to think that each species appears fully fledged as if by magic. Few of these people have any scientific qualifications, but most of them are sincere, well-meaning people acting from the best possible motives. Some of the astrologers are less desirable; and there are some cults—mostly quasi-religious—which are to be deplored: they do immense harm by influencing gullible people and breaking up families. But fortunately these are the exceptions, and they are easy to detect.

Generally, the Independent Thinker has one particular theme, and one only. (It was once said that every crank thinks that every other person is a crank.) His exceptional belief does not debar him from accepting all the conventional facts of life: thus President Kruger of South Africa was a Flat Earther, while Gladstone believed so firmly in the lost continent of Atlantis that he asked the Treasury to finance an expedition to the sea-bed— a request which was turned down. Furthermore, he does not deliberately set out to be different from his fellows; he believes that he has a message, and he will do all he can to propagate it, usually for motives which are entirely altruistic.

What are regarded as erratic ideas are generally greeted with ridicule; but there are occasions when the Independent Thinker has been proved right. Only a few decades ago the concept of flight to the moon was regarded with contempt; some time after the Wright brothers had made their first 'hop' in a heavier-than-air machine, the famous astronomer Simon Newcomb was stating that nothing of the sort could ever be achieved, and that a raft pulled by birds was a more rational idea; and in pre-Stephenson days it was maintained that no human being could possibly stand up to the strain of being carried along at thirty miles per hour. To be dogmatic is always dangerous, and science fiction has the uncanny habit of changing into science fact.

P. M.

Evans, J. (1975). *Cults of Unreason*. London.
Moore, P. (1978). *Can You Speak Venusian?* London.

**THINKING: HOW IT CAN BE TAUGHT.** Is thinking simply IQ in action, or is it a separable skill that can be developed just as we develop *skill at cooking, skiing, or riding a bicycle? It seems that when asked to think about matters within their own experience, children of relatively low IQ do much better than expected when compared with children of high IQ. It seems that the practical operating skills of thinking (decision, judgement, assessment of priorities, breadth of scan) are not the same as the knowledge-absorbing skills (perceiving relationships, attention skills, ordering information, memorizing).

If thinking is a skill, then it seems likely to be a natural skill that we can pick up in the ordinary course of events just as we pick up the skill of walking, talking, or breathing. We may indeed pick up the skill, but as a 'two-finger skill'. The expression comes from the world of typing. Someone who has to pick up the skill of typing as he goes along acquires a fair degree of skill using two fingers, but the skill never develops much beyond this point of coping with immediate needs. Someone else who sets out to train to be a secretary learns touch-typing from the start, and within eight weeks has a greater skill than the two-finger operator. Quite soon the skill of the touch-typist is far ahead. A skill that is built up by coping with the immediate situation may never develop beyond this level. For example, 'prejudice' is an excellent two-finger thinking skill since it allows action without reflection and removes the need for decision. But in a wider field prejudice can be inhibiting.

Twenty-four groups of children, aged 9 to 10, from six London primary schools with widely differing social backgrounds, were asked to consider the suggestion that 'bread, fish, and milk should be made freely available'. The discussions were tape-recorded and analysed. Some of the children came from families that were too poor to afford milk on a regular basis. Yet twenty-three out of the twenty-four groups decided that the suggestion was a bad one. Their reasoning went something like this:

'If bread, fish, and milk are free the shops will be overcrowded.'
'So the buses going to the shops will be overcrowded.'
'The drivers will ask for more pay.'
'They won't get more pay so they will go on strike.'
'Other people will join the strike and there will be chaos.'
'So it is a bad idea.'

This is a typical example of 'point-to-point' thinking in which one point becomes the starting-point for the next idea and so on. It often occurs with younger children. Teaching some scanning strategy allows the child to broaden his area of attention and to avoid getting pulled along a point-to-point track.

At the other extreme is the highly skilled, highly intelligent, highly articulate thinker. He makes up his mind instantly on an issue and then uses his skill of argument to support the position that he has taken up. The sheer brilliance of this supporting effort makes it unlikely that the thinker will ever feel the need to change his position. And yet at no time has he ever tried to *explore* the subject. Similarly we put a lot of emphasis on debating skills, with the assumption that if you can prove the other fellow wrong, somehow that proves you right. In terms of thinking skill both these strategies are highly inefficient and indeed dangerously so.

In the past, attempts have been made to teach thinking by teaching the rules of logic or the rules of the syllogism. Taught this way, logic can become an abstract, idealized system with little relevance to everyday life. More importantly, logic can only process the material presented to it by perception, and it is at the perception stage that most ordinary thinking has to take place. The general approach to teaching thinking is not to teach it directly but to criticize pupils when they make logical errors. Unfortunately, thinking that is free from logical errors is by no means necessarily good thinking. Bad logic makes for bad thinking, but good logic makes for good thinking *only* if the starting perceptions are themselves appropriate. Logic is only a servicing device for perception. It is far too much part of our culture to assume that a logical argument proves a point.

In education we also assume that from an interested discussion on some subject, pupils will abstract certain habits and skills of thinking and transfer them to new situations. This does not seem to happen. Such discussions increase fluency but seem to provide little transferable skill. If, rather, we create, quite deliberately, various attention-directing tools, these tools can then be practised on a rapidly changing variety of situations. This change is necessary so that attention stays on the tool and does not drift to the content—as it would if the content remained constant.

In the perception stage, much of thinking is concerned with directing attention. After all, a question is only a device for directing attention. The very first lesson might introduce the PMI device. This requires the pupils deliberately to look for the Plus, Minus, and Interesting points in a situation. It is intended to prevent the instant-judgement habit and to encourage exploration before decision rather than after it. Most people would of course claim to carry out this simplistic procedure, and no doubt they do in doubtful situations. But very few people carry out the procedure if they have a firm opinion on the matter. In one

experiment two random groups of adults were asked to consider the suggestions 'that marriage should be a five-year contract' and 'that currency should be dated so that at the year end the exchange with the new currency could be altered according to the rate of inflation'. In the first group 23 per cent were in favour of the five-year marriage contract and in the second group 35 per cent were in favour of the dated currency. The questions were then switched over and each group was asked to do a deliberate PMI on the matter. The 23 per cent in favour of the contract marriage now rose to 37 per cent in favour. The 35 per cent in favour of the dated currency now fell to 11 per cent. So asking people to do what they would have claimed to do anyway made a huge difference. A group of thirty children, aged 9 to 11, was given the suggestion that all children should be paid some money each week for going to school. Each one of them was in favour of the idea. They were then asked to do a PMI on it. Five minutes later twenty-nine out of the thirty had changed their minds and decided it would be a bad idea.

Eight groups of primary-school children were asked to consider the problem of a girl whose parents were being posted abroad. The girl wanted to continue her studies to be a teacher: should she stay behind or go with her parents? The four groups who had had no special training considered the following number of aspects of the situation: 3, 5, 5, and 5. The four groups who had had ten thinking lessons considered 17, 17, 13, and 19 aspects.

It is not really surprising that skill can be developed by direct attention and practice.

See also INTELLIGENCE; PROBLEM-SOLVING.  E. B.

Bono, E. de (1977). *Teaching Thinking*. Albuquerque, New Mexico.

**THORNDIKE,** EDWARD LEE (1874–1949), born in Williamsburg, Massachusetts, is best known for his contributions to the psychology of *learning, and secondarily for his work in educational psychology and mental testing (see INTELLIGENCE). While doing graduate work with William *James at Harvard in the 1890s, he became interested in animal intelligence; he studied the intelligence of chicks in James's own basement. For financial reasons he soon transferred to Columbia University, where he studied under James McKeen *Cattell. His thesis, 'Animal Intelligence: an experimental study of the associative processes in animals', became one of the most influential works ever written in American psychology. In it are described the famous 'puzzle-box' experiments with cats, dogs, and chicks. In a typical experiment, a cat could escape from a box by clawing down a rope, lifting a latch, or engaging in a series of different manipulations; and escape would give the cat access to food. From trial to trial, Thorndike plotted the times it took for an animal to escape; over trials, animals were found to require less and less time to make the escape response.

These data composed the first 'learning curves', and were said to show something fundamental about the nature of learning.

As formalized in his later works (notably *Animal Intelligence*, 1911), Thorndike's theory of learning may be summarized as follows. Learning occurs 'by trial and error, and accidental success', or, as we have come to simplify this view, by *trial and error*. Correct movements—for example, movements toward a door-latch in a puzzle-box—will lead to a 'satisfying state of affairs' and be 'stamped in'. Wrong movements will lead to an 'annoying state of affairs' and be 'stamped out'. Over time, only correct movements will survive; a cat at this point would have learned the correct response to the puzzle-box and could escape quickly. The learning process could be reduced to a number of 'laws'. The *law of effect* describes the trial-and-success process noted above: a response is more or less likely to occur depending on whether it produces a satisfying or annoying state of affairs. The *law of exercise* states that learning improves with practice. Other laws and sub-laws were presented, and occasionally changed, over the course of Thorndike's career.

Thorndike's work on learning was a step away from the earlier psychology of mind and towards the *functionalist and *behaviourist movements that came to dominate American psychology. Prior to Thorndike's work, all learning, even in simple animals, was said to show some sign of *consciousness. But for Thorndike, learning occurred simply as the result of the satisfying or annoying effects of instinctive movements. Though he described the learning process as affecting associative bonds between stimuli and responses, in the tradition of the British associationists, his emphasis on the trial-and-error nature of learning and on observable movement made consciousness seem a less important factor in the learning process.

From 1899 to 1940 Thorndike taught at Teachers College of Columbia University, and his contributions to educational psychology are many. His textbook, *Educational Psychology* (1903, later revised and expanded), became a classic in that field. In 1901 he published a paper with Robert Sessions *Woodworth dispelling the myth that training on one task necessarily transfers to training on a different task (SEE TRANSFER OF TRAINING); this paper foretold the end of traditional classical education in schools. He also did work on mental measurements and the study of individual differences, applied animal learning theories to human education, constructed a scale to measure children's handwriting, and with I. Lorge compiled an important table of word-frequency counts. By far America's most prolific psychologist, he published more than 450 articles and many books in his lifetime.                                    R. E.

**THOULESS,** ROBERT HENRY (1894–1984). British psychologist, born in Norwich and educated at Corpus Christi College, Cambridge. He became a lecturer in psychology at Manchester and later at Glasgow before returning to Cambridge as a lecturer, later Reader, in educational psychology, a post which he occupied with distinction for almost thirty years.

Thouless is best known for his experimental work on size and brightness constancy, to which his approach differed substantially from that of the *Gestalt psychologists. He laid the emphasis not on constancy of appearance of objects *per se* but on the element of compromise which he thought to be involved in its genesis. If, for example, a subject is required to match a circular disc placed obliquely so that its retinal image is elliptical, with a series of ellipses placed at right angles to his line of sight, he was found invariably to choose an ellipse which is less elliptical, i.e. more circular, than the retinal image. This Thouless described as phenomenal regression to the 'real' object, and it appeared to indicate that a property of an object, such as its size, shape, or brightness, is intermediate between that of the peripheral stimulus pattern on the one hand and the actual property of the object on the other. At the same time, Thouless insisted that phenomenal regression, although it might show marked individual differences, could not be assigned to learning. Although his work attracted considerable interest, he was not without his critics, in particular Kurt *Koffka.

Thouless had wide interests in general and social psychology, among them psychical research and the psychology of religion. He was for many years a consultant to the National Foundation for Educational Research and was president of both the British Psychological Society and the Society for Psychical Research.                                    O. L. Z.

**THURSTONE,** LOUIS LEON (1887–1955), American pioneer in psychometrics (mental measurement). Thurstone was born in Chicago of Swedish ancestry, obtained his doctorate at the University of Chicago, and taught there until he retired to Chapel Hill, North Carolina. Earlier he had studied as an electrical engineer, and worked with Edison on cine projection; but in 1914 he turned to psychology, and became involved in the production of tests for army recruits in the First World War.

From then on the main goal of his researches was the measurement of mental qualities, whereby psychology could become a quantitative and rational science. This was not merely an academic exercise; he succeeded in developing and applying his new techniques to a wide variety of practical problems.

The earliest attempts at mental measurement were the so-called *psychophysical methods, developed by German psychologists in the nineteenth century for studying people's sensitivity to touch, sound, and other sensations. For example, what was the smallest difference in pitch between two tones that people could detect? Thurstone showed that such methods could be extended to much more complex qualities, such as the strength of attitudes, e.g. like or dislike of communism, capital punishment, negroes, or the Church. He published a number of such attitude scales, and used them for measuring the effects of propaganda on people's prejudices. Many subsequent research workers in social psychology have constructed, and made use of, Thurstone-type scales.

Another topic was the measurement of progress in learning (i.e. the plotting of learning 'curves'), and in mental development generally. He showed how to express such development in absolute units, comparable to physical measurements. This made it possible to predict the zero point of mental growth, namely around three months before birth.

Thurstone was prolific in the construction of *intelligence tests, and, being dissatisfied with current definitions of intelligence, he published a thoughtful book, *The Nature of Intelligence* (1924). This he approached from the biological angle, rather than the logical or statistical. In the 1930s he contested Charles *Spearman's view of intelligence as a unitary, general or 'g' factor. He proposed that it is a combination of several distinctive abilities, e.g. verbal comprehension, reasoning, memory. And he superseded Spearman's statistical technique of measuring g with a much more flexible procedure known as multiple factor analysis, which could handle numerous ability factors simultaneously. With his Primary Mental Abilities tests, constructed for various age-groups, he could obtain a profile of each person's strengths and weaknesses (see *Vectors of the Mind*, 1935, and *Multiple Factor Analysis*, 1947). It is for this work on factor analysis that he is most widely known; and it was applied by him, or his numerous followers, to many practical problems: for example, isolating the main distinguishable types of mental illness, analysing human perceptual abilities, or developing new tests of such special aptitudes as mechanical ability.

Thurstone was interested too in the measurement of personality characteristics, and published a widely used test of psychoneurotic tendencies. In each of the many areas that he touched he produced original ideas, and innovative techniques of measurement. He also advanced the study of his subject by founding the outstanding journal *Psychometrika*, and guiding it for nearly twenty years, until his death.    P. E. V.

**TIME-GAP EXPERIENCE.** Quite frequently, during the course of a long-distance journey, motorists reach some point—a crossroads for instance—and find they have no conscious recollection of covering the miles since the last village. They usually interpret this in terms of time, reporting, for example, 'a lost half hour'. Having consulted their watches, they may reflect, bemusedly, 'How did it jump to three o'clock?' For this reason, the term 'time-gap experience' has been coined for discussion of the phenomenon (Reed, 1972).

The sudden awareness of a 'time gap' is usually experienced as 'waking up'; part of the puzzlement felt by the individual is due to the experience of 'waking up' when one is already awake. But more perturbing is the belief that there has been an inexplicable blank in one's awareness of the passage of time. In part this is due to the strict temporal structuring of our civilization. For most of us, our workaday lives demand continual reference to clock time, and assessment of temporal duration. Only in certain occupations or during holidays can we enjoy release from the constant need to be aware of the passage of time. But more importantly, our sense of self is intimately related to the subjective awareness of the continuity of life. Any break in personal time is alarming, because it suggests some disintegration of psychic synthesis.

There is considerable evidence to suggest that our awareness of temporal duration is determined by *events*. These can be of both external and internal origin. What the time-gapper describes as his failure to register a period of time is really a failure to register a series of external events which would normally have functioned as his time-markers. The problem is primarily one of *attention*. The question, then, is how he could fail to register so many sequential events. How can a person completely fail to 'pay attention' over a prolonged period while successfully performing a very complex task like driving a car, which itself is largely dependent on reactions to external events?

The answer may be found by considering the nature of skilled behaviour. (See SKILL.) This is hierarchically organized, so that its elementary components become progressively automatized. The skilled driver does not need to pay conscious attention to such basic matters as the position of the controls, or the movements of his hands and feet. He can afford to reserve his attention for the assessment of input at a strategic level. If the situation is relatively undemanding, and external events routine or predictable, he may require only a low level of conscious attention. He will deploy his attentional resources elsewhere—typically, to his own thoughts. In one sense, he has 'switched to automatic pilot'. But any significant change in the situation will involve the processing of new information, the assessment of probabilities and the making and implementation of decisions. All this requires heightened conscious awareness, a switching back to 'manual control'. The crossroads, for example, introduces a sudden increase in information load, which demands the sharp refocusing of our motorist's attention. And this is the moment when the time-gapper describes himself as 'waking up'.    G. F. R.

Reed, G. (1972). *The Psychology of Anomalous Experience*. London.

**TITCHENER,** EDWARD BRADFORD (1867–1927). Born at Chichester, Sussex, he studied philosophy at Oxford and took his doctorate under Wilhelm *Wundt at Leipzig. He moved to Cornell in 1892, where he spent the rest of his life. Much influenced by Wundt's psychological outlook, he translated a large part of the 5th edition of his *Physiologische Psychologie*, published in America as *Principles of Physiological Psychology* in 1904. His own work was mainly on sensation and *attention. Although highly respected, he never felt really at home with American psychology, and wholly rejected *behaviourism as irrelevant to psychology as he understood it. (None the less, he liked and respected J. B. *Watson and, unlike his colleagues, supported him warmly after he lost his post at Johns Hopkins University in consequence of a personal indiscretion.)

Titchener's principal works are: *Experimental Psychology: a manual of laboratory practices* (1901, 1905); *Lectures on the Elementary Psychology of Feeling and Attention* (1908); *Lectures on the Experimental Psychology of the Thought Processes* (1909); and *A Text-Book of Psychology* (1909–10).                      O. L. Z.

**TOLMAN,** EDWARD CHASE (1886–1959). American psychologist, born at Newtown, Massachusetts and educated at the Massachusetts Institute of Technology and at Harvard, where he obtained his doctorate in 1915. He spent almost the whole of his active academic life at the University of California at Berkeley, where he evolved a theory of *learning which, while behaviouristic, owed little to J. B. *Watson; though the theory was formulated in purely behavioural terms, reflexes were not central to his ideas. Tolman, who worked almost exclusively with rats, placed much emphasis on the importance of latent learning, reward expectancy, and the formation of hypotheses in animal learning. He also placed emphasis on spatial orientation and cognitive maps in maze-learning.

Tolman's most important book was *Purposive Behavior in Animals and Men* (1932). Jointly with the former Viennese psychologist Egon *Brunswik, he wrote an influential article entitled 'The Organism and the Causal Texture of the Environment' (1935).

**TOUCH.** Objects in contact with the skin can arouse a variety of tactile sensations, of which introspection allows several qualities to be distinguished: for example, vibration, steady pressure, light touch. The sensations can be graded in intensity in a predictable manner in relation to the magnitude of the stimulus, as described quantitatively by the *Weber–Fechner and *Stevens's power law relations (see PSYCHOPHYSICS). The position of an applied stimulus, both absolute for a single point and relative with respect to two loci of stimulation, can be detected, with varying degrees of accuracy, in different parts of the body surface.

The physiological mechanisms underlying these perceptual properties can be analysed in a systematic manner, starting with the neural receptor elements in the skin. These are at the ends of axons

connected with the spinal cord and brain stem. Neural processing occurs at the spinal, brain stem and thalamic levels on the pathway from the skin to the cerebral cortex. Further processing in the somatosensory area of the cerebral cortex and in the adjacent association areas of the cortex leads to final elaboration of sensation, where perception is assumed to occur.

The groundwork of knowledge, as of other sensory systems, was laid in experiments on anaesthetized or conscious animals, in which very precise studies of morphology, physiology, and behaviour could be made. This knowledge has recently been extended, in a dramatic way by electrophysiological and correlated psychophysical studies, to conscious human subjects, with a remarkable degree of concordance with the animal studies.

**Cutaneous sensory tactile receptors.** The skin contains several kinds of encapsulated mechanoreceptors (tactile receptors) innervated by myelinated dorsal root nerve fibres, and each kind is specialized to detect particular parameters of a mechanical stimulus. The *Pacinian corpuscle*, the first cutaneous receptor to be discovered, is relatively large, up to 2 mm long and 1 mm in diameter, and is present in the deeper layers of both hairy and hairless (glabrous) skin. It is pearl-shaped and comprises a lamellated structure, with an outer capsule, outer lamellae, inner lamellae, and in its core the specialized rod-like nerve terminal. The corpuscle is adapted to respond to vibration, with maximal sensitivity at 200–300 hertz and a range (band width) of 20 to 1,500 hertz. It is capable of detecting movements smaller than a micrometre (about one-twenty-fifth of one-thousandth of an inch). The lamellae are high-pass filters that prevent steadily maintained pressure from penetrating to the nerve terminal in the core, but allow rapidly changing pressures to, so that vibrations can be detected, even in the presence of maintained pressure.

*Meissner's corpuscles* are encapsulated and present in the glabrous skin of Primates, including man. They lie in rows just below the epidermis, in dermal papillae. The papillae correspond to the familiar surface ridges of the fingers and toes that form each individual's distinctive fingerprint. Meissner's corpuscles are innervated by myelinated axons and, like Pacinian corpuscles, also detect vibration, but at lower frequencies and with lesser sensitivity. Their maximal sensitivity is at 20–40 hertz and their frequency range from about 1 to 400 hertz. The corresponding receptors in non-Primates are the Krause end bulbs, which also detect changing stimuli.

In hairy skin, the *hair follicles* are innervated by myelinated fibres that have terminals arranged in a 'palisade' round the hair shaft. They too respond to changing stimuli, and can be subdivided into at least three sub-categories, with different band widths for maximal sensitivity to hair movement and different thresholds of movement sensitivity.

All these kinds of mechanoreceptors have one feature in common—they do not respond to a steadily maintained displacement of the skin, and thus are incapable of detecting steady pressure. On the other hand, they can encode with great precision the magnitude and wavelength of vibratory stimuli of different frequencies, covering a range from less than 1 hertz to greater than 1,500 hertz.

Static or steadily maintained mechanical stimuli are detected by two other specialized cutaneous receptors. The first and more numerous are the *Merkel* cells, which occur in small clusters in the lower margin of the epidermis. In hairy skin these clusters are scattered, each innervated by a single myelinated axon, and form Iggo–Pinkus domes visible at the skin surface, especially after depilation of the skin. The receptors form *Sa I* mechanoreceptors that can sustain a discharge during static deformation, as well as during superimposed vibrations. The mechanical thresholds in hairy skin are about 1 micrometre, and the receptors can fire at rates higher than a thousand a second when the skin is stroked. The Sa I receptors are also present in glabrous skin, the Merkel cells there lying in the so-called rete pegs of the epidermis.

The other slowly-adapting receptor, the *Sa II*, has the *Ruffini ending* as its receptor. These are present in the dermis. They are spindle shaped, up to 2 mm long, with a distinct capsule, and a densely branched nerve ending in the central core of the receptor. These receptors are structurally similar to the Golgi tendon organs, and have the similar property of responding with a sustained discharge to maintained displacement of the skin. The mechanical sensitivity of the Sa II receptors is less than that of the Sa I.

**Receptive fields.** Each of these receptors occupies a small region of skin, from about 100–300 micrometres in diameter for the Sa I and Meissner's corpuscles in the fingertip, to several centimetres for hair follicle receptors in the arm and trunk skin. These small spots are the *receptive fields from which a discharge of impulses can be evoked by an appropriate stimulus. The sizes of individual receptive fields and the density of innervation (the number of receptive fields per unit area) are important factors in determining the location of a stimulus, and for two-point discrimination, the ability to distinguish two stimuli applied simultaneously.

**Central processing.** This array of mechanoreceptors provides the central nervous system with a great deal of information about the characteristics of mechanical stimuli (intensity, duration, band width, location) that is further processed at spinal, brain stem, and thalamic levels before it reaches the cerebral cortex.

*Direct pathways.* The most direct routes go via the dorsal columns of the spinal cord to the lower end of the brain stem, where the ascending branches of the incoming sensory nerve fibres make synaptic connections with neurones that in turn send axons to the ventro-basal thalamus. Thalamic neurones in their turn send their axons to the somatosensory region of the cerebral cortex. An important feature of this direct system is that it can preserve, to an astonishing degree, the information encoded by the cutaneous receptors—the system has the property of specificity. Individual neurones of the somatosensory cerebral cortex may have characteristics analogous to the different kinds of primary cutaneous sensory receptors, in terms of their responses to mechanical stimuli, encoding parameters such as amplitude, static/dynamic aspects, and frequency response range; but supplemented by additional properties, such as feature extraction, e.g. location of stimulated skin and direction of a moving object.

*Indirect pathways.* There are several other sensory pathways in addition to those via the dorsal column, medial lemniscus system. These others are more elaborate, since additional neurones are present in them, and may also be non-specific, because an admixture of inputs from different touch receptors, as well as from thermoreceptors and nociceptors, can interact. The ascending information in these pathways (such as the spinothalamic tract) may have lost, to varying degrees, some of the spatial and specific attributes of the dorsal column system. Their role in 'touch' is still open to question, but they provide sensory pathways in parallel with the direct dorsal column routes.

**Central control of sensation.** A further important feature of tactile sensation, also present in other senses, is that not all the stimuli delivered to the skin surface necessarily cause excitation in the somatosensory cortex and an associated sensory awareness. There are very potent control systems, usually originating in the brain, that can modify the transmission of excitation from the skin on its way to the cerebral cortex. This is achieved through descending inhibition that interacts on neurones, at several levels in the sensory pathway, with the incoming excitatory information. This inhibition can totally or partially prevent the onflow of information, and may be used to enhance contrast between a stimulated area and adjacent regions, or to admit only certain inputs to higher levels. In this latter context it is analogous to 'attention'—a familiar capacity to attend to certain stimuli and disregard others. These interactions are based on excitatory and inhibitory synapses playing against each other on individual neurones and, therefore are accessible to pharmacological manipulation, although this has been little exploited in relation to cutaneous touch.

**Recent studies in man.** In the past there was considerable controversy about the cutaneous sensory mechanisms, including the existence and function of cutaneous receptors. Although experimental evidence from animal studies leads to the conclusion that the general rules of specificity operate, it has only recently become possible to provide direct evidence from studies on conscious man. When a thin insulated tungsten wire electrode is inserted through the human skin and into a peripheral nerve it can, by suitable adjustment, record the impulses in a single axon coming from a cutaneous mechanoreceptor. This technique has been applied most rigorously to analyse cutaneous receptors in the hand, by recording from the median nerve in the arm. Four principal kinds of mechanoreceptor, with myelinated axons, exist in human glabrous skin, corresponding to: Pacinian corpuscles, Meissner's corpuscles, Sa I (Merkel receptors), and Sa II (Ruffini endings). The general characteristics of the receptors closely match those already well known from animal studies. The sensory function of the receptors was assessed by comparing the subject's report of his sensations with the responses of individual afferent fibres recorded at the same time. Criticism of this approach has been directed at the likelihood that a mechanical stimulus, even though controlled with great precision, could excite other receptors in addition to the one recorded from electrically, so that a one-to-one correspondence of sensation and unit receptor activity would be difficult to assert. In a refinement of the technique, electrical stimulation through the recording electrode was used as a means of precise excitation of a single, functionally identified, sensory axon. The exciting, and fundamentally important, result of this approach has been to establish in a quite convincing way, that the different kinds of receptor can indeed cause perceptually distinct sensation. Thus, the Pacinian corpuscle receptors caused a sense of tickling or vibration when stimulated at frequencies above 20–50 hertz, with a sensation of vibration related to the actual frequency of stimulation. Meissner corpuscles (Fa I) evoked a sense of tapping, flutter, buzzing, or vibration (related to the frequency of stimulation) that did not change its sensory quality if the stimulation continued for several seconds. Sa I (Merkel receptor) units did not evoke a sensation if only two or three electrically induced impulses were evoked at frequencies of 5–10 hertz, and for larger numbers of impulses at higher frequencies they evoked a sense of sustained pressure or sustained contact, lacking either the vibratory or tapping quality of the Pacinian and Meissner units. In contrast, activity in Sa II units did not give rise to any sensation, and so may be more concerned with muscle reflexes and proprioception which are not in consciousness.

These results brilliantly confirm the suggestions coming from the correlative studies in man and make possible the restatement of Muller's now ancient Law of Specific Nerve Energies. As originally stated, this asserted that excitation of a sense organ, by whatever means, always gave rise to the same modality of sensation, whether—in the case of, say, vision—the stimulus was the normal one of light acting on the retina or was an abnormal one, such as pressure on the eyeball. In late nineteenth-century elaborations, the Law came to be restated as asserting that every kind of sensation required its own kind of nerve fibre, and that each kind of nerve fibre with its end organ had a 'specific energy', giving rise to a certain definite sensation and no other. The experimental results cited above give credence to Muller's original proposal—namely, that a given kind of receptor or its nerve fibre, when excited by whatever means, gives rise to a certain sensation. The sensation resulting from the simultaneous excitation of several kinds of receptor, such as mechanoreceptors and thermoreceptors, can, however, yield a sensation that arises from central interactions among the sensory inflow.

A further consequence of this new work is that the old controversy between 'specificity' and 'pattern' theories of cutaneous sensation has been resolved in favour of the 'specificity' theory.

**Relation to other skin senses.** This review of the 'tactile' sensory system has concentrated on the sensory receptors because it is in that area of knowledge that dramatic progress has been made in the last two decades, with the resolution of the long-standing controversy about the nature and role of the sensory receptors. Two other cutaneous sensory systems that coexist with the tactile system provide specific information about nociception (painful stimuli) and thermoreception (temperature sensation). Each is served by its own set of specific sensory receptors. The central processing of sensory information from these receptors is by the indirect route through the dorsal horn of the spinal cord. The three systems, tactile, nociceptive and thermal, do however interact. A striking example is the reduction in pain that can, in appropriate conditions, be achieved by the concurrent application of a tactile stimulus and a noxious stimulus. A familiar instance is provided by the instinctive act of rubbing a sore place on the skin. Rubbing or stroking excites sensitive tactile receptors that interact on neurones in the spinal cord with an inflow from the nociceptors and block or reduce the excitatory action of the latter. TENS (transcutaneous electrical nerve stimulation) is a method of pain relief, now in clinical use, that is based on this interaction. A. I.

Euler, C. von, Franzen, O., Lindblom, U., and Ottoson, D. (eds.) (1984). *Somatosensory Mechanisms* (Wenner-Gren Symposium no. 41). London.

Handwerker, H. O. H. (1984). Nerve fibre discharges and sensation. *Human Neurobiology*, **3**, 1–58.

Iggo, A. (1982). Cutaneous sensory mechanisms. In Barlow, H. B. and Mollon, J. D. (eds.), *The Senses*. Cambridge.

**TRANSFER.** This essential concept for appreciating learning concerns the benefit of, or impairment from, what has been learned on later performance. Where there is resulting improvement, transfer from the past experience is *positive*; when impairment, the transfer is *negative*. The same learned knowledge or components of skill may transfer to be helpful (Positive) in some situations, but may impair (be negative transfer) in other situations, or for some other skills. Thus transfer from practising table tennis may impair one's ability to hit a tennis ball with the appropriate arm movements. To understand the concept, it is important to note that the neural mechanisms for positive and negative transfer are exactly the same: the only difference is whether what has transferred is useful or not.

Transfer tends to be thought of in general terms, rather than for particular items of knowledge. Thus the skill of learning Latin is generally supposed to transfer positively to the learning of other languages, although it may transfer negatively to differently constructed languages. A commonly experienced transfer problem occurs when driving in a different country, on the opposite side of the road from that to which one is used. Accidents from negative transfer are particularly likely to occur when starting off in the morning on the wrong side, and when faced with situations such as complicated crossings. It is remarkable that complete reversal of accustomed patterns of behaviour is not more difficult than it generally is.

Precisely what it is that transfers, and why it transfers, are far from understood, though these are essential questions for education. They are also extremely important in appreciating the difficulties a pilot may experience in transferring from one type of aircraft to another, and in designing flight simulators to give as much positive transfer in training, with as little negative transfer as possible. There may be features of a simulator (such as horizontal raster lines on a video screen) which allow 'flight' with cues that are not available in actual flying, and which may be dangerous.

It is interesting that perceptual abilities and skills can transfer from one part of the body to other parts. Thus, discrimination of two-point touch practised on the back of one hand (with a pair of dividers) can transfer to improved two-point discrimination on the corresponding region of the other hand.

See also TRANSFER OF TRAINING.

**TRANSFERENCE.** A patient in psychotherapy tends to transfer into his relationship with the therapist the sometimes intense feelings he experienced at an earlier stage in his life, in his relationship with his mother or father or other important figure. The formation of a transference relationship thus facilitates the overcoming of resistances to the recall of painful experiences from his past. The transference relationship (entirely different from *transfer above) is said to be positive if the patient is compliant, negative if he is

defiant. The formation of a positive relationship may by itself relieve symptoms, but this is no more than a false 'transference cure'. If it is strong and persistent, and the patient becomes dependent on the therapist, the relationship amounts to a 'transference neurosis'. By 'counter-transference' is meant the transfer by the therapist of feelings derived from his past into his relationship with the patient: such feelings have to be recognized and overcome.

Sigmund *Freud described transference in 1895 in one of his first papers on psychoanalysis. Seeing the trouble that was caused to his colleague, Josef *Breuer, when he became the object of the erotic feelings of his patient 'Anna O.', he argued that these feelings referred not to his colleague personally but to a fantasy figure. He was later to encourage the development of fantasy about the therapist by his habit of sitting unseen behind the patient lying on a couch. The therapist thus becomes a blank screen on to which the patient projects his feelings. However, the emphasis in psychoanalytic treatment gradually moved from the analysis of dreams (see FREUD ON DREAMS) and the overcoming of resistances to the opening up of communication between therapist and patient through the analysis and elucidation of the transference relationship. This was the main therapeutic tool of psychoanalysis, and its hallmark, during the years between the wars. The transference relationship is an inevitable necessity, Freud argued. Psychoanalysis does not create it. It brings it to light so that it can be combated at the appropriate time. It has to be dissolved before treatment ends so that the patient can reassert his independence and resume an adult role. Dissolution proves difficult in some cases.

Schools of psychotherapy differ in the balance they seek to achieve between the advantages and disadvantages of the transference relationship. (See FREUDIANISM: LATER DEVELOPMENTS.) Some modern schools counteract the tendency from the beginning and regard the re-enactment of the conflicts of the past within the relationship with the therapist as inessential. More important is what happens in the patient's relationships with members of his family and others. The relationship with the therapist is then regarded as mediating, and interpretations are concerned with the difficulties the patient experiences outside the treatment sessions, or in his relationships with others in a therapeutic group.                    D. R. D.

Freud, S. (1901). Fragment of an analysis of a case of hysteria ('Dora'). (Trans. Strachey, A. and J., Pelican Freud Library, **8**, 157–61.) Harmondsworth.
Melan, D. H. (1963). *A Study of Brief Psychotherapy*. New York.

**TRANSFER OF TRAINING.** It is often evident in *transfer situations that a very considerable amount of learning has been carried from one task to another. For both theoretical and for practical

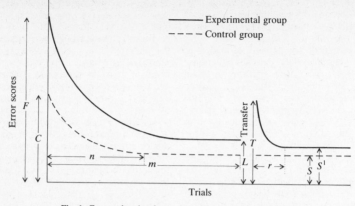

**Fig. 1.** Curves showing form of typical transfer experiment.

reasons, it is desirable to be able to measure the amount of this transfer.

Let us consider a typical transfer experiment or situation. An experimental group of subjects learns some task or skill A. Initially, as we might expect, their errors are many; but after some time, or number of trials, they reach a satisfactory and stable level of performance characterized by few errors. They then attempt some new task B; and again proceed, more or less rapidly, from making many errors to making only a few. (The mean performance of this group is shown, smoothed for the sake of argument, as the continuous line in Fig. 1, whose notation will henceforth be used.) A control group has learned task B *ab initio* (dashed line in figure), and it is generally the case that the final error levels of performance of the two groups ($S$ and $S'$) are virtually indistinguishable—and may, indeed, be zero.

All the quantities labelled in the figure can be measured. $F$, $C$, $L$, $T$, $S$, and $S'$ are all measures of performance in terms of error; while $m$, $n$, and $r$ are either numbers of trials or elapsed time. Since all these are available, it is natural to ask how they may best be used and combined to express the amount of learning transferred by the experimental group from task A to task B.

The number of expressions and formulae that has been proposed is very large (Gagne et al., 1948; Murdock, 1957); but they all fall into one of two categories: there are those which measure the saving of training time, or number of trials (i.e. which in some way compare $r$ with $n$), and those which are concerned with the initial performance of subjects immediately after transfer (i.e. which evaluate $T$). The former class we may call *savings* measures; the latter we may call *first-shot* measures. Unfortunately, although the contrary was often tacitly assumed, these two classes of measures can give sharply contrasting impressions; for it is quite possible to save a great deal of training time on the second task ($r < n$) while still finding a marked transient decremental effect of

transfer ($T > C$) (Hammerton, 1967; Hammerton and Tickner, 1967). The measure selected must answer the question the user wishes to put; and he must always be aware that it may not answer any other question.

The simplest question is: What proportion of training time in task B is saved by prior training on task A? This is clearly and straightforwardly measured by the quantity $a$, given by:

$$a = (n-r)/n \qquad (1)$$

It is worth pausing to note how difficult it is to apply even the simplest psychological findings in a practical situation. Suppose someone was being trained to use some complex industrial equipment (task B) by practice on a simulator (task A). The proportional saving of time is given by (1); but in practice the following questions arise: What is the running cost per hour of the simulator as compared to that of the real equipment? Does even a poor operator of the real equipment produce some useful output which can be set against cost? Is he, on the other hand, likely merely to waste raw materials or damage the equipment itself? Evidently the practical utility of a training programme or device cannot be measured by any simple expression, but is a complex psychological and economic question.

If we recall that there is often a brief but marked impairment in performance immediately after transfer, it will be evident that there are many practical situations in which some measure of first-shot transfer is necessary. Again, more than one question may be asked about this. One is: How does the learning immediately after transfer compare with that required by the control group to reach a stable performance? This comparison may be given by:

$$b = (F-T)/(F-S) \qquad (2)$$

But a user may raise a practical objection to this;

for he may not be concerned with the comparative measurement of learning, however interesting that may be theoretically. He generally needs to know whether expensive equipment is liable to be misused when first handled: in other words, how does first-shot transfer performance ($T$) compare with the stable performance of the control group ($S$)? The information required may be given as a simple percentage:

$$c = 100(1 - T/S) \qquad (3)$$

Another question which can arise in practice is this. Suppose that you have no control group—i.e. suppose that all trainees start on some simulator device, and that no man is allowed to begin with task B. How much of the skill acquired with the simulator (A) will be retained upon first transfer? This is not the question answered either by (2) or by (3) above, and it is more precisely answered by:

$$d = (F - T)/(F - L) \qquad (4)$$

However, in pursuit of understanding, a quite different question may be put, namely: How does the learning shown by the first-shot performance of the experimental group compare with that acquired by the control group? A measure for this is:

$$e = (C - T)/(C - S) \qquad (5)$$

It is by no means claimed that the expressions given here are the only, or necessarily the best, answers to the questions discussed; and certainly many other questions can be put, of both theoretical and economic significance. As we have shown, it is important to be clear about what question is being asked, and especially important to be clear about the extent and limitations of the information obtained from the answer. For example, an answer to a question on saving of training time—such as (1)—gives no information at all about first-shot performance: the one may be excellent and the other deplorable. In one particular case (Hammerton and Tickner, 1967) the several expressions given here yielded values (rendered as percentages) from 92 to minus 54. If any one had been taken as 'the' measure of transfer, the over-simple question 'How much learning was transferred?' could have received any answer in the range from 'almost all' to 'less than none'.

Evidently there is no such thing as 'the' measure of transfer; but if a specific question concerning transfer is precisely formulated, expressions exist for answering it, and a useful and informative numerical measure can be obtained.     M. H.

Gagne, R. M., Foster, H., and Crowley, M. E. (1948). The measurement of transfer of training. *Psychology Bulletin*, **45**, 97–103.

Hammerton, M. (1967). Measures for the efficiency of simulators as training devices. *Ergonomics*, **10**, 63–5.

Hammerton, M. and Tickner, A. H. (1967). Visual factors affecting transfer of training from a simulated to a real situation. *Journal of Applied Psychology*, **51**, 46–9.

Murdock, B. B. (1957). Transfer designs and formulas. *Psychology Bulletin*, **54**, 313–26.

**TRUTH.** There are three main epistemological theories: *correspondence*, that a proposition is true when it corresponds to some kind of reality; *coherence*, that propositions are true when they cohere to form a consistent body of what is taken to be knowledge; and *pragmatism* (or pragmaticism), that propositions are true when useful. Undoubtedly coherence and usefulness are very generally accepted *criteria* for truth; but they are not normally what is *meant* by 'truth'. Some kind of correspondence is what is meant; but it is ultimately impossible to observe correspondences between appearance and reality. It would require a kind of God's-eye view to see that the observations of a man, or the understanding of science, correspond to the world. So, although what we generally mean by 'truth' is correspondence with reality, correspondence is not, ultimately, an available criterion for truth.

Most empiricists have supposed that propositions can be individually tested for truth, by suitable observation or experiment. This is a tenet of 'logical atomism'. But the now current view is, rather, that not all can be tested at all directly and that perceptions, observations, and experiments require assumptions (which may be hidden) in order for us to interpret them. The American philosopher Thomas Kuhn (1962) has put forward the highly influential notion of scientific *paradigms: that there are accepted, though often implicit, assumptions in all 'normal' sciences. For example, *Darwinian natural selection is, or sets, a paradigm for current biology. *Newton's and Einstein's accounts are paradigms for physics and cosmology. One of the problems of modern psychology is the difficulty of making explicit the ruling paradigms and assumptions in terms of which its day-to-day experiments are assessed and interpreted. Where these assumptions are regarded as *'common sense', they may in fact reflect the philosophical and scientific presuppositions of previous centuries, which may change with changes of assumptions or paradigms. But only God knows what the next paradigm will be.

R. L. G.

Kuhn, T. (1962; enlarged edn. 1970). *The Structure of Scientific Revolutions*. New York.

**TURING, ALAN MATHISON (1912–54).** British mathematician, born in London, and educated at King's College, Cambridge, graduating in mathematics. He was the key figure in the conception of electronic digital computers and *artificial intelligence (AI), the only other contender being the brilliant American mathematician John *Von Neumann. Working almost entirely independently, they set the stage and wrote the script for the computer revolution; and concepts of mind in terms of artificial intelligence are based on the technology of the electronic digital computer, of which they were the principal inventors.

Turing made a fundamental contribution, shortly after graduating, with his paper 'On computable numbers with an application to the Entscheidungsproblem' (1937). In this he showed that there are classes of mathematical problems that cannot be proved by any fixed definite process or heuristic procedures. At the same time he proposed an automatic problem-solving machine that is the starting point of philosophies, and practical hopes, of digital computer-based AI. The Turing machine, as it is now called, is abstract in the sense that its description defines all possible operations though not all may be realizable in practice. Although the notion in its original form is clumsy, it encapsulates the essentials of modern digital computers.

The Turing machine can be visualized as an indefinitely long tape of squares on which are numbers, or a square may be blank. The machine reads one square at a time, and it can move the tape to read other squares, forwards or backwards. It can print new symbols, or erase symbols. Turing showed that his very simple machine (which had as its ancestor Charles *Babbage's 'analytical engine' of the 1830s) can specify the steps required for the solution of any problem that can be solved by instructions, explicitly stated rules, or procedures.

Turing considered whether a human being, or rather the human mind, can be described by analogy with such a machine, or can be simulated by one with appropriate programs. The essential idea, which he was among the first to see clearly, is that the physical construction of the machine is unimportant. Turing pointed out that Babbage's computer was mechanical, and though in the twentieth century electricity could be used, as faster and more reliable, it mattered nothing whether a computer was mechanical, electrical, or worked in any other way provided it could carry out the necessary instructions. It is a short step from this to saying that the biological material of the brain, protoplasm, or the way in which the brain is constructed, is not particularly important for intelligence or perhaps for anything else. If we were constructed differently we would in some ways be different; but we might still be intelligent, perceiving, conscious beings.

Turing suggested how we could recognize whether a simulation of the human mind had succeeded or failed. His paper, 'Computing machinery and intelligence' (1950) remains the clearest short account of the philosophy of artificial intelligence, as it came to be called, and 'Turing's test' for judging the adequacy of a simulation of mind remains the best criterion for recognizing intelligence in a machine. The 'test' is the Imitation Game, which Turing describes in these words: 'It is played with three people, a man (A), a woman (B), and an interrogator (C), who may be of either sex. The interrogator stays in a room apart from the other two. The object of the game for the interrogator is to determine which of the other two is the man and which the woman.' The interrogator is allowed to put questions to A and B, though not of physical characteristics such as length of hair, and he is not allowed to hear their voices. He is allowed to experience or question only *mental* attributes. The next step of the game is to substitute a machine for one of the humans. The machine communicates with a teletype. The question is whether the interrogator can distinguish the remaining human from the machine. Turing points out that for some questions, such as problems in arithmetic, the humans would show up revealingly poorly, and that this is perhaps an objection to the test; but it seems as good a test as any so far suggested for distinguishing between man and intelligent machines. It is of course behaviouristic; but, as Turing says, we cannot 'get inside' another human being, to know directly whether he or she has conscious experience, such as sensations of colour and emotional state. He leaves it open whether we should assume that the machine which passes the test of the Imitation Game is conscious.

Alan Turing was the master code breaker who succeeded in reading the German highest-level secret codes during the Second World War. This was not revealed until thirty years after the war, when his true importance as the originator of the first practical programmed computer—the Colossus (electronic cryptanalytic machine)—which, with human intelligence and a good deal of luck, broke the German codes and showed just how powerful information-handling machines can be. He died tragically at the height of his remarkable powers, as mathematician, biologist, and supreme creative philosopher of computing by machine and brain.

Feigenbaum, E. A. and Feldman, J. (1963). *Computers and Thought*. New York. (Contains a reprint of Turing's Imitation Game paper.)

Hodges, A. (1983). *Alan Turing: the enigma*. London.

Randell, B. R. (1972). On Alan Turing and the Origins of Computers. In Meltzer, B. and Michie, D. (eds.), *Machine Intelligence 7*. Edinburgh.

Turing, S. (1959). *Alan M. Turing*. Cambridge. (A Life by his mother.)

Von Neumann, J. (1958). *The Computer and the Brain*. New Haven.

**TWINS.** See GENETICS OF BEHAVIOUR.

# U

**UNCONSCIOUS, THE.** According to Sigmund *Freud a large part of the mind is unconscious—though essentially similar to the conscious mind in having wishes and fears and so on. This Freudian theory is very different from the notion which forms a part of many, more recent psychological theories, that the brain processes accept and analyse information unconsciously, as one might expect of a computer—lack of *consciousness is not the same as the unconscious.

Opinion is probably moving away from the Freudian view, to something closer to this *artificial intelligence notion that unconscious processing is basic to behaviour. This view, however, is not that of extreme *behaviourism, which claims that there is no consciousness whatever.

The notion of unconscious inference was developed by Hermann von *Helmholtz, when he considered perception as given by inferences ('Unconscious Inferences') from features of the world as signalled by the senses. This gave rise to a very complex historical controversy, with Helmholtz and Freud as major figures, which even now has not been resolved in detail. At the time, the Helmholtz view was highly unpopular, as it was considered that inference requires consciousness, and this argument was associated with the moral position that consciousness is required for ethical judgement. So the notion of unconscious inference threatened morality and justification of praise, blame, and punishment.

See CONSCIOUSNESS AND CAUSALITY.     R. L. G.

**UNIVERSALS.** We experience particulars but not universals. Thus we *see* a *particular* triangle, but geometry depends upon generalized concepts of 'triangularity'—which is never seen by the senses. Universals are mental constructs based on inductive inference or hypotheses from the experience of particulars. They are essential for explanation.

**UTILITARIANISM.** See BENTHAM, JEREMY; MILL, JOHN STUART.

# V

**VASOPRESSIN.** See NEUROPEPTIDES.

**VERSTEHEN.** This German term means 'to understand'. A *Verstehen* approach to the study of human beings is any which assumes that the enquiry cannot be modelled on natural science: any 'non-scientistic' approach, to use another term in common employment. Nineteenth-century German opponents of scientism often expressed their claim in the assertion that making sense of human beings was a matter of *Verstehen*, that making sense of natural things was one of *Erklären*, and that the two operations were fundamentally distinct.

The *Verstehen* tradition is often traced to the work of the Italian thinker Giambattista Vico (1668–1744). He countered *Descartes's emphasis on the certainty available in the natural sciences with his *verum factum* principle, according to which the true—what we can know for certain—is coextensive with the made—what we have ourselves created. The idea was that we are in a better position to understand human actions, artefacts, and institutions, the products of the mind, than we are to grasp material phenomena that are not of our making. Whether or not through Vico's influence, this idea was an important component in the German Romantic movement at the beginning of the nineteenth century, and was taken up in the thought of Wilhelm Dilthey (1833–1911), the influential philosopher of history. Through Dilthey it passed on to the sociologist Max Weber (1864–1920) and since his time it has been a staple discussion topic among practitioners and philosophers of social science.

In the twentieth century the dominant expression of the scientistic approach to the study of human beings has been *logical positivism. Positivist methodology, which derives from the work of the Vienna Circle in the 1920s, lays great stress on the unity of method across respectable cognitive disciplines, and it insists that so far as the understanding of people is respectable, the method followed must be the same as in natural science. *Verstehen* theorists have had to argue against this that the positivist characterization of explanation does not apply in the human case, and in particular that it does not fit explanations of action. Positivists have been prepared to concede that in thinking up explanations for action we can rely on clues not available in the non-human case, and the issue has been whether we also have some special aids at our disposal for corroborating those explanations (see Abel, 1948).

Putting aside the lineaments of the anti-positivist debate, and also the details of the earlier tradition, we can say that there are two claims which distinguish any *Verstehen* position. The first, a thesis as often assumed as it is argued, says that our common fashion of explaining what we each say and do is an indispensable explanatory practice. More exactly, the idea is that the working conception of agents which guides us in our interpretation of one another's actions cannot be displaced by a different approach. The conception is identified by its essentially mentalistic concepts, such as those of intention, desire, decision, perception, judgement, and belief. What is supposed is that such concepts cannot be discarded without emasculating the understanding of human beings.

This indispensability thesis is not an easy one to defend. Perhaps the most natural line for the *Verstehen* theorist to argue is that our working conception of agents is tied to the interactive attitude which we adopt *vis-à-vis* one another, and that it is as entrenched as that attitude. (For other lines, see MacDonald and Pettit, 1981, ch. 2.) The tie to the interactive attitude is easy enough to argue: when we interact we project the responses of the other person, through assuming that he forms mental states on much the pattern that we do, through assuming that he takes us to form mental states on the same pattern, and so on through an indefinite series of mutual replications. It is arguable that such accommodation towards one another is essentially linked with the application of the loose conception of agents embodied in our everyday explanatory practice (see Pettit, 1978, part 2).

But if we grant this link, we still have to argue that the interactive attitude is indispensable; otherwise the indispensability of the associated conception will not have been established. Could we think of giving up this attitude in favour of something like the interventionist disposition that we normally adopt towards natural systems? Some have argued that we could not, short of contemplating a total transformation of our sensibility, and a morally repugnant transformation at that (see Strawson, 1962). Others have argued a similar line from the following sort of consideration. Suppose that we are playing chess with a computer. We are in a position to give up treating the computer in the ordinary half-interactive way, wondering what it is up to and what it thinks that we are up to; if we wish, we may adopt the viewpoint of the electronics engineer and attempt to predict its every move for certain. The situation is much as it might be with a human being, if we could have recourse to a thorough neurophysiology (or even behaviouristic theory) which would allow us to predict every action of a colleague (see Dennett, 1973). With the computer we would not normally give up the interactive stance, at least so long as our interest was in the game of chess, and the suggested moral is that even if there were a theory available which permitted an interventionist attitude towards human beings, in most instances this would not displace the regular interactive disposition. The reason is that just as the interventionist attitude towards the computer would make chess impossible, so it would undermine important interpersonal exchanges if we adopted it towards people (see Habermas, 1972, appendix).

The second claim, which anyone espousing a *Verstehen* position must embrace, is a distinctiveness thesis: a claim to the effect that our working conception of agents is not only indispensable but distinctive. Specifically, the thesis is that the conception is distinguished by the fact of not allowing the sort of amendment and development which characterizes scientific theory. Unless such a proposition is written into the *Verstehen* charter, the position will be indiscernible from that of enthusiasts for decision theory and game theory, who acknowledge that their preferred approach derives from our everyday conception of agents, but who think that this starting-point will soon be a distant memory.

There are many ways in which the distinctiveness thesis may be argued, and they make for different versions of the *Verstehen* view. One, and it is the most traditional, is to say that people have a special non-inferential access to the human mind, whether in introspection or empathy, and that this intuitive base gives our working conception of agents the required distinctiveness (see Outhwaite, 1974). Another, deriving mainly from the later work of Ludwig *Wittgenstein, says that applying the everyday conception in explaining what agents do and say is not a matter of hypothesizing mental causes, but one of redescribing the actions in a manner which makes them unproblematic, and that a descriptive conceptual framework is naturally less malleable than an explanatory scientific theory (see Melden, 1961). Recent developments in hermeneutics and semantics have generated further arguments for the distinctiveness of our working conception of agents. On the hermeneutic, side it has been argued that in explaining human action we cannot rely on theory-independent data for arguing our preferred interpretation, and that this looseness makes our conception of agents immune to the ordinary pressures of theory refinement (see Taylor, 1971). On the semantic side it has been claimed that such immunity comes from the necessity of assuming a minimum of rationality in accounting for what is taken to be properly human action; the assumption of such rationality, it is said, militates against the possibility that our conception of agents could be rad-

ically transformed (see MacDonald and Pettit, 1981, ch. 2).

Any of these arguments, if successful, would suggest that the corroboration of action explanation is different from the corroboration available in the explanation of the natural event: this is the point which *Verstehen* theorists sought to establish against positivism. More generally, any would combine with the argument for the indispensability of our working conception of agents and return us to the point of view of something like Vico's *verum factum* principle. It would leave us secure in the humanistic assumption that where the material world has readily submitted itself to the yoke of scientific theory, the mental will prove in some respects to be resistant and recalcitrant. Whether this assumption is reasonable depends on whether any of the arguments is valid, and this question will be with us for some time.                    P. P.

Abel, T. (1948). The operation called 'Verstehen'. *American Journal of Sociology*, **54**.

Dennett, D. (1973). Mechanism and responsibility. In Honderich, T. (ed.), *Essays on Freedom of Action*. London.

Habermas, J. (1972). *Knowledge and Human Interests*. London.

MacDonald, G. and Pettit, P. (1981). *Semantics and Social Science*. London.

Melden, A. I. (1961). *Free Action*. London.

Outhwaite, R. W. (1974). *Understanding Social Life*. London.

Pettit, P. (1978). Rational man theory. In Hookway, C. and Pettit, P. (eds.), *Action and Interpretation*. Cambridge.

Strawson, P. F. (1962). Freedom and Resentment. *Proceedings of the British Academy, 1962*. (Repr. in Strawson, P. F., ed., *Studies in the Philosophy of Thought and Action*, Oxford, 1968.)

Taylor, C. (1971). Interpretation and the sciences of man. *Review of Metaphysics*, **25**.

**VISION: THE EARLY WARNING SYSTEM.** It is only recently that demands on sophisticated electronics and computing systems have become as severe as those with which our sensory systems must cope. It is interesting to see whether, say, our visual processes and radar systems evolved in similar ways. Radar engineers a generation or so ago became aware that the requirements of early warning of approaching targets are very different from their detailed identification and tracking at close range. The first demanded the rapid detection of many targets appearing simultaneously in a vast space, rather than pin-pointing. The second demanded the ability to zoom in on a selected target with great precision and follow it continuously. So it is with the visual system. There are two distinct processes involved: a pre-attentive one for the almost instantaneous detection of textural changes in our environment that indicate the occurrence of objects, and an attentive, serial one that can shift focal attention to any of the objects detected by the pre-attentive process. The pre-attentive process can detect textural changes in a brief flash (less than 150 milliseconds) throughout the entire visual field, but is unable to tell apart individually objects that appear very different when inspected with focal attention.

**Limits of global (statistical) processing in texture discrimination.** Discriminable texture pairs in real life seem to differ both in their local elements and in their global properties. Figs. 1a and 1b show discriminable texture pairs that differ in their local elements: in Fig. 1a the elements are of different sizes, whereas in Fig. 1b the orientation differs. Moreover, one can also demonstrate texture discrimination in their global properties: in Fig. 1a the first-order statistics are different in the two textures, whereas in Fig. 1b the first-order statistics agree but the second-order statistics are different.

What do we mean by first- and second-order statistics? If we randomly throw confetti on a texture of different colours and count the frequencies with which the dots fall on certain colours (black, grey, white, red, etc.), a first-order statistic is obtained. If we randomly throw needles (their end-points having certain length and orientation) and count the frequencies that they fall on certain colour combinations (for example, both on black, or one on white, the other on black, etc.), we obtain a second-order statistic. If a triangle is randomly thrown on a texture, and we count the frequencies that the three vertices of this triangle fall on certain colour combinations, a third-order statistic is obtained. Of course, all possible triangles in all possible orientations have to be tried in order to obtain the full third-order statistic. Finally, the throwing of $n$gons at random on a texture, and summing the frequencies that the $n$ vertices of the $n$gons land on certain colours, yields the $n$th-order statistic. Thus the first-order (confetti) statistics differ for the two textures in Fig. 1a, while for the two textures in Fig. 1b their first-order statistics are identical, though their second-order (needle) statistics differ.

These examples are typical of naturally occurring textures. Since the discriminable texture pairs differ globally in their first- or second-order stat-istics, it is impossible to assess the role played by *local* differences in element features, as opposed to that played by *global* differences in their statistics. In order to separate local from global influences, a research paradigm was proposed in 1962 to generate and study texture pairs with identical second- (hence also first-) order statistics, but different third- and higher-order statistics (Julesz, 1962). In the years since then, many such iso-second-order texture classes have been discovered, and many of these texture pairs are indistinguishable, in spite of the fact that their elements in isolation are easily told apart. A typical indistinguishable texture pair with identical second-order statistics is shown in Fig. 2a, generated by a method of Julesz et al. (1973).

The texture pair in Fig. 2a is presented outside the region of foveal attention (such that the boundaries between the texture pair are 1–2 degrees of arc outside of fixation) for a brief flash (under 150 milliseconds, to prevent scanning eye-movements) followed by an erasing field (to prevent shifting focal attention to various areas of an after-image). The texture pair appears indistinguishable, but a square-shaped area in Fig. 2a is composed of *R*s while its neighbourhood is composed of mirror-image *R*s. Any texture pair composed of randomly thrown identical micropatterns (in all possible orientations and without overlap) has the same second-order, but different third- or higher-order statistics as a texture generated in similar ways, though without throwing the mirror-image of the original micropattern.

Another almost indistinguishable texture pair with identical second- but different third- and higher-order statistics is shown in Fig. 2b. This texture pair appears indistinguishable in spite of the fact that the elements by themselves look very different. When they are presented a few degrees of arc left and right from the centre of fixation point, for 150 milliseconds with erasure, they can easily be told apart.

These experiments, and many others that yield indistinguishable iso-second-order textures, clear-

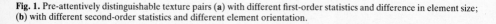

a                    b

**Fig. 1.** Pre-attentively distinguishable texture pairs (**a**) with different first-order statistics and difference in element size; (**b**) with different second-order statistics and different element orientation.

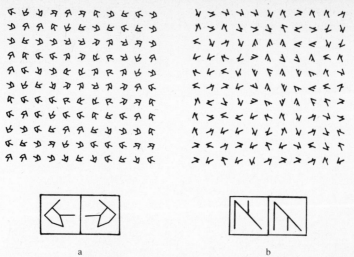

**Fig. 2.** Pre-attentively indistinguishable texture pairs with identical second-order statistics but different third- and higher-order statistics: (**a**) composed of randomly thrown and not overlapping similar micropatterns and their mirror-images, respectively; (**b**) composed of dual micropatterns that have the same line segment length and width; the number of their terminators (end-points) also agrees.

ly suggest that pre-attentive texture discrimination cannot utilize third- and higher-order statistical parameters. So, if discriminable textures with identical second-order statistics are to be found, their discrimination can be based not on global processing but rather on the local processing of some conspicuous local features. We will call these conspicuous local features 'textons', and will show that they are limited to only a few, perhaps only three, kinds (Julesz, 1980).

**Textons, the basic units of texture perception.** In 1978 several iso-second-order texture classes were found that yielded strong discrimination (Caelli and Julesz, 1978; Caelli et al., 1978; Julesz et al., 1978). In Figs. 3a and 3b two such examples are demonstrated. In Fig. 3a the four-dot micropatterns in one texture are quasi-collinear, whereas their four-dot partners in the other texture are not. The texture pair of Fig. 3a is strongly discriminable, so the local conspicuous feature of quasi-collinear structures—and *elongated blobs* in general—prove to be of a texton class. In Fig. 3b the left and right areas have identical third-order statistics (hence identical second- and first-order statistics), and strong discrimination is again due to elongated blob textons that have different width and orientation in the two textures.

It was believed for a while that corner, closure, and connectivity might also be different texton classes. However, as shown by Julesz (1980), if one generates texture pairs in which the dual elements are either connected open line segments, or disconnected closed ones (Fig. 4a, inserts), the texture pair formed by these elements is indistinguishable. It seems that if the elongated blobs (line segments) agree and the *terminators* (*end-points*) of these

elongated blobs (line segments) total the same number, as in Fig. 4a, no texture discrimination can be experienced. That the difference in number of terminators is a crucial parameter is shown in the strongly discriminable texture pair of Fig. 4b, where one of the texture elements contains two terminators while its dual contains five, and this terminator difference of three yields strong texture discrimination. This contrasts with Fig. 2b, where the dual elements have the same number of terminators, and these iso-second-order textures are indistinguishable.

In addition to elongated blobs (particularly line segments) of given colour, width, orientation, and length and their terminators, the third texton class is their crossings. Whether some additional textons will be found remains to be seen.

*Only the first-order statistics of textons are used in texture perception.* So long as the number of terminals remains identical, whether the small line segments in Fig. 4a form an S-shaped or 10-shaped micropattern passes unnoticed in pre-attentive texture perception. Thus it seems that only the differences between first-order statistics of textons (perhaps only their density gradients) are computed by the textural system; the pre-attentive process is unable to compute even second-order statistical parameters (Julesz, 1981)—a conclusion that can be derived from Fig. 5a. Here the top image shows a $4 \times 4$ micropattern of eight black and eight white dots, repeated periodically at eight-dot intervals both horizontally and vertically. The gaps between these periodic patterns are filled with grey (a chequerboard screen) in the left bottom array, and the whole is flanked by random-dot regions. In the right array, the gaps in the same

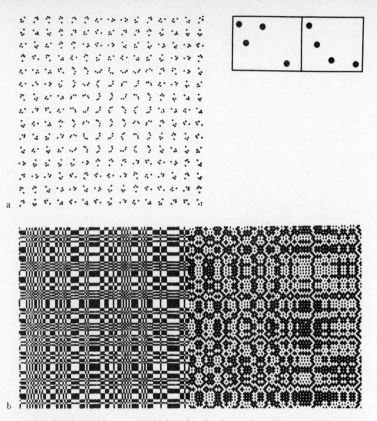

**Fig. 3.** Pre-attentively distinguishable texture pairs based on local conspicuous features of (**a**) elongated blobs (here quasi-collinear discs) that are absent in the iso-second-order dual texture; (**b**) elongated blobs of different width, length, and orientation, in spite of the fact that both half-fields have identical third-order (and hence identical second- and first-order) statistics.

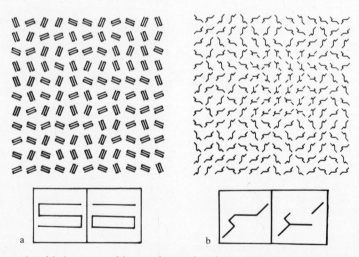

**Fig. 4.** Demonstration of the importance of the second texton class, the terminators (end-points) of elongated blobs (line segments). **a.** Since the number of terminators (two) is the same in each texture, the textures are indistinguishable, in spite of the fact that one contains open-connected and the other closed-unconnected elements. **b.** In this pair of identical second-order statistics, the number of terminators differs, and hence the textures are strongly discriminable.

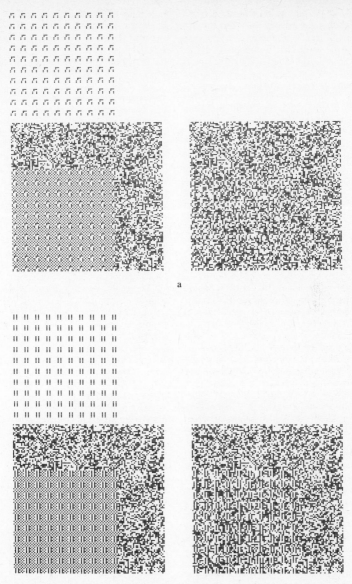

**Fig. 5.** Demonstration that the pre-attentive system cannot process globally differences in second-order statistics, and only first-order statistical differences in textons yield texture discrimination. **a.** Periodically repeated 4 × 4 dot micropattern that does not contain textons, flanked by randomly dotted areas. The blank four-dot-wide columns and rows between the periodic micropatterns are filled in by a chequerboard screen in the lower left half, and by random dots in the right half. No texture discrimination is obtained. **b.** Similar to **a** except that the 4 × 4 repeated micropatterns are texton-rich. Texture discrimination is now strong. The autocorrelation difference is the same between the periodic areas and their random neighbours in **a** and **b**; therefore the textural system cannot detect differences in autocorrelation (a second-order statistical parameter), only differences in the density of textons.

periodic region are filled with randomly selected black and white dots, rendering the periodicity invisible. Although the autocorrelation (a second-order statistical parameter that for black and white patterns is the second-order statistics) has periodic peaks at eight-dot intervals in the periodic array, while no such periodicity exists in the flanking random regions, the two regions appear equally random. One could argue that perhaps the difference in autocorrelation is too slight for detection.

However, in Fig. 5b the same procedure is repeated, except that the periodic 4 × 4 micropattern is not texton-free, but contains vertical bars and thus is rich in textons. In the right image of Fig. 5b the periodic area is distinctly different from its random neighbourhood, although the maximum autocorrelation difference is the same as in Fig. 5a. It is the density difference between textons that yields texture discrimination, and differences in second-order statistical parameters are not perceived.

**The two visual processes.** So we have two visual processes. The first, the pre-attentive process, can inspect a complex texture all over the visual field in parallel, and can detect changes in the kind and density of textons. Only if such changes occur in certain regions does it summon up the attentive, serial process to scrutinize one of these regions by focal pin-pointing. Thus the pre-attentive process acts as an early warning system; for itself it cannot evaluate positional shifts in textons (as long as these shifts do not change the terminator density or yield crossings), although it can look for texton changes throughout the entire visual field during very brief glimpses. If there is an equilibrium of textons—called ideal camouflage—(as in Figs. 2a, 2b, and 4a), then it is most unlikely that focal attention would notice that certain areas contain elements very different from the rest. Very different texture elements can yield camouflaged textures, as long as the density of their constituent textons agrees.

Work on the texton theory since 1981 has produced further refinements. It has become clear that pre-attentive texture discrimination operates only if the texture elements are dense, such that the distance between these elements is within about twice the distance of the average element size. The essence of serial scrutiny has also been clarified by presenting patterns very briefly, followed by a masker. It was found that observers could shift a small aperture of focal attention in steps of 20–50 milliseconds (almost an order of magnitude faster than scanning eye-movements). Only in this 'searchlight of attention' would the observers know 'what' the textons were and be able to connect them together into shapes. Outside the aperture of focal attention, the pre-attentive system could only tell 'where' texton gradients occurred but could not connect them. It is this independence between textons that permits them to act as the fundamental elements of the pre-attentive system.

The pre-attentive/attentive dichotomy exists only when the texton gradients are high, and the entire visual field can be inspected in parallel. With reduced texton gradients, observers are forced to reduce their visual field to one that can be inspected in parallel in size, hence increasing the coupling between the textons more and more (Bergen and Julesz, 1983). So, there is a continuum between scrutiny-free vision when the textons are independent elements and vision with scrutiny when the textons become more and more connected together, ultimately forming shapes (Gestalten). Obviously when shapes are formed, no perceptual elements exist, and the enigmatic problems of form recognition are encountered.

The texton theory shows many similarities with the trigger features found in the visual cortex of monkeys by neurophysiologists, particularly Hubel and Wiesel (1968). The pre-attentive/attentive dichotomy also resembles some theories posed by cognitive psychologists, particularly Anne Treisman (Treisman and Gelade, 1980), and the 'primal sketch' of David Marr (1982), who did his research in the framework of artificial intelligence.

In summary, it was shown that prior to form recognition an important, early visual system exists, that can effortlessly locate some conspicuous local feature differences (texton gradients), and in turn can direct the searchlight of attention to these locations. This is in essence how the 'ground' state is segmented into the 'figure' one, if not the fundamental problem of perception.

The second visual process is to inspect regions where the density of textons is different. In so doing, it can perform the prodigious feats of human form recognition. Whether the fundamental elements of form recognition are some complex combination of textons, or whether they are based on some entirely different constituents, remains to be seen. However, the finding that pre-attentive texture perception can be explained by elongated blobs, particularly line segments, their terminators, and their crossings—which in turn are probably the simple and complex cortical units of the neurophysiologist—and that these units are not coupled (only differences in their histograms are taken), might be the first step toward understanding human vision. B. J.

Bergen, J. R. and Julesz, B. (1983). Rapid discrimination of visual patterns. *IEEE Transactions on Systems, Man and Cybernetics*, **13**, 857–63.

Caelli, T. and Julesz, B. (1978). On perceptual analyzers underlying visual texture discrimination, part I. *Biological Cybernetics*, **28**, 167–75.

Caelli, T., Julesz, B., and Gilbert, E. N. (1978). On perceptual analyzers underlying visual texture discrimination, part II. *Biological Cybernetics*, **29**, 201–14.

Hubel, D. H. and Wiesel, T. N. (1968). Receptive fields and functional architecture of monkey striate cortex. *Journal of Physiology*, **195**, 215–43.

Julesz, B. (1962). Visual pattern discrimination. *IRE Transactions on Information Theory*, **IT–8**, 84–92.

Julesz, B. (1980). Spatial nonlinearities in the instantaneous perception of textures with identical power spectra. *Philosophical Transactions of the Royal Society of London, B*, **290**, 83–94.

Julesz, B. (1981). Textons, the elements of texture perception, and their interactions. *Nature*, **290**, 91–7.

Julesz, B. (1984). Toward an axiomatic theory of preattentive vision. In Edelman, G. M., Cowan, W. M., and Gall, W. E. (eds.), *Dynamic Aspects of Neocortical Function*, pp. 585–612. New York.

Julesz, B. (1986). Texton gradients: the texton theory revisited. *Biological Cybernetics*. New York.

Julesz, B. and Bergen, J. R. (1983). Textons, the fundamental elements in pre-attentive vision and perception of textures. *Bell Systems Technical Journal*, **62**, 1,619–45.

Julesz, B., Gilbert, E. N., Shepp, L. A., and Frisch, H. L. (1973). Inability of humans to discriminate between visual textures that agree in second-order statistics—revisited. *Perception*, **2**, 391–405.

Julesz, B., Gilbert, E. N., and Victor, J. D. (1978). Visual discrimination of textures with identical third-order statistics. *Biological Cybernetics*, **31**, 137–40.

Marr, D. (1982). *Vision*. San Francisco.

Sagi, D. and Julesz, B. (1985). 'Where' and 'What' in vision. *Science*, **228**, 121–9.

Sagi, D. and Julesz, B. (1986). Enhanced detection in the aperture of focal attention during simple discrimination tasks. *Nature*, **321**, 693–5.

Treisman, A. and Gelade, G. (1980). A feature-integration theory of attention. *Cognitive Psychology*, **12**, 97–136.

**VISUAL ADAPTATION.** Photographers know that to get a good picture they must have the right light intensity. If the light is too dim the picture will be 'underexposed', a dark scene with only the brightest parts showing detail. If the light is too bright, on the other hand, the picture will be 'overexposed', and detail will again be lacking, swallowed, this time, in a kind of luminous fog. Modern cameras often have an automatic device to regulate the light so that the film receives about the right average light intensity. This is usually achieved by automatic adjustment of the iris stop which controls the intake of light.

It is common experience that our eyes act in the same general way. Without any conscious effort we find that we can appreciate detail over a very great range of light intensities, and indeed the (blue or brown) iris stop of our eyes may be seen to shut down in bright light, leaving the small black entrance pupil of only 2 mm diameter, or in twilight of 10 mm. This mechanism of the iris stop can cause a change in pupil area of 25 times; but since the change in illumination over which the eye can operate well exceeds 10,000 times, it contributes rather little towards it.

Birds that are active by day and go to roost at sundown have a retina very different from night birds. Those that use bright daylight to detect tiny insects and attack ripe, red fruit among green leaves possess good *visual acuity* and colour vision, a faculty often displayed by their coloured plumage. Night birds on the other hand are mainly concerned with distinguishing something from nothing, for at night there is not enough light entering the eye to afford detailed information. The human retina has two types of light-sensitive cells: *cones* that function best in bright light and are essential for acute vision, and *rods* that are necessary for seeing in dim light. (See COLOUR VISION.)

It may be wondered how the eye-camera can manage to handle two types of film at the same time, since a single picture is all that we perceive. The analogy is faulty, of course, for the eye is more like a TV camera. The retinal image is not 'snapped' and fixed as a permanent picture; the living scene is encoded in a moving pattern of nerve signals which are transmitted to the brain for further processing.

Human retinas consist of a mosaic of rods and cones, each receptor having its separate nerve. The assemblage of rod nerves encodes the twilight picture, the cone nerves encode the daylight picture. Rod messages and cone messages coexist all the time and are combined in varying degrees to form one picture whose composition depends upon the level of adaptation. The brighter the light, the more detailed the picture. Thus the dependence of perception upon the level of illumination and the way that contrast is preserved over such an enormous luminance range is chiefly achieved by the processing of these nerve signals.

The exact way that this is done, of course, is exceedingly complex. Nerve fibres from the million cones and the hundred million rods of each human retina converge upon about one million fibres of the optic nerve. As Lord *Adrian has said, the 'copy' furnished by these hundred-and-one million reporters is severely edited and condensed, and only the more dramatic features are telegraphed in code from the retina to the central offices in the brain.

To get a good picture with a photographic camera it is necessary to control the amount of light actually falling on the film. With a TV camera or eye, however, a more flexible control is possible, namely the 'scaling' of the encoded signals. Radio sets possess an *automatic gain control* (AGC) that keeps the sound output at a constant level despite changes in radio input. The AGC in the eye likewise adjusts the encoded signals to about the same average size whatever the brightness of the scene. The retinal image is encoded in terms of contrast (i.e. the brightness of each part compared with the average brightness), a code which has the advantage of being independent of the constantly changing overall brightness level in nature. This intelligible and purposeful adaptation is very different from the way that eyes seem to be temporarily blinded by exposure to a very bright light. The recovery from this state is called *dark adaptation*.

Dark adaptation happens when we go from bright sunlight into a darkened lecture-room or cinema, or leave a brilliantly lit room to walk a dark lane. At first the eye is so insensitive that we can hardly see anything, though improvement rapidly begins. It takes half an hour, however, to reach full dark-adapted sensitivity. What is going on that takes all this time for its accomplishment? Are not the nerves very slow in reorganizing themselves? It is chemicals, not nerves, that are responsible for the delay. The sensitive pigments of our retinal film are bleached away by strong light; and we cannot regain full sensitivity until they have been restored by the eye's chemical regenerative process.

The course of recovery in the dark may be measured and displayed as in the curve of Fig. 1. In this experiment the subject looked directly at a

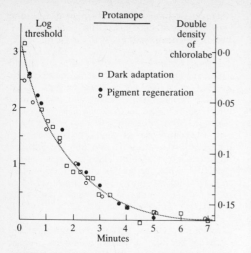

**Fig. 1.** Foveal dark adaptation curve from a protanope. The subject had only green-sensitive cones on the central retinal region where the test flash fell. These had their pigment bleached away by a strong light that was extinguished at zero minutes. At various subsequent times the strength of the test flash, so weak as to be only just visible, was measured. Its logarithm is plotted (scale on the left) by the squares. Black and white circles (two runs) show the amount of green cone pigment present during regeneration (scale on right). The fact that all the 'points' lie on the same curve means that recovery of sensitivity waits upon the regeneration of pigment.

very bright light, which after a short time was extinguished, and then, in darkness, he transferred his gaze to a repeatedly flashing, weak test light of adjustable intensity. This was reduced so that the flash was only just perceptible, and the logarithm of this threshold intensity was noted (ordinate in Fig. 1 with scale to the left); the time since the adapting light was extinguished is plotted horizontally.

The results shown by the squares refer to the recovery of cones, since there are no rods at the fovea, the central fixation point of the retina, where the test flash fell. It is seen that immediately after this strong light adaptation the threshold was $10^3$ (= a thousand times) as high as the fully dark-adapted level, reached seven minutes later. By our reflection densitometer it is possible to measure at each moment the amount of visual pigment in the cones. It is plotted by the black and white circles (two sets of measurements) read by the scale on the right. The adapting light was so strong that initially all the cone pigment had been bleached away. But in the dark it immediately began to be regenerated and returned along the curve that fits the return of the visual threshold. This means that at every moment during recovery the visual threshold was raised above the fully dark value by an amount proportional to the amount of pigment still in the bleached state.

The subject of this experiment was 'colour-blind' and possessed only green-sensitive cones on the fovea. So these results are uncomplicated. But just the same results occur with normal subjects when the adapting light is white and bleaches red- and green-sensitive cones equally.

Fig. 2 shows the dark adaptation curve in a subject defective in all types of cone, so her threshold depended entirely upon the rods of twilight vision. The irregular line is an automatic plot of visual threshold by a device which made the series of light flashes get continually brighter when a switch was up, and continually dimmer when down. When the subject could see the flashing test she depressed the switch and when the flashes consequently became too faint to see she lifted the switch. There is no irregular line before seven minutes, because until then she saw no flash though it was a million times above the final dark threshold (log scale on the left).

The dotted curve in Fig. 2 shows the threshold in a *normal* eye when the test flash falls off-centre upon a place where both rods and cones are present. The cones recover much faster, and the dotted curve, like the cone curve in Fig. 1, recovers completely in seven minutes. But when the continually falling rod curve reaches this cone level, the dotted curve is seen to join it. For after this point it is the rods that are the more sensitive, and consequently they define the threshold for vision.

The black circles of Fig. 2 show the pigment content of the rods throughout regeneration. The scale on the right gives the proportion of pigment in the bleached state, and we see again that this is

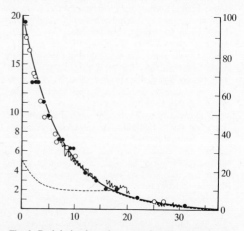

**Fig. 2.** Rod dark adaptation curve from a subject nearly devoid of cones. Irregular line plots the log intensity of a threshold flash at various times after extinction of bleaching light (scale on left: horizontal time-scale in minutes). Black circles: time course of regeneration of rod pigment in this subject (scale on right shows fraction of pigment in the bleached state). White circles: regeneration in a normal subject whose visual threshold is indicated by the dotted curves, cones to the left, rods where this meets the heavy curve.

proportional to the rise in visual threshold over the millionfold range where this can be measured. The white circles plot the pigment regeneration of a normal eye, to show that our subject who lacked cones had nothing abnormal with her rod pigment.

It may be asked, 'Why is the rod threshold raised ten to one hundred times (1–2 log units) when the rods still contain 90 per cent of their pigment?' This seems a crippling loss of performance from so small a loss of pigment. We have no very clear answer to this but it must lie along the following lines.

If a bright light is observed for a short time with steady gaze it leaves a persistent *after-image. For instance, the bars of a window seen against the sky may be observed floating across the ceiling with the drift of the observer's eye. Against the white ceiling the bright sky image appears black, and the bars white in contrast (negative after-image). The contrast is reversed if the eyes are now shut or the gaze shifted to some black background (positive after-image).

H. B. Barlow and J. M. B. Sparrock in an elegant experiment compared the positive after-image of a flash with the brightness of a real light held fixed (stabilized) upon a neighbouring retinal region. They found that when the stabilized light was made equal to the after-image in brightness, it was also equal in raising the threshold of a superposed test flash. Now the threshold rise of a test flash when it falls upon the after-image of a bright light is identical to what is plotted in the dark adaptation curve, following bleaching by the bright light. Thus a rather small pigment loss causes a large threshold rise because it generates a strong and persistent after-image that forms a bright background against which weak lights will be quite invisible.

Visual adaptation is one of the most marvellous features of that marvellous organ, the eye. In common usage it automatically sets the sensitivity so as to extract the best contrast from the retinal picture over a millionfold range of illumination. But when a dazzlingly bright bleaching light throws the normal mechanism out of adjustment, the receptor activity is prolonged and gives rise to the after-image. The eye adapts to this situation as though it was a real light flooding the scene, and the normal retinal picture fades into darkness by contrast.                                     W. A. H. R.

Rushton, W. A. H. (1956). The Rhodopsin Density in the Human Rods. *Journal of Physiology*, **124**, 1, 30–46.

Rushton, W. A. H. (1962). Visual Pigments in Man. *Scientific American*, November.

**VISUAL ILLUSIONS.** See ILLUSIONS.

**VISUAL INFORMATION RATE.** Let us first estimate the information capacity of the visual system, then see how much of this capacity is used in a decision based solely on visual information, and finally discuss what are the factors that determine the capacity. Accurate data are available only for the central region of the retina (a circle whose diameter is 2° in the visual field) and

this area is considered below. The total information capacity of the visual system is about 10 times that of this central circle, known as the fovea.

The number of points that can be resolved within the central 2° circle is about $10^4$. When the eye is working near the limit of resolution, contrast discrimination is poor. Jacobson (1951) assumed that, at the limit of resolution, a person could distinguish black from white but not discriminate any intermediate shades of grey. He thus associated one bit of information with each small area surrounding one of the resolved points. (One bit is the amount of information required to decide between two equally probable alternatives: see BIT; INFORMATION THEORY.) For the central region the flicker-fusion frequency is about 50 cycles per second, so that the information capacity is $50 \times 10^4 = 5 \times 10^5$ bits per second.

Ditchburn and Drysdale (1973) calculated the information capacity from measurements of the variation of contrast sensitivity with number of lines per degree of visual angle for targets which were sinusoidal gratings. This calculation also yields a value of $5 \times 10^5$ bits per second, though their method includes capacity in terms of targets with different shades of grey. Neither of these estimates includes colour information, but it is unlikely that the additional information due to colour is more than about 20 per cent, making $6 \times 10^5$ bits per second in all.

Jacobson estimated the capacity for the ear at about $10^4$ bits per second. Thus the central region of the retina has about 50 times the capacity of the ear and the whole visual system has about 500 or 600 times the aural capacity.

Vernier acuity judgements are probably the most precise decisions based on visual information. Foley-Fisher (1972) found that 4 to 5 bits of visual information were used in this judgement. For other visual tasks, values of 3 and less have been found (Crossman, 1969). Experiments on rates of response have yielded values of up to 50 bits per second (Klemmer, 1957). Some allowance must be made for unutilized spare capacity—for instance, when a subject makes a vernier acuity judgement on whether two lines are correctly aligned he could simultaneously make judgements on the width, length, and colour of the lines. When considerations like this are taken into account, the information used may rise to between 10 and 20 bits in a single judgement and the rate to about 200 bits per second, but even these values are very small compared with a capacity of $10^4$ bits for a single judgement or $6 \times 10^5$ bits per second for the rate.

Ditchburn and Drysdale calculated that, for the lower illuminances at which foveal vision operates, nearly one bit of information was obtained for every photon absorbed by the cone-detectors. This was true both for steady illumination and for brief flashes of light. At higher luminances the efficiency (measured in bits per photon absorbed) fell so that at daylight level about $10^4$ photons must be absorbed to yield one bit. Thus at the lower luminances purely physical considerations determine the efficiency, but at higher levels it is determined by properties of the visual system. The relevant properties are (i) the aperture and quality of the lens of the eye, (ii) the number, and hence the spacing, of the photon-detectors, (iii) the number of associated nerve fibres, and (iv) the neural processes by which information is transformed so that it is most readily appreciated by the higher centres of the brain.

The first three of these properties are matched in such a way that each by itself would give a limit of about $10^4$ resolved points in the central $2°$. The neural processes include an edge-sharpening device (lateral inhibition), an arrangement by which an object appears to be about the same size over a range of distances (size constancy scaling), and many similar manipulations of the basic information. Some loss of information in these processes is inevitable, but the system is very economical and the loss may only be about 20 per cent.

In the situation involved in the evolution of the higher animals, decisions vital to survival had to be made mainly or solely on visual information. A wide variety of situations was encountered, so a vast information capacity was needed. Yet the amount used in making a decision had to be limited to the minimum required for a correct decision. This limited amount had to be processed to yield an action as rapidly as possible. If too little information was processed so that there was a considerable chance of a wrong decision, or if too much was processed so that the decision came too late, the animal did not survive. Those species which did survive usually had a large visual information capacity but were able to select a small number of bits for processing towards an action-decision.

The amount of information actually used in a decision is determined by limitations of *short-term memory and other aspects of brain processing which are not strictly part of the visual system.

R. W. D.

Crossman, R. H. S. (1969) in Meetham, A. R. and Hudson, R. A. (eds.), *Encyclopaedia of Linguistics, Information and Control*. Oxford.
Ditchburn, R. W. and Drysdale, A. E. (1973). *Vision Research*, **13**, 2435.
Jacobson, H. (1951). *Science*, **113**, 292.
Klemmer, E. T. (1957). *Journal of Experimental Psychology*, **49**, 89.

**VISUAL SPACE.** The space that appears to us visually at any moment was defined by Ewald *Hering as *visual space*. It is a manifold of three dimensions in which objects are located in an ordered fashion. What metrical properties it has do not make it a space of constant curvature, because free movability of objects, an important characteristic of such a space, does not occur in visual space: sun and moon vary in apparent size with elevation. Nor is visual space unbounded like infinite Euclidean space: the sky forms a dome.

An individual's concept of spatial relationships is not an exact replica of the 'outside world'. Physical transduction in the eye and neural transformation of impulses arising in retinal receptors shape sensory signals in genetically pre-programmed ways that match pre-programmed neural response patterns (for example, eye movements); visual *illusions have their origin in many ambiguities and mismatches.

By abstractions, and by logical deductions from moment-to-moment sensory input and from memory traces, a concept of spatial relationships is built up, transcending immediate visual space and containing fewer contradictions: perceptual processes are now involved that are described by laws such as size constancy, i.e. distances are estimated by the size (and relative sizes) of known objects.

The physicist takes these abstractions and logical deductions from experience (he calls them theories based on experiments) many steps further, and constructs edifices like *Newton's absolute space or the more esoteric spaces of modern views of the universe (SEE MACH). But, as *Poincaré pointed out, the geometry of the physicist's space is a part of his theory, it being a matter of convention what are regarded as the laws of physics and what are the properties of the space within which they operate.

In contrast to visual space, a product of the individual's sensory processes, the mathematician's formal spaces are analytical structures of relationships developed from axioms and merely need to satisfy the condition of not containing internal contradictions. Attempts to express the properties of visual space in formal mathematical terms (for example, postulating a hyperbolic metric for visual space) have generally not met with success. The many restrictive conditions which are built in during the formulation of a mathematical space cannot immediately be assumed to apply to visual space, which may, for example, be non-Archimidean and often features internal contradictions—witness the logico-deductive process necessary to detect illusions of the type found in the graphic works of M. C. Escher.

G. W.

Carnap, R. (1922). *Der Raum. Kant-Studien Ergänzungsheft*, **56**.

**VISUAL SYSTEM: ENVIRONMENTAL INFLUENCES.** Experience in early life influences the organization of the visual system. That is, a specific set of environmental conditions seems to modify the properties of the visual system in a way that reflects these conditions. The best-known example of this is the changes produced by 'monocular deprivation'. If in infancy the input to one eye is selectively impaired, either due to a severe refractive error or squint (see EYE DEFECTS AND THEIR CORRECTION), there is a loss of visual capability in the affected eye, which persists in adult life even after the original disorder has been corrected. This is a type of 'amblyopia' and it has been investigated experimentally by rearing animals (cats or monkeys) from eye-opening time with one eye sutured closed. If after a period of three months or more of this monocular deprivation, the eye is opened, it looks perfectly normal, but the animal appears to be behaviourally blind in it. Examination of the visual cortex of animals reared in this way reveals dramatic changes in the distribution of ocular dominance columns (see VISUAL SYSTEM: ORGANIZATION). Instead of the normal bands of alternating left- and right-eye ocular dominance columns, virtually all the cells outside layer IV are driven only by the non-deprived eye. Within layer IV, the number of cells receiving an input from the deprived eye is greatly reduced, and the number receiving an input from the normal eye greatly increased. In other words, in layer IV the deprived-eye ocular dominance columns appear to shrink, and the non-deprived (normal) columns expand. Moreover, the cells still receiving an input from the deprived eye in layer IV seem to lose the capability to drive the cells in the other layers of the cortex.

**Critical period and binocular competition.** In animals, the marked changes in cortical organization following monocular deprivation are seen only if the deprivation occurs during the first three months of life. After that age, even extended periods of deprivation seem to have little effect. There is thus a critical period in early life in which the visual system is particularly susceptible to environmental influences. Moreover, within this critical period it is possible to reverse the effects of monocular deprivation. For example, even one week of monocular deprivation can result in the changes described above but, if at this stage the deprived eye is opened and the other closed, after another week or so the situation reverses, and the cortex becomes dominated by the initially deprived eye. A competitive interaction between the inputs from the two eyes therefore seems to be an important factor in producing the changes in cortical organization that can occur within the critical period. If both eyes are closed at eye-opening time, so that there is binocular as opposed to monocular deprivation, both eyes retain equal access to the visual cortex although there is a reduction in the number of binocularly driven cells. It appears that only when the input from one eye is selectively decreased, with respect to the other, does it lose the ability to drive cortical cells. This suggests a competition between the excitatory nerve terminals for synaptic sites on cortical cells (see NERVOUS SYSTEM). Thus, during monocular deprivation there would be a reorganization of excitatory terminals within the cortex, so that the lateral geniculate neurones and cortical interneurones relaying the input from the non-deprived eye take over the synaptic sites normally occupied by terminals from the deprived eye. However, things are not quite this simple. Recent work has shown that it is possible under some conditions to reveal inputs from the deprived eye in monocularly deprived animals, in a way which suggests that at least some synapses are present but ineffective.

The cortical changes occurring during monocular deprivation may thus involve a change in synaptic effectiveness, or some form of synaptic suppression, as well as the redistribution of terminals.

**Other factors influenced in the critical period.** So far, a large part of the discussion has been concerned with environmental influences on ocular dominance columns in the cortex. However, other aspects of visual cortical organization also seem to be influenced by the environment. The subset of orientation columns crossing the ocular dominance columns appears to be sensitive to the distribution of the orientation of the contours in the visual world in early life. Thus, rearing an animal in an environment where it only 'sees' vertical stripes results in a population of cortical neurones which, instead of representing all orientations, are biased to orientations in the region of the vertical, and not to others. Precisely organized binocular inputs to cortical cells render them sensitive to retinal image disparity, and form the basis of normal *stereoscopic vision. This is a more subtle level of organization than that seen in the gross distribution of ocular dominance columns, and it is very sensitive to abnormal environments. Even relatively mild squints seem to be able to upset the formation of these connections, and possibly result in loss of binocular connection altogether.

**Significance of the critical period.** Taken as a whole, it seems that the visual system is set up during early life to match the visual environment. A 'normal' set of connections appears only if the environment is normal. There has been considerable debate as to whether the normal cortical organization is innately determined, but can be distorted by abnormal experience in the critical period, or whether it is mainly experience which determines connections in a system that is 'designed' simply to match the environment. Present evidence suggests that genetic constraints predispose the cortex to a certain pattern of development, whilst the environment determines whether this is fully realized or not. One important reason for the plasticity in binocular connections may be the need to match these to the changing pattern of input as the separation of the eyes increases in the growing head.

This is an exciting area of brain research with a number of important implications. There are many questions to follow up. For example, are other aspects of brain function so dependent on experience in early life? (See, for instance, SPATIAL CO-ORDINATION OF THE SENSES.) Why is the brain only susceptible in this particular way to its environment in the critical period? Indeed, what factors determine the critical period? Recent evidence has raised the possibility that non-specific inputs to the cortex from the cholinergic and noradrenergic 'neuromodulatory systems' may play an important role in the plasticity seen in the critical period. If this is so, it may be possible to use some type of pharmacological manipulation to regenerate plasticity in the adult brain. The potential clinical implications of this are considerable. We have here an example of how scientific study of fundamental neurobiological problems can produce wide-reaching conclusions of pragmatic value, which strongly influence the way we understand our own development.                                                    A. M. S.

Barlow, H. (1975). Visual experience and cortical development. *Nature*, **258**, 199–204.

Kuffler, S. W. and Nicholls, J. G. (1984). *From Neuron to Brain*. New York.

Lund, R. D. (1978). *Developmental plasticity of the brain*. Oxford.

Sherman, S. M. and Spear, P. D. (1982). Organization of visual pathways in normal and visually deprived cats. *Physiology Review*, **62**, 738–855.

Sillito, A. M. (1986). Conflicts in the pharmacology of visual cortical plasticity. *Trends in Neuroscience*, **9**, 301–3.

Wiesel, T. N. and Hubel, D. H. (1963). Single cell responses in striate cortex of kitten deprived of vision in one eye. *Journal of Neurophysiology*, **26**, 1,003–17.

**VISUAL SYSTEM: ORGANIZATION.** At the most simple level the visual system may be considered as comprising the eyes and a long chain of neural connections extending from the retinal receptors at the back of the eye through the visual pathway to the cerebral cortex. The optics of the eye produce an image of the external world on the *retina. This results in a patterned excitation of retinal receptors which is then processed by the neuronal machinery of the visual system to form a representation of the external world in our brain. The representation does not seem to be formed in any one region but in a series of interacting regions that process different aspects of the input in parallel.

**Retina.** The retinal receptors convert the pattern of light that is the visual image, into a neural signal. This is then processed by the neuronal network of the retina and transmitted to the brain by the *axons of the 'retinal ganglion cells'. The retinal receptors make synaptic contact with bipolar cells, which in turn make synaptic contact with the retinal ganglion cells—these are serial connections. At the same time, two other groups of cells, the horizontal cells and ammacrine cells, make laterally directed connections that control the transfer of information through the serial connections (see Sterling et al., 1986). The neural organization of the retina is summarized in Fig. 1.

**Retinal receptors** fall into two groups: the cones, which are associated with daylight vision and colour vision, and the rods, which are associated with night vision. The cones can be subdivided into three types each responding best to light from a different part of the visible spectrum. These are essential to normal colour vision and a loss or deficiency in the operation of one of the three categories leads to a corresponding deficiency in colour vision. People referred to as 'protanopes'

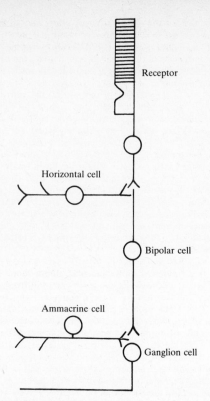

**Fig. 1.** Interconnections between cells in the retina. The receptors respond to changes in the level of the light falling on them, and synaptically activate bipolar cells which in turn activate the retinal ganglion cells. Lateral connections are made by horizontal cells and ammacrine cells. These modify the transmission of information from receptor to ganglion cells and result in the ganglion cell response being influenced in a complex way by the activity of a large number of receptors.

lack the cones sensitive to the red end of the spectrum, 'deuteranopes' those to the green portion, and 'tritanopes' those sensitive to the blue end of the spectrum.

**Retinal activity.** Whilst it is commonly accepted that most nerve cells in the brain generate action potentials (see NERVOUS SYSTEM), this is not the case in the retina. Only the retinal ganglion cells generate action potentials; the other cells in the retina and the retinal receptors exhibit graded shifts in membrane potential, in response to changing levels of illumination without developing a propagating action potential. If one views an action potential as a mechanism for transmitting information over *long* nerve axons, this is not surprising. The retina is a thin structure, with correspondingly short connections, and the electrotonic spread of potential change is adequate for the length of the neural processes involved. When a retinal receptor is exposed to light the membrane of the receptor 'hyperpolarizes', and the amount of *neuro-transmitter released by the synaptic process of the receptor goes down. Receptors depolarize and release more neurotransmitter when the level of light decreases. The potential changes in the receptor are mediated by the action of light on the photopigment contained in the outer segment, and involve a series of chemical interactions leading to a reduction in the level of cyclic GMP, and a consequent decrease in the sodium conductance of the membrane (Lamb, 1986). The transmitter released by the retinal receptors produces potential changes in bipolar cells; these can be subdivided into two groups—one is hyperpolarized by the transmitter and the other depolarized. This difference in the response of bipolar cells leads in turn to two categories of retinal ganglion cells.

**Responses of retinal ganglion cells.** The various synaptic interactions occurring in the neural circuits of the retina determine the response of retinal ganglion cells to visual stimuli. Since the retinal ganglion cells provide the output from the eyes to the brain, how they respond to visual stimuli tells us something of the nature of the message the brain is receiving. The visual response properties of retinal ganglion cells can be demonstrated in a very simple experiment. An electrode is implanted into the optic nerve of an eye, which is focused on a projector screen. The electrode records the activity (action potentials) of the axons of retinal ganglion cells in the optic nerve. A spot of light is then shone on to the screen and moved over it. As the image of this spot in turn moves over the retina, a point is reached at which the light excites the receptors providing the input to the ganglion cell under study. This induces an action potential discharge in the ganglion cell, which is detected by the electrode recording from its axon. The area over which responses can be elicited from the ganglion cell constitutes its *receptive field. Although these receptive-field properties can appear quite complex, they can be simply understood if one considers the 'problem' they have to deal with. The retinal image consists of a set of variations in light intensity above and below the background illumination level (this ignores *colour vision). Following from the bipolar cells, retinal ganglion cells exhibit two types of receptive field. In one, the cell is excited by an *increase* in light intensity above background level and, in the other, it is excited by a *decrease* in light intensity below the background level. The receptive fields consist of a concentrically organized centre and surround region. Broadly speaking, in each cell's receptive field the amount of light falling on the centre is compared with that falling on the surround, by lateral synaptic interactions, mediated by the horizontal and ammacrine cells. For one type of cell, a relative increment in the amount of light falling on the receptive field centre, with respect to the surround, causes an increase in firing, whilst the converse applies to the other type of cell.

Obviously, the relative amount of light falling on the centre, with respect to the surround, can be varied by changes in the absolute light level on either centre or surround. The comparison of

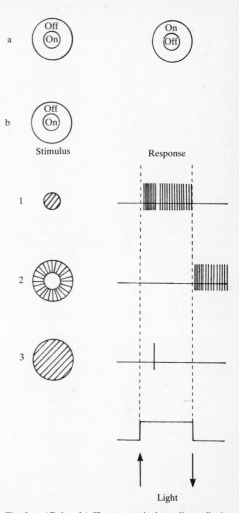

**Fig. 2. a.** 'On' and 'off' centre retinal ganglion cells. **b.** Responses of 'on' centre retinal ganglion cell to: 1. Spot of light illuminating centre of the receptive field only. 2. Annulus of light illuminating receptive field surround. 3. Large spot of light illuminating both receptive field centre and surround. In each case the light is briefly flashed on and then off as indicated at the bottom of the records. The records show the spikes elicited by each of the three stimuli. In 1 the spot of light elicits a response while it is *on*; in 2 the annulus produces no apparent response while it is on, but a vigorous response when it goes *off*. Illumination of both centre and surround as in 3 produces very little response either while the illumination is on or when it goes off, thus demonstrating the mutual antagonism between the centre and the surround. See also RECEPTIVE FIELD, Fig. 2, for a simplified view of the neuronal connections that may form the inhibitory surround of the concentric receptive field.

illumination levels on the receptive field of centre and surround is important to maintaining optimal sensitivity to change in illumination over a wide range of background illumination levels. For a discussion of the process of adaptation and dark adaptation, see VISUAL ADAPTATION.

In one type of retinal ganglion cell, an increment in the relative amount of light falling on the centre (light 'on') causes an increased discharge, whilst in the other a decrement (light 'off') causes a discharge; thus, neurophysiologists describe the two types of cell as 'on' and 'off' centre cells. Because the cells actually compare the light falling on the centre and surround, changes in the surround illumination of the opposite polarity to that exciting the centre, cause an increased response; hence 'on' centre cells are said to have 'off' surrounds, and 'off' centre cells have 'on' surrounds. Contrast in the retinal image is not only defined by luminance but also by colour. Thus, the retinal circuitry also processes the input from the three types of cone in a way which allows different classes of retinal ganglion cell to transmit details of the chromatic properties of the image. In some ways, the receptive-field properties of retinal ganglion cells, transmitting information about colour contrast, follow a similar logic to that outlined above for luminance contrast.

**Types of retinal ganglion cell.** Retinal ganglion cells fall into a range of different types. In addition to the 'on' and 'off' centre cells already mentioned, there are further subdivisions in terms of the chromatic sensitivity of the cells and the type of spatial summation shown in the receptive field. With respect to spatial summation, some cells show a linear summation of the components of a distribution of varying luminance across their receptive field, others a non-linear summation (Enroth-Cugell and Robson, 1966). These are referred to as X and Y cells respectively, and show distinctions in a range of other properties, including receptive field size, sensitivity to stimulus velocity, and spatial frequency (see PSYCHOPHYSICS) (Sherman, 1985). In particular, X cells can resolve finer visual patterns (higher spatial frequencies) than Y cells. They are also distinguished on anatomical grounds; the Y cells correspond to the alpha retinal ganglion cells distinguished by anatomists; they are larger and have thicker axons than the beta cells which correspond to X cells. One important point to note is that the Y cells have faster conducting axons than X cells. These distinctions cut across the broad subdivision into 'on' and 'off' centre types.

**The visual pathway.** The axons of the retinal ganglion cells travel in the optic nerve to the brain. Each retina can be considered as subdivided into two halves in the vertical plane—a nasal half and a temporal half. The axons from the nasal half of each retina, after travelling in the optic nerve, cross over to the other side of the brain in the optic chiasma. They join fibres, from the temporal half

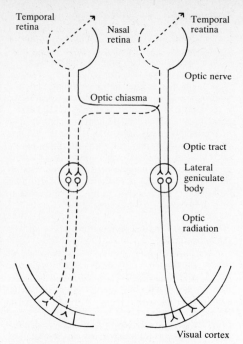

**Fig. 3.** Schematic diagram of the visual pathway as seen by looking down from above the head. Note that, because of the crossing in the optic chiasma, the right side of the brain 'sees' the left side of the visual world, and vice versa.

of the other retina, which encompass the same half of the visual field, and pass with these to the lateral geniculate body (a group of cells in the thalamus). The lateral geniculate body is a laminated structure with six separate layers, four parvocellular and two magnocellular. The inputs from the two eyes synapse in separate layers. The axons of the lateral geniculate cells project via the optic radiation to the visual cortex. One can view the visual cortex as a folded 'slab' of grey matter containing nerve cells, with an underlying layer of white matter formed by the nerve fibres entering and leaving the grey matter. The grey matter of the cortex is commonly subdivided into six layers. The projection from the lateral geniculate body terminates most densely in the vicinity of layer IV of the visual cortex. In this layer, the input from the two eyes is kept separate (or approximately so). There are thus alternating bands in layer IV of cells dominated respectively by the ipsilateral (same-side) and contralateral (opposite-side) eyes. This forms the basis of the so-called 'ocular dominance' columns in the cortex. In the cortical layers above and below layer IV, there are laterally spreading connections which result in binocularly driven cells. The crossing in the optic chiasma thus ultimately enables the retinal inputs relating to the two views of the same part of the visual world to be brought together.

In the visual projection there is an orderly map of each half retina on the lateral geniculate body, and then again in the cortex. Each retinal ganglion cell 'looks' at a particular part of the retinal image, and hence a point in *visual space, and its neighbour at an adjacent or overlapping point, and so on. This sequence of sampling of visual space is reflected in the projection to the lateral geniculate nucleus, and from there to the cortex. The inputs from the two half retinae are in register; thus there is a double mapping of the same view of the visual world, firstly in the separate geniculate layers, and then again through the ocular dominance columns in the visual cortex. The 'slab' of grey matter forming the left visual cortex is thus a 'map' of the right visual world as seen from two slightly different viewpoints. Moreover, the various categories of retinal ganglion cell all sample the visual field more or less uniformly. They convey different types of information to the central visual system, and the patterns of termination of the inputs relaying this information are distinctive. The input to the visual cortex, thus, not only reflects the visual world seen from two slightly different viewpoints, but also the visual world sampled several times over by elements with differing sensitivity to the properties of the retinal image.

**Receptor density and the central visual map.** The density of retinal receptors is not uniform over the retina, but is highest in the fovea and falls off towards the periphery of the retina. The higher the density of receptors, the smaller their size and the greater the visual acuity. Broadly, one can equate receptor size with the grain size in a photographic emulsion. The proportion of the map in the central visual system devoted to each retinal area reflects the density of receptors, rather than the dimensions of the area. Thus, in terms of the area of the visual field, the visual cortical representation of the fovea is much larger than that for peripheral parts of the retina.

**Processing of the visual input.** Our knowledge of the way in which the visual input is first processed within the brain owes a great deal to the work of *Hubel and Wiesel. They studied the response properties of cells in the lateral geniculate nucleus and visual cortex, utilizing the same overall technique as that described for the analysis of retinal ganglion cell response properties. The eyes of an anaesthetized animal were focused on a projector screen and the activity of cells in the lateral geniculate nucleus and visual cortex recorded. Because of the orderly visual projection, as an image moves over the projector screen and hence over the retina, it also moves in a similar fashion over the map of the retina in the lateral geniculate nucleus and visual cortex. When examined this way, cells in the lateral geniculate nucleus were found to have receptive fields that were very similar to those seen in retinal ganglion cells. They were well activated by flashing spots of light, and fell into the same broad categories (e.g. 'on' and 'off' centre X and Y cells). Conversely, the majority of cells in the visual cortex were not best activated by flashing

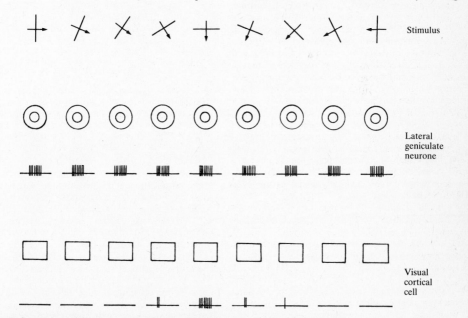

**Fig. 4.** Comparison of the response of a lateral geniculate neurone and a visual cortical cell to a bar of light moving over their receptive field. The lateral geniculate neurone responds to the bar at all orientations. The visual cortical cell is very selective to the orientation of the stimulus. As visual cortical cells get their excitatory input from lateral geniculate neurones, this implies that there is some specific organization of inhibitory and excitatory interconnections within the cortex generating this orientation selectivity.

spots of light, but by an elongated stimulus moving over their receptive field at a particular orientation. This selectivity to the orientation of the 'contour' of a stimulus is a characteristic feature of visual cortical cells (Hubel, 1963). A retinal ganglion cell, or a cell in the lateral geniculate nucleus, responds to a bar of light moving over its receptive field at all orientations. In the light of this evidence, Hubel and Wiesel proposed that visual cortical cells were concerned with the detection of specific features of the visual environment. The selectivity to stimulus orientation appears to be an important component of the way in which nervous systems throughout the animal kingdom encode the visual input; it is seen, for example, in the higher visual centres of mammals, cephalopods, and birds. Although selectivity to stimulus orientation seems to be a particularly important facet of the neuronal machinery in the visual cortex, cells exhibit selectivity to a range of other properties of the visual input. This includes direction of stimulus motion, the colour, the length, and the depth in visual space. The latter property underlies stereopsis (see STEREOSCOPIC VISION) and involves cells that are driven by both eyes, but are sensitive to the disparity of the image location on the two retinae.

**Columnar organization of visual cortex.** One of the major discoveries made by Hubel and Wiesel was that the visual cortex is divided into a sequence of columns or sheets of neurones, with common functional properties. The ocular dominance columns have been described elsewhere (see HUBEL AND WIESEL: JOINT WORK). These run from the surface of the cortex to the white matter, and are themselves subdivided into a further subset of columns, which appear to be concerned with stimulus orientation. These are the 'orientation columns', containing cells with common orientation selectivity. Adjacent orientation columns are sensitive to slightly different orientations and this process repeats as a series of approximately 10° steps from one column to the next. The portion of an ocular dominance column, representing one location in visual space, contains a series of orientation columns that, on average, cover an entire 180° range. Each location in visual space is thus represented by two ocular dominance columns (for the right and left eye), and their subsets of orientation columns. The orientation and ocular dominance columns can be envisaged as crossing each other at right angles as shown in Fig. 5. However, the true situation is not as orderly as this and it is possibly better to envisage the two sets of columns as intersecting in a pseudo-random fashion, but one which broadly ensures that each location in visual space is represented by a full complement of orientation columns.

**Laminar organization of the visual cortex.** There is a difference between the input and output connections of the cells in each layer of the visual cortex. Consequently, in addition to the columnar

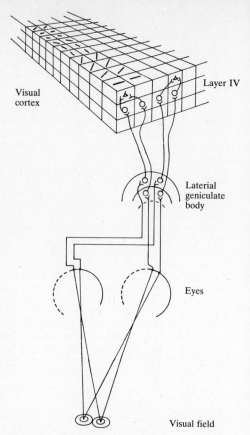

**Fig. 5.** Detailed view of the organization of the visual perception through the lateral geniculate body to the visual cortex. This shows the projection of two adjacent regions in the visual field on to adjacent groups of neurones in the lateral geniculate body and visual cortex. Note that the input relating to the corresponding points in the two eyes ends on separate layers in the lateral geniculate body and on separate bands (ocular dominance columns) of neurones in layer IV of the cortex. However there is binocular convergence on to single neurones in the cortex, mainly outside layer IV.

organization, there is a differentiation of function in the vertical domain, i.e. within an orientation column. In their early work on this matter, Hubel and Wiesel proposed three types of cell in a column—simple cells, complex cells, and hypercomplex cells. The term 'simple' was applied to the cells in layer IV receiving their input directly from the lateral geniculate body. Orientation selectivity was thought to be set up in this layer by the organization of the geniculate cell connections to simple cells. Each simple cell was conjectured to receive an excitatory input from several geniculate cells, with their receptive fields extending in a row through visual space (see RECEPTIVE FIELD, Fig. 2). Only a bar of the appropriate orientation would simultaneously activate all the input cells, and hence produce a maximal response in the simple cell. A group of simple cells were then thought to provide the drive out of layer IV to complex cells, and complex cells, in turn, to provide a drive to hypercomplex cells. Each of these cell types was considered to have a receptive field organization elaborating successively more complex features of the visual environment.

The strictly hierarchical view of the organization of cells in a column has not been supported by subsequent findings. Present evidence emphasizes parallel processing of different facets of the visual input in the cortex, utilizing a circuitry that is much more complex than originally envisaged (Sherman, 1985, Rose and Dobson, 1985, Martin, 1984). Extensive excitatory and inhibitory connections mediate lateral interactions in the visual cortex, which generate many aspects of the stimulus select-ivity of the cells. Indeed, experiments inducing a localized blockade of intracortical inhibitory pro-cesses have demonstrated that inhibitory connec-tions play a critical role in the generation of some receptive field properties; these include sensitivity to the direction of stimulus motion and, for some cells, stimulus orientation (Sillito, 1984). The direct comparison here is with the retina, where hori-zontal and ammacrine cell connections generate the concentric receptive field of ganglion cells, not just the direct connections from the receptors via the bipolar cells. However, in the central visual system, the heavy reciprocal interconnections between each level in the system suggest that any analysis of its function must take note of the fact that the levels constitute interacting components of a circuit, rather than just a stage in a sequence. For example, the projection from the visual cortex to the lateral geniculate nucleus is as dense, or even denser, than that from the retina, and yet, remark-ably, the function of the former is largely ignored. Obviously the cortex is potentially capable of exerting a powerful control over the response of geniculate cells, and yet at the same time the cortical activity is dependent on the geniculate input. Similar comments apply to the interactions between the cortical laminae and the different cortical areas. Further progress in our understand-ing, at this level of analysis, requires a hypothesis regarding visual-system function that needs the synaptic complexity we now know to exist.

**'Blobs' and colour processing in the visual cortex.**
Recent evidence in the Primate has shown that, in addition to the columnar organization of the visual cortex, there is a sequence of regularly repeated blob-like structures. These can be distinguished anatomically by virtue of the fact that they stain very densely for the mitochondrial enzyme, cyto-chrome oxidase. They are most conspicuous in layers II and III of the cortex, and are notable in a functional sense because they contain cells that seem to be primarily concerned with processing colour information, and they lack cells sensitive to stimulus orientation. The blobs show a regular distribution in the tangential plane, in relation to the ocular dominance columns, in a way which suggests that there is a blob for each location in visual space as well as a full complement of orienta-tion columns. The pattern of the output from the blobs, and columnar regions of the primary visual cortex, suggests that colour information and orien-tation are processed in parallel through separate channels.

**Cortical pathways processing the visual input.**
The processing of the visual input, after the pri-mary visual cortex, appears to proceed through distinct, although interlinked, groups of cortical areas. The regions of cortex most strongly domin-ated by the visual input are often labelled in sequence as V1 (primary visual cortex or area 17), through V2, up to V5. There seem to be two major channels of processing. One passes from V1 to V2, from there to V4, and eventually to the inferotemporal cortex. This seems to be involved in object recognition and colour. The other chan-nel passes from V1 to V2, and from V2 to V5 (V5 is also referred to as 'MT'), and the inferior parietal cortex; it seems to be involved in object location and movement in visual space. Within these broad channels, various aspects of the input are likely to be processed in parallel for all, or part, of the sequence of connections, as for example for colour and orientation, in the sequence of connections passing to V4. Neurones in the inferotemporal cortical region can have highly selective response properties, some for example seem to respond only to faces. However, it is far from clear that this represents a general case for the sequential elaboration of more and more complex fields deal-ing with specialized elements of our environment. Many would suggest that in general this level of representation involves ensemble encoding in a matrix of interacting neurones. The presence of face-specific neurones in Primates may have more to do with the biological importance of faces than the general rules underlying visual processing.

A. M. S.

Enroth-Cugell, C. and Robson, J. G. (1966). The contrast sensitivity of retinal ganglion cells of the cat. *Journal of Physiology*, **187**, 517–52.

Essen, D. C. and Maunsell, J. H. R. (1983). Hierarchical organization and functional streams in the visual cortex. *Trends in Neuroscience*, **6**, 370–5.

Hubel, D. H. (1963). The visual cortex of the brain. *Scientific American*, November.

Kuffler, S. W. and Nicholls, J. G. (1984). *From Neurone to Brain*. Sunderland, Massachusetts.

Lamb, T. D. (1986). Transduction in vertebrate photo-receptors: the roles of cyclic GMP and calcium. *Trends in Neuroscience*, **9**, 224–8.

Martin, K. A. C. (1984). Neuronal circuits in cat striate cortex (1984). In Peters, A. A. and Jones, E. G. (eds.), *The Cerebral Cortex*, vol. 2. New York.

Rose, D. and Dobson, V. G. (eds.) (1985). *Models of the Visual Cortex*. New York.

Sherman, S. M. (1985). Functional organization of the W-, X-, and Y-cell pathways in the cat: A review and hypothesis. *Progress in Psychobiology and Physiolo-gical Psychology*, vol. **II**, 234–314.

Sillito, A. M. (1984). Functional considerations of the operation of GABAergic inhibitory processes in the visual cortex. In Peters, A. A. and Jones, E. G. (eds.), *The Cerebral Cortex* vol. 2. New York.

Sterling, P., Freed, M., and Smith, R. G. (1986). Microcircuitry and functional architecture of the cat retina. *Trends in Neuroscience*, **9**, 186–92.

**VOLLEY THEORY.** The transmission of sound by the ear to the brain presents a special problem, because sound frequencies greatly exceed the maximum frequency of action potentials in a nerve fibre. The volley theory, based on electrical recordings of action potentials in auditory nerves, states that for frequencies up to perhaps 500 hertz each cycle of a sound wave produces a single neural spike (actually at the zero energy cross-over of the wave), but, at frequencies beyond those that a nerve can follow, other nerve fibres are recruited to code higher frequencies by combinations of spikes from co-operating nerves.

For still higher frequencies, the cochlea analyses the various frequencies into different positions along the basilar membrane, so that different hair cells are activated, and different neural channels employed, to transmit each frequency. There are thus three ways, depending on frequency, in which sounds are represented and transmitted by the ear.

See HEARING.

**VOLUNTARY CONTROL.** See BIOFEEDBACK.

**VON BÉKÉSY,** GEORG (1899–1972), Hungarian physicist and physiologist. See BÉKÉSY.

**VON EHRENFELS,** CHRISTIAN (1859–1933), Austrian philosopher and psychologist. See EHRENFELS.

**VON FREY,** MAX (1852–1932), German physiologist. See FREY.

**VON FRISCH,** KARL RITTER (1886–1983), Austrian ethologist. See FRISCH.

**VON HELMHOLTZ,** HERMANN LUDWIG FERDINAND (1821–94), German physiologist and physicist. See HELMHOLTZ.

**VON KRAFFT-EBING,** RICHARD, BARON (1840–1902), German neurologist. See KRAFFT-EBING.

**VON NEUMANN,** JOHN (1903–57), a mathematician of international repute, born in Budapest, and later an American citizen. His work touched on most branches of both pure and applied mathematics. During the 1920s and 1930s his work included quantum theory, mathematical logic, ergodic theory, continuous geometry, and abstract algebra; his interest then turned to theoretical hydrodynamics. He became well known as a member of the Atomic Energy Commission, having been professor in the school of mathematics at the Institute for Advanced Study at Princeton from 1933 until 1954.

Von Neumann first became known internationally for his work in developing the digital computer. It was at the Moore School of Electrical Engineering in Philadelphia in 1946 that he led a team that completed ENIAC, the first digital computer. His work gave publicity to the subject under the title *The Theory and Techniques of Electronic Digital Computers*, and set out the design principles that in essentials remain unchanged today. Then, immediately the ENIAC was complete, the design was set out for a smaller and much more powerful computer, with a store of 1,000 words each of ten decimal digits—fifty times that of ENIAC. New storage methods were designed and new programming techniques suggested, leading to the present digital computer with a store capacity for millions of words. The work fitted in with that of Alan *Turing. Von Neumann worked primarily from the standpoint of the engineer and was concerned with the hardware realization, while Turing worked on the algorithmic approach to define what was computable. The first four generations of computers are now called Von Neumann machines since they all followed the essential features of Von Neumann's earliest design; as a result nearly all the computer languages in existence are essentially Von Neumann languages.

The most famous of his many contributions to mathematics was embodied in *The Theory of Games and Economic Behavior* (1944; revised edn. 1953), which he wrote in collaboration with the American economist Oskar Morgenstern. It was concerned to develop a general theory of the rational behaviour of two or more people in what are basically conflicting or competing situations, although coalitions are also considered. First he developed the theory of two-person, zero-sum games, in which one player's gain is the other player's loss; he then suggested the concept of equilibrium, known as the *minimax* solution, in which one player minimizes the maximum loss the other player can impose on him. The solution of a game depended on the players using mixed strategies where the actual moves are chosen at random. Later, games for many players were devised, not necessarily zero-sum; here coalitions were possible, and a number of solution concepts were developed. The special case of 'the prisoner's dilemma' was made explicit, where neither player would wish to change his move given the strategy of the other—a pair of strategies that is worse for both players than any alternative. The development of the theory of games since Von Neumann has been considerable and involves decision making (especially under conditions of uncertainty), games against nature, and the very important interpretation of the theory known as linear programming.

Von Neumann's next major work was *Probabilistic Logics* (1952). In this he was primarily concerned with the role of error in logical nets, which are particular examples of finite automata and designed to be abstract models of the central nervous system. He was interested in the technique of *multiplexing*, which is multiplication of neural connections between neural type elements, so that if a certain number of fibres fail, the system is still operable. The basic element of the Von Neumann automata, unlike the usual use of conjunction and negation, was the Sheffer stroke element. This element fires when either of its two input elements fire, but not when both do, for if they fire together they inhibit the element and stop an output firing. The or-element, and-element, and not-element are then defined in terms of the Sheffer stroke. This in turn leads to the majority organ whose output fires if and only if the majority of the inputs fire. The multiple line trick was used to provide the needed multiplexing. This is done by setting a fiducial level $k$ to the number of lines of the bundle to be stimulated; then, for $0<k<\frac{1}{2}$ at least $(l-k)N$ lines being stimulated is said to be in a positive state—and conversely, when no more than $kN$ are stimulated, it implies a negative state. Building on this multiplexing method, Von Neumann examined in detail the notion of error.

The final phase of Von Neumann's work was represented by the Silliman lectures which he was to have given at Yale in 1956 and which were embodied in his posthumous *The Computer and the Brain* (1958). His terminal illness made the lectures impossible but the book made clear the form they would have taken. The work was that of the mathematician operating in the field of brain studies and emphasized the differences and similarities between brains and computers. The nerve impulse is primarily electrical, apparently digital, and has time characteristics not unlike the pulses in a computer. Overall, computer speeds then were slower at performing the range of functions performed by the brain—a state of affairs that has gradually changed. The languages of the brain involve mathematical, logical, and statistical methods, and Von Neumann foresaw that in describing the brain and the nervous system new forms of mathematics would be developed. This has occurred in the forms of uncertainty logics and empirical logics. The precision of brain operation he thought of as logical, its computational working as arithmetic, and the functional description as statistical.

See also ARTIFICIAL INTELLIGENCE; CRAIK; McCULLOCH; PATTERN RECOGNITION; TURING; WIENER.                    F. H. G.

**VYGOTSKY,** LEO (Lev Semionovich, 1896–1934). The most outstanding Soviet psychologist, and founder of the most influential school of Soviet psychology, Vygotsky was born in Orsha (Belorussia), and began his work in psychology after leaving Moscow University (faculty of letters) in 1919. As a young man he wrote the subsequently well-known pieces that were included in the *Psychology of Art* (1965; Eng. trans. 1971). Psychological analysis of the personality of Hamlet, as well as studies in the psychology of fables, were central to the work of this outstanding young scholar. After a few years in Gomel (Belorussia), where he taught psychology and wrote *Pedagogical Psychology* (1926; in Russian), he moved to Moscow, where his most important work began. He soon became a leading figure of the Institute there, and the central figure in a group of young scholars (including A. N. Leontiev and A. R. *Luria) who became his first co-workers and followers.

At the time of his early studies, psychology was in a state of crisis. It was split into two independent sciences. The first was the *explanatory or physiological psychology* of *Wundt and *Ebbinghaus, who tried to explain complex psychological phenomena by reducing them to elementary physiological components. They refused to deal scientifically with the highest, specifically human forms of conscious behaviour—motives, abstract thinking, active memorizing, voluntary actions, etc. The second school attempted a *descriptive psychology* which did consider the highest forms of conscious experiences, treating them as spiritual forms of mental life, and supposing that these phenomena may be described in *phenomenological terms but not explained scientifically.

Vygotsky assumed that the basic goal of scientific psychology was to overcome this division, and to try to explain scientifically not only the elementary but also the highest forms of psychological processes. This—he thought—could be done by reducing the complex psychological phenomena not to physiological 'elements', but rather to more complex psychological 'units', which would preserve all the properties of the complex forms of conscious behaviour and which could serve as its models, making the more complicated forms of mental life accessible for scientific analysis.

Supposing the highest forms of mental life and conscious behaviour to be not of a spiritual nature but a product of social development, Vygotsky saw tool-using and sign-using ('significative') behaviour as essential for all higher forms of psychological processes. He also considered forms of sign-using behaviour, its rules, and the stages of its development. Studies in sign-using, as a model of complex active *memory, were his first attempt to approach experimentally the most complicated psychological processes. (The results of these studies were published by A. N. Leontiev.)

His work on simple 'units' of tool- and sign-using behaviour led Vygotsky to investigate the role that language (the most universal system of signs) plays in human behaviour, and to a careful analysis of its development during the life of the individual. The main purpose was to describe the semantic structure of words. His famous experiments with artificial words (the Vygotsky–Sakharov technique) were published later by Hanfman and Kasanin and became known as the Vygotsky–Hanfman–Kasanin tests.

These investigations led Vygotsky to one of his

main discoveries—that the meaning of words undergoes a complex development, and that words starting as emotional soon become concrete designations of objects later to acquire abstract meaning. (See LANGUAGE: LEARNING WORD MEANINGS.) This conclusion was followed by the statement that the whole of mental development can be understood as a profound change of psychological systems which mediate the basic forms of activities; and that with each new stage the leading function changes. So, Vygotsky supposed, the child is thinking by memorizing, whereas the adult is memorizing by thinking. This systemic approach to complex psychological functions was one of the most important steps in contemporary psychology.

The idea that the higher psychological processes have a social origin brought Vygotsky to a new approach in the evaluation of the child's mental development, and to the assumption that not only the actual 'mental age' of the child has to be measured, but also its potential capacities—what he called 'the zone of potential development'. This can be done by comparing how the child solves certain problems by itself with a second indicator: how it can solve similar tasks with the help of the teacher—representing here the ability to acquire social prompting. The principles proposed by Vygotsky were of the highest importance for practical educational and clinical psychology.

During his short life in science (he died at the age of 37 from tuberculosis, and worked actively in experimental psychology only for about ten years), Vygotsky was active in many fields of scientific psychology: general psychological problems, child psychology, the problems of retarded and deaf children, the psychological analysis of local brain injuries, and a series of related fields. Although his career was very brief, his influence on Soviet and world psychology has become more and more significant with the passing years. In addition to the two works mentioned, his most important books are *Thought and Language* (1937; Eng. trans. 1962); *Selected Psychological Studies* (1956; in Russian); and *Development of the Higher Mental Processes* (1960; in Russian).   A. R. L.

# W

**WALLACE,** ALFRED RUSSEL (1823–1913). British naturalist, born at Usk, Monmouthshire. He made extensive natural history collections in the Amazon basin (though a large part of these were lost when the ship he was on caught fire) and later in the Malay Archipelago.

Independently of Charles *Darwin (and, like him, to some extent inspired by reading *Malthus's *Essay on Population*), he conceived the notion of evolution by survival of the fittest. On 18 June 1848 Darwin received a letter from Wallace which expressed the key concept that he had been working on for over twenty years. Darwin wrote to Charles Lyell:

Your words have come true with a vengeance—that I should be forestalled. You said this, when I explained to you here very briefly my views on 'Natural Selection' depending on the struggle for existence. I never saw a more striking coincidence; if Wallace had my MS. sketch written out in 1842, he could not have made a better short abstract! Even his terms now stand as heads of my chapters.

The problem of priority was solved by the two of them in the most gentlemanly fashion with a joint paper presented to the Linnean Society on 1 July 1858. Nevertheless, Wallace's letter prompted Darwin into writing *The Origin of Species*, which was finished on 19 March 1859.

Though unfortunate in being anticipated by Darwin and overshadowed by him, Wallace was an excellent naturalist and a careful, original thinker. In later life, however, he became an advocate of *spiritualism. He was elected Fellow of the Royal Society in 1893 and appointed to the Order of Merit in 1910.

Among Wallace's main works are *Contributions to the Theory of Natural Selection* (1870); *The Malay Archipelago* (1869); *Darwinism* (1889); *On Miracles and Modern Spiritualism* (1881); and, for solid scientific work, *Geographical Distribution of Animals* (1876) and *Island Life* (1880). See also *Man's Place in the Universe* (1903) and *My Life, an Autobiography*, 2 vols. (1905).

**WALTER,** WILLIAM GREY (1910–76), Anglo-American physiologist, was born in Kansas City and educated at Westminster School, London, and at Cambridge. As a postgraduate student with E. D. *Adrian, he worked on muscle contraction before joining Frederick Lucien Golla at the Maudsley Hospital in London in 1935, to start his work on the electrical activity of the brain by recording the *electroencephalogram (the EEG) that was to continue for the next forty years. In 1939 he moved with Golla to Bristol, to open a research laboratory and clinic called the Burden Neurological Institute. In addition to his work on the EEG, Grey Walter was much concerned with the development and use of *electroconvulsive therapy (ECT), and the first shock treatment on patients in Britain was done at the Institute, with apparatus he designed and constructed.

In about 1940 Grey Walter started work on two aspects of the EEG that were to occupy his efforts for many years—frequency analysis, and mental attributes such as imagery (see IMAGING). Then came a period of several years when he turned to the construction of electromechanical models to simulate brain-function behaviour. This was the time of the birth of *cybernetics. The publicity that these fascinating models received tended to distract attention from their scientific value. The famous electromechanical tortoise (*M. speculatrix*) was designed to see how many sensory systems had to interact before complex behaviour patterns were produced. This turned out to require very few active elements, with only two control systems (one light-sensitive and the other touch-sensitive). The simplicity of the model was the mark of its value: a fact that many imitators did not appreciate, and thus they merely produced elaborate toys. Grey Walter was the first to show that simple control devices could produce lifelike behaviour, with learning.

While all this was going on, the 22-channel toposcope was being made to examine aspects of the rhythmic electrical activity of the brain that the frequency analyser was unable to achieve. The helical scan 'Topsy' was useful for measurement and display of frequency and phase relationships on a short time-scale at many electrode sites.

Then, at about this time, two events occurred at the Institute that were to change the course of the work. First was the use of implanted electrodes for investigation of *epilepsy and treatment of psychiatric illness, which allowed recording from local brain regions in conscious humans; and second was the development of a 2-channel *evoked potential averager. This gave Grey the chance he had been waiting for—the opportunity of studying the functioning brain in its complexity, particularly interactions between associated stimuli. He had attempted these conditioning experiments on several occasions since the 1930s, probably stimulated in the early days by meeting Ivan *Pavlov. In 1962 a study was undertaken of a group of *autistic children, using scalp electrodes, and it was during this work that Grey Walter first noticed a negative shift between the associated stimuli. The contingent negative variation (CNV)—brain activity occurring just before a decision—was made public at a meeting of the EEG Society in 1964.

His highly productive work on evoked potentials for the rest of that decade was tragically halted in 1970 by a severe head injury from which he never fully recovered. Grey Walter was a pioneer and an intellectual leader of world renown; but he was never fully accepted by the British scientific establishment. He wrote some 200 research papers and a uniquely stimulating book: *The Living Brain* (1953), which attracted many students to follow in his footsteps.                                    R. C.

**WARD,** JAMES (1843–1925), English philosopher, educated at Cambridge and later at the universities of Göttingen and Berlin. While in Germany, he acquired considerable understanding of both physiology and *psychophysics, and after his return to Cambridge published an article on *Fechner's law in the first volume of the neurological journal *Brain*.

Ward's major interest in later life lay almost wholly in philosophy, but this did not deter him from writing a celebrated article on psychology for the ninth edition of the *Encyclopaedia Britannica* in 1886, which he expanded and largely rewrote for the eleventh edition in 1911. His other major contribution to psychology was an impressive, if difficult, treatise on *Psychological Principles* (1918). Although he did not contribute further to experimental psychology, he did much to foster its development in Cambridge through the activities of such men as W. H. R. *Rivers, C. S. *Myers, and F. C. *Bartlett.

A bibliography of Ward's writings by E. B. Titchener and W. S. Foster was published in the *American Journal of Psychology*, **23**, 457–60 and reprinted in 1926, with some extensions to the date of Ward's death, in the *Moniest*, **36**, 170–6.

                                                   O. L. Z.

**WATSON,** JOHN BROADUS (1878–1958) was the founder of the American school of psychology known as *behaviourism. The movement was launched in 1913 with his paper 'Psychology as the Behaviorist Views It', and was bolstered by many subsequent papers and popular articles, as well as by his four influential books: *Behavior: an introduction to comparative psychology* (1914), *Psychology from the Standpoint of a Behaviorist* (1919), *Behaviorism* (1924), and *The Psychological Care of Infant and Child* (1928). Reacting against the influential introspective psychology of his day, which even he had practised early in his career, Watson declared that behaviour should be the only subject-matter of psychology. Though psychology had long been concerned with the study of mind, Watson believed that such an endeavour had proved fruitless. Psychology could become a productive science like other natural sciences only by being objective and dealing with the observable; the study of mind could never be accomplished objectively, but the study of behaviour could. The goal of psychology would become the prediction and control of behaviour. *Consciousness, mind, and mental states were to be ignored.

Soon after *Pavlov's reflexology became prominent in America, Watson adopted the reflex as the basic unit by which all behaviour was to be explained. He believed that all complex human behaviour was the sum of simple conditioned reflexes. So powerful did he see the *conditioning process that he eventually promoted a staunch environmentalism, a philosophical belief that all behaviour is learned. In advocating this position, Watson made many extreme statements about the power of conditioning. The best known is:

Give me a dozen healthy infants . . . and my own specified world to bring them up in and I'll guarantee to take any one at random and train him to become any type of specialist I might select—doctor, lawyer, artist, merchant-chief and, yes, even beggar-man and thief, regardless of his talents, penchants, tendencies, abilities, vocations, and race of his ancestors.

Though Watson qualified this statement and others like it, his qualifying statements have often been overlooked and his views simplified. For example, he is usually credited with the simplistic notion that thinking is merely subvocal speech or laryngeal movement, though he repudiated such a view on several occasions (for example, in *The Battle of Behaviorism*, published in 1928 with William *McDougall).

Watson's work had an immeasurable impact on American psychology. The tenets of behaviourism dominated the field until perhaps the 1950s, and psychology is still often known as the science of 'behaviour' rather than the science of 'mind'. It was Watson's behaviourism that inspired B. F. Skinner's early work in psychology, though Skinner, in developing the modern version of behaviourism, abandoned Watson's environmentalism and his aversion to a consideration of mind (SEE BEHAVIOURISM: SKINNER ON).

Though his impact was long-lasting, Watson only remained active in academic psychology until 1920, when, as a result of a personal scandal, he was forced to resign from his position at Johns Hopkins University. His subsequent successful career was in advertising.                        R. E.

Bergmann, G. (1956). The contributions of John B. Watson. *Psychological Review*, **63**, 265–76.
Skinner, B. F. (1959). John Broadus Watson, behaviorist. *Science*, **129**, 197–8.
Watson, J. B. (1967). *Behavior: An Introduction to Comparative Psychology*, with an Introduction by R. J. Herrnstein. New York.
Woodworth, R. S. (1959). John Broadus Watson: 1878–1958. *American Journal of Psychology*, **72**, 301–10.

**WEBER,** ERNST HEINRICH (1795–1878). German physiologist, born at Wittenberg; professor of anatomy and later of physiology at Leipzig. He is celebrated for developing methods of measuring the sensitivity of the skin which, together with the work of Gustav *Fechner, resulted in the Weber–Fechner law ($\Delta I/I$ = constant), where $I$ is the intensity of the sensation and the constant is known as Weber's constant. The constant is different for each sense (for intensity of light, sound, etc.) and tends to increase with ageing, as sensory discrimination becomes impaired. (See AGEING: SENSORY AND PERCEPTUAL CHANGES.) It represents the smallest stimulus intensity difference that can be distinguished, and is a constant proportion (generally about 3 per cent) of the stimulus. This logarithmic relation is basic to almost all sensory discrimination, so that larger differences are required for greater intensities. (For a detailed account of the psychophysics that is the basis of experimental psychology and is still rooted in the work of Weber and Fechner, see PSYCHOPHYSICS; see also SIZE–WEIGHT ILLUSION.)

**WERNICKE,** CARL (1848–1905), German neurologist and psychiatrist, qualified at the University of Breslau and returned to it many years later as a professor after spending several years in Berlin. He trained under the distinguished neuropathologist Theodor Meynert, who had great influence on Sigmund *Freud. Indeed Freud's early work in neurology betrays an outlook which had much in common with that of Wernicke and he likewise wrote a monograph on *aphasia.

At the early age of 26, Wernicke published the monograph that won him lasting fame. Its title was *Der Aphasische Symtomencomplex* (The Aphasic Syndrome) and it appeared in 1874. The syndrome described by Wernicke was quite different from—and in many ways much more interesting than—that described a few years earlier by Paul *Broca and which had become known as *motor aphasia*. Whereas the latter involved essentially a loss or defect in the expression of speech, the form of aphasia described by Wernicke was marked by a severe defect in the understanding of speech, and correspondingly became known as *sensory aphasia*. This term, however, is by no means totally appropriate as expressive disorders undoubtedly occur in Wernicke's aphasia, but they are disorders in word usage and word choice rather than disorders in the articulation or expression of speech. In severe cases, indeed, the patient's speech approximates to incomprehensible jargon. In such cases, it is the phonemic structure of language rather than its formulation and expression that is at fault.

Wernicke was further able to demonstrate that there are important differences between these two forms of aphasia, not only in clinical features but also in the site of the responsible lesions; whereas in Broca's aphasia the lesion as a rule involves the posterior portion of the left frontal lobe, Wernicke's aphasia is typically localized in the left temporal lobe, though bilateral lesions are not uncommon in cases in which the receptive loss is severe.

Wernicke's interest in aphasia was far from limited to its phenomenology and localization. He made a most creditable attempt to tie together anatomical and functional findings in order to produce a general theory of language and its disorders. This approach was well represented in the fact that his monograph bore the subtitle: 'A psychological study on an anatomical basis'. By bringing together the cortical localizations of the two major speech areas, namely those of Broca and himself, Wernicke evolved what we should no doubt today describe as a flow diagram for language in the brain, and his theory provided a major stimulus to the discovery and understanding of new syndromes, for example his pupil Hugo Liepmann's work on apraxia and its relation to lesions of the corpus callosum.

Although the type of thinking exemplified by Wernicke and his pupils, with its strong emphasis on brain centres and the connections between them, went out of fashion between the two world wars, in modified form it has once again become a foundation stone in the work of many present-day investigators. (See also LANGUAGE AREAS OF THE BRAIN; LANGUAGE: NEUROPSYCHOLOGY.)

Apart from his papers on aphasia, Wernicke wrote on a variety of neurological issues, and is still remembered for his description of a form of encephalopathy resulting from thiamine deficiency (common among alcoholics), which bears his name. He also wrote a textbook entitled *Foundations of Psychiatry*, which he himself regarded as his most important work, though it failed to achieve the popularity of Emil *Kraepelin's textbook.

N. G.
O. L. Z.

Wernicke, C. (1895). *Gesommelte Aufsätze und Kritische Referate zur Pathologie des Nervensystems.* Berlin.

**WERTHEIMER,** MAX (1880–1943). Born in Prague, Wertheimer is conventionally regarded as the founder of *Gestalt psychology. Working under F. Schumann at the University of Frankfurt, he carried out an important study on apparent visual motion, published in 1912 (see KORTE'S LAWS). His colleagues at that time included Wolfgang *Köhler and Kurt *Koffka, who acted as subjects in his experiments. Wertheimer's report of this work was a seminal paper in the evolution of Gestalt theory: 'Experimentelle Studien über Sehen von Bewegung', *Zeitschrift für Psychologie*, **61**, (1912), 161–265.

Wertheimer later transferred to Berlin and subsequently emigrated to the United States, where he later reported original experimental work on learning, described in a book entitled *Productive Thinking* (1945; enlarged edition 1959). O. L. Z.

**WHITEHEAD,** ALFRED NORTH (1861–1947). Born in London and educated at Sherborne and Trinity College, Cambridge, Whitehead was both mathematician and philosopher. He was co-author, with Bertrand *Russell, of *Principia Mathematica* (1910–13), yet he differed greatly from Russell in his philosophy, as he was an *idealist. His main works are: *Process and Reality* (1929); *Adventures of Ideas* (1933); and *Modes of Thought* (1938). He was elected Fellow of the Royal Society in 1903 and appointed to the Order of Merit in 1945.

**WIENER,** NORBERT (1894–1964), American mathematician of international stature, born at Cambridge, Massachusetts. He joined the faculty of the Massachusetts Institute of Technology at the age of 25, and worked extensively on problems in the mathematics of electrical engineering, and especially on non-linear problems. Much of this work was later published in *Nonlinear Problems in Random Theory* (1958). His exceptional talents as a mathematician were evident very early; he graduated from Tufts University at the age of 14 and won his doctorate from Harvard at 18. His range of activities included work on assemblages, functions of a real variable, mathematical logic, relativity, quantum theory, and the Fourier integral and many of its applications. Late in the 1930s he became increasingly interested in biological and social problems, and formed a group with Arturo Rosenblueth, who was then at the Harvard Medical School. The group included philosophers, anthropologists, sociologists, psychologists, physiologists, mathematicians, and electrical engineers. Their meetings were concerned with scientific method and the unification of science; they continued until 1944, when Rosenblueth went to Mexico, and from them came the concept of *cybernetics. This dates from 1942 but was not named 'cybernetics' until 1947. It was defined generally as 'the science of control and communication in the animal and the machine', but the clear idea was that 'animal' included human being.

The idea of cybernetics arose not only from the integration of science to include all aspects of scientific activities; it was inspired also by the development of the computer which was taking place at the same time under the influence of *Von Neumann, *Turing, and others. It was affected too by the development of *information theory, work on which had emanated from the Bell Telephone Company under the influence of C. E. Shannon and W. Weaver. This work described the principles involved in communication between any 'source' and 'sink'. Meaning was irrelevant to the measurement of information encoded, transmitted, and decoded, in a possibly noisy channel. Channel capacity and optimum coding procedures were all considered, and the whole development was incorporated into the cybernetic mode of thought.

Wiener himself made use of time series and other statistical techniques, also involving Gibbsian theory. Information and its processing, in all its aspects, was seen to apply to a wide range of phenomena both organic and inorganic, including human speech, genetics, the nervous system, and the muscular system. Philosophical issues were involved in cybernetics, since vitalism was brought into the cybernetic view and its world was thought of as one of Bergsonian time rather than Newtonian. Mathematically, Wiener brought group theory and statistical mechanics into the picture and made it a part of the bulwark of what was primarily an attempt to show that man was a complex 'machine'. The language of the computer (originally binary code) was likened to the language of the nervous system and gave rise to the development of automata known as logical nets. This was carried out by two other members of the cybernetic group, Warren *McCulloch and Walter Pitts.

Yet another component of the cybernetic viewpoint was that of servo-systems. It was recognized that *feedback was essential to learning, and that the sort of adaptive control typified by a thermostat must operate in all animals, and especially human beings. It was recognized too that there were higher-level feedbacks which, as it were, adjusted the thermostat settings. The idea of man being a 'machine' had existed for years before Wiener's cybernetics. Democritus in early Greek times, Diderot, *Helvetius, *La Mettrie, and many others, including Mark Twain, had thought the same, but Wiener was the first person to give genuine evidence to support such a view. He saw human beings as encompassed by the same basic principles as other animals, and this included self-organization and self-reproduction.

Wiener pointed out some of the social dangers of cybernetics in *The Human Use of Human Beings* (1950); and it is now well known that science and technology have contributed, as he foresaw, to unemployment and to the need to reconstruct our society to allow for social evolution. He spent his last years working on the applications of cybernetics to human thinking, notably in areas where the detail was immensely complicated. Not only did he see the need for economic and social change, but he worked in more immediately practical fields, particularly in artificial limbs, thus showing the enormous range of cybernetics. This range of application, from the abstract to the particular, led to fragmentations such as biocybernetics, engineering cybernetics, neurocybernetics, and sociocybernetics.

Wiener also wrote a number of articles, with Rosenblueth and Julian Bigelow, on the philosophical aspects of cybernetics. The most controversial of these dealt with teleology as purposiveness, and attempts to justify a relatively simple feedback control system as necessary to scientific explanation. That teleological explanation is now widely accepted, as part of scientific explanation, is due mainly to him, even if the precise detail of such a form of explanation is still controversial and goes beyond what he originally envisaged. There are now new subdivisions of cybernetics in which automata theory is more developed mathematically, though the close association with philosophy is maintained. The central core of Wiener's cybernetics has been developed under the label *'artificial intelligence'. This has taken over the concept of 'man as a machine' and, with it, extensive theories of *sensation, *perception, *learning, *thinking, *problem-solving, and language, have been built up, all in mathematical and 'machine-like' terms. Wiener's most famous book, Cybernetics (1947; revised edn. 1961), started a scientific revolution which has, as he would have wished, evolved and grown, and yet retains the central idea that human beings, however highly complex and sophisticated they might be, are 'machines' in that they can, in principle, be built in the laboratory.

See also MIND–BODY PROBLEM: PHILOSOPHICAL THEORIES.                                                    F. H. G.

**WIESEL,** TORSTEN NILS (1924–   ), Swedish-born physiologist. See HUBEL AND WIESEL: JOINT WORK.

**WILLED ACTION.** See FREE WILL for references.

**WINNICOTT,** DONALD (1896–1971), British paediatrician, child psychiatrist and psychoanalyst. See FREUDIANISM: LATER DEVELOPMENTS.

**WITTGENSTEIN,** LUDWIG JOSEF JOHANN (1889–1951). Born in Vienna, the son of a wealthy engineer, he studied engineering at Berlin and at Manchester (1908–11), where he designed a propeller. Here he became interested in mathematics and logic, which he studied under Bertrand *Russell at Cambridge from 1912 to 1913. He served in the Austrian artillery during the First World War, was captured, and ended the war in a prisoner-of-war camp near Monte Cassino, where he wrote the Tractatus Logico-Philosophicus (Leipzig, 1921; published with parallel English–German text in 1922 with an introduction by Russell). Wittgenstein taught in a village school in Austria from 1920 to 1926, worked in a monastery garden, and then, after designing a house for his sister, returned to philosophy at Cambridge. He was a Fellow of Trinity College from 1930 to 1936, and professor from 1939 to 1947. For part of this time he did war service as a porter in Guy's Hospital, London. He became a naturalized British subject in 1938.

He lived austerely in his college rooms. It is said that he only dined once in the college hall, finding the conversation dull. His room was furnished with deck-chairs for his students and a fireproof safe for his papers. After a lengthy illness, during much of which he lived in Ireland, he died in Cambridge on 29 April 1951.

Wittgenstein's main works are: Notebooks 1914–16 (repr. 1961); Tractatus Logico-Philosophicus (1922); Philosophical Remarks (1930; repr. 1975); Philosophical Grammar (1974; completed in 1933); The Blue and Brown Books (1958; compiled from lecture notes of the period 1933–5); Remarks on the Foundations of Mathematics (1956; compiled from notes of the period 1937–44); Philosophical Investigations (1953).

Anscombe, G. E. M. (1959). An Introduction to Wittgenstein's Tractatus. London.
Bartley, W. W. (1973). Wittgenstein. Philadelphia.
Kenny, A. (1973). Wittgenstein. Harmondsworth.
Malcolm, N. (1958). Ludwig Wittgenstein: a memoir. London.
Pears, D. (1970). Wittgenstein. London.

**WITTGENSTEIN'S PHILOSOPHY OF LANGUAGE.** The philosophy of language gives a general account of the nature and function of language. The central question that it tries to answer is, 'What is meaning?' It is closely connected with the philosophy of mind, because language expresses things that are in the mind, such as thoughts and intentions. More generally, whatever the functions of language, their performance depends on constancy of meaning, and the preservation of this constancy is an intellectual achievement.

*Wittgenstein's philosophy developed in two stages. His first theory of language is set out in Tractatus Logico-Philosophicus, and his second in Philosophical Investigations. The first theory is mainly concerned with statements of fact, while the second is equally concerned with other uses of language. The first theory gives a very abstract account of factual discourse and says little about what goes on in the minds of its producers, whereas the second presents language, in all its uses, as part of human life, so that questions about meaning lead inevitably to questions about what goes on in people's minds.

It may seem surprising that Wittgenstein focused his first study on to factual discourse, because he certainly did not regard religion and morality as unimportant, or their statements as meaningless. The explanation is that his interest in the philosophy of language began when he was working on the foundations of logic and mathematics (see WITTGENSTEIN'S PHILOSOPHY OF LOGIC AND MATHEMATICS). For anyone who wants to understand how logical formulae achieve necessary truth must first understand how ordinary statements achieve contingent truth. The work already done by Gottlob Frege and Bertrand *Russell on the foundations of logic and mathematics had made that very clear. Now factual statements are the most perspicuous kind, because the conditions under which they achieve truth are most easily understood. So given Wittgenstein's approach, it was natural for him to concentrate on them. He treated them in a very abstract way, because that is what logicians always do to language.

Factual discourse is also the dominant kind, and we tend to construe other kinds of discourse by reference to it, making either an assimilation or a contrast. According to the Tractatus, it mirrors the actual world by presenting it as it is, and alternative possible worlds by presenting them as they might be. Since it expresses everything that can be said, it sets a limit to what can be imagined or conceived. Beyond that limit there is nothing—i.e. nothing of the same kind, only better. There are facts and possibilities, and, beyond them, nothing.

This seems to imply that all non-factual discourse is meaningless. But Wittgenstein distinguished two ways of understanding. In order to understand a factual statement, you have to know its sense, i.e. the possibility which, if it were actualized, would make it true. Other kinds of statement lack sense, but they are not, therefore, meaningless, like jumbled factual messages. They achieve meaning by revealing certain features of the world and human life. This is the mystical element in Wittgenstein's early philosophy.

His reconciliation of the competing claims of scientific understanding and other modes of apprehension is *Kantian in spirit. The novelty is that it is presented as part of a theory of language. Factual discourse stretches to the extreme limit of what we can understand, but only on one level. There is also another, deeper level of discourse, which can be construed only by contrast with factual discourse, because assimilation would render it meaningless. For example, religious statements must not be construed as factual statements of a special kind.

The distinguishing mark of a factual statement is, according to the *Tractatus*, its pictorial character. The words that make up the statement are correlated with things in the world, just as the points on a map are correlated with points on the ground. The arrangement of the words reveals how the things are arranged, if the statement is true, and the statement says that they are so arranged, truly, if they are. The analogy with the kind of picture that is used to convey factual information is obvious. But Wittgenstein generalized the obvious analogy, because he did not think that the words and their arrangement have to be *like* the things and their arrangement. All that he thought necessary is that the statement should have the same form as the fact that it reports. The shared form is spatial in the case of a map, but it need not be spatial, because it could be purely logical. So the analogy between factual statements and informative pictures is a very abstract one.

This theory differs from Frege's, because Wittgenstein takes assertion to be an essential part of a statement, which possesses sense only because it is a shot at the truth. It also differs from Russell's theory, which treated logical forms as things with which we are acquainted, albeit in a Platonic way. The central point of Wittgenstein's theory is that logical form can neither be named nor described. It is inherent in reality, and it can only be revealed in language. So his mysticism touches the centre of his theory of factual discourse.

His later philosophy of language is very different. It does not draw a single line dividing factual discourse from the rest. Language is now presented as something multiply variegated, the nature of each variety being determined by its function. There is no longer any attempt to impose a system on the phenomena. All theorizing is avoided and its place taken by careful description of different uses of language ('language games'). Although the description is untheoretical, it is not undirected, because it is designed to check our endemic tendency to misunderstand the logic of our language. That had been one of the aims of the *Tractatus* too. What is new is the method, which is not to seek a profound, abstract theory, but, rather, to sift the details that lie open to view on the surface of language. So *Philosophical Investigations* is a contribution to *Geisteswissenschaft*. The enquiry traverses some of the territory of psychology, and even sociology, but the purpose is philosophical, viz. to understand how we mean what we mean by what we say.

When language is examined in its natural setting, as a part of human life, questions about meaning lead inevitably to questions about what goes on in people's minds. What does someone else mean by those words? How do you know what he means? How do you even know what you yourself meant by a particular word in the past? These questions all lead into the subject that dominates Wittgenstein's later philosophy of language, the preservation of constancy of meaning by individuals and by cultures.

The early account of factual language relied on correlations between words and things. But how were the correlations to be maintained? A natural answer is that the speaker must follow a rule. However, Wittgenstein makes the important point that a rule is not like the mechanism of a clock, which forces the hands to move as they do. You may have internalized a rule governing the use of a particular word, but the internalized rule still needs to be interpreted, and any interpretation will be verbal and so will need to be interpreted in its turn. Perhaps it looks as if we could cut out all problems of interpretation by going straight to your actual applications of the word. But many of them lie in the future, and Wittgenstein argues that nothing that is in your mind now determines exactly how you will apply the word in the future. What you have internalized is not a programme of the kind that can be inserted in a machine.

If what is in your mind now does not rigidly predetermine your use of the word, the same will be true of other people too. But this seems to threaten communication. For how can you be sure that what is in the mind of someone who claims to understand you is the same as what was in your mind when you spoke? Would not improvisation make all communication impossible?

Wittgenstein rejects the theory on which these questions are based. If the meaning of a word, as used by you, had to conform to a kind of template in your mind, communication would indeed be impossible. For when you were using the word, the difference between fidelity and improvisation could not be detected by others. Even you could not be sure of it, because the template might have changed without your noticing the change. So he suggests, instead, that two people agree about the meaning of a word when they agree, and see that they agree, in their applications of it. This may sound like *behaviourism, but in fact there is no repudiation of mental events and processes. The point is only that the contact that keeps the meaning of a word the same for different people is public and part of the life that they live together.

It follows that communication about what occurs in people's minds is possible only if they already share a language for describing what occurs outside their minds. For a vocabulary with the first of these two functions necessarily depends on a vocabulary with the second one (see WITTGENSTEIN'S PHILOSOPHY OF MIND). This argument against the possibility of a 'private language'—i.e. a completely independent language for describing the contents of the mind—is the key to Wittgenstein's later theory of meaning.                     D. F. P.

**WITTGENSTEIN'S PHILOSOPHY OF LOGIC AND MATHEMATICS.** Both logic and mathematics are concerned with connections of thought—for example, the connection between the information that there are two heaps of walnuts on the table, each containing twelve nuts, and the conclusion that there are twenty-four nuts on the table. This is a necessary connection. It is, perhaps, discovered by experience, but it certainly is not vulnerable to experience. Anyone who claimed to have found that it broke down in certain cases would be told that he did not understand arithmetic. The necessity of a mathematical equation, such as $12 + 12 = 24$, is quite different from the universal truth of the contingent statement that no walnut weighs a pound. The same is true of the necessities of logic. Experience could never upset the hypothetical statement that, if no walnut weighs a pound, and if you have chosen a walnut, then what you have chosen does not weigh a pound.

If a discipline invokes special ideas, or things of a special kind, its philosophy must explain them. Logic and mathematics evidently do introduce new kinds of things, such as numbers and the logical forms of sentences. But the most fundamental idea that is peculiar to these two disciplines is the idea of necessity. What is the nature of the necessity of a mathematical equation or a logical formula? And how do we know about it? Wittgenstein's philosophy of logic and mathematics is mainly a search for answers to these two questions.

Like his other philosophy, it divides into two stages. His first account of logic and mathematics is given in the *Tractatus Logico-Philosophicus*, and his later ideas are developed in *Philosophical Remarks*, *Philosophical Grammar*, and *Remarks on the Foundations of Mathematics*. The most striking feature of both accounts is his preoccupation with applied logic and mathematics. In the examples used above, a mathematical equation enabled us to answer the question, how many nuts there were on the table, without combining the two heaps and counting again, and a logical formula enabled us to answer the question, whether a particular nut weighed a pound, without actually weighing it. Wittgenstein always kept this kind of application in the centre of the picture. In fact, it is arguable that he did not pay enough attention to pure mathematics or pure logic.

His preoccupation with applied logic and mathematics is most conspicuous in his later work, which treats language as part of human life and investigates it in its natural setting (see WITTGENSTEIN'S PHILOSOPHY OF LANGUAGE). But though his early work is more abstract, and, therefore, less concerned with the actual uses of language, one of its leading ideas already points towards the later developments. Logicians often assume that their job is to prove the formulae that are used in everyday life, but in the *Tractatus* Wittgenstein argues that such proofs achieve nothing, and, anyway, are not needed. This is directed against Gottlob Frege and Bertrand *Russell, who both assumed that applied logic relies on pure logic to ratify its formulae by deducing them from the smallest possible set of axioms.

First, consider what, if anything, such proofs achieve. Suppose that the candidate to be proved is the logical formula used above, viz. 'If no A is B, and if this is an A, then this is not B'. You choose a set of axioms, and, using them as premises, you set out to prove this particular formula. But even if you are successful, Wittgenstein points out that your achievement will be limited. You will know that, if your axioms are necessary truths, then this formula too is a necessary truth. But how will you know whether your axioms are necessarily true? It is no good saying that they are self-evident, as Russell did. For we have no criterion of self-evidence, and, if we are going to rely on it in the end, we might as well appeal to it immediately and say that the formula itself is self-evident.

Wittgenstein's second thesis, that in any case such proofs are not needed, is based on the idea that the necessary connection between premises and conclusion in an ordinary valid argument, like the one set out above, is guaranteed by their structures. They simply fit together, like the pieces of a jigsaw puzzle, and there is no need for any formula, or instruction for fitting them together, still less for a proof of the formula itself. Such devices seem to be needed only because ordinary language is not perspicuous and does not reveal the structures of the thoughts that it expresses. Consequently, we feel unable to do the jigsaw puzzle without more apparatus. But Wittgenstein regards this as an illusion. If we had a perspicuous language, we would see that 'logic takes care of itself'. If $q$ follows from $p$, this can be read off from the structures of the two sentences, once they have been made perspicuous.

The idea of a perfectly perspicuous language is one that Wittgenstein borrows from Frege and Russell and uses against them. He also rejects their theory that mathematics is an extension of logic, involving no new ideas and dealing with no new kinds of things (the theory known as 'logicism'). He thinks that mathematics too takes care of itself. For the necessary connection expressed by an equation is guaranteed by the structures of the expressions flanking the sign for equality.

This assignment of an autonomous status to mathematics is another feature that points towards later developments. His hostility to logicism continued, and he came to see mathematics itself as a group of separate, autonomous disciplines, or, to use his word for it, 'a motley'. The new view was a consequence of the general reorientation of his philosophy. He gave up the idea that philosophers should seek systematic theories, and came to think that their task is to describe our modes of thought, or 'language games', in all their variety. In each of them it is possible to distinguish correct from incorrect performances, but the appeal is always to a criterion that is internal to the practice, and never to one that is fixed independently of it.

The new conception of the philosophy of logic and mathematics led to changes that are difficult to assess. His emphasis on application is increased, but there seems to be a complete change in his account of necessity. His early theory was that necessity depends on structure, and we give a sentence its structure by determining its truth-conditions, i.e. the contingencies that would make it true. The early theory was that, when we have fixed the semantics of sentences in this way, we have already determined whether they are necessarily connected with one another or not, and there is nothing more that we can do about it. His later view seems to be that there is something more that we can do about it: we can ratify, or refuse to ratify, the connection as a necessary one.

If we really do have this option, proof is not what it seems to be. In the argument about the weight of the nut it seems to trace a necessary connection that is predetermined by the semantics of three sentences. This is, of course, a proof in the application of logic (or of mathematics in the other example). But proofs in the pure disciplines seem to run on equally predetermined lines. However, Wittgenstein appears to be denying predetermination in both kinds of case. If he meant the denial literally, he would be making logic and mathematics completely unsystematic. Every move would be autonomous, and the theory would be extreme conventionalism.

It is difficult to divine the precise meaning of his new, paradoxical view of necessity. This is partly because we try to relate it to other contemporary theories, such as intuitionism or strict finitism. But the chief reason is that he is making a profound suggestion, which is designed to change our whole conception of language and thought, without changing the ways in which we actually speak and think. His suggestion is that the concept of following a rule, which is fundamental in the philosophy of language, is not what it seems to be. It seems that there is something in the mind of a person who is following a rule which determines what will count as following it in the future. But Wittgenstein regards this as an illusion. If he is right, we were wrong in thinking that, when we fix the semantics of a sentence, we predetermine everything. On the contrary, there will still be options left open. So the later development of Wittgenstein's philosophy of language is the key to his new philosophy of logic and mathematics. Some problems of interpretation still remain baffling, but it does open many doors.

D. F. P.

**WITTGENSTEIN'S PHILOSOPHY OF MIND.** Psychology occupies a central position among the sciences, because everything about which we know anything is filtered through the mind. For the same reason the philosophy of mind stands at the centre of all philosophy. The difference between psychology and the philosophy of mind is that the latter is not concerned with scientific questions but concentrates on questions of the utmost generality. For example, the question why people are aggressive is for psychologists to answer, but the philosopher asks, 'What is a motive?' and, 'What sort of thing is an unconscious motive?' For his interest is in the general nature of mental phenomena. He also asks how we know what goes on in people's minds, and the history of *behaviourism shows that the two questions are, at least, connected.

Given the central position of the philosophy of mind, it is surprising how little discussion it gets in *Wittgenstein's early works (*Notebooks 1914–16*, and *Tractatus Logico-Philosophicus*). This is because they are concerned mainly with the philosophy of language, approached through logic and mathematics (see WITTGENSTEIN'S PHILOSOPHY OF LANGUAGE and WITTGENSTEIN'S PHILOSOPHY OF LOGIC AND MATHEMATICS). In them Wittgenstein developed a theory of meaning based on an analogy between sentences and pictures. These things mirror the world, but he said very little about what goes on in the minds of people who use them. He believed that their unspoken thoughts must have the same structure as their sentences, but he made no attempt to explain what a thought is. Such details, he supposed, could be left to psychologists. The philosopher only had to produce an abstract model of language and logic, without bothering about the way in which the model is exemplified in real life.

After he had published the *Tractatus* his view of philosophy changed. He came to think that it is impossible to understand the nature of language or of logical necessity without going down into the market-place and finding out about people who use sentences and arguments. How do they endow them with meaning? And how do they succeed in understanding what is going on in each other's minds? His later work (*Philosophical Remarks*, *Philosophical Grammar*, *The Blue and Brown Books*, and *Philosophical Investigations*) is mainly an attempt to find answers to these questions.

This may seem surprising, because the questions appear to be for psychologists rather than philosophers. Surely if you want to know what goes on in the minds of people who use language, you should construct a scientific theory about it and test it against the empirical evidence. So how does the philosopher come into it? The short answer, already given, is that he is concerned with very general problems about mental phenomena. But though this is true, it does not tell us about the specific character of Wittgenstein's philosophy of mind. It is equally true of the philosophy of mind of *Spinoza, whose procedure was to define the mental and its various forms.

Wittgenstein's method is completely different. One of the dominant themes of his later philosophy is the futility of definitions. He accepted the fact that the philosopher's interest in mental phenomena is general, but he did not draw the conclusion that his results should be general too. A philosopher who starts investigating meaning or understanding should not expect to be able to pack up his discoveries in neat definitions. On the contrary, he will find the answers to his general questions in individual cases. What he discovers will not be new facts, because he is not a scientist, but, rather, the significance of familiar facts. He will find the essence in its particular exemplifications, like an artist.

This method is well adapted to the philosophy of mind. For the distinctive characteristic of the mental is its infinitely subtle variegation. How else could it hold up a mirror to the world? If someone asks,'How do people endow sentences with meaning and succeed in understanding one another?' the reaction might well be, 'It depends on what they are talking about'. This simple reaction is a natural one, because there is no reason to expect the same answer when they are talking about objects in their environment and when they are talking about their feelings. The aim of Wittgenstein's new method is to put us back in touch with familiar things—in this case, with the familiar facts of our mental lives—from which we are so often alienated by false analogies.

This introduces two more themes which dominate his later philosophy. One is the variety of different modes of meaning, and the other is the therapeutic character of philosophy, which frees us from the grip of false analogies.

The second theme is especially important in the philosophy of mind. Take, for example, his treatment of the phenomenon of understanding. It is only too easy to be misled by the following piece of analogical reasoning. If A uses an ordinary word like 'blue', and B understands it, his understanding must be a mental process because it is not a physical one. Now we can often explain a physical process by pointing to some physical event that produces it. So in order to explain understanding, we should look for an introspectible mental event. The most likely candidate is the occurrence of an image of the colour in B's mind. So we are led to conclude that understanding essentially involves mental images.

Wittgenstein's therapeutic treatment of this case starts from the familiar fact, forgotten by this theory, that quite often B has no mental image. Then he argues that, even when B has one, its occurrence does not explain his understanding. For in order to get the right image and know that he has got it, B must already understand the word 'blue', unless, of course, he got the right image by luck. But in that case he might have taken the word 'blue' to mean 'coloured' or anything under the sun.

More generally, Wittgenstein claims that understanding is not really a mental process at all. If you silently run through the dates of the kings of England, that is a mental process. But often there is nothing introspectible to mark the achievement of understanding. What counts is B's ability to operate with the word 'blue'. The idea that at the moment of understanding there must be mental events too quick to be introspected is a myth. It is the false analogy with physical phenomena that generates the myth, and the cure is to remind ourselves of the familiar facts of our mental lives, from which the analogy has alienated us. This is not behaviourism. Wittgenstein's point is not that there are no mental events or processes, but rather that we exaggerate their frequency, because we credit them with more explanatory power than they actually possess.

If philosophy is a kind of therapy designed to free us from bewitchment by false analogies, it will help us to recognize the variety of different modes of meaning, which was the first of the two themes mentioned just now. For we should be misled if we construed sentences about emotions or sensations on the analogy with sentences about physical phenomena. Wittgenstein's explanation of the differences between these two types of sentences is his main contribution to the philosophy of mind.

It begins, characteristically, with a thesis about meaning (see WITTGENSTEIN'S PHILOSOPHY OF LANGUAGE). Meaning must be kept constant, not only in order that A should be able to communicate with B, but also in order that A should be able to communicate with himself across an interval of time—for example, in his diary. But A's use of the word 'blue' cannot be kept constant by reference to anything fixed in his mind, because there are no reliable mental templates. If A's template were a mental image of the colour, it could change without his noticing any change. Even if it did not change, it would not rigidly predetermine his applications of the word 'blue' to other things. It is really the other way round: his public applications of the word to physical objects determine the character of the images that he accepts as 'blue'. So even if he did rely on a private image when he applied the word to a physical object, his appeal to it would not be final, because there would always be the further question, whether he had appealed to the right image, viz. to a blue one, rather than to one that he was inclined, rightly or wrongly, to call 'blue'.

If the meaning of the word 'blue' is kept constant by its public applications, B's understanding of A's meaning is no longer the unverifiable miracle that it would be on the theory of private mental templates. But what about words like 'pain' and 'anger', which, unlike the word 'blue', are applied exclusively to mental phenomena? Wittgenstein argues that here too constancy of meaning is preserved by public criteria. But in these cases, which are typical cases of mental phenomena, there is a complication. The words 'pain' and 'anger' are not used to *describe* their public criteria, and yet it is the meanings of *these* words that their public criteria keep constant. Much of Wittgenstein's philosophy of mind is devoted to explaining how this feat is achieved.                D. F. P.

**WOODWORTH**, ROBERT SESSIONS (1869–1962). American psychologist, born in Belcher Town, Massachusetts, and educated at Amherst College, where he graduated in philosophy. He proceeded to Harvard for his graduate studies, where he worked with William *James, Josiah Royce, and George Santayana, and completed his doctoral thesis *On the Accuracy of Voluntary Movement*. After working for a time as assistant in physiology at Harvard, Woodworth worked briefly in Sharpey-Schäfer's laboratory in Edinburgh and returned to England two years later as a senior demonstrator in physiology and as an assistant to C. S. *Sherrington at Liverpool, where he published a paper on 'The Electrical Conductivity of Mammalian Nerve'.

On his final return to Amerca, Woodworth was appointed to an instructionship in psychology under James McKeen *Cattell at Columbia University, where he collaborated with E. L. *Thorndike, who shared his interest in the measurement of individual differences. He became professor of psychology in 1909 and was elected president of the American Psychological Association in 1914.

Apart from his work on individual differences and his attempt during the First World War to devise objective tests of emotional stability, Woodworth's contributions to research were somewhat meagre. He was, however, a prolific writer, his *Dynamic Psychology* appearing in 1918 and his massive *Experimental Psychology* in 1938 (revised edition 1954). His popular, though thoughtful, *Contemporary Schools of Psychology* was first published in 1931 and went into several editions. Woodworth edited a monograph series from Columbia entitled *Archives of Psychology* from 1906 to 1948. He published one book in French, *Le Mouvement*, in 1903.

**WORD-BLINDNESS.** See ALEXIA.

**WUNDT**, WILHELM MAX (1832–1920). Wilhelm Wundt, the 'father' of experimental psychology, was born at Neckerau in Baden and educated at Tübingen and Heidelberg. He studied physiology at Berlin with Johannes *Müller and Du Bois-Reymond before qualifying in medicine at Heidelberg, where he became a *docent* in physiology shortly before Hermann von *Helmholtz's arrival as professor and head of the physiology department. Although Wundt held Helmholtz in high esteem, it seems probable that the two men were never close. Whereas Helmholtz did not regard himself explicitly as a psychologist, Wundt became increasingly preoccupied with philosophical and psychological issues and for many years held lectures on psychology directed primarily at students of philosophy.

Wundt's most important book is *Grundzüge der Physiologische Psychologie*, which was first published in 1873–4 and went into six editions. It presented psychology as an independent scientific discipline complementary to anatomy and physiology though in no sense reducible to them. The first and largest part of the fifth edition was translated into English by his former doctoral student and great admirer, Edward *Titchener, under the title of *Principles of Physiological Psychology*. Although it has been said that, in this book, anatomy and physiology were only marginally related to psychology, the book none the less established the principle that experimental psychology will find its future in close alliance with the anatomy and physiology of the central nervous system.

Wundt was appointed professor of physiology at Leipzig in 1875 and, in the same year, established the first laboratory in the world expressly dedicated to the advancement of experimental psychology: the Institute for Experimental Psychology. This laboratory very soon became a focus for those who held a serious interest in psychology, at first mainly for those who had studied philosophy and psychology in other German universities, but soon for graduates of several American and a few British universities. All subsequent psychological laboratories were closely modelled in their early years on the Wundt model.

Understandably, the activities of Wundt's laboratory closely reflected both the physiological background and the more recent philosophical preoccupations of its founder. On the more philosophical side, these were represented by the study of attention and what, following J. F. *Herbart, was termed *apperception; on the more psychological side, one might specify the study of sensory processes, psychophysics, and the measurement of reaction times.

In this approach to experiment in psychology, Wundt's subjects were invariably adults who had undergone an intensive training in the technique of introspection (as it was understood by Wundt) in order that the facts of immediately apprehended conscious experience should not be contaminated by previous knowledge or anticipation. Even though this alleged purity of introspective report was taken to extremes, bordering on the ridiculous, there is no doubt that it did provide a genuine training in precise and consistent subjective observation that contrasted strongly with the often haphazard and poorly controlled observations that had characterized much earlier work on sensory thresholds and *psychophysics. Whether, however, such an approach to scientific psychology is truly applicable to the investigation of human personality and its development, or to abnormal states of mind, is an altogether different and far more controversial affair. None the less, it is important to bear in mind that Wundt did not himself believe that experimental method is applicable to all aspects of human psychology. In particular, he had no doubt that our understanding of language and its development must be sought through our understanding of history and culture rather than through experimental analysis. Wundt himself wrote voluminously on such issues in his later years, though very little of this work has appeared in English. It is, however, clear that the 'founder of experimental psychology' was neither a reductionist nor a dualist and that he believed that the field of application of experiment in psychology was distinctly limited.

Wundt's autobiography, *Erlebtes und Erkanntes* (1920), gives a straightforward account of his life and career and describes in some detail the establishment of his Institute for Experimental Psychology. This narrative outlines in a most interesting way Wundt's relations with a number of his contemporaries, not least E. H. *Weber and G. T. *Fechner, both of whom resided in Leipzig and both of whom he came to know well, despite the fact that Weber was a very old man at the time when Wundt first made his acquaintance. Fechner, on the other hand, was still active and directly inspired some of the experimental work in psychophysics that Wundt set in train in his new laboratory.                                    O. L. Z.

For a reassessment of Wundt seen through modern eyes, see A. L. Blumenthal, 'A Re-Appraisal of Wilhelm Wundt', *American Psychologist* (1975), pp. 1,081–8. Also relevant is R. W. Rieber (ed.) *Wilhelm Wundt and the Making of Modern Psychology* (1980); of particular interest is K. Danziger's chapter in this volume on 'Wundt's Theory of Behaviour and Volition'. An older, if possibly unduly fulsome, account of Wundt's psychological system and the work of his laboratory is to be found in E. G. Boring, *History of Experimental Psychology*, 1st edn. (1925), ch. 15.

# Y

**YELLOW** appears to be a primary or simple colour; but in fact it is signalled at the retina by a mixture of red- and green-sensitive (cone) receptors having overlapping spectral sensitivity. This is a warning that it is not possible to infer the simplicity of physiological mechanisms from the simplicity or apparent complexity of experience. It shows indeed the fallibility of introspection for understanding functions of the nervous system, if not of the mind.

See COLOUR VISION; YOUNG.

**YOUNG,** THOMAS (1773–1829), British physician, physicist, and Egyptologist. Born at Milverton in Somerset he was, as the plaque to his memory in Westminster Abbey says, 'a man alike eminent in almost every branch of human learning, endowed with the faculty of intuitive perception, who, bringing an equal mastery to the most abstruse investigations of letters and science, first established the undulatory theory of light, and first penetrated the obscurity which had veiled for ages the hieroglyphics of Egypt'. This last he accomplished by studying the Rosetta stone in the British Museum.

Young suggested that *colour vision, as we might put it, is given by neural mixture from three retinal channels, tuned to different but overlapping spectral bands. The notion was developed by *Helmholtz into the Young–Helmholtz trichromatic theory of colour vision, which is now generally accepted as an account of the first stage of colour analysis. Young also was the first to measure (on his own eyes) astigmatism, which he (wrongly) accounted for by supposing the eye's lens to be tilted. He showed by experiments (correctly) that accommodation to different distances is given by changing curvature of the anterior surface of the lens, and not by changes of curvature of the cornea.

He studied medicine at London, Edinburgh, Göttingen, and Cambridge, and he practised in London; but his main work was in research at the newly founded Royal Institution, where he became professor of natural philosophy in 1801. His optical experiments set the wave theory of light and phenomena of interference on a sound experimental and theoretical basis.

Young's classic paper 'On the Theory of Light and Colours' was delivered to the Royal Society, as the Bakerian lecture, on 12 November 1801, and printed in 1802 (*Philosophical Transactions*, **92**, 12). His argument for only a few (three) primary colours is based on the consideration that visual acuity is almost normal in coloured light:

Now, as it is almost impossible to conceive each sensitive point of the retina to contain an infinite number of particles, each capable of vibrating in perfect unison with every possible undulation, it becomes necessary to suppose the number limited, for instance, to the three principal colours, red, yellow, and blue, of which the undulations are related in magnitude nearly as the numbers 8, 7, and 6; and that each of the particles is capable of being put in motion less or more forcibly, by undulations differing less or more from a perfect unison; for instance, the undulations of green light being nearly in the ratio of $6\frac{1}{2}$, will affect equally the particles in unison with yellow and blue, and produce the same effect as a light composed of those two species: and each sensitive filament of the nerve may consist of three portions, one for each principal colour.

In later papers, Young changed his 'principal' colours to red, green, and violet. The concept of 'principal' or 'primary' colours is a treacherous one, and he never fully grasped its multiple ambiguities. He was not, however, ensnared by one common error, that of supposing that the retinal receptors must have their greatest sensitivities at wavelengths which subjectively appear to us as 'pure' or 'unmixed' hues; but he did fall into a second common error, that of supposing that the three spectral regions that are conveniently used as primaries in colour-mixing experiments are those which produce maximal activity in the three kinds of receptor. We now know that the cone receptors have their peak absorbances in the violet, the green, and the yellow–green parts of the spectrum (see COLOUR VISION). A light that looks red is not a light that optimally excites the last of these three types of cone; rather it is a light that produces the maximum *ratio* of absorptions in the last two of these types, and such a light lies at a wavelength much longer than the wavelength of peak sensitivity of either of them. This realization did not come until the second half of the nineteenth century, and to this day the term 'primary colour' continues to obstruct the proper understanding of colour among non-specialists.

Young's *A Course of Lectures on Natural Philosophy and the Mechanical Arts* (1807); new edition edited by Kelland in two volumes in 1845 is a useful source. His complete papers were edited in three volumes in 1854 by Peacock and Leitch: *Miscellaneous Works of Dr. Thomas Young*.

R. L. G.

Morse, E. W. (1976). Entry in Gillespie, C. C., *Dictionary of Scientific Biography*, **14**, 562–72. New York.
Wood, A. (1954). *Thomas Young: natural philosopher*. Cambridge. (A Life, with a full bibliography of Young's books and papers.)

# Z

**ZENO OF ELEA** (5th century BC). Greek philosopher, celebrated for his Paradoxes of motion. These are: Achilles and the tortoise, the Flying Arrow, the Stadium, and the Row of Solids. They are well described by J. Burnet in *Early Greek Philosophy* (4th edn., 1930).

Zeno introduced the philosophical technique of trying to establish characteristics of reality—or at least of what cannot be real—from paradoxes.

The basis of the Paradoxes is that if a distance between *A* and *B* can be subdivided an infinite number of times, and an object travels from *A* to *B* by crossing successive points (subdivisions), then it must cross an infinite number of points—which would take an infinite time. Therefore, motion is impossible! The Paradoxes derive from the manner of expressing the problem. This is itself interesting, indicating the extreme importance of finding appropriate mathematical and logical kinds of description, as well as appropriate conceptual models for describing or explaining the physical world and mind.

# INDEX

Compiled by Richard Raper

*Note*: Subjects and first names to cited references are listed as well as authors of initialled articles. Only where an author has contributed more than two entries are the titles given in full. Page numbers in **bold** type refer to main articles.

Aaron, R. I. 440
abacus **1**
Abdulwahab Emiri 20
Abeelen, J. H. F. 286
Abel, T. 787
Abercrombie, M. L. J. 139
abilities
　heredity question 286
　intelligence measurement 377, 381
abnormal behaviour/event **1**
aboutness, *see* intentionality
Abraham, Karl **1**, 274
abreaction **1**
　hypnotic therapy 332
absolute concept (Hegel) 308
abstract, symbolic representation 764
abstraction in art **40–7**
acceleration **1**
accidental property, *see* contingent property
accidents
　amnesia problems 21
　out-of-the-body experience 571–3
　proneness **1–3**
　shock effect 713
accommodation (of the eye) **3**, 249
acetylcholine **3**
　memory association 462
　neuromuscular function 498–9
　physiological processes 555
acquaintance, knowledge origin theory 412
action
　instinct element 374–5
　mechanisms 170
　muscle mechanisms 497–9
　neuropsychological disorders 545–9
　reaction times 671–2
　reflex 676–7
　schema 695–7
action potential
　nervous system 516, 517
　refractory period 677
　*see* nervous system
acupuncture, pain control 575
Adam, K. 719
Adams, C. D. 160
Adams, M. 469
adaptation of the eyes 166–8, 793–5
addiction **3–5**
　opium 570–1
Adler, Alfred **5–7**, 368, 404
Adler, G. 405
adolescence 134
　human growth changes 316, 317

Rousseau's views 686–7
　sexual development 703–7
adrenaline (epinephrine) **7**
　neuroanatomical training 538
　neurotransmitter 552, 554
　synthesis and action 126–7
adrenal medulla, catecholamines 126
Adrian, Edgar Douglas **7–8**
Adrian, Richard H. **497–9**
adults
　agoraphobia 617
　height 316–17
adversity, diver performance **198–9**
aesthetics **8–10**
　empathy theory 220–1
　Kant's judgement of taste 408
　music 504
　Newton's ideas 561
　perception link 600
　psychological approaches **10–12**
affection, attachment theory 57–8
affect term in pyschology 12
afferent **12–13**
afferent impulses 86
Affifi, A. E. 335
after-effects, *see* contingent perceptual...
after-image **13**
　Emmert's law 218–19
　ghost explanation 293
　iconic effect 336
　Newton's notion 562
　retinal constancy 683
ageing **13–14**
　accident proneness 1–3
　arousal behaviour 40
　bereavement 80
　memory deterioration phenomenon 461
　memory and learning 14
　personality, apparent changes 14
　sensory and perceptual changes **14–16**
　sleep loss 718–19
　smell sensitivity 721
　speed of performance 13–14
aggressive behaviour **16–19**
　animal–human comparisons 26
　brain stimulation 435, 529–30
　military psychology 484–7
　negotiation strategy 509
　sex differences in childhood 701–3
agnosia **19**, 751
agnostic, Huxley's term 327–8
agnosticism 245
agoraphobia 30, 616–17

agraphia **19**, 426
agreement, negotiating process 508–10
Ågren, Hans **146–7**
Ahuja, N. 593
AI, *see* artificial intelligence
aims, purpose element 664–5
akinesia **19**
alarm calls, danger recognition 178
Albert, M. L. 88, 425
alcohol
　amnesia effect 20
　aphrodisiac effect 33
alcoholism 4, 5
　delirium tremens 184
　Korsakoff syndrome association 413–14
Aldridge, J. W. 732
Alexander, F. 659
Alexander, Peter **438–9, 439–41**
alexia (word-blindness) **19**, 205, 426
Al-Farabi 19
Al-Ghazzali **19**
algorithm **19–20**
　feedback/feedforward strategies 259–61
　program and planning 644–6
Al-Hashimi, *see* Hashimi, A. Al- ...
Al-Kindi **20**
Allen, E. L. 410
Allen, G. W. 396
Allman, John M. **633–9**
allotropy **20**
Allport, F. H. 614
Allport, G. W. 722
alpha rhythm
　Berger's EEG investigation 81
　brain 215–16
　evoked potential discovery 231–2
altered states of consciousness
　hypnosis 328–33
　out-of-the-body experience 571–3
ambiguity
　figure–ground (visual) 263–4
　Gestalt theory 288–90
　illusions 339–40
　Necker cube 508
ambition, purpose 664–5
amblyopia 314, 796–8
American Psychiatric Association 467
Amerine, M. A. 721
amino acids 543–5, 552–4
amnesia **20–2**
　brain function 111–12
　concussion link 158
　*déjà vu* explanation 183

amnesia *(cont.)*:
  epilepsy 225
  forgetting 264–5
  hypnotic suggestion 329, 330
  memory, experimental approaches
    460–3
  post-hypnotic 478
  short-term memory 713–14
amnesic syndrome (Korsakoff
    syndrome) 413–14
amygdala, brain 40, 528
anaesthesia **22–4**
  hypnosis 329, 331
  laughing gas origin 429–30
  nothingness experience 564–5
anaglyph **24**
analgesia
  neuropeptides association 544–5
  opioid mechanisms 222
  opium effects 570–1
  pain control analgesics 574–5
analogue mechanism 192–3
  internal models 170, 387
analogy, metaphor 478–480
analytic proposition **24–5**
anatomy
  brain 520–9
  brain development 101–10
  corpus callosum 740–7
  cortical cells, for vision 314
  ear 305
  eye 248
  images, brain in action 347–53
  limbic system 435
  neuroanatomical study techniques
    534–9
  neurones 514–15
  synapses 551
Anderson, A. R. 223
Andrews, D. P. 130
Angell, James Rowland **25**
anger
  bereavement situations 79–80
  child abuse 132
animal **25**
animal behaviour
  *see also* social behaviour
  ethology **228–30**
  food preference 123
  instinct 374–5
  invertebrate learning 389–92
  Watson's studies 71, 72
animal electricity 283–4
animal–human comparisons **25–7**
animal magnetism 477–8
  *see also* mesmerism
  hypnosis, history 330–3
animal psychology, Morgan's study
    496
animals, brain graft technique 104
animism 27
Anna O. (Pappehheim, Bertha) 118
Annas, J. 629
Annett, J. 302
annihilation, nothingness effect
    564–5
anoesis 27
Anokhin, Piote Kuzmich **27–8**
anorexia nervosa **28–9**
  neuropeptide association 544
  symptoms and abnormalities 472

anorthoscopic visual perception
    **29–30**
anosmia 30
Ansbacher, H. L. 7, 368
Anscombe, G. E. M. 811
Anstey, E. 388
anticipation (or prediction) **30**
  Anokhin's studies 27
  observer error 611
  size–weight illusion 714–15
antidepressants 188, 654–5
antisocial behaviour cause 651–3
anxiety **30–1**
  aversion therapy 66
  biofeedback therapy 90–2
  blinking indicator 96
  fear effects 257–8
  hysteria involvement 333
  Janet's contribution 398
  mental illness frequency 471
  neurosis 549–50
  pain factor 575
  personality disorder 613–14
  phobia element 616–17
  projective techniques 646–7
  pseudodementia type depression
    647–8
  psychosomatic association 659
aphasia **31–2**, 185
  brain processes 733–4
  Broca's discoveries 119
  Freud's contribution 268
  Jackson's study 395
  language functions 423–6
  neurolinguistic ideas 539–40, 541
  neuropsychology 546, 549
  sensory (Wernicke) 809
  stroke cause 751
aphrodisiac **32–3**
apparent movement, perception 414,
    604–5
apparent term **33**
apparitions, *doppelgänger*
    experiences 200
appearance, phenomenology theory
    614–16
apperception **33–4**, 816–17
appetite mechanisms 323–5
apprehension 256, 257
apraxia **34–6**, 426, 751
*a priori* **36**
  axiom concept 67
Apter, J. 444
Aquila, R. E. 386
Aquinas, St Thomas **36–8**
'Arabi or Al-'Arabi, Ibn, *see* Ibn
    'Arabi
Arberry, A. J. 59
Arbib, Michael A.
  feedback and feedforward **259–61**
  McCulloch, Warren Sturgis **443**
  McCulloch on brain theory **443–4**
  programs and planning **644–6**
  schemas **695–7**
  synergies **765–6**
Arendt, H. 568
argument
  deduction process 180–2
  negotiating process 508–10
Argyle, Michael
  eye-contact **247–8**

Hawthorne effect **303**
Ariam, S. 755
Aries, P. 134
Aristotle **38–40**, 630
  axiom notion 67
  cause function 128
  deduction treatment 180–2
  dissection-based evidence
    296–7
  dreams 203–4
  psyche theory 649
arithmetic
  Gödel's theorem 294–5
  Husserl's philosophy 326
Armitage, A. 409
Armstrong, D. M.
  consciousness and causality 164
  knowledge **410–12**
  mental concepts **464–5**
  mind–body problem **490–1**
Arnheim, Rudolf 46, **47–8**
arousal **40**
  emotion 219–20
  extraversion–introversion 246
  female sexuality 261–2
  humour theory 322
  sexual problems 707–11
art
  aesthetics **8–12**
  children's drawings **135–9**
  illusion component 337
  perceptual experience **47–8**
  psychology, Vygotsky's work
    805–6
  visual abstraction **40–7**
    colour 42–3
    contour/linear contours 40–6
    motion effects 41, 45–6
    structural axes 41, 45–6
Artemidorus 204
artificial intelligence **48–50**
  Butler's notion 122
  functionalist approach 280
  Gödel's theorem 295
  heuristic approach 312
  homunculus sub-systems 313
  imaging function 353–4
  intention problems 383
  laws of thought 430
  meaning interpretations 450–4
  other minds 571
  pattern recognition 591–4
  problem-solving 641, 646
  programs and planning 644–6
  schemata use 696–7
  speech recognition 734–5
  thinking, mechanistic theory 170
  Turing's work 783–4
  Von Neumann's contribution
    804–5
  Wiener's work 810–11
Ashby, W. R. 313
Ashton, H. 5
Asperger, H. 65
association
  behaviourism 74, 76–7
  ideas 276, 303, 419
  imprinting process 355
  intelligence assessment 381–3
  Locke 439–40
  symbols 266–9, 763–5

assumptions
  metaphysics application 481
  size–weight illusion 714–15
astigmatism **50**, 169
  cause and correction 251–2
  Young's measurement 818
astral projection theory, OBE 572
astrobiology evidence 50–2
astrology **50–2**
  independent thinkers 772–4
  Kepler's views 408–9
  paranormal explanation 577–9
astronauts, space psychology 725–7
astronomy, music link 505–6
asylums
  historical survey **52–4**
  necessity question **54–6**
  psychiatric use 649
  schizophrenia treatment 699
asymmetry, mirror reversal effect
    491–3
ataxia **56–7**
atheism, humanist approach 317–19
atoms of consciousness 71
attachment **57–8**
  bonding relationship 100
  infancy 368
  mental health need 469–70
  Oedipus complex 569–70
  psychoanalytic theory 273
  sexual development, effect on 704
Attardi, D. G. 628
Attar, Fariduddin **58–9**
attention **59–61**
  accident proneness factor 2
  arousal apperception 34
  blink index measure 96
  'cocktail party' effect 149
  lapses of **61**
  neurolinguistic theory 539–40
  pre-attentive visual processes
    787–93
  receptor mechanisms 515–16
  set (intention to act) 701
  sleep-deprivation 719
  subliminal perception 752–5
  time-gap experience **777**
Attili, G. 18
Attneave, F. 94, 291
audiometer **61**
  Békésy's invention 77
auditory illusions 61–3, 88
Auerbach, C. 732
aura experience 225
authority, obedience factor 566–8
autism **63–5**, 142, 468
automatic control systems 170,
    174–7
automation **65**
automatism **65–6**
  time-gap experience **777**
autonomic nervous system **66**,
    219–20, 524
autoradiography 536–9
autoscopy (*doppelgänger*) **200–1**
auto-suggestion, Coué's therapy 169
Averbach, E. 336
aversion therapy **66**
Avicenna **66**, 392
awareness
  attention 59

brain function 110–13
mind and body 487–9
neuropsychology study 547
perception association 598–9
split-brain effects 740–7
subliminal perception 752–5
time-gap experience 777
axiom **67**, 231
axon **67**
  brain development 101–10
  growth and development 511–14
Ayer, Sir Alfred J.
  Hume, David 320
  meaning 441, 454
  mind and body **487–9**
  Russell, Bertrand 688
Azouvi, F. 447
Azrin, N. H. 18

*ba* (term), Egyptian thought 212
Babbage, Charles 1, **68**
babbling **68**
Babinski reflex **68**
Babkin, B. P. 596
baby, *see* infancy...
Bacon, Francis **68–9**, 362
Baddeley, Alan D.
  amnesia **20–2**
  diver performance **198–9**
  forgetting **264–5**
  memory and context 456, **463–4**
  nitrogen narcosis **563–4**, 564
  remembering 680
  short-term memory 714
  skills, memory for **716–17**
Baerends, G. P. 18
Bahrick, H. P. 265
Bailey, J. S. 732
Bain, Alexander **69**
Bajjah, Ibn, *see* Ibn Bajjah
Bakan, D. 660
balance
  fear and courage 257
  insanity traditions 372
  labyrinths of the ear 69, 416
Balint, M. 274
Ballard, D. H. 593
Bandura, A. 18
Bárány, Robert **69**
Barber, F. X. 330
Barber, T. X. 92
barbiturates 653–4
  addiction 4
  anaesthetic effects 23
bargaining, negotiating process
    508–10
Barker, J. L. 545
Barlow, Horace B.
  Hubel & Wiesel: joint work
    **313–15**
  intelligence **381–3**
  perception 601, 798
Barnes, Jonathan
  Aristotle **38–40**
  metempsychosis **481–2**
  perception: early Greek theories
    **603–4**
  Plato **628–9**
  pre-Socratic philosophers **631**
  psyche **648–9**
Barnett, H. J. N. 752

Baron-Cohen, S. 142
Barrios, R. R. 732
Barsley, M. 302
Bartak, L. 65
Bartlett, Sir Frederic Charles **69–70**
  aesthetics 12
  Craik, Kenneth John William 170
  Freud on dreams 275
  internal models 387
  memory 456
  remembering 680
  schemas 696, 697
Bartley, W. W. 811
Bary, W. T. de 147
basal ganglia **70**
  blinking 96
  Parkinsonism link 587–91
Bastian, H. C. 425
Bate, C. M. 513
Bateson, G. 658
Bateson, P. P. G. **228–30, 355–7,**
    459
battle neurosis, shock effect 713
Beach, F. A. 428
Beardslee, D. C. 687
Beattie, Geoffrey **99–100**
beautiful, aesthetics discussion 8–10
bedlam **70**
behaviour
  *see also* social behaviour
  abnormal 1
  Adlerian treatment 6–7
  animal–human comparisons 27
  anorexia nervosa 28–9
  Darwin's contribution 179
  displacement activity **195–7**
  evolution position 242
  Hull's contribution 315
  laws of thought 430
  nervous system basis 527–32
behaviour genetics, *see* genetics...
behaviourism **71–5**
  attention studies 59
  conditioning **159–60**
  covarant concept **169**
  emotion issue 219
  mind–body problem 490–1
  Ryle's ideas **691–2**
  Skinner on **74–5**
  Watson's system **808–9**
behaviour therapy **75–7**
  neurosis 472–3
Behr, C. A. 204
Beidler, L. M. 769
being, Sartre's ideas 693–5
Békésy, Georg von **77**, 308
Bekhterev 76, 416
belief
  animism **27**
  doubting philosophy **201**
  Gnosticism **294**
  Hume's views 319–20
  independent thinkers **772–4**
  intentionality **383–6**
  Japanese multi-faith approach
    399–401
  knowledge association 410–12
  metempsychosis idea 481–2
  omens in dreams 203
  religion **677–9**
Bell, Sir Charles **77–8**

Beloff, John **585–7**
Bendall, D. S. 244
bends (nitrogen narcosis) 563–4
Benedek, T. 262
Benedict, H. 423
Benedict, R. 614
Benham, C. E. 79
Benham's top **78–9**
Beninger, R. J. 112
Bennet, Glin **255–6**
Bennett, A. G. 252
Bennett, J. 320
  Berkeley, George **82**
  Kant, Immanuel **406**
  meaning 454
  mirror reversal 493
Benson, A. J. 727
Benson, D. F. 32
Bentham, Jeremy 79
Bentley, D. 513
benzodiazepines 653–4
  addiction 4–5
  sleep inducing 719
bereavement **79–81**
  mental health problem 470
  pseudohallucination incidence 648
Bergen, J. R. 792
Berger, Hans 81
Bergin, A. E. 663
Bergmann, G. 808
Bergson, Henri Louis **81–2**
Berkeley, George **82–3**
  mind, views on **84–5**
  perception, views on **83–4**, 601
  vision 96
Berkowitz, L. 18
Berlot, J. 513
Berlyne, D. E.
  aesthetics 12
  music 505
  problems: their appeal 641
Bernheim, H. 333
Bernstein, Nicholas **85–6**, 766
Berridge, V. 571
Berry, C. 56
Bertalanffy, L. von 387
'beside oneself' **86**
Bettelheim, B. 134
*Bhagavad Gītā* 359
Bidwell, R. G. S. 487
Bidwell's ghost 79
Bidwell, Shelford 79, **86**
bilingualism **86–8**
Billig, M. 722
Bills, A. G. 40
Bills' blocks (attention) 61
binary digit (bit) **93–4**
binaural hearing **88**
Binet, Alfred, **88**, 157, 477
binocular vision **88**
  *see also* stereoscopic vision
  anomalies 252
  cortical neurones 314
  neural plasticity experiments
    626–8
  primate brain evolution 636
biofeedback **88–92**
  autonomic nervous system 66
  learning theory 432
  pain control 575

biological clock **92–3**
  jet lag problem 403
  sleep 718–19
  space effect 725–7
biological form, evolution issues
    241–2
biopolitics, Laing's interest 418
Biran, Maine de, *see* Maine de
    Biran
Birdwhistel, R. L. 36
Birnbaum, M. H. 670
Birren, J. E. 14
birth, brain development 106–7
bit **93–4**, 369
black **94**
Black, M. 480
Blacker, C. 403
Blackman, D. E. **431–2**
Blackmore, Susan J. **571–3**
Blakemore, C. 732
blame, responsibility association
    681–2
Bleuler, Eugen **94**, 699
blindness
  Braille system 101
  brain function 111, 112, 522
  colour vision 153–4
  recovery from **94–6**
blindsight capacity 111, 112
blinking **96–7**
blood myth **97**
blushing **97–8**
  Darwin's theory 180
  physiognomy example 621
Bobrow, D. G. 697
Boden, M. 622
Boden, Margaret A.
  artificial intelligence **48–50**
  concept 157–8
  functionalist theories 280
  intention 383
  purpose **664–5**
bodily responses, James–Lange
    emotion theory 219
Bodis-Wollner, Ivan **214–17**
body
  human growth 315–17
  mind and body dualism 487–9,
    490–1
body build and personality **98–9**
body interface, Sherrington's theory
    712
body language **99–100**
  facial expression 253
  gestures 293
body–mind problem, *see*
    mind–body...
body schema 728
Boethius 506
Bogen, J. E. 746
boggle 100, 543
Bonaparte, M. 278
bonding **100**
  attachment 57
  infant relationships 365
Bonhoeffer, F. 513
Boole, G. 430
boredom, problem appeal 639–41
Boring, Edwin Garrigues **100–1**
  Angell, James Rowland 25
  Bell, Sir Charles 78

Emmert's Law 219
Frey, Max von 278
intelligence 378
Korte's Laws 414
Kulpe, Oswald 415
laboratories of psychology 416
personal equation 611
Borst, C. V. 691
Boskind-Lodahl, M. 29
Boston Women's Health Book
    Collective 707
Bottome, P. 7
Bower, G. H. 464
Bower, T. G. R. 368
Bowerman, M. 423
Bowlby, John
  attachment **57–8**
  bereavement 80
  Freudism 274
  mental health 470
  phobias, **616–17**
Bowler, P. J. 244
Boyd, W. 687
Boyer, C. B. 288
Boynton, R. M. 154
Braddick, O. 130
Bradford, H. F. **550–60**
Bradley, Francis Herbert **101**
Bradley, I. J. 701
Braid, James **101**, 333
Braille **101**
brain
  anaesthetic effects 23
  anatomy 520–9
  animal–human comparisons 25
  asymmetries 425, 547–9
  basal ganglia 70
  behaviour 547
  centres **129**
  cerebellum **129**
  cerebral cortex **129**
  cerebral dominance 425
  circuit studies 114–17, 443–4
  corpus callosum **169**, 741–2
  cortical maps 436–8
  development **101–10**
    anatomical 102–9
    maternal influences 104, 109
    sociological effects 108
  digital operation 192–3
  dopamine neurones 199–200
  drug therapy benefits 653–5
  electrical activity 81, 231–2,
    807–8
  electrical stimulation 527, 529–30
  electroencephalography 81,
    **214–17**
  endorphins 221, 222
  evoked potentials **231–2**
  extirpation term 244
  function 541–3
    learning (memory) 455
    localization 436–8
    neural networks (McCulloch)
      443–4
    parapsychology research 586
  function and awareness **110–13**
  Greek investigations 297
  hemispheres (Sperry) 114–17
  hypothalamus 527–30, 531, 533,
    544

brain *(cont.)*:
  images of action **347–53**
  imprinting 355–7
  language areas 425–6
  limbic lobes 521, 528, 531, 532
  limbic system 119, **435–6**
  manipulation ethics **113–14**
  maps 723
  mechanisms 347–53, 428, 541–3
    attention 60
    cerebral functions, localization
      129, 217–18, 262
    colour vision **150–5**
    consciousness 162–6
    contingent after-effects 166–8
    *déjà vu* phenomenon 182–4
    developing structures 101–10
    Emmert's law on after-images
      218–19
    extraversion–introversion
      theory 246–7
    handedness 300–2
    humour appreciation 322–3
    image rotation 347
    intellect 375
    localization of function theories
      436–8
    memory 455–64
    mental imagery 475
    neural plasticity 623–8
    opioid systems 222–3
    perception 524–7
    sleep 718–19
    speech 119, 733–4
    stereoscopic vision 88
    thinking 530–1
  mind relationship 204, 489–91,
    740–7
  neuroanatomical techniques
    **534–9**
  neuromodulators **550–60**
  neuronal connectivity 511–14,
    541–3
  neuron number estimates 458
  neuropeptides **543–5**
  neuropsychology **545–9**
  neurotransmitters 550–60
  primate evolution **633–9**
  psychosurgery **660–1**
  schema systems 695–7
  somatotopic maps 723
  Sperry's contribution **114–17**
  split-brain effects 163, 164, 740–7
  synergies 765–6
  visual system 313–15, 798–804
  waves (EEG) 214–17
brain disorders/injuries
  amnesia 20–2
  aphasia 31–2
  apraxia 34–6
  ataxia 56–7
  autism 63–4
  brain manipulation 113–14
  Capgras' syndrome 125
  concussion syndrome 158
  dementia 185–6
  development periods 108, 109
  epilepsy 223–5
  Goldstein's contribution 295–6
  hallucination causes 300
  Huntington's chorea 325–6

hysteria symptoms 334
Korsakoff syndrome 413–14
language: neuropsychology 423–5
migraine 483–4
neurolinguistic study 540–1
neuropsychology role 546–7
Parkinsonism **587–91**
strokes 750–2
war wounds 770
Bramwell, J. M. 333, 478
Braude, S. E. 579
Bréal, M. J. A. 480
breathing, anaesthesia 22
breeding techniques 285
Bregman, A. 505
Brentano, Franz **117–18**, 386
Bretherton, I. 133
Breuer, Joseph **118**, 333
  abreaction 1
Brewer, W. F. 159
Brewster, Sir David 79, **118–19**, 562
brightness 119
Brindley, G. S. 154
British Society of Psychical
  Research 577–9, 585–6, 740
Broadbent, D. E.
  arousal 40
  attention 59, 61
  behaviourism 74
  Kulpe, Oswald 415
Broad, Charlie Dunbar **119**
  'emergence' and 'reduction' 217
  Leibniz, G. W., Freiherr von 433
  mind–body problem 491
  paranormal 579
  parapsychology 586
Broca, Paul Pierre **119**, 546
Broca's aphasia 31, 424
Bromley, D. B. 14
Bronfenbrenner, U. 134, 446
Brothwell, D. R. 12
brown **119**
Browne, E. G. 397
Brown, J. A. C. 475
Brown, John 264–5, **713–14**
Brown, P. T., female sexuality
  **261–2, 703–11**
Brown, R. 723
Brown, T. 440
Bruce, D. 549
Bruce, R. V. 92
Bruch, H. 29
Bruner, J. S. 368, 416
Brunswik, Egon **120**, 291
Bryant, P. 674
Buddhism 677–9
  Indian concepts **357**, 358–61
  Japanese interpretation 399–401
  mind concepts 146–7
Budge, E. A. 212
Budzynski, T. 92
bulimia nervosa **28–9**
Bullock, M. 142
bundle dualism theory of mind 490
Burke, O. M. 758
Burnet, B. 286
Burnet, J. 770
Burns, E. 505
Burr, H. S. 52
Burt, Sir Cyril Lodowic **120–1**
  aesthetic preferences 12

intelligence 381
parapsychology 596
Burton, Robert 121
Butcher, H. J. 381
Butler, Samuel **121–2**
Butterworth, Brian Lewis
  language: neuropsychology **423–5**
  neurolinguistics **539–40**
  phonetics **617–18**
Bynum, William 54, 649

Caelli, T. 792
CAEs, *see* contingent after-effects
cafeteria experiments **123**
Cajal, Santiago Ramon Y, *see*
  Ramon...
*cakras*, Indian concept 357
calcium, neurotransmitter release
  559–60
calculate **123**
  abacus process 1
  algorithm process 19–20
  Babbage's machines 68
  geniuses **123–4**
  nulling technique 565
  programs and planning approach
    644–6
calibrate **124–5**
  feedback loop system 176–7
  illusory figures 338–9, 344–6
  neural channels 130, 168
Campbell, K. K. 465, 491
Campbell, R. N. 423
Campbell, T. D. 255
cancer, pain alleviation 575
cannabis addiction 4–5
Cannon, Walter Bradford **125**, 220,
  313
Capgras' syndrome **125**
Caplan, G. 470
Card, S. K. 228
care-givers
  attachment behaviour 58
  brain development effects 108
Carmichael, Leonard 78, **125–6**
Carnap, R. 796
Carr, Harvey **126**
Carritt, E. F. 221
Carroll, J. B. 378
Carroll, Lewis **126**
Carterette, E. C. 149
Cartesianism 189–90
  *see also* Descartes, René
  mind–body problem 490–1
  mind–brain dualism 204
Cartmill, M. 639
cartoon concept **126**
case histories
  amnesia 21–2
  Anna O. 118
  children's drawings 135–9
  'Clever Hans' horse 149
  danger recognition **178**
  inventors 389
  invertebrate learning 390–2
  multiple personalities 197–8
  split-brain tests 163, 164, 740–7
Caspar, M. 409
Castleman, K. R. 593
catecholamines **126–7**, 538
Catell, R. B. 614, 816

Cattell, James McKeen **127**
causality
  conditioning mechanisms 159–60
  consciousness **164–6**
  emergence/reduction arguments
    217–18
  mental concepts 464–5
causal theory **464–5**
  children's understanding 141–2
  empiricist view (Hume) 319–20
  meaning theory 452
cause account of knowledge 411
causes **127–9**
  aggressive behaviour 17–18
  extraversion–introversion 246–7
  fear 257–8
Cazden, N. 505
Cecil, D. 125
cell physiology, memory
  mechanisms 458–64
central nervous system
  brain development 101–10
  Flourens's findings 264
  spinal cord and brain 520–4
centres in the brain **129**
cerebellum **129**, 521, 522–4
cerebral cortex **129**
  neuropsychology 545–9
cerebral dominance 425
  split-brain study 743–4
cerebral haemorrhage (stroke) **750**
cerebral hemispheres
  anatomy 520–4
  asymmetries 547–9
  brain development 107–8
  Sperry's work 114–17
  split-brain effects 740–7
cerebrovascular disease 750–2
certainty, Vico's views 318
Cézanne, G. 601
chakras, see cakras
chance, see possibility
change, future shock term 280
Changeux, J. P. 110
channels, neural **129–30**, 168
  'cocktail party' effect 149
  colour vision 150–1
  knowledge association 411
  memory process 455
Chapman, Anthony J. **320–3**
character
  see also personality
  obedience factor 566–8
  physiognomy assessment 620–1
Charcot, Jean Martin **130**, 581
charisma, see halo effect
Charness, N. 14
Charniak, E. 50
Chase, W. G. 157
chemical processes
  anaesthesia 23
  brain 102, 104, 113
  muscular action 497–9
  nerve connections 511–14, 518–19
  neurotransmitters (list) 554–60
Chen, C. H. 593
Cheney, Dorothy L. **178**
Cheselden, William **130**
Cheshire, N. M. 221
chess, computer-based **155–7**
Child, I. L. 12

child abuse **131–3**
childhood **133–4**
  Gestalt therapy 291–3
  mental development (Vygotsky)
    805–6
  Rousseau's views 686–7
  sex differences 701–3
  visual system development 796–8
children **134**
  attachment behaviour 58
  autism 63–5
  calculating geniuses 123
  child abuse **131–3**
  creativity **171–2**
  critical learning periods 173
  dyslexia **205–6**
  education **207–10**
  eye-contact behaviour 247
  Freud, Anna's contribution 268
  Freudianism, later developments
    271–2
  growth **315–17**
  human figure drawings **135–9**
  humour 322
  hypnotic susceptibility 328–9
  infancy **362–8**
  intelligence tests (Binet) 88
  Klein's work 410
  language development 419–23,
    **426–7**
  learning word meanings 421–3
  Makarenko's work 447–8
  mental handicap 467–9
  mental health 469–70
  mental world/understanding
    **139–42**
  metaphors claim 479–80
  Montessori teaching method 495
  Neill's influence 510
  perceptual skills 602–3
  play-learning approach (Froebel)
    279
  reasoning, development **672–4**
  school phobia 616–17
  sex differences **701–3**
  somnambulism 723
  thinking skills, learning how
    774–5
China
  ideas of mind **146–7**
  language evolution, evidence
    **142–6**
Chin, R. 147
Chisholm, R. 386
chlorpromazines 653–4, 699
choice
  biological **147–8**
  bit (binary) system **93–4**
  brain function 527
  Jamesian theme 396
  quantifying judgements **667–70**
choleric temperament 246
Chomsky, A. Noam **419–21**, 499
Christianity 677–9
  Japanese acceptance 400–1
  theological approach 770–2
Christianson, S. 664
chromosomes
  composition 236
  sexual development 701, 703–7
  speciation role 239–41

chunking **148**
  bit rates 93
  musical performance 503–4
circadian rhythms, biological clock
  93
Cirlot, J. E. 765
cladistics **148–9**
clairvoyance 245
  see also extra-sensory perception
  paranormal reports 577–9
Claparède, Édouard 21, **149**
Clare, A. 475, 661
Clarke, A. M. 757
classical conditioning, see
  conditioning
classification
  aphasic syndromes 424
  biological and evolution 234–5
  cladistics **148–9**
  depression 188
  dyslectic symptoms 206
  ethology structure 230
  gestures 293
  mental disorders 465–7
  mind–body relationship 490–1
  neurotransmitters 552–4
  pattern recognition **591–4**
  personality disorders **613–14**
  personality types 98–9
  psychoses 657
Claudius Galenus, see Galen
'Clever Hans' horse **149**
clock, see biological clock
Clouston, T. C. 470
Clutton-Brock, T. H. 639
CNS, see central nervous system
Cobb, S. 353
cocaine 4
'cocktail party' effect **149**
code-breaking, Turing's work 784
code/coding **149**
  chunking **148**
  memory hypothesis 457–8
codeine, opium derivative 570–1
cognition **149**
  ageing, effects of 13–14
  autistic impairment 63–4
  children 139–42, 672–4
  consciousness concepts 162–4
  emotion theory 219–20
  illusions 338–41
  Indian ideas of mind **357–61**
  language neuropsychology **423–5**
  pain control 575
  pragmatism **630–1**
Cohen, David, **71–4**
Cohen, J., Bell, Sir Charles **77–9**
Cole, F. J. 78
Cole, M. 674
collapse, shock cause 713
collective unconscious 404–5
Collins, J. D. 410
Collins, Steven **357–61**
colour-blindness 153–4, 798
colour Mondrian 684–5
colour perception 592, 599–600, 602
  aesthetic preferences 11–12
  art and visual abstraction 42–3
colours
  Benham's top effect 78–9
  black 94

colours *(cont.)*:
brown 119
yellow 818
colour vision
brain mechanisms **150–2**
colour-blindness 153–4, 798
colour television analogy 151–2
cortical analysis 152
dichromatic 192
eye mechanisms **150–2**
Goethe's shadows 295
Helmholtz's contribution 309–10
Hering's theories 311
luminance 151
McCollough effect 166–8
Müller's studies 496
perception 599–600, 602
retinex theory 419, 684–5
sensations **700–1**
trichromatic theory (Young) 818
visual system 798, 803–4
Coltheart, M. 425
Comfort, A. 568, 707, 711
commisurotomy, *see* split-brain...
common sense **154**
doubting method of reasoning 201
intelligence association 382
communication
animal–human comparisons 26
body language **99–100**
brain function 110
cybernetics 174
displacement activity 195–8
gestures 293
information theory **369–71**
negotiating **508–10**
paranormal **577–9**
primate language **631–3**
speech and brain processes **733–4**
Wittgenstein's philosophy **811–13**,
**814–16**
compatibilism **154**
compensation concept (Adler) 5–6
complex (Jung) **154–5**
behaviour therapy use 76–7
free association testing 267
inferiority form 368
compositional semantics 451, 453
compulsions 568–9
*see also* obsessions and...
drug dependence 204, 571
neurosis 549–50
computed tomography (CT) 347–8,
352–3
computers
AI functions 48–50
astrology claims 51
Babbage's pioneer work 68
chess **155–7**
ergonomics of use 227–8
memory concept 455
other minds discussion 571
pattern recognition 591–4
programs and planning 644–6
speech recognition 734–5
Turing's work 783–4
Von Neumann's work 804–5
Comte, Auguste **157**
concentration
attention property 59–61
blink rate measure 96

concept **157–8**
conclusion, inductive procedure 361
concussion 21, **158**
Condillac, Étienne de **158**
conditioned emotional responses
76–7
conditioned reflexes, extinction **244**
conditioning **159–60**
amnesia effects 21
Anokhin's experiments 27–8
anxiety drive 31
autonomic nervous system **66**
behaviour therapy **75–7**
biofeedback alternative 89
brain development 102
fear theory 258
Humphrey's contribution 323
imprinting effect 355–7
Konorski's studies 413
learning theory 430–2
memory theory 455
Pavlov on 595–6
reductionism 675–6
Watson's ideas 808
Condon, W. S. 100
cones, visual receptors 153–4
conflict
aggressive behaviour case 17
Luria's study 441–2
negotiating process 509–10
Confucian views 146
Connolly, Kevin J. **284–6**
conscience, obedience (Milgram)
566–8
consciousness **160–4**
altered states 328–33, 571–3
anaesthesia effects 22–4
anoesis state 27
attention 59
behaviourist ideas 72
biofeedback application 89
blushing (Darwin) 97–8, 180
brain function 113–14, 116,
121–2
Brentano's views 117, 118
causality **164–6**
concussion disability 158
external world identity 244
free association approach 266–8
Husserl's philosophy 326–7
Indian ideas 357–61
Jamesian interest 395–6
out-of-the-body experience
571–3
perception association 598–9
personal identity 611–13
phenomenology theory 614–16
Sartre's ideas 693–5
soul question 724
split-brain effects 740–7
subliminal perception 752–5
synaesthesia (confusion) 765
time-gap experience 777
unconscious theory 785
construction, information
component 369
contingent perceptual after-effects
**166–8**
contingent property **168–9**
contraception, sexual problem link
710

contradiction
possibility element 630
problem appeal 639–41
control theory
ethology of behaviour 228
feedback/feedforward strategies
259–61
feedback mechanisms **174–7**
obedience factor **566–8**
convergers, creativity role 172
conversation
manners 449
primate language 631–3
conversion hysteria 333
Conze, E. 401
Cook, A. M. 573
Cook, David Angus Graham **266–8**,
**403–5**
Cooke, D. 505
Cooper, Arthur R. V. **142–6**
Cooper, J. E. 467
Cooper, J. R. 545, 560
Cooper, Ray 216, **807–8**
co-ordination, stroke disorders 751
Cope, Z. 96, 130
coping behaviour (displacement) 196
Copleston, F. C. 38
Corcoran, D. W. J. 487
cornea **169**
Corning, W. C. 392
corpus callosum **169**, 522, 528–9
development 107, 108–9
division 740–7
correlation **169**, 173–4
Corso, J. L. 16
Corteen, R. S. 755
cortex of brain
*see also* split-brain
colour analysis 152
development 107–8, 109
Cottingham, John G.
animal **26**
apparent **33**
compatibilism **154**
Descartes, René **189–90**
doubting **201**
entelechy **223**
epistemology **225–6**
essence **228**
functionalist theories of the mind
**280**
hedonism **308**
Hobbes, Thomas **312**
homunculus **313**
innate idea **371**
Kant, Immanuel **406**
Platonic forms **629**
*qualia* **666**
qualities **666–7**
Coué, Emile **169**
counselling
bereavement therapy 80
mentally ill, services for the 475–7
counter-conditioning, behaviour
therapy 77
courage **256–8**
courtship, displacement activity 195,
196
Cousins, J. 707
coverant **169**
Cowan, W. M. 539

Cowey, Alan 112, **436–8**, **534–9**
Cowley, J. J. 755
Craft, M. J. 653
Craik–Cornsweet illusion 656
Craik, Kenneth John William 70,
  **169–70**
  interactional approach 387
  internal models 387
  schemas **695–7**
Cranefield, P. 78
cranial formation (phrenology)
  618–20
cranioscopy (lumps) 618–20
Cranston, M. 439
Craske, B. 732
Crawford, A. 40
creativity **171–2**
  ideas 337
  lateral thinking **428–9**
Creed, R. S. 766
cretinism 172
Crick, Francis 234
criminology **172–3**
  crime responsibility factors 681–2
  diminished responsibility **193–5**
  genetic determinism belief 373
  mental illness question 651–3
crises
  mental health 469–70
  negotiating process 508–10
Crisp, A. H. 29
Critchley, M. 206, 732
critical periods 173
Croall, J. 510
Cromer, R. 427
cross-cultural studies, perception
  601–3
Crossman, R. H. S. 796
cross-modal sensory integration
  **173–4**
Crown, June **475–7**
Crown, Sidney **661–3**
cruelty 693
CT, see computed tomography
Cuckle, H. S. 469
cue theory
  biological clock rhythms 93
  forgetting **265–7**
  interviews **387–8**
  memory recall (retrieval)
    component 456
culpability, responsibility 681–2
cultural influences
  aesthetic preferences 10–12
  behaviourism 71
  Indian ideas of mind **357–61**
  intelligence meaning 375–81
  manners **448–9**
  music 499–506
  paranormal phenomena 577–85
  perception 601–3
  sex differences in childhood 701–3
  taste 768
curiosity
  infancy 365–6
  problem appeal 639–41
Curran, D. 614
cutaneous sensation (touch) 778–80
cybernetics
  biofeedback 88–92

brain function models
  (McCulloch) 443–4
heuristic approach 312
history of **174–7**
homeostasis component 313
interactional approach 386–7
musical performance 503–4
Walter's tortoises 807–8
Wiener on 810–11
cyclothymic, personality disorder
  614

Dahl, M. E. 772
Dally, P. 29
Dalmane 653
Daltonism, see colour-blindness
Dalton, John 178
danger, courage training 256–8
danger recognition **178**
Daniels, L. 266
Danziger, Kurt **33–4**
dark, adaptation 793–5
Darwin, Charles Robert **179–80**, 293
  see also neo-Darwinian theory
  emotion study 97–8, 219
  facial expression study 253
  Huxley's support 327–8
  Lamarckianism acceptance 419
Darwin, Erasmus **180**
Davies, D. L. 5
da Vinci, see Leonardo da Vinci
Davis, D.R. see Russell Davis
Davis, F. H. 397
Dawkins, R. 190, 575
Dawood, N. J. 336
day-dreaming, see hypnagogic
  hallucination
dead, communication claims 579–81
deafness, audiometer test **61**
death
  bereavement 79–81
  humanist scepticism 318
  metempsychosis belief 481–2
  out-of-the-body experience 571–3
  spiritualist ideas 739–40
  theological approach 770–2
Deaux, K. 723
De Boer, T. J. 393
de Bono, Edward **428–9**, **774–5**
decibels (dB) 303
decision-making
  bit information measure 93–4
  computer application 49, 644–6
  lateral thinking 428–9
  negotiating process 508–10
  problem-solving process 641–4
  projective techniques 646–7
  skills **715–16**
  thinking skill approach 774–5
  visual information rate 93, 795–6
decoding 149
de Condillac, Étienne, see
  Condillac...
deduction **180–2**
defence, Freudian concepts 270
defiance, obedience factor 566–8
deities, religion 677–9
déjà vu **182–4**
delirium 184, 473
  hallucination symptom 300
  psychosis element 657–8

De Long, G. R. 65
Delphic oracle 583–4
delusion **184–5**
  Capgras' syndrome 125
  fatigue association 256
  paranoia symptoms 576–7
  schizophrenic 697–9
dementia **185–6**
  amnesia component 22
  Huntington's chorea 325–6
  language/speech disorders 423–5
  neuroanatomical study 538
  Parkinsonism link 589–90
  pseudodementia 647–8
dementia-like illness 186
dementia praecox, Jung's study 404
Dement, W. 203
dendrite **186**, 514
Dennett, Daniel C.
  consciousness **160–4**
  functionalist theories 280
  homunculus 313
  intentionality **383–6**
  other minds **571**
  verstehen 786–7
denotation **186**
dependence, see addiction
dependency theory, attachment 57,
  58
depersonalization **186–7**
  delusion symptoms 184–5
  Laing's study 417–18
depression **187–8**
  anxiety states 30
  delusion symptoms 184–5
  dementia-like illness 186
  depersonalization symptom 186–7
  drug therapy 654
  ECT treatment 207
  epilepsy proneness 225
  fatigue association 256
  Huntington's chorea 325–6
  hysteria explanation 333
  manic depressive personality 187,
    448
  melancholy study (Burton) 121
  mental illness frequency 471
  neurotic features 472
  pain factor 575
  Parkinsonism symptom 587–91
  phobia element 616–17
  pseudodementia 647–8
  suicidal behaviour 759–61
deprivation, nothingness **564–5**
depth perception **188–9**
derealization state 186
Deregowski, J. B. **601–3**
Descartes, René 96, **189–90**, 201
description, knowledge origin
  theory 412
desensitization
  behaviour therapy 77
  fear 257–8
  phobia treatment 616
design
  argument on deity **190**
  ergonomics 226–8
  nature **190**
desire, purpose element 664–5
desires and needs 308, 527–30
detection **190**
determinism 147–8, 154, **190–2**

Deutsch, Diana **61–3, 505–6**
Deutsch, J. A. 60, **323–5, 460–3**
De Valois, R. L. 152
development, ethology questions
        228–30
Devereux, G. 274
Devijver, P. A. 593
Dewhurst, K. 763
diagnosis **192**
dichromatic vision 153, **192**
Dickinson, A. **159–60, 413**
diet, brain evolution influence 633–9
digital 93–4, **192–3**
diminished responsibility **193–5**, 658
    Doe–Ray tests 193
    English treatment 194–5
    legal interpretation 681–2
    McNaghten Rules 193
    Scottish treatment 193–4
Dimond, S. J. 302
diopter unit **195**
diplopia **195**, 252
disability (handicap) 302
disablement, stroke cause 750–2
discrimination categories 318
    brain function 110–12
    just-noticeable differences 405
    nulling technique 565
    quantifying judgements 667–70
    reaction times 671–2
    skill expertise 715–16
    visual 787–93
disease
    Hippocrates's belief 312
    psychosomatic 658–60
disorientation, derealization state
        186
displacement activity **195–7**
disposition theory, humour 322
dissection, Greek investigations
        296–7
dissociation of the personality
        **197–8**
    hypnotic effects 329–30
    hysteria component 333–4
    hysterical mechanism 472
    possession phenomenon 403
    trance states 403
distortion **198**
    calibrate channels 130
    contingent after-effects 166–8
    depth perception 189
    illusion effects 340–2
    movement (parapraxia) 34–5
distraction
    attention loss 59–61
    blink rate measure 96
Ditchburn, Robert William **682–4,
        795–6**
Divac, I. 591
Divenyi, P. 505
divergers, creativity role 172
diver performance **198–9**
    helium effect 563–4
    nitrogen narcosis 563–4
Dixon, N. F. **484–7, 752–5**
DNA
    composition 233, 236
    natural selection process 237–8
    neuropeptide activity 544
Dobbing, J. 110

Dodds, E. R. 204, 584
Dodge, Raymond **199**
Dodgson, Charles L., *see* Carroll,
        Lewis
Dodson, B. 707
Doerner, K. 649
Dollard, J. 18
dominance, hand, *see* handedness
Dominian, J. 707
Donaldson, Margaret **421–3, 672–4**
Donnelly, Michael 54
Doolittle, Hilda 268
dopamine
    centres in the brain 129
    neuroanatomical study techniques
        538
    neurones sensitive to **199–200**
    neurotransmitter 552, 554
    schizophrenia link 698–9
    synthesis and action 126–7, 519
*doppelgänger* **200–1**
Dore, J. 423
double vision (diplopia) **195**
doubting **201**
    thinking [Descartes's] method 189
Douglas, J. 763
Downes, C. P. 560
Downes, D. 173
Down's syndrome 142, **201**
    genetic abnormality cause 467
    Penrose's work 597–8
    subnormality aspect 756–7
dowsing
    evidence 51, 52
    paranormal claims 579–81
Doyle, A. Conan 740
Drake, S. 282
drawing
    children **135–9**
    neurological processes 40–6
dreaming **201–3**
    ancient Greece **203**
    animals, evidence 26
    creativity element 171–2
    *déjà vu* experiences 182
    Dunne's views on time 205
    ESP evidence 245
    free association therapy 267
    Freudian psychology **274–5**
    hypnagogic hallucination 328
    hypnotic experience 329, 330
    Jung's interpretation 403–5
    psychoanalysis use 649–50
    sleep **718–19**
Dretske, F. I. 412
Drever, J. 440
Dreyfus, H. L. 644
drug **204**
    addiction 3–5
    aphrodisiacal claims 32–3
    psychoactive 653–5
drug addiction 3–5, 570–1
drug dependence, opiates 570–1
dualism **204**
    Chinese approach 146–7
    Descartes's dualism 189–90
    matter **450**
    mind and body argument 487–9
    mind–body philosophies 490–1
    Russell's views 688–91
    Spinoza's challenge 737–9

Dublin, L. 763
Du Bois-Reymond, Emil Heinrich
        **204**
Duda, R. O. 593
Dunbar, F. 3, 660
Duncker, Karl **205**
Dunne, John William **205**, 582, 584
Dunnington, G. W. 284
Durkheim, E. 760
Dusen, W. van 293
dysgraphias, language
        neuropsychology 423–5
dyslexias **205–6**, 423–6
dysphasia, stroke cause 751

ear
    anatomy and physiology 304–6
    Békésy's investigations 77
    hearing impairments 307–8
    labyrinth functions (Bárány) 69
    labyrinths 416
    perception functions 306–7
Eastwick, E. B. 758
eating, food intake regulation **323–5**
eating disorders **28–9**
Ebbinghaus, Hermann **207**
Eccles, J. C. 677
ecstacy, fatigue association 256
ECT (electroconvulsive therapy) **207**
    depression 188
ectomorphic physique 98–9
Edge, H. L. 586
education **207–10**
    behaviourism application 75
    brain manipulation ethic 113–14
    Burt's work 120–1
    calculating ability 123
    dyslexia treatment 205–6
    Locke's views 440
    Makarenko's work 447–8
    Montessori method 495
    Neill's contribution 510–11
    perception 'hands on' 610
    Piaget's contribution 622–3
    Rousseau's views 686–7
    self-discovery method (Freubel)
        **279**
    Spencer's contribution **735–7**
    thinking as skill(s) 774–5
    transfer concepts/training 780–1,
        782–3
Edwards, G. 56
EEG, *see* electroencephalography
effect, law of **430**
efferent impulses 86, 516–19
efferent term **210**
efficiency, working environment
        226–8
effort after meaning (Bartlett) 69–70
Efron, D. 36
ego-psychology 270–1, 689
ego and super-ego **210–11**
    *déjà vu* for events 182
    female sexuality **261–2**
Egyptian concepts of mind **211–13**
Ehrenfels, Christian von **213**
eidetic imagery (Bergson) 354
*élan vital* notion 81–2
elderly
    ageing effects **13–16**
    dementia disorders 185
    pseudodementia **647–8**

Electra complex 155, **213**
electricity, nervous system 516–36
electroconvulsive therapy, *see* ECT...
electrodermal activity **213–14**
  anxiety 30–1
electroencephalography **214–17**
  autism abnormalities 63
  Berger's discovery 81
  epilepsy symptoms 224
  evoked potentials 231–2
  Fourier analysis 265
  hypnosis measurement 329
  sleep patterns 719
  Walter's work 807–8
electromyography, *see* EMG...
Eliade, M. 361, 679
Eliot, Sir C. 401
Ellenberger, H. F.
  dissociation of personality 198
  Freudianism 274
  Janet, Pierre 399
  paranormal phenomena and the unconscious 583
Ellerstein, N. S. 133
Ellison, C. W. 114
Ellis, W. D. 291
embarrassment
  blinking indicator 96
  blushing 97–8
embedding, language/action association 422–3
embryology, evolution of form 241–2
emergence and reduction **217–18**
EMG (electromyograph)
  biofeedback 89–91
Emmert, E. 219
Emmert's law **218–19**
emotion **219–20**
  affect term 12
  anxiety **30–1**
  attachment theory 57–8
  autonomic nervous system 524
  bereavement complex **79–81**
  'beside oneself' emotion 86
  blushing indicator 97–8
  brain function 527
  Cannon's study 125
  Darwin's contribution 179–80
  *déjà vu* explanation 183–4
  empathy 220–1
  fear 256–8
  Gestalt therapy 291–3
  hypnosis therapy 332
  James–Lange theory 219–20, 419
  Luria's study 441–2
  music association 504
  paralysis theory 576
  psychoanalytic transference 650
  sexual problems 709–11
  Spinoza's view 738–9
  split-brain implications 746
  stress 748–50
empathy **220–1**
empiricism
  Brentano's study 117–18
  Hume's contribution 319–20
  induction term 361–2
  Kant's philosophy of mind 406–8
  learning studies 430–2

meaning definition 451
encephalins 221, 222
  neuropeptides 544–5
  neurotransmitters 553–4
encephalitis, memory loss side-effect 20
enclosedness, law of 289
encounter group **221**
endocrine glands, opioid involvement 222
endomorphic physique 98–9
endorphins **221–3**
  neuropeptides 544–5
  neurotransmitters 553–4
Engen, T. 721
Engfer, A. 18
engram **223**, 356, 456–60
enlightenment, Indian concepts 357–61
Enoch, M. D. 125
Enroth-Cugell, C. 803
entailment **223**, 355
entelechy **223**
environment
  behaviour effect 73, 74
  ergonomics application 226–8
  genetic interaction 286
  human growth 317
  imprinting influence 356
  natural selection argument 237–9
  stress 749–50
  visual system association 796–8
enzymes
  neurotransmitter function 556–7
  Pavlov's ideas 594–5
ephemera, parapsychology research 584–5
Epicurus **223**
epilepsy **223–5**
  autistic connection 63
  automatism 66
  corpus callosum association 169
  *déjà vu* experiences 182, 184
  Jackson's study 395
  neuroanatomical study 538
  split-brain treatment 111–12, 116, **740–7**
epiloia, genetic studies (Penrose) 597–8
epiphenomena **225**
epistemology **225–6**
  Husserl's contribution 326–7
  induction term 361–2
  Piaget's foundation 621–3
  truth theories 783
Epstein, Robert
  coverant **169**
  Skinner box **718**
  Thorndike, Edward Lee **775–6**
  Watson, John Broadus **808**
ergonomics **226–8**
ergotropic behaviour 533
Erickson, R. 505
Ericsson, K. A. 494, 714
Erikson, E. H. 134, 470
erotic **228**
errors, fatigue effect 255
escape behaviour
  danger recognition 178
  fear response 257
  Indian ideas of destiny 357–61

ESP, *see* extra-sensory perception
essence **228**
  Avicenna's concepts 66
  cause explanation 128
  phenomenology 326–7
Essen, D. C. 803
essentialism, essence debate 228
eternal life, Egyptian concepts 211–12
ethics
  brain manipulation **113–14**
  diminished responsibility 193–5
  Hippocratic oath 312
  Moore's contribution 495–6
ethology **228–30**
  attachment **57–8**
  displacement activity 196
Ettlinger, G. **173–4**
Euclid **230–1**
Euler, C. von 780
Evans, Christopher **244–5**, **584–5**
Evans, J. 774
events
  compatibilism standpoint 154, 244
  correlation links 118, 169
  future shock 280
  information theory 369
evoked potential **231–3**
evolution **233–4**
  aggressive behaviour view 16–18
  Bergson's *élan vital* idea 81–2
  Darwin/Wallace discovery 179
  ethology questions 228
  Galton's studies 283
  Lamarck's contribution 418, 419
  language, Chinese evidence **142–6**
  neo-Darwinian theory **234–44**
    background, historical 234
    behaviour 242
    classification 148–9, 234–5
    current status 242–3
    embryology 241–2
    natural selection 237–9
    origin of species 239–41
    variation 235–7
  origin of species problem 239–41
  primate brains 633–9
  Spencer's views 735–7
  Wallace's contribution 807
excitation, nervous system 517–19
existence
  idealism (Husserl) approach 327
  personal identity 611–13
  Sartre's ideas 693–5
existentialism
  depersonalization concept **186–7**
  essence debate 228
expectancy
  attention factor 60
  behaviourism studies 74
  brain potential 232
  musical perception 503
experience
  Berkeley's ideas 83–4
  brain development 106–7, 108
  Brentano's philosophy 117–18
  consciousness state 164–6
  external world 244
  illusory figures 344–7
  impression concept 355

experience *(cont.)*:
matter 450
mind and body **487–9**
nothingness 564–5
Oriental philosophy **401**
pain **574–5**
phenomenology 326–7
reaction times factor 671
sexuality 261–2
transfer (knowledge) 780–1,
782–3
visual system, development
314–15
willed effort argument 447
experimental studies
aesthetics 11, 12
animal–human comparisons
25–7
association-of-ideas 283
attention 59–60
behaviourism **71–4**
body build correlations 98–9
brain 110–12, 114–16
brain in action 347–53
Brentano's contribution 117–18
cerebral cortex (Lashley) 427–8
children
drawing ability 135–9
mental world 139–40, 142
circulation physiology (Pavlov)
594–5
colour vision 150, 152–3, 684–5
complex term 154–5
consciousness 163, 164
cross-modal sensory integration
173–4
digestion physiology (Pavlov)
594–5
emergence/reduction arguments
217
ethology 229, 230
experimental design (Fisher) 264
Galton's methodology 282–3
genetics of behaviour 284–6
Hawthorne effect **303**
humour **320–2**
hypnosis **328–30**, 332
image rotation **347**
imprinting **355–6**
interactional approach **386–7**
invertebrate learning 390–1
isolation experiments **393–4**
laboratory facilities **416**
learning **430–2**
memory 459–60, 460–3
metaphors 479
nervous system plasticity 623–8
neuroanatomical study techniques
**534–9**
neuroses (Pavlov) 596
obedience (Milgram) 566–8
paranormal claims 580
perception (Helmholtz) 308–9
perceptual causality (Michotte)
482–3
quantifying judgements **667–70**
reaction times 671–2
Skinner box technique 718
social psychology **721–3**
space psychology **725–7**
spatial co-ordination 729–32

split-brain and mind 740–7
transfer measurement **781–3**
explanation
aggressive behaviour **16–19**
cause approach 127–8
criminology **172–3**
*déjà vu* experiences **182–3**
dreams, ancient Greece **203**
'emergence' and 'reduction'
**217–18**
intentionality element **383–6**
internal models term **387**
mental concepts problem 464–5
purpose element 664–5
thinking, Craik's theory 170
expression, *see* facial expression
external world **244**
idealism (Husserl) 327
extinction, conditioned reflexes **244**
extirpation **244**
extracampine hallucination events
200–1
extra-sensory perception **244–5**
*déjà vu* explanation 182
paranormal research 577–9,
584–5
extraterrestrial intelligence (Kepler)
409
extraversion–introversion **245–7**
eye-contact **247–8**
eyes
accommodation by lens focus 3,
249
adaptation mechanism 793–5
after-image effect 13
anaglyphs 24
anatomical features 248
anorthoscopic perception **29–30**
astigmatism 50, 818
ataxia, **56–7**
binocular vision 88, 747–8
blindness recovery **94–6**
blinking **96–7**
brightness sensation 119
childhood development 796–8
colour constancy 684–5
colour receptors (Benham) 78–9
colour vision **150–2**
defects and their correction
**248–52**
depth perception **188–9**
dichromatic vision 192
eye–brain nerve plasticity 623–6
Greek investigations 296, 297
Helmholtz's contribution 309–10
iconic image 336
iris 392
Leonardo's views 434–5
light receptors 516, 682
neural networks (McCulloch)
443–4
primate brain evolution 635–6
retina **682**
retinal images 250, 682–4
retinex theory 684–5
saccades **693**
spatial co-ordination 729–33
squint 195, 252, 796
visual information rate **795–6**
visual system organization
**798–804**

Ey, H. 399
Eysenck, Hans J.
aesthetics 12
astrology 52
behaviour therapy **75–7**
extraversion–introversion **245–7**
personality test **614**
psychotherapy, assessment of
662–3

Fabre, Jean Henri **253**
facial expression **253**
blushing 97–8
Darwin's contribution 179
fear 257
physiognomy 620–1
primate evolution 639
faculty psychology **253–4**, 439–40,
618–20
insanity theory 373
Fairbairn, Ronald **254**, 274, 658
faith-healing, mesmerism link 478
Falkner, F. 317
Fallside, F. 735
falsification **254–5**
familiarity
fear desensitization 257–8
remembering mnemonic 679–80
family behaviour, child abuse 131–3
fantasies, post-Freudian
psychoanalysis 271–2
Farabi, Al-, *see* Al-Farabi
Farber, M. 616
Farmer, E. 3
Farrell, B. A. 164
Fatemi, N. S. 758
fatigue **255–6**
over-arousal 40
Fatmi, H. A. 383
fear **256–8**
aggressive behaviour 16, 17
aversion therapy 66
nothingness 564
phobia responses 616–17
psychosomatic effects 659
terror **770**
Fechner, Gustav Theodor **258–9**
Fechner's law, psychophysics 655–7
feeble-mindedness (idiot) 337
feedback and feedforward **259–61**
biofeedback **88–92**
cybernetics 174–7
Wiener's concepts 810
feelings, *see* emotion; sensations
Feigenbaum, E. A. 50, 784
Fel'dman, A. G. 261
female children, childhood traits
701–3
female sexuality **261–2**
Fenichel, O. 334
Ferguson, E. J. 354
Ferrier, Sir David **262–3**
Feshbach, S. 18
Feuerstein, R. 378
Feynman, R. 430
Field, H. 386
Field, T. M. 368
figural after-effects **263**
figure-ground **263–4**
Gestalt theory 288–90
figures, illusory **344–7**

film-making, motion picture
  perception 604–8
filter theory, attention 59–60
Fish, F. 648
Fisher, G. H. 732
Fisher, R. 510
Fisher, Sir Ronald Aylmer **264**,
  383
Fite, K. V. 444
Fitts, P. M. 228
Fitzpatrick, F. J. **36–8**
fixed-action patterns 230, 374
Flaster, M. S. 513
flat-earth believers 772
Flavell, J. H. 142, 622
flavour, taste 767–9
Fleishman, E. A. 717
Fletcher, P. 427
flooding therapy 79–80
Floud, J. 173
Flourens, (Marie Jean) Pierre 264
flow charts, feedback 259–61
Flowers, K. A. **300–2, 587–91**
Flugel, John Carl 264
fluorescence, neuroanatomical
  technique 537–8
flying saucers 773–4
focal (epileptic) seizures 182, 223–5
Fodor, J. A.
  faculty psychology 254
  intentionality 386
  meaning 454
  phrenology 620
foetus, brain development 101–9
Folstein, S. 65
food, taste 767–9
food intake regulation **323–5**
food preference 123
forgetting **264–5**
form
  Aquinas's concepts 36, 37
  art and visual abstraction 40–1
  cause explanation 128
  evolution issues 241–2
  geometry 286–8
  Gestalt concept 288–91
  irradiation effect 392
  Platonic theory of Forms 629
  recognition, neural basis 115,
    591–4
  visual perception 294, 608–10
Forrest, D. W. 283
Foster, J. 82
Foulkes, D. 203
Fourier analysis **265**
Fouts, D. H. **631–3**
Fouts, R. S. **631–3**
Fox, P. T. 353
Francès, R. 12
Frankenhaeuser, Marianne **748–50**
Frankenstein [monster] **265–6**
Frankens, W. 210
Frank, J. D. 663
Frankl, V. 583
Franz, Shepherd Ivery 266
Fraser, Colin, **721–2**
Frazer, Sir James George 266
free association **266–8**
  creativity role 171–2
  Freudianism, later developments
    270

psychoanalysis 649–50
  repression **681**
freedom, Sartre's conception 693–5
Freeman, Norman H. **135–9**
free will
  choice element 147–8
  choice questions 147–8
  compatibilism contrast **154**
  determinism argument **190–2**
  mentalist approach 165
Frege, G.
  analytic proposition **25**
  *a priori* 36
  deduction 180–2
  denotation **186**
  symbols 763–5
French, P. A. 586
Freud, Anna 211, 274, **268**
Freudianism: later developments
  **270–4**
Freud, Sigmund **268–70**
  Adler, A. 7
  anxiety 30–1
  aphasia 268
  dreams **274–5**
  ego and super-ego concepts
    210–11
  fear and courage 258
  female sexuality 262
  free association 266–7, 268
  grief 80
  humour 321
  hypnosis **275–6**
  id **336–7**
  mental structure **276–8**
  neurology studies 268
  Oedipus complex 569–70
  paranoia 576–7
  psychoanalysis 649–50
  repression **681**
  sexual development 707
  transference **781**
  unconscious 162–3, 581
Frey, Max von **278**
Friedman, L. 711
frigidity, sexual problems 707–11
Frisch, Karl Ritter von **278–9**
Froebel, Friedrich Wilhelm August
  **279**
Fromm, E. 568
frontal lobes, brain 521–3, 532
frustration
  behaviourist observations 71
  displacement activity 196
  fatigue association 256
fugues 197
Fukanaga, K. 593
Fu, K. S. 593
Fukurotani, K. 152
Fulton, J. F. 353
function
  ethology interest 228, 229
  learning word meanings 422
functionalism **279–80**
  theories of mind 280
functional psychoses 657–8
future shock 280
Futuyma, D. 244

Gabriel, C. 505
Gackenbach, J. 573

Gagne, R. M. 783
Gainer, H. 545
Galen **281**
  dissection-based evidence 297
  four temperaments system 246
Galileo (Galileo Galilei) **281–2**
Gall, Franz Joseph **282**
Gallup, G. G. 493
Galton, F.
  free association 268
  hallucination 300
  mental imagery **475**
Galton, Sir Francis **282–3**
galvanic skin response (GSR) 213
galvanic stimulation **283–4**
games, Neumann on 804–5
Ganser syndrome 648
Gardiner, A. 212
Gardner, B. T. 27
Gardner, H. 32, 139
Gardner, M. 493
Gardner, R. A. 633
Garmo, C. de 310
Garner, W. 505
Gauquelin, M. 52
Gauss, Karl Friedrich **284**
gaze behaviour 247–8
Gaze, R. M.
  brain development 110
  nerve connections **511–14**
  neuronal connectivity **541–3**
  plasticity, nervous system **623–8**
Gazzaniga, M. S. 112, 549
Geach, P. T. 38
Gel'fand, I. M. 766
Geller, Yuri 578, 585
Gellner, E. A. 154, 336
gender identity, sexual development
  **703–7**
gene-pool concept 234
generalizing **284**
genes
  brain development 104, 106, 108
  causal theory 464–5
  choice in biology 147–8
  definition 236
  Huntington's chorea 325–6
genetics of behaviour 234, **284–6**
  brain function theory, Sperry on
    116
  Down's syndrome 201, 467,
    597–8
  endorphins **221**
  handedness theories 302
  insanity due to 373
  intelligence affected by 378
  language: Chomsky's theory
    **419–21**
  mental retardation 467–8
  neuropeptide hypothesis 544
  schizophrenia, contribution to
    473–4
  subnormality (Penrose) 597–8
genius 283, **286**
  calculating 123–4
  creativity 171
genotypes 284–6
geometry **286–8**
  axiom concept **67**
  Euclid's contribution **230–1**
  illusory figures 344–6

geometry *(cont.)*:
  Kepler on 408–9
  Lobachevski's contribution 436
  Thales's contribution 770
George, Frank **804–5, 810–11**
George, W. 244
Gescheider, G. A. 657
Geschwind, Norman
  apraxia 36
  language areas, brain **425–6**
  neuropsychology 549
  Wernicke, Carl **809**
Gestalt theory **288–91**
  aesthetics 11, 500
  apperception 34
  Ehrenfels's contribution **213**
  Hering's ideas 311
  isomorphism concept **394**
  Köhler's contribution 412–13
  obsession 546
  problem-solving 641
Gestalt therapy **291–3**
gestures **293**
Getzels, J. W. 172, 641
Ghazzali, Al-, *see* Al-Ghazzali
ghosts **293–4**
  problem of proof 579–81
  research 584
Gibson, J. 440
Gibson, James Jerome **294**
  depth perception 189
  illusions 343
  schemas 697
  theory of perception 601
gift of tongues reports 583–4
Gillespie, W. H. 262
Gill, M. M. 330
Giorgi, A. 327
glial cells 541
gnostic concepts **294**
goals
  movement theory (Bernstein) 86
  purpose element 664–5
goals in learning **294**
  feedback mechanisms 176, 177
Godden, D. R. 199, 464
Gödel, Kurt **294–5**
God/gods
  Aquinas's views 36–8
  Avicenna's view 66
  Berkeley's view 84
  Egyptian beliefs 211
  humanist rejection 317–18
  Indian ideas 357–61
  Jung's writings 405
  Leibniz's view 433
  Newton's ideas 561–2
  religion **677–9**
  Spinoza's philosophy 738–9
Goethe, Johann Wolfgang von **295**
golden mean 9
Goldman, A. 412
Goldman-Rakic, P. S. 110
Goldstein, Kurt **295–6**, 425
Golgi, Camillo **296**
Golgi staining technique 535–6
Golomb, C. 139
Gombrich, E. H.
  aesthetics 10
  art/visual abstraction 46

illusions 343
perception 601
Gonzalez, R. C. 593
good, aesthetics discussion 8–10
good continuation, law of 289–90
Gooderson, R. N. **193–5**
Goodman, L. S. 571
Goodnow, J. J. 139
Gordon-Taylor, G. 78
Gorer, G. 80
Gouhier, H. 447
Gould, S. J. 244
*grand-mal* seizures 224
Graves, R. 125
gravity, space psychology 725–7
Gray, J. A. 258, 596
Greece
  doubting as a method of
    reasoning 201
  dream mysticism 203
  metempsychosis belief 481–2
  paranormal phenomena 583–4
  perception ideas 603–4
  pre-Socratic philosophers 631
  Zeno of Elea's philosophy 819
Greek investigations of mind **296–8**
Green, C. E. 573
Greene, J. 427
Greene, P. 261
Greenwood, M. 3
Gregory, Richard L.
  aesthetics **8–10**
  automation **65**
  Benham's top **78–9**
  bit **93–4**
  blindness, recovery from **94–6**
  blushing **97–8**
  channels, neural **129–30**
  Darwin, Charles Robert **179–80**
  depth perception 189
  design in nature 190
  Egyptian concepts of mind
    **211–13**
  'emergence' and 'reduction'
    **217–18**
  Emmert's Law 218–19
  facial expression **253**
  faculty psychology **253–4**
  falsification **254–5**
  figure–ground **263–4**
  Galileo **281–2**
  Gestalt theory 291
  Hegel, G. W. L. **308**
  Helmholtz, H. L. F. von, **308–10**
  Herbart, Johann Friedrich **310**
  Hume, David **319–20**
  illusions **337–43**, 343
  illusory figures 346
  Kepler, Johannes 408–9
  knowledge **412**
  laboratories of psychology **416**
  laws of thought **430**
  McCulloch's contribution **443–4**
  metaphysics **481**
  mirror reversal **491–3**
  Necker cube 508
  Newton on mind **560–2**
  nulling 565
  paradigm **575–6**
  paranormal **577–9**
  perception **598–601**

perception as hypotheses **608–11**
perception of motion pictures 608
personal equation **611**
phrenology **618–20**
physiognomy **620–1**
Piaget, Jean **621–2**
Russell, Bertrand Arthur William
  **687–8**
scanning 695
sensations **700–1**
size–weight illusion **714–15**
telekinesis 769
Teuber, Hans-Lukas **770**
truth **783**
unconscious, the **785**
Young, Thomas **818**
Gregory, W. K. 639
Grene, M. 244
Grice, H. 608
grief, bereavement reaction 79–81
Griffiths, P. D. 423
Griggs, R. A. 644
Grigorian, N. A. 596
Grimsley, R., Rousseau 686
Grindle, G. C. 496
Groddeck, G. 660
Groeger, J. A. 755
Groot, A. de 157
Grosskurth, P. 410
Grossman, C. M., and S. 660
Grossman, H. J. 469
groups, encounter group 221
Gruber, H. E. 172
Grylls, R. G. 266
Guilford, J. P. 378
Guillain, G. 130
Guillaume, A. 335, 393
guilt
  bereavement 79–80
  blushing indicator 97–8
  childhood experience 134
Gunderson, V. M. 174
Guntrip, H. 7, 273, 274
Guthrie, W. K. C. 723

Haack, S. 355
Habermas, J. 787
habit 73, (neurotic) 549–50
habituation 244, **299**, 389–40
Hadamard, J. 172
Haddon, W. 3
Haeberle, E. J. 707
Hagerty, M. 670
Hajime, N. 401
Haldane, E. S. 190
Hall, C. S. 203, 247
Hall, D. C. 336
Hall, E. L. 594
Hallett, M. 591
Hall, Granville Stanley **299**
Halliday, A. M. **231–3**, 330
Hallie, P. P. 447
Hall, T. H. 507, 740
hallucination **299–300**
  delirium **184**
  delusion symptom 184
  extracampine 200–1
  fatigue association 256
  hypnagogic 202, 328
  hypnosis investigations 329, 331
  isolation experiments 393–4

hallucination *(cont.)*:
    organic psychosis symptom 473
    pseudohallucination events 648
    schizophrenia 697–9
    sleep-deprivation 719
hallucinogens, addiction 4
halo effect **300**, 388
Hammerton, M. **486–7, 781–3**
Hammond, R. 19
Hampshire, S. 739
hand, significance to mind **300**
handedness **300–2**
    cerebral dominance 425
    infancy evidence 366, 367
    split-brain 744
handicap (origin) **302**
    *see also* mental handicap
    apraxia 34–6
Handwerker, H. O. H. 780
Hannam, Charles
    childhood **133–4**
    Makarenko, Anton Semyonovitch
        **447–8**
    Neill, Alexander Sutherland
        **510–11**
    Rousseau and education **686–7**
Hannam, Pam **467–9**
Hansel, C. E. M. 579–80
Hanson, A. R. 646
Hanson, Norwood Russell 320, 481
haptic touch **302–3**
Hardyck, C. 302
Harlow, H. F. 641
Harré, R. 129
Harrer, G. 505
Harris, H. 598
Harris, John P. **166–8**
Harris, T. A. 707
Hart, H. L. A. 682
Hartley, David **303**
Hartmann, H. 211
Hartman, W. E. 711
Hartnell, A. 210
Hartshorne, C. 430, 772
Hartston, W. R. 644
Hashimi, A. Al- 393
Haugeland, John C. **383–6**
Haugen, E. 88
Hawkins, Sir J. 506
Hawthorne effect **303**
Hay, D. A. 286
Hayes, J. E. 157
headache, migraine association
    483–4
Head, Sir Henry **303**, 425, 546, 697
head shape, phrenology notion
    618–20
health, mental 469–70
health, stress factor 749–50
hearing **303–8**
    ageing induced changes 14–16
    attention 60
    audiometer tests 61
    auditory illusions 61–3
    Békésy on 77
    binaural 88
    cerebral hemisphere function 548
    ear, anatomy and physiology
        304–6
    impairments 307–8
    labyrinth functions (Bárány) 69

music 499–506
perception theories 306–7
sound characteristics 303–4
spatial location use 727–32
synaesthesia 184, 765
volley theory 804
Hearnshaw, Leslie S. **120–1**
Heard, Dorothy H. **131–3**
Hebb, D. O.
    blindness, recovery from 95, 96
    phase sequences 387
    memory 458, 460, 546
Hécaen, H. 540, 549
hedonism **308**
Hegel, Georg Wilhelm Friedrich **308**
height, human adults 316–17
Heim, Alice W. **379–81**
Heimer, L. 539
Held, R. 732
helium, diver use 563–4
Helmholtz, Herman Ludwig F. von
    **308–10**
    art/visual abstraction 46
    music 502, 505, 506
    perception as unconscious
        inferences 601, 610, 611
helplessness, stress factor 749–50
Helvétius, Claude-Adrien **310**
hemianopia, stroke cause 751
hemiplegia, stroke cause 750, 751
Henderson, D. 653
Hendin, H. 763
Henle, M. 674
Henley, S. H. A. 755
Henn, Volker **174–7**
Henry, M. 447
Heraclitus **310**
Herbart, Johann Friedrich 33, **310**,
    816
heridity, variation 235–7
Hering, Ewald 46, **310–11**
heritability 285
Hermelin, Beate, autism **63–5**
hermetic term **311**
heroin
    addiction 4, 5
    opium derivative 570–1
    pain contol 574–5
Herophilus **311**
Herriot, Peter **426–7**
Hess, W.R. 533
Heston, L. L. 469
Heterophoria 252
heterosexuality, development 706–7
heuristics 312
Hewson, S. N. P. 674
Hick, John **770–2**, 672
Hick, W. E. 94, 371
Hicks, R. E. 302
Higgins, M. B. 660
Hilgard, E. R.
    Freud on hypnosis 276
    habituation (adaptation) 299
    hypnosis 330
Hill, O. W. 659
Hill, P. 475
Hindemith, P. 506
Hinde, Robert A.
    aggressive behaviour **16–19**
    animal–human comparison **25–7**
    ethology 230

intelligence 381
invertebrate learning 392
Hinduism 677–9
    Indian concepts 357
    Japanese interpretation 400–1
Hinshelwood, J. 206
hippocampus **312**
Hippocrates **312**
    behavioural studies 246
    dreams in Ancient Greece 203–4
    epilepsy 225
    Greek investigations 297
    histological techniques 535–6
Hitti, P. K.
    Al-Kindi 20
    Avicenna 66
    Ibn Hazm 335
    Islamic philosophy 393
Hobbes, Thomas **312**
Hobson, P. 65
Hochberg, Julian **288–91, 604–8**
Hodges, A. 784
Hofstadter, D. R.
    'emergence' and 'reduction' 217,
        218
    Gödel, Kurt 295
    sensations 701
Hogg, J. 748
holism
    aphasia theory 546
    Chinese outlook 146–7
    Gestalt theory 288–91
    Gestalt therapy 291–3
    mind–brain concept 164–6
    religious philosophy 677–9
Holmes, Sir Gordon Morgan
        **312–13**
holographic memory theories 458
Holt, Edwin Bissell **313**
Holt, R. R. 486
Home, Daniel Douglas **313**
    levitation report 578
homeostasis 125, 176, **313**
Homme, L. E. 169
homologies in classification 148–9,
    235
homosexuality 706
homunculus **313**
Honeck, R. P. 480
Honoré, Deborah Duncan
    Du Bois-Reymond, Emil Heinrich
        **204**
    Ferrier, Sir David **262–3**
    Holmes, Sir Gordon Morgan
        **312–13**
    Home, Daniel Dunglas **313**
    Magendie, François **445**
Hook, S. 371
Hooper, A. 707, 711
Hopkins, A. 225
hormones
    brain development factors 107,
        109
    brain function 527, 530
    catecholamines 126
    neuropeptides 544
    neurotransmitters 553–4
    sexual development 703–7
    sleep 719
    stress induced imbalance 749–50
Horn, G. 459, 460

Horridge, G. A. 543
Houtsma, W. T. 393
Howard, David 423–5, 539–40
Howard, Ian P. 727–32
Howard, J. 244
Howe, E. 52
Hubel, D. H.
  see also Hubel and Wiesel...
  art/visual abstraction 46
  perception 601
  vision 792
  visual system: organization 803
Hubel and Wiesel: joint work
  313–15
  visual system 798
Hubley, P. 368
Hudson, Liam 171–2
hue, colour identification 151, 152
Hughes, G. E. 223
Hughes, Miranda 701–3
Hull, Clark Leonard 315, 330
human engineering (ergonomics)
  226–8
human figures, children's drawings
  135–9
human growth 315–17
  brain development 101–10
  childhood 133–4
  mental faculties (mental organs)
    419–21
  mental health 469–70
  nerve connections, development
    511–14
  sex differences in childhood 701–3
  sexuality 703–11
  sleep 719
humanism 317–19
Hume, David 319–20
  causality 128
  induction 362
  paranormal 579
  possibility 630
humour 320–3
humours
  Hippocrates's views 312
  insanity theory 373
Humphrey, George 299, 323, 415,
  416
Humphrey, N. K. 112
hunger and food intake 28, 323–5
Hunkin, O. J. W. 677–9
Hunt, E. 378
Hunt, F. V. 506
Hunter, Ian M. L.
  calculating geniuses 123–4
  Galton, Sir Francis 282–3
  James, William 395–7
  mnemonics 493–4
Hunter, R. 763
Huntington's chorea 325–6
Hurvich, L. M. 152
Husserl, Edmund Gustav Albert
  326–7
Hutt, Corinne 701–3
Huttenlocher, J. 423
Huxley, Thomas Henry 327–8
Hyman, A. 68
hyperaesthesia (term) 328
hyperopia 251
hypertension, stroke avoidance 750
hypnagogic hallucination 202, 328

hypnosis history 330–3
  automatism 66
  Binet's contribution 88
  Brentano's work 118
  experimental 328–30
  forgetting control 265
  Freudian views 275–6
  Freud's studies 268–9
  mesmerism association 477–8
  mesmerism origin 578
  multiple personality cases 197–8
  pain control 575
  post-hypnotic dissociation 197
  somnambulism 478
hypochondria, delusion symptom
  185
hypokinesia 200
hypothalamus 527–30, 531, 533, 544
hypothesis
  falsification approach 254–5
  perception 608–10
  problems 640–1
hysteria 333–4
  abreaction treatment 1
  Brentano's contribution 118
  extraversion–introversion links
    245–6
  hypnosis effects 331, 332
  Janet's contribution 397, 398
  neurotic features 472
  paralysis 576
  Sydenham's contribution 763
  vulnerable personalities 614
hysterical dissociation states 197–8
hysterical pseudodementia 647–8

iatrogenic disorders, drugs cause
  204
Ibn'Arabi 335
Ibn Bajjah 335
Ibn Hazm 335
Ibn Khaldun 335–6
Ibn Sina, see Avicenna
iconic image 336
  function of mental imaging 353–4
iconographic symbols 763–5
id 162, 336
  ego, difference from 210–11
  ego-psychology 270–1
ideal 337
idealism 337
  Chinese thought 146
  Kant's philosophy of mind 406–8
  matter notion 450
  metaphysics approach 481
  realism comparison 672
ideas 337
  association experiments 283
  Berkeley's arguments 83, 84–5
  innate theory 371
  Locke's views 439–40
  symbolic form 763–5
  unconventional 772–4
ideational apraxia 35–6
identity
  contingent property 168–9
  mind and body 488–9
  personal 611–13
  pyschophysical theory 164
  theological question 770–2
ideomotor apraxia 34–5

idiot (definition) 337
Idries Shah
  Al-Farabi 19
  Al-Ghazzali 19
  Al-Kindi 20
  Attar, Fariduddin 58–9
  Avicenna 66
  Ibn 'Arabi 335
  Ibn Bajjah 335
  Ibn Hazm 335
  Ibn Khaldun 335–6
  Islamic philosophy 392–3
  Jami 397
  Rumi, Jalaluddin 687
  Sanai, Hakim 693
  sufism 757–8
Iggo, Ainsley 303, 778–80
illness, psychosomatic cause 658–60
illusions 337–43
  auditory 61–3
  constancies 342
  Craik–Cornsweet 656
  cultural influences 602
  depth perception 188–9
  distortion effects 198
  Emmert's laws 218–19
  figural after-effects 263
  figure–ground (visual) 263–4
  ghosts 293–4
  hallucination 299–300
  Necker cube 340, 508
  paranormal reports question 578
  Pepper's ghost 598
  pseudohallucination 648
  Pulfrich's pendulum 663–4
  size–weight 714–15
  sleep-deprivation 719
  stereoscopic vision 747–8
  visual space 796
illusory figures 344–7
illustrations, illusions 338–346
imageless thought 415
image rotation 347
images
  after-images 13
  artistic objectivity 47–8
  behaviourist approach 75
  brain in action 347–53
    computed tomography 347–8,
      352–3
    nuclear magnetic resonance
      347–8, 351–2
    positron emisssion tomography
      348–53
  hypnagogic hallucination 328
  iconic 336
  illusions 338–9
  memory theory 463–4
  mirror reversal puzzle 491–3
imagination
  creativity 171, 172
  internal models concept 387
  Kantian concepts 407
  OBE explanations 572
  Sartre's ideas 693–5
imaging (mental) 353–5
  children, human figure 135–9
  image rotation 347
  mental 475, 691
  mnemonics 493–4
Imberty, M. 12

immortality, theological approach 770–2
immunohistofluorescence technique 538–9
implication 223, **355**
impossibility, *see* possibility
impotence 549–50, 707–11
impression **355**
imprinting **355–7**
  attachment 57
  ethology 230
  learning physiology 459
impulses, afferent/efferent 7–8, 12, 86, 210, 516–19
incompatible behaviour, *see* displacement...
incongruity, in humour 322
incredulity (boggle) 100
Indian ideas of mind **357–61**
individuality, Jamesian theme 396
individual psychology school 5–7
induction **361–2**, 630
industrial psychology
  automation 65–6
  Burt's contribution 120–1
  ergonomics 226–8
  Hawthorne effect 303
  intelligence assessment 379–83
  interviews 387–8
  skill 715–16
infancy **362–8**
  brain development 106–8, 109
inference, deduction concept 180
  induction concept 361–2
inferiority complex 155, **368**
inferiority viewpoints 5
information theory **369–71**
  accident proneness 3
  aesthetics 11
  attention 59–61
  bit (binary digit) 93–4
  brain storage capacity 458
  channels role 129–30, 458
  choice 147–8
  'chunking' 148
  'cocktail party' effect 149
  colour vision 150
  computer chess 155–7
  conditioning, contemporary view 159–60
  deduction 180–2
  displacement activity 195–7
  evolution 233–4
  forgetting 264–5
  Gestalt approach 288–91
  gestures 293
  iconic image phenomenon 336
  image rotation 347
  intelligence question 377–8
  knowledge 410–12
  memory, biological basis 456–8
  memory mechanisms 455–6
  mnemonics 493–4
  models, explanatory 494–5
  paradigms approach 575–6
  pattern recognition 591–4
  perception 598–601, 610
  problem-solving 641–4
  programs and planning 644–6
  remembering 679–80
  Shannon and Weaver on 369–71

vision characteristics 795–6
Wiener's cybernetics 810–11
inheritance
  acquired characteristics 418, 419
  intelligence 378
  nativism 508
  neo-Darwinian theory 234–44
inhibition, Pavlov's work 595–6
inhibitors, nervous system 517–19
injury
  nervous system, response 520
  pain experiences 574–5
  shock effects 713
ink-blot test (Rorschach) 686
innate abilities, language: Chomsky's theory 419–21
innate behaviour, instinct explanation 374–5
innate ideas **371**
innovation, *see* creativity
inquisitiveness **371**
insanity
  *see also* mental illness
  asylums 52–6
  diminished responsibility **193–5**
  early theories **371–3**
  psychopathic link 651–3
insight learning in invertebrates 391
insomnia 718–19
inspiration **373–4**
instinct 336, **374–5**
  classification 230
instinct-response, terror 770
instrumental conditioning 159–60
  behaviour therapy 76
instruments, calibrate (term) 124–5
intellect (term) **375**
  Aristotle's view 39
  phrenology claim 618–20
intelligence **375–9**
  art of good guesswork **381–3**
  assessment 378, **379–81**
  autism association 63–5
  bilingualism 87
  brain function discussion 543
  creativity aspect 171–2
  dyslexia 205–6
  Egyptian notion 212
  halo effects 300
  innate ability view (Burt) 120–1
  invertebrate 389–92
  perception role 599
  Spearman's ideas 733
  split-brain evidence 744–6
  subnormality statistics 755–7
  tests 375–8, 379–81, 769–70
  Thurstone's view 777
  trial-and-error (Lloyd Morgan) 496
intelligence quotient
  Binet's pioneer work 88
  Down's syndrome sufferers 201
  evaluation 171
  good guesswork as alternative 381
  subnormality statistics 755–7
  thinking skills 774–5
intention **383**
  behaviourism 74
  purpose 664–5
  social psychology 721–3

intentionality **383–6**
  Aquinas 36–8
  Husserl 326–7
  meaning 450–4
  phenomenology 614–16
  Russell's rejection 691
  Sartre's ideas 693–5
intention tremor **386**
interactional approach **386–7**
  mind and body 487–9
  negotiating process 508–10
interactional synchrony 99–100
internal models (Craik) **387**
interpersonal experience (Laing) 417–18
interviews **387–8**
intoxication, hallucination 300
introspection 72–3, 75, **388–9**, 414–15
introversion–extraversion **245–7**
intuition **389**
  creativity 171–2
  Hindu tradition 400
  implication paradox 355
invention **389**
invertebrate learning/intelligence **389–92**
involuntary action
  blushing 97–8
  pupil changes 392
involuntary nervous system (autonomic) 66, 88–92
IQ, *see* intelligence quotient
IRCAM Rapports 505
iris **392**
irradiation **392**
irrationality, instinct concept 374
irritability **392**
Islamic philosophy **392–3**, 677–9
  scholars 335–6
  Sufi influence 757–8
isolation experiments **393–4**
isomorphism concept **394**
Isserlin, M. 540
iterative procedures **394**
Iversen, S. D. 655
Iverson, L. L. **653–5**
Ives, Lawrence Alfred **205–6**

Jackendoff, Ray 421
Jackson, C. V. 732
Jackson, H. J. 425
Jacksonian seizure 224
Jackson, John Hughlings **395**, 532, 546
Jacobi, J. 405
Jacobson, H. 796
Jahoda, G. 603
Jainism, Indian concepts 357
Jakobson, R. 540, 734
James, William **395–7**, 816
  attention 61
  emotion 220
  Freud on mental structure 278
  religion 679
Jami **397**
Janet, Pierre 333, **397–9**
Janis, I. L. 486
Japanese concept of mind
  new religions **401–3**
  traditional views **399–401**

Jastrow, Joseph **403**
Jaynes, J. 164, 583
Jeeves, Malcolm A. **545–9**
Jennings, Herbert Spencer **403**
Jensen, A. R. 378
Jerison, H. J. 639
Jesus Christ 677–9
jet lag 92–3, **403**
Johansson, G. 46
Johnson-Laird, P. N. 641, 644
Johnston, R. S. 727
Jones, E.
  Breuer, Joseph 118
  Freud, Sigmund 270
  Oedipus complex 570
  psychoanalysis 650
Jones, J. 571
Jones, M. 505
Jorden, N. 74
Joseph, H. W. B. 433
judgement
  *see also* reasoning
  aesthetics study 10, 11
  Berkeley's view 83
  deductive argument 181–2
  fatigue impairment 255
  Kantian philosophy 406
  Moore's contribution 495–6
  psychophysics 655–7
  quantifying 667–70
  statistics 284, 733
Julesz, Bela
  contingent after-effects 168
  illusory figures 346
  primates, evolution of the brain
    in 639
  stereoscopic vision 748
  vision **787–93**
Jung, Carl Gustav **403–5**
  Adler, A. 7
  aesthetics 10
  complex 155
  dementia precox 404
  extraversion–introversion theory
    245–6
  free association 267
  Freud's influence 269
  paranormal phenomena and the
    unconscious 582–3
  religion 679
  word association studies 266–7
Jung, R. **40–7**
just-noticeable differences **405**, 655

Kaczmarek, L. K. 560
Kahl, R. 310
Kahneman, D. 61
Kamali, S. A. 19
Kamin, L. J. 160, 379
Kandel, E. R. 460
Kandinsky, V. 648
Kanizsa, G.
  illusions 343
  illusory contours 346
  sensations 701
Kanner, L. 65
Kant, Immanuel **406**
  analytic propositions 24–5
  *a priori* 36
  deduction 182
  humour 323

Külpe's study 414–15
  philosophy of mind **406–8**
Kaplan, H. S. 707, 711
*karma* 357, 400
Katan, N. J. 212
*ka* term, Egyptian thought 212
Katz, David **408**
Katz, S. E. 12
Kay, Harry **1–3**
Kazdin, A. E. 77
Keith-Spiegel, P. 323
Keller, Helen Adams **408**
Kellogg, R. 139
Kendall, J. 430
Kendell, R. E. 188, **697–9**
Kendler, T. S. 674
Kendon, A. 100
Kennard, C. **483–4**
Kennedy, P. 760
Kenny, A. 313, 811
Kepler, Johannes **408–9**, 505
Kety, S. S. 719
*khaibit* term, Egyptian thought 212
*khu* (shining one/glorious) 212
Kierkegaard, Søren Aaby **410**
Kilmer, W. L. 444, 646
Kimura, D. I. 549
Kimura, M. 244
kinaesthesis 727–32
kindergarten schools 279
Kindi, Al-, *see* Al-Kindi
King-Hele, D. 180
Kinsey, A. C. 707, 711
Kirk, G. S. 770
Kirk-Smith, M. 755
Kirman, B. 757
Kirwan, C. 169
Kitcher, P. 244
Klein, Melanie 274, **410**
Kleint, B. 47
Klemmer, E. T. 796
Klima, E. 633
Klopfer, B. 686
Klüver, Heinrich **410**, 546
Kneale, W. and M. 182, 630
knowledge **410**
  anticipation 30
  artificial intelligence 49
  Berkeley's views 83, 84
  bilingualism influence 87–8
  Brentano's views 117–18
  by acquaintance **412**
  by description **412**
  Chinese concepts 146
  education: theory and practice
    207–10
  empirical (Kant) 407
  epistemology 225–6
  falsifying hypotheses (Popper)
    254–5
  generalizing (induction) 284
  geometry 287
  gnostic concepts 294
  heuristic methods 312
  Humes's views 319–20
  Indian ideas 357–61
  innate ideas 371
  Islamic philosophy 392–3
  Kant's philosophy 407–8
  language 419–23
  Maine de Biran's views 445–7

musical perception 505–6
  naturalistic analyses **410–12**
  paradigms (Kuhn) 575–6
  phenomenology view 326–7
  Piaget's views 621–2
  possibilities 630
  pre-Socratic philosophy 631
  schemas theory 695–7
  Sufism 757–8
  thinkers, independent 772–4
  transfer 780–1, 781–3
Kockelmans, J. J. 327, 616
Koenigsber, L. 310
Koestler, A.
  creativity 172
  Kepler, Johannes 409
  obedience 568
Koffka, Kurt 291, **412**
Köhler, Wolfgang 263, 291, **412–13**
Kolb, B. 549
Kolers, Paul A.
  bilingualism **86–8**
  imaging **353–4**
  perception of movement 608
Konorski, Jerzy **413**
Korsakoff's syndrome 20, **413–14**
Korte's laws (of movement) 414
Koyré, A. 288
Kraepelin, Emil **414**
Krafft-Ebing, Baron Richard von
  **414**
Kragh, U. 755
Kramer, M. 203
Kramer, S. N. 213
Kräupl-Taylor, F. 569, 648
Krause, E. 180
Krebs, J. R. 197
Kreitman, N. **758–60**, **761–3**
Kretschmer, Ernst **414**
Kripke, S. 228, 454
Kruk, Z. L. 560
Kuffler, S. W. 798, 803
Kühn, C. G. 281
Kuhn, Thomas S. 320, 481
  paradigms 576
  problem-solving 644
  truth 783
Külpe, Oswald **414–15**
Kumar, R. 464
Kurtz, R. 469

laboratories of psychology **416**
labyrinths (of the ear) **416**
Lack, D. 18
Lackner, J. R. 164
Ladd, George Trumbull **417**
La Fave, L. 323
Laing, R. D. 187, **417–18**, 658
Lake, Brian **5–7**
Lakoff, G. 480
Lamarck, Jean-Baptiste de **418**
Lamarckianism **419**
Lamb, T. D. 803
La Metrie, Julien Offray de **419**
Laming, Donald R. J. **655–7**, **748**
Lanczos, C. 288
Land colours (retinex theory) **419**,
  684–5
Land, E. H. 685, 701
Lange, Carl Georg **419**
Langley, J. N. 514

Langton-Hewer, Richard **750–2**
language
  AI, in 49–50
  ancient Egypt 211
  animal–human comparisons 27
  animal limits 25
  autistic disorder 63, 64
  babbling 68
  bilingualism 86–8
  body language 99–100
  Braille system 101
  brain areas for **425–6**
  brain development for 108
  brain function for 546
  children, development 419–23,
    **426–7**, 673–4
  Chomsky's theory **419–21**
  computer programs 644–6
  consciousness 164
  cross-modal function 174
  denotation 186
  dyslectic conditions 205
  education theory 209
  evolution, Chinese evidence **142–6**
  intentionality 385–6
  learning word meanings **421–3**
  meaning 451–4
  memory, context-dependence
    463–4
  metaphor application 478–81
  nativism **508**
  neurolinguistics **539–41**
  neuropsychological disorders
    545–9
  neuropsychology **423–5**
  phonetics 617–18
  Primate **631–3**
  reasoning development 673–4
  speech **733–4**
  split-brain studies 740–7
  stroke-induced disorders 751
  symbolism, in origins 764
  taste vocabulary 767–8
  Vygotsky's pychological elements
    805–6
  Wernicke's area 809
  Wittgenstein's philosophy 811–14
Lashley, Karl Spencer **427–8**, 546
  mass action 428
  memory (engram) 460
  music 505
  programs and planning 646
latent learning 294
lateral thinking **428–9**
Latta, R. 96
laughing gas **429–30**
laughter, humour association 320–3
law of effect **430**
law-enforcement, nomological
    studies 173
laws of nature **430**
laws of thought **430**
laxatives, abuse 28
Leach, Edmund R. **317–19**
Leahy, T. H. 34
learning **430–2**
  ageing effects 14
  amnesia defects 21–2, 265
  appetite selectivity 325
  arousal and efficiency 40
  attachment 57

autistic problems 64–5
behaviour therapy 75–7
biofeedback use 90–1
biological processes 456–60
blindness, recovery from 95–6
brain development effects 107
brain function theories 116,
    531–2
calculating procedures 123–4
conditioning 159–60
courage training 257–8
Craik's theory 170
critical periods 173
cross-modal transfer 173, 174
education: theory and practice
    207–10
facial expression paradox 253
generalizing (term) 284
goals 294
Humphrey's account 323
imprinting process 355–7
induction 362
infancy 362–8
inquisitiveness 371
instinct, confusion with 375
intelligence component 375–6
invertebrates 389–92
maturation, confusion with 430–2
mnemonics 493–4
neurosis 549–50
Olds's studies 570
Pavlov's concepts 594–6
perception involvement 608–10
Piaget's work 621–3
reading difficulties (dyslexia)
    205–6
remembering 206, 679–80
Rousseau's views 686–7
skill transfer 780–1, 782–3
thinking skills 774–5
Thorndike's ideas 775–6
transfer experiments 781–3
trial-and-error 496
word meanings 68, 421–3
least effort principle **432**
Lea, W. A. 735
Lecours, A. R. 540
Leenders, K. L. 353
Lee, V. 221
Le Fanu, W. R. 78
Leff, G.
  Al-Kindi 20
  Ibn Bajjah 335
  Islamic philosophy 393
left-handedness 300–2
Legge, D. 716
legislation, asylums, 52–6
Leibniz, G. W. F. von **432–3**
  philosophy of mind 33, **433–4**,
    630
Leonardo da Vinci **434–5**
Leontiev, A. N. 676, 805
Lerdahl, F. 505
Leslie, Alan M. **139–42**
Lettvin, J. Y. 443, 444
leucotomy **435**, 660–1
Levinson, D. J. 707
levitation **435**, 578, 579–81
levodopa, Parkinson's disease
    treatment 200
Levy, J. 302, 746

Lewin, L. 758
Lewis, A. J. 334, 569
Lewis Carroll, see Carroll, Lewis
Lewis, C. I. 223
Lewis, D. K. 465
Lewis, I. 740
Libet, B. 755
libido (term) **435**
Lichteim, K. 425
Liddell, E. G. T. 677
Lieber, A. L. 52
lie-detectors, see electrodermal
    activity
Liepmann, H. 36
life
  choices 147–8
  evolution, purpose question 233
  Maine de Biran's views 445–7
  psyche meaning 648
life after death, theology question
    770–2
life-force, blood myth 97
light
  corpuscular theory (Newton)
    561–2
  undulatory theory (Young) 818
  visual adaptation 793–5, 800
Lightfoot, David 421
Lighthill, Sir James 274
Lilge, F. 446
Lilley, I. M. 279
L'illusion des sosies, see Capgras'
    syndrome
limbic lobes, brain 521, 528, 531,
    532
limbic system **435–6**
  amnesia 20
  Broca's area 119
  centres, stimulation 129
  dopamine neurones 200
Lindemann, E. 80
Lindsay, J. 52
Lindzey, G. 723
linguistic analysis 441, 571, 691–2,
    811–13
linguistics
  bilingualism 86–8
  Chinese language characters
    142–6
  Chomsky's theory 419–21
  intentionality role 386
  learning word meanings
    421–3
  Leibniz's views 432–3
  logical positivism 441
  meaning 451–4
  metaphor 478–81
  neurolinguistics 539–41
  neuropsychology 423–5
  phonetics, use of 617–18
  speech codes 733–4
  symbols 763–5
Lipps, T. 221
Lishman, W. A. 186, 648
Lloyd, Geoffrey Ernest Richard
    **296–8**
Lobachevski, Nikolai Ivanovich **436**
Lobitz, W. C. 262
localization, brain function **436–8**
location, spatial co-ordination
    727–33

Locke, John **438–9**
  blindness, recovery from 96
  perception 601
  primary and secondary
    characteristics 438–9
  psychology of mind **439–41**, 765
  self-consciousness idea 162
Lodge-Patch, I. C. 56
Loeb, Jacques **441**, 748
logic
  algorithms 19–20
  brain function models
    (McCulloch) 443–4
  deduction process 180–2
  digital computing techique 192–3
  empiricism (Hume) **319–20**
  entailment of propositions 223
  Gödel's theorem 294–5
  Husserl's philosophy 326–7
  idea chains 337, 439
  implication theories 355
  induction 361–2
  inductive 68–9, 487
  inference (term) 361
  intentionality approach 383–6
  intuition contrast 389
  Kantian approach 406–8
  knowledge patterns 410–12
  lateral thinking method 428–9
  Leibniz's account 432–3
  logical positivism philosophy 441
  meaning problem 450–4
  metaphor 478–81
  problem appeal 639–41
  Russell's contribution 687
  tautology 769
  Von Neumann's contribution 805
  Wittgenstein's philosophy 813–14
logical ability, children 140
logical positivism **441**
  meaning, definition of 451
Logie, R. H. 564
Lonergan, B. J. F. 38
long-term memory 457–8, 461
Longuet-Higgins, C. 502, 505
LoPiccolo, J. 711
Lotter, V. 65
Lovaas, O. I. 65
love, erotic term, meaning 228
Low-Beer, Ann **735–7**
LSD (lysergic acid) 4
LTM, *see* long-term memory
Luborsky, L. 663
Lucas, J. R. 295
Luce, A. A. 83
Luce, G. G. 719
Ludovici, A. M. 323
Ludwig, J. 579, 586
luminance 655–6
Lumsden, A. G. S. 514
lunacy 52–6, 371–3, **441**
Lund, R. D. 798
Luria, Alexander Romanovich
    **441–2**
  Anokhin, Piotre Kuzmich **27–8**
  aphasia 32
  Bernstein, Nicholas **85–6**
  language 425
  memory 460
  mind and brain **489–90**
  mnemonics 494

neurolinguistics **540–1**
neuropsychology 549
published works 442
reductionism in psychology **675–6**
speech and brain processes **733–4**
Vygotsky, Leo **805–6**
lyceum 442
lying **442**
Lyons, W. 692
lysergic acid (LSD) 4

McAdams, S. 505
Macalpine, I. 54
McCann, J. J. **684–5**
McCarthy, P. 763
McCleery, R. H. **195–7**
Maccoby, E. E. 703
McCollough effect 166–8
McCulloch, Warren Sturgis **443–4**
MacDonald, G. 787
McDougall, William 416, **444–5**,
    584, 686
McDowall, J. J. 100
McEwan, P. 263
McFarland, D. J. **374–5**
McFarland, N. 403
McGarrigle, J. 674
McGhee, P. E. 323
McGinn, Colin **693–5**
McGuffin, Peter **470–5**
McGuire, W. 405
Mach, Ernst **445**
  aesthetics 10
  physics based on perceptions 611
  sensations 701
Macintosh, N. 416
MacKay, Donald M.
  brain manipulation **113–14**
  determinism and free will **190–2**
  feedback and feedforward 261
  information theory **369–71**
  soul, brain science and the **723–5**
McKendrick, J. G. 310
Mackensie Davey, D. 388
MacKenzie, N. 203
Mackie, J. 129
Macmurray, J. 679
McNaghten Rules (insanity) 193
McNally, Raymond T. **97**, **770**
McNamara, J. and B. 469
Macnamara, J. 423
'mad as a hatter' **445**
madhouses, *see* asylums, history
madness 52–6, 653–5
Magendie, François **445**
magic, aphrodisiacal claims 33
magical processes, *déjà vu* 182
magnetic fields, astrology
    association 51
magnitude judgement 667–70
Magoun, M. H. 490
Maine de Biran **445–7**
Makarenko, Anton Semyonovitch
    **447–8**
Malan, D. 663
Malcolm, N. 811
male children, childhood traits
    701–3
male sexuality 261–2
malingering, mental illness
    association 472

Malthus, Thomas Robert **448**
  Darwin's and Wallace's
    inspiration 179
mammals, brain evolution **633–9**
mandala symbol 405
Mandler, George **219–20**, **679–80**
mania (term) **448**
  drug therapy 654
manic-depressive psychosis 414, **448**,
    474
  classification 466
  mental illness, frequency of 471
manikin concept (homunculus) 313
manners **448–9**
Manning, M. 18
Manuel, F. E. 562
maps, somatotopic 723
'maps' in the brain **436–8**
marijuana (cannabis) 5
Mark, R. F. 110
Marks, I. M. 258, 617
Markwick, B. 580
Marr, D. A.
  artificial intelligence 50
  perception 601
  stereoscopic vision 748
  vision 793
Marr, David Courtenay **449–50**
marriage, sexual problems 707–11
Marriott, F. H. C. 154
Marshack, A. 52
Martin, K. A. C. 803
Martin, R. D. 639
masochism **450**
  Sartre's views 695
Masterman, M. 576
Masters, W. H.
  female sexuality 262
  sexual development 707
  sexual problems 711
masturbation 262, 705–6
materialism
  consciousness concept 164–6
  ESP implications 244–5
  functionalist ideas 280
  mental concepts view 465
  mind–body problem 490–1
materiality, corpuscular theory 440
maternal behaviour, attachment 57,
    58
mathematics
  ancient Egypt 211
  Euclid **230–1**
  geometry **286–8**
  Gödel's theorem 294–5
  Husserl's philosophy 326
  Leibniz's account 432–3
  Poincaré's ideas 629
  Russell and Whitehead 688
  Turing's concepts 783–4
  Von Neumann's work 804–5
  Wiener's work 810–11
  Wittgenstein's philosophy 813–14
Mattaei, R. 295
matter **450**
  Berkeley's denial 82
  Descartes's theory 189
Matthews, A. 711
Mause, L. de 134
May, E. 399
Mayer-Gross, W. 188, 707

Maynard Smith, J. 18
Mayr, E. 244
Mayr, O. 177
Mead, G. H. 454, 723
Mead, M., sexual development 707
Meadows, S. A. C. 623
meaning **450–4**
  essence 228
  implication 355
  language semantics 805–6
  metaphors 478–81
  music interpretation 502–3
  qualities 666–7
  symbol use 763–5
  Wittgenstein's picture theory
    811–13, 814–16
Medawar, P. 255, 737
medical services, mentally ill 475–7
medicine, Hippocratic oath 312
medicines (drugs) 204
  opium use 570–1
  psychoactive 653–5
mediumship claims 583, 584,
  739–40
medulla **454**
medulla oblongata 521, 522, 523
Mehler, J. 368
Meisel, W. S. 594
Meiselman, H. L. 769
melancholic temperament 246
melancholy
  Burton's treatise 121
  insanity: early theories 372
Melan, D. H. 781
Melden, A. I. 787
Meltzoff, A. N. 174
Melzack, Ronald, pain **574–5**
memory **455–6**
  acquisition 456
  ageing effects 14
  amnesia effects 20–2
  anaesthesia effects 24
  bereavement reaction 80
  biological basis **456–60**
  brain functions 111–12
  chunking 148
  context role **463–4**
  *déjà vu* experiences 182–4
  dementia effects 185–6
  dyslectic conditions 205
  Ebbinghaus's studies 207
  emotion linked cues 220
  engram concept **223**
  experimental approaches **460–3**
  forgetting 264–5
  Hering's views 311
  holographic theories 458
  hypnosis effects 328, 329
  iconic image accuracy 336
  imaging 353–5
  impression concept (seal on wax)
    355
  long-term 457–8, 461, 713–14
  loss, dissociations 197
  mnemonics 493–4
  molecular storage theory 458–60,
    461–2
  neural function questions 543
  neuropsychological studies 547
  recall (retrieval) component 456
  remembering 679–80

short-term 713–14
skills, learned 716–17
sleep, enhancement by 719
synaptic function theory 455–60,
  462
Vygotsky's ideas 805–6
Mendel, Gregor 234
mental concepts
  ageing 13–16
  boggle 100
  causal analysis **464–5**
  cause **127–9**
  children **139–42**
  faculties (mental organs)
    (Chomsky) 419–21
  imaging, brain function during
    475
  imagery **475**
  implication 355
  impression 355
  intelligence 375–9
  intentionality 383–6
  Japanese approaches 399–403
  responsibility 681–2
  subnormality (Penrose) 597–8
mental development, Vygotsky's
  ideas 805–6
mental handicap **467–9**
  Down's syndrome 201, 597–8
  education 208, 210
  extrinisic causes 467–8
  intrinsic causes 467
  treatment 468–9
mental health **469–70**
  asylums 54–6
  historical survey 52–4
mental illness **470–5**
  *see also* asylums
  Adlerian treatment 6
  asylums, necessity question
    54–6
  body build 98–9
  classifications of **465–7**
  delusion symptoms 184–5
  depersonalization symptoms
    186–7
  depression 187–8
  drug treatment
    (psychopharmacology) 653–5
  dyslexia 205–6
  functional psychoses 473–5
  insanity: early theories 371–3
  interactional approach 387
  Kraepelin's contribution 414
  legal definition 195
  mania (term) 448
  moon cycles effect 51
  neuroses 471–3
  organic psychoses 473
  psychopathic disorders 651–3
  psychosis 657–8
  psychosurgery 660–1
  psychotherapy assessment 661–3
  schizophrenia 697–9
  services and after-care **475–7**
  simulated, pseudodementia
    condition 647–8
mental image phenomena (imaging)
  353–5
mental impairment 755–7
mentalism 165–6, 490–1

mental measurement (Thurstone)
  776–7
mental structure, Freud's view 270,
  **276–8**
Merskey, H. 334
Merton, P. A. **676–7**
mescaline 4
Mesmer, Franz Anton, mesmerism
  477–8
mesmerism **477–8**
  hypnosis, history 330–1
  paranormal notion 578
mesomorphic physique 98–9
mesopic vision **478**
metaphor **478–81**
metaphysics **481**
  Buddhist doctrine 401
  ideals 337
  innate ideas theory 371
  Leibniz's ideas 432–4
  logical positivism, attack on 441
  Spinoza's ideas 737–9
metempiric(al) (term) **481**
metempsychosis **481–2**
Method of Loci 493–4
Metter, E. J. 353
Mettrie, J. O. 96
Meyer, R. L. 514
Michaels, D. D. 252
Michie, Donald **155–7**, 645
Michotte, Albert **482–3**
Midgley, M. 244
migraine **483–4**
Miles, T. R. **691–2**
Milgram, Stanley 330, **566–8**
military incompetence **484–6**
military mind **486–7**
Milkman, R. 244
Miller, D. 134
Miller, E. 186
Miller, G. A.
  chunking 148
  programs and planning 646
  taste 769
Miller, K. W. 24
Miller, N. E. 92
Miller, R. J. 560
Mill, James **487**
Mill, John Stuart **487**
  denotation 186
  education 208, 209
  induction in reasoning 362
Millodot, Michel **248–52**
Milner, B. 549
Milner, M. 274
Milner, Peter M. 40, **570**
mind and body **487–9**
mind–body problem **490–1**
  psychosomatic disease 658–60
  purpose question 664–5
  theological approach 770–2
mind and brain: Luria's philosophy
  **489–90**
mind–brain problem
  behaviour, nerve basis view 115
  consciousness 164–5
  dualism 204
  functionalist argument 280
  paranormal phenomena 579,
    585–6
  theological issues 770–2

mind-reading, paranormal claims 579–81
Minsky, M. L.
  artificial intelligence 50
  feedback and feedforward 261
  frames 697
Minuchin, S. 29
mirror reversal **491–3**
mirror-writing 434–5
Mishkin, M. 112
Misiak, H. 616
Mitchell, F. D. 124
Mitchell, J. 410
mnemonics **493–4**, 679–80
models, explanatory **494–5**
Mogadon 653
mokṣa, Indian ideas 357–8
Moles, A., aesthetics 12
Mollon, J. D. 152
monad concept 433–4
Money, J. 707
mongolism, *see* Down's syndrome
Monod, J. 148
Montessori, Maria **495**
mood
  forgetting, influence of 265
  memory factor 463
Moore, B. E. 262
Moore, Brian C. J. **77**, **303–8**
Moore, Francis C. T. **446–7**
Moore, George Edward **495–6**
Moore, Patrick **772–4**
Moore-Ede, M. C. 93
moral issues
  animal, treatment of 25
  brain manipulation 113–14
  education 209
  humanist viewpoint 319
  obedience 566–8
  religion 677–9
Moran, R. 682
Moray, Neville **59–61**
More, L. T. 562
Morgan, Conwy Lloyd 217, 230, **496**
Morgan, M. J. 158, **663–4**
Morley, I. E. 510
morphine
  opium derivative 570–1
  pain control 574–5
Morris, D. 100, 293
Morris, J. M. 206
Morris, M. 433
Morris, R. L. 573
Morse, E. W. 818
Moruzzi, S. 755
Moscovici, S. 723
mother–infant relationship 26–7, 273
motion pictures, perception 604–8
motion sickness 725–6
motivation
  aggressive behaviour 16–17
  courage 258
  displacement activity 195–6
  infancy patterns 368
  invertebrate learning 390
  purpose 664–5
motor function
  nervous system 519–20

paralysis 576
  synergies 765–6
motor nerves
  efferent neural signals **210**
  sensory signals **12–13**
motor skills 715–16
  memory 716–17
  schema concept 695–7
motor gyrus or strip, brain 521
motor system, Bernstein's view 85–6
mourning (bereavement) 80
movement
  acceleration perception 1
  akinesia disorder 19
  aphasic syndromes 426
  apparent 604–8
  apraxia disorders 34
  Aristotle's account 39
  art, in 41, 45–6
  Bernstein's investigation 85–6
  body language 99–100
  brain, control of 522–4
  feedback/feedforward 259–61
  gestures 293
  hypokinesia symptom 200
  intention tremor 386
  Korte's laws 414
  muscular action 497–9
  nerve mechanisms 78
  nervous system involvement 519–20
  Parkinsonism disorder 587–9
  programs for 644–6
  saccades (eye flicks) 693
  schemas theory 695–7
  synergies 765–6
  touch sensitivity 778–80
Moyer, K. E. 18
Muhammad 677–9
Muldoon, S. 573
Müller, Johannes Peter **496**
Müller-Lyer, Franz Carl **497**
multiple personalities **197–8**
multiplexing 804–5
Murdock, B. B. 783
Murphy, G. 441
Murray, Robin M. **470–5**
Murti, T. R. V. 401
muscles
  ataxia disorder 56–7
  movement mechanisms 86
muscle sense, Bell's ideas 78
muscle types 524
muscular action **497–9**
music
  aesthetic preferences 10, 11
  auditory illusion effects 62
  Kepler's study 408–9
music, psychology of **499–505**
  aesthetic aspects 504
  language function 502–3
  pattern characteristics 499–500
  perception, history **505–6**
  performance of 503–4
  psychoacoustic factors 500–2
mutations 285
mutual gaze phenomena 247–8
myelin nerve sheaths 514–17
Myers, Charles Samuel **506–7**
Myers, C. S. 207, 686

Myers, F. W. H. **507**
  ghosts 294
  paranormal 579
  parapsychology and the mind–body problem 587
  spiritualism interest 507
myopia 250–1
Myrianthopoulos, N. C. 326
mysticism
  dream interpretation 203
  Kepler's views 408–9
  metempsychosis belief 481–2
  out-of-the-body experience 571–3
  Sufism 757–8
  Wittgenstein on 812

Nagel, T. 27, 164
naloxone, opiate antagonist 222–3
narcissism, paranoia 577
narcosis, nitrogen ('the narcs') 563–4
narcotic drugs, addiction 4–5
Nathar., Peter W., tutorial article on structure and function of the nervous system **514–34**
nativism **508**
natural selection
  Darwin, Darwinism 179–80
  neo-Darwinian theory 234, 237–9
  Wallace's joint discovery 807
nature, Spinoza's philosophy 738–9
Nauta staining technique 535–6
Nebylitsyn, V. D. 247
necessary properties 168–9
necessity concept 630
Necker cube **508**
Necker, L. A. 508
Needham, J. 147
needs and desires 527–30, 664–5
negative feedback 174–7, 313
neglect, child abuse 131
negligence, responsibility 681–2
negotiating **508–10**
  aggressive factor 18
Neill, A. S. 134, **510–11**
Neisser, U.
  children's drawings 139
  intelligence 379
  schemas 697
Nelson, G. K. 740
Nelson, K. 423
neo-Darwinian theory **234–44**
Nerlich, G. 288
nerve-cells, staining techniques 535–6
  Golgi **296**
  Nauta 535–6
  Ramon y Cajal **671**
nerve fibre (axon) 516–19
nerves
  afferent 12–13
  efferent 210
  electricity role 283–4
  myelin sheaths 414–17
  neuromodulators 550–60
  neurotransmitters 550–60
  refractory period 677
nervous system **514–34**
  acetylcholine function 3
  anticipation 30

nervous system *(cont.)*:
autonomic 524, 531
basal ganglia **70**
Bell's discoveries 78–9
brain 520–4
brain development 101–10
disorders (Jackson) 395
dopamine neurones 199–200
Galen's investigation 281
Gall's ideas 282
genetic factors 284–5
message transmission 516–19
mind question 533–4
movement 519–20, 532
muscular action 498–9
nerve connections
brain function 541–3
formation of **511–14**
nerve path routing studies 114–15
neuroanatomical techniques
**534–9**
neurone structure 514–15
neuropeptides 543–5
neurotransmitter **550–60**
nulling notion **565**
perception **524–7**
plasticity **623–8**
receptors 515–16
reflex action **676–7**
speaking 531
spinal cord and brain 520–4
synapse 765
thinking 530–1
total conceptions (overview)
531–4
Netheim, N. 505
Neumann, John Von *see* Von
Neumann
neural activity, electrical component
(Galvanic) 283–4
neural channels, *see* channels...
neuroanatomical techniques **534–9**,
541–2
neurohormones 553–4
neurolinguistics **539–40, 540–1**
neurology, neuropsychology **545–9**
neuromodulators 557
neuronal connectivity 538–9, **541–3**
catecholamine functions **126–7**
channels, neural **129–30**
neurones
brain development **101–10**
dendrites 186
dopamine 199–200
nervous system 514–15
neuroanatomical study techniques
534–9
neurotransmitters 550–2
number estimated in brain 542
opioid sensitive 221–3
receptive fields 674–5
staining techniques 535–6
visual cortex 313–15
neuropeptides **543–5**
analgesic effects 24
neurotransmitters 552–4
neuropsychology **545–9**
cerebral asymmetries 547–9
language 423–5
speech study 733–4
neuroreceptors 553, 555–7, 559

neurosis 471–3, **549–50**
behaviour therapy 75–7
cause and treatment 472–3
complex types 154–5
compulsions 568–9
delusion 184
depression **187–8**
fear in 257
Freud's treatment ideas 269–70
mental illness (term) 466
obsessions 568–9
Pavlov's experimental 596
personality disorders in **613–14**
psychoanalysis, use of 650
psychosis element **657–8**
psychotherapy assessment 661–3
neurotransmitters **550–60**
acetylcholine 3
adrenaline 7
catecholamines 126–7
chemical identity (list) 552–4
dopamine neurones 199–200
drug therapy effects 654
endorphins **221–3**
functions 554–60
memory involvement 462
message transmission 518–19
migraine association 484
neuromodulators 557–8
neuropeptides 544
neutral monism 491, **688–91**
Newell, A. 379, 644
Newson, J. 134
Newton, Sir Isaac **560–2**, 601
Nicholson, Nigel **508–10**
Nicholson, R. A. 393, 687
Nicogossian, A. E. 727
nicotine addiction 4–5
Niemann, 594
Nietzsche, Friedrich Wilhelm **562–3**
nightmares, dreaming 202
*nirvāṇa* concept 357
nitrogen narcosis **563–4**
nitrous oxide (laughing gas) 429–30
NMR, *see* nuclear magnetic
resonance
'noise', information theory 369
nomic (gnomic) account of
knowledge 411–12
nominalism 228
nomological (law) studies 173
non-materialism, ESP suggestions of
244–5
noradrenaline
neuroanatomical techniques 538
neurotransmitters 552, 554
synthesis and action 126–7, 519
Norman, D. A. 680
North, Joanna **737–9**
nose, smell 719–21
nothingness **564–5**
novelty, appeal of 639–41
Nowell Jones, F. **13–16, 719–21**
NREM sleep (non-rapid eye
movements) 202, 718
nuclear magnetic resonance (NMR),
for brain imaging 347–8,
351–2
nulling **565**, 714–15
numerology, Chinese concepts
146

OBE, *see* out-of-the-body
experience
obedience 330, **566–8**
objectivity 598–601
object–relations (Freud) 270
objects
causal theory 464
neutral monism 690–1
perception of **568**
spatial location 727–32
symbolic forms 763–5
obsessions and compulsions
**568–9**
Janet's contribution 398
mental illness frequencies 471
neuroses 471–2, 549–50
personality disorders 614
Occam's razor 218
occipital lobes, brain 521–4
occult, paranormal ideas 577–9
O'Connor, Neil
autism **63–5**
Penrose, Lionel Sharples **597–8**
subnormality **755–7**
Oedipus complex 155, 213, **569–70**
Ogden, C. K. 765
Ogle, K. 748
O'Hare, D. 12
Oldfield, R. C.
Bartlett, Sir Frederick Charles 70
handedness 302
schemas 697
Olds, James **570**
O'Leary, D. 393
Olesen, J. 484
olfactory system 521, 523, 719–21
Olton, D. S. 92
O'Mahoney, Michael, taste **767–9**
omens belief, dreams 203
one/many problem 217
*On the Origin of Species...* (Darwin)
179
ophthalmoscope, Babbage's and
Helmholz's invention 68
opiate-like substances 221
opiates 4–5, 653–5
opinions, doubting reasoning
method 201
opioids 221, 222–3
opium **570–1**, 574–5
Oppenheim, Ronald W. **125–6**
opponent colour theory 150–1
Oram, J. 719
Orbach, J. 428
Ordy, J. M. 16
organic psychoses, 657–8
orgasm, female sexuality 261–2
originality, creativity effect 171
Orlansky, J. 608
orthodoxy and eccentricity 772–4
Ortony, Andrew **478–81**
Osborne, H. 12, 139
Osgood, C. E. 263
Osler, W. 549
Oswald, Ian
dreaming **201–3**
sleep **718–19**
somnambulism 723
other minds (J. Wisdom) **571**
Otto, R. 679
Outhwaite, R. W. 787

out-of-the-body experience **571–3**
*doppelgänger* episodes 201
Owen, I. M. 583
Owen, Sir Richard **573**
Oxbury, John M. **223–5**

Padel, John Hunter **270–4**
Paget, Sir R. 765
Paillard, J. 112
pain **574–5**
  anaesthesia 22
  anxiety response 31
  biofeedback therapy 90–1
  endorphin relief mechanisms 222
  masochism 450
  migraine 484
  opium treatment 570–1
  relief, neuropeptides 544–5
  sadism 693
  touch, related to 780
Paley, William **575**
Palmer, J. 573
panic, fear 257
Pannenberg, W. 772
panpsychism doctrine 27, 491
Pap, A. 630
Pappehheim, Bertha (Breuer's Anna
  O.) 118
Pappenheimer, J. R. 545
paracognitive phenomena 586
paradigms (T. Kuhn) **575–6**
paradoxes
  illusions 342–3
  material implication 355
  Zeno's philosophy 819
paradoxical sleep (REM sleep) 202
paralysis **576**
  neurosis causes 549–50
  stroke, cause of 750–2
paramnesia, *déjà vu* events 182–3
paranoia **576–7**
paranoid personality disorders 614
paranormal phenomena **577–9**
  ancient Greece **583–4**
  out-of-the-body experience 571–3
  proof, problem of **579–81**
  spiritualism evidence 739–40
  telekinesis 769
  unconscious **581–3**
paraphysical phenomena 586
parapraxia 34–5
parapsychology
  *doppelgänger* episodes 200–1
  ESP claims 245
  ghosts 293–4
  Home's mediumship 313
  mind–body problem **585–7**
  psychic possession reports 403
  research history **584–5**
parasuicide 760
parents
  attachment behaviour 57, 58
  autism disorder 64
  child abuse 131–3
  child rearing problems 133, 134
  sex differences in childhood **701–3**
Parfitt, D. 772
parietal cortex **587**
parietal lobes, brain 521–2
Parker, J. F. 228
Parker, R. C. T. **203–4, 583–4**

Parkes, Colin Murray
  attachment 58
  bereavement **79–81**
  mental health 470
Parkinsonism 200, **587–91**
  akinesia, term 19
  intention tremor symptom **386**
  mental changes in 589–91
  motor symptoms 587–9
  neuroanatomical changes 538
  pseudodementia symptoms 647
Parks, Theodore E.
  anorthoscopic visual perception
    **29–30**
  iconic images **336**
  illusory figures **344–7**
Pascal, Blaise **591**, 677, 679
Pascal, Blaise, calculating machine 1
Passons, W. R. 293
Paton, Sir William D., anaesthesia
    **22–4**
pattern recognition **591–4**
Patterson, Colin 149, **234–44**
Pavlov, Ivan Petrovich 160, **594–6**
  biographicy 594
  circulation and digestion
    physiology 594–5
  conditional reflexes 595–6
  experimental neuroses 596
  learning theory 431
P.D.P. (Parallel Distributed
  Processing) 48–50, 101–110, 387,
  458, 462
Pearce, J. M. S. 484
Pears, David F.
  Russell's philosophy **688–90**,
    **690–1**
  Wittgenstein's philosophy **811–16**
Pearson, K. 283
Peatfield, R. 484
Peirce, Charles Sanders **596**
  induction, definition 362
  laws of nature 430
  symbols 765
Penfield, Wilder Graves **596–7**
  'emergence' and 'reduction' 217
  epilepsy 225
  primates, evolution of brain 639
penological research 172–3
Penrose, Lionel Sharples 343,
    **597–8**, 757
Pepper's ghost **598**
peptides
  *see also* neuropeptides
  neurotransmitters 553–4
perception **598–608**
  acceleration 1
  adaptation 793–5
  aesthetic preferences 8–10, 11–12
  ageing induced changes 14–16
  agnosia (loss) 19
  anorthoscopic vision 29–30
  Aristotle's views 39
  artistic experience 47–8
  attention, selective 59–60
  auditory illusions 61–3
  Bartlett's ideas 69
  behaviourist approach 75
  Berkeley's arguments 83–4
  blindness, recovery from 94–6
  brain development, on 107

brain mechanisms 115
cartoon techniques 126
causality 482–3
channels, neural 129–30
chunking 148
'cocktail party' effect 149
colour vision 150–4
contingent after-effects 166–8
cross-modal sensory effects 173–4
cultural differences **601–3**
depth, visual 188–9
detection, energy patterns 190
distortion effects 198
dyslectic conditions 205
empiricist views (Hume) 319–20
external world 244
fatigue, producing errors 255
figural after-effects 263
figure–ground (visual) **263–4**
Galileo's writings on 281–2
Gestalt theory 288–91
Greek theories **603–4**
hallucination imagery 299–300
hands, significance of 300
haptic (Bell) 78
Helmholtz's contribution 308–10
hypotheses concept **608–11**
illusions 337–47
illusory figures 344–7
infancy, in 362–8
isolation experiment effects 393–4
motion pictures phenomena
    **604–8**
music 503–6
nervous system, given by 524–7
objects 568
organization laws 288–91
paralysis influence 576
realism and 672
schema theory 695–7
sensations 700–1
skill 715–16
sound 306–7
Spinoza's views 738–9
split-brain studies 744
stereoscopic vision 747–8
subliminal 752–5
taste 767–9
touch 778–80
unconscious inference
    (Helmholtz) 308–10
visual 787–96
perceptual causality (Michotte)
    482–3
Perenin, M. T. 112
Perera, K. 423
performance, transfer experiments
    bit, and skill 93–4, 715–16
    781–3
peripheral neuritis 413
Perls, Fritz 293, **611**
Perner, J. 142
Perry, J. R. 613
persecution, paranoia diagnosis
    576–7
personal equation **611**
personal identity **611–13**
personality
  accident proneness 2, 3
  ageing, effects 14
  astrology claims 50

personality *(cont.)*:
'beside oneself' 86
body build effects 98–9
disorders 466, **613–14**
dissociation **197–8**
dream hypotheses 203
ego-psychology criticism 271
epileptic 225
extraversion–introversion 245–6
Gestalt therapy 291–3
hysteria based disorders 333
Jung's studies 404–5
manic depressive type 448
obedience 566–8
Pavlov's ideas 596
phrenology theory 618–20
psychopathic 651–3
psychotherapy assessment 661–3
tests **614**
perspective, Emmert's law 218–19
PET, *see* positron emisssion
tomography
Peters, R. S. 210, 441
*petit mal* seizures 224
Pettit, Philip **786–7**
Pfungst, O. 149
phantom limbs 728
phantoms
*doppelgänger* episodes 200–1
illusory figures 344–5
pharmacology 204, 653–5
Phelps, M. E. 353
phenomenology **614–16**
Husserl's philosophy 326–7
intentionality 383
Laing's psychology 417–18
qualia (sensations) 666
phenotypes 284–6
pheromones 516, 719–21
Phillips, D. Z. 772
Phillipson, O. T.
catecholamines **126–7**
dopamine neurones **199–200**
endorphins **221–3**
limbic system **435–6**
schizophrenia: organic cause **699**
philosophy
Ayer 487–9
Brentano 117–18
Chinese tradition 146–7
Comte 157
Descartes 189
education, of 209–10
emergence/reduction 217–18
empiricism (Hume) 319–20
Epicurus's views 223
functionalism approach
**279–80**
hedonism 308
Hegel 308
Hemholtz 308–10
Indian ideas 357–61
innate ideas 371
Japanese tradition 399–401
Leibniz 433–4
linguistics 142–6, 419–21, 421–3,
441, 596, 691–2, 763–5,
811–13
McDougall's psychology 444–5
Mach 445
metaphysics 481

mind–body problem 164–6,
**490–1**
objectivity 598–601
personal identity 611–13
phenomenology 326–7, **614–16**
Pierce 596
Plato **628–9**
Poincarré 629
Popper 254–5
pragmatism 395–6, 596, **630–1**
pre-Socratic 631
qualia (sensations) 666
qualities 666–7
Quine (symbols) 763--5
realism 672
reductionism 675–6
Russell 687–91
Sartre 693–5
Socrates 723
Spencer 735–7
Spinoza 737–9
Thales 770
*verstehen* approach 786–7
Wittgenstein 209, 454, 811–16
Zeno of Elea **819**
phlegmatic temperament 246
phobias **616–17**
anxiety **30–1**
aversion therapy 66
behaviourist approach 72
fear in 257
Janet's contribution 398
neuroses 471, **549–50**
phonemes 617–18
phonetics **617–18**, 734–5
phrenology 527, **618–20**
cerebral dominance 425
faculty psychology view 253–4
Gall's notions 282
physiognomy **620–1**
physiological changes
in fear 257
James–Lange theory 220
physique, personality association
98–9
Piaget, Jean **621–2**, 697
education **622–3**
reasoning in childhood 672–5
Pick, A. 540
Pick, H. L. 732
Pickford, R. W. **10–12**, **69–70**
Pien, D. 323
Pieron, Henri **623**
pigments, vision 153
pineal gland (psychology) 526,
530
interface to soul 190, 724
pining 80
Pirsig, R. M. 217
pitch
absolute 500
auditory illusion 62–3
hearing 303–8
Helmholtz 308–10
music 499–505
Pitcher, G. W. 83
Pitts, W. H. 443, 444
placebos as analgesia 222
planetary influences 50–2
plasticity in the nervous system
**623–8**

Plato 10, **628–9**, 629
aesthetics 8–9
psyche theory 648–9
Platonic Forms 327, **629**
play, infancy activity 365–7
pleasure
brain centres 129
Epicurus's philosophy 223
eye-contact effects 247, 248
female sexuality 261–2
hedonism 308
male sexuality 261–2
masochism form 450
sadism 693
Pleydell-Pearce, I. W. **88–92**
Plowden Report (education) 208
pneuma concept 373–4
Poeck, Klaus **34–6**
Poincaré, Jules Henri **629**
Pollard, J. W. 244
Pollen, D. A. 216
poltergeists 581–3
Polyak, S. 639
polyglossia, *see* bilingualism
polygraphy, *see* electrodermal
activity
POMC, *see* propiomelanocortin
Ponder, E. 96
pons 522, 523–4
Pöppel, E. 113
Popper, Karl R.
Descartes, René 190
epiphenomena 225
falsification **255–6**
Hume, David 320
metaphysics 481
soul and brain science 725
population, Malthus's principles 448
positivism 157, 326, 441, 451, 454,
786–7
positron emisssion tomography
(PET) 348–53
possession phenomena 403, 739–40
possibility **630**
postulates 231
posture
ataxia disorder 56
body language 99–100
gestures 293
Potts, M. J. 168
Poulton, E. C.
blinking 96
ergonomics **226–8**
quantifying judgements **667–70**
pragmatism 395–6, 596, **630–1**
Pratt, W. K. 594
precognition 579–81
ESP defined phenomenon 245
prediction
anticipation 30
falsifying question 254–5
generalizing basis 284
perceptual hypotheses 609–10
reaction times element 671–2
Preece, M. A. **315–17**
prefrontal leucotomy 660
pregnancy, foetal brain 104, 106
Premack, D. 27, 633
premeditation, responsibility 681–2
presbyopia 249–50
pre-Socratic philosophers **631**

pretence 329, 330, 334
Pribram, K. H. 278, 549
Price, H. H. 587, 772
Price, S. R. F. 204
Prichard, J. W. 353
primary colours, Young's 818
primate language **631–3**
primates, evolution of the brain **633–9**
Prince, Morton 197–8
prison psychosis 648
problems: their appeal **639–41**
problem-solving **641–4**
  AI in 49
  attention factors 61
  intelligence, related to 377–8
  knowledge, contribution of 410
  Köhler's ideas 412–13
  lateral thinking 428–9
  naturalistic analyses 410–12
  thinking skills 774–5
programs and planning **644–6**
  algorithms 19–20
  artificial intelligence 48–50
  fuctionalism 280
  Gödel's theorem 295
projective techniques **646–7**
prophecies, dream reports 203, 205
propiomelanocortin (POMC) 221, 222
propositions
  analytic 24–5
  axiom concept 67
  definition of 361
  meaning 450–4
  Quine 763–5
psychotherapy
  *see also* psychoanalysis
  assessment 661–3
  behaviour 75–7
  fear induced disorders 258
  Gestalt 291–3
pseudodementia 186, **647–8**
pseudohallucination 299, **648**
psi 586
psyche **648–9**
  Aristotle's views 38–9
  Plato's views 628–9
psychiatric disorders 470–5
psychiatric hospitals (asylums) 52–6
psychiatry **649**
  Chinese approach 147
  Freud's work 268–78
  psychotherapy assessment 661–3
psychical research
  *see also* parapsychology
  British Society for 577, 579, 585–6
  spiritualism 739–40
psychoacoustics, music 500–3
psychoactive drugs 475–7, 653–5
psychoanalysis **649–50**
  fear therapy 258
  Freud and Freudianism, later developments 268–270, 270–4
  phobia 616–17
  psychosis 658
  repression 681
  sexual development theory 704, 705

sublimation (term) 752
suppression (term) 763
transference 781
psychogalvanic skin response (PGR) 213
psychokinesis (PK) 582, 586
psycholinguistics 540
  bilingualism 86–8
psychology **650–1**
  laboratories of 69–7, **416**
  Wundt (the first laboratory) 816–17
psychopathic personality 195, **651–3**
  disorders 613–14
psychopharmacology 4, **653–5**
psychophysics **655–7**, 816–17
  audiometer test 61
  Békésy 77
  consciousness 164–6
  experimental design 264
  Galton's methodology 282
  illusions 337–43
  information theory 369–71
  just noticeable differences 405
  mind and body problem 490–1
  nulling 565, 714–15
  quantifying judgements 667–70
  reaction times 671–2
  sensations 700
  size–weight illusion 714–15
  Stevens 748
  transfer experiments 781–3
  Weber–Fechner law 258–9
  Weber's ideas 808–9
psychoses 300, 473–5
psychosexuality, women 261–2
psychosis **657–8**
  depression 188
  mental illness term 466
  paranoia 576–7
  personality disorder cause 613–14
psychosomatic disease **659–60**
  biofeedback 88–92
  fear 257
  medical view **658–9**
  phobias **616–17**
psychosurgery **660–1**
  ethics of 113–14
psychotherapy
  assessment of treatment **661–3**
  behaviour therapy association 75–6
  free association 267–8
  Gestalt 291–3
  hypnosis method 332
  mentally ill, services 475–7
puberty, sexual development 703–7
Pulfrich's pendulum **663–4**
Pullan, J. M. 1
punch-drunk syndrome (concussion) 158
punishment, behaviourism 71–4, 76
purpose 533, **664–5**
  behaviourism (Skinner) 74
  evolution 233–4
  Jamesian theme 396
  McDougall's contribution 444–5
puzzles
  computer chess 155–7
  problem appeal 639–41
  problem-solving 641–4

Pythagoras 481–2, 500, 505–6, **665**

qualia (sensations) **666**
qualities **666–7**
quantifying judgements 667–70
quarrelling, paranoia pattern 576–7
Quetelet, Lambert Adolphe Jacques **670**
Quine, Willard V.
  analytic propositions 25
  intentionality 386
  meaning 451, 454
  symbols 763–5
Quinton, A. 691

Rabbitt, P. A. M. **671–2**
Rachman, S. 77, **256–8**
racial difference, aesthetics 11–12
Radinsky, L. 639
radioactive tracers, neuroanatomical study 536–9
Raichle, Marcus E. **347–53**
Rakic, P. 110, 514
Rameau, J. P. 505
Ramon y Cajal 513, **671**
Ramsay, R. W. 81
Randell, B. R. 784
Raper, J. A. 514
Raphael, B. 81
Ratcliff, F. 47
Ray, O. S. 655
Ray, W. J. 92
reaction times **671–2**
  Angell's discoveries 25
  apperception 33–4
  Külpe's study 414–15
  personal equation 611
  skill 715–16
  sleep period correlation 718
readiness, brain potential 232
reading
  Braille system 101
  brain activity 531
  dyslexia 205–6
reading-machines, pattern recognition 591–4
realism 228, 452, **672**
reality
  absolute unity (Hegel) 308
  aesthetics of expression 8–10
  Avicenna's view 66
  flux (Bergson) 81–2
  children's understanding 140–1
  Chinese concepts 146–7
  contingent properties 168–9
  depersonalization 186–7
  Descartes's account 189–90
  emergence/reduction arguments 217–18
  external world 244
  geometry view 287
  idealism approach 327
  illusions 337–43
  internal models concept 387
  Leibniz's views 433–4
  Spinoza's conception 738–9
reasoning
  *see also* logic
  artificial intelligence 48–50
  behaviourism approach 75
  children, development **672–4**

reasoning *(cont.)*:
  deduction 180–2
  doubting 201
  entailment 223
  falsifying hypotheses 254–5
  Hippocrates's contribution 312
  implication 355
  induction 68–9, 362
  inductive (Mill) 487
  intelligence in 378, 379–83
  intuition 389
  lateral thinking 428–9
Reason, J. 727
rebirth, Indian ideas 357–8
recall
  *see also* memory
  ageing effects 14
  dream experiences 718–19
  forgetting association 265
receptive field **674–5**
receptors
  *see also* hearing, smell, taste, touch, vision
  nervous system 515–16, 543
  peptide recognition 543
  receptive field 674–5
  Sherrington's work 711–13
recklessness, responsibility 681–2
recognition
  *see also* memory
  context-dependence memory 463–4
  danger **178**
  *déjà vu* experiences 182–4
  imprinting 357
  machine recognition 591–4, 734–5
  speech patterns (machines) 734–5
reduction and emergence **217–18**
reductionism in psychology **675–6**
redundancy, information theory 369
Reed, Graham F.
  *déjà vu* **183–4**
  *doppelgänger* **200–01**
  time-gap experience **777**
Reeve, E. G. 487
reference, *see* denotation
reflexes **676–7**
  *see also* behaviourism
  Babinski 68
  biofeedback 91
  blinking, 96
  extinction 244
  habituation (adaptation) 299
  instinct explanation 374
  Müller's studies 496
  nervous system 519–20, 532
  Pavlov's discoveries 595–6
  Sherrington on 711–13, 765–6
refractory period of nerve 677
rehabilitation, mentally ill 475–7
Reich, P. A. 423
Reid, Thomas, **677**
reincarnation
  Bhuddist philosophy 400
  *déjà vu* explanation 182
  Indian ideas 357–8
  metempsychosis belief 481
reinforcers 159–60
  *see also* behaviourism
Reisz, K. 608

religion **677–9**
  blood myth symbols 97
  humanist scepticism 317–19
  Indian 357–61
  Japanese 399–403
  Sufi 757–8
  theology and mind–brain identity 770–2, 723–5
remembering **679–80**
  *déjà vu* 182, 183
  Ebbinghaus's studies 207
  forgetting causes 264–5
  mnemonics 493–4
REMs, *see* rapid eye movements
repetition, remembering aid 679–80
repression **681**
Rescoria, R. A. 160
response time, *see* reaction time
responsibility 193–5, 653, **681–2**
resting potential 516
resurrection 723–5, 770–2
reticular formation, brain 525
retina **682**
  visual function 793–5, 798–804
retinal images, stabilization **682–4**
retinex theory (colour) 419, **684–5**
retrograde marking — histology techniques 536–8
revelation experiences, dreams 203
revenge, suicide threats 760
reward 71–4, 532, 776
Rhine, Joseph Banks, ESP 584–5
rhodopsin (in retina) 153
rhythms
  biological clocks 92–3
  music 499–505
  sleep 718
ribonucleic acid 93, 544
Ribot, Théodule **685–6**
Richards, I. A. 481
Ridley, Mark 244, **594–6**
Ridpath, I. 727
Rieber, R. W. 34
Rivers, William Halse Rivers 275, **686**
RNA, *see* ribonucleic acid 544
Roazen, P. 650
Robertson, J. D. S. 12
Robins, E. 760
Robins, L. N. 653
Robinson, J. O. 343
robots, programming 280, 645–6
Rock, I.
  anorthoscopic visual perception 29–30
  perception 601
  spatial co-ordination 732
rods, visual receptors 153–4
Rogers, C. R. 221
Rogo, D. S. 573
Rollin, H. R. **54–6**
Rooth, Graham F. **291–3**, **397–9**
Rorschach, Hermann **686**
Rorschach ink-blots test 646–7, 686
Rose, A. 383
Rose, D. 803
Rose, Stephen **456–60**
Rosenblatt, P. C. 81
Rosenfield, A. 594
Rosner, B. 505

Ross, Helen E.
  Fechner, Gustav Theodor 259
  size–weight illusion 715
  space psychology **725–7**
Ross, O. 763
Ross, W. D. 297
Rothbart, M. K. 323
Roth, M. 186
Rothman, David 54
Rousseau, Jean-Jacques **686**
  education 207–8, **686–7**
Roy, C. S. 353
Rubin, Edgar **687**
Rubin, J. Z. 510
Rumi, Jalaluddin **687**
Ruse, M. 244
Rushton, William A. H.
  colour vision **152–4**
  visual adaptation **793–5**
Russell, Bertrand Arthur William **687–91**
  dualism views **688–90**
  Hume, David 320
  knowledge by aquaintance and by description 412
  mathematical logic 688
  neutral monism **690–1**
  sense data perception 688
Russell Davis, Derek
  anxiety **30–1**
  complex **154–5**
  delusion **184–5**
  depersonalization **186–7**
  ego and super-ego **210–11**
  electra complex **213**
  encounter groups **221**
  hallucination **299–300**
  Huntington's chorea **325–6**
  inferiority complex **368**
  interactional approach **386–7**
  Korsakoff syndrome **413–14**
  mental disorders: classification **465–7**
  mental health **469–70**
  Morgan, Conwy Lloyd **496**
  neurosis **549–50**
  Oedipus complex **569–70**
  personality tests **614**
  psychiatry **649**
  psychoanalysis **649–50**
  psychology **650–1**
  psychosomatic disease **658–9**
  repression **681**
  shock **713**
  somnabulism **723**
  sublimation **752**
  transference **781**
Russell, G. F. M. 29
Russell, W. R. 32
Rutter, M. 65, 210
Ruzicka, L. T. 763
Rycroft, Charles
  dissociation of the personality **197–8**
  Freudianism 274
  paranoia **576–7**
  psychosis **657–8**
  psychosomatic disease **659–60**
Ryle, Gilbert 217, **691–2**

saccades (eye movements) **693**
Sachs, E. 664
Sacks, Oliver **564–5**, 591
sacrifices, religious 677–9
sadism **693**, 695
  masochism comparison 450
sadness, bereavement cause 79–80
Sagi, D. 793
Sahakian, Barbara J. **28–9**
Sainsbury, P. 763
St Thomas Aquinas, *see* Aquinas,
  St Thomas
salivation, Pavlov's experiments 595
*saṃsāra*, Indian ideas 357
Samuels, I. 755
Sanai, Hakim 693
sanguine temperament 246
Sartre, Jean-Paul, **693–5**
Satterly, D. J. **622–3**
Saussure, F. de 454
Savage, C. W. 701
Savage-Rumbaugh, E. 633
Sayce, R. N. 12
scanning **695**
scans of the brain 347–53
scepticism (Hume) 319–20
Schachter, S. 220
Schacht, J. 393
Schafer, R. 274
Schank, R. C. 50
Schatzman, M. 577
Scheflen, A. E. 100
Scheibel, A. B. 444
schemas 69, **695–7**, 728
Schiller, Francis **119**
schizophrenia 473–4, **697–9**
  asylum treatment 55–6
  autism resemblance 63
  Bleuler's term 94
  body build link 98–9
  classification 466
  delusion symptoms 184–5
  depersonalization 187
  dopamine neurones link 200
  drug therapy 653–5
  Jung on 404
  Kraepelin on 414
  Laing on 417–18
  mental illness, frequency 471
  organic cause, evidence of **699**
  paranoia 576–7
  pseudodementia link 648
Schmidt, J. T. 514, 628
Schmölders, Claudia **448–9**
Schneider, K. 653
Schoen, M. 505
Schofield, M. 5
school phobia 616–17
Schopenhauer, Arthur 323,
  **699–700**
Schumann, F. 346
Scott, Christopher **579–81**
Scott, R. 56
scripts
  Braille 101
  picture (Chinese) 142–6
Scruton, R. 406, 739
Scull, Andrew 54
seances
  paranormal phenomena 579–81
  spiritualism 739–40

Searle, J. R.
  functionalist theories 280
  intentionality (meaning) 386
  perception of motion pictures 608
Seashore, C. 505
sedatives 653–5
Sedman, G. 648
Segall, M. H. 12, 603
seizures, epileptic 223–5
*sekhem* term, Egyptian thought 212
Sekuler, R. 16
selection of information 369–70
self
  'beside oneself' notion 86
  ego psychology 271
  Indian concepts 358–60
  multiple personality 197–8
  personal identity 611–13
  psyche 648–9
  unconscious, theory of the 785
self-consciousness 162, 163, 180,
  388–9
self-discovery 640–1
self-image, social psychology 721–3
semantics 451, 478–81
Semeonoff, B. **646–7**
semicircular canals (labyrinths) 416
senility 16
  memory problems 14, 22
  dementia 185–6
  pseudodementia, incidence 647–8
sensationalism (Condillac) 158
sensations **700–1**
  behaviourist approach 75
  black as a colour 94
  blindness, recovery from 94–6
  brightness 119
  brown as a colour 119
  centres in the brain for 129
  cerebral studies (Flourens) 264
  colour vision 154, 419, 599–600,
    602
  cutaneous (Rivers) 686
  emotion theory 219
  empathy 220–1
  fatigue 255–6
  Galileo's writing 281–2
  hunger 323–5
  just-noticeable differences *see*
    psychophysics
  measurement (Fechner) 258–9
  migraine 483
  perception association 598–601
  qualities of 666–7
  retinex theory (colour) 684–5
  satiety from hunger 324–5
  sense-data (Russell) 688–90
  Spinoza's view 738–9
  taste 767–9
  touch 778–80
  yellow as a colour 818
sense-data (qualia) 688–90, **701**
senses
  *see also* perception
  Aquinas on 36–8
  Aristotle on 39
  blindness, recovery from 94–6
  common sense 154
  cross-modal integration 173–4
  discrimination 809
  Greek investigations 296–8

hearing **303–8**, 804
  humour 320–3
  Indian ideas 358–9
  object perception 568
  perception function 598–601
  quality concept 666–7
  smell 719–21
  spatial co-ordination 727–33
  taste 767–9
  touch 302–3, 778–80
  vision 787–804
separation
  anxiety patterns 31
  bereavement 80
Serban, G. 27
serial time, Dunne's idea 205
set (attention) **701**
sex differences in childhood **701–3**
sex pheromones 516
sexual behaviour
  aggression 18
  anxiety 30
  aphrodisiacs 32–3
  child abuse 131–3
  conversion hysteria 333
  female sexuality 261–2
  masochism 450
  sadism 693
sexual development **703–7**
sexuality
  chromosome difference 701,
    703–4
  female patterns **261–2**
  Freud's ideas 269
  human growth 316
  libido element 435
  Oedipus complex 569–70
  pheromone attractants 719–20
sexual problems **707–11**
Seyfarth, Robert M. **178**
Shaffer, D. 18
Shah, Idries, *see* Idries Shah
*shakras*, see *cakras*
Shallice, T. 22
*shamans* 402, 678
Shannon, C. E.
  bit 94
  computer chess 157
  information theory 371
  'noise' 369
shape
  geometric identity 287
  Gestalt theory 288–91
  split-brain, perception of 740–7
Shapiro, D. A. and D. 663
Sharpe, M. R. 727
Shaw, L. 3
Sheehan, P. W. 354
Sheehy, Noel P. **320–3**
Sheikh, M. S.
  Al-Farabi 19
  Al-Ghazzali 19
  Al-Kindi 20
  Islamic philosophy 393
shell-shock 686, 713
Shepard, R. N. 347
Shepherd, I. L. 293
Sherman, S. M. 798, 803
Sherrington, Sir Charles Scott 217,
  677, **711–13**
Sherwood, J. J. 40

Shinto religion 399–400, 402
shock **713**
    opioid blocking therapy 222–3
Shoemaker, S. 613
Shontz, F. C. 139
Short, R. 18
short-term memory 457–8, 461,
    **713–14**
Shushtery, A. M. A. 758
Sidney, E. 388
Siegel, R. K. 300
Siegfried, J. 591
sight
    amblyopia 314
    blindness, recovery from 94–6
    colour 150–4
    dyslexia 205–6
    optical disorders 248–52
    receptors 515–16
    visual system 798–804
sign stimulus 230
    blushing 97–8
    body language 99–100
    invertebrate learning 389
    meaning association 450–4
sign theory (Peirce) 596
sign-using, Vygotsky's work 805–6
Sillito, A. M.
    receptive fields**674–5**
    visual system: environmental
        influences **796–8**
    visual system: organization
        **798–804**
Silverman, L. H. 755
Silverstone, T. 188
similarity, metaphor 478–81
Simkin, J. S. 293
Simms, A. C. P. 663
Simon, H. A. 157
Simpson, W. K. 213
Sims, H. V. 152
sin 678–9
Singer, C. 312
Singer, P. 25
Singer, W. 110, 113
Singleton, W. T. 716
sinistrality 300–2
Siva, Indian god 358, 360–1
size constancy (in illusion) Thouless'
    work 776
Sizemore, C. 198
size–weight illusion 714–15
Sjöval, B. 583
Skidelski, R., 510
Skilbeck, C. E., stroke 752
skill
    accident proneness 2
    ageing effects 13–14
    apraxias, inhibition effect 34
    arousal effects 40
    automation resentment 65
    bit rates 93–4
    brain development for 109
    critical learning periods 173
    diver performance **198–9**
    handedness characteristics 300–2
    human **715–16**
    interactional approach 386–7, 610
    interviews 387–8
    memory for **716–17**
    negotiating 508–10

obsessions and compulsions
    568–9
problem-solving appeal 639–44
thinking 774–5
transfer (knowledge) 780–1,
    782–3
skin
    electrodermal activity 213–14
    touch mechanisms 778–80
Skinner, B. F.
    behaviourism 74, **74–5**
    conditioning 160
    Watson, John Broadus 808
Skinner box **718**
Skowbo, D. 168
skull bumps (phrenology) 618–20
Skultans, Vieda
    asylums **52–4**
    insanity: early theories **371–3**
    spiritualism **739–40**, 740
Skylab space programme 725
Slater, E. 334
sleep **718–19**
    arousal 40
    dream experiences 201–3
    EEG patterns 216
    hypnosis 329
    neuropeptides 544–5
    REM and NREM types 202
sleeping, isolation experiment effects
    394
sleeping pills 719
sleep learning myth 719
sleep-walking 723
    automatism condition 66
Slobin, D. I. 427
Slobodon, R. 686
Sloman, A. 50
Small, J. G. 65
Smart, N. 679
smell **719–21**
    ageing changes 16
    anosmia (loss) 30
    flavour 767
    perception of 525
    receptors for 515–16
Smith, H. 505
Smith, J. M. 244
Smith, S. B. 124
Smith, S. J. 661
Smith, S. M. 133
smooth muscle 524
Smythies, J. R. 587
Smyth, M. M. 641
Soal, S. C. 580
Sober, E. 244
social behaviour
    aggression 16, 17–18
    animal–human comparisons 26
    attachment 57–8
    autism (lack of) 63
    bereavement 79–80
    blushing 97–8
    body language 99–100
    childhood sex differences 701–3
    displacement activities 195–6
    eye-contact 247–8
    facial expression 253
    fear expression 256–8
    gestures 293
    halo effect 303

Hawthorne effect 300
humour 320–3
hysteria 333–4
imprinting 355–7
infancy development 362–8
interactional approach 386–7
interpersonal experience 417–18
interviews 387–8
manners 448–9
needs and desires 527–30
negotiating 508–10
obedience 566–8
paranoics 576
personality disorders 613–14
phobias 616–17
psychopathic personality 651–3
social psychology studies 721–3
social psychology **721–3**
social services, for the mentally
    handicapped 468–9
Society for Psychical Research 507,
    740
sociobiology, evolution position 242
Socrates **723**
Sokal, M. M. 127
somatotopical **723**
somnambulism 478, 719, **723**
    automatism 66
    dreaming 202
sonograph, phonetics use 617–18
Sorabji, R. 129
soul
    Aquinas's account 36, 37–8
    Aristotle's psychology 38–40
    Berkeley's views 84–5
    brain science question **723–5**
    Descartes's views 190
    dreams explanation 201, 203
    Egyptian ideas 211–12
    faculty psychology in 373
    Greek investigations 296, 297
    Ibn Bajjah's teaching 335
    metempsychosis belief 481–2
    Plato's views 628–9
    psyche association 648–9
    science/religion conflict 585–7
    spiritualism view 584
    theology, on the 770–2
sound
    binaural hearing 88
    Fourier analysis 265
    hearing **303–8**
    loudness measure 655–7, 667
    musical psychoacoustics 500–3
    memory for 713–14
    phonemes 617–18
    volley theory 804
space
    geometric theory 286–8
    nothingness experience 564–5
    objects 568
    perception 598–608
space psychology **725–7**
spatial co-ordination **727–33**
    intersensory 728–9
    sensorimotor 729–32
    sensory integration 727–8
    stroke induced disorder 751
    visual space 796
Spearman, Charles Edward 379,
    **733**

species
definitions 234
heredity principle 235–7
origin, Darwin and neo-
Darwinian theory 179–80,
239–41
spectacles 3
speech
aphasia **31–2**
autistic impairment 63
babbling 68
bilingualism 86–8
body movement association
99–100
brain mechanisms (Broca's area
and Wernicke's area) 119,
426
brain processes 531, **733–4**
cerebral specialization 301, 302
cognitive competence 426–7
Fourier analysis 265
language areas, in the brain 425
loss (aphasia) 185
machine recognition **734–5**
neurolinguistics 540–1
phonetics 617–18
shadowing technique 59, 60
short-term memory 713–14
split-brain effect 743–7
Spencer, Herbert 323, **735–7**
Spender, Natasha **499–505**
Sperry, Roger Walcott
brain development 110
brain function 113
brain science **114–17**
consciousness **164–6**, 166
engram (term) 223
neuronal connectivity and brain
function 514, 543
neuropsychology 549
paranormal phenomena and the
unconscious 583
split-brain and the mind 746–7
Spiegelberg, H.
Brentano, Franz 118
Husserl, Edmund Gustav Albert
327
phenomenology 616
spinal cord
nervous system 514, 520–4
neuropeptide action 543–5
Spinoza, Benedict (Baruch) de
**737–9**
spirit
Berkeley's view 84–5
ESP 244–5
Galen's system 281
spiritualism **739–40**
Home's mediumship 313
suggested evidence 584
splenetic disorders (temperament)
372
split-brain and the mind 542, **740–7**
brain function 111, 115–16
cerebral asymmetries 548
consciousness 163, 164, 741
epilepsy treatment 741–3
visual effects 744–5
Spock, B. 134
spontaneous remission, of mental
illness 661–3

Springer, S. P. 302
squint (strabismus) 195, 252, 796
Squire, L. R. 113, 460
Stafford Clark, D. 334, 475
staining techniques
nerve-cells (neurones) 535–6
Raman y Cajal's histology 671
starvation, anorexia/bulimia nervosa
28–9
statistical psychology, Spearman's
views 733
statistics, Gaussian distribution 284
status, social psychology studies
722–3
Stauffer, R. C. 244
Steinthal, H. 540
Stengel, E. 761
Stephenson, A. F. 560
Stephenson, Norman
childhood **133–4**
Froebel, Friedrich Wilhelm
August **279**
Makarenko, Anton Semyonovitch
**447–8**
Rousseau and education **686–7**
stereoscopic vision **747–8**
anaglyphs 24
binocular vision 88
depth perception 188–9
eye defects 252
Pulfrich pendulum 663–4
squint 195, 252, 796
Sterling, P. 804
Sternberg, Robert J. **375–9**, 383
Stern, D. N. 368
Stevens, Stanley Smith 670, **748**
Stich, S. 371
stimulants, addiction 4
stimulus **748**
*see also* perception, senses
cerebral hemisphere function 548
intersensory co-ordination 728–9
just-noticeable differences 405
measurement of effects, Stevens's
work 748
object perception 568
perception 598–601
psychophysics 655–7
quantifying judgements 667–70
reaction times 671–2
reflex action 595–6, 676–7
sensations effect 700–1
weight-size illusion effect 714–15
stimulus-response theory 159
STM, *see* short-term memory
Stoller, R. J. 707, 711
Stone, A. A. 56
Stone, J. 469
Storr, A. 405
Stout, G. F. 310, 416
strabismus (squint) 195, 252, 796
Strasser, S. 616
Stratton, G. M. 733
Straus, E. 713
Strauss, A. 510
Strawson, Peter F. **406–8**, 787
stress **748–50**
*see also* anxiety
abreaction 1
arousal 40
blink rate indicator 96

fatigue 256
fear 257–8
migraine 483–4
neurosis 472–3
opioid relief mechanisms 222
psychosomatic disease, causes
658–60
schizophrenia trigger 698
striate cortex 314
striated muscle 524
stroboscopic movement 604–8
stroke **750–2**
alpha rhythm 216
aphasia 31
Stromeyer, C. F. 168
Strongman, K. T. 220
Stroop test 60
structural axes in art 41, 45–6
structuralism, definition 453
Strupp, H. H. 663
Stumpf, Carl **752**
Subhan, J. A. 758
subjective colours 78–9
subject've experience
consciousness 165
illusions 337
introspection, reliability of 388–9
sublimation 276–8, **752**
subliminal perception **752–5**
subnormality **755–7**
Sufism 58–9, 335, **757–8**
Islamic philosophy 393
Jami's contribution 397
Rumi's ideas 687
Sanai's ideas 693
suggestibility
Binet's discoveries 88
hypnosis 328–33
hysteria 334
suicidal behaviour **758–61**
depression hazard 188
international statistics **761–3**
Sundberg, J. 505
sun signs, *see* astrology
super-ego **210–11**
supernatural
Chinese tradition 146
humanist rejection 318
supernatural phenomena 577–9
superstition, obsessions 568–9
suppression (term) **763**
surgery (psychosurgery) 660–1
ethics of 113–14
leucotomy 435
survival
diver performance **198–9**
fatiguing situations 256
inquisitiveness 371
suspiciousness, paranoia 576–7
Sutherland, Stuart **449–50**
Suzuki, D. T. 401
Svare, B. B. 19
Svedelins, C. 734
Swinburne, R. 362
Sydenham, Sir Thomas **763**
syllogistic inference, *see* deduction
symbolic logic
Boole's laws of thought 430
Leibniz on 432–3
Quine on 763–5
Russell on 687–8

symbolism
  *see also* meaning
  Freud and Freudianism 270,
    274–5
  humour ingredient view 322
  primate language 631–3
  musical patterns 499–500
symbols **763–5**
  *see also* thinking
  artistic 48
  blood myth 97
  Chinese language characters
    142–6
  Piaget's views on 621–2
  sign-using behaviour 805–6
sympathetic nervous system 524,
  531
synaesthesia 184, **765**
synapse **765**
  brain development 101–9
  memory theories 455–60, 462
  neurotransmitters 550–60
  transmission mechanisms 511–14,
    517–19
syndromes **765**
synergies **765–6**
systems
  automatic control 170
  biofeedback 88–92
  biological clocks 92–3
  brain functions 489–90
  choice in 147–8
  cybernetic 174–7
  extraversion–introversion 245–7
  feedback and feedforward 259–61
  feedback loop concept 176
  Gödel's theorem 295
  homeostasis 313
  interactional approach 386–7
  mental faculties (mental organs)
    253–4, 419–21, 618–20
  nervous **514–34**

table manners 449
tachistoscope **767**
tactile receptors (touch) 778–80
Tajfel, H. 19, 723
Tanner, J. M. 317, 659
Tanner, W. P. jr. 383
Taoist ideas of the mind 146
taste 16, 515–16, **767–9**
tautology 180–2, **769**
Taylor, C. 787
Taylor, I. 173
Taylor, Jeremy S. H.
  nerve connections: formation
    **511–14**
  neuronal connectivity/brain
    function **541–3**
  plasticity in the nervous system
    **623–8**
teaching
  artificial intelligence use 49
  creativity concept 171
  critical periods 173
  educational theories 208–9
  'hands-on' interaction 608–11
  play element (kindergarten) 279
  thinking skills 774–5
telekinesis **769**
teleology, goal-directed systems 176

telepathy
  'Clever Hans' horse sense 149
  *déjà vu* 182
  ESP defined 245
  paranormal theories 577–9
television
  colour vision analogy 151–2
  picture perception 604–8
temperament
  astrological debate 50, 51
  body build relations 98–9
  extraversion–introversion
    245–7
  four humours tradition 372
  irritability (term) 392
  personality tests 614
Templeton, W. B. 733
temporal lobes, brain 521–3, 531
Tenney, J. 505
tension 88–90, 575
Teplov, B. 505
Terman, Lewis Madison **769–70**
Terrace, H. 633
terror **770**
Teuber, Hans-Lukas 546, **770**
textons 787–93
Thales **770**
Thatcher, R. W. 164
Thayer, H. S. 631
thematic apperception test 646–7
theology and mind–brain identity
    **770–2**
  ethics of brain manipulation
    113–14
thermoreception, touch system 780
thiamine deficiency, amnesia 20
Thiéry, J.-P. 514
Thinès, Georges
  Brentano, Franz **117–18**
  Husserl, Edmund **326–7**
  Michotte, Albert **482–3**
  phenomenology **614–16**
  Sherrington, Charles **711–13**
thinkers, independent **772–4**
thinking/thought
  algorithmic 19–20
  anoesis (absence) state 27
  Aristotle's views 39
  artificial intelligence 48–50
  bereavement urge 80
  brain function in 530
  brain scans 347–53
  Chinese ideas 146–7
  computer chess 155–7
  concept term 157–8
  deduction process 181
  doubting 189
  free association 266–8
  humanism 318
  imageless 415
  imaging 353–5
  implication 355
  independent thinkers 772–4
  infancy 363–8
  intentionality 383–6
  lateral thinking 428–9
  laws **430**
  Locke's views 439–40
  Maine de Biran's views 445–7
  mechanistic theory 170
  mind and body 487–9

neurolinguistic ideas (Luria)
    540–1
  problem-solving 641–4
  reductionism method 675–6
  symbols as tools 763–5
  teaching methodology **774–5**
Thomas, A. J. 16
Thomas Aquinas, St, *see* Aquinas,
    St Thomas
Thomas, D. A. 173
Thompson, K. 157
Thomson, G. H. 379
Thomson, H. 403
Thomson, M. E. 206
Thorndike, Edward Lee **775–6**
  conditioning 160
  Freud on mental structure 278
  intelligence 383
  law of effect 430
  Morgan, Conwy Lloyd 496
Thouless, Robert 219, 587, **776**
Thurstone, Louis Leon 379, **776–7**,
    816
Ticklenberg, J. R. 19
Tiles, J. E.
  analytic propositions **24–5**
  *a priori* **36**
  causes **127–9**
  contingent properties **168–9**
  denotation **186**
  induction **361–2**
  meaning **450–4**
  Peirce, Charles Sanders **596**
  possibility **630**
  pragmatism **630–1**
Tiles, Mary Elizabeth
  axioms **67**
  deduction **180–2**
  entailment **223**
  Euclid **230–1**
  geometry **286–8**
  Gödel, Kurt **294–5**
  implication **355**
time
  *see also* reaction times
  biological clocks 92–3
  Dunne's theory of 584
  perception of 23, 205
time-gap experience 60, **777**
Tinbergen, N. 230
Tipton, I. C. 83
tiredness 255–6
Tisserand, P. 447
Titchener, E. B. 61, **777–8**
Tobias, J. 505
Toffler, Alvin 280
Tolman, Edward Chase **778**
Tomlin, E. W. F. 399–401, **402–3**
Tooke, J. H. 765
Tooth, G. C., asylums 56, 661
Torjussen, T. 113
Totman, R. G. 660
touch **778–80**
  blindness, recovery from, in 94–6
  cerebral hemisphere function 548
  haptic **302–3**
  irritability response 392
  short-term memory 713–14
  spatial location use 727–32
Tou, J. T. 594
Toulmin, S. E. 255

training
  astronauts 725
  interviewing 388
  military mind 486–7
  skill 715–16
  transfer 781–3
trance 197, 583, 584
  hypnosis 329–33
  Japanese reports 403
  spiritualism evidence 739–40
tranquillizers 653–4
transcendence theory (Husserl) 327
transcendental idealism (Kant) 406, 408
transcendental phenomenology 582–3
transfer (of knowledge, skill) 780–1, 781–3
transference 197–8, 270, 781
transmigration of souls 481–2
transparency drawings 139
traumas
  amnesia 21–2
  future shock 280
Travel, D. 113
travel sickness 725–6
Treisman, A. 60, 793
trembling, terror stimulus 770
tremor, intention 386
Trends in Neuroscience 560
Trevarthen, Colwyn
  brain development 101–10
  brain science (Sperry) 114–17
  handedness 302
  infancy, mind in 362–8
  split-brain and the mind 740–6, 747
trial-and-error learning 496
Triandis, H. 603
trichromatic theory, colour vision 150, 153
trophotropic behaviour 533
Troscianko, Tom 150–2
trpytamine, neuroanatomical training 538
truth 783
  see also epistemology, logic
  aesthetics of expression 8–10
  a priori concept 36
  deductive reasoning 181
  doubting 201
  falsification 254–5
  illusions 337
  implication 355
  independent thinkers 772–4
  knowable 287
  lying 442
  meaning 450–4
  phenomenology 614–16
  possibility 630
  pragmatism 630–1
Turing, Alan Mathison 444, 783–4
Turing, S. 784
Turnbull, H. W. 562
twilight vision (mesopic) 478
Tyler, C. W. 664
Tyrer, P. 5, 755

UFOlogists 773–4
Ullman, Julian R. 591–4, 734–5
Ullman, L. P. 77

Ulrich, R. E. 19
unconscious 171, 785
  see also id
  Berkeley's view 85
  Chinese ideas 146
  concussion syndrome 158
  electrodermal activity 213
  Freudian concept 162, 270
  inference (Helmholtz) 308–10, 598
  Leibniz's idea 433–4
  paranormal claims 579–83
  repression 681
unconventional ideas 772–4
understanding
  children's mental world 139–42
  creativity 171–2
  doubting 201
  humanist approach 318
  Japanese approach 399
  meaning 451
  verstehen position 786–7
  Wittgenstein's views 812, 815
Underwood, G. 61
unity
  Avicenna's view 66
  Heraclitus on 310
  one/many problem 217
  Sufi teaching 335
universals 443–4, 785
universe
  Descartes's system 189
  mechanistic philosophy (Herbart) 310
  Newton's concept 561–2
  one/many problem 217
  Pythagorean view 506
uproar state (bedlam) 70
utilitarianism 79, 487

Valenstein, E. S. 114
Valium 653
values
  aesthetics of expression 8–10
  human states of mind 233
Valvo, A. 96
Van Cott, H. P. 228
Van Toller, C. 16
variation, Darwinian theory 235–7
vasopressin 544
Venables, Peter H. 213–14
verbal disorders, speech 733–4
verification, meaning interpretation 326, 441, 451, 811–16
Verillo, R. T. 16
Vernon, M. D. 206
Vernon, Philip E. 379, 381, 776–7
Verstehen 786–7
Vesey, Godfrey N. A. 611–13
vibration, touch sensitivity 778–80
Victor, M. 414
vigilance, see attention
Vinci, Leonardo da, see Leonardo...
violence
  aggressive behaviour 16
  child abuse 131
  military psychology 484–7
vision 787–93
  adaptation 793–5
  after-image effects 13, 218–19
  ageing induced changes 14–16

apparent movement 604–8
artificial (Marr) 449–50
attentional, pre-attentional processes 60
binocular 88, 314
black as a colour 94
blindness, recovery from 94–6
blindsight 111
brain development 106, 107
brain function 110–11
colour 150–4, 192, 684–5
contingent after-effects 166–8
cortical neurones, selectivity 314
depth perception 188–9
diopter unit 195
dyslexia 205–6
eye defects and correction 248–52
Fourier analysis 265
iconic images and memory 336, 713–14
illusions 337–46
irradiation effect 392
Land colours (retinex) 419, 684
mesopic 478
neural plasticity 623–8
perception 525–6, 602, 604–6
primate brain evolution 633–9
Pulfrich's pendulum illusion 663–4
retina 682
retinex colour theory 684–5
spatial location 727–32
split-brain studies 740–6
stabilization of retinal images 682–4
stereoscopic 747–8
striate cortex, arrangement 314
stroke induced defects 750–2
system 796–804
tachistoscope 767
texture discrimination 788–92
visual cortex 313–15, 525–6
visual function 793–5, 798–802
visual aesthetics 10–12
visual cortex
  Hubel and Weisel 313–15
  organization 525–6, 802–4
  primate brain evolution 633–9
visual hypotheses 608–11
visual information rate 370–1, 795–6
visual perception 525–6, 602
  figural after-effects 263
  figure–ground 263–4
  illusions 337–43
  motion pictures 604–6
visual purple 153
visual space 796, 801
visual system
  environmental influences 796–8
  organization 798–804
vitamin deficiency, amnesia symptom 20
vocabulary, learning word meanings 421–3
volley theory 804
von Békésy, G., see Békésy
von Ehrenfels, C., see Ehrenfels
von Frey, M., see Frey
von Frisch, K. R., see Frisch

von Helmholtz, H. L. F., *see*
    Helmholtz
von Krafft-Ebing, R., *see* Krafft-
    Ebing
Von Neumann, John 784, **804–5**
Vorkapich, S. 608
Voutsinas, D. 447
Vygotsky, Leo 423, 675, **805–6**

Wade, D. T. 752
Wade, N. J. 118
Walker, Nigel D.
    criminology **172–3**
    psychopathic personality 653
    responsibility and mental states
        **681–2**
Walker, Ralph C. S.
    Kant, Immanuel 406
    Leibniz, G. W., Freiherr von
        **432–3**
    Leibniz's philosophy of mind
        **433–4**
Wallace, Alfred Russel 179, 584,
    **807**
Walmsley, D. M. 478
Walter, William Grey, **807–8**
    electroencephalography 217
    homeostasis 313
    mind and brain 490
Walton, R. E. 510
Wanner, E. 427
war—suicide statistics 759, 762
Ward, James **808**
Ward, W. D. 505
Warner, S. J. 12
war neuroses, Rivers' work 686
Warnock, Geoffrey **82–5**
Warnock, M. **207–10**, 469
Warren, R. 505
Warren, R. M. 310, 502
Warrington, E. K. 21, 113
Warr, P. B. 510
Warr, Roger J. **387–8**
Wason, Peter Cathcart **639–41**,
    **641–4**
Wasserman, G. S. 152
water, taste 769
water-divining 51, 52, 579–81
Watson, James 234
Watson, John Broadus 71–2, 74,
    765, **808**
Watt, Roger J. **129–30**
Watt, W. M. 19
Watzlawick, P. 387
Wavell, A. 487
Weber, Ernst Heinrich **808–9**
Weber–Fechner law 258, 655, 809
weight, obsession over 28–9
weightlessness 725–7
weight–size illusion 714–15
Weigl, E. 540
Weiner, N. 313
Weinreich, U. 88
Weisenburg, T. H. 425
Weisheipl, J. A. 38
Weiskrantz, L. 21, **110–12**, 113, 416
Weitzenhoffer, A. M. 330
Weizenbaum, J. 644
Welford, A. T. **13–16**, 40, **715–16**
Wellman, H. M. 142
Wells, Martin John **92–3, 389–92**

Werner, H. 423
Wernicke, Carl 32, 425, **809**
Wernicke's aphasia 426
Wertheimer, Max 644, **809**
West, D. J. 173
Westfall, R. S. 562
Westheimer, Gerald **310–11, 796**
Weston, M. J. 125
Wheatley, J. M. 587
Wheatstone, Sir Charles 747
Wheeler, W. M. 217
Whinfield, E. H. 687, 758
Whitaker, H. A. 540
White, B. L. 733
Whitehead, Alfred North 310, 688,
    **809–10**
White, P. T. 65
White, R. W. 641
Whitlock, F. A. **660–1, 763**
    addiction **3–5**
    aphrodisiacs **32–3**
    automatism **65–6**
    Capgras' syndrome **125**
    concussion **158**
    depression **187–8**
    drugs **204**
    hysteria **333–4**
    obsessions and compulsions
        **568–9**
    opium **570–1**
    personality disorder **613–14**
    pseudodementia **647–8**
    pseudohallucination **648**
    psychopathic personality **651–3**
Whitty, C. W. M. 22, 414
WHO (World Health Organization)
    Expert Committee on Drug
        Dependence 571
    mental disorders, classification
        467
Wickers, G. M. 66
Wiener, Norbert **810–11**
    cybernetics, history 177
    information theory 371
    interactional approach 387
Wiesel, Torsten Nils **313–15**
Wilkins, Arnold J. **483–4**
will
    *see also* free will
    Dennett on 383–6
    Locke's views 439–40
    Maine de Biran on 445–7
    soul concept (Berkeley) 85
will to power urge 5–6, 368
Williams, B. 190, 613, 772
Williams, J. M. G. 188
Williams, L. F. R. 758
Williams, Moyra **31–2, 185–6**
Wills, W. D. 510
Wilson, Colin **50–2, 581–3**
Wilson, E. O. 230
Wilson, M. 190
Wimmer, H. 142
Windrow, M. 487
wine, taste 769
Wing, J. 699
Wing, J. K. 65
Wing, L. 65
Winnicott, Donald 274, **811**
Winograd, T. 50, 502, 505
Winston, P. H. 50

Wisdom, J. 571
wish-fulfilment 267
Witten, I. 735
Wittgenstein, Ludwig Josef Johann
    **811–16**
    biography 811
    education 209
    language 811–14
    logic and mathematics **813–14**
    meaning 454
    mind **814–16**
    Russell's influence 688, 691
Wittig, M. A. 703
Wolfe, T. 727
Wollheim, R. 101, 275, 278
Wolman, B. B. 581, 587
Wolstencroft, John H. **543–5**
Wood, A. 818
Woodfield, A. 665
Wood, O. P. 692
Woodworth, Robert Sessions **816**
    Locke on the mind 441
    Watson, John Broadus 808
Wootton, B. 470, 653
word-association tests (Jung) 403–4
word-blindness (alexia) 19, 205, 426
words
    aphasic disorders 425–6
    association tests 647
    dyslexia 205–6
    learning meanings 421–3
    meaning problem 453–4
    semantic structure (Vygotsky)
        805–6
    symbolic use 763–5
World Health Organization, *see*
    WHO... 467
writing ability, agraphia disorder 19
Wundt, Wilhelm Max 33, 34,
    **816–17**
Wyss, D. 650

Yahr, M. D. 591
Yakovlev, P. I. 110
yang and yin 146
Yarbus, A. L. 684
Yates, A. J. 92
Yates, F. A. 680
yellow as a colour **818**
Yolton, J. W. 440
Young, J. Z.
    choice, biological **147–8**
    evolution **233–4**
    memory **455–6**
    mind and brain 490
Young, M. 210
Young, Thomas **818**
Young, T. Y. 594

Zangwill, O. L.
    Adrian, Edgar Douglas **7–8**
    Anokhin, Piotre Kuzmich **27–8**
    Bartlett, Sir Frederick Charles 70
    Binet, Alfred **88**
    body language **99–100**
    Breuer, Joseph 118
    Brunswik, Egon 120
    Carr, Harvey 126
    Cattell, James McKeen **127**
    centres in the brain **129**
    Claparède, Édouard **149**

Zangwill, O. L. *(cont.)*:
    Craik, Kenneth John William
        169–70
    delirium 184
    Dodge, Raymond 199
    Duncker, Karl 205
    Ebbinghaus, Hermann 207
    Ehrenfels, Christian 213
    Fairbairn, Ronald 254
    Fechner, Gustav Theodor 258–9
    figural after-effects 263
    Flugel, John Carl 264
    Freud, Anna 268
    Freud, Sigmund 268–70
        dreams 274–5
        hypnosis 275–6
        mental structure 276–8
    Frisch, Karl Ritter von 278–9
    functionalism 279–80
    Gall, Franz Joseph 282
    Goldstein, Kurt 295–6
    handedness 302

Humphrey, George 323
hypnagogic images 328
hypnosis 328–33
isolation experiments 393–4
Jackson, John Hughlings 395
Katz, David 408
Klüver, Heinrich 410
Köhler, Wolfgang 412–13
Kraeplin, Emil 414–15
Kretschmer, Ernst 414
Külpe, Oswald 414
Lange, Carl Georg 419
language 425
Lashley, Karl Spencer 427–8
Leonardo da Vinci 434–5
Luria, Alexander Romanovich
    441–2
mesmerism 477–8
Myers, Charles Samuel 506–7
neuropsychology 549
Penfield, Wilder Graves, 596–7
Ribot, Théodule 685–6

Rivers, William Halse Rivers
    686
Rubin, Edgar 687
Spearman, Charles Edward
    733
split-brain and the mind 747
Stumpf, Carl 752
Teuber, Hans-Lukas 770
Thoules, Robert Henry 776
Titchener, Edward Bradford
    777–8
Ward, James 808
Wernicke, Carl 809
Wertheimer, Max 809
Wundt, Wilhelm Max 816–17
Zeki, Semir 152, 601
Zen doctrines, Japan 401
Zeno of Elea 819
Zihl, J. 113
Zillman, D. 323
zodiac, *see* astrology
Zotterman, Y. 7–8

# ACKNOWLEDGEMENTS

The publishers are grateful to the following for their permission to reproduce illustration material. Although every effort has been made to contact copyright holders, it has not been possible to do so in every case and we apologize to any that may have been omitted. For permission to reproduce figures not listed below, please apply to Oxford University Press.

ADRIAN: Fig. 1 from E. D. Adrian, *Basis of sensation* (Christophers, 1928). By permission of Grafton Books, a Division of the Collins Publishing Group.

AGEING: Fig. 1 after A. Duane, 'Studies in monocular and binocular accommodation with their clinical applications', in *American Journal of Ophthalmology*, **122**, 3(5), 865–77. Copyright © by the Ophthalmic Publishing Company. By permission of the *American Journal of Ophthalmology*.

Fig. 2 from C. P. Lebo & R. C. Reddell, 'The presbycusis component in occupational hearing loss', in *Laryngoscope*, **82** (1972). By permission of the *Laryngoscope*.

BIOFEEDBACK: Figs. 1, 2 & 3 from T. H. Budzynski et al., 'EM9 biofeedback and tension headache: A controlled outcome study', originally in *Psychosomatic Medicine*. Copyright © by The American Psychosomatic Society, Inc. By permission of Elsevier Science Publishing Company, Inc.

BRAILLE: Fig. 1 from J. Roblin, *Louis Braille* (1960), p. 33.

BRAIN DEVELOPMENT: Fig. 2a from D. P. Purpura, *Morphogenisis of Visual Cortex in Development of the Brain: Nutritional, Genetic and Environmental Factors, Vol. 1*, International Brain Research Organization (1975). By permission of the publishers, Raven Press, New York.

Fig. 2b, c, & d, from J. le Roy Conel, *Postnatal Development of the Human Cerebral Cortex* (Harvard U.P., 1939–63). By permission of the publishers.

CHILDREN'S DRAWINGS: Fig. 5 from *Nature*, **254**, 417 (1975). Copyright © 1975 Macmillan Journals Ltd. By permission of the publishers.

Fig. 7 from fig. 2–4 in N. Freeman, *Strategies of Representation in Young Children*, (Academic Press, Inc., 1980). By permission of the publishers.

ELECTROENCEPHALOGRAPHY: Fig. 1a by permission of Dr R. Jaffe.

EVOKED POTENTIAL: Fig 1 from H. Berger, 'On the electroencephalogram of man: 10th report', in P. Gloor (ed.) *Hans Berger on the Electroencephalogram of Man*, *Electroenceph. Clin. Neurophysiol.* supp. 28: 243 (1935). By permission of Elsevier Scientific Publishers, Ireland, Ltd.

Fig. 2 from E. D. Adrian, 'Brain rhythms', in *Nature*, **153** (1944). Copyright © 1944 Macmillan Journals Ltd. By permission of the publishers.

Fig. 3 from T. W. Picton & S. A. Hillyard, 'Human auditory evoked potentials. II: Effects of attention' in *Electroenceph. Clin. Neurophysiol.* **34**: 191 (1974). By permission of Elsevier Scientific Publishers, Ireland, Ltd.

FEEDBACK AND FEEDFORWARD: Figs. 1, 2 & 3 from V. B. Brooks (ed.), Handbook of physiology, section on Neurophysiology, *Motor Control*, Vol. II (Williams & Wilkins), for the American Physiological Society.

HEARING: Fig. 1 from P. H. Lindsay & D. A. Norman, *Human Information Processing*, copyright © 1972 by Harcourt Brace Jovanovich, Inc. By permission of the publisher.

Fig. 2 from G. von Békésy, *Experiments in Hearing*, trans. and ed. by E. G. Wever, (McGraw-Hill, 1960). By permission of the publishers.

Fig. 3 from R. M. Arthur et al., 'Properties of "two-tone inhibitions" in primary auditory neurones', *Journal of Physiology*, **212** (1971). By permission of the Physiological Society.

Fig 4 data from Egan & Hake in *Journal of the Acoustical Society of America*, **22**, 622–30 (1950). By permission of the American Institute of Physics.

HUMAN GROWTH: Fig. 1 from J. M. Tanner, *Foetus into Man* (Open Books, 1978). By permission of the publishers.

IMAGES OF THE BRAIN IN ACTION: Fig. 1c by permission of M. E. Phelps, E. J. Hoffman, & J. Mazziotta, University of California, Los Angeles.

Fig. 2 from M. E. Raichle, 'Positron emission tomography', in *Annual Review of Neuroscience*, **6** (1983). Copyright © 1983 by Annual Reviews, Inc, By permission of the *Annual Review of Neuroscience*.

Fig. 7 from E. J. Metter et al., 'Comparison of glucose metabolism, X-ray CT, and postmortem data in a patient with multiple cerebral infarcts', in *Neurology*, **35**, (1985).

LOCALIZATION OF BRAIN FUNCTION AND CORTICAL MAPS: Fig. 1 from W. Penfield & T. Rasmussen, *The Cerebral Cortex of Man* (Macmillan, New York, 1950). Copyright © 1950 by Macmillan Publishing Company, renewed 1978 by T. Rasmussen. By permission of the publishers.

MUSIC PSYCHOLOGY: Figs. 2 & 3 from McAdams & Bregman in *Computer Music Journal*, 3(4).

NERVOUS SYSTEM: Fig. 1 from H. Mannen in *British Medical Journal*, **18**: 2, 101. By permission of the author and the publishers.

Figs. 2 & 3 from H. Ford & J. P. Schade, *Basic Neurology* (Elsevier). By permission of the authors and of Elsevier Science Publishers, BV, Amsterdam.

Figs. 4 & 5 from D. Landon, *The Peripheral Nerve*, ed. D. N. Landon (Chapman & Hall Ltd.). By permission of the author and of Associated Book Publishers.

Figs. 9 & 10 from E. Ludwig & J. Klinger, *Atlas Cerebri Humani* (S. Karger AG, Switzerland). By permission of the publishers.

Figs. 11 & 12 from N. Gluhbegovic & T. H. Williams, *The Human Brain* (Harper & Row). By permission of the authors and publishers.

NEUROANATOMICAL TECHNIQUES: Fig. 3 from P. Milner, *Physiological Psychology*, (Holt, Rinehart & Winston, 1970).

Fig. 7 from fig. 4, Hokfelt & Ljungdahl, and Fig. 8 from fig. 15, Ljungdahl et al., both in W. M. Cowan & M. Cuenod (eds.), *The Use of Axonal Transport for Studies of Neuronal Connectivity* (Elsevier, 1975). By

# ACKNOWLEDGEMENTS

permission of Elsevier Science Publishers, BV, Amsterdam.

Fig. 9 from D. H. Hubel et al., 'Anatomical demonstration of orientation columns in Macaque monkey', in *Journal of Comparative Neurology*, **177** (1978). By permission of Alan R. Liss, Inc., publishers.

NEUROTRANSMITTERS: Fig. 1 after a figure in S. R. Cajal, *Degeneration and Regeneration in the Nervous System*, trans. R. May (OUP, 1928). By permission of the publisher.

Fig. 2 from A. Peters & I. R. Kaiserman-Abramof in *Z. Zellforsch*, **100** (1969).

Fig. 6 from J. Linstrom et al., in *Cold Harbor Symposium on Quantitative Biology*, **48** (1983). By permission of the Cold Spring Harbor Laboratory.

Fig. 7 from C. F. Stevens, 'The neuron', in *Scientific American*, **241** (1979). Micrograph produced by Dr John E. Heuser of Washington University School of Medicine, St Louis, Mo. Used by permission.

Fig. 11 redrawn from H. F. Bradford, *Chemical Neurobiology* (W. H. Freeman & Co., 1986).

Fig. 12 from G. Burnstock, *Dale's Principle and Communication Between Neurones*, ed. N. N. Osborne (Pergamon Books Ltd., 1983). By permission of Pergamon Press.

PARKINSONISM: Fig. 1 after fig. 4–18 from J. C. Eccles, *The Understanding of the Brain* (McGraw-Hill, 1977). By permission of the publishers.

Fig. 2 drawn by A. E. Brotman in L. Iverson, 'The chemistry of the brain', *Scientific American*, Sept. 1979. Copyright © 1979 by Scientific American, Inc. All rights reserved. By permission of W. H. Freeman & Co., publishers.

PRIMATES: Fig. 1 from W. K. Gregory, 'Mongolian mammals of the "age of reptiles"', *Scientific Monthly*, **24** (1927).

Fig. 2 after J. J. Kaas et al., 'Cortical visual areas I & II in the hedgehog', *Journal of Neurophysiology*, **33** (1970).

Fig. 3 from L. B. Radinsky, 'The oldest primate endocast', *American Journal of Physical Anthropology*, **27** (1967). By permission of Wistar Press.

Figs. 4, 5, 6, & 7 (fig. 6 photograph by J. Tigges), from J. M. Allman, 'Evolution of the visual system in the early primates', *Progress in Psychobiology and Physiological Psychology*, **7** (1977). By permission of Academic Press.

Fig. 8 drawn by L. Wolcott after J. M. Allman & J. H. Kaas, 'Representation of the visual field on the medial wall of occipital-parietal cortex in the owl monkey', *Science*, **191** (1976); W. T. Newsome & J. M. Allman, 'The interhemispheric connections of visual, cortex in the owl monkey (*Aotus trivirgatus*), and the bushbaby (*Galago senegalensis*)', *Journal of Comparative Neurology*; M. M. Merzenich et al., 'Double representation of the body surface within cytoarchitectonic areas 3G and 1 in SI in the owl monkey (*Aotus trivirgatus*)', *Journal of Comparative Neurology*, **181**, (1978); and T. G. Imig et al. 'Organization of auditory cortex in the owl monkey (*Aotus trivirgatus*)', *Journal of Comparative Neurology*, **171** (1977).

PROBLEM SOLVING: Fig. 1 from P. C. Wason, 'Self-contradictions' in Johnson-Laird & Wason (eds.), *Thinking: Readings in Cognitive Science* (Cambridge, 1977). By permission of the author and publishers.

PSYCHOPHYSICS: Fig. 1 from D. Laming, *Sensory Analysis*, (Academic Press, 1986). By permission of the publisher.

QUANTIFYING JUDGEMENTS: Fig. 1 from E. C. Poulton, 'Models for biases in judging sensory magnitude', *Psychological Bulletin*, **86** (1979). Copyright © 1979 by the American Psychological Association. By permission of the author.

RETINAL IMAGES: Fig 1a & b from the *Thomas Young Oration* of the (now defunct) Physical Society, by permission of the Institute of Physics.

Fig. 2 after fig. 1 from C. R. Evans, 'Pattern perception using a stabilized retinal image', *British Journal of Psychology*, **56** (1965). By permission of the author and the British Psychological Society.

Fig. 4 after H. Bennett-Clark & C. R. Evans, in *Nature*, **199**, 1215 (1963). Copyright © 1963 by Macmillan Journals Ltd. By permission of the authors and the publisher.

SPACE PSYCHOLOGY: Fig. 1 from Young et al., 'Spatial orientation in weightlessness and readaptation to Earth's gravity', *Science*, **225** (1984). Copyright © 1984 by the AAAS. By permission of the American Association for the Advancement of Science.

Fig. 2 photograph by permission of the European Space Technology Centre.

SPATIAL CO-ORDINATION OF THE SENSES: Fig. 1 from G. H. Fisher, 'Intersensory localization' (1962). By permission of the author.

Figs. 2 & 6 from I. P. Howard, *Human Visual Orientation* (Wiley, 1982). Copyright © 1982 I. P. Howard. By permission of John Wiley and Sons Ltd.

Fig. 3 from R. Held & A. Hein, 'Movement-produced stimulation in the development of visually guided behaviour', *Journal of Comparative and Physiological Psychology*, **56** (1963). Copyright © 1963 by the American Psychological Association. By permission of the authors.

Figs. 4 & 5 from A. Hein & R. Held, 'Dislocation of the visual placing response into elicited and guided components', *Science*, **158** No. 3799 (1967). Copyright © 1967 by the AAAS. By permission of the American Association for the Advancement of Science.

TRANSFER OF TRAINING: Fig. 1 after a fig. from M. Hammerton, 'Measures for the efficiency of simulators as training devices', *Ergonomics*, **10** (1967). By permission of the author and Taylor & Francis Ltd. as publishers.